1

Encyclopedia of
American Radio,
1920–1960

Second edition

Encyclopedia of American Radio, 1920–1960

Second edition

LUTHER F. SIES

Volume 1 : Introductions, How to Use, Entries 1–28040 (A–R)

McFarland & Company, Inc., Publishers
Jefferson, North Carolina, and London

To my family:
My mother and father, Hilda and Frank Sies,
my brother, Roger,
and especially my wife, Leora M. Sies,
without whose love, understanding, encouragement
and assistance it never could have been written.
The book is also dedicated
to those countless pioneering broadcasters,
many of whom, unfortunately, have been overlooked
and forgotten for too long.

ALSO OF INTEREST
The Encyclopedia of Women in Radio, 1920–1960,
by Luther F. Sies and Leora M. Sies
(McFarland, 2003)

Volume 1

LIBRARY OF CONGRESS CATALOGUING-IN-PUBLICATION DATA

Sies, Luther F.
Encyclopedia of American radio, 1920–1960 / Luther F. Sies — 2nd ed.
p. cm.
Includes bibliographical references and indexes.

ISBN 978-0-7864-2942-4
2 volume set : library binding : 50# alkaline paper ♾

1. Radio brodcasting — United States — Encyclopedias.
I. Title.
PN1991.2.S57 2008 791.44097303 — dc22 2007036686

British Library cataloguing data are available

Manufactured in the United States of America

McFarland & Company, Inc., Publishers
Box 611, Jefferson, North Carolina 28640
www.mcfarlandpub.com

Acknowledgments

This book is the result of more than thirty years of collecting printed materials about broadcasting and its performers and tape recordings of radio programs and their performers from its early "pioneer days through its golden age." The author is privileged that his audio research materials are preserved in the Luther F. Sies Radio Collection of the Rodgers and Hammerstein Archive of Recorded Sound, New York Library of the Performing Arts at Lincoln Center (Don McCormick, curator). Many people have helped me over the years and deserve my thanks.

I begin by acknowledging several significant sources that contained valuable information. First, there was Eric Barnouw's masterful three-volume history of American broadcasting: *A Tower in Babel*, *The Golden Web* and *The Image Empire*. Second, Gleason Archer's basic radio histories, *The History of Radio to 1926* and *Big Business and Radio*, were landmarks in scholarship that proved invaluable to me. Finally, the book that probably best captures the flavor and spirit of Radio's Golden Age is *I Looked and I Listened* by Ben Gross.

The contemporary periodicals and annuals used most frequently were:

Broadcast Listener (1926–1927)
Broadcast Programs & News — San Francisco/Los Angeles (1939)
Broadcast Program for the Pacific Coast (1923)
Broadcast Weekly (1925–1931)
Broadcasting (1931–1960)
Radio Age (1924–1927)
Radio Broadcasting News (1922–1923)
Radio Digest (in its various formats from 1922 to 1932)
Radio Guide: The Blue Book of Radio (1925–1926)
Radio Guide (later *Movie Radio Guide* and, still later, *Television-Radio Guide*
Radio Listeners' Guide and Call Book (1928)
Radio Stories (1925)
Radio Weekly Post (1925)

Various issues were also used from such papers as the New York *Times*, New York *Herald-Tribune* and the *Christian Science Monitor* when available. The same was true for certain issues of *Rural Radio, Radio Varieties, Microphone, Tune-In, Fan-Fare, Tower Radio, Radioland, Radio-Movie Guide, Radio Album, Radio Stars, Radio Mirror* and *Radio-TV Mirror*.

This work was also enhanced by the assistance provided me by the librarians at Columbia University's Oral History Division; Broadcast Pioneers Library at the University of Maryland; Yivo Institute for Jewish Research; the Library of Congress; New York City's Library of the Performing Arts at Lincoln Center, New York City; and the Research Division of the New York City Public Library.

In addition, Ms. Kathryn Moore Stucker, Curator of the Lum and Abner Society Collection; George McWhorter, Curator of the Edgar Rice Borroughs' Memorial Archive at the University of Louisville; George French of the Metropolitan Washington Old-Time Radio Organization; Mike Mashon, Library of American Broadcasting, University of Maryland; Ronnie Pugh, Country Music Foundation; and Amelia Todd, Research Assistant, Oral History Research Division, Columbia University generously provided me with their time, help and knowledge. Most important, my wife, Leora, provided me valuable advise and assistance that made this book possible. Her help was indispensable.

Useful information about old-time radio programs can be found in Swartz and Reinehr's *Handbook of Old-Time Radio: A Comprehensive Guide to Golden Age Radio Listening and Collecting;* Buxton and Owens' *The Big Broadcast—1920–1950*; and Dunning's *Tune in Yesterday: The Ultimate Encyclopedia of Old-Time Radio, 1925–1970.* The most accurate guide to program dates and comprehensive information about network programming can be found in Hickerson's *New Revised Ultimate History of Network Programming and Guide to all Circulating Shows*, Harrison B. Summers' *Thirty-Year History of Programs Carried on National Networks in the United States—1926–1956.*

My gratitude to quote is due: WBBM — News Radio, Copyright 1988: *WBBM Radio—Yesterday and Today* by Chuck Shaden; May Broadcasting Company, Copyright 1985: *KMA Radio—The First Sixty Years* by Robert Birkby; and Rosemary Thurber, Copyright ©1948 James Thurber, Copyright ©1976 by Rosemary Thurber from "Soapland," *The Beast in*

Me and Other Animals, published by Harcourt Brace & Company.

Many broadcasters have helped me by generously providing information and encouragement. Among these professionals were: Mark Halverson, WHO-TV; Mike Stocklin, General Manager, KGEZ-AM; Joe Davis, Vice-President, WMCA; Don Hansen, Station Manager and Jackie Willcoxon, Administrative Assistant, KMA; Chris Berry, Director, News and Programming, WBBM; Roy Shapiro, Vice-President-General Manager, KYW; Dan Fabian, Vice-President-General Manager, WGN; Ricci Filiar, Programming Administrator, WJR; Debbie Billinslea, Administrative Assistant, WHAS; James J. Carter, Vice President-General Manager, WTAE; Gregory Skaltas, Manager, KGU; Herndon Hasty, President, WDAF; Ed Greaney, WMC-TV News; Bob Meyer, Vice-President, WSM; Bruce Still Operations-Compliance Director, WCKY; Jane Graber, Promotions Director, KCMO; Jennifer Lawhorn, Public Relations Officer, WNYC; Judith Rose, Listener Service, WHA; Dave Pavlock, WWRO; Jeffrey D. Greenhawt, WQAM; Granville Klink, Jr., Engineering Consultant, WTOP-Radio; Dick Pust, General Manager, KGY; Anne Dieters, WWJ; Ray Watson, Senior Vice-President-Division General Manager, KXL; Ken Fearnow, Vice President-General Manager, WOW; Maria L. Soll, Administrative Assistant, WOW; Rick Lewis, General Manager, WOI; Jill Schroth, Promotions Director, WAAM; Randy Brown, Creative Director, KRLD-Texas State Network; Bob Meyer, Vice-President-General Manager, WSM; Cindy Wood, Administrative Assistant, WSM; Dennis Sturtz, General Manager, KFUO; Doug Brown, Program Director, WOI, Bob Bruno, Vice-President-General Manager, WOR; John A. Gambling, formerly WOR; John R. Gambling, WOR; and Philip Eberly.

Other professionals who made significant contributions to my work include: Mel Blanc, Norman Corwin, Bing Crosby, Benny Goodman, Brent Gunts, Quincy Howe, Granville Klink, Jr., Ward Quaal, Harry Richman, Robert Lewis Shayon, Frank Sinatra, Rudy Vallee, Eddie Walker, Ireene Wicker and Polly Willis. Their help and well wishes were greatly appreciated. My contacts with these pioneer broadcasters helped me put a human face on Radio's Golden Age. Regrettably, not all of them are now able to accept my thanks.

The author is also grateful to the special assistance many others gave me. I am particularly appreciative of the data on stations tirelessly supplied to me by Jim Roggentine and the information about Iowa's pioneer radio stations given to me by broadcast historian Rick Plummer. Hugh Carlson, Marsha Washington George, Frank Bequaert of Rainy Day Books, Ada Fitzsimmons, Dale Manesis, David G. Hintz, Radio Coordinator of the Rock and Roll Hall of Fame and Museum and Mrs. Tommy Smalls also were generous with their assistance. Dick Judge, Peter Kanze and Max Schmeid supplied me with some important recorded materials. Dave Siegel also provided me with hard to find program recordings and helpful advice. Finally, my special thanks go to Glenn McDonald, the grandson of Gleason Archer and Polly Willis Archer, two broadcasting pioneers. McDonald, a radio correspondent for United Press, who covered the Viet Nam War among other assignments, is not included in this book, because he was too young to have broadcast during Radio's Golden Age. He was very helpful to me by supplying me with many of the writings of Gleason Archer and, equally important, arranged for me to speak with his grandmother, Polly Willis Archer, who sang and played the piano on Chicago's KYW in 1923. My talks with her were both inspiring and informative.

The author also appreciates the assistance provided me for the second edition by Bobb Lynes, Martin Tytun, Arthur Robinson of LaGrange College, John Mainelli, program director, WOR, New York, New York. Katherine Cassels, Lori Cassels, Jeanne Toomey, Marjorie Weinberg, Michael Henry, Robert C. Carroll and Harry Miller, who also were generous with their time and generosity in providing information. Thanks also to Tom Davis and Bryan College Finally, I appreciate the valuable advice and assistance given me by my brother and sister-in-law Roger F. Sies and Dr. Andrea Wargo.

Unfortunately, even in its expanded second edition the book is still far from complete. It remains only a representative sample of broadcasters' work from 1920 to 1960. The same is true of the listings of broadcasters by category in Appendix B. The book, however, and the categories included demonstrate the diversity of the work of pioneer broadcasters. The author welcomes other information about broadcasters and programs, as well as the correction of any errors of omission or commission. Those with additions and corrections should send them to the author in care of the publisher. All responses will be answered with thanks.

Table of Contents

— Volume 1 —

— Volume 2 —

Introduction to the First Edition

Radio was magic. There were no wires or phonograph records. Music and voices just came out of the air into the home. For many Americans in 1922, at least, it seemed like magic to hear these enchanted sounds pulled out of the air and coming from a piece of living room furniture. Other listeners picked the sounds from out of the air by delicately tuning the "cat's whiskers" of their tiny crystal receivers. These crystal receiving sets worked most of the time. If the set did go dead, the owner frantically moved the "cat's whisker" to another part of the crystal. If he still couldn't hear anything, he added a drop of rubbing alcohol to the crystal and, as a last resort, he might even bake the crystal in the oven for a few minutes.

Radio provided an exciting new experience for listeners. Many Americans found romance, thrills and excitement in it. Nothing caught the imagination of Americans in the second decade of the twentieth century as much as radio. *Variety's* front page headline on March 10, 1922 read: **RADIO SWEEPING COUNTRY—1,000,000 SETS IN USE.** Frederick Lewis Allen has noted that although there was no such thing as radio in the autumn of 1920, by 1922 radio had become a craze (Allen, 1931, p. 165).

Early radio stations broadcast for only a few hours each day and many of them didn't broadcast during daytime hours. Others for many years didn't broadcast on Sunday. Although at first Americans could only listen a few hours a day, they found what they heard fascinating and wanted more. Soon they got it. *Dunston's Radio Log and Call Book* for 1926 reported that station WEAF (New York, NY) was broadcastings an average of seven hours a day, excluding Sunday, and that hundreds of stations were on the air.

DX-ing, the practice of listening for stations from distant cities, became a popular pastime for many listeners. Variations on the practice of Radio Golf also became popular. *Radio Broadcasting News* (January 6, 1923, p.14) described Radio Golf for its readers in this way:

> The game [Radio Golf] was suggested by Frank H. Jones of Tuinucu, Cuba. It is a gentlemen's game and each person keeps his own score. The method of scoring is as follows:
>
> Let each person make a list of the stations he has heard, and opposite each station give the distance in miles from his location. The total score is found by adding up the miles thus listed. In order to make the game interesting, and permit a great number of persons to participate, it is suggested that only such stations be listed as have been heard on detector tube, without amplification except that obtained by regenerative action of tickler coil or similar regeneration. The distance between your station and the one heard can be easily estimated by scaling the distance on an ordinary map.

Some of the radio golf scores the issue contained were:

Milton L. Johnson, Atchison, Kansas	83,470
L.C. Davis, Berea, Kentucky	71, 345
Frank H. Jones, Tuinucu, Cuba	65,000

DX-ing in its many forms excited radio's listeners.

Annual radio sales soared. The $842,548,000 sales of radio sets in 1929 was an increase over the 1922 figures of 1,400 per cent (Allen, 1931, p. 165):

1922	$60,000,000	1926	$506,000,000
1923	$136,000,000	1927	$425,600,000
1924	$358,000,000	1928	$650,550,000
1925	$430,000,000	1929	$842,548,000

Always aware of the changing patterns of show business and entertainment in general, *Variety* began to carry articles about broadcasting from radio's earliest days. The first formal reviews of radio programs, however, did not begin until January 7, 1931, when their "Radio Reports" page first appeared with reviews of Phil Spitalny and his orchestra, Ted Lewis, Gus Van and others.

If radio reflected the life-styles of Americans, it also changed the way they thought, acted and, even, how they spoke. Taken for granted until it had virtually disappeared, radio's Golden Age was a cornucopia of creativity and talent that both entertained a people and reflected their life-styles for almost 50 years. Radio broadcasting entertained, informed and maintained morale during the Great Depression, World War II and into the burgeoning post-war period. In the Fifties, radio fought an unsuccessful rear guard action against television, only to lose its stars, programs, advertisers and much of its audience to that medium, much as vaudeville years before had succumbed to radio and motion pictures.

For many Americans, mystery, adventure and some children's programs provided vicarious thrills and excitement, being virtual auditory comic strips. Radio was at its best with its comedy, music and dramatic programming. The birth of broadcast journalism as we know it today can be found in the development of great radio news gathering organizations and the broadcasting of momentous events (the Munich Crisis, D-Day and FDR's death, etc.). Not only did radio entertain, inform and maintain morale through both the vicissitudes and happy periods of four decades, but it did so at no charge to its listeners other than the initial purchase of a receiver.

Some critics have suggested that radio introduced greater informality into national life. If so, a similar transformation can also be seen in the transition of radio's formal manners (performing in full-dress to broadcast) and the use of overly precise articulation in its early days to the changes reflected by Bing Crosby's floral sports shirts, his casual conversational broadcast style and his use of magnetic recording tape on his broadcasts. In some instances radio programs appeared to change listener behavior. One example is that of daytime serials ("soap operas"), where the Behavior Modification technique known as "modeling" provided some possible solutions for many women facing their own *real* personal problems.

Radio, like comic strips and jazz, was an uniquely American contribution, although other nations did make a few notable contributions to its development. American radio's Golden Age entertained, transmitted information and maintained morale with an efficiency and elan never duplicated before or since. For example, neither radio, nor television broadcasting during the Korean or Viet Nam wars provided a fraction of the positive morale boosting that radio provided during World War II.

Although the work of famous radio performers such as Jack Benny, Fred Allen and Bing Crosby and their programs have been preserved on recordings and discussed extensively, there were thousands of other performers and hundreds of programs that have gone largely unnoticed. Unfortunately, as time passes memories fade and printed records disappear or deteriorate. The author has seen many important printed source materials literally crumble into dust, because they were not preserved by microfilming for the use of future scholars. This book attempts to record the work of some of those broadcasters and the programs they broadcast from 1922 to 1960. It arbitrarily ends at 1960, because it ends a significant era in American radio history. By that time, not only had many comedians and programs made the transition from radio to television. Almost all the old favorite radio shows had gone off the air. Then, too, when the radio was turned on instead of hearing the music of Les Brown or Benny Goodman, it was more likely to be a group with a name like Mama Ego and the Little Ids. One era of radio clearly had ended. By that time, not only had many comedians and programs made the transition from radio to television, but almost all the old favorite radio shows had gone off the air. Perhaps this book will help to preserve the memories of that era.

A note on the book's organization: American radio began with the work of *individual* performers. There were few, if any, programs in the beginning. Singers, musicians, readers, monologists and announcers were some of the varied performers who broadcast in radio's early years. Announcers were the first important figures. They seemed to be glamorous, romantic and mysterious figures. In the early days they were identified only by initials — not always their own. Famous announcer Tommy Cowan, for example, identified himself on the air as AAC.

There were only a few programs broadcast during radio's first decade. Individual performers predominated. True, there were a few early programs such as the *Eveready Hour* and the *Nighthawk Frolic*, but they were exceptions. It was the growth and development of network radio — what they called "chains" in the early days — that helped usher in the use of the "program" format. It was not until the end of the medium's first decade that the networks began to play a major role in broadcasting. Although the network programming concept was well established by 1929, some unaffiliated stations continued to present individuals as their basic programming unit. In order to reflect the nature of American radio as it developed, this book arbitrarily assigned that year (1929) as the last one that individual performers were a significant programming unit. Beginning with 1930, *programs* are considered the basic programming unit.

Entries prior to 1930, therefore, reflect the work of announcers, singers, musicians, vocal and instrumental groups, newscasters and commentators and actors *individually*. Program entries, on the other hand, are included from their *earliest* appearance to 1960. After 1929, *individual* entries are made only for newscasters, commentators, female commentators and home economists, DJs, singers, musicians, vocal groups and bands providing *they had their own programs*. If they appeared on another program, their work is recorded as part of the entry for that programming unit. Such a pattern of organization reflects the structure of the growth and development of American radio from its beginning.

Separate entries are included for special topics* such as:

Black Radio
Border Radio
Charlatans, Demagogs and Politicians
Chronology, 1906–1960 (Appendix A)
Commercials
Country-Western (CW) Music
Daytime Serials ("Soap Operas")
Drama
Foreign Language Broadcasts
Music on Radio
Networks
News on Radio

**See Intoduction to the Second Edition, following, for additional special topics.*

OPERA
RELIGIOUS BROADCASTING
ROCK AND ROLL HALL OF FAME AND MUSEUM
SOUND EFFECTS
SPORTS
STATIONS—GROWTH AND DEVELOPMENT
TRANSCRIPTIONS
WARTIME RADIO

Further information on format may be found in the "How to Use This Book" section.

Introduction to the Second Edition

The present volume is a revised, expanded and corrected edition of the *Encyclopedia of America Radio, 1920–1960*. This second edition includes 10 additional extended entries: American Traitors on Radio; Comediennes; Gender Discrimination on Radio; Holidays on Radio; Husband and Wife Talk Shows; Minstrel Shows, Vaudeville, Burlesque and Radio; Scopes "Monkey" Trial Broadcasts (1925); Singers — Crooners, Canaries, Country Belles, Cow Girls and Hillbillies; Superheroes on Radio; and Women Pioneers of Radio.

Other additions are various supplementary information included in the Chronology (Appendix A) and Appendix B that includes 83 categories of broadcasters: Actors; Actresses; Advice to the Lovelorn; Announcers and Program Hostesses (women); Announcers and Program Hosts (men); Astrologists, Mentalists and Numerologists; Aunts; Aviation Talks; Band and Orchestra Leaders (women); Band and Orchestra Leaders (men); Book Reviewers; Bridge Experts; Children' Program Performers; Choral Directors; Choruses; COM-HE; Comedians and Comic Actors; Comedy Teams; Comediennes and Comic Actresses; Corillion Players; CW Singers (men); CW Singers (women); CW Vocal and Instrumental Groups; Dancers; Dancing Lessons; Daytime Serial Actors (men); Daytime Serial Actresses (women); DJs (men); DJs (women); Dramatic Companies; Educational and Self-Improvement; Executives and Management; Gardening and Agriculture; Graphologists; Health and Nutrition; Hunting and Exploration; Husband and Wife Teams; Imitators and Impersonators; Inspirational Talks; Interviewers, Moderators and Panelists; Investment Advice; Language Teachers; Miscellaneous Philosophers; Monologists; Music Appreciation and Music Talks; Musical Comb Performers; Musical Glass Virtuoso; Musical Saw Performers; Musicians (men); Musicians (women); Newscasters and Commentators (men); Newscasters and Commentators (women); Orchestras and Bands; Parent Education and Child Guidance; Personal Problems Advisers; Pets; Piano Lessons; Popular Singers (men); Popular Singers (women); Producers and Directors; Publicity; Quiz and Talk Panelists; Quiz Masters; Radio, Broadway and Hollywood News and Gossip; Readers; Religious; Singers — Concert and Operatic; Singing Lessons; Singing Teams — Duets, Trios, Quartets and Quintets; Small Music Groups; Sound Effects; Sportscasters; Station Owners; Studio Hostesses; Swimming Lessons; Travel Talks; Ukulele Lessons; Uncles; Weathermen; Women's Exercise Programs; World War II Information; Writers; and Yodelers.

Unfortunately, even in its second edition the book is far from complete. It remains only a representative sample of broadcasters' work from 1920 to 1960. The same is true of the listings of broadcasters by category in Appendix B. The categories, however, demonstrate the diversity of the work of pioneer broadcasters. The author welcomes other information about broadcasters or programs, as well as correction of any errors of omission or commission. Those with additions and corrections should send them to the authors in care of the publisher. All responses will be answered with thanks.

How to Use This Book

An explanation of the selection, content and the order of this book's entries should be useful when seeking information on specific performers or programs. Entries for all individual performers prior to 1930 and newscasters, commentators, singers, vocal and instrumental groups, DJs, female commentators and home economists with their own programs are listed alphabetically by surname:

Bertha Brainard	as	**Brainard, Bertha**
Thomas Cowan	as	**Cowan, Thomas**
Alan Freed	as	**Freed, Alan**

All programs are listed alphabetically by title, excluding articles such as *a, an* and *the*:

A Date with Judy	as	***(A) Date with Judy***
The Chamber Music Society of Lower Basin Street	as	***(The) Chamber Music Society of Lower Basin Street***
The Fred Allen Show	as	***(The) Fred Allen Show***
Grand Central Station	as	***Grand Central Station***

The work of individual performers after 1929 without a program of their own are included in the specific entries for the programs on which they worked. Many broadcasters used professional names instead of their own given names. When known their given surname is provided in parentheses:

Alan Reed (Teddy Bergman)
Mike Wallace (Myron Wallace)
Lee Stevens (Ad Weinert)

The index should always be used in case there are several entries that might provide information about an individual's work.

Radio stations during the years covered appeared, disappeared and changed locations only to reappear later with different call letters. The initial listing of a station in any entry includes its geographical location at the time it is discussed:

WBAL (Baltimore, MD)
WGN (Chicago, IL)
WJZ (New York, NY)
WEAF (New York, NY)
WMAQ (Chicago, IL)

During radio's first decade, individual broadcasters such as announcers, musicians, singers, readers, etc. are given individual entries, because performers, not programs, were the *basic broadcasting unit.* There were few programs listed as such in the 1920s. Later, when programs became the basic unit, entries are made for programs, with any individuals who appeared on them included in the entry.

For example, in the 1920s **Will Rogers** receives an individual entry for his broadcast appearances. In the next decade, however, when he was a regular performer on the *Gulf Oil Program* in 1933, his work is included in the ***Gulf Oil Program*** entry. Another example should suffice: The ***Jack Benny Show*** entry includes mention of Mary Livingstone, Phil Harris, Dennis Day, Mel Blanc, Don Wilson and, of course, Benny. The program's announcer, **Don Wilson**, receives a separate entry because of his work in the 1920s.

Entries for newscasters, news commentators, sportscasters and orchestra leaders are not biographical. Instead, entries focus primarily on their verified professional broadcasting appearances. In some instances, chronological gaps in a broadcaster's work might reflect job changes, military service or illness.

A note about a program's duration, time and date of broadcast and the network or station on which it appeared is necessary. A typical information line in a program entry includes information such as duration, day of broadcast, time of broadcast, station and its location and year of broadcast, when the information is available. Typically, it would be:

(15 min., Tuesday, 6:00–6:15 P.M., WBAL, Baltimore, MD, 1935).

Finally, the length of time a program was broadcast is supplied when available. The best source for the years the programs were on the air is Jay Hickerson's (1996) *The New Revised Ultimate History of Network Radio Programming and Guide to All Circulating Shows* and Harrison B. Summers' (1958) *Thirty-Year History of Programs Carried on National Networks in the United States—1926–1956.*

Style and abbreviations used in entries usually follow standard practices with few exceptions. Musical programming, the instrumentation of radio bands and program types are exceptions.

Programs are designated as:

inst. mus. prg.	Instrumental Music Program
vcl. mus. prg.	Vocal Music Program
syn.	Syndicated
trans.	Transcribed

Abbreviations used to identify orchestral instrumentation are as follows:

a.	arranger
acc.	accordion
as.	alto saxophone
bar.	baritone saxophone
bj.	banjo
bh.	bass horn
bss.	bassoon
bsx.	bass saxophone
cnm.	concertmaster
con.	conductor
c.	cornet
clr.	clarinet
dir.	director or directed by
d.	drums
eh.	English horn
elg.	electric guitar
f.	flute
g.	guitar
h.	horn
ha.	harmonica
hp.	harp
ldr.	leader
m.	melophone
o.	oboe
or.	organ
p.	piano
pac.	piano accordion
pe.	percussion
pi.	piccolo
s.	saxophone
sb.	string bass
ss.	soprano saxophone
stg.	steel guitar
t.	trumpet
tba.	tuba
tb.	trombone
ts.	tenor saxophone
ty.	tympani
u.	ukulele
v.	violin
vc.	violoncello
vb.	vibraphone
vl.	viola
vcls.	vocals
x.	xylophone

Network abbreviations used were:

AFRS	Armed Forces Radio
ABC	American Broadcasting Company
ABS	Amalgamated Broadcasting System
CBS	Columbia Broadcasting System
MBS	Mutual Broadcasting System
NBC	National Broadcasting Company
TN	Texas Network
TQN	Texas Quality Network
YN	Yankee Network

Women in early radio did not always receive the recognition they deserved. At times, knowledgeable female commentators were lumped together and designated as "home economists," when they conducted "women's programs." In order to alleviate this somewhat, the designation—COM/HE—is used here to identify the broadcaster as either/or a "commentator," "home economist," or both.

An explanation of the language found in this book may be useful for those who think some of it insensitive. The language used reflects that found in the original sources or periodical accounts. An example is the weekly broadcast schedule published for its listeners by station KSTP (St. Paul, MN). It illustrates the language that was in general use in 1928:

> Uncle Tom, baritone soloist, will sing two Negro spirituals on the Dusk in Dixie program to be broadcast from KSTP, the National Battery Station, Sunday, November 15 between 8:00 and 8:30 P.M. He has selected "Going Up" and "Ride On Moses" as his offerings for this weekly period of southern music.
>
> As usual the program will open with the stirring strains of "Dixie" and the half hour will include:
>
> Orchestra—The Racoon and the Bee—Beyer
> Orchestra—Reminiscences of the South—Solomon
> Baritone Solo—Going Up
> Orchestra—A Little Bit of Honey—Bond
> Orchestra—A Pickaninny Patrol—Strauss
> Baritone Solo—Ride on Moses
> Orchestra—Frolic of the Coons

In quoting such sources the intent is not to disregard significant changes to our language that have occurred through the twentieth century, but to record broadcasting history with the greatest possible accuracy. At times, however, even original sources should be questioned as to their accuracy.

Although original sources are considered the most accurate basis for information, at times it was necessary to attempt verification by cross-checking sources. Sometimes even well respected sources contained obvious errors. For example, one of them had a listing for the D'Orsey Orchestra that *actually* was for a Tommy Dorsey remote broadcast. When original sources were in conflict about the spelling of a name and no definitive verification was available, possible spelling variations are provided; for example:

Gabrilowitsch, Ossip [Ossyp]
Gaslight Gayeties [*Gaities*]
Goodelle, Niela [Nina].

The Encyclopedia

1 ***(The) A&P Bandwagon.*** "Song Bird of the South" Kate Smith was host of the *A&P Bandwagon*, a variety program sponsored by the A&P Food Company. *Variety* said the program's chief purpose was to break the time-spot supremacy long held by Rudy Vallee's *Fleishmann Hour.* Although never a serious threat to Vallee's popularity, the *A&P Bandwagon* did present entertaining variety fare along with Smith's beautiful singing voice. Comedians Clyde Hager and Henny Youngman appeared on the program as guests. Jack Miller's orchestra and announcers Andre Baruch and Ted Collins were also program regulars (60 min., Thursday, 8:00–9:00 P.M., CBS, 1936).

2 ***A&P Coffee Time.*** Kate Smith sang and hosted the variety program, backed by the Jack Miller Orchestra. Frank Galop was the announcer (15 min., Tuesday through Thursday, 7:30–7:45 P.M., CBS, 1935).

3 ***(The) A&P Gypsies (Orchestra).*** WEAF (New York, NY) broadcast the first radio appearance of the pioneer radio orchestra in 1923. When they played on WOO (Philadelphia, PA) in 1925, the A&P Gypsies contained only five string players led by Henry Horlick. The Gypsies eventually grew into a 32-piece concert orchestra sponsored, of course, by the A&P Food Company. Jessica Dragonette occasionally sang with the orchestra in 1927. The program was announced, first, by Phil Carlin and, later, by Ed Thorgersen. Typical songs featured were "Shadows of the East" and "Black Eyes."

In 1930, the *A&P Gypsies* were a 27-piece concert orchestra with vocalists, including tenor Oliver Smith, a male vocal quartet and a string sextet. Milton J. Cross was the announcer (60 min., Monday, 8:30–9:30 P.M., NBC-Red, 1930). Later, tenor Frank Parker and bass Emile Cote sang with the Gypsies. Tenor Jan Peerce and the blackface comedy team of Molasses and January were program regulars in 1932. Tenor Ben Klassen replaced Jan Peerce in 1935.

4 ***A&P Gypsy String Ensemble.*** Classical music group composed of members of the A&P Gypsies Orchestra (WCAE, Pittsburgh, PA, 1925.)

5 ***A.L. Alexander's Good Will Court*** (aka ***Goodwill Court***). A.L. Alexander conducted the informative program on which free legal advice was provided persons who were willing to tell their stories on the air. The program was sponsored by Chase and Sanborn Coffee. After only a short time on the air, the New York State Supreme Court issued a statement that prevented all New York lawyers and judges from appearing on the program. The show then left the air (30 min., Weekly, NBC, 1936). *See* ***A.L. Alexander's Mediation Board***

6 ***A.L. Alexander's Mediation Board*** (aka ***A.L. Alexander's Arbitration Program***). Alexander, who had previously produced and moderated *A.L. Alexander's Good Will Court* program, conducted this one where a judgment was reached by a board of four arbitrators. Instead of the lawyers he had used in his previous series, Alexander this time used a panel of educators and social workers, since a New York lawyers' group had protested against his previous *Alexander's Good Will Court* program. The sustaining program originated from New York City (60 min., Friday, 9:00–10:00 P.M., WHN, New York, NY, 1939).

7 **Aaker, Tom.** Newscaster (KROC, Rochester, MN, 1960).

8 **Aalbu Sisters.** Veteran vaudeville singing team, Vera and Aileen, were radio pioneers (WCCO, Minneappolis–St. Paul, MN, 1925).

9 **Aanderson, Bob.** Sports (*The Sports Show*, WNOP, Newport, KY, 1960).

10 **Aaroe, Alden.** Newscaster (WCHV, Charlottesville, VA, 1939–1941).

11 **Aaronson, Irving.** Orchestra leader (*Irving Aaronson and his Commanders*, KFWB, Hollywood, CA, 1929; *Irving Aaronson Orchestra*, NBC, 1935; WOR , Newark, NJ, 1936; WOR, 1942).

12 **Abaray, John.** DJ (WBIS, Bristol, CT, 1960).

13 **Abas, Nathan.** Director, Nathan Abas's Hotel Pennsylvania Orchestra (WJZ, New York, NY, 1925). Violin soloist (KPO, San Francisco, CA, 1927).

14 **Abas String Quartet.** Instrumental group including Nathan Abas, violinist; Julian Brodetzky, violinist; Michel Penha, cellist; Roman Joseph Verney, viola (KPO, San Francisco, CA, 1929).

15 **Abbe, James.** Newscaster (KWYO, Sheridan, WY, 1940–1941; KGW, Portland, OR, 1944; *James Abbe Observes*, KGO, San Francisco, CA, 1946–1947; *James Abbe Observes the News*, KSJO, San Jose, CA, 1949).

16 **Abbey, Eleanor.** Actress in the *Aunt Jenny* daytime serial.

17 **Abbey, Jean.** COM-HE (*Shopping Talk,* 15 min., Monday, 9:00–9:15 A.M., WJR, Detroit, MI, 1935).

18 **Abbott, Ade.** Sportscaster (KGAR, Tucson, AZ, 1938–1939).

19 **Abbott, Betty.** "Girl baritone" (KHJ, Los Angeles, CA, 1925).

20 **Abbott, Bill.** Announcer (WMBD, Peoria, IL, 1925).

21 **Abbott, Bob.** DJ (*1480 Club*, KAUS, Austin, MN, 1948–1952; KMMT Austin, MN, 1955. Newscaster: KMMT, 1955).

22 **Abbott, Bud.** DJ (*Abbott Habit*, WHAS Louisville, KY, 1949).

23 **Abbott, Carroll.** Sportscaster (KERV, Kerrville, TX, 1956).

24 **Abbott, Dotty.** COM-HE (KIMO, Independence, MO, 1955–1958).

25 **Abbott, Ed.** Newscaster (WCCO, Minneapolis, MN, 1939).

26 **Abbott, George.** Sportscaster (*Speaking of Sports*, KOLN, Lincoln, NE, 1949).

27 **Abbott, George.** DJ (KDFM, Beaumont, TX, 1960).

28 **Abbott, Grace.** Miss Abbott broadcast talks for mothers on her *Your Child* program (WJZ, New York, NY, 1927).

29 **Abbott, Gregory.** Newscaster (WINS, New York, NY, 1942).

30 **Abbott, Jim.** DJ (*Money for Music*, KFDA, Amarillo, TX, 1954. Newscaster (KTVT Dallas-Fort Worth, TX, 1960). Sportscaster (KFDA, 1954).

31 **Abbott, Judith.** Newscaster (WNEW, New York, NY, 1938).

32 **Abbott, Nellie G.** Violinist (WFI, Philadelphia, PA, 1923).

33 **Abbott, Tom.** Newscaster (WNOE, New Orleans, LA, 1946; WJMR, New Orleans, LA, 1952–1954). DJ (*1450 Radio Row*, WNOE, 1948).

34 Abbott, Walt. DJ (*Morning Varieties*, KCSB San Bernardino, CA, 1952; *Sentimental Journey*, KFOX , Long Beach, CA, 1954).

35 *(The) Abbott and Costello Show*. The ex-vaudeville and burlesque team of Bud Abbott and Lou Costello survived and flourished during the age of radio and television. They also starred in numerous motion pictures, often doing little more than repeating their old vaudeville routines. One of the typical burlesque gags they used was:

> LOU: Where do all the little bugs go?
> BUD: Search me.

The boys began working as a team in 1936. They made their radio debut on the *Kate Smith Show* in 1938 and continued appearing there through 1940, when their own show first appeared as a summer replacement. It became a network feature in 1942.

They introduced their famous "Who's on First?" routine in 1938, a routine they had used years before on stage. Costello's trademark was his plaintive call: "H-e-y-y Abb-ott." Writers for the program were: Ed Cherkose, Paul Conlan, Pat Costello, Don Pringle, Martin A. Ragaway and Len Stern. The orchestras that performed on their NBC program were led by Will Osborne, Leith Stevens and Skinnay Ennis, featuring such vocalists as Marilyn Maxwell and Connie Haines. Ken Niles was the announcer. Sound effects were produced by Floyd Caton (30 min., ABC and NBC, 1940–1949). On their ABC program, they featured vocalist Susan Miller and the Matty Malneck Orchestra. Michael Roy was the announcer.

36 *(The) Abbott and Costello Kids Show*. Abbott and Costello hosted the Saturday morning program for children. Young talent appeared on the program that also included quizzes and games (30 min., Saturday A.M., ABC, 1947–1949).

37 *(The) Abbott Mysteries*. Helbros Watch Company sponsored the mystery program that *Variety* called a weak imitation of *The Thin Man*. Adapted from the "Pat Abbott" novels of Frances Crane, Howard Merrill wrote the radio scripts and Roger Bower directed the program. The program began as Helbros' summer replacement for *Quick as a Flash* on MBS. When the program returned to the air on NBC in 1954, it was renamed *The Adventures of the Abbotts*. Chuck Webster and Julie Stevens were the first to play Pat Abbott, a smart-aleck private detective and his wife, Jean, who managed each week to bicker their way to the successful solution of a murder mystery. Les Tremayne and Alice Reinheart later played the title roles. Also in the cast were: Elspeth Eric, Ted Osborne, Jean Ellyn, Luis Van Rooten, Sidney Slon and Louis Sorin. Music was supplied by Albert Burhman's orchestra. Cy Harrice was the announcer (30 min., P.M., MBS and NBC).

38 Abbott Worsted Band. Commercially sponsored band (WEEI, Boston, MA, 1925).

39 *Abbott's Radio Star Revue*. Baritone Martin Bills and operatic soprano Josephine Lucchese appeared weekly on the music program sponsored by Abbott's Diaries. Arthur Morgan was the announcer (15 min., Monday, 7:45–8:00 P.M., KYW, Philadelphia, PA, 1936).

40 *ABC Safety Club*. The program, intended for children ages three to twelve, sought to teach the need for safety. Emphasis was placed on watching out for traffic on the way to school, not playing with matches and avoiding scalding hot water from the faucet (KVOO, Tulsa, OK, 1927).

41 Abdou, Gloria. COM-HE (WCAE, Pittsburgh, PA, 1956–1957).

42 *(The) Abe Burrows Show*. Versatile comedian-writer-composer Burrows was featured on the 15-minute comedy program. The talented Burrows mixed his funny commentary with performances of his own compositions. He performed his comedy routines and sang his song creations accompanied by the Milton DeLugg Quartet. The program ran for only 29 weeks (15 min., P.M., CBS, 1948).

43 Abee, James. Newscaster (KGW-KEX, Portland, OR, 1942).

44 Abel, Chuck. DJ (*Tuneville Trolley*, KAMD, Camden, AR, 1955).

45 Abel, Thelma. Soprano (WEMC, Barrien Springs, MI, 1925).

46 Abele, Dorothy. Vocalist (*Dorothy Abele*, vcl. mus. program, WMBD, Peoria, IL, 1936).

47 Abell, Fran. DJ (*G.A. Bargain Show*, KBOX, Modesto, CA, 1952; KMOD, Modesto, CA, 1954).

48 Abell, Mike. DJ (*Sunday Serenade*, WLBN, Lebanon, KY, 1960).

49 Abell, O.L. Announcer (WWL, New Orleans, LA, 1925).

50 Abeloff, Irvin G. Newscaster (WRVA, Richmond, VA, 1937–1938).

51 Abels, Ed. Newscaster (*Comments on Local Affairs*, KLWN, Lawrence, KS, 1952–1955). DJ (KLWN, 1955).

52 Abels, Richard. Newscaster (WPAR, Parkersburg, WV, 1941).

53 Aber, E.D. Announcer (WMBH, Joplin, MO, 1925).

54 Abercrombie, (Mrs.) C.W. Organist-pianist (KMA, Shenandoah, IA, 1928).

55 Abergh's Concert Ensemble. Popular radio group (WLS, Chicago, IL, mid–1920s).

56 Abernathy, Helen. COM-HE (WKSR, Pulaski, TN, 1957).

57 Abernathy, Matsy. COM-HE (WEEB, Southern Pines, NC, 1954).

58 Abernethy, Robert. Newscaster (*News on the Hour*, NBC, 1950).

59 Abeyta, Vergie. COM-HE (KGGM, Albuquerque, NM, 1956–1957).

60 *Abie's Irish Rose*. The situation comedy sponsored by Drene shampoo was first broadcast in 1942. It was based on the popular, long-running Broadway play by the same name written by Anne Nichols. The premise and the basis for most of its humor was the courtship and marriage of a Jewish boy with an Irish Catholic girl. Sidney Smith and Betty Winkler originated the roles of Abie and his Rosemary. Actors who appeared on the program were: Bill Adams, Charme Allen, Anna Appel, Joe Boland, Richard Bond, Clayton "Bud" Collyer, Richard Coogan, Paul Douglas, Carl Eastman, Florence Freeman, Dolores Gillen, Walter Kinsella, Mercedes McCambridge, Amanda Randolph, Alan Reed (Teddy Bergman), Marion Shockley, Menasha Skulnik, Sydney Smith, Julie Stevens, Fred Sullivan, Ann Thomas, Marion White and Betty Winkler. The writer was Morton Friedman. The directors were Joe Rines and Rip Van Runkle. Paul Douglas was the announcer (30 min., Saturday, 8:00–8:30 P.M., NBC-Red, New York, NY, 1942).

61 Abiowich [Ablowich], Jr., Dave. Announcer (KFPM, Greenville, TX, 1926).

62 Ableman, Berwyn. Sportscaster (WPDR, Portage, WA, 1953). Newscaster (WPDR, 1960). DJ (WPDR, 1955).

63 "ABN." Designation for Bertha Brainard, announcer at WJZ in the early 1920s. It was during this period that announcers were known only as initials, not always their own. When listeners inquired as to the identify of announcers, they might receive a letter such as that typically sent by WHAS, Louisville, KY (Harris, 1937, p. 86).

> Dear Madam:
> It is against the rules of this radio station to divulge the name of our announcer.
> With deep regret, I am — —.

See **Brainard, Bertha.**

64 Abner, A.K. Newscaster (*Round Town Reporter*, KFJI, Klamath Falls, OR, 1954).

65 Aborbasell, Lisa. Miss Aborbasell was an opera star who appeared on the *Edison Hour Program* (WRNY, New York, NY, 1926).

66 Abramchik, William. Newscaster (WEDC, Chicago, IL, 1944).

67 Abramo, Joe. Leader (*Joe Abramo's Strings*, mus. prg., WHDH, Boston, MA, 1939).

68 Abrams, Jr., Al. Newscaster (WEDO, McKeesport, PA, 1957).

69 Abrams, Irwin. Leader-violinist (Irwin Abram's Band broadcasting from New York's Hotel Manger in 1927). Abram's band was a popular recording orchestra whose personnel included: Julian Hess, t.; Louis Harmin, tb.; Les Crumbacher, Otto Tucker and James Imberman, ts.; Jules Towers and Glenn Wakeman, clr.; Fred Bilotti, violin; Elliott Jacoby, p.; Joe Fellini, bj.; Albert R. Smith, tba.; and Fred Bauer, d.

70 Abrams, Morrie. Vocalist billed as *Maurice, The Singer of Romance* on his vcl. mus. prg. (NBC, 1935).

71 Abrams, Terry. Sportscaster (WHIM, Bloomsburg, PA, 1956).

72 Abramson, Mildred J. COM-HE (WROW, Albany, NY, 1960).

73 Abrens, Walter. Baritone (*Walter Abrens*, vcl. mus. prg., WOR, Newark, NJ, 1934).

74 Abromavich, Karin. DJ (*Coffee with Karin*, WTCN, Minneapolis, MN, 1949).

75 *Absorbine Jr. Setting-Up Exercise Program*. Robert Burdette conducted the exercise program appropriately sponsored by Absorbine Jr., a product for sore muscles (WLW, Cincinnati, OH, 1930).

76 (The) Abundant Life Mixed Chorus. The vocal group directed by John Henry Bodkin appeared on the *Operatic Night* programs (KOA, Denver, CO, 1925).

77 Accoke [Accola], Dorothy. COM-HE

(KASL, Newcastle, WY, 1956). DJ (KASL, 1960).

78 ***Accordiona.*** Phillips Dental Magnesia tooth paste sponsored the music program that featured soprano Vivienne Segal, tenor Oliver Smith and the Abe Lyman Orchestra (30 min., Tuesday, 8:30–9:00 P.M., CBS, 1934).

79 Ace, Goodman. Comedian-writer Ace was born Jan 15, 1899. He worked twelve years as a reporter, drama critic and columnist for the Kansas City *Journal Post.* A radio version of his column was broadcast as *The Movie Man* over a Kansas City station. A year later he originated the *Easy Aces* program. *see* ***Easy Aces***

80 Acevedo, Francisco. Newscaster (WKAQ, San Juan, PR, 1939–1942; WORA, Mayaguez, PR, 1948–1949).

81 Achor, Dave. Newscaster (WBIJ, Dalton, GA, 1941; WCHI, Chillicothe, OH, 1957). DJ (*Plow Jockey*, WBEX, Chillicothe, OH, 1954). Sportscaster (*Sportsman*, WBEX, 1953).

82 Ackerly, Gene. Newscaster (KID, Idaho Falls, ID, 1944; KFRE, Fresno, CA, 1947). Sportscaster (KID, 1945).

83 Ackerly, Robert J. "Bob." Newscaster (KGO, San Francisco, CA, 1938; KGO and KPO, San Francisco, CA, 1939; KJR, Seattle, WA, 1939; and KXA, Seattle, WA, 1951–1952). DJ (KOMO, Seattle, WA, 1955).

84 Ackerman, Al. Sportscaster (*Sports Notebook*, WHTC, Holland, MI, 1953; *Looking at Sports*, WHTC, 1954; WOOD, Grand Rapids, MI, 1956–1960).

85 Ackerman, Bernice. Soprano (*Bernice Ackerman,* voc. mus. prg., WOR, Newark, NJ, 1936).

86 Ackerman's Orchestra. Local band (WOAW, Omaha, NE, 1923).

87 Ackley, Howard. Chief announcer (WOWO, Fort Wayne, IN and WGL, Fort Wayne, IN, 1928.) Ackley began work as a bookkeeper for the Main Auto Supply Company of Fort Wayne, the owner of both WOWO and WGL. His first broadcasting career step occurred when he was forced to make an emergency announcement about a lost dog on station WOWO.

88 Ackley, Mildred H. Pianist (WIP, Philadelphia, PA, 1926).

89 Ackley, Wayne. Newscaster (KSO, Des Moines, IA, 1940–1941).

90 Ackroyd, June. Soprano on the *Nite Caps on Lake Erie* program (WJAX, Cleveland, OH, 1924).

91 Ackroyd, Lorraine. COM-HE (KGFL, Roswell, NM, 1951).

92 ***Acme Sunshine Melodies.*** Acme White Lead and Color Works sponsored the music program that featured singing star, Smiling Ed McConnell. McConnell was supported by organist Irma Glen and Palmer Clark's Orchestra (30 min., Sunday, 4:30–5:00 P.M. C.S.T., WMAQ, Chicago, IL, 1936).

93 Acosta, Joseph. Leader (*Joseph Acosta Orchestra,* instr. mus. prg., WCAO, Baltimore, MD, 1936; WCAO, 1942).

94 ***(The) Acousticon Hour.*** The quality light concert music program was sponsored by Dictaphone, It was a 30-minute network show (30 min., Sunday, 5:30–6:00 P.M., NBC, 1927–1928).

95 Acree, Jimmy. DJ (WAGF, Dothan, AL, 1949; *The Wax Works*, WAGF, 1954).

96 Actor, Allen. DJ (WHIY, Orlando, FL, 1957).

97 Acuff, Roy. CW musician and leader (*Roy Acuff and the Smokey Mountain Boys*, CW mus. prg, WSM, Nashville, TN, 1938). Acuff was a leading performer on *the Grand Ole Opry* for many years, where he gained national prominence. Before gaining fame on the *Grand Ole Opry*, Acuff began working with such CW musicians as Pete Kirby and Lonnie Wilson, both of whom continued to play with him for years. Their group broadcast frequently on Nashville, TN, stations WROH and WNOX. Although rebuffed by George D. Hay on his first attempt to join the *Opry*, he eventually gained acceptance and great popularity on the program with his rendition of "The Great Speckled Bird." Acuff eventually starred in such networks segment of the *Opry* as the *Prince Albert Show* and the *Royal Crown Program. See* ***The Grand Ole Opry***

98 Adair, Alyce. COM-HE (WCLI, Corning, NY, 1956–1957).

99 Adair, Billy. Leader (Billy Adair's Orchestra., WDAF, Kansas City, MO, 1926).

100 Adair, Frances. Soprano (*Frances Adair,* vcl. mus. prg., NBC, 1935 and 1938).

101 Adair, James. Violinist (KOA, Denver, CO, 1926).

102 Adair, Peggy. Singer (WPCH, New York, NY, 1932).

103 Adair, Robert. Sportscaster (WPMT, Portland, ME, 1954).

104 Adair, Sam. Announcer (WOQ, Kansas City, MO, 1924).

105 Adams, Archie. DJ (*Platter Chatter*, WTWA, Thomson, GA, 1952).

106 Adams, Ben. Newscaster (WOV, New York, NY, 1940).

107 Adams, Bernie. DJ (*Musical Clock*, WPDQ, Jacksonville, FL, 1948; WJAX, Jacksonville, FL, 1955). Newscaster (WJAX, Jacksonville, FL, 1955).

108 Adams, Bette. COM-HE (WKEI, Kewanee, IL, 1955).

109 Adams, Bill. Actor Adams appeared in *Abie's Irish Rose*, *Adventures of Mortimer Meek*, *Big Town*, *The Career of Alice Blair*, *Cavalcade of America*, *The Collier Hour*, *The Gibson Family*, *Let's Pretend*, *The Light of the World*, *The March of Time*, *Pepper Young's Family*, *Rosemary* and *The Story of Mary Marlin* programs.

110 Adams, Bill. Sportscaster (KGW, Portland, OR and KEX, Portland, OR, 1937–1939; *Ice Hockey*, KWJJ, Portland, OR, 1947). Newscaster (*Farm Reporter*, KGO, San Francisco, CA, 1952).

111 Adams, Bob. Newscaster (KMPC, Los Angeles, CA, 1946).

112 Adams, Carol. COM-HE (WHBC, Canton, OH, 1956–1957).

113 Adams, Cedric. Newscaster (WCCO, Minneapolis, MN, 1937–1942, 1952; CBS, 1953; WCCO, 1957–1960).

114 Adams, Charles "Chuck." DJ (*Sunrise Salute*, WTAN, Clearwater, FL, 1952–1955; *Morning Show*, WAZE, Clearwater, FL, 1960).

115 Adams, Charles F. Newscaster (WMVA, Martinsville, VA, 1942–1947; *Charles F. Adams and the News*, WMVA, 1948, 1955). DJ (WHEE, Martinsville, VA, 1955).

116 Adams, Charlotte. COM-HE (*Charlotte Adams,* a local homemaking show, 15 min., WOR, Newark, NJ, 1948).

117 Adams, Clara Acuff. Soprano (KOA, Denver, CO, 1925).

118 Adams, Clarence. Newscaster (KBTM, Jonesboro, AK, 1938; *Arkansas Traveler*, KBTM, 1948; *Morning Herald*, KBTM, 1953–1955). DJ (KBTM, 1955).

119 Adams, Cliff. Newscaster (KYSM, Mankato, MN, 1960).

120 Adams, Dana. DJ (*990 Club*, KFDX, Wichita Falls, TX, 1947; *Club 600*, KTBB, Tyler, TX, 1948).

121 Adams, Deborah. COM-HE (WFIL, Philadelphia, PA, 1956).

122 Adams, Dr. Talked about canines on his *Dog Talk* program (WLW, Cincinnati, OH, 1928).

123 Adams, Don. Newscaster (KVOD, Denver, CO, 1957).

124 Adams, Dorothy. Contralto (WAAF, Chicago, IL, 1935).

125 Adams, Eddie. DJ (*Clock Spinner*, WDAR, Savannah, GA, 1952).

126 Adams, Edith. Actress in the *Today's Children* and *Those Happy Gilmans* programs,

127 Adams, Edna. Singer billed as "The Sweetheart of the Air" (KPRC, Houston, TX, 1926).

128 Adams, Elinor Riggs. Soprano (KOIL, Council Bluffs, IA, 1927).

129 Adams, Evangeline. Astrologer Adams broadcast weekly "horoscope talks" (1929). She was sponsored by Forhan's toothpaste in 1931. For those listeners who sent in a toothpaste box top, their birth date and a description of their personal problem, Adams would provide them with advice on how to solve it. Adams was one of the country's most successful astrologers. David Ross was the announcer on her 1931 CBS program, which was said to produce more mail than any other in the country. No radio astrologer, it was said, approached Evangeline Adams' popularity. *See* ***Evangeline Adams.***

130 Adams, Felix. Sportscaster (WIBC, Indianapolis, IN, 1942). Newscaster (WHOT, South Bend, IN, 1945).

131 Adams, Frank. Sportscaster (WNHC, New Haven, CT, 1948).

132 Adams, (Mrs.) Fred Winslow. Singer (WBZ, Boston-Springfield, MA, 1924).

133 Adams, Garret. Newscaster (WRJN, Racine, WI, 1941).

134 Adams, Georgia. COM-HE (WMFG, Hibbing, MN, 1955)

135 Adams, Glen. Sports (*Hudiphone Sports Column*, WMRC, Greenville, SC, 1940).

136 Adams, Guila. Actress Adams played **Dorothy Dix** and provided advice to the lovelorn (WMAQ, Chicago, IL, 1928). She also appeared on the *Stepmother* daytime serial.

137 **Adams, Harry.** Newscaster (WWRL, Woodside, NY, 1939).

138 **Adams, Hazel.** COM-HE (WKAI, Macomb, IL, 1958).

139 **Adams, Helen.** COM-HE (*It's Fun to Keep House* or *Let's Help You Keep House).* Home economist Adams tried to do the convincing and helping (15 min., Wednesday, 1:00–1:15 P.M. CST, KWK, St. Louis, MO, 1939–1940).

140 **Adams, Henry.** Newscaster (KTIM, San Raphael, CA, 1948).

141 **Adams, Inga [Inge].** Actress Adams appeared on *Ellen Randolph* aka *The Story of Ellen Randolph* and the *Our Gal Sunday* daytime serial.

142 **Adams, (Mrs.) J. Homer.** Contralto (WBAP, Fort Worth, TX, 1928).

143 **Adams, Jerry.** Newscaster (WIMA, Lima, OH, 1955). DJ (WIMA, 1955).

144 **Adams, Jim.** DJ (*The Jim Adams Show,* WNOP, Newport, KY, 1952).

145 **Adams, Jim.** DJ (*The Nite Club of the Air,* WSTV, Steubenville, OH, 1952; *Daybreaker,* WSTV, 1954).

146 **Adams, Jim.** Sportscaster (KWWL, Waterloo, IA, 1960).

147 **Adams, Joan (Joan Whitehead).** Whitehead dispensed movie gossip as "Joan Adams" on her *Hollywood Sketchbook* program (WEEI, Boston, MA, 1941).

148 **Adams, Joe.** DJ (KOWL, Los Angeles, CA, 1949; *Mayor of Melody,* KOWL, 1952–1955).

149 **Adams, John.** Newscaster (CBS, 1944; WTOP, Washington, DC, 1946–1947; CBS, 1947–1948.

150 **Adams, Johnnie.** Vocalist (*Johnnie Adams,* vcl. mus. prg., KMOX, St. Louis, MO, 1936).

151 **Adams, Johnny.** Sportscaster (WQQW, Washington, DC, 1947).

152 **Adams, Julia D.** COM-HE (WGCD, Chester, SC, 1951).

153 **Adams, Kay.** COM-HE (WQUA, Moline, IL, 1954–1955).

154 **Adams, Larry.** Sportscaster (WVJS, Owensboro, KY, 1955).

155 **Adams, Lee [Lew].** Leader (*Lee Adams Orchestra,* instr. mus. prg., KARK, Little Rock, AR, 1939).

156 **Adams, Leslie.** Announcer (KFI, Los Angeles, CA, 1928).

157 **Adams, Loretta.** Soprano (*Loretta Adams,* vcl. mus. prg., WPG, Atlantic City, NJ, 1935- 1936).

158 **Adams, Louise.** COM-HE (WCMB, Harrisburg, PA, 1956).

159 **Adams, Marion.** Contralto (WOR, Newark, NJ, 1925).

160 **Adams, Mary.** Pianist (WHAS, Louisville, KY, 1923).

161 **Adams, Mason.** Actor Adams appeared on the *Big Sister, Gasoline Alley* and *Pepper Young's Family* programs.

162 **Adams, Merry.** COM-HE (KNDC, Hettinger, ND, 1956).

163 **Adams, Norris "Norey."** Sportscaster (KVOS, Bellingham, WA, 1945; KGY, Olympia, WA, 1947; *Sports of the Day with NA,* KPUG, Bellington, WA, 1950–1952).

164 **Adams, Opal.** COM-HE (WMBC, Macon, MS, 1954).

165 **Adams, Ron.** Newscaster (KVOD, Denver, CO, 1957).

166 **Adams, Ruth.** COM-HE (WSKI, Montpelier-Barre, VT, 1960).

167 **Adams, Sally.** COM-HE (*Sally Adams at the Market,* WHB, Kansas City, MO, 1941).

168 **Adams, Tony.** Sportscaster (*Tony Adams' Roundup,* WMUR, Manchester, NH, 1947; *Headlines in News and Sports,* WMUR, 1949; *Sports Extra,* WFDF, Flint, MI, 1950; *Sports Tonight,* WCAX, Burlington, VT, 1951–1956.

169 **Adams, Van.** Sportscaster (*Sports* and *High School Hi Lites,* KMIX, Portageville, MO, 1960).

170 **Adams, W. Clarence.** Newscaster (KBTM, Jonesboro, AR, 1946, 1957).

171 **Adams, Wally.** Sportscaster (WAGA, Atlanta, GA, 1937).

172 **Adams, Ward.** Newscaster (WRVA, Richmond, VA, 1937–1938).

173 **Adams, Warren.** DJ (*Hillbilly Hits,* WIHL, Hammond, LA, 1952).

174 **Adams, Wesley "Wes."** Sportscaster (*Sports Show,* WKRT, Cortland, NY, 1954). DJ (WKRT, 1955).

175 **Adams, William.** Actor-announcer Adams was born May 9, 1987. His first radio appearance was on *Collier's Radio Hour,* where he originated the character of "Uncle Henry," a role he played on the program for six-and-a-half years from 1926 to 1932. He also acted on the *Wayside Cottage* serial drama broadcast by CBS in 1929.

176 **Adams, William.** Newscaster (WDAN, Danville, IL, 1939).

177 **Adamson, Ernie.** Newscaster (WGBB, Freeport, NY, 1939–1940).

178 **Adamson, Norma.** COM-HE (KWIK, Pocatello, ID, 1951).

179 **Adamson, Shirley.** COM-HE (KAFY, Bakersfield, CA, 1955).

180 **Adcock, Sue.** COM-HE (WKCT, Bowling Green, KY, 1951).

181 **Addington, (Mrs.) Blanche.** Singer (KWSC, Pullman, WA, 1926).

182 **Addington, Don.** DJ (*Sandman Serenade,* WHTB, Talladega, AL, 1954).

183 **Addington, Harold.** Newscaster (*Roundup of Editorial Opinion,* KFKU, Lawrence, KS, 1947).

184 **Ade, George.** American author-humorist (WJZ, New York, NY, 1925).

185 **Adell, Ray.** DJ (*Journey into Melody,* WGSM, Huntington, NY, 1954–1955).

186 **Adelman, Lisa.** DJ (WSET, Glen Falls, NY, 1960).

187 **Adelman, Pat.** Sportscaster (KNOW, Austin, TX, 1942).

188 **Adelphia Hotel Dinner Dance Orchestra.** Hotel dance orchestra (WOO, Philadelphia, PA, 1926).

189 **Adelson, James (Jim).** Sportscaster (KCJB, Minot, ND, 1952; *Today in Sports,* KCJB, 1953).

190 **Adelstein, Vera.** Pianist (KJBS, San Francisco, CA, 1925).

191 **Ademy, John.** Baritone-Bass (*John Ademy,* voc. mus. prg., WCAO, Baltimore, MD, 1936).

192 **Aders, Edna M.** COM-HE (WLSI, Pikeville, KY, 1956–1957).

193 **Adkins, Alice.** Soprano (KFXF, Colorado Springs, CO, 1926).

194 **Adkins, Denise.** COM-HE (KMAE, McKinney, TX, 1951).

195 **Adkins, Bob.** DJ (*1420 Favorites,* WVOT, Wilson, NC, 1960).

196 **Adkins, Gales M.** Newscaster (WSAT, Salisbury, NC, 1953).

197 **Adkins, John.** Newscaster (WETB, Johnson City, TN, 1952).

198 **Adkins, Robert D. "Bob."** DJ (*Western Requests,* KLER, Lewiston, ID, 1954; KNEW, Spokane, WA, 1957–1960).

199 **Adkins, Spritter.** Sportscaster (WRVA, Richmond, VA, 1937).

200 **Adlam, Barbara.** COM-HE (WKEN, Dover, DE, 1960).

201 **Adlam, Buzz.** Leader (*Buzz Adlam Orchestra,* instr. mus. prg., Network, 1935).

202 **Adler, Clarence.** Pianist, a member of the New York Trio (WNYC, New York, NY, 1925).

203 **Adler, Henry.** Leader (Henry Adler Orchestra, WFAA, Dallas, TX, 1925).

204 **Adler, Jessie.** Adler broadcast talks on such topics as "A Lawyer's Argument in Favor of Home Budgets" (WLW, Cincinnati, OH, 1925–1926).

205 **Adler, Lou.** Sportscaster (WESB, Bradford, PA, 1956).

206 **Adler, Stella.** Actress Adler appeared on the *John's Other Wife* daytime serial.

207 ***Admiral Richard E. Byrd Antarctica Expedition.*** See **Byrd Antarctica Expedition.**

208 **Admire, Margaret.** Singer (*Margaret Admire,* vcl. mus. prg., WJBC, Bloomington, IN, 1936).

209 **Admon, Yedidyah.** Baritone (WBAL, Baltimore, MD, 1926).

210 **Adolph, Katherine.** Soprano (KGCP, New York, NY, 1926).

211 **Adolph and Rudolph.** The comic team of Adolph (Ned Becker) and Rudolph (Bill Doyle) appeared on the *KYW Follies* program (KYW, Chicago, IL, 1927).

212 **Adolphus Hotel Orchestra.** Band that broadcast from the Adolphus Hotel, Dallas, Texas, (WFAA, Dallas, TX, 1923–1925).

213 **Adonis, Harold John.** Singer-announcer (*Michaels Department Store Program, Celebrity Hour,* WNEW, New York, NY, 1937; WHOM, Jersey City, NJ, 1938).

214 **Adrian, Vic.** DJ (*Man About Manhattan,* WQBC, Vicksburg, MS, 1949).

215 **Adrienne.** Singer (WNEW, New York, NY, 1939).

216 ***Adventure Stories for Boys.*** Fred J. Turner selected and told tales for boys (WEAF, New York, NY, 1924).

217 ***(The) Adventurer.*** ABC in cooperation with MacFadden Publications produced the sustaining dramatic adventure show based on stories that first appeared in MacFadden's *Adventure* magazine. Music was provided by Bobby Christian's Orchestra. Burgess Meredith, Barry Kroeger and Ralph Bell were in the cast. Don Wittig wrote and Warren Bryan produced the show (30 min., Sunday, 9:30–10:00 P.M., ABC, 1953).

218 ***(The) Adventurers' Club.*** True adventure stories were dramatized on the program sponsored by the Sheaffer Products company and produced in cooperation with the Adventurers Club of Chicago. The cast members were Roy Engel, Johnny Coons, Paul Barnes, Marianne Bertrand and Arthur Young. Ken Nordine was the announcer (30 min., Saturday, 11:30 A.M. to noon, CBS, 1946).

219 ***Adventures in Good Music.*** Ted Cassidy, later famous for his role on TV's *The Addams Family* program, acted as DJ on the fine music show broadcast five nights a week in the 50s (Pensacola, FL, 1959).

220 ***Adventures in Travel.*** Henry Mico delivered talks on the sustaining program about the thrills and pleasures of travel (Wednesday, 10:45–11:00 P.M., WINS, New York, NY, 1949).

221 ***Adventures in Words.*** Dr. Frank Vizetelly, Dictionary Editor at Funk and Wagnall, told interesting tales that provided fascinating information about words (15 min., Tuesday, 5:15–5:30 P.M., WABC, New York, NY, 1931).

222 ***(The) Adventures of Captain Diamond.*** Burr Cook wrote and Lester O'Keefe produced the dramatic adventure series sponsored by Diamond Crystal Salt Company. Al Swenson and Florence Malone played the roles of Captain and Mrs. Diamond. Tiny Ruffner and Howard Claney were the program's announcers. First broadcast in 1932, the format had the program's announcer visiting Captain and Mrs. Diamond at their light house residence. The Captain would then tell his weekly story (30 min., Sunday, 3:00–3:30 P.M., NBC-Blue, 1936).

223 ***(The) Adventures of Casanova.*** Even Errol Flynn in the title role failed to lift the dramatic series above the level of the average adventure program. William Robson wrote, produced and directed the program. Music was supplied by Walter Schumann (30 min., Thursday, 8:00–8:30 P.M., MBS, 1952).

224 ***(The) Adventures of Dr. Doolittle.*** The 15-minute daytime children's serial program was based on the Dr. Doolittle stories of Hugh Loftus (Transcribed, 15 min., Tuesday & Thursday, 5:30–5:45 P.M.).

225 ***(The) Adventures of Frank Merriwell.*** The exploits of Frank Merriwell, the fictional creation of author Phil Strong, formed the basis for the dramatic serial for children. Lawson Zerbe, Jean Gillespie, Harold Studer and Al Hodge were in the cast (30 min., Saturday, 10:00–10:30 A.M., NBC-Red, New York, NY, 1946).

226 ***(The) Adventures of Frank Race.*** Buckley Angell wrote and Joel Murcott produced the transcribed dramatic adventure series loosely based on the life of adventurer Frank Race. Tom Collins played the title role on the program that unfortunately never provided the excitement a good adventure series needed to attract listeners (30 min., Saturday, 10:00–10:30 P.M., WINS, New York, NY, 1949).

227 ***(The) Adventures of Helen and Mary.*** An early serial drama for children (30 min., Saturday, 12:00–12:30 P.M., CBS, 1929).

228 ***(The) Adventures of Judge Quaker State.*** Quaker State Oil Company sponsored the weekly daytime serial that told the story of a genial old judge played by John Ince (KFAC, Los Angeles, CA, 1932).

229 ***(The) Adventures of Maisie.*** Ann Sothern played the role of secretary Maisie Revere, whose funny escapades made this a popular show. Written by Arthur Phillips and John L. Green, the music was provided by Harry Zimmerman. In addition to Sothern, the cast included: Lurene Tuttle, Howard McNear, Gerald Mohr, Peter Leeds, William Conrad, Hans Conreid, Frank Nelson, Stanley Waxman, Herb Butterfield, Elvia Allman, Hal Gerard, Hy Averback, Bea Benadaret, Bob Cole, Will Wright, Sandra Gould, Sheldon Leonard, Joan Banks, Byron Kane, Edgar Barrier, Stanley Miller, Tommy Bernard, Griff Bernard, Sammy Hill, Ernest Whitman, Roy Glenn, GeGe Pearson, Arthur Q. Bryan, Marvin Miller, Earl Lee, Wally Maher, Pat McGeehan, John McGovern, Jerry Hausner, Barney Phillips, Henry Bartel, Isabel Randolph, Ed Macks, Donald Woods and Norman Fields (30 min., CBS & MBS, 1945–1952).

230 ***(The) Adventures of Mr. Meek.*** Lever Brothers Company sponsored the dramatic series that was virtually a reverse mirror image of *One Man's Family.* The program portrayed the life of a milquetoast, Mortimer Meek. Meek was played by Frank Readick and his wife by Adelaide Klein. Jack Smart and Doris Dudley also appeared as members of the Meek family (30 min., Wednesday, 7:30–8:00 P.M., WABC-CBS, 1940).

231 ***(The) Adventures of Philip Marlowe.*** Pepsodent Toothpaste sponsored the program that was originally broadcast as a summer replacement for the *Bob Hope Show* in 1947 on NBC. Van Heflin originated the role of Raymond Chandler's tough private eye on the exciting dramatic series. When the program went on the CBS regular schedule, Marlowe was played by Gerald Mohr. The program's writers were Gene Levitt and Robert Mitchell. Norman Macdonnell was the producer-director. Sound effects were produced by Clark Casey and Cliff Thorsness (30 min, P.M. weekly, NBC and CBS, 1947–1951. When Gerald Mohr played Marlowe the program began with him saying: "Get this and get it straight! Crime is a sucker's road and those who travel it wind up in the gutter, the prison or the grave." In a later version, the announcer followed this opening statement by saying: "From the pen of Raymond Chandler, outstanding author of crime fiction, comes his most famous character in *The Adventures of Philip Marlowe* ... now with Gerald Horn starring as Philip Marlowe we bring you tonight's transcribed story "The Headless Peacock."

232 ***(The) Adventures of Pinocchio.*** The quarter-hour transcribed serial program for children was based on the story of a puppet who turned into a mischievous little boy. Music was supplied by Paul Sawtelle.

233 ***(The) Adventures of Sam and Dick.*** Children's serial drama (15 min., Monday, 4:45–5:00 P.M., NBC).

234 ***(The) Adventures of Sonny and Buddy.*** The daytime children's serial told the story of two talented young singers who were kidnapped by a traveling medicine show operator. The operator's daughter, Beth, and Charcoal, a black helper, also appeared in the story. Sonny and Buddy performed in blackface as Rastus and Sambo, accompanied by Beth who played the piano with Charcoal on banjo. While traveling with the medicine show, the children experienced many adventures (Transcribed, 15 min., probably mid–1930s).

235 ***(The) Adventures of the Falcon.*** The program opened with the announcement: "Once again the National Broadcasting Company brings you *The Adventures of the Falcon* starring Les Damon. The transcribed *Adventures of the Falcon* are dedicated to private investigators everywhere, who, like Mike Waring, risk their lives to aid law enforcement agencies. So join him now when the Falcon solves *The Case of the Amorous Bookkeeper*" (30 min, 1950–1952). Originally introduced in a short story by Michael Arlen as Gay Stanhope Falcon, the main character's name was changed several times when he appeared in motion pictures and on radio. In the movies he was known as Gay Lawrence and Tom Lawrence. Tom took over the role of the Falcon when his brother, Gay, was killed. On the radio, however, he was known as Michael Waring. On the earlier programs he was introduced as "that freelance detective who's always ready with a hand for oppressed men and an eye for repressed women." The other actors who played the title role over the years were: Barry Kroeger, Les Damon, James Meighan, George Petrie and Les Tremayne. Music was provided by the orchestras of Emerson Buckley and Harry Sosnik and organist Bob Hamilton. Ross Dunbar and Ed Herlihy were the announcers. The program appeared on ABC, MBS and NBC at various times between 1943 and 1954.

236 ***Adventures with Stamps.*** Ernest A. Kehr and his guests talked about stamps and stamp collecting on the weekly sustaining program. Dick Bradley was the announcer (15 min., Tuesday, 9:00–9:15 P.M., WNEW, 1949).

237 **Aeolian Ensemble.** Musical group (*Aeolian Ensemble,* instr. mus. prg., CBS, 1939).

238 **Aeolian Quartet of the Kold and Dill Company.** Vocal group (KGY, Lacey, WA, 1922).

239 **Aeolian Trio.** Instrumental trio comprised of violinist Jeanete Rauhut, cellist Doris Eckler and pianist-organist Harriett Poole (KFWM, Oakland, CA, 1929).

240 **Aerial Serenaders.** Instrumental trio consisting of Minnie von Bremen, zither; Berthl Schaerberle, zither; and Carl Schaerberle, violin (KPO, San Francisco, CA, 1927).

241 **Aerials.** The Aerials were a popular male quartet that included tenors Eugene Dressler and Paul Mallory, baritone Fred Hunty and bass Frank Collins (WMAQ, Chicago, IL and WQJ, Chicago, IL, 1928).

242 ***(The) Affairs of Ann Scotland.*** Arlene Francis played the title role of Ann Scotland, a female detective who combined great personal charm with a breezy manner. The program was written by Barbara Owens and directed by Helen Mack. In addition to Francis, the cast included: Howard McNeer, David Ellis, Cathy Lewis and Howard Duff (30 min., Wednesday, 9:00–9:30 P.M., WJZ, New York, NY, 1946).

243 ***(The) Affairs of Peter Salem.*** Louis Vittes wrote the interesting sustaining program about a clever small town detective played by Santos Ortega. Also in the cast were Jack Grimes, Everett Sloane, Luis Van Rooten, Ann Sheperd and Jean Ellyn. The program was produced by Himan Brown and directed by Mende Brown. Adrian Penner produced the sound effects (30 min., Saturday, 2:30–3:00 P.M., MBS, 1949).

244 ***(The) Affairs of Roland.*** Romantic singer Harry Stockwell was featured on the program sponsored by Sensation (Calipygian) Corsets (15 min., Tuesday evening, WOR, Newark, NJ, 1935).

245 ***(The) Affairs of the Heart.*** Betsy Logan offered advice to lovelorn listeners on this program (WDAR, Philadelphia, PA, 1923).

246 ***(The) Affairs of Tom, Dick and Harry.*** Marlin Hurt along with Bud and Harry Vandover were a popular Chicago vocal trio. On the sustaining program the trio sang and presented clever comedy sketches. Guest female vocalists made regular appearances. Robert Trendler's orchestra provided the music (30 min., Monday, 9:30–10:00 P.M. C.S.T., MBS, 1941).

247 ***Affectionately Yours.*** Tenor Ken Ward, accompanied by organist Shirley Fenne , presented romantic songs on the local music program broadcast five times weekly (15 min., weekdays, 11:00–11:15 A.M., WTAM, Cleveland, OH, 1947).

248 **Affick, Mary.** Actress Affick appeared on the *Sue and Irene* daytime serial (WGN, Chicago, IL, 1930).

249 ***Afield with Ranger Mac.*** Ranger Mac, portrayed by Wakelin McNeel, conducted the program of nature lore and woodland stories for 17 years on WHA (Madison, WI).

250 **Afman, Fred.** Sportscaster (WMUU, Greenville, SC, 1952).

251 **Afriston, John.** Newscaster (*Observations*, KCSB, San Bernardino, CA, 1948).

252 **Afspung, William.** Reader (WLW, Cincinnati, OH, 1923).

253 ***(The) After TV Show.*** This show brings back memories of television's early days when television stations went off the air at midnight. The radio program supposedly was designed for those who had shut off their TV sets and wanted to listen to some pleasant cowboy-western music. Tex Ferguson and his western musical group provided that music (60 min., Saturday and Sunday, 12:00 midnight to 1:00 A.M., WOKO, Albany, NY, 1952).

254 ***(The) Afternoon News.*** Newscasters on the daily program were Wallace Fanning, Joseph McCaffrey, Les Higbe and Everett Holles (15 min., Weekdays, MBS, 1954).

255 ***Against the Storm.*** Sandra Michael wrote the Peabody Award winning daytime serial that began in 1939 on NBC. Sponsored by Procter & Gamble, the story was about Professor Jason Allen's attempts to warn of the danger of fascism. Shortly after winning the Peabody Award in 1942, the serial went off the air due to a dispute about program content. Roger De Koven played Professor Allen and May Seymour his wife in the first version of the program.

In 1949 when the program returned on MBS, it was sponsored by Phillip Morris cigarettes. This time the story was about Professor Allen and the struggle of liberal faculty members against the conservatives at the college at which he taught. When the program returned for still a third time in 1951, once again it was sponsored by Phillip Morris. This time the program was carried by ABC and told the story of Allen, a professor of English, beginning employment at a new college. His problems were both academic and domestic, as he worried about his daughter's romantic life and his colleagues' antics. Members of the cast over the years included: Joan Alexander, Leslie Bingham, Sarah Burton, Philip Clarke, Edward Corben, Roger DeKoven, Alan Devitt, Jane Erskine, Delores Gillian, Charlotte Holland, Mona Hungerford, Mary Hunter, Rex Ingram, Michael Ingram, Lenore Kingston, Florence Malone, Ian Martin, Ruth Matteson, Eddie Mayehoff, James Meighan, James Monks, Claudia Morgan, Arnold Moss, Ethel Waite Owen, William Quinn, Katherine Raht, Elliott Reid, Alexander Scourby, Anne Seymour, May Davenport, Robert Shayne, Lotte Stavsky, Chester Stratton, Joan Tompkins, Walter Vaughn, Sam Wanamaker, Gertrude Warner, and Lawson Zerbe. The announcers were Nelson Case, Ralph Edwards and Richard Stark. Gifted Sandra Michael was the writer and Axel Gruenberg the director (15 min, NBC, MBS and ABC).

256 **Agard, Frederick.** Tenor (WEBH, Chicago, IL, 1924 and WHT, Chicago, IL, 1925).

257 ***Agatha Christie's Poirot.*** Poirot, Christie's famous Belgian detective, was presented in the half-hour mystery program (30 min., Thursday, 8:30–9:00 P.M., MBS, 1945). An interesting feature was the introduction of each program by Agatha Christie via shortwave from London (30 min., Thursday, 8:30–9:00 P.M., MBS, 1945). Sometimes the program is referred to simply as *Hercule Poirot.*

258 **Agee, Bob.** Newscaster (WBIR, Knoxville, TN, 1953). DJ (WBIR, 1954–1955).

259 **Agee, Jewell.** Pianist on experimental station 5 ACW (Fort Smith, AR, 1922).

260 **Agee, Olivia.** Violinist who also performed on the Fort Smith, Arkansas, experimental station, 5 ACW in 1922.

261 **Agee, Lester "Les."** DJ (*Melody Market*, KRHD, Duncan, OK, 1952–1955).

262 **Agee, Tom.** DJ (WINA , Charlottesville, VA, 1957).

263 **Agnew, Charlie.** Leader (*Charlie Agnew Orchestra,* instr. mus. prg., WGN, Chicago, IL, 1939; WMAQ, Chicago, IL, 1939; MBS, 1940; WLW, Cincinnati, OH, 1942).

264 **Agnew, Theodore J. "Ted."** Sportscaster (*Sportsbook Sportscope*, KUBC, Montrose, CA, 1948). DJ (*Club 43*, KSMA, Santa Maria, CA, 1949).

265 **Agnew, Sam.** Sportscaster (WKRC, Cincinnati, OH, 1940).

266 **Agrait, Gustavo.** Newscaster (WIPR, San Juan, PR, 1952).

267 **Agresta, Phil.** Sportscaster (WBT , Charlotte, NC, 1951–1954). Newscaster (WBT, 1953–1956).

268 **Agronsky, Martin.** News commentator (NBC-Blue, 1944; ABC and WMAL, Washington, DC, 1945–1954; *Events of the Day*, WABC, New York, NY, 1955; *News of the Hour* and *Emphasis*, NBC, Washington, DC, 1960). Agronsky was an extremely liberal news commentator during his entire career.

269 **Agusty, Joaquin.** Announcer (WKAQ, San Juan, P.R., 1927.

270 **Ahearn, Jack.** Sportscaster (*Scholastic Sports*, WITH, Baltimore, MD, 1947).

271 **Ahearn, Richard.** DJ (*Bandstand*, WKRT, Cortland, NY, 1954).

272 **Ahearne, Dick.** Actor Ahearne appeared on the *Stepmother* daytime serial.

273 **Ahern, (Mrs.) Clara.** Leader (Hotel Chisca Philhamonic Orchestra, WMC, Memphis, TN, 1923–24).

274 **Ahern, John.** Newscaster (KYJC, Medford, OR, 1953).

275 **Ahern, Michael.** Sportscaster (WIRE, Indianapolis, IN, 1960).

276 **Aherns, Crystal.** COM-HE (KRFS, Superior, NE, 1960).

277 **Ahlers, Emma.** Soprano (WJZ, New York, NY, 1924).

278 **Ahmann, Mark.** Sportscaster (*Today's Sports*, KTIV, Sioux City, IA, 1960).

279 **Ahrens, B.A.** Baritone (WJZ, New York, NY, 1925).

280 **Ahrens, Walter.** Baritone (*Walter Ahrens,* vcl. mus. prg., WOR, Newark, NJ, 1935–1936).

281 **Aichele Novelty Dance Orchestra.** Popular local band (WLW, Cincinnati, OH, 1923).

282 **Aigeltinger, Lester.** Singer (*Lester Aigeltinger,* vcl. mus. prg., WORK , York, PA, 1936).

283 **Aiken, Bill.** Leader (*Bill Aiken Orchestra,* instr. mus. prg., KVOR, Colorado Springs, CO, 1940).

284 **Aiken, June.** COM-HE (WMSC, Columbia, SC, 1960).

285 **Aiken, Larry.** DJ (WEOA, Evansville, IN, 1957).

286 **Aiken, Louis.** Newscaster (WINX, Washington, DC, 1945–1946).

287 **Aikman [Aiklman], Leola.** Soprano (WHT, Chicago, IL, 1926).

288 **Ailau, Nubs.** Contralto (WLS, Chicago, IL, 1925).

289 **Ainsworth, Arthur R.** Announcer (WMH, Cincinnati, OH, 1925; WSAI, Cincinnati, OH, 1927).

290 ***Air Cyclopedia.*** Walter Casey, who conducted the program, claimed that it was the first quiz program for listeners (WMCA, New York, NY, 1930).

291 ***(The) Air Scout Hour.*** Marian and Jim Jordan were featured on this show before they achieved popularity on their own *Fibber McGee and Molly* program (WENR-WBCN, Chicago, IL, 1929–1930).

292 **Aird, Tommy.** Leader (*Tommy Aird Orchestra,* instr. mus. prg., WPG, Atlantic City, NJ, 1938).

293 **Airliners Orchestra.** Musical group (*Airliners Orchestra,* instr. mus. prg., MBS, 1939).

294 ***Airport Reporter.*** An airport waiting room served as a studio for Herb Harris and Bob Pollock, where they interviewed passengers arriving in Atlanta (WSB, 1941). When Pollock entered service in World War II, Elmo Ellis took his place. After leaving service, Pollock produced several successful programs before eventually becoming the manager of WSB-AM-FM.

295 **Aitkens, Gailes.** Newscaster (WAYS. Charlotte, NC, 1944).

296 **"AJN."** First designation of Milton Cross, when he began announcing at WJZ (New York, NY) and WJY (New York, NY) in 1925. In early radio, announcers and performers were often identified only by initials, incidentally, not necessarily their own. *See* **Milton J. Cross**

297 **Ake, Allan.** DJ (KSRC, Socorro, NM, 1960).

298 **Aker, Dick.** DJ (KTFY, Brownfield, TX, 1954).

299 **Akerley, Eugene A.** Sportscaster (KID, Idaho Falls, IA, 1948).

300 **Akers, Bob.** Newscaster (KRIC, Beaumont, TX, 1939–1941; KRIC, 1949; *World News,* KRIC, 1951).

301 **Akers, Carl.** Newscaster (KLZ, Denver, CO, 1953).

302 **Akers, Dick.** Sportscaster (WKBL, Covington, KY, 1956).

303 **Akridge, Bing.** Sportscaster (WMSD, Muscle Shoals City, AL, 1941).

304 ***Al and Lee Reiser.*** Instr. mus. prg. with the popular piano duo of Al and Lee Reiser (NBC, 1935–1938).

305 **Al and Pete.** Al Cameron from Anderson, Indiana, and Pete Bontsema, who was born in the Netherlands, formed the comedy singing team. Cameron had been a vaudeville performer before teaming with Pete Bontsema on radio. Bontsema was a genuine radio pioneer, one of the original five members of the *Red Apple Club* program that was broadcast by WCY-WCX. Later in 1929, Al and Pete appeared on KYW (Chicago, IL) and on WBBM (Chicago, IL). They also broadcast in 1929 as the Inspiration Boys on WMAQ (Chicago, IL) and made numerous network appearances. *See* ***The Red Apple Club.***

306 ***Al Bernard and the Merry Minstrels.*** Veteran radio minstrel man Al Bernard hosted and provided comic turns on the show with such performers such as Emil Casper and tenor Mario Cozzi (NBC, 1935).

307 ***Al Bernard, Minstrel.*** Bernard, who previously had broadcast as one of the Raybestos Twins in the 1920s, sang and told jokes on the quarter-hour program (15 min., 11:45 A.M. to 12:00 noon, NBC-Red, 1934).

308 ***(The) Al Jolson Lifebuoy Show.*** Lever Brothers sponsored the weekly program, sometimes known as *The Lifebuoy Show.* Comics Martha Raye, Harry Einstein and Sid Silvers were featured. The star, Al Jolson, was known as the "World's Greatest Entertainer." Music was provided by Lud Gluskin's Orchestra. Tiny Ruffner was the announcer. *Variety's* critics praised little about the show other than Jolson's singing (30 min., Tuesday, 8:30–9:00 P.M., CBS, 1936–1939).

309 ***Al Pearce and His Gang.*** Pearce, who first gained recognition and popularity on West Coast radio, was a comedian blessed with a talented supporting cast. His first version of the "Gang" program, begun in 1932, was 15-minutes in length, although most members of his "gang" had been active since 1927 on West coast radio. After six years of coaxing, Pearce, his brother, Cal, and the gang left California to begin network broadcasting. They came to the NBC-Blue network in 1933. A later network program was broadcast three times a week (15 min., Monday-Wednesday-Friday, 4:00–4:30 P.M. C.S.T., NBC-Red, 1935). Over the years the program's length changed, as did the days it was broadcast. By 1938, for example, Pearce's show was broadcast in two versions by NBC. There was a Friday evening show (30 min., Friday, 8:00–8:30 P.M. C.S.T., NBC-Blue, 1938) and a Monday afternoon version (30 min., Monday, 4:00–4:30 P.M., C.S.T., NBC-Red, 1938).

Pearce created the character of Elmer Blurt, a bumbling door-to-door salesman, whose memorable lines were uttered as he rapped on the door of a prospective customer, "Nobody home. I hope, I hope, I hope." Bill Comstock created the "Tizzie Lish" role. Tizzie gave listeners ridiculous recipes. Other comediennes who added to the fun were Arlene Harris (The Human Chatterbox) and Kitty O'Neil. The other cast members were: Morey Amsterdam, Andy Andrews, Orville Andrews, Artie Auerbach, Harry Foster, Kitty O'Neil, Parker Jennison, Tony Romano, Harry Stewart, Mabel Todd (The Little Ray of Sunshine), Monroe Upton, Hazel Werner and Bill Wright. The program's vocal groups included Marie Green and her Merrie Men and the Three Cheers (E.J. Derry, Travis Hale and Phil Hanna). Pearce's show, in one version or another, was broadcast until 1946. Earlier versions of the show were sometimes called *Watch the Fords Go By, Fun Valley* and *Watch the Fun Go By.*

310 ***Al, Pete and Dorothy Miller.*** Vocal trio (WBBM, Chicago, IL, 1934).

311 ***(The) Al Trahan Revue.*** Hudson Motor Car Company sponsored the variety show starring comedian Al Trahan. Graham McNamee hosted the program that also featured music by the singing Saxon Sisters (Grace and Beatrice) and a male singing group consisting of Scrappy Lambert, Randolph Weyant, Leonard Stokes, Robert Moody and Kenneth Christie. Lennie Hayton conducted the orchestra (30 min., Saturday, 10:00–10:30 P.M., NBC-Red Network, New York, NY, 1934).

312 **Al X's Dance Orchestra.** California band (KMIC, Inglewood, CA, 1928).

313 ***Alabama Hayloft Jamboree.*** CW music program hosted by Ralph Rogers who called it a "jollification by all the greatest hillbilly stars on records." Happy Wilson and His Golden River Boys were featured (WAPI, Birmingham, AL, 1948).

314 **Alabama Melody Boys.** Jazz band (KYW, Chicago, IL, 1923).

315 ***(The) Alabama Minstrels.*** Walter Melber, Matthew Mahoney, James Hill, Hank Miller and Eugene O'Haire performed on the radio minstrel show (WGY, Schenectady, NY, 1932).

316 **Alabama Troubadours.** Vocal group (*Alabama Troubadours,* vcl. mus. prg., WJR, Detroit, MI, 1935).

317 ***Aladdin Barn Dance.*** The early barn dance program presented CW music performed by tenor Hugh Cross (The Smokey Mountain Boy); Karl Davis on mandolin; Hartford Connecticut Taylor on guitar; Slim Miller on violin; and John Lair. Lair, who "played" jug, was the group's leader. The Mantle Lamp Company, manufacturer of Aladdin Lamps, sponsored the program (30 min., Saturday, 8:30–9:00 P.M., WLS, Chicago, IL, 1932).

318 ***Aladdin Lamp Dramas.*** Homer Griffith played the part of Jim Higgins, owner, manager, actor and ticket taker at the Aladdin Hayloft Theater where the Aladdin Players performed brief dramatic sketches. The actors included Dorothy McDonald, Agnes Hedrick, Hazel Dopheide, Les Pugh, Al Halus and, of course, Homer Griffith (30 min., Saturday, 9:30–10:00 P.M., C.S.T., WLS, Chicago, IL, 1935–1936).

319 **Aladdin Orchestra.** Popular local band (WOR, Newark, NJ, 1923).

320 **Alameda Scots' Band.** Music group directed by Adolph F. Nelson (KGO, San Francisco, CA, 1926).

321 **Alamo Theater Orchestra.** House band broadcasting from the Alamo Theater, Louisville, Kentucky led by Harry S. Currie; (WHAS, Louisville, KY, 1923–1924).

322 **Alampi, Phil.** Newscaster (*Farm News,* ABC, 1948; *Freedom Gardener,* WJZ New York, NY, 1948–1951).

323 **Alan, Lee.** DJ (WKMH , Dearborn, MI, 1960).

324 **Alan, Marc.** Sportscaster (WMPS, TN, 1953).

325 **Alan, Pat.** Newscaster (WCLO, Janesville, WI, 1945–1946).

326 ***Alan Courtney.*** Courtney, a popular New York DJ, conducted his three-hour all-night sustaining recorded music program with many special attractions. He frequently interviewed guests such as Bea Wain and Andre Baruch. Courtney also conducted a job search for the unemployed on his program and offered listeners membership in his *All Night Club.* Inspirational talks by various ministers and organ interludes rounded out his show (180 min.,

Sunday, 12:00 midnight to 3:00 A.M., WMCA, New York, NY, 1941).

327 ***(The) Alan Courtney Show.*** After previously conducting a three-hour DJ show, Courtney returned in 1948 to host a live, half-hour music show locally broadcast five times weekly. Singer Marilyn Towne and the Ray Ross Orchestra were featured (30 min., Monday through Friday, 12:00 noon to 12:30 P.M., WNEW, New York, NY, 1948).

328 ***(The) Alan Young Show.*** On January 19, 1949, comedian Alan Young's program took the place of *A Date with Judy.* Comedian Young was joined on the program by Jim Backus and Minerva Pious. The Peter Van Steeden Orchestra and Four Chicks and a Chuck provided the music on the half-hour show (30 min., Weekly, 1949). An earlier run had appeared on NBC in 1944–1947, after a successful summer replacement assignment for the *Eddie Cantor Show.* Also appearing with Young were Charlie Cantor, Ed Begley, Ruth Perrott, Doris Singleton, Ken Christy and Jean Gillespie. The Smart Set Quintet (Mike Corrigan, Patricia Corrigan, Leo Dukehorn, Gerry Salathiel and Gloria Wood) also appeared frequently. The program's announcers were Larry Elliott, Michael Roy and Jimmy Wallington. The writers were Sam Packard, Norman Paul, Dave Schwartz and Jay Sommers, and the director was Eddie Pola. On the shows, Young always was the target of someone who wished to take advantage of him.

329 **Alarie, Dick.** Sportscaster (WPCT, Putnam, CT, 1956).

330 **Alban, Dave.** DJ (WALK, Patchogue, NY, 1957; *Carnival of Music,* WJNO, West Palm Beach, FL, 1960).

331 **Alban, Theo.** Tenor (WOR, Newark, NJ and WMCA, New York, NY, 1925).

332 **Albanese, Lisa.** Operatic soprano (ABC, MBS, NBC). Soprano Albanese was heard in many opera broadcasts from the Metropolitan Opera stage on NBC and ABC. In addition, she starred with Jan Peerce on the *Treasure Hour of* Song on MBS in 1940.

333 **Albanese, Margaret.** DJ (*Arrows in the Air,* KTIM, San Raphael, CA, 1948).

334 **Albani, (Countess) Olga Megolago.** Mezzo-soprano (NBC, New York, NY, 1929).

335 **Albany College of Pharmacy Orchestra.** Collegiate band (WHAZ , Troy, NY, 1926).

336 **Albany Community Chorus.** Local vocal group (WGY, Schenectady, NY, 1923).

337 **Albavalde, Abraham A.** Newscaster (KTOH, Lihue, HA, 1942).

338 **Albee, Doris.** Pianist (WEAF, New York, NY, 1925).

339 **Alberghini, Harold.** DJ (*Krackpot Kollege,* WCOU, Lewiston, ME, 1949–1955). Newscaster (WCOU, 1955).

340 **Albert, Barton G.** Announcer (WSAR, Fall River, MA, 1925).

341 **Albert, Bill.** DJ (WLS, Chicago, IL, 1954; WLW, Cincinnati, OH, 1957).

342 **Albert, Dave.** Accordion soloist (KFI, Los Angeles, CA, 1925).

343 **Albert, Don.** Leader (*Palace Theatre String Orchestra,* WFAA, Dallas, TX, 1923–1924).

344 **Albert, Don.** Leader (*Don Albert Orchestra,* instr. mus. prg., WGN, Chicago, IL and MBS, 1935).

345 **Albert, Freddie.** DJ (*Ranch House Roundup,* WJAT, Swainsboro, GA, 1952).

346 **Albert, Grace and Eddie Albert.** Vocal team (*Grace and Eddie Albert,* vcl. mus. prg., NBC, 1934). Eddie Albert later went on to have a successful career in motion pictures and on television.

347 **Albert, Harry.** Leader (*Harry Albert Orchestra,* instr. mus. prg., WJSV, Washington, DC, 1939).

348 **Albert, Maude.** Contralto (WBAL, Baltimore, MD, 1928).

349 **Albert, Mildred.** COM-HE (WVDA, Boston, MA, 1956).

350 **Alberton, George.** Sportscaster (WJIM, Lansing, MI, 1951).

351 **Alberts, Don.** Sportscaster (KHUB, Watsonville, CA, 1949).

352 **Alberts, Mal.** Sportscaster (*Sports Camera,* KATL, Houston, TX, 1950; KPUG, Bellingham, WA, 1953).

353 **Alberts, Nicky.** DJ (*1490 Club,* WAZL, Hazleton, PA, 1949).

354 **Albertson, Don.** Sportscaster (KGDE, Fergus Falls, MN, 1952).

355 **Alberty, Bob.** Announcer (WREC, Memphis, TN, 1925).

356 **Albin, Jack.** Leader (*Jack Albin Orchestra,* instr. mus. prg., WOO, Philadelphia, PA and WEAF, New York, NY, 1925).

357 **Albin, Mary Christine.** Leader of the Mary Christine Albin Trio consisting of violinist Evelyn Pickrell, cellist Hazel Babbadge and pianist Mary Christine Albin (KFI, Los Angeles, CA, 1926).

358 **Albinger, Albert.** Newscaster (WKWK, Wheeling, WV, 1941).

359 **Albion, Peggy.** Singer-program director Albion conducted the *Children's Hour* program (WRC, Washington, DC, 1925).

360 **Albion, Peggy and Mary Frances Gunn.** The vocal team sang songs and told stories for children (WRC, Washington, DC, 1924).

361 **Albrecht, Ken.** DJ (*Yawn Patrol,* KVOB, Alexandria, LA, 1949).

362 **Albrecht, Paul.** Sportscaster (WJMC, Rice Lake, WI, 1950). DJ (*Music with Paul,* WBIZ, Eau Claire, WI, 1952).

363 **Albridge, Ken.** Sportscaster (WPOR, Portland, ME, 1960).

364 **Albright, Bob.** CW singer (*Bob Albright the Oklahoma Cowboy,* CW vcl. mus. prg., WLW, Cincinnati, OH, 1932 and *Bob Albright the Singing Cowboy,* CW vcl. mus. prg., WLW, Cincinnati, OH, 1935).

365 **Albright, Dave.** DJ (KCRG, Cedar Rapids, IA, 1954).

366 **Albright, Eddie.** Announcer known as "The Town Crier of the Day Watch" (KNX, Los Angeles, CA, 1920).

367 **Albright, Johnny.** Crooner (*Johnny Albright,* vcl. mus. prg., WGY, Schenectady, NY, 1935).

368 **Albright (Allbright) Nat M.** Sportscaster (WEAM , Arlington, VA, 1948; *Sports Hi-Way,* WEAM, 1949; *Albright Sports,* WEAM, 1950; *Sports Hi-Way,* WEAM, 1951–1952; *Sports Highway,* WEAM, 1954–1956; WINX, Washington, DC, 1955).

369 **Albright, (Dr.) Robert E.** Newscaster (WBEN, Buffalo, NY, 1944).

370 **Albritton, Dave.** DJ (*The Dave Albritton Show,* WING, Dayton, OH, 1952).

371 **Albritton, Leo.** Sportscaster (KGFI, Brownsville, TX, 1938).

372 **Alburty, Bob.** Sportscaster (WHBQ, Memphis, TN, 1938–1942).

373 **Alby, Wynn.** Sportscaster (*Sports Shots,* WWOD, Lynchburg, VA, 1952 , KECK, Odessa, TX, 1954).

374 **Alck, Bven L.** Newscaster (KVOA, Tucson, AZ, 1953).

375 **Alcock, Dorothy.** Concert pianist (KFI, Los Angeles, CA, 1927).

376 **Alcott, Carroll.** Newscaster (WLW-WSAI, Cincinnati, OH, 1941; WLW, 1942; WCAU, Philadelphia, PA, 1944; WINS, New York, NY, 1948–1950; *Carroll Alcott and the News,* WINS, 1951; KNX, Los Angeles, CA, 1954–1957).

377 **Alcott, Mary.** Blues singer (*Mary Alcott* vcl. mus. prg.; WLW, Cincinnati, OH, 1935–1936).

378 **Alda, Frances.** Operatic soprano (*Atwater Kent Hour,* 1927; *Frances Alda,* vcl. mus. prg., NBC Red and Blue, 1933–1934).

379 **Alden, Ann.** COM-HE (KFJZ, Fort Worth, TX, 1951).

380 **Alden, George.** Newscaster (KWBW, Hutchinson, KS, 1948).

381 **Alden, Irene.** Vocalist (*Irene Alden,* vcl. mus. prg., WIP, Philadelphia, PA, 1936).

382 **Alden, Jane.** Contralto (*Jane Alden,* vcl. mus. prg., WOR, Newark, NJ, 1934).

383 **Alden, Jerry.** Sportscaster (WSNJ, Bridgeton, NJ, 1939; WSNJ, 1945–1946; *Sports Roundup,* WSNJ, 1947; *Sports Picture,* WSNJ, 1948–1960).

384 **Alden, Norm.** DJ (*Rhythm Caravan,* KXOL, Fort Worth, TX, 1948).

385 **Alden, Tom.** DJ (*You Name It,* KOLS, Pryor, OK, 1952).

386 **Alder, W.F.** Broadcast travelogues (KNX, Los Angeles, CA, 1925, 1928).

387 **Alderman, James S. "Jim."** Newscaster (*Avalon Big Ben News,* WFAA, Dallas, TX, 1937–1938; WRR, Dallas, TX, 1942–1946).

388 **Alderman, W.E.** Announcer (WEBW, Beloit, WI, 1925).

389 **Alderson, John.** Newscaster (WFBR, Baltimore, MD, 1941–1951; *Shell News Digest,* WFBR, 1952).

390 **Aldrich, Darrah.** COM-HE (*Calling All Women,* WCCO, Minneapolis, MN, 1942–1954). Aldrich conducted the *Calling All Women* program from 1942 through 1954. She preceded Florence Lehmann as the director of Women's Activities at WCCO.

391 **Aldrich, Laura E.** Pianist-accordionist (WLW, Cincinnati, OH, 1925).

392 **Aldrich, Les.** Newscaster (KICA, Clovis, NM, 1957).

393 **Aldrich, Philip.** Violinist (KTAB, Oakland, CA, 1925).

394 ***(The) Aldrich Family.*** Clifford Goldsmith's play, *What a Life,* was the source for this highly successful family situation comedy about an upper- middle class family, not so joyfully experiencing the adolescent growing pains of their son, Henry. Ezra Stone as Henry became a star of stage and radio when he weakly answered his mother's call of "HENRY—HENRY ALDRICH," by croaking, "Coming, Mother." Rudy Vallee first introduced the family's story on his *Fleischmann Hour Program.* It was then heard for many weeks on the *Kate Smith Hour,* before premiering as its own program on NBC-Blue in 1939. Despite the show's many cast changes over the years, it remained one of the funniest situation comedies on radio. The cast included: Judith Abbott, Jone Allison, Charita Bauer, Ed Begley, Lenrow Bernard, Ethel Blume, Eddie Bracken, Bobby Ellis, Betty Field, Clyde Fillmore, Jean Gillespie, Raymond Ives, Joan Jackson, House Jameson, Dickie Jones, Jackie Kelk, Ann Lincoln, Mary Mason, Agnes Moorehead, Lea Penman, Charles Powers, Leona Powers, Katherine Raht, Thelma Ritter, Mary Rolfe, Pat Ryan, Mary Shipp, Howard Smith, Ezra Stone, Norman Tokar, Dick Van Patten, Ward Wilson, Ethel Wilson and Alice Yourman. The program's directors were Edwin Duerr, Sam Fuller, George McGarrett, Joseph Scibetta, Lester Vail, Day Tuttle and Bob Welsh. George Bryan, Ralph Paul, Dan Seymour, Harry Von Zell and Dwight Wiest were the announcers. The writers were Clifford Goldsmith, Ed Jurist, Pat and Ed Joudry, Phil Sharp, Sam Taylor, Frank Tarloff and Norman Tokar. Jack Miller conducted the orchestra. Sound effects were produced by Bill Brinkmeyer (30 min., Weekly, NBC-Blue, CBS, 1939–1953).

395 **Aldridge, Charlie.** Sportscaster (*Mississippi Sports,* WNAG, Grenada, MS, 1950). DJ (WCRS, Greenwood, SC, 1954).

396 **Aldridge, Jay.** DJ (*Meet the Artists,* WROB, West Point, MS, 1948).

397 **Aldridge, Mahlon.** Newscaster (KXOX, St. Louis, MO, 1944). Sportscaster (KFRU, Columbia, MO, 1948; *Play by Play,* KFRU, Columbia, MO, 1949–1951; *Sports Page,* KFRU, 1952–1954).

398 ***(The) Alec Templeton Show.*** Templeton returned once more to radio from 1947 to 1948. The program, sponsored by Standard Brands, essentially reprised his earlier one. The brilliant performer was assisted this time by singer Eugenie Baird and Dan Daldenberg's orchestra (30 min., Sunday, 8:00–8:30 P.M., NBC, 1947).

399 ***Alec Templeton Time.*** Blind British pianist-comedian Templeton first appeared on network radio as a summer replacement for the *Fibber McGee and Molly* program. Templeton's stock in trade was his witty treatment of the classics and popular songs that he loaded with heavy doses of satire. Additional music was supplied by the Billy Mills Orchestra and vocalist Edna O'Dell. Former motion picture star Conrad Nagel was the announcer (30 min., Tuesday, 9:30–10:00 P.M., NBC-Red, 1939). After leaving the air in 1941, the program returned to the network briefly from 1943 to 1944.

400 **Aleman, Joe.** DJ (KPRL, Paso Robles, CA, 1952).

401 ***(The) Alemite Half-Hour.*** The Horace Heidt Orchestra was featured on the weekly program (Monday, 8:00–8:30 P.M., 193

402 ***(The) Alemite Hour.*** The Alemite Company sponsored the variety hour, whose major attraction was the fact that Texas Guinan made frequent appearances (CBS, 1930).

403 **Alemite Orchestra (aka Alemite High Pressure Orchestra).** Band led by saxophonist Jack Crawford (WBBM, Chicago, IL, 1926).

404 ***(The) Ales of Hoffman.*** Hoffman Ginger Ale Company sponsored the program of light opera, folk, popular and classical music performed by an orchestra directed by Josef Pasternack. Soprano Lois Bennett and contralto Veronica Wiggins were featured (WOR, Newark, NJ, 1932).

405 **Aleshin, Vlacha.** Balalaika soloist (NBC, 1928).

406 **Alex, Steve.** Newscaster (KSIL, Silver City, NM, 1946).

407 **Alex, Susan.** COM-HE (KSAN, San Francisco, CA, 1951).

408 **Alexander, A.L.** An announcer in 1925, Alexander later originated and conducted *A.L. Alexander's Good Will Court* in the 1930s. *See **A.L. Alexander's Good Will Court.***

409 **Alexander, Alex.** Sportscaster (*Coachella Valley Sports Round-Up,* KREO, Indio, CA, 1951–1954).

410 **Alexander, Barbara.** COM-HE (KVNI, Coeur d'Alene, ID, 1954).

411 **Alexander, Ben.** Announcer-MC and actor Alexander appeared on the *Anniversary Club* (Announcer-MC), *Brent House* (actor), *Edgar Bergen-Charlie McCarthy Show* (announcer), *Heart's Desire* (MC, audience participation) and *Little Ol' Hollywood* (host, gossip) programs.

412 **Alexander, Ben.** Newscaster (*This Moving World,* NBC, 1939).

413 **Alexander, Bernie.** DJ (WIBR, Baton Rouge, LA, 1957).

414 **Alexander, (Col.) Boris.** Newscaster (WMC, Memphis, TN, 1938).

415 **Alexander Brothers.** Piano duo (*Alexander Brothers* instr. mus. prg., WFBR, Baltimore, MD, 1936).

416 **Alexander, Connie.** Sportscaster (*Previews,* KVER, Albuquerque, NM, 1949; *Sports Call,* KCRC, Enid, OK, 1954; *Sports Call,* KDEF, Albuquerque, NM, 1955).

417 **Alexander, Denise.** Actress featured on *A Tree Grows in Brooklyn* daytime serial.

418 **Alexander, Dick.** DJ (*Dick's Den,* WICC, Bridgeport, CT, 1952).

419 **Alexander, Ed.** Sportscaster (*Sports Roundup* and *Speaking of Sports,* KXOX, Sweetwater, TX, 1950; *Highlights,* KXOX, 1951; *Gridiron Parade,* KXOX, 1954–1955).

420 **Alexander, Elsie.** Alexander taught radio music lessons (WFI, Philadelphia, PA, 1924).

421 **Alexander, (Mrs.) Florence.** Violinist (KFWM, Oakland, CA, 1927).

422 **Alexander, Jack.** Sportscaster (WINN, Louisville, KY, 1942).

423 **Alexander, Jeanne.** COM-HE (WBT, Charlotte, NC, 1954–1955).

424 **Alexander, Joan.** Busy radio actress Alexander appeared on the daytime serials *Lone Journey, Against the Storm, Rosemary, The Second Mrs. Burton, This is Nora Drake, A Woman of Courage, Young Dr. Malone, Bright Horizon* and *Brighter Day.*

425 **Alexander, John.** Newscaster (KFBB, Great Falls, MT, 1940–1941, 1945).

426 **Alexander, John.** Newscaster (WFPG, Atlantic City, NJ, 1942). Sports (WFPG, 1942).

427 **Alexander, Kurt [Curt].** DJ (*Roll Jordan,* WEAS, Decatur-Atlanta, GA, 1952–1954).

428 **Alexander, Lee.** DJ (KECK, Odessa, TX, 1957).

429 **Alexander, Leo.** DJ (WCAO, Baltimore, MD, early 1950s).

430 **Alexander, Lois.** Reader Alexander specialized in "novelty readings" (KTHS, Hot Springs National Park, AR, 1927).

431 **Alexander, Marion.** COM-HE (WADC, Akron, OH, 1951–1958).

432 **Alexander, Maxime.** Whistler (KTBI, Los Angeles, CA, 1926).

433 **Alexander, Mildred.** COM-HE (WTAR, Norfolk, VA, 1956–1957).

434 **Alexander, Owen.** Sportscaster (WAPI, Birmingham, AL, 1942). Newscaster (WSAV, Savannah, GA, 1949).

435 **Alexander, (Mrs.) Robert L.** Pianist (WSM, Nashville, TN, 1928).

436 **Alexander, Ross.** Baritone (WBZ, Springfield, MA, 1926).

437 **Alexander, Van.** Leader (*Van Alexander Orchestra* mus. prg., NBC, 1939; WOR, Newark, NJ, 1942).

438 **Alexander, (Mrs.) Virginius.** Vocalist (WOK, Pine Bluff, AR, 1922).

439 **Alexander, William C.** Newscaster (*Noon News,* WTIK, Durham, NC, 1948).

440 **Alexanderova, Sascha.** Soprano (WMEX, Boston, MA, 1939).

441 **Alexandria, Elenora.** COM-HE (WBAX, Wilkes-Barre, PA, 1954).

442 **Alexandria Tailors Orchestra.** Band on the *Alexandria Tailors' Program* (KFWF, St. Louis, MO, 1926).

443 **Aley, Albert.** Writer-actor Aley worked on the *Don Winslow of the Navy* (writer), *Hop Harrigan* (writer), *Let's Pretend* (actor), *Stella Dallas* (actor), *Sunday Mornings at Aunt Susan's* (actor) and the *Superstition* (writer) programs.

444 **Aley, Carl Jack.** Newscaster (WGTC, Greenville, NC, 1941–1942).

445 **Alfonso, Antonio.** Sportscaster (WIAC, San Jose, PR, 1942).

446 **Alford, Dale.** Sportscaster (KARK, Little Rock, AR, 1938).

447 **Alford, Dick.** DJ (*Strollin' with Alford,* KXLR, Little Rock, AR, 1949–1957).

448 **Alford, Ken.** DJ (KULA, Honolulu, HI, 1949).

449 **Alfred, Jerry.** DJ (KPQ, Wenatchee, WA, 1948).

450 Alfred, Kitty. COM-HE (WRGA, Rome, GA, 1951).

451 Alfred, Milton. Sportscaster (WICA, Astabula, OH, 1937).

452 Alfred, Rusty. DJ (*Woodchoppers Ball*, KTRE, Lufkin, TX, 1948).

453 Alfredo, Don. Leader (*Don Alfredo's Blue and White Marimba Band,* instr. mus. prg., NBC, 1933 and *Don Alfredo's Marimba Orchestra*, NBC, 1934–1936; WOR, Newark, NJ, 1936; *Don Alfredo's Orchestra*, instr. mus. prg., WOR, Newark, NJ, 1942).

454 Alger, E. Bella. Talked on "The Care of Clothing" (KFAE, Pullman, WA, 1923).

455 *Alias Jane Doe.* A complete story was presented weekly on the 30-minute program sponsored by Toni Home Permanent. The program's title came from the premise that on each program a lovely magazine editor posed as different characters in order to research a story. Written by Kay Phillips, John M. Hayes and E. Jack Newman, the cast included: Tudor Owens, Eric Sinclair, Lamont Johnson and the Starlighters. Frank Martin was the announcer (30 min., Saturday, 1:30–2:00 P.M., CBS, 1951).

456 *Alias Jimmy Valentine.* Bert Lytell played the title role on the program, loosely based on the fictional character created by O. Henry. Sponsored by Larus & Brothers Company, the story focused on Jimmy Valentine, an expert safe cracker just out of prison. The suspense grew out of Jimmy's attempt to go straight. As the story began, Jimmy got a job as a bank clerk and met the banker's daughter, who immediately has faith in him. However, another bank clerk who had his eye on the same young woman, began to make trouble for Jimmy. Can he go straight and overcome his troubles? That was the question constantly posed by the program (15 min., Thursday, 7:30–7:45 P.M., NBC-Blue 1937–1938).

457 *(The) Alice Foote MacDougal Hour.* The music program was broadcast Tuesday evenings (6:30–7:00 P.M., WABC-CBS, 1929). The Candlelight Dance Orchestra conducted by Bela Loblo was featured.

458 *(The) Alice Hutchins Drake Program.* Miss Drake broadcast more than 100 programs on which she presented book reviews and talked about art works and sight-seeing in the Washington, DC, area (WRC, Washington, DC, 1931).

459 *(The) Alice Jane McHenry Program.* A twelve-year-old singer described by *Variety* as a good soprano, McHenry was billed as "the upside-down tummy girl," because she had experienced a series of operations to correct an inverted stomach. International Diamond Appraising and Gold Buying Company sponsored her weekly 15-minute program (WHN, New York, NY, 1935).

460 *Alicia McElroy String Quartet.* String quartet mus. prg. (KGW, Portland, OR, 1926).

461 Aliga, Laszlo. Hungarian tenor featured on *Roxy and His Gang* program (NBC, 1928).

462 Alinoch, William. Newscaster (WCQS, Alma, GA, 1960).

463 Alisky, Marvin. Newscaster (KMAC, San Antonio, TX, 1949).

464 Alison, Hugh. DJ (WJBF, Augusta, GA, 1949).

465 *(The) Alistair Cooke Show.* British journalist Cooke broadcast the weekly sustaining series of talks on various aspects of American life. These intellectually stimulating programs were taped repeats of programs he made for BBC transmission (15 min., Sunday, 9:45–10:00 P.M., ABC, 1952).

466 Alizier, Joan. Alizier was one of the intelligent "kids" on the *Quiz Kids* program (NBC, ABC, CBS, 1940–1953).

467 *Alka-Seltzer Time* (aka *Herb Shriner Time*). Hoosier comedian-philosopher Herb Shriner provided a homey, rural commentary on his weekday quarter-hour program sponsored by Alka-Seltzer. The Raymond Scott Quintet supplied the music and guest stars, such as Jack Haley, frequently appeared. Durward Kirby was the announcer (15 min., Five time weekly, 5:45–6:00 P.M., CBS, 1948).

468 *Alka-Seltzer Time.* The quarter-hour music show featured singers Curt Massey and Martha Tilton with music by County Washburn (Transcribed, 1953).

469 Alkman, Leola. Soprano (WHT, Chicago, IL, 1926).

470 *All About Stamps.* Sylvan Levin, musical director of station WOR, Newark, NJ, conducted the program about stamps for collectors young and old (15 min., Saturday, 10:15–10:30 A.M., WOR, 1948).

471 *All About You.* Author-psychologist Harold Sherman broadcast inspirational self-help advice to listeners on the program broadcast three times weekly (8:30–8:45 A.M., WABC-CBS, 1934).

472 All American (Male) Quartet. The vocal group was accompanied by pianist Alice Williams (WNAX, Yankton, SD, 1928).

473 *All Night International Program.* Ted Lewis and his orchestra were the major attraction on the music-variety program (WHB, Kansas City, MO, 1923).

474 All Star College Inn Orchestra. Band directed by Maurie Sherman (WLS, Chicago, IL, 1928).

475 Allabaugh [Allabough], Joe. Ukulele soloist-tenor (WIBO, Chigago, IL, 1925 and WBBM, 1926). Announcer (WEHS, Evanston, Il, 1927).

476 Allain, Orren. Sportscaster (WKAN, Kankakee, IL, 1947–1949; *Sizing Up Sports*, WKAN, 1950–1956).

477 Allan, Bob. Newscaster (WTSP, St. Petersburg, FL, 1955). DJ (WTSP, 1955).

478 Allan, Frank. Newscaster (KECK, Odessa, TX, 1949). DJ (*Make Believe Ballroom*, KECK, 1949).

479 Allan, Mark. DJ (*Wake Up Atlanta*, WAOK, Atlanta, GA, 1954).

480 Allan, Nubs. Contralto (WLS, Chicago, IL, 1925).

481 Allan, Stan. Sportscaster (WPAC, Patchogue, NY, 1952–1954). DJ (*This is Music*, WPAC, 1954–1956).

482 Allanson, Ruth. Pianist (WJJD, Mooseheart, IN, 1926).

483 Allard, James. DJ (*Gospel Melodies*, WABO, Waynesboro, MS, 1955).

484 Allbaugh, Bill. Sportscaster (*Sports*, KASI, Ames, IA, 1949).

485 Allbrook, Robert. Newscaster (WLB, Minneapolis, MN, 1944).

486 Allcorn, Bill. Sportscaster (*Football News*, KBWD, Brownwood, TX, 1951).

487 Allday, Jim. Sportscaster (*Sports Parade*, WOWL, Florence, AL, 1954).

488 Alldredge, Jay. DJ (WBRC, Birmingham, AL, 1957).

489 *Allegheny Mountain Jamboree.* CW music show featuring Dick Smith and His Rhythm Pals (Coudersport, PA, 1955).

490 Allegro Mandolin Sextet and Company. Instrumental music group directed by Percy Lichtenfels (KDKA, Pittsburgh, PA, 1923).

491 Allegro Saxophone Band. *See* **Allen, Joseph**.

492 Allen, Ada. Soprano (WOK, Chicago, IL, 1925).

493 Allen, Agnes May. COM-HE Allen delivered home economics talks (KFWB, Hollywood, CA, 1926).

494 Allen, Al. DJ (*Al's Jive Til Five*, KXLR, North Little Rock, AR, 1952–1954).

495 Allen, Anne. Soprano (WGBS, New York, NY, 1926).

496 Allen, Art. DJ (WABJ, Adrian, MI, 1957; *Dial M for Music*, WKNX, Sagninaw, MI, 1960).

497 Allen, Arthur. Character actor Allen was born April 8, 1881. His first radio appearances were in 1927. He also appeared in several Broadway productions. His radio career in the following decades mainly consisted of portraying "rural" characters. Among the many programs in which he appeared were *Four Corners, U.S.A.*, *Gibbs and Finney*, *General Delivery*, *Mother of Mine*, *The Simpson Boys of Sprucehead Bay*, *Snow Village*, *The Stebbins Boys* and *Uncle Abe and David*. See ***Snow Village Sketches (Snow Village)***.

498 Allen, Audrey. COM-HE (WKRC, Cincinnati, OH, 1951).

499 Allen, Barbara. COM-HE (WCOS, Columbia, SC, 1951).

500 Allen, Barbara Jo [Vera Vague]. Actress-comedienne Allen appeared on *The Hawthorne House* daytime serial and the *Bob Hope Show*. Also see ***(The) Vera Vague Show.***

501 Allen, Bert. Sportscaster (WNCT, Greenville, NC, 1960).

502 Allen, Betty. DJ (WLIZ, Fort Worth, FL, 1960).

503 Allen, Bettye. DJ (WCMI, Ashland, KY, 1954). COM-HE (WCMI, 1956–1957).

504 Allen, Bill. Sportscaster (*Sport Spotlight*, WHIN, Gallatin, TX, 1948).

505 Allen, Bill. DJ (*Tempo and Time*, KXLE, Ellensburg, WA, 1952).

506 Allen, Bill. DJ (KWFC, Hot Springs, AR, 1952).

507 Allen, Bill. DJ (WHTC, Holland, MI, 1954–1955).

508 Allen, Bob. Piano "novelties" (KPO, San Francisco, CA, 1928).

509 **Allen, Bob.** Sportscaster (WEAU, Eau Claire, WI, 1942).

510 **Allen, Bob.** Newscaster (*Listen America*, MBS, 1939; KFAB, Lincoln, NE, 1944).

511 **Allen, Bob.** Leader (*Bob Allen Orchestra,* instr. mus. prg., KMA, Shenandoah, IA and WLW, Cincinnati, OH, 1942).

512 **Allen, Bob.** Newscaster (KPAZ, Pottstown, PA, 1951–1952).

513 **Allen, Bob.** DJ (*Radio Ranch*, KPAS, Banning, CA, 1954).

514 **Allen, Bob.** DJ (*630 Club*, KMAC, San Antonio, TX, 1954).

515 **Allen, Bob.** DJ (KOOK, Billings, MT, 1960).

516 **Allen, Bobo.** DJ (*Musical Clock*, KIOX, Bay City, TN, 1948).

517 **Allen, Boyd.** Sportscaster (*Sports in Review*, KROY, Sacramento, CA, 1948).

518 **Allen, Buddy.** DJ (WSIG, Mt. Jackson, VA, 1960).

519 **Allen, Burritt.** DJ (WKBN, Youngstown, OH, 1960).

520 **Allen, (Mrs.) C.J.** Eighty-two-year-old pianist Allen played with her daughter, M.A. Cox, violinist; grand daughter, Mrs. George Tarlton, cellist; and banjoist Mrs. Victor Taylor. The group was billed as "three generations playing melodies of a half century ago" (WSB, Atlanta, GA, 1924).

521 **Allen, Carl.** Leader (Carl Allen's Orchestra, KFI, Los Angeles, CA, 1926).

522 **Allen, Carl.** DJ (*Musical Clock,* WLBK, DeKalb, IL, 1954).

523 **Allen, Casey.** Actor Casey appeared on the *Big Town* and *Ma Perkins* programs.

524 **Allen, Charles.** Sportscaster (WTAL, Tallahasee, FL, 1956).

525 **Allen, Charme.** Versatile actress Allen appeared on the *Backstage Wife* aka *Mary Noble, Backstage Wife, Mary Marlin* aka *The Story of Mary Marlin, The O'Neills, Pretty Kitty Kelly, Valiant Lady, We Love and Learn;* and *David Harum.*

526 **Allen, Chuck.** Newscaster (*News From Here*, WJPR, Greenville, MS, 1947). DJ (WKHM, Jackson, MI, 1957).

527 **Allen, Claire.** Singer (WEVD, New York City, NY, 1936).

528 **Allen, Claire.** Newscaster (WEBR, Buffalo, NY, 1951, 1957).

529 **Allen, Claude.** Leader (Claude Allen and his Original California Collegiate Orchestra, KGER, Long Beach, CA, 1927).

530 **Allen, Cliff.** Newscaster (WWVA, Wheeling, WV, 1942; WTOP, Washington, DC, 1945; WNOX, Knoxville, TN, 1948).

531 **Allen, Chris.** Sportscaster (WELI, New Haven, CT, 1945).

532 **Allen, Creighton.** Pianist (*Creighton Allen*, instr. mus. prg., NBC, 1935).

533 **Allen, Cyril.** Cellist (KYW, Chicago, IL, 1925).

534 **Allen, Dan.** DJ (*Stuff and Nonsense*, WRUF, Gainesville, FL, 1949).

535 **Allen, Dave.** DJ (*The Afternoon Show*, KILO, Grand Forks, ND, 1960).

536 **Allen, Dell.** DJ (*Melody Til Midnite*, KROS, Clinton, IA, 1952; KSO, Des Moines, IA, 1954).

537 **Allen, Dick.** Sportscaster (WJHO, Opelika, AL, 1956). DJ (WLCY, St. Peterburg, FL, 1960).

538 **Allen, Dolores.** COM-HE (WDOR, Sturgeon Bay, WI, 1956).

539 **Allen, Don.** Leader (*Don Allen Orchestra,* instr. mus. prg., WJJD, Chicago, IL, 1936; WADC, Talmadge-Akron, OH, 1942).

540 **Allen, Don.** Newscaster (KIMN, Denver, CO, 1957).

541 **Allen, Don.** DJ (*The Band Box*, WATH, Athens, OH, 1952).

542 **Allen, Don.** DJ (*The Alarm Clock Club*, KMOD, Modesto, CA, 1954; *Allen's Alley*, KWTC, Barstow, CA, 1960).

543 **Allen, Dorothy.** COM-HE (KAND, Corsicicana, TX, 1958).

544 **Allen, Dorothy.** COM-HE (WBNL, Booneville, IN, 1958).

545 **Allen, Ed.** Newscaster (WGN, Chicago, IL, 1941). DJ (*The Early Bird* and *400 Hour*, WMAQ, Chicago, IL, 1949).

546 **Allen, Edward "Ed,"Jr.** Newscaster (WDOR, Sturgeon Bay, WI, 1954–1955). DJ (WDOR, 1955).

547 **Allen, Eleanor.** Organist Allen, who studied piano and organ at Oberlin Conservatory of Music, was the first woman organist to play at Loew's State Theater, New York City. She also appeared frequently on San Francisco radio in 1929.

548 **Allen, Emily.** Pianist (WSM, Nashville, TN, 1928).

549 **Allen, Ernie.** DJ (*Ernie's Choice* and *Stardust Time*, KFAB, Omaha, NE, 1948; *Ernie's Apron Club*, KFAB, 1949).

550 **Allen, Eve.** COM-HE (WNAK, Wilkes-Barre, PA, 1958).

551 **Allen, Florence.** Soprano (WGHB, Clearwater, FL, 1926).

552 **Allen, Frank.** Sportscaster (WEMP, Milwaukee, WI, 1946). DJ (*All Set for Music*, WOW, Omaha, NE, 1954–1955). Newscaster (KOWH, Omaha, NE, 1957).

553 **Allen, Fred.** *See* ***The Fred Allen Show.***

554 **Allen, Fred.** Organist — not the radio comedian (WHAD, Milwaukee, WI, 1927).

555 **Allen, Fred.** DJ (*It Pays to Listen*, KCLE, Cleburne, TX, 1952).

556 **Allen, Fred.** Newscaster (KSRO, Santa Rosa, CA, 1957).

557 **Allen, Gene.** DJ (*Turntable Terrace*, WTAN, Clearwater, FL, 1954).

558 **Allen, George.** Sportscaster (WBVP, Beaver Falls, PA, 1949–1954). Newscaster (WBVP, 1952). DJ (*Listen While You Work*, WBVP, 1952–1954).

559 **Allen, George, Jr.** Newscaster (KHMO, Hannibal, MO, 1948).

560 **Allen, George W.** Announcer (WOK, Chicago, IL, 1926–1927).

561 **Allen, Gladys.** COM-HE (WDOC, Prestonburg, KY, 1958).

562 **Allen, Gordon.** Sportscaster (KYAK, Yakima, WA, 1948).

563 **Allen, Helene.** COM-HE (KLEA, Lovington, NM, 1956).

564 **Allen, Herb.** Newscaster (KECA-KFI, Los Angeles, CA, 1939–1941; WCKB, Dunn, NC, 1955). DJ (*Top Tunes*, KMPC, Los Angeles, CA, 1948; WCKB, 1955; WESA, Charleroi, PA; WMCK, McKeesport, PA, 1960). Sportscaster (WCKB, 1954).

565 **Allen, Herbert.** Allen was an announcer on the *Guiding Light* program.

566 **Allen, Hoyt.** Director-actor Allen worked on the *Backstage Wife* (actor), *Little Orphan Annie* (actor), *Perry Mason* (director), *Portia Faces Life* (director), *Rosemary* (director) and *Wendy Warren and the News* programs. He also appeared on the *National Barn Dance* as Pokey Martin.

567 **Allen, Ida Bailey.** Known as "The Happy Homemaker," Allen was a pioneer broadcaster of women's programs. Her early programs were called *Hospitality Talk* (WGI, Medford Hillside, MA, 1923); *The Homemakers Hour* (WMCA, New York, NY, 1926) and the *National Radio Homemakers Hour* (CBS, 1929). Allen was a trained dietician, cooking school instructor and cookbook author before becoming a radio cooking instructor. She was said to have been one of the three best known conductors of women's programs in the 1920s. It is interesting to note that the other two were fictional — Aunt Sammy and Betty Crocker. Allen's listener popularity was due in large part to her perceived integrity. Her statement on her program's sponsors in 1929, for instance, reflects her philosophy: "I have always felt that I must give to my readers and listeners-in — the best. When the time came to invite several food manufacturers to sponsor the National Radio Home-Makers Club air meetings, the whole country was scoured to find the best. That is why the Royal Baking Power Company, the Pillsbury Flour Mills Company and the Beech-Nut Packing Company are mentioned in our broadcasts, and why I am proud to tell you about their products and the place they occupy in the Balanced Ration."

Allen was one of the most talented and respected women working in early radio. She was the author of twenty-three books on foods, cooking and home economics. Her successful radio career lasted well into the 1930s: *Visiting with Ida Bailey Allen* (15 min., Thursday, CBS, 1933). In the late 1920s, in conjunction with her National Radio Home-Makers Club, she edited a weekly newsletter (*The Radio Home-Makers)* that sold for the price of 50 cents per year. This newsletter contained a front page article written by Allen on such topics as "Buying for Two," several recipes, dates and topics of Allen's future broadcasts and many of her sponsor's advertisements.

568 **Allen, Irwin.** Newscaster (*Hollywood Merry-Go-Round*, KMTR, Los Angeles, CA, 1944).

569 **Allen, Irwin.** Newscaster (KFIZ, Fond du Lac, WI, 1944).

570 **Allen, J.T.** DJ (*Coffee Cup Review*, KXOX, Sweetwater, TX, 1948).

571 **Allen, Jack.** Newscaster (MBS, 1960).

572 **Allen, Jerry.** DJ (KVNU, Logan, UT, 1960).

573 **Allen, Jim.** DJ (*Back of the Hit Parade*, KVER, Albuquerque, NM, 1952; *Listen While You Work*, KCJB, Minot, ND, 1954).

574 **Allen, Jim.** DJ (*A Whiz of a Weekend*, WWIZ, Lorain, OH, 1960).

575 **Allen, John.** Newscaster (KGKO, Fort Worth, TX, 1946).

576 **Allen, John.** Newscaster (WFAA, Dallas, TX, 1946–1949).

577 **Allen, Joseph.** Allen was the director of the Allen Saxophone Band, a popular radio band of the middle 1920s that was composed of 60 pieces of which 44 were saxophones.

578 **Allen, Judie.** COM-HE (KLAS, Las Vegas, NV, 1951).

579 **Allen, Judith.** Theater newscaster (WPAT, Paterson, NJ, 1942). Allen broadcast stage and screen gossip and news.

580 **Allen, Jules Verne (aka Lonesome Luke).** A singer of cowboy songs, Allen began working as a cowboy at the age of ten in Texas and spent ten years at the work. Allen actually had performed regular ranch chores and conducted cattle drives. He sang real cowboy songs on early radio (WOAI, San Antonio, TX, 1925–1926). His Victor recordings of "Little Joe the Wrangler" and "The Cowboy's Dream" brought him national prominence. Later, Allen appeared on network radio on his *Songs of the Plains* program (NBC, 1934).

581 **Allen, June.** Vocalist (*June Allen,* vcl. mus. prg., WGY, Schenectady, NY, 1942).

582 **Allen, Kay.** Vocalist (*Kay Allen,* vcl. mus. prg., WCAU, Philadelphia, PA, 1935 and WIP Philadelphia, PA, 1936).

583 **Allen, Kirby.** Sportscaster (KXEO, Mexico, MO, 1950–1956).

584 **Allen, Larry.** Newscaster (WJOC, Jamestown, NY, 1960).

585 **Allen, Lee.** Leader (*Lee Allen Orchestra,* instr. mus. prg., WHK , Cleveland, OH and MBS, 1938).

586 **Allen, Lee.** Sportscaster (*Lee Allen Sports Show*, WSAI, Cincinnati, OH, 1949; *Inside Angle on Sports*, KYW, Philadelphia, PA, 1951).

587 **Allen, Lee.** DJ (*Musical Bazaar*, WSCR, Scranton, PA, 1952).

588 **Allen, Len.** DJ (*Dawn Busters*, KLO, Ogden, UT, 1948–1954).

589 **Allen, Leon.** Newscaster (WTRL, Bradenton, FL, 1955). Sportscaster (WTRL, 1955).

590 **Allen, Lewis.** Newscaster (KSAN, San Francisco, CA, 1940).

591 **Allen, Lilly Belle.** Singer (KLDS, Independence, MO, 1926).

592 **Allen, Lloyd.** DJ (*Music Round Table*, KIGW, Alamosa, CA, 1948).

593 **Allen, Lorraine.** Pianist (KUOA, Fayetteville, AR, 1925–1926 and KLRA, Little Rock, AR, 1927–1928). Allen was a 19-year-old university senior in 1925, when she was billed as "The Queen of the Ivories." She composed such songs as "Lonesome Blues," "Radio Mama," "Golfer's Blues" and "The Sig Ep Reverie." Bill Mann was her announcer when she appeared later on KFMQ (Fayetteville, AR).

594 **Allen, Madeline.** COM-HE (WGAL, Lebanon, OR, 1956).

595 **Allen, Marc.** Sportscaster (KLEO, Wichita, KS, 1960).

596 **Allen, Margaret.** COM-HE (KSLM, Salem, OR, 1951).

597 **Allen, Mark.** DJ (KPOJ, Portland, OR, 1960).

598 **Allen, Mattie Brown.** COM-HE (WOHS, Shelby, NC, 1956).

599 **Allen, Mel.** Sportscaster (CBS sustaining, 1938; *Mel Allen's Sports Review*, *Mel Allen's Football Previews*, WMCA, New York, NY, 1939 and the *Kentucky Derby* and *Brooklyn Dodgers football broadcasts*, CBS, 1939; *Camel Baseball*, WMCA, New York, NY and CBS, 1940; CBS, 1941; CBS, WMCA, WOR-MBS, New York, 1942; WINS, New York, NY, 1945–1946; *White Owl Sports Smoker* was sponsored by White Owl Cigars featuring both Allen and Russ Hodges; NBC, 1947; MBS, 1949; *New York Yankees baseball play-by-play*, WINS, New York, NY and *Sports Daily*, NBC, 1953–1955). In addition to his sports work Allen performed some announcing chores on such programs as *Truth or Consequences.*

600 **Allen, Nancy.** COM-HE (WLAU, Laurel, MA, 1956–1957).

601 **Allen, Nina.** Soprano (*Nina Allen,* vcl. mus. prg., WGY, Schenectady, NY, 1936).

602 **Allen, [Allan] Nuba.** Singer (WEBH, Chicago, IL, 1925).

603 **Allen, Pat.** Newscaster (WBOW, Terre Haute, IN, 1937).

604 **Allen, Perry.** DJ (Morning man, WKBW, Buffalo, NY, mid–1950s; KRLA, Los Angeles, CA, 1959–1960 and KHJ, Los Angeles, CA, 1960). In the fall of 1960 an unusual event took place when DJ Allen was "traded" to station KHJ for another young DJ by the name of Wink Martindale.

605 **Allen, Phil.** Newscaster (KFBB, Great Falls, WT, 1939; KIDO, Boise, ID, 1942; KOIL, Omaha, NE, 1948–1954). Sports (KIDO, 1941–1942).

606 **Allen, Prescott.** *See **The Wife Saver—Allen Prescott.***

607 **Allen, Reginald.** Newscaster (WBT, Charlotte, NC, 1937–1938). Allen was also a talented vocalist on his own *Reginald Allen,* vcl. mus. prg. (WBT, 1936).

608 **Allen, Rex.** CW singer (*Rex Allen*, vcl. mus. prg., WLS, Chicago, IL, 1947). Allen, who also starred on the *National Barn Dance*, went on to become a singing cowboy movie star.

609 **Allen, Robert.** DJ (*Music in the Air*, KOVE, Lander, WY, 1954).

610 **Allen, Robert S.** News analyst Allen was a long-time columnist, who along with Drew Pearson, wrote a column and appeared on their radio program (*The Washington Merry-Go-Round,* 15 min., Weekly, MBS, 1935). He later conducted his own news program (WOR, New York, NY, 1947–1949).

611 **Allen, Roger.** Newscaster (WLAV, Grand Rapids, MI, 1942).

612 **Allen, Roger.** DJ (WTON, Staunton, VA, 1960).

613 **Allen, Ron.** DJ (WARM, Scranton, PA, 1960).

614 **Allen, Ron.** DJ (WSAI, Cincinnati, OH, 1960).

615 **Allen, Rosalie (Julie Marlene Bedra).** Allen, a popular CW singer, became New York City's first country-western music DJ (*Prairie Stars*, WOV, New York, NY, 1944–1956). Allen was popularly known as the "Hillbilly Yodeling Star of the 40s." She gained fame initially when she sang and recorded with Denver Darling's band (Denver Darling's Swing Billies) in 1944. Later, when she joined the Zeke Clements band she began singing popular duets with Elton Britt.

616 **Allen, Roy.** Newcaster (KTRI, Sioux City, IA, 1945).

617 **Allen, Ruth.** COM-HE (WGAR, Cleveland, OH, 1956–1957).

618 **Allen, Samuel L.** Allen performed on the tower chimes of a Pasadena Church. He was the owner and operator of station KPPC (Pasadena, CA, 1926).

619 **Allen, Shannon.** News commentator (*Education in the News*, NBC, 1938).

620 **Allen, Spencer.** Newscaster (KTAT, Fort Worth, TX, 1938; WGN, Chicago, IL, 1939–1954).

621 **Allen, Steven "Steve."** Sportscaster (*Spotlight on Sports*, KOKX, Keokuk, IA, 1950–1951; *Sports Parade*, KICD, Spencer, IA, 1953–1954).

622 **Allen, Taylor.** Daytime announcer (KMOX, St. Louis, MO, 1928).

623 **Allen, Ted.** DJ (*Allen's Frolics*, KATE, Albert Lea, MN, 1948).

624 **Allen, Tom.** Sportscaster (KWBC, Fort Worth, TX, 1948).

625 **Allen, Tom.** DJ (*OK Ballroom*, WOKZ, Alton, IL, 1954–1955).

626 **Allen, Tommy.** DJ (*Tommy's Variety Store*, KOMA, Oklahoma City, OK, 1948–1949).

627 **Allen, Tony.** Newscaster (WUSJ, Lockport, NY, 1954). Sportscaster (WUSJ, 1955).

628 **Allen, Vera.** Actress-comedienne Allen entered radio in 1928 doing dialect portrayals on the *Socony-Vacuum Hour* program. She appeared on many network shows during the following decades, including such daytime serials as: *Hilltop House, Joyce Jordan, Girl Interne, Thanks for Tomorrow, Big Sister, Wendy Warren and the News, and Young Dr. Malone.*

629 ***Allen, Virginia.*** Singer on the *Wynken, Blynken, and Nod* group program (KDYL, Salt Lake City, UT, 1929).

630 **Allen, Wayne.** Sportscaster (*Sports Cast*, KSEL, Lubbock, TX, 1947–1951).

631 **Allen, Webb.** Sportscaster (WELO, Taupelo, MS, 1945).

632 **Allen Saxophone Band.** *See* **Allen, Joseph.**

633 **Allenby, Peggy.** Busy daytime serial actress Allenby appeared on such programs as: *Aunt Jenny* aka *Aunt Jenny's Real Life Stories, Kate Hopkins, Angel of Mercy, Life Can Be Beau-*

tiful, Pages of Romance, Rich Man's Darling, The Road of Life, Claudia and David, David Harum, and *Dot and Will.*

634 **Allen's Serenaders.** Dance orchestra (WFAA, Dallas, TX, 1924).

635 **Allenson, Dorothy.** Vocalist (*Dorothy Allenson,* vcl. mus. prg, WIP, Philadelphia, PA, 1935).

636 **Allesee, Bob.** DJ (WNDU, South Bend, IN, 1960).

637 **Alletto, Vince.** DJ (*Driver's Digest,* WWL, New Orleans, LA, 1960).

638 **Alleva, Harry.** Newscaster (WBUD, Morrisville, PA, 1951).

639 **Alley, Ben.** Irish singer Alley was known as the "Blue Grass Tenor" (WKRC, Cincinnati, OH, 1926;. WSAI, Cincinnati, OH, 1927 and WMAQ, Chicago, IL, 1929). He was also active in the next decade (*Ben Alley,* vcl. mus. prg., CBS, 1934, 1937–1938).

640 **Alley, Clint.** Sportscaster (WKOY, Bluefield, WV, 1955–1956).

641 **Alley, George.** DJ (*Early Bird Show,* WIPS, Ticonderoga, NY, 1955).

642 **Alley, J. Landsey.** Newscaster (*Week in Review,* WKOY, Blueville, WV, 1951).

643 **Alley Pat.** *See* **Patrick, James.**

644 **Alley, Shelly Lee.** Tenor (WFAA, Dallas, TX, 1928).

645 **Alley, Vernon.** DJ (*Down in Vernon's Alley,* KROW, Oakland, CA, 1948).

646 **Alliger, Dick.** DJ (*Alliger's Almanac,* WBUX, Doylestown, PA, 1952).

647 **Allinger, Ralph.** Sportscaster (*Today in Sports,* WFAS, White Plains, NY, 1947–1948; *Sports Roundup,* WIBX, Utica, NY, 1954). DJ (*Musical Clock,* WIBX, 1952).

648 **Allis, Sarah.** Newscaster (*Turners Falls News,* WHAI, Greenfield, MA, 1951).

649 ***(The) Allis-Chalmers Family Party.*** Allis-Chalmers farm machinery company sponsored the half-hour variety program with a rural flavor added by the commentary of Joe DuMond, playing the role of "Josh Higgins of Finchville." Josh Higgins was a philosopher-singer-composer who was "typical of all that was finest in rural America." He supplied a practical common sense approach to life. DuMond became manager of station WMT (Waterloo, IA) in 1928. While there he was known as "The Singing Salesman." and creator of "Josh Higgins" at WMT (NBC, 1930s).

A later version of the program featured the music of the Joseph Gallicchio Orchestra and the songs of Annette King—"The Queen of Melody" (30 min., Saturday, 9:30–10:00 P.M., C.S.T., NBC-Blue, 1939).

650 **Allison, Bill.** Newscaster (WNNT, Warsaw, VA, 1955). Sportscaster (WNNT, 1955).

651 **Allison, Dan "Danny."** DJ (*Shop and Save,* KCLE, Cleburne, TX, 1952). Newscaster (KCUL, Fort Worth, TX, 1953).

652 **Allison, Fran.** Actress-singer (*Fran Allison,* vcl. mus. prg., NBC, Chicago, IL, 1939–1940s). Although Fran Allison sang on the NBC network and starred on the *Breakfast Club* program on that network, she gained her greatest fame by talking with the Kuklapolitan puppets on the *Kukla, Fran and Ollie* NBC television program. *See* ***The Breakfast Club.***

653 **Allison, Gene.** Newscaster (WPEN, Philadelphia, PA, 1955).

654 **Allison, Joe.** CW DJ (WMAK, Nashville, TN, 1947; KXLA, Pasadena, CA, 1950s). After leaving California, Allison worked on Nashville's WSIX and WSM.

655 **Allison, John and Lucy.** The folk song singing team broadcast a weekly sustaining local program (*John and Lucy Allison,* 15 min., Weekly, WQXR, New York, NY, 1938).

656 **Allison, Jone.** Actress Allison appeared on the daytime serial programs *The Guiding Light, Hearts in Harmony, Home of the Brave, Rosemary, When a Girl Marries, and Young Dr. Malone.*

657 **Allison, Ken.** Sportscaster (*Sportscope,* WANS, Anderson, SC, 1960).

658 **Allison, Mayme.** COM-HE (KBON, Omaha, NE, 1956).

659 **Allison, O.** News reporter (*News From Over the World,* KFWM, Oakland, CA, 1926).

660 **Allison, Paul.** Reader of poetry with an organ background (*Paul Allison,* instr. mus. prg., MBS, 1942).

661 **Allison, Robert.** Sportscaster (WNYC, New York, NY, 1941).

662 **Allison, Steve.** Newscaster (WPEN, Philadelphia, PA, 1955). DJ (WPEN, 1955).

663 **Allison, Tab.** DJ (*E-Z Listening,* WANS, Anderson, SC, 1960).

664 **Allman, Bob.** Sportscaster (*On the Sports Horizon,* KYW, Philadelphia, PA, 1947–1948).

665 **Allman, Claudia.** Singer (WIBO, Chicago, IL, 1926).

666 **Allman, Elvia.** Actress Allman appeared on the *Adventures of Ozzie and Harriet* situation comedy.

667 **Allmand, Joyce.** Contralto (*Joyce Allmand,* vcl. mus. prg., NBC, 1935).

668 **Allmon, Lucille.** COM-HE (KWBB, Wichita, KS, 1954).

669 **Allredge, Jay.** Newscaster (WJJJ, Montgomery, AL, 1953). DJ (*Today's Top Five,* WBRC, Birmingham, AL, 1954).

670 **Allwood, James I.** Newscaster (WSTS, Southern Pines, NC, 1949).

671 **Allyn, Harriet.** Actress Allyn appeared on the *Clara, Lu and Em* and *In Care of Aggie Horn* daytime serials.

672 **Allyn, Jack.** DJ (WAZF, Yazoo City, MS, 1949; WROV, Roanoke, VA, 1957).

673 **Allyn, Kay.** COM-HE (WSAN, Allentown, PA, 1958).

674 **Allyn, Rita.** Actress Allyn appeared on the *Empire Builders* program sponsored by Great Northern Railroad program broadcast on NBC-Blue in the late 1920s. *See* ***Empire Builders.***

675 **Alm, Jeanne.** Singer (WDAY, Fargo, ND, 1937).

676 **Alm, Ross C.** Newscaster (KBIM, Roswell, NM, 1954).

677 **Alman, Richard.** Sportscaster (WKAT, Miami Beach, FL, 1942).

678 ***(The) Almanac.*** The early morning program of music and jokes was conducted by Clellan Card "the Working Girls' Friend." Noted for his Scandanavian dialect routines, Card is probably best remembered for his annual parody in dialect of "The Night Before Christmas."

679 **Almen, E.L.** Newscaster (NBC, 1946).

680 **Almesan, Madame.** Pianist (WCSH, Portland, ME, 1934).

681 **Almon, Joseph.** Violinist (WMCA, New York, NY, 1925).

682 **Almon (Joseph) and Bower.** Instrumental duo of violin and piano (WAHG, Richmond Hill, NY, 1925).

683 **Almond, Becky.** Pianist (KSL, Salt Lake City, UT, 1942).

684 **Almond, Joyce.** Contralto (NBC, 1935).

685 **"ALN."** Designation for announcer J. Lewis Reed (WJZ, New York, NY and WJY, New York, NY, 1925).

686 ***Aloha Hawaiians Orchestra.*** Instr. mus. prg. (WHAS, Louisville, KY, 1933).

687 **Aloi, Fred.** Newscaster (*Views on the News,* WHIL, Medford, MA, 1953).

688 ***Along the Great White Way.*** Colin O'Moore narrated the quarter-hour Sunday evening music program with soprano Erva Giles and tenor Robert Simmons (15 min., Sunday, 6:30–6:45 P.M., WJZ-Blue, New York, NY, 1930).

689 **Alonzo, Ivo Luis.** DJ (KIFN, Phoenix, AZ, 1957).

690 **Alpen Brau Boys.** Musical group (*Alpen Brau Boys,* instr. mus. prg., KWTO, Springfield, MO, 1939).

691 ***(The) Alpen Brau Swingsters.*** Orchestra (*Alpen Brau Swingsters,* instr. mus. prg., KFH, Wichita, KS, 1940).

692 **Alpert, Marvin.** DJ (WOLF, Syracuse, NY, 1960).

693 **Alpert, Mickey.** Leader (*Mickey Alpert Orchestra,* instr. mus. prg., KFOR, Lincoln, NE, 1942).

694 **Alpert, Mildred.** COM-HE (WBZ, Boston, MA, 1958).

695 **Alpert, Pauline.** Pianist (*Pauline Alpert,* instr. mus. prg., WOR, Newark, NJ, 1934–1942). Alpert was known as "The Whirlwind Pianist."

696 **Alpha Omega Glee Club.** African-American singing group directed by N.W. Ryder (WLW, Cincinnati, OH, 1923).

697 **Alsing, Nellie Clark.** Soprano (KLX, Oakland, CA, 1929).

698 **Alsop, Carlton.** Director Alsop was a director of the *Don Ameche Show.*

699 **Alspach, Dave.** Sportscaster (KYUM, Yuma, AZ, 1960).

700 **Alstock, Bernice.** Staff contralto (KGW, Portland, OR, 1927).

701 **Alston, J. Robert "Bob."** Sportscaster (WKOY, Bluefield, WV, 1954–1955).

702 **Alstott, Sally.** COM-HE (WBCM, Bay City, MI, 1960).

703 **Alsup, Charles C.** Newscaster (KICA, Clovis, NM, 1937–1941). Sportscaster (KICA, 1939–1941).

704 Alt, Natalie. Singer on the *Major Bowes Capitol Family* program (NBC, 1929).

705 *(The) Alt Vien (Old Vienna) Orchestra.* Instr. mus. prg. (WLW, Cincinnati, OH, 1936; WLW, 1942).

706 Alta and Opal. The singing team was also known as the Dixie Girls of KMA (KMA, Shenandoah, IA, 1927).

707 Alta Ladies Band. Band directed by Mort Herron (WFAA, Dallas, TX, 1925).

708 Altenburg, James. DJ (WCCN, Nielsville, WI, 1960).

709 Alter, Lou. Singer (WNYC, New York, NY, 1925).

710 Alter, Sarah. Pianist Alter was a member with Mary C. Hoffman of a popular piano team (WEAF, New York, NY, 1926).

711 Alterman, James. Newscaster (WFAA, Dallas, TX, 1940).

712 Althouse, Lillian. Saxophonist (KFI, Los Angeles, CA, 1925).

713 Althouse, Paul. Tenor (WEAF, New York, NY, 1926–1927).

714 Altizer, Betsy. COM-HE (WRIC, Richlands, VA, 1955).

715 Altizer, Billy. Leader (*Billy Altizer's String Band*, WDBJ, Roanoke, VA, 1935).

716 Altman, Gary. Sportscaster (KORN, Mitchell, SD, 1955).

717 Altman, Les [Len]. Newscaster (WSAR, Fall River, MA, 1955). DJ (WSAR, 1955).

718 Altman, Richard "Dick." Sportscaster (WJHL, Johnson City, TN, 1938; WSAV, Savannah, GA, 1941; WTHT, Houston, TX, 1945–1946).

719 Altmiller, Jess. Leader (*Jess Altmiller Orchestra,* instr. mus. prg., WIP, Philadelphia, PA, 1936; WIP, 1942).

720 *(The) Altruists.* The Dallas, Texas, Rotary Club produced and performed on the dramatic program that was said to have been the first drama broadcast in 1922 by WFAA (Dallas, TX).

721 Altschuler, Bernard. Conductor of the Sylvania Foresters orchestra (NBC-Blue, New York, NY, 1929).

722 Alvarado, Leo. Violinist (WRC, Washington, DC, 1925).

723 Alvarez, Don. Vocalist (*Don Alvarez,* vcl. mus. prg., CBS, 1935).

724 Alvarez, Enrique. Newscaster (*Commentaries,* WAEL, Mayaguez, PR, 1949). Sportscaster (*Commentarios Deportivos,* WAEL, 1949).

725 Alvarez, Gustravo. Newscaster (KCOR, San Antonio, TX, 1957).

726 Alvern, Michael. Singer (WEEI, Boston, MA, 1925).

727 Alves, Bob. Sportscaster (*Spotlight on Sports,* KPRK, Livingston, MT, 1947). Newscaster (KSTV, Reno, NV, 1954).

728 *Always Be Careful Club.* The children's radio club was so successful that it led to the organization of the Lehigh Valley Junior Safety Council (WSAN, Allentown, PA, 1927).

729 Alwyn, Alice. Alwyn broadcast talks on investments (KJBS, San Francisco, CA, 1929).

730 Alwyn, Eve. COM-HE (WEAT, West Palm Beach, FL, 1957).

731 Alwyn, Lauri. COM-HE (WEAT, W. Palm Beach, FL, 1958).

732 Alyn, Kay. COM-HE (WSAN, San Francisco, CA, 1957).

733 Amadon, Arthur. DJ (WBZ-WBZA, Boston-Springfield, MA, 1948).

734 Amador, Charlie. Newscaster (KEPO, El Paso, TX, 1953).

735 *Amaizo's Gitanos.* Spanish orchestra (Instr. mus. program, NBC, 1928).

736 (The) Amalgamated Broadcasting System (ABS). In 1935, six small Atlantic Coast radio stations joined together as a network to "revolutionize" broadcast operations. Ed Wynn, the major stockholder called it a "New Deal in broadcasting." He said actors would be "unhampered." Advertising would be limited to ten words *before* and *after* each program. There was little attention paid to the new network, however, by either sponsors or listeners. Wynn, who was the president of the organization, left most of its management to others. He soon, however, saw evidence of fraudulent dealings and graft. Since he had invested $250,000 in the company, one day he simply walked out. A great deal of gossip swirled around Wynn. Some 300 law suits were filed against him. The Amalgamated Broadcast System's life was a short one. It went bankrupt after only a few months.

737 Aman, Lloyd. DJ (*Nite Owl,* KALE, Richland, WA, 1952).

738 *Amanda of Honeymoon Hill.* Another of the Frank and Anne Hummert daytime serial productions, *Amanda of Honeymoon Hill* was written by Elizabeth Todd. The story concerned Amanda, a "beauty with flaming hair" from a working class family married to Edward Leighton, a man from a wealthy old southern family. The show opened with the announcer saying: "This is the story of Edward and Amanda who now, in spite of the hatred of both their families, seek happiness on Honeymoon Hill in Virginia, in a world that few Americans know." The program's cast over the years included: Edward Andrews, Sanford Bickart, John Brown, John Connery, Paul Conrad, Staats Cotsworth, Boyd Crawford, Roger DeKoven, Florence Edney, Elizabeth Eustis, Ruth Gates, Joy Hathaway, Rod Hendrickson, Juano Hernandez, Irene Hubbard, John M. James, Lamont Johnson, Evelyn Juster, Jackie Kelk, George Lambert, Elizabeth Love, John (Jack) MacBryde, Florence Malone, Jay Meredith, John Raby, Richard Rider, Cecil Roy, Helen Shields, Muriel Starr, Chester Stratton, Reese Taylor, Linda Watkins, Patricia Wheel and Ruth Yorke. The program announcers were Frank Gallop, Hugh Conover and Howard Claney. The directors were Arnold Michaelis and Ernest Ricca (15 min., Monday through Friday, NBC-Blue, CBS, 1940–1946).

739 *Amateur Authors.* Matley Kemp produced the sustaining program on which amateur writers were given an opportunity to have their scripts broadcast (30 min., Tuesday, 9:00–9:30 P.M., KFWB, Los Angeles, CA, 1938).

740 *Amateur Night on Beale Street.* Memphis, Tennessee, listeners enjoyed the unusual amateur program presented by six co-op sponsors. Unlike the *Major Bowes Amateur Hour,* where a gong was used, this show stopped unlucky amateurs mid-performance by a gun shot (WNBR, Memphis, TN, 1935).

741 *Amateur Try-Out Hour.* KEX (Portland, Oregon) broadcast the unique program on Monday afternoons from 5:00–6:00 P.M. in 1928, for the sole purpose of finding amateur talent for their broadcast schedule.

742 Amauli, Guilio. Newscaster (WHOM, Jersey City, NJ, 1941).

743 *(The) Amazing Mrs. Danbury.* When Martin Hurt, who portrayed *Beulah,* died in 1946, Tums sponsored Agnes Moorehead in *Calamity Jane* as a replacement program. Although Moorehead was bright and funny on the program as she twisted men around her finger with ease, it lasted for only one season. Tums replaced it with *The Amazing Mrs. Danbury.* On this program, Miss Morehead played Mrs. Jonathon Danbury, the widowed owner of a town's leading department store. Cathy Lewis and Dan Wolfe were also in the cast and Ken Niles was the announcer. *Variety* called it good entertainment with Moorehead performing at her best as a sharp-tongued old lady (30 min., Sunday, 8:00–8:30 P.M., CBS, 1946).

744 Ambassador Hotel Concert Orchestra. Orchestra directed by Josef Rosenfeld (KNX, Hollywood, CA, 1925–1926).

745 Ambassador Hotel Dance Orchestra. Hollywood dance band (KNX, Los Angeles, CA, 1926).

746 Amber's Dance Orchestra. Band that broadcast from the Amber Ballroom of the Portland Elks' Temple (KOIN, Portland, OR, 1927).

747 Ambert Dance and Concert Orchestra. Popular dance band (WDAF, Kansas City, MO, 1924).

748 Ambler, Frena. Announcer-Associate Program Director (KMA, Shenandoah, IA, 1928).

749 Ambrose, John V. "Johnny." Sportscaster (*Speaking of Sports,* WTAG, Worcester, MA, 1948–1956).

750 Ambrose, Joyce. COM-HE (WTAN, Clearwater, FL, 1958).

751 Ambrose, Roy. DJ (WTUX, Wilmington, DE). Newscaster (WBKV, West Bend, WI, 1954).

752 Ambrose, Tom. DJ (WTRC, Elkhart, IN, 1960).

753 *(The) Ambrosius Sisters.* Vcl. mus. prg. featuring two singing Ambrosius sisters (WTAQ, Green Bay, WI, 1937).

754 Amburg, Van. Sportscaster (KPIX, San Francisco, CA, 1960).

755 Ameche, Don. Before his successful motion picture career, Ameche had a varied radio career as actor, comedian and MC. Among the many programs on which he appeared were *Betty and Bob* (actor), *The Don Ameche Show* (actor), *First Nighter* (actor), *Grand Hotel* (actor), *National Farm and Home Hour* (actor), *The Bickersons* (comedian), *Edgar Bergen and Charlie McCarthy Show* (MC) and the *Old Gold Show* (comedian).

756 **Ameche, Jim.** DJ (KLAC, Los Angeles, CA, 1954; WNJR, Newark, NJ, 1955; WJVA, South Bend, IN, 1960; KXIV, Phoenix, AZ, 1960). Although he never was as nationally prominent as his brother Don, Jim Ameche had a long successful career as announcer, actor and DJ. Probably his best known acting jobs were in the title roles of *Jack Armstong the All-American Boy* and *Silver Eagle, Mountie*. In addition, he acted on the *Attorney-at-Law, Big Sister* and *Grand Hotel* programs. He also was MC on *Hollywood Playhouse*.

757 **Ameche, Jim, Jr.** Young Ameche appeared on the *Big Sister* daytime serial program.

758 **Amend, Eddie.** DJ (*Rhythms by Request*, KHON, Honolulu, HI, 1949).

759 ***America Calling.*** During the Korean War, Regent cigarettes sponsored the music program hosted by Rebel Randall on which records were played from servicemen's requests. In addition, wives and sweethearts of overseas servicemen were allowed to place telephone calls to them during the program. The same idea was used previously during World War II on the *Transatlantic Call* program. Guest stars such as Dinah Shore frequently appeared on the program. The announcer was George Walsh (30 min., Sunday, 4:00–4:30 P.M., CBS, 1952).

760 ***America Flies.*** Dick Bircher broadcast the flying lessons he was giving to stenographer Ursula Carroll (WCAU, Philadelphia, PA, 1940).

761 ***America in Music.*** John Trasker Howard narrated the musical series that its announcer claimed "depicted the panorama of American life as painted in native melodies." Howard was supported by a concert orchestra with instrumental and vocal soloists (NBC-Blue, 1935).

762 ***America Sings.*** S.C. Johnson Company sponsored the variety program that was a summer replacement for *Fibber McGee and Molly* in 1940. Comedian Cliff Nazarro and Meredith Willson's orchestra were featured (30 min., Tuesday, 9:00–9:30 P.M., NBC-Red, 1940).

763 **American Dye Works Orchestra.** Popular California radio band (KFWB, Hollywood, CA, 1926).

764 **American LaFrance Orchestra.** Commercial radio band (WFAA-NBC, Dallas, TX, 1927).

765 **American Legion Band of Little Rock, Arkansas.** Legion Commander Lloyd Judd directed the hour program featuring a local American Legion post band (WLBN, Little Rock, AR, 1928).

766 **American Orchestral Society's Orchestra.** Orchestra directed by Chambers Clifton (WJZ, New York, NY, 1923).

767 **American Philharmonic Orchestra.** Symphonic orchestra directed by F. Longo (KYA, San Francisco, CA, 1929).

768 **(The) American Singers.** Popular male quartet (WLW, Cincinnati, OH, 1929).

769 **American Salon Orchestra.** Francesco Longo directed the orchestra (KJR, Seattle, WA, 1928).

770 ***American Ace Coffee Time.*** Grant Turner hosted the CW music program broadcast from Nashville's Ryman Auditorium, the home of the *Grand Ole Opry*. The American Ace Coffee Company was the sponsor. Roy Acuff and the Smokey Mountain Boys were featured (WSM, Nashville, TN, 1948–1949).

771 ***American Adventure.*** Dr. Stanley High was the commentator on the weekly series of 13 programs that presented the saga of a typical American family. The program's theme was the epic of America and American life (NBC-Blue, 1935).

772 ***American Album of Familiar Music.*** The long-running good music program, sponsored by Bayer Aspirin, was broadcast by NBC from 1931 through 1951. The show concluded its broadcast run in 1952 on ABC. Over the years Frank Munn, Vivian Della Chiesa, Evelyn MacGregor, Jean Dickenson, Daniel Lieberfeld, Arden and Arden, Donald Dame and the Bertrand Hersch, Gustave Haenschen and Abe Lyman orchestras were featured. Frank and Anne Hummert were the show's producers, James Haupt the director and Andre Baruch, Roger Krupp and Howard Claney the announcers (30 min., Sunday, NBC and ABC, 1931–1952).

773 ***(The) American Company of Arkansas Hour.*** Music for the program was provided by singer Sue Bearnoff, pianist Mrs. W.B. Goetz and Lloyd Hemphill on banjo (KGHI, Little Rock, AR, 1927–1928).

774 ***American Family Robinson.*** The transcribed series was broadcast in the midst of the Great Depression. It stressed family values, hard work and the strength of the American economic system. The program was funded and produced by an organization of industrial manufacturers (15-min., Transcribed, Monday through Friday, WIND, Chicago, IL, 1935; WCBD, Waukegan, IL, 1936; WWVA, Wheeling, WV, 1935).

775 ***American Fireside — A Half-Hour of Civilization.*** Although the program's title was somewhat pretentious, it did present a series of talks by "men and women who have contributed to the mental life of the nation." The first speaker was novelist Dorothy Canfield Fisher (9:30–9:45 P.M., NBC-Blue, 1934).

776 ***American Home Banquet.*** A half-hour music program, *American Home Banquet* was broadcast five times weekly (30 min., Monday through Friday, 6:30–7:00 P.M., WEAF, New York, NY, 1929).

777 ***(An) American in England.*** Written, produced and directed by Norman Corwin, this was a World War II production that emphasized the contribution England had and was making in the war against Hitler. The series was a combination of dramatic and documentary elements. Some programs were broadcast from England, others from the United States. Their casts included such British and American performers as: David Baxter, Edna Best, Leslie Bradley, Laidman Browne, John Bryning, Clifford Buckton, Gwen Day Burrows, Gerald Cooper, Phillip Cunningham, Terence deMarney, Tommy Duggan, Olga Edwards, Lyn Evans, Paul Fierro, Richard George, Dorothy Greene, Angela Gynne, Betty Hardy, Nicholas Joy, Joseph Julian, Curigwen Lewis, Frank Lovejoy, Robert Marsden, James McKechnie, Joan Miller, Edward R. Murrow, Tommy Palmer, MacDonald Parke, Harry Ross, Alfred Shirley, Everett Sloane, Dorothy Smith, John Snagge, Julian Somers, Thorley Walters, Arthur Young and Gladys Young.

778 ***American Legion Championship Band.*** American Legion musical group (*American Legion Championship Band,* instr. mus. prg., NBC, 1939).

779 ***(The) American Melody Hour.*** Frank and Anne Hummert produced the good music program that featured such performers as Bob Hannon, Evelyn MacGregor, Stanley McClelland, the Knightsbridge Chorus and Victor Arden's orchestra. The announcer opened it this way: "Next — the *American Melody Hour* dedicated to the druggists of America, who supply you with Bayer Aspirin. Ladies and gentlemen, here's the *American Melody Hour* bringing you the songs of the day so you can know them all, sing them all your self." It was an excellent musical program (Weekly, 30 min., CBS, 1947).

780 ***American Music Hall.*** Leonard Blair produced and Joe Graham directed the sustaining music program that featured such performers as Paul Whiteman, Larry Douglas, June Valli and Glen Osser's Orchestra. John Hicks was the announcer (60 min., Sunday, 8:00–9:00 P.M., ABC, 1952).

781 ***(The) American Musical Festival.*** The program, begun in 1940, was a musical celebration of American values, tradition and heritage. Broadcast annually between the birthdays of Lincoln and Washington, it presented symphony, swing, opera, popular music, folk music, jazz, chamber music, marches and ballads. Among the famous musicians, music groups, guest conductors and composers that appeared on the program were Morton Gould, Deems Taylor, Oscar Levant, Aaron Copeland, Richard Hale, Roy Harris, Jules Bledsoe, the Kolisch Quartet, Ralph Kirkpatrick, the American Ballad Singers, Benny Goodman, Burl Ives, Tommy Dorsey, Earl Robinson, Lucas Foss, Leonard Bernstein and Virgil Thomson (WNYC, New York, NY, 1940).

782 ***American Musical Review.*** Soprano Vivienne Segal, tenor Frank Munn and violinist Bertrand Hirsch appeared on the half-hour music program with an orchestra directed by Gus Haenschen (30 min., Sunday, 8:30–9:00 P.M., NBC, 1935).

783 ***American Pageant of Youth.*** Youthful performers, at least one of whom later enjoyed great success on radio, were featured on the program. They included comedian Pinky Mitchell, the Four Bars Quartet, hillbilly singer Billy Pape, baritone Cy Bofird, soprano Margaret Laren, comedians Ginger Snap, Ezra Stone and Sandy Douglas plus the music of Johnny Johnston's orchestra (30 min., NBC, 1936).

784 ***(The) American Radiator Musical Interlude.*** The music program sponsored by the American Radiator Company featured bass Sigurd Nilssen. Graham McNamee was the announcer (Saturday, 30 min., 7:30–8:00 P.M., NBC, 1935).

785 ***(The) American Radio Warblers.*** Canaries chirped and sang their hearts out ac-

companied by background organ music on the *American Radio Warblers*, a pleasant 15-minute program that had been on the air in one form or another since 1937. Sometimes the program was called *Hartz Mountain Canaries*, the *Master Radio Canaries* or *American Radio Canaries*. Individual birds, such as "Frankie the Crooner" were often featured (15 min., Sunday, 2:15–2:30 P.M., MBS, 1952).

786 ***(The) American Review.*** The variety show featuring the music of the Freddy Martin Orchestra and the comedy of the Marx Brothers was sponsored by the American Oil company (30 min., Sunday, 7:00–7:00 P.M., CBS, 1934).

787 ***(The) American School of the Air.*** CBS broadcast the *American School of the Air*, one of the finest educational programs presented by network radio during Radio's Golden Age. Written by Harry Granich, Edward Mabley and Howard Rodman, topics on history, literature, geography and current affairs were covered. Many schools made the program, broadcast Monday through Friday, required listening for their students. One of the popular features used to teach geography was the program's "Hamilton Family" segment, on which pieces of geographical information were provided by the dramatic segments that portrayed the family's fictional world tour. The members of the Hamilton family were portrayed by Albert Aley, Betty Garde, Gene Leonard, John Marks, Ruth Russell and Walter Tetley. Knowles Entriken and Kirby Hawkes directed the Hamilton Family segment.

One of the program's most stimulating programs was on Tuesday, November 16, 1937, when the Sage of Baltimore, H.L. Mencken, spoke on "Americanisms" to differentiate American English from that spoken in Great Britain. Lexicographer Cabell Greet also discussed American Dialects on the program. The next day's program was devoted to a geography lesson — "Ireland and Its High Civilization."

Among the program's various hosts and frequent performers were Lyman Bryson, Ray Collins, Parker Fennelly, Mitzi Gould and Chester Stratton. The program's various directors were

Howard Barnes, Oliver Daniel, John Dietz, Robert B. Hudson, Leon Levine, Marx Loeb, Earle McGill, Richard Sanville and Albert Ward. The music was directed by Channon Collinge and Dorothy Gordon. Robert "Bob" Trout was the announcer (CBS, 1930–1948).

788 ***(The) American Theater Wing Lecture Hall.*** The sustaining quarter-hour lecture program presented distinguished critic Harold Clurman discussing various aspects of American theater news and trends. Paul Brentson was the announcer (15 min., Wednesday, 10:00–10:25 P.M., WNEW, New York, NY, 1949).

789 **American Traitors on Radio.** Radio was not always a medium that broadcast messages of truth, morality and patriotism. There were such charlatans as John R. Brinkley and Huey Long, and at times the airwaves carried messages of intolerance and hatred. However, no more poisonous messages were beamed to the American public than those broadcast by such traitors as "Lord Haw Haw," "Axis Sally," "Paul Revere," "Mr. O.K.,""Mr. Guess Who," the "Georgia Peach" and "Tokyo Rose" during World War II. If the venomous messages of Tokyo Rose never reached listeners in the continental United States, they were nevertheless heard by many American GIs serving in the Pacific War Theater. All the others *could have been* and *were* heard in the United States on even the cheapest shortwave radios. The story of these American traitors is a fascinating and often a disturbing one.

Not all Nazi propaganda broadcasts originated outside the United States. Frances Chase, Jr. reported on some of the techniques that were used by Germany to use pre-war American radio to spread their propaganda, some of which were directly paid for by the German government (*Movie and Radio Guide*, August 24–30, 1940, pp. 38–39).

In May, 1940, for example, Ernest Ten Eichen, president of the German-American Alliance (Deutsche-Amerikansche Einheitsfront) spoke over station WHIP (Hammond, Indiana)and played the "Horst Wessel" and "Badenweiller March," both favorites of Adolf Hitler.

Ten Eichen previously had broadcast in Germany. Speaking in English, he spoke of the supposedly poor treatment of Germans in the United States: "It is not enough that Americans of German extraction are made the victims of undeserved suspicion, defamation, oppression and persecution. It is not enough that they are deprived of this honor, social and economic welfare. They are now to be made political criminals, free to be hunted, arrested, prosecuted, sentenced and imprisoned." These were charges similar to those directed against the Austrians and Czechs before the German annexation of their countries.

The German-American Alliance broadcast their programs six times a week over WHIP for $750 a week. In San Francisco the Dies Committee investigated similar broadcasts by Henry Lage and discovered they were paid for by the German counsul — Baron Manfred von Killinger.

The following year it was reported that the German Library of Information, located at 17 Battery Place in New York City, distributed their publication, *Germany Calling*, that contained weekly schedules of Nazi shortwave propaganda broadcasts directed at American listeners. These weekly programs included talks, news and music. Programs such as the *Women's Club*, news reports in English, Lord Haw Haw, the Berlin Philharmonic Orchestra, *Easter Bells are Ringing*, *O.K Speaking* and *Soldiers' Songs* were broadcast regularly.

Charlie and His Orchestra

During the Thirties when the Nazis came to power, swing music and jazz were strictly *verboten*, it was considered *unerwunscht musik* (undesirable music), because it was degenerate because of its non–Aryan origins. A law was passed in 1935 banning jazz from being played on German radio. Even though the Nazis tried to suppress it in Germany, they used this music as an important part of their propaganda efforts against the United States and Great Britain. The major instrument by which jazz and swing was used by the German propaganda ministry was Charlie and his Orchestra.

Charlie and His Orchestra was founded in 1939 to disseminate anti–British and anti–American propaganda more effectively. The chief German propaganda program on their North American (shortwave) Service was *Germany Calling*, featuring such American traitors as Lord Haw Haw, Axis Sally, Paul Revere and Mr. O.K. Regardless of who was on the particular program, however, invariably there was music played by Charlie and his Orchestra with vocals by Charlie. Although the band was patterned after those of Glen Miller, Tommy Dorsey and Benny Goodman, it never reached the musical level of any of these three bands.

Two major misconceptions remain about Charlie and his Orchestra. First, even the name is a misnomer. Although the featured vocalist was Karl "Charlie" Schwedler, who delivered the propaganda message, the band actually was that of Lutz Templin. Second, the band did not consist of ex-members of concentration camps or citizens of countries conquered by the Germans, nor were there any Americans among its members.

The band typically would play popular American songs and "Charlie" [Karl Schwedler] would sing the original lyric's first verse to be followed later by the second altered to contain lyrics derogatory of Americans, British and Jews. Frequently, Schwedler would stop singing to deliver a monolog chastising President Roosevelt, Prime Minister Winston Churchill or the Jews. An example of the altered lyrics most of whom were written by Schwedler himself is that for "Slumming on Park Avenue." "Charlie" in virtually accent free English would sing:

> Let's go smelling where they're dwelling,
> Sniffing everything the way they do.
> Let us go to it, let's do it.
> Why can't we do it too?
> Let's go slumming, nose thumbing on Park Avenue.

Typical of the songs Charlie and His Orchestra played with altered lyrics were:

"You're Driving Me Crazy,"
"Stormy Weather,"
"I Want to be Happy,"
"I'm Putting All My Eggs in One Basket,"
"F.D.R. Jones,"
"After You've Gone,"
"Japanese Sandman."

Born on August 13, 1902 in Germany, Schwedler rose to prominence in 1939 as a member of the USA Section of the Foreign Minister's broadcasting section, writing the anti–British, anti–Semitic and anti–American lyrics that he later sang with Charlie's Orchestra. When World War II ended, he worked as a croupier in a Berlin casino. By 1960, Schwedler, his wife and two children settled into anonymity in the United States, where few, if any, of his neighbors or co-workers knew of the prominent propaganda role he played during World War II. Many of his 90 recordings are still available, and it must be admitted that their cleverness and mean spirit are still evident.

The lyrics sung or spoken by Charlie frequently were targeted at Winston Churchill and Franklin D. Roosevelt. They also contained vicious attacks on Jews whenever possible. For example, Charlie said Churchill's latest tear-jerker was "You're Driving Me Crazy" in which he complains, "You Germans are driving me crazy." Furthermore, he complains, "The Jews are the friends who are near me to cheer me, but the Jews are not the kind of heroes who will fight for me. You Germans are driving me crazy."

"Stormy Weather" also has Churchill complaining. This time it is his navy that worries him: "Stormy weather since my ships and German planes got together. Can't keep my poor ships together. They're sinking all the time. Even my true friends are gone. I'm beaten all the time. I'm beaten all the time." London's people supposedly are singing in Charlie's version of "When Day is Done." They sing: "When day is done, we dream of peace. London's life has lost its charm. The air raids are getting us down. This is Churchill's war. It's not too late to get rid of him. Churchill is the world's enemy number one."

A major theme of Charlie's propaganda was how Churchill was exploiting Americans. This can be heard in the lyrics he wrote for "I Want to be Happy" and "I'm Putting All My Eggs in One Basket." In the former, Churchill said, "I want to be happy, but I won't be happy until I get the USA into the war, too. I need money, ships and tanks from you. I want to be happy, but I won't be happy until I get the United States in this muddle,too. Just give me all your money. England always pays her debts as you know."In the latter, Churchill sang to the Americans, "I'm putting all my eggs in one basket. I'm betting everything I've got on you. I'm giving my British Empire to you, Yankee. I'm betting everything I've got on you."

Sometimes Charlie combined attacks on Churchill with his comments about how the British people were suffering in the war. Churchill is condemned in "Goody, Goody," as one who never fought in France and doesn't know how it feels and, furthermore, "would like to put the whole world on a barrel of dynamite." Adapting "St. Louis Blues," a "Negro from the London docks" sings "The Blackout Blues." He sings, "I hate to see the evening sun go down, cause the Germans done bombed this town. Churchill and his "bloody war" is a bad man."

No theme, however, was repeated more frequently than that of the particularly bitter attacks on Jews. The most venomous of these attacks were Charlie's lyrics in "Mr. F.D.R., Jones" and "Makin' Whoopee." Adaptations of these songs enabled him to engage in virulent anti–Semitic attacks. "Mr. F.D.R. Jones," as adapted by Charlie began by announcing, "It's a Hebrew holiday everywhere for the Jewish family has a brand new heir — Mr. Franklin D. Roosevelt Jones." Later, the U.S.A. was charged with aggressive intervention by Roosevelt: "He sends troops everywhere to engage in foreign wars — Mr. Franklin D. Roosevelt Jones. He's aggressive, as aggressive can be. If he could he'd like to be known as the great emperor — Franklin D. Roosevelt Jones."

Introducing the song "Makin' Whoopee," Charlie said, "The Jews of the U.S.A. have asked Eddie Cantor to write a new version of his famous old favorite, "Makin' Whoopee." The supposed result included these lyrics sung by "Cantor," "Another war, another profit. A lot of gold. The British Empire is being sold. Another Jewish Christmas rich, another season another reason for making whoopee. We're in the money. Washington is our ghetto. Roosevelt is our king. Democracy is our motto. Think what a war will bring. We're the kikes of the U.S.A. . You are the goy folk, we are the boy folk. We're in the money." Anti-Jewish attacks were a staple of German propaganda, but only Lord Haw Haw (William Joyce) combined the wit and viciousness that frequently outdid Charlie and his Orchestra in that endeavor.

Charlie and his orchestra along with such American traitors as Lord Haw Haw and Axis Sally were regularly heard on the *Germany Calling* program broadcast on Germany's North American Service shortwave schedule. *Germany Calling* was broadcast Tuesday and Thursday evening at 7:15 P.M. Eastern War Time. Another American traitor, Mr. Guess Who (Robert Guest), on the other hand, broadcast many weekday evenings at 8:15 P.M. Eastern War Time. Of all the traitorous broadcasters the most famous — or infamous — was William Joyce, who broadcast as Lord Haw Haw.

Lord Haw Haw

American born William Joyce, known to the British as Lord Haw Haw, was the best known German propagandist of World War II. Ironically, it was his claim of American citizenship that was the chief defense in his British trial for treason.

Joyce was born in the United States in Brooklyn. When he was three his family moved to Ireland. At 15 his family moved again. This time to England. Two years later, he joined the British Fascisti Ltd., a movement that praised Mussolini and virulently condemned "Jewish Communists." He soon left the group, however, to join the Conservative Party. In 1932, he left the Conservatives and became a dedicated party member of Sir Oswald Mosley's British Union of Fascists.

Warned that he would be interned during the impending war, Joyce moved to Berlin in 1939, a week before the outbreak of World War II. At the age of 33, he began broadcasting German propaganda to British listeners, who immediately nicknamed him Lord Haw Haw. During the war Joyce's anti–Semitic attacks never faded, for he always blamed the war on international Jewish financiers. His propaganda efforts were particularly effective early in the war, as he spoke of a Fifth Column in Britain and accurately described town clocks that had stopped and the number of steps needed to reach the steeples in various churches. His accuracy on these details caused dismay, anxiety and sometimes panic among British listeners.

The combined effects of advancing Allied armies and the persistent effects of his alcoholism caused Joyce to move from Berlin to Hamburg as the Russian armies advanced closer to the Reich's capital. He was probably drunk when he made his last broadcast from Hamburg on April 30, 1945, as British troops entered the city.

In his last broadcast Joyce warned that Britain would be poor following the war, having lost her wealth and power during the six years of war. His final broadcast carried a much different tone than his previous ones. The old confidence and arrogance of his earlier broadcasts were gone. To the end, however, he was a committed Nazi and continued apologist for Germany and her war aims.

"We might have avoided the hatred [war]," he said, "if Germany and England had decided to preserve the welfare of this continent, I would have been happy." Germany alone, Joyce proclaimed, had attempted to stem the Bolshevik advance. It was the German legions, according to him, that saved England by attacking Russia. If there can not be an alliance between Germany and Great Britain, he stated, my work has been a failure. Praising and explaining Germany's present condition, Joyce said that in Germany there was a spirit of unity and strength. "We [the Germans] have a unified people. They do not want to take what is not there's. They only want to live peacefully without outside influences."

Rambling, disjointed and lacking both logic and truth, Joyce went on to explain that Poland was merely a pretense for Great Britain's declaration of war. Furthermore, he prophesied that the people of Britain would deserve what they get, since they now must make terms with the Bolsheviks. The end of the war, he insisted, might bring a greater World War than was ever thought possible. With a shrillness and strident tone, he insisted that whatever happens, "Germany will live. No measures of oppression or tyranny will shatter Germany. Germany will live. Because the people of Germany have in them the secret of life. In these last words, you may not hear from me again for a few months. I say [in German] Live Germany, Heil Hitler and farewell." Unrepentant, shrill and strident it was his last broadcast. Joyce escaped capture for some time, until he was spotted and taken into custody by British troops near the Danish border.

Although he was born in the U.S.A., raised in Ireland, and lived in England with a passport, he was nevertheless tried in a British court for treason, convicted and sentenced to death by hanging. When executed on January 3, 1945, Joyce was still defiant, criticizing the Jews and the "power of darkness they represent."

Joyce made his first broadcast as Haw Haw on September 18, 1939 and continued until April 30, 1945. The *first* Lord Haw Haw was Wolf Mitler, but before his first month was over Joyce took over the role. Joyce's program became very popular in British Isles, claiming more than six million listeners. Mitler eventually appeared with Mildred Gillars on the Axis Sally program. After the war ended Mitler had a successful career in German television.

Joyce's propaganda was effective, because he was very different from the BBC. He used direct plain ordinary English, sneers, parody, rumor, gossip and frequently humor. The BBC, by contrast, was formal. Joyce was anything but. He was by far the most brilliant of all the propagandists broadcasting from Germany.

Joyce and other German propaganda was

sent by short wave to North and South America. To England and the continent of Europe it was broadcast over a medium (middle) wave station. British listeners, therefore, heard Lord Haw Haw nightly on that station.

Frederick Wilhelm Kaltenbach

Frederick Wilhelm Kaltenbach, not nearly as well known as William Joyce, was another American broadcasting on Radiofunk for the Third Reich. Known as "Lord Hee Hee" by British listeners, Kaltenbach was born in Dubuque, Iowa on March 29, 1895. In addition to broadcasting, Kaltenbach wrote numerous dramas broadcast on German radio attacking the British and American war effort. He also wrote and personally broadcast a series of talks, "British Disregard for American Rights," in which he satirized the American Lend-Lease Bill and viciously attacked President Roosevelt.

He visited Germany in 1932 and became convinced that the Nazis did not deserve the condemnation they often received in the United States. Kaltenbach, after observing the conditions in Nazi Germany, said the Communists worked at the expense of good German workers who were unemployed, while the Jews lived a life of luxury. After he returned to the United States, he resumed high school teaching in Dubuque, his home city. But he soon ran into trouble at the school when he formed a boys' hiking club, organized on the pattern of the German Hitler's Youth Movement. After losing his teaching job for forming the boys' club, he returned to Germany to seek a Ph.D. degree at the University of Berlin. While working toward the degree he was employed by the German government as translator and writer.

After receiving his Ph.D. degree in 1936, he began a series of "Dear Harry" broadcasts, so named because they were supposedly directed to a friend in his native state of Iowa, in which he expressed his strong sympathy for German National Socialism and his hatred of Jews. Throughout the war he railed loudly against the British and Americans. He said that he was proud that the British called him the "American Lord Haw Haw" and gave him the "Lord Hee Hee" nickname.

In addition to his own broadcasts, Katenbach regularly appeared on several dramatic propaganda programs and also wrote the Saturday night "Military Review" and "British Disregard for American Rights" programs. Notably, he wrote an infamous radio drama intended for D-Day invasion forces readying to storm Fortress Europe, for which Mildred Gillars (Axis Sally) was convicted of treason.

After broadcasting throughout the war and protesting to the end Germany's righteous cause, he was captured by British soldiers in July 1945 when they took Berlin. Kaltenbach died in a Russian concentration camp three months later of natural causes.

Axis Sally

Mildred Elizabeth Sisk ("Axis Sally") was born in Portland, Maine on November 29, 1900. After her parents divorced in 1907, her mother married Robert B. Gillars, the name she used from then on. She moved to New York after attending Ohio Wesleyan to pursue a career in the theater. Her effort to become an actress brought her only limited success, although she did find some work in musical comedies, stock companies and vaudeville. Significantly, while living in New York she studied music at Hunter College, where she fell in love with her music professor, Max Otto Koischewitz, later known as German propagandist "Mr. O.K."

Gillars moved to France in 1933, where she worked as a sales girl and a governess. She moved to Germany two years later to teach English at the Berlitz School of Languages in Berlin. At the urging and assistance of Max Otto Koischewitz, she went to work for the Radio Berlin Reichsrundfunk Overseas Service as actress and announcer. During World War II she conducted her daily program, *Home Sweet Home*, which combined good music from back home in America with sultry voiced propaganda aimed at GI's. She was particularly vicious as she regularly signed-off by telling them she had a hot date, and that she wondered if their sweethearts and wives back home were going to have the same thing with some 4-F's.

Some GI's began to call her "Axis Sally," but others scornfully called her the "Bride of Lord Haw Haw." On some of her broadcasts, Gillars would give the names and serial numbers of some captured and wounded American GI's. Sometimes her description of some wounded soldiers would be particularly cruel by implying that perhaps they would not survive their wounds by asking, "Who knows?"

A frequent trick used by Gillars was to pose as an International Red Cross representative to record interviews with American prisoners, telling them she would broadcast their uninterrupted messages to their family and friends at home. She often used this ruse in an effort to get them to produce "happy" messages to indicate they were being well treated as prisoners of war in Germany.

Although she had promised the GI's messages would be broadcast uninterrupted, they frequently were presented with her outbursts of such propagandas: "It's disgrace to the American public that they don't wake to the fact of what Franklin D. Roosevelt is doing to the gentiles of your country and my country."

After the Axis was defeated Gillars remembered her country by seeking aid from American forces in Germany. She was detained after spending several weeks in an American hospital in 1946. Even then, however, she was soon released from an internment camp and given a pass that allowed her to live in the French Zone of Germany. When she soon returned to the American Zone to get her pass renewed, she was detained by the American Army. After a year of detention, Gillars was returned to the United States and charged with 10 counts of treason. The number was later dropped to eight when she went on trial. The prosecutor brought out the fact that she had signed an oath of allegiance to Germany when she went to work for Radio Berlin Reichsrundfunk. Furthermore, Gillars was charged with posing as a representative of the International Red Cross in order to obtain cheerful interviews with American prisoners of war. The prosecutor pointed out their messages were combined with Nazi propaganda that was far from cheerful.

A number of veterans who had heard her broadcasts , or been interviewed by Gillars while a German prisoner of war, testified against her. Her defense rested primarily on the contention that she was not responsible for acts, since she was little more than a puppet of her lover — Max Otto Koischewitz. Furthermore, her counsel argued that under freedom of speech guarantees it was not treasonous to express anti–Semitic opinions or criticize an American president.

Despite all the evidence presented, Gillars was convicted on the basis of only one of the many broadcasts she made for Germany. She was convicted in 1949 on only one count of treason for acting in the *Vision of Invasion*, a radio drama written, produced and directed by Koischewitz. A particularly vicious drama, it was beamed both to the United States and American forces in England preparing to invade the German held continent. Koischewitz insisted that Gillars play the leading role in the drama, that of an Ohio mother who dreams of her soldier son in England waiting to invade Fortess Europe.

Gillars was sentenced to from 10 to 30 years, fined $10,000 and made eligible for parole after 10 years. She was paroled in 1961. After teaching music in a Catholic school for girls in Ohio, she returned to Ohio Wesleyan to receive her bachelor's degree. She died at 87 in 1988.

Max Otto Koischwitz

Dr. Max Otto Koischwitz, Axis Sally's so-called Svengali, broadcast for the Nazis under such names as "Mr. O.K.," "Dr. Anders" and "Fritz." of the *Fred and Fritz, the Friendly Quarrelers*. He was born February 19, 1902, in the German Silesian village of Jauer. He achieved an excellent academic record and accepted a teaching position, but he was not willing to accept the poor teaching pay in Germany and emigrated to the United States in 1924. After brief adjunct teaching positions at Columbia University, New York University and Hunter College, he eventually attained a full-time position in the latter school's German department. He gained academic credibility by publishing numerous professional articles and was considered to be a good teacher. By 1937 he had been a visiting scholar at West Virginia and the University of Berlin and received Hunter College's "Outstanding Teacher" award. The following year, despite the recognition he had received, Koischwitz did not believe that the college was fully according him what he deserved.

Although Koischwitz's academic reputation was solid and he enjoyed popularity with students, his strong pro–German sentiments brought him to the attention of the Hunter College administration and New York City's Board of Higher Education. Nevertheless, he had became an American citizen in 1935, hoping this would help him be tenured as a full professor at Hunter. He was particularly frustrated, therefore, in 1938, when the college granted him tenure at only the assistant professor level.

With the beginning of World War II in 1939, his pro–German writings and speeches had made him extremely controversial, causing New York City's Board of Higher Education to place him on leave of absence without pay. Fearing his arrest, he resigned his position January 22, 1940, returned to Germany and immediately began his propaganda broadcasting career.

During his first radio series as "Dr. Anders" or "Dr. Otherwise," he appeared with "Little Margaret," supposedly an American girl living in Germany. The little girl would answer letters from her friends in America, with extravagant praise for the Third Reich, always describing the plentiful, good food she enjoyed. Soon, however, "Margaret" disappeared from the program, leaving only "Dr. Anders" to provide his own negative observations about life in the United States.

Koischwitz later teamed with Frederick W. Kaltenbach in their own conversational program known at *Fritz and Fred, the Friendly Quarrelers*. At the same time, his role at Radio Berlin quickly expanded to that of commentator, writer, director and producer. In the role of "Mr. O.K.," he was an angry, opinionated propagandist for Germany. All this time, Koischwitz carried on his romance with Mildred Gillars, even though he was married with four children. The long-lived romance provided the intellectual Gillars with the romance she had always longed for during a rather ordinary life.

As World War II was winding down with Allied armies closing the vise on the Axis forces and Allied guns not too far behind him, Koischwitz fled from his Paris assignment to return to Berlin, where he became ill and died in a Berlin hospital of tuberculosis and heart failure on August 31, 1944. An intellectual who failed as an academic, Koischwitz used his many talents in the service of the native country he had previously abandoned, before returning to her to serve in what he saw as a glorious cause. Some, however, would say his life mainly demonstrates extreme egocentricity and opportunism. Nevertheless, it is difficult to determine whether he was working for Germany as much as he was working against the United States.

Robert Henry Best

Robert Henry Best ("Mr. Guess Who"), the son of a Methodist minister, was born April 16, 1896. After Best received his Batchelor's and Master's degrees in 1916, he taught school before volunteering for service when the United States entered World War I. Rising to the rank of Lieutenant, he remained in service until 1920 when he resigned his commission and moved to New York to pursue a career in journalism. He traveled to Europe with funds he received from a Pulitzer scholarship after graduating from the Columbia University School of Journalism. When his scholarship funds ran out, he accepted a job as stringer with the United Press covering central and southern Europe. In addition to his United Press work, he also did occasional jobs for such British and American newspapers and periodicals as the Chicago *Tribune*, Manchester *Guardian*, New York *Post*, *Newsweek* and *Time*.

A member of Vienna's café society, Best's politics gradually changed after Germany took Austria (the Anchluss). He began expressing Nazi sentiments with greater frequency, but there is no agreement as to exactly why or when Best decided to defect. Various elements might have influenced him. First, his employment by British and American periodicals was now greatly restricted. Second, the Japanese attack on Pearl Harbor meant that he was now an enemy alien in Germany. Eventually, Best along with other newsmen and diplomats was interned.

Best successfully petitioned the German Propaganda Ministry for permission to remain in Germany. After his release, he immediately began broadcasting for the Nazis as "Mr. Guess Who." These broadcasts vehemently attacked President Roosevelt as a Jewish dupe, frequently using such words as "Christocrat" and "Jewdocrat." His most vicious propaganda was broadcast on his *Best's Berlin Broadcasts* series.

After moving from Berlin to broadcast from Vienna in early 1945, he found himself in the line of fire of the advancing Russian army. Escaping to the British zone after the war was over, Best grew a beard and hid on a farm before he was apprehended by British army forces. He was convicted of treason in 1947, fined $10,000 and sentenced to life imprisonment. In 1951 he suffered a cerebral hemorrhage and died the following year. Always denying he was a traitor, Best maintained he was merely carrying on a battle against the deadly dangers Communism posed for the United States. That he was carrying on the good fight for the United States in Germany was his unconvincing defense argument.

Douglas Chandler

One of Robert Best's friends was fellow broadcast propagandist Douglas Chandler, "Alias Paul Revere." Chandler was born May 26, 1889, in Chicago, Illinois. After attending Baltimore Public Schools, he moved to New York City to enter advertising. After serving in the Navy, at the end of World War I, he began to work for several newspapers and do free lance writing for magazines.

Achieving little professional success and suffering what probably was a nervous breakdown, Chandler and his family moved to France in 1931. Shortly thereafter they moved to Germany, settling first in Munich before moving on to Austria the following year.

Chandler and his family traveled extensively in Europe up to 1939. Enjoying some success with his writing, Chandler cultivated many friendships with Nazi leaders and increasingly began publicly to warn of the menace of Communism. After World War II began, the U.S. Consul in Florence instructed all American citizens to return home. Chandler and his family, however, decided to remain. Through the intercession of a friend, Chandler began broadcasting for the Reichrundfunk under the name "Paul Revere."

Chandler apparently never considered himself a traitor, but instead thought of himself as a critic attempting to reform American society and culture. He saw himself as a throwback to the early days of American history — a modern day Paul Revere warning of peril ahead for the nation.

Within weeks of V-E in 1945, Chandler was detained by the U.S. Army. Tried for treason in 1947, his defense was that he merely was exercising his First Amendment free speech rights in Germany. Convicted of treason, fined $10,000 and sentenced to life imprisonment, Chandler was incarcerated at Danbury and Lewisburg prisons in the United States. He was released and allowed to join his daughter in Germany in 1963. President Kennedy commuted his sentence that same year.

Donald Day

One of the last Americans employed to broadcast German propaganda was Donald Day. A sometime correspondent for British and American newspapers such as the *Daily Mail* and Chicago *Tribune*, Day spent most of the World War II years in Finland, before moving to Berlin in 1944 to broadcast Nazi propaganda.

After the conclusion of the war, Day was interrogated by the U.S. Army and soon released. Citing the content of his broadcasts and the brief period of his propaganda broadcasting career, American officials agreed they had no convincing case against him. He remained in Europe after World War II to work as a stringer for the Chicago *Tribune*. He died of a heart attack in 1966.

Ezra Pound

An unlikely American who broadcast for the Axis during World War II was famous poet Ezra Pound. A promoter of avant-garde literature, Pound settled in Italy during the early 1920s and soon achieved world wide acclaim for his poetry, particularly for his *Cantos*, in which he attacked war profiteers and imperialist politicians. Pound began a ten-minute segment broadcast three times a week on Radio Rome's *American Hour*. It was a rambling feature that included everything from poetry and health topics to warnings against the menace of Communism and attacks on Jews. After the war, he was arrested, but never tried for treason. Instead, he was committed to St. Elizabeth's Hospital for the Criminally Insane, outside Washington, DC. After his commitment, Pound once remarked in an interview that an insane asylum was the only place he could stand to live in the United States. After his release from St. Elizabeth's in 1958, Pound returned to Italy where he died in 1972.

Burgman, Monti and Delancy

Three other lesser known American traitors who broadcast for the Nazis were Martin James Monti, Edwin Leopold "Leo" Delancy and Dr. Herbert John Burgman. Dr. Burgman was working at the U.S. Embassy in Berlin, when the United States entered World World War II. Refusing repatriation, he decided, instead, to broadcast propaganda for the German government.

Burgman, as "Joe Scanlan," began broadcasting in 1942 on Germany's "STATION DEBUNK" to agitate vigorously against President Roosevelt's "catastrophic policies" (Bergmeier and Lotz, 1997, p. 220). When he joined the German radio propaganda service, Burgman took the name "Helmuth Bruckman."

Station Debunk — "The Station of All Free Americans," claimed to be broadcasting from rural Iowa, but few were taken in by the claim, although Burgmann on STATION DEBUNK opened his program by playing "Carry Me Back to Old Virginny" and closed it with "The Star Spangled Banner." As Scanlan on Station

Debunk, Burgman broadcast such falsehoods as: The Russian Foreign Minister had arrived in Berlin to seek a negotiated peace *and* While driving a car General MacArthur hit and killed several American soldiers (Bergmeier and Lotz, 1997, p. 220). It was such broadcast claims as these that at the conclusion of the war caused Burgman to be indicted, convicted and sentenced to between six and twenty years in prison for treason. He died in prison.

The only American commissioned officer that broadcast German propagranda was Second Lieutenant Martin James Monti. Early in 1943, Monti enlisted as an Air Force cadet. After completing flight school, he was eventually assigned to Karachi, India, as a P-38 replacement pilot.

Feeling increasing resentment against American participation in the war, Monti went AWOL. After reaching an airbase near Naples, Italy, he persuaded an Air Force mechanic to allow him to test fly an P-38. He immediately flew into German air space and landed his plane behind enemy lines. When he was taken prisoner, Monti persuaded his captors to allow him to broadcast German propaganda. After broadcasting only a few small talks for the Nazis under the name of "Martin Weithaupt," Monti went AWOL once more. This time he sought the zone of American control where he told authorities a false story of his capture and imprisonment by the Germans. Since the American authorities were not impressed by his story, he was taken into custody. He eventually pled guilty to treason in 1949, was convicted and sentenced to prison, where he served 11 years before being released in 1960.

An American traitor who escaped punishment was Edwin Leopold Delancy. Delancy was born in Olney, Illinois, in 1885. Early in life he began a successful acting and singing career. The Great Depression that began with the 1929 stock market crash, dealt a serious blow to Delancy's career, forcing him to seek work in Europe. In 1939, he was hired to broadcast German propaganda under the name of "E.D. Ward." During Germany's early triumphs, Ward's broadcasts boasted of the Nazi battlefield successes and how comfortable life on the home front remained for German citizens, while frequently inserting anti–American tirades.

With the change of Nazi fortunes in 1945, Delancy's also deteriorated, since his particular brand of anti–American propraganda then seemed particularly ill-timed and irrelevant. At that point he quit broadcasting and moved to Prague, where he eventually was taken into custody by U.S. Army Counter-Intelligence. After twice being detained, he eventually was allowed to return to New York City, where he was arrested. At his trial, Delancy was able to convince his jury that he was being prosecuted only because of writing anti–Communist, anti–Russian literature. Although he clearly was guilty of broadcasting German propaganda, his indictment was dismissed.

Iva Ikuki Toguri D'Aquino

Justice, however, probably was meted out to most Americans who broadcast for the enemy in World War II. One exception was the possible injustice suffered by Iva Ikuki Toguri D'Aquino, frequently referred to as "Tokyo Rose." Iva Ikuki Toguri was born in 1916. She married Felipe D'Aquino in 1945.

Actually there was no "Tokyo Rose," but a dozen or more female Japanese broadcasters to whom GI's gave the name. None of these female broadcasters were ever identified by Tokyo Radio as "Tokyo Rose." D'Aquino, for example, identified herself as Orphan Ann on the air. "Orphan" because she called the Gi's in the Pacific War Theater orphans and "Ann" for announcer. Supposedly, she was forced to broadcast under duress on the Japanese *Zero Hour* program. Foumy ("Madame Tojo") Saisho and Myrtle ("Little Margie") Lipton were other Tokyo Radio's female broadcasters and the names given them by their GI listeners.

D'Aquino was a first generation Japanese-American, who had the misfortune to be visting a sick relative at the time of the outbreak of World War II. Forced to stay in Japan after Pearl Harbor and unable to speak Japanese, she took a job as a typist at Radio Tokyo. D'Aquino was pressured by the Japanese to renounce her American citizenship and, finally, to appear on their propaganda broadcasts. She called her radio work "sweet propaganda," since it consisted only of seductive talk and American music directed at the GI's.

Although some of them might have become homesick and depressed as the result of her broadcasts, most GI's listened to hear the good music her programs contained. At war's end, when experiencing great financial hardships, she was paid by an American newspaper man for an interview. As a result of the interview, she was arrested and returned to the United States, where she was tried and convicted of treason in 1949. Her conviction was based solely on one broadcast in which she mentioned the sinking of American ships.

She received a ten-year sentence and fined $10,000. She was released from prison early in 1956 for good behavior. Many observers and journalists believed she was not given a fair trial. After her release from prison, she returned to Chicago to work in a family owned import store in that city. Since her husband was never able to join her, they eventually divorced. Although President Gerald Ford pardoned her in 1977, the question of her guilt is still uncertain.

790 ***(The) American Way.*** Horace Heidt conducted his orchestra and hosted the program on which young amateur performers competed against each other. John Morris was the producer-director of the show sponsored by Lucky Strike cigarettes (30 min., Thursday, 10:00–10:30 P.M., CBS, 1953).

791 ***(The) American Weekly Program.*** The transcribed quarter-hour program presented dramatized stories from the Hearst newspapers' Sunday supplement. Begun in 1933, after 36 programs the name was changed to *Front Page Drama* and broadcast for 5 more years (15 min., transcribed on various stations, 1933). *See* ***Front Page Drama.***

792 ***American Women.*** David Hannon, Frank and Doris Hursley wrote the series that was designed to encourage the recruitment of women for the World War II war effort. The series was narrated by Eliose Kummer and Charlotte Manson. The producers and directors were Bob Brown and Ted Robertson (30 min., CBS, 1943). *See* **Wartime Radio.**

793 ***Americanization.*** The Key Men of America, a "patriotic organization," sponsored the 30 week series in which they argued against the presence of "undesirable immigrants and Reds" in the United States (KTHS, Hot Springs National Park, AR, 1928).

794 ***America's Flying Rhythm Symphony.*** Actor DeWolf Hopper narrated the good music program that presented symphonic music performed by 86 musicians from the Kansas City Philharmonic Orchestra (30 min., NBC, 1935).

795 ***America's Grub Street Speaks.*** Thomas L. Stix, head of the Book League of America, conducted the program on which he discussed current books and their authors. Blair Niles later took over the program (15 min., Saturday, 6:00–6:15 P.M., CBS, 1933).

796 ***America's Music.*** Henry Cook narrated the sustaining music program on which Joseph Gallicchio's orchestra provided the music and mezzo-soprano Lois Ray and baritone Bill Snary the vocals (30 min., Sunday, 2:00–2:30 P.M., NBC, 1951).

797 ***America's Town Meeting*** **(aka *America's Town Meeting of the Air*).** Topics of social significance were discussed by panels comprised of distinguished political personages on the program broadcast from 1935 to 1956. George V. Denny, Jr., was the moderator of the program that emanated from New York's Town Hall. Marion Carter, radio director of Town Hall, assisted Denny. Over the years the program was on the air, the directors were Wylie Adams, Leonard Blair and Richard Ritter. George Gunn, Ed Herlihy and Gene Kirby were the announcers (30 min, Thursday, 8:30–9:00 P.M., ABC, 1947).

798 **Ames, Adrienne.** News analyst and commentator (*Kitchen Kapers*, WHN, New York, NY, 1942).

799 **Ames, Don.** Sportscaster (KXEL, Waterloo, IA, 1945).

800 **Ames, Edward C.** Newscaster (WSPD, Toledo, OH, 1938–1939).

801 **Ames, Jane Ellen.** COM-HE (WKIP, Poughkeepsie, NY, 1955).

802 **Ames, Marlene.** Actress Ames was in the cast of *The Adventures of Ozzie and Harriet* situation comedy and the *Holly Sloan* daytime serial program.

803 **Ames, Mary Ellis.** COM-HE (*Mary Ellis Ames*, 15 min., Monday through Friday, 11:00–11:15 A.M., CBS, 1933).

804 **Ames, Toni.** COM-HE (WTUX, Wilmington, DE, 1951).

805 **Ames, Wilson.** Organist (*Wilson Ames,* instr. mus. prg., WKBW, Buffalo, NY, 1942).

806 **Amick, Dolly.** Singer (*Dolly Amick*, vcl. mus. prg., WPAR, Parkersburg, WV, 1937).

807 **Amidon, Walter L.** Announcer (WKEN, Buffalo, NY, 1925).

808 **Amlung, Jack.** Leader (*Jack Amlung Orchestra,* instr. mus. prg., WBAP, Fort Worth, TX, 1939).

809 Ammerman, Mel. DJ (*AM Music*, KVLG, La Grange, TX, 1960).

810 Amole, F.E. Newscaster (KDEN, Denver, CO, 1960).

811 Amole, Gene. DJ (*Meet the Boys in the Band*, KMYR, Denver, CO, 1949).

812 Amols, Mervyn. DJ (*Anything Goes*, WJLS, Beckley, WV, 1948).

813 Amoo, Lloyd. Newscaster (KRMC, Jamestown, ND, 1938).

814 Amores, Estrella. Soprano (WRC, Washington, DC., 1925).

815 Amory, Joe. DJ (*Off the Record*, KWIL, Albany, OR, 1952).

816 Amos, Fred. Newscaster (KGHF, Pueblo, CO, 1944).

817 *Amos 'n' Andy.* Two of radio's most memorable characters, Amos Jones and Andrew J. Brown, made their appearance when the *Amos 'n' Andy* program premiered March 19, 1928. No program enjoyed greater popularity or generated greater controversy. From its first broadcast the listening public made it an instant all-time favorite. No radio program before or since has matched its popularity. Motion picture theaters, for example, stopped their movies and piped the program into the theaters for their patrons. If they had not done so, many members of their audience would have stayed home to hear *Amos 'n' Andy*. It was said that in warm weather when windows were open, one could walk along city streets when the program was on the air and not miss a word of the broadcast.

Freeman Gosden and Charles Correll, two white men, developed and played all the show's characters in 1928. The men first met when both worked for the Joe Bren Company, which produced local shows throughout the country, furnishing the script, costumes, scenery, music and direction to the amateur talent involved. When Gosden first joined the company, he was sent to Durham, North Carolina, to meet an experienced director who was to help him learn the nuts and bolts of how to produce the local shows. That was Charles Correll, who soon became a good friend.

During the next six years Gosden and Correll frequently worked together. When both were promoted to head complimentary divisions of the company in Chicago, they shared an apartment and found that they made a good harmony singing team while accompanying themselves with piano and ukulele. Although still working for the Joe Bren Company, the men were anxious to explore the new and exciting medium of radio. They auditioned as a "song and chatter" team for Chicago's station WEBH, owned by the Edgewater Beach Hotel. Still maintaining their jobs with the Bren Company, the men sang and chattered once a week for WEBH without any remuneration other than the free meals they received at the Edgewater Beach Hotel. Their WEBH program was sometimes listed as *The Kinky Kids Parade*, the title of a popular song they had written. During this time, Gosden and Correll wrote a few other songs and made a successful personal appearance tour in the greater Chicago area.

In 1926 when they were about to attempt a vaudeville career, they were offered a WGN (Chicago, IL) staff position at $50 a week for both. A year before WGN had hired Jim and Marion Jordan — later famous for their *Fibber McGee and Molly* program — for their *The Smiths* program, which might have been radio's first serial drama (soap opera). The potential value of a program with a continuing story to attract a large listening audience was not lost on WGN executives, who planned to develop another series based on a comic strip such as *The Gumps*. When Gosden and Correll were approached with the idea, they suggested they use their talent and experience to create an original show called *Sam 'n' Henry*, which they first broadcast on January 12, 1926.

In *Sam 'n' Henry*, Gosden (Sam) and Correll (Henry) used their previous experience with blackface comedy to tell the story of two uneducated black men who left their Birmingham, Alabama, home to travel to Chicago seeking employment. *Sam 'n' Henry* began with the two men riding in a mule drawn buckboard traveling to the Birmingham railroad station:

> SAM: Henry, did you evah see a mule as slow as dis one?
>
> HENRY: Oh, dis mule is fas' enough. We gonna git to de depot alright.
>
> SAM: You know dat Chicago train don't wait fo' nobody. It jes' goes on. Jes' stops and goes right on.
>
> HENRY: Well, we ain't got but two mo' blocks to go. Don't be so 'patient. Don't be so 'patient.
>
> SAM: I hope dey got fastah mules dan dis up in Chicago.
>
> HENRY: You know some o' de boys said dey was goin' to be down dere to de depot to tell us go'bye and take dis mule back.
>
> SAM: Not only some o' de boys, but Liza goin' to be down dere too and she's gonna kiss me go'bye she said. You know, Henry, I kin'a hate to leave dat dere gal.

After reaching Chicago, Sam and Henry encountered adventures similar to those found on the *Amos 'n' Andy* program a few years later. For example, they joined a lodge, the Jewels of the Crown, whose head man was the Most Precious Diamond. Later in *Amos 'n' Andy*, the leading characters joined the Mystic Knights of the Sea Lodge headed by George "Kingfish" Stevens.

Sam 'n' Henry's popularity in the Chicago area arose more from the humorous characters portrayed than from a funny plot or comic situations with which they were confronted. In retrospect it can be seen that *Sam 'n' Henry* was the means by which Gosden and Correll developed and polished their writing and performing skills, unknowingly preparing themselves for the good fortune and popularity they would soon enjoy with *Amos 'n' Andy*. After 586 episodes of *Sam 'n' Henry*, Gosden and Correll left WGN for greater opportunities at WMAQ (Chicago, IL). When Gosden and Correll left WGN, they were forced to leave *Sam 'n' Henry* behind, because WGN and the *Chicago Tribune* owned the copyright. Using the same voices and similar characterizations as before, Gosden and Correll developed *Amos 'n' Andy.*

Their new program made its first appearance on Chicago's WMAQ on March 19, 1928. *Amos 'n' Andy* began as a 15-minute program broadcast six times a week at 11:00 P.M., before being moved to a 7:00–7:15 P.M. slot five times weekly. On November 19, 1929, it was announced that NBC had signed Gosden and Correll at the rate of $1,000 a week for their daily program. In 1943, the format changed to a weekly 30-minute program.

When it first appeared, *Amos 'n' Andy* became the first syndicated radio program. It was broadcast by many stations from two 12" transcription disks of five minutes each per program. By summer it became a sensation wherever it was heard, and on August 19, 1929, NBC placed it on its Blue network. Two months after it first appeared, Pepsodent toothpaste began sponsoring *Amos 'n' Andy* on one of the earliest coast-to-coast networks. Although some stations broadcast the program by transcription, the announcer, Bill Hay, always introduced it as "Amos *'n' Andy*, in person."

The program's national acceptance was immediate. Merlin Aylesworth, president of NBC, observed that Gosden and Correll had developed a "new art form" that combined the elements of a magazine serial with those of a newspaper comic strip. Some of the credit, however should go to the creative planning performed long before at WGN headquarters. By 1931–1932, the program was said to reach 40 million listeners.

Some of the program's trademark lines became famous such as Andy's "I'se regusted," when frustrated and upset. When Amos was surprised and bewildered, a frequent occasion in the early broadcasts, he would exclaim, "Awa! Awa!" As any long-running program must, *Amos 'n' Andy* showed some changes in the characters portrayed and the language used. It can be noted that throughout the program's long life the southern accents were retained, but standard grammar and correct pronunciation always used, unless for specific comic purpose. The most obvious character development was that of Amos, for he was transformed into an intelligent, family man who was also a successful business man. The most important line that was added over the years was the Kingfish's quizzical expression of surprise, "Holy Mackerel!"

Amos 'n' Andy in its early years broadcast serial stories that lasted two or three weeks. In those early years it frequently presented trials, in which Andy was confronted by women with breach of promise suits. Although the charges lodged against Andy by Madame Queen in 1931 saw the introduction of one of his greatest nemesis who would return over the years to bother him, she was not the first lady who charged him with tampering with her affections. In 1928, it was the Widow Parker who charged in court that Andy had promised to marry her.

On the witness stand, Mrs. Parker testified how Andy had come into her life, led her on and then tossed her aside. After a testimony filled with tearful intermissions, Mrs. Parker fainted and had to be carried from the witness stand. It was at this time that Andy's lawyer (Mr. Spielman) had his last attempt to counsel Andy before he took the witness stand in his own defense:

SPIELMAN: (quietly to Andy) And Brown, when you get on the witness stand, admit nothing.

ANDY: Do what to nuthin'?

SPIELMAN: I say, when you get on the witness stand, admit nothing.

His lawyer further counseled Andy as to what he should say on the witness stand:

SPIELMAN: Now, Brown, you can occasionally use the expression, "I don't remember." Now don't forget that. Now, what are you going to say?

ANDY: Now don't forget dat.

SPIELMAN: No, no. You don't remember.

ANDY: Oh, dat's right. You don't remember.

SPIELMAN: No, no. "*I* don't remember."

Andy faithfully followed his lawyer's advice when asked to raise his right hand and even when asked his name, he repied, "I don't remember." After finally taking the witness stand, he was asked by the plaintiff's lawyer, "Your name is Andrew Brown?" Following Mr. Spielman's advice faithfully, Andy, of course, replied, "I don't remember." As in his other trials, Andy escaped more by fate than by his own good behavior or sense.

Despite the program's popularity from its earliest years, controversy soon arose because of the claim it presented unfavorable stereotypes of Blacks as uneducated and shiftless. True enough, *Amos 'n' Andy* grew out of the blackface minstrel show tradition when it first started. Yet, when the program is viewed in the context of the show business of 1920s and 1930s, its humor appears much milder than most of the other comedy styles and routines of the time. Blackface comedy teams and minstrel shows were staples of both vaudeville and early radio. Molasses and January (Pick Malone and Pat Padgett, who had first performed on radio as Pick and Pat) and Honey Boy and Sassafras (George Fields and Johnnie Walsh) were but two of the many blackface teams that appeared on early radio. Some of the many minstrel shows that were listener favorites were: *The Burnt Cork Review* (WLW, Cincinnati, OH, 1926), *Haymaker's Minstrels* (WLS, Chicago, IL, 1920s), *Sealy Air Wavers Minstrels* (NBC, 1927–1928), *Dutch Masters Minstrels* (1928–1932), *Sinclair Weiner Minstrels* (NBC, 1932–1936) and *Molle Minstrels* (1934–1935). Minstrel shows were frequently broadcast until the late 1930s, when the format practically disappeared (Wertheim, 1979, p. 28). The *Dutch Masters Minstrels* program demonstrates what the minstrel show comedy was like. (*See* the *Dutch Masters Minstrels* program entry for examples of their humor.)

Even before *Amos 'n' Andy* became a successful television program, it was heavily criticized by the N.A.A.C.P. and some other critics for its portrayal of African-Americans. Although some characters on *Amos 'n' Andy* were indeed shiftless, lazy and not too intelligent, they were presented in a situation comedy, much as had been done with the Irish, Jews, Italians and Germans. Other radio programs of the time frequently carried ethnic and racial portrayals that combined these comic elements without attracting much attention or criticism. Some examples of this were: Mrs. Nussbaum on the *Fred Allen Show* portrayed by Minerva Pious; Bert Gordon as the Mad Russian on the *Eddy Cantor Show;* Eddie Anderson as Rochester on the *Jack Benny Show;* and Eddie Green as Eddie the Waiter on *Duffy's Tavern*.

After the program made a transition to television in 1951, criticism began to escalate until the network decided to cancel it in 1953. When the uproar continued against the program's constant reruns and world wide syndication, the network banned its use entirely. Gosden and Correll, who never appeared on the television show, remained on radio as DJs on their *Amos 'n' Andy Music Hall* program that was broadcast from 1954 to 1960. By this time Gosden and Correll had broadcast more than 10,000 programs.

One of the most touching moments of the *Amos 'n' Andy* program always was the annual Christmas program. Repeated some 30 times, the program had Amos talking to his little daughter, Arabella, before she went to sleep on Christmas Eve. He told her the Christmas message and ended the program by reciting *The Lord's Prayer* for her.

Throughout its entire run, Gosden supplied the voices of Amos, the Kingfish and Lightning, while Correll those of Andy and Henry Van Porter. Other valuable contributors to the program's humor were Eddie Green as Stonewall the lawyer and Ernestine Wade as Saphire, Kingfish's wife. Other cast members included: Elinor Harriot, Terry Howard, Johnny Lee, Madaline Lee, Lou Lubin and Harriette Widmer. The orchestra and choir was conducted by Jeff Alexander. The Jubalaires singing group (Theodore Brooks, Caleb Ginyard, John Jennings and George MacFadden) sometimes appeared, and organ interludes by Gaylord Carter were frequently used. The producers were Bob Connolly and Bill Moser and the directors were Andrew Love and Glenn Middleton. In addition to Gosden and Correll, the writers were Bob Connolly, Octavus Roy Cohen, Bob Fisher, Paul Franklin, Harvey Helm, Shirley Illo, Bill Moser, Bob Moss and Arthur Slander. The program's first and best remembered announcer was Bill Hay, whose "Here they are" (*"Heah they ah")* in his pleasant southern accented speech became a program trademark. The other announcers were Olan Soule, Del Sharbutt and Harlow Wilcox. The executive producers were Bob Connolly and Bill Moser. Glenn Middleton and Andrew Lowe were the program's directors. Sound effects were created by Frank Pittman, Gus Bayz, Dave Light and Ed Ludes.

The program appeared on CBS television from 1951 to 1953, the first TV show to feature an all Black cast. It was seen in syndication until 1966, when it was pulled from circulation by CBS because of protests by such groups as the National Association of Colored People (NAACP). CBS had begun selling the program to various African countries, causing the Kenyan government to ban the program in 1963. Two years later the show was finally pulled from circulation. *See* **Correll, Charles; Gosden, Freeman** *and* ***The Kinky Kids Parade***.

818 ***Amos 'n' Andy Minstrels*** (aka ***The Mystic Knights of the Sea Friday Night Minstrel Show***). Gosden and Correll shattered radio tradition by adding a minstrel show segment each Friday. On their first show Amos sang, as did their first guest, Frank Parker. Also on that first show was the Vagabond Male Quartet, a group that sounded suspiciously like the Mills Brothers. Noble Cain's a capella choir also appeared with the NBC Orchestra conducted by Joseph Gallicchio. Bill Hay was the interlocutor and Basil Loughrane the announcer (15 min., Friday, 7:00–7:15 P.M., NBC-Red, 1936).

819 ***(The) Amos 'n' Andy Music Hall.*** By this time in their careers, Gosden and Correll had become little more than glorified DJs, who occasionally interviewed special guests who appeared with them. Harlow Wilcox was their announcer (25 min., Monday through Friday, 9:30–9:55 P.M., CBS, 1954). Gosden and Correll's first show in this format was broadcast September 23, 1954.

820 **Amphian Quartet.** Singing group consisting of baritone H.C. Wisler, bass Joseph Mersey, and tenors T.G. Wilson and Robert Ream (WTAM, Cleveland, OH, 1923).

821 **Amphion Ensemble.** The Amphion Ensemble included Lydia Harlow, cellist; Doris Tirrell, pianist; Davis Leavitt, clarinetist; William Toris, flutist; and William Benson, violinist (WBC, Boston-Springfield, MA, 1925).

822 ***(The) Ampico Hour of Music.*** The Ampico Company sponsored the program of good music (Thursday, 8:30 P.M., NBC-Blue, 1927–1928). One performer on the program was Russian pianist Leo Ornstein.

823 **(The) Amrad Banjo-Mandolin Club Orchestra.** Music group directed by W. Eugene Hammett (WGI, Medford Hillside, MA, 1923).

824 ***(The) Amrad's Women's Club Talk.*** May Bliss Dickinson conducted the early woman's program (WGI, Medford Hillside, MA, 1923).

825 **Amsberry, Bob.** DJ (*Squirrely Bird*, KEX, Portland, OR, 1948).

826 **Amsdell, William.** Actor Amsdell appeared on the *Houseboat Hannah* daytime serial program.

827 **Amsler, Barbara.** COM-HE (KATV, Pine Bluff, AR, 1955).

828 **Amspaugh, Faith.** COM-HE (WMTC, Vancleve, KY, 1954–1955).

829 **Amstel, Felix.** Leader (*Felix Amstel Orchestra*, instr. mus. prg., WCAU, Philadelphia, PA and WTIC, Hartford, CT, 1935).

830 **Amsterdam, Morey.** Entertainer Amsterdam was billed as the "Original Radio Mimic" (KGO, Oakland, CA, 1926). DJ (*For People Only*, WHN, New York, NY, 1947).

831 **Amsterdam Concert Orchestra.** Local band (WGY, Schenectady, NY, 1925).

832 **Amundsen [Amundson], Margaret.** Pianist (KWSC, Pullman, WA, 1926).

833 ***Amy Lou Shopping Hour.*** "Amy Lou" hosted the hour-long program, broadcast 10:00–11:00 A.M., in which shopping tips, sales and specials were discussed (KFSD, San Diego, CA, 1927).

834 ***An Analysis of Propaganda.*** The *Analysis of Propaganda* program was broadcast during World War II. Each week on the informative sustaining program, Siegfried Wegener analyzed several foreign propaganda broadcasts (15 min., Friday, 6:15–6:30 P.M., KFEL, Denver, CO, 1941).

835 **Anastapolis, John.** Sportscaster (WGGH, Marion, IL, 1955).

836 **Ancell, Bob.** DJ (WTVN, Columbus, OH, 1960).

837 ***Ancient and Honorable Order of the Hoot Owls.*** This was one of the many variety shows that flourished and persisted on early American radio. One of the featured acts on the show was Forrest Berg and George Smith ("The Village Blacksmith"). It was broadcast weekly (KGW, Portland, OR, 1930).

838 **Andelin, James "Jim."** Actor Andelin appeared on the *Arnold Grimm's Daughter, Houseboat Hannah* and *Og, Son of Fire* programs.

839 **Anderly, B.H.** Newscaster (*Noontime News*, KLIZ, Brainer, MN, 1947). DJ (*Concert Miniatures*, KLIZ, 1947).

840 **Anders, Bill.** Sportscaster (KFYO, Lubbock, TX, 1950).

841 **Andersen, Bert.** DJ (KTAC, Tacoma, WA, 1957).

842 **Andersen, Betty.** Soprano (KGA, Spokane, WA, 1930).

843 **Andersen, Robert "Bob."** Newscaster (KGO, San Francisco, CA and KPO, San Francisco, CA, 1938–1939; KSFO, San Francisco, CA, 1940–1941).

844 **Anderson, A. Robert.** Newscaster (WSTV, Steubenville, OH, 1944–1946; *The Week's News in Review*, WSTV, 1948).

845 **Anderson, Ace.** DJ (WRMA, Montomery, AL, 1957).

846 **Anderson, Al.** Newscaster (WSDR, Sterling, IL, 1953; KTRH, Houston, TX, 1957; KGVO, Missoula, MT, 1960).

847 **Anderson, Allen "Al."** Sportscaster (WASA, Havre de Grace, MD, 1948–1956).

848 **Anderson, Andy.** Baritone (WMBB, Chicago, IL, 1926). Pianist (KJBS, San Francsico, CA, 1929).

849 **Anderson, Andy.** Sportscaster (*Saturday Review of Sports*, WCNU, Crestnew, FL, 1950).

850 **Anderson, Andy.** DJ (*Dance Date*, KENI, Anchorage, Alaska, 1952; *Starline Swingtime*, KCIM, Carroll, IA, 1954–1955; KLGA, Algona, IA, 1960).

851 **Anderson, Andy.** Newscaster (*Long Island Beat*, WFYI, Garden City, NY, 1960).

852 **Anderson, Arthur C.** Announcer (KFAB, Lincoln, NE, 1926; KFAD, Phoenix, AZ, 1927). Sportscaster (KTAR, Phoenix, AZ, 1940).

853 **Anderson, Arvid.** Baritone (WMBB, Chicago, IL, 1926).

854 **Anderson, Axel.** DJ (*Record Rondezvous*, WDEV, Waterbury, VT, 1947).

855 **Anderson, Beth.** COM-HE (WMDN, Midland, MI, 1951).

856 **Anderson, Betty.** COM-HE (WSRC, Durham, NC, 1957).

857 **Anderson, Bill.** CW singer, composer and DJ (DJ, WJJC, Commerce, GA, early 50s). After a successful recording career, Anderson joined the *Grand Ole Opry* in 1961.

858 **Anderson, Bill.** Sportscaster (KVWO, Cheyenne, WY, 1956).

859 **Anderson, Blanche.** COM-HE (WLOA, Braddock, PA, 1956).

860 **Anderson, Bob.** Sportscaster (KRLC, Lewiston, ID, 1937).

861 **Anderson, Bob.** Newscaster (WJHI, Johnson City, TN, 1938).

862 **Anderson, Bob.** Newscaster (KNX, Los Angeles, CA, 1942). Sports (KWBR, Oakland, CA, 1947).

863 **Anderson, Bob.** DJ (KWLK, Longview, WA, 1947; *Harmony House*, KWIE, Kennewick, WA, 1954–1955).

864 **Anderson, Bob.** Sportscaster (WAZF, Yazoo City, MS, 1948).

865 **Anderson, Bobby.** Sportscaster (WMTA, Central City, KY, 1955–1956).

866 **Anderson, Bruce F.** Newscaster (*The Editor Speaks*, KWYO, Sheridan, WY, 1947).

867 **Anderson, Carl.** Tenor (KFWM, Oakland, CA, 1926).

868 **Anderson, (Mrs.) Carl.** Singer (WOC, Davenport, IA, 1926–1927).

869 **Anderson, (Mrs.) Carl and Roy Cortsen.** Popular vocal team of a contralto and tenor accompanied by Esta Marvin Pomeroy (WTAB, Oakland, CA, 1925).

870 **Anderson, Carl R.** Sportscaster (KFNF, Shenandoah, IA, 1955).

871 **Anderson, Carl and Clarence Oliver.** Vocal duet team (KGO, Oakland, CA, 1924).

872 **Anderson, Carol.** COM-HE (WBYS, Canton, IL, 1051; KAYS, Hays, KS, 1955).

873 **Anderson, Cecilia.** Singer (KLX, Oakland, CA, 1923).

874 **Anderson, Charlene.** COM-HE (WJOL, Joliet, IL, 1960).

875 **Anderson, Chuck.** DJ (WHTC, Holland, MI, 1960).

876 **Anderson, (Mrs.) Cyrus.** Contralto (KGO, Oakland, CA, 1924).

877 **Anderson, Dale.** Sportscaster (KUOA, Siloam Springs, AR, 1948).

878 **Anderson, David.** Newscaster (NBC, 1942).

879 **Anderson, Dick.** Sportscaster (WEOA, Evansville, IN, 1947; *Dick's on at Six*, WEOA, 1948–1953).

880 **Anderson, Don.** DJ (*Record Party*, KTFS, Texarkana, TX, 1947; *199 Club*, KUBC, Montrose, CO, 1949).

881 **Anderson, Doug.** Sportscaster (*Spotlight on Sports*, KDIX, Dickinson, ND, 1950; *Reports on Sports*, KFYR, Bismark, ND, 1951).

882 **Anderson, Ed.** Sportscaster (WQDM, St. Albans, VT, 1938–1939).

883 **Anderson, Eddie.** DJ (*Night Hawk*, KIKI, Honolulu, HI, 1952).

884 **Anderson, Edilberto G.** Baritone (KGO, Oakland, CA, 1924).

885 **Anderson, Eric.** Tenor (WBZ, Boston-Springfield, MA, 1924).

886 **Anderson, Ernie.** DJ (*Melody Time*, WSKI, Montpelier, VT, 1949).

887 **Anderson, Fran.** COM-HE (KXRA, Alexandria, MN, 1956–1957).

888 **Anderson, Frances.** Soprano (KGO, Oakland, CA, 1926).

889 **Anderson, Frank.** Baritone (WJZ, New York, NY, 1925).

890 **Anderson, Gary.** DJ (*1430 Club*, WLAK, Lakeland, FL, 1954).

891 **Anderson, Gaston.** DJ (*Request Parade*, WGWD, Gadsden, AL, 1948).

892 **Anderson, George.** Sportscaster (*Sports Whirl*, WANS, Anderson, SC, 1960).

893 **Anderson, Gordon.** DJ (*Up 'N' Atom*, WAUG, Augusta, GA, 1952).

894 **Anderson, Harold.** Accordionist (WBBM, Chicago, IL, 1925).

895 **Anderson, Harry.** Sportscaster (WSIV, Pekin, IL, 1948).

896 **Anderson, Helen.** COM-HE (KDIX, Dickinson, ND, 1951).

897 **Anderson, Herb.** DJ (WPIN, St. Petersburg, FL, 1960).

898 **Anderson, Herb Oscar.** DJ (*Make Believe Ballroom*, WABC, New York, NY, 1957).

899 **Anderson, Howard.** Newscaster (WMT, Cedar Rapids, IA, 1948).

900 **Anderson, Ina P.** Singer (WOC, Davenport, IA, 1927).

901 **Anderson, Jack.** Sound effects specialist Anderson worked on the *Brighter Day* and *The Light of the World* programs.

902 **Anderson, Jack.** Sportscaster (WKIM, Mayfield, KY, 1952).

903 **Anderson, James "Jim."** DJ (*Platter Party*, WIRK, West Palm Beach, FL, 1947–1949).

904 **Anderson, Jane.** Pianist (*Jane Anderson*, instr. mus. prg., WGN, Chicago, IL, 1942).

905 **Anderson, Jane.** COM-HE (KIOA, Grand Island, NE, 1954–1958).

906 **Anderson, Jane.** COM-HE (KMMJ, Grand Island, NE, 1957).

907 **Anderson, Janestra.** Soprano (*Janestra Anderson*, vcl. mus. prg., WICA, Astabula, OH, 1942).

908 **Anderson, J.E.** Announcer (WMAN, Columbus, OH, 1925).

909 **Anderson, Jennie.** Soprano (WLAG, Minneappolis–St. Paul, MN, 1924).

910 **Anderson, Jo.** COM-HE (KVOX, Moorhead, MN, 1955).

911 **Anderson, John.** Newscaster (*Local News*, WPNF, Brevard, NC, 1954).

912 **Anderson, Judith.** COM-HE (*Cooking Chat*, on which she talked about such topics as "Pies That Men Like," WLW, Cincinnati, OH, 1925–1926).

913 **Anderson, K.L.** DJ (WPBC, Minneapolis, MN, 1954).

914 **Anderson, Kirk.** DJ (*A.M. Alley*, WFGM, Fitchburg, MA, 1952). Sportscaster (*Spotlight on Sports*, WFGM, 1953–1956).

915 **Anderson, (Mrs.) Knox W.** Singer of old songs and "southern melodies" (WBAP, Fort. Worth, TX, 1925).

916 **Anderson, Laura Kemp.** Contralto (KOA, Denver, CO, 1925).

917 **Anderson, Leonard.** DJ (*Roger Roundup*, KTRB, Modesto, CA, 1947).

918 **Anderson, Leonard G.** Sportscaser (WJMC, Rice Lake, WI, 1945).

919 **Anderson, Lois Edra.** Seven-year-old pianist (KFWM, Oakland, CA, 1926).

920 **Anderson, Lorena.** Soprano (WQJ, Chicago, IL, 1926).

921 **Anderson, Luella.** Violinist (KOIL, Council Bluffs, IA, 1927).

922 **Anderson, Lyle.** Tenor (KWTC, Santa Ana, CA, 1928).

923 **Anderson, Margaret.** Pianist (KYW, Chicago, IL, 1925).

924 **Anderson, Marguerite.** Actress Anderson appeared on the *Masquerade* daytime serial.

925 **Anderson, Marjorie.** Concert pianist (KFOA, Seattle, WA, 1927).

926 **Anderson, Mary.** Pianist (KGW, Portland, OR, 1923).

927 **Anderson, Mary Ann.** Anderson was one of the intelligent "kids" on the *Quiz Kids* program.

928 **Anderson, Mary B.** COM-HE (WAPG, Arcadia, FL, 1958).

929 **Anderson, Max.** Sportscaster (*World of Sports*, WKRG, Mobile, AL, 1949). Newscaster (WPFA, Pensacola, FL, 1953).

930 **Anderson, Millie.** COM-HE (WNAW, Warren, PA, 1957).

931 **Anderson, Millard.** DJ (*Breakfast Time*, WRKD, Rockland, ME, 1954).

932 **Anderson, Millie.** COM-HE (WNAE, Warren, PA, 1957).

933 **Anderson, Milton.** DJ (*11th Hour Dance Time*, WMCK, McKeesport, PA, 1948; *Platter Party*, WJAS, Pittsburgh, PA, 1952).

934 **Anderson, Myrtle.** COM-HE (WMOU, Berlin, NH, 1951).

935 **Anderson, Nancy.** DJ (*Princess Midnight*, 105 min., Monday through Friday, 11:30–1:05 A.M., WCOP, Boston, MA, 1952). Anderson was the first late-night female DJ on Boston radio and a local favorite.

936 **Anderson, Norwood.** DJ (WFMC, Goldsboro, NC, 1957; *Town and Country Party Line*, WFTC, Kinston, NC, 1960).

937 **Anderson, Orval.** Newscaster (WWL, New Orleans, LA, 1940; ABC, Los Angeles, CA, 1960). Sportscaster (WDBO, Orlando, FL, 1939).

938 **Anderson, Phil.** Newscaster (WLS, Chicago, IL, 1935).

939 **Anderson, Roger.** Sportscaster (KIVA, Yuma, AZ, 1954).

940 **Anderson, Roy.** Baritone (*Roy Anderson*, vcl. mus. prg., 15 min., Saturday, 6:15–6:30 P.M., CST, WLS, Chicago, IL, 1936). Anderson was accompanied by organist Ralph Waldo Emerson.

941 **Anderson, Ruth.** Newscaster (*Last Minute News*, KFRC, San Francisco, CA, 1942).

942 **Anderson, Sam.** DJ (*Music Matinee*, WNAR, Norristown, PA, 1954–1957).

943 **Anderson, Sam W.** Newscaster (KFFA, Helena, AR, 1941).

944 **Anderson, Stella.** Pianist (NBC, 1929).

945 **Anderson, Sue.** CO-HE (WMOX, Meridian, MS, 1960).

946 **Anderson, Tom.** DJ (*1340 Club*, WLDY, Ladysmith, WI, 1948). Sportscaster (*Sports Parade*, WLDY, 1949; *Sports Roundup*, WLDY, 1951; *Sports Roundup*, WGEZ, Beloit, WI, 1952–1956).

947 **Anderson, Tommy.** Sportscaster (*Let's Go Fishing*, WLCO, Eustis, FL, 1956).

948 **Anderson, Trezvant W.** Newscaster (*Pittsburgh Courier News*, WUST, Bethesda, MD, 1952).

949 **Anderson, Virginia.** COM-HE (WGMA, Hollywood, FL, 1958).

950 **Anderson, Warren.** Leader (Warren Anderson Orchestra, KOMO, Seattle, WA, 1928).

951 **Anderson, Warren.** Newscaster (WING, Dayton, OH, 1944; WJIM, Lansing, MI, 1946; WBEL, Rockford, IL, 1953). DJ (KBIZ, Ottumwa, IA, 1947; *Ramblin' Around*, KSTT, Davenport, IA, 1948).

952 **Anderson, Wayne.** Newscaster (KDON, Monterey, CA, 1946)

953 **Anderson, (Dr.) William M.** Dr. Anderson conducted a radio Bible class (WFAA, Dallas, TX, 1926).

954 **Anderson, William.** Steel guitarist (WBBM, Chicago, IL, 1926).

955 ***(The) Anderson Family.*** A 30-minute syndicated program, *The Anderson Family* told of the funny adventures of an "average" American family. The cast included Dick Lane, Louise Arthur and Walter Tetley (30 min., weekly, 1947).

956 ***(The) Andersons.*** Rosemary Smith wrote the slow-moving, short-lived sustaining daytime serial about the "true to life story of a family." Ben Grauer was the announcer (15 min., Monday through Friday, 5:30–5:45 P.M., NBC-Red, 1942).

957 **Andonegui, Professor.** Spanish violinist (WRVA, Richmond, VA, 1926).

958 **Andre, Pierre.** Famous announcer Andre worked on the *Captain Midnight*, *Little Orphan Annie* and *Romance of Helen Trent* programs.

959 **Andreasen, Reid.** DJ (KVNU, Logan, UT, 1960).

960 **Andree, Betty.** COM-HE (KWKC, Abilene, TX, 1951).

961 **Andree, Jan.** DJ (*The Jazz Jamboree*, WWSW , Pittsburgh, PA, 1949; WPIT, Pittsburgh, PA). Newscaster (WACB, Kittanning, PA, 1960).

962 **Andregg, Don.** Newscaster (KSLM, Salem, OR, 1941).

963 **Andres, Joe.** Newscaster (*Today's News*, WMAW, Milwaukee, WI, 1948). DJ (*Serenade*, WMAW, 1949; *Music Til Dawn*, WBBM, Chicago, IL, 1954). Sports (*Sports News*, WMAW, Milwaukee, WI, 1948).

964 **Andreson, Orville.** DJ (*Klub Kwik*, KWIK, Burbank, CA, 1948).

965 **Andrew, Bert.** Newscaster (ABC, 1949).

966 **Andrew, Bob.** DJ (*Holiday for Strings*, WDUK, Durham, NC, 1947).

967 **(The) Andrew Jackson Orchestra.** Popular Nashville band (WSM, Nashville, TN, 1928).

968 **Andrews, Arch.** DJ (KTLN, Denver, CO, 1960).

969 **Andrews, Betty.** COM-HE (WJEJ, Hagerstown, MD, 1957).

970 **Andrews, Bob.** Newscaster (*Farm Reporter*, KWKH, Shreveport, LA, 1942).

971 **Andrews, Bob.** DJ (WLOF, Orlando, FL, 1960).

972 **Andrews, Cameron.** Actor Andrews worked on the *Lone Journey* and *Terry and the Pirates program*.

973 **Andrews, Carl.** Newscaster (*Carl Andrews Reports*, WDBJ, Roanoke, VA, 1951). DJ (WDBJ, 1955).

974 **Andrews, Caroline.** Coloratura soprano (NBC-Red, New York, NY, 1926–1927 and singer in 1928 on the *Major Bowes Capitol Family* program). Bowes called her "The Lark."

975 **Andrews, Chester.** Newscaster (KIDD, Monterey, CA, 1960).

976 **Andrews, Clark.** Director Andrews worked on the *Famous Jury Trials* and *Rogue's Gallery* programs.

977 **Andrews, David.** DJ (*Night Beat*, KOLN, Lincoln, NE, 1948).

978 **Andrews, Don.** DJ (*Coffee Time*, WKNX, Saginaw, MI, 1948; *Country Junction*, WSGW, Saginaw, MI, 1954–1957).

979 **Andrews, Earl.** Newscaster (WAUD, Auburn, AL, 1952).

980 **Andrews, Ed.** Leader (Ed Andrews Orchestra, WEEI, Boston, MA, 1925; Ed Andrews' Nautical Dance Orch., WEEI, 1926).

981 **Andrews, Edward.** Actor Edwards appeared on the *Amanda of Honeymoon Hill* program.

982 **Andrews, Ernie.** Leader (*Ernie Andrews Orchestra*, WTIC, Hartford, CT, 1935).

983 **Andrews, Freida.** Newscaster (WHBI, Newark, NJ, 1955). DJ (WHBI, 1955).

984 **Andrews, Gene.** Newscaster (WHAR, Clarksburg, WV, 1947; *Preview of Tomorrow*, WVEC, Hampton, VA, 1949).

985 **Andrews, Herb.** DJ (*Sunny Side of the Street*, WEBO, Owego, NY and WTTC, Towanda, PA, 1960).

986 **Andrews, Hiram G.** Newscaster (*Dispelling the Fog*, WARD, Johnstown, PA, 1948–1954).

987 **Andrews, Jean.** Sportscaster (*Play by Play*, WINX, Rockville, MD, 1952).

988 **Andrews, Jim.** DJ (*Cousin Andy*, WINX, Rockville, MD, 1952).

989 **Andrews, Jo.** Announcer (WING, Dayton, OH, 1942). Jo Andrews was a full-time announcer on the Ohio station.

990 **Andrews, John "Johnny."** Newscaster (KOCA, Kilgore, TX, 1945, 1953).

991 **Andrews, John "Johnny."** DJ (*Music in the Night* and *WHOT's Cooking*, WHOT, South Bend, IN, 1949; WTRC, Elkhart, IN, 1957).

992 **Andrews, Johnny.** DJ (*Morning Bandwagon*, WTAM, Cleveland, OH, 1952; *Easy Does It*, WTAM, 1955).

993 **Andrews, Joseph.** Announcer (WICC, Bridgeport, CT, 1925).

994 Andrews, Larry. Newscaster (*Column of the Air*, KRUX, Phoenix and Glendale, AZ, 1947–1948.

995 Andrews, Leonard. Announcer (WICC, Bridgeport, CT, 1925).

996 Andrews, M. Carl. Newscaster (*Over the Editor's Desk*, WDBJ, Roanoke, VA, 1947–1954).

997 Andrews, Martin "Marty." Director Andrews directed the *Casebook of Gregory Hood, My True Story* and *Terry and the Pirates* programs.

998 Andrews, Miriam. COM-HE (WRUF, Gainesville, FL, 1954).

999 Andrews, Neil. DJ (*Request Time*, WKRT, Cortland, NY, 1948).

1000 Andrews, Nick. DJ (*Music on the Sunny Side*, WNRC, New Rochelle, NY, 1954–1955).

1001 Andrews, Perry. DJ (*Open Road, USA*, KYW, Philadelphia, PA, 1954–1955; WBAL, Baltimore, MD, 1957).

1002 Andrews, Ralph. Sportscaster (WAUX, Waukesha, WI, 1948).

1003 Andrews, Robert Hardy. Talented writer Andrews was the writer and director of the *Jack Armstrong* program. He also worked on the *Just Plain Bill* (writer), *Ma Perkins* (creator and writer), *Skippy* (writer), *Stolen Husband* and *Terry and the Pirates* programs. He also was the first actor to play the part of the Shadow on radio.

1004 Andrews, Russ. Newscaster (WFBR, Baltimore, MD, 1944).

1005 Andrews, Ted. Sports commentator (*Rambling Round Sports* and play-by-play of Centenary College football games, KWKH, Shreveport, LA, 1937–1938; KOCY, Oklahoma City, OK, 1939–1941; WJBW, New Orleans, LA, 1946; WSMB, New Orleans, LA, 1956).

1006 Andrews, Vic. DJ (*Kopp's Carnival*, KEIO, Pocatello, ID, 1948).

1007 Andrews, William J. From a job as a "radio expert" in the Oakland, California branch store of Montgomery Ward, Andrews went on to become a staff announcer at San Francisco (NBC, 1928).

1008 *(The) Andrews Sisters Program.* The Andrews Sisters presented many guests on their show including Xavier Cugat, George Jessel, Ray Noble, Al Pearce, Eddy Duchin, Hoagy Carmichael, the Charioteers and Gene Austin (15 min. & 30 min., 1944–1946, ABC). The sisters also appeared on the *Eight-to-the-Bar Ranch* program, sponsored by Kelvinator in 1944 on ABC with George "Gabby" Hayes and the orchestra of Vic Schoen. This was similar to their *Nash-Kelvinator Showroom* program broadcast in 1946 on CBS. The latter featured the Vic Schoen band, baritone Curt Massey and weekly guests such as Morton Downey and Ethel Merman.

1009 Andrian, Elsie. Pianist (KGO, Oakland, CA, 1926).

1010 Andrick, Bill. DJ (*Lamplighter's Serenade*, WPAR, Parkersburg, WV, 1954).

1011 Andriese, Ted. Newscaster (WFUR, Grand Rapids, MI, 1957).

1012 Andrus, Walt. DJ (KOLE, Port Arthur, TX, 1960).

1013 Angel, Bill. DJ (*1450 Club*, KSVP, Artesia, NM, 1947).

1014 Angel, Jack. DJ (KOLO, Reno, NV, 1960).

1015 Angell, J. Herb. Newscaster (WHJB, Greensburg, PA, 1939; KQV, Pittsburgh, PA, 1939–1940).

1016 Angell, Jack. Newscaster (WNBQ, Chicago, IL, 1952–1954).

1017 Angelo. Unidentified tenor who broadcast as the *Italian Troubadour* (vcl. mus. prg., WLW, Cincinnati, OH, 1937).

1018 Angelo, Bettina. COM-HE (*Home Decoration* program, KTAB, Oakland, CA, 1929).

1019 *Angelo Patri.* Child psychologist Patri was known as a "wise and tolerant" counselor who provided information on child rearing. He was sponsored by Cream of Wheat cereal (30 min., Sunday, 10:00–10:30 P.M., CBS, 1933).

1020 *Angels in Blue.* Captain W.G. Moore and Bob Burtt, who wrote *The Air Adventures of Jimmy Allen*, wrote this sustaining dramatic program that told of the experiences of an airline hostess. Audrey McGrath starred on the program (30 min., Sunday, 4:00–4:30 P.M., WHB, Kansas City, MO, 1938).

1021 *Angelus.* Tony Wons conducted the five-minute program as a time for "rest and reflection." It contained the sound of chimes, violin and cello music, a brief prayer and an "inspiration thought" segment delivered by Wons. Harlow Wilcox eventually succeeded Wons as the program's host (WLS, Chicago, IL, 1924). *See* ***Tony Wons.***

1022 Angelus String Trio. Instrumental group including violinist Fred Bosman, cellist Lela Davies and pianist Helen Davies, that broadcast from Sister Aimee Semple McPherson's Angelus Temple (KFSG, Los Angeles, CA, 1926).

1023 Angelus Temple Children's Orchestra. Helen McNaughton directed the orchestra from the Angelus Temple (KFSG, Los Angeles, CA, 1925).

1024 Angelus Temple Choir. Vocal group directed by Gladwyn N. Nichols (KFSG, Los Angeles, CA, 1925–1926).

1025 Angelus Temple Silver Band. Instrumental group directed by Gladwyn N. Nichols (KFSG, Los Angeles, CA, 1925–1926).

1026 Angelus Temple Ukulele Band of Thirty. String band directed by Essie Binkley (KFSG, Los Angeles, CA, 1925).

1027 Angle, Mel. Newscaster (KRKD, Los Angeles, CA, 1941).

1028 Anglin, Margaret. Actress Anglin was featured in the *Orphans of Divorce* daytime serial.

1029 Anglin, Mary Louise. A script buyer for Compton Advertising, Inc., Anglin handled a large number of daytime serial programs daily. She directed programs, supervised others and generally readied new programs for broadcast. She started in radio in 1932.

1030 Anglin, Walter. DJ (*Ebony Express*, WJLD, Birmingham, AL, 1960).

1031 Anglo-Persians. Popular ten-man radio and recording orchestra led by Louis Katzman. Varied in its programs, the band played popular, folk music, operatic, and operetta selections. The band sometimes used the names of **The Ambassadors** or **Lou Katzman and his Kittens** (CBS, New York, NY, 1929).

1032 Angst, B.A. Sportscaster (WPAM, Pottsville, PA, 1952).

1033 Angwin, Percy. Sportscaster (*Just Outdoors*, WSKI, Montpelier, VT, 1951).

1034 Anikeef, Wasily. Operatic basso profundo (WGBS, New York, NY, 1928).

1035 *Animal Bedtime Stories.* Florence Smith Vincent told stories for children (WJZ, New York, NY, 1923).

1036 *(The) Animal Farm.* A program modeled after children's motion picture cartoons, each broadcast told a complete nursery story. All parts were played by Art Faust and Harriet Harris, who also were the authors (15 min., KOIL, Omaha, NE, 1935).

1037 *Animals in the News.* Dr. W.A. Young, the managing director of the Anti-Cruelty to Animals Society of Chicago, IL, broadcast amusing pet stories and valuable information about the care and feeding of animals (15 min., Weekly, WAIT, Chicago, IL, 1942).

1038 Anisman, Doc. DJ (*1490 Club*, KCIL, Houma, LA, 1948).

1039 Anker, Sigmund. Violinist (KFRC, San Francisco, CA, 1925).

1040 Ankner, Helen. Pianist (*Helen Ankner*, instr. mus. prg., WHAM, Rochester, NY, 1942).

1041 *Ann Butler.* Veteran vaudevillian Butler was an entertaining comedienne. Music on her sustaining program was provided by xylophonist Sam Herman and pianist Frank Banta (15 min., Thursday, 11:15–11:30 A.M., NBC-Blue, 1933).

1042 *Ann Leaf at the Organ.* Miss Leaf broadcast an organ recital for listeners three times weekly (30 min., three times weekly, 2:30–3:00 P.M., CBS, 1929). *See* **Leaf, Ann.**

1043 *Ann Masters' Celebrity Notebook.* Miss Masters interviewed celebrities who were visiting Chicago on her local weekday program sponsored by the Evans Fur Company. Guests including movie star Joe. E. Brown were frequently interviewed (15 min., Monday through Friday, 6:00–6:15 P.M., WGN, Chicago, IL, 1945).

1044 *Ann of the Airlanes.* The transcribed daytime serial concerned the adventures of Ann, who entered stewardess training. When she completed her training, she became involved with spies, political intrigue and diamond smugglers (15 min., transcribed, mid–1930s).

1045 *Ann Warren's Home Chats.* Home economics information was broadcast by Miss Warren (KPO, San Francisco, CA, 1929).

1046 Annand, Shirley. COM-HE (WTIP, Charleston, WV, 1960).

1047 Anne, Lillie. DJ (*Carolina Barndance*, WIRC, Hickory, NC, 1954–1955).

1048 Anno, Mary Jean. COM-HE (WATW, Ashland, WI, 1954).

1049 Annstaett, Anne. COM-HE (WHDL, Olean, NY, 1951).

1050 Anscome, (Dr.) Frances. Newscaster (WAIR, Winston Salem, NC, 1939).

1051 Anselmo, Vince. Sportscaster (KJRL, Pocatello, ID, 1952).

1052 Ansley, Brad. Newscaster (WIOD, Miami, FL, 1941). Sports (WIOD, 1941).

1053 Anson, Bill. DJ (*Hollywood Bandstand*, KFWB, Hollywood, CA, 1947–1952; WAIT, Chicago, IL, 1954).

1054 Anson, Bob. DJ (KBAM, Longview, WA, 1960).

1055 Anson, Bruce. DJ (*Dancin' with Anson*, KWIK, Burbank, CA, 1948).

1056 Anspach, W. Leroy. Announcer (WIBG, Elkins Park, PA, 1925).

1057 Ansbro, George. Famous announcer Ansbro worked on such diverse programs as *Chaplain Jim, Ethel and Albert, Home Sweet Home, Mrs. Wiggs of the Cabbage Patch, Singo, When a Girl Marries* and *Young Widder Brown.*

1058 Ansell, George. Actor Ansell appeared on the *Backstage Wife* daytime serial.

1059 Anstaett, Carroll. Newscaster (WHDL, Olean, NY, 1951).

1060 *(The) Answer Man.* Trommers' Premium White Label beer sponsored the program on which the Answer Man (Albert Mitchell) answered questions sent in by listeners. Some typical questions and Mitchell's answers were:

Q: Is it true the male cricket chirps?
A: Yes, only the male cricket chirps.
Q: How high does an airplane skywriter make his letters?
A: The skywriter makes his letters a mile high.

Despite Mitchell's pedantic manner, the program attracted a large audience (15 min., Monday through Friday, 7:15–7:30 p.m, WOR, New York, NY, 1945).

1061 Anter, Elaine. Singesr (*Elaine Anter*, vcl. mus. prg., WHLS, Port Huron, MI, 1942).

1062 Antes, Marian. COM-HE (WRAK, Williamsport, PA, 1955).

1063 Anthony, Al. DJ (KAFY, Bakersfield, CA, 1957).

1064 Anthony, Anthony [Ashley]. Announcer (KFJR, Portland, OR, 1927).

1065 Anthony, Beatrice. Pianist (WAHG, Richmond Hill, NY, 1926).

1066 Anthony, Bill. Newscaster (*Cella News*, KJEO, Fresno, CA, 1953).

1067 Anthony, Bill. DJ (WMC, Memphis, TN, 1960).

1068 Anthony, Bob. DJ (*Sleepwalker's Serenade*, KVOO, Tulsa, OK, 1952).

1069 Anthony, Carmine. DJ (WOC, Davenport, IA, 1955; WJJD, Chicago, IL, 1957).

1070 Anthony, Charles "Chuck." Sportscaster (WBCM, Bay City, MI, 1941, WKAR, East Lansing, MI, 1942). Newscaster (WKAR, MI, 1942–1946).

1071 Anthony, Dick. Newscaster (*Morning Editor*, KDAL, Duluth, MN, 1948–54, 1957–1960).

1072 Anthony, Earle. Announcer and station owner (WFI, Los Angeles, CA, 1925).

1073 Anthony, George. Sportscaster (WOND, Pleasantville, NJ, 1951; *Sports Parade*, WOND, 1953). Newscaster (WOND, 1954).

1074 Anthony, Ida May. Pianist (WOC, Davenport, IA, 1928).

1075 Anthony, Jerry. Newscaster (*Past and Present*, KDAL, Duluth, MN, 1960).

1076 Anthony, Joe. DJ (*Harlem Serenade*, KMAC, San Antonio, TX, 1960).

1077 Anthony, John. Actor Anthony appeared on *The O'Neills* and *Road of Life* daytime serials.

1078 Anthony, Julian. Newscaster (*Headline Edition* and *News ofTomorrow*, ABC, 1946–1953; *Events of the Day* and *This Year Around the World*, WABC, New York, NY, 1955–1960).

1079 Anthony, Lee. Newscaster (WTAD, Quincy, IL, 1947–1948; *Community News*, WTAD, 1952).

1080 Anthony, Marv. DJ (*Marv Anthony Show*, WSPT, Stevens Point, WI, 1952; WDLB, Marshfield, WI, 1954).

1081 Anthony, Mike. Sportscaster (*The Sports Page*, WMOD, Moundsville, WV, 1960).

1082 Anthony, Mildred. Pianist (1925).

1083 Anthony, Robert. DJ (*Juke Box Review*, WMIX, Mt. Vernon, IL, 1948).

1084 Anthony, Vincent. Newscaster (WCNW, Brooklyn, NY, 1937).

1085 Anthony, W. E. Announcer (KFDX, Shreveport, LA, 1927).

1086 Anthony, Jr., William D. DJ (WEED, Rocky Mount, NC, 1957).

1087 *Anthony Ewwer—the Philosopher of the Crossroads.* The Amalgamated Broadcasting System presented the program of homey philosophy in 1933. Unfortunately, the Amalgamated Broadcasting System lasted only several months as did the Philosopher.

1088 *(The) Antique Record Shop.* Joe Franklin interviewed great performers of the past including Belle Baker and Gus Van on his hour-long weekday program. He would then play their recordings on the nostalgic local program (60 min., Monday through Friday, 8:00–9:00 A.M., WMCA, New York, NY, 1948).

1089 *Antobal's Cubans Orchestra.* Instr. mus. prg. (NBC-Red, 1936).

1090 Antoine, Frances. COM-HE (WVIM, Vicksburg, MS, 1954–1955).

1091 Antoine, Tex. DJ (WRCA, New York, NY, 1957). He later became a TV weatherman.

1092 Antoine, Valerie B. COM-HE (KFQD, Anchorage, AK, 1957–1958).

1093 Anton, Anita. Actress featured on the *Backstage Wife* aka *Mary Noble, Backstage Wife* daytime serial.

1094 Antone, Jerry. Leader (Jerry Antone Orchestra, WOR, Newark, NJ, 1925).

1095 Antone's Circle Orchestra. Popular local band (WGBS, New York, NY, 1925).

1096 Antonetti, Clara. COM-HE (WTSA, Brattelboro, VT, 1957).

1097 Antonini, Alfred. Leader (*Alfred Antonini Orchestra,* instr. mus. prg., WOR, Newark, NJ, 1939).

1098 *Antonio's Continentals Orchestra.* Instr. mus. prg. (WGN-MBS, Chicago, IL, 1935).

1099 Antonsen, Evelyn. Violinist (WCCO, Minneappolis–St. Paul, MN, 1925).

1100 Antony, Eleanor. Pianist (WRC, Washington, DC, 1924).

1101 Antos, R. DJ (WSYB, Rutland, VT, 1960).

1102 Anway, Joseph. Reader (WLDS, Independence, MO, 1925).

1103 *(The) Anybodys.* The story of an "average American family" was broadcast each weekday evening. The family included a husband and wife (George and Gertrude) and their children (Buddy and Junior). All the show's characters were played by Bob Herrick and Hazel Dopheide on the 10 minute program (10 min., Monday through Friday, KMOX , St. Louis, MO, 1930).

1104 *Anything Goes.* Gene Rayburn and Jack Lescoulie, one time trombonist in the Ben Bernie orchestra, jointly hosted the early morning show. They gave time signals, weather reports, news summaries, funny skits and lively patter. The program began with an introduction by Rayburn and Lescoulie: "I'm Jack.... I'm Gene.... and *Anything Goes*" (120 min., Monday through Friday, 7:00–9:00 A.M., WNEW, New York, NY, 1947). After the program went off the air, Rayburn teamed with DJ Dee Finch to conduct another popular New York early morning show. When Gene Rayburn left Dee Finch, the latter was joined by witty comedian-DJ Gene Klavan, who had previously conducted a successful morning show in Baltimore (210 min., Monday through Saturday, 7:00–9:10 A.M., WNEW, New York, NY, 1952).

1105 Anz, Johnny. Leader (*Johnny Anz Orchestra,* instr. mus. prg., WESG, Elmira, NY, 1937).

1106 Anzivino, Joe. Sportscaster (KGMB, Honolulu, HI, 1945; *Sports Parade*, KGMB, 1950–1951).

1107 "AOC." Designation for announcer Asa O. Coggeshall (WGY, Schenectady, NY, 1923).

1108 "AON." Designation for announcer Norman E. Brokenshire (WJZ, New York, NY, and WJY, New York, NY, 1925). *See* **Norman Brokenshire**.

1109 Aparicio, Ray. DJ (KBUC, Corona, CA, 1960).

1110 Apfel, Adelaide. Pianist (WLW, Cincinnati, OH, 1923–1924).

1111 Apollo Club Orchestra. Club band directed by Robert Boice Carson (KVOO, Tulsa, OK, 1928).

1112 Apollo Country Club Orchestra. Society dance orchestra (WOR, Newark, NJ, 1923).

1113 Apollo Little Symphony Orchestra. Classical music organization (WRNY, New York, NY, 1925).

1114 App, James. DJ (*Second Breakfast*, WWOD, Lynchburg, VA, 1952).

1115 Appel, Mabel. Cellist (WOC, Davenport, IA, 1923).

1116 Appel, Pearl. Pianist (WLS, Chicago, IL, 1926).

1117 Apple, Bill. DJ (*Stay Up Stan*, KXA, Seattle, WA, 1948–1949).

1118 Apple, Marie. COM-HE (KWCB, Searcy, AR, 1956).

1119 (The) "Apple Sauce Twins." Comedy singing team of "Doc" Bellamy and Grady Forte (KMA, Shenandoah, IA, 1928).

1120 Applebaum, Dora Jean. Soprano (WOR, Newark, NJ, 1924).

1121 "Appleblossom and Moonshine." Blackface comedy team (WBAP, Fort Worth, TX, 1928).

1122 *(The) Appleburys.* Murray and Harris were featured in the serial drama written by Harry Colwell (NBC-Pacific Coast Network, 1929).

1123 Appleby, Roy. Actor Appleby appeared on the *Young Dr. Malone* daytime serial program.

1124 Applegate, George. Newscaster (KMJ, Fresno, CA, 1941).

1125 *(The) Applesauce Club.* Ransome ("Rans") Sherman was one of the comedians who performed on the popular local variety show (Chicago radio, 1925). The program included a little bit of everything but its emphasis was mainly on zany comedy. The show probably originated from Chicago's station WMAQ.

1126 Appleton, Ray. Actor Appleton appeared on the *Myrt and Marge* daytime serial program.

1127 Appy, Jerry. Sportscaster (KXXX, Colby, KS, 1948).

1128 *Arabesque.* A play within a play format was used on the dramatized series of "Arabian Desert" stories. Written by Yolanda Langworthy, the romantic series was inspired by the memories of Valentino and the popularity of "harem" stories. Frank Knight played Dr. Gilbert, the masculine lead, in *Arabesque.* Georgia Backus, Reynolds Evans and Geneva Harrison were also in the cast. Music was supplied by Emery Deutsch and his Gypsy Violins. The narrator was David Ross (30 min., Sunday,10:30–11:00 P.M. in 1930 and Wednesday, 9:30–10:00 P.M. in 1931, CBS).

1129 *Arabian Nights.* Charles Martin produced the sustaining oriental fantasy, a dramatic program targeted for young listeners. Romance, intrigue and mystery were the main ingredients as Scherezade told the stories of Aladdin, Ali Baba and the Forty Thieves, the Magic Carpet and other exotic themes. Music was directed by Robert Hood Bowers (30 min., Tuesday, 8:30–9:00 P.M., WMCA, New York, NY, 1933).

1130 Araki, S. COM-HE (KOHO, Honolulu, HA, 1960).

1131 Aranzamendi, Francisco. DJ (WAPA, San Juan, PR, 1954–1955).

1132 *Arbogast.* Robert Louis Arbogast and his assistant Peter Robinson were a zany Chicago DJ team. Their humor was something similar to that of *Bob and Ray* (30 min., Monday through Friday, 10:30–11:00 P.M., WMAQ, Chicago, IL, 1951).

1133 Arbogast, Bob. Sportscaster (WEAW, Evanston, IL, 1954).

1134 Arbuckle, Bryant. DJ (*Clock Spinner*, WAIR, Winston-Salem, NC, 1948–1949; *Tunes From Texas*, KURV, Edinburg, TX, 1952; KRIO, McAllen, TX, 1955).

1135 Arcadia Cafe Orchestra (aka the Arcadia Concert Orchestra). Directed by Howard Lanin (WDAR, Philadelphia, PA, 1923); directed by Feri Sarkozi and Salvatore Pizza, (WDAR, PA, 1923–25 and WLIT, Philadelphia, PA, 1926).

1136 Arcadia Cafeteria Orchestra. Popular restaurant band directed by Jack Cronshaw (KHJ, Los Angeles, CA, 1925).

1137 Arcadia Dance Orchestra. Dance band led by Salvatore Pizza (WLIT, Philadelphia, PA, 1925).

1138 Arcadians Orchestra. Popular local band directed by Harry Lang (WNOX, Knoxville, TN, 1928).

1139 *Arcadians Orchestra.* Instr. mus. prg. (WWVA, Wheeling, WV, 1935).

1140 Arcady Orchestra. Radio dance orchestra (WNYC, New York, NY, 1925).

1141 Arcady Trio. The instrumental trio of Idell Moye, Hazel Shively and Eleanor Maegle (KFI, Los Angeles, LA, 1929).

1142 Arch, Shirley. COM-HE (WHLD, Niagra Falls, NY, 1951–1954; WJJL, Niagra Falls, NY, 1958).

1143 Archambault, (Madame) Blanche. Pianist (WBZ, Boston-Springfield, MA, 1926).

1144 *Archer, (Dean) Gleason.* Legal scholar, educator, broadcaster and radio historian Archer was the president of Boston's Suffolk Law School and author of many reference works for lawyers and students of the law and history books for children. For several seasons he broadcast a series of weekly lectures on the law for laymen on his *Laws That Safeguard Society* program. The scholarly series presented with clarity and precision was carried by 40 NBC stations on Saturday evening in the early 1930s. On January 16, 1932, Archer delivered his 77th lecture program. His subject on that broadcast was "Marriage Law." Archer's widow, Polly Willis Archer, was a pioneer broadcaster who had performed on KYW (Chicago, IL) in 1923. *See* ***Laws That Safeguard Society*** *and* **Willis, Polly**.

1145 Archer, Edward. Actor Archer appeared on the *Brent House* daytime serial program.

1146 Archer, Gene. DJ (WRC, Washington, DC, 1955).

1147 Archer, Graham. DJ (*Wax Museum*, KGW, Portland, OR, 1949).

1148 Archer, John. DJ (*Dial-a-Tune*, WCMB, Lemoyne, PA, 1948).

1149 Archer, Vance. Sportscaster (*Sports for All*, KNEX, McPherson, KS, 1950).

1150 Archer, Ward. Musician Archer was a featured drummer in the Ben Bernie orchestra on the *Ben Bernie Show.*

1151 Archibald, Vernon. Baritone (CBS, New York, NY, 1928 and WEAF, New York, NY, 1929).

1152 *Archie Andrews.* First heard in 1943 on MBS in a 15-minute format, the comedy show had become 30-minutes in length by the time it went off the air in 1953. The program was based on the comic strip of the same name by Bob Montana. The sponsor was Swift Premium Meats, makers of Swift Premium franks "in the sanitary, flavor saving cellophane wrapped one-pound package." *Variety* critically commented that the acting and writing of the *Archie Andrews* program was below the standards of such other teenage shows as the *Aldrich Family* and *A Date with Judy.* Over the years the program's cast included: Peggy Allenby, Cameron Andrews, Fred Barron, Burt Boyer, Maurice Franklin, Joy Geffen, Paul Gordon, Bill Griffis, Jack Grimes, Doris Grundy, Bob Hastings, Vinton Hayworth, Grace Keddy, Arthur Kohl, Joe Latham, Arthur Maitland, Gloria Mann, Charles Mullen, Rosemary Rice, Vivian Smolen, Harlan Stone, Jr., Reese Taylor and Alice Yourman. Created by John L. Goldwater, the program was written by Carl Jampel and Howard Merrill. The producers and directors included Floyd Holm, Kenneth W. MacGregor and Herbert M. Moss. Ken Banghart and Dick Dudley were the announcers (30 min., NBC, 1945).

1153 Archinard, Paul. Newscaster (NBC, 1942–1946).

1154 Arcieri, Joseph. Banjo soloist (WRNY, New York, NY, 1927).

1155 *(The) Arco Birthday Party.* A combination of music and drama, the program, sponsored by the American Radiator Company, dramatized events in the life of a famous historical person. The novel format had listeners supposedly attending a birthday party of some long dead famous person. Tenor Mario Chamlee, a male quartet, a string quartet, trumpet trio and orchestra supplied the music (30 min., Thursday, 9:00–9:30 P.M., NBC-Red, 1930).

1156 *(The) Arco Dramatic Musicale.* The program featured old-time musical selections played by the Jeffrey Harris Orchestra (30 min., weekly, 9:00–9:30 P.M., NBC-Red, 1932).

1157 Ardell, June. Soprano (*June Ardell*, vcl. mus. prg., WOR, Newark, NJ, 1935).

1158 Arden, Harold. Leader (*Harold Arden Orchestra*, instr. mus. prg., KTHS, Hot Springs, AR, 1940).

1159 Arden, Joan. Pianist (*Piano Moods*, KFI, Los Angeles, CA, 1930).

1160 Arden, Robert. Newscaster (WATI, Atlanta, GA, 1938; KFWB, Los Angeles, CA, 1940; *Your Foreign Correspondent*, KWIK, Burbank, CA, 1948).

1161 Arden, Victor. Pianist and member of a famous piano duo with Phil Ohlman (WJZ, New York, NY) Arden later was the conductor of a busy studio orchestra and musical director (Armstrong Quakers orchestra, NBC-Blue, New York, NY, 1929; leader, *Victor Arden Orchestra*, instr. mus. prg, WMAL, Washington, DC, 1936; WGAR, Cleveland, OH, 1937; WJR, Detroit, MI, WHAM, Rochester, NY and WDEL, Wilmington, DE, 1938; KFEL, Denver, CO, 1939; MBS, 1940; WMAL, Washington, DC, 1942). Arden played the piano on the *Hearts in Harmony* daytime serial program and conducted the orchestra on the *Harry and Esther* show, *Manhattan Merry-Go-Round* and *Mr. Chameleon* programs.

1162 Arden (Victor) and Ohman (Phil). Popular piano duo (NBC-Red, New York, NY, 1929).

1163 Ardis, William I. Newscaster (KGKL, San Antonio, TX, 1946; *Phillips 66 News*, KGKL, 1948).

1164 Ardre, Bob. DJ (*Jukebox Jamboree*, WNAR, Norristown, PA, 1947).

1165 Arehart. A. Z. Announcer (WRBC, Valpariso, IN, 1927).

1166 Arena, Vincent. Newscaster (KEEW, Brownsville, TX, 1941).

1167 Arends, Cecile. Violinist (WBCN, Chicago, IL, 1926).

1168 Arends, Johanna. Pianist (WBCN, Chicago, IL, 1926).

1169 Arenson, Saul B. Professor of chemistry at the University of Cincinnati, Arenson delivered talks on various scientific topics (WLW, Cincinnati, OH, 1928–1929).

1170 Aresoni, Enrico. Tenor (WCAU, Philadelphia, PA, 1926).

1171 Aretta, Tony. Pianist (KFI, Los Angeles, CA, 1928).

1172 Argall, Phyllis. Newscaster (WGBS, Miami, FL, 1945).

1173 *(The) Argentine Orchestra.* Instr. mus. prg. (NBC, 1935).

1174 Argiewicz, Arthur. Violinist on the *Eveready Hour* (KGO, Oakland, CA, 1926).

1175 Argo, Verla. COM-HE (KARY, Prosser, WA, 1960).

1176 Argumedo, Oscar. DJ (KCOR, San Antonio, TX, 1954).

1177 Ariel, Lilyan. Pianist (KFI, Los Angeles, CA, 1927).

1178 Ariel Four. The quartet included soprano Barbara Blanchard, contralto Ruth W. Anderson, tenor Albert E. Gross and baritone Desaix McCloskey (KLX, Oakland, CA, 1927).

1179 Ariens, Phyllis. COM-HE (WLBH, Matoon, IL, 1955).

1180 Arim, Thomas. DJ (*Birthday Party*, WSTV, Steubenville, OH, 1948).

1181 Arion Male Chorus. Vocal music group (WJZ, New York, NY, 1923).

1182 Arion Trio. The instrumental trio consisting of Margaret Avery, cello; Joyce Barthelson, pianist, and Josephine Holub, violinist began their radio appearances in 1924 on the Pacific coast. The music supervisor of the Oakland Technical High School in 1918 suggested the women form a trio and helped them organize it. They specialized in light classics (KGO, San Francisco, CA, 1924–1925). When they appeared on the NBC-Pacific Network in 1929, the trio was composed of Joyce Barthelson, pianist-arranger; Josephine Holub, violinist; and cellist Auro Craverot. Throughout the 1930s, the Arion Trio were regular performers on San Francisco radio.

1183 *Aristocratic Rhythm.* Harold Levey's Orchestra appeared on the popular music program (NBC, 1936).

1184 *Arizona Hayride* aka *Baby State Jamboree.* CW music program that changed its name to the *Baby State Jamboree* (KOY, Phoenix, AZ, 1956). The show featured the Bob Casey Band, the Sweethearts and the Buckskins.

1185 Arkansas, Phillip. Saxophonist, billed as a "full-blooded Ute Indian" from the Cherokee reservation, who specialized in playing the "blues" (WWNC, Ashville, NC, 1929).

1186 *Arkansas Jamboree Barndance.* CW music program featuring the Armstrong Twins and Frank Dungeon (KLRA, Little Rock, AR, 1946

1187 (The) Arkansas Log Rollers. CW music group (*The Arkansas Log Rollers,* CW mus. prg., WJJD, Chicago, IL, 1937).

1188 *Arkansas Ramblers.* CW mus. prg. (KUOA, Fayetteville, AR, 1933–1934).

1189 *(The) Arkansas Traveler.* Lever Brothers, makers of Lifebuoy soap, sponsored the comedy show on which Bob Burns was featured (30 min., Wednesday, 9:00–9:30 P.M., CBS, 1942).

1190 *(The) Arkansas Treasure Hour of Literature.* Literary topics were discussed and various literary selections read by Dr. Charles H. Brough (KLRA, Little Rock, AR, 1929).

1191 (The) Arkansas Troubadours. CW music group (*The Arkansas Troubadours,* CW mus. prg., WBZ, Boston-Springfield, MA, 1939).

1192 (The) Arkansas Valley Boys. CW music group (*The Arkansas Valley Boys*, KFH, Wichita, KS, 1939).

1193 (The) Arkansas Woodchopper (aka "Arkie"). CW entertainer (KMBC, 1929). *See* **The National Barn Dance** *and* **Ossenbrink, Luther**.

1194 Arkell, Bud. DJ (*Rise and Hot Sauce*, WSIR, Winter Haven, FL, 1952; WANS, Anderson, SC, 1957).

1195 Arkell, (Mrs.) Lillian. Organist on the the faculty of the Cincinnati College of Music (WLW, Cincinnati, OH, 1926).

1196 Arkell, Rod. Newscaster (WSUN, St. Petersburg, FL, 1939).

1197 "Arkie." *See* ***The National Barn Dance*** *and* **Ossenbrink, Luther**.

1198 Arkison, Jim. Sportscaster (*Speaking of Sports*, WALE, Fall River, MA, 1949; *Sports Beat*, WALE, 1953–1954).

1199 Arlas, Jose. Leader (Jose Arlas and his Orchestra, WOAW, Omaha, NE, 1924). Two years later he was in San Francisco with a band billed as Joe Arlas and his Mexican Orchestra (KFI, San Francisco, CA, 1926).

1200 Arledge, Irene. Contralto (KFDM, Beaumont, TX, 1928).

1201 Arledge, Mabel. COM-HE (KIVY, Crockett, TX, 1954).

1202 Arlen, Jimmy. Baritone (*Jimmy Arlen*, vcl. mus. prg., WLW, Cincinnati, OH, 1934).

1203 Arlen, Joan. Vocalist (*Joan Arlen,* vcl. mus. prg., WIP, Philadelphia, PA, 1938).

1204 Arlen, Judith. Vocalist (*Judith Arlen,* vcl. mus. prg, CBS, 1939, 1942). Even though papers and other publications of the time list both a Judith Arlen and a Joan Arlen, they may indicate the same performer.

1205 Arlin, Harold W. Famous pioneer announcer (KDKA, Pittsburgh, PA, 1925). Arlin, considered to have been the first full-time announcer on the KDKA staff, was one of the great pioneers of early American radio. His training was as an electrical engineer. When he entered a Westinghouse training program, he attracted the attention of Leo Rosenberg, who offered him an announcing job at KDKA. He accepted and became one of early radio's most popular announcers. Soon after starting at KDKA, Arlin *most likely* became the first DJ when he played phonograph records on the air. Although at first he announced neither their titles or their performers, he soon began to do so in response to listener requests. Immediately after he began giving this information, the sale of phonograph records in his area greatly increased.

On August 5, 1921, Arlin on KDKA broadcast the *first* baseball play-by-play from Forbes Field. Later, on August 6, 1921, he became the first man to broadcast a tennis match. Approximately two months later, he broadcast the Pittsburgh-West Virginia football game. KDKA claimed that Arlin was the first to broadcast football play-by-play with the University of Pittsburgh-West Virginia University game.

1206 Arlington, Charles. Newscaster (WWJ, Detroit, MI, 1939; KQW, San Jose, CA, 1944).

1207 Arlington Concert Orchestra. Local popular music group (KTHS, Hot Springs National Park, AR, 1928).

1208 Arlington Hotel Ensemble. Musical group conducted by Dan LeBow (KTHS, Hot Springs National Park, AR, 1928).

1209 *(The) Arlington Hotel Show.* The fine music program originated from Hot Springs, Arkansas. Performers included the Eddie Rogers Orchestra, Arlington Glee Club, Frank Simeone, George Frewert, Troy Watkins, Tosi Brandenberg, Walter Brown, John Cardia and Jack Coffin (30 min., Saturday, 10:30–11:00 P.M., KWFC, Hot Springs, AR, 1958).

1210 Arlington Orchestra. Musical group (*Arlington Orchestra*, KTHS, Hot Spings, AR, 1939–1940).

1211 Arliss, Joan. Singer (KFVE, University City, MO, 1925).

1212 Arlitt, (Dr.) Ada. Director of the Department of Child Care and Training at the University of Cincinnati, Arlitt hosted the *Mother's Discussion Group* program (WLW, Cincinnati, OH, 1929).

1213 Arm Chair Quintet. The music group included tenors, Milton J. Cross and Maurice Tyler, baritone Walter Preston and bass Marley R. Sherris. In their broadcasts they were assisted by Keith McLeod, vibraphonist. Milton J. Cross was also the announcer (NBC-Blue, New York, NY, 1929).

1214 Arman, Marion. COM-HE (WGAP, Maryville, TN, 1955–1957).

1215 Armand, Dorothy. COM-HE (WCOV, Montgomery, AL, 1951–1955).

1216 Armand, Ray. Newscaster (WARL, Arlington, VA, 1953). DJ (*Hillbilly Star*, WARL, 1953).

1217 *(The) Armand Program.* Armand Cosmetics sponsored singers Jane Froman and Don Ross on the quarter-hour program of romantic songs. Lennie Hayton's Orchestra provided the accompaniment (15 min., Monday, 9:45–10:00 P.M., WOR, Newark, NJ, 1934).

1218 Armatta, Wilbur. Newscaster (*Penthouse Journal*, WCOH, Houston, TX, 1951).

1219 Armbrister, Randy. DJ (WYVE, Whytheville, VA, 1954).

1220 Armbruster, Joe. Leader (Joe Armbruster's Orchestra, WGR, Detroit, MI, 1926 and WMAK, Buffalo, NY, 1928).

1221 Armbruster, Robert. Conductor-pianist Armbruster started on radio in its earliest days, playing the piano for NBC. He joined NBC when it first was formed and appeared on its inaugural program. Armbruster conducted the orchestra on the *Enna Jettick Melodies* program (WJZ, New York, NY, 1928).

1222 Armchair Quartet. Vocal group (*Armchair Quartet,* vcl. mus. prg., WJZ, New York, NY, 1938).

1223 *(The) Armco Ironmaster Program.* Frank Simon's 51-piece Armco Band broadcast for 15 years. Simon, who had been a cornet soloist and the assistant conductor for John Philip Sousa's band, first broadcast with the Armco band in 1925. Armco Steel Company sponsored the program (30 min., Sunday, 2:30–3:00 P.M., C.S.T., 1938).

1224 Armen, Kay. Singer (*Kay Armen—Songs*, vcl. mus. prg. 15 min., Saturday, 11:45–12:00 noon, NBC-Blue, 1947). DJ (*The Kay Armen Story,* Miss Armen became a DJ who also dispensed household and kitchen hints on the program that replaced Pegeen Fitzgerald's *Strictly Personal* show 15 min., 9:30–10:00 A.M., WRCA, New York, NY, 1955).

1225 Armentrout, Charles. Sportscaster (WJLS, Beckley, WV, 1941).

1226 Armer, Allan. DJ (*Hits for Mrs.*, KEEN, San Jose, CA, 1947).

1227 Armer, Austin. Flutist (KTAB, Oakland, CA, 1925).

1228 Armes, George. Saxophonist (WMAZ, Macon, GA, 1926).

1229 Armey, Joe. Sportscaster (KBRC, Mount Vernon, WA, 1955).

1230 Armistead, Bea. COM-HE (WHBQ, Memphis, TN, 1958).

1231 Armitage, Dave. DJ (*Take It Easy Time*, KFOX, Long Beach, CA, 1955).

1232 Armond, William. Newscaster (*News and Views*, WBLJ, Dalton, GA, 1947).

1233 *(The) Armour Hour of Music.* Armour Meat Packing Company sponsored this 60-minute program of concert music. Tenor Fred Aldner, a male vocal trio, an 18-voice mixed choir and a 30-piece orchestra conducted by Josef Koestner were featured. Thomas Green, Jr., was the announcer (60 min., Friday, 9:30–10:30 P.M., NBC, 1929).

1234 *(The) Armour Jester.* Comedian Phil Baker was the jester on the comedy show (NBC-Blue, 1933). *See* ***The Phil Baker Show***.

1235 *Armour Menuettes.* Armour Meat Packing Company sponsored the local music program (30 min., Monday, 6:30–7:00 P.M., WKY, Oklahoma City, 1930).

1236 *(The) Armour Program.* Soprano Edna Kellogg appeared on the variety program sponsored by the Armour Meat Packing Company. Irvin S. Cobb and the orchestras of Josef Koestner and Frank Shields also performed. Sen Kaney was the announcer. The program was on the air from 1929 through 1933 (30 min., Friday, 9:30–10:00 P.M., NBC-Blue, 1930).

1237 Armstead, George. Newscaster (WDRC, Hartford, CT, 1944).

1238 Armstrong, (Mrs.) A. Scott. Pianist (WQJ, Chicago, IL, 1925).

1239 Armstrong, Bernie. Organist (*Bernie Armstrong,* instr. mus. program, WJAS, Pittsburgh, PA, 1935 and KDKA, Pittsburgh, PA, 1936–1938).

1240 Armstrong, Betty. COM-HE (WBPZ, Lock Haven, PA, 1951).

1241 Armstrong, Bill. Newscaster (WRAL, Raleigh, NC, 1952–1953; WNCA, Siler City, NC, 1955). DJ (WNCA, 1955).

1242 Armstrong, Bob. Leader (*Bob Armstrong Orchestra,* instr. mus. prg., NBC, 1942).

1243 Armstrong, Bob. DJ (*WCNT Bandwagon*, WCNT, Centralia, IL, 1952). Newscaster (WIBV, Belleville, IL, 1960).

1244 Armstrong, Bud. DJ (*Mr. Music*, KOWH, Omaha, NE, 1947).

1245 Armstrong, Carl B. Sportscaster (*Togos Men Shop Sports*, WHED, Washington, DC, 1949; *Sports Digest,* WHED, 1950; *Sports Views*, WIAM, Williamston, NC, 1951). Newscaster (WIAM, 1951).

1246 Armstrong, Don. DJ (WQAM, Miami, FL, 1960).

1247 Armstrong, Edwin Howard. Inventor Armstrong pioneered in radio by inventing and developing the superheterodyne circuit that produced clearer reception and better tonal quality for listeners. Although frustrated much of his life by undeserved setbacks in patent infringement cases, Armstrong is now generally recognized as one of the most important contributors to the development of American radio. His significant contributions include such radio circuitry improvements as the development of regenerative, super-regenerative and superheterodyne circuits. These improvements provided greater amplification of signals received without the howling noise usually associated with signal regeneration. Armstrong became wealthy when he sold the rights to his superheterodyne circuit to RCA in 1922. Eleven years later Armstrong demonstrated his wideband FM (frequency modulation) system that is recognized as the beginning of multiplexing and high fidelity (Lewis, 1993, p. 259). Despite his several significant contributions, Armstrong committed suicide in 1954, believing himself a failure. Throughout his life, the introverted Armstrong contributed as much or more than did his counterpart and bitter rival—the extroverted Lee DeForest.

1248 Armstrong, Frank. Sportscaster (WJPR, Greenville, MS, 1942; *Sports Parade*, WDSG, Dyersburg, TN, 1947).

1249 Armstrong, Harry. Armstrong told tales and recounted his "Reminiscences of Minstrel Days" (WBAY, New York, NY, 1922).

1250 Armstrong, Helen. Contralto (WGBS, New York, NY, 1925).

1251 Armstrong, Jean Belle. COM-HE (WSYR, Syracuse, NY, 1954–1955).

1252 Armstrong, (Dr.) John. Newscaster (*John Armstrong Reviews the News*, WHDL, Olean, NY, 1940–1944, 1957–1960).

1253 Armstrong, Ken. Newscaster (*News with Ken Armstrong*, WKBZ, Muskegon, MI, 1949).

1254 Armstrong, Louis. Pianist, not the famous jazz trumpet artist (KOIL, Council Bluffs, IA, middle or late 1920s).

1255 Armstrong, Louis. Leader (*Louis Armstrong Orchestra*, instr. mus. prg., WIP, Philadelphia, PA, 1935–1936; WENR, Chicago, IL, 1938–1939). Armstrong was a great American jazz musician.

1256 Armstrong, Mary. COM-HE (WTNJ, Trenton, NJ, 1958).

1257 Armstrong, Nellie. Contralto (WFI, Philadelphia, PA, 1925).

1258 *Armstrong Quakers.* The weekly musical program presented soprano Lois Bennett, "The Quaker Girl," the Armstrong Quakers Orchestra, contralto Mary Hopple, a male vocal quartet and Victor Arden conducting the orchestra (30 min, Friday, 10:00–10:30 P.M., NBC-Blue, 1928–1931).

1259 Armstrong, Robert "Bob." Newscaster (WGBR, Goldsboro, NC, 1939).

1260 Armstrong, Stuart "Stu." Sportscaster (WWXL, Peoria, IL, 1950; *According to the Coach*, WSIV, Pekin, IL, 1952).

1261 Armstrong, Tom. DJ (WGAR, Cleveland, OH, 1954–1960).

1262 Armstrong, William "Army." Sportscaster (WOMI, Owensboro, KY, 1946; *Sports News and Views*, WOMI, 1948–1951).

1263 *Armstrong of the S.B.I.* Most of the characters that originally appeared on the popular children's daytime serial, *Jack Armstrong*, also appeared on this show. Unlike the original program, this one ran 30-minutes in length and was broadcast twice weekly. A complete story was told each time. Jack appeared on the program as an investigator for the Scientific Bureau of Investigation—an organization roughly mirroring the FBI. Charles Flynn played the title role assisted by: Patricia Dunlap, Ken Griffin, Carlton KaDell and Dick York. The announcers were Ed Prentiss and Ken Nordine. James Jewell was the show's producer-director and chief writer. Other writers who contributed to the show were Paul Fairman, Alan Fishburn, Thomas Elvidge, Donald Gallagher, Jack Lawrence and Kermit Slobb (30 min., Tuesday and Thursday, 7:30–8:00 P.M., ABC, 1950).

1264 Armstrong Quaker Oats Orchestra. Band featured on the *Parisian Vocal Concert* program (WABC , New York, NY, 1928; WLW , Cincinnati, OH and WJZ, New York, NY, 1929).

1265 *(The) Army Hour.* The *Army Hour* program, an official broadcast report of the United States War Department, began during the World War II era. At that time numerous soldier interviews were broadcast along with generally upbeat Army news. Ed Herlihy was the announcer. In the following years the program broadcast various news features about the Army and its achievements (NBC, 1944).

1266 Arnall, Curtis. Actor Arnall played the title role in the *Buck Rogers in the 25th Century* program and in the *Just Plain Bill* and *Pepper Young's Family* daytime serial programs.

1267 Arndt, (Professor) William. Professor Arndt conducted a series of radio Bible classes (WFUO, St. Louis, MO, 1925–1926).

1268 Arnesen, Arne. Violinist (WLS, Chicago, IL, 1924 and KSD, St. Louis, MO, 1924–1926). Arnesen was also the leader of Arne Arnesen's Concert Orchestra (KSD, St. Louis, MO, 1925).

1269 Arneson, Esther. Pianist (WORD, Batavia, IL, 1925).

1270 Arnett, Eddie. DJ (WIZE, Springfield, OH, 1960).

1271 Arnheim, Gus. Popular California band leader, Arnheim formerly was a pianist with the Abe Lyman Orchestra before starting his own band. His programs often originated from Hollywood's Coconut Grove and featured songs by Bing Crosby. Arnheim's 1928 band included: Arnheim, ldr. and p.; Walter Holzhaus, t. and vcls.; Stanley Green, t.; Marlo Imes, tb.; Nelson Hall, g. and vcls.; Joe Krechter and Tom Sandvall, cl. and as. During the early days of radio, the Arnheim band, playing from the Coconut Grove in Los Angeles, broadcast every evening other than Sunday (KNX, Los Angeles, CA, 1927–1929). The band also appeared on the *Gus Arnheim Orchestra* instr. mus. prg. (CBS, 1932–1936; WMAQ, Chicago, IL, 1936 and WLW, Cincinnati, OH, 1942).

1272 Arno, George. Leader (*George Arno Orchestra,* instr. mus. prg., WWJ, Detroit, MI, 1942).

1273 Arnold, Al. Newscaster (KOBH, Rapid City, SD, 1939). Sportscaster (KOBH, 1939).

1274 Arnold, Alice. Singer (KFAE, Pullman, WA, 1925).

1275 Arnold, Art. DJ (*Pap's Tunes, Bar None Ranch* and *Cactus Classics,* KCKY, Coolidge, AZ, 1948).

1276 Arnold, Arthur. Sportscaster (KOBH, Rapid City, SD, 1940).

1277 Arnold, Betty. Actress Arnold appeared on the daytime serials *The Guiding Light, The Road of Life* and *Stepmother.*

1278 Arnold, Bill. Announcer (KTUE, Houston, TX, 1927).

1279 Arnold, Bill. DJ (*Platter Party,* WHSY, Hattiesburg, MS, 1949).

1280 Arnold, Bill. Newscaster (*Buckeye Viewpoint,* WRFO, Worthington, OH, 1952).

1281 Arnold, Bruce. DJ (WCCM, Lawrence, MA, 1960).

1282 Arnold, Charles. DJ (KBBA, Lufkin, TX, 1960).

1283 Arnold, Chuck. DJ (WIRL, Peoria, IL, 1957).

1284 Arnold, Chuck. DJ (WSOK, Nashville, TN, 1957).

1285 Arnold, Dick. Newscaster (KOAC, Coravallis, OR, 1946).

1286 Arnold, Don. DJ (*Sunday Serenade,* WDHL, Bradenton, FL, 1948).

1287 Arnold, Earl. Leader (*Earl Arnold Orchestra,* instr. mus. prg., WCKY, Cincinnati, OH, 1939).

1288 Arnold, Ed. DJ (KIEM, Eureka, CA, 1947).

1289 Arnold, Eddy (Richard Edward Arnold). Smooth CW and folk singer, Arnold crossed from CW performer to popular recording star, regularly working in Las Vegas in the 1950s. He first appeared on the *Grand Ole Opry* as part of Pee Wee King's Golden West Cowboys. In the late 1940s Arnold appeared on a network segment of the *Grand Ole Opry* and the Mutual Network's *Checkerboard Jamboree* with Ernest Tubb. Arnold's reputation grew with his many syndicated, recorded programs and the *Hometown Review* (CBS, 1948) on which he starred with the Duke of Paducah. One of country music's most successful crossover stars, Arnold was elected to the Country Music Hall of Fame in 1966.

1290 Arnold, Edna. Singer (WGBS, New York, NY, 1925).

1291 Arnold, Elsie Earp. Pianist (WBAL, Baltimore, MD, 1926).

1292 Arnold, Ethel. Leader (KMOX Rambler Orchestra, an all girl band, KMOX, St. Louis, MO, 1928).

1293 Arnold, Eugenia Earp. Contralto (WBAL, Baltimore, MD, 1926).

1294 Arnold, Fulton. Sportscaster (WTNJ, Trenton, NJ, 1941; WTTM, Trenton, NJ, 1945; *Arnold Sports,* WTTM, 1947–1948; *Sports Roundup,* WTTM, 1949–1954).

1295 Arnold, Gary. DJ (WDUN, Gainesville, GA, 1949). Sports (WDUN, 1949).

1296 Arnold, Gene. Interlocutor on the *Weener Minstrel Show* broadcast by WENR (Chicago, IL, 1929).

1297 Arnold, Gene. DJ (*Gospel Train,* WBMT, Black Mountain, NC, 1960).

1298 Arnold, Gere. COM-HE (KUGN, Eugene, OR, 1951).

1299 Arnold, George. Sportscaster (KWFC, Hot Springs, AR, 1949).

1300 Arnold, Gertrude. Mezzo-soprano (WSAI, Cincinnati, OH, 1927).

1301 Arnold, Harry. Newscaster (*Harry Arnold Views the News,* KLIX, Twin Falls, ID, 1947).

1302 Arnold, Helen. COM-HE (WCRI, Scottsboro, AR, 1956).

1303 Arnold, (Dr.) J. Sportscaster (*The Sports Picture,* WCWC, Ripon, WI, 1960).

1304 Arnold, Joe. DJ (*Rise and Shine,* KIBS, Bishop, CA, 1960).

1305 Arnold, John. Arnold broadcast safety talks (WKRC, Cincinnati, OH, 1925).

1306 Arnold, Joseph. Newscaster (*Current Events,* WAAB-Yankee Network, Boston, MA, 1931).

1307 Arnold, Kay and Buddy Arnold. Harmony singing team (WMCA, New York, NY, 1936).

1308 Arnold, Paul. Singer (*Paul Arnold,* vcl. mus. prg., WLW, Cincinnati, OH, 1942).

1309 Arnold, Ted. Sportscaster (*Sports Roundup,* WHTN, Huntington, WV, 1948).

1310 Arnold, Walter. Newscaster (KFOX, Long Beach, CA, 1940).

1311 *Arnold and McNatt.* Country music star-to-be Eddy Arnold brought his smooth singing style to the program on which he teamed with country fiddler Speedy McNatt (WTJS, Jackson, MI, 1938). The men teamed together until Arnold left to join Pee Wee King's Golden West Cowboys and appear on the *Grand Ole Opry* in 1938–1939.

1312 Arnoldi, Florence Lake. Coloratura soprano (WOAW, Omaha, NE, 1925).

1313 Arnoldi, Virginia. Pianist (WABC, New York, NY, 1932).

1314 Arnold's Seven Aces. Popular local orchestra (WWNC, Ashville, NC, 1928).

1315 Arnoux, G.C. ("Uncle Billy," "GCA" or "CAM"). Arnoux began his announcing career at station WGI (Medford Hillside, MA, 1923), where he also told "Peter Rabbit and Johnny Chipmunk" stories on his *Uncle Billy* children's program (WGI, 1923). After WGI, where he was known as "GCA," he went to WBAP (Dallas, TX) as an announcer from 1923 to 1924 and told tales of cowboys and western life. Arnoux was WBAP's first announcer. Known for his excellent diction and well modulated voice, Arnoux had made a successful transition from newspaper man to pioneer announcer. He left the Dallas station to become the manager-announcer-director at KTHS (Hot Springs National Park, AR) in 1924.

Arnoux was the announcer on KTHS's inaugural broadcast, a remote broadcast from Hot Springs' New Arlington Hotel ballroom featuring the Meyer Davis Orchestra. He began that program with, "Greetings to radioland. Station KTHS in Hot Springs National Park, Arkansas, is now on the air."

Arnoux also did many sports' re-creation broadcasts in the late 1920s such as: The 1925 World Series between the Washington Senators and Pittsburgh Pirates; the Dempsey-Tunney fight in 1926; the Dixie Minor League Series between Dallas and New Orleans; the Jack Sharkey-Jack Dempsey bout and Jack Demsey-Gene Tunney fight in 1927.

Arnoux became manager of KTAR (Norfolk, VA) in 1931 and, later, the president and general manager of the station. During a talent search in 1931, Arnoux found two young Mena, Arkansas, businessmen, who entertained friends with their blackface act. The pair he found was "Chet" Lauck and Norris "Tuffy" Goff. After the two men appeared on KTHS (Hot Springs, AR,1931) with musicians Oleu Wilhite and Cliff and Bill Beavers, they went on to network fame as *Lum and Abner.* Anroux died in 1966 at the age of 71 after serving as president of the National Association of Broadcasters.

1316 Arnoux, Natalie. Violinist (KFDM, Beaumont, TX, 1928).

1317 Arnow, Ed. Newscaster (NBC, San Francisco, CA, 1960). Sportscaster (NBC, 1960).

1318 Arnow, Kroll. Pianist (WIP, Philadelphia, PA, 1926).

1319 Aro, Bob. DJ (*Finnish Folk Songs,* WHLB, Virginia, MN, 1952).

1320 Aro, Sam. DJ (*Top O' the Morning*, WNDB, Daytona Beach, FL, 1949). Sports (WROD, Daytona Beach, FL, 1948; *Sports Roundup*, WNDB, 1949–1950; *Giant Jottings*, WMCA, New York, NY, 1951, 1954; *Sports Jottings*, WMCA, 1952–1956).

1321 Aronson, Bob. DJ (WMFG, Hibbing, MN, 1960).

1322 Aronson, Samuel S. Pianist (WJZ, New York, NY, 1924).

1323 Arough, Harry. Sportscaster (KPRC, Houston, NY, 1955). Newscaster (KPRC, 1960).

1324 *Around the Melodian.* "The days of yesteryear" were depicted in music on the popular local program directed by Frederick R. Huber and supervised by Gustav Klemm. The continuity script was written by Broughton Tall. The featured singers were Jane Kirby, soprano; Maud Albert, contralto; John Wilburn, tenor; Walter Linthicum, bass; Charlie Grace, tenor; and Charlie Thorp, tenor. John H. Elterman was the program's organist (30 min., Saturday, 9:00–9:30 P.M., WBAL, Baltimore, MD, 1929–1930). The favorites of its listening public were "Annie Laurie," "O Susanna," and "My Darling Nellie Gray."

1325 *Around the Old Parlor.* Organist Bill O'Connor and vocalist Howard Peterson appeared on the quarter-hour music program (15 min., Saturday, 10:15–10:30 A.M., WLS , Chicago, IL, 1938).

1326 *Around the Samovar.* Concert singer Mme. Dora Boescher, soprano Mme. Zinaida Nicolina, baritone Eli Spivak, violinist Mlle. Elaine Kazanova and Peter Biljou's Balalika Orchestra, conducted by M. Biljou, appeared on the program that presented primarily Russian music (Saturday, 9:30–10:00 P.M., CBS, 1929–1930).

1327 *Around the Town.* The evening show toured various New York night clubs and broadcast music directly from their dance floors (180 min., nightly, 11:00 P.M.-2:00 A.M., WMCA, New York, NY, 1932).

1328 *Around the Town with WDAF.* Every Saturday nights from 8:00–10:00 P.M., the station presented remote musical broadcasts from various Kansas City hotels, theaters and dining rooms (WDAF, Kansas City, MO, 1926).

1329 *Around the World with Betty Ross.* Journalist Ross talked about her adventures that had taken her from the Russian steppes to the Arabian desert (NBC, early-1930s).

1330 *Around the World with Libby.* Libby-McNeil-Libby sponsored the weekly series of musical tours around the world. Songs of many countries were performed by vocal soloists and the orchestra conducted by Josef Pasternack. Toscha Seidel also conducted the orchestra at times. Alwyn E.W. Bach was the announcer (NBC-Blue, 1929). A Pacific Coast version was also broadcast in the same year with Alois Havrilla as the announcer.

1331 *Arpeako Minstrel Show.* The old-fashioned radio minstrel show broadcast by WHAM (Rochester, NY, 1932) presented the usual gags, blackface jokes, songs, and skits.

1332 Arquette, Cliff. Veteran radio actor-comedian Arquette turned DJ on his *Carnival* program (WAMR, Venice, FL, 1960). Previously, he had appeared on *The Dick Haymes Show*, *Fibber McGee and Molly* show, *Glamor Manor*, *Lum and Abner*, *Myrt and Marge*, *Point Sublime* and *Welcome Valley*.

1333 Arrasmith, Herb. DJ (*West by Request*, KERN, Bakersfield, CA, 1948).

1334 Arreola, Olivia. COM-HE (KDJI, Holbrook, AZ, 1956).

1335 Arriga, Arno. Director of the critically praised Crosley Moscow Art Orchestra, a group equally proficient with the classics and the modern standard repertoire of the period (WLW, Cincinnati, OH, 1927).

1336 Arrington, Bill. Newscaster (WGTC, Greenville, SC, 1940).

1337 Arrington, Dera. COM-HE (KTVE, Longview, TX, 1955).

1338 Arrington, Pat. DJ (KWYK, Farmington, NM, 1960).

1339 Arrowhead Inn Orchestra. The popular ten-man Meyer Davis music unit worked out of New York City. The orchestra, led by Harold Veo, broadcast Saturday nights and Sunday afternoons (WGBS, New York, NY, 1926).

1340 Art, Bobby. DJ (*Country Clubhouse*, WRFW, Eau Claire, WI, 1954.)

1341 *Art in America.* NBC broadcast the half-hour program Saturday evenings (7:00–7:30 P.M., 1935). It was devoted to the work of various artists as its broadcast schedule indicates:

Oct. 20: Portrait Painters Fashionable and Unfashionable: Sargent and Eakins.

Oct. 27: American Sculpture Since the Civil War.

Nov. 3: Henry Hobson Richardson: America's First Modern Acchitect.

Nov. 10: The Architecture of Public Buildings.

Nov. 17. Frank Lloyd Wright and the International Style in Architecture.

Nov. 24: Theater Art: Stage Design in the American Theater.

Dec. 1: The Impressionists.

Dec. 8: The Impact of Modern Art — The Armory Show.

Dec. 15: The Contemporary American World: Social and Political Caricature.

1342 *Art Moger's Cartoon School.* Cartoonist Moger taught his craft on the series of sustaining programs (15 min., Saturday, 11:45–12:00 noon, WCOP, Boston, MA, 1937).

1343 *Art Mooney's Talent Train.* Band leader Mooney conducted his band and hosted the network amateur show, one of the last in the once extremely popular format (30 min., Tuesday, 8:00–8:30 P.M., ABC, 1949).

1344 *(The) Art of Living.* Dr. Norman Vincent Peale's inspirational sermons were broadcast on the late Saturday afternoon series by CBS in 1936.

1345 Artale, Vince. Newscaster (*Morning News*, WOVE, Welch, WV, 1960).

1346 Arter, Malcom "Mel." DJ (*You Name It*, WKOK, Sunbury, PA, 1948–1952).

1347 Arth, Hazel. Soprano Arth was the second place winner of Atwater-Kent's 1928 National Radio Auditions. She later was featured on her own *Hazel Arth*, vcl. mus. prg., accompanied by guitarist Andy Sanella (NBC, 1934–1935).

1348 Arthur. DJ (*This is Arthur*, WHAM, Rochester, NY, 1947). This DJ was not otherwise identified.

1349 Arthur, Bob. DJ (*The Wax Museum*, WOMT, Manitowoc, WI, 1947).

1350 Arthur, Bob. Newscaster (KFH, Wichita, KS, 1949; *Voice of the News*, WEEK, Peoria, IL, 1952–1953, 1957).

1351 Arthur, Charline. CW singer, composer and DJ, Arthur was born in 1929. She began her singing career at KPLT, Paris, TX in the 1940s. Later she appeared on KERM, Kermit, TX, as a DJ.

1352 Arthur, Chuck. Sportscaster (KTOX, Bay City, TX, 1956).

1353 Arthur, Don. DJ (*Arthur's Etchings*, WDUZ, Green Bay, WI, 1949). Sportscaster (*Shell Sports Review*, WDUZ, 1949; *Sportscast*, WDUZ, 1950; *Gettelman Sports*, WDUZ, 1951–1952; *Sports Edition*, WDUZ, 1953).

1354 Arthur, Doug. DJ (*Danceland*, WBIG, Philadelphia, PA, 1947,1952–1954; WCAU, Philadelphia, PA, 1960).

1355 Arthur, Ed. Newscaster (KOAC, Corvallis, OR, 1946).

1356 Arthur, Frank. Sportscaster (KSAN, San Francisco, CA, 1938–1940, 1948; KMJ, Fresno, CA, 1942; KLX, Oakland, CA, 1945; *Sports Review*, KSAN, 1949–1951; *Sports Report*, KSAN, 1952). Newscaster (*News at Thirty*, KSAN, 1952–1954; KYNO, Fresno, CA, 1960).

1357 Arthur, Fred. DJ (KVOC, Casper, WY, 1954–1955).

1358 Arthur, George. DJ (WHOW, Clinton, IL, 1954).

1359 Arthur, Harold. Newscaster (WPAV, Portsmouth, OH, 1946).

1360 Arthur, Harry. Sportscaster (WSMB, New Orleans, LA, 1947; *Sports Whirl*, KNOE, Monroe, LA, 1953).

1361 Arthur, Jack. Baritone (*Jack Arthur*, vcl. mus. prg., WOR, Newark, NJ, 1934–1937). Singer-actor Arthur also appeared on *The Callahans*, *Collier Hour*, *The Cuckoo Hour*, *Death Valley Days*, *Gay Nineties Revue*, *Grand Central Station*, *Harv and Esther*, *Light of the World*, *Lincoln Highway*, *Little Old New York*, *Maxwell Coffee Time*, *Stories of the Black Chamber*, *Texaco Star Theater*, *When a Girl Marries* and *Ziegfeld Follies of the Air*.

1362 Arthur, Jay. Sportscaster (WATS, Sayre, PA, 1955).

1363 Arthur, Jerry. DJ (*Make Merry with Jerry*, WLAD, Danbury, CT, 1949).

1364 Arthur, Jon. Newscaster (WIBC, Indianapolis, IN, 1942; *Woman's Side of the News*, WSAI, Cincinnati, OH, 1947). DJ (*The Jon Arthur Show*, WSAI, 1948–1949).

1365 Arthur, Louise. Actress Arthur appeared on *The Woman in White* and *Holly Sloan* daytime serials.

1366 Arthur, Zin. Leader (*Zin Arthur Orchestra*, instr. mus. prg., WFIL, Philadelphia, PA, 1938).

1367 *Arthur Godfrey.* Godfrey talked and sang on his entertaining morning program, sponsored by Cornation Milk. *Billboard* (June 20, 1940) suggested that few one-man shows reached Godfrey's quality and concluded: "The guy's good." Millions of listeners in later years agreed (15 min., Wednesday, 9:00–9:15 A.M., MBS, 1940). When Godfrey conducted an early morning music and weather show on WJSV (Washington, DC) in the 1930s, he often kidded a furrier sponsor by the name of Zlotnick, whose shop was located on G Street just above 10th Street in downtown Washington, DC. Godfrey often referred disparaging to Zlotnick's shop and the sign of the large white bear that marked its location. Since everyone in Washington knew where it was located, Godfrey seldom gave the shop's exact address when doing a commercial for Zlotnick. Merely saying it was located "at the sign of the dirty white bear" was enough. Klink (1996) tells an amusing story about the time when Godfrey was leaving Washington to go to work in New York and the station gave him a going away luncheon at the Federal Club. As Godfrey was saying farewell to everyone, the "dirty white bear" was rolled on the stage behind him without him noticing. When the audience broke out in laughter, Godfrey wondered what was going on, until he turned, saw the bear and laughed loudly.

Godfrey probably was the most popular radio personality of the Golden Age. People liked him and bought his sponsor's products. At the peak of his popularity he had an estimated audience of 82 million for both his radio and television programs. His $150 million dollar commercial billings represented 12 per cent of the total CBS yearly revenues (Tollin, 1997, p. 30). However, Godfrey's popularity began to wane on October 19, 1952, when he fired a young singer — Julius LaRosa — on the air during his *Arthur Godfrey Time* morning show. Godfrey's image for many of his faithful listeners was damaged irreparably. *See* ***Arthur Godfrey Time.***

1368 ***Arthur Godfrey Time.*** Godfrey was at the peak of his radio career with this program and his *Arthur Godfrey's Talent Scouts* program that ran concurrently. Godfrey warbled, played his uke and exchanged small talk with cast members Jeanette Davis, the Mariners and members of the Archie Bleyer Orchestra. Tony Marvin was the announcer. Over the years Godfrey's performers included: the Chordettes vocal quartet (Janet Erlet, Carol Hagedorn, Jinny Osborn and Dottie Schwartz), Patti Clayton, Bill Lawrence, the Mariners vocal quartet (Nathaniel Dickerson, Martin Karl, James Lewis and Thomas Lockard), Frank Parker, Marion Marlowe and Lu Ann Simms (60 min., Monday through Friday, 10:30–11:30 A.M., CBS, 1948). Earlier in 1946, his gang included Marshall Young, Frank Saunders, James Van Dusen, Janette Davis and the Lud Flatow Orchestra (CBS, 1946).

In 1947, Tony Marvin opened the program with these words: " Yes, it's *Arthur Godfrey Time* with all the little Godfreys — Janette Davis, the Mariners, Archie Bleyer and his orchestra and a studio of wonderful people. And here's that man himself— Arthur Godfrey." Godfrey's tremendous popularity arose from a variety of things. First, it probably was his homey, down-to-earth conversational style and his "just folks" approach. Second, and probably equally important, was his knack of kidding his sponsors. This began early in his career while he was doing the morning progam at WJSV (Washington, DC) and he started to tease Zlotnick, one of his favorite sponsors. Godfrey enjoyed talking about Zlotnick the Furrier at the sign of the big Polar Bear, one of the strangest signs in the nation's capital. Godfrey is best remembered for an incident that occurred on the *Arthur Godfrey Time* broadcast of October 19, 1952, when he fired singer Julius LaRosa on the air. *See* **Arthur Godfrey**.

1369 ***Arthur Godfrey's Digest.*** The "best" of Godfrey's weekly morning shows were rebroadcast on the weekly transcribed program (30 min., Saturday, 9:30–10:00 P.M., CBS, 1950).

1370 ***Arthur Godfrey's Talent Scouts.*** Godfrey presented many young and talented performers to the listening audience on the half-hour sustaining network program (30 min., Tuesday, 9:00–9:30 P.M., CBS, 1946).

1371 ***Arthur Hopkins Presents.*** Broadway producer Hopkins presented a series of five plays with distinguished performers. He opened the series by presenting Thornton Wilder's *Our Town* with Frank Craven, Helen Carew, Philip Coolidge, Evelyn Varden, Thomas W. Rors, John Thomas, Mary Patton and Howard Smith. Wynn Wright directed the excellent sustaining program (60 min., Wednesday, 11:30–12:30 P.M., NBC-Red, 1943).

1372 ***Arthur Murray's Course in Ball Room Dancing by Radiophone.*** Murray, although a stutterer, was a gifted salesman of himself and his product (WGI, Hillside, MA, 1924). Another program by Murray broadcast that year on many stations was listed as *Arthur Murray's Dancing Lesson # 5* (WHAS, Louisville, KY; WOC, Davenport, IA; WNAC, Boston, MA; WLW, Cincinnati, OH; WGY, Schenectady, NY; WMC, Memphis, TN; WRC, Washington, DC; WGI, Medford Hillside, MA; WBZ, Boston-Springfield, MA; WCAE, Pittsburgh, PA; WHAM, Rochester, NY; WGR, Buffalo, NY; KYW, Chicago, IL; and WSAD, Providence, RI). This was an impressive group of stations in 1924.

1373 ***Arthur Smith and His Cracker Jacks.*** CW mus. prg. (15 min., transcribed, various stations, 1948). Smith was a popular CW musician who enjoyed a long successful career on various shows.

1374 ***Arthur Smith's Carolina Corner.*** CW mus. prg. (15 min., transcribed, various stations, 1950).

1375 **Arthurs, Winifred C. "Bill."** Newscaster (*Buckeye Briefs*, WRFD, Worthington, OH, 1951–1960).

1376 **Artist, Michael.** Actor Artist appeared on the *Brighter Tomorrow* daytime serial program.

1377 **Artman, Paul.** DJ (*Bandstand*, WJPR, Greenville, MS, 1947; *Big Jamboree*, WNLA, Indianola, MS, 1955).

1378 ***Arturo's Caballeros Orchestra.*** Popular local orchestra (instr. mus. prg., WLW, Cincinnati, OH, 1942).

1379 ***Arty Hall's Southern Rubes.*** The network CW music program was performed by a group of "musical farmers" (15 min., Monday through Friday, 6:15–6:30, P.M. C.S.T., NBC-Blue, 1936).

1380 **Artzt, Bill "Billy."** Artzt was the orchestra leader on the *Planters Pickers* program (NBC-Red Network, New York, NY, 1929). He was also the musical director of the *Conti Gondoliers*, *House of Glass* and *Mysteries of Paris* programs.

1381 **Arundel, Arthur W.** News analyst (*Editorial Commentary*, WAVA, Arlington, VA, 1960).

1382 **Arvin, Ray.** Sportscaster (KORN, Fremont, NE, 1945). News analyst (*Commentary*, WREN, Topeka, KS, 1949).

1383 ***As the Twig Is Bent.*** Barbara Terrell and George Coulouris starred in the daytime serial sponsored by Post Toasties cereal. The story concerned a young school teacher working in a rural community. The program was revived twice. Once as *We Love and Learn* and, later, as *The Story of Ruby Valentine*. The latter was unique in that it was the first network African-American "soap opera." The cast members who worked on the program are listed in the *We Love and Learn* entry (15 min., Monday through Friday, 1:15–1:30 P.M., WNAC, Boston, MA, 1941). *See* ***We Love and Learn and The Story of Ruby Valentine.***

1384 ***As We Are.*** The discussion program of the early 1950s presented a positive view of the American scene (15 min., Monday, 11:00–11:15 P.M., NBC-Red Network, early 1950s).

1385 ***As You Like It.*** This broadcast of Shakespeare's play is thought to be one of the first dramatic presentations of the work of that genius ever to be broadcast (WCAL, Northfield, MN, 1922).

1386 **Asbell, Ferrell.** Newscaster (WDVH, Gainesville, FL, 1960).

1387 **Asbury Park Dance Orchestra.** Amusement park dance orchestra (WMCA, New York, NY, 1925).

1388 **Ascarelli, G.** Newscaster (WHOM, Jersey City, NJ, 1940–1942).

1389 **Ascher, Sally.** Soprano (WBBC, WCBU, Brooklyn, NY, 1929).

1390 **Ascot, Rita.** Actress Ascot was in the *Ma Perkins* daytime serial.

1391 **Ash, Edith.** Singer (WTIC, Hartford, CT, 1925).

1392 **Ash, Harry.** Leader (Harry Ash and his Royal Novelty Orchestra, WNYC, New York, NY, 1924; Ash's Canadian Orchestra, WNYC, New York, NY, 1925).

1393 **Ash, Ken.** Sportscaster (*Sports Quiz*, WHAV, Haverhill, MA, 1948–1951).

1394 **Ash, Merrill.** Newscaster (KOMO, Seattle, WA, 1946, 1953–1954).

1395 **Ash, Paul.** Ash was the orchestra leader and host of the *Merry Mad Gang* program broadcast from Chicago's Oriental Theater (WGN, Chicago, IL, 1926).

1396 **Ashard, Dick.** Newscaster (Cedar City, UT, 1946).

1397 **Ashbaugh, Don.** Newscaster (KBNE, Boulder City, NV, 1946).

1398 Ashbaugh, Don. Sportscaster (KBNE, Boulder City, NV, 1946).

1399 Ashbeck, Lois Jean. Ashbeck was one of the intelligent "kids" on the *Quiz Kids* program (NBC, ABC, CBS, 1940–1953).

1400 Ashburn, Bonnie. Sportscaster (KOWH, Omaha, NE, 1942).

1401 Ashburn, Ron. DJ (WNOX, Knoxville, TN, 1952).

1402 Ashburn, Virginia. COM-HE (WLNA, Peekskill, NY, 1955).

1403 Asbury Park Dance Orchestra. Amusement park dance orchestra (WMCA, New York, NY, 1925).

1404 Ashby, Dick. DJ (*940 Special*, WMAZ, Macon, GA, 1952).

1405 Ashby, Fanny. Singer known as "The Sunshine Radio Girl" (KFSG, Los Angeles, CA, 1925).

1406 Ashcroft, Frank. Singer (*Frank Ashcroft*, vcl. mus. prg., KLRA, Little Rock, AR, 1930s).

1407 Ashenbrenner, Walter. Violinist (WJAZ, Chicago, IL, 1923).

1408 Ashenfelder, Louis (The Louis Aschenfelder Company). Louis Ashenfelder directed the grand opera company that broadcast "Manon" and "La Boheme" (WRNY, New York, NY, 1926).

1409 Asher, Frederick M. Newscaster (WDCR, Hanover, NH, 1960).

1410 Asher, James D. Newscaster (WJDA, Quincy, MA, 1957–1960).

1411 Asher, Warren. DJ (*Rural Roundup*, WFOR, Hattiesburg, MS, 1947).

1412 Asher and Little Jimmy (Sizemore). Father and son CW singing team (*Asher and Little Jimmy*, CW vcl. mus. prg., WDZ, Tuscola, IL, 1937; WSM, Nashville, TN, 1938–1939 and WHAS, Louisville, KY, 1935, 1939). The father and son act recorded numerous transcribed programs broadcast by many stations. They also appeared on the *Grand Ole Opry*.

1413 Ashford, Ed. Sportscaster (WLAP, Lexington, KY, 1937).

1414 Ashley, Arthur "Art." Newscaster (WNGC, New Haven, CT, 1946). DJ (*Club Midnight*, WONS, Hartford, CT, 1947). Sportscaster (*Sports Edition*, WONS, 1950).

1415 Ashley, Charles. Newscaster (WEEI, Boston, MA, 1941, 1948; CBS, 1949; WEEI, 1952–1957). DJ (WEEI, 1955). Ashley once teamed with Bill Campbell to report sports on a weekly show (*Saturday Sports Review*, 15 min., Saturday, CBS, 1947).

1416 Ashley, Doris. COM-HE (WESC, Greenville, SC, 1957).

1417 Ashley, Ernie. Sportscaster (WOWO, Fort Wayne, IN, 1953–1954).

1418 Ashley, Henry. Leader (*Henry Ashley Orchestra*, instr. mus. prg., WBIG, Greensboro, NC, 1936 and KFEL, Denver, CO, 1939).

1419 Ashley, Ira. Producer-director Ashley worked on the *Grand Central Station* (director), *Second Mrs. Burton* (producer-director) and *Young Dr. Malone* (director) programs.

1420 Ashley, Lorraine. Singer Ashley was one of the three sisters of the Prairie Daisies vocal trio (WLS, Chicago, IL, 1929).

1421 Ashley, Paul. Leader (Paul Ashley's Texas Cowboys, WFAA, Dallas, TX, 1923–1924; director of the Dallas Band, WFAA, 1925; and leader of the Paul Ashley Orch., WRR, Dallas, TX, 1927).

1422 Ashley Sisters. Popular harmony singing team (KFWB, Hollywood, CA, 1925).

1423 Ashman, Butch. Leader (Butch Ashman Chinese Garden Orchestra, KFI, Los Angeles, CA, 1926).

1424 Ashmore, Dorothy. COM-HE (WCAT, Orange, MA, 1956–1957).

1425 Ashmore, Harry. Newscaster (WFBC, Greenville, SC, 1940).

1426 Ashton, Adelaide. Operatic soprano (KTAB, Oakland, CA, 1926).

1427 Ashton, Keith. DJ (KRAK, Stockton-Sacramento, CA, 1957).

1428 Ashton, Ruth. COM-HE (KNX, Los Angeles, CA, 1957).

1429 Ashworth, Ernie. CW singer and songwriter Ashworth performed on WBHP, Huntsville, AL, 1948). He enjoyed a successful recording career and joined the *Grand Ole Opry* in 1964.

1430 Asia Orchestra. WGY (Schenectady, NY, 1925).

1431 *Ask Eddie Cantor.* One of Cantor's last radio appearances was on this transcribed program. He answered questions from listeners, sang a capella and played a few records. Examples of the topics discussed were: August 2, 1961, "Lucy and Desi's Divorce"; October 2, 1961, "Dull Speakers"; and October 18, 1961, "Sophie Tucker's Weight." The show was sponsored by Montgomery Ward (5 minutes, Transcribed, 1961). *See* ***The Eddie Cantor Show.***

1432 Asker, Virginia. COM-HE (WDOV, Dover, DE, 1955).

1433 Askey, Bob. DJ (KFOR, Lincoln, NE, 1954).

1434 Askins, Allen. DJ (*Savannah River Rag*, WAKN, Aiken, SC, 1954).

1435 Askowith, Herbert. "Herbert Askowith's Talks on Books" and "Books as Gifts" are examples of the talks given by Askowith (WGI, Medford Hillside, MA, 1923).

1436 Asmundson, Helen. Soprano (WHAD, Milwaukee, WI, 1925).

1437 Aspe, John V. Tenor (WHN, New York, NY, 1925).

1438 Aspen, Stew. Leader (Stew Aspen's Mt. Wilson Five Dance Orchestra, KFQJ, Hollywood, CA, 1926).

1439 Asper, Myrtle. COM-HE (KID, Idaho Falls, ID, 1951–1955).

1440 Aspinwall, Hugh. Tenor (WHT , Chicago, IL, 1926). Announcer (WJJD, Chicago, IL, 1925; WHT, Chicago, IL, 1928). In 1928, Aspinwall became station WHT's chief announcer. He was previously employed by Chicago radio stations WLS, KYW, WHT and WOK.

1441 Assaf, Woody. Newscaster (WSKB, McComb, MS, 1939–1940). Sportscaster (WLBT, Jackson, MS, 1955; WJOX, Jackson, MS, 1956; *The Sports Show*, WLBT, 1960).

1442 *(The) Associated Spotlight.* The entertaining program, sponsored by the Associated Oil Company, contained comedy, music and dramatic episodes. Cecil Underwood was the program's host. Producer and continuity writer Caryl Coleman also performed in many of the program's comedy skits. Playwright and orchestra leader Walter Beban wrote over 200 skits for the show and was also the musical director. Bobbe Deane played "hundreds of characters" in Beban's skits, including the "Sassy Little" role. Imelda Montagne played "Sophie Svenson" in Beban's *School Days* skits. Tenor Irving Kennedy, who previously had worked with the Marx Brothers in their stage hit *Cocoanuts*, played the role of "Ikey Lechinsky" in *School Days*. Monroe Upton played "Lord Bilgewater."

Many of the popular "School Days" segments were written by Captain William Royle, who also played "Ishud Sokitoyou" and "Spud McGuire" in them. Max Waizman played "Herr Fitzmeyer the Schoolteacher" and Bennie Walker played "Bennie Fischel. Musical selections were also performed by bass Armand Girard; "Miss Ethyl Associated," a beautiful unidentified soprano; Alice Joy; Welsh tenor Gwynfi Jones; the versatile Annette Hastings, who played the piano, organ and sang; and the Cycol Four vocal quartet that included Marjorie Primley singing and playing the piano. Another interesting performer on the *Associated Spotlight* was Harold Perez (later famous as Harold Peary), who played the parts of "George Washington U.S. Lee" and the "Laughing Villain." Don Thompson wrote and narrated the program's "Champions of the West" segment that presented biographies of various sports champions. Thompson also broadcast football play-by-play for the Associated Oil Company. The program was broadcast on the NBC-Pacific Coast network in 1932.

1443 Astell, Helen P. Soprano (WQJ, Chicago, IL, 1925).

1444 Aster, Alex. Pianist Aster was a former concert pianist with the Royal Orchestra at St. Petersburg, Russia (KTHS, Beaumont, TX, 1928).

1445 Astor Coffee Dance Orchestra. Radio band sponsored by the B. Fischer and Company (WEAF, New York, NY, 1923–1925).

1446 Astrup, Grace. Violinist (WGY, Schenectady, NY, 1923).

1447 Aswell, James B. Newscaster (KALB, Alexandria, LA, 1939).

1448 *At Eight-Thirty.* Bob Short hosted the popular Pittsburgh early morning sustaining variety show. Earl Truxell's orchestra and various vocalists supplied the musical selections (45 min., Monday through Friday, 8:30–9:15 A.M., WCAE, Pittsburgh, PA, 1936).

1449 *At Home with Faye and Elliott.* One of the many husband-and-wife talk shows so popular during this period, the transcribed quarter-hour show was unique in that it was conducted by actress Faye Emerson and Elliott Roosevelt, FDR's son. Jim Ameche was the announcer. *Variety* reported that the program, carried by 42 stations, was particularly appealing because of the quality of guests interviewed by Emerson and Roosevelt. These guests included Orson Welles, Jan Struthers, Lucille Ball, Desi Arnez, Earl Wilson and Toots Shor (15 min., 1946).

1450 ***At Home with Music.*** Sigmund Spaeth was a classical music DJ, who played the music and provided informative commentary about it. Ed Michael was the program's announcer (30 min., Saturday, 10:00–10:30 P.M., ABC, 1950).

1451 ***At the Baldwin.*** The instr. mus. prg. was broadcast Sunday afternoons with various performers including Brazilian pianist Alfredo Oswald and Jose Iturbi (NBC, 1930).

1452 ***At the Sign of Green and White.*** The Quaker Oil Company sponsored the musical program hosted by Norman Brokenshire (30 min., Friday, 10:00–10:30 P.M., CBS, 1930).

1453 ***At the Theatre.*** Theatrical reviews were broadcast by A.L.S. Wood (WBZ, Boston-Springfield, MA, 1924).

1454 **Atcher, Bob (Robert Owen Atcher).** CW singer (WHAS, Louisville, KY, 1935). CW singer Atcher was probably best known for his appearances on the *National Barn Dance* after appearing earlier on several Louisville, KY, programs. Atcher's early recording career featured duets with Bonnie Blue Eyes (Laeta Applegate). Atcher was featured on the Chicago originated *Wrigley's Spearmint Show* (CBS,1942–1943) He also appeared on the *Faultless Starch Time* (NBC, 1953) program. Before joining the *National Barn Dance* show, Atcher had several network show of his own. *See* ***National Barn Dance.***

1455 **Atcher, Randy.** DJ (*Atcher Service*, WKLO, Louisville, KY, 1949).

1456 **Atchison, Charles.** Newscaster and sportscaster (WDEF, Chattanooga, TN, 1941–1942). DJ (*Magic Valley Jamboree*, WKAX, Birmingham, AL, 1948).

1457 **Atchison, Dorothy.** Newscaster (WCBI, Columbus, MS, 1940).

1458 **Atchison, Wendell.** Sportscaster (WOTN, Pine Bluff, AR, 1956).

1459 **Ater, Tom.** DJ (*Later with Ater*, WKAB, Mobile, AL, 1948–1949).

1460 **Ates, Roscoe.** Leader (*Roscoe Ates Orchestra,* instr. mus. prg., WABC-CBS, New York, NY, 1936–1938).

1461 **Athaide, Johnnie.** Tenor (KGB, San Diego, CA, 1929).

1462 **Athens Athletic Club Orchestra.** Club band (KLX, Oakland, CA, 1926).

1463 **Atkerson, Paul.** Newscaster (KPHO, Phoenix, AZ, 1946).

1464 **Atkin, Carol.** Pianist (KPLA, Los Angeles, CA, 1927).

1465 **Atkins, Bill.** DJ (KFRD, Rosenberg, TX, 1954; KDOK, Tyler, TX, 1957).

1466 **Atkins, Dorothy.** Singer (*Dorothy Atkins,* vcl. mus. prg., WCBM , Baltimore, MD, 1934.)

1467 **Atkins, Chet.** CW musician Atkins in 1924 after completing high school worked with singer Bill Carlisle and comedian Archie Campbell on station KNOX (Knoxville, TN). Guitarist Atkins was soon featured on the station's daily barn dance program, *Midday Merry-Go-Round* (KNOX, Knoxville, TN). In 1945 he worked with Johnny and Jack on a Raleigh, NC, station, before going on to work with Red Foley on the *Prince Albert Show* segment of the *Grand Ole Opry.* During the late 1940s and early 1950s, Atkins worked at KWTO (Springfield, MO), before returning to KNOX. He later added to his performance schedule by working as a highly successful record producer for the Capitol, Decca and Columbia Record divisions.

1468 **Atkins, Eddie.** DJ (WJEH, Gallipolis, OH, 1954).

1469 **Atkins, Eva Gruninger.** Contralto (KGO, Oakland, CA, 1925; KPO, San Francisco, CA, 1927).

1470 **Atkins, Glen.** Newscaster (CBS, 1944).

1471 **Atkins, Jimmy.** DJ (*Musical Alarm Clock*, WSSB, Durham, NC, 1948).

1472 **Atkins, Thomas B.** DJ (WOOB, Anniston, AL, 1949).

1473 **Atkins, Tom.** Newscaster (KVOR, Colorado Springs, CO, 1955; WPTA, Fort Wayne, IN, 1957). DJ (KVOR, 1955).

1474 **Atkinson, Dorothy.** Newscaster (KWLK, Longview, WA, 1950.)

1475 **Atkinson, Helen, Louise.** Contralto (WOR, Newark, NJ, 1923).

1476 **Atkinson, J.C.** DJ (*KVKM Record Party*, KVKM, Monahans, TX, 1947; *Wake Up With J.C.*, WBBQ, Augusta, GA, 1948–1949; *Wake with WAKN*, WAKN, Aiken, SC, 1950).

1477 **Atkinson, Marie.** Singer (WOK, Pine Bluff, AR, 1922).

1478 **Atkinson, Marion.** COM-HE (KXLA, Pasadena, CA, 1951).

1479 **Atkinson, Nancy I.** COM-HE (WJZM, Clarkville, TN, 1957).

1480 **Atkinson, Walter.** Bass (WWJ, Detroit, MI, 1923).

1481 **Atkinson, William L.** Announcer (WCAO, Baltimore, MD, 1927).

1482 ***(The) Atlanta Army Reports.*** The daily program broadcast during the World War II era answered questions about the war that were submitted by listeners (WSB, Atlanta, GA, World War II period). *See* **Wartime Radio.**

1483 ***(The) Atlantic Family on Tour*** (aka ***The Atlantic Family***). A variety show that emphasized comedy starred a young comedian by the name of Bob Hope, who appeared with Frank Parker, Margaret Johnson and Red Nichols' lively jazz group. The announcer was Del Sharbutt. The sponsor was the Atlantic Oil Company (30 min., Thursday, 7:00–7:30 P.M., CBS, 1936).

1484 **Atlantic Ladies Trio.** Female vocal group (WABC, New York, NY, 1928).

1485 **Atlas, Don.** Sportscaster (*Sports Tabloid*, KLOK, San Jose, CA, 1947).

1486 **Atlass, Leslie.** Atlass was the first announcer on WBBM (Lincoln, NE) in 1925, a station that later moved to Chicago. Atlass continued as announcer with WBBM (Chicago, IL) the following year.

1487 **Atlass, Pauline Stiffler.** Pianist (WBBM, Chicago, IL, 1926).

1488 **"ATN."** Designation for announcer Herbert B. Glover (WJZ, New York, NY and WJY, New York, NY, 1925).

1489 **Attearn, Connie.** Announcer (WHO, Des Moines, IA, 1925).

1490 **Atteberry, Larry.** Sportscaster (WNMP, Evanston, IL, 1955).

1491 **Atteberry, Terry.** DJ (*Teen-Age Tunes*, KCOL, Fort Collins, CO, 1954; *Popular Music*, KCOL, 1960).

1492 **Atter, Virginia.** COM-HE (WJXT, Jacksonville, FL, 1958).

1493 **Atterberry, Mona.** COM-HE (KCOL, Fort Collins, CO, 1958–1960).

1494 **Atterbury, Barbara.** COM-HE (WROY, Carmi, IL, 1951).

1495 **Atterbury, Doris.** COM-HE (WTJS, Jackson, TN, 1951).

1496 **Attl, Katejan.** Harpist (KPO, San Francisco, CA, 1923).

1497 ***Attorney at Law.*** S.C. Johnson sponsored the summer replacement for the *Fibber McGee and Molly* program. Young attorney Terry Regan, his assistant and his efficient secretary, played respectively by Jim Ameche, Arthur Jacobson and Fran Carlon, successfully battled to secure justice for Regan's clients. Sometimes known as *Terry Regan—Attorney at Law*, the program originally was a daily 15-minute daytime serial before expanding to half an hour. Other members of the cast were Lucy Gilman, Grace Lockwood, June Meredith and Fred Sullivan (30 min., Tuesday, 8:30–9:00 P.M., NBC, 1938).

1498 ***Attorney for the Defense.*** Al Hodge played the role of Roger Allen, a successful lawyer, who battled each week against an aggressive, politically ambitious DA on the sustaining program. Milton Kramer wrote, Herb Rice produced and Ernest Rice directed the summer replacement for *The Shadow.* A few early episodes were broadcast that featured two old comrades from the *I Love a Mystery* program, Michael Raffetto and Barton Yarborough, in the leading roles (30 min., Sunday, 5:00–5:30 P.M., MBS, 1946).

1499 **Atwater, Edith.** COM-HE (KERG, Eugene, OR, 1951).

1500 **Atwater, Gilbert.** Newscaster (WCNW, Brooklyn, NY, 1941–1942).

1501 **Atwater, Kent.** Newscaster (WJRI, Lenoir, NC, 1954).

1502 ***Atwater Kent Artists Orchestra.*** Instr. mus. prg. featuring a group directed by Ernest Ingold (KPO, San Francisco, CA, 1925).

1503 ***Atwater Kent Auditions.*** Atwater Kent Company sponsored and Graham McNamee hosted the program during the late 1920s. Talented amateurs were allowed to compete before a national radio audience on the NBC program. Talented singer Hazel Arth first appeared on the show.

1504 **Atwater Kent Boys (Doug and Fred).** Song and comedy patter team (KFOA, Seattle, WA, 1926).

1505 ***(The) Atwater Kent Dance Orchestra.*** Atwater Kent, the radio manufacturing company, sponsored the popular network music program (60 min., Thursday, 10:00–11:00 P.M., NBC-Blue Network, 1929–1930).

1506 Atwater Kent Orchestra. The commercially sponsored (Atwater Kent Radio Company) orchestra was conducted by Paul Finstein (KNX, Los Angeles, CA, 1925) and by Nicoli Berezowski, (KNX, 1926). Later, Louis Edin conducted the orchestra on the Atwater Kent Hour network program (NBC-Red, New York, NY, 1927).

1507 *(The) Atwater Kent Program.* Atwater Kent sponsored the distinguished weekly musical program that featured sopranos Mabel Garrison, Hulda Lashanska and Edith Mason; baritones George Cehanovsky, Alfredo Gandolfi, WIlliam Simmons and Lawrence Tibbett; tenors Beniamino Gigli, Frederick Jagel and Allen McQuhae; violinists John Corigliano and Efrem Zimbalist; pianist Kathleen Stewart; and other singers including Harold Nason and Genevieve Rowe. The Atwater Kent orchestra was conducted by Louis Edin.

The program was first broadcast October 4, 1925 on WEAF. On May 2, 1926, the program concluded its first series of broadcasts with a Music Week Festival program that was broadcast that day. The special program included performances by contralto Kathryn Meisle, tenor Allen McQuhae, pianist John Powell and violinist Albert Spalding. Frances Alda, Louise Homer and Josef Hoffman also appeared. The following year (1927), the Atwater Kent Company sponsored its first National Radio Auditions. Agnes Davis won the first contest with her performance of "Pace, Pace, Mio Dio" from Verdi's *La Forza del Destino* and Wilbur Evans took second place by singing Flegier's "Le Cor." In the following years, the Atwater Kent auditions [*see* ***The Atwater Kent Auditions***] brought recognition to and furthered the musical and radio careers of Hazel Arth (1928), Josephine Antoine (1929) and Thomas L. Thomas and Lydia Summers (1932), along with others (60 min., Sunday, 9:15–10:15 P.M., NBC-Blue Network, 1925–1931). Programs of this nature brought good music and many talented performers to listeners. For example, the program was often used in schools as a means to encourage music appreciation by pupils. As part of the music appreciation program in the Dallas, Texas, schools students were assigned to listen to the program and write a review of it.

1508 Atwater Kent Quartette. Members of the singing group were Victor Edmonds, 1st tenor; George Rasply, 2nd tenor; James Davies, bass; and Erwyn Mutch, baritone (NBC, 1929).

1509 *Atwater Kent Summer Series.* The summer musical program featured among others the Atwater Kent Quartette; soprano Frances Peralto; bass William Gustafson; baritone George Cehanovsky; soprano Jane Carroll; tenor Allen McQuhae; baritone William Simmons; soprano Thalia Sabenieve; baritone Graham McNamee; soprano Pearl Besuner; violinist Leonora Collette; pianist Leonara Cortes; contralto Grace Devine; violinist Ruth Breton and tenor Max Bloch. (NBC, late-1920s and early 1930s).

1510 *Atwater Kent Sunday Concerts.* These weekly commercially sponsored good music programs originated on station WEAF (NBC Network-New York, NY, 1925).

1511 Atwell, Howard. DJ (*The Timekeeper*, WVPO, Stroudsburg, PA, 1949).

1512 Atwell, Martha. Actress Atwell appeared in the *Young Widow Brown* daytime serial. She was also successful as a writer, producer and director, directing such daytime serial programs as *Editor's Daughter* and *Linda's First Love*.

1513 Atwood, Brad. Sportscaster (*Sports Roundup*, KWIK, Burbank, CA, 1947).

1514 Atwood, Jack S. Announcer (WLBZ, Bangor, ME, 1925). Newscaster (WRDO, Augusta, MA, 1939). Sportscaster (WRDO, 1939–1941).

1515 Atwood, Russ. DJ (WMAS, Springfield, MA, 1957).

1516 Atwood, Ted. Sportscaster (*The Sports Page*, WCNT, Centralia, IL, 1953; WSOW, Saginaw, MI, 1954).

1517 Auburn Dance Orchestra. Local radio band (WLW, Cincinnati, OH, 1929).

1518 Aubrey, Bob. Newscaster (WHAT, Philadelphia, PA, 1957).

1519 Aubrey, Will. Singer Aubrey was billed as *The Wandering Minstrel* (voc. mus. prg., NBC-Blue Network, 1936).

1520 *Auction Bridge Game.* The program presented a series of talks about bridge. The sponsor was the Work-Whitehead Company (30 min., Tuesday, 10:00–10:30 P.M., NBC, 1926–1931).

1521 Audley, Eleanor. Actress Audley was featured in the *By Kathleen Norris* daytime serial.

1522 Audubon Terrace Meadowlarks Orchestra. Club orchestra (WGR, Detroit, MI, 1926)

1523 Auerbach, Arthur "Artie." Talented comic actor Auerbach appeared on the *Al Pearce Show*, *The Goldbergs*, *Jack Benny Show* and the *Phil Baker Show* programs.

1524 Aufderheide, Doris. COM-HE (KNUJ, New Ulm, MN, 1955).

1525 Augello, Joseph. DJ (*Hub Cap Caravan*, WJLB, Detroit, MI, 1952; WOHO, Toledo, OH, 1957).

1526 August, Edwin. Drama critic (KFI, Los Angeles, CA, 1929).

1527 Augusta Military Academy Orchestra. Scholastic band (WRVA, Richmond, VA, 1926).

1528 Augustine, Johnny. Leader (*Johnny Augustine Orchestra*, instr. mus. prg., CBS, 1935).

1529 Augustine, Percy. Tenor (WEMC, Berrien Springs, MI, 1926).

1530 Augustus, H. T. Announcer (WJBK, Ypsilanti, MI, 1927).

1531 Aulick, June. Publicist Aulick was a member of the CBS publicity staff.

1532 Ault, Carroll. Baritone (WOR, Newark, NJ, 1929).

1533 *Aunt Abby Jones.* Marie Nelson and Dorothy Day MacDonald appeared on the short-lived daytime serial broadcast weekdays in 1938.

1534 Aunt Anne. The "aunt" told tales and sang songs for children (WAAM, Newark, NJ, 1927).

1535 Aunt Betty. Ruth Thompson in the role of Aunt Betty told stories for children (KGO, Oakland, CA, 1925–1926). Thompson regularly appeared on the Aunt Betty segment of the *KGO Kiddies Club* program.

1536 *Aunt Carrie.* Mrs. Carlotta Stewart Watson, a high school teacher and counselor, provided counsel and comfort to her lovelorn listeners (15 min., Monday through Friday, 10:45–11:00 A.M., WDIA, Memphis, TN, mid-1950s).

1537 Aunt Elsie. An unidentified performer who told children's stories, her program was known as *Aunt Elsie's Sunset Matinee* (KLX, Oakland, CA, 1925).

1538 *Aunt Em.* Aunt Em Lanning read poetry and broadcast inspirational bits of wisdom. Musical accompaniment was supplied by organist Elsie Mae Emerson (15 min., Sunday, 9:15–9:30 A.M., WLS, Chicago, IL, 1937). *See* ***Everybody's Hour***.

1539 *Aunt Emmy and Bert.* Cliff Arquette was Aunt Emmy and Harold Isbell was Bert on the daily comedy show (15 min., Monday through Friday, 10:00–10:15 P.M., KNX, Hollywood, CA, 1932).

1540 *Aunt Harriet's Nieces and Nephews.* Harriet Gustin (as Aunt Harriet) produced, directed and co-hosted the children's amateur hour sponsored by the R.H. White Company. Uncle Roy (Roy Girardin), a WEEI announcer, co-hosted the program with Gustin (60 min., Saturday, 10:00–11:00 A.M., WEEI, Boston, MA, 1937).

1541 Aunt Jane. Another Aunt who told stories for children (WOC, Davenport, IA, 1928).

1542 *Aunt Jemima.* Singer Tess Gardella first played the role after Lew Leslie named her "Aunt Jemima" and brought her to vaudeville. She performed in blackface. Famous before coming to radio, Gardella had played the Palace in 1922 (CBS, 1928). Harriette Widmer also played the stereotypical "blackface mammy" portrayed on the Aunt Jemima pancake mix box. She entertained by singing and performing comedy routines (15 min., Saturday 9:45–10:00 A.M., NBC-Blue, 1937). The Quaker Oats Company later broadcast the program in a five-minute format (1942–1944). Over the years the program's cast included: Harriette Widmer in the title role, Bill Miller and Mary Ann Mercer as vocalists and the Old Plantation Sextet. Harry Walsh was musical director and Marvin Miller the announcer. The program was written by Mason Ancker and directed by Palmer Clark.

In later years Aunt Jemima was played by Amanda Randolph.

1543 *(The) Aunt Jemima Man.* Comic Phil Cook sang and joked his way through the quarter-hour early morning program sponsored by Quaker Oats and broadcast six times weekly (15 min., Monday through Saturday, 8:00–8:15 A.M., NBC-Blue, 1930).

1544 *Aunt Jemima on the Air.* Buck and Wheat, a blackface comedy team, were featured on this Quaker Oats sponsored program broadcast by NBC in 1937. Vance McCune played Wheat, one member of the comedy team.

1545 ***Aunt Jenny*** **(aka *Aunt Jenny's Real Life Stories*).** The daytime serial presented a series of stories. Over the years the cast included: Peggy Allenby, Henry Boyd (as the whistling canary), Alfred Corn (Alfred Ryder), Tom Darnay, Virginia Dwyer, Maurice Franklin, Franc Hale, Ed Jerome, Nancy Kelly, Ed MacDonald, Eddie O'Brien, Ann Pitoniak, Helen Shields, Edith Spencer, Ruth Yorke, and Agnes Young. The writers included Eleanor Abbey, Carl Alfred Buss, David Davidson, Edwin Halloran, Doris Halman, Lawrence Klee, Elinor Lenz, Elizabeth McLean and Bill Sweets. Dan Seymour was the announcer who capably assisted Aunt Jenny. Ralph Berkey, John Loveton, Bill Steel, Robert S. Steele, Thomas F. Victor, Jr. and Tony Wilson were the directors. Elsie Thompson was the organist. Sound effects were produced by Jim Dwan and Harold Forry (15 min., CBS, 1937–1954). Aunt Jenny was a small town philosopher who passed out tips on both cooking and living. Not surprising, many of her cooking tips suggested the use of Spry, her sponsor's product.

1546 Aunt Martha and Uncle George. This broadcast team sang and told children's stories (*Lullaby Time*, WLS, Chicago, IL, 1925).

1547 ***Aunt Mary.*** An unidentified woman delivered talks on child rearing and training (WOR, Newark, NJ, 1936).

1548 Aunt Nell. This unidentified Aunt told children's stories (KGW, Portland, OR, 1923–1924).

1549 Aunt Sally. Mrs. Pasco Powell, as "Aunt Sally," told stories for children (WBT, Charlotte, NC, 1929).

1550 Aunt Sammy. On October 4, 1926, 50 different women on 50 stations across the country became "Aunt Sammy," (Uncle Sam's wife) and began to read identical scripts prepared by the U.S. Department of Agriculture to provide American women with cooking and home making information. A typical 15-minute program contained poetry, how to care for kitchen linoleum, a definition of vitamins, a description of the five essential foods for daily consumption and a daily menu that included scalloped potatoes, carrots, sliced tomatoes, meat loaf with green beans and lemon jelly desert. The Department of Agriculture, using the name of Aunt Sammy, also prepared and distributed many cooking pamphlets during this and the following decade. In 1928, "Aunt Sammy" for KFWB (Hollywood, CA) was Florence Israel and Evelyn Kitts on KOIL (Council Bluffs, IA). "Aunt Sammy" and Betty Crocker were the two most popular fictional cooking experts of the era. Ida Bailey Allen provided the only "real" competition for those two fictional characters.

1551 Aunt Vivian [Elsie Olmstead]. This Aunt also broadcast children's bedtime stories (KSND, Seattle, WA, 1925). This "Aunt" broadcast children's bedtime stories, but also allegedly broadcast encoded messages. *See* **Olmstead, Elsie.**

1552 ***Aunty Blossom.*** Aunty Blossom read the newspaper comics and as "Winnie Winkle" sang on the children's program (KGW, Portland, OR, 1927).

1553 Aunty Jack (Jacquinot). A multi-talented performer, Aunty Jack was an organist, pianist, harpist and composer (WMOX, St. Louis, MO, 1928).

1554 ***Aunty-Tell-a-Tale.*** The unidentified performer told children's stories on her late afternoon program (WPG, Atlantic City, NJ, 1936).

1555 Aurandt, Dick. Leader (*Dick Aurandt Orchestra,* instr. mus. prg., CBS, 1939).

1556 Aurandt, Paul H. Newscaster (KXOK, St. Louis, MO, 1939; WRZO, Kalamazoo, MI, 1941–1942).

1557 Ausenbaugh, Glenda. COM-HE (WFMW, Milwaukee, WI, 1958).

1558 Ausland, John. Newscaster (KWFT, Wichita Falls, TX, 1940).

1559 Ausley, Wally. Sportscaster (*Speaking of Sports*, WSSB, Durham, NC, 1948–1949; *Sports Bandstand*, WRTM, Danville, VA, 1950; WNAO, Raleigh, NC, 1951). DJ (*The Bandstand*, WSSB, 1948; WDNC, Durham, NC, 1955).

1560 Austad, Mark. Newscaster (WWDC, Washington, DC, 1945–1947).

1561 Austin, Anne. Soprano (WBZ, Boston-Springfield, MA, 1923; WBZ-WBZA, Boston-Springfield, MA, 1928).

1562 Austin, Axel. Swedish pianist-composer (WHN, New York, NY, 1926).

1563 Austin, Bill. Newscaster (WPLH, Huntington, WV, 1952).

1564 Austin, Bob. DJ (KSDO, San Diego, CA, 1952).

1565 Austin, Carl. DJ (WOPF, McComb, MS, 1949).

1566 Austin, Caryle. Sportscaster (KEVR, Seattle, WA, 1941).

1567 Austin, Coleman. DJ (*Rub-Scrub Music Club*, WROV, Roanoke, VA, 1947). Sportscaster (*Roanoke Boxing Bouts*, WROV, Roanoke, VA, 1947–1948).

1568 Austin, Don. Newscaster (KJR, Seattle, WA, 1942).

1569 Austin, Don. DJ (WHOW, Clinton, IL, 1954; WSIV, Pekin, IL, 1955).

1570 Austin, Edmund. Baritone (*Edmund Austin,* vcl. mus. prg., WOR, Newark, NJ, 1935).

1571 Austin, Frances. COM-HE (WWNC, Asheville, NC, 1956).

1572 Austin, Frank. Sportscaster (KDYL, Salt Lake City, UT, 1937).

1573 Austin, Gene. Tenor (WHN, New York, NY, 1924). Austin broadcast as "The Man in the Diamond Mask" (WSMB, New Orleans, LA, 1927). He later was featured on the *Maxwell Coffee Hour* in 1928 and 1929 on NBC. Austin had his own programs in the following decades: (*Gene Austin*, vcl. mus. prg., 15 min., Wednesday, 7:00–7:15 P.M., NBC-Red, 1931). Austin later fronted a band and sang on the *Gene Austin Show* (vcl. mus. prg., WLW, Cincinnati, OH, 1940).

1574 Austin, Harold. Leader (*Harold Austin Orchestra,* instr. mus. prg., WGR, Detroit, MI, 1936–1938).

1575 Austin, Harvey. Baritone (KFRC, San Francisco, CA, 1927).

1576 Austin, James. Saxophonist (WLS, Chicago, IL, 1926).

1577 Austin, Jim. Sportscaster (KNCO, Garden City, KS, 1955).

1578 Austin, Kay. "Crooning xylophonist" (KMOX, St. Louis, MO, 1929).

1579 Austin, Lee. Singer (*Lee Austin,* vcl. mus. prg., WIP, Philadelphia, PA, 1936).

1580 Austin, Mabel. Singer (WGY, Schenectady, NY, 1925).

1581 Austin Male Quartet. Male vocal group (WGN, Chicago, IL, 1928).

1582 Austin, Marie. Singer (*Marie Austin,* vcl. mus. prg., WPG, Atlantic City, NJ, 1936).

1583 Austin, Mel. Sportscaster (WATL, Atlanta, GA, 1938; WCSC, Charleston, SC, 1941).

1584 Austin, Rusty. DJ (WBUD, Morrisville, PA, 1948).

1585 Austin, Steve. Sportscaster (*Sports Page*, WKID, Urbana, IL, 1954).

1586 Austin, Ted. Sportscaster (*Sports Edition*, WFAI, Fayetteville, NC, 1952).

1587 Autels, Van. Sportscaster (KTAR, Phoenix, AZ, 1960).

1588 Authier, Irene. Blues singer (KFWB, Hollywood, CA, 1925).

1589 ***Author/Author.*** Humorist and author S.J. Perelman conducted the sustaining panel show on which an incomplete mystery plot sent in by a listener was read to a group of four authors. After a few moments each author attempted to complete the story. The panel of authors included the Ellery Queen writing team, Frederic Dannay and Manfred Lee, as regulars. Poet Ogden Nash later replaced Perelman as program host (30 min., Friday, 8:30–9:00 P.M. MBS, 1939).

1590 ***Author Meets the Critics.*** The interesting program ran at various times from 1946 to 1951 with Barry Gray and John McCaffery as host on MBS, NBC and ABC. The format brought together two critics — one pro and one con — to review a book during the first half of the program. During the second half the author was allowed to respond directly to their comments (30 min., Wednesday, 10:30–11:00 P.M., MBS, 1947).

1591 ***(The) Author Speaks His Piece.*** On the sustaining program an author was allowed to read one of his contemporary articles. For example, Walter White appeared on the program in 1947 to read his "Why I Remain a Negro" from the *Saturday Review of Literature* (15 min., Monday, 10:00–10:15 P.M., WNEW, New York, NY, 1947).

1592 ***Autobiographies of Infamous Bugs and Rodents.*** Unique in concept, the program was devoted to household pests and their eradication (15 min., Tuesday, 6:30–6:45 P.M., KQW, San Jose, CA, 1927).

1593 Automatic Disc Duo Orchestra. Commercial dance band (WJZ, New York, NY, 1928 and WLW, Cincinnati, OH, 1929).

1594 Autry, Gene (aka The Oklahoma Yodeling Cowboy). Cowboy singer-actor Autry, born Sept 29, 1908, first appeared on KVOO (Tulsa, OK, 1927–1929), billed as "Oklahoma's Yodeling Cowboy" and "The Oklahoma Yodeling Cowboy." After recording for Sears' Conqueror label, he appeared on the company's Chicago station (*Conqueror Record Time,* WLS, Chicago, IL,1930–1931). From 1930 to 1934 Autry appeared on the *National Barn Dance* (WLS, Chicago, IL). After enjoying great success on the show, Autry left for Hollywood to star in numerous western movies. His first motion picture for Republic Pictures was made in 1934. *See* ***Melody Ranch*** *and* **Singers: Crooners, Song Birds, Country Belles, Cow Girls and Hillbillies.**

1595 ***Autumn in New York.*** Alfredo Antonini's orchestra was featured on the sustaining music program with singers Jimmy Carroll and Frances Greer (30 min., Friday, 9:30–10:00 P.M., CBS, 1952). In January, 1953, *Autumn in New York* became *There's Music in the Air.* See ***There's Music in the Air.***

1596 **Auulea, H.** Leader of the H. Auulea School of Hawaiian Music Orchestra (WFAA, Dallas, TX, 1926).

1597 ***A.U.V. Dixies Circus.*** Bob Sherwood was joined on the 15-minute show by a 12-year-old girl who listened to his tales of his interesting experiences in the circus (15 min., Saturday, 7:15–7:30 P.M., NBC, 1930).

1598 **Auxer, Ed.** DJ (WSBT, South Bend, IN, 1960).

1599 **Avalon Club Orchestra.** New York jazz band (WHN, New York, NY, 1926).

1600 ***Avalon Time Program.*** Comedian Red Skelton made his radio debut on the program. He was assisted by Edna Stilwell, Del King, singers Curt Massey and Red Foley and the Bob Strong Orchestra. Skelton's show was sponsored by Raleigh Cigarettes in 1947 and Tide from 1950–1952.

1601 **Averitt, Helen.** Singer (KFRU, Columbia, MO, 1926).

1602 **Avery, Ann Matheson.** Contralto (KOIN, Portland, OR, 1928).

1603 **Avery, Bob.** Sportscaster (WTHT, Hartford, CT, 1942).

1604 **Avery, Charles.** Newscaster (WFPG, Atlantic City, NJ, 1951).

1605 **Avery, Chuck.** DJ (*Top of the Morning,* WLNA, Peekskill, NY, 1954).

1606 **Avery, Don.** Newscaster (KROW, Oakland, CA, 1939).

1607 **Avery, Gaylord "Gay."** Newscaster (KFAB, Lincoln, NE, 1946–1948).

1608 **Avery, Leslie Hart.** DJ (*Evening Concert,* KRE, Berkeley, CA, 1960).

1609 **Avery, Marc.** DJ (KAIR, Tucson, AZ, 1960).

1610 **Avery, Margaret.** Musician Avery was a member of the popular Arion Trio (NBC, 1929).

1611 **Avery, Martin.** Newscaster (WLNH, Laconia, NE, 1940).

1612 **Avey, Gary M.** DJ (KYOS, Merced, CA, 1960).

1613 **Avey, (Mrs.) Thomas.** Soprano (KTHS, Hot Springs National Park, AR, 1928).

1614 **Avila, Bill.** Sportscaster (KXOA, Sacramento, CA, 1954).

1615 **Avila, Jose.** DJ (KSBW, Salinas, CA, 1954).

1616 **Avila, Manuel.** DJ (*Mexican Canta,* KWBC, Fort Worth, TX, 1952).

1617 **Avirett, William C.** Newscaster (WHAI, Greenfield, MA, 1940).

1618 **Avon Society Orchestra.** Popular New York band (WHN, New York, NY, 1923).

1619 **Avon String Quintet.** The instrumental group's members were J.H. Harrison, ukulele; M.A. Hardin, mandolin; Harold McDonald, guitar; R.L. Owen, ukulele; and E.S. Flynn, director and mandolin (KPO, San Francisco, CA, 1925).

1620 **Avram, Bud.** DJ (*Bud's Platter Party,* KWFC, Hot Springs, AR, 1948).

1621 **Axelson, Joe.** Sportscaster (WWNS, Statesboro, GA, 1960).

1622 **Axley, Bob.** DJ (*Night Train,* KWRW, Guthrie, OK, 1960).

1623 **Axt, Edward.** Twelve-year-old saxophonist Axt played on the *Major Bowes Capitol Family* program. He was the son of Dr. William Axt, arranger for Bowes' Capitol Orchestra (NBC, 1928).

1624 **Axtell, Carolee [Carol].** COM-HE (KNOR, Norman, OK, 1957; KLRP, Oklahoma City, OK, 1958).

1625 **Axtell, Nancy.** Sportscaster (*Bowling with Nancy,* WMBM, Miami Beach, FL, 1948).

1626 **Axton, Bailey.** Tenor (*Bailey Axton,* vcl. mus. prg., WLW, Cincinnati, OH, 1935–1936, NBC, 1938–1939).

1627 **Axton, Louise.** COM-HE (KTOP, Topeka, KS, 1955).

1628 **Aya, Bill.** Sportscaster (KEVE, Seattle, WA, 1941).

1629 **Ayala, Marcus Garcia.** DJ (KIFN, Phoenix, AZ, 1957).

1630 **Ayarse, Joseph.** Newscaster (*Delaware Valley Review,* WTTM , Trenton, NJ, 1952).

1631 **Aycock, Bob.** DJ (*Commuters Special,* WMPS, Memphis, TN, 1952).

1632 **Aycrigg, Ben.** Newscaster (WLOF, Orlando, FL, 1955). DJ (WLOF, 1955).

1633 **Ayer, Esther.** COM-HE (WMUR, Manchester, NH, 1951).

1634 **Ayers, Bill.** Newscaster (WSBT, South Bend, IN, 1944).

1635 **Ayers, Cesta.** Black DJ (*Doctor Daddy,* KNUZ, Houston, TX, 1953).

1636 **Ayers, Rusty.** Sportscaster (*Sports News,* KSWS, Roswell, NM, 1949).

1637 **Aylward, Bill.** DJ (WMTR, Morristown, NJ, 1957).

1638 **Aylward, Jim.** DJ (WREB, Holyoke, MA, 1957).

1639 **Ayner, Rutherford H.** Announcer (WHAZ, Troy, NY, 1924).

1640 **Ayoob, Ki.** Newscaster (WABI, Bangor, ME, 1938).

1641 **Ayres, Betsy.** Soprano (WEAF, New York, NY, 1923); Ayres later was billed as "The Texas Nightingale" (WJAX, Cleveland, OH, 1928–1929).

1642 **Ayres, (Mrs.) Charles Stewart.** Soprano (KTAB, Oakland, CA, 1926).

1643 **Ayres, Frank.** Actor Ayres appeared on the *Young Dr. Malone* daytime serial program.

1644 **Ayres, Gene.** DJ (*Open House,* WDSG, Dyersburg, TN, 1949).

1645 **Ayres, James.** DJ (KLKC, Parsons, KS, 1949).

1646 **Ayres [Ayers], Kirby.** DJ (WEEX, Easton, PA, 1957–1960). In the early 1940s, Ayres was a director of the *Grand Slam* radio quiz.

1647 **Ayres, (Miss) Mabel Norton.** Miss Norton of Cincinnati, Ohio, sang with phonograph record accompaniment on September 23, 1920 on WWJ (Detroit, MI).

1648 **Ayres, Margaret.** Singer (WSUI, Iowa City, IA, 1927).

1649 **Azar, Rick.** Sportscaster (*The Sports Program,* WHLD, Niagra Falls, NY, 1954).

1650 **Azine, Harold.** Newscaster (WLS, Chicago, IL, 1939).

1651 ***(The) Aztecs.*** Luis Zamuido led the popular band. Georgia Backus also appeared on the program with them (1939).

1652 ***B.A. Rolfe and his Lucky Strike Orchestra.*** Lucky Strike cigarettes sponsored the popular radio band. Edward "Ed" Thorgersen was the program announcer (60 min., Saturday, 10:00–11:00 P.M., NBC-Red, 1930).

1653 **Baacke, Gladys.** COM-HE (WJKO, Springfield, MA, 1954).

1654 **Baar, Bill.** Actor Baar appeared on the *Grandpa Burton* and *Jane Arden* programs.

1655 **Babb, Jr., Hugh Webster.** Sportscaster (WPOR, Portland, ME, 1953).

1656 **Babbee, Owen.** Newscaster (KMTH, Los Angeles, CA, 1939; KMPC, Beverly Hills, CA, 1940).

1657 **Babcock, Bill.** DJ (*Platter Party,* WJAS, Pittsburgh, PA, 1951; *Bing Crosby Time,* WJAS, 1952).

1658 **Babcock, Charlie.** Newscaster (WTAW, College Station, TX, 1941). Sportscaster (WTAW, 1941).

1659 **Babcock, Franklin "Frank."** Newscaster (KTRH, Houston, TX, 1942). DJ (*The Mail Bag,* KXYZ, Houston, TX, 1949).

1660 **Babcock, Marianne Powell.** Soprano (WOK, Chicago, IL, 1925).

1661 **Babcock, Sam.** DJ (*Teen Town,* KWEM, West Memphis, AR, 1947; KFSB, Joplin, MO, 1951).

1662 **Babcock, William.** Sportscaster (WMMN, Fairmont, WV, 1942). Newscaster (WMMN, 1942).

1663 ***Babe Ruth Boy's Club.*** The great baseball star told stories of his baseball career, conducted this radio boy's club and promoted the many contests conducted on the program. Standard Oil of New Jersey sponsored the transcribed program (15 min., Wednesday, 6:30–6:45 P.M., MBS, 1934).

1664 **Baber, (Mrs.) R.E.** Harpist (WSM, Nashville, TN).

1665 ***Babes in Radio.*** Created by Grant Maxwell, who also produced and directed the program like an old "Hollywood campus movie." A "line" of 18 girls, who sang, danced and told jokes, were featured. A studio audience always witnessed the weekly show (30 min., Weekly, KTAB, San Francisco, CA, 1934).

1666 Babette. Singer (WPCH, New York, NY, 1932).

1667 Babington, Stan. Newscaster (WGRC, New Albany, IN, 1942).

1668 Bab's Lady Orchestra. The orchestra often broadcast with soprano Mary Lane and tenor J. Leslie Pitcher (KJR, Seattle, WA, 1927–1928).

1669 Babson, Roger. Economist Babson broadcast his weekly *Babson Reports* (WLW, Cincinnati, OH, 1924). He also gave business talks (WDAF, Kansas City, MO, 1925).

1670 *Babson Finance Period* (aka *The Babson Finance Program*). Distinguished economist Roger Babson provided financial and general economic information on the unusual program that also included musical selections by an orchestra directed by Harry Salter. The music played was selected because they were favorites of various highly successful American corporation officers. For example, one program featured the favorite music of the president of the Welch Grape Juice Company (15 min., Saturday, 8:15–8:30 P.M., CBS, 1929–1930).

1671 *(The) Baby Corner.* Baby care topics were the subjects discussed on the 15-minute program (15 min., Monday through Friday, 1:15–1:30 P.M., WROW, Albany, NY, 1949).

1672 Baby Rose Marie. *See* **Rose Marie.**

1673 *Baby Snooks.* Fanny Brice (Fannie Borach) played the role of Snooks, a mischievous little girl who kept her bedeviled father, played by Hanley Stafford (Alfred John Austin), in a constant state of agitated frustration. Brice began her career as a comedienne-singer in vaudeville and on the Broadway stage, where she starred in several versions of the *Ziegfeld Follies.* Brice's repertoire ranged from torch songs like "*My Man*" to the comic "*Second Hand Rose.*" Fanny had performed a baby routine in vaudeville many years before she did on radio. She introduced Snooks on CBS radio on the *Ziegfeld Follies* [radio] *Show* of February 29, 1936. After that she played Snooks on the *Good News of 1938* and the *Maxwell House Coffee Time* programs on NBC. She returned to CBS for the *Baby Snooks Show,* which ran until 1949, when she went back to NBC.

Over the years in addition to Stafford her cast members included: Gale Gordon, Hans Conried, Sara Berner, Georgia Ellis, Arlene Harris and Lalive Brownell. Music was conducted by Carmen Dragon and Meredith Willson. Songs were performed by Bob Graham. The announcers were John Conte, Ken Roberts and Harlow Wilcox. Ted Bliss, Walter Bunker and Roy Rowlan were the directors. The program was produced by Mann Holiner and written by Bill Danch, Devary Freeman, Everett Freeman, Jess Oppenheimer and Jerry Seelen.

1674 *Baby Yvonne.* Baby Yvonne, a great Tennessee favorite, was a six-year-old mentalist, who appeared on this sustaining program with her mother, Princess Yvonne (15 min., Monday-Wednesday-Friday, 5:15–5:30 P.M., WNOX, Knoxville, TN, 1936).

1675 Bacal, Dave. Organist, pianist and novachord Bacal first appeared on radio in 1929 (WIP, Philadelphia, PA). He also played with the Charlie Gaylord, Al Kavelin and Leo Zollo orchestras.

1676 Bach, Alwyn E.W. Baritone-announcer (WBZ, Boston-Springfield, MA, 1924 and NBC, New York, NY, 1928). Bach was the announcer on such network programs as *Moment Musicale, Freed Orchestradians, Echoes of the Orient, Heroes of the World, Old Man Sunshine, Lehn and Fink Serenaders, Famous Loves, Maxwell House Melodies, Around the World with Libby* and *Three Kings and a Queen.* Bach later was a newscaster (KYW, Philadelphia, PA, 1947–1948).

1677 Bach, H.E. Announcer (WBZ, Springfield, MA, 1925).

1678 Bach, Joe. Sportscaster (WHLD, Niagara Falls, NY, 1940).

1679 Bach, Richard. Organist (*Richard Bach,* instr. mus. prg., WIP, Philadelphia, PA, 1935).

1680 Bacha, Robert. DJ (*Rise 'N' Shine,* WNCC, Barnesboro, PA, 1960).

1681 *(The) Bachelor of Song.* A vcl. mus. prg. by an unidentified romantic tenor (WLW, Cincinnati, OH, 1935).

1682 *(The) Bachelor Poet.* Norman Pearce read romantic poetry written for the program in his rich, baritone voice. The Lipton Tea Company sponsored this version of the program that also featured contralto Annette King. Donald Dowd was the announcer; (15 min., Monday-Wednesday-Friday, 10:15–10:30 P.M., WMAQ, Chicago, IL, 1937). Another version of the *Bachelor Poet* program presented Norman Pearce alone reading his romantic poetry. *Billboard* was none too kind in a review that said Pearce made Eddie Guest look good (15 min., Thursday, 8:00–8:15 P.M., WMCA, New York, NY, 1938).

1683 *Bachelor's Children.* Bess Flynn wrote the long running (1936–1946) daytime serial that centered on Dr. Robert Graham, his friend Sam Ryder and his adopted twin daughters, Ruth Ann and Janet Dexter. After Graham reared the adopted twin sisters, who were the daughters of a deceased World War I friend, he eventually married one of them. His friend, Sam, married the other. Old Dutch Cleanser was the original sponsor of the interesting daytime drama.

Old Dutch Cleanser delivered this message about the program in 1939:

> This story of *Bachelor's Children* is dedicated to the radio audience of America by the makers of Old Dutch Cleanser in the interest of better cleaning. The loyalty and friendly interest of this great audience is evidenced by the thousands upon thousands of letters we have received. We trust that *Bachelor's Children* will entertain you in the future as it has in the past, and that Old Dutch Cleanser will merit your continued use.

The author, Bess Flynn, was one of the most skilled writers of daytime serials [*See* **Daytime Serials**]. She explained the program's beginning in this way:

> Dr. Robert Graham was a bachelor — 35 years old — the only surviving child of a father who had spent his life in the practice of medicine. Dr. Graham had been brought up by his father with the ideals of the old-time family physician, and had learned to love his profession as something more than merely a means to earn a livelihood. To him it means a creed — the privilege of giving to his fellow human beings not only of professional skill, but of his personal interest as well. Men and women from all classes of society found their way to his office which he maintains in a part of the home where he was born and raised and where his father had also practiced his profession.
>
> In place of the mother whom he lost at the age of eight, Dr. Graham had been reared by Miss Ellen Collins who came to them as a housekeeper and stayed to fill the place of mother as well, to her "Dr. Bob." After the death of the "old doctor," as she always called him, her whole life was centered about the young doctor whom she had come to love as her own son, and whom she alternately spoils and scolds.
>
> At the beginning of the program, Dr. Graham, while entertaining his closest friend, Sam Ryder — likewise a bachelor, but eight years younger than the doctor — received a letter from James Dexter, his top sergeant during the war. He was greatly surprised as he had lost all contact with Dexter since they had returned home at the close of the war. Dexter had written from his death bed asking Dr. Graham to take his motherless twin children under his care, since he was dying penniless and knew of no one else to whom he might turn in his necessity.

When Dr. Graham agreed, he was surprised to learn that Dexter's children were two attractive twin girls — eighteen years old! Many interesting complications and adventures arose from the intriguing beginning.

Movie Radio Guide gave the program its award for the best daytime radio serial of 1942. The performers on the program over the years were: Ruth Bailey, Muriel Brenner, Frank Dane, Dorothy Denver, Patricia Dunlap, Laurette Fillbrandt, Charles Flynn, Janice Gilbert, David Gothard, Marjorie Hannan, Alice Hill, Peg Hillias, John Hodiak, Raymond Edward Johnson, Ginger Jones, Art Kohl, Sunda Love, Marie Nelson, Nelson Olmstead, Mary Patton, Arthur Peterson, Marion Reed, Olga Rosenova, Olan Soule, Hugh Studebaker, Helen Van Tuyl, Beryl Vaughn, and Kay Westfall. The program was directed by Burt Lee and Russ Young. Don Gordon and Russ Young were the announcers (15 min., Monday through Friday, CBS, 1936–1946).

1684 Bacher, Jeanne. COM-HE (KGST, Fresno, CA, 1956–1957).

1685 Bachman, Charlie. DJ (*Football Predictions,* WILS, Lansing, MI, 1947).

1686 Bachman's Million Dollar Band. Local radio band (WLS, Chicago, IL, 1926).

1687 Bacho, Bob. DJ (*Memorable Music,* WNCC, Barnesboro, PA, 1954).

1688 Bachrad, Marv. Sports (WNAR, Norristown, PA, 1960).

1689 Bachus, Ellen. Soprano (WHAS, Louisville, KY, 1927).

1690 **Back, Gunnar.** Newscaster (WJNO, West Palm Beach, FL, 1938; WJSV, Washington, DC, 1939; WTOP, Washington, DC, 1945–1946; *Events of the Day* and *The World and You*, ABC, Washington, DC, 1955).

1691 **Back, Howard.** Newscaster (WERC, Erie, PA, 1948).

1692 ***Back Bay Matinee.*** Bob Elliot, a popular Boston DJ, conducted the program before he met Ray Goulding and joined with him to create the *Bob and Ray* team. *Back Bay Matinee* was broadcast six times per week (120 min., Monday through Saturday, 2:00–4:00 P.M., WHDH, Boston, MA, 1948). *See* ***Bob and Ray.***

1693 ***(The) Back Home Hour.*** A large symphony orchestra and chorus performed on the weekly radio religious service. Famous evangelist Billy Sunday occasionally preached the program's sermon (60 min., Saturday, 11:00–12:00 midnight, CBS, 1929). Although he had not achieved his national fame on radio, Sunday at 69 began broadcasting in 1929 at the peak of his career. Even in his old age, the dynamic Sunday was aggressive "in the service of the Lord." The *Back Home Hour* remained on the network until Sunday's death in 1935. *See* **Sunday, Billy.**

1694 ***Back of the News in Washington.*** Newspaper correspondent William Hard broadcast the early network program of political analysis (15 min., Monday, 7:45–8:00 P.M., NBC-Red, 1930).

1695 ***Back to God Hour.*** In 1947, Harry Schultze, followed by Peter Eversheld and Joel Nederland, conducted the network religious program that later moved to television (MBS, 1947).

1696 ***Back to the Bible.*** Theodore Epp inaugurated the religious program in Lincoln, NE, in 1939. Each daily program included a Bible lesson. The program was still on radio in the 1980s.

1697 ***Back Where I Come From.*** Nicholas Ray wrote and Alan Lomax researched the informative sustaining program. Clifton Fadiman was the host. He was joined by the Luther Layman Singers and the Golden Gate Quartet (15 min., Monday, 10:30–10:45 P.M., CBS, 1940).

1698 **Backes, Lee.** COM-HE (WSBS, Great Barrington, MA, 1958).

1699 **Backlin, Jim.** DJ (KCJB, Minot, ND, 1951; KFYR, Bismark, ND, 1957).

1700 **Backman, John.** DJ (*All Star Dance Party*, KWAL, Wallace, ID, 1947).

1701 **Backman, Lillian.** Singer Backman appeared on *The Cathedral Hour*, *The Musical Album, The Voice of Columbia* and *The Grand Concert Opera Concert* (WABC, New York, 1930).

1702 **Backmann, Art.** DJ (WKUL, Cullman, AL, 1956).

1703 **Backmann, Barton.** Pianist (KYW, Chicago, IL, 1924).

1704 ***Backstage Review.*** Earl Nightingale was the host of the sustaining musical review program. Charlie Agnew's Orchestra, the Skylarks vocal group and vocalists Don Orlando and George Ramsby were regular performers (30 min., Monday through Friday, 11:00–11:30 P.M., WBBM, Chicago, IL, 1949).

1705 ***Backstage Wife*** **(aka** ***Mary Noble, Backstage Wife*****).** The well-known opening of the daytime serial told of the trials and tribulations faced by Mary Noble, the backstage wife. It went like this: "*Backstage Wife*, the story of Mary Noble, and what it means to be the wife of a famous Broadway star — dream sweetheart of a million other women." The role of Mary was played by Vivian Fridell and Claire Niesen.

Mary, a stenographer from Iowa, faced many difficult times married to a romantic Broadway star, and the program presented everyone of them in detail. Because the program was broadcast from 1935 to 1959, the cast members involved were many: Hoyt Allen, Charme Allen, George Ansell, Anita Anton, Luise Barclay, Anne Burr, Helen Claire, Donna Creade, Leo Curley, Frank Dane, Susan Douglas, Patricia Dunlap, Virginia Dwyer, Louise Fitch, Dorothy Francis, Vivian Fridell, Don Gallagher, Maxine Garenas, Norman Gottschalk, Ken Griffin, Joyce Hayward, Rod Hendrickson, Gail Henshaw, Wilda Hinkel, John M. James, Ginger Jones, Carlton KaDell, Bonita Kay, Charlotte Keane, Mandel Kramer, Eloise Kummer, John Larkin, Paul Luther, Ken Lynch, Alan MacAteer, Charlotte Manson, Sherman Marks, Bess McCammon, John McGovern, Malcolm Meecham, James Meighan, Marvin Miller, George Niese, Claire Niesen, Ethel Waite Owen, Eileen Palmer, George Petrie, Kay Renwick, Bartlett Robinson, Elmira Roessler, Dorothy Sands, Betty Ruth Smith, Guy Sorel, Dan Sutter, Henrietta Tedro, Phil Truex, Vicki Vola, Andree Wallace, Charles Webster, Ethel Wilson and Lesley Woods. The several announcers were: Sandy Becker, Harry Clark, Ford Bond and Roger Krupp. Lou Jacobson, Les Mitchel, Joe Mansfield, Richard Leonard and Blair Walliser were the directors. Frank and Anne Hummert were the producers-writers. Other writers who worked on the program included: Ruth Borden, Ned Calmer, Phil Thorne and Elizabeth Todd (15 min., Monday through Friday, MBS and NBC, 1935–1939).

1706 **Backstedt, William.** Leader (William Backstedt's Old-Timers Orchestra, KFRC, San Francisco, CA, 1925; KJR, Seattle, WA, 1927).

1707 **Backsu, Ethel Waring.** Soprano (WMC, Memphis, TN, 1926).

1708 **Backus, Georgia.** Actress Backus took part in the *Columbia Experimental Laboratory* broadcasts (CBS, 1930s). She also appeared in the *Brent House* and *Holly Sloan* daytime serials.

1709 **Bacon, Anne D.** Soprano (WMC, Memphis, TN, 1926).

1710 **Bacon, Bob.** DJ (*Bacon for Breakfast*, WBRE, Wilkes-Barre, PA, 1947–1951; *Jive After Five*, WBRE, 1949; *Rhythm and Rhyme*, WBRE, 1955).

1711 **Bacon, Katherine.** Pianist (WOR, Newark, NJ, 1928, *Katherine Bacon*, instr. mus. prg., WOR, 1935).

1712 **Bacon, Leona.** Soprano (WNAC, Boston, MA, 1925).

1713 **Bacon, Norman.** DJ (*Playing Favorites*, WOC, Davenport, IA, 1949). Sportscaster (*Hamm's Spotlight*, WOC, 1949–1950).

1714 **Bachrad, Marv.** Sportscaster (WNAR, Norristown, PA 1960).

1715 **Baddour, Glenda.** COM-HE (WCOR, Lebanon, TN, 1958).

1716 **Badeaux, Ed.** DJ (*The Mail Bag*, KXYZ, Houston, TX, 1948).

1717 **Badger, Bob.** Newscaster (*The Editor Speaks*, WEDO, McKeesport, PA, 1947–1948).

1718 **Badger Four.** Male vocal quartet (WHT, Chicago, IL, 1926).

1719 **Badger's Hollywood Californians.** Popular local orchestra (KFI, Los Angeles, CA, 1926).

1720 **Badham, Mary.** COM-HE (WBRC, Birmingham, AL, 1954–1958).

1721 **Badillo, Samuel.** Newscaster (WIAC, San Juan, PR, 1942).

1722 **Baebler, Phil.** Tenor (WEAF, New York, NY, 1925).

1723 **Baer, A.E. [E.A.].** Announcer (KFBB, Havre, MT, 1927).

1724 **Baer, Arthur "Bugs."** Humorist-newspaper columnist Baer delivered funny stories and commentary on his quarter-hour show. Lou Jacobson, Joe Mansfield, Les Mitchel, Blair Walliser and Fred Weihe were the directors. Chet Hill supplied sound effects. Some examples of Baer's remarks about lawyers illustrate his type of humor: "Always count your fingers after shaking hands with a lawyer." Speaking to an audience of lawyers, he once addressed them as the "Consolidated Ambulance Chasers of America" (15-min., WJZ, New York, NY, 1925).

1725 **Baer, Beulah.** Soprano (WBBC & WCBU Brooklyn, NY, 1929).

1726 **Baer, Emanuel.** Assistant Conductor (Rivoli Orchestra, WNYC, New York, NY, 1925).

1727 **Baer, Johnny.** Vocalist (*Johnny Baer*, vcl. mus. prg., KDKA, Pittsburgh, PA, 1936).

1728 **Baer, Max.** DJ (*Max Baer Show*, KFBK, Sacramento, CA, 1951–1952). On this program ex-heavyweight champion Baer tried his hand at radio again as a DJ. Much earlier he had appeared in an adventure series. *See* ***Lucky Smith.***

1729 **Baer, Mid.** COM-HE (WGRD, Grand Rapids, MI, 1958).

1730 **Baer, Moe.** Leader (*Moe Baer Orchestra*, instr. mus. prg., WDBJ, Roanoke, VA, 1935).

1731 **Baerg, Royce.** DJ (*Musical Varieties*, KNEX, McPherson, KS, 1952).

1732 **Baffa, Emil.** Leader (*Emil Baffa Orchestra*, instr. mus. prg., NBC, 1939).

1733 **Bagdasarian, Albert.** Newscaster (*Behind the News*, WNBZ, Saranac Lake, NY, 1949–1955).

1734 **Bagg, Chester.** Baritone (WCBD, Zion, IL, 1926).

1735 **Bagg, Mary.** Reader (WCBD, Zion, IL, 1925).

1736 **Bagg, Minnie.** Soprano (WBZ, Boston-Springfield, MA, 1923).

1737 **Baggiore, Attilio.** Leader (*Attilio Baggiore Concert Orchestra*, instr. mus. prg., WGN, Chicago, IL, 1935).

1738 Bagley, Carl E. Announcer (KFVN, Welcome, MN, 1926).

1739 Bagley, Hariet. COM-HE (KOVE, Lander, WY, 1954–1955).

1740 Bagley, Orlo. Sportscaster (KOMB, Cottage Grove, OR, 1955).

1741 Bagli, Guy. Sportscaster (WALT, Tampa, FL, 1953; WTVT, Petersburg, FL, 1955).

1742 Bagli, Vince. Sportscaster (WBAL, Baltimore, MD, 1956).

1743 Baglino, Rafaela. COM-HE (WGNS, Murfeesboro, TN, 1958).

1744 Bagnal, Frank. DJ (*Magic of Music*, WFIG, Sumter, SC, 1960).

1745 Bagwill, Gladys. Blues singer (KTHS. Hot Springs National Park, AR, 1928).

1746 Bahakel, Cy. Newscaster (WJRD, Tuscaloosa, AL, 1941).

1747 Bahakel, Dia. COM-HE (WKIN, Kingsport, TN, 1958).

1748 Bahman, Alice. COM-HE (WIZE, Springfield, OH, 1957).

1749 Bahn, Carl. DJ (WCSS, Amsterdam, NY, 1960).

1750 Bahnsen, Alvin C.W. Newscaster (WWRL, New York, NY, 1955).

1751 Bahnsen, Linden D. DJ (WPLX, Dales, OR, 1955).

1752 Bahntge, Eleanor Perez. Pianist (KYW, Chicago, IL, 1925–1926).

1753 Bahwell, Marilyn. COM-HE (WKTY, LaCrosse, WI, 1956).

1754 Baier, Grace. COM-HE (WIZE, Springfield, OH, 1957–1960).

1755 Bailard, Jean. Contralto (WBCN, Chicago, IL, 1925).

1756 Bailes Brothers (Walter Butler Bailes, Kyle O. Bailes, John Jacob Bailes and Homer Abraham, Jr.). Although there were four brothers they were most famous for performing duets. After years of performing on WCHS (Charleston, WV), WPAR (Parkersburg, WV), WJLS (Beckley, WV), WWVA (Wheeling, WV) and WHIS (Bluefield, WV), they gained great popularity on WSAZ (Huntington, WV). After joining the *Grand Ole Opry* in 1944, two years later they moved to KWKH (Shreveport, LA) to appear on the *Louisian Hayride*.

1757 Bailey, Angus. Newscaster (WSAR, Fall River, MA, 1944).

1758 Bailey, Ann D. COM-HE (WSIP, Paintsville, KY, 1956–1957).

1759 Bailey, Bertha. COM-HE (WRMA, Montgomery, AL, 1957).

1760 Bailey, Betty Brown. Soprano (WOR, Newark, NJ, 1924).

1761 Bailey, Bill. Leader (*Bill Bailey Orchestra*, instr. mus. prg.,WOR, Newark, NJ, 1939, 1942).

1762 Bailey, Bill. DJ (*Welcome Inn*, KRIZ, Phoenix, AZ, 1952).

1763 Bailey, Bill. DJ (*Smilin' Time*, WMIX, Mt. Vernon, IL, 1952).

1764 Bailey, Bob. DJ (*Good Music in Hi-Fi*, WECL, Eau Claire, WI, 1960).

1765 Bailey, Buck. Sportscaster (KWSC, Pullman, WA, 1939).

1766 Bailey, Carl. DJ (*Juke Box*, KXLA, Los Angeles, CA, 1947; KBIG, Avalon, CA, 1954).

1767 Bailey, Charles. Newscaster (WHBU, Anderson, IN, 1948). Sportscaster (*Sports Roundup* and *Sports in Brief*, WHBU, 1948–1950). DJ (*Meet the Band*, WHBU, 1948).

1768 Bailey, Dave. DJ (*Tops in Pops*, WBRV, Boonville, NY, 1960).

1769 Bailey, DeFord. Bailey was a Black harmonica soloist on the *Grand Ole Opry*, who was highly praised by *Variety* for his playing (WSM, Nashville, TN, 1925–1927). *See* ***The Grand Ole Opry***.

1770 Bailey, Don. Sportscaster (KWLK, Longview, WA, 1947). DJ (KWLK, 1947; *Open House*, KWLK, 1948).

1771 Bailey, Don Lee. DJ (WESC, Greenville, SC, 1954; *1450 Club*, WCRS, Greenwood, SC, 1960).

1772 Bailey, Edith. Soprano (WEAF, New York, NY, 1924).

1773 Bailey, Francille. COM-HE (KWOS, Jefferson City, MO, 1955).

1774 Bailey, Frederick. Baritone (WTIC, Hartford, CT, 1936).

1775 Bailey, Gene. DJ (*Trading Post*, KGBC, Galveston, TX, 1952).

1776 Bailey, Helen. Violinist (WNAD, Norman, OK, 1926).

1777 Bailey, Jack. DJ (WEEP, Pittsburgh, PA, 1960).

1778 Bailey, Jim. DJ (*1240 Jukebox*, KRDU, Dinuba, CA, 1951; KBIF, Fresno, CA, 1954).

1779 Bailey, Jim. DJ (*I Dee Clare*, WCEN, Mt. Pleasant, MI, 1953).

1780 Bailey, L. H. Announcer (WKJC, Lancaster, PA, 1925).

1781 Bailey, LeRoy. Writer Bailey wrote the *Thanks for Tomorrow* and *When a Girl Marries* programs.

1782 Bailey, Liz. COM-HE (KWBU, Corpus Christi, TX, 1956; KATR, Corpus Christi, TX, 1957).

1783 Bailey, Lynn. COM-HE (WNOG, Naples, FL, 1956–1957).

1784 Bailey, Maude. COM-HE (KRCO, Prineville, OR, 1951).

1785 Bailey, Mildred. The talented singer known as "The Rocking Chair Lady" sang with the Paul Whiteman band. Bailey and her husband, xylophonist Red Norvo, left Whitman to form their own band. Bailey was the sister of Al Rinker, a member of Whiteman's Rhythm Boys vocal group. At various times in the 1930s and 1940s, Bailey had programs on both NBC and CBS.

1786 Bailey, Mildred. COM-HE (WCOP, Boston, MA, 1951–1954).

1787 Bailey, Mitzi. DJ (*Time of Milady*, KMUR, Murray, UT, 1954).

1788 Bailey, Norman. DJ (*Smile Awhile*, WKXL, Concord, NH, 1947; WKBR, Manchester, NH, 1954).

1789 Bailey, Pat. COM-HE (KXRO, Aberdeen, WA, 1957).

1790 Bailey, Parker. Pianist (WTAM, Cleveland, OH, 1927).

1791 Bailey, Ray. Leader (Ray Bailey's Concert Orchestra, KMTR, Hollywood, CA, 1926).

1792 Bailey, Ray. DJ (*Melody Matinee*, KATY, San Luis Obispo, CA, 1952).

1793 Bailey, Robert "Bob." Busy actor Bailey appeared on the *Chicago Theater of the Air, Holly Sloan, Mary Marlin, Mortimer Gooch, One Man's Family, Road of Life, Scattergood Baines, That Brewster Boy, Today's Children* and *Your Truly, Johnny Dollar* programs.

1794 Bailey, Russ. DJ (KSOO, Sioux Falls, SD, 1957).

1795 Bailey, Ruth. Soprano (KDKA, Pittsburgh, PA, 1924).

1796 Bailey, Ruth. Actress Bailey appeared on the daytime serials *The Guiding Light, Bachelor's Children*; and *The Right to Life* daytime serials.

1797 Bailey, Seth T. Announcer designated as "STB" (KLX, Oakland, CA, 1924).

1798 Bailey, Ukulele. Singer (WHN, New York, NY, 1925).

1799 Bailey, Virginia M. COM-HE (WPME, Punxsutawney, PA, 1957).

1800 Bailey, William C. DJ (WIBV, Belleville, IL, 1954).

1801 Bailey, William D. DJ (*Pop Shop*, WFLB, Fayetteville, NC, 1951).

1802 Bailey, William J. Announcer (WCAU, Philadelphia, PA, 1928).

1803 Bailey, William S. "Bill." Newscaster (KTHS, Hot Springs, AR, 1945). Sportscaster (KTHS, 1945–1946).

1804 Bailey, Yancy. COM-HE (WHMA, Anniston, AL, 1951).

1805 Bailie, Ron. DJ (KEEP, Twin Falls, ID, 1956.)

1806 Baily, Bud. DJ (*Treasure Chest*, KGCX, Sidney, MT, 1948).

1807 Baily, Cliff. DJ (*Music Hour*, KVEC, San Luis Opispo, CA, 1948).

1808 *Baim's Novelty Five.* Baim's novelty band combined music and comedy on the early radio program. Each program also contained news bulletins, local police bulletins and state and local news. Music and humorous monologs were performed by members of the Baim group: violinist Aaron Baim; pianist Margaret Riat; cornetist Irwin Scott; trombonist Clifton Wingood; and drummer Ezra Cochran (WOK, Pine Bluff, AR, 1922).

1809 Bain, Beth. COM-HE (WKRT, Cortland, NY, 1958).

1810 Bain, Leslie Balogh. Newscaster (WIOD, Miami, FL, 1941–1942; WKAT, Miami Beach, FL, 1946).

1811 Bain, Sara. Soprano (WRNY, New York, NY, 1926).

1812 Baine, Lee. COM-HE (WNCO, Ashland, OH, 1958).

1813 Baines, Beverly. COM-HE (KPDN, Pampa, TX, 1951).

1814 Baino, Salvine. Violinist (KFWB, Hollywood, CA, 1927).

1815 Bainter, Jack. DJ (*Lucky Dance Time*, KHQ, Spokane, WA, 1954).

1816 Bainter, William "Bill." DJ (*Just

Released, KIT, Yakima, WA, 1951–1954). Newscaster (KIT, 1954).

1817 **Bair, Stewart.** Baritone (KYW, Chicago, IL, 1928).

1818 **Baird, Don.** Leader (*Don Baird Orchestra*, instr. mus. prg., WAIU, Columbus, OH, 1935).

1819 **Baird, Donna.** COM-HE (*Shopping News*, WSM, Nashville, TN, 1936).

1820 **Baird, Jeanne.** COM-HE (KEYT, Santa Barbara, CA, 1954).

1821 **Baird, Margaret.** COM-HE (WDLP, Panama City, FL, 1956).

1822 **Baird, Neal.** DJ (*Off the Record* and *Ballroom Melody*, KFFA, Helena, AR, 1948; *In the Groove*, KFFA, 1949).

1823 **Baird, Virginia.** COM-HE (WDLP, Panama City, FL, 1956).

1824 **Baisden's Bon Ton Ballroom Orchestra.** Popular radio dance band (KHJ, Los Angeles, CA, 1923).

1825 **Bakaleinkoff, Vladimir.** Conductor (Cinncinnati Symphony Orchestra, WLW, Cincinnati, OH, 1929).

1826 **Baker, (Mr.) A.F.** Flutist (KLS, Oakland, CA, 1923).

1827 **Baker, Albert S.** Newscaster (*ASB Reports*, WKXL, Concord, NH, 1949).

1828 **Baker, Alberta M.** Contralto (KDKA, Pittsburgh, PA, 1925).

1829 **Baker, Alan.** DJ (*Platter Party*, WLBN, Lebanon, KY, 1954).

1830 **Baker, Allan.** DJ (WNOK, Columbia, SC, 1954–1955).

1831 **Baker, Ann.** COM-HE (WAND, Canton, OH, 1958).

1832 **Baker, Anna Pinkerton.** Singer (WFAA, Dallas, TX, 1926).

1833 **Baker, Arleen.** COM-HE (KRAL, Rawlins, WY, 1954).

1834 **Baker, Arline.** Child pianist, a pupil of Erwin Swindell, broadcast pianologues (WOC, Davenport, IA, 1925).

1835 **Baker, Art.** Newscaster (*Never Too Old* and *Art Baker's Note Book*, KFI, Los Angeles, CA, 1944–1945; NBC, 1945–1947; KECA, Los Angeles, CA, 1948–1949).

1836 **Baker, Arthur T.** Piccolo and flute soloist Baker was a member of the KGO Little Symphony Orchestra (KGO, Oakland, CA, 1925).

1837 **Baker, Babe.** DJ (*In the Groove*, WSAI, Cincinnati, OH, 1952).

1838 **Baker, Barbara.** COM-HE (WTOD, Toledo, OH, 1951).

1839 **Baker, Belle.** One of vaudeville's great singing stars, whose songs of humor and pathos were equally well received. After her Palace appearance in 1913, she immediately became a popular recording star. She made many radio appearances in both the 1920s and the 1930s.

1840 **Baker, Betty.** COM-HE (*Betty Baker's Cooking School*, KGW, Portland, OR, 1929).

1841 **Baker, Betty.** COM-HE (WHO, Des Moines, IA, 1954).

1842 **Baker, Beverly.** COM-HE (KRWC, Forest Grove, OR, 1958).

1843 **Baker, Beverly.** COM-HE (WTKO, Ithaca, NY, 1958).

1844 **Baker, Bill.** DJ (*560 Club*, WMIK, Middleboro, KY, 1951).

1845 **Baker, Bill.** DJ (*Hillbilly Jamboree*, WEBQ, Harrisburg, IL, 1951). Sportscaster (WROY, Carmi, IL, 1952–1953).

1846 **Baker, Bill.** DJ (*Burnt Toast and Coffee*, WIOU, Kokomo, IN, 1955; WIBC, Indianapolis, IN, 1960).

1847 **Baker, Bill.** Newscaster (WBTH, Williamson, WV, 1940).

1848 **Baker, Bob.** DJ (*Sun Side Serenade*, KORK, Las Vegas, NV, 1952).

1849 **Baker, Bobby B.** Leader (*Bobby Baker Orchestra*, instr. mus. prg., WCKY, Cincinnati, OH, 1942).

1850 **Baker, Bruce.** DJ (*Spin the Platter*, WTTS, Bloomington, IN, 1960).

1851 **Baker, Buddy.** Banjoist-singer (KYW, Chicago, IL, 1928).

1852 **Baker, C.W.** Newscaster (KLPM, Minot, ND, 1942).

1853 **Baker, Charles.** Newscaster (KOA, Denver, CO, 1944).

1854 **Baker, Dan.** Announcer (WMBB, Chicago, IL, 1927).

1855 **Baker, Danny.** *Variety* said saxophonist Baker was a "wicked sax tooter" on the *Village Grove Nut Club* program (WMCA, New York, NY, 1929).

1856 **Baker, Dean.** DJ (*550 Roundup*, KCRS, Midland, TX, 1951).

1857 **Baker, Della.** Soprano (CBS, 1929).

1858 **Baker, Dick.** DJ (WGN, Chicago, IL, 1951; WPIN, St. Petersburg, FL, 1955–1957).

1859 **Baker, Donald H.** Organist (WOR, Newark, NJ, 1926)

1860 **Baker, Dorothy.** COM-HE (KGKO, Dallas, TX, 1955).

1861 **Baker, Edna.** Pianist (WNAC, Boston, MA, 1923).

1862 **Baker, Ellen.** Singer (WGBI, Scranton, PA, 1937).

1863 **Baker, Elsie.** Contralto (NBC, New York, NY, 1928; WEAF, New York, NY, 1929).

1864 **Baker, Eugene.** Announcer (KEX, Portland, OR, 1928).

1865 **Baker, Evangeline.** COM-HE (KNBC, San Francisco, CA, 1960).

1866 **Baker, Evelyn J.** Mezzo-soprano (WJZ, New York, NY, 1925).

1867 **Baker, Florence.** Actress Baker was featured on the *Glorious One* and *Brent House* daytime serials.

1868 **Baker, Florence.** Nine-year-old pianist (KOIL, Council Bluffs, IA, 1928).

1869 **Baker, Frank.** Newscaster (WALA, Mobile, AL, 1949). DJ (WALA, 1951).

1870 **Baker, (Col.) Frayne.** Newscaster (KFYR, Bismark, ND, 1940).

1871 **Baker, Gene.** Announcer Baker worked on the *Houseboat Hannah*, *Lum and Abner*, *Midstream* and *Queen for a Day* programs.

1872 **Baker, Gene.** Leader (*Gene Baker's Rhythm* [orchestra], instr. mus. prg., WTAM, Cleveland, OH, 1935).

1873 **Baker, George.** Newscaster (WKBW, Buffalo, NY, 1949; *By George*, WESA, Charleroi, PA, 1951; *Polka Party*, WESA, 1952).

1874 **Baker, Gertrude.** COM-HE (WBUT, Butler, PA, 1956–1957).

1875 **Baker, Gordie.** DJ (WSPR, Springfield, MA, 1954–1956).

1876 **Baker, Harold.** Newscaster (KCRC, Enid, OK, 1939–1940; WSM, Nashville, TN, 1955; WTRB, Ripley, TN, 1956). DJ (WTRB, 1955).

1877 **Baker, Helen.** COM-HE (WDMG, Douglas, GA, 1956).

1878 **Baker, I.** Announcer (KGEX, Muscatine, IA, 1927).

1879 **Baker, Jack.** Tenor (*Jack Baker*, vcl. mus. prg., NBC, 1936; WOWO, Albany, NY, 1942).

1880 **Baker, Jack.** DJ (*Musical Clock*, WFKY, Frankfort, KY, 1947; *Jack Baker Show*, KTOK, Oklahoma City, OK, 1949).

1881 **Baker, James.** DJ (*Coffee Caravan*, KBWD, Brownwood, TX, 1948).

1882 **Baker, Jane.** COM-HE (KNTV, San Jose, CA, 1958).

1883 **Baker, Jeff.** Announcer (WMAK, Buffalo, NY, 1925).

1884 **Baker, Jerry.** Vocalist (*Jerry Baker*, vcl. mus. prg., WCBM , Baltimore, MD, 1934). Leader (*Jerry Baker Orchestra*, instr. mus. prg., WMEX, Boston, MA, 1939).

1885 **Baker, Jim.** DJ (*Stroll Through the Village*, KVOC, Casper, WY, 1956).

1886 **Baker, Joe.** DJ (*Nighthawk*, WATG, Ashland, OH, 1948).

1887 **Baker, John.** DJ (*Ramblin' Review*, KWPM, West Plains, MO, 1948).

1888 **Baker, June.** COM-HE (*Home Management*, 15 min., Monday, 12:45–1:00 P.M., WGN, Chicago, IL, 1934–1936).

1889 **Baker, Mary.** Soprano (WGBS, New York, NY, 1926).

1890 **Baker, Mary.** COM-HE (*Mary Baker's Shopping Basket*, WTMJ, Milwaukee, WI, 1935).

1891 **Baker, Mary.** Conducted her *Album of Beauty* program (WOW, Omaha, NE, 1936. Reader (*Mary Baker's Poetry Album*, WOW, Omaha, NE, 1936).

1892 **Baker, Mary V.** COM-HE (WAIT, Chicago, IL, 1958).

1893 **Baker, Melvin.** Newscaster (KUSD, Vermillion, SD, 1939). Sportscaster (KUSD, 1939; KABR, Aberdeen, SD, 1940–1941).

1894 **Baker, Merrill.** DJ (WOAP, Owosso, MI, 1952).

1895 **Baker, Mildred.** COM-HE (KNAK, Salt Lake City, UT, 1954–1958).

1896 **Baker, Milton.** Tenor (*Milton Baker*, vcl. mus. prg., WBAL, Baltimore, MD, 1935).

1897 **Baker, Nelson.** Sportscaster (WFBR, Baltimore, MD, 1939–1941; WCAO, Baltimore, MD, 1946; *Hamburger's Sports News*, WFBR, 1947; *Sports Page of the Air*, WFBR, 1948–1949; *The Nelson Baker Show*, WFBR, 1950–1951; *Melody Scoreboard*, WFBR, 1952–1954; WWIN, Baltimore, MD, 1955).

1898 **Baker, Norman.** The former vaudevillian and businessman headed the Baker Institute and broadcast a program known as *Mr. Baker Himself* on which one of his topics was, "Cancer is Curable" (KTNT, Muscatine, IA, 1928). *See* **Border Radio** *and* **Charlatans, Demagogs and Politicians.**

1899 Baker, Paul. DJ (*800 Club*, WLAD, Danbury, CT, 1948–1949; *Singing Stars*, WLAD, 1952–1954). Sportscaster (*Good Morning Sports*, WLAD, 1953–1955; *Early Sports Review*, WLAD, 1960).

1900 Baker, (Mrs.) R.E. Harpist of the Nashville Symphony Orchestra (WLAC, Nashville, TN, 1928).

1901 Baker, Ray. Newscaster (WCNW, Brooklyn, NY, 1939; WITH, Baltimore, MD, 1942).

1902 Baker, Roger. Announcer (WGR, Buffalo, NY, 1925).

1903 Baker, Roland. DJ (*The Clock Watcher*, WKYZ, Houston, TX, 1949). Newscaster (WKYZ, 1955).

1904 Baker, Sanford. Newscaster (WWRL, Woodside, NY, 1940).

1905 Baker, Sue. COM-HE (WJJL, Niagara Falls, NY, 1957).

1906 Baker, Susan Lacey. COM-HE (WGAU, Athens, GA, 1957).

1907 Baker, Tom. Tenor (*Tom Baker*, vcl. mus. prg., KMOX, St. Louis, MO, 1935–1937).

1908 Baker, Tony. DJ (*Juke Box Saturday Night* and *Music Matinee*, WELI, New Haven, CT, 1948–1949).

1909 Baker, Virginia. COM-HE (KCKY, Coolidge, AZ, 1955).

1910 Baker, W. M. Fiddler on the *WSM Barn Dance* (WSM, Nashville, TN, 1928).

1911 Baker, William. DJ (*Tunes for Teens*, WGRP, Greenville, PA, 1960).

1912 Baker and Anderson. Harmony singing team (KSO, Clarinda, IA, 1926).

1913 *Baker Chocolate Program.* The Boswell Sisters sang with the Bob Haring Orchestra on the program sponsored by Baker's Chocolate (15 min., Monday-Wednesday-Friday, 7:30–7:45 P.M., CBS, 1932).

1914 *(The) Baker's Broadcast.* Fleischmann's Yeast sponsored the half-hour program starring comedian Joe Penner, the Ozzie Nelson Orchestra and vocalist Harriet Hilliard. Penner's trademark was his persistent query, "Do you want to buy a duck?" Although some called him "The Charlie Chaplin of Radio," his tenure with the program lasted only from 1933 to 1935 (30 min., Sunday, CBS). In a later format of the *Baker's Broadcast,* Robert "Believe it or Not" Ripley was featured as host. In addition to the music of the Ozzie Nelson Orchestra and Harriet Hilliard, Ripley's odd, hard to believe oddities were featured on the program. The Werner Janssen Orchestra also was heard on some programs (30 min., CBS, 1937). *See* ***Believe It or Not.***

1915 Baker Hotel Symphony Five. A Dallas hotel orchestra (WFAA, Dallas, TX, 1926).

1916 *(The) Baker's Theatre of Stars.* Producer-director Norman MacDonald presented a different dramatization weekly acted by guest stars. For example, on one program Joan Fontaine and John Dana appeared in "The Guardsman." The sponsor was the American Bakers Association (30 min., Sunday, 6:00–6:30 P.M., CBS, 1953).

1917 Bakey, Ed. DJ (WTOW, Towson, MD, 1956).

1918 Bakke, Hal. Sportscaster (*S.W. Football Preview*, WBAP, Fort Worth, TX, 1947). DJ (*Talkin' of Tunes*, KLIF, Dallas, TX, 1948; KGKO, Dallas, TX, 1954).

1919 Baklor, Elsa. Soprano (WBAL, Baltimore, MD, 1929).

1920 Bako, Joe. Leader (Joe Bako's Gypsy Band, WADC, Akron, OH, 1928).

1921 *Balaban and Katz Theatre Program.* Various musical and theatrical performers were presented on the variety program. David Lipton was the program's announcer (WMAQ, Chicago, IL; WGN, Chicago, IL and WEBH, Chicago, IL, 1926).

1922 Balakshin, Natalie. Pianist (KFAE, Pullman, WA, 1925).

1923 Balas, Clarece. Pianist (WJAX, Cleveland, OH, 1924).

1924 Balazs, Francis. Baritone (KPO, San Francisco, CA, 1926).

1925 *Balboa Hilarities.* Veteran vaudevillian Rod Corcoran was the MC of the entertaining variety show. Singer Mary Lind and Archie Vance's Balboa Playhouse Band were regulars on the program. The sponsor was the Balboa Brewing Company (30 min., Monday through Friday, 9:00–9:30 P.M., PST, KFWB, Hollywood, CA, 1935).

1926 Balch, Bill. DJ (*Dawnbuster*, WKYB, Paducah, KY, 1948).

1927 Balch, Marie. Pianist (WBAP, Fort Worth, TX, 1925).

1928 Balch, Vesta. Ballad singer (WSWS, Chicago, IL, 1926).

1929 Balchuck, La Vona. COM-HE (KGHF, Pueblo, CO, 1960).

1930 Balcomb, Carl. Balcomb conducted the *Poet's Corner* program (WOC, Davenport, IA, 1928).

1931 Baldi, Diana. Newscaster (*Women's World*, WOV, New York, NY, 1942). COM-HE (WOV, New York, NY, 1951).

1932 Balding, Chuck. Sportscaster (*Sports Whirl*, WOAY, Oak Hill, WV, 1947–1955). DJ (*Juke Box Review*, WOAY, 1954).

1933 Baldrica, Merv. Sportscaster (*Sports from the Sidelines*, WMIQ, Iron Moutain, MI, 1947–1948). DJ (*Fat Merv—the Record Man*, WMIQ, 1948).

1934 Baldridge, Elois. COM-HE (WHSM, Hayward, WI, 1958).

1935 Baldridge, Fanny May. Actress Baldridge played all the roles in *Miracles of Magnolia* (NBC, 1931–1933). She later appeared on the *Ellen Randolph* aka *The Story of Ellen Randolph* and *The Man I Married* daytime serials.

1936 Baldridge, Gene. DJ (*Gene's Record Shop*, WSIP, Paintsville, KY, 1952).

1937 Baldsen, Harry. Leader (Harry Balsden's Venice Ballroom Orchestra, KFI, Los Angeles, CA, 1924).

1938 Baldwin, Bettie [Bette] S. COM-HE (KMMO, Marshall, MO, 1951; KSIS, Sedalia, MO, 1956–1957).

1939 Baldwin, Bill. Vocalist (*Bill Baldwin*, vcl. mus. prg., WPG, Atlantic City, NJ, 1935).

1940 Baldwin, Bill. DJ (*Baldwin's Music Shop & Tea Time Serenade*, KSO, Des Moines, IA, 1947).

1941 Baldwin, Birdie. Soprano (KMA, Shenandoah, IA, 1928).

1942 Baldwin, Bruce. DJ (*Western Jamboree*, KCRC, Enid, OK, 1954).

1943 Baldwin, Bud. DJ (*Breakfast in Bedlam*, WHIO, Dayton, OH, 1947–1949; *Bud Baldwin Show*, WING, Dayton, OH, 1952–1957).

1944 Baldwin, Carolyn Cone. Pianist (KPO, San Francisco, CA, 1929).

1945 Baldwin, Cy. Singer (WRR, Dallas, TX, 1926).

1946 Baldwin, Dick. DJ (*Melody Corner*, WJOY, Burlington, VT, 1954).

1947 Baldwin, Earl. DJ (KXIV, Phoenix, AZ, 1960).

1948 Baldwin, Gene. DJ (*Silver Dollar Time* and *Time to Dance*, KFKA, Greeley, CO, 1952).

1949 Baldwin, J. Gordon. Organist (WHAM, Rochester, NY, 1927–1928).

1950 Baldwin, Jim. Newscaster (KALL, Salt Lake City, UT, 1946).

1951 Baldwin, Joy. COM-HE (KFJI, Klamath Falls, OR, 1956).

1952 Baldwin, Madge. Pianist (*Piano Novelties*, instr. mus. prg., KOL, Seattle, WA, 1929).

1953 Baldwin, Mel. DJ (KNX, Los Angeles, CA, 1954).

1954 Baldwin, (Dr.) Samuel. Organist Baldwin was a pioneer broadcaster (WEAF, New York, NY, 1922).

1955 Baldwin, Ted. DJ (*Afternoon of Music*, WLEA, Hornell, NY, 1960).

1956 Baldwin, Tom. DJ (WIEL, Elizabethtown, KY, 1948).

1957 *(The) Baldwin Program.* A vocal quartet accompanied by a pianist was featured on the music program (30 min., Sunday, 7:30–8:00 P.M., NBC-Blue, 1929).

1958 Bale, Frank. DJ (KIDD, Monterey, CA, 1960).

1959 Bale, Norm. DJ (*Ark-La-Tex Jubilee*, KWKH, Shreveport, LA, 1954–1956).

1960 Balfe, Kiernan. Newscaster (WISR, Butler, PA, 1941).

1961 Balgian, Rose. Soprano (WHN, New York, NY, 1925).

1962 Balhatchet, William. Tenor (WHT, Chicago, IL, 1928).

1963 Balinger, Art. Newscaster (KMTH, Hollywood, CA, 1940).

1964 *Balkin Success Charts.* Bost toothpaste sponsored the show that sold "success" in the form of charts that promised "how-to-get-it" (Weekly, WMCA, New York, NY, 1930s).

1965 *(The) Balkiter.* The *Balkiter* program was part of a network opera series initiated by NBC-Blue on November 3, 1927. The first opera presented was "La Traviata."

1966 Ball, Arthur. Tenor (WGR, Detroit, MI, 1928).

1967 Ball, Don. Announcer and ukulele virtuoso (WABC, New York, NY, 1929).

1968 Ball, Dorothy. Soprano (WCBD, Zion, IL, 1925).

1969 Ball, Eddie. Pianist Ball was a member of the Syrian Shrine Band Trio (WLW, Cincinnati, OH, 1923).

1970 Ball, Ernie. Singer (1921).

1971 Ball, Harvey. Leader (Harvey Ball and his U.S. Grant Hotel Orchestra, KFSD, San Diego, CA, 1926).

1972 Ball, Jack C. DJ (*Jack the Ball Boy*, KROP, Brawley, CA, 1947).

1973 Ball, Jane Ellen. COM-HE (WJAS, Pittsburgh, PA, 1956).

1974 Ball, Lilah Older. Reader (WQJ, Chicago, IL, 1924).

1975 Ball, Margaret. Pianist (KQW, San Jose, CA, 1926).

1976 Ball, Marnie. COM-HE (WNOK, Columbia, SC, 1958).

1977 Ball, Noel. DJ (*Eight Ball Show*, WSIX, Nashville, TN, 1954–1956).

1978 Ball, Rae Eleanor. Violinist (*Rae Eleanor Ball*, instr. mus. prg., CBS, 1936). Miss Ball had played earlier in 1922 on experimental station 5 ACW at Fort Smith, Arkansas.

1979 Ball, Ralph. Blind pianist (*Ralph Ball*, instr. mus. prg., WGBI, Scranton, PA, 1937).

1980 Ball, Roger [Rodger]. Sportscaster (WALT, Tampa, FL, 1947). DJ (*Roger*, WALT, 1947–1948).

1981 *(The) Ballad Hour.* A quarter-hour light music program with an orchestra and guest vocalists (15 min., Sunday, 1:45–2:00 P.M., WCAO, Baltimore, MD, 1930).

1982 *(The) Balladeers.* Vcl. mus. prg. with a male chorus (NBC, 1935–1936).

1983 (The) Balladiers. Male quartet (KYW, Chicago, IL, 1928). Although the name is spelled differently this may be the Balladeers vocal group that later appeared on NBC (1935–1936). *See* ***The Balladeers.***

1984 *Ballads of the Hills and Plains.* CW mus. prg. (WGH, Newport News, VA, 1939).

1985 Ballagh, Bill. Newscaster (KBIZ, Ottumwa, IA, 1940).

1986 Ballant, Dennis. DJ (WJAG, Norfolk, NE, 1949).

1987 Ballard, B. Earnest. Organist (KFSG, Los Angeles, CA, 1925–1926).

1988 Ballard, Bobbye. Soprano (WSM, Nashville, TN, 1928).

1989 Ballard, David. Newscaster (KGFJ, Hollywood, CA, 1945–1946).

1990 Ballard, Edna Wheeler. Harpist (WBBM, Chicago, IL, 1926).

1991 Ballard, George. Newscaster (WAYS, Charlotte, NC, 1945–1946). DJ (*Dancing Party*, WJHL, Johnson City, TN, 1948).

1992 Ballard, Jean. Contralto (WQJ, Chicago, IL, 1925).

1993 *Ballard Chefs.* Ballard Foods sponsored the weekly quarter-hour program broadcast Monday evenings. The *Ballard Chefs* offered two groups of "Negro boys." One group was a jug band with two banjos, a violin and a jug. The second group was a vocal quartet with four boys "none of whom had ever studied music" (*What's on the Air?*, April, 1930, p. 18).

1994 Ballew, Betty. COM-HE (KFTM, Ft. Morgan, CO, 1954).

1995 Ballew, Smith. Ballew was the tall, handsome, popular singer and leader of the Smith Ballew Band that frequently broadcast from Whyte's Restaurant on Fifth Avenue, New York City. Ballew also recorded frequently in 1929 with the following personnel: Jack Purvis, t.; Pete Pumiglio, clr; Babe Russin, as.; Bruce Yantis, v.; Bobby Van Epps, p.; Carl Kress, g.; Ward Lay, bass; and Stan King, d. (WJZ-NBC-Blue, New York, NY, 1929). Ballew was a western movie star and band singer, who once sang with the Freddie Rich, Ted Fiorito, Ben Pollack and George Olsen bands. Ballew appeared for a short time as host of the *Shell Chateau* program in 1936.

1996 Ballin, Robert and Oscar Race. Popular piano duo (WOR, Newark, NJ, 1925).

1997 Ballinger, Kenneth. Newscaster (*Home News*, WTAL, Tallahassee, FL, 1947–1948).

1998 Ballmer, Anne. COM-HE (WESA, Charleroi, PA, 1951).

1999 Ballman, Louise. Violinist on experimental station 5 ACW (Fort Smith, AR, 1922).

2000 Ballon, Florence. Pianist (WOR, Newark, NJ, 1925).

2001 Ballyn, (Chief Steward) William. A singer of sea songs, Ballyn worked on the ocean liner *Berengaria* (WJZ, New York, NY, 1924–1926).

2002 Balmer, Clinton C. News commentator (*The World of Books*, WLVA, Lynchburg, VA, 1947.

2003 Balmert, Francis C. Newscaster (WPAY, Portsmouth, OH, 1948–1955)

2004 Balogh, Erno. Pianist (WEAF, New York, NY, 1926).

2005 Balsam, (Dr.) Sol. Newscaster (WCNW, Brooklyn, NY, 1941).

2006 Balter, Sam. Sportscaster (MBS and WFIL, Philadelphia, PA, 1937; WCPO, Cincinnati, OH, 1941; KLAC, Los Angeles, CA, 1946–1955). Newscaster (KECA, Los Angeles, CA and KFWB, Los Angeles, CA, 1944; *Sam Balter Commentary*, ABC, 1945; KLAC, 1953–1960).

2007 Balthis, Elmore. Newscaster (KCOK, Tulare, CA, 1946).

2008 Baltimore, Ed. DJ (WISE, Asheville, NC, 1947).

2009 Baltimore, Louis G. Announcer (WBRE, Wilkes-Barre, PA, 1927).

2010 Baltimore City Park Orchestra. Municipal music organization (WBAL, Baltimore, MD, 1926).

2011 Baltimore Hotel Orchestra. Atlanta hotel band (WSB, Atlanta, GA, 1926).

2012 *(The) Baltimore Municipal Band.* The sustaining program featured an excellent brass band (Sunday, 6:30–7:00 P.M., NBC-Blue, 1934).

2013 Baltin, Charles. Newscaster (WHOM, Jersey City, NJ, 1941).

2014 Baltzer, Larry. DJ (*Please Play*, KHUZ, Borger, TX, 1948–1960).

2015 Balwin, Bud. DJ (WPFB, Middletown, OH, 1960).

2016 Bamberger, Carl. Pianist (WLW, Cincinnati, OH, 1923).

2017 Bamberger, Clara. Reader (WLW, Cincinnati, OH, 1924).

2018 Bamberger Little Symphony Orchestra. Classical music group sponsored by Newark, New Jersey's Bamberger Department Store, the owner of station (WOR, Newark, NJ, 1929; *Bamberger's Symphony Orchestra*, instr. mus. prg., WOR, Newark, NJ, 1936).

2019 *Bambi.* General Foods' Sanka Coffee sponsored the story of an over confident wife, who was trying to sell her writer husband's play. Her many difficulties were detailed on the show. Mark Warnow's orchestra provided the music. Helen Hayes played the title role of the helpful wife (30 min., Monday, 8:00–8:30 P.M., NBC-Blue, 1936).

2020 Bamboo Gardens Orchestra. Restaurant orchestra directed by Emerson Gill (WTAM, Cleveland, OH, 1928).

2021 Bambrick, Gordon. DJ (KGON, Portland, OR, 1956).

2022 Bammann, Glen. Sportscaster (*Outdoors Ohio*, WGAR, Cleveland, OH, 1952).

2023 Bampton, Rose. Contralto (WABC, New York, NY, 1929).

2024 Bancroft, Griffing. Newscaster (CBS, 1949–1955).

2025 *Bancroft Hotel Ensemble.* Instr. mus. prg. (WTAG, Worcester, MA, 1932).

2026 Band of a 1,000 Melodies. Led by Larry Funk, the versatile band was sometimes known as the Village Grovers. The band consisted of four members doubling, tripling, and quadrupling on various instruments (WMCA, New York, NY and WPCH, New York, NY, 1928). *See* ***Village Grovers.***

2027 *(The) Band of America.* The fine band was directed by Paul LaValle. In radio's earliest days the music group was known as the Cities Service Band. In 1948 with this program, LaValle's 48-piece Band of America gained even greater prominence and popularity (30 min., Friday, 8:00–8:30 P.M., NBC, 1948). *See* **Cities Service Band.**

2028 Band of Saxophones. Harry J. Waters directed the instrumental group (KTAB, Oakland, CA, 1927).

2029 *(The) Band Wagon.* Vicks Chemical Company and the Huppmobile Automobile Company co-sponsored the musical program that featured Benny Kyte's Golden Tower Band (30 min., Monday, 9:00–9:30 P.M., WJR, Detroit, MI, 1933).

2030 Bandell, Gail. Contralto (WQJ, Chicago, IL, 1926).

2031 Bandell, (Gail) and Chiddix (Frank). Gail and Frank were a harmony vocal team (WHT, Chicago, IL, 1928).

2032 Bandis, Edward. Pianist (WIP, Philadelphia, PA, 1926).

2033 Bangert, Randolph. Accordionist (WCOC, Columbus, MS, 1928).

2034 Banghart, Kenneth. Newscaster (NBC, New York, NY, 1946–1949). DJ (WRCA, New York, NY, 1957). Announcer Banghart also announced the *Archie Andrews* and *Katie's Daughter* daytime serial programs.

2035 Banfield, Bob. DJ (*Sunrise Serenade*, WEIR, Weirton, WV, 1948).

2036 Banjo Harmony Team. The Banjo Harmony Team of "Inky" Henneberg and Joe Sherman (KOIL, Council Bluffs, IA, 1928).

2037 *Banjoleers.* Instr. mus. prg. (WLW, Cincinnati, OH, 1935).

2038 *(The) Banjoleers and the Radio Sweethearts.* Instrumental and vocal music program (WGY, Schenectady, NY, 1935).

2039 Bank, Gail. DJ (*Time Out for Melody*, KWBB, Wichita, KS, 1952).

2040 Banker, Fred. Newscaster (KJR, Seattle, WA, 1938).

2041 Bankers Life Corn Sugar Orchestra. The popular Des Moines, Iowa, orchestra featured vocalists Virginia Groome Maurrine, Leona Martindate and Pauline Payton (WHO, Des Moines, IA, 1924–1926).

2042 Bankers Life Little Symphony Orchestra. Light classics group (WHO, Des Moines, IA, 1926).

2043 Bankey, Jack. Guitarist, banjoist and vocalist (WMAK, Buffalo, NY, 1928).

2044 Banks, Ann. COM-HE (WGOA, Winter Garden, FL, 1957).

2045 Banks, Bill. DJ (*Bill's Bull*, KSPT, Sandpoint, ID, 1948).

2046 Banks, Billie. DJ (*Music to Work By*, WVNA, Tuscumbria, AL, 1960).

2047 Banks, Dave. Sportscaster (*B.C. Sports Review*, a program that Banks began by announcing, "This is DB for BC," KLRA, Little Rock, AR, 1941). Newscaster (*News of the Hour on the Hour*, WDXI, Jackson, TN, 1948; *Dixie Doings*, WDXI, 1949). DJ (WLOX, Biloxi MS, 1955).

2048 Banks, Dolly. COM-HE (WINX, Washington, DC, 1951).

2049 Banks, Doris. Contralto (WILL, Urbana, IL, 1939).

2050 Banks, Joan. Busy actress Banks appeared on the daytime serials *Her Honor, Nancy James, Home of the Brave, House in the Country, John's Other Wife, Mary Foster—the Editor's Daughter, Portia Faces Life, This Day is Ours, Valiant Lady* (title role), *We Love and Learn, Young Dr. Malone* and *By Kathryn Norris.* She also appeared in the cast of the *Bringing Up Father* situation comedy.

2051 Banks, Lew. DJ (*Lunchtime Hillbilly Parade*, WJIV, Savannah, GA, 1948).

2052 Banks, Margaret. Organist (*Margaret Banks*, instr. mus. prg., WBIG, Greensboro, NC, 1936).

2053 Banks, Mary Ruth. Singer of "Negro spirituals" (KFSG, Los Angeles, CA, 1927).

2054 Banks, Pat. COM-HE (WBKB, Chicago, IL, 1958).

2055 Bankson, Russell. News commentator (*Russell Bankson*, KHQ, Spokane, WA, 1932).

2056 Bankston, Kathryn D. COM-HE (WRFC, Athens, GA, 1956).

2057 Banner, Ande. DJ (KIUP, Durango, CO, 1947).

2058 Banner, Bill. Newscaster (*Bill Banner and the News*, WSPA, Spartanburg, SC, 1947).

2059 Bannett, Wilda. Singer (NBC, 1927).

2060 Bannon, Bob. DJ (*One Nite Stand*, WSKI, Montpelier, VT, 1949).

2061 Bannon, Richard "Dick." DJ (*Western Serenade*, KIYI, Shelby, MT, 1947–1949).

2062 Bannwart, Carl. Religous broadcaster Bannwart was the Superintendent of the Olivet Sunday School and the ex-President of the Presbyterian Union. He broadcast "uplifting" talks (WOR, Newark, NJ, 1922).

2063 Banowich, Lorraine. COM-HE (WGMA, Hollywood, FL, 1957).

2064 Banquet Rhythm Pounders Orchestra. Popular Pacific Coast band (KMIC, Inglewood, CA, 1928).

2065 Banta, Dean. Newscaster (KGO, San Francisco, CA, 1945; KLX, Oakland, CA, 1946–1947).

2066 Banton, Bill. DJ (*Starlight Souvenirs*, KSBW, Salinas, CA, 1954).

2067 Banyard, Frank. Baritone (WOR, Newark, NJ, 1927).

2068 *Bar Nothing Ranch.* CW mus. prg.(WIBW, Topeka, KS, 1939).

2069 *Bar X Ranch Boys.* CW mus. prg. (WCBM, Baltimore, MD, 1939).

2070 Barager, Robert. DJ (*Supper Serenade* and *Waltz Time*, WNBZ , Saranac Lake, NY, 1948).

2071 Barakian, Lusinn. Soprano (KFAE, Pullman, WA, 1925).

2072 Baran, Henry. DJ (*Designs for Dancing*, WVEC, Hampton, VA, 1948–1952).

2073 Barath, Ray. DJ (*Grin 'n' Barath*, WKIX, Columbia, SC, 1949; *The Grab Bag*, WAIM, Anderson, SC, 1955).

2074 *Barbara Gould.* Miss Gould broadcast a weekly 15-minute program about beauty and beauty products (15 min., CBS, 1929–1932).

2075 *Barbara Wells.* Miss Wells, whose name was Florence Pritchett, conducted interviews with various personalities who lived in or were traveling through New York City. She also discussed various topics of interest to women. Miss Pritchett was also a regular panel member of Mutual's *Leave It to the Girls* program, where the feminine point of view was expressed. George Hogan was the program's announcer (15 min., Monday through Friday, 3:00–3:30 P.M., WOR, Newark, NJ, 1947). In 1948, her program moved to a Saturday 11:15–11:30 A.M. broadcast slot.

2076 Barbash, Anna. Soprano Barbash appeared on the *Memories of Jennie Lind and Claire Schumann* program with pianist Alice Warren Sachse (WPG, Atlantic City, NJ, 1926).

2077 Barbe, Charles. Newscaster (KGW, Portland, OR, 1944).

2078 Barbee, Belle. Spanish guitarist (KGO, Oakland, CA, 1926).

2079 Barbee, Bud. Sportscaster (WJPF, Herrin, IL, 1940).

2080 Barbee, Olivia. COM-HE (WJBB, Haleyville, AL, 1951).

2081 Barber, Bill. DJ (WOOD, Grand Rapids, MI, 1955–1960).

2082 Barber, Dick. DJ (*Two on the Aisle*, KVNU, Logan, UT, 1948).

2083 Barber, Don. DJ (*Jive at Five*, WAGA, Atlanta, GA, 1947; *Today's Top Five*, WGBS, Miami, FL, 1948; *Hillbilly Hits*, WGBS, 1948–1954).

2084 Barber, Don. DJ (*Record Review*, WGNI, Wilmington, NC, 1947).

2085 Barber, Elizabeth. Soprano (WEVD, New York, NY, 1930).

2086 Barber. Elizabeth. COM-HE (WNUZ, Talladega, AL, 1960).

2087 Barber, George. Newscaster (WDEF, Chattanooga, TN, 1941–1942).

2088 Barber, Joyce. Pianist (WBAL, Baltimore, MD, 1926).

2089 Barber, Julian. DJ (WAYS, Charlotte, NC, 1949).

2090 Barber, Mary. DJ (KOPP, Ogden, UT, 1947).

2091 Barber, Rowland. Newscaster (KVSF, Santa Fe, NM, 1940).

2092 Barber, Samuel. Baritone (*Samuel Barber*, vcl. mus. prg., NBC, 1935).

2093 Barber, Tom. DJ (*Midnight Serenade*, WLAK, Lakeland, FL, 1948).

2094 Barber, Walter "Red." Barber began his career by broadcasting football games on his school's (University of Florida) broadcasting station in 1929. His busy career as sportscaster included: WSAI, Cincinnati, OH, 1934–1937 and WLW, 1937–1938; New York Giants and Brooklyn Dodger baseball play-by-play, WHN, New York, NY, 1942, assisted by Alan Hale; WOR, Newark, NJ, 1939–1944; MBS-WHN , New York, NY, 1945; WHN, 1946; *CBS Presents Red Barber,* 15 min., Monday through Friday, 6:30–6:45 P.M., CBS, 1946; *Red Barber Sports*, 15 min., Monday through Friday, 6:30–6:45 P.M., CBS, 1947; *Red Barber's Club House* and *The Catbird Seat*, WMGM, New York, NY, CBS, WHN, 1948; *Red Barber's Club House,* 30 min., Saturday, 10:00–10:30 A.M., CBS, 1949; *Football Roundup* and *Senior Bowl Football* broadcast, CBS, 1953; *Football Roundup, Orange Bowl Football* game and *New York Yankees baseball,*CBS, 1955.

Barber began broadcasting major league baseball on WSAI in 1934 for a $25 a week salary. Incidentally, the first game he broadcast on the station was the first professional baseball game he had ever seen. *See* **Sports.**

2095 *Barber Shop Blues.* Vernon Dahlhart, the popular recording star of the 1920s, was "Barbarsol Ben" and his female singing companion, Adelyn Hood, was "Cutiecle Barbara" on the 15-minute program of songs and old-time ballads sponsored by Barbasol shaving cream. Dahlhart and Hood were joined on the show by the Barber Shop Quartet (CBS, 1931).

2096 Barber Shop Orchestra. Commercial radio band (WBBM, Chicago, IL, 1926).

2097 *(The) Barbison [Barbizon] Recital.* Operatic and instrumental selections were performed on the program by various guest stars (60 min., Wednesday, 9:00–10:00 P.M., WOR, Newark, NJ, 1930).

2098 Barborka, J.V. Bohemian harpist (KMA, Shenandoah, IA, 1928).

2099 Barbosa, Perfecto. Newscaster (KMAC, San Antonio, TX, 1941).

2100 Barbour, Hershel "Hersh." DJ (*Musical Varieties*, WCKB, Dunn, NC, 1952; WTYC, Rock Hill, SC, 1955; WCPS, Tarboro, NC, 1956). Sportscaster (WCKB, Dunn, NC, 1952).

2101 Barbour, June. Pianist (WOW, Omaha, NE, 1927).

2102 Barbour, Oliver. Actor-producer-director Barbour was born October 23, 1904. He began work as actor and producer at WHAM (Rochester, NY, 1929). Among the many programs he directed were *Life Can Be Beautiful*, *Light of the World*, *The Man I Married*, *The Parker Family*, *We Love and Learn* and *When a Girl Marries.*

2103 Barclay, Al. DJ (*Sunday Serenade*, WHAT, Philadelphia, PA, 1947; *Al Barclay's Danceland*, WAMS, Wilmington, DE, 1952). Sportscaster (WAMS, 1952).

2104 Barclay, Fran. COM-HE (WJNC, Jacksonville, NC, 1951).

2105 Barclay, George. Newscaster (KWKW, Pasadena, CA, 1942).

2106 Barclay, Luise. Actress Barclay appeared in *Backstage Wife* aka *Mary Noble, Backstage Wife*, *A Tale of Today*, *Woman in White* (title role) and *Portia Faces Life* daytime serials.

2107 Barco, Ralph. Leader (*Ralph Barco Orchestra*, instr. mus. prg., WHK, Cleveland, OH, 1942).

2108 Barcroft, Barbara. COM-HE (WMMB, Melbourne, FL, 1951–1955).

2109 Barcroft, Wendell. Newscaster (KGGM, Albuquerque, NM, 1942–1942).

2110 Barcus, Cyrus. Cornetist (WFAA, Dallas, TX, 1926).

2111 Bard, Katherine. Radio actress Bard was featured on the *Claudia and David* daytime serial.

2112 Bardill, Martha Backes. Soprano (KYW, Chicago, IL, 1925).

2113 Bardo, Bill (Wilbur P. Bardo). Musician Bardo was born September 24, 1906. A Columbia University graduate, he first appeared on radio with the George Olsen orchestra in 1927 before forming his own radio band.

2114 Bardwell, Anne. COM-HE (WKLX, Paris, KY, 1958).

2115 Baret, (Madame) Berthe. Violinist (KGO, Oakland, CA, 1927).

2116 Bareteletti, Juliette. Soprano (WGBS, New York, NY, 1925).

2117 Barfield, Harry. Newscaster (WAYS, Charlotte, NC, 1948). Sportscaster (WAYS, 1948).

2118 Barfield, Ruth. COM-HE (COM-HE, WJOR, Port St. Joe, FL, 1958).

2119 Barg, Myron. DJ (*1230 Club*, WJBC, Bloomington, IN, 1947).

2120 Barge, Elsie. Pianist (KYW, Chicago, IL, 1924).

2121 Barger, Carl. DJ (WFDF, Flint, MI, 1960).

2122 Barger, Darel. DJ (WEAR, Pensacola, FL, 1948).

2123 Baret, (Mme.) Berthe. French violinist (KGO, San Francisco, CA, 1927).

2124 *Bargin' Around with Boulton.* Acme Markets sponsored DJ Mike Boulton's popular program (60 min., Monday through Friday, 11:00–12:00 noon, WPAT, Paterson, NJ, 1950).

2125 Bari, Joe. DJ (WLBK, DeKalb, IL, 1956).

2126 Bari, Vern. DJ (*Hale Kula*, KULA, Honolulu, HI, 1952).

2127 Barile, Diane. Singer (WELI, New Haven, CT, 1937).

2128 Barile, Lou. DJ (*Words and Music*, WKAL, Rome, NY, 1949–1954; *Hall of Records*, WKAL, 1955).

2129 Barile, Michael. Barile broadcast recitations with "descriptive" background music played by Maurice Popkin (WMCA, New York, NY, 1925).

2130 Barill, Gene. DJ (*Midnight Matinee,* WJEF, Grand Rapids, MI, 1954–1956).

2131 Barkdoll, Gary. DJ (*Melody Lane*, WAYZ, Waynesboro, PA, 1960).

2132 Barker, Al. Actor Barker appeared on the *Don Winslow of the Navy*, *Kitty Foyle* and *Terry and the Pirates* programs.

2133 Barker, Betty. COM-HE (KTUC, Tucson, AZ, 1958).

2134 Barker, Bill. DJ (*Morning Jamboree*, WSIP, Paintsville, KY, 1952).

2135 Barker, Bobbye. COM-HE (KIFI, Idaho Falls, ID, 1958).

2136 Barker, Bradley "Brad." Actor and animal imitator Barker used his acting and animal imitations during the early years of talking motion pictures, skills that he had first used in radio during his appearances on the *Eveready Hour* late in the 1920s. *See* **Sound Effects.**

2137 Barker, Eddie. Sportscaster (KMAC, San Antonio, TX, 1945; *Sports Editor* and *Scoreboard*, 1947–1948, KMAC; KRLD, Dallas, TX, 1956). News analyst (KMAC, 1945; *Problems and Solutions*, KBRZ, Freeport, TX, 1960). DJ (KWFT, Wichita Falls, TX, 1957).

2138 Barker, George A. Bass-baritone (WBZ, Boston-Springfield, MA, 1924).

2139 Barker, Helen Gordon. Conducted an *Art Talks* program (KPO, San Francisco, CA, 1926–1929).

2140 Barker, John. Baritone (*John Barker*, vcl. mus. prg., WLW, Cincinnati, OH, 1934–1935).

2141 Barker, Kermit. DJ (*Morning Serenade*, KCHR, Charleston, MO, 1954).

2142 Barker, Louise Foskett. Pianist (KFWM, Oakland, CA, 1926).

2143 Barker, Mark, Jr. DJ (*Luncheon on the Hill*, WDUK, Durham, NC, 1949).

2144 Barker, Pepper. DJ (WCMB, Harrisburg, PA, 1960).

2145 Barker, Raymond. Baritone (WIBO, Chicago, IL, 1925).

2146 Barker, Sam. DJ (*In the Mood*, KVOU, Uvalde, TX, 1947).

2147 Barker, Ted. DJ (*Parade of Hits*, WJOY, Burlington, VT, 1954–1956).

2148 Barkey's Mandolin Orchestra. String music group (KFON, Long Beach, CA, 1927).

2149 Barkley, James "Jim." DJ (*News & Music from the Boys*, KSUM, Fairmont, MN, 1948; *News and Music*, WSUM, 1952–1956).

2150 Barkley, Ron. DJ (*Relaxin' on Waxin'* and *Ark Valley Record Review*, KGAR, Garden City, KS, 1949).

2151 Barkowitz, Milton. Newscaster (WNBC, New Britain, CT, 1937).

2152 Barkwell, Patsy. COM-HE (KOOS, Coos Bay, OR, 1956).

2153 Barlow, Chuck. Singer (*Chuck Barlow*, vcl. mus. prg., WMBD, Peoria, IL, 1935).

2154 Barlow, Howard. Conductor (23-piece concert orchestra, CBS, New York, NY, September 18, 1927; Columbia Symphony Orchestra, CBS, New York, NY, 1928; United Symphony Orchestra, WABC-CBS, New York, NY; conductor of the *Voice of Firestone* orchestra, CBS, 1929).

2155 Barlow, Jack. DJ (*Penthouse Party*, WTOL, Toledo, OH, 1952; WQUA, Moline, IL, 1954).

2156 Barlow, Jay. Sportscaster (WHLN, Harlan, KY, 1945–1946). DJ (*1230 Club*, WHLN, 1947–1951; *Mantrap*, WHLN, 1952–1954).

2157 Barlow, John. DJ (*Turntable Time*, KGEM, Boise, ID, 1948).

2158 Barlow, Ralph. Leader (*Ralph Barlow Orchestra*, instr. mus. prg., WBBM, Chicago, IL, 1942).

2159 *Bar-N-Frolic.* *Woman's World* magazine sponsored the show that replaced the *Meet the Folks* program. The host was Hal Culver. Culver sang western songs and also interviewed visitors to the *National Barn Dance* program (30 min., Saturday, 7:00–7:30 P.M., WLS, Chicago, IL, 1938).

2160 *(The) Barn Dance.* Max Terhune, later famous as a B-movie comic, hosted the CW music program (Weekly, WCCO, Minneappolis–St. Paul, MN, 1935).

2161 *Barn Dance Frolic.* Many of the WLS *National Barn Dance* crew were featured on the CW music program sponsored by the Gillette Razor Company (15 min., Saturday, 9:00–9:15 P.M., WLS, Chicago, IL, 1936).

2162 *Barn Dance Frolic.* CW mus prg. (KFH, Wichita, KS, 1939).

2163 *Barnacle Bill the Sailor.* Cliff Soubier played the title role on the humorous serial drama (1934).

2164 Barnaby, Beatrice. COM-HE (WDCL, Tarpon Springs, FL, 1955).

2165 Barnard, Frank. Sportscaster (WHBL, Sheybogen, WI, 1939).

2166 Barnard, Maude Reeves. Mezzo-soprano (KFI, Los Angeles, CA, 1925).

2167 Barnes, Alma Lou. Soprano (KFWB, Hollywood, CA, 1925).

2168 Barnes, Binnie. Movie actress Barnes conducted a husband-and-wife talk show, *Breakfast with Binnie and Mike* (KFVD, Los Angeles, CA, 1947). *See* **Husband and Wife Teams.**

2169 Barnes, E. Known as "The Wolverine Fiddler," Barnes was the leader of E. Barnes and his Old Time Dance Orchestra (KGO, San Francisco, CA, 1926).

2170 Barnes, Eleanor. Barnes interviewed guests on the *California Melodies* program (CBS, 1933–1934).

2171 Barnes, Estelle. Pianist (WAAF, Chicago, IL, 1935–1939).

2172 Barnes, Harriet. COM-HE (KSRO, Santa Rosa, CA, 1951).

2173 Barnes, Hugh. DJ (WDNT, Dayton, TN, 1960).

2174 Barnes, Jackie. COM-HE (WWGP, Sanford, NC, 1955).

2175 Barnes, Jo Ann. COM-HE (WJRD, Tuscaloosa, AL, 1955).

2176 Barnes, Josey. COM-HE (KTVT, Salt Lake City, UT, 1956).

2177 Barnes, Kelly. Announcer (WTFI, Toccoa, GA, 1925).

2178 Barnes, Mabel. COM-HE (KMIC, Inglewood, CA, 1928).

2179 Barnes, Patrick Henry "Pat." A veteran theatrical and radio performer, Barnes joined WHT, Chicago, IL, in 1925 as the chief announcer and program director. Barnes had come from WGN, Chicago, IL. While at WHT, he directed, adapted and acted in their first electrically transcribed program (Poindexter, 1978, p. 65). He also was a talented tenor who often sang on the station. Barnes won the *Radio Digest* Silver Cup awards for announcers in both 1926 and 1927. In 1927, he also added comic touches to his performances with female impersonations, Hamlet comic routines and by playing the role of Lord Helpus (WHT, Chicago, IL, 1927). He also performed announcing chores and read the news on WHT in 1927–1928. Barnes later starred on radio in the 1930s in various roles. His later career included his own *Pat Barnes and his Barnstormers* program featuring singer Marjorie Hendricks and the Jimmy Shields Orchestra (30 min., Saturday, 8:00–8:30 P.M., MBS, 1938).

2180 Barnes, Paul. Newscaster (WHJB, Greensburg, PA, 1941).

2181 Barnes, Ralph. Tenor (WGCP, New York, NY, 1925).

2182 Barnes, Russell. Newscaster (WWJ, Detroit, MI, 1941).

2183 Barnes, Teddy. DJ (*Rhythm by Request*, WHAL, Shelbyville, TN, 1949).

2184 Barnes, Vic. Newscaster (WCFL, Chicago, IL, 1949).

2185 Barnet, Charlie. Leader (*Charlie Barnet Orchestra*, instr. mus. prg., WOR, Newark, NJ, and NBC, 1939).

2186 Barnet, [Barrett] Hugh. Leader (Hugh Barnet Orchestra, WEAF, New York, NY, 1926).

2187 Barnet, Jewel and Freda Leonard. The harmony singing team Barnet and Leonard were known as the "Humming Birds of the Air" (WGN, Chicago, IL, 1926).

2188 Barnett, Barbara. Lyric soprano (KLS, Oakland, CA, 1923).

2189 Barnett, Bob. DJ (*Night Sounds*, WOPI, Bristol, TN, 1960).

2190 Barnett, Dan. Leader (Dan Barnett's Orchestra, WEBJ, New York, NY, 1925–1926).

2191 Barnett, Don. DJ (*Don's Dance Date*, KENI, Anchorage, AK, 1948).

2192 Barnett, Joseph. (Newark, NJ, 1925).

2193 Barnett, Joseph M. "Joe." Announcer, vocalist and station manager Barnett created and conducted a morning exercise program, *The Daily Dozen*. In addition, he also pioneered with remote broadcasts and the presentation of several shortened Broadway musicals and operas. On April 1922, after Barnett sang for 70 minutes at a studio audition, he was offered a job as announcer and "emergency singer." Three months later at age 22 he became announcer and manager of station WOR (WOR, Newark, NJ, 1922–1927).

2194 Barnett, Josephine. COM-HE (KGON, Oregon City, OR, 1954).

2195 Barnett, Lorraine. Singer-violinist (WHN, New York, NY, 1939).

2196 Barnett, Mary Joan. COM-HE (WLOH, Princeton, WV, 1954).

2197 Barnett, Melvin F. Sportscaster (WHIS, Bluefield, WV, 1940–1941). Newscaster (WLOH, Princeton, WV, 1949).

2198 Barnett, Paul. DJ (*970 Club*, WNEA, Jonesboro, AR, 1952).

2199 Barnett, Stanley. Announcer-program director Barnett as an announcer was designated as "BMX" (WOC, Davenport, IA, 1925–1926). When he moved to Baltimore the following year, Barnett announced his station's slogan, "The Station of Good Music"(WBAL, Baltimore, MD, 1927).

2200 Barney, Jay. Actor Barney appeared on the *Romance of Helen Trent* daytime serial program.

2201 Barney, Marion. Versatile radio actress Barney appeared on the daytime serials *Pepper Young's Family, Red Davis, Rosemary, When a Girl Marries* and *Marriage for Two*.

2202 Barney, Rex. Former Brooklyn Dodger pitcher Barney turned sportscaster and baseball color man (*Game of the Day*, MBS, 1955–1956).

2203 Barnhardt, Bonnie. Miss Barnhardt sang songs and told bedtime stories for children (WSB, Atlanta, GA, 1923).

2204 Barnhart, Harry. Leader (Harry Barnhart Orchestra, WOR, Newark, NJ, 1928).

2205 Barnhart, L.D. Newscaster (WKAR, East Lansing, MI, 1939).

2206 Barnhart, Mary. COM-HE (WLEU, Erie, PA, 1960).

2207 Barnhill, Pat. DJ (KDRS, Paragould, AR, 1956).

2208 Barnhouse, Donald Grey. The Reverend Grey Barnhouse participated in the first network religious service broadcast from the Tenth Presbyterian Church, Philadelphia, PA. He began broadcasting in the early 1920s. Barnhouse was the first to purchase network time for a religious program. His program, *The Bible Study Hour*, was syndicated in 1949 before moving to NBC in 1956.

2209 Barnhouse, Nancy "Nan." COM-HE (WTIG, Massillon, OH, 1957).

2210 Barnitz, Anna. Vocalist (*Anna Barnitz*, vcl. mus. prg., WORK, York, PA, 1936).

2211 Barnitz, Walter. Tenor (WJAZ, Chicago, IL, 1924).

2212 Barnouw, (Mme.) Anne. Barnouw broadcast recitations with a music background (WEAF, New York, NY, 1925).

2213 Barns, Teddy. DJ (*Juke Box Review*, WHAL, Shelbyville, TN, 1948).

2214 *Barnyard Follies.* CW mus. prg. (KMOX, St. Louis, MO, 1939). Billed as "Music from the Ozarks," it featured songs by Roland Gaines, Tommy Watson and the Range Riders among others.

2215 *(The) Barnyard Jamboree.* A transcribed CW music show, the *Barnyard Jamboree* was broadcast in the 1940s. Some of the great pioneer CW musicians such as singer-comedian-composer Peg Moreland and the Farm Hands vocal group were featured. Texas Slim called the square dances and Jimmy "Round Boy" Jeffries was the program's host (Transcribed, Various Stations, 1930s).

2216 (The) Barnyard Twins. The instrumental team of Walter Stohlman and Ray Denham, who played many musical instruments while performing old-time musical selections, were the Barnyard Twins (KOIL, Council Bluffs, IA, 1925–1928).

2217 Baron, Dorothy. Miss Baron broadcast "physical exercises for women" (KRE, Berkeley, CA, 1925).

2218 Baron, Karl. Newscaster (KYA, San Francisco, CA, 1945).

2219 *(The) Baron and the Bee.* Jack Pearl as the "Baron," assisted by his long-time stooge, Cliff "Sharlie" Hall, conducted the spelling bee. Ken MacGregor was the producer and Billy K. Wells and Fred Lightner the writers of the sustaining program. Fred Collins was the announcer. Organ interludes were performed by Paul Taubman (30 min., Tuesday, 9:00–9:30 P.M., NBC, 1935).

2220 *Baron Munchausen.* Jack Pearl created the long-winded Baron Munchausen, a character immediately popular with listeners. An example of the Baron's tall tales was this one: "In 1602, I was sitting starving in my tent in the middle of the Sahara Desert, when a Scotch musician came along. He was a sand piper you know. He was on his way to the ocean to go to court. He wanted to get a herring. So I said to him, 'Have you got anything to eat?' And he said, 'Why don't you eat the sand that is here?' I ate the sand, and I was so hungry that pretty soon I had made a hole ten miles deep and there was a whale in it. The whale was sitting there saying, 'I'm a great guy. I'm a great guy.' He was an awful blow hard. So I ate the whale, too. And when I cut him up, I found a man sitting in his stomach, reading. The man said, 'Hello. What are you doing in my house?' I said, 'You're not in a house.

You're in a whale's stomach.' He just said, 'Well, well. Anyway, I was so interested in this magazine I didn't know it.' So I took the magazine away from him." *See **The Jack Pearl Show**.*

2221 Barondess, Harriet. COM-HE (WMIE, Miami, FL, 1954).

2222 Baross, Jack. Violinist (KPO, San Francisco, CA, 1925).

2223 Barr, B. DJ (WKMI, Kalamazoo, MI, 1954).

2224 Barr, Claudia. Mezzo-soprano (WJZ, New York, NY, 1923).

2225 Barr, Dwight. DJ (*Teen Time Tunes*, WLBC, Muncie, IN, 1948).

2226 Barr, Fred. DJ (*1600 Club*, WWRL, Woodside, NY, 1947–1951; *Spiritual Time*, WWRL, 1952–1960).

2227 Barr, Helen. Soprano Barr appeared on the *Salicon Vanities* program (WEEI, Boston, MA, 1928).

2228 Barr, (Mrs.) J. Victor. Pianist (WSM, Nashville, TN, 1928).

2229 Barr, Joseph. Baritone (*Joseph Barr*, vcl. mus. prg., WOR, Newark, NJ, 1934).

2230 Barr, Marie. COM-HE (WGSA, Ephrata, PA, 1956).

2231 Barr, Melba French. Soprano (KPPC, Pasadena, CA, 1926).

2232 Barr, Richard. Newscaster (WARL, Arlington, VA, 1946).

2233 Barr, Winifred T. Pianist (WEAF, New York, NY, 1923–1924). Barr was the station's first staff accompanist. She also broadcast many 15-minute programs of solo piano music.

2234 Barrat, Maxine. COM-HE (WCKT, Miami, FL, 1956).

2235 *Barrel of Fun*. Rubsam and Harryman Brewing Company sponsored the program featuring Charlie Ruggles and Benny Rubin. *Variety* called it a mediocre comedy show (30 min.,Thursday, 8:30–9:00 P.M., MBS, 1941).

2236 Barrere, George. Conductor (George Barrere's Little Symphony Orchestra, WJAR, Providence, RI, 1926).

2237 Barrett, Art. DJ (WSIG, Mount Jackson, VA, 1954).

2238 Barrett, B.J. Leader (B.J. Barrett Orchestra, WLAG, Minneapolis, MN, 1924).

2239 Barret, Beulah. Pianist (WLW, Cincinnati, OH, 1925).

2240 Barrett, Betty. Vocalist (*Betty Barrett*, vcl. mus. prg., KSD, St. Louis, MO, 1939).

2241 Barrett, Bill. DJ (*Alarm Clock*, KVOP, Plainview, TX, 1947–1948).

2242 Barrett, Dick. DJ (WSHE, Sheboygan, WI, 1956).

2243 Barrett, Ethel Van Riper. Soprano (WEAF, New York, NY, 1925).

2244 Barrett, John. Newscaster (WIKY, Evansville, IN, 1948; *Music Out of the Night*, KLMS, Lincoln, NE, 1954).

2245 Barrett, Lawrence. Newscaster (WAYX, Waycross, GA, 1938).

2246 Barrett, Monty. Actor Barrett appeared on the *Jane Arden* daytime serial program.

2247 Barrett, Myrtle. COM-HE (WHDF, Houghton, MI, 1954).

2248 Barrett, Pat. Announcer Barrett was first heard on WTMJ (Milwaukee, WI) in the 1920s. He created his Uncle Ezra character on the *National Barn Dance* program in 1932 on WLS, Chicago, IL, and got his own network show in 1938 on the NBC-Red network. *See **Uncle Ezra**.*

2249 Barrett, Phil. Vocalist (*Phil Barrett*, vcl. mus. prg., WPG, Atlantic City, NJ, 1935–1936).

2250 Barrett, Rick. DJ (*On the Sunny Side of the Street*, KTMS, Santa Barbara, CA, 1948).

2251 Barrett, Ronald A. "Ronnie." DJ (WDOK, Cleveland, OH, 1956–1957).

2252 Barrett, Tony. Actor Barrett appeared on the *Adventures of Topper*, *Boston Blackie*, *Pepper Young's Family* and *This Life is Mine* programs.

2253 Barrett, Tony. Sportscaster (WRBL, Columbus, OH, 1942; KENT, Shreveport, LA, 1954–1956; KRMD, Shreveport, LA, 1960). Newscaster (WRBL, 1945).

2254 Barrett, William R. Sportscaster (*Quarterback Club*, WJLS, Beckley, WV, 1947; *Sports Line*, WJLS, 1948–1950).

2255 Barrick, Eldon. DJ (*Old Time Tunes*, KTRB, Modesto, CA, 1947; *Sunrise Serenade*, KTRB, 1948).

2256 Barricks, Johnny. DJ (*1490 Club*, WKAY, Glasgow, KY, 1948).

2257 Barrie, Clyde. Baritone (*Clyde Barrie*, vcl. mus. prg., CBS, 1935–1937; KUOA, Siloam Springs, AR, 1939).

2258 Barrie, Dick. Leader (*Dick Barrie Orchestra*, instr. mus. prg., MBS, 1935; CBS, 1939).

2259 Barrie, Elaine. Actress Barrie appeared in the cast of the *Dear John* daytime serial program.

2260 Barrie, Wendy. Former motion picture star Barrie was a regular on the *Direct and Collect* quiz program (NBC, 1946). She became a DJ on her own transcribed *Wendy Barrie Show* (30 min., Monday through Friday, 10:30–11:00 P.M., WMGM, New York, NY, 1956).

2261 *Barrie Crain, Confidential Investrigator*. The sustaining program, originally known only as *Barrie Crain*, was written by George Lefferts, produced by Van Woodward and directed by Ed King. The title role was played by William Gargan. He was supported by an excellent cast that included Ralph Bell, John Gibson, Jan Miner, Arnold Moss and Byrna Raeburn (NBC,1951–1955).

2262 Barrier, Edgar. Actor Barrier appeared on the *Young Dr. Malone*, *One Man's Family*, *Romance* and *The Saint* (title role) programs.

2263 Barringer, Louise. COM-HE (WQXI, Atlanta, GA, 1957).

2264 Barrington, Bruce. Newscaster (WEBQ, Harrisburg, IL, 1937; KXOK, St. Louis, MO, 1939–1940; *Early Edition News*, *Overnight News*, and *Final News with Bruce Barrington*, KXOK, 1947; *Inside the Headlines*, KXOK, 1948).

2265 Barrington, Charles. Newscaster (KOB, Albuquerque, NM, 1941; KDYL, Salt Lake City, UT, 1945).

2266 Barrios, Jose. DJ (*Exitos Y Novedades*, KUBO, San Antonio, TX, 1960).

2267 Barroff, Lenny. Newscaster (*News Around the World*, WISR, Butler, PA, 1948).

2268 Barron, Bill M. DJ (*Music Unlimited*, KXGI, Fort Madison, IA, 1948).

2269 Barron, Billy. Leader (Billy Barron's Dance Orchestra, KPLA, Los Angeles, CA, 1929).

2270 Barron, Blue. Leader (*Blue Barron Orchestra*, instr. mus. prg., WTAM, Cleveland, OH, 1936; KWK, St. Louis, MO and NBC, 1937; WHP, Harrisburg, PA, KFEQ, St. Louis, MO, 1939; WGR, Detroit, MI and KMOX, St. Louis, MO, 1942).

2271 Barron, Bob (Dr. Robert Henri Barron). Actor Barron was born April 3, 1898. Originally a physician, he appeared in stock and vaudeville before working on Seattle, Washington, radio in 1927.

2272 Barron, George. DJ (KCRT, Trinidad, CO, 1949).

2273 Barron, Lee. DJ (*Hello Beautiful*, KSWI, Council Bluffs, IA, 1948; *The Lee Barron Show*, KSWI, 1949).

2274 Barron, Lou. Leader (*Lou Barron Orchestra*, instr. mus. prg., WFBR, Baltimore, MD, 1935).

2275 Barron, Martha. Barron was the KGHI program director and station pianist. When she was on the air she took requests. Barron was often billed as "The Queen of the Ivories" (KGHI, Little Rock, AR, 1928).

2276 Barron, Russ. Sportscaster (*Down the Line*, WKLV, Blackstone, ME, 1953).

2277 Barron, Stan. Sportscaster (*Sports Extra*, WKBW, Buffalo, NY, 1955).

2278 Barron, Tommy. DJ (KTEM, Temple, TX, 1954).

2279 Barrows, Richard. Actor Barrows appeared on the *Young Dr. Malone* daytime serial program.

2280 Barrus, Gabby. Sportscaster (KODI, Cody, WY, 1953–1955).

2281 Barry, Alice. Newscaster (KTSM, El Paso, TX, 1941; *Woman's World*, KTSM, 1945–1947; *Today's World*, KEPO, El Paso, TX, 1949).

2282 Barry, Bert. Newscaster (KROY, Sacramento, CA, 1940). DJ (KGMS, Sacramento, CA, 1956).

2283 Barry, Bob. DJ (*Bob Barry Show*, KOWH, Omaha, NE, 1948).

2284 Barry, Dan. Tenor (*Dan Barry*, vcl. mus. prg., WIP, Philadelphia, PA, 1935).

2285 Barry, Donald J. Sportscaster (WIKE, Newport, VT, 1953). DJ (*Sandman's Matinee*, WIKE, Newport, VA, 1954).

2286 Barry, Edward. Classic piano virtuoso Barry taught radio piano lessons and also broadcast concerts (WGN, Chicago, IL, 1928).

2287 Barry, Frank. Tenor (KFI, Los Angeles, CA, 1925).

2288 Barry, Gene. Newscaster (WING, Dayton, OH, 1946). DJ (*Swing with WING* and *Lonesome Gal*, WING, Dayton, OH, 1947–1957).

2289 Barry, George. DJ (WHOT, Youngstown, OH, 1960).

2290 Barry, Guy. Sportscaster (*National Sports Parade*, WCOJ, Coatesville, PA, 1951–1952; WLAN, Lancaster, PA, 1956). DJ (*Spinner Sanctum*, WLAN, Lancaster, PA, 1954).

2291 Barry, Jack. Sportscaster (WHEC, Rochester, NY, 1942–1946; *Atlantic Football*, WHEC, 1948). DJ (*Musical Clock*, WHEC, 1949).

2292 Barry, Jack. Newscaster (WTTM, Trenton, NJ, 1944).

2293 Barry, Jack. DJ (*The Jack Barry Show*, WKAT, Miami Beach, FL, 1948).

2294 Barry, Jack. DJ (*You Asked For It*, WJOY, Burlington, VT, 1949). Sportscaster (*Sports Notebook*, WJOY, 1949–1950).

2295 Barry, Jim. Tenor (*Jim Barry*, vcl. mus. prg., WOR, Newark, NJ, 1936).

2296 Barry, John. Newscaster (WBZ-WBZA, Boston-Springfield, MA, 1944, 1948).

2297 Barry, John D. Newscaster (*What's Happening in the World?*, KGO, San Francisco, CA, 1928).

2298 Barry, Lee. Newscaster (KBUR, Burlington, IA, 1941).

2299 Barry, Les. DJ (*Luncheon Club*, WBEN, Buffalo, NY, 1947).

2300 Barry, Madeline. COM-HE (WAGC, Chattanooga, TN, 1956).

2301 Barry, M.K. "Mike." Sportscaster Barry broadcast horse race news on his *Horse Sense* program (WKLO, Louisville, KY, 1959–1960).

2302 Barry, Nick. DJ (*Tip Top Tunes*, WCMW, Canton, OH, 1948).

2303 Barry, Norman. Newscaster (WENR, Chicago, IL and WMAQ, Chicago, IL, 1939–1942). Sportscaster (WIBO, Chicago, IL, 1933; WMAQ, 1954).

2304 Barry, Phil. Newscaster (WFBR, Baltimore, MD, 1941).

2305 Barry, Sylvia. Singer (*Sylvia Barry*, MBS, 1939).

2306 Barry, Tom. DJ (WOL, Washington, DC, 1956).

2307 *Barry Cameron.* Richard Leonard and Peggy Blake wrote the daytime serial. Spencer Bentley played the title role. Rolly Bester, King Calder, Helen Carew, Elsie Hitz, Mary Hunter, Scott McKay, Doris Rich, Dorothy Sands, Colleen Ward and Florence Williams were also in the cast. Larry Elliott was the announcer (NBC, 1945).

2308 *Barry Gray on Broadway.* Gray, who at the time was also doing a late-night DJ program on WOR, stirred up considerable controversy with the guests he interviewed and the topics discussed on his sustaining program. His guests included Jack Barrett, Marion Colby, Walter Gross, Olsen and Johnson and Al Jolson (30 min., Monday, 10:00–10:30 P.M., WOR, New York, NY, 1946).

2309 *Barry Gray Show.* Gray later continued his popular talk show format with this sustaining weekly program (30 min., Friday, 8:30–9:00 P.M., WOR, New York, NY, 1950). The show soon expanded to two hours. This version of Gray's earlier late-night show gave him an opportunity for more talk and extended interviews with personalities on the New York scene (120 min., 12:00–2:00 A.M., Monday through Friday, WOR, New York, NY, 1950).

2310 *Barry Wood.* Popular baritone Wood was featured on his weekly transcribed program accompanied by the Hank Silvern Orchestra (15 min., Transcribed, late 1940s).

2311 Barrymore, Ethel. Actress Barrymore was introduced as "The Laughing Lady" (WJZ, Boston-Springfield, MA, 1923). The distinguished Broadway star was respectfully known as "The First Lady of the American Stage." Although well known for her work on stage in *The Corn is Green*, it was her performance in the motion picture *None But the Lonely Heart* that won her an Oscar as best Supporting Actress in 1944. Ethel Barrymore was the great aunt of current motion picture star Drew Barrymore, who reflects some of her great aunt's beauty.

Ethel Barrymore and her equally famous brothers, Lionel and John, frequently appeared on radio, occasionally in comedy skits, but usually in dramatic productions. Ethel most often appeared as a guest star on programs, but did perform in a short-lived situation comedy, *Miss Hattie*, with young Dick Van Patten on ABC (1944–1945). Brother Lionel, who was also a talented stage and film star, won the motion picture's Academy Award in 1931 for his work in *A Free Soul*. He was best known as a radio actor for his annual portrayal of "Ebenezer Scrooge" in Dickens' *Christmas Carol* and as "Dr. Gillespie" in the *Dr. Kildare* dramatic series with Lew Ayres.

Major Broadway and motion picture star John Barrymore was known variously as "The Great Profile" and "The Greatest Lover on the Screen." Perhaps he is best known on radio for his comedy role on the *Rudy Vallee Show*. All the members of the Barrymore family made major contributions to the American theater. According to a family legend, the Barrymores had acting in their blood since the time of Shakespeare (*Biography*, April 1998, p. 36).

2312 Barsby, Stuart. Announcer and business manager (KLZ, Dupont, CO, 1928).

2313 Barshard, Henetta. Violinist (*Henetta Barschard*, instr. mus. prg., CBS, 1935).

2314 Barsky, Ted. Newscaster (WILM, Wilmington, DE, 1941).

2315 Barstow, Dorothy. Producer-writer Barstow worked for McCann-Erickson, Inc., advertising agency. She was in charge of some of the agency's earliest programs. Specifically, she was responsible for the programs *Death Valley Days* and *Dr. Christian*.

2316 Barstow, Vera. *Variety* said violinist Barstow was "one of the top ten violinists" (KHJ, Los Angeles, CA, 1925).

2317 Bart, Belle. Astrologist Bart conducted her *The Stars and You* program (WOR, Newark, NJ, 1922–1924).

2318 Bartell, Ed. Newscaster (WPGH, Pittsburgh, PA, 1948). DJ (*The Golden Triangle*, WPCH, 1948; *Mr. Music*, KQV, Pittsburgh, PA, 1952).

2319 Bartell, Melvin. Newscaster (WHAM, Rochester, NY, 1939).

2320 Bartell, Paul. Newscaster (WFOX, Milwaukee, WI, 1946, 1948). DJ (*Fox Club*, WFOX, 1947–1952; WFOX, 1957).

2321 Bartell, Ted. Leader-trumpeter (Ted Bartell's Orchestra, a nine-man band that broadcast frequently from Yoeng's Chinese Restaurant in New York City, WJZ, New York, NY, 1928).

2322 Bartelli, Ingrid. COM-HE (WLUC, Marquette, MI, 1960).

2323 Bartelt, Mary Ann. COM-HE (WJPG, Green Bay, WI, 1954).

2324 Barth, Alvina. Soprano (KFRC, San Francisco, CA, 1926).

2325 Barth, Bernard C. "Bernie." Newscaster (KOBM, Rapid City, SD, 1939; *Bernie Barth's Commentary*, WLOS, Asheville, NC, 1947). Sportscaster (KOBM, 1939).

2326 Barth, Hans. Concert pianist (WOO, Pittsburgh, PA, 1925–1926; WEAF, New York, NY, 1925). Conductor (Gold Spot Orchestra, NBC-Red, New York, NY, 1929).

2327 Barthel, Burr. DJ (*Club 1090*, KING, Seattle, WA, 1948).

2328 Barthell, Elizabeth [Betty]. Singer (*Betty Barthell*, vcl. mus. prg., CBS, 1934–1936).

2329 Barthell, Lois. COM-HE (WZIP, Covington, KY, 1951).

2330 Barthelson, Joyce Holloway. Pianist (KGO, Oakland, CA, 1926).

2331 Bartholomew, Marshall. Tenor (NBC, 1928).

2332 Bartimus, Bernice. Pianist (WMAK, Buffalo, NY, 1928).

2333 Bartl, Bob. DJ (*Nite Patrol*, WFMD, Frederick, MD, 1954).

2334 Bartle, (Mrs.) Richard. Pianist (KPO, San Francisco, CA, 1923).

2335 Bartlett, Bob. DJ (KFJI, Klamath Fall, OR, 1954).

2336 Bartlett, Edna. COM-HE (WENY, Elmira, NY, 1957).

2337 Bartlett, Forrest. Newscaster (KGER, Long Beach, CA, 1938).

2338 Bartlett, Louis. Pianist (KYW, Chicago, IL, 1925).

2339 Bartlett, Marcus. Sportscaster (WSB, Atlanta, GA, 1941). Prior to 1931, Bartlett did all types of announcing jobs before doing sports color with Red Cross on prep football games. Later he broadcast George Tech football play-by-play. The Atlanta *Journal* called Bartlett "the best football reporter in the South."

2340 Bartlett, Marie. Reader (WEEI, Boston, MA, 1925).

2341 Bartlett, Marjorie. Scriptwriter Bartlett worked for the Ruthrauff & Ryan Inc., advertising agency. One of the daytime serials she wrote was *Big Sister*.

2342 Bartlett, Michael. Tenor (*Michael Bartlett*, vcl. mus. prg., WOR, Newark, NJ, 1934).

2343 Bartlett, Ray. DJ (*Groovie's Boogie*, KWKH, Shreveport, LA, 1948).

2344 Bartlett, Tom. Newscaster (WBBM, Chicago, IL, 1939).

2345 Bartlett, Virginia. COM-HE (WNET, Providence, RI, 1954).

2346 Barto, Frances. Nine-year-old reader (KHJ, Los Angeles, CA, 1924).

2347 Barton, Ada. Soprano (KPO, San Francisco, CA, 1925).

2348 Barton, Barbara. Actress Barton was featured on the *Stella Dallas* daytime serial.

2349 Barton, Betty. COM-HE (WNBH, New Bedford, MA, 1951).

2350 Barton, Bob. Newscaster (*Billy Barton — Hollywood Reporter*, movie news and gossip, WAAF, Chicago, IL, 1935).

2351 Barton, Dale. Newscaster (KIOA, Des Moines, IA, 1949). Sportscaster (KCIM, Carroll, IA, 1951–1952; *Sports Parade*, KCIM, 1953–1954).

2352 Barton, Emily. COM-HE (KFRC, San Francisco, CA, 1956).

2353 Barton, Frances Lee. COM-HE (*Food Talks*, 15 min., Tuesday and Thursday, 11:15–11:30 A.M., NBC-Red, 1933).

2354 Barton, Fred. DJ (WANE, Fort Wayne, IN, 1957).

2355 Barton, George. Saxophonist (WCCO, Minneappolis–St. Paul, MN, 1928).

2356 Barton, Hal. Sportscaster (KLUF, Galveston, TX, 1941). DJ (*Syncopation Time* and *Coffee Time*, WTAD, Quincy, IL, 1948; *Off the Record*, WTAD, 1949; *Syncopation Time*, WTAD, 1952.)

2357 Barton, John. DJ (WHOW, Clinton, IL, 1948–1954).

2358 Barton, Kearney. DJ (KTW, Seattle, WA, 1957).

2359 Barton, Ken. Sportscaster (KMTR, Los Angeles, CA, 1939). Newscaster (KWKW, Pasadena, CA, 1946).

2360 Barton, Marie. COM-HE (WLDS, Jacksonville, IL, 1960).

2361 Barton, Vera. Leader (*Vera Barton Orchestra*, instr. mus. prg., WKBW, Buffalo, NY, 1942.)

2362 Barton, William. Newscaster (KVEC, San Luis Obispo, CA, 1940, 1945).

2363 Barton-Smith, Susie. Reader (WCDB, Zion, IL, 1926).

2364 *(The) Bartons.* The daytime serial told the story of a boy and his family living in a small, Midwestern river town (15 min., Monday through Friday, NBC, 1941).

2365 Bartow, (Captain) D.M. Bartow spoke on such topics as, "Shooting as a Sport" (KFAE, Pullman, WA, 1923).

2366 Bartter, Bob. DJ (*Musical Varieties*, KNEX, McPherson, KS, 1954).

2367 Baruch, Andre. Newscaster-announcer (*Liberty News Commentator*, CBS, New York, NY, 1937). DJ with wife **Bea Wain** (*Mr. and Mrs. Music*, WMCA, New York, NY, 1947–1948; WABC, New York, NY, 1956). As an announcer Baruch was busy announcing such programs as *The American Album of Familiar Music, Bobby Benson's Adventures, Just Plain Bill, Kate Smith Show, Linda's First Love, Marie the Little French Princess, Myrt and Marge, Second Husband, The Shadow* and *Your Hit Parade*. See ***Mr. and Mrs. Music***.

2368 Baruth, Jack. DJ (WGVM, Greenville, MS, 1948).

2369 Barzelay, Benar. Polish violinist (WMCA, New York, NY, 1925).

2370 Barzen, Katherine. COM-HE (KTRF, Thief River, MN, 1951).

2371 Basch, Frances Scott (aka Faith Fortune, Frankie Basch and Frances Scott). News commentator (*Rating the News*, WAAT, Jersey City, NJ, 1930s). Pioneer female Basch covered current newspaper stories on her program. She later did interview shows for WMCA (New York, NY). She also worked under the names of Faith Fortune, Frankie Basch and Frances Scott.

2372 *Baseball News.* Frederick G. Lieb broadcast scores and the latest baseball news (WNYC, New York, NY, 1925).

2373 *Baseball with Clay Bryant.* Bryant, formerly a big league pitcher, talked baseball on his sports show (15 min., WMIN, St. Paul, MN, 1952).

2374 Basehore, John. DJ (*The John Basehore Show*, WGET, Gettysburg, PA, 1948).

2375 Bash, Otto. DJ (*Jump School*, WHOP, Hopkinsville, KY, 1948).

2376 Bashara, Lester. Newscaster (KGFW, Kearney, NE, 1940).

2377 Bashein, Nancy. Actress Bashein appeared on the *Second Husband* daytime serial.

2378 Basil, Athena. COM-HE (WCAV, Norfolk, VA, 1951).

2379 Basile, Frances. COM-HE (WBOY, Clarksburg, WV, 1960).

2380 *Basin Street.* Over the years the variety show presented talented performers including vocalists Dick Todd, Gertrude Niessen, Georgia Gibbs, Johnny Johnson, Cab Calloway, Delores Gray and the Mills Brothers. Motion picture and Broadway stars such as Bonita Granville and Ethel Merman sometimes appeared, as did musicians such as John Sebastian and Carmen Cavallaro. Comedians George Jessel, Milton Berle and Frank Fay were also featured (30 min., Weekly, NBC, 1944, 1947–1948).

2381 Baskerville, Nancy. Soprano (WSM, Nashville, TN, 1928).

2382 Baskos, George. DJ (KLMO, Longmont, CO, 1956).

2383 Basnight, Catherine. COM-HE (WCAV, Norfolk, VA, 1951).

2384 Bass, Beatrice. COM-HE (WHBI, Newark, NJ, 1958).

2385 Bass, George. Violinist (*George Bass*, instr. mus. prg., WMAQ, Chicago, IL, 1936).

2386 Bass, Grady. DJ (*Musical Clock*, KTBB, Tyler, TX, 1949). Sportscaster (KSFA, Nacogdoches, TX, 1950).

2387 Bass, H. Victor. Singer (KTAB, Oakland, CA, 1925).

2388 Bass, Marguerite and Mildred Waddey. Piano duo (WREC, Memphis, TN, 1929).

2389 Bass, Martin. Newscaster (KANS, Wichita, KS, 1940).

2390 Bass, M. R. Announcer (WHDI, Minneapolis, MN, 1925).

2391 Bass, Sam. DJ (KWRO, Coquille, OR, 1960).

2392 Bass, Terry. DJ (KOPR, Butte, MT, 1960).

2393 Bassell, Aleda J. Pianist (KSD, St. Louis, MO, 1923).

2394 Bassett, Robert E. "Bob." DJ (WHIM, Providence, RI, 1956–1957).

2395 Bassi, Kathryn. Harpist (KYW, Chicago, IL, 1925).

2396 Basso, Nick. Sportscaster (WNAR, Norristown, PA, 1946). Newscaster (WNAR , 1946). DJ (*Rise and Shine*, WAJR, Morgantown, WV, 1947–1949).

2397 Bast, Merwin. DJ (WKOA, Hopkinsville, KY, 1956).

2398 Bastianelli Trio. The trio included Helen Bastianelli, cellist; Hazel May, violinst; and Louise Woodruff, pianist (WHAM, Rochester, NY, 1928).

2399 Bataess, Michael. Bass (WGBS, New York, NY, 1925).

2400 Batch, Lee. DJ (KCSB, San Bernardino, CA, 1956).

2401 Batchelder, Charles. Sportscaster (WDBO, Orlando, FL, 1937–1941).

2402 Batcheller, Ruth. COM-HE (WACE, Springfield-Chicopee, MA, 1957).

2403 Batchellor, Bob. DJ (*Magic Carpet*, WCNX, Middletown, CT, 1960).

2404 Batchelor, Ernest. DJ (WDAX, McRae, GA, 1960).

2405 Batchelor, Richard "Dick." Newscaster (WTRR, Sanford, FL, 1947). DJ (WTRR, 1947; WDBO, Orlando, FL, 1948).

2406 Batdorf, Carol. COM-HE (KVOS, Bellingham, WA, 1957).

2407 Bate, Dick. DJ (*Record Breakers*, WNDB, Daytona Beach, FL, 1949).

2408 Bate, (Dr.) Humphrey. A harmonica player and surgeon from Tennessee, Bate led the Dr. Humphrey Bate and his Possum Hunters country string band that played on WDAD (Nashville, TN, 1924). On October 24, 1925, the group joined the *Grand Ole Opry* (WSM, Nashville, TN). This group was the first string band featured on the *Grand Ole Opry*. The CW group included fiddler Stringbean, banjoist Walter Liggett, bass violinist Oscar Albright and guitarists Stanley Walton and Paris Pond. Burt Hutcherson and James Hart also played in Bate's early band at various times.

2409 Bateman, Douglas. DJ (*Pleasure, Inc.*, WLIO, East Liverpool, OH, 1948).

2410 Bateman, Frank. DJ (*Hi Fi Club*, KDRS, Paragould, AR, 1960).

2411 Bateman, June. COM-HE (WLIO, East Livepool, OH, 1951).

2412 Bateman, Ray. DJ (*The Ray Bateman Show*, 1952).

2413 Bates, Bill. Newscaster (KWOC, Poplar Bluff, MS, 1938). Sportscaster (KTBB, Modesto, CA, 1939).

2414 Bates, Carl. Newscaster (WKST, New Castle, PA, 1939).

2415 Bates, Jeanne. Actress Bates was a member of the *Today's Children* daytime serial cast.

2416 Bates, Karl. Newscaster (WKBN, Youngstown, OH, 1942).

2417 Batey, Hubert "Hugh." Sportscaster (WGPC, Albany, GA, 1938; *Sports Roundup*, WRBL, Columbus, OH, 1949; WLTG, Thomasville, GA, 1956). Newscaster (WGPC, 1938–1939; *Feature Story*, WRBL, 1948). DJ (*Music 'Til Midnight*, WPDQ, Jacksonville, FL, 1947; *Record Session*, WRBL, 1949; *Music 'Til Midnight*, WPDQ, 1952).

2418 Bath, Gomer. Newscaster (WMDB, Peoria, IL, 1938).

2419 Bath, Helen. COM-HE (WITZ, Jasper, IN, 1958).

2420 Bathe, C.E. Announcer Bathe proclaimed his station to be "The Voice of Sooner Land" (WNAD, Norman, OK, 1926).

2421 Batione, (Prof.) Benicia. A Professor of Spanish at the University of Denver, Benicia broadcast the instruction of conversational Spanish (KOA, Denver, CO, 1925).

2422 Batozech, Ron. DJ (WJOL, Joliet, IL, 1956–1960).

2423 Batson, Charles A., Jr. Newscaster (WFBC, Greenville, SC, 1940; WFNY, Fayetteville, NC, 1941).

2424 Batters, Charles. Sportscaster (WBRY, Waterbury-New Haven, CT, 1940; WFBL, Syracuse, NY, 1942). DJ (*Batters Platters*, WRC, Washington, DC, 1948–1950).

2425 Battery Boys of WNAX. The Boys were a singing team that also played piano and guitar (WNAX, Yankton, SD, 1929).

2426 Battey, Bess Beatrice. Pianist (KOIL, Council Bluffs, IA, 1928).

2427 Battin High School Orchestra. Scholastic music group (WJZ, New York, NY, 1923).

2428 Battisti, Paul. DJ (*Musical Clock*, KRSN, Los Alamos, NM, 1952).

2429 Battle, Lisa. COM-HE (WTMA, Charleston, SC, 1951).

2430 Battle, Rex. Leader (*Rex Battle Ensemble*, instr. mus. prg., WXYZ, Detroit, MI, 1935; NBC-Red, New York, NY, 1937).

2431 Battles, Frank. DJ (KOCA, Kilgore, TX, 1960).

2432 Batton, V.S. Assistant announcer (WDAF, Kansas City, MO, 1928).

2433 Batts, Helen. COM-HE (WPET, Greensboro, NC, 1957).

2434 Bauby, Cathy. COM-HE (WMCT, Memphis, TN, 1957).

2435 Bauer, A.J. DJ (*Alarm Clock Melodies*, WINK, Fort Myers, FL, 1948–1949).

2436 Bauer, Bill. DJ (*Nitewatch*, KYSM, Mankato, MN, 1960).

2437 Bauer, Charita. Busy actress Bauer appeared on the *Lora Lawton*, *Orphans of Divorce* (evening program), *Right to Happiness*, *Rose of My Dreams*, *Our Gal Sunday*, *Second Husband* and *Young Widder Brown* daytime serials.

2438 Bauer, Frederick. Newscaster (*Six O'Clock News*, WINN, Louisville, KY, 1944–1948).

2439 Bauer, Harold. Distinguished concert pianist (NBC, 1926).

2440 Bauer, Ione M. COM-HE (KSPT, Sandpoint, ID, 1957).

2441 Bauer, Joe. DJ (*Hi Fi for Cincy*, WZIP, Cincinnati, OH, 1960).

2442 Bauer, Mary Jo. DJ (*Fandels Disc Jockey Show*, KRAM, St. Cloud, MN, 1949).

2443 Bauer, Russ. DJ (*Alarm Clock Club* and *County Party Line*, KJFJ, Webster City, IA, 1948).

2444 Baughman, George. Newscaster (KWSC, Pullman, WA, 1939).

2445 Baughn, Ted. Sportscaster (WELL, Battle Creek, MI, 1937).

2446 Baukhage, H.R. Respected news analyst and commentator (*National Farm and Home Hour*, NBC, 1932; WMAL, Washington, DC and WRC, Washington, DC, 1937; *Four Star News* and *News from the Nation's Capitol*, NBC, 1939; NBC, 1939–1944; *Baukhage Talking*, ABC, 1945; WMAL, 1946–1947; ABC, 1948–1949; MBS, 1951–1953). Newspaper man and magazine editor, Baukhage began his broadcasting career in 1932 as a commentator on the famous *National Farm and Home Hour* program broadcast Monday through Friday on the NBC-Blue network (1932). He became a national commentator on NBC-Blue in 1937. When NBC's Blue Network became ABC, he became the Washington correspondent for that network. Baukhage was an objective commentator with no discernable bias. He moved to MBS in 1951, where his *Baukhage Talking* program was carried by 545 stations. In 1953, he retired from commercial radio when the program was canceled. He returned to radio on AFRS from 1963 to 1967 with a weekly commentary program.

2447 Baum, Charles. Leader (*Charles Baum Orchestra*, instr. mus. prg., CBS, 1939, 1942).

2448 Baum, Clare. Actress Baum was featured on the *Ma Perkins*, and *Mary Marlin* aka *The Story of Mary Marlin* daytime stories.

2449 Baum, Harry. DJ (*Request Party*, WSSB, Durham, NC, 1948).

2450 Baum, Oscar. Conductor-violinist of the Capitol Orchestra (WCCO, Minneapolis, MN, 1928).

2451 Baum, Robert. DJ (WOKW, Sturgeon Bay, WI, 1954).

2452 Baum, Russell. Pianist (*Russell Baum*, instr. mus. prg., WGR, Buffalo, NY, 1937).

2453 Bauma, George. DJ (WBMD, Baltimore, MD, 1955).

2454 Bauman, Bill. DJ (*1140 Club*, KSOO, Sioux Falls, SD, 1952).

2455 Bauman, Bob. DJ (*Club 1060*, WHFB, Benton Hour-St. Joseph, MI, 1960).

2456 Bauman, Marjorie. COM-HE (WHOL, Allentown, PA, 1951).

2457 Baumann, Everett. Newscaster (NBC, 1942).

2458 Baumann, George. DJ (WBMD, Baltimore, MD, 1954).

2459 Baumann, Ken. DJ (WKKO, Cocoa, FL, 1960).

2460 Baumgardt, (Dr.) Mars. Dr. Baumgardt broadcast talks on astronomy (KHJ, Los Angeles, CA, 1925–1927).

2461 Baumgart, Red. DJ (*1240 Club*, KRAL, Rawlins, WY, 1948).

2462 Baur, Franklyn. Tenor (NBC, 1928; *Franklyn Baur*, vcl. mus. prg., NBC, 1934). Baur was a popular recording artist.

2463 Bausch & Lomb Concert Ensemble. Commercially sponsored music group directed by Bernard Kaun (WHAM, Rochester, NY, 1927).

2464 Bauscha, Billie. Miss Bauscha was known as the "singing jazzette" (WBAX, Wilkes-Barre, PA, 1929).

2465 Bave, Louise. Lyric soprano Bave sang with the *Major Bowes Capitol Family* and on her own program (*Louise Bave*, vcl. mus. prg., WGR, Detroit, MI, 1934). *See* ***Major Bowes Capitol Family***.

2466 Baver, Milton. Tenor (*Milton Baver*, vcl. mus. prg., WBAL, Baltimore, MD, 1935).

2467 Bawden, Clarence K. Organist (WOO, Philadelphia, PA, 1925).

2468 Baxter, Andrew. Baritone (*Andrew Baxter*, vcl. mus. prg., WOR, Newark, NJ, 1934).

2469 Baxter, Bee. News analyst (*The Woman's Side of the News*, KSTP, St. Paul, MN, 1937).

2470 Baxter, Betty. COM-HE (WLBG, Laurens, SC, 1951).

2471 Baxter, Betty. COM-HE (KWJJ, Portland, OR, 1955).

2472 Baxter, Charles. Newscaster (WTOL, Toledo, OH, 1942). DJ (*12:30 Record Club*, WTOL, 1948–1949).

2473 Baxter, Dorothy. Singer (*Dorothy Baxter*, vcl. mus. prg., WJAG (Norfold, NE, 1937).

2474 Baxter, Ed. Sportscaster (KCHV, Indio, CA, 1960).

2475 Baxter, Frances. COM-HE (WDXE, Lawrenceburg, TN, 1956).

2476 Baxter, Frank. Newscaster (WSSB, Durham, NC, 1949).

2477 Baxter, George. Actor Baxter appeared on the *Career of Alice Blair* daytime serial program.

2478 Baxter, George. DJ (*Housewives Blues*, WKTM, Mayfield, KY, 1949). Sportscaster (*Monday Morning Quarterback*, *Gridiron Preview* and *Football Forecasts*, WKTM, 1949).

2479 Baxter, Gordon, Jr. DJ (*Baxter's Garden*, KPAC, Port Arthur, TX, 1948; *Talk of the Town*, KPAC, 1949; *Jambalaya*, KTRM, Beaumont, TX, 1952–1954). Sportscaster (KPAC, 1948).

2480 Baxter, Lionel. Sportscaster (WAPI, Birmingham, AL, 1938–1942). Newscaster (WAPI, 1938–1942; *News 'Til Now*, WAPI, 1944–1947; *WAPI News*, 1948; *Headlines From the News*, WAPI, 1949).

2481 Baxter, Lowell. Organist (*Lowell Baxter*, instr. mus. prg., WCKY, Cincinnati, OH, 1933).

2482 Baxter, Phil. Leader (Phil Baxter and his Southern Entertainers Orchestra,

WOK, Pine Bluff, AR, 1922; Phil Baxter and his Singing Orchestra broadcasting from the DeSota Japanese Ballroom, KTHS, Hot Springs National Park, AR, 1924.)

2483 Baxter, Raymond. Announcer Baxter proclaimed station WTAL to be "The Gateway to the Sea" (WTAL, Toledo, OH, 1926).

2484 Baxter, Raymond. DJ (*Time to Wake Up*, WHUZ, Borger, TX, 1949).

2485 Baxter, Tom. Director Baxter directed the *When a Girl Marries* daytime serial program.

2486 Baxter, Roy. DJ (WBNX, New York, NY, 1954).

2487 Bay, Peter. DJ (*Spotlighting the Stars*, KVCV, Reading, CA, 1954).

2488 Bay, Victor. Leader (*Victor Bay Orchestra*, instr. mus. prg., CBS, 1936).

2489 Bayer, Florence. Radio actress (WMAQ, Chicago, IL, 1927).

2490 Bayes, Nora. Vaudeville star Bayes appeared on the *General Motors Family Party* (NBC, 1927).

2491 Bayles, George. Announcer (KFAE, Pittsburgh, PA, 1925).

2492 Bayles, J. C. Announcer (WILL, Urbana, IL, 1925).

2493 Bayley, Arthur K. Tenor (WEEI, Boston, MA, 1924).

2494 Bayley, Travers. DJ (KDAL, Duluth, MN, 1949).

2495 Bayliss, Edgar. Bayliss broadcast organ recitals from Bragton's Theater (KFON, Long Beach, CA, 1925).

2496 Bayliss, Grant. Actor Bayliss appeared on the *House of Glass* program.

2497 Baylor, Berlyn. Leader (Berlyn Baylor's Troubadours Orchestra, the regular Rainbow Gardens' Orchestra that originated its broadcasts from the Little Rock, Arkansas, club, WLBN, Little Rock, AR, 1928). It was unusual programming, but station WLBN frequently broadcast the band throughout the entire evening from 8:00 p.m to 3:00 A.M. in the morning.

2498 Baylor, David. Newscaster (WGAR, Cleveland, OH, 1944).

2499 Baylor, Glen. Announcer (WDBS, Roanoke, VA, 1925).

2500 Baylor, O.W. News analyst (*As I See It*, WVLK, Versailles, KY, 1948).

2501 Baylor Dallas Glee Club. Edwin Lisman directed the vocal group (WFAA, Dallas, TX, 1925).

2502 Baymiller, W.H. Baymiller broadcast interesting travelogues (KFON, Long Beach, CA, 1927).

2503 Bayne, Barbara. COM-HE (WLOL, Minnapolis, MN, 1951–1954).

2504 Baytown Band of the Humble Oil and Refining Company. Humble Oil Company sponsored this brass band (KPRC, Houston, TX, 1926).

2505 Bazyn, Wally. DJ (WJAG, Norfolk, NE, 1956).

2506 Bazzare [Bazzare], Gail. COM-HE (WCHV, Charlottesville, VA, 1957).

2507 *Be Kind to Announcers.* Members of station WLS appeared on this unique program that showcased the talent and personality of its announcers. Pat Buttram, Joe Kelly, Jack Holden and Howard Chamberlain were featured (15 min., 11:30-ll:45 P.M., WLS, Chicago, IL, 1935).

2508 *Bea Wain and Andre Baruch.* Husband and wife team Wain and Baruch engaged in domestic talk with a few ideas thrown in for good measure on their popular local talk show. Mel Parnell contributed tasteful piano selections (60 min., Monday through Friday, 1:00–2:00 P.M., WABC, New York, NY, 1955).

2509 Beach, Alan. DJ (*Beach Party*, KNEZ, Lompoc, CA, 1960).

2510 Beach, Charles Bradford. Singer (WBZ, Boston-Springfield, MA, 1924).

2511 Beach, Dick. DJ (*Wax Works*, WICA, Ashtabula, OH, 1948).

2512 Beach, Dorothy. Soprano (WHT, Chicago, IL, 1928).

2513 Beach, Isabelle. COM-HE (NBC, 1936). This may be the same Isabelle Beach who co-hosted a quiz show with Warren Hull.

2514 Beach, Isabelle. Beach co-hosted with Warren Hull the *Mother Knows Best* quiz program (CBS, 1950).

2515 Beachboard, Kenneth. Newscaster (WISE, Asheville, NC, 1941–1942).

2516 Beachwood, Bud. DJ (*Magic Valley Stampede*, KVMV, Twin Falls, ID, 1949).

2517 Beadles, J. Robert. Announcer and piano accompanist (WRVA, Richmond, VA, 1925–1928).

2518 Beagle, Maude Stewart. COM-HE (WBBC, Flint, MI, 1951–1954).

2519 Beaglem, Barbara. COM-HE (WLOL, Minneapolis, MN, 1954).

2520 Beal, Bill. Newscaster (KDKA, Pittsburgh, PA, 1938).

2521 Beal, Bob. Leader (Hotel Claremont Orchestra, KRE, Berkeley, CA, 1926).

2522 Beal, Bud. Sportscaster (WMAK, Nashville, TN, 1960).

2523 Beal, Clyde. DJ (*Operation Music*, WCPM, Cumberland, KY, 1954).

2524 Beal, George Brenton. Editor, critic and philosopher Beal broadcast weekly on his *Bits of Wisdom* program (WGI, Medford Hillside, MA, 1923).

2525 Beale, George. Newscaster (WHO, Ames, IA, 1941–1942).

2526 Beale, Patricia. COM-HE (WRGS, Rogersville, TN, 1956).

2527 *(The) Beale Street Boys.* This singing group had their own programs on the networks in 1934.

2528 Bealin, Frank. Actor Bealin appeared on the *Young Dr. Malone* daytime serial program.

2529 Beall, Howard. Beall broadcast golf instruction (KFWB, Hollywood, CA, 1925).

2530 Beall, Jack. Newscaster (WLW, Cincinnati, OH, 1944; WJZ, New York, NY, 1945; WMAL, Washington, DC and ABC, 1946–1948; ABC, 1949).

2531 Beals, Ray. Newscaster (KVGB, Great Bend, KS, 1946). DJ (*The Sammy Duck Show*, KVGB, 1954).

2532 Beamer, Florence. Pianist (KFKU, Lawrence, KS, 1926).

2533 Beamer, Mildred. COM-HE (WATA, Boone, NC, 1951).

2534 Beamont, Perry. DJ (*Musical Clock*, WOLK, Lima, OH, 1948).

2535 Bean, Bob. Newscaster (WGBG, Greensboro, NC, 1946). Sportscaster (WGBG, 1946). DJ (*Bob Bean's Big Barn Bands*, WBIG, Greensboro, NC, 1949).

2536 Bean, Don. DJ (*Matinee Ballroom*, WFRP, Savannah, GA, 1954). Sportscaster (WFRP, 1954).

2537 Bean, Harold. Baritone (*Harold Bean*, vcl. mus. prg., KYW, Philadelphia, PA, 1933; WMBD, Peoria, IL, 1936).

2538 Bean, Jane. COM-HE (KMAQ, Maquoketa, IA, 1958–1960).

2539 Bean, Mildred. COM-HE (KLIX, Twin Falls, ID, 1951).

2540 Bean, Tom. Leader (Tom Bean Fiddle Band, WBAP, Ft. Worth, TX, 1924).

2541 Bean, Wilma. COM-HE (KRXK, Rexbury, ID, 1954).

2542 Beane, Jacqueline. COM-HE (WNES, Central City, KY, 1955).

2543 Beans, Wesley. Baritone (KFSG, Los Angeles, CA, 1925).

2544 Bear, Chet. DJ (*First Call*, WILS, Lansing, MI, 1949).

2545 Bear, Ella. Pianist (WHO, Des Moines, IA, 1926).

2546 Bear Cafe Jazz Orchestra. Popular West Coast band (KFON, Long Beach, CA, 1927–1928).

2547 Beard, Billy. Singer Beard performed with Al Bernard as one of the Raybestos Twins, a popular comedy singing team on *The Raybestos Hour* program (NBC, 1928).

2548 Beard, Charles. Baritone (*Charles Beard*, vcl. mus. prg., WDBJ, Roanoke, VA, 1935).

2549 Beard, Helen. Singer (ABS, 1935).

2550 Beard, Jeanette. Contralto (WEAF, New York, NY, 1925).

2551 Beard, Lance. DJ (*Club 900*, WCOR, Lebanon, TN, 1952).

2552 Beard, Naomi. COM-HE (WTCO, Campbellsville, KY, 1954).

2553 Beard, Pat. DJ (WSTP, Salisbury, NC, 1947; *Rare Old Records Session*, WSTP, 1948; *Strictly From Dixie*, WSTP, 1949–1952).

2554 Beard, Pearl. Pianist (WEAF, New York, NY, 1926).

2555 Beard, Sam H. Newscaster (WOPI, Bristol, TN, 1939; WPTF, Raleigh, NC, 1942). DJ (*The Sam Beard Show*, WPTF, 1948; *Breakfast with Beard*, WPTF, 1949).

2556 Beardsley, Basil. DJ (*Polka Time*, WJER, Dover, OH, 1948). Sportscaster (WPAY, Portsmouth, OH, 1950).

2557 Beardsley, C.L. Announcer (WHBF, Rock Island, IL, 1925–1927).

2558 Beardsley, Harry. Sports announcer (WMAQ, Chicago, IL, 1928).

2559 Beardsley, Harry James. Baritone Beardsley was known as "Cousin Jim" (KHJ, Los Angeles, CA, 1923; KFSG , Los Angeles,

CA, 1925). Beardsley was accompanied by pianist Eugene Lamb.

2560 Beardsley, Leonard "Len." Newscaster (KINY, Juneau, AK, 1941; KXA, Seattle, WA, 1945).

2561 Beardsley, Miltonella. Pianist (WJZ, New York, NY, 1923).

2562 Bearman, Marion Bernstein. Singer (WLAG, Minneapolis, MN, 1924).

2563 Beasley, Bob. DJ (*Yawn Patrol*, WFKY, Frankfort, KY, 1952).

2564 Beasley, Buzz. DJ (*Man on the Beat*, WUST, Bethesda, MD, 1948; KATZ, St. Louis, MO, 1957).

2565 Beasley, Irene. Blues singer (*Irene Beasley*, vcl. mus. prg., NBC, 1934; CBS, 1937). Miss Beasley was often referred to as "The Long Tall Gal from Dixie." She also broadcast programs for children on CBS as "Aunt Zelena." Beasley and Dwight Weist later conducted the *Grand Slam* quiz program sponsored by Wesson Oil. The 15-minute program was broadcast five times weekly (CBS, 1946–1953). *See* ***Aunt Zelena***.

2566 Beasley, Josephine. Pianist (WBAL, Baltimore, MD, 1926).

2567 Beasley, Marlene. COM-HE (WIRO, Ironton, OH, 1956–1957).

2568 Beasley, Ray. DJ (*Western Hits*, KGVL, Greenville, TX, 1954).

2569 Beasley, Suzie Mai. Pianist (WLAC, Nashville, TN, 1927).

2570 ***Beat Our Band.*** Jack Stillwell hosted the show that featured the WLS Rangers, a CW music group, that had gained popularity on the *National Barn Dance*. They attempted to play the songs requested by listeners. If the group couldn't play the song, the listener received a small prize (30 min., Monday through Friday, 1:30–2:00 P.M., WLS, Chicago, IL, 1950).

2571 ***Beat the Band.*** General Mills sponsored the lively music quiz. Announcer Ford Bond opened the program by saying: "General Mills, makers of Kix, invites you to *Beat the-Band*— if you can. General Mills, makers of Kix, that delicious new ready to eat breakfast cereal that comes in delicious sound bubbles brings you another session of that novel radio game, *Beat the Band*, featuring Ted Weems and his music, Perry Como, Marvell Maxwell [later known as Marilyn Maxwell], Elmo Tanner, Orm Downes, Country Washburn and Red Ingle, who join with Garry Moore to bring you this opportunity to *Beat the Band*." In this format the show ran on NBC for a year (NBC, 1940–1941). Two years later it returned sponsored by Raleigh cigarettes and hosted by vocalist Hildegarde (Hildegarde Loretta Sell). Music was provided by the Harry Sosnik orchestra (NBC, 1943–1944).

2572 ***Beatrice Fairfax.*** Marie Manning, as Beatrice Fairfax, dispensed advice to lovelorn listeners on the program sponsored by the Gold Dust Corporation (15 min., Thursday, 2:45–3:00 P.M., MBS, 1937). On an earlier 1934 version of the *Beatrice Fairfax* program, Warren Hull and Billy Blankenship appeared in dramatized episodes about the personal problems submitted by listeners to Miss Fairfax (30 min., Saturday, 9:30–10:00 P.M., NBC, 1934). The typical letters to Miss Fairfax were in this vein: "I love him. How can I win him?"

2573 Beatte, William "Bill." DJ (*Tempo Time*, WGL, Fort Wayne, IN, 1948; *Million Dollar Ballroom*, WBIW, Bedford, IN, 1949).

2574 Beattie, Dorothy. Soprano (WHT, Chicago, IL, 1928).

2575 Beatty, Bessie [Beattie, Betty]. COM-HE (*Bessie Beatty Women's Hour*, WOR, Newark, NJ, 1941). For a short time in 1940 Beatty played the role of Martha Deane at WOR, after the departure of Mary Margaret McBride. When McBride left the Deane role, she personally selected Beatty to replace her. *See* **McBride, Mary Margaret** *and* ***Martha Deane***.

2576 Beatty, Ed. DJ (*Tim and Ed*, WNMP, Evanston, IL, 1949).

2577 Beatty III, George. DJ (KWBY, Colorado Springs, CO, 1957).

2578 Beatty, Harlan. Newscaster (KBRL, McCook, NE, 1949).

2579 Beatty, Harold. Newscaster (WBML, Macon, GA, 1945).

2580 Beatty, Jim. DJ (*Night Shift*, WBRY, Waterbury, CT, 1948–1949).

2581 Beatty, Louise. Violinist (WJAZ, Chicago, IL, 1923).

2582 Beatty, Morgan. Newscaster (WRC, Washington, DC and WMAL, Washington, DC, 1941; *Military Analysis of the News*, NBC-Blue and WRC, 1942; WRC, 1944–1945; NBC and WRC, 1945–1948; *News of the World*, NBC, 1949). Conservative news analyst Beatty joined the Associated Press after he left NBC in 1967.

2583 Beatty, Ross. DJ (*Coffee and Crumpets Club*, WELM, Elmira, NY, 1947). Sportscaster (*Sports Parade* and *Sports Pages of the Air*, WELM, 1947–1949; *Sports with Beatty*, WELM, 1950–1952).

2584 ***Beau Bachelor.*** Don Ameche played the title role of Beau, a handsome bachelor who encountered adventures in various night club locales in North America, Europe and South America (30 min., Friday, 10:00–10:30 P.M., CBS, 1932–1935).

2585 Beauchamp, Charles. Tenor (KFWB, Hollywood, CA, 1925).

2586 Beauchamps, Dennis. DJ (WMAM, Marinette, WI, 1960).

2587 Beaudette, Carlton. Newscaster (WLW, Cincinnati, OH, 1942). DJ (*1490 Club*, WLCX, LaCrosse, WI, 1947).

2588 Beaumont, Joe. DJ (*Hep Parade*, WJAT, Swainsboro, GA, 1948–1952; WBHB, Fitzgerald, GA, 1953; WWGS, Tifton, GA, 1955).

2589 Beaumont, Perry. DJ (*Musical Clock*, WLOK, Lima, OH, 1949–1951; *Music Shop*, WLOK, 1952).

2590 Beaumont [Texas] Band of the Magnolia Petroleum Company. Dr. Harry Cloud directed the company band (WFAA, Dallas, TX, 1925).

2591 Beaupre, Bob. Newscaster (*Local News*, WJOY, Burlington, VT, 1949).

2592 Beaupre, Walter. Newscaster (WCOU, Lewiston, ME, 1946). DJ (*Music For Folks Who Get Lonesome*, WCOU, 1948).

2593 Beauregard, (Mme.) Yvonne. Pianist (WBZ, Boston-Springfield, MA, 1925).

2594 ***Beauty and Personality.*** Elsie Pierce conducted the program whose major topic was "charm" (WRC, Washington, DC, 1925).

2595 ***Beauty and the Beast.*** The variety show featured stage actress Mimi Shelton as the "Beauty" and vaudeville comedian Harry Tighe as "the Beast" (WLWL, New York, NY, 1932).

2596 ***Beauty Box Theater.*** Baritone John Barclay, a chorus and guest stars entertained with the musical backing of Al Goodman conducting the program's orchestra and chorus. Colgate-Palmolive Company sponsored the show (60 min., Friday, 8:00–9:00 P.M., NBC, 1935).

2597 ***Beauty Hints.*** M. Pearl Newman talked about beauty and facial care (KFI, Los Angeles, CA, 1927).

2598 ***Beauty on a Budget.*** Jeanne Brady wrote and Margaret Seitz delivered weekday beauty talks for women (5 min., Monday through Friday, WGR, Buffalo, NY, 1939).

2599 ***Beauty Parade.*** Victor Arden conducted the orchestra and soprano Connie Gates and baritone Richard Norton sang on the program that combined music with dramatic segments (CBS, 1935).

2600 ***Beauty Talk.*** Georgia O. George conducted the informative program on various beauty topics (KFON, Long Beach, CA, 1927).

2601 Beaux Arts Orchestra. Popular New York band (WJZ, New York, NY, 1925).

2602 Beaver, Horace. Announcer (WMSG, New York City, NY, 1925).

2603 Beaver, Win. DJ (WRAG, Carrollton, AL, 1956).

2604 Beaver, Winifred. Pianist (WBZ, Springfield, MA, 1926).

2605 Beaver Falls High School Girls Quartet. School singing group (WCAE, Pittsburgh, PA,1927).

2606 Beavers, Wallace. Newscaster (WCOL, Columbus, OH, 1940).

2607 Beban, Walter. Leader Walter Beban and his "Talking Saxophone" fronted his own 14-piece orchestra that performed on various stations in the late 1920s. Musician and playwright Beban was an important contributor to the *Associated Spotlight* program. *See* ***The Associated Spotlight***.

2608 Bechtel, Ethel. COM-HE (WACB, Kittanning, PA, 1956).

2609 Bechtel, Harold Dwight ("Uncle Harry"). Short, 5' 5½" tall, and jovial, Uncle Harry was a popular comedian on San Francisco radio (1929).

2610 Bechtel, Jay. Sportscaster (WTBO, Cumberland, MD, 1946–1948; WHOL, Allentown, PA, 1950).

2611 Beck, Al. DJ (*Stamps for Shoppers*, KXOL, Fort Worth, TX, 1948; *Melody Matinee*, WKBZ, Muskegon, MI, 1949).

2612 Beck, Albin. Newscaster (WKBZ, Muskegon, MI, 1941).

2613 Beck, Alma. Contralto (WLWL, New York, NY, 1928).

2614 Beck, Anna Buxton. Reader and story teller (WFAA, Dallas, TX, 1928).

2615 Beck, C.C. DJ (*On the Record*, WLDY, Ladysmith, WI, 1948).

2616 Beck, Carlton. Newscaster (KOMA, Oklahoma City, OK, 1941). DJ (*Around the Town*, WKBW, Buffalo, NY, 1948).

2617 Beck, Cecil. DJ (WEIR, Weirton, WV, 1960).

2618 Beck, Claudia. COM-HE (KFSA, Fort Smith, AR, 1957).

2619 Beck, Don. DJ (*At the Inn*, KAVR, Apple Valley, CA, 1954).

2620 Beck, Fred. Organist (*Fred Beck*, instr. mus. prg., WJJD, Chicago, IL, 1936).

2621 Beck, Fred. DJ (KABC, Hollywood, CA, 1955–1956).

2622 Beck, George. Announcer (WTAR Norfolk, VA, 1925).

2623 Beck, Jack. Newscaster (CBS, 1949).

2624 Beck, Jackson. Versatile announcer-narrator-actor Beck appeared on the *Brownstone Theater* (actor), *Casey Crime Photographer* (actor), *Cisco Kid* (actor-title role), *Dimension X* (actor), *FBI in Peace and War* (actor), *Hop Harrigan* (actor), *Joe and Ethel Turp* (actor), *Man Behind the Gun* (narrator), *Mark Trail* (announcer), *Milton Berle Show* (actor), *Myrt and Marge* (actor), *My Son and I* (actor), *Mysterious Traveler*, *Philo Vance* (actor-title role), *Quick as a Flash* (actor), *Superman* (actor), *The Timid Soul* (actor) and *Woman of America*.

2625 Beck, Martha Bond. Mezzo-soprano (WOC, Davenport, IA, 1928).

2626 Beck, Otto. Organist (WRC, Washington, DC, 1925–1926).

2627 Beck, Richard. Organist (*Richard Beck*, instr. mus. prg., WIP, Philadelphia, PA, 1935).

2628 Beck, Spook. DJ (WTVN, Columbus, OH, 1956).

2629 Beckel, L. Carroll. Pianist (WJZ, New York, NY, 1923).

2630 Becker, A.W. Steel guitarist (KDKA, Pittsburgh, PA, 1924).

2631 Becker, Al. Announcer (WOWO, Fort Wayne, IN, 1925).

2632 Becker, Al. Newscaster (WORD, Spartanburg, SC, 1946).

2633 Becker, Alice Rose. COM-HE (KMHT, Marshall, TX, 1951).

2634 Becker, Alvina. Soprano (WQJ, Chicago, IL, 1924–1925).

2635 Becker, Barbara. Actress Becker was in the cast of *The Road of Life* daytime serial.

2636 Becker, Bill. DJ (*Record Review*, WINZ, Hollywood, FL, 1949). Sportscaster (WPFC, Panama City, FL, 1955).

2637 Becker, Bruce. Leader (*Bruce Becker Orchestra*, instr. mus. prg., NBC, 1942).

2638 Becker, Don. Musician, script writer producer and director Becker was born May 28, 1907. He made his first radio appearance as a ukulele player, after he had worked as a "Boy Wonder" performer in night clubs and vaudeville (WLW, Cincinnati, OH, 1926). He became assistant general manager, announcer, sound engineer, writer and publicity man at WLW four years later. In addition, he taught radio ukulele lessons on the station in 1928–1929.

Becker in the years that followed wrote more than 2,000 radio scripts. While writing scripts at WSAI (Cincinnati, OH) before returning to WLW, he created such fictitious sponsors on his programs as "The Dolly Dimple Steam Roller Corporation of Podunk," makers of the Flatenmflat 8, whose motto was "A steam roller in every home."

Among Becker's many network programs were: *Beyond these Valleys* (writer), *Life Can be Beautiful* (producer-director), *Life of Mary Sothern* (writer), *Light of the World* (creator-writer), *The Man I Married* (writer), *Parker Family* (creator-producer), *This Day is Our's* (writer) and *We Love and Learn* (producer-writer).

2639 Becker, Emma. Soprano (*Emma Becker*, vcl. mus. prg., KSD, St. Louis, MO, 1937).

2640 Becker, Fred. Newscaster (KARM, Fresno, CA, 1939).

2641 Becker, George. DJ (*Evening Heatwave*, WEDC, Chicago, IL, 1948).

2642 Becker, Gertrude. Mezzo-soprano (WBNX, Bronx, NY, 1956).

2643 Becker, H.J. Bass (KMA, Shenandoah, IA, 1928).

2644 Becker, Harry. Newscaster (KWBW, Hutchinson, KS, 1948).

2645 Becker, Harry L. Newscaster (KVSF, Santa Fe, NM, 1946). DJ (*Morning Theater*, KIMO, Independence, MO, 1948–1954; *This is Becker*, KIMO, 1948).

2646 Becker, Helen Margaret. COM-HE (KIMO, Independence, MO, 1954.

2647 Becker, Howard. Leader (*Howard Becker Orchestra*, instr. mus. prg., KVOD, Denver, CO, 1939).

2648 Becker, Jack. DJ (*Jack and Jill*, WHIO, Dayton, OH, 1949).

2649 Becker, Jeanne. COM-HE (KRSL, Russell, KA, 1958–1960).

2650 Becker, Johnnie "Johnny." COM-HE (KIUP, Durango, CO, 1954–1960).

2651 Becker, Marie. Pianist (WGBB, Freeport, NY, 1928).

2652 Becker, Marie and Francis Volich. Piano duo (KFWM, Oakland, CA, 1927).

2653 Becker, Ned. Comedian (WOK, Chicago, IL, 1925).

2654 Becker, O.E. Announcer (1925).

2655 Becker, Otto. Announcer (WGR, Buffalo, NY, 1924–1925).

2656 Becker, Sandy. Announcer-actor Becker announced such programs as *Backstage Wife* and *The Shadow*. In addition, he played the title role in *Young Dr. Malone*.

2657 Beckers, Norb. DJ (*Open House Party*, WDSG, Dyersburg, TN, 1947).

2658 Beckett, Hal. Organist (*Hal Beckett*, instr. mus. prg., WOR, Newark, NJ, 1935).

2659 Beckett, Ralph. DJ (*Juke Box Review*, KWIN, Ashland, OH, 1948).

2660 Beckloff, Dorothea. "Soft crooning contralto" Beckloff performed on the *Major Bowes Capitol Theater Family* program (NBC, 1929).

2661 Beckman [Beckmann], Anna. Soprano (WIP, Philadelphia, PA, 1926–1927; KFVE, St. Louis, MO, 1927).

2662 Beckman, Fred. DJ (WTVN, Columbus, OH, 1960).

2663 Beckman, Harvey. Tenor (WWJ, Detroit, MI, 1928).

2664 Beckman, Joan. COM-HE (WWCA, Gary, IN, 1951).

2665 Beckman, Meredith C. Tenor (KMOX, St. Louis, MO, 1928).

2666 Beckner, Ray. Newscaster (KIUP, Durango, CO, 1941, 1946). Sportscaster (*Sports Roundup*, KRLN, Canon City, CO, 1947).

2667 Becktel, Earl. DJ (WSNJ, Bridgeton, NJ, 1947; *1240 Night Club*, WSNJ, 1948–1949).

2668 Beckwith, Kathleen. COM-HE (WLSV, Wellsville, NY, 1956).

2669 Beckwith, Sam. DJ (*$1,000,000 Ballroom*, KEEN, San Jose, CA, 1952–1954).

2670 Beddoes, Don. Actor Beddoes appeared on the *John's Other Wife* daytime serial program.

2671 Beddome, Bob. Baritone (KFWI, San Francisco, CA, 1926).

2672 Bedell, A. Douglas. Newscaster (WCAP, Asbury Park, NJ, 1939). Sportscaster (WCAP, 1940–1942).

2673 Bedell, A.W. News commentator Bedell on his *Timely Topics* program focused chiefly on news and events in Asbury Park (15 min., Weekly, WCAP, Asbury Park, NJ, 1938).

2674 Bedell, Diane. COM-HE (WRAL, Raleigh, NC,1958).

2675 Bedell, Robert. Organist (*Robert Bedell*, instr. mus. prg., NBC-Blue, 1934).

2676 Bedford, Paul. DJ (WFMJ, Youngstown, OH, 1947).

2677 Bedford, Rachel. Reader (WNAD, Norman, OK, 1926).

2678 Bedford Municipal Band. City band directed by W.W. Mitchell (KFNF, Shenandoah, IA, 1925).

2679 Bedlam, Eloise. Pianist (KYW, Chicago, IL, 1923).

2680 *Bedtime Stories.* Miss Mary Carter told stories for children on the early evening program (WFAA, Dallas, TX, 1925).

2681 *Bedtime Stories.* Miss Peggy Cooper conducted a program for children presented by WFAA (Dallas, TX, 1925).

2682 *Bedtime Stories.* Walter Wilson broadcast bedtime stories for young Chicago listeners (KYW, Chicago, IL, 1925).

2683 *Bedtime Stories and Fairy Tales.* Miss Mary C. Toomey conducted the early evening children's program (WFAA, Dallas, TX, 1923).

2684 "Bee Bee." A tropical thrush who warbled for the microphone, "Bee Bee" was accompanied by his master, George B. Ashton (WCCO, Minneapolis–St. Paul, MN, 1926 and WMCA, New York, NY, 1926).

2685 Beebe, Chester. Organist (WOR, Newark, NJ, 1926).

2686 Beebe, Florence. Pianist (WTAM, Cleveland, OH, 1926).

2687 Beebe, Jon. Newscaster (KCOK, Tulare, CA, 1948).

2688 Beebe, Wallace. Newscaster (KIT, Yakima, WA, 1938).

2689 Beebout, George. Newscaster (WHKC, Columbus, OH, 1940–1941).

2690 Beech, Harold. Xylophonist (WLS, Chicago, IL, 1926).

2691 Beecham, (Sir) Thomas. DJ (WQXR, New York, NY, 1948). The distinguished British orchestra conductor also served as a "good music DJ" on New York radio.

2692 Beecham, Wallace "Wally." Newscaster (WAPI, Birmingham, AL, 1945). DJ (*Anything Goes*, WBRC, Birmingham, AL, 1947; *Alarm Clock Club*, WHOS, Decatur, AL, 1948).

2693 Beecher, Don. DJ (*Music Unlimited*, WJPS, Evansville, IN, 1948; *Start with a Whistle*, WEOA, Evansville, IN, 1952; WKLO, Louisville, KY, 1955; WIL, St. Louis, MO, 1956).

2694 Beecher, Gene. Leader (*Gene Beecher Orchestra*, instr. mus. prg., NBC, 1935–1936; KVOO, Tulsa, OK, 1940).

2695 Beecher, Janet. Actress Beecher was in the cast of the *Dear John* daytime serial program.

2696 Beecher, Ralph. Leader (*Ralph Beecher Orchesrtra*, instr. mus. prg., CBS, 1935).

2697 Beechinor, Bob. DJ (*Campus Serenade*, KEEN, San Jose, CA, 1947).

2698 *(The) Beechnut Hour.* Beechnut Chewing Gum sponsored comedian Phil Baker on the variety show (30 min., Weekly, 1932). *See **The Phil Baker Show**.*

2699 Beeley, Helen. COM-HE (WORD, Spartanburg, SC, 1954–1955).

2700 Beem, Art. DJ (*Hillbilly Hit Parade*, KLRA, Little Rock, AR, 1957).

2701 Beem, George. Marimba soloist (WCBD, Zion, IL, 1926).

2702 Beeman, Cora. COM-HE (*Diet for a Nervous Person*, WQJ, Chicago, IL, 1924).

2703 Beemer, Brace. Later famous for playing the role of the Lone Ranger, Beemer began his career as an actor and announcer on an Indianapolis, Indiana, radio station in 1922. *See **The Lone Ranger**.*

2704 Been [Beem], Beatrice. Reader (WCBD, Zion, IL, 1925–1926). Soprano (WCBD, 1926).

2705 Beers, Betty. DJ (WEAB, Greer, SC, 1955). COM-HE (WEAB, 1956).

2706 Beers, Bobby. DJ (*Bobby's Bandstand*, KOA, Denver, CO, 1952).

2707 Beers [Boers], Hazel. Soprano (WBZ, Springfield, MA, 1924).

2708 *Bee's Prairie Crooners.* CW mus. prg. (WMMN, Fairmont, WV, 1938).

2709 Beethoven Trio. The Beethoven Trio included Maurice Greenberg, violinist; Samuel Aldaman, violinist; and Dorothy Marino, pianist (WBZ, Boston-Springfield, MA, 1924).

2710 Begg, Jeanie. Actress Begg appeared on the *Moonshine and Honeysuckle* dramatic program.

2711 *Beggar's Bowl.* Basil Ruysdael wrote and narrated the dramatic program about a British Secret Service man in India, who plied his trade while disguised as a beggar. George Shackley provided oriental background music (30 min., Thursday, 10:30–11:00 P.M., WOR, Newark, NJ, 1932).

2712 Beggs, Hugh. Pianist (WHO, Des Moines, IA, 1925).

2713 Beghold, Kenneth "Ken." Newscaster (WBAX, Wilkes-Barre, PA, 1939–1940). DJ (*Early Bird*, WGBI, Scranton, PA, 1948–1949).

2714 Begich, Celia. COM-HE (WEVE, Eveleth, MN, 1951).

2715 Begley, Ed. Later a theater and motion picture star, radio actor Begley appeared on such diverse programs as: *The Allen Young Show, Aldrich Family, Big Sister, Charlie Chan* (title role), *Ethel and Albert, The Fat Man, Joyce Jordan, Girl Interne, Life Can Be Beautiful, Myrt and Marge, Mysterious Traveler, Official Detective, Richard Diamond, Private Detective* and *Stella Dallas.*

2716 Begon, Jack. Newscaster (NBC, 1946).

2717 Begue, John. DJ (*John Begue Show*, WTAX, Springfield, IL, 1948; *Be Gay*, WTAX, 1949).

2718 Behan, Dennis. Sportscaster (*The World of Sports*, KLMR, Lamar, CO, 1953).

2719 Behan, John. Tenor (*John Behan*, vcl. mus. prg., WHO, Des Moines, IA, 1935).

2720 Behike, Helen Jane. Vocalist (*Helen Jane Behike*, cvl. mus. prg., NBC, 1936–1937). She was accompanied by the Harry Kogan orchestra.

2721 *Behind Prison Bars.* Sloane's Liniment, manufactured by the William R. Warner Company, sponsored the dramatic program about prison life. *Variety* said this was an improvement over Warden Lewis E. Lawes' former prison show — *Twenty Thousand Years in Sing Sing*— because its budget was enlarged. After the dramatic portion of the program was completed, Warden Lawes answered questions about crime and prison life that were asked by the audience (30 min., Monday, 10:00–10:30 P.M., NBC-Blue, 1938). Later in 1946–1947, a similar program — *The Crime Cases of Warden Lawes*— was broadcast by MBS.

2722 *Behind the Mike.* Pioneer radio announcer Graham McNamee hosted the program that took listeners behind the scenes of radio. Even McNamee could not keep a potentially interesting concept from becoming lack luster. For example, the May 18, 1941, program superficially treated sound effects; radio columnist Al Simon provided a few funny broadcasting stories focusing on fluffs; McNamee and announcer Gilbert Martin conducted a question-and-answer session based on listener letters; and Alma Kitchell told a human interest story about a potential juvenile delinquent, whose life was "changed" when he became interested in listening to radio. The program ended with Sylvia Foos singing a song. Mort Lewis wrote the program. Ernie Watson composed and conducted the original music for the program (30 min., NBC-Blue, 1941).

2723 Behlke, Helen Jane. Vocalist (*Helen Jane Behlke*, vcl. mus. prg., NBC, 1936).

2724 Behm, Bernice. Soprano (KMA, Shenandoah, IA, 1928).

2725 Behmiller, Helen. Actress Bemiller appeared on the *Mary Marlin* aka *The Story of Mary Marlin* daytime serial.

2726 Behner, Dick. Newscaster (KCLO, Leavenworth, KS, 1948–1949).

2727 Behrend, Florence. Soprano (WEBH, Chicago, IL, 1925).

2728 Behrends, Earle D. Conductor, violinist and tenor (WFAA Little Symphony Orchestra, WFAA, Dallas, TX, 1925–1926).

2729 Behrendt, (Mme.) Lydia Hoffman. Classical pianist (*Mme. Lydia Hoffman Behrendt*, instr. mus. prg., CBS, 1936)

2730 Behrens, Frank. Actor Behrens appeared on *Arnold Grimm's Daughter, The Guiding Light, Joyce Jordan, Girl Interne, Lorenzo Jones, The Right to Happiness, The Road of Life* and *Woman in White.*

2731 Behrens, Marvin. Newscaster (WBZ-WBZA, Boston, MA, 1944–1948).

2732 Behrer, Mary Shaw. Soprano (KDKA, Pittsburgh, PA, 1924).

2733 Behrman, Ethel Knapp. Conducted a children's program (*The Story Lady*, WSAI, Cincinnati, OH, 1925).

2734 Behrman, W.W. Newscaster (WBOW, Terre Haute, IN, 1938).

2735 Beichl, Bruce. Newscaster (WFHR, Wisconsin Rapids, WI, 1946).

2736 Beighley, Sidney. Newscaster (WJAX, Jacksonville, FL, 1941).

2737 Beinert, Ted. DJ (*Sophisticated Swingtime*, WIBV, Belleville, IL, 1948; WDZ, Decatur, IL, 1952).

2738 Beiper, Harry. Leader (Harry Beiper's Movieland Dance Orchestra, KFI, Los Angeles, CA, 1926).

2739 Beitermeister, Fritz. Baritone (WHAZ, Troy, NY, 1923).

2740 Beitz, (Mrs. Blanche. COM-HE (KIE, Palo Alto, CA, 1951).

2741 Bekas, Tony. DJ (*Shellac Stack*, WKAP, Allentown, PA, 1954; WNAR, Norristown, PA, 1955–1957). Sportscaster (WKAP, 1952).

2742 Bel Canto Quartet. This male quartet was featured on a weekly program (WFAA, Dallas, TX, 1928). *See* **Folger Male Quartet**.

2743 Belancio, Gloria. COM-HE (WSJV, Elkhart, IN, 1954).

2744 Belaney, Bill. DJ (*Home Songs*, WCOL, Columbus, OH, 1947; *Rise and Shine*, WCOL, 1949).

2745 Belanger, Go Go. Blues singer (KFI, Los Angeles, CA, 1926).

2746 Belanger, Phyllis. COM-HE (WFST, Caribou, ME, 1960).

2747 Belasco, Leon. Leader (*Leon Belasco Orchestra*, instr. mus. pr., WAAB, Boston, MA, 1932; NBC, 1936; WCCO, Minneappolis–St. Paul, MN, 1937).

2748 **Belbesheimer, Evelyn.** Pianist (KFRC, San Francisco, CA, 1926).

2749 **Belcher, Rod.** Sportscaster (KGVO, Missoula, MO, 1942; *Echoes from the Grandstand*, KMO, Tacoma, WA, 1947–1949; KOL, Seattle, WA, 1952–1955; KING, Seattle, WA, 1960). DJ (*The Jazz Show*, KMO, 1947).

2750 **Belden, Virginia.** COM-HE (KCKY, Coolidge, AZ, 1954).

2751 **Belding, Lee.** DJ (*You Name It*, KXLO, Lewiston, ME, 1948).

2752 **Belding, (Mrs.) Violet.** Contralto (KTHS, Hot Springs National Park, AR, 1928).

2753 **Belgrad, Madeline.** Actress Belgrad was featured on the *Second Husband* daytime serial.

2754 **Belham, William.** Reader (WHAG, New York, New York, 1925).

2755 ***Believe It or Not.*** Robert L. "Believe It or Not" Ripley presented dramatizations and told stories about the oddities and strange facts he discovered. The program was broadcast on a sustaining basis (15 min., Monday through Friday, 1:45–1:00 P.M., NBC, 1947). Ripley for many years was famous for his syndicated newspaper "Believe It or Not" cartoon feature. After replacing Joe Penner on *The Baker's Broadcast*, he became a nationally known personality who frequently appeared on radio as a purveyor of oddities and strange events. Ripley's programs included dramatic vignettes and the individuals involved in the oddities. Ripley made the transition to television with *Believe It or Not* on March 1, 1949. After his death in 1950, radio veteran Robert St. John succeeded his as host on the television show.

Ripley always sought notable "broadcast firsts." It is claimed that in 1940 he presented the Duke of Windsor on his first American broadcast. Edward, the Duke of Windsor, incidentally, figured in another significant event in American radio history. His broadcast as Edward VIII abdicating the British crown was broadcast December 10, 1936, and heard in the United States via short wave. On one of radio's most dramatic moments, he said that he was unable to carry the burden of the crown without the "love of the woman ... [he] loved."

A popular figure during his younger years, Prince Edward became King when his father died in January 1936. Edward had caused some eyebrows to be raised previously by his playboy reputation and independence, but it was his romance with Wallis Warfield Simpson, a married American, who had previously been divorced, that caused the crisis that led to his abdication.

When Mrs. Simpson instituted divorce proceedings and word spread that the King planned to marry her and make her queen, the crisis resulted that led to his dramatically memorable broadcast. Americans listened enthralled as the British King renounced his throne. All of this, of course, made Ripley's broadcast of the Duke significant. *See* ***The Baker's Broadcast*** *and* ***The Joe Penner Show***.

2756 **Belka, Blanche.** Mezzo-soprano (WLS, Chicago, IL, 1925).

2757 **Belkin, Beatrice.** Soprano Belkin sang on the *Roxy's Gang* program (NBC, 1927; WEAF, New York, NY, 1929).

2758 **Belknap, Al.** DJ (*Sunrise Serenade*, WESX, Salem, MA, 1947).

2759 **Belknap, Patricia.** COM-HE (WSIG, Mt. Jackson, VA, 1958).

2760 **Bell, Andy.** Newscaster (KAND, Corsicana, TX, 1946). Sportscaster (KAND, 1946).

2761 **Bell, Bernice.** Conducted a program on French cooking and a household hints program (WLAG, Minneapolis, MN, 1924).

2762 **Bell, Bill.** Sportscaster (WRAK, Williamsport, PA, 1940; WMRF, Lewistown, PA, 1945).

2763 **Bell, Billy.** DJ (WBHP, Huntsville, AL, 1954).

2764 **Bell, Bob.** DJ (*Club Sterling*, WHOT, South Bend, IN, 1947; *Suppertime Serenade*, WHKY, Hickory, NC, 1948–1949; *Hit the Road*, WSIX, Nashville, TN, 1960).

2765 **Bell, Boots.** DJ (WHOT, Youngstown, OH, 1960).

2766 **Bell, Caroline.** COM-HE (KLWN, Lawrence, KS, 1960).

2767 **Bell, Charlie.** DJ (*In the Groove*, WIS, Columbia, SC, 1947).

2768 **Bell, Corine.** Pianist (KDKA, Pittsburgh, PA, 1924).

2769 **Bell, Dan.** DJ (WJAN, Spartanburg, SC, 1956; WNOK, Columbia, SC, 1957).

2770 **Bell, Deno.** Accordionist (*Deno Bell*, instr. mus. prg., WJAS, Pittsburgh, PA, 1935).

2771 **Bell, Don.** DJ (*Off the Record*, WGH, Newport News, VA, 1947; *Don Bell Matinee*, KRNT, Des Moines, IA, 1948–1949).

2772 **Bell, Dorothy.** Harpist Bell was a member of the Chicago Civic Orchestra and a pupil of Tramonti, the famous harpist of the Chicago Symphony Orchestra (KYW, Chicago, IL, 1923).

2773 **Bell, Gabby.** DJ (*Best by Request*, WTNB, Birmingham, AL, 1948). Sportscaster: WILD, Birmingham, AL, 1952–1955).

2774 **Bell, Geneva Willoughby.** Soprano (KFRC, San Francisco, CA, 1926).

2775 **Bell, George.** Leader (*George Bell Orchestra*, instr. mus. prg., WOR, Newark, NJ, 1935).

2776 **Bell, George.** Sportscaster (*Let's Look 'em Over*, WJRD, Tuscaloosa, AL, 1947; WILD, Birmingham, AL, 1955–1956).

2777 **Bell, Glen.** DJ (KGMC, Englewood, CO, 1954).

2778 **Bell, Hanna.** Pianist (WBZ, Boston-Springfield, MA, 1926).

2779 **Bell, Helena.** COM-HE (WTYC, Rock Hill, SC, 1957).

2780 **Bell, Hillis F.** Sportscaster (KVSO, Ardmore, OK, 1942). Newscaster (KSIL, Silver City, NM, 1946).

2781 **Bell, Howard.** Newscaster (KRKD, Los Angeles, CA, 1941).

2782 **Bell, Jack.** Sportscaster (*Jack Bell's Review*, WIOD, Miami, FL, 1939–1940).

2783 **Bell, John.** DJ (WDOG, Marine City, MI, 1956).

2784 **Bell, Johnny.** Sportscaster (WCMA, Corinth, MS, 1948). DJ (*1230 Club*, WCMA, 1949).

2785 **Bell, Joseph.** Director-actor Bell worked on *Big Town* (director), *Bishop and the Gargoyle (director), Collier Hour (actor), East of Cairo (director), New Penny (actor), Orange Lantern* (director), *Right to Happiness* (actor), *Sherlock Holmes* (director) and *20,000 Years in Sing Sing* (actor).

2786 **Bell, Ken.** Newscaster (WSAY, Rochester, NY, 1945). DJ (*Music 'Til Midnight*, WPDQ, Jacksonville, FL, 1947–1948).

2787 **Bell, Lauren.** Baritone (*Lauren Bell*, vcl. mus. prg., WGY, Schenectady, NY, 1935).

2788 **Bell, Lou.** Pianist (*Lou Bell*, instr. mus. prg., WBZ-WBZA, Boston-Springfield, MA, 1934).

2789 **Bell, Monte.** DJ (*Songs of the Range* and *Homemakers Music*, KADA, Ada, OK, 1949–1954). Sportscaster (KADA, 1951–1954; KTEN, Ada, OK, 1960).

2790 **Bell, Muriel M.** COM-HE (WBOB, Galax, VA, 1956).

2791 **Bell, Nick.** DJ (*Hillbilly Hit Parade*, WGUY, Bangor, ME, 1955).

2792 **Bell, Peggy.** COM-HE (KFYO, Lubeck, TX, 1951–1954).

2793 **Bell, Ralph.** Actor Bell appeared on the *Big Sister, Columbia Presents Corwin, Dick Tracy, Evelyn Winters, FBI in Peace and War, Superstition* and *This is Nora Drake.*

2794 **Bell, Ridley.** Newscaster (WGBA, Columbus, OH, 1949).

2795 **Bell, Shirley.** Actress-singer Bell was born February 21, 1921. She first appeared on WGN (Chicago, IL, 1927). In the 1930s she appeared in several serial dramas and network sustaining productions. Perhaps her most famous role was playing "Annie" on the *Orphan Annie* program.

2796 **Bell, Skip.** DJ (WOKY, Milwaukee, WI, 1960).

2797 **Bell, Stanley.** Stanley Bell was known as the "President's announcer," since he was the one who introduced that dignitary whenever he broadcast to the nation in the late 1920s (WMAL-CBS, Washington, DC, 1927).

2798 **Bell, Steve.** DJ (*Luncheon Club*, WNMP, Evanston, IL, 1960).

2799 **Bell, Ted.** Newscaster (KRSC, Seattle, WA, 1939, 1945). Sportscaster (KRSC, 1939–1951; KAYO, Seattle, WA, 1956).

2800 **Bell, Victor.** Newscaster (KUTA, Salt Lake City, UT, 1938).

2801 **Bell, Wayne.** DJ (*Ding's Merry Go Round* and *Cornbread Jamboree*, WFTM, Maysville, KY, 1949).

2802 **Bell, William Orton.** Tenor (WJZ, New York, NY, 1925).

2803 **(The) Bell Boy.** Announcer Ted Hedeger, who also was known as Fred Herman, was a favorite St. Louis announcer (KWK, St. Louis, MO, 1928).

2804 **Bellah, Milton.** Sportscaster (WDAR, Savannah, GA, 1946). DJ (*The Bandstand*, WDAR, 1947).

2805 **Bellairs, Mal.** DJ (WBBM, Chicago, IL, 1956).

2806 **Bellamy, Aline.** Solo pianist Bellamy was also an accompanist for the Dixie Quartet (WLAC, Nashville, TN, 1928).

2807 Bellamy, (Dr.) J.D. and Grady Fort. The singing team of Bellamy and Fort often broadcast variously as the How Do You Do Boys, the Applesauce Twins and Doc's Red Hot Serenaders (KMA, Shenandoah, IA, 1927).

2808 Bellamy, Joe. DJ (*Country Club*, WPKO, Waverly, OH, 1960).

2809 Belle, Mme. Fashion talks (WHN, New York, NY, 1925).

2810 Belle, Zura E. Director of the Oakland Realtors' Glee Club (KGO, Oakland, CA, 1925).

2811 Belleglade Orchestra. Popular St. Louis radio band (KSD, St. Louis, MO, 1923).

2812 Bellevue-Stratford Hotel Orchestra (aka Bellevue-Stratford Roof Garden Orchestra). Philadelphia hotel band (WFI, Philadelphia, Pa, 1926).

2813 Bellin, Morton. Organist (*Morton Bellin*, instr. mus. prg., WIP, Philadelphia, PA, 1935).

2814 Bellinger, Fred. Saxophonist (WMAK, Buffalo, NY, 1928).

2815 Bellinger, Steve. Sportscaster (WTCJ, Tell City, IN, 1948; *Highlights from the Sidelines*, WTCJ, 1949; *Sports Sidelights*, WVMC, Mt. Carmel, IL, 1951). DJ (*Pop Shop*, WTCJ, 1948–1949).

2816 Belloise, Mike. Newscaster (WMAN, Mansfield, OH, 1945).

2817 Bellows, H.A. Announcer and station manager (WCCO, Minneappolis–St. Paul, MN, 1928).

2818 Belman, Dave. DJ (KNGS, Handford, CA, 1948; KONG, Visalia, CA, 1956). Sportscaster (KNGS, 1955).

2819 Belman, Jerry. DJ (*1350 Club*, WPDR, Portage, WI, 1954).

2820 Belmore, Rita. Singer (WNYC, New York, NY, 1932).

2821 Beloit College Choir. College singing group led by Mrs. Erma H. Miranda (WBBW, Norfolk, VA, 1925).

2822 Belote, Willard. Newscaster (WMJM, Cor, GA, 1946). Sportscaster (WGAF, Valdosta, GA, 1952).

2823 Belshaw, Florence. Pianist (KFAB, Lincoln, NE, 1928).

2824 Belshaw, George. Guitarist and leader (George Belshaw's KFAB, Lincoln, NE, 1926). Belshaw's orchestra was a ten-man group that included Frankie Roberts on clr. and ss., Pete Peterson, ts., George Piper, c.; Frank Silvano, v.; and messers Triego on tb. and Durand bj. and g. Belshaw also directed the Buick Studio Orchestra and the Master Six Orchestra; (KFAB, Lincoln, NE, 1928).

2825 Belson, Gordon. DJ (*Party Line*, KXO, El Centro, CA, 1954).

2826 Beltcher, Florence. Contralto (KFSG, Los Angeles, CA, 1925).

2827 Belton, Norma. COM-HE (WHEY, Millington, TN, 1958).

2828 Beltran, Alma Leonor. COM-HE (KALI, Pasadena, CA, 1954).

2829 Bemis, Elizabeth. Newscaster (WLW-WSAI, Cincinnati, OH, 1941; KNX, Los Angeles, CA, 1942; WLW, 1944; CBS, 1945). Elizabeth Bemis was one of the first newscasters hired by CBS.

Specifically, she was hired as CBS's first West Coast woman news analyst in 1942. Previously she had conducted a regular news program at WLW. Despite her experience, CBS let her go in 1944 with the implication that they couldn't sell a newscast by a woman (Hosley and Yamada, 1947, p. 41). After her CBS employment, Bemis worked for the Office of War Information during the second World War.

2830 Bemis, Katherine Prescott. Singer (KOA, Denver, CO, 1926).

2831 Benac, Henry "Hank." DJ (*Rhapsodies in Rhythm*, WGLN, Glens Falls, NY, 1947). Sportscaster (*Speaking of Sports*, WWSC, Glens Falls, NY, 1948).

2832 Benadaret, Bea. Singer (KGO, Oakland, CA, 1926). Miss Benadaret later enjoyed a long successful career as a comic actress on many comedy shows including *A Day in the Life of Dennis Day*, *The Adventures of Ozzie and Harriet*, *Fibber McGee and Molly*, *The Great Gildersleeve*, *The Jack Benny Show* and *The Mel Blanc Show*. She also appeared on the evening dramatic program — *The Other Woman*.

2833 Benante, Irene. Pianist (WCDA, Brooklyn, NY, 1928).

2834 Benard, R. DJ (WSYB, Rutland, VT, 1960).

2835 Benavie, Samuel. Leader (*Samuel Benavie Orchestra*, instr. mus. prg., WJR, Detroit, MI, 1930s).

2836 Bence, Bob. DJ (*Rise & Shine*, KHJ, Los Angeles, CA, 1948).

2837 Benci, Charles. Leader (*Charles Benci Orchestra*, instr. mus. prg., WIP, Philadelphia, PA, 1935).

2838 Bendall, Sallie. COM-HE (WBTM, Danville, VA, 1956).

2839 Bendel, Fred J. Bendel broadcast sports news weekly on his *Sports News Up To The Minute* program (WOR, Newark, NJ, 1924).

2840 Bendel, Robert. Announcer (WEBH, Chicago, IL, 1925).

2841 Bender, Bill. Singer (*Bill Bender*, vcl. mus. prg., KOA, Denver, CO, 1939).

2842 Bender, Bob. DJ (*Cowboy Rhythm*, KWBU, Corpus Christi, TX, 1947). Sportscaster (*Sports Roundup*, WGY, Schenectady, NY, 1952–1955).

2843 Bender, Carol. COM-HE (WILA, Danville, VA, 1958).

2844 Bender, Charles. Operatic tenor (WMSG, New York, NY, 1926).

2845 Bender, Chief. Sportscaster (*Sports Parade*, WGPC, Albany, GA, 1951).

2846 Bender, Leona. Newscaster (WOAI, San Antonio, TX, 1938–1941).

2847 Bender, Myra. Soprano (WSM, Nashville, TN, 1928).

2848 Bender, Ted. DJ (*Hits & Headlines*, KTSM, El Paso, TX, 1948–1951; *Open Mike*, KTSM, 1952). Sportscaster (*This Week in Sports*, KTSM, 1951).

2849 Bendig, Irving. Actor Bendig appeared in the *Houseboat Hannah* daytime serial program.

2850 Bendix, Millie. COM-HE (WNAE, Warren, PA, 1951).

2851 Benecke, Robert. DJ (*Almanac*, WGBB, Freeport, NY, 1960).

2852 Benedict, Barbara. Newscaster (WBYN, Brooklyn, NY, 1944).

2853 Benedict, Edward. Organist (WGN, Chicago, IL and WJBT, Chicago, IL, 1928).

2854 Benedict, Nita. DJ (*Wishing Well*, KPOA, Honolulu, HI, 1952).

2855 *Benei's Gypsies*. Popular Philadelphia radio band (instr. mus. prg., WIP, Philadelphia, PA, 1936).

2856 Benell, Julie. COM-HE (WFAA, Dallas, TX, 1951). Actress Bennell also appeared on the *Stella Dallas* daytime serial.

2857 Benes, Joseph. Newscaster (WRZO, Kalamazoo, MI, 1944; KCOY, Santa Maria, CA, 1949).

2858 Bengston, Celeste. Pianist-organist (KFLV, Rockford, IL, 1929).

2859 Bengston, Charles. DJ (*Melody Time*, WATR, Waterbury, CT, 1947; *Afternoon Capers*, WATR, 1949).

2860 Benham, Dick. DJ (WBET, Brockton, MA, 1956–1959; *Platter Patter*, WBET, 1960).

2861 Benioff, Millicent. Russian mezzo-soprano (KTAB, Oakland, CA, 1926). In 1926, a broadcast listing of Benioff's appearance on KFWI, San Francisco, CA identified her as a contralto.

2862 Benjamin, Bruce. Tenor (WEAF, New York, NY, 1926).

2863 Benjamin, Charles. DJ (*Matinee Dancetime*, WHK, Cleveland, OH, 1949).

2864 Benjamin, Phyllis. COM-HE (WKAM, Gosden, IN, 1958).

2865 Benjamin Franklin Hotel Concert Orchestra. Philadelphia hotel orchestra (WLIT, Philadelphia, PA and WIP, Philadelphia, PA, 1926).

2866 Benkert, Max. Reader (KPO, San Francisco, CA, 1925).

2867 Benneche, Freda. Coloratura soprano (WOR, Newark, NJ, 1924).

2868 Benner, Hazel. COM-HE (KCLS, Flagstaff, AZ, 1954).

2869 Benner, Lee. Singer (*Lee Benner*, vcl. mus. prg., WORK, York, PA, 1936).

2870 Bennet, Mercedes. Pianist (WRVA, Richmond, VA, 1934).

2871 Bennett, Bing. Newscaster (WAYS, Charlotte, NC, 1946). DJ (*WAYS Ballroom*, WAYS, 1947; *Bing's Merry-Go-Round*, WSKY, Asheville, NC, 1949).

2872 Bennett, Bob. Pianist and celeste soloist Bennett performed piano novelties and celeste specialties (WMBB, Chicago, IL, 1926).

2873 Bennett, Bill. Sportscaster (KODL, The Dalles, OR, 1940).

2874 Bennett, Bill. DJ (*The Bill Bennett Show*, WPTR, Albany, NY, 1952). DJ Bennett was a popular Albany favorite.

2875 Bennett, Don. DJ (*1450 Club*, KSEM, Moses Lake, WA, 1949).

2876 Bennett, Donn. Newscaster (WNBF, Binghampton, NY, 1937–1939).

2877 Bennett, Edward. Newscaster (KEX-KGW, Portland, OR, 1945).

2878 Bennett, Eldean. Sportscaster (*Sports Review*, KCSU, Provo, UT, 1948; KSL, Salt Lake City, UT, 1953–1954). DJ (*Hi-Time*, KCSU, 1949; KSL, Salt Lake City, UT, 1954).

2879 Bennett, (Mrs.) Elmer. COM-HE (WPCO, Mt. Vernon, IN, 1958).

2880 Bennett, Ford. DJ (*AM Party*, WAOV, Vincennes, IN, 1949).

2881 Bennett, Fred. DJ (*Fred Bennett Show*, WPEN, Philadelphia, PA, 1948–1949).

2882 Bennett, Helen. Violinist in the Marylin Trio (KNX, Hollywood, CA, 1929).

2883 Bennett, Iva. COM-HE (WNYC, New York, NY, 1951).

2884 Bennett, Jack. DJ (WHWB, Rutland, VT, 1956; *Night Watch*, WCTW, New Castle, IN, 1960).

2885 Bennett, James. Newscaster (WWSO, Springfield, OH, 1948).

2886 Bennett, Jay. DJ (*Round-Up Ranch*, KGAR, Garden City, KS, 1954; KSYD, Wichita Falls, TX, 1960).

2887 Bennett, Jerry. DJ (KTIM, San Rafael, CA, 1960).

2888 Bennett, Joe. Leader (Joe Bennett's Moonlight Syncopators [orchestra], WMC, Memphis, TN, 1925).

2889 Bennett, Joe. Sportscaster (WBRB, Red Bank, NJ, 1939).

2890 Bennett, John. Sportscaster (KHUB, Watsonville, CA, 1938). Newscaster (KHUB, 1938).

2891 Bennett, John L. DJ (WNNJ, Newton, NJ, 1955–1957).

2892 Bennett, Ken. Newscaster (KPDN, Pampa, TX, 1946). Sportscaster (KPDN, 1946).

2893 Bennett, Lee. Sportscaster (WAGA, Atlanta, GA, 1939–1942).

2894 Bennett, Len. DJ (*Saturday Nite Jamboree*, WNHC, New Haven, CT, 1948).

2895 Bennett, Lois. Soprano Bennett was known as "The Quaker Girl" on the *Armstrong Quakers Program* (WJZ-NBC, New York, NY, 1929). She also appeared on the *Fada Hour* (CBS, New York, NY, 1929). Miss Bennett was both a talented mezzo-soprano and radio actress.

2896 Bennett, M.J. DJ (*MJB*, KSO, Des Moines, IA, 1948).

2897 Bennett, Margaret. DJ (*Tiny Tot Time*, WESC, Greenville, SC, 1954).

2898 Bennett, Maude. Contralto (WJAZ, Cleveland, OH, 1923).

2899 Bennett, Mickey. COM-HE (WWOK, Charlotte, NC, 1955).

2900 Bennett, Myron. Newscaster (KDAL, Duluth, MN, 1939). DJ (*MJB Show*, WIL, St. Louis, MO).

2901 Bennett, Nancy. COM-HE (KTAR, Phoenix, AZ, 1957).

2902 Bennett, Oscar. Baritone (KFAB, Lincoln, NE, 1928).

2903 Bennett, (Mrs.) R.B. Dramatic soprano (WLAC, Nashville, TN, 1927).

2904 Bennett, Ralph. Leader (Ralph Bennett's Seven Aces Orchestra, KOA, Denver, CO, 1929; *Ralph Bennett Orchestra*, instr. mus. prg., NBC, 1935).

2905 Bennett, Ray. DJ (*Records with Ray*, KGA, Spokane, WA, 1948).

2906 Bennett, Teri L. COM-HE (WHWB, Rutland, VT, 1956).

2907 Bennett, Theron. Composer, pianist and leader (Theron Bennett Dance Orchestra, KFI, Los Angeles, CA, 1923–1924; Theron Bennett's Packard Six Orchestra, KFI, Los Angeles, CA, 1925–1926; Theron Bennett's Hollywood Footlifters Orchestra, KFI, 1926).

2908 Bennett, Thurston. Sportscaster (WRDW, Augusta, GA, 1938–1942; *Baseball play-by-play broadcasts*, WBBQ, Augusta, GA, 1947; *Sports Special*, WBBQ, 1948–1950). Newscaster (WRDW, 1939).

2909 Bennett, Zane. DJ (*Alarm Clock Club*, WHJC, Matewan, WV, 1952).

2910 *(The) Bennetts.* A dramatic show created by Carlton E. Morse, the cast included Dean Jagger, William Holden, Nan Grey, Jack Edwards, Tommy Cook and the Opie Cates Orchestra (30 min., Weekly, 1946).

2911 Bennick, Dick. DJ (WSGN, Birmingham, AL, 1956; WTOB, Winston-Salem, NC, 1957).

2912 Bennigson, Ray. DJ (*Saturday Date*, KALI, Pasadena, CA, 1949).

2913 Benning, Bill. Leader (Bill Benning's Milwaukee Athletic Club Orchestra, WHAD, Milwaukee, WI, 1926).

2914 Benning, Joan. COM-HE (WMEG, Eau Gallie, FL, 1956).

2915 Bennitt, Russell. Newscaster (KXOX, Sweetwater, TX, 1939–1942; KGRH, Fayetteville, AR, 1946).

2916 Benny, Julia. Singer (Pianist, WHA, Madison, WI, 1939).

2917 *Benny Fields and Blossom Seeley.* Fields and Seeley, two veteran vaudevillians, were the DJ's on their show. They played records and engaged in nostalgic conversation. The show replaced DJ *Ted Husing* (120 min., Monday through Saturday, 11:00–12:00 noon and 6:00–7:00 P.M., CBS, 1953).

2918 *Benny Ford's Arkansas Travelers.* CW music group (CW mus. prg., WHAS, Louisville, KY, 1935).

2919 *(The) Benny Meroff Review.* Benny Meroff led his band and hosted the program sponsored by Plough, Inc., manufacturers of Penetro Salve, Penetro Nose and Throat Drops and St. Joseph's Aspirin. Various guest performers sang with the Meroff band (15 min., Tuesday, 7:00–7:15 P.M. CST, 1934).

2920 *(The) Benny Rubin Show.* Vaudeville veteran Rubin was the comedian-host on the entertaining variety show that also featured singer Don Ward and the Rex Mauphin Orchestra (25 min., Monday through Friday, 2:00–2:25 P.M., ABC, 1951).

2921 *Benny Rubin's Whirligig Revue.* Comedian Rubin performed his dialect routines and hosted this sustaining comedy revue. *Variety* said that Rubin's comic talent seldom was in evidence on radio (30 min., Wednesday, 8:30–9:00 P.M., NBC-Blue, 1936).

2922 Benoist, Bill. DJ (*Country Music Time*, WBSC, Bennettsville, SC, 1954–1955).

2923 Benoit, J.T. Newscaster (WFEA, Manchester, NH, 1941).

2924 Benoit, Joan. COM-HE (WJAR, Providence, RI, 1941).

2925 Benoit, Virginia. HE-COM (Kitchen Helps and *Virginia Benois Style Talk*, WIND, Gary, IN, 1935; *Fashionette*, WIND, 1935).

2926 Bensen, Albert. Violinist (KVOS, Bellingham, WA, 1928).

2927 Bensen, Edna. Soprano (WEBH, Chicago, IL, 1924; KYW, Chicago, IL, 1925).

2928 Bensen, Frederick. Leader (Frederick Bensen Orchestra, WNYC, New York, NY, 1925).

2929 Benson, Al (Arthur Leaner). Black DJ (*Al Benson Show*, WGES, Chicago, IL, 1930s; WJJD, Chicago, IL, 1948–1956; *Spinning the Shellacs*, WGES, 1960). Benson introduced himself as "Your old friend and swing master." He came onto the Chicago radio scene from Mississippi. Benson respected the street culture he knew so well and the experience of southern immigrants who had come to Chicago. He created an effect that was entirely different from that of the other DJs.

His real name was Arthur Leaner. Before entering radio he conducted church services. Entering broadcasting when a station owner came to him and urged him to do a DJ show, Leaner changed his name to Al Benson, accepted the station owner's offer and began a successful DJ career. Benson became an effective commercial salesman and was a powerful influence in the music industry until he retired from radio in 1963. Along with Jack Leroy Cooper, Benson helped Chicago to become known as the "Black Radio Capital of the World." *See* **Black Radio.**

2930 Benson, Barbara. COM-HE (WJOC, Jamestown, NY, 1957).

2931 Benson, Bob. DJ (*Bob Benson Show*, WBIZ, Eau Claire, WI, 1948–1952; KYW, Philadelphia, PA, 1954).

2932 Benson, Bobo. DJ (*On the Sunny Side*, KYW, Philadelphia, PA, 1947–1948).

2933 Benson, Buzz. DJ (*Top 'o the Morning*, WSIX, Nashville, TN, 1960).

2934 Benson, C. W. Announcer (WIL, St. Louis, MO, 1925).

2935 Benson, Gordon. DJ (*Hits for the Mrs.*, KEEN, San Jose, CA, 1954).

2936 Benson, Hal. DJ (*Around the Town*, WMPS, Memphis, TN, 1949).

2937 Benson, Helen. CW singer (WROK, Rockford, IL, 1939).

2938 Benson, Jerry. DJ (*Western Roundup*, WGAT, Utica, NY, 1948).

2939 Benson, Joe. Pianist (KFRC, San Francisco, CA, 1927).

2940 Benson, Johnny. Leader (*Johnny Benson Orchestra*, instr. mus. prg., WFIL, Philadelphia, PA, 1935).

2941 Benson, Lester Arthur. Benson broadcast the first baseball games and boxing bouts presented by WEB (St. Louis, MO, 1922). Announcer (WIL, St. Louis, MO, 1925).

2942 Benson, Mimi. Singer (*Mimi Benson*, WMEX, Boston, MA, 1939; WMCA, New York City, NY, 1939).

2943 Benson, Ray. Leader (*Ray Benson Orchestra*, instr. mus. prg., WMAQ, Chicago, IL, 1942).

2944 Benson, Red. DJ (WINS, New York, NY, 1947; WPEN, Philadelphia, PA, 1957).

2945 Benson, Reuben. Banjo soloist (WCAL, Northfield, MN, 1925).

2946 Benson, Richard H. "Dick." DJ (*RFD 630*, WIRC, Hickory, NC, 1948; *Wake Up Club*, WIRC, 1949). Sportscaster (*Sports Digest*, WIRC, 1949–1950).

2947 Benson, Robert. DJ (*Gambles' Suppertime Serenade*, KFAM, St. Cloud, MN, 1949).

2948 Benson, Stella. Miss Benson appeared on the *To an Unamed Listener* program with such British celebrities as Max Beerbohm, Evelyn Waugh and George Bernard Shaw on the British Broadcasting Corporation's program broadcast by CBS (1932). Each celebrity discussed whatever topics they wished.

2949 Benson Chicago Orchestra. A popular Chicago recording and radio band (WDAR, Philadelphia, PA, 1924).

2950 Bensonians Orchestra. Popular local dance orchestra (WAHG, Richmond Hill, NY, 1925).

2951 Bent, Marian. Bent, an actress at the Rosalie O'Grady theater company, was interviewed on the *Interview—A.R. Plough* program (WLW, Cincinnati,OH, 1925–1926).

2952 Bentley, Julian. News analyst (WLS, Chicago, IL, 1933). Bentley headed the WLS news department when he came to the station in 1933. His deliberate factual treatment of the news earned him a large enthusiastic audience. Bentley's customary sign-off was, "73 until tomorrow morning." The "73" was the telegrapher's short handed "Best Regards" message. His *Julian Bentley News* program was broadcast in the late morning and late evening (*Julian Bentley*, 15 min., Monday through Friday, 10:45–11:00 A.M., WLS, Chicago, IL, 1935; 15 min., Monday through Friday, 10:45–11:00 P.M., WLS, Chicago, IL, 1935; WLS, Chicago, IL, 1936–1942, 1944–1946; WBBM, Chicago, IL, 1947; CBS, 1949). In 1937, Bentley's busy schedule shows that he broadcast brief daily news reports at 7:00, 8:15, 9:45, 11:55 A.M. and 2:10 P.M.

2953 Bentley, Lyn. DJ (*Lyn's Jukebox*, KVOB, Alexandria, LA, 1949). Sportscaster (KVOB, 1949).

2954 Bentley, Max. Newscaster (KRBC, Abilene, TX, 1937).

2955 Bentley, Ray. DJ (*That's My Favorite*, WROV, Roanoke, VA, 1947).

2956 Bentley, Spencer. Actor Bentley appeared on *Barry Cameron* (title role), *Betty and Bob*, *Hilltop House*, *Jane Arden*, *The Man I Married*, *Our Gal Sunday*, *Romance of Helen Trent* and *Stella Dallas*.

2957 Bentley, Stanley. Organist (KNX, Los Angeles, CA, 1928).

2958 Bentley, Thomas W. Newscaster (WAVZ, New Haven, CT, 1949).

2959 Bentley, (Doctor of Divinity) W.B. Dr. Bentley delivered his sermons on church services broadcast from San Francisco's First Christian Church (KPO, San Francsico, CA, 1923).

2960 Benton, Bill. DJ (WLFA, Lafayette, GA, 1956; WAPX, Montgomery, AL, 1960).

2961 Benton, Fal. Violinist (WOR, Newark, NJ, 1925).

2962 Benton, Fats. DJ (*Ebony Rhapsody*, WMAP, Monroe, NC, 1949).

2963 Benton, Jack. Newscaster (KMBC, Kansas City, MO, 1946–1947).

2964 Benton, Violet C. Soprano (KPSN, Pasadena, CA, 1925).

2965 Bentz, Judy. COM-HE (WADP, Kane, PA, 1956).

2966 Bentz, Morey. DJ (*Off the Record*, WDVX, Waupaca, WI, 1960).

2967 *(The) Bentztown Bard*. Folger McKenzie, a Maryland poet regularly published in Baltimore newspapers, read his own poetry on his popular local program (WBAL, Baltimore, MD, 1934).

2968 Benum, Arnold. DJ (*The Music Room*, KMO, Tacoma, WA, 1947; *Benum's Beanery*, KITO, San Bernardino, CA, 1948).

2969 Beppart, Marguerite. Pianist (WOR, Newark, NJ, 1923).

2970 Berch, Jack. Leader (*Jack Berch Orchestra*, instr. mus. prg., WLW, Cincinnati, OH, 1935; WOR, Newark, NJ, 1936).

2971 Bercovici, B.S. Newscaster (WSAY, Rochester, NY, 1940–1941; MBS-WHN, New York, NY, 1942; KFEL, Denver, CO, 1944–1945).

2972 Bercovitz, Abe. Violinist and concert master (KGW, Portland, OR, 1928).

2973 Berdan, Bird. DJ (*960 Club*, WEAV, Plattsburg, NY, 1948).

2974 Berding, Andre. Newscaster (WEBR, Buffalo, NY, 1941).

2975 Bereford, Arthur B. Announcer (WLCI, Ithaca, NY, 1927).

2976 Berend, David. Banjoist (WEAF, New York, NY, 1925).

2977 Berendt, Mildred. Soprano (WFBH, New York, NY, 1925).

2978 Berens, Cecile M. Pianist (WEAF, New York, NY, 1925).

2979 Berensen's Riverview Band. Midwestern orchestra (WHT, Deerfield, IL, 1925).

2980 Berenson, Jessie. Soprano (WGBS, New York, NY, 1925).

2981 Berentsen. Organist (WHAM, Rochester, NY, 1928).

2982 Berentsen, Marguerite. COM-HE (WDON, Wheaton, MD, 1955; KLRA, Little Rock, AR, 1958).

2983 Berezowski, Nicoli. Orchestra conductor on the *Atwater Kent Orchestra* program (NBC, 1926).

2984 Berg, Allan. DJ (*Turn Table Time*, KSBW, Salinas, CA, 1948; *The Allan Berg Show*, KALI, Pasadena, CA, 1949; KWOW, Pomona, CA, 1956).

2985 Berg, Bill. DJ (WASK, Lafayette, IN, 1960).

2986 Berg, Carl. DJ (KWBB, Wichita, KS, 1956).

2987 Berg, Gertrude. Actress-writer Berg was so closely identified with the Molly Goldberg character she created, her fans and many of her co-workers called her "Molly." Famous for creating *The Goldbergs*, she first wrote its forerunner *The House of Glass* (NBC-Blue, 1929). *The Goldbergs*, broadcast with strong Yiddish dialect influences, told the story of a Bronx Jewish family that lived on East Tremont Avenue in the Bronx, living lives much like those who really lived in that neighborhood. *The Goldbergs* was the first major Jewish comedy on network radio (Dunning, 1976, p. 238). The program was accepted by NBC because network executive Bertha Brainard vigorously argued for its acceptance, insisting that it would not insult Jewish listeners.

The highly successful daytime serial was broadcast on NBC-Blue, MBS and CBS from 1929 to 1945 and from 1949 to 1950. In addition to writing and acting in *The Goldbergs*, the busy Mrs. Berg also wrote the *Kate Hopkins, Angel of Mercy* daytime serial.

2988 Berg, Hal. DJ (*Curfew Club*, KOLN, Lincoln, NE, 1947).

2989 Berg, Hal. DJ (*Club Swingtime*, WILK, Wilkes-Barre, PA, 1947–1948; *Clubtime*, WILK, 1948–1952.

2990 Berg, Hal and Buddy Brode. DJ team (*Club Swing Time*, WILK, Wilkes-Barre, PA, 1948).

2991 Berg, Herb. DJ (WWOK, Charlotte, NC, 1956).

2992 Berg, Johnny. DJ (*Dance Time*, KGDE, Fergus Falls, MN, 1949).

2993 Berg, Lee. Sportscaster (*Speaking of Sports*, KOLN, Lincoln, NE, 1947).

2994 Berg, Marilyn. COM-HE (WEDO, McKeesport, PA, 1951).

2995 Berg, Mildred. Pianist Berg was a pupil of Professor Kruger (KPO, San Francisco, CA, 1923).

2996 Berg, Mildred. COM-HE (KGHI, Little Rock, NY, 1956).

2997 Berg, Si. Ukulele soloist (WOK, Chicago, IL, 1925).

2998 Bergamo, Giulia. Soprano (WEVD, New York, NY, 1936).

2999 Bergen, Candice. Candice, the daughter of Edgar Bergen, appeared as a child with her "brother," Charlie McCarthy, on her father's *Maxwell Hour Coffee Time* aka the *Edgar Bergen-Charlie McCarthy Show*.

3000 Bergen, Catherine. Violinist (WEMC, Berrien Springs, MI, 1925).

3001 Bergen, Edgar and Charlie McCarthy. *See **The Chase and Sanborn Hour***.

3002 Bergen, Jack. Leader (*Jack Bergen Orchestra*, instr. mus. prg., WLW, Cincinnati, OH, 1934).

3003 Bergen, Ron. DJ (*Coffee Pot*, WHOL, Allentown, PA, 1948).

3004 Bergen County Veterans' Band. Veterans' band (WGBS, New York, NY, 1926).

3005 Bergener, Walt. Organist (*Walt Bergener*, instr. mus. prg., WTAM, Rochester, NY, 1942).

3006 Bergeon, Clarke. DJ (*Request Club*, WION, Ionia, MI, 1954–1955).

3007 Berger, C.A. Announcer (KHQ, Spokane, WA, 1928).

3008 Berger, Jack. Leader (*Jack Berger Orchestra*, instr. mus. prg., WOR, Newark, NJ and NBC, 1934).

3009 Bergere, Max. Leader (*Max Bergere Orchestra*, instr. mus. prg., WCBM, Baltimore, MD, 1934).

3010 Bergeron, Eleanor. COM-HE (KREL, Baytown, TX, 1951; KTIB, Thibodaux, LA, 1957).

3011 Bergeron, Jolly. DJ (*Sweet Music Time*, WSLB, Ogdensburg, NY, 1947).

3012 Bergeron, Marie. COM-HE (KTIB, Thibodaux, LA, 1957).

3013 Bergeron, Mary Servino. COM-HE (KTIB, Thibodaux, LA, 1957).

3014 Bergeson, Chuck. DJ (WSOO, Sault Ste. Marie, MI, 1949). Sportscaster (WSOO, 1950; WJBK, Detroit, MI, 1954–1955; WJR, Detroit, MI, 1956).

3015 Berggren, A. Announcer (WMES, Boston, MA, 1925).

3016 Bergie, Bob. DJ (*Melody Matinee*, KWBE, Beatrice, NE, 1952).

3017 Bergin, Freddie. Leader (*Freddie Bergin Orchestra*, instr. mus. prg., Network, 1935).

3018 Bergin, P. COM-HE (WVOS, Liberty, NY, 1951).

3019 Bergman, Alan. DJ (*Midnight in Syracuse*, WNDR, Syracuse, NY, 1948).

3020 Bergman, Arthur "Dutch." Sportscaster (WRC, Washington, DC, 1947–1948; *Bergman on Sports*, WRC, 1949–1950).

3021 Bergman, Professor. A professor from the University of Cincinnati, Bergman delivered a series of geography talks on his *ABC of South America* program (WLW, Cincinnati, OH, 1928–1929).

3022 Bergman, Ruth. Soprano (KSL, Salt Lake City, UT, 1928).

3023 Bergman, Teddy (Alan Reed). Comic actor and announcer Bergman acted on such varied programs as *Abie's Irish Rose*, *Big Sister*, *Eddie Cantor Show*, *Eveready Hour*, *Falstaff Fables*, *Flash Gordon*, *Fred Allen Show* (as Falstaff Openshaw), *Harv and Esther*, *Hilltop House*, *Joe Palooka* (title role), *Life with Luigi*, *Manhattan at Midnight*, *Maxwell House Coffee Time* (as Daddy Higgins opposite Fanny Brice), *Mel Blanc Show*, *Meyer the Buyer*, *My Friend Irma*, *Myrt and Marge*, *Pages of Romance*, *Phillip Morris Playhouse*, *The Shadow*, *The Tim and Irene Show*, *True Detective Mysteries*, *Valiant Lady* and *The Ziegfeld Follies of the Air* (as Daddy Higgins opposite Fanny Brice). He also was an announcer on the *Duffy's Tavern* show. After 1939, he used the name—**Alan Reed.** *Also see* ***The Fred Allen Show*** *and* **Reed, Theodore Alan.**

3024 Bergner, Carl. DJ (*Early Risers*, WLAV, Grand Rapids, MI, 1952; *Early and Late Risers*, WLAV, 1954).

3025 Bergsoll, Hilda. Mezzo-soprano (WGBS, New York, NY, 1926).

3026 Bergstrom, Arthur "Art." Newscaster (WNBC, Hartford-New Britain, CT, 1940). DJ (*The Timekeeper*, WMMW, Meriden, CT, 1948; *Mailman Matinee*, WMMW, 1949).

3027 Bergstrom, John. Baritone (WJAZ, Chicago, IL, 1924).

3028 Berigan, Bunny. Leader (*Bunny Berigan's Blue Boys*, instr. mus. prg., CBS, 1935; *Bunny Berigan's Blue Boys*, instr. mus. prg. CBS, 1935; *Bunny Berigan's Orchestra*, instr. mus. prg., NBC-Blue, New York, NY, 1937).

3029 Beringer, Bob. DJ (*Afternoon Show*, WDUZ, Green Bay, WI, 1960).

3030 Berjstresser, Harriet Brown. Soprano (WEAF, New York, NY, 1924).

3031 Berkes, Billy. Baritone (WHN, New York, NY, 1923).

3032 Berkey, Ralph. Director-writer Berkey worked on such programs as *Aunt Jenny* (director), *Joyce Jordan, Girl Interne* (director) and *Radio Reader's Digest* (writer).

3033 Berkley Carteret Dance Orchestra. Club band (WMCA, New York, NY, 1925).

3034 Berkovits, Clara. Violinist (KPO, San Francisco, CA, 1925).

3035 Berkowitz, Gussie. Pianist (WJAX, Cleveland, OH, 1923).

3036 Berkowitz, Milton "Milt." Newscaster (WHNC, Hartford-New Britain, CT, 1938–1941; 1945; WONS, Hartford, CT, 1949). Sportscaster (WNHC, 1942; WONS, 1949–1950).

3037 Berkowitz, Ralph. "Boy concert pianist" (WNYC, New York, NY, 1925).

3038 Berlin, Ed. Leader (Ed Berlin and his Moonglo Orchestra, WEBJ, New York, 1926).

3039 Berlin, Paul. DJ (*Dinner Date* and *Mission in Music*, KNUZ, Houston, TX, 1948; *Dinner Date*, KNUZ, 1952; *Mission in Music*, KNUZ, 1954; *Dinner Date*, KNUZ, 1955).

3040 Berlitz, V. Harrison. Berlitz taught radio Spanish language lessons (WNYC, New York, NY, 1925).

3041 *Berlitz Weekly French Lessons.* Foreign language program series (WJY, Hoboken, NJ, 1924).

3042 Berliza, Raphael. Newscaster (WNEL, San Juan, PR, 1938).

3043 Berly, Sadie. Cellist (WEAF, New York, NY, 1925).

3044 Bermain, George. DJ (*Chapel in the Sky* and *Musical Roundup*, WKTM, Mayfield, KY, 1947).

3045 Berman, Al. Sportscaster (WEVD, New York, NY, 1951).

3046 Berman, Averill. Newscaster (WLB, Minneapolis, MN, 1940; KWTK, Burbank, CA, 1947).

3047 Berman, Ben. Tenor (KPO, San Francisco, CA, 1925).

3048 Berman, Grace. Pianist (*Grace Berman*, instr. mus. prg., WJR, Detroit, MI, 1935).

3049 Bern, Stanislas [Stanislaus]. Leader (Stanislas Bern's Little Symphony Orch., KFRC, San Francisco, CA,1925–1927; KBO, Oakland, CA, 1927).

3050 Bernard, Al. Blackface comedian and singer Al Bernard was a popular vaudeville performer before beginning his long radio career. He first appeared on radio in 1922 on WEAF (New York, NY). Bernard was a featured soloist on the *Dutch Masters Minstrels* (NBC-Blue, 1928–1930), a program sponsored by Dutch Masters Cigars. He also teamed with Billy Beard as one of the Raybestos Twins, a comedy singing team featured on the *Raybestos Hour* (NBC-Red, 1929–1930); *Al Bernard* (vcl. mus. prg. with Bernard billed as "The Boy from Dixie," NBC, 1934). *See* ***The Dutch Masters Minstrels.***

3051 Bernard, Ben. Singer (WMCA, New York, NY, 1925).

3052 Bernard, Charles. DJ (*Harmony Hall*, KPOJ, Portland, OR, 1954).

3053 Bernard, Dick and Flo. Singing team (WGCP, New York, NY, 1925).

3054 Bernard, Don. Singer Bernard was born August 9, 1903. He first appeared on radio on a program with Mary Garden during the first week Chicago's KYW went on the air. Announcer (WAW, Columbus, OH, 1927). Bernard later worked as a successful producer, director and writer in radio.

3055 Bernard, Dudley. DJ (KLFT, Golden Meadow, LA, 1956).

3056 Bernard, Elizabeth. Soprano (WNAC, Boston, MA, 1923).

3057 Bernard, Fred. DJ (*1240 Club*, WDNE, Elkins, WV, 1954). Sportscaster (WDNE, 1954).

3058 Bernard, Herman. Bernard, the editor of *Radio World*, delivered weekly talks on various radio topics as "Radio Hookups—Questions and Answers" (WGBS, New York, NY, 1925).

3059 Bernard, Jerry. DJ (*Night Flight*, WJQS, Jackson, MS, 1960).

3060 Bernard, Johnny. Sportscaster (WJRL, Decatur, IL, 1939).

3061 Bernard, Leo. Singer (KFWM, Oakland, CA, 1929).

3062 Bernard, Leo. DJ (KCKY, Coolidge, AZ, 1955; KCLF, Falstaff, AZ, 1956)

3063 Bernard, Lucy. Pianist (WOR, Newark, NJ, 1926).

3064 Bernard, Mel. DJ (*Music Shop*, WHSC, Hartsville, SC, 1947). Sportscaster (*The Sportsman*, WHSC, 1947).

3065 Bernard, Paul. DJ (*Musically Yours*, KWAT, Watertown, SD, 1952).

3066 Bernard, Peter. Bagpipe soloist (KLDS, Independence, MO, 1926).

3067 Bernard, Rocky. Singer (KFI, Los Angeles, CA, 1928; KFVD, Culver City, CA, 1929).

3068 Bernard, Wilda. Soprano (KFWB, Hollywood, CA, 1925).

3069 *Bernard Levitow and His Commodore Ensemble.* Music program featuring the Levitow instrumental group (CBS, 1929).

3070 Bernardy, Leroy. DJ (*Four B's*, KLCB, Libby, MT, 1954).

3071 *Bernarr McFadden's Editorial Program.* Magazine editor and physical culturist McFadden used this 15-minute program to expound his theories of health and physical culture (15 min., MBS, 1936).

3072 Berndt, Irving "Bud." Sportscaster

(WRAK, Williamsport, PA, 1939; WRAK, 1955).

3073 Bernero, Louise. Pianist Bernero was a member with Anne Sorkin of a piano duet team (KSD, St. Louis, MO, 1923).

3074 Bernhardt, Bonnie. Pianist (WSB, Atlanta, GA, 1925).

3075 Bernhardt, Elmer. Baritone (WBAL, Baltimore, MD, 1929; *Elmer Bernhardt*, vcl. mus. prg., WBAL, 1934).

3076 Bernhardt, Homer. Tenor (WSAI, Cincinnati, OH, 1925).

3077 Bernhardt, Roy. Flutist (WJAZ, Chicago, IL, 1923).

3078 Bernhardt, Zetta. Contralto (WSAI, Cincinnati, OH, 1925).

3079 "Bernice." Sixteen-year-old pianist "Bernice" was one of the earliest popular stars created by their radio appearances (WCX, Detroit, MI, 1923).

3080 Bernie, Ben (Bernard Anzelevitz or Benjamin Ancellowtiz). Popular New York orchestra leader Bernie's band was busy broadcasting from radio's earliest days (Ben Bernie Orchestra, Monday and Friday evenings from the Mayflower Grill of the Hotel Roosevelt, WGI, New York, New York, 1924; WNYC, New York, NY, 1925; WRNY, New York, NY, 1925–1926; Ben Bernie and his Berkeley Cartaret Orchestra, WOR, Newark, NJ, 1926). Prior to his radio career, Bernie was a vaudeville solo violinist who later teaming up with Phil Baker in a vaudeville act. His first network show was *Ben Bernie and all the Lads*, broadcast by CBS. Bernie led his fine band and hosted this variety show. Weekly guests stars such as Ethel Shutta, Frank Parker, Jackie Heller, Sophie Tucker, Phil Baker, Benny Fields and Blossom Seeley appeared with him. Bernie's trademark was his "Yaw-sah, Yaw-sah" and his "feud" with Walter Winchell (30 min., Weekly, CBS, 1931–1934). Perhaps his best known network show was the *Ben Bernie Pabst Blue Ribbon Show*. One of Bernie's best radio and recording orchestras included: Donald Bryan, t. and Bill Moore, t.; Frank Sarlo, tb.; Len Kavash and Norman Ronemous, as. and clr.; Jack Pettis clr. and as.; Nick Gerlach, v.; Oscar Levant and Al Goering, p.; Paul Nito, bj. and v.; and Sam Fink, d.

3081 Bernie, Dave. Bernie directed the music on the *Ciro Orchestra* program (WOR, Newark, NJ, 1925).

3082 *Bernie Bierman.* Bierman, probably the University of Minnesota's most famous football coach, broadcast a weekly program of football news and commentary (WCCO, Minneappolis–St. Paul, MN, 1936). During the 1940s on his *Bernie Bierman Show*, he was assisted by Halsey Hall. The show included college football songs and music interspersed with football post-mortems. Music was supplied by Bob Link, Hal Garvin, Ernie Garvin, Toby Prin and Dick Link. The show's announcer was Gordon Eaton (WCCO, 1940s and 1950s).

3083 *Bernie Cummings and His Hotel New Yorker Orchestra.* Instr. mus. prg. (60 min., Wednesday, 6:00–7:00 P.M., NBC-Blue, 1930; WGN, Chicago, IL, 1933; CBS, 1936; WLW, Cincinnati, OH, 1937; WBAL, Baltimore, MD, 1938; MBS, 1939; KFOR, Lincoln, NE, 1942).

3084 Bernier, Don. DJ (KMEL, Wenatchee, WA, 1960).

3085 Berns, Bill. Hollywood news reporter (WNEW, New York, NY, 1942).

3086 Bernstein, Florence. Soprano (WCFL, Chicago, IL, 1935).

3087 Bernstein, Jerry. Newscaster (KTHS, Hot Springs, AR, 1939, 1945).

3088 Bernstein, M. Newscaster (WMBC, Detroit, MI, 1938).

3089 Bernstein Sisters Trio. Instrumental trio consisting of piano, bass viol and violin played by Minna, Deborah and Selma Bernstein (WGCP, Newark, NJ and WRNY, New York, NY, 1926).

3090 Berntsen, Kathryn. COM-HE (KMRS, Morris, MN, 1957).

3091 Bernzen, (Mrs.) Ben. Reader (KOA, Denver, CO, 1926).

3092 Beronio, Dave. Sportscaster (*What Do You Know About Sports?*, KVON, Napa, CA, 1953).

3093 Berquist, Dewey. DJ (KVOX, Moorhead, MN, 1949; *Dewey's Follies*, KVOX, 1954, WDAY, Fargo, ND, 1955).

3094 Berrens, Freddie. Leader (*Freddie Berrens Orchestra*, instr. mus. prg., CBS, 1935).

3095 Berres, Ken. DJ (WKAN, Kankakee, IL, 1954–1957; WCGO, Chicago, IL, 1960).

3096 Berresford, A.B. Announcer (WLCI, Ithaca, NY, 1927).

3097 Berrill, Larry. DJ (*Swing Shift*, WCAE, Pittsburgh, PA, 1949). Sportscaster (KBIG, Avalon, CA, 1953–1956).

3098 Berry, Al. DJ (WPLA, Plant City, FL, 1956).

3099 Berry, Bill. DJ (*Whoot'n Antics*, WHOO, Orlando, FL, 1947; *Berry's Bandstand*, WDBO, Orlando, FL, 1948–1957).

3100 Berry, Bill. DJ (KWCO, Chickasha, OK, 1955).

3101 Berry, Bob. DJ (*Wake-Up Baltimore*, WITH, Baltimore, MD, 1947; *Melody Time*, WOTW, Nashua, NH, 1948–1954).

3102 Berry, Bud. Sportscaster (WRC, Washington, DC, 1936).

3103 Berry, Chick. DJ (KFDA, Amarillo, TX, 1960).

3104 Berry, Clara. Singer (WCOH, Yonkers, NY, 1932).

3105 Berry, Diane. COM-HE (WLAD, Danbury, CT, 1951).

3106 Berry, Dick. Newscaster (WEBQ, Harrisburg, IL, 1944). DJ (*Grin and Berry It*, WFIW, Fairfield, IL, 1954–1955).

3107 Berry, Doris. COM-HE (KOLT, Scottsbluff, NE, 1957).

3108 Berry, Doris Irene. Contralto (WJAZ, Chicago, IL, 1926).

3109 Berry, Edith. Soprano (WLS, Chicago, IL, 1925).

3110 Berry, Esther. Pianist (WEBH, Chicago, IL, 1924).

3111 Berry, Fatso. DJ (*Loose Wig*, KSAN, San Francisco, CA, 1949).

3112 Berry, Genevieve. Soprano (WHT, Chicago, IL, 1925).

3113 Berry, Jack. Newscaster (WORL, Boston, MA, 1938). DJ (*Berry-Go-Round*, WIOD, Miami, FL, 1954).

3114 Berry, (Miss) Jean. Vaudeville singer-pianist (KSB, Tacoma, WA, 1923).

3115 Berry, John. Newscaster (WEBQ, Harrisburg, IL, 1946).

3116 Berry, (Miss) Jean. Vaudeville singer-pianist (KSB, Tacoma, WA, 1923).

3117 Berry, Jimmie. At the age of fifteen, Berry had the task each evening of beginning the daily broadcast program of station WGAR by saying: "This is WGAR, the Southwest American station located in Fort Smith, Arkansas, the playground of America. We have just come on the air and we wonder if anyone is listening." Berry would then broadcast the names of various people and ask them if they were listening. If they heard the broadcast, listeners would call the station and report how well they were receiving the broadcast (WGAR, Fort Smith, AR, 1922).

3118 Berry, Lester. Newscaster (KVOV, Redding, CA, 1945).

3119 Berry, Lowell. Leader (Lowell Berry and his Rhythm Boys, KSL, Salt Lake City, UT, 1929).

3120 Berry, Marilou [Mari Lou]. COM-HE (WJPS, Evansville, IN, 1954–1957).

3121 Berry, Norman. Announcer Berry announced the *Dan Harding's Wife* daytime serial program.

3122 Berry, Spike. DJ (*Juke Box Time*, KEYJ, Jamestown, ND, 1955–1956).

3123 Berry, Stan. DJ (*Be Merry with Berry*, WBET, Brockton, MA, 1952).

3124 Berry, Thomas Davis. Newscaster (WGCM, Biloxi-Gulfport, MS, 1945).

3125 Berry, W.K. DJ (*Ballroom Melody Time*, KFFA, Helena, AR, 1949).

3126 Berry, Wilfred. COM-HE (WHHH, Warren, OH, 1958).

3127 Berryhill, Ken. DJ (WDIA, Memphis, TN, 1947; *Old Record Shop*, WNAG, Grenada, MS, 1960).

3128 Berryman, Edward "Ed." DJ (*Majestic Ballroom*, WHOT, South Bend, IN, 1947; *Sagebrush Slim*, WBBC, Flint, MI, 1949). Sportscaster (*Sports Roundup*, WBBC, 1953; WTAC, Flint, MI, 1955).

3129 Berryman, Lew. Sportscaster (*Bowling Bonanza* and *Kegler's Korner*, WGRD, Grand Rapids, MI, 1950).

3130 Bert, (Professor). Bert broadcast a series of French lessons (KFKB, Sacramento, CA, 1927–1929).

3131 *Bert Lahr Show.* Standard Brands sponsored the replacement for the *Chase and Sanborn Hour*. Teddy Bergman, later known as Alan Reed, played straight man to comedian Lahr. "Rasputin the Heckling Child" was on hand to heckle Lahr. Rubinoff's orchestra and the piano team of Lee Sims and Lomay Bailey provided the music (60 min., Sunday, 8:00–9:00 P.M., NBC-Red, 1933). When the format of the program was changed later in the year, the music was supplied by the George Olsen

Orchestra (30 min., Wednesday, 8:00–8:30 P.M., NBC-Red, 1933).

3132 ***Bert Lane Fiddlers.*** CW mus. prg. (WIND, Gary, IN, 1937).

3133 **Berthoff, Stella.** Berthoff held an executive position in the Artists Bureau Staff at WOR (New York NY, 1940s).

3134 **Bertram, Erna.** COM-HE (WQJ, Chicago, IL, 1924). Bertram talked on such topics as "Sixty Ways of Serving Ham."

3135 **Bertrand, Bob.** DJ (*Bob Bertrand Show*, KIOA, Des Moines, IA, 1948).

3136 **Bertrand, Jackie Todd.** COM-HE (KJEF, Jennings, LA, 1956).

3137 **Bertschy-Krohn, La Veta.** Pianist (KOA, Denver, CO, 1925).

3138 **Berwick, Viola.** Talented radio actress Berwick appeared in the cast of the *Scattergood Baines, Lonely Women* and *The Road of Life*.

3139 **Berwin, Bernice.** Dramatic actress Berwin appeared on the *Roads to Romance* program sponsored by the Associated Oil Company (NBC, New York, NY, 1928–1932). She also appeared on the *Memory Lane* program sponsored by General Petroleum (NBC, 1929–1934).

3140 ***(The) Beseda School of Music and Dramatics of St. Wencelaus Church Program.*** The program featured the Beseda Band conducted by Rev. Edward Chapman. The band's members included: Emil Cermak, Jr., John Kotera, Louis Foral, Joseph Skola, Agnes Foral, Antonia Fillipsic, Joe Herman and Albert Schenk (WOAW, Omaha, NE, 1923).

3141 **Beseth, Muriel H.** COM-HE (WNBZ, Saranac Lake, NY, 1956–1957).

3142 **"Bess."** DJ (*Siesta Session*, WKBI, St. Marys, PA, 1948). "Bess" was not otherwise identified.

3143 ***Bess Kelmer's Hints to Housewives.*** Women's homemaking program (KFI, Los Angeles, CA, 1929).

3144 **Besse, Harry.** DJ (*Main Stem Derby*, KSWI, Council Bluffs, IA, 1948–1949).

3145 **Bessemer Hawaiian Orchestra.** H.O. Phillips conducted the band (WAPL, Auburn, AL, 1929).

3146 **Besser, Ted.** DJ (WGL, Ft. Wayne, IN, 1960).

3147 **Besserer, Charles T.** Organist Besserer played the Scottish Rite organ from the new Los Angeles' Scottish Rite Temple (KLX, Oakland, CA, 1928).

3148 **Best, Bobbe.** COM-HE (WTAX, Springfield, IL, 1954).

3149 **Best, Doug.** DJ (*Best on Wax*, WFMB, San Diego, CA, 1948).

3150 **Best, Gerald.** Editor of both *Radio* and *Radiocast Weekly* magazines, Best answered questions from listeners about radio and radio broadcasting (KFRC, San Francisco, CA, 1925).

3151 **Best, Laverne.** COM-HE (WTAX, Springfield, IL, 1954).

3152 **Best, Marvin.** Newscaster (WTZP, St. Petersburg, FL, 1941).

3153 **Best, Natalie.** COM-HE (KNX, Los Angeles, CA, 1955).

3154 ***(The) Best Bands in the Land.*** Paul Whiteman hosted the music show that featured various big bands playing from different venues throughout the country. For example, the bands of Russ Morgan, Lawrence Welk, Tommy and Jimmy Dorsey, Ralph Flanigan and Ralph Marterie appeared on the series (25 min., Monday through Friday, 9:30–9:55 P.M., ABC, 1956).

3155 ***Best of All.*** George Voutsas produced the good musical program that replaced *The Voice of Firestone* program. Skitch Henderson and singers Robert Merrill and Elizabeth Doubleday were program regulars (30 min., Monday, 8:30–9:00 P.M., NBC, 1954).

3156 ***Best Plays.*** John Chapman narrated the series of dramatized plays selected from Burns Mantle's *Best Plays* annuals. One play presented in the series was *Mr. Roberts* with Arthur Kennedy, Leon Janney, Wendell Holmes and Steve Hill in the cast. Edward King directed, William Welch produced and Ernest Kinoy wrote the scripts and adapted the plays for radio (30 min., Friday, 8:30–9:00 P.M., NBC, 1953).

3157 **Bester, Rolly.** Actor Bester appeared on the *Barry Cameron* program.

3158 **Bestor, Beulah.** COM-HE (WSTC, Stamford, CT, 1956–1957).

3159 **Bestor, Don.** Pianist-leader (Don Bestor's Recording Orchestra, WLW, Cincinnati, OH, 1925; Don Bestor's Drake Dance Orchestra, WGN, Chicago, IL, 1925–1926). On radio and recording sessions Bestor's band included: Ray Raymond, c.; Joe Quartell, tb.; Jack Forsythe, clr. and as.; John Hibner, as.; Guy Shrigley, clr. and ts.; Cloyd Griswold, bj. and v.; James Roth, tba.; and Ray Rohle, d. The band's programs frequently appeared on the networks; (*Don Bestor Orchestra*, mus. prg., CBS, 1936; WLW, Cincinnati, OH, 1937; MBS, 1939).

3160 **Betancourt, Louis.** Leader (*Louis Betancourt Orchestra*, instr. mus. prg., KFEL, Denver, CO, 1940).

3161 **Bethel, Al.** DJ (*Club 690*, WHLM, Bloomsburg, PA, 1952).

3162 **Bethmann, Carl.** Baritone (NBC, 1928).

3163 ***Betsy Logan's Household Hints.*** As the title implied, Miss Logan broadcast various bits of information of interest to women (WDAR, Philadelphia, PA, 1923).

3164 **Betsy Ross.** Betsy Ross was the name used by Marie Rogge when she broadcast costume sewing lessons (KPO, San Francisco, CA, 1926).

3165 **Better Ole Club Orchestra.** Popular club band (WRC, Washington, DC, 1924).

3166 ***Better Reception.*** H.C. Burr provided the information on the program designed to help listeners get the best possible reception from their radio sets. This is an indication of the great interest in DX radio during the 1920s (WMCA, New York, NY, 1925). *See* **DX-ing.**

3167 **Betters, Mitchell C. "Mitch."** Sportscaster (WTHT, Hartford, CT, 1948–1950). DJ (*Bandstand*, WTHT, 1948–1949).

3168 **Bettinson, Winslow "Win."** Newscaster (WHEB, Portsmouth, NH, 1944). Sportscaster (WHEB, 1946; *Sports Billboard*, WHEB, 1947). DJ (*Alarm Clock Club*, WHEB, 1947; *Breakfast Show*, WLYN, Lynn, MA, 1949).

3169 **Bettis, Jim.** DJ (KUMA, Pendleton, OR, 1956).

3170 **Bettis, Rex G.** Announcer (WOO, Kansas City, MO, 1925).

3171 ***Betty and Bob.*** A product of Chicago radio, *Betty and Bob* was the first Frank and Anne Hummert daytime serial. The Hummerts came to be known as a veritable "soap opera factory." During the program's run from 1932 to 1940, the title roles were played by Betty Churchill, Edith Davis, Arlene Francis, Alice Hill, Mercedes McCambridge, Elizabeth Reller, Don Ameche, Spencer Bentley, Carl Frank, Van Heflin, J. Anthony Hughes, and Les Tremayne. Others in the cast were: Bill Bouchey, Don Briggs, Francis X. Bushman, Marion B. Crutcher, Frank Dane, Eleanor Dowling, Ethel Kuhn, Eloise Kummer, Forrest Lewis, Grace Lockwood, Herbert Nelson, Ethel Waite Owen, Frankie Pacelli, Loretta Poynton, Henry Saxe, Dorothy Shideler, Peggy Wall, Ned Wever, and Betty Winkler (15 min., Monday through Friday, NBC-Blue and CBS, 1932–1940). During the World War II era the program was broadcast by transcription. This portion of the story told how Bob returned to his country home after a miraculous operation allowed him to walk once again after suffering a terrible accident. The title roles were played by Arlene Francis and Karl Swenson respectively. Other cast members included Everett Sloane, Mary Mason and Edmund O'Brien. *See* **Daytime Serials.**

3172 ***Betty and Buddy.*** Vcl. mus. prg. with songs and patter (MBS, 1939).

3173 ***Betty Budget.*** H. Blanche Frederickson, known as Betty Budget, broadcast weekly shopping hints (30 min., Wednesday, 9:00–9:30 P.M., WHDH, Boston, MA, 1936).

3174 ***Betty Crocker*** **(aka *The Betty Crocker Magazine of the Air*).** Several actresses played the Betty Crocker role, Zella Layne among them. They presented household hints and recipes on the General Mills sponsored program. Originally broadcast in a 15-minute format on NBC from 1928 to 1931, the program was known as the *National Home Hour*. During its 24-year broadcast history the program was carried by NBC, CBS and ABC (15 min., Monday through Friday, 9:45–10:00 A.M., NBC-Red, 1933).

3175 ***Betty Crocker Gold Medal Hour Home Service Talk.*** Betty Crocker, sponsored by General Mills Gold Medal Flour, gave talks on such foods as "The Gold Medal Plum Pudding" and "The Versatile Potato" (KFI, Los Angeles, CA, 1925).

3176 ***Betty Moore Triangle Club.*** The long-running women's program was sponsored by Benjamin Moore Paint Company. Over the years it was conducted by several unidentified women (NBC and CBS, 1929–1944).

3177 ***Betty Sue.*** Vcl. mus. prg. by an otherwise unidentified female performer (KGB, San Diego, CA, 1929).

3178 ***Between the Bookends.*** Ted Malone (Alden Russell) broadcast popular poetry readings on this program that was broadcast in one format or another for more than 21 years (15 min., Sunday, 1:30–1:45 P.M., CBS, 1935).

3179 ***Between Us Girls.*** Automatic Soap Flakes sponsored the weekly program for women conducted by Betty Ames (15 min., Monday, 2:15–2:30 P.M., WBBM, Chicago, IL, 1942).

3180 **Betz, Carl.** DJ (*Swing Shift*, WCAE, Pittsburgh, PA, 1948).

3181 **Beuder, Bert.** Singer (WHB, Kansas City, MO, 1926).

3182 ***Beulah.*** White singer-actor Marlin Hurt created the role of Beulah, a black maid, on the *Fibber McGee and Molly* program. Hurt's own *Beulah* show of 30-minutes duration began its run on CBS in 1945, when he played both Beulah and her boy friend, Bill. After his death in 1947, the program was broadcast by ABC. It later returned to CBS. After Hurt's death, Beulah was played by Bob Corley, Hattie McDaniel, Louise Beavers and Lillian Randolph. Other cast members included: Henry Blair, John Brown, Lois Corbett, Mary Jane Croft, Vivian Dandridge, Ruby Dandridge, Roy Glenn, Jester Hairston, Jess Kirkpatrick, Butterfly McQueen, Marvin Miller, Amanda Randolph, Nicodemus Stewart, Hugh Studebaker, Lee "Lasses" White and Ernest Whitman. Buzz Adlam and Al Sack conducted the orchestra. Carol Penny Piper and Carol Stewart were the vocalists. Johnny Jacobs, Marvin Miller, Ken Niles and Hank Weaver were the announcers. The writers were Seaman Jacobs, Hal Kanter, Phil Leslie, Arthur Phillips, Sol Saks, Charles Stewart and Sol Stewart. Steve Hatos, Jack Hurdle, Helen Mack and Tom McKnight were the directors. Vic Livoti provided sound effects. *Beulah's* last revival on CBS in the mid–1950s was in a fifteen minute format with Hattie McDaniel in the title role (15-min., Monday-Wednesday-Friday, 7:00–7:15 P.M., CBS, mid–1950s).

3183 **Beutel, Edith.** Contralto of the Cleveland Opera Company (WJAX, Jacksonville, FL, 1924).

3184 **Beveridge, Albert J., Jr.** Newscaster (WIRE, Indianapolis, IN, 1940).

3185 **Beverly.** DJ (KBOL, Boulder, CO, 1947; *Time for Beverly*, KDB, Santa Barbara, CA, 1952).

3186 **Beverly Bearcats Dance Orchestra.** Lively jazz band (KHJ, Los Angeles, CA, 1928).

3187 ***(The) Beverly Hillbillies.*** The popular CW music group was popularized by Glen Rice, the KMPC (Los Angeles, CA) station manager, in 1928. The group not only attracted a large radio audience, but also performed at parties for such personalities as Tom Mix, Mary Pickford, Jimmy Cruze, Carrie Jacobs Bond and others. The Beverly Hillbillies were the most popular CW act when country-western music first became popular in southern California. Popular music on radio previously had been dominated by jazz until the early and mid–1930s, when the "hillbilly music craze" began. On Los Angeles radio stations alone, there were 21 "hillbilly" music programs in 1935. The trend could also be found on many other stations throughout the country.

Announcer John McIntire Rice joined with station manager Glen Rice to make up a story that this band consisted of a group of hillbillies found in Beverly Hills. The story went that they were brought in each evening to KMPC to broadcast. The fabrication included stories about Zeke "Craddock"Manners (accordionist Leo Mannes), guitarist Tom "Pappy" Murray, Ezra Longnecker (singer Cyprian Paulette) and Hank Skillet (fiddler Henry Blaeholder). Other sometime members of the group were Elton Britt (singer Jimmy Baker), Lem H.Giles (guitarist Aleth Hansen), Charlie Slater (guitarist Charles Quirk), Aaron Judd (bass, fiddler Shug Fisher) and singers Ashley Dees (Jad Scroggins), Hubert Walton, Mirandy (Marjorie Bauersfeld), Stuart Hamlen (Dave Donner), Kaleb Winbush (Ken Carson) and Lloyd Perryman.

The group to KTM (Los Angeles, CA) in 1932. They made many recordings and appeared in Gene Autry and Tex Ritter western movies. In Los Angeles two other groups, the Sons of the Pioneers and Stuart Hamlen's Lucky Stars were their main radio competitors.

3188 **Beverlyridge Hawaiians Orchestra.** Hawaiian radio band (KFWB, Hollywood, CA, 1925).

3189 **Bevier, Joan C.** COM-HE (KGHM, Brookfield, MO, 1956).

3190 **Bewick, Doug.** DJ (*Trading Post*, WSPR, Springfield, MA, 1948–1951; *Top O the Morning*, WSPR, 1952).

3191 **Bewik, M. H.** Announcer (WDBI, St. Petersburg, FL, 1924).

3192 **Beyer, Anita.** Singer (*Anita Beyer*, vcl. mus. prg., WGN, Chicago, IL, 1936).

3193 **Beyer, Otto.** Pianist (WORD, Batavia, IL, 1925).

3194 **Beynon, Jack.** Sportscaster (WDWS, Champaign, IL, 1939).

3195 **Bezoff, Ben.** Newscaster (WKY, Oklahoma City, OK, 1938; WHLD, Niagra Falls, NY, 1940; KMYR, Denver, CO, 1941–1942, 1945; WKY, Denver, CO, 1946; KLZ, Denver, CO, 1947).

3196 **Biagini, Henry.** Leader (*Henry Biagini Orchestra*, instr. mus. prg., WXYZ, Detroit, MI, 1935).

3197 **Biamonte, Louis.** Saxophonist-flutist (WEAF, New York, NY, 1925).

3198 **Bibbins, Betty.** Soprano (KGO, Oakland, CA, 1925).

3199 ***Bible Class Course of KFUO.*** Professor Kretzmann conducted radio Bible Class lessons. When the program began, 1,246 persons from 29 different states enrolled (KFUO, St. Louis, MO, 1927).

3200 ***Bible Dramas.*** NBC in 1935 presented the series of dramatized episodes from the Bible (15 min., Sunday, 1:00–1:15 P.M., NBC, 1935).

3201 ***(The) Bible Fellowship Hour.*** T. Myron Webb, his wife, Cecilia Webb, and William J. Roberts created the *Bible Fellowship Hour* in Glendale, California in the 1930s. Another Webb associate, Theodore Epp, eventually created his own *Back to the Bible* program. Both programs were still being broadcast in the 1980s.

3202 ***Bible Lover's Meditation Hour.*** Begun on July 26, 1926 by Don R. Falbenburg, the Sunday evening vespers program continued to be broadcast well into the 1930s (60 min., Sunday, WAIU, Columbus, OH, 1930).

3203 ***Biblical Drama.*** Wilda Wilson Church directed the series of religious dramas originally broadcast on the NBC-Pacific Coast Network and later was carried on the national network (30 min., Sunday, 10:30–11:00 P.M., NBC-Red, 1927–1929). *See* **Church, Wilda Wilson**.

3204 ***Biblical Dramas.*** A series of weekly dramatic religious episodes, that were broadcast on Sunday evenings (30 min., Sunday, 10:30–11:00 P.M., NBC-Red, 1927–1929).

3205 **Bice, Max.** Newscaster (KMO, Seattle, WA, 1939).

3206 **Bichl, Elizabeth Monson.** Contralto (KHJ, Los Angeles, CA, 1924).

3207 **Bickart, Sanford.** Actor Bickart appeared on the *Amanda of Honeymoon Hill* daytime serial program.

3208 ***(The) Bickersons.*** Don Ameche and Frances Langford played a bickering husband and wife for some five years for various sponsors, after first appearing as a comedy segment of the *Chase and Sanborn Hour* with Bergen and McCarthy. The program sometimes was known as *The Old Gold Show* or *Drene Time*. Philip Rapp was the program's writer-producer. Other cast members included: Marsha Hunt, Danny Thomas and Pinky Lee. Philip Morris was the sponsor on the show's last network appearance (30 min., Tuesday, 9:30–10:00 P.M., CBS, 1951).

3209 **Bickel, Helen.** COM-HE (WMMN, Fairmont, WV, 1959).

3210 **Bickford, Charles.** DJ (*Merry Merchant*, WOHS, Shelby, NC, 1947).

3211 **Bickford, Louise.** Lyric coloratura (WGBS, New York, NY, 1928).

3212 **Bickman, Lisa.** Soprano (WHN, New York, NY, 1923).

3213 **Bicknell, Max.** DJ (*Club Carousel*, KIUL, Garden City, KS, 1948; *Lakin Hour*, KIUL, 1949).

3214 ***Bicycle Party.*** Music by the Hugo Mariani Orchestra and performers such as singer-pianist Grace Blaine were featured on the variety show. Bill Slater was the host (30 min., Sunday, NBC-Red Network, 1938).

3215 **Bicycle Playing Card Sextet.** A commercially sponsored Cincinnati vocal group (WSAI, Cincinnati, OH, 1926).

3216 ***Bide Dudley's Dramatic Review.*** Newspaper columnist and critic, Dudley (Walter Bronson Dudley) rushed back to the WMCA studio to broadcast his critical review of the play immediately after the curtain fell on the Broadway production that he had just attended (15 min., daily, WMCA, New York, NY, 1932).

3217 ***Bide Dudley's Theater Club.*** Critic Dudley (Walter Bronson Dudley) broadcast a program of Broadway and Hollywood gossip (15 min., Monday, 12:30–12:45 P.M., MBS, 1933–1939).

3218 **Biddick, Walter.** Announcer (KFWB, Hollywood, CA, 1928).

3219 Biddle, Adelaine. Pianist (KDKA, Pittsburgh, PA, 1926).

3220 Biddle, Franklin. Reader (KDKA, Pittsburgh, PA, 1926).

3221 Biddle, Mary. COM-HE (WIP, Philadelphia, PA, 1951).

3222 Bidlack, C.S. Announcer (WMAN, Columbus, OH, 1925)

3223 Bidle, Jerry. DJ (*Alarm Clock Club*, KBRS, Springdale, AR, 1948).

3224 Bidne, Bernell. Under the direction of a faculty member, Bidne, an engineering student at the South Dakota State College of Agriculture and Mechanic Arts, built the station's transmitter and did most of the announcing when it first went on the air in 1923 (KFDY, Brookings, SD, 1923).

3225 Bidwell, Doris. COM-HE (WBLG, Lexington, KY, 1958–1960).

3226 Bidwell, H. F. Announcer (WKBO, Jersey City, NJ, 1925).

3227 Bieber, Frederick. Newscaster (WTHT, Hartford, CT, 1939).

3228 Biebesheimer, Evelyn. Pianist (KGO, Oakland, CA, 1925; KFWI, San Francisco, CA, 1926).

3229 Bieloh [Bielch], Ival. COM-HE (KTFS, Texarkana, TX, 1957).

3230 Bier, Joseph A. Announcer (WLWL, New York City, NY, 1927). Baritone (*Joseph Bier*, vcl. mus. prg., WOR, Newark, NJ, 1934).

3231 Bierfeldt, Jack. DJ (*Club 1500*, WGGO, Salamanca, NY, 1960).

3232 Bierkamp, (Mrs.) A.H. Soprano (WOC, Davenport, CT, 1927).

3233 Biers, Marvin. DJ (KROD, El Paso, TX, 1956).

3234 Bierstadt, Edward. Announcer-writer Bierstadt conducted a news program (WOR, Newark, NJ, 1925) and also wrote the *Empire Builders* series sponsored by Great Northern Railroad (NBC-Blue Network, 1927–1930). *See* ***Empire Builders***.

3235 Big Bethel Methodist Episcopal Church Choir. A fine African-American singing group that specialized in "Negro spirituals" (WSM, Nashville, TN, 1923; WSB, Atlanta, GA, 1926; WSUN, St. Petersburg, FL, 1928).

3236 Big Brother *see* **Emery, Claire Robbins**

3237 Big Brother of KFWB. The unidentified performer spoke on educational subjects, told stories and provided answers from the *The Book of Knowledge* to children's questions (KFWB, Hollywood, CA, mid-1920s).

3238 Big Brother of KPO. The unidentified station employee Big Brother conducted a children's program (KPO, San Francisco, CA, 1924–1925).

3239 Big Brother Uncle Jack. Uncle Jack provided stories and musical entertainment for children (KPO, San Francisco, CA, 1925).

3240 ***Big Chief Gumbo.*** Sixteen-year-old Sherrie Gootkin played the role of Mary Jane on the popular local children's program (WLS, Chicago, IL, 1937).

3241 ***(The) Big City Parade.*** Lillian Gordoni assisted by Wesley Burke wrote and directed the program designed to "help modern youth solve its problems" (15 min., Friday, 1:45–2:00 P.M., WLS, Chicago, IL, 1938).

3242 ***Big D Jamboree*** **aka** ***Lone Star Barn Dance*** **and KRLD Big D Jamboree.** A popular CW music show, the *Big D Jamboree* featured among others the Shelton Brothers, the Callahan Brothers, Billy Walker, Sonny James and Lefty Frizell (KRLD, Dallas, TX, 1947). After starting in 1947 as the *Lone Star Barn Dance*, it became known as the *Big D Jamboree*. Al Turner, the show's MC, along with the owner of Sportatorium, Ed McLemore, were the producers. The show was presented weekly to a live audience of some 6,300 people in the Sportatorium. The show started at 8:15 P.M. and ended at midnight. The *Big D Jamboree* was one of the first CW shows presented on the CBS network's Saturday Night Country Style program series broadcast from 1951 to 1956. Some regular members of the *Jamboree* were Marvin and Charlie Morris, Otis West, Riley Crabtree, Billy Jack Saucier, Red Gilliam, Al Turner, Tony Miller, Ray Munroe, Buddy Griffin, Roy Wiley, Sonny James, Artie Glenn, Hank Locklin and Billy Walker aka "The Travelin' Texan." Guest stars such as Homer and Jethro, Floyd Tillman, Hank Thompson, Moon Millican, Hank Snow, Lefty Frizzell, Carolina Cotton, Jimmy Wakely, Carl Smith and Webb Pierce frequently appeared on the show. The show thrived into the 1950s and beyond.

3243 ***Big Freddie Miller.*** National Oil Products sponsored Miller, who entertained with songs and patter (15 min., Monday through Friday, 11:15–11:30 A.M., CBS, 1933).

3244 ***(The) Big Guy.*** The *Big Guy*, a private investigator, solved crimes and caught the bad guys on the interesting adventure show. The cast included Henry Calvin in the title role joined by David Anderson, Joan Lazer, Bill Zuckert, Linda Watkins and Sandy Strauss. Organ interludes were provided by Jim Ward. Peter Roberts was the announcer (30 min., Weekly, NBC, 1950).

3245 ***Big Jeff Bass and the Radio Playboys.*** Big Jeff Bass headed the CW music group on his local early morning show. The program featured his wife, singer-comedienne Tootsie Bass (90 min., Weekdays, WLAC, Nashville, TN, World War II era).

3246 ***(The) Big Show.*** Professor Herman "Und Come It Now" Schnitzel was the zany host-comedian on the weekly variety program that also featured Frank and Charlie — the Hill Billy Boys, accordionist Johnny Toffoli, saxophonist Walter Beban, the blues singing crooner, Joziena Van der Ende and the Trocaderans Orchestra directed by Vinton LaFerrera. (120 min.,10:00 P.M. to midnight, KFI-NBC-Pacific Coast Network, San Francisco, CA, 1928).

3247 ***(The) Big Show.*** A weekly network variety show sponsored by Ex-Lax, the program featured the songs of Gertrude Niesen and the comedy team of Block and Sully. Lud Gluskin's orchestra provided the music (30 min., CBS, 1934). An earlier version, also sponsored by Ex-Lax laxatives, had presented comedienne Lulu McConnell, contralto Niesen and the Isham Jones Orchestra. Future motion picture actor Paul Douglas was the announcer. The program was written by David Freeman (30 min., Monday, 9:30–10:00 P.M., CBS, 1933–1934).

3248 ***(The) Big Show.*** In an unsuccessful attempt to compete with the inroads of television, NBC radio presented this costly series broadcast from 1950 to 1952. Program costs each week were reported to be at least $50,000. Writers on the 90-minute variety show were Goodman Ace, Selma Diamond, Mort Green, George Foster, Welbourn Kelley and Frank Wilson. The announcer was Ed Herlihy. At times Tallulah Bankhead and Fred Allen served as the hosts who greeted a number of guest stars including: Clive Brooks, Portland Hoffa, Frankie Laine, Ethel Merman, Margaret Phillips, Hugh Reilly, Herb Shriner, Margaret Truman, Joan Davis, Judy Holliday, Dennis King, Lisa Kirk, Groucho Marx, Fran Warren, Luerene Boyer, George Jessel, Joe Frisco, Peter Lorre, Sheppard Strudwick and Fibber McGee and Molly (90 min., Sunday, 6:00–7:30 P.M., NBC, 1950–1952).

3249 ***Big Sister.*** One of the most popular daytime serials, *Big Sister* was sponsored by both Rinso and Procter & Gamble, two of the country's largest soap producers, while the program was on the air. Filled with many cliches of daytime serials, the show nevertheless featured many talented radio actors, some of whom gained considerable fame on the Broadway stage and in motion pictures. The title character, originated by Alice Frost, experienced problems both with her romance and marriage and with her attempts to care for her younger sister and brother.

The cast included: Mason Adams, Vera Allen, Jim Ameche Jr, Marjorie Anderson, Ed Begley, Alan Reed (Ted Bergman), Horace Braham, Patsy Campbell, Fran Carden, Peggy Conklin, Staats Cotsworth, Guy deVestel, Susan Douglas, Eric Dressler, Helene Dumas, Elspeth Eric, Louise Fitch, Arlene Francis, Alice Frost, Martin Gabel, David Gothard, Charlotte Holland, Joe Julian, Teri Keane, Alexander Kirkland, Adelaide Klein, Richard Kollmar, Barry Kroeger, Elizabeth Love, Nancy Marshall, Ian Martin, Grace Matthews, Mercedes McCambridge, Paul McGrath, Dorothy McGuire, Arnold Moss, Erin O'Brien-Moore, Michael O'Day, Santos Ortega, Oscar Polok, Carl Benton Reid, Ruth Schafer, Ann Shepherd (Scheindel Kalish), Everett Sloane, Haila Stoddard, Chester Stratton, Joan Tompkins, Evelyn Varden, Harold Vermilyea, Charles Webster, Ned Wever, and Richard Widmark. The announcers were Jim Ameche and Hugh Conover. The show was created by Lillian Lauferty and written by Carl Bixby, Julian Funt, Robert Newman and Bill Sweets. Mitchell Grayson, Theodore T. Hunton and Thomas F. Vietor, Jr. were the directors. The musical director was William Meeder. Sound effects were produced by Bill Brown. Richard Liebert was the organist. The program was first broadcast in 1936 (15 min., Monday through Friday, CBS, 1936–1952).

3250 ***(The) Big Six of the Air.*** The six attractions presented each week on this lively half-hour show were the Frank Black Orchestra; the piano team of Phil Ohman and Victor Arden; tenor Lewis James; contralto Welcome Lewis; and a male quartet consisting of tenors Henry Shope and Frank Parker, baritone John Sleagle and bass Elliott Shaw. Jimmy Wallington was the announcer (30 min., Thursday, 9:00–9:30 P.M., NBC-Red Network, 1932).

3251 ***Big Time.*** Comic Johnny Hart presented humorous sketches and the Joseph Bonime Orchestra the music on the weekly network program (15 min., 8:00–8:15 P.M., WEAF, New York, NY, 1932).

3252 ***Big Town.*** Jerry McGill was the producer, writer and director of the series about Steve Wilson, the fighting editor of the *Illustrated Press*, a crusading newspaper. Edward G. Robinson created the role of Steve Wilson, who was ably assisted by Lorelei Kilbourne, the newspaper's society editor, played by Claire Trevor. These roles were played later by Edward Pawley, Walter Greaza, Ona Munson and Fran Carlon. The program was broadcast by both CBS and NBC during the years it was on the air (1937–1954). The cast members during these years included: Mason Adams, Casey Allen, Helen Brown, Fran Carlon, Ted deCorsia, Robert Dryden, Gale Gordon, Walter Greaza, Larry Haines, Jerry Hausner, Cy Kendall, Donald MacDonald, Ed MacDonald, Ona Munson, Michael O'Day, Edward Pawley, George Petrie, Thelma Ritter, Edward G. Robinson, Jack Smart, Claire Trevor, Dwight Weist, Robbie Winkler, Paula Winslowe and Lawson Zerbe. Dwight Weist was the narrator and Ken Niles the announcer. Joseph Bell, William N. Robson, Richard Uhl and Crane Wilbur were the directors. Leith Stevens was the musical director and John Gart the organist. Sound effects were by John Powers.

The program was first broadcast in 1937 over CBS. The show opened with a newsboy's cries of "EXTRA! EXTRA!" That was followed by the announcer saying: "Lever Brothers, makers of Lifebuoy health soap, are proud to present *Big Town*— the story of fighting editor Steve Wilson of the *Illustrated Press*, whose newspaper creed stands for freedom and justice against the forces of intolerance and evil. Now *Big Town* and Steve Wilson's story headlined 'Murder in the Snow.'"

3253 ***Big Yank.*** Red Foley was the host and featured singer on this CW music program sponsored by the Reliance Manufacturing Company, makers of Big Yank overalls. Tommy Tanner, Reggie Cross, Howard Black and Dan Hosmer played the roles of Jimmy, Jonas, Jasper and Uncle Buster on the show (15 min., 6:30–6:45 A.M. CST, WLS, Chicago, IL, 1937).

3254 **Bigbee, Nell [Nelle].** COM-HE (WOWL, Florence, AL, 1958).

3255 **Bigelow, Bill.** DJ (*WJTN Music Hall*, WJTN, Jamestown, NY, 1960).

3256 **Bigelow, Don.** Leader (Don Bigelow Orchestra, KDKA, Pittsburgh, PA, 1929; *Don Bigelow Orchestra*, instr. mus. prg., NBC, 1934).

3257 **Bigelow, Earl.** Pianist (WIBO, Chicago, IL, 1926).

3258 **Bigelow, Paul.** Newscaster (WBML, Macon, GA, 1948).

3259 ***(The) Bigelow Twins.*** Jim and Mel Bigelow were a talented pair of harmony singing brothers (15 min., WELI, New Haven, CT, 1937).

3260 **Biggler, Lynn.** Newscaster (KWFT, Wichita Falls, TX, 1941).

3261 **Biggs, John.** Newscaster (WPOB, Hammond, IN, 1948).

3262 **Biggs, Marion.** COM-HE (KLO, Ogden, UT, 1956).

3263 **Bigler, Bernice.** COM-HE (WCSS, Amsterdam, NY, 1960).

3264 **Bigler, Tom.** DJ (*Whistlin' in the Dark*, WILK, Wilkes-Barre, PA, 1949).

3265 **Bigley, Bill.** Leader (*Bill Bigley Orchestra*, instr. mus. prg., WNAC, Boston, MA, 1934).

3266 **Bigley, Bill.** Newscaster (WJZM, Clarksville, TN, 1945).

3267 **Bigley, Dave "Sun River Dave."** DJ (*Melody Round-Up*, KMON, Great Falls, MT, 1948–1949; *Rickey's Request Time*, KFJI, Klamath Falls, OR).

3268 **Bigley, David E.** DJ (*Requestfully Yours*, WJOI, Florence, AL, 1947–1948).

3269 **Bigley, Patricia.** COM-HE (WSNY, Schenectady, NY, 1955).

3270 **Bignell, Frank.** Newscaster (WJJD, Chicago, IL, 1939; WIBA, Madison, WI, 1945).

3271 **Bilbee, Rodney.** DJ (KWON, Bartlesville, OK, 1956).

3272 **Bilea, Edna.** Contralto (KFI, Los Angeles, CA, 1927).

3273 **Bilger, Anson.** Reader (KGO, Oakland, CA, 1924).

3274 **Bilger, Bill.** Leader (*Bill Bilger Orchestra*, instr. mus. prg., WIP, Philadelphia, PA, 1935).

3275 **Bilincoff, Al.** Director (Al Bilincoff and his Green Acre Lodge Orchestra; WJAR, Providence, RI, 1926).

3276 **Biljou's [Biljo's] Balalaika Orchestra.** Peter Biljou directed his popular string orchestra that was featured on the *Around the Samovar* program (WABC-CBS, 1929) and *In a Russian Village* (WABC-CBS, New York, NY, 1929).

3277 **Bill, Glen.** DJ (*The Sundial*, WTSP, St. Petersburg, FL, 1948).

3278 **Bill, Edgar L.** Announcer (WLS, Chicago, IL, 1928).

3279 ***Bill and Ginger.*** Bill (Lynn Murray) and Ginger (Virginia Baker) engaged in bright chatter and sang on their popular sustaining program (15 min., Monday, Wednesday and Friday, CBS, 1933).

3280 ***Bill and Henry.*** Veteran radio performers Al Cameron and Pete Bontsema took the name of Bill and Henry when the comedy team broadcast in 1933. *See **Al and Pete**.*

3281 **Bill and His Uke.** Bill was an ukulele performer who appeared on *The Sandman* program (KMBC, Kansas City, MO, 1928).

3282 **Bill Boyd's Cowboy Ramblers.** *See* **Boyd, Bill.**

3283 ***(The) Bill Goodwin Show.*** Announcer turned actor Goodwin starred in his short-lived situation comedy (30 min., Saturday, 9:00–9:30 P.M., CBS, 1947).

3284 ***Bill Judge's Celtic Minstrels.*** The sustaining program of Irish reels and hornpipes was according to *Billboard*, "the answer to an Irishman's prayer." Singer George Gilmore, pianist Johnnie Peters and flutist Jack Monohan accompanied by Elizabeth Koerner, performed the stirring Irish music (15 min., Sunday, 12:00–12:15 P.M., WELI, New Haven, CT, 1937).

3285 ***Bill, Mack and Johnny.*** Vcl. mus. prg. by a male trio not otherwise identified (KFH, Wichita, KS, 1939).

3286 ***Bill Schudt's Going to Press.*** Various reporters, editors and publishers had their say on this interesting weekly news program (15 min., Wednesday, 6:00–6:15 P.M., WABC, New York, NY, 1931).

3287 ***Bill Stern's Sports Newsreel.*** Famous sportscaster Stern presented dramatic sports stories, often exaggerated and sometimes fictitious, on his weekly show. He always presented a guest star on each program and related some sports event or activity to them. Some of Stern's guests included: Tommy Dorsey, Elsa Maxwell, Babe Ruth, Ezra Stone, Lucille Ball, Joan Edwards, Dinah Shore, Vivian Blaine, Cab Calloway, Mischa Auer, Sammy Kaye, Roddy MacDowell, Mickey Rooney, Guy Lombardo, Eddie Cantor, Morton Downey, Rudy Vallee, Spike Jones and Frankie Frisch. (15 min., Sunday, NBC, 1945–1947). Bill Stern was famous for exaggerating the effects of sports on the life of famous people and, sometimes, of even manufacturing "facts" for the sake of a more dramatic impact. Even during his play-by-play of sports events, Stern frequently was thought to make the games exciting, no matter what was happening on the playing field. David Brinkley (1995, p. 18) tells the story of how Grantland Rice one day was sitting in the press box watching a baseball game and listening to Bill Stern, who was sitting nearby broadcasting it. Although the ball game was exciting, Sterns's broadcast of it was "frenzied with excitement." Rice wrote: "There were two entirely different games played here today— one on the field and another on the radio."

3288 **Billich, George.** DJ (*Campus Clambake*, WOLF, Syracuse, NY, 1947). Sportscaster (*Sportscoop*, WOLF, 1947).

3289 **Billin, Reginald.** Baritone (WHAS, Louisville, KY, 1925).

3290 **Billings, Frank.** DJ (*Wax Museum*, KGW, Portland, OR, 1949).

3291 **Billingsley, Bob.** DJ (*K-Bar Roundup*, KVET, Austin, TX, 1954).

3292 **Billingsley, William "Bill."** DJ (WADE, Wadesboro, NC, 1947; *After Hours*, WADE, 1948). Newscaster (WTOB, Winston-Salem, NC, 1949).

3293 **Billingsly, Virginia.** COM-HE (KPIN, Casa Grande, AR, 1957).

3294 **Billmeyer, Doug.** Newscaster

(KMO, Tacoma, WA, 1942; KFPY, Spokane, WA, 1944).

3295 **Billquist, Art.** Baritone (WCFL, Chicago, IL, 1928).

3296 **Bills, Dick.** DJ (*Dick Bills Show*, KOB, Albuerque, NM, 1952).

3297 ***Bill's Hawaiian Players Orchestra.*** Instr. mus. prg. (KFEQ, St. Joseph, MO, 1939).

3298 **Billsbury, Rye (Michael Rye).** Actor Billsbury appeared on the *Ma Perkins* daytime serial program.

3299 ***Billy and Betty.*** James McCallion and Audrey Egane played the title roles on the daytime serial program for adolescents sponsored by the Sheffield Farms Company. They played a brother and sister of high school age, who published an amateur newspaper and experienced the usual problems faced by adolescents (15 min., Monday through Friday, 6:45–7:00 P.M., WEAF, New York, NY, 1935).

3300 ***Billy and Helen.*** The husband and wife singing team of Harold Marshall and Helen Wilson was a great local favorite (KOIL, Council Bluffs, IA, 1928). Their program also contained brief skits based on the normal events that occur in married life.

3301 **Billy and His Uke.** An otherwise unidentified ukulele performer, Billy crooned as he played (KFJZ, Fort Worth, TX, 1928).

3302 ***Billy Bachelor.*** A dramatic series consisting of small town sketches (NBC, 1932–1933). *See **Wheatenaville.***

3303 ***Billy Gleason and His Gang.*** Singing comedian Gleason, who billed himself in vaudeville as "Just Songs and Sayings," appeared on the comedy show with his wife, Paula (WMCA, New York, NY, 1939).

3304 **"Billy Lang."** "Billy" was a white rooster whose crowing was used to sign on and off station WLAG (Minneapolis, MN, 1924).

3305 ***Billy Walters and Her Texas Longhorns.*** CW mus. prg. (WJAS, Pittsburgh, PA, 1936).

3306 **Billy's Hawaiian Trio.** Instrumental group (KOIL, Council Bluffs, IA, 1928).

3307 **Bilson, Elizabeth.** Soprano (*Elizabeth Bilson*, vcl. mus. prg., WBAL, Baltimore, MD, 1934).

3308 ***Biltmore Boys Orchestra.*** Instr. mus. prg. (NBC, 1939).

3309 **Biltmore Hotel Dance Orchestra.** Hotel band led by Don Clark (KHJ, Los Angeles, CA, 1925; WSB, Atlanta, GA, 1926; KNX, Los Angeles, CA, 1928).

3310 **Binegar, Lewis.** Newscaster (WCAT, Rapid City, SD, 1942).

3311 **Bing, Herman.** Tenor (WOK, Chicago, IL, 1925).

3312 ***Bing Crosby Philco Time*** (aka ***Philco Radio Time***). The program included the usual high quality blend of music and comedy that Crosby always provided. It was most noteworthy because it was the first major transcribed network show ever broadcast. Usually network prohibitions against the broadcast of recorded major programs had banned such performances. Crosby resented the demands of broadcasting the *Kraft Music Hall* live. When NBC refused him the right to record it, Crosby moved to ABC in 1947 with a transcribed show for Philco. For the 1947–1948 season, he used magnetic recording tape and, in effect, was influential in bringing magnetic tape recording to broadcast production and, later, to use in the home.

3313 **Bingenheimer, W.A.** Bingenheimer was an announcer who proudly proclaimed WNJ, Newark, NJ, to be "The Voice of Newark," (WNJ, Newark, NJ, 1925–1927).

3314 **Bingham, Bob.** Sportscaster (*Bob Bingham's Nightly Sports Review, The Human Side of Sports, Kellogg Baseball Reports, Coca-Cola Football games, Saturday Evening Football Review,* boxing bouts, golf and tennis tournaments, WWNC, Asheville, NC, 1939; WITH, Baltimore, MD, 1941; WFTC, Kinston, NC, 1945; *The Human Side of Sports*, WCNC, Elizabeth City, NC, 1948; WAHR, Miami Beach, FL, 1955).

3315 **Bingham, Constance.** COM-HE (WOHI, East Liverpool, OH, 1956–1957).

3316 **Bingham, Dick.** Sportscaster (WTSP, St. Petersburg, FL, 1950). DJ (*Alarm Klok Klub*, KEEP, Twin Falls, ID, 1954).

3317 **Bingham, Earl.** DJ (*Best on Wax*, KWIK, Pocatello, ID, 1948).

3318 **Bingham, Irwin Drake.** Newscaster (WKY, Oklahoma City, OK, 1937; KTUL, Tulsa, OK, 1938); Sportscaster, WKY, 1937.

3319 **Bingham, Leslie.** Actor Bingham appeared on the *This Day is Ours* daytime serial program.

3320 **Bingham, Pete.** DJ (*Atomic Boogie*, WJOL, Florence, AL, 1947–1952).

3321 **Bingham's Dance Orchestra.** Local dance band (WGR, Buffalo, NY, 1926).

3322 **Bink, Rose.** Soprano (WCAY, Milwaukee, WI, 1924).

3323 **Binkey, Essie.** Cornetist (KFSG, Los Angeles, CA, 1925–1926).

3324 **Binkin, Syl.** Newscaster (WEW, St. Louis, MO, 1938).

3325 **Binkin, Wyl.** DJ (WMAY, Springfield, IL, 1960).

3326 **Binkley, Essie.** Cornetist (KFSG, Los Angeles, CA, 1925–1926).

3327 **Binkley Brothers Barn Dance Orchestra.** CW band (WSM, Nashville, TN, 1928; *Binkley Brothers*, CW mus. prg., WSM, 1938; *Binkley Brothers Dixie Clodhoppers*, a CW music program featuring banjoist Gale Binkley and his brother, fiddler Amos Binkley, WSM, 1930s). The brothers were watchmakers and jewelry repairmen were pioneer performers on the *Grand Ole Opry*, making their first appearance on October 30, 1926.

3328 **Binns, Barbara.** COM-HE (WVCG, Coral Gables, FL, 1956).

3329 **Binns, (Dr.) Frazier.** Tenor (WSM, Nashville, TN, 1928).

3330 **Bintliff, Tom.** DJ (*1490 Club*, KORN, Mitchell, SD, 1952).

3331 **Binyon, Conrad.** Actor Binyon appeared on such diverse programs as *The Life of Riley, Masquerade, Mayor of the Town, The Nebbs* and *One Man's Family.*

3332 ***Biography in Sound.*** This distinguished program presented carefully researched and produced audio biographies of famous Americans. Compelling sound pictures were presented of such famous Americans as Stan Kenton, Fred Allen, H.L. Mencken, George M. Cohan, General George Marshall, John L. Lewis and Ethel Barrymore. Kenneth Banghart was the narrator (60 min., NBC Network, 1955–1958).

3333 **Biondi, Dick.** DJ (*The Timekeeper*, KSYL, Alexandria, LA, 1954; WHOT, Campbell, OH, 1956; WSBA, York, PA, 1959; WLS, Chicago, IL, 1960). Sportscaster (KSYL, 1954).

3334 **Birch, Ray.** Newscaster (KPRO, Riverside, CA, 1941).

3335 **Birch, Tommy [Tommye].** Actor Birch appeared on the *Dan Harding's Wife* daytime serial program.

3336 **Birch, Vic.** Leader (Vic Birch Orchestra, KFBK, Sacramento, CA, 1928).

3337 **Bircher, Bill.** DJ (WTNJ, Trenton, NJ, 1957; *Commuter's Special*, WBCB, Levittown, PA, 1960).

3338 **Bird, Al.** DJ (*Early Bird Serenade*, WJAC, Johnstown, PA, 1954).

3339 **Bird, Bud.** DJ (*Musical Mailbox*, KISD, Sioux Falls, SD, 1952). Sportscaster (KISD, 1952; *Bird's Eye on Sports*, KISD, 1953).

3340 **Bird, Charles, Jr.** DJ (*Showcase of the Stars*, WKBZ, Muskegon, MI, 1952).

3341 **Bird, Muriel.** Singer (*Muriel Bird*, vcl. mus. prg., WIP, Philadelphia, PA, 1936).

3342 **Bird, Theodore H.** Reader (KOA, Denver, CO, 1925).

3343 **Bird, Tommy.** DJ (WAXU, Georgetown, KY, 1960).

3344 **Birdas, George.** DJ (*Record Varieties*, WLNA, Peekskill, NY, 1948–1956).

3345 **Birder, Cecil.** Tenor (WCCO, Minneappolis–St. Paul, MN, 1928).

3346 ***Bird's Eye Open House.*** Bird's Eye frozen foods sponsored this entertaining variety show that featured Dinah Shore, Wally Brown, Cornelia Otis Skinner, Roland Young, Frank Nelson, the Ken Lane Singers and the Robert Emmett Dolan orchestra. The announcer was Harry Von Zell (30 min, Weekly, CBS, 1943–1944).

3347 **Bird's Jazz Orchestra.** Popular six piece band (WKY, Oklahoma City, OK, 1922).

3348 **Birdsell, John.** DJ (*Top O' the Morning*, KWAT, Watertown, SD, 1948; *Melody, Inc.*, KWAT, 1952).

3349 **Birkeland, Jorgen M.** Newscaster (WOSU, Columbus, OH, 1945).

3350 **Birkenholz, Arcadie.** Violinist-orchestra leader (NBC-Blue Network, New York, NY, 1929).

3351 **Birkenholz, Axel.** Violinist (NBC, 1927).

3352 **Birkhahn, Marie.** Pianist (WJZ, Boston-Springfield, MA, 1925).

3353 **Birleffi, Larry.** Sportscaster (KFBC, Cheyenne, TN, 1952–1955).

3354 **Birmingham, Helen.** Pianist (WHO, Des Moines, IA, 1925).

3355 **Birmingham, John.** DJ (*1450 Club*, WNBZ, Saranac Lake, NY, 1948–1949).

3356 **Birnbach, Meta Ashwin.** Soprano (WCCO, Minneappolis–St. Paul, MN, 1928).

3357 **Birnbaum, Emil.** Leader-violinist

(KOMO Orchestra, KOMO, Seattle, WA, 1927–1928).

3358 Birrell, Harry. DJ (*Beaver Valley Serenade*, WBVP, Beaver Falls, PA, 1949; *Day Breaker*, WSTV, Steubenville, OH, 1952).

3359 Bischoff, (Dr.) Jules. Singer of "character songs" (KMOX, St. Louis, MO, 1926).

3360 Bisgard, Jo Anne. COM-HE (KXO, El Centro, CA, 1956).

3361 Bish, Don. DJ (*At Your Request*, KGEM, Boise, IA, 1948).

3362 Bishop, Barney. Leader (*Barney Bishop Orchestra*, instr. mus. prg., WPG, Atlantic City, NJ, 1935).

3363 Bishop, Billy. Leader (*Billy Bishop Orchestra*, instr. mus. prg., WCLE, Cleveland, OH, 1942).

3364 Bishop, Bob. DJ (*Open House Party*, KUBA, Yuba City, CA, 1949).

3365 Bishop, Burton. Sportscaster (KTEM, Temple, TX, 1938–1942; *Sports play-by-play*, KTEM, 1948). Newscaster (WTEM, 1940).

3366 Bishop, Clay. DJ (*Boots and Saddles*, KSEM, Moses Lake, WA, 1948).

3367 Bishop, Don. DJ (*Alarm Klock Klub*, KGEM, Boise, ID, 1947).

3368 Bishop, Dorothy. COM-HE (WDSV, Viroqua, WI, 1960).

3369 Bishop, E. Ellworth. Announcer (WGH, Newport News, VA, 1925).

3370 Bishop, Eddie. DJ (*Hillbilly Fever*, WVMI, Biloxi, MS, 1948).

3371 Bishop, Elizabeth MacKay. Soprano (WNAC, Boston, MA, 1923).

3372 Bishop, Ethel. COM-HE (WXOK, Baton Rouge, LA, 1954).

3373 Bishop, Forrest. DJ (KWLK, Longview, WA, 1947).

3374 Bishop, (Mrs.) Fred. Organist (WHB, Kansas City, MO, 1926).

3375 Bishop, Gordon. Pianist (WFAA, Dallas, TX, 1925).

3376 Bishop, J. Dige. DJ (*All Request Hour*, WCTA, Andalusia, AL, 1947).

3377 Bishop, Jack. DJ (WLBG, Laurens, SC, 1955–1956).

3378 Bishop, Jill. Pianist (WJJD, Chicago, IL, 1939).

3379 Bishop, Joan. Bishop was one of the intelligent "kids" on the *Quiz Kids* program (NBC, CBS, 1940–1953).

3380 Bishop, Kathryn. Actress Bishop appeared on the *Ellen Randolph* aka *The Story of Ellen Randolph* daytime serial.

3381 Bishop, Ken. Sportscaster (*Sports Highlights*, KXIT, Dalhart, TX, 1948; KDDD, Dumas, TX, 1955). DJ (*Show Time*, KFDA, Amarillo, TX, 1954).

3382 Bishop, Pat. Newscaster (KECA, Los Angeles, CA and KFI, Los Angeles, CA, 1937–1942; KFI, 1948). Sportscaster (KECA and KFI, 1938–1942).

3383 Bishop, Phyllis. COM-HE (WMBR, Jacksonville, FL, 1956).

3384 Bishop, Stan. DJ (*Platter Palace*, KDIX, Dickinson, ND, 1954).

3385 Bishop, Ted. DJ (*Saturday Date*, KFJB, Marshalltown, IA, 1955).

3386 Bisping, Hubert. Newscaster (KUTA, Salt Lake City, UT, 1939).

3387 Bissett, Billy. Leader (*Billy Bissett Orchestra*, instr. mus. prg., NBC, 1935).

3388 Bissell, Evelyn. Pianist (KFXF, Colorado Springs, CO, 1926).

3389 *Bits of Life.* Newspaper correspondent Linton Wells inaugurated the series of programs in 1937, on which he broadcast the personal anecdotes of a wandering newspaperman. He also discussed the trends and events that he saw shaping the world of tomorrow (15 min., weekly, NBC-Red, 1937).

3390 Bittel [Bittell], Sam. Leader (*Sam Bittel Orchestra*, instr. mus. prg., WBZ-WBZA, Boston-Springfield, MA, 1932; WNAC, Boston, MA, 1934).

3391 Bitterman, Jack. DJ (*Best on Wax*, WABB, Mobile, AL, 1948; *Jive, Jam'n Jump* and *Pipe Rack Parade*, WABB, 1949). Sportscaster (WABB, 1948; *Sports Page of the Air*, WABB, 1949–1956).

3392 Bittinger, Lucie. COM-HE (KAWL, York, NE, 1956).

3393 Bittke, Frederic. Baritone (KPO, San Francisco, CA, 1929). Bittke, an American citizen, was born in Germany. He appeared in motion pictures before he performed on radio.

3394 Bittong, Artie. Director of the *Midnight Follies* program (WCAU, Philadelphia, PA, 1928).

3395 Bivans, Robert. DJ (WITY, Danville, IL, 1956).

3396 Bivens, Jack. Actor Bivens appeared on the *Captain Midnight*, *Road of Life*, *Silver King*, *Mountie* and *Sky King* programs.

3397 Bivens, James. Sportscaster (WMOZ, Mobile, AL, 1954).

3398 Bivens, Virginia. Soprano (WHLS, Bluefield, WV, 1938).

3399 Biviano, Joe. Accordion virtuoso (NBC-Blue Network, New York, NY, 1929).

3400 Bixby, Carl. Writer Bixby wrote the *Big Sister*, *Life Can Be Beautiful*, *The Man I Married*, *Mrs. Minniver*, *Radio Reader's Digest* and *This Day is Ours* programs.

3401 Bjornson, Bjorn. Newscaster (NBC, 1942; WRC, Washington, DC, and NBC, 1945; NBC, 1945–1948).

3402 Blacak, Ted. Leader (*Ted Blacak Orchestra*, instr. mus. prg., WBZ-WBZA, Boston-Springfield, MA, 1934).

3403 Blachford, Frank. Violinist (WGY, Schenectady, NY, 1925).

3404 Blachson, Ida. Actress who appeared frequently on WLW (Cincinnati, OH, 1925).

3405 Black, Alan. DJ (*Polka Party*, WJPA, Washington, PA; WPIT, Pittsburgh, PA, 1948; WPIT, 1955).

3406 Black, (Dr.) Algernon. Newscaster (WQXR, New York, NY, 1944–1945).

3407 Black, Ben. Leader (Ben Black's Orchestra broadcasting from Tait's Dancing Palace, KGO, Oakland, CA, 1925).

3408 Black, Bernie. DJ (*For You By Request*, KGEM, Bethlehem, PA, 1948; *Disc's and Data*, WGPA, Bethlehem, PA, 1949).

3409 Black, Bill. Sportscaster (KGAR, Tucson, AZ, 1939).

3410 Black, Bob. Leader (Bob Black Orchestra, instr. mus. prg.; WMBD, Peoria, IL, 1936).

3411 Black, Bud. Sportscaster (WMMB, Melourne, FL, 1955).

3412 Black, Buddy. DJ (WGN, Chicago, IL, 1956).

3413 Black, Charles. Newscaster (WSAI, Cincinnati, OH, 1945). DJ (*Charlie Black Show*, WSAI, 1952).

3414 Black, Dave. DJ (*Record Room*, WLET, Toccoa, GA, 1954; *Turn Table Two*, WTPR, Paris, TN, 1955; KOCY, Oklahoma City, OK, 1956).

3415 Black, Ed. DJ (KBMY, Billings, MT, 1954; KLUB, Salt Lake City, UT, 1956).

3416 Black, Emil. Pianist (WOK, Pine Bluff, AR, 1922).

3417 Black, Fellicia Lavender. Soprano (KFSG, Los Angeles, CA, 1925).

3418 Black, Frank. Pianist (WJZ, New York, NY, 1927; arranger-conductor on the *Palmolive Hour*, NBC, 1927; orchestral conductor and composer, NBC-Red Network, New York, NY, 1929; *Happy Wonder Bakers*, WEAF-NBC-Red, New York, NY, 1929; the *Edison Hour*, WJZ-NBC-Blue, New York, NY, 1929).

3419 Black, George. Bass (KJBS, San Francisco, CA, 1925).

3420 Black, Helen. Contralto (WIND, Gary, IN, 1935).

3421 Black, Howard. DJ (*Rise and Shine*, KAY, Phoenix, AZ, 1948).

3422 Black, (Dr.) James M. Leader (Chevrolet Motors Band of St Louis, KSD, St. Louis, MO, 1923).

3423 Black, Jay. DJ (*Matinee with Jay*, WDXI, Jackson, TN, 1948). Sportscaster (WDXI, 1951; WHHM, Memphis, TN, 1956; WSUN, St. Petersburg, FL, 1960).

3424 Black, John. Newscaster (KGGF, Coffeyville, KS, 1941).

3425 Black, John "Johnnie." DJ (*Dawn O'Day*, KGB, San Diego, CA, 1948–1949).

3426 Black, Joseph. Leader (Joseph Black's Sexton Cafe Concert Orchestra, WDAF, Kansas City, MO, 1924).

3427 Black, Mabel. COM-HE (WMGY, Montgomery, AL, 1955).

3428 Black, Martin. DJ (*Martin Black Show*, KRAM, Las Vegas, NV, 1952). Sportscaster (KRAM, 1952–1953).

3429 Black, Russell. Newscaster (WJNR, Newark, NJ, 1949).

3430 Black, Sherman. Leader (*Sherman Black Orchestra*, instr. mus. prg., WIND, Chicago, IL, 1935).

3431 Black, Ted. Leader (*Ted Black Orchestra*, instr. mus. prg., NBC, 1934; WOR, Newark, NJ, 1936).

3432 *Black America Speaks.* Nat D. Williams conducted the pioneering Sunday afternoon show that explored social and political subjects (WDIA, Memphis, TN, late 1940s). *See* **Williams, Nat D.**

3433 *(The) Black and Gold Room Or-*

chestra. Club orchestra (NBC-Red Network, New York, NY, 1929; *Black and Gold Orchestra*, a program of dinner music from New York City, 30 min., Monday, 7:00–7:30 P.M., WEAF-Red, 1930).

3434 ***(The) Black and Orange Orchestra.*** Instr. mus. prg. (WBZ-WBZA, Boston-Springfield, MA, 1932).

3435 **Black Cat Orchestra.** Pittsburgh jazz band (KDKA, Pittsburgh, PA, 1924 and WTAY, Oak Park, IL, 1925).

3436 ***(The) Black Flame of the Amazon.*** Some portions of the dramatic adventure series were based on the expedition led by explorer Harold Noise in the mountains of Colombia, where he found gold. The announcer proudly proclaimed the program was based on "the adventures of Harold Noise, adventurer, explorer and scientist in the darkest jungles of South America." The characters in the story were Noise; Pedro, Noise's assistant; Jim and Jean Brady, two of the explorer's old friends; and a friendly native by the name of Keyto. The program claimed that it contributed to the listeners' knowledge of the "strange savage customs, fierce animals and the weird tropical plants found in South America." Hi-Speed Gasoline and Melrose Ham sponsored the transcribed program (15 min., Transcribed, 1930s).

3437 ***(The) Black Mask Serenaders.*** A masked male vocal quartet whose identities remained a secret were featured (WCKY, Covington, KY, early 1930s).

3438 ***(The) Black Museum.*** Orson Welles was the narrator of this BBC production that was written by Ira Marion and produced by Harry Alan Towers. The sustaining show was based on items related to various crimes that were found in Scotland Yard's museum. The show appeared to have been copied, *Variety* said, from NBC's *Whitehall 1212*. Welles' narration always added interest to the show (30 min., Tuesday, 8:30–9:00 P.M., MBS, 1952).

3439 **Black Radio.** No more important aspect of radio history or American culture has been more neglected than Black Radio, its programs, performers and their positive effects upon American life. Fortunately, this too long neglected topic was researched, described and portrayed in an excellent 13-week series *Black Radio: Telling It Like It Was*, produced by Radio Smithsonian with Jacquie Gales Webb as series director. Other recent contributions have included books such as Cantor's *Wheelin' on Beale Street*, Palmer's *Deep Blues* and Lornell's *Happy in the Service of the Lord: African-American Sacred Vocal Harmony Quartets in Memphis*. Nevertheless, more intensive studies should be undertaken on this important topic.

All too often studies of Black radio have concentrated on the negative aspects. As they correctly concluded, many Blacks felt that the stereotypes of them presented in early radio were demeaning. The few exceptions were seldom noted. Nashville's WSM, for example, frequently presented such fine African-American groups as the Fiske Jubilee Singers among others in the early 1920s. Even that station's *Grand Ole Opry* had as one of its earliest stars Black harmonica virtuoso, DeFord Bailey. Hampton Roads, Virginia, radio stations in the early years presented the Sterling Jubilee Singers as the CIO Singers on a program sponsored by the Congress of Industrial Organizations. The fine Golden Gate Quartet, who began singing together as high school students, had their own program on WIS (Columbia, SC) in 1936. In the 1930s, black gospel groups such as the Utica Jubilee Quartet were on a syndicated series and the Southernaires were on network shows that gained national recognition for both groups. The number of positive Black images and featured performers on radio, however, were all too few. Demeaning radio portrayals far outnumbered them. Even when sophisticated Duke Ellington's band played at Harlem's Cotton Club, it was introduced on the air as a *Jungle Orchestra*, a term rightfully resented. Negative stereotypes that probably carried the greatest hurt can be traced to the minstrel show forms of entertainment that were often broadcast in the middle 1920s and extended into the following decade, when the popularity of this program type eventually faded.

In 1947, *Ebony* magazine estimated that there were some 3,000 DJs on radio in the United States and only 16 of them were Black. A notable event occurred in 1949 that set in motion a reversal of this situation. That was when station WDIA, Memphis, Tennessee, became the first American station to have an entirely Black announcing staff that included such talented broadcasters as B.B. King and Rufus Thomas. Known as the "Mother Station of the Negroes," WDIA was the first station in the United States to have all-Black DJs playing all-Black music with programming led by Nat D. Williams' *Tan Town Jamboree*. WDIA was renowned for its service to the Black community, which earned it the title of "The Goodwill Station." Shortly after WDIA increased its power to 50,000 watts, it justifiably advertised itself as: "WDIA, The Goodwill Station, is the FIRST—and the only 50,000 watts station programmed exclusively for Negroes,—truly one of America's GREAT stations!"

Another important contribution of stations like WDIA and Black DJs, not always fully appreciated, is that of the religious influence exerted by such groups as the Wings Over Jordan Choir and the First Church of the Deliverance group when their music was played by DJs on these stations. The many contributions of Black Radio, its talented broadcasters and astute executives to American culture should be recognized. All played an important role *in* and made significant contributions *to* American radio history. *See* ***An Open Letter on Race Relations; Aunt Carrie; Camp Meeting of the Air;*** **Ayers, Cesta; Benson, *Al (Al Leaner)*;** ***Black America Speaks;*** **Bondu, Dave and Mayme; Brown, Gatemouth; Chattie Hattie; C.I.O. Singers (Sterling Jubilee Singers); Cooper, Jack Leroy;** ***Destination Freedom;*** **Dizzy Lizzie; Durst, Lavada; Fairfield Four; Four Harmony Kings;** ***Freedom's People;*** **Garner, Robert "Honeymoon"; Gibson, Jack; Golden Crown Quartet; Golden Gate Quartet; Gospel Travelers; Henderson, Douglas "Jocko"; Hill, Gladys; Hulbert, Maurice "Hot Rod"; John R.; I.C. Glee Club;** ***King Biscuit Flour Show;*** **KWEM Black Gospel Quartet Programming; M.N. Gospel Singers; Monroe, Willa; N&W Imperial Quartet; Nelson, Ford;** ***New World*** **A** ***Coming;*** **Nobles, Gene; Poppa Stoppa; Prater, George; Ruchon, Lonnie; Selah Jubilee Singers; Smith, Novella Doe; Steinberg, Martha Jean "The Queen"; Silver Leaf Quartet of Norfolk; Song Birds of the South; Southern Jubilee Singers; Southern Wonders; Southernaires; Spirit of Memphis Gospel Singers; Spiritual Four; Sunset Travelers; Thomas, Robert "Honeyboy"; Thomas, Rufus; Utica Gospel Quartet; Wade, Theo; Williams, A.C. "Moohah"; Williams, Nat D.;** *and* **Winslow, Vernon.**

3440 ***(The) Black Rock Boys.*** The half-hour music program featured Brennan and Shaw's songs and patter (30 min., Tuesday, 7:30–8:00 P.M., CBS, 1928).

3441 **Blackburn, Arline.** Actress Blackburn was featured in the daytime serials *House of Glass*, *Linda's First Love* (title role), *The O'Neills*, *Pretty Kitty Kelly* (title role) and *Young Widder Brown*.

3442 **Blackburn, Billy.** DJ (*Music Till Sundown*, WKHC, Mashville, AR, 1960).

3443 **Blackburn, Bob.** Sportscaster (*Sports Edition*, KEX, Portland, OR, 1951–1956; KPOJ, Portland, OR, 1960). Sportscaster (KEX, 1953–1955).

3444 **Blackburn, Lucy.** Bridge expert Blackburn appeared on the *Auction Bridge* program (WLW, Cincinnati, OH, 1925).

3445 **Blackburn, Merl.** Announcer (WTMJ, Milwaukee, WI, 1925).

3446 **Blackford, H. W.** Announcer (WEAM, North Plainfield, NJ, 1925–1927).

3447 **Blackman, Alexander.** Viola and violin soloist (WBZ, Springfield, MA, 1926).

3448 **Blackman, Dave.** Leader (Dave Blackman Orchestra, KFWI, San Francisco, CA, 1927).

3449 **Blackmon, Teddy.** DJ (WJMO, Cleveland, OH, 1948).

3450 **Blackson, Ida.** Soprano Blackson was featured on the *Crossley Gem Box Hour* program (WLW, Cincinnati, OH, 1928).

3451 **Blackstone, Reid.** DJ (*Sunrise Serenade*, WMVA, Martinsville, WV, 1947).

3452 ***(The) Blackstone Plantation Party.*** Blackstone Cigars sponsored the weekly musical variety show that featured Frank Cumit and his wife, Julia Sanderson. Their songs and gentle humor provided pleasant entertainment (30 min., Tuesday, 8:00–8:30 P.M., CBS, 1929–1930).

3453 ***Blackstone String Quartet.*** Classical music group (WGN, Chicago, IL, 1926–1928).

3454 **Blackwell, G.C.** Newscaster (WBLK, Clarksville, WV, 1945).

3455 **Blackwell, H.B. "Burt."** Newscaster (WAVE, Louisville, KY, 1937–1942, 1945).

3456 **Blacquiere, Bob.** DJ (KRCK, Ridgecrest, CA, 1960).

3457 **Blade, Jim.** Leader (*Jim Blade Orchestra*, instr. mus. prg., WMAQ, Chicago, IL, 1942).

3458 Blades, Pat. COM-HE (WFUN, Huntsville, AL, 1957).

3459 Bladmond, Vernon. DJ (*House of Blue Lights*, WSID, Baltimore, MD, 1952).

3460 Bladon, Doyle. DJ (*Happy Time*, KFOR, Lincoln, NE, 1952.)

3461 Blagg, Bob. DJ (*Record Reveille*, WDNE, Elkins, WV, 1948).

3462 *(The) Blah Club.* The *Blah Club* was one of the earliest of the zany variety programs that were so appealing to listeners of early radio. Credit for originating the program and acting as master of ceremonies and comedian was "Dizzy Izzy," otherwise known as "EKC" (Eugene Konecky).

Dizzy Izzy was the official poet laureate and humorist of stations WOAW and WOW (Omaha, NE). Dizzy Izzy's philosophy maintained that the "world was full of blah and that he [Izzy] was a little wild flower getting wilder every hour (*On the Air—A Magazine of Radio*, April, 1926, p. 11).

The program broadcast sessions of the Blah Club, whose residents included Dizzy Izzy, of course, Cy Perkins, Fred Jensen, Bill Goodrich, Eddie Stewart, Gus Swanson and Mac Ohman, all of whom were residents of Podunk Center. The broadcasts came from Cy Perkins' combined post office, grocery, barber shop, beauty parlor, drug store, restaurant, shoe shine parlor and undertaker's parlor. Other entertainers who added to the mid-afternoon mahem and madcap antics were Lew Ferris the "Eiffel Tower of Radio, Sid Jolson and pianist Louise Race. Another featured performer was composer Barry J. Sisk, who played the piano with his knuckles. Sisk was the acclaimed composer of the official American Legion march, "Armistice Day Forever."

The *Blah Club's* slogan was: "A little nonsense now and then is relished by the wisest men." The program was one of the earliest "nutty club" shows broadcast (*On the Air*, April, 1926, p.12).

The *Blah Club* was unique in that it was broadcast in the afternoon. The size of the Club's "membership" is an indication of how many listeners agreed with its philosophy of BLAH. During the first four months it was on the air, the Club attracted more than 35,000 members and had 25,000 applications still on file waiting for action. Dizzy Izzy boasted that he conducted the program with the other "inmates of the Omaha Psychopathic Institution known as the *Blah Club* (WOAW, 120 min., Friday, 4:00–6:00 P.M., WOAW, Omaha, NE, 1926).

3463 Blailock, Bill. Baritone (*Bill Blailock*, vcl. mus. prg., WCFL, Chicago, IL, 1937).

3464 Blaine, Betty. COM-HE (KDWT, Stamford, TX, 1957).

3465 Blaine, Gene. Sportscaster (*Today's Games*, WGST, Atlanta, GA, 1953). DJ (WAKE, Atlanta, GA, 1956; WPLO, Atlanta, GA, 1960).

3466 Blaine, Grace. Miss Blaine, a pianist, banjo soloist and singer appeared on the Bicycle Playing Card company station (WSAI, Cincinnati, OH, 1925).

3467 Blaine, Jerry. Leader (*Jerry Blaine Orchestra*, instr. mus. prg., WOR, Newark, NJ, 1934–1937).

3468 Blaine, Joan. Narrator and reader of prose selections (*Music Magic*, NBC, 1936. Actress Blaine was also a major daytime serial actress, who appeared on *Mary Marlin* aka *The Story of Mary Marlin* (title role) , *Tale of Today* and *Valiant Lady* (title role).

3469 Blaine, Lee. Newscaster (WBML, Macon, GA, 1945). DJ (*Requestfully Yours*, WGAD, Gadsden, AL, 1947). Sportscaster (WGAD, 1948).

3470 Blaine, Martin. Actor Blaine appeared on the *Evelyn Winters, FBI in Peace and War, Katie's Daughter, The Open Door, Valiant Lady* and *Young Dr. Malone* programs.

3471 Blaine, Mary. COM-HE (KCUL, Fort Worth, TX, 1956).

3472 Blaine, Mary. COM-HE (WGNY, Newburgh, NY, 1957–1958).

3473 Blaine, Mary. COM-HE (KOEL, Oelwein, IA, 1957).

3474 Blaine, Mary. COM-HE (WRTA, Altoona, PA, 1957).

3475 Blaine, Mary. COM-HE (WAFC, Staunton, VA, 1957).

3476 Blair, Anne. COM-HE (WGMS, Washington, DC, 1951–1954).

3477 Blair, Barbara. COM-HE (WEAM, Arlington, VA, 1957).

3478 Blair, Don. DJ (*This is the Hour*, WNBZ, Saranac Lake, NY, 1952–1953; WOC, Davenport, IA, 1954; WPOP, Hartford, CT, 1960).

3479 Blair, Ed. DJ (WQXI, Atlanta, GA, 1948).

3480 Blair, Elaine. Organist (WSUI, Iowa City, IA, 1927).

3481 Blair, Harry. DJ (*Late Date*, WGL, Fort Wayne, IN, 1952–1956).

3482 Blair, Henry. Actor Blair appeared on the *Adventures of Ozzie and Harriet, Beulah, Burns and Allen, One Man's Family* and *Red Ryder* programs.

3483 Blair, Jimmy. Singer (*Jimmy Blair*, vcl. mus. prg., 15 min., Saturday, 6:00–6:15 P.M., ABC, 1947).

3484 Blair, Kenny. DJ (*Noontime Tunes*, WKBI, St. Marys, PA, 1954).

3485 Blair, Les. DJ (*Dance Date*, WGET, Gettysburg, PA, 1952).

3486 Blair, Liz. COM-HE (KMBY, Monterey, CA, 1955).

3487 Blair, Merle. Sportscaster (KIND, Independence, MO, 1954). DJ (KTOP, Topeka, KS, 1956.)

3488 Blair, Michael. Sportscaster (Hollywood Legion Stadium boxing bouts and Gilmore Stadium boxing bouts, KFWB, Los Angeles, CA and CBS, 1939; football, baseball and horse racing broadcasts, CBS, 1939).

3489 Blair, Ray. DJ (*Night Watch Show*, WLAV, Grand Rapids, MI, 1954–1956; WRRR, Rockford, IL, 1957).

3490 Blair, Russell. Announcer (WLW, Cincinnati, OH, 1922).

3491 Blair, Ted. Newscaster (WCLS, Joliet, IL, 1945).

3492 Blair, Walter. Reader (KPO, San Francisco, CA, 1925).

3493 Blais, Dan. DJ (WLAU, Laurel, MS, 1949).

3494 Blake, Alix. DJ (*Stardreams*, WABY, Albany, NY, 1948; *Wake with Blake*, WENT; Gloversville-Johnstown, NY, 1949; WABY, 1954; *Star Dreams*, WABY, 1955).

3495 Blake, Bill. Tenor (KFWB, Hollywood, CA, 1925) Leader (Bill Blake and the Auburn Orchestra, KFWB, 1926–1928).

3496 Blake, Bruce. DJ (*Music for Ohio*, WHKK, Akron, OH, 1948–1949).

3497 Blake, Charles. DJ (*Goodtime Charlie*, WSON, Henderson, KY, 1952). Sportscaster (*Parade of Sports*, WSON, 1952).

3498 Blake, Doris. Lovelorn columnist (WMCA, New York, NY, 1940). Blake conducted a lovelorn column of the air, *Dear Doris Blake*, on which she provided solutions to the letters sent her by listeners.

3499 Blake, Florence. Soprano (KGO, Oakland, CA, 1928).

3500 Blake, Judy. Actress Blake appeared on the daytime serials *Mary Marlin* aka *The Story of Mary Marlin* and *Second Husband*.

3501 Blake, Julia [Julie]. COM-HE (WFEA, Manchester, NH, 1954–1958).

3502 Blake, Martha. Pianist (WTIC, Hartford, CT, 1926).

3503 Blake, Mary. Miss Blake broadcast talks on cooking (KOMO, Seattle, WA, 1929).

3504 Blake, Nancy. COM-HE (WHOL, Allentown, PA, 1954–1955).

3505 Blake, Peggy. Writer Blake worked on the *Barry Cameron, David Harum, Evelyn Winters* and *Just Plain Bill* programs.

3506 Blake, Randy. DJ (WJJD, Chicago, IL, 1940s). Blake was one of the first popular CW DJ's.

3507 Blake, Win. DJ (WKXL, Concord, NH, 1948).

3508 Blakeley, Arthur. Blakeley was an internationally known organist who broadcast recitals from the First Methodist Church, of Los Angeles (KHJ, Los Angeles, CA, 1923–1925).

3509 Blakely, Clint. DJ (*Time to Rise*, WAPI, Birmingham, AL, 1949; *Musical Clock*, WAPI, 1952).

3510 Blakeslee, Margaret. Violinist (WGR, Buffalo, NY, 1923).

3511 Blakiston, T.B. Newscaster (KMJ, Fresno, CA, 1945).

3512 Blanca, Flor. Leader (Flor Blanca and her Spanish Serenaders, KHJ, Los Angeles, CA, 1927).

3513 Blanchard, Barbara. Soprano (NBC-Pacific Coast, 1927).

3514 Blanchard, Lowell. Sportscaster (WNOX, Knoxville, TN, 1938–1942). DJ (*Musical Clock*, WNOX, 1947–1954).

3515 Blanchard, Red. DJ (WLS, Chicago, IL, 1954–1955).

3516 Blanchard's Dance Orchestra. Club band (KPRC, Houston, TX, 1926).

3517 *Blanche Sweet Beauty Talk.* Actress Sweet broadcast beauty help and hints (15 min., 10:15–10:30 A.M., CBS, 1935).

3518 Blanckey, Viola. Coloratura soprano (WRNY, New York, NY, 1926).

3519 Blanco, Eumenio. Baritone (WKY, Oklahoma City, OK, 1924; WGBS, New York, NY, 1927).

3520 Bland, Artie. DJ (KWBU, Corpus Christi, TX, 1956).

3521 Bland, Cecil. DJ (*Cowboy Jamboree*, KTBS, Shreveport, LA, 1949).

3522 Bland, Marjorie. Pianist (WSAI, Cincinnati, OH, 1925).

3523 Bland, Sam. DJ (WCEC, Rocky Mount, NC, 1948).

3524 Blane, Lee. DJ (*Morning Show*, WMSR, Manchester, TN, 1960).

3525 Blanford, Mary. COM-HE (WGRC, Louisville, KY, 1956).

3526 Blank, Hulda. Soprano (WHT, Chicago, IL, 1928).

3527 Blankenship, Marion. Harpist (WDAR, Philadelphia, PA, 1924).

3528 Blanton, Wally. Newscaster (KFJZ, Fort Worth, TX, 1940).

3529 Blasco, Frank. "Boy tenor" (WQJ, Chicago, IL, 1925).

3530 Blasey, Esther R. COM-HE (WCVI, Connellsville, PA, 1957).

3531 Blashill, John. DJ (*Hot Cake Club*, KVOE, Santa Ana, CA, 1949).

3532 Blaske, Art. DJ (*Musical Almanac*, KFAM, St. Cloud, MN, 1952–1954).

3533 Blauar, Estelle. COM-HE (KVOO, Tulsa, OK, 1951).

3534 Blaufuss, Walter. Leader (*Walter Blaufuss Orchestra*, instr. mus. prg., NBC, 1936). Balufuss for many years led the band on the long running *Breakfast Club* program.

3535 Blatz, Bill. Sportscaster (*Ten Pin Tattler*, WHKC, Colmbus, OH, 1940).

3536 Blayke, Bettye. COM-HE (WFGN, Gaffney, SC, 1958).

3537 Blazak, Joseph. Newscaster (KGFJ, Los Angeles, CA, 1945).

3538 Blazer, Eleanor J. COM-HE (WHOK, Lancaster, OH, 1954–1960).

3539 Bleck, Don. DJ (WBAT, Marion, IN, 1960).

3540 Bleck, Ruth. COM-HE (WIMS, Michigan City, IN, 1956–1957).

3541 Bleckley, W. John. DJ (*Crescent City Carnival*, WJMR, New Orleans, LA, 1949).

3542 Bledsoe, Jules. Singer on *The Theater Magazine* program (WGBS, New York, NY, 1928; *Jules Bledsoe*, vcl. mus. prg., WIP, Philadelphia, PA, 1935).

3543 Bleich, Selma. Pianist (WNYC, New York, NY, 1936).

3544 Blessey, Earl. Sportscaster (WVMI, Biloxi, MS, 1953). DJ (WVMI, 1954).

3545 Blessing, Sam. DJ (*Top Rail*, KMAN, Manhattan, KS, 1954; KDEN, Denver, CO, 1960).

3546 Blevens, Pat. COM-HE (KVNA, Flagstaff, AZ, 1960).

3547 Blevins, Kenneth "Ken." DJ (WTTH, Port Huron, MI, 1948; *Ken's Korner*, WTTH, 1952; WTTH, 1957).

3548 Blewett's Orchestra. Band from Denton, Texas (WBAP, San Antonio, TX, 1923).

3549 Bleyer, Archie. Leader (*Archie Bleyer Orchestra*, instr. mus. prg., WIP, Philadelphia, PA, and NBC, 1934; *Archie Bleyer and his Commodore Hotel Orchestra*, instr. mus. prg., WMCA, New York, NY, 1934; CBS, 1939).

3550 *Blind Date.* Arlene Francis was the hostess on this game show on which six servicemen competed with each other for dates with three women. General Foods, manufacturers of Maxwell House Coffee, sponsored the program written by Arlene Francis and Kenneth Rouight and directed by Tom Wallace (30 min., Thursday, 8:00–8:30 P.M., NBC-Red, 1943).

3551 Bliss, Beryl Brown. Soprano (KVOO, Tulsa, OK, 1928).

3552 Bliss, Edna. Blind pianist (KSO, Clarinda, IA, 1926).

3553 Bliss, Ted. Newscaster (KHJ, Los Angeles, CA, 1939).

3554 Bliven, Leona. Pianist (WOC, Davenport, IA, 1928).

3555 Blizzard, Junior. DJ (*Mail Train*, WMJM, Cordele, GA, 1954).

3556 Blizzard, Marie. Miss Blizzard was Columbia's fashion director. She conducted a show that presented fashion news (15 min., Monday and Friday, 3:30–3:45 P.M., CBS, 1930).

3557 Bloch, Ray. Pianist (*Ray Bloch*, inst. mus. prg., CBS, 1935–1938). Leader (*Ray Bloch Orchestra*, instr. mus. prg., CBS, 1939; *Ray Bloch's Swing Fourteen* [orchestra], instr. mus. prg., KWK, St. Louis, MO, 1942).

3558 *Bloch Party.* The Ray Bloch Orchestra was featured on his sustaining music program. Singers Judy Lynn, Russ Emery and a chorus also appeared on this entertaining show (30 min., Friday, 8:30–9:00 P.M., CBS, 1951).

3559 Block, Bert. Leader (*Bert Block Orchestra*, instr. mus. prg., CBS, 1935; WHK, Cleveland, OH, 1937).

3560 Block, Josephine. Leader of the KOA orchestra, she conducted *A Lesson in the Newest Dance Steps* program (KOA, Denver, CO, 1926).

3561 Block, Marie. Blizzard was Columbia's fashion director. She conducted a show that presented fashion news (15 min., Monday and Friday, 3:30–3:45 P.M., CBS, 1930).

3562 Block, Martin. DJ (*Make Believe Ballroom*, WNEW, New York, NY and ABC, 1947–1957; *The Martin Block Show*, MBS, 1948). Block's show with an imaginary ballroom format created the illusion for listeners that they were actually listening to "live" big bands. Block's career as an announcer included work on the *Chesterfield Supper Club*, *Make Believe Ballroom*, *Pepper Young's Family* and *Your Hit Parade* programs.

3563 Block, Mickey. Leader (Mickey Block and the Carolina Buccaneers Orchestra; WPTK, Raleigh, NC, 1928).

3564 Block, Rose. Soprano (KGEF, Los Angeles, CA, 1929).

3565 Block, Rosemary. COM-HE (KWPC, Muscatine, IA, 1955).

3566 Block, Roy. Leader (*Roy Block Orchestra*, instr. mus. prg., KOIL, Omaha, NE, 1939).

3567 Blocki, Fritz. Writer-director Blocki directed the *Chick Carter, Boy Detective* program.

3568 Blocki, Louise. Actress Blocki appeared on the *Rich Man's Darling* daytime serial.

3569 Blodgett, Hope. Violinist (WBZ, Springfield, MA, 1927).

3570 Bloemaker, Clarence. Tenor (WOR, Newark, NJ, 1926; WJR, Detroit, MI, 1926).

3571 *Blondie.* A long-running situation comedy, *Blondie* was based on the Chic Young comic strip by the same name. The title role was created by Penny Singleton, who also played it in a series of movies. She was followed in the role on radio by Ann Rutherford, Patricia Van Cleve and Alice White. Arthur Lake played her husband, Dagwood, in the movies and throughout the entire run of the radio program. Dagwood's boss, the blustering Mr. Dithers, was played by Hanley Stafford. The other members of the cast included: Elvia Allman, Marlene Ames, Arthur Q. Bryan, Conrad Binyon, Tommy Cook, Mary Jane Croft, Dix Davis, Harry Lang, Leone Ledoux, Frank Nelson, Norma Jean Nilsson, Howard Petrie, Joan Rae, Jeffrey Silver, Larry Sims, Lorene Tuttle and Veola Vonn. Bill Goodwin and Howard Petrie were the announcers. The show was written by Johnny Greene and directed by Eddie Pola. The producer-director was Don Bernard. Sound effects were by Parker Cornell (30 min., Monday, 7:30–8:00 P.M., CBS, 1939; NBC; ABC, 1950)

3572 Blood, Blanche. Leader (Hotel LaSalle Orchestra, WMAQ, Chicago, IL, 1924).

3573 Bloodworth, Bill. DJ (*Coffee Pot Parade*, WMVG, Milledgeville, GA, 1949–1952).

3574 Bloom, Edna Beatrice. Soprano (WEAF, New York, NY, 1925).

3575 Bloom, Mary. Sportscaster (WCED, Dubois, PA, 1946–1948; *Sports Review*, WCED, 1949).

3576 Bloom, Maury. DJ (WXRA, Buffalo-Kenmore, NY, 1954).

3577 Bloomquist, Saima. Pianist (KGO, Oakland, CA, 1926).

3578 Blossom Heath Serenaders. Popular radio band (WGBS, New York, NY, 1925).

3579 Blotcky, Anna K. Contralto (KTAB, Oakland, CA, 1926).

3580 Blotkofsy, Pauline. Pianist (WBKN, New York, NY, 1927).

3581 Blough, Bill. DJ (WBEL, Beloit, WI, 1956).

3582 Blount, Bob. Sportscaster (KPAN, Hereford, TX, 1951).

3583 Blount, James. DJ (WMSN, Raleigh, NC, 1956).

3584 Blount, Morrel. DJ (WDBF, Delray Beach, FL, 1960).

3585 Blower, Chuck. DJ (KTKT, Tucson, AZ, 1954).

3586 ***Blubber Bergman.*** Teddy Bergman, who later changed his name to Alan Reed, starred on the quarter-hour comedy program (15 min., Tuesday, 10:15–10:30 P.M., WGN, Chicago, IL, 1934).

3587 ***(The) Blubber Bergman Revue.*** Bigelow-Sanford Weavers and Schottenfeld's Carpet Store sponsored the transcribed comedy show featuring Teddy "Blubber" Bergman, who later changed his name to Alan Reed. Bergman performed in several brief comedy sketches assisted by Arlene Francis, Ray Collins, Paul Stewart and Katherine Renwick. The program was written by Hi Alexander (15 min., Tuesday, 8:00–8:15 P.M., WNEW, New York, NY, 1937).

3588 **Blue, Alice.** Organist-pianist (KTAB, Oakland, CA, 1929; *Alice Blue*, pianist, instr. mus. prg., WGN, Chicago, IL, 1935).

3589 **Blue, Bonnie.** A beauty, 5 feet 5 inches in height, Miss Blue had blue eyes and auburn hair. The blues singer gained fame for her appearance as the "Television Girl of the 1929 Radio Show" held in Chicago. A veteran radio performer, she had previously sung at WBAP, Fort Worth, TX, WFAA, Dallas, TX, and KPRC, Houston, TX, before working at Chicago's WBBM, Chicago, IL, in 1928–1929. She left Chicago to appear frequently on Pacific Coast radio in the early 1930s (*Bonnie Blue*, vcl. mus. prg., KRKD, Los Angeles, CA, 1933).

3590 **Blue, Dave.** DJ (*Twin Tune Hits*, WTEL, Philadelphia, PA, 1947).

3591 **Blue, Harriet.** COM-HE (KRE, Berkeley, CA, 1960).

3592 **Blue, Ira.** Sportscaster (*California Sports Searchlight*, *Football Scoreboard* and *Sports Graphic*, KGO-KPO, San Francisco, CA, 1938–1945; KGO, 1945–1946; *Adventures in Sports*, KGO, 1947–1949; *Blue Streak Final*, KGO, 1949–1951; ABC, 1951; KNBC, San Francisco, CA, 1953–1954; *Adventures in Sports*, KNBC, 1955; KGO, 1960).

3593 **Blue, Tommy.** Leader (*Tommy Blue Orchestra*, instr. mus. prg., MBS, 1939).

3594 ***Blue and Silver Orchestra.*** Instr. mus. prg. (WCAO, Baltimore, MD, 1936).

3595 ***Blue and White Marimba Band.*** The novelty band that specialized in Spanish music was led by Alfred Jamesworth (NBC, 1929).

3596 ***(The) Blue and White Minstrels.*** Frank Singhiser was the announcer of the typical radio minstrel show (NBC, 1929).

3597 ***(The) Blue Beetle.*** Frank Lovejoy played the title role of the super hero who fought crime and criminals on the transcribed adventure serial (Transcribed, Various Stations, 1930s).

3598 **Blue Bird Hawaiian Trio.** Hawaiian music group (WGN, Chicago, IL, 1926).

3599 **Blue Bird Orchestra.** Local radio band (WRW, Tarrytown, NY, 1925).

3600 ***Blue Birds.*** Vcl. mus. prg. by female vocal trio (CBS, 1935).

3601 **Blue Bonnet Serenaders.** Local radio orchestra (WFAA, Dallas, TX, 1925).

3602 **Blue Boy (a canary).** Leader on the *Blue Boy Canaries* program, he was said to "know" three hundred songs. "The World is Waiting for the Sunshine" was the canary's most popular selection, **Big Boy**, another canary, played a secondary role to **Blue Boy** on the program. Both birds were said to be Blue Forest Rollers (NBC, 1929–30).

3603 **Blue Grass Serenaders.** Country music group (WSM, Nashville, TN, 1926).

3604 **Blue Room Dance Orchestra.** Club dance band (WJR, Detroit, MI, 1925).

3605 ***Blue Belles.*** Vcl. mus. prg. by a female vocal trio (WLW, Cincinnati, OH, 1936).

3606 ***(The) Blue Coal Minstrels.*** Glen Alden was the interlocutor on the old fashion transcribed minstrel show. It opened with the traditional command: "Ladies and gentlemen be seated." Tambo and Bones were the End Men. Vocal selections were provided by the Blue Coal Quartet (15 min., Transcribed, Various Stations, Middle 1930s).

3607 ***Blue Coal Radio Revue.*** The first half-hour of the program featured the George Earle Orchestra. The second half was the *Shadow* mystery program (60 min., Sunday, 5:30–6:30 P.M., CBS, 1932). *See* ***The Shadow.***

3608 ***Blue Correspondents Abroad.*** World War II news correspondents of the NBC-Blue network reported daily on events from their particular part of the world (15 min., Weekdays, 1:15–1:30 P.M., NBC-Blue, 1944–1945).

3609 ***Blue Correspondents at Home and Abroad.*** Blue network correspondents reported the news on the weekly program (15 min., Sunday, 9:00–9:15 A.M., NBC-Blue, 1945).

3610 ***Blue Flames Quartet.*** Male quartet (vcl. mus. prg., CBS, 1936).

3611 ***Blue Grass Roy.*** CW singer-musician (CW voc. mus. prg., WTIC, Hartford, CT, 1936; WTIC, Hartford, CT, 1938).

3612 ***(The) Blue Jacket Choir.*** The U.S. Navy choir performed stirring songs on their weekly sustaining program (25 min., Sunday, 11:05–11:30 A.M., CBS).

3613 ***Blue Melody Hour.*** Joseph Honti conducted the orchestra on the good music program (30 min., Sunday, 8:00–8:30 A.M., NBC-Blue, 1937).

3614 ***Blue Monday Jamboree.*** The *Blue Monday Jamboree* was a West Coast variety show that contained music, comedy and a dramatic sketch (a detective story). The music was provided by baritone Harvey Austin and the Hawaiians and Mac's Haywire Orchestra (Monday evening, 8:00–10:00 P.M., KFRC, San Francisco, CA, 1927). A 1930 version, broadcast from 8:00 to 10:00 P.M., starred Harry "Mac" McClintock and virtually all of station KFRC's talent. Jazz singer Abe Bloom, known as the "Joy Boy of KFRC," was featured on this version, along with pianist Edna Fischer, comedians Monroe Upton (Simpy Fits), Harold Watanabe, Pedro (Eugene Hawes), Dippy and Morey Amsterdam; contraltos Margaret O'Dea and Lucille Atherton Harger; singers Edna Hazel Warner, Juanita Tennyson, Jean Wakefield and Edna O'Keefe; tenors Bob Olsen, Raymond Marlowe, Tommy Harris and Norman Neilsen; baritone Harold Dane; the vocal team of the Pearce Brothers; and a band led by saxophonist Mickey Gillette.

In 1931, the *Blue Monday Jamboree* added hilarious comedy sketches performed by Al Pearce as Silas Solomon; Eugene Hawes as Pedro; Monroe Upton as Lord Bilgewater; Tommy Monroe as Lem; and Arnold McGuire as Lafe. Edna O'Keefe assisted the comics in their routines and singer Norma Schiller was added as a regular cast member. Harrison Halloway was the host on the *Blue Monday Jamboree*, a genuinely pioneering radio program that was still going strong in 1935. Cast regulars on the last version of the show were singers Jean Ellington and Midge Williams, an 18-year-old Black blues singer; Murray and Harris, a team known as "The Crackpots of Comedy" and Claude Sweetan's Orchestra (60 min., Monday, 9:00–10:00 P.M., KFRC-CBS-Pacific Coast Network, 1935). *See* **Al Pearce** *and* **Simpy Fits.**

3615 ***(The) Blue Moon Orchestra.*** Local radio band (instr. mus. prg., WORK, York, PA, 1936).

3616 ***(The) Blue Mountain Boys.*** CW music group (CW mus. prg., WTNJ, Trenton, NJ, 1936).

3617 ***(The) Blue Ribbon Malt Jester.*** Richie Craig, Jr., the "Jest for Fun," man appeared on the comedy show sponsored by Blue Ribbon Malt liquor (15 min., 10:15–10:30 P.M., WABC, 1931).

3618 ***(The) Blue Ribbon Sports of Kings.*** Chicago's Arlington Park race track was the locale for the horse racing program. Don Ameche and sportscaster Jack Drees provided the color, conducted interviews and called the races on the program sponsored by Pabst Blue Ribbon Beer (37 min., Saturday, 4:30–5:07 P.M., CDT, NBC, 1950).

3619 ***(The) Blue Ridge Buddies.*** CW music group (CW mus. prg., WTIC, Hartford, CT, 1936).

3620 ***(The) Blue Ridge Harmonizers.*** CW music group (CW mus. prg., WMMN, Fairmont, WV, 1942).

3621 ***(The) Blue Ridge Mountain Boys.*** CW music group (CW mus. prg., KWTO, Springfield, MO, 1939).

3622 ***(The) Blue Ridge Mountain Girls.*** CW music group (CW mus. prg., WIRE, Indianapolis, IN, 1936–1937).

3623 ***(The) Blue Ridge Ramblers.*** CW music group (CW mus. prg., WWVA, Wheeling, WV, 1942).

3624 **Blue Sky Boys (William and Earl Bollick).** CW team featuring harmony duets accompanied by mandolin and guitar. They appeared on station WGST (Atlanta, GA) in 1946. They also appeared on the *Louisiana Hayride* (KWKH, Shreveport, LA).

3625 ***Blue Velvet.*** Coloratura soprano Hollace (Vivien) Shaw and Mark Warnow's Orchestra were featured on the sustaining music program (30 min., 9:30–10:00 P.M., CBS, 1938).

3626 ***(The) Bluebirds.*** Vcl. mus. prg. by a female vocal trio (WABC-CBS, New York, NY, 1934–1936).

3627 **Blueboys Orchestra.** Local radio band (WAMD, Minneappolis–St. Paul, 1926).

3628 ***(The) Blues Chasers.*** Harry Baker

planned and produced the program and directed the orchestra on the popular Pittsburgh music show. Vocalists Ralph (Hector) Hubertson, Cutty Buthall and Bill Rose were featured (60 min., Wednesday, 10:00–11:00 A.M., KQV, Pittsburgh, PA, 1936).

3629 **Bluett, Spots.** DJ (WWCO, Waterbury, CT, 1947).

3630 **Bluettes.** A female singing trio known in 1926 as the Three Coeds changed their names to the Bluettes in 1929. The trio included Theresa Aezer who sang, played piano and arranged songs for the other two members of the group, Marian Peck and Meredith Gregor. The Bluettes were popular Pacific Coast radio favorites in 1929.

3631 ***Bluff Creek Round Up.*** CW the show originated at KOMA (Oklahoma City, OK) in 1944. Its creator was KOMA station manager, Kenyon Brown. The program was broadcast from Oklahoma City's Shrine Auditorium before a crowd of more than 2,000. When Brown originated the show, he brought in veteran singer, comedian and MC Hiram Higsby. Higsby had just come from WLS (Chicago, IL). Prior to that he had appeared on the *Brush Creek Follies* (KMO, Kansas City, MO), the *Iowa Barndance* (WHO, Des Moines, IA), the *Renfro Valley Barn Dance* (WLW, Cincinnati, OH), *National Hillbilly Champion Show* (KMOX, St. Louis, MO) and the *Grand Ole Opry* (WSM, Nashville, TN). The featured performers on the show included cowboy singing star Dick Reinhart, Mary Lou "America's Most Beautiful Cowgirl Singer," singer Ann Bond, country comedian Lem Hawkins and a comic-musician from vaudeville Fred Fauntleroy. The veteran vaudevillian did pantomime comedy and played such weird musical instruments as the musical saw and the one string broom fiddle. Others on the show were the Carl Jones Quartette, whose specialty was spiritual songs; Billy Taylor, who was identified as "a sensational Negro tap dancer"; the Songbirds and a band known as Guy Sanderson and His Bluff Creek Rounders. Alan Page was the announcer. One indication of the show's success was that in 1946, just two years after its inception, it was estimated to have been seen by more than 200,000 audience members and heard over the radio by tens of thousands.

3632 **Blu-Green Gas Boys.** Male vocal group (vcl. mus. prg., KTM , Santa Monica, CA, 1928).

3633 **Blum, (Mme) Alice.** Blum taught French lessons on the *Radio Echo French Lessons* program (WRNY, New York, NY,1926).

3634 **Blum, Dorothy Herman.** Soprano (WEBH, Chicago, IL, 1925).

3635 **Blum, George.** Newscaster (KWAT, Watertown, SD, 1946). DJ (*Alarm Clock Club*, KORN, Mitchell, SD, 1948–1952).

3636 **Blum, Monte.** Tenor (WMBB, Chicago, IL, 1926).

3637 **Blum, Vaunceil.** COM-HE (KMMO, Marshall, MO, 1957).

3638 **Blumberg, Dorothy.** Pianist (WOR, Newark, NJ, 1934).

3639 **Blume, Ethel.** Blume appeared on the daytime serial programs *John's Other Wife*, *Joyce Jordan*, *Girl Interne* and *Red Davis*.

3640 **Blume, Mabel.** Soprano (WGCP, New York, NY, 1925).

3641 **Blumenstock, Carolyn.** COM-HE (WINI, Murphysboro, IL, 1958).

3642 **Blundon, George.** Baritone (WEAF, New York, NY, 1923).

3643 **Blunt, Carolyn.** COM-HE (WOKJ, Jackson, MS, 1956).

3644 **Blythe, Betty.** Motion picture actress Blythe provided advice on how to get into the movies (WGR, Buffalo, NY, 1923).

3645 **Blythe, Richard B.** Announcer (WEBJ, New York, NY, 1925).

3646 **Blytheville (Arkansas) Colored Glee Club.** Vocal music group (KLCN, Blytheville, AR, 1925).

3647 **"BMX."** Designation for announcer Stanley W. Barnett (WOC, Davenport, IA, 1925–1926).

3648 **"BN."** Announcer-singer Robert H. Nolan (WDAE, Tampa, FL, 1926).

3649 **Boaden, E. T.** Announcer (KSEI, Pocatello, ID, 1927).

3650 **Board, Helen.** Vocalist (*Helen Board*, vcl. mus. prg., WCBM, Baltimore, MD, 1934).

3651 **Boardman, Barry.** DJ (*Dance on the Down Beat*, WKOZ, Kosciusko, MS, 1954).

3652 **Boardman, Epley.** Singer (KWSC, Pullman, WA, 1925).

3653 **Boardman, Frank.** Sportscaster (*Sports Roundup*, KSWO, Lawton, OK, 1947). DJ (*1380 Club*, KSWO, 1948; *Frank Boardman Show*, KWFT, Wichita Falls, TX, 1949).

3654 **Boarman, Patrick.** Newscaster (CBS, 1947).

3655 **Boas, Jack.** Boas, the "Hunting and Fishing Scout" of the New York Hardware and Trading Company, talked about his specialty (KFWB, Hollywood, CA, 1925).

3656 ***Boating for Fun.*** H.E. Jamison talked about sailing, safety and boat maintenance (15 min., Thursday, 10:15–10:30 P.M., KIRO, Seattle, WA, 1948).

3657 **Boaz, Joan.** Blues singer (*Joan Boaz*, vcl. mus. prg., WLW, Cincinnati, OH, 1935).

3658 **Bob and Babe.** Unidentified performers who specialized in "singing and clogging" (KMA, Shannandoah, IA, 1926).

3659 **Bob and Ray.** Ray Goulding started as an announcer and newscaster at WHDH (Boston, MA), where he met Bob Elliott. They both began joking on the air and soon were given a show of their own. Their gentle satire and innovative comedy included the creation of such comic characters as Mary McGoon, Charles the Poet and Wally Ballou. Their show included such comic interludes as Mary Backstayge Wife; Hawaii Eye, Ear, Nose and Throat Man; One Feller's Family; The Gathering Dusk; and Linda Lovely. The team's formal debut was on Boston's WHDH broadcasting prior to the Red Sox baseball games. They later did their show on NBC in 1951.

After appearing on various other network shows, they performed regular five-minute comedy spots on *Monitor* in 1954; a DJ show for Mutual in 1956, and later a 15-minute Monday through Friday show for CBS (*Bob and Ray*, 15 min., Monday through Friday, 5:45–6:00 P.M., NBC, 1951; *The Bob and Ray Show*, NBC, CBS & Mutual, 1956). Always funny, their satire never cruelly skewered their targets. *See* **Comedy and Humor** *and* ***Matinee with Bob and Ray***.

3660 ***Bob Atcher Presents.*** Cowboy singer Bob Atcher hosted the CW music program featuring Don White, the Benson Valley Sweethearts and Lou Clatt's Orchestra (30 min., Monday through Friday, 1:30–2:00 P.M., WLS, Chicago, IL, 1951).

3661 ***Bob Barton — Hollywood Reporter.*** Barton discussed motion pictures and their stars (WAAF, Chicago, IL, 1935).

3662 ***Bob Becker's Dog Chats.*** Becker talked about all aspects of dog care and appreciation (15 min., 4:30–4:30 P.M., NBC, 1935).

3663 ***(The) Bob Burns Show* (aka *The Arkansas Traveler*).** Campbell Soup sponsored the dramatic series that presented Burns as a loveable hobo, who rode the rails all over the country. Each week he became involved in the lives of the people he tried to help. The announcers were Verne Smith and Gayne Whitman (25 min., 8:30–8:55 P.M., CBS, 1941). Burns first appeared on radio on Rudy Vallee's *Fleischmann Hour*, before he became a regular for five years on the *Kraft Music Hall* with Bing Crosby for five years. Burns is remembered for the invention of a "musical instrument" called the bazooka, an odd-looking and weird sounding, strangely shaped piece of pipe that he played too frequently. R.G. Dun Cigars sponsored Burns in a later format (*The Bob Burns Show*, 15 min., Tuesday, 6:30–6:45 P.M., CBS, 1942) that *Variety* said was more effective than his previous one had proved to be. This time Burns delivered his humorous dialogue more effectively. Frank Burke was the show's announcer In 1944, Burns hosted his *Bob Burns Lifebuoy Show* with Cass Daley, Spike Jones and the City Slickers and guest stars that included Frank Sinatra.

3664 ***Bob Byron.*** Music and comedy by Byron, a whistling pianist, made his program an entertaining one (CBS, 1937).

3665 ***(The) Bob Crosby Show.*** Singer Kay Armen, the Emil Cote Choir and Gus Haenschen's Orchestra were featured in addition to singer Crosby (30 min., Sunday, 10:30–11:00 P.M., NBC, 1950).

Formerly, the program was called the *Pet Milk Show*. Later, Crosby, his band and vocalist Joanie O'Brien were featured on a show by the same name sponsored by the U.S. Marine Corps. Jimmy Wallington was the announcer (15 min., Transcribed, middle or late 1950s).

3666 ***Bob Crosby's Night Shift.*** Bob Crosby joined the large number of celebrities and musical performers who became DJs (60 min., 9:00–10:00 P.M., ABC, 1950).

3667 ***(The) Bob Eberle Show.*** Popular singer Eberle performed live and played recorded music (15 min., Monday through Friday, 11:45–12:00 noon, WABC, 1957).

3668 ***(The) Bob Hawk Show.*** Quizmaster Bob Hawk conducted the quiz on which members of the studio audience answered increasingly difficult questions in order to become a L-E-M-A-C (Camel spelled backward) and win prizes offered by sponsor Camel Cigarettes (30 min., Weekly, CBS, NBC, 1945–1953). Bob Hawk made his reputation by conducting several popular radio quiz shows. *See* ***Quixie Doodles*** *and* ***Take It or Leave It***.

3669 ***(The) Bob Hope Show.*** Bob Hope was another vaudeville and Broadway comedian who found great success on radio. A quick-witted comic unafraid to gently tweak authority figures, he was praised for entertaining servicemen at various training camps from World War II through Viet Nam. Hope always had an excellent supporting ensemble that included talented second bananas, vocalists and a first-rate band.

Best known for his breezy, irreverent humor, Hope also appeared in many motion pictures. He was most famous for the "Road" pictures that also starred Bing Crosby. Hope began in vaudeville, starred in the *Follies*, and appeared on Broadway in the Jerome Kern musical, *Roberta*. Hope made his first radio appearance on Rudy Vallee's *Fleischmann Hour* in 1934. On September 27, 1938, Hope began his Pepsodent show for NBC that ran until 1950. From 1951 to 1958 Chesterfield cigarettes sponsored the show Hope broadcast from various military bases where he entertained service personnel. The show featured Jimmy Wakely, Marilyn Maxwell and Jerry Colonna (30 min., NBC, 1951–1958).

For many years during the run of Hope's shows, Barbara Jo Allen played the role of the distracted and somewhat disturbed comedy character of Vera Vague. "Professor" Jerry Colonna played the maniacal stooge who frequently upstaged Hope. Over the years Hope's cast members included: Barbara Jo Allen, Elvia Allman, Jerry Colonna, Frank Fontaine, Claire Hazel, Irene Ryan, Blanche Stewart and Patricia Wilder. The various orchestras on the show were Les Brown, Al Goodman, Skinnay Ennis and Red Nichols. His vocalists were Doris Day, Trudy Erwin, Frances Langford, Judy Garland and Gloria Jean. The vocal groups on the show were: Three Hits and a Miss (eventually changed to Six Hits and a Miss to include Pauline Byrnes, Marvin Bailey, Vincent Degen, Howard Hudson, Mack McLean, Jerry Preshaw and Bill Seckler. His writers included: Jack Douglas, Fred S. Fox, Hal Block, Al Josefsberg, Samuel Kurtzman, Larry Marks, Ted McKay, Albert Schwartz, Mel Shavelson and Norman Sullivan. The program's announcers were Hy Averback, Art Baker, Bill Goodwin, Larry Keating, Jackson Weaver and Wendell Niles (CBS, NBC, 1938–1958). Hope made a successful transition from radio to television. His 1996 television special, *Laughing with the Presidents*, marked Hope's 58th year on NBC radio and television.

3670 ***Bob Johnson and Ilene Woods.*** The vocal team of Johnson and Woods made this a pleasant daily musical feature (15 min., 11:45–12:00 noon, NBC-Blue, 1945).

3671 ***Bob Wills and the Texas Playboys.*** Wills' fine western swing band appeared on several stations before broadcasting on KXLA (Los Angeles, CA), during his appearance at the Harmony Ballroom in Los Angeles. At the time his group included Jack Lloyd, Keith Coleman and vocalist Louise Rowe. Wills attracted guest stars such as Molly Bee and Patsy Montana (30 min., Monday through Friday, 12:30–1:00 P.M., KXLA, Los Angeles, CA, 1953).

3672 **Bobb, Charles J.** DJ (*Sunset and Vine*, KVOB, Alexandria, LA, 1948; *Music Shop*, KVOB, 1949).

3673 **Bobbitt, Happy.** DJ (*Coffee Time*, WBOB, Galax, VA, 1947).

3674 ***Bobby Benson and the B-Bar-B Riders*** **(aka** ***Bobby Benson and Sunny Jim*** **and** ***Bobby Benson's Adventures*****).** The daytime serial first appeared in several formats with different names (15 min., Monday through Friday, 5:15–5:30 P.M., CBS, 1935). The program returned in 1949 on MBS as a summer replacement for *Straight Arrow*. In its first format sponsored by H-O Oats cereal, the program offered its young listeners a large number of premiums for package tops or a single top alone and cash such as: Ranger's badge for 2 box tops or 1 and 5 cents; Rodeo rope with directions how to spin it for 5 box tops or 1 box top and 15 cents; Ranger's bandanna for 2 box tops or 1 box top and 5 cents; Cartridge belt for 5 box tops or 1 and 15 cents; Ranger's gun for 5 box tops or 1 and 15 cents; Gun holster for 5 box tops or 1 and 15 cents; Ranger's cuffs for 8 box tops or 1 and 30 cents; Ranger's spurs for 10 box tops or 1 box top and 35 cents; Ranger's hat for 20 box tops or 1 box top and 85 cents; and Ranger's chaps for 25 box tops or 1box top and $1.45. It should be remembered that money in the Great Depression era was scarce for many listeners.

The later sustaining western adventure series featured 12-year-old Bobby as the leading character. *Variety* noted that somehow this later version never seemed to be as entertaining as the version broadcast earlier. The cast of the latter program included: Ivan Curey, Craig McDonnell, Charles Irving and Don Knotts. Bob Emerick was the announcer (30 min., Tuesday and Thursday, 5:00–5:30 P.M., MBS, 1949). Don Knotts as Wally Wales provided entertaining comic relief.

3675 ***(The) Bobby Breen Show.*** Ex-child film star Breen displayed a good tenor voice on his local New York local radio show (15 min., WHN, New York, NY, 1947). Breen first gained popularity from his appearances as a child singer on the *Eddie Cantor Show*.

3676 ***Bobby Hackett and the Best Jazz Band in the Land.*** Brilliant jazz cornetist Hackett led his little band from Nick's Restaurant in New York's Greenwich Village (30 min., Networks, 1940s).

3677 ***(The) Bobby Sherwood Show.*** Band leader Sherwood played piano and trumpet on his show, as well as performing DJ duties (30 min., Monday through Friday, 5:00–5:30 P.M., 1955).

3678 **Bobcok, May E.** Pianist (WGR, Buffalo, NY, 1925).

3679 **Bobisud, Walt.** DJ (KBKR, Baker, OR, 1947).

3680 **Bobrow, Norm.** DJ (*Jazz at the Philharmonic*, KOMO, Seattle, WA, 1952).

3681 **Bocco, Joseph M.** Tenor (WEBJ, New York, NY, 1926).

3682 **Bocelli, Luigi.** Lyric tenor (NBC, 1928).

3683 **Bocho, Rudolph.** Violinist (*Rudolph Bocho*, instr. mus. prg., NBC, 1934–1935).

3684 **Bock, Bob.** DJ (KLAS, Las Vegas, NV, 1960).

3685 **Bockley, Taylor.** Baritone (WGBS, New York, NY, 1928).

3686 **Bockstein [Blockstein], Edna.** Pianist (WAHG, Richmond Hill, NY, 1926).

3687 **Boda, Lou.** DJ (*Good Morning*, WJER, Dover, OH, 1952). Sportscaster (WMBH, Joplin, MO, 1953–1954).

3688 **Boden, (Miss) Rose.** Miss Boden sang on WLW's inaugural program (WLW, Cincinnati, OH, 1922).

3689 **Bodge, Dave.** DJ (WOTW, Nashua, NH, 1949).

3690 **Bodgen [Bogden], Hilary.** Newscaster (WJAS, Pittsburgh, PA, 1948). DJ (*Old Timer's Party*, WJAS, 1954). Sportscaster (WJAS, 1954).

3691 **Bodkin, Larry.** DJ (*Light Flash*, WTAL, Tallahassee, FL, 1947).

3692 **Bodner, George.** DJ (*Melody Mill*, WRFD, Worthington, OH, 1948).

3693 **Bodycombe, Aneurin.** Newscaster (KDKA, Pittsburgh, PA, 1945).

3694 **Boe, Shari.** COM-HE (WLDL, LaCrosse, WI, 1956).

3695 **Boehm, Lucian.** DJ (*1490 Club*, WCPM, Cumberland, KY, 1952).

3696 **Boehm, Marion.** COM-HE (KBTM, Jonesboro, AR, 1955).

3697 **Boehm, Mary Kay.** COM-HE (WITZ, Jasper, IN, 1956).

3698 **Boelter, Erwin.** DJ (*Concert Miniature*, KJAM, Vernal, UT, 1947).

3699 **Boerstein, Irving.** Leader (Irving Boerstein Trio, WRC, Washington, DC, 1924; Irving Boerstein's Hotel Washington Orchestra, WRC, 1926).

3700 **Boesch, Roy.** DJ (WIOU, Kokomo, IN, 1960).

3701 **Boettcher, Edmund P.** Tenor (WFAA, Dallas, TX, 1926).

3702 **Boettiger, C.O.** Announcer (KFBB, Havre, MT, 1926).

3703 **Bogard (Dr.) Ben.** Bogard, minister of the Antioch Missionary Baptist Church, was one of Little Rock's most dynamic preachers. He broadcast sermons on such topics as, "Man or Monkey, Which?" Hymns were performed by the Antioch Choir (WLBN, Little Rock, AR, 1928).

3704 **Bogard, Tillie I.** COM-HE (COM-HE, KOKY, Little Rock, AR, 1958).

3705 **Bogardus, R.E.** Announcer (WQAO, New York City, NY, 1925).

3706 **Bogarte, Howard.** Newscaster (KRDD, Dallas, TX, 1938). DJ (*Music in the Night*, WFAA, Dallas, TX, 1948).

3707 **Boger, Dorothy.** Violinist (KYW, Chicago, IL, 1923).

3708 Boger, Eugene. DJ (*Gene's House Party*, KWYO, Sheridan, WY, 1947).

3709 Boggess, John. Newscaster (WMSL, Decatur, IL, 1939). Sportscaster (WLAG, LaGrange, GA, 1946–1947, 1953–1955; WPCF, Panama City, FL, 1956). DJ (*Request Hour*, WLAG, 1948–1952).

3710 Boggess, Bill. Tenor crooner (WFAA, Dallas, TX, 1929).

3711 Boggs, Bill. DJ (WJPA, Washington, PA, 1956).

3712 Boggs, Catherine. Soprano (WCAE, Pittsburgh, PA, 1924).

3713 Boggs, Otis. Sportscaster (WRUF, Gainesville, FL, 1940–1946; WFAA, Dallas, TX, 1947; *Speaking of Sports*, WRUF, 1948; *Sports Matinee*, WRUF, 1949–1953; *Sports Review*, WRUF, 1954–1955).

3714 Boggs, Ran. DJ (*Music of the Masters*, WMTC, Vancleve, KY, 1952).

3715 Bogolub, Sally. Bogolub was one of the intelligent "kids" on the *Quiz Kids* program (NBC, ABC, CBS, 1940–1953).

3716 Boguslawski, Lillian and Moissaye Boguslawski. Popular piano team (NBC, New York, NY, 1929).

3717 Boguslawski, Moissaye. Pianist (*Moissaye Boguslawski*, instr. mus. prg., WIND, Gary, IN, 1936).

3718 Bohack, Bill. Newscaster (WPAT, Paterson, NJ, 1944). DJ (*Band Box*, WPAT, 1948).

3719 Bohannan, John. Announcer (WMAK, Buffalo, NY, 1926).

3720 Bohannon, Florence. Soprano (KJR, Seattle, WA, 1930).

3721 Bohannon, J.K. Announcer who introduced his Norfolk station as "Down in old Virginia" (WTAR, Norfolk, VA, 1926).

3722 Bohannon, Ray. DJ (KATO, Reno, NV, 1947).

3723 Boheke, Vera. Singer (KFAE, Spokane, WA, 1925).

3724 *Bohemian Nights.* An early 1930s music program, *Bohemian Nights* was filled with atmosphere as the announcer said in opening: "Atmosphere is the prevailing quality at Pietro's Bohemian Cafe. The sightseer in New York may find the artist and the would-be artist talking across the same table, inhaling the same tobacco fumes and after 3:00 A.M. drinking Pietro's famous dago red. A few bottles of this liquid and everybody in the cafe is your friend. Tonight, Pietro has fairly outdone himself with caviar and Russian olives... ." (15 min., Transcribed, Various stations, early 1930s).

3725 *Bohemian Orchestra.* Local Nebraska band (instr. mus. prg., KFAB, Lincoln, NE, 1940).

3726 Bohl, Charlene. COM-HE (KDOV, Medford, OR, 1958).

3727 Bohlsen, Martha. COM-HE (WOW, Omaha, NE, 1951).

3728 Bohman, Dorothy. Pianist (WOW, Omaha, NE, 1927).

3729 Bohman, Ronnie. Newscaster (WKBS, Oyster Bay, NY, 1948).

3730 Bohn, Adolph. Bohn was the conductor of the Corps de Ballet of the Chicago Civic Opera Company (KYW, Chicago, IL, 1923).

3731 Bohn, Hal. Newscaster (WGN, Chicago, IL, 1941).

3732 Bohne, Marion. COM-HE (KBTM, Jonesboro, AR, 1957).

3733 Bohnsack, Christie E. Announcer (WNYC, New York City, NY, 1927).

3734 Bohrer, Alphonse. Pianist (WJZ, New York, NY, 1923).

3735 *Bohumer Kryl Band.* Instr. mus. prg. (CBS, 1936).

3736 Boislair, Stephen E. Organist (WGY, Schenectady, NY, 1925–1926 and WGR, Buffalo, NY, 1926).

3737 Boivin, Jay. DJ (*1370 Streamliner*, WFEA, Manchester, NH, 1946–1949).

3738 Boker, Bill. DJ (*Western Caravan*, WMIK, Middleboro, KY, 1952). Sportscaster (WMIK, 1952).

3739 Bolan, Bert. Violinist-vocalist Bolan appeared on the *Musical Mirth Makers* program (WBZ, Springfield, MA, 1926).

3740 Boland, Joe. Sportscaster (WFAM-WSBT, South Bend, IN, 1939; *Football*, WCFL, Chicago, IL, 1948–1951; *Joe Boland on Sports*, WCFL, 1947–1957).

3741 Boland, Joe. Sportscaster (KTLN, Denver, CO, 1954; KWBY, Colorado Springs, CO, 1955).

3742 Boland, Myrtle. Vocalist Boland was billed as "The Love Racketeer" (*Myrtle Boland*, vcl. mus. prg., NBC-Blue Network, New York, NY, 1934).

3743 Bolby, Bob. DJ (*Record Rodeo*, KOVE, Lander, WY, 1947–1949).

3744 Bolding, Pat. COM-HE (WCGC, Belmont, NC, 1955).

3745 Boldt, Vic. DJ (*Polka Time*, KVIC, Victoria, TX, 1952; KVIC, 1955).

3746 Bolek, George. Pianist (WBAL, Baltimore, MD, 1926–1928).

3747 Bolen, Jim. DJ (*1020 Club*, WCIL, Carbondale, IL, 1947–1949). Sportscaster (WCIL, 1949).

3748 Bolen, Merrill O. Announcer (KFMX, Northfield, MN, 1926).

3749 Bolender, Richard "Dick." DJ (*Concert Hall*, WBRK, Pittsfield, MA, 1947; WBBK, 1947).

3750 Bolero, Leon. Leader (*Leon Bolero Orchestra*, instr. mus. prg., WIP, Philadelphia, PA, 1936).

3751 Boles, Jerry J. DJ (*Battle of Baritones*, WMON, Moundsville, WV, 1952).

3752 Boles, Jim. Actor Boles worked on the *Best Sellers, Fishing and Hunt Club, Gene Autry'Melody Ranch (Melody Ranch), I Love a Mystery, Land of the Lost, Mr. Fix-It, The O'Neills, Tennessee Jed* and *Two on a Clue* programs.

3753 Boles, Martha Jane. COM-HE (WTRC, Elkhart, IN, 1951).

3754 Boles, Paul. DJ (*Don't Look Now*, WFUR, Grand Rapids, MI, 1948; *Doc Boles Show*, WKBZ, Muskegon, MI, 1949).

3755 Boley, Ray. Newscaster (WLEU, Erie, PA, 1940).

3756 Bolger, Anna. Mezzo-soprano (WOR, Newark, NJ, 1923).

3757 Bolich, Mary. COM-HE (WKVA, Lewistown, PA, 1960).

3758 Bolin, Art. DJ (*Swing Session* and *Uncle Art's Almanac*, WARM, Scranton, PA, 1947–1948; *The Borden Show*, WARM, 1949).

3759 Bolin, Lee. Tenor (KFI, Los Angeles, CA, 1925).

3760 Bolinks, Link. Leader (Link Bolinks and his Cowboy Band, KVOO, Tulsa, OK, 1928).

3761 Boll, Linus. Pianist (1925).

3762 Boller, Phil. DJ (WKHM, Jackson, MI, 1957; *Sunriser*, WKNX, Sagninaw, MI, 1960).

3763 Boller, Wally. DJ (WDLB, Marshfield, WI, 1956).

3764 Bolley, Leo. Sportscaster (WGY, Schenectady, NY, 1937; WFBL, Syracuse, NY, 1939–1942).

3765 Bollinger, Gene. DJ (*Musical ABC's*, KCSJ, Pueblo, CO, 1948; *As You Like It* and *Hillbilly Holiday*, WEGO, Concord, NC, 1949; WLET, Toccoa, GA, 1956).

3766 Bollinger, Jim DJ (*Jim Bollinger Time* and *Parade of Hits*, WINN, Louisville, KY, 1948; *Saturday Morning Swing*, WINN, 1949).

3767 Bollwinkel, Calvin "Cal." DJ (*Great Day Show*, WHFB, Benton Harbor, MI, 1948; *Hayloft Jamboree*, WHUC, Hudson, NY, 1949).

3768 Bolognini, Ennio. Cellist (*Ennio Bolognini*, instr. mus. prg., NBC, 1934). Leader (*Ennio Bolognini Orchestra*, instr. mus. prg., WENR, Chicago, IL, 1939).

3769 Bolokovic, Z. Violinist (WJZ, New York, NY, 1925).

3770 Bolt, Arthur. Tenor (WGR, Buffalo, NY, 1923).

3771 Bolt, Mary. COM-HE (WROZ, Kosciusko, MS, 1957).

3772 Bolten, Geneva. COM-HE (KREL, Baytown, TX, 1954).

3773 Bolton, Bill. DJ (*Number Please*, KSYL, Alexandria, LA, 1947). Sportscaster (*Tendercrust Sports Review* and *Football Play-by-Play*, KSYL, 1947).

3774 Bolton, George. Newscaster (KTBI, Tacoma, WA, 1945).

3775 Bolton, Jack. DJ (KHEY, El Paso, TX, 1960).

3776 Bolton, Joe. Sportscaster (WMCA, New York, NY, 1937).

3777 Bolton, Virginia. COM-HE (WUSN, Charleston, SC, 1951).

3778 Boltz, Irene. Vocalist (KVOO, Tulsa, OK, 1928).

3779 Bomer, Bill. DJ (KBCH, Oceanlake, OR, 1956).

3780 Bon Bon. Vocalist (*Bon Bon*, vcl. mus. prg., WCAU, Philadelphia, PA, 1936).

3781 Bonaldi, Nino. Baritone (WHAM, Rochester, NY, 1928).

3782 Bonapart, Allan. DJ (*This Afternoon*, WIBX, Utica, NY, 1954–1955).

3783 Bonar, Leon. DJ (*Morning Music Hall*, KAWT, Douglas, AZ, 1947).

3784 Bonasso, Russ. DJ (*Meet the Missus*, WBLK, Clarksburg, WV, 1949). Sportscaster (*Muntzing Newscast*, WBLK, 1939).

3785 Bonawitz, Karl. Organist and pianist (WIP, Philadelphia, PA, 1925; WPG, Atlantic City, NJ, 1926; *Karl Bonawitz*, instr. mus. prg., KYW, Philadelphia, PA, 1936).

3786 Boncoeur, Vade. Newscaster (WSYR, Syracuse, NY, 1945).

3787 Bond, Bernard. DJ (*Platter Chatter*, KCHS, Hot Springs, NM, 1947).

3788 Bond, Betty. Singer (WOR, Newark, NJ, 1932).

3789 Bond, Betty. COM-HE (WSLS, Roanoke, VA, 1955).

3790 Bond, Billie. COM-HE (WIKC, Bogalusa, LA, 1956).

3791 Bond, Bryce. DJ (*Memo Pad*, WVOX, New Rochelle, NY, 1960).

3792 Bond, Curley. Pseudonym for announcer Stanley Houston. *See* **Houston, Stanley**.

3793 Bond, Edna. Singer (KFON, Long Beach, CA, 1928).

3794 Bond, Ford. Singer Bond, who in later years became an announcer-sportscaster-commentator, was born October 23, 1904. He toured as an oratorio soloist after he graduated from college, before making his first radio appearance on WHAS, Louisville, KY, in 1921. He joined NBC (New York) in 1929. Bond appeared on many *General Motors* programs broadcast on the NBC-Red Network (1928–1930) and the *Collier's Hour* program also on the NBC-Red network (1929–1931). He was a sportscaster later on his *Ford Bond—Sports Program* (WEAF, New York, NY, 1934). Early in his professional career, Bond often teamed with Graham McNamee to announce various sports events. Among the many other programs he announced were *Backstage Wife*, *Cities Service Concert*, *David Harum*, *Easy Aces*, *Manhattan Merry-Go-Round* and *Stella Dallas*.

3795 Bond, Jane. COM-HE (KLWN, Lawrence, KS, 1955).

3796 Bond, Jean. COM-HE (KEEN, San Jose, CA, 1956).

3797 Bond, Lyle. Sportscaster (KHJ, Los Angeles, CA, 1953).

3798 Bond, Margaret. Violinist (KMTR, Hollywood, CA, 1926).

3799 Bond, Marjorie Irene. Journalist Bond appeared three times a week discussing the experiences and ideas of a newspaper woman (KOA, Denver, CO, 1926). Bond also wrote regularly for the Denver *Express* newspaper as Cynthia Grey.

3800 Bond, Richard. DJ (KEEO, Springfield-Eugene, OR, 1960).

3801 *(The) Bond Bread Show.* Frank Crumit and Julia Sanderson starred on the musical variety show (CBS, 1934–1935).

3802 Bondietti, Helene. Violinist (WCOH, New York, NY, 1932).

3803 Bonds, Buddy. Organist (*Buddy Bonds*, instr. mus. prg., WIP, Philadelphia, PA, 1935).

3804 Bonds, Hoyt. DJ (*South Forty*, WTCB, Flomaton, AL, 1960).

3805 Bondshu, Neil. Leader (*Neil Bondshu Orchestra*, instr.mus. prg., WWL, New Orleans, LA, 1942).

3806 Bondu, Dave. Black DJ (*Bondu's Rendez-Vous*, WERD, Atlanta, GA, 1949).

3807 Bondu, Dave and Mayme Bondu. Black husband-and-wife DJ team (*Mr. and Mrs. Swing*, WERD, Atlanta, GA, 1940s).

3808 Bone, Billy. DJ (*Record Party*, WHSC, Hartsville, SC, 1949). Sportscaster (WHSC, 1949; WNOK, Columbus, SC, 1956).

3809 Boner, Ester. COM-HE (KWNA, Winnemucca, NV, 1960).

3810 Boner, Lee. DJ (*Saturday Night Swing Session*, KAWT, Douglas, AZ, 1948; *Easy Rhythm*, KAWT, 1949).

3811 Bonet, John. DJ (*Dial for Music*, KPHO, Phoenix, AZ, 1954).

3812 Bongiorno, Michael. DJ (WHOM, New York, NY, 1947).

3813 Boni, Elvira. Soprano (WEAF, New York, NY, 1926).

3814 Bonick, Lou. Leader (*Lou Bonick Orchestra*, instr. mus. prg., WNAC, Boston, MA, 1932.)

3815 Boniel, Robert D. Announcer and director (WEBH, Chicago, IL, 1928).

3816 Bonime, Josef. Musical conductor Bonime was born in Vilna, Poland. He first appeared on radio directing a small ensemble (WJZ, New York, NY, 1925).

3817 Bonin, Donald. Sportscaster (*Sports Review* and *Football Final*, KANE, New Iberia, LA, 1948–1955). DJ (*Alarm Clock Club*, KANE, New Iberia, LA, 1949).

3818 Bonligny, Myrza Mayer. Concert pianist (WSMB, New Orleans, LA, 1928).

3819 Bonn, Ted. DJ (*The Ted Bonn Show*, WKLV, Blackstone, VA, 1948).

3820 Bonneau, Robin. DJ (WTSV, Claremont, NH, 1954).

3821 Bonnell, George. DJ (*Juke Box Review*, WIHL, Hammond, LA, 1949; *Kitchen Club*, WJBO, Baton Rouge, LA, 1955). Sportscaster (WIHL, 1953).

3822 Bonnelly [Bonnelle], Eddy. Leader (*Eddy Bonnelly Orchestra*, instr. mus. prg., WIP, Philadelphia, PA, 1935).

3823 Bonner, Crenshaw. Sportscaster (WAGA, Atlanta, GA, 1940–1941).

3824 Bonner, Ed. DJ (*St. Louis Ballroom*, KXOK, St. Louis, MO, 1948–1957).

3825 Bonner, Ed. DJ (*Spin 'N' Chin*, WNJR, Newark, NJ, 1949; KXOK, St. Louis, MO, 1955).

3826 Bonner, Frank A. Cornetist (WCOA, Pensacola, FL, 1926).

3827 Bonner, (Captain) M.J. A Confederate veteran of the Civil War, Bonner was an old-time fiddler who appeared on WBAP's square dance program's first broadcast on January 4, 1923 (WBAP, San Antonio, TX, 1923).

3828 Bonner, Wimmer. Contralto (KPO, San Francisco, CA, 1923).

3829 Bonnett, Jim. DJ (*Hillbilly Hits*, KALB, Alexandria, LA, 1952).

3830 Bonnett, Lee. COM-HE (KTOO, Henderson, NV, 1958).

3831 *Bonnett Sisters.* Vcl. mus. prg. by harmony trio (WMAQ, Chicago, IL, 1935).

3832 *Bonnie and the Boys.* Mixed vocal group (Vcl. mus. prg., KMBC, Kansas City, MO, 1939).

3833 (The) Bonnie Laddies. Vocal trio consisting of Charles Kenny, Lou Noll and Jimmie Whalen (NBC-Blue Network, New York, NY, 1927).

3834 Bonnie Lou (Mary Kath). CW singer Bonnie Lou made her radio debut in 1939 (WMBD, Peoria, IL). She went on to sing on WJBC (Bloomington, IL, 1940–1942). She later sang on the *Brush Creek Follies* as Sally Carson. She became Bonnie Lou when she sang on the *Midwestern Hayride* (WLW, Cincinnati, OH) in 1945.

3835 Bono, Victor. Newscaster (WPAB, Ponce, PR, 1944).

3836 *Bono's Orchestra.* Local band (instr. mus. prg., WKBW, Buffalo, NY, 1937).

3837 Bonrel, Robert. Announcer (WEBH, Chicago, IL, 1927).

3838 Bontay, Ruth. Blues singer (WSWS, Chicago, IL, 1926).

3839 Bontempo, Michele. Baritone (WEBJ, New York, NY, 1925–1926).

3840 Booen, Sherman "Sherm." Sportscaster (KATE, Albert Lea, MN, 1940). Newscaster (KATE, 1940). DJ (*Holsum Time* and *Friendly Time*, WDGY, Minneapolis, MN, 1948–1949).

3841 Boogar, Marian. Boogar performed pianologues (KFQZ, Hollywood, CA, 1926).

3842 *Book Chats.* WOI, the station of Iowa State University, originated the program about books and their authors. It was rebroadcast by the State University of Iowa's station (WSUI) in 1936.

3843 *(The) Book Club.* The *Book Club* program arose from the need of many rural Iowans to gain access to books at a time when county roads were unpaved and local libraries few. At that time station WOI in cooperation with the Iowa State University Library invited listeners to borrow certain books by mail from the university library. Each month club members received a booklet listing the titles available to them. The program was broadcast daily from Monday to Friday, 10:05 to 10:30 A.M. In 1940, the lending library function was discontinued, but the radio program continued. After the lending operation ceased, the program's format changed to one on which a reader each day would read a portion of a book. *Bambi* was the first book read on the program. It was read a few pages a time over a period of seven weeks. The readers during the program's run included Andy Woolfries, Ruth Galvin, Betty Wells, Marjorie Donaldson, Victoria Hargrave, Lucille Gibb, Charlotte Peterson, Ed Wegner, Martha Duncan, Ray Giese and Erik Warren. Program Director Doug Brown took over as reader in 1964 and continues in that role today (WOI, Ames, IA).

3844 *(The) Book House Story Man.* Don Carney (later Uncle Don) starred on the early comedy show (WOR, Newark, NJ, 1930).

3845 *(The) Book of the Week.* Book reviewer George Douglas discussed various literary topics and a recently published books (KPO, San Francisco, CA, 1924).

3846 ***(The) Book Parade.*** Critic Harry Hansen discussed books and their authors (15 min., Thursday, 5:00–5:15 p.m, CBS, 1935).

3847 ***Books.*** Levere Fuller discussed current books (15 min., Friday, WGY, Schenectady, NY, 1934).

3848 ***Books.*** Critic Rosalind Jewet broadcast her critical opinions on the weekly program (15 min.,Wednesday, 1:30–1:45 P.M., WOR, Newark, NJ, 1934).

3849 ***Books in the Limelight.*** Book news and reviews were broadcast on the program weekly (15 min., Friday, 6:00–6:15 P.M., WJZ, New York, NY, 1930).

3850 ***Books with Lewis Gannett.*** Critic Gannett broadcast book reviews (CBS, 1936).

3851 **Bookspan, Martin.** DJ (*Off the Record,* WBMS, Boston, MA, 1949).

3852 **Bool, L.E.** Announcer (WRAL, Ithaca, NY, 1927).

3853 **Boom, Jane.** DJ (*Package from Parkers,* WOC, Davenport, IA, 1948).

3854 **Boon, Charlie.** DJ (KFGO, Fargo, ND, 1956; WCCO, St. Paul, MN, 1960).

3855 **Boone, Joe.** DJ (*Moonlight Melodies,* WMVG, Milledgeville, GA, 1948–1956). Sportscaster: WMVG, 1955).

3856 **Boone, Mildred.** Organist (KTBI, Los Angeles, CA, 1927).

3857 **Boone, Robert.** DJ (WBYS, Canton, IL, 1947).

3858 ***Boone County Jamboree.*** Harold Carr produced and Bob Lacey hosted the popular CW music program sponsored by Pinex Cough Syrup. The featured performers were the Boone County Bucaneers, Sunshine Sue and her Rangers, the Happy Valley Girls and the Girls of the Golden West — Millie and Polly Good. Comedy was supplied by Merle Travis as "Possum Gossip" (30 min., Saturday, 8:00–8:30 P.M., WLW, Cincinnati, OH, 1938; MBS, 1939). The program became *The Midwestern Hayride* and continued well into the 1960s. The Drifting Cowboys, Merle Travis, Bill Brown, Morris "Sleepy" Marlin and Walter Brown were featured. Other performers on the show were ventriloquist Kenny Carson with his "pal," Scrappy O'Brien, Hugh Cross and His Radio Pals, the Boone County Buccaneers, Grandpa Jones, Grandpappy Doolittle, Lafe Harkness and the Williams Brothers group that included a young Andy Williams. *See the* ***Midwestern Hayride.***

3859 **Boose, Dana.** Sportscaster (WTSP, St. Petersburg, FL, 1946–1947). DJ (*The 1380 Local,* WTSP, 1947).

3860 **Booth, Bette Mills.** COM-HE (KLWN, Lawrence, KS, 1954).

3861 **Booth, Dick.** DJ (*The Morning Show,* WKTJ, Farmington, ME, 1960).

3862 **Booth, Mary.** Contralto (KPPC, Pasadena, CA, 1926).

3863 **Booth, Richard.** Newscaster (KNOW, Austin, TX, 1937).

3864 **Booth, Ted.** Newscaster (KSOK, Arkansas City, KS, 1948). DJ (*Call the Spin* and *The Music Booth,* WJVB, Jacksonville, FL, 1952).

3865 **Boothby, John.** DJ (*Sweet Music,* WEBR, Buffalo, NY, 1947).

3866 **Booton, Fran.** Newscaster (WDZ, Tuscola, IL, 1939–1941). Sportscaster (KCID, Caldwell, ID, 1954).

3867 **Boots, Granville Ray.** Announcer (KFFP, Moberly, MO, 1926).

3868 ***Boots and the Bachelors.*** Mixed vocal group (Vcl. mus. prg., WKBW, Buffalo, NY, 1936).

3869 **Booze, Virginia.** Virginia Booze was one of the intelligent "kids" on the *Quiz Kids* program (NBC, CBS, ABC, 1940–1955).

3870 **Borden, Jack.** DJ (*910 Club,* WHAY, New Britain, CT, 1952).

3871 **Borden, Ruth.** Writer Borden wrote radio commercial copy for the Ruthrauff & Ryan Company agency.

3872 ***(The) Borden Program.*** Soprano Barbara Blanchard and a male vocal quartet performed musical selections accompanied by Joseph Hornik leading the Blue and White Band (9:00–9:30 P.M., NBC-Pacific Coast Network, 1929).

3873 **Borden Quartet.** Male vocal quartet including Harry Stanton, Myron Niesley, Ben Klassen and Austin Mosher (NBC-Pacific Coast, 1929).

3874 **Border Radio.** Lax enforcement and the absence of adequate Mexican broadcasting regulations and unlimited transmission power allowed some broadcasters to blanket the United States without any possible control from Washington, DC. Twelve of these virtually unregulated high powered stations were in operation by 1934, two of whom were operated by Americans Norman E. Baker and John Romulus Brinkley (Sterling and Kitross, 1978, p. 134).

Baker's station in Nuevo Loredo, Mexico, boasted with the slogan that said it "Covers America like a blanket." By October 15, 1934, Brinkley's XER (XERA) began to transmit with 500,000 watts power. As early as 1931, *Broadcasting* magazine (November 1, 1931, p. 10) warned against Brinkley's XER, located at Villa Acuna, Mexico, and the interference it was causing Atlanta's WSB and Montreal's CKAC, among others, but the situation only worsened.

Although Mexican border stations existed all the way from California to the Gulf of Mexico, the most famous ones were located across the Rio Grande adjacent to Texas in such places as Villa Acuna and Nuevo Loredo. All these stations changed call letters and transmitting power frequently. Almost all the stations' programming was in English and much of it was by transcription.

Unhampered and unregulated by the Mexican government and not limited by adherence to any international broadcasting agreements, the stations frequently expanded their transmitting power, sometimes to as much as 500,000 or 1,000,000 watts. This booming power could be heard all over the United States and Canada. Their transmitting power attracted advertisers of all types in an effort to spread their messages across the North American continent day and night. These advertisers included patent medicine salesmen, evangelical preachers, medical quacks, fortune tellers, numerologists and diverse charlatans of all types. Unregulated both as to content, broadcast practices and transmitter power, the stations boomed out their commercials for baby chicks, hair-dye, Bibles, song books and patent medicines.

Professional broadcasters said that most of the Mexican border station's broadcasts were by "spooks." In radio terminology, "spooks" meant commercial charlatans. Many of these "spooks" began their broadcasts in this way: "Ladies and gentlemen, I do not claim to be infallible, but if anything is troubling you, if there are any questions related to love, marriage, romance or the future — write to me and enclose one dollar. I will answer your troubling questions." The broadcasters who used such spiels were astrologer Koran, Brandon the Man of Destiny, psychic Gayle Norman the Second, Hindu mentalist Marijah and Ethel Dunan "the Good Samaritan." Norman, who broadcast from XEAW and WEPN, reportedly received 2,000 letters a day. Each of these psychics were said to have received from $400 to $2,000 a day from listeners in the the United States, the Philippines, Greenland, Cuba and Alaska, because the super power Mexican stations boomed their messages all over the world to gullible listeners.

Country-western (CW) music was a staple program element sandwiched between the hard-sell commercials. Reaching all over the continent during the Great Depression, the Border Stations played a major role in popularizing CW music and its performers. Many CW performers moved to Texas and produced transcriptions there for use on the border stations. The famous Carter Family was one of the best known.

The Carter Family resided in San Antonio, Texas, and Del Rio, Texas, for three years in the late 1930s. Like most other country-western performers, the Carters stayed in the United States and *sent* the transcriptions they made in Texas across the border to Mexican stations like XERA and XEG. Another CW group that traveled to Texas was the Pickard Family. Obed "Dad" Pickard and his family can be heard on still existent recordings extolling the virtues of Pe-Ru-Na tonic to build up resistance against colds and combat them if already present. Pickard also warned that you could lose your job and look old if you didn't use Kolor-Bak hair dye. The Pickards also provided entertaining gospel and country music between commercials [*See* **Pickard, Obed "Dad"**].

By far the worst offenders on Border Radio were medical quacks such as Dr. John Romulus Brinkley and Norman Baker, both of whose medical and broadcasting licenses had previously been suspended in the United States. Brinkley's claims for the cure of impotence and prostate cancer and his goat gland operation were blatantly untrue, but many gullible sufferers responded to his attacks on the medical profession and its practitioners. Listening to transcriptions of his broadcasts still in existence provides ample evidence of both Brinkley's persuasive skill and menace [*See* **Charlatans, Demagogs and Politicians** *and* **Baker, Norman**].

Two particular chilling Brinkley techniques

were demonstrated in his dramatizations of "ordinary folks" with medical problems and his "Letter to Johnny" broadcast. During his dramatized episodes, he launched particulary virulent attacks against the medical profession, while boasting of his [Brinkley's] success and skill in treating disease. For example, one dramatized episode included such lines as, "They intend to take out your prostate gland, just like they did Uncle John." Following this line, a description was given of how Uncle John died. Continuing with virulent attacks on medical professionals as money grabbers, the actors stopped just short of calling doctors killers. Mixed with this vitriol was much praise for Brinkley: "They say Dr. Brinkley is a quack. Well he's the doctor I want. Thank God for such quacks. The Hell with ethics. Dr. Brinkley, here we come." Radio never carried any more savage attacks against doctors in general, nor so much self-praise for one in particular.

When he was 48, Brinkley addressed a radio message to his six-year-old son. He began by saying: "Johnny boy, Johnny boy. This is daddy talking to you on August 23, 1933. I'm sitting here in the offices of the Radio Victor Company in Chicago making this record, because I believe you would like to hear daddy's voice after he is gone. I have wanted to hear the voice of my own daddy, who passed away when I was ten years of age." Since Johnny's birthday was soon coming up, Dr. Brinkley said he was sure Johnny would receive many gifts from relative and friends — an alert to his listeners to send his son a few presents. Egotistical and self-righteous, Brinkley in this broadcast was not above comparing himself to Lincoln, when he was not ranting against the "powers" that were arrayed against him. Brinkley cleverly and highly effectively mixed emotion and family values with his self-advertisement.

Brinkley's broadcasting, however, was eventually terminated [*See* **Charlatans, Demagogs and Politicians**]. As the result of the North American Regional Broadcast Agreement (NARBA) among countries of North and Central America, the Mexican Border stations were shut down in 1941, but they were not gone forever. In a few years they were broadcasting again, but this time the country music they had popularized gradually began to be replaced by rock-and-roll. Many American DJs, including Wolfman Jack, got their experience on these stations. By 1986, agreements between Canada, Mexico and the United States finally muted the effects of broadcasts by powerful border stations by granting local American stations the right to broadcast on clear channel frequencies.

3875 ***Border Riders.*** CW music group (CW mus. prg., WWVA, Wheeling, WV, 1936–1938; 1942).

3876 ***Border Town Barbecue.*** CW mus. prg. (WBIG, Greensboro, NC, 1938).

3877 **Borders, Johnny.** DJ (KBOX, Dallas, TX).

3878 **Bordner, Frank.** Singer (WEBH, Chicago, IL, 1926).

3879 **Boree, Vic.** Newscaster (KTRI, Sioux City, IA, 1938).

3880 **Boren, Charles C.** DJ (*Sunrise Salute*, WELO, Tupelo, MS, 1949).

3881 **Boretz, Alvin.** Writer Boretz wrote the *Front Page Farrell* daytime serial program.

3882 **Borg, Emil.** Pianist (WMAQ, Chicago, IL, 1923).

3883 **Borg, Marge.** COM-HE (WDZI, Jackson, TN, 1957).

3884 **Bori, Lucrezia.** Italian opera singer (WMBB, Chicago, IL, 1925).

3885 **Bories, Merton.** Pianist (WMAQ, Chicago, IL, 1923; KPO, San Francisco, CA, 1926).

3886 ***Boris Karloff's Treasures.*** Playing his own charming self on the sustaining program, Karloff, the movie horror star, acted as a children's DJ and also told bedtime stories (30 min., Sunday, 7:00–7:30 P.M., WNEW, New York, NY, 1950).

3887 **Borman, Frances.** Soprano (WDAF, Kansas City, MO, 1928).

3888 **Bormann, Jim.** Newscaster (WMT, Cedar Rapids, IA, 1947).

3889 **Borne, Gladys.** Newscaster (WISR, Butler, PA, 1944). COM-HE (WISR, 1951).

3890 **Borner, J. O.** Announcer (WGBC, Memphis, TN, 1927).

3891 **Bornesti, Violetta.** Italian opera singer (WMBB, Chicago, IL, 1924).

3892 **Bornsch, Ruby Freeman.** Blues singer (WSB, Atlanta, GA, 1925).

3893 **Boroughs, Doug.** DJ (WAPX, Montgomery, AL, 1960).

3894 **Borovac, Joyce.** COM-HE (WMFG, Hibbing, MN, 1954).

3895 **Borow, Beatrice.** Soprano (WJZ, New York, NY, 1925).

3896 **Borowsky, Yascha.** Leader (*Yascha Borowsky's String Ensemble*, instr. mus. prg., KFWB, Los Angeles, CA, 1933).

3897 ***Borowsky's Gypsies Orchestra.*** Instr. mus. prg. (WFIL, Philadelphia, PA, 1935).

3898 ***Borrah Minevitch and the Harmonica Rascals.*** Minevitch led the novelty harmonica band on his program. The Rascals later became motion picture performers (15 min., Sunday, 7:00–7:15 P.M., WJZ, New York, NY, 1933).

3899 **Borreman, Lois.** COM-HE (KNDC, Hettinger, ND, 1957).

3900 **Borroff, Edward "Eddie."** Announcer (KYW, Chicago, IL, 1924–1925).

3901 **Borrosso, Senor.** Cellist (KOMO, Seattle, WA, 1928).

3902 **Borrow, Norman.** Newscaster (KFQD, Anchorage, AK, 1945; KOMO, Seattle, WA, 1946).

3903 **Borst, Hansell.** Musical saw performer (WIP, Philadelphia, PA, 1926).

3904 **Bort, Ken.** DJ (*Snake River Stampede*, KFXD, Nampa, ID, 1948).

3905 **Bortwick, Bill.** DJ (*Anything Goes*, WBRC, Birmingham, AL, 1948).

3906 **Borwick, Harry.** Newscaster (WINX, Washington, DC, 1941).

3907 ***Bosch Radio Hour.*** Broadcast at various times, this program combined musical selections and informative talks that provided an interesting view of Arkansas life. For example, Mrs. Sayre Leach talked on "Arkansas in Song and Story." Other performers on the program included the Sunny Side Male [vocal] Quartet; tenor Emmett McMurray; Hawaiian guitarist Dale Crotchett; violinists Byron Schriver and Charles Cook; pianists Lillian Barnes and Eugenia Schriver; and Ted Wood's Orchestra. At times, a cantata by a group from the First Methodist Church of Little Rock was performed. Mrs. Joe Sexton was the program's musical director (KLRA, Little Rock, AR, 1928).

3908 **Bosche, David.** Newscaster (KGGM, Alburuerque, NM, 1946).

3909 ***Boscul Moments.*** William Scull Company, makers of Boscul chocolate drink, sponsored this program featuring Metropolitan Opera prima donna Frances Alda and piano accompanist Frank LaForge (15 min., Wednesday, 7:15–7:30 P.M., NBC-Red, 1931)

3910 **Boselly, Elinore.** Singer (WNYC, New York, NY, 1936–1939). .

3911 **Bosher, Katy.** Singer (*Katy Bosher*, vcl. mus. prg., WRVA, Richmond, VA, 1934).

3912 **Bosley, Roberta.** Vocalist (WEVD, New York, NY, 1929). Bosley was a popular Black singer who won a 1929 WEVD listeners' popularity poll.

3913 **(The) Bosley Family.** The family singing group specialized in religious songs (KSO, Clarinda, IA, 1928).

3914 **Bossard, Alan.** DJ (*The Big Beat*, KSVC, Richfield, CA, 1960).

3915 **Bosse, Bill.** DJ (KWHI, Brenham, TX, 1954).

3916 **Bossell, (Mrs.) L.H.** Soprano (KPO, San Francisco, CA, 1926).

3917 **Bossert Lumber Jacks.** Local musical group (WFBH, New York, NY, 1925).

3918 **Bossert Marine Orchestra.** New York band (WEAF, 1925).

3919 **Bossery, George.** Bossery specialized in singing songs made famous by Sir Harry Lauder (KPO, San Francisco, CA, 1925).

3920 **Bossing, (Mrs.) S.D.** Organist (WHAS, Louisville, KY, 1925).

3921 **Bossong, Charles.** DJ (*Musical Clock* and *Tea and Trumpets*, WOGB, West Yarmouth, MA, 1949).

3922 **Bost, Cecile.** COM-HE (WIRC, Hickory, NC, 1954).

3923 **Bost, W.T.** Newscaster (WRAL, Raleigh, NC, 1940).

3924 **Bostic, Joe.** DJ (*Harlem Serenade*, WLIB, New York, NY, 1948–1952).

3925 **Bostick, M.N.** Newscaster (KLRA, Little Rock, AR, 1939).

3926 **Bostick, Ozella.** Pianist (KJBS, San Francisco, CA, 1925).

3927 **Boston Civic Grand Opera Company.** The opera company broadcast a performance of "Aida" featuring Clara Jacobo as Aida; Antonio Marquez as Radames; and Rhea Toniola as Amneris (WJZ, New York, NY, 1925).

3928 **Boston Collegians Band.** Popular band led by George P. Rupert (WGI, Medford Hillside, MA, 1923).

3929 ***(The) Boston Edison Big Brother Club.*** Leona May Smith conducted the children's safety club sponsored by the Boston Edison Electric Company (WEEI, Boston, MA, 1925).

3930 ***Boston Police Reports.*** Boston's police reports were broadcast daily (WGI, Medford Hillside, MA, 1923).

3931 ***(The) Boston "Pops" Concert.*** The "Pops" light music program was a great favorite of listeners (60 min., 6:30–7:30 P.M., NBC-Blue Network, 1936).

3932 **Boston Symphony Orchestra.** The famous classical music organization, conducted by Serge Koussevitsky, was a pioneer from the earliest days of radio in providing classical music for its listeners (WEEI, Boston, MA, 1926, NBC, 1926).

3933 ***Boston Tune Party.*** The weekly program featured popular dance music (15 min., Saturday, 6:45–7:00 P.M., NBC, 1947).

3934 **Bostwick, Arthur.** Newscaster (WQBM, St. Albans, VT, 1938).

3935 **Bostwick, (Dr.) Arthur E.** Bostwick broadcast "library talks" (KMOX, St. Louis, MO, 1928).

3936 **Bostwick, (Mrs.) Norris.** Soprano (KFI, Los Angeles, CA, 1923).

3937 **Boswell, Laura.** Newscaster (WHMA, Anniston, AL, 1939).

3938 **Boswell, Naomi.** COM-HE (KJBC, Midland, TX, 1960).

3939 ***Boswell Lynch.*** Lynch conducted the sustaining program for youthful amateur performers (30 min., Saturday, 10:00–10:30 A.M., WMCA, New York, NY, 1934).

3940 ***(The) Boswell Sisters.*** The Boswell Sisters — Martha Meldania, Constance ("Connie") and Helvetia("Vet") — were an entertaining rhythm and harmony vocal group. They first appeared on radio as winners of an amateur talent contest broadcast by WSMB, New Orleans, LA, in 1922. From 1922 to 1929, they sang on Los Angeles' KFWB. They left KFWB in 1931 to travel to New York and appear on *The Pleasure Hour.* The following year they sang on the *Music that Satisfies* show and, later, on their own *Boswell Sisters* program on CBS (1933). The following year they sang with Bing Crosby on the *Woodbury Hour.* The sister act broke up in 1936, when Vet left to have a baby. Connie, who was crippled as a child with polio, continued to perform alone after the act dissolved.

3941 **Bosworth, Chet.** DJ (*Alarm Clock* and *1340 Club*, WIRY, Plattsburg, NY, 1948–1954).

3942 **Bosworth, Grant.** DJ (*Hay Loft Hit Parade*, KJAM, Vernal, UT, 1948).

3943 **Bosworth, Helen.** Soprano (WBCN, Chicago, IL, 1925).

3944 **Botkin, Celia.** Singer (WEVD, New York, NY, 1936).

3945 **Botkin, Freda.** COM-HE (KNCA, Tucson, AZ, 1951).

3946 **Botstick, Buddy.** Sportscaster (WACO, Waco, TX, 1939).

3947 **Bott, Mabel.** Soprano (WHAZ, Troy, NY, 1925).

3948 **Botta, Ruth.** Contralto (WCCO, Minneappolis–St. Paul, MN, 1927).

3949 **Bottger, Bob.** Leader (Bob Bottger and his Venetians orchestra, KFI, Los Angeles, CA, 1926).

3950 **Bottoms, Jeanette.** COM-HE (KXJK, Forrest City, AR, 1957).

3951 **Bouarne, Charles.** Jazz pianist (WHN, New York, NY, 1923).

3952 **Bouchard, George Albert.** Organist (WGR, Buffalo, NY, 1923–1924).

3953 **Boucher, George.** DJ (KNBX, Kirkland, WA, 1960).

3954 **Boucher, Walter.** DJ (KXRX, San Jose, CA, 1952).

3955 **Bouchey, Bill (Willis B.).** Announcer Bouchey was born May 24, 1907. He began work as an announcer in 1926 (KFAC, Los Angeles, CA). He later became an actor, appearing during the following decades in many dramatic radio serials, including *Arnold Grimm's Daughter, The Barton Family, Captain Midnight (juvenile), Guiding Light, Kitty Keene, Midstream, One Man's Family, Romance of Helen Trent, Those Happy Gilmans* and *Woman in White.*

3956 **Bouchier, Eugene P.** DJ (*Bouchier's Ballroom*, KCOM, Sioux City, ID, 1948).

3957 **Bouchier, Gene.** DJ (*Musical Clock*, WPDQ, Jacksonville, FL, 1947; *600 Club*, WPDQ, 1948).

3958 **Bouchier, Robert "Bob."** Newscaster (KOBH, Rapid City, SD, 1942; WLOL, Minneapolis, MN, 1945).

3959 **Boudreau, Edna.** COM-HE (WLST, Escanaba, MI, 1960).

3960 **Boudreau, Verna.** COM-HE (WHIL, Boston-Medford, MA, 1957).

3961 **Bouer, Georgia.** COM-HE (WHIT, New Bern, NC, 1951).

3962 **Boulanger, Charles "Charlie."** Leader (*Charles Boulanger Orchestra*, instr. mus. prg., WCAE, Pittsburgh, PA; WENR, Chicago, IL; NBC, 1935).

3963 **Bouldin, Arthur "Art."** Sportscaster (KFAD, Fairfield, IA, 1954). DJ (WICH, Norwich, CT, 1956–1957).

3964 **Bouldin, Betty Ruth.** COM-HE (WZOB, Fort Payne, AL, 1957–1960).

3965 **Boulevard Players.** The dramatic group was directed by Wilbur S. Tupper. One of their presentations in 1926 was "In Toscanna Tavern" with Helen Holmes, Richard Nething, Adeline O'Brien and John Warfel (KTAB, Oakland, CA, 1926).

3966 **Bouley, Bob.** DJ (*Musical Grab Bag*, WACE, Springfield-Chicopee, MA, 1948).

3967 **Boult, Reber.** Baritone (WSM, Nashville, TN, 1928).

3968 **Boulton, Milo.** Actor-host Boulton appeared on such network programs as *Ellen Randolph* (actor), *John's Other Wife* (actor) and *We the People* (host).

3969 **Boulton, Milo "Mike."** DJ (*Bargin' Around with Boulton*, 60 min., Monday through Friday, 11:00–12:00 noon, WPAT, Paterson, NJ, 1949–1950). Mike Boulton was a popular DJ sponsored by Acme Markets.

3970 **Bounerba, Dick.** DJ (WNLK, Norwalk, CT, 1954).

3971 ***(A) Bouquet for You.*** Lee Vines and Franklyn MacCormack were the announcers on the popular sustaining music program that originated from New York on Monday, Wednesday and Friday and on Tuesday and Thursday from Chicago. The talented performers included: singers Patti Clayton, Billy Williams, Louise King and Billy Leach. Howard Smith and Caesar Pettrillo conducted the orchestras (30 min., Monday through Friday, 5:30–6:00 P.M., CBS, 1946).

3972 ***(A) Bouquet of Music.*** William Brallowsky conducted his all string orchestra on the transcribed program. Gene Kirby was the announcer (15 min., Transcribed, 1947).

3973 **Bouquet's Southland Serenaders Orchestra.** Radio band (KHJ, Los Angeles, CA, 1923).

3974 **Bourbon, Ruth.** Writer, newscaster, producer and broadcast executive Bourbon began as an actress in England before becoming Paris correspondent for the *New York Times.* In addition to her newspaper work, she wrote fiction for many national magazines and screen plays for both English and American motion picture companies such as Columbia, Warner's and Gaumont. She produced *Life Begins* and *Double or Nothing* programs. She also served as writer-producer on the *Amos 'n' Andy* and *Hollywood Hotel* shows while an executive for the Ward Wheelock Company advertising agency.

3975 **Bourbonnais, James.** Leader (*James Bourbonnais Orchestra*, instr. mus. prg., WBCM, Bay City, MI, 1942).

3976 **Bourdon, Rosario.** Leader (Rosario Bourdon's Orchestra featured on *The Cities Service Concert* program as the City Service Concert Orchestra, NBC-Red, New York, NY, 1927–29). Rosario suceeded Edwin Franko Goldman as musical director on the *City Service Concert Orchestra* program in 1927. For many years, Bourdon was a versatile staff musician for the Victor Talking Machine Company, where he worked as solo cellist, arranger, and frequent accompanist on many Victor recordings in addition to his work on NBC. His name as conductor is found on many radio transcriptions produced in the 1930s. Later, he broadcast on many stations by transcription (*Rosario Bourdon Orchestra*, instr. mus. prg., WHP, Harrisburg, PA, 1936; WIRE, Indianapolis, IN, 1937; WGH, Newport News, VA, 1939; KFEQ, St. Joseph, MO, 1940).

3977 ***Bourjois' Evening in Paris.*** Bourjois Cosmetics sponsored the program that combined music and a dramatic sketch with humor. Woods Miller and Mary McCoy sang romantic duets accompanied by an orchestra conducted by Nat Shilkret. Agnes Moorehead provided "country girl" comic relief. *Variety* criticized the program for its weak story line (30 min., Monday, 9:30–10:00 P.M., CBS, 1931–1932).

3978 **Bourland, Minnie.** COM-HE (KICN, Blytheville, AR, 1958).

3979 **Bourne, Charles A.** Jazz pianist (WHN, New York, NY, 1923).

3980 **Bourne, Gene.** COM-HE (KNGS, Hanford, CA, 1958).

3981 Bourne, Helen. Singer (WBAL, Baltimore, MD, 1926).

3982 Bourne, Porter. Sportscaster (WEXL, Royal Oak, MI, 1939).

3983 Bourque, Warren. DJ (WSTS, Southern Pines, NC, 1949; *Club 1230*, WERI, Westerly, RI, 1952; WNLC, New London, CT, 1957).

3984 Boutay, Ruth. Blues singer (WSWS, Chicago, IL, 1926).

3985 Boutin, Marie. Boutin taught radio French lessons (KPO, San Francisco, CA, 1926).

3986 Bovard, Bob. DJ (*Dixieland Jamboree*, KWBR, Oakland, CA, 1947).

3987 Bovay, Don. Singing guitarist (*Don Bovay*, instr. and vcl. mus. prg., WCAU , Philadelphia, PA, 1936–1938; WGR, Detroit, MI, 1942).

3988 Bove, Dick. Sportscaster (*Marine Sports Review*, WJNC, Jacksonville, NC, 1954). DJ (WNAE, Warren, PA, 1956).

3989 Bove, William. Leader (William Bove and his Royal Palm Orchestra, WOO, Pittsburgh, PA, 1924).

3990 Bow, Frank. Newscaster (WHBC, Canton, OH, 1945).

3991 Bowater, Peggy. COM-HE (WEEP, Pittsburgh, PA, 1960).

3992 Bowden, J.L. Newscaster (WKBN, Youngstown, OH, 1939).

3993 Bowden, Jane, Jr. COM-HE (WGBR, Jesup, GA, 1955).

3994 Bowden, R.H. Newscaster (WMFD, Wilmington, NC, 1940).

3995 Bowe, Morton. Tenor (*Morton Bowe*, vcl. mus. prg., NBC, 1936).

3996 Bowen, Al. DJ (WADK, Newport, RI, 1956).

3997 Bowen, Charles. Pianist (KVOS, Bellingham, WA, 1928).

3998 Bowen, Frank. Newscaster (WGFJ, Los Angeles, CA, 1945).

3999 Bowen, Garth. Newscaster (WTAL, Tallahassee, FL, 1946).

4000 Bowen, Jerry. COM-HE (KXOC, Chico, CA, 1951).

4001 Bowen, Rex. Newscaster (KYCA, Prescott, AZ, 1940).

4002 Bowen, T.O. Newcaster (WFIG, Sumter, SC, 1941).

4003 Bowen, Worcester. DJ (*Teen-Time*, KWTC, Barstow, CA, 1947).

4004 Bowen, Ysabel. Soprano (KFI, Los Angeles, CA, 1925).

4005 Bower, Bill. DJ (WFAI, Fayetteville, NC, 1960).

4006 Bower, Bob. DJ (*Music in the Nite*, WTIP, Charleston, WV, 1948). Sportscaster (WTIP, 1949–1960).

4007 Bower, Dick. DJ (*Dance Roundup*, WRAK, Williamsport, PA, 1948).

4008 Bower, Larry. DJ (KASI, Ames, IA, 1960).

4009 Bower, Roger. Actor (WOR, Newark, NJ, 1929). Bower went on to have a busy radio career.

4010 Bower, Wayne. DJ (*KSEM House Party*, KSEM, Moses Lake, WA, 1960).

4011 Bowers, Bill. Newscaster (WJKT, Springfield, MO, 1945–1946). DJ (*Coffee Time*, KAKC, Tulsa, OK, 1947).

4012 Bowers, Budd. DJ (KTAR, Phoenix, AZ, 1956).

4013 Bowers, Charlie. Leader (*Charlie Bowers Orchestra*, instr. mus. prg., NBC, 1935).

4014 Bowers, Charlie. DJ (*Hillbilly Hit Parade*, WKDK, Newberry, SC, 1947).

4015 Bowers, Dan. Newscaster (KOMA, Oklahoma City, OK, 1940; WJZM, Clarksville, TN, 1941).

4016 Bowers, Floye. COM-HE (WISE, Asheville, NC, 1951).

4017 Bowers, Jerome. Newscaster (WJHO, Opelika, AL, 1941).

4018 Bowers, Lois. COM-HE (WHIZ, Zanesville, OH, 1956).

4019 Bowers, Newton. DJ (WAAB, Worcester, MA, 1954).

4020 Bowers, Robert Hood. Leader (*Robert Hood Bowers Band*, instr. mus. prg. of military band selections, WHP, Harrisburg, PA, 1936, 1939). Most of this band's programs were transcribed.

4021 Bowers, Tom. DJ (*Little Ole Opry*, WLAG, LaGrange, GA, 1954).

4022 Bowery, Joanne E. COM-HE (KOJM, Havre, MT, 1956).

4023 *(The) Bowery Mission*. Golden Crust Bread sponsored this series of religious programs conducted by Charles St. John. Music was provided by organist Harold Clark, xylophonist Irene Forbes, baritone Horace Nichols, child singer Bobby Britton and Frank S. Harrison's Jubilee Singers. Charles Hanson Towne, a critic known as New York's unofficial poet laureate, frequently read some of his verses. St. John often asked listeners for clothes and jobs for his mission's members. This program was first made famous by its creator, Tommy Noonan (60 min., Sunday, 3:00–4:00 P.M., WHN, New York, NY, 1938).

4024 Bowes, (Major) Edward. Most famous in the decade of the 30s and 40s for conducting his *Original Amateur Hour*, Bowes took over the *Roxy and his Gang* program from S.L. "Roxy" Rothafel and transformed it into the *Capitol Theater Program*. It was broadcast from the stage of New York City's Capitol Theater as Roxy's was before it. *See* ***The Original Amateur Hour, Capitol Theater Program*** *and* ***Roxy and His Gang***.

4025 Bowick, Bill. DJ (*Sweet and Swing*, WALB, Albany, GA, 1947; *Coffee with Bill*, WALB, 1949–1954; WGBA, Columbus, OH, 1956).

4026 Bowin, Martin. Newscaster (KWK, St. Louis, MO, 1941).

4027 Bowker, Garth. DJ (*T.N.T.*, WPDR, Portage, WI, 1954).

4028 Bowler, James. DJ (*Club 990*, WJMR, New Orleans, LA, 1947).

4029 Bowles, Johnnie. Leader (Johnnie Bowles Napoli Four vocal group, WEEI, Boston, MA, 1925).

4030 Bowles, Shannon. DJ (*Grapevine Party Line*, KELD, El Dorado, AR, 1948).

4031 *Bowling Tips*. Local bowling champion Mary Jane Huber and sports commentator Hal Totten supplied the bowling tips (15 min., Wednesday afternoon, WCFL, Chicago, IL, 1940).

4032 Bowman, (Mrs.) Bertha. Pianist (WGY, Schenectady, NY, 1923).

4033 Bowman, Burl. DJ (*Club Coeur D'Alene*, KVNI, Coeur D'Alene, ID, 1949).

4034 Bowman, Carl. Announcer (WBBP, Petoskey, MI, 1927).

4035 Bowman, Carleton. Baritone (KOA, Denver, CO, 1925).

4036 Bowman, Dee. DJ (KVSP, Lubbock, TX, 1954).

4037 Bowman, Dick. DJ (*Working People*, WELS, Kinston, NC, 1954). Sportscaster (WELS, 1954; WFNS, Burlington, SC, 1956).

4038 Bowman, Jeanne. Bowman on her *Jeanne Bowman* program told animal stories for children (WIBA, Madison, WI, 1941). Her program was sponsored by Bowman's Diary.

4039 Bowman, Helen. COM-HE (WIKE, Newport, VT, 1956).

4040 Bowman, Joe. DJ (WIRO, Ironton, OH, 1955–1956).

4041 Bowman, John Duke. DJ (WLOH, Princeton, WV, 1949).

4042 Bowman, Lillian. Singer (*Lillian Bowman*, vcl. mus. prg., KYW, Philadelphia, PA, 1936).

4043 Bowman, Margie. COM-HE (WSFB, Quitman, GA, 1956).

4044 Bowman, Maury. DJ (WDIA, Memphis, TN, 1947).

4045 Bowman, Maxine. COM-HE (KBRS, Springdale, AR, 1957).

4046 Bowman, Patricia. Bowman was a featured dancer on the *Roxy and His Gang* program (NBC, 1923–1931).

4047 Bowman, Phil. DJ (WMAQ, Chicago, IL, 1960).

4048 Bowman, Phillip "Phil." Director Bowman directed the *Dear Mom* and *Ma Perkins* programs.

4049 Bowman, Roy Joe. Newscaster (KGFF, Shawnee, OK, 1941, 1945–1946). Sportscaster (KGFF, 1947–1948).

4050 Bowman, Sam. DJ (KOBY, San Francisco, CA, 1956).

4051 Bowman, William M. DJ (*Spiritual Parade*, WOIC, Columbia, SC, 1954).

4052 Bowne, Sarah Steward. Soprano (WHN, New York, NY, 1924).

4053 Bowser, Bill. DJ (*3-B Time*, WFLB, Fayetteville, NC, 1948).

4054 Bowton, Don. DJ (*Musical Clock*, WROK, Rockford, IL, 1948).

4055 Box, Mary Jane. COM-HE (WFRX, W. Frankport, IL, 1954–1955).

4056 Box, Ves. Sportscaster (KRLD, Dallas, TX, 1940–1942, 1946). Newscaster (KRLD, 1945–1948).

4057 Boxcar Willie (Lecil Travis Martin). CW Singer and DJ Boxcar Willie was a creation that began to take shape in 1960. As Lecil Martin, he became a regular at age 16 on the *Big D Jamboree* (KRLD, Dallas, TX, 1947). While working as a DJ on KGEM (Boise, ID) in 1960, he began working on the Boxcar Willie character when he took the name Marty Martin and gradually expanded it. He later became a member of the *Grand Ole Opry.*

4058 **Boxell, Carlton.** Tenor (WJZ, New York, NY, 1928).

4059 ***(A) Boy, A Girl, A Band.*** The sustaining music show starred tenor Howard Poice, soprano Betty Cook and Earl Truxell's band (30 min., Saturday, 4:30–5:00 P.M., WCAE, Philadelphia, PA, 1940).

4060 ***Boy Meets Girl.*** Tenor Pat Haley wooed sultry voiced Carol Mansfield on the sustaining music program that intertwined the threads of a romantic story with the songs they sang (15 min., Thursday, 11:15–11:30 A.M., KDKA, Pittsburgh, PA, 1940).

4061 **(The) Boy with a Smile.** The "Boy with a Smile" was the name given to Len Finch, who sang with Slater's Squirrel Dodgers Orchestra (WFQB, Ft. Worth, TX, 1927).

4062 **Boyce, Malton.** Concert pianist (WCAP, Washington, DC, 1924).

4063 **Boyd, Betty.** COM-HE (KOTV, Tulsa, OK, 1956).

4064 **Boyd, Bill.** Boyd led his Cowboy Ramblers, a country-western string band that eventually moved from country to western jazz and dance music. Boyd and brother Jim first performed on Greenville, Texas, radio in 1926. He later had his own *Bill Boyd's Cowboy Ramblers* program (WRR, Dallas, TX, mid–1930s).

4065 **Boyd, Bill.** DJ (*Music of the Masters*, WTXC, Big Spring, TX, 1948).

4066 **Boyd, Buddy.** Singer (KMIC, Inglewood, CA, 1928).

4067 **Boyd, Don.** Sportscaster (*World of Sports*, WCLO, Janesville, WI, 1947; *World of Sports*, WCLO, 1948–1955). DJ (*Sunrise Roundup*, WCLO, 1949–1952).

4068 **Boyd, Eleanor.** Newscaster (WMOB, Mobile, AL, 1941).

4069 **Boyd, Forrest.** Newscaster (WMBI, Chicago, IL, 1945).

4070 **Boyd, Harold J.** Newscaster (KYA, San Francisco, CA, 1942).

4071 **Boyd, Harvey.** Sportscaster (KPLT, Paris, TX, 1942). DJ (*Boyd's Nest*, KWBC, Fort Worth, TX, 1948–1949).

4072 **Boyd, Helen.** Accordionist (WSM, Nashville, TN, 1926).

4073 **Boyd, Henry.** Sound effects man, whistler and animal imitator Boyd worked on the *Aunt Jenny* program whistling and imitating a canary and providing the famous bob-white (Rinso white) sound on the soap flakes commercial.

4074 **Boyd, Ingrid Arneson.** Soprano (KFI, Los Angeles, CA, 1925).

4075 **Boyd, Jack.** Newscaster (WMFH, High Point, NC, 1945).

4076 **Boyd, Jim.** DJ (WOC, Davenport, IA, 1960).

4077 **Boyd, Jimmie.** Leader (*Jimmie Boyd's Lucky Devils Orchestra*, a CW music program featuring Boyd's group of musicians and singers from Ripley, TN, KLCN, Blytheville, AR, 1930).

4078 **Boyd, Jo.** DJ (*Listen Ladies*, WMPA, Aberdeen, MS, 1954).

4079 **Boyd, John.** DJ (*Showcase*, WTOD, Toledo, OH, 1948).

4080 **Boyd, Lep.** DJ (*Turn Table Spin*, WSSO, Starkville, MS, 1960).

4081 **Boyd, Lex.** DJ (*Date at the Krowsbah*, KROW, Oakland, OK, 1947; *The Boyd's Nest*, KROW, 1949).

4082 **Boyd, Lillian.** Pianist (KROW, Oakland, CA, 1929).

4083 **Boyd, Nelle.** Pianist (WSM, Nashville, TN, 1928).

4084 **Boyd, Tom.** DJ (*Juke Box Saturday Nite*, WCHV, Charlotteville, VA, 1948).

4085 **Boyd's Cameo Six Orchestra.** Radio dance band (WCAE, Pittsburgh, PA, 1924).

4086 **Boyer, Carl.** Actor Boyer appeared on the *We are Four* program.

4087 **Boyer, Dean.** DJ (*Ham 'N' Eggs*, WBLK, Clarksburg, WV, 1949). Sportscaster (WCOL, Columbus, OH, 1952).

4088 **Boyer, Emmeline.** Soprano (WSM, Nashville, TN, 1928).

4089 **Boyer, Hazel.** Leader (Hazel Boyer's Twentieth Century Girls Orchestra, a six-woman band, WBAP, San Antonio, TX, 1926).

4090 **Boyer, Herb.** DJ (KLGA, Algona, IA, 1960).

4091 **Boyer, John.** Newscaster (KTSA, San Antonio, TX, 1938–1941; KTRB, Modesto, CA, 1944).

4092 **Boyer, John F. "Johnny."** Sportscaster (*Meet Your Neighbor* and *Today's Sports*, KQV, Pittsburgh, PA, 1939; KDKA, Pittsburgh, PA, 1941, 1946–1947; *Johnny Boyer Sports*, KDKA, 1948–1953; *Whirl Around the World of Sports*, KDKA, 1954). Newscaster (KDKA, 1941).

4093 **Boyer, Leo.** Leader (Leo Boyer and his Tangoland Syncopators [orchestra], WHN, New York, NY, 1925).

4094 **Boyer, William.** Tenor (WPG, Atlantic City, NJ, 1925).

4095 **Boyett, Pat.** DJ (*Rhythm Express*, KONO, San Antonio, TX, 1948).

4096 **Boyette, Martha.** COM-HE (WTRP, La Grange, GA, 1954–1955).

4097 **Boylan, Lydia.** COM-HE (WDXB, Chattanooga, TN, 1960).

4098 **Boylay, Robert.** DJ (*Say It With Music*, WHYN, Holyoke, MA, 1948).

4099 **Boyle, Ed.** DJ (*Romance in the Night*, KBIZ, Ottumwa, IA, 1954).

4100 **Boyle, Ed.** DJ (*Wax Works*, KFBK, Sacramento, CA, 1955).

4101 **Boyle, Gertrude Hess.** Contralto (WPG, Atlantic City, NJ, 1928).

4102 **Boyle, Jim.** DJ (WFVA, Fredericksburg, VA, 1960).

4103 **Boyle, John J.** Announcer (WJAR, Providence, RI, 1925).

4104 **Boyle, Patricia.** Blind pianist (WJZ, New York,NY, 1923; *Patricia Boyle*, inst. mus. prg., WIBX, Utica, NY, 1936; KWBW, Buffalo, NY, 1936). Singer (*Patricia Boyle*, vcl. mus. prg, WGR, Buffalo, NY, 1936).

4105 **Boyle, Robert.** Newcaster (KUOM, Minneapolis, MN, 1946).

4106 **Boyle, William W.** DJ (*Journeys into Jazz* and *Comin' Right Up*, WGRD, Grand Rapids, MI, 1948; *Platter Party*, WGRD, 1949).

4107 **Boyles, Chuck.** DJ (WKY, Oklahoma City, OK, 1960).

4108 **Boyles, Letitia R.** COM-HE (WGVM, Greenville, MS, 1951).

4109 **Boyles, Lois.** Soprano (WBAL, Baltimore, MD, 1926).

4110 **Boyne, Jerry.** DJ (*Music in the Afternoon*, WNBZ, Saranac Lake, NY, 1960).

4111 **Boynton, Dick.** Sportscaster (KFMB, San Diego, CA, 1954). DJ (KSDO, San Diego, CA, 1956).

4112 **Boynton, Percy.** Critic Boynton broadcast a *Book Reviews* program (WGN, Chicago, IL, 1935).

4113 **Boynton, Wesley.** Lyric tenor (WOR, Newark, NJ, 1926). Boynton also appeared on the *Major Bowes Capitol Theater Family* program (NBC, 1929).

4114 **Boys, Gladys.** Pianist (KPO, San Francisco, CA, 1925).

4115 ***Boys and Girls 4-H Club Program.*** Begun in October, 1926, the program was broadcast for decades on the station of Kansas State University. Inspirational, practical and informative talks were featured on music, travel information and news of 4-H activities (KSAC, Manhattan, KS, 1926).

4116 **Boys' Industrial Training School Band [Golden, CO].** Scholastic band directed by B.B. Givens (KOA, Denver, CO, 1927).

4117 **Boysen, James P.** DJ (*Alarm Clock Club*, WTCN, Minneapolis, MN, 1947; *Jim Boysen Show*, WTCN, 1948–1949).

4118 **Boyum, G.W.** DJ (*4:00 O'Clock Special*, WLBJ, Bowling Green, KY, 1947).

4119 **Bozarth, Dick.** DJ (*Requestfully Yours*, WEBQ, Harrisburg, IL, 1952).

4120 **Bozeman, Jerry.** DJ (KTBS, Shreveport, LA and KWKH, Shreveport, LA, 1940).

4121 **B.P.O.E. Band.** Fraternal [Benevolent Protective Order of Eagles] lodge band (KGW, Portland, OR, 1924).

4122 **Brabant, Louise.** Soprano (WTAM, Cleveland, OH, 1931; WGN, Chicago, IL, 1934–1935). Brabant had previously sung on other Chicago stations as WBBM and WMAQ.

4123 **Brabson, Bill.** DJ (WVKO, Columbus, OH, 1954).

4124 **Braca, Elia.** Radio actress Braca was a cast member of the *Mainstream* daytime serial.

4125 **Bracanovitch, Tom.** DJ (*Juke Box Review*, KWIN, Ashland, OR, 1947).

4126 **Brace, Celia.** Violinist (WBAL, Baltimore, MD, 1926–1928).

4127 **Brachocki, Alexander.** Pianist (WJZ, New York, NY, 1925).

4128 **Bracken, Dennis "Denny."** DJ (*Jukebox Serenade*, WOLF, Syracuse, NY, 1954; KFMB, San Diego, CA, 1960).

4129 **Bracken, Tom and Bob King.** Popular singing team (WHN, New York, NY, 1925).

4130 **Bracken, Virginia.** COM-HE (WDOV, Dover, DE, 1954–1955).

4131 Brackett, Lulu. Pianist (KWTC, Santa Ana, CA, 1928).

4132 Brackin, John. DJ (*Mail Order Music* and *Howdy Neighbors*, WTBF, Troy, AL, 1948).

4133 Bradbury, Grace Lowell. Soprano (WBZ, Boston-Springfield, MA, 1924).

4134 Bradby, Ken. DJ (*Bright and Early*, WBCI, Williamsburg, VA, 1960).

4135 Braddley, Mary. COM-HE (WMTR, Morristown, NJ, 1955).

4136 Braden, Mary E. COM-HE (KSMN, Mason City, IA, 1960).

4137 Braden, Paul. DJ (*560 Club*, WMIK, Middleboro, KY, 1960).

4138 Bradfield, R. Max. Leader (Max Bradfield's Versatile Band broadcasting from the Palace Hotel Rose Bowl Room, KPO, San Francisco, CA, 1923–1925; KGO, Oakland, CA, 1925; Max Bradfield's Orchestra playing from the Senator Theater, KFBK, Sacramento, CA, 1925).

4139 Bradford, Anne. Home service features broadcaster (WEEI, Boston, MA, 1928).

4140 Bradford, Betty. COM-HE (WESB, Bradford, PA, 1954).

4141 Bradford, Esther. COM-HE (*Fashions*, WJJD, Chicago, IL, 1934–1935).

4142 Bradford, John. DJ (WJPS, Evansville, IN, 1960).

4143 Bradford, Johnny. DJ (*The Johnny Bradford Show*, WRC, Washington, DC, 1948).

4144 Bradford, Larry. Leader (*Larry Bradford Orchestra*, instr. mus. prg., WBIG, Greensboro, NC, 1936).

4145 Bradford, Phil. DJ (*Rise and Shine*, WCOL, Columbus, OH, 1947; *Phil Bradford Show*, WCOL, 1949).

4146 Bradford, Ray. Leader (*Ray Bradford Orchestra*, instr. mus. prg., KSL, Salt Lake City, UT, 1939).

4147 *(The) Bradford Orchestra.* Instr. mus. prg. (WBZ-WBZA, Boston-Springfield, MA, 1932).

4148 Bradley, Bill. DJ (KLAC, Hollywood, CA, 1960).

4149 Bradley, Bob. DJ (*Platter Time*, WDAY, Fargo, ND, 1947; *Patter and Platter Time*, WDAY, 1948; *Browsing with Bradley*, WMIL, Milwaukee, WI, 1949; WLOL, Minneapolis, MN, 1954).

4150 Bradley, Bruce. DJ (*Night Beat*,165 min., Monday through Saturday, 8:00–10:45 P.M., WBZA, Boston, MA, 1956; WBZA, 1960).

4151 Bradley, Curtis P. "Curt." DJ (*WCNT Bandwagon*, WCNT, Centralia, IL, 1948; *Requestfully Yours*, WCRA, Effingham, IL, 1952; WMIX, Mt. Vernon, IL, 1954).

4152 Bradley, Dick. DJ (WQXR, New York, NY, 1948).

4153 Bradley, Don. DJ (*Fanfare*, WKAN, Kankakee, IL, 1948).

4154 Bradley, Etta. Soprano (WBZ, Springfield, MA, 1925).

4155 Bradley, George. DJ (*Hits and Encores*, KTUC, Tucson, AZ, 1954).

4156 Bradley, Jim. DJ (KIHR, Hood River, OR, 1956).

4157 Bradley, Junita. COM-HE (WOPI, Bristol, TN, 1951).

4158 Bradley, Lem. DJ (KENA, Mena, AR, 1952).

4159 Bradley, Leroy. Leader (*Leroy Bradley Orchestra*, instr. mus. prg., KDKA, Pittsburgh, PA, 1936).

4160 Bradley, Lyle C. DJ (*Request Club*, WSSV, Petersburg, VA, 1947; WRVA, Richmond, VA, 1960). Sportscaster (*Sportsman*, WSSV, 1947; WTRY, Troy, NY, 1948–1949).

4161 Bradley, Lynn. DJ (KTTN, Trenton, MO, 1956).

4162 Bradley, Mack. DJ (*Musical Spree*, WQBC, Vicksburg, MS, 1948).

4163 Bradley, Nick. DJ (*Easy Rhythm*, WABI, Bangor, ME, 1947).

4164 Bradley, Pat. DJ (*Bradley's Workshop*, KXLW, St. Louis, MO, 1949).

4165 Bradley, (Dr.) Preston. Newscaster (WBBM, Chicago, IL, 1938; *News*, 15 min., Monday through Friday, 7:15–7:30 P.M., NBC, 1943).

4166 Bradley, Robert E. DJ (*Bradley's Bandstand*, KCOM, Sioux City, IA, 1948).

4167 Bradley, Sam. DJ (KCHS, Hot Springs, NM, 1949).

4168 Bradley, Truman. Newscaster (WBBM, Chicago, IL, 1937; KNX, Los Angeles, CA, 1942, 1945).

4169 Bradley, Wesley "Wes." DJ (*Good Morning*, KRDO, Colorado Springs, CO, 1948–1951; *Yawn Patrol*, KRDO, 1952–1956).

4170 Bradley, Will. Leader (*Will Bradley Orchestra*, instr. mus. prg., NBC, 1935, 1940–1942).

4171 Bradley, William V. Sportscaster (WHEB, Portsmouth, NH, 1946; *College Cheer* and *Pigskin Review*, WHEB, 1947). DJ (*Platter Parade*, WHEB, 1947).

4172 Bradner, C.C. Newscaster (WWJ, Detroit, MI, 1932–1939).

4173 Bradshaw, Claray. COM-HE (WTRO, Dyersburg, TN, 1958).

4174 Bradshaw, Dick. DJ (*Morning Mail* and *Caro Coffee Time*, WCEC, Rocky Mount, NC, 1947). Sportscaster (WCEC, 1947–1948).

4175 Bradshaw, Dorothy Emelyn. Soprano (WJZ, New York, NY, 1924).

4176 Bradshaw, John. DJ (*Melody Mart*, WIRK, West Palm Beach, FL, 1954; WBOF, Virginia Beach, FL, 1957). Sportscaster (WIRK, 1954).

4177 Bradshaw, Justin. Newscaster (KFBI, Wichita, KS, 1942).

4178 Bradshaw, Tom. DJ (*550 Club*, KOPR, Butte, MT, 1948; WLOW, Norfolk, VA, 1956)

4179 Brady, Alice. Actress (WJZ, New York, NY, 1926).

4180 Brady, Betty. COM-HE (WHO, Des Moines, IA, 1951).

4181 Brady, Bill. Sportscaster (WPRC, Lincoln, IL, 1953). DJ (WDZ, Decatur, IL, 1960).

4182 Brady, Bob. DJ (*Melody Matinee*, WTTM, Trenton, NJ, 1960).

4183 Brady, Ed. Newscaster (KOA, Denver, CO, 1941).

4184 Brady, Florence. Singer Brady appeared on *The Oriental Theater Revue* (WGN, Chicago, IL, 1927).

4185 Brady, J. Henry. Brady was a guitar soloist and a member with Georgia Price and Ruth Elder of an instrumental trio (WHAS, Louisville, KY, 1923).

4186 Brady, Josh. DJ (WBBM, Chicago, IL, 1954).

4187 Brady, Toni. COM-HE (WABY, Albany, NY, 1951–1960).

4188 Brae, Anne [Anna]. Singer (*Anne Brae*, vcl. mus. prg., MBS, 1935).

4189 Braemore Dance Orchestra. Radio band (WJAR, Providence, RI, 1925).

4190 Bragdon, Emily Kauffeld. Pianist (KTAB, Oakland, CA, 1926).

4191 Bragg, Bobby. DJ (WNEX, Macon, GA, 1960).

4192 Bragg, Charles. DJ (*Breakfast on the Farm*, WHAL, Shelbyville, TN, 1949).

4193 Bragg, Dean. DJ (*Club 1230*, WAYX, Waycross, GA, 1952).

4194 Bragg, Marion. DJ (*Alarm Clock Club*, WNEX, Macon, GA, 1947).

4195 Bragg, Nelson. DJ (WBBM, Chicago, IL, 1954).

4196 Bragg, W. F. Announcer (KMJ, Fresno, CA, 1927).

4197 Braggiotti, Mario. Leader (*Mario Braggiotti Orchestra*, instr. mus. prg., WLW, Cincinnati, OH, 1936; NBC, 1937). *See* ***Fray and Braggiotti***.

4198 Braham, Adele. Soprano (WEEI, Boston, MA, 1926).

4199 Braham, Horace. Busy actor Braham appeared on the *Big Sister*, *Joyce Jordan, Girl Interne*, *We Love and Learn*, *Wendy Warren and the News* and *Woman of Courage*.

4200 Brahm, Helene. Pianist (*Helene Brahm*, instr. mus. prg., 15 min., Monday through Friday, 12:30–12:45 P.M., WLS, Chicago, IL, 1936).

4201 Brailes, Luther. Newscaster (KSAL, Salma, KS, 1938).

4202 Brailowsky, Alexander. Operatic singer (WEAF, New York, NY, 1927).

4203 Brainard, Bertha. One of the first women announcers, Brainard was known as "ABN" and the "First Lady of Radio." She was a regular on the WJZ (New York, NY) announcing staff in the mid–1920s with colleagues Milton J. Cross and Norman Brokenshire. Brainard also reviewed plays and discussed theater news and events when she initiated a series of programs of dramatic criticism on WJZ, May 9, 1922.

When she presented the idea of a newspaper column of the air, WJZ accepted it immediately. She opened her program with the announcement: "Bertha Brainard broadcasts Broadway." Her program, *Broadcasting Broadway*, was heard over WJZ-WJY, New York, NY and Schenectady, NY, 1922–1924. She soon got the idea of interviewing various people on her program. Her first interviewee was Nellie Ravell. Brainard became the program manager of the National Broadcasting Company when it was formed in 1926, the beginning of her highly successful executive career in broadcasting.

4204 **Brainard, Gladys Ives.** Pianist (WTAQ, Green Bay, WI, 1938).

4205 **Brainard, Kay.** COM-HE (KORT, Grangeville, ID, 1957).

4206 **Braine, Robert.** Pianist-composer (WOR, Newark, NJ, 1928). Braine was also the pianist on the popular *Slumber Hour* program (NBC, New York, 1928).

4207 **Bralson, William.** DJ (WFPG, Atlantic City, NJ, 1948).

4208 **Braly, Bill.** DJ (*On the Q.T.*, KVSF, Santa Fe, NM, 1947).

4209 **Bramberg, Ruth.** Violinist (WOAC, Corvallis, OR, 1926).

4210 **Bramblett, Gladys V.** COM-HE (WSAR, Fall River, MA, 1954).

4211 **Bramhall, Bill.** DJ (*Old Timers Party*, WEMP, Milwaukee, WI, 1949–1954).

4212 **Bramley, Raymond "Ray."** Actor Bramley appeared on the *David Harum* and *Stella Dallas* daytime serial programs.

4213 **Bramstedt, A.D.** Newscaster (NBC, 1942; 1946).

4214 **Branch, Blanche.** Soprano (KOA, Denver, CO, 1926).

4215 **Branch, Frances.** Musical saw performer (KTAB, Oakland, CA, 1925).

4216 **Branch, George.** DJ (*Yours for the Asking*, WELC, Welch, WV, 1952; *Boogie and Blues*, WELC, 1954–1955).

4217 **Branch, Marion.** DJ (*Free For All*, KVAN, Vancouver, WA, 1948).

4218 **Branch, Neal.** DJ (*Branchin' Out*, WJHL, Johnson City, TN, 1947; *1240 Club*, WBIR, Knoxville, TN, 1948–1954).

4219 **Branch, Sandra.** Branch was a musical saw performer (KTAB, Oakland, CA, 1925).

4220 **Branch, W.E.** Announcer (1925).

4221 **Brand, Chuck.** DJ (WOOD, Moundsville, WV, 1960).

4222 **Brand, (Mr.) Dixie.** Entertainer (WHR, Cleveland, OH, 1926).

4223 **Brand, Lucille.** COM-HE (WETB, Johnson City, TN, 1958).

4224 **Brand, Luther.** Newscaster (WOWO, Fort Wayne, IN, 1946).

4225 **Brand, Paul.** DJ (*Dance Time*, WKNY, Kingston, NY, 1954).

4226 **Brandborg, Gustav.** Baritone (KVOO, Tulsa, OK, 1928).

4227 **Brandenburg, Catharine.** COM-HE (WREN, Topeka, KS, 1956–1957).

4228 **Brandenburg, Karl.** Tenor (KHJ, Los Angeles, CA, 1926). Announcer (KWC, Stockton, CA, 1927).

4229 **Brandt. Adele.** Contralto (WHT, Deerfield, IL, 1925). She sang a daily morning hymn on WLS (Chicago, IL) in 1939.

4230 **Brandt, Albert.** Newscaster (WEVD, New York, NY, 1948).

4231 **Brandt, Bill.** Sportscaster (*Inside of Sports*, MBS, 1945–1948).

4232 **Brandt, Del.** Newscaster (KPOW, Powell, WY, 1941–1942). Sportscaster (KPOW, 1942).

4233 **Brandt, Frances.** Violinist (WOC, Davenport, IA, 1923).

4234 **Brandt, Jack.** DJ (*Club Matinee*, WITZ, Jasper, IN, 1954). Sportscaster (WITZ, 1954–1960).

4235 **Brandt, Joseph.** DJ (*You Asked For It*, WTPR, Paris, TX, 1947).

4236 **Brandt, Lynn.** Sportscaster (College football play-by-play, NBC, 1937; WMAQ-WENR, Chicago, IL, 1938–1942). Newscaster (WMAQ-WENR, 1938–1942).

4237 **Brandywine, Nat.** Leader (*Nat Brandywine Orchestra*, instr. mus. prg., WLW, Cincinnati, OH, 1937).

4238 **Branham, Edna.** COM-HE (WKTG, Thomasville, GA, 1960).

4239 **Branham, Jimmy.** DJ (*Best at Dawn*, WTCW, Whiteburg, KY, 1960).

4240 **Brannagan, Art.** Leader (Art Brannagan's Orchestra, KPO, San Francisco, CA, 1926).

4241 **Brannan, Dan.** DJ (KEYJ, Jamestown, ND, 1960).

4242 **Brannen, Bertha.** COM-HE (WWNS, Statesboro, GA, 1960).

4243 **Brannen, (Mrs.) Ernest H.** COM-HE (WWNS, Statesboro, GA, 1956–1957).

4244 **Brannigan, Gertrude.** Organist (WOC, Davenport, IA, 1928).

4245 **Brannon, Bob.** DJ (*Brannon's Open House*, KLOU, Lake Charles, LA, 1947; KRAK, Stockton, CA, 1956).

4246 **Brannon, (Col.) Earl.** Newscaster (WHIZ, Zanesville, OH, 1945–1946).

4247 **Brannon, Jerry.** Singer (*Jerry Brannon*, vcl. mus. prg., NBC, 1936).

4248 **Branson, Bruce.** DJ (*Branson Show*, KOH, Reno, NV, 1948; KXOA, Sacramento, CA, 1954).

4249 **Branson, Todd.** Sportscaster (*Sports Show*, WWCA, Gary, IN, 1953; *Northwestern University Football*, WNMP, Evanston, IL, 1960).

4250 **Brant, Bill.** DJ (*Midnighter's Club*, KDKA, Pittsburgh, PA, 1947–1948; WJAS, Pittsburgh, PA, 1955–1956).

4251 **Brant, Roy.** Newscaster (WCCO, Minneappolis–St. Paul, MN, 1938).

4252 **Branton, Roy.** Newscaster (WGRB, Goldsboro, NC, 1940).

4253 **Branz (Brawz), Celia.** Contralto Branz was featured on the *Roxy and his Gang* program (WJZ, New York, NY, 1927; *Celia Branz*, vcl. mus. prg., NBC, 1936).

4254 **Branzell, Karin.** Mezzo-soprano (WJZ, New York, NY, 1927).

4255 ***Braqiutti Orchestra.*** Instr. mus. prg. (WOR, Newark, NJ, 1936).

4256 **Brard, Magdeleine.** Pianist (WRNY, New York, NY, 1927).

4257 **Brascia, Vince.** DJ (*Top Five*, KCRT, Trinidad, CO, 1952).

4258 **Brasfield, Rod (Rodney Leon Brasfield).** CW comedian joined the *Grand Ole Opry* in 1944. Brasfield worked with Red Foley on the *Opry's* NBC segment in 1947. Known as "The Hohenwald Flash," Brasfield replaced the Duke of Paducah (Benjamin Francis Ford), the famous country comedian, on the *Grand Ole Opry*. From time to time on the *Opry*, Brasfield showed some interest in pursuing Cousin Minnie Pearl and the predictable laughter that resulted.

4259 **Brasher, James.** DJ (*Radio Ranch Roundup*, KTXJ, Jasper, TX, 1954).

4260 **Brass, Sadie.** Violinist (WMEX, Boston, MA, 1940).

4261 **Bratton, Genevieve.** Violinist (WOS, Jefferson City, MO, 1925).

4262 **Braum, Morris.** Violinist (*Morris Braum*, instr. mus. prg., WIP, Philadelphia, PA, 1936).

4263 **Braun, Charles.** Announcer (WFAA, Dallas, TX, 1928).

4264 **Braun, Florence.** Soprano (WSAI, Cincinnati, OH, 1925).

4265 **Braun, Jerome.** DJ (KXRA, Alexandria, MN, 1954).

4266 **Brauninger [Brauning], Stanley.** Swimming instructor at the Central Park YMCA, Cincinnati, Ohio, Brauninger broadcast an eight-week series of swimming lessons (WLW, Cincinnati, OH, 1922).

4267 **Braver, Philip.** Baritone (WJZ, New York, NY, 1924).

4268 **Braviroff, Harry.** Pianist (WOAW, Omaha, NE, 1926).

4269 **Brawner, Onalee.** COM-HE (KWYN, Wynne, AR, 1958).

4270 **Bray, Bob.** DJ (*Bob Bray Show*, WINR, Binghampton, NY, 1948).

4271 **Bray, Dick.** Singer (*Dick Bray*, vcl. mus. prg., WSAI, Cincinnati, OH, 1942). Sportscaster (WCKY, Cincinnati, OH, 1950–1954).

4272 **Bray, Ed.** DJ (*Sunrise Serenade*, WKTG, Thomasville, GA, 1954; WALT, Tampa, FL, 1956–1957).

4273 **Bray, Gene.** DJ (*Clockwatcher* and *Hi Gene*, WRYO, Rochester, PA, 1949).

4274 **Braymer, Clara V.** Reader (WHAZ, Troy, NY, 1925).

4275 **Brayton, Margaret.** Actress Brayton appeared on the *Brent House* daytime serial.

4276 **Brazeau. Henrietta.** COM-HE (WPAW, Pawtucket, RI, 1951).

4277 **Brazier, Hal.** DJ (*Breakfast Club*, WSTP, Salisbury, NC, 1948).

4278 **Brazil, Jules.** Brazil performed pianologues (NBC, 1929).

4279 **Brazil Orchestra of Bellows Falls, VT.** Local band (WLAK, Bellows Falls, VT, 1922).

4280 **Brazillian Mandoliers.** Latin music group whose program was sponsored by the United Coffee Company (WGY, Schenectady, NY, 1927).

4281 **Brazzell, Jim "Jimmy."** DJ (*Music Shop*, WHSC, Hartsville, SC, 1947; *You Name It—We Play It*, WGFN, Gaffney, SC, 1949). Sportscaster (*The Sportsman*, WHSC, 1947).

4282 **Brazzle, Ernest.** *See* ***The Farm Show.***

4283 **Breakers Hotel Orchestra.** Hotel band (KFON, Long Beach, CA, 1927).

4284 ***Breakfast at the Brass Rail.*** Carleton Fredericks combined yoga, calisthenics and nutritional tips on the program originating from New York's Brass Rail restaurant. Dick DeFreitas was the announcer (30 min., Monday through Saturday, 9:00–9:30 P.M., WMGM, New York, NY, 1948).

4285 ***Breakfast Bandstand.*** DJ Ray Olson conducted the early morning program of recorded music sponsored by Nabisco (7:15 A.M., Tueday, Thursday and Saturday, WOW, Omaha, NE, 1948).

4286 ***Breakfast Club*** **(aka *The Pepper Pot Program* and *The Smile Before Breakfast Program*).** Don McNeill hosted the long-running (1933–1968) variety program that appeared in a 60-minute format on both NBC and ABC. Originating from Chicago on June 23, 1933, with genial McNeill as host, the program projected an atmosphere of warmth and sincerity from its inception. Before McNeill took over in 1933, the program had been called *The Pepper Pot,* hosted by announcers Bill Kephart and King Bard and featuring the music of Walter Blaufuss and a small orchestra. When McNeill took over as host, the program's name was changed to *Smiles Before Breakfast.* Later the same year the name was changed once more to *The Breakfast Club.*

McNeill's 1933 cast included violinist Sleepy Joe Englehart and singer Dick Teela. Among the features introduced that year was "Memory Time." The following year Marion and Jim Jordan (later famous as Fibber McGee and Molly) appeared often as "Toots and Chickie," along with other performers such as the Merry Macs, the Songfellows, Three C's, the Morin Sisters, the Ranch Boys, Bill Thompson, guitarist Jack Rose and Jack Owens.

Small talk, jokes, songs and comedy skits were featured on every show, but it was the personality of McNeill and his cast members that attracted a large audience of devoted listeners. The program always included a great deal of sentimental talk about old folks in "homes" and lots of sentimental poetry. The early version of the program featured Evelyn Lynn, who sang and read poetry; singer Nancy Martin; Jack Owens, singer and second banana; and guitarist Jack Rose. Fran Allison joined the program in 1937 with her comic character of Aunt Fanny.

A regular feature of the show was "Memory Time," an uplifting sentimental segment of poetry and inspirational stories. Then, too, there was "Prayer Time," a segment begun during World War II and the "Sunshine Shower" featuring cards and letters to residents in rest and nursing homes. During McNeill's summer vacations he was replaced by such show business veterans as Ole Olsen, Peter Donald and Joe E. Brown. Special features of the program included the daily march around the breakfast table and the morning prayer. Sam Cowling regularly offered his "Fiction and Fact from Sam's Almanac" and Fran Allison, hilarious as Aunt Fanny, contributed gossip, small talk and still more gossip.

The program's cast over the years was extensive and contained many who would attain great popularity and professional success. Fibber McGee and Molly, Homer and Jethro, Fran Allison and Johnny Desmond are a few examples. The other performers included: Eugenie Baird, Jack Baker, Helen Jane Behilke, the Cadets (Jack Halloran, Al Scheibe, Al Stracke and Homer Snodgrass), Ted Claire, Douglas Craig, Janette Davis, Clark Dennis, the Escorts and Betty (Douglas Claire, Douglas Craig, Floyd Holm, Cliff Peterson and Betty Olson), Johnny Johnson, Annette King, Evelyn Lynn, Marion Mann, Nancy Martin, the Merry Macs (Cheri McKay, Joe McMichael, Judd McMichael and Ted McMichael), the Morin Sisters, Ranch Boys, Edna O'Dell, Jack Owens, Gale Page, Cliff Peterson, Russell Pratt, the Ranch Boys, Jack Rose, the Songfellows, Mildred Stanley, Dick Teela, Bill Thompson, Johnny Thompson, the Three C's, the Three Romeos (Sam Cowling, Gil Jones and Louie Perkins), the Vagabonds (Ray Grant, John Jordan and Robert O'Neil), and Ilene Woods. The program announcers included: Bob Brown, Don Dowd, Franklyn Ferguson, Charles Irving, Fred Kasper, Durward Kirby, Bob McKee, Bob Murphy, Ken Nordine and Louis Roen. At various times the orchestra was led by Eddie Ballantine, Walter Blaufuss, Joe Gallichio, Harry Kogen and Rex Mauphin. The program was directed by Cliff Peterson, who earlier had performed comedy routines using a Swedish accent (60 min., Monday through Friday, 8:00–9:00 P.M., NBC, 1935).

An example of the material that McNeill presented during the World War II era was "A Letter From a Son to his Dead Father":

> Dear Dad:
>
> I am writing this to you, though you have been dead thirty years. I feel I must say some things to you, things I didn't know when I was a boy in your house, and things that I was too stupid to say.
>
> It is only now, after passing through the long, hard school of years, only now when my hair is grey, that I understand how you felt. I must have been a bitter trial to you. I believed my own petty wisdom, and I know now how ridiculous it was compared to the calm, ripe, wholesome wisdom that was yours.
>
> Most of all, I want to confess my worst sin against you. It was the feeling I had that you didn't understand; you understood me better than I did myself. Your wisdom flowed around mine as an ocean around an island.
>
> How patient you were with me; how full of long suffering and kindness. How pathetic, it now comes home to me, were your efforts to get close to me, to win my confidence, to be my pal. I wouldn't let you. I couldn't. What was it held me aloof? I didn't know, but it was tragic, that wall that rises between a boy and his father, and their frantic attempts to see through it and climb over it.
>
> I wish you were here now, across the table from me, just for one hour, so that I could tell you how there's no wall anymore. I understand you now, Dad, and God how I love you and wish I could go back and be your boy again. I know now how I could make you happy every day. I know how you felt. It took a good many years for this prodigal son, and all sons are in a measure prodigal, to come to himself. I've come. I see it all now. I know what a rich and priceless thing, and one least understood, is that mighty love and tenderness and craving to help, which a father feels toward his boy, for I have a boy of my own.
>
> It is he that makes me want to go back to you and get down on my knees and ask you to hear me, Dad, and believe me.

McNeill frequently used material of this nature to appeal to his large listening audience.

4287 ***(The) Breakfast Club Review.*** Ball Brothers sponsored the reprise of Don McNeill and his gang's *Breakfast Club* program on the weekly digest of his daily program (25 min., Saturday, 9:30–9:55 P.M., ABC, 1955).

4288 ***Breakfast Express.*** Recorded music, time checks, numerous contests and giveaways plus some comedy chatter were the main ingredients of the Chicago early morning show. Don Norman was the host and Edna Erne his willing foil (120 min., Monday through Friday, 7:00–9:00 A.M., WAAF, Chicago, IL, 1938).

4289 ***Breakfast in Hollywood*** **(aka *Breakfast at Sardi's* and *Breneman's Hollywood*).** The show opened with the announcer's greeting: "Good morning. From America's newest fine restaurant, Tom Breneman's on Vine Street between Hollywood and Sunset Boulevard, Kellogg's Pep and Procter & Gamble's Ivory Flakes serves you *Breakfast in Hollywood."* Breneman gave corsages to visiting ladies, passed out silly prizes to the oldest, tallest, etc., and he made them laugh by trying on their hats. When Breneman died, Garry Moore tried to take his place as host in 1948 without much success. (30 min., Monday through Friday, NBC, ABC, NBC, 1943–1954). *See* **Tom Breneman, *Tom and* Wash *and Tom and His Mule Hercules.***

4290 ***Breakfast in the Blue Ridge.*** CW singing stars Lulu Belle and Scotty, stars of the *National Barn Dance* for many years, appeared on the transcribed series of programs (15 min., Transcribed, Various stations, late 1940s).

4291 ***Breakfast with Binnie and Mike.*** Motion picture actress Binnie Barnes and Mike Frankovitch conducted the local early morning husband-and-wife talk show (30 min., Monday through Friday, 8:30–9:00 A.M., KFVD, Los Angeles, CA, 1947).

4292 ***Breakfast with Jimmy O'Keefe.*** Three times a week, restaurateur O'Keefe broadcast from his Jimmy O'Keefe restaurant. On his program, which he also wrote and produced, he interviewed such sports personalities as Jumpin' Joe Dugan, Clipper Smith, Jack Britten, footballer Bobby Green, writer Dave Egan and columnist Allan Frazier (WLAW, Boston, MA, 1949). He also broadcast blow-by-blow accounts of boxing bouts from the Boston's Callahan Athletic Club.

4293 ***Breakfast with the Brooks.*** Irma Lemke and David Kroman were the first local husband-and-wife talk team in the Schenectady area (30 min., Monday through Friday, 9:30–10:00 A.M., WGY, Schenectady, NY, 1946).

4294 ***Breakfast with the Lynns.*** Movie star Jeffrey Lynn and his wife, Robin Chandler, were vacation replacements for *Dorothy and Dick* and supplied the same type of husband-and-wife talk as Dorothy Kilgallen and her spouse, Richard Kollmar (45 min., Monday through Friday, 8:15–9:00 A.M. and Sunday, 11:15–12:00 noon, 1951). *See* **Husband-and-Wife Shows.**

4295 Breakley, Clara. New York University lecturer in Home Economics Breakley broadcast a *Cooperative Economics* course in 1925 (WEAF, New York, NY, 1925).

4296 Bream, Louis. Pianist Bream appeared on the first program broadcast by WDY (Roselle Park, NJ, December 14, 1921).

4297 Brearley, Grace Senior. Pianist (KHJ, Los Angeles, CA, 1923).

4298 Breault, Rita. Concert pianist (WNAC, Boston, MA, 1933).

4299 Breaux, Emily Locke. Violinist (WHAS, Louisville, KY, 1923).

4300 Breaux, Jerry. Sportscaster (WLCS, Baton Rouge, LA, 1952–1954).

4301 Brecht, Lester. DJ (*Pitchin' Kurvs*, KURV, Edinburg, TX, 1947).

4302 Breck, Edward S. Classical pianist and announcer (WOR, Newark, NJ, 1925–1926).

4303 Breck, Ward S. Concert pianist (WOR, Newark, NJ, 1926).

4304 Breckinridge, Mary Marvin. Newscaster (CBS, 1939). Breckinridge, a friend of Edward R. Murrow from their student years, was in Europe when World War II began. During her stay in Europe, she was given a photographic assignment to cover the Nazi Nuremberg Rally. When war broke out she sought other photographic assignments in London, where once again she met Murrow. After appearing on his program, Murrow asked her to work for him. Her first broadcast from Amsterdam, Holland, was on December 10, 1939, reporting on Dutch preparations for war. She later appeared on the CBS *The World This Week* program, following such veteran radio reporters as Eric Sevareid from Paris; Warren Sweeney from New York; William L. Shirer in Berlin; and Edward R. Murrow from London. When she married in 1940, she resigned her CBS position, although the reason for her leaving has sometimes been questioned. *See* **Gender Discrimination.**

4305 Breckner, Gary. Sportscaster (Sports news and football play-by-play broadcasts, KHJ, Los Angeles, CA, 1932; KNX , Los Angeles, CA, 1939; *Pigskin Predictions*, KMPC, Beverly Hills, CA, 1940; KNX, CA, 1940).

4306 Bredmeter, August. Tenor (WOK, Chicago, IL, 1925).

4307 Breece, Chuck. DJ (WFBM, Indianapolis, IN, 1954–1955).

4308 Breed, Tony. DJ (KFTS, Texarkana, TX, 1960).

4309 Breedlove, Judy. COM-HE (WAMW, Washington, IN, 1956).

4310 Breeland, Ed. Newcaster (WAML, Laurel, MS, 1945).

4311 Breeland, Tom. DJ (*Hello World*, WCHL, Chapel Hill, NC, 1960).

4312 Breen, Edward, Jr. Announcer (WHO, Des Moines, IA, 1925).

4313 Breen, Edwin. Baritone (WLWL, New York, NY, 1928).

4314 Breen, May Singhi ("The Ukulele Lady"). Instrumentalist-singer Breen was also a banjo soloist (WJZ, New York, NY, 1924). Leader (May Singhi Breen and her Syncopators orchestra, WGBS, New York, NY and WEAF, New York, NY, 1925) . Breen became the "Ukulele Lady," when she teamed with husband Peter DeRose on WEAF (New York, NY). Breen and DeRose first began broadcasting as a team on WEAF as the "Sweethearts of the Air" in June, 1923. They were on the air consecutively from 1923 to 1939 with the exception of only two weeks. They appeared together on the *Three Kings and a Queen* program (NBC-Blue, New York, NY, 1929). Their sponsors over the years included: Listerine, Kraft-Phenix Cheese, Conti Soap, Breyer's Ice Cream, Valspar, Elgin Watch Company, Humphrey's Homeopathic Medicines, Pennzoil and Wrigley Chewing Gum. They were busy in the following decade as well: *Breen and DeRose (*1935). Bob Emery, "The Big Brother of Boston," also appeared on their program as announcer and "household counselor." Emery sometimes also recited poetry (15 min., Wednesday, 10:30–10:45 P.M., NBC-Red, 1934–1935; 1936–1939).

4315 Breen, Thomas, Jr. Announcer on the *Yeast Foamers* program (NBC-Blue, New York, NY, 1929).

4316 Breene, Elizabeth. Pianist (WSM, Nashville, TN, 1928).

4317 Breene, Pat. DJ (*The Whittier Square Matinee* and *Record Roundup*, KTUL, Tulsa, OK, 1948; *The Pat Breene Show* and *The Record Roundup*, KTUL, 1949).

4318 Brees, Anton. A native of Antwerp, Belgium, Brees was a carillonneur who played the carillon at Mountain Lake Singing Tower (WFLA, Clearwater, FL, 1929).

4319 Brees, Bud. DJ (WPEN, Philadelphia, PA, 1956).

4320 Breese, Alice. Singer (*Alice Breese*, vcl. mus. prg., WMCA, New York, NY, 1939).

4321 Breese, Beth. COM-HE (KNOE, Monroe, LA, 1951).

4322 Breese, Lou. Leader (*Lou Breese Orchestra*, instr. mus. prg., NBC, 1936–1939).

4323 Breese, Sidney. Actor Breese worked on the *Guiding Light* and *Road of Life* daytime serial programs.

4324 *Breezing Along.* Phillip Morris cigarettes sponsored this musical revue that replaced the *Guess Where* quiz show. Music was supplied by Johnny Green's orchestra, singer Jack Smith and Beverly and her Bel-Airs, a talented singing group of six girls and three boys. Charles O' Connor was the program's host (30 min., Friday, 8:00–8:30 P.M., MBS, 1939).

4325 Breezy, Chuck. DJ (*Rhythm Roundup*, KDLK, Del Rio, TX, 1948).

4326 Bregman, Kitty. COM-HE (WWLP, Springfield, MA, 1955–1958).

4327 Breher, Harry. Breher was a xylophone soloist on the *Cliquot Club Eskimos* program in 1927.

4328 Brehm, C.M. Violinist (KVOO, Tulsa, OK, 1928).

4329 Breidenstein, Grace. Mezzo-soprano (KOMO, Seattle, WA, 1928).

4330 Breining, Paul. Newscaster (WRAK, Williamsport, PA, 1939).

4331 Breitenfeld, Emil. Singer (KTAB, Oakland, CA, 1925).

4332 Breitenmoser, Don. Sportscaster (KMLB, Monroe, LA, 1939).

4333 Breland, Betty. COM-HE (WIKC, Bogalusa, LA, 1957).

4334 Breland, Ed. DJ (*Record Review*, WAML, Laurel, MS, 1947).

4335 *Bremer E. Tully.* Singer Tully presented a half-hour program of popular songs (30 min., Friday, 10:00–10:30 P.M., CBS, 1929).

4336 Bremmer, Muriel. Busy actress Bremner appeared on the daytime serials *The Guiding Light*, *The Woman in White*, *The Road of Life*, *In Care of Aggie Horn* and *Bachelor's Children*.

4337 Bremser, Lyell. Sportscaster (KFOR-KFAB, Lincoln, NE, 1941, 1945–1946; *Sports Director*, KFOR-KFAB, 1947–1955). Newscaster (KFOR-KFAB, 1945–1951).

4338 Bren, Joe. Leader, Joe Bren's Minstrel Company (WLS, Chicago, IL, 1925).

4339 Bren, Sheldon. Sportscaster (KCMJ, Palm Springs, CA, 1946). DJ (KIFI, Idaho Falls, ID, 1949; *Night Mayor of Honolulu*, KULA, Honolulu, HI, 1950s).

4340 Brenard, George. DJ (*Melody Cruise*, WLIP, Kenosha, WI, 1947). Sportscaster (*Sports Lineup*, WLIP, 1947–1948).

4341 *Brenda Curtis.* The Campbell Soup Company sponsored this daytime serial that told the story of Brenda Curtis, a promising actress who gave up her career for house and home. Vicki Vola played the title role. Also in the cast were: Charlie Cantor, Helen Choate, Matt Crowley, Parker Fennelly, Hugh Marlowe, Agnes Moorehead and Kathleen Niday. Kenneth Roberts was the announcer (15 min., Monday through Friday, 11:15–11:30 A.M., CBS, 1939).

4342 Brendel, Gretchen. Contralto (KPO, San Francisco, CA, 1929).

4343 Brendt, Jack. Newscaster (WINN, Louisville, KY, 1940).

4344 Breneman, Tom. Announcer-MC Breneman was born June 18, 1902. He began his radio career on KFWB, Hollywood, CA in 1925 and demonstrated his tenor singing voice on that station in 1925 and 1926. He originated and starred on his own *Tom and his Mule Hercules* program on KNX, Los Angeles, CA in 1929. In 1939, Breneman conducted *Sports Pop-Offs* and *Sports Huddle* on CBS. His greatest fame, however, came from his *Breakfast in Hollywood* program that he hosted in the 1940s. *See* ***Breakfast in Hollywood, Tom and His Mule Hercules*** *and* ***Tom and Wash.***

4345 Brengel, Bill. Sportscaster (WWL, New Orleans, LA, 1953).

4346 Brengel, George. Newscaster (WSCC, Charlotte, NC, 1939).

4347 Brennan, Bill. DJ (*Disc Time*, KOLT, Scottsbluff, NE, 1947).

4348 Brennan, Bob. Tenor (KFWI, San Francisco, CA, 1926).

4349 Brennan, Bob. DJ (*Bob and Chris*, WRGM, Newport, RI, 1949; *Morning Line*, KYMA, Yuma, AZ, 1954).

4350 **Brennan, Dan.** DJ (*Autumn Serenade* and *Hillbilly Hits*, WVOK, Birmingham, AL, 1949; *Breakfast Jamboree*, WVOK, 1952). Sportscaster (WVOK, 1948).

4351 **Brennan, Libby.** COM-HE (WILK, Wilkes-Barre, PA, 1954).

4352 **Brennan, Morey.** Leader (*Morey Brennan Orchestra*, instr. mus. prg., WHAM, Rochester, NY and MBS, 1939).

4353 **Brennan, Peter.** Newscaster (NBC, 1942, 1945).

4354 **Brennan, Tommy.** Brennan was a harmonica soloist who, *Variety* said, "played torrid blues and pop songs on the harmonica" (WBBC, Brooklyn, NY, 1928).

4355 **Brenneman, Hugh.** Newscaster (WTCM, Traverse City, MI, 1941).

4356 **Brenner, Bill.** Sportscaster (KGY, Olympia, WA, 1950s).

4357 **Brenner, Bob.** DJ (*Green Room*, WCOP, Boston, MA, 1947).

4358 **Brenner, Paul.** DJ (*Requestfully Yours*, WAAT, Newark, NJ, 1947–1954).

4359 **Brenner, Shiela.** Brenner was one of the intelligent "kids" who appeared on the *Quiz Kids* program (NBC, ABC, CBS, 1940–1953).

4360 **Brenner, Vladimir.** Pianist (*Vladimir Brenner*, instr. mus. prg., NBC, 1936).

4361 **Brent, Blackie.** DJ (*Man About the House*, WKBW, Buffalo, NY, 1954).

4362 **Brent, Larry.** Sportscaster (*Sports Parade*, WAJF, Decatur, AL, 1953).

4363 ***Brent House.*** In this daytime serial, Brent House was a publishing company run by Portia Brent, a role played by Georgia Backus before being taken over by Kathleen Fitz. The intrigues and conflicts of publishing provided many plot twists and turns. Other cast members of this daytime serial included: Ben Alexander, Edward Archer, Georgia Backus, Florence Baker, Grant Bayliss, Margaret Brayton, Al Cameron, Ernest Carlson, Kathleen Fitz, Gavin Gordon, Frederic MacKaye, Wally Maher, Jane Morgan, Larry Nunn, Naomi Stevens, Anne Stone, Lurene Tuttle and Jack Zoller (NBC-Blue, 1938–1940).

4364 **Brentholtz, George.** DJ (WSSB, Durham, NC, 1956).

4365 **Brenton, William.** Actor (CBS, New York, NY, 1928).

4366 **Brentson, Cheer.** Actress Brentson was a cast member of the daytime serial programs *Kitty Keene* aka *Kitty Keene, Incorporated*, *Ma Perkins* and *The Woman in White*.

4367 **Brescia, Pete.** Leader (*Pete Brescia Orchestra*, instr. mus. prg., WBEN, Buffalo, NY, 1942).

4368 **Bresette, Charles.** DJ (WOBT, Rhinelander, WI, 1949).

4369 **Bresky, Albert.** Tenor (WEAR, Cleveland, OH, 1925).

4370 **Bressen, Helen.** Hawaiian guitarist (WBZ, Springfield, MA, 1927).

4371 **Bressler, Bob.** DJ (*1400 Club*, WARD, Johnstown, PA, 1947).

4372 **Bressler, Rube.** Sportscaster (*Today's Baseball*, WCKY, Cincinnati, OH, 1940).

4373 **Breton, Ruth.** Violinist (NBC, 1929).

4374 **Bretschneider, (Mrs.) H.C.** Soprano (KOA, Denver, CO, 1925).

4375 **Bretton Hall String Quartet.** Broadcasting from the Bretton Hall Hotel, the music group specialized in playing classic, standard and jazz selections (WOR, Newark, NJ, 1926).

4376 **Bretz, Woody.** DJ (*Rhythm in Blues*, KWIL, Albany, OR, 1955; KOCO, Salem, OR, 1956).

4377 **Breuner String Trio.** The instrumental group included Orley See, violinist; Wenceslao Villalvande, cellist; and Emil Breitenfeld, pianist (KTAB, Oakland, CA, 1925).

4378 **Breur, Julie.** Soprano (WJAZ, Chicago, IL, 1926).

4379 **Brevard, Edna.** Singer (*Edna Brevard*, WHN, New York, NY, 1936).

4380 **Brewbaker, Jeannette.** Soprano (WOC, Davenport, IA, 1925).

4381 **Brewer, Charles W.** DJ (*1340 Club*, WKRM, Columbia, TN, 1947).

4382 **Brewer, Dan.** DJ (*Mail Bag*, WMRN, Marion, OH, 1948).

4383 **Brewer, Ed.** Newscaster (WHOP, Hopkinsville, KY, 1941).

4384 **Brewer, Eugenia.** Newscaster (WGGA, Gainesville, GA, 1941).

4385 **Brewer, Gage.** Leader (Gage Brewer's Hawaiians [orchestra], KFH, Wichita, KS, 1928).

4386 **Brewer, Hugh.** DJ (WKSR, Pulaski-Lawrenceburg, TN, 1947). Sportscaster (*Sports Roundup*, WKSR, 1947).

4387 **Brewer, Jack.** DJ (KIEM, Eureka, CA, 1956).

4388 **Brewer, (Mrs.) Jerry.** COM-HE (WMIS, Natchez, MS, 1956).

4389 **Brewer, Kay.** Contralto (WLS, Chicago, IL, 1950).

4390 **Brewer, (Prof.) Lucille.** COM-HE Brewer spoke on "Home Canning" (WGY, Schenectady, NY, 1925).

4391 **Brewer, Marion.** Soprano (WGY, Schenectady, NY, 1924–1925).

4392 **Brewer, Sam.** Newscaster (WCAE, Pittsburgh, PA, 1942).

4393 **Brewer, Ted.** Leader (*Ted Brewer Orchestra*, instr. mus. prg., WOWO, Fort Wayne, IN, 1935.

4394 **Brewer, Vernon.** DJ (WKOA, Hopkinsville, KY, 1960).

4395 **Brewster, (Mrs.) G.A.** Pianist (KFAE, Pittsburgh, PA, 1924).

4396 **Brewster, George Ashley.** Tenor (WFAA, Dallas, TX, 1925–1928).

4397 **Brewster, John.** Actor Brewster appeared on the *Stella Dallas, Valiant Lady* and *Woman of Courage* programs.

4398 **Brewster, Marion.** Singer (WFAA, Dallas, TX, 1925).

4399 ***(The) Breyer Leaf Boys.*** Comic Raymond Knight and the Landt Trio and White musical group appeared on this show (15 min., Thursday and Satruday, 6:30–6:45 P.M., NBC-Red, 1931).

4400 **Breyer's Ice Cream Quartet.** Male vocal quartet (WCAU, Philadelphia, PA, 1925).

4401 **Briar, Steve.** DJ (*Requestfully Yours*, KENT, Shreveport, LA, 1947).

4402 ***(The) Briar Hopper Boys.*** CW mus. prg. (WBT, Charlotte, NC, 1936–1939).

4403 **Brice, Bee.** DJ (*Anything Goes and Does*, WTPR, Paris, TN, 1948).

4404 **Brice, Don.** Newscaster (KSAL, Salina, KS, 1939; WKBN, Youngstown, OH, 1947–1948).

4405 **Brice, James A.** DJ (*Disc Jockey's Choice*, WTPR, Paris, TN, 1947).

4406 **Brickell, Ad.** Singer (*Ad Brickell*, vcl. mus. prg., WCAE, Pittsburgh, PA, 1935).

4407 **Bricker, Lena Weber.** Contralto (WIP, Philadelphia, PA, 1925).

4408 **Brickert, Carlton.** Actor Brickert appeared on the *Joyce Jordan, Girl Interne*, *Lum and Abner*, *Show Boat*, *Story of Mary Marlin*, *Tale of Today* and *Thurston the Magician* programs.

4409 **Brickhouse, Jack.** Sportscaster (WMBD, Peoria, IL, 1937–1939; WGN, Chicago, IL, 1941–1942; *Sports play-by-play*, WGN, 1949–1951; WGN, 1952–1955; *Man in the Street*, WGN, 1956). Early in his career, Brickhouse conducted an interview program on which he covered many subjects other than sports (*Jack Brickhouse Interviews*, WMBD, 1935).

4410 **Bricks, Phil.** Leader (Phil Bricks and his Yorke Tea Room Orchestra, WHO, Des Moines, IA, 1927).

4411 **Bride, Esther Lee.** COM-HE, (*Homemakers' Music Hall*, 1937, local St. Louis stations). From 1937 to 1977, Bride produced and broadcast cooperative programs for five different St. Louis stations for the Adult Council of St. Louis, Washington University, St. Louis University, the Metropolitan Nutrition Council and the St. Louis Public Library. She also was the Director of Home Economics for the St. Louis Union Electric Company.

4412 **Bridge, Agnes.** Soprano (KTBI, Los Angeles, CA, 1929).

4413 ***Bridge Lessons.*** Wynn Ferguson was the instructor on the weekly program (WQJ, Chicago, IL, 1925).

4414 ***Bridge Party Hour.*** George Taylor, Helen Troy, Nita Mitchell, Henry Lieberknecht and Bonnie Walker played and discussed their bridge hands (60 min, Monday, 3:00–4:00 P.M., KYA, San Francisco, CA, 1928). In 1929, the station broadcast the program in the morning (60 min., Monday, 11:00 A.M. to 12:00 noon). Most of the original bridge players remained on the show when the broadcast time was changed.

4415 ***Bridge Talk.*** Mrs. Guy U. Purdy discussed bridge and its problems (WAAW, Omaha, NE, 1924–1925).

4416 ***Bridge Talk.*** Edward Marshall conducted the bridge talk show (15 min., Saturday, 3:00–3:15 P.M., WMCA, New York, NY, 1934).

4417 **Bridges, Art.** Leader (Art Bridges Orchestra, KFQJ, Hollywood, CA, 1927).

4418 **Bridges, Doris.** COM-HE (WKMT, Kings Mountain, NC, 1956).

4419 **Bridges, Evelyn.** COM-HE (KGAL, Lebanon, OR, 1955).

4420 **Bridges, Glen.** Tenor (WYW, Chicago, IL, 1925).

4421 **Bridges, J.E.** "Daytime" announcer (WBAP, Fort Worth, TX, 1928).

4422 **Bridges, Ray.** DJ (KID, Idaho Falls, ID, 1956).

4423 **Bridwell, Betty.** COM-HE (WHUB, Cookville, TN, 1955).

4424 **Briegel, George F.** Director, 22nd Regiment Band broadcasting from the Central Park Mall in New York City (WNYC, New York, NY, 1924–1925).

4425 **Brien, Payton [Peyton].** DJ (WJIG, Tullahoma, TN, 1948; *Breakfast with Brien*, WDXB, Chattanooga, TN, 1948).

4426 **Brienen, Donald "Don."** DJ (*Record Party*, WHSC, Hartsville, SC, 1948–1952).

4427 **Brierly, Jimmy.** Tenor (*Jimmy Brierly*, vcl. mus. prg., WOR, Newark, NJ, 1933; *Jimmy Brierly*, vcl. mus. prg., CBS, 1936). Leader (*Jimmy Brierly Orchestra*, instr. mus. prg., CBS, 1936).

4428 **Briggs, Donald "Don."** Busy actor Briggs worked on such diverse programs as *Betty and Bob*, *City Desk*, *David Harum*, *Dick Daring's Adventures*, *First Nighter*, *Girl Alone*, *Grand Hotel*, *Hilltop House*, *Perry Mason*, *The Sheriff*, *Story of Bess Johnson* and *Welcome Valley.*

4429 **Briggs, Finney.** Actor Briggs was born January 11, 1891. He made his radio debut on Chicago radio (WBCN, Chicago, IL, 1924). He appeared on the *Woman in White* daytime serial.

4430 **Briggs, Fred.** DJ (*Open Line*, WSAZ, Huntington, WV, 1960).

4431 **Briggs, John.** Reader (WCCO, Minneappolis–St. Paul, MN, 1925).

4432 **Briggs, Ralph E.** Announcer (WPCC, Chicago, IL, 1925).

4433 **Briggs, Vera.** Musical comedy singer (WGBS, New York, NY, 1928).

4434 **Brigham, Natalie Adeline.** Violinist Brigham was the wife of station manager, G.C. Arnoux (KTHS, Hot Spings National Park, AR, 1924–1925).

4435 **Brigham, Paul.** DJ (*Get-Up-and-Go Show*, WBLR, Batesburg, SC, 1960).

4436 **Bright, Betty.** COM-HE (KUTV, Salt Lake City, UT, 1955).

4437 **Bright, Harry.** Sportscaster (*Bright Lites of Sports*, WGBR, Goldsboro, NC, 1940–1942; WETZ, New Martinsville, WV, 1956). Newscaster (WGBR, 1940–1942, 1944–1945). DJ (*Bright & Early*, WSAL, Loganport, IN, 1952).

4438 **Bright, Howard.** DJ (*Alarm Clock Club*, WKMO, Kokomo, IN, 1948).

4439 **Bright, Robin.** DJ (WIBC, Indianapolis, IN, 1956).

4440 **Bright, Weldon.** DJ (KGNC, Amarillo, TX, 1960).

4441 ***Bright Horizon.*** Michael West, the daytime serial's main character, originated on the *Big Sister* program, which was a spin-off from that program. *Bright Horizon*, in turn, was transformed into *A Woman's Life* in 1945. *Bright Horizon* was first broadcast on CBS in 1941. The cast included: Marjorie Anderson, Joan Alexander, Lon Clark, Alice Frost, Will Geer, Alice Goodkin, Jackie Grimes, Sammie Hill, Alice Hubbard, Joe Julian, Dick Keith, Richard Kollmar, Ronald Liss, Frank Lovejoy, Santos Ortega, Stefan Schnabel, Sid Slon, Chester Stratton, Renee Terry, Audrey Totter and Lesley Woods. Henry Hull, Jr. and Day Tuttle were the directors and Stuart Hawkins, Kathleen Norris and John M. Young the writers. Marjorie Anderson was the announcer and John Gart the organist.

4442 ***Bright Lights.*** Local entertainers from the Philadelphia area were featured on the CBS variety program (30 min., Wednesday, 10:30–11:00 A.M., CBS, 1935).

4443 ***(The) Brighter Day.*** With the demise of *Joyce Jordan, M.D.* on Friday, October 8, 1948, Procter and Gamble substituted the daytime serial *The Brighter Day*, which premiered Monday, July 11, 1949. "A story of human hearts — like yours and mine," concerned Papa Dennis, a minister, who was on the verge of losing his church. He was widowed with five daughters and a son. Further complications arose when his 25-year-old daughter was wooed by a young man. The program was a spin-off from the *Joyce Jordan, M.D.* daytime serial, where the character of the minister's daughter, Liz Dennis, first appeared. Members of the program's cast over the years included: Inge Adams, Joan Alexander, Joe DiSantis, Margaret Draper, Ann Hilary, Pat Hosley, John Larkin, Judith Lockser, Lorna Lynn, Charlotte Manson, Grace Matthews, Paul McGrath, Jay Meredith, Bob Pollock, John Raby, Billy Redfield, Dick Seff, and Bill Smith. Bill Rogers and Len Sterling were the announcers. Bill Meeder was the organist and music director. The writers were Irna Phillips and Orin Tovrov, who also wrote *Ma Perkins.*

The program was produced by David Lesan and directed by Ted Corday. Arthur Hanna and Ed Wolfe. Jack Anderson and Bill Brown produced the sound effects. When the program first aired in 1948, it was broadcast weekdays from 10:45–11:00 A.M. on NBC. The following year it was shifted to CBS (15 min., Monday through Friday, 2:45–3:00 P.M., CBS, 1949).

4444 ***(A) Brighter Tomorrow.*** Gabriel Heatter, who is best remembered for the customary "There's good news tonight" opening on his nightly newscast during World War II, was in a similar mood as he hosted this program sponsored by the Mutual Benefit Association. The program dramatized episodes demonstrating how various Americans had overcome physical or social handicaps. Actors on the program were Michael Artist, Amzie Strickland, Jules Getlon, Paul Mann and Ian Martin. The announcer was Cy Harrice (30 min., Sunday, 10:00–10:30 P.M., WOR, Newark, NJ, 1946).

4445 **Brignall, Roy Reid.** Organist (KFSG, Los Angeles, CA, 1925).

4446 **Brigode, Ace.** Leader (Ace Brigode and his Ten Virginians [orchestra], WIP, Philadelphia, PA, 1923; WJY, Schenectady, NY, 1924 and WKRC, Cincinnati, OH; Ace Brigode and his Fourteen Virginians, WKRC, 1926; *Ace Brigode Orchestra*, instr. mus. prg., WLW, Cincinnati, OH, 1935; WCAE, Pittsburgh, PA, 1935; WLW, 1942). Brigode led a busy radio and recording band that included the following personnel: Brigode, ldr.-clr.-as.; Lucien Criner and John Poston, t.; Jimmy Freeshour, tb.; Eddie Allen, clr. and ts.; Nick Cortez, f. and pac.; Gene Fogarty, v.; Penn Fay, p.; Fred Barber, bj.; Happy Masefield, tba.; and Billy Hayes, d. and c.

4447 **Briley, Larry.** DJ (WKDL, Clarksdale, MS, 1960).

4448 **Brill, Anita.** Hymn singer (*Anita Brill*, vcl. mus. prg., WMMN, Fairmont, WV, 1942).

4449 **Brill, Leonardo.** Leader (Leonardo Brill's Concert Trio [instrumental group], KHJ, Los Angeles, CA, 1928).

4450 **Brillhart, Janice.** COM-HE (KXXX, Colby, NE, 1957).

4451 **Brimm, Claude.** DJ (KOL, Seattle, WA, 1956).

4452 **Brimmer, Josephine.** Soprano (KXA, Seattle, WA, 1929).

4453 **Brindle, Karl.** DJ (*Let's Listen*, KVEC, San Luis Obispo, CA, 1949).

4454 **Brine, Ruth.** Newscaster (WBBM, Chicago, IL, 1938). Brine previously had broadcast a movie gossip and motion picture news program (KMOX, St. Louis, MO and WFBM, Indianapolis, IN).

4455 **Bring, Lou.** Leader (*Lou Bring Orchestra*, instr. mus. prg., NBC, 1935).

4456 ***Bring and Crystal.*** Vernon Dahlhart and Adelyn Hood starred in this daytime serial that included a dramatic sketch with frequent humorous bits. Dahlhart and Hood also occacionally were a vocal recording team (WOR, Newark, NJ, 1934). *See* **Dahlhart, Vernon**.

4457 **Bringas, Consuelo.** COM-HE (KCCT, Corpus Christi, TX, 1955).

4458 **Bringham, Marguerite.** Singer billed as "The Nightingale of KHJ" (KHJ, Los Angeles, CA, 1926.)

4459 **Bringier [Bringer], Ernest "Ernie."** DJ (*Ernie the Whip*, WMRY, New Orleans, LA, 1948–1956).

4460 **Brink, Arthur.** DJ (KSPR, Casper, WY, 1956).

4461 **Brink, Don.** DJ (WTKO, Ithaca, NY, 1960).

4462 **Brink, Norma S.** COM-HE (WGRD, Grand Rapids, MI, 1954).

4463 **Brinker, Kay.** Actress Brinker appeared on such daytime serials as *Kitty Keene* aka *Kitty Keene, Incorporated*; *Our Gal Sunday*; *Ma Perkins* and *The Woman in White.*

4464 **Brinkley, Amy.** COM-HE (WHKY, Hickory, NC, 1954).

4465 **Brinkley, David.** Newscaster (WRC, Washington, DC and NBC, 1943–1948). Brinkley became the NBC Washington correspondent in 1943.

4466 **Brinkley, Jack.** Actor-announcer Brinkley worked on the *Couple Next Door* (actor) and *Ma Perkins* (announcer) programs. DJ (WLS, Chicago, IL, 1948–1953; *Stars of the Barn Dance*, WLS, 1954).

4467 **Brinkley, John Romulus.** *See* **Charlatans, Demagogs and Rogues.**

4468 **Brinkman E.N.** Contralto (KLDS, Independence, MO, 1925).

4469 **Brinkman, Harry.** Newscaster (WTCM, Traverse City, MI, 1944).

4470 **Brinn, Jack.** Newscaster (WCBI, Columbus, MS, 1942, 1945).

4471 **Brinnon, Virgil.** DJ (*Moon Dog Matinee*, WJW, Cleveland, OH, 1954).

4472 **Brisandine, Robert "Bob."** Newscaster (WRRF, Washington, DC, 1942). Sportscaster (WRRF, 1942; WERD, Atlanta, GA, 1950). DJ (*Bouncing with Bob*, WERD, 1950s). Brisandine, was the only white DJ who worked at WERD, an all-Black station. Paul E.X. Brown, the station's program director and DJ, called Brisandine "one of the boys." When Brown moved on to Florida, Brisdandine became the station's program director.

4473 **Briscoe, George.** Tenor (KGO, Oakland, CA, 1926).

4474 **Briscoe, Helen.** Singer (*Helen Briscoe*, vcl. mus. prg., NBC, 1939).

4475 **Briscoe, Roy.** DJ (*Nite Club of the Air*, WSTV, Steubenville, OH, 1948–1949).

4476 **Briscoe, Wally.** Sportscaster (KCLA, Pine Bluff, AR, 1953). DJ (KCLA, 1954–1955).

4477 **Brissette [Brisett], Dol.** Leader (*Dol Brissette Orchestra*, instr. mus. prg., WTAG, Worcester, MA and NBC, 1939).

4478 **Brissey, Grace M.** COM-HE (WHPB, Belton, SC, 1957).

4479 **Bristow, Dude.** Leader (Dude Bristow's Oklahoma Orchestra, KVOO, Tulsa, OK, 1927).

4480 **Bristow [OK] Lions Club Quartet.** Civic club vocal group (KVOO, Tulsa, OK, 1928).

4481 **Britain, Ron.** DJ (WSAI, Cincinnati, OH, 1960).

4482 **Britling's Cafeteria Orchestra.** Popular band directed by Lou Goldberg (WFAA, Dallas, TX, 1923; WHO, Des Moines, IA, 1925; WMC, Memphis, TN, 1926). This band was sometimes known as Britling's Novelty Orchestra.

4483 **Britling's Novelty Orchestra.** *See* **Britling's Cafeteria Orchestra.**

4484 **Brito, Alfredo.** Leader (*Alfredo Brito Orchestra*, instr. mus. prg., WOR, Newark, NJ, 1934).

4485 **Brito, Phil.** Tenor (*Phil Brito*, vcl. mus. prg., NBC, 1939, 1942). Crooner Brito later became a DJ (*The Phil Brito Show*, WKAT, Miami Beach, FL, 1952).

4486 **Britt, Andy.** Baritone (WHAS, Louisville, KY, 1924).

4487 **Britt, Jim.** Sportscaster (WBEN, Buffalo, NY, 1937; WAAB-WNAC , Boston, MA, 1939–1941; WNAC ,Boston, MA, 1945–1947; WHDH, Boston, MA, 1950; MBS, 1951; *Jim Britt's Sports Report*, ABC, 1953).

4488 **Britt, Paul.** DJ (*Matinee for Mama* and *Teen Time*, KCOL, Fort Collins, CO, 1947; KOAT, Albuquerque, NM, 1949).

4489 **Britt, Weston.** Newscaster (WCOV, Montgomery, AL, 1945).

4490 **Brittain, Zaidee.** COM-HE (KTRE, Lufkin, TX, 1951).

4491 **Britten, Patsy.** Miss Britten was "The Sandman's Little Helper" on the early evening children's program (WOL, Seattle, WA, 1929).

4492 **Britton, Bashful Red or Red.** DJ (*The Red Britton Show*, KCSB, San Bernardino, CA, 1952–1954).

4493 **Britton, Bill.** DJ (*The Bill Britton Show*, WNLK, Norwalk, CA, 1948; WNDB, Daytona Beach, FL, 1952).

4494 **Britton, Harriet.** Soprano (WBAL, Baltimore, MD, 1935).

4495 **Britton, J.A.** Newscaster (KGBU, Ketchikan, AK, 1941).

4496 **Britton, Jack.** DJ (*Morning Express*, WKGN, Knoxville, TN, 1947; KTRN, Wichita Falls, TX, 1954). Sportscaster (WHBQ, Memphis, TN, 1949–1951; KTRN, 1953–1955; KSYD, Wichita Falls, TX, 1960).

4497 **Brixley, Frances.** Pianist (WNAD, Norman, OK, 1926).

4498 ***Broadcasting Broadway.*** Bertha Brainard reviewed plays and talked about the current Broadway scene and season. She always opened her program with "Bertha Bernard broadcasts Broadway." The program was a great New York favorite (WJZ, New York, NY, 1922). *See also* **Brainard, Bertha.**

4499 **Broadhurst, Walt.** DJ (WMOD, Moundsville, WV, 1960).

4500 **Broadmoor Rhythm Rustlers.** Local music group (KOA, Denver, CO, 1926).

4501 **Broadstone, Don.** DJ (*The Mailbag*, WJAG, Norfolk, NE, 1955).

4502 **Broadstreet, Lucy Hearn.** Singer Broadstreet specialized in such songs as "Four Leaf Clover" and "Land of the Sky Blue Waters,." Miss Broadstreet was accompanied by pianist Mrs. Ray Paterson (WOK, Pine Bluff, AR, 1922).

4503 **Broadwater, Bob.** DJ (KARR and KFBB, Great Falls, MT, 1960).

4504 **Broadwater, Elwood.** Newscaster (WCMW, Canton, OH, 1948).

4505 ***(The) Broadway Bandwagon.*** Northampton Brewing Company, makers of Tru-Blu Beer and Ale, sponsored the half-hour variety show hosted by vaudeville veteran Pat Rooney. George Hall's Orchestra with vocalist Dolly Dawn performed regularly. Singers Anthony and Rogers, contralto Margaret Young, Freddy Lightner and Roscella were also featured (30 min., Wednesday, 8:30–9:00 P.M., WOR, Newark, NJ, 1935).

4506 ***Broadway Lights.*** The dual piano team of Muriel Pollack and Vee Lawnhurst were featured on the music program with baritone Earl Oxford (15 min., Saturday, 9:00–9:15 P.M., NBC-Blue, 1929–1930).

4507 ***Broadway Melodies.*** NBC staff singers and musicians were featured on the West Coast music program that presented operatic and light classic music. Margaret O'Dea and Edna May Hamilton, contraltos; Ethel Wakefield, soprano; Gwynfi Jones, tenor; and baritone John Warner were featured. Joseph Hornik conducted the program's orchestra (60 min., Friday evenings, 10:00–11:00 P.M., NBC-Pacific Coast Network, 1929).

4508 ***Broadway Melodies.*** Torch singer Helen Morgan and the band and chorus of Jerry Freeman were featured on the entertaining music show sponsored by American Home Products (30 min., Sunday, 2:00–2:30 P.M., CBS, 1934).

4509 ***Broadway Melody Hour.*** Versatile Jay C. Flippen, ex-vaudevillian and former band leader, who later became a TV and motion picture star, hosted the local variety program sponsored by Pioneer Ice Cream Company. Irving Aaronson's Commodores Orchestra supplied the music and Rose Marie and Ethel Shepard sang the songs on the program broadcast by two New York stations (30 min., Wednesday, 8:00–8:30 P.M., WOR, New York, NY and WHN, New York, NY, 1937).

4510 ***Broadway Vanities.*** The music show featured the Victor Arden Orchestra and singer Everett Marshall (30 min., Wednesday, 8:30–9:00 P.M., CBS, 1934).

4511 ***Broadway Varieties.*** Vocalists Oscar Shaw and Elizabeth Lennox sang with an orchestra directed by Victor Young on the music program (30 min., Friday, 7:30–8:00 P.M., CBS, 1936).

4512 ***Broadways and Boulevards.*** Soprano Gail Taylor and tenor Irving Kennedy sang on the music program (60 min., Monday, 10:00–11:00 P.M., NBC-Pacific Coast Network, 1928).

4513 ***Broadway's Greatest Thrills.*** Each week newspaper columnist Ed Sullivan hosted dramatizations of the life of some outstanding figure in the theatrical world. Jack Berger directed the orchestra (15 min., Tuesday, 8:45–9:00 P.M., CBS, 1932). *See* ***The Ed Sullivan Show.***

4514 ***Broadway's My Beat.*** Larry Thor starred as a tough New York detective on the dramatic series. He was assisted in his adventures by Charles Calvert. The program began with Thor saying, "From Times Square to Columbus Circle — the grandest, the most violent, the lonesomest mile in the world. Broadway is my beat." Elliot Lewis produced and directed the half-hour dramatic adventure series (CBS, 1949–1954).

4515 **Broadwell, Fay.** COM-HE (KXOX, Sweetwater, TX, 1954).

4516 **Brocaw, C.W.** DJ (*Your Request*, KGIW, Alamosa, CO, 1948).

4517 **Brock, Art.** DJ (*Melody Matinee*, KCOK, Tulare, CA, 1948; *Cavalcade of Sports*, KAFY, Bakersfield, CA, 1948; KTVK, Phoenix, AZ, 1955).

4518 **Brock, Arthur** Announcer (WKBN, Youngstown, OH, 1925).

4519 **Brock, Buddy.** Leader (*Buddy Brock's Swingsters*, instr. mus. prg., WHAS, Louisville, KY, 1939).

4520 **Brock, Elliott.** Violinist (*Elliott Brock*, instr. mus. prg., WLW, Cincinnati, OH, 1935).

4521 **Brock, Grace.** COM-HE (WABB, Mobile, AL, 1951).

4522 **Brock, Johnny.** DJ (*Yawn Patrol*, WWKY, Winchester, KY, 1960).

4523 **Brock, Leland.** Pianist (*Leland Brock*, instr. mus. prg., WHAS, Louisville, KY, 1936).

4524 **Brock, Mabel.** COM-HE (WMTS, Murfreesboro, TN, 1956–1957).

4525 **Brock, Mary.** Newscaster (NBC, 1942).

4526 **Brock, Ray.** DJ (*Fox Club*, WHBY, Appleton, WI, 1948–1952; WHBY, 1955).

4527 **Brock, William.** DJ (WRLD, West Point, GA, 1949).

4528 **Brockerman [Brockman], Mary Elizabeth.** Soprano (*Mary Elizabeth Brockerman*, vcl. mus. prg., KFEL, Denver, CO, 1939).

4529 **Brockham, Charles.** Sportscaster (*Kingham's Klubhouse*, WIRE, Indianapolis, IN, 1953–1955).

4530 **Brockhurst, Claire.** Concert contralto (WHN, New York, NY, 1926).

4531 **Brockman, Don.** Sportscaster (KLIZ, Brainerd, MN, 1948–1949). DJ (KBUN, Bemidji, MN, 1949; WJON, St. Cloud, MN, 1951).

4532 **Brockway, Beaman.** DJ (*1460 Club*, KIMA, Yakima, WA, 1947).

4533 **Brodbury, V. W.** Announcer (WABZ, New Orleans, LA, 1927).

4534 **Brode, Buddy.** DJ (WILK, Wilkes-Barre, PA, 1947; *Juke Box Jamboree*, WNAR, Norristown, PA, 1948–1957). Sportscaster (WNAR, 1950–1960).

4535 **Brodemeir, August.** Tenor (WHT, Decatur, IL, 1925).

4536 **Broderick, Helen.** Cellist (WBZ, Springfield, MA, 1924).

4537 **Broderick, J. William.** Pianist (*J. William Broderick*, instr. mus. prg., WMMN, Fairmont, WV, 1938).

4538 **Broderick, Laura.** Soprano (KGO, Oakland, CA, 1925).

4539 **Broders, Spank.** DJ (*Platter Party*, KCBG, Cedar Rapids, IA, 1948; KXIC, Iowa City, IA, 1954–1960).

4540 **Brodey, Sherm.** DJ (WKAL, Rome, NY, 1954).

4541 **Brodsky, Vera.** Pianist (*Vera Brodsky*, instr. mus. prg., 15 min., Sunday, 11:15–11:30 A.M., CBS, 1945).

4542 **Brodsky, Vera and Harold Triggs.** Duo piano team (WOR, Newark, NJ, 1934).

4543 **Brodt, Dale.** DJ (KCHE, Cherokee, IA, 1960).

4544 **Broeg, Heloise.** COM-HE (WEEI, Boston, MA, 1955).

4545 **Broemer, Helene [Helen].** Cellist (WBAL, Baltimore, MD, 1928).

4546 **Broholm, Norman.** Pianist (WHO, Des Moines, IA, 1926).

4547 **Broilers, Mark.** DJ (*Dance Club*, KGNO, Dodge City, KS, 1948).

4548 **Broiles, Luther.** Newscaster (KSAL, Salina, KS, 1939).

4549 **Brokenshire, Norman.** Distinguished announcer Brokenshire was born in Canada in 1898. He was first known as "AON" (WJZ, New York, NY, 1923). When he joined WJZ in 1923, the announcing staff included Tommy Cowan, Milton J. Cross and Lewis Reid. Brokenshire became nationally famous in 1925, when he competed against WEAF's Graham McNamee in covering Calvin Coolidge's presidential inauguration. His description of the event with his emphasis on the colorful elements brought him great popularity. In 1926, he left WJZ to become the first free lance announcer, but then reversed his professional choice by joining WFBH (New York, NY)—a station whose call letters were eventually changed to WPCH—to join the other staff announcers: Alois Havrilla, Walter Neff and Lewis Reid. In 1927, he joined WPG (Atlantic City, NJ) and then moved to WCAU (Philadelphia, PA). He left WCAU in 1929 to join station WABC (New York, NY) and the CBS organization. Announcing such CBS programs as the *La Palina Hour*, Brokenshire's customary opening was, " How do you do, ladies and gentlemen. How *DO* you *DO?"* It was this distinctive opening trademark that listeners remembered once they heard it. Later, Brokenshire became a DJ, hosting *The Norman Brokenshire Show* (WNBC, New York, NY, 1947–1948) and the *Brokenshire Broadcasting* program (WNBC, New York, NY, 1949).

4550 **Broks, Harold.** DJ (WMRE, Monroe, GA, 1956).

4551 **Broman, Carol.** Pianist (WJAZ, Chicago, IL, 1923).

4552 **Broman, Catherine.** COM-HE (WREN, Topeka, KS, 1956; WWLP, Springfield, MA, 1957).

4553 **Broman [Bromon], Kitty.** COM-HE (WWLP, Springfield, Ma, 1955–1960).

4554 **Bromberg, Vern.** DJ (*Melody Merchant*, KCHA, Charles City, IA, 1948). Sportscaster (*Hawkeye Sports Journal*, KCHA, 1951).

4555 ***(The) Brome-Llewellyn Program.*** A 30-minute program of songs and comic patter (CBS, 1928).

4556 ***(The) Bromo-Seltzer Program.*** Eddie Garr was the host on the program, whose basic format was an imaginary visit to a nightclub, an idea that already had successfully been used by the *Manhattan Merry-Go-Round* program. Sidney Skolsky provided movie gossip and Yascha Bundchuk's Orchestra the music (15 min., Wednesday, 9:30–9:45 P.M., NBC-Blue, 1938).

4557 **Brondfield, Jerry.** Sportscaster (*Football Interviews*, WCLE-WHK, Cleveland, OH, 1940).

4558 **Bronson, George.** Newscaster (WELI, New Haven, CT, 1944–1946).

4559 **Brook, Bill.** DJ (WRJN, Racine, WI).

4560 **Brook, Mary.** COM-HE (KOFO, Ottowa, KS, 1951).

4561 **Brook, Nat.** DJ (*K'Mon Along & Listen*, KMON, Great Falls, MT, 1948–1952).

4562 **Brook, Phil.** DJ (WTAY, Robinson, IL, 1956).

4563 **Brooke, Kirby.** DJ (*The Dreambuster*, WIOD, Miami, FL, 1947; *Babbling Brooks*, WQAM, Miami, FL, 1948–1951; *The Kirby Brooke Show*, WQAM, 1952).

4564 **Brooker, Cracker Jim.** CW DJ (1950s).

4565 **Brooker, King.** DJ (*Diggin' the Grooves*, KXO, El Centro, CA, 1947).

4566 **Brookhart, Gary.** DJ (WCOM, Parkersburg, WV, 1956; WCEF, Parkersburg, VA, 1957).

4567 **Brookins, Carrie B.** Pianist (WEAF, New York, NY, 1924).

4568 **Brookins, Don.** DJ (*Brookins Incorporated*, WDLP, Panama City, FL, 1948).

4569 **Brookins, Frances.** COM-HE (*WGY, Schenectady, NY, 1925).*

4570 ***(The) Brooklyn Eagle Travel Talks.*** The Brooklyn *Eagle* newspaper sponsored this program on which the newspaper's travel editor was featured (15 min., Saturday, 5:45–6:00 P.M., WMCA, New York, NY, 1938).

4571 ***(The) Brooklyn Mark Strand Stage and Studio Program.*** A Sunday evening program, that presented information by many prominent speakers about Broadway plays and motion pictures. One program, for example, offered D.W. Griffith, the director-producer of "The Birth of a Nation" and "Intolerance" motion pictures, discussing his work and the movie industry. The program also contained several musical selections (WNYC, New York, NY, 1925). *See* **Griffith, D.W.**

4572 **Brooks, Al.** DJ (*Late Date*, WIBC, Indianapolis, IN, 1954–1955; WISH, Indianapolis, IN, 1957).

4573 **Brooks, Arthur Scott.** Organist (WPG, Atlantic City, NJ, 1925–1926).

4574 **Brooks, Beatrice and Harriet Brooks.** Singing team (WBX, Newark, NJ, 1925).

4575 **Brooks, Bess [Besse].** COM-HE (KSFA, Nacogdoches, TX, 1957).

4576 **Brooks, Bob.** Announcer (WREC, Memphis, TN, 1925).

4577 **Brooks, Bob.** Newscaster (KTRH, Houston, TX, 1947).

4578 **Brooks, Bob.** DJ (*Musicology*, WSCR, Scranton, PA, 1950).

4579 **Brooks, Bobby.** COM-HE (KVOW, Littlefield, TX, 1958).

4580 **Brooks, Bonnie Jean.** COM-HE (KBHS, Hot Springs, AR, 1954–1955).

4581 **Brooks, Carol.** COM-HE (KSLY, San Luis Obispo, CA, 1960).

4582 **Brooks, Clifton "Cliff."** Newscaster (WEOA, Evansville, IN, 1945; WGBF, Evansville, IN, 1947; *Our Town*, WGBF, 1948).

4583 **Brooks, Don.** DJ (KDEF, Albuquerque, NM, 1960).

4584 **Brooks, Donald.** News commentator and news editor (WORL, Boston, MA, 1942).

4585 **Brooks, Ed.** DJ (*Coffee Time*, WMIX, Mt. Vernon, IL, 1947).

4586 **Brooks, Ed.** Newscaster (*Farm Information*, WBBB, Burlington, NC, 1948; WBAG, Burlington, NC, 1960).

4587 **Brooks, Edward.** Baritone (WOR, Newark, NJ, 1927).

4588 **Brooks, Farrell.** DJ (*Juke Box Review*, KHRD, Duncan, OK, 1949).

4589 Brooks, Foster. DJ (*The Foster Brooks Show*, WAVE, Louisville, KY, 1946; *Melody, Inc.* and *Million Dollar Ballroom*, WKBW, Buffalo, NY, 1947; *Million Dollar Ballroom*, WKBW, 1950). Brooks was a popular DJ before he later achieved national prominence on television as a comedian.

4590 Brooks, George. Newscaster (WNEW, New York, NY, 1945–1947).

4591 Brooks, George. DJ (*Swing Symphony*, KDIX, Dickinson, ND, 1949).

4592 Brooks, (Mrs.) George. COM-HE (KMRS, Morris, MN, 1958).

4593 Brooks, Happy. DJ (KRNO, San Bernardino, CA, 1956).

4594 Brooks, Helen. COM-HE (WFBR, Baltimore, MD, 1951–1955).

4595 Brooks, Jack. Singer (*Song Souvenirs*, 15 min., Weekly, CBS, early 1930s; *Jack Brooks*, vcl. mus. prg., CBS, 1933–1935).

4596 Brooks, Jack. DJ (*Make Mine Music*, WCCC, Hartford, CT, 1954).

4597 Brooks, Jane. COM-HE (WTVR, Richmond, VA, 1956).

4598 Brooks, Jean. Newscaster (WGAA, Cedartown, GA, 1942).

4599 Brooks, Joan. Singer (*Joan Brooks*, vcl. mus. prg., WAKR, Akron, OH, 1942; CBS, 1945).

4600 Brooks, Julie. COM-HE (WREN, Topeka, KS, 1951).

4601 Brooks, Ken. DJ (*Off the Record*, KWIL, Albany, OR, 1948).

4602 Brooks, Lou. DJ (*1150 Club*, WCOX, Middletown, CT, 1952).

4603 Brooks, Martha. COM-HE (WGY, Schenectady, NY, 1956–1957).

4604 Brooks, Ned. Newscaster (NBC, 1947–1948).

4605 Brooks, Norman "Norm." Sportscaster (*Sports Hilites of the Air*, WMID, Atlantic City, NJ, 1948). DJ (*Open House*, WMFJ, Daytona Beach, FL, 1955–1956).

4606 Brooks, Pat. COM-HE (KVAS, Astoria, KS, 1954).

4607 Brooks, Phil. DJ (WKPA, New Kensington, PA, 1954).

4608 Brooks, Ray. DJ (WHIS, Bluefield, WV, 1956).

4609 Brooks, Renee. Singer-pianist (WBIL, New York, NY, 1937).

4610 Brooks, Richard. Newscaster (WNEW, New York, NY, 1937–1938; *Little Things in Life* and *Sensation and Swing*, WNEW, 1939).

4611 Brooks, Robert. Singer (*Robert Brooks*, vcl. mus. prg., WHAS, Louisville, KY, 1935).

4612 Brooks, Russell. Newscaster (WORC, Worcester, MA, 1938).

4613 Brooks, Ruthye. Singer (WDRC, Hartford, CT, 1939).

4614 Brooks, Shirley. COM-HE (WKDL, Clarksdale, MS, 1957).

4615 Brooks, Tex. DJ (*Top Tunes*, WSLI, Jackson, MS, 1954).

4616 Brooks, Tom. DJ (*Easy Rhythm*, KAWT, Douglas, AZ, 1947; *Merry Go Round*, KAWT, 1950). Sportscaster (KAWT, 1948–1949).

4617 Brooks, Tom. DJ (*Babbling Brook*, WHAW, Weston, WV, 1950; WSAZ, Hunting, WV, 1952).

4618 Brooks, Vance. DJ (WGCD, Chester, SC, 1949).

4619 Brooks, William. Newscaster (NBC, 1945).

4620 Brookshire, Gloria. COM-HE (KRDO, Colorado Springs, CO, 1951–1960).

4621 Brophy, Allen. Newscaster (WROK, Rockford, IL, 1938–1939).

4622 Brophy, Bill. DJ (*Number Please*, WKNY, Kingston, NY, 1947; *Brunch with Brophy*, WKNY, 1948; *Melody Lane*, WTHT, Hartford, CT, 1949).

4623 Brophy, Ethel. Soprano (WGBS, New York, NY, 1925).

4624 Brosche, Hank. DJ (*Party Line*, WKCT, Bowling Green, KY, 1954).

4625 Brose, Bob. Leader (Bob Brose Orchestra, WCCO, Minneappolis–St Paul, MN, 1928).

4626 Brosnan, Jack. DJ (WMBO, Auburn, NY, 1954).

4627 Broster, Bernard. Newscaster (WJZM, Clarksville, TN, 1947).

4628 Broth, Clarewell. Pianist (WSMB, New Orleans, LA, 1925).

4629 *Brother Bill.* Sam Serota, as "Brother Bill," read comics including *Dick Tracy* and *Mickey Mouse*, all of whom appeared in the newspaper of their sponsor, the Philadelphia *Public Ledger* (15 min., Monday, 6:00–6:15 P.M., WIP, Philadelphia, PA, 1937).

4630 Brother Bob. Ray Raymond was "Brother Bob," who broadcast stories for children (KTAB, Oakland, CA, 1929–1930).

4631 *Brother Ken's Kiddie Hour.* A weekday children's program (30 min., Monday through Friday, 5:15–5:45 P.M., KNX, Los Angeles, LA, 1929).

4632 Brothers, Bill. DJ (*800 Club*, WHNC, Henderson, NC, 1947).

4633 Brott, Lou. Newscaster (WOL, Washington, DC, 1945).

4634 Brotzman, Mildred. Blues singer (KGFJ, Los Angeles, CA, 1929).

4635 Broughman, Don. DJ (KAYE, Puyallup, WA, 1956).

4636 Broun, Heywood. Motion picture and theater critic, newspaper man Broun was his critical self (*Seeing Things At Night*, WOR, Newark, NJ, 1935).

4637 Brous [Brouse], Ellen. Soprano (*Ellen Brous*, vcl. mus. prg., WIP, Philadelphia, PA, 1935; WFIL, Philadelphia, PA, 1936).

4638 Brower, Florence. Soprano (WGN, Chicago, IL, 1925).

4639 Browing, Johnny. DJ (WWNS, Statesboro, GA, 1960).

4640 Brown, A.D. DJ (*Collegiate Parade*, KSFA, Nacogdoches, TX, 1949).

4641 Brown, A. Shirley. Newscaster (WTIK, Durham, NC, 1946).

4642 Brown, Al. DJ (WICC, Bridgeport, CT, 1954).

4643 Brown, Albert C. Newscaster (KMJ, Fresno, CA, 1945).

4644 Brown, Allen. Newscaster (WFOY, St. Augustine, FL, 1942). Sportscaster (WFOY, 1942).

4645 Brown, Alray. Newscaster (KHAS, Hastings, NE, 1940).

4646 Brown, Anderson B. Newscaster (WGBG, Greensboro, NC, 1941, 1945–1946; *Behind the Headlines*, WGWR, Asheboro, NC, 1947). Sportscaster (*Sports Review*, WGWR, 1947–1948).

4647 Brown, Art. Organist (*Art Brown*, instr. mus. prg., WRVA, Richmond, VA, 1934).

4648 Brown, Art. DJ (WOL, Washington, DC, 1947; WWDC, Washington, DC, 1960).

4649 Brown, Barbara. COM-HE (WINA, Charlottesville, VA, 1951–1954).

4650 Brown, (Mrs.) Barton. Contralto (WSM, Nashville, TN, 1928).

4651 Brown, Bernard. DJ (*At Sundown*, WAPO, Chattanooga, TN, 1947; *Sittin' In*, WAPO, 1948–1952; *Atlanta Carousel*, WGST, Atlanta, GA, 1954).

4652 Brown, Betty. Newscaster (KGKL, San Antonio, TX, 1940).

4653 Brown, Betty. COM-HE (WGBF, Evansville, IN, 1957).

4654 Brown, Betty Jane. COM-HE (WHHH, Warren, OH, 1957).

4655 Brown, Betty Jo. COM-HE (WJOT, Lake City, SC, 1954).

4656 Brown, Bill. Newscaster (KWTO-KGBX, Springfield, MO, 1938; WCNC, Elizabeth City, NC, 1940). DJ (*Sleepy Bill*, WMSC, Columbia, SC 1946; *Modern Harmonies*, WSTP, Salisbury, NC, 1947; WSTP, 1949; WMSC, 1960). Sportscaster (*Sports Journal*, WSTP, 1947–1953; *Sports Parade*, WSTP, 1954; WMSC, 1956).

4657 Brown, Bill. DJ (*AM 1230 Club*, WNEB, Worcester, MA, 1948; 1952–1957).

4658 Brown, Bill. DJ (*Request Club*, WCNH, Quincy, FL, 1949).

4659 Brown, Bill. DJ (*The Nut Club*, WIKK, Erie, PA, 1950; *Melody Go-Round*, WJAC, Johnstown, PA, 1954–1956). Sportscaster (*Time Out for Sports*, WIKK, 1948).

4660 Brown, Bill. Sound effects man and producer-director Brown produced sound effects for the *Big Sister* and *Ma Perkins* daytime serials programs. He produced and directed the *American Women* program.

4661 Brown, Bob. Performer Brown was billed as "Bob Brown and his Ukulele" (WDAP, Chicago, IL, 1924).

4662 Brown, Bob. DJ (*Turntable Matinee*, WEPM, Martinsburg, WV, 1947–1950). Sportscaster (WEPM, 1950).

4663 Brown, Bob. DJ (*Breakfast Jamboree*, WLBK, De Kalb, IL, 1949).

4664 Brown, Bob. DJ (KTHS, Hot Springs, AR, 1949).

4665 Brown, Bob. DJ (*1450 Club*, WFPG, Steel Pier, Atlantic City, NJ, 1947; *The Punch Bowl Show*, WMID, Atlantic City, NJ, 1950; *Music Room*, WMID, 1949–1950).

4666 Brown, Bob "Bobby." Announcer-producer-director Brown worked on such diverse programs as *American Women* (producer-director), *Ben Bernie Show* (announcer), *Breakfast Club* (announcer), *Dear Mom* (director), *Myrt and Marge* (producer-director), *Service to the Front* (producer-director), *The Singing Lady* (announcer) and *Vic and Sade* (announcer).

4667 **Brown, Bruce.** DJ (WKVA, Lewistown, PA, 1960).

4668 **Brown, Carleton.** Announcer-DJ Brown conducted a daily 60-minute program of recorded music. On Sunday, Brown for many years also hosted a popular program of music performed by the Waterville Military Band (WLBZ, Bangor-Waterville, ME, 1930s).

4669 **Brown, Cecil.** Newscaster (WJR, Detroit, MI and CBS, 1942; MBS, 1944–1947; WMCA, New York, NY, 1948). When liberal commentator Brown left CBS after executive criticism of his work, he joined MBS. Brown's wartime experience included being aboard the British cruiser *Repulse* when it was sunk by the Japanese.

4670 **Brown, Chuck.** DJ (*Morning Melodies*, WJMA; Orange, VA, 1952).

4671 **Brown, Clare.** DJ (WTTH, Port Huron, MI, 1954).

4672 **Brown, Cleo.** Pianist (*Cleo Brown*, instr. mus. prg., NBC, 1935; WMAQ, Chicago, IL, 1937).

4673 **Brown, Dale C.** DJ (*Platter Party*, KGSU, Provo, UT, 1949; *Songs of our Times*, KLO, Ogden, UT, 1952).

4674 **Brown, Dennis.** Sportscaster (*Sports Area*, WMLT, Dublin, GA, 1950s). DJ (*Georgia Jamboree*, WBGR, Jesup, GA, 1952).

4675 **Brown, Dick.** Newscaster (WINN, Louisville, KY, 1944).

4676 **Brown, Don.** DJ (*The Big Show*, KGBX, Springfield, MS, 1960).

4677 **Brown, Douglas.** DJ (KNEL, Brady, TX, 1948).

4678 **Brown, Dwight.** Organist (WFAA, Dallas, TX, 1924–1925).

4679 **Brown, Ed.** DJ (*Wax-Works*, WMGY, Montgomery, AL, 1947; *Boogie Man*, WCOY, Montgomery, AL, 1954). Sportscaster (*Sports Hi-Lights*, WMGY, 1947; *Sports Parade*, WJJJ, Montomery, AL, 1948).

4680 **Brown, Eddy.** Violinist (*Eddy Brown*, instr. mus. prg., WOR, Newark, NJ, 1934–1935).

4681 **Brown, Edna.** Singer (WLBZ, Bangor, ME, 1941).

4682 **Brown, Elizabeth A.** COM-HE (KBMX, Coalinga, CA, 1954).

4683 **Brown, Ethel.** Lyric soprano (KHJ, Los Angeles, CA, 1923).

4684 **Brown, Evans.** Accordionist (WFWB, Hollywood, CA, 1929).

4685 **Brown, Everett.** Announcer (WGN, Chicago, IL, 1925).

4686 **Brown, F. Fred, Jr.** Newscaster (*Fred Brown News*, WNCA, Asheville, NC, 1947; *Skyway Serenade*, WLOS, Asheville, NC, 1948). Sportscaster (WLOS, NC, 1951–1956).

4687 **Brown, Fay.** Sportscaster (KFYR, Bismark, ND, 1939; KFYR, 1942).

4688 **Brown, Florence Ruth.** Contralto (KGO, Oakland, CA, 1925).

4689 **Brown, Floyd.** Tenor (KFI, Los Angeles, CA, 1925).

4690 **Brown, Frances Roche.** Violinist (KFSG, Los Angeles, CA, 1925).

4691 **Brown, Frank.** "Evangelistic singer" (KFSG, Los Angeles, CA, 1925).

4692 **Brown, (Mrs.) Frank.** Contralto (KGO, Oakland, CA, 1925).

4693 **Brown, Frank J. "Hylo."** CW singer Brown was one the premier Bluegrass singers in the 1950s. During World War II, he worked in a war plant and sang on WPFB (Middleton, OH, 1940s). He later appeared on the *WWVA Jamboree* and became the opening act for the Flatt and Scruggs touring group.

4694 **Brown, Frank Robinson.** DJ (KHUM, Eureka, CA, 1950).

4695 **Brown, G. Crystal.** Singer (WBAN, Paterson, NJ, 1922).

4696 **Brown, Gatemouth.** Black gospel DJ (*Light of the World*, WDIA, Memphis, TN, 1950–1951). Popular DJ Brown left WDIA in 1951 to continue his distinguished career as a gospel DJ at WERD (Atlanta, GA, 1951).

4697 **Brown, Gene.** DJ (KOLS, Pryor, OK, 1956).

4698 **Brown, George.** Cellist (WBZ, Springfield, MA, 1926).

4699 **Brown, George.** DJ (*Music on the Upbeat*, WTYC, Rock Hill, SC, 1960).

4700 **Brown, George Frame.** Writer, producer and actor Brown starred in *Main Street Sketches* (WOR, Newark, NJ) as Luke Higgins, before moving on to write, produce and act in the *Real Folks* program (NBC, New York, NY). Brown had worked in Greenwich Village theaters before writing and acting in *Main Street Sketches*. In *Real Folks,* he wanted to present a "Thanksgiving rural sketch"—a sort of "barn dance with high jinks." The program's fun grew out of the problems faced by and the trouble in which small town characters found themselves. Brown also played the role of Captain Peterson of the ship *Silver Wave* on the program of the same name (WABC, New York, NY). *See* ***Main Street Sketches*** *and* ***Real Folks***.

4701 **Brown, Gerald.** DJ (*Brown's Derby*, WGRC, Louisville, KY, 1950).

4702 **Brown, Gerry.** COM-HE (KDKD, Clinton, MO, 1955).

4703 **Brown, Gloria.** Organist (*Gloria Brown*, instr. mus. prg., WCAU, Philadelphia, PA, 1936).

4704 **Brown, Gloria.** COM-HE (WNBK Cleveland, OH, 1951: KYW, Chicago, IL, 1956–1958).

4705 **Brown, Gordan.** DJ (*Mountain Music*, WVLK, Lexington-Versailles, KY, 1949).

4706 **Brown, Gordman.** DJ (*Dinner Date*, KKIN, Visalia, CA, 1948).

4707 **Brown, Gordon.** Newscaster (KSRO, Santa Rosa, CA, 1939–1940).

4708 **Brown, Grace.** Singer Brown was known as "The Ukulele Lady" (KTHS, Hot Springs National Park, AR, 1927).

4709 **Brown, Grace B.** Soprano (WCAE, Pittsburgh, PA, 1924).

4710 **Brown, Hal.** Musician, guitar and harmonica, performed on the *Just Plain Bill* daytime serial program.

4711 **Brown, Harry.** DJ (*Name Your Nitecap*, WBEC, Pittsfield, MA, 1949; WHUC, Hudson, NY, 1954; WKIS-WORZ, Orlando, FL, 1956; *Brown Hound Show*, WOTR, Corry, PA, 1960). Sportscaster (*Sports Extra*, WKIP, Poughkeepsie, NY, 1951).

4712 **Brown, (Mrs.) Harry K.** Director of the KFI Oratorio Society (KFI, Los Angeles, CA, 1925). One of their notable broadcasts was that of Handel's *Messiah*.

4713 **Brown, (Mrs.) Harry S.** Contralto (WCOA, Pensacola, FL, 1926).

4714 **Brown, Harvey.** DJ (*Platter Party*, WLFB, Leesburg, FL, 1950).

4715 **Brown, Hazelene.** COM-HE (WLON, Lincolnton, NC, 1958).

4716 **Brown, Helen.** Actress Brown worked on the *Big Town* program.

4717 **Brown, Himan.** Talented actor, writer, producer and director Brown was born July 21, 1910. He performed in little theater groups before acting in dramatic sketches on WMCA (New York, NY, 1928). His extensive work included *Affairs of Peter Salem* (producer), *Bulldog Drummond* (producer), *City Desk* (director), *Grand Central Station* (producer), *Green Valley, USA* (producer-director), *The Gumps* (writer), *Hilda Hope, M.D.* (writer), *Joyce Jordan, Girl Interne* (producer), *Little Italy* (actor-producer-director), *Marie the Little French Princess* (producer-director) and *The Thin Man* (producer-director).

4718 **Brown, Honey.** DJ (WBCO, Birmingham-Bessemer, AL, 1948).

4719 **Brown, Hudie.** DJ (*Cuzzin Al*, WDAK, Columbus, GA, 1949).

4720 **Brown, Hugh.** Newscaster (*Days of '49*, KGFN, Grass Valley, CA, 1947).

4721 **Brown, Irwin.** DJ (WREN, Topeka, KS, 1956).

4722 **Brown, Ivy.** Soprano (WBBR, New York, NY, 1927).

4723 **Brown, Jack.** Leader (*Jack Brown and the Lumberjacks*, CW mus. prg., WROK, Rockport, IL, 1936).

4724 **Brown, Jack.** DJ (*Tops in Pops*, WLTC, Gastonia, NC, 1949; *Tempo*, WCOS, Columbia, SC, 1960).

4725 **Brown, Jere.** COM-HE (WELO, Toledo, OH, 1956).

4726 **Brown, Jim.** Newscaster (KCRC, Enid, OK, 1945).

4727 **Brown, Jim Ed.** Popular CW baritone Brown while still in high school with older sister, Maxine Brown, had their own program on KCLA (Pine Bluff, AK, 1950) and eventually became regulars on the *Barnyard Frolic* conducted by Dutch O'Neal. The Browns became regulars on the *Louisiana Hayride* (KWKH, Shreveport, LA) before moving on to KWTO (Springfield, MOP), where they appeared on the *Ozark Jubilee*. When sister Bonnie joined Jim Ed and Maxine, the group became known as the Browns. After a successful career the group disbanded in 1967 and Jim Ed went on alone as a solo act. He successfully teamed with singer Helen Cornelius in 1976 and recorded many hits, causing them to be named Country Music "Duo of the Year." Brown has been a longtime member of the *Grand Ole Opry.*

4728 **Brown, Jimmy.** DJ (*Night Owl Parade*, KCLV, Clovis, NM, 1960).

4729 **Brown, Joan.** COM-HE (KWG, Stockton, CA, 1958; KRKC, King City, CA, 1960).

4730 **Brown, Joe.** Newscaster (WGBR, Goldsboro, NC, 1939). Sportscaster (WGBR, 1939).

4731 **Brown, John.** Pianist (*John Brown*, instr. mus. prg., 5 min., Thursday, 12:30–12:35 P.M., WLS, Chicago, IL, 1937 and 8 min., Monday through Friday, 12:52–1:00 P.M., WLS, Chicago, IL, 1937).

4732 **Brown, John.** Versatile comic actor Brown appeared on such diverse programs as *The Adventures of Ozzie and Harriet, Amanda of Honeymoon Hill, Amazing Mr. Smith, Beulah, Charlotte Greenwood Show, Date with Judy, Day in the Life of Dennis Day, Eddie Cantor Show, Fred Allen Show, Life of Riley, Lorenzo Jones, Maisie, My Friend Irma, The Saint* and *Tillie the Toiler.*

4733 **Brown, John E.** Evangelist Brown founded the John E. Brown College in Siloam Springs, Arkansas. He bought station KUOA (Fayetteville, AR), previously owned and operated by the University of Arkansas, and moved it to Siloam Springs in 1936.

4734 **Brown, John T.** Musician John T. Brown was billed as a "master harmonica player of popular songs and ballads" (KPO, San Francisco, CA, 1923).

4735 **Brown, Johnny.** Leader (*Johnny Brown Orchestra*, instr. mus. prg., WIP, Philadelphia, PA, 1935).

4736 **Brown, Johnny.** DJ (WROK, Rockford, IL, 1956–1957).

4737 **Brown, Josephine.** Pianist (KTHS, Hot Springs National Park, AR, 1927).

4738 **Brown, Josephine.** COM-HE (KWBU, Corpus Christi, TX, 1951).

4739 **Brown, L. Marion.** Soprano (WBBR, Rossville, NY, 1925–1926).

4740 **Brown, La Rue.** Pianist (Pianist, WMMN, Fairmont, WV, 1937–1939).

4741 **Brown, Larry.** DJ (*Rhythm Club*, WPEN, Philadelphia, PA, 1952–1956).

4742 **Brown, Lana.** COM-HE (WGRO, Lake City, FL, 1960).

4743 **Brown, Leila.** Soprano (WOR, Newark, NJ, 1925).

4744 **Brown, Leonard.** Newscaster (KGFW, Kearney, NE, 1940).

4745 **Brown, Les.** Leader (*Les Brown Orchestra*, instr. mus. prg., MBS, 1935; WTAM, Cleveland, OH, 1937, 1942). The band was frequently billed as "The Band of Renown — Les Brown."

4746 **Brown, Lettye.** COM-HE (WDRX, Hamlet, NC, 1958).

4747 **Brown, Liz.** COM-HE (KDAL, Duluth, MN, 1951).

4748 **Brown, Lorne.** DJ (WAIK, Galesburg, IL, 1960).

4749 **Brown, Louise Kimble.** Soprano (KGO, Oakland, CA, 1924).

4750 **Brown, Lucy.** Pianist (WATR, Waterbury, CT, 1936).

4751 **Brown, Mae.** COM-HE (WMAS, Springfield, MA, 1951).

4752 **Brown, Margot and Earl Brown.** Piano team (WMCA, New York, NY, 1936).

4753 **Brown, Mary Sullivan.** Dramatic readings (WLW, Cincinnati, OH, 1922).

4754 **Brown, Maurice.** Cellist (*Maurice Brown*, instr. mus. prg., CBS, 1935).

4755 **Brown, Max.** Newscaster (WHAS, Hastings, NE, 1945).

4756 **Brown, Maxine.** A singer billed as "The Sweetheart of the Air," Brown was said to have sung more than a thousand songs on the air by 1925 (WCX, Detroit, MI, 1925).

4757 **Brown, Mel.** DJ (*Hillbilly Matinee*, WGAU, Athens, GA, 1949).

4758 **Brown, Mende.** Director Brown directed the *Affairs of Peter Salem* and *Joyce Jordan, Girl Interne* programs.

4759 **Brown, Milton.** Leader (*Milton Brown and his Musical Brownies*, CW mus. prg., KTAT, Fort Worth, TX, 1935–1936). Brown was one of the originators of western swing. Before coming to KTAT, he had appeared on WBAP, Fort Worth, TX, with guitarist Herman Arnspiger and violinist Bob Wills. That group used such names as the *Aladdin Laddies* and the *Light Crust Doughboys.* The 1935 band included: Cecil Brown and Cliff Bruner, v; Bob Dunn, g; W. Coffman, sb; Ocie Stockard, bj; and Durward Brown, g.

The Alladin Laddies broadcast on WBAP (Fort Worth, TX, 1930), before going to work for the Light Crust Flour Company and becoming the Light Crust Doughboys on KFJZ (Fort Worth, TX).Their program was moved back to WBAP (Fort Worth, TX), where it became even more popular. Brown left the Light Crust Doughboys in 1932 to form his own band — the Musical Brownies. The band consisted of Jess Ashlock, Wanna Coffman, Durward Brown, Ocie Stockard, Fred Calhoun, Cecil Brower, Cliff Bruner and Bob Dunn. The popular band popularized "western swing" on their programs on KTAT (Fort Worth, TX, 1932–1935) and WBAP (Fort Worth, 1935–1936). Brown died in 1936 from injuries received in an automobile accident.

4760 **Brown, Naomi Sweeney.** Whistler (KHJ, Los Angeles, CA, 1923). A versatile singer and whistler, Miss Brown was called "The California Mocking Bird" (KHJ, Los Angeles, CA, 1926).

4761 **Brown, Ned.** Newscaster (*News and Farm Review*, WORZ, Orlando, FL, 1947).

4762 **Brown, Neil.** Leader (*Neil Brown Orchestra*, instr. mus. prg., WJAS, Pittsburgh, PA, 1935).

4763 **Brown, Nelson.** DJ (WNLC, New London, CT, 1948–1949).

4764 **Brown, Pat.** DJ (*Quartet Time*, KAPK, Minden, LA, 1954–1955).

4765 **Brown, Pat.** DJ (*University Hour*, KVET, Austin, TX, 1954; KWBY, Colorado Springs, CO, 1956).

4766 **Brown, Paul.** Sportscaster Brown, a famous professional football coach, was a popular Cleveland sportscaster (WGAR, Cleveland, OH, 1948).

4767 **Brown, Paul.** DJ (*Housewife Special*, WMGW, Meadville, PA, 1948–1955).

4768 **Brown, Paul.** DJ (*Morning Clock Watcher*, KVMC, Colorado City, TX, 1948; KOLO, Reno, NV, 1955–1956).

4769 **Brown, Paul E.X.** Black DJ and Program Director (WERD, Atlanta, GA, 1950). A native Mississippian, Brown had worked for years on Illinois local radio before moving to Atlanta's WERD in 1950 as DJ, announcer and program director. *See* **Black Radio.**

4770 **Brown, Pen.** DJ (*The Pen Brown Show*, WTAG, Worcester, MA, 1948). Sportscaster (*Sports Parade*, WTAG, 1948–1949).

4771 **Brown, Perry J.** DJ (WNDR, Syracuse, NY, 1949; WTAO, Boston, MA, 1955–1956).

4772 **Brown, Phil.** DJ (*Midnight Jamboree*, WGBA, Columbus, GA, 1948; *Breakfast with Brown*, WGBA, 1952; WPBC, Minneapolis, MN, 1960).

4773 **Brown, R. Fred, Jr.** DJ (*Platter Party*, WLOS, Asheville, NC, 1949–1950). Sportscaster (WLOS, 1949–1950).

4774 **Brown, R.J.** Announcer (WEW, St. Louis, MO, 1925).

4775 **Brown, (Reverend) R.R.** The Reverend Brown broadcast church and chapel services (WOAW, Omaha, NE, 1926). Brown's *World Radio Congregation* was first broadcast on April 8, 1923, by WOAW — a station that later became WOW. When Brown was asked to give a religious service the first Sunday station WOAW was on the air, his sermon became the first non-denominational religious service broadcast (Ward, 1994, p. 31). After a short time, Brown recognized that his radio services were in effect a "kind of church" and formed a "World Radio Congregation" that by 1925 had attracted a listening audience of more than 100,000. Less than ten years later, he had a weekly national audience of half a million. Brown was considered by many to be the minister of the first American radio church and was called "The Billy Sunday of the Air." In 1948, WOW stated that the program had never missed a Sunday service since its inception.

4776 **Brown, Ray.** DJ (*Swingtime & Night Patrol*, WDSG, Dyersburg, TN, 1947).

4777 **Brown, Red.** Sportscaster (WFOY, St. Augustine, FL, 1945).

4778 **Brown, Rhoda.** DJ (WMGM, New York, NY, 1954).

4779 **Brown, Richard.** DJ (*Brown's Waxworks*, WSNY, Schenectady, NY, 1948).

4780 **Brown, Richard Rolland.** Announcer (KOA, Denver, CO, 1928).

4781 **Brown, Robert.** DJ (*Curfew Club*, WJLS, Beckley, WV, 1947; *Off the Record*, WANE, Fort Wayne, IN, 1949). Sportscaster (WSBT, South Bend, IN, 1953).

4782 **Brown, Robert V. "Bob."** *See* **Brown, Robert Vahey "Bob."**

4783 **Brown, Robert Vahey "Bob."** Staff announcer Brown conducted a series of programs from a plane for the U.S. Army Signal Corps in 1927. A year later he became chief announcer at WLW (Cincinnati, OH, 1928). Chief station announcer, writer and producer (WLW, 1928–1932).

4784 Brown, Ron. DJ (KGAL, Lebanon, OR, 1955; KASH, Eugene, OR, 1956).

4785 Brown, Rose. Miss Brown was a radio actress and leading lady with the KGO Players (KGO, San Francisco, CA, 1924).

4786 Brown, Roy. DJ (WJET, Beaumont, TX, 1960).

4787 Brown, Ruby. Leader (Ruby Brown and his Orchestra, WSB, Atlanta, GA, 1928).

4788 Brown, Russell "Russ." Singer (*Russell Brown*, vcl. mus. prg., WMOX, St. Louis, MO, 1936; KNX, Los Angeles, CA, 1939; WBBM, Chicago, IL, 1942).

4789 Brown, Russell and Edith Karen. Popular vcl. mus. team (KMOX, St. Louis MO, 1936).

4790 Brown, Sam. Leader (Sam Brown's Devon Park Hotel Orchestra, WOO, Philadelphia, PA, 1926).

4791 Brown, Sam. DJ (*Music Hall*, WARL, Arlington, VA, 1948; *Music Hall*, WINX, Washington, DC, 1948–1949; *Music Hall*, WARL, 1954).

4792 Brown, Sandy. COM-HE (KOBE, Las Cruces, NM, 1957; KMAM, Tularosa, NM, 1958).

4793 Brown, Saundra. Singer (*Saundra Brown*, vcl. mus. prg., CBS, 1935).

4794 Brown, Sherm. DJ (WJAR, Providence, RI, 1960).

4795 Brown, Shirley. COM-HE (KMED, Medford, OR, 1954).

4796 Brown, Sylvia. Soprano (WHN, New York, NY, 1924).

4797 Brown, (Dr.) T. Floyd. Plastic and facial surgeon Brown spoke on his medical specialty (KFWB, Hollywood, CA, 1925).

4798 Brown, Ted. Leader (*Ted Brown Orchestra*, instr. mus. prg., WOR, Newark, NJ, 1934).

4799 Brown, Ted. DJ (KRES, St. Joseph, MO, 1954).

4800 Brown, Ted. DJ (*The Ted Brown Show*, WMGM, New York, NY, 1948–1956; *Ted Brown and the Redhead*, WMGM, 1957).

4801 Brown, (Mrs.) Thompson. Singer (WSM, Nashville, TN, 1928).

4802 Brown, Tillie. Fifteen-year-old pianist (KGO, Oakland, CA, 1925; violinist, KFRC, San Francisco, CA, 1926).

4803 Brown, Tom. DJ (WWOK, Charlotte, NC, 1956).

4804 Brown, Tom. DJ (WHK, Cleveland, OH, 1956–1957; *The Late Afternoon Show*, WIP, Philadelphia, PA, 1960).

4805 Brown, Tracy. Leader (Tracy Brown Orchestra, WOW, Omaha, NE, 1927).

4806 Brown, Virgil A. "Virge." DJ (WFAR, Farrell, PA, 1955; *Milkman's Parade*, WGRP, Greenville, PA, 1960).

4807 Brown, Vivian. COM-HE (KREX, Grand Junction, CO, 1956).

4808 Brown, W.C. Baritone (KTHS, Hot Springs National Park, AR, 1928).

4809 Brown, W.M. DJ (*Spiritual Parade*, WOIC, Columbia, SC, 1960).

4810 Brown, Walberg. Leader (*Walberg Brown String Quartet*, instr. mus. prg., NBC, 1935).

4811 Brown, Warren. DJ (*Warren Brown Show*, KPQ, Wenatchee, WA, 1948).

4812 Brown, William. Newscaster (KYA, San Francisco, CA, 1945).

4813 Brown, William H. Sportscaster (WHO, Des Moines, IA and WOC, Davenport, IA, 1937).

4814 Brown, Win. DJ (*6 to 8 Special*, WWSW, Pittsburgh, PA, 1947).

4815 Brown, Wylbert. Violinist (WBAP, Fort Worth, TX, 1928).

4816 (The) Brown Brothers Saxophone Sextet. Popular instrumental group that appeared on many stations in the middle 1920s.

4817 *Brown County Jamboree* aka *Bean Blossom Jamboree*. CW music show that was broadcast weekly from 1941 through 1957 over stations WIBC (Indianapolis, IN) and WIRE (Indianapolis, IN). Located in Bean Blossom, Indiana, the radio program evolved from a free show performed weekly during seven months of the year. Some of the performers on the program were Asher and Little Jimmy Sizemore, Laddy Moore and the Allen County Boys, the Kentucky Boys, Prairie Songbirds, the Campbell Sisters, Marion Martin, Jack Cox, Shorty Sheehan, Loren Parker, Maxine Montgomery. and Judy Perkins. Some of the nationally known CW performers who appeared on the *Jamboree* was Rex Allen, Little Jimmy Dickens, Uncle Dave Macon, Pee Wee King, Curly Fox and Texas Ruby, Minnie Pearl and Roy Acuff.

4818 *Brown County Revelers*. CW music group (CW mus. prg., WLW, Cincinnati, OH, 1938).

4819 Brown Palace String Orchestra. Howard Tillotson conducted the Denver music group (KOA, Denver, CO, 1925–1926).

4820 Brown Ritz Theater Ensemble. Theater band (WEBJ, New York, NY, 1926).

4821 Browne, Anita. Reader (*Anita Browne's Poetry Hour*, WNYC, New York, NY, 1936).

4822 Browne, Bill. Newscaster (KPDN, Pampa, TX, 1941). Sportscaster (KPDN, 1941).

4823 Browne, Bradford. Versatile and multi-talented actor, announcer, singer, producer, writer, director and producer Browne first entered radio as a member of a harmony singing team with Al Llewelyn (WOR, Newark, NJ, 1925). That same year he joined WGCP (New York, NY) as program director and announcer. He became announcer, writer and studio manager of WABC (New York, NY) in 1928. Browne joined CBS as a writer and announcer in 1929, where he created the *Nit Wit Hour* and *The Cellar Knights* programs. He later took the role of Captain Kid on the *Kid Boots Show*.

4824 Browne, Dave. DJ (KIEM, Eureka, CA, 1956).

4825 Browne, Frank. Newscaster (KTHS, Hot Springs, AR, 1945). Sportscaster (KWFC, Hot Springs, AR, 1950).

4826 Browne, Gerald. DJ (*Request Matinee*, KIFI, Idaho Falls, ID, 1947).

4827 Browne, Harry C. Announcer (WGHP, Clemens, MI, 1927; Senior announcer (CBS, 1928).

4828 Browne, Kathryn. Australian contralto (KYW, Chicago, IL, 1926).

4829 Browne, Olivia. COM-HE (WMC, Memphis, TN, 1941–1956). Although she wanted to be a dramatic actress, Browne was hired at WMC to broadcast a women's program. Only 17 years old, she went to WMC at the close of the school day to do her program. Despite knowing nothing about cooking, she was hired because they liked her "low voice" that made her sound "very mature" (Browne, 1977).

When a Memphis department store began to sponsor her show, it eventually became an interview program broadcast six times a week at 8:15 A.M. (WMC, Memphis, TN). This was Memphis radio's first interview program. On the show Browne interviewed such personalities as Benny Goodman, Bob Hope and Dorothy Parker. During World War II, she began to do newscasts for 30 minutes, five times a day on WMC.

Browne qualifies as one of the pioneers of Memphis radio. Incidentally, Browne (Browne, 1977) said that she never encountered the problems and treatment in broadcasting about which some women complained.

4830 Browne, Paul. Newscaster (WAIM, Anderson, SC, 1940).

4831 Browne, Tom. DJ (*Platter Party*, WMEV, Marion, VA, 1948; *WIST Soundtrack*, WIST, Charlotte, NC, 1960).

4832 Browne, Zona DeLong. Soprano (KFWM, Oakland, CA, 1926).

4833 Brownell, Elspeth. Pianist (WAHG, Richmond Hill, NY, 1926).

4834 Brownell, Jim. DJ (*Brownell for Breakfast*, WCEN, Mt. Pleasant, MI, 1948). Sportscaster (WCEN, 1948).

4835 Brownell, Kurt. Tenor (*Kurt Brownell*, vcl. mus. prg., NBC, 1935).

4836 Brownell, Larry. DJ (*The Larry Brownell Show*, WHHH, Warren, OH, 1948–1952; *Easy Does It*, WKBW, Buffalo, NY, 1954–1956).

4837 Brownell, Mabel. Director Brownell founded her own Mabel Brownell Players. They performed in *Polly with a Past* (WOR, Newark, NJ, 1923).

4838 Browning, Ada Redd. COM-HE (WSJS, Winston-Salem, NC, 1956).

4839 Browning, Allan. DJ (WKIX, Raleigh, NC, 1956).

4840 Browning, Bill. DJ (*Best by Bill*, KUTA, Salt Lake City, UT, 1952; *The Music Box*, KFMB, San Diego, CA, 1955–1957).

4841 Browning, Doug. DJ (*The Doug Browning Show*, ABC, New York, NY, 1954).

4842 Browning, Ed. Newscaster (WLAT, Conway, SC, 1946).

4843 Browning, J.C. Newscaster (*Local News*, WKNY, Kingston, NY, 1948).

4844 Browning, Jim. Newscaster (KGVO, Missoula, MT, 1937).

4845 Browning, Lillian. COM-HE (WESB, Bradford, PA, 1951).

4846 Browning, Robert F. "Bob." Newscaster (WRNY, Kingston, NY, 1946).

4847 Browning King Orchestra. The orchestra began its famous *Wednesday Night Dance* programs April 12, 1923 (WEAF, New York, NY, 1923). Commercial salesman, Harry C. Smith created the show at WEAF. Anna Byrne was the conductor of the orchestra.

4848 Brownless, Carolyn. COM-HE (KUSH, Cushing, OK, 1958).

4849 Brownlow, Joe. Newscaster (KPQ, Wenatchee, WA, 1946). Sportscaster (*Cascade Sports*, KPQ, 1947).

4850 Brown's Ferry Four. Popular CW gospel quartet that originally included Grandpa Jones, Merle Travis and the Delmore Brothers—Alton and Rabon. They broadcast daily on WLW (30 min., Cincinatti, OH, 1943). The original group was broken up when two members entered service. The original members were reunited in 1946. When Travis and the Delmore Brothers left the group, it was reformed with the addition of Clyde Moody, Lige Turner, Louis Innes and Red Foley. Other members of the quartet at times included Dolly Good, Zeke Turner, Wayne Ranney and Red Turner.

4851 Brownsell, Jim. DJ (*Turntable Terrace* and *Sun Dial Club*, WKDK, Newberry, SC, 1949).

4852 Brownstein, Anne. Pianist (WQJ, Chicago, IL, 1926).

4853 *(The) Brox Sisters.* The singing Brox sisters (Dagmar, Loraine and Kathryn) first appeared on local radio in 1928. It is interesting to note that in some contemporary magazines the sisters' names were given as Lorna, Patsy and Gloria without further explanation. During the 1920s they appeared in the *Ziegfield Follies,* movies and at the Palace. Their NBC network program *(The Brox Sisters)* debuted in 1931.

4854 Broyles, Clara E. COM-HE (KBLO, Hot Springs, AR, 1954).

4855 Broza, Stan Lee. Announcer and Program Director (WCAU, Philadelphia, PA, 1923–1928).

4856 Brubaker, Ray. Newscaster (WMBI, Chicago, IL, 1945–1946).

4857 Bruce, Al. DJ (*Morning Mirth*, WLBR, Lebanon, PA, 1947; *Pattern*, WLBR, 1960).

4858 Bruce, Ann. COM-HE (WGUY, Bangor, ME, 1954).

4859 Bruce, Bill. Newscaster (KGHF, Pueblo, CO, 1945).

4860 Bruce, Dick. DJ (*1280 Reveille* and *1280 Matinee*, WDSU, New Orleans, LA, 1949).

4861 Bruce, Don. Newscaster (WIRE, Indianapolis, IN, 1948).

4862 Bruce, Edwin. Busy actor Bruce appeared on *Coast-to-Coast on a Bus*, *Death Valley Days*, *Hilltop House*, *Joyce Jordan, Girl Interne*, *The Open Door* and *Portia Faces Life.*

4863 Bruce, Evelyn. COM-HE (WLET, Toccoa, GA, 1956–1957).

4864 Bruce, Frances "Fran." COM-HE (KVCV, Redding, CA, 1951–1958).

4865 Bruce, Glenn. Bruce told bedtime stories and read to young listeners (WTAY, Oak Park, IL, 1925).

4866 Bruce, Jack. DJ (*Barn Dance*, WNAX, Yankton, SD, 1952–1960).

4867 Bruce, Jay. Bruce, the "State lion hunter of the Fish and Game Commission of California," spoke on the topic of "My Most Thrilling Experiences Hunting Mountain Lions" (KGO, Oakland, CA), 1925).

4868 Bruce, Lathrop. DJ (*Designs in Harmony*, KTIM, San Raphael, CA, 1950).

4869 Bruce, Lucretia. Mezzo-soprano (KLS, San Francisco, CA, 1923).

4870 Bruce, Margaret. Pianist (WWJ, Detroit, MI, 1923–1924).

4871 Bruce, Mildred. Mezzo-soprano (WIP, Philadelphia, PA, 1925).

4872 Bruce, Ramon. DJ (*Snap Club* and *Ravin' With Ramon*, WHAT, Philadelphia, PA, 1947–1951; *Snap Club*, WHAT, 1952).

4873 Bruckner, Skip. DJ (*1350 Platter Party*, WGAU, Athens, GA, 1947). Sportscaster (*Sports Final*, WGAU, 1947).

4874 Bruder, Peggy. Bruder was a member of the *Juvenile Jury* program's panel that provided the opinion of juveniles on questions sent in by listeners (MBS, NBC, 1946–1953).

4875 Bruemmer, Mary. COM-HE (WCVS, Springfield, IL, 1951).

4876 Bruer, Julie. Operatic soprano (WIBO, Chicago, IL, 1927).

4877 Bruffett, (Reverend) Bert. The Reverend Bruffett delivered sermons and prayers for the sick on Sister Aimee Semple McPherson's station (KFSG, Los Angeles, CA, 1925).

4878 Bruggeman, Vern. Newscaster (KALL, Salt Lake City, UT, 1945; *Intermountain Empire News*, KALL, 1947). DJ (*Melody Mac & Vern*, KALL, 1947; KULA , Honolulu, HI, 1948).

4879 Bruhl, Martin. Pianist (WOC, Davenport, IA, 1928).

4880 Bruley, Fred. Bruley performed musical saw solos (KFWB, Hollywood, CA, 1925).

4881 Brumet, Reba. COM-HE (WFHG, Bristol, VA, 1960).

4882 Brumlett, Louise. COM-HE (WANY, Albany, KY, 1958–1960).

4883 Brumsey, Jerry. COM-HE (WMBG, Richmond, VA,1954).

4884 Brunby, Mary. Leader (The Mandolin Club Orchestra, WSB, Atlanta, 1923).

4885 Brunch, Taylor. DJ (WIRR, Dallas, TX, 1950).

4886 Brundage, Jack. Newscaster (KLZ, CO, World War II era).

4887 Brundige, Bill. Sportscaster (WAVE, Louisville, KY, 1938; KSFO, San Francisco, CA, 1945; WOL, Washington, DC, 1946; *Sports Parade*, WOL, 1947; WOIC, Washington, DC, 1948; WINX, Washington, DC, 1949; WPEN, Philadelphia, PA, 1950; KHJ, Los Angeles, CA, 1960).

4888 Bruner, Bob. DJ (*Variety Hour*, WISH, Indianapolis, IN, 1947; WKKO, Cocoa, FL, 1956).

4889 Bruner, Cliff. CW fiddler-song writer and band leader. Early in his career in 1934, Bruner became a member of the Milton Brown and His Musical Brownies, billed at that time as the "Greatest String Band on Earth." After the death of Milton Brown in 1936, Bruner formed his own band, the Texas Wanderers. Broadcasting on KDFM (Beaumont, TX, 1936), the band featured CW and Cajun swing music. It included Bob Dunn, Moon Mullican, Leo Raley and vocalist Dickie McBride.

4890 Bruner, Flora Howell. Soprano (KFRC, San Francisco, CA, 1926).

4891 Bruner, Paul A. Newscaster (KBIX, Muskogee, OK, 1945–1946).

4892 Bruner, Robert. Newscaster (WSOY, Decatur, IL, 1946).

4893 Bruner String Trio. Instrumental group consisting of violinist Orley See, cellist Wenceslao Villalpando and pianist Emil Breitenfeld (KTAB, Oakland, CA, 1925).

4894 Brunes, Larry. DJ (*You Asked For It* and *Western Request*, KTIL, Tillamook, OR, 1949). Sportscaster (KTIL, 1949).

4895 Brunesco, Jean [Jan]. Leader (*Jean Brunesco Orchestra*, instr. mus. prg., WOR, Newark, NJ, 1934; CBS, 1935).

4896 Brunet, Carlos. DJ (KIWW, San Antonio, TX, 1956).

4897 Brunet, Paul. Tenor (WHN, New York, NY, 1928).

4898 Bruno, H.A. Announcer (WEBJ, New York, NY, 1925–1927).

4899 *Bruno Richard Haupmann.* The sustaining dramatic series based on the life of the convicted kidnapper of the Lindbergh baby was presented in *March ofTime* style and based on material developed by the New York *Mirror*, a William Randolph Hearst tabloid paper. On the program, Hauptmann's "voice" was heard and then the drama enfolded. None of the actors who appeared in the topical dramatic serial were identified (15 min., Monday-Wednesday-Friday, 9:15–9:30 P.M., WNEW, New York, NY, 1935).

4900 Bruns, Darleen. DJ (*Date with Darleen*, KIST, Santa Barbara, CA, 1952).

4901 Bruns, Gene. DJ (*Diggin*, KWED, Seguin, TX, 1948–1952).

4902 *(The) Brunswick Hour.* Tenor Mario Chamlee was one of the featured performers on *The Brunswick Hour*, an early variety program (WJZ, New York, NY, 1924).

4903 *Brunswick Night.* A two-hour music program, *Brunswick Night* featured such San Francisco–Oakland performers as organist Iris Vining of the Grenada Theater; Harold Johnson, melophone soloist; Harold Pracht, baritone; George Madison, bassist; Maurice Michael, pianist; Alice Guthrie Poyner, violinist; Allan Wilson, tenor; Albert Aldersley, clarinetist; and Lydia Sturtevant, contralto. The program was broadcast weekly. Paul Ash's Grenada Theater Orchestra also appeared regularly (KGO, Oakland, CA, 1925).

4904 Brunswick Orchestra. Radio band (WBZ, Springfield, MA, 1925).

4905 Bruntlett, George E. Newscaster (KOBH, Rapid City, SD, 1940, 1945). Sportscaster (KOBH, 1942).

4906 Brunton, Alberta. COM-HE (KXIC, Iowa City, IA, 1957).

4907 ***(The) Brush Creek Follies*** aka ***KMBC Brush Creek Follies.*** CW music-variety show first broadcast in 1937 from the Ivanhoe Temple, Kansas City, MO, before a live audience, the program lasted more than 20 years, still going strong into the 1950s. Performers varied over the years. The 1946 version, sponsored by Four-Way Cold Tablets, had Danny Slofoot as MC and Jack Butler as announcer. The CW music performers included: popular singer Eddie Arnold and his gang including fiddler Speedy McNatt, steel guitarist Little Roy Wiggins, bassist Lloyd George (Ken Marvin), rhythm guitarist Rollin Sullivan, the Texas Rangers, Rhythm Riders, Mildred and Sue, Jed Starkey, Ted Ross, Colorado Pete, Dan Sullivan and George Washington White and the Square Dancers (15 min., Saturday, 9:15–9:30 P.M., KMBC-CBS, Kansas City, MO, 1946). Louise Massey and Rex Allen later appeared on the *Brush Creek Follies* in 1951.

The early version featured Hiram Higsby as MC, singer, guitarist, comedian, straight man, harmonic player, and staff writer. Another performer on the *Follies* was Dole Hensley "Tex" Owens. Singer Owens, the brother of Texas Ruby Owens, was one of the program's earliest stars. A composer, Owens wrote the popular "Cattle Call." Other performers were the Texas Rangers, Curt Massey, Allen Massey, Captain Bob Crawford, Hugh Studebaker, Gomer Cool, Herb Kratoska, the Oklahoma Wranglers, Kit and Kay the singing cowgirls, Crouse Sisters Quartet, Colorado Pete (Pete Martin), Millie and Sue (Bybee Sisters), ventriloquist Kenny Carlson and his partner Scrappy O'Brien. comic Frank Wiziarde, Jed Starkey and comic team Bud and Spud (Ralph Hunt and Earl Bledsoe.

4908 **Bruton, Bill.** DJ (*Rhythm on the Range*, KBMY, Billings, MT, 1948).

4909 **Bruton, Bob.** DJ (KXOL, Fort Worth, TX, 1956).

4910 **Bruun, Paul.** Newscaster (WKAT, Miami Beach, FL, 1946).

4911 **Bruvald, Leonard.** Latvian baritone (WFI, Philadelphia, PA, 1926).

4912 **Bryan, Arthur Q.** Announcer (WOR, Newark, NJ, 1925).

4913 **Bryan, Bill.** Newscaster (WIBW, Topeka, KS, 1942; KOMA, Oklahoma City, OK, 1944; KMOX, Oklahoma City, OK, 1945; KTOW, Oklahoma City, OK, 1950–1952; KTOK, Oklahoma City, OK, 1960).

4914 **Bryan, Charles.** Newscaster (KVI, Tacoma, WA, 1941, 1945). Sportscaster (KVI, 1946).

4915 **Bryan, Claflin.** Pianist (KVOO, Tulsa, OK, 1928).

4916 **Bryan, George.** Announcer Bryan worked on such network programs as *Aldrich Family, Armstrong Theater of Today, Arthur Godfrey's Talent Scouts, Helen Hayes Theatre* and *The Road of Life.* Newscaster (CBS, 1947–1948).

4917 **Bryan, Gil.** DJ (*Bandstand*, WTNS, Coshocton, OH, 1952).

4918 **Bryan, Glen.** DJ (*Ocean Watch*, KURY, Brookings, OR, 1960).

4919 **Bryan, Ralph.** Newscaster (KVCV, Redding, CA, 1944).

4920 **Bryan, Tony.** DJ (*Klock Request*, KNPT, Newport, OR, 1952).

4921 **Bryan, Warren.** Actor Bryan appeared on the *Orphans of the Storm* and *Stella Dallas* daytime serial programs.

4922 **Bryan, William "Bill."** Newscaster (WHAS, Louisville, KY, 1937–1941).

4923 **Bryan, William Jennings ("The Great Commoner").** Bryan broadcast a sermon from Pittsburgh's Point Breeze Presbyterian Church (KDKA, Pittsburgh, PA, 1922). He also delivered two speeches on WFAA (Dallas, TX) in 1924. One of these "Why I Believe the Bible" was delivered at the Dallas First Presbyterian Church. He also played a prominent role in the Scopes "Monkey" Trial shortly before his death. *See* **Ryan, Quin.**

4924 **Bryan, Wright.** Newscaster (WSB, Atlanta, GA, 1941).

4925 **Bryant, Al.** DJ (*Polk County Express*, WSIR, Winter Haven, FL, 1948).

4926 **Bryant, Clay.** Sportscaster Bryant, a former baseball pitching star, tried his hand at sports reporting (15 min., WMIN, St. Paul, MN, 1952).

4927 **Bryant, Floyd.** DJ (*Early Bird*, KFXD, Nampa, ID, 1948–1950).

4928 **Bryant, George.** DJ (*The George Bryant Show*, WSAI, Cincinnati, OH, 1948; *The Starduster*, WCON, Atlanta, GA, 1949; *George Bryant Record Show*, WSAI, 1952).

4929 **Bryant, Georgia.** Announcer (WSY, Birmingham, AL, 1923).

4930 **Bryant, Ken.** DJ (*1400 Club*, KMHK, Mitchell, SD, 1947; *Austin Radio Clock*, KAUS, Austin, MN, 1948–1952).

4931 **Bryant, Kenneth L. "Kenny."** DJ (WKEY, Covington, VA, 1947–1950).

4932 **Bryant, Pressley.** Newscaster (WBAP, Fort Worth, TX, 1938–1939; WBAP, 1940–1941).

4933 **Bryant, Robie.** COM-HE (KTAC, Tacoma, WA, 1960).

4934 **Bryant, Rosemary.** COM-HE (WJPF, Herrin, IL, 1955).

4935 **Bryant, Rudolph.** Bryant was billed as Rudolph Bryant and his Banjo (WLS, Chicago, IL, 1925).

4936 **Bryant, Sen Bristoe.** DJ (*Hub Cap Caravan*, WJLB, Detroit, MI, 1954–1956).

4937 **Bryant, Slim.** CW guitarist-band leader Bryant in his early career worked on local radio in Pittsburgh, Louisville, Richmond, Cincinnati and Chicago. He formed his own band in 1939 consisting of Kenny Norton, Jerry Wallace and his brother, Loppy Bryant. After appearances on *The National Barn Dance*, Bryant had his own radio show, *The Slim Bryant Show* (NBC, 1950).

4938 **Bryant, Ted.** DJ (*The Ted Bryant Show*, WDXB, Chattanooga, TN, 1949).

4939 **Bryant, Vivian.** Pianist (KFWI, San Francisco, CA, 1926).

4940 **Bryant, Willie.** Leader (*Willie Bryant Orchestra*, instr. mus. prg., NBC, 1935).

4941 **Bryant, Willie.** DJ (WHOM, New York, NY, 1948–1949; *After Hours Swing Session*, WHOM, 1950–1954).

4942 **Bryar, Robert.** Sportscaster (*Sportraits*, WHIP, Hammond, IN, 1940–1941).

4943 **Bryden, Charles.** Tenor (WGBS, New York, NY, 1925).

4944 **Bryden, Keith.** DJ (KUBC, Montrose, CO, 1954).

4945 **Bryon, Bob.** Vocalist (*Bob Bryon*, vcl. mus. prg., CBS, 1942).

4946 **Bryson, John.** Sportscaster (KFPY, Spokane, WA, 1941, 1946). Newscaster (NBC-Blue, 1944; *Sports Review*, WENR, Chicago, IL, 1951).

4947 ***Bryson-Conney Orchestra.*** Instr. mus. prg. (WOR, Newark, NJ, 1935).

4948 **Brzinsky, Frank.** Pianist (WCCO, Minneappolis–St. Paul, MN, 1928).

4949 **Bubb, Miriam.** Pianist (KGO, Oakland, CA, 1925).

4950 **Bubbett, Mary.** COM-HE (WENC, Whiteville, NC, 1956).

4951 **Bubeck, Harry.** Director Bubeck directed *The Guiding Light* daytime serial program.

4952 **Bublert, F.A.** Announcer Bublert was known as "Spark Plug" (KFJC, Junction City, KS, 1924).

4953 **Bublig, Richard.** Concert pianist (NBC, 1928).

4954 **Bubp, Bob.** DJ (WPTW, Piqua, OH, 1949–1950). Sportscaster (WPTW, 1952).

4955 ***(The) Buccaneers.*** Vcl. mus. prg. sponsored by the Imperial Tobacco Company (KVOR, Colorado Springs, CO, 1939).

4956 **Bucchin, Yolanda.** COM-HE (WGPA, Bethlehem, PA, 1956).

4957 **Buchan, Alex.** Sportscaster (WEW, St. Louis, MO, 1937; KXOK, St. Louis, MO, 1939; KMOX, St. Louis, MO, 1946; *Bulletin Clock*, KXLW, St. Louis, MO, 1947).

4958 **Buchanan, Bruce.** Sportscaster (*Sports Review*, KVI, Tacoma, WA, 1947; *Candid Pictures of the World of Sports*, WMFD, Wilmington, NC, 1948–1949). DJ (*Dixie Jamboree*, WMFD, 1949–1951.

4959 **Buchanan, Dean.** DJ (*610 Club*, KVNU, Logan, UT, 1949; *Platter Party*, KCSU, Provo, UT, 1950). Sportscaster (KCSU, Provo, UT, 1948).

4960 **Buchanan, Paul.** DJ (*School & College Matinee*, WSUA, Bloomington, IN, 1947).

4961 **Buchanan, Frances.** COM-HE (WJMS, Michigan City, IN, 1951).

4962 **Buchanan, Stuart.** Newscaster (KNX, Hollywood, CA, 1931). Director Buchanan directed *The Falcon* and *Jungle Jim* programs. In addition, he was the voice of Goofy on the *Mickey Mouse Theater of the Air* program. Incidentally, Walt Disney was the voice of Mickey Mouse on the show.

4963 **Buchil, Agnes.** Soprano (WIBO, Chicago, IL, 1926).

4964 **Buchwald, Charlotte.** Theater critic (*On Theatre*, WIP, Philadelphia, PA, 1937; *The Playgoer*, WMCA, New York, NY, 1939).

4965 **Buck, Anita E.** COM-HE (WAVN, Stillwater, MN, 1956).

4966 **Buck, Ashley.** Writer Buck wrote the *Tennessee Jed* and the *We Are Always Young* programs.

4967 **Buck, George, Jr.** DJ (WJNO, West Palm Beach, FL, 1954).

4968 Buck, Harvey. Newscaster-announcer (WSBA, York, PA, 1946).

4969 Buck, Jack. Sportscaster (*Sports Digest*, WCOL, Columbus, OH, 1949–1950; KTVI, St. Louis, MO, 1955).

4970 Buck, Keith. DJ (WTCO, Campbellsville, KY, 1954).

4971 Buck, Louis "Louie." Sportscaster (WAGA, Atlanta, GA, 1938; WSM, Nashville, TN, 1941–1942). Newscaster (WSM, TN, 1945). "Cousin Louie" Buck for many years was the chief announcer on the *Grand Ole Opry* program.

4972 Buck, Owen E. Newscaster (WGIL, Galesburg, IL, 1946).

4973 Buck, Steve. Newscaster (*News of the World*, KWSC, Pullman, WA, 1947).

4974 Buck, Verne. Violinist-leader (Verne Buck Orchestra, KYW, Chicago, IL, 1926).

4975 Buck and Wing. The blackface comedy team of Phil Cook and Vic Fleming were network favorites (15 min., Monday, 7:00–7:15 P.M., NBC-Red Network, New York, NY, 1929).

4976 *Buck Rogers in the 25th Century.* Buck Rogers was a fighter pilot in World War I, who was trapped in a cave-in and over come by its gas. Centuries later he awoke from a state of suspended animation to find himself *Buck Rogers in the 25th Century*. Assisted by his female friend, Wilma Deering and the brains of Dr. Huer, the super scientist, Buck overcame the villainies concocted by Killer Kane and friends. Based on the comic strip written by Phil Nowlan and drawn by Phil Calkins, the dramatic daytime serial for children appeared from 1932 to 1947 in various formats with many different sponsors. The earliest version featured Matt Crowley and Curtis Arnall playing the title role (15 min., Monday through Friday, 5:00–5:15 P.M., CBS, 1935). *Variety* reported the show's reincarnation in 1946 with John Larkin, Virginia Vass and Edgar Stehli playing the leading roles of Buck, Wilma Deering and Dr. Huer. Tom Dougall was the writer. General Foods' Post Toasties was the sponsor (15 min, Monday through Friday, 4:45–5:00 P.M., MBS, 1946).

The many performers who appeared on the program in its various formats over the years were: Curtis Arnall, Matt Crowley, Carl Frank, Alice Frost, Joe Granby, Walter Greaza, Henry Gurvey, John Larkin, Ronald Liss, Junius Matthews, Elaine Melchoir, John Monks, Dan Ocko, Frank Readick, Adele Ronson, Jack Roseleigh, Bill Shelley, Everett Sloane, Edgar Stehli, Paul Stewart, Walter Tetley, Fred Uttal, Walter Vaughn, Arthur Vinton, Vicki Vola, Dwight Weist and Eustace Wyatt. The announcers were Paul Douglas, Jack Johnstone and Fred Uttal. The later writers were Dick Calkins, Joe A. Cross and Albert G. Miller. Jack Johnstone was the versatile producer, director and writer.

4977 *(The) Buckaroos.* The CW singing team of Ted Maxwell and Charles Marshall (KGO, San Francisco, CA, 1932).

4978 Buckland, Jack. Leader (*Jack Buckland's Serenaders*, CW mus. prg., WFBL, Syracuse, NY, 1938).

4979 Buckle, Bob. Sportscaster (*Sports Fare*, WRDW, Augusta, GA, 1953).

4980 *(The) Bucklebusters.* Gene Autry was the featured singer on the CW music program (WJJD, Chicago, IL, 1932).

4981 Buckley, Alice. Soprano (WJZ, New York, NY, 1924).

4982 Buckley, Bill. Newscaster (KGGM, Albuquerque, NM, 1941).

4983 Buckley, Dick. Sportscaster (*Sportsworld*, WANE, Fort Wayne, IN, 1948). DJ (*11th Hour*, WANE, IN, 1950).

4984 Buckley, Floyd. Actor Buckley began his radio career in 1929 on various NBC sustaining programs. In the next decade his most important role was that of "Popeye" on the *Popeye the Sailor* program. *See* ***Popeye***.

4985 Buckley, Neil. DJ (*Requestfully Yours*, WPFB, Middletown, OH, 1948–1952; *Tailgate Ramblings*, WPFB, 1954).

4986 Buckley, Taylor. Baritone (WJZ, New York, NY, 1928).

4987 Buckley, Teresa. Singer (WLBZ, Bangor, ME, 1941).

4988 Buckley, Thad. DJ (KBAK, Bakersfield, CA, 1954; KGEE, Bakersfield, CA, 1956).

4989 Buckman, Florence. Pianist (WIP, Philadelphia, PA, 1924).

4990 Bucknam, Lillian. Soprano (*Lillian Bucknam*, vcl. mus. prg., NBC, 1934).

4991 Buckner, Fred. Leader (Fred Buckner's Band was featured on the *Van Heusen Program*, a popular half hour music program, 30 min., Weekly, Network, 1929).

4992 Buckwalter, John. Director Buckwalter directed the *David Harum*, *Front Page Farrell* and *Pepper Young's Family* programs.

4993 *Bud Birmingham's Music.* CW mus. prg. (WFIL, Philadelphia, PA, 1936).

4994 Budd, Joe. DJ (*Sunday Show*, WGFS, Covington, GA, 1960).

4995 Budd, Milton H. Singer (*Milton Budd*, vcl. mus. prg., WMBD, Peoria, IL, 1935). DJ (WMBD, 1947; *Musical Clock*, WMBD, 1949; WMBD, 1957).

4996 Buddies in Harmony. Vocal team of Larry and Verne Cannon (KFQZ, Hollywood, CA, 1927).

4997 *Buddy Cantor.* In his discussion of theatrical news, Cantor provided a multitude of details both old and new. *Billboard* even criticized him for giving too much casting news on the program sponsored by Bartel Liquors. Cantor perhaps could be forgiven for wanting to give the impression that every one of his items were exclusive with him. Certainly this behavior was not limited to Cantor (15 min., Saturday, 6:00–6:45 P.M., WMCA, New York, NY).

4998 *(The) Buddy Rogers Show.* Rogers, the former motion picture star and band leader, became a DJ on the sustaining program. He also conducted celebrity interviews (30 min., Monday through Friday, 5:00–5:30 P.M., WOR, Newark, NJ, 1950).

4999 Buddy's Blue Melody Boys Orchestra. Popular Texas band (WFAA, Dallas, TX, 1925).

5000 Budget, Betty. COM-HE (*Betty Budget, Food Reporter*, KWK, St. Louis, MO, 1939).

5001 *(The) Budget Stretcher.* Dale Cooper conducted the program designed to save shoppers time and money (WAAF, Chicago, IL, 1935).

5002 *Bud 'n' Wiser.* The comedy singing team, formerly known as the Red Wagon Boys, moved to Georgia and changed their name (WMAZ, Macon, GA, 1934).

5003 Buechler, Jack. DJ (*Madison Top Tunes* and *Billboard Hit Parade*, WKOW, Madison, WI, 1948; *Juke Box Review*, WEKT, Milwaukee, WI, 1950).

5004 Bueckman, Gene. DJ (WMMB, Melbourne, FL, 1956).

5005 Buehler, Carl. DJ (*The Carl Buehler Show*, WCAP, Asbury Park, NJ, 1949).

5006 Buehler, George. Baritone (*Gene Bueler*, vcl. mus. prg., NBC, 1934).

5007 Buehlman, Clint. DJ (WGR, Buffalo, 1940s; *Clint Buehlman*, WBEN, Buffalo, NY, 1947–1952; WBEN, 1957).

5008 Buenning, Paul. Newscaster (KTOK, Oklahoma City, OK, 1941).

5009 Buest, Ruth. Violinist (WHAS, Louisville, KY, 1926).

5010 Buettner, Al. DJ (*Music 'Til Past Midnight*, 120 min., Monday through Saturday, 10:30–12:30 P.M., WTMJ, Milwaukee, WI, 1949–1950).

5011 Buff and Van. Musical team of Forrest Buffington and Jack Van Cleve, who together played a dozen instruments (WJBL, Decatur, IL, 1928).

5012 *Buffalo Trailers.* CW mus. prg. (WMBD, Peoria, IL, 1937).

5013 *(The) Buffalo Variety Show* (aka *The Buffalo Variety Workshop*). Following a trend for affiliates to provide local programs for full network transmission, the entertaining variety show featured the Harold Austin Orchestra, blues singer Olive Adams and baritone Jack Quinlan (30 min., Saturday, 3:30–4:00 P.M., CBS, 1934–1935).

5014 Buffalodians Dance Orchestra. Popular radio band (WEAF, New York, NY, 1926).

5015 Buffay, Jerry. DJ (*Second Cup of Coffee Time*, WCVA, Culpepper, VA, 1952; *Music in the Night*, WCVA, 1955).

5016 Buffington, H.E. DJ (WTWA, Thomson, GA, 1954).

5017 Buffum, Ray. Writer Buffum wrote *The Casebook of Gregory Hood*, *Hawthorne House* and *Rogue's Gallery* programs.

5018 *Bug House Rhythm.* A group of unidentified musicians played hot and swinging music on the show (15 min., Monday through Friday, 7:15–7:30 P.M., NBC-Blue, 1936).

5019 Bugdanowitz, Bob. Newscaster (KFEL, Denver, CO, 1945).

5020 Bugg, Eugene. Bass (WSM, Nashville, TN), 1928).

5021 Buhl, Lucile. Miss Buhl presented weekly beauty talks (WJZ, New York, NY, 1928).

5022 Buhl, Ruth. Reader (KYW, Chicago, IL, 1924; WEBH, Chicago, IL, 1924).

5023 Buick, Johnny. Leader (Johnny Buick's Cabirians orchestra and Johnny Buick's Amphians, KPO, San Francisco, CA, 1925).

5024 Buick Little Symphony. Commercially sponsored good music organization (KFAB, Lincoln, NE, 1928).

5025 *(The) Buick Program.* Humorist Robert Benchley, tenor Howard March, a mixed vocal chorus and an orchestra conducted by Andre Kostelanetz provided the entertainment on the program sponsored by Buick Motor Cars (15 min., Monday and Wednesday, 9:15–9:30 P.M., CBS, 1934).

5026 *(The) Buick Revelers.* The Revelers, cited by *Radio Digest* as one of radio's foremost quartets, were featured on the weekly program. They were joined by soprano Countess Olga Albani and Frank Black conducting the orchestra (15 min., Sunday, 9:45–10:00 P.M., NBC-Blue, 1932). *See* **(The) Revelers.**

5027 *(The) Buick Show.* The Buick-Olds-Pontiac Sales Company sponsored the entertaining variety show featuring the piano duo of Ohman and Arden, baritone Conrad Thibault, soprano Arlene Jackson, comedian Arthur Boran and the Gus Haenschen Orchestra (30 min., Monday, 10:30–11:00 P.M., NBC-Red, 1933).

5028 (The) Buick Studio Orchestra. George Belshaw conducted the studio band (KFAB, Lincoln, NE, 1928).

5029 Buisseret, Armand. Leader (*Armand Buisseret Orchestra*, instr. mus. prg., WIND, Gary, IN, 1936).

5030 Buker, Norman K. DJ (*Melody Matinee*, WLAM, Lewiston, ME, 1948).

5031 Bull, Bulkeley Thad. DJ (KREO, Bakersfield, CA, 1947).

5032 Bull, Clarence. Newscaster (WBTA, Batavia, NY, 1941).

5033 Bull, Dorothy. Soprano (WCDB, Zion, IL, 1923).

5034 Bull, Frank. Sportscaster (KHJ, Los Angeles, CA, 1937; KECA-KFI, Los Angeles, CA, 1939; KMPC, Los Angeles, CA, 1946 and KHJ, 1946). DJ (*America Dances*, KFWB, Hollywood, CA, 1947–1948).

5035 Bull, Peggy. COM-HE (WCMJ, Palm Springs, CA, 1955–1957).

5036 Bull, Robert. Newscaster (WSBT, South Bend, IN, 1944).

5037 Bullard, Iris. COM-HE (WTAW, College Station, TX, 1956).

5038 Bullen, Reed. Newscaster (KVNU, Logan, UT, 1941, 1945).

5039 Bullington, William "Bill." DJ (*Music Madness*, KSGM, Ste. Genevieve, MO, 1947; *Melody Time*, KREI, Farmington, MO, 1948; *1450 Club*, KSGM, 1950).

5040 Bullock, Sheldon "Shel." DJ (WWSC, Glens Falls, NY, 1954–1960).

5041 Buloff, Joseph. Actor Buloff appeared on the *House of Glass* program.

5042 Bulotti, Charles. Tenor (KFRC, San Francisco, CA, 1928–1929).

5043 Bulow, Harry. DJ (*Musical Clock*, WJPR, Greenville, MS, 1947). Sportscaster (WJPR, 1947).

5044 Bumbaugh, Howard. DJ (KMAC, San Antonio, TX, 1956).

5045 Bumgardner, Neida. COM-HE (KGAS, Carthage, TX, 1957).

5046 Bump, Bill. DJ (WOTW, Nashua, NH, 1954).

5047 Bumpers, Marita. COM-HE (KEVA, Shamrock, TX, 1958).

5048 Bunce, Alan. Talented actor Bunce appeared on the *Ethel and Albert*, *Hello, Peggy*, *Home of the Brave*, *John's Other Wife*, *Pepper Young's Family*, *Young Dr. Malone* (title role) and *Young Widder Brown*.

5049 Bunch, Coyita. Singer (*Coyita Bunch*, vcl. mus. prg., KSD, St. Louis, MO, 1936).

5050 Bunch, Pete. Sportscaster (WRNL, Richmond, VA, 1939).

5051 Bunchuk, Yascha. Cellist (NBC, 1929). Orchestra leader (*Major Bowes Family*, NBC-Red Network, New York, NY, 1929).

5052 Bundy, Jack. Announcer (WGHP, Detroit, MI, 1925).

5053 Bundy, Rudy. Leader (*Rudy Bundy Orchestra*, instr. mus. prg., WHAS, Louisville, KY, 1934; MBS, 1936; KFEL, Denver, CO, 1942).

5054 Bunkhardt, Emma. Contralto (WEAF, New York, NY, 1924).

5055 *Bunkhouse Bill.* CW vcl. mus. program by an otherwise unidentified performer (KFEQ, St. Joseph, MO, 1939).

5056 *Bunkhouse Jamboree.* Jerry Campbell was the DJ on this recorded music show that specialized in CW music (120 min., Monday through Friday, 3:00–5:00 P.M., WLS, Chicago, IL, 1942).

5057 *Bunkhouse Serenade.* CW music program featuring Carson Robison and his music makers (15 min., Tuesday, 5:15–5:30 P.M., CBS, 1935).

5058 Bunn, Bill. DJ (*Bunn's Bunny Hop*, WGTM, Wilson, NC, 1954–1955).

5059 Bunn, Jim. DJ (*Meet Mr. Music*, KCMO, Kansas City, MO, 1947).

5060 Bunn, Neal. Newscaster (WTJS, Jackson, TN, 1945). Sportscaster (KNEA, Jonesboro, AR, 1952; WDXL, Lexington, TN, 1956).

5061 Bunnell, Barbara. Blues singer (KFWB, Hollywood, CA, 1925).

5062 Bunnell, Merrill J. Sportscaster (KLO, Ogden, UT, 1939).

5063 Bunnell, Roberta Scott. COM-HE (WKLO, Louisville, KY, 1956).

5064 Bunston, Cliff: Actor Bunston appeared on the *Myrt and Marge* daytime serial program.

5065 Bunting, J. Whitney. Newscaster (WELI, New Haven, CT, 1938).

5066 Bunyan, Paul, Jr. DJ (*Paul Bunyan, Jr.*, 55 min., Monday through Friday, 6:05–7:00 P.M., KXA, Seattle, WA, 1948).

5067 Burati, Vivian. COM-HE (WIST, Charlotte, NC, 1955).

5068 Burbank, Howard. DJ (*Evening Symphony*, KARM, Fresno, CA, 1960).

5069 Burbank, Marie Keber. Contralto (WHAM, Rochester, NY, 1928).

5070 Burbank, (Mrs.) Luther. The wife of the famous horticulturist, Luther Burbank, appeared on her *Gardening the Luther Burbank Way* transcribed program (Transcribed, 1933).

5071 Burbank, Sara. COM-HE (WNBF, Binghampton, NY, 1951–1955).

5072 Burbank, Vannie. COM-HE (KODY, North Platte, NE, 1951).

5073 Burbank Choral Club. Community chorus (KFI, Los Angeles, CA, 1923).

5074 *Burbig's Rhythm Boys.* Henry Burbig was a veteran dialect comedian of radio's early years. On this show sponsored by the Gillette Sports Razor Company, Burbig appeared with the Rhythm Boys, a group that only recently had left Paul Whiteman's employment (15 min., Monday, 6:45–7:00 P.M., NBC-Red, 1934). *See* ***The CeCo Couriers*, Singers: Crooners, Canaries, Cow Girls and Hillbillies.**

5075 Burbridge, Maybelle A. Miss Burbridge broadcast beauty talks (WGBS, New York, NY, 1925).

5076 Burch, Bob. DJ (KGHF, Pueblo, CO, 1948; *Discatorially Yours*, KCSJ, Pueblo, CO, 1952).

5077 Burch, Edward. Newscaster (WRNL, Richmond, VA, 1937). Sportscaster (WPID, Petersburg, VA, 1941).

5078 Burch, Harrison. Pianist (WWJ, Detroit, MI, 1923).

5079 Burch, Leo. DJ (KORC, Mineral Wells, TX, 1954).

5080 Burchell, Gene. Leader (*Gene Burchell Orchestra*, instr. mus. prg., WLW, Cincinnati, OH, 1934–1935).

5081 Burchett, Edwina. Singer (WQJ, Chicago, IL, 1925).

5082 Burchett, Lillian. COM-HE (WBMS, Boston, MA, 1955).

5083 Burchfield, Marlene. COM-HE (WTIV, Titusville, Pa, 1960).

5084 Burdett, James H. Broadcast talks on gardening (WMAQ, Chicago, IL, 1925).

5085 Burdett, Winston. Newscaster (CBS, 1944; WTOP, Washington, DC and CBS, 1946–1948). A frequent criticism made of Burdett was that he sometimes blurred the lines between reporter and analyst without warning his listeners.

5086 Burdette, Robert. Director of the WLW Dramatic Staff (WLW, Cincinnati, OH, 1928–1929).

5087 Burdick, Cornelia. Actress Burdick was in the cast of the *Dr. Kate* (title role) daytime serial program.

5088 Burdick, Ella May. Soprano (WBZ, Springfield, MA, 1926).

5089 Burdick, Hal. Writer Burdick wrote the *Dr. Kate* daytime serial program.

5090 Burdick, Kenneth. Baritone (WJY, New York, NY, 1925).

5091 Burditt, Flora Hardie. Singer (WMAZ, Chicago, IL, 1927).

5092 Burdow, Miriam. Soprano (WHPP, Bronx, New York, 1927).

5093 Burdy, Bob. Newscaster (WSKB, McComb, MS, 1940).

5094 Burford, Ken. DJ (*Come On, Coffee's On*, KWIL, Albany, OR, 1954).

5095 Burford, William H. "Bill." DJ (*Morning on the Mahoning*, WHHH, Warren, OH, 1948–1954; *The Nut Club*, WHHH, 1949).

5096 Burgan, Barbara. COM-HE (WCYN, Cynthiana, KY, 1960).

5097 Burge, Dale. DJ (KWBG, Boone, IA, 1954).

5098 Burge, Harry. Newscaster (WTAM, Cleveland, OH, 1940). DJ (*Juke Box Serenade*, WQAM, Miami, FL, 1952; WGBS, Miami, FL, 1956).

5099 Burge, Ralph. DJ (*Rhythm Express*, *Ralph's Record Shop* and *Let's Get Up*, WMPS, Memphis, TN, 1947; *Breakfast with Burge*, WJBO, Baton Rouge, LA, 1950–1954; WIBR, Baton Rouge, LA, 1956).

5100 Burgeen, Patricia. COM-HE (WBAR, Bartow, FL, 1957).

5101 Burgeni, Edward. Newscaster (WNBZ, Saranac Lake, NY, 1938).

5102 Burger, Frank. Newscaster (WAOV, Vincennes, IN, 1940).

5103 Burgess, Frank. DJ (*Request Performance*, WHMA, Anniston, AL, 1947–1952). Newscaster (*First Edition*, WGAA, Cedartown, GA, 1948).

5104 Burgess, Harry C. DJ (WISE, Asheville, NC, 1947).

5105 Burgess, Ralph. DJ (*Breakfast with Burgess*, WGBA, Columbus, GA, 1948; *Midnight Serenade*, WGBA, 1949; *Party Line*, WGBA, 1952).

5106 Burgess, S.A. Contralto (KLDS, Independence, MO, 1925).

5107 Burgess, Smoky. Sportscaster (*Sports Report*, WGBA, Columbus, GA, 1953).

5108 Burgess, Thornton. Burgess, a famous author of children's books, broadcast a regular weekly children's story program July 14, 1922 (WJZ, New York, NY). A naturalist-author, Burgess founded the Radio Nature League of WBZ-WBZA on January 7, 1925. He said he formed the League to "preserve and conserve all desirable wild life, including birds, animals, trees, flowers and other living things together with the natural beauty spots and scenic wonders of all America." After the second week of his announcement of the League's formation, he had 2,000 members and 50,000 by 1928.

5109 Burgess, Tom. DJ (*Saturday Matinee*, WMSC, Columbia, SC, 1948–1952).

5110 Burgevin, Margaret McKay. Soprano (WBZ, Boston-Springfield, MA, 1925).

5111 Burgin, (Mrs.) James. Violinist (KMOX, St. Louis, MO, 1926).

5112 Burgin, Robin. DJ (KDAC, Fort Bragg, CA, 1952).

5113 Burgmann, Mitzi. Vocalist (*Mitzi Burgmann*, vcl. mus. prg., WPG, Atlantic City, NJ, 1936).

5114 Burheman [Burhemm], Edna. Broadcasting during the *Sandman Hour*, Burheman told stories of "Peter Rabbit" and the "Three Bears." Her work was a forerunner of Ireene Wicker's *The Singing Lady* program that began in the next decade (WBAL, Baltimore, MD, 1929).

5115 Burick, Si. Sportscaster (WHIO, Dayton, OH, 1937–1942; 1945–1956).

5116 Burka, Bud. DJ (*The Daybreaker Matinee*, WTIP, Charleston, WV, 1948).

5117 Burkarth, Johnny. Leader (*Johnny Burkarth Orchestra*, instr. mus. prg., KMOX , St. Louis, MO, 1935).

5118 Burke, Agnes. COM-HE (WALY, Herkimer, NY, 1960).

5119 Burke, Andy. Sportscaster (WARD, Brooklyn, NY, 1938).

5120 Burke, Billy. Ukulele soloist (WLW, Cincinnati, OH, 1928).

5121 Burke, Charles. Newscaster (KFBC, Cheyenne, WY, 1946).

5122 Burke, Dorothy. Singer (KJBS, San Francisco, CA, 1925).

5123 Burke, Edmund. Metropolitan Opera bass-baritone Burke appeared on the *Atwater Kent Hour* (NBC, 1926).

5124 Burke, Elizabeth. Newscaster (WCLS, Joliet, IL, 1939).

5125 Burke, Gene. Actor Burke appeared on the *Mary Marlin* daytime serial program.

5126 Burke, Georgia. Actress Burke was a cast member of the *When a Girl Marries* daytime serial program.

5127 Burke, Gordon. Newscaster (KGMB, Honolulu, HI, 1948). Sportscaster (KULA, Honolulu, HI, 1951–1952).

5128 Burke, Hilda Hopkins. Soprano (WBAL, Baltimore, MD, 1926–1929).

5129 Burke, J. Frank. Newscaster (KFVD, Los Angeles, CA, 1941–1942, 1944–1945).

5130 Burke, Jack. DJ (*1490 Club*, WICY, Malone, NY, 1947–1949; *Spinner's Sanctum*, WICY, 1950).

5131 Burke, Jessie. COM-HE (WVMC, Mount Carmel, IL, 1956–1957).

5132 Burke, John. Tenor (WGBS, New York, NY, 1926).

5133 Burke, Kathleen Hopkins. Soprano (WBAL, Baltimore, MD, 1926).

5134 Burke, Kathleen J. Pianist (WHN, New York, NY, 1924).

5135 Burke, Kathy. COM-HE (WDLC, Port Jervis, NY, 1957).

5136 Burke, Larry. Tenor (*Larry Burke*, vcl. mus. prg., NBC-Blue, 1936).

5137 Burke, Lucille. Soprano (WGHP, Detroit, MI, 1926).

5138 Burke, Lucy. COM-HE (*Pennywise*, WBTA, Batavia, NY, 1951).

5139 Burke, Ray. DJ (*Late Date*, WAIR, Winston-Salem, NC, 1947–1949).

5140 Burke, Rio. Singer (*Rio Burke*, vcl. mus. prg., WLW, Cincinnati, OH, 1936).

5141 Burke, Sheldon. DJ (*Invitation*, WNAM, Neenan-Menasha, WI, 1954).

5142 Burke [Burkes], Spider. DJ (*The Spider Burke Show*, KXLW, St. Louis, MO, 1949–1955; KSTL, St. Louis, MO, 1957–1960).

5143 Burke, Verna. Contralto (*Verna Burke*, vcl. mus. prg., NBC, 1935).

5144 Burke, Walter. Tenor (WOR, Newark, NJ, 1925).

5145 Burke, Walter. Actor Burke appeared on the *Ellen Randolph* daytime serial program.

5146 Burke and Ferrar's Kirkland Serenaders [Orchestra]. Local radio band (KFOA, Seattle, WA, 1926).

5147 Burkes, Steve. DJ (WMOX, Meridian, MS, 1957–1960).

5148 Burkhardt, Emma. Contralto (WEAF, New York, NY, 1924).

5149 Burkhart, E. W. Announcer (WLAL, Tulsa, OK, 1927).

5150 Burkharth, Johnny. Leader (*Johnny Burkharth Orchestra*, instr. mus. prg., WLW, Cincinnati, OH, 1935; WHAS, Louisville, KY, 1937).

5151 Burkhead, Willie. DJ (*Morning Melodies*, KTTR, Rolla, MO, 1950).

5152 Burklund, Ted. Newscaster (WEDC, Chicago, IL, 1940–1941, 1945; WKMO, Kokomo, IN, 1948).

5153 Burkow, Louis Y. Violinist (WNYC, New York, NY and WMCA, New York, NY, 1925).

5154 Burk's Orchestra. The popular radio band presented a "program of the latest ditties" (WMC, Memphis, TN, 1924).

5155 *Burl Ives' Show.* Folksinger Burl Icle Ivanhoe Ives after several successful Broadway appearances, first appeared on NBC on his own program *The Wayfaring Stranger* aka *Burl Ives' Show* (1940–1941). At the same time CBS featured Ives in *Back Where I Come From* (1940–1941) and a Saturday morning half-hour program, *The Burl Ives Coffee Club Show* (1940–1942). He frequently appeared with Bing Crosby on the latter's *Philco Radio Time.* Starred for Philco on NBC on the *Burl Ives, Philco's Friendly Troubadour* program (NBC, 1946–1947).

5156 Burleigh, Ernest. Cellist (WGY, Schenectady, NY, 1923).

5157 Burleigh, Wilbur C. Pianist (WEEI, Boston, MA, 1928).

5158 Burlen, Robert. Announcer and continuity writer (WEEI, Boston, MA, 1928).

5159 Burleson, Lois. COM-HE (KION, Pecos, TX, 1955).

5160 Burley, Don. DJ (*Teen Age Jamboree*, WBBZ, Ponca City, OK, 1948; KCKN, Kansas City, MO, 1960).

5161 Burling, Lamar. Pianist (KFAB, Lincoln, NE, 1928).

5162 Burlingame, Lloyd. Newscaster (*The Farming Business*, WRFD, Worthington, OH, 1948).

5163 Burlingame, Robert "Bob." Newscaster (WHO, Des Moines, IA, 1940–1942; KIOA, Des Moines, IA, 1948).

5164 Burman, Ned. Newscaster (KGDM, Stockton, CA, 1938).

5165 Burne, Al. DJ (*Turntable Terrace*, WHEE, Boston, MA, 1949).

5166 Burnell, Ruth. Pianist (WSWS, Chicago, IL, 1926).

5167 Burnes, Bob. Sportscaster (KMOX, St. Louis, MO, 1955).

5168 Burnett, Earl. Leader (Earl Burnett's Biltmore Hotel Orchestra, KHJ, Los Angeles, 1924–29). Burnett's band was a popular California group broadcasting from the Los Angeles' Biltmore Hotel.

5169 Burnett, Jim. DJ (WHBC, Canton, OH, 1956–1957).

5170 Burnett, Julietta. Soprano (KFOX, Long Beach, CA, 1929).

5171 Burnett, Nickey. Newscaster (WHK, Cleveland, OH and WCLE, Cleveland, OH, 1939–1940).

5172 Burnette, Bill. Newscaster (WFIG, Sumter, SC, 1945). Sportscaster (WFIG, 1945).

5173 Burnette, (Mrs.) Glade. Soprano (KFAE, Pullman, WA, 1924).

5174 Burnette, Jack. Singer Burnette was described as "the dark and handsome tenor with the high-pitched voice" (WBBM, Chicago, IL, middle–1930s).

5175 Burnette, Jack. DJ (WALT, Tampa, FL, 1947). This might be singer Jack Burnette described in the previous entry.

5176 Burnette, Lester Alvin "Smiley." CW singer, guitarist, accordionist, song writer and comedian Burnette was born March 8, 1911. Although best known as "Frog Millhouse" in the 55 western movies he did with Gene Autry for Republic and Columbia, Burnette also worked with western stars Ken Maynard, Charles Starrett and Roy Rogers. He began his radio career on WDZ (Tuscola, IL, 1932–1933), where he sang and played accordion and piano. (Supposedly, Burnette played some 100 instruments.) His big break came when he was hired by Gene Autry to appear on *The National Barn Dance* on Christmas Eve, 1933 (McCloud, 1995, p. 116.). In addition to his busy motion picture career, Burnette had two syndicated radio shows.

5177 Burnham, Charles E. Concert singer (WWNC, Asheville, NC, 1928).

5178 Burnham, Genevieve Barry. Soprano (WOK, Chicago, IL and WHT, Chicago, IL, 1925).

5179 Burnham, John. Concert pianist (WEAF, New York, NY, 1924).

5180 Burns, Al. DJ (*1360 Club*, WLYN, Lynn, MA, 1949; WMEX, Boston, MA, 1955).

5181 Burns, Allen. DJ (*Household Quizzer*, WMPS, Memphis, TN, 1952).

5182 Burns, Baron. DJ (WCLS, Columbus, OH, 1956).

5183 Burns, Bill. DJ (*Club 560*, WQAM, Miami, FL, 1948; *Jukebox Serenade*, WQAM, 1954).

5184 Burns, Darrel. DJ (*Seven to Two*, KXLE, Ellensburg, WA, 1948–1949; *Five Five Club*, KXLE, 1950).

5185 Burns, Dick. Newscaster (WTTM, Trenton, NJ, 1944).

5186 Burns, Dolly. COM-HE (KDDD, Dumas, TX, 1956).

5187 Burns, Ed. DJ (*On the Bandstand*, WGNY, Newburgh, NY, 1947).

5188 Burns, Fred. Sportscaster (WSAZ, Huntington, WV, 1939).

5189 Burns, Gene. DJ (*Music Till Midnight*, KICK, Springfield, MO, 1954).

5190 Burns, Hal. DJ (WILD, Birmingham, AL, 1954).

5191 Burns, Jack. DJ (*All Night*, KTUC, Tucson, AZ, 1955–1956).

5192 Burns, Jane. Soprano (KGW, Portland, OR, 1928).

5193 Burns, Jerry. Sportscaster (KDYL, Salt Lake City, UT, 1945–1946).

5194 Burns, Louella. Soprano (WMCA, New York, NY, 1925).

5195 Burns, Lucille. DJ (*Listen to Lucille*, KAKC, Tulsa, OK, 1949).

5196 Burns, May Clark. Soprano (KPO, San Francisco, CA, 1924).

5197 Burns, Monty. COM-HE (KNEL, Brady, TX, 1958).

5198 Burns, Ray. DJ (*Record Review*, KVRC, Arkadelphia, AR, 1954–1957).

5199 Burns, Roberta. COM-HE (KBOE, Oskaloosa, IA, 1951).

5200 Burns, Roger. Sportscaster (*Sports Spotlight* and *Sports Nitecap*, WBEL, Beloit, WI, 1948). DJ (*Melody Time*, WBEL, Beloit, WI, 1950).

5201 Burns, Stan. DJ (WINS, New York, NY, 1947–1956; *The Spinner*, WINS, 1956; *The Stan Burns Show*, 1957–1959; *The Stan Z. Burns Show*, WINS, 1960). Burns also hosted a local New York quiz program, *Kashbox Quiz*, on station WINS.

5202 Burns, Tommy. DJ (KMA, Shenandoah, IA, 1956–1957).

5203 Burns, W.M., Jr. Newscaster (KQV, Pittsburgh, PA, 1948).

5204 Burns, Walt. DJ (KYOR, Blythe, CA, 1956; KOCS, Ontario, CA, 1957).

5205 Burns, Walter. Newscaster (WBOW, Terre Haute, IN, 1940).

5206 Burns, William. Singer on the *Kenrad Cabin Nights* program (NBC-Blue, New York, NY, 1929).

5207 *Burns and Allen.* The veteran vaudeville comedy team of George Burns and Gracie Allen made their first national network appearance on the *Robert Burns Panatella Program* in 1932. Two years later they had their own network radio show on CBS. One of the famous routines of this endearing pair was George's familiar closing of "Say good night, Gracie" and her immediate response, "Good night, Gracie." Music was supplied by the bands of Ray Noble and Meredith Willson. The program's announcers were Bill Goodwin and Harry Von Zell. When the program left radio in 1950, Burns and Allen began a successful run on television (CBS, NBC, 1932–1950).

Nathan Birnbaum (George Burns), a lack luster dancer and former seal trainer, and Grace Ethel Cecile Rosalie Allen (Gracie Allen), half of a sister dancing act, became a vaudeville team in 1922. George once said of their act, "We had a hunger for something more important than fame — food!" Although George started as the comedian with Gracie playing the "straight man," he soon realized that she was the one who got the laughs and reversed the roles. They became a highly successful team, soon winning the coveted next to last closing spot on the vaudeville bill and they stayed there.

George's voice often conveyed the frustration he felt as Gracie played the "dumb female" role Clearly, the audience loved Gracie's sweet innocence, no matter how bewildered or unknowing her behavior might be. They never would allow George to verbally attack or abuse Gracie, for they *loved* her. This audience reaction persisted throughout their entire show business career.

Two of the team's vaudeville routines demonstrate their style of humor:

> GEORGE: You're so smart. Name three kinds of nuts.
> GRACIE: Walnuts, chestnuts and forget-me-nuts.
>
> —
>
> GEORGE: What did you take up at school?
> GRACIE: Everything that wasn't nailed down.

Gracie was radio's most beloved comedienne, whose sweet innocence superseded the "dumb female" she portrayed. Only Jack Benny surpassed her excellent sense of timing. George, on the other hand, became radio's best straight man. Like their friend Jack Benny, Burns and Allen were one of the few vaudeville acts to make the successful transition, first, to radio and, later, to television. Bob Hope, on the other hand, although enjoying a long run on television did so only with "specials," not on a series with permanent characters and plot line.

Two of Burns and Allen's most famous running gags were Gracie's search for her "lost" brother in 1933 and her campaign as candidate of the Surprise Party for President in 1940. Their typical gags are exemplified by three examples:

> GEORGE: Gracie, why should I give your mother a bushel of nuts?" What did she ever do for me?
> GRACIE: Why George, she gave you me, and I'm as good as nuts.
>
> —
>
> GEORGE: Did the nurse ever happen to drop you on your head when you were a baby?
> GRACIE: Oh, no, we couldn't afford a nurse, my mother had to do it.
> GEORGE: You had a smart mother.
> GRACIE: Smartness runs in my family. When I went to school I was so smart my teacher was in my class for five years.
>
> —
>
> GRACIE: Where do you keep your money?
> GEORGE: In a bank.
> GRACIE: What interest do you get?
> GEORGE: Four percent.
> GRACIE: Ha! I get eight.
> GEORGE: You get eight?
> GRACIE: Yep — I keep it in two banks.

George worked almost until the time he died on March 9,1996 at age 100. He outlived Gracie by 32 years, but he continued to mention her when he performed stand-up. George played the role of God in his last two films. In retrospect, no radio team has been more appreciated than Burns and Allen. Their long successful career warrants their recognition as the best comedy team in American Radio's Golden Age. *See **Comediennes**.*

5208 *Burns Panatella Country Club.* Panatella Cigars sponsored the music program with the Guy Lombardo Orchestra playing from an imaginary country club setting (30 min., Monday, 10:00–10:30 P.M., CBS, 1930).

5209 **Burnside, Curtis.** DJ (KYJC, Medford, OR, 1950).

5210 **Burnside, Jane.** COM-HE (WBLK, Clarksburg, WV, 1956).

5211 **Burnstein, Martin A.** Newscaster (WOLF, Syracuse, NY, 1940).

5212 ***(The) Burnt Cork Review.*** *The Burnt Cork Review* was a 60-minute combination minstrel and variety show that featured instrumentalists, singers, and comics (WLW, Cincinnati, OH, 1926).

5213 **Burr, Anne.** Actress Burr was a cast member of the daytime serials *Backstage Wife* aka *Mary Noble, Backstage Wife* and *Wendy Warren and the News.*

5214 **Burr, Bob.** DJ (WDOG, Marine City, MI, 1956)

5215 **Burr, Ellen T.** COM-HE (WIBX, Utica, NY, 1956).

5216 **Burr, Fred.** Newscaster (KEYS, Corpus Christi, TX, 1945).

5217 **Burr, George.** Burr talked about "Sound Investments" on the *Educational Hour* program (KGW, Portland, OR, 1925).

5218 **Burr, Gwen W.** COM-HE (KSUE, Susanville, CA, 1958).

5219 **Burr, H.C.** On his program, Burr talked about the problems of radio listeners getting "Better Reception" (WMCA, New York, NY, 1925).

5220 **Burr, Henry.** Famous tenor Burr sang on the *Little Brown Church of the Air* program (WLS, Chicago, IL, 1935–1937). Burr's first radio appearance was in 1921 on a Denver, Colorado, station. He had started in the 1920s as second tenor in the Peerless Quartet before he became famous as a soloist. Burr later sang on WEAF (New York, NY, 1925). While singing on the *National Barn Dance* in 1937, it was reported that Burr had sold 3,000,000 records. He also appeared on the *Henry Burr's Book of Ballads* program, a vocal music show (WLS, 1935). *See* ***The National Barn Dance.***

5221 **Burr, Osceola Hall.** Pianist (KSAC, Manhattan, KS, 1925).

5222 **Burr, Ruth.** Pianist (KSAC, Manhattan, KS, 1925).

5223 **Burr, (Dr.) Wayne B.** Dr. Burr delivered child care talks (KNX, Los Angeles, CA, 1925).

5224 ***Burr McIntosh.*** McIntosh conducted a program of inspirational and cheerful talk. For this reason, he was known as "The Cheerful Philospher" (KFWB, Hollywood, CA, 1930).

5225 **Burrell, Ferne.** Singer (*Ferne Burrell*, vcl. mus. prg., WHP, Harrisburg, PA, 1942).

5226 **Burress, H. Freda.** COM-HE (WWIT, Canton, OH, 1960).

5227 **Burril, Scott.** Newscaster (WCAT, Rapid City, SD, 1945).

5228 **Burris, Dick.** Newscaster (KSO, Des Moines, IA, 1945; *Ten O'Clock News*, KSO, 1947).

5229 **Burris, Jackie.** Radio evangelist (WDBJ, Roanoke, VA, 1936).

5230 **Burris, Vina.** COM-HE (KNAL, Victoria, TX, 1955).

5231 **Burroughs, Edmond.** Newscaster (*Yale News*, WICC, Bridgeport, CT, 1938).

5232 **Burroughs, James.** Comic opera tenor (KFI, Los Angeles, CA, 1927–1929).

5233 **Burroughs, Larry.** DJ (WDAN, Danville, IL, 1954–1955; KPHO, Phoenix, AZ, 1957).

5234 **Burroughs, Tom.** DJ (*Catalina Clubtime*, KCNA, Tucson, AZ, 1954).

5235 **Burt, Bill.** DJ (*For Shut-Ins*, WCOL, Columbus, OH, 1950).

5236 **Burt, Bob.** DJ (*1320 Club*, WFHR, Wisconsin Rapids, WI, 1960).

5237 **Burt, Elizabeth.** Lecturer (*Famous Figures in History*, WAAM, Newark, NJ, 1924).

5238 **Burt, Ellen T.** COM-HE (WIBX, Utica, NY, 1956).

5239 **Burt, Garland.** DJ (*SSL Hillbillies*, WJOI, Florence, AL, 1947; *1430 Club*, WLAK, Lakeland, FL, 1948).

5240 **Burt, Jim.** Sportscaster (KELO, Sioux Falls, SD, 1955).

5241 **Burt, Lyle.** Newscaster (*World Revue*, KRSC, Seattle, WA, 1947).

5242 **Burt, Marion.** Newscaster (WGAU, Athens, GA, 1938).

5243 **Burt, Richard.** DJ (*The Timekeeper*, WSAY, Rochester, NY, 1947).

5244 ***Burt Repine's Dominos.*** CW mus. prg. (WRVA, Richmond, VA, 1939).

5245 **Burtnett, Earl.** Leader (Earl Burtnett Orchestra, KHJ, Los Angeles, CA, 1928–1929; *Earl Burtnett Orchestra*, instr. mus. prg., WLW, Cincinnati, OH, 1935).

5246 **Burton, Benny.** Leader (*Benny Burton Orchestra*, instr. mus. prg., WJAS, Pittsburgh, PA, 1935–1939).

5247 **Burton, Billy.** Leader (Billy Burton's Melodists, WFBH, New York, NY, 1925).

5248 **Burton, Cecile.** Miss Burton broadcast readings of "popular poems and essays" (WDAF, Kansas City, MO, 1924–1925).

5249 **Burton, Daisy.** COM-HE (KGVL, Greenville, TX, 1958).

5250 **Burton, Linn.** DJ (*The Linn Burton Show*, WAAF, Chicago, IL, 1947; *Platter Party*, WENR, Chicago, IL, 1950).

5251 **Burton, Lucille.** Pianist (KFWI, San Francisco, CA, 1926).

5252 **Burton, Marion.** Baritone (KFI, Los Angeles, CA, 1925).

5253 **Burton, Mutt.** Newscaster (WFRC, Reidsville, NC, 1947).

5254 **Burton, Paul.** Leader (*Paul Burton Orchestra*, instr. mus. prg., WTAM, Cleveland, OH, 1934–1936).

5255 **Burton, Phyllis.** Violinist (WOR, Newark, NJ, 1925).

5256 **Burton, Robert "Bob."** DJ (*Juke Box Review*, WEEK, Peoria, IL, 1947; *Breakfast with Burton*, WEEK, 1948–1952; *Rhythm by Request*, WEEK, 1950; *620 Jamboree*, KNGS, Hanford, CA, 1954).

5257 **Burton, Ruth.** Newscaster (WHO, Des Moines, IA, 1945).

5258 **Burton, Sara.** Actress Burton was a cast member of the daytime serial programs *Against the Storm, Romance of Helen Trent* and *We Love and Learn.*

5259 **Burton's Melody Orchestra.** New York band (WHN, New York, NY, 1925).

5260 **Burtson, Eddy.** Leader (*Eddy Burtson Orchestra*, instr. mus. prg., WHAS, Louisville, KY, 1936).

5261 **Burwell, Ed.** Newscaster (WHIT, New Berne, NC, 1942; *Final Edition*, WCKB, Dunn, NC, 1947). Sportscaster (WHIT, 1942).

5262 **Burwell, H. W.** Announcer (WBT, Charlotte, NC, 1927).

5263 **Burwell, Ted.** DJ (WCKB, Dunn, NC, 1948).

5264 **Burzell, Ken.** Leader (Ken Burzell Orchestra with vocalist Margie Ring, KFQZ, Hollywood, CA, 1926).

5265 **Busch, Leopold.** Violinist (WJY, New York, NY, 1924).

5266 **Busch, Roy.** Vocalist (*Roy Busch*, vcl. mus. prg., KMOX, St. Louis, MO, 1936).

5267 **Buschle, Hubert.** Leader (Hubert Buschle's Orchestra, WLW, Cincinnati, OH, 1925).

5268 **Busek, Anita.** COM-HE (KNBX, Kirkland, WA, 1958).

5269 **Busconi, Philip.** Baritone (WBZ, Boston-Springfield, MA, 1923).

5270 **Busfield, Roger M.** Newscaster (KNOW, Austin, TX, 1938–1940; KTBC, Austin, TX, 1942, 1945).

5271 **Bush, A.E.** Announcer (WKAF, Milwaukee, WI, 1927).

5272 **Bush, Charles.** DJ (*The Charm*, WAXX, Chippewa Falls, WI, 1960).

5273 **Bush, Derrick.** Sportscaster (WGEM , Quincy, IL, 1960).

5274 **Bush, (Mrs.) Guy.** Music appreciation talks (KFI, Los Angeles, CA, 1926).

5275 **Bush, Helen.** COM-HE (KCVR, Lodi, CA, 1956).

5276 **Bush, Janet.** COM-HE (KGVL, Greenville, TX, 1951).

5277 **Bush, Nancy.** Bush was one of the intelligent "kids" who appeared on the *Quiz Kids* program (NBC, ABC, CBS, 1940–1953).

5278 **Bush, Owen.** Sportscaster (WDAF, Kansas City, MO, 1956).

5279 **Bush, Ricci.** COM-HE (KVER, Albuquerque, NM, 1951).

5280 **Bush, Ruth.** Singer (WDRC, Hartford, CT, 1939).

5281 **Bush-Hecht, Janet.** Pianist (WEAF, New York, NY, 1925). Contralto (WOR, Newark, NJ, 1932).

5282 **Bushman, Francis X.** Silent motion picture star Bushman talked about motion pictures and the theater on his program (*Francis X. Bushman*, 15 min., Tuesday, 12:00–12:30 P.M., WGN, Chicago, IL, 1935). His career as a radio actor included work on such programs as *Betty and Bob, Johnny Modero, Pier 23, Rin-Tin-Tin, Mary Marlin* and *Those We Love.*

5283 **Bushnell, Georgiana.** COM-HE (WPIN, St. Petersburg, FL, 1957).

5284 **Buslee, Henry.** DJ (*Top O' the Morning*, WISC, Madison, WI, 1948).

5285 **Buss, Carl Alfred.** Writer Buss

wrote the *Aunt Jenny* and *Woman of Courage* programs.

5286 **Bussard, Adaline.** COM-HE (KTEL, Walla Walla, WA, 1958).

5287 **Busse, Al.** DJ (WSUA, Bloomington, IN, 1950).

5288 **Busse, Henry.** Leader (*Henry Busse Orchestra*, instr. mus. prg., CBS, 1934; NBC, 1936–1937, 1939; KGHF, Pueblo, CO, 1942). Born in Germany in 1894, Busse played trumpet in the Paul Whiteman band before forming his own popular orchestra in the late 1920s.

5289 **Busse, Henry, Jr.** DJ (*Music Shop*, KYSM, Mankato, MN, 1954). Busse, the son of Henry Busse, played his music as a DJ.

5290 **Busse, Rob.** DJ (*Robin's Nest*, WTTH, Port Huron, MI, 1952).

5291 **Bussey, Gorden.** DJ (WAVY, Norfolk, VA, 1960).

5292 ***Buster Brown and His Dog Tighe.*** Beverly Brown was the announcer on the comedy program sponsored by Buster Brown Shoes. Unidentified actors performed on this entertaining show that was based on a cartoon strip (30 min., Thursday, 5:15–5:45 P.M., CBS, 1937). An earlier version of the program was broadcast by CBS in 1929.

5293 **Buston, Benjamin.** Pianist (WBZ, Boston-Springfield, MA, 1924).

5294 ***(The) Busy Mr. Bingle.*** John Brown played the title role in the comedy drama. Bingle, the zany head of the J.B. Bingle Pin Company and his staff mortgaged everything they owned in order to finance a gold mine located in the building next door to their factory. Foolishness of this nature was typical on the short-lived program (30 min., Thursday, 8:30–9:00 P.M., MBS, 1942).

5295 **Butcher, Blayne R.** Announcer-program director Butcher was born December 20, 1902. He began his radio career as an announcer and program director on WTAR (Norfolk, VA, 1927).

5296 **Butcher, Dwight.** CW singer Butcher was also leader of a popular music group (Dwight Butcher and his Cedar Ridge Boys, CW mus. prg., 15 min., Weekdays, 6:30–6:45 A.M., WBAP, Fort Worth, TX, 1940s).

5297 **Butcher School of Music Hawaiian Players.** Instrumental music school performers (WBAP, Dallas, TX, 1923).

5298 **Buteau, Herb.** Leader (*Herb Buteau Orchestra*, instr. mus. prg., WENR, Chicago, IL, 1937).

5299 **Butera, Sal.** DJ (*Hi Fi Club*, WJER, Dover, OH, 1960).

5300 **Butherus, Ed.** Sportscaster (KUJ, Walla Walla, WA, 1937). DJ (*Hodge Podge*, KGW, Portland, OR, 1949).

5301 **Butler, (Prof.) Alfred.** Organist (KJS, Los Angeles, CA, 1925) Butler also broadcast recitals from the Church of the Open Door (KTBI, Los Angeles, CA, 1925).

5302 **Butler, Alfred G.** Butler talked about "The Art of Billiards" (WOR, Newark, NJ, 1922).

5303 **Butler, Carole.** COM-HE (WTPA, Harrisburg, PA, 1956).

5304 **Butler, Cliff.** DJ (WLOU, Louisville, KY, 1956–1957).

5305 **Butler, Don.** DJ (WGBS, Miami, FL, 1947).

5306 **Butler, Donald.** DJ (KANO, Anoka, MN, 1960).

5307 **Butler, Emma.** Contralto (WGES, Oak Park, IL, 1925).

5308 **Butler, Eugenia.** COM-HE (WGAU, Athens, GA, 1956).

5309 **Butler, Frank.** DJ (*Record Room*, WRFC, Athens, GA, 1954).

5310 **Butler, Grant.** Sportscaster (WHFC, Cicero, IL, 1939–1941).

5311 **Butler, Gwyneth.** COM-HE (KBUN, Bemidji, MN, 1951).

5312 **Butler, Homer.** Newscaster (WEBQ, Harrisburg, IL, 1939–1942; 1948).

5313 **Butler, Howard.** NBC announcer who worked on such programs as the *Black and Gold Orchestra*, the *Park Central Hotel Orchestra*, *The Family Goes Abroad*, *Godfrey Ludlow and Mrs. Lolita Cabrera Gainsborg* and the *Jewish Hour* (NBC, 1929).

5314 **Butler, Ina Mitchell.** Soprano (KFWB, Hollywood, CA, 1925–1927).

5315 **Butler, Jack.** Sportscaster (*Sports Afield and Afloat*, KENO, Las Vegas, NV, 1950).

5316 **Butler, James W.** Newscaster (WGBR, Goldsboro, NC, 1942; *Town News and Views*, WGBR, 1944–1947).

5317 **Butler, Jane.** COM-HE (WGBS, Miami, FL, 1956).

5318 **Butler, Jesse.** Xylophonist (WLAK, Bellows Falls, VT, 1922).

5319 **Butler, Jim.** DJ (*Records Til Dawn*, KMOX, St. Louis, MO, 1952–1955).

5320 **Butler, Joe.** Newscaster (WGCM, Gulfport, MS, 1940).

5321 **Butler, John.** Newscaster (WSAP, Norfolk, VA, 1945).

5322 **Butler, John.** DJ (WCTC, New Brunswick, NJ, 1956).

5323 **Butler, Joseph.** DJ (WKZO, Kalamazoo, MI, 1950).

5324 **Butler, Katherine.** COM-HE (KUZN, West Monroe, LA, 1960).

5325 **Butler, Luke.** DJ (KHUZ, Borger, TX, 1960).

5326 **Butler, Ralph.** Director Butler directed the *Perry Mason* and *Rosemary* programs.

5327 **Butler Hotel Dance Orchestra.** Hotel band led by Vic Meyer (KJR, Seattle, WA, 1928).

5328 **Butterfield, Bruce.** DJ (KASI, Ames, IA, 1960).

5329 **Butterfield, Catherine.** COM-HE (WLOX, Biloxi, MS, 1957).

5330 **Butterfield, G.** Announcer (WEAM, North Plainfield, NJ, 1924).

5331 **Butterfield, Herbert "Herb."** Actor Butterfield appeared on *Dan Harding's Wife*, *Girl Alone*, *Halls of Ivy*, *Jack Armstrong*, *Kitty Keane*, *Lonely Women*, *Ma Perkins*, *One Man's Family*, *Today's Children* and *Woman in White* daytime serial programs.

5332 **Butterfield, Ray.** Sportscaster (WLOX, Biloxi, MS, 1955).

5333 **Butterfield, Roland.** Actor Butterfield appeared on the *Jack Armstrong* and *Road of Life* programs.

5334 **Butterly, Walter.** Baritone (KELW, Burbank, CA, 1928).

5335 **Butters, Harley.** DJ (*News and Music Till Midnight*, WROK, Rockford, IL, 1948).

5336 **Butterworth, Bert.** Leader (*Bert Butterworth and his Airdales Orchestra*, instr. mus. prg., KNX, Los Angeles, CA, 1929).

5337 **Butterworth, Wallace "Wally."** Announcer Butterworth was a talented baritone who became a NBC staff announcer in 1929. He conducted the popular *Rise and Shine* morning program each weekday (WMAQ-NBC, Chicago, IL, 1929) and later worked as a sportscaster (*Wallace Butterworth—Sports*, NBC, 1931). In 1938, Butterworth conducted the *Radio Newsreel* on NBC. He also worked for some time with Parks Johnson on the popular *Vox Pop* program. *See* ***Vox Pop***.

5338 **Butterworth, Wilfred.** Comedian (KFI, Los Angeles, CA, 1928).

5339 **Buttner, (Pauline) Hope.** Pianist (KYA, San Francisco, CA, 1927).

5340 **Buttolph, Al.** DJ (*Requestfully Yours*, KTEL, Walla Walla, WA, 1960).

5341 **Button, Dave.** Newscaster (KODY, North Platte, NE, 1945). Sportscaster (KSVP, Artresia, NM, 1949). DJ (*Uncle Dave Makin' with Music*, KSVP, Artesia, NM, 1952–1955).

5342 **Button, Veri.** COM-HE (KSVP, Artesia, NM, 1956).

5343 **Butz, Bob.** Newscaster (*News Editor*, KBOL, Boulder, CO, 1948).

5344 **Butzin, Henrietta.** COM-HE (WCWC, Ripon, WI, 1957).

5345 **Buuck [Buck], Winifred.** Newscaster (WMBO, Austin, NY, 1939).

5346 **Buxbaum, Jr., Philip L.** Sportscaster (WELI, New Haven, CT, 1939–1941).

5347 **Buzzard, Dick.** DJ (*1400 Club*, WELM, Elmira, NY, 1952).

5348 **Buzzini, Bert.** Newscaster (KQW, San Jose, CA, 1945).

5349 **"BWS."** Designation for announcer S.W. Barnett (WOC, Davenport, IA, 1924).

5350 ***By Kathleen Norris.*** Phillips H. Lord produced the daytime drama series based on the fiction of Kathleen Norris. The "author," played by Ethel Everett was the narrator. The cast members in the several stories that were broadcast in the series included: Eleanor Audley, Joan Banks, Teresa Dale, Ethel Everett, Irene Hubbard, House Jameson, Ed Jerome, James Meighan, Jay Meredith, Nancy Sheridan, Helen Shields, Chester Stratton and Anne Teeman. The announcer was Dwight Weist. A typical story was one like "The Love of Julie Borel," in which "the advisability of American girls marrying titled foreigners, even though the titled foreigner professes genuine love and is in no sense a fortune hunter" was addressed (CBS and NBC, 1939–1941).

5351 ***By Popular Demand.*** Ray Bloch's orchestra accompanied singers Little Mary Small and Harry Babbitt on the pleasant music program sponsored by Conti Castille Shampoo. Clayton "Bud" Collyer was the announcer

(30 min., Thursday, 9:30–10:00 P.M., MBS, 1946).

5352 **Byam, Helen.** COM-HE (KBND, Bend, OR, 1956).

5353 **Bybee, Elayne.** COM-HE (KID, Idaho Falls, ID, 1958).

5354 **Byer, Hal.** Sportscaster (KWSC, Pullman, WA, 1938; KWIL, Albany, OR, 1941–1942, 1945–1952; *Sports Slants*, KWIL, 1953). Newscaster (KBND, Bend, OR, 1939).

5355 **Byerly, Jeannine.** COM-HE (WTNC, Thomasville, NC, 1956).

5356 **Byers, Billie.** Actress Byers appeared on the *Hawthorne House* daytime serial program.

5357 **Byers, Geneva.** Whistler (KWSC, Pullman, WA, 1926).

5358 **Byers, Hale "Pee Wee."** Leader of "Pee Wee" Byers and his Jazzists who, *Variety* said, offered a "smooth style of syncopation." The orchestra played from the Club Barney located on West Third Street, New York City (WOR, Newark, NJ, 1928). The Byers' radio and recording band included: Byers, ldr.-as.-clr.; Jack Mayhew and Nye Mayhew, clr.-as.-ts.; Wayne Euchner, p.; Perry Botkin, bj. and Emory Kenyon, d.

5359 **Byers, Hale.** Newscaster (WHLB, Virginia, MN and WEBC, Duluth, MN, 1939; WCCO, Minneapolis–St. Paul, MN, 1940–1942).

5360 **Byers, Marvin.** Newscaster (KCRA, Sacramento, CA, 1945).

5361 **Byers, Wayne C.** Sportscaster (WHLB, Virginia, MN, 1938–1939; WJW, Akron, OH, 1941; WATG, Ashland, OH, 1951; *Panorama of Sports*, WATG, 1953–1955).

5362 **Byington, Norma.** Soprano (KFI, Los Angeles, CA, 1928).

5363 **Byng, (Dr.) Edward.** Newscaster (WEVD, New York, NY, 1945–1948).

5364 **Byrd, Betty.** COM-HE (WNAG, Grenada, MS, 1960).

5365 **Byrd, Bob.** DJ (WCPK, College Park, MD, 1956–1960).

5366 **Byrd, Charles M.** Leader (Charles M. Byrd's Atlantic Stompers Orchestra, KTBR, Portland, OR, 1929).

5367 **Byrd, Clark.** DJ (WHAR, Clarksburg, WV, 1956).

5368 **Byrd, Earl.** DJ (WTRX, Bellaire, OH, 1956).

5369 **Byrd, Herbert "Herb."** Newscaster (KXLR, North Little Rock, AR, 1946). DJ (*After Hours* and *Boogie and Blues*, KXLR, North Little Rock, AR, 1947–1951).

5370 **Byrd, Jim.** DJ (KTBC, Austin, TX, 1954).

5371 **Byrd, Muriel.** Singer (WHN, New York, NY, 1937).

5372 **Byrd, Russell.** Leader (*Russell Byrd Orchestra*, instr. mus. prg., WIP, Philadelphia, PA, 1939).

5373 **Byrd, Ted.** DJ (WCIN, Cincinnati, OH, 1954).

5374 ***Byrd Expedition Broadcasts.*** Radio carried regularly scheduled broadcasts by Admiral Richard E. Byrd during his several exploratory trips to Antarctica. In 1930, Byrd spoke from the "South Pole" to Lloyd Thomas on station KDKA (Pittsburgh, PA, February 24, 1930). On a later expedition they had a regularly scheduled program sponsored by Grape Nuts Flakes cereal. The programs emanated from Byrd's camp in Little America near the South Pole (30 min., Wednesday, 10:00–10:30 P.M., CBS, 1933–1934).

5375 **Byrne, Anna C.** Leader (Anna C. Byrne and her Orchestra, WEAF, New York, NY, 1925). Byrne began broadcasting for Browning King clothing manufacturers in April, 1925, although no mention of the sponsor was allowed at that time on broadcasts other than the name of the band — the Browning King Orchestra. These 1925 programs were said to be the first series of musical programs that were not merely one-shot broadcasts. Byrne previously had directed the B. Fischer Astor Coffee Orchestra (WEAF, New York, NY, 1923) and, later, the La France Radio Band (WEAF, 1926).

5376 **Byrne, Betty.** COM-HE (WSKI, Montpelier, VT, 1951).

5377 **Byrne, Bobby.** Leader (*Bobby Byrne Orchestra*, instr. mus. prg., MBS, 1935; KMA, Shenandoah, IA, 1942).

5378 **Byrne, Bud.** Singer (*Bud Byrne*, vcl. mus. prg., WTNJ, Trenton, NJ, 1936).

5379 **Byrne, Harry.** Sportscaster (*Spotlight on Sports*, KCSJ, Pueblo, CO, 1947; *Sports Extra*, KTLN, Denver, CO, 1948).

5380 **Byrne, Maggi.** COM-HE (WNBK, Cleveland, OH, 1951–1955).

5381 **Byrne, Mike.** DJ (WALF, Fall River, MA, 1949).

5382 **Byrnes, Syd.** DJ (*The Alarm Clock Club*, WCPS, Tarboro, NC, 1947; *1290 Club*, WCCC, Hartford, CT, 1949).

5383 **Byron, Delma.** Actress Byron appeared on the *Kate Hopkins, Angel of Mercy* and *Our Gal Sunday* daytime serial programs.

5384 **Byron, Edward.** Director-writer-producer Byron worked on the *Adventures of Christopher Wells* (creator-director), *Mr. District Attorney* (writer), *Pot of Gold* (creator-producer) and *What's My Name?* programs.

5385 **Byron, Eva.** COM-HE (WALT, Tampa, FL, 1951; WTVT, Petersburg, FL, 1955).

5386 **Byron, Gene.** Actor Byron appeared in the title role on the *Molly of the Movies* daytime serial program.

5387 **Byron, James A. "Jimmie."** Sportscaster (WBAP, Fort Worth, TX, 1938; WBAP and KGKO, Fort Worth, TX, 1940; WBAP, 1941, 1945–1948).

5388 **Byron, Louis.** Newscaster (WRBL, Columbus, GA, 1937).

5389 **Byrum, Howard.** Newscaster (WLBJ, Bowling Green, KY, 1941). Sportscaster (WLBJ, 1941; *Sports Spotlight*, WGNS, Murfreesboro, TN, 1947).

5390 **"C" Company Dance Orchestra.** Military dance band (WLW, Cincinnati, OH, 1922).

5391 ***C-Sharpe Minor.*** A music program that featured a talented organist, who was identified only by the program's name, *C-Sharpe Minor (*KNX, Los Angeles, CA, 1929).

5392 **Caballero, Lupe.** COM-HE (KOYE, El Paso, TX, 1958).

5393 ***Cabin at the Crossroads.*** Hariette Widmer as Aunt Jemima was the hostess on the program of fun and music sponsored by the Quaker Oats Company. Tenor Roy Brown, the Noble Cain a Capella Choir, Vance McCune, Forrest Lewis and the Sammy Williams band were program regulars (15 min, Monday through Friday, 8:00–8:15 A.M., NBC-Blue, 1938).

5394 ***(The) Cabin Door.*** A dramatic program with instrumental and vocal music of the South, the cast included Phyllis Campbell, Clarence Hayes, Jack Curtiss and Harold Peary. The harmony singing team of Ted and Art Miller provided vocal interludes (NBC-Pacific Network, 1929).

5395 ***Cabin Nights.*** Don Bernard wrote the series of dramatic sketches about Southern life. The program originated in Chicago. Ken-Rad was the sponsor (NBC-Blue, 1929).

5396 **Cabiness, Travis.** Newscaster (KRMD, Shreveport, LA, 1938).

5397 **Cable, Gail Watson.** Violinist (WTAM, Cleveland, OH, 1924).

5398 **Cabot, Caroline.** "Shopping reporter" (15 min., Monday through Saturday, 9:00–9:15 A.M., WEEI, Boston, MA, 1928–1932).

5399 **Cabirians Orchestra.** Johnny Buick directed the California music group (KPO, San Francisco, CA, 1925–26). The band was sometimes known as the Cabiria Cafe Dance Orchestra.

5400 ***Cactus Pete and His Ranch Ravellers.*** CW music program (WXYZ, Detroit, MI, 1938).

5401 **Caddell, Graham.** Newscaster (WHSC, Hartsville, SC, 1946). DJ (*Sunrise Serenade* and *Hillbilly Jamboree*, WOLS, FLorence, SC, 1947).

5402 **Caddell, Jan.** DJ (WHSC, Hartsville, SC; *Record Party*, WHSC, 1960).

5403 **Cade, Margaret.** Soprano (WIBO, Chicago, IL, 1926).

5404 **Cade, Marvin.** Newscaster (WCHS, Charleston, WV, 1939; WFBM, Indianapolis, IN, 1941–1942).

5405 **Cade, Miriam.** COM-HE (KTSW, Emporia, KS, 1951).

5406 **Cadell, Raymond.** Newscaster (WFIG, Sumter, SC, 1942; WOLS, Florence, SC, 1945; WHSC, Hartsville, SC, 1946; *Raymond Cadell and the News*, WHSC, 1948).

5407 ***The Cadets.*** Male vocal quartet (NBC-Blue, New York, NY, 1936).

5408 **Cadill, John.** DJ (*Soft Sounds and Sweet Music*, KCRG, Cedar Rapids, IA, 1960).

5409 **Cahill, Marie.** Vaudeville star Marie Cahill appeared on the *General Motors Family Party* program (NBC, 1927).

5410 **Cadillac-LaSalle Symphony Orchestra.** Classical music organization (WFAA, Dallas, TX, 1927).

5411 **Cadman, Charles.** Distinguished clergyman Cadman delivered inspirational talks and recitations on character and morality (WGY, Schenectady, NY, 1925).

5412 **Cadman, (Dr.) S. Parkes.** Brooklyn minister and syndicated columnist Cadman broadcast a weekly religious service to thousands of listeners on NBC in the late 1920s. Cadman began broadcasting his series of religous talks from the Bradford Avenue YMCA over WEAF (New York, NY) in January 7, 1923. He is remembered for calling the Woolworth Building "the cathedral of commerce." This radio minister became nationally known for his preaching on the *Cathedral Hour* (Sunday, NBC-Red, New York, NY, 1929). He later broadcast the *Dr. S. Parkes Cadman* program, on which he delivered a sermon, the Oratorio Choristers sang and the orchestra was directed by George Dilworth. Milton J. Cross was the announcer (60 min., Sunday, 5:00–6:00 P.M., NBC-Red, 1930).

5413 **Cadwell, Clyde.** DJ (*Morning Call*, KFVD, Los Angeles, CA, 1949–1952).

5414 **Cafarelli, (Mme.) Helen.** Dramatic soprano (KYW, Chicago, IL, 1928).

5415 ***Cafe DeWitt Orchestra.*** Instr. mus. prg. (WABC, New York, NY, 1931).

5416 ***Cafe Istanbul.*** Marlene Dietrich starred as "Mlle. Madow," the owner of Cafe Istanbul, located in the center of Istanbul, Turkey, where spies and intrigue always swirled around her. Dietrich opened and closed each sustaining program by seductively singing a few bars of "La Vie en Rose." Arnold Moss and Ken Lynch also appeared on the entertaining program. Leonard Blair was the producer and Murray Bennett the director (30 min., Sunday, 9:15–9:45 P.M., ABC, 1952–1953). The following season the show moved to CBS, renamed *Time for Love* and the locale changed to San Francisco. Diedrich still starred although her name was also changed. *See* ***Time for Love.***

5417 **Cafferty, Tom.** Newscaster (KDYL, Salt Lake City, UT, 1940) DJ (*Roundup*, KOH, Reno, NV, 1949).

5418 **Caffey, Bob.** Newscaster (WMC, Memphis, TN, 1944; WMPS, Memphis, TN, 1946).

5419 **Caffey, Rudolf.** Tenor (WFAA, Dallas, TX, 1928).

5420 **Caffrey, Harry J.** Tenor (WAHG, Richmond Hill, NY, 1925).

5421 **Cagle, Gene L.** DJ (KFJZ, Fort Worth, TX, 1940).

5422 **Cahill, Allan.** Announcer (WKBQ, New York City, NY, 1925).

5423 **Cahill, Ed.** Sportscaster (*Cahill on Sports* (WLYN, Lynn, MA, 1948–1949).

5424 **Cahill, Marie.** Vaudeville star Marie Cahill appeared on the *General Motors Family Party* program (NBC, 1927).

5425 **Cahoon, Fred.** Leader (Fred Cahoon's WBAP Southern Serenaders [orchestra], WBAP, Fort Worth, TX, 1923).

5426 **Caille, Jeannette.** Pianist (*Jeannette Caille*, instr. mus. prg., WBZ, Boston-Springfield, MA, 1936).

5427 **Cain, Ben.** Newscaster (*Raising Cain*, KAFY, Bakersville, CA, 1947).

5428 **Cain, Bennet F.** Newscaster (WNOE, New Orleans, LA, 1939–1940).

5429 **Cain, Bob.** DJ (WSKY, Asheville, NC, 1956; WJW, Cleveland, OH, 1957).

5430 **Cain, Claude.** Sportscaster (*Basketball on the Air*, KID, Idaho Falls, ID, 1951).

5431 **Cain, Doyle.** Sportscaster (KFXD, Nampa, ID, 1937–1952; *Sports Roundup*, KFXD, 1953).

5432 **Cain, Harriet.** Actress Cain appeared on the *Today's Children* daytime serial.

5433 **Cain, Helen Virginia.** Contralto (WTIC, Hartford, CT, 926).

5434 **Cain, Jeanne.** COM-HE (KKTV, Colorado Springs, CO, 1955).

5435 **Cain, Judy.** COM-HE (KTBS, Shreveport, LA, 1951–1954).

5436 **Cain, Sandra.** COM-HE (WBLF, Bellefonte, PA, 1958).

5437 **Caine, Betty.** Busy actress Caine appeared on the daytime serial programs *Girl Alone, Life of Mary Southern* (title role), *Mary Marlin* aka *The Story of Mary Marlin, Mollie of the Movies, The O'Neills, The Second Mrs. Burton, A Tale of Today, There was a Woman* and *We Love and Learn.*

5438 **Caine, Conway.** Newscaster (WOPI, Bristol, TN, 1937–1938).

5439 **Cain's Castle Orchestra.** Club orchestra (WGY, Schenectady, NY, 1923).

5440 **Cair, Doyle.** Sportscaster (KFXD, Nampa, ID, 1939).

5441 **Cairney, Jim.** Newscaster (*News in Review*, WDSG, Dyersburg, TN, 1947). DJ (*Night Patrol*, WDSG, 1947).

5442 **Cairns, George.** Sportscaster (WORC, Worcester, MA, 1939).

5443 **Cajal, Al.** Leader (Al Cajal's Greenwich Village Orchestra, KHJ, Los Angeles, CA, 1926).

5444 **Cajano, Pasquale.** Newscaster (WHOM, Jersey City, NJ, 1941).

5445 ***Cal King's Country Store.*** Cal King conducted the noon time radio shopping show (KYA, San Francisco, CA, 1931).

5446 ***Cal Tinney.*** Tinney was featured in the role of a rural news commentator (WCAU, Philadelphia, Pa, 1940). Later, Tinney had a network sustaining program where his homespun humor was at its best (15 min., Sunday, 4:45–5:00 P.M., ABC, 1948). *See* ***Call for Cal Tinney.***

5447 ***Calamity Jane.*** "Tums for the Tummy" sponsored the comedy drama starring Agnes Moorehead in the title role of a shrewd female reporter, whose father owned a newspaper. Each week Moorehead outwitted assorted racketeers and criminals. Also in the cast were Dan Wolfe, Bill Johnstone and Cathy Lewis. Ken Niles was the announcer (30 min., Sunday, 8:00–8:30 P.M., CBS, 1946).

5448 **Calbi, Louis.** Banjoist-cellist (WCDA, New York, NY, 1929).

5449 **Calder, C. Wylie.** Sportscaster (WTMA, Charleston, SC, 1939).

5450 **Calder, Crane.** Baritone (*Crane Calder*, vcl. mus. prg., WCBM, Baltimore, MD, 1934).

5451 **Calder, King.** Actor Calder appeared on *Barry Cameron, Hearts in Harmony, Second Mrs. Burton* and *When a Girl Marries.*

5452 **Calder, Thomas A.** Baritone (WOR, Newark, NJ, 1928).

5453 **Caldwell, Bob, Jr.** Newscaster (WHB, Kansas City, MO, 1941).

5454 **Caldwell, (Mrs.) Charles.** Contralto (KTHS, Hot Springs National Park, AR, 1928).

5455 **Caldwell, Chuck.** DJ (*All Star Parade*, WPAD, Paducah, KY, 1951; WJPS, Evansville, IN, 1955).

5456 **Caldwell, Ennis.** DJ (*Nite Show*, WJHO, Opelika, AL, 1960).

5457 **Caldwell, Evelyn.** COM-HE (KCSJ, Pueblo, CO, 1957).

5458 **Caldwell, Fred.** Newscaster (KTBC, Austin, TX, 1941). DJ (*Music Matinee*, KVET, Austin, TX, 1947). Sportscaster (KTBC, 1941).

5459 **Caldwell, Gladys.** Banjo soloist (WWJ, Detroit, MI, 1924).

5460 **Caldwell, (Mrs.) Jo Clark.** Newscaster (WRDW, Augusta, GA, 1940–1941).

5461 **Caldwell, Larry.** DJ (*Breakfast Varieties*, WAVL, Appolo, PA, 1950).

5462 **Caldwell, Melba.** Singer (WJBT, Chicago, IL, 1928).

5463 **Caldwell, Nate.** Announcer (KNRC, Los Angeles, CA, 1926; chief announcer, WBBM, Chicago, IL, 1928).

5464 **Caldwell, (Dr.) Orestes H.** Newscaster (*New York on Parade*, NBC, 1938).

5465 **Caldwell Sisters.** The sisters were a singing team known as the "Sweetest Singers on Earth" (WJBY, Gadsden, AL, 1929).

5466 **Calfee, Burke S.** Leader (Burke Calfee's Banjo Orchestra, KLX, Oakland, CA, 1929).

5467 **Calhoun, Adams.** Announcer (WFAA, Dallas, TX, 1925).

5468 **Calhoun, Allston.** Newscaster (WBBQ, Augusta, GA, 1948).

5469 **Calhoun, Bob.** DJ (KCLA, Pine Bluff, AR, 1957).

5470 **Calhoun, Bruce.** Newscaster (KIRO, Seattle, WA, 1945).

5471 **Calhoun, Cal.** Sportscaster (KHSL, Chico, CA, 1939).

5472 **Calhoun, Nora.** Soprano (KTAB, Oakland, CA, 1925).

5473 ***Cal-I-Bama Coeds.*** The band and vocal group were featured on a transcribed quarter-hour series broadcast by various stations in the early 1930s.

5474 **Calich, Bob.** Sportscaster (*Sports at Five*, WTCS, Fairmont, WV, 1960).

5475 **California Blue Boys.** Charles Hamp played piano and kazoo and sang with banjoist Earl Reynolds as the California Blue Boys (KFWB, Hollywood, CA, 1925).

5476 ***California Carry On.*** As part of the World War II war effort, the Bank of America sponsored this program in an effort to help employers sell more U.S. War Bond. Elsie Janis, the "Sweetheart of the A.E.F." during the first World War, was the program's hostess. She entertained by singing World War I songs and interviewing war heroes. The orchestra was conducted by Al Sack (30 min., Thursday, 7:30–8:00 P.M., CBS-Pacific Coast Network, 1943).

5477 ***California Concert.*** Ernest Gill conducted the orchestra on the good music program (30 min., Sunday, 7:30–8:00 P.M., NBC, 1938).

5478 ***California Hayride.*** CW music program begun in 1956 was broadcast from Richmond, CA. Performers on the *Hayride* included singer Mary Orlando, Mike Calkins, Eddie Kirk, Jerri Jones, Black Jack Wayne, Cottonseed Clark and Glenn Stepp.

5479 ***California Melodies.*** A music program broadcast Sunday evenings from 6:00 to 6:30 P.M., *California Melodies* presented the Raymond Paige Orchestra, vocalist Joan Marsh, Sam Coslow, Hazel Waters, Nora Schiller and Ray Hendricks. Reporter Eleanor Barnes interviewed various guest stars. One of her coups was the program on which she interviewed Jean Harlow and convinced her to sing (30 min., Sunday, 6:00–6:30 P.M., CBS, 1933–1934).

5480 ***California Melodies.*** A pleasant weekly music show introduced by announcer Bill Gordon in this way: "Out of the west to you." Leo Arneaux conducted and Maxine Gray sang on the entertaining feature from the Don Lee Studios in Hollywood (30 min., Weekly, KHJ, Los Angeles, CA, Don Lee Broadcasting System, 1942–1943).

5481 **California Mixed Quartet.** Vocal group consisting of soprano Zilpha Ruggles Jenkins, contralto Ruth Waterman, tenor Carl Anderson and bass Albert Gillette (KGO, San Francisco, CA, 1925).

5482 **California Night Hawks.** Popular jazz band of the period (WIP, Philadelphia, PA, 1925).

5483 **California Ragadores Orchestra.** Los Angeles radio band (KFQZ, Hollywood, CA, 1926).

5484 **California Ramblers.** The California Ramblers were a popular recording orchestra that broadast from New York City's Hotel Almanac (WHN, New York, NY, 1925; WMCA, New York, NY, 1926). Sometimes the band played under the name of the Golden Gate Orchestra. The 1925 band included such famous musicians as Frank Kush and Red Nichols, t.; Arnold Brilhart and Jimmy Dorsey, clr. and as.; Tommy Dorsey, tb.; Freddy Cusick, clr. and as.; Adrian Rollini, bsx.; Tommy Felline, bj.; Stan King, d.; and Irving Brodsky, p.

5485 **California Russian Trio.** Chico DeVerdi directed the instrumental musical group (KFQZ, Hollyood, CA, 1926).

5486 **California Sunshine Boys.** Vocal team of Jay Hurley and Glenn Putnam (KFWI, San Francisco, CA, 1927).

5487 **California Syncopators Orchestra.** F.L. Worrell directed the popular band (KJBS, San Francisco, CA, 1925).

5488 **California Trio.** Violinist Cecil Rauhut; cellist-vocalist Laura Ann Cottan and pianist S. Sydonia McKinley were the instrumental group that played from the Hotel Claremont Hotel, Berkeley, CA (KRE, Berkeley, CA, 1925).

5489 ***California's Hour.*** Chain Stores of California sponsored this gala variety show hosted by motion picture star, Conrad Nagel. Soprano Jane Froman, comedian Yogi Yorgenson the "Yogi Mystic," and the Dan Broekman orchestra were regular participants. In addition, six guest performers previously selected by community auditions were presented each week (60 min., Monday, 9:00–10:00 A.M., KFRC, San Francisco, CA, 1936).

5490 **Calkins, Jo Anne.** COM-HE (WRNY, Rochester, NY, 1954).

5491 **Call, Audrey.** Miss Call, a 17-year-old violinist made her debut with the Chicago Symphony Orchestra play-ing the D'Ambrosia Concerto. She appeared both as a soloist and as a member of the Edison String Trio daily (KYW, Chicago, IL, 1927).

5492 **Call, June.** Violinist (KDKA, Pittsburgh, PA, 1924).

5493 ***Call for Cal Tinney.*** Humorist Tinney answered queries called in by listeners on his sustaining program. Most often he was asked to discuss state and local New York City events; (15 min., Wednesday, 8:00–8:15 P.M., WMCA, New York, NY, 1941). *See* ***Cal Tinney.***

5494 ***Call for Music.*** Dinah Shore and Johnny Mercer sang and the Henry Jones Orchestra played on the musical program designed for young listeners sponsored by Philip Morris Cigarettes. Jack Rourke was the announcer (30 min., Friday, 10:00–10:30 P.M., CBS, 1948). This was the 1948 format of what eventually became the *Dinah Shore Show. See* ***The Dinah Shore Show.***

5495 ***Call the Police.*** Joe Julian played the role of Police Commissioner Bill Grant, a college educated World War II Marine, who returned from the war to pursue criminals in the summer replacement for *Amos 'n' Andy.* Lever Brothers, manufacturers of Lifebuoy soap, sponsored the dramatic series that was billed as "glorifying the policemen of the country." Ed Jerome, Mandel Kramer, George Matthews, Bill Smith, Alice Reinheart and Joan Thompkins were cast members. The program's announcer was Jay Sims (30 min., Tuesday, 9:00–9:30 P.M., NBC, 1947).

5496 **Callaghan, Jack.** Newscaster (WKAR, East Lansing, MI, 1940).

5497 **Callahan, Chris.** Sportscaster (*Sportlight,* WNOC, Norwich, CT, 1947).

5498 **Callahan, Donald.** Newscaster (KWAL, Wallace, ID, 1946).

5499 **Callahan, Elaine.** COM-HE (WYTI, Rocky Mount, VA, 1957).

5500 **Callahan, Ellen.** COM-HE (WWNC, Asheville, NC, 1951).

5501 **Callahan, Judy.** COM-HE (KWKC, Abilene, TX, 1951).

5502 **Callahan, Rosellen.** Publicist Callahan worked on the CBS publicity staff.

5503 **Callahan, Wanda.** COM-HE (KTTR, Rolla, MO, 1951).

5504 **Callan, R.L.** Newscaster (WHKY, Hickory, NC, 1941). Sportscaster (WHKY, 1941).

5505 **Callarman, John.** DJ (KCOV, Corvallis, OR, 1955). Sportscaster (*Football Scoreboard,* KTUE, Tulia, TX, 1960).

5506 **Callaway, Edwin.** Sportscaster (KTEM, Temple, TX, 1939).

5507 **Callebbs, Nora.** COM-HE (WAJR, Morgantown, WV, 1957).

5508 **Callegan, Charles.** DJ (*Lucky Seven,* WESB, Bradford, PA, 1955).

5509 **Callen, Joseph.** Newscaster (WATR, Waterbury, CT, 1947).

5510 ***Calling All Cars.*** Rio Grande Oil Company sponsored the weekly half-hour dramatic program that told the stories of various fictional police operations. The program, one of the most popular West Coast programs of the time, was similar to *Gangbusters* with its depiction of the rough and rugged treatment of crime and criminals. Frederick Lindsley was the narrator. Guest performers such as Charles Bickford were often featured (30 min., Wednesday, 9:00–9:30 P.M. PST, KHJ-Don Lee Network, Los Angeles, CA, 1936–1939).

5511 ***Calling All Detectives.*** The syndicated crime-adventure series told of the adventures of private detective Jerry Browning (15 min., WGN, Chicago, IL, 1949).

5512 ***Calling All Stamp Collectors.*** The National Federation of Stamp Clubs sponsored the program on which famous stamp collectors such as Lauritz Melchoir, Theodore Steinway and Adolph Menjou were interviewed (15 min., weekly, NBC-Red, 1938).

5513 ***Calling America.*** E.R. Squibb & Sons sponsored the attempt to bolster public morale during World War II. Bob Trout read letters from American servicemen at the front on the patriotic music program. Victor Bay's orchestra and baritone Walter Cassel performed (30 min., Sunday, 8:00–8:30 P.M., CBS, 1943).

5514 ***Calliope and Mis' Kath'rine.*** Talented Katherine Tift-Jones delivered humorous monologs on the weekly program. Alwyn E.W. Bach was the program's announcer (15 min., Sunday, 11:00–11:15 P.M., NBC-Blue, 1930).

5515 **Callow, Frances.** Harpist (WJZ, New York, NY, 1923).

5516 **Calloway, Blanche.** Leader (*Blanche Calloway Orchestra,* instr. mus. prg., WCAU, Philadelphia, PA, 1933; WLW, Cincinnati, OH, 1934; NBC, 1935).

5517 **Calloway, Cab.** Leader (*Cab Calloway Orchestra,* instr. mus. prg., CBS, 1932, 1935–1939).

5518 **Calloway [Callaway], Elizabeth.** COM-HE (KTRE, Lufkin, TX, 1956–1960).

5519 **Calloway, Ermine.** Popular radio singer Calloway was billed as "The Baby Vamp Singer" NBC, 1928–1929).

5520 **Calloway, Joe.** Sportscaster (WSIX, Nashville, TN, 1939).

5521 **Calloway, Magdalene.** COM-HE (KEY, Jamestown, ND, 1957).

5522 **Calmer, Ned.** Newscaster (CBS, 1941, 1944–1948). Writer Calmer wrote the *Backstage Wife* daytime serial program.

5523 ***Calpet Hour.*** Condensed versions of operettas were broadcast on the Thursday evening music program (60 min., Thursday, 8:00–9:00 P.M., NBC-Pacific Coast Network, 1928). For example, Offenbach's "The Grand Dutchess" was presented with soprano Barbara Blanchard, contralto Margaret O'Dea, tenor

Harold Spaulding and baritone James Isherwood.

5524 (The) Calpet Orchestra. Chico DeVerde directed his orchestra on the *California Petroleum Corporation* music program (KFI, Los Angeles, CA, 1926).

5525 Calsamalia, William J. Announcer (KRSC, Seattle, WA, 1927).

5526 Calusen, Magdalene. COM-HE (KEYJ, Jamestown, ND, 1957).

5527 *Calvary Episcopal Church Services.* These services were said to be the first *regularly scheduled* church [religious] broadcasts (KDKA, Pittsburgh, PA, 1921).

5528 Camacho, Carlos. DJ (KALI, Pasadena, CA, 1956).

5529 Camacho, Cesar. DJ (KXOE, San Antonio, TX, 1954; KCOR, San Antonio, TX, 1957).

5530 Camaday, Ewing. Newscaster (KELD, El Dorado, AR, 1942; WKY, Oklahoma City, OK, 1944).

5531 Camargo, Ralph. Actor Camargo appeared on the *Road of Life* daytime serial.

5532 *(The) Camay Soap Program.* Camay Soap sponsored a program of romantic music performed by baritone Barry McKinley (15 min., Thursday, 3:00–3:15 P.M., NBC-Red, 1934).

5533 Camb, Bill. DJ (*Just for Breakfast* and *The Bill Camb Show*, WBBC, Flint, MI, 1949).

5534 Cambell, Marian. Contralto (KLDS, Independence, MO, 1925).

5535 Cambria Serenaders. New Jersey jazz group (WGCP, Newark, NJ, 1925).

5536 Cambridge Sisters. Vocal trio (WDAR, Chicago, IL, 1923).

5537 *(The) Camel Caravan.* The first version of the *Camel Caravan* was a variety show that featured Glen Gray's Casa Loma band, Stoopnagle and Budd and singer Connie Boswell. R.J. Reynolds was the sponsor (15 min., Tuesday and Thursday, 10:15 P.M., CBS, 1934). A later musical format featured Vaughn Monroe and his orchestra (Weekly, CBS, 1953).

5538 *(The) Camel Caravan with Vaughn Monroe.* Baritone Monroe performed on this entertaining music program sponsored by Camel cigarettes (30 min., Saturday, 7:30–8:00 P.M., CBS, 1949). *See* **Monroe, Vaughn.**

5539 *(The) Camel Hour Program.* The Charles Previn Orchestra with singers Willard Robison, Reinald Werrenrath and Mary McCoy were presented on the music program sponsored by Camel cigarettes. Gordon Whyte was the announcer (NBC, 1930).

5540 *(The) Camel Quarter Hour.* Tony Wons read poetry, tenor Morton Downey sang and Jacques Renard led the orchestra on a quarter-hour program of music and poetry (15 min., Monday through Friday, 7:45–8:00 P.M., CBS, 1931).

5541 *Camera and Sound.* Originating from Warner's Enright Theatre in Philadelphia, the sustaining program featured the theater's organist, Johnny Mitchell. Walter Framer was also on hand to discuss theatrical topics (30 min., Tuesday, 11:30–12:00 noon, WWSW, Philadelphia, PA, 1936).

5542 *Camera Club of the Air.* Len Beardsley and John Condon provided photographic tips and information for their Seattle listeners (15 min., Thursday, 6:45–7:00 P.M., KJR, Seattle, WA, 1948).

5543 Cameo Collegians Orchestra. College band directed by Dick Shipley (WGBS, New York, NY, 1925).

5544 *Cameos of New Orleans.* Each week the show presented a complete dramatic vignette based on the history of New Orleans. The sponsor was the Illinois Central Railroad. Written by William Murphy, the first program was "Drums of Destiny," a historic romance about a Native American princess who was married in the Notre Dame Cathedral in Paris, before returning to her native Louisiana (15 min., Sunday, 2:30–2:45 P.M., NBC-Red, 1930s).

5545 *(The) Cameo Serenaders.* Link Porter directed the local orchestra (WTAG, Worcester, MA, 1932).

5546 Cameron, Al. Singer, comedian and writer Cameron was a member of a comedy singing team, Son and Tron, featured on a program by the same name, *Son and Tron,* sponsored by Sonatron Tubes (CBS, 1928–1929). He also acted on the *Brent House* daytime serial program

5547 Cameron, Barbara. COM-HE (WKRC, Cincinnati, OH,1954; WCPO, Cincinnati, OH, 1928).

5548 Cameron, Jane Holland. Contralto (WCCO, Minneappolis–St. Paul, MN, 1928).

5549 Cameron, Layman Wesley. Newscaster (*Gooch Products News Program* and *The Omar Flour Company News Program*, WOW, Omaha, NE, 1937).

5550 Cameron, Mabel M. Harpist (KGO, Oakland, CA, 1925).

5551 Cameron, Phil. Newscaster (WENY, Elmira, NY, 1941).

5552 Cameron, Winifred Eva. Flutist (KGO, Oakland, CA, 1925).

5553 Cammerota, Ed. Sportscaster (WEEU, Reading, PA, 1953).

5554 Camp, Del. Sportscaster (WDEV, Waterbury, VT, 1937).

5555 Camp, Mel. Newscaster (WIBA, Madison, WI, 1945).

5556 Camp, Raymond R. Sportscaster (*Angler and Hunter*, NBC, 1938).

5557 *Camp Crossroads.* In an effort to boost World War II civilian morale, this program presented interviews with men in service from all over the country (WSB, Atlanta, GA, World War II era).

5558 *Camp Meeting of the Air.* The Reverend W. Herbert Brewster conducted a religious program of preaching and gospel music that was broadcast in the late 1940s and early 1950s. The program featured singer Queen C. Anderson and the Brewsteraires singing group that at various times included Queen C. Anderson, Gurice Malone, Dorothy Ford, Hessie Ford, Nancy Jerome, Odell Rice, Nathaniel Peck, Henry Reed, Solomon Alson, Ella Clark Willians and Nina Jai Daugherty (WDIA, Memphis, TN, 1940–1950). *See* **Black Radio.**

5559 Campanieskaja, Glukerja. Soprano (WHY, Hoboken, NJ, 1924).

5560 Campbell, Anne. Poet (WWJ, Detroit, MI, 1923–1925).

5561 Campbell, Archie. Talented CW singer, songwriter and comedian, Campbell began his radio career as an announcer on WNOX (Knoxville, TN, 1936). At that station he sang and provided comedy bits with Roy Acuff's Crazy Tennesseans and that the station's *Mid-Day Merry Go Round* (1936) and *Barn Dance* (1936) with such future stars as Roy Acuff, Eddie Hill, the Carlisles, Pee Wee King, Chet Atkins and Homer and Jethroe. Campbell later had his own programs on WOPI (Bristol, TN) and WDOD (Chatanooga, TN). When comedian Rod Brasfield died in 1958, he became a member of the *Grand Ole Opry*, appearing on the *Prince Albert* segment (NBC, 1958) of the Opry. He gained national prominence as a member of television's *Hee Haw* program in 1969. Campbell, incidentally, was chief writer for the TV show.

5562 Campbell, Bernice. COM-HE (WBBB, Burlington, NC, 1960).

5563 Campbell, Betty. Campbell broadcast items about show business and interviewed visiting personalities.

5564 Campbell, Bettye. COM-HE (KPET, Lamesa, TX, 1956).

5565 Campbell, Bill. Sportscaster (WCAU, Philadelphia, PA, 1946–1947; 1960).

5566 Campbell, (Mrs.) Blanche Bingham. Contralto (WSM, Nashville, TN, 1926–1928). In some local papers she was identified as a mezzo-soprano. .

5567 Campbell, Bob. Newscaster (WCCO, Minneappolis–St. Paul, MN, 1939).

5568 Campbell, Bud. Sportscaster (WIND, Chicago, IL, 1951–1953; KARK, Little Rock, AR, 1955).

5569 Campbell, Cecil. CW musician made his radio debut on WSJS (Winston-Salem, NC, 1932). He later worked on WSB (Atlanta, GA, 1938–1939) and WBT (Charlotte, NC, mid–1930s to 1950). He appeared on such network programs as *Carolina Hayride* (CBS, 1944–1945), *Carolina Calling* (CBS, 1946) and *Dixie Jamboree* (ABC, 1950–1951) and in motion pictures with such stars as Roy Acuff, Charles Starrett, Tex Ritter and Gene Autry.

5570 Campbell, Charles. Sportscaster (KGEZ, Kalispell, MT, 1947).

5571 Campbell, Claude N. Newscaster (WCLA, Baton Rouge, LA, 1948). Sportscaster (WCLA, 1948).

5572 Campbell, Constance. Reader (KHJ, Los Angeles, CA, 1923).

5573 Campbell, Craig. Newscaster (WOC, Davenport, IA, 1941).

5574 Campbell, Cynthia. COM-HE (WKY, Oklahoma City, OK, 1958).

5575 Campbell, D.C. Sportscaster (KCRC, Enid, OK, 1937).

5576 Campbell, Dave. DJ (*Matinee in Birmingham*, WAPI, Birmingham, AL, 1947–1951). Sportscaster (WAPI, 1949–1951, WBRC, Birmingham, AL, 1955–1956).

5577 Campbell, Dick. Sportscaster (KGGF, Coffeyville, KS, 1937–1941). Newscaster (KGGF, 1940–1941; KOME, Tulsa, OK, 1937, 1946).

5578 Campbell, Don. Newscaster (*Campbell Calling*, WTSP, St. Petersburg, FL, 1947).

5579 Campbell, Donald. Leader (Donald Campbell's Orchestra, KHJ, Los Angeles, CA, 1923).

5580 Campbell, Dorothy. COM-HE (WRDO, Augusta, ME, 1957).

5581 Campbell, (Mrs.) F. Graham. (KFAB, Lincoln, NE, 1925).

5582 Campbell, Flora. Actress Campbell was a cast member of the *Evelyn Winters* aka *The Strange Romance of Evelyn Winters* daytime serial.

5583 Campbell, Fran. COM-HE (WFNS, Burlington, NC, 1957).

5584 Campbell, Frank. Newscaster (*Today's World*, KVSM, San Mateo, CA, 1947).

5585 Campbell, Gladys Mary. Soprano (KFUU, Oakland, CA, 1925).

5586 Campbell, Howard. Newscaster (KDNT, Denton, TX, 1941).

5587 Campbell, Jack. DJ (KVOO, Tulsa, OK, 1955; *Sleepwalker*, KVOO, 1960).

5588 Campbell, Jean. Pianist (KPO, San Francisco, CA, 1926).

5589 Campbell, John T. Sportscaster (KGVO, Missoula, MT, 1939; *Sports Review*, KXLI, 1951–1956; KYSS, Missoula, MT, 1960). Newscaster (KGVO, 1942, KXLI, 1949; *Coach's Corner*, KXLI, 1953–1955).

5590 Campbell, Johnnie. Leader (Johnnie Campbell's Kansas City Club Orchestra, WDAF, Kansas City, MO, 1925; Johnnie Campbell's Orchestra, WDAF, 1926).

5591 Campbell, Joyce. COM-HE (KWAL, Kellogg-Wallace, ID, 1958).

5592 Campbell, Juanita. COM-HE (KVIP, Redding, CA, 1956).

5593 Campbell, Kay. Actress Campbell appeared on the *Ma Perkins* program.

5594 Campbell, (Mrs.) Lanthe R. COM-HE (WHKY, Hickory, NC, 1956–1957).

5595 Campbell, Lois. COM-HE (WPEP, Park Falls, WI, 1956).

5596 Campbell, Malcolm, Jr., "Mal." Sportscaster (*National Sports Parade*, WCUM, Cumberland, MD, 1950–1952; WNAV, Annapolis, MD, 1955–1956).

5597 Campbell, Marianne B. COM-HE (WJEH, Gallipolis, OH, 1956–1957).

5598 Campbell, Martin. Newscaster (ABC, 1946).

5599 Campbell, Mary Jane. COM-HE (WMRE, Monroe, GA, 1956).

5600 Campbell, (Mrs.) Melvin A. Singer (WLAG, Minneapolis, MN, 1924)

5601 Campbell, Naomi. Actress Campbell was a member of the *Young Dr. Malone* daytime serial.

5602 Campbell, Neenie. Sportscaster (*Caravan of Sports*, WMCK, McKeesport, PA, 1947–1956).

5603 Campbell, Olin. DJ (*Dawnbusters*, WFNS, Burlington, NC, 1955–1957).

5604 Campbell, Patsy. Versatile radio actress Campbell appeared on the daytime serial programs *Home in the Country*, *Rosemary*, *Second Mrs. Burton* (title role) and *Big Sister*.

5605 Campbell, Phyllis. Contralto (KFI, Los Angeles, CA, 1928).

5606 Campbell, Robert. Pianist (WLW, Cincinnati, OH, 1923).

5607 Campbell, (Mr. and Mrs.) Robert. Vocal duets (KFKQ, Conway, AR, 1923). Piano accompaniment was provided by Evelyn Patchell.

5608 Campbell, Roy. Leader (*Roy Campbell Orchestra*, instr. mus. prg., NBC-Red Network, 1936).

5609 Campbell, Sterling "Soup." DJ (*Soup's On*, WWOL, Buffalo, NY, 1948–1951).

5610 Campbell, Walter N. Announcer-director (WLAC, Nashville, TN, 1928).

5611 Campbell, Wanda. COM-HE (WBOW, Terre Haute, IN, 1951).

5612 *(The) Campbell Playhouse.* Campbell Soups sponsored this fine dramatic program and Orson Welles produced it during the first two years it was on the air The 1940–1941 series was directed by George Zachary. The scripts were written by John Houseman and Willis Cooper. Lyn Murray conducted the orchestra.

The first series (1938–1939) was directed by Paul Stewart, Orson Welles, John Houseman and Howard Koch wrote the scripts. The announcer was Niles Welch. The cast members over the years included: Luther Adler, Fred Allen, Amos 'n' Andy, Ruth Anderson, Mary Astor, Fay Bainter, Lucille Ball, Tallulah Bankhead, Wendy Barrie, Lionel Barrymore, John Beal, Noah Beery, Joan Bennett, Jack Benny, Gertrude Berg, Joan Blondell, Humphrey Bogart, Eddie Cantor, Madeleine Carroll, Ilka Chase, Ruth Chatterton, Ronald Colman, Donald Cook, Jackie Cooper, Joseph Cotton, John Craven, Frances Dee, Florence Eldridge, Jean Ellyn, Douglas Fairbanks, Jr., Frances Farmer, Geraldine Fitzgerald, Arlene Francis, William Gargan, Grace George, Tamara Geva, Paulette Goddard, Jack Grimes, Sigrid Gurie, Ann Harding, Helen Hayes, Katherine Hepburn, Arthur Hopkins, Miriam Hopkins, Hedda Hopper, Walter Huston, George M. Kaufman, Beatrice Kay, Elissa Landi, Warden Lewis E. Lawes, Gertrude Lawrence, Sam Levine, David Lewis, Beatrice Lillie, Ida Lupino, Jeanette MacDonald, Aline MacMahon, Frederic March, Herbert Marshall, Burgess Meredith, Philip Merivale, Agnes Moorehead, Frank Morgan, Helen Morgan, Alan Mowbray, Paul Muni, Edna May Oliver, Laurence Olivier, Gale Page, Dick Powell, William Powell, George Raft, Gene Raymond, Rosalind Russell, Randolph Scott, Hiram Sherman, Sylvia Sydney, Cornelia Otis Skinner, Everett Sloane, Margaret Sullivan, Nan Sunderland, Regis Toomey, Helen Twelvetrees, June Walker, Linda Watkins, Marie Wilson, Anna May Wong and Jane Wyatt. Some of the authors whose work was adapted for the series were: Daphne duMaurier, Charles Dickens, Ernest Hemingway, Elmer Rice, Sinclair Lewis, Arthur Hopkins, Charles MacArthur, Ben Hecht, Edna Ferber, Victor Hugo, Pearl Buck, Noel Coward, John P. Marquand, Thornton Wilder, Orson Welles, Gerald duMaurier, Eugene O'Neill, J.M. Barrie, Alexander Dumas, John Galsworthy, John Howard Lawson, Agatha Christie, Hugh Walpole, Nordhoff and Hall, William Thackeray, A.J. Cronin, George S. Kaufman, Kenneth Roberts, Mark Twain, George Kelly, Ring Lardner, Charlotte Bronte, George Bernard Shaw, Clifford Odets, Ellery Queen, Norman Corwin, John Van Bruten and Somerset Maugham (60 min., Friday, 9:00–10:00 P.M., CBS, 1938–1939; 60 min., Sunday, 8:00–9:00 P.M., CBS, 1939–1940; 30 min., Friday, 9:30–10:00 P.M., CBS, 1940–1941).

5613 *(The) Campbell Room.* The *Raleigh Room* program changed its name, sponsor (Campbell soups) and network. Each week Hildegarde presented such guests as Brooklyn baseball star Dixie Walker, comedian Bert Lahr and actress Tallulah Bankhead. Paul Barron's orchestra and announcer Ernest Chappell were program regulars (30 min., Sunday, 9:00–9:30 P.M., CBS, 1946).

5614 *(The) Campbell Sisters.* Female vocal trio (vcl. mus. prg., MBS, 1934).

5615 *Campbell's Orchestra.* Instr. mus. prg. (WEEI, Boston, MA, 1932).

5616 Campchero, Bob. DJ (*You Name It—We Play It*, WABY, Albany, NY, 1948).

5617 Campenella, Joe. Sportscaster (WMRF, Lewiston PA, 1949).

5618 Campo, Del. Leader (*Del Campo Orchestra*, instr. mus. prg., NBC, 1934).

5619 Campofreda, Nick. Sportscaster (WFBR, Baltimore, MD, 1946). Campofreda was a star college football player at Western Maryland College, who later played professional football with the Washington Redskins.

5620 Campos, Lalo. DJ (*Noche de Fiesta*, KVET, Austin, TX, 1947–1951).

5621 *Campus Capers.* Clarence Fuhrman's orchestra, organist Arthur Hinnett and singers Eve Knight and Larry Lane were featured on the weekly sustaining program; (30 min., Saturday, 4:00–4:30 P.M., NBC, 1940).

5622 *Campus Cut-Ups.* The vocal music program featured the singing team of Tommy Kyle and Floyd Terry (WCKY, Covington, KY, early 1930s).

5623 Campus Flirts. Harmony vocal trio (WLS, Chicago, IL, 1928).

5624 *Campus Review.* Music and sports news were the major features of the weekly network program. Hal Totten delivered sports news and the music was supplied by the Art Kassel and his Kassels in the Air Orchestra, soprano Grace Dunn and the Mills Brothers (30 min, Friday, 9:30–10:00 P.M. CST, NBC-Red, 1935).

5625 Campus Serenaders. Students' dance orchestra from Renssaelaer Polytechnic Institute (WHAZ, Troy, NY, 1924).

5626 *Campy's Corner.* After Brooklyn Dodger catcher Roy Campanella was severely injured in an automobile accident, New York *Herald-Tribune* sports columnist Bob Cook suggested the idea of taping a sports news program at Campanella's bedside. Chris Schenkel and sports guests appeared regularly with Campanella on the five-minute transcribed program sponsored by P. Ballentine beer and R.J. Reynolds cigarettes (5 min., Monday through Friday, 6:00–6:05 P.M., WINS, New York, NY, 1958).

5627 ***Can You Top This?*** Ward Wilson hosted the often raucous comedy show that gave listeners the opportunity to "top" the panel of comedians with their jokes and win a prize of $25 if they successfully topped all four panelists. Peter Donald, with his skillful use of dialects, told the jokes submitted by listeners. A "Laugh Meter," actually a volume indicator meter, registered the "laugh" achieved by Donald and each of the panel members when they told their jokes. The funny panelists included Harry Hershfield, Joe Laurie, Jr. and "Senator" Ed Ford.

Originated by Senator Ford (Edward M. Ford), the program was broadcast on MBS, NBC and ABC from 1940 to 1954. Ward Wilson was the program's host and Charles Stark the announcer. Alan Dingwall, Jay Clark and Roger Bower were the directors. The show also enjoyed a brief television run.

5628 ***(The) Canada Lee [DJ] Show.*** Distinguished Broadway actor Canada Lee as a DJ played only records made by Black artists (30 min., Saturday, 8:00–8:30 P.M., WNEW, New York, NY, 1948).

5629 **Canaday, Ewing.** Newscaster (KELD, El Dorado, AR, 1941; WKY, Oklahoma City, OK, 1946).

5630 **Canaday, Ralph.** Pianist (*Ralph Canaday,* instr. mus. prg., WDBJ, Roanoke, VA, 1935).

5631 ***Canadian Grenadier Guards.*** The distinguished Canadian band appeared on a series of fine military music programs (NBC, 1935–1939).

5632 **Canady, Ann.** COM-HE (KWBB, Wichita, KS, 1955).

5633 **Canady, John.** Sportscaster (KMPC, Los Angeles, CA, 1938; KECA, Los Angeles, CA, and KFI, Los Angeles, CA, 1939).

5634 ***(The) Canary Pet Show.*** Hartz Mountain Products sponsored the program devoted to canaries in all their glory. Nannette Sargent and the Master Radio Canaries were featured. Background music was provided by violinist David Bohme and organist Porter Heaps (15 min., Sunday, 1:15–1:30 P.M., MBS, 1950).

5635 **Canata [Cannata], A.** Clarinetist (WBZ, Boston-Springfield, 1925).

5636 **Canavan, Robert.** Newscaster (KROD, El Paso, TX, 1946). Sportscaster (KROD, 1946–1949; KSET, El Paso, TX, 1950–1951).

5637 **Canby, Edward T.** DJ (*New Recordings,* WNYC, New York, NY, 1949).

5638 **Candelori, Anthony.** Leader (*Anthony Candelori Orchestra,* instr. mus. prg., NBC, 1936; WFIL, Philadelphia, PA, 1938–1939; MBS, 1942).

5639 ***Candelori Dance Orchestra.*** Instr. mus. prg. (WOO, Philadelphia, PA, 1925).

5640 ***Candid Microphone.*** Allen Funt's *Candid Microphone* moved to CBS with Philip Morris cigarettes as sponsor, after first having been heard as a sustaining program on ABC. Unsuspecting persons were placed in strange, mostly humorous, situations and their reactions recorded. Later, Funt transformed the program into a successful television program. *Variety* commented that when the program was really unrehearsed, it was somewhat annoying to hear unwary persons being harassed merely to get a laugh at their expense. This criticism was equally applicable to the television version that appeared years later. The radio program was first heard on ABC in 1947. The narrators were Alan Funt and Don Hollenbeck. Ken Roberts was the announcer. Music was supplied by Bernie Green's orchestra (30 min., Tuesday, 9:00–9:30 P.M., CBS, 1950).

5641 **Candler, Barbara.** COM-HE (WQXI, Atlanta, GA, 1951).

5642 **Candlyn T. Frederick.** Pianist (WGY, Schenectady, NY, 1923).

5643 **Candullo [or Candulla], Harry.** Leader (*Harry Candullo Orchestra,* instr. mus. prg., WCAE, Pittsburgh, PA, 1938–1939; WSB, Atlanta, GA, 1939).

5644 **Candullo, Joel.** Leader (*Joel Candullo Orchestra,* instr. mus. prg. (NBC-Red, 1935–1936).

5645 **Candy, Jane C.** COM-HE (WNOW, York, PA, 1951).

5646 **Candy, Lou.** COM-HE (KITE, San Antonio, TX, 1956).

5647 ***(The) Candygram Frolic.*** The music program featured the Edgewater Beach Orchestra directed by Frank Kuhl (WSOE, Milwaukee, WI, 1926).

5648 **Cane, Allene W.** COM-HE (WKSR, Pulaski, TN, 1954).

5649 **Cane, Lenny.** Sportscaster (WENT, Gloversville, NY, 1953).

5650 **Cane, Stella.** COM-HE (WSEE, Erie, PA, 1954).

5651 **Cane, Sugar.** Singer (WOR, Newark, NJ, 1935).

5652 **Canepari, Alessandra.** Singer (KOA, Denver, CO, 1936).

5653 **Canfield, Iris.** Cellist (KJR, Seattle, WA and KFOA, Seattle, WA, 1927).

5654 **Canfield, Loretta.** COM-HE (WEKY, Richmond, KY, 1957).

5655 **Canham, Erwin.** Newscaster (*The Christian Science Monitor Views the News,* ABC, 1944–1947; *Canham Views the News,* ABC, 1948). Sportscaster (ABC, 1951).

5656 **Caniglia, Phil.** DJ (*Italian Hour,* KSWI, Council Bluffs, IA, 1948).

5657 **Canine, Margaret.** Soprano (WBAA, West Lafayette, IN, 1939).

5658 ***Canine Comment.*** George Michael talked about dogs on the sustaining quarter-hour program (15 min., Sunday, 12:15–12:30 P.M., WGY, Schenectady, NY, 1947).

5659 ***Canine Forum.*** George Michael and his guests talked about dogs and their care (30 min., Wednesday, 8:30–9:00 P.M., WROW, Albany, NY, 1948).

5660 **Cann, Peggy.** COM-HE (WNAG, Grenada, MS, 1957).

5661 **Cann, Wesley.** Singer, (*Wesley Cann,* vcl. mus. prg., WMAL, Washington, DC, 1936).

5662 **Cannaday, Bill.** DJ (*Swing with Bill,* WJMO, Cleveland, OH, 1947).

5663 **Cannaday, Ralph.** Pianist (*Ralph Cannaday,* instr. mus. prg., WDBJ, Roanoke, VA, 1936).

5664 ***(The) Canning House.*** The homemakers' program provided information about canning techniques for fruits and vegetables (WCTS, Worchester, MA, 1925).

5665 **Cannon, Don.** DJ (KDAL, Duluth, MN, 1960).

5666 **Cannon, Dorsey.** COM-HE (WDAD, Indiana, PA, 1951).

5667 **Cannon, Sarah Ophelia (Cousin Minnie Pearl).** Country comedienne and singer (*Grand Ole Opry,*WSM, Nashville, TN). Cousin Minnie Pearl first appeared on radio in 1940. The Cousin Minnie Pearl character was originated in 1938 on personal appearances, but not on the air. Cousin Minnie Pearl was an unmarried lady of between 25 and 35, who came from Grinder's Switch, Tennessee. Her trademark greeting "Howdee-e-e-e, I'm just so proud to be here," when she first started was spoken relatively softly. While on NBC's Prince Albert segment of the *Grand Ole Opry,* she was told she should be louder. When she got louder she found that the audience did the same. After rejecting it at first, she soon realized the audience loved to shout, "Howdy" back at her (Cannon, 1977). A price tag hanging from her $1.98 hat became her most familiar trademark.

5668 **Cannon, Win.** DJ (*Radio Rancher,* KPQ, Wenatchee, WA, 1949–1954).

5669 **Canova, Anna.** Pianist Canova was called the "Queen of the Ivories" (WJAX, Jacksonville, FL, 1927).

5670 **Canova, Juliette "Judy."** CW "hillbilly" comedienne Canova began performing with family members Leon and Diane as the Three Georgia Crackers with character names of "Judy, Zeke and Anne" in 1932. The following year the singing comedy act appeared on WJAX (Jacksonville, FL, 1933). The trio moved to New York in 1934, and as Leon and the Happiness Girls worked in Manhattan clubs. Judy soon went off on her own to do some motion picture work and appeared on Broadway in the *Calling All Stars*in 1934 and the *Ziegfeld Follies of 1936.* From 1936 to 1937 she rejoined the family group to appear regularly on programs with Edgar Bergen and Paul Whiteman. She had her own programs, earlier known as *Rancho Canova* (CBS, 1943–1944) and later as the *Judy Canova Show* (NBC, 1945–1951). Judy continued her motion picture and Broadway work before beginning a successful television career. *See* **Comediennes** ***and the Judy Canova Show.***

5671 **Cantanese, Vincent.** Leader (Vincent Cantanese and his Hotel Almanac Orchestra (WHN, New York, NY, 1925).

5672 **Canter, Russell E.** Newscaster (WBNS, Columbus, OH, 1945).

5673 **Canterbury, Clare Perkins.** Singer (KOIL, Council Bluffs, IA, 1926).

5674 **Cantfort, Van.** Sportscaster (WAVY, Norfolk, VA, 1960).

5675 Cantiell, Lloyd. Saxophonist (KFWM, Oakland, CA, 1929).

5676 Canton, Louis. Singer Canton was known as "The Steel Mill Tenor" (WOR, Newark, NJ, 1926).

5677 Cantor, Charlie. Comic actor Cantor appeared on the *Adventures of Mortimer Meek, Alan Young Show, Amazing Mr. Smith, Duffy's Tavern, Flash Gordon, Fred Allen Show, Life of Riley, Phillip Morris Playhouse* and *Terry and the Pirates* programs.

5678 Cantor, Eddie. A famous comedian-singer, who starred in vaudeville and musical comedy, Cantor appeared on the *Eveready Hour* program (WEAF, New York, NY, 1925). Earlier the banjo-eyed comedian had appeared on the inaugural broadcast of station WDY (Roselle Park, NJ, December 14, 1921). Cantor's first regularly scheduled radio appearances were on the *Chase and Sanborn Hour*, a program frequently known merely as the *Eddie Cantor Show*. His most famous show, however, was called *Time to Smile*, named to remind listeners of his toothpaste sponsors. The Ipana sponsored program was on the air from 1940 to 1946. Cantor was known both for his authoritarian manner and his advancement of the careers of many young performers such as Burns and Allen, Deanna Durbin, Bobby Breen and Dinah Shore. He also popularized the work of Bert Gordon, whose hilarious antics deservedly earned him the designation of "The Mad Russian" and Harry Einstein, whose "Parkyarkarkas" characterization of genial stupidity earned him a loyal following. Over the years, the Cantor program's cast included: John Brown, Maude Davis, Shirley Dinsdale, Harry Einstein, Sidney Fields, Bert Gordon, Frank Nelson, Nan Rae, Alan Reed (Teddy Bergman), Dave Rubinoff, Lionel Stander and Veola Vonn. The announcers were Harry Von Zell and Jimmy Wallington. The talented singers who appeared on the program included Bobby Breen, Dianna Durbin, Nora Martin, Dinah Shore and Margaret Whiting and the Sportsman Quartet (male vocal group). The orchestras over the years were Cookie Fairchild, Louis Gress, Jacques Renard and George Stoll. Ed Beloin, Matt Brooks, Carroll Carroll, Bob Colwell, Eddie Davis, Izzy Elinson, David Freedman, Everett Freeman, Barbara Hotchkiss, Sam Moore, Bobbie O'Brien, PhiL Rapp, John Quillen and Phil Rapp were the writers. The directors were Vic Knight, Manning Ostroff and Abbott K. Spencer. Like many other personalities, Cantor eventually became a DJ (NBC, 1951–1954). His daughter Marilyn also performed DJ duties in 1952. *See* **Cantor, Eddie** *and* **Cantor, Marilyn**.

5679 Cantor, Marilyn. Marilyn Cantor, Eddie's daughter, took over for DJ Bea Kalmus on the *Republic Star Time* program sponsored by Republic Stores. In addition to playing records, Miss Cantor interviewed celebrity guests such as Delores Gray. Bill Lang was the program's announcer (30 min., Monday through Saturday, WMGM, New York, NY, 1952).

5680 Cantor, Mary and Sarah Alter. Piano duet team (WEAF, New York, NY, 1924).

5681 Cantrell, Jane. COM-HE (KWAL, Wallace, ID, 1951–1954).

5682 Cantrell, Margaret and Miss Neal. Harmony singing team known as Neal and Contrell (WOR, Newark, NJ and WHN New York, NY, 1924).

5683 Cantrell, Pat. DJ (*Big Beat*, KBYP, Shamrock, TX, 1960).

5684 Canup, Red. Sportscaster (WAIM, Anderson, SC, 1937–1940).

5685 Caparo, Joe. Leader (*Joe Caparo Orchestra*, instr. mus. prg., KTHS, Hot Springs, AR, 1939–1940).

5686 Capell, Peter. Actor Capell appeared on *Front Page Farrell, Portia Faces Life, Right to Happiness, Thanks for Tomorrow, Wendy Warren and the News* and *When a Girl Marries*.

5687 Capen, Ginger. COM-HE (KJAN, Atlantic, IA, 1958–1960).

5688 *Capitol Family Program* (aka *Major Bowes Capitol Family*). As a partner, Major Edward Bowes helped build New York's Capitol Theater, where showman Samuel Lionel Rothafel originated and conducted his *Roxy and His Gang* program in the early 1920s. When Roxy left the Capitol Theater, Bowes took over his show and transformed it into the *Capitol Family Program*. The program continued to enjoy enthusiastic listener response (60 min., Sunday, 11:30–12:30 P.M., NBC-Red, 1934). *See* ***Roxy and His Gang***.

5689 Capitol Orchestra. Oscar Baum conducted the Capitol Orchestra (WCCO, Minneappolis–St. Paul, MN, 1928).

5690 *Capitol Schnitzel Bankers*. Music and gags were supplied by Otto Schultz, Fritz Schott and Vic Lyon on the popular local program sponsored by the Capitol City Brewing Company (15 min., Sunday, 12:45–1:00 P.M., KMOS, Jefferson City, MO, 1938).

5691 *Capitol Theater Concert*. The two-hour concert music show was broadcast weekly (120 min., Sunday, 7:30–9:30 P.M., WJZ-Blue Network, 1926).

5692 *Capitol Theater Family*. *See* ***Roxy and His Gang***.

5693 Capitol Theater Jazz Orchestra. Popular theater orchestra that played on station WLW's inaugural program March 1922 (WLW, Cincinnati, OH, 1922).

5694 Capitol Theater Orchestra. WBZ (Springfield, MA, 1925–1926).

5695 *(The) Capitol Theater Symphony*. This was a 60-minute program of symphonic music originating from New York's Capitol Theater (60min., Sunday, 12:00–1:00 P.M., NBC-Red, 1927).

5696 (The) Capitolians. S.L. Rothafel developed the Capitolians Orchestra to perform on his *Roxy and his Gang* program. It is thought the band was organized and trained by Paul Specht (NBC, 1926–1928). *See* ***Roxy and His Gang***.

5697 Caplan, Sam. Violinist (WHO, Des Moines, IA, 1925).

5698 Capland, Letha Lee. COM-HE (KPAC, Port Arthur, TX, 1954–1955).

5699 Capodiferro, Pietro. Trumpet soloist (WEAF, New York, NY, 1927).

5700 Capouilliez, Francois. Bass (WGCP, New York, NY, 1925).

5701 Capozucchi, James. Newscaster (WOV, New York, NY, 1938; WHOM, Jersey City, NJ, 1941–1942).

5702 Cappell, (Miss) Angie. Vaudeville singer-entertainer Angie Cappell was affectionately known to veterans of World War I, whom she had entertained frequently, as "The Little Wop" (KGY, Lacey, WA, 1922).

5703 Cappell, Bootsy. Sportscaster (KVPI, Ville Platte, LA, 1955).

5704 Cappellini, Edgar R. Newscaster (KALB, Alexandria, LA, 1939–1945).

5705 Capps, Bob. DJ (*Rhythm Roundup*, KRUX, Phoenix, AZ, 1951; *Night Riders*, KOY, Phoenix, AZ, 1954–1955).

5706 Capps, Jimmy. DJ (*Our Best to You*, WPTF, Raleigh, NC, 1951;1954–1955).

5707 Capra, Jimmy. Leader (*Jimmy Capra Orchestra*, instr. mus. prg., KTHS, Hot Springs National Park, AR, 1938–1939).

5708 Capraro, Mike. Leader (Mike Capraro and his Bellmont Harmony Kings Orchestra, KJBS, San Francisco, CA, 1926).

5709 Capron, Paul. Newscaster (*Gazette Review*, WASA, Havre de Grace, MD, 1948).

5710 *Captain Danger*. None of the actors were identified on the exciting children's dramatic series sponsored by Wilshire Club Beverages. The program followed the adventures of Captain Danger, Dan and Diana Dangerfield and Doolittle Nohow Jones fighting Malay Pirates in the South Seas (15 min., 5:15–5:30 P.M., KHJ, Los Angeles, CA, 1941).

5711 *Captain Dobbsie's Ship of Joy*. *See* **Dobbs, Hugh Barrett**.

5712 *Captain Henry's Showboat*. Charles Winninger, as Captain Henry, played a Mississippi showboat captain and hosted the show sponsored by Maxwell House Coffee. His verbal trademark was "You ain't seen nothing yet." The show's talented cast included Jules Bledsoe, the Hall-Johnson Choir, Mabel Jackson, Molasses and January, Lanny Ross, Annette Henshaw and the Don Voorhees Orchestra (60 min., Thursday, 9:00–10:00 P.M., NBC-Red, 1932).

5713 *Captain Jack*. Don Ameche played the title role in the dramatic network adventure series broadcast in 1935.

5714 *Captain Midnight*. The sound of a gong and an airplane swooping toward the earth alerted young listeners that the *Captain Midnight* daytime adventure series was on the air. After experiencing many daring adventures in the first World War, the fictional Captain Red Albright assumed the role of Captain Midnight, commander of the Secret Squadron. The Squadron was a super secret government organization with a mission to fight evil throughout the world. Although the Captain fought several arch villains, but by far his most dangerous adversary was Ivan Shark.

Captain Midnight was assisted by his mechanic, Ichabod Mudd, and his two young helpers, Chuck Ramsey and Joyce Ryan. Over the years Captain Midnight was played by Ed Prentiss, Bill Bouchey and Paul Barnes. The villainous Ivan Shark was played by Boris

Aplon. The program'scast included: Paul Barnes, Joe Bivens, Bill Bouchey, Johnny Coons, Maurice Copeland, Earl George, Sharon Grainger, Art Hern, Sherman Marks, Marvin Miller, Marilou Neumayer, Angeline Orr, Ed Prentiss, Rene Rodier, Bill Rose, Olan Soule and Hugh Studebaker. The announcers were Pierre Andre and Don Gordon. The directors were Kirby Hawkes, Alan Wallace and Russell Young. The program was first broadcast on MBS in 1940.

5715 ***Captains of Industry.*** This program dramatized the lives of successful businessmen such as Elbert Gary, Marcus Hanna, Philip Danforth Armour, John Davis Rockefeller, King Champ Gillette, Henry Clay Frick, Henry Morrison Flagler, P.T. Barnum, Edward L. Doheny, Julius Rosenwald, Jay Gould and Mark Hopkins (15 min., Weekly, Transcribed, mid–1930s).

5716 ***Captain Stubby and the Bucaneers.*** CW musical group under the direction of Captain Stubby (Tom. C. Fouts) first appeared on WDAN (Danville, IL, 1938–1940). The group broadcast on the *Boone County Jamboree* on WLW (Cincinnati, OH) from 1940 to 1944. The entire group joined the Navy in 1944 and for two years traveled around the world entertained American troops. When they left the Navy the group played at various clubs before they became regulars on the *National Barn Dance* (1949–1958). Members of the group over the years in addition to Fouts included: Sonny Fleming, Jerald Richards, Dwight "Tiny" Stokes, Peter Kunatz, Curly Myers, Buddy Ross, Tony Walberg, Chuck Kagy, Peter Kaye and Ralph "Rusty" Gill.

5717 ***Captain Tim Healy's Ivory Soap Stamp Club.*** During the years from 1938 to 1945, Healy conducted many programs for stamp collectors—young and old, but the best known was *Captain Tim Healy's Ivory Stamp Club*. Healy was a world traveler, skillful lecturer and engrossing storyteller. In his effort to interest young listeners in stamps, he frequently reminded them that, "You never know when a fortune might be lying around your own home." After telling his fascinating stamp stories, he offered stamp albums and packets as premiums. He closed his show by saying, "And so, good night boys and girls from 8 to 80. Next Wednesday night I will bring you another fascinating story behind a stamp." Healy knew precisely how to appeal to both adults and children (15 min., Monday, Wedesday and Friday, 5:45–6:00 P.M.,NBC-Blue, 1935). He was on the air from 1933 to 1945 for various sponsors with essentially the same format on his *Adventures with Captain Tim, Captain Tim's Adventures* and *Captain Tim's Adventure Stories* programs.

5718 ***(The) Captivators Orchestra.*** Instr. mus. prg. (WABC-CBS, New York, NY, 1936).

5719 **Caputo, Dominick.** French horn soloist (NBC, 1928).

5720 **Caputo, Edward.** DJ (*Top Twenty Club*, WNHC, New Haven, CT, 1954–1955).

5721 **Caracel [Caracl], Rennie.** Singer (WCAU, Philadelphia, PA, 1925).

5722 **Caraker, George.** Newscaster (KOLN, Lincoln, NE, 1947).

5723 **Caramella, Bobby.** COM-HE (WWBZ, Vineland, NJ, 1957).

5724 ***Caravan.*** Walter O'Keefe was the host and Ted Husing the announcer on this popular music program. Annette Henshaw sang with the Glen Gray Casa Loma Orchestra on the twice weekly (Tuesday and Thursday) CBS program in 1934–1935. A later summer series by the same name featured novelist-playwright Rupert Hughes as host and two famous bands—Benny Goodman's and Nat Shilkret's (30 min., Tuesday, 7:30–8:00 P.M. CST, CBS, 1936).

5725 **Caray, Harry.** Sportscaster (WCLS, Joliet, IL, 1940; *Sports Extra*, WKZP, Kalamazoo, MI, 1941–1942; KXOK, St. Louis, MO, 1946; *Harry Caray Sports Review*, KXOK, 1947; *Sports Extra*, KXOK, 1948; WIL, St. Louis, MO, 1949–1952; KMOX, St. Louis, MO, 1955–1956).

5726 **Carazo, Castro.** Conductor (Strand Theater Concert Orchestra, WSMB, New Orleans, LA, 1926).

5727 **Carbauh, Earl.** Baritone (WEAF, New York, NY, 1924).

5728 **Carbauh, Robert.** Xylophonist (WEAF, New York, NY, 1924).

5729 **Carbonnell, Celeste.** Soprano (WGBS, New York, NY, 1927).

5730 ***Carborundum Band.*** The sponsor of the 55-piece band was the Carborundum Abrasives Company. The evening program was broadcast weekly from Niagra Falls, New York (WABC-CBS, New York, 1929). From 1937 to 1939 the band was directed by Edward D'Anna (instr. mus. prg.,WABC-CBS, New York, NY, 1937–1939).

5731 **Card, Clellan.** Newscaster (KSTP, St. Paul, MN, 1945). DJ (*Card's Midnight Show*, WCCO, Minneapolis, MN, 1947).

5732 **Card, Dexter "Dex."** DJ (*Wax Works*, WGAN, Portland, ME, 1955–1957).

5733 **Card, (Mrs.) G.W.** Pianist (WSM, Nashville, TN, 1928).

5734 **Card, (Mrs.) Harper.** Whistler (WSM, Nashville, TN, 1928).

5735 **Card, Kathryn.** Actress Card was a cast member of the daytime serial programs *Girl Alone, Helpmate* and *The Woman in White*.

5736 **Card, Norman R.** DJ (*Music for Lonely Folks*, WCOU, Lewiston, ME, 1948–1951; *WLAM Bandstand*, WLAM, Lewiston, ME, 1949).

5737 **Carde, Leo.** Baritone (KOL, Seattle, WA, 1929).

5738 **Carden, Frances (Fran).** Actress Carden appeared on the daytime serials *Big Sister* and *The Man I Married*.

5739 **Carden, John.** DJ (*Owl Club*, WROK, Rockford, IL, 1954–1957).

5740 **Cardiasco, Jimmy and Frank Maloney.** Banjo duet team (WAAM, Newark, NJ, 1923).

5741 **Cardinals [University of Louisville] Orchestra.** University radio orchestra (WHAS, Louisville, KY, 1926).

5742 ***(The) Cardoba Sisters.*** Vocal music prg. (MBS, 1935).

5743 **Cardwell, Leigh.** Newscaster (KLRA, Little Rock, AR, 1945).

5744 **Care, Norman.** Leader (*Norman Care Orchestra*, instr. mus. prg., WIND, Gary, IL, 1935).

5745 ***(The) Career of Alice Blair.*** Standard Oil Company sponsored this transcribed daytime serial that told the trials and tribulations of Alice Blair, a small town girl who journeyed to the big city to seek career opportunities. Innocently, she became involved in a scandal with a prominent man. When she returned to her home town, she received a cool reception from her old friends, who considered her guilty of what the vicious gossips said about her. Despite the scandal, Tom Harrington asked to marry her. The program dramatized Alice's problems and how she coped with them. The cast members included: Bill Adams, George Baxter, Helaine Freeman, Betty Moran, Martha Scott and Lawson Zerbe. The announcer was Alan Kent (15 min., Monday through Friday, 9:30–9:45 A.M., WOR, Newark, NJ, 1939).

5746 ***Carefree Carnival.*** Ned Tollinger was MC of the entertaining variety show that featured tenor Tommy Harris, comedian Cliff Nazarro, contralto Nola Day, comedienne Helen Troy, Perry the Playwright, Charles Mars and his Boys, Nuts and Bolts and the Meredith Willson Orchestra (30 min., Saturday, 9:30–10:00 P.M., NBC, 1935). The following year the show's format changed to present Tim and Irene Noblette (Tim and Irene), Ben Klassen, Helen Troy, singer GoGo Delys and Charlie Marshall's Mavericks (30 min., Saturday, 9:00–9:30 P.M. PST, NBC, 1936). In an earlier 1933 version, Gene Arnold, Nuts and Bolts and Vera Vague (Barbara Jo Allen) appeared.

5747 ***Careful Children's Club.*** Safety Sam, Reddy Eddie and Handy Andy were the safety mentors featured on the show for young listeners (KMOX, St. Louis, MO, 1928).

5748 **Carel, Connie.** COM-HE (KROP, Brawley, CA, 1956).

5749 ***Careless Love.*** Sketches of African-American life in the South were presented in the dramatic series. The cast included Georgia Burke, Monty Hurley, Carlton Moss, Eva Taylor and Edna Thomas. Carlton Moss was the writer. The Southernaires supplied the beautiful vocal music (15 min., Saturday, 9:00–9;30 P.M., NBC-Red, 1931).

5750 **Caren, Pete.** Harmonica soloist (WBZ, Springfield, MA, 1926).

5751 **Carew [Carewe] , Helen [Helene].** Actress Carew appeared on the *Barry Cameron* and *Stella Dallas* daytime serial programs.

5752 **Carey, Edith.** Cello (WCBD, Zion, IL, 1925).

5753 **Carey, Macdonald.** Television and motion picture star Carey had a successful career acting on the *Ellen Randolph, Family Theater, First Nighter, John's Other Wife, Just Plain Bill, Stella Dallas, Woman in White* and *Young Hickory* programs.

5754 **Carey, Marion.** Reader (WGY, Schenectady, NY, 1925).

5755 **Carey, William.** Newscaster (*Herald Reporter*, WQAM, Miami, FL, 1948).

5756 **Carfagne String Quartet.** Popular instrumental group (KPLA, Los Angeles, CA, 1927).

5757 **Cargen, Marion.** Singer (WGBS, New York, NY, 1927).

5758 **Cargill, E. K.** Announcer (WMAZ, Macon, GA, 1925).

5759 **Cargill, John.** Newscaster (WHB, Kansas City, MO, 1941).

5760 **Cargill, S.H.** Marimba soloist (WCCO, Minneapolis–St. Paul, MN, 1928).

5761 **Carhart, Ruth.** Contralto (Vcl. mus. prg., 15 min., CBS, 1934). Singer Carhart's program began with this announcement: "Once again the lyric strains of "Stars in My Eyes" introduces the voice of Ruth Carhart, Columbia's charming melody hostess in another of her morning recitals of the songs you like to hear. The first number is a tuneful refrain from the current Broadway revue *Pins and Needles*. It's 'Sunday in the Park.'"

5762 **Cariker, Ken.** Sportscaster (KDUB, Lubbock, TX, 1953).

5763 **Carioti, Freddy.** Leader (*Freddy Carioti Orchestra*, instr. mus. prg., WGBI, Scranton, PA, 1938–1939).

5764 **Carl, Leonard.** Sportscaster (*Sports Parade*, KMA, Shenandoah, IA, 1951).

5765 **Carl, Walter R.** Newscaster (KINY, Juneau, AK, 1941; KPRK, Livingston, MT, 1946).

5766 ***Carl and Hardy.*** Popular CW musical team (CW music prg., WJJD, Chicago, IL, 1936).

5767 ***Carl Haden's Hillbillies.*** CW music program with the Haden group (WIBW, Topeka, KS, 1936).

5768 **Carlay, Colette.** Singer (*Colette Carlay*, vcl. mus. prg., NBC-Blue, New York, NY, 1934).

5769 **Carlberg, Loren.** Newscaster (KWBG, Hutchinson, KS, 1939).

5770 **Carley, Jack.** Newscaster (WMC, Memphis, TN, 1938).

5771 **Carley, Marian [Marion].** Pianist (*Marian Carley* instr. mus. prg., CBS, 1934–1936; WGBI, Roanoke, VA, 1938).

5772 **Carlin, Frances.** Sportscaster (WHP, Harrisburg, PA, 1936).

5773 **Carlin, Herb.** Leader (*Herb Carlin Orchestra*, instr. mus. prg., NBC-Blue, 1936).

5774 **Carlin, Phillips "Phil."** Famous pioneer announcer (WEAF, New York, NY), Carlin was the first announcer on the *A&P Gypsies* program that began in 1923. He was a New York City native, who had demonstrated his gift for oratory by winning honors in elocution, first, at Public School 65 and, later, in debating contests at DeWitt Clinton High School. Later, at New York University, Carlin won several prizes in oratory. He was called "The Voice with a Smile at the National Broadcasting Company."

5775 **Carlino, William.** Banjoist (NBC, 1928).

5776 **Carlisle, Alexandra.** Actress Carlisle spoke on "Voice Production, Diction and English Literature" (WMAQ, Chicago, IL, 1924).

5777 **Carlisle, Charles.** Tenor (*Charles Carlisle*, vcl. mus. prg; CBS, 1934).

5778 **Carlisle, Cookie.** Singer (WNYC, New York, NY, 1936).

5779 **Carlisle, Margaret.** Singer (*Margaret Carlisle*, vcl. mus. prg., WLW, Cincinnati, OH, 1934).

5780 **Carlisle, Una Mae.** Singer (*Una Mae Carlisle*, vcl. mus. prg., WIP, Philadelphia, PA, 1936).

5781 **Carlisle and London.** Dual piano team (*Carlisle and London,* instr. mus. prg., NBC, 1934; CBS, 1935; NBC, 1937–1938).

5782 **Carlo, Michael.** Newscaster (*Behind the News*, WKAL, Rome, NY, 1946–1947).

5783 **Carlon, Fran.** Busy actress Carlon appeared on the *Girl Alone*; *Joan and Kermit*; *Joyce Jordan, Girl Interne*; *Kitty Keene* aka *Kitty Keene, Incorporated* (title role), *Lone Journey*; *Lora Lawton*; *Ma Perkins*; *Mary Marlin* aka *The Story of Mary Marlin*; *Our Gal Sunday*; *Today's Children*; and the *Woman of America* daytime serial programs.

5784 **Carlon, Linda.** Actress Linda Carlon appeared on the daytime serial programs *Life of Mary Southern* (title role), *Mary Marlin* aka *The Story of Mary Marlin* (title role) and *Valiant Lady.*

5785 **Carlon-Reid, Linda.** Talented radio actress Carlon-Reid was featured on the daytime serials *Evelyn Winters* aka *The Strange Romance of Evelyn Winters* and *The O'Neills.*

5786 **Carlsen [Carlson], Bill.** Leader (*Bill Carlsen Orchestra,* instr. mus. prg. *(* MBS, 1939–1940).

5787 **Carlsen, Norma.** Soprano (KJBS, San Francisco, CA, 1926).

5788 **Carlson, Ade.** Sportscaster (*Your Sports Round-Up*, WEBC, Duluth, MN, 1947).

5789 **Carlson, (Mrs.) Aino.** COM-HE (WEAT, West Palm Beach, FL, 1954).

5790 **Carlson, Betty.** COM-HE (WBCB, Levittown, PA, 1958–1960).

5791 **Carlson, Beverly.** COM-HE (KVFD, Fort Dodge, IA, 1951).

5792 **Carlson, Carl.** Violinist (WJAR, Providence, RI, 1925).

5793 **Carlson, Charlotte.** COM-HE (WRRR, Rockford, IL, 1957).

5794 **Carlson, Edward A.** Newscaster (*Editors View the News*, WGAN, Portland, ME, 1947–1948).

5795 **Carlson, Ernest.** Actor Carlson appeared on the *Brent House* daytime serial program.

5796 **Carlson, (Mrs.) Henning.** Pianist (KOMO, Seattle, WA, 1927).

5797 **Carlson, Hugo.** Newscaster (KECA, Los Angeles, CA, 1944–1946).

5798 **Carlson, Jean.** Soprano (WOK, Chicago, IL, 1925).

5799 **Carlson, Jim.** Newscaster (KFXD, Nampa, ID, 1939).

5800 **Carlson, Joel F.** Newscaster (WGH, Newport News, VA, 1945–1947).

5801 **Carlson, Linda.** Actress Carlson, who was born January 22, 1900, appeared on the *Eveready Hour* in 1928 (NBC).

5802 **Carlson, Mary Alice.** COM-HE (KGBX, Springfield, MA, 1955).

5803 **Carlson, Merle.** Leader (*Merle Carlson Orchestra*, instr. mus. prg., CBS, 1935).

5804 **Carlson, Mildred.** COM-HE (WBZ, Boston, MA, 1954–1956). After graduating from the University of Connecticut, Carlson took a graduate dietician's course at Hartford (CT) Hospital. She then went to New York to become the kitchen manager of Alice Foote MacDougall's tearoom. After a year in New York City, she went to Boston in 1930 to teach at Alice Bradley's School of Cookery. In the summer of 1930 she tried out at WBZ (Boston, MA) as a substitute to conduct Westinghouse's *The Home Forum* program. Westinghouse had the program on their three stations in Boston, MA, Seattle, WA, and Pittsburgh, PA. The woman who conducted the Boston program was going to New York to start the program there. After Carlson tried out for ten days she was hired. She stayed on the job for 26 years, ending in 1956. Her radio show was on for 30-minutes in the morning.

From 1949 to 1956, she conducted the *At Home with Mildred Carlson* television show for the Salada Tea Company. In addition to her daily radio and television shows, she also became Food Editor of the Boston *Post* and Contributing Editor of the *New England Home Magazine.*

5805 **Carlson, Neva.** Mezzo-soprano (WMBB, Chicago, IL, 1926).

5806 **Carlson, Norah B.** COM-HE (WLYC, Williamsport, PA, 1956–1957).

5807 **Carlson, Ted G., Jr.** Newscaster (KWH, Albany, OR, 1944). Sportscaster (KRUL, Corvallis, OR, 1950; KCOV, Corvallis, OR, 1955).

5808 **Carlson, Virginia.** COM-HE (KERG, Eugene, OR, 1951).

5809 **Carlson, W. Richard.** Newscaster (WELI, New Haven, CT, 1941; WAVZ, New Haven, CT, 1947).

5810 **Carlson, Will.** Newscaster (*Carlson News*, WTOD, Toledo, OH, 1947). DJ (*Yours For the Asking*, WTOD, 1947).

5811 **Carlton, H.A. and Mrs. H.A. Carlton.** Folk singing team (WFHH, New York, NY, 1927).

5812 **Carlton, Henry Fisk.** Writer Carlton wrote the following programs: *Vivian the Coca Cola Girl*, (NBC, 1927); *Soconyland Sketches*, (NBC-Red, 1928); *The General Motors Hour*, (NBC-Red, 1928); *Gus and Looie*, (NBC-Red, 1929); and *Mr. and Mrs. (*CBS, 1929). During radio's first decade the team of Henry Fisk Carlton and William Ford Manley were considered to be the deans of radio writing. On one of their most successful collaborations, they took several O. Henry stories and successfully adapted them for radio. Together they wrote and produced *Soconyland Sketches,* the popular *Biblical Drama* series and the *Mr. and Mrs.* program.

5813 **Carlton, Hollis.** Newscaster (WCOV, Montgomery, AL, 1945).

5814 Carlton, Peter. Newscaster (WRCS, Ahoskie, NC, 1948).

5815 Carlton, Robert. Newscaster (WMRO, Aurora, IL, 1940).

5816 Carlton and Shaw. Dual piano team (*Carlton and Shaw*, istr. mus., prg.; CBS, 1935).

5817 *Carlton Fredericks.* Nutritionist Fredericks talked on health and nutrition (WMGM, New York, NY, 1956). *See* **Fredericks, Carlton.**

5818 Carlyle, Bob. Newscaster (WHP, Harrisburg, PA, 1942).

5819 Carlyle, Cathryn. Newscaster (KTUL, Tulsa, OK, 1939–1941).

5820 Carlyle, Hugh. Sportscaster (WRVA, Richmond, VA, 1946; *Sports Album*, KSWI, Council Bluffs, IA, 1947; *Sports Roundup*, WHAP, Hopewell, VA, 1949).

5821 *(The) Carlyle Sisters.* Female singing team (vcl. mus. prg., KUOA, Siloam Springs, AR, 1939).

5822 Carlyn, Tommy. Leader (*Tommy Carlyn Orchestra* instr. mus. prg., WLAV, Grand Rapids, MI, 1942).

5823 Carman, Lois. Violinist (KMIC, Inglewood, CA, 1928).

5824 Carman, William. Announcer and baritone soloist (WBAL, Baltimore, MD, 1928).

5825 Carmean, Ormah. Announcer (KMA, Shenandoah, IA, 1926–1928).

5826 Carmella, Larry. DJ (*Midnight Merry Go Round*, KMO, Tacoma, WA, 1949).

5827 Carmichael, Edith Marie. Soprano-pianist (KFWM, Oakland, CA, 1927).

5828 Carmichael, H. Newscaster (*On File,* KUIN, Grants Pass, OR, 1947). Sportscaster (KUIN, 1947).

5829 Carmichael, Lee. Sportscaster (*Jax Beer Sports Review*, KRMD, Shreveport, LA, 1940).

5830 Carmichael, Les. Newscaster (WJZM, Clarksville, TN, 1941). Sportscaster (WJZM, 1941; *Sports Time*, KWDM, Des Moines, IA, 1948).

5831 Carmichael, Margaret. Pianist (WOAW, Omaha, NE, 1924).

5832 Carmona, Al. Newscaster (KVEC, San Luis Obispo, CA, 1942). Sportscaster (KVEC, 1942).

5833 Carnas-Barker Orchestra. Local musical group (WMC, Memphis, TN, 1926).

5834 *Carnation Contented Hour* (aka *The Contented Hour*). The Carnation Milk Company, producers of condensed milk that they boasted came from contented cows, sponsored the popular musical program. On the air from 1931, the show presented such performers as soprano Josephine Antoine, baritone Buddy Clark, singers Dinah Shore and Jo Stafford and bass Reinhold Schmidt. The announcers were Vincent Pelletier and Jimmy Wallington. C.H. Cottington and Harry K. Gilman were the producers. During the 1930s, Opal Craven, Kathryn Harris and Isabel Zehr appeared as the Lullaby Lady. On the show's last version before going off the air, Tony Martin, Jo Stafford, the Ken Lane Singers and Victor Young's Orchestra were the featured performers. Jimmy Wallington was the announcer (30 min., Sunday, 10:00–10:30 P.M., CBS, 1950).

5835 Carne, Bert. Newscaster (KGFJ, Los Angeles, CA, 1945).

5836 Carneal, Herb. Sportscaster (WSYR, Syracuse, NY, 1945–1947; WHYN, Holyoke, MA, 1950; WSPR, Springfield, MA, 1952; KYW, Philadelphia, PA, 1953–1955; WRCV, Philadelphia, PA, 1956).

5837 Carnegie, Dale. Commentator (*How to Win Friends and Influence People*, NBC, 1938). Best selling author Carnegie gained national prominence with his advice on improving personal relationships, personality development and achieving business success.

5838 Carnegie, Tom. Sportscaster (WIRE, Indianapolis, IN, 1949–1952; WFBM, Indianapolis, IN, 1953–1956).

5839 *Carnegie Hall.* An interesting blend of classical and folk music was presented on the program sponsored by the American Oil Company. Various distinguished guest performers appeared with an orchestra conducted by Frank Black. Gene Hamilton was the announcer (30 min., Sunday, 7:30–8:00 P.M., ABC, 1948).

5840 Carnegie Tech Glee Club. Collegiate singing group (KDKA, Pittsburgh, PA, 1924).

5841 Carnes Richards Hotel Portage Orchestra. Hotel dance orchestra (WADC, Akron, OH, 1926).

5842 Carney, Al. Organist (WHT, Chicago, IL, 1925–1928).

5843 Carney, Art. Actor and comedian gained fame for his motion picture and television work, but previously he had enjoyed a successful career acting on such radio programs as *Casebook of Gregory Hood, Dimension X, Gangbusters, Henry Morgan Show, Joe and Ethel Turp, Land of the Lost, Lorenzo Jones* and *The March of Time.*

5844 Carney, Don (Howard Rice). Although famous for his "Uncle Don" role, his real name was Howard Rice. Before starting his radio career, he had enjoyed a successful vaudeville career playing the piano while standing on his head as "Don Carney, the Trick Pianist." Carney gained fame by conducting his popular children's radio program each weekday evening as "Uncle Don." When he began his *Uncle Don* program in September, 1928, he was initiating a format that would last for 21 years; (30 min., Monday through Friday, 6:00–6:30 P.M., WOR, Newark, NJ, 1928).

Carney began his radio career as an announcer at WMCA, New York, NY, in 1928 before moving to WOR. He appeared on the *Book House Story Man* comedy show on WOR in 1930. In addition, he played the role of Luke Higgins on the *Main Street Sketches* show. For a relatively short time in 1933, Carney conducted a program about animals known as the *The Don Carney Show,* sponsored by Spratt's Dog Food, Fish Food and Bird Seed. It was first broadcast on CBS, then WOR (Newark, NJ) and, finally, the NBC-Blue Network. On the program Uncle Don talked about the friendship between dogs and man and then told a story about some animal, usually a dog (15 min., Monday, 8:30–8:45 P.M., NBC-Blue Network, 1933). Carney has been followed by a story, perhaps apocryphal, that supposedly occurred after he had concluded one of his children's programs. The story goes that, unknowingly, he said into an open microphone, "That will hold the little bastards" and it was broadcast. *See* **Rice, Howard** *and* ***Uncle Don.***

5845 Carney, Jack. DJ (WIL, St. Louis, MO, 1957–1958). Carney was a popular rock-and-roll DJ in the St. Louis area during the late 1950s.

5846 Carney, Joe. Leader (Joe Carney Cowboy Band, KTCL, Seattle, WA, 1926).

5847 Carney, Kenneth. Hawaiian guitarist (WCAU, Philadelphia, PA, 1925).

5848 Carney, Pat. COM-HE (WLBH, Mattoon, IL, 1957).

5849 *Carnival.* "Barkers" gave the program a carnival atmosphere. Many guest stars appeared with Professor Schonberg's Concert Orchestra (60 min., Saturday, 8:00–9:00 P.M., NBC-Pacific Coast Network, 1929).

5850 *Carnival.* Contralto Gale Page and tenor Clark Dennis sang with the Roy Shields Orchestra on the music program (30 min., Weekly, NBC, 1935).

5851 Carol, Anita. Singer (*Anita Carol*, vcl. mus. prg., KNX, Los Angeles, CA, 1942).

5852 Carol, Ann. COM-HE (WWTV, Cadillac, MI, 1955).

5853 Carol [Caroll], Elaine. COM-HE (WKBN, Youngstown, OH, 1954).

5854 Carola, Herma. Soprano (*Herma Carola*, vcl. mus. prg., WNYC, New York, NY, 1939).

5855 Caroli Singers. Female vocal trio of Mary Gretchen Walsh, soprano; Ruth Sammet, mezzo-soprano; and Louise Ryder, contralto (WLW, Cincinnati, OH, 1926).

5856 *Carolina Calling.* Grady Cole hosted the long-running sustaining CW music and comedy program that originated from Charlotte, North Carolina. Harry Blair, the Briarhoppers, Claude Casey, the Johnson Family, Fred Kirby, the Swanee River Boys, Howard Turner and the comic team of Whitey Grant and Arval Hogan were featured performers (30 min., Saturday, 9:30–10:00 A.M., CBS, 1946). The program began as *Carolina Hayride* aka *WBT Carolina Hayride* in 1945. When the show first went on the CBS network as *Carolina Calling* it featured: the Johnson Family, Grady Cole, Arthur "Guitar Boogie" Smith and His Crackerjacks, Claude Casey, the Briarhoppers, Fred Kirby, Fiddlin' Hank Warren, Big Bill Davis, Whitey and Hogan and Mr. Crutchfield, the station manager. The Johnson Family, incidentally, made their first broadcast on WBT (Charlotte, NC, 1940) in 1940, billed as "Radio's Sweetest Singing Family." Arthur "Guitar Boogie" Smith got his nickname from his famous instrumental composition.

5857 *Carolina Hayride* aka *WBT Carolina Hayride.* *See* ***Carolina Calling.***

5858 *(The) Carolina Hillbillies.* CW music program (WBIG, Greensboro, NC, 1936).

5859 *Carolina Trio.* CW mus, prg. (WDZ, Tuscola, IL, 1937).

5860 "Carolina's Lyric Tenor." *See* **Cornwall, Arthur.**

5861 (The) Carolinians. Charles M. Koch directed the orchestra (WOR, Newark, NJ, 1926).

5862 Carolinians Orchestra. James J. Sheeran directed the dance band (WEAF, New York, NY, 1924).

5863 Carota, Fred. Newscaster (*Local Happenings*, WWSC, Glens Falls, NY, 1947–1948).

5864 Carothers, Isobel. Carothers was one of the original cast members of the *Clara, Lu and EM* daytime serial.

5865 Carpenter, Boyden ("The Hillbilly Kid"). CW singer-guitarist Carpenter was the well-travelled country performer, the Hillbilly Kid. He sang on numerous stations during the 1930s and 1940s (WHAS, Louisville, KY; WKRC, Cincinnati, OH; WFBM, Indianapolis, IN; WJJD, Chicago, IL; WIOD, Miami, FL; WDBO, Orlando, FL; WJAX, Jacksonville, FL; WMBR, Jacksonville, FL; WFBC, Greenville, NC; WGST, Atlanta, GA; WSB, Charlotte, NC; WPTF, Raleigh, NC; and WMFR, High Point, NC).

5866 Carpenter, C.R. Soprano (KLDS, Independence, MO, 1925).

5867 Carpenter, Cliff. Actor Carpenter appeared on the *Amazing Mr. Smith*, *County Seat*, *Just Plain Bill*, *Prairie Folks*, *Terry and the Pirates* and *We the Abbotts* programs.

5868 Carpenter, Irma Louise. Soprano (KDKA, Pittsburgh, PA, 1924).

5869 Carpenter, James. Announcer (WKBF, Indianapolis, IN, 1925).

5870 Carpenter, James D. "Jim." DJ (WKBB, Dubuque, IA, 1940). Sportscaster (WKBB, 1941–1945; WKBB, 1949–1952).

5871 Carpenter, Jane. Pianist (*Jane Carpenter*, instr. mus. prg., WGN, Chicago, IL, 1934).

5872 Carpenter, John "Johnny." Sportscaster (*Speaking of Sports*, KALE, Portland, OR, 1940; *Speaking of Sports*, KOIN, Portland, OR, 1948–1953; *Sports Desk*, KOIN, 1960).

5873 Carpenter, Louise. Violinist (WMBH, Joplin, MO, 1937).

5874 Carpenter, Pat. COM-HE (WHFB, Benton Harbor, MI, 1955; WBCK, Battle Creek, MI, 1957).

5875 Carpenter, Peg. COM-HE (KAYE, Puyallup, WA, 1956).

5876 Carpenter, Ruth. COM-HE (WCEF, Parkersburg, WV, 1957).

5877 Carpenter, Skip. DJ (*Fundial*, WDNC, Durham, NC, 1960).

5878 Carpenter, Wiley. DJ (*Teenage Jury*, WWIT, Canton, NC, 1955).

5879 Carper, Hallie. COM-HE (KXLW, St. Louis, MO, 1955).

5880 Carpet City Male Quartet. Male vocal group (WGY, Schenectady, NY, 1925).

5881 Carr, Bessie Ruth. Pianist (WSM, Nashville, TN, 1928).

5882 Carr, Betty. COM-HE (WBBZ, Ponca City, OK, 1956–1957).

5883 Carr, D.C. Announcer (WTAR, Norfolk, VA, 1925).

5884 Carr, Dave. Sportscaster (*Sports Spotlight*, WMAN, Mansfield, OH, 1960).

5885 Carr, Elizabeth "Betty." Pianist (WSM, Nashville, TN, 1928).

5886 Carr, Gene. Newscaster (WHBQ, Memphis, TN, 1941). DJ (*Breakfast Club*, WDOD, Chattanooga, TN, 1948–1951).

5887 Carr, George. Sportscaster (WFEB, Sylacauga, AL, 1953).

5888 Carr, Jan. COM-HE (WWL, New Orleans, LA, 1960).

5889 Carr, Jerry. Newscaster (WLIB, Brooklyn, NY, 1946).

5890 Carr, Jimmy. Leader (Jimmy Carr and his Frolic Cafe Frolickers Band; WMCA, New York, NY, 1927 and Jimmy Carr's Hollywood Orchestra, WMCA, 1929; *Jimmy Carr Orchestra*, instr. mus. prg., NBC and CBS, 1935). The radio and recording band included the following musicians in the 1920s: Jimmy Carr, ldr.-v.; Tony Vilanova and Don Moore, t.; Maurice Wiley, tb.; Don McIntyre, clr. and as.; Charles McIntyre, clr. and ts.; Manny Prager, as.; Sam Brown, p.; Al Sheff, bj.; Jimmy Cirina, d.; Morton Clavner, tba.; and Jerry Macy and Joe O'Callahan, v.

5891 Carr, Katherine. Newscaster (KNX, Los Angeles, CA, 1943). Carr was the first woman newscaster at station KNX in 1943. She eventually had her own 15-minute news program on that station.

5892 Carr, Larry. Sportscaster (WNCT, Greenville, NC, 1953).

5893 Carr, Lorraine. COM-HE (KTRC, Santa Fe, NM, 1960).

5894 Carr, Mary. Soprano (WJZ, New York, NY, 1925).

5895 Carr, Paula. COM-HE (WIRE, Indianapolis, IN, 1951; WMOA, Marietta, OH, 1954).

5896 Carr, Roy. Newscaster (WLOL, Minneapolis, MN, 1946).

5897 Carr, Thomas. Newscaster (WGAA, Cedartown, GA, 1945). Sportscaster (WGAA, 1945).

5898 Carr, Wesley "Wes." Newscaster (KTNM, Tucumcari, NM, 1945).

5899 Carrabba, P.J. Clarinetist (KOMO, Seattle, WA, 1927).

5900 Carraway, Howard. Sportscaster (KFJZ, Fort Worth, TX, 1938). Newscaster (KFRO, Longview, TX, 1941).

5901 Carregan, E.F. "Radio mimic" (WCAU, Philadelphia, PA, 1926).

5902 Carreras, Maria. Pianist (WGY, Schenectady, NY, 1925).

5903 Carrier, M.E. Announcer (KTBI, Los Angeles, CA, 1927).

5904 Carrillo, Leo. After years of newspaper work, Carrillo became a radio character actor who presented a series of sketches and humorous stories in Italian dialect (WOR, Newark, NJ, 1925). Carrillo appeared on the *General Motors Family* program in 1927. He later became a successful motion picture actor, usually specializing in comic roles.

5905 Carrington, Elaine. Writer of daytime serials Carrington earned one of the largest salaries in radio in 1939. She came to radio from a successful background of writing for the stage, magazines and motion pictures. Her first popular daytime serial was *Red Davis*. After four years the program became *Pepper Young's Family*. Very prolific, Carrington said she wrote stories about everyday things that listeners could identify with easily.

5906 Carrington, Elizabeth. Soprano (*Elizabeth Carrington* vcl. mus. prg., WCAO, Baltimore, MD, 1936).

5907 Carrington, George. Announcer (WSV, Little Rock, AR, 1922).

5908 Carrington, John. Newscaster (WORD, Spartanburg, SC, 1945).

5909 Carroll, Adam. Pianist-composer Carroll accompanied the *Gold Dust Twins* (WEAF, New York, NY, 1925–1926), played on the *Ampico Hour* (WEAF, 1927) and the *Majestic Hour;* (CBS, 1929).

5910 Carroll, Bob. Leader (*Bob Carroll Orchestra*, instr. mus. prg., WRVA, Richmond, VA, 1936).

5911 Carroll, Brooke. DJ (*The Brooke Carroll Show*, KGVL, Greenville, TX, 1947). Sportscaster (KGVL, 1947).

5912 Carroll, Carroll. Prolific writer Carroll worked on the *Bob Crosby Show*, *Chase and Sanborn Hour*, *The Circle*, *Club Fifteen*, *Double or Nothing*, *Edgar Bergen and Charlie McCarthy Show*, *Frank Sinatra Show*, *Melody Ranch*, *Joe Penner Show*, *Kraft Music Hall*, *Lux Radio Theater*, *Robert Burns Panatella Show (Burns and Allen)*, *Rudy Vallee Show* and *Shell Chateau.*

5913 Carroll, Charles. Actor Carroll appeared on the *Margot of Castlewood*, *The O'Neills* and *Valiant Lady* daytime serial programs.

5914 Carroll, Claire. Singer (*Claire Carroll*, vcl. mus. prg., WMCA, New York, NY, 1936).

5915 Carroll, Cleora M. COM-HE (WWBG, Hornell, NY, 1957).

5916 Carroll, Dick. Leader (*Dick Carroll Orchestra*, instr. mus. prg., WRVA, Richmond, VA, 1936–1937).

5917 Carroll, Floyd. Newscaster (WEIM, Fitchburg, MA, 1941).

5918 Carroll, Frances. Vocalist (*Frances Carroll*, vcl. mus. prg.; NBC-Red, 1934).

5919 Carroll, Gail. COM-HE (WTWB, Auburndale, FL, 1960).

5920 Carroll, Gene. *See* **Gene and Glenn** *and* ***Jake's Juke Box.***

5921 Carroll, George. Leader (George Carroll and his Merrymakers Orchestra; KXA, Seattle, WA, 1928–1929). The band broadcast from Seattle's Claremont Hotel.

5922 Carroll, George C. Newscaster (WEEU, Reading, PA, 1945–1946). Sportscaster (WEEU, 1945; *Sports Final*, WEEU, 1955).

5923 Carroll, Gloria. Singer (*Gloria Carroll*, vcl. mus. prg., WHDH, Boston, MA, 1941).

5924 Carroll, Harry. Sportscaster (*Sports Round Up*, WLTC, Gastonia, NC, 1948–1951). DJ (*Carolina in the Morning*, WANS, Anderson, SC, 1949).

5925 Carroll, Helen. COM-HE (WILO, Frankfort, IN, 1956).

5926 Carroll, Howard A. Tenor (WOC, Davenport, IA, 1926).

5927 Carroll, Irene. Soprano (KGO, Oakland, CA, 1925).

5928 Carroll, Jeanne. Singer (*Jeanne Carroll*, vcl. mus. prg., WMCA, New York, NY, 1932).

5929 Carroll, Jim. Newscaster (KWYO, Sheridan, WY, 1938–1942). Sportscaster (KWYO, 1942–1949).

5930 Carroll, Jimmy. Singer (*Jimmy Carroll*, vcl. mus. prg., 15 min, 6:15–6:30 P.M., CBS, 1945.

5931 Carroll, Jimmy. Newscaster (WSTP, Salisbury, NC, 1945).

5932 Carroll, Jo. A children's story teller (WNYC, New York, NY, 1932).

5933 Carroll, Jo. COM-HE (WBCM, Bay City, MI, 1951).

5934 Carroll, Joan. COM-HE (*Joan Carroll's Shopping Service*, WSPR, Springfield, MA, 1939).

5935 Carroll, Joan. COM-HE (WBIS, Bristol, CT, 1955).

5936 Carroll, John. Baritone (WMCA, New York, NY, 1925).

5937 Carroll, Leslie. COM-HE (WSSB, Durham, NC, 1951).

5938 Carroll, Lynn. COM-HE (WCAO, Baltimore, MD, 1954).

5939 Carroll, Marion. COM-HE (WICS, Springfield, IL, 1956–1957).

5940 Carroll, Martha. Violinist (WSM, Nashville, TN, 1928).

5941 Carroll, Mary. COM-HE (KCRA, Sacramento, CA, 1951).

5942 Carroll, Mildred. Pianist-soprano on the Marylin Trio (KNX, Los Angeles, CA, 1929).

5943 Carroll, Mildred. COM-HE (WILM, Wilmington, DE, 1951).

5944 Carroll, Parke. Sportscaster (WHB, Kansas City, MO, 1937–1938).

5945 Carroll, Ray. Newscaster (WHOP, Hopkinsville, KY, 1941).

5946 Carroll, Ray. Sportscaster (WWRL, Woodside, NY, 1946). DJ (*After Hours*, WHOM, New York, NY, 1947–1952; WMCA, New York, NY, 1954).

5947 Carroll, Robert C. "Bob." Chief announcer (WRHI, Rock Hill, SC. 1944).

5948 Carroll, Roger. DJ (*Roger's Corral*, KGER, Long Beach, CA, 1948–1951).

5949 Carroll, Tim. Sportscaster (*Sports Page of the Air*, KELP, El Paso, TX, 1947).

5950 Carroll, Winifred. Soprano (WRNY, New York, NY, 1928).

5951 Carroll's Palais Royal Dance Orchestra. Club dance orchestra (WTIC, Hartford, CT, 1926).

5952 Carron, Jeldo. Accordionist (KOA, Denver, CO, 1926).

5953 Carruth, William W. Pianist (KGO, Oakland, CA, 1925).

5954 Carruth (Mr. and Mrs.) William W. Piano duet team (KGO, Oakland, CA, 1924).

5955 Carsen, Bill. Leader (*Bill Carsen Orchestra*, instr. mus. prg.; MBS, 1942).

5956 Carson, Fiddlin' John. Carson, a violinist and pioneer country music artist, was the winner of several Old Time Fiddlers Championships in the 1920s. He recorded his famous rendition of "The Old Hen Cackled and the Rooster Crowed" for Okeh records in 1923. His first radio appearances began in 1922 (WSB, Atlanta, GA, 1922–1925).

5957 Carson, Fiddlin' John and Uncle Am Stewart. Country-western instrumental team (WSB, Atlanta, GA, 1925). *See* **Carson, Fiddlin' John.**

5958 Carson (Carlson), Hugh. Singer (*Hugh Carlson*, vcl. mus. prg.; WGN, Chicago, IL, 1942).

5959 Carson, John "Johnny." DJ (*The John Carson Show*, WOW, Omaha, NE, 1948). Johnny Carson graduated from his DJ job on radio to great prominence with his classic *Tonight Show* on TV. Carson's television work makes him well deserving of the recognition accorded him as a broadcasting genius.

Johnny Carson was born in Norfolk, Nebraska. It was his Midwestern All-American *persona* that helped him achieve stardom on television's *Tonight Show*. Carson consistently communicated a warm, genial friendliness to which his audience readily responded. His pleasant manner and comic skills enabled him to appeal to the broadest possible public. In addition, it was Carson's interviewing skills that made him seem sincerely interested in all his guests on *The Tonight Show*.

He acknowledged the influences of Jack Benny, particulary the great radio comedian's masterful sense of timing that was evident in Carson's performances. Another influence was Fred Allen's Mighty Allen Art Players adopted as Carson's Mighty Art Players. Carson's own early show business interests and experience also contributed to his eventual television stardom. He began doing magic tricks for money as "The Great Carsoni," while still a teenager. During his service in the Navy, he added skills as a ventriloquist. His brief radio career at WOW (Omaha, NE) was his first step toward a great broadcasting career.

After hosting several network television programs, Carson was selected by NBC to become the permanent host of *The Tonight Show*, replacing a series of interim hosts who had filled in when Jack Paar left the show. On *The Tonight Show*, Carson clearly demonstrated his understanding of comedy and television. His vast audience certainly appreciated his many talents and pleasant manner. For example, Carson's last *Tonight* show reached an estimated audience of 50 million, the largest ever attracted by a late night program

5960 Carson, Kit. DJ (*Late Dancing Party*, WFEB, Sylacauga, AL, 1954; *Number Please*, WFEB, 1955).

5961 Carson, Lillian. COM-HE (WPIT, Pittsburgh, PA, 1951).

5962 Carson, Martha (Irene Ethel Amburgey). CW gospel singer Carson was born in the coal mining country of Kentucky. She sang with her sisters, Bertha and Opal as the Sunshine Sisters (WLAP, Lexington, KY, 1938). The sisters later joined the WSB *Atlanta Barn Dance* (WSB, Atlanta, GA, 1938) as the Hoot Owl Holler Girls. After marrying James Roberts, Martha sang with him on the *Barn Dance* as the "Barn Dance Sweethearts,"before moving on to sing on WNOX (Nashville, TN, 1940s).

After divorcing Roberts in the early 1950s, she recorded as a soloist and appeared on the WNOX *Mid-Day Merry-Go-Round* (WNOX, Knoxville, TN, 1950s). She then began to feature country-western gospel at eastern clubs and on the television programs of Arthur Godfrey, Steve Allen and Tennessee Ernie Ford.

5963 Carson, Pam. COM-HE (WKY, Oklahoma City, OK, 1954).

5964 Carson, Paul. San Francisco radio organist Carson was known as "The Musing Organist Builder of the Bridge to Dreamland" (1929).

5965 Carson, Rusty. DJ (KBYE, Oklahoma City, OK, 1955).

5966 Carson, William S. Tenor (WCAE, Pittsburgh, PA, 1925).

5967 Carson Brothers Saxophone Quartet. Insr. music group (KDKA, Pittsburgh, PA, 1923).

5968 *Carson Robison's Buckaroos.* Robison was the leader of a busy CW music group that did much to popularize CW music on radio. His theme usually was "Home Sweet Home on the Range." His programs and sponsors in the 1930s were many: (*Carson Robison's Buckaroos* (CW mus. prg. sponsored by Asper Gum, 15 min., Monday, 8:00–8:15 P.M., CBS, 1935; *Carson Robison's Buckaroos*, CW mus. prg. sponsored by Servel by transcription, WLS, Cincinnati, OH, 1936; *Carson Robison and his Buckaroos,*a transcribed CW program sponsored by Crazy Water Crystals (laxative), 15 min., Monday, Tuesday, Thursday and Friday, Transcribed, Various Stations and Times, 1936; *Carson Robinson and His Buckaroos*, sponsored by Musterole Ointment, presented a popular band of CW musicians and singers that included Bill Pearl, John Mitchell, Dick Sawyer and Dick van Hallburg. *Variety* praised the program as an outstanding country-western music group, 30 min., Monday, 8:00–8:30 P.M., NBC-Red, 1938–1939).

5969 *Carson Robison's Pioneers.* Carson Robison hosted the early CW music program with his group of singers and musicians that included Bill Mitchell, Pearl Pickens (Mrs. Bill Mitchell) and John Mitchell. Robison earlier had teamed with Vernon Dahlhart, the famous recording artist, before leading his own group (NBC-Blue, 1932).

5970 *Carson Robison's Triple Bar X Program.* Carson Robison combined CW music with comedy sketches on the entertaining show. Millie June played most of the program's female roles (1933).

5971 Carswell, Tom. DJ (*Matinee in Rhythm*, WCOA, Pensacola, FL, 1947; *Studio Party*, WORZ, Orlando, FL, 1950). Sportscaster (WORZ, 1948).

5972 Cart, Anita. COM-HE (KEUN, Eunice, LA, 1958).

5973 Cartasso, Dena. Soprano (KGO, Oakland, CA, 1924).

5974 Carter, Albert. Tenor (WGBS, New York, NY, 1927).

5975 Carter, Boake. News analyst (WABC, New York, NY, 1933; CBS 1934–1939; WMCA, New York, NY, 1939; WOR, Newark, NJ and MBS, 1940–1942, 1945). Conservative analyst Carter made his radio debut in 1930, when a rugby football game was scheduled at the Philadelphia Navy Yard and no member of the WCAU (Philadelphia, PA) staff knew the game. Englishman Carter, who knew rugby, was the ideal choice of the station to handle the match. He then became a regular member of the WCAU news staff. The kidnaping of the Lindbergh baby in 1932 provided him with an opportunity to make his network debut (15 min., Monday through Friday, 7:45–8:00 P.M.,CBS, 1932).

Born in Baku, Russia, where his father was in the British Consular Service, Carter eventually worked as a free lance correspondent for the London *Daily Mail.* After joining CBS as a newscaster, he was no stranger to controversy. He soon began to attack FDR's policies and earn the enmity of big labor. CBS removed him from the air August 26, 1938. He returned to broadcast for Mutual intermittently from 1939 until his death in 1944.

5976 Carter, Callis "Cal." DJ (*Musical Clock*, KAMD, Camden, AR, 1947–1952). Sportscaster (KAMD, 1947–1950; *Sports Roundup*, KAMD, 1952–1953).

5977 Carter, Cecile. COM-HE (KALB, Alexandria, LA, 1954).

5978 Carter, Charles. Singer (*Charles Carter*, vcl. mus. prg., WJAS, Pittsburgh, PA, 1935).

5979 Carter, Charlotte. COM-HE (KSEL, Lubbock, TX, 1951; KFYO, Lubbock, TX, 1958).

5980 Carter, Florence. COM-HE (WJBF, Augusta, GA, 1956).

5981 Carter, Francis "Fran." COM-HE (WAZL, Hazleton, PA, 1956–1957).

5982 Carter, Freda. COM-HE (KAMD, Camden, AR, 1954).

5983 Carter, Hattie. Pianist (WGY, Schenectady, NY, 1925).

5984 Carter, Joan. COM-HE (KTSM, El Paso, TX, 1957).

5985 Carter, John E. Tenor (WSM, Nashville, TN, 1928).

5986 Carter, John T. Announcer Carter proudly identified his station as the "Wonderland Dynamo of Dixie" (WDOD, Chattanooga, TN, 1927).

5987 Carter, Katherine. COM-HE (WLOU, Louisville, KY, 1954).

5988 Carter, LeRoy. DJ (*Carter's Clambake*, KCTX, Childress, TX, 1947–1954). Sportscaster (KCTX, 1950).

5989 Carter, (Miss) Mary. Miss Mary broadcast children's bedtime stories (WFAA, Dallas, TX, 1925).

5990 Carter, Myles. Leader (*Myles Carroll Orchestra,* instr. mus. prg. (KMOX, St. Louis, MO, 1937).

5991 Carter, Robert "Bob." Sportscaster (WMCA, New York, NY, 1937–1940). Newscaster (WNEW, New York, NY, 1938; WMCA, 1940).

5992 Carter, Sheelah. Newscaster (MBS, Cleveland, OH, 1942; KFEL, Denver, CO, 1944; WTCN, Minneapolis, MN, 1948).

5993 Carter, Tony. DJ (*Wake Up East Alabama*, WAUD, Auburn, AL, 1949; WBHB, Fitzgerald, GA, 1955).

5994 Carter, Val. DJ (*Joy a la Carter*, WJOY, Burlington, VT, 1948–1949; *You Asked For It*, WJOY, 1950–1951; *Joy a la Carter*, WJOY, 1952).

5995 Carter, William. Leader (*William Carter Orchestra*, instr. mus. prg., KUOA, Siloam Springs, AR, 1934, 1939).

5996 *(The) Carter Family.* The famous CW mus. group's program probably was broadcast by transcription (WBT, Charlotte, NC, 1939). *See* **Border Radio**.

5997 Carthage College Glee Club. Collegiate vocal group (KSD, St. Louis, MO, 1926).

5998 Carthay, Smiling Billie. Leader (Smiling Billie and his California Syncopators [orchestra], WGAR. Fort Smith, AR, 1922). The band played at the Joyland Dance Pavilon and enjoyed an enthusiastic response from their listeners when they broadcast a noon program of songs they were "plugging" for publishers.

5999 Carthy, William. Newscaster (WCAM, Camden, NJ, 1939).

6000 Carton, Crete. Soprano (WGBS, New York, NY, 1925).

6001 *Carton of Pleasure.* Raleigh Cigarettes sponsored this program of music and comedy starring comedian Henny Youngman, singer Carol Bruce and the Eddy Howard Orchestra (30 min., Weekly, NBC-Red, 1945).

6002 Cartright, Stephen D. Blind-deaf news commentator (*Stephen D. Cartright*, KFOR, Lincoln, NE), 1937).

6003 Cartwright, Christine. COM-HE (WCCM, Lawrence, MA, 1951–1954).

6004 Caruso, Enrico. Great Italian operatic tenor Caruso made radio history when Dr. Lee De Forest's broadcast featured him singing the role of Turiddu in *Cavalleria Rusticana* from the New York Metropolitan Opera's stage on January 12, 1910.

6005 Caruso, Guiseppe. Operatic tenor (WMAQ, Chicago, IL, 1926).

6006 Caruso, Harriet. Singer Caruso was known as the "Oriole of the Air" (KFAB, Lincoln, NE, 1926).

6007 Caruso, J.A.N. Leader (J.A.N. Caruso Orchestra featured on *The White Rock Concert* program, WOR, Newark, NJ, 1928).

6008 Caruso, James. Director (James Caruso and his Concert Ensemble, WOR, Newark, NJ, 1924).

6009 Carver, Hugo. Tenor (KTAB, Oakland, CA, 1928).

6010 Carver, Cynthia May. *See* **Cousin Emmy**.

6011 Carver, Louise. COM-HE (WKZO, Kalamazoo, MI, 1956).

6012 Carver, Phyllis. Carver conducted a children's show with husband Burrill Smith.

6013 Carver, Wally. DJ (*Plastic and Shellac*, WGPA, Bethlehem, PA, 1948).

6014 Cary, Sally. COM-HE (WSNO, Barre, VT, 1960).

6015 *(The) Casa del Rio Orchestra.* Spanish music group (instr. mus. prg., WIND, Gary, IN, 1935).

6016 *(The) Casa Loma Orchestra.* Instr. mus. prg. featuring the swinging band led by Glen Gray; (WCBD, Waukegan, IL, 1935). The Casa Loma crew appeared on many stations by transcription.

6017 Casanova, Eve. COM-HE (*Fashions*, WMCA, New York, NY, 1937).

6018 *Casanova.* Violinist (Instr. mus. prg., WCPO, Cincinnati, OH, 1936).

6019 Cascio, Carmelo. Pianist (*Carmelo Cascio,* instr. mus. prg., WGY, Schenectady, NY, 1934).

6020 Cascioli, Ann. COM-HE (WIKB, Iron River, MI, 1956).

6021 Case, Ack. Sportscaster (WWNY, Watertown, NY, 1941).

6022 Case, Anna. A popular recording artist, Miss Case made her debut on WJZ (New York, NY) in 1921.

6023 Case, Doris. COM-HE (KARM, Fresno, CA, 1958).

6024 Case, Florence. Singer (WOR, Newark, NJ, 1932).

6025 Case, George and Marilu. DJ team (WSAI, Cincinnati, OH, 1957).

6026 Case, (Reverend) George H. The Reverend Case preached on religious service programs (WLW, Cincinnati, OH, 1925–1926).

6027 Case, George T. Newscaster (WRAL, Raleigh, NC, 1939; WTMV, East St. Louis, MO, 1940; *World in Review*, WINK, Ft. Myers, FL, 1947). Sportscaster (WTMV, 1940).

6028 Case, Jane. Soprano (WDAP, Chicago, IL, 1924).

6029 Case, Ken. Sportscaster (*Sports Folio*, KTBS, Shreveport, LA, 1948–1955).

6030 Case, Lee. DJ (*Alarm Clock Club*, WCHA, Chambersburg, PA, 1947; *Your Grocer*, WITH,

6031 Baltimore, MD, 1949; WCBM, Baltimore, MD, late–50s). Sportscaster (WCHA, 1947).

6032 Case, Nelson. Announcer, singer and pianist Case was born February 3, 1910. He began his radio career as a pianist at KFON (Long Beach, CA, 1925). The following year he formed his own orchestra and appeared with it on KFON. Case became announcer and singer for KGER (Long Beach, CA) in 1927. He enjoyed a distinguished announcing career for the next several decades, working on such programs as *Against the Storm*, *Charlie and Jessie*, *Ford Theater*, *Lone Journey* and *Mary Marlin.*

6033 Case, (Mrs.) Robert. Pianist (WBZ, Springfield, MA, 1924).

6034 Case, Sarah. Pianist (WJZ, New York, NY, 1923).

6035 Caseboom, Adeline. COM-HE (WFEA, Manchester, NH, 1951).

6036 *(The) Casebook of Gregory Hood.* Petri Wine sponsored this dramatic adventure program, a summer replacement for *Sherlock Holmes.* Gregory Hood was a gentlemen detective, who infuriated the police because he solved their crimes. The tough, debonair Hood was first played by Gale Gordon in the 1946 version. The format featured actor-announcer Harry Bartell visiting Mr. Hood each week to hear him tell of his latest adventure. Written by Dennis Green and Anthony Boucher, the show was produced by Ned Tollinger (30 min., Monday, 8:30–9:00 P.M., MBS, 1946). When the show was broadcast later by ABC as a sustaining feature, its format was changed. Known as *The Casebook of Jeffrey Hood*, the leading character, played by Jackson Beck, not only changed his name, but also became a San Francisco importer by day and criminologist by night. *Variety* praised the latter version as an interesting mystery series (30 min., Saturday, 8:30–9:00 P.M., ABC, 1950). Anthony Boucher, Dennis Green and Ray Buffum were the writers and Frank Cooper the producer. Martin Andrews, Lee Bolen and Ray Buffum were the directors and Art Sorrance produced the sound effects.

6037 Casel, Maude Reese. COM-HE (WCOH, Yonkers, NY, 1932).

6038 Casey, Cass. DJ (*Angelus*, WWOL, Buffalo, NY, 1949).

6039 Casey, Claude. CW singer-band leader Casey was born September 13, 1912. His western swing band—Claude Casey and the Pine State Playboys—played on WFTC (Kinston, NC, 1938). He worked on WBT (Charlotte, NC, 1941–1953) appeared on such programs as *Briarhopper Time*, *Carolina Hayride* and *Dixie Jamboree*.

6040 Casey, Daniel W. Newscaster (WICY, Malone, NY, 1946).

6041 Casey, Eddie. Sportscaster (WAAB, Boston, MA and WNAC, Boston, MA, 1937).

6042 Casey, J.C. Casey conducted his "morning gym exercise" program on KNX (Los Angeles, CA, 1925).

6043 Casey, Jim. DJ (*Tower of Smiles*, WRMT, Rocky Mount, NC, 1960).

6044 Casey, Kenneth. Singer (WNYC, New York, NY, 1925).

6045 Casey, Mary. Director of the *Women's Hour* program (KYW, Chicago, IL, 1926).

6046 Casey, Mary. DJ (*For the Ladies*, WJPG, Green Bay. WI, 1950).

6047 Casey, Wynne. COM-HE (WJOY, Burlington, VT, 1956–1957).

6048 *Casey at the Mike.* Casey, not otherwise identified, but supposedly a famous Harvard football coach talked about that sport each week (15 min., WNAC, Boston, MA, 1937).

6049 *Casey Crime Photographer* (aka *Flashgun Casey* and *Crime Photographer*). Casey, a photographer, who often played detective, and his girl friend, Annie Williams, were kept busy each week catching criminals on the popular crime show. Staats Cotsworth and Alice Reinheart originated these roles. Casey and Annie, when not pursuing criminals seemed to spend the balance of their time at the Blue Note Cafe talking with Ethelbert the bartender, played by John Gibson. Other members of the cast included: Jone Allison, Jackson Beck, Art Carney, Robert Dryden, Betty Furness, John Griggs, Jack Hartley, Bernard Lenrow, Jan Miner, Byrna Raeburn and Leslie Woods. The announcers on the program were Bob Hite, Bill Cullen and Tony Marvin. The writers were Alonzo Deen Cole, Gail Ingram, Harry Ingram and Milton J. Kramer and John Dietz was the director. Sound effects were by Jerry McCarthy and Art Strand. Music was supplied by Archie Bleyer's Orchestra. The talented pianists who played at the Blue Note Cafe during the program's long run were Herman Chittison and Teddy Wilson (CBS, 1943–1955).

6050 Cash, Al. Sportscaster (WCPM, Cumberland, KY, 1953).

6051 Cash, Benny. Leader (*Benny Cash Orchestra*, instr. mus. prg., WCAE, Pittsburgh, PA, 1935).

6052 Cash, Cyril G. Tenor (WGCP, New York, NY and WHN, New York, NY, 1925).

6053 Cashman, Edmund. Announcer (WNAC, Boston, MA, 1925).

6054 Casino, Del. Vocalist (*Del Casino*, vcl. mus. prg., CBS, 1934, 1937).

6055 Casley (Dr.) John F. Dr. Casley broadcast inspirational talks (KMOX, St. Louis, MO, 1928).

6056 Casmus, Al. Yodeler (WLW, Cincinnati, OH, 1927).

6057 Cason, Barbara. COM-HE (WMPS, Memphis, TN, 1954).

6058 Cason, Bob. Pianist (WSM, Nashville, TN, 1928).

6059 Cason, Marion. COM-HE (WAIR, Winston-Salem, NC, 1957).

6060 Casper, Cy. Sportscaster (KMOX, St. Louis, MO, 1938; KXOK, St. Louis, MO, 1940; WKY, Oklahoma City, OK, 1946 KTOK, Oklahoma City, OK, 1949).

6061 Casper, Tee. Sportscaster (KGKO-WBAP, Fort Worth, TX, 1941; WGKO-WBAP, 1946; KCUL, Fort Worth, TX, 1951–1953).

6062 Casriel, Gertrude. Pianist (WEAF, New York, NY, 1925).

6063 Cass, Betty. COM-HE (WIBA, Madison, WI, 1956–1957).

6064 *(The) Cass Daley Show* (aka *The Cass Daley Bandwagon* or *The Fitch Bandwagon*). Singer-comedienne Daley starred on the situation comedy that was originally sponsored by Fitch Shampoo from 1945 to 1947. The program returned to the air in 1950 on a sustaining basis. Most of the show's humor arose from the attempts by Daley to help others, but her efforts usually backfired. Other cast members were Fred Howard, Lurene Tuttle and Willard Waterman. Music was supplied by Robert Armbruster's orchestra. The announcer was Arch Presby (30 min., Thursday, 9:00–9:30 P.M., NBC, 1950).

6065 Cassell, Pete. Blind CW singer Cassell first appeared on WDOD (Chatanooga, TN, 1937), before going to Atlanta to broadcast on WAGA (Atlanta, GA) and WSB (Atlanta, GA). He appeared on the WSB *Barn Dance* on the latter station. In the 1940s, Cassell sang on WWVA (Wheeling, WV, 1940s) before going on to work for Connie B. Gay on WARL (Arlington, VA) In between times, he worked on radio stations in Georgia, Wisconsin, Pennsylvania and Missouri.

6066 Cassell, Walter. Baritone (*Walter Cassell*, vcl. mus. prg., NBC, 1935–1936).

6067 Cassella, Alfredo. Italian pianist (NBC, 1929).

6068 Casselle, Jeanne. Prima donna soprano (WMSG, 1926).

6069 Casselman, Chet. DJ (*Time Out for Music*, KERN, Bakersfield, CA, 1950).

6070 Casseux, Millie. Soprano (WGR, Buffalo, NY, 1925).

6071 Cassidy, John. Cassidy sang the songs of Scotland and Ireland (WJZ, New York, NY, 1925).

6072 Cassidy, John. Singer (WHY, Martinsville, IL, 1925).

6073 Cassidy, Ted. DJ (*Adventures in Good Music*, WCOA, Pensacola, FL, 1959). DJ Cassidy later became famous for his role of Lurch on television's *Addams Family* show.

6074 Cassidy, Viola. Pianist (WFAA, Dallas, TX, 1926).

6075 Cassin, Marigold. Actress-monologist Cassin was born February 7, 1903. She began her radio career as a member of an amateur theatrical group on WOC, Davenport, IA in 1926. She remained with that station as secretary, hostess, announcer, continuity writer and performer from 1926 to 1931.

6076 Cassinelli, Delores. Lyric soprano (WJZ, New York, NY, 1928–1929).

6077 Cassinelli, Elizabeth. Miss Cassinelli specialized in old-fashioned songs on her *Never to be Forgotten Songs by Elizabeth Cassinelli* program (KGHI, Little Rock, AR, 1927).

6078 Castagna, Bruna. Contralto (CBS, 1936).

6079 Castebury, Joanne M. COM-HE (WMPT, Williamsport, PA, 1958).

6080 Castleberry, Roy. DJ (*Coffee Time*, KFTV, Paris, TX, 1960).

6081 Castee, Ellamae. COM-HE (WKBN, Youngstown, OH, 1958).

6082 Castello, Carmen. Soprano (KFWB, Hollywood, CA, 1928).

6083 Casteneda, Les. Sportscaster (KNGS, Hanford, CA, 1953).

6084 Castile, Lynn. COM-HE (WMFS, Chattanooga, TN, 1955).

6085 Castillian Orchestra. Mexican string band (WFAA, Dallas, TX, 1926–1928).

6086 Castillo, Louis J. DJ (*Record Review*, KSLO, Opelousas, LA, 1952).

6087 Castillo, Oscar. Sportscaster (KGFI, Brownsville, TX, 1938).

6088 Castle, Bert. Leader (*Bert Castle Orchestra*, instr. mus. prg., KFEL, Denver, CO, 1934–1939).

6089 Castle, Clyde. Sportscaster (WFIE, Evansville, IN, 1953).

6090 Castle, Lee. Leader (*Lee Castle Orchestra*, instr. mus. prg., WBBM, Chicago, IL, 1942).

6091 Castlen, Betty. Accordionist (*Betty Castlen*, inst. mus. prg., WSM, Nashville, TN, 1934).

6092 Castner, Huntley. Pianist (KFRC, San Francisco, CA, 1926).

6093 Castognola, Babe and Louis De-Valle. Dual accordion team (KLX, Oakland, CA, 1930).

6094 Caston, Dorothy. COM-HE (WHEC, Rochester, NY, 1957–1958).

6095 "Castor Oil Clarence." Harmonica soloist Clarence was mentioned by *Variety* as a "harmonica artist in country music" (KFDM, Beaumont, TX, 1925).

6096 Castrodale, Dave. DJ (WDBQ, Dubuque, IA, 1956–1958)

6097 Caswell, Herbert. Tenor (KTAB, Oakland, CA, 1925).

6098 Caswell Coffee Company Quartet. Commercially sponsored instrumental group consisting of violinist Mischa Gluschkin; cellist H. Wallace; cellist George von Hagel and pianist E. Suennen (KPO, San Francisco, CA, 1925).

6099 Caswell Coffee Company Radio Eight Symphony Orchestra. Studio band directed by cellist George von Hagel (KPO, San Francisco, CA, 1925).

6100 Caswell Coffee Company Vocal Quartet. Singing group sponsored by the Caswell Coffee Company that consisted of Hugh Williams, 1st tenor; Robert Saxe, 2nd tenor; Clarence Oliver, 1st bass; and Henry L. Perry, 2nd bass, KPO (San Francisco, CA, 1925).

6101 Catalina, Francesca. Soprano (WJY, Hoboken, NJ, 1924;WGBS, New York, NY, 1927).

6102 *Catch Me If You Can.* Bill Cullen conducted a sustaining quiz program that challenged phone-in contestants. George Bryan was the announcer (30 min., Sunday, 9:00–9:30 P.M., CBS, 1948).

6103 Cater, Jean. COM-HE (WAAX, Gadsden, AL, 1960).

6104 Cates, Jim. Sportscaster (KWEI, Kennewick, WA, 1950).

6105 Cates, Mary Kathryn. Cellist (WLW, Cincinnati, OH, 1924).

6106 *(The) Catfish String Band from Polecat Creek.* The Catfish String Band was a great Oklahoma radio favorite on the CW program (KOME, Tulsa, OK, 1939).

6107 Cathay Tea Garden Dance Orchestra. Popular Philadelphia band (WCAU, Philadelphia, PA, 1926).

6108 Cathcart, Bob. DJ (*Cheerful Earful*, WOKO, Albany, NY, 1960).

6109 *(The) Cathedral Hour.* A sacred music program, *The Cathedral Hour* featured tenor Willard Amison (60 min., Sunday, 4:00–5:00 P.M., WMAL, Washington, DC, 1930).

6110 *(The) Cathedral Hour.* The religious program broadcast Sunday afternoons (90 min., Sunday, 1:00–2:30 p.m, NBC). Typically, the program contained a sermon by Dr. S. Parkes Cadman, a question-and-answer session conducted by Dr. Cadman and musical selections presented under the direction of George Dilworth. Milton J. Cross was the announcer. Later, on the NBC-Red network the program was broadcast at 4:00–5:30 P.M. (NBC, 1930s and 1940s).

6111 Cathers, Chet. Baritone (KFI, Los Angeles, CA, 1928–1929).

6112 Cathey, Jim. Sportscaster (*Fisherman's Corner*, WJBO, Baton Rouge, LA, 1955).

6113 *(The) Catholic Hour.* When this sustaining religious program began, its purpose was to present "priests of noted scholarship and eloquence." The Paulist Choir led by Father Finn provided music of composers such as Bach, Pastrina and Frescobaldi. Father Fulton J. Sheen deservedly gained a national reputation from his masterful preaching on the *Catholic Hour* (60 min., Sunday, 6:00–7:00 P.M., NBC-Red, 1930). Rev. William S. Kirby preached on the program in 1935 (30 min., Sunday, 5:00–5:30 P.M., NBC, 1935). The program ran continuously until 1956.

6114 Cathryn and Caroline. Known as "The Ukulele Girls," Cathryn and Caroline were great local favorites (KVOO, Tulsa, OK, 1928).

6115 Catizone, Billy. Leader (*Billy Catizone Orchestra,* instr. mus. prg., WCAE, Pittsburgh, PA, 1942).

6116 Catlett, Betty. COM-HE (WKOA, Hopkinsville, KY, 1957–1958).

6117 Cato, Evelyn. DJ (*Guest Dee-Jay*, WMFS, Chattanooga, TN, 1952; WMFS, 1955). COM-HE (WMFS, 1956).

6118 Caton, Earl, Jr. DJ (*Waiting for Caton*, WKDK, Newberry, NC, 1950).

6119 Caton, Louis. Tenor (WEAF, New York, NY, 1925; WAHG, Richmond Hill, NY, 1926).

6120 Catricia, (Mrs.) Norma V. Soprano (WGY, Schenectady, NY, 1923).

6121 *Cats 'n' Jammers.* Vocal and instrumental mus. prg. (MBS, 1939)

6122 Cattell, Margaret. COM-HE (WEIR, Weirton, WV, 1958–1960). .

6123 Catteruci, Angelo. Accordionist (WBZ, Springfield, MA, 1926).

6124 Cattle Farm Orchestra. Instr. mus. prg. (WKRC, Cincinnati, OH, 1933).

6125 Caudill, Carl R., Jr., DJ (WGTL, Kannapolis, NC, 1947; *Caudill's Carnival*, WFTC, Kinston, NC, 1949; WWNF, Fayetteville, NC, 1950; *Caudill's Coffee Club*, WFTC, 1952; *Coffee Shoppe*, WGNI, Wilmington, NC, 1954). Sportscaster (WFTC, 1949–1952).

6126 Cauffman, Dick. Sportscaster (WTEL, Philadelphia, PA, 1941).

6127 Cauglin, Patricia. "Radio's shopping consultant" (KOIL, Council Bluffs, IA, 1928).

6128 Caulk, Worthy. COM-HE (COM-HE, WAGE, Leesburg, VA, 1958).

6129 Caulkins, Lynn. COM-HE (KHJ, Los Angeles, CA, 1955).

6130 Causer, Bob. Leader (*Bob Causer Orchestra,* instr. mus. prg., WHAM, Rochester, NY, 1942).

6131 Causey, Grace Parker. Reader (KVOO, Tulsa, OK, 1928).

6132 Causier, John. DJ (*Matinee*, ABC, 1960).

6133 Cauthen [Cathen], John. Newscaster (WIS, Columbia, SC, 1938–1940).

6134 Cavagnero, Marie. Soprano (WFBH, New York, NY, 1925).

6135 *Cavalcade.* Hugo Mariani and the Mediterraneans Orchestra were featured on the instrumental music program (60 min., Saturday, NBC-Pacific Coast Network, 1929).

6136 *(The) Cavalcade of America.* DuPont Company sponsored these distinguished dramatizations of important American historical figures and events. The program began October 9, 1935 and ran on radio for 18 years. It ended on March 31, 1953, after 781 broadcasts on CBS and NBC. The company-famous slogan, "Better living through chemistry," was proudly announced frequently.

The *Cavalcade of America* was conceived as a series of historical dramas of epic proportion and quality. The broadcasts were supposed to be accurate to the smallest detail. In the beginning at least, war and political subjects were taboo. Instead, the program sought to deal with persons or institutions that had made substantial contributions to American progress.

One of the early dramatic episodes, "The Seeing Eye" by Ruth Knight, was introduced in this way: "This evening the DuPont Calvacade brings you the story of the Seeing Eye, a school in Morristown, New Jersey, where German shepherd dogs are educated as guides for the blind, bringing new opportunities, independence and faith in life to those who walk in darkness. Our scene is Highland Hospital. In a room on the second floor, Donald Dean, college freshman, is recovering from the effects of an automobile accident. His mother meets the doctor outside the door." The drama then began.

Over the years the program featured such performers as: Bill Adams, Ray Collins, Staats Cotsworth, Joseph Cotten, Ted De Corsia, Edwin Jerome, Ted Jewett, Raymond Edward Johnston, Bill Johnstone, John McIntire, Agnes Moorehead, Jeanette Nolan, Frank Readick, Everett Sloane, Jack Smart, Paul Stewart, Luis Van Rooten and Orson Welles. The announcers were Clayton "Bud" Collyer and Gabriel Heatter. Roger Pryor was the producer. Homer Fickett, Paul Stewart, Bill Sweets, John Zoller were the program's directors. Stuart Hawkins, Russ Hughes, Ben Kagan, Peter Lyon, Arthur Miller, Paul Peters, Virginia Radcliffe, Norman Rosten, Edith Sommer, Robert Tallman and Milton Wayne were the writers. Dr. Frank Monaghan was the program's historical consultant and Rosa Rio the organist.

6137 *(The) Cavalcade of Music.* Host John Connelly played recordings on this program of American popular songs from 1620 to 1950 in their historical and cultural setting. The program was based on the *Variety's Musical Calvacade* book (30 min., Monday through Saturday, 9:00–9:30 P.M., WMGM, New York, NY, 1953).

6138 *(The) Cavalcade of 1950.* This was one of an annual series of programs sponsored by the United Press. Editors of United Press selected the year's biggest news stories and discussed them on the transcribed program. Earl J. Johnson, Vice-President and General News Editor of the United Press, was the narrator. The major stories presented were: the Brinks' armored car robbery; the Alger Hiss conviction for perjury; Florence Chadwick setting a new women's record for swimming the English Channel and the North Koreans crossing the 38th parallel to start the Korean War (15 min., Transcribed, Many Stations, 1950).

6139 ***(The) Cavalcade Players.*** Horace Taylor recited poetry and prose selections (NBC-Red, 1927).

6140 ***(The) Cavaliers.*** Orchestral mus. prg. (WLW, Cincinnati, OH, 1933).

6141 **Cavall, Jean.** Singer (*Jean Cavall*, vcl. mus. prg., WXYZ, Detroit, MI, 1942).

6142 **Cavallo, Peter.** Leader (*Peter Cavallo Orchestra*, instr. mus. prg., KFEL, Denver, CO, 1939).

6143 **Cavanagh, Gloria B.** COM-HE (WJIM, Lansing, MI, 1957).

6144 **Cavanaugh, Eddie and Fannie.** The Cavanaughs, a husband and wife singing team known as "The Gaelic Twins," often appeared together. Wife Fanny played the piano (WOK, Chicago, IL, 1925 and KYW, Chicago, IL, 1926–1928).

6145 **Cavanaugh, Jo.** COM-HE (WGLV, Easton, PA, 1955).

6146 **Cavanaugh, Joseph.** Sportscaster (WJAC, Johnstown, PA, 1941; WARD, Johnstown, PA, 1947–1950). DJ (*Jr. Disc Jockeys*, WENE, Endicott, NY, 1948; *Hi Neighbor*, WARD, 1950–1951; *Joe Cavanaugh Show*, WARD, 1952–1960).

6147 **Cavanaugh, Marian Patricia.** Singer (KFI, Los Angeles, CA, 1928).

6148 **Cave, Walter H.** Sportscaster (KMJ, Fresno, CA, 1944–1946; *Sports Arena* and *Football Scoreboard*, KMJ, 1947).

6149 **Caverlee, (Dr.) Robert.** Sportscaster (WFVA, Fredericksburg, VA, 1944).

6150 **Cavin, Patty.** COM-HE (WRC, Washington, DC, 1957).

6151 **Cavitt, Don.** Newscaster (WIBA, Madison, WI, 1945; KFOR, Lincoln, NE, 1946). DJ (*Waxing Wise*, WHB, Appleton, WI, 1950).

6152 ***CBS Is There.*** The excellent program of historical recreations had the added element that they were "covered" by CBS news reporters as though the events were actually taking place at the time of broadcast. The first program in the series was broadcast July 7, 1947, when it "covered" the assassination of Lincoln at Ford's Theater (30 min, Monday, CBS, 1947). The following year the program's title was changed to *You Are There*. *See* ***You Are There.***

6153 ***CBS Presents Red Barber.*** Barber, one of radio's greatest sports broadcasters, reported sports news on his program. George Bryan was his announcer (15 min., Monday through Friday, 6:30–6:45 P.M., CBS, 1946) *See* **Barber, Walter "Red."**

6154 ***CBS Radio Roundup.*** Singer Dorothea James was featured on the music program (CBS, 1931).

6155 ***CBS Views the Press.*** Douglas Edwards replaced Don Hollenbeck on the program that many considered to be somewhat pretentious. How, many critics asked, could CBS attempt a critical review of other news gathering organizations? The program's attempt, at any rate, was short-lived 15 min., weekly, CBS, 1950).

6156 **Cecil, Chuck.** DJ (KFI, Los Angeles, CA, 1957; *Swinging Years*, KFI, 1960).

6157 **Cecil, Herman.** Sportscaster (KDNT, Denton, TX, 1940; KCMC, Texarkana, TX, 1942–1949). Newscaster (KCMC, 1942–1946).

6158 **Cecil, Mary.** Actress Cecil was fetured on such daytime serials as *John's Other Wife* and *The Life and Loves of Dr. Susan*.

6159 ***Cecil and Sally.*** Johnny Patrick and Helen Troy played the title roles in the comedy sketch (KPO, San Francisco, CA, 1930). The team later worked at KYA (San Francisco, CA, 1932). Earlier in 1929, the comedy team had appeared on a show called *The Funniest Things* broadcast on KLRA (Little Rock, AR). Patrick sang and wrote the scripts. Troy sang and played the organ and piano. They were a prolific recording team.

6160 **Cecka, Arnold.** Newscaster (WHO, Des Moines, IA, 1945).

6161 ***CeCo Couriers.*** The weekly musical variety show featured dialect comedian Henry Burbig, who played such characters as "Levy at the Bat," "De Willage Chastnut" and "Dangerous Jake the Jew" (30 min., Monday, 8:00–8:30 P.M., CBS, 1928–1929).

A typical interchange between Burbig and Norman Brokenshire, the program's announcer, was as follows: "Hello, Mr. Brokenwire. It's a werry werry nice evening, ain't it?" Brokenshire would respond: "Why it's Henry Burbig." Burbig would then recite one of his poems (*Radio Digest*, April, 1930, p. 25):

> Leetle Jakey Rosenbloom set in de leeving room
> Eating some motziss end herring.
> He stock in his fork end took out some prok
> End ate it end said: "Vot I'm careing!"

Burbig's also broadcast his own version of inside "heestory"(*Radio News*, June, 1930, p. 106):

> Vunce opon ah time ago ... dare lieved in de hold contree, de Pilgrimmees. Each day was dissatiefactioned from de vay de Kink was treating dam, so dey made ah union end wowed dot de Kink was loosing de pipple's monee on de shock market end dey couldn't bear no shorter.

In 1923, Burbig was the chief physical instructor at the Hotel McAlpin, the home of station WMCA. While there he met WMCA announcer Snedden Weir, who persuaded him to broadcast his comedy routines on local radio stations. Burbig's dialect humor appealed to many listeners.

6162 ***Cedar Valley Hillbillies.*** CW mus. prg. (WMT, Cedar Rapids–Waterloo, IA, 1936).

6163 **Cederberg, Cecil.** Newscaster (WWJ, Detroit, MI, 1946).

6164 **Cedrick, Sir.** DJ (*Sir Cedric*, KTRM, Beaumont, TX, 1950).

6165 **Cehanovsky, George.** Metropolitan Opera baritone Cehanovsky sang on the *Atwater Kent Hour* program (NBC, 1929).

6166 ***Celebrity Night.*** George Olsen, his orchestra and his wife, singer Ethel Shutta, hosted the weekly variety program. The hosts supplied good music and each week presented famous guests who were nationally known stars of radio, stage or screen (30 min., Saturday, 9:30–10:00 P.M., NBC-Red, 1936).

6167 ***Celebrity Table.*** Ray Heatherton interviewed various guests on the entertaining local talk show (45 min., Monday through Friday, 11:15–12:00 noon, local New York City radio, 1958).

6168 ***(The) Celebrity Train.*** DJ Marty Hogan conducted a popular Chicago program of recorded music (120 min., Monday through Saturday, 11:30–1:30 P.M. CST, WCFL, Chicago, IL, 1948).

6169 ***(The) Cellphane Program.*** Emily Post dispensed information on manners as part of the early variety program. Music was supplied by Edward Neil and the Harding Sisters (15 min., Various times, NBC-Blue, 1933).

6170 **Cencig, Lucy.** COM-HE (WGES, Chicago, IL, 1958).

6171 ***Central Church Service.*** Dr. Frederick F. Shannon conducted the radio church service (60 min., Sunday, 11:00–12:00 noon, WENR, Chicago, IL, 1930).

6172 ***Central Methodist Episcopal Church Services.*** These church service broadcasts originated from Detroit's Central Methodist Episcopal Church (WCX, Detroit, MI, 1922).

6173 **Central Park Casino Orchestra.** Dance music was played by Flo Richardson and her girls (WOR, Newark, NJ, 1925).

6174 ***(The) Central Park Casino Orchestra.*** Leo Reisman's orchestra provided the music on the program. The announcer was Edward Thorgerson (30 min., Wednesday, 11:30–12:00 midnight, NBC-Red, 1930). This may be the orchestra listed below.

6175 ***(The) Central Park Casino Orchestra.*** Instr. mus. prg. (WNAC, Boston, MA, 1932).

6176 **Central State Hospital Orchestra.** Institutional band (WHAS, Louisville, KY, 1926).

6177 **Century Orchestra.** WGR (Detroit, MI, 1925; WMAK, Buffalo, NY, 1928).

6178 **Ceppos, Mac.** Leader (*Mac Ceppos Orchestra*, instr. mus. prg., MBS, 1945).

6179 **Cepuran, Rose.** Pianist, organist and hostess (WOW, Omaha, NE, 1929). Cepuran began her study of the piano at the age of 12 with Clara Hoffman Morearty and continued later with Jean Duffield and Dorothy Cogswell.

6180 **Cerea, Madeline.** Pianist (WOR, Newark, NJ, 1925).

6181 **Cermak, Emil, Jr.** Flutist (WOAW, Omaha, NE, 1923).

6182 **Cerri, Bill.** Newscaster (WGAT, Utica, NY, 1947). DJ (WGAT, 1948).

6183 **Cervi, Samueline.** COM-HE (WCNT, Centralia, IL, 1956).

6184 **Cerwin, Connie.** Ballad singer (WSWS, Chicago, IL, 1926).

6185 **Cerwin, Herbert.** Critic Cerwin on

his broadcasts discussed a good "book diet" (KQW, San Jose, CA, 1928).

6186 Cesana, Renzo. DJ (*The Continental*, 60 min., Monday through Saturday, 11:00–12:00 noon, WMGM, New York, NY, 1953). Cesana, known as "The Continental," was a DJ who projected romance with such lines as, "Don't be afraid, darling. You're in a man's apartment."

6187 "CFK." Designation for announcer Corley F. Kirby (WWJ, Detroit, MI, 1924).

6188 Chace [Chase], Arthur R. Announcer (WDWM, Asbury Park, NJ, 1927).

6189 Chadbourne, Mortimer. Tenor (WJZ, New York, NY, 1928).

6190 Chadwin, Minerva Tose. Soprano (WIP, Philadelphia, PA, 1926).

6191 Chaffee, Darlene. COM-HE (KOSI, Aurora, CO, 1955).

6192 Chaffey, C.M. Announcer (WRAN, Reading, PA, 1925; Chaffey identified the following station as "The Schuylkill Valley Echo" WRAW, Reading, PA, 1926).

6193 Chaimovitz, Annette. Soprano (WRNY, New York, NY, 1926).

6194 Chalbeck, Jack. Actor Chalbeck appeared on the *Girl Alone* daytime serial program.

6195 Chalfant, Lucille. Coloratura soprano (WEAF, New York, NY, 1923).

6196 Chalfant Sisters. Harmony singers (WCAU, Philadelphia, PA, 1926).

6197 Chalk, Sonny. Sportscaster (WMOX, Meriden, MS, 1960).

6198 Chalk, Wesley. Sportscaster (WCOA, Pensacola, FL, 1938).

6199 *(The) Challenge of the Yukon.* George W. Trendle and Fran Striker, who previously had developed *The Lone Ranger* and *The Green Hornet,* created the story of Sergeant Preston of the Northwest Mounted Police and his adventures in the Yukon. The program made its debut on Detroit's WXYZ in a 15-minute format before being extended to 30 minutes. After some 260 episodes were broadcast on MBS and ABC, the series ended on June 9, 1955. The program opened with the announcer's dramatic: "Now as the howling winds echo across the snow covered reaches of the wild northwest, we present Sergeant Preston of the Yukon brought to you by the Quaker Oats Company, makers of Quaker Puffed Wheat and Quaker Puffed Rice, the delicious cereal shot from guns. It's Yukon King, the swiftest and strongest lead dog of the northwest, breaking the trail for Sergeant Preston of the Northwest Mounted Police in his relentless pursuit of law breakers." *A whip cracked.* Sergeant Preston was then heard calling, "On King! On you huskies." The cast included: Brace Beemer, Jay Michael, Paul Sutton and John Todd. The program was directed by Al Hodge. The announcers were Bob Hite and Fred Foy (ABC, 1947–1955).

6200 Challenger, Lilyan May. Mezzo-soprano (WOR, Newark, NJ, 1923; KFWB, Hollywood, CA, 1927).

6201 Chalmers, Eleanor. Miss Chalmers broadcast talks on style and fashion (WQJ, Chicago, IL, 1924).

6202 Chalmers, Jim. Newscaster (WEIM, Pittsburgh, PA, 1946). Sportscaster (*Speaking for Sports*, WEIM, 1951–1953).

6203 Chalmers, Thomas. Actor Thomas appeared on the *Pepper Young's Family* daytime serial program.

6204 (The) Chalmont Sisters. Singing team (WCAU, Philadelphia, PA, 1926).

6205 *(The) Chamber Music Society of Lower Basin Street.* The entertaining music program offered good jazz served with a generous dose of tongue in cheek humor. In 1943, the program took the place of *The Gibson Family.* Milton Cross and Gene Hamilton were most often the announcers. Many fine jazz musicians and singers appeared as guests on the show. Regulars at various times were Dinah Shore and Lena Horne and the bands of Henry "Hot Lips" Levine and Paul "Woodwindy" LaValle (30 min., Weekly, ABC, NBC, 1940–1952). The program went on and off the air many times. Most often the program was broadcast on a sustaining basis or as a public service program with appropriate announcements.

6206 Chamberlain, Carl. Sportscaster (WARC, Rochester, NY, 1950–1952).

6207 Chamberlain, Gus. Sportscaster (WDEF, Chattanooga, TN, 1950–1952; WAPO; Chattanooga, TN, 1955–1956).

6208 Chamberlain, Howard. Newscaster (*World Front,* WLW, Cincinnati, OH, 1946–1948). Chamberlain began his career as a singer at station WHOG (Huntington, IN) in 1926.

6209 Chamberlin, Francis S. Announcer (WMC, Memphis, TN, 1926–1927). Sportscaster (WMPS, Memphis, TN, 1938–1940).

6210 Chambers, Dudley. Tenor Chambers organized, sang with and arranged songs for the Rounders singing group (NBC-Pacific Coast Network, 1928).

6211 Chambers, Garde. Newscaster (WHK, Cleveland, OH, 1945).

6212 Chambers, George R. Minister Chambers conducted nondenominational church services (KLS, Oakland, CA, 1923).

6213 Chambers, Harry. Tenor (WWJ, Detroit, MI, 1924).

6214 Chambers, Hugh. Newscaster (WIP, Philadelphia, PA, 1942).

6215 Chambers, Jo Elyn. COM-HE (KVOL, Lafayette, LA, 1955).

6216 Chambers, Lenoir. Newscaster (WTAR, Norfolk, VA, 1944–1945).

6217 Chambers, May. Soprano (WOC, Davenport, IA, 1926).

6218 Chambers, Pat. DJ (*Gulf Coast Serenade,* WFLA, Tampa, FL, 1949–1952; WMBL, Morehead, NC, 1955).

6219 Chamblee, Ruth. COM-HE (WETC, Wendell-Zebulon, NC, 1960).

6220 Chamburs [Chambers], Pat. DJ (*Radioactivity,* WDAE, Tampa, FL, 1960).

6221 Chames, Nick. Sportscaster (*Sports Reel,* KMOR, Oroville, CA, 1953; KSDA, Redding, CA, 1955).

6222 Chamlee, Mario. Tenor Chamblee was featured on the *Brunswick Hour* (WJZ, New York, NY, 1924).

6223 Champagne, Loretta. Pianist (WBZ, Boston-Springfield, MA, 1924).

6224 Champenois, Ruth. Delivered talks on "Health and Beauty" (WJZ, New York, NY, 1925).

6225 Champion, Myron. Pianist (KGW, Portland, OR, 1923).

6226 Champion, Ned. DJ (*Wax Train,* WNAO, Raleigh, NC, 1948).

6227 *(The) Champion Sparklers.* Singers Frank Munn, Vaughn deLeath and Ed Smalle were featured with popular singing comedian Irving Kaufman. The Studebaker Champions Orchestra was also a program regular (NBC-Blue, 1926–1929).

6228 Champlin, Charles. Baritone (WIBO, Chicago, IL, 1926).

6229 Chan, Gus. Newscaster (WWRL, Woodside, NY, 1941).

6230 Chancellor, John. Newscaster Chancellor first gained radio fame for his on-the-spot recording of a killer's capture by the Chicago police during a running gun fight. Chancellor's account was broadcast by WMAQ (Chicago, IL, 1955).

6231 Chandler, Arthur, Jr. Organist (*Arthur Chandler,* instr. mus. prg., WLW, Cincinnati, OH, 1934–1942).

6232 Chandler, Bess. Singer (WIP, Philadelphia, PA, 1936; NBC, 1937).

6233 Chandler, Edna. Newscaster (WHLB, Virginia, MN, 1940).

6234 Chandler, Elaine. COM-HE (WPEP, San Angelo, TX, 1956).

6235 Chandler, Gloria. Reader (KYW, Chicago, IL, 1925). Later Miss Chandler was identified as the "Leading Lady of WMAQ players [dramatic group]," a Chicago radio favorite (WMAQ, Chicago, IL, 1927).

6236 Chandler, Mario. Leader (*Mario Chandler Orchestra,* instr. mus. prg., WJAG, Norfolk, NE, 1939).

6237 Chandler, Mimi. DJ (*Coffee Time,* WVLK, Lexington-Versailles, KY, 1948–1952).

6238 *Chandu the Magician.* The well-written adolescent adventure drama was based on the characters created by Harry A. Earnshaw. Gayne Whitman, a star of the stage and silent movies, originated the role of Chandu in 1932. The program was first broadcast on the West Coast in 1932. The sponsor was Beechnut. The producers were Harry A. Earnshaw and Vera M. Oldham of the Earnshaw-Young Advertising Agency, both of whom had previously collaborated in writing the *Adventures of Detectives Black and Blue. Chandu* was broadcast live and by transcription on 77 stations in 1932–1933. When it began *Chandu the Magician* was entirely transcribed. The popularity of the program did much to increase the broadcast use of electrical transcriptions.

The program was revived in 1948 on West Coast radio with White Cloud soap as sponsor. It closely followed the original scripts. In 1950, writers Vera Oldham and Sam Dann along with producer-director Cyril Armbrister brought the program to network radio. At that time Tom Collins played the title role of Chandu, who actually was an American by the name of Frank Chandler. Chandler was an

American secret agent, who had learned the arts of magic from a Hindu yogi. Members of the cast in the final format were Tom Collins, Carl Emory, Peter Griffith, Roger DeKoven, Susan Thorne, Luis Van Rooten, Viola Vonn, Lee Millar, Irene Tedrow, Gertrude Warner. The program was directed by Blair Wallster. Music was provided by Juan Rolando (30 min., Saturday, 8:00–8:30 P.M., ABC, 1949). In previous years, when it was broadcast in a 15-minute format, the title role was played by Gayne Whitman, Jason Robards, Sr. and Howard Hoffman. Others in the cast included Leon Janney, Ian Martin, Margaret MacDonald, Cornelia Osgood, Byrna Raeburn and Olan Soule.

6239 Chaney, Bill. DJ *(1,00,000 Ballroom,* KEEN, San Jose, CA, 1949).

6240 Chaney, Charles. DJ (*Moonlight Ballroom*, KMYC, Marysville, CA, 1947).

6241 Chaney, Frances. Actress Chaney appeared on the *House in the Country* daytime serial.

6242 Chang, Phillip. Billed as "Phillip Chang and his Uke," Mr. Chang was a local radio favorite KJBS, San Francisco, CA, 1926).

6243 Chanley, Mabel. Songs (WHN, New York, NY, 1925).

6244 Channing, Maura. Contralto (WGBS. New York, NY, 1926).

6245 Chapeau, Ted. DJ (*Lazy Bones*, WMBR, Jacksonville, FL, 1947; *Sky Commuter*, WMBR, 1948–1950; *Lazy Bones*, WMBR, 1950; WJHP, Jacksonville, FL, 1956; WJOK, Jacksonville, FL, 1957).

6246 Chapel, John K. Newscaster (KROW, Oakland, CA, 1940–1942; *Bond News*, KROW, 1944–1948).

6247 Chapin, Patti. Singer (*Patti Chapin*, vcl. mus. prg., WABC-CBS, New York, NY, 1935–1937).

6248 *Chaplain of the Old Church.* Bill Vickland conducted this religious program (WMBD, Peoria, IL, 1938).

6249 Chapleau, E. Oliver. Tenor (WLS, Chicago, IL, 1925).

6250 Chaples, Lorayne. COM-HE (KBYG, Big Spring, TX, 1958).

6251 Chaplin, Connie. COM-HE (WLBZ, Muskegon, MI, 1960).

6252 Chaplin, William "W.W." News analyst (NBC, 1941, 1945–1948).

6253 Chapline, Lois. Pianist (WHAG, New York, NY, 1925).

6254 Chapman, Arlene. Pianist (WTIC, Hartford, CT, 1927).

6255 Chapman, Clayton. Leader (Clayton Chapman Orchestra, KJR, Seattle, WA, 1928).

6256 Chapman, Dave. Sportscaster (KWFT, Wichita Falls, TX, 1940–1942; KCMC, Texarkana, TX, 1949; *The Old Armchair Athlete*, KFTS, Texarkana, TX, 1950; KALB, Alexandria, LA, 1952). Newscaster (KWFT, 1946). DJ (*Let's Play Records*, KCMC, 1948; KNOE, Monroe, LA, 1954).

6257 Chapman, Fred. DJ (*Whistling in the Dark*, WILK, Wilkes Barre, PA, 1947–1950).

6258 Chapman, Howard. Sportscaster (*Spotlight on Sports*, KONP, Port Angeles, WA, 1954).

6259 Chapman, Jack. Leader (Jack Chapman's Dance Orchestra, WDAP, Chicago, IL, 1923; Jack Chapman and his Rainbow Gardens Orchestra, WQJ, 1926). Chapman's eight man orchestra in 1923 included: Chapman, ld.-p.; Clark Meyer, as. and v.; and Raymond Davis, v. and vcls.

6260 Chapman, Jack. DJ (*Songs You Remember*, KTSM, El Paso, TX, 1949).

6261 Chapman, James "Jim." Newscaster (KSAC, Manhattan, KS, 1938, WHO, Des Moines, IA, 1945). Sportscaster (KSAC, 1938–1941).

6262 Chapman, Lillie. COM-HE (KAML, Kenedy, TX, 1958–1960).

6263 Chapman, Margaret. COM-HE (WCDL, Carbondale, PA, 1956).

6264 Chapman, Marion. COM-HE (WNOX, Knoxville, TN, 1958).

6265 Chapman, Martha. COM-HE (WCDL, Carbondale, PA, 1955).

6266 Chapman, Minerva Rose. Singer (WIP, Philadelphia, PA, 1926).

6267 Chapman, Myrtle C. Pianist (WBZ, Springfield, MA, 1924).

6268 Chapman, Patee. Actress Chapman was a cast member of the daytime serials *Mother of Mine* and *Young Dr. Malone*.

6269 Chapman, Ralph. DJ (*Call to Breakfast*, WHAV, Haverhill, MA, 1954–1955).

6270 Chapman, Reid. DJ (*Chuckles Open House*, WISH, Indianapolis, IN, 1949; *Breakfast with Chuckles*, WISH, 1950–1954).

6271 Chapman, Sylvia. COM-HE (WMOX, Meridian, MS, 1956).

6272 Chappell, Ernest. Announcer (Syracuse, NY, 1925–1927 and WHAM, Rochester, NY, 1928). Newscaster (*Headlines*, MBS, 1938).

6273 *(A) Chapter a Day.* This program consisted of readings from a classic book. It began broadcasting in 1927 and was still on the air in 1997 (WHA, Madison, WI, 1927).

6274 Charette, (Mrs. George L. Soprano (KHJ, Los Angeles, CA, 1924).

6275 *(The) Charioteers.* Vocal music group (CBS, 1935–1936; WOR, Newark, NJ, 1937; NBC, 1939).

6276 *(The) Charis Musical Review.* The Charis Corporation presented the music show with singers Ben Alley and Helen Nugent, "The Little Sweethearts of the Air," organist Ann Leaf and a string trio (15 min., Tuesday, 2:15–2:30 P.M., NBC, 1932).

6277 Charlatans, Demagogues and Politicians. American radio in its earliest years provided listeners with a wide variety of programs and performers. It presented amateurs with varying degrees of skill and semi-professionals plus a number of talented professionals. Birds, children, mentalists, ministers and fortune tellers shared air time with various doctors, professors and self-proclaimed authorities, who happily expounded their knowledge and theories. Not all of them, however, possessed the best character or the purest of motives. Some of them were charlatans, others demagogues and many were both. At times the various politicians who appeared on radio were also guilty of excessive rhetorical zeal bordering on outright prevarication.

As interesting and engaging as charlatans and demagogues may seem, the mischief they caused and the potential damage they produced may never be completely excused. Unfortunately, not all the damage inflicted upon listeners was financial. The lasting effects upon thought, attitudes and behavior might have been where the most damage was inflicted by those dynamic demagogic personalities.

One of the most remarkable figures in American radio was John Romulus Brinkley. After dropping out of medical school, Brinkley bought medical diplomas from schools in St. Louis and Kansas City. Setting up a medical office in Greenville, North Carolina, he began to buy newspaper advertising asking men if they were "manly" and "vigorous." It was the beginning of an idea that brought him fame and fortune.

In 1917, Brinkley moved to Milford, Kansas, where he bought a house and an empty drug store. From the drug store he supplied the citizens of Milford with a flood of patent medicines and cure-alls, some of his own making. A major incident in Brinkley's life occurred when one of his patients complained to him of "failing manhood." Brinkley, by chance, commented that if he had some goat glands he wouldn't have this trouble. The patient anxiously asked Brinkley if he could accomplish the transplantation of goat glands. Brinkley performed the operation on the patient in the kitchen of his Milford home. Many other men came to Brinkley when news of his promises of "renewed manhood" spread. Soon, the entire nation became aware of Brinkley's "goat gland" operation.

After returning from a profitable California excursion made under the aegis of Henry Chandler, owner of the Los Angeles *Times* and radio station KHJ, Brinkley founded and obtained a license for KFKB (Milford, KS) in 1923. This provided him with a powerful means of self-promotion that he soon learned to use masterfully.

With his "southern rural-accented speech," Brinkley began to use his station to extol the miraculous virtues of his goat gland operations for men. He would begin his advertising spiel with a series of barnyard allusions that also frequently appeared in his diagnoses.

Brinkley appeared on his station six days a week. He talked about prostate cancer, masculine rejuvenation and men who were geldings. It is believed that his "rejuvenation work" brought him about 12 million dollars in his 25 years of activity. One of Brinkley's major promotional programs was *The Medical Question Box*, on which he diagnosed the ailments of listeners who wrote him about their symptoms. In order to profit from the program, he organized some 1500 druggists into the Brinkley Pharmaceutical Association. Brinkley would read the symptoms of the listeners who wrote in and then prescribe by prescription number what they needed. His listeners could then buy either from his mail order pharmacy, or from any of the 1500 druggists he'd organized in his Brinkley Pharmaceutical Association.

An example of *The Medical Question Box* and how Brinkley diagnosed and prescribed by radio is as follows:

> You are listening to Doctor Brinkley speaking from his office over station KFKB. We must dig into our question business this morning. The first question is from somewhere in Missouri. She says she enjoys our talks. She states her case briefly, which I appreciate. She had an operation, with her appendix, ovary and tubes removed a few years ago. She is very nervous and has dizzy spells. She says the salt solution and constipation and liver medicine has already benefitted her. In reply to your question Number 1, I am more or less of the opinion that while the symptoms are to a great extent those of a premature menopause, I think they are not, but yet they are due to the fact that you have a very small amount of ovarian substance remaining. In my practice in such cases as this I have for many years used [prescribed] Prescription Number 61 for women. I think you should, as well use Prescription Number 50 and I think if you would go on a vegetable diet, a salt-free diet for a while and use Prescriptions Number 64, 50 and 61, you would be surprised at the benefit you would obtain.

Egocentric, boastful, vulgar and paranoid all are terms that have been used to describe Dr. Brinkley. When a listener wrote to Brinkley requesting birth control information, he used some of the barnyard allusions he often fell back upon: "I suggest that you have your husband sterilized and then you will be safe from having more children, providing you don't get out in anybody else's cow pasture and get in with some other bull."

The doctor rarely was modest about his medical skills or his use of them:

> I believe that I have found my place in the world. I believe that I am here for the purpose of performing surgery, advanced surgery and curative surgery. I believe that my surgery work is fifty years ahead of times when it comes to curing insanity, diseases of old age, assisting bright minds and valuable men and women to remain here and finish work of value to the coming generation (Resler, 1958, p. 180).

Nor did Brinkley hesitate to compare himself to Christ. The Kansas City *Star* quoted him on October 27, 1930, as saying: "I am being persecuted even as Jesus Christ was persecuted. If I am a quack, Dr. Luke was a quack, too, for he did not belong to the American Medical Association."

Brinkley played upon the animosities held by many of his listeners toward doctors and the belief that they practiced medicine with the chief aim to "get their patients on the operating table." He broadcast *The Medical Question Box* program three times a day. He opened these programs with a confident, "Greetings to my friends in Kansas and elsewhere." He talked his listeners' language and they liked him and his station. They sent him a steady stream of money to purchase items from his pharmacy. His station also prospered.

Station KFKB had other attractions in addition to Dr. Brinkley. Although they also broadcast numerous cowboy singers, yodelers, story tellers, fundamentalist preachers, musicians and music groups of all types to attract listeners, Brinkley remained the station's star attraction. Despite the many attacks on Brinkley by the American Medical Association, station KFKB was voted the most popular station in 1925 and again in 1930 in *Radio Digest* polls.

Gross (1954, p. 68) has observed that Brinkley opened the floodgates to provide access to radio by all types of diploma mill owners, fortune tellers, clairvoyants, quacks and "assorted nuts and dreamers." Brinkley discovered how radio could be used effectively to sell himself, his operations and his medicines. He used his rural, accented speech to communicate effectively with his audience (Barnouw, 1966, p. 172). His techniques were also used effectively by others, but none more effectively than Huey Long.

Although nationally prominent and controversial, Brinkley was considered a model citizen by his small town neighbors in Milford, Kansas. He contributed financially to support the Milford Sunday school — the Brinkley Methodist Sunday School — and the Brinkley Goats, a local baseball team, in addition to developing a relationship with Kansas State College to offer college courses by radio. Despite his various good works, serious trouble lay ahead for Brinkley.

In 1925, the American Medical Association began shutting down the medical diploma mills that had sold Brinkley his medical degrees. Furthermore, the medical association said that his operations were a fraud (Barnouw, 1966, p. 171). Fighting back, Brinkley used KFKB to attack the A.M.A. and the various states that had revoked his medical license.

The Federal Radio Commission (FRC), the forerunner of the Federal Communication Commission, responded to various newspaper exposes of Brinkley's practices and the pressure exerted by the A.M.A. by refusing to renew KFKB's license in 1930. Brinkley sued, claiming that he was being censored. The court ruled against him, holding that the FRC ruling was not based on Brinkley's broadcasts, but the nature of the programs he broadcast. Despite this controversy and legal setbacks, his station KFKB once more won the *Radio Digest's* poll as the nation's most popular station.

After refusing to renew Brinkley's station license, the FRC followed its action by refusing renewals to others engaged in questionable broadcast activities. Dr. Norman Baker's station, KTNT (Muscatine, Iowa) was refused license renewal because of Baker's sale of a cancer cure on his programs and his attacks on physicians in general. The Los Angeles station of the Reverend Robert E. Shuler was also refused renewal because of the minister's attacks on various religions and cultural institutions. Norman Baker, one of Brinkley's greatest rivals among the quacks and charlatans of radio's early years, had been a vaudeville performer, mentalist and steam calliope manufacturer. After a successful experience of selling a ten-lesson oil painting course by mail, Baker began operating station KTNT in Muscatine, Iowa. He quickly ventured into the medical field by offering a veterinary medicine for horses as a cancer cure for humans. When his station's license was denied renewal, Baker moved to Mexico to sell his wares and safely promote his various "cures" from across the Rio Grande.

The Reverend Bob Shuler, whose station's license renewal had also been denied, has been characterized as combining the attributes of Aimee Semple McPherson with those of Huey Long (Carson, 1960, p. 92). Despite his skillful use of these attributes, Shuler was refused license renewal because of his hate broadcasts against other persons and religions.

After his station was refused renewal, Brinkley began broadcasting on XER (later XERA) located in Villa Acuna, Mexico, three miles from Del Rio, Texas. In addition, he still broadcast from Milford, Kansas on KFBI — the successor to KFKB. Although he did not own the Mexican station, Brinkley appeared on it regularly, becoming a regular part of border radio. Brinkley found himself broadcasting on XER (XERA) with its newly expanded power of 500,000 watts that made it the most powerful station in North America.

Brinkley in his later years — the middle 1930s — broadcast his version of fireside chats, in which he praised Ku Klux Klan leader, Gerald B. Winrod; Fritz Kuhn, the leader of the German-American Bund; and Gerald L.K. Smith and William D. Pelley, both leaders of fascist inspired American groups and solid Father Coughlin supporters.

The final blow to Brinkley was the destruction of XERA, by action of the North American Regional Broadcasting Agreement. After traveling to Mexico City in an effort to save the station, he suffered a severe heart attack that eventually led to his death. Brinkley was undoubtedly one of radio's greatest salesmen. Pure charlatan, he opened the door to the fortune tellers, car dealers, lawyers and real estate salesmen who today still operate just within the limits of the law on radio and television. He also assisted the progress of a powerful religious figure — Father Coughlin.

Father Charles E. Coughlin, known as the "Radio Priest," had his own church, the Shrine of the Little Flower of Royal Oak, Michigan in 1925, when he first went on radio. Leo Fitzpatrick, manager of WJR (Detroit, MI), persuaded the priest to try radio as a funds raising technique. Coughlin was given free air time on the station, but had to pay the line charges incurred by broadcasting from his Shrine of the Little Flower.

Coughlin's first broadcasts were designed for children, but when he began to discuss adult topics, he was deluged with letters from listeners praising his work. From that time on, recognizing the power of his broadcasts, Coughlin began to emphasize political and economical topics and attack Communism as poisonous and unregulated Capitalism as evil. His attack on unregulated Capitalism was based on his claim that it operated without respect for human rights. His broadcasts appealed to the populist feelings of many of his listeners. Many Americans suffering under the grim economic conditions of the Great Depression fell under the radio priest's spell, when he began preaching politics. Coughlin blamed the country's economic ills on "international bankers" and the "money changers in the temple." When he further identified them as the "wolves in sheep's clothing who want to shake hands with Russia," he was laying the foundation for his strong anti-Semitic tirades that would soon follow. Encouraged by listener enthusiasm, Coughlin organized the Radio League of the Little Flower with dues of a dollar for a year's membership. His weekly broadcasts were carried by CBS during the early years of the depression. An early supporter of Roosevelt, Coughlin severely criticized President Herbert Hoover's failure to take action to alleviate the nation's poor economic health. When Roosevelt defeated Hoover in the 1932 presidential election, he found a staunch supporter in the Radio Priest. Coughlin remained a strong supporter of FDR and his New Deal until 1934, when his previously enthusiastic comments began, first, to show ambivalence and, later, open hostility. In the summer of 1934 he called President Roosevelt a "liar" and "betrayer." Forced to issue a public apology to the President by the Vatican, Coughlin said that he would have showed more restraint if he had not uttered those words in "the heat of civic interest and righteous anger." His use of the phrase "*righteous anger*" is particularly significant.

The Vatican's rebuke did not stop Coughlin from his continued tirades and personal attacks. He once called Will Rogers "a millionaire court jester of the billionaire oil men." Still later, Coughlin voiced a near rebellious note when in one of his broadcasts he said, "When the ballot becomes useless, I shall have the courage to stand up and agitate the use of bullets." Before long, Coughlin added anti-Semitic and various other hate messages to his network broadcasts. Warren (1966, p. 155), in his study of Coughlin's radio career, quotes the priest's apologetic explanation of the persecution in Germany by suggesting that the Jews were an aggressively powerful minority that had attained great influence by means of their success in journalism, finance, radio, art and science, despite the many obstacles they had encountered.

One of Coughlin's earliest anti-Semitic attacks carefully couched in "coded language" occurred in a broadcast he made in the fall of 1933, when he blamed the Depression on the " ... international bankers who perverted to their selfish ends an economic system which was predicated upon debts and upon payments of those debts in gold." Later in the same broadcast, he condemned, "The liars, the Judases, the high priests, Annas and Calphas, [who]were at work crucifying the brothers of Christ." Saying that there had been a successful conspiracy against the English and the American people, Coughlin went on to say: "The Rothchilds had tricked us." From this point on, Coughlin began to blame Jews for many of the existing economic and social ills. Furthermore, Coughlin explained that Nazism was hostile to Jews because they were responsible for the economic and social ills experienced by Germany after the Treaty of Versailles. Like any skillful demagogue, he had learned how to arouse passions by means of words that were both spoken and left unspoken.

Coughlin frequently said that Nazism was a strong shield against Communism, a product he said was not produced by the Russians, but by a Jewish group that dominated the country (Warren, 1996, p. 156). If Coughlin was not a Fascist, many of his ideas certainly were in accord with that particular philosophy. He consistently harangued against the "contentedness" of persons of "wealth and power." International bankers also came in for their share of the blame for causing the suffering of the "common people" during the depression years. His resonant voice and trilled "r's" helped him proclaim these ideas interspersed with his anti-Semitic messages.

The powerful radio priest was not without his critics. Dr. John Haynes Holmes, a Protestant minister, was one who praised Coughlin's style, but condemned his use of propaganda techniques and its potential dangers. In his condemnation of Coughlin, Holmes also sounded a warning about the possible dangerous misuse of radio. Adolf Hitler in Europe during the same period was a prime example of how the insidious poison of a demagogue could be spread by a skillful broadcaster.

Coughlin's outright anti-Semiticism probably was the main reason CBS dropped his program at the end of the 1930–1931 season, when the network decided to replace it with a *Church of the Air* program that presented rotating speakers of different Christian denominations. When Warren in the course of his research asked Paley for information about the priest's cancellation, he was told he [Paley]would not discuss the matter. This is precisely the same response the author received several years ago when he queried Paley about the Coughlin cancellation.

Paper (1987, p. 61) in a biography of Paley suggests it was Ed Klauber [a CBS executive], who initiated the requirements of fairness and equal presentation of varying points of view for listeners who were not fully informed about the topics under discussion. After Coughlin was dropped from the CBS schedule, he asked his listeners to write Paley requesting his freedom of speech rights, they responded by writing some half million letters to the CBS chief executive.

World War II caused Coughlin's popularity to wane, for some of his ideas were clearly unpatriotic. From a once potent political force, he became merely another small voice critical of capitalism and the government. Not only the priest's anti-semiticism, but also his antagonism toward FDR and his veiled pro-Axis and anti-Allied sympathies caused him to lose public favor. Coughlin was officially "silenced" in 1942 by an agreement he reached with Archbishop Mooney. In effect, he was forbidden public utterances for the next quarter of a century. Unable to continue his broadcasts, he still fulfilled his priestly duties at the Shrine of the Little Flower and the schools for boys and girls associated with it. Father Coughlin died in 1979 at the age of 88 with little public notice. When he was silenced in 1942, perhaps radio's most powerful and dangerous demagogue vanished from the scene and was soon forgotten. Some of Coughlin's defenders argue that he was not anti-Semitic. *See* **Coughlin, (Father) Charles.**

While active, Coughlin showed great skill in inciting and inflaming public opinion, a lesson that was not lost on United States Senator Huey Long. Long learned his lessons well from both John Romulus Brinkley and the Radio Priest. Huey Long—the Kingfish of Louisiana—combined the skills of a charlatan with the power of a demagogue.

Barnouw (1968, p. 72) correctly points out that Huey Long followed the trail blazed by Dr. Brinkley. Long used radio as effectively as any American demagogue ever had with his heavily accented Southern speech, liberally laced with "down home" references. He used the language of the ordinary man and particularly that of the people of Louisiana. Many Americans fell under his spell after hearing his radio speeches.

First as governor and, later, as Senator from Louisiana, the Kingfish quickly became a popular populist spokesman. Like Father Coughlin, Huey Long was an effective radio speaker despite his relatively poor voice and speech patterns. His radio messages carried the siren song of his "Every man a king" slogan and "Share the wealth" idea. One of Huey's radio techniques was to begin his broadcast with a greeting and suggestion that the listener should call some friends to tell them that "Huey was on the radio."

Although a Democrat like Coughlin, Long also became a bitter enemy of Roosevelt and his administration. His criticisms were so strong that prominent Democrats took to the radio to criticize him. General Hugh Johnson, for one, criticized him on NBC in 1934:

> You can laugh at Huey Long—you can snort at Father Coughlin—but this country was never under a greater menace.... Added to the ful-de-rol of Senator Long, there comes burring over the air the dripping brogue of the Irish-Canadian priest ... musical, blatant back from the very rostrum of religion, it goes straight home to simple souls weary in distress.... Between the team of Huey Long and the priest we have the whole bag of crazy and crafty tricks ... possessed by Peter the Hermit, Napoleon Bonaparte, Sitting Bull, William Hohenzollern, Hitler, Lenin ... boiled down to two with the radio and the newsreel to make them effective. If you don't think Long and Coughlin are dangerous, you don't know the temper of the country in this distress!

For a short period in the early 1930s, Huey Long had gained strong popular support by means of his frequent radio speeches, for which he bought his own air time. Appearing before the microphone at every opportunity, Long launched strong personal attacks against Roosevelt. An example of his style and the content of his messages is this one:

> So it has been that while millions have starved and gone naked. So it has been that while babies have cried and died for the lack of milk, the Roosevelt administration has sailed merrily along plowing under and destroying the things to eat and wear.

Later, when preparing to run for president, Long called upon the people to wage a class war, seize the fortunes of the rich and to divide it equally among all the people.

Democrats became increasingly wary of his harsh criticisms of FDR, but on September 10, 1935, Long's threat disappeared when he was assassinated in Baton Rouge, Louisiana. Although some Louisianans were saddened by his loss, there were many others who shed no tears for the dead Kingfish.

Brinkley, Coughlin and Huey Long all were involved in politics. Long was a powerful politician, Brinkley an unsuccessful candidate for governor of Kansas and Coughlin an influential national figure. Fortunately, only Long ever achieved public office. Charlatans and demagogues are still to be found in American life, but there are now higher legal and ethical standards and increased restraints imposed by broadcasters on those who would practice fraud and deception. It is still necessary, however, that radio listeners and television viewers critically think about what they see and hear, for there still are politicians and salesmen of various ideas who wish to sing their own particular siren song to the gullible.

6278 Charles, Al. Sportscaster (WAYB, Waynesboro, VA, 1953).

6279 Charles, Ann. Violinist (WEAO, Columbus, OH, 1925–1927).

6280 Charles, Bert. Newscaster (WAKR, Akron, OH, 1946). Sportscaster (WAKR, 1947; WVKO, Columbus, OH, 1952–1955).

6281 Charles, Claire. COM-HE (*Homemaker Chats*, KMTR, Hollywood, CA, 1926).

6282 *Charles Courtney.* The sustaining dramatic adventure show was based on the life of Charles Courtney, a locksmith and deep sea diver. When the show began it told how Courtney joined the Marines and was sent to Nicaragua. He found adventure there. One of his first adventures involved a perilous dive into the ocean to free a snarled ship's rudder (30 min., Tuesday, 9:30–10:00 P.M., WHN, New York, NY, 1934).

6283 Charles, Mrs. F.G. Announcer (WEAO, Columbus, OH, 1925).

6284 Charles, Gordon. Newscaster (WTCM, Traverse City, MI, 1947).

6285 Charles, Larry. Tenor Charles was known as "The Voice of the State Police" (*Larry Charles*, vcl. mus. prg., WPG, Atlantic City, NJ, 1935–1936).

6286 Charles, Lewis. Newscaster (*Remington-Rand News Program*, WINS, New York, NY, 1937; WOV, New York, NY, 1944).

6287 Charles, Milton. Organist (*Milton Charles*, instr. mus. prg., WBBM, Chicago, IL and CBS, 1935).

6288 Charles, Perry. Announcer (WPAP, Palisades, NJ, 1925; WNYC, New York City, NY, 1925).

6289 Charles, Robert. Newscaster (KWTX, Waco, TX, 1946). DJ (*Request Club*, KWTX, 1947).

6290 *(The) Charles Boyer Show.* Romantic motion picture star Boyer played the role of a Parisian panhandler on the sustaining romantic drama series. He earned his living by telling stories to tourists. In addition to telling the stories, Boyer also appeared in a variety of roles in the dramatic episodes presented. Hanley Stafford was the announcer (30 min., Tuesday, 9:30–10:00 P.M., NBC, 1950).

6291 *Charlie and Jessie.* Donald Cook and Florence Lake played the title roles on the scatterbrain daytime comedy series about two newlyweds. Diane Bourbon also played a leading feminine role. The sponsor was Campbell Soups. Red Cooper was the writer. Nelson Case was the announcer (15 min., Monday through Friday, 11:00–11:15 A.M., CBS, 1940).

6292 *Charlie Chan.* Tom Curtin used the character created by Earl Derr Biggers as the basis for the radio mystery series. Other writers for the program over the years included Alfred Bester, Judith Bublick, John Cole and James Erthein. The producer-directors were Alfred Bester and Chick Vincent. When first broadcast in 1932 on the NBC-Blue network, the title role was created by Walter Connolly. After Connolly, the great Chinese detective was played by Ed Begley in one version and Santos Ortega in another. Leon Janney played the role of the Number One Son in support of both Begley and Ortega (NBC, MBC, ABC, 1932–1938; 1944–1945).

6293 *Charlie Freshwater's Cowboy Band.* CW mus. prg. (MBS, 1939).

6294 *Charlie Hamp Goes to Town.* Hamp sang and played the piano on his lively music program sponsored by Morrell's Packing Company (15 min., 10:30–10:45 P.M. PST, KNX, Los Angles, CA, 1939).

6295 *Charlie Hamp — the Voice of Hollywood.* Hamp, a former band leader, was at the piano on his program. He played, sang, ad libbed and gossiped about Hollywood and its stars (KNX, Los Angeles, CA, 1935).

6296 *Charlie Wellman's Chasin' the Blues.* Charlie Wellman, pioneer radio entertainer, hosted his daily afternoon variety program (60 min., Monday through Friday, 3:00–4:00 P.M., KFRC, San Francisco, CA, 1929). *See* **Wellman, Charlie**.

6297 *Charlie Wellman's Liquocold Program.* Wellman conducted the weekly program of music and comedy (30 min., Monday, 1:30–2:00 P.M., KHJ, Los Angeles, CA, 1928). *See* **Wellman, Charlie**.

6298 *Charlie Wellman's Saturday Afternoon Frolic.* The versatile Wellman hosted the popular weekly variety show (240 min., Saturday, 2:00–6:00 P.M., KHJ, Los Angeles, CA, 1924). The program later was carried by KFWB, Hollywood, CA, in 1925. See **Wellman, Charlie**.

6299 *Charlie Wild, Private Eye.* The mystery-adventure program sponsored by Wildroot Hair Tonic had the misfortune of following the popular *Sam Spade* program. Private investigator Wild, originally played by George Petrie, dictated his adventures to a tape recorder when the show opened. Peter Hobbs played Wild's assistant. The program was written by Peter Barry and directed by Carlo DeAngelo. Bill Rogers was the announcer. Kevin O'Morrison and John McQuade played the title role when the program moved to CBS the following year (30 min., Sunday, 5:30–6:00 P.M., NBC, 1950; CBS, 1951).

6300 *Charlotte Greenwood Show.* Hallmark Cards sponsored the combination situation comedy and variety show featuring movie comedienne Charlotte Greenwood as eccentric Aunty Ellen from Oklahoma (Weekly, 30 min., NBC & ABC, 1944–1946).

6301 Charlton, Frederick. Musical hand saw performer (WFLA, Clearwater, FL, 1928).

6302 Charlton, James. Newscaster (WHO, Des Moines, IA, 1946).

6303 Charlton, R.M. "Dick." Newscaster (WTOC, Savannah, GA, 1945–1947; WFRP, Savannah, GA, 1948).

6304 *Charm School.* Assisted by popular models, John Robert Powers broadcast "charm" information that paid special attention to the beauty problems of the under-twenty age group (15 min., 1:15–1:30 P.M., NBC-Red, 1947).

6305 *Charm School of the Air.* Virginia Clark broadcast beauty and charm hints and Forrest Lewis provided the comic relief on the weekday show from Chicago. Lee Bennett was the announcer (30 min., Monday through Friday, 9:30–10:00 A.M., WGN, Chicago, IL, 1936).

6306 Charnley, Mabel. Soprano (WGCP, New York, NY, 1925).

6307 Charvat, Jack. Sportscaster (KTUL, Tulsa, OK, 1944–1953).

6308 Chase, Bob. Newscaster (WIL, St. Louis, MO, 1941–1942). Sportscaster (WOWO, Fort Wayne, IN, 1956–1960). DJ (WOWO, 1955).

6309 Chase, Brandon. DJ (WNLC, New London, CT, 1948–1950). Sportscaster (WNLC, New London, CT, 1948).

6310 Chase, Bud. DJ (*Breakfast Biscuits*, WHOT, South Bend, IN, 1948; *1290 Club*, WMLO, Milwaukee, WI, 1950).

6311 Chase, Frank. Sportscaster (*For Men Only*, NBC, 1938).

6312 Chase, Frank. Actor Chase appeared on the *Front Page Farrell* daytime serial program.

6313 Chase, Glenn E. Announcer (WSAZ, Pomeroy, OH, 1925–1927).

6314 Chase, Howard. Sportscaster (WWOR, Worcester, MA, 1953).

6315 Chase, Ilka. DJ (*Ilka Chase Show*, ABC, 1949).

6316 Chase, Janet. COM-HE (KITN, Olympia, WA, 1957).

6317 Chase, Julie. COM-HE (WTAG, Worcester, MA, 1956–1957).

6318 Chase, Kay. COM-HE (WTAG, Worcester, MA, 1955–1960).

6319 Chase, Mary Wood. Pianist (WJAZ, Chicago, IL, 1923).

6320 Chase, Milton. Newscaster (*World Front*, WLW, Cincinnati, OH, 1944–1947).

6321 Chase, Sam. Sportscaster (KFBB, Great Falls, MT, 1938).

6322 Chase, Thomas B. Announcer and bass soloist Chase was a member for seven years of the Radio Double Quartette, a popular vocal group that broadcast Sunday mornings on WOW (Omaha, NE, 1929).

6323 Chase, Vicki. Soprano (*Vicki Chase,*

vcl. mus. prg., WLW, Cincinnati, OH, 1937; NBC, 1939).

6324 ***(The) Chase.*** The premise of the sustaining dramatic show was that at one time or another everyone — physically or psychologically — was either the hunter or the hunter. Each dramatic episode told the story of someone in just such circumstances. The program opened with this announcement: "The National Broadcasting Company invites you by transcription to join *The Chase.* There is always the hunter and the hunted, the pursuer and the pursued. It may be the voice of authority or a race with death and destruction, the most relentless of the hunters. There are times when laughter is heard as counterpoint and moments when sheer terror is the theme ... but always there is *The Chase.*" Lawrence Klee wrote and Walter McGrew directed the program. Cameron Andrews, Ruth Gilbert, Larry Haines, Kermit Murdock, Karl Swenson and Lucille Wall were in the cast (30 min., Sunday, 8:30–9:00 P.M., NBC, 1952–1953).

6325 ***(The) Chase and Sanborn Choral Orchestra.*** The good music program sponsored by Chase and Sanborn Coffee was broadcast in 1929. In addition to the orchestra conducted by either Frank Black or Gustave Haenschen, performers on the program included female crooner Welcome Lewis, the piano team of Phil Ohman and Victor Arden, soprano Mary McCoy and a male quartet. Neil Enslen was the announcer (30 min., Sunday, 8:30–9:00 P.M., NBC-Red, 1930).

6326 ***(The) Chase and Sanborn Hour.*** The Chase and Sanborn Coffee Company sponsored several popular entertainers in various formats on the show generically designated as the *Chase and Sanborn Hour.* The program premiered September 13, 1931. Each week the program included an original dramatic episode written by Louis Joseph Vance. Another of the stars featured in its early format was the famous French entertainer, Maurice Chevalier, who was paid the astounding sum for 1931 of $5,000 weekly. Eddie Cantor became one of radio's most popular stars when he appeared on the show. Cantor sang, clowned and introduced the various guest stars that appeared with him each week. The *Chase and Sanborn Hour* was written by David Freedmen, Carroll Carroll, Bob Colwell, Everett Freeman, Sam Moore and Phil Rapp and directed by Abbott K. Spencer (60 min., Weekly, 8:00–9:00 P.M., NBC, 1935).

Comedian-singer Jimmy Durante and the great torch singer, Ruth Etting, took over when Cantor went on vacation (60 min., Sunday, 8:00–9:00 P.M., NBC-Red, 1933). Later that year when star Eddie Cantor took a summer vacation, the cast that replaced him included vaudeville headliner Bert Lahr assisted by the vocal team of Lee Sims and Ilomay Bailey and the Dave Rubinoff Orchestra. It was the 1937 version of the program with host Don Ameche that featured the characters most frequently associated with the program: Edgar Bergen and Charlie McCarthy, W.C. Fields, Dorothy Lamour and Ray Noble. Although the show continued to be sponsored by Chase and Sanborn, the program also became to be known as *The Edgar Bergen and Charlie McCarthy Show, The Edgar Bergen Hour* and *The New Edgar Bergen Hour.* When Chase and Sanborn's sponsorship ended in 1948, the show's name continued to be associated with Bergen and McCarthy for the remainder of their radio career. During the years the program was broadcast (1937–1956) the cast and guest stars included: Barbara Jo Allen (Vera Vague), Don Ameche, Jim Backus, John Barrymore, Ethel Barrymore, Edgar Bergen, Bob Burns, Nelson Eddy, Norman Fields, W.C. Fields, Richard Haydn, Marsha Hunt, Dorothy Lamour, Frances Langford, Eddie Mayehoff, Pat Patrick, Jane Powell, George Raft, Basil Rathbone, Rosalind Russell, Barbara Stanwyck, Rudy Vallee, Orson Welles and the Stroud Twins. The announcers were Ben Alexander, Bill Baldwin, Ken Carpenter and Bill Goodwin. Donald Dixon, Anita Ellis, Dale Evans and Anita Gordon were vocalists who sang with the Robert Armbruster and Ray Noble orchestras. The writers were Alan Smith, Carroll Carroll, Joe Connelly, Royal Foster, Zeno Klinker, Roland MacLane, Dick Mack, Robert Mosher and Stanley Quinn. Earl Ebi was the director.

Edgar Bergen was a radio phenomenon, since it was always thought that a ventriloquist on radio would have no appeal whatsoever for listeners. But Bergen's humor and the character he created — Charlie McCarthy, the world's most famous ventriloquist "dummy"him great popularity. Bergen (Edgar Berggen) had starred at the Palace in 1926. His big break came on December 17, 1936, when he appeared on Rudy Vallee's *Fleishmann Yeast Hour* on NBC. He continued to appear with Vallee until April, 1937. The next month he joined the *Chase and Sanborn Hour.* In addition to Charlie McCarthy, who was always dressed in a tuxedo with a top hat and monocle, Bergen introduced other characters such as the hayseed hick, Mortimer Snerd (Catch phrase: "Yup ... Yup ... Yup.") and the prim Effie Klinker (Catch phrase: "That's a witty one."). It is interesting to speculate whether or not the name of writer, Zeno Klinker, inspired Bergen to name his female "dummy," Effie Klinker. Regardless of who appeared on the *Chase and Sanborn Hour,* the star was always wise-guy Charlie McCarthy. W.C. Fields (Claude William Dukenfield) once commented that "Charlie McCarthy is the finest piece of timber I've ever known. In fact, nothing would give me greater pleasure on an evening to be here by my fireside with a good book, a couple of lemonades and Charlie. Yeah, me here in my easy chair and Charlie in the fireplace." Fields described how Charlie abused him: "He [Charlie] alludes to my proboscis as being fashioned of redwood. He was referring, of course, to the slight tinge of carmine which graces my nose. It's ruddy glow, I'm proud to say is the gift of Mother Nature, what a woman. Why, with nothing but my nose to guide me, I once lighted the way for Stanley through darkest Africa." And philosophically, almost reverentially, Fields added, "Listeners get the feeling that Charlie is human, and so does everyone around the studio. Sometimes I get it myself, when I see Edgar Bergen and Charlie off in a corner enjoying a heart to heart talk with themselves. All I know is that the more I hate him the more I love him. But I won't know he's human until he bites me." Charlie's spirit is best caught in his reply to Bergen's admonition: "Young man, women will be the ruination of you" to which Charlie immediately replied, "Can I actually depend on that?" Bergen was a ventriloquist whose lips moved somewhat, making his act an ideal one for radio. Charlie, in fact, often mischievously teased him about how much his lips moved.

The *Chase and Sanborn* broadcast of December 12, 1937, included one of the most interesting moments in radio history, because of what occurred as the result of it. Written by Arch Oboler, the eight-minute sketch featured Mae West and Don Ameche, as Adam and Eve, in the Garden of Eden. The lines and the situation that caused the furore seem innocuous by today's standards, but the dialog between Eve and the Snake may have smoldered somewhat because of West's sultry voice (Wertheim, 1979, p. 365–366). At any rate, after listening to the program it is impossible to find anything in the sketch that seems objectionable or obscene. Because of the furore that resulted, NBC banned Mae West from appearing on the network and even refused to allow her name to be mentioned. It all seems to have been blown too far out of proportion.

Bergen's daughter, Candice, continues the family's theatrical tradition in films and on television (*Murphy Brown*). She has written an interesting and informative autobiography describing growing up in the Bergen household with her "brother" Charlie in *Knock Wood* (1984).

6327 ***(The) Chase and Sanborn Opera Guild.*** When Eddie Cantor left the *Chase and Sanborn Hour* on NBC for a program on CBS that was broadcast opposite it, the coffee company tried to compete by broadcasting operas in English (1935, NBC). Deems Taylor was selected as host and narrator. The orchestra was conducted by Maestro Wilfred Pelletier of the Metropolitan Opera with a chorus of 40 plus various guest stars. At first the program attracted an audience, but with Cantor's competition on the CBS schedule opposite it, the listening audience dropped and the program was eventually replaced by *Major Bowes Family* program (1935, NBC).

6328 ***Chasins' Music Series.*** Abram Chasins, a distinguished American composer-pianist, broadcast a series of lecture-recitals (30 min., Saturday, 10:00–10:30 A.M. CST, NBC-Red, 1936).

6329 **Chasnoff, Hal.** Leader (Hal Chasnoff's String Ensemble, KPLA , Los Angeles, CA, 1927).

6330 **Chassy, Lon.** Director and violinist (Meyer Davis Orchestra, 1925). Solo violinist (KTHS, Hot Springs National Park, AR, 1926).

6331 **Chastain, Tony.** Newscaster (KRIC, Beaumont, TX, 1941). DJ (*The Nightwatch,* WGBS, Miami, FL, 1947). Sportscaster (WORZ, Orlando, FL, 1949–1950).

6332 **Chateau Baltusrol Orchestra.** Popular club orchestra (WOR, Newark, NJ, 1925).

6333 ***Chats About New Books.*** Joseph

Henry Jackson broadcast book reviews (KGO, Oakland, CA, 1925).

6334 Chatterton, Betty. COM-HE (KWIP, Merced, CA, 1958).

6335 Chauncey, Marie. Writer (KVOO, Tulsa, OK, 1942). Chauncey worked as a rewrite women in the news department of KVOO during World War II.

6336 *Chautauqua Summer Concert.* Zona Gale performed readings on the summer program of light concert music (60 min., Sunday, 3:30–4:30 P.M., NBC-Red, 1934).

6337 *Chautauqua Symphony Orchestra.* Symphonic music program directed by Albert Stoessel (NBC, 1935).

6338 Chaves, Corrine. COM-HE (KFLY, Corvallis, OR, 1960).

6339 Cheatham, Robert. Baritone (KTWB, Hollywood, CA, 1928).

6340 Check, Nell. COM-HE (WKRM, Columbia, TN, 1955).

6341 *(The) Checker Cabbies.* Murray Kellner's Orchestra supplied the music. The sponsor was the Checker Cab Company (WOR, Newark, NJ, 1929).

6342 Checker Inn Orchestra. Boston music group (WNAC, Boston, MA, 1924).

6343 *Checkerboard Jamboree* (aka *Checkerboard Fun Festival, Checkerboard Square Jamboree* or simply *Checkerboard Square*). Such talented performers as Eddie Arnold, Hal Horton, Chick Martin and Ernest Tubb were featured on the CW music program broadcast daily by MBS. The Oklahoma Wranglers (Vic, Skeeter and Guy Willis) were also featured. In various formats, the program was still on the air five years after its inception in 1946 (15 min., Monday through Friday, 12:00–12:30 P.M., MBS, 1946–1951).

6344 Chedwick, Craig "Porky." Sportscaster (*Sports Round Up*, WHOD, Homestead, PA, 1948–1952). DJ (WHOD, 1954).

6345 Chee Wee [a dog]. The four-year-old canine owned by Mrs. Jacob Greenberg was a "comedian," who gave "barking recitals" on cue (KFI, Los Angeles, CA, 1928).

6346 *Cheer Up, America.* Dialect comedian Henry Burbig, Ray Murray, the Funnyboners and the Frank Novak Orchestra appeared on the variety show sponsored by Mennen Shaving Cream (15 min., Wednesday, 7:45–8:00 P.M., NBC-Red, 1938).

6347 *Cheer Up Jamboree.* Pee Wee King and the Golden West Cowboys played lively country music and Don Hill broadcast sports news on the popular local progam. Bob Kay was the announcer. The program was sponsored by the Oertel Brewing Company (30 min., Monday through Friday, 5:15–:45 P.M. and Saturday, 6:30–7:00 P.M., WAVE, Louisville, KY, 1949).

6348 *Cheerio.* Cheerio was the radio name used by the popular broadcaster, Charles K. Field. He read poetry and delivered inspirational talks to his large audience. Probably Cheerio's earliest program was *Daily Strength* (KGO, Oakland, CA, 1925).When he began broadcasting on the NBC network in 1926, Cheerio had Russell Gilbert's orchestra provide music for the show and Geraldine Rigger sing. At this time, his program was 15 minutes in length. It soon expanded to half an hour (30 min., Monday through Saturday, 8:00–8:30 A.M. and 8:30–9:00 p.m, NBC-Red, 1927–1933). In 1930, Cheerio enlarged his cast to 12 performers, including soprano Lovina Gilbert, known variously as "Gil" and "The Sweet Lady," Pat Kelly and Harrison Isles and his Five Little Peppers Orchestra. A special feature of the show was Miss Lizzie and her canaries—Blue Boy and Dickie. When the canaries sang with "The Sweet Lady," they were known as the Lovebirds. In 1935, the program was broadcast six times per week by NBC-Red in the 8:30–9:00 A.M. time slot. *See* **Field, Charles K.**

6349 *Cheeseborough Real Folks.* Dramatic sketches of small town life were presented on the program sponsored by Vaseline. The cast included George Frame Brown, who also wrote the show, Tommy Brown, Elsie May Gordon, Phoebe MacKaye, G. Underhill Macy and Edwin Whitney. A novelty band supplied the music. Alwyn E.W. Bach was the announcer (30 min., Monday, 9:30–10:00 P.M., NBC-Blue, 1930–1931).

6350 Chekova, Jesofa. Chekova sang the songs of "Old Bohemia" (WRNY, New York, NY, 1926).

6351 *(The) Cheloni Skin Program.* Cheloni Cosmetics sponsored the transcribed program of music and beauty and tips (15 min., Transcribed, Various stations, 1932).

6352 Chelton, Gerard. Newscaster (WRDW, Augusta, GA, 1946).

6353 Chenault, Evelyn. COM-HE (WHIN, Gallatin, TN, 1957).

6354 Chenault, Frances. Newscaster (KFRE, Fresno, CA, 1942).

6355 Chenault, Mary Emily. Pianist Chenault was a member with Annette Waring of a dual piano team (WHAS, Louisville, KY, 1923).

6356 Chenee, Alec. DJ (*60 Silver Minutes*, KITE, San Antonio, TX, 1948).

6357 Cheney, David M. News commentator Cheney discussed current events on his broadcast (WGI, Medford Hills, MA, 1924).

6358 Cheney, H.P. Saxophonist (WGY, Schenectady, NY, 1923).

6359 Cheney, Mary Alice. Contralto Cheney composed and sang children's songs on her *Children's Hour* program (WSAI, Cincinnati, OH, 1927–1928).

6360 Chenoweth, Mary Curtis. COM-HE, director and news commentator (WMBH, Joplin, MO, 1939). Versatile Chenoweth doubled as a program director and news commentator on WMBH and also conducted a daily women's show, *The Woman's Viewpoint*, in 1939.

6361 Chenoweth, W.B. Leader (W.B. Chenoweth and his Cornfield Symphony Orchestra of Old Fiddlers, a Dallas, Texas, country music group, WFAA, Dallas, TX, 1924–1925).

6362 Chenoweth, Wilbur. Pianist-pipe organist (KFAB, Lincoln, NE, 1928).

6363 *Cheri and the Three Notes.* Vcl., mus. prg. (WABC, New York, NY, 1934–1936).

6364 Cherkassky, Shura. "Boy piano prodigy" (WBAL, Baltimore, MD, 1928).

6365 Cherne, Leo. Commentator (MBS-WOR, New York, NY, 1945).

6366 Cherninsky, Hyman. Violinist (WFAA, Dallas, TX, 1928).

6367 Chernoff, (Dr.) Lewis. Director (KOA Orchestra, KOA, Denver, CO, 1925).

6368 Cherry, Hugh. Popular CW DJ Cherry worked on WKAY, (Glasgow, KY,1946); WKDA (Nashville, TN, 1949); WMPS (Memphis, TN, 1950–1951); WMAK (Nashville, TN, 1951–1955); WLW (Cincinnati, OH, 1955–1957) and KFOX (Long Beach, CA, 1959–1960).

6369 Cherry, Marilyn. COM-HE (WLOF, Orlando, FL, 1960).

6370 Cherry, Opal E. COM-HE (WKAY, Glasgow, KY, 1955).

6371 Cherviavsky [Cherniavsky], Josef. Leader (*Josef Cherviavsky Orchestra,* instr. mus. prg., CBS, 1936, WOR-MBS, Newark, NJ, 1937).

6372 Chesebraugh, Beatrice. Chesebraugh conducted a children's program. She was known as the "Princess of the Air" on her *Novelty Children's Hour* (WOW, Omaha, NE, 1927).

6373 Cheshire, Pappy. Leader (*Pappy Cheshire's National Hillbilly Champions* CW mus. prg., CBS, 1939).

6374 Cheskin, David. Leader (*David Cheskin Orchestra,* instr. mus. prg., WBBM, Chicago, IL, 1942).

6375 Chessher, Faye. COM-HE (KWED, Seguin, TX, 1956).

6376 Chester, Bob. Leader (*Bob Chester Orchestra*, instr. mus. prg.; NBC, 1935; WLW, Cincinnati, OH, 1935).

6377 Chester, Bob. DJ (*Bob Chester Show*, WKMH, Dearborn, MI, 1950).

6378 Chester, Giraud. Newscaster (WHA, Madison, WI, 1942).

6379 *Chesterfield Dance Show.* Liggett and Myers, manufacturers of Chesterfield cigarettes, sponsored the excellent music program on which David Ross announced the musical selections performed by the Andre Kostelanetz orchestra, baritone Ray Heatherton, Kay Thompson and a mixed vocal group (30 min., 10:00–10:30 P.M., CBS, 1936).

6380 *(The) Chesterfield Show.* Comedians Lou Holtz and Shawowsky, stooge Benny Baker, soprano Grace Moore and the Lenny Hayton Orchestra were featured on the program sponsored by Chesterfield cigarettes. Norman Brokenshire was the announcer (30 min., Friday, 9:00–9:30 P.M., CBS, 1933).

6381 *(The) Chesterfield Supper Club.* The popular music show was broadcast in 1944 from New York on Monday, Wednesday and Friday with Perry Como and Lloyd Shaffer's Orchestra and from Hollywood on Tuesday and Thursday with Jo Stafford. The announcers were Martin Block, Tom Reddy and Ben Grauer. Between musical numbers the announcers would read baseball scores.

Over the years the various vocalists and vocal groups on the show included: Mary Ashworth, Perry Como, Don Cornell, Dick Edwards, Fontaine Sisters (Gert, Marge and Bea), Frankie Laine, Bill Lawrence, Peggy Lee, Laura

Leslie, the Pied Pipers, the Satisfiers (Art Lambert, Helen Carroll, Bob Lange and Kevin Gavin), Jo Stafford and Kay Starr. The orchestras were Fred Waring and the Pennsylvanians, Mitchell Ayres, Dave Barbour, Sammy Kaye, Glenn Miller, Lloyd Schaefer and Ted Steele. Ward Byron and Eldridge Packham were the program directors and Bob Moss and Eldridge Packham were the producers. The writers were Mike Dutton, Dave Harmon, Frank Moore and Bob Weiskopf.

6382 ***Chesterfield Time with Johnny Johnson.*** Romantic baritone Johnson was featured on the quarter-hour program (15 min., Monday through Friday, 7:15–7:30 P.M., CBS, 1945).

6383 **Chestnut, D. Lee.** Trombonist (WBZ, Boston-Springfield, MA, 1924).

6384 **Chestnut, Virginia.** Soprano (*Virginia Chestnut,* vcl. mus. prg., MBS, 1942).

6385 **Chestnut, (Mrs.) Stanley.** Soprano (WFHH, New York, NY, 1927).

6386 **Chevigny, Hector.** Writer Chevigny wrote the *Mr. and Mrs. North, Portia Faces Life* and *The Second Mrs. Burton* programs.

6387 **Chevrolet Little Symphony Orchestra.** Classical music group (KGW, Portland, OR, 1926).

6388 **Chevrolet Motors Band of St. Louis.** Band directed by Dr. James M. Black (KSD, St. Louis, MO, 1923).

6389 **Chew, Mansie.** Pianist (KGW, Portland, OR, 1925).

6390 **Cheyne, Arthur.** Sportcaster (KIT, Yakima, WA, 1937–1941).

6391 **Chez Pierre Orchestra.** Earl Hoffman led this club band (WCFL, Chicago, IL, 1928).

6392 ***(The) Chez Show.*** Mike Wallace and his wife, Buff Cobb, conducted the husband-and-wife talk show and played record requests phoned in by listeners. The show originated from the Sapphire Bar of Chicago's Chez Paris and was sponsored in part by Fox Head 400 Beer (90 min., Tuesday through Sunday, 11:30–1:00 P.M., NBC, 1951). Jack Eigen took over the program the following year and transformed it into an interview show. Jack Eigen was a pioneer in New York radio talk shows from restaurants and clubs where he interviewed their patrons. He inaugurated this type of programming in Chicago, broadcasting from Chez's Sapphire Bar. The program featured interesting celebrity interviews (105 min., Tuesday through Sunday, 11:15–1:00 P.M., WMAQ, Chicago, IL, 1951). Mike Wallace left Chicago for New York, where he later became a prominent television reporter on *Sixty Minutes.*

6393 ***Chicago Amateur Hour.*** A first prize of $75 and a watch was given to the winner of the weekly radio amateur show. One of the winning contestants in late 1937 was 13-year-old Curtiss Damrell, an imitator of birds and animals, who previously had won a $25 prize on the Coleman-Act-of-the-Week Contest on WLS (Chicago, IL). Many amateurs with interesting human interest stories appeared on the weekly amateur show (WENR, Chicago, IL, 1937).

6394 ***(The) Chicago Civic Opera.*** The opera company, directed by Charles Moore, broadcast a weekly program of operatic selections (Friday, NBC-Blue, Chicago, IL, 1929). For an account of the opera company's role in the development of early radio in Chicago. *See* **Opera on Radio.**

6395 ***Chicago Gospel Tabernacle.*** The Reverend Dr. Paul Rader, a popular radio evangelist, conducted the weekly religious service (30 min., Sunday, 9:30–10:00 A.M. CST, WBBM, Chicago, IL, 1930).

6396 **Chicago Philharmonic Trio.** Classical instrumental trio of violinist Theordore Katz; cellist Lois Colburn Richi; and pianist Doris Wittich (WHT, Chicago, IL, 1928).

6397 **Chicago Symphony Orchestra.** The distinguished symphony orchestra appeared on the *Opera VS. Jazz Program* competing against Maurie Sherman's Jazz Band (WLS, Chicago, IL, 1927). Their own concert broadcasts were numerous (*Chicago Symphony Orchestra,* instr. mus prg. conducted by Dr. Frederick Stock, Sunday, 3:00–4:00 P.M.; WTMJ, Milwaukee, WI, 1930, 30 min.; Sunday, 3:00–4:00 P.M., CBS, 1930; and 30 min., Saturday, 9:30–10:00 P.M.; NBC-Red, 1934; MBS, 1937–1938).

6398 ***(The) Chicago Theatre of the Air.*** One of the most popular and distinguished musical programs on radio, the *Chicago Theatre of the Air* broadcast from 1940 to 1954 on MBS. The program's creator was William A. Bacher. Originating from Chicago's WGN, the program was broadcast live before a large audience from Chicago's Shrine Auditorium. Each week operettas, musical comedies or popular operas were presented. In addition to stellar vocalists, a talented dramatic cast performed the speaking roles for the singers. The performers on the program included soprano Marion Claire, tenor Attilio Baggiore, baritones Bruce Foote and Earl Wilkie and contralto Ruth Slater. Distinguished guest singers included: John Brownlee, John Carter, Igor Gorin, Frederick Jagel, Allan Jones, Felix Knight, James Melton, Robert Merrill, Jan Peerce, Thomas L. Thomas and Richard Tucker. The dramatic cast during the program's years on the air included: Rita Ascot, Bob Bailey, John Barclay, Luise Barclay, Muriel Bremner, Fran Carlon, Everett Clarke, Hazel Dopheide, Patricia Dunlap, Laurette Fillbrandt, Rosemary Garbell, Betty Lou Gerson, John Goldworthy, Norman Gottschalk, Ken Griffin, Alice Hill, Bob Jellison, John Larkin, Phil Lord, Barbara Luddy, Marvin Miller, Bret Morrison, Marilou Neumayer, Charles Penman, Donna Reade, Olan Soule, Les Tremayne, Willard Waterman, Kay Westfall and Betty Winkler. Marvin Miller and John Weigle were the announcers. The directors were Joe Ainley, Fritz Blocki, Jack LaFrandrem and Kenneth W. MacGregor. The choral director was Bob Tendler. Ray Charles was the assistant choral director. When the program first went on the air in 1940, *Variety* called it one of the finest musical programs in radio history. Its quality was maintained throughout (60 min., Thursday, 9:00–10:00 P.M., MBS, 1940).

6399 ***Chicago Varieties.*** Carl Hohengarten's Orchestra and singer Shirley Sadler performed on the sustaining variety show (15 min., Friday, 3:15–3:30 P.M., CBS, 1938).

6400 ***Chick Carter, Boy Detective.*** Young Chick, the adopted son of the fictional master sleuth, Nick Carter, was the central figure in the serial drama targeted for adolescents, a spinoff of the *Nick Carter, Master Detective* program. Chick battled against a crime lord known only as the Rattler, a master villain played by Stefan Schnabel. The role of Chick was originated by Billy Lipton. Other members of the cast were: Bill Griffis, Leon Janney, Gilbert Mack, Jean McCoy and Joanne McCoy. Fritz Blocki and Nancy Webb were the writers. Fritz Blocki was the director (MBS, 1943–1945).

6401 ***Chicken Every Sunday.*** Billie Burke and Harry Von Zell provided an entertaining half-hour on the sustaining situation comedy (30 min., Wednesday, 8:00–8:30 P.M., NBC, 1949).

6402 **Chickene, Joseph.** Leader (Joseph Chickene and his Clover Club Orchestra, WGY, Schenectady, NY, 1924).

6403 **Chickering, Bart.** Leader (Bart Chickering and his Melody Boys orchestra, KFI, Los Angeles, CA, 1928).

6404 ***Chickie.*** Fritz Blocki wrote the daytime serial that *Variety* (February 23, 1933, p. 50) said presented a "plausible picture of the younger generation struggling with the impulses of adolescence" with "dialog that rings true." Although the program contained a little more sex than was usually found on the air, it also got some sugar-coated treatment, *Variety* (February 23, 1933, p. 50). The cast included Ireene Wicker, Jack Daley, Cornelia Osgood, Marie Nelson, Willard Farnum, Vincent Coleman and Tom Shirley (WBBM, Chicago, IL, 1933).

6405 **"Chief" [dog].** Chief, a canine owned by Meanette Miller, appeared regularly in order to bark and "call together all dogs of the nation to the annual Atlantic City Dog Show" (WPG, Atlantic City, NJ, 1928).

6406 **Chief Gonzales and his Arabian Room Orchestra.** Club orchestra (KOA, Denver, CO, 1928).

6407 ***Chief Gumbo.*** Bill Roth, as Chief Gumbo, hosted the quarter hour comedy show sponsored by Campbell Cereal (WLS, Chicago, IL, 1937).

6408 **Chief Lone Eagle.** A native American, Chief Lone Eagle sang genuine Indian songs of love and battle and hymns to the gods of rain and sunshine (KOA, Denver, CO, 1926).

6409 **Chief Lost Angel (Charlie Wellman).** Announcer, singer, entertainer and Brunswick recording star Wellman hosted the popular variety program. He was a great favorite with Los Angeles listeners (KFWB, Los Angeles, CA, 1925). *See* **Wellman, Charlie.**

6410 **Chief Razzberry's Orchestra.** Popular local band (KOIL, Council Bluffs, IA, 1927–1928).

6411 **Chief Roaring Thunder.** The Chief was an American Indian who led an U.S. Indian band that appeared on various radio stations (1929).

6412 **Chief Shunatuna.** A full-blooded Pawnee Indian, Chief Shunatuna directed an U.S. Indian band (KSTP, Minneappolis–St. Paul, MN, 1929).

6413 **Chiesa, Don.** Leader (*Don Chiesa Orchestra*, instr. mus. prg., WMBD, Peoria, IL, 1936).

6414 **Chilcott Family Quartet.** The Chilcott Family Quartet was a singing group that included a father and three sons from the Sheik Temple D.O.K.K (WCAE, Pittsburgh, PA, 1925).

6415 **Childe, Robert.** Pianist-announcer Childe was born in January 10, 1899. He joined WJZ (New York, NY) as a staff pianist in 1923, before moving to Detroit (WGHP, Detroit, MI, 1928).

6416 **Childers, Louise.** COM-HE (WJAN, Spartanburg, SC, 1956).

6417 **Childers, Marge.** COM-HE (KDEF, Alburquerque, NM, 1957).

6418 **Childre, Lew.** Childre was a popular CW singer-musician (*Lew Childre*, CW mus. prg.,WWL, New Orleans, LA, 1937). A product of the medicine show and vaudeville circuit, Childre gained national recognition on the *Grand Ole Opry* (WSM, Nashville, TN, 1940s-1950s). He had several transcribed radio series, as well as performing on WWVA (Wheeling, WV), WAGA (Atlanta, GA), WWL (New Orleans, LA) and on border radio at XERA (Del Rio, Texas).

6419 ***Children's Birthday Program.*** Pat Flanagan conducted the program that was broadcast Monday through Friday. He wished a happy birthday to members of his listening audience. Organist Al Melgard supplied the music (Weekdays, WBBM, Chicago, IL, 1930).

6420 ***Children's Corner.*** Dorothy Gordon conducted the Monday afternoon children's program that presented fairy stories, animal stories and tales about children of other countries (Weekly, Monday P.M., CBS, 1935).

6421 ***Children's Corner.*** Frank Luther sang to and talked with ten-year-old Lois Volkman on the pleasant sustaining local children's show (25 min., Sunday, 8:35–9:00 A.M., WNEW, New York, NY, 1946).

6422 ***(The) Children's Friend.*** Uncle Robert, not otherwise identified, conducted the early evening program for children (WHN, New York, NY, 1925).

6423 ***Children's Hour.*** Uncle John Daggett hosted the early children's show that was unique in that it contained a quiz portion, probably a first on radio. Uncle John welcomed to his program such guest stars as Pollywinkle, a famous talking cockatoo, and Babe (Baby Napoleon), a movie chimpanzee who "talked." Harry "Mac" McClintock was also featured on the program (KHJ, Los Angeles, 1922). *See* **Daggett, Uncle John** and **McClintock, Harry "Mac."**

6424 ***Children's Hour.*** Peggy Albion conducted the children's show (WRC, Washington, DC, 1925).

6425 ***Children's Hour.*** A program for young listeners, the *Children's Hour* featured musical selections by the Rose Kindergarten Orchestra and other young performers (KLRA, Little Rock, AR, 1928).

6426 ***(The) Children's Hour.*** Paul Reichenbach, a 12-year-old singer, was a featured performer on the show that featured many young performers (KSTP, St. Paul, MN, 1929)

6427 ***(The) Children's Hour.*** The Sunday morning show was designed to be performed by children and heard by them. They sang and acted in the plays presented on the show (60 min., Sunday, NBC, 1931). The NBC program featuring young performers eventually became *Coast to Coast on a Bus* (NBC, Weekly, 1930s). *See* ***Coast to Coast on a Bus.***

6428 ***(The) Children's Hour Entertainment.*** Harry "Mac" McClintock was the featured performer on the children's show. He sang and told stories. Probably his most popular song was "The Wreck of the Old 97" (KFRC, San Francisco, CA, 1930). *See* **McClintock, Harry "Mac."**

6429 ***(The) Children's Safety Club.*** Duke Messer directed and conducted the children's program (KLRA, Little Rock, AR, 1928).

6430 ***(The) Children's Story Hour.*** Aunt Jenny (Jenny Garrett) conducted the children's program WLBN, Little Rock, AR, 1928).

6431 ***Children's World.*** Helen Parkhurst, the founder and director of New York City's Dalton School, discussed various children's problems and their solutions. George Hicks was the announcer (30 min., Sunday, 7:00–7:30 A.M., ABC, 1947).

6432 **Childs, Big Bill.** End man on the *Weener Minstrel Show (*WENR, Chicago, IL, 1929).

6433 **Childs, Georgia.** Contralto (WEAF, New York, NY, 1925).

6434 **Childs, Leland.** Sportscaster (WBRC, Birmingham, AL, 1940–1942; WSFA, Montgomery, AL, 1944–1945; WMGY, Montgomery, AL, 1946; WBRC, 1956). Newscaster (WJLD, Bessemer, AL, 1942). DJ (*Musical Clock*, WSFA, 1949).

6435 **Childs, Marquis.** Childs was a newspaper columnist and a news analyst on his *Washington Report* program broadcast by the Labor-Liberal FM Network (Washington, DC, 1950).

6436 **Childs, Reggie.** Leader (*Reggie Childs Orchestra*, instr. mus. prg., NBC, 1934–1935 WTAR, Norfolk, VA, 1935; NBC, 1939).

6437 **Childs, Robert.** Newscaster (KMA, Shenandoah, IA, 1939–1942, 1944–1948).

6438 ***(The) Chili Beaners.*** Juan Haidrigo led the Mexican band (WBBM, Chicago, IL, 1936).

6439 **Chilton, Ruth.** COM-HE (WJMJ, Philadelphia, PA, 1951).

6440 **Chimera, J.** Chimera was billed as the "World's premier trombone soloist" (KYW, Chicago, IL, 1926).

6441 **China Royal Orchestra.** Popular New York band (WGCP, New York, NY, 1926).

6442 **Chindbloom, (Mrs.) Carl [Christine Nilsson].** Pianist (WRC, Washington, DC, 1925).

6443 **Chinese Garden Orchestra.** Restaurant band (KFI, Los Angeles, CA, 1926).

6444 ***Chinese Night.*** On this special program Edward H. Smith personally conducted listeners on a radio tour through New York City's Chinatown of a quarter century before. Chinese music was played by the WGY Orchestra (WGY, Schenectady, NY, 1924).

6445 **Chinley, Jeannette.** Actress Chinley was a member of *The Goldbergs* cast.

6446 **Chinn, Genevieve.** Miss Chinn was a singer billed as "The Sweetheart of Song" (KFWI, San Francsico, CA, 1927).

6447 **Chinn, Mary Jane.** COM-HE (KRNT, Des Moines, IA, 1955).

6448 **Chipman, June.** COM-HE (KOVO, Provo, UT, 1951).

6449 ***Chips Davis, Commando.*** The action drama told the story of Commando Davis who operated exclusively behind enemy lines during World War II. Carleton Young played the title role (15 min., CBS, 1943).

6450 ***(The) Chiropractic Hour of Music.*** Weekly music program (60 min., Tuesday, 10:00–11:00 p.m, WMCA, New York, NY, 1925).

6451 **Chisholm, D. Scott.** Chisholm broadcast golf talks (KNX, Los Angeles, CA, 1925).

6452 **Chisholm, Frances.** COM-HE (WGMS, Washington, DC, 1951).

6453 **Chittick, Cline.** Harmonica soloist (KFOX, Long Beach, CA, 1929).

6454 **Chittick, H.R.** Newscaster (KGEZ, Kalispell, MT, 1941). Sportscaster (KGEZ, 1941).

6455 **Chittison, Herman.** Leader (*Herman Chittison Trio*, inst. mus. prg., 15 min., Saturday, 6:15–6:30 P.M., ABC, 1947).

6456 **Choate, Helen.** Daytime serial actress Choate appeared on the daytime serial programs *Pretty Kitty Kelly*, *Rosemary*; and *Brenda Curtis*.

6457 **Choate, Robert A. "Bob."** Newscaster (KWFC, Hot Springs, AR, 1945–1946; *Headline News*, KWFC, 1948).

6458 ***(The) Choice of a Lifetime.*** John Reed King and Janie Ford hosted the transcribed quiz program. The announcer was Ken Roberts (30 min., Sunday, 9:30–10:00 P.M., ABC, 1949).

6459 **Choir of the University Christian Church.** Mrs. Leonard C. Brown directed the vocal group assisted by Miss Bernice Hargrove (KTBI, Los Angeles, CA, 1925).

6460 ***Cholly Knickerbocker.*** Maury H.H. Paul became Cholly Knickerbocker in 1934 (CBS, 1934). He specialized in society gossip. Igor Cassini, the society columnist of the New York *Journal American*, later became Cholly and broadcast social (society) news and interviewed celebrities (15 min., Monday through Saturday, 11:45–12:00 midnight, WJZ, 1951).

6461 **Chong, Peter.** *See* **Goo Chong, Peter.**

6462 **Chopin Singing Society.** Seth Clark directed the 40 voice male choir (WGR, Buffalo, NY, 1925).

6463 ***(The) Choraliers.*** Longine-Wittnauer Watches sponsored this transcribed program of choral music. Frank Knight was the program's announcer (30 min., Sunday, 2:30–3:00 P.M., CBS, 1950).

6464 **Chowen, Betty.** Pianist (WJAZ, Chicago, IL, 1926).

6465 ***(A) Christmas Carol.*** *See* **Holidays on Radio.**

6466 ***(The) Christ Episcopal Church [Glenridge, NJ] Service.*** In 1922, the Reverend George P. Dougherty delivered a Christmas Eve message that supposedly was the *first* church service broadcast in the New York City area (WJZ, New York, NY, 1922).

6467 **Chriss, Nadine.** Pianist (KFWI, San Francisco, CA, 1930).

6468 **Christian, Ann.** COM-HE (KKAN, Phillipsburg, KS, 1960).

6469 **Christian, Guy.** Sportscaster (KSBW, Salinas, CA, 1953).

6470 **Christian, Jo.** COM-HE (KFAL, Fulton, MO, 1956).

6471 **Christian, Tommy.** Leader (Tommy Christian Orchestra, KMOX, St. Louis, MO, 1929). The fine radio and recording band included the following personnel: Christian, ldr. and bar.; Phil and Ted Fisher, t.; Harold Lawson and Art Manners, clr. and as.; James DeAngeles, clr. and ts.; Victor DeAngeles, pac.; Carl Pickel, p.; Art Barnett, t. and d., Harry Rich, tba.; and Paul Close, bj.

6472 **(The) Christian School Kindergarten Orchestra of North Little Rock.** Miss Mildred Oates directed the "band" of little ones (KGHI, Little Rock, AR, 1929).

6473 ***(The) Christian Science Monitor Views the News.*** The *Christian Science Monitor* newspaper sponsored an authoritative news commentary program drawn from the pages of the paper. Erwin D. Canham broadcast the news. Phelps Gates was the announcer (15 min., Thursday, 8:15–8:30 P.M., NBC, 1946).

6474 **Christiansen, Axel.** Pianist known as the "Czar of Ragtime" (WHT, Chicago, IL, 1927).

6475 **Christiansen, Betty.** Pianist (WGY, Schenectady, NY, 1923).

6476 **Christiansen, Chris.** Leader (*Chris Christiansen Orchestra*, instr. mus. prg.,WLW, Cincinnati, OH, 1942).

6477 **Christiansen, K.** Newscaster (KUSD, Vermillion, SD, 1944).

6478 **Christiansen, Loraine.** COM-HE (KOGA, Ogallala, NE, 1960).

6479 **Christiansen, Meta.** Contralto (WJZ, New York, NY, 1925).

6480 **Christiansen, Sharon.** COM-HE (KSVC, Richfield, UT, 1960).

6481 **Christianson [Christenson], Paul.** Leader (*Paul Christianson Orchestra*, instr. mus. prg., NBC, 1935; WENR, Chicago, IL, 1937–1938).

6482 **Christie, George.** Sportscaster (*Christie's Sports Page*, WFEA, Manchester, NH, 1944; WFEA, 1947–1952).

6483 **Christie, Lewis B.** Newscaster (KOCA, Kilgore, TX, 1945). DJ (*Eye Opener*, KOCA, 1950).

6484 **Christine.** Singer-pianist (NBC, 1936).

6485 **Christofferson, Al.** Sportscaster and play-by-play announcer (KTRF, Thief River Falls, MN, 1949–1951).

6486 **Christopher, Bob.** DJ (*Rise 'N Shine*, WSAR, Fall River, MA, 1960).

6487 **Christopher, Gage.** Bass-baritone (KFI, Los Angeles, CA, 1923).

6488 **Christopher, Robert.** Newscaster (WMAN, Mansfield, OH, 1944).

6489 ***Christopher London.*** Motion picture star Glenn Ford played Christopher London, a private-eye created by Earle Stanley Gardner. Written by Les Crutchfield and directed by William N. Robson, the interesting series was short lived (30 min., Sunday, 7:00–7:30 P.M., NBC, 1950).

6490 ***Christopher Wells.*** DeSoto-Plymouth dealers sponsored this show on which Myron McCormick and Charlotte Laurence played a Winchell-type columnist and his girl Friday. They encountered many adventures as they traveled their news hunting rounds. Music was supplied by Peter Van Steeden's Orchestra. The cast members also included: Joe DeSantis, Wendell Holmes, Jane Lauren and Peter Sapell (30 min., Sunday, 10:00–10:30 P.M., CBS, 1947).

6491 **Christy, Al.** DJ (*Syncopated Clock*, WDAF, Kansas City, MO, 1949).

6492 **Christy, Kenneth "Ken."** Actor Christy appeared on the *Alan Young Show*, *Jack Armstrong*, *The Saint* and *Stepmother* programs.

6493 **Christy, R. Jack.** Newscaster (KASA, Elk City, OK, 1940).

6494 **Chromis, Joe.** Leader (*Joe Chromis Orchestra*, instr. mus. prg., WLW, Cincinnati, OH, 1935).

6495 **Chrystie, Bob.** Sportscaster (WPAL, Charleston, WV, 1948–1950).

6496 **Chubb-Steinberg Orchestra.** Popular radio band (WLW, Cincinnati, OH, 1924).

6497 **Chuck and Ray.** Harmony singing team of Chuck Harris and Ray Ferris (WMBB, Homewood, IL and WOK, Chicago, IL, 1928). These veterans of the *Weener Minstrel Show* later sang as the *Old Harmony Slaves*, vcl. mus. prg. (WLS, 1935–1936). They also appeared on other stations such as WHN (New York, NY); WOK (Chicago, IL); WGES (Chicago, IL); and WQJ (Chicago, IL). Frequently they also appeared on the *Grand Ole Opry.*

6498 ***(The) Chuck Wagon Boys.*** CW singing group that consisted of Reggie Cross, Red Foley, Hal O'Halloran and Howard Black (15 min., Tuesday and Thursday, 6:45–7:00 A.M., WLS, Chicago, IL, 1936; WWVA, Richmond, VA, 1942).

6499 ***(The) Chuck Wagon Gang.*** CW music group specializing in religious and gospel music (WWVA, Wheeling, WV, 1942). Children Lola, Effie and Ernest sang with Dave "Dad" Carter on Texas local radio in 1935 as the Carter Quartet (KFYO, Lubbock, TX, 1935). The quartet sang cowboy, American and Irish folk ballads, along with some gospel songs. They were sponsored first by Martin's Bakery and, later, by Conoco Oil Company. After moving to WBAP (Fort Worth, TX) in 1936, they sang on a Saturday morning show sponsored by Morton Salt Company.

The Brewley Flour Mills Company persuaded the Carter Quartet to become the radio version of the Brewley's Chuck Wagon Gang. Cy Leland was the group's announcer and manager at the time. Over the years, the group added and lost family members. They engaged in the "flour war" of the 1930s, when other Fort Worth stations featured such other outstanding CW groups as the Light Crust Doughboys, sponsored by Light Crust Flour and Ernest Tubb, sponsored by Gold Chain Flour. When their sponsor offered a picture of the Chuck Wagon Gang, they received 100,000 requests. By 1940, the group sang gospel songs exclusively. They made their first recordings in 1936 and produced 408 masters for Columbia Records by the time they completed their last recording session on September 23, 1975. David P. "Dad" Carter, mother Carrie and, at one time or another, all of their children, with the exception of Clellon sang with the group: Effie, Ernest, Rose, Lola, Anna, Ruth, Ellen, Roy, Eddie and Bettye.

6500 ***Chuck Wagon Time.*** The CW mus. prg. featured the Chuckwagon Gang (WGN, Chicago, IL, 1937). *See* **Chuck Wagon Gang.**

6501 ***(The) Chuckle Chronicle.*** Russell Pratt and Don McNeill starred in the daytime comedy series as editors for a daily newspaper called the *Chuckle Chronicle.* One of the paper's campaigns conducted by Pratt and McNeill was "BE-CLEAN-FOR-ONCE-IN-YOUR-LIFE." The paper also employed Professor Marmaduke Courtleigh Twitchett as the children's editor; sports editor Speed O'Blatz; reporter T. Thomas Toofins; and copy boy Nutsy O'Swish (15 min., Monday through Friday, 12:45–1:00 P.M. CST, WMAQ, Chicago, IL, 1936).

6502 **Chudnow, Dave.** Leader (Dave Chudnow's Ensemble, KFQZ, Hollywood, CA, 1926).

6503 **Chumasero, Kathryn.** Contralto (*Kathryn Chumasero*, vcl. mus. prg., WOR, Newark, NJ, 1934).

6504 **Chumley, Charles.** Newscaster (KRBC, Abilene, TX, 1941–1942). Sportscaster (KRBC, 1941).

6505 **Church, Arthur B. [R.].** Announcer (KLDS, Independence, MO, 1925–1927).

6506 **Church, Betty.** COM-HE (WARL, Arlington, VA, 1956).

6507 **Church, Christine.** Soprano (WGBS, New York, NY, 1925).

6508 **Church, Joyce.** COM-HE (WARL, Arlington, VA, 1956).

6509 **Church, Ross.** Leader (*Ross Church Orchestra*, instr. mus. prg., WHP, Harrisburg, PA, 1936).

6510 **Church, Wilda Wilson.** Director of the KGO Players (KGO, San Francisco, CA, 1924).The following year Church conducted a program dedicated to "the improvement of our native tongue," *A Lesson in English*, as well as other programs on which she talked about various aspects of music (KGO, 1925).

6511 ***(The) Church in the Hills.*** Religious program (30 min., Sunday, 1:30–2:00 P.M., WLW, Cincinnati, OH, 1934).

6512 ***(The) Church of the Air.*** The program was broadcast in two half-hour segments. The first service from 8:00–8:30 a.m was conducted by Rev. Z.T. Phillips, Rector of the Epiphany Episcopal Church, Washington, DC, and the second from 11:00–11:30 A.M. by Rabbi Jonah B. Wise of New York City's Central Synagogue (CBS, 1934).

6513 **Church of the Open Door Choir.** Professor J.B. Trowbridge directed the vocal group (KTBI, Los Angeles, CA, 1925).

6514 **Churches, Glenn.** DJ (*Jazz, Rhythm and Blues*, KCRA, Sacramento, CA, 1954–1957).

6515 **Churchill, Audrey.** COM-HE (KRLC, Lewiston, ID, 1960).

6516 **Churchill, Betty.** Actress Churchill was a cast member of the *Betty and Bob* daytime serial.

6517 **Churchill, Dorothy.** Soprano (KJBS, San Francisco, CA, 1929)

6518 **Churchill, Nelson.** News Analyst (*Nelson Churchill Views the News*, WAAB-WNAC, Boston, MA, 1939; WNAC, 1945). Sportscaster (*Digest of Sports*, WNAC, Boston, MA, 1939).

6519 **Churchill, Stuart.** Tenor (*Stuart Churchill*, vcl. mus. prg., CBS, 1936).

6520 **Churchill, Ted.** Newscaster (WCOP, Boston, MA, 1944).

6521 **Churchman, Caroline.** COM-HE (KTTV, Bloomington, IN, 1958).

6522 **Cianca, Alberto.** Newscaster (WOV, New York, NY, 1942).

6523 **Cianci, Mirella.** Soprano (WFI, Philadelphia, PA, 1926).

6524 **Ciccone, Al.** Leader (Al Ciccone and his Harlem Tea Garden Orchestra, WGBS, New York, NY and WEBJ, New York, NY, 1926).

6525 **Cicero, Tendaro.** Tenor (WEBJ, New York, NY, 1926).

6526 **Cieciuch, Leon.** Newscaster (WHOM, Jersey City, NJ, 1941).

6527 **Cierpke, (Dr.) Alfred.** Newscaster (WDXB, Chattanooga, TN, 1948).

6528 ***(The) Cigar Band.*** Versatile Walter Beban conducted the program's orchestra with vocals by Clarence Hayes (Monday, 9:30–10:00 P.M., NBC-Pacific Network, 1929).

6529 **Cimers, Jaroslav.** Cimers was billed as a "Trombonist ace" (KYW, Chicago, IL, 1928).

6530 **Cincinnati String Quartet.** A classical music group that included Ernest Park, first violin; Herbert Silbersack, second violin; Herbest Weiss, cello; and Gordon Kahn, viola (WLW, Cincinnati, OH, 1923).

6531 ***Cincinnati Symphony Orchestra.*** The Cincinnati Symphony broadcast a weekly program of symphonic music for adults, as well as an irregularly scheduled series of concerts for children (Tuesdays, 2:30–3:00 P.M., 1936–1937). Another series for adults was also broadcast weekly (Fridays, 1936–1939). Guest performers who appeared with the orchestra included: Simon Barer, pianist; Gregor Piatigorsky, cellist; pianist Jose Iturbi; violinist Josef Szigeti; organist Charles M. Courboin; Rudolf Ganz, pianist; Severin Eisenberger, pianist; violinist Bronislaw Huberman; and pianists E. Robert Schmitz and Alexander Tansman.

6532 **Cincinnati Zither Players.** Zither music group (WLW, Cincinnati, OH, 1926).

6533 ***Cinderella.*** Cinderella, not otherwise identified, was a DJ who played records. *Variety* said she had a poor "radio voice" and had to "leave at midnight" (60 min., Wednesday, 11:00–12:00 midnight, WHN, New York, NY, 1940).

6534 **Cinderella Ballroom Orchestra.** Los Angeles dance orchestra (KFI, Los Angeles, CA, 1924).

6535 **Cinderella Cafe Orchestra.** Popular dance band (WHT, Chicago, IL, 1926).

6536 **(The) "Cinderella from Georgia."** An unidentified female "crooner" (WFAA, Dallas, TX, 1928).

6537 **Cinderella Wolverines.** Popular local jazz band (WOR, Newark, NJ, 1924).

6538 ***Cindy's Cabin Door.*** *Cindy's Cabin Door* was a variety show that featured a "colored quartet" and readings by a "colored girl" from the works of Paul Laurence Dunbar (WCKY, Cincinnati, OH, 1934).

6539 **Cinecone, Genevieve.** Soprano (KYW, Chicago, IL, 1922–1924).

6540 ***(The) Cinnamon Bear.*** First broadcast in 1937 and repeated at Christmas on many stations for several years, *The Cinnamon Bear* became a children's holiday classic. The first program of the 26 episode serial was first broadcast November 29, 1937. The program's 26th and final episode's happy ending was broadcast on December 24, 1937.

Written by Glanville "Glen" Heisch, it was narrated by Bud Heistand. Its cast included such talented veteran radio performers as Buddy Duncan, Joseph Kerns, Verna Felton, Hanley Stafford, Howard McNear, Elvia Allman, Barbara Jean Wong, Elliot Lewis, Lou Merrill, Frank Nelson, Cy Kendall, Gale Gordon, Ted Osborne, Ed Max, Joe DuVal, Martha Wenthworth, Bud Thompson and Dorothy Scott. Music was provided by Felix Mills.

Glanville Heisch's inspiration came from a favorite stuffed bear of his childhood. When he began writing light verse stories for his daughter, Catherine, one of them featured his childhood favorite stuffed bear. When he was asked to write a Christmas program for children, he created *The Cinnamon Bear*, and an annual children's classic was produced.

The story tells of the adventures of Judy and Jimmy Barton, who search for the silver star that always was placed on the top of their Christmas tree. While searching in their attic for the star, they find a teddy bear — Paddy O'Cinnamon, who sets out with them to help them search. Their silver star, it seems, was stolen by the Crazy Quilt Dragon and taken to Maybeland. The Cinnamon Bear guides them on their successful search that ended on Christmas Eve.

6541 **(The) Cino Singers Quartet.** Richard Fluke directed the vocal group that also consisted of Russell Dunham, Fenton Pugh and Ralph Hartzell. Walter de Vaux was the group's accompanist (WLW, Cincinnati, OH, 1929).

6542 ***(The) C.I.O. Singers*** **(aka *Sterling Jubilee Singers*).** The talented Black singing group was sponsored by the Congress of Industrial Organizations (C.I.O.). They appeared on a Hampton Roads, VA, station in the 1930s.

6543 **Ciraldo, Al.** Sportscaster (*Sports Column*, WGLS, Decatur, GA, 1953–1955).

6544 ***(The) Circle.*** Kellogg Company sponsored the program that probably was the first network "talk show" to feature prominent stars. Ronald Colman presided over the show whose regular participants included: Madeleine Carroll, Cary Grant, Carole Lombard, Chico and Groucho Marx, Basil Rathbone, Lawrence Tibbett, the Foursome and Bobby Dolan's Orchestra. The regulars discussed a variety of topics, sang, gossiped, traded quips, told jokes and appeared in dramatic sketches. Several ghost stories were dramatized and significant topics such as the freedom of speech and propaganda were discussed. Carroll Carroll, George Faulkner and Dick Mack were the writers and Cal Kuhl the director. Although it was entertaining and highly literate, the show received an undeserved barrage of negative criticism. *Variety* reported that the show soon disappeared despite its creativity and unique appeal or perhaps because of it (60 min., Sunday, 10:00–11:00 P.M., NBC-Red, 1939).

6545 ***(The) Circle Bar Ranch Boys.*** CW mus. prg. (KYW, Philadelphia, PA, 1934–1937).

6546 **(The) Circle Theater Symphony Orchestra.** The symphonic group was directed by Caril D. Elinor (KNX, Los Angeles, CA, 1926).

6547 ***(The) Circuit Rider.*** The Circuit Rider, an unidentified CW singer, was featured on the CW mus. prg. (WIRE, Indianapolis, IN, 1937).

6548 ***Circus Days.*** Courtney Riley Cooper wrote the dramatic series sponsored by the Harold F. Ritchie Company, makers of Scott's Emulsion. The story told of Shoestring Charlie, a circus owner, played by Jack Roseleigh, who was a strong proponent of clean shows. His circus rival, Bill Hayden, on the other hand, was a gyp artist. The program's cast included: Betty Council, Bruce Evans, Griffin Grafts, Henry Gurvey, Milton Herman, Walter Kinsella, Wally Maher, Jack Roseleigh, Ernest Whitman and Frank Wilson (15 min., Friday, 7:30–7:45 P.M., NBC-Red, 1933).

6549 ***Circus Night in Silvertown.*** Comedian Joe Cook was the barker on the "circus" program. B.A. Rolfe conducted the orchestra. Phil Duey, Lucy Monroe and Peg LaCentra sang and Tim and Irene Ryan, Teddy Bergman (Alan Reed) and Lew Hearn provided the comedy routines on the simulated circus show (NBC, 1935).

6550 **Ciro Orchestra.** Dave Bernie directed the club band (WOR, Newark, NJ, 1925).

6551 **Cisler, Steve.** Nightly at 8:00 P.M. in 1929, announcer Steve Cisler signed station WLW, (Cincinnati, OH) off the air by saying, "All right, Homer, pull the big switch and let's go home." When hearing this, young listeners knew it meant bedtime for them. Cisler began his radio career after completing high school by taking a summer announcing job at KTHS (Hot Springs National Park, AR). Enrolling at the University of Arkansas in 1925, he began working at the university's station, KFMQ (Little Rock, AR). On his first program Cisler read an agricultural report on "The Castration of Spring Pigs." By 1925, he had moved on to WLS (Chicago, IL) and, later to WLW, where he originated his unique trademark sign-off. Cisler returned to manage station KTHS in 1937 and stayed until 1939.

6552 Cisne, Dick. Leader (*Dick Cisne Orchestra,* instr. mus. prg., WHAS, Louisville, KY, 1942).

6553 *Cities Service Band of America* (aka *Band of America Program*). Paul LaValle conducted the excellent 48-piece band sponsored by Cities Service Company (30 min., Friday, 8:00–8:30 P.M., NBC, 1948).

6554 *Cities Service Concert.* The excellent weekly musical program was first broadcast on February 18, 1927, and remained on the air in one format or another until 1956. That first program featured Edwin Franko Goldman's brass band performing the following musical selections: "The William Tell Overture," "The Overture to Mignon," exerpts from *Faust* and Liszt's "Second Hungarian Rhapsody." Many guests appeared on the program (NBC-Red, 1927).

When the Rosario Bourdon Orchestra replaced the Goldman band later in the first year, the Cavaliers [male] singing group joined them as regular cast members. Other singers, musicians and conductors appearing later on the program were: Jessica Dragonnette, the piano team of Frank Banta and Milton Rettenberg, conductor Frank Black, baritone John Seagle, the Men About Town [male quartet], Lucille Manners, Ross Graham and Paul LaValle's band. Sportswriter Grantland Rice gave football scores on some programs. Ford Bond and Edward Thorgerson were the announcers. When the program celebrated its 19th year on the air in 1946, it was reported to be the oldest commercial radio program on the air. Incidentally, Paul LaValle played clarinet in the orchestra on the program's first broadcast in 1927. Nineteen years later LaValle conducted the orchestra on the *Cities Service Highways in Melody* program. A few years after that he conducted the band on *The Cities Service Band of America* program, which later became *The Band of America* show. The *Cities Service Concert* program's name had changed to *Highways of Melody* in 1944, when Paul LaValle replaced orchestral conductor Frank Black. Still another name change to *The Cities Service Band of America* occurred when the Paul LaValle's brass band became the featured attraction in 1948.

6555 Cities Service Salon Orchestra. Salon music group (NBC, 1927).

6556 *City Delivery Hour.* Bobbie Benedict and "Smokey Joe" Brown sang on the vocal program (30 min., Daily, 6:30–7:00 P.M., WLBN, Little Rock, AR, 1928). The two men who were billed as "The Musical Ice Men," ironically, in real life actually were ice delivery men.

6557 *(The) City Delivery Ice Men Orchestra.* The program was sponsored by the same City Ice Delivery Company that sponsored the *City Delivery Hour.* The band broadcast regularly (KGHI, Little Rock, AR, 1928).

6558 *City Desk.* Frank Gould wrote the dramatic series sponsored by Colgate Brushless Shave Cream. The story focused on two star reporters, played by Charles Stratton and Gertrude Warner, who each week tracked down murderers and other vicious criminals. The other cast members included: Donald Briggs, George Coulouris, Jimmy McCallion, James Meighan, Karl Swenson and Ethel Owen. The writers were Frank Dahm, Frank Gould and Stuart Hawkins and the directors were Himan Brown and Kenneth W. MacGregor. Incidental music was composd by Charles Paul (25 min., Wednesday, 8:30–8:55 P.M., NBC, 1940–1941).

6559 *Civic Calendar.* Bill Herson was the announcer-host on the program that was devoted to broadcasting community notices free of charge. Entertainment was provided by a tenor and musical interludes by an unidentified pianist (15 min., Monday through Friday, Morning, WFBR, Baltimore, MD, 1936).

6560 *Civic Repertory Theater.* Eve LaGallienne and associates presented weekly dramatic productions on the interesting show (30 min., Thursday, 6:30–7:00 P.M., CBS, 1930).

6561 Civic Symphony Orchestra of Denver. Horace E. Tureman conducted the hundred-piece orchestra (KOA, Denver, CO, 1925).

6562 Civille, Roy. Newscaster (KIDO, Boise, ID, 1939–1940; KFIO, Spokane, WA, 1941). Sportscaster (KIDO, 1940; KFIO, Spokane, WA, 1941).

6563 "CJ." Designation for announcer Carl Jester (WBY, Charlotte, NC, 1923).

6564 Clahan, John. Sportscaster (*Marin Sports,* KTIM, San Raphael, CA, 1953).

6565 Claiborne, Everett. Newscaster (KLX, Oakland, CA, 1946).

6566 Claire, Bernice. Soprano (*Bernice Claire,* vcl. mus. prg., CBS, 1936).

6567 Claire, Dorothy. Singer (*Dorothy Claire, Songs,* vcl. mus. prg., 30 min., Sunday, 2:00–2:30 P.M., ABC, 1945).

6568 Claire, Helen. Busy actress Claire appeared on such daytime serials as *Backstage Wife* aka *Mary Noble, Backstage Wife, The O'Neills, Stella Dallas,* and *Evelyn Winters* aka *The Strange Romance of Evelyn Winters.*

6569 Claire, Rose. COM-HE (*Woman's Page with Rose Claire,* KXOK, St. Louis, MO, 1941).

6570 Claire Trio. Instrumental trio with Ruth Niedholt, violinist; Janet Richards, cellist; and Ruth Howard, pianist (KFRC, San Francisco, CA, 1926).

6571 Clancy, Jim. Clancy was the announcer on the *Vaudeville Program,* a variety show that originated from the Hartford [Connecticut] Theater (WTIC, Hartford, CT, 1928).

6572 Clancy, Josephine. Singer (WFRL, New York, NY, 1936).

6573 Clancy, Nancy. Singer (WMCA, New York, NY, 1936).

6574 Clancy, Ray. Newscaster (WMFJ, Daytona Beach, FL, 1945–1946). Sportscaster (WMFJ, Daytona Beach, FL, 1945–1950).

6575 Claney, Howard. Announcer Claney worked on the *Amanda of Honeymoon Hill, American Album of Familiar Music, Mr. Chameleon* and *Stella Dallas* programs.

6576 Clapham, D. COM-HE (KNBA, Vallejo, CA, 1958).

6577 Clapp, Nona. Four-year-old reader Nona Clapp appeared with her sister, Paulie Clapp (KHJ, Los Angeles, CA, 1924).

6578 Clapp, Sandy. Sportscaster (WWSR, St. Albans, VT, 1956).

6579 Clapper, Kenneth "Kenny." Sportscaster (*Sports Page,* WRTA, Altoona, PA, 1952–1953; WRTA, 1956).

6580 Clapper, Raymond. Newscaster (MBS, 1930s-1940s; WMAL, Washington, DC, 1941; MBS-WOR, New York, NY, 1942).

6581 *Clara, Lu and Em.* This daytime serial was an entertaining mix of drama and comedy (15 min., Monday through Friday, 10:00–10:15 P.M., NBC-Red, 1934). The program originated as a dramatic sketch when Louise Starkey, Isobel Carothers and Helen King were students at Northwestern University. These women in the roles of Clara, Lu and Em, respectively, first broadcast on WGN (Chicago, IL) in 1930, before it appeared on the NBC-Blue network. When Carothers died in 1936 the show went off the air. It returned on CBS in 1942 with Harriet Allyn, Dorothy Day and Fran Harris in the title roles.

6582 Clardy, Gilda. Contralto (KLDS, Independence, MO, 1926).

6583 Clare, Bob. Newscaster (*News Roundup,* KTIP, Porterville, CA, 1947). DJ (*Here Comes Charlie,* KYNO, Fresno, CA, 1949).

6584 Clare, Val. Newscaster (CKLW, Detroit, MI/Ontario, Canada, 1942, 1946).

6585 Clare, Virginia. COM-HE (KIHO, Sioux Falls, SD, 1954).

6586 Claridge, Gay. Leader (*Gay Claridge Orchestra,* instr. mus. prg., WENR, Chicago, IL, 1939, 1942).

6587 (The) Clarion Trio. The popular vocal group consisted of soprano Vera Hamann; contralto Hazel Potter; and alto Claire Jones. Their accompanist was Flora Zimmerman (KYA, San Francisco, CA, 1927).

6588 Clark, Adele. Panelist on *This is Broadway* show (CBS, 1949).

6589 Clark, Bernie. DJ (*Wonderful World of Music,* WSNO, Barre, VT, 1960).

6590 Clark, Bill. DJ (*Caravan of Music* and *Hoosier Ho-Down,* WJCD, Seymour, IN, 1949).

6591 Clark, Bob. Sportscaster (KULE, Ephrata, WA, 1960).

6592 Clark, Bruce. Pianist (*Bruce Clark,* instr. mus. prg., WWVA, Richmond, VA, 1935).

6593 Clark, Bud. Sportscaster (WIL, St. Louis, MO, 1960).

6594 Clark, Buddy. Baritone (*Buddy Clark,* vcl. mus. prg., CBS, 1935–1937).

6595 Clark, Carl. Newscaster (WTAQ, Green Bay, WI, 1940; WINN, Louisville, KY, 1941).

6596 **Clark, Chris.** Sportscaster (*In the Sportlight*, WBSM, New Bedford, MA, 1953).

6597 **Clark, Cottonseed.** DJ (*Cottonseed Clark*, a six-hour program of recorded CW music daily, KVSM, San Mateo, CA, 1949; 1952; KEEN, San Jose, CA, 1955–1956).

6598 **Clark, David C.** Announcer Clark was sometimes known only as "DC" (WHAM, Rochester, NY, 1924).

6599 **Clark, Dick.** DJ (WFIL, Philadelphia, PA, 1955).

6600 **Clark, Dick.** DJ (KTEM, Temple, TX, 1956).

6601 **Clark, Don.** Leader (Don Clark La Monica Orchestra, KNX, Hollywood, CA, 1924–1925; Biltmore Hotel Dance Orchestra, KHJ, Los Angeles, CA, 1926). Clark recorded on Victor records in 1924 as Don Clark and his LaMonica Ballroom Orchestra that included: Clark, ldr., clr., as. and bar.; Aime Reinwald and Kenneth Howard, t.; Art Ginder and Frank Jenks, tb.; Dick Dickinson and Whitney Stayner, clr. and as.; Howard Jackson, p.; Everett McLaughlin, clr. and ts.; Harold McDonald, d.; and Leonard Mojica, bj. On some sessions, Clark recorded with Bing Crosby and Al Rinker.

6602 **Clark, Don.** Newscaster (KFDA, Amarillo, TX, 1945).

6603 **Clark, Donald.** Announcer (NBC, 1928).

6604 **Clark, Douglas.** DJ (*Western Trails*, KWEM, West Memphis, AR, 1947).

6605 **Clark, Edna.** COM-HE (WWGP, Sanford, NC, 1954).

6606 **Clark, Elwood L.** Bass (WGY, Schenectady, NY, 1925).

6607 **Clark, Eunice.** Singer (WAAF, Chicago, IL, 1938–1939).

6608 **Clark, F.** Tenor (WQJ, Chicago, IL, 1926).

6609 **Clark, Frances.** COM-HE (KROG, Sonora, CA, 1957).

6610 **Clark, Freddie.** Leader (*Freddie Clark Orchestra*, instr. mus. prg., KTHS, Hot Springs, AR, 1940).

6611 **Clark, Gordon.** DJ (*Moods in Melody*, KRAL, Rawlins, WY, 1947–1951; *Afternoon Variety*, KRAL, 1952).

6612 **Clark, Gordon L.** Newscaster (KFKA, Greeley, CO, 1939). DJ (*Revolving Bandstand*, KPBX, Beaumont, TX, 1947; *Gordon's Recordings*, KPBX, 1948; *Gordon's Recordings*, KRIC, Beaumont, TX), 1949–1955; KOGT, Orange, TX, 1957).

6613 **Clark, Harper.** DJ (*Hillbilly Hits*, KALB, Alexandria, LA, 1948).

6614 **Clark, Harry.** Newscaster (*CBS News*, CBS, 1944–1947). Sportscaster (WVOM, Boston, MA, 1952). Announcer (*Backstage Wife*, network).

6615 **Clark, Hazel.** Violinist (WBZ, Springfield, MA, 1924).

6616 **Clark, Helen.** Contralto (WJZ, New York, NY, 1927). Clark appeared on the *Royal Hour* program (NBC, New York, NY, 1928).

6617 **Clark, Helen.** COM-HE (KXXX, Colby, KS, 1951).

6618 **Clark, Herbert "Herb."** Newscaster (KWBW, Hutchinson, KS, 1942; KHAS, Hastings, NE, 1946). Sportscaster (KWBW, 1942).

6619 **Clark, Herbert M.** Newscaster (NBC-Blue, 1944).

6620 **Clark, Howard.** Announcer (WJAS, Pittsburgh, PA, 1925; KQV, Pittsburgh, PA, 1927).

6621 **Clark, Howard E.** Announcer (WMT, Waterloo, IA, 1925).

6622 **Clark, J.B.** Sportscaster (WPTF, Raleigh, NC, 1938; WRAL, Raleigh, NC, 1940; WDNC, Durham, NC, 1942; WBT, Charlotte, NC, 1945; WAYS, Charlotte, NC, 1946–1947). Newscaster (WDNC, 1941–1942; WAYS, 1946).

6623 **Clark, J. Mabel.** Newscaster (KTBC, Austin, TX, 1942).

6624 **Clark, James E.** Newscaster (WMMN, Fairmont, WV, 1942).

6625 **Clark, Jimmy.** Leader (Jimmy Clark and his White Way Entertainers band, WHN, New York, NY and WGBS, New York, NY, 1925). Pianist (WEAF, New York, NY and WGCP, New York, NY, 1925–1926).

6626 **Clark, (Miss) Jo.** Newscaster (WRDW, Augusta, GA, 1938–1939).

6627 **Clark, Joan.** COM-HE (WLEU, Erie, PA, 1951).

6628 **Clark, John.** Announcer (KYW, Chicago, IL, 1927). Announcer and continuity writer (WBZ, Springfield, MA, 1928).

6629 **Clark, John.** Producer-director Clark worked on the *We Love and Learn* daytime serial program.

6630 **Clark, Katherine.** Newscaster (WCAU, Philadelphia, PA, 1945).

6631 **Clark, Kathleen.** Station staff pianist (WKAF, Milwaukee, WI, 1926).

6632 **Clark, Keith.** Sportscaster (KUTA, Salt Lake City, UT, 1946).

6633 **Clark, Kenneth.** Guitarist (WLS, Chicago, IL, 1925).

6634 **Clark, Lee.** DJ (KMBY, Monterey, CA, 1955). Sportscaster (*San Diego Today*, KGB, San Diego, CA, 1960).

6635 **Clark, Lon.** Actor Clark appeared on *Bright Horizon*, *Earth Born*, *Mysterious Traveler*, *Nick Carter, Master Detective* (title role) and *Wilderness Road*.

6636 **Clark, Lou.** Leader (*Lou Clark Orchestra*, instr. mus. prg., WLLH, Lowell, MA, 1939).

6637 **Clark, Lowell.** Newscaster (KTMC, McAlester, OK, 1946). DJ (*Dinner Dance*, KGFF, Shawnee, OK, 1947–1950). Sportscaster (KGFF, 1947).

6638 **Clark, Maurice.** Announcer (WABO, Rochester, NY, 1927).

6639 **Clark, Norman.** Leader (Norman Clark and his South Sea Islanders Orchestra, NBC, 1928).

6640 **Clark, Palmer.** Leader (*Palmer Clark Orchestra*, instr. mus. prg., WGN, Chicago, IL, 1934).

6641 **Clark, Paul.** Sportscaster (WGBF, Evansville, IL, 1937; WEOA, Evansville, IL, 1937; WGBF, 1938).

6642 **Clark, Randy.** Newscaster (WMMJ, Peoria, IL, 1947).

6643 **Clark, Ray.** Newscaster (WNAX, Yankton, SD, 1939; WOW, Omaha, NE, 1948). Sportscaster (WOW, 1941).

6644 **Clark, Raymond.** Tenor (KFI, Los Angeles, CA, 1926).

6645 **Clark, R. E.** Announcer (KFBC, Sacramento, CA, 1927).

6646 **Clark, Robert T.** Tenor (WSM, Nashville, TN, 1928).

6647 **Clark, Rocky.** Newscaster (WICC, Bridgeport, CT, 1941).

6648 **Clark, Sim.** Newscaster (KFDM, Beaumont, TX, 1941). Sportscaster (KFDM, 1941).

6649 **Clark, Sylvia.** Monologist (NBC, 1937).

6650 **Clark, Temple.** COM-HE (WITN, Washington, DC, 1937).

6651 **Clark, Tom.** Sportscaster (*Let's Talk Sports*, WTAP, Parkersburg, WV, 1955).

6652 **Clark, Victoria.** Organist (WJSV, Washington, DC, 1937).

6653 **Clark, Virginia.** COM-HE (Beauty and charm hints were broadcast on her *Charm School of the Air* program, WGN, Chicago, IL, 1936). She also appeared on *The Romance of Helen Trent* (title role) daytime serial.

6654 **Clark, Walter C.** Announcer (KFEY, Kellogg, ID, 1926–1927).

6655 **Clark, Willard.** Baritone (WBZ, Boston-Springfield, MA, 1924).

6656 ***(The) Clark Carbon Paper Quartet.*** Tenors Don Dinty and Bob Benedict appeared with baritone Harry Wigenton and bass Virgil Ward on the popular local music show (KGHI, Little Rock, AR, 1929).

6657 **Clark University Colored Glee Club.** Talented collegiate vocal group (WSB, Atlanta, GA, 1924).

6658 **Clarke, Betty.** COM-HE (WFDF, Flint, MI, 1956–1957).

6659 **Clarke, Ellen.** Pianist (KGO, Oakland, CA, 1926).

6660 **Clarke, Helen.** COM-HE (KMMJ, Grand Island, NE, 1951)

6661 **Clarke, Jack.** Newscaster (*7:00 AM News*, KTIP, Porterville, CA, 1948).

6662 **Clarke, Jimmy.** DJ (*Melody Hour*, WAZL, Hazleton, PA, 1947).

6663 **Clarke, Johnny.** DJ (*Three Corner Club*, WINS, New York, NY, 1950).

6664 **Clarke, Mike.** Newscaster (WGST, Atlanta, GA, 1940; WWL, New Orleans, LA, 1942).

6665 **Clarke, Paul J.** Newscaster (WMT, Cedar Rapids, IA and KRNT-KSO, Des Moines, IA, 1945). DJ (*Borden's Ballroom*, WMT, 1947).

6666 **Clarke, Phillip "Phil."** Actor Clarke appeared on *Against the Storm* and *Mr. Keen, Tracer of Lost Persons* programs.

6667 **Clarke, Robert G. "Bob."** Organist Clarke was born February 9, 1891. He first appeared on WWJ (Detroit, MI, 1928).

6668 **Clark's Hawaiians.** Hawiian music group (WJZ, New York, NY, 1925).

6669 **Clarkson, Harry.** DJ (*Saturday Af-*

ternoon Sports Parade, WBBC, Bethesda-Chevy Chase, MD, 1950).

6670 Clarkson, Harry Irving. Bass (KVOO, Tulsa, OK, 1928).

6671 Clarkson, Margaret. Soprano (WOR, Newark, NJ, 1923).

6672 Clary, Mike. Newscaster (WXKW, Albany, NY, 1948).

6673 Clary, Skeet. DJ (*Melody Shop*, KOSA, Odessa, TX, 1947).

6674 *Classical Music for People Who Hate Classical Music.* Host George R. Marek and announcer Gene Hamilton introduced recorded music and commented upon the classical music selections played on the program, whose chief purpose seemed to be to sell RCA classical records (30 min., Monday, 9:30–10:00 P.M., NBC, 1957).

6675 *Classroom Instruction of the Oakland Public Schools.* Vivian Gorman, University High School, presented a radio course for sixth graders, "Story Writing — California Themes" (KGO, Oakland, CA, 1925).

6676 *Claude Hopkins Show.* Jazz band leader Hopkins was joined by the Mills Brothers and pianist Maurice Rocco on the show that originated from New York's Club Zanzibar (30 min., 1930s).

6677 *Claudia* (aka *Claudia and David*). Rose Franken's popular story was the basis for the daytime serial that originally starred Patricia Ryan and Richard Kollmar in the title roles that later were filled by Katherine Bard and Paul Crabtree. Also in the cast were: Peggy Allenby, Jane Seymour and Frances Starr. Music was by the Peter Van Steeden orchestra. The announcers were Charles Stark and Joe King. The 1947 transcribed version of the show was sponsored by Coca-Cola (15 min., Monday through Friday, 11:15–11:30 A.M., WGN, Chicago, IL, 1947). CBS had previously broadcast the show in 1941.

6678 Clausen, Bob. DJ (*Borden's Bouquet*, WHDH, Boston, MA, 1949).

6679 Clausen, (Major) Walter B. Newscaster (WCKY, Cincinnati, OH, 1944).

6680 Clauser, Al. CW musician and vocalist (*Al Clauser*, CW mus. prg., KFEL, Denver, CO, 1939). Clauser later worked as a DJ (*Coffee Call* program, KTVL, Tulsa, OK, 1948–1951; *Morning Ramble*, KTVL, 1952).

6681 Claussen, Clarence. Tenor (WQJ, Chicago, IL, 1926).

6682 Claussen, Gene. Newscaster (WMT, Cedar Rapids, IA, 1945–1946; KMOX, St. Louis, MO, 1947). Sportscaster (WMT, 1946; KMOX, 1947; KXIC, Iowa City, IA, 1950–1960).

6683 Clavier Trio. The instrumental trio consisted of Ruth Bailey, Mary Josephine Cooke and Mildred Carlile. Pianist Ettadel Hall was the director (KFWM, Oakland, CA, 1926).

6684 Clawson, Lew. Newscaster (WWVA, Wheeling, WV, 1945). Sportscaster (WWVA, 1946–1951; WWVA, 1955–1956).

6685 Clay, Blanche. Pianist (KFSG, Los Angeles, CA, 1925).

6686 Clay, Gene. Sportscaster (WHSY, Hattiesburg, MS, 1960).

6687 Clay, Randall. Sportscaster (WOAI, San Antonio, TX, 1960).

6688 Claycomb, Hugh. Announcer (KFDX, Shreveport, LA, 1926).

6689 Claypoole, Elizabeth. Singer (WOV, New York, NY, 1936).

6690 Clayton, Bob. DJ (*Waitin' for Clayton*, WPIN, St. Petersburg, FL, 1949–1955).

6691 Clayton, Bovard. Newscaster (WEBQ, Harrisburg, IL, 1939–1942). Sportscaster (WEBQ, 1940–1942).

6692 Clayton, Dave. Tenor (*Dave Clayton*, vcl. mus. prg., KMOX, St. Louis, MO, 1936).

6693 Clayton, (Aunt) Ida. COM-HE (WSAM, Saginaw, MI, 1951).

6694 Clayton, Oliver. Newscaster (WJMC, Rice Lake, WI, 1942). Sportscaster (WJMC, 1942).

6695 Clayton, Patti. Singer (*Waitin' for Clayton*, vcl. mus. prg., 15 min., Saturday, 7:00–7:15 P.M., CBS, 1947).

6696 Clayton, Reba. COM-HE (WQXI, Atlanta, GA, 1955).

6697 Clayton, Robert "Bob." DJ (*Boston Ballroom*, 120 min., Monday through Friday, 4:00–6:00 P.M., WHDH, Boston, MA, 1947–1949; WHDH, 1955).

6698 Clayton, Robert. DJ (*Tunes and Trivia*, WJAS, Pittsburgh, PA, 1948–1950).

6699 Clayton, Tom. Sportscaster (WLLH, Lowell-Lawrence, MA, 1953).

6700 Clear, William. Sportscaster (*Clearly for Sports*, WRTA, Altoona, PA, 1952).

6701 Clearman, Sylvia. COM-HE (WMOX, Meridian, MS, 1957).

6702 Clearwater Belleair Estate Orchestra. Commercially sponsored band (WGHB, Clearwater, FL, 1926).

6703 Cleary, Ed. DJ (*Yawnin' in the Morning*, KOSE, Oseola, AR, 1949).

6704 Cleary, Joseph M. Newscaster (*News Review*, WESB, Bradford, PA, 1947–1948).

6705 Cleary, Leo T. Singer-actor Cleary, who was born January 15, 1894, began his career as a singer (KFVD, Los Angeles, CA, 1924) before he became the station's manager. Announcer (KFVD, 1925–1927).

6706 Cleaver, Marshall. DJ (*Down on the Farm*, *Polka Dots* and *Yawn Patrol*, WKAP, Allentown, PA, 1947–1950).

6707 Clegg, Agnes. Violinist (KFUU, Oakland, CA, 1925).

6708 Clemens, Loretta and Jack Clemens. Brother and sister vocal team (*Loretta and Jack Clemens*, vcl. mus. prg., NBC, 1934–1937). The Clemens mixed light chatter with their pleasant vocal selections.

6709 Clement, DeWitt. Sportscaster (WCAU, Philadelphia, PA, 1936).

6710 Clement, Earle. Newscaster (WEIM, Fitchburg, MA, 1944–1946).

6711 Clement, Elsa. Miss Clement sang songs for children (WRNY, New York, NY, 1926).

6712 Clement, Elsie. Pianist (WEBH, Chicago, IL, 1925).

6713 Clement, Elwayne. DJ (*Music for a Lazy Afternoon*, KIBS, Bishop, CA, 1960).

6714 Clement, Gordon. DJ (*Yawning at Dawning*, WBCK, Battle Creek, MI, 1949).

6715 Clement, John. DJ (*Carnival of Rhythm*, KELO, Sioux Falls, SD, 1949–1951; *Time, Temp and Tunes*, KELO, 1952).

6716 Clements, Carter. DJ (*WHAY Open House*, WHAY, New Britain, CT, 1949).

6717 Clements, Joe. Sportscaster (KLIX, Twin Falls, ID, 1953).

6718 Clements, Laurel. COM-HE (WLBZ, Bangor, ME, 1951).

6719 Clements, Mary Lou. COM-HE (WLBN, Lebanon, KY, 1956).

6720 Clements, Zeke. CW vocalist (*Zeke Clements*, CW mus. prg., KFEL, Denver, CO, 1939). Billed variously as the "Oklahoma Cowboy" and the "Dixie Yodeler," Clements made his first radio appearances on WLS (Chicago, IL) in 1929. He began an early morning program on WSM (Nashville, TN) in 1931. Leading his group — the Bronco Busters — he became a regular member of the *Grand Ole Opry* (Nashville, TN, 1933). The group eventually broadcast on WHAS (Louisville, KY) , the *Iowa Barn Dance Frolic* (WHO, Des Moines, IA) and WBAP (Fort Worth, TX), before becoming a featured act on the *Hollywood Barn Dance* (CBS-Pacific). It was about that time that Clements was selected to provide the voice of Bashful in Walt Disney's *Snow White and the Seven Dwarfs*. He also appeared in more than 100 other motion pictures, including the Durango Kid series of westerns with Charles Starrett. Clements later returned to the *Grand Ole Opry* and remained there through the 1940s.

He was a highly successful songwriter and busy performer all his life, eventually playing and singing all types of music, including Dixieland jazz, on cruise ships. Clements also headlined TV variety shows in Atlanta, Georgia; New Orleans, Louisiana; Madison, Tennessee; Birmingham, Alabama; and Nashville, Tennessee.

6721 Clemons, Connee. COM-HE (WFJB, Marshalltown, IA, 1955).

6722 Clemons, Frances. COM-HE (WTRP, LaGrange, GA, 1957).

6723 Clemons, Howard. Tenor (WPG, Atlantic City, NJ, 1928).

6724 Clemons, Lucille. Organist (WBZ, Springfield, MA, 1926).

6725 Clemson, Christine Miller. Mezzo-soprano (KDKA, Pittsburgh, PA, 1924).

6726 Cleugh, Sophie. Cleugh along with Mitchell Benson delivered interesting book chats on their weekly *WHN Bookshop* program (WHN, New York, NY, 1936).

6727 Cleveland, Bill. DJ (*Bill Cleveland's Bandstand*, KMYC, Marysville, CA, 1947).

6728 Cleveland, Carlton. DJ (*Evening Serenade*, WCRW, Chicago, IL, 1947).

6729 Cleveland, (Reverend) D.E. The Reverend Cleveland broadcast weekly religious services (WNAX, Yankton, SD, 1929).

6730 Cleveland Orchestra. Symphonic orchestra directed by Nicolai Sokoloff (WJAX, Cleveland, OH, 1923).

6731 ***(The) Cleveland Symphony Orchestra.*** Symphonic music program (60 min., Tuesday, 1:00–2:00 P.M., NBC-Red, 1935). The orchestra later broadcast a series of ten network programs (CBS, 1937–1938; NBC, 1939; 60 min., Saturday, 6:00–7:00 P.M., MBS, 1947).

6732 ***(The) Clevelanders.*** Announcer Jay Miltner introduced this music show by saying, "Thirty minutes of good music styled in the distinctive fashion of Walberg Brown and his orchestra with vocals by Ken Ward." Fred Wilson produced the show (30 min., Weekly, NBC, 1950).

6733 ***Cliff and Lolly.*** Cliff Arquette and Lolly Gookins, sometimes known as the "Nuts of Harmony," combined piano selections and vocals with their zany humor on the entertaining quarter- hour transcribed show (15 min., Transcribed, Various stations, August 3, 1930).

6734 ***Cliff Edwards, Ukulele Ike.*** Vaudeville singer and recording star Edwards, known as Ukulele Ike, probably was best remembered as the voice of Jiminy Cricket in Disney's *Pinocchio* and his singing of "When You Wish Upon a Star." Edwards played the Palace and was featured in motion pictures as early as 1929. He claimed to have sold some seventy-four million records during his life time. His radio show featured both his songs and genial patter in 1932. Later in 1945 and 1947, he appeared on a show with the same name (*Cliff Edwards, Ukulele Ike*, vcl. mus. prg. 15 min., Monday through Friday, 10:30–10:45 A.M., NBC-Blue, 1945; 15 min., Monday through Friday, 4:30–4:45 P.M., ABC, 1947).

6735 **Clifford, Bill.** Leader (Bill Clifford Orchestra, instr. mus. prg., NBC, 1935).

6736 **Clifford, Dorothy.** Pianist (KFWI, San Francisco, CA, 1926).

6737 **Clifford, Kathleen.** COM-HE (*Beauty Talk*, KHJ, Los Angeles, CA, 1930).

6738 **Clifford, Mary.** Pianist (WBZ, Springfield, MA, 1925).

6739 **Clifro, Charlie.** Sportscaster (KRKD, Los Angeles, CA, 1953).

6740 **Clift Hotel Concert Orchestra.** Musical group directed by Sollie Heilbronner (KPO, San Francisco, CA, 1926).

6741 **Clifton, Arthur.** Organist (WBZ, Springfield, MA, 1926).

6742 **Clifton, Chambers.** Director (American Orchestral Society's Orchestra, WJZ, New York, NY, 1923).

6743 **Clifton, Jack.** DJ (*Music Hour*, KPRL, Paso Robles, CA, 1947; *Clifton's House Party*, WJW, Cleveland, OH, 1949; *Clifton Comes Calling*, WJMO, Cleveland, OH, 1950–1951; *Clifton's House Party*, WJW, 1952).

6744 **Clifton, Mary.** COM-HE (KJFJ, Webster City, IA, 1958).

6745 **Cline, Caldwell.** Newscaster (WWNC, Asheville, NC, 1941).

6746 **Cline, Clay.** DJ (*Midnight Masquerade*, WJZM, Clarksville, TN, 1947).

6747 **Cline, Cynthia.** Cline was one of the intelligent "kids" on the *Quiz Kids* program (NBC, CBS, ABC,1940–1953).

6748 **Cline, Louise.** Soprano (WBAL, Baltimore, MD, 1926).

6749 **Cline, Patsy.** CW singer (WSM, Nashville, TN, 1957). Born Virginia Patteron Hemsley, she became one of country music's greatest singers using her professional name Patsy Cline. She played a particularly important role in advancing the opportunities for women in country music. Tragically, Cline died in a plane crash with other country music greats Hawkshaw Hawkins and Cowboy Copas. She was the *first* woman to be elected to the Country Music Hall of Fame in 1973.

6750 **Clinnick, Frederick A.** Cornetist (WGY, Schenectady, NY, 1923–1924).

6751 **Clint, Fred.** Violinist (KPLA, Los Angeles, CA, 1927).

6752 **Clinton, Larry.** Leader (*Larry Clinton Orchestra,* instr. mus. prg., NBC-Blue, 1938–1939; 1942). Clinton began his music career as arranger for the bands of Tommy Dorsey and Glen Gray.

6753 ***Clipper Gang Plank.*** The unique quarter-hour program was sponsored by the Wisconsin and Michigan Steamship Company. Bob Heiss recorded interviews with persons taking the S.S. Milwaukee Clipper [a ship] to Muskegon, Michigan. He gave them picture postcards for participating. These interesting interviews were broadcast the same evening they were recorded (15 min., Monday, Wednesday and Friday, 10:15–10:30 P.M., WTMJ, Milwaukee, WI, 1941).

6754 ***Cliquot Club Eskimos.*** The popular radio band was led by virtuoso banjoist Henry Reser and named for its sponsor, Cliquot Club ginger ale (1925). In the early days of radio, the sound of a barking dog and sleigh bells were the trademark of the Cliquot Club Eskimos. The band set a record for consecutive broadcasts by an orchestra that extended from 1925 to 1932 on NBC. During that span of years the show was always sponsored by Cliquot Club ginger ale (30 min.,Wednesday, 8:00–8:30 P.M., NBC-Red, 1927). Merle Johnson and Jimmy Brierly were early members of the band. The personnel remained fairly constant over the years: Reser, ldr., a., and bj.; Matthew Collen, tb.; Joe Davis, clr. and as.; Clarence Doench, clr. and ts.; Paul Rickenbach, p.; Maurice Black, tba.; Paul Raymond, bj.; and Tom Stacks, d. and vcls. In later years the time slot changed (*Cliquot Club Eskimos*, instr. mus. prg., Weekly, 7:00–7:30 P.M., NBC, 1932). Cliquot Club beverages brought the program back on the air in 1951 with Reser once more leading the band. Vocals on this particular show were performed by Virginia Hauer. The announcer was Murray Lowe (25 min., Sunday, 8:30–8:55 P.M., Yankee Network, 1951). *See* **Reser, Harry.**

6755 **Clisbee, Emma J.** Leader (Emma J. Clisbee's California Ramblers [orchestra], KGER, Long Beach, CA, 1927).

6756 **Clive, Thomas.** Leader (Fraternity Tango Orchestra, WJY, New York, NY, 1924).

6757 ***Cloak and Dagger.*** Winifred Wolfe wrote the sustaining spy series based on Corey Ford's book, *Cloak and Dagger*. Joe Julian played the role of the chief OSS agent. (The OSS was the forerunner of the CIA.) Raymond Edward Johnson, Barry Kroeger, Ross Martin and Carl Webber were also in the cast as either agents or villains (30 min., Sunday, 4:00–4:30 P.M., NBC, 1950). The show opened with an announcer asking: "Are you willing to undertake a dangerous mission behind enemy lines, knowing you may never return? What you have heard is the question asked during the war of agents of the OSS — ordinary citizens who to this question answered, 'Yes.' This is *Cloak and Dagger*. Black warfare, espionage, international intrigue. Those are the weapons of the OSS. Today's adventure — The Norwegian Incident."

6758 **Clock, Charlie.** DJ (*Saturday Nite Record Party*, WMFT, Florence, AL, 1949).

6759 **(The) Clod Hoppers.** An early country string band featured on the *Grand Ole Opry* (WSM, Nashville, TN, 1927–1930).

6760 **Clooney, Josephine.** COM-HE (WFBG, Altoona, PA, 1951).

6761 **Close, Bill.** Sportscaster (*Close Up in Sports*, KOY, Phoenix, AZ, 1948–1950). DJ (*Close to You*, KOY, 1949; *Close Up in Sports*, KOY, 1952–1955).

6762 **Close, Dean.** DJ (*Close to You*, WLEM, Emporium, PA, 1960).

6763 **Close, Upton.** News analyst (*World Parade*, WOR, Newark, NJ, 1936; NBC, 1942; *World News Parade*, WOR, New York, NY, 1942; *World News Parade*, NBC, 1944; KHJ, Los Angeles, CA, 1945–1946; *World News Parade*, MBS, 1945–1948). Close was an extremely conservative news analyst. Opposition to the United Nations was one of the major themes of his programs.

6764 **Close, Vivian.** DJ (*Close to You*, KPDR, Alexandria, LA, 1947).

6765 **Cloud, (Dr.) Harry.** Leader (Magnoleum Petroleum Band, KFDM, Beaumont, TX, 1925).

6766 **Cloudy, Ida May.** Soprano (KDKA, Pittsburgh, PA, 1925).

6767 **Clough, Edwin M.** Newscaster (KOY, Phoenix, AZ, 1941–1942, 1945).

6768 **Clough, Forrest.** Newscaster (KFJZ, Fort Worth, TX, 1941).

6769 **Clough, Lee D.** Newscaster (KLUF, Galveston, TX, 1940). Sportscaster (WLUF, 1940–1941).

6770 **Cloutier, Norman L.** Leader (*Norman Cloutier Orchestra,* instr. mus. prg., NBC, 1934–1936; NBC-Red, 1937; NBC, 1938–1939).

6771 **Clover, Bob.** Newscaster (KVCV, Redding, CA, 1938).

6772 **Clover, Carlos.** Sportscaster (*Evening Sportscast*, KRIG, Odessa, TX, 1947–1951).

6773 **Clover, Cotton.** Sportscaster (KECK, Odessa, TX, 1949–1950).

6774 **Clover Gardens Orchestra.** Popular restaurant band (WHN, New York, NY, 1923).

6775 **Clow, Irma.** Harpist (WOAW, Omaha, NE, 1923).

6776 **Clow, Ken.** DJ (*The Night Mayor*, KBIZ, Ottumwa, IA, 1955).

6777 ***(The) Clown of the Air.*** Bert Davis provided gags and witty chatter on this comedy show (WQJ, Chicago, IL, 1925).

6778 **Cloyd, Blanche.** Soprano (WFHH, New York, NY, 1927).

6779 Club Arcady Orchestra. New York club band (WNYC, New York, NY, 1925).

6780 Club Deauville Orchestra. Chicago club band (KYW, Chicago, IL, 1925).

6781 *Club 15* (aka ***Bob Crosby's Club 15***). This program appeared in several different formats with various singers featured. An early *Club 15* version had Margaret Whiting broadcasting Monday, Wednesday and Friday and Patti Clayton on Tuesday and Thursday (15 min., Monday through Friday, 7:30–7:45 P.M., CBS, 1947). Later that year when Bob Crosby was featured, the program was sometimes known as *Bob Crosby's Club 15*. After Crosby left the show, he was replaced by Dick Haymes. Campbell Soups sponsored the Haymes version. Evelyn Knight, the Modernaires and the Andrews Sisters were sometimes featured with Haymes. The music was provided by Jerry Gray's Orchestra (1949, CBS).

6782 *Club Hollywood Orchestra.* Instr. mus. prg. (WTIC, Hartford, CT, 1932).

6783 *Club Matinee.* A popular hour-long variety program, *Club Matinee* featured veteran radio wit Ransom Sherman as host. *Club Matinee* grew out of an earlier network program, *The NBC Club Matinee*. Sherman eventually was joined on the show as co-host by Thomas Garrison Morfit, who had begun his career on Baltimore's station WBAL, before changing his name to Garry Moore. Music, songs and comedy were also supplied by the Three Romeos (Louise Perkins, Sam Cowling and Gil Jones), guitarist "Sunny Jim" Wolverton, singer Betty Bennett, bassist Bill Short and announcer Durward Kirby. The featured vocalists who appeared on the program were Johnny Johnston, Evelyn Lynne and Phil Shukin. One of the best remembered comedy features of the program was Rex Mauphin's orchestra playing out-of-tune, off-beat and off-key arrangements of such familar musical selections as the "William Tell Overture." Ransom Sherman was the show's writer. After a five-year run and three year hiatus, the program reappeared on ABC in a 30-minute version (1937–1942, NBC and 1945–1946, ABC).

6784 *Club Mayfair Orchestra.* Instr. mus. prg. (WAAB, Boston, MA, 1932).

6785 *Club of Hearts of the Berean Bible Class, Division of Pulaski County Baptist Brotherhood.* The organization sponsored the first KGHI (Little Rock, AR) program that was broadcast on April 27, 1928. O.A. Cook was the announcer who presented the Pulaski Heights Christian Church Choir directed by A.L. Woolfolk and the First Baptist Church Double Quartet under the direction of Miss Martha McAnich. The Double Quartet included Eleanor Stronga and Vera Wyatt, sopranos; Mrs. L.M. Sipes and Ruth Neile, altos; W.C. Ware and W.E. Rhodes, tenors; and H.S. Hale and M. Audrey Blankenship, basses.

Also on the program was the Missouri Pacific Quartet with L. Spann, B.M. Gibson, E.L. Hunt and L.L. Gibson; Mamie Jones, reader; and singer Mrs. L.P. Coleman. Popular music was provided by Lloyd Hemphill and his Entertainers with Mrs. W.B. Gietzman on the piano. Among the band's selections on that program were "Let a Smile Be Your Umbrella," "The Girl of My Dreams" and "Some of These Days." The program also included talks by Henry Donham ("The Layman's Responsibility to the Denomination") and Claude L. Durrett. The program's sponsorship made this an unusual inaugural broadcast.

6786 *Club Romance.* A night club setting and a romantic story told between songs was the format used on the entertaining program sponsored by Lehn & Fink Products. Baritone Conrad Thibault and soprano Lois Bennett sang the romantic songs accompanied by the Don Voorhees Orchestra (30 min., Sunday, 8:00–8:30 P.M., CBS, 1935).

6787 *Club Valspar.* Norman Sweetser was the host on the music program that featured soprano Aileen Clark and the William Wirges Orchestra (30 min., Saturday, 9:30–10:00 P.M., NBC-Red, 1931).

6788 Club Virginia Orchestra. Popular club band (WEBJ, Chicago, IL, 1925).

6789 Club Wigwam Orchestra. Jazz club band (WLW, Cincinnati, OH, 1925).

6790 Club Worthy Hills Orchestra. Hartford club band (WTIC, Hartford, CT, 1928).

6791 Cluff, E. Curtis. Newscaster (WGH, Newport News, VA, 1938).

6792 Cluney, John A. Sportscaster (WATR, Waterbury, CT, 1938; WBRY, Waterbury, CT, 1947–1955).

6793 Clute, Dorothy. Mezzo-soprano (KGO, Oakland, CA, 1926).

6794 Clyborne, Mildred. Contralto (WCCO, Minneappolis–St. Paul, MN, 1928).

6795 Clyde, Sylvia. Soprano (*Sylvia Clyde*, vcl. mus. prg., WOR, Newark, NJ, 1934–1936).

6796 *(The) Clyde Beatty Show.* The sustaining children's adventure serial supposedly was based on the life of famous animal trainer and circus performer, Clyde Beatty. Tim Graham, Byron Kane, Eva McVeagh, Vic Perrin and Eric Snowden were in the cast. Larry Thor was the announcer (30 min., Monday-Wednesday-Friday, 5:30–6:00 P.M., MBS, 1951).

6797 Clyman, Beatrice. Singer (WBBC and WCBU, Brooklyn, NY, 1929).

6798 Clymer, George. Clymer broadcast a *Dog Talks* program (WIP, Philadelphia, PA, 1936).

6799 Coakley, Jack. Leader (Jack Coakley Orchestra, KPO, San Francisco, CA, 1926).

6800 Coakley, Tom. Leader (*Tom Coakley Orchestra,* instr. mus. prg., WHAM, Rochester, NY, 1934; WOR, Newark, NJ, 1935; NBC, 1935–1936).

6801 Coan, Marion. Reader of poetry (Local radio, 1925).

6802 Coarley [Coaley], Jack. Leader (Jack Coarley's Cabirians Orchestra playing from the Cabira Cafe, KPO, San Francisco, CA, 1925). He possibly could be Jack Coakley. *See* **Jack Coakley**.

6803 Coast (Mrs.) Preston. Organist (WSUI, Iowa City, IA, 1926).

6804 *Coast to Coast.* Malcolm Childs broadcast Hollywood gossip and Lou James performed the same function for Broadway. Both men conducted guest interviews on the program (15 min., Monday, 11:45–12:00 midnight, Network, mid–1930s).

6805 *Coast-to-Coast-on-a-Bus.* The successor to *The Children's Hour*, this program was first broadcast in 1927. Milton J. Cross was the conductor on the "bus" that supposedly transported its young crew around the country. Audrey Egan and Madge Tucker portrayed "Mumsy Pig" and "The Lady Next Door," respectively. Like *The Children's Hour* before it and Philadelphia radio's *Horn and Hardart Children's Hour*, the program provided the first opportunity for many children who later became major show business performers. Each program began with the sound of a bus horn and a young voice announcing, "The White Rabbit Line — Jumps anywhere, anytime." The cast members over the years included: John Bates, Ann Blyth, Edwin Bruce, Carmina Cansino, Gwen Davies (Estelle Levy). Diana Jean Donnenwirth, Jeanne Elkins, Peter Fernandez, Jean Harris, Bob Hastings, Helen Holt, Tommy Hughes, Jackie Kelk, Donald Kelly, Bill Lipton, Ronald Liss, the Mauch Twins (Billy and Bobby), Jimmy McCallion, Michael O'Dea, Pam Prescott, Billy Redfield, Lawrence Robinson, Niels Robinson, Susan Robinson, Laddie Seaman, Renee and Joy Terry, Joan Tetzel and Eddie Wragge. Madge Tucker was the program's producer, director and writer assisted by Ethel Hart and Hilda Norton. The director was Tom DeHuff and Walter Fleischer the musical director. The 60-minute program was heard on both NBC and ABC from 1927 to 1948.

6806 Coates, C.L. Newscaster (WNOE, New Orleans, LA, 1939).

6807 Coates, Irma. COM-HE (WDLB, Marshfield, WI, 1954; WCCN, Neillsville, WI, 1960).

6808 Coates, Pattison. Baritone (WNYC, New York, NY, 1925; WLIB, Chicago, IL, 1926.

6809 Coates, Tommy. Announcer-baritone (WGN, Chicago, IL, 1928).

6810 Coates, Vivian. COM-HE (WATH, Athens, OH, 1951).

6811 Cobb, Dick. Newscaster, WAAB-WNAC (Boston, MA), 1940.

6812 Cobb, Buff. Cobb with husband Mike Wallace conducted the *Chez Show* program (WMAQ, Chicago, IL, 1951). *See* **Husband and Wife Teams.**

6813 Cobb, Grover C., Jr. Newscaster (KSAL, Salinas, KS, 1945).

6814 Cobb, Irvin S. Cobb was a famous humorist who appeared frequently on many radio programs of the 1920s. He appeared often with Will Rogers. On one of those occasions when Rogers interviewed Cobb this exchange took place:

> ROGERS: What do you do to keep your weight down?
>
> COBB : I don't keep my weight down. It's my weight that is keeping me down.
>
> ROGERS: Do you find yourself going Hollywood?
>
> COBB : Well, I find that I'm talking to myself and worse than that, I'm answering back.

ROGERS: Kind of saying your own yesses?
COBB : Yes, I'm living in Yes Man's Land, which is worse than No Man's Land during the war.

Cobb later was featured on his own program (*Irwin S. Cobb*, 30 min., Monday and Friday, 9:00 P.M., CBS, 1933), on which he was assisted by Allan Joslyn, as "Chris," who ran a Gulf filling station and acted as a straight man who fed lines to Cobb. Cobb told stories on the show. He did not do gags or one-liners. The show was sponsored by the Gulf Oil Company.

6815 **Cobb, Muriel.** COM-HE (KCON, Conway, AR, 1951).

6816 **Cobb, Tye "Ty."** Newscaster (KRGV, Weslaco, TX, 1937–1942; *News and Views*, KRGV, 1947).

6817 **Cobb, Wally.** DJ (*Wally's Follies*, WWPB, Miami, FL, 1952).

6818 **Cobb, Wilton.** Newscaster (WMAZ, Macon, GA, 1938–1941, 1946).

6819 **Cobbledeck, (Mrs.) James H.** Soprano (KGO, San Francisco, CA, 1926).

6820 ***Cobina Wright.*** Socialite Wright interviewed famous personalities and sang on her weekly afternoon show (60 min., Monday, 3:00–4:00 P.M., CBS, 1935).

6821 **Coburn, Hugh.** Sportscaster (*Let's Look 'Em Over*, WBLJ, Dalton, GA, 1951; WRBL, Columbus, GA, 1953).

6822 **Coburn, Jolly.** Leader (*Jolly Coburn Orchestra*, instr. mus. prg., NBC, 1935). The Coburn program featured tenor Harold Van Emburg and the Roy Campbell Singers.

6823 **Coburn, Paul.** Sportscaster (KVNU, Logan, UT, 1945; KLO, Odgen, UT, 1948; KVNU, 1950; *Coburn's Corner*, KNAK, Salt Lake City, UT, 1952). DJ (*Coburn's Carousel*, KVNU, 1948–1949; KNAK, 1954; KOL, Seattle, WA, 1955).

6824 **Coca-Cola Orchestra.** Singer Jessica Dragonette, as "Vivian the Coca-Cola Girl, was accompanied by the popular radio band led by Eros Schmit (NBC, 1927).

6825 ***(The) Coca-Cola Song Shop.*** Frank Crumit, Reed Kennedy and Alice Cornett were featured on the entertaining music show. Music was provided by the Gus Haenshen Orchestra (30 min., Friday, 10:00–10:30 P.M., CBS, 1938).

6826 ***(The) Coca-Cola Sports Casts.*** Coca-Cola Bottling Company sponsored the interesting program of sports features and music. Grantland Rice, the dean of American sports writers, conducted interviews with outstanding sports figures. Len Joy's String Orchestra provided the music (30 min., 10:30–11:00 P.M., CBS, 1930).

6827 ***(The) Coca-Cola Summer Show.*** Nestor Chayres and the Los Panchos singing with Charles Laichter's orchestra were the featured performers on the music show (30 min., 7:30–8:00 P.M., CBS, 1948).

6828 ***(The) Coca-Nut Club Meeting.*** The zany late night variety program broadcast weekly was a popular one with West Coast listeners (120 min., Weekly, 9:00–11:00 P.M., KJBS, San Francisco, CA, 1927).

6829 **Cocconi, Eugene and Edna Davis.** Harmony singing team (KFOB, Burlingame, CA, 1926).

6830 **Coce, Francisca.** Lyric soprano (WOR, Newark, NJ, 1926).

6831 **Cochens, Adelaide.** Pianist (KWTC, Santa Ana, CA, 1928).

6832 **Cochran, Harry.** Sportscaster (WSTV, Steubenville, OH, 1945–1946). Newscaster (WSTV, 1946).

6833 **Cochran, J.T.** COM-HE (WAIN, Columbia, KY, 1955).

6834 **Cochran, Paul.** Newscaster (KICA, Clovis, NM, 1939).

6835 **Cochran, Ron.** Newscaster (WCOP, Boston, MA, 1945–1946; *The Civil Defense Reporter*, CBS, 1952).

6836 **Cochran, Ronald.** Newscaster (WHOM, Jersey City, NJ, 1944).

6837 **Cochran, William "Bill."** Sportscaster (*Bill Cochran Sports News*, WIOD, Miami, FL, 1946–1947; *The Bill Cochran Show*, WNBC, New York, NY, 1949; NBC, 1956).

6838 **Cochrane, Betty Rae.** COM-HE (WTOD, Toledo, OH, 1955).

6839 **Cochrane, Jane.** Singer (WGBS, New York, NY, 1927).

6840 **Cochrane, Mickey.** Sportscaster Cochrane, a former baseball star of the Detroit Tigers, discussed baseball and its players (*Mickey Cochrane,* CBS, 1934).

6841 **Cock-a-Doodle-Do Orchestra.** Novelty band led by Floyd Taylor (KTHS, Hot Springs National Park, AR, 1928).

6842 **Cocke, C. Alton.** Newscaster (KGKB, Tyler, TX, 1946).

6843 **Cockerill, Clem** DJ (*Readin' Ritin' Rhythm*, WKCT, Bowling Green, KY, 1952).

6844 **Coconut Grove Orchestra.** Night club band led by Jacques Renard (WEEI, Boston, MA, 1929; *Coconut Grove Orchestra*, WAAB, Boston, MA, 1932). These broadcasts originated from Boston's famous Coconut Grove night club.

6845 **Coddon, Hal.** DJ (*Cheatin' on the Sandman*, KFMB, San Diego, CA, 1947–1950; *Cotton Tales*, KFMB, 1950).

6846 **Codolban, Cornelius.** Leader (*Cornelius Codolban Orchestra,* instr. mus. prg., KDKA Pittsburgh, PA, 1936).

6847 **Cody, Del Rio.** Sportscaster (KGA, Spokane, WA and KHQ, Spokane, WA, 1941; KGA, 1945–1946). DJ (*Western Serenade*, KGA, 1948; *The Korn Krib*, KGA, 1949).

6848 **Coe, Bud.** Sportscaster (WIL, St. Louis, MO, 1960).

6849 **Coe, Donald.** Newscaster (NBC-Blue, 1944–1945).

6850 **Coe, F. Robert.** Baritone; (KDKA, Pittsburgh, PA, 1924).

6851 **Coe, Jay.** Leader (*Jay Coleman Orchestra*, instr. mus. prg., WTNJ, Trenton, NJ, 1939).

6852 **Coe, June T.** COM-HE (WWTB, Tampa, FL, 1958).

6853 **Coe, Winn.** Pianist (KHQ, Spokane, WA, 1928).

6854 **Coeff, Howard.** Violinist (*Howard Coeff*, instr. mus. prg., WLW, Cincinnati, OH, 1934).

6855 **Coelho [Cochio], Olga.** Vocalist (*Olga Coelho,* voc. mus. prg., WJR, Detroit, MI, 1942).

6856 **Coe's Orchestra.** Popular radio band (WBZ, Sprinfield, MA, 1925).

6857 **Coeur, Jerry.** Newscaster (*Log and Saw*, KIEM, Eureka, CA, 1948).

6858 **Coffee, Dick.** Newscaster (KORN, Freemont, NE, 1944).

6859 ***Coffee Time.*** The Department of Norwegian at St. Olaf's College presented this unique educational program. Members of the department and their guests met in the radio studio over coffee. Their conversation — both humorous and serious — was broadcast entirely in Norwegian. They talked about well known persons, places and things. In addition, they sang Norwegian songs (WCAL, Northfield, MN, 1939).

6860 **Coffer, Eddy.** Leader (*Eddy Coffer Orchestra,* instr. mus. prg., WHIO, Dayton, OH, 1942).

6861 **Coffey, Edward J.** Violinist (WBZ, Boston-Springfield, MA, 1924).

6862 **Coffey, Jack.** Leader (*Jack Coffey Orchestra*, instr. mus. prg., CBS, 1940).

6863 **Coffin, Frank.** Newscaster (KWLK, Longview, WA, 1941; KXRO, Aberdeen, WA, 1942). Sportscaster (KXRO, 1942).

6864 **Coffin, (Professor) Harrison C.** Newscaster (WSNY, Schenectady, NY, 1944).

6865 **Coffin, Margaret.** COM-HE (WEGP, Presque Isle, ME, 1960).

6866 **Coffin, Tris.** Newscaster (CBS, 1944; WTOP, Washington, DC, 1945–1946; ABC, 1948).

6867 **Coggeshall, Asa O.** Announcer Coggeshall was sometimes designated as "AOC," (WGY, Schenectady, NY, 1923–1925). Coggeshall began his career in radio when Kolin Hager established an announcers' school at station WGY. Coggeshall attended the summer school and after finishing began a long, successful radio career at WGY.

6868 **Coggeshall, H.B.** Violinist (WGY, Schenectady, NY, 1923).

6869 **Coggeshall, Joe.** Newscaster (KOB, Albuquerque, NM, 1944).

6870 **Coggeshall, Nancy.** Coggeshall was one of the intelligent "kids" on the *Quiz Kids* program (NBC, CBS, ABC, 1940–1953).

6871 **Coggin, Joyce.** COM-HE (WCOH, Newman, GA, 1954).

6872 **Coggins, Marcia P.** COM-HE (WKDK, Newberry, SC, 1951–1960).

6873 **Coggle, Myrtle.** Cellist (KTAB, Oakland, CA, 1926).

6874 **Coghan, Rose and Lita Coghan.** Vocal duets and solos (KFWM, Oakland, CA, 1927).

6875 **Cogley, Helen Sprague.** Mezzo-soprano (KOIL, Council Bluffs, IA, 1926).

6876 **Cogswell, Dorothy.** Pianist-hostess (WOW, Omaha, NE, 1929).

6877 **Cohan, George M.** Famous vaudeville song-and-dance man Cohan was a beloved performer. When Lindbergh returned home from Europe after flying the Atlantic solo, NBC established a fifty station network to broadcast the homecoming. Graham Mc-

Namee described the event, and at the conclusion of the ceremony, Cohan sang "When Lindy Comes Marching Home" to commemorate it (NBC, 1927). He later appeared on the *Colliers Hour* program (NBC, 1929).

6878 Cohan, John. Sportscaster (KNET, Palestine, TX, 1944).

6879 Cohen, Carrie. Pianist (WHN, New York, NY, 1924).

6880 Cohen, Dorothy. Soprano (WDWM, Newark, NJ, 1927).

6881 Cohen, Elise Lee. Actress and program director (WBAL, Baltimore, MD, 1929).

6882 Cohen, Esther M. Pianist (WLIT, Philadelphia, PA, 1925).

6883 Cohen, Jack. Jazz pianist (WHY, New York, NY, 1925; WGBS, New York, NY, 1925; WMCA, New York, NY, 1926).

6884 Cohen, Joann. Cohen was one of the intelligent "kids" on the *Quiz Kids* program (NBC, CBS, ABC, 1940–1953).

6885 Cohen, (Cantor) Max. Singer (WHN, New York, NY, 1924).

6886 Cohen, Miriam. Violinist (WLIT, Philadelphia, PA, 1925).

6887 Cohen, Sid. Pianist (WAHG, Richmond Hill, NY, 1925).

6888 Cohen, Walter. Fifteen-year-old violinist (WHO, Des Moines, IA, 1925).

6889 *Cohen and Casey.* The tribulations of two old pals — Mike Casey and Abe Cohen — were presented on the comedy series. The story began with Mike rescuing Abe from some menacing gangsters (15 min., Monday through Friday, WBZ-WBZA, Boston, MA, 1931).

6890 Cohn, Al. Violinist (*Al Cohn*, instr. mus. prg., WTIC, Hartford, CT, 1935).

6891 Cohn, Harold. DJ (*Hillbilly Hoedown*, WPDQ, Jacksonville, FL, 1948).

6892 Cohn, Harriet. COM-HE (WJVA, South Bend, IN, 1958).

6893 *Coke Time with Eddie Fisher.* Coca-Cola sponsored the music show that starred Eddie Fisher and the Axel Stordhahl Orchestra. The announcer was Fred Robbins (15 min., ABC, 1954–1956). A program by the name of *Coke Time* (aka *Songs by Morton Downey*) was broadcast from 1943 to 1951.

6894 Coker, Will. DJ (*Pony Express*, KFDM, Beaumont, TX, 1949–1952; WPTR, Paris, TN, 1955).

6895 Colbert, Jeanne. COM-HE (WTIC, Hartford, CT, 1951–1960). Colbert also appeared on the *Young Dr. Malone* and *The Life of Mary Southern* daytime serials.

6896 Colbert, John. Newscaster (KFWB, Los Angeles, CA, 1939).

6897 Colbron, Grace. Book reviewer (*Book Reviews*, WJZ, New York, NY, 1925).

6898 Colburn, H.C. Announcer (KFUU, Sacramento, CA, 1926).

6899 Colby, Brooks. Violinist (WLS, Chicago, IL, 1925).

6900 Colby, Ethel. Drama critic (WMCA, New York, NY, 1942).

6901 Coldren, Phil. Newscaster (WMBH, Joplin, MO, 1945).

6902 Cole, Betty. COM-HE (WICH, Norwich, CT, 1955).

6903 Cole, Bob. DJ (KRLA, Los Angeles, 1939; KABC, Los Angeles, CA, 1957).

6904 Cole, Brad. DJ (*Mixing Bowl*, KOOS, Coos Bay, OR, 1949). Sportscaster (*Western Sportsman*, KOOS, 1950).

6905 Cole, Buddy. Leader (*Buddy Cole Orchestra*, instr. mus. prg., KFEL, Denver, CO, 1940; WAKR, Akron, OH, 1942).

6906 Cole, Carol. COM-HE (WJUD, St. Johns, MI, 1960).

6907 Cole, Charlie. Singer (Hollywood, CA, 1925).

6908 Cole, D.B. Announcer (WTAC, Johnstown, PA, 1925).

6909 Cole, (N.) Dean. Announcer Cole was known as "Old King Cole" (WHO, Des Moines, IA, 1924).

6910 Cole, Don. Announcer (WJBK, Ypsilanti, MI, 1925).

6911 Cole, Don. Sportscaster (KCCX, Sidney, MT, 1953–1955).

6912 Cole, E. Rae. COM-HE (WPMP, Pascagoula, MS, 1957).

6913 Cole, Fred B. DJ (*Carnival of Music*, WHDH, Boston, MA, 1947–1960).

6914 Cole, George. Tenor (WIP, Philadelphia, PA, 1925).

6915 Cole, George. DJ (*Cole-Cuts*, KFOX, Long Beach, CA, 1950).

6916 Cole, Gerry. COM-HE (WHOC, Philadelphia, MS, 1956).

6917 Cole, Grace. Soprano (KJBS, San Francisco, CA, 1926).

6918 Cole, Grady. Newscaster (WBT, Charlotte, NC, 1938–1939; *Grady Cole's Farm Club*, 1940). DJ (WBT, 1955).

6919 Cole, Harry. Newscaster (WJAX, Jacksonville, FL, 1941; WBIZ, Ottumwa, IA, 1942).

6920 Cole, Hilda. Publicist-script analyst (CBS). Publicist Cole first worked for CBS before leaving the network to do publicity for Kate Smith and Fred Waring.

6921 Cole, Howard. Newscaster (KCRC, Enid, OK, 1939).

6922 Cole, Jean. COM-HE (WWGS, Tifton, GA, 1956).

6923 Cole, Leon and Red Hawn. Singing team (*Cole and Hawn*, vcl. mus. prg., WSM, Nashville, TN, 1934–1938).

6924 Cole, Marth Lee. Cole discussed "interior decorating" topics (NBC, 1934).

6925 Cole, Max. DJ (*Wake Up, New York*, WOV, New York, NY, 1948–1952).

6926 Cole, Mildred. Contralto (*Mildred Cole*, vcl. mus. prg., WOR, Newark, NJ, 1934).

6927 Cole, Pauline. Pianist (KFKQ, Conway, AR, 1923).

6928 Cole, Phil. Leader (Phil Cole's Nebraskan Orchestra, WHN, New York, NY, 1925).

6929 Cole, Reg. Singer (KPO, San Francisco, CA, 1925).

6930 Cole, Rex. Leader (*Rex Cole Mountaineers*, CW music group, NBC, 1934).

6931 Cole, Richard. Leader (*Richard Cole Orchestra*, instr. mus. prg., WGN, Chicago, IL, 1933; WFAA, Dallas, TX, 1934).

6932 Cole, Rodney. Leader (*Rodney Cole Orchestra*, instr. mus. prg., KUOA, Siloam Springs, AR, 1939).

6933 Cole, Ron. DJ (*Discathon*, KGFF, Shawnee, OK, 1960).

6934 Cole, Tracy. DJ (*Disc Digest*, WWSR, St. Albans, VT, 1949; WWMJ, Rochester, NY, 1955).

6935 Cole, Vera. COM-HE (KSLO, Opelousas, LA, 1956).

6936 Colee, Donn Ramon. DJ (*Platter Party*, WLBF, Leesburg, FL, 1947; *1240 Club*, WLBF, 1950).

6937 Coleman, Bernice. Singer (WBRY, Waterbury, CT, 1939).

6938 Coleman, Bill. DJ (*Bill Coleman Calling*, WEEI, Boston, MA, 1948).

6939 Coleman, Carl. Organist (*Carl Coleman*, instr. mus. prg., WKBW, Buffalo, NY, 1942).

6940 Coleman, Carlyn. COM-HE (WHLI, Wheeling, WV, 1957).

6941 Coleman, Charles. Pianist (WGCP, Newark, NJ, 1926).

6942 Coleman, Charlotte. COM-HE (KCEE, Tucson, AZ, 1958).

6943 Coleman, Dick. DJ (*Dick Coleman Show*, WCBM, Baltimore, MD, 1948; *Let's Get Acquainted*, WLBE, Leesburg, FL, 1949).

6944 Coleman, Dottie. COM-HE (WGTH, Hartford, CT, 1955).

6945 Coleman, Earl. Leader (Earl Coleman and his Ambassador Orchestra, WDAF, Kansas City, MO, 1926).

6946 Coleman, Emil. Leader (Emil Coleman Orchestra, WDAF, Kansas City, MO, 1925. *Emil Coleman Orchestra*, instr. mus. prg., NBC, 1934–1939; WCAE, Pittsburgh, PA, 1936; KLZ, Denver, CO, 1939; WMAQ, Chicago, IL, 1940).

6947 Coleman, Hal. Sportscaster (*Sports Spotlight*, KOLY, Mobridge, SD, 1960).

6948 Coleman, Jerry. Sportscaster (CBS, 1960).

6949 Coleman, Joseph. Violinist (*Joseph Coleman*, instr. mus. prg., WOR, Newark, NJ, 1936).

6950 Coleman, Ken. Sportscaster (*Sports Journal*, WNEB, Worcester, MA, 1951; *The Cleveland Browns*, WTAM, Cleveland, OH, 1953; WHK, Cleveland, OH, 1956; WDOK, Cleveland, OH, 1960).

6951 Coleman, Leon. Violinist (*Leon Coleman*, instr. mus. prg., CBS, 1938).

6952 Coleman, Milt. Singer (NBC, 1928).

6953 Coleman, Nancy. Actress Coleman appeared on the *Young Dr. Malone* daytime serial.

6954 Coleman, Paul. DJ (*Timekeeper*, WINR, Binghampton, NY, 1947–1952).

6955 Coleman, Robert J. Announcer (WEAO, Columbus, OH, 1926–1927).

6956 Coleman, Roger. Leader (*Roger Coleman Orchestra*, instr. mus. prg., WCBM, Baltimore, MD, 1939).

6957 Coleman, Vincent. Actor Coleman appeared on the *Chickie* program.

6958 Coleman, Ward A. Newscaster (WSLI, Jackson, MS, 1942; WAML, Laurel, MS, 1945; *Columbus Commentary*, WENC, Whiteville, NC, 1947).

6959 *Coleman Cox — The Morning Philosopher.* Cox delivered early morning inspirational talks (NBC, 1935).

6960 Coleman String Quartet. Musical group of Ivan Steed, Terry Ferrel, Edward Turner and Frank Hallowell (KFH, Wichita, KS, 1926).

6961 Colendesky, Gertrude. Singer (WTIC, Hartford, CT, 1926).

6962 Coles, Ed. Sportscaster (*The Sports Roundup*, KMCO, Conroe, TX, 1953).

6963 Coles, Elizabeth P. Violinist (KDKA, Pittsburgh, PA, 1924).

6964 Coley, Hal. Newscaster (KPRC, Houston, TX, 1945–1946). Sportscaster (KMCO, Conroe, TX, 1955).

6965 Coley, Lem. Newscaster (WRFS, Alexander City, AL, 1948). Sportscaster and play-by-play announcer (WRFS, 1949–1950).

6966 Colf, Howard. Violinist (*Howard Colf*, instr. mus. prg., WLW, Cincinnati, OH, 1936).

6967 Colgate, J. Tenor (WCAU, Philadelphia, PA, 1925).

6968 *Colgate House Party* (*aka The Colgate Home Party*). Hostess Peggy Allenby introduced featured vocalists, Conrad Thibault and Frances Langford. Musical selections were played by the Al Goodman Orchestra. The program was sponsored by Colgate-Palmolive Company (30 min., Monday, 9:30–10:00 P.M., NBC-Red, 1934). Another version of the program was broadcast later in the year featuring singers Donald Novis and Frances Langford, host-comedian Joe Cook and the Don Voorhees Orchestra (NBC-Red, 1934).

6969 *(The) Colgate Show.* Otto Harbach wrote the musical drama and also appeared in the cast with Peggy Allenby, Eunice Howard, Jerry Macy, Florence Malone and Francia White (60 min., Monday, 9:30–10:30 P.M., NBC-Red, 1935).

6970 Colhoun, Adams. Announcer Colhoun was known as "The Voice of WFAA" (WFAA, Dallas, TX, 1925–1928).

6971 Colie, Anita. COM-HE (WCME, Brunswick, ME, 1956).

6972 Coliet, Claude C. Minister Coliet conducted interdenominational services programs (WEAF, New York, NY, 1925).

6973 Colini, Aroldo. Concert tenor who performed with the Florentine String Trio (KPLA, Los Angeles, CA, 1927).

6974 Colkers, Oscar. Singer on WLW's inaugural program (WLW, Cincinnati, OH, 1922).

6975 Colkitt, Jerry. Sportscaster (KALE, Richland, WA, 1953).

6976 Coll, Ben. Newscaster (WJAC, Johnstown, PA, 1939).

6977 Collander, Ruth. COM-HE (WICA, Ashtabula, OH, 1958).

6978 Collar, (Mrs.) Floyd. Soprano (KTAB, Oakland, CA, 1926).

6979 Collar, Helen. Pianist (WIBO, Chicago, IL, 1926).

6980 *Collector's Item.* Designed for the literate, sophisticated listener, the sustaining program was broadcast in 26 segments as a part of the network's *Monitor* programming. The segments were devoted to music, theater, the graphic arts and the physical and social sciences. The first show of the series was broadcast January 10, 1954, with a cast that included Dr. Edward P. Alexander, Homer Croy, James Fleming, Earl Godwin, Roger Kennedy, Hans Konigsberger, Dr. Norman Vincent Peale and Leon Pearson (120 minutes, Sunday, 10:30–12:30 P.M., NBC, 1954). *See* ***Monitor***.

6981 *College Courses by Radio.* The State University of Iowa was a pioneer in broadcasting courses for college credit over the university's station (WSUI, Iowa City, IA, 1925).

6982 *College Days.* Singer Greta Gahler was featured on the West Coast variety program (KYA, San Francisco, CA, 1935).

6983 *(The) College Inn Dance Orchestra.* Instr. mus. prg. (WEAF, New York, NY, 1933).

6984 College of Industrial Arts [Denton, Texas] Choir. Scholastic vocal group (WFAA, Dallas, TX, 1929).

6985 College of Industrial Arts Girls Orchestra of Texas. Female music group (WBAP, San Antonio, TX, 1923).

6986 *College of the Air.* Kansas State University broadcast what some believe to be the *first* series of college courses on American radio (KSAC, Manhattan, KS, 1924).

6987 *College of the Air.* The station of Michigan State University offered radio courses in Home Economics, Animal Husbandry, Poultry, Veterinary Medicine, Horticulture, Dairy Husbandry and Farm Crops in a series of programs (WKAR, East Lansing, MI, 1925).

6988 *College Prom.* Red Nichols and his band performed with vocalist Ruth Etting and guests on the music program (NBC, 1935).

6989 *College Quiz Bowl.* Teams from two colleges competed for prizes on the quiz program hosted by Allen Ludden (30 min., Saturday, 8:00–8:30 P.M., NBC, 1953).

6990 *College Views and News.* Ernie Neff conducted interviews and broadcast news from colleges in the greater Pittsburgh area on the sustaining program (30 min., Thursday, KQV, Pittsburgh, PA, 1938).

6991 (The) Collegians. Charles M Raidon directed the popular orchestra (WSM, Nashville, TN, 1928).

6992 (The) Collegians. College orchestra (WFAA, Dallas, TX, 1928).

6993 Collegiate Aeolians Dance Orchestra. Scholastic dance band (KFI, Los Angeles, CA, 1927).

6994 Collette, Lucille. French violinist (WRNY, New York, NY, 1926).

6995 Colletti, Anthony. Director (*Anthony Colletti Trio*, vcl. mus. prg. (WPG, Atlantic City, NJ, 1935).

6996 Colletti, Marjorie. Pianist (KFRC, San Francisco, CA, 1928).

6997 Collie, Bill "Biff." DJ (*Mailman's Matinee*, KSIX, Corpus Christi, TX, 1947; *Collie's Corral* and *Houston Hoedown*, KNUZ, Houston, TX, 1948; *Collie's Corral*, KNUZ, 1952).

6998 Collie, Hiram Abiff "Biff." Influential CW DJ Collie broadcast at the age of 16 on KMAC (San Antonio, TX, 1943); KNUX (Houston, TX, 1948; and KFOX (Long Beach, CA, 1954–1969). Collie was inducted into the DJ Hall of Fame in 1978.

6999 Collie, Sunshine. COM-HE (WCBL, Benton, KY, 1957).

7000 Collier, Arlene. COM-HE (WGNI, Wilmington, NC, 1955).

7001 Collier, Constance. Actress Collier appeared in the cast of *Kate Hopkins, Angel of Mercy*.

7002 Collier, Dorothy. COM-HE (WCOL, Fort Collins, CO, 1955).

7003 Collier, (Mrs.) J.T. Whistler (WOK, Pine Bluff, AR, 1922).

7004 Collier, June. Leader (June Collier's Orchestra, KVOO, Tulsa, OK, 1928).

7005 Collier, Laura. COM-HE (KUBC, Montrose, CO, 1951)

7006 Collier, Willie. Vaudeville star Collier appeared on the *General Motors Family Party* (NBC, 1927).

7007 *(The) Collier Radio Hour (Collier Hour).* One of the first variety programs on American radio, *The Collier Hour* was sponsored by *Collier's* magazine, which had a weekly circulation of 1,500,000 and was published by the Crowell-Collier Publishing Company. The program was broadcast by the NBC-Blue network on Sunday evening at 8:15 P.M. One of its memorable features was a dramatization of the evil doings of the villainous Dr. Fu Manchu, the memorable fictional creation of Sax Rohmer. Although John C. Daly played the role of the hero, it was Arthur Hughes as the arch criminal — Fu Manchu — who is best remembered. Sunda Love played one of Fu Manchu's slave girls. In a later story by Sax Rohmer, Parker Wilson played the role of Yu An Hee See, another of the villain's pawns. Curt Peterson was the announcer in the program's early years (60 min., Sunday, 8:15–9:15 P.M., NBC-Blue, 1927–1932). The *Collier Hour* was successful from its beginning. Each program contained some dialogue between Uncle Henry and the editor, John B. Kennedy. The program always included a series of dramatizations interspersed with musical interludes. Distinguished speakers and the magazine's staff writers also provided informative commentaries. Each weekly program was representative of that week's magazine fiction, articles and special features such as Grantland Rice's sports articles and Rube Goldberg's "Inventions of Professor Lucifer G. Butts." When editor John B. Kennedy, acting as host and announcer, introduced the appearance of Professor Lucifer Gamaliel Butts, he said: "If the greatness of a man is indicated by the number of cigars named after him, what shall we say of Professor Butts? For after him all cigars are named — eventually if not now." Years after the program left the air, the exploits of Professor

Butts still appeared frequently in *Collier's Magazine.* Music on the program was performed by musicians of the New York Philharmonic Orchestra. Performed before a large live audience, each member of the audience received an elaborate program for each broadcast.

The *Collier Radio Hour* of October 11, 1931 was broadcast by the National Broadcasting Company from the New Amsterdam Roof, "the Auditorium of the Air." Listed as "A radio adaptation of the issue of *Collier's* for October 17, 1931," it was directed by John B. Kennedy and dramatist Malcolm La Prade assisted by Casting Director Philip Barrison and Musical Director Ernest La Prade. After the Collier Hour Band played Goldman's "On the Road," there was a brief dialog between Mr. Editor (Kennedy) and Uncle Henry; a talk by Eliot Wadsworth, Chairman of the National Committee on Cooperation on Unemployment; the radio debut of Spanish soprano Lucita Romero singing "Clavelitos" accompanied by the Collier Hour Band; a dramatization of the first chapter of J.P. McElvoy's serial, "Are You Listening?"; a visit to the scientific laboratory of Professor Lucifer G. Butts; another vocal selection by soprano Romero; a final musical selection by the band; and closing remarks by John B. Kennedy. The first episode of the "Are You Listening?" serial included performances by Porter Hall, Wendell Hart, Harold Van Amburgh, Adele Ronson, Rose Keane, Eunice Howard, Georgette Harvey, Edward Pawley, Bob Lynn, George Spelvin, Ivan Firth, John Spelvin, Ernest LaPrade and Skippy Barrison.

7008 Colling, E.S. Movie critic Colling broadcast his *Personal Chats of the Stage and Screen* (WHN, New York, NY, 1925).

7009 Collingwood, Charles. Newscaster (CBS, 1944–1948). A criticism that was sometimes raised against Collingwood was that he blurred the lines between reporter and commentator.

7010 Collins, Al "Jazzbo." DJ (*Happy Al*, KALL, Salt Lake City, UT, 1948; *Collins on a Cloud* and *Purple Grotto*, WNEW, New York, NY, 1949–54; WRCA, New York, NY, 1954–1956; KALL, 1957).

7011 Collins, Artie. Leader (*Artie Collins Orchestra,* instr. mus. prg., WHAM, Rochester, NY, 1934).

7012 Collins, Bill. Sportscaster (*At Bat*, KTAN, Sherman, TX, 1948).

7013 Collins, Brad. Leader (*Brad Collins Orchestra*, instr. mus. prg., WIP, Philadelphia, PA, 1936).

7014 Collins, C.B. Tenor (WEEI, Boston, MA and WNAC, Boston, MA, 1925). Collins later headed a group known as "Hiram and the Hired Hands" (WEEI, 1928).

7015 Collins, Dave. Newscaster (*Local News*, WBYS, Canton, IL, 1948). Sportscaster (WHOK, Lancaster, OH, 1949–1950; WRFD, Worthington, OH, 1952–1956).

7016 Collins, Eddie. Saxophonist (WCOA, Pensacola, FL, 1926).

7017 Collins, Edna. COM-HE (KCIM, Carroll, IA, 1956–1957).

7018 Collins, (Mrs.) H.P. Soprano (WBZ, Boston-Springfield, MA, 1924).

7019 Collins, Helen. COM-HE (KTTN, Trenton, MO, 1955).

7020 Collins, Jan. COM-HE (KFTM, Ft. Morgan, CO, 1957).

7021 Collins, Jean. Singer (WMEX, Boston, MA, 1939).

7022 Collins, Joe. Sportscaster (KGNC, Amarillo, TX, 1953).

7023 Collins, Joy. COM-HE (WGUY, Bangor, ME, 1958).

7024 Collins, Juanita. Pianist (WDAF, Kansas City, MO, 1928).

7025 Collins, Judson "Jud." Newscaster (WSGN, Birmingham, AL, 1938). Sportscaster (WSM, Nashville, TN, 1941–1942; WSM, 1945–1947).

7026 Collins, Kay. COM-HE (WIS, Columbia, SC, 1956–1957).

7027 Collins, Ken. DJ (KCSB, San Bernardino, CA, 1955).

7028 Collins, Ken. DJ (*The Night Scene*, KXYZ, Houston, TX, 1955).

7029 Collins, Leonard. Newscaster (WTTM, Trenton, NJ, 1944).

7030 Collins, Madeleine. Operatic prima donna from London's Covent Garden (WMCA, New York, NY, 1925).

7031 Collins, Marge. COM-HE (WTRL, Bradenton, FL, 1956).

7032 Collins, Margo. COM-HE (WWNC, Asheville, NC, 1955).

7033 Collins, Marjorie. COM-HE (WTRL, Bradenton, FL, 1936).

7034 Collins, Ovid. Baritone (WSM, Nashville, TN, 1928).

7035 Collins, Ray. Actor Collins once was called by Orson Welles as "the greatest of all radio actors." He appeared on *The American School of the Air, Bulldog Drummond, Cavalcade of America, County Seat, Eno's Crime Club, Flash Gordon, Just Plain Bill, Life Begins, Mercury Theater (on the air), Philip Morris Playhouse, Trouble House* and *Wilderness Road.*

7036 Collins, Rose. COM-HE (WKDL, Clarksdale, MS, 1960).

7037 Collins, Sid. Sportscaster (*Fox's Den*, WIBC, Indianapolis, IN, 1952–1960).

7038 Collins, Ted. Newscaster (CBS, 1942; MBS, 1948).

7039 Collins, Tex. DJ (*Nightly Serenade*, WAZL, Hazleton, PA, 1954–1956).

7040 Collins, Tom. "Song stylist" (*Tom Collins*, vcl. mus. prg., KWK, St. Louis, MO, 1936).

7041 Collins, Tom. Actor-announcer-MC Collins appeared on the *Aunt Mary, Chandu the Magician, Dear John, One Man's Family* and *The Saint* (title role) programs.

7042 Collins, Tom D. Mandolin soloist (WFAA, Dallas, TX, 1922). Leader (Harmony Five [Orchestra], WFAA, Dallas, TX, 1924).

7043 Collins, Tommy (Leonard Raymond Sipes). CW Singer-Composer and DJ, Collins began work as a DJ on KLPR (Oklahoma City, OK, 1950). He later wrote songs that were popularized and recorded by Buck Owens, Ferlin Husky, Faron Young and Merle Haggard.

7044 Collins, Virginia. COM-HE (KFMO, Flat River, MO, 1956).

7045 Collins, Walter. Violinist and leader (Walter Collins' Fiddlers of Cleburne, Texas, WBAP, Ft. Worth, TX, 1924).

7046 Collins, Whispering Will. Singer (WCX, Detroit, MI, 1923).

7047 Collness, Judy. COM-HE (KATL, Miles City, MT, 1960).

7048 Collyer, Clayton "Bud." Busy and versatile Collyer was an actor, announcer and MC on such programs as *Abie's Irish Rose* (actor), *Break the Bank* (MC), *Cavalcade of America* (announcer), *Guiding Light* (announcer), *High Places* (actor), *Just Plain Bill* (actor), *Kate Hoplins, Angel of Mercy* (actor), *Kitty Foyle* (actor), *Life Can Be Beautiful* (actor), *Listening Post* (actor), *Man I Married* (actor), *Pretty Kitty Kelly* (actor), *Road of Life* (accouncer), *Superman* (actor — title role), *Terry and the Pirates* (actor), *Truth or Consequences* (announcer), *Winner Take All* (MC) and *Young Widder Brown* (actor).

7049 Colon, Jack. Sportscaster (KIST, Santa Barbara, CA, 1948; KCOY, Santa Maria, CA, 1953).

7050 Colon, Royce. Newscaster (KRLD, Dallas, TX, 1938–1940). Sportscaster (KRLD, 1938–1940). Colon had earlier joined the staff of KLRA (Little Rock, AR) in 1929 as salesman and "crooning tenor."

7051 *Colonel Bill.* William C. Gallaher of Leesburg, Virginia, conducted this children's program of Southern legends and folklore sponsored by Suplee Ice Cream. Colonel Bill told charming stories about Jack Rabbit, Billie Possum and Tessie Beaver (15 min., Wednesday, 6:00–6:15 P.M., WIP, Philadelphia, PA, 1935).

7052 *Colonel Combs and the Ramblers.* CW mus. prg. (WIBW, Topeka, KS, 1939).

7053 *Colonel Humphrey Flack.* Wendell Holmes played Colonel Humphrey Flack, a pompous confidence man with a walrus mustache, who often helped outwit other confidence men to aid "marks." Frank Maxwell played the role of Garvey, the Colonel's assistant. The program was based on the *Saturday Evening Post* magazine stories of Everett Rhodes Castle (30 min., Thursday, 8:00–8:30 P.M., NBC, 1947).

7054 *Colonel Jack and Shorty's Hillbillies.* The Alabama CW string band was sponsored by Crazy Water Crystals on the transcribed music show (Transcribed, Various stations, 1933).

7055 *Colonel Shafter Parker's Circus.* Los Angeles local children's show starring Hal Berger (KHJ, Los Angeles, CA/Don Lee Network ,West, 1939–1940; MBS, 1941).

7056 Colonial Dance Orchestra. Local dance band (WOKO, Peekskill, VA, 1925).

7057 Colonial Dance Orchestra of Brooklyn. Brooklyn jazz band (WHN, New York, NY, 1923).

7058 Colonial Inn Orchestra. Club dance band (WHN, New York, NY, 1923).

7059 Colonna, Victor. DJ (*The Night Owl*, WMTW, Portland, ME, 1950).

7060 ***(The) Colorado Cowboys.*** CW music prg. (KOA, Denver, CO, 1931).

7061 **Colorado School of Mines Band.** College band directed by A.E. Bellis (KOA, Denver, CO, 1925).

7062 ***Colorado School of Mines Open Air Twilight Concert.*** Instr. prg. (KOA, Denver, CO, 1925). These open air concerts were broadcast from Denver's Greek Theater.

7063 **Colorado Theater Orchestra.** Theater band (KOA, Denver, CO, 1928).

7064 ***(The) Colored Kiddies Hour.*** The Nixon Grand Theater sponsored the radio amateur show by and for "colored children." Harry Slatko hosted the show. Lucky Millinder's band accompanied the amateurs (60 min., Sunday, 3:00–4:00 P.M., WIP, Philadelphia, PA, 1936).

7065 **Colson, Bob.** DJ (WOLF, Syracuse, NY, 1960).

7066 **Colson, Howard.** Pianist (WOC, Davenport, IA, 1925).

7067 **Colston, Harriet Zell.** Soprano (WBAL, Baltimore, MD, 1927).

7068 **Colston, Warren.** Actor Colston appeared on the *Young Widder Brown* daytime serial program.

7069 **Colt, Dorothy.** Violinist (KLDS, Independence, MO, 1926).

7070 **Colt Park Municipal Orchestra.** Local music group (WTIC, Hartford, CT, 1925–1926).

7071 **Colton, Kingsley.** Actor Colton appeared on *John's Other Wife*, *Let's Pretend*, *My Son and I*, *Prairie Folks* and *Valiant Lady* daytime serial programs.

7072 **Colton, Larry.** Sportscaster (*In this Corner*, WGUY, Bangor, ME, 1953).

7073 **Colton, Lavern.** Newscaster (WCOU, Lewiston, ME, 1945). Sportscaster (WCOU, Lewiston, ME, 1947).

7074 **Colton, Tom.** Newscaster (WWSR, St. Albans, VT, 1941–1942). Sportscaster (WWSR, 1942; WARE, Ware, MA, 1950).

7075 **Colucio, Mildred.** Blues singer (WSWS, Chicago, IL, 1927).

7076 **Colum, Padraic.** Reader (WEAF, New York, NY, 1926).

7077 **Columbati, Virginia.** Coloratura soprano (WRNY, New York, NY, 1926).

7078 **Columbia Broadcasting System Dance Band.** Don Voorhees led the network dance band that included such outstanding musicians as: Vic Berton, ty.; Philip Gleason, clr.-as.; Jack Hansen, tba; Leo McConville, t.; Dick McDonough, bj-g.; Miff Mole, tb.; Red Nichols, t.; Joseph Raymond, v.; and Arthur Schutt, p. (CBS, New York, NY, 1928).

7079 **Columbia Broadcasting System Symphony Orchestra.** Conductor Howard Barlow and assistant conductor Alexander Semmler led the excellent symphony orchestra that included: Henry Baker, pe.; Carl Barnick, t.; Victor Bay, v.; Gregory Beerodny, cnm.; Guy D'Iseri, clr.; Walter Edelstein, v.; J.L. Fonteyn, o-eh.; Ossip Giskin, ce.; Harry Glantz ,t.; Edward Horwitz, h.; Egon Kornstein, vl.; John J. Perfetto, tb.; E. Roelofsma, clr.; Oscar Walther, v.; Adolph Weiss, bss.; and R. Meredith Willson, f.-pi. (CBS, New York, NY, 1927). The young Meredith Willson later gained fame as composer of the popular Broadway musical, *The Music Man*.

7080 **Columbia Broadcasting System's All-Soloist Radio Symphony Orchestra.** Network studio orchestra (CBS, New York, NY, 1928).

7081 ***Columbia Experimental Laboratory.*** The show's content was strange indeed. Actress Georgia Backus demonstrated a technique for radio drama in which everyone spoke to himself and thought for everyone else (30 min., 10:00–10:30 P.M., early 1930s, CBS). Perhaps this was one of the experiments carried out as a forerunner of the *Columbia Workshop*. *See* ***(The) Columbia Radio Workshop***.

7082 ***(The) Columbia Male Chorus.*** Freddie Rich conducted the orchestra on a program of semi-classical instrumental and popular choral music (60 min., Sunday, 3:00–4:00 P.M., CBS, 1930).

7083 **Columbia Orchestra.** New York dance band (WMCA, New York, NY, 1925).

7084 ***Columbia Phonograph Hour.*** Columbia Records sponsored the hour long program of concert music (60 min., Wednesday, 10:00–11:00 P.M., CBS, 1927).

7085 ***Columbia Presents Corwin.*** The 30-minute anthology series was written, produced and directed by Norman Corwin. Many believe it presented Corwin at his very best. The program premiered on CBS March 7, 1944. Some of the cast members included: Joan Alexander, Charme Allen, Michael Artist, Jim Backus, Harry Bartell, Jackson Beck, Ralph Bell, Roland Bottomley, Bob Bruce, Walter Burke, Kathleen Carnes, Peter Chong, Dane Clark, Lon Clark, Betty Comden, Hans Conreid, Ed Cullen, Shannon Day, Ted de Corsia, Oliver Deering, John Dehner, Peter Donald, Allan Drake, Robert Dryden, Laura Duncan, Jay Malcolm Dunn, Alex Englander, Roy Fant, Norman Field, Joseph Forte, Margaret Foster, Carl Frank, Maurice Franklin, Martin Gabel, Frank Gallop, Tana de Gamez, Ruth Gilbert, the Golden Gate Quartet, Joe Granby, Adolph Green, John Griggs, Larry Haines, Berford Hamden, Robert Harris, Nora Howard, Yung Ying Hsu, Richard Huey, Earl Hyman, Michael Ingram, Burl Ives, Nicholas Joy, Joseph Julian, Byron Kane, Sid Kassell, Donna Keith, Betsy Kelly, Adelaide Klein, Mordecai Kossover, Charles Laughton, Raymond Lawrence, Canada Lee, Peter Leeds, Rosetta Lenoir, Gene Leonard, Elliott Lewis, Katherine Locke, Joan Lorring, Frank Lovejoy, Wally Maher, Paul Mann, Harry Marble, Frederic March, Edward Marr, Tony Marvin, Mercedes McCambridge, Myron McCormick, John McGovern, Paul McVey, Peggy Miller, John Moore, Arnold Moss, Kermit Murdock, Franklin Parker, Hank Peters, Minerva Pious, Samuel Raskyn, Ken Renard, Earl Ross, Cecil Roy, Billy Roy, Dick Ryan, Alfred Ryder, James Scott, Eleanor Sherman, William L. Shirer, Everett Sloane, Hester Sondergaard, Giulana Taberna, Bertram Tanswell, Robert "Bob" Trout, Lurene Tuttle, Arthur Vinton, Regina Wallace, Josh White, Horace Willard, Mary Lou Williams, Martin Wolfson, Will Wright and Roland Young. *See* **Drama**.

7086 ***Columbia Presents Shakespeare.*** During a three month period in 1937, CBS broadcast a series of Shakespearean plays featuring major Hollywood stars. Some of the plays broadcast were: *The Taming of the Shrew* with Edward G. Robinson; *Much Ado About Nothing* with Leslie Howard and Rosalind Russell; *Julius Caesar* with Walter Abel, Thomas Mitchell and Claude Rains; *Henry IV* with Humphrey Bogart; and *Twelfth Night* with Tallulah Bankhead, Orson Welles and Sir Cedric Hardwicke.

7087 ***Columbia Record Shop.*** The program of recorded music was said by *Variety* (January 15, 1947, p. 32) to be a "watered down version of Fred Robbins' evening jive session (30 min., Saturday, 10:00–10:30 A.M., WCBS, New York, NY, 1947).

7088 ***Columbia Salon Orchestra.*** Vincent Sorey conducted the orchestra on the good music program (15 min., Saturday, 2:30–2:45 P.M., CBS, 1931; WNAC, Boston, MA, 1932; CBS, 1934).

7089 **Columbia String Quartet.** A small instrumental group, the Columbia String Quartet included Ivor Karman, Walter Edelstein, Samuel Stillman and Ossip Giskin (Columbia, 1927).

7090 ***Columbia Variety Hour.*** Edith Murray, Vera Van, the Eton Brothers and Little Jack Little were featured on the show (45 min., Sunday, 8:00–8:45 P.M., CBS, 1934). Another version was broadcast late Sunday afternoon, featuring Cliff "Ukulele Ike" Edwards, the Do Re Mi Trio, Vera Van, Jerry Cooper, Fray and Braggiotti and the Singing Spinsters sextet (WABC, 1934). A later 1935 version featured the piano duo of Fray and Braggiotti, orchestra conductors Johnny Green, Freddy Rich and Mark Warnow, singers Nick Lucas, Vera Van, Betty Barthell and Loretta Lee (60 min., Tuesday and Thursday, 3:00–4:00 P.M., CBS, 1935).

7091 ***(The) Columbia Workshop.*** CBS inaugurated the program in 1936 to stimulate good writing for radio. Although the series did offer many new writers and their work to the listening audience, it was the arrival of Norman Corwin in 1938 at the age of 27 that both invigorated the program and introduced to network radio a genuine creative genius. His contributions were many, including his "We Hold These Truths," a program that celebrated the 150th anniversary of the Bill of Rights in 1941, broadcast eight days after Pearl Harbor. See **Drama.**

7092 ***Columbia's Gay Nineties Revue (aka The Gay Nineties Review).*** Frank Lovejoy, Beatrice Kay, the Elm City Four, Elizabeth Newberger and the Ray Bloch Orchestra were featured on the popular music show (30 min., Weekly, CBS, 1939–1941). Joe Howard and Lillian Leonard joined the cast later.

7093 ***Columbia's Magazine of the Air.*** Broadcast three times a week, the program featured guests of special interest to women. For example, one week's schedule in 1936 included the following guests: Monday, Grand Duchess Marie of Roumania; Wednesday, authors Walter Pitkin and Ethel Cotton; and Friday, columnists Cholly Knickerbocker and Shelah Graham (30 min., Monday, Wednesday and Friday, CBS, 1936).

7094 Columbo, Russ (Ruggerio). Russ Columbo was a popular crooner of the early 1930s, who was a contemporary and rival of both Rudy Vallee and Bing Crosby before he was killed by an accidental shot from an antique pistol (*Russ Columbo,* vcl. mus. prg., 15 min., Tuesday through Saturday, NBC-Blue, 1931). Columbo later was featured with the Jimmy Grier Orchestra (15 min., Sunday, 12:15–12:30 P.M., NBC-Blue, 1934).

7095 Columbus, John A. DJ (*Requestfully Yours,* WPUV, Pulaski, VA, 1952).

7096 *(The) Column of the Air.* Lisa Sergio filled her sustaining radio column with information mainly of interest to women (30 min., Thursday, 10:00–10:30 P.M., WQXR, New York, NY, 1939).

7097 Colvig, Robert. Newscaster (KALE, Portland, OR, 1940).

7098 Colvin, Don. Sportscaster (KSFO, San Francisco, CA, 1937–1939).

7099 Colwell, Terry. Newscaster (WACE, Chicopee, MA, 1947). Sportscaster (WACE, 1947).

7100 Colwell, Virginia. COM-HE (WLDS, Jacksonville, IL, 1951).

7101 Colyar, (Mrs.) George. Pianist (WSM, Nashville, TN, 1928).

7102 Coman, Tom. DJ (*Uncle Tom's Gabbin',* WTIP, Charleston, WV, 1948).

7103 Combes, Jack. DJ (*Insomniac Serenade,* WFUN, Huntsville, AL, 1947).

7104 Combs, George, Jr. Newscaster and commentator (WHN, New York, NY, 1938; *Editorial Slant of the News,* WHN, 1939–1942; 1944–1947; WMGM, New York, NY, 1948).

7105 Combs, Hance and Vance Combs. Old time vocal music team (KMA, Shenandoah, IA, 1928).

7106 Combs, Joe. Tenor (WSM, Nashville, TN, 1928).

7107 Combs, Laura. Soprano (WOR, Newark, NJ, 1927).

7108 Combs, Virgil W. Bandmaster of the Missouri State Prison Concert Band, a popular music group on early radio (WOS, Jefferson City, MO, 1923).

7109 *Come On, Let's Sing* (*aka The Palmolive Community Sing*). Colgate-Palmolive sponsored this community sing program. Homer Rodeheaver was the program's songleader. (Rodeheaver had performed a similar function earlier for evangelist Billy Sunday at his revival meetings.) Music on the show was provided by Joe Green and his Cloister Bells Orchestra. Tiny Ruffner was the announcer (30 min., Wednesday, 9:30–10:00 P.M., CBS, 1936). After Rodeheaver left the program it was sometimes conducted by veteran vaudevillian and recording star Irving Kaufman as "Lazy Dan."

7110 Comediennes. Many women successfully worked in early radio as singers, musicians and actors, but relatively few as comedians. Although there were many talented comic actresses, only a few achieved major star status. In fact, even the funniest comediennes often did their best work in ensemble program situations, as opposed to a strictly stand-up comedy format. For many years an old show business adage from vaudeville and burlesque held that: Women couldn't be comedians. They could do a few comic bits, perhaps, a funny song now and then, but they couldn't possibly be major comedians. They could be part of a comedy team or comic ensemble, yes, but not funny alone. True, there was the old stereotyped role of the "dumb blonde" or "silly wife," but women were really good only as a "second banana," stooge, or foil. The "dumb role" was skillfully played on radio by Marie Wilson in the movies and early television. Carol Wayne did the same for many years on Johnny Carson's *Tonight Show* even in an era of Women's Lib. Each of these women represented only a continuation of the familiar show business staple of the "dumb female role."

Although Lucille Ball made a major break through for female comediennes on television, it was in radio that women first demonstrated they could be more than foils or second bananas. Certainly we can recognize this now, but it was not generally realized in the 1930s. Jack Benny, Fred Allen and Goodman Ace all were accepted as talented comics and comedy writers, but Mary, Portland and Jane were not always respected for their roles in making their husbands funny. These women were contributors and, sometimes, excellent comedians in their own right.

Women in comedy traditionally played the "foil," "straight man," or "second banana," generally as a "scatterbrain," "dumb dora," or "dumb dame" character. This tradition had been the case in vaudeville and it was carried over into the early years of radio. When radio began, the vaudeville format could be seen in the roles assigned to Gracie Allen, Mary Livingstone and Jane Ace on the *Burns and Allen, Jack Benny* and *Easy Aces* programs and their antecedents. However, in all three of these cases of husband-and-wife teams, there was never any doubt as to which performers on the program was delivering the strong laugh lines. Clearly, it was Gracie and Jane, not George or Goodman. The women were often the source of laughs, while the men were the brunt of the jokes.

When radio first began the "dumb dora" or "scatterbrain girl" tradition became a staple, typified by Burns and Allen, the Easy Aces and in the beginning Jack Benny and Mary Livingstone, as well as Fred Allen and Portland Hoffa. Husband-and-wife teams were popular in vaudeville with wife usually playing the foil or "dumb dame." One of the major exceptions to the husband-and-wife comedy team on radio was that of Marian and Jim Jordan (Fibber McGee and Molly). With the McGee's it was always Molly who was the smartest, straight thinking member of the team.

Burns and Allen were probably the most beloved of all radio's comedy teams. George Burns (Nathan Birnbaum) was born January 20, 1896 on New York's Lower East Side. He began in small time vaudeville and sang with the Pee Wee Quartette at stag parties, smokers, saloons and in the popular amateur night entertainments. He also worked as a dance instructor, seal trainer and in a dress factory. Before he met Gracie, he tried vaudeville with several partners including Sid Gary and Billy Lorraine, but he always left the acts. In New York, George and Gracie both were both looking for new partners when they decided to work together.

Grace Ethel Cecile Rosalie Allen was born July 26, 1905, into a show business family that included her song and dance man father who had worked in vaudeville successfully. She and her three older sisters formed a song and dance team and toured the West Coast vaudeville circuit.

Gracie was an excellent dancer, who also did various stage bits. After attempting a show business career in New York, Gracie was about to start secretarial school when she met George. She teamed with Burns as the "dumb female" in their comedy act, and they got their first in Newark, New Jersey, in 1923. George once said of their first act, "We had a hunger for something more important than fame — food." Although George started as the comedian and Gracie the foil, he soon realized that she was the one who got the laughs so he reversed their roles.

George had gotten no laughs whatsoever, but whenever Gracie said a word the audience laughed. Even Gracie's straight lines got laughs, while George's jokes did not. The audience loved Gracie and felt that she needed their protection. Burns quickly understood and after reversing their roles the team became one of vaudeville's most popular acts. A typical example of Gracie's lines was, "When I was born, I was so surprised I couldn't talk for a year and a half."

It was during an European trip in the summer of 1929, when they frequently broadcast on the BBC that George first realized that radio was a good medium for them. Returning to the United States, they resumed their successful vaudeville appearances. Eddie Cantor saw them at the New York's Palace Theater and had them appear on his *Chase and Sanborn Hour* program on November 15, 1931. Following that network broadcast they made guest appearances on Rudy Vallee's *Fleischmann Hour* and the *The Guy Lombardo* program. The next year Burns and Allen had their own half-hour show on CBS, *The Robert Burns Panatella Program,* with the Guy Lombardo orchestra. They began using their vaudeville format on radio, but in the 1941–1942 season they changed their routine to one of domestic situation comedy.

Some examples of the team's routines demonstrate their style of humor:

> GEORGE: Did you ever hear silence is golden?
>
> GRACIE: No, what station are they on?
>
> GEORGE: It's an adage, you know what an adage is.
>
> GRACIE: Oh sure, that's where you keep you old trunks.

—

> GRACIE: I'm going into the department store business. I made up my mind.
>
> GEORGE: What mind?
>
> GRACIE: Somebody told you to say that.

I'm going to open up five or six deparment stores, of course, that's only for a start.

GEORGE: No doubt in a few months, you will have several hundred department stores.

GRACIE: Well, I don't want to count my chickens before they're department stores.

Gracie was radio's most beloved comedienne, whose sweet innocence and naivete superseded the "dumb female" she portrayed. Only Jack Benny surpassed Gracie's excellent sense of timing. George, on the other hand, became radio's best straight man. Like their friend Jack Benny, Burns and Allen were one of the few vaudeville acts to make the successful transition, first, from vaudeville to radio and, later, to television Although Bob Hope also made the same transition, his long run on television was with "Specials," not on a series with permanent characters and a plot line like that of George and Gracie's program. Two of Burns and Allen's most famous running gags were Gracie's search for her "lost" brother in 1933 and her campaign as candidate of the Surprise Party for President in 1940.

After 18 years on radio, they made their successful transition to television on October 12, 1950. With them, on their TV show were Harry Von Zell, Bea Benadaret as neighbor Blanche Morton and their adopted son, Ronnie Burns.

Gracie retired in 1958 and died in 1964. George worked almost until the time he died on March 9,1996 at age 100. He outlived Gracie by 32 years, but he continued to mention her whenever he performed stand-up routines. He made several motion picture appearances, playing the role of God in his last two films. In retrospect, no radio team was more appreciated than Burns and Allen. Their long successful career warrants their recognition as the best comedy team in American Radio's Golden Age.

The act of veteran husband-and-wife vaudeville team Block and Sully was similar to that of Burns and Allen, since both had the same writer Al Boasberg. Herman Wouk also wrote some jokes for them. Despite the similarity with Burns and Allen there was no rivalry, but genuine friendliness. Two Block and Sully gags demonstrate the similarity.

BLOCK: Why were you late?

SULLY: I was watching the show and I had to change my seat six different times.

BLOCK: Why, were you molested?

SULLY: Yes, finally.

—

BLOCK: I saw your sister on the street today, but she didn't see me.

SULLY: Yes, I know. She told me.

Jesse Block (1900–1982) and Eve Sully (1902–1990) were a great vaudeville team with Block playing the straight man and she the "dumb dame." They played the Palace in 1929 and as Block said, "We played all the theaters on Broadway except the Roxy." In the early 1930s they had their own network radio program broadcast on Monday evening. Arlene Francis portrayed Eve's sister. Songs were performed by Gertrude Niesen. Paul Douglas was the announcer. In 1941 they returned as *Joe and Ethel Turp*, two Damon Runyon characters on WMCA (New York, NY). In addition, Block and Sully appeared on such network radio shows as Vallee's *Fleishmann Hour* and the *Magic Key of Radio*, as well as in the movies and Broadway revues. This veteran comedy team was one of the last acts working on vaudeville bills.

Jane and Goodman Ace were another famous husband-and-wife comedy team. Their program, *Easy Aces*, brilliantly written by Goodman Ace, began as a skit about a husband and wife who teamed together in a bridge game. The skit was developed into a show and first broadcast on Kansas City radio in 1930.

Goodman Ace (Goodman Aiskowitz) was born in Kansas City in 1899. By the age of 18, he was a drama, movie and vaudeville critic on the Kansas City *Post*. For years he supplied Jack Benny with jokes for his vaudeville act. Realizing the importance of radio, Ace broadcast two programs on KMBC (Kansas City, MO). On Sunday morning he read the comics for children, while on Saturday night he hosted the *Ace Goes to the Movies* program.

He met Jane Epstein, the daughter of a successful clothing merchant, and married her in 1922. They became a comedy team by accident. One evening in 1929 Jane was waiting in the KMBC studio for Ace to finish his Saturday night show. When the KMBC engineer could not pick up a scheduled CBS program that was scheduled for broadcast, he signaled Ace. After Ace began talking to fill the air time, he motioned to Jane to come in where he was broadcasting. Introducing her to the listening audience, they began talking about various subjects, including bridge and an incident that recently occurred, ad libbing about a wife who murdered her husband over a bridge game argument. Jane innocently asked Ace, "Would you care to shoot a game of bridge, dear?" Some other examples of Jane's linguistic scrambles were: "You have to take the bitter with the batter"; "We're insufferable friends"; "Familiarity breeds attempt"; "Time ends all heels"; "We're all cremated equally"; and "Things are going to Hades in a handbag." Poor Ace would frequently comment in a suffering tone, "Isn't that awful?"

The radio audience loved the husband-and-wife talk and *Easy Aces* was born. Goodman and Jane Ace portrayed the comedy roles of a "dumb" wife and her long suffering, sarcastic husband. Jane's malaprops, language scrambles and words of doubtful wisdom were hilarious. On those occasions when she agreed with her husband, her typical response was: "I'll tell the world."

Goodman Ace soon recognized that Jane was the comedian who got the laughs. He provided the brilliant writing, but she delivered the lines with skillful comedic timing. Ace confessed the situation in a short article he wrote for *Radio Guide* (March 24, 1934, p. 3).

GOODMAN ACE'S STORY OF HOW HE LOST HIS WHIP

I am a stooge. Groucho's Zeppo, Clark's McCullough — Mussolini's Emanuel — all these I am and I know it.

In short, I am a radio husband.

Like Fred Allen, Jack Benny and George Burns, I have called upon my roommate to aid and abet me in creating a radio program. Four years ago she was a girl. She made her own hats. She sewed on a button. She even threw together a victual of no mean delicacy. But like Fred, Jack and George I got an idea for radio.

Now, I am a stooge.

For years — a dozen to be exact — I wrote a daily column for a newspaper. People knew me. My head was high, a sparkle was in my eye and a spring in my tread.

"He writes for the paper," they said and: "Oh, she? She's his wife."

Then came radio.

Like Fred, Jack and George, I bend over a typewriter and make it say funny things. I speak them aloud as I pound away — fashioning them for her to say — muttering at my work. And she, from above her bottle of Cutex says: "What on earth are you muttering about?" A man's best friend is his mutter — but not in my house.

I am a stooge.

Four days a week I come to my typewriter and grind out funny things to say, weaving them into homey little situations, vaguely remembered from a home that was a home — before radio.

And once in a while, a very great while, I try to sneak in a little laugh for myself— not a big laugh, more of a suppressed snicker, just for auld lang syne and the days when I was somebody and cracked a whip. And I know that somewhere up in their Central Park apartments, Fred, Jack and George are trying to slip in little laughs somewhere for themselves, too. But not too many laughs — laughs are not for us — not for me anyhow. Laughs are for her, so the fans can write and say: "We love Jane ... she is so funny. She is so dumb. She is so delightfully dumb."

Yes ... she's so dumb.

Whose picture is that on the page with this story? [It was that of Jane Ace.] I am a stooge.

After their initial success the *Easy Aces* were signed for a 13 week run. In 1931–1932 they began another 13 week trial on CBS three times weekly, 10:15–10:30 P.M. They returned the following season. Without a sponsor they traveled to New York, where Frank Hummert liked their slick, sophisticated brand of humor. They began broadcasting four times a week on CBS from 1933 to 1935. In the fall of 1935 they began appeared for Anacin, their long time sponsor, on a 15 minute show opposite *Amos 'n' Andy*. Despite this tough competition the Aces developed a loyal following. Their quarter-hour format was extended through 1942.

On *Easy Aces*, "radio's distinctive laugh novelty," they played a prosperous couple living in an upper class Manhattan neighborhood. Ace played an advertising agency executive. Jane was busy finding a husband for her girl friend, getting Ace to buy her a fur coat or two and even making a little extra money at various odd jobs. Jane's best friend Marge was played by Mary Hunter. Their 21-year-old adopted son, Cookie, was portrayed by Ken Roberts. Their maid was played by Helene Dumas and Ace's secretary by Ann Thomas.

When they broadcast, the cast simply sat around a card table with a concealed microphone to achieve a spontaneous, conversational sound. Beginning in 1943, the show went to a

30-minute format, but it proved not as successful as the quarter-hour program. One of Goodman's favorite remarks always was, "We have our Crossley's [listener ratings] to bear." After broadcasting in this format on Wednesday night, 7:30–8:00 P.M., for two years, the program went off the air. The Aces returned once more in the half-hour format during the 1948–1949 season as *Mr. Ace and Jane.* This was their last program.

Some of the best examples of the Aces' comedy can be found in a World War II program on which Jane wanted to start a community victory garden:

> JANE: I think I'll start a community victory garden in that empty lot on the corner there. Wouldn't it be wonderful to get all our tomatoes, radishes, beans, peas and corn au gratin?
>
> ACE: What do you mean au gratin?
>
> JANE: Free.
>
> —
>
> MARGE [Jane's best friend]: Jane, I hear you're going to start a victory garden.
>
> JANE: Yes, Marge, I am — a community victory garden. I'll get all the other women in the neighborhood to dig the garden with me. It's for the war you know — the boys in the army. We must all put our shoulders to wheel to wheel until the duration is over.

When the neighborhood women won't help, Jane says: "So they won't help with the community victory garden. Well, I'll figure out a way to make them help, if I have to work my head to the bone." And: "Of course, a community victory garden is only a kick in the bucket, but it'll help. And I'm going to get all the women around here to help dig that garden. You just leave it to your Uncle Dulcy. I've got a scheme. I'll have those women eating out of the hollow of my head and we'll have that community victory garden going quicker than you can say Bill Robinson."

Jane retired from radio in 1949 and died in 1974. Goodman Ace went on to write for many television shows and periodicals, and for awhile in the 1960s was heard on the WPAT (Paterson, NJ) *Tempo* morning program giving his view of the world. Much like Goodman Ace, Fred Allen also wrote for his wife, Portland Hoffa, and incorporated her into his radio program. Only a part-time scatterbrain on *The Fred Allen Program*, Portland Hoffa also came from the vaudeville tradition that had developed the stereotyped dumb female character. When the two first teamed up, Allen used her early to play the dumb dame. Portland was gifted with a funny, high-pitched voice, which Allen said sounded like "two slate pencils mating or a clarinet reed calling for help."

In many respects, when Portland Hoffa played the "dumb female" role on the *Fred Allen Show*, it was that of a smarter more astringent version of Gracie Allen playing off Fred's much more capable, worldly wise and worn version of George Burns. None of this implies that they copied or imitated the Burns and Allen routines, for this, of course, was far from the case. George and Gracie merely portrayed familiar show business types — as did Fred and Portland — characters that were later portrayed over and over in radio, television and movies.

Portland Hoffa was the daughter of Frederick Hoffa, an optometrist. She was an excellent dancer, who became a Broadway chorus girl. Portland met Fred Allen when both were appearing in Broadway's *The Passing Show of 1922.* Their marriage on May 4, 1927 began a happy, lifetime partnership. During their radio years, her call of "Mis-ter A-l-l-en" and "Tally ho, Mr. Allen" became familiar trademarks. Catchwords and phrases always were the marks of a successful radio series. *The Fred Allen Show* had several of them that mostly resulted when the Allen's Alley segment was added. "Tally ho," always said by Portland, was used in early Allen programs as a means of closing one segment and providing a transition into another. It indicated to listeners that something was finished and that the program was moving onto something else, usually a song or instrumental selection by the orchestra. At other times, the phrase served as a philosophical "so be it" to close the program.

After completing a two-year run on Broadway with Clifton Webb and Libby Holman in *Three's a Crowd,* Allen found himself out of work with only a promised role in another Broadway show not scheduled to open for six months. It was the spring of 1932, deep in the economic gloom of the Great Depression. The gold rush of vaudeville comedians moving into radio had begun. Comics such as Ed Wynn, Eddie Cantor and Joe Penner already were enjoying some success in the new medium, due chiefly to the funny costumes and rough-house physical antics they used to make studio audiences laugh. Although they achieved some amount of success, they gave no real evidence of fully understanding radio and its unique possibilities as a medium for comedy.

Facing weeks of inactivity, Allen planned a series of radio programs, assembled a cast that featured Portland and, eventually, auditioned it for the Corn Products Company. The successful audition marked the beginning of the *Linit Bath Club Review*, whose first program was broadcast on CBS on October 23, 1932. It was on the *Linit Bath Club Review* that Portland began playing the scatterbrain comedy role. She continued to play a major role on all the various programs she and Allen broadcast together until their last network radio show in 1949. Portland Hoffa played a vital role in the long running success of radio's brightest comedian.

If Fred Allen was radio's brightest, Jack Benny was one of American radio's most beloved comedians, despite his adopted persona of stinginess and vanity. An important reason for Benny's success was the contribution made to the "Benny ensemble" by his wife, Mary Livingstone. Other important members of the ensemble were Eddie "Rochester" Anderson, Don Wilson, Phil Harris, Dennis Day and Mel Blanc. Although the success of the Benny program was primarily due to the ensemble, certainly Jack and Mary as a comedy team made a significant contribution.

Mary Livingstone was born Sadie Marks in 1908, the daughter of a wealthy Vancouver, British Columbia, businessman. She was working in a Los Angeles department store when she first met Jack Benny, and she was not impressed by him. Benny at that time was already a successful vaudevillian, working the circuit around the country. Whenever he was working in Los Angeles, he made it a point to see Mary. Benny would pretend to be interested in hosiery if that was the item she was selling. He began dating her whenever he returned to Los Angeles.

On one of Benny's trips to Los Angeles he discovered that Mary was about to marry another boy friend. Spurred into action by this development, Benny proposed and they were married in 1927. Mary joined Benny's act as a singer and "foil." She played "Marie Marsh," a "dumb Dora" stereotype. She got laughs in the act by putting down the egotistical Benny in the routine, a staple that continued to get laughs when they went on the radio. When reluctantly she appeared with Benny on his first radio show, the *Canada Dry Program*, she was extremely nervous. As she had begun in vaudeville, she continued to make cutting remarks whenever Benny bragged about his good looks, clothes or generosity. Mary's role was greatly diminished and finally disappeared altogether when Jack made his successful transition to television. Although always an extremely nervous radio performer, she never came across as the "dumb dame." Instead, she seemed to be a perceptive observer whose comments reflected reality, where none existed before.

Another comedy team that played husband-and-wife, although never married in real life, was the hilarious Don Ameche and Francis Langford playing *The Bickersons.* Ameche, a talented, show business veteran, was one of the stars of early radio in *The Chase and Sanborn Show* and the *The First Nighter* program, among many, many others. As the bumbling, somewhat egotistical John Bickerson, he was always the foil of his wife, Blanche Bickerson, skillfully played by Frances Langford.

Langford gained national prominence as a popular singer when she made her first national network appearance with Rudy Vallee on his *Fleishmann Yeast Hour* program. From 1933 to1935, she starred on her own program on NBC, *The Spartan Hour,* sponsored by the Spartan Radio Corporation. She also appeared on *The Chase and Sanborn Hour* with Charlie McCarthy, W.C. Fields and Don Ameche. In later years she was the long time singer on the *Bob Hope Show.* During World War II, Langford made many numerous trips overseas with Hope to entertain service men and women.

The Bickersons act was a spin-off from a skit on the *Chase and Sanborn Hour.* Their program was first called *Drene Time* and, later, *The Old Gold Show.* It was broadcast on NBC and CBS from 1946 through 1951. The 1951 version of *The Bickersons* had Lew Parker playing John Bickerson, but the humor this time never reached that of the comic sparks that flew between Langford and Ameche.

Jim and Marian Jordan as *Fibber McGee and Molly* were another husband-and-wife comedy team that for many years also portrayed the wife as the sensible voice of reason, attempting to keep her boastful husband down to earth. James Edward Jordan was born November 16, 1896 near Peoria, Illinois. His wife to be, Marian Driscoll, was born April 5, 1898. Marian and Jim met at a church choir practice in 1915.

Tenor Jim toured the Western Vaudeville Circuit from September 1917 to April 1918 with the "A Night with the Pacific Musical Quartet" act. He and Marian were married in 1918 when Jim was drafted into the army at the close of World War I. After he was discharged from the army, he and pianist Marian became a successful concert act in vaudeville billed as the Metropolitan Musical Entertainers. They also traveled at times as a harmony singing team. At other times, tenor Jim appeared alone on the vaudeville circuits.

After the Jordans made their Chicago radio audition in 1925 at Chicago's station WIBO, they were hired by the station for 10 weeks. On these appearances they didn't say a word, only sang and played the piano. They began talking on their broadcasts the following year. Between 1925 and 1927, they averaged broadcasts on three different Chicago local stations per night. They soon were heard on regularly scheduled programs, including *The Air Scouts*, a quarter-hour children's program on Chicago's WENR. On this program Marian first began experimenting with her "Teeny" voice, that of a curious little girl with many questions. Jim also experimented with various characters on the program. When they appeared on the station's *Grab Bag* program, Marian was doing a dozen voices. By 1929, they were playing a rural couple *Luke and Mirandy* on Chicago radio station WENR.

Later in 1929, Marian had a leading role on the *Smith Family* show, a program that depicted "an average middle class family." Jim was also featured in the cast, along with Bud Morris, Thora Martens, Daisy Dugan, Joe Smith and Joe Warner. The show's organist was Irma Glen. It ran from 1929 to 1932.

In the 1930s, Jim and Marian appeared on WENR's *Farmer Ruck—Top of the Morning Show*. When the program moved to WMAQ, Chicago's NBC outlet, the Jordans moved with it. The popular morning show featured country-western singer Doc Hopkins and the Joseph Gallichio orchestra.

At about this time the couple met Don Quinn, who was to play an important role in their later professional lives. Quinn wrote the *Smackout Show* broadcast by WMAQ from 1931 to 1935. The program told the story of a small, country store featuring Jim as the proprietor. Marian did the voice of "Teeny," as well as many of the store's other customers. *Smackout* was announced as the store down at the Crossroads of the Air. The country store supposedly was located in a rural area in a valley near Smackout Corner. On the show, Jim was the store's owner and Marian a little girl, "Teenie," who was frequently sent to the store by her mother, only invariably to be told by Jim that he was "smack out" of everything she asked for.

The program, incidentally, pre-dated Lum and Abner's Jot Em Down Store by a few months. After the theme was played by either the Harry Kogen, Joseph Gallichio or Walter Blaufuss orchestras, the entire show was carried on by Jim and Marian with a few customers dropping in occasionally. The announcers were Bob White, Alfred Saxe, Jack Negley and Everett G. Mitchell.

The *Smackout* show eventually went on the NBC network on a sustaining basis. During this time Jim and Marian made frequent guest appearances on the *The Saturday Night Jamboree*, *The Breakfast Club* and *The National Farm and Home Hour*, all favorite NBC network features. Jim and Marian were also regular performers on the hilarious juvenile comedy, *Kaltenmeyer's Kindergarten* in the roles of Mickey Donovan and Gertie Gump. *See **Kaltenmeyer's Kindergarten**.*

Don Quinn wrote, polished and developed the Fibber and Molly roles. When the Jordans premiered on their own *Fibber McGee and Molly* show on April 16, 1935, Quinn continued to write for them along with Phil Leslie until 1950, when he left for other pursuits.

Molly left the program in 1937 after she suffered a serious illness. She was able to return to the show on April 18, 1939. While she was gone the program was called *Fibber McGee and Company*. During this time a featured member of the cast was Hugh Studebaker, who played "Silly" (Silus Leviticus Deuteronomy Watson). Silly often drawled on about his sweetheart Rosebud Jackson. Also appearing on the show during Molly's absence was Betty Winkler, Bernardine Flynn and ZaSu Pitts.

When *Fibber McGee and Molly* went off the air in 1953, they continued to do guest spots on radio, including many on *Weekend Monitor* on NBC. Their last appearance together on *Weekend Monitor* was September 6, 1959, exactly 24 years, 4 months and 19 days after they first debuted as *Fibber McGee and Molly* (Stumf and Price, 1987, p. 225).

After Molly died in 1961, Jim continued to work, appearing occasionally on *Weekend Monitor*, but the genial good humor the team once generated was gone. When the voice of "Teeny" and "Sis" was stilled, only an echo remained of Molly's famous, "Tain't funny, McGee." Most of the laughter had died.

One of the greatest female comedians, Fannie Brice, also came to radio from burlesque and vaudeville. She was born Fannie Borach on New York City's Lower East side on October 29, 1891. Entering many amateur night contests in Brooklyn and Manhattan, Fannie won most of them. Singing and dancing extremely well, she joined burlesque and became a chorus girl. Fannie sang with an exaggerated Jewish accent, accompanied by stereotyped body movements and the audience loved it.

After starring in burlesque, Fannie moved on to Broadway. She was already a headliner when she opened in the *1910 Follies* with Bert Williams and Lillian Lorraine, but in its June 18, 1910 issue, *Variety* proclaimed Fannie was "the star" of *The Follies*. She starred in comedy turns in the 1911, 1916, 1917, 1920, 1921 and 1925 versions of *The Follies*. Singing at the Palace she showed the range of her talent by performing "The Song of the Sewing Machine," a lament about the plight of the women in sweat shops. She often also came up with some funny lines off-stage such as: "I've been poor and I've been rich. Rich is better." Although often attributed to others, apparently it was Brice's original line.

For 15 years Fannie starred in *The Ziegfeld Follies* as a gifted singer and comedian. Her best known songs were "Becky's Back in the Ballet," "Second Hand Rose" and "My Man," a song her fans thought she sang about her tragic marriage to gangster Nicky Arnstein, since she performed it with such great tragic style and feelings. In many of her songs, she showed her skill by first singing straight, then starting to use a Yiddish word here and there, before ending the song with a strong Yiddish accent. She could change the audience reaction to a song quickly by the nuances she made with her voice.

Fannie portrayed a little girl on the stage long before she did Baby Snooks on radio. Snooks actually began in vaudeville where Fannie developed a Babykins character. Supposedly, she first tried Snooks out at a party after the opening of the 1910 version of *The Follies*. Snooks first appeared on the radio on the *Ziegfeld Follies of the Air* program in 1936 on CBS.

Appearing on radio frequently in 1932, Fannie sang songs and performed monologues. She was popular on radio in both the 1930s and 1940s on the *Good News* program (1938–1939) and *Maxwell House Coffee Time* (1940–1944). Latter she appeared on the *The Baby Snooks Show* (1944–1951) with Hanley Stafford as Daddy, Arlene Harris as her Mother and Leone Ledoux as her brother Robespierre. Snooks' pranks included planting a bees' nest in the meeting room of her mother's club, putting marbles into their piano and glue on baby brother Robespierre.

Brice planned to retire from radio after her NBC contract ended on June 21, 1951. But on May 29, 1951, she died of a cerebral hemorrhage on the day before a Snooks program was to be broadcast

Many comedians and comic actors regularly performed on network radio. One of the busiest was Barbara Jo Allen, best known for her "Vera Vague" character on the *The Bob Hope Show*, but who also played straight dramatic roles. New Yorker Allen studied at Stanford and the University of California before enrolling at the University of Paris. She traveled extensively through Europe and Africa before returning to appear on the New York stage. Eventually, she moved to San Francisco where she began her radio career. Although one of her major dramatic roles was that of "Beth Holly" in *One Man's Family*, she became most famous for playing the man-chasing "Vera Vague" on *The Bob Hope Show*.

Allen also appeared on *The Edgar Bergen-Charlie McCarthy Show* and *The Jimmy Durante Show*. Her "Vera Vague" character, always on the lookout for men, was a particularly valuable comic asset during World War II, when *The Bob Hope Program* was broadcast each week from a different Navy base or Army camp.

Other regular comic performers on *The Bob Hope Show* were "Brenda and Cobina," played by Blanche Stewart and Elvia Allman. This comedy pair were parodies of two prominent, real-life social debutantes, Brenda Frazier and Cobina Wright, Jr. In addition to appearances on the Hope program, Stewart also broadcast frequently on *The Jack Benny Program*. Elvia Allman, who played "Cobina," began her network radio career by doing sketches with W.C. Fields on the earliest versions of *Your Hit Parade*. Allman was born in Spencer, North Carolina in 1905. Her first radio appearance was on Chicago's KYW as a reader of various literary passages. After leaving Chicago, she traveled to Los Angeles to further her radio career as a comedian. In addition to *The Bob Hope Show*, she also appeared regularly on *Glamour Manor*, *The Burns and Allen Show*, *The Ray Bolger Show* and *The Jimmy Durante Show*.

Eve Arden, with her contrasting comic style of wise cracks mixed with insightful observations, played the title role on *Our Miss Brooks* (CBS, 1948–1957) an English teacher at Madison High School. Although she yearned for the attention of Mr. Boynton, the biology teacher played by Jeff Chandler, there was no doubt that *Our Miss Brooks* was much smarter than the bashful biology teacher. In the role of English teacher Connie Brooks, Arden provided a straight-faced, down-to-earth monotone delivery of good common sense, except when it came to her unrequited affection for Mr. Boynton.

Arden's radio career also included regular appearances on the *The Ken Murray Program* (1939); *The Danny Kaye Show* (1945–1946); and *The Village Store* (1945–1948) program with Jack Haley, who was replaced by Jack Carson in 1947. She also had a long successful motion picture career that included her brilliant performance as a wise cracking side kick to star Joan Crawford in *Mildred Pierce*. Arden also enjoyed a successful television career when *Our Miss Brooks* made a successful transition to television in 1952 (CBS, 1952–1956). Jeff Chandler was replaced by Robert Rockwell, the only regular not a member of the original radio cast. Richard Crenna played her favorite student, Walter Denton. Arden won an award as the Best Female Star of a Regular Series in 1952. She also appeared in television on *The Eve Arden Show* (1957–1958) and *The Mothers-in-Law* (1967–1967, 1969).

Another versatile comic actress who had a long and varied radio career was Bea Benadaret. Among her best known work were the dual roles of Gloria the maid and Mrs. Waddington on *The Adventures of Ozzie and Harriet*, Wanda Werewolf on *Glamour Manor*, and telephone operator Gertrude Gearshifton on *The Jack Benny Show*. In addition, Benadaret performed regularly on a *Day in the Life of Dennis Day*, *Fibber McGee and Molly* and *The Mel Blanc Show*.

Three other versatile comic actresses were Verna Felton, Arlene Harris and Fran Allison. Verna Felton's three most prominent roles were those as Junior's mother on *The Red Skelton Show*, Aunt Aggie on *The Judy Canova Show* and Dennis Day's mother on *The Jack Benny Show*. She also appeared regularly on *The Village Store* program, *The Tommy Riggs and Betty Lou Show* and *The Ray Bolger Show*. Fran Allison, also a talented singer and actress, supplied rural comic commentary as "Aunt Fanny" on *The Breakfast Club*. Allison later gained greater prominence appearing with Burr Tillstrom's puppets on television's *Kukla, Fran and Ollie*. Arlene Harris, a "motor mouth," was "the Human Chatterbox" on the *Al Pearce and His Gang* show and "mommy" on *The Baby Snooks Show*.

Joan Davis was a comedienne who enjoyed more success in motion pictures and television than in radio. The comedienne-singer was born Madonna Josephine Davis in St. Paul, MN, on June 29, 1907. After appearing on the stage as a child, she teamed with her husband, comedian Sy Wills to form the Wills and Davis vaudeville act. By 1934, she began appearing in comedy shorts in Hollywood. The following year she made her first feature film, *Millions in the Air* (1935). She enjoyed popularity on the radio on the *Leave It to Joan* situation comedy and the *Village Store* (1943–1948, NBC) sometimes known as *The Sealtest Village Store* with Jack Haley, Eve Arden and Verna Felton. For the 1947–1948 season Jack Carson replaced Haley. The talented Miss Davis appeared on early television when she starred on *I Married Joan* (1952–1955) co-starring with Jim Backus as her husband, Judge Bradley Stevens. Davis usually presented a nervous, nasal, highly excitable persona on most of her shows. *See* ***It's Joan Davis Time, Leave It to Joan*** *and* ***(The) Village Store***.

Joan Davis appeared in the following feature films: *Millions in the Air* (1935); *The Holy Terror* (1937); *On the Avenue* (1937); *Wake Up and Live* (1937); *Angel's Holiday* (1937); *Thin Ice* (1937); *Life Begins in College* (1937); *Love and Hisses* (1937); *Sally, Irene and Mary* (1938); *Josette* (1938); *My Lucky Star* (1938); *Hold That Coed* (1938); *Just Around the Corner* (1938); *Tail Spin* (1939); *Daytime Wife* (1939); *Free, Blonde and 21* (1940); *Hold that Ghost* (1941); *Sun Valley Serenade* (1941); *Two Latins from Manhattan* (1941); *Yokel Boy* (1942); *Sweetheart of the Fleet* (1942); *Two Senoritas from Chicago* (1943); *Around the World* (1943); *Beautiful But Broke* (1944) *Show Business* (1944); *Kansas City Kitty* (1944); *She Gets Her Man* (1945); *George White's Scandals* (1945); *She Wrote the Book* (1946); *If You Knew Susie* (1948); *Make Mine Laughs* (1949); *Traveling Salesman* (1950); *Love that Brute* (1950); *The Groom Wore Spurs* (1951); and *Harem Girl* (1956).

Lucille Ball, the beautiful motion picture and television star appeared on radio on the popular *My Favorite Husband* program (1948–1951), as a guest panelist on *Leave It to the Girls* and made frequent guest appearances on the *Screen Guild Theater* and *Suspense* programs. It was on television, however, with the *Lucille Ball Show* she enjoyed her greatest comic success.

Of all radio's comediennes and comic actresses, however, probably none was more beloved than Minerva Pious, who was famous for her "Mrs. Nussbaum" role on *The Fred Allen* programs and *The Henry Morgan Show, Columbia Presents Corwin, The Goldbergs*, and *Life Can Be Beautiful*.

Minerva Pious performed on Allen's programs for many years in different roles. She was a regular denizen of Allen's Alley as Pansy Nussbaum, a Bronx Jewish housewife. When Allen knocked on her apartment door, Pansy Nussbaum typically answered, "Nu," a Yiddish colloquial expression roughly translated as "All right" or "Now what?" When Allen greeted her with, "Well — Mrs. Nussbaum," she would answer with such responses as:

> You were expecting the Fink Spots?
> You were expecting Weinstein Churchill?
> You were expecting Cecil B. Schlemiel?
> You were expecting Emperor Shapiro-Hito?
> You were expecting the King Cohen Trio?

Pansy Nussbaum was an active urban housewife, busy in her garden growing "rutabagels" and reading the poetry of Heinie Wadsworth Longfellow. She liked to remind Allen that in her earlier days she had been Miss Low Tide at Far Rockaway Beach. Skillfully played by Minera Pious, Mrs. Nussbaum was one of Allen's funniest creations.

There were many other comediennes and comic actresses who worked alone or as a team on early radio whose work has been lost and generally overlooked. Whether famous or forgotten, however, these funny women made many lives brighter by providing the valuable gift of laughter to their audience.

Two unique performers — Judy Canova and Cousin Minnie Pearl (Sarah Ophelia Cannon) — two educated, intelligent and sophisticated women, adopted a hillbilly persona to entertain millions of radio listeners. The first of these talented comediennes, Judy Canova, began her own radio career on CBS with *The Judy Canova Show*, aka *Rancho Canova*, wearing her hair in pigtails as the "Queen of the Hillbillies."

Born Juliette [Julia] Etta Canova in Jacksonville, FL, in 1916, the comedienne-singer first appeared professionally with brother Zeke and sister Anne as the Singing Canovas. After appearing in the Flo Ziegfeld's *Calling All Stars on Broadway*, Judy's first radio appearance was on the *Paul Whiteman Show* in the 1930s. Her own radio program, the *Judy Canova Show* broadcast from 1943 to 1953 on CBS and NBC. Its cast included: Mel Blanc, Joe Kearns, Sheldon Leonard, Ruby Dandridge and Verna Felton. *See* ***(The) Judy Canova Show***. Judy also made numerous World Transcriptions on which she delivered monologs, consisting mainly of tall tales and yarns. In addition to her radio career, she also enjoyed a busy motion picture career, always portraying a raucous hillbilly character who yodeled loudly. She is the mother of actress Diana Canova.

Judy's first motion picture was Busby Berkeley's *In Caliente* in 1935. Her other films include: *Going Highbrow* (1935); *Artists and Models* (1937); *Thrill of a Lifetime* (1937); *Scatterbrain* (1940); *Sis Hopkins* (1941); *Puddin' Head* (1941); *Sleepytime Gal* (1942); *True to the Army* (1942); *Joan of Ozark* (1942); *Sleepy Lagoon* (1943); *Chatterbox* (1943); *Louisiana Hayride* (1944); *Hit the Hay* (1945); *Singing in the Corn* (1946); *Honeychile* (1951); *Oklahoma Annie* (1952); *The WAC from Walla Walla* (1952); *Untamed Heiress* (1954); *Carolina Cannonball* (1955); *Lay That Rifle Down* (1953); *The Adventures of Huckleberry Finn* (1960); and *Cannonball* (1976). At the age of 60, she returned to appear in the *Cannonball* film with Burt Reynolds.

Any discussion of comediennes should also include "rural" or "country" performers, most of whom appeared on programs such as *The Grand Ole Opry, The Louisiana Hayride* and *The National Barn Dance*. Although rural listeners undoubted comprised their largest audience, there were many urban and suburban listeners who enjoyed the antics of the greatest country comedienne of them all — Cousin Minnie Pearl, whose long career outlasted such great comic stars of the *Grand Ole Opry* as Rod Brasfield and the Duke of Paducah (Benny "Whitey" Ford).

Sarah Ophelia Cannon was born in Centerville, TN, in 1912, the daughter of a prospeous business man. She attended a finishing school for two years, before she was forced to leave because of her father's problems encountered during the business slow down of the Great Depression.

Traveling throughout the South working for the Sewell Company, Minnie organizing dramatic performances and amateur musicals. When she lost her job in 1940, she returned to Tennessee and successfully auditioned for a job at WSM (Nashville, TN), using the Minnie Pearl character, a persona she had been developing professionally since 1938.

Cousin Minnie Pearl first appeared on *The Grand Ole Opry* in 1940. Playing an unmarried lady between the ages of 25 and 35, she soon developed her trademark greeting to the audience — "Howdee." Incidentally, she began greeting the audience in a relatively soft voice, but soon realized that the louder she greeted the audience the louder was their response.

Her other trademark of a $1.98 price tag dangling from the flowers on her hat was the result of an accident. Once she inadvertently left a price tag attached after she had purchased flowers from a five-and-dime store and found that the audience loved it. The audience reaction was so favorable that she made it a regular part of her costume. A member of the Country Music Hall of Fame, Cousin Minnie Pearl played Madison Square Garden, Carnegie Hall, Houston's Astrodome, Berlin's Titania Palace and the Vienna Music Hall, in addition to the *Grand Ole Opry*. *Also see* **Women in Country Music** *and* **Pearl, Cousin Minnie**.

If the performances of sophisticated and educated women like Judy Canova and Cousin Minnie Pearl as "hillbillies" seem unusual, motion picture star Mae West caused a scandal in one of radio's truly unique events. It was Arch Oboler's script on *The Chase and Sanborn-Edgar Bergen-Charlie McCarthy Show* that made her the central figure on the "Garden of Eden" incident.

Oboler's script was innocuous enough, but it was West's seductive delivery that produced the condemnation of many religious organizations and incurred the wrath of Federal Communications Commissioner, Frank R. McNinch. The dialogue between Adam and Eve, played by Don Ameche and Mae West, respectively, does not sound as suggestive as does that between Eve and the Snake.

Eve asks the "palpitating python" to pick her a forbidden apple, since Mr. Snake was skinny enough to slither through the fence that surrounded the tree containing the forbidden fruit. After Eve entices him to do so, the snake becomes stuck in the fence, she advises him to "shake your hips" and praises him when he gets through, "There, there now, you're through."

> MR. SNAKE: I shouldn't be doing this.
>
> EVE: Yeh, but you're doing all right now. Get me a big one. I feel like doing a big apple.
>
> MR. SNAKE: Here you are, Missus Eve.
>
> EVE : Mm — oh I see. Huh — nice goin' swivel hips.
>
> MR. SNAKE: Wait a minute. It won't work. Adam'll never eat that forbidden apple.
>
> EVE : Oh, yes he will — when I'm through with it.

After the Adam and Eve skit was over, West sizzled in a brief comedy dialogue with Charlie McCarthy. She asks Charlie to come up to her apartment, "Why don't you come home with me now, honey, I'll let you play in my woodpile." When Charlie refuses, Bergen learns the young man had already been up at Mae's place, when she explains, "Charlie came up and I showed him my etchings and he showed me his stamp collection." Furthermore, she chided Charlie about his reluctance to come back.

> MAE: You didn't need any encouragement to kiss me.
>
> CHARLIE: Did I do that?
>
> MAE : You certainly did and I've got the marks to prove it and the splinters, too.

As the skit continued Charlie still attempted to resist Mae's advances, but he clearly was weakening.

The aftermath of the program was a barrage of protests against this "vulgar" and "sacrilegious" program. The show was debated on the floor of the House of Representatives in Washington as part of a discussion of obscenity on radio. FCC Chairman Frank McNinch condemned the program's "objectionable character." The show's advertising agency, J. Walter Thompson, apologized to NBC, who in turn on the following Sunday's program apologized to its listeners if the broadcast offended them. Bowing to the objections raised, NBC banned Miss West from further radio appearances and, furthermore, ordered that her name should not even be mentioned on the air (Wertheim, 1970, pp. 365–366).

Certainly Mae West left a lasting mark on radio comedy. A victim of criticism for what today would hardly have caused a stir, Mae clearly had the last laugh for she knew precisely what she was doing and how well she did it. *Also see* **Comedy and Humor**.

7111 Comedy and Humor. The United States emerged victorious from the First World War a vigorous young nation, keenly aware for the first time that it was a world power. Confident and energetic the nation and its people eagerly entered the decade that appropriately has been called the Roaring Twenties. Blending a curious mix of hedonism and puritanism, they were years of flappers, free love, religious Fundamentalists and Prohibitionists. Restless, aggressive and innovative, the decade produced a burst of artistic activity along with great technological advances. It was an era of explosive growth and change, it was strongly influenced by the automobile, airplane and radio.

Early radio humor in the giddy decade of the 1920s can best be characterized by lone performers reading funny literary pieces, delivering monologues or performing blackface minstrel routines that tended to be broad, none too subtle and, intentional or not, frequently insensitive and cruel. There were also late night "variety" programs broadcast by many stations for the pleasure of listeners who enjoyed hearing the music and wisecracks from such night spots in New York's Greenwich Village as *Village Grove Nut Club* to the merriment hosted by the Merry Old Chief on *The Nighthawk Frolic* from Kansas City, Missouri.

As the 1920s ended the gaiety faded. The laughter stopped with the Stock Market Crash of 1929 and the onset of the Great Depression. A depressed army of Americans were unemployed. Many once prosperous citizens were going hungry for the first time. National morale was low. It was at this time that radio began to play a major role to improve its listeners' spirits.

Franklin Delano Roosevelt was elected President in 1932 and immediately began to use radio to boost morale by broadcasting his reassuring message that, "The only thing we have to fear is fear itself." His effective Fireside Chats also provided rhetorical reassurance to a nation sorely in need of it. Radio also contributed to national morale with the nightly comedy programs it provided. As the Depression grew ever more grim, radio comedy seemed to get better. The harder the country's economic conditions became, it seemed, the funnier and more entertaining was the humor broadcast.

During the Great Depression, radio brought at least a little joy into homes where it was greatly needed. With the coming of World War II, the best of radio comedy served a somewhat different purpose. Entertaining servicemen far away from home and brightening the spirits of civilians on the home front took precedence. Once more radio made an important contribution to national morale with its bright good humor.

Who provided the radio comedy and humor that meant so much to Americans? Many of the comics and their writers never received the credit their work deserved. But some can be identified. First, there were the comedians who came from vaudeville to achieve success in radio. Among these were Fred Allen, Jack Benny, Burns and Allen, Eddie Cantor and Red Skelton. Then, too, there were the burlesque comics such as Joe Penner and Abbott and Costello. Finally, there were the comedians who gained their fame entirely from their radio work such as Henry Morgan, Jean Shepherd, Stan Freberg and Bob Elliott and Ray Goulding. In a class by himself was Edgar Bergen, a ventriloquist, whose Charlie McCarthy "dummy" became a "real" comic character. Another interesting group were the more visual comics, whose funny costumes, facial expressions or pantomime made them more effective on television than on radio. For one of them, Ed Wynn, who achieved some radio popularity, television came too late. Red Skelton, on the other hand, while funny on radio, was much more successful on television.

Radio comedians, such as Henry Morgan, Jean Shepherd and Stan Freberg, understood the medium best and achieved their success precisely because of this understanding. Not only that, but at their best they could also be considered great humorists like Mark Twain and Will Rogers. Radio listeners enjoyed the critical barbs and good-natured jesting of Rogers for years.

Later, in 1937 Henry Morgan's *Here's Morgan* program was a 15-minute broadcast, on which he played strange records and made acerbic comments about his sponsors, New York customs and life in general. In many respects, Morgan's monolog format was a forerunner of Jean Shepherd's rambling talks about city life and his nostalgic reminiscences of growing up in a happy Midwestern working family. Shepherd's many talents brought him a large cult following and financial rewards, but his achievements in the many fields in which he worked might have been larger if he could have remained focused on any one of them.

Fred Allen, on the other hand, produced almost all his work for radio. Although only a small part of it has been preserved, enough of his programs survive to demonstrate his comic mastery. Perhaps Johnny Carson expressed it best. When asked by Kenneth Tynan who was the wittiest man he ever knew. Carson named Fred Allen without hesitation. Citing the old vaudeville adage, "A comic is someone who says funny things, and a comedian is one who says things funny," Carson went on to explain his answer. Allen, he said, was a comic, while Jonathan Winters and Mel Brooks were comedians. Although he thought all were funny, Carson's distinction was an important one. Allen stands out as arguably the finest radio comic of them all.

Fred Allen was born John Florence Sullivan on May 31, 1894, in Cambridge, Massachusetts. After completing high school he entered show business as a juggler, performing as an amateur at every possible opportunity. Since it was the era of the "paid" amateur, his juggling immediately brought him financial rewards. He became Fred Allen at the age of 23, purely as the result of an agent's whim. The gift of a name was the only thing anyone ever gave him, for he reached the heights of success in radio entirely on his own. Like another juggler—W.C. Fields—who became a great comedian, Allen's transition from juggling to comedy was a slow, gradual one.

Although radio brought him fame and fortune, he never found it emotionally satisfying. Radio for Allen was big business and hard work, for which he never felt the great affection he had for vaudeville. The comic became *Fred Allen* in 1917, as the result of an agent's casual phone call. After getting a booking for him at the City Theater, Edgar Allen, a Fox booking agent in Boston, told the theater's manager the name of the juggler for his bill was *Fred Allen*, and that it remained for the rest of his life. The act of the new Fred Allen depended on his ability to make people laugh with the line of patter he added to augment his juggling skills. Extremely successful in the vaudeville of his day, Allen played New York's Palace Theatre in 1919. From there, he went on to appear in such long-running Broadway shows as *The Passing Show of 1922*, the *Greenwich Village Follies* in 1924, and, later, in such reviews as *The Little Show* and *Three's a Crowd*, the latter with Libby Holman and Clifton Webb.

While working in *The Passing Show*, Allen met an attractive chorus girl in the show named Portland Hoffa. Their marriage on May 4, 1927, began a happy lifetime partnership. During the radio years, her call of "Mis-ter A-l-l-en" and "Tally ho, Mr. Allen" became familiar trademarks. Catchwords and phrases were the marks of a successful radio series. The *Fred Allen Show* had several of them that mostly resulted when the Allen's Alley was added. "Tally ho," always said by Portland, was used in the early Allen programs as a means of closing one segment and providing a transition into another. It indicated to listeners that something was finished, and that it was then proper to go onto something else, usually a song or instrumental selection by the orchestra. At other times, the phrase served as a philosophical "so be it" to close the program.

Repetition of words and phrases for comic effect, of course, is an important element whether it appears in radio comedy or children's nursery rhymes. Allen, himself, took a rather dim view of the need for repeated catch phrases, although many of them naturally grew out of his shows and were continued successfully for years. For Allen, repetition seemed to be little more than a form of pandering to mass taste.

In many respects, when Portland played the "dumb female" role on the *Fred Allen* program, it was that of a smarter more astringent version of Gracie Allen playing off Fred's much more capable, worldly wise and worn version of George Burns. None of this implies that they copied or imitated the Burns and Allen routines, for this, of course, was far from the case. George and Gracie merely portrayed familiar show business types—as did Fred and Portland—that were later portrayed over and over in radio and television. The "dumb role" was later played on radio by Marie Wilson and in early television. Carol Wayne did the same for years on Johnny Carson's *Tonight Show* even in the Women's Lib era. All of them represented only a continuation of a familiar show business stereotype of the "dumb female role."

After completing a two-year run with Clifton Webb and Libby Holman in *Three's a Crowd*, Allen found himself out of work with only a promised role in a show not scheduled to open for six months. It was the spring of 1932, deep in the economic gloom of the Great Depression. The gold rush of vaudeville comedians into radio had begun. Comics such as Ed Wynn, Eddie Cantor and Joe Penner already were enjoying some success in the new medium, due chiefly to the funny costumes and rough-house physical antics they used to make studio audiences laugh. Although they achieved some success, they gave no real evidence of fully understanding radio and its unique possibilities as a medium for comedy.

Allen, facing weeks of inactivity, planned a series of radio programs, assembled a cast and, eventually, auditioned it for the Corn Products Company, who manufactured a beauty bath powder called Linit. His successful audition marked the beginning of the *Linit Bath Club Review*, whose first program was broadcast October 23, 1932, on the Columbia Broadcasting Company network.

The Linit program established a pattern that was continued until Allen's last network show in 1949. When asked by the sponsor who would write the show, Allen replied, "I will." He wrote everything for the *Linit Bath Club Review*, and, in fact, almost all the other material he used for the rest of his professional life in radio. Even in later years when there were other writers to help him with the formidable task of writing his weekly program and keeping it both topical and funny, ninety per cent of the writing was done by Allen.

Among the writers who wrote for Allen was Nat Hiken, later famous as the creator of television's *Sgt. Bilko*; Arnold Auerback, writer of such Broadway hit revues as *Bless You All*, *Inside USA* and *Call Me Mister* and Herman Wouk, probably best known for his novel, *The Caine Mutiny*. Wouk, recalling that Allen was the show's major writer, remembered that young writers like himself worked only to flesh out the great volume of material that was needed for the weekly programs. Perhaps it was the ever increasing pressure upon Allen of writing the weekly shows and the cumulative effects of hundreds of deadlines successfully met, that aggravated the hypertension that eventually killed him in 1956.

Even though the *Linit Bath Club Review* received critical praise and better than average audience survey ratings, it ended after only 26 weeks. The following year, while vacationing in Maine, Allen received an urgent call from New York. He learned that Hellmann's Mayonnaise had hired a comedian whose estimated potential far out-weighed his actual performance, and that the company wanted him to return to New York immediately to take over the radio program.

In 1933, *The Salad Bowl Review* starring Fred Allen was launched. In December, when the show's contract was completed, a new sponsor was eagerly waiting. Allen's next program, *The Sal Hepatica Review* (*The Hour of Smiles)*, sponsored by Bristol-Myers, was the show that brought him even more favorable critical notice and listener popularity. The *Sal Hepatica Review*, first broadcast in 1934, became *Town Hall Tonight* in 1938, when Bristol-Myers decided to use it to sell Ipana toothpaste as well as the laxative Sal Hepatica, and the *Texaco Star Theater* in 1941, when the Texas Company became its sponsor. Later, several other companies including Blue Bonnet Margarine, Tenderleaf Tea and the Ford Motor Company sponsored Allen. After *The Texaco Star Theater* ended, regardless of who sponsored it, the program became and continued to be known as *The Fred Allen Show*, until finally leaving the air June 26, 1949.

Fortunately, recordings of more than sixty hours of Allen's radio programs still exist. After listening to these programs that represent his 17 years of broadcasting, some conclusions are inescapable. There is a pattern running through all the shows. Their content, performances and general over-all quality testify to Allen's astute professionalism and rich comic genius.

The format for each hour program, other than the early ones, contain the newsreels, musical selections, the Portland Hoffa segment, the guest spot and dramatizations of the Mighty Allen Art Players. Some transformations occured along the way, as the newsreels, for instance, became, first, Allen's Alley and, later, Walking Down Main Street. Guests in the early years were "unknowns" with strange occupations, amateur performers or participants in a roundtable discussion drawn from the studio audience. Whenever a change in format was made, the result invariably was a general improvement in program pace and quality. Except as guest stars, few individual singers performed on the show. One notable exception was Kenny Baker, a talented tenor, who had first gained popularity on *The Jack Benny Show*. Baker's short stint on the program occurred during the early World War II years.

One program (March 8, 1942), in particular, illustrates the high quality of entertainment that radio brought into American homes during its great years. Kenny Baker on that program sang two selections. The first was "I'll Follow My Secret Heart" and the second, "It Ain't Necessarily So" from Gershwin's *Porgy and Bess*. After listening to programs of this era, one can readily understand how much a part of this cultural milieu George Gershwin and Fred Allen were. In the maturity of their professional achievements, they can be understood best in light of the spirit and energy we hear in those broadcasts of the 1930s and 1940s. There is a breezy, irreverence there, along with an open, friendly hale-fellow well-met quality in them. A free and lively spirit in spite of the Depression continually emerges. Much of this temperament of the times is displayed in these broadcasts for any listener still able to savor them.

Guests appeared regularly on Allen's early programs with such unusual or interesting occupations as an organ grinder, who naturally brought his monkey with him; an assistant to the Superintendent of the Statue of Liberty; a "stockyard Selznick," as Allen called him, a big man at the Paramount Studios, who was the talent scout responsible for casting all cows and horses in their pictures; and a man who ran a pushcart on the Warner Brothers' motion picture studio lot and knew all the hot dog and hamburger peccadillos of famous movie stars.

The radio audience in the 1930s and early 1940s idolized Major Edward Bowes and his amateur show, perhaps vicariously enjoying the frequent stories of overnight popularity, fame and success achieved by a few of the winning amateur performers. Consequently, many radio programs, incorporated amateurs in some way, hoping to win extra listeners and higher poll ratings by their addition. Allen's true feelings about amateur shows, caused in part, perhaps, by his own "amateur" experience, were not very favorable. Only the giveaway quiz shows annoyed him more. Allen cleverly parodied amateur shows when he played the role of Admiral Crow on one of his own programs.

Allen's burlesque of Major Bowes' program began with an announcer proclaiming, "Station HISKIMNOP presents Admiral Crow and his Amateur Hour." The wildly hilarious antics began when Allen, as Admiral Crow, stepped to the microphone.

> Admiral Crow: All right! All right! [Exactly in the style of Major Bowes]
> *PHONE RINGS*
>
> Admiral Crow: Oh, yes. Thank you. [*Phone is hung up*] Well — the first telephone bulletin is in. 400 votes for Trundle Pulp the Yodeling Taxidermist. Trundle hasn't even been on yet. The votes are coming in from California. There's a difference in time, you know. They say the program is coming over beautifully out there. And here's a message from the Governor of the Thousand Islands. They're making me an honorary beachcomber on Island 702. And thanks to Mr. and Mrs. Pomfret of New Orleans for the corn pone receipt.

As Admiral Crow continued to take call-in votes from around the country, a steady vote-getter was the Whistling Mousetrap Maker.

No doubt hounded by ad agency vice-presidents and network executives, the early *Fred Allen Show* even contained some amateur contests! One notable contest, whose contestants were winners of a series of amateur competitions in Boston, presented a lyric soprano, a boy-girl "sweetheart singing team," an Irish tenor, a tap-dancer, a trick violin player, a Boston hillbilly trio and a "sneeze expert," who managed to display all the different sneezes he knew.

Another feature of the *Fred Allen Show* in which "unknowns" participated was Mr. Average Man's Roundtable. The Roundtable feature logically led directly to the asking of questions to such zany products of Allen's imagination as Senator Bloat, poet Thorndyke Swinburne, a low-wattage, itinerant philosopher named Socrates Mulligan and the proverbial "average man," Mr. John Doe, played by Jack Smart, Harry Von Zell, Charlie Cantor and John Brown, respectively. A Jewish-sounding Bronx housewife, Mrs. Prawn — who sounded like, but was not played by Minerva Pious — also appeared occasionally. These burlesque characterizations of politician, poet, philosopher, average man and Bronx housewife, in time, eventually became the Allen's Alley feature.

Dramatizations by the Mighty Allen Art Players — the inspiration for the Mighty Carson Art Players on television's *Tonight Show*— remained a constant feature of the program and one of its most effective vehicles for satire. Murder mysteries were popular dramatic fare for the Players, who romped through many of them. Their early mysteries featured an Inspector Bungle, who did exactly that most of the time. A little later, Allen introduced the masterful Chinese detective One Long Pan, who often introduced himself by saying, "Ah, greeting and Shalom, kiddies. One Long Pan, oriental Dick Tracy on the job." When a murder victim had been shot, and even sometimes when he apparently had been killed by some other means, this wily sleuth searched dilligently for the "le-wah-law-wah" with which the victim had been dispatched.

When the program went from an hour to a thirty-minute format, the amateurs and the people with unusual occupations were replaced by "name" guests. Therefore, the Mighty Allen Art Players were sometimes joined by celebrities when they presented their epic dramas. Some of the presentations of the Players had such engaging titles as: "The Psychopathic Speculator or He Made a Killing But They Called it Murder," "Admiral Allen was Leading a Dog's Life, So They Left Him at the South Pole," "Santa Sits Down, or Jingle Bells Won't Ring Tonight," and "The Hardy Family in the Penitentiary, or Life With Father."

Among the memorable guests who joined the Mighty Allen Art Players were Bea Lillie, who romped through Allen's musical "Picadilly," sung to the music of Rodgers and Hammerstein's musical hit of the day, *Oklahoma*. Another was Tallulah Bankhead, who joined Fred in a classic spoof of husband-and-wife broadcasting teams entitled "Talu and Fred," a skit that deserves recognition as one of radio's best comedy routines.

In 1937, Ed and Pegeen Fitzgerald on New York's station WOR inaugurated the husband-and-wife talk show, a format that was soon copied by several other married couples such as Tex McCrary and Jinx Falkenburg (*Tex and Jinx*), Dorothy Kilgallen and Richard Kollmar (*Dorothy and Dick*), Andre Baruch and Bea Wain and, still later, Peter Lind Hayes and Mary Healy. At one time there was said to be 78 imitators of the Fitzgeralds' format on the air. At its worst, this type program degenerated into little more than a saccharin parade of commercials without much information or entertainment provided for listeners.

As early as 1945, when Tallulah Bankhead visited his program, Fred Allen directed his barbs against inferior husband-and-wife shows. Fred and Tallulah combined as "Talu and Fred" to deliver one of the most devastating radio satires ever perpetrated. Its format was a "regular" segment to illustrate what these programs normally were like, followed by a "grumpy" portion, in which one morning both spouses awoke testy and out of sorts.

At the opening and close of a program on which the James Masons appeared, there was a strange element that was part of Allen's struggle against the *Stop the Music* program and similar giveaway quiz shows of the time. The program opened and closed with a promise to reimburse any listener who missed a quiz show prize because he was listening to Fred Allen. A curiosity now, the device didn't stop the quiz program, but it remains a novel maneuver in the struggle against them. At the beginning of the program, this announcement was made:

> Ladies and Gentlemen, stay tuned to the *Fred Allen Show*. For the next 30 minutes you are guaranteed that if you — any listeners in the United States — are called on the telephone during the next thirty minutes by any giveaway radio program, and because you are listening to Fred Allen you miss an opportunity to win a refrigerator, a television set, a new car or any amount of cash prize, the National Surety Corporation guarantees that Fred Allen will perform his agreement to reimburse you for any amount of prize money you may have lost up to $5,000. Notice of any claim under this guarantee must be mailed to Mr. Fred Allen by registered mail, care of the National Broadcasting Company, Radio City, New York, and postmarked no later than midnight Monday, March 29, 1948. Relax! Enjoy the

Fred Allen Show. For the next thirty minutes you are protected under the terms of a guarantee bond covering all valid claims up to a total of $5,000.

This announcement with slight variation was made at the close of the program as well. No valid claim was ever collected under the guarantee and the competing quiz shows rolled on unchecked.

Many famous guests appeared on the *Fred Allen Show.* Some of them were Tony Martin, Boris Karloff, Edward Everett Horton, Charlie McCarthy, George Jessel and, of course, most often the aspiring violinist-comedian — Jack Benny.

Benny and Allen, actually the best of friends, participated in what perhaps was radio's greatest "feud." One of the popular radio gimmicks of the time was the "phony feud" between radio performers. Two of the other major "feuds" were those of Ben Bernie-Walter Winchell and Charlie McCarthy-W.C. Fields. What triggered the Allen-Benny feud was an accidental remark made by Allen on a 1937 program that soon grew to be a major topic of jokes for both comedians.

The famous Allen's Alley feature was an outgrowth of his encounters on the early programs with poet Thoryndyke Swinburne, coyly played by announcer Harry von Zell. On one program on which they were discussing the New York housing shortage, the poet read a poem about overcrowded housing conditions. Influenced by Edgar Guest, the popular homespun radio poet of the time, whose familiar line was, "It takes a heap of living to make a house a home," Thorndyke let fly by beginning, "It takes a heap of people to make a house a heap." Sad to say, his poetic vision sank even lower after that ambitiously promising beginning.

After Allen left the poet he often would run into John Doe the Average Man. John Brown, the great radio supporting actor whose most famous role probably was that of Digger O'Dell on the William Bendix radio show, *The Life of Riley*, played the role of John Doe the Average Man. Characteristically, Mr. Doe would angrily carry on a noisy discussion with Allen, only eventually to completely lose control and end by slamming his door shut in a rage, an interesting comment indeed on the "average man." Although both a Socrates Mulligan and John Doe were used as devices for commentary upon topical questions, neither of them survived to be part of Allen's Alley. Even closer to what eventually became Allen's Alley, however, was the introduction of a windbag politician, Senator Bloat; an obviously Jewish housewife, Mrs. Prawn; and the flaky poet, Thorndyke Swinburne. In the beginning, none of these roles were played by Kenny Delmar, Minerva Pious or Alan Reed, whose portrayals later made these prototypes famous as Senator Claghorn, Pansy Nussbaum and Fallstaff Openshaw.

O.O. McIntyre, writer of a daily newspaper column that sometimes contained the feature, "Thoughts While Strolling," was credited by Allen as the precise inspiration for Allen's Alley. Most of the elements for it, however, obviously came as the culmination of the comedian's own creative efforts. When in 1945, after three years of experimentation, the Alley's complete cast of Senator Claghorn, Titus Moody, Mrs. Nussbaum and Falstaff Openshaw was finally assembled, the listeners responded enthusiastically.

When he walked down Allen's Alley with Portland, Allen appeared as a thoughtful, inquiring reporter, a peripatetic commentator on American life. Sometimes, however, he was portrayed as an innocent, picked-on and occasional recipient of attacks by the Alley's residents, but most often a victim of the frequently scheming and manipulating guests who appeared on his show. Each program contained cogent comments on the news, weather, radio, show business and the American scene. With the inception of Allen's Alley, the tone of the comments changed somewhat, and the focus placed upon the Alley's characters themselves. Regardless of what Allen, himself, said, Allen's Alley may have had its beginnings, partially at least, in 1942, because of the pressures of wartime censorship to play down criticism of American life and the national scene. In the great Alley characters he developed, Allen focused directly on individuals, not stereotypes or representatives of any group or race. When Allen began his last season on the air with the January 4, 1949, program, he changed *in name only* the Allen's Alley feature to Walking Down Main Street in response, no doubt, to a demand made by some network executives who equated any change with progress. Nevertheless, the great characters remained unchanged and continued to perform in their own unique manner.

Senator Claghorn was a Southerner, first, and a politician second. His catch phrase was, "That's a joke, son," and it habitually followed a pun of magnificent, if sometimes horrendous proportions. Claghorn's feelings about the South are indicated by some of his more characteristic statements:

SENATOR CLAGHORN: I can't say "No."
ALLEN: Why not, Senator?
SENATOR CLAGHORN: Because "No" is the abbreviation for north.

—

SENATOR CLAGHORN: When I leave New York I always take the South Ferry.

—

SENATOR CLAGHORN: I don't even go to a ballgame unless a southpaw's pitching. I don't even go to see the Dodgers unless Dixie Walker is playing.

The Senator's loyalty to the South was unquestioning and constant, and he felt it necessary to ensure everyone knew exactly what part of the country he preferred. Continuously and loudly, he would offer such gems as, "Where I live, we call the people in Alabama — *Yankees.*" Claghorn's favorite drink, he said, was the Memphis Martini, a tall drink that featured a wad of cotton floating in it with two boll weevils riding on top. Then, too, there was his expression of supreme love for his home region,"I'm from the South. Nobody can make me wear a union suit."

Claghorn's typical puns, always used with his familiar catch phrases, of course, were those based on the names of members of Congress:

CLAGHORN : (Talking about President Truman's recommendation of a National Health Insurance Plan in 1948.) We had a big debate in Congress. Somebody was running down Senator Hill [Lister Hill, D., Alabama.] Running down Senator Hill, that's a joke, son.

—

CLAGHORN : I was glad to see Senator Aiken back. Senator Aiken [George D. Aiken, R., Vermont]. Senator Aiken back, see that's a joke, son.

Senator Claghorn's dislike for Yankees extended even to baseball, as his account of a game he attended at Yankee Stadium clearly shows:

CLAGHORN : I saw a ball game today. I saw the Yankees beaten. Wahoo!
ALLEN : How could the Yankees lose?
CLAGHORN : The umpire was from the South.
ALLEN : How do you know?
CLAGHORN : Well, after he called three balls, he called a weevil.
ALLEN : You must have had a great day.
CLAGHORN : I hooted those pigeon-plucking Yankees to a fare-thee-well. I gave Bill Dickey the bird. Dickey bird, get it? That's a joke, son.

The joke had considerable meaning on March 20, 1947, for the Yankees seldom lost in those days.

Titus Moody was usually the next character Allen encountered in the Alley. Moody, a crusty old rural New Englander, was played by veteran radio actor, Parker Fennelly. Moody's dry wit and wily skepticism allowed Allen to use his own New England background for this character. After greeting Allen with his customary, "Hello, Bub," Titus was always glad to provide his uniquely idiosyncratic view of the world.

Talented dialectician Peter Donald was also encountered in Allen's Alley playing Ajax Cassidy, who was frequently in an alcoholic haze. Ajax usually greeted Allen with a noisy, "Well — how do ye do?" Cassidy's tales of his countrymen seldom portrayed them in a good light. For example, Ajax once told of a Dumb David Dineen, who came from Ireland on a cattle boat and felt right at home there.

Minerva Pious, another veteran radio actor, who had performed on Allen's programs for many years in different roles, was a regular denizen of Allen's Alley as Pansy Nussbaum, a Bronx Jewish housewife. When Allen knocked on her apartment door, Pansy Nussbaum answered, "Nu," a Yiddish colloquial expression roughly translated as "All right" or "Now what?" When Allen greeted her with, "Well — Mrs. Nussbaum," she would answer with such responses as: You were expecting the Fink Spots? You were expecting Weinstein Churchill? You were expecting Cecil B. Schlemiel? You were expecting Emperor Shapiro-Hito?" Pansy Nussbaum was an active urban housewife, busy in her garden growing "rutabagels" and reading the poetry of Heinie Wadsworth Longfellow. She liked to remind Allen that in her earlier days she had been Miss Low Tide at Far Rockaway Beach. Pansy Nussbaum, skillfully played by Minera Pious, was one of Allen's funniest creations.

Usually the last resident of Allen's Alley that Allen encountered was Falstaff Openshaw, played by Allan Reed. Allen variously introduced Falstaff by calling him "The Shoddy Swinburne" or "The Vagabond Voltaire." Although poet Openshaw specialized in "mother poetry," such as "Those Ain't Spots on the Sugar, Mother, You're Putting Your Dice in My Tea," he also produced such epic poems as "Said the Horse Hair to the Violin String, May I Be Your Beau?" These Allen Alley characters and his Mighty Allen Art Players might be radio's most memorable comic routines, but they came at the final years of his great radio humor.

A major change in radio humor came late in the 1920s, when Freeman Gosden and Charles Correll revolutionized radio comedy with their introduction of comic characterization in a serial format with their *Sam 'n' Henry* and *Amos 'n' Andy* programs originating from Chicago. Much of the best warm, gentle radio humor came from the midwest and clearly showed its influence. Jean Shepherd was one of its late practitioners. Earlier, there had been Jim and Marian Jordan (*Fibber McGee and Molly*) and the brilliantly written contribution of Paul Rhymer (*Vic and Sade*). *Fibber McGee and Molly* are best remembered for a hall closet that noisily collapsed whenever it was opened. It was perhaps the program that produced more successful spin-offs than any other radio show with *Beulah* and *The Great Gildersleeve*. Paul Rhymer's inhabitants of the little house halfway up the next block, on the other hand, however, probably produced the best low-keyed radio humor ever broadcast. It was warmly human and humane.

Fred Allen, on the other hand, was a social critic who took a leisurely, day-at-a-time approach, somewhat in the Will Rogers manner, but he also showed many flashes of the dark, sardonic humor displayed by Mark Twain in his latter years. Had not Mark Twain once observed that Americans enjoyed three precious things: the freedom of speech, freedom of conscience and the prudence never to practice either. Much of Twain's dark humor is echoed in Allen's best work.

Although he never attained the pinnacle of public popularity enjoyed by Jack Benny, Fred Allen enjoyed the admiration of a diverse group of listeners that included intellectuals, artists, news stand dealers and factory workers. His humor — often sardonic and bristling with satire — was one that children and adolescents usually did not enjoy or understand. While youngsters enjoyed Jack Benny's antique wheezing Maxwell car, his adventures with Carmichael the ferocious polar bear that he kept as a pet in his basement, or his infrequent trips to his money vault. Allen's assaults against network and advertising executives meant relatively little to them.

Josh Billings, Mark Twain and Will Rogers were writers with whom Allen most often has been compared, Although such comparisons are valid, there are two others to whom he also bears some resemblance: William Cowper Brann and Ambrose Bierce. Brann the Iconoclast and Bitter Bierce also tossed literary thunderbolts at the hypocrisies and stupidities of their day. Satirists, who are almost inevitably moralists, although most would vehemently deny the accusation, are seldom popular among their fellows. In fact, such social critics may be considered fortunate if they are merely tolerated and not actually banished from the company of all decent men.

Fred Allen, in his own way, was banished from broadcasting when TV finally brought about the end of network radio. Broadcasting's banishment of Allen took the form of refusing to use the comedian's many gifts, because the newer medium of sight and sound made strict demands of conformity — a characteristic attitude of mind and expression that never was Fred's long suit. With the advent of television, rigid demands to conform and avoid experimentation became stronger and stronger. Unfortunately, television, except in rare instances as in the late *Omnibus* series and on the current *Masterpiece Theater* programs, have remained bound by the same confining and stuffy restraints.

In 1956, shortly after Allen's death, NBC rebroadcast *Conversation*, a program in which Fred talked with Clifton Fadiman and Gilbert Seldes about how, if they were given the opportunity, they would live their lives over. Allen continually made the point of how much material radio demanded. He said that although he was well rewarded financially, he had been forced to produce a tremendous amount of material during his 17 years on radio. While in vaudeville, he said, five routine monologues would have lasted a comedian a lifetime. A radio program's demands, on the other hand, were insatiable. "In 39 weeks on radio," he said, "we used more jokes than Weber and Fields used in a lifetime." Continuing he added, "At sixty or so you wind up in a rickety chair with the debris of your aspirations around you."

In response to the question posed by Fadiman, Allen said he would have chosen wealthy parents, so he could have obtained a better education. Furthermore, he confided he would have liked to have been a writer. When Fadiman objected that Allen *was* a writer. Fred responded, "I never could have been able to support myself in that way."

Most of Allen's writing had been to entertain and enlighten, but some of it was done also to apologize to sensitive souls who didn't always think he was funny. During his lifetime, he had written seven or eight hundred radio scripts and many explanatory letters to NBC vice-presidents. He had also written apologetic letters to the Mayor of Pottstown, Pennsylvania, for supposedly derogatory references to that thriving metropolis; the Philadelphia Hotel Association for making references to the small hotel rooms in that city ("The hotel rooms in Philadelphia are so small, the mice in them are humpbacked."); and to the estate of Earl Derr Biggers for killing off the venerable Chinese sleuth, Charlie Chan, in one of the Mighty Allen Art Players' dramatic presentations.

The major ills of radio and television, as Allen diagnosed them, were advertising agency executives, network vice-presidents and quiz shows. Oddly enough, all three are closely related to each other and to our society. Commenting on "The State of American Humor" on NBC's *Living 1949* program, Allen traced its developments from its beginnings in New England and on the frontier. American humor, he said, had its beginnings in a leisurely time and it clearly manifested that characteristic.

Any definition of humor was tricky, Allen insisted. Mark Twain had insisted that sorrow was a secret source of humor, while Josh Billings had said it was, "Wit with a rooster's tail feathers stuck in its cap." Agreeing with both humorists, Allen went on to note that humor makes a man feel good all over. Frequently it was the unexpected, the incongruous present in any situation that was responsible for the laughter. An important role of humor, according to Allen, was that it could be used as a safety valve against the world and its problems. Humor in America soon became attacking and provocative, striking out against pretensions in high and low places. From the time when Artemus Ward wise-cracked, "Most of the girls in Utah marry young, Brigham Young that is" to the gaiety of the minstrel show, the pace was slow and easy, as was the humor. "It was a leisurely age of humor uncorrupted by the Hooper ratings," said Allen.

Soon, however, conditions changed, as vaudeville became the chief vehicle for comedy and the quick one- or two-liners took over. The pace become increasingly frenetic. Snappy humor arrived, yet, there still were some humorists who operated in the old tradition. One was Will Rogers, who seemed to be a wise and witty commentator from another era. Perhaps it was his rapid climb to national popularity on radio in the midst of the Great Depression that enabled Rogers to retain the style, pace and values of an earlier age. When many people were unemployed and doing without, the old values looked particularly good and well worth considering again. Will Rogers supplied that need.

Nothing could be more American than the leisurely delivery and manner of Rogers who said, "Americans are getting just like Ford cars. They all have the same parts, the same upholstery and all make the same noises." When introduced to President Calvin Coolidge, Rogers with his folkiest irreverence and innocence, shook the President's hand and said, "I'm sorry. I didn't get the name." Will Rogers' encounters with the famous was a far cry from how Johnny Carson interviewed presidential candidates on the old *Tonight Show,* or how Bob Hope hobnobbed with the residents of the White House.

Individual sham, hypocrisy and advertising were not the only factors that destroyed radio comedy. Network executives straining for maximum profits also share the responsibility, but, essentially, it was the change in American society that did the most damage, Allen contended. "Radio humor," Allen said, "has lost all its spontaneity. It is the victim of the times — mechanized and urbanized — produced in such quantities, it's downright chaotic." Furthermore, he added, "Radio wit tends to be the product of tired gag-writers. The star comedians are rarely more than a mouthpiece for their writers. Too many comedians survive on the brains of others." He went on to point out there was too much pressure on the comedian to produce too much material, since he not only had to be funny each week, but every moment he was on the air as well.

As to the future of American humor, Allen said, it all depended on whether we slowed down. "If the pace of life slows down, there may then be some hope." On humor in general, he commented, "Laughter is an universal language of mankind. A little nonsense now and then is relished by the wisest men."

Fred Allen, first on *Town Hall Tonight*, later while making trips down Allen's Alley, and, finally, during the Walks Down Main Street, served as an early warning system to detect the nonsense prevalent in American society. Once during one of his last programs, Fred and Portland walked down Main Street as usual and asked the question of the day of Sentator Claghorn, Titus Moody, Mrs. Nussbaum, Ajax Cassidy and Falstaff Openshaw. After getting their amusing, but generally non-responsive answers, Fred, with a line, perhaps more self-revealing than even he realized, noted, "It's the same every week, Portland. All you get out of a walk down Main Street is the exercise." The closing sentence of Allen's autobiographical *Treadmill to Oblivion* serves both as prophecy and epitaph: "All that the comedian has to show for his years of work and aggravation is the echo of forgotten laughter."

One bright spot after Allen's departure from radio was the success he enjoyed as an author. His longtime desire to be a *real* writer must have been partially gratified, at least, by the critical acclaim given *Treadmill to Oblivion*, his personal account of his radio career. A detailed autobiography of his life up to the time he entered radio, *Much Ado About Me*, unfinished at his death, was published posthumously and also received lavish critical praise.

Fred Allen died March 17, 1956, St. Patrick's Day, while taking his evening walk on 57th Street in New York City, a fitting date and place for an Irishman who loved New York so much he spent much of his time satirizing it. Much of what Allen said was inescapably right. He was appreciated, but not nearly as much as he deserved.

When the *Fred Allen Show* left the air in 1949, an era of radio comedy ended and a great vaudevillian, perhaps radio's greatest comedian of them all, was silenced. Radio programming in the 1950s changed drastically. Recorded music and the DJ were mostly heard during the daytime and evening hours. Most daytime serials and comedy shows faded and eventually disappeared. By January 1956, the only comedy show still broadcast weekly was the *Charlie McCarthy Show* and that only on a sustaining basis.

Some radio comedians such as Jack Benny and Red Skelton made a successful transition to television. Fred Allen did not. Whether it was fatigue, deteriorating health or his disenchantment with the medium, his insightful wit and satirical skill never came through on television. Only two interesting comedy shows were heard on radio by the late 1950s—*Bob and Ray* and the *Stan Freberg Show*. Bob Elliott and Ray Goulding, as *Bob and Ray* had survived with their gentle satire from their modest beginnings on Boston's WHDH in 1946. Elliott and Goulding enjoyed a long, successful career. Freberg's case was different. After many popular recordings, Freberg was given an opportunity to star in his own 15-week *Stan Freberg Show* series in the summer of 1957. Freberg's show was the biggest budgeted CBS radio show in ten years. The gifted Freberg has claimed that since his show was the last network comedy show broadcast, it made him the last network radio comedian. Jean Shepherd survived on local radio (WOR, New York, NY). Few others survived even on local radio. *See* ***Amos 'n' Andy, Comediennes, The Baker Broadcast, Beulah, Bob and Ray, Fibber McGee and Molly, Fred Allen Show, Great Gildersleeve, Here's Morgan, Hour of Smiles, Jack Benny Show, Linit Bath Club Review, Red Skelton Show, Sal Hepatica Revue, Salad Bowl Review, Sam 'n' Henry, Stan Freberg Show, Town Hall Tonight, Vic and Sade, Texaco Star Theater*** *and* ***Shepherd, Jean.***

7112 ***(The) Comedy Caravan*** **(aka** ***The Camel Caravan*****).** Jimmy Durante and Garry Moore provided the fun on the comedy show sponsored by Camel cigarettes. Music was supplied by Georgia Gibbs and Jeri Sullivan singing with the Roy Bargy Orchestra. Howard Petrie was the announcer (30 min., 1944).

7113 ***(The) Comedy of Errors.*** Jack Bailey hosted the quiz on which contestants attempted to identify errors they spotted in various skits. Fort Pearson was the announcer. Eddie Dunsteder provided organ interludes (25 min., Saturday, 7:30–7:55 P.M., MBS, 1950).

7114 ***(The) Comedy Theater with Harold Lloyd.*** Movie comedian Lloyd starred on his comedy program (30 min., Sunday, 10:30–11:00 P.M., NBC-Red, 1945).

7115 **Comer, Carol.** COM-HE (WABJ, Adrian, MI, 1956).

7116 **Comer, Charlotte.** Singer Comer was known as the "Female Baritone" (WPCH, New York, NY, 1931).

7117 **Comer, Connie.** COM-HE (KBCH, Ocean Lake, OR, 1956).

7118 **Comer, Sybil.** Soprano (KYW, Chicago, IL, 1924).

7119 **Comfort, Mary.** COM-HE (KTRC, Santa Fe, NM, 1955).

7120 **Comfort, Roy.** Leader (*Roy Comfort Orchestra* and *Roy Comfort's Ensemble*, WIP, Philadelphia, PA, 1935).

7121 **Comfort's Orchestra.** New York jazz band (WGBS, New York, NY, 1925).

7122 ***Comic Strip of the Air.*** The comedy sketch was performed by Cecil and Sally, who were not otherwise identified (KUOA, Fayetteville, AR, 1933).

7123 ***(The) Comic Weekly Man.*** Hearst newspapers sponsored the transcribed quarter-hour program. An unidentified actor as the Comic Weekly Man read the Sunday comics to a small child ("little honey"). As the narrator, he described the action in the comic strip, but one or two actors delivered most of the comic strip character's lines. Comic strips including *Prince Valiant, Hopalong Cassidy, Donald Duck, Dagwood and Blondie* and *Roy Rogers* were read each week. The program opened and closed with a male voice singing, "I'm the Comic Weekly Man—the Jolly Comic Weekly Man" (Transcribed, Many Stations, 1940s and 1950s).

7124 **Comin, (Senorita) Julita.** Spanish prima donna (WGMS, 1928).

7125 **Comly, Sam.** Movie reviewer (*Sam Comly's Movie Chats*, WGBS, New York, NY, 1924).

7126 ***Commencement Program, University of Vermont.*** The historic broadcast took place June 16, 1922. It was unique in that a receiving set was installed on the steamer *Ticonderoga* during an alumni boat ride, in order that the passengers could hear the ceremonies that were taking place on the University of Vermont campus (WCAS, Burlington, VT, 1922).

7127 **Commer, Carol.** COM-HE (WABJ, Adrian, MI, 1955).

7128 **Commercials.** In 1923, WEAF (New York, NY) announced they would broadcast advertisements at the rate of $100 for ten minutes or $10 per minute. Their first ten-minute commercial was for the Queensborough Reality Corporation attempting to sell units of Long Island's Jefererson Heights Development. At the same time, the station offered a music program sponsored by the Browning King Clothing Company featuring Anna Byrne conducting the Browning King Orchestra. The only commercial announcement on the program was: "You are listening to an hour of dance music by the Browning King Orchestra through the courtesy of Browning King and Company of New York City." Not too many years later the pattern was established of a three-minute commercial every 15 minutes or six minutes an hour.

The sale of commercial time established a precedent that allowed stations to use the best possible entertainers on their broadcasts. In addition, it allowed broadcasters sufficient funds to increase their educational offerings and coverage of public affairs. Advertising made great strides, adding such sales gimmicks as clever slogans and, most entertaining of all, the singing commercial. A few examples of familiar commercial slogans used were:

> LS—MFT. Lucky Strikes means fine tobacco.
> Smoke Chesterfields. They satisfy.
> Use Ipana for the Smile of Beauty and Sal Hepatica [a laxative] for the Smile of Health.

One of the most famous singing commercials was the Pepsi-Cola jingle:

> Pepsi-Cola hits the spot,
> Twelve full ounces, that's a lot.
> Twice as much for a nickel, too.
> Pepsi-Cola is the drink for you.

This jingle, one of radio's earliest singing commercial, was first broadcast in 1939. Written by Austin Herbert Croon, it was sung by the Tune Twisters vocal trio, consisting of Gene Lanham, Andy Love and Bob Walker.

7129 **Commerford's Serenaders Orchestra.** Local radio band (WHN, New York, NY, 1923).

7130 ***Community Sing*** **(*aka The Gillette Community Sing*).** At times the community sing originated from two different locations:

Milton Berle and Wendell Hall conducted the New York portion while Billy Jones and Ernie Hare broadcast from Philadelphia. Announcer Paul Douglas frequently used a portable microphone to walk out into the audience and catch their singing. In reviewing the program, *Variety* shrewdly pointed out the old show business wisdom, "The ideal act is one in which the audience entertains itself." That was precisely the basis of this program (45 min., 9:00–9:45 P.M., Sunday, CBS, 1936).

7131 ***Community Synagogue of the Air.*** Each Friday at Sunday, Rabbi Mayer Winkler conducted services assisted by Cantor Paul Lambott and a Hebrew choir (KNX, Los Angeles, CA, 1931).

7132 ***Commuters.*** Emery Deutsch conducted the orchestra on the music show (15 min., Monday through Saturday, 9:00–9:15 A.M., CBS, 1940s).

7133 **Como, Hunter.** DJ (KDAL, Duluth, MN, 1948).

7134 **Como Roof Gardens Orchestra.** Club orchestra (KTHS, Hot Springs National Park, AK, 1926).

7135 **Compagno, Grace M. and Eleanore Compagno.** Piano duet team (*Siot Minstrel Program*, KPO, San Francisco, CA, 1926).

7136 ***Companion.*** ABC in cooperation with *Woman's Home Companion* magazine developed the unusual daytime serial. The program dramatized stories based on the cases of counselor Dr. David R. Mace, who wrote a column for the magazine. Each week a new case from Dr. Mace's files was dramatized. Lon Clark, Martha Greenhouse and Warren Parker were in the cast. Virginia Travers and Hetta Ripley were the writers and Drexel Hines the director (15 min., Monday through Friday, 11:15–11:30 A.M., 1954).

7137 **Co. C., 121st Engineers, National Guard Band.** Military dance orchestra (WCAP, Washington, DC, 1926).

7138 ***(The) Compinsky Trio.*** Instr. mus. prg. (WWVA, Wheeling, WV, 1935).

7139 ***(The) Complete Sayings of Jesus.*** The Agency for Practical Christianity sponsored the transcribed series of five-minute broadcasts (WNAX, Yankton, ND; KRNT, Des Moines, IA; WMT, Cedar Rapids, IA; KMJ, Fresno, CA; WWVA, Wheeling, WV; WBT, Charlotte, NC; and KFBK, Sacramento, CA, 1942).

7140 **Compton, Betty.** Singer (WJZ broadcast of *Vogues* from the Schubert Theater, WJZ, New York, NY, 1924).

7141 **Compton, George C.** Newscaster (WJPS, Evansville, IN, 1948).

7142 **Compton, Homer.** Tenor (KFAB, Lincoln, NE, 1928).

7143 **Compton, Ranulf C.** Newscaster (WELI, New Haven, CT, 1939).

7144 **Compton, Walter.** News analyst (WOL, Washington, DC, 1937–1941; MBS, 1942–1944).

7145 **Comstock, Evelyn.** Pianist (KFOB, Burlingame, CA, 1926).

7146 **Comstock, Uncle Frank.** Violinist Comstock was an "old-time" country music radio pioneer on radio (KFNF, Shenandoah, IA, 1925).

7147 ***Comy Time.*** Lucy Jane Kielman and Mary Jane Morrison played the uke and sang on this entertaining show (WIBW, Topeka, KS, 1930).

7148 **Comyn, Amy.** Contralto (WABC, New York, NY, 1929).

7149 **Conant, A.O.** Pianist (WGY, Schenectady, NY, 1923).

7150 **Conard, Grace.** Vocalist (*Grace Conard*, vcl. mus. prg., WFIL, Philadelphia, PA and WIP, Philadelphia, PA, 1936).

7151 **Conaway, Ray.** Newscaster (*Ten O'Clock News*, KXYS, Houston, TX, 1948).

7152 **Conboy [Coboy], Sarah.** Pianist (WGY, Schenectady, NY, 1923).

7153 ***Concert in Miniature.*** Musical selections were performed by soprano Gloria Marcus, tenor Jack Barkin and violinist Nathan Swartz, who also conducted the orchestra on the program (30 min., Sunday, 5:00–5:30 P.M., WFIL, Philadelphia, PA, 1941).

7154 ***Concert Jewels.*** Musical selections on *Concert Jewels* were performed by an orchestra conducted by Max Dolin and guest vocalists (30 min., Sunday, 10:00–10:30 P.M., NBC-Pacific Coast network, 1930).

7155 ***Concert Kings.*** Forty stations carried the series of 156 transcribed programs featuring the Hoosier Hot Shots, a novelty music group that consisted of Paul "Hezzie" Trietsch, Gabe Ward, Ken Trietsch and Gil Taylor. The Hoosier Hotshots got their start on the *National Barn Dance* in 1933 (15 min., Transcribed, Various Times and Stations, 1946).

7156 ***(The) Concert Orchestra.*** Josef Stopak conducted the orchestra on the music program (30 min., Sunday, 12:30–1:00 P.M., NBC-Blue, 1945).

7157 ***(The) Conclave of Nations.*** Ranking diplomats from four countries delivered talks about their home countries on the April, 1930, series. The diplomats were: Herr Friedrich Wilhelm von Prittautz Gaffron, German Ambassador; Mr. Katrsuji Debuchi, Japanese Ambassador; Senor Don Juan Enciso, Counselor of the Argentine Embassy; Senor Don Manuel C. Tellez, Mexican Ambassador; and Vicount d'Alte, Portugese Ambassador (30 min., Sunday, 3:30–4:00 P.M., CBS, 1930).

7158 **Condon, Eva.** Actress Condon appeared on the daytime serial *Mrs. Wiggs of the Cabbage Patch* (title role) and *David Harum.*

7159 **Condon, Glenn.** Newscaster (WGAR, Cleveland, OH, 1939; KTUL, Tulsa, OK, 1941, 1944–1945; *City Desk* and *Home Town News*, KARC, Tulsa, OK, 1947–1948).

7160 **Condon, Maurice.** Newscaster (WGAR, Cleveland, OH, 1941–1942).

7161 **Condon and Rogers.** The vocal team was known as the "Harmony Pair," (WGN, Chicago, IL, 1928).

7162 **Condra, (Dr.) G.E.** Dr. Condra, the manager of the Chicago, Burlington and Quincy Railroad, spoke on the topic of "Seeing by Radio the Territory Covered by the Burlington Route" (WOAW, Omaha, NE, 1925).

7163 **Coney, Lee.** Newscaster (WLCS, Baton Rouge, LA, 1948).

7164 ***Confession.*** A sustaining documentary-type program, *Confession* was produced and directed by Homer Canfield. Based on the files of various correctional agencies, the program was a summer replacement for *Dragnet.* The general theme that was emphasized over and over was that "Crime does not pay." Paul Frees played the leading role assisted by Sam Edwards, Virginia Gregg, Stacy Harris, Joyce McCluskey and Marvin Miller. The show began with a criminal's statement: "The confession you're about to hear is an actual recording. I made this confession of my own free will because it is true." The program then went on with the crime drama. (30 min., Sunday, 9:30–10:00 P.M., NBC, 1953).

7165 ***Confidential Close-Ups.*** Hunt Club Dog Meal sponsored the program of Hollywood gossip reported by George Fisher, who also interviewed guests ranging from Bob Hope to Sabu (15 min., Saturday, 5:45–6:00 P.M., 1950).

7166 ***Confidentially Yours.*** Jack Lait, editor of the New York *Daily Mirror*, hosted the sustaining show on which he introduced his favorite crime stories that were then dramatized. David Harmon was the writer. Peter Capell, Ethel Everett and Joe Julian were in the cast. Jack Miller's orchestra provided the music. Bob Warren was the announcer (30 min., Thursday, 9:30–10:00 P.M. NBC, 1950).

7167 **Confrey, Zez.** Leader (Zez Confrey Orchestra, WDAF, Kansas City, MO, 1926). Confrey was a pianist who composed the popular novelty tune, "Kitten on the Keys."

7168 **Congdon, Kenyon.** Baritone (WWJ, Detroit, MI, 1928; WABC, New York, NY, 1928–1929).

7169 **Conger, Bob.** DJ (WHBK, Detroit, MI, 1947).

7170 **Conger, Fred.** DJ (*Variety Matinee*, WREN, Topeka, KS, 1947).

7171 **Congress, Joe.** Newscaster (WBYN, Brooklyn, NY, 1941).

7172 **Conine, Bill.** Newscaster (WMBH, Joplin, MO, 1939). Sportscaster (KOME, Tulsa, OK, 1941).

7173 ***Conjur and Caroline.*** Caroline was a cook and Conjur a general handyman, who worked in a Southern hotel, on the sustaining program that combined music and a dramatic sketch. The program included brief dramatic interludes that soon led to the pair singing a song (15 min., Thursday, 9:45–10:00 P.M., MBS, 1936).

7174 **Conklin, Peggy.** Actress Conklin was featured on the *Big Sister* daytime serial.

7175 **Conlee, L.T.** Newscaster (*News to Now*, WHBQ, Memphis, TN, 1947).

7176 **Conley, Jerry.** Leader (Jerry Conley's Blackstone Dance Orchestra, WGN, Chicago, IL, 1925).

7177 **Conley, Patty.** Actress Conley was a member of the *Scattergood Baines* daytime serial cast.

7178 **Conley, William J.** Leader (William J. Conley's Washington Park Exposition Orchestra, WLTH, Brooklyn, NY, 1928). *Variety* called it a "fair Brooklyn orchestra."

7179 **Conlin, Dee.** COM-HE (KJOE, Shreveport, LA, 1957).

7180 **Conlon, Shiela.** Conlon was one of the intelligent "kids" on the *Quiz Kids* program (NBC, CBS, ABC, 1940–1955).

7181 **Conn, Irving.** Leader (*Irving Conn Orchestra*, instr. mus. prg., WOR, Newark, NJ, 1936).

7182 **Conn, Marvin "Marv."** Sportscaster (WMT, Cedar Rapids–Waterloo, IA, 1941; WOWO, Fort Wayne, IN and WGL, Fort Wayne, IN, 1942; WTCN, Minneapolis, MN, 1946; WCCO, Minneapolis, MN, 1949; KFGO, Fargo, ND, 1950).

7183 **Conne, Ruth.** Conne broadcast fashion and decoration information on WRNY's *Women's Hour* (WRNY, New York, NY, 1926).

7184 ***(The) Connee Boswell Show.*** Singer Boswell, who had earlier gained popularity as part of the Boswell Sisters singing team, was accompanied by George Wright on the 15-minute network show (15 min., NBC-Blue Network, 1944). She later spelled her name "Connie."

7185 **Connell, James.** Newscaster (WHDL, Olean, NY, 1941).

7186 **Connell, Kay.** COM-HE (KCOM, Sioux City, IA, 1951).

7187 **Connell, Pat.** DJ (*Let's Go Places*, KGVO, Missoula, MT, 1949–1952).

7188 **Connelly, Brooks.** Newscaster (WIND, Gary, IN, 1939).

7189 **Connelly, Jack.** DJ (*Java Jive*, KLMR, Lamar, CO, 1955).

7190 **Connelly, Jeanne.** COM-HE (WNEB, Worcester, MA, 1956–1957).

7191 **Connelly, John.** Newscaster (WCBS, Springfield, IL, 1938; WMBD, Peoria, IL, 1941–1942; WHAS, Louisville, KY, 1944).

7192 **Conner, Bill.** Sportscaster (*Standard Oil Sports News*, WEBC, Duluth, MN, 1947–1948).

7193 **Conner, Dorothy.** COM-HE (WGL, Fort Wayne, IN, 1955).

7194 **Conner, Eddie.** Banjo soloist on the popular *Nite Caps in Lake Erie* program (WJAX, 1924).

7195 **Conner, George.** Newscaster (*The Man Next Door*, KVAN, Vancouver, WA. 1948).

7196 **Conner, William.** Newcaster (WEAU, Eau Claire, WI, 1942).

7197 **Conners, Dorsey.** COM-HE (WNBQ, Chicago, IL, 1956–1957.

7198 **Connery, John.** Actor Connery appeared on the *Amanda of Honeymoon Hill* daytime serial program.

7199 **Connet, Paul.** Announcer (KOIN, Portland, OR, 1928).

7200 **Connett, Helen.** Soprano (*Helen Connett*, vcl. mus. prg., WMBD, Peoria, IL, 1935).

7201 ***Connie Moffatt.*** Peggy (Pegeen) Fitzgerald played "Connie Moffatt" on this talk and music show. Peggy and Ed Fitzgerald engaged in light banter, presenting the masculine and feminine points of view. Peggy sang occasionally accompanied by the Claude Sweetan Orchestra.

Peggy was a good salesperson on the show for the O'Connor Moffatt Department Store, the sponsor. She also worked as the store's Advertising Director (KFRC, San Francisco, CA, 1933). Ed and Peggy (Pegeen) eventually moved to New York and enjoyed a long, successful radio career. *See* **Husband and Wife Talk Teams.**

7202 **Connolly, Dud.** Announcer (WBRC, Birmingham, AL, 1927).

7203 **Connolly, James P.** Newscaster (WITH, Baltimore, MD, 1947–1948).

7204 **Connolly, Kathryn.** Soprano (WHN, New York, NY, 1924–1925; WEBJ, New York, NY and WFBH, New York, NY, 1925; WMSG, New York, NY, 1927).

7205 **Connolly, Vincent.** Newscaster (WOR, Newark, NJ, 1935; *Women Make the News*, WOR, Newark, NJ, 1937–1938).

7206 **Connor, Dave.** Newscaster (WITH, Baltimore, MD, 1942).

7207 **Connor, Hugh "Hughie."** Leader (*Hugh Connor Orchestra*, instr. mus. prg., WBZ-WBZA, Boston-Springfield, MA, 1932–1934).

7208 **Connor, Joe.** Newscaster (WKRZ, Oil City, PA, 1948). Sportscaster, WKRZ, 1948).

7209 **Connor, Louis.** Leader (Louis Connor and his LeClaire Hotel Orchestra, WOC, Davenport, IA, 1925).

7210 **Connor, Whitfield.** Actor Connor appeared on *The Romance of Helen Trent* and *When a Girl Marries* daytime serial programs.

7211 **Connors, Eddie.** Banjoist (*Eddie Connors*, instr. mus. prg., WOR, Newark, NJ, 1935).

7212 ***Conoco Adventurers.*** Conoco Oil Company sponsored the series devoted to dramatic episodes in the history of the West. Music was supplied by the Josef Koestner Orchestra (15 min., Thursday, 11:00–11:15 P.M., NBC, 1930–1931).

7213 ***Conoco Presents.*** Conoco Oil Company sponsored the variety show that featured singer Harry Richman, the Jack Denny Orchestra and newsman-announcer John B. Kennedy (15 min., Monday, Wednesday and Friday, NBC, 1934).

7214 **Conover, Hugh.** Newscaster (WJSV, Washington, DC, 1939–1941). Announcer (*Amanda of Honeymoon Hill*, *Big Sister* and *Right to Happiness.*)

7215 **Conover, Willis.** DJ (*Willis Conover Show*, WWDC, Washington, DC, 1948; *1260 Club*, WWDC, 1949; WEAM, Arlington, VA, 1954).

7216 ***Conqueror Record Time.*** Gene Autry was featured on the CW music program sponsored by Conqueror Record Company. After Autry joined the *National Barn Dance*, he was given his own show on WLS. He soon moved on to Hollywood to star in western movies (WLS, Chicago, IL, 1931).

7217 **Conrad, Bob.** Sportscaster (WWL, New Orleans, LA, 1944).

7218 **Conrad, Carolyn.** COM-HE (KCOY, Santa Marria, CA, 1955).

7219 **Conrad, Chris.** COM-HE (WAGC, Chattanooga, TN, 1951).

7220 **Conrad, Dorothy.** Leader (*Dorothy Conrad Orchestra*, instr. mus. prg., WGN, Chicago, IL, 1934).

7221 **Conrad, (Dr.) Frank.** Conrad, an assistant engineer of Westinghouse Electrical Company, East Pittsburgh, Pennsylvania, received his 8XK radio license to begin experimental work in the summer of 1916. Conrad's experimental broadcasts led to the origin and development of station KDKA (East Pittsburgh, PA). *See also* ***Appendix A — Chronology, 1906–1960.***

7222 **Conrad, Gladys.** Contralto (WABC, New York, NY, 1929).

7223 **Conrad, Heyde C.** Organist (WHAS, Louisville, KY, 1923).

7224 **Conrad, Joseph.** Singer of "character songs" (WCCO, Minneappolis–St. Paul, MN, 1924).

7225 **Conrad, Lew.** Leader (*Lew Conrad Orchestra*, instr. mus. prg., WEEI, Boston, MA, 1932).

7226 **Conrad, Margaret.** Violinist (WMBB, Chicago, IL, 1926).

7227 **Conrad, Michael.** Newscaster (WFIN, Findlay, OH, 1945).

7228 **Conrad, Paul.** Actor Conrad appeared on the *Amanda of Honeymoon Hill* and *Cimarron Tavern* programs.

7229 **Conrad, Richard.** Newscaster (WSAU, Wausau, WI, 1939).

7230 **Conrad, Russ.** DJ (KEX, Portland, OR, 1948–1960).

7231 **Conrad, Stan.** Newscaster (WCPO, Cincinnati, OH, 1937; WMFR, High Point, NC, 1941–1942; WGBG, Greensboro, NC, 1945). DJ (*Carolina Reveille*, WSJS, Winston-Salem, NC, 1950). Sportscaster (WMFR, 1942; WGBG, 1945).

7232 **Conrad, Steve.** Sportscaster (WAPO, Chattanooga, TN, 1953).

7233 **Conrad's Society Orchestra.** Boston dance band (WNAC, Boston, MA, 1925).

7234 **Conried, Hans.** Comedian-actor Conried appeared on such diverse programs as *Burns and Allen*, *Great Gildersleeve*, *Judy Canova Show*, *Life of Riley*, *Mel Blanc Show*, *My Friend Irma* and *One Man's Family.*

7235 **Conshaw, Jack.** Leader (Leighton Arcade Cafeteria Orchestra, KHJ, Los Angeles, CA, 1925).

7236 **Considine, Bob.** Sportscaster (WNEW, New York, NY, 1941–1942).

7237 **Constantineau, Joe.** Leader (Joe Constantineau and his Buckeye Serenaders, WHK, Cleveland, OH, 1927).

7238 **Constantino, Joe.** DJ (*Off the Record*, KDB, Santa Barbara, CA, 1948; KIST, Santa Barbara, CA, 1952).

7239 **Constable, Anita.** COM-HE (KFXD, Nampa, ID, 1958).

7240 ***Consumer Tips.*** NBC in cooperation with the General Federation of Women's Clubs produced the program of consumer information (NBC, 1933).

7241 **Conte, Helen.** Singer (WELI, New Haven, CT, 1937).

7242 ***Contemporary Composers Concert.*** Paul Whiteman hosted and conducted the orchestra on the program devoted to modern American composers and their compositions (30 min., 1944).

7243 **Content, Mona.** Pianist (KHJ, Los Angeles, CA, 1929).

7244 ***(The) Contented Hour*** *See* ***Carnation Contented Hour.***

7245 **Conti, Anthony.** Newscaster (WLEU, Erie, PA, 1945).

7246 **Conti, Eddy.** Leader (*Eddy Conti Orchestra,* instr. mus. prg., WLW, Cincinnati, OH, 1938).

7247 ***(The) Conti Gondoliers.*** The romantic atmosphere of Southern Italy was captured on the pleasant vocal music program. Tenor James Haupt played the role of Giacomo, a singing gondolier. Billy Artzt conducted the orchestra (15 min., Wednesday, 6:00–6:15 P.M., WJZ, 1931).

7248 **Contrares [Contrera], Manual.** Leader (*Manual Contrares Orchestra,* instr. mus. prg., NBC, 1936; KDKA, Pittsburgh, PA, 1939).

7249 **Conture, Edward J.** Newscaster (WDLP, Panama City, FL, 1942).

7250 ***Convention Hall Organ.*** The City of Asbury Park, NJ, sponsored the program featuring Howard Scott, organist at the Asbury Park Convention Hall, and baritone George Horne (30 min., Saturday, 8:30–9:00 P.M., WCAP, Asbury Park, NJ, 1938).

7251 **Converse, Nell.** Actress Converse appeared on the *Prairie Folks* program.

7252 ***Conversation.*** Clifton Fadiman hosted the interesting panel talk show. *Variety* called it *Can You Top This?* for intellectuals. The regular revolving guest panel included Bennett Cerf, Marc Connelly and Allan Green. Louis G. Cowan produced and Arnold Sagalyhn directed the transcribed talk show that provided equal amounts of fun and information (30 min., Sunday, 7:30–8:00 P.M., NBC, 1954).

7253 ***Conversation with the Stars.*** Edwin Schallert interviewed various Hollywood stars on this sustaining evening show (15 min., Sunday, 9:45–10:00 P.M., KHJ, Los Angeles, CA, 1937).

7254 **Conway, Cleve.** Newscaster (WMAQ-WENR, Chicago, IL, 1941).

7255 **Conway, Jimmy.** Newscaster (WISN, Milwaukee, WI, 1939).

7256 **Conway, Joseph.** Newscaster (WMIN, St. Paul–Minneapolis, MN) 1938).

7257 **Conway, Julie.** COM-HE (KIDD, Monterey, CA, 1960).

7258 **Conway, Pat.** Conductor (Pat Conway's Band, WPG, Atlantic City, NJ and WIP, Philadelphia, PA, 1926). Conway was a famous bandmaster during the 1920s. He recorded both for Victor and Okeh records.

7259 **Conway, Patricia and Margaret.** Violin and piano duets (WLW, Cincinnati, OH, 1925).

7260 **Conway, Stewart.** Newscaster (WBIR, Knoxville, TN, 1944).

7261 **Conway, Tom.** DJ (*Time for Dancing,* WHIS, Bluefield, WV, 1947–1950).

7262 **Conway, William.** Tenor (KPO, San Francisco, CA, 1925).

7263 **Conwell, Jennie.** Dramatic reader (KFWM, Oakland, CA, 1927).

7264 **Conzelman, Willa.** Director, KRE Players Ensemble (KRE, Berkeley, CA, 1925).

7265 **Coogan, Art.** Leader (Art Coogan and his Club Madrid Orchestra, WIP, Philadelphia, PA, 1925).

7266 **Coogan, Richard.** Actor Coogan appeared on the *Abie's Irish Rose* and *Young Dr. Malone* programs.

7267 **Cook, Alice Newhall.** Organist (WBZ, Boston-Springfield, MA, 1924).

7268 **Cook, Art.** Announcer (WHK, Cleveland, OH, 1925).

7269 **Cook, Aubrey Waller.** Mrs. Cook began a series of piano recitals in 1926 on KMBC (Kansas City, MO) that continued to be broadcast for the next 26 years.

7270 **Cook, Bill.** Newscaster (*UP World News Roundup,* KVKM, Monahans, TX, 1947).

7271 **Cook, Bobby.** DJ (*Mountain Jamboree,* WHTN, Huntington, WV, 1947).

7272 **Cook, Boe.** Sportscaster (KICA, Clovis, NM, 1953).

7273 **Cook, Carl.** DJ (*Bar None Roundup,* KTMS, Santa Barbara, CA, 1947).

7274 **Cook, Chack.** DJ (*Chack Cook Show,* WEBR, Buffalo, NY, 1948).

7275 **Cook, Charlie.** DJ (*Country Boy,* WHHT, Durham, NC, 1948).

7276 **Cook, Chuck.** Newscaster (KFJB, Marshalltown, IA, 1937). Sportscaster (KFJB, 1937).

7277 **Cook, Clark.** DJ (*Afternoon Agenda,* KTMS, Santa Barbara, CA, 1950).

7278 **Cook, Connie.** COM-HE (WOW, Omaha, NE, 1956–1957).

7279 **Cook, Dick.** Newscaster (KQV, Pittsburgh, PA, 1946; KSFO, San Francisco, CA, 1955–1956). Sportscaster (WMPS, Memphis, TN, 1953).

7280 **Cook, Doc.** Leader (Doc Cook's Orchestra, WLS, Chicago, IL, 1928).

7281 **Cook, Donald.** Actor Cook appeared on *Charlie and Jessie, Life Begins* and *Mother of Mine* daytime serial programs.

7282 **Cook [Cooke], Edmund.** Violinist (WBAL, Baltimore, MD, 1928). Leader (Edmund Cook's Elite String Quartet, WBAL, 1928).

7283 **Cook, Edna.** Blues singer (KFI, Los Angeles, CA, 1927).

7284 **Cook, Edwin.** Baritone (KJR, Seattle, WA, 1928).

7285 **Cook, Elmer.** Leader (Elmer Cook's New Monterey Society Orchestra, WOR, Newark, NJ, 1926).

7286 **Cook, Erlene.** COM-HE (KENM, Portales, NM, 1958).

7287 **Cook, Eve.** COM-HE (WSBA, York, PA, 1955).

7288 **Cook, Frank.** Singer of old-time songs (WCAU, Philadelphia, PA, 1926).

7289 **Cook, Frank.** DJ (*Frank the Musical Cook,* KXRN, Renton, WA, 1949).

7290 **Cook, Freddie.** Leader (Freddie Cook Orchestra, WHO, Des Moines, IA, 1927).

7291 **Cook, H.M.** Guitarist Cook was a member of a country string band that appeared on the *WSM Barn Dance* program (WSM, Nashville, TN, 1927).

7292 **Cook, Harold.** Newscaster (WTRC, Elkhart, IN, 1940).

7293 **Cook, Herb.** Announcer (WKY, Oklahoma City, OK, 1927).

7294 **Cook, Hope Jackson.** Sopranlo (WCSH, Portlant, ME, 1933–1934).

7295 **Cook, (Mrs.) I. Milton.** Violinist (WSM, Nashville, TN, 1928).

7296 **Cook, Ira.** Newscaster (KMTR, Los Angeles, CA, 1939; KFI, Los Angeles, CA, 1944; *The Record,* KMPC, Los Angeles, CA, 1944). DJ (*Lucky Lager Dance Time,* KFAC, Los Angeles, CA, 1947; ABC, 1948; *Sunday Record Session,* KMPC, 1950; *Dance Time,* KFAC, 1950; KMPC, 1954–1955).

7297 **Cook, Irene.** COM-HE (KGER, Long Beach, CA,1955).

7298 **Cook, Jack.** Veteran vaudevillian Cook appeared on the initial broadcast of WDY (New Rochelle, NY, December 14, 1921).

7299 **Cook, Jim.** DJ (WHBU, Anderson, IN, 1956).

7300 **Cook, Joe.** DJ (*Open House,* KDAL, Duluth, MN, 1947).

7301 **Cook, Joyce.** COM-HE (KFDM, Beaumont, TX, 1957).

7302 **Cook, Laetitia.** COM-HE (KXGI, Fort Madison, WI, 1951).

7303 **Cook, Lucille.** Pianist (KSD, St. Louis, MO, 1923).

7304 **Cook, Lynn.** Newscaster (WKBH, La Crosse, WI, 1942). Sportscaster (WKBH, 1942).

7305 **Cook, Mal.** DJ (*Ebony Bandstand,* WAUG, Augusta, GA, 1954–1955).

7306 **Cook, Marion.** COM-HE (WFDF, Flint, MI, 1960).

7307 **Cook, Mary Lou.** COM-HE (WCOH, Newman, GA, 1956).

7308 **Cook, Mildred.** Soprano Cook appeared on *The Lamplit Hour* (WGAR, Cleveland, OH, 1932).

7309 **Cook, Milton.** Newscaster (KARM, Fresno, CA, 1940; KCOK, Tulare, CA, 1946).

7310 **Cook, O.A.** Announcer and station manager (KGHI, Little Rock, AR, 1928).

7311 **Cook, Ollie D.** Newscaster (KFYO, Lubbock, TX, 1937–1939; KWFT, Wichita Falls, TX, 1945).

7312 **Cook, Patti.** COM-HE (KPOJ, Portland, OR, 1956).

7313 **Cook, Phil.** Dialect comedian (NBC, 1929). Cook appeared on many programs during the first two decades of American radio. He was known variously, depending on the program on which he was appearing, as "The Quaker Crackles Man" or the "Aunt Jemima Man." An example of a Cook joke can be seen with this exchange with Graham McNamee:

> GRAHAM: You look unusually prosperous tonight.
>
> COOK: I am prosperous, Graham. I'm like a raisin inside a cake.
>
> GRAHAM: A raisin inside a cake? I get it. You're in the dough.

7314 **Cook, R.R.** Leader (R.R. Cook and his Melody Bunch Orchestra, WLBN, Little Rock, AR, 1928).

7315 **Cook, Richard.** DJ (*Cookie's Capers,* WMDN, Midland, MI, 1949).

7316 **Cook, Robbye.** Fourteen-year-old female singer (WCOA, Pensacola, FL, 1927).

7317 **Cook, Sid.** Sportscaster (*Aroostook Sportscast*, WAGM, Presque Isle, ME and WABM, Houlton, ME, 1950).

7318 **Cook, T.G. "Van."** Conducted "exercises over the air" (KTCL, Seattle, WA, 1925).

7319 **Cook, Vella.** Contralto (WMBB, Chicago, IL, 1926; *Vella Cook*, vcl. mus. prg., WCFL, Chicago, IL, 1937).

7320 **Cook, Vern.** DJ (*Martha and Vern*, WGY, Schenectady, NY, 1948; *Timekeeper & 980 Melody Lane*, WTRY, Troy, NY, 1949; *Vern Cook Show*, WGY, 1950; *980 Melody Lane*, WTRY, 1952; *Time Keeper*, WTRY, 1954; *Melody Lane*, WOKO, Albany, NY, 1955).

7321 **Cook, Warren.** DJ (*Blob's Bandstand*, KWIV, Douglas, WY, 1960).

7322 **Cook, William.** Violinist (KDKA, Pittsburgh, PA, 1924).

7323 **Cooke, Alistair.** Distinguished British writer-commentator Cooke became an American citizen and enriched both American radio and television programming (15 min., Wednesday, 10:45–11:00 P.M., NBC-Red, 1938). Cooke commented upon stage and film productions and American life and culture in general.

7324 **Cooke, Eric Russell.** Baritone (WHT, Chicago, IL, 1928).

7325 **Cooke, Joyce.** COM-HE (KFDM, Beaumont, TX, 1957).

7326 **Cooke, Kay B.** COM-HE (WKBW, Buffalo, NY, 1956).

7327 **Cooke, Mary.** COM-HE (KYA, San Francisco, CA, 1929).

7328 **Cooke, Patti.** COM-HE (KPOJ, Portland, OR, 1955).

7329 **Cooke, Polly [Betty].** COM-HE Cooke broadcast on women's topics while billed as the "Better Homes girl" (KEX, Portland, OR, 1928).

7330 **Cooke, Russell.** DJ (WWNR, Beckley, WV, 1956).

7331 **Cooke, Sally.** COM-HE (*Sally Cooke—The Better Homes Girl*, KYA, San Francisco, CA, 1929).

7332 ***Cooking Hints.*** Home economist Frances Lee Barton broadcast cooking tips and recipes for women on her program (NBC, 1934).

7333 ***(The) Cooking School.*** Mrs. Ada H. Swann conducted the cooking show (WAAM, Newark, NJ, 1925).

7334 **Cooks, Naomi.** Cooks was one of the intelligent "kids" on the *Quiz Kids* program (NBC, CBS, ABC, 1940–1953).

7335 **Cook's Dreamland Orchestra.** Chicago club band (KYW, Chicago, 1923).

7336 ***Cook's Travelogue.*** Malcolm LaPrade delivered a descriptive monologue about the joys of travel. Ralph Freese was the announcer. The program was sponsored by Thomas Cook & Sons Travel Company (30 min., Sunday, 7:00–7:30 P.M., NBC-Blue, 1926–1930). The program was switched to CBS in 1931 and later to ABC in 1939, the year it went off the air.

7337 **Cool, Peggy.** Soprano (KFUU, Oakland, CA, 1925).

7338 **Coolbrith, Ina.** Poet Coolbrith read her original poetry (KPO, San Francisco, CA, 1925).

7339 **Cooledge, James.** Violinist (KDKA, Pittsburgh, PA, 1924).

7340 **Cooley, Anita.** Soprano (KFRC, San Francisco, CA, 1925).

7341 **Cooley, Irene.** Pianist (WGY, Schenectady, NY, 1924).

7342 **Cooley, Frank.** Newscaster (KIRO, Seattle, WA, 1941). DJ (*Frank Cooley Show*, KWJJ, Portland, OR, 1949).

7343 **Cooley, Irene.** Pianist (WGY, Schenectady, NY, 1923).

7344 **Cooley, John.** Sportscaster (*A Cool Look at Sports*, WGAY, Silver Spring, MD, 1955). DJ (WGAY, 1957).

7345 **Cooley, John B.** Newscaster (KLMP, Minot, ND, 1938–1942, 1945).

7346 **Cooley, Spade.** Leader (*Spade Cooley and his Orchestra*, transcribed and network shows, middle 1940s). Cooley was instrumental in popularizing western swing.

7347 ***Coolidge String Quartet.*** Instr. mus. program (CBS, 1937). The string quartet played the chamber works of Johannes Brahms on a series of programs (60 min., Tuesday, 2:00–3:00 P.M., CBS, 1938).

7348 **Coombs, Aileen.** Mezzo-soprano (KPO, San Francsico, CA, 1923).

7349 **Coombs, Jim.** Basso featured on the *Roxy and his Gang* program (WJZ-NBC-Red, New York, NY, 1927).

7350 **Coon [Coons], Del.** Leader (*Del Coon Orchestra*, instr. mus. prg., CBS, 1935).

7351 **Coon, Dorothy.** COM-HE (WTOL, Toledo, OH, 1951).

7352 **Coon Creek Girls.** CW string band (WLW, Cincinnati, OH, 1937). Lily May Ledford formed this popular CW group, the first all-female string band. Its original members included leader Lily May Ledford; Rose Ledford; Esther "Violet" Koehler; and Evelyn "Daisy" Lange. A member added later was Minnie Ledford ("Black Eyed Susan"). The band was first broadcast on the *WLS Barn Dance* (WLS, Chicago, IL, 2936) and featured on the *National Barn Dance.* They became long time regulars on the *Renfro Valley Barn Dance.* *See* **Ledford, Lily May.**

7353 **Coons, Ray.** Leader (Ray Coons' Orchestra broadcast from the Kansas City Athletic Club, WDAF, Kansas City, MO, 1927).

7354 **Coon-Sanders Nighthawks Orchestra.** The Nighthawks, one of the best "hot" dance bands of the 1920s, was a famous pioneer radio band (WOAF, Kansas City, MO, 1922–1923; WGN, Chicago, IL, 1923–1924; KYW, Chicago, IL, 1925–26; WBBM, Chicago, IL, 1927–1928). Carlton Coon ("Coonie") was born Feb. 5, 1894 in Rochester, Minnesota. Before serving in the Army during World War I, he led bands in and around Kansas City. His friend and co-director of the band, Joe Sanders ("The Old Left Hander") was a promising amateur baseball pitcher. During World War I, Sergeant Sanders formed a band called the Camp Bowie Jazz Hounds. After the war he became friends with Coon, and together they formed the Coon-Sanders Novelty Orchestra that included Clyde Hendrick, t.; Carl Nordberg, tb; Harold Thiell and Hal McLain, sax-clr.; Bob Norfleet, bj.; Joe Sanders, p.-vcl. and Carlton Coon, d.-vcl.

The band began broadcasting on December 5, 1922, from the Plantation Grill in Kansas City's Hotel Muehlehach. The band was heard over the entire North American continent and became the first one to broadcast nightly. They became the "Nighthawks" because their broadcast started at midnight. The Kansas City *Star* on December 4, 1923 wrote: "With more than 1,500 telegrams of congratulation from every state in the Union and Mexico, the WOAF Nighthawks celebrated their first birthday last night, signing off at two o'clock in the morning."

The band began broadcasting on WGN from Chicago's Blackhawk Restaurant in 1923. Their theme was "Nighthawk Blues" composed by Joe Sanders. In 1925, under the aegis of MCA, their booking agency, the band began to tour. They played in 86 cities in four months during the summer of 1927. By the end of 1927, the band was broadcasting several nights each week from the Blackhawk Restaurant. When Florsheim shoes began to sponsor the orchestra's broadcasts, their sponsorship raised the weekly salary per musician from $150 to $200. Musicians in the band at this time included: Carlton Coon, ldr. and vcls.; Joe Sanders, p. and vcls.; Joe Richolson and Bob Pope, t.; Rex Downing, tb; Harold Thiell and John Thiell, clr. and as.; Floyd Estep, clr. and ts.; Elmer Krebs, tba.; and Bill Haid, bj. The band performed on the *Maytag Frolic Radio Program*, using the theme "Nighthawk Blues," in 1929. A later program also attracted many listeners (*Coon-Sanders Orchestra*, instr.mus. prg., WEAF, New York, NY, 1931). After the death of Carleton Coon, Joe Sanders led the band for the next two decades.

7355 **Cooney, Carroll.** Leader (Carroll Cooney Orchestra, WJZ 1928).

7356 **Cooney, Ed.** Newscaster (KGHI, Billings, MT, 1937).

7357 **Cooney, (Mrs.) Harry.** Cooney was a soprano member of the Just a Song at Twilight Quartet (KFH, Wichita, KS, 1929).

7358 **Coontz, Eddie.** Sportscaster (KVOO, Tulsa, OK, 1938). DJ (*Morning Watch*, KTUL, Tulsa, OK, 1947 and *Eddie's Corner Store*, KOMA, Oklahoma City, OK, 1947; *Morning Watch*, KTUL, 1949; *Eddie's Country Store*, KOMA, 1950; KTUL, 1955–1956, KOMA, 1957).

7359 **Cooper, Al.** Sportscaster (*Sports Digest*, WPAM, Pottsville, PA, 1955).

7360 **Cooper, Alex.** DJ (KLAC, Los Angeles, CA, 1955).

7361 **Cooper, Alice Nason.** Soprano (WOR, Newark, NJ, 1928).

7362 **Cooper, Ann.** COM-HE (WBCA, Bay Minette, AL, 1958–1960).

7363 **Cooper, Ben.** Actor Cooper appeared on the *Mark Trail* and *Second Mrs. Burton* programs.

7364 Cooper, Christine. Soprano (WOV, New York, NY, 1932).

7365 Cooper, Clyde. Leader (Clyde Cooper's Roof Garden Orchestra, KFWI, San Francisco, CA, 1927).

7366 Cooper, Delores. COM-HE (KPAT, Pampa, TX, 1956).

7367 Cooper, Drayton. DJ (*Old Potentate*, WLBG, Laurens, SC, 1949).

7368 Cooper, Ed. Newscaster (WMBD, Peoria, IL, 1942).

7369 Cooper, Hedley. Violinist (WFAA, Dallas, TX, 1922).

7370 Cooper, Hoyt. Announcer (KFAU, Boise, ID, 1926).

7371 Cooper, J. Van Cleft. Pianist Cooper appeared on the *Musical Travelog* program (WRNY, New York, NY, 1925).

7372 Cooper, Jack Leroy. Black DJ (*All Negro Hour*, WSBC, Chicago, IL, 1929; *Rug Cutters Special* and *Search for Missing Persons*, Chicago radio, 1940s-1960s; *Jivin' with Jack Cooper*, WAAF, Chicago, IL, 1947; *Rug Cutters Special*, WSBC, Chicago, IL, 1948). Although he despised the term DJ, Cooper and fellow DJ, Al Benson, were chiefly responsible for Chicago's reputation as the "Capital of Black Radio" (*See* **Benson, Al**). Cooper was also an announcer, program host, newscaster and broadcast executive, but above all he was an innovative pioneer broadcaster.

Cooper was the first Black DJ with a commercially sponsored program. He began his radio career in Washington, DC, in the 1920s on station WCAP, where he appeared as a straight man on a comedy show. In 1929, he moved on to Chicago and bought time on WSBC, an ethnic radio station, where he broadcast variety shows featuring Black talent. One of Cooper's best remembered shows was his *All Negro Hour* broadcast regularly in 1929. Cooper first went on the air in Chicago on November 23, 1929 with his 15-minute *All Negro Hour* that was eventually expanded to 30 minutes before finally being broadcast for a full hour in 1935. *Broadcasting* magazine (November 15, 1935, p. 39) said that Cooper was thought to be the only Negro announcer on commercial radio in the United States in 1935. Four years later, Cooper was broadcasting 5½ hours of black-oriented programming.

His DJ career apparently began in 1931, when a union pianist was not allowed to play on one of Cooper's non-union programs. At that point, he began playing records and discussing the music. His *Rug Cutters Special* made him one of radio's first DJs, a reputation that did not please him. Although he did not want to be known as a DJ, he began to play rhythm and blues recordings in 1947. Another of his contributions to Chicago radio was his promotion of religious broadcasting and gospel music. On one of his religious programs he introduced the great gospel singer, Mahalia Jackson.

He bought time from six stations and sold numerous advertising spots on all his shows. Cooper was not only a creative broadcaster, but also a highly successful businessman. His many contributions include his broadcasts of Negro League baseball games and those describing missing persons that helped locate more than 20,000 persons in 12 years. He is usually credited as both pioneering in the DJ format and providing news and sports coverage that was targeted specially for Black radio audiences.

7373 Cooper, James G. Newscaster (KVOL, Lafayette, LA, 1939, 1945).

7374 Cooper, Jane. Gardening expert (*Your Garden with Jane Cooper*, KARK, Little Rock, AR, 1940).

7375 Cooper, (Mrs.) Jean Lyman. Mezzo-soprano (WHAZ, Troy, NY, 1925).

7376 Cooper, Jerry. Baritone (*Jerry Cooper*, vcl. mus. prg., CBS, 1933–1934).

7377 Cooper, Jim. Newscaster (WBNS, Columbus, OH, 1938–1942, 1944–1946).

7378 Cooper, John M. Newscaster (KDKA, Pittsburgh, PA, 1940–1941; WBAL, Baltimore, MD, 1946).

7379 Cooper, Juanita. COM-HE (WRPB, Warner Robins, GA, 1958).

7380 Cooper, Madge. COM-HE (WMRN, Marion, OH, 1956–1957).

7381 Cooper, Mildred. COM-HE (KCRT, Trinidad, CO, 1958).

7382 Cooper, (Miss) Peggy. Miss Cooper told bedtime stories for children as "The Story Lady" (WFAA, Dallas, TX, 1925–1928). She also worked with "Uncle Billy" on a weekly *Book-of-Knowledge* feature. *See* **"Uncle Billy."**

7383 Cooper, Ralph. DJ (WMCA, New York, NY, 1948; WNRC, New Rochelle, NY, 1956).

7384 Cooper, Robert. Cooper was a part-time announcer and host of the *Fifty-Third National Bank Report* and the *Weather Forecasts* features (WLW, Cincinnati, OH, 1922–1923).

7385 Cooper, Robert. Bass (WGBS, New York, NY, 1925).

7386 Cooper, Tom. Leader (Tom Cooper's Country Club Orchestra, *Music While You Dine,* Wednesday, 6:15–7:30 P.M., WOR, Newark, NJ, 1924).

7387 Cooper, Violet Kemple. Legitimate actress Cooper appeared in William Brinsley Sheridan's *School for Scandal* (WEAF, New York, NY, 1926).

7388 Cooper, (Mrs.) W.J. Soprano (KDKA, Pittsburgh, PA, 1923).

7389 Cooper, Wayne. Performer who played the bells (KLDS, Independence, MO, 1925).

7390 Cooper, Wilma Lee and Stoney Cooper. CW husband and wife team, considered to be one of the best, Wilma and Stoney Cooper in the 1940s worked on WWVA (Wheeling, WV), KMMJ (Grand Island, NE), WIBC (Indianapolis, IN), WMMN (Fairmont, WV), KLCN (Blytheville, AR) and WWNC (Asheville, NC). Their long, successful career consisted of some 20 years on the *Grand Ole Opry.*

7391 Coote, Leonard F. Announcer (WOR, Newark, NJ, 1925).

7392 Coots, Fred and Benny Davis. Coots and Davis were a singing team of popular songwriters, who also sang many of their own songs (CBS, New York, NY, 1929).

7393 Cope, Dan. Producer-director Cope worked on the *Lincoln Highway* (director), *Portia Faces Life* (producer), *Mary Marlin* (director) and *Woman of America* (producer) programs.

7394 Cope, Donald. Violinist (KSL, Salt Lake City, UT, 1929).

7395 Cope, Frank. Cope conducted one of the earliest early morning programs of music, weather and news (*The Alarm Klok Klub,* KJBS, San Francisco, CA, 1929). The program was still being conducted on the West Coast by Cope in 1952).

7396 Cope, Happy Bill. Cope was a British born banjo, guitar and accordion soloist (WSM, Nashville, TN, 1929).

7397 Cope, Joe. DJ (KREX, Grand Junction, CO, 1956).

7398 Cope, (Mrs.) Joe. Soprano (KLDS, Independence, MO, 1926).

7399 Cope, Kitty. COM-HE (WSAV, Savannah, GA, 1957).

7400 Cope, Susan B. COM-HE (WMRB, Greenville, SC, 1957).

7401 Copenhaver, Carley. COM-HE (KWIL, Albany, OR, 1951).

7402 Copenhaver, Marie. Pianist (KFQW, Seattle, WA, 1928).

7403 Copeland, Jack. Newscaster (KOY, Phoenix, AZ, 1938–1939; KSUN, Lowell, AZ, 1939; KGLU, Safford, AZ, 1940; WWWB, Jasper, AL, 1946). DJ (*Flip the Platter*, WWWB, 1947). Sportscaster (KGLU, 1940).

7404 Copeland, Maurice. Actor Copeland appeared on *Captain Midnight, Ma Perkins, Silver Eagle, Mountie* and *Woman in White.*

7405 Copeland, S. Royal. Dr. Copeland broadcast health talks four days per week (NBC-Blue, New York, NY, 1927–1930).

7406 *Copeland Ceresota Flour Program.* Dr. S. Royal Copeland delivered a series of health talks on his program (15 min., Thursday, 10:00–10:15 A.M., CBS, 1932). *See* **Copeland, S. Royal.**

7407 Coplantz, Lillian. Pianist (KGO, San Francisco, CA, 1926).

7408 Copley Plaza Orchestra. Musical group directed by Edward Boyle (WBZ, Springfield, MA, 1926).

7409 Copley Plaza Trio. Instr. mus. group (WNAC, Boston, MA, 1925).

7410 Copp, Charles A. Newscaster (WDLB, Marshfield, WI, 1947).

7411 Coppens, Nancy. COM-HE (WMAM, Marinette, WI, 1955).

7412 Coppin, Grace. Actress Coppin appeared on the *Katie's Daughter* daytime serial.

7413 Coppola, Carmine. Flutist (WGBS, New York, NY, 1926).

7414 Cops, C. W. Announcer (WHBB, Stevens Point, WI, 1925).

7415 *Coral Islanders Orchestra.* Instr. mus. prg. (WNAX, Yankton, SD, 1939).

7416 Corbein, M. "Famous Belgian organist" (KSD, St. Louis, MO, 1924).

7417 Corben, Edwards. Actor Corben appeared on the *Against the Storm* daytime serial program.

7418 **Corbett, Beatrice.** Soprano (WOV, New York, NY, 1932).

7419 **Corbett, James J. "Gentleman Jim."** Former heavyweight boxing champion Corbett appeared as a special summer feature on *Thornton Fisher's Sports* program (WAHG, Richmond Hill, NY, 1925).

7420 **Corbett, Jean.** COM-HE (WCAU, Philadelphia, PA, 1951).

7421 **Corbett, Jim.** Newscaster (WNAX, Yankton, SD, 1945–1946).

7422 **Corbett, Selma.** Singing entertainer Corbett was known as "The Laughing Mammy" (WCAU, Philadelphia, PA, 1929).

7423 **Corbin, Henry.** Baritone (WIBO, Chicago, IL, 1926).

7424 **Corbin, Jimmy.** Pianist (*Jimmy Corbin*, instr. mus. prg., WJJD, Chicago, IL, 1935).

7425 **Corbin, Lou.** Sportscaster (WFBR, Baltimore, MD, 1953).

7426 **Corbin, Paul [C. Paul Corbin].** Newscaster (KELA, Centralia-Chebalis, WA, 1937–1939). Sportscaster (KELA, Centralia-Chebalis, WA, 1938–1939; KIEM, Eureka, CA, 1941; KIEM, 1948).

7427 **Corbin, Slim.** DJ (*Hillbilly Hoedown*, KTFY, Brownfield, TX, 1954; KHOB, Hobbs, NM, 1956).

7428 **Corby, Mabelanna.** Soprano (WEAF, New York, NY, 1925).

7429 **Corday, Ted.** Director Corday worked on the *Brighter Day* and *Joyce Jordan, Girl Interne* daytime serial programs.

7430 **Cores, Alexander.** Violinist (*Alexander Cores*, instr. mus. prg. .CBS, 1936).

7431 **Corin, Sabin.** Poetry reader (*Sabin Corbin* prg., WHLS, Port Huron, MI, 1942).

7432 **Corca, Armando.** Leader (*Armando Corca Orchestra*, instr. mus. prg., WLBZ, Bangor, ME, 1934).

7433 **Corcoran, John.** Newscaster (WPEN, Philadelphia, PA, 1938–1939; WSAI, Cincinnati, OH, 1942; WFIL, Philadelphia, PA, 1944–1945).

7434 **Corcoran, Rosamond Eustis.** Pianist (WJZ, New York, NY, 1925).

7435 **Corcoran, Tony.** Singer (WEBH, Chicago, IL, 1924; WHT, Chicago, IL, 1925).

7436 **Corcoran, William.** Newscaster (KIRO, Seattle, WA, 1945).

7437 **Cordell, Ann.** News analyst (*Column of the Air*, KELD, El Dorado, AR, 1945–1948).

7438 **Cordell, Bob.** DJ (*Corn Till Morn*, WKBK, Detroit, MI, 1947).

7439 **Cordell, Kathleen.** Busy radio actress Cordell was a cast member of such daytime serials as *The Romance of Helen Trent*, *Second Husband*, *Second Mrs. Burton* and *Valiant Lady*.

7440 **Cordes and Marks Dance Orchestra.** WEAF (New York, NY, 1924).

7441 **Cordier, Andrew.** Newscaster (*Your United Nations*, NBC, 1947).

7442 **Cordler, Clarine.** Soprano (WLTH, Brooklyn, NY, 1930).

7443 **Cordner, Blaine.** Actor Blaine appeared on the *Pepper Young's Family* daytime serial program.

7444 **Cordray, Don.** DJ (*Goodwill Dawnbuster*, WJR, Detroit, MI, 1948).

7445 **Corduroy Tire Orchestra.** Commercially sponsored band (KFWB, Hollywood, CA, 1926).

7446 ***Corea's Orchestra.*** Instr. mus. prg.(WEEI, Boston, MA, 1932).

7447 **Cores, Alexander.** Violinist (*Alexander Cores*, instr. mus. prg., CBS, 1936).

7448 **Corey, Tom.** Banjo soloist (WGN, Chicago, IL, 1926).

7449 **Corey, Virgil.** Sportscaster (KANS, Wichita, KS, 1938–1939).

7450 **Corigliano, John.** Violinist featured on the *Atwater Kent Hour* (NBC, New York, NY, 1927).

7451 **Cork, Frank.** Leader (Frank Cork Orchestra and Frank Cork's Luna Park Orchestra, WEBJ, New York, NY, 1925).

7452 **Corkum, Joan.** COM-HE (WBHC, Conway, NH, 1960).

7453 **Corlew, Mabel.** Soprano (WEAF, New York, NY, 1925–1928).

7454 **Corley, Beth.** COM-HE (WILN, Atlanta, GA, 1960).

7455 **Corley, Bill.** Sportscaster (Ohio State football play-by-play, WBNS, Columbus, OH, 1942, 1950–1955).

7456 **Corley, Bob.** DJ (*Cuzzin Lem*, WQXI, Atlanta, GA, 1952).

7457 **Corley, (Dr.) Buren L.** Dr. Corley broadcast talks on chiropractic, diet and health topics (KJBS, San Francisco, CA, 1925–1927).

7458 **Corley, Jim.** Sportscaster (*Saturday's Sports Page*, KIXL, Dallas, TX, 1950; WBNS, Columbus, OH, 1956).

7459 **Corley, Stan.** Newscaster (KBIZ, Ottumwa, IA, 1940). Sportscaster (KBIZ, 1940).

7460 **Cormack, Rennie.** Singer (WCAU, Philadelphia, PA, 1925).

7461 **Cormier, Aurelia.** Soprano (WBZ, Springfield, MA, 1927).

7462 **Corn, Alfred.** *See* **Ryder, Alfred.**

7463 ***Cornbelt Jamboree.*** CW variety show 30 minutes in length (KMA, Shenandoah, IA,1945–1946). The half-hour broadcast was part of the weekly 90 minute show performed at the Council Bluffs, IA, City Auditorium. Hosts for the show were Lou Black and Steve Wooden. Featured performers were the West Sisters, Eddie Comer, Ike Everly and the Everly Brothers — Phil and Don — Zeke Williams and comedian Elmer Axelbender.

7464 ***Corn Belt Peepers.*** Henry Hornsbuckle read unusual and interesting poulty and egg anecdotes sent him by his listeners. His unusual show was sponsored by Corn Belt Hatcheries (5 min., Tuesday and Thursday, 12:30–12:35 P.M., WLS, Chicago, IL, 1938).

7465 ***(The) Corn Cob Pipe Club Program* (aka known as *The Corn Cob Pipe Club of Dutch Gap Center*).** Edgeworth Pipe Tobacco sponsored the entertaining program of country music and humor. Host Pat Binford opened the show with the warning and promise: "If hokum's what you want, hokum's what you're gonna get cause that's what we've got plenty of." Supposedly a meeting of a rural club, the program's characters included crossroads philosophers Strickland Gillilan, Squire Hicks and Jim Grapevine. Also on hand was the blackface team of Sawdust and Moonshine. Musical selections were provided by the Crossroads Quartet, the Tobacco Boys (a "Negro vocal ensemble"), Jake and the Crossroads Symphony, Little Margie and Aunt Sarah, who specialized in singing the ballads of the Virginia hills (30 min., Wednesday, 10:00–10:30 P.M., NBC-Red, 1932–1933).

7466 **Corne, Rene.** Oboe soloist (WLW, Cincinnati, OH, 1925).

7467 ***Cornelia Otis Skinner.*** Talented actress-monologist Skinner conducted her entertaining one-woman show. Andrew Jergens Lotion sponsored the program (15 min., Sunday, 9:30–9:45 P.M., NBC-Blue, 1935).

7468 **Cornelius, Glen.** DJ (WJRD, Tuscaloosa, AL, 1956).

7469 **Cornelius, L.B.** Announcer (KGRS, Amarillo, TX, 1927).

7470 **Cornelius, Y.M.** Announcer (WOAN, Lawrenceburg, TN, 1925).

7471 **Cornell, Henrietta [Henryetta] Letitia.** Soprano (KGO, San Francisco, CA, 1926).

7472 **Cornell, John.** Newscaster (WSAI, Cincinnati, OH, 1942).

7473 **Cornell, Ken.** DJ (WBRV, Boonville, NY, 1956).

7474 **Cornell, Lillian.** Vocalist (*Lillian Cornell*, vcl. mus. prg., NBC, 1939).

7475 ***The) Cornell Musical Clubs.*** Three university music clubs — the Cornell Glee Club, the Cornell Male Quartet and the Cornell Mandolin Club — performed on the program (WGR, Buffalo, NY, 1923).

7476 **Cornely, Paula.** Soprano (KGO, Oakland, CA, 1926).

7477 **Corner, Eulah.** Contralto (WMAQ, Chicago, IL, 1927).

7478 **Cornett, Alice.** Vocalist (*Alice Cornett*, vcl. mus. prg., WREN, Buffalo, NY, 1939).

7479 ***(The) Cornhuskers.*** CW vcl. mus. prg. (WLS, Chicago, IL, 1935; KFEL, Denver, CO, 1939). A lively music group, the Cornhuskers first gained popularity on the *National Barn Dance.* The Cornhuskers included Roy Knapp, Chris Steiner, Emilio Silvestre, Lou Klatt and Howard Chamberlain.

7480 **Cornhuskers Orchestra.** Popular local band (WGY, Schenectady, NY, 1926).

7481 **Corning-Wilson, Isabelle.** Soprano (KFSG, Los Angeles, CA, 1924).

7482 **Cornish, Worthen C. "Bud."** Sportscaster (WGAN, Portland, ME, 1938–1940; WGAN, 1944–1947; *On the Main Stem*, WGAN, 1948–1953).

7483 **Cornish School Artistic Ensemble.** The school's instrumental group included violinist Peter Mereblum; cellist Kola Levienne; and pianist Mme. Berthe Poincy Dow (KJR, Seattle, WA, 1926).

7484 **Cornwall, Albion S.** Baritone (WHAS, Louisville, KY, 1923).

7485 **Cornwall, Arthur.** "Carolina's lyric tenor" (WBT, Charlotte, NC, 1928).

7486 **Cornwall, Burton.** Baritone (WBZ, Boston-Springfield, MA, 1924).

7487 **Cornwall, Ruth.** Writer Cornwall's major program was her *Death Valley Days*. She was best known for her careful research of atmosphere and detail. Before coming to radio she had done advertising agency work.

7488 **Cornwell, Blaine.** Sportscaster (KVOO, Tulsa, OK, 1937). DJ (*Top Ten and First Fifteen*, KWFT, Wichita Falls, TX, 1948; *First Five*, KWFT, 1949).

7489 **Cornwell, Bob.** Newscaster (KFBC, Cheyenne, WI, 1951).

7490 **Cornwell, Frank.** Director (Crusaders Orchestra, WEAF, New York, NY, 1926).

7491 **Corona Presbyterian Church Quartet.** A religious vocal group, the quartet's members were soprano Mrs. Richard Osenbaugh; contralto Mrs. Irving Green; tenor Ralph Freese; and baritone Dr. Clyde England. George Richie was the group's accompanist (KGO, San Francisco, CA, 1925).

7492 **Coronadians Orchestra.** St. Louis band led by Joe Johnson (KMOX, St. Louis, MO, 1928).

7493 **Corray, Fred.** Sportscaster (WILL, Urbana, IL, 1938–1941; WILL, 1944–1945).

7494 **Correa, Eric.** Leader (*Eric Correa Orchestra*, instr. mus. prg., WOR, Newark, NJ, 1936).

7495 **Correll, Charles.** *See* ***Amos 'n' Andy.***

7496 **Correll, (Mr. and Mrs.) Sidney.** The husband and wife team sang vocal duets (KFSG, Los Angeles, CA, 1925).

7497 **Correlli, Alfonso.** Director of the Vienna Concert Orchestra (KNX, Los Angeles, CA, 1928).

7498 ***The Correspondents' Scratch Pad.*** Don Hohlenbeck hosted the meeting of such CBS correspondents as Tony Craveri, Rex Davis, George Herman and Howard K. Smith. They occasionally interviewed prominent persons in the news (15 min., CBS, 1950).

7499 **Corris, Allyn.** Newscaster (WRDW, Augusta, GA, 1938).

7500 **Corsover, Sidney.** Lyric baritone (WOR, Newark, NJ, 1927).

7501 **Cortez, Carlos.** DJ (*Monacita*, KDIA, Auburn, CA, 1949).

7502 **Corum, Bill.** Sportscaster (WOR, Newark, NJ, 1936). Corum later broadcast blow-by-blow accounts of boxing bouts (ABC, New York, NY, 1945–1948).

7503 **Corwin, Byron.** Newscaster (KKIN, Visalia, CA, 1946).

7504 **Corwin, Connie.** Ballad singer (WSWS, Chicago, IL, 1926).

7505 **Corwin, Madeline.** COM-HE (WCRB, Boston, MA, 1957).

7506 **Corwin, Norman.** *See* **Drama.**

7507 **Corwin, W. P.** Announcer (KSD, St. Louis, MO, 1927).

7508 **Corwine, Tom.** Pioneer sound effects man Corwine could imitate dog fights, farm animals, steam boats, chickens, etc. (WLS, Chicago, IL, 1928). *See* **Sound Effects.**

7509 **Cory, Uncle Dave.** Cory conducted a children's program (WNYC, New York, NY, 1925).

7510 **Cosa, Jim.** DJ (*Sentimental Journey*, KFOX, Long Beach, CA, 1955).

7511 ***Cosmopolitan Singers.*** Vcl. mus. prg. (KUOA, Siloam Springs, AR, 1939).

7512 **Coss, Paul.** DJ (WAAB, Worcester, MA, 1956).

7513 **(The) Cossacks.** Male vocal group directed by William Stace (WLW, Cincinnati, OH, 1928).

7514 **Cosell, Howard W.** Sportscaster (*The World and You*, *Sports Kaleidoscope* and *Soundmirror*, WABC, New York, NY, 1955; *Speaking of Sports*, ABC, New York, NY, 1956–1960). Years later Cosell became famous or infamous — depending on your point of view — with his television appearances on various programs including *Monday Night Football* on ABC.

7515 **Cosentino, Nicholas.** Writer Cosentino worked on the *We Are Always Young* daytime serial program.

7516 **Cossiter, Don.** Sportscaster (WFBG, Altoona, PA, 1953).

7517 **Costa, Esther.** COM-HE (WESO, Southbridge, MA, 1956–1957).

7518 **Costain, Harry M.** Tenor (KXA, Seattle, WA, 1928).

7519 **Costello, Beverly C.** COM-HE (WGAY, Silver Spring, MD, 1955).

7520 **Costello, Bill.** Newscaster (WJWC, Hammond, IN, 1942; CBS, 1944–1948; WDBF, Delray Beach, FL, 1960).

7521 **Costello, Ed.** Newscaster (*Willis News*, KOSA, Odessa, TX, 1947). Sportscaster (KOSA, 1947–1952).

7522 **Costello, Jack.** Announcer Costello announced the *Fitch Bandwagon*, *Stella Dallas* and *What Would You Have Done?* programs.

7523 **Costello, Jack.** DJ (*Morning Mayor*, KBKW, Aberdeen, WA, 1960).

7524 **Costello, Kay.** Singer (*Kay Costello*, vcl. mus. prg., WOR, Newark, NJ, 1933–1934).

7525 **Costello, Len.** DJ (WGHN, Grand Haven, MI, 1956).

7526 **Costigan, Howard.** Newscaster (KOL, Seattle, WA, 1942, 1946).

7527 **Costley, Jan.** Newscaster (WJTN, Jamestown, NY, 1937).

7528 **Cot, Roger.** Newscaster (KUOA, Siloam Springs, AK, 1937).

7529 **Cote, Emile.** Bass Cote sang with the A&P Gypsies in the 1920s (NBC).

7530 **Cothran, Fanny Mae.** COM-HE (WXTN, Lexington, MS, 1960).

7531 **(The) Cotillions Dance Orchestra of Concord, New Hampshire.** The dance band and the 72nd Field Artillery Band appeared on WBRL's first broadcast (WBRL, Manchester, NH, 1926).

7532 **Cotsworth, Staats.** Busy actor Cotsworth appeared on such diverse programs as *Amanda of Honeymoon Hill*, *Big Sister*, *Casey, Crime Photographer* (title role), *Cavalcade of America*, *Front Page Farrell* (title role), *Lone Journey*, *Man from G-2*, *The March of Time*, *Mr. and Mrs. North*, *The Right to Happiness*, *Second Mrs. Burton* and *When a Girl Marries*.

7533 **Cotton, Carolina (Helen Hagstrom).** Carolina Cotton, a CW yodeling cowgirl, worked on San Francisco local radio (KYA, San Francisco) with Dude Martin before starring with Roy Acuff in the *Sing, Neighbor, Sing* motion picture in 1944. She appeared in many other motion pictures with such stars as Ken Curtis, Charles Starrett, Eddy Arnold and Gene Autry. During the 1950s, Cotton starred on her Armed Forces Radio program, *Carolina Calls*.

7534 **Cotton, Dorothy.** COM-HE (WHEC, Rochester, NY, 1956).

7535 **Cotton, Larry.** Tenor (*Larry Cotton*, vcl. mus. prg., NBC, 1936).

7536 **Cotton, Laura Ann.** Cellist (KFRC, San Francisco, CA, 1927).

7537 **Cotton, Liz.** COM-HE (KGFL, Roswell, NM, 1958).

7538 **Cotton, Sarah.** COM-HE (KGFL, Roswell, NM, 1957).

7539 **Cotton, Wint.** Tenor (KFRC, San Francisco, CA, 1928).

7540 ***(The) Cotton Blossom Minstrels.*** Barry Hopkins was the interlocutor on the old-fashioned 60-minute minstrel show program whose cast included Harold Peary, Bobbie Deane, Captain Bill Royle, Clarence Hayes and the Southern Harmony Four (a "colored quartet"). One of the most popular parts of the program was Sylvano Dale's tap dancing specialty act (NBC-Pacific Coast Network, 1929). In a later 1929 format, bass Harry Stanton was the interlocutor and the music was supplied by Jerry and his Dixie Melodists. The other cast members remained the same (30 min., Wednesday, 10:00–10:30 P.M. PST, NBC-Pacific Coast Network, 1929).

7541 ***(The) Cotton Club Dance Orchestra.*** Mus. prg. (WEAF, New York, NY, 1933).

7542 **Cotton Club Orchestra.** The hot jazz band broadcast from the Cotton Club, a famous Harlem, New York, night club (WHN, New York, NY, 1926).

7543 ***(The) Cotton Pickers Orchestra.*** Instr. mus. prg. (WFBE, Cincinnati, OH, 1933). This was the well known McKinney's Cotton Pickers band.

7544 ***(The) Cotton Queen Show Boat Review.*** An old-fashioned variety program (WLW, Cincinnati, OH, 1935).

7545 **Cottongim, Earl K.** DJ (*Saturday Night Session*, WSFC, Somerset, KY, 1952–1954).

7546 **Coty, Bill and Jack Armstrong.** Harmony singing team (WBZ, Boston-Springfield, MA, 1924).

7547 ***(The) Coty Playgirl.*** Irene Bordoni sang on the program sponsored by Coty Cosmetics. Eugene Ormandy and Ray Noble conducted the orchestra at various times (15 min., Sunday, 9:00–9:15 P.M., WABC, New York City, NY, 1931).

7548 Cougar Coed Band of Washington State University. Unique college band (KWSC, Pullman, WA, 1926–1927).

7549 Cougle, Bob. Pianist (WDAP, Chicago, IL, 1923).

7550 Coughlin, (Father) Charles E. Father Charles E. Coughlin, the famous radio priest made his first appearance on station WJR (Detroit, MI), broadcasting from his Shrine of the Little Flower in Royal Oak, Michigan, on October 17, 1926. When the station owner of KWK (St. Louis, MO) in 1934 asked his listeners if they wanted to hear Father Coughlin, who at that time found himself in the midst of a controversy caused by his broadcasts, KWK listeners responded dramatically in favor of Coughlin. They responded strongly in the affirmative: YES —1,485, NO —129.

Later that year when Alfred E. Smith criticized the New Deal by talking about "baloney dollars," Coughlin criticized him for his attacks on FDR. In 1934, Coughlin called for a managed and flexible currency that would expand to "bring prices and values in line." It appears that he was appeasing Roosevelt by advancing this inflationary policy of currency expansion. His approach, however, soon changed and he began attacking FDR's policies. Father Coughlin frequently ventured into news analysis and social commentary on his later programs (MBS, 1937). He combined religious talks with social criticism, and there is strong evidence of radical anti–Semitic propaganda in his broadcasts.

The charges of anti–Semitism against Coughlin were answered in a booklet, *An Answer to Father Coughlin's Critics* published in 1940 by the Radio League of the Little Flower. It presented a reasoned defense of Coughlin. Some relevant observations included in *An Answer to Father Coughlin's Critics* were as follows:

a. Father Coughlin made negative statements about those Jews who were prominent persons during the 1917 Bolshevik revolution in Russia. One example of the evidence included is an extensive list of Russian revolutionaries active in the 1917 Bolshevik revolution. The list contains 50 revolutionaries with their assumed names, actual names, race and or religion. Only seven of them were not Jews.

b. Chief among the organizations accusing Father Coughlin of being an "anti–Semite, pro–Nazi, a falsifier of documents and a priest in bad standing" was the Jewish People's Committee. The leader of that organization was William Warszoer, alias William Weiner, who was the "third in command of the Communist Party in America" (p.121). Weiner was tried, convicted and sentenced for the "fraudulent securing of a document [passport](p.121).

c. Clear statements, his defenders said, indicate that Coughlin's attacks were against Jews who supported the Communist Party and its objectives. This proves, they suggested, that since his attacks were only against some Jews, he was NOT anti–Semitic.

d. Coughlin attacked the Nazi party and its brutal acts against Jews in Germany.

e. Coughlin's strong attacks against Communism in Russia and the Loyalist Government and troops in the Spanish Civil War often included criticism against individual Jews and Jewish organizations that became the basis for the charges of anti–Semitism against him. [The Spanish Civil War pitted the Communist forces of the Loyalist Government against the rebels led by Generalissimo Francisco Franco backed by Nazi Germany.]

Although the judgement of history appears to be against Couglin, the question of his anti–Semitism is an interesting one, raising as it does his *intentions.* A constant theme of Coughlin's radio broadcasts was: The Russian Revolution brought about the elevation of Karl Marx and the degradation of Jesus Christ. Among Coughlin's listeners in the turmoil and social stress of the Great Depression's dark years, unfortunately, were many in both the pro– and anti–Coughlin groups anxious to hear strong anti–Semitic opinions expressed. *See* **Charlatans, Demagogs and Politicians.**

7551 Coughlin, (Mrs.) Tom. Singer (WBAP, Fort Worth, TX, 1927).

7552 Coukart, Fred. News analyst (WHBC, Canton, OH, 1945; WMBI, Chicago, IL, 1946). DJ (*A Man and His Music*, WWCA, Gary, IN, 1955).

7553 Coule, Helen. Actress Coule appeared on the daytime serials *Hilltop House* and *The Second Mrs Burton.*

7554 Coulehan, (Miss) M.E. Newscaster (WTBO, Cumberland, OH, 1939).

7555 Coulouris, George. Actor Coulouris appeared on the *We Love and Learn* daytime serial program.

7556 Coulson, (Major) Thomas. Newscaster (WCAU, Philadelphia, PA, 1940–1941).

7557 Coulston, Elmer. Pianist (WEMC, Berrien Springs, MI, 1925).

7558 Coulter, Esther. Soprano (KYW, Chicago, IL, 1923).

7559 Coulter, Lydia. COM-HE (WAKU, Latrobe, PA, 1956).

7560 Coulter, (Dr.) T.J. Coulter was a veterinarian who talked about "cats and dogs" (KMTR, Hollywood, CA, 1925).

7561 Counce, Lois. COM-HE (WCMA, Corinth, MS, 1956–1957).

7562 *Count Basie.* Leader (Count Basie Orchestra, an excellent jazz band, NBC and CBS, 1937–1948).

7563 *(The) Count of Monte Cristo.* Based on the characters created by Alexander Dumas. The entertaining, swashbuckling dramatic series told the story of Edmond Dantes and his servant Rene, who fought injustice and evil. Carleton Young played the title role assisted by Anne Stone and Parley Baer. The weekly program probably was broadcast by transcription (MBS, Chicago, IL, 1946). A 1949 version of the show was written by Anthony Ellis and produced and directed by Jaime Del Valle. Carleton Young once again played the title role. Other cast members in this format were Parley Baer, Virginia Gregg, Jay Novello, Howard McNear, John Dehner and Victor Redman. Charles Arlington and Dick Wynn were the announcers. Music was supplied by Dean Fossler's orchestra (30 min., Sunday, 9:00–9:30 P.M., MBS, 1949). A much earlier version was broadcast daily in 1933 featuring Betty Webb on such stations as WOR (Newark, NJ), WBBM (Chicago, IL), and KNX (Los Angeles, CA).

7564 *Counterspy (aka David Harding, Counterspy).* First heard in 1942 on the ABC network, *Counterspy* was the creation of Phillips H. Lord, who also produced the program. The adventure series told the story of David Harding, a specialist in counter espionage. Harding and his assistant were played by Don MacLaughlin and Mandel Kramer. They battled first against Nazis and Japanese agents during World War II and, later, against Communists when the war ended. The program's writers included: Edward J. Adamson, Arva Everitt, Morton Friedman, Milton J. Kramer, Phillips H. Lord, Peggy Lou Mayer, John Mole, Stanley Niss, John Roeburt, Emile C. Tepperman, Palmer Thompson, Jacqueline W. Palmer and Jacqueline W. Trey. The directors were: Leonard Bass, Max Loeb, Victor Seydel, Robert Steen and Bill Sweets. Lionel Rico, Bob Shepherd and Roger Krupp were the announcers.

7565 *Countess Olga Medlolago Albani.* George Hicks was the announcer on the music program featuring the lovely mezzo-soprano (15 min., Sunday, 6:15–6:30 P.M., NBC-Blue, 1930).

7566 *Country Carnival Barn Dance* aka *KMPC Country Carnival Barn Dance.* CW barn dance program that broadcast two hours of a complete four hour stage show (KMPC, Los Angeles, CA, 1948). Cottonseed Clark, Billy Starr and Billy Walker were the MC's. Featured on the program were T. Texas Tyler, Shug Fisher, Doyle O'Dell, Carolina Cotton and Max Terhune.

7567 *(The) Country Church.* Rev. W.B. Hogg conducted the popular religious program (30 min., Thursday, 11:30–12:00 noon, CBS, 1935). *See* ***The Country Church of Hollywood.***

7568 *(The) Country Church of Hollywood.* The transcribed religious program was broadcast by numerous st-ations in the 1930s. Sponsored by the May Company Footware Department, the serial was broadcast before a live audience with the cast members dressed in the authentic costumes of the period. Former Army Chaplian the Reverend W.B. Hogg played the role of old time circuit parson Joseph Hopkins, the central character in the series (Transcribed, Weekly, Various Stations, 1933). The program later appeared on the CBS network. *See* ***The Country Church.***

7569 *(The) Country Club.* Richfield Oil Company sponsored the entertaining variety program (30 min., Weekly, 10:00–10:30 P.M., CBS, 1933). This was the same program format broadcast as *The Richfield Country Club* on NBC (30 min., Weekly, 10:30–11:00 P.M. and CBS, 1933). *See* ***The Richfield Country Club.***

7570 Country Club Arcadians Orchestra. The club dance band was led by Bill Schaeffer (WAPI, 1929).

7571 *Country Journal.* Burl Ives was the featured singer on the music show (15 min., Saturday, 9:30–9:45 A.M., CBS, 1945).

7572 *Country Store.* A large studio audience paid a quarter each to attend the weekly country and western music broadcast (KTHS, Hot Springs, AR, 1937).

7573 **Country-Western (CW) Music on Radio.** Country and western music for many persons was, and too often still is, looked down upon. Many consider it unsophisticated and uncultured to listen to and enjoy "hillbilly" music. Even before the public's general recognition that CW music was a genuine form of expression in American culture, there already was an expansion of its popularity on American radio during the late 1930s and early 1940s. But this faded as did those later cycles of public popularity for calypso and folk music.

Despite the popularity of CW today, it really was there from radio's earliest days for a large number of avid listeners. A large audience enjoyed the *Grand Ole Opera* from Nashville's WSM and Chicago's WLS production of the *National Barn Dance*. Then, too, there were various other "barn dances" and "old fashion fiddling" programs broadcast from other parts of the country. Several CW singing stars in the 1930s reached national prominence by means of their network broadcasts. One example is Bradley Kincaid, one of the most admired CW singers of the period, who, incidentally despised being called a "hillbilly, " unlike Uncle Dave Macon, who prided himself on being called exactly that. By their radio broadcasts and records Jimmie Rodgers and a young Gene Autry reached a large audience with their yodeling skills and often tragic story songs. Carson Robison, a composer-performer who brought much fun to CW music, sometimes teamed with Vernon Dahlhart, another tremendously popular recording star, to entertain listeners.

Not all CW music was "old fashioned." There were also "sophisticated hillbillies and cowboys," such as the Zeke Manners Gang, an outgrowth of the Beverly Hillbillies group; Louise Massey and the Westerners; and the Hank Keene gang. Eventually, the music broadcast by the *National Barn Dance* became more sophisticated, often featuring the popular songs of the day along with old favorites smoothly performed.

During the pre–World War II years, the only network CW music shows were the *National Barn Dance*, the *Grand Ole Opry* and Gene Autry's *Melody Ranch* (Pugh, 1997). Several individual stations were "hotbeds of country music" with a large amount of local programming devoted to the music and its performers. These were WSB (Atlanta, GA); WBT (Charlotte, NC); KMOX (St. Louis, MO); WWVA (Wheeling, WV); WHO (Des Moines, IA); WLW (Cincinnati, OH); KVOO (Tulsa, OK); KWKH (Shreveport, LA); WNOX (Knoxville, TN); WROL (Knoxville, TN); WHAS (Louisville, KY); WCKY (Covington, KY); and the collection of Mexican border stations (Pugh, 1997).

One steadfast group, almost invariably the largest and most loyal listeners to CW radio programs, was the farmers and their families, who listened early in the morning and at lunch time. Country-western music programs were presented live to fit the work schedules of these hard working farm workers. Not only large metropolitan stations such as Chicago's WLS met the farmers' needs and wishes, but hundreds of smaller stations throughout the country did the same. Singers and musicians worked the circuit of these stations that supplied the bulk of CW music for their rural listeners. As Pugh (1997) suggests country-western artists would work these local stations until they had "milked" one territory, before moving on to another. The pattern was a familiar one that can be recognized in the career of most CW artists of the time. It was a rarity for an artist or group to remain at one station for many years.

Although CW music during the 1930s and 1940s was often looked down upon by cultural snobs as "hillbilly," urban audiences soon heard it and enjoyed it. It remained for perceptive critics such as Gilbert Seldes to point out the importance of American popular arts, and this music certainly was an important part of American life. Although the first influential CW barn dance programs are generally thought to be the *National Barn Dance* and the *Grand Ole Opry*, probably the first radio barn dance was broadcast by WBAP (San Antonio, TX) beginning on January 4, 1922. The station at that time presented a 90-minute program of square dance music. Confederate veteran and old-time fiddler Captain M.J. Bonner directed the program. In addition to fiddler Bonner, music was also supplied by Fred Wagner's Hilo Five Hawaiian orchestra. Another group that later appeared on the WBAP program was the Peacock Fiddle Band of Cleburne, Texas. The program was broadcast irregularly two or three times a month before it became a regularly scheduled Friday night feature in 1929.

The audience for CW music rapidly grew because of local programs. By 1949, there were at least 650 stations broadcasting live CW music talent (Malone, 1985, p. 199) The listening audience also heard it on such programs in the 1930s and 1940s as the *Wheeling Jamboree* (Wheeling, WV, 1933); the *Crazy Barn Dance* (WBT, Charlotte, NC, 1934); the *Old Fashion Barn Dance* (KMOX, St. Louis, MO, 1930); the *Boone County Jamboree*—which later became the *Midwestern Hayride* (WLW, Cincinnati, OH, 1936); the *Renfro Valley Barn Dance* (WHAS, Louisville, KY, 1937); the *Saddle Mountain Round-Up* (KVOO, Tulsa, OK, 1940s); the *Old Dominion Barn Dance* (WRVA, Richmond, VA, 1938); the *WSB Barn Dance* (WSB, Atlanta, GA, 1940); the *KWKH Roundup* (Shreveport, LA, 1939); the *Iowa Barn Dance* (WHO, Des Moines, IA, 1930s); the *Saturday Night Shindig* (WFAA, Dallas, TX, 1932); the *Big D Jamboree* (KRLD, Dallas, TX, 1940s-1950s); and the *Louisiana Hayride* (KWKH, Shreveport, LA, 1948). The *Louisiana Hayride* was often known as "The Cradle of the Stars." Some of the stars that first gained national prominence by appearing on the program were Hank Williams, Slim Whitman, Jim Reeves, Kitty Wells, Faron Young and Johnny and Jack (Johnny Wright and Jack Anglin).

Various trends in CW music can be identified. For example, there were the "cowboy singers," such as Jules Verne Allen, Gene Autry and Carl T. Sprague. Another was the "western swing movement" exemplified by the music of Milton Brown and Bob Wills. The popularity of the music increases as the years pass. That can best be seen by the growth in country music stations that grew from 1,116 in 1975 to 2,402 in the late 1980s.

See **Allen, Jules Verne; Autry, Gene; Brown, Milton; Dahlhart, Vernon; Rodgers, Jimmie; Kincaid, Bradley; Macon, Uncle Dave; Monroe, Bill; McClintock, Harry "Mac"; Robison, Carson; Wills, Bob; Border Radio; *Grand Ole Opry; Melody Ranch; National Barn Dance, Louisiana Hayride, The Saturday Night Shindig, The Renfro Valley Gathering and* Singers: Crooners, Canaries, Cow Girls and Hillbillies.**

7574 ***(The) Couple Next Door.*** The funny serial drama started as a local radio comedy sketch on WGN (Chicago, IL), where it was produced by Frank and Anne Hummert. Olan Soule, Eleanor Harriot and Jack Brinkley appeared in the original version that was sponsored by the Holland Furnace Company (15 min, Monday, 8:15–8:30 P.M., WGN, Chicago, IL, 1935). When the program was moved to New York and broadcast on MBS in 1937, Lillian Gish and Harold Vermilyea played the leading roles. A still later version was broadcast from 1957 to 1960 with Peg Lynch and Alan Bunce in the title roles.

7575 **Couppee, Al.** Sportscaster (KRNT, Des Moines, IA, 1949–1953).

7576 ***Courant Comics.*** Uncle Ed, not otherwise identified, read the Sunday comics from the Hartford *Courant* newspaper (25 min., Sunday, 12:35–1:00 P.M., WCCC, Hartford, CT, 1948).

7577 **Courchene, (Mme.) Calita Dupont.** Pianist and dramatic reader (WBJ, 1923).

7578 **Coursey, Alex "Alec."** Newscaster (WQDM, St. Albans, VT, 1938–1939).

7579 **Court, Ted.** DJ (*Morning Digest*, WSLS, Roanoke, VA, 1955).

7580 ***(The) Court of Human Relations.*** Simulated court proceedings were dramatized on which the attempt was made to adjudicate thorny problems of human relationships. Sponsored by *True Story* magazine, the program was directed mainly toward women. Percy Hemus played the Judge of the court assisted by such famous actors as Porter Hall, Allyn Joslyn and Brian Donlevy who, at one time or another, played the role of the Court Clerk. It has been said that Van Heflin made his first radio appearance on the *Court of Human Relations* (Buxton and Owen, 1973, p. 63). The program was first broadcast in 1933 (30 min., Friday, 7:30–8:00 P.M., CBS, 1935).

7581 ***(The) Court of Missing Heirs.*** Each week the program dramatized stories of interesting persons who had died without leaving a will. The program attempted to find the missing heirs to these unclaimed fortunes. They once claimed that they had helped missing heirs collect almost a million dollars previously unclaimed. The cast included: Dorothy Day, Jim Goss, Elizabeth Heller, Burr Lee, Tom Shirley and Dick Wells. Music was performed by the orchestra of Peter A. Cavallo, Jr. Fritz Blocki was the producer (30 min., CBS, 1937). A similar program, *Are You a Missing Heir?* was carried by ABC in 1946.

7582 **Courtland, Jane.** Pianist (NBC, 1937).

7583 **Courtland, Mary.** Contralto (*Mary Courtland*, voc. mus. prg., NBC, 1934).

7584 **Courtmamche, Ray.** DJ (KQTY, Everett, WA, 1960).

7585 **Courtnay, Don.** Newscaster (KIRO, Seattle, WA, 1948).

7586 **Courtney, Alan.** DJ (*Courtney Record Carnival*, MBS, 1947–1950; WNEW, New York, NY, 1950). *See* ***The Alan Courtney Show***.

7587 **Courtney, Del.** Leader (*Del Courtney Orchestra*, instr. mus. prg., NBC, 1939; CBS, 1942). Courtney later worked as a DJ (KSFO, San Francisco, CA, 1956).

7588 **Courtney, Diane.** Singer (NBC, 1942).

7589 **Courtney, Don.** Courtney was a popular Salt Lake City DJ (*KALL for Music* show, 60 min., Monday through Thursday, 12:00–1:00 P.M., KALL, Salt Lake City, UT, 1947).

7590 **Courtney, Ed.** Newscaster (WDGY, Minneappolis–St. Paul, MN, 1939).

7591 **Courtney, Johnny.** Leader (*Johnny Courtney Orchestra*, instr. mus. prg. (WLW, Cincinnati, OH, 1935).

7592 **Coury, Connie.** COM-HE (WMOU, Berlin, NH, 1957).

7593 **Coury, Roselle.** Newscaster (WCOU, Lewiston, ME, 1945).

7594 **Cousin Betty.** Cousin Betty, not otherwise identified, conducted the *World's Best Stories* program (WEVD, New York, NY, 1930).

7595 ***Cousin Clare's Children's Program.*** Cousin Clare, not otherwise unidentified, broadcast the early evening children's program (KFBK, Sacramento, CA, 1926).

7596 **Cousin Dorothy and Barbara.** CW singing team (WEBC, Duluth, MN, 1937).

7597 **Cousin Emmy (Cynthia May Carver).** Versatile CW singer, comedienne and musician Cousin Emmy was a talented and versatile musician, playing banjo, violin, guitar, harmonica, ukulele, trumpet, accordion, piano, jew's harp, saw and dulcimer. Carver and her cousins — Noble and Warner Carver — appeared on WHB (Kansas City, MO) in the 1920s. She gained popularity on WHAS (Louisville, KY, 1935–1937).

7598 ***Cousin Emmy's Kinfolks.*** CW mus. prg. (WWVA, Wheeling, WV, 1937; *Cousin Emmy's Band*, WHAS, Louisville, KY, 1938).

7599 ***Cousin Jim.*** James Beardsley (Cousin Jim) conducted the children's program (KFSG, Los Angeles, CA, 1925). Beardsley both hosted and sang lively songs for his young listeners.

7600 ***Cousin Lee.*** CW vocalist (*Cousin Lee*, vcl. mus., prg., WORK, York, PA, 1934–1937).

7601 ***Cousin Lee and the Boys.*** CW mus. prg. (WORK, York, PA, 1938).

7602 **Cousin Minnie Pearl.** *See* **Cannon, Sarah Ophelia** and ***(The) Grand Ole Opry***.

7603 ***Cousin Willie.*** Bill Idelson played the title role on the sustaining situation comedy. On the program Cousin Willie moved into the home of his California relatives "until he could get settled." Many hilarious complications arose from the arrangement. Dawn Bender, Pattie Chapman, Patricia Dunlap, Marvin Miller, Frank Nelson, Stuffy Singer and Bob Sweeney were also in the cast. Music was supplied by the Robert Armbruster Orchestra. Jimmy Wallington was the announcer. The sustaining program was written by Doris and Frank Hursley and produced and directed by Homer Canfield (30 min., Tuesday, 9:30–10:00 P.M., NBC, 1953).

7604 ***Covered Wagon Jamboree.*** Stuart Hamblen hosted the early morning CW music show (KFVD, Culver City, CA, 1932).

7605 ***Covered Wagon Jubilee.*** CW mus. prg. (KUOA, Siloam Springs, AR, 1939).

7606 **Covert, Effie.** COM-HE (WWGP, Sanford, SC, 1951).

7607 **Covert, Jean.** COM-HE (KTBC, Austin, TX, 1958).

7608 **Covert, Mary A.** Home management specialist (KDFY, Brookings, SD, 1937).

7609 **Covington, Thomas B.** Newscaster (*Local and State News*, WHOP, Hopkinsville, KY, 1948).

7610 ***Cowtown Jamboree.*** CW variety program broadcast a portion of the four and a half-hour show held Saturday evening at the Ivanhoe Temple in Kansas City, MO, by KCMO (Kansas City, MO, 1950–1953). Dal Stallard, a KCMO DJ, hosted the program with an assist from Hoby Shepp, who also was its producer. Milt Dickey, a singer, also served as announcer. Others who appeared on the program were Peggy Clark, Neal Burris, Jimmy Dallas and the Sons of the Golden West quartet.

7611 **Cowan, Dick.** Sportscaster (*Fishing and Hunting Tips*, KWIL, Albany, OR, 1948).

7612 **Cowan, Elbert.** Organist (KGO, Oakland, CA, 1925). Announcer (KGO, Oakland, CA, 1927).

7613 **Cowan, Emily.** Singer (WNYC, New York, NY, 1936).

7614 **Cowan, Geraldine.** COM-HE (WKKS, Vanceburg, KY, 1958).

7615 **Cowan, Jean [Jeanne].** Blues singer (KFI, Los Angeles, CA, 1927; KFON, Long Beach, CA, 1928; KFWB, Hollywood, CA, 1929).

7616 **Cowan, Ruby.** Singer (WHN, New York, NY, 1925; WGCP, New York, NY, 1926).

7617 **Cowan, Steve.** Newcaster (KGKL, San Angelo, TX, 1941).

7618 **Cowan, Thomas "Tommy."** When he was assigned by Westinghouse Electric Company as Chief Announcer at the newly established WJZ (New York, NY), Cowan became the first radio announcer in the greater New York area. He inaugurated the station's first broadcast with the announcement, is WJZ, WJZ, WJZ, the radio telephone station located in Newark, New Jersey. This is announcer Cowan, Newark." Soon he began to identify himself as "ACN."

In the fall of 1921, WJZ decided to broadcast the World Series between the Yankees and Giants of New York, using the same technique Major Andrew White had used previously to broadcast the Dempsey-Carpentier heavy weight championship boxing bout. Unable to use a remote line from either baseball parks, they decided to have Sandy Hunt sit in a box at the Polo Grounds and telephone a play-by-play account back to Cowan at the WJZ studio. Cowan's exciting delivery of the play-by-play brought an enthusiastic response from his listeners. Cowan also worked as the station's program director. In this role, he was responsible for bringing a great variety of talented performers into the WJZ studios to broadcast. Cowan was hired away from WJZ in 1924 and persuaded to join the WNYC announcing staff (New York, NY). *See* **deLeath, Vaughn**.

7619 **Cowanova, Florence.** Cowanova was an internationally famous ballet dancer who performed "novelty clog dances" on radio (WDAR, Philadelphia, PA, 1924).

7620 ***(The) Coward Comfort Hour.*** Coward Comfort Shoe Company sponsored the music program that featured an orchestra directed by Fritz Forsch. Martin [Marthin] Provensen was the announcer (30 min., Thursday, 7:30–8:00 P.M., NBC-Red, New York, NY, 1926–1929).

7621 **Cowbell Boys.** Country music group (KFAB, Lincoln, NE, 1926).

7622 **Cowbell Four and the Village Orchestra.** Vocal quartet and orchestra (WGY, Schenectady, NY, 1924).

7623 ***(The) Cowboy Band.*** CW mus. prg. (MBS, 1939).

7624 ***(The) Cowboy Caravan.*** Hosmer Motor Sales sponsored the program of cowboy songs and music. John E. Reilly was the program announcer. Oklahoma Buck Nation was featured (15 min., Tuesday, Thursday and Saturday, 8:15–8:30 P.M., WMEX, Boston, MA, 1937).

7625 ***Cowboy Jamboree.*** CW mus. prg., KUOA, Siloam Springs, AR, 1939).

7626 ***Cowboy Jamboree.*** Bristol-Myers sponsored the local western music program that originated from Kansas City, MO. The talented cast included Frank Wiziarde, Tiny Tillman, Jimmy Dallas, Cora Rice, Charley Stewart, Mickey Cottil, the Nash Sisters, Goo Goo and Lenny, and Hoby Shepp with the Cow Town Wranglers (60 min., Saturday, 8:30–9:30 P.M., KMBC, Kansas City, MO, 1955).

7627 ***Cowboy Jim.*** Unidentified CW singer (vcl. mus. prg., WORK, York, PA, 1936).

7628 ***Cowboy Loye.*** CW singer (vcl. mus. prg., WWVA, Wheeling, WV, 1933–1934; WMMN, Fairmont, WV, 1934–1938). Cowboy Loye D. Pack was a great listener favorite. He first appeared on WWVA November 11, 1933. When his son was born in 1934, he asked his listeners to help name him. After six days, the Cowboy had received 11,235 names that listeners suggested, an indication of the loyalty listeners felt for their local radio favorites.

7629 ***Cowboy Loye and the Blue Bonnet Troupe.*** CW mus. prg. (WMMN, Fairmont, WV, 1938).

7630 ***Cowboy Tim's Roundup.*** The "wild west" variety show began as *Tom Keene's Roundup*. Later, the format was changed with George Martin in the title role perfoming dramatic sketches. Comedian Doug McTague also appeared along with Joe Shonatona, who played "Snookum" for comedy relief. When McTague returned to Canada, Tex Ritter replaced him and the show became *The Lone Star Cowboy*, later once again to be renamed *Cowboy Tom* (15 min., Monday through Friday, WHN, New York, NY, 1933).

7631 ***Cowboy Tom* (aka *Cowboy Tom's Roundup*).** An early western drama series with Tex Ritter and "Chief" Shonatona telling interesting western stories for children. The sponsor was Remington-Rand Company (15 min., Tuesday, 5:45–6:00 P.M., CBS, 1933).

7632 **Cowell, Edward J. "Eddie."** Newscaster (WJHL, Johnson City, TN, 1942; 1945, WJHL) DJ (*Breakfast Club*, WJHL, 1952; WETB, Johnson City, TN, 1954). Sportscaster (WJHL, 1941; WJHL, 1945; *Speaking of Sports*, WJHL, 1947–1951).

7633 **Cowgill, Helen.** Lecturer (*What Oregon Girls Will Do This Summer*, KOAC, Corvallis, OR, 1926).

7634 **Cowie's Juvenile Bag Pipe Band.** Unique young peoples' band (KFI, Los Angeles, CA, 1926).

7635 **Cowl, Jane.** Talented actress Cowl appeared in several Shakespearian plays that were broadcast in the 1920s. *Romeo and Juliet*, for example, was broadcast from the Henry Miller Theater (WEAF, New York, NY).

7636 **Cowles, A.L.** Announcer (WGBC, Memphis, TN, 1925).

7637 **Cowles, Ethelyn.** Soprano (*Ethelyn Cowles*, vcl. mus. prg., WCAO, Baltimore, MD, 1935).

7638 **Cowley, Bee.** COM-HE (WIEL, Elizabethtown, KY, 1957).

7639 **Cowley, Paul.** DJ (*Cowley's Alley*, WNOP, Newport, KY, 1948; WKLO, Louisville, KY, 1955–1956).

7640 **Cowly, Sam.** Baritone (WOR, Newark, NJ, 1924).

7641 **Cox, Bill.** Country music performer Cox sang and played the guitar and harmonica (WOBU , Charleston, WV, 1928).

7642 **Cox, Bill.** DJ (WLOS, Baton Rouge, LA, 1956).

7643 **Cox, Billy.** Leader (Billy Cox and his Packard 8 Orchestra, KFI, Los Angeles, CA, 1927).

7644 **Cox, Bob.** Newscaster (WJHL, Johnson City, TN, 1942).

7645 **Cox, Dorothy.** COM-HE (KRRV, Sherman, TX, 1955).

7646 **Cox, Ed.** Newscaster (WJNC, Jacksonville, NC, 1945–1946).

7647 **Cox, Harry Richard.** Tenor (*Harry Cox*, vcl. mus. prg., WIP, Philadelphia, PA, 1936).

7648 **Cox, Houston, Jr.** Newscaster (WCBI, Columbus, MS, 1940; WTJS, Jackson, TN, 1941; WCBI, 1944). Sportscaster (WCBI, 1941; WCBI, 1944).

7649 **Cox, James.** Newscaster (KCMO, Kansas City, MO, 1945).

7650 **Cox, (Father) James R.** Father Cox began to broadcast religious services from Old St. Patrick's Catholic Church, Pittsburgh, PA, in 1925 and continued broadcasting them into the 1940s (WJAS, Pittsburgh, PA, 1925).

7651 **Cox, Leslie D. "Les."** Newscaster (KVAK, Atchinson, KS, 1939, 1945).

7652 **Cox, Mildred.** Contralto (WOR, Newark, NJ, 1933).

7653 **Cox, R. Gratz.** Cox broadcast voice lessons (KFXF, Colorado Springs, CO, 1926).

7654 **Cox, Stan.** DJ (*Saddle Pals*, KONO, San Antonio, TX, 1949).

7655 **Cox, Warren R.** Announcer (WHK, Cleveland, OH, 1924).

7656 **Coy, Alice B.** Broadcast book reviews (WKRC, Cincinnati, OH, 1925).

7657 **Coy, Jim.** DJ (WOR, New York, NY, 1960).

7658 **Coykendall, Frank.** Coykendall spoke on topics of interest to Iowa farmers (KMA, Shenandoah, IA, 1928).

7659 **Coyle, Bert.** DJ (WHBO, Tampa, FL, 1954–1956).

7660 **Coyle, Matthew.** Leader (Coyle's Orchestra, WGI, 1923).

7661 **Coyne Electrical School Orchestra.** Training school band (WGES, Oak Park, IL, 1925).

7662 ***Coyotes Frolic from KHQ.*** This zany, late hour variety program attracted a large following among West Coast listeners (90 min., Weekly, 10:30–12:00 midnight, KHQ, Seattle, WA, 1927).

7663 **Cozad, Floyd V.** Sportscaster (WDYK, Cumberland, MD, 1951).

7664 **Cozad, Sammy "Sam."** Sportscaster (WTBO, Cumberland, MD, 1937–1939; WFMD, Frederick, MD, 1940).

7665 ***(The) Cozy Corner.*** Allen Franklin read poetry on his sustaining radio show (15 min., Tuesday, 10:30–10:45 A.M., WHN, New York, NY, 1937).

7666 **Cozzens, Jane.** Soprano (*Jane Cozzens*, vcl. mus. prg., NBC, 1941; WHIS, Bluefield, VA, 1942).

7667 **Cozzi, Mario.** Baritone (*Mario Cozzi*, vcl. mus. prg., NBC, 1934–1936).

7668 **Crabaugh, Marjorie "Marge.** COM-HE (KXRJ, Russellville, AR, 1956–1960).

7669 **Crabtree, Charles "Chic."** Sportscaster (KIFI, Idaho Falls, ID, 1940). Newscaster (*Farm News*, KIFI, 1947).

7670 ***(The) Cracraft Electonestra.*** Andre Monici conducted the first electronic orchestra on this sustaining program. The orchestra was organized by scenic designer Adrian Cracraft. Milton Cross was the announcer (30 min., Thursday, 10:30–11:00 P.M., NBC-Blue, 1939).

7671 **Craddock, Fred.** Leader (*Fred Craddock's Cornhuskers*, CW music group, WRVA, Richmond, VA, 1935).

7672 **Craft, A.B.** Newscaster (KVOL, Lafayette, LA, 1938–1940, 1945). Sportscaster (KVOL, 1940–1941).

7673 **Craft, Stan.** Newscaster (KXRO, Aberdeen, WA, 1946–1948). Sportscaster (KXRO, 1950–1951).

7674 **Crager, Leon W.** Sportscaster (WJHO, Opelika, AL, 1941).

7675 **Craeger, Mack.** Sportscaster (KRMG, Tulsa, OK, 1953).

7676 **Crago, Dick.** Sportscaster (WCBI, Columbus, MS, 1948–1952).

7677 **Crago, William.** Sportscaster (WMAL, Washington, DC and WRC, Washington, DC, 1938–1939).

7678 **Crahan, Mary Kaye.** COM-HE (KDTH, Dubuque, IA, 1955).

7679 **Craig, Ada W.** Soprano (WIP, Philadelphia, PA, 1926).

7680 **Craig, Archie.** Violinist (*Archie Craig*, instr. mus. prg. KGHI, Little Rock, AR, 1929).

7681 **Craig, Benny.** Sportscaster (*Passing Parade of Sports*, KARK, Little Rock, AR, 1940–1941; football play-by-play (KELD, El Dorado, AR, 1950; KARK, 1955; KTHS, Little Rock, AR, 1960).

7682 **Craig, Carval.** Leader (*Carval Craig Orchestra*, instr. mus. prg., WHAS, Louisville, KY, 1937).

7683 **Craig, Charles.** Newscaster (KFXM, San Berardino, CA, 1944; *Four Bells News Round-Up*, KODY, North Platte, NE, 1947).

7684 **Craig, Francis.** Leader of the popular Francis Craig Orchestra (WSM, Nashville, TN, 1926–1928). The band's musicians included, among others: Malcolm Crain and Clarence "Cool" Morrison, t. and tb.; Kenny Sargent, clr., as. and ss.; Newton Richards, clr. and ts.; Jess Jessup, p., bj., and tba.; and Powell Adams, d. In the next decades the band broadcast frequently (*Frances Craig Orchestra*, instr. mus. prg., WSM, Nashville, TN, 1935–1939; NBC-Red, 1936–1937; WGN, Chicago, IL, 1940). Craig became a DJ in 1947 (*Featured by Frances Craig*, WSM, Nashville, TN, 1947).

7685 **Craig, George B.** Newscaster (KOCA, Kilgore, TX, 1946). DJ (*Coffee with Craig* and *Varsity Drag*, KFDX, Wichita Falls, TX, 1948–1950, 1954; WSYD, Wichita Falls, TX, 1956).

7686 **Craig, Glenn.** DJ (*All Hillbilly Show*, KCLE, Cleburne, TX, 1947).

7687 **Craig, Hubert.** Guitarist (*Hubert Craig*, instr. mus. prg., KGHI, Little Rock, AR, 1929).

7688 **Craig, Julie.** COM-HE (WICS, Springfield, IL, 1954–1955).

7689 **Craig, Louise M.** COM-HE (WSFC, Somerset, KY, 1956–1957).

7690 **Craig, Mel.** Leader (Mel Craig and his Spanish Grillers Orchestra broadcasting from the Spanish Grill of Brooklyn's Leverich Tower Hotel, WLTH, Brooklyn, NY, 1928).

7691 **Craig, Nancy.** COM-HE (ABC, 1949).

7692 **Craig, Robert S.** Newscaster Craig broadcast a "digest of world news" (KFWM, Oakland, CA, 1927).

7693 **Craig, Virgie.** Newscaster (KUOA, Siloam Springs, AR, 1939).

7694 **Craig, W.** Concert soprano (WGHB, Clearwater Beach, FL, 1926).

7695 Craigan [Craigin], Eunice Hogan. Soprano (KFSG, Los Angeles, CA, 1925).

7696 Craik, Robert. Bass-baritone (WJY, New York, NY, 1925).

7697 Crain, Dick. Newscaster (WHHM, Memphis, TN, 1946).

7698 Crain, Marvin. DJ (*Almanac and Portfolio*, KNET, Palestine, TX, 1960).

7699 Crain, Paul. Sportscaster (KEX, Portland, OR, 1945; KNEW, Spokane, WA, 1947).

7700 Craker, P.J. Organist (KRFU, Columbia, MO, 1925).

7701 Cram, Bill. Announcer (WNAD, Norman, OK, 1925).

7702 Cram, Richard. Newscaster (WMAN, Mansfield, OH, 1945).

7703 Cram, Rosemary. COM-HE (*The Women's Hour*, WGY, Schenectady, NY, 1925).

7704 Cramb, Beryle. COM-HE (KLMR, Lamar, CO, 1957).

7705 Cramb, (Mrs.) William C. Announcer known as "Mrs. WJC" (WGY, Schenectady, NY, 1923).

7706 Cramer, Alma. COM-HE (WARD, Johnstown, PA, 1951–1960).

7707 Cramer, Carol. Newscaster (WIP, Philadelphia, PA, 1937).

7708 Cramer, Edward. Violinist (WFAA, Dallas, TX, 1926).

7709 Cramer, Elise. Mezzo-soprano (KGW, Portland, OR, 1924).

7710 Cramer, Ernest. Newscaster (WMSL, Decatur, AL, 1944).

7711 Cramer, Jeanette Putnam. Home economics editor of the Portland *Oregonian*, Cramer broadcast talks on home economics with "household helps" (KGW, Portland, OR, 1923–1926). She also contributed household hints on the *Town Crier* program (KGW, Portland, OR, 1927).

7712 Cramer, Marjorie. COM-HE (WJSW, Altoona, PA, 1951).

7713 Cramer, Ted. Newscaster (WKY, Oklahoma City, OK, 1944; KCRC, Enid, OK, 1945). DJ (*Time and Tune Parade*, WKY, 1947).

7714 Crandall, Mark. Newscaster (*The Pace of the World Today*, KFEL, Denver, CO, 1945–1948).

7715 Crandall, Paul. Newscaster (WDEF, Chattanooga, TN, 1941). DJ (*Breakfast Express*, WBLJ, Dalton, GA, 1947; *Yawn Patrol*, WROM, Rome, GA, 1950).

7716 Crandall, Ruth Hall. Contralto (KTAB, Oakland, CA, 1926).

7717 Crandall, Violet. Organist (WIP, Philadelphia, PA, 1925).

7718 Crandall's Orchestra. Popular District of Columbia band (WRC, Washington, DC, 1925).

7719 Crane, Bob. DJ (*The Town Crier*, WICC, Bridgeport, CT, 1952–1955).

7720 Crane, Carolyn. COM-HE (KRMO, Monett, MO, 1957).

7721 Crane, Claire Forbes. Concert pianist (KHJ, Los Angeles, CA, 1924–1925).

7722 Crane, Dick. Newscaster (KBTM, Jonesboro, AR, 1937).

7723 Crane, Elise Banta [Banata]. Contralto (KGO, Oakland, CA, 1924; KTAB, Oakland, CA, 1926).

7724 Crane, Martha. Miss Crane conducted the women's *Homemakers' Hour* with Lois Schenck for a time before taking on the job alone (WLS, Chicgo, IL, 1928–1934). She held the position until 1934, when she and Helen Joyce initiated a similar program, *Feature Foods*.

7725 Crane, Miriam. Soprano (WHN, New York, NY, 1925).

7726 Crane, Philip. Baritone (*Philip Crane*, vcl. mus. prg., CBS, 1936).

7727 Crane, Ruth (Ruth Franklin). COM-HE (WJR, Detroit, MI, 1929; WMAL, Washington, DC, 1940s). Crane began her 26-year broadcasting career as a commercial writer at WJR, Detroit, Michigan, before becoming both women's and commercial editor. She had graduated from Northwestern University's School of Journalism and previously worked in advertising at the Hart Publishing Company. She became "Mrs. Page" to conduct WJR's *Mrs. Page's Home Economies* program. Crane went to WMAL, Washington, DC, in the 1940s, where she was the director of women's activities and hostess of the daily *Modern Woman* program. The program went on television in 1947 with Crane writing its skits, modeling fashions and conducting the program.

7728 Craney, E.R. [B]. Announcer (KFPY, Spokane, WA, 1926).

7729 Crans, Christine. Actress Crans appeared on the *Pa and Ma Smithers* program (KFBI, Medford, KS, 1931; WLS, Chicago, IL, 1935).

7730 Crans, Hazel P. COM-HE (WVMI, Biloxi, MS, 1956).

7731 Crans, Richard. Sportscaster (WGNY, Newburgh, NY, 1940). Newscaster (WGNY, 1941).

7732 Crary, Clarence. Announcer (KFON, Long Beach, CA, 1928).

7733 Crary, Guy and Mrs. Guy Crary. Piano duets (WEMC, Berrien Springs, MI, 1927).

7734 Craven, Carl. Tenor (WLS, Chicago, IL, 1925).

7735 Craven, Carol. Leader of Carol Craven's Ladies Chorus (WLS, Chicago, IL, 1936).

7736 Craven, Harold. Newscaster (WMFR, High Point, NC, 1945–1946). DJ (*Off the Record*, WMFR, 1947; WHPE, High Point, NC, 1948–1950).

7737 Craven, Helen Marie. COM-HE (WGBG, Greensboro, NC, 1957).

7738 Craven, Opal. Soprano (*Opal Craven*, vcl. mus. prg., WBBM, Chicago, IL, 1936).

7739 Cravens, Kathryn (Kathryn Cochran). News analyst (*News Through a Woman's Eyes*, CBS, 1937–1941; *Kathryn Cravens Broadcasts the News*, WNEW, 1942–1944; MBS, 1945). Cravens was said to be radio's first sponsored woman commentator on a nation wide network. She worked briefly for Fox Films in Hollywood in 1919 and in stock companies for the next five years. She was a radio actress at KWK (St. Louis, MO) in 1928. She became director of the station's *Women's Hour* in 1931. Cravens became the first coast-to-coast news commentator in 1936 for CBS. She inaugurated her *News Through a Woman's Eyes* sponsored by Pontiac the following year. Her syndicated newspaper column was begun in 1938. She moved her quarter-hour news program to WNEW (New York) in the 1940s, later worked on WOL (Washington, DC) and as foreign correspondent for WOR (New York, NY) during World War II, when she sent shortwave news reports back for her *Europe Through a Woman's Eyes* program.

7740 Crawford, Alexander. Organist (WJZ, New York, NY, 1925).

7741 Crawford, Blackie. DJ (*Radio Ranch Party*, KPEP, San Angelo, TX, 1960).

7742 Crawford, Bob. Newscaster (WTOC, Savannah, GA, 1939).

7743 Crawford, Boyd. Actor Crawford appeared on the *Amanda of Honeymoon Hill* and *Joyce Jorday, Girl Interne* daytime serial programs.

7744 Crawford, Carolyn. Contralto (*Carolyn Crawford*, vcl. mus. prg., WCFL, Chicago, IL, 1935).

7745 Crawford, Estelle. COM-HE (KSET, El Paso, TX, 1951).

7746 Crawford, Eugene "Bob." Newscaster (WEBQ, Harrisburg, PA, 1940–1941). Sportscaster (WEBQ, 1940–1941).

7747 Crawford, George. DJ (*District Matinee*, WOL, Washington, DC, 1949–1952).

7748 Crawford, Georgia A. COM-HE (KCNI, Broken Bow, NE, 1957).

7749 Crawford, Helen. Pianist (KGO, San Francisco, CA, 1926).

7750 Crawford, Jack (Foster). Saxophonist-Leader (Jack Crawford's Orchestra, WBBM, 1926; Alemite Orchestra, WBBM, 1926). Crawford's radio and recording band of this period included: Crawford, ldr-clr., as. and ss.; Joe Snyder, clr., as. and ss.; Carroll Willis, clr. and ts; Harry Sosnik, p.; Earl Center, tba.; Joe Bucher, bj.; Paul McKnight, d.; and Lewis James, vcls. The Crawford band continued to broadcast in the following decade (*Jack Crawford Orchestra*, mus. prg., KMPC, Beverly Hills, CA, 1931; CBS, 1937–1938; KOA, Denver, CO, 1939).

7751 Crawford, Jesse. Organist Crawford was called the "The Poet of the Organ" (WABC-CBS, New York, NY, 1929). He had a long, distinguished radio career that continued into the 1930s and 1940s (*Jesse Crawford*, instr. mus. program, NBC, 1934–1936). Among the many programs for which he provided music was *Valiant Lady*.

7752 Crawford, (Mrs.) Jesse. Organist, wife of Jesse Crawford (CBS, New York, NY, 1929).

7753 Crawford, John. DJ (*Musical Jamboree*, KRXK, Rexburg, ID, 1954; KTFS, Texarkana, TX, 1956).

7754 Crawford, Mildred C. COM-HE (WCDT, Winchester, TN, 1956).

7755 Crawford, Rice. DJ (*Tops in Hillbilly*, WAPX, Montgomery, AL, 1949).

7756 Crawford, Robert P. DJ (*Western

Request Hour, KNAK, Salt Lake City, UT, 1948). Sportscaster (*Early Edition*, KNAK, 1949).

7757 **Crawford, Ruth.** Pianist (WLW, Cincinnati, OH, 1925).

7758 **Crawford, Sam.** Newscaster (KGY, Olympia, WA, 1932–1942; *News and Views*, KGY, 1949). Crawford began broadcasting the news on KGY in 1932 and continued for more than 16 years. One of his earliest shows at KGY was *The Voice of the News*.

7759 **Crawford, Vern.** Sportscaster (*Fish 'N' Tackle*, WJNO, West Palm Beach, FL, 1951).

7760 **Crawford, Vernon.** Newscaster (KTAR, Phoenix, AZ), 1938).

7761 ***Crazy Capers.*** Crazy Water Crystals [laxative] and Folger's Coffee sponsored the popular country-western music show that featured Ray Whitley (WMCA, New York, NY, 1933–1934).

7762 ***(The) Crazy Mountaineers.*** The transcribed CW music program was one of the many sponsored by Crazy Water Crystals laxatives (WPTF, Raleigh, NC, 1939).

7763 ***Crazy Water Hotel.*** The country-western music program was also sponsored by Crazy Water Crystals and loaded with hard sell commercials for that laxative product (Transcribed, WHB, Kansas City, MO, 1936).

7764 **Creade, Donna.** Actress Creade was a cast member of the daytime serial program *Backstage Wife* aka *Mary Noble, Backstage Wife*.

7765 **Creager, Mack.** Sportscaster (*Sports Parade* and football, hockey and wrestling play-by-play, KAKC, Tulsa, OK, 1947–1950; KRMG, Tulsa, OK, 1952–1960).

7766 **Creagh, Ed.** Newscaster (WHDL, Olean, NY, 1941).

7767 **Creamer, James Arthur "Art."** Newscaster (WAGF, Dothan, AL, 1940; WGOV, Valdosta, GA, 1941–1941). Sportscaster (WAGF, 1948–1950).

7768 **Creamer, Professor W. J.** Announcer (WABI, Bangor, ME, 1927).

7769 **Creasman, James "Jimmy."** Newscaster (KTAR, Phoenix, AZ, 1939–1941). Sportscaster (KTAR, 1940).

7770 **Creasy, Alma.** Violinist (WLWL, New York, NY, 1936).

7771 ***Creasy's Hawaiians Orchestra.*** Instr. mus. program (WDBJ, Roanoke, VA, 1936).

7772 **Creatore.** Leader (Creatore's Band, WFAA, Dallas, TX, 1922; Metropolitan Theatre Orchestra, KFI, Los Angeles, CA, 1925).

7773 **Creekmore, Bruce.** DJ (WETC, Wendell-Zebulon, NC, 1960).

7774 **Creemer's Old Fiddlers.** CW string band directed by W.B. Nichols (WFAA, Dallas, TX, 1925).

7775 ***Creeps by Night.*** Boris Karloff frequently appeared on the series that dramatized human anxiety and fear. The opening announcement began: "We bring you *Creeps by Night*. The Blue Network presents a series of dramatic exploitations into the vast and unknown documents of the tortured human mind. Tonight, *Creeps by Night* presents your host, the master of mystery, Dr. X." The show was transcribed (15 min., Weekly, NBC-Blue, 1944).

7776 **Creese, Irving.** Pianist (WEAF, New York, NY, 1926).

7777 **Creig, Virgil E.** Newscaster (KIUL, Garden City, KS, 1940).

7778 **Creighton, Harry.** Sportscaster (WAAF, Chicago, IL, 1937–1940; WGN, Chicago, IL, 1951).

7779 **Creighton, Sally.** Actress Creighton appeared on the *Those We Love* daytime serial program.

7780 **Cremeens, George.** Newscaster (WISN, Milwaukee, WI, 1941; KXEL, Waterloo, IA, 1945).

7781 ***Cremo Presents Bing Crosby.*** Cremo cigars was the sponsor of Crosby's first network show (15 min., Monday through Saturday, 7:15–7:30 P.M., CBS, 1931). *See* ***The Kraft Music Hall*** *and* **Singers: Crooners, Canaries, Cow Girls and Hillbillies.**

7782 **Creone, Phyllis.** Actress Creone was a cast member of the *Hollywood Dreams* daytime serial.

7783 **(The) Crescent Graham Cracker.** A tenor, not otherwise identified, sang regularly on the Friday afternoon *Crescent Hour of Music* program (WOC, Davenport, IA, 1928).

7784 **Crescent Male Quartet.** Metropolitan vocal group (WMCA, New York, NY, 1925).

7785 **Cresent Orchestra.** Music group directed by Bernie Schultz (WOC, Davrenport, IA, 1925).

7786 **Crewe, Dorothy.** Singer (KFH, Wichita, KS, 1926).

7787 **Crews, Bill.** Sportscaster (WTAD, Quincy, IL, 1953).

7788 **Crews, Laura Hope.** Actress interviewed by **Teresa Rose Nagel** (WGBS, New York, NY, 1925).

7789 ***Crime and Peter Chambers.*** Dane Clark starred on the slow moving transcribed crime drama. Peter Chambers, played by Clark, was a private investigator, who frequently became embroiled in various adventures when asked for help by some beautiful female client. Chambers was frequently assisted by Lt. Louie Parker, "a straight cop and a good friend." Elaine Rost and Leon Janney were also in the cast. The date of the program's last broadcast was September 7, 1954 (30 min., Weekly, NBC, 1954).

7790 ***Crime Classics.*** The sustaining summer replacement for *Suspense* was written by Morton Fine and David Friedkin. Lou Merrill, playing the role of a "connoisseur of crime," narrated these true crime story dramatizations. The cast members included: Herb Butterfield, Mary Jane Croft, Sam Edwards, Georgia Ellis, Bill Johnstone, Tudor Owen and Ben Wright. Elliott Lewis produced and directed. The program opened with the announcement: "*Crime Classics*, a new series of transcribed crime stories from the records and newspapers of every land — from every time. Your host each week is Thomas Hyland, connoisseur of crime, student of violence and teller of murders." Hyland then said: "Good Evening. This is *Crime Classics*. I am Thomas Hyland with another true story of crime. Listen." Music was provided by Bernard Hermann. Bob Lemond was the announcer (30 min., Monday, 8:00–8:30 P.M., CBS, 1953–1954).

7791 ***Crime Doctor.*** Psychiatrist Dr. Benjamin Ordway solved many difficult cases on the dramatic crime series. Ordway was an amnesiac who became a psychiatrist and criminologist. He eventually learned that he previously — unknown to him — had been a criminal gang leader. Ordway overcame his problems, made suitable amends and went ahead to combat crime. John McIntire created the title role in the original 1940 version. In the several versions broadcast later, Ordway was played by Ray Collins, House Jameson, Hugh Marlowe and Everett Sloane. Other cast members included Edith Arnold, Edgar Stehli, Walter Vaughn and Walter Graeza. Max Marcin was the program's writer and Paul Monroe the director (CBS, 1940–1947).

7792 ***Crime Does Not Pay.*** Ira Marion wrote and Max Loeb directed the fast-paced transcribed dramatic program. Donald Buka was the featured actor. After running for several years as a local program (WMGM , New York, NY), it ran on MBS during the 1952 season. The cast included Joseph Wiseman, Richard Hart, Margo, Frank Albertson, Horace McMahon, John Loder, Charles Corbin, Donald Curtis, Mary Wickes, Ward Wilson, Ralph Forbes, Ian Keith, Philip Reed, Diana Barrymore, John Sheridan, Ralph Meeker, Una O'Connor and Robert Lowery (30 min., Monday, 7:30–8:00 P.M., WMGM, New York, NY, 1950; MBS, 1952).

7793 ***(The) Crime Files of Flamond.*** The program ran for five years on WGN (Chicago, IL) with Myron (Mike) Wallace as Flamond and Patricia Dunlap as Sandra, his assistant in criminal investigation. Flamond's voluminous files of the crimes he had solved supposedly served as the basis for these programs. Flamond was introduced as the "most unusual detective in history — "a famous psychoanalyst and personality analyst." When the program returned to the air as a network show, the title role of private investigator Flamond was played by Everett Clarke. In the cast with him were: Muriel Bremmer, Maurice Copeland, Harry Elders and Ben Younger. Bob Cunningham was the announcer. George Anderson wrote, W.B. Lewis produced and Myron Golden directed the program (30 min., Wednesday, 8:00–8:30 p.m, MBS, 1953).

7794 ***(A) Crime Letter from Dan Dodge.*** Myron McCormick played the title role on the crime drama that used flashbacks to tell the story. Toni Home Permanents sponsored the show on which private investigator Dan Dodge always began by dictating a letter describing one of his recent cases to his secretary, who was played by Shirley Eggleston. Harold Swanton wrote the program that was directed by Charles Irving and Donald Painter (30 min., Friday, 8:00–8:30 P.M., ABC, 1952).

7795 ***(The) Crimson Trail.*** CW mus. prg. (KGNF, North Platte, NE, 1939).

7796 **Crisler, Fritz.** Fritz Crisler, the famous University of Michigan football coach, broadcast football news and talked about sports (NBC, 1935).

7797 **Criss, Verna.** COM-HE (WEEU, Reading, PA, 1951).

7798 **Crist, Phil.** DJ (*Morning in Maryland*, WFBR, Baltimore, MD, 1948–1950). Crist was a tenor, who previously had his own vocal music program (WJSV, Washington, DC, 1933).

7799 ***Critic at Large.*** Critic Leon Pearson discussed books and the theater (15 min., weekly, NBC, 1951).

7800 **Croatian Tamburica Orchestra.** Ethnic musical group (WSOE, Milwaukee, WI, 1926).

7801 **Crocker, Betty.** "Betty Crocker" was one of the most famous fictional personages who broadcast homemaking information. When she first went on the air, "Betty Crocker" was played by five different actresses. After the program became a network feature, she was portrayed by one woman speaking from station WCCO (Mineapolis-St. Paul, MN). On the network she appeared on the *National Home Hour* sponsored by General Mills (NBC-Red, New York, NY.)

7802 **Crocker, Harold.** Leader (Harold Crocker's Gator Orchestra, WGHB, Clearwater, FL, 1926).

7803 **Crocker, Jerry.** DJ (*Crocker's Clambake*, WISR, Butler, PA, 1948).

7804 **Crocker, Sid.** DJ (*Sad Sack*, KLFY, Lafayette, LA, 1952).

7805 **Crockett, Charlie.** DJ (*The Charlie Crockett Show*, 150 min., Monday through Friday, 7:30–10:00 P.M., KIKI, Honolulu, HI, 1953).

7806 **Crockett, David.** Newscaster (KBST, Big Springs, TX, 1945).

7807 **Crockett, Hudley.** Sportscaster (WSIX, Nashville, TN, 1956–1960).

7808 **Crockett, John H. "Dad."** *See* **(The) Crockett Family.**

7809 **Crockett, Owen.** Leader (Owen Crockett's Texans Supreme Orchestra, WBAP, San Antonio, TX, 1929).

7810 **(The) Crockett Family.** John H. "Dad" Crockett and his five sons, said to be descendants of Davie Crockett, played country music on several California radio stations (KNJ; KMJ, Fresno, CA; and KHJ, Los Angeles, CA, from 1925 to 1929. The family's program was known as the *Crockett Mountaineers*. *See* ***The Crockett Mountaineers.***

7811 ***(The) Crockett Mountaineers (aka Crockett's Kentucky Mountaineers*** **and** ***Crockett Family).*** On this CW music prg., the music was produced by a father and his five sons said to be descendents of Davie Crockett (15 min., Monday through Saturday, 6:15–6:30 P.M., CBS, 1930). The group remained on CBS for several years. *See* **The Crockett Family.**

7812 **Crococo, Katherine DeWitt.** Soprano (WJY, New York, NY, 1925).

7813 **Croes, Ken.** Newscaster (KERO, Bakersfield, CA, 1946).

7814 **Croft, Beulah.** Singer (*Beulah Croft*, vcl. mus. prg., NBC, 1934–1935).

7815 **Croft, Mary Jane.** Actress Croft appeared on the situation comedy programs *The Adventures of Ozzie and Harriet* and *Blondie*.

7816 **Croft, Vera.** COM-HE (KENA, Mena, AR, 1960).

7817 **Crogan, Joe.** Sportscaster (*Sports Special*, WANN, Annapolis, MD, 1947; WBAL, Baltimore, MD, 1949–1960).

7818 **Crohan, John F.** DJ (*Hospitality House*, WICE, Providence, RI, 1954).

7819 **Croker, W.J.** Newscaster (KDEC, Decorah, IA, 1947–1948).

7820 **Crombie, Dick.** Newscaster (KJR, Seattle, WA, 1946). DJ (*Dance Time*, KJR, 1952).

7821 **Cromer, Morris.** Baritone (WBAL, Baltimore, MD, 1926).

7822 **Cromer, Sturgeon.** Sportscaster (KWJB, Globe, AZ, 1941).

7823 **Cromwell, Chauncey.** Leader (*Chauncey Cromwell Orchestra*, instr. mus. prg., WHAM, Rochester, NY, 1937–1938).

7824 **Cromwell, Chuck.** DJ (*Musicman*, KERG, Eugene, OR, 1960).

7825 **Cromwell, Dean.** Sportscaster (*Game Room*, KNBH, Hollywood, CA, 1948).

7826 **Cromwell, Richard.** Actor Cromwell appeared on the *Those We Love* daytime serial program.

7827 **Cromwell, Rex.** Newscaster (KAND, Corsicana, TX, 1946).

7828 **Cronan, Carey.** Newscaster (WELI, New Haven, CT, 1940–1941; WNHC, New Haven, CT, 1946).

7829 **Crone, Herman "Herm."** Leader (*Herm Crone Orchestra*, instr. mus. prg., NBC, 1935; WFIL, Philadelphia, PA, 1936).

7830 **Cronican, Lee.** Newscaster (WHP, Harrisburg, PA, 1941–1942, 1945–1948).

7831 **Cronin, Dan.** Newscaster (WROV, Roanoke, VA, 1946).

7832 **Cronin, Francis J.** Organist (*Francis Cronin*, instr. mus. prg., WNAC, Boston, MA, 1934–1935).

7833 **Cronin, George.** Newscaster (WKBV, Richmond, IN, 1945).

7834 **Cronin, James F.** Announcer Cronin proclaimed his station's slogan, "For God and Country" (WLWL, New York, NY, 1926).

7835 **Cronin, Marion.** COM-HE (KFJI, Klamath Falls, OR, 1951).

7836 **Cronk, George.** Leader (George Cronk's California Ramblers Orchestra, KFWB, Hollywood, CA, 1925).

7837 **Cronk [Cronck], Gladys.** Singer accompanied by pianist Paul Nelson (KFOB, Burlingame, CA, 1925–1926).

7838 **Cronkhite, Madeline [Marguerite].** Singer (WLBZ, Buffalo, NY, 1936).

7839 **Cronkite, Walter Leland, Jr.** Newscaster (KCMO, Kansas City, MO and WKY, Oklahoma City, OK, 1937). Sportscaster (KCMO and WKY, 1937). Cronkite went on to become one of television's most respected newsman.

7840 **Cronshaw, Jack.** Leader (Jack Cronshaw's Orchestra, instr. mus. prg., KMTR, Hollywood, CA, 1926–1927).

7841 **Cronyn, Hume.** Motion picture actor Cronyn appeared on *The Marriage* program.

7842 **Crook Brothers Barn Dance Orchestra.** CW instrumental group (WSM, Nashville, TN, 1928). The CW music group enjoyed great popularity on the *Crook Brothers* show (CW mus. prg., WSM, Nashville, TN, 1937) and from their appearances on the *Grand Ole Opry*.

7843 **Crook, Marian.** COM-HE (KOWH, Omaha, NE, 1951).

7844 **Crooks, Helen.** COM-HE (WOOK, Meridian, MS, 1960).

7845 **Crooks, Richard.** Distinguished tenor Crooks appeared on the *Maxwell House Coffee Hour* (NBC, New York, NY, 1927).

7846 **Crooks, William.** Newscaster (WFMJ, Youngstown, OH, 1945–1947).

7847 ***(The) Crooner.*** Vcl. mus. prg. by an unidentified vocalist (WHB, Atlanta, GA, 1939).

7848 ***(The) Crooning Guitarist.*** Vcl. mus. prg. by an unidentified crooning instrumentalist (WFBE, Cincinnati, OH, 1933).

7849 **Crosbie, Cameron.** Organist (*Cameron Crosbie*, instr. mus. prg., KFAC, Los Angeles, CA, 1931).

7850 **Crosby, Bing.** Crooner (*Bing Crosby*, vcl. mus. prg., 15 min., Tuesday, Thursday and Saturday, 6:30–6:45 P.M., CBS, 1932; *Bing Crosby*, vcl. mus. program, 30 min., Monday, 8:30–9:00 P.M., CBS, 1933–1934). The latter show also featured the Boswell Sisters and was sponsored by Woodbury facial soap. One *Billboard* review praised Woodbury for selecting Crosby, since "he is in the midst of a brilliant career." Crosby went on from this beginning to fashion a great radio career with such programs as the *Kraft Music Hall* and *Bing Crosby Philco Time*. He concluded his radio career with *The Bing Crosby Show* (15 min., Monday through Friday, 9:15–9:30 P.M., CBS, 1954). Bing sang and bantered with announcer Ken Carpenter on his transcribed program. Music was supplied by the Buddy Cole Trio. *See* ***Cremo Presents Bing Crosby, Bing Crosby Philco Time,*** *and* ***Kraft Music Hall.***

7851 **Crosby, Bob.** Leader (*Bob Crosby Orchestra*, instr. mus. prg., NBC, 1935 and CBS, 1935–1939; WGN, Chicago, IL, 1939–1942). Bing's younger brother Bob later joined the large number of musical stars and celebrities who became DJs late in their careers (60 min., Saturday, 9:00–10:00 P.M., ABC, 1950).

7852 **Crosby, Charles.** Sportscaster (WNHC, New Haven, CT, 1945).

7853 **Crosby, Chuck.** Sportscaster (*Sports Scrapbook*, WCOP, Boston, MA, 1947–1948).

7854 **Crosby, Ernest.** Tenor (KOIN, Council Bluffs, IA, 1928).

7855 **Crosby, Lee.** DJ (KTIM, San Raphael, CA, 1956).

7856 **Crosby, Louise.** Pianist (KLDS, Independence, MO, 1927).

7857 **Crosby, Phoebe.** Operatic concert singer appeared on the *Roxy and His Gang* was also a guest on the *Something for Everyone* program.

7858 **Crosby, W.F.** Violinist (KFOB, Burlingame, CA, 1926).

7859 **Crosiar, Frank.** Sportscaster (WHOT, South Bend, IN, 1944–1946; *Spots in*

Sports, WHOT, 1947–1951; WNDU, South Bend, IN, 1956; WJVA, South Bend, IN, 1960).

7860 Crosland, Dan. Newscaster (WFBC, Greenville, SC, 1937–1939; *News of the World*, WMRC, Greenville, SC, 1940).

7861 *Crosley Arabian Nights.* The music program featured the Lange-McKay Orchestra (WLW, Cincinnati, OH, 1924).

7862 *Crosley Burnt Corkers.* Elmer Hinkle and G.W. Ross as end men Hink and Dink were featured on the radio minstrel show (WLW, Cincinnati, OH, 1926).

7863 Crosley, E. Powel, Jr. Crosley built a radio receiver for $35 in 1921, when sets had previously sold for $130 and higher. He then decided to manufacture these moderately priced radios on a mass production basis. When he became the owner, announcer and operator of station WLW, he personally broadcast the opening day baseball game between the Cincinnati Reds and the Chicago Cubs on Monday, April 12, 1926 (WLW, Cincinnati, OH, 1926).

7864 Crosley Ensemble. Instrumental group directed by Emil Heermann, (WLW, Cincinnati, OH, 1928).

7865 *Crosley Follies.* Soprano Edith Karen, tenor Adrien O'Brien and a 30-voice choir were featured on the entertaining variety show (30 min., Tuesday, 9:00–9:30 P.M., WLW, Cincinnati, OH, 1936).

7866 Crosley Moscow Art Orchestra. Directed by Arna Arriga, this orchestra played both classical and modern standard selections. *Variety* called it "one of the class instrumental groups on the air" (WLW, Cincinnati, OH, 1927; NBC-Red, 1928).

7867 *Crosley Saturday Knights.* The *Crosley Saturday Knights* was one of Cincinnati's most interesting variety programs (60 min., Saturday, 8:30–9:30 P.M., WLW, Cincinnati, OH, 1930).

7868 Crosley's Cossacks Orchestra. Station orchestra (WLW, Cincinnati, OH, 1928).

7869 *Crosley's Woman's Hour.* Edna Silverton conducted the show targeted for women (WLS, Cincinnati, OH, 1928).

7870 Cross, Hugh. CW singer and leader (*Hugh Cross and the Radio Pals*, CW mus. prg., WWVA, Wheeling, WV, 1938).

7871 Cross, Hugh and Shug Fisher. CW singing team (*Hugh Cross and Shug Fisher*, CW vcl. mus. prg., WWVA, Wheeling, WV, 1935–1937).

7872 Cross, (Dr.) Lawrence L. A minister, whose *Cross-Cuts From the Log of the Day* program attracted a large Pacific Coast audience, Cross was praised as "the preacher who doesn't preach" (Various Pacific Coast radio stations, 1923–1930).

7873 Cross, Maury. Leader (*Maury Cross Orchestra*, instr. mus. prg., WTAM, Cleveland, OH, 1936).

7874 Cross, Milton J. Tenor and announcer (WJZ, New York, NY and WJY, New York, NY, 1925–1930). Cross was known as "AJN" on both WJZ and WJY in radio's early days. He also was a tenor on the *Champion Sparklers* program sponsored by Champion Spark Plugs (WJZ, New York, NY, 1927). Cross, who played the Ampico organ, frequently sang the song his listeners requested of him most, "Little Mother of Mine." In 1929, Cross announced such NBC network programs as *The Jeddo Highlanders, The Roxy Symphony Concert, Old Man Sunshine, The Cathedral Hour, The Sylvania Foresters, Philco Theatre Memories, Salon Singers* and *The Old Company Singalongue.*

When he first began his radio career, Cross was a talented singer. He had completed the Music Supervisor's course at the Damrosch Institute of Musical Art and toured for several seasons with the Paulist Choristers, covering the entire eastern United States. After touring, Cross worked extensively on church and concert work. He was a soloist at the First Presbyterian Church and a member of the Brooklyn Progressive Synagogue's quartet. His first radio appearance as a vocal soloist was on September 15, 1921.

After joining WJZ on March 13, 1922, as "second announcer," Cross divided his time between singing and announcing before deciding to devote his entire time to announcing. Cross was particularly famous for the announcing and narration duties he performed for many years onTexaco's *Metropolitan Opera* broadcasts. After the Metropolitan Opera season was over in 1949, Cross acted as DJ and opera recording critic-teacher on his *Milton Cross Opera Album* program. *See* ***The Milton Cross Opera Album*** *and* **Opera on Radio**.

7875 Cross, Monte. Sportscaster (*Radio Broadcast Dope*, WIP, Philadelphia, PA, 1923).

7876 Cross, Phillip S. Sportscaster (*Cross Kickoff*, KDKA, Pittsburgh, PA, 1950).

7877 Cross, Red (Fred Crowther). Sportscaster, WSB, Atlanta, GA, 1930; WMAZ, Macon, GA, 1942; WMAZ, 1946–1948). In his early days at WSB, Cross broadcast many prep football games play-by-play.

7878 Crossland, Marjorie. Acress Crossland was a cast member of the *Myrt and Marge* daytime serial program.

7879 Crossley, Alice M. Coloratura soprano (WIP, Philadelphia, PA, 1926).

7880 Crossman, (Mrs.) Edward C. Contralto (KFI, Los Angeles, CA, 1927).

7881 Crossman, Estelle. Pianist (WTIC, Hartford, CT, 1926).

7882 *Crossroads of the Nation.* Don Kelley interviewed passengers coming and going at the Omaha airport on the somewhat immodestly titled program (KOIL, Omaha, NE, 1937).

7883 *Crossroads Store.* Campbell Cereal Company, makers of Campbell Corn Flakes and Malt-O-Meal cereals, sponsored the daytime serial that told about the "average" day-to-day events that took place in a small village store (15 min., Monday, Wednesday and Friday, KGBX, Springfield, MO, 1942).

7884 *(The) Crossroads Troubadour.* Elwyn Cross was the Troubadour, whose theme was "You Can't Take Dixie from Me." The transcribed vocal music program was sponsored by Chooz for acid indigestion and Four-Way Cold Tablets (15 min., Transcribed, Various Stations, 1940).

7885 *Crossword Quiz.* Alan Prescott and Les Griffith conducted this ingenious sustaining radio version of a crossword puzzle (30 min., Sunday, 5:00–5:30 P.M., NBC, 1947).

7886 Crouch, Al. DJ (*Coffee Time*, WJBO, Baton Rouge, LA, 1954).

7887 Crouchet, George. Newscaster (KPAC, Port Arthur, TX, 1945).

7888 Crow, Clarence. Whistler (KSD, St. Louis, MO, 1924).

7889 Crow, Jimmie. Leader (Jimmie Crow's Orchestra, WFAA, Dallas, TX, 1927).

7890 Crow, Leslie. Newscaster (KTMV, East St. Louis, MO, 1939).

7891 Crowder, Constance "Connie." Busy radio actress Crowder appeared on such daytime serial programs as *The Woman in White, Ma Perkins, Right to Happiness* and *Mary Marlin* aka *The Story of Mary Marlin.*

7892 Crowder, Ralph. Announcer (KOA, Denver, CO, 1925).

7893 Crowe, Elmer. Leader (*Elmer Crowe's Boys*, CW mus. prg., WWVA, Wheeling, WV, 1938).

7894 Crowe, Hilton. Newscaster (WALT, Tampa, FL, 1947–1948). Sportscaster (WALT, 1948).

7895 Crowe, John. Sportscaster (*The Old Angler*, WJAC, Johnstown, PA, 1956). Crowe hosted this informative program for fishermen.

7896 Crowe, Wanda. COM-HE (WMMH, Marshall, NC, 1957).

7897 Crowell, Dorothy. Violinist (KGO, San Francisco, CA, 1926).

7898 Crowell, George. Newscaster (WORL, Boston, MA, 1938).

7899 Crowl, Lester. Announcer (WSCO, Springfield, OH, 1927).

7900 Crowle, George. Newscaster (KROW, Oakland, CA, 1946).

7901 Crowley, Dick. Newscaster (WIBA, Madison, WI, 1945; WSAM, Sagninaw, MI, 1946). DJ (*1–2–3 Club*, WCLO, Janesville, WI, 1948; WSAM, Saginaw, MI, 1954; WAMM , Flint, MI, 1956).

7902 Crowley, Lois. COM-HE (WAGG, Franklin, TN, 1958).

7903 Crowley, Matt. Talented actor Crowley appeared on *Buck Rogers in the 25th Century* (title role), *Dick Tracy* (title role), *John's Other Wife, Mark Trail* (title role), *Myrt and Marge, Perry Mason, Pretty Kitty Kelly, Road of Life* and *Superman.*

7904 Crowley, Mort. DJ (KIMN, Denver, CO, 1957; WLS, Chicago, IL, 1960).

7905 Crowley, Paul C. Sportscaster (WJPD, Ishpeming, MI, 1953).

7906 Crowley, Virginia. Organist (WDBJ, Roanoke, VA, 1942).

7907 Crowson, Shirley. COM-HE (KTMC, McAlester, OK, 1960).

7908 Croxton, Charles. Program director and baritone (WBAL, Baltimore, MD, 1928).

7909 Croxton, Frank. Bass-baritone (CBS, 1928).

7910 Croxton, Olive. Soprano (WBAP, Fort Worth, TX, 1928).

7911 Cruger, George S. "Concert announcer" (WOO, Philadelphia, PA, 1923).

7912 Cruise [Crusise], Harriet. Singer Cruise was billed as "That shy little girl from Nebraska" (WBBM, Chicago, IL, mid–1930s). Earlier in Nebraska, she was called "The Oriole of the Air" (KFAB, Lincoln, NE, 1926–1929).

7913 Crum, Bill. Sportscaster (WCHS, Charleston, WV, 1944).

7914 Crum, Frank. Leader (*Frank Crum Orchestra*, instr. mus. prg., WOR, Newark, NJ, 1935).

7915 Crum, Glen. Leader (*Glen Crum's Musical Trio*, WISN, Milwaukee, WI, 1935).

7916 Crum, James "Jimmy." Sportscaster (WMAN, Mansfield, OH), 1945; WRFD, Worthington, OH, 1951; WLWC, Columbus, OH, 1955–1960).

7917 Crum, Jay. Newscaster (KOME, Tulsa, OK, 1938).

7918 Crumbaugh, Catherine. COM-HE (Crumbaugh broadcast home decoration hints on the *Duco Decorators* program (NBC-Pacific Network, 1929).

7919 Crumit, Frank. Tenor (WJZ, New York, NY, 1927; *Frank Crumit*, vcl. mus. prg., NBC, 1936) *See* **Crumit, Frank and Julia Sanderson.**

7920 Crumit, Frank and Julia Sanderson. Popular husband and wife singing team of vaudeville and radio whose "class" was first noted by *Variety* in 1925. The couple made their radio debut as a team in 1928. From 1929 to 1933, they starred on the *Blackstone Plantation* program on CBS. In the 1930s, they starred in several other programs such as *Frank Crumit and Julia Sanderson* (vcl. mus. prg. with Crumit, Sanderson, the Three Jesters and the Nat Shilkret Orchestra, 30 min., Sunday, 4:30–5:00 P.M., CBS, 1934–1935). Later, they worked on *The Battle of the Sexes* quiz (NBC, 1938), *The Crumit-Sanderson Quiz* (1942) and *The Singing Sweethearts* programs. After Crumit's death, Sanderson worked on the *Let's Be Charming* show (MBS, 1944–1945).

7921 Crump, George. Sportscaster (*Speaking of Sports*, WCRO, Johnstown, PA, 1947).

7922 Crumrine, Ruth. Singer (WLW, Cincinnati, OH, 1925).

7923 Crunte, Earl. Mandolin soloist (KDKA, Pittsburgh, PA, 1924).

7924 Crusaders Orchestra. Orchestra led by Frank Cornwell (WEAF, New York, NY, 1926).

7925 Crusinberry, Jane. Daytime serial writer whose major program was *The Story of Mary Marlin.*

7926 Crusise, Harriet. *See* **Harriet Cruise.**

7927 Crutcher, Marion B. Actress Crutcher was a cast member of the *Betty and Bob* daytime serial.

7928 Crutchfield, Charles H. Sportscaster (WBT, Charlotte, NC, 1937–1939).

7929 Crutchley, W.F. DJ (*Hillbilly Hit Parade* and *740 Club*, WPAQ, Mt. Airy, NC, 1948).

7930 Cruz, Marie. Pianist (WFAA, Dallas, TX, 1926).

7931 Crystal Palace Orchestra. New York club orchestra (WGBS, New York, NY and WNYC, New York, NY, 1926).

7932 Crystal Tea Room Orchestra. Philadelphia dance band directed by Robert E. Golden (WOO, Philadelphia, PA, 1923).

7933 Crystall, Martha Jane. COM-HE (KOLD, Tucson, AZ, 1960).

7934 C.T.S. and His Performing Elks. Fraternal [Elks Lodge] orchestra (WWJ, Detroit, MI, 1926).

7935 *(The) Cub Reporter.* Peter Dixon and Aline Berry starred in the situation comedy (15 min., 9:15–9:30 P.M., NBC-Blue, 1930).

7936 *(The) Cuban Biltmore Orchestra.* Instr. Mus. prg., WNAC, Boston, MA, 1932).

7937 Cubberly, Dan. Newscaster (KGY, Olympia, WA, 1938; KOY, Phoenix, AZ, 1940). Announcer: *Romance* and *Whispering Streets*, network.

7938 *(The) Cuckoo Hour.* Raymond Knight, a lawyer, actor and playwright, was asked by NBC network executive Bertha Brainard to write a 30-minute comedy show. Knight, who had been a student at Harvard in George Pierce Baker's famous 47 Workshop, was up to the task. *The Cuckoo Hour* program was the result. The show was considered to be one of the finest satires on radio. Any and all topics and persons were suitable targets for Knight. An example of the show's humor follows:

> KNIGHT: Toomey is the favorite soft drink of China. And the theme song on the Toomey Radio Program is heard on all the radios of the country. We now present Miss Lotus Flower singing the Toomey theme song.
>
> LOTUS FLOWER (singing): Drink Toomey only with thine eyes. The show was first broadcast January 1, 1930. Ambrose J. Weems, played by Knight, was the show's chief character. As manager of radio station KUKU, Weems was always at the center of the program's zany burlesque skits. Mrs. Pennyfeather, a parody of radio's home economists, appeared regularly in these skits. One of her suggestions for baby care was that a toupee should be placed on the baby's head to ward off colds and other upper respiratory illnesses. Alwyn E.W. Bach was the announcer (30 min., Wednesday, 9:30–10:00 P.M., NBC-Blue, 1930). After *The Cuckoo Hour* went off the air in 1937, Knight became a successful director and network executive at NBC.

7939 Cuetara, Rick. DJ (*Juke Box Review*, KCOY, Santa Maria, CA, 1947).

7940 Cuff, Samuel. Newscaster (WNEW, New York, NY, 1942).

7941 Cugat, Xavier. Spanish violinist (WRNY, New York, NY, 1926; CBS, New York, NY, 1927; KFWB, Hollywood, CA, 1928). Leader (Xavier Cugat Orchestra, *Xavier Cugat Orchestra*, instr. mus. prg, WTAR, Norfolk, VA, 1935; WOR, Newark, NJ, 1936 and NBC, 1936–1939. *Music by Cugat*, instr. mus. prg., KDKA, Pittsburgh, PA, 1937). Cugat and his orchestra were featured in many motion pictures.

7942 Culber, Nelson. Newscaster (*Suburban League News*, WNMP, Evanston, IL, 1948).

7943 Culbertson, (Dr.) J.C. Pastor Culbertson broadcast sermons from the Plymouth Congregational Church of Los Angeles (KHJ, Los Angeles, CA, 1923).

7944 Culbertson, (Prof.) J.L. A professor in the Department of Chemical Engineering at Washington State College, Culbertson presented talks on topics such as "New Developments in Industrial Chemistry" (KWSC, Pullman, WA, 1925).

7945 Culbertson, (Mrs.) Oma. Pianist (KSD, St. Louis, MO, 1923).

7946 Culbertson, Ron. DJ (WJCW, Johnson City, TN, 1960).

7947 Culbertson, Sasha. Leader (Sasha Culbertson's String Quartet, WJZ, New York, NY, 1926).

7948 *Culinary Hints.* Mrs. Helen Harrington Downing, Home Service Editor of the Denver *Evening News*, broadcast cooking hints (KOA, Denver, CO, 1927).

7949 Culkin, Ann. COM-HE (WSCR, Scranton, PA, 1951).

7950 Cull, Dean. DJ (KAGR, Yuba City, CA, 1956).

7951 Cull, Richard. Newscaster (WHIO, Dayton, OH, 1938–1941, 1944–1947).

7952 Cullen, Bill. Newscaster (WWSW, Pittsburgh, PA, 1942). Cullen later enjoyed considerable success on network television.

7953 Cullen, Cecilia. Pianist (WCAY, Milwaukee, WI, 1924).

7954 Cullen, Hazel. Violinist (WCAY, Milwaukee, WI, 1924).

7955 Cullen, Joy. COM-HE (KUDU, Ventura, CA, 1958).

7956 Cullen, Tommy. Leader (*Tommy Cullen Orchestra*, instr. mus. prg., WIP, Philadelphia, PA, 1936).

7957 Culley, Fred. Leader (*Royal Oak Orchestra*, instr. mus. prg., WJZ, New York, NY, 1930).

7958 Cullinan, W. Howell. Newscaster (WEEI, Boston, MA, 1937–1941, 1945).

7959 Cullinane, Joe. Sportscaster (*The Locker Room*, KWIK, Pocatello, ID, 1955).

7960 Cullings, Bob. Sportscaster (*Five Star Final*, WINR, Binghampton, NY, 1948–1949; *Sports Parade*, WINR, 1950–1952).

7961 Cullitan, Bill. Leader (*Bill Cullitan Orchestra*, instr. mus. prg., WTAM, Rochester, NY, 1942).

7962 Cullivan, Joe. Sportscaster (KROY, Sacramento, CA, 1938–1939).

7963 Cullum, Dick. Sportscaster (WDGY, Minneappolis–St. Paul, MN, 1944).

7964 Culpepper, Helen. Singer Culpepper was called the "Blues singing ukulele lady" (WRR, Dallas, TX, 1926).

7965 Culpepper, Joan. COM-HE (WTAL, Tallahassee, FL, 1958).

7966 Culver, Cal. DJ (*Saturday Swing Session*, KFYR, Bismark, ND, 1947).

7967 Culver, Hal. Singer (*Hal Culver,* vcl. mus. prg., WMBD, Peoria, IL, 1935; WLS, Chicago, IL, 1942).

7968 Culver, J.P. Sportscaster (*Sports Hi-Lites,* WDIG, Dothan, AL, 1948).

7969 Culver, Katherine. Soprano (WOR, Newark, NJ, 1929).

7970 Cumberland Ridge Runners. The CW music group led by John Lair included Slim Miller, Hugh Cross, Karl Davis and Hartford "Hardy" Taylor. The group had several early morning shows (WLS, Chicago, IL, mid–1930s;15 min., Monday through Saturday, 8:00–8:15 A.M., WLS,Chicago, IL, 1935; WIND, Gary, IN, 1937; WJJD, Chicago, IL, 1938; WLS, Chicago, IL, 1942).

7971 Cumberworth, Elva. COM-HE (WHSY, Hattiesburg, MS, 1951).

7972 Cumming, Richard. Baritone (WBAL, Baltimore, MD, 1926).

7973 Cummings, Al. DJ (KING, Seattle, WA, 1955–1956).

7974 Cummings, Bob. Motion picture and television star Cummings appeared on the *Those We Love* program.

7975 Cummings, Bob. Newscaster (KTYW, Yakima, WA, 1944).

7976 Cummings, Don. Newscaster (KGY, Olympia, WA, 1950s).

7977 Cummings, Harry. Harmonica soloist (WBZ, Boston-Springfield, MA, 1924).

7978 Cummings, J.G. Station manager and chief announcer Cummings proclaimed his station's slogan, "The winter playground of America, where the sunshine spends the winter" (WOAI, San Antonio, TX, 1925–1927).

7979 Cummings, Katherine Dorcas. Soprano (WHAZ, Troy, NY, 1925).

7980 Cummings, Leo. Leader (Leo Cummings Orchestra, WFBH, New York, NY, 1925).

7981 Cummins, Charlie. Newscaster (KEEW, Brownsville, TX, 1945). DJ (KURV, Edinburg, TX, 1954).

7982 Cummins, Charlotte. COM-HE (WROY, Carmi, IL, 1954; WSTR, Sturgis, MI, 1958).

7983 Cummins, Hilda. COM-HE (WBMA, Beaufort, NC, 1958).

7984 Cummins, Howard. Sportscaster (KGFI, Brownsville, TX, 1937).

7985 Cummins, Jack. Sportscaster (*Pigskin Predictions,* WPDQ, Jacksonville, FL, 1947–1949; *Jack of All Sports,* WTVJ, Miami, FL 1950–1960).

7986 Cummins, John H. Newscaster (WFOY, St. Augustine, FL, 1939).

7987 Cummins, Steff. DJ (KXRA, Alexandria, MN, 1960).

7988 Cummins, Tait. Sportscaster (WMT, Cedar Rapids, IA, 1947–1949; *Sports with Tait* and *Sports Digest,* WMT, 1950–1956).

7989 Cummiskey, Joe. Sportscaster (WHOM, Jersey City, NJ, 1944; *Inside of Sports,* MBS, 1947–1948; *Sports Extra,* WPAT, Paterson, NJ, 1949).

7990 Cunningham, Bill. Newscaster (KWLK, Longview, WA, 1940; MBS, 1944–1948).

7991 Cunningham, Bob. Newscaster (WBBM, Chicago, IL, 1939, 1945).

7992 Cunningham, Don. DJ (KROS, Clinton, IA, 1956).

7993 Cunningham, Etta. Soprano (KDKA, Pittsburgh, PA, 1925–1926).

7994 Cunningham, (Mrs.) H.A. Pianist (WFAA, Dallas, TX, 1924).

7995 Cunningham, Homer. Sportscaster (WIBW, Topeka, KS, 1940). Newscaster (WIBW, 1942.)

7996 Cunningham (Reverend) J.G. The Reverend Cunningham broadcast a series of lectures on public speaking (KFAU, Boise, ID, 1926).

7997 Cunningham, J.M. Employed in the Bond Department of the Anglo-California Trust Company, Cunningham broadcast talks on investments (KFRC, San Francisco, CA, 1925).

7998 Cunningham, Jessie. COM-HE (WYTH, Madison, GA, 1958).

7999 Cunningham, P.H. Newscaster (KWOC, Poplar Bluff, MO, 1940–1942). Sportscaster (KWOC, 1940–1942).

8000 Cunningham, Roy. Baritone (KVOO, Tulsa, OK, 1928).

8001 Cunningham, William. DJ (*Insomnia Inn,* WARC, Rochester, NY, 1948).

8002 *Cupid Interviews.* Walter Framer, playing Don Cupid, asked contestant couples various questions related to romance and marriage. Sometimes the couples were confronted with such questions as, "Should the husband or the wife walk the floor at night with the crying baby?" and "Is it all right for the girl to buy the engagement ring?" Spear & Company sponsored the program (15 min., Monday, 7:00–7:15 P.M., WJAS, Pittsburgh, PA, 1936).

8003 *(The) Curb Is the Limit.* Uncle Bob (Walter Wilson) conducted the radio safety club program for Chicago area children (KYW, Chicago, IL, 1928).

8004 Curet, Marge. COM-HE (WVMI, Biloxi, MS, 1954–1955).

8005 Curlee, Dick. Sportscaster (WSIC, Charlotte, SC, 1953).

8006 Curlee, Zeke. Newscaster (*Around Town with Zeke,* KWBU, Corpus Christi, TX, 1947).

8007 Curley, Leo. Actor Curley appeared on *Backstage Wife, Dear Mom, Silver Eagle, Mountie* and *Tom Mix.*

8008 Curley, Margaret. COM-HE (WJEF, Grand Rapids, MI, 1956).

8009 *Curley and His Saddle Pals.* CW mus. prg. (KWTO, Springfield, MO, 1939).

8010 *Curley and Zeke.* CW mus. prg. with otherwise unidentified performers (KWTO, Springfield, MO, 1939).

8011 *(The) Curley Bradley Show.* Western singer Bradley was joined by the M-B Bar Ranch Boys on the sustaining program. Franklyn MacCormack was the announcer (15 min., Monday through Friday, 5:45–6:00 P.M. MBS, 1949).

8012 *Curley Bradley — the Singing Marshal.* Bradley played himself on the summer replacement for the *Roy Rogers* program. Don Gordon was the program's narrator. The cast members included: Muriel Bremmer, Maurice Copeland, Leo Curley, Forrest Lewis, Fred Smith and Arthur Young. Billie and Bob McKee were the writers (30 min., Sunday, 5:00–5:30 P.M., MBS, 1950).

8013 *Curley Fox and Texas Ruby.* CW mus. prg. (WSM, Nashville, TN, 1938). Old-time champion fiddler Curley Fox acted as host on the popular country music program that also featured his wife, Texas Ruby, who was billed as "The Queen of the Cowgirls." The South Texas Cotton Oil Company sponsored the program (15 min, Tuesday, Thursday and Saturday, 11:45–12:00 noon, WOAI, San Antonio, TX, 1949).

8014 *Curley Miller's Plow Boys.* CW mus. prg. (KDKA, Pittsburgh, PA, 1935).

8015 Curlin, George. Sportscaster (KOTN, Pine Bluff, AR, 1938- 1941).

8016 Curran, Harry. Sportscaster (*Sports Final,* WXGI, Richmond, VA, 1950).

8017 Curran, Mattie. Leader (*Mattie Curran Orchestra,* instr. mus. prg., WCAU, Philadelphia, PA, 1934).

8018 Curran, Vin. DJ (*Deuces Wild,* WKAT, Miami Beach, FL, 1949).

8019 Curran, Vincent. Tenor (WPCH, New York, NY, 1929; *Vincent Curran,* vcl. mus. prg., WGY-NBC, 1934). In a 1934 listing, Curran was identified as a baritone.

8020 *Current Events.* A series of talks were delivered on the program by Dr. George Earle Raigvel, an "international traveler and lecturer" (WLIT, Philadelphia, PA, 1925).

8021 *Current History Comments.* Professor Clyde Egleston of Southern Methodist University conducted the news program (WFAA, Dallas, TX, 1922).

8022 *Current Topics (aka Current Events).* H.V. (Hans von) Kaltenborn conducted the lively, sometimes controversial, news program (WAHG, New York, NY, 1925). *See* **Kaltenborn, H.V.**

8023 Currey, Grace. Harpist (KHJ, Los Angeles, CA, 1926).

8024 Currie, Bill. Sportscaster (WHPE, High Point, NC, 1948–1951).

8025 Currie, Carlton E. Newscaster (WLOX, Biloxi, MS, 1948)

8026 Currie, Donelda. Actress Currie appeared on the *Stepmother* daytime serial program. .

8027 Currie, Eben. DJ (*Sunrise Serenade,* WABM, Houlton, ME, 1949).

8028 Currie, Harry. Leader (*Harry Currie Orchestra,* instr. mus. prg., WHAS, Louisville, KY, 1935–1936).

8029 Currier, Bernice. COM-HE (KMA, Shenandoah, IA, 1957).

8030 Curris, Leonard. Banjoist (WOR, Newark, NJ, 1923).

8031 Curry, Cathy. COM-HE (WLOU, Louisville, KY, 1955).

8032 Curry, Ernest "Butch." Sportscaster (*Big Town Sports,* WMRY, New Orleans, LA, 1953).

8033 Curry, Ethel. Soprano, (WBZ, Boston-Springfield, MA, 1925).

8034 Curry, J. Winfred. Pianist (KPO, San Francsico, CA, 1925).

8035 Curry, Marion. Pianist (KJBS, San Francisco, CA, 1928–1929).

8036 Curry, Ray. Sportscaster (WAYE, Baltimore, MD, 1960).

8037 Curt, Kenneth. Boy soprano (KFO, Oakland, CA, 1928).

8038 *(The) Curt Massey Show.* Popular CW singer-violinist Curt Massey hosted and performed on his music show (15 min., Monday, 10:30–10:45 P.M., ABC, 1949). When he was later joined by singer Martha Tilton, the program was known either as *The Curt Massey and Martha Tilton Show* or *The Curt Massey Show.* The quarter-hour program was sponsored by Alka-Seltzer (15 minutes, Monday through Friday, 2:45–3:00 P.M., 1953).

8039 *Curtain America.* Virginia Mae Cooke wrote the variety program sponsored by the Western Conference of Teamsters. Edward Robinson was the show's producer and Felix Mills the musical director (30 min., Thursday, 6:30–7:00 P.M. PCT, Mutual-Don Lee Network, 1942).

8040 *Curtain Time.* Similar to the *First Nighter* program, this dramatic program was hosted by Patrick Allen and starred Harry Elders, Nanette Sargent and Mike Wallace. The sponsor was Milky Way candy (30 min., Weekly, MBS, 1938). The program in a similar format was later presented on both ABC and NBC as late as 1950.

8041 Curtin, David. DJ (*Clock Watcher,* WRNY, Rochester, NY, 1947). Sportscaster and play by play of the Rochester Royals baseball games (WRNY, 1950).

8042 Curtin, Joseph "Joe." Busy actor Curtin appeared on *David Harum, Her Honor, Nancy James, Hilltop House, John's Other Wife, Mr. and Mrs. North, Myrt and Marge, Our Gal Sunday, Second Husband, The Story of Bess Johnson* and *The Thin Man.*

8043 Curtin, Marc. DJ (KFYO, Lubbock, TX, 1956).

8044 Curtis, Betty D. COM-HE (KIPA, Hilo, HI, 1960).

8045 Curtis, Bill. DJ (*Jazz in Review,* WDGY, Minneapolis, MN, 1948).

8046 Curtis, Bill. DJ (*Moondial,* KALL, Salt Lake City, UT, 1954).

8047 Curtis, Bill. DJ (*Timekeeper,* WRAP, Norfolk, VA, 1954–1956).

8048 Curtis, Bob. Sportscaster (KWSC, Pullman, WA, 1945; KCLX, Calfax, WA, 1954–1955).

8049 Curtis, Dan. DJ (*C'mon and Dance Bandwagon,* WIP, Philadelphia, PA, 1949).

8050 Curtis, Dorothy. Pianist (WBZ, Boston-Springfield, MA, 1925).

8051 Curtis, E.H. "Elmer." Newscaster (WIBW, Topeka, KS, 1939–1942, 1944–1945).

8052 Curtis, Evelyn. COM-HE (KSYC, Yreka, CA, 1951).

8053 Curtis, Francis [Frances]. Pianist (KFXF, Colorado Springs, CO, 1926).

8054 Curtis, Gene. Sportscaster (*Sports Scoreboard* and *Sports Reel,* KGLN, Glenwood Springs, CO, 1952).

8055 Curtis, George E. Newscaster (WGAN, Portland, ME, 1945). DJ (*560 Revue,* WGAN, 1949–1950).

8056 Curtis, Guy. DJ (WADK, Newport, RI, 1956).

8057 Curtis, Jack. Singer (*Jack Curtis,* voc. mus. prg., WIP, Philadelphia, PA, 1936).

8058 Curtis, James R. Newscaster (KFRO, Longview, TX, 1938).

8059 Curtis, Ken. DJ (*All Alone Club,* KPST, Preston, ID, 1949–1949; *All Alone Club,* KELK, Elko, NV, 1950).

8060 Curtis, Margaret. Actress Curtis appeared on the *Hilltop House* daytime serial.

8061 Curtis, Marge [Margaret]. COM-HE (KTYL, Mesa, AZ, 1951).

8062 Curtis, Norman. Pianist (WEAF, New York, NY, 1925).

8063 Curtis, Paul. Tenor (*Paul Curtis,* vcl. mus. prg., WGY, Schenectady, NY, 1934).

8064 Curtis, Peggy. COM-HE (WJLK, Asbury Park, NJ, 1951–1954).

8065 Curtis, Ronald Ezzo "Ron." Newscaster (*WFBL News,* WFBL, Syracuse, NY, 1947). DJ (*Coffee with Curtis,* WFBL, 1948–1951; *Musical Matinee,* WFBL, 1952).

8066 Curtis, Russell. Pianist (WFAA, Dallas, TX, 1922).

8067 Curtis, Sandusky. Newscaster (WTAR, Norfolk, VA, 1939).

8068 Curtis, Virginia. Singer (WPG, Atlantic City, NJ, 1928).

8069 Curtis, Virginia and Margaret Siracusa. Mandolin and guitar instrumentalists who played and sang Italian folk songs (WPG, Atlantic City, NJ, 1927).

8070 *Curtis Institute of Music* (aka ***Curtis Institute Musicale*** or the ***Curtis Institute Recitals***). Faculty artists and students from the Curtis Institute appeared on the fine music series (30 min., Friday, 10:30–11:00 P.M., NBC-Red, 1929–1930).

8071 Curtner, Virginia. Pianist (KGO, Oakland, CA, 1924).

8072 Curzon, Bob. Sportscaster (WTTB, Vero Beach, FL, 1956).

8073 Cusack, William. Sportscaster (WOTW, Nashua, NH, 1960).

8074 Cushing, George. Newscaster (WJR, Detroit, MI, 1945).

8075 Cushing, Kerby [Kirby]. Sportscaster (KYW, Philadelphia, PA, 1935–1937; *Kerby Cushing Sportscaster,* KYW, 1940–1941, WHDH, Boston, MA, 1947).

8076 Cushing Military Band. Oklahoma brass band (KVOO, Bristow, OK, 1926).

8077 Cushman, R.A. Announcer (WFAV, Lincoln, NE, 1925).

8078 Cushman's Serenaders. New York jazz band (WEAF, New York, NY, 1925).

8079 Cusiamano, Tony. Sportscaster (WJOC, Jamestown, NY, 1960).

8080 Cusich, Jack. Performer Cusich was billed as "Jack and His Uke" (WMBB, Homewood, IL and WOK, Chicago, IL, 1928).

8081 Cusick, Fred. DJ (*Platter Patter,* WBET, Brockton, MA, 1947). Newscaster (*The News Right Now,* WVOM, Boston, MA, 1948). Sportscaster (WVOM, 1948; WEEI, Boston, MA, 1953).

8082 Cusick, L. S. Announcer (WGBN, LaSalle, Il, 1925).

8083 Custara, Rick, Sr. Newscaster (*Home Town News,* KCOY, Santa Maria, CA, 1947).

8084 Custer, Bob. DJ (KLOK, San Jose, CA, 1955–1960).

8085 Cutbirth, (Mrs.) O.L. Leader of the Sweetwater Violin Club (WHO, Des Moines, IA, 1925).

8086 Cutchin, Esther Marvin. Pianist (WBZ, Boston-Springfield, MA, 1925).

8087 Cuthbert, Frank. Bass-baritone on the *Willys Overland Hour* (NBC, New York, NY, 1927).

8088 Cuthbert, Margaret. COM-HE, executive (WEAF, New York, NY, NBC) Cuthbert joined WEAF when it was the pioneer station of the American Telephone Company before it became the key NBC station. Before coming to WEAF, she had worked in the Home Economics Department of Cornell University. At the station Cuthbert announced and scheduled daytime programs, particularly the talk and interview programs. Her first guest on the air was John Galsworthy. One of her major contributions was to expand "women's interests" programs to include consideration of art, literature, theater, national and international affairs. Among the programs she recognized and argued for placement on the network schedule was *Town Meeting of the Air,* although it was another woman, Marian Carter, who supervised its actual development.

8089 Cutland, Henry. Newscaster (KLZ, Denver, CO, 1945).

8090 Cutler, Ben. Leader (*Ben Cutler Orchestra,* instr. mus. prg., NBC, 1939).

8091 Cutler, Helen. Soprano (KTAB, Oakland, CA, 1925).

8092 Cutler, Miles. Cellist (KTAB, Oakland, CA, 1925).

8093 Cutler, (Mrs.) Will H. Soprano, KOIL, Council Bluffs, IA, 1926; soprano in the Mona Mixed Quartet.

8094 Cutrer, T. Tommy (Tommy Clinton Cutrer). Although early in his career Cutrer did som singing, it was as CW host, DJ, promoter and announcer that he was best known. Specifically, it was his ten years at WSM when he hosted the *Grand Ole Opry* and conducted the station's all-night *Opry Star Spotlight* that was the high point of his radio career. DJ (*930 Club,* WSLI, Jackson, MS, 1947; WSM, Nashville, TN, 1955). Cutrer also worked at WSKB (McComb, MS); WJDK (Jackson, MS); KARK (Little Rock, AR); WMC (Memphis, TN); WREC (Memphis, TN); WSW (Jackson, MS); WSW (Jackson, MS); KWYZ (Houston, TX); KNUZ (Houston, TX); and KCU (Shreveport, LA). Sportscaster (*Sports Page,* KXYZ, Houston, TX, 1949).

8095 Cutter, (Mme.) Belle Forbes. Soprano (WEBH, Chicago, IL, 1925–1927; WABC, New York, NY, 1932).

8096 Cuyler, Louise. Violinist (KOIL, Council Bluffs, IA, 1926).

8097 Cuzad, Sam. Sportscaster (WLPM, Suffolk, VA, 1941–1942).

8098 Cuzenza, Salvatore. Mandolin soloist (WNYC, New York, NY, 1926).

8099 Cyde [Clyde], Sylvia. Soprano Cyde sang with the Raoul Nadeau Orchestra (MBS, 1937).

8100 Cyganero, Nathan. Pianist (WOR, Newark, NJ, 1923).

8101 Cythiana High School Orchestra. Scholastic orchestra (WHAS, Louisville, KY, 1926).

8102 Czechoslovakian Band. Local ethnic band (WEBJ, New York, NY, 1925).

8103 Czerniak, Elaine. COM-HE (WIGM, Medford, WI, 1958).

8104 Czuwara, William. Newscaster (WEDC, Chicago, IL, 1944).

8105 D'Accardo, Gene. Newscaster (KTRB, Modesto, CA, 1940, 1946; *Top Story*, KTRB, 1948). Sportscaster (KTRB, 1947; KMOD, Modesto, CA, 1953).

8106 Daboul, Joe. DJ (*Melody Time*, WIRY, Plattsburg, NY, 1949; WMAS, Springfield, MA, 1960). Sportscaster (*Sports Hi-Lights*, WIRY, 1951).

8107 Da Costa, Blanche. Soprano (KOA, Denver, CO, 1929).

8108 Dacre, George. DJ (*George's Orgy*, WFNC, Fayetteville, NC, 1948).

8109 *Dad Differ.* Clarence B. Mooney, a Kansas City newspaperman, wrote the dramatic serial and played the title role. Lee Roberts and Lillian Faust played his daughters, who listened to his homey advice and philosophy. The announcer was Larry Proctor (15 min., Wednesday, 6:45–7:00 P.M. CST, KCMO, Kansas City, MO, 1938).

8110 *Daddy and Rollo.* Author J.P. McAvoy wrote the interesting story about a father and his son. Nick Dawson and 11-year-old Donald Hughes played father and son on the literate program sponsored by La Palina Cigars (15 min., Tuesday-Wednesday-Thursday, 7:45–8:00 P.M., CBS, 1931). A later version featuring Craig McDonnell and George Ward returned to the air on MBS in 1942 with Frank Knight as the announcer.

8111 Daddy Winkum. Daddy told bedtime stories for children (KDKA, Pittsburgh, PA, 1924).

8112 D'Adalena, Helen. Soprano (KGO, Oakland, CA, 1926).

8113 Dadisman, Amos. Announcer (WEAH, Wichita, KS, 1925).

8114 Dady, Ray E. Newscaster (KWK, St. Louis, MO, 1936–1942, 1945–1946).

8115 Daehler, Polly. COM-HE (WPAY, Portsmouth, OH, 1956–1957).

8116 Daffron, Polly. Newscaster (WRNL, Richmond, VA, 1946–1949).

8117 Daffy and Gloomy. Blackface comedy team (KTNT, Muscatine, IA, 1928).

8118 Daga. Cowboy singer and composer (WOR, Newark, NJ, 1926).

8119 Dagenais, Rene. Organist and leader (Rene Dagenais and the South Capitol Theater Orchestra, WBZ, Springfield, MA, 1926).

8120 Dagg, William. Sportscaster (WELL, Battle Creek, MI, 1955).

8121 Daggett, Uncle John. Uncle John Daggett was an announcer known as the "King of Hosts." He interviewed such stars and personalities as Mary Garden, Douglas Fairbanks and Mary Pickford (KHJ, Los Angeles, CA, 1925). In 1922, he was the conductor of *Children's Hour*, a popular children's program on which he told children's stories. The program also contained a quiz feature, certainly one of the first on radio. Daggett's skill as announcer was demonstrated after the sudden death of President Warren G. Harding. Thirty minutes after the Associated Press bulletin reported President Hardings's death on August 2, 1923, Daggett went on the air with an extemporaneous twenty-minute speech, while pianist Claire Forbes Crane provided background music (KHJ, Los Angeles, CA, 1922–1927). *See **The Children's Hour** and **Uncle John (Daggett)***.

8122 DaGrossa, John "Ox." Sportscaster (*Speaking of Sports*, WCAU, Philadelphia, PA, 1950–1951).

8123 Dahl, Arnold. Tenor (WCCO, Minneapolis–St. Paul, MN, 1928).

8124 Dahl, Don. Sportscaster (KDAL, Duluth, MN, 1948–1951). DJ (*Open House*, KDAL, 1952–1953; *On the Sidelines*, KDAL, 1954).

8125 Dahl, Jon. DJ (*Jon's Juke Box*, WDMJ, Marquette, MI, 1948).

8126 Dahlberg, Jerry. DJ (*Gotta Match*, KROX, Crookston, MN, 1948). Sportscaster (*Accent on Local Sports*, KROX, 1948; *Sports Page of the Air*, KROX, 1949–1960).

8127 Dahlgren, Babe. Former Yankee baseball star Dahlgren worked as a sportscaster on his *Sports Panorama* program (KWKW, Pasadena, CA, 1954).

8128 Dahlhart, Vernon (Marion Try Slaughter). Dahlhart was a RCA recording artist, whose early training as a concert singer helped make him become one of the most popular male singers of the 1920s. He picked his name from two west Texas towns. During his career it was said that he recorded under more than 100 different names (Palmer, 1994, p. 54). He specialized in songs of catastrophes and tragedies such as "The Death of Floyd Collins," "The Wreck of the Shenandoah," "Little Marian Parker," and "The Santa Barbara Earthquake" (WEAF, New York, NY, 1927–1928; KFON, Long Beach, CA, 1928). Dahlhart teamed with Carson Robison, a versatile singer-whistler-songwriter-composer from 1925 to 1928. Together they recorded and broadcast such songs as "The John T. Scopes Trail," "Golden Slippers," and "Lucky Lindy [Lindbergh]." The popular team broke up after performing together for some three years. Dahlhart also broadcast and recorded with CW singer, Adelyn Hood (*Vernon Dahlhart and Adelyn Hood*, CW vcl. mus. prg., WOR, Newark, NJ, 1934).

8129 Dahm, Frank. Sports announcer Dahm broadcast both football and baseball games (WGN, 1925–1928). Dahm, a veteran newsman from the Chicago *Tribune*, before coming to WGN, wrote the early scripts for *Little Orphan Annie*. He later moved to New York to write such daytime serials as *City Desk, Pretty Kitty Kelly* and *The Sea Hound*.

8130 Dahners, H.L. Announcer (KGCU, Mandan, ND, 1927).

8131 Daiger, Fred. Newscaster (WAPI, Birmingham, AL, 1939). Sportscaster (WAPI, 1939; WSUN, St. Petersburg, FL, 1940; WXKW, Albany, NY, 1948).

8132 Dail, Ambert. Newscaster (Danville, VA, 1946–1947).

8133 Dailey, Bob. Newscaster (WTAM, Cleveland, OH, 1938–1939).

8134 Dailey, Frank. Leader (Frank Dailey Orchestra, WAAM, Newark, NJ, 1925; *Frank Dailey Orchestra*, instr. mus. prg., CBS, 1935; WLW, Cincinnati, OH, 1939).

8135 Dailey, Hartwell. Newscaster (WLAW, Lawrence, MA, 1945).

8136 Dailey, Joe. Leader (*Joe Dailey Orchestra*, instr. mus. prg., CBS, 1934).

8137 Dailey, Paul. Newscaster (KOAM, Pittsburg, KS, 1945).

8138 Dailey, Tom. Sportscaster (WDOD, Chattanooga, TN, 1937; KVOO, Tulsa, OK, 1939; *Sports Time with Falstaff*, WOW, Omaha, NE, 1940–1945). DJ (KWK, St. Louis, MO, 1947; *Recall It and Win*, KWK, 1948; *Recall It and Win It*, WEW, St. Louis, MO, 1960).

8139 *Dailey Paskman Minstrels.* One of the most memorable early radio minstrel shows was originated and produced by broadcast executive, Dailey Paskman (WGBS, 1928). Paskman was an innovative broadcast pioneer, who became enough of an authority on the minstrel show form of entertainment to collaborate with Sigund Spaeth and write an history of that entertainment form. *See* **Paskman, Dailey**.

8140 Daily, Dick. DJ (*1240 Club*, WFOY, St. Augustine, FL, 1947).

8141 Daily, John. Newscaster (*John Daily*, WKBW, Buffalo, NY, 1942).

8142 *(The) Daily Dozen.* Joe Barnett conducted his early physical exercise program (WOR, Newark, NJ, 1922). This type of program became very popular in the early days of radio.

8143 *Daily Health Drill.* An early radio exercise program, the *Daily Health Drill* was conducted by Wiley Winsor (7:00–7:30 A.M. and 8:00–8:30 A.M., KPO, San Francisco, CA, 1925).

8144 *Daily Tattler.* Daytime romantic sketch with Genevieve Sherlock and actor-writer Vic Whitman (15 min.,WEEI, Boston, MA, 1931).

8145 Dain, Roland "Rollie." Sportscaster (KWLC, Decorah, IA, 1942; KWLC, 1947; KAUS, Austin, MN, 1951–1953; KMMT, Austin, MN, 1954). Newscaster (*Noon News*, KWLC, 1947).

8146 *Dakota Jamboree.* CW mus. prg. (KCJB, Minot, ND, 1955).

8147 *Dakota Roundup.* CW mus. prg. (WNAX, Yankton, SD, 1939).

8148 Dale, Alan. DJ (WOAI, San Antonio, TX, 1960).

8149 Dale, Betty. COM-HE (WMRA, Myrtle Beach, SC, 1951).

8150 Dale, Carlotta. Singer (*Carlotta Dale*, vcl. mus. prg., WCAU, Philadelphia, PA, 1934; NBC-Red, New York, NY, 1935).

8151 Dale, Curly. DJ (KFNF, Shenandoah, IA, 1955).

8152 Dale, Cyr. Baritone (KFWM, Oakland, CA, 1928).

8153 Dale, Dorothy. COM-HE (WBET, Brockton, MA, 1956).

8154 Dale, George. Newscaster (WJLS, Beckley, WV, 1939). Sportscaster (WJLS, 1939).

8155 Dale, Harold. Sportscaster (WGTC, Greenville, NC, 1940–1942; WABZ, Albemarle, NC, 1947). Newscaster (WGTC, 1941–1942).

8156 Dale, Jerry. COM-HE (WNRC, New Rochelle, NY, 1954).

8157 Dale, Kay. Singer and whistler (WBAL, Baltimoe, MD, 1926).

8158 Dale, Marvin. Leader (*Marvin Dale Orchestra*, instr. mus. prg., MBS, 1940 and WBBM, Chicago, IL, 1942).

8159 Dale, Pat. COM-HE (WCAW, Charleston, WV, 1949).

8160 Dale, Rex. DJ (*Make Believe Ballroom*, WCKY, Cincinnati, OH, 1948–1955).

8161 Dale, Stan. DJ (*Dale's Gulch*, WCOL, Columbus, OH, 1948).

8162 Dale, Stephanie. Singer (*Stephanie Dale*, vcl. mus. prg., WOR, Newark, NJ, 1936).

8163 Dale, Sylvano. Dale was billed as the "only tap dancer on the air in the west" (*Sylvano Dale,* NBC-Pacific Coast Network, 1930).

8164 Dale, Teresa. Actress Dale appeared in the *By Kathleen Norris* daytime serial.

8165 *Dale Carnegie.* Carnegie, a best selling author well known for his *How to Win Friends and Influence People* book, told inspirational human interest stories about famous persons on his program. Music was supplied by Harold Sanford's orchestra (30 min., Weekly, 5:30–6:00 P.M., NBC-Red, 1933). Carnegie later broadcast a series of dramatic sketches that made the point he always wished to emphasize. For weary Great Depression listeners his inspirational message was reassuring: "Success is a matter of the approach. You can do it, too." The show was sponsored by the Colgate-Palmolive Company (*Dale Carnegie*, 15 min., Monday, 10:45–11:00 P.M., NBC-Red, 1938). A still later version, *Interesting Persons*, reiterated the same theme.

8166 *(The) Dale Trio.* Singer Eve Casanova joined the Dale Trio [instrumental group] on this music program (WEVD, New York, NY, 1933).

8167 Dale's Blue Melody Blues. Trombonist L.L. Dale led the band known as "one of the South's finest jazz orchestras." The orchestra's other members included Hugh "Pickles" Hines on drums; saxophone-clarinetist Roy McGowan; trombonist Jimmie Freshour; and pianist Al Marney. The band frequently appeared on WSV (Little Rock, AR, 1922).

8168 Daley, Don. Newscaster (WABI, Bangor, ME, 1938).

8169 Daley, Tom. Sportscaster (KVOO, Tulsa, OK, 1938).

8170 Dalheim, Rayner. Leader (Rayner Dalheim's Orchestra, WHT, Chicago, IL, 1926).

8171 Dallas, Carlos. Leader (*Carlos Davis Orchestra*, instr. mus. prg., WTAM, Cleveland, OH, 1934).

8172 *Dallas First Baptist Church.* The Reverend Dr. George W. Truett conducted regular church services on the program (WFAA, Dallas, TX, 1924).

8173 Dallas Male Chorus. Members of the Dallas Scottish Rite (Masonic) Temple sponsored and performed on the vocal music program, a favorite of Dallas listeners. The president of the chorus was E.C. Blesi (WFAA, Dallas, TX, 1929).

8174 Dallavo, Bill. Leader (Bill Dallavo and his Orchestra, WOOD, Grand Rapids, MI, 1926).

8175 Dalton, Bob. DJ (WTOP, Washington, DC, 1957).

8176 Dalton, Doris. Doris Dalton was a cast member of the *King's Row* daytime serial program.

8177 Dalton, Ham. Newscaster (WIP, Philadelphia, PA, 1936–1936).

8178 Dalton, Irene. Pianist (KFI, Los Angeles, CA, 1928).

8179 Dalton, Jane. Conducted children's program (*Children's Theatre*, WSPA, Spartanburg, SC, 1949). COM-HE (WSPA, 1949).

8180 Dalton, Kenneth G. Newscaster (WBET, Brockton, MA, 1947–1948).

8181 Dalton, Wanda. COM-HE (KCLW, Hamilton, TX, 1956).

8182 *(The) Dalton Brothers.* Male vocal group (voc. mus. prg., CBS, 1933, 1935).

8183 Daly, Anne. COM-HE (WPDQ, Jacksonville, FL, 1956).

8184 Daly, Bud. DJ (*930 Melody Lane*, WSAZ, Huntington, WV, 1952).

8185 Daly, Duke. Leader (*Duke Daly Orchestra*, instr. mus. prg., MBS, 1934, 1939).

8186 Daly, John. Irish tenor (WJR, Detroit, MI and WWJ, Detroit, MI, 1928).

8187 Daly, John. Actor in the Fu Manchu dramatic segment of the *Collier Hour* (NBC, New York, NY, 1927–1930). *See* ***The Collier Hour***.

8188 Daly, John Charles. Newscaster (WJSV, Washington, DC, 1940–1941; *Report to the Nation* and *The World Today*, CBS, 1942, 1944–1948).

8189 Daly, Linda. COM-HE (WLOU, Louisville, KY, 1949).

8190 *Daly Brothers Orchestra.* Instr. mus. prg. (WRVA, Richmond, VA, 1938).

8191 Dalzell, John. DJ (*Saturday Nite Juke Box*, WOWO, Fort Wayne, IN, 1954).

8192 Dalzell, Madge. COM-HE (WIOU, Kokomo, IN, 1954).

8193 Dalziel, George. Tenor (WCGU, Chicago, IL, 1927).

8194 Damarin, Joan. COM-HE (WCVS, Springfield, IL,1960).

8195 Dame, Paula. COM-HE (WDOT, Burlington, VT, 1956).

8196 Dameron, Charles "Charlie." Comedian on the *Crosley Burnt Corkers* minstrel show program (WLW, Cincinnati, OH, 1928–1929). Dameron later began a radio singing career (*Charlie Dameron*, vcl. mus. prg., WLW, Cincinnati, OH, 1934).

8197 Dameron, Charles. Newscaster (WFVI, Hollywood, FL, 1946). DJ (*Charlie's Top Ten*, WFTL, Fort Lauderdale, FL, 1952). He *could* be the Charlie Dameron who began his career as a comedian and singer.

8198 D'Amico, Nick. Leader (*Nick D'Amico Orchestra*, instr. mus. prg., WXYZ, Detroit, MI, 1942).

8199 Damman Ladies Trio. Female music group (WKAF, Milwaukee, WI, 1926).

8200 *(The) Damon Runyon Theatre.* Russell Hughes wrote the comedy program based on Damon Runyon's Broadway characters. John Brown was the narrator of the funny show that contained an excellent cast that included: William Conrad, Larry Dobkin, Sandra Gould, Sheldon Leonard, Frank Lovejoy and Luis Van Rooten (30 min., Saturday, 2:30–3:00 P.M., Syndicated, 1949).

8201 Damrosch, Dr. Walter. Conductor of the New York Symphony Orchestra (NBC, 1926). Damrosch was a much beloved and respected conductor, who played an important role in advancing the public's appreciation of serious music. His first radio appearance was on October 29, 1923, when he presented a lecture-recital on Beethoven (WEAF, New York, NY, 1923). By 1929, his *Music Appreciation Hour* (often known as *Damrosch's Music Appreciation Hour*) was broadcast by NBC on both the Red and Blue networks simultaneously (Friday, 11:00 A.M. to 12:00 noon, NBC-Red & Blue, 1929).

NBC claimed that the program had an audience of 6,000,000 school children. The distinguished singer Mme. Ernestine Schumann-Heink said of Damrosch's endeavors: "Never have I seen such promise of a great musical future for this country. One man is responsible for it all — Walter Damrosch. From the children who are learning at his feet will come the artistry of tomorrow. Perhaps he will also improve the audience so they are less snobbish about American art" (*Radio Digest*, December, 1933, p. 52). Damrosch's father, composer-conductor Dr. Leopold Damrosch, founded the New York Oratorio Society, the organization that was partially responsible for providing the foundation of the New York Philharmonic Society.

Damrosch's customary opening on the *Music Appreciation Program* was, "Good morning, my dear young friends." School children liked both his manner and his music. Some classes on the Pacific Coast came to school an hour earlier (at eight o'clock) in order to hear the program (*Radio Digest*, December, 1933, p. 71). Charles H. Farnsworth, Professor of Music Education at Columbia University, and Ernest La Prade, Damrosch's assistant, prepared manuals to accompany the program. The children's manuals sold for a dime and the teachers' manuals for a quarter. Damrosch's work can best be summarized by saying he proved that it was possible to educate without being dull.

8202 Damski, Henri. Director (Puget Sound Savings and Loan Association Band, KJR, Seattle, WA, 1926; KJR Orchestra, KJR, 1928; Imperial Grand Orchestra, KGS, Spokane, WA, 1929).

8203 Damsky, Leah. Dramatic reader (WGY, Schenectady, NY, 1924).

8204 ***Dan Dunne, Secret Operative.*** The 15-minute adventure series was based on a comic strip written by Manurice Zinn. Lou Marcelle played the title role assisted by Lucille Meredith, Myron Gary, Jerry Mohr, Hans Conreid and David Sterling (15 min., Transcribed, Various stations, 1948).

8205 ***Dan Harding's Wife.*** Isabel Randolph played the title role on the daytime serial drama written by Ken Robinson. Because his wife was a widow, Dan Harding never appeared on the program. Mrs. Harding bravely carried on after the death in a mining accident of her engineer husband. Her twin children, Donna and Dean Harding, played by Loretta Poynton and Merrill Fugit, were at the center of many of the program's twists and turns of plot. Other members of the cast included: Tommy Birch, Herb Butterfield, Willard Farnum, Templeton Fox, Alice Goodkin, Robert Griffin, Carl Hanson, Judith Lowry, Herbert Nelson, Hugh Rowlands, Marguerette Shanna and Cliff Soubier. Les Griffith and Norman Berry were the announcers (NBC, 1936–1939).

8206 ***Dan Healy.*** Dan Healy hosted the novel sustaining program that gave Broadway chorus girls an opportunity to perform on radio. They sang accompanied only by a piano. Incidentally, Healy's program apparently was the first to use this concept, since NTG's program, which was identical, came on the air a month later (30 min., Friday, 10:00–10:30 P.M., WNEW, New York, NY, 1935). *See* ***NTG and the Chorus Girls.***

8207 Dana, E. Harold. Dana was a singer who was said to have been "selected by Titto Ruffo as [the] finest baritone in San Francisco" (KPO, San Francisco, CA, 1923; KTAB, Los Angeles, CA, 1925; KPO, 1928).

8208 Dana, Joe. Newscaster (KOY, Phoenix, AZ, 1937–1940; KSUN, Lowell, AZ, 1939).

8209 Dana, Les. DJ (*Show Time*, WSPD, Toledo, OH, 1947).

8210 Danald, Ruth. COM-HE (KGVO, Missoula, MO, 1960).

8211 ***(The) Dancepators Ochestra.*** Instr. mus. prg. (CBS, 1939 and WNAC, Boston, MA, 1939).

8212 Danero, Camilla. Soprano (KYA, San Francisco, CA, 1927).

8213 Dancey, Charles. Newscaster (*The World at Large*, WSIV, Pekin, IL, 1947–1948).

8214 ***Dancing in the Twin Cities.*** Two bands, the Jimmy Joy Orchestra and that of Cecil Golly, were featured on the program that presented both bands. One band broadcast from Minneapolis, MN, and the other from St. Paul, MN (NBC, 1935).

8215 ***Dancing Instruction.*** Dancing master-entrepreneur Arthur Murray conducted this radio dancing instruction program (WHO, Des Moines, IA, 1924). Murray was prominent in the early days of radio for teaching dancing and actively promoting his business activities by the new medium.

8216 ***Dandies of Yesterday.*** The Dandies of Yesterday sang old-time ballads. They were a male quartet not otherwise identified (15 min., Saturday, 6:15–6:30 P.M., NBC-Blue, 1930).

8217 Dandorand, Tommy. Dandorand, the country violinist and leader of Tommy Dandorand and his Barn Dance Fiddlers group, was from Kankakee, Illinois. His group first appeared on the *National Barn Dance* on April 19, 1924 (WLS, Chicago, IL, 1924).

8218 Dane, Dudley. DJ (*Birthday and Anniversary Club*, KFAM, St. Cloud, MN, 1948–1949; KTFI, Twin Falls, ID, 1952). Sportscaster (KFAM, 1949).

8219 Dane, Tom. Newscaster (WBAL, Baltimore, MD, 1939).

8220 Danenbring, Ray. DJ (*Alarm Clock Club*, KASI, Ames, IA, 1948).

8221 Danero, Camilla. Soprano (KYA, San Francisco, CA, 1927).

8222 Danforth, Ed. Sportscaster (WSB, Atlanta, GA, 1940).

8223 Danforth, Harold Potter. Announcer (WTOC, Savannah, GA, 1925–1927). Announcer-director (WDBO, Orlando, FL, 1928).

8224 ***Danger Fighters.*** Based on Paul de Kruif's best selling *Microbe Hunters*, the dramatic series presented dramatizations in which medical researchers attempted to alleviate or eliminate various diseases. *Radio Digest* critics praised the program and the cast. The Gordon Harris Orchestra provided the music (30 min., Saturday, 8:00–8:30 P.M., NBC-Blue, 1932).

8225 ***Dangerous Assignment.*** Brian Donlevy as secret agent Steve Mitchell traveled to Greece, the Belgian Congo, North Borneo, Munich, Damascus and Havana on various dangerous assignments. The program opened with his admission: "Yeah, danger is my assignment. I get sent to a lot of places I can't even pronounce. They all smell of something though — trouble." Donlevy's rugged depiction of Mitchell was always entertaining and exciting (30 min., Weekly, NBC, 1950).

8226 ***Dangerous Paradise.*** Elsie Hitz and Nick Dawson played the leading roles in the dramatic serial sponsored by Woodbury Soap. The story centered around Gale Brewster, an American newspaper woman who was covering stories in the Philippines. After she hired a plane to fly to another island, her pilot was mortally wounded when the plane developed engine trouble and crashed into the sea. When Dan, an American beachcomber, came by in his boat, the badly wounded pilot told her to go on and save herself. Dan took her to an island that was inhabited only by himself and three other men. The plot centered about the potential romance between Elsie and Dan (15 min., Wednesday, 8:30–8:45 P.M., NBC-Red, 1933). Two years later the day of broadcast was changed (Monday, 6:45–7:00 P.M., NBC-Red, 1935).

8227 Daniel, Alfred P. Announcer (KPRC, Houston, TX, 1927).

8228 Daniel [Daniels], Betty. COM-HE (WDVH, Gainesville, FL, 1956–1957).

8229 Daniel, Clay. Newscaster (WDNC, Durham, NC, 1939).

8230 Daniel, Dan. Sportscaster (*Sports Journal*, WHOO, Orlando, FL, 1947–1953; WABT, Birmingham, AL, 1954).

8231 Daniel, Jacqueline. COM-HE (KFBK, Sacramento, CA, 1954).

8232 Daniel, John. Newscaster (KWSC, Pullman, WA, 1945).

8233 Daniel, John H. Announcer (WRC, Washington, DC, 1927).

8234 Daniel, Nathan. DJ (*Date with Nate*, KTFY, Brownfield, TX, 1949).

8235 Daniel, Nell. COM-HE (WBGR, Jesup, GA, 1951).

8236 Daniels, Bebe. Motion picture star (NBC, 1929).

8237 Daniels, Betty. COM-HE (WDVH, Gainesville, FL, 1957–1958).

8238 Daniels, Bob. DJ (KDAL, Duluth, MN, 1948).

8239 Daniels, Catherine. COM-HE (WISH, Indianapolis, IN, 1949).

8240 Daniels, Clara [Clare]. COM-HE (KWIN, Ashland, OH, 1949).

8241 Daniels, Ed. DJ (*Luncheon Melodies*, WGRV, Greenville, TN, 1947).

8242 Daniels, Edna. Contralto (KLDS, Independence, MO, 1926).

8243 Daniels, Elizabeth. Newscaster (KDAL, Duluth, MN, 1945–1949).

8244 Daniels, Grant. Newscaster (WSLB, Ogdensburg, NY, 1941, 1945).

8245 Daniels, Helene. Blues singer (MBS, 1937).

8246 Daniels, John. Newcaster (WLOK, Lima, OH, 1945). Sportscaster (WLOK, 1945).

8247 Daniels, John B. Senior announcer (WJZ, New York, NY, 1924–1925; WRC, Washington, DC, 1928).

8248 Daniels, Mary Ellen. Blues singer (WCFL, Chicago, IL, 1932).

8249 Daniels, Merill. DJ (*Tunes, Time and Shopping Tips*, WRRF, Washington, NC, 1947).

8250 Daniels, Nan. COM-HE (WLEA, Hornell, NY, 1956–1957).

8251 Daniels, Paul. DJ (*Matinee*, WWNH, Rochester, NH, 1948–1949).

8252 Daniels, Stuart. Newscaster (KLO, Ogden, UT, 1939).

8253 Daniels, William. Tenor (WJZ, New York, NY, 1929).

8254 Daniels, Yvonne. COM-HE (WOBS, Jacksonville, SC, 1956–1957).

8255 Danielson, Jim. DJ (*Drugstore Cowboy*, KSLM, Salem, OR, 1949).

8256 Dann, Harvey. DJ (WJAG, Norfolk, NE, 1957; *Man About Music*, KRMD, Shreveport, LA, 1960).

8257 D'Anna, Edward. Leader (*Edward D'Anna Orchestra*, instr. mus. prg., CBS, 1936).

8258 Dannis, Mel. Newscaster (WCOP, Boston, MA, 1942).

8259 ***Danny and August.*** Jackson Beck and Paul Daniels wrote, produced and played all the roles on this sustaining program that dramatized the news. Danny, the cop on the beat, bought a paper each time at his friend August's shop. After the headlines were read, various news events were dramatized (15 min., Wednesday, 12:25–12:30 P.M., WBNX, New York, NY, 1935).

8260 ***(The) Danny Kaye Show.*** (30 min., Friday, 10:30–11:00 P.M., CBS, 1945). Although frenetic movie comic Kaye was assisted by a fine writing, production and acting team on the program, he never achieved great success on radio. The program was directed by Goodman Ace and written by Ace and Sylvia Fine, Kaye's wife. The cast included: Goodman Ace, Eve Arden, Jim Backus, John Brown, Everett Clark, Jane Cowl, Joan Edwards, Rush Hughes, Butterfly McQueen and Lionel Stander. Music was by the Four Clubmen vocal group and the orchestras of Harry James, Lyn Murray, David Terry and Harry Sosnik (CBS, 1944–1946).

8261 ***(The) Danny Thomas Show.*** Danny Thomas (Amos Jacobs) was the comedian host on the sustaining variety show that *Variety* called "unimaginative." The show first appeared on NBC as a sustaining program in 1942. Guitarist George Barnes, vocalist Marion Mann, Hans Conreid, Marvin Miller and Rex Mauphin's Orchestra were featured. Ben Gage was the announcer (30 min., Wednesday, 9:15–9:45 P.M.). When revived in 1947, the sponsor was Pabst Blue Ribbon Beer. In this version, Thomas was assisted by Eve Arden, Jim Backus and Kenny Delmar. The various orchestras that provided the music were Harry James, Lyn Murray, Harry Sosnik and David Terry. Ken Niles and Dick Joy were the announcers (30 min., Weekly, ABC, 1942–1943; CBS, 1947–1948).

8262 **Dan's Musical Dons.** Dan's orchestra broadcast from Denver's Arena Club (KOA, Denver, CO, 1927).

8263 **Dant, Charles.** Leader (*Charles Dant Orchestra*, instr. mus. prg., NBC, 1940; WMAQ, Chicago, IL; KFI, Los Angeles, CA, 1942).

8264 ***Dantro the Planet Man.*** In the early 1950s, this science-fiction adventure series appeared briefly on several stations by transcription. The opening was as follows: "This is the fascinating story of Dantro the Planet Man, troubleshooter for the League of Planets organization, the law enforcement body for peace and justice in the celestial world, whose headquarters and center of operations are situated in the capital of all the planets — Planeteria Rex. From Mercury to Pluto, wherever danger threatens the universe, you will find Dentro the Planet Man fighting for fair play. In a moment — the planet man." The program was not one of the strongest adventure series on the air (15 min., Transcribed, 1950s).

8265 **Dantzig, Eli.** Leader (*Eli Dantzig Orchestra*, instr. mus. prg., CBS, 1935; NBC, 1937).

8266 **Dantzler, Rex.** Tenor (WGHB, Clearwater, FL, 1926).

8267 **Dantzler, Taurance.** Leader (*Taurance Dantzler Orchestra*, instr. mus. prg, KMTR, Los Angeles, CA, 1932).

8268 **Danus, Anna.** Pianist (WELI, New Haven, CT, 1937).

8269 **Darby, Bill.** Leader (Bill Darby's Cotillion Hotel Orchestra, KGW, Portland, Oregon, 1924).

8270 **Darby, Madaliene.** Soprano (KGO, Oakland, CA, 1926).

8271 **Darby, Ruth.** COM-HE (WILK, Wilkes-Barre, PA, 1951).

8272 **D'Arcy, Constance.** COM-HE (WBZ-WBZA, Boston-Springfield, MA, 1928). Miss D'Arcy specialized in Broadway news and gossip.

8273 **D'Arcy, Don.** Baritone (*Don D'Arcy*, vcl. mus. prg., WOR, Newark, NJ, 1935–1936).

8274 **Dare, Virginia.** Singer (WHO, Des Moines, IA, 1937).

8275 **D'Arezzo, Buddy.** Newscaster (KROW, Oakland, CA, 1941).

8276 **Dariens, Frank, Jr.** DJ (*Hits and Misses for the Mrs.* and *Seven Till Bedlam*, KSJO, San Jose, CA, 1948–1949; *Frank's Juke Box*, KSJO, 1952–1954). Sportscaster (KSJO, 1949).

8277 **Dark, Glenn.** DJ (KIST, Santa Barbara, CA, 1960).

8278 ***Dark Destiny.*** The weekly dramatic series presented weird stories of the occult and the supernatural. Each story was based on the idea that: "There are lives foredoomed from the beginning. There are souls born beneath dark stars who must travel by strange and terrible roads to meet their destinies." Robert Arthur and David Kogan wrote the sustaining horror drama advancing the unlucky, if not the bad seed, theory of heredity. Jack Johnstone was the producer (30 min., Wednesday, 9:30–10:00 P.M., WOR, Newark, NJ, 1942).

8279 ***Dark Enchantment.*** Marion Parsonnet produced the unique sustaining program written by William Lennox. It dramatized, *Variety* said, "Negro versions of fairy tales." Lennox said he had "heard the stories from an elderly Negro." The entertaining program featured unidentified African-Armerican performers. Robert Armbruster composed and conducted the program's special music (30 min., Tuesday, 9:30–10:00 p.m, WOR, Newark, NJ, 1935).

8280 ***Dark Fantasy.*** This anthology program, first aired in 1941, dramatized various stories of encounters with the supernatural (30 min., Weekly, NBC, 1941–1942).

8281 **Dark Town Wanderers.** Singing group specializing in southern melodies and spirituals, they were a great listener favorite (NBC-Red, New York, NY, 1929).

8282 ***(The) Darkey Jubilee Program.*** The Melody Club singers were presented on the local program accompanied by the Virgil Howard Orchestra (WOK, Pine Bluff, AR, 1922).

8283 **Darktown Orchestra.** Popular club band (KFWB, Hollywood, CA, 1925).

8284 **Darley, Larry.** Newscaster (*The Town Crier*, KVOP, Plainview, TX, 1946). DJ (*All-Request*, KVOP, Plainview, TX, 1947).

8285 **Darling, Dixie.** COM-HE (WTVM, Columbus, GA, 1957).

8286 **Darling, Sue.** COM-HE (KCRG, Cedar Rapids, IA, 1954).

8287 **Darling, Velva.** Broadcast "chats about movies" (KNX, Los Angeles, CA, 1932).

8288 **Darlington, (Dr.) Thomas.** Dr. Darlington began a series of health talks, *Health and Efficiency* on March 4, 1922 (WJZ, New York, NY).

8289 **Darmonte, Jerome.** Accordionist (KTAB, Oakland, CA, 1926).

8290 **Darnay, Toni.** Versatile radio actress Darnay appeared on the daytime serials *Nona from Nowhere*, *When a Girl Marries* and *The Strange Romance of Evelyn Winters.*

8291 **Darnell, Lyndell Decker.** Soprano (WJAX, Cleveland, OH, 1924).

8292 **Darogan, Clara.** Pianist (WFAA, Dallas, TX, 1926).

8293 **Darrie, Dick.** Leader (*Dick Darrie Orchestra*, instr. mus. prg., KLZ, Denver, CO, 1939).

8294 **Darrow, Ben H.** Darrow hosted the *Ohio School of the Air* series of programs (WLW, Cincinnati, OH, 1928–1929).

8295 **Darvas, Lillie.** Actress Darvas was a cast member of the daytime serials *Hilltop House* and *We Love and Learn.*

8296 **Darville, Jessie.** Soprano (WHN, New York, NY, 1924).

8297 **Darwin, Glen.** Baritone (*Glen Darwin*, vcl. mus. prg., NBC, 1939).

8298 **Dary, Alan.** DJ (*Stardust in the Afternoon*, WBRY, Waterbury, CT, 1948; *Dary Go Round*, WORL, Boston, MA, 1949–1955; WBZ-WBZA, Boston, MA, 1957; WBZ, Boston, MA, 1960).

8299 **D'Asalena, Helen.** Soprano (KGO, San Francisco, CA, 1926).

8300 **Dash, (Captain) V.A.** Newscaster (*The News Behind the Headlines,* WFNC, Fayetteville, NC, 1940).

8301 **Dasher, Russell.** Leader (*Russell Dasher Orchestra*, instr. mus. prg., WHP, Harrisburg, PA, 1938–1939, 1942).

8302 **Dat, George.** DJ (*Daytime,* KERO, Bakersfield, CA, 1949).

8303 **D'Attali, Clauco.** Eight-year-old pianist (WOR, Newark, NJ, 1929).

8304 **Daub, Jack.** Sportscaster (WAPO, Chattanooga, TN, 1941).

8305 **Daubenspeck, Ed.** Newscaster (*Empire Builder*, KIYI, Shelby, MT, 1948).

8306 **Daubenspeck, Eloise.** Producer (CBS, 1939). Daubenspeck produced the *School of the Air* program.

8307 **Daugherty, Bert.** DJ (*Yours For the Asking* and *Music for You*, KWAL, Wallace, ID, 1947–1949).

8308 **Daugherty, Catherine.** COM-HE (WKBI, St. Mary's, PA, 1954).

8309 **Daugherty, Deacon.** DJ (*Reveille Round-Up*, KREL, Baytown, TX 1948).

8310 **Daugherty, Dick.** DJ (*Coffee Time*, WFIN, Findlay, OH, 1952–1955).

8311 **Daugherty, Harold "Doc."** Director (Hotel Traymore Dance Orchestra, WPG, Atlantic City, NJ, 1928).

8312 **Daugherty, Harold.** DJ (*1250 Luncheon Club*, WNOW, York, PA, 1948).

8313 Daugherty, Jim. DJ (*Pop Parade*, KWPC, Muscatine, IA, 1952).

8314 Daugherty, Nell aka Anne Davenport. COM-HE (WSTC, Stamford, CT, 1949).

8315 Daugherty, Stan. Leader (*Stan Daugherty Orchestra*, instr. mus. prg., KXOK, St. Louis, MO, 1942).

8316 Daugherty, Vivian. COM-HE (WGBA, Columbus, GA, 1951).

8317 Daulton, Jack. Leader (Jack Daulton and his Orchestra, KVOO, Tulsa, OK, 1928).

8318 Daum, Eleanor. COM-HE (WTRW, Two Rivers, WI, 1958–1960).

8319 Daum, Margaret. Soprano (*Margaret Daum*, vcl. mus. prg., CBS, 1935).

8320 Daunt, Charles. Tenor (*Charles Daunt*, WCKY, Covington, KY, early 1930s).

8321 Dauscha, Billie. Contralto (WOR, Newark, NJ, 1929).

8322 Davallo, Bill. Leader (Bill Davallo Orchestra, WOOD, Grand Rapids, MI, 1926).

8323 Dave and Evelyn. Singing team of Dave Morris and Evelyn Kitts (KOIL, Council Bluffs, IA, 1928).

8324 *Dave Vine Show.* Comic Dave Vine told gags and introduced various guest vocalists such as James Barton on his half-hour variety show (30 min., Tuesday, 8:30–9:00 P.M., WOR, Newark, NJ, 1934). Vine also hosted a quarter-hour comedy show on WOR the same year. Later, comedian Vine and various guest stars performed on another local variety show (*The Dave Vine Show*, 30 min., Sunday, 8:00–8:30 P.M., WMCA, New York, NY, 1936).

8325 Davenport, (Mrs.) C.W. Contralto (KWWG, Brownsville, TX, 1926).

8326 Davenport, Eddie. Sportscaster (*Sports Review*, WWPB, Miami, FL, 1953).

8327 Davenport, Frank. Leader (Frank Davenport and his Orchestra, WFAA, Dallas, TX, 1925).

8328 Davenport, James A. Newscaster (WRDW, Augusta, GA, 1938–1939).

8329 Davenport, John. Newscaster (WAIM, Anderson, SC, 1945).

8330 Davenport, Len. DJ (*Nightwatch*, KRUX, Phoenix, AZ, 1948).

8331 Davenport, May. Actress Davenport appeared on the *Against the Storm* daytime serial.

8332 Davenport, Uncle Dave. Uncle Dave was a popular teller of bedtime stories for children (KHQ, Spokane, WA, 1929).

8333 Davenport Hotel Dance Orchestra. Hotel orchestra directed by Emil Couture (KHQ, Spokane, WA, 1926–1928).

8334 Davey, C.V. Newscaster (KQW, San Jose, CA, 1937).

8335 Davey, Joe. Pianist (WGN, Chicago, IL, 1925).

8336 *(The) Davey Hour.* The Davey Tree Experts Company sponsored the program that featured organist and music director, Chandler Goldwaithe; violinist Arcadie Birkenholtz; actress Paula Heminghaus; instrumental soloists and a mixed vocal quartet on this eclectic program of classical, semi-classical and folk music. John S. Young was the announcer (30 min., 5:30–6:00 P.M., NBC-Red, 1932).

8337 David, Art. DJ (*Early Worm*, KGYW, Vallejo, CA, 1947).

8338 David, Avery. DJ (*Jive Til Five*, WPLI, Jackson, TN, 1949).

8339 David, Gil. DJ (WSBA, York, PA, 1959).

8340 David, Louise. COM-HE (WFIS, Fountain Inn, SC, 1958–1960).

8341 David, Lowe. Movie reviewer (WNEW, New York, NY, 1939).

8342 David, Russ. Leader (*Russ David Orchestra*, instr. mus. prg., WMAQ, Chicago, IL and KSD, St. Louis, MO, 1942).

8343 David, Tinny. Sportscaster (WYNK, Baton Rouge, LA, 1960).

8344 David, Toby. DJ (WJR, Detroit, MI, 1947).

8345 *David Harum.* Frank and Anne Hummert produced this daytime serial that told the story of David Harum, played consecutively by Wilmer Walter, Craig McDonnell and Cameron Prud'Homme. David, a small town banker with a kind heart, helped all those he could by trying to hold in check the scheming citizens of his little town of Hometown. He has been described as a lovable character with a keen mind, who willingly interfered with fate to soften the blows that were intended for his friends.

The program's opening was notable for its theme, "Sunbonnet Sue," that was hummed and strummed by guitarist Stanley Davis. Over the years the cast included: Charme Allen, Peggy Allenby, Ray Bramley, Donald Briggs, Eva Condon, Joseph "Joe" Curtin, Marjorie Davies, Ethel Everett, Roy Fant, Paul Ford, Bennett Kilpack, Florence Lake, Arthur Maitland, Junius Matthews, Richard McKay, Claudia Morgan, Billy Redfield, Philip Reed, William Shelley, Paul Stewart, Joan Tompkins, Gertrude Warner and Ken Williams. The announcer was Ford Bond. Martha Atwell, John Buckwalter, Arthur Hanna, Ed King and Lester Vail were the directors. Peggy Blake, John DeWitt, Noel B. Gerson, Charles J. Gussman, Johanna Johnston and Mary W. Reeves were the writers.

8346 *David Lawrence.* Newspaperman-columnist Lawrence broadcast a weekly program of news analysis and commentary (15 min., Sunday, 9:00–9:15 P.M., 1927–1928).

8347 *David Rose.* Procter and Gamble sponsored the music program featuring David Rose and his orchestra as a summer replacement for the *Red Skelton show.* Fort Pearson was the announcer (30 min., Sunday, 8:30–9:00 P.M., CBS, 1950).

8348 Davidoff, George. Russian pianist (WOR, Newark, NJ, 1926).

8349 Davidoff, Yasha. Baritone (*Yasha Davidoff*, vcl. mus. prg., NBC, 1934; WOR, Newark, NJ, 1935).

8350 Davids, Lou. Newscaster (WFMJ, Youngstown, OH, 1944–1945).

8351 Davidson, Bryan. DJ (*Melody Time*, WSON, Henderson, KY, 1947).

8352 Davidson, Bryon. DJ (*1450 Club*, WAOV, Vincennes, IN, 1947).

8353 Davidson, Dave. Singer and musician Davidson was billed as the "Crooning trumpador," perhaps a misspelling of "troubadour" (KTHS, Hot Springs Natural Park, AR, 1928).

8354 Davidson, Gretchen. Actress Davidson was cast member of the daytime serial program *Life Begins* aka *Martha Webster.*

8355 Davidson, Kay. Singer (WBBM, Chicago, IL, 1925).

8356 Davidson, Meade. Newscaster (WWRL, Woodside, NY, 1942, 1944–1945; *News Analysis*, WWRL, 1947; *Leaders in Exile*, WWRL, 1948).

8357 Davidson, Randall. Newscaster (WAIM, Anderson, SC, 1945). Sportscaster (WAIM, 1945).

8358 Davidson, Thelma. COM-HE (KCRV, Caruthersville, MO, 1958).

8359 Davidson, Tom. Newscaster (WBIX, Muskogee, OK, 1946). Sportscaster (KBIX, 1946).

8360 Davidson, Trump. Leader (*Trump Davidson Orchestra*, instr. mus. prg., NBC-Red, New York, NY, 1937).

8361 Davidson, Vee. Leader (*Vee Davidson Orchestra*, instr. mus. prg., WHAS, Louisville, KY, 1933).

8362 Davie, Victoria. Contralto (WWJ, Detroit, MI, 1924).

8363 Davies, Alden E. Tenor (WBZ, Boston-Springfield, MA, 1924).

8364 Davies, Bill. Newscaster (WBLJ, Dalton, GA, 1940; WDOD, Chattanooga, TN, 1941).

8365 Davies, Bob. Sportscaster (KARM, Fresno, CA, 1938–1939; KFRE, Fresno, CA, 1942; KOL, Seattle, WA, 1946; KMUR, Murray, UT, 1951). Newscaster (KARM, 1938–1939; KSAN, San Francisco, CA, 1940; KRFE, 1942; KVAK, Atchison, KS, 1945; KOL, 1946).

8366 Davies, Clara Novello. Leader (Clara Novello's Choir, WBZ, Boston-Springfield, MA, 1925).

8367 Davies, Dave. Newscaster (WAZL, Hazleton, PA, 1946).

8368 Davies, Doug. Newscaster (WTCN, Minneapolis–St. Paul, MN, 1944).

8369 Davies, Douglas. Newscaster (WDOD, Chattanooga, TN, 1945).

8370 Davies, Edward. Baritone (*Edward Davies*, vcl. mus. prg., NBC, 1933, 1939).

8371 Davies, Edward A. Announcer-director (WIP, Philadelphia, PA, 1925–1928).

8372 Davies, Gwen. Singer (WBBM, Chicago, IL, 1942).

8373 Davies, Jack. Newscaster (KSL, Salt Lake City, UT, 1941). Sportscaster (KSL, 1941).

8374 Davies, Lawson S.C. DJ (*Diggin' the Discs with Davies*, KCSU, Provo, UT, 1947).

8375 Davies, Lew. Leader (*Lew Davies Orchestra*, instr. mus. prg., WHAM, Rochester, NY, 1937; MBS, 1938).

8376 Davies, Lynn. Newscaster (WAIR, Winston-Salem, NC, 1941).

8377 Davies, Marion. When motion picture star Davies spoke about "How I Made Up for the Movies" (WEAF, New York, NY, January 17, 1923), she received an avalanche of mail from listeners. Before the Davies' broadcast, station WEAF usually received only one or two letters a day. After her broadcast so much mail poured into the station that its commercial manager rushed off to tell advertisers about it. Before the end of 1923, the station was receiving 800 letters a day.

8378 Davies, Marjorie. Daytime serial actress (*Today's Children* and *David Harum*).

8379 Davis, Al. Sportscaster (*Scoreboard Forecast*, KTVO, Ottumwa, IA, 1960).

8380 Davis, Alma. COM-HE (WCSC, Charleston, SC, 1956–1957).

8381 Davis, Anne. COM-HE (WJHO, Opelika, AL, 1949).

8382 Davis, Art. DJ (*Western Roundup*, KEPO, El Paso, TX, 1952).

8383 Davis, Bert. Comedian Davis was billed as "The Clown of the Air" (WQJ, Chicago, IL, 1925).

8384 Davis, Bette. COM-HE (WTHE, Spartanburg, SC, 1957–1958).

8385 Davis, Betty. COM-HE (KOIN, Portland, OR, 1960).

8386 Davis, Betty. COM-HE (WSON, Henderson, KY, 1960).

8387 Davis, Bill. DJ (*Sheriff Davis*, WLOW, Norfolk, VA, 1949). Sportscaster (WLOW, 1951–1953).

8388 Davis, Bob. Newscaster (KWLK, Longview, WA, 1946).

8389 Davis, Bobbie Lee. DJ (*Record Room*, KTMS, Santa Barbara, CA, 1952).

8390 Davis, Britt. DJ (*Musical Roundup*, KOWB, Laramie, WY, 1948).

8391 Davis, Buzz. Sportscaster (WDAS, Philadelphia, PA, 1938–1940).

8392 Davis, C. James. DJ (*All Colored Review*, WHNC, Henderson, NC, 1949).

8393 Davis, Charlie. Ukulele soloist (KGFJ, Los Angeles, CA, 1929).

8394 Davis, Charlie. Leader (*Charlie Davis Orchestra*, instr. mus. prg., CBS, 1933–1934; ABS, 1935).

8395 Davis, Charlie. DJ (*Rock 'N Roll*, WAPX, Montgomery, AL, 1948).

8396 Davis, Clyde. Popular singer and violinist (KFAB, Lincoln, NE, 1928).

8397 Davis, Clyde C. DJ (*Morning Rise 'n' Shine*, WAYX, Waycross, GA, 1947–1948).

8398 Davis, Count Connie. DJ (*Highway of Melody*, KWRE, Warrenton, MO, 1949).

8399 Davis, Dan. DJ (WMCA, New York, NY, 1960).

8400 Davis, Don. Sportscaster (KEVE, Everett, WA, 1942). Newscaster (KWLK, Longview, WA, 1946). DJ (*Flying Discs*, KFRC, San Francisco, CA, 1947-1950; *Open House*, KFRC, 1952–1955).

8401 Davis, Don. DJ (*Jamboree* and *Old Time Hit Parade*, WCKY, Cincinnati, OH, 1948; *Saturday Nite Dance Party*, WLW, Cincinnati, OH, 1949).

8402 Davis, Dorothy. COM-HE (*Dorothy Davis Advice on Cleaning Clothes*, WEEI, Boston, MA, 1934).

8403 Davis, Dorothy. COM-HE (KIST, Santa Barbara, CA, 1958–1960).

8404 Davis, Earl. Sportscaster (KPAT, Pampa, TX, 1956). DJ (*Evening Serenade*, KPDN, Pampa, TX, 1960).

8405 Davis, Earle. DJ (KTHS, Little Rock, AR, 1957).

8406 Davis, Ed. DJ (*Midnite Platter Party*, WFPG, Steel Pier, Atlantic City, NJ, 1947–1950).

8407 Davis, Eddie. Sportscaster (WTOC, Savannah, GA, 1946). DJ (*The Alarm Clock Club*, WTOC, 1947).

8408 Davis, Edith. Singer (*Edith Davis*, voc. mus. prg., WOR, Newark, NJ, 1936).

8409 Davis, Edward. Baritone (*Edward Davis*, vcl. mus. prg., NBC-Blue, New York, NY, 1936).

8410 Davis, Edward and Olga Kargon. Vocal team (*Edward Davis and Olga Kargon*, vcl. mus. prg., NBC-Blue, 1935).

8411 Davis, Elizabeth. Pianist (*Elizabeth Davis*, instr. mus. prg., WCAO, Baltimore, MD, 1935).

8412 Davis, Elmer. Davis was a distinguished news analyst and commentator (CBS, 1939–1942; WMAL, Washington, DC and ABC, 1946–1947). Hoosier Davis began his career at the New York *Times*, where he worked for ten years before leaving to become a free lance writer. A liberal, who was a strong supporter of socialist Norman Thomas in 1932, Davis supported FDR after he became president. His strong anti–Fascist views and liberal philosophy made him a patriotic commentator precisely right for his time and place.

Davis previously had a brief career in radio, but returned in 1939 to join CBS to do an uncensored nightly commentary (8:55–9:00 P.M., CBS, 1939). He continued at CBS until 1942, when FDR asked him to head the OWI (Office of War Information), a task he performed admirably throughout the remainder of World War II. After the war's conclusion he returned to broadcasting until 1953, when poor health forced him to retire. Davis was a strong advocate of and spokesman for the freedom of thought and speech. He believed both should be free and completely unhampered. He proved to be one of Senator Joseph F. McCarthy's staunchest foes.

8413 Davis, Emma. Whistler (KFSG, Los Angeles, CA, 1926).

8414 Davis, Ernie. DJ (*Clover Club*, WCSS, Amsterdam, NY, 1948; *Ernie Davis Show*, WABY, Albany, NY, 1952).

8415 Davis, Ethel. Music discussion programs (*Music Chats*, WCAE, Pittsburgh, PA, 1925).

8416 Davis, Etheldra. COM-HE (WLET, Toledo, OH, 1951).

8417 Davis, Eva. COM-HE (WQBC, Vicksburg, MS, 1949).

8418 Davis, Gary. Newscaster (WMFR, High Point, NC, 1941, 1945–1946).

8419 Davis, Gene. DJ (WDOK, Cleveland, OH, 1949; *Requests Review*, WAKR, Akron, OH, 1952–1954; *Coffee Time*, KWK, St. Louis, MO, 1960). Sportscaster (*Sportlight*, WDOK, 1949).

8420 Davis, Genevieve. Singer Davis was a member of the Wynken, Blynken and Nod vocal trio (KDYL, Salt Lake City, UT, 1929).

8421 Davis, Geoff. DJ (*Singing Battle Royal*, WINS, New York, NY, 1947–1948; *Battle of the Baritones*, WINS, 1949). Sportscaster (WINS, 1947–1951).

8422 Davis, George T. Sportscaster (KFW, San Francisco, CA, 1927).

8423 Davis, Glen. Evangelist (WIP, Philadelphia, PA, 1942).

8424 Davis, Gwen. Singer (*Gwen Davis*, vcl. mus. prg., WBBM, Chicago, IL, 1942).

8425 Davis, Hal. DJ (*Music for the Party*, KCMJ, Palm Springs, CA, 1947; *Songs of Enchantment*, KRAM, Las Vegas, NV, 1948).

8426 Davis, Hal. DJ (*Easy Listening*, WDUZ, Green Bay, WI, 1948).

8427 Davis, Harold. Davis was billed as "Harold Davis and his Banjo" (KFI, Los Angeles, CA, 1928).

8428 Davis, Harry. Baritone (WEBH, Chicago, IL, 1924).

8429 Davis, Harry. Leader (Harry Davis and his Ballroom Entertainers [orchestra], KLX, Oakland, CA, 1925).

8430 Davis, Hassoldt. Newscaster (NBC, 1942).

8431 Davis, Helen. Banjo soloist (WJZ, New York, NY, 1924–1926).

8432 Davis, Helen. COM-HE (KIBE-KDFC, San Francisco, CA, 1960).

8433 Davis, Helen. COM-HE (*Stichin' Time*, KGNO, Dodge City, KS, 1949).

8434 Davis, Helen C. COM-HE (WCUM, Cumberland, MD, 1951).

8435 Davis, Hy. DJ (*Ranch Party*, WJXN, Jackson, MS, 1949). Sportscaster (WJXN, 1949).

8436 Davis, Jack. Leader (Jack Davis Orchestra, WFAA, Dallas, TX, 1924).

8437 Davis, (Mrs.) Jack. Mezzo-soprano (KTAB, Oakland, CA, 1925).

8438 Davis, Jack. Singer (WGBH, Clearwater, FL, 1926).

8439 Davis, Jack. Sportscaster (WCAU, Philadelphia, PA, 1944).

8440 Davis, Jack. Sportscaster (WEAU, Eau Claire, WI, 1944). DJ (*Music Shop*, WBIZ, Eau Claire, WI, 1948).

8441 Davis, Jack. DJ (*Turntable Time*, WWXL, Peoria, IL, 1948).

8442 Davis, Jack. Sportscaster (WALL, Middletown, NY, 1944).

8443 Davis, James Houston "Jimmie." Louisiana born country singer and composer Jimmie Davis went on to become twice governor of his home state in 1944 and 1960. He began his radio career on KWKH (Shreveport, LA, 1928). Radio always played a large part in both his political and music career. Davis is best known as composer and singer of his most famous composition, "You Are My Sunshine."

8444 Davis, Jean. Harpist-singer (WMAQ, Chicago, IL, 1923).

8445 Davis, Jean. COM-HE (WGIG, Brunswick, GA, 1955–1957).

8446 Davis, Jerry. Newscaster (WCAP, Asbury Park, NJ, 1938).

8447 Davis, (Mrs.) Jerry. COM-HE (WGIG, Brunswick, GA, 1957).

8448 Davis, Jim. Newscaster (WORD, Spartanburg, SC, 1946). Sportscaster (WORD, 1946).

8449 Davis, Jim. DJ (*Kowboy Kapers*, KOWB, Laramie, WY, 1960).

8450 Davis, Joan. Singer (*Joan Davis with the Laddies*, vcl. mus. prg., WHAS, Louisville, KY, 1935).

8451 Davis, Joan. *See* **Comediennes.**

8452 Davis, John Lee. DJ (WKEY, Covington, VA, 1947).

8453 Davis, John. Newscaster (WWSW, Pittsburgh, PA, 1937–1942, 1945–1947).

8454 Davis, Johnny. Leader (*Johnny Davis Orchestra*, instr. mus. prg., WGN, Chicago, IL, 1934, 1939).

8455 Davis, (Miss) Johnye. Pianist (WFAA, Dallas, TX, 1925).

8456 Davis, Kennie. DJ (*Platter Parade*, WHOC, Philadelphia, MS, 1948).

8457 Davis, Lane. Newscaster (*Phillips Petroleum Company Program*, *RCA News Broadcast* and *McDaniel Milling Company Broadcast*, WMBH, Joplin, MO, 1937; KWTO-KGBX, Springfield, MO, 1938–1939).

8458 Davis, Les. Sportscaster (*Today in the World of Sports*, WNAX, Yankton, SD, 1948–1960).

8459 Davis, Les. Sportscaster (WAVY, Norfolk, VA, 1956).

8460 Davis, Lillian. COM-HE (WSSC, Sumter, SC, 1954).

8461 Davis, Louise. COM-HE (KBOI, Boise, ID, 1960).

8462 Davis, Lulubelle. COM-HE (KPAC, Port Arthur, TX, 1960).

8463 Davis, Margie. DJ (*Jack and Jill*, WHIO, Dayton, OH, 1948).

8464 Davis, Marguerite. COM-HE (KXOB, Stockton, CA, 1954).

8465 Davis, Marion. Soprano (KTAB, Oakland, CA, 1926).

8466 Davis, Mark. Leader (Mark Davis Orchestra, WEAF, New York, NY, 1924).

8467 Davis, Meyer. Leader (Meyer Davis Orchestra, WFI, Philadelphia, PA, 1923; Meyer Davis Society Orchestra, WJZ, New York, NY, 1924; Meyer Davis New Arlington Orchestra; New Arlington Ensemble directed by Jacques Renard, KTHS, Hot Springs National Park, AK, 1925; Meyer Davis Le Paradis Orchestra, WRC, Washington, DC, 1926; Meyer Davis Swannee Syncapators, WPG, Atlantic City, NJ, 1926; Meyer Davis Orchestra, WEAF, New York, NY, 1926). Meyer Davis had many units playing simultaneously on different radio stations and in various clubs around the country in the following decade (*Meyer Davis Orchestra*, instr. mus. prg.,MBC. 1933; *Meyer Davis's Hotel St. Regis Orchestra*, instr. mus. prg., NBC, 1933; WCAU, Philadelphia, PA, 1934).

8468 Davis, Mildred. Miss Davis conducted a radio cooking school (KDKA, Pittsburgh, PA, 1928).

8469 Davis, Ovide. DJ (*1490 Club*, KCIL, Houma, LA, 1947–1949).

8470 Davis, Pat. COM-HE (KCLW, Hamilton, TX, 1957).

8471 Davis, Pearl Calhoun. Singer (WBAP, Fort Worth, TX, 1925).

8472 Davis, Phil. Leader (*Phil Davis Orchestra*, instr. mus. prg., WLW, Cincinnati, OH, 1937).

8473 Davis, Rex. Sportscaster (WCKY, Cincinnati, OH, 1937–1940). Newscaster (WCKY, 1938–1945; KMOX, St. Louis, MO, 1947–1948).

8474 Davis, Richard Harding. Newscaster (WGTM, Wilson, SC, 1945).

8475 Davis, Robert. Newscaster (KVOR, Colorado Springs, CO, 1941; *Report to the Valley*, KSRV, Ontario, OR, 1947).

8476 Davis, Rodney. Leader (*Rodney Davis Orchestra*, WBBM, Chicago, IL, 1935).

8477 Davis, Roy E. Announcer Davis worked for the Reo Motor Car Company's station (WREO, Lansing, MI, 1925–1926) and proudly announced its slogan, "Watch REO."

8478 Davis, Rubi. Violinist (WEAF, New York, NY, 1925).

8479 Davis, Sara. COM-HE (KAGR, Yuba City, CA, 1956–1957).

8480 Davis, Sig. Sportscaster (WMIN, St. Paul, MN, 1937–1938).

8481 Davis, Stanley. Sportscaster conducted a program for golfers (*Down the Fairways with Stanley Davis*, WOW, Omaha, NE, 1935).

8482 Davis, Sue. COM-HE (WACE, Springfield-Chicopee, MA, 1958).

8483 Davis, Suzanne. Violinist (KGB, San Diego, CA, 1929).

8484 Davis, Suzi. COM-HE (KICK, Springfield, MS, 1960).

8485 Davis, Tex. DJ (*All Star Record Roundup*, WELS, Kinston, SC, 1952).

8486 Davis, Tom. Tenor (*Tom Davis*, vcl. mus. prg., WOR, Newark, NJ, 1934–1935; WIP, Philadelphia, PA, 1935).

8487 Davis, Tom. DJ and sportscaster (WCBM, Baltimore, MD, late 1950s).

8488 Davis, Velda. COM-HE (KSPI, Stillwater, OK, 1954).

8489 Davis, Verna. Singer (WROK, Rockford, IL, 1957).

8490 Davis, Wendy. Sportscaster (WBZ-WBZA, Boston and Springfield, MA, 1941–1942).

8491 Davis, Wilbur. Baritone (*Wilbur Davis*, vcl. mus. prg., WPG, Atlantic City, NJ, 1936).

8492 Davis, Willard. Newscaster (KRKD, Los Angeles, CA, 1941).

8493 Davis, Zona B. COM-HE (WCRA, Effingham, IL, 1957).

8494 Davis Baking Powder Saxophone Octet. Popular instrumental group (WBAP, San Antonio, TX, 1926).

8495 Davis Radio Orchestra. Kansas City radio band (WDAF, Kansas City, MO, 1924).

8496 *(The) Davis Saxophone Octette.* Led by Clyde Davis, this small instrumental group was widely praised by critics. The octette appeared on its own weekly programs (WJZ, New York, NY and WEAF, New York, NY, 1926).

8497 Davison, Janet. COM-HE (WCON, Cornelia, GA, 1958).

8498 Davison, Randy. Sportscaster (WAIM, Anderson, SC, 1945). Newscaster (WAIM, 1945).

8499 Davison, Janet. COM-HE (WKIP, Poughkeepsie, NY, 1958–1960).

8500 Davison, (Dr.) W.T. A health officer of the city of Dallas, Texas, Davison delivered health talks (WFAA, Dallas, TX, 1927).

8501 Davison Sisters. A singing sisters team (WHAG, New York, NY, 1925).

8502 Davitt, Barbara. COM-HE (WKIP, Poughkeepsie, NY, 1958–1960).

8503 Davy, Fred. DJ (*Just for You*, WJAS, Pittsburgh, PA, 1948). Sportscaster (WJAS, 1951).

8504 Daw, Edna. Drummer (KWSC, Pullman, WA, 1925–1926).

8505 Dawdy, Maurine. COM-HE (WLIK, Jefferson City, MO, 1956).

8506 Dawes, Bill. Newscaster (WCKY, Cincinnati, OH, 1945). DJ (*Bill Dawes Show*, WCPO, Cincinnati, OH, 1948–1957).

8507 Dawes, Clara. Soprano (WTAQ, Green Bay, WI, 1938–1939).

8508 Dawley, Dorothy. COM-HE (WSLI, Jackson, MS, 1957).

8509 Dawley, Walter. Organist (WTIC, Hartford, CT, 1928; *Walter Dawley*, instr. mus. prg., WTIC, Hartford, CT, 1935).

8510 Dawn, Dolly (Theresa Maria Stabile). Singer-leader (*Dolly Dawn Orchestra*, instr. mus. prg, NBC, 1935). Born Theresa Maria Stabile in Newark, NJ, February 3, 1919, as Dolly Dawn she became one of radio's best known female singers and band leaders. George Hall's good band with vocalist Loretta Lee frequently was heard on many remote broadcasts in the early 1930s. Vocalist Lee was replaced in 1935 by Dolly Dawn. Dawn's vocals on the band's many Bluebird recordings and numerous radio remotes from New York's Hotel Taft brought her national popularity. (Hall's band broadcast six times a week for 30 minutes on CBS.) On July 4, 1941, Hall, who functioned as the band's manager, turned the band over to Dawn. Although she achieved success, Dolly Dawn and Her Dawn Patrol disbanded in 1942, due to the many problems caused by World War II. Nevertheless, she continued singing and recording.

8511 Dawn, Julia. Singing organist (WGR, Buffalo, NY, 1929).

8512 Dawn, Marian. Singer (WFBR, Baltimore, MD, 1942).

8513 Dawson, Anne. COM-HE (WGKV, Charleston, WV, 1949).

8514 Dawson, Bill. DJ (*Housewives' Requests*, WPAY, Portsmouth, OH, 1947; *Burnt Toast and Coffee Time*, WNXT, Portsmouth, OH, 1954–1955; WAZY, Lafayette, IN, 1960).

8515 Dawson, Bud. Sportscaster (WQUA, Moline, IL, 1953–1955).

8516 Dawson, Edward. Newscaster (KVCV, Redding, CA, 1939).

8517 Dawson, Frances. Lyric soprano (WOR, Newark, NJ, 1927).

8518 Dawson, Helen. COM-HE (WVMC, Mt. Carmel, IL, 1954).

8519 Dawson, J. Moody. Violinist (KPRC, Houston, TX, 1926).

8520 Dawson, Jack. Dawson was a singer of cowboy songs and teller of western tales (*Jack Dawson*, CW vcl. mus. prg., WIP, Philadelphia, PA, 1939).

8521 Dawson, Jack. DJ (WWIN, Baltimore, MD, 1955).

8522 Dawson, James. Newscaster (WFBC, Greenville, SC, 1940–1941).

8523 Dawson, John. Newscaster (KGDE, Fergus Falls, MN, 1948).

8524 Dawson, R.L. Newscaster (KBIZ, Ottumwa, IA, 1944). Sportscaster (KBIZ, 1944).

8525 Dawson, Roy. Newscaster (WHIT, New Berne, NC, 1942).

8526 Dawson, Stuart. Singer (WHT, Chicago, IL, 1927). Announcer (WIBO, Chicago, IL, 1925–1928).

8527 Dawson, Tom. Vocalist (*Tom Dawson*, vcl. mus. prg., WCAU, Philadelphia, PA, 1934).

8528 Dawson, Tom. DJ (*Critter Jamboree*, KGBC, Galveston, TX, 1948–1949; KTXN, Austin, TX, 1950).

8529 Dawson, Virginia. COM-HE (WGEA, Geneva, AL, 1955).

8530 Dawson, (Captain), W.H. Leader (Captain W.H. Dawson and his String Orchestra, WFAA, Dallas, TX, 1925).

8531 Day, Ada. Beauty expert Day broadcast beauty tips for women (WBBM, Chicago, IL, 1928).

8532 Day, Allison. COM-HE (WTVL, Waterville, ME, 1949).

8533 Day, Bobby. Leader (*Bobby Day Orchestra*, instr. mus. prg., CBS, 1940).

8534 Day, Charles. Newscaster (WGAR, Cleveland, OH, 1944–1945; 1947–1948).

8535 Day, Collett. Violinist (KVOO, Tulsa, OK, 1928).

8536 Day, Dean. DJ (*Man Around the House*, KRAK, Sacramento, CA, 1960).

8537 Day, Delores. News analyst (WEAN, Providence, RI, 1936).

8538 Day, Dorothy. Actress Day was a cast member of the daytime serial programs *Myrt and Marge* and *Clara, Lu and Em*.

8539 Day, Ed. Leader (*Ed Day Orchestra*, instr. mus. prg., WHK, Cleveland, OH, 1933).

8540 Day, Elizabeth. Actress Day appeared on the daytime serials *Just Plain Bill* and *Five Star Jones*.

8541 Day, Emily. Soprano (WEAF, New York, NY, 1926).

8542 Day, Erin. COM-HE (KGVO, Missoula, MT and WMSO, Missoula, MT, 1957).

8543 Day, Francis. Violinist (KVOO, Tulsa, OK, 1928).

8544 Day, George. Newscaster (KPAB, Laredo, TX, 1942).

8545 Day, Helen. COM-HE (WMIL, Milwaukee, WI, 1954–1960).

8546 Day, Jack. Newscaster (WFBR, Baltimore, MD, 1944).

8547 Day, Jane. Announcer (WASN, Boston, MA, 1927).

8548 Day, June. COM-HE (KWBB, Wichita, KS, 1960).

8549 Day, Louise. COM-HE (WFRS, Alexander City, LA, 1954–1955).

8550 Day, Lucy. Soprano (KYA, San Francisco, CA, 1929).

8551 Day, Margaret. Cellist (WBAL, Baltimore, MD, 1926).

8552 Day, May. Beauty talks were broadcast by Miss Day (KFOX, Long Beach, CA, 1929).

8553 Day, Nola. Singer (*Nola Day*, vcl. mus. prg., NBC-Blue, New York, NY, 1935).

8554 *(A) Day on the Old Plantation.* The early variety program featured "Uncle Remus and company" (KHJ, Los Angeles, CA, 1923).

8555 *(A) Day in the Life of Dennis Day* (aka *The Dennis Day Show*). Colgate-Palmolive Company sponsored the situation comedy that allowed tenor Dennis Day to show his considerable comic skill. The cast included: Bea Benadaret, John Brown, Barbara Eiler, Betty Miles and Frances "Dink" Trout. Ken Carson sang the Lustre Creme Shampoo commercials. Frank Galen was the writer and Frank O'Connor the show's director. Bill Harding was the producer-director (30 min., Thursday, 7:30–8:00 P.M., NBC-Red, 1946).

8556 Day, Richard "Dick." Newscaster (WDGY, Minneapolis–St. Paul, MN, 1942–1945).

8557 Day, Suzy. COM-HE (WJOT, Lake City, SC, 1960).

8558 Day, Verna Larraine. Contralto (KRE, Berkeley, CA, 191925; KPO, San Francisco, CA, 1925).

8559 Daye, Doris. COM-HE (KWAT, Watertown, SD, 1949).

8560 Daye, Sunny. COM-HE (WLOS, Asheville, NC,1949).

8561 Dayk, John. DJ (*Musical Mail Box*, KISD, Sioux Falls, SD, 1948).

8562 Daylie, D. DJ (*Daddy-O Show*, WAFF, Chicago, IL, 1960).

8563 Day-Ray-O (or Da-Ra-O). A children's story teller, Day-Ray-O broadcast from the "Land-O-Health," where he was the ruler. He would go walking through Slumber Forest with his young listeners and tell them his tales (KGO, San Francisco, CA, 1927).

8564 Daytime Serials ("Soap Operas"). Although they were usually called soap operas, everyone who listened to radio from 1930 to1950 knew exactly what daytime serials were. Almost everyone knew about *Mary Noble, Backstage Wife, Our Gal Sunday* and *Ma Perkins*. Although the 15-minute programming format was often laughed at and even scorned by some critics, the "soaps" did receive some critical study and even praise. Above all, they enjoyed such great popularity with their large, intensely loyal listening audience, that the daytime serial became an unique creation and influential innovation of American radio.

James Thurber in a famous series of *New Yorker* articles (Thurber, 1973, pp. 191–260) treated daytime serials with a mock serious tone, but studied them carefully with a critical seriousness that had been rarely attempted before. Thurber's articles indicate he was a student of soap opera. His study began with a tongue in cheek definition of a soap opera (Thurber, 1973, p. 191):

> A soap opera is a kind of sandwich, whose recipe is simple enough, although it took years to compound. Between thick slices of advertising, spread twelve minutes of dialogue, add predicament, villiany, and female suffering in equal measure, throw in a dash of nobility, sprinkle with tears, season with organ music, cover with a rich announcer sauce, and serve five times a week

The term *soap opera* probably arose because most of the programs were sponsored by soap companies. However, the shows were also sponsored by many other companies wanting to sell their products to the programs' predominantly female audience. It may have also been the case that the term *soap opera* was used with the derogatory connotation of the supposed low intelligence and inferior judgement of the women who comprised their audience. Neither Jim and Marian Jordan (*Fibber McGee and Molly*), nor Gertrude Berg (author of and performer on *The Goldbergs*) were pleased with the term *soap opera*. As Berg put it, "The kind of writing that has ended up being played mostly in the daylight hours is the soap opera, an unfortunate nom-de-guerre, by the way, for it unfairly carries an unmistakable aroma with it" (Berg, 1944, p. 123). Use of the term *daytime serial* helps avoid both the confusion of sole sponsorship of the programs and any derogatory connotation the term may have conveyed in the past for the women who listened to them. Moreover, the term *daytime serial* more accurately reflects the major characteristics of the programs — the time of their broadcast and their continuing nature.

In the New York City area alone, the amazing number of 36 daytime serials were broadcast from 10:30 A.M. in the morning until 6:00 P.M., Monday through Friday (1947–1948). Ten other serials broadcast outside the New York area brought the number to almost 50 running in the United States at the time. Most likely this was the high water mark for daytime serials, for television soon made its inroads, adding to the reasons that eventually caused their demise. During their golden years, a few top daytime serial actors earned $700 a week. Many stage and screen stars such as Van Heflin, Frank Lovejoy, John Hodiak, Art Carney, Richard Widmark, Macdonald Carey and Ed Begley began as daytime radio serial performers.

Daytime serials had their origin in 1925 on Chicago radio, probably with Jim and Marian Jordan's program, *The Smith Family*, an early serial drama with comic elements. It was a continuing story of the Smith family and their daily adventures. Later, after gaining fame as *Fibber McGee and Molly*, the Jordans denied *The Smith Family* was a "soap opera," because of its broad humor content. Nevertheless, the popularity of *The Smith Family* program's apparently motivated WGN (Chicago, IL) to present Gosden and Correll's *Sam 'n' Henry*, the forerunner of *Amos 'n' Andy*. The latter, one of radio's all time most popular programs, used a daytime serial format. Other sources contend that Pat Barnes had an earlier daytime serial drama, *Henry Adams and His Book*, on Chicago's WHT in 1925.

Quin Ryan (1965) says the daytime serial was essentially an attempt to transform comic strips into a radio programming format. WGN, it should be noted, was highly successful with such daytime serials as *We Are Four, Bachelor's Children* and *Painted Dreams*, the Irna Phillips creation that has been called the first "true" daytime serial.

Ryan (1965) says that *Painted Dreams* had its origins in 1930, when Irna Phillips came to WGN manager Henry Selinger to propose a program of poetry and inspirational messages for shut-ins. When Selinger hired her on a trial basis, she told him of her idea for a daily radio serial called *Sue and Irene*, the story of two young girls. When it went on the air the cast included Bess Flynn, Mary Afflick, Alice Hill, Ed Smith and Loni and Lucy Gilman, the daughters of Henry Gilman, WGN's production manager. The program eventually evolved into *Painted Dreams* first broadcast on September 30, 1930, with Phillips still the writer. The cast remained the same with the addition of author Phillips playing Mother Moynihan, the show's central figure. After Phillips left WGN following a business dispute, Bess Flynn took over both the chores of writing *Painted Dreams* and playing the leading role of Mother Moynihan. Flynn, the mother of Charles Flynn, radio's *Jack Armstrong*, became a prolific writer of daytime serials and a busy radio actress.

When *The Romance of Helen Trent* went on the air in 1933, there were 30 daytime serials being broadcast — most originating from WGN with many of them produced by the Blackett, Sample and Hummert advertising agency. At this early stage in the format's development, Frank Hummert had already begun to play an important role. WGN became a testing ground for many comic strip and daytime serial programs, such as *Easy Aces*, which Blackett, Sample and Hummert brought to Chicago from Kansas City, before they went on the network. Other important influences on daytime serial writing and production were Elaine Carrington, Anne Hummert and Bess Flynn.

Elaine Carrington in the 1920s had been a prolific writer of fiction for women's magazines and motion pictures. Deciding that radio might be a more lucrative market, she took the opportunity to write *Red Adams*, a half-hour weekly drama broadcast by NBC. At the end of three months, *Red Adams* became a 15-minute daytime series sponsored by Beechnut. Noting a similarity in the program's title to a competitor's product, Beechnut insisted the program's title be changed to *Red Davis*. Procter & Gamble eventually took over sponsorship of the program and once again changed the title to *Pepper Young's Family*, the name that lasted as long as the show remained on the air.

Carrington's wit and intelligence made her a successfully prolific writer, second only to Irna Phillips in the amount of material she wrote for these weekly programs. Among her other successful daytime serials were *Rosemary, Marriage for Two* and *When a Girl Marries*. It was said that in 1938 Carrington produced some 38,000 words a week (Edmonson and Brooks, 1973, p. 51). She explained the success of her stories in this way:

> All my scripts are written so that listeners can imagine themselves in the same situations as people in the cast. The daytime serials fill a tremendous hole in lonely people's lives. Listeners take the characters to heart and suffer, live, love and laugh with them.

Women did live vicariously with the daytime serials and probably did some empathic problem solving while they listened.

Frank and Anne Hummert, without doubt, were the two most dominant figures in radio's daytime serials and were the format's major influences in the 1930s and 1940s. At its peak, their production company created and produced most of the daytime serials that were broadcast. One reason often cited as the chief factor for the Hummert's success was their strict control over every aspect of their programs from writing to all other phases of their production. The Hummerts were a veritable daytime serial factory, employing some 200 writers over the years (Thurber,1973, p. 205). Among the Hummert's programs were *Amanda of Honeymoon Hill, Backstage Wife, David Harum, Evelyn Winters, Front Page Farrell, John's Other Wife, Just Plain Bill, Lora Lawton, Lorenzo Jones, Mrs. Wiggs of the Cabbage Patch, Nona from Nowhere, Orphans of Divorce, Our Gal Sunday, Real Stories from Real Life, The Romance of Helen Trent, Second Husband, Skippy, Stella Dallas, Stolen Husband* and *Young Widder Brown*.

At the height of their enterprise, the Hummerts produced 50 different program scripts weekly, a total of some 6,500,000 words yearly. They developed plot lines for each show four to six weeks in advance. After they dictated the plot trends for each show, their ghost writers fleshed out the dialogue and prepared the scripts. As an indication of how well the Hummerts' work was received by listeners and sponsors alike, they could boast in 1941 that some of their shows had been on the air eight years without a change of sponsor, a radio rarity. During World War II, the Hummerts and daytime serials successfully contributed to the war effort [*See* **Wartime Radio**].

The Hummerts' programs were not only popular in the United States, but also in England where they were broadcast by transcription with appropriate words anglicized for that market. They received some 75,000,000 letters a year from their listeners. Frank Hummert explained their programs in this way (Chase, 1942, p. 191):

> We write successful stories about unsuccessful people. This means our characters are simply unsuccessful in the material things of life, but highly successful spiritually. Our characters are everyday people and our stories can be understood on Park Avenue and on the prairies.

When Irna Phillips left WGN after a business dispute, Bess Flynn not only took over writing *Painted Dreams* but also the role of Mother Moynihan. Flynn wrote and produced many other successful daytime serials at WGN such as *Bachelor's Children* and *We Are Four* at WGN. She was a skillful writer and versatile radio actress, whose behavior can be contrasted with those of modern broadcasters.

In contrasting early daytime serial broadcasters and their performers with their present day (1998) radio and television counterparts, one similarity and one difference becomes apparent. Contemporary radio listeners and television viewers show a similarity to their earlier predecessors in the way they still strongly identify with the performers and the central characters they play on their programs, often treating them as though they were real persons. The marked difference is that in radio's early days when listeners wrote to their favorite daytime serials, they frequently received warm, personal responses to their letters. Today radio and television performers seldom even look at or read their fan mail and, rarely, if ever, answer it personally, although sponsors and broadcast executives still pay considerable attention to the mail for commercial reasons.

Radio listeners 50 or 60 years ago received considerable attention and often personal replies. Bess Flynn, busy radio writer and actress, took a great personal interest in her listeners' reactions to her shows and their suggestions. This can be seen in the letters Flynn wrote to fans in 1935, 1937 and 1939. Notice should be given that the three letters — the first handwritten — were four years apart. None were form letters. All were personally signed. Today very few fans of contemporary radio, television or motion picture personalities would receive such personal attention, and most likely they would receive none whatsoever.

When Flynn's show, *Painted Dreams*, was canceled, she expressed disappointment in a handwritten letter to one of her fans:

> February 17, 1935
> Dear Mary:
>
> Many thanks for the lovely valentine! Your letters and cards have made you very dear to me, although I've never seen you!
>
> Now I have a little surprise to tell you. Cal-Aspirin has canceled "Painted Dreams" to go into effect March 24 for a wild and wooly show called "Mary Sothern," and unless our "Painted Dreams" friends come to the front in a big way, before that date, we may go off the air! But, if enough pressure is brought to bear, they may reconsider, for a sponsor knows well, that our listeners are apt to stop using their product, if they cancel a favorite program. Will you and any of your friends, stand by us? Address Cal-Aspirin — above address [company letterhead].
>
> Many thanks and write to me soon.
> Affectionately yours,
> *(Signed)* Mother Moynihan

Two years later, Flynn wrote to the same fan to explain why the story line of *Bachelor's Children* had taken a certain turn:

> September 22, 1937
> Dear Mary:
>
> This isn't a regular letter. As you know, I always write those to you personally, but wanted

to get a note off and will take care of that letter myself at a later date when I'm not as busy as I am right now.

I'm going to answer only the last part of the letter, and that is your questions. "Bachelor's Children" and "We Are Four" both took to the air for the first time on September 9, 1935 and have been on continuously ever since. There have been no changes in the cast of "Bachelor's Children." Cornelia Osgood was Nancy, but she was replaced by Alice Hill in January of this year. Marjorie Hannon also replaced Elinor Harriot when the latter went to Hollywood.

Yes — but don't whisper it to a soul because its a secret — the wedding will take place on October 12th. However, I'm sorry to have to tell you that no visitors will be allowed on that day. We have had so many hundreds of requests to be permitted to see the broadcast on the day of the wedding that the sponsors have decided that they will have to bar all. However, any other day but that one, I would be delighted to have you see the show. For the night shows — yes, you have to have tickets which I can secure for you, but all the morning shows, that is, any of mine, all you have to do is let me know when you're going to be here and I will take care of you. I hope you can make it.

With kindest regards, I am

As ever,

(Signed) Bess Flynn

bf; cb

In 1939, Flynn once more responded to her fan's comment about the plot twists in *Bachelor's Children*:

March 7, 1939

Dear Mrs. Smith (*not fan's name)*:

Thank you for your letter of March 1st in regard to "BACHELOR'S CHILDREN."

Yes, I am receiving a few letters every day of complaint against the trend my story is taking just now — but, surprisingly enough — not as many as I had expected. And — before I go further, I want you to know that I am glad to hear from our listeners and to have them voice their views — even though they differ from mine.

In explanation of my reasons for writing the story as I have recently, I believe that, much as we might wish it didn't — life does have its ups and downs for all of us, and since I have always tried to make my story true to life, with characters — not over-drawn — but with the human frailities common to us all, we must expect them to have periods in their lives when it looks as if a kind Providence turned its face away from them.

In the years I have been writing "BACHELOR'S CHILDREN" — the characters have come to be real to me — and their problems are mine. I think of them — not as fictional characters, but as real people and as such, I love them, [feel] sorry about them — am irritated by them [and] suffer with them.

So won't you, please, bear with me just now and believe me when I say that I am not going to spoil the story for you — but have a very definite — and I trust, most interesting sequence of events coming up during the coming months?

Again — may I thank you for your letter — and I hope that you will always feel free to write to me when something in the story occurs which you feel is not as it should be. Please remember that without the cooperation of the listening audience no script can long survive.

Sincerely yours

(Signed) Bess Flynn

BF:tat

After Flynn signed the letter, she recognized that she knew this longtime fan and added a brief note in her own handwriting to it:

Dear Mary: My secretary got this — along with a bunch of fan mail — and answered it — not understanding that I answer your letters personally. So please forgive the formal tone — and do send for our B&C book. Good picture of the author in it — and the other less important characters like Dr. Bob, the twins, etc.

Love

(Signed)

Bess

The personal attention given by sponsors to fan mail can be seen in a 1932 letter to the same fan that was sent by a Battle Creek Food Company's advertising manager:

December 7, 1932

Dear Madam:

With this letter, we are enclosing an autographed photograph of Mother Moynihan which you requested. This manifested interest on your part is deeply appreciated by all of us — and especially by Mother Moynihan. It is our sincerely wish that you will continue to enjoy the "Painted Dreams" program. If at any time you have suggestions that would help us in continuing to make this program interesting and entertaining to you, please feel perfectly free to write us.

In a few words preceding and following the program, the announcer, Ed Smith, will continue to give you a brief message on Battle Creek Health Foods. In order to give you more complete information regarding these delicious Health Foods, we are enclosing with our compliments a copy of "Healthful Living" the Battle Creek Diet Book. We hope you will read it carefully because it tells you definitely how to eat, to build and maintain good health. The Battle Creek Health Foods recommended are palatable, easy-to-prepare foods which satisfy a specific need. The health food chart inserted in "Healthful Living" gives you an indication of the wide scope of these famous health building foods.

For your convenience, we enclose the name of the Battle Creek dealer in your community. You will find him a progressive merchant who will gladly help you to select the Battle Creek Health Foods best suited to your needs.

In closing, let us chime in with Ed Smith in saying that Battle Creek Health Foods cost you no more as they replace some of the foods and drugs which would ordinarily be purchased.

Sincerely yours,

THE BATTLE CREEK

FOOD COMPANY

(Signed) L.E. Bauer

Advertising Manager

LEB D

Daytime serial actors also responded personally to their fan mail. Actress Alice Hill — already referred to by Bess Flynn in a previous letter — sent a handwritten letter to a fan on April 6, 1937:

April 6, 1937

Dear Mrs. Smith (*not fan's name)*:

Thank you so much for your lovely Easter card. I never cease being surprised as well as terribly pleased to think that our radio friends think enough of us to remember us at the different seasons.

I hope you like the new picture of all of us with our new baby. How is your new little "Ken" getting along?

I am so happy to be working on Mrs. Flynn's show "We Are Four" at 11:45 A.M. as Nancy. Hope you'll listen to it and enjoy it.

Sincerely yours

Alice Hill

(Signed)

W.G.N.

Chicago

Producer-actor Walter Wicker and his actress wife, Ireene, later famous as *The Singing Lady,* also wrote to their fans by sending them typed and personally signed post cards. Notice that these actors kept a file of the fans who wrote them. Although the cards are undated, they were mailed in 1934 when the program went on the air:

Dear Friend:

Because you have been kind enough, during the past, to tell us of your interest in our radio programs, we want you to know in advance about our new program. It is called "SONG OF THE CITY" and is a serial story about the life, adventures and romance of two young women in a big city. We hope you are going to enjoy it a lot. On this program you will hear Ireene Wicker as "Rosemary," Irna Phillips as "Ann," Lucy Gillman as "Mary Lou," and myself as "Phillip Lawrence."

"SONG OF THE CITY" will start August 14th, on N.B.C. Station — WMAQ, WLW, WHO, WOW, WIBA, KSTP, and WDAF.

Thank you again for your past interest and support. All of us appreciate it tremendously.

Sincerely — *(Signed)* Walter Wicker

And later both he and Ireene signed this card to the same fan:

Dear Friend — Just a note to thank you very much for your friendly and loyal support of our "Song of the City" Program. Starting April 30th, we go on the air in the mornings, and we hope this new time will make it easier for you and your friends to follow the program. Will you be kind enough to tell all your friends about this new time, and also that on May 7th and 8th there will be synopsis of the story so far, so that a new listener can easily follow it from then on.

Don't forget — we're always very happy to hear from you. We would especially appreciate hearing what you think of this program, we want to do everything we can to make it thoroughly enjoyable to you. So please do write — just address "Song of the City" care National Broadcasting Company, Chicago. And thanks a lot for your friendly interest and help. We do appreciate it so much. Sincerely,

(Signed) Ireene Wicker Walter Wicker

"Song of the City" is heard each Tues., Wed. And Thurs., over WLW at 11:30 A.M.

E.S.T.—and over WMAQ, WSTP, WHO, WOW, WDAF, WIBA at 10:30 A.M., C.S.T. or 11:30 A.M. Daylight Savings Time.

Joe Kelly, host of the *Jolly Joe's Junior Jamboree* program at WLS (Chicago, IL) also answered his fans personally [*See* ***Jolly Joe's Junior Jamboree***]:

September 12, 1933
Dear Friend:

Your kind letter at hand. Would have answered sooner but have been completely swamped with letters from (little kids) and (big kids) like yourself. Your suggestions in the case of little Earl Bonnes is a very good one. However, there are so many letters from mothers and daddies concerning their children, some of them just as pitiful as Earl's unfortunate accident that I am unable to carry on in one instance only a certain length of time. Earl is home from the hospital now and getting along splendidly. I gave your note to Jolly Joe, Jr., and he is very proud of it. Thanking you for your kind interest and hoping to hear from you again real soon, I beg to remain.

Sincerely yours,
(*Signed*) Joe Kelly
JK:SG JOLLY JOE

Personal attention to listeners and their requests was not the only factor that attracted daytime listeners. The programs' content also evoked favorable response. Exactly what were daytime serials about and why did listeners enjoy them so much?

First and foremost, daytime serials focused on family life. The families they portrayed for the most part were identified as "average" people, who most often lived in an "average small town." Usually, the characters were Protestant and middle class. Money seldom seemed to be a problem for them. Housewives did their own work. There were no maids and no nannies. The opening announcement on *Rosemary* succinctly described its purpose and that of other daytime serials as well: "This is your story. This is your life. This story is about you and your life. Listen and live vicariously the everyday problems faced by women just like you." Many listeners — mostly women — believed that sufficiently to become faithful listeners. Women apparently did live vicariously by listening and were able to solve some of the problems they either faced themselves or thought they might encounter in the future.

Who were daytime serial listeners? Summers (1943, pp. 3–4) in cooperation with the Office of Radio Research, Columbia University, summarized the data collected by Dr. Forest L. Whan from 5,324 Iowa women who listened to daytime serials. Ten major conclusions were drawn on the basis of the data collected:

1. Approximately one-half of all women who lived in "radio homes" were regular listeners to daytime serials.
2. There was no recognizable "daytime serial listening types" identified.
3. Minor differences existed between regular listeners and non-listeners of daytime serials in the proportions of women in various age, educational and place of residence groups.
4. There was evidence of a close relationship between the amount of daytime serial listening and magazine reading.
5. The listening to programs of classical music, audience participation programs and discussions of current affairs decreased as the amount of daytime serial listening increased.
6. No evidence of any major psychological or social difference between regular daytime serial listeners and non-listeners was found.
7. Forty percent of the women who listened regularly to daytime serials believed that serial listening "help them solve the problems of their everyday lives."
8. The audience size of any individual daytime serial was affected by such physical factors as station coverage, time of broadcast and position in the broadcast schedule.
9. Audiences of individual daytime serials varied widely in the proportions of listeners falling within age, educational and place of residence classifications.
10. Audience make-up of individual daytime serials was affected by such factors as setting, plot type and age of the leading character.

Scorn against the much maligned radio "soap operas" and their female listeners came not only from cultural snobs, but from some well-meaning feminists as well. The feminists implied in their criticism that female listeners to daytime serials were uneducated, naive or both. Criticism of this nature, of course, overlooked the many Ph.Ds and business executives who eagerly looked forward to hearing their favorite daily radio serial. Not all daytime serials were scorned. For example, no scorn was directed against Sondra Michaels' *Lone Journey* and *Against the Storm*. *Against the Storm* was praised for its broadcast of poet Edgar Lee Masters reading from his *Spoon River Anthology* and John Masefield reading his poetry from London by shortwave. Critical praise for these programs, however, was quite rare.

Criticisms often were leveled against the programs' claims that they portrayed the "real life stories" of women living in small towns. If the shows portrayed passionate love affairs, amnesia, violent jealousy, revenge, murders, blindness, automobile accidents and rare life-threatening diseases, presumably these, too, were possible ingredients in the everyday life of American women. Despite these incongruities, one major emphasis that the daytime serials *always* provided was a positive statement best expressed by one program's name—*Life Can Be Beautiful*. They unequivocally proclaimed the search for personal happiness was an individual's right and responsibility. The names of the daytime serials indicating this were: *Portia Faces Life*, *Valiant Lady*, *Lone Journey*, *Love of. Life*, *One Life to Live*, *Against the Storm* and the *Right to Happiness*.

Regardless of the positive messages of these programs, scorn against them and their listeners never faded. Females — who comprised the largest part of their listening audience — were ridiculed by both male and female critics for believing the program's characters were "real people." There were hundreds of stories printed about the personal letters and gifts listeners sent to Mary Noble, Ma Perkins and Amanda of Honeymoon Hill. Certainly the acceptance of fictional characters as "real" did not begin or end with daytime serial listeners. Letters are still addressed to Sherlock Holmes of 221B Baker Street, London, asking for his help in solving a case of some sort. As noted before, when listeners wrote to actors or writers, they often received warm personal responses, even if the listeners' letters were critical.

Regardless of the harsh criticism leveled against them, it was neither the scorn nor the onslaught of television that was solely responsible for the disappearance of the daytime radio serial. Economic factors also played a role. At the height of their popularity in the post–World War II period, there were thirty network serials, producing an impressive bargain for advertisers at a cost per thousand listeners of 49 cents (Edmondson and Brooks, 1973, p. 119). When their listening audience decreased, this meant an advertising rate increase per thousand listeners.

Television's impact and the action of network affiliates to increase local radio programming did combine to hasten the downfall of daytime radio serials. Seeking to increase the advertising rates they could charge, local network affiliates took less and less network programming, an action that allowed them more free time for local recorded music programming. Networks, in response, cut back on the amount of programming they produced. For example, CBS in 1959 reduced network programming from 63 to 30 hours weekly, including the discontinuance of such long-running daytime serials as *This is Nora Drake*, *Backstage Wife*, *Our Gal Sunday* and *The Road of Life*. Many local DJ shows were used by affiliate stations to fill these time slots. In Thanksgiving week of 1960, the last remaining daytime radio serials left the air when *Ma Perkins*, *The Road to Happiness*, *The Second Mrs. Burton* and *Young Dr. Malone* disappeared.

8565 Dayton, Eddie. Ukulele soloist (WMAK, Buffalo, NY, 1928).

8566 "DC." Designation for announcer David C. Clark (WHAM, Rochester, NY, 1924).

8567 DeAbna [DeAhna], Leontine. Contralto (KFI, Los Angeles, CA, 1925).

8568 ***(The) Deacon.*** John Howard by means of monologs and stories reconstructed the entire life of a small Midwestern town on the unique program (15 min., Monday, Wednesday and Friday, WGN, Chicago, IL, 1940).

8569 Deal, H. B. Announcer (WOI, Ames, IA, 1925).

8570 Deal, John H. Newscaster (WHCU, Ithaca, NY, 1944–1946). DJ (*Time Service*, WHCU, 1947; *Dial to Deal*, WHCU, 1948).

8571 Deal, William "Bill." DJ (*Clock O' the Morning*, WCAM, Camden, NJ, 1948–1954).

8572 ***Dealer in Dreams.*** Phil Stewart, the "Dealer," delivered soft, dreamy talks for women, read poetry to them and provided solutions for their personal problems on the program sponsored by the Holland Furnace Company (15 min., 9:00–9:15 A.M., WGN, Chicago, IL, 1942).

8573 Dean, Austin. Newscaster (WGGA, Gainesville, GA, 1941).

8574 **Dean, Bev.** Newscaster (WCKY, Cincinnati, OH, 1939).

8575 **Dean, Bill.** DJ (*Turntable Terrace*, KBIX, Muskogee, OK, 1947). Sportscaster (KBIX, 1947).

8576 **Dean, Bill.** DJ (*The Ossining Hour*, WLNA, Peekskill, NY, 1948).

8577 **Dean, Bob.** Newscaster (WHB, Kansas City, MO, 1944).

8578 **Dean, Bobbye.** Actress Dean appeared in the *Hawthorne House* daytime serial.

8579 **Dean, Doris.** COM-HE (WBTM, Danville, VA, 1951).

8580 **Dean, Dorothy.** COM-HE (*Shopping with Dorothy Dean*,WAAB, Boston, MA, 1936).

8581 **Dean, Eddie.** Singing with a rich baritone voice and accompanying himself on guitar, Dean performed on KMA (Shenandoah, IA) and WNAX (Yankton, SD) in the middle and late 1920s before moving to WLS (Chicago, IL) in 1929. Dean sang as one of the "Sunshine Coffee Boys" and "The Hawaiians" before emerging as a solo performer. Eddie, who really could sing and ride a horse, starred in several "singing cowboy" movies in the late 1930s and early 1940s.

8582 **Dean, Eleanor.** Leader (*Eleanor Dean Orchestra*, instr. mus. prg., WIP, Philadelphia, PA, 1935).

8583 **Dean, Eulala.** Blues singer (KJR, Seattle, WA, 1929).

8584 **Dean, Ina Mae.** COM-HE (KYSM, Mankato, MN, 1954).

8585 **Dean, Jan.** COM-HE (KICO, Calexico, CA, 1957).

8586 **Dean, Jerome Hanna "Dizzy."** Former baseball great Dizzy Dean turned in fine play-by-play baseball broadcasts on the MBS *Game of the Day* (1951–1953). Dean also co-hosted some interesting sports programs. *See* ***Dizzy Dean***.

8587 **Dean, Marie.** Singer (WOKO, Mt. Beacon, NY, 1925).

8588 **Dean, Martha.** DJ (*Early Risers*, WJJD, Chicago, IL, 1949).

8589 **Dean, Nina.** Soprano (*Nina Dean*, vcl. mus. prg., NBC, 1939, 1942).

8590 **Dean, Pat.** COM-HE (WFMD, Frederick, MD, 1957).

8591 **Dean, Saralee.** Newscaster and announcer (WSBA, York, PA, 1942).

8592 **Dean, Stewart [Stuart].** Newscaster (KOMA, Oklahoma City, OK, 1938–1939).

8593 **Dean, Wesley "Wes."** DJ (*Farmfolks Jamboree*, KGRI, Henderson, TX, 1952). Sportscaster (KTVE, Longview, TX, 1954).

8594 **Deane, Beth.** COM-HE I(WGUY, Bangor, ME, 1951).

8595 **Deane, Bobbe.** Comedienne and mimic (KFI, Los Angeles, CA, 1929).

8596 **Deane, Buddy.** DJ (*Club 1340*, WHHM, Memphis, TN, 1948; *Wake Up Baltimore,* 120 min., Monday through Saturday, 6:30–8:30 P.M., WITH, Baltimore, MD, 1951–1952).

8597 **Deane, David C.** Pianist (*David Deane*, instr. mus. prg., WCKY, Cincinnati, OH, 1942).

8598 **Deane, Joe.** DJ (*Open House*, WHEC, Rochester, NY, 1947–1952; WBBF, Rochester, NY, 1955–1957).

8599 **Deane, Martha.** COME-HE (WOR, New York, NY, 1956–1957). This was a generic name owned by WOR for the performers who conducted women's programs. One of the earliest was Mary Margaret McBride before she left to create her own network program.

8600 ***(The) Deane Sisters.*** Sisters Berna and Vera were a harmony singing team featured on the network show (15 min., Sunday, 10:45–11:00 P.M., NBC, 1930).

8601 ***Dear Columbia.*** The unique program was devoted to letters listeners sent to the network. The host of the program supplied the network's comments and answers (Friday, 8:15–8:45 A.M., CBS, 1935).

8602 ***Dear Doris Blake.*** Ms. Blake conducted her lovelorn column of the air. She supplied solutions to the letters sent her by listeners that were often signed with such indications of distress as "Bored," "Worried" and "Perplexed" (15 min., Tuesday, 9:15–9:30 P.M., WMCA, New York, NY, 1940).

8603 ***Dear Margy.*** The clever sustaining comedy-mystery program was produced and directed by Cyril Armbruster. The plot concerned an American woman studying in England under the GI Bill of Rights, who met and became a friend of a Scotland Yard Inspector. These roles were played by Mason Adams and Ian Martin, respectively. As might be expected, the American helped the British inspector solve many baffling crimes. The title comes from the American's explanatory letters to her girl friend back home (30 min., Sunday, 4:30–5:00 P.M., MBS, 1953).

8604 **Dearing, G. L.** Announcer (WMC, Memphis, TN, 1925).

8605 **Dearth, Jacqueline G.** COM-HE (WBEX, Chillicothe, OH, 1954–1955).

8606 ***Death Fighters.*** The Wayne County Medical Society and the Detroit *News* sponsored this program that dramatized various medical discoveries and how they were achieved. Myron Golden wrote the programs, some of which were based on the writings of Paul de Kruif. There were some similarities found in the program to the *Danger Fighters* network show that was broadcast in 1932 (30 min., Wednesday, 7:00–7:30 P.M., WWJ, Detroit, MI, 1937).

8607 ***Death Valley Days*** **(sometimes incorrectly referred to as *Death Valley Sheriff* and *The Sheriff*).** When it first went on the air in 1930, the program opened with the singing of John White, "The Lonesome Cowboy." Later, the more familiar opening began with announcer Dresser Dahlstead introducing the narrator,"The Old Ranger," who was played by John MacBryde, as a bugle call sounded in the background. Sponsored by the Twenty Mule Team Borax Company, the makers of Boraxo, the program was created and originally written by Ruth Woodman, who later was assisted by Ruth Adams Knight. The talented cast included: Jack Arthur, Rosemarie Broncato, Edwin Bruce, Geoffrey Bryant, Frank Butler, Helen Claire, Tim Daniel Frawley, Robert Haag, Harvey Hays, Milton Herman, Harry Humphrey, Jean King, Olyn Landick, Michael Rafetto, George Rand and cowboy singer, John White. The announcer was George Hicks. Music was supplied by Joseph Bonime, who, incidentally, composed the original music for the bugle call heard at the opening of each program. The producer was Dorothy McCann. When *Death Valley Days* went off the air in 1944, *Death Valley Sheriff*, a related program, also sponsored by Boraxo, took its place. One of the interesting cast members, who both acted in and directed some of the later programs, was Michael Rafetto (Elwyn Creighton). Raffetto, who practiced law before beginning his acting career, attained his greatest fame as Paul in *One Man's Family* and Jack Packard in *I Love a Mystery*. Rafetto was an important member of Carleton E. Morse's radio repertory company (30 min., Monday, 8:30–9:00 P.M., NBC-Red, 1932). *See* ***Death Valley Sheriff***.

8608 ***Death Valley Sheriff.*** The western adventure drama was the story of a modern sheriff, Mark Chase, played over the years by Robert Haag, Don Briggs and Bob Warren. Sponsored by Boraxo, the program opened with the same bugle call that had always opened the *Death Valley Days* program, but the similarity ended there. After being on the air for a year, its name was changed to *The Sheriff* (*CBS, ABC,* 1944–1951).

8609 **DeBabary, Joska.** Leader (Joska de Babary Orchestra, KYW, Chicago, IL, 1925–1926).

8610 **DeBaun, Irma.** Soprano DeBraun (*Irma DeBraun*, voc. mus. prg.,WABC, New York, NY, 1928–1929) also played the role of "Peaches" on the popular *Evening in Paris* program (CBS, New York, NY, 1929).

8611 **De Benedetto, Giuseppe.** Tenor (WEAF, New York, NY, 1925).

8612 **Debering, Harv.** DJ (*10 O'Clock Special*, KSRV, Ontario, OR, 1947).

8613 **DeBie, Dick.** Newscaster (KSIG, Crowley, LA, 1947; *Tic Tock Tunes*, KSIG, 1947).

8614 **Debnam, Bob.** DJ (*Pastel Room*, WCOG, Greensboro, NC, 1952).

8615 **Debnam, W.E.** Newscaster (WTAR, Norfolk, VA, 1940; WPTF, Raleigh, NC, 1941–1945; *Debnam Views the News*, WPTF, 1947–1948).

8616 **DeBoer, H.O.** Tenor (WOC, Davenport, IA, 1928).

8617 **DeBoer, Ruth.** Contralto (WBBR, New York, NY, 1925).

8618 **DeBou, George N.** DeBou broadcast reminiscences of the old South on the *Southern Night Program* (WLW, Cincinnati, OH, 1922–1923). *See* ***The Southern Night Program***.

8619 **DeBraun, Irma.** Soprano DeBraun (WJZ, New York, NY, 1927; WABC, 1928–1929) also played the role of "Peaches" on the popular *Evening in Paris* program (CBS, New York, NY, 1929).

8620 DeBrine, (Minister) John. DJ (25 min., Monday through Friday, 10:05–10:30 P.M., WMEX, Boston, MA, 1953). Minister DeBrine was probably the first religious DJ on radio.

8621 Debris, Earl. Violinist (WLW, Cincinnati, OH, 1923).

8622 DeBueris, John. Clarinetist (WEAF, New York, NY and WGBS, New York, NY, 1928).

8623 DeBueris, Josephine. Pianist (WNYC, New York, NY, 1936).

8624 DeCamp, Rosemary. Although DeCamp appeared on the *Dot and Will* daytime serial, it was as nurse "Judy Price" on the *Dr. Christian* evening show that she gained national prominence.

8625 DeCampo, Mario. Tenor (*Mario DeCampo*, vcl. mus. prg., WCAU, Philadelphia, PA, 1934).

8626 *December Bride.* A sustaining situation comedy, *December Bride* told the story of a couple married eight years, who were confronted with problems presented by a mother-in-law who came to visit them. Spring Byington starred as the mother-in-law. She was assisted by such other cast members as: John Brown, Hans Conried, Hal March, Alan Reed and Doris Singleton. Reuben Ship and Paul Sharp produced and directed the show (30 min., Sunday, 7:00–7:30 P.M., CBS, 1952).

8627 DeChing [DeCichiny], Baroness. Soprano (*Baroness DeChing*, vcl. mus. prg., WCAU, Philadelphia, PA, 1934).

8628 Decker, A. Thomas. Newscaster (KALE, Portland, OR, 1944–1946).

8629 Decker, Della West. Actress Decker was featured on the *Woman of America* program.

8630 Decker, Dimond. Leader (Decker Instrumental Trio, KFQZ, Hollywood, CA, 1926).

8631 Decker, Doris. Blues singer (KFI, Los Angeles, CA, 1928).

8632 Decker, Harry. Leader (Harry Decker's Hawaiians [orchestra], KFWB, Hollywood, CA, 1926).

8633 Decker, Kay. COM-HE (KODI, Cody, WY, 1957).

8634 Decker, Leon. Newcaster (NBC-Blue, 1944).

8635 Decker, Paul. Leader (*Paul Decker Orchestra*, instr.mus. prg., MBS, 1934–1935, 1939; WLAV, Grand Rapids, MI, 1942).

8636 Decker, Tom. Newscaster (KALE, Portland, OR, 1945).

8637 Decker, Vic. Sportscaster (WHBC, Canton, OH, 1938; *Clean Sports for Good Sports*, WCMW, Canton, OH, 1947). Newscaster (WCMW, 1946; *Timken Time*, WCMW, 1947).

8638 de Cordova, Pedro. Musical director (*Westinghouse Salute*, NBC-Blue, 1929).

8639 DeCoy, Robert. DJ (*Diggin with Ducky*, WMRY, New Orleans, LA, 1949).

8640 Dedrick, Ann. Contralto (WFBH, New York, NY, 1925).

8641 Dee, Danny. Radio philosopher (WLW, Cincinnati, OH, 1937).

8642 Dee, Joni. COM-HE (KSHO, Las Vegas, NV, 1960).

8643 Dee, June. COM-HE (WWBB, Wichita, KS, 1956).

8644 Dee, Mary. DJ (*Rise and Shine*, WSBT, South Bend, IN, 1949; *Mary Dee Show*, WHOD, Homestead, PA, 1952–1954).

8645 Dee, Sally. COM-HE (Miss Dee conducted a *Fashion Review* program (KOA, Denver, CO, 1926). She also was *Aunt* Sally on her children's program (WOW, Omaha, NE, 1949).

8646 Dee, Squire. DJ (*Good Morning*, WTRL, Bradenton, FL, 1960).

8647 Dee, Tommy. DJ (*Rise and Shine*, WBST, South Bend, IN, 1947–1952).

8648 Dee, Yolanda. COM-HE (KTER, Terrel, TX, 1951).

8649 Deeble, Charlotte. Organist (WPAR, Parkersburg, WV, 1937).

8650 Deegan, Johnny. DJ (KYW, Philadelphia, PA, 1948).

8651 Deem, Warren. Newscaster (WKBH, LaCrosse, WI, 1940).

8652 *(The) Deems Taylor Musical Series.* Both NBC divisions — Blue and Red — broadcast the educational course in grand opera with examples sung in English. Although the program originally was broadcast in a 45-minute format, it eventually was reduced to 30-minutes. The program's partial schedule in 1931was as follows:

May 3: The Second Reformation
May 10: The Revolution
May 17: Verdi
May 24: The Opera After Wagner
May 31: American Composers and American Opera.

8653 *(The) Deep River Boys.* Vcl. mus., prg. (CBS, 1939; KDKA, Pittsburgh, PA, 1942). The good vocal group's early program began with the announcer proclaiming: "Columbia presents the Deep River Boys singing the spirituals of the old South ... songs of faith and yearning ... songs full of hard trials, great tribulations and glory in the day to come. Deep River songs by the Deep River Boys. First, the boys sing an old-time song of faith and help — "Don't Get Weary."

8654 Deer [Dear], Dottie. COM-HE (WFMC, Goldsboro, NC, 1957).

8655 Deering, Henry. Concert pianist (*Henry Deering*, instr. mus. prg., NBC, 1934).

8656 Deering, Olive. Actress Deering was a cast member of the *Lone Journey* daytime serial.

8657 Dees, Grace. COM-HE (WAJF, Decatur, AL, 1955).

8658 Dees, James. Baritone (*James Dees*, vcl. mus. prg., WPTF, Raleigh, NC, 1936).

8659 Dees, Mildred. COM-HE (KXYZ, Houston, TX, 1949).

8660 Deever, Hayes. Tenor (*Hayes Deever*, vcl. mus. prg., WJAS, Pittsburgh, PA, 1935).

8661 DeFao, Harmonica Joe. Harmonica soloist (KFWM, Oakland, CA, 1927).

8662 *Defense Attorney* (aka *Defense Rests*). The program was loosely based on the work of successful female attorney, Martha Ellis Bryan. The writers were Bill Johnston, Cameron Blake , Kay Wiley and Joel Murcott. Warren Lewis was the producer. Mercedes McCambridge played the leading role of the successful attorney. Other cast members included: Howard Culver, Paul Frees and co-authors Bill Johnston and Kay Wiley (30 min., Friday, 8:00–8:30 P.M., ABC, 1951).

8663 Defilipo, Kim. COM-HE (WNOK, Columbia, SC, 1956).

8664 DeForest, Ed. Sportscaster (*Ed DeForest's Inside of Sports*, KRUX, Phoenix-Glendale, AZ, 1947–1949; KOY, Phoenix, AZ, 1953). DJ (*Platter Party*, KRUX, Phoenix, AZ, 1948).

8665 De Forest, (Dr.) Lee. Lee De Forest was an early pioneer of radio with an eye for the dramatic event. In the summer of 1908, for instance, he broadcast from the Eiffel Tower in Paris and achieved reception of his signal in Marseilles, exactly 500 miles away. A little more than a year later on January 10, 1910, De Forest broadcast Enrico Caruso singing the role of Turridou in *Cavalleria Rusticana* from the stage of the Metropolitan Opera. Although probably not more than 50 people heard the Caruso broadcast, public awareness and enthusiasm for radio increased. Next came his development of the "audion" amplifying tube, a modification of John Fleming's vacuum tube. De Forest's invention produced a more powerful tube that strengthened the detection and amplification of radio signals, improved long distance signal reception and helped to create modern electronics (Lewis, 1993, p. 53).

After years of litigation involving patent infringement, De Forest once more began his experimental broadcasts. He made radio history in 1916 with broadcasts transmitted from his experimental station located in New York City. Miss Vaughn deLeath, who from this point on was known as the "original radio girl," agreed to sing "Old Folks at Home" before his microphone. After climbing three flights of creaky stairs to reach De Forest's Highbridge laboratory, the broadcaster dramatically announced to her, "You are about to become the first woman ever to sing for people and continents invisible."

During the summer and fall of 1916, De Forest began broadcasting what some consider to be the first regular radio broadcasts (Archer, 1938, p. 133). Emanating from the Columbia Phonograph Records Laboratory in New York City, his broadcasts consisted entirely of Columbia's new recordings. De Forest's programming was praised by the New York press and enthusiastically received by listeners.

After De Forest moved his experimental station from the borough of Manhattan to Highbridge in the Bronx, he demonstrated what may have been the first radio broadcasts of the news, when he personally presented hourly bulletins of the 1916 presidential election results. Unfortunately, he closed his broadcast with the announcement that Charles Evans Hughes had been elected president, an embarrassing error that the next morning's papers corrected. Nevertheless, De Forest's creativity both in invention and actual broadcasting make him one of

American radio's pioneering giants. *See also* **Appendix A — Chronology, 1906–1960** *and* **deLeath, Vaughn.**

8666 ***(The) De Forest Audions.*** The De Forest Radio Company sponsored this Sunday evening music program (CBS, 1928–1929). The Audions, named after the radio tube invented by Lee De Forest, were a talented brass band.

8667 DeFrange, Anita. COM-HE (KTMC, McAlester, OK, 1956).

8668 deFremercy, Virginia. Pianist (KGO, Oakland, CA, 1924).

8669 Defreitas, Dick. DJ (*It's a Woman's World*, WMGM, New York, NY, 1955–1958).

8670 DeGaray, Lydia. COM-HE (KCOR, San Antonio, TX, 1954).

8671 deGarmo-Peck, Olive. Singer (WDAF, Kansas City, MO, 1925).

8672 Degele, Charles. Violinist (WHN, New York, NY, 1924).

8673 Degerman, Amy. Pianist (KYW, Chicago, IL, 1923).

8674 DeGonitch, Marianne. Russian opera singer (WGBS, New York, NY, 1928).

8675 De Graf, Belle. COM-HE (*Household Hour*, KPO, San Francisco, CA, 1929).

8676 DeGraff, Margaret. Harpist (WGY, Schenectady, NY, 1923).

8677 DeGrasse, (Signor) Antonio. Violinist (KTAB, Oakland, CA, 1925–1926).

8678 DeGraw, Louise. COM-HE (KATL, Miles City, MT, 1956–1957).

8679 DeGre, Muriel. COM-HE (WKNY, Kingston, NY, 1956).

8680 DeGrood, Elise. Violinist (WGR, Buffalo, NY, 1923).

8681 DeHarrack, Charles. Concert pianist (*Charles DeHarrack*, instr. mus. prg., WHK, Cleveland, OH, 1931).

8682 DeHaven, Bob. Sportscaster (KVOO, Tulsa, OK, 1937; WTCN, St. Paul, MN, 1938). DJ (*DeHaven Date* and *Friendly Time*, WCCO, Minneapolis, MN, 1948–1949). *See* ***DeHaven's Date.***

8683 ***DeHaven's Date.*** Popular announcer, sportscaster and radio personality Bob DeHaven hosted the variety show that was one of the most popular local programs of the 1940s. Frankie Roberts, Burt Hanson, Kenny Spears, Biddy Bastian, Irv Wickner, Ernie Garvin and Sally Foster were in the cast (WCCO, Minneapolis, MN, 1940s).

8684 Dehn, Doris. Soprano (*Doris Dehn*, vcl. mus. prg., WPG, Atlantic City, NJ, 1935–1936).

8685 Deihl, A. Newscaster (KVOE, Santa Ana, CA, 1937).

8686 Dein, Cowell. Pianist-banjoist (KFWI, San Francisco, CA, 1927).

8687 Deines, Nay. Sportscaster (KMMJ, Grand Island, NE, 1941–1956).

8688 Deiro, Pietro. Accordionist (WOR, Newark, NJ, 1929).

8689 Deis, Carol. Contralto (*Carol Deis*, vcl. mus. prg., NBC, 1935–1937).

8690 Deis, Edward. Singer (WFBH, New York, NY, 1925).

8691 DeJean, Louis. DeJean delivered aviation talks (KFI, Los Angeles, CA, 1928).

8692 DeJon, Lythe Orme. Newscaster (WRON, Ronceverte, WV, 1948).

8693 DeJong, Samuel. Leader (*Samuel DeJong Orchestra*, instr. mus. prg., CBS, 1934).

8694 DeJonge, Robert. Saxophonist DeJonge was a member with Robert Hazenberg of a saxophone duo (WOOD, Grand Rapids, MI, 1926).

8695 ***(The) DeJurik Sisters.*** Carolyn and Mary Jane De Jurik was a popular Chicago harmony singing team (WLS, Chicago, IL, 1937–1938). They were great audience favorites on the *National Barn Dance* program (WLS).

8696 Dekyle, Ben H. DJ (*Yawnin' in the Morning*, WGSW, Greenwood, SC, 1954).

8697 Delacourt, Tom E. DJ (*Morning Digest*, WSLS, Roanoke, VA, 1954.)

8698 Del and, Jim. DJ (WWJ, Detroit, MI, 1957).

8699 Delacroix, Richard. DJ (WJBW, New Orleans, LA, 1957).

8700 Delaney, Bob. Sportscaster (*Inside Story on Sports*, WHDN, Boston, MS, 1953).

8701 Delaney, Jim. Sportscaster (WMCA, New York, NY, 1954).

8702 Delaney, Verner. Tenor (KPCB, Seattle, WA, 1927).

8703 DeLano, Martha aka Susan Smith. COM-HE (WCUM, Cumberland, MD, 1949).

8704 Delaporte, Ray. Leader (*Ray Delaporte Orchestra*, instr. mus. prg., WBZ, Boston-Springfield, MA, 1932; 1935).

8705 de la Torre, Rey. Guitarist (WQXR, New York, NY, 1939).

8706 ***De La Rosa Orchestra.*** Instr. mus. prg. (WIP, Philadelphia, PA, 1935).

8707 Delcoglin, Frank. CW vocalist (*Frank Delcoglin*, CW vcl. mus. prg., WDEL, Wilmington, DE, 1938).

8708 de Leeuw, Hendrik. Violinist who performed on the *Flying Dutchman* weekly dramatic program (WOR, Newark, NJ, 1931).

8709 deLeath, Vaughn (Leonore Vonderleith). A singer, composer and pianist, DeLeath was born in Mt. Pulaski, Illinois, September 26, 1900 and known as "The Original Radio Girl." She claimed she was the first to broadcast *live* vocal music and that she was the "first lady announcer." In 1916, Lee De Forest broadcast deLeath singing from the World Tower Building in New York City. De Forest called her "the first woman to sing for people and continents invisible" (Archer, 1933, p. 133).

Whenever Tommy Cowan needed a singer for WJZ (New York, NY) programming, it is said, he immediately summoned deLeath to the studio [*See* **Cowan, Tommy**]. She is generally credited with originating the "crooning" style of singing. Some contend that deLeath sang in this manner in order to prevent damage to the delicate radio transmitting tubes used in early radio. *Non-Skid* (January 29, 1930, p. 3), the house journal of the Firestone Tire Company, described deLeath's voice in this way: "Then came the low contralto of deLeath like the low moan of the wind, the break of the sea, the mother's lullaby — undistorted to the pioneer radio audience."

For a time in 1923, she was the leader of Vaughn deLeath's Merry Melody Makers Orchestra (NBC, 1923) and Vaughn deLeath's Marshland Orchestra (NBC, 1923). She sang on WGBS (New York, NY, 1925) and appeared on such programs as *The Voice of Firestone* and the *Forhan's Tooth Paste Show.* She continued to have her own programs into the next decade: *Vaughn de Leath*, vcl. mus. prg. (WTAM, Cleveland, OH, 1930; CBS, 1932; NBC, 1935–1936).

Tommy Cowan (1950–1951) said that deLeath was a performer he could always count on to broadcast on short notice in radio's early days, whenever he was "caught short"or "disappointed with another artist." Cowan (1950–1951, p. 46) said that he would go to her 38th Street apartment just off Sixth Avenue and find her in the middle of a dinner party. As he recounted it: "I would grab her arm and say, 'Come on. You're going to Newark.' There would be a scene, but she'd finally put on her hat and start for Newark — completely unscheduled. She built up a tremendous radio following." He [Cowan, 1950–1951, p. 46] went on to explain why she was such an excellent radio singer in those early days: "She had a marvelous microphone technique. It was all the more marvelous since the microphone had to be humored, and she knew how to humor it."

DeLeath enjoyed a varied career, appearing on Broadway in *Laugh, Clown, Laugh* at the Belasco Theater; becoming a successful composer; and performing on early television in 1939. A talented composer, she wrote some two hundred published songs. Some of her compositions were played on *The Voice of Firestone* during the first years it was on the air. She also hosted a program for aspiring composers, *Want to Write a Song?* (NBC, 1935).

8710 Delehanty, Katherine. Pianist (WBZ, Boston-Springfield, MA, 1924).

8711 DeLeon, Pedro. Leader (*Pedro DeLeon Orchestra*, instr. mus. prg., KLZ, Denver, CO, 1934, 1939).

8712 Delfino, Frank. DJ (*The Man Around the House*, WICC, Bridgeport, CT, 1954).

8713 Delgado, Felipe. Baritone (KFI, Los Angeles, CA, 1928).

8714 Delia, Mildred. Soprano (WHY, New York, NY, 1924).

8715 DeLima, Pete. Newscaster (KFI-KECA, Los Angeles, CA, 1942; KFI, 1945).

8716 Dell, Winifred. Mezzo-soprano (WWJ, Detroit, MI, 1923).

8717 Della Chiesa, Vivian. Soprano (*Vivian Della Chiesa*, vcl. mus. prg., WCAU, Philadelphia, PA and NBC, 1936; CBS, 1937). Miss Della Chiesa was also featured on the *American Album of Familiar Music* and the *American Melody Hour* programs.

8718 Delma [Delna], Mildred. Metropolitan Opera soprano (WJY, Hoboken, NJ and WOR, Newark, NJ, 1926).

8719 Delman, Hattie. Singer (WBBC & WCBU, Buffalo, NY, 1929).

8720 Delmar, Jack. Leader (*Jack Delmar*

Orchestra, instr. mus. prg., WIP, Philadelphia, PA, 1934, 1936; KYW, Philadelphia, PA, 1938).

8721 **Delmerjian, Haig.** Newscaster (WKBS, Oyster Bay, NY, 1948).

8722 **Delmonico's Dreamers Dance Orchestra.** Restaurant band (KMA, Shenandoah, IA, 1926).

8723 **Delmont, James "Jimmy."** Sportscaster (WMIN, St. Paul, MN,1940; KATE, Albert Lea, MN, 1941–1944; KATE, 1948). Newscaster (KATE, 1945). DJ (*Five O'Clock Club*, WTCN, Minneapolis, MN, 1952).

8724 ***Del Monte Musical Comedy.*** The California Packing Company, producers of Del Monte food products, sponsored the music program featuring soprano Vivienne Segal and Emil Polak, who conducted the orchestra. The program presented condensed versions of Hollywood features, claiming they were "direct from the sound stages." For example, Victor Herbert's *Mlle. Modeste* with Helen Claire and Walter Pidgeon was one of the many presentations (30 min., Saturday, 8:30–9:00 P.M., NBC-Red, 1930).

8725 ***(The) Delmore Brothers (Alton and Rabon Delmore).*** CW mus. prg., (WSM, Nashville, TN, 1936–1938). From 1932 to 1950, the brothers performed on 13 stations and made personal appearances in 37 states. They later recorded as part of Brown's Ferry Four, a gospel quartet that at times also included Red Foley, Merle Travis and George Jones.

8726 **Delmunzio, Richard.** Violinist (WAHG, Richmond Hill, NY, 1926).

8727 **DeLoach, Gayle.** COM-HE (WIBJ, Humboldt, TN, 1957).

8728 **DeLoca, Adelaide.** Contralto DeLoca appeared on the *Roxy and His Gang* program (NBC, New York, NY, 1928).

8729 **Deloneloce, Charlotte.** Singer (KFWB, Hollywood, CA, 1928).

8730 **DeLong, Howard.** Dramatic tenor (WDOD, Chattanooga, TN, 1927).

8731 **Delores.** Singer (*Songs by Delores*, vcl. mus. prg., KYW, Philadelphia, PA, 1939).

8732 **DeLovelace, Charlotte.** Singer (WFWB, Hollywood, CA, 1929).

8733 **Delperdang, Charles.** DJ (*Fun with the Classics*, KSUM, Fairmont, MN, 1954).

8734 **Del Pino, Paoli.** Busy tenor (WGBS, New York, NY; WGCP, New York, NY and WRNY, Richmond Hill, NY, 1925).

8735 ***(The) Delta Rhythm Boys.*** Vcl. mus. prg. (WJR, Detroit, MI, 1942).

8736 **DeLuca, Guiseppe.** Metropolitan Opera baritone (NBC, New York, NY, 1928).

8737 **DeLuca, Paula.** Pianist (KFUU, Oakland, CA, 1925).

8738 **DeLys, Go Go.** Vocalist (*Go Go DeLys*, vcl. mus. prg., CBS, 1935–1936).

8739 **DeMacchi Opera Company.** Grand opera company that broadcast *Rigoletto* (WRNY, New York, NY, 1926).

8740 **DeMaire, Josephine.** Singer (WGBS, New York, NY, 1927).

8741 ***DeMarco Orchestra.*** Instr. mus. prg. (WOR, Newark, NJ, 1936, 1942).

8742 **DeMaree, John.** Leader (John DeMaree's Original Bellhops [Orchestra], WGBS, New York, NY, 1928).

8743 **DeMarse, Willard.** DJ (*Melody Matinee*, WRNY, Rochester, NY, 1947).

8744 **DeMartini, Count.** Leader (Count Martini and his Concert Orchestra, WEAF, New York, NY, 1924).

8745 **Deme, Hazel R.** COM-HE (WINF, Manchester, CT, 1955).

8746 **Demeny, Laszlo.** Cellist (KPO, San Francisco, CA, 1926).

8747 **Demerest, Ada Rose.** Miss Demerest was a reader of children's stories (KRE, Berkeley, CA, 1925).

8748 **DeMichele, Henry.** Vocalist (*Henry DeMichele*, vcl. mus. prg., WGES, Chicago, IL, 1935–1936).

8749 **Demick, Dean.** Pianist (WEBH, Chicago, IL, 1924).

8750 **DeMille, Stan.** DJ (*Columbia Record Shop*, KSUB, Cedar City, UT, 1947).

8751 **DeMiller, E. Pierre.** Newscaster (WLBC, Muncie, IN, 1937).

8752 **de Minchen, Helen.** Singer (WMAK, Buffalo, NY, 1926).

8753 **Demler, Mary Eaton.** Soprano (WOR, Newark, NJ, 1924).

8754 **deMoss, Lyle.** Baritone (KFAB, Lincoln, NE, 1928).

8755 **Dempsey, Bob.** DJ (*Operation Moonbeam*, KTMC, McAlester, OK, 1960).

8756 **Dempsey, Jack.** Heavyweight champion boxer Dempsey acted as the announcer for his father, oldtime fiddler Hiram Dempsey, who performed on KTHS (Hot Springs Natural Parks, AR, 1926).

8757 **Dempsey, Pearl.** Pianist (KJR, Seattle, WA, 1929).

8758 **Dempster, Carole.** Silent picture star Dempster was a leading lady with D.W. Griffith's "stock company" (WBOQ, Richmond Hills, NY, 1925). *See* **Griffith, D.W.**

8759 **DeNario, Rose.** Soprano (WIP, Philadelphia, PA, 1926).

8760 **DeNegron, Fredda S.** COM-HE (WORA, Mayaguez, PR, 1960).

8761 **Dengler, Bob.** Sportscaster (*Headpin Headlines*, KSYL, Alexandria, LA, 1947).

8762 **Dengler, Clyde.** Tenor (WJZ, New York, NY, 1929).

8763 **Denham, (Mrs.) Edwin.** Pianist (KHJ, Los Angeles, CA, 1923).

8764 **Denham, Jean.** COM-HE (WJBS, DeLand, FL, 1957).

8765 **Denison, Clifford B.** Newscaster (WMRC, Greenville, NC, 1941–1945; *Between the Lines*, WMRC, 1946–1948).

8766 **Denkema, Eddie.** Newscaster (KOPP, Ogden, OR, 1947).

8767 **Denman, Dot.** COM-HE (WPKO, Waverly, OH, 1960).

8768 **Denman, John L.** Newscaster (WJR, Detroit, MI, 1944–1947).

8769 **Denman, Mert.** Performer Denman was billed as "Mert Denman and his Ukulele" (KFI, Los Angeles, CA, 1926).

8770 **Denman, Nell.** COM-HE (KBWD, Brownwood, TX, 1954).

8771 **Dennenger, Esther.** Pianist (KPO, San Francisco, CA, 1923).

8772 **Denney, Roland.** DJ (*Cowboy Rhythms*, KPLT, Paris, TX, 1947).

8773 **Denning, Eloise.** COM-HE (WCOJ, Coatesville, PA, 1954).

8774 **Denning, John R.** Announcer (KFQB, Fort Worth, TX, 1926).

8775 **Denning, Robert.** Organist (WGR, Buffalo, NY, 1925).

8776 **Dennis, Albert.** Newscaster (WJSV, Washington, DC, 1939; WTOP, Washington, DC, 1945–1946).

8777 **Dennis, Belmont.** Newscaster (*The World This Week*, WMOC, Covington, GA, 1948).

8778 **Dennis, Clark.** Tenor (*Clark Dennis*, vcl. mus. prg., NBC, 1936–1937).

8779 **Dennis, Dinty.** Sportscaster (WQAM, Miami, FL, 1937–1939; *Dugout of the Air*, WQAM, 1940–1942; WQAM, 1946; WGBS, Miami, FL, 1945; *Sports Dugout*, WKAT, Miami Beach, FL, 1947).

8780 **Dennis, Don.** Newscaster (WMAZ, Macon, GA, 1946).

8781 **Dennis, Dorothy.** COM-HE (KTTN, Trenton, MO, 1956–1957).

8782 **Dennis, E. R.** Announcer (WFAN, Hutchinson, MN, 1924).

8783 **Dennis, Gene [Jean].** Vocalist Dennis was known as "The Kansas City Wonder Girl," who sang with the American Salon Orchestra (KYA, San Francisco, CA, 1929).

8784 **Dennis, Horace.** Dennis delivered talks on such topics as, "Why I'm a Patriot" (WOR, Newark, NJ, 1922).

8785 **Dennis, Joyce.** COM-HE (KRHD, Duncan, OK, 1955).

8786 **Dennis, Lorell.** COM-HE (WTRF, Bellaire, OH, 1949).

8787 **Dennis, Marjorie.** Newscaster (WAPI, Birmingham, AL, 1940–1941).

8788 **Dennis, Mimi.** COM-HE (WAPI, Birmingham, AL, 1949).

8789 **Dennis, Mort.** Leader (*Mort Dennis Orchestra*, WCAO, Baltimore, MD, 1939).

8790 **Dennison, Eugene R.** Announcer (WHAR, Atlantic City, NJ, 1924–1927).

8791 **Denny, Earl.** Leader (*Earl Denny Orchestra*, instr. mus. prg., WFIL, Philadelphia, PA, 1935; WIP, Philadelphia, PA, 1935–1936, 1942).

8792 **Denny, Jack.** Leader (Jack Denny Orchestra broadcasting from New York's Frivolity Club, WJZ, New York, NY, 1926; WMCA, New York, NY, 1926). Denny's early band included: Denny, ldr.-p.; Moe Selzer and Archie Jarry, t.; Jack Kendle, tb.; Joe Ruscheck, tba.; Tudy Kendle and Harold Noble, clar. and as.; Gus Sharp, clr. and ts.; Mort Dennison, v.; Fred Rich, 2nd. p.; Floyd Campbell, bj.; and Harry Burkhardt, d. The Denny band was also active the following decade on radio: (*Jack Denny Orchestra*, instr. mus. prg.,NBC, 1931; *Jack Denny Orchestra*, WOR, Newark, NJ, 1933–1936; CBS, 1939).

8793 **Dent, Lillian.** Contralto (WSAI, Cincinnati, OH, 1925).

8794 Denti, Robert. Trumpet soloist (*Major Bowes Capitol Theater Family*, NBC, 1928–1929).

8795 Dentler, Warren. Newscaster (KEYS, Corpus Christi, TX, 1945).

8796 Denton, Bill. Sportscaster (*Football Prophet*, *Marching Thru Sports* and *Rainier Sports Reel*, KPQ, Wenatchee, WA, 1951–1955).

8797 Denton, Elsa. Contralto (WLW, Cincinnati, OH, 1926).

8798 Denton, Pat. COM-HE (KGNC, Amarillo, TX, 1956–1957).

8799 Denver, Dee, Jr. Newscaster (KFEQ, St. Joseph, MO, 1946–1947).

8800 Denver, Dorothy. Actress Denver appeared on the *Bachelor's Children* daytime serial program.

8801 Denver Darling. CW vocalist (*Denver Darling*, CW voc. mus. prg., WWVA, Wheeling, WV, 1935). Denver Darling, the lanky cowboy singer, was a great favorite on the *WWVA Midnight Jamboree* (WWVA, Wheeling, WV, 1930s), where he appeared with Marshall "Grandpa" Jones.

8802 Denver Municipal Band. Brass band directed by Henry Everett Sachs (KOA, Denver, CO, 1928).

8803 Denver Union Pacific Shop Employees Band. Otis L. Lewis directed this company band (KOA, Denver, CO, 1926).

8804 Denye, Dalma. Musical comedy singer (WGBS, New York, NY, 1928).

8805 Deollibus, Nicholas. Violinist (WLIT, Philadelphia, PA, 1925).

8806 DePasca, Signor. Marimba soloist (WOC, Davenport, IA, 1928).

8807 DePew, Alexander. Flutist (WCBD, Zion, IL, 1926).

8808 DePew, J. H. Announcer (WCBD, Zion, IL, 1927).

8809 DePlesses [duPlesses], Marie. Pianist (KFWM, Oakland, CA, 1926).

8810 Deppe, Grace. Director of the Louisville and Jefferson County Children's Home Glee Club and Orchestra (WHO, Des Moines, IA, 1925).

8811 Deppen, Stan. DJ (*Literature on Request*, WSBA, York, PA, 1947; *Tunes in Tempo*, WSBA, 1949).

8812 dePolenzske, (Baroness) Helena. News commentator (*Women in the News of the War*, WBNY, Brooklyn, NY, 1942).

8813 DePrimero, Santo. Tenor (*Santo DePrimero*, vcl. mus. prg., WOR, Newark, NJ, 1935).

8814 Derbridge, Pearl. Contralto (KGO, Oakland, CA, 1926).

8815 Der Lar, Eleanor. Soprano (WJY, New York, NY, 1925).

8816 Derks, R. Announcer (WCAZ, Cathage, IL, 1928).

8817 Derniann, Rose. Soprano (WGBS, New York, NY, 1925).

8818 DeRodriguez, (Madame) Maria Pedroti. Soprano (WRC, Washington, DC, 1925).

8819 DeRoliesser, Rosemary. COM-HE (KLIZ, Brainerd, MN,1949).

8820 DeRose, Peter. Pianist and leader (Peter DeRose and his Four Jack Roses [instrumental group], WAHG, Richmond Hill, NY, 1926). DeRose was the husband of May Singhi Breen and appeared with her on the *Three Kings and a Queen* and other programs (NBC-Blue, New York, NY, 1929). *See* **Breen, May Singhi.**

8821 Derr, John. Sportscaster (*Saturday Sports Review* and the *Olympic Games*, CBS, 1948; *Sports Roundup*, CBS, 1951; *Orange Bowl football game*, *Senior Bowl football game* and the *Sports Roundup* program, CBS, 1952; *John Derr's Scoreboard*, CBS, 1953; CBS, 1955).

8822 Derrick, Elta. COM-HE (KNOG, Nogales, AZ, 1954).

8823 Derwin, Hal. Singer (*Hal Derwin*, vcl. mus. prg., WAAF, Chicago, IL, 1935).

8824 DeSales, Francis. Actress DeSales appeared on the *King's Row* daytime serial.

8825 DesAutels, Van. Newscaster (KTSM, El Paso, TX, 1938; KFAC, Los Angeles, CA, 1940, 1945). Sportscaster (KTSM, 1938).

8826 Desch, Jack. Newscaster (KFRC, San Francisco, CA, 1945).

8827 deSeversky, Alexander. Aviation authority and inventor deSeversky broadcast his informative *The War in the Air* program during World War II (WMAQ, Chicago, IL, 1942).

8828 *Design for Melody.* Music program featuring soprano Florence Vickland, baritone Raoul Nadeau and chorus (Sunday evening, 30 min., WOR, Newark, NJ, 1939).

8829 DeSilva, Adrian. Tenor DeSilva was featured on the *Roxy and His Gang* program broadcast (NBC, 1927).

8830 Desimone, Gene. Newscaster (KFBK, Sacramento, CA, 1939).

8831 de Simone, Rita. Dramatic soprano (WOR, Newark, NJ, 1925).

8832 Deskins, Delores Ann. COM-HE (WPKE, Pikesville, KY, 1960).

8833 Desmond, Connie. Sportscaster (WSPD, Toledo, OH, 1937–1939; WCOL, Columbus, OH, 1940–1941; WHN, New York, NY, 1946–1947; WMGM, New York, NY, 1948; *Dodgers' Baseball*, CBS, 1949–1951; WMGM, 1954).

8834 Desmond, Dan. Sportscaster (*Sport Static of the Air*, KSCJ, Sioux City, IA, 1940).

8835 Desmond, Helen. Pianist (WCSH, Portland, OR, 1927).

8836 Desmond, Johnny. Popular singer Desmond became a network DJ, who spun records and conducted interviews on his weekly show (*Phonarama*, 25 min., Saturday, 11:30–11:55 A.M., MBS, 1954).

8837 Desmond, Mae. Actress Desmond gave dramatic readings on her Philadelphia local program (*Mae Desmond*, 15 min., Monday, Wednesday and Friday, 7:45–8:00 P.M., WIP, Philadelphia, PA, 1935).

8838 Desmond, Mary Frances. Versatile radio actress Desmond appeared on the *Ma Perkins* and *The Romance of Helen Trent* daytime serial programs.

8839 Desmond, Warren. DJ (*Musical Train*, KLO, Ogden, UT, 1949).

8840 DeSola, Vincent. Pianist (WJZ, New York, NY and WJY, New York, NY, 1924).

8841 Despard, Wilfred. Newscaster (WHEC, Rochester, NY, 1942, 1944).

8842 Dessauer, Leo A. Violinst (KOMO, Seattle, WA, 1927).

8843 DeStefano, Salvatore. Harpist (*Salvatore DeStefano*, instr. mus., prg., WTIC, Hartford, CT, 1935).

8844 DeStevens, Mario. Leader (*Mario DeStevens Orchestra*, instr. mus. prg., MBS, 1942).

8845 *Destination Freedom.* Destination Freedom was a weekly series of half-hour programs broadcast on Chicago local radio for two years (30 min., Weekly, WMAQ, Chicago, IL, 1948–1950). Written by Richard Dunham, the program was announced as being dedicated to the presentation of "the great democratic heritage of the Negro people [and] brought to you by station WMAQ as a part of the pageant of history and of America's own *Destination Freedom.*" Comedy, drama and documentaries were presented as part of the series. Liberal Chicago newspaper columnist Studs Terkel was a frequent participant. Oscar Brown, Jr., was a permanent member of the show's repertory stock company.

8846 DeStkvara, Beatrice. COM-HE (*How to Be Charming*, WOR, Newark, NJ, 1936).

8847 Destor, Don. Leader (*Don Destor Orchestra*, instr. mus. prg., WGH, Newport News, VA, 1938).

8848 DeSylva, Richard. Violinist (WHAM, Rochester, NY, 1928).

8849 *Detect and Collect.* Fred Uttal and Wendy Barrie initially were the hosts on the audience participation quiz sponsored by B.F. Goodrich Company, before they were replaced by movie comic Lew Lehr. Music was supplied by Teddy Raph's orchestra. Don Gardiner was the announcer. The program was written by Mildred Fenton and directed by Walter Tibbals (25 min., 9:30–9:55 P.M., NBC-Blue, 1946).

8850 DeTemple, Mimi. DJ (*Studio Party*, KASH, Eugene, OR, 1948).

8851 Detienne, Lillian. Reader (WCBD, Zion, IL, 1925).

8852 *Detour.* *Variety* noted the crime drama was similar to *The Clock* program. Although *Variety* said the sustaining program was thrilling, it also stated that, unfortunately, Dr. Richard Hoffman, the psychiatrist on the program, sometimes appeared to offer only cliche commentary and interpretation (30 min., 9:30–10:00 P.M., ABC, 1950).

8853 Detroit News Orchestra. Newspaper sponsored band (WWJ, Detroit, MI, 1924).

8854 *(The) Detroit News Poet—Anne Campbell.* Poetess Campbell, who was claimed by the Detroit *News* as its own, read her original poetry (WWJ, Detroit, MI, 1924). Station WWJ at the time was owned by the Detroit *News* paper.

8855 Detroit News String Quartet. The instrumental group's musicians included: Maurice Warner, violin; Valhert P. Coffey, viola;

Herman Goldstein, violin; and Frederick Broeder, cello (WWJ, Detroit, MI, 1923).

8856 Detroit Symphony Orchestra. Symphonic orchestra (WWJ, Detroit, MI, 1928).

8857 *Detroit Symphony Orchestra.* CBS presented the weekly program of symphonic music (60 min., Sunday, 3:00–4:00 P.M., CBS, 1934). The orchestra later appeared on ABC (60 min., Sunday, 8:00–9:00 P.M., ABC, 1947).

8858 Dettinger, Alma. COM-HE (WQXR, New York, NY, 1949–1957).

8859 DeTurk, Leroy. DeTurk performed pianologues (WWJ, Detroit, MI, 1923).

8860 DeVault, Charles. Newscaster (WOWO, Fort Wayne, IN, 1942; 1945).

8861 Detwiler [Detweiler], Joe. Baritone (KFWI, San Francisco, CA, 1926–1927).

8862 Deutsch, Emery. Violinist (WAHG, New York, NY, 1925; WABC-CBS, New York, NY, 1929). Deutsch sometimes was known as the "Golden Boy of Radio." He also was an orchestra leader (Merideans Orchestra, WABC, New York, NY, 1929; Emery Deutsch and his Gypsy Orchestra, CBS, New York, NY, 1929). In the following decade his band was equally busy: *Emery Deutsch Orchestra*, instr. mus. prg. (CBS, 1934, 1938–1939; WJR, Detroit, MI, 1937). Deutsch in later years worked as a DJ (*Gypsy Melodies,* WQXR, New York, NY, 1947).

8863 Deutsch, (Professor) Harold. Newscaster (*Backgrounding World News*, WCCO, Minneapolis–St. Paul, MN, 1940–1945).

8864 Deutsch, Violet. Pianist (WOAW, Omaha, NE, 1925).

8865 DeValley, Antoine. Lyric tenor (KGO, San Francisco, CA, 1927).

8866 DeVaney, Carolyn. COM-HE (WMBH, Joplin, MO, 1951–1954).

8867 Devaney, Frank. Newscaster (WMIN, St. Paul, MN, 1940).

8868 Devel, Gervin. Leader (Gervin Devel's California Collegians Orchestra, KGO, Oakland, CA, 1925).

8869 DeVende, Chico. Leader, Chico DeVende's Russian String Trio (KFQZ, Hollywood, CA, 1926).

8870 De Veritch, Victor. Yugoslavian pianist (WEVD, New York, NY, 1939).

8871 DeVictor, Marty. Sportscaster (WBNS, Columbus, OH, 1945–1946). DJ (*Marty's Party,* WBNS, 1947).

8872 Devigneau, Antone. Violinist (KFUU, Oakland, CA, 1925).

8873 DeVille, Marie. Vocalist (*Marie DeVille*, vcl. mus. prg., NBC, 1935).

8874 *Devils, Drugs and Doctors.* Dr. Howard W. Haggard, Professor of Physiology at Yale University, conducted the program that was devoted to providing authoritative medical information and identifying and combating misinformation (15 min., Sunday, 8:00–8:15 P.M., CBS, 1931).

8875 Devine, Barry. Baritone (NBC and CBS, 1929).

8876 DeVine, Marguerite. Concert pianist (WGBS, New York, NY, 1929).

8877 Devine, Ott. Newscaster (WSM, Nashville, TN, 1941).

8878 DeVivier, Jeanne. COM-HE (KFBK, Sacramento, CA, 1951)

8879 Devlin, Andrew. DJ (WWBZ, Vineland, NJ, 1947).

8880 Devlin, Doris. COM-HE (KSRC, Socotto, NM, 1960).

8881 Devlin, Marion. COM-HE (KVON, Napa, CA, 1951).

8882 DeVodi, Don. Leader (*Don DeVodi Orchestra*, instr. mus. prg., NBC, 1934, 1938).

8883 *DeVoe-Reynolds Redskins.* Ben Selvin's orchestra and vocalists were featured on this music program sponsored by the DeVoe-Reynolds Paint Company (30 min, 9:30–10:00 P.M., CBS, 1930).

8884 DeVol, Eva. Operatic soprano (KPO, San Francisco, CA, 1929).

8885 DeVon, Dovel. DJ (KREM, Spokane, WA, 1948; *Music in the Morning* and *The Spinning Wheel*, KWNW, Wenachee, WA, 1949).

8886 DeVon, Pru. DJ (*Nights in Latin America*, WQXR, New York, NY, 1948–1955).

8887 Devonchik, Joe. DJ (*Musical Reveille*, WMBL, Morehead City, NC, 1947).

8888 Devore, Tom. DJ (*Music Room*, KVOO, Tulsa, OK, 1947).

8889 DeVorzon, Jules. Violinist (WEBJ, New York, NY, 1926).

8890 Devoto, Angela. Violinist-singer (WMH, Cincinnati, OH, 1924).

8891 DeVrees, Henrik. Flutist (NBC, 1928).

8892 Devron, George. Leader (*George Devron Orchestra*, instr. mus. prg., NBC, 1934–1935).

8893 DeWald, Don. Newscaster (KHUB, Waysonville, CA, 1944). DJ (*Music Box Revue*, KHUB, Watsonville, CA, 1947).

8894 Dewart, James. Newscaster (WERC, Erie, PA, 1945–1948).

8895 DeWeese, Dallas. Newscaster (WTOL, Toledo, OH, 1945; *Sohio Reporter*, WLW, Cincinnati, OH, 1947).

8896 DeWeese, Tex. Newscaster (KPDN, Pampa, TX, 1937–1945).

8897 Dewey. DJ (KVOX, Moorhead, MN, 1949).

8898 DeWire, Bunny. COM-HE (WITT, Lewisburg, PA, 1957).

8899 De Wit, Jacqueline. Actress De Wit appeared on the *Second Husband* daytime serial.

8900 DeWitt, Gladys. Miss DeWitt talked on travel topics such as "The Romance of the Santa Fe Trail" (KHJ, Los Angeles, CA, 1925).

8901 Dewitz, Golda Helen. Contralto (KTAB, Oakland, CA, 1926).

8902 DeWolfe, Marie. Actress DeWolfe was a cast member of the *Rosemary* daytime serial program.

8903 DeWoody, Ruth. Soprano (*Ruth DeWoody*, vcl. mus. prg., WIP, Philadelphia, PA, 1935).

8904 Dexter, Ron. DJ (KCBD, Lubbock, TX, 1957).

8905 DeYoannes, Armondo M. Sportscaster (WHLB, Virginia, MN, 1942; WHLB, 1947–1951).

8906 DeYoung, Gene. Newscaster (KARM, Fresno, CA, 1940). Sportscaster (*Midget Auto Races*, KARM, 1940–1941).

8907 DeYoung, John. Newscaster (WISH, Indianapolis, IN, 1942).

8908 DeYoung, Lucy. Contralto (WLW, Cincinnati, OH, 1924).

8909 Dhossche, (Professor) R.A. Professor Dhossche was a flute and piccolo soloist and leader of the Magnolia Refinery Band (KFDM, Beaumont, TX, 1928).

8910 Dial, Linda. COM-HE (WESA, Charleroi, PA, 1957).

8911 *Dialing with Luscretia.* Luscretia Davidson pretended to use the phone to talk to a friend on the novel program, as she reported what was happening of interest to women in Charlotte, NC (15 min., Monday, 10:45–11:00 A.M., WSOC, Charlotte, NC, 1941).

8912 *(The) Dialist.* Radio critic Charlotte Greer, author of *Silas of the Hill Country*, commented on radio and radio programming (WOR, 1933).

8913 Diamond, Bill. Newscaster (WHO, Des Moines, IA, 1946).

8914 Diamond, Charles, Jr. Saxophonist (WBZ, Boston-Springfield, MA, 1925).

8915 Diamond, Leo. Leader (*Leo Diamond and His Harmonaires Orchestra*, instr. mus. prg., NBC, 1943).

8916 Diamond, Lew. Leader (*Lew Diamond Orchestra*, instr. mus. prg., WGN, Chicago, IL, 1933; WGN, 1939; MBS, 1940; WGN, 1942–1943).

8917 *Diamond Dance Orchestra.* Instr. mus. prg. (WTIC, Hartford, CT, 1932).

8918 Diana-Moon Dance Orchestra. KFWB (Hollywood, CA, 1925).

8919 Diana Trio. The trio was an instrumental group that included violinist Willa Conzelman; pianist Bernice Parrott; and cellist Solomon Chilton (KRE, Berkeley, CA, 1926).

8920 Diane. DJ (*The Diane Program*, WBEN, Buffalo, NY, 1952).

8921 *Diane and Her Lifesaver.* Life Savers sponsored the program that told the story of two singers played by Lucille Wall and John Diggs. When they sang to the music of the Meyer Davis Orchestra, however, it was the singing voices of soprano Rhoda Arnold and baritone Alfred Drake that the audience heard. (15 min., Monday, 8:15 P.M., CBS, 1935).

8922 *(The) Diary of Jimmy Mattern.* Darrell Ware wrote the daytime children's serial about the story of globe trotting Hollywood stunt pilot, Jimmy Mattern. Sponsored by the Pure Oil Company, the program was a popular juvenile daytime serial. The Pure Oil Company gave away three small hardbound books as a premium that described Mattern's radio adventures. The program was produced by Bob White (15 min., Monday through Friday, 5:15–5:30 P.M. CST, WLW, Cincinnati, OH, 1936). Mattern's *real* aviation feats included a July 4–5, 1932 flight with Bennett Griffin from New York City to Berlin, Germany, by way of Newfoundland. This flight set a transatlantic record of 10 hours 15 minutes plus four other world records. Mattern also attempted the first solo flight around the world. He broke all speed records three-fourths of the way around the world before crashing in Siberia. After borrowing another plane, Mattern flew on to New York to complete his flight.

8923 DiBendetto, Giuseppe. Tenor (WEAF, New York, NY, 1926; WJZ, New York, NY, 1929).

8924 Dick, John. Baritone (WGY, Schenectady, NY, 1923).

8925 *Dick and Denny.* Dick and Denny, not otherwise identified, were a harmony singing team (15 min., 4:00–4:15 P.M., CBS, 1931).

8926 *Dick Daring, a Boy of Today* (aka ***Dick Daring's Adventures***). The daytime juvenile serial drama was sponsored by the Quaker Oats Company. Merrill Fugit played the title role. Joan Blaine, Donald Briggs, Art Van Harvey and Billy Yea were also in the cast (15 min., Monday through Friday, 6:15–6:30 P.M. and Sunday, 6:45–7:00 P.M., NBC-Blue, 1933).

8927 *(The) Dick Haymes Show.* Crooner Haymes was the host on his entertaining music show sponsored by Autolite. He was joined by vocalist Helen Forrest, the Four Hits and a Miss [vocal group] and Gordon Jenkins' Orchestra. Frank Martin was the announcer (30 min., Thursday, 9:00–9:30 P.M., NBC-Red, 1946). When Forrest left the show late in 1946, comedian Cliff Arquette joined the cast. The Andrews Sisters frequently appeared with Haymes on the show.

8928 *Dick Steele, Boy Reporter.* Merrill Fugit played the title role on the children's daytime serial program that featured, among others, Charlie Calvert, who played many gangster roles on the show. The sponsor was Hammered Wheat Thinsies cereal (NBC, 1935).

8929 Dickason, Deane H. Dickason was the announcer on *The Musical Travelog Program* (KPO, San Francisco, CA, 1926). Newscaster (KGO, San Francisco, CA, 1942).

8930 Dickens, Dean. COM-HE (WGST, Atlanta, GA, 1951–1955).

8931 Dickens, Jimmy. DJ (*Melody Ranch*, WKNX , Saginaw, MI, 1947).

8932 Dickenson, (Mrs.) Grace Gilmore. Contralto (WTIC, Hartford, CT, 1925).

8933 Dickenson, Jean. Singer (*Jean Dickenson*, vcl. mus. prg., NBC-Blue, 1935–1937). Miss Dickenson also sang on the *American Album of Familiar Music* program.

8934 Dickenson, Millie. COM-HE (WTLO, Somerset, KY, 1960).

8935 Dicker, Martin. Tenor (WMOX, St. Louis, MO, 1928).

8936 Dickerman, Carlton H. Announcer (WEEI, Boston, MA, 1928–1929).

8937 Dickerson, Doris. COM-HE (WOXF, Oxford, NC, 1954).

8938 Dickerson, Nancy. Newscaster-producer (CBS, late 1950s-1960). Although most famous for her television newscasting, Dickerson began in radio. After graduating from the University of Wisconsin, she did graduate work at Harvard on Foreign Relations. Before going to work for CBS, Dickerson wrote speeches for several senators. At CBS she first produced radio and television programs before being allowed to go on the air herself. After covering stories in Europe, she considered herself a "foreign correspondent" (Dickerson, 1976). When she returned to the United States and began to broadcast political news, a first for a woman, she met some resistance (Dickerson, 1976): "You're not married. You're not supporting a family. Why do *you* want to go on the air?" The comments implied that men needed the work. She even remembers a call she received from a CBS vice president in charge of news in 1960 the first time she was to appear on the *Face the Nation* program. He told her, "Listen, you're going to go on the program and we've never had a woman on it before. Now don't giggle" (Dickerson, 1976). She went on the program and did well.

8939 Dickey, Ellen Rose. Announcer (WJJD, Chicago, IL, 1925).

8940 Dickey, Milton. Newscaster (KDRO, Sedalia, MO, 1941).

8941 Dickinson, Ed. DJ (KELK, Elko, NV, 1949).

8942 Dickinson, Florence. COM-HE (WOKW, Sturgeon Bay, WI, 1954).

8943 Dickinson, May Bliss. Miss Dickinson was the hostess of the *Amrad's Women's Club Talk* program (WGI, Medford Hillside, MA, 1923).

8944 Dickler, Sid. DJ (*Meet the Maestro*, WMCK, McKeesport, PA, 1947; *Disc Diggin'*, WMCK and WHOD, McKeesport, PA, 1948–1949; WEDP, McKeesport, PA, 1954).

8945 Dickman, Harry. Leader (*Harry Dickman Orchestra*, instr. mus. prg., WHAS, Louisville, KY, 1936).

8946 Dickoff, Charles. DJ (*Top O' the Morning*, WISC, Madison, WI, 1948). Sportscaster (WISC, 1949).

8947 Dickson, Artells. Singer (*The Street Singer*, WAAB, Boston, MA, 1931; as the "Singing Vagabond" on the *Vitality Personalities* program, CBS, 1932).

8948 Dickson, Bill. Newscaster (KFDA, Amarillo, TX, 1941).

8949 Dickson, Bobbie. Singer (*Bobbie Dickson*, vcl. mus. prg., WJJD, Chicago, IL, 1935).

8950 Dickson, Bryce. Newscaster (KPRC, Houston, TX, 1939).

8951 Dickson, Dick. Organist (KFON, Long Beach, CA, 1927).

8952 Dickson, Dick. Leader (*Dick Dickson Orchestra*, instr. mus. prg., WIP, Philadelphia, PA, 1936, 1942).

8953 Dickson, Dick. DJ (*Today's Top Tunes*, WARS, Wilmington, DE, 1947). He could be the orchestra leader listed previously.

8954 Dickson, Evangeline. Soprano (WORD, Batavia, IL, 1925).

8955 Dickson, Frank. Newscaster (WNBH, New Bedford, MA, 1939–1940).

8956 Dickson, Georgia Lowe. Contralto (KFI, Los Angeles, CA, 1928).

8957 Dickson, John Paul. Newscaster (MBS, 1942). Dickson served as Berlin correspondent for the Mutual Broadcasting Company during the early years of World War II.

8958 Dickson, Ray. Singer (*Ray Dickson*, vcl. mus. prg., WIND, Chicago, IL, 1935).

8959 Dickson, Robert. DJ (KBRZ, Freeport, TX, 1955).

8960 Dickson, S.B. Dickson recited "coded limericks" (KPO, San Francisco, CA, 1925).

8961 Dickson, Stewart. Pianist (KFKU, Lawrence, KS, 1925).

8962 *(The) Dictograph Orchestra.* The Dictograph Orchestra, a popular radio band, broadcast a weekly program of dance music (30 min., Sunday, 6:00–6:30 P.M., NBC-Red, 1929).

8963 Diddle, Clyde. Bass (KPO, San Francisco, CA, 1925).

8964 Didrichsen, Hugo. Danish-American baritone (KSD, St. Louis, MO, 1924).

8965 Didur, Adam. Metropolitan Opera singer (WMCA, New York, NY, 1927).

8966 Dieckman, Herbert. Flutist (WLW, Cincinnati, OH, 1923).

8967 Diehl, Bill. Sportscaster (WGH, Newport News, VA, 1944–1953; WLOW, Norfolk, VA, 1955). Newscaster (WGH, 1945–1946).

8968 Diehl, John and Henry Diehl. Zither and piano instrumental team (WAHG, Richmond Hill, NY, 1926).

8969 Diehl, Johnny. Leader (*Johnny Diehl Orchestra*, instr. mus. prg., WHP, Harrisburg, PA, 1936, 1942).

8970 Diehl, Vic. Sportscaster (WAZL, Hazleton, PA, 1937).

8971 Dien [Diem], Al. Leader (*Al Dien Orchestra*, instr. mus. prg., CBS, 1934–1935; WBBM, Chicago, IL, 1936).

8972 Dies, Bob. DJ (*At Peace with Dies*, WADC, Akron, OH, 1948).

8973 Dietrich, Helen Jenks. Pianist (WEAF, New York, NY, 1924).

8974 Dietrich [Dietrick], Mary. Leader (*Margaret Dietrich Orchestra*, instr. mus. prg., NBC, 1942).

8975 Dietrich, Ray. DJ (*Sun-KIST Show*, KIST, Santa Barbara, CA, 1947).

8976 Dietz, Hulda. Soprano (KPLA, Los Angeles, CA, 1928).

8977 Dietz, (Mrs.) Kenneth. Newscaster (WBRB, Red Bank, NJ, 1939).

8978 Dietzel, Al. Leader (*Al Dietzel Orchestra*, instr. mus. prg., KWK, St. Louis, MO, 1936).

8979 Dietzen, John. Newscaster (WDAN, Danville, IL, 1944).

8980 DiFant, Luigi. Newscaster (WNBC, New Haven, CT, 1945).

8981 DiFilippo, Kim. COM-HE (WNOK, Coljumbia, SC, 1954–1956).

8982 DiFiore, Lina. Pianist (*Lina DiFiore*, instr. mus. prg., WOR, Newark, NJ, 1934).

8983 Digesu, Fred. DJ (*All-College Review*, WJHO, Opelika, AL, 1947). Sportscaster (WJHO, 1949; WHBS, Huntsville, AL, 1952–1953).

8984 Dighton, John. Newscaster (WJRD, Tuscaloosa, AL, 1940–1941). Sportscaster (WJRD, 1941).

8985 DiGiorgia Orchestra of Italy. The DiGiorgia Orchestra included a father, mother and their two daughters playing trombone, mandolin, cornet and violin (KMA, Shenandoah, IA, 1927).

8986 DiLalla, Eddie. Leader (Eddie DiLalla's Ideal Novelty Orchestra, WHN, New York, NY, 1923).

8987 di Lascia, Anthony. Flutist (WCDA, New York, NY, 1928).

8988 DiLeo, Foca. Leader (Foca DiLeo and his Accordian Symphony Orchestra, WSOE, Milwaukee, WI, 1926).

8989 DiLeo, Lew. Sportscaster (WGAT, Utica, NY, 1947).

8990 Dill, Clive. Newscaster (WBTA, Batavia, NY, 1942).

8991 Dill, Glen. DJ (*The Sundial*, WTSP, St. Petersburg, FL, 1947–1956).

8992 Dillahunty, Thomas. Newscaster (KCMC, Texarkana, TX, 1938). Sportscaster (KCMC, 1938–1939).

8993 Dillehay, Gene. DJ (*Western Swingtime*, KTOW, Oklahoma City, OK, 1948).

8994 Dilley, Mary. COM-HE (WCVS, Springfield, IL, 1949).

8995 Dillin, Alberta. COM-HE (WFOY, St. Augustine, FL, 1954).

8996 Dilling, Mildred. Harpist (*Mildred Dilling*, instr. mus. prg., NBC, 1934–1935). On her August 18, 1935, program, Dilling performed the following selections: Saint-Saens' "Fantasie," Beethoven's "Minuet in G," D'Yvetot's "Le Bon Petit-Roi" and Hazzelmans' "Fireflies" (15 min., Sunday, 1:00–1:15 P.M., NBC, 1935).

8997 Dillingham, Alex. Newscaster (WKAR, East Lansing, MI, 1942). DJ (*Record Time*, WILS, Lansing, MI, 1947–1949; *Club 1430*, WILS, Lansing, MI, 1949).

8998 Dillingham, Frances. COM-HE (WTAB, Tabor City, NC, 1956).

8999 Dillingham, Frank. DJ (WBLJ, Dalton, GA, 1949).

9000 Dillingham, Harry. Newscaster (WTAW, College Station, TX, 1945).

9001 Dillner, Bill. DJ (*Midnight Flyers*, WEDC, Chicago, IL, 1947–1949).

9002 Dillon, Alice. Harpist (KPO, San Francisco, CA, 1927).

9003 Dillon, Carl. Conductor (Third Infantry Band, WCCO, Minneapolis–St. Paul, MN, 1928; KSTP, St. Paul–Minneapolis, MN, 1929).

9004 Dillon, Claire. Singer (WMEX, Boston, MA, 1938–1939).

9005 Dillon, Dorothy Davis. Soprano (WJQ, Chicago, IL, 1924; WIBO, Chicago, IL, 1926).

9006 Dillon, Gene. Sportscaster (WCMW, Canton, OH, 1960).

9007 Dillon, James. Saxophonist (KFWI, San Francisco, CA, 1927).

9008 Dillon, Joe. Newscaster (WHAT, Philadelphia, PA, 1942).

9009 Dillon, John. Newscaster (KVOR, Colorado Springs, CO, 1938).

9010 Dillon, Len. Sportscaster (NBC, 1960).

9011 Dillon, Michael "Mike." Newscaster (KVOR, Colorado Springs, CO, 1940–1941).

9012 Dillon, Rosemary. Actress Dillon appeared on the *Modern Cinderella* daytime program.

9013 Dillon, Zita. Pianist, xylophonist and vibraphonist (KOMO, Seattle, WA, 1927–1928).

9014 Dillworth, Billy. CW DJ Dilworth was a great Georgia favorite (15 min., Daily, WLET, Toccoa, GA, 1960).

9015 Dilson, Burt. DJ (*Club Playhouse*, WJW, Cleveland, OH, 1948).

9016 Dilworth, George. Leader (George Dilworth's Sixteen Salon Singers, Network, 1929). Dillworth led a singing group that specialized in old time songs.

9017 Dilworth, Scot. Newscaster (WBOW, Terre Haute, IN, 1942).

9018 *Dimension X.* An excellent adult science-fiction drama series, *Dimension X* set a high standard that few other programs of its type achieved. The show's first presentation was "The Outer Limits," adapted from Graham Doar's story by Ernest Kinoy. The cast members over the years included: Joan Alexander, Jackson Beck, Ralph Bell, Art Carney, Joyce Gordon, Jack Grimes, Larry Haines, Raymond Edward Johnson, Mandel Kramer, Joan Lazer, Peter Lazer, Jack Lemmon, Ronald Liss, Jan Miner, Claudia Morgan, Santos Ortega, Byrna Raeburn, Norman Rose, Everett Sloane and Patricia Wheel. Bob Warren and Fred Collins were it announcers. The program's writers were Ray Bradbury and Earl Hammner, Jr. Ed King, Danny Sutter and Fred Weihe directed the show. Each week a new story was dramatized (30 min., Saturday, 8:00–8:30 P.M., NBC, 1950). A later version of the program known as *X Minus One* was broadcast in 1955. *See* ***X Minus One.***

9019 *Dimmick's Orchestra.* Instr. mus. prg. (WLW, Cincinnati, OH, 1934).

9020 Dimpel, Dorothy. COM-HE (WLAV, Grand Rapids, MI, 1951).

9021 *Dinah Shore's Open House* (aka ***Dinah Shore Show***). Dinah Shore's excellent singing was the chief ingredient of her entertaining variety show (NBC-Red, 1945). Wally Brown assisted Dinah by adding his comic bits. Toby Reed was the program's announcer. Various guest stars such as Akim Tamiroff, Charles Laughton and Groucho Marx frequently appeared. For other examples of Shore's work. *See* ***Call for Music, The Chamber Music Society of Lower Basin Street*** *and* ***The Ford Show.***

9022 Dineen, Joseph F. "Joe." Newscaster (WORL, Boston, MA, 1942, 1944–1947).

9023 Dingman, Bob. DJ (*Date with a Disc*, WCSS, Amsterdam, NY, 1948; *Dunkin' with Dingman*, WENT, Gloversville, NY, 1949; WSPN, Saratoga Springs, NY, 1955–1957).

9024 *Dinner Bell Time* (aka ***The Dinner Bell***). This long-time WLS favorite was broadcast each weekday at noon and presented several segments of information for farmers, music, humor and religious elements. *Dinner Bell Time* was conducted by gregarious Arthur Page. Each program opened with the sound of cowbells and the playing of the "National Anthem."

Farm news and devotional talks were intermixed with entertainment features. Many newlyweds visited the program, and when they did the "Wedding March" was played in their honor. Dr. John Holland, a Methodist minister, appeared regularly on the program for many years. Another popular feature was the Allotted Time Quartet of Elgin, Illinois, whose members were bass E.D. Cooke, tenor Caleb Marlowe, tenor O.R. Hasty and second bass Mayo Haas (WLS, Chicago, IL, 1937). *Dinner Bell Time* first went on the air March 2, 1926, with organist-pianist Martha Meier Whyland playing three piano solos and Marquis Smith singing "Loch Lomand."

9025 *Dinner Music from the Rose Room of the Hotel Astoria.* Joseph Knecht conducted the Astoria Hotel Orchestra on the program of classical music. One program that was broadcast in the spring of 1924 included the following selections: "Marche Lorraine" by Ganne; Selections from "Les Huguenots" by Meyerbeer; "The Arlesienne Suite" by Bizet; "Caprice Viennois" by Kreisler; "Entr'acte and Valse" from *Copelia* by DeLibes; "Habaniera" by Chabrier; "Lob der Fraven" by Strauss; and "Madame Sherry" by Hoshna (WEAF, New York, NY, 1924).

9026 Dinning Sisters. Popular close harmony singing group from the Chicago area (*The Dinning Sisters*, vcl. mus. prg., NBC, 1939; WJR, Detroit, MI, 1942). The sisters often performed on the *National Barn Dance* program (WLS, Chicago, IL, 1944). *See* ***The National Barn Dance.***

9027 Dinsdale, Alfred. Newscaster (WATN, Watertown, NY, 1941–1942).

9028 Dinsmore, Dorothy. Violinist (WHO, Des Moines, IA, 1926).

9029 Dinsmore, Ed. Newscaster (WORL, Boston, MA, 1942, 1944–1947). DJ (WCOP, Boston, MA, 1947; *Luncheon Club*, WBEN, Buffalo, NY, 1948–1952).

9030 Dinsmore, Ray. Cellist (WCOA, Pensacola, FL, 1926).

9031 Dinsmore, Wayne. Dinsmore spoke on such intriguing topics as "The Horse — Next to Woman — God's Greatest Gift to Man" (WGY, Schenectady, NY, 1925).

9032 DiPardo, Tony. Leader (*Tony DiPardo Orchestra*, instr. mus. prg., WOAI, San Antonio, TX, 1942).

9033 D'Ippollito, Lewis. Saxophonist (KFSG, Los Angeles, CA, 1926).

9034 Dipson, Diana. Ten-year-old violinist (WGR, Buffalo, NY, 1927).

9035 Director, Anne. An executive in the radio department of the San Francisco office of the J. Walter Thompson advertising agency, Director bought and developed programming for the agency (1930).

9036 Dirman, Rose. Soprano (WQXR, New York, NY, 1937).

9037 DiServi, Dorothy. Pianist (WELI, New Haven, CT, 1939).

9038 Dishinger, Mary. COM-HE (WITZ, Jasper, IN, 1960).

9039 Diskay [Discay], Joseph. Hungarian tenor (KNX, Los Angeles, CA, 1928).

9040 Disney, Rufus. Newscaster (*Time for News*, WCTT, Corbin, KY, 1947).

9041 Disque, Ruth. COM-HE (WCNT, Centralia, IL, 1957).

9042 Ditmer, Beverly. COM-HE (WHGR, Houghton Lake, MI, 1956–1957).

9043 Dittus, (Mrs.) Addie. Soprano (KFWM, Oakland, CA, 1926).

9044 DiTullio, Joseph. Cellist (KPLA, Los Angeles, CA, 1928).

9045 Ditzler, Harry. Blind pianist-composer (NBC, 1928).

9046 Divine, Grace. Soprano (WOR, Newark, NJ, 1925).

9047 *Divine Healing Service.* Sister Aimee Semple McPherson conducted this radio healing service from her Angelus Temple in Los Angeles (KFSG, 1925). *See* **McPherson, Aimee Semple.**

9048 Dix, Jack. Newscaster (WGBI, Columbus, MS, 1946). Sportscaster (WGBI, 1946; WFOR, Hattiesburg, MS, 1948; *Speaking of Sports*, WFOR, 1949; WHSY, Hattiesburg, MS, 1951). DJ (*Mr. Beesure's Waxworks*, WHBQ, Memphis, TN, 1947).

9049 Dix, Richard. DJ (*Midnight Flyers*, WEDC, Chicago, IL, 1948).

9050 Dixie Banjo Trio. Popular instrumental group (WTAM, Cleveland, OH, 1926).

9051 *Dixie Beeliners.* CW mus. prg. (WORK, York, PA, 1936).

9052 Dixie Bluegrass Serenaders. Henry L. Dixon directed the popular band (WHAS, Louisville, KY, 1925).

9053 *Dixie Boy Jordan.* Singer (*Dixie Boy Jordan*, voc. mus. prg., KMOX, St. Louis, MO, 1932).

9054 Dixie Boys Orchestra. Music group that broadcast a Sunday afternoon program of tea dance music (WBBM, Chicago, IL, 1925).

9055 *Dixie Circus.* Uncle Bob Sherwood told tales that were designed to bring the thrill to "modern children" so they could experience what their fathers did "when the circus came to town." Uncle Bob Sherwood, an old time circus clown, told entertaining stories, a novelty band supplied the music, a calliope played and numerous animal sounds were produced by Bradley Barker. Ralph Freese was the announcer (30 min., Friday, 7:30–8:00 p.m, NBC-Blue, 1928–1929). The program was revived in 1934.

9056 *Dixie Circus.* This music program had a circus theme. Sponsored by Dixie Cups, the cast included Marcella Shields, Phillips Carlin and a "circus band" directed by Ludwig Laurier (30 min., Saturday, 8:00–8:30 P.M., WJZ-Blue, 1930). The program might have been another version of the *Dixie Circus* program described above.

9057 (The) Dixie Clodhoppers. *See* **Binkley Brothers' Dixie Clodhoppers.**

9058 *(The) Dixie Dandies.* Al Bernard and Paul Dumont, veteran radio entertainers, performed songs and patter on their lively show (NBC, 1934).

9059 Dixie Devil Demons. The Dixie Devil Demons hot jazz band broadcast from New York's Cinderella Dance Hall (WHN, New York, NY, 1924).

9060 *Dixie Echoes.* J. Rosamund Johnson directed the program of "Negro spirituals" that were sung by a talented "Negro vocal group" (15 min., Saturday, 8:30–8:45 P.M., CBS, 1930).

9061 Dixie Girls. The female singing team included Alta and Opal, who were not otherwise identified (KMA, Shenadoah, IA, 1928).

9062 *Dixie Jamboree.* A CW music program, the *Dixie Jamboree* featured the Tennessee Ramblers and a talented group of performers that included Fred Kirby the Victory Cowboy, the Rangers Quartet, Vernon Hyles, Arthur Smith and singer Kitty Clyde (WBT-CBS, Charlotte, NC, 1944). It enjoyed a brief network run.

9063 Dixie Jubilee. *Variety* said they were a talented "Negro spiritual" singing group (WABC, New York, NY, 1927).

9064 *Dixie Liners.* CW mus. prg. (WSM, Nashville, TN, 1936). This might be the Dixielanders group described below.

9065 Dixie Melody Boys. Orchestra managed (directed) by L.H. Feiling (KDKA, Pittsburgh, PA, 1922).

9066 *Dixie Plowboys.* CW mus. prg. (WHAM, Rochester, NY, 1936; WCAU, Philadelphia, PA, 1938).

9067 *Dixie Ramblers.* CW mus. prg. (WGH, Newport News, VA, 1938).

9068 *Dixie Serenaders.* CW mus. prg. (CBS, 1936, 1938).

9069 *Dixie Spiritual Singers.* *What's on the Air?* magazine (March, 1931, p. 13) praised their vocal music program for presenting "genuine Negro folk songs" sung in "genuine Negro fashion." The group consisted of 17 male voices (15 min., Monday, 10:30–10:45 P.M., WRVA, Richmond, VA, 1931).

9070 Dixie Twins. Soprano Minnie Mae Moore and singing pianist Mrs. Harry Close were called the Dixie Twins (WSMB, New Orleans, LA, 1925).

9071 *Dixieland Music Shop.* Bob Crosby's Bob Cats band played good dixieland jazz on the lively show. Mildred Bailey and Bonnie King were the vocalists. The show was sponsored by the R.J. Reynolds Tobacco Company (30 min., Thursday, 9:00–9:30 P.M., NBC-Red Network, 1940).

9072 *Dixieland Song Shop.* Bob Crosby's fine dixieland band performed on the show (15 min., CBS, 1939). The following year the program was expanded to a 30-minute format and broadcast on NBC as *The Dixieland Music Shop* (NBC, 1940). *See* ***Dixieland Music Shop.***

9073 *(The) Dixielanders.* Brothers Sam and Kirk McGee teamed with Arthur Smith to play banjo, violin and guitar on the CW music show (WSM, Nashville, TN, middle 1930s). The group appeared frequently on the *Grand Ole Opry (WSM).*

9074 Dixola Novelty Orchestrta. Eight-man jazz band (WSMB, New Orleans, LA, 1928).

9075 Dixon, Bert. Announcer (WAAT, Jersey City, NJ, 1927).

9076 Dixon, Betty. Pianist (*Betty Dixon*, instr. mus. prg., WJTN, Trenton, NJ, 1937).

9077 Dixon, Bill. DJ (*Record Lounge*, WTCB, Flint, MI, 1947).

9078 Dixon, Bob. Sportscaster (WTAG, Worcester, MA, 1942).

9079 Dixon, Bobby. Leader (*Bobby Dixon Orchestra*, instr. mus. prg., WENR, Chicago, IL, 1936).

9080 Dixon, Christine. COM-HE (WONG, Oneida, NY, 1960).

9081 Dixon, Darrell E. DJ (*The Best in Music*, WSLM, Salem, IN, 1955–1960).

9082 Dixon, Dick. Organist (KFON, Long Beach, CA, 1928).

9083 Dixon, Don. Vocalist (*Don Dixon*, vcl. mus. prg., WGY, Schenectady, NY, 1940s).

9084 Dixon, Henry. Leader (Henry Dixon's Hawaiians [orchestra], WGN, Chicago, IL, 1928).

9085 Dixon, Homer L. Sportscaster (*Sports Final*, WNOG, Naples, FL, 1960).

9086 Dixon, J.C. DJ (*Nightbeat*, WACL, Waycross, GA, 1960).

9087 Dixon, John. Sportscaster (WROK, Rockford, IL, 1939). Newscaster (*News Plus*, WROK, 1947).

9088 Dixon, Kenneth. Newscaster (KWEW, Hobbs, NM, 1938). Sportscaster (KWEW, 1938).

9089 Dixon, Lee. Leader (*Lee Dixon Orchestra*, instr. mus. prg., WIP, Philadelphia, PA, 1934–1935).

9090 Dixon, Martha. COM-HE (WJIM, Lansing, MI, 1960).

9091 Dixon, Mason. Newscaster (WFBC, Greenville, SC, 1938; WNOX ,Knoxville, TN, 1939–1940; KICD, Spencer, IA, 1946–1949). Sportscaster (WNOX, 1939–1940; KICD, 1946–1951).

9092 Dixon, (Mrs.) N.V. Pianist (KSD, St. Louis, MO, 1923).

9093 Dixon, Nancy. COM-HE (WEEI, Boston, MA, 1949).

9094 Dixon, Norwood. Vocalist (*Norwood Dixon*, vcl. mus. prg., WAKR, Akron, OH, 1942)

9095 Dixon, Paul. Newscaster (WCPO, Cincinnati, OH, 1945). DJ (WCPO, 1947–1952).

9096 Dixon, Randy. Sportscaster (*Toast to Sports*, WTEL, Philadelphia, PA, 1947–1948). DJ (*Ebony Hall of Fame*, WDAS, Philadelphia, PA, 1952–1955).

9097 Dixon, Ray. Leader (*Ray Dixon Orchestra*, instr. mus. prg., WMBD, Peoria, IL, 1936).

9098 Dixon, Roy. DJ (*Mixin' with Dixon*, KTRM, Beaumont, TX, 1948; *Top of the Trail*, KTRM, 1952).

9099 Dixon, Stanley. Lyric tenor (KOMO, Seattle, WA, 1927–1928).

9100 Dixon, Stanley [Stanton]. Newscaster (MBS, 1944; KICD, Spencer, IA, 1945;

KSO, Des Moines, IA, 1945; *Five Star Final*, KSWI, Council Bluffs, IA, 1947; *Stanley Dixon and the News*, WBEX, Chillicothe, OH, 1948).

9101 Dixon, Vonda. COM-HE (WARN, Fort Pierce, FL, 1957).

9102 *Dizzy Dean.* Former baseball great Jay Hanna "Dizzy" Dean talked baseball with announcer Frank Eschen in his inimitable, frequently ungrammatical style and answered questions sent in by listeners. On this program sponsored by Johnson's Wax, Dean was an entertaining broadcaster. (15 min., Saturday, 5:00–5:15 P.M., NBC, 1948). When Dean was criticized for using *aint*, he answered his critics by saying, "A lot of people who don't say *aint, aint* eating." Two other examples of the Dean broadcasting style are:

> The runners had to go back to their respectable bases.
>
> The pitcher and catcher are meeting to see if they're going to have nice cold Falstaff [beer] and a steak after the game.

Even if "Old Diz" sometimes suffered with his syntax, he still was more informative, interesting and entertaining than most other players who followed him on radio and television.

9103 *Dizzy Fingers and Bud Taylor.* An entertaining music program by an unidentified pianist and singer (WWVA, Wheeling, WV, 1935).

9104 Dizzy Four. Popular jazz combo (WFAA, Dallas, TX, 1922).

9105 *Dizzy Lizzy.* *See* **Hill, Gladys** *and* **Smith, Novella.**

9106 *(The) Djer Kiss Recital.* Djer Kiss Cosmetics sponsored the program of romantic music featuring contralto Cyrena Van Gordon and her accompanist, Walter Golde (15 min., Wednesday, 7:30–7:45 P.M., NBC, 1933).

9107 Dnaprova, Maria. Russian soprano (WOK, Chicago, IL, 1925, KYW, Chicago, IL, 1925; WQJ, Chicago, IL, 1926).

9108 *Do Re Mi.* Vcl. mus. prg. featuring a talented female harmony trio, (15 min., 5:45–6:00 P.M., WABC, New York, NY, 1933; CBS, 1934–1935).

9109 *Do You Know the Answer?* The unique combination of newscast and quiz program was conducted by Alan Courtney, a DJ best known as host of *The 1280 Club*. In between news announcements, Courtney would call various persons chosen at random from the phone book. If they answered the phone, they got a small prize. If they could correctly answer a question about some news event, they received an even larger prize (WOV, New York, NY, 1942).

9110 *Doakes and Doakes.* Mr. and Mrs. Harry Gibson were a popular vaudeville singing team before they turned to radio and became San Francisco favorites in 1932.

9111 Doan, Douglas. Newscaster (KRBC, Abilene, TX, 1937).

9112 Doan, Ed. Newscaster (WOSU, Columbus, OH, 1940).

9113 Doan, Margie. COM-HE (KBMO, Benson, MN, 1960).

9114 Doane, Dorothy. COM-HE (WILS, Lansing, MI, 1957).

9115 Doane, Elgin. Baritone (KYA, San Francisco, CA, 1927; KYA, San Francisco, CA, 1928).

9116 Doane, Francis C. Soprano (WBZ, Boston-Springfield, MA, 1923).

9117 Dobbert, Shirley. Violinist (KGO, Oakland, CA, 1925).

9118 Dobbins, Joe. DJ (*Yawn Patrol*, WBNS, Columbus, OH, 1947).

9119 Dobbs, Dar. DJ (*Pop Parade*, KDSH, Boise, ID, 1948).

9120 Dobbs, Hugh Barrett. Affectionately known as "Dobbsie" and "Captain Dobbsie," Hugh Barrett Dobbs first went on the air conducting morning health exercises and "pep club" programs (*Health Exercises* and *Pep Class*, KGO, Oakland, CA, 1925). In the evenings Dobbs would deliver talks on *Physical Culture for the Family* on KGO. His early morning exercise program in July, 1925, was called *Energetics*. He delivered what the station called *Dobbsie's Daily Chat in 1929* assisted by William H. Hancock (30 min., Monday through Friday, KPO, 9:30–10:00 A.M., San Francisco, CA, 1929). That same year Dobbs began his *Shell Happy Time* program, an inspirational variety show that became a great Pacific Coast favorite (60 min., Monday through Friday, KPO, San Francisco, CA, 1929). The show was known by such varied names as *Captain Dobbs Ship of Joy, Shell Happy Time, Shell Ship of Joy* or merely *The Ship of Joy*.

The Ship of Joy (30 min., NBC, 1931) was an inspirational variety program that consisted of poetry for the young and old, but, somehow it mostly seemed to be addressed to those who were alone and needed friends. It contained good music, cheerful patter and inspiring poetry. Captain "Dobbsie" was talented at providing exactly what his listeners needed. As the skipper of the *Ship of Joy*, he featured violinist Max Dolin; organist "Wee Willie" Hancock; Negro tenor William Powers; soprano Helen Lowe; contralto Eileen Elman; actor Arnold McGuire; concert pianist Eleanor Bernard; pianist Dixie Marsh; violinist Caesar Linden; blind cellist John Faivre; flutist Antonio Linden; and harpist Kathryn Thompson. A comic team of Sambo (Sam Moore) and Ed (Ed Evans) also entertained, sometimes joined by Mrs. Sam Moore playing the role of Mandy. Also featured on the show were: the Whispering Cowboys (tenor Clarence Tollman and Curley David); baritone Edward Radell; Irish tenor Dan O'Brien; tenor Ricardo Jose; soprano Emily Hardy; and singer Annabelle Lee. Theodore Strong was the program's musical director and Edmund "Ed" Evans the staff continuity writer.

The program had one of the largest casts on radio, featuring as it did more than 50 singers, musicians and entertainers plus large orchestras and singing groups. Another of its regular features was Charles Kellogg's singing birds. The orchestras of both Cyrus "Cy" Trobbe and Walt Roesner were featured at times. Orthocut Coffee sponsored a later network version of the show (*The Ship of Joy*, 30 min., Monday, 9:30–10:00 A.M., NBC-Red, 1933). Later, when the show was sponsored by the Stewart-Warner Company (Alemite) a commercial was delivered by Captain Dobbs as the orchestra played "Ave Maria" in the background; *(The Ship of Joy*, 15 min., Tuesday and Thursday, 10:30–10:45 P.M., CBS, 1935). This version of the show was sponsored by Stewart-Warner Company (Alemite). Captain Dobbsie still hosted the show with music provided by the Radio Ramblers, a mixed quartet and Horace Heidt's orchestra. Dobbs always closed all his shows by joyfully admonishing his listeners, "Happy Day."

9121 Dobbs, Jack. DJ (*Platter Party*, WZOB, Fort Payne, AL, 1952). Sportscaster (WZOB, 1953).

9122 Doblens, Frank R. Baritone (WHAS, Louisville, KY, 1923).

9123 Dobratz, Delphine. COM-HE (KDUZ, Hutchinson, MN, 1956).

9124 Dobson, Delores. COM-HE (KSLM, Salem, OR, 1954).

9125 Dobson, Ethel. Coloratura soprano (WPG, Atlantic City, NJ, 1925–1929).

9126 Dobson, George. Sportscaster (KTFS, Texarkana, TX, 1948; 1956). DJ (*Alarm Clock Club*, KALT, Atlanta, TX, 1949; KTFS, 1954; *Rise and Shine*, KTFS, 1955).

9127 Dobyn's Shoestring Orchestra. California dance band (KGER, Long Beach, CA, 1929).

9128 Doc and Grady. Doc Bellamy and Grady Forte were popular country entertainers (KMA, Shanandoah, IA, 1927). Although the team broadcast on KMA with various names, they were always great listener favorites.

9129 *Doc Applesauce.* Arthur A. Frudenfeld conducted a novel show as Doc Applesauce, who read from his book of inspirational poetry, proverbs and philosophy (WIL, St. Louis, MO, 1930). He began in radio as a pioneer announcer (WOAW, Omaha, NE, 1925).

9130 *Doc Barclay's Daughter.* Frank and Anne Hummert produced the 15-minute daytime serial drama broadcast daily Monday through Friday. It told the story of a father's effort to raise his three daughters and assist them with the various problems they encountered. Bennett Kilpack played the role of Doc Barclay, a widowed druggist. Doc's three daughters were played by Elizabeth Reller, Mildred Robin and Vivian Smolen. Janice Gilbert and Albert Hayes were also in the cast. The program's announcer was Tom Shirley (1938–1940, CBS).

9131 *Doc Hopkins.* Hopkins led a spirited music group on the CW music show (WJJD, Chicago, IL, 1937). Doc Hopkins starred previously on the *WWVA Midnight Jamboree* (1935).

9132 *Doc Hopkins and the Cumberland Ridge Runners.* CW music program (WLS, Chicago, IL, 1942).

9133 *Doc Savage the Man of Bronze.* Doc Savage, "the man of bronze," fought criminals wherever he found them on the sustaining adventure show. The super hero possessed a great power that resided in a magic ring that immediately cast an evil eye over any and all villains that were encountered. The show was written by Ed Gruskin, produced by Charles Michaelson and directed by Garrett E. Hallihan (30 min., Wednesday, 8:00–8:30 P.M., WMCA, New York, NY, 1942).

9134 ***Doc Schneider [Snyder] and his Texans.*** Schneider's music group entertained on the lively CW music show presented by various sponsors (15 min., Monday through Saturday, 6:15–6:30 P.M., NBC, 1938).

9135 ***Doc Schneider's [Snyder's] Yodeling Cowboys.*** CW mus. prg. (WGY, Schenectady, NY and NBC, 1935).

9136 ***Doc Whipple.*** Whipple was a talented jazz pianist (15 min., NBC, 1936).

9137 **Dochee, Jacob.** DJ (*Opera Favorites*, WWJ, Detroit, MI, 1948).

9138 **Doerfler, Hilary.** Announcer (WFBJ, Collegeville, MN, 1925–1927).

9139 ***Dr. Allan Roy Dafoe.*** Dr. Dafoe, whose main claim to fame was his medical care of the Dionne Quintuplets — Yvonne, Annette, Emile, Cecile and Marie — broadcast this program from his hospital at Callender, Ontario, Canada. The program was sponsored by Lysol (15 min., Monday, Wednesday and Friday, 10:45–11:00 A.M., CBS, 1936).

9140 ***Dr. Arthur Torrance.*** Torrance, a famous explorer, related his many thrilling experiences on the quarter-hour program (15 min., Saturday, 8:00–8:15 P.M., CBS, 1930).

9141 ***Dr. Bones and Company.*** Paul Dumont and Jim Dandy were featured with their songs and patter on this radio minstrel show (15 min., Saturday, 5:30–5:45 P.M., WEAF, New York, NY, 1935).

9142 ***Dr. Bundesen's Magazine of the Air.*** President Bundesen of Chicago's Board of Health started each of his programs with an editorial. Following the editorial, news events were reported by Dr. Hayden Roberts and then dramatized. Dr. Roberts followed the dramatization with another editorial comment. After musical interludes by pianist John Brown and organist Ralph Waldo Emerson, informative talks on nutrition and child rearing were provided and a daily serial drama presented. The daily drama was written by Hayden Roberts, John Welch and Herbert Futran, who also directed. Actors in the program's dramatizations were Al Halus, Maxine Garner, Jack Holden and Joe Kelly. The announcer was Les Tremayne (60 min., Monday through Friday, 9:00–10:00 A.M. CST, WLS, Chicago, 1934).

9143 ***Doctor Christian.*** Jean Hersholt played the title role of wise, kind-hearted Doctor Christian, who practiced medicine and performed good deeds in the small town of River's End. The program was suggested by and developed from *The Country Doctor*, a motion picture in which Hersholt played Dr. Allan Roy Defoe, a physician who gained fame by being the Dionne Quintuplets' doctor. An unusual event occurred in 1941, when the program solicited manuscripts from listeners for program scripts and were deluged with more than 10,000 responses. The announcer at the time stated that *Dr. Christian* was the "only show on radio where the audience writes the script." Listeners could earn $2,000 in the writing competition by winning the Dr. Christian Award. Other members of the *Dr. Christian* cast were: Helen Claire, Rosemary DeCamp, Kathleen Fitz, and Lurene Tuttle. Art Gilmore was the announcer. The writer was Ruth Adams Wright. Florence Ortman and Neil Reagan were the directors.

9144 ***Dr. Diamond's Medicine Show of the Air.*** A large cast provided the entertainment on the weekly mix of music, comedy and melodrama (WOAI, San Antonio, TX, 1932).

9145 ***Dr. Clyde Fisher.*** Dr. Fisher delivered astronomy talks on his sustaining program (15 min., Wednesday, 10:45–11:00 P.M., CBS, 1936).

9146 ***Dr. D.R. Hodgdon.*** Dr. Hodgdon broadcast talks on food and nutrition on his half-hour program four times weekly (30 min., Monday through Thursday, 5:00–5:30 P.M., CBS, 1928).

9147 ***Doctor Dollar.*** Unusual success stories about the odd ways men and women had used to make money were dramatized on this novel program (15 min., Tuesday, 6:45–7:00 P.M. CST, WMAQ, Chicago, IL, 1937). Success and money making were popular topics in the midst of the severe economic Depression then in progress.

9148 ***Dr. Edward Parrish.*** Parrish, an M.D., broadcast weekly health talks (15 min., MBS, 1938).

9149 ***Doctor Gino's Musicale.*** Once again — as in previous years on the *Chamber Music Society of Lower Basin Street* program — Gene Hamilton, as Doctor Gino, hosted an entertaining program of Dixieland jazz. Henry "Hot Lips" Levine led the band, and many great jazz performers appeared each week as guest artists on the sustaining program (30 min., Monday, 10:30-11:00 P.M., MBS, 1950). Although the program followed the format of the *Chamber Music Society of Lower Basin Street* and presented good Dixieland jazz, it never equaled the sharp satire of that entertaining show (ABC, 1951–1952).

9150 **Dr. Humphrey Bate and his Possum Hunters.** *See* **Bate, (Dr.) Humphrey.**

9151 ***Dr. Jazz.*** The jazz music program was hosted by Harry E. Seyer, then a local school superintendent. Seyer later became a Pennsylvania state senator (WSBA, York, PA, 1950).

9152 ***Dr. John Holland.*** The Reverend Dr. Holland conducted a weekly religious program with the assistance of station organist Ralph Waldo Emerson and, sometimes, by singer "Little George" Goebel (15 min., Saturday, 6:45–7:00 A.M. CST, WLS, Chicago, IL, 1937). George Goebel later enjoyed success as a television comedian.

9153 ***Dr. Julius Klein.*** Klein discussed various topics related to national and world business (CBS, 1928–1929).

9154 ***Dr. Karl Reiland.*** The Reverend Dr. Reiland, formerly the pastor of New York City's St. George Church, was one of the few regularly ordained ministers who appeared on commercially sponsored programs. His religious program was sponsored by the Pepperell Manufacturing Company (15 min., Friday, 7:15–7:30 P.M., NBC-Blue, 1937).

9155 ***Dr. Kildare*** **(aka *Calling Dr. Kildare* and *The Story of Dr. Kildare*).** The *Dr. Kildare* radio series was based on the stories of Max Brand (Frederick Schiller Faust), whose inspiration was prominent urologist George Winthrop Fish. The program appeared after the release of the popular series of motion pictures about Kildare that began with *Young Dr. Kildare* (1938) starring Lew Ayres as Kildare and Lionel Barrymore as Dr. Gillespie. The first *Dr. Kildare* picture was followed by several others including: *The Secret of Dr. Kildare* (1939); *Dr. Kildare's Strange Case* (1940); *Dr. Kildare Goes Home* (1940); *Dr. Kildare's Crisis* (1940); *Dr. Kildare's Victory* (1941); and *Calling Dr. Gillespie* (1942).

Dr. Kildare on radio starred Lew Ayres in the title role of a young doctor mentored by the gruff Dr. Gillespie, played by Lionel Barrymore. Both doctors worked at a large New York City hospital. The cast also included Ted Osborne and Virginia Gregg (30 min., Weekly, MBS, 1951–1952). The popular medical series made a successful transition to NBC television, beginning September 28,1961, with Richard Chamberlain in the title role and Raymond Massey as his demanding mentor.

9156 **Dr. Mu.** A "mysterious Chinese philosopher," Dr. Mu provided sage comment and soothing music on his popular program, *The Music and Musings of Dr. Mu* (WABC, New York, NY, 1928). Dr. Mu was played by George Frame Brown, who also wrote the program on which he dispensed "ancient" precepts and various other choice bits of wisdom with an accompaniment of "oriental" music. Brown later was the creator and writer of the *Real Folks* program, in which he also played the leading role. *See* **Brown, George Frame** *and* ***Real Folks.***

9157 **Dr. Palmer's Happy Hour Twins.** Singing comedy team consisting of Pat Flanagan and Sunshine, his female piano-playing partner (WOC, Davenport, IA, 1928).

9158 ***Dr. Paul.*** Russell Thorson was in the title role on this program that was identified as "radio's wonderful story of love and service to humanity," As Dr. Paul, Thorson faced the tensions created by his ambitious wife, who wanted him to leave the small town hospital where he worked to establish a practice in New York City. In addition to Thorson, the cast included: Henry Blair, Sam Edwards, Gloria Gordon, Bob Holton, Janet Logan, Jean Olivet, Willard Waterman and Peggy Webber. Virginia Crosby wrote and Gil Faust directed the daytime serial sponsored by Wesson Oil and Snow Drift soap flakes. The announcer was Vincent Pelletier (15 min., Monday through Friday, 11:00-11:15 A.M., NBC, 1949).

9159 ***Dr. Pepper Parade.*** The blackface comedy team of Molasses and January, singers Jack Arthur and Margaret McCrea and the music of the Peter Van Steeden orchestra were featured on the variety show (30 min., Weekly, late-1930s).

9160 **Doctor Q.** The "Doctor" was a "mysterious masked man" who served as announcer-host (KSTP, St. Paul–Minneapolis, MN, 1929).

9161 ***Dr. Royal S. Copeland.*** Weekly 15-minute talks were broadcast by the popular physician (15 min., Monday through Friday, 10:00–10:15 A.M., NBC-Blue, 1927–1930). *See* **Copeland, Royal S.**

9162 ***Dr. Scholl's Ramblers.*** The California Ramblers, the Rodeliers Male Quartet and singer Iona Mull appeared on the music show (15 min., Tuesday and Thursday, 7:45–8:00 P.M., NBC, 1931).

9163 ***Doctor Six Gun.*** Karl Weber played the role of Dr. Ray Matson, a frontier doctor who combined the righting of wrongs with the practice of healing in the western adventure drama. William "Bill" Griffis played Weber's assistant. The show was written by George Lefferts and Ernest Kinoy and directed by Fred Weihe (30 min., Thursday, 8:30–9:00 P.M., NBC, 1954).

9164 ***Dr. Standish Medical Examiner.*** Gary Merrill played the title role of a doctor interested in crime. The sustaining program was a summer replacement for *The FBI in Peace and War*. Audrey Christie and Eric Dresser joined Merrill on the breezy, mystery drama. Lee Vines was the announcer (30 min., weekly, CBS, 1948).

9165 ***(The) Dr. Talks with his Children.*** An informative monthly program, the Doctor was sponsored by the Hartford Medical Association. Dr. William Lane talked things over with his own adolescent children, Jack and Babs. Their conversations were always directed toward specific health topics (15 min., Saturday, 6:45–7:00, WTIC, Hartford, CT, 1939).

9166 ***Dr. West's Celebrity Night.*** Band leader George Olsen and his wife, singer Ethel Shutta, hosted and performed on the entertaining program sponsored by Dr. West's tooth powder. Joe Cook was the guest on the first show of their series (30 min., Saturday, 9:30–10:00 P.M., NBC, 1936).

9167 ***Dr. Wynne's Food Forum.*** The American Institute of Food Products sponsored Dr. Shirley Wynne to talk about food, health and her sponsor's products. Dr. Wynne was formerly New York City's Health Commissioner, and, later, president of the Home Institute of Food Products. Ella Mason, the program's home economist, also participated each week. The announcer was Joe O'Brien (30 min., Tuesday, 9:30–10:00 P.M., WMCA, New York, NY, 1940).

9168 **Dodd, Esther K.** DJ (WNCA, Silver City, NC, 1957).

9169 **Dodd, Sam.** DJ (*Sad Sam—the Record Man*, WAOV, Vincennes, IN, 1947).

9170 **Dodd, Virginia.** COM-HE (WDEV, Waterbury, VT, 1951).

9171 **Dodds, Dar.** DJ (WGTO, Cypress Gardens, FL, 1956–1957).

9172 **Dodds, Everett.** Dodds was a singer of the songs of Scotland (WOW, Omaha, NE, 1928).

9173 **Dodge, Bill.** Leader (*Bill Dodge Orchestra*, instr. mus. prg., WBIG, Greensboro, NC, 1936, 1942).

9174 **Dodge, Fred.** Newscaster (WNBF, Binghampton, NY, 1937).

9175 **Dodge, Jane.** COM-HE (KVOR, Colorado Springs, CO, 1957).

9176 **Dodge, Otis.** DJ (*Yawnbusters*, WHTB, Talladega, AL, 1947).

9177 **Dodge, Ruth.** COM-HE (WHWB, Rutland, VT, 1954).

9178 **Dodge, Virginia.** Contralto (WLWL, New York, NY, 1936).

9179 **Dodge, Will.** Leader (*Will Dodge Orchestra*, instr. mus. prg., WNAC, Boston, MA, 1934).

9180 **Dodge, William C., Jr.** Newcaster (WMCA, New York, NY, 1940).

9181 **Dodge Sedan Cars Orchestra (aka The Dodge Sedan Serenaders).** A commercially sponsored band featured on *The Dodge Hour* program (WOR, Newark, NJ, 1927).

9182 **Dodier, Verna.** COM-HE (WHIL, Medford, MA, 1955).

9183 **Dodsworth, John.** Reader (WGR, Buffalo, NY, 1924).

9184 **Doe, Doris.** Contralto (WJZ, New York, NY, 1926). Miss Doe also sang on the *Philco Hour of Theater Memories*, (NBC-Blue, New York, NY, 1927–1931).

9185 **Doerr, Clyde.** Leader (Clyde Doerr Orchestra broadcasting from the Congress Hotel, KYW, Chicago, IL, 1924; Davis Saxophone Octet, WEAF, New York, NY, 1926; White Rock Saxophone Orchestra, NBC, 1928; *Clyde Doerr's Saxophone Octet*, inst. mus. prg., NBC, 1933). Famous saxophonist Doerr was also a soloist on the *Major Bowes Capitol Theater Family* program (NBC, 1928).

9186 ***Dog Dramas.*** Canine authority Bob Becker hosted the dramatic series that presented dramatic episodes in the lives of man's best friend (WGN, Chicago, IL, 1935).

9187 ***Dog Heroes.*** Modern Food Products sponsored the program that dramatized the stories of heroic dogs. Henry Swan wrote the script for the show and also played all the male roles. A National Dog Medal was awarded each week for some heroic canine deed. Pat Kelly provided organ interludes (15 min., Sunday, 3:00–3:15 min., NBC-Blue, 1938).

9188 ***Dog Talks.*** This was another program that appealed to dog owners by presenting various experts on canines discussing the care and training of dogs. One such expert was Dr. George Little who talked about "Airdales" (WOR, Newark, NJ, 1925).

9189 **Dogey, John.** Violinist (WSWS, Cincinnati, OH, 1926).

9190 ***Dogs.*** Information about various breeds of dogs was broadcast by the New York *Herald-Tribune's* Frank Dole (NBC-Blue, 1925).

9191 ***Dogs.*** Daisy Miller conducted the weekly program for dog lovers (15 min., Saturday, 1:45–2:00 P.M., WMCA, New York, NY, 1934).

9192 **Doherty, Annette.** Doherty taught radio French lessons (KFI, Los Angeles, CA, 1929).

9193 **Doherty, Mel.** Leader (Mel Doherty Orchestra and the Doherty Melody Boys [orchestra], WLW, Cincinnati, OH, 1929).

9194 **Dohnanyi, Ernest Van.** Hungarian pianist-composer (WEAF, New York, NY, 1926).

9195 **Doke, Dell.** COM-HE (KWTO, Springfield, MO, 1956–1957).

9196 **Dokey, Okey.** DJ (*The Okey Dokey Show*, WBOK, New Orleans, LA, 1952).

9197 **Dolan, Bert.** Leader (Bert Dolan's Orchestra, WBZ, Boston-Springfield, MA, 1926).

9198 **Dolan, Doris.** Studio pianist (KFON, Long Beach, CA, 1928).

9199 **Dolan, Eddie.** DJ (*Platter Party*, KLOK, San Jose, CA, 1947).

9200 **Dolan, Fran.** Newscaster (KGCX, Wolf Point, MT, 1940).

9201 **Dolan, Frank.** Sportscaster (*All Outdoors*, WKOP, Binghampton, NY, 1953).

9202 **Dolan, George.** Singer (WGBS, New York, NY, 1925).

9203 **Dolan, Jimmy.** Sportscaster (*That's What I Said*, 1939, CBS; 1940–1944).

9204 **Doland, Mildred (Mrs. E.L).** Soprano (KSD, St. Louis, MO, 1925; KMOX, St. Louis, MO, 1926).

9205 **Dolberg, Eugenia.** Pianist (WEBH, Chicago, IL, 1926).

9206 **Dole, Frank.** An employee of the New York *Herald-Tribune*, Dole spoke on various topics about dogs, i.e., "Beagles" (WJZ, New York, NY, 1925). *See* ***Dogs.***

9207 **Dolin, Max.** Musical director (Pacific Coast Network, NBC, 1928). Leader (Max Dolin Kylectroneers, NBC-Pacific, 1929; *Max Dolin Orchestra*, instr. mus. prg., WFIL, Philadelphia, PA, 1934–1935; *Max Dolin's Grenadiers Orchestra*, WMAQ, Chicago, IL and NBC, 1935).

9208 **Doll, Bob.** DJ (*The 1450 Club*, WDLB, Marshfield, WI, 1949; *Doll House*, WCSI, Columbus, IN, 1952).

9209 **Doll, Charlie.** DJ (*Journey on a Cloud*, WGAT, Gate City, VA, 1960).

9210 **Doll, Eugenia Coert.** Soprano (KPO, San Francisco, CA, 1926).

9211 **Doll, Johnny.** Leader (*Johnny Doll's Dixielanders* [orchestra], instr. mus. prg., WTNJ, Trenton, NJ, 1936).

9212 **Dollar, Russell.** Sportscaster (WAIR, Winston-Salem, NC, 1940).

9213 ***(A) Dollar a Minute.*** Bill Goodwin hosted the sustaining weekly quiz (30 min., Wednesday, 6:30–7:00 P.M., CBS, 1950).

9214 **Dolphin, Nancy.** COM-HE (WHWL, Nanticoke, PA, 1949).

9215 **Domas, Roland.** Newscaster (WMAS, Springfield, MA, 1944). Sportscaster (WMAS, 1944).

9216 **Dombey, Ken.** Leader (*Ken Dombey Orchestra*, instr. mus. prg., WHK, Cleveland, OH, 1942).

9217 **Domina, Chappy.** Sportscaster (WKNE, Keene, NH, 1947).

9218 ***Domino Hillbillies.*** CW mus. prg. (WRVA, Richmond, VA, 1936, 1938–1939).

9219 **(The) Domino Lady.** Unidentified singer (WRVA, Richmond, VA, 1933–1934).

9220 **Don, Jack.** Don was a guitarist specializing in Hawaiian music (KMTR, Hollywood, CA, 1927; KSL, Salt Lake City, UT, 1928).

9221 ***Don Alfredo Orchestra.*** Instr. mus. prg. (WOR, Newark, NJ, 1936).

9222 ***Don Amazio, Wizard*** **(aka *Don Amazio the Unknown Violinist*).** A combination musical serial drama and travelog. The program featured an announcer telling the story of a handsome violinist. At the conclusion of each program, Don Amazio, the young violinist, played a violin solo (30 min., Sunday, 8:30–9:00 P.M., NBC-Blue, 1926–1927). The following year the program was broadcast daily in a 15-minute format.

9223 ***Don Ameche's Real Life Stories.*** Patterned after the *My True Story* program, the dramatic series dramatized the stories of men and women with personal problems. Ameche narrated and also played the leading role in each dramatic episode. Other cast members were: Ralph Bell, Jack Grimes, Evelyn Juster, Santos Ortega, Ruth Warwick and Lawson Zerbe. The program was written by David Driscoll. The producer and director was Himan Brown (30 min., Monday through Friday, 10:30–11:00 A.M., NBC, 1958).

9224 ***(The) Don Ameche Show.*** Drene shampoo sponsored this series of dramatic sketches that replaced the *Rudy Vallee Show* in 1946. Each of the sketches starred veteran motion picture and radio actor Ameche. The program was directed by Carlton Alsop and Howard Wiley. The announcer was Marvin Miller (30 min., Weekly, CBS, 1946–1947). Ameche began his professional career by appearing on some of radio's most popular programs: *Betty and Bob*, *The Bickersons*, *Maxwell House Coffee Show* (*Bergen and McCarthy*), *First Nighter*, *Grand Hotel*, *Jack Armstrong the All-American Boy* and *The National Farm and Home Hour*

9225 ***Don and Helen.*** An entertaining singing team, Helen also played the piano (Saturday, 6:15–6:30 P.M., WLS, Chicago, IL, 1937 and Saturday, 1:45–2:00 P.M., WLS, 1937).

9226 **Don and Sleepy.** CW comedy and singing team (WROK, Rockland, IL, 1938).

9227 ***(The) Don Becker Original Weak End Satires.*** Some idea of the Becker humor can be judged by the names of the characters he used on his program, supposedly broadcast by the Irrational Broadcasting Company. The announcers were A. Large Gorilla, Graham Smackatmee, Fullof Carbon and Fence Picket. One of the "station's" most memorable characters was Kinda Kross "the Silver Flask Tinner" (WLW, Cincinnati, OH, 1930).

9228 ***Don Carlos Marimba Band.*** Instr mus. prg. (NBC-Blue, 1930).

9229 ***Don Jose.*** Vcl. mus., prg. featuring an otherwise unidentified vocalist (NBC, 1935).

9230 ***(The) Don Juan Hour.*** The program of semi-classical and chamber music was conducted by George Earle (WOR, Newark, NJ, 1929).

9231 ***(The) Don Lang Animal Stories.*** The Christian Hanson Laboratories sponsored the series of true animal tales told with a dramatic flair by Don Lang. Lang also conducted a club for his young listeners (15 min., Tuesday and Thursday, 5:45–6:00 P.M., WABC, New York, NY, 1933).

9232 ***(The) Don Lee Symphony Orchestra.*** Instr. mus. prg. (KHJ, Los Angeles, CA, 1928).

9233 ***Don Pedro Orchestra.*** Instr. mus. prg. (WBZ-WBZA, Boston-Springfield, MA, 1932; NBC, 1936).

9234 ***Don Winslow of the Navy.*** Frank Martinek's action packed comic strip was the basis for the serial drama. Bob Guilbert originally played the title role during the program's 1937–1938 run. When it returned on ABC in 1943, Raymond Edward Johnson played the role. Assisted by his loyal sidekick, Red Pennington, Don Winslow fought a constant battle against the Scorpion, an evil crime lord. Other members of the program's cast were: Ruth Barth, Edward Davison, Betty Lou Gerson, John Gibson, Betty Ito and Lenore Kingston. Albert Aley and Al Barker were the writers and Ray Kremer the director (NBC-Blue, 1937–1938; ABC, 1943).

9235 **Donahoo, Del.** Sportscaster (WKIZ, Ottumwa, IA, 1946–1948).

9236 **Donahoo, Puss.** Leader (Puss Donahoo Orchestra, KGO, Oakland, CA, 1926 and KFRC, San Francisco, CA, 1926).

9237 **Donahue, Al.** Leader (*Al Donahue Orchestra*, instr. mus. prg., NBC, 1934–1935; NBC-Red, New York, NY, 1937–1939, 1942–1943).

9238 **Donahue, Donald.** Sportscaster (KDLR, Devils Lake, ND, 1939–1941; KDLR, 1945).

9239 **Donahue, Jack.** Newscaster (KCMJ, Palm Springs, CA, 1946).

9240 **Donahue, Joseph.** Newscaster (*Naugatuck Valley News*, WATR, Waterbury, CT, 1948).

9241 **Donahue, Mary.** Contralto (WDAF, Kansas City, MO, 1936).

9242 **Donahue, Ruth.** COM-HE (WLOF, Orlando, FL, 1949).

9243 **Donahue, Tom.** Leader (Tom Donahue's Bamboo Village Orchestra, WJAX, Cleveland, OH, 1924).

9244 **Donald, Vivian.** COM-HE (WAIP, Pritchard, AL, 1956). DJ (WAIP, 1957).

9245 ***Donald Novis Sings.*** Tenor Novis was the star of the transcribed 15-minute show (Transcribed, Various stations, mid–1930s).

9246 **Donaldson, Al.** Sportscaster (KRIC, Beaumont, TX, 1939; KOMA, Oklahoma City, OK, 1944; KENT, Shreveport, LA, 1948–1953). Newscaster (KOMA, 1945; KPDN, Pampa, TX, 1946).

9247 **Donaldson, Barton.** Baritone (WDAF, Kansas City, MO, 1928).

9248 **Donaldson, Bob.** DJ (*Wax-Works*, WMGY, Montgomery, AL, 1947; WJJJ, Montgomery, AL, 1949).

9249 **Donaldson, Chris.** DJ (*Today's Music*, WOI, Ames, IA, 1947).

9250 **Donaldson, Dean.** Violinist (KTAB, Oakland, CA, 1928).

9251 **Donaldson, E.** Announcer (WHAR, Atlantic City, NJ, 1925).

9252 **Donaldson, Earn [Earl].** DJ (*Melody Mac and Vern*, KALL, Salt Lake City, UT, 1947).

9253 **Donaldson, Frank.** DJ (*Ladies Matinee*, WLEE, Richmond, VA, 1954).

9254 **Donaldson, Herbert.** Pianist (*Herbert Donaldson*, instr. mus. prg., CBS, 1942).

9255 **Donaldson, Ruth.** Contralto (WEAF, New York, NY, 1925).

9256 **Donaldson, Sam.** DJ (*Sam's Show*, KEPO, El Paso, TX, 1952–1954).

9257 **Donat, Esther.** COM-HE (KFEQ, St. Joseph, MO, 1957).

9258 **Donath, Jeno.** Leader (*Al Donath Orchestra*, instr. mus. prg., WCAU, Philadelphia, PA and WIP, Philadelphia, PA, 1939).

9259 **Donato, Louis.** Singer (KFWI, San Francisco, CA, 1926).

9260 **Donegan, Bill.** DJ (*Music Shop*, WSAV, Savannah, GA, 1948).

9261 **Donges, Cathy.** COM-HE (WATG, Ashland, OH, 1949–1956).

9262 **Donham, Betty Jo.** COM-HE (KWEX, McPherson, KS, 1954–1956).

9263 **Donley, Bob.** Newscaster (WCAE, Pittsburgh, PA, 1940).

9264 **Donley, Red.** Sportscaster (*Let's Talk Sports*, WSTV, Steubenville, OH, 1951–1960).

9265 **Donnan, Carol.** Violinist (KFWM, Oakland, CA, 1926).

9266 **Donnell, Darrell.** Newscaster (KFRC, San Francisco, CA, 1938; KYA, San Francisco, CA, 1939–1941; KFRC, 1945).

9267 **Donnell, Jack.** Newscaster (WGRC, New Albany, IN, 1942). Sportscaster (WGRC, 1948. DJ: WGRC, Louisville, KY, 1955). Note that the station's call letters moved from an Indiana to a Kentucky location.

9268 **Donnell, Philip S.** Announcer (1926).

9269 **Donnell, William A.** Newscaster (KDON, Monterey, CA, 1939).

9270 **Donnelly, Eddie.** Leader (*Eddie Donnelly Orchestra*, instr. mus. prg., WIP, Philadelphia, PA, 1934–1935).

9271 **Donnelly, James.** Leader, James Connelly and His Colorado University Serenaders, KLZ, Denver, CO, 1929–1932).

9272 **Donnelly, Jim.** DJ (*Red Rooster*, WCOJ, Coatesville, PA, 1952). Sportscaster (WCOJ, 1955).

9273 **Donnerberg, Ruth.** Cellist, WMH String Trio (WMH, Cincinnati, OH, 1924).

9274 **Donnery, Lillian.** Contralto (KOA, Denver, CO, 1926).

9275 **Donoran, Eddy.** Pianist (KFOB, Burlingame, CA, 1925).

9276 **Donovan, Dan.** DJ (WMEX, Boston, MA, 1960).

9277 **Donovan, Gregg.** Newscaster (WDGY, Minneapolis–St. Paul, MN, 1939–1942).

9278 **Donovan, Joyce P.** COM-HE (WTRY, Troy, NY, 1954–1955).

9279 **Donovan, (Mrs.) T.C.** Soprano (KDKA, Pittsburgh, PA, 1924).

9280 **Donovan, Warde.** Singer (*Songs by Warde Donovan*, vcl. mus. prg., 30 min., Tuesday, 7:30–8:00 P.M., NBC, 1948).

9281 **Donst, Esther.** COM-HE (KFNF, Shenandoah, IA, 1954).

9282 ***Don't Listen, Men.*** This was a 90-minute block of programming devoted entirely to broadcasts for women. It included a feminine news commentary, a shopping advice program, a physical fitness broadcast, Hollywood news column, nutrition program, a quiz and music with feminine appeal (WSBA, York, PA, 1942).

9283 ***(The) Doodlesockers.*** A novelty comedy-music program, *The Doodlesockers* featured the Jugheads, an instrumental trio consisting of Duckwell (George Hall) on fiddle; Purlosa (Hortense Rose) on piano; and Cletus (Carl Clauve) on guitar. Sydney Ten Eyck was the program announcer (15 min., Monday through Friday, 11:30–11:45 A.M. and Saturday 12:30-1:00 A.M., WLW, Cincinnati, OH, 1930).

9284 **Dooley, Charles.** Newscaster (*Kentucky News*, WFKY, Frankfort, KY, 1947).

9285 **Dooley, Eddie "Ed."** Sportscaster (*Football Forecasts*, CBS, 1936–1937). Eddie Dooley was a popular sports writer and former All-American quarterback who broadcast this twice weekly show. On Thursday, he analyzed forthcoming college games and predicted the results. On Saturday, he gave the games' scores and analyzed them (15 min, Thursday and Saturday, 4:30–4:45 P.M., CBS, 1936–1937; NBC, 1939; WNEW, New York, NY, 1941).

9286 **Dooley, Jim L.** Sportscaster (WSTV, Steubenville, OH, 1940; WHBC, Canton, OH, 1941–1942). Newscaster (WHBC, 1946).

9287 **Dooley, Margaret.** Soprano (WDRC, Hartford, CT, 1936).

9288 **Dooley, Peter.** DJ (*Dance with Dooley*, WFKY, Frankfort, KY, 1947; *Coffee Cup Parade*, WVJS, Owensboro, KY, 1948; *Top Tunes*, WOMI, Owensboro, KY, 1952; WEOA, Evansville, IN, 1955).

9289 **Doolittle, Ellen.** Cellist (WQJ, Chicago, IL, 1925).

9290 **Doolittle, F. M.** Announcer (WDRC, New Haven, CT, 1927).

9291 **Doolittle, Jessie.** Doolittle played banjo solos on the first *National Barn Dance* program (WLS, Chicago, IL, April 19. 1924).

9292 **Doolittle, Mabel.** Contralto (WHT, Chicago, IL, 1928).

9293 **Doom, Johnny.** Leader (*Johnny Doom Orchestra*, instr. mus. prg., WHIO, Dayton, OH, 1942).

9294 **Doonan, Kate.** COM-HE (WCHS, Charleston, WV, 1957).

9295 **Doonan, Thomas J.** Announcer (WIAS, Ottumwa, IA, 1925).

9296 **Doran, Irene.** Leader (Irene Doran's Little Symphony Orchestra, WHO, Des Moines, IA, 1926).

9297 **Doran, Jeanne.** COM-HE (WMRO, Aurora, IL, 1955).

9298 **Doran, Marion.** Singer (WFBH, New York, NY, 1925).

9299 **Doran, Morrell.** Banjoist (KFAB, Lincoln, NE, 1928).

9300 **Doran, (Mrs.) O.D.** Soprano (WIP, Philadelphia, PA, 1927).

9301 **Doremus, John.** DJ (*Melody Bandstand*, KRMG, Tulsa, OK, 1952). Sportscaster (WKY, Oklahoma City, OK, 1956).

9302 **Dorey, Ray.** Newscaster (WBRK, Pittsfield, MA, 1941). DJ (*Turntale Terrace*, 45 min., Saturday, 9:15–10:00 A.M., WBZ, Boston, MA, 1947–1950; WHDH, Boston, MA, 1952).

9303 ***Dorian String Quartet.*** Instr. mus. prg. (CBS, 1934, 1939).

9304 **Doris (Dolan) and Clarence.** Blackface comedy sketch with piano selections by Doris Dolan (KFOX, Long Beach, CA, 1929).

9305 ***(The) Doris Day Show.*** Singer Day and various guest stars entertained on this show written by David Greggory, directed by Sam Pierce and produced by Marty Melcher (30 min., Friday, 9:00–9:30 P.M. CBS, 1952).

9306 **Dorlag, (Mrs.) Lou.** COM-HE (KFVS, Cape Girardeau, MO,1949).

9307 **Dorland, Nan.** Singer-actress (NBC, 1932). Actress Dorland was a cast member on the *Keeping Up with Daughter* program.

9308 **Dorman, Emmet.** Violinist (KTAB, Oakland, CA, 1929).

9309 **Dormont Ladies Trio.** The Dormont Ladies Trio included Mrs. Donald Maxwell, violin; Mrs. Rudy D. MacCurdy, cello; and Mrs. Elizabeth F. Evans, piano (KDKA, Pittsburgh, PA, 1923).

9310 **Dorn, Bill.** DJ (*Tune Inn*, WHAN, Charleston, SC, 1948).

9311 **Dorn, Bill.** DJ (*The Bill Dorn Show*, WEEK, Peoria, IL, 1952).

9312 **Dorn, Patricia.** Singer (WPCH, New York, NY, 1932).

9313 **Dorn, William.** Xylophonist (*Major Bowes Capitol Theater Family*, NBC, 1928).

9314 ***Dorn and Kirschner.*** Instr. mus. prg. by a saxophone duo (WOR, Newark, NJ, 1935).

9315 **Dornberger, Charles.** Leader (Charles Dornberger's Orchestra, KTHS, Hot Springs National Park, AR, 1928; *Charles Dornberger Orchestra*, instr. mus. prg., CBS and NBC, 1935).

9316 **Dorner, Heinie.** Tenor (KFOX, Long Beach, CA, 1929).

9317 **Dornwell, Roy.** Newscaster (KTEM, Temple, TX, 1937).

9318 **D'Oro, Medagalia.** Sportscaster (WBIL, New York, NY, 1938).

9319 ***Dorothy Dix.*** Miss Dix supplied advice for the lovelorn listeners who requested it on this program sponsored by Sabaka Company (15 min., Monday through Friday, 11:45–12:00 noon, KECA, Los Angeles, CA, 1946).

9320 ***Dorothy Dix at Home.*** The unusual daytime serial, sponsored by Sealtest Dairies, supposedly was based on the life of Dorothy Dix. Barbara Winthrop once again played the title role. of Dorothy Dix. Along the way it seems that problems of the lovelorn always seemed to pop up for Miss Dix to solve. Each program opened with some homey bit of philosophy in the form of a Dorothy Dix-O-Gram such as: "Money is important, but some things are more important." In addition to Winthrop, the cast included: Jo Gilbert, Mitzi Gould, Joan Lorring and Lyle Sudrow (15 min., Monday through Friday, 10:45–11:00 A.M., NBC, 1950).

9321 ***Dorothy Dix on the Air.*** Dorothy Dix, played by Barbara Winthrop, proposed solutions for those enmeshed in romantic problems. The program was sponsored by Sealtest Diaries. Perry Lafferty was the director (15 min., Monday through Friday, 1:45–2:00 P.M., ABC, 1948).

9322 ***Dorothy Gordon.*** Pioneer broadcaster Gordon was said to have created the first children's program for WEAF (New York, NY, 1924). She made significant contributions both in children's and educational programming. Later, on the *Dorothy Gordon* sustaining program she broadcast literate book reviews for an adult audience (15 min., Tuesday, 10:45–11:00 A.M., WQXR, New York, NY, 1941).

9323 ***Dorothy Gordon's Children's Corner.*** Dorothy Gordon presented songs and stories on the popular children's program (CBS, 1936).

9324 **Dorr, Russell.** Baritone (*Russell Dorr*, vcl. mus. prg., CBS, 1935–1936).

9325 **Dorrance, Nyra.** Prima donna soprano (WOR, Newark, NJ, 1929).

9326 **Dorris, Dave.** DJ (KYA, San Francisco, CA, 1952).

9327 **Dorris, Lee.** DJ (*Red, Hot and Blue*, WSOK, Nashville, TN, 1952; *Rock and Rise*, WILY, Pittsburgh, PA, 1954–1955; WBEE, Chicago, IL, 1957).

9328 **Dorsett, Elenore.** COM-HE (WFNC, Fayetteville, NC, 1957).

9329 **Dorsett, Grace.** COM-HE (WBOF, Norfolk, VA, 1960).

9330 **Dorsett, Mildred.** COM-HE (WRJW, Picayune, MS, 1957).

9331 **Dorsey, Bill.** DJ (*Rhythm Ranch*, WSKY, Asheville, NC, 1947–1949).

9332 **Dorsey, Fred and Helen Dailey.** Singing team (*Fred Dorsey and Helen Dailey*, vcl. mus. prg., WCAU, Philadelphia, PA, 1936).

9333 **Dorsey, Howard.** Newscaster (WMBD, Peoria, IL, 1938; WHAS, Louisville, KY, 1940–1941). DJ (*Clock Watcher*, KMOX, St. Louis, MO, 1948).

9334 **Dorsey, Jimmy.** Leader (*Jimmy Dorsey Orchestra*, instr.mus. prg., NBC, 1937; MBS, 1939; CBS, 1938–1939). Saxophonist Jimmy was the younger brother of Tommy Dorsey. *See* ***The Dorsey Brothers Orchestra*** *and* **Dorsey, Tommy**.

9335 **Dorsey, Joe.** DJ (*Wire Request*, WEMP, Milwaukee, WI, 1947–1954).

9336 **Dorsey, Polly.** COM-HE (WBMD, Baltimore, MD, 1956–1957).

9337 **Dorsey, Rod.** Newscaster (WOLS, Florence, SC, 1941–1942). DJ (*Nightowl Serenade*, WJNC, Jacksonville, SC, 1952–1954).

9338 **Dorsey, Ruth.** COM-HE (WAPX, Montgomery, AL, 1956).

9339 **Dorsey, Thelma.** COM-HE (WTAY, Robinson, IL, 1957).

9340 **Dorsey, Tommy.** Leader (*Tommy Dorsey Orchestra*, instr. mus. prg., CBS, 1935–1937, 1939; NBC-Red, 1937–1938, 1940–1942). Dorsey later hosted and acted as a DJ on his *Tommy Dorsey Show* (WMCA, New York, NY, late 1940s). Tommy Dorsey, Jimmy's brother, was one of the finest jazz trombonist of all time. *See **The Dorsey Brothers Orchestra** and* **Dorsey, Jimmy.**

9341 ***(The) Dorsey Brothers Orchestra.*** Instr. mus. prg. (NBC, 1934–1935). Brothers Tommy and Jimmy Dorsey, between their spats and angry outbursts, frequently joined to front a swinging band. After breaking up and enjoying great success separately, the brothers once again formed a big band together in the 1950s (*Dorsey Brothers Orchestra*, from New York's Statler Hotel, 1955, CBS; and the *Dorsey Brothers* from the Cafe Rouge of the Hotel Pennsylvania, CBS, 1956).

9342 **Doscher, George.** Tenor (WFAA, Dallas, TX, 1928).

9343 **Doson, Robert.** DJ (*Breakfast in Texas*, KURV, Edinburg, TX, 1954).

9344 ***Dot and Will.*** A daytime dramatic serial, *Dot and Will* told the story of the daily life of an average young married couple. Will, played by James Meighan, worked in the real estate business. His wife, Dot, played by Florence Freeman, was a typical young housewife attempting to make a slender budget cover both their household expenses and social ambitions. The cast also included: Peggy Allenby, Rosemary DeCamp, Helene Dumas, Irene Hubbard, Allyn Joslyn, Ralph Locke, Agnes Moorehead, Effie Palmer, Sidney Smith and Nora Stirling (15 min., Monday through Friday, 5:30–5:45 P.M., NBC-Blue, 1935).

9345 ***Dot Meyerberg.*** Meyerberg, the film editor of station KELW, broadcast a daily program of film studio gossip (15 min., Monday through Friday, 11:45–12:00 noon, KELW, Burbank, CA, 1931).

9346 **Dotson, Doris.** COM-HE (WPMP, Pascagoula, MS, 1960).

9347 **Dotson, Perry.** Sportscaster (KSTP, St. Paul–Minneapolis, MN, 1941).

9348 **Doty, Dick.** Newscaster (WEBR, Buffalo, NY, 1944; WCOP, Boston, MA, 1945–1946; WHAM, Rochester, NY, 1954).

9349 **Doty, J. Wilson.** Accordionist (KOIL, Omaha, NE, 1928).

9350 **Doty, Lockwood.** Newscaster (WCON, Atlanta, GA, 1948).

9351 **Doty, Mary.** COM-HE (WTRL, Bradenton, FL, 1957).

9352 **Doty, Wilson.** Pianist (KOIL, Council Bluffs, IA, 1926).

9353 **Doub-Kerr, William.** Doub-Kerr conducted an *Elementary French Lessons* program (WEAF, New York, NY, 1923).

9354 ***Double or Nothing.*** Various hosts such as Walter Compton, John Reed King, Todd Russell and, finally, Walter O'Keefe posed the questions to contestants on the quiz show. On their last question, contestants were able to either double their winnings or lose them all. The sponsor when it first went on the air in 1940 was Feenamint laxative. The announcer was Fred Cole. The producer was Diana Bourbon and the writers were Harry Bailey, Carroll Carroll and Gerald Rice. The final version of the program broadcast in 1953 was sponsored by Campbell Soups (30 min., Monday through Friday, 3:00–3:30 P.M., CBS, 1953). The long-running show was broadcast on three major networks at one time or another (MBS, CBS, NBC, 1940–1953).

9355 ***Double Suds Review.*** Conducted by Home Economist Jane Hamilton, this supposedly was the "first" program of news specially broadcast for women. The sponsors were the American Family Soap Flakes and American Family Soap (WMAQ, Chicago, IL, 1931).

9356 ***Double Voiced News Commentary.*** Don Pryor, CBS Special Events Director in San Francisco and Carroll Hansen appeared on the unusual news program for an informal conversation about the news of the day (15 min., 11:45–12:00 noon, KQW, San Francisco, CA, 1942).

9357 **Doublier, Marcel.** Saxophonist (WGCP, New York, NY, 1925).

9358 **Dougherty, Chuck.** DJ (KQV, Pittsburgh, PA, 1957).

9359 **Dougherty, Chuck.** DJ (WQAM, Miami, FL, 1957).

9360 **Dougherty, Emory.** Leader (*Emory Dougherty Orchestra*, instr. mus. prg., WJSV, Washington, DC, 1935–1936; CBS, 1935).

9361 **Dougherty, (Reverend) George P.** The Reverend Dougherty, minister of the Christ Episcopal Church of Glen Ridge, New Jersey, broadcast a Christmas message on Christmas Eve, 1921 (WJZ, New York, NY). The following month, he inaugurated weekly Sunday afternoon religious services broadcast (45 min., 3:00 to 3:45 P.M., WJZ, New York, NY). Dougherty frequently invited other clergymen to participate in the broadcasts.

9362 **Dougherty, Henrietta.** Singer (WAAM, Newark, NJ, 1925).

9363 **Dougherty, J.T.** Newscaster (WOPI, Bristol, TN, 1938).

9364 **Dougherty, Martin.** Baritone Dougherty sang on many stations during radio's early days. He sang at Denver stations, KOA, KLZ and KFEL from 1922 to 1927; San Francisco station KFRC in 1927; and on KHJ in Los Angeles, CA, from 1928 to 1929. Dougherty organized a vocal trio in Denver in 1922 that was brought to California by the Piggly Wiggly Company in 1927 to broadcast there.

9365 **Doughit, (Mrs.) Lucille H.** Black COM-HE (WAAA, Winston-Salem, N.C., 1950).

9366 **Doughty, Mildred.** Pianist (KFRC, San Francisco, CA, 1927).

9367 **Douglas, Anita.** COM-HE (KGFF, Shawnee, OK, 1951).

9368 **Douglas, Donna.** COM-HE (WTOP, Washington, DC, 1956).

9369 **Douglas, Doug.** Newscaster (KRKD, Los Angeles, CA, 1937–1940; 1944).

9370 **Douglas, Eileen.** Actress-writer Douglas first appeared on the *Eileen and Bill* program (WABC, New York, NY; WJZ, New York, NY and WOR, Newark, NJ, 1928–1931).

9371 **Douglas, Ernie.** Newscaster (*Dinnerbell*, KOY, Phoenix, AZ, 1948).

9372 **Douglas, Francis P.** Newscaster (KMOX, St. Louis, MO, 1941).

9373 **Douglas, Harriet.** COM-HE (WOSC, Fulton, NY, 1951).

9374 **Douglas, Hugh.** Newscaster (WCFL, Chicago, IL, 1945). DJ (*Tops in Town*, WCFL, 1949). .

9375 **Douglas, Jan.** COM-HE (WEOK, Poughkeepsie, NY, 1957).

9376 **Douglas, John.** DJ (*Name This Program*, KCSJ, Pueblo, CO, 1952).

9377 **Douglas, Mary.** Pianist (WGHB, Clearwater, FL, 1926).

9378 **Douglas, Merl.** DJ (*The Merl Douglas Show*, KMA, Shenandoah, IA, 1952).

9379 **Douglas, Nancy.** Busy radio actress Douglas appeared on the daytime serial programs *Houseboat Hannah, Ma Perkins, Portia Faces Life* and *Woman of America.*

9380 **Douglas, Paul.** Sportscaster (*Paul Douglas, Sports,* CBS, 1936). Douglas became a successful network announcer before going on to Hollywood to begin a successful career in motion pictures.

9381 **Douglas, Richard.** Tenor (WHN, New York, NY, 1924).

9382 **Douglas, Rod.** DJ (*Juke Box*, KSDN, Aberdeen, SD, 1954).

9383 **Douglas, Sharon.** Versatile radio actress Douglas appeared on the daytime serial programs *Backstage Wife* aka *Mary Noble, Backstage Wife* and *Big Sister.*

9384 **Douglas, Steve.** Sportscaster (WWNC, Asheville, NC, 1938; WRC, Washington, DC, 1942; WRC, 1947–1949). Newscaster (WWNC, 1939).

9385 **Douglas, Van.** DJ (*Harlem on Parade*, WKBK, Detroit, MI, 1947).

9386 **Douglas, W.D.** Newscaster (*News and Views*, WCNU, Crestview, FL, 1948).

9387 **Douglas, Will.** Newscaster (WKBN, Youngstown, OH, 1940).

9388 ***Douglas Shoemakers.*** Guitarist Earle Nelson, a crooning MC, and baritone John Herrick. were featured on the music show. The program had an unusual close that the announcer said was performed by "a real colored tap dancer." Gordon Graham was the dancer who was said to have "singing feet." The show was sponsored by the Douglas Shoe Company (30 min., Thursday, 8:30–9:00 P.M., CBS, 1930).

9389 **Douglass, Ken.** Newscaster (KTOK, Oklahoma City, OK, 1939).

9390 **Douglass, Marie.** COM-HE (WDSP, DeFuniak Springs, FL, 1960).

9391 **Douglass, Win.** Sportscaster (*Sports Spotlight*, WCMA, Corinth, MS, 1947; KTRI, Sioux City, IA, 1948–1949).

9392 **Douglass, Winnifred.** Reader (WNAC, Boston, MA, 1923).

9393 **Dour, (Mrs.) John C.** Pianist (WBZ, Springfield, MA, 1927).

9394 **Douthat, Louis.** Newscaster (WHIS, Bluefield, WV, 1939–1940).

9395 **Dove, Elsbeth.** Pianist (KGO, Oakland, CA, 1924).

9396 **Dover, Hal J.** Baritone (KPO, San Francsico, CA, 1925).

9397 **Dow, Grace Eaton.** Pianist (KPI, Los Angeles, CA, 1927).

9398 **Dow, Marjorie.** COM-HE (WTWN, St. Johnsbury, VT, 1951).

9399 Dow, Peg. COM-HE (WKTQ, South Paris, ME, 1957).

9400 Dow, William. DJ (*Turntable Terrace*, WCAX, Burlington, VT, 1952).

9401 Dowagiac High School Orchestra. Scholastic band (WEMC, Boston, MA, 1926).

9402 Dowd, Barbara. COM-HE (KOKX, Keokuk, IA, 1951).

9403 Dowd, Donald. Baritone (*Donald Dowd*, vcl. mus. prg., WLW, Cincinnati, OH, 1934).

9404 Dowd, John. Baritone (WSM, Nashville, TN, 1928).

9405 Dowds, (Mrs.) Ella. Soprano (WAAM, Newark, NJ, 1925).

9406 Dowdy, Alice. COM-HE (WROA, Gulfport, MS, 1960).

9407 Dowell, Saxie. Big band musician Dowell turned DJ on his *Sincerely Yours* program (WGN, Chicago, IL, 1952).

9408 Dower, Irene Grant. Soprano (WTIC, Hartford, CT, 1927).

9409 Dowling, Albert. Tenor (WTAM, Cleveland, OH, 1927).

9410 Dowling, Bernice. Newscaster (KWAT, Watertown, SD, 1946).

9411 Dowling, Jack. Newscaster (WWNC , Asheville, NC, 1940)

9412 Dowling, Jeanette. Actress Dowling appeared on the daytime serial programs *Road of Life* and *When a Girl Marries*. .

9413 *Down a Country Lane.* Radio veteran Hugh Aspinwall read poetry and conducted the program of verses, songs and instrumental music (WCCO, Minneapolis, MN, 1935).

9414 *Down at Grandpa's.* Dan Hosmer, the Hoosier Hot Shots, the Hoosier Sod Busters and the Girls of the Golden West (Dolly and Millie Good) appeared on the homey program of CW music and inspirational philosophy (15 min., Saturday, 9:30–9:45 A.M. CST, WLS, Chicago, IL, 1936–1937).

9415 *Down Lover's Lane.* Henry M. Neely narrated the morning musical program featuring soprano Gloria LaVey and the piano duo of Al and Lee Reiser (NBC, 1935).

9416 *Down on the Farm.* CW mus. prg. on which Luke and Mark Hignight played old-time hoedown melodies and French harp selections (KTHS, Hot Springs National Park, AR, 1924).

9417 *Down You Go.* Bergen Evans, the word maven, was the host of the interesting quiz show, whose transition from TV to radio, *Variety said*, was none too successful. Panelists Robert Breen, Fran Coughlin, Toni Gilman, Carmelita Pope, Pat Tobin and vocalist Katie Carnes were program regulars. Listeners sent in linguisic puzzles in an attempt to stump the panelists (30 min., 6:30–7:00 P.M. CST, MBS, 1952).

9418 Downes, E. Hall. Downes taught bridge lessons on his *E. Hall Downes Bridge Talk*, bridge instruction program (KDKA, Pittsburgh, PA and CBS, 1934).

9419 Downey, Jack. DJ (*Music Shop and Wax Works*, WONS, Hartford, CT, 1949–1951; *Jack's Wax Works*, WONS, 1952).

9420 Downey, Joe. Newscaster (*Headline Parade*, KOCS, Ontario, CA, 1948).

9421 Downey, Morton. A popular tenor (WEAF, New York, NY, 1927), Downey made his network debut on a four times a week quarter-hour sustaining program (CBS, 1929). He enjoyed a successful career for several decades (*Morton Downey*, vcl. mus. prg., WLW, Cincinnati, OH, 1935; *Songs By Morton Downey*, vcl. mus. prg, KGNF, North Platte, NE, 1939). Downey was also sponsored by Coca-Cola later in his career. *See **Coke Time**.*

9422 Downey, Vivian. Soprano (WGHP, Detroit, MI, 1926).

9423 Downing, Helen Harrington. Mrs. Downing talked on various home economics topics (WQJ, Chicago, IL, 1924–1925).

9424 Downing, Irene. Pianist-organist (WLW, Cincinnati, OH, 1926).

9425 Downing, James. Tenor (KHQ, Spokane, WA, 1928).

9426 Downing, Tom. Newscaster (WLAP, Lexington, MA, 1940).

9427 Downs, Bob. Leader (*Bob Downs Orchestra*, instr. mus. prg., WMMN, Fairmont, WV, 1934, 1938).

9428 Downs, Lee. DJ (KNET, Palestine, TX, 1949).

9429 Downs, Vera. Pianist (KOMO, Seattle, WA, 1928).

9430 Downs, William R. "Bill," Jr. Newscaster (CBS, 1937, 1944, 1948).

9431 Dowrick, Thomas. Tenor (KYA, San Francisco, CA, 1927).

9432 Dowst, Kay. COM-HE (WDAE, Tampa, FL, 1960).

9433 Dowty, Byron. Sportscaster (WDSU, New Orleans, LA, 1946–1948).

9434 Doyfoos, Leon. Newscaster (WLEU, Erie, PA, 1937).

9435 Doyle, Dick. Newscaster (WELO, Tupelo, MS, 1946). Sportscaster (WELO, 1946; WHBQ, Memphis, TN, 1947).

9436 Doyle, Elaine. COM-HE (KVSM, San Mateo, CA, 1955).

9437 Doyle, Ginny. Singer (*Ginny Doyle*, vcl. mus. prg., WHP, Harrisburg, PA, 1936).

9438 Doyle, Jim. Newscaster (NBC, 1944; *Hollywood Mystery Time*, ABC, 1946–1947).

9439 Doyle, John. DJ (*Johnny Comes Early*, KIT, Yakima, WA, 1947).

9440 Doyle, Larry. DJ (*Dancing Party*, KGA, Spokane, WA, 1948). Sportscaster (*Great Moments in Sports*, KGA, 1948).

9441 Doyle, Leonard. Tenor (WQJ, Chicago, IL, 1926).

9442 Doyle, Victor. Tenor (KTAB, Oakland, CA, 1927).

9443 Dozier, Kathryn. COM-HE (WGAU, Athens, GA, 1960).

9444 Dozier, Lydia. Dozier was an operatic soprano with the Cincinnati Civic Opera Company, WLW, Cincinnati, OH, 1928).

9445 *Dragnet.* Although the program supposedly was drawn from the files of the Los Angeles Police Department with the cooperation of its Chief, William Parker, *Variety* said it glamorized the lives of police detectives. On the other hand, others considered it to be a highly successful attempt to depict police work realistically. There were attempts to make the program realistic by having Sergeant Joe Friday, played by Jack Webb, frequently refer to the time: "Twelve-fifteen. We were working the day watch out of homicide." Friday's assistant was played by Barton Yarborough. Charles McGraw was also in the cast.

After the death of Yarborough in 1951, Friday's assistant, Frank Smith, was played by Ben Alexander. Although *Dragnet* started as a summer replacement for *The Life of Riley*, *Variety* noted that it became, first, one of radio's and, later, television's most popular programs. Initially sponsored by Fatima cigarettes, the sponsorship was later taken over by Chesterfield. In addition to Webb, Yarborough, Alexander and McGraw, the other cast members included: Richard Boone, Ken Peters, Raymond Burr, Harry Morgan, Stacy Harris, Virginia Gregg, Vic Perrin, Georgia Ellis, Barney Phillips and Marvin Miller. The program was directed by Bill Rousseau. The announcers were George Fenneman and Hal Gibney (30 min., Friday, 10:00–10:30 P.M., NBC, 1949).

9446 Drago, Lou. Ukulele (WAHG, Richmond Hill, NY, 1926).

9447 Dragon, Wilda. Violinist (WBAP, Fort Worth, TX, 1927).

9448 Dragonette, Jessica. Miss Dragonette was a singer who enjoyed great popularity from her earliest appearances on radio. Dragonette was first known as "Vivian the Coca-Cola Girl" when she appeared on CBS in 1927. She later broadcast under her own name on the *Cities Service Concert* program, (NBC-Red, New York, NY, 1927–1930); the *A&P Gypsies* program (NBC, New York, NY, 1927); *The General Motors Family Party* (NBC, New York, NY, 1927); *The Philco Theater Memories* (CBS, New York, 1927–1930); and the *Hoover Sentinels* program (NBC-Blue, 1929). One time when on tour, she attracted 150,000 people to her concert in Chicago's Grant Park — an indication of her great popularity with the listening public.

9449 Drake, Al. Sportscaster (WELL, Battle Creek, MI, 1937).

9450 Drake, Alice Hutchins. On her, more than 100 programs, Drake presented book reviews along with comments on art in general and painting in particular. In addition, she discussed sight-seeing in Washington (WRC, Washington, DC, 1930).

9451 Drake, Dale. Sportscaster (WRR, 1939–1941). Newscaster (WRR, Dallas, TX, 1939).

9452 Drake, Francis B. Newscaster (NBC-Blue, 1945).

9453 Drake, Frank. DJ (WGH, Norfolk-Newport News, VA, 1957).

9454 Drake, Galen. Newscaster (ABC, 1945–1947). *See **Galen Drake**.*

9455 Drake, John. Newscaster (KCKN, Kansas City, KS, 1941).

9456 Drake, Myron. Newscaster (KTAR, Phoenix, AZ, 1938–1941, 1946). Sportscaster (KTAR, 1940–1941; KTAR, 1946–1954).

9457 **Drake, Nellie.** COM-HE (WCAV, Norfolk, VA, 1949).

9458 **Drake, Patti.** COM-HE (WORC, Worcester, MA, 1957).

9459 **Drake Concert Ensemble.** Henry Selinger directed this talented ensemble that included Leon Benditsky, Armand Buisseret, Frank Kiesca, Fred Meinken and Leon Lichtenfeld (WDAP, 1923; WGN, Chicago, IL, 1928).

9460 **Drake Hotel Dance Orchestra.** Hotel band led by Bobby Meeker (WGN, Chicago, IL, 1928).

9461 **Drama.** Dramatic productions in radio's early days were few. One of the earliest was the WGY (Schenectady, NY) full length two and a half-hour August 3, 1922, broadcast of Eugene Walter's melodrama, *The Wolf* directed by Edward H. Smith. Later, *The Old Soak* was broadcast from New York's Plymouth Theater by WJZ (New York, NY). From these modest beginnings numerous dramatic productions eventually were broadcast, but not all were of high quality.

Norman Corwin, writing as a radio critic in 1935 for the Springfield, MA, *Republican* observed: "There is about as much creative genius in radio today as there is in a convention of plasterers and plumbers." Certainly a major exception to Corwin's criticism were the pioneering efforts of WGY (Schenectady, NY) and the *Eveready Hour* broadcasts of the early and middle 1920s. Sponsored by the National Carbon Company, the *Eveready Hour* was first broadcast by WEAF (New York, NY) in December 4, 1923. A variety program, it was one of the first network programs to attract critical praise and wide spread popularity. The program at various times presented minstrel shows, full length dramatic productions and one-act plays with Broadway casts. One of its finest productions was a dramatization of Edna Ferber's *Show Boat* that was broadcast when the book was first published. In addition to the many famous performers presented on the *Eveready Hour*, many of its productions featured the *first* and perhaps *greatest radio actress*— Rosaline Greene.

Born Rosaline Greenberg in Hempstead, Long Island, she attended New York University, before transferring to Albany State College in her sophomore year to complete her studies. Her first radio acting job came about almost by accident. When station WGY in Schenectady was attempting to assemble a stock company of radio actors, Edward Smith, who wanted to produce and direct dramatic productions, put out a call to area colleges for acting talent. Although only a sophomore at Albany State, Greene was sent to Schenectady by a professor who told her, "You might as well go along, Rosaline. You've got a nice voice" (Greene, 1951, p. 2). She was hired by WGY immediately and appeared the following week in the station's production of Shakespeare's *Merchant of Venice*. Plays at WGY were broadcast weekly on its regular *Theatre Night* Friday evening program from 8:00 P.M. to 10:30 or 11:00 P.M., depending upon the play's length. Greene went on to be acclaimed as the leading WGY actress, while working for the magnificent salary of five dollars a week. After she worked at WGY for two years and received even more critical acclaim, her salary was raised to seven dollars and fifty cents a week.

After graduating from Albany State, Greene returned to New York City, where she soon appeared in dramatic productions on Broadway. Returning to radio, she became a regular on *The Eveready Hour*, one of early radio's most distinguished programs. After playing the leading role in *Joan of Arc*, she continued on *The Eveready Hour* for the next three years. Greene said the first real director on radio who had a Broadway background was Gerald Stopp, who had been brought into radio by Bertha Brainard.

After the *Eveready Hour*, Greene went on to play in many other radio productions — large and small — including daytime serial programs. Incidentally, she always resented the term "soap opera," considering it demeaning to both performers and their audience (Greene, 1951, p. 27). She appeared in one of New York's first daytime serial programs, *The Luck of Joan Christopher*, in 1930 sponsored by Hecker's Flour on station WOR (Newark, NJ) three nights a week. Pauline Lord and Lou Tellegen appeared on the program with Greene. In her long radio career, Greene played many roles in all types of programs from heroine in dramatic productions to comedy stooge for Eddie Cantor. Arguably, she was the first and finest actress ever developed by radio [*See* **Greene, Rosaline**].

The quality of early radio's dramatic productions varied greatly, but entertainment was always guaranteed. One writer-producer-director who combined entertainment with a firm philosophical frame of reference was Carleton E. Morse, a veritable one man fiction factory, equally famous for his enormous energy. Morse went to work for NBC in September 1929, the month of the disastrous stock market crash that preceded the Great Depression. Despite the somber economic conditions, Morse was kept busy writing for the many shows that emanated from NBC-San Francisco for many years.

Morse's most memorable program was *One Man's Family*, an early dramatic serial that ran for some 20 years without losing any of its principal cast members, remarkable proof of its listener popularity and the loyalty and mutual respect that existed between its writer and cast. Morse's suggestions on how to write dramatic radio serials precisely described his own successful approach and the good chemistry that existed between the writer and his actors. Few writers were more prolific than Morse. Most famous for *One Man's Family* and *I Love a Mystery*, Morse was fond of using the same actors in all his programs. He often said that the actors he cast in his programs helped him write his shows. Morse felt that there was a definite interaction between his actors playing certain roles and the show's on-going plot.

Morse said that he knew the actors playing the roles so well, that he was not only writing fiction, but something of each actor into the plot (Morse, 1945, p. 116). Since he knew the actors who played in *One Man's Family* for several years, their personal characteristics, mannerisms and professional skills helped him plot the story. For instance, he thought of actors on the show and their special characteristics in this way:

> Father Barber (J. Anthony Smythe) was a Republican conservative with strong upper-middle class values;
>
> Mother Barber (Minetta Ellen) was a quiet, warmly sympathetic woman whose exchanges with her children were particularly engaging;
>
> Paul Barber (Michael Raffetto), the eldest son, had a rich, resonant voice and a cooly controlled serious manner;
>
> Hazel (Bernice Berwin) was the oldest daughter whose warm, gentle and serene manner made her an excellent mother;
>
> Claudia (Kathleen Wilson) was a light-hearted comedy actress; and
>
> Clifford (Barton Yarborough) was an easy going person who sometimes demonstrated a moody disposition.

Writer-director-producer Morse was innovative, prolific and highly successful, not merely because of his own considerable talent and high energy level, but also because he was insightful enough to keep what, in effect, was a repertory company of radio actors together for many years. Between 1931 and 1944 alone, it was estimated that he wrote between 18 and 20 million words for radio. When *One Man's Family* finally ended in 1959, it was with Book 189. Each "book" was an 80,000 to 100,000 word novella, meaning that millions of words had been written for and spoken on the program. Even if he lacked the versatility of an Arch Oboler or the artistic achievements of a Norman Corwin, no radio writer enjoyed greater listener popularity or remained prolific as long as Carleton E. Morse.

Probably the *Columbia Workshop* (later the *Columbia Radio Workshop*) was the most creative series ever broadcast. Originally conceived, developed and produced by Irving Reis, the only criterion for inclusion of a writer's work in the series was that it be creative in concept and innovative in production technique. Begun in 1936, the program became a training ground and testing space for new writing styles and experimental techniques. Sound effects and music became an integral part of the series' productions. Bernard Hermann composed and conducted most of the music for the programs. Erik Barnouw, who saw the 1930s as a renaissance period in American radio, noted that the *Columbia Workshop* played a major role by its many significant contributions. Orson Welles, Norman Corwin and Arch Oboler were among the major movers in the dramatic changes that occurred and the first two dramatists came out of the *Columbia Workshop* programs.

After the broadcast of Archibald MacLeish's "The Fall of the City" on April 11, 1937, the program presented the work of such other distinguished writers as Norman Corwin, Lord Dunsany, Steven Vincent Binet, Alfred Kreymborg, Pare Lorentz, Dorothy Parker, Irving Reis, William Saroyan, Wilbur Daniel Steele and Max Wylie. After Reis, William N. Robson took over production of the program. The program was one of William Paley's considerable cultural contribution, but its frequent cancellations and renewals were unfortunate (1936–1941; 1946–1947; 1956–1957). The program became the *Columbia Radio Workshop* when it was revived in 1956. It is estimated that more than 318 programs were broadcast in the series.

Orson Welles, who gained radio experience on the *Columbia Workshop*, first attracted national attention as a "boy genius," responsible for the Mercury Theater productions on Broadway. He came to radio with his *Mercury Theater* program series in 1938. It was on this series that his "Martian Panic" broadcast made radio history. For Welles, the program was the earthshaking radio achievement that *Citizen Kane* was for him in motion pictures. Artistic and critical merit aside, the "Panic Broadcast" was significant for its demonstration of the widespread hysterical reactions a radio broadcast could produce.

Many examples of individual and group hysteria were reported during and after the broadcast. Some listeners who tuned in during the middle of the program believed they were hearing actual news bulletins and battle scene reports of Martian armies invading New Jersey. The hysteria of many others, however, resulted from hearing by word-of-mouth the news that hostile Martians had landed and were terrorizing the country side. Anyone who had been listening from the program's beginning should have known better, for they were clearly told what they were about to hear.

The program's opening announcement was: "CBS presents Orson Welles and the *Mercury Theatre of the Air* in a radio play by Howard Koch suggested by H.G. Wells' novel, *The War of the Worlds.*" Welles then came on to explain further: "We know now that in the early years of the twentieth century the world was being watched closely by intelligences greater than man's, but as mortal as his own, who regarded this earth with envious eyes and surely drew their plans against us. In the thirty-eighth year of the twentieth century came the great disillusionment."

Despite this opening and three announcements made during the program itself to tell listeners this was an adaptation of H.G. Wells' *War of the Worlds*, some listeners responded with irrational hysteria. After the program was over and Welles understood what had transpired, he feigned surprise as to what all the fuss was about. At a press conference the next day, Wells was asked if he was aware of the terror the broadcast would cause. He answered, "Definitely not. The technique I used was not original with me. It was not even new. I anticipated nothing unusual."

After all, it was true that Welles had concluded the program by saying that it all had been nothing but a *Mercury Theatre* Halloween prank: "The *Mercury Theatre's* own radio version of dressing up in a sheet and jumping out of a bush and saying, 'Boo.'" He then went on to say, "Remember please, for the next day or so, the terrible lesson you learned tonight. The grinning, global invader of your living room is an inhabitant of the pumpkin patch, and if your doorbell rings and there's no one there, that was no Martian. It's Halloween." Listening to a recording of the "War of the World" broadcast makes one wonder how so many people could believe it was "real" and react as hysterically as some did.

Social psychologist Hadley Cantril in his study of the incident, *The Invasion from Mars*, noted that in 1938 that of 32,000,000 American families, 27,500,000 had radios. This, he concluded, meant that for many families radio was their major source of information, and, furthermore, one that they had come to trust explicitly.

Another equally reasonable explanation for the hysterical reactions of so many was the state of mind of most Americans in 1938. The year of 1938 had been one in which there was the constant threat of an European war—an almost constant state of crisis that built to a climax only at the last minute giving way to a momentary resolution. Nerves for many citizens were at a breaking point. Hitler and Mussolini in Europe and the Japanese in Asia were menacing forces. A trust in radio combined with the state of the world's tensions made the American public particularly susceptible to such an erroneous over reaction.

Among the hysterical reactions the program produced was the one in Concrete, Washington, when that city's power plant failed in the middle of the program and its inhabitants fled frightened into the surrounding hills. On the eastern seaboard, hundreds of doctors and nurses telephoned police stations to volunteer their services. Many officers and men of the National Guard, believing they had been mobilized to battle the Martians, telephoned New Jersey headquarters to ask where they should report for duty.

There was a great diversity of opinion about the event the following day. Welles said he was sorry. Columnist Dorothy Dunbar Bromley scorned the public reaction:

> The United States must be the laughing stock of Europe today. To populations who have really been endangered by air raids or the immediate threat of air raids, it will be to laugh that countless Americans were driven into a panic by a make believe radio dramatization of an H.G. Wells' gas attack on this planet by the Martians.

The New York *World-Telegram* editorialized:

> If so many people could be misled unintentionally, when the purpose was merely to entertain, what could designing politicians not do through control of broadcasting stations? The dictators of Europe use radio to make their people believe falsehoods. We want nothing like that here. Better have American radio remain free to make occasional blunders then start on a course that might, in time, deprive it of freedom to broadcast uncensored truth.

It remained for columnist Heywood Broun to provide the most perceptive comment of all:

> I doubt that anything of the sort would have happened four or five months ago. The course of world history has affected national psychology. Jitters have come to roost. We have just gone through a laboratory demonstration of the fact that the peace of Munich hangs heavy over our heads like a thundercloud. If many sane citizens believed that Mars had jumped us suddenly they were not quite as silly as they seemed.

Welles at first was reluctant to accept any responsibility for the program, although he had produced and directed it, but eventually he did say he was sorry. A few years later in 1940, however, Welles tried to take writing credit away from Koch and take it for himself (Callow, 1996, p. 406). No one ever disputed the fact that Welles' ego was as large as his considerable talent. As a radio actor, probably to his discomfort, he was best known for his short-lived portrayal in the title role of *The Shadow*. Perhaps Mrs. Hans V. Kaltenborn put the Mars Panic Broadcast in its proper prospective when she said, "Why, anybody should have known it was not a real war. If it had been, the broadcaster would have been Hans."

A radio dramatist whose body of work has never been equaled was Norman Corwin. A gifted poet with words and sound, he explored radio's possibilities and used them to their fullest to produce many memorable programs. Corwin was convinced of the value of radio and its unique possibilities. Although early in his career as newspaper man, Corwin had been critical of radio drama and its practitioners, he understood early the uniqueness of radio, its nature and potential. He said that he believed radio would someday develop a literature as great as that of the theater. Corwin's assessment and prediction was accurate. Welles, Oboler and Corwin were the newcomers to radio who understood the medium's nature and potential. If Welles had not spread his time and talent in so many different areas, he might have made as many significant contributions to radio as did Norman Corwin and Arch Oboler.

It is no exaggeration to say that Corwin's work was an important part of radio's golden age. One of his most memorable programs was his *On a Note of Triumph*," broadcast on VE Day, May 8, 1945, for which he was credited as writer, director and producer. *Billboard* magazine described the broadcast as, "The single greatest radio program we have ever heard." They called Corwin the "poet laureate of radio." Martin Gabel narrated *On a Note of Triumph.*" The cast included Harry Bartell, Euba Deal, Johnny Bond, Ludwig Donath, Fred Essler, June Foray, Alex Hartford, Ramsey Hill, Merton Koplin, Raymond Lawrence, Elliott Lewis, Joan Lorring, Pat McGeehan, Lucille Meredith, Norbert Muller, Dick Nelson, Jim Nusser, George Sorel, Irene Tedrow, Peter Witt and Joe Worthy. The program's music was composed by Bernard Hermann and conducted by Lud Gluskin. *On a Note of Triumph* was a prime example of Corwin's poetic drama at its best.

Another powerful Corwin program, *We Hold These Truths*, was a celebration of the United States Constitution. It was broadcast December 15, 1941, only eight days after the Japanese attack on Pearl Harbor. Narrated by Jimmy Stewart, the cast included: Edward Arnold, Lionel Barrymore, Walter Brennan, Bob Burns, Walter Huston, Elliott Lewis, Marjorie Main, Edward G. Robinson, Rudy Vallee and Orson Welles.

During Corwin's long career, he showed respect for radio by providing it with some of its finest moments and contributing such series as *The Columbia Workshop* and his own *So This Is Radio* (1939); *26 by Corwin* (1941); *This is War* (1942), *An American in England* (1942); *Columbia Presents Corwin* (1944); and *One World Flight* (1947).

An assessment of Corwin's work can only be made when it is *heard*, since his medium was spoken words and sounds. After World War II, some of Corwin's work began to sound shrill and repetitive, but when his words sang, and most of them did, especially when his performers delivered them with an emotional gamut ranging from anger to hysteria, the superior nature of Corwin's work was apparent.

When Corwin first joined CBS, Arch Oboler had already enchanted and challenged his listeners with his *Lights Out* program, and Orson Welles had scared his listeners out of their wits with his "War of the Worlds" broadcast. Oboler's style was uniquely different from that of the other two. One of Oboler's characteristics was his stream of consciousness dialogue that gave his programs a great sense of reality combined at times with an imagery of fantasy.

Although he was best known for his *Lights Out* series and *Arch Oboler's Plays* on NBC, Oboler also wrote the famous lines delivered by Mae West on the Bergen-McCarthy *Maxwell House Coffee Hour* that resulted in the actress being banned from the air. After working on *Lights Out*, Oboler was eager to try his hand at experimental drama by writing, producing and directing it. NBC gave him an opportunity on his *Arch Oboler's Plays* series broadcast on the network from 1939 to 1940. Experimental in all its dramatic and technical techniques, the program was critically acclaimed as successful. It was so successful that many stars asked to perform on it. Alla Nazimova frequently performed for Oboler, along with others such as: Jimmy Cagney, Bette Davis, Edmund O'Brien and Frank Lovejoy. Probably his best remembered program of the series was his production of the tragic "Johnny Got His Gun" written by Dalton Trumbo.

A revival of the program in the format of *Oboler's Plays* was broadcast by Mutual Broadcasting System in 1945 [*See also* ***Lights Out***, ***Plays for Americans***, ***Arch Oboler's Plays***, ***Everyman's Theater***, ***Treasury Star Parade***, ***Free World Theater*** *and* ***Oboler's Plays***].

The work of Carleton E. Morse, Norman Corwin and Arch Oboler was similar in that in their best work all three served as writer, producer and director. All three, although varying in style, were *radio writers* in the strictest and best sense. All had prodigious energy, a love and respect for words and a facility with language. Although different from each other in style, content and substance, all pocessed the highest ethical standards and consistently portrayed a strong, consistent point of view.

9462 ***Dramas of Everyday Life.*** The Indemnity Insurance Company of North America sponsored the dramatic program about how persons were saved from the dire consequences of automobile accidents, fire, broken windows, etc., by their insurance policies. Margaret (Mike) Schaeffer wrote and played small roles in the dramatized portions of the program. Others in the cast were: Alma Mackenzie, Sam Serota and Al Woods (15 min., Tuesday and Thursday, 8:15–8:30 P.M., WIP, Philadelphia, PA, 1936).

9463 **Drane, Mary Endicott.** Violinist (KLDS, Independence, MO, 1926).

9464 **Drane, Virginia.** Violinist (KLSA, Independence, MO, 1926).

9465 **Drapeau, Barbara.** COM-HE (WACE, Chicopee, MA, 1949).

9466 **Draper, Margaret.** Actress Draper appeared on the daytime serial programs *Ma Perkins* and *The Brighter Day.*

9467 **Draughton, F. O.** Announcer (WDBW, Columbia, TN, 1924).

9468 ***Dream Boat.*** Emery Deutsch's Orchestra was featured on the pleasant music show (30 min., Thursday, 11:00–11:30 P.M., CBS, 1930).

9469 ***Dream Daddy.*** Harry Ehrhart told bedtime stories on his *Dream Daddy* program (WDAR, Philadelphia, PA, 1923; WLIT, Philadelphia, PA, 1926).

9470 ***Dream Drama.*** The veteran radio team of Arthur Allen and Parker Fennelly appeared in the quarter-hour dramatic sketch (NBC, 1935).

9471 ***(The) Dream Singer.*** Ralph Kirbery was the popular *Dream Singer* (15 min., Monday through Friday, 12:00–12:30 P.M., NBC-Red, 1932).

9472 ***Dream Valley.*** Reginald King read poetry on the weekly sustaining program (15 min., Tuesday, 11:45–12:00 midnight, WPEN, Philadelphia, PA, 1941).

9473 ***Dreams Come True.*** Baritone Barry McKinley and the Ray Sinatra Orchestra provided the program's romantic music (15 min., Tuesday, 2:45–3:00 P.M., NBC, 1935).

9474 ***Dreams of Long Ago.*** After being off the air for some time, Ethel Park Richardson's dramatizations of sentimental ballads, heart songs and old folk songs returned to NBC in 1936. The program presented dramatic versions of songs such as "The Old Oaken Bucket." The songs were sung by the Vass Trio — Frank, Virginia and Sally — and dramatized by a cast of five actors (30 min., Wednesday, 4:00–4:30 P.M. CST, NBC-Red, 1936).

9475 **Dreamtime Lady.** Children's program (*Visit to the Little Folks,* Pittsburgh, PA, 1923).

9476 **Drebing, Carl.** Newscaster (KGFX, Pierre, SD, 1937).

9477 **Dreeben, Rose.** Soprano (WEAF, New York, NY, 1925).

9478 **Dreer, Walter.** Cello (WIP, Philadelphia, PA, 1926).

9479 **Drees, Jack.** Sportscaster (WJJD, Chicago, IL, 1938; WIND, Chicago, IL and WJJD, 1939–1941; WIND, 1945; *Drees on Sports*, WJJD, 1953; WBKB, Chicago, IL, 1955).

9480 **Drehr, Marjorie Mott.** Soprano (WJZ, New York, NY, 1925).

9481 **Dreier, Alex.** Newscaster (*News of the World*, *World News Parade*, *Dreier Comments*, and *News at Noon*, NBC, 1942; WMAQ, Chicago, IL, 1942–1944; NBC, 1945; WMAQ, 1945–1946; *Skelly News*, NBC, 1947–1948).

9482 **Dreis, Dave.** DJ (KENT, Shreveport, LA, 1955).

9483 ***(The) Drene Show.*** Don Ameche hosted, sang and clowned on this variety show sponsored by Drene Shampoo. Other regular cast members were singer Joanell James and comic Pinky Lee. Each week guest stars such as Ida Lupino appeared. Truman Bradley was the announcer (30 min., 10:00–10:30 P.M., NBC-Red, 1946).

9484 **Drennan, Lee.** DJ (*Number Please*, KCLV, Clovis, NM, 1954).

9485 ***Dreno's Orchestra.*** Instr. mus. prg. (WOR, Newark, NJ, 1935).

9486 **Drepperd, Bob.** DJ (*Morning in Norfolk*, WLOW, Norfolk, VA, 1947; *PM Club*, WLOW, 1948–1949).

9487 **Drescher, Bertha.** Organist (WGR, Buffalo, NY, 1924).

9488 **Dreschler, Gerry.** Newscaster (WISC, Madison, WI, 1948).

9489 **Dresden, Rosalie.** Singer (*Rosalie Dresden*, vcl. mus. prg., WSBC, Chicago, IL, 1935).

9490 **Dreskell, Lucille.** Soprano (KPO, San Francisco, CA, 1926).

9491 **Dreslin [Dreslein], Dorothy.** Soprano (*Dorothy Dreslin*, vcl. mus. prg., NBC, 1935–1937, 1939).

9492 ***Dress Rehearsal.*** The program's novel format pretended to take listeners behind the scenes as though they were present at a radio program's rehearsal. Singers Mabel Albertson and Morton Bowe was featured along with comedian Joe Rines (30 min., Sunday, 10:30–11:00 P.M., NBC-Blue, 1936).

9493 **Dresselhuys, Tom.** DJ (*Night Watch*, KSDN, Aberdeen, SD, 1952).

9494 **Drew, Albert "Al."** Sportscaster (WBTM, Danville, VA, 1939–1941; WBBB, Burlington, NC, 1942; WCBT, Roanoke Rapids, NC, 1945). Newscaster (WCBT, 1945).

9495 **Drew, Dave.** DJ (WTAX, Springfield, IL, 1955).

9496 **Drew, Deborah.** Soprano (WEVD, New York, NY, 1937).

9497 **Drew, Ed.** Leader (*Ed Drew Orchestra*, instr. mus. prg., WPRO, Providence, RI, 1939).

9498 **Drew, Sally.** COM-HE (WJER, Dover, OH, 1956–1957).

9499 **Drew, Virginia.** Graphologist (WBEN, Buffalo, NY, 1936).

9500 **Drew, Wendy.** Actress Drew appeared on the *Young Widder Brown* daytime serial.

9501 **Dreyer, Ruth Ann.** COM-HE (WKIP, Poughkeepsie, NY, 1951).

9502 **Dreyfuss, Dick.** DJ (*Pop Melody Time*, WAGM, Presque Isle, ME, 1947–1949).

9503 ***Drifting Pioneers.*** CW mus. prg. (WLW, Cincinnati, OH, 1938, 1942).

9504 **Drilling, Joe C., Jr.** Newscaster (*Peter Paul News*, KCOK, Tulare, CA, 1946–1947). Sportscaster (KCOK, 1946–1947; KMJ,

Fresno, CA, 1949–52; KJEO, Fresno, CA, 1953). DJ (*Date with a Disc*, KCOK, 1947).

9505 **Driscoll, Dave.** Newscaster (WOR, Newark, NY, 1938; *The Show of the Week*, MBS, 1939). Sportscaster (WOR, 1938–1940).

9506 **Driscoll, Dick.** DJ (*Music Before Midnight*, KXRA, Alexandria, MN, 1952).

9507 **Driscoll, Maurice.** Newscaster (KGEZ, Kalispell, MT, 1945–1946).

9508 **Driscoll, Peggy.** Singer (KDYL, Salt Lake City, UT, 1929).

9509 **Driscoll, Richard V.** Newscaster (WBTA, Batavia, NY, 1942).

9510 **Driscolo, Richard.** Newscaster (WLIP, Kenosha, WI, 1948).

9511 **Driskell, Jim.** DJ (WINN, Louisville, KY, 1955).

9512 **Driury [Drury], Bernard.** Driury conducted one of the earliest physical exercise programs on his *Daily Dozen* program (KPO, San Francisco, CA, 1925).

9513 **Drivas, Chris.** COM-HE (*The Jane Colby Show*, WIDE, Biddleford, ME, 1949).

9514 ***Drive East.*** As a recognition of the importance of radio to drivers, the drive time show presented the humor of Jean Shepherd and the music of the Tommy Reynolds Orchestra. The program premiered Monday, November 7, 1955 (60 min., Monday through Friday, WOR, New York, NY, 1955). *See **Jean Shepherd**.*

9515 **Drohlich, Robert "Bob."** Newscaster (KDRO, Sedalia, MO, 1939–1942).

9516 **Drollet, David.** Drollet was a tenor on the *Roxy and His Gang* program (NBC, 1929).

9517 **Drooz [Drooze], Elaine.** COM-HE (WROW, Albany, NY, 1951; WPTR, Albany, NY, 1955).

9518 **Drucker, Mikeshina.** Pianist (KGO, Oakland, CA, 1925).

9519 **Drucker, Vladimir.** Trumpet soloist (KGO, Oakland, CA, 1925–1926).

9520 **Druley, Lulu Trier.** Soprano (WDAP, Chicago, IL, 1924).

9521 **Drum, Dewey.** DJ (*Early Risers Club*, WSOC, Charlotte, NC, 1949–1955).

9522 **Drusilla.** Drusilla was the *Radio Dancer*, who performed tap dancing numbers before the microphone (WBGS, New York, NY, 1925).

9523 **Druxman, Bob.** Newscaster (KOL, Seattle, WA, 1946).

9524 **Dryden, Wheeler.** Cockney monologist (WEAF, New York, NY, 1926).

9525 **Dryfoos, Leon.** Newscaster (WLEU, Erie, PA, 1941–1945; WERC, Erie, PA, 1945–1948).

9526 **Duakte, Gwen.** COM-HE (WPFC, Panama City, FL, 1955).

9527 **Duane, Bob.** Newscaster (WKY, Oklahoma City, OK, 1942).

9528 **DuBard, (Mme.) Homer.** Soprano (WWJ, Detroit, MI, 1924).

9529 ***DuBarry Beauty Talk.*** The quarter-hour east coast version of the DuBarry show was broadcast on Thursday evenings (CBS, 1929–1930).

9530 ***DuBarry Radio Program.*** Dorothy Hale broadcast talks on "beauty culture" (15 min., Friday, 10:00–10:15 A.M., NBC-Pacific Coast Network, 1929).

9531 **DuBois, Charles "Chuck."** DJ (KBMY, Billings, MT, 1947–1949).

9532 **DuBois, Joellen.** COM-HE (WTNS, Coshocton, OH, 1954).

9533 **DuBois, Robert.** Pianist (*Robert DuBois*, instr. mus. prg., WFIL, Philadelphia, PA, 1936).

9534 **DuBois Californians Orchestra.** Pacific Coast jazz band (KFI, Los Angeles, CA, 1923).

9535 **Dubus, Alma.** Actress Dubus appeared on *The Woman in White* daytime serial program.

9536 **Duchin, Eddy.** Leader (*Eddy Duchin Orchestra*, WABC, New York, NY, 1931; WNAC, Boston, MA and WAAB, Boston, MA, 1932; NBC, 1934–1937, 1939; CBS, 1937; NBC-Blue, New York, NY, 1938).

9537 **Duck, Orm.** DJ (KPLT, Paris, TX, 1957).

9538 **Duck, Robert.** DJ (*Operation Music*, WCHK, Canton, GA, 1960).

9539 **Duck, Tommy.** DJ (*Mail Order Music*, WTBF, Troy, AL, 1954).

9540 **Duckett, Carl E.** Newscaster (WLOE, Leesville, NC, 1946; WBOB, Galax, VA, 1947).

9541 **Duckett, Mattie.** "Colored soprano" (KFSG, Los Angeles, CA, 1925).

9542 **Duckwitz, Dorothy Miller.** Pianist (WEAF, New York, NY, 1925).

9543 ***Duco Decorators.*** The quarter-hour show presented home decoration hints by Catherine Crumbaugh, readings by Charles McAllister and music by the Duco Orchestra (NBC-Pacific Coast Network, 1929).

9544 **Ducommun, Jesse C.** Announcer (KFMR, Sioux City, IA, 1926–1927).

9545 ***Dude Ranch.*** Louise Massey and the Westerners were featured on the popular CW music show (NBC, 1936).

9546 **Dudley, Bide.** Broadcast theatre news and comment, *Bide Dudley's Theatre Club of the Air* and *Bide Dudley Spotlights the Stage* (WHN, New York, NY, 1939).

9547 **Dudley, Bill.** DJ (*Club AM*, WMLS, Sylacauga, AL, 1952).

9548 **Dudley, Clara.** COM-HE (KCLW, Hamilton, TX, 1949).

9549 **Dudley, Dick.** DJ (*Rockabye Dudley*, WNBC, New York, NY, 1948–1949).

9550 **Dudley, James R. "Jimmy."** Sportscaster (WCFL, Chicago, IL, 1939–1941; WKAR, East Lansing, MI, 1942; WJW, Cleveland, OH, 1946–1949; WERE, Cleveland, OH, 1951–1956).

9551 **Dueringer, Bert.** Tenor (KOA, Denver, CO, 1925).

9552 **Duerr, Florence.** Pianist (KOIL, Council Bluffs, IA, 1926).

9553 **Duff, Allene Patterson.** Singer (WBAP, Fort Worth, TX, 1926).

9554 ***(The) Duffer's Club.*** Toni Williams talked about golfers and golfing on this sustaining program (15 min., Saturday, 6:45–7:00 P.M., KCMC, Texarkana, TX, 1949).

9555 **Duffy, Bob.** DJ (*At Your Request*, WLNH, Laconia, NH, 1947). Sportscaster (WLNH, 1947).

9556 **Duffy, George.** Leader (*George Duffy Orchestra*, instr. mus. prg., WFBR, Baltimore, MD, and WTAM, Cleveland, OH, 1935; MBS, 1940).

9557 **Duffy, George.** Sportscaster (WICE, Providence, RI, 1953).

9558 **Duffy, Jon.** DJ (*Rhythm in the Rockies*, KDYL, Salt Lake City, UT, 1954).

9559 **Duffy, Kathleen.** Soprano Duffy was featured on the late night *Hoot Owls* program (KGW, Portland, OR, 1925).

9560 **Duffy, Karrin.** COM-HE (WCOW, St. Paul, MN, 1954).

9561 **Duffy, Lee.** DJ (*Will Creek Hoedown*, WTBO, Cumberland, MD, 1952).

9562 **Duffy, Ray.** Leader (*Ray Duffy Orchestra*, instr. mus. prg., WDEL, Wilmington, DE, 1938).

9563 **Duffy, Tom.** Newscaster (WTMV, East St. Louis, IL, 1946).

9564 ***Duffy's Tavern.*** Ed Gardner, as Archie, the manager of Duffy's Tavern, "Where the Elite Meet to Eat," was the focal point around which all the comedic action swirled on this popular situation comedy. The Archie character first appeared on a CBS sustaining program, *So This Is New York*, created by Gardner and George Faulkner. Archie appeared again on *Forecast*, thanks to Abe Burrows. *Forecast* was an hour-long show, on which CBS presented pilot and preview versions of programs that were being considered for later network broadcast. Because of the favorable listener response, *Duffy's Tavern* was placed on the CBS schedule in 1941. During its 11-year run, the show featured many talented comics, notably Shirley Booth as Duffy's daughter, Miss Duffy; Alan Reed (Teddy Bergman) as Clancy the Cop; Charlie Cantor as Finnegan, whose IQ was even below counting or measuring; and Eddie Green as Eddie the waiter in a funny role, somewhat reminiscent of Jack Benny's Rochester. Other members of the cast were: Gloria Erlanger, Sandra Gould, Florence Halop, Florence Robinson, Hazel Shermet, Lurene Tuttle and Dickie Van Patten. Its announcers were: Jack Bailey, Marvin Miller, Rod O'Connor, Jimmy Wallington and Perry Ward. Among the show's many talented writers were Abe Burrows, Raymond Ellis, Ed Gardner, Alan Kent, Bill Manhoff, Larry Marks, Lew Meltzer, Norman Paul, Ed Reynolds and Manny Sachs. Mitchell Benson, Rupert Lucas, Jack Roche and Tony Stanford were the producers. Bob Graham, Tito Guizar, Benay Venuta and Helen Ward sang on the show with the orchestras of Matty Malneck, Reet Veet Reeves and Joe Venuti (CBS, ABC, NBC, 1941–1951).

9565 **Dugan, Dan.** Leader (Dan Dugan's Melody Boys Orchestra, WSAI, Cincinnati, OH, 1927). *Variety* called the group "a peppy" orchestra.

9566 **Dugan, Jack.** DJ (*The 590 Ballroom*, 120 min., Monday through Friday, 1:15–3:15 A.M., WROW, Albany, NY, 1952).

9567 **Dugdale, Charles.** DJ (*Melody-Go-Round*, KOIL, Omaha, NE, 1947; KFOR, Lincoln, NE, 1948; *Here's Charlie*, KFOR, 1952).

9568 **Dugdale, Walter.** DJ (KVOL, Lafayette, LA, 1948).

9569 **Duggan, Tom.** DJ (*KEEN Kapers*, KEEN, San Jose, CA, 1947). Sportscaster (*Sports World*, KEEN, 1947).

9570 **Duggers, Melvin.** DJ (*Hillbilly Melodies*, WKRM, Columbia, TN, 1947).

9571 **Duhme, Frank.** Newscaster (WTSP, St. Petersburg, FL, 1945).

9572 **Dukas, Jim.** DJ (*Moonlight Savings Time*, WPAR, Parkersburg, WV, 1952).

9573 **Dukate, Elbert.** Newscaster (KTBC, Austin, TX, 1940).

9574 **DuKate, Gwen.** COM-HE (WPCF, Panama City, FL, 1956).

9575 **Duke, Ann.** COM-HE (WDBL, Springfield, TN, 1954–1955).

9576 **Duke, Elmer.** Baritone (WSM, Nashville, TN, 1928).

9577 **Duke, Jerry.** COM-HE (KDDD, Dumas, TX, 1951).

9578 **Duke, Marilyn.** Contralto (*Marilyn Duke*, voc. mus. prg., WOR, Newark, NJ, 1935).

9579 **Duke, Marion.** COM-HE (WENE, Endicott, NY, 1949).

9580 **Duke, Paul.** Sportscaster (WMBG, Richmond, VA, 1944–1946).

9581 **Duke, Tommy.** DJ (*WMLT Dancing Party*, WMLT, Dublin, GA, 1947; *Country Store*, WULA, Eufaula, AL, 1949).

9582 ***Duke and Duchess Orchestra.*** Instr. mus. prg. (NBC, 1939).

9583 ***(The) Duke of Paducah and the Opry Gang.*** The Locke Stove Company sponsored the excellent program of country music and humor originating from Nashville, TN. Whitey Ford (the Duke of Paducah), Anne Lou and Danny, George Morgan and Moon Mulligan's band supplied fun and lively music. Jud Collins was the announcer of the show that was written and produced by Noel Digby (30 min., Saturday, 10:30–11:00 P.M., NBC, 1952).

9584 **Dukehart, Tommy.** Sportscaster (*Scholastic Scrapbook*, WFBR, Baltimore, MD, 1948–1949).

9585 **Dukeshire, William.** Newscaster (WICC, Bridgeport, CT, 1938; WELI, New Haven, CT, 1940).

9586 **Dulane, Chuck.** Sportscaster (*Sports Circus*, WGAY, Silver Spring, MD, 1948). DJ (*Chuck Dulane Show*, WGAY, 1952–1955).

9587 **Dulaney, Carroll.** Newscaster (*Our Town*, WCBM, Baltimore, MD, 1947).

9588 **Dulaney, Maude Martin.** COM-HE (WALT, Tampa, FL, 1949).

9589 **Dulfer, Ary.** Violinist (WBZ, Springfield, MA, 1926).

9590 **Dulin, Alfred.** Swedish concert pianist (WHN, New York, NY, 1923–1924; WGBS, New York, NY, 1925).

9591 **Dulin, Martha.** Newscaster (WBT, Charlotte, NC, 1939).

9592 **Dull, Johnny.** Leader (Johnny Dull and his Melody Boys with vocalist Rocky Bernard, KFI, Los Angeles, CA, 1928).

9593 **Dulles, Foster Rhea.** News analysis (WOSU, Columbus, OH, 1945). Dulles later became the Secretary of State during the Eisenhower administration.

9594 **Dumas, Helene.** Actress in *Blue Coal Radio Revue* and the *Blue Coal Radio Mysteries* programs (WNAC, Boston, MA, 1931). Busy and versatile actress Dumas also appeared on the *House of Glass*; *Jane Arden*; *John's Other Wife*; *Life Begins* aka *Martha Webster*; *Right to Happiness*; *Romance of Helen Trent*; *Big Sister*; *When a Girl Marries*; *Woman of America*; *Young Dr. Malone*; *Dot and Will*; and *Ellen Randolph* aka *The Story of Ellen Randolph* daytime serials.

9595 **Dumas, Roland.** Sportscaster (WMAS, Springdfield, MA, 1947–1949). DJ (*Tops in Pops*, WMAS, 1952–1955).

9596 **Dumesnil, M. Maurice.** French pianist (WOR, Newark, NJ, 1926).

9597 **Dumm, Bob.** Sportscaster (KROW, Oakland, CA, 1940; KXOA, Sacramento, CA, 1945).

9598 **DuMond, Irene.** COM-HE (*For Women, About Women*), KXEL, Waterloo, IA, 1949).

9599 **Dumont, Adolphe.** Orchestra conductor (*Twilight Melodies,* instr. mus. prg., NBC-Blue, New York, NY, 1929).

9600 **Dumont, Jeanne.** COM-HE (WTWO, Bangor, ME, 1956).

9601 **Dumont, Paul.** Announcer (WMCA, New York City, NY, 1925; WEAF-NBC, New York, NY, 1928).

9602 **Dumont, Phyllis.** COM-HE (WHEB, Portsmouth, NH, 1951).

9603 **Dumont, Virginia Brown.** Pianist (WIP, Philadelphia, PA, 1925).

9604 **Dunan, Earline.** COM-HE (WPNX, Phoenix City, AL, 1955).

9605 **Dunaway, Al.** Sportscaster (*World of Sports*, KFDA, Amarillo, TX, 1960).

9606 **Dunaway, Chuck.** DJ (*The Chuck Dunaway Show*, WABC, New York, NY, 1960).

9607 **Dunaway Sisters.** Harmony singing duo (WHT, Chicago, IL, 1928).

9608 **Dunbar, Ed.** DJ (*The Night Watch*, WBBQ, Augusta, GA, 1948; *Cousin Ed*, WBBQ, 1949–1952).

9609 **Dunbar, Walt.** Sportscaster (WBET, Brockton, MA, 1953; *Time for Sports*, WBET, 1954–1956).

9610 **Dunbar, (Dr.) Willis F.** Newscaster (WKZO, Kalamazoo, MI, 1944–1948).

9611 **Duncan, Cornelia.** Duncan told bedtime stories on her children's program (WGES, Oak Park, IL, 1925).

9612 **Duncan, Coyal "Dusty."** CW DJ (*Dusty Duncan*, KXOB, Stockton, CA, 1949).

9613 **Duncan, Dopey.** DJ (*Crossroad Store*, WKAP, Allentown, PA, 1952).

9614 **Duncan, Eleanor.** COM-HE (WSOY, Decatur, IL, 1956–1957).

9615 **Duncan, Hip Pockets.** DJ (*Western Roundup*, KDAV, Lubbock, TX, 1954).

9616 **Duncan, J. Al.** DJ (*Jam the Boogie Man*, WJAM, Marion, AL, 1952).

9617 **Duncan, Jean.** Contralto (WSWS, Chicago, IL, 1926).

9618 **Duncan, Jean.** COM-HE (WSOY, Decatur, IL, 1957).

9619 **Duncan, Jean.** COM-HE (WGGH, Marion, IL, 1957).

9620 **Duncan, Jim.** Sportscaster (WEBQ, Harrisburg, IL, 1945–1949). DJ (*Requestfully Yours*, WEBQ, 1947–1950; WGGH, Marion, IL, 1955–1957).

9621 **Duncan, Lee.** DJ (*Lucky Lager Dance Time*, KRAM, Las Vegas, NV, 1952).

9622 **Duncan, Novin.** Newscaster (WFBC, Greenville, SC, 1942, 1948).

9623 **Duncan, Priscilla.** COM-HE (WSIL, Silver City, NM, 1957).

9624 **Duncan, Rosetta and Vivian Duncan.** The Duncan Sisters were the comedy singing team known as "Topsy and Eva" of musical comedy fame (WCAE, Pittsburgh, PA, 1926). They were one of vaudeville's greatest sisters act. They first appeared on radio in 1924 (KYW, Chicago, IL).

9625 **Duncan-Marin Orchestra.** Texas dance band (WBAP, Fort Worth, TX, 1926).

9626 **Dunham, Bob.** Newscaster (KMOX, St. Louis, MO, 1940).

9627 **Dunham, Dick.** Newscaster (WITH, Baltimore, MD, 1942; CBS, 1945).

9628 **Dunham, Don.** Leader (*Don Dunham Orchestra*, instr. mus. prg., WLW, Cincinnati, OH, 1939).

9629 **Dunham, E. Lewis.** Organist (WLAC, Nashville, TN, 1928).

9630 **Dunham, Florence Clayton.** Organist (WMMN, Fairmont, WV, 1937).

9631 **Dunham, "Sonny."** Leader (*Sonny Dunham Orchestra*, instr.mus. prg., CBS, 1935; KMOX, St. Louis, MO, 1942).

9632 **Dunham, Walter.** Pianist (WOAI, San Antonio, TX, 1925).

9633 **Dunkirk, Millard.** Newscaster (WDAY, Fargo, ND, 1937).

9634 **Dunlap, Helen Morrison.** Pianist (WBZ, Boston-Springfield, MA, 1924).

9635 **Dunlap, Howard.** Organist (KFON, Long Beach, CA, 1926).

9636 **Dunlap, Patricia.** Busy actress Dunlap appeared on the daytime serial programs *Bachelor's Children*, *Backstage Wife* aka *Mary Noble*, *Backstage Wife*, *Ma Perkins*, *Romance of Helen Trent*, *This Day Is Ours* and *Today's Children*.

9637 **Dunlap, Wallace "Wallie."** Newscaster (WMOB, Mobile, AL, 1941–1942). DJ (*Dial Dunlap*, WLIZ, Bridgeport, CT, 1947–1949; *Dial Dunlap*, WICC, Bridgeport, CT, 1952).

9638 **Dunlea, E.A.** Newscaster (WMFD, Wemington, NC, 1940).

9639 **Dunlop, Ruth.** COM-HE (KPHO, Phoenix, AZ, 1955).

9640 **Dunn, Adeline.** COM-HE (*Aunt Em's Homemakers*, WCLO, Janesville, WI, 1949).

9641 **Dunn, Artie.** Dunn teamed with Les Reis as the "Wandering Minstrels" on the *Major Bowes Capitol Theater Family* (NBC, 1929). Dunn later was a leading member of the Three Suns musical group.

9642 Dunn, Billie. Pianist (KFWB, Hollywood, CA, 1926).

9643 Dunn, Bob. DJ (*1240 Club*, KRAL, Rawlins, WY, 1952).

9644 Dunn, Bob. DJ (*Night Watch*, KWBR, Oakland, CA, 1952–1954; KLX, Oakland, CA, 1955).

9645 Dunn, Edward "Eddy." Assistant Announcer (WFAA, Dallas, TX, 1927). Sportscaster (WFAA, 1938).

9646 Dunn, Grace. Soprano (WCFL, Chicago, IL, 1935).

9647 Dunn, Jack. Leader (Jack Dunn Orchestra, KFQJ, Hollywood, CA, 1929; *Jack Dunn and His Rainbow Gardens Orchestra*, KTM, Santa Monica, CA, 1931).

9648 Dunn, Jack. Newcaster (WDAY, Fargo, ND, 1938–1945)

9649 Dunn, Jean Ann. COM-HE (KSPR, Casper, WY, 1949).

9650 Dunn, Jeanne. Female "crooner" (KFI, Los Angeles, CA, 1929).

9651 Dunn, Jo Anne. COM-HE (WTRF, Bellaire, OH, 1951; WTRX, Bellaire, OH, 1954–1955).

9652 Dunn, Juliette. Soprano (KFRC, San Francisco, CA, 1927).

9653 Dunn, Kenneth. Pianist (WOK, Chicago, IL, 1925).

9654 Dunn, Margaret. Pianist (*Margaret Dunn*, instr. mus. prg., WMMN, Fairmont, WV, 1937).

9655 Dunn, Ron. DJ (WSBA, York, PA, 1954).

9656 Dunn, Ruth. Pianist (WIP, Philadelphia, PA, 1925).

9657 Dunn, Ura. COM-HE (WJLK, Asbury Park, NJ, 1957).

9658 Dunn, Violet. Actress Dunn appeared on *The O'Neills* daytime serial.

9659 Dunn, Walter F. Tenor (WEEI, Boston, MA, 1925).

9660 Dunn, William. Euphonium soloist (WCBD, Zion, IL, 1926).

9661 Dunn, (Mrs.) William. Soprano (WSM, Nashville, TN, 1926–1927).

9662 Dunn, William J. Newscaster (CBS, 1944).

9663 *(The) Dunn Sisters.* Vcl. mus. prg. (KARL, Little Rock, AR, 1939). The Dunn Sisters were a harmony singing team.

9664 Dunnagan, Ken. DJ (*The Cat's Meow*, KANE, New Iberia, LA, 1948).

9665 Dunnavant, Bob. DJ (*Juke Box Revue* and *Echoes from the Hills*, WJMW, Athens, AL, 1948–1949).

9666 Dunnavant, Homer. DJ (*Pappy's Roundup* and *Uncle Bob*, WJMW, Athens, AL, 1948).

9667 Dunnaway, Al. Sportscaster (WALT, Tampa, FL, 1960).

9668 Dunne, Bert. Sportscaster (NBC and CBS, 1942).

9669 Dunne, Frank. Newscaster (WTAG, Worcester, MA, 1940).

9670 Dunning, Harlan. Newscaster (KFRC, San Francisco, CA, 1941).

9671 Dunning, Owen. Newscaster (KOIN, Portland, OR, 1945).

9672 Dunninger, Joseph. Dunninger was a mentalist who "projected telepathic images to NBC listeners," (NBC, 1929). *See **Dunninger the Modern Mentalist**.*

9673 Dunninger, (Mrs.) William. Pianist (WLW, Cincinnati, OH, 1923).

9674 *Dunninger the Modern Mentalist.* Although there were many skeptical of Dunninger's "mind reading feats," his show enjoyed great popularity (30 min., ABC, 1943). Dunninger previously had been recognized as a master magician and illusionist.

9675 Dunn's Orchestra. North Carolina dance band (WWNC, Ashville, NC, 1928).

9676 Dunphy, Don. Sportscaster (WINS, New York, NY, 1938–1940; WOR, New York, NY and MBS, 1941; WOR, MBS and WINS, New York, NY, 1942; WINS, 1944–1946; WHN, New York, NY and ABC, 1947; WMGM, New York, NY and ABC, 1948; ABC, 1949). Dunphy's reputation is based on his blow-by-blow broadcasts of famous boxing bouts. His first fight broadcasts were of amateur bouts for WINS in the 1940s. He got his network break when he was selected to broadcast the first Louis-Conn heavyweight championship bout in June 1941.

9677 Dunphy, Geraldine. Soprano (WNAC, Boston, MA, 1925).

9678 Dunstedter, Eddie. Organist (WCCO, Minneapolis–St. Paul, MN, 1925–1928; *Eddie Dunstedter*, instr. mus. prg., WWVA, Wheeling, WV, 1935).

9679 Duo Disc Duo. Singing team (NBC-Pacific Network, 1929; *Duo Disc Duo*, vcl. team accompanied by the Walter Blaufuss Orchestra, 30 min., Sunday, 4:30–5:00 P.M., NBC-Blue, 1930).

9680 Duo-Ikesters. The comic female singing team of Gay and Lou (KYW, Chicago, IL, 1928).

9681 *Duo Piano Flashes.* Music program featuring the piano team of Clem Kennedy and Virginia Spencer (KYA, San Francisco, CA, 1930).

9682 DuPont, Larry. Newscaster (WBAP, Fort Worth, TX, 1945; WBAP-KGKO, Fort Worth, TX, 1946).

9683 Dupre, Henry Phillips. Sportscaster (WWL, New Orleans, LA, 1937–1941).

9684 Dupree, Wayne. DJ (KALT, Atlanta, TX, 1955).

9685 Dupree, (Dr.) William. DJ (*Jazz Show*, WMFS, Chattanooga, TN, 1954).

9686 Dupres, Betty. Singer (WBRY, Waterbury, CT, 1939).

9687 Dupuich, Helen. Soprano (KGO, Oakland, CA, 1926).

9688 DuPuy, Monty. DJ (*Requestfully Yours*, WNCA, Asheville, NC, 1947; WFBC, Greenville, SC, 1954–1955).

9689 DuPuy, (Mrs.) William Atherton. COM-HE (*What Women are Doing Today*, WTAM, Cleveland, OH, 1924).

9690 Duque, Ernest. Newscaster (KTMS, Santa Barbara, CA, 1945).

9691 Duquenne, Marti. Singer (*Marti Duquenne*, vcl. mus. prg., WMBD, Peoria, IL, 1935).

9692 Duran, Ted. Newscaster (KBUC, Corona, CA, 1948).

9693 Durand, Tom. DJ (*Tom Durand Show*, WTTM, Trenton, NJ, 1952–1955).

9694 Durbin, Frank. Flutist (KWSC, Pullman, WA, 1926).

9695 Durdelberger, Charles. Tenor (WOR, Newark, NJ, 1923).

9696 Durham, Dean. DJ (*Let's Get Together with Records*, KOGT, Orange, NM, 1954; *Best on Wax*, KOGT, 1955).

9697 Durham, Dorothy. Singer (KFSD, San Diego, CA, 1929).

9698 Durham, Ernie. DJ (*Records with Ernie*, WMRP, Flint, MI, 1954; WJLB, Detroit, MI, 1957–1960).

9699 Durham, Gladys. Soprano (WEAF, New York, NY, 1924).

9700 Durham, Murray. Newscaster (KLBM, LaGrande, OR, 1945).

9701 Durkee, Bob. Newscaster (WFVL, Hollywood, CA, 1946).

9702 Durkee, C.A. Leader (C.A. Durkee and his Novelty Harmonica Orchestra, KPRC, Houston, TX, 1926).

9703 Durkee, Jennie M. Ukulele-guitarist soloist (KFSG, Los Angeles, CA, 1924).

9704 Durkin, Sherwood (Ralph). Sportscaster (KCKN, Kansas City, KS, 1940; WDAF, Kansas City, MO, 1951). Newscaster (WMT, Cedar Rapids–Waterloo, IA, 1941).

9705 Durney, Bill. Sportscaster (WIL, St. Louis, MO, 1937–1945).

9706 Durno, Jeanette. Pianist (WMAQ, Chicago, IL, 1925).

9707 Durrett, (Mrs.) W.E., Jr. COM-HE (KELD, El Dorado, AR, 1956).

9708 Durso, Mike. Leader (*Mike Durso Orchestra*, instr. mus. prg., WCBM, Baltimore, MD, 1935).

9709 Durst, Lavada. Black DJ (*Rosewood Ramble*, KVET, Austin, TX, 1947–1948; *Dr. Hepcat*, KVET, Austin, TX, late 1940s to early 1960s). Durst was a popular rhythm and blues and rock-and-roll DJ. Most likely he was the first Black DJ in Texas. Typically, Durst closed his program by saying: "This is Dr. Hepcat, Lavada Durst, in the cool of evening, wishing you a very warm good night." An expert practitioner of jive talk, Durst wrote his own jive dictionary, *The Jives of Dr. Hepcat*. At the height of his popularity in the early 1960s, he left radio to become a minister of an Austin, Texas, church.

9710 Durst, Ralph. Tenor (WGBS, New York, NY, 1928).

9711 Dutch and his Uke. Unidentified ukulele soloist (KFWB, Hollyood, CA, 1924).

9712 *(The) Dutch Masters Minstrels.* Dutch Masters Cigars sponsored the radio minstrel show. On the 1930 version, William Shelley was the interlocutor with Paul Dumont and Al Bernard acting as end-men. Singers on that show included Carson Robison, bass Harry Donaghy, tenor Steele Jamison, baritone Carl Bethmann and tenor Harold Branch. Instrumental novelties were performed by Charles Magnante, James Boyd and William Carlino (30 min., Saturday, 9:30–10:00 P.M., NBC-Blue, 1930). A year before the cast of the show also had included Percy Hemus, Al Bernard, Steve Porter and Leon Salanthiel and an orchestra conducted by Hugo Mariani. The program was broadcast on a different day the previous year (30 min., Tuesday, 9:30–10:00 P.M., NBC-Blue, 1928–1929). An example of the show's humor from the 1929 version was this exchange between interlocutor Steve Porter and end-man Percy Hemus:

HEMUS: Mistah Porter, that niggah Al Bernard axe me somepin I kant understand.

PORTER: What was it you asked Percy, Al?

BERNARD: I says if a brick mason lays brick, why kaint a plumber lay plums? (*Radio Digest*, p. 33, December, 1929).

An example of an exchange between interlocutor William Shelley and end-man Al Bernard on the 1930 show was as follows:

SHELLEY: How's you father, Al?

BERNARD : Laziest man livin', Mistuh Shelley.

SHELLEY : Well, Al, I happen to know that your father is a hard working man.

BERNARD : Well, Ah'll tell you why you're wrong. They's 365 days in the year. Father don't work but eight hours a day — that's one third of the time, or 122 days. Well, they's 52 Sundays — that takes off 26 days and leaves 44. He gets two weeks' vacation — that's 14 more days to come off— that makes 30 days. Then there's 11 holidays, so that makes 19. Well, he gets an hour for lunch every day, that's 365 hours or 15 days, and that leaves only 4 days. Look here, Mistuh Shelley, if father goes and gets sick and has to stay home, he's goin' to owe that man money for lettin' him work for him.

A 1936 version presented Al Bernard and Paul Dumont as end-men, tenor Steele Jamison and music by Harold Sanford's Orchestra.

9713 ***(The) Dutch Masters Program.*** Dutch Masters cigars sponsored the good music show featuring baritone Nelson Eddy, soprano Lillian Taiz and Jack Smart. Music arrangements were made by William Spielter for the orchestra directed by Eugene Ormandy (30 min., Thursday, 8:30–9:00 P.M., CBS, 1931).

9714 **Dutch the Boy Blues Singer.** Dutch was a young male singer, not otherwise identified (KFKB, Milford, KS, 1925–1926).

9715 **Dutton, Chuck.** Leader (Chuck Dutton's Hotel Oakland Dance Band, KLX, Oakland, CA, 1927).

9716 **Dutton, Hazel.** COM-HE (KNGS, Hanford, CA, 1954).

9717 **Dutton, Ivy.** COM-HE (WSBS, Great Barrington, MA, 1960).

9718 **Dutton, Marie.** Comedienne (WBZ, Springfield, MA, 1925).

9719 **Duva, Marion Bennett.** Soprano (KOIN, Council Bluffs, IA, 1928).

9720 **Duval, Gaby.** Soprano (KGO, Oakland, CA, 1928).

9721 **Duvall, Carol.** COM-HE (WOOD, Grand Rapids, MI, 1956–1957).

9722 **Dux, Walter.** Newscaster (WOPI, Bristol, TN, 1937).

9723 **Dvorak, George.** DJ (*George Dvorak's Bandstand*, KFI, Los Angeles, CA, 1949).

9724 **Dvorak, Madelin.** Singer (KOMO, Fisher's Bend, WA, 1929).

9725 **Dvorak, Madelin and Dorothea Wel.** Vocal team (KOMO, Seattle, WA, 1929).

9726 **Dvorak, Melissa.** Pianist (WOOD, Grand Rapids, MI, 1926).

9727 **Dwelley, Dale.** DJ (*Lasson Roundup*, KSUE, Susanville, CA, 1949; *Cheerful Earful*, KATO, Reno, NV, 1954).

9728 **Dwyer, Donn.** DJ (*Watching the Grooves*, KFNF, Shenandoah, IA, 1947).

9729 **Dwyer, Eddie.** Newscaster (*Headline News*, WASA, Havre de Grace, MD, 1948).

9730 **Dwyer, Gertrude.** Blues singer (WRNY, New York, NY, 1932).

9731 **Dwyer, Margaret.** Reader (WBZ, Boston-Springfield, MA, 1924).

9732 **Dwyer, Mary.** COM-HE (WRDW, Augusta, GA, 1954–1955).

9733 **Dwyer, Pearl.** Dwyer was the station's staff pianist. She was known as "The Rhythm Girl" (KFJF, Oklahoma City, OK, 1928).

9734 **Dwyer, Virginia.** Busy actress Dwyer appeared on the *Houseboat Hannah, Aunt Jenny* aka *Aunt Jenny's Real Life Stories, Joyce Jordan, Girl Interne, Backstage Wife* aka *Mary Noble, Backstage Wife, Second Husband* and *Front Page Farrell.*

9735 ***(The) DX Club.*** This local program was devoted to the quest for and enjoyment of receiving long distance radio broadcasts (15 min., Saturday, 12:00–12:15 A.M., KDKA, Pittsburgh, PA, 1935).

9736 **DX-ing.** *See* **Appendix A — Chronology, 1906–1960.**

9737 ***(The) Dyas Girl.*** Blues singer Jo Ann Stone was the B.H. Dyas Department Store Girl who had her own popular local Los Angeles program (KFAC, Los Angeles, CA, 1932).

9738 **Dyckman, W.A.** Basso (WHT, Chicago, IL, 1926).

9739 **Dye, Charlotte Van Grinkle.** Pianist (WHO, Des Moines, IA, 1924).

9740 **Dye, Robert.** Sportscaster (*Sports Today*, KSRV, Ontario, OR, 1960).

9741 **Dye, Tom.** DJ (KTTR, Rolla, MO, 1955; *Soest Holler Time*, KTTR, 1960).

9742 **Dyer, Arthur.** Former Southwest Conference football official Dyer broadcast weekly football talks (WFAA, Dallas, TX, 1928).

9743 **Dyer, Bill.** Dyer was a veteran sportscaster who gained prominence in Philadelphia for his play-by-play broadcasts of the hapless A's and Phils' baseball games (WCAU, Philadelphia, PA, late 1920s and early 1930s). He also broadcast sports news on several programs, one of which was sponsored by the Adam Scheidt Brewing Company (*The Sporting Extra,* 30 min., Monday, 10:30–11:00 P.M., KYW, Philadelphia, PA, 1936). Soon thereafter, Dyer went to Baltimore where he broadcast the baseball games of the Baltimore Orioles of the International League for many years (WITH, Baltimore, MD, 1937–1939; *Sports Special,* WITH, 1947–1949).

9744 **Dyer, Bob.** DJ (*Hall of Records*, WKNX, Sagninaw, MI, 1949–1952).

9745 **Dyer, Braven.** Sportscaster (KNX, Los Angeles, CA, 1938; *Sports Huddle,* CBS, 1939; *Rose Bowl football game,* CBS, 1953, NBC, 1960).

9746 **Dyer, Don.** DJ (*Your Choice*, WAYB, Waynesboro, VA, 1947).

9747 **Dyer, Harold F.** Sportscaster (WCSH, Portland, ME, 1944; WCSH, 1947).

9748 **Dyer, John.** Sportscaster (*Sports Final*, KSTV, Stephenville, TX, 1953–1954).

9749 **Dyer, Maurine.** Soprano (KFI, Los Angeles, CA, 1925).

9750 **Dyer, Roy.** Leader (Roy Dyer's El Nido Cafe Orchestra, KLX, Oakland, CA, 1927).

9751 **Dyke, Esther.** Soprano (WSUI, Iowa City, IA, 1926).

9752 **Dymale, Nancy.** COM-HE (WBKV, West Bend, WI, 1954).

9753 **Dynacone Dance Orchestra.** Commercial radio band (WLW, Cincinnati, OH, 1929).

9754 **Dynes, Charles.** Sportscaster (KGIW, Alamosa, CA, 1948–1949).

9755 **Dyrdal, Vernon.** Sportscaster (KWLC, Decorah, IA, 1940–1941).

9756 **Dyson, Leola.** COM-HE (WRAP, Norfolk, VA, 1957).

9757 **Dziedzic, Mike.** DJ (*Polka Time,* WGAT, Utica, NY, 1954).

9758 ***E. Gunn's Fashion Feature.*** Gunn focused on fashion news on her women's program news (WLIT, Philadelphia, PA, 1925).

9759 **Eager, Clay.** DJ (*Clay's Country Capers*, WLOK, Lima, OH, 1952).

9760 **Eagon, Bruce.** Newscaster (KRLD, Dallas, TX, 1944).

9761 **Eaker, Forrest.** Newscaster (*News Round-Up*, WMFT, Florence, AL, 1948).

9762 **Eakin, Vera.** Pianist (ABS, 1935).

9763 **Eakins, Phil.** Sportscaster (*The Sports Broadcast*, KSIL, Silver City, NM, 1947; *Sportsreel*, KEPO, El Paso, TX, 1950–1951).

9764 **Earl, Grace.** Beauty expert (*Beauty Talk*, WMAQ, Chicago, IL, 1924).

9765 **Earl, Jean.** COM-HE (KONP, Port Angeles, WA, 1949).

9766 **Earl, Mary Winfrey.** Contralto (KFWM, Oakland, CA, 1927).

9767 ***(The) Earl Wilson Show.*** Newspaper columnist Wilson conducted a radio gossip column (15 min., weekly, 10:00–10:15 P.M., MBS, 1945).

9768 ***Earl Wilson's Column of the Air.*** Broadway columnist Wilson broadcast show business gossip and interviewed celebrities (30 min., Monday-Wednesday- Saturday, 30 min., 9:30–10:00 P.M., NBC-Blue, 1950).

9769 **Earle, Allan.** Newscaster (WJJD, Chicago, IL, 1946).

9770 **Earle, Bob.** DJ (*Midnight in Madison*, WKOW, Madison, WI, 1947; KSO, Des Moines, IA, 1949–1956).

9771 Earle, C.A. Leader (*C.A. Earle Orchestra,* instr. mus. prg., NBC, 1930).

9772 Earle, George. Newscaster (KWTO, Springfield, MA, 1946).

9773 Earle, Lowell. DJ (*Dixie Jubilee,* WGBA, Columbus, GA, 1949).

9774 Earle, Stanley. DJ (*Anything Goes,* KAYL, Storm Lake, IA, 1950).

9775 Earle, William "Bill." Sportscaster (WASL, Annapolis, MD, 1949–1952).

9776 Earley, Charles. Newscaster (KDKA, Pittsburgh, PA, 1945–1946).

9777 Earley, Thomas A., Jr. DJ (*Polka Dots,* WKAP, Allentown, PA, 1948).

9778 Early, Bob. DJ (WKNX, Saginaw, MI, 1955).

9779 Early, Christmas. COM-HE (WGMA, Hollywood, FL, 1954).

9780 Early, Michele. COM-HE (KVOG, Ogden, UT, 1956).

9781 ***Early American Dance Music.*** Historically correct musical scores were used in the production of the interesting program that presented early American musical selections (30 min., Saturday, 8:00–8:30 P.M., NBC-Blue, 1945).

9782 ***Early Bird Exercises.*** Dr. P.M. Seixas conducted the early morning exercise program (95 min., Monday through Saturday, 6:45–8:00 A.M., KNX, Hollywood, CA, 1928).

9783 ***(The) Early Bird Program.*** Comedian host Simpleton (Simpy) Fits was featured on the morning show (KFRC, San Francisco, CA, 1927). *See* **Simpleton (Simpy) Fits.**

9784 ***(The) Early Birds.*** An early *Breakfast Club*-type variety program (WFAA, Dallas, TX, 1930).

9785 ***(The) Early Birds Club.*** Professor Full-O-Pep led the exercises on the early morning show (WLBN, Little Rock, AR, 1928).

9786 ***(The) Early Bookworm.*** Alexander Woolcott reviewed books on his weekly program (15 min., Saturday, 8:00–8:15 P.M., CBS, 1931).

9787 ***(The) Early History of Little Rock.*** The Albert Pike Hotel sponsored the series of dramatized episodes of local history. The cast included W.T. "Billy" Briggs, Alleene Roberson, Louis Cohen, Mauel F. Shue and Ogden S. Williams (KLRA, Little Rock, AR, 1932).

9788 ***Early Risers Club.*** The Physical Director of the St. Paul, Minnesota, YMCA conducted the early morning setting-up exercise program (KSTP, Minneapolis–St. Paul, MN, 1930).

9789 ***Earn Your Vacation.*** Former vaudevillian Jay C. Flippen conducted the audience participation quiz, a summer replacement for the *Helen Hayes Electric Theatre Show.* Flippen's contestants won vacations as prizes. The announcer was Johnny Jacobs. Steve Allen later replaced Flippen as quizmaster on the show (30 min., Sunday, 9:00–9:30 P.M., CBS, 1949).

9790 ***Earth Born.*** Walter "Hank" Richards wrote and produced the sustaining program that dramatized the problems faced by Cindy Bennett, a city girl who had to make the necessary adjustments when she moved to a rural area after her marriage to Darrell Bennett. The daytime serial told how the couple went to live on Blue Belle Farm. Complications arose when Darrell's childhood sweetheart appeared on the scene. Laura Fraser and Ken Peters played the roles of Cindy and Darrell. Other members of the cast included: Minabelle Abbott, Lon Clark, Wilda Hinkel, Ray Shannon and Virginia Temple (30 min., Sunday, 3:00–3:30 P.M., WLW, Cincinnati, OH, 1940).

9791 Eason, Imogene. COM-HE (WGAI, Elizabeth City, NJ, 1956).

9792 Eason, Lib. COM-HE (WVOT, Wilson, NC, 1956).

9793 East, Fred. Baritone (WRC, Washington, DC, 1925).

9794 East, Grace Adams. Cornetist (KGO, Oakland, CA, 1928).

9795 East, Harry. DJ (*Talk of the Town,* WDAK, Columbus, GA, 1947).

9796 East, Henry. Newscaster (WRBL, Columbus, GA, 1939; WGPC, Albany, GA, 1942; WRBL, 1945). DJ (*Hank's Alarm Clock,* WGBA, Columbus, GA, 1948; *Noontime Frolic,* WLAG, LaGrange, GA, 1952).

9797 East, Len. DJ (*Melody Mill,* KRVN, Lexington, NE, 1949; KIOA, Des Moines, IA, 1954).

9798 East Bay Trio. The instrumental group's members were violinist Florence Scranton; cellist Malcolm Rolls; and pianist Maria Chamblin Himes (KGO, Oakland, CA, 1925).

9799 Eastcott, Elmitt M. Newscaster (WOOD-WASH, Grand Rapids, MI, 1941–1942).

9800 Eastern States Exposition Orchestra. Musical group (WBZ, Boston-Springfield, MA, 1925).

9801 Eastman, Howard. Eastman was the pianist-leader of the Lorraine Trio that broadcast weekly luncheon concerts (KTAB, Oakland, CA, 1926).

9802 Eastman, Mary. Soprano (*Mary Eastman,* vcl. mus. prg., CBS, 1934–1935; NBC, 1935).

9803 Eastman, Morgan L. Conductor (Edison Symphony Orchestra, KYW, Chicago, IL, 1921–1937). The *Edison Symphony Orchestra* program was a popular Chicago feature in the 1920s and 1930s.

9804 Eastman, Robert "Bob." Newscaster (KGBK, Tyler, TX, 1937; WKY, Oklahoma City, OK, 1938–1940).

9805 Eastman Hotel Orchestra. "Smiling Charlie" Fisher directed the hotel band that broadcast frequently in the mid–1920s.

9806 ***(The) Eastman-Kodak Hour.*** Tenor Victor Edwards, bass James Davies, soprano Della Baker and contralto Helen Oelheim sang on the good music program with David Mendoza's orchestra (60 min, Thursday, 9:00–10:00 P.M., CBS, 1930).

9807 Easton, Florence. Metropolitan Opera soprano (WJZ, New York, NY, 1927). Easton appeared on the *Brunswick Hour* (CBS, 1925).

9808 Easton, Sally. COM-HE (WBIS, Bristol, CT, 1951–1954).

9809 ***(The) East-West Shrine Football Game.*** The Shriners sponsored this annual charity football game that probably was first broadcast December 26, 1925 (KPO, San Francisco, CA, 1925).

9810 ***Easy Aces.*** *Easy Aces,* brilliantly written by Goodman Ace, began as a burlesque skit about a husband and wife who teamed together in a bridge game. The show was developed and first broadcast in 1930 on Kansas City radio. The following year it moved to WBBM (Chicago, IL).

By the age of 18, Goodman Ace was already a movie and drama critic on the Kansas City *Post.* One night, while Ace was broadcasting a Hollywood gossip program, the actors in the show that was to follow his failed to appear. To fill the time slot, Ace and his wife, Jane, ad libbed silly talk about a bridge game. The listeners loved it and *Easy Aces* was born. On the program, Goodman Ace and his wife, Jane, portrayed the comic roles of the "dumb" wife and the long-suffering, sarcastic husband. Jane's hilarious malapropism was interspersed with her words of doubtful wisdom. When she agreed with her husband she often would respond, "I'll say the world." The Aces produced some of the finest comedy ever broadcast (15 min., Monday-Wednesday-Friday, 9:00–9:15 P.M., WGN, Chicago, IL, 1932). Later the show was broadcast on NBC and CBS. The program left the air after a long run in 1945. Another version returned in 1948 as *Mr. Ace and Jane. See* ***Mr. Ace and Jane*** *and* **Comediennes.**

9811 Eaton, Amy Marcy. Pianist (WEEI, Boston, MA, 1934).

9812 Eaton, Elsie. Soprano (WIBO, Chicago, IL, 1927).

9813 Eaton, Glen. Tenor (KGA, Spokane, WA, 1929).

9814 Eaton, Gordon. Newscaster (WTFL, Fort Lauderdale, FL, 1939). DJ (*Music Made in the USA,* WCCO, Minneapolis, MN, 1947–1957).

9815 Eaton, Howard. Newscaster (*Between You and Me,* WNAD, Norman, OK, 1947).

9816 Eaton, Jack. DJ (WMC, Memphis, TN, 1957). Sportscaster (*Today in Sports,* WMCT, Memphis, TN, 1960).

9817 Eaton, Joe. Announcer (WOW, Omaha, NE, 1925).

9818 Eaton, Lonnie. Leader (*Lonnie Eaton Orchestra,* instr. mus. prg., WGBI, Scranton, PA, 1937).

9819 Eaton, Richard. Newscaster (WSIX, Nashville, TN, 1942).

9820 Eaton, Richard. Newscaster (WOL, Washington, DC, 1941; WWDC, Washington, DC, 1942–1945; WOOK, Silver Spring, MD, 1947).

9821 Eaton, Tom. Sportscaster (WREB, Holyoke, MA, 1951–1953).

9822 ***Eb and Zeb.*** *Eb and Zeb* was written by John Hasty. The story was about two old residents of Corn Center, the owners and operators of a service station located along the highway where their small town was located. The syndicated rural comedy sketch was a weak and not very funny imitation of *Lum and Abner*. The program was first broadcast on the West Coast by the Don Lee Network. In what was probably its first broadcasts, Harrison Holloway, the manager of station KFRC (San Francisco, CA), was the announcer. Shell Oil Company was the sponsor. The program's performers were not identified (15 min., Tuesday, Wednesday and Friday, 9:15–9:30 P.M., PCT, KFRC, San Francisco, CA, 1932). Later broadcasts probably were by transcription (WTAR, Norfolk, VA, 1935 and WIND, Gary, IN, 1936).

9823 Ebbert, Dick. DJ (*Coffee Club*, KTIP, Porterville, CA, 1949).

9824 Ebbin(s), Milton. Leader (*Milton Ebbin Orchestra*, instr. mus. prg., WBZ-WBZA-NBC, Boston-Springfield, MA, 1934).

9825 Ebbs, Jessie Worth. Soprano (WTIC, Hartford, CT, 1927).

9826 Ebel, Ethel. Soprano (WMCA, New York, NY, 1926).

9827 Ebel, Hana. Pianist (WBZ, Springfield, MA, 1926).

9828 Ebel, Jim. Sportscaster (WILL, Urbana, IL, 1937–1945).

9829 Ebel, Walter. Newscaster (*News and Views*, KWFC, Hot Springs, AK, 1948).

9830 Ebeling, Betty. COM-HE (WCBD, Lubbock, TX, 1954).

9831 Ebeling, Ellie Marion. Soprano (WJZ, New York, NY, 1925).

9832 Ebeling, Rella. Pianist (KVOS, Bellingham, WA, 1928).

9833 Ebell, Hans. Russian pianist (WBZ, Springfield, MA, 1929).

9834 Ebener, Freddie. Leader (*Freddie Ebener Orchestra*, instr. mus. prg., WTAM, Cleveland, OH, 1942).

9835 Eberhardt, (Prof.) Walter C. DJ (WEW, St. Louis, MO, 1957).

9836 Ebersole, Red. Sportscaster (WKOY, Bluefield, WV, 1950).

9837 Ebert, Larry. Sportscaster (WFRV, Green Bay, WI, 1960).

9838 Ebony and Ivory. Unidentified piano duo (KGW, Portland, OR, 1926).

9839 Ebright, Harriette. Soprano (KFWM, Oakland, CA, 1927).

9840 Eby, Rena. Flutist (WEMC, Berrien Springs, MI, 1925).

9841 Eccles, John B. Announcer (WJR, Detroit, MI, 1925).

9842 Echner, Larry. Leader (Larry Echner and the Original Collegiate Serenaders, WGBS, New York, NY, 1927).

9843 *Echoes of Cairo* (aka ***East of Cairo***). Sven and Gene von Hallberg developed and directed the show, as they had done previously with the *Echoes of the Orient* program. The show differed from the former in that it contained a dramatic sketch with interesting musical interludes. Once again the von Hallbergs composed all the music used on the program and also performed it. Arthur Hughes, Tim Frawley, John McGovern, Agnes Moorehead, Harry Neville and Bill Skelly were cast members. The writer was Ray Scudder and the director, Joseph Bell. Neal Enslen was the announcer (30 min., Wednesday, 8:00–8:30 P.M., NBC-Red, 1930). *See* ***Echoes of the Orient***.

9844 *Echoes of New York*. Consolidated Edison Electric Company sponsored the good local variety program hosted by John Reed King. Jane Pickens, Mason Adams, Al Gallodore, the Edisoneers, James Van Dyk, Jeffrey Ryan and Charles Herbert Martin performed on the show. Music was supplied by Josef Bonime's orchestra. George Hicks was the announcer (30 min., Tuesday, 9:00–9:30 P.M., WJZ, New York, NY, 1946).

9845 *Echoes of the Orient*. The intriguing music program was originated, developed and produced by Sven von Hallberg and his brother, Gene. Both performed on the show and composed the music played. The program was first broadcast in 1929 (15 min., Sunday, 6:00–6:15 P.M., NBC-Blue, 1929–1930). *See* ***Echoes of Cairo***.

9846 Echols, Odis. Leader (*Odis Echol's Melody Boys Orchestra*, KFBI, Wichita, KS, 1942).

9847 Echols, Pat. COM-HE (KCLV, Clovis, NM, 1960).

9848 Eckels, Damon. Newscaster (WTSP, St. Petersburg, FL, 1946).

9849 Eckert, Charles. A minor league pitcher with the Little Rock Travelers baseball club, Eckert broadcast on Saturday evenings. He played the harmonica and accordion. Fittingly enough, the first musical number he played on his first broadcast was "Take Me Out to the Ball Game" (KLRA, Little Rock, AR, 1929).

9850 Eckert, Dutch. Leader, (Dutch Eckert Orchestra, WSM, Nashville, TN, 1927).

9851 Eckert, Elise. Pianist (WOR, Newark, NJ, 1932).

9852 Eckert, Ralph. Baritone (KTAB, Oakland, CA, 1925).

9853 Eckhart, George. Leader (George Eckhart Orchestra, KPLA, Los Angeles, CA, 1928).

9854 Eckler, Dora. Cellist (KFWM, Oakland, CA, 1928).

9855 Eckler, Doris. Cellist (KFWM, Oakland, CA, 1928; also cellist in the Aeolian Trio (KFWM, 1929).

9856 Eckles, Damon. DJ (*Junior DJ Club*, WTSP, St. Petersburg, FL, 1947).

9857 Eckles, Pop. DJ (WBGE, Atlanta, GA, 1947).

9858 Ecklund, Victor. Newscaster (WGMB, Honolulu, HI), 1945).

9859 Eckstein, Donna. COM-HE (KTRF, Thief River Falls, MN, 1956).

9860 Eckstine, Charles. Sportscaster (*Sports Today*, WARK, Hagerstown, MD, 1949).

9861 Eclipse Clippers of Melody Lawn. The Eclipse Lawn Mower Company sponsored the ten-man dance orchestra (WOC, Davenport, IA, 1927; WBAP, San Antonio, TX, 1928).

9862 Economides, Constantin. Mandolin soloist (WNYC, New York, NY, 1925).

9863 *Ed and Polly East* (aka ***Ed East and Polly***). Contests, interviews and quizzes were regular features of the couple's audience participation program (45 min., Monday through Friday, 9:00–9:45 A.M., NBC-Red, 1945). The program became *Ladies Be Seated* when Ed and Polly East left the show.

9864 *Ed Fitzgerald*. Fitzgerald, a former World War I fighter pilot, discussed a wide variety of topics and news events. He always inserted his own interesting commentary on each of the many topics he discussed (15 min., Weekly, MBS, 1938).

9865 *Ed Fitzgerald and Company*. Fitzgerald the variety show featuring baritone Walter Ahrens, soprano Grace Perry and popular singer Barbara LaMarr (WOR, Newark, NJ, 1937).

9866 *Ed Sullivan Entertains*. Mennen Shave Cream sponsored newspaper columnist Sullivan, who broadcast show business gossip and conducted interesting celebrity interviews (15 min., Monday, 7:15–7:30 P.M., CBS, 1943). The format on this program was a forerunner Sullivan's highly successful *Toast of the Town* television show of the 1950s and 1960s.

9867 *(The) Ed Sullivan Show*. Broadway columnist Sullivan hosted his program of show business news, gossip and celebrity interviews. In addition, each week entertainment was provided by guest performers. Sullivan's show introduced such future comic stars as Jack Pearl and Jack Benny (30 min., Tuesday, CBS, 1932). Sullivan tried radio again in 1942 with a similar format on his *Ed Sullivan Entertains* show.

Ed Sullivan Entertains was a forerunner of Sullivan's highly successful *The Toast of the Town* television program. Sullivan once compared his radio and television work by saying (New York *Times*, May 11, 1997, p. 43): "I was on the ground floor of radio and dropped out of it like a dope. Now I'm on the ground floor of TV, and I'm not giving up on my lease until my landlord evicts me." *See* ***Ed Sullivan Entertains***.

9868 *Ed Sullivan Show* (aka ***Ed Sullivan***). Columnist Sullivan broadcast show business gossip (15 min., Weekly, NBC-Blue, New York, NY, 1946).

9869 *Ed Wynn's Uncle Taylor Holmes*. Comic Taylor Holmes subbed for Ed Wynn on the variety show that also featured the comic team of Wimp Carlsen and Larry Butler, the Fire Chief Quartet and the Don Voorhees Orchestra. Graham McNamee was the announcer (30 min., Tuesday, 9:30–10:00 P.M., NBC-Red, 1933).

9870 *Eddie and Jimmy*. The male harmony team of Eddie and Jimmy, the singing Dean Brothers, was also known as "The Deans of Harmony" (WGN, Chicago, IL, 1936). Eddie Dean later moved to Hollywood to star as a singing cowboy in many western movies.

9871 *(The) Eddie Cantor Show* (aka ***Time to Smile***). The great banjo-eyed vaudevillian, Eddie Cantor, sang, told jokes and introduced weekly guest stars on his variety program. One featured performer on the early Cantor program was Bert Gordon "the Mad Russian." The manic Russian who first appeared on *The Eddie Cantor Show* in 1935 continued with him for many years. Gordon later was featured with Milton Berle on radio. Gordon's famous greeting was, "How do-o-o you do?" Cantor was instrumental in introducing young talent and giving them national network exposure. For example, Bobbie Breen, Deanna Durbin and Dinah Shore first appeared on the network and became regulars on Cantor's program (30 min., Weekly, CBS & NBC, 1931–1946). Cantor's sponsors on his early shows were Chase and Sanborn coffee and Ipana toothpaste. On a later version of *The Eddie Cantor Show,* sponsored by Philip Morris Cigarettes, Cantor performed DJ duties and shared his entertaining reminiscences of show business. Cantor wrote and directed the show. Archie Scott was the producer (30 min., Sunday, 9:30–10:00 P.M., NBC, 1951). Cantor's last radio program was his *Ask Eddie Cantor,* a five-minute show on which he answered questions sent in by his listeners (5 min., Transcribed, 1961). *See* **Cantor, Eddie.**

9872 ***Eddie Condon Jazz Concert.*** Jazzman Condon hosted the excellent music show. Many famous jazz performers appeared on the entertaining show with Condon. Among many others were: Billy Butterfield, Bobby Hackett, Jonah Jones and Gene Krupa (30 min., Saturday, 1:30–1:00 P.M., NBC-Blue, 1945). Condon also broadcast a transcribed Dixieland jazz show the same year (*Eddie Condon All-Stars,* Transcribed, 1945).

9873 ***Eddie Dowling's Revue.*** Dowling and Ray Dooley were featured on the comedy-music show. Music was supplied by Benny Goodman's orchestra and vocalist Helen Ward (30 min., Tuesday, 9:00–9:30 P.M., NBC-Red, 1936). Another version of the show was *The Eddie Dowling Elgin Revue,* sponsored by the Elgin Watch Company, on which Ray Dooley and Arthur Kay assisted Dowling with comedy routines. Helen Ward and the Goodman band once again provided good swing music (30 min., Thursday, 10:00–10:30 P.M., NBC-Red, 1936).

9874 **Eddie the Wandering Pianist.** Eddie was a pianist not otherwise identified (WEEI, Boston, MA, 1925).

9875 **Eddinfield, Sgt.** Sportscaster (*Army Sports Show,* WJLD, Bessemer, AL, 1948).

9876 **Eddy, Carl.** Leader (*Carl Eddy Orchestra,* instr. mus. prg., WJAS, Pittsburgh, PA, 1935–1936).

9877 **Eddy, Clarence.** Organist (WQJ, Chicago, IL, 1926).

9878 **Eddy, Cliff.** Leader (Cliff Eddy and the La Boheme Cafe Orchestra, KFQZ, Hollywood, CA, 1926).

9879 **Eddy, Elmer Newton.** Newscaster (WESX, Salem, MA, 1941; WMEX, Boston, MA, 1945; WBZ-WBZA, Boston, MA, 1945–1946).

9880 **Eddy, Hope.** Miss Eddy was a "mind reader" who demonstrated her powers on radio (WEEI, Boston, MA, 1926).

9881 **Eddy, Maxine.** Newscaster (KGFF, Shawnee, OK, 1944).

9882 **Eddy, Nemo.** Leader (*Nemo Eddy Orchestra,* instr. mus. prg., WLW, Cincinnati, OH, 1936).

9883 **Eddy, Ralph.** Newscaster (WGN, Chicago, IL, 1941).

9884 ***(The) Eddy Arnold Show.*** Country singing star Arnold hosted his transcribed program originating from Nashville. Singers Marvin Hughes, Joan Hager, the Anita Kerr Vocal Quintet and comedienne Dotty Dillard appeared with Arnold (30 minutes, Monday through Friday, 8:00–8:30 P.M., CBS, 1956).

9885 ***(The) Eddy Duchin Show.*** Handsome maestro Duchin led his band and acted as host on the summer replacement for the *Life of Riley* program. Canadian comedians Johnny Wayne and Frank Shuster also appeared on the variety show. Georgia Day and Samuel Harzenboren were also cast regulars. Hugh May was the announcer (30 min., Saturday, 8:00–8:30 P.M., NBC, 1947). *See* **Eddy Duchin.**

9886 ***(The) Eddy Duchin-Eddy Foy, Jr., Music Hall.*** Duchin hosted and Foy provided the humor on the variety show. Vocalist Milena Miller and the Mills Brothers sang and Russ Cates conducted the music (30 min., Thursday, 9:00–9:30 P.M., NBC, 1947).

9887 **Edelen, Ilva.** COM-HE (WBBZ, Ponca City, OK, 1949).

9888 **Edelson, (Dynamic Dr.) Dave.** Announcer (WJKS, Gary, IN, 1925). Director and announcer of the *Motorist Studio Program* (WSBC, Chicago, IL, 1928).

9889 **Edelson, William.** Bass (WRNY, Richmond Hill, NY, 1925).

9890 **Eden, Hope.** Miss Eden was a "mind reader" who demonstrated her powers on radio (WEEI, Boston, MA, 1926).

9891 **Edes, Arthur F.** Chief announcer and program director (WEEI, Boston, MA, 1927–1928). Edes began his radio career as an announcer in the early 1920s (WBZ, Springfield-Boston, MA, 1924) using the designation of "EFA." He reversed his initials to avoid confusion with another pioneer announcer at the station. Edes became the chief announcer at WEEI (Boston, MA) in 1926, where he later became program director and studio manager.

9892 **Edgar, Bill.** DJ (WBEJ, Elizabethton-Johnson City, TN, 1950; *Hillbilly Hits,* KTRN, Wichita Falls, TX, 1952–1954).

9893 **Edgar, George.** DJ (*Klan Klub,* KLAN, Renton, WA, 1952.) Sportscaster (KLAN, 1955).

9894 ***(The) Edgar Bergen Show.*** Richard Hudnut Company sponsored the comedy show with music. Although the program came at the end of Bergen's radio career, his comedy routines with Charlie McCarthy, Mortimer Snerd and Effie Clinker were still hilarious. Ray Noble's orchestra and weekly guests, such as Dorothy Kirsten, made this a thoroughly entertaining show. Bill Baldwin was the announcer (30 min., Sunday, 8:00–8:30 P.M., CBS, 1952). To the end, Charlie's brash character still showed through with his familiar jibe still heard quite frequently: "I'll murder you. So help me, I'll mow you down." *See* ***Maxwell House Coffee Time.***

9895 **Edge, Bob.** Sportscaster (*Sports Afield with Bob Edge,* ABC, 1954). Edge broadcast hunting and fishing lore.

9896 ***(The) Edgewater Beach Dance Orchestra.*** Instr. mus. prg.(WEAF, New York, NY, 1933).

9897 **Edgewater Beach Hotel Oriole Orchestra.** Popular hotel band (WEBH, Chicago, IL, 1924–1926).

9898 **Edgeworth Male Quartet.** Male vocal group sponsored by Edgeworth Tobacco Company (WRVA, Richmond, VA, 1926).

9899 **Edington, Bob.** DJ (*Redskin Rhapsodies,* KGYW, Vallejo, CA, 1954).

9900 **Edington, John.** DJ (*John's Jockey Journal,* KTFI, Twin Falls, ID, 1948; KLAS, Las Vegas, NV,1956).

9901 **Edison, Guy.** Edison broadcast poetry and prose selections (*Guy Edison,* WCAO, Baltimore, MD, 1936).

9902 **Edison, Harry.** Vibraphonist (NBC, 1928).

9903 **Edison, Joe.** Newscaster (WIBC, Indianapolis, IN, 1945).

9904 **Edison, Thomas.** Edison in the 1920s donated a set of recorded hymns and Bible readings recorded by his company to help fill and improve the broadcast schedule of WJZ (New York, NY).

9905 **Edison Ensemble.** The ensemble was a ten-piece instrumental group that specialized in both classical and semi-classical music (WRNY, New York, NY, 1926).

9906 ***(The) Edison Hour.*** The Edison Electric Orchestra and singer Frank Luther were featured on the weekly program (NBC-Blue, 1929).

9907 ***Edison Phono and Records.*** Early program of recorded music from phonograph and records of J.E. Bumbera, Swiss Valley, PA (KDKA, 1922).

9908 **Edison Recording Orchestra.** Herman Newell led the talented commercial band that was featured on the *Judson Radio Corporation Program* (WABC, New York, NY, 1928).

9909 **Edison String Quartet.** Jack Baus, violinist; Sierra Feigen, cellist; and Sally Menkes, director-pianist were members of the string quartet (WENR, Chicago, IL and WBCN, Chicago, IL, 1928).

9910 **(The) Edison Symphony Orchestra.** A popular Chicago program of the 20s and 30s, the orchestra was conducted by Morgan L. Eastman (KYW, Chicago, IL, 1921–1937).

9911 ***(The) Editor's Desk.*** Nathan Straus, the owner of the station, broadcast his weekly editorial commentary on the program (15 min., Weekly, WMCA, New York, NY, 1955).

9912 **Edkins, Alden.** Bass-baritone (*Alden Edkins,* vcl. mus. prg., NBC, 1933, 1935–1936).

9913 **Edlin, Louis.** Edlin was the conductor of the orchestra on the *Atwater Kent Hour* program (WEAF, New York, NY, 1927).

9914 **Edman, Herbert.** Newscaster (WMAS, Springfield, MA, 1940).

9915 **Edmonds, Bill.** Singer (*Bill Edmonds,* vcl. mus., prg., WOC, Davenport, IA, 1937).

9916 **Edmonds, Bill.** DJ (*Barnyard Jamboree,* WMGM, New York, NY, 1955).

9917 Edmonds, (General) James E. Newscaster (WLW, Cincinnati, OH, 1944).

9918 Edmonson, Neal. Newscaster (KROW, Oakland, CA, 1945). DJ (Edmonson was a popular Seattle DJ on his *KING'S Ballroom,* 120 min., Monday through Friday, 10:00–12:00 noon, KING, Seattle, WA, 1947).

9919 Edmondson, William, Jr. Tenor (WSUI, Iowa City, IA, 1926).

9920 Edmunds, Glenn. Leader (Glenn Edmunds and his Collegians [orchestra], KFI, Los Angeles, CA, 1927).

9921 Edmunds, June. COM-HE (WKGN, Knoxville, TN, 1956).

9922 Edmunds, Mildred. Singer who specialized in college songs (KOA, Denver, CO, 1927).

9923 Edney, Grady. DJ (*Skyland Ballroom,* WLOS, Asheville, NC, 1947).

9924 Edney, Florence. Actress Edney appeared on the *Amanda of Honeymoon Hill* daytime serial.

9925 Edridge, Carlton. Tenor (*Carlton Edridge,* vcl. mus. prg., WKAR, East Lansing, MI, 1942).

9926 Edrington, M. Ann. COM-HE (KOSE, Osceola, AR, 1951).

9927 Edson, Katherine. Soprano (*Katherine Edson,* vcl. mus. prg., WMCA, New York, NY, 1936).

9928 Edward, Erle Emery. Tenor (KVOO, Tulsa, OK, 1928).

9929 Edward, Gene. DJ (*Falstaff Serenade,* WOW, Omaha, NE, 1950).

9930 Edwards, A.F. Newscaster (KWFT, Wichita Falls, TX, 1942; *World Affairs,* KWFT, 1947–1948).

9931 Edwards, Albert. Baritone (WBZ, Boston-Springfield, MA, 1924).

9932 Edwards, Allan. DJ (WRCA, New York, NY, 1954).

9933 Edwards, Bill. Sportscaster (*Sportscast,* KGNC, Amarillo, TX, 1951).

9934 Edwards, Carrie G. Pianist (WEEI, Boston, MA, 1925).

9935 Edwards, Charles. DJ (WMAL, Washington, DC, 1948).

9936 Edwards, Charles D. Sportscaster (*Highlights of Sports,* WBBZ, Ponca City, OK, 1947).

9937 Edwards, Charlotte. Contralto (WIBO, Chicago, IL, 1926).

9938 Edwards, Chuck. DJ (*Recordially Yours,* WIZZ, Streator, IL, 1954; KSET, El Paso, TX, 1957).

9939 Edwards, Clifton. Tenor (KSD, St. Louis, MO, 1925).

9940 Edwards, Curtis. Newscaster (WTCN, Minneapolis, MN, 1945–1946).

9941 Edwards, Dolores. Contralto (WQJ, Chicago, IL,1926).

9942 Edwards, Dorothea. Contralto Dorothea Edwards, the sister of Gus Edwards, appeared o the *Roxy and His Gang* program (NBC, 1929).

9943 Edwards, Douglas. Newscaster (WAGA, Atlanta, GA, 1937; WXYZ, Detroit, MI, 1939; WSB, Atlanta, GA, 1940–1942; CBS, 1942–1947). He was the first anchor man on CBS-TV.

9944 Edwards, Eleanor. COM-HE (WCLI, Corning, NY, 1955).

9945 Edwards, Elsie. Organist (WBZ, Springfield, MA, 1927).

9946 Edwards, Evelyn K. COM-HE (WWGS, Tifton, GA, 1955).

9947 Edwards, Forrest. Sportscaster (KGCU, Mandan, ND, 1939).

9948 Edwards, Frank. Newscaster (WIBC, Indianapolis, IN, 1945–1947; *Edwards' Miniatures* and *Frank Edwards News,* WISH, Indianapolis, IN, 1948; MBS, 1950).

9949 Edwards, (Mrs.) Gloss [Glass]. Conducted a program of interviews with celebrities (WRNY, New York, NY, 1926).

9950 Edwards, Gus C. Leader (Gus Edwards Orchestra, WSWS, Chicago, IL, 1926; WBBM, Chicago, IL, 1927). The Edwards' band included: Rick Adkins and Eddie Copeland, t. and tb.; Joe Falvo, as. and v.; and Cliff Covert, bj. and vcls.

9951 Edwards, Howard. Newscaster (KBWD, Brownwood, TX, 1947). DJ (KONO, San Antonio, TX, 1957).

9952 Edwards, Hulda Helen. Soprano and director of afternoon programs (KOA, Denver, CO, 1926).

9953 Edwards, Jill. Actress Edwards appeared on the *Jill and Judy* dramatic sketch (NBC, 1932).

9954 Edwards, Joan. Singer, (*Joan Edwards, Songs,* vcl. mus. prg., NBC, 1938).

9955 Edwards, John. Newscaster (KFOR-KFAB, Lincoln, NE, 1937; WMAL, Washington, DC and ABC, 1946–1948).

9956 Edwards, Johnny. Singer (*Johnny Edwards,* vcl. mus. prg., WPG, Atlantic City, NJ, 1935).

9957 Edwards, Johnny. DJ (*Chuckwagon Call,* KATL, Houston, TX, 1947; KXYZ, Houston, TX, 1956; KPRC, Houston, TX, 1960). Sportscaster (KTRN, Wichita Falls, TX, 1950).

9958 Edwards, Lyn. COM-HE (WFOM, Marietta, GA, 1954).

9959 Edwards, Mac. Newscaster (WSBA, York, PA, 1945–1946). Sportscaster (WSBA, 1945–1946).

9960 Edwards, Martin. DJ (*Wake Up Baltimore,* WITH, Baltimore, MD, 1952).

9961 Edwards, Mary Lou. COM-HE (WORZ, Orlando, FL, 1954–1955).

9962 Edwards, Merle. DJ (*Caravan,* WMIN, St. Paul, MN, 1954).

9963 Edwards, Patricia Kier. COM-HE (WJDX, Jackson, MS, 1949).

9964 Edwards, Ralph Livingstone. Beginning his radio career as a part-time announcer and actor (KROW, Oakland, CA, 1929), Edwards later became famous for creating radio's *Truth or Consequences* and television's *This Is Your Life.* As a high school junior, Edwards wrote a short play and acted in it when it was broadcast on KROW (Oakland, CA, 1929). As a result, the station manager hired young Edwards as a writer and part-time actor-announcer. *See* ***Truth or Consequences.***

9965 Edwards, Ruby. COM-HE (WHAT, Philadelphia, PA,1951).

9966 Edwards, Sarah. Musical monologues (WOR, Newark, NJ,1925).

9967 Edwards, Stanley. Announcer (KFBU, Laramie, WY, 1927).

9968 Edwards, (Mrs.) V.E. Soprano (WOC, Davenport, IA, 1926).

9969 Edwards, Webley "Web." Sportscaster (KGMB, Honolulu, HI, 1940–1941; *Sports Roundtable,* KPOA, Honolulu, HI, 1951). Newscaster (CBS, 1944). Edwards gained national prominence by hosting his long running *Hawaii Calls* program. *See* ***Hawaii Calls.***

9970 Edswardsen, Bill. DJ (WQBK, Albany, NY, 1950s).

9971 Edwoods, Prince L. Newscaster (WPEN, Philadelphia, PA, 1938).

9972 *(The) Effervescent Trio.* Dr. Miles Laboratory, the maker of Alka-Seltzer, sponsored Tom, Dick and Harry, the popular Chicago singing trio, on the local show (15 min., Tuesday, 7:00–7:15 P.M. ST, WGN, Chicago, IL, 1936). *See* ***Tom, Dick and Harry.***

9973 Egan, Audrey. Actress Egan appeared on the daytime serial programs *Just Plain Bill, We the Abbotts* and *When a Girl Marries.*

9974 Egan, Dorothy. Pianist (WQJ, Chicago, IL, 1925).

9975 Egan, Gail. Sportscaster (*The Sports Desk,* WXEL, Cleveland, OH, 1951–1952).

9976 Egan, Jack. Irish tenor (WSM, Nashville, TN, 1926).

9977 Egan, Leo. Newscaster (WOR, New York, NY, 1944). Sportscaster (WHDH, Boston, MA, 1949; *Leo Egan Sports,* WHDH, 1950; *All About Sports,* WBZ, Boston, MA, 1952–1960).

9978 Egan, Parnell. Sportscaster (*Memory Book of Sports* and *Sports Spotlight,* WCLT, Newark, OH, 1950).

9979 Egenroad, Charles. Newscaster (WSBT, South Bend, IN, 1941).

9980 Eggert, George. DJ (*Dawn Patrol,* WFBG, Altoona, PA, 1949–1954).

9981 Eggert, J.H. Cellist (KSD, St. Louis, MO, 1923).

9982 Eggert, Jimmie. Baritone (WMBB, Chicago, IL, 1926).

9983 Eggleston, Charles. Character and comic actor Eggleston was born on July 16, 1882. After twenty years of working in the theater, he began working on WLW (Cincinnati, OH, 1929). Eggleston in later years played a major role in the long-running dramatic serial *Ma Perkins. See* ***Ma Perkins.***

9984 Eggleston, Ken. Newscaster (KKST, New Castle, PA, 1940).

9985 Eggleston, Kent. Baritone (WCCO, Minneapolis–St. Paul, MN, 1925).

9986 Egner [or Egnor], Nate. Newscaster (WJBL, Decatur, IL, 1936; WJPF, Herrin, IL, 1942). Sportscaster (WLDS, Jacksonville, IL, 1946).

9987 *Egyptian Choral Club.* This vocal group presented a popular weekly music show (30 min., Sunday, 1:00–1:30 P.M., NBC, 1935).

9988 ***Egyptian Room Orchestra.*** Instr. mus. prg. (WBZ-WBZA, Boston-Springfield, MA, 1932).

9989 **Ehlers, Henry.** Baritone Ehlers was billed as "The Crooning Mountaineer" (KFOA, Seattle, WA, 1928–1929).

9990 **Ehmborn, Evelyn.** Harpist (WHT, Deerfield, IL, 1925).

9991 **Ehnert, Al.** Leader (Hot Manitowac Jazzters Orchestra, WOMT, Manitowac, WI, 1929). *Radio Digest* (November, 1930) called Ehnert "The Paul Ash of Manitowac, Wisconsin."

9992 **Ehrenzeller's Concert Orchestra.** New York concert band (WHN, New York, NY, 1924).

9993 **Ehrhart, Harry E.** Announcer, sometimes designated as "HEE" (WDAR, Philadelphia, PA, 1923–1924). Ehrhart also broadcast bedtime stories for children as "Dream Daddy" (WLIT, Philadelphia, PA, 1925–1927). *See* **Dream Daddy**.

9994 **Ehrhart, Riley.** Leader (Riley Ehrhart Orchestra, WDAF, Kansas City, MO, 1924).

9995 **Ehrlich, George.** Sportscaster Ehrlich broadcast play-by-play of the University of Connecticut basketball games (WHAY, New Britain, CT, 1956).

9996 **Ehrman, Robert W.** Newscaster (WRTD, Richmond, VA, 1939).

9997 **"EHS."** Designation for announcer Edward H. Smith who was also director of the WGY Players (WGY, Schenectady, NY, 1923).

9998 **Eichelberger, Clark M.** News commentator (*The UN Is My Beat*, WNBC, 1949). Eichelberger reported on United Nations' activity on his transcribed program.

9999 **Eichler, Fran.** Leader (*Fran Eichler Orchestra*, instr. mus. prg., WJAS, Pittsburgh, PA, 1935–1936).

10000 **Eichler, Lillian.** Miss Eichler broadcast talks on etiquette (WGBS, New York, NY, 1925).

10001 **Eichorn, Anna.** Violinist (WGI, Medford Hillside, MA, 1922).

10002 **Eichorn, Dorothy.** COM-HE (WLAM, Lewiston, ME, 1960).

10003 **Eid, Leaf.** Newscaster (WRC, Washington, DC, and NBC, 1944–1947; WRC, 1948). Norwegian newsman Eid worked on NBC's Washington staff during World War II and broadcast a daily ten-minute newscast from 6:05–6:15 P.M. during that period.

10004 **Eifert. Dorothy.** COM-HE (WHLM, Bloomsburg, PA, 1960).

10005 **Eigen, Jack.** DJ and talk-show host Eigen broadcast his *Meet Me at the Copa* program (WINS, New York, NY, 1947; WMGM, New York, NY, 1948) from the New York night club. It was one of the forerunners of the "talk" show format. His later shows further developed the format (*The Jack Eigen Show*, WMGM, New York, NY, 1949–1950; WMAQ, Chicago, IL, 1956–1957).

10006 **Eight Bright Boys Orchestra.** Local Philadelphia dance band (WCAU, Philadelphia, PA, 1926).

10007 **Eight Saxomaids.** Female novelty orchestra (KFH, Wichita, KS, 1927).

10008 ***Eight Sons of Eli Orchestra.*** Instr. mus. prg. (WNAC, Boston, MA, 1932).

10009 ***1847 Musical Camera.*** Singer Willie Morris and an orchestra conducted by Josef Cherniavsky were featured on the program presenting a musical recreation of an era (NBC, 1936).

10010 **Eiken, Al.** Newscaster (KYA, San Francisco, CA, 1945).

10011 **Eilers, Bill.** DJ (*Saddle Pals*, KEEN, San Jose, CA, 1947).

10012 **Einsig, Percy.** Leader (*Percy Einsig and the Gypsies Orchestra*, instr. mus. prg., WSAN, Allentown, PA, 1939).

10013 **Eiseman, Mort.** Eiseman discussed actors and plays on his *Glimpses Through the Stage Door* program (WHAR, Atlantic City, NJ, 1926).

10014 **Eiseman, Robert.** Newscaster (WSAV, Savannah, GA, 1940).

10015 **Eisen, Rosa.** Pianist (*Rosa Eisen*, instr. mus. prg., NBC, 1935).

10016 **Eisenbeisz, Albert.** Newscaster (KWAT, Watertown, SD, 1945).

10017 **Eisenburg [Eisenbourg], Dok.** Leader (Dok Eisenburg and his Sinfonians [orchestra], WEEI, Boston, MA, 1925; WNAC, Boston, MA, 1928).

10018 **Eisenman, Bob.** Sportscaster (WCOS, Columbia, SC, 1940–1941).

10019 **Eisert, Annabelle.** COM-HE (WHDL, Olean, NY, 1949).

10020 **Eishin, Donna.** Pianist (KFWI, San Francisco, CA, 1926).

10021 **Eisner, Jack.** DJ (WMAS, Springfield, MA, 1955–1956).

10022 **Eix, (Miss) Milton.** Soprano (KGHI, Little Rock, AR, 1929).

10023 **Eken, Ann.** "Girl baritone" (WSBC, Chicago, IL, 1928).

10024 **Ekins, H.R.** Newscaster (WSYR, Syracuse, NY, 1944–1946; *Ekins Views the News*, WKRT, Cortland, NY, 1948).

10025 **Ekolf, Margaret.** Pianist (*Piano Moods*, WROK, Rockford, IL, 1937).

10026 **Ekman, Minnie.** Pianist (KHJ, Los Angeles, CA, 1924).

10027 **El Patio Ballroom Dance Orchestra.** California dance band (KNX, Los Angeles, CA, 1925).

10028 **El Patio Dance Orchestra.** Club dance band (WIP, Philadelphia, PA, 1926).

10029 ***El Sidelo Minstrels.*** Consolidated Cigar Corporation sponsored the program patterned after old time minstrel shows (30 min., Saturday, NBC-Pacific Coast Network, 1941).

10030 ***El Tango Romantico.*** Tangos and other romantic rhythms were featured on the music program (30 min, Thursday, 9:00–9:30 P.M., NBC-Blue, New York, NY, 1929). Soprano Dolores Cassinelli sang with the orchestra under the direction of Frank Vanoni. Martin [Marthin] Provensen was the announcer.

10031 **"ELA."** Designation for announcer E.L. Olds (WBAP, Fort Worth, TX, 1923).

10032 **Elardo, Helen.** COM-HE (KMON, Great Falls, MT, 1956).

10033 **Elder, Don.** Sportscaster (WMAQ, Chicago, IL, 1945–1946; *Sports Final*, WMAQ, 1947–1948).

10034 **Elder, Ruth.** Elder was a member with Georgia Pope and J. Henry Brady of a popular guitar trio (WHAS, Louisville, KY, 1923).

10035 **Eldert, Alan Kent.** DJ (WAIK, Galesburg, IL, 1960).

10036 **Eldon, Polly.** Newscaster (*Local News Round-Up*, WSTP, Salisbury, NC, 1948–1949).

10037 **Eldridge, Florene.** Actress (KHJ, Los Angeles, CA, 1929–1930).

10038 **Eldridge, Roy.** Leader (*Roy Eldridge Orchestra*, instr. mus. prg., NBC, 1934; WBBM, Chicago, IL, 1937; NBC, 1939).

10039 ***Eleanor and Anne Roosevelt.*** The Roosevelts — mother and daughter — discussed current affairs on their morning show (15 min., Monday through Friday, 10:45–11:00 A.M., ABC, 1948). *See the* ***Eleanor Roosevelt*** *program entry.*

10040 ***Eleanor Howe's Homemakers Exchange.*** Miss Howe broadcast homemaking information of interest to her many women listeners (CBS, 1936).

10041 ***Eleanor Roosevelt.*** Mrs. Roosevelt, one of America's most respected First Ladies, was a distinguished magazine and newspaper columnist and UN diplomat, in addition to her extensive broadcasting career. The *Ponds' Program*, sponsored by Ponds' Facial Cream, featured a brief commentary by Mrs. Roosevelt, vocals by Lee Wiley and Leo Reisman's orchestra (NBC, 1932). *It's a Woman's World* (CBS, 1935) gave her an opportunity to discuss at length various problems faced by women. She conducted a discussion of current events alone on her final show (*Eleanor Roosevelt*, 45 min., Monday through Friday, 12:30–1:45 P.M., ABC, 1950), which followed her earlier *Eleanor and Anne Roosevelt* program. *See* ***Eleanor and Anne Roosevelt.***

10042 **Eleazer, J.M.** Newscaster (WFIG, Sumter, SC, 1941).

10043 ***(The) Electric Hour.*** Nelson Eddy and Jeanette MacDonald were the featured singers on the variety show. Music was supplied by Robert Armbruster's orchestra. The program was sponsored by the Electric Companies of America. On the program's special 1945 Christmas Show the featured guests were Walt Disney, Mickey Mouse and Donald Duck. Soprano Anne Jamison and baritone Bob Shanley appeared in a later version of the program (CBS, 1944–1946).

Eddy's rousing baritone and MacDonald's soaring soprano voice blended perfectly. The co-starring of Eddy and MacDonald in a series of MGM musical films brought them lasting fame and great popularity: *Naughty Marietta* (1935); *Rose Marie* (1936); *Maytime* (1937); *The Girl of the Golden West* (1938); *Sweethearts* (1938); *New Moon* (1940); *Bitter Sweet* (1940); and *I Married an Angel* (1942). Miss MacDonald was known as Hollywood's "First Lady of Song." Although happily married to motion picture actor, Gene Raymond, many of her fans mistakenly thought she was married to Eddy, because of the series of romantic pictures in which they appeared together.

10044 ***Electric Park Band.*** Instr. mus. prg. (WMT, Cedar Rapids–Waterloo, IA, 1937).

10045 ***Elementary French Lessons.*** William Doub-Kerr taught French language lessons (WEAF, New York, NY, 1925).

10046 ***(The) 1160 Club.*** Dave Garroway played jazz records and became the idol of many jazz aficionados on his recorded music show. Garroway entered radio as a studio page boy and worked his way up to announcer before finally becoming a successful DJ. With the coming of television, he had a brief, but impressive career there as well. The *1160 Club* program was one of Garroway's peak radio performances (120 min., Monday through Saturday, 12:00–2:00 P.M., WMAQ, Chicago, IL, 1947).

10047 ***(The) 11:30 Clubhouse.*** Chris Schenkel broadcast sports news and interviewed guests on the local New York program. Howard Cosell and Ed Silverman produced the show (30 min., Monday through Friday, 11:30–12:00 midnight, WABC, New York, NY, 1955).

10048 **Elger's Creole Roof Orchestra.** Hot club jazz band (WHAS, Louisville, KY, 1925).

10049 **Elgin, Jack.** Sportscaster (KENT, Shreveport, LA, 1948–1950).

10050 **Elgin, John.** Newscaster (WHBQ, Memphis, TN, 1939).

10051 ***(The) Elgin Football Review.*** Ed Thorgersen hosted the novel sports show. While the Kay Kyser Orchestra played from Chicago, Thorgersen in New York talked about forthcoming football games and interviewed famous coaches (30 min., Saturday, 7:30–8:00 P.M. CST, CBS, 1936).

10052 **Elias, Albert.** Elias was an authority on baseball statistics (WHN, New York, NY, 1924).

10053 **Elias, Bob.** Sportscaster (*Inside Football*, KUTV, Salt Lake City, UT, 1955; *Armchair Quarterback*, KPMC, Bakersfield, CA, 1960).

10054 **Elinor, Caril D.** Leader (Caril Elinor's Circle Theater Concert Orchestra, KNX, Hollywood, CA, 1926).

10055 **Eliot, (Major) George Fielding.** Newscaster (CBS, 1942–1945).

10056 **Elite Orchestra.** Local New York club band (WMCA, New York, NY, 1925).

10057 **(The) Elite Trio.** Violinist-vocalist Louise Sullivan; cornetist Florence Sullivan; and pianist Georgia Booth comprised this trio (KFWB, Hollywood, CA, 1925).

10058 ***Elizabeth Philharmonic Orchestra.*** Instr. mus. prg. (MBS, 1939).

10059 **Elkin, Charles.** Violinist and saxophonist. *See* **The Pasadena Orchestra DeLuxe.**

10060 **Elkins, Eddie.** Leader (Eddie Elkins Orchestra broadcasting from New York City's Club Richman, WGBS, New York, NY, 1924; *Harry Richman Entertainers Program*, WHN, New York, NY, 1925; *Eddie Elkins Orchestra*, instr. mus. prg., WOR, Newark, NJ, 1936).

10061 **Elkins, Frank.** Sportscaster (WHN, New York, NY, 1947).

10062 **Elkins, Hubert.** Drummer (WHAS, Louisville, KY, 1923).

10063 **Elkins, Jeanne.** Actress Elkins appeared on the *Hilltop House* daytime serial program.

10064 **Elkins, Liston.** Sportscaster (WAYX, Waycross, GA, 1939–1941).

10065 **Elkins, Mildred.** COM-HE (KGHF, Pueblo, CO, 1949).

10066 **Elkins, Tom.** DJ (WOC, Davenport, IA, 1957).

10067 **Elks' Band from Dallas Lodge No. 71.** Fraternal [Elks' Lodge] organization band (WFAA, Dallas, TX, 1923).

10068 **Elks' Glee Club of San Francisco.** Fraternal [Elks] vocal group directed by Maynard S. Jones (KPO, San Francisco, CA, 1926).

10069 **Elks' Home Dance Orchestra.** Fraternal [Elks' Lodge] band (WPG, Atlantic City, NJ, 1926).

10070 **Elks' Municipal Band.** Local lodge [Elks] band (KMA, Shennandoah, IA, 1928).

10071 **Elks' Quartet.** Fraternal [Elks] group included Ernest Crosby, 1st tenor; Ross Fargo, 2nd tenor; Charles Thomson, 1st bass; and Walter Harwich, 2nd bass, accompanied by pianist Matt Howard (KGW, Portland, OR, 1924).

10072 **Ellen, Joan.** COM-HE (WOKE, Oak Ridge, TN, 1956).

10073 **Ellen, Kaytee.** COM-HE (KGHF, Pueblo, CO, 1951).

10074 **Ellen, Nanny.** COM-HE (WWNR, Beckley, WV, 1954).

10075 ***Ellen Randolph*** **(aka** ***The Story of Ellen Randolph*****).** Colgate-Palmolive Company sponsored the daytime serial about Ellen Randolph. While traveling in China, Miss Randolph met and married a missionary. When they returned to America, they lived in the home of her wealthy brother. Her trials and tribulations centered about her husband's own feelings of failure and her sister-in-law's allegations that Ellen had an affair with a local resident. The leading roles were originated by Elsie Hitz and John McGovern. Other cast members included: Inge Adams, Fanny May Baldridge, Kathryn Bishop, Milo Boulton, Walter Burke, Macdonald Carey, Ken Daigneau, Helene Dumas, Parker Fennelly, Maurice Franklin, Florida Friebus, Ted Jewett, Jackie Jordan, Bernard Lenrow, John McIntire, Jay Meredith, Effie Ellis Palmer, Robert Regent, Bart Robinson, Edward Trevor, George Wallach, Colleen Ward and Gertrude Warner. Carlo De Angelo was the program's director. Margaret Sangster was the writer (15 min., Monday through Friday, 1:15–1:30 P.M., NBC-Red, 1939).

10076 **Ellen Rose (Dickey).** Ellen Rose Dickey broadcast advice and helpful hints for housewives on *The Homemakers' Hour* (WLS, Chicago, IL, 1926). *See* **Dickey, Ellen Rose.**

10077 **Ellerbrock, Mary.** Pianist on the WLW Trio (WLW, Cincinnati, OH, 1925).

10078 **Ellerman, Carmen.** COM-HE (WZIP, Covington, KY, 1951).

10079 **Ellers, Richard.** Newscaster (KYA, San Francisco, CA, 1939).

10080 ***Ellery Queen.*** Queen, an intellectual master detective, helped his police inspector father solve baffling mysteries on the entertaining mystery series. The program was based on the fictional creation of Frederic Dannay and Michael Bennington. *Ellery Queen* first appeared on CBS in 1939 with a novel idea known as "The Armchair Detective," in which a prominent weekly guest tried to solve the mystery before Ellery Queen announced the solution. When the program returned to air on June 1, 1947, sponsored by Anacin, it was as a summer replacement for the *Bob Burns Show* (30 min., Sunday, 6:30–7:00 P.M., CBS, 1947). No cast credit was given for the role of Ellery Queen, as *Variety* (June 4, 1947, p. 29) explained, "... in an effort to perpetuate the fiction that Ellery is a real character." Despite that, we now know that Queen was played at various times by Hugh Marlowe, Larry Dobkin, Carleton Young and Sidney Smith. The other cast members over the years included: Ted deCorsia, Virginia Gregg, Charlotte Keane, Ed Latimer, Santos Ortega, Marion Shockley, Howard Smith, Bill Smith, Barbara Terrell and Gertrude Warner. The program's directors were Phil Cohen, William P. Rousseau, Robert S. Steele and George Zachary. The producer in 1947 was Don Victor and the announcer was Roger Krupp.

10081 **Ellett, Duane.** CW singer known as the "Masked Cowboy" on the *Iowa Barn Dance Frolic* (KRNT, Des Moines, IA, 1952).

10082 **Ellin, Marvin.** DJ (*Varieties*, WCAO, Baltimore, MD, 1947; *Afternoon Carousel*, WCAO, 1948).

10083 **Ellington, Duke.** Leader (Duke Ellington Orchestra playing from Harlem's Cotton Club and Duke Ellington's Jungle Band, WMCA, New York, NY and CBS, New York, NY, 1928–1929; *Duke Ellington Orchestra*, instr. mus. prg., WTAR, Norfolk, VA, 1935, 1938; NBC, 1936; KFEL, Denver, CO, 1942). Ellington's fine orchestra consistently received good reviews from *Variety.* Like so many other musicians and show business personalities, Ellington tried his hand as a DJ (CBS, MBS, NBC, 1947–1948; WMCA, New York, NY, 1950).

10084 **Ellington (Ellingson), Ed.** Singer Ellington was billed as the "Original Song Bird" (KFAB, Lincoln, NE, 1926).

10085 **Ellington, Jean.** Singer (*Jean Ellington*, vcl. mus. prg., NBC-Blue, 1936; NBC, 1939).

10086 **Ellington, Steve.** DJ (*Ride 'Em Cowboy*, KOAC, Corvallis, OR, 1947).

10087 **Elliot, Tanya.** Pianist (WEVD, New York, NY, 1936).

10088 **Elliott, Baron.** Leader (*Baron Elliott Orchestra*, instr. mus. prg., WJAS, Pittsburgh, PA, 1935, 1937–1938; KDKA, Pittsburgh, PA, 1936; WCAE, Pittsburgh, PA, 1940; WWVA, Wheeling, WV, 1942).

10089 **Elliott, Bea.** COM-HE (WGAW, Gardner, MA, 1960).

10090 **Elliott, Bob.** DJ, *Back Bay Matinee*, WHDH (Boston, MA), 1947. Elliott was a popular Boston DJ on his *Back Bay Matinee* program before he joined Ray Goulding to form the *Bob and Ray* comedy team. *See* ***Bob and Ray*** *and* ***Matinee with Bob and Ray***.

10091 Elliott, Bob. DJ (WTOD, Toledo, OH, 1948).

10092 Elliott, Bob. DJ (*Night Beat*, KENT, Shreveport, LA, 1954–1957).

10093 Elliott [Eliot], Bruce. DJ (*Bruce and Dan Show*, MBS, 1954; MBS, 1955–1956; WOR, New York, NY, 1960).

10094 Elliott, Carroll. Pianist (WKY, Oklahoma City, OK, 1928).

10095 Elliott, Don. DJ (*Mike Fright*, WEAS, Decatur, GA, 1947; WCON, Atlanta, GA, 1950).

10096 Elliott, Doyce. DJ (*Coffee Cup Review*, KXOX, Sweetwater, TX, 1947; *Yours Til Midnight*, KOSA, Odessa, TX, 1952). Sportscaster (*Tonight's Sports Review*, KXOX, 1947; KCRS, Midland, TX, 1951; KOSA, 1955).

10097 Elliott, Evelyn. Contralto (WIBO, Chicago, IL, 1926).

10098 Elliott, Frances. COM-HE (KGNO, Dodge City, KS), 1956).

10099 Elliott, Franklin. Newscaster (KORN, Freemont, NE, 1944).

10100 Elliott, Hazel. Organist (WOC, Davenport, IA, 1928).

10101 Elliott, Irwin. Newscaster (WFBR, Baltimore, MD, 1941–1945).

10102 Elliott, Jay. DJ (*Tommy Dorsey Show*, WBBC, Flint, MI, 1947).

10103 Elliott, Jean. COM-HE (WCUE, Akron, OH, 1956).

10104 Elliott, Jim. Newscaster (WHOM, Jersey City, NJ, 1944; WCOP, Boston, MA, 1945).

10105 Elliott, Larry. Newscaster (*Headlines and Bylines*, CBS, 1938).

10106 Elliott, Martha. COM-HE (WHIR, Danville, KY, 1955).

10107 Elliott, Mary. COM-HE (WKEE, Huntington, WV, 1960).

10108 Elliott, Melvin. Newscaster (WNYC, New York, NY, 1939; WOR, New York, NY, 1946–1948).

10109 Elliott, Pat. COM-HE (WAGF, Dothan, AL, 1951–1955).

10110 Elliott, Perry. Newscaster (WDAK, West Point, GA,1940). Sportscaster (WDAK, 1941). DJ (*Round-Up Time*, WDAK, 1947).

10111 Elliott, Tim. Newscaster (WCPO, Cincinnati, OH, 1941; WKRC, Cincinnati, OH, 1942; *News as it Happens*, WAKR, Akron, OH, 1947–1948).

10112 Elliott, William "Bill." Newscaster (*Bill Elliott Reporting*, WLIZ, Bridgeport, CT, 1948).

10113 Elliott, William. Newscaster (*News and Views*, WCBT, Roanoke Rapids, NC, 1948).

10114 Elliott, Win. Sportscaster (WMGM, New York, NY, 1954; NBC, 1960).

10115 *Elliott Thurston — Washington News.* Thurston broadcast political news and commentary (15 min., Monday, 7:45–8:00 P.M., NBC-Red, 1929).

10116 Ellis, Bill. DJ (WBMD, Baltimore, MD, 1948).

10117 Ellis, Bud. Singer (*Bud Ellis*, vcl. mus. prg., WMBD, Peoria, IL, 1936).

10118 Ellis, Caroline Crockett. Newscaster (KMBC, Kansas City, MO, 1945–1949).

10119 Ellis, Cornelia. Singer (WNYC, New York, NY, 1936).

10120 Ellis, Dorothy. COM-HE (WLOI, LaPorte, IN, 1956).

10121 Ellis, Frank. Leader (Frank Ellis and his St. Francis Orchestra, KGO, Oakland, CA, 1927).

10122 Ellis, Frankie Jo. COM-HE (KOY, Phoenix, AZ, 1954).

10123 Ellis, Judy. COM-HE (WJHO, Opelika, AL, 1956).

10124 Ellis, Lavon. Baritone (*Lavon Ellis*, vcl. mus. prg., WMBD, Peoria, IL, 1936).

10125 Ellis, Lee. DJ (*Breakfast with the Ellises*, WSPR, Springfield, MA, 1948).

10126 Ellis, Lorraine. DJ (*Saturday Night House Party*, WSPR, Springfield, MA, 1950). COM-HE (KFSD, San Diego, CA, 1956).

10127 Ellis, Muriel. Reader (WMSG, New York, NY, 1927; WCBU, New York, NY, 1927).

10128 Ellis, Ruth. Singer (WBRB, Monmouth, NJ, 1941).

10129 Ellis, Seeger. Leader (*Seeger Ellis Orchestra*, instr. mus. prg., WIBX, Utica, NY, 1937; NBC, 1942).

10130 Ellis, Steve. Sportscaster (WMCA, New York, NY, 1944–1945, 1947; boxing blow-by-blow, WHN, New York, NY, 1945; WMCA, 1946–1947; *Giant Jottings*, WMCA, 1948–1951; WFTL, Ft. Lauderdale, FL, 1953; ABC, 1956).

10131 Ellis, Suzy. COM-HE (WCPM, Cumberland, KY, 1955).

10132 Ellis, Ted. Newscaster (WFNC, Fayetteville, NC, 1940).

10133 Ellis, Winona. Ukulele soloist (KFI, Los Angeles, CA, 1928).

10134 Ellison, Bill. Newscaster (*Business Review*, WJBC, Bloomington, IN, 1947). Sportscaster (*Sports Page* and *Great Moments in Sports*, KXO, El Centro, CA, 1949).

10135 Ellsworth, Al. Newscaster (WLAV, Grand Rapids, MI, 1942).

10136 Ellsworth, Bill. Announcer (WIL, St. Louis, MO, 1925).

10137 Ellsworth, Jack. DJ (*Record Review*, WHIM, Providence, RI, 1947; *Memories in Melody*, WALK, Patchogue, NY, 1952–1957).

10138 *Ellsworth Vines, Jr.* Tennis star Vines talked about his sport and how to play it well (15 min., Sunday, 9:30–9:45 P.M., NBC-Red, 1934).

10139 Ellyn, Jean. Actress Ellyn appeared in the *Valiant Lady* daytime serial.

10140 Elman, Evelyn [Eileen Eddleman]. COM-HE (KSTT, Davenport, IA, 1956; KSTT and KTHS, Davenport, IA, 1957).

10141 Elmandt, Robert. Violinist (WJY, New York, NY, 1925).

10142 Elmer, Bob. Sportscaster (WCAU, Philadelphia, PA, 1939; WFTL, Fort Lauderdale, FL, 1940; *Speaking of Sports*, WQAM, Miami, FL, 1940–1941).

10143 *Elmer Everett Yess.* Hal K. Dawson and John Eldredge played the title role on the situation comedy at various times. The sponsor was the Plymouth Car Corporation. The sketches focused mostly on the car business. In fact, there was so much talk about buying and selling cars that *Variety* noted that most of the program seemed like little more than a company promo (15 min., Thursday, 8:00–8:15 P.M., CBS, 1933).

10144 Elmer Orchestra. Popular radio band (WFBH, New York, NY, 1925).

10145 *Elmo Roper.* Roper, a distinguished pollster, broadcast information that he had elicited about the opinions and attitudes of Americans. Robert Denton was the announcer (15 min., Sunday, 3:30–3:45 P.M., NBC, 1952). NBC committed an embarrassing error on the program's premiere by playing the audition tape. The network corrected their goof by playing the correct program later the same night.

10146 Else, Mickey. DJ (KSD, St. Louis, MO, 1957).

10147 Elsie Jean. Not otherwise identified, Elsie Jean conducted her *Elsie Jean's Children's Hour* WJZ, New York, NY, 1922).

10148 *Elsie Lichtenshul.* Miss Lichtenshul conducted interviews on her popular Pittsburgh program (15 min., Weekly, WCAE, Pittsburgh, PA, 1935).

10149 Elsmore, Ralph. Singer (*Ralph Elsmore*, vcl. mus. prg., WCAU, Philadelphia, PA, 1942).

10150 Elsner, Hal. Sportscaster (*Major and Minor Sports*, WWRL, Woodside, NY, 1947).

10151 Elsner, Roy. DJ (*920 Special*, KECK, Odessa, TX, 1947–1952).

10152 Elson, Bob. After working as an announcer (WGN, Chicago, IL, 1925; WAMD, Milwaukee, WI, 1927; KWK, St. Louis, MO, 1928; WGN, 1929), Elson began a long, successful career as a sportscaster and play-by-play baseball announcer (*Bob Elson Sports*, 15 min., Monday, 6:00–6:15 P.M., WGN, 1935; football play-by-play and World Series games, MBS and WGN, 1939–1940; WGN, 1945; WIND, Chicago, IL, 1946; WJJD, 1946–1949; WBKB, Chicago, IL, 1951; WIND, 1954; *Sports Comments*, WCFL, Chicago, IL and NBC, 1960).

10153 Elson, Isabel. Actress Elson appeared in the *Young Dr. Malone* daytime serial program.

10154 Elstner, Anne. Actress Elstner first appeared on radio in 1923 when she performed in an act from *Sun Up,* a Broadway play in which she was then working (WEAF, New York, NY, 1923). In the years that followed, she was a busy radio actress appearing on such programs as *Stella Dallas* and *Brenda Curtis.*

10155 Elston, Bob. Sportscaster (KFVD, Fort Dodge, IA, 1941; 1944; KXEL, Waterloo, IA, 1946–1949; KIOA, Des Moines, IA, 1951; *Elston on Sports*, KIOA, 1952–1953).

10156 Elstun, C.K. DJ (*Carousel*, WZIP, Cincinnati, OH, 1960).

10157 ***Elton Britt and his Pals.*** Yodeler Britt and his country music group appeared on the popular CW music program (15 min., Monday through Friday, 7:00–7:15 P.M. WMCA, New York, NY, 1938).

10158 Elvin, Ralph. Announcer (WKBF, Indianapolis, IN, 1925).

10159 Elwell, Jeva. COM-HE (WLYN, Lynn, MA, 1951).

10160 Elwell, Roy. DJ (KRLA, Los Angeles, CA, 1959).

10161 ***Elwood's German Band.*** Instr. mus. prg. (KFEL, Denver, CO, 1934, 1939).

10162 Ely, Albert. Announcer, staff organist and actor Ely played "Grandpa" on the *Children's Hour* program broadcast by KSTP (Minneapolis–St. Paul, MN), before he moved on to use his many talents on station KGA (Spokane, WA, 1928).

10163 Ely, Hugh. DJ (*The Poor Man's Alarm Clock*, WNVA, Norton, VA, 1950).

10164 Ely, Mollie Chapin. Contralto (WOR, Newark, NJ, 1924).

10165 Elysian Symphony Orchestra. Local symphonic group (KMA, Shenandoah, IA, 1928).

10166 Elysian Trio. The Elysian Trio members were violinist Modesta Mortensen, cellist Elsa Melville and pianist Constance Yates. Vocalist Millicent Benioff often sang with the trio (KTAB, Oakland, CA, 1928).

10167 Ember, George G. Newscaster (*Under the Capitol Dome*, KSEM , Moses Lake, WA, 1948).

10168 Embody, Dick. DJ (*Western Jamboree*, KGGF, Coffeyville, KS, 1948–1954).

10169 Embry, Dink. DJ (*Early Bird Show*, WHOP, Hopkinsville, KY, 1955).

10170 Emerald, Gene. DJ (*The Gene Emerald Show*, KRNT, Des Moines, IA, 1948–1950).

10171 Emerick, Billy. Singer (KOMO, Seattle, WA, 1927).

10172 Emerick [Emerich], Bob. The *Christian Science Monitor* (April 25, 1925, p. 6) identified Emerick in its broadcast schedule as the "radio pianist" (WHN, New York, NY, 1924; WGBS, New York, NY, 1925).

10173 Emerick, Frank. Newscaster (KEVR, Seattle, WA, 1941).

10174 Emerson, E.B. Newscaster (KGIV, Alamosa, CO, 1948).

10175 Emerson, Elsie May. Organist (*Elsie May Emerson*, instr. mus. prg., 13 min., Sunday, 10:45–10:58 A.M., WLS, Chicago, IL, 1937).

10176 Emerson, James. Singer (*James Emerson*, vcl. mus. prg., WLW, Cincinnati, OH, 1936).

10177 Emerson, Jane. Soprano (*Jane Emerson*, vcl. mus. prg., WLW, Cincinnati, OH, 1936).

10178 Emerson, Joe. Baritone (*Joe Emerson*, vcl. mus. prg., WLW, Cincinnati, OH, 1934–1936).

10179 Emerson, Lillian. Pianist (KGHI, Little Rock, AR, 1929).

10180 Emerson, Olive. Soprano (WCCO, Minneapolis–St. Paul, MN, 1925).

10181 Emerson, Ralph Waldo. Organist (WDAP, Chicago, IL, 1924; WLS, Chicago, IL, 1924–1937; *Ralph Emerson*, 15 min., Monday, Wednesday, Thursday and Friday, 10:30–10:45 A.M., WLS, Chicago, IL, 1937).

10182 ***(The) Emerson Effervescent Hour.*** The Emerson Company sponsored the 30-minute variety program broadcast on Sunday evenings (30 min., Sunday P.M., CBS, 1927).

10183 Emery, Claire Robbins "Bob." Announcer Emery, also known as "Uncle Bob" and "Brother Bob," told stories for children (WEEI, Boston, MA, 1925). Emery began his radio career years before playing the ukulele and singing on station WGI (Medford Hillside, MA). When he was asked to be Santa Claus at WGI, he devised a program that was "broadcast" to Santa Claus.

At WEEI, Emery appealed to children of the area by starting his Big Brother Bob club, on which he promoted safety and good manners. His Big Brother Club enrolled 30,000 members. A member's dues was one letter a week, in which they described to him some "Big Brother" act (a good deed or safety action) they performed. Emery's ingenuity in advancing child safety brought WEEI considerable public praise in 1928. Big Brother Emery's popularity caused many young listeners to lose interest in the other "aunts, uncles and brothers" broadcasting at the time.

10184 Emery, Marge. COM-HE (KOPR, Butte, MT, 1949).

10185 Emery, Ralph. DJ (WMAK, Nashville, TN, 1956). Emery's career in Nashville radio provided him an opportunity to exert a major influence on country music. His all-night DJ show on WSM was one of CW music's major showcases and it made him a great national favorite. An innovative DJ, Emery discovered and promoted many CW performers who went on to gain national fame. Emery combined the skills of a journalist with those of an excellent DJ (*Opery Star Spotlight*, 285 min., Monday through Saturday, 10:15–3:00 A.M., WSM, Nashville, TN, 1957–1960).

10186 Emes, Marion. Pianist (KFWM, Oakland, CA, 1928).

10187 ***(The) Emily Kimbrough Show.*** Actress-author Kimbrough interviewed celebrities in the arts, letters, labor and politics on her weekday show (30 min., Monday through Friday, 9:30–10:00 A.M., CBS, 1959). Cornelia Otis Skinner's amusing account of traveling through Europe during the 1920s with Kimbrough was made into the popular 1944 motion picture *Our Hearts Were Young and Gay* starring Diana Lynn as Kimbrough and Gail Russell as Skinner. A sequel, *Our Hearts Were Growing Up*, became a film in 1946.

10188 ***Emily Post.*** Miss Post, a famous expert on etiquette, presided over this quarter-hour program (15 min., Friday, 11:00–11:15 A.M., CBS, 1931).

10189 Emm, Jack. DJ (*Kaffee Klatsch*, WHIO, Dayton, OH, 1952; *Breakfast in Bedlam*, WHIO, 1954–1960).

10190 Emm, Lou. DJ (*Dialing M for Music*, WHIO, Dayton, OH, 1950s).

10191 Emma, Tony. Leader (*Tony Emma Orchestra*, instr. mus. prg., WHK, Cleveland, OH, 1942).

10192 Emmel, Lou. Baritone (KFRC, San Francisco, CA, 1927).

10193 Emmerich, Lee. DJ (*Date with a Disc*, WKOX, Framingham, MA, 1948–1950). Sportscaster (*Tops in Sports*, WKOX, 1947–1950).

10194 Emmet, Christopher. Newscaster (WEVD, New York, NY, 1945–1946).

10195 Emmett, George. Newscaster (KMJ, Fresno, CA, 1941).

10196 Emmet, Katherine. Actress Emmet appeared on such daytime serial programs as *The Romance of Helen Trent*, *Our Gal Sunday* and *Front Page Farrell*.

10197 Emmons, Marion. Violinist (WLS, Chicago, IL, 1926).

10198 Emmy, Cousin (Cynthia May Carver). CW entertainer (WHAS, Louisville, KY, 1935–1937). Platinum blonde Carver was a talented bundle of energy who enjoyed performing her comedy bits, yodeling, eccentric dancing and displaying her musicianship. She was born in Lamb, Kentucky in 1903, and the story is told that she decided to be an entertainer after she heard a radio for the first time in a general store.

She learned music from that she often heard her family members play and sing. As a teenager she joined the Carver Boys, a band formed by her two cousins, Noble and Warner, then playing on WHB (Kansas City, MO). Her first break came with her appearance on WHS, Louisville, KY, from 1935 to 1937. By this time she had developed her Cousin Emmy character for which she is best known. Cousin Emmy mixed eccentric dancing, yodeling and comedy bits with her instrumental music skills. Carver's long successful career included starring appearances on the *Midnight Jamboree* on WWVA (Wheeling, WV); *The Crossroads Follies* on WSB and WAGA in Atlanta, GA; and *The WSB Barn Dance* (WSB, Atlanta, GA). Although Cousin Emmy was never a member of *The Grand Ole Opry*, she was one of country music's genuine pioneers.

10199 ***Emmy and Ezra.*** The "Pennsylvania Dutch" comedy team, not otherwise identified, was a local radio favorite (15 min., Weekly, 12:00–12:15 P.M., WGAL, Lancaster, PA, 1932).

10200 Empey, (Mrs.) Billie. Saxophonist (KTAB, Oakland, CA, 1926).

10201 ***Empire Builders.*** The Great Northern Railroad sponsored this critically acclaimed drama series in 1929. The railroad surprised many when they hired Edward Hale Bierstadt for the sole purpose of writing the dramatic serial about incidents related to the railroad's growth and development. The adventure, thrills and romance of various railroad stories were presented by the Old Timer, played by Harvey Hays. The distinguished cast also included Don Ameche, Edward Hale Bierstadt, Bernardine Flynn, Virginia Gardner, Lucille Husting, Raymond Knight and Bob MacGinsey. During the program's broadcast run from 1929 through 1931, the featured orchestras were led by Andy Sanella and Josef Koestner. Harold Sims was the busy sound effects man. John S. Young and Ted Pearson were the announcers.

Edward Hale Bierstadt, who later produced a series called *Historic Trails*, wrote most of the programs based on real historic incidents. One of the most interesting performers on *Empire Builders* was whistler Bob MacGinsey (30 min., Monday, 10:30–11:00 P.M., NBC-Blue, 1930). An interesting note is that actress Lucille Husting, who also wrote some of the program's scripts, played the role of her own great-grandmother on one program. In 1928–1929, the program was broadcast only by the Midwestern portion of the NBC network. The first story presented on the program was that of James J. Hill, the builder of the Great Northern Railroad.

10202 Empire State Novelty Orchestra. Metropolitan novelty band (WEAF, New York, NY, 1924).

10203 Empress of Scotland Orchestra. Ocean liner's orchestra (WJZ, New York, NY, 1926; KPO, San Francisco, CA, 1927).

10204 *Encore.* Robert Merrill, Marguerite Piazza, the Meredith Willson Orchestra and the Ray Charles Singers performed on the sustaining music program. Ken Banghart was the announcer (30 min., Monday,10:00–10:30 P.M., NBC, 1952).

10205 *(The) Encore Theatre.* Schlendley Laboratories sponsored the series of dramatic stories that told of great advances in medicine and of its skillful practitioners. The program began with the following announcement: "The Schlendley Laboratories, producers of Penicillin — Schendley and Schendley Pharmaceuticals — presents *The Encore Theatre.* Tonight Schendley Laboratories presents another in a new series of great dramatic programs. Some of our stories are fact. The struggles and accomplishments of great men of medicine. Others are fiction — stories of devotion to an ideal, individual heroism or great courage. By these programs, Schendley Laboratories would remind you that medical science and progress is not cold impersonal records or pages of statistics, but a warm human story told in loving terms, whether in the life of medicine's immortals, or the everyday record of service rendered by your own physician. The *Encore* play tonight 'The Life of Louis Pasteur.'" The actors who appeared in the series included: Ronald Colman, Robert Young, Virginia Bruce, Robert Taylor, Charles Bickford, Lionel Barrymore, Ida Lupino, Zachary Scott, Hume Cronyn, George Zucco. Franchot Tone and Susan Peters.

10206 Ender, Chic. Singer of specialty songs (WABC, New York, NY, 1929).

10207 Enderly, Lucille. Contralto (WLS, Chicago, IL, 1925).

10208 *(The) Endicott-Johnson Hour.* Endicott-Johnson Shoe Company sponsored the music program that featured a male quartet and orchestra (30 min., Sunday, CBS, 1930).

10209 *Endorsed by Dorsey.* Tommy Dorsey was the host on his swinging music show that featured his own band, Buddy Moreno, Sy Oliver, the Herman Chittison Trio, the Clark Sisters and Vera Holly. Tiny Ruffner was the announcer (30 min., late-1940s).

10210 Endresen, R.M. Clarinet and saxophone soloist (KEBY, Portland, OR, 1925).

10211 Engel, Bob. Sportscaster (*Sports Capsules*, WHK, Cleveland, OH, 1960).

10212 Engel, Harold A. Engel initiated and directed the *Wisconsin School of the Air*, a program that became the *College of the Air* in 1933. After still another name change, it became the *University of the Air.* The program presented lectures by various professors from the University of Wisconsin (WHA, Madison, WI, 1933).

10213 Engel, J.O. Newscaster (WIBV, Belleville, IL, 1946).

10214 Engel, Luella. Agricultural writer-newscaster (WKBV, Richmond, IN, 1935). Engel began volunteer broadcasting for John Slade on his small station in Richmond, IN. She wrote and broadcast on many topics, not merely rural and farming ones. After doing this for five years in World War II, she also began broadcasting for the Emergency Radio Service. In 1944, she was recognized as the first of the women "farm broadcasters" for her *Voice of Butler County* program broadcast five times a week. She also conducted a *4-H Radio Club* program that included 15 to 20 boys and girls who wrote their own program.

She had become a recognized farm authority by the 1940s. She broadcast on WMLH (Worthington, OH); WRFD (Worthington, OH); and WMOH (Worthington, OH) during the late 1940s and 1950s.

When asked in 1980 about how women could get better status, pay and responsibility in broadcasting, Engel (1980) said: Plan and be completely prepared when you come to get a broadcasting job. "I don't want men to be any less dominant, but I want them to accept me as an equal." In order to achieve this, she said, you must be knowledgeable. In 1945 she got $45 a week while the men were paid $75 for the same job. "I did it in an age when women were not accepted at all, and I just walked in where angels feared to tread."

10215 Engelbach, Dee. Engelbach was the director of the *Rogue's Gallery* and *This is Nora Drake* programs and the producer-director of the *Hallmark Playhouse.*

10216 Engelbrecht, Bettie. COM-HE (WTVK, Knoxville, TN, 1956).

10217 Engelbrecht, Katherine. Contralto (KFI, Los Angeles, CA, 1925).

10218 Engelbretson, John. Sportscaster and play-by-play man Engelbretson broadcast Flathead County High School's football and basketball games (KGEZ, Kalispell, MT, 1958–1960).

10219 Engelhardt, Wally. Sportscaster (KVFD, Fort Dodge, KS, 1949).

10220 Engelhart, Katherine. Contralto (KFI, Los Angeles, CA, 1925).

10221 Enger, Phyllis. Singer (WHN, New York, NY, 1925).

10222 England, Edythe. Violinist (WOK, Chicago, IL, 1925).

10223 England, Gladys G. COM-HE (WSMT, Sparta, TN, 1954).

10224 England, John. Tenor (KPO, San Francisco, CA, 1925).

10225 Engle, Holland. Newscaster (WGN, Chicago, IL, 1942). DJ (*Today's the Day,* 15 min., Monday through Friday, 8:45–9:00 A.M., WGN, Chicago, IL, 1949). Engle was a DJ who conducted a cheerful wake-up program of music, time, temperature and news on a sustaining basis.

10226 Engle, Lura. COM-HE (WLPO, LaSalle, IL, 1951).

10227 Engle, Rita. COM-HE (KIJV, Huron, SD, 1954).

10228 Engle, Roy. Tenor (WLS, Chicago, IL, 1925).

10229 Engle, Thaine. Newscaster (WBAP, Fort Worth, TX and KGKO, Fort Worth, TX, 1946; *What Happened Last Night?*, WBAP, 1947).

10230 Englehart, Joe. Leader (*Joe Englehart Orchestra*, instr. mus. prg., CBS, 1934).

10231 Engler, Bill. Newscaster (WNAD, Norman, OK, 1941).

10232 Engler, Bob. Newscaster (*News of the Hour*, WMIN, St. Paul, MN, 1947).

10233 Engler, Enid. Soprano (WMCA, New York, NY, 1925).

10234 Englert, Ray. Leader (*Ray Englert Orchestra*, instr. mus. prg., WJAS, Pittsburgh, PA, 1935).

10235 English, Al. Newscaster (WAML, Laurel, MS, 1945).

10236 English, Bertha Miller. Pianist (KFI, Los Angeles, CA, 1927).

10237 English, Don. Comedian (KFI, Los Angeles, CA, 1928).

10238 English, Jim "Jimmy." DJ (*Saturday Session,* WKYB, Paducah, KY, 1947). Sportscaster (*Sportlight*, WKYB, 1949).

10239 English, Pat. COM-HE (WSEE, Erie, PA, 1954).

10240 English, Ray. Newscaster (WNBZ, Seranac Lake, NY, 1938).

10241 English, Tom. Sportscaster (*The Tom English Sports Review*, WRLC, Toccoca, GA, 1947).

10242 *English Literature Series.* Hoxie N. Fairchild, Supervisor of Home Studies Courses at Columbia University, offered an interesting perspective on English literature on this series that began July 17, 1923, on WEAF, New York, NY. By the spring of 1924, Fairchild's program was heard on a three station network that consisted of WEAF (New York, NY), WCAP (Washington, DC) and WJAR (Providence, RI).

10243 Enich [Emich], Howard L. Newscaster (*Noon News Edition*, WMAM, Marinette, WI, 1945–1947).

10244 *Enna Jettick Melodies.* Singers Betsy Ayres and Bessie Wynn appeared on the popular music show with a mixed quartet, an instrumental ensemble and orchestra directed by George Dilworth (15 min., Sunday, 8:00–8:15 P.M., NBC-Blue, 1930). Two years earlier the program's orchestra was conducted by

Robert Armbruster. Enna Jennick [shoes] was the sponsor.

10245 Ennis, H. Drummer (Swanee Orchestra, WJZ, New York, NY, 1923).

10246 Ennis, Skinnay. Leader (*Skinnay Ennis Orchestra*, instr. mus. prg., MBS, 1935–1939).

10247 Eno, Jack. DJ (*One for the Money*, WEBR, Buffalo, NY, 1949; *Musical Market Basket*, WEBR, 1952–1954; *Night Patrol*, WEBR, 1960).

10248 *Eno Crime Club* (aka *Crime Club, Crime Clues, Eno Crime Clues*). Eno laxative sponsored the mystery-adventure program written by Albert G. Miller and Stewart Sterling. The cast included: Georgia Backus, Helen Choate, Ray Collins, Spencer Dean, Brian Donlevy, Helene Dumas, Gloria Holden, Jack MacBryde, Elaine Melchoir, Clyde North, Edward Reese, Adele Ronson and Ruth Yorke (15 min, Monday through Friday, CBS and NBC-Blue, 1931–1933). When the program's format changed in 1934, the name became *Eno Crime Club Clues*. Sometimes the show was referred to simply as *Crime Club* or *Crime Clues*. In its new format, a mystery was dramatized the first night and its solution the second (30 min., Monday and Tuesday, 8:00–8:30 P.M., NBC-Blue, 1934). The following year the program was broadcast on Tuesdays and Thursdays at the same time. Edward Reese originated the role of the man hunting detective, Spencer Dean, who solved heinous crimes. (CBS, NBC-Blue, 1931–1936).

10249 Enos, Corinne. COM-HE (KPAC, Port Arthur, TX, 1951).

10250 Enroth, Dick. Sportscaster (WLOL, Minneapolis, MN, 1947–1948; *Morning Slant on Sports*, WLOL, 1949–1951; *Newsports*, WLOL, 1952–1953; WCCO, Minneapolis, MN, 1954–1960).

10251 Ensemble Aeolienne. Marie Hughes Macquarret directed this unusual music group consisting of nine harpists. They appeared on many Pacific Coast stations in 1924.

10252 Ensign, George. Newscaster (KJBS, San Francisco, CA, 1945; KLX, Oakland, CA, 1945).

10253 Ensign, Jean T. COM-HE (WKIS, Orlando, FL, 1957).

10254 Enslen, Neal. Announcer Enslen worked on such NBC programs in 1929 as *The Nomads, The New Yorker Orchestra, Slumber Music, Park Central Hotel Orchestra, Duo Disc Duo, Personalities at 711, At the Baldwin, The Campus Carrollers, Mystery House* and *Songs of the Season*.

10255 Ensley, Harold. Sportscaster (*Fisherman's Friend*, KIMO, Independence, MO, 1952).

10256 Entee, Edith. COM-HE (WKIS-WORZ, Orlando, FL, 1956; WKIS, 1957).

10257 Epinoff, Ivan. Leader (*Ivan Epinoff Orchestra*, instr. mus. prg., WMAQ, Chicago, IL, 1936).

10258 Epley, Malcolm. Newscaster (KFLW, Kiamath Falls, OR, 1946; *Managing Editor's Report*, KFLW, 1947).

10259 Epperson, Grace. Singer Epperson was a member of the National Battery Girls Vocal Trio (KOIL, Council Bluffs, IA, 1929).

10260 Epps, Lew. Newscaster (WORD, Spartanburg, SC, 1940).

10261 Epps, Paul. Leader (Paul Epps Revelers Orchestra, WFBH, New York, NY, 1925).

10262 Epstein, Beinish. Newscaster (WBBC, Brooklyn, NY, 1938).

10263 Epstein, Joe. Sportscaster (WNOX, Knoxville, TN, 1937–1940).

10264 Epstein, Ruth. COM-HE (KSTT, Davenport, IA, 1956).

10265 Equires, Eddie. *Radio Digest* in 1927 called Equires the "Ace announcer of the Southland" (WJAX, Jacksonville, FL, 1927).

10266 *(The) E.R. Squibb Program.* E.R. Squibb, the pharmaceutical company, sponsored this mid–1930s program that combined dramatic sketches of "gripping moments in medical history" with music intervals supplied by the Revelers Quartet and the symphony orchestra of Frank Black. The announcer was Graham McNamee (30 min., Sunday, 4:40–5:00 P.M., NBC-Red, mid–1930s).

10267 Erbstein, Charles. Announcer and owner of Station WTAS (Chicago, IL,1925), Erbstein was sometimes called "The Ha Ha Man."

10268 Erckenbrach, Bernice. Soprano (KVOO, Tulsa, OK, 1928).

10269 Erdman, George H. Newscaster (WOMT, Manitowac, WI, 1946–1948).

10270 Erdmann, Hildegarde. Soprano (*Hildegarde Erdmann*, vcl. mus. prg., NBC-Blue, 1936).

10271 Erdmann, Jake. Sportscaster (*Sports Special*, WRAC, Racine, WI, 1954).

10272 Erdody [Erlody], Leo. Leader (*Leo Erdody Orchestra*, instr. mus. prg., WIP, Philadelphia, PA, 1937–1938).

10273 Erdossy, Bill. Sportscaster (*Sports Extra*, WHP, Harrisburg, PA, 1960).

10274 Erdstrom, Eleanor Olive. Contralto (*Hildegarde Erdstrom*, vcl. mus. prg., NBC, 1936).

10275 Eric, Elspeth. Eric, a busy actress appeared in such daytime serial programs as *Joyce Jordan, Girl Interne, Life and Loves of Dr. Susan, Rosemary, The Second Mrs. Burton, This Is Nora Drake, Valiant Lady, Big Sister, Young Dr. Malone, Ever Since Eve* and *Front Page Farrell*.

10276 Erickson, Carl. Newscaster (WWJ, Detroit, MI, 1942; *Esso Reporter*, WBEN, Buffalo, NY, 1949).

10277 Erickson, Catherine L. COM-HE (WJOC, Jamestown, NY, 1951).

10278 Erickson, Esther. Soprano (WCAL, Northfield, MN, 1924).

10279 Erickson, Gladys Arbeiter. Newscaster (WCLS, Joliet, IL, 1939).

10280 Erickson, R.C. Saxophonist (Swanee Orchestra, WJZ, New York, NY, 1923).

10281 Erickson, Selma. Singer (WCCO, Minneapolis–St. Paul, MN, 1925).

10282 Erickson, Wallie. Leader (Wallie Erickson's Coliseum Orchestra, WCCO, Minneapolis–St. Paul, MI, 1925–28).

10283 Ericson, Bette. COM-HE (WRJM, Newport, RI, 1951).

10284 Erika, Olga. Danish soprano (WGBS, New York, NY, 1925).

10285 Erisman, A.J. "Al." Tenor and program director (WGR, Buffalo, NY, 1924–1926 and WMAK, Buffalo, NY, 1927–1928).

10286 Erisman, Jean Webster. Soprano (WJAX, Cleveland, OH, 1924).

10287 Erk, Christy E. Newscaster (WBRY, Waterbury, CT, 1940–1942, 1944–1947, *Survey of the News*, WBRY, 1948).

10288 Erlandson, Alice. COM-HE (KJRG, Columbus, NE, 1954).

10289 Erlandson, Marian. COM-HE (KXOB, Stockton, CA, 1955).

10290 Erlenback, Lester. Leader (Lester Erlenback's Knights of Columbus Concert Orchestra, WGR, Buffalo, NY, 1926).

10291 Erlman, Dora. Pianist (KGO, Oakland, CA, 1925).

10292 Erlody's Park Lane Orchestra. Restaurant band (WJZ, New York, NY, 1925). This could be the Leo Erdody band previously listed.

10293 Ermete, Ann. Soprano (WOV, New York, NY, 1932).

10294 *Ern Westmore.* Make-up expert Westmore delivered beauty talks for women on his program (15 min., Weekly, WMCA, New York, NY, 1940).

10295 Ernest, Frank. Pianist (WGES, Oak Park, IL, 1925).

10296 Ernest, Ken. Sportscaster (*Sports Today*, WPMP, Pascagoula-Moss Point, MS, 1960).

10297 Ernest, Lois and Joe Ernest. Vocal team (*Lois and Joe Ernest*, vcl. mus. prg., KFBI, (Abilene, KS, 1939).

10298 Ernest, Mildred. COM-HE (KWRL, Riverton, WY, 1949).

10299 *Ernest Tubb's Record Shop.* *See* **Tubb, Ernest** *and* **Singers: Crooners, Song Birds, Country Belles, Cow Girls and Hillbillies.**

10300 Ernie, Little. DJ (*WGAY Story Time*, WGAY, Silver Spring, MD, 1949).

10301 Ernie [Erney], Val. Leader (*Val Ernie Orchestra*, instr. mus. prg., WIP, Philadelphia, PA, 1935; ABS, 1935; WOR, Newark, NJ, 1936).

10302 *(The) Ernie Lee Show.* Lee was the singing host on the CW music program sponsored by the Cole Milling Company. He was joined by Donna Jean, the Trailblazers, Brown's Ferry Four and Doc Wildeson's orchestra. Hank Fisher was the announcer (30 min., Sunday, 4:00–4:30 P.M., WLW, Cincinnati, OH, 1947).

10303 Ernst, Mildred. COM-HE (WRTH, Thermopolis, WY, 1957).

10304 Erp, Johnny. Sportscaster (WMAQ, Chicago, IL, 1960).

10305 Erpenbeck, Beverly. COM-HE (WMUS, Muskegon, MI, 1955).

10306 Errico, Mike. Sportscaster (*Sports Roundup*, WNLK, Norwalk, CT, 1948–1949).

10307 Errol, Leon. Actor-comedian Errol broadcast humorous songs and stories (WENR, Chicago, IL, 1926).

10308 Erskine, Jane. Actress Erskine was a member of the cast of the *Against the Storm* daytime serial.

10309 *Erskine Johnson's Hollywood.* Hollywood columnist Johnson broadcast news and gossip about movies and their stars in several different formats from 1945 to 1949 (15 min., Monday through Friday, 4:00–4:15 P.M., MBS, 1947). Sometimes his programs were broadcast as *Erskine Johnson in Hollywood, Erskine Johnson — Hollywood Reporter* and *Erskine Johnson's Hollywood.* .

10310 Erskine, Kay. COM-HE (KSVP, Artesia, NM, 1954).

10311 Erskine, Marilyn. Versatile actress Erskine appeared on the daytime serials *Lora Lawton, The Romance of Helen Trent* and *Young Widder Brown.*

10312 Erstinn, Gitla. Soprano Erstinn specialized in light opera selections (NBC, 1929).

10313 Ervin, Bill. Sportscaster (*Sports Special*, KARE, Atchison, KS, 1953–1960).

10314 Ervin, C.E. "Shorty." Announcer (WOAI, San Antonio, TX, 1923).

10315 Ervin, Puss. Sportscaster (KCUL, Fort Worth, TX, 1952–1960).

10316 Erwin, George. DJ (KFIZ, Fort Wayne, IN, late 1930s). Erwin was a pioneering DJ morning man.

10317 Erwin, Lew [Louis]. Organist (*Lew Erwin*, instr. mus. prg., WLW, Cincinnati, OH, 1936).

10318 Erwin, McConnell. Blind pianist (WEAF, New York, NY, 1925).

10319 Erwin, Skip. DJ (*Shipper's Showboat*, WMOK, Metropolis, IL, 1951–1952).

10320 Erwin, Tommy. Newscaster (*7:30 Commentary*, KVLF, Alpine, TX, 1947). Sportscaster (*Sports Highlights*, KVLF, 1947; *World of Sports*, KARE, Alexandria, LA, 1954).

10321 Esberger, Walter. Leader (Walter Esberger Concert Orchestra, WLW, Cincinnati, OH, 1923; Walter Esberger Orchestra, WLW, 1929).

10322 Escabedo, Gilbert E. Vocalist (*Gilbert Escabedo the Mexican Troubadour*, WIP, Philadelphia, PA, 1936).

10323 Escagne, Kearney. DJ (*Hayride Jamboree*, KANE, New Iberia, LA, 1949).

10324 *Escape.* This horror-adventure series probably represents the last program of its kind. An extremely fine group of actors performed in the sometimes original, often classic, always exciting stories, written for radio by E. Jack Newman, John Dehner and others. The program was directed by Anthony Ellis and Richard Sanville. The producers and directors were Norman Macdonnell and William N. Robson. Richard Sanville directed some of the programs. Roy Rowan, Paul Frees and William Conrad were the announcers. Among the many fine cast members to appear over the years were: Parley Baer, Anthony Barrett, John Dehner, Ramsey Hill, Jack Kruschen, Charlie Lung, Jeanette Nolan, Alan Reed (Teddy Bergman), Eric Snowden, Ben Wright, Dave Young and Paula Young. Music was supplied by organist Ivan Ditmars and the orchestra conducted by Leith Stevens (CBS, 1947–1954).

10325 *Escape with Me.* Kathi Norris hosted the sustaining series of complete romantic dramas broadcast weekly. Alice Frost, Fran Laferty and Paul McGrath were in the program's cast (30 min., Thursday, 8:00–8:30 P.M., ABC, 1952).

10326 Escobar, Hugo. Senor Escobar taught Spanish language lessons (KFI, Los Angeles, CA, 1929).

10327 *(The) Escorts and Betty.* Vcl. mus. prg. on which the popular male harmony singing team was joined by vocalist Joan Olson replacing Joan Drake, who had received a MGM movie contract. On a later show Betty Winkler replaced Olson (15 min., Weekly, WENR, Chicago, IL and NBC, 1937).

10328 Escudier, R.A. Sportscaster (KVOL, Lafayette, LA, 1939–1941).

10329 Esgate, Leslie. COM-HE (WRAD, Radford, VA, 1951).

10330 Eskin, Sadie. Pianist (WEAF, New York, NY, 1924).

10331 Eskin, Vera. Pianist (*Vera Eskin*, instr. mus. prg., WCBM, Baltimore, MD, 1934–1936).

10332 Eskridge, Neal. DJ (WCBM, Baltimore, MD, late 1950s).

10333 Esmong, Marcile. Soprano (WGY, Schenectady, NY, 1933–1934).

10334 *Especially for You.* Tenor Billy Leech teamed with Faye Parker to sing romantic songs on the weekly sustaining local program (15 min., Sunday, 6:15–6:30 P.M., KDKA, Pittsburgh, PA, 1940).

10335 Esser, Wright. Newscaster (KJR, Seattle, WA, 1942).

10336 Esssers, Hendrik. Violinist (WBAL, Baltimore, MD, 1926).

10337 Esson [Essin], Sonia. Contralto (*Sonia Esson*, vcl. mus. prg., WJZ-NBC-Blue, 1936).

10338 Esterbrook, Winifred. Soprano (KQW, San Jose, CA, 1925).

10339 Esterline, Berne. Newscaster (WMBD, Peoria, IL, 1942). DJ (*Berne's Bandstand*, WMMJ, Peoria, IL, 1947).

10340 Esterly, Helen B. Contralto (KFI, Los Angels, CA, 1923).

10341 Estes, Bernard. Newscaster (*Copydesk*, WINS, New York, NY, 1941).

10342 Estes, Dave. DJ (*The Bestes with Estes*, KWTO, Springfield, MA, 1952–1955).

10343 Estes, Frank. DJ (*Top Fifty on 1150*, WDIX, Orangeburg, SC, 1960).

10344 Estes, Gene. DJ (KONG, Visalia, CA, 1956).

10345 Estess, James. Sportscaster (*Along the Sports Trail*, WAIM, Anderson, SC, 1949; WRHI, Rock Hill, SC, 1950–1951).

10346 Esther, Mary. COM-HE (KDEC, Decorah, IA, 1949).

10347 Estornelle, Virginia. COM-HE (WQBC, Vicksburg, MS, 1956).

10348 Estrella, Blanca. Newscaster (WIOD, Miami, FL, 1942; *Latin American News* [in Spanish], WIOD, 1945–1948).

10349 Etelka, Mrs. Mrs. Etelka spoke on various music appreciation topics (WLW, Cincinnati, OH, 1925–1926).

10350 *(The) Eternal Light.* The Jewish Theological Seminary provided research and some production costs and NBC the air time for this distinguished program that dramatically portrayed incidents from the Bible and Jewish history (Swartz and Reinehr, 1993, p. 318). Begun in 1946, the program was broadcast well into the 1970s. The cast included: Roger DeKoven, Adelaide Klein, Bernard Lenrow, Norman Rose, Alexander Scourby, Edgar Stehli and Morton Wishengrad. Some of the writers were: Virginia Mazer, Joe Mindel and Morton Wishengrad. Anton M. Leader and Frank Papp were the directors.

10351 *(The) Eternal Question.* The Wilbur Coon Players presented religious dramas on the local program (30 min., Weekly, 7:00–7:30 P.M., WHO, Davenport, IA, 1930).

10352 *Ethel and Albert* (aka *The Private Life of Ethel and Albert*) Ethel and Albert Arbuckle lived in Sandy Harbor, another of those average American small towns on the daytime comedy serial. The show's writer, Peg Lynch, played Ethel during the program's entire run. Alan Bunce played her husband, Albert. Although Peg Lynch and Alan Bunce are best remembered in the title roles, Richard Widmark originated the role of Albert. With the exception of Madeleine Pierce in the role of Baby Suzy, Ethel and Albert were usually the show's only characters. Dolph Gobel, Rosa Rio and Lew White provided organ music. The announcers were George Ansbro, Fred Cole, Cy Harrice, Don Lowe, Glenn Riggs and Herb Sheldon (ABC, 1944–1950). In its sixth year (1950), the show changed from a quarter-hour daytime serial to a 30-minute format and an evening time slot. The humor was always warm hearted and low keyed on the pleasant family show.

Interestingly enough, Baby Susy was talked about for two years before her voice was heard. Although Ethel and Albert usually were the show's only characters heard, occasionally there were appearances by Ed Begley, Leon Janney, Raymond Edward Johnson, Don MacLaughlin, Julie Stevens and Paul Whiteman. The program was first broadcast in 1944 on ABC. The directors were Bob Cotton and William Hamilton (ABC, NBC-Blue, 1944–1950).

10353 *Ethel Merman Show.* Great Broadway star Merman was joined by Leon Janney and Allen Drake on her sustaining variety show (30 min., Sunday, 9:30–10:00 P.M., NBC, 1949).

10354 *Etiquette.* Lillian Eichler talked about good manners and how to get them (WGBS, New York, NY, 1925).

10355 *Eton Boys (Male Quartet).* Popular vcl. mus. prg., (15 min., Wednesday, 3:45–4:00 P.M., CBS, 1933). This program was on the network schedule from 1933–1936. A popular CBS quartet, the Eton Boys' members were Charlie and Jack Day, Art Gentry and Earl Smith. Ray Bloch was their pianist and arranger.

10356 Etris, R. W. Announcer (WDBD, Martinsburg, WV, 1924).

10357 Etting, Ruth. Singer (WLS, Chicago, IL, 1925). Before coming to radio, Ruth Etting first gained popularity as a vaudeville and night club singer in the middle 1920s. In addition, she starred in the 21st edition of the "Ziegfeld Follies" and was known as the "Sweetheart of Columbia Records." In the early 1930s and the 1940s, when she made many radio appearances, she was sometimes called "The Shine on Harvest Moon Girl."

10358 Ettinger, Janet. Soprano (KJBS, San Francisco, CA, 1925–1926).

10359 Etzenhouser, Pauline. Pianist (KLDS, Independence, MO, 1926).

10360 Eubank, Mabelle. Organist (KLDS, Independence, MO, 1927).

10361 Eubanks, Bill. DJ (*Dawn Patrol*, WABY, Albany, NY, 1955).

10362 Eubanks, Blair. Newscaster (WCHS, Charleston, WV, 1938). Sportscaster (WCHS, 1939–1940; WTAR, Norfolk, VA, 1941; WTAR, 1945–1946; *Coca-Cola Sports Revue*, WTAR, 1947–1951; *Sports Revue*, WTAR, 1952–1955).

10363 Eubanks, Bob. DJ (*North's Melody Inn*, KORE, Eugene, OR, 1947; KRLA, Los Angeles, CA, 1959).

10364 Eubanks, George. Sportscaster (WRGA, Rome, GA, 1945). DJ (WEAT, Lake Worth, FL, 1948; WETZ, New Martinsville, WV, 1955).

10365 Eubanks, Lani. COM-HE (WETZ, New Martinsville, WV, 1957).

10366 Eubanks, Pat. COM-HE (KLOU, Lake Charles, LA, 1949).

10367 Eubanks, Velma. COM-HE (WMUU, Greenville, SC, 1956–1957).

10368 Euchell, Lela. Coantralto (WEMC, Berrien Springs, MI, 1925).

10369 Eugene, Les. DJ (KTFS, Texarkana, TX, 1946).

10370 *Eugene Ormany Presents.* Musical program (WBZ, Boston, MA, 1931).

10371 Eugene's Singing Orchestra. Novelty music group (WEEI, Boston, MA, 1926).

10372 Eureka Vacuum Cleaners Male Quartet. Male vocal group including 1st tenor Edwin Draper; 2nd tenor George Jones; baritone Robert Baxter Todd; and bass Richard Lundgren (KPO, San Francisco, CA, 1925).

10373 Eustis, Elizabeth. Actress Eustis appeared on the *Amanda of Honeymoon Hill* daytime serial.

10374 Euwer, Anthony. Leader (Anthony Euwer and his Golden Hour Orchestra (WABC, 1929).

10375 Evan, Evan E. Sportscaster (*Sports of All*, WWRJ, White River Junction, VT, 1960).

10376 *Evangeline Adams.* Astrologer Evangeline Adams was said to been one of America's most successful radio astologers. Her 1931 program, for example, was said to have produced more mail than any other show on the air at that time. David Ross was the program's announcer (CBS, 1931). If her listeners sent in a Forhan's toothpaste box top, their birth date and a letter describing their personal problems, astrologer Adams would then provide them with advice to help them solve all their problems.

10377 Evans, Alan. DJ (*Heavens It's Evans*, WHOK, Lancaster, OH, 1952). Sportscaster (WHOK, 1952).

10378 Evans, Alfred. Saxophonist on the *Wrigley Review* program (WJZ, New York, NY, 1928).

10379 Evans, Beth. Soprano (*Beth Evans*, vcl. mus. prg., WPG, Atlantic City, NJ, 1935–1936).

10380 Evans, Bill. DJ (WGN, Chicago, IL, 1947; *Record Reveille*, 1948–1951; *The Bill Evans Show*, WGN, 1952).

10381 Evans, Bill. DJ (WCFL, Chicago, IL, 1948–1949; *Wax and Needle Club*, WCFL, 1950).

10382 Evans, Bob. Newscaster (KXRO, Aberdeen, WA, 1938; WTOP, Washington, DC, 1945).

10383 Evans, Bob. Sportscaster (WKAT, Miami Beach, FL, 1952–1955).

10384 Evans, Carlisle. Leader (Carlisle Evans Orchestra, WMAQ, 1923).

10385 Evans, Cecile. Actress Evans was a member of *The Goldbergs* cast.

10386 Evans, Charles M. Newscaster (WTSP, St. Petersburg, FL, 1941).

10387 Evans, Charlie "Chick." Newscaster (WCSH, Portland, ME, 1922).

10388 Evans, Christine. COM-HE (WHDH, Boston, MA, 1949–1956).

10389 Evans, Clifford "Cliff." Newscaster (WLIB, Brooklyn, NY, 1942–1945).

10390 Evans, Claude. DJ (*Rural Rhythm*, KSWM, Joplin, MO, 1950).

10391 Evans, Don. Newscaster (WIBA, Madison, WI, 1945).

10392 Evans, Eddie. Newscaster (KWFT, Wichita Falls, TX, 1939).

10393 Evans, Elizabeth. Soprano (WJZ, New York, NY, 1922).

10394 Evans, Evan. Baritone (*Evan Evans*, vcl. mus. prg., CBS, 1934).

10395 Evans, Flem. Newscaster (WCHS, Charleston, WV, 1938–1939).

10396 Evans, Franklin. Newscaster (WDNC, Durham, NC, 1941). Sportscaster (KPO, San Francisco, CA, 1945).

10397 Evans, G.W. Announcer (WGH, Newport News, VA, 1925).

10398 Evans, Gregory. DJ (*Putting on Airs*, WFAU, Augusta, ME, 1955).

10399 Evans, J.E. "Jeff." DJ (*Musical Clock*, WLDY, Ladysmith, WI, 01949–1950). Sportscaster (WLDY, 1950–1952).

10400 Evans, Jan. COM-HE (WOHP, Bellefontaine, OH, 1954).

10401 Evans, Jimmy. Sportscaster (*Sports Resume*, WIND, Gary, IN, 1935).

10402 Evans, Joan. COM-HE (WIBC, Indianapolis, IN, 1956–1957).

10403 Evans, Joe. Newscaster (*Washington Correspondent*, WGNS, Murfeesboro, TN, 1948).

10404 Evans, Joe William. Newscaster (KFRU, Columbia, MO and KWTO-KGBX, Springfield, MO, 1937–1938).

10405 Evans, John W. DJ (*Johnny Calling*, WIS, Columbia, SC, 1952–1956).

10406 Evans, Jones. Newscaster (WBAX, Wilkes-Barre, PA, 1945–1946). Sportscaster (WBAX, 1945–1949; *Top of the Sports*, WHWL, Nanticoke, PA, 1949; *Top of the Sports News*, WBAX, 1950–1960).

10407 Evans, Joseph. Newscaster (CBS, 1947).

10408 Evans, Josephine. Soprano (WJY, Hoboken, NJ, 1924).

10409 Evans, Julie. COM-HE (WRUN, Utica, NY, 1949).

10410 Evans, Ken. Newscaster (WOIC, Washington, DC, 1948).

10411 Evans, L. Paul [Powell]. Evans directed the *Opera Night in the Studio* program (WPG, Alantic City, NJ, 1925).

10412 Evans, (Mrs.) Laureen English. Violinist (WHAS, Louisville, KY, 1923).

10413 Evans, LeRoy. Pianist (WBAL, Baltimore, MD, 1928).

10414 Evans, Lloyd. Newscaster (KIUL, Garden City, KS, 1942).

10415 Evans, Marjorie. Soprano (KFKU, Lawrence, KS, 1926).

10416 Evans, Mark. DJ (*Sunrise Salute*, WTOP, Washington, DC, 1948–1951; *The Housewives Protective League*, WTOP, 1952).

10417 Evans, Mary. COM-HE (WKIP, Poughkeepsie, NY, 1949).

10418 Evans, Mel. Sportscaster (*KLUB Sports Corner*, KLUB, Salt Lake City, UT, 1960).

10419 Evans, Mike. Newscaster (WSAI, Cincinnati, OH, 1946).

10420 Evans, Mildred. Soprano (WMBB, Homewood, IL and WOK, Chicago, IL, 1928).

10421 Evans, Milton. Sportscaster (*Pigskin Prevue*, KNET, Palestine, TX, 1954).

10422 Evans, Paul. Leader (Paul Evans' Orchestra, WDAF, Kansas City, MO, 1926).

10423 Evans, Robbie. COM-HE (WKBJ, Milan, TN, 1956–1957).

10424 Evans, Robert B. Newscaster (WBZ-WBZA, Boston-Springfield, MA, 1939; CBS, 1944–1945). Sportscaster (WBZ-WBZA, 1939; WSPD, Toledo, OH, 1948–1950).

10425 Evans, Sally. COM-HE (WMT, Cedar Rapids, IA, 1956).

10426 Evans, Shirl. Newscaster (WDZ, Tuscola, IL, 1946; *Kenny the Kirby Man*, WXLW, Indianapolis, IN, 1948).

10427 Evans, Tommy. Tenor (WJR, Detroit, MI, 1928).

10428 Evans, V.G. Newscaster (KALB, Alexandria, LA, 1937).

10429 Evans, Virgil. Newscaster (WCOA, Pensacola, FL, 1939–1941; WDLP, Panama City, FL, 1942).

10430 Evans, Wick. Newscaster (KMOX, St. Louis, MO, 1945; WTMV, East St. Louis, MO, 1946; *Good News*, KXLW, St. Louis, MO, 1947).

10431 Evans, Wilbur. Baritone Evans frequently appeared on the *Atwater Kent Hour* (NBC, 1927–1928 and 1931–1932).

10432 Evanson, Edith. Actress Evanson appeared on the *Myrt and Marge* program.

10433 Evarts, Marta. Leader (Marta Evarts Orchestra, KFI, Los Angeles, CA, 1926).

10434 Evelyn, Gertrude. Soprano (WEAF, New York, NY, 1924).

10435 Evelyn, Judith. Actress Evelyn appeared on the *Helpmate* program.

10436 *Evelyn and the Hilltoppers.* A popular early morning CW music program (15 min., Monday through Friday, 6:15–6:30 A.M. CST, WLS, Chicago, IL, 1937).

10437 *Evelyn Winters* (aka *The Strange Romance of Evelyn Winters*). Frank and Anne Hummert produced the daytime serial. Toni Darnay played the heroine who was faced by romantic problems. Evelyn's strange romance was her attraction for her playwright guardian, 15 years her senior, with whom she lived. Although courted by other suitors, her so-called "strange" yearnings for her guardian persisted. Members of the program's cast included: Ralph Bell, Martin Blaine, Flora Campbell, Linda Carlon-Reid, Helen Claire, Stacy Harris, Vinton Hayworth, James Lipton, Mary Mason, Kate McComb, John Moore and Karl Weber. Larry Elliott was the announcer and H.L. Algyir and Peggy Blake the writers. The program was directed by Ernest Ricca (15 min., Monday-through-Friday, 1944–1948, CBS).

10438 *(The) Evening Concert.* The Pacific Gas and Electric Company in association with its advertising agency, McCann-Erickson, and station KYA presented the two-hour program of transcribed music each evening. The recorded selections included orchestral, instrumental, solo and choral vocal music. It was estimated that in the first two years on the air the program had presented approximately 5,000 musical selections (KYA, San Francisco, CA, 1941–1942).

10439 *Evening Echoes.* *Evening Echoes* was a good music program that presented soprano Betty Cooke, violinist Charles Riley and the KDKA Salon Orchestra conducted by Aneurin Bodycombe on a sustaining basis (30 min., Wednesday, 9:00–9:30 P.M., KDKA, Pittsburgh, PA, 1940).

10440 *(An) Evening Entertainment.* The early variety program combined music, comedy and poetry. Organist Ralph Waldo Emerson, the comedy singing team of Ford and Glenn and the Isham Jones Orchestra supplied the music, and Tony Wons read poetry and prose selections (WLS, Chicago, IL, 1924).

10441 *Evening Herald Radiolians Dance Orchestra.* Commercially sponsored band (KFI, Los Angeles, CA, 1925).

10442 *Evening in Paris.* Bourjois Perfume Company sponsored the variety show that combined music and a dramatic sketch with fashion news from Paris. Pierre Brugnon hosted the program and added his pleasant tenor voice to the musical accompaniment of an orchestra directed by Max Smolen. Soprano Irma DeBraun sang and played the role of "Peaches" in the dramatic sketches (30 min., Monday, 9:30–10:00 P.M., CBS, 1930–1932). Earlier (1928–1929) the format was similar, but tenor Frank Parker and actress Agnes Moorehead starred. In a 1933 version that featured soprano Mary McCoy and Nat Shilkret's orchestra, each program was in the form of a miniature musical comedy (30 min., Monday P.M., CBS, 1933). A later format featured Milton Watson, the Pickens Sisters, musical comedy star Odette Hyrtil (or Myrtil), Claire Majette, Katherine Carrington and Mark Warnow's Orchestra (30 min., Monday, 8:30–9:00 P.M., NBC-Blue, 1934–1935). Tenor Morton Downey replaced Milton Watson the following year and the program's time slot was changed (30 min., Monday, 7:30–8:00 P.M., NBC-Blue, 1936).

10443 *Evening Musicale.* Soprano Marguerite Roas and organist Uda Waldrop performed on the fine music program (KPO, San Francisco, CA, 1929).

10444 *Evening Stars.* Contralto Paula Heminghaus and baritone Theodore Webb were featured on the network music show (NBC-Red Network, 1929).

10445 *Evenings with Papa Haydn.* The four-program music series featured an actor with a German accent taking the part of composer Haydn, who answered questions asked of him by the program's announcer. Musical examples were played when appropriate. The last program of the series included a performance of Haydn's F-Sharp Minor Symphony, No. 45. It was introduced this way: "Yes, Papa Hayden, the symphony we're going to play this evening was written at Esterhaz. The one in F Sharp Minor, No. 45. It dates from 1772."

Haydn responded: "Yes, yes, I remember—the 'Farewell Symphony.' I had some fun with that one too. The Prince had decided to stay at Esterhaz for two more months before moving to Vienna for the winter. My poor musicians were frantic. They were tired of staying out in the country and wanted to go home to their wives and children. I was at that time young and lively, and consequently not any better off than the others. They all came to me in despair, and of course I sympathized with them in full. They even thought of presenting a petition to the Prince." The announcer then interrupted by saying: "What could *you* do, Papa Haydn?"

Haydn responded by saying: "Well, I am sure that the Prince knew of our disappointment, so I decided to give him a hint with my music. That's how I came to write the 'Farewell Symphony.' We played it at our next concert. Right in the midst of the music, one player snuffed out his candle, folded up his score and silently walked out. Soon another instrument ceased, and the player walked off the stage. Then a third and a fourth—all snuffing out the candles on their music stands and taking their instruments away. The Prince and his guests just sat still in silent wonder. Finally, everyone was gone but Tomasini, the first violinist. I got up myself and went out. With that even Tomasini folded up his music and followed me away." The program humanized Haydn and displayed both his good humor and the genius of his music (CBS, 1933).

10446 *Ever Since Eve.* Keith Morrison narrated the stories of love and romance dramatized Monday through Friday. Each story was completed in a week. An idea of how love was treated on the show can be understood by the manner in which one story was introduced: "Pat was in love with Brad, and when a woman's in love, she'll do anything." The cast included Elspeth Eric, Leon Janney, John Larkin and Vicki Vola. Bette Ripley was the writer and Dick Hines the show's producer (15 min., Monday through Friday, 11:40–11:55 A.M., ABC, 1954).

10447 Eveready Chamber Orchestra. Max Jacobs conducted the orchestra featured on the distinguished *Eveready Hour* program (WEAF, New York, NY, 1923–1931).

10448 *(The) Eveready Hour.* This was unquestionably radio's first super program. Since its first broadcast December 4, 1923, on WEAF (New York, NY) *The Eveready Hour* entertained, thrilled and informed its audience each week. The first program included a concert orchestra, jazz band and a one-act play starring Gene Lockhart, Lawrence Grattan and Eva Taylor (Buxton and Owen, 1973, p. 79).

Sponsored by the National Carbon Company, the manufacturers of Eveready batteries, the *Eveready Hour* was a spectacular variety program. Its typical opening was: "Tuesday evening means the Eveready Hour, for it is on this day that the National Carbon Company, makers of Eveready flashlight and radio batteries, engages the facilities of these fourteen radio stations. Tonight, the sponsors have included on the program Elsie Janis, who will present hits and bits of former years and guest, Arthur N. Young, who will talk of his experiences while hunting wild animals in Alaska and Africa with bow and arrow." The *Eveready Hour* contained elements from minstrel shows, comedy, drama, classical music, informative lectures, opera and jazz. Stars from Broadway dramas, musical comedies and the Metropolitan Opera were frequently the program's guest entertainers, as were other interesting and well-known personalities of the time.

Guests on the program could be paid as much as $1,000 for a single performance, a large sum at that time. Guest performers on the program included Will Rogers, Ed Wynn, Wendell Hall, Arthur Argiewicz, Van and Schenk, Weber and Fields, Moran and Mack and the Hall-Johnson Singers among many others. Music was provided by the Eveready Chamber Orchestra conducted by Max Jacobs and the Eveready Orchestra conducted by Nathaniel "Nat" Shilkret (WEAF-NBC-Red, 1923–1931). The program premiered on WEAF (New York, NY) on December 4, 1923.

10449 Eveready Mixed Quartet. Soprano Ethel Wakefield, contralto Mary Groom, tenor Gwynfi Jones and baritone Harold Dana comprised this vocal group (NBC, 1928).

10450 Eveready Orchestra. Nathaniel (Nat) Shilkret conducted the orchestra on the *Eveready Hour (* NBC, 1923–1931).

10451 Eveready Salon Orchestra. Max Dolin conducted the orchestra on this program of light classical music broadcast over the NBC-Pacific Coast network (30 min., Tuesday, 8:00–8:30 P.M., 1929).

10452 Everett, Cecil Dunavant. Singer (WFAA, Dallas, TX, 1926).

10453 Everett, Ethel. Busy actress Everett appeared on the daytime serial programs *Hilltop House, The O'Neills, Road of Life, Stella Dal-*

las, We Love and Learn, We the Abbotts, Young Dr. Malone, By Kathleen Norris and *David Harum.*

10454 ***Everett Marshall's Broadway.*** Marshall broadcast theatrical news and gossip (CBS, 1934).

10455 ***Everett Marshall's Varieties.*** American Home Products sponsored the interesting variety show hosted by baritone Everett Marshall. In addition to Marshall, contralto Elizabeth Lennox, a blackface comedian-singer and the Ohman-Arden orchestra performed (30 min., Wednesday, 8:30–9:00 P.M., CBS, 1934).

10456 **Everglades Orchestra.** Music group (WHN, New York, NY, 1926).

10457 **Everhart, Billie.** COM-HE (WSAT, Salisbury, NC, 1956).

10458 **Evering, Margaret.** Contralto (*Margaret Evering,* vcl. mus. prg., WCAO, Baltimore, MD, 1936).

10459 **Everinghorn, Ann.** Seven-year-old pianist (KGO, Oakland, CA, 1926)

10460 **Everit, Janice.** COM-HE (WBRN, Big Rapids, MI, 1954).

10461 ***(The) Eversharp Penmen.*** Eversharp Pens sponsored the network music program (30 min, Friday, 8:30–9:00 P.M., CBS, 1929).

10462 **Eversole, T. Jack.** COM-HE (WKCT, Bowling Green, KY, 1954).

10463 **Everson, Bob.** Sportscaster (KGKO-WBAP, Ft. Worth, TX, 1946).

10464 **Everson, Chris.** DJ (*Solid Senders,* WMOX, Meriden, MS, 1947–1950; *Red, Hot and Blue,* WCBI, Columbus, MS, 1952; *Wake Up Time,* WCBI, 1954).

10465 ***Every Day Speech.*** Professor Mayne conducted his self-improvement program designed to assist listeners improve their speech (WAHG, New York, NY, 1925).

10466 ***Everybody Wins.*** Phil Baker conducted the audience participation quiz program. The announcer was Ken Roberts (30 min., Friday, 10:00–10:30 P.M., CBS, 1948).

10467 ***Everybody's Hour.*** One of Chicago's favorite Sunday morning programs, *Everybody's Hour* was hosted by Don Chisholm, known on the program only as Don C. It contained several segments, including music by the Hilltoppers vocal group, organist John Brown, singer Tommy Tanner and the WLS Orchestra. Other segments included the host's discussion of "oddities," ten minutes of news delivered by George Harris, a children's song feature, interviews about hobbies, an almanac of anniversaries and historical events and interviews with prominent men and women (60 min., Sunday, 8:30–9:30 A.M. CST, WLS, Chicago, IL, 1935). The following year John Baker replaced Chisholm as host and organist Ralph Waldo Emerson replaced John Brown. Singer Glen Welty was added to the regular cast. The length and time slot was also changed (30 min., Sunday, 7:30–8:00 A.M. CST, WLS, Chicago, IL, 1936).

The format and cast underwent still more changes in 1937. Host Baker presented new ideas and new inventions, and each week an inventor appeared to discuss his invention. New cast members included organist Elsie Mae Emerson, wife of WLS staff organist Ralph Waldo Emerson; announcer Herb Morrison, later to become famous for his recorded broadcast of the Hindenburg dirigible disaster; baritone Ray Anderson; veteran singer Grace Wilson, the Lawson WMCA Glee Club and the WLS Orchestra conducted by Herman Felber. Finally, 72-year-old Aunt Em Lanning was also added. Aunt Em started her radio career late in life in the mid–1930s. She read her own original stories and poems on station WROK (Rockford, IL), while appearing as the Grandmother on *Uncle Jerry's Story Hour* broadcast by a Grand Rapids, MI, station. She joined WLS as a member of the *Everybody's Hour* cast in 1937 to read her original poetry.

10468 ***Everybody's Night.*** Both amateurs and professionals were featured on this variety show (180 min., Weekly, 9:00–12:00 midnight, KFON, Long Beach, CA, 1927).

10469 ***Everyman's Theater.*** Some of Hollywood's biggest stars appeared on the series written, produced and directed by Arch Oboler. Sponsored by Oxydol Soap Powder, the program presented a series of dramatic productions, some of which were Oboler's originals. Some of the guest stars who appeared on the program were: Alla Nazimova, Joan Crawford, Ronald Colman, Walter Huston, Mary Astor, Charles Laughton, Elsa Lanchester, Bette Davis, Marlene Dietrich, Raymond Massey, Katherine Hepburn and Boris Karloff. Cast regulars were Betty Caine, Raymond Edward Johnson, Bill Lipton, Gilbert Mack, Ann Shepherd (Sheindel Kalish) and Martin Gabel. Some adaptations broadcast were: *Ivory Tower, Baby, Lust for Life, None But the Lonely Heart, The Laughing Man, The Ugliest Man in the World, A Drink of Water, The Battle Never Ends, Cat Wife, Mr. and Mrs. Chump, I'll Tell My Husband, The Flying Yorkshireman, Of Human Bondage* and *Madame Affamee* (NBC, 1940–1941).

10470 ***Everything for the Boys.*** Ronald Colman hosted the program dedicated to the entertainment of men in service. The show presented such guest stars as Janet Blair, Greer Garson, Dennis Day, Bob Burns, Ginger Rogers, Bette Davis, Anne Baxter, Ida Lupino, Ella Logan, Barbara Stanwyck and Ingrid Bergman (30 min., Weekly, NBC, 1944).

10471 ***Everything Goes.*** Singer Georgia Gibbs (Fredda Gibson) was featured on the music show (15 min., Saturday, 9:00–9:15 A.M., NBC, 1943).

10472 **Eward, Fran.** COM-HE (WKBV, Richmond, IN, 1951–1960).

10473 **Ewell, Katherine.** COM-HE (WMSR, Manchester, TN, 1960).

10474 **Ewell, Robert.** Announcer (WDBS, Dayton, OH, 1924).

10475 **Ewer, Mabel Swint.** Trumpet soloist and announcer (WFI, Philadelphia, PA, 1924). Ewer also conducted the *Housewives' Radio Exchange* program (WFI, Philadelphia, PA, 1925).

10476 **Ewing, Charles.** Newscaster (WBIR, Knoxville, TN, 1941).

10477 **Ewing, Clifford E. "Cliff."** Newscaster (KVOC, Casper, WY, 1948). DJ (*Kookin at Coffee Time,* KOOK, Billings, MT, 1949–1952).

10478 **Ewing, David.** Baritone (KDKA, Pittsburgh, PA, 1926).

10479 **Ewing, LaVerne.** COM-HE (KIOX, Bay City, TX, 1949).

10480 **Ewing, William.** Newscaster (WCMB, Honolulu, HI, 1942; NBC-Blue, 1944–1945).

10481 ***Ex-Lax Program.*** The show combined the comedy of the team of Block and Sully with the music of Lud Gluskin's orchestra (30 min., CBS, 1935). The Ex-Lax [laxative] Company was the program's sponsor.

10482 ***Exploring Music.*** Bernard Hermann conducted the Columbia Concert Orchestra in short classical selections on the sustaining music program (15 min., Monday, 10:30–10:45 P.M., CBS, 1940).

10483 **Exum, Bill.** DJ (*Music Hall,* WJEM, Valdosta, GA, 1960).

10484 **Exum, F.F.** Announcer (WDAD, Nashville, TN, 1927).

10485 **Exum, Loretta.** COM-HE (WDAK, Columbus, OH, 1954–1955).

10486 **Eyberg, Mel.** Newscaster (KFNF, Shenandoah, IA, 1941).

10487 **Eyck, Sid Ten.** DJ (*The Sid Ten Eyck Show,* KSAN, San Francisco, CA, 1947).

10488 **Eyre, Al.** DJ (*Shoppers Special,* WTOR, Torrington, CT, 1949). Sportscaster (*Sports Extra,* WTOR, 1952–1953).

10489 **Eyrich, Richard "Dick."** Newscaster (WSVA, Harrisonburg, VA, 1945). DJ (*Matinee Frolic,* WSIR, Winter Haven, FL, 1949–1956).

10490 **Ezell, Ivanell.** COM-HE (WDXE, Lawrenceburg, TN, 1960).

10491 ***Ezio Pinza's Children's Show.*** Operatic singer Pinza became a children's DJ on this program that replaced *The Jackie Robinson Show.* Pinza's daughter, Celia, appeared on his sustaining show with him to introduce some of the recordings he played (30 min., Saturday, 9:30–10:00 A.M., NBC, 1953).

10492 **Fabelo, Ruben.** Spanish DJ Fabelo was a popular feature in the Tampa area (WALT, Tampa, FL, 1949).

10493 **Faber, Minnie.** Pianist, WBAL (Baltimore, MD), 1926.

10494 **Fabiani, Rozell Fair.** Receptionist, writer, producer, director, announcer (WRBL, Columbus, GA, 1949). When Fabiani applied for a receptionist position at WRBL in 1949, she was asked, "Can you write?" When she was given a job as a receptionist and assistant copywriter, she wrote a "birthday poem" daily for the station's *Birthday Party* program. She also did copywriting. Fabiani appeared on many of the station's programs before going to TV in the early 1950s as producer-director.

10495 **Fabien, Louis.** Newscaster (WSAY, Rochester, NY, 1945). DJ (*Dawn Patrol,* WARC, Rochester, NY, 1952).

10496 **Fabing, Joe.** Leader (Joe Fabing Orchestra, KFUU, Oakland, CA, 1925).

10497 **(The) Fable Lady.** Otherwise unidentified broadcaster conducted a weekday program for children (6:15–6:30 P.M., Weekdays, WCFL, Chicago, IL, 1926).

10498 Fabley, Andrew. Pianist (WRW, Tarrytown, NY, 1925).

10499 Fabre, Numa Frank. Newscaster (WAJR, Morgantown, WV, 1945).

10500 *Face to Face.* Arnold Michaelis hosted a radio program similar to Edward R. Murrow's *Person to Person* television program. On one of his earliest shows Michaelis interviewed Mike Todd (30 min., Wednesday, 9:30–10:00 P.M., CBS, 1957).

10501 Facemeyer, Roy. DJ (*Jersey Jamboree*, WSNJ, Bridgeton, NJ, 1947).

10502 Facenda, John. Newscaster (WIP, Philadelphia, PA, 1940–1942, 1948).

10503 Facer, Carol. COM-HE (KVOG, Ogden, UT, 1960).

10504 Facey, Stan. DJ (*Anything for You*, WFPG, Atlantic City, NJ, 1948).

10505 *Fada Hour.* Fada [radio] Manufacturing Company sponsored the hour of music broadcast by CBS from July 9, 1929, to December 31, 1929. Soprano Lois Bennett was one of the regular cast members.

10506 Fadal, Eddie. Newscaster (KWBU, Corpus Christi, TX, 1946).

10507 Fadaol, Bill. Sportscaster (*Sports Reports*, KSLO, Opelousas, LA, 1960).

10508 Fadden, Art. Pianist (KJBS, San Francisco, CA, 1928).

10509 (The) Fadettes. The Fadettes were an all-girl orchestra, one of the first on radio (WEEI, Boston, MA, 1925).

10510 Fadiman, Clifton. Book reviewer Fadiman was born May 15, 1904. In the 1930s and 1940s he was most famous for his radio appearances as moderator of the *Information Please* program. He began his broadcasting career as a book reviewer for NBC in 1924. *See* ***Information Please.***

10511 Fadley, Louise. COM-HE (WSIG, Mt. Jackson, VA, 1960).

10512 Faerber, Joseph. Violinist (KMOX, St. Louis, MO, 1928).

10513 Faffe, Jack. Humorist (KYW, Chicago, IL, 1925).

10514 Fagan, Bill. Sportscaster Fagan broadcast football scores on his *Bill Fagan* show (CBS, 1931).

10515 Fagan, Bill. DJ (*Start with a Whistle*, WEOA, Evansville, IN, 1949).

10516 Fagan, Frank. DJ (*Block Party*, WGTC, Greenville, NC, 1947). Sportscaster (*The Sports Parade*, WGTC, 1947).

10517 Fagan, Sybil Sanderson. Whistler (WEAF, New York, NY, 1925).

10518 Fahey, John R. Newscaster (KNEW, Spokane, WA, 1947). DJ (*Melody Matinee*, KHQ, Spokane, WA, 1954).

10519 Fahrlander, Harry W. Singer (WSRO, Hamilton, OH, 1926).

10520 Fahs, Robert. Newscaster (KYNO, Fresno, CA, 1948).

10521 Fahy, A.A. Newscaster (KABR, Aberdeen, SD, 1941, 1945–1946).

10522 Fain, Norma. COM-HE (KNEL, Brady, TX, 1951).

10523 Fair and Warmer. Piano duo, not otherwise identified (WBBM, Chicago, IL, 1926).

10524 Fair, Harold. Formerly a radio musician, Fair became a popular announcer (KOIL, Council Bluffs, IA, 1927).

10525 Fair, Jack. Conductor (Jack Fait's Entella Cafe Orchestra, KPO, San Francisco, CA, 1924; Jack Fair's Canary Cottage Orchestra, KFRC, San Francisco, CA, 1926).

10526 Fair, Jim. Sportscaster (WLEE, Richmond, VA, 1945–1947). DJ (*Spotlite on Music*, WLEE, 1947).

10527 Fairbanks, Douglas. Famous silent movie star Fairbanks was hired by KHJ (Los Angeles, CA) to report on the Rotary International Convention held in that city in 1921.

10528 Fairbanks, Lucille. COM-HE (KFIZ, Fond du Lac, WI, 1954).

10529 Fairchild, Helen. Pianist (WGHP, Detroit, MI, 1926).

10530 Fairchild, Ken. Sportscaster (KAMQ, Amarillo, TX, 1956).

10531 Fairchild, Pearl. Pianist (KYW, Chicago, IL, 1925).

10532 Fairchild, Prescott. Violinist (WEMC, Berrien Springs, MI, 1926).

10533 *Fairchild and Carroll.* Instr. mus. prg. that featured a talented piano duo (15 min., Monday through Friday, 7:30–7:45, NBC-Red, 1937).

10534 Faircloth, Peanut. DJ (WRDW, Augusta, GA, 1954; WAPO, Chattanooga, TN, 1956).

10535 Fairfield, W.R. Evangelist Fairfield conducted the *Radio Church of America* program (KLS, Oakland, CA, 1925).

10536 *Fairfield Four.* The Fairfield Four were a talented Black gospel quartet that traveled throughout the country to broadcast on various stations (WLAC, Nashville, TN, 1942).

10537 Fairleigh, Paul. Sportscaster (*Mid-South Sportsman*, WMPS, Memphis, TN, 1939).

10538 Fairley, Bill. Newscaster (KUOA, Siloam Springs, AR, 1939; KBIX, Muskogee, OK, 1942).

10539 Fairmont Hotel Orchestra. San Francisco hotel orchestra (KPO, San Francisco, CA ,1926).

10540 Fairmount Symphony Orchestra. Fine symphony orchestra (WLIT, Philadelphia, PA, 1925).

10541 Fairtrace, Bess. Miss Fairtrace was the director of station WFAA's Radio Players (WFAA, Dallas, TX, 1927).

10542 Faith, Percy. Leader (*Percy Faith Orchestra*, instr. mus. prg., MBS, 1934, 1942).

10543 Falcon, Bob. DJ (WGMS, Washington, DC, 1949; *Bay Window*, WGRO, Bay City, MI, 1952; WNAV, Annapolis, MD, 1957).

10544 *(The) Falcon.* The detective serial program that appeared on MBS in 1945 grew out of a motion picture series. The radio adventures of the Falcon, a suave detective-adventurer were written by Jay Bennett, Bernard Dougall, Palmer Thompson and Eugene Wang. The role of the Falcon on radio was first played by Barry Kroeger. The program's cast included: Joan Alexander, Joan Banks, Les Damon, Robert Dryden, Ethel Everett, Mandel Kramer, James Meighan, George Petrie and Les Tremayne. The producer was Bernard Schubert, Jr. The announcer was Ed Herlihy. Jay Bennett, Bernard Dougall, Stanley Niss, Palmer Thompson, Stuart Buchanan, Carlo DeAngelo and Richard Lewis were the directors (MBS, ABC, NBC, 1945–1954)

10545 Falconer, W. Alfred. Teller of dialect stories (WRC, Washington, DC, 1925).

10546 Falconnier, L.H. Sportscaster (*Hook, Line and Sinker*, WTAN, Clearwater, FL, 1955).

10547 Faler, Dick. Newscaster (WTAD, Quincy, IL, 1942, 1947–1948).

10548 Fales, Marguerite. Contralto (WOR, Newark, NJ, 1934).

10549 Falk, Ed "Eddie." Sportscaster (KABR, Aberdeen, SD, 1938–1941).

10550 Falk, Edna. Monologist (WOR, Newark, NJ, 1925).

10551 Falk, Florence. COM-HE (KMA, Shenandoah, IA, 1960).

10552 Falkenburg, Jinx. Talk show host. *See* **Husband-and-Wife Talk Shows; McCrary, "Jinx" Falkenburg** and ***Tex and Jinx.***

10553 Falkenstein, Cecile. Pianist (WLW, Cincinnati, OH, 1927).

10554 Falkenstein, Max. Sportscaster (WREN, Lawrence, KS, 1946–1948; *The Sports Scene*, WREN, 1949–1950; *Tops in Sports*, WREN, 1951–1952; *Speaking of Sports*, WREN, 1953–1958; WREN, 1959–1960).

10555 *(The) Fall of the City.* Archibald MacLeish wrote the critically praised program that attacked fascism and dictatorships. The program was unique in that it was the first poetic work written specifically for radio. Orson Welles and Burgess Meredith participated in the production broadcast in 1937 as part of the *Columbia Workshop* series. The story dramatically told of the take over of a city [country] by Fascist forces. As right-minded as the program's warning undoubtedly was, it was one of the strongest propaganda pieces ever broadcast in the United States. *See* ***Columbia Workshop (Columbia Radio Workshop).***

10556 Fallert, Ralph. Newscaster (WCAE, Pittsburgh, PA, 1940).

10557 Fallet, (Mlle.) Marcella. French singer and violinist (WOR, Newark, NJ, 1928–1929).

10558 Fallon, Bob. Leader (*Bob Fallon Orchestra*, instr. mus. prg., WCBM, Baltimore, MD, 1934).

10559 Fallon, Eugene [Eugen] P.O. Announcer (KFEL, Denver, CO, 1926).

10560 Fallon, Frank. Newscaster (WMEX, Boston, MA, 1941). Sportscaster (WMEX, 1941; WMEX, 1945–1953; *Sports Roundup*, WMEX, 1954–1956; *Sports of the Day*, WBOS, Boston, MA, 1960).

10561 Fallon, Frank. Sportscaster (KITE, San Antonio, TX, 1948–1952; *Last Word in Sports*, KWTX, Waco, TX, 1954–1956).

10562 Fallon, Lee. COM-HE (KTRH, Houston, TX, 1949).

10563 Fallon, Owen. Leader (Owen Fallon's Californians, KFI, Los Angeles, 1926). Fallon's band included the following musicians: Fallon, ldr. and d.; Robert Stevenson, t. and fh.; Warren Smith, tb. and eph.; Max Kressich and Eddie Thomas, clr. and as.; Norman Rathert, bj. and v.; Bud Kleinhall, p.; and Hartmann Angst, tba.

10564 Falsonnier, Harold. Newscaster (WTSP, Minneapolis–St. Paul, MN, 1941–1945).

10565 *Falstaff's Fables.* Alan Reed (Teddy Bergman), playing the role of Falstaff the Poet, told stories that were humorously fractured versions of such classics as Longfellow's "The Village Blacksmith." Reed first portrayed the role in Allen's Alley on the *Fred Allen Show*. *Variety* noted that Don Johnson wrote the show that sometimes was in "questionable taste." Mars Candy Company was the sponsor (5 min., Monday through Friday, 5:55–6:00 P.M., ABC, 1950).

10566 Falta, Joseph. Newscaster (WEDC, Chicago, IL, 1945; *Czech Breakfast*, WEDC, 1948).

10567 *(The) Family Goes Abroad.* Katherine Seymour wrote the comedy sketch about the adventures of a typical American family on an European tour. Incidental music was conducted by Frank Vagnoni (30 min., Friday,7:00–7:30 P.M., NBC-Red, 1930).

10568 *Family Hotel.* Billy K. Wells wrote this situation comedy the starred Jack Pearl in the role of Peter Pfeiffer. Pfeiffer ran a small, country hotel and faced, mostly successfully, his many problems. Cliff Hall, Pearl's long time stooge from *Baron Maunchausen* days, was also in the cast. Frigidaire Corporation sponsored the show (30 min., Wednesday, 10:00–10:30 P.M., CBS, 1935).

10569 *(The) Family Hour* (aka ***The Capitol Family Hour, The Major Bowes Family Hour*** and ***The Ted Mack Family Hour***).

10570 *Family Skeleton.* Mercedes McCambridge starred in the story of a girl with a dark past and highly uncertain future. Carleton E. Morse wrote, produced and directed the daytime serial sponsored by Sweetheart Soap and Prom Home Permanents. Although *Variety* praised the program, its time on the air was relatively short. Other members of the cast were John Dehner, Forrest Lewis, James McCallion, Marvin Miller, Marilyn Steiner and Russell Thorson (15 min., Monday through Friday, CBS, 1953).

10571 *Family Theater.* Buddy Rogers hosted the music program and led his Green Stripe Orchestra on it. Singer Jeanne Lang, the Three Rascals and various guest stars were featured (CBS, 1934). This should not be confused with the *Family Theater* dramatic program broadcast by NBC from 1947 to 1963.

10572 *Family Theater.* Father Patrick Peyton hosted the dramatic series that emphasized the importance of love and religion in family life. One enduring slogan that came from the series was: "The family that prays together stays together." Guests who appeared on the show were: Fred Allen, Ethel Barrymore, Ann Blyth, Macdonald Carey, Perry Como, Gary Cooper, Bing Crosby, Irene Dunne, Bob Hope, Ray Milland, Marvin Miller, Maureen O'Sullivan, Spencer Tracy and Loretta Young. The program was written by John Kelley and Robert O'Sullivan and directed by John Kelley, Robert O'Sullivan, Mel Williamson and Dave Young. The announcer was Tony LaFranco (MBS, 1947–1963).

10573 *Famous Babies.* Former New York City Health Commissioner Dr. Louis I. Harris conducted the weekly program, whose purpose was to promote child health by providing parents with the latest medical information (WABC-CBS, 1935).

10574 *Famous Jury Trials.* Famous trials were dramatized on the series that featured narrators Roger DeKoven and DeWitt McBride. Maurice Franklin presided as the judge. Other cast members were: True Boardman, Raymond Edward Johnson, Byron Kane, Jean Paul King, Mandel Kramer and Frank Readick. The writers were Daisy Amoury, Stedman Coles, Len Finger, Ameel Fisher, Joseph L. Greene, Milton J. Kramer, Jerry McGill, Lawrence Menkin, Paul Monash, Bill Rafael and Martin H. Young. Wylie Adams, Clark Andrews, Carl Eastman, Robert H. Nolan and Charles Powers were the directors. The program's announcers were Peter Grant, Hugh James and Roger Krupp (MBS, NBC-Blue, ABC, 1936–1949).

10575 *Famous Loves* (aka ***Famous Loves of History***). Famous love stories of history were dramatized on the program. Built around actual characters and incidents, the interesting show was written by Katherine Seymour. Sponsored by Natural Bridge shoes, the opening went this way:

> Another in the series of Natural Bridge Romances — a series of dramatic sketches based on *Famous Loves*—is presented by the nationwide distributors of Natural Bridge Arch Shoes for the smart feminine foot. These shoes are modern — fashionable — and retain the natural loveliness of dainty feet — naturally. Dealers of Natural Bridge Arch Shoes can fit almost any foot smartly, comfortably — and at moderate expense. Their slogan is "Good to the foot — good to the eye — good to the pocketbook."

After a portion of the theme was played, the announcer provided an introduction to the evening's story:

> In many an Irish cottage, on many a night during the past century, a favorite topic of conversation has been the brave lad Robert Emmet, a youthful martyr to the cause for which he fought — the independence of his native land, Ireland. Robert Emmet, who lived during the latter half of the eighteenth century, was a brilliant student at the University of Dublin, until he left college as a protest against the political restrictions imposed by the English governors. For three years he roamed on the Continent, meeting other exiled Irishmen, and completing plans to free Ireland from the yoke of England. Finally, after an interview with Napoleon and a promise of French aid, he returned to Ireland to carry out his plans, and also — to see again Sarah Curran, the girl he loved. This beautiful girl, daughter of the distinguished lawyer John Curran, had twice rejected him, and after his return he lost all hope that she would ever love him. Nevertheless, he had always been a welcome guest in her father's house, and although he was absorbed in secret plans for Ireland, he could not forget Sarah nor could he resist dropping in from time to time to chat with her. One afternoon in the early spring of 1803, Sarah was strolling in the garden, as Robert Emmet opened the wicket gate and greeted her, "Good day, Sarah. May I stroll with you in the garden?"

Their love story was then dramatized. The program was critically praised for the quality of its writing (15 min., Friday, 8:45–9:00 P.M., NBC-Blue Network, 1929–1931).

10576 Famous Owls Orchestra. The Famous Owls Orchestra, an eight-man group, broadcast from the New Orleans' Roosevelt Hotel (WSMB, New Orleans, LA, 1926).

10577 *Famous Trials in History.* National Dairy Products sponsored the dramatic series that portrayed a different trial each week (30 min., Sunday, 10:15–10:45 P.M., NBC-Red).

10578 Fanchon, Miss. A member of the KTAB Players Group (KTAB, Oakland, CA, 1929).

10579 Fann, Linda. COM-HE (WMBC, McMinnville, TN, 1960).

10580 *Fannie Hurst.* Famous novelist Fannie Hurst broadcast weekly dramatic criticism (15 min., Weekly, WJZ, New York, NY, 1946).

10581 Fanning, (Major) John J. Announcer and program director Fanning was known as "JJF" (WNAC, Boston, MA, 1923–1927). The September 8, 1923, issue of *Radio Digest* said: "The most popular voice on [the] air in the East is Major J.J. Fanning of WNAC."

10582 Fanning, Larry. Newscaster (KGO, San Francisco, CA, 1945).

10583 Fanning, Wallace. Newscaster (MBS, 1954).

10584 Fansler, Dick. Fansler was called the "Hoosier singer " (WISH, Indianapolis, IN, 1947)

10585 Fant, Julian. DJ (*Julian's Bandstand*, WFOY, St. Augustine, FL, 1948; *Breakfast Party*, WFOY, 1954). Sportscaster (WFOY, 1950–1951; *Sports Roundup*, WFOY, 1952–1954).

10586 Fantasia, Nick [Jack]. Sportscaster (*Sports Preview* and *Sports Review*, WHAR, Clarksburg, WV, 1948; WVVW, Fairmont, WV, 1952; WJPB, Fairmont, WV, 1953; WVVW, 1954; WTCS, Fairmont, WV, 1955–1960).

10587 *Far Lands.* The educational program that was devoted to the geography and culture of other lands originated on the Iowa State University's station (WOI, Ames, IA, 1936). It was rebroadcast by the State University of Iowa's station (WSUI, Iowa City, IA, 1936).

10588 Farber, Burt. Leader (*Burt Farber Orchestra*, instr. mus. prg., NBC, 1934; WSAI, Cincinnati, OH, 1942; WLW, Cincinnati, OH,

1944). DJ (*The Burt Farber Show,* 40 min., Monday through Friday, 12:50–1:30 P.M., WSAI, Cinncinnati, OH, 1947).

10589 Farber, Katheryn. Soprano (WCBD, Zion, IL, 1925).

10590 Farelle, Betty. COM-HE (WSDA, Redding, CA, 1957).

10591 Farese, Angela. COM-HE (WBOS, Boston, MA, 1957).

10592 Farham, Ruth. Director of the Shenandoah High School Chorus (KFNF, Shenandoah, IA, 1925).

10593 Faris, Clinton. Newscaster (WGTM, Wilson, NC, 1939–1940).

10594 Farkas, Charles W. "Chuck." DJ (*Platter Party,* KBKI, Alice, TX, 1952). Sportscaster (KBKI, 1952–1955).

10595 Farkas, Remy. DJ (*Record Rarities,* WQXR, New York, NY, 1947–1949).

10596 Farlender, (Reverend) A.W. Newscaster (*A Parson Views the News,* KSRO, Santa Rosa, CA, 1947).

10597 Farley, Edward. Pianist (WOR, Newark, NJ, 1924.)

10598 Farley, Grace. COM-HE (KCID, Caldwell, ID, 1957).

10599 Farley, June. Soprano (WHK, Cleveland, OH, 1924).

10600 Farley's Gold Star Rangers. The CW group later became the Sons of the Pioneers (30 min., Monday through Saturday, 5:30–6:00 P.M. and Sunday, 2:30–3:00 P.M., KFSD, San Diego, CA, 1935). *See* ***Sons of the Pioneers.***

10601 Farlow, Stubby. DJ (*Four Corners Rodeo,* KIUP, Durango, CO, 1954).

10602 Farly, Tom. Sportscaster (KRMD, Jamestown, ND, 1937).

10603 *(This) Farm Business.* Lloyd "Doc" Burlinglam, who was said to have been the first sponsored news commentator on radio, conducted the agricultural news show. The program for farmers was sponsored by the J.L. Case Farm Equipment Company (15 min., Monday-Wednesday-Friday, 12:45–1:00 P.M., WLS, Chicago, IL, 1938).

10604 *(The) Farm Digest.* Don Tuttle broadcast farm news on the Ralston-Purina Company sponsored program (30 min., 8:30–9:00 A.M., WGY, Schenectady, NY, 1953).

10605 *Farm Fiddlers* (aka *Farmers' Fiddlers Hour*). The CW program featured a group of old-time fiddlers and singer-dancer Mary Lynch (WCFL, Chicago, IL, 1929).

10606 *(The) Farm Front.* The public affairs program focused on the problems found in agriculture and rural economics (30 min., Sunday, 9:00–9:30 A.M., WLW, Cincinnati, OH, 1947).

10607 *(The) Farm Hour.* The long-running program of information for farmers and their families was first broadcast in 1924. Milt Bliss and Maury White conducted the program (WHA, Madison, WI, 1924–1944).

10608 *(The) Farm Paper of the Air.* Don Tuttle and Enoch Squires broadcast farm news (30 min., Monday through Saturday, 12:30–1:00 P.M., WGY, Schenectady, NY, 1955).

10609 (The) *Farm Question Box.* George C. Wheeler, editor of *Western Farm Life* magazine conducted the informative program for farmers (KOA, Denver, CO, 1927).

10610 *(The) Farm Show.* In the 1950s, Black farm editor Ernest Brazzle conducted *The Farm Show* on station WDIA (Memphis, TN). At the same time he served in the Shelby County Agricultural Extension Service and conducted research on how to improve crop and livestock production. By 1991, Brazzle had broadcast more than 10,000 shows during his 41 years at WDIA.

10611 Farmer, Chick. Singer (WHN, New York, NY, 1928).

10612 Farmer, Chuck. DJ (*Chuck Wagon,* KVVC, Ventura, CA, 1948).

10613 Farmer, Helen. COM-HE (WMAZ, Macon, GA, 1949; WBML, Macon, GA, 1956).

10614 Farmer, John. Newscaster (KMBC, Kansas City, MO, 1939–1942, 1947).

10615 Farmer, Johnny. Vocalist-pianist (WWNC., Ashville, NC, 1928).

10616 Farmer, Jon. DJ (*Early Worm* and *Hillbilly Hit Review,* WAGA, Atlanta, GA, 1947–1952).

10617 Farmer, Judy. DJ (KBMI, Henderson, NE, 1955).

10618 Farmer, Pat. COM-HE (WBML, Macon, GA, 1955).

10619 Farmer, William "Willie." Leader (*William Farmer Orchestra,* instr. mus. prg., WOR, Newark, NJ, 1934–1936, MBS, 1942).

10620 *Farmer's Night.* In 1925, station KFMQ (Fayetteville, AR) scheduled its Thursday night programs specifically for farmers and their families. Dr. A.M. Harding, KEMQ's program director, directed and planned a series of 18 University of Arkansas Extension courses specifically for them. On Tuesday evening the station presented a series of music programs by Owens Mitchell's orchestra (KFMQ, 1925).

10621 *Farmer's Noon Hour.* In 1922, KFBB (Great Falls, MT) initiated a weekday program of information for farmers and their family members. Some suggest this program was a radio "first."

10622 Farnam, Lynwood. Organist (WMAK, Buffalo, NY, 1926).

10623 Farnum, Bud. Sportscaster (WFLA, Tampa, FL, 1939–1941).

10624 Farnsworth, Sally. Singer Farnsworth was a member of the Melody Trio (KNX, Hollywood, CA, 1929).

10625 Faro, Frank. Newscaster (WCED, DuBois, PA, 1945).

10626 Farquhar, Walter. Newscaster (WPAM, Pottsville, PA, 1947).

10627 Farr, Floyd. Newscaster (KGO-KPO, San Francisco, CA, 1941).

10628 Farr, Hilda Butler. Pianist (WMAQ, Chicago, IL, 1924).

10629 Farrar, Art. Leader (*Art Farrar Orchestra,* instr. mus. prg., KDKA, Pittsburgh, PA, 1934).

10630 Farrar, Florence. Contralto (WCBD, Zion, IL, 1923–1924).

10631 Farrar, Jack. DJ (*Kilocycle Klambake,* KTFI, Twin Falls, ID, 1954).

10632 Farrar, Mary. COM-HE (WLMJ, Jackson, OH, 1955).

10633 Farrell, Charles. Newscaster (WMBC, Detroit, MI, 1940).

10634 Farrell, Dick. DJ (*Swinging '70,* KDZA, Pueblo, CO, 1960).

10635 Farrell, Eileen. Singer (*Eileen Farrell, Songs,* CBS, 1945).

10636 Farrell, Frank. Leader (Frank Farrell Orchestra, WEAF, New York, NY, 1926). The following year the band became Frank Farrell and his Greenwich Village Inn Orchestra. Members included: Farrell, ldr.-p.; Hymie Farberman and Red Nichols, t.; Sammy Lewis, tb.; Larry Abbott and Arnold Brilhart, clr. and as.; Alfie Evans, clr., as., ts. and bar.; Louis Condell, bj.; Irving Leonard, v.; August Helleberg, tba.; and Sonny Tudor, d.

10637 Farrell, Jerry. DJ (*Road Show,* WJJL, Niagara Falls, NY, 1960).

10638 Farrell, Jimmy. Baritone (*Jimmy Farrell,* vcl. mus. prg., CBS, 1935–1936).

10639 Farrell, Johnny. Golf professional Farrell broadcast a weekly program of golf instruction (WDAE, Tampa, FL, 1926).

10640 Farrell, Maury. Sportscaster (WAPI, Birmingham, AL, 1939–1940; WAPI, 1945–1946; *Speaking of Sports* and *Sports Headlines,* WAPI, 1947–1954). Newscaster (*WAPI News,* WAPI, 1940, 1947–1948). DJ (*Matinee in Birmingham,* WAPI, 1947–1952).

10641 Farrell, Reed. DJ (*Spins and Needles,* KGBC, Galveston, TX, 1949; WAIT, Chicago, IL, 1956).

10642 Farrell, Roberta. COM-HE (WJBC, Bloomington, IL, 1960).

10643 Farrell, Skip. Singer (*The Skip Farrell Show,* vcl. mus. prg., with crooner Farrell with the Honeydreamers vocal group and the George Barnes Trio. Jack Lester was the announcer (15 min., Monday, Tuesday and Wednesday, 7:15–7:30 P.M., ABC, 1947; *Skip Farrell,* vcl. mus. prg., WCFL, Chicago, IL, 1950).

10644 Farrelle, Paul S. Newscaster (KPMC, Bakersville, CA, 1939).

10645 Farren, William. Sportscaster (KDKA, 1932; NBC, 1940). Newscaster (NBC, 1940).

10646 Farrington, Fielden. Newscaster (WXYZ, Detroit, MI, 1937; CBS, 1947–1948).

10647 Farrington, Frank. Sportscaster (KFAM, St. Cloud, MN, 1945–1949; *Frank Farrington Sports,* KFAM, 1950–1954; *Sports Hi-Lites,* KFAM, 1955).

10648 Farrington, Vivian. COM-HE (WPKO, Waverly, OH, 1955).

10649 Farris, Joe. Newscaster (*Purity News,* WGKV, Charleston, WV, 1947). Sportscaster (*Today's Luck in Sports,* WGKV, 1947; *Sports Billboard* and *Sports Tips,* WGKV, 1949–1952).

10650 Farris, Wayne. DJ (*680 Club,* WCLE, Clearwater, FL, 1950).

10651 *(The) Fashion Review.* Sally Dee conducted this fashion program for women (KOA, Denver, CO, 1926).

10652 ***Fashionette.*** Virginia Benoit broadcast fashion news and information (WIND, Gary, IN, 1935).

10653 **Faske, Arthur.** Newscaster (WCNW, Brooklyn, NY, 1939).

10654 **Fassen [Faasen], "Uncle Joe."** Announcer Fassen, affectionately known as "Uncle Joe," won the 1927 Silver Cup Announcer Award (KSO, (Clarinda, IA, 1927–1928).

10655 **Fat Daddy.** DJ (WWIN, Baltimore, MD, 1960). Fat Daddy, not otherwise identified, was a morning man specializing in rhythm and blues. He started in 1960 and continued at the Baltimore station for two decades.

10656 ***Father Knows Best.*** A situation comedy that became a television staple, *Father Knows Best* was written by Ed James. The story told of the everyday life and problems of an "average" suburban American family headed by a warm and wise father played by Robert Young. The program's other cast members included: Eleanor Audley, Ted Donaldson, Sam Edwards, Norma Jean Nilsson, Herb Vigran, June Whitley and Rhoda Williams. The directors were Murray Bolen, Ken Burton and Fran Van Hartesfeldt. Music was supplied by the Roy Bargy Orchestra (30 min., Thursday, 8:30–9:00 P.M., NBC, 1949).

10657 ***Father Ricard's Sun Spot Weather.*** An early weather program conducted by Father Ricard (KFI, Los Angeles, CA, 1925).

10658 **Fatman, Lloyd.** DJ (WHAT, Philadelphia, PA, 1957).

10659 ***Fats Waller's Rhythm Club.*** Waller, the great jazz pianist, hosted the quarter-hour program and also provided the good music (CBS, 1934).

10660 **Faucon, Albert.** Violinist (WBZ, Boston-Springfield, MA, 1924).

10661 **Faulconer, J.B.** Sportscaster (WLAP, Lexington, KY, 1947–1954).

10662 **Faulk, John Henry.** DJ (*The John Henry Faulk Show*, WCBS, New York, NY, 1951–1952). *See* ***John Henry Faulk.***

10663 **Faulk, Pauline E. "Polly."** COM-HE (WCKB, Dunn, NC, 1957).

10664 **Faulkner, Dick.** Newscaster (WAPI, Birmingham, AL, 1938).

10665 **Faulkner, Georgene.** A teller of *Stories for Children* in the late afternoon, Faulkner was known as the "Story Lady" (WMAQ, Chicago, IL, 1924). Her program emphasized the Mother Goose stories.

10666 **Faulkner, Mary.** COM-HE (WRDO, Augusta, ME, 1951).

10667 **Faulkner, Ruth.** Pianist (KWSC, Pullman, WA, 1925–1926).

10668 **Faulkner, Werthe.** Singer (WGBS, New York, NY, 1925).

10669 **Faulkner, William "Bill."** DJ (*Whoosier Request Time*, WISH, Indianapolis, IN, 1947–1948; *Bill Faulkner Show*, WISH, 1949–1954).

10670 ***Faultless Starch Time.*** Faultless Starch sponsored the CW music program hosted by cowboy singer Bob Atcher, who had replaced the original host, Ernie Lee. Mary Jane Johnson and Caesar Giovannini's Combo were cast regulars. The announcer was Franklyn Ferguson. The program was first broadcast on the network in 1949 (15 min., Sunday, 10:00–10:15 A.M., NBC, 1953).

10671 **Faust, Leone.** Leading lady of the WAMD Players (WAMD, Minneapolis, MN, 1926).

10672 **Faverly, George.** Baritone (WJAZ, Chicago, IL, 1923).

10673 ***Favorite Story*** **(aka *My Favorite Story*).** Ronald Colman hosted and sometimes acted in the excellent series of dramatized classics. Jerry Lawrence and Robert Lee wrote and directed the transcribed show. Music was directed by Claude Sweetan and Robert Mitchell. *Variety* called the series one of the best of its kind (30 min., Transcribed, Various stations, 1947).

10674 **Fawcett, Letitia.** Soprano (KFWI, San Francisco, CA, 1926).

10675 **Fay, Barbara.** COM-HE (WMPO, Middleport-Pomeroy, OH, 1960).

10676 **Fay, Chauncey.** Newscaster (WMT, Cedar Rapids–Waterloo, IA, 1938).

10677 **Fay, Elita.** Soprano (WIBO, Chicago, IL, 1926).

10678 **Fay, Florence S.** Violinist (WBZ, Springfield, MA, 1925).

10679 **Fay, Joe.** Sportscaster (WPRO, Providence, RI, 1940; *Joe Fay's Sports Slants*, WPRO, 1947).

10680 **Fay, Lew.** DJ (*Rhythm and Romance* and *10 O'Clock Tunes*, KONO, San Antonio, TX, 1947).

10681 **Fay, Mabel.** Contralto (KFSG, Los Angeles, CA, 1925).

10682 **Fay, Margaret.** Singer (WSM, Nashville, TN, 1926).

10683 **Fay, Maria.** Soprano (WIBO, Chicago, IL, 1926).

10684 **Fay, Romelle.** Organist (*Romelle Fay*, instr. mus. prg., 30 min., Sunday, 8:00–8:30 A.M., WLS, Chicago, IL, 1935).

10685 **Fay, William.** Talented announcer Fay also directed the station's light opera company; played bass fiddle in the WGY orchestra; sang baritone solos and performed in the Radio Four male quartet (WGY, Schenectady, NY, 1924–1927). When he moved to WMAK (Buffalo, NY) in 1928, he performed both announcing and directing duties. Fay was the announcer on the *Stromberg-Carlson Program* (NBC-Blue, New York, NY, 1929).

10686 **Faye, Dorothy.** COM-HE (WDAF, Kansas City, MO, 1951–1955).

10687 **Faye, Farol.** COM-HE (WAPO, Chattanooga, TN, 1956–1957).

10688 **Faye, Marty.** DJ (WAAF, Chicago, IL, 1954–1960).

10689 **Fayre, Kay.** Singer (WBZ, Boston, MA, 1933).

10690 ***Fay's Orchestra.*** Instr. mus. prg. (WIP, Philadelphia, PA, 1935).

10691 **Fazer, Marlene.** COM-HE (KCVR, Lodi, CA, 1951).

10692 **Fazzin, Art.** Sportscaster (*Sports Spotlight*, WDUK, Durham, NC, 1947). DJ (*Top O' the Morning*, WAKR, Akron, OH, 1949).

10693 **Feagan, Earl.** Leader (Earl Feagan's Orchestra, KFSD, San Diego, CA, 1926).

10694 **Feagan, Robert R. "Bob."** Newscaster (WBML, Macon, GA, 1940–1941; WPDQ, Jacksonville, FL, 1942, 1945; *News Final*, WPDQ, 1947; *Headline News*, WPDQ, 1948).

10695 **Feagler, Dave.** DJ (WANE, Ft. Wayne, IN, 1955).

10696 **Feagley, Charles W.** Announcer (WGAL, Lancaster, PA, 1927).

10697 **Fealy, Aileen and Phyllis Ashley.** Piano duo (KPO, San Francisco, CA, 1927).

10698 **Feather, Leonard.** DJ (*Jazz at its Best*, WMGM, New York, NY, 1948–1950). Distinguished jazz critic Feather was also a DJ on his sustaining *Leonard Feather Show* (60 min., Saturday, 4:00–5:00 P.M., WOR, New York, NY, 1951).

10699 **Featherstone, Charlie.** DJ (WWSC, Glen Falls, NY, 1947; WNDR, Syracuse, NY, 1948).

10700 ***Feature Foods.*** Martha Crane and Helen Joyce replaced the station's long running *Homemaker's Hour* in 1934 with their women's show. In its early years music was supplied on the program by Otto's Tunetwisters and organist Ralph Waldo Emerson (30 min., Monday through Saturday, 10:00–10:30 A.M., WLS, Chicago, IL, 1935). During World War II, one of the program's most praised features was its 16-month series of reports from a London homemaker who described her life during the period of the London Blitz.

10701 ***Feature Story — Bob Trout.*** News commentator Trout was featured on his weekday news show (30 min., Monday through Friday, 5:15–5:30 P.M., CBS, 1945).

10702 **Fechner, Margaret.** Soprano (WCAY, Milwaukee, WI, 1924).

10703 ***Federal Chamber Orchestra.*** Instr. mus. prg. (WESG, Elmira, NY, 1937).

10704 ***Federal Concert Orchestra.*** Instr. mus. prg.(WHB, Kansas City, MO, 1934).

10705 ***(The) Federal Radio Division.*** This government produced program dramatized various cultural topics such as "The True Story of Swing" on this Depression era program (15 min., Sunday, 4:00–4:15 P.M., WMCA, New York, NY, 1939).

10706 ***(The) Federal Theater Project of the Air.*** The sustaining program broadcast adaptations of plays from various Federal Theater Project productions. For example, Sylvia Altman adapted for radio *One Third of a Nation*, the Project's first successful play that the Living Newspaper Unit had previously presented. Webb Lawrence directed the radio version (45 min., Thursday, 9:00–9:45 P.M., WEVD, New York, NY, 1939).

10707 **Feeney, Eugene.** DJ (*Club 690*, WHLM, Bloomsburg, PA, 1949).

10708 **Feezor, Betty.** COM-HE (WFMY, Greensboro, NC, 1943). After studying Home Economics at the University of Tennessee, Feezor began a homemaking program on WFMY during the World War II era. She later went on to do a TV show on WBTV (Charlotte, NC).

10709 **Fehner, Alma.** Pianist (WWJ, Detroit, MI, 1924).

10710 Feibel, "Fred" Frederick. Organist (*Fred Feibel Organ Recital,* instr. mus. prg., CBS, 1934–1936) Leader (*Fred Feibel Orchestra,* instr. mus. prg., WDBJ, Roanoke, VA, 1936; CBS, 1936–1939). Organist Feibel's program in the 1930s began with the announcer saying: "We bring you—*Fred Feibel at the Organ* in a sparkling program of console impressions culled from the music of today and yesterday. We hear first four lovely excerpts from the work of Rudolf Friml."

10711 Feibenbaum, F. Violinist (KDKA, Pittsburgh, PA, 1923).

10712 Feibusch, Mischa. Pianist (WFAA, Dallas, TX, 1926).

10713 Feinman, Samuel. Pianist (WEJB, New York, NY, 1925).

10714 Feirman, Herb. Leader (Herb Feirman and his Orchestra, WOAW, Omaha, NE, 1926).

10715 Feistel, John. Newscaster (WHOM, Jersey City, NJ, 1941).

10716 Feld, Ben. Leader (*Ben Feld Orchestra,* instr. mus. prg., KMOX, St. Louis, MO, 1934; CBS, 1936–1937).

10717 Feldkamp, Lorraine. Violinist (WLW, Cincinnati, OH, 1923).

10718 Feldman, Arthur. Newscaster (NBC-Blue, 1944–1945).

10719 Feldman, Robert M. "Bud." Sportscaster (WMAS, Springfield, MA, 1937–1940; WMAS, 1944–1946).

10720 Felgar, Gerald. Singer (WGBS, New York, NY, 1927).

10721 Felimer, Frank. DJ (*890 Club,* WHNC, Henderson, NC, 1949).

10722 Felix, Delia. COM-HE (KEVT, Tucson, AZ, 1957).

10723 Felix, Winslow. Leader (Winslow Felix's Chevrolet Orchestra, KHJ, Los Angeles, CA, 1928).

10724 Felkner, Gail. Sportscaster (KPAB, Laredo, TX, 1945).

10725 Fell, Hans. Organist (WHB, Kansas City, MO, 1926).

10726 Feller, Sherman "Sherm." DJ (*Club Midnight,* 60 min., Monday through Saturday, 12:00–1:00 A.M., WEEI, Boston, MA, 1947–1950; WLAW, Boston, MA, 1952).

10727 Fellow, Homer. Baritone (WEMC, Berrien Springs, MI, 1926).

10728 Fellows, Barton. Newscaster (WMCA, New York, NY, 1938).

10729 Felming, D.F. Newscaster (WSM, Nashville, TN, 1940).

10730 Felton, Barbara. COM-HE (WROV, Roanoke, VA, 1957; WEET, Richmond, VA, 1960).

10731 Felton, Happy. Leader (*Happy Felton Orchestra,* instr. mus. prg., WGY, Schenectady, NY, 1934; NBC-Red, 1937–1938).

10732 Felton, Maggie. COM-HE (WFAI, Fayetteville, NC, 1955).

10733 Felton, William "Bill." Newscaster (WOSH, Oshkosh, WI, 1945). DJ (*Valley Varieties,* WNAM, Neenah, WI, 1947; *Recreation Room,* WHBY, Appleton, WI, 1949).

10734 Felton's Orchestra. Local New York jazz band (WFBH, New York, NY, 1925). Possibly this was the Happy Felton Orchestra listed previously.

10735 Fender, William. Newscaster (WHOM, Jersey City, NJ, 1941).

10736 Fenger, Austin. Newscaster (KSFO, San Francisco, CA, 1944–1945).

10737 Fenk [Fink], Mary Muller. Harpist (WBAL, Baltimore, MD, 1926).

10738 Fenley, Maurine. COM-HE (KMCO, Conroe, TX, 1955).

10739 Fennell, George. DJ (WHIL, Medford, MA, 1955–1957).

10740 Fenno, Ralph. Sportscaster (*Fish and Game Club of the Air* and *Ralph Fenno on Sports,* WKXL, Concord, NH, 1947–1949; WPOR, Portland, OR, 1950–1951; *Sports Roundup,* WPOR, 1952).

10741 Fensel, Irma. Lyric soprano (WOR, Newark, NJ, 1925).

10742 Fenster, Lajos. Violinist (KGO, Oakland, CA, 1925).

10743 Fenstermacher, Bruce. DJ (WGPA, Bethlehem, PA, 1954).

10744 Fenton, Carl. Leader (*Carl Fenton Orchestra,* instr. mus. prg., WIP, Philadelphia, PA, 1935–1936)

10745 Fenton, Eddie. Sportscaster (WCBM, Baltimore, MD, 1940; WCBM, 1945; *All Sports Special,* WCBM, 1947–1949; *Scoreboard,* WCBM, 1960).

10746 Fenton, Lee. Baritone (KMIC, Inglewood, CA, 1928).

10747 Fenton, Lucille. Actress Fenton appeared on the *Myrt and Marge* daytime serial program.

10748 Fenton, Thelma E. COM-HE (KWRL, Riverton, WY, 1960).

10749 Fenton, Ward. Newscaster (WENY, Elmira, NY, 1940).

10750 Fentress, Aline. Violinist (WSM, Nashville, TN, 1928).

10751 Fentress, Daisy. Singer (WSM, Nashville, TN, 1928).

10752 Fenwick, Virginia. Soprano (WJY, New York, NY, 1924).

10753 Ferch, Harriet. Pianist (KOL, Seattle, WA, 1929).

10754 Ferda, Osman. Newscaster (NBC, 1946).

10755 Ferdi, Don. Leader (*Don Ferdi Orchestra,* instr. mus. prg., WBZ, Boston-Springfield, MA, 1936).

10756 Ferdinando, Angelo. Leader (*Angelo Ferdinando Orchestra,* instr. mus. prg., NBC, 1934).

10757 Ferdinando, Felix. Leader (*Felix Ferdinando Orchestra,* instr. mus. prg., WOR, Newark, NJ, 1934–1935).

10758 Fergus, Leon. Leader (Leon Fergus and his Venetians [orchestra], KFH, Wichita, KS, 1926).

10759 Ferguson, Alice Knox. Pianist (WFAA, Dallas, TX, 1928).

10760 Ferguson, Andrew B. Sportscaster (*The Sports Desk,* WBOW, Terre Haute, IN, 1947–1949).

10761 Ferguson, Bert. Sportscaster (WHBQ, Memphis, TN, 1939; WJPR, Greenville, MS, 1941). Newscaster (WJPR, 1942; WDIA, Memphis, TN, 1947).

10762 Ferguson, Bess. Singer (WGN, Chicago, IL, 1924).

10763 Ferguson, Bill. DJ (*Midnight Serenade,* WHHT, Durham, NC, 1947; *Moments of Melody,* WRUF, Gainesville, FL, 1948; *Wake Up with WONN,* WONN, Lakeland, FL, 1952).

10764 Ferguson, David. Irish tenor Ferguson was known as "The Limerick Minstrel" (WGBS, New York, NY, 1927).

10765 Ferguson, Donald L. Newscaster (NBC, 1946).

10766 Ferguson, Ed. Tenor (KGO, Oakland, CA, 1926).

10767 Ferguson, Elizabeth Alexander. Singer (WOW, Omaha, NE, 1927).

10768 Ferguson, Faye. Pianist (WLW, Cincinnati, OH, 1925).

10769 Ferguson, Gene. Newscaster (WEW, St. Louis, MO, 1942–1945).

10770 Ferguson, Jim. DJ (*Especially for You,* WCBT, Roanoke Rapids, NC, 1947; WPFA, Pensacola, FL, 1957). Sportscaster (*Sports Parade,* WCBT, 1948).

10771 Ferguson, Karen. COM-HE (WAKO, Lawrenceville, IL, 1960).

10772 Ferguson, Marion. Violinist (KOMO, Seattle, WA, 1928).

10773 Ferguson, Paula. COM-HE (WJOI, Florence, KY, 1954).

10774 Ferguson, Terry. COM-HE (KOWB, Laramie, WY, 1960).

10775 Ferguson, (Mrs.) W.D. and Mrs. Alta LaRowe. Soprano Ferguson and contralto LaRowe sang duets (WOK, Pine Bluff, AR, 1922).

10776 Ferguson, Wynn. Ferguson broadcast *Bridge Lessons* (WQJ, Chicago, IL, 1925).

10777 Ferlinger, F.C. Organist (KFOA, Seattle, WA, 1928).

10778 Fernando, Don. Leader (*Don Fernando Orchestra,* instr. mus. prg., WCFL, Chicago, IL, 1937).

10779 Ferneau, Frank. Leader (*Frank Ferneau Orchestra,* instr. mus. prg., MBS, 1938).

10780 Feroglio and His Accordion. Accordionist not otherwise identified (WFKB, Chicago, IL, 1924).

10781 Ferra, Cressy. Pianist (KLX, Oakland, CA, 1929).

10782 Ferrand, Marion. Member with Jimmy Keith of the comedy singing team of Jimmy and Ann (KSTP, St. Paul, MN, 1929).

10783 Ferrar, Smith. Violinist (WLW, Cincinnati, OH, 1923).

10784 Ferrebee, Sally. COM-HE (WVPO, Stroudsburg, PA, 1957).

10785 Ferreci, Baci. DJ (KROG, Sonora, CA, 1956).

10786 Ferrentino, Theresa. Pianist (WEAF, New York, NY, 1925).

10787 Ferrette [Ferretti/Ferretto], Carlo. Baritone (WPG, Atlantic City, NJ, 1926) Ferrette also performed on the *Major Bowes Capitol Theater Family* (NBC, New York, NY, 1928).

10788 Ferri, Gaetano. Newscaster (WBIL, New York, NY and WOV, New York, NY, 1938).

10789 Ferrie, Robert "Bob." Newscaster (WOI, Ames, IA, 1945; KABC, San Antonio, TX, 1945–1946).

10790 Ferris, Jill. COM-HE (KBTV, Denver, CO, 1956).

10791 Ferris, Ray. End man on the *Weener Minstrel Show* (WENR, Chicago, IL, 1929).

10792 Ferris, Robert. Newscaster (KJR, Seattle, WA, 1940). Sportscaster (KJR, 1940).

10793 Ferris-Hinz [Heintz], Beatrice. Director, Jubilee Singers (KFWM, Oakland, CA, 1929).

10794 Ferruci's Orchestra. Local New York dance band (WRNY, New York, NY, 1925).

10795 Ferruza, Grace. Soprano (WNYC, New York, NY, 1924).

10796 Ferry, Charles T. Pianist (WRC, Washington, DC, 1923–1924).

10797 Ferry, Dexter. DJ (*Ramblin' Rhythm*, KENA, Mena, AR, 1949).

10798 Ferry, Ruth. Singer (WICC, Bridgeport, CT, 1939).

10799 Ferte, Joe. Tenor (WTAM, Cleveland, OH, 1925).

10800 Feruzza, Michael. DJ (*Half 'n' Half*, WJER, Dover, OH, 1949).

10801 Fessenden, Reginald Aubrey. Fessenden, was an engineer-chemist, who worked as chief chemist for Thomas Alva Edison. He later focused his interest on the wireless transmission of messages. By experimentation, Fessenden discovered a means to improve Marconi's wireless system and adapt it to the transmission of voice. His first "voice broadcast" took place Christmas Eve, 1906, when he broadcast poetry, a woman singing Christmas carols and his own violin solo of "O, Holy Night."

10802 *(The) Festival of Music.* Martin Bookspan was a classical music DJ, who provided erudite critical commentary along with good music (390 min., Sunday, 5:30–12:00 midnight, WCOP, Boston, MA, 1951).

10803 Fettis, Jim. Leader (*Jim Fettis Orchestra*, instr. mus. prg., WFIL, Philadelphia, PA, 1935–1936; CBS, 1936, 1939; WCAU, Philadelphia, PA, 1934–1935).

10804 Fetzer, John E. Announcer (WEMC, Barrien Springs, MI, 1925).

10805 Fey, Phillip. Tenor (WAHG, Richmond Hill, NY, 1926).

10806 Feyhl, W. H. Announcer who broadcast his station's slogan, the "Penn City Station" (WWAD, Philadelphia, PA, 1925–1926).

10807 *Fibber McGee and Molly.* After singing on radio as "The O'Henry Twins" in 1925, Jim and Marian Jordan (Fibber McGee and Molly) appeared in the *Smith Family*, an early serial drama with comic elements (WJBO, Chicago, IL, 1925–1926), later on the *Airscout Hour* in 1930 (WENR, Chicago, IL) and, finally, on network radio in 1930 with *The Smackouts*. They also were comic favorites on *Kaltenmeyer's Kindergarten* (WMAQ, Chicago, IL & NBC, 1932–1933).

On *Fibber McGee and Molly*, they played the roles of a lovable windbag and his level headed wife. The program was sponsored by Johnson Wax throughout its long broadcast run from 1935 to 1952. Old softy Fibber spoke with a loud mouth that was nevertheless driven by a warm heart. The *Fibber McGee and Molly* characters were developed on their first network show, *The Smackouts* [*see* ***The Smackouts***]. Both *The Smackouts* and *Fibber McGee and Molly* were written by Don Quinn. Phil Leslie eventually joined Quinn to assist him in writing the latter.

Fibber and Molly, the long time residents of 79 Wistful Vista, were popular radio favorites for many years. Marian Jordan took on various roles on the show such as those of Teeny, Geraldine and Mrs. Wearybottom. The show's excellent ensemble cast included Bill Thompson playing Wallace Wimple; Arthur Q. Bryan as Doc Gamble; and Isobel Randolph as Mrs. Uppington. Also included were Hal Peary as the Great Gildersleeve and [Mr.]Marlin Hurt as Beulah. Both later played these title roles in successful radio spin-off shows. Other cast members included: Cliff Arquette, Bea Benaderet, Gene Carroll, Gale Gordon, Jess Kirkpatrick, Shirley Mitchell, Ransom Sherman and Hugh Studebaker. The King's Men Vocal Quartet (Ken Darby, Jon Dodson, Bud Linn, and Rad Robinson) also made frequent appearances. Music was supplied by the orchestras of Rico Marchielli, Billy Mills and Ted Weems. Director Frank Pitman produced the program's sound effects. Harlow Wilcox was the program's announcer.

The couple who lived at 79 Wistful Vista are probably best remembered for the sound effect produced when McGee's hall closet's contents noisily spilled out each week after its door was opened. That disaster and McGee's many ridiculous statements frequently caused Molly to utter her famous catch-phrase, "Heavenly days, McGee." At other times when McGee thought he was being exceptionally witty, she would bring him down to earth with her, "Tain't funny, McGee." *See* ***The Smack Outs, Beulah, Kaltenmeyer's Kindergarten, The Great Gildersleeve*** and **Comediennes**.

10808 Fichthorne, Kathryn. Contralto (WCAU, Philadelphia, PA, 1926).

10809 Fick, Donna Demerel. Actress Fick played one of the title roles in *Myrt and Marge*, the famous daytime serial first broadcast by CBS in 1931. Her mother, Myrtle Vail, who played the role of "Myrt," also wrote the program. Tragically, Fick who played "Marge" died during childbirth on February 15, 1941. *See* ***Myrt and Marge***.

10810 Fickert, Kenneth. Announcer (WGR, Buffalo, NY, 1927).

10811 Fiddler [Fidler], Dick. Leader (*Dick Fiddler Orchestra*, instr. mus. prg., WGY, Schenectady, NY, 1934, NBC, 1935; WTAM, Cleveland, OH, 1937).

10812 Fiddlers from Muscatine and Riverside. Local musicians performed "old-time fiddle music" (WOC, Davenport, IA, 1924).

10813 Fidler, James Marion. Newscaster (*Luden Cough Drops Program* and *Drene Shampoo Program*, NBC, 1937).

10814 Fidler, Mark. DJ (*Sam's Songs*, WJBC, Bloomington, IN, 1954).

10815 Fidleroff, Raiya and Gena. The Fidleroff siblings—10 and 14 years of age respectively—played violin solos and duets (KFBK, Sacramento, CA, 1926).

10816 Fiedler, Arthur. DJ (WCRB, Boston, MA, 1955). Fiedler, the distinguished orchestra conductor, became a classical DJ in 1955.

10817 Field, Charles "Chuck." DJ (*Wake Up Rogue Valley*, KWIN, Ashland, OR, 1947; *Flying Discs*, KMED, Medford, OR, 1952; KBOY, Medford, OR, 1955).

10818 Field, Charles K. ("Cheerio"). Field, using the name of "Cheerio," began broadcasting on KGO, San Francisco, CA, in 1926, with his message of faith and good cheer. His inspirational talks, homey philosophy and soothing background music brought him many listeners. Cheerio began a six-times weekly network program March 14, 1927, on NBC. His inspirational morning show, containing poetry, music and up-lifting messages, quickly became one of the most popular programs on the network. Regular features on his programs were the singing canaries, pianist Harrison Isles, the Parnassus Trio and Emil Seidel's Little Peppers.

In 1934, Cheerio claimed that he never received a penny for broadcasting. "I'll make my money some other way," he said. It should be noted, that he authored many best selling books containing the poetry and aphorisms used on his programs, for which he was well compensated. Cheerio tried to keep his identity a secret, refusing for many years to give interviews. A unique feature of the program was the "Cheerio Exchange," in which his staff maintained a fund to purchase radios at a discount to be lent to shut-ins. Field's program continued to enjoy great popularity well into the 1930s. From 1937 to 1940, Cheerio broadcast in the evening one day per week as *Cheerio's Musical Maniacs*. *See* ***Cheerio***.

10819 Field, Erna. Cellist (WGCP, Newark, NJ, 1925).

10820 Field, Henry. Announcer and owner of station KFNK (Shenandoah, IA, 1925). Field provided his Henry Field Seed Company ample advertising on his station. Field was one of the most colorful pioneer broadcasters. *See* **Stations Growth and Development**.

10821 Field, Iris. COM-HE (WLOH, Princeton, WV, 1957).

10822 Field, Thomas. Newscaster (WTAM, Cleveland, OH, 1940; 1952).

10823 Fielder, Joseph J. Newscaster (*The Taxpayer*, WDLP, Marshfield, WI, 1947).

10824 Fielder, Lena Holland. Lyric coloratura soprano (WFAA, Dallas, TX, 1923).

10825 Fielding, Jules. DJ (*Juke Box Revue*, WMBM, Miami Beach, FL, 1948).

10826 Fielding, (Captain) Michael. Newscaster (WIND, Gary, IN, 1941–1945).

10827 Fielding, Romaine. Fielding hosted the *Radiocast Review* program (KFVE, University City, MO, 1925).

10828 Fields, Barbara. COM-HE (KTOW, Oklahoma City, OK, 1951).

10829 Fields, Benny. Entertainer known as "The Minstrel Man" (*Benny Fields*, vcl. mus. prg., CBS, 1936).

10830 Fields, Bill. CW leader of Billy Fields' Cowboys (WNBC, New Britain, CT, 1937).

10831 Fields, Bill. Newscaster (WMBS, Uniontown, PA, 1940).

10832 Fields, Buddy. Leader (*Buddy Fields Orchestra*, instr. mus. prg., NBC, 1934; WXYZ, Detroit, MI, 1935).

10833 Fields, Catherine. Soprano (WJZ, New York, NY, 1932).

10834 Fields, Don. CW leader Don Fields' Pony Boys (WCAX, Burlington, VT, 1931).

10835 *Fields, Dorothy and Jimmy McHugh*. Dorothy, daughter of Lew Fields sang and Jimmy McHugh played the piano on the critically praised program. The composing team performed both their own songs and those of other composers (15 min., Friday, 10:15–10:30 P.M., NBC-Blue, 1933).

10836 Fields, Edna. Mezzo-contralto (WEAF, New York, NY, 1924–1926).

10837 Fields, Eric. Newscaster (WTND, Orangeburg, SC, 1948).

10838 Fields, Geraldine. CLOM-HE (WAYX, Waycross, GA, 1951).

10839 Fields, Joe. Newscaster (WTOL, Toledo, OH, 1940–1941).

10840 Fields, Lew. Vaudeville comedian Lew Fields was a member of the famous Weber and Fields vaudeville team (WWJ, Detroit, MI, 1921).

10841 Fields, Mildred. COM-HE (WLRP, Albany, IN, 1949).

10842 Fields, Pat. COM-HE (WBMD, Baltimore, MD, 1960).

10843 Fields, Shep. Leader (*Shep Fields Orchestra*, instr. mus. prg., CBS, 1934; WOR, Newark, NJ and NBC, 1936; MBS, 1939). Orchestra leader Fields became a DJ on his *Ripplin' Rhythm Rendezvous* program (KTHT, Houston, TX, 1955). During his years as a big band leader, his orchestra was known as Shep Fields and his Rippling Rhythm.

10844 *Fields and Hall Mountaineers*. CW mus. prg. (NBC, 1935–1936). The Mountaineers combined CW songs with comic patter on their popular program.

10845 Fiengold, Blanche. Newscaster (*Timely Topics*, WALB, Albany, GA, 1947).

10846 *Fiesta*. Pancho (Anthony Barrett) was the comic host of the sustaining music show that featured singer Olga St. Juan, Bob Graham, the Samba Kings Trio and Wilbur Hatch's orchestra (30 min., Sunday, 7:30–8:00 P.M., CBS, 1951).

10847 Fiesta De Las Rosas Instrumental Quartet. Ethnic music group (KGO, Oakland, CA, 1926).

10848 *Fiesta Rancho*. Comedian Ransom Sherman owned the Grapevine Ranch, where the situation comedy show supposedly took place. The program's talented cast included motion picture stars Leo Carrillo, Mary Astor and Carlos Ramirez. Lud Gluskin's orchestra was also featured on this show sponsored by Roma Wines (30 min., Thursday, 8:00–8:30 P.M., CBS, 1942).

10849 Fife, Otto. Newscaster (KSUB, Cedar City, UT, 1948).

10850 Fifer, Margaret. Leader (Margaret Fifer Orchestra, WFAA, Dallas, TX, 1924).

10851 Fifield, Georgia. Reader (KFI, Los Angeles, CA, 1925). Miss Fifield later was the director of the *KNX Playlets (*KNX, Los Angeles, CA, 1928).

10852 Fifield, (Dr.) James W. World traveler Fifield talked about his travels (WHB, Kansas City, MO, 1928).

10853 Fifield, Marie. Piano accompanist Fifield appeared on the *Big Brother Club* program (WEEI, Boston, MA, 1928).

10854 *Fifteen Minutes of Sunshine*. Band leader Charlie Hamp provided the sunshine on the quarter-hour program with his talk and songs (KMTR, Hollywood, CA, 1926).

10855 Fifth Avenue Club Orchestra. Metropolitan club band (WOR, Newark, NJ, 1926).

10856 Fifth Avenue Knights. Enrique Madriquera directed this New York orchestra (WJZ, New York, NY, 1928).

10857 *Fifty Flying Fingers*. Five typists on each program competed for a $5 prize that was awarded to the fastest one. Each contestant typed unfamiliar copy for three minutes and then read it on the air. The program was sponsored by the Remington-Rand Typewriter Company (30 min., Weekly, KFOR, Lincoln, NE, 1937).

10858 *Fights of Yesteryear*. Peter King broadcast blow-by-blow accounts of re-creations of great boxing matches. Bob Clement assisted him by providing between rounds "color." The "bouts" included realistically simulated crowd noises when appropriate. This interesting show for boxing fans was sponsored by the Erie Brewing Company. Al Zink was the writer. An example of the show's creativity was provided when the Dempsey-Firpo fight ended in the early rounds with a knock out by Dempsey, and the announcers "returned it to the studio" for an interview with Jimmy Goodrich, a former lightweight champion, to fill the time (30 min., Wednesday, 10:00–10:30 P.M., WEBR, Buffalo, NY, 1939). For an earlier show that recreated famous boxing bouts see the program described by Quin Ryan. *See* **Ryan, Quin**.

10859 Figueroa, Conrad. DJ (*Morning Serenade*, KYOR, Blythe, CA, 1954).

10860 Figueroa, Frank. DJ (WHOM, New York, NY, 1955).

10861 Filardi, Madeline. Singer (WIP, Philadelphia, PA, 1937).

10862 File, August A., Jr., " Augie." DJ (*Records for Rising*, WLOX, Biloxi, MS, 1952; *Top of the Dial*, WLOX, 1954; WALA, Mobile, AL, 1957).

10863 Files, Bert. DJ (WCAW, Charleston, WV, 1954–1956).

10864 Files, Norma K. COM-HE (WCAW, Charleston, WV, 1954).

10865 Filipino Novelty Orchestra. Ethnic band (WMCA, New York, NY, 1925).

10866 Filipino Orchestra. A popular ethnic orchestra (WIP, Philadelphia, PA, 1926).

10867 Fillbrandt, Laurette. Busy actress Fillbrandt was a cast member of such daytime serial programs as *The Guiding Light*, *Bachelor's Children*, *Ma Perkins*, *Girl Alone*, *Midstream*, *Tale of Today* and *Today's Children*.

10868 Fillingham, Joan. COM-HE (KANS, Wichita, KS, 1951).

10869 Fillmore, Henry. Fillmore, was one of the greatest American brass bandmasters and composers. He probably was exceeded in popularity only by John Philip Sousa. Fillmore conducted his band on many network programs in the 1930s and 1940s.

10870 Fillmore, Hildegarde. COM-HE (*Beauty Talk*, CBS, 1936).

10871 *Final Edition*. Bob Ryf and Larry Marcus wrote the revised version of the network's *Front Page* program. The good dramatic adventure show featured Dick Powell and Bill Conrad in an exciting story of a newspaper columnist (30 min., Thursday, 7:30–8:00 P.M., ABC, 1948).

10872 Finch, Bertha. Blues singer (NBC-Pacific Network, 1928–1929).

10873 Finch, Bud. DJ (*Coffee Club*, WELI, New Haven, CT, 1947–1950).

10874 Finch, Durwood "Dee." DJ (Partner of **Gene Rayburn** on their popular New York morning program, *Anything Goes with Rayburn & Finch*, WNEW, New York, NY, 1949–1950).

10875 Finch, Francis. Announcer (WKBF, Indianapolis, IN, 1925).

10876 Finch, George. Leader (*George Finch Orchestra*, instr. mus. prg., WIP, Philadelphia, PA, 1936).

10877 Finch, Howard K. Newscaster (WJIM, Lansing, MI, 1939–1941). Sportscaster (WJIM, 1939–1940; WJIM, 1947–1952; *Sports Column*, WJIM, 1953).

10878 Finch, Len. Singer Finch was called "The Boy with a Smile." He sang with Slater's Squirrel Dodgers Orchestra (KFQB, Fort Worth, TX, 1927).

10879 Finch, Louise. Finch, a busy radio actress, was a cast member of such daytime serial programs as *Ma Perkins*; *Joyce Jordan, Girl Interne*; *Kitty Keene* aka *Kitty Keene, Incorporated*; *Backstage Wife* aka *Mary Noble, Backstage Wife*; *Road of Life*; *Scattergood Baines*; *Big Sister*; and *The Woman in White*.

10880 Findling, Arthur. Baritone (WHAS, Louisville, KY, 1924).

10881 Fine Arts Trio. Director-pianist Geraldine McNeely, violinist Edward Lurton and flutist William Fries comprised the musical group (WHAS, Louisville, KY, 1924).

10882 Fine, Hy. Leader (*Hy Fine Orchestra*, instr. mus. prg., WEEI, Boston, MA, 1932).

10883 Fine, Jack. Newscaster (WAYX, Waycross, GA, 1940).

10884 Finestone, Edna. Pianist Finestone was called by *Variety* "a charming piano soloist" (WDAR, Philadelphia, PA, 1923).

10885 Finey, Milo. Leader (Milo Finey String Trio, WHB, Kansas City, MO, 1926).

10886 Finger, Art. DJ (*Sun Dial*, KXYZ, Houston, TX, 1948–1950).

10887 Finger, Len. Sportscaster (KTAT, Ft. Worth, TX, 1939; KFDM, Beaumont, TX, 1940). Newscaster (KFDM, 1940).

10888 Fink, Henry. Leader (Henry Fink Orchestra, WGBS, New York, NY, 1928).

10889 Fink, Maurice. Sportscaster (WQAM, Miami, FL, 1937).

10890 Finkeldey, William. Sportscaster (*Sports Newsreel* and *Rod and Gun Club*, WLAM, Lewiston, ME, 1949).

10891 Finklea, Jacquelynn. COM-HE (WATP, Marion, SC, 1960).

10892 Finklestein, Ethel. COM-HE (WRSA, Sarasota Springs, NY, 1960).

10893 Finley, Elmer A. Newscaster (*Home Edition*, WLBJ, Bowling Green, KY, 1948).

10894 Finley, Larry. DJ (*The Larry Finley Show*, KFWB, Los Angeles, CA, 1952; *Strictly Informal*, KTLA, Los Angeles, CA, 1954).

10895 Finley, Stuart. Newscaster (KYW, Philadelphia, PA, 1940). DJ (*Capitol Scrapbook*, WRC, Washington, DC, 1949).

10896 Finn, Gregg. DJ (*Turntable Terrace*, WORL, Boston, MA, 1954–1957). Sportscaster (WORL, 1955).

10897 Finn, Leo. DJ (*Spin with Finn* and *The Leo Finn Show*, WMMW, Meriden, CT, 1949–1952).

10898 Finn, Lillian. Pianist (WLW, Cincinnati, OH, 1923).

10899 Finn, Margaret. Pianist (WLW, Cincinnati, OH, 1926).

10900 Finn, Michael. DJ (*Finn Fare*, WEOA, Evansville, IN, 1948–1952).

10901 Finnegan, Bob. Sportscaster (WJZ, New York, NY, 1952; boxing and football play-by-play, ABC, 1953–1955).

10902 Finnerty, Hugh J. Sportscaster (KCRC, Enid, OK, 1945; *Time Out for Sports*, KCRC, 1947; KOTV, Tulsa, OK, 1954–1956). DJ (*Screen Song Hits* and *Matinee Time*, KCRC, 1947; KBYE, Oklahoma City, OK, 1948).

10903 Finnie, "Piper." Scots bagpiper (KDKA, Pittsburgh, PA, 1922).

10904 Finstein, Paul. Leader (*Paul Finstein's Concert Orchestra*, instr. mus. prg., KNX, Los Angeles, CA, 1926). Finstein became director of the KNX studio orchestra in 1928.

10905 Finty, Evelyn. Violinist (WFAA, Dallas, TX, 1928).

10906 Finucane, Bob. Newscaster (*News and Sports*, WVCH, Chester, PA, 1948).

10907 Finzel's Dance Band. Popular local jazz band (WWJ, Detroit, MI, 1928).

10908 Fiora, Catherine. COM-HE (WCUM, Cumberland, MD, 1954).

10909 Fiorella, Mario. Italian baritone (*Mario Fiorella*, WBBM, Chicago, IL, mid–1930s).

10910 Fiorito and Gordy. Harmony vocal team (WCCO, Minneapolis–St. Paul, MN, 1928).

10911 Fiorito, Ernie. Leader (*Ernie Fiorito Orchestra*, instr. mus. prg., MBS, 1934, 1942).

10912 Fiorito, Ted. Pianist (WIBO, Chicago, IL, 1926). Fiorito later became the leader of the popular Ted Fiorito Orchestra (WIBO, Chicago, IL, 1926). Fiorito's popular orchestra made frequent broadcasts from Chicago's Edgewater Beach Hotel (NBC, Chicago, IL, 1929). The band was also busy in the next decade: (*Ted Fiorito and His Maytag Orchestra*. Fiorito's band was joined by a male trio and the piano team of Retting and Platt on the lively music show, 15 min., Monday, 9:30–9:45 P.M., NBC-Blue, 1930; *Ted Fiorito Orchestra*, instr. mus. prg., CBS, 1934–1939; MBS, 1937; KXOK, St. Louis, MO, 1939).

10913 *Fire Alarms.* The series of dramatized stories about firemen was the fire department's version of the police's *Calling All Cars* program. The sustaining local program, however, lacked the professional polish of the police show (15 min., Monday, 8:45–9:00 P.M., PST, KFAC, Los Angeles, CA, 1936).

10914 *Fire Prevention.* Real life incidents were dramatized on the program designed to promote safety and the prevention of fires. Smokey Rogers, the fire clown, was the fire chief of the mythical town of Asheville on the program. Others in the cast were Eddie Allan and Della Anne Ragland (15 min., Saturday, 8:15–8:30 A.M. CST, WLS, Chicago, IL, 1936).

10915 (The) Fireman's Orchestra of Oakland (California). B. Russo directed the municipal band (KTAB, Oakland, CA, 1926).

10916 *Fireside Party.* Henry Hornsbuckle, Patsy Montana, the Kentucky Girls, Hilltoppers and the Prairie Ramblers provided CW music on the weekly show (60 min., Saturday, 10:00–11:00 P.M., WLS, Chicago, IL, 1938).

10917 *Fireside Recital.* Graham McNamee hosted the program of classical music. Bass Sigurd Nilssen, Willie Morris and tenor Hardesy Johnssen were regular performers. The orchestra was conducted by Frank St. Leger. When St. Leger was on vacation, his place was taken by Vladimir Padwa (30 min., Sunday, 5:30–6:00 P.M. CST, NBC-Red, 1936). Two years later, the program featured Sigurd Nilssen and soprano Helen Marshall (30 min., Sunday, 7:30–8:00 P.M., NBC-Red, 1938).

10918 *Fireside Songs.* Tenor Phil Dewey was featured on the weekly music program (15 min., 10:00–10:15 P.M., NBC-Blue, 1933).

10919 *Fireside Thoughts for Men.* June Merrill read poetry and gave advice intended to enhance the male ego. Interludes of romantic music added to the sustaining program's atmosphere (30 min., Monday through Friday, 12:30–1:00 A.M., WENR, Chicago, IL, 1947).

10920 First Baptist Church Male Trio. Vocal group included DeWitt Pugh, Charles A. Pugh and Dudley Wendt (KQW, San Jose, CA, 1925).

10921 First Baptist Church Orchestra (Ft. Worth, TX). A 25-piece concert orchestra (WBAP, Fort Worth, TX, 1923).

10922 First Baptist Church (San Jose, CA) Sextet. The religious vocal group's members were Margaret Algar, Mrs. Nylin, Miss Brown, Mrs. Curtis, Mrs. Rasmussen and Mrs. Downer (KQW, San Jose, CA, 1925).

10923 *(The) First Hundred Years.* The situation comedy about the problems faced by a young married couple was written by Jean Holloway. Bea Benadaret, Sam Edwards, Barbara Eiler, Joseph Kearns, Myra Marsh and Earle Ross were in the cast. The announcer was Owen James (30 min., Weekly, 8:30–9:00 P.M., ABC, 1949).

10924 *First Love.* Rosalind Russell and Jimmy Stewart played the leads in the romantic story of a boy and girl in Hollywood. Grover James wrote and Conrad Nagel directed the interesting romantic drama sponsored by Rogers 1947 Silverware. Coincidentally, one of the company's silverware patterns just happened to be called First Love (30 min., Sunday, 5:00–5:30 P.M., CBS, 1937).

10925 First Methodist Church (Dallas, Texas) Choir. Church vocal group (WFAA, Dallas, TX, 1922).

10926 *First Nighter.* When the program first went on the air, producer Charles Hughes, himself, played the role of Mr. First Nighter. The Eric Sagerquist Orchestra and actors Don Ameche, June Meredith and Cliff Soubier were featured. Originally, Hughes wanted the program to be a vehicle for 40-word advertisements for ten advertisers. Searching for the ninth advertiser, an associate suggested to Hughes that he contact Campana's Italian Balm Company of Batavia, Illinois. He gave the company a free ad on the following Saturday night program and by Monday, the company committed themselves to sponsor the entire show.

The program presented all types of productions: melodramas, comedies, historical shows, costume dramas, romantic and adventure dramas. Although no scenery was ever used, producer-actor Hughes in an opera cloak, cane and silk top hat sat in an elaborate box to view the show. First broadcast in 1929, the program pretended to be a visit by Mr. First Nighter to a performance at the "Little Theatre just off Times Square." Traffic and crowd noises added to the realism, as did those sounds that were generally heard in a Broadway theater. After Mr. First Nighter was shown to his seat by an usher, a complete story was dramatized on each program. Don Ameche was the male lead from the program's beginning until 1936. Later, the lead was played by Les Tremayne and Olan Soule. The female leads were June Meredith, Betty Lou Gerson and Barbara Luddy. During the period the program was on the air (1929–1953), the cast included: Don Ameche, Don Briggs, Macdonald Carey, Jack Doty, Betty Lou Gerson, Charles P. Hughes, Raymond Edward Johnson, Barbara Luddy, June Meredith, Marvin Miller, Bret Morrison, Michael Rye (Rye Billsbury), Cliff Soubier, Olan Soule, and Les Tremayne. The writers were Edwin Halloran, Virginia Safford Lynne, Arch Oboler and Dan Shuffman. Frank Smith composed the program's original music. The final producer-director was Joe Ainley and Vincent Pelletier was the announcer (30 min., Friday, 9:00–9:30 P.M., NBC-Blue, 1935). While on the air *The*

First Nighter was broadcast by all major networks, NBC, CBS and MBS.

10927 ***(The) First Piano Quartet.*** Several pianists comprised the "quartet" on the fine music program: Edward Edson, Adam Garner (Adam Gelbtrunk), Hans Horwitz, Frank Mittler, Vee Padwa and George Robert. Edwin Fadiman was the show's writer-producer and Arthur Austin, James E. Kovach and Paul Knight the director. The announcer was Gene Hamilton (30 min., NBC, 1947).

10928 **First Presbyterian (San Jose, CA) Church Choir.** Homer DeWitt Pugh directed the sixty-voice church choir that was accompanied by pianist Elizabeth A. Pugh (KQW, San Jose, CA, 1925).

10929 **Firstenberg, Irving.** Pianist (WGCP, Newark, NJ, 1926).

10930 **Fischer, Barbara.** Soprano (WNYC, New York, NY, 1925).

10931 **Fischer, Bill.** DJ (*1440 Club*, WROK, Rockford, IL, 1948).

10932 **Fischer, Charles L.** Leader (Charles L. Fischer Orchestra, WGBS, New York, NY, 1928).

10933 **Fischer, Dick.** Newscaster (WHAS, Louisville, KY, 1941–1945).

10934 **Fischer, Donald F.** Newscaster (*Morning Edition*, WGEM, Quincy, IL, 1948).

10935 **Fischer [Fisher], Edna.** Pianist (KFRC, San Francisco, CA, 1929; *Edna Fischer*, instr. mus. prg., KFRC, San Francisco, CA, 1930–1931).

10936 **Fischer, George.** Motion picture newscaster and commentator (*Hollywood Commentator*, MBS, 1937; *Jergens Lotion Program*, NBC, 1937).

10937 **Fischer, Larry.** Newscaster (KVKM, Monahans, TX, 1947). DJ (*Record Shop*, WLOL, Minneapolis, MN, 1952; *Music with Larry Fischer*, 150 min., Monday through Friday, 9:15–10:15 P.M. and 10:30–12:00 midnight, WTCN-FM, Minneapolis, MN, 1954; WNOE, New Orleans, LA, 1957). Sportscaster (KVKM, 1950).

10938 **Fischer, Leora E.** Soprano who specialized in children's songs (WJZ, New York, NY, 1922).

10939 **Fischer, Lou.** Newscaster (WCAM, Camden, NJ, 1938).

10940 **Fischer, Phyllis.** COM-HE (KALB, Alexandria, LA, 1951).

10941 **Fischer, Richard.** Newscaster (WHAS, Louisville, KY, 1940).

10942 **Fish, Harriett Beecher.** Organist (KYA, San Francisco, CA, 1928).

10943 **Fishback, Clifton M.** Announcer (WFBE, Seymour, IN, 1925).

10944 **Fishel, Raymond.** Singer (WGCP, Newark, NJ, 1925).

10945 **Fishell, Richard Edward "Dick."** Sportscaster (*General Mills Sports Resume* and *Sobol Brothers Sports Resume*, WMCA, New York, NY, 1937; WHN, New York, NY, 1939; NFL Giants' football play-by-play, New York Rangers' hockey and *Sports Resume*, WHN, 1940–1941; KFWB, Hollywood, CA, 1946–1947).

10946 **Fisher, Alice E.** COM-HE (KBIZ, Ottumwa, IA, 1951).

10947 **Fisher, Bill.** DJ (*Fisher 'Til One*, WOWO, Ft. Wayne, IN, 1949).

10948 **Fisher, Bud.** Leader (*Bud Fisher's Happy Players* [musical comedy band], WGBS, New York, NY, 1926; WOR, Newark, NJ, 1934; WHAS, Louisville, KY, 1936).

10949 **Fisher, Buddy.** Leader (*Buddy Fisher Orchestra*, instr. mus. prg., WLW, Cincinnati, OH, 1939; NBC, 1939).

10950 **Fisher, Cecil.** Singer (WOR, Newark, NJ, 1925).

10951 **Fisher, Charles "Smiling Charlie."** Leader (Eastman Hotel Orchestra, broadcast frequently during the mid–1920s).

10952 **Fisher, Earl.** DJ (*1450 Club*, WFUN, Hunstville, AL, 1948).

10953 **Fisher, Edith.** COM-HE (WLSE, Wallace, NC, 1954).

10954 **Fisher, Ernest.** Fisher was the leader of the Tenth Infantry Band of Fort Thomas (WLW, Cincinnati, OH, 1923).

10955 **Fisher, Ethel R.** COM-HE Fisher, using the name Nancy Lee, appeared on the *Homemaker's Club*, a popular weekly program (KMOX, St. Louis, MO, 1931).

10956 **Fisher, Hank.** Sportscaster (WDZ, Tuscola, IL, 1939; WMBD, Peoria, IL, 1940–1941; *Sports Review*, WLW, Cincinnati, OH, 1947; *6:25 Sports*, WIRL, Peoria, IL, 1949–1950; *Hank Fisher on Sports*, WIRL, 1951; WEEK, Peoria, IL, 1952–1954).

10957 **Fisher, Howard.** Newscaster (KFDA, Amarillo, TX, 1940).

10958 **Fisher, Jack.** Leader (*Jack Fisher Orchestra*, instr. mus. prg., WNAC, Boston, MA, 1934).

10959 **Fisher, Jerry.** Newscaster (KNOW, Austin, TX, 1941; KVIC, Victoria, TX, 1945). Sportscaster (KNOW, 1941; KRIO, McAllen, TX, 1948).

10960 **Fisher, Jim.** DJ (*Ham 'n' Eggs*, WFOY, St. Augustine, FL, 1947; *Jive to Five*, WGGG, Gainesville, FL, 1950). Sportscaster (WGGG, 1949).

10961 **Fisher, Joe.** DJ (*Hillbilly Shindig*, KRHD, Duncan, OK, 1949).

10962 **Fisher, Jonilee.** Reader (KGHI, Little Rock, AR, 1929).

10963 **Fisher, Kelson.** DJ (WWIN, Baltimore, MD, 1954). Fisher specialized in rhythm and blues.

10964 **Fisher, Larry.** DJ (*Alarm Clock Club*, KVKM, Monahans, TX, 1947).

10965 **Fisher, Leon.** Announcer (WKEN, Buffalo, NY, 1925).

10966 **Fisher, Margaret.** Pianist (WCAE, Pittsburgh, PA, 1924).

10967 **Fisher, Marian.** Coloratura soprano (WOAW, Omaha, NE, 1926).

10968 **Fisher, Mark.** Leader (*Mark Fisher Orchestra*, instr. mus. prg., KYW, Chicago, IL, 1934; WLW, Cincinnati, OH,1934; CBS, 1935; WBBM, Chicago, IL, 1937).

10969 **Fisher, Martha.** Harpist (KFUU, Oakland, CA, 1925).

10970 **Fisher, Max.** Leader (*Max Fisher Orchestra*, KFAC, Los Angeles, CA, 1932).

10971 **Fisher, Phil.** Leader (*Phil Fisher and His Ten Eyck Hotel Orchestra*, instr. mus. prg. WABC, New York, NY, 1931; WNAC, Boston, MA, 1932).

10972 **Fisher, Rolly.** Leader (Rolly Fisher's Cosmos Club Orchestra, WGBS, New York, NY, 1925).

10973 **Fisher, Scott.** Leader (*Scott Fisher Orchestra*, instr. mus. prg., CBS, 1935).

10974 **Fisher, Sterling.** Newscaster (*Our Foreign Policy*, NBC, 1947–1948).

10975 **Fisher, Steve.** Newscaster (WWNR, Beckley, WV, 1946).

10976 **Fisher, Thornton.** Sports columnist (WAHG, Richmond Hill, NY, 1925; WNEW, New York, NY, 1937; *The Briggs Sports Review*, 15 min., Saturday, 5:45–6:00 P.M.; CBS, 1935; *Sports Parade of the Air*, 15 min., 6:45–7:00 P.M.; NBC, 1935).

10977 **Fisher, Tiny.** DJ (*Clockwatcher*, WEIR, Weirton, WV, 1949).

10978 ***(The) Fishfinder.*** Al Accardi, editor of the *Sportsmen Review*, conducted this "talking bulletin board" that advised fishermen where the fish were running and biting. The sponsor was the Golden Glow Beer Company of San Francisco, California (KROW, Oakland, CA, 1940).

10979 **Fisk, Jim.** DJ (*Anything Can Happen*, KGFN, Grass Valley, CA, 1947; *Lucky Lager Dance Time*, WCKA, Tucson, AZ, 1949).

10980 **Fisk, Pauline.** Pianist (KYW, Chicago, IL, 1923).

10981 **Fiske, Fred.** DJ (WWDC, Washington, DC, late1940s-1960). Fiske combined music, news and sports on his program.

10982 ***Fiske Jubilee Singers (aka Fiske Jubilee Choir).*** The Fiske Jubilee Singers, a talented African-American singing group, frequently appeared on WSM during radio's early years (WSM, Nashville, TN, 1920s and 1930s).

10983 ***Fiske-Time-to-Retire Boys.*** An otherwise unidentified vocal group appeared on the program of popular songs. The vocal group and an orchestra were featured (Monday, 9:30–10:00 P.M., NBC-Pacific Coast Network, 1928).

10984 **Fiske University Student Quartet.** Excellent African-American university vocal group (WSM, Nashville, TN, 1928).

10985 **Fitch, Gail.** Leader (Gail Fitch Orchestra, WHO, Des Moines, IA, 1925).

10986 **Fitch, Helen.** Movie critic (WBBM, Chicago, IL, 1934–1935).

10987 **Fitch, Marcie.** COM-HE (WGLN, Glenwood Springs, CO, 1954).

10988 **Fitch, (Dr.) W.E.** Fitch was an M.D., who frequently broadcast health talks (WEAF, New York, NY, 1924).

10989 ***(The) Fitch Bandwagon.*** Originally, the program featured a different name band each week playing their current hits. A new format was introduced in 1945, when Cass Daley's comedy was featured and music relegated to a secondary role. After Miss Daley left the following year, Phil Harris and his wife, Alice Faye, became the program's stars and transformed the show into a situation comedy. In addition to its stars, the Phil Harris-Alice

Faye format of the *Fitch Bandwagon* featured the following performers: Arthur Q. Bryan, June Foray, Sheldon Leonard, Elliott Lewis, Jane Morgan, Robert North, Jeanine Roos, Walter Tetley and Anne Whitfield. The writers were: Dick Chevillat, George D. Faber, Milton Josefsberg, Martin A. Ragaway and Ray Singer. The Phil Harris and the Walter Sharp bands occasionally performed. Jack Costello, Bill Forman and Tobe Reed were the announcers. Ward Byron was the producer-writer (NBC, 1937–1948).

10990 ***(The) Fitch Professor.*** This program was designed to both entertain and sell Fitch Shampoo. Tenor Jack Brooks and an instrumental trio provided the entertainment, while "Professor" Carl Way talked about hair care and sold Fitch Shampoo (CBS, 1930).

10991 Fitts, Lou. DJ (*Music in the Air*, WLNH, Laconia, NH, 1949).

10992 Fitz, Kathleen. Actress Fitz appeared on the *Brent House* daytime serial.

10993 Fitz Sisters. Harmony singing team of Mary and Geneva Fitz (WBAL, Baltimore, MD, 1927).

10994 Fitz, Stephen. Sportscaster (WSNY, Schenectady, NY, 1948–1954).

10995 Fitzcharles, H.V. Sportscaster (*Twentieth Century Bowling*, WHIP, Hammond, IN, 1940).

10996 Fitzer, H. Dean. Chief announcer (WDAF, Kansas City, MO, 1927–1928).

10997 Fitzgerald, Charles. Leader (Rhythm Kings Jazz Band, WJR, Detroit, MI, 1928–1929).

10998 Fitzgerald, Ed. DJ (*Discs and Dollars*, WOOD, Grand Rapids, MI, 1952; WMAX, Grand Rapids, MI, 1960).

10999 Fitzgerald, Edward. Newscaster (WMUR, Manchester, NH, 1942).

11000 Fitzgerald, Ella. Vocalist and leader (*Ella Fitzgerald Orchestra*, instr. mus. prg., WENR, Chicago, IL, 1934; *Ella Fitzgerald*, vcl. mus. prg., NBC, 1942). Ella Fitzgerald was one of the greatest jazz singers of her era.

11001 Fitzgerald, Gordon. DJ (*Time and Tempo*, WBAP, Fort Worth, TX, 1947; *Rendezvous with Melody*, WBAP, 1948; *570 Matinee*, WBAP, 1950).

11002 Fitzgerald, Jack. Newscaster (WSPD, Toledo, OH, 1937).

11003 Fitzgerald, Jacqueline. COM-HE (WKLZ, Kalamazoo, MI, 1957).

11004 Fitzgerald, John Frances. Told stories of the old sailing ship days on his *The Ancient Mariner* program (WLWL, New York, NY, 1931–1932).

11005 Fitzgerald, Josephine. Reader (KFAE, Pullman, WA, 1925).

11006 Fitzgerald, Pat. DJ (*Fitz Parade*, WNOK, Columbia, SC, 1952).

11007 Fitzgerald, Pegeen. COM-HE (*Pegeen Prefers*, WOR, Newark, NJ, 1942; WRCA, New York, NY, 1955–1956). *See* **Husband-and-Wife Talk Shows** and ***(The) Fitzgeralds.***

11008 ***(The) Fitzgeralds.*** Ed and Pegeen Fitzgerald broadcast their entertaining and lively version of a husband-and-wife talk show conducted over the breakfast table (15 min., Monday through Friday, 6:45–7:00 A.M., WJZ, New York, NY, 1947). John A. Gambling says that he believes that the Fitzgeralds were the first "Mr. and Mrs." broadcasters on New York radio. John B. Gambling had an early "Mr. and Mrs." show from Macy's department store, but the format for the show was scripted and the "Mrs." was an actress. Perhaps the Fitzgeralds were the first authentic husband and wife team on radio.

In addition to their popular husband-and-wife breakfast show in 1947, Ed and Pegeen also broadcast an evening show with a dinner table setting (*The Fitzgeralds*, 15 min., Monday through Friday, 6:45–7:00 P.M., WJZ, New York, NY, 1947). Ed and Pegeen were great favorites on New York radio for many years with their interesting husband-and-wife talk shows. *See* **Husband-and-Wife Talk Shows**.

11009 Fitzgibbons, John M. Newscaster (WSAR, Fall River, MA, 1938–1942).

11010 Fitzjohn, Olive. Soprano (WGY, Schenectady, NY, 1925).

11011 Fitzpatrick, Aiden. Newscaster (WWSW, Pittsburgh, PA, 1940; WSM, Nashville, TN, 1946).

11012 Fitzpatrick, Ed. Leader (Ed Fitzpatrick and his Hotel St. Francis Concert Orchestra, KGO, San Francisco, CA, 1927). Later his band was introduced as, "Music for moderns with Eddie Fitzpatrick and his orchestra from the Del Mar Club in Santa Monica, California" (Network, 1940).

11013 Fitzpatrick, Jack. Newscaster (KLZ, Denver, CO, 1937–1941; KFEL, Denver, CO, 1946). Sportscaster (KLZ, 1939–1941; KFEL, 1946–1949).

11014 Fitzpatrick, Les. Sportscaster (*Sports Spotlight*, KHQ, Spokane, WI, 1949).

11015 Fitzpatrick, Leo ("The Merry Old Chief"). Leo Fitzpatrick was not only the "Merry Old Chief," the broadcaster famous for presenting the Coon-Sanders Nighthawks band, but also the Radio Editor of the Kansas City *Star*. While he was hosting the famous *Nighthawks Frolic* program, he also appeared as "Mr. R.A. Dio" on station WDAF's (Kansas City, MO) weekly minstrel show. *The Nighthawks Frolic* was one of the first attempts to broadcast a program regularly at midnight six nights a week. It ran nightly except Sunday for over two years (90 min., Monday through Saturday, 11:30–1:00 A.M., WDAF, 1922). Fitzpatrick claimed that about two million listeners were members of the Nighthawks Club.

Fitzpatrick left WDAF in 1925 to join WJR, Detroit, MI. He soon organized *The Jewett Jesters Program*, a show similar to *The Nighthawks Frolic* he had created previously at WDAF. At the Detroit station, Fitzpatrick initiated the famous *Red Apple Club* program. "Bernice" was the official accompanist for six years, until blues singer-pianist Thelma Bow took over the task. *See* ***Nighthawk Frolic and Red Apple Club.***

11016 Fitzsimmons, Rodney. Baritone (*Rodney Fitzsimmons*, vcl. mus., WPG, Atlantic City, NJ, 1935).

11017 Fitzsimmons, (Mrs.) W.E. Contralto (WCCO, Minneapolis–St. Paul, MN, 1928).

11018 Fitzwater, Jean. COM-HE (KGEZ, Kalispell, MT, 1949).

11019 Fitzwilson, Ethel. COM-HE (KSWO, Lawton, OK, 1956).

11020 Five Billikens. The Five Billikens were a popular five-piece orchestra consisting of students from St. Louis University (WEW, St. Louis, MO, 1929).

11021 ***Five By Five.*** In one of the best examples of innovative programming, five popular Baltimore DJ's — Al Ross, Jay Grayson, Lee Case, Galen Fromme and Martin Edwards — alternated to play their favorite recordings. They played their "pick of the week tunes" (30 min., Monday through Friday, 7:00–7:30 P.M., WBAL, Baltimore, MD, 1955).

11022 ***555 Dinner Music Program.*** This special series of music programs presented various bands and musicians such as Joseph Dunn's Marigold Orchestra; the Al Amin 60-piece Shrine Band directed by R.B. "Scrubby" Watson; White City's Rose Garden Orchestra; violinist Fredericka Chappell; and pianist Florence Federer (KLRA, Little Rock, AR, 1929).

11023 ***507 Boys Dance Orchestra.*** Instr. mus. prg. (KFWB, Hollywood, CA, 1929).

11024 Five Little Eskimos Orchestra. Joe Martin directed the small dance band (KFWB, Hollywood, CA, 1925).

11025 Five Messner Brothers Orchestra. Popular local band (WMCA, New York, NY, 1925).

11026 ***Five O'Clock Revue.*** Budd Carter (Powell Clark) broadcast Hollywood gossip. Nat Brusiloff's orchestra and singers Jane Clifton and Jerry Baker supplied the music on the program. sponsored by Min-Aqua. The announcer was Don Kerr (30 min., Monday, 5:00–5:30 P.M., WMCA, New York, NY, 1938).

11027 ***Five Star Final.*** News events were dramatized on the popular New York program (15 min., Wednesday, 8:15–8:30 P.M., WMCA, New York, NY, 1934).

11028 ***Five Star Jones.*** Frank and Anne Hummert produced the daytime serial program about a young newspaperman and his wife played by John Kane and Elizabeth Day. Bill Johnstone was also in the cast (15 min., Monday through Friday, 11:45–12:00 noon, CBS, 1935).

11029 ***Five Star Theater.*** Standard Oil of New Jersey sponsored the variety show that featured veteran German dialect comedian Solly Ward, the music of Josef Bonime's orchestra and singers Barbara Blair and Frank Luther (30 min., Weekly, CBS, 1933).

11030 Fjelde, Astride. Norwegian mezzo-soprano (WJZ, New York, NY, 1926).

11031 Flaenzer, Anila Gibson. Concert mezzo-soprano (WOR, Newark, NJ, 1928).

11032 Flaget, L.E. *See* **Palace Theatre String Orchestra.**

11033 Flagg, Elizabeth. Pianist (WTIC, Hartford, CT, 1927).

11034 Flagg, Gertrude. Singer (WFMD, Frederick, MD, 1942).

11035 Flagg, Nellie. Blind pianist (KOIL, Council Bluffs, IA, 1927).

11036 Flagler, Robert. Assistant announcer (KOMO, Seattle, WA, 1928).

11037 Flaherty, Bob. DJ (*Melody Matinee*, WSKY, Asheville, NC, 1947; *Nighthawks*, WCKY, Cincinnati, OH, 1952).

11038 Flaherty, Pat. Sportscaster (WOAI, San Antonio, TX, 1937–1940; KPRC, Houston, TX, 1941). Newscaster (KPRC, Houston, TX, 1945–1946).

11039 Flahive, Ella. COM-HE (WDEW, Westfield, MA, 1960).

11040 Flamm, Donald. Flamm was a drama critic for station WMCA (New York, NY,1925). Later, he led Donald Flamm's Frolickers, a popular New York band (WMCA, 1926). Flamm also was an announcer at WMCA from 1925 to 1929.

11041 Flanagan, Alvin. Newscaster (WRUF, Gainesville, FL, 1940).

11042 Flanagan, Pat. Flanagan was a busy sportscaster at WBBM, Chicago, IL, in 1929 and in the next decade as well: (*Flanagan's Football Winners*, WBBM, 1935, each week Flanagan predicted the scores of next Saturday's games*; Pat Flanagan Sports*, WBBM, Chicago, IL, 1937; WBBM, 1938–1939; KOOL, Phoenix, AZ, 1948). Newscaster (KOOL, 1948).

11043 Flanagan, Paul E. DJ (*Tri-City Ballroom*, WTRY, Troy, NY, 1948; *Record Man*, WTRY, 1949–1956).

11044 Flanders, Lydia. COM-HE (WTAG, Worcester, MA, 1949).

11045 Flanders, Sandra. COM-HE (WMEN, Tallahassee, FL, 1960).

11046 Flanders, Walt. Leader (Walt Flanders and his Commanders [orchestra], KFBK, Sacramento, CA, 1928).

11047 Flanerty, Pat. Newscaster (KPRC, Houston, TX, 1945–1946).

11048 Flanner, Janet. Newscaster (NBC-Blue, 1944). Her broadcasts originated from Paris, France, where she owned a book store.

11049 Flannery, Agnes. Pianist (WHO, Des Moines, IA, 1925).

11050 Flannery, Harry W. Newscaster (KMOX , St. Louis, MO, 1938–1939; KNX, Los Angeles, CA, 1942, 1945; CBS, 1944–1947).

11051 Flannigan, Lon. DJ (*Really the Blues*, WGVA, Geneva, NY, 1947).

11052 *Flash Gordon.* In the adventure serial based on the Alex Raymond comic strip of the same name, space ships and interplanetary travel were common elements, as Flash battled the villainous Ming the Merciless on the planet Mongo. Flash, played first by Gale Gordon and later by James Meighan, was assisted in his adventures by Dr. Zarkoff, played by Maurice Franklin. Other cast members included: Alan Reed (Teddy Bergman), Charlie Cantor, Ray Collins and Everett Sloane. Bruno Wick played the villainous Ming the Merciless. The producer was Himan Brown (15 min., Transcribed, Various Stations, 1935). The series concluded after 26 programs and was replaced by *Jungle Jim*, another Alex Raymond comic strip creation that also appeared in the Hearst newspapers.

11053 *Flashes from the Films.* Betty Ann Pointer and Norvell Slater broadcast film gossip (15 min., Weekly, WHB, Kansas City, MO, 1938).

11054 Flatau, K. Louis. Newscaster (KMTR, Hollywood, CA, 1944).

11055 Flath, H.E. Announcer Flath for WRAK (Escanaba, MI, 1926–1927) broadcast his station's slogan, "The Gateway to Cloverland."

11056 Flautt, (Mrs.) Meredith. Contralto (WSM, Nashville, TN, 1928).

11057 Flayhaven, Alice. Xylophone soloist (WTAM, Cleveland, OH, 1924).

11058 Flecey, Jerry. DJ (*Let's Dance*, WGAM, Presque Isle, ME, 1947). Sportscaster (WGAM, 1948).

11059 Fledderman, Doc. Leader (Doc Fledderman's Jazz Artists orchestra, 60 min., Friday, KLS, Oakland, CA, 1923). Their Friday, November 9, 1923, broadcast included these selections: "Carolina Mammy," "Annabelle," "Beale Street Mama," "Indiana Moon," "I Cried For You," "Cat's Whiskers," "Bebe," "Dreamy Melody," "Banana Blues," "Love Tales," "No, No, Nora," "Ala Moana," "That Old Gang of Mine" and "After Every Party." Doc Fledderman's Jazz Artists band in 1923 included, among others, this personnel: Lyle Ingersoll, p.; Harry Day, bj.; Leroy Cerrudo, as.-clr.; Jack Freitas, t.; and Doc Fledderman, ldr.-dr.

11060 Fledstedt, Henry J. Fledstedt discussed thrift topics (WLW, Cincinnati, OH, 1925–1926).

11061 Fleeger, Paul. Organist (KDKA, Pittsburgh, PA, 1924).

11062 Fleet, Tom. Sportscaster (WELO, Tupelo, MS, 1950; *Radio Relay Quiz*, KCNY, San Marcos, TX, 1952).

11063 Fleetwood, Harry. DJ (WRCA, New York, New York, 1956).

11064 Fleg, Julian. Newscaster (WLAP, Lexington, KY, 1944).

11065 Fleischer, Edith. Opera singer (WEAF, New York, NY, 1927).

11066 Fleischer, Nathan. Newscaster (WDAS, Philadelphia, PA, 1938–1940, 1945).

11067 Fleischer, Wilifred. Newscaster (WMAL, Washington, DC, 1945; CBS, 1947–1948).

11068 Fleischman, Charles. Violinist (WJZ, New York, NY, 1925).

11069 Fleischman, Sol J. Sportscaster (WDAE, Tampa, FL, 1937–1941; WDAE, 1946; *Thrills for Sportsmen*, WDAE, 1947; *Sol's Sports Slants*, WDAE, 1948; *Sports Slants*, WDAE, 1952; *Florida Fishing*, WTVT, Tampa, FL, 1960). DJ (*Wake Up Tampa*, WDAE, 1947).

11070 Fleischmann, Betty. COM-HE (KVEC, San Luis Obispo, CA, 1949)

11071 Fleishman, Alfrieda. Miss Fleishman was a reader whose specialty was performing "My Mom" as a pianologue accompanied by pianist Alice McClelland (KPO, San Francisco, CA, 1925).

11072 *(The) Fleishmann Yeast Program* (aka *The Fleishmann Sunshine Hour, The Fleishmann Hour, The Sunshine Hour, Rudy Vallee Show* and the *Royal Gelatin Hour*). Standard Brands, maker of Fleishmann's Yeast, sponsored the popular show hosted by orchestra leader-crooner, Rudy Vallee. This program set the pattern for the variety show format that was later copied on both radio and television. Few shows, however, could match the high standards the show consistently maintained. One week, for example, Vallee presented the Louis Armstrong orchestra, a drama written by Octavius Roy Cohen, an appearance by a prominent African-American author, an instrumental group called the Four Nuts of Rhythm and the comedy team of Eddie Green and Gee Gee Jones. Dr. R.E. Lee was the spokesman for Fleischmann's Yeast and its health promoting attributes and Graham McNamee was the announcer (60 min., Friday, 9:00–10:00 P.M., NBC-Blue, 1937).

Among the stars that appeared on the program were Weber and Fields, Bert Lahr, Mae West, Adolphe Menjou, Helen Hayes, Moran and Mack, Robert Montgomery, Jimmy Durante, Katherine Hepburn, Marie Dressler, Borrah Minevitch and his Harmonica Gang, Lou Holtz, Jules Bledsoe, the Yacht Club Boys, Milton Berle, Peggy Flynn, Chic Sale, Lynwood "Schoolboy" Rowe, Brad Browne and Al Llewelyn, Grace Moore, Blossom Seeley and Benny Fields, the Keller Sisters, Walter Huston, Fannie Brice, saxophonist Benny Kreuger, Dorothy Stone, Charles Collins, Lila Lee, Robert Armstrong, Mr. and Mrs. Ernest Truex with son Philip, Cornelia Otis Skinner, Ilka Chase, Edward Everett Horton, Peggy Conklin, Roger Pryor, Noah Berry, Claude Raines, pianist Henrietta Schumann, George and Howard Shelton, the Duncan Sisters, Monroe Silver, the Good Sisters (Girls of the Golden West), Katherine Perry, Earl "Fatha" Hines, the Stewart Sisters and Ethel Waters.

Another major accomplishment of the Vallee program was the great number of stars who made their first network appearance on the show such as Phil Baker, Milton Berle, Edgar Bergen, Bob Burns, Eddie Cantor, Alice Faye, Red Skelton, Teddy Bergman (later famous as Alan Reed) and Bert Gordon. Vallee (1976) was proud of the quality and variety he presented on his program. He claimed that he had only one guest who appeared more than three times during his first three years on the air. *The Fleischmann Hour* and the following shows hosted by Vallee presented several features that later were spun-off to become separate programs. Three examples of these spin-offs were the *Edgar Bergen and Charlie McCarthy, We the People and The Aldrich Family* programs. Each week the show was broadcast from the Variety Theater located in New York City's RCA Building before a large appreciative audience.

11073 Fleming, Bill. Newscaster (KWYO, Sheridan, WY, 1938). Sportscaster (*Today in Sports*, WHRV, Ann Arbor, MI, 1952; WWJ, Detroit, MI, 1953–1956).

11074 Fleming, Bruce. DJ (*Guess-a-Tune*, KSON, San Diego, CA, 1948).

11075 Fleming, (Dr.) D.F. Newscaster (WDAS, Philadelphia, PA and WSM, Nashville, TN, 1944).

11076 Fleming, Dorothy "Dot." COM-HE (WDSC, Dillon, SC, 1954–1956).

11077 Fleming, Douglas. Newscaster (WCPO, Cincinnati, OH, 1942).

11078 Fleming, Ed. Sportscaster (WIBA, Madison, WI, 1937). Newscaster (CBS, 1942).

11079 Fleming, Gordon. Organist (*Gordon Fleming*, instr. mus. prg., MBS, 1938).

11080 Fleming, Jack. Sportscaster (WAJR, Morgantown, WV, 1947–1947; *Today in Sports*, WAJR, 1948–1955). DJ (*Tea and Trumpets*, WAJR, 1949–1951).

11081 Fleming, Jacobus. Fleming broadcast talks on books (WGR, Buffalo, NY, 1925).

11082 Fleming, James. Newscaster (KYA, San Francisco, CA, 1945).

11083 Fleming, Joel. DJ (*Anthracite Club*, WPAM, Pottsville, PA, 1947).

11084 Fleming, Lurine. Soprano (*Lurine Fleming*, vcl. mus. prg., NBC-Red, New York, NY, 1936).

11085 Fleming, Mae Jacobs. Miss Fleming was a book reviewer (WOR, Newark, NJ, 1925).

11086 Fleming, Robert. DJ (*The Fleming Show* and *Swingtime*, KID, Idaho Falls, ID, 1947; KIFI, Idaho Falls, ID, 1954).

11087 Fleming, Rosemary. Newscaster (WBSR, Pensacola, FL, 1947).

11088 Fleming, Thomas. Newscaster (WLEU, Erie, PA, 1942).

11089 Fleming, Woody. Sportscaster (*Let's Go Hunting*, WCSI, Columbus, IN and KLIX, Twin Falls, ID, 1952).

11090 (The) Fleming Trio. *Variety* said the trio consisting of three attractive girls playing cello, piano and violin (WEAF, New York, NY, 1923).

11091 Flemming, Mary Lou. COM-HE (KGRH, Fayetteville, NC, 1957).

11092 Flenniken, Jim. Newscaster (WBRW, Welch, WV, 1942).

11093 Fletcher, Elbie. Sportscaster (WBZ, Boston, MA, 1952).

11094 Fletcher, Fred. DJ (*Tempus Fugit*, WRAL, Raleigh, NC, 1947–1949;1954).

11095 Fletcher, (Mrs.) George B. Pianist (KTHS, Hot Springs National Park, AR, 1927).

11096 Fletcher, Gordon. Newscaster (WLAK, Lakeland, FL, 1938). Sportscaster (WLAK, 1939).

11097 Fletcher, Graeme. Newscaster (KFH, Wichita, KS, 1938–1945; NBC, 1946–1947; KAKE, Wichita, KS, 1948).

11098 Fletcher, Louise. Singer (KWSC, Pullman, WA, 1926).

11099 Fletcher, Louise. COM-HE (WSOK, Nashville, TN, 1954).

11100 Fletcher, Lucille. Writer (CBS). Fletcher wrote various feature programs for CBS.

11101 Fletcher, Marian. COM-HE (WLOK, Lima, OH, 1951).

11102 Fletcher, Olive. Pianist (KFAB, Lincoln, NE, 1925).

11103 Fletcher, Ruth [Ruthe] A. COM-HE (KSEI, Pocatello, ID, 1954–1955).

11104 Fletcher, Tex. CW vocalist Fletcher was billed as *Tex Fletcher the Lonely Cowboy* (CW vcl. mus. prg., WOR, Newark, NJ, 1935; *Tex Fletcher Orchestra*, instr .mus. prg., MBS, 1947).

11105 Fletcher, (Mrs.) Vera. Soprano (KTHS, Hot Springs National Park, AR, 1928).

11106 Fletcher, Wilfred. Tenor (WHO, Des Moines, IA, 1925).

11107 *Fletcher Wiley* (aka *The Housewives Protective League*). Wiley, without using a script, conducted his Housewives' Protective League, on his popular talk show for women sponsored by the California Prune and Apricot Growers Association (30 min., Tuesday, 4:00–4:30 P.M. CST, CBS, 1938). In 1940 with Campbell Soups as sponsor, the program devoted to human interest topics was broadcast daily. Wiley enjoyed a particularly large following on the Pacific Coast (15 min., Monday through Friday, 2:30–2:45 P.M., CBS, 1940).

11108 Flett, Deanne. Newscaster (KTRI, Sioux City, IA, 1938; KFBB, Great Falls, MT, 1940). Sportscaster (KFBB, 1940).

11109 Flettrich, Terry. COM-HE (*Helen Holmes*, WDSU, New Orleans, LA, 1949).

11110 Fleur-de-Lis Dance Orchestra. Club band (KLX , Oakland, CA, 1929).

11111 Flexon, Anna D. Announcer (WRAX, Gloucester City, NJ, 1925–1926).

11112 Flick, C. Roland. Violinist (WSM, Nashville, TN, 1928).

11113 Flick, George A. Announcer (KFWM, Oakland, CA, 1927).

11114 Flick, Ruth Buhl. Reader (WEBH, Chicago, IL, 1926).

11115 *Flight with Music*. Thirty stations carried the transcribed program in 1946 sponsored by Rensie Watches. Comedian Herb Sheldon, singer Marion Hutton and the music of Nat Brusiloff's orchestra were featured (15 min., Transcribed, Various Stations, 1946).

11116 Flint, Julian. Newscaster (WATL, Atlanta, GA, 1939–1940). Sportscaster (WATL, 1940).

11117 Flint, Walter H. DJ (*Platter Party*, WGPC, Albany, GA, 1948; *Musical Clock*, WGPC, 1960).

11118 *Flint Order of Phillyloobirds*. This program was an example of early radio's zany late night variety programs. James H. MacLafferty and Miss Teddy Jerome were the directors (KFUU, Oakland, CA, 1925).

11119 Flitecraft, W.S. Newspaper sports editor Flitecraft broadcast play-by-play football games weekly (WJZ, New York, NY, 1922).

11120 Floe, Mert. Accordionist, (WCCO, Minneapolis–St. Paul, MN, 1929) Leader (*Mert Floe Orchestra*, instr. mus. prg., WCCO, Minneapolis–St. Paul, MN, 1936).

11121 Flohr, Mildred. COM-HE (KYSM, Mankato, MN, 1949).

11122 Flohri, Virginia. Singer Flohri was billed as "Radio's Nightingale" (KFI, Los Angeles, CA, 1925). She was a busy West Coast radio performer who broadcast frequently, including regular appearances with a string quartet on the weekly *Walter M. Murphy Motors Program* (KFI, Los Angeles, CA, 1925).

11123 Flood, Dorothy. COM-HE (WHLP, Centerville, TN, 1960).

11124 Flood, Harold. DJ (WKRM, Columbia, TN, 1957).

11125 Flood, Joe. DJ (*Upsee Daisy*, KTLN, Denver, CO, 1948–1957).

11126 Florea, Louise. Soprano (*Louise Florea*, vcl. mus. prg., NBC, 1935; WRVA, Richmond, VA, 1936).

11127 Florence. DJ (*Florence, Girl Disc Jockey*, WGAY, Silver Spring, MD, 1947).

11128 Florence, Dick. DJ (WCMR, Elkhart, IN, 1957).

11129 Florence, George. DJ (*Dancing in the Dark*, WGAU, Athens, GA, 1952).

11130 (The) Florentine Quartet. Semi-classical music group (WHN, New York, NY, 1925).

11131 Flores, Mary. COM-HE (WGST, Atlanta, GA, 1957).

11132 Floria the Flapper. Radio personality, not otherwise identified, also known as the "Cincinnati Post Mystery Girl" (WLW, Cincinnati, OH, 1925).

11133 Florian, Joe. Leader (Joe Florian's Vikings Orchestra, WGBS, New York City, NY, 1927).

11134 *Florida Citrus Music*. The Florida Citrus Growers sponsored the program of light music (NBC-Red, 1926).

11135 Florida Footwarmers Orchestra. Popular Pensacola, Florida band (WCOA, Pensacola, FL, 1926).

11136 *Florida Treats*. Harry Richman hosted and sang on the transcribed program that boasted of the pleasures of Florida living. Richman was joined on each program by such guests as Julia Sanderson and Frank Crumit, Eve Beck, the Sisters of the Skillet, Cliff Edwards, the Revelers, Pick and Pat, Connie Boswell, Lee Wiley and Mildred Bailey (15 min., Transcribed, Various Stations, 1935–1936).

11137 Floridians' Orchestra. Popular music group, sometimes a pseudonym for Irwin Abrams Orchestra (WCAE, 1926). *See* **Abrams, Irwin.**

11138 *Florsheim Frolic*. The popular Coon-Sanders Orchestra was featured on the program sponsored by Florsheim Shoes (30 min., Tuesday, 8:00–8:30 P.M., NBC-Red, 1931).

11139 *Florsheim Frolics*. Florsheim Shoes sponsored the Two Perfect Heels comedy team of Ransom Sherman and Russell Pratt — two-thirds of the "Three Doctors" team (NBC, 1932).

11140 Flournoy, Rose. COM-HE (WRBL, Columbus, GA, 1949–1955).

11141 Flournoy's Californians. Popular Pacific Coast dance band (KHJ, San Francisco, CA, 1923).

11142 *Flow Gently Sweet Rhythm*. John Kirby's excellent little band that included Charlie Shavers, Russell Procope and Buster Bailey providing the sweet rhythms. Songs were sung by Maxine Sullivan and the Golden Gate Boys (30 min., CBS, 1940).

11143 Flower, Elsie. Newscaster (*City Journal*, KGDM, Stockton, CA, 1947). COM-HE (KGDM, Stockton, CA, 1954–1955; KRAK, Stockton-Sacramento, CA, 1957).

11144 Flowers, Eleanor. COM-HE (WHSC, Hartsville, SC, 1954).

11145 Flowers, Elizabeth. COM-HE (WHSC, Hartsville, SC, 1956–1957).

11146 Flowers, George. Newscaster (WAYS, Charlotte, NC, 1945). Sportscaster (WAYS, 1945; WJRI, Lenoir, NC, 1956).

11147 Flowers, Helen. COM-HE (WHOD, Moundsville, WV, 1956).

11148 Flowers, Sally. Singer (WGH, Newport News, VA, 1942).

11149 Flowers, Tiger. DJ (*Coffee Club*, WDSA, New Orleans, LA, 1952).

11150 Floyd, Chic. Leader (*Chic Floyd Orchestra*, instr. mus. prg., WKBN, Youngstown, OH, 1942).

11151 Floyd, Margo. COM-HE (WTWO, Bangor, ME, 1954).

11152 Floyd, Odell. COM-HE (WCEH, Hawskinsville, GA, 1956–1957).

11153 Floyd, Troy. Leader (Troy Floyd Orchestra, WFAA, Dallas, TX, 1926).

11154 Fluegel, Marie. Soprano (WRNY, New York, NY, 1928).

11155 Fluke, Richard. Baritone (WLW, Cincinnati, OH, 1926).

11156 Fly, (Dr.) T.M. Dr. Fly read entertaining selections from the "Uncle Remus" stories (KGHI, Little Rock, AR, 1929).

11157 *Flyin' X Roundup*. CW mus. prg. (CW group, not otherwise identified, WWVA, Wheeling, WV, 1942).

11158 *Flying Adventures of Roscoe Turner*. The daytime children's serial was loosely based on the adventures of pilot Roscoe Turner (15 min., Monday, 6:30–6:45 P.M., WHK, Cleveland, OH, 1935).

11159 *Flying Red Horse Tavern*. Socony Oil Company (Moboil) sponsored the musical program, whose cast included host "Colonel" Jim Harkins — later replaced by Walter Woolfe King, singer Jean Marsh, the Tavern Singers, the Four Red Horsemen male quartet and Lennie Hayton's band. Guests stars appeared on the program each week (30 min., Friday, 8:00–8:30 P.M., CBS, 1936).

11160 *Flying Time*. *Flying Time* was a dramatic series that emphasized aviation thrills and adventures. The cast included: Sidney Ellstrom, Willard Farnum, Betty Lou Gerson, Billy Lee, Phil Lord, Ted Maxwell, Hal Peary and Loretta Poynton (NBC, 1935).

11161 Flynn, Arthur "Art." Sportscaster (WHAI, Greenfield, MA, 1939; WLAW, Lawrence, MA, 1944–1952). Newscaster (*Round the Town*, WLAW, Lawrence, MA, 1948).

11162 Flynn, Bernardine. Newscaster Bernardine Flynn, a veteran radio actress, whose most famous role was that of Sade on the *Vic and Sade* program, broadcast the news daily on her own program, *Bernardine Flynn the Girl Reporter* (Monday through Friday, 1:30–1:45 P.M., CBS, 1945). Flynn always claimed that she broadcast a program of *news for women*, not a *women's news* program.

11163 Flynn, Bess. Writer-actress Flynn was a cast member in *Sue and Irene* (WGN, Chicago, IL, 1930) and *The Gumps* (CBS, 1934). She also played "Mother Monahan" in *Painted Dreams* (WGN, Chicago, IL, 1930s), a program that she also wrote. Among the other daytime serials she wrote were *Bachelor's Children; Life Begins*; and *We Are Four*. She was particularly attentive and responsive to the fan letters from her listeners. *See* **Daytime Serials**.

11164 Flynn, Fahey. Newscaster-sportscaster-announcer (WEMP, Milwaukee, WI, 1940). Sportscaster (*The Sports Roundup*, WEMP, 1940; WCBM, Chicago, IL, 1941–1956).

11165 Flynn, Gail. COM-HE (WAOV, Vincennes, IN, 1956–1957).

11166 Flynn, George "Skipper." Tenor Flynn was a Brunswick recording artist (WGES, Chicago, IL, 1928).

11167 Flynn, Howard. DJ (*The Howard Flynn Show*, KMPC, Los Angeles, CA, 1949).

11168 Flynn, Eileen. COM-HE (WRGB, Schenectady, NY, 1954).

11169 Flynn, Gail. COM-HE (WAOV, Vincennes, IN, 1956–1957).

11170 Flynn, J.A. Conductor (Salvation Army Band, KYW, Chicago, IL, 1923).

11171 Flynn, Jimmy. Tenor (WHN, New York, NY, 1924–1925).

11172 Flynn, Paul. Newscaster (WFEA, Manchester, NH, 1940).

11173 Flynn, Peggy. COM-HE (WTAL, Tallahassee, FL, 1956).

11174 Flynn, (Captain) Robin. Newscaster (KFPY, Spokane, WA, 1938; WCAU, Philadelphia, PA, 1945; KHQ, Spokane, WA, 1948).

11175 Flynn, Roy. Newscaster (WAPI, Birmingham, AL, 1945; *Final Edition*, WAPI, 1947).

11176 Flynn, Tony. Sportscaster (WDBC, Escanaba, MI, 1948; WJPG, Green Bay, WI, 1951–1952).

11177 Flynt, Mary Ellen. COM-HE (KSAM, Huntsville, TX, 1951).

11178 *Flywheel, Shyster and Flywheel*. Two of the Marx brothers, Groucho and Chico, played the roles of lawyer Waldorf T. Flywheel and his assistant, Emmanuel Ravelli. This was one of a series of weekly programs sponsored by the Standard Oil Company and Colonial Beacon Oil on NBC in the *Five Star Theatre* series. Another program in the series was *Charlie Chan*.

Flywheel, Shyster and Flywheel was developed and written by Nat Perrin and Arthur Sheekman, two writers who worked for the Marx brothers on their two highly successful recent motion pictures. George Oppenheimer and Tom McKnight assisted Perrin and Sheekman with the writing chores after the thirteenth program. Although the ratings were never high, the program provided good examples of vintage Marx Brothers' humor.

The program for its first three broadcasts was known as *Beagle, Shyster and Beagle*. The name was changed to *Flywheel, Shyster and Flywheel*, when a lawyer named Beagle called to threaten a libel suit. With the exception of a later short-lived series with Groucho and Chico broadcast by NBC in 1934, this was the only Marx Brothers radio show. On the later program sponsored by the American Oil Company, Groucho played Ulysses H. Drivel, an "eagle-eyed" news hound and Chico his "doughty Panelli" (30 min., Monday, 7:00–7:30 P.M., NBC-Blue, 1932–1933).

11179 Fobes, Allan. Newscaster (KYSM, Mankato, MN, 1948).

11180 Foden, Charles W. Tenor (KDKA, Pittsburgh, PA, 1924).

11181 Foerch, Ole B.J. Organist (*Ole B.J. Foerch*, instr. mus. prg., WWJ, Detroit, MI, 1932).

11182 Foerstel, Edmund. Conductor (KMTR Concert Orchestra, KMTR, Hollywood, CA, 1926).

11183 *(The) Fog Lifts*. The Bahai World Faith sponsored the transcribed series of dramas with a religious theme. Joe DeSantis, John Griggs, Bob Quigley, William Sears and Les Tremayne appeared in the cast. Bernard Lanpaw was the announcer (15 min., Transcribed, 1947).

11184 Fogarty, Jack [John]. Newscaster (WCPO, Cincinnati, OH, 1941–1942, 1945).

11185 Foland, Merrill. Pianist (WIND, Gary, IN, 1935).

11186 Foland, Myles. DJ (*Foland Revue*, WWXL, Peoria, IL, 1947; *Myles Foland Show*, WMBD, Peoria, IL, 1949; WSIV, Pekin, IL, 1950; WIRL, Peoria, IL, 1952; WCOL, Columbus, OH, 1954).

11187 Foley, Elsa Zelinda. Coloratura soprano (KNX, Los Angeles, CA, 1928).

11188 *Folger's Male Quartet* (aka *The Bel Canto Quartet*). Folger Coffee Company sponsored this male quartet. The group had two weekly programs on Dallas radio, one as the *Folger Male Quartet* and the other as *The Bel Canto Quartet* (WFAA, Dallas, TX, 1927).

11189 Folger's Serenaders [Orchestra]. Commercially sponsored orchestra (WDAF, Kansas City, MO, 1928).

11190 *(The)Folies Bergere of the Air* (aka *The Folies Bergere* or *Folies de Paree*). Veteran vaudeville comedians Willie and Eugene Howard were featured on the variety program sponsored by Dr. Lyons' Tooth Powder. The story concerned two American entertainers living in the midst of Paris night life. The program's format consisted of musical numbers and comedy sketches. Fifi D'Orsay sang and acted on the weekly show. Ford Bond was the announcer (30 min., Wednesday, 8:00–8:30 P.M., NBC-Blue, 1936–1937). When the program's name was changed to the *Folies de Paree* the following year, the cast remained the same.

11191 Folies Bergere Orchestra. Night club orchestra (WHAR, Atlantic City, NJ, 1926).

11192 Foljambe, Charlotte Tyson. Soprano (KFSG, Los Angeles, CA, 1925–1926).

11193 *(The) Folk Song Festival*. Oscar Brand began the long-running music series in the 1940s. The program continued on the air well into the 1990s (WNYC, New York, NY, 1940s).

11194 ***(The)Folk Song Lady.*** Vcl. mus. prg. conducted by an otherwise unidentified performer (WIP, Philadelphia, PA, 1936).

11195 ***Folk Songs From England, Wales, Norway and France.*** Tenor Paul Reese, baritone Andre DeHaaf, soprano Florence Wilde and contralto Mary Richards were the talented performers on the folk music program (Weekly, 9:00–10:00 P.M., KFI, Los Angeles, CA, 1925).

11196 **Foll, Charles.** Newscaster (KMO, Tacoma, WA, 1940).

11197 **Folley, Lois.** COM-HE (KWEW, Hobbs, NM, 1956).

11198 **Follis, Jimmy.** DJ (*Records at Radio Ranch*, WFPA, Ft. Payne, AL, 1960).

11199 **Follis, Woody.** DJ (KTUE, Tulia, TX, 1960).

11200 **Follott, Doris.** Actress Follott appeared on the *Woman of America* program.

11201 ***Follow the Moon.*** First broadcast in 1936 by the NBC-Red network, the daytime serial featured Elsie Hitz and Nick Dawson in leading roles as husband and wife. Hitz and Dawson had appeared previously as leads in an evening serial drama, *Dangerous Paradise*. Other cast members of *Follow the Moon* were: Alan Devitt, Rosaline Greene, Georgette Harvery, William Pringle and Alfred Swenson (15 min., Monday through Friday, NBC-Red, 1937).

Although *Variety* called the program a routine daytime serial (January 13, 1937, p.40), the story moved fast enough. Before two programs were finished, Elsie Hitz had left one man at the altar and shot the hero, Nick Dawson. The sponsor was Jergens-Woodbury.

11202 **Followill, Murray.** DJ (*Western Hit Parade*, KDSX, Denison, TX, 1952).

11203 **Folsom, Charlotte.** COM-HE (WJBS, DeLand, FL, 1956).

11204 **Folsom, Martha Jane.** Newscaster (WAYX, Waycross, GA, 1938).

11205 **Folster, George Thomas.** Newscaster (NBC, 1941, 1945–1946).

11206 **Fomeen, Basil.** Leader (*Basil Fomeen Orchestra*, instr. mus. prg., MBS, 1936, 1942).

11207 **Fonariova, Genia.** Mezzo-soprano (NBC, New York, NY and WEAF, New York, NY, 1928; *Genia Fonariova*, vcl. mus. prg., WJZ, New York, NY, 1935–1936).

11208 **Fontaine, Bill.** Leader (*Bill Fontaine Orchestra*, instr. mus. prg., WJAG, Norfolk, VA, 1940).

11209 **Fontaine, Pat.** COM-HE (KARK, Little Rock, AR, 1955–1957).

11210 **Fontenelle Orchestra.** Sometimes the band was also known as the Royal Fontenelle Orchestra (WOAW, Omaha, NE, 1926).

11211 **Fontenont, Leonard.** DJ (*Popathon*, KSLO, Opelousas, LA, 1960).

11212 **Fontenont, Rene.** DJ (*Cajun Frolics*, KSLO, Opelousas, LA, 1960).

11213 **Fonticoli, Michele.** Tenor (WIP, Philadelphia, PA, 1926).

11214 **Foote, Herbert.** Organist (*Herbert Foote*, instr. mus. prg., WBBM, Chicago, IL, 1936).

11215 **Foote, Maude.** Pianist (WEAF, New York, NY, 1924).

11216 ***Footlight and Lamplight.*** Oliver M. Sayler broadcast play reviews on the weekly program (WGBS, New York, NY, 1927).

11217 ***Footlight Echoes.*** An orchestra, vocalists and instrumental soloists appeared on this pleasant music program (30 min., Monday, 8:00–8:30 P.M., WOR, Newark, NJ, 1930).

11218 ***For Women Only.*** Rosaline Greene, the talented pioneer radio actress, conducted her interesting program of commentary and news for women (15 min., Monday through Friday, 3:30–3:45 P.M., WOR, Newark, NJ, 1935). *See* **Greene, Rosaline.**

11219 **Foral, Agnes.** Pianist (WOAW, Omaha, NE, 1923).

11220 **Foral, Louis.** Saxophonist (WOAW, Omaha, NE, 1923).

11221 **Foran, Margaret H.** COM-HE (WAAF, Chicago, IL, 1956).

11222 **Forbes, Bob.** DJ (*Alarm Clock*, WJMX, Florence, SC, 1947–1955).

11223 **Forbes, Don.** Newscaster (*The Richfield Reporter*, NBC, 1940–1941).

11224 **Forbes, E. Gilbert.** Newscaster (WFBM, Indianapolis, IN, 1937–1939, *Gilbert Forbes and the News,* WFBM, 1940–1945).

11225 **Forbes, Joanne E.** COM-HE (KWIL, Albany, OR, 1954).

11226 **Forbes, Kathryn (Katjerome).** Soprano (WGES, Oak Park, IL, 1925; WEBH, Chicago, IL, 1926).

11227 **Forbes, Rosita.** Miss Forbes told of her experiences as explorer and lion hunter (KMOX, St. Louis, MO, 1926).

11228 **Forbes, Ruth.** Newscaster (KXRO, Aberdeen, WA, 1942).

11229 ***Forbidden Cargo.*** A transcribed adventure show, *Forbidden Cargo* presented dramatic episodes that focused on smugglers and their capture by law enforcement agents. It began: "By ship, by plane, by road. Goods are smuggled dangerously out of one country into another. Goods which are *Forbidden Cargo*" (30 min., Transcribed, Various Stations, 1950s).

11230 **Ford, (Mrs.) A.** Mezzo-soprano (KGO, Oakland, CA, 1926).

11231 **Ford, Ann.** Newscaster (WSM, Nashville, TN, 1939). COM-HE (WSM, Nashville, TN, 1949).

11232 **Ford, Art.** DJ (WNEW, New York, NY, 1947; *Milkman's Matinee*, WNEW, 1948–1957; WNTA, New York, NY, 1960).

11233 **Ford, Beverly.** COM-HE (KNOX, Grand Forks, ND, 1957).

11234 **Ford, Dean.** Ballad singer (KVOS , Bellingham, WA, 1928).

11235 **Ford, Ernest J.** DJ (*Dude Ranch Party*, KFXM, San Bernardino, CA, 1947).

11236 **Ford, Esther.** COM-HE (WBET, Brockton, MA, 1949).

11237 **Ford, Fenton.** Newscaster (KLSM, Salem, OR, 1942).

11238 **Ford, Franklin.** Announcer (WHAP, New York City, NY, 1925–1927).

11239 **Ford, Gerry.** COM-HE (WLTC, Gastonia, NC, 1957).

11240 **Ford, Gilbert.** Tenor Ford along with Mark Love, Bryce Talbot and a Mr. Pontius comprised the WGN Male Quartet (WGN, Chicago, IL, 1928).

11241 **Ford, Honeyboy.** DJ (WSRC , Durham, NC, 1957).

11242 **Ford, Jackie.** COM-HE (KSAN, San Francisco, CA, 1955).

11243 **Ford, John.** Newscaster (WTCN, Minneapolis, MN, 1945; *John Ford News*, WTCN, 1947; *Breakfast News* and *Noontime News*, WTCN, 1948). DJ (*The John Ford Show*, WTCN, 1947–1948; *Grampappy Gramaphone*, WTCN, 1950).

11244 **Ford, Lloyd.** DJ (*Western Frolic*, KAYS, Hays, KS, 1948–1949).

11245 **Ford, Milton Q.** DJ (*The Morning Show*, WWDC, Washington, DC, 1947–1948; *The Milton Q. Ford Show*, WWDC, 1949–1950; *The Milton Q. Ford Show,*60 min., Saturday, WOR, New York, NY, 1950; WWDC, 1954; WMAL, Washington, DC, 1955; WOL, Washington, DC, 1957).

11246 **Ford, Paul W.** Baritone (KFI, Los Angeles, CA, 1923 and KNRC, Los Angeles, CA, 1925).

11247 **Ford, Ruth.** Contralto (WIBO, Chicago, IL, 1926).

11248 **Ford, Ted.** DJ (KREX, Grand Junction, CO, 1957).

11249 **Ford, Walter.** Leader (Walter Ford's Orchestra, WDT, Decatur, IL, 1925).

11250 **Ford, Whitey (Benjamin F. Ford).** CW comedian-musician Ford was known as the "Duke of Paducah." He began his radio career in 1925 by leading his own band (KTHS, Hot Springs National Park, AR, 1925). In later decades, Ford appeared regularly on the *Renfro Valley Barn Dance* and the *Grand Ole Opry* as a country comic.

11251 ***Ford and Glenn Time.*** These early radio pioneers — Ford Rush and Glenn Howell — were a popular team that performed songs and patter (WLS, Chicago, IL, 1924–1926). Ford possessed a pleasant baritone voice. Glenn who was a good tenor also played the piano. Ford and Glenn as the Lullaby Boys moved on to WJR (Detroit, MI) in 1927 after broadcasting stints at WLS (Chicago, IL) and WLW (Cincinnati, OH). Before joining the WLS staff, the harmony singing team made a highly successful theatrical tour, where they often performed their specialties: "The Woodshed Theater," "Lullaby Time" and the "Radio Song Shop." *Radio Digest* (October 29, 1927) asked: "Was there ever a pair that could entwine their hearts around the hearts of radio fans like Ford and Glenn?" Their answer was, "*No.*"

11252 ***(The) Ford Hour*** **(aka *The Ford Sunday Evening Hour* or the *Ford Summer Hour*).** The first program in this music series featured the 70-piece Ford Symphony Orchestra [the Detroit Symphony Orchestra]. Five of the world's most eminent conductors (Fritz Reiner, Eugene Ormandy, Alexander Smallens, Jose Iturbi and Victor Kolar) conducted the orchestra. Baritone John Charles Thomas appeared on the first program. During the first season guest soloists who appeared were violinist Misha Elman, soprano Josephine Antoine, pianist Jose Iturbi, pianist Vladimir Horowitz and baritone Nelson Eddy (60 min., Sunday, CBS, 1936). The program ran from 1934 through 1946 with only a few breaks in continuity.

11253 ***(The) Ford Program.*** The Ford Motor Company sponsored the program featuring the pleasant music of Fred Waring and his Pennsylvanians [orchestra] on CBS (1934).

11254 ***(The) Ford Rhythm Revue.*** Ferde Grofe conducted the orchestra and soprano Marguerite Howard and the Buccaneers vocal group performed on the half-hour music show (30 min., Weekly, NBC, 1936).

11255 ***(The) Ford Showroom.*** Meredith Willson hosted the program and conducted his orchestra on the pleasant music show that also featured singers Ben Gage and Paulene Carter (30 min., Wednesday, 9:30–10:00 P.M., CBS, 1947).

11256 ***(The) Ford V8 Revue.*** *See* ***Ford Rhythm Revue.***

11257 **Fordan [Firdon], Leo [Lou].** Tenor (WHN, New York, NY, 1924–1925).

11258 **Forde, Nina Mae.** Soprano (WBZ, Springfield, MA, 1925).

11259 **Fordham, Howard and Jimmie White.** Fordham and White were a vocal team known as the "Singing Serenaders" (KFH, Wichita, KS, 1928).

11260 **Fordham, Louise.** Ballad singer (WKO, San Francisco, CA, 1928).

11261 **Fordling, Ida M.** Organist (KTAB, Oakland, CA, 1925).

11262 **Ford's Texas Trumpeters Orchestra.** Brass instrumental group (WFAA, Dallas, TX, 1925–1926).

11263 **Fordyce, Gerry.** Newscaster (WGRC, Louisville, KY, 1944).

11264 ***(The) Forecast School of Cooking.*** The early morning cooking show was a weekly Saturday morning feature (15 min., Saturday, A.M., NBC-Red, 1933). Earlier, the *Forecast School of Cooking* program was broadcast four times weekly (NBC-Blue, 1928–1929).

11265 **Forehand, Ruth.** COM-HE (WDKN, Dickson, TN, 1955).

11266 **Foreign Language Broadcasts.** In all large cities there usually were stations that provided their listening audience with foreign language broadcasts. As early as 1927, Chicago's WEDC began broadcasting instrumental music and vocal selections along with talks in such foreign languages as Polish, Czech and Russian. In New York, stations WEVD and WOV began extensive broadcasting in several foreign languages with Yiddish and Italian predominating. Pittsburgh stations broadcast programs in Slovak and Detroit stations in Polish. WHOM (Jersey City, NJ) carried programs in ten languages in the early 1930s. During the same period, WCDA (New York, NY), known as the "Italian Station," broadcast four grand operas with such prominent artists as soprano Alba Novella with an orchestra under the direction of maestro Carlo Peroni. (WCDA was owned and operated by the Italian Educational Alliance.) John Belluci was the program's director. In 1942, WWRL (New York, NY) added a 45-minute Lithuanian language program to their schedule making a total of eight different foreign language programs broadcast by the station.

New York stations in the mid–1940s offered a wide variety of foreign language broadcasts:

WOV (New York, NY) presented Italian language broadcasts during the day and English ones at night.

WBNX (Bronx, NY) carried programs in German, Yiddish, Lithuanian, Armenian, Spanish, Polish, Greek, Ukranian, French and English.

WHOM (New York, NY) was unique in that in addition to its usual foreign language programs, it added ones in Norwegian for the 100,000 plus Norwegian speaking listeners in the Greater New York Area.

WBYN (Brooklyn, NY) featured Russian, Hungarian and Lithuanian DJs. It also presented the "Jewish Mark Twain," not otherwise identified, who told stories and "The American Court for Peace and Justice."

Some examples of Yiddish programs broadcast in the New York area were:

American Jewish Hour: Yiddish Swing Musical Review. Sponsored by Edelstein's Tuxedo brand cheese, the program was produced and directed by Sam Medoff. It was broadcast in both Yiddish and English and featured Alan Chester, the Dairy Maids, the Barry Sisters and Sam Medoff and his Yiddish Swing Orchestra. The announcer was Lewis Charles (15 min., WHN, New York, NY, July 28, 1940). The program ran into 1955 with its name changed to *Yiddish Melodies in Swing*. The sponsor in latter years was B. Manischewitz Company, but its format remained the same through the years. A special 1945 program broadcast from the top of Loew's State building featured the Barry Sisters, Seymour Rechtzeit and the Benny Goodman orchestra (WHN, New York, NY, 1945).

Bei tate manes tish (Round the Family Table). This radio drama was written and directed by Nuchen Stutchkoff. The sponsor was a matzoh company. A programming example from 1939 featured dramatized excerpts from the 1931 diary of a young playwright who marries his sweetheart against the wishes of his parents. He then begins to doubt his artistic abilities and encounters family pressures that lead him to divorce his wife. The young man succeeds in Hollywood, although he thought he would fail. His ex-wife raises their child, but is unable to forget him (WEVD, New York, NY, 1939). The program was broadcast in both Yiddish and English.

(The) Congress for Jewish Culture Program. At various times the distinguished program presented social commentary, dramatic readings, biography, poetry and dramatizations in Yiddish (WEVD, New York, NY, 1948–1950).

Der Grammeister. The Yiddish-English language program was sponsored by the *Jewish Daily Forward* newspaper. At times the format was entirely narrative, but at other times the programs were presented in dramatic form that might contain commentary, poetry or drama (WEVD, New York, NY, 1947–1952).

Der Yiddisher Filosof (The Yiddish Philosopher). Israel Lutsky read letters from listeners and offered them advice for their personal problems. The sponsor was Carnation Milk (New York radio, 1950s).

Fashions in Song with Don Dennis. B. Manischewitz Company and Levine and Smith, the Fashion Headquarters for Well Dressed Women, sponsored the entertaining show on which Dennis sang and casually talked to his listeners (WHN, New York, NY, late 1940s).

Freedom Train: Delayed Pilgrims of 1948–1949. The program developed and presented by the National Council of Jewish Women was presented in both English and Yiddish. It told chiefly survivor stories (WCOP, Boston, MA, 1949).

Golden's Mustard Program. Victor Packer told stories on his show about people and their accomplishments. The sponsor was Golden's Mustard (WLTH, New York, NY, 1940s).

(The) Hammer's Beverage Program. This program was conducted by Victor Packer with cohosts Raisele and Shaindele, a popular vocal team and the comic patter of the Gay Twins. The sponsor was the Hammer Beverage Company (WLTH, New York, NY, 1940).

It Happened This Week (aka *The American Jewish Hour*). Stuhmer's Pumpernickel Bread Company and Zion Kosher Meat Products sponsored this program, produced by the Jewish Broadcasting Company and directed by Maurice Rapel. Usually four news events were presented in short dramatizations. One 1940 contest on the program offered booklets of admission tickets to the New York World's Fair for completing the sentence: "I prefer Stuhmer's Pumpernickel bread because...." The announcer was Lewis Charles (WHN, New York, NY, 1940). Another 1940 program contained these four brief news dramatizations: (1) Charges made against England's prime minister Neville Chamberlain of anti–Semitism; (2) Bella Futterman brought back to life by a physician in her Bronx apartment; (3) The leading independent candidate for the Mexican presidency survives a train ambush and makes an inspirational speech; and (4) The crew of the French submarine *Pascal* takes eight German refugees from an Italian ocean liner to Casablanca where they were questioned as spies.

Jewish Festival and Other Jolly Functions. Seymour Rechtzeit narrated the program honoring Jewish holidays and celebrations in words and music. The sponsor was Pabst Beer (15 min., Weekly, WEVD, New York, NY, 1942).

*Jewish Refugee Theater (*aka *Refugee Theater of the Air).* The show premiered December 12, 1938. The dramatic series broadcast in Yiddish and English was unique in that every featured performer was a refugee (30 min., Weekly, WMCA, New York, NY, 1938).

Life is Funny with Harry Hershfield. Zion Kosher Meat Products and Simon Ackerman Clothing Store sponsored comedian Hershfield on his quarter hour program (15 min., WHN, New York, NY, late 1940s).

Music by New Americans. The music program featuring refugee performers was broadcast weekly (30 min., Weekly, WNYC, New York, NY, 1948).

News of the Week in Review. B. Manischewitz Company sponsored the Yiddish-English program with commentator Mordecai Danzis discussing current events (Weekly, Sunday, WEVD, New York, NY, 1947–1948). The 1952 format of the *News of the Week in Review* featured Leon Crystal, editorial writer and UN correspondent for the *Jewish Daily Forward* as commentator (WEVD, New York, NY, 1952).

(The) Quiz Master. A quiz program in English and Yiddish featured teams from two schools competing to demonstrate their knowledge of Jewish history, music, art, etc. Sponsored by B. Manischewitz, the program's announcer was Henry Gladstone (WHN, New York, NY, 1940). The February 9, 1940, program presented an all male team from the Abbey Institute competing against an all female team from the Training School for Secretaries.

Reunion. This English-Yiddish program broadcast live reunions of refugees with their families (WOR, New York, NY, 1947).

(The) Sarah Gorby Show. Another program sponsored by Stuhmer's Bread Company, this one was hosted by Sarah Gorby. Broadcast in Yiddish and Russian, the program featured songs by Goldie Moskowitz (WEVD, New York, NY, 1945).

(The) Sterling Salt Interviews. The Yiddish *Vox Pop*-type program conducted by Victor Packer presented discussions of various "issues that interest everyone" and interviews from various Brooklyn business locations. Once Packer visited Borenstein Brothers Butchers Market where he interviewed shoppers about Jewish holiday foods. Various songs were mixed in with the program's commercials and interviews. On another program originating from Mr. Epstein's Dairy on Church Avenue in East Flatbush, he asked shoppers: "Should beautiful young women wear make-up on the street?" Still another program was broadcast from Mr. Tannenbaum's Public Market of Brooklyn (WBYN, Brooklyn, NY and WLTH, New York, NY, 1941).

Variety Show. Madame Bertha Hart was the hostess on the program that offered entertainment by singers Dvorele Wasserman, Mr. Redding and Eleanor Kramer accompanied by pianist Jean Rubin. Sometimes political speeches by Rabbi Myron Magnet were included (WCNW, Brooklyn, NY, 1936).

Vi di flegt zugn (As Mother Used to Say). B. Manischewitz Company sponsored the Yiddish-English program conducted by Nuchem Stutchkoff. It discussed Yiddish etymology and presented questions and answers about the Yiddish language and expressions. Commercials were delivered in English (15 min., Weekly, WHN, New York, NY, 1943).

The preceding list contains only a few of the many foreign language programs that appeared on radio from 1920 to 1960. The topic should receive the attention of researchers in order to catalog the many other programs broadcast during these years and describe their featured performers.

11267 Foreman, Bill. Leader (The Foreman Banjo Sextet, WFAA, Dallas, TX, 1924).

11268 Foreman, R.I. DJ (*Musical Forum*, WLDY, Ladysmith, WI, 1952).

11269 Forester, Dorothy. COM-HE (KSWS, Roswell, NM, 1949).

11270 *Forever Ernest*. Bromo-Seltzer sponsored the situation comedy that starred Jackie Coogan in the title role. *Variety* gave it only faint praise when it replaced the *Vox Pop* program. Arthur Q. Bryan and Lurene Tuttle supported Coogan on the show. Music was supplied by Billy May's Orchestra. Dick Joy was the program's announcer (30 min., Monday, 8:00–8:30 P.M., CBS, 1946).

11271 Forgue, Sonia. COM-HE (WLAM, Lewiston, ME, 1955).

11272 *Forhan's Song Shop*. Forhan's Tooth Paste sponsored the weekly half-hour variety program (NBC-Blue, 1928).

11273 Forker, Alice. Pianist (*Alice Forker*, instr. mus. prg., WTNJ, Trenton, NJ, 1936).

11274 Forman, Don. DJ (*Magical Carpet of Music*, WMFD, Wilmington, NC, 1954).

11275 Forman, Lynn. COM-HE (WARM, Scranton, PA, 1951).

11276 Forman, Win. DJ (*Sunny Side of the Street*, WARM, Scranton, PA, 1947).

11277 Formica Band and Orchestra. Commercially sponsored orchestra (WLW, Cincinnati, OH, 1924–1926).

11278 Forno, Leandro. Newscaster (WBIL, New York, NY, 1938 and WOV, New York, NY, 1938).

11279 Forrest, Charles. Newscaster (WPID, Petersburg, VA, 1940).

11280 Forrest, Helen. A busy young singer, Forrest began singing on WNEW in 1933 using four different names on four different broadcasts. The names she used were Marlene, Bonnie Blue and Helen Forrest (WNEW, New York, NY, 1933). Forrest in later years was the featured band singer with both the Artie Shaw and Harry James orchestras.

11281 Forrest, Johnny. Newscaster (KIRO, Seattle, WA, 1938–1939; KOL-KIRO, Seattle, WA, 1940). DJ (KOL, 1954).

11282 Forrester, Eddie. Forrester was a talented and busy flamenco guitarist, station announcer and manager of the local Mayfair Theater (KMS, Shenandoah, IA, 1926).

11283 Forrester, Roy. DJ (*Hillbilly Hoedown*, KPOC, Pocahontas, AR, 1949).

11284 Forrester, (Dr.) Wade. Singer billed as the "Singing Chiropractor" (KROW, Oakland, CA, 1931).

11285 Forsans, Bob. Tenor (*Bob Forsans*, vcl. mus. prg., WGN, Chicago, IL, 1934).

11286 Forsch, Fritz. Orchestra leader on the *Coward Comfort Music* program (NBC-Red, New York, NY, 1929).

11287 Forshaw, James R. Singer (KTBI, Los Angeles, CA, 1927).

11288 Forssell, Gene. DJ (*Sun-KIST Show*, KIST, Santa Barbara, CA, 1950; KDB, Santa Barbara, CA, 1957).

11289 Forst, Howard. Saxophonist (WOR, Newark, NJ, 1923; WAHG, New York, NY, 1925).

11290 Forstat, Jacob. Cellist (WGBS, 1925).

11291 Forster, Bob. DJ (*Wake Up and Scream*, WICA, Ashtabula, OH, 1947–1950; WEBQ, Harrisburg, IL, 1955; WITH, Baltimore, MD, 1957). Sportscaster (WICA, 1949).

11292 Forster, Bobbie. COM-HE (KXLR, North Little Rock, AR, 1948).

11293 Forster, Gertrude. Contralto (NBC, 1929).

11294 Forster, Ilse. Mezzo-contralto (WJJD, Chicago, IL, 1926).

11295 Forster, Lee. DJ (*The Lee Forster Show*, WHLD, Niagara Falls, NY, 1949).

11296 Forster, Roger. DJ (WEOA, Evansville, IN, 1947; *Forster's Follies*, WEOA, 1948; WIBA, Madison, WI, 1949).

11297 Forsyth, Jim. Newscaster (WDSU, New Orleans, LA, 1944).

11298 Forsyth, Melva. Contralto (WBAL, Baltimore, MD, 1926).

11299 Forsythe, Jim. DJ (*In the Groove*, WDSO, New Orleans, LA, 1947).

11300 Forsythe, Slim. Sportscaster (WEEB, Southern Pines, NC, 1948).

11301 *Fort Devens' Radio Party*. The program was broadcast during the early years of World War II from an army base (Ft. Devens, Massachusetts) featuring Army personnel and professional entertainers in 1941. *See* **Wartime Radio.**

11302 *Fort Laramie*. Raymond Burr and Vic Perrin starred in the transcribed sustaining western adventure series. Burr played "Lee Quince, Captain of U.S. Calvary," in the dramatic story, a "saga of fighting men." In one of the early episodes, Burr, the hero, discovered that it was white men who were burning frontier settlers' cabins and scalping victims, not Indians. John Meston wrote and Norman Macdonnell produced and directed the show, whose cast members also included Harry Bartell and Jack Moyles. Music was supplied by Amerigo Moreno. Don Cubberly was the announcer (30 min., Sunday, 5:30–6:00 P.M., CBS, 1955).

11303 *Fort Worth Barn Dance*. Station WBAP (Fort Worth, TX) first broadcast the program January 4, 1923. It probably was the first barn dance ever broadcast. The *National Barn Dance* on WLS (Chicago, IL) and the *Grand Old Opry* on WSM (Nashville, TN) came on the air within the next two years after the *Fort Worth Barn Dance* was first broadcast. *See* **Country-Western (CW) Music.**

11304 Fort Worth Club String Orchestra. Club orchestra (WBAP, San Antonio, TX, 1928).

11305 Forth Worth Police Band. Forty-five piece municipal brass band (WBAP, Dallas, TX, 1924).

11306 Forte, Sally. DJ (WSOC, Charlotte, NC, 1954).

11307 Fortescue, Priscilla. COM-HE (WEEI, Boston, MA, 1949–1957).

11308 Fortier, Roselle Coury. Newscaster (WCOU, Lewiston, ME, 1946). COM-HE (WCOU, 1957).

11309 Fortson, John L. Newscaster (*Religion in the News*, NBC, 1947–1948).

11310 *Fortune Builders*. Newsman Douglas Gilbert interviewed various successful business leaders on the weekly program (15 min., Sunday, 10:45–11:00 A.M., CBS, 1931).

11311 *Forty Fathom Trawlers*. An old sea captain told sea adventure stories on this show that attracted a large listening audience. The sponsor was the Bay State Fishing Company. Frances Collette was one of the actresses who appeared frequently on the program (30 min., Wednesday, 8:30–9:00 P.M., CBS, 1930).

11312 ***Forty-Five Minutes in Hollywood.*** A different motion picture star, such as Claudette Colbert, appeared as a guest each week in condensed versions of motion pictures. *Variety* noted that many stars were impersonated each week by the program's talented cast that included: Peggy Allenby, Porter Hall and Marion Hopkinson. Peter Yorke broadcast movie gossip on the show each week, and Mark Warnow's Orchestra and the Eton Boys [vocal group] provided the music. The program was sponsored by the Borden Company (45 min., Saturday, 8:00–8:45 P.M., CBS, 1934).

11313 ***Forty-Five Minutes on Broadway.*** Broadway columnists Danton Walker and Hy Gardner interviewed show business personalities and reported the latest gossip on the weekly sustaining show (45 min., Sunday, 10:00–10:45 P.M., WOR, Newark, NJ, 1948).

11314 ***Forum of Liberty.*** Each week the program presented a leading national figure discussing current industrial and public problems. Music was provided by baritone Edward Nell and the orchestra was conducted by Arnold Johnson (WABC-CBS, New York, NY, 1934).

11315 **Fosdick, Harry A.** Newscaster (KIST, Santa Barbara, CA, 1946).

11316 **Fosdick, Harry Emerson.** Minister Fosdick conducted the long running *National Vespers* religious program that began on February 6, 1927, and continued to 1954 (WJZ, New York, NY, 1927).

11317 **Foss, Bill.** Announcer-salesman Foss became "Uncle Billy" on the *Kids Klub Program* (WCSH, Portland, ME, 1920s). "Uncle Jimmy" Nicholson eventually took over the program from Foss.

11318 **Foss, Ellen.** COM-HE (KATE, Albert Lea, MN, 1949).

11319 **Fossenkemper, Marius.** Clarinetist (WGHP, Detroit, MI, 1926).

11320 **Fossey, Harry E.** Bass (KGO, Oakland, CA, 1925).

11321 **Foster, Barbara.** COM-HE (KDON, Monterey, CA, 1949).

11322 **Foster, Bill.** DJ (*Radio Juke Box*, WARJ, Adrian, MI, 1947).

11323 **Foster, Carroll.** Sportscaster (KIRO, Seattle, WA, 1939). Newscaster (KIRO, 1940).

11324 **Foster, Cedric W.** News analyst (WTHT, Hartford, CT, 1938–1940; WAAB, Boston, MA, 1941; MBS, 1942–1944; WNAC, Boston, MA and MBS, 1945; MBS, 1947–1948).

11325 **Foster, Chuck.** Newscaster (KGW, Portland, OR, 1946).

11326 **Foster, Chuck.** Leader (*Chuck Foster Orchestra*, instr. mus. prg., 30 min., Saturday, 5:00–5:30 P.M., MBS, 1934; NBC, 1940; CBS, 1949). The Foster band in 1940 was introduced in this manner: "Music in the Foster Fashion from the Peacock Court of the Mark Hopkins Hotel in San Francisco."

11327 **Foster, Cy.** Announcer (WHAD, Milwaukee, WI, 1925).

11328 **Foster, Day.** Newscaster (KORE, Eugene, OR, 1941).

11329 **Foster, Dorothy.** Pianist (WGN, Chicago, IL, 1938).

11330 **Foster, Everett.** Baritone (KOA, Denver, CO, 1929).

11331 **Foster, Faye.** Singer (WNYC, New York, NY, 1936).

11332 **Foster, Fran.** COM-HE (WHKK, Akron, OH, 1951).

11333 **Foster, Gertrude.** Singer on the *Popular Bits* program (NBC, 1931).

11334 **Foster, Homer.** Newscaster (WSOO, Sault St. Marie, MI, 1947).

11335 **Foster, Jack.** Newscaster, WCKY (Cincinnati, OH, 1938–1942, 1945). Sportscaster (WCKY, 1940).

11336 **Foster, Jean.** COM-HE (KMA, Shenandoah, IA, 1949).

11337 **Foster, Joan.** COM-HE (WVOK, Birmingham, AL, 1955).

11338 **Foster, Joanne.** COM-HE (WCHV, Charlottesville, VA, 1955).

11339 **Foster, John "Johnny."** DJ (*Requestfully Yours*, WBAX, Wilkes-Barre, PA, 1948–1956). Sportscaster (WILK, Wilkes-Barre, PA, 1960).

11340 **Foster, Joseph.** DJ (*Request Party*, WSSB, Durham, NC, 1948).

11341 **Foster, Kay.** Singer (*Kay Foster*, vcl. mus. prg., NBC, 1935).

11342 **Foster, Kay.** COM-HE (KTYL, Mesa, AZ, 1956).

11343 **Foster, Lucille.** Whistler (WLW, Cincinnati, OH, 1924).

11344 **Foster, Marilyn.** COM-HE (WDEH, Sweetwater, TX, 1955).

11345 **Foster, Mark.** DJ (*Western Swingtime*, KIMO, Independence, MO, 1949). Sportscaster (KIMO, 1952).

11346 **Foster, R. D.** Announcer (KGBX, St. Joseph, MO, 1927).

11347 **Foster, Sid.** DJ (*Sunrise Musical* and *Hillbilly Hit Parade*, KSTB, Breckenridge, TX, 1948).

11348 **Foster, Terry.** DJ (*Home Folks Frolics*, WHBL, Sheybogan, WI, 1949–1950). Sportscaster (*Sports Parade*, WHBL, 1951).

11349 **Foster, Walton.** News analyst (*Between the Lines*, KTXL, San Angelo, TX, 1948).

11350 **Foster, Will.** Organist (WBAP, Fort Worth, TX, 1925).

11351 **Foster, Wilson K.** Newscaster (KFAR, Fairbanks, AK, 1941–1942).

11352 **Foulis, Bill.** Newscaster (KFEL, Denver, CO, 1942).

11353 **Fountain, Bill.** DJ (*Time and Tune Parade*, WKY, Oklahoma City, OK, 1950).

11354 **Fountain, Jean.** COM-HE (WMFD, Wilmington, NC, 1956).

11355 **Fountain, Mary.** Organist Fountain performed on her *Organalities* program (instr. mus. program, WHP, Harrisburg, PA, 1936–1939).

11356 ***Four Aces.*** Four leading bridge experts — Burnsteine, Schenken, Gottlieb and Jacoby — appeared on the transcribed program. A bridge hand was dealt to the experts and they began bidding. A contest question was then posed to the listening audience. Listeners wrote in their correct answers in order to win the prize, a book written by the bridge aces (5 min., Wednesday, 11:00–11:05 P.M., CBS, 1935).

11357 **Four Aces of Harmony.** Male quartet (WIL, St. Louis, MO, 1926).

11358 ***Four Barons—Aristocrats of Harmony.*** Vcl. mus. prg., by an otherwise unidentified vocal group (WCAE, Pittsburgh, PA, 1935).

11359 ***Four Clubmen.*** Vcl. mus. prg., performed by a male vocal group directed by Leith Stevens (15 min., Saturday, 11:30–11;45 A.M., CBS, 1932; CBS, 1935).

11360 **Four Deuces Quartet of the AP and L Company.** The members of the commercially sponsored vocal group were tenors Francis Boyle and W.J. Colburn, baritone Wesley Bean and bass Herbert Sutherland (KLRA, Little Rock, AR, 1928).

11361 ***Four Hand Work.*** An instrumental music program that presented the dual piano team of Pauline Sternlicht and Etta Kabram (WJY, New York, NY, 1925).

11362 ***Four Harmony Kings.*** The Black gospel quartet changed its name to the Swan Silvertone Singers, when their program was sponsored by the Swan Bread Company (WNOX, Knoxville, TN, 1938).

11363 **Four Indians.** Nate Caldwell, Evelyn Kitts, John Wolfe and Mrs. Nate Caldwell made up the busy vocal quartet (KOIL, Council Bluffs, IA, 1928).

11364 **Four Jazz Hounds.** Instrumental group specializing in "syncopation" (KFBK, Sacramento, CA, 1927).

11365 **Four Kings of Harmony.** Male vocal group of Arthur Thomas, Renus Lytle, Ben Jordan and Clair Marshall (WHO, Des Moines, IA, 1928).

11366 **Four Legionaires.** Male quartet (WLS, Chicago, IL, 1928).

11367 ***(The) Four of Us.*** The vocal quartet's members were Geraldine Ayres, Carl Koch, Alice Brearey and Loretta Clemens (15 min., Weekly, WBEN, Buffalo, NY, 1932).

11368 ***Four Showmen.*** Vcl. mus. prg., by an otherwise unidentified male vocal group (NBC-Red, 1935).

11369 ***Four Tempos.*** Vcl. mus. prg., by an otherwise unidentified vocal group (WOR, Newark, NJ, 1935).

11370 ***(The) Foursome.*** Del Porter, Ray Johnson, Dwight Snyder and Marshall Smith made up the popular vocal quartet (15 min., Weekly, CBS, 1935).

11371 **Foust, Bob.** Sportscaster (*Bob Foust's Sports Page*, KYA, San Francisco, CA, 1948).

11372 **Fouts, Xenia.** Pianist (WOW, Omaha, NE, 1927).

11373 **Fowden, Florence.** Mezzo-soprano (KGO, Oakland, CA, 1926).

11374 **Fowle, Bob.** Sportscaster (WHED, Washington, DC, 1955–1956).

11375 **Fowle, Farnsworth.** Newscaster (CBS, 1944–1948).

11376 Fowler, Bernard. Leader (*Bernard Fowler Orchestra*, instr. mus. prg., WBIG, Greensboro, NC, 1938).

11377 Fowler, Bill. Sportscaster (*Sports Time*, WBAT, Marion, IN, 1948; *The Field of Sports*, WBAT, 1951; *Sports Review*, WBAT, 1960). DJ (*Bill's Band Box*, WBAT, 1949).

11378 Fowler, Bill. DJ (*Musical Clock*, WGPC, Albany, GA, 1949).

11379 Fowler, Bob. DJ (*Ham With Your Eggs*, KBOR, Brownsville, TX, 1952).

11380 Fowler, Cecil. Newscaster (WGPC, Albany, GA, 1941). DJ (WGPC, 1954).

11381 Fowler, Ethel R. COM-HE (*Fashions*, WPG, Atlantic City, NJ, 1926).

11382 Fowler, Evelyn. Pianist (WHO, Des Moines, IA, 1925).

11383 Fowler, Fred. Newscaster (WATL, Atlanta, GA, 1941).

11384 Fowler, Frosti [Frosty]. DJ (*Jive at Five*, KWSC, Pullman, WA, 1947; KLOQ, Yakima, WA, 1956; *King's Klock*, KING, Seattle, WA, 1960).

11385 Fowler, J.B. DJ (*Platter Parade*, WPAD, Paducah, KY, 1947; *After Hours*, WKYB, Paducah, KY, 1954). Sportscaster (*Pigskin Parade*, WNGO, Mayfield, KY, 1948).

11386 Fowler, Jim. DJ (*Record Shop*, WGPC, Albany, GA, 1947–1958; *Musical Caravan*, WGPC, 1949–1952; *The Stars Sing*, WGPC, 1954–1957).

11387 Fowler, Lucille. Contralto (KOA, Denver, CO, 1928).

11388 Fox, Alden "Al" L. Newscaster (WHLD, Niagara Falls, NY, 1944; WIS, Columbia, SC, 1945).

11389 Fox, Bill. DJ (KGY, Olympia, WA, 1947; *Melody Ranch*, KXRO, Aberdeen, WA, 1949).

11390 Fox, Bill. Newscaster (WPTW, Piqua, OH, 1948).

11391 Fox, Blanche Hamilton. Mezzo-soprano Fox was a member of the KFRC Opera Company (KFRC, San Francisco, CA, 1926). Some local periodicals identified her as a contralto.

11392 Fox, Dick. Sportscaster (*Sports Parade*, KCHS, Truth or Consequences, NM, 1955).

11393 Fox, Don L. Announcer (WMBC, Detroit, MI, 1927).

11394 Fox, Ethel. Soprano (WGBS, New York, NY, 1925).

11395 Fox, Franke. DJ (*Doghouse Program*, WHLN, Harlan, KY, 1947).

11396 Fox, Gary. DJ (*Band of the Day*, KILO, Grand Forks, ND, 1947).

11397 Fox, J. Leslie. Chief announcer (KFH, Wichita, KS, 1927–1928).

11398 Fox, Jack. Leader (Jack Fox and his Melody Belles (orchestra), WHN, New York, NY, 1923 and Jack Fox's Clover Garden Orchestra, WHN, New York, NY, 1923).

11399 Fox, Jack. DJ (WEOA, Evansville, IN, 1960).

11400 Fox, Josephine. Actress Fox appeared on the *Prairie Folks* program in the 1930s.

11401 Fox, Leon H. Violinist (WEBJ, New York, NY, 1925).

11402 Fox, Les. DJ (*Music Box*, WMMW, Meriden, CT, 1948).

11403 Fox, Maryjean. COM-HE (KTUL, Tulsa, OK, 1949).

11404 Fox, N.L. COM-HE (KCHS, Truth or Consequences, NM, 1955).

11405 Fox, Peggy. Singer (WIP, Philadelphia, PA, 1937).

11406 Fox, Rae. Violinist known as the "Lady of Strings" (WPCH, New York, NY, 1932).

11407 Fox, Ray. Violinist (KTAB, Oakland, CA, 1925).

11408 Fox, Robert. Newscaster (WLBJ, Bowling Green, KY, 1944).

11409 Fox, Roger. Leader (*Roger Fox Orchestra*, instr. mus. prg., KWK, St. Louis, MO, 1936–1937).

11410 Fox, Sylvan. DJ (*1400 Melody Lane*, KSYL, Alexandria, LA, 1947; *Spotlight Rhythm*, KSYL, 1950).

11411 Fox, William F., Jr. Sportscaster (WIBC, Indianapolis, IN, 1945–1948; *Fox's Den*, WIBC, 1949–1956).

11412 *Fox Fur Trappers*. L.J. Fox Furriers sponsored the musical program that featured operatic singer Ganna Walska and vaudeville star, Belle Baker (30 min., Sunday Afternoon, NBC-Red, 1928). In a later musical format, Earle Nelson, the "Crooning Fur Trapper," was featured (30 min., 7:00–7:30 P.M., NBC-Blue, 1930).

11413 Fox Fur Trappers Orchestra. Commercial dance band (WJZ, New York, NY, 1929).

11414 *(The) Foxes of Flatbush*. Mignon Schreiber and Murray Forbes appeared in the daytime serial that *Variety* called an "absorbing true-to-life story of a Jewish family in Brooklyn" (15 min., Monday through Friday, 2:00–2:15 P.M. CST, NBC-Blue, 1936).

11415 Foy, Evelyn. COM-HE (WCIN, Cincinnati, OH, 1955).

11416 Foy, Fred. DJ (*Sunrise Serenade*, WXYZ, Detroit, MI, 1947). Foy for many years enjoyed his greatest popularity as the resonant voiced announcer of the *Lone Ranger* program.

11417 Foy, Jack. CW singer known as the "Hill Billy Boy," Foy first appeared on the radio in Memphis, TN, in 1923 (KDKA, Pittsburgh, PA, 1931).

11418 *Foy Willing and the Riders of the Purple Sage*. The well liked syndicated CW music show featured the popular Willing group that included Kenny Driver and Al Sloey (15 min., KABC, San Antonio, TX, 1949).

11419 Frackman, Beatrice. Singer (*Beatrice Frackman*, vcl. mus. prg., WMBD, Peoria, IL, 1935).

11420 Fraim, John. DJ (*Wabash Avenue Serenade*, WTHI, Terre Haute, IN, 1948).

11421 Frain, Edna Hall. Pianist (WMAQ, Chicago, IL, 1927).

11422 Fraker, Willard W. Newscaster (WFBG, Altoona, PA, 1938–1939; WKPA, New Kensington, PA, 1940).

11423 Frakes, Ellis. Leader (*Ellis Frakes Orchestra*, instr. mus. prg., WLW, Cincinnati, OH, 1937).

11424 France, Shirley May. DJ (*Juke Box Matinee*, WSAR, Fall River, MA, 1949).

11425 *Frances Ingraham*. Miss Ingraham conducted a weekly 15-minute cooking show (15 min., Tuesday, 10:15–10:30 A.M., NBC-Blue, 1929).

11426 Francesco, Longo. Director (American Salon Orchestra, KJR, Seattle, WA, 1928).

11427 Francher, Isobel. Soprano (KGU, HI, 1929).

11428 Francis, Al. DJ (*Name the Program*, WKST, New Castle, PA, 1947–1948; *Fun with Francis*, WKST, 1949–1950).

11429 Francis, Ann. Actress Francis appeared on the *When a Girl Marries* daytime serial program.

11430 Francis, Arlene. Versatile actress, host and announcer, Arlene Francis came to WOR (New York, NY) in 1960 and spent many successful years at the station, primarily conducting excellent celebrity interviews. She also was famous for her television work. She also appeared on such daytime serials as *Helpmate*, *Second Husband*, *Betty and Bob* and *Big Sister*.

11431 Francis, Della Hoover. Violinist (KOA, Denver, CO, 1926).

11432 Francis, Dorothy. Actress Francis appeared on the daytime serials *Backstage Wife* aka *Mary Noble, Backstage Wife* and *The Road of Life*.

11433 Francis, Joe. DJ (*Musical Mail Call* and *Night Club of the Air*, WNHC, New Haven, CT, 1947–1948).

11434 Francis, Lee. Pianist (*Lee Francis*, instr. mus. prg., WBBM, Chicago, IL and CBS, 1936).

11435 Francis, Nora. Soprano (WEAF, New York, NY, 1929).

11436 Francisco, Chuck. DJ (WJJD, Chicago, IL, 1957).

11437 Francisco Mixed Quartet. The members of the mixed quartet included soprano Florence Ringo; contralto Orvilla de Pauw; tenor James Gerard and baritone Albert Gillette (KPO, San Francisco, CA, 1926). At other times in 1926, Ringo was joined by contralto Nina Campbell; tenor Georges Simondet and bass Ed Thomas (KPO, 1926).

11438 Franck, Mary Anne. COM-HE (WVNA, Tuscumbia, AL, 1960).

11439 Franck, Stanley. Baritone (*Stanley Franck*, vcl. mus. prg., WRVA, Richmond, VA, 1936).

11440 Franconi, Terri. Tenor (*Terri Franconi*, vcl. mus. prg., NBC, 1936).

11441 Frandini, Edna. Soprano (WHN, New York, NY, 1924).

11442 Frandsen, Tom. Newscaster (KECA-KFI, Los Angeles, CA, 1939–1941).

11443 Frank, Arnold. Leader (Arnold Frank's Casino Orchestra, WCCO, Minneapolis–St. Paul, MN, 1925).

11444 Frank, Beecher. Newscaster (KFMB, San Diego, CA, 1941). DJ (*Continental Room*, WKLO, Louisville, KY, 1949–1953; *Showcase*, WKLO, 1954; WGRC, Louisville, KY, 1956–1957).

11445 Frank, Bernard. Harmonica soloist (WHN, New York, NY and WOR, Newark, NJ, 1925).

11446 Frank, Betty. COM-HE (WLIB, New York, NY, 1924).

11447 Frank, Bob. Newscaster (WOC, Davenport, IA, 1939; WRAK, Williamsport, PA, 1945).

11448 Frank, Harold J. Newscaster (WSLB, Ogdensburg, NY, 1944).

11449 Frank, Howard. Concert baritone (WGBS, New York, NY, 1929).

11450 Frank, J. Elliott. Frank was known as the "Poet Laureate of WRR" (WRR, Detroit, MI, 1926).

11451 Frank, Leon. Pianist Frank was the director of the *Leon Frank's Advanced Piano Students* program (WSM, Nashville, TN, 1926).

11452 Frank, Margaret H. COM-HE (WHNC, Henderson, NC, 1956).

11453 Frank, Noble. Sportscaster (WHP, Harrisburg, PA, 1937–1941).

11454 Frank, Paul B. Newscaster (WHKC, Columbus, OH, 1945–1948).

11455 Frank, Val. Newscaster (WAAT, Newark, NJ, 1938–1942; *Breakfast Reporter*, WAAT, 1944–1947).

11456 Frank, William. Commentator (*Around the Town* ,WILM, Wilmington, DE, 1947).

11457 Frank and Dina. Vocal team (WHN, New York, NY, 1924).

11458 *Frank and Jackson* (aka *Harden and Weaver*). Frank Harden and Jackson Weaver were popular comic DJ's, whose program originated from Washington, DC (30 min., Saturday, 2:30–3:00 P.M., ABC, 1952). Harden and Weaver were still at it more than 25 years later — probably a longevity record for DJ's in one city.

11459 *Frank Black's Recording Orchestra.* Maestro Black conducted his popular orchestra (WTIC, Hartford, CT, 1931).

11460 *Frank Buck.* Explorer Buck, billed as Frank "Bring 'Em Back Alive" Buck, told of his adventures with appropriate sound effects added to simulate the atmosphere of the jungle. Radio-Keith-Orpheum Motion Picture Company sponsored the program in order to promote their movie showing Buck's exploits. On the program, Buck also interviewed various authorities on animals, such as Dr. Raymond L. Ditmars, curator of the New York Zoological Gardens (30 min., Thursday, 11:30–12:00 midnight, WEAF-Red, 1932). *See* ***Frank Buck's Adventures.***

11461 *Frank Buck's Adventures* (aka *The Jungle Adventures of Frank Buck* or *Bring 'em Back Alive*). The serial drama was based on the exploits of Frank "Bring 'em Back Alive" Buck (15 min., Monday through Friday, 6:45–7:00 P.M., NBC-Red, 1934). Buck was famous for capturing animals for zoos and circuses. Several movies were made in the form of documentaries showing his animal capturing exploits, but his radio program was not well produced.

11462 *(The) Frank Campbell Funeral Parlor Program.* Campbell's, the famous New York funeral parlor, sponsored a program of quiet recorded music (15 min., Wednesday, 10:00–10:15 A.M., WMCA, New York, NY, 1934).

11463 *Frank Crumit and Julia Sanderson.* Crumit and Sanderson sang and joked on their pleasant Sunday afternoon program (30 min., Sunday, 5:30–6:00 P.M., CBS, 1934). The husband-and-wife team also appeared together on other programs including: *The Blackstone Plantation*, *Universal Rhythm* and the *Battle of the Sexes*.

11464 *(The) Frank Fay Show.* Veteran vaudeville comedian Fay wrote, directed and hosted this variety show sponsored by Standard Brands' Royal Gelatine. Music was supplied by either Eddie Kay's or Bobby Dolan's Orchestra (30 min., Saturday, 9:00–9:30 P.M., NBC-Red, 1936). Fay's later show, also known as *The Frank Fay Show*, was sponsored by Tums for the Tummy in 1941 on the NBC-Blue network. The latter show was unique in that the comedian was also the program's writer, producer and host. Harry Salter's Orchestra, tenor Bob Hannon and Beverly and her Boy Friends singing group provided the music.

11465 *(The) Frank Fontaine Show.* Frank Fontaine, who was first heard on *The Original Amateur Hour*, was joined on his show by vocalist Helen O'Connell, Mary Jane Croft, announcer Harry Von Zell and Lud Gluskin's Orchestra. S. Rose wrote the sustaining show with Al Schwartz, who was also director and producer (30 min., Sunday, 8:00–8:30 P.M., CBS, 1952).

Fontaine later gained fame playing tipsy Crazy Guggenheim on *Jackie Gleason's American Scene Magazine* television program on CBS in 1962. Fontaine, as Guggenheim, would greet Gleason, as Joe the Bartender, with a drunken, "Hiya, Mr. Dunahy." After he and Gleason traded a few pointless quips, Fontaine would sing a ballad in his beautiful baritone voice.

11466 *(The) Frank Luther Show.* Tenor Luther, who was sometimes joined by his wife, Dorothy Knox, entertained on this sustaining children's music show (30 min., Saturday, 8:30–9:00 A.M., WNBC, New York, NY, 1947).

11467 *(The) Frank Parker Show.* Tenor Parker was joined by Paula Kelly, Kay Lorraine and the Modernaires on the transcribed program. Paul Barron's Orchestra supplied the music. Andre Baruch was the announcer (15 min., Transcribed, WNEW, New York, NY, 1947–1949). Parker was also a featured singer on Arthur Godfrey's radio and television programs singing duets with Marion Marlowe.

11468 *Frank Simon's Concert Band.* Bandmaster Simon conducted his excellent band (NBC, 1935).

11469 *(The) Frank Sinatra Show.* Toni Home Permanents sponsored Sinatra's return appearance as a DJ. Jerry Laurence was the program's announcer (15 min., Wednesday and Friday, 8:15–8:30 P.M., NBC, 1954). Sinatra also starred in such programs as *Songs by Sinatra*, *Light-Up Time* and *To Be Perfectly Frank* among others during the 1950s.

Sinatra first gained fame in the 1940s as one of the great crooners of the era, singing with the Tommy Dorsey and Harry James bands. His successful movie career was marked by his Academy Award winning performance in James Jones' *From Here to Eternity*.

Radio played a prominent role in the singer's career. From his earliest radio appearance with the Hoboken Four in 1935 on *Major Bowes' Original Amateur Hour* through the many big band remote broadcasts on which he starred with the Tommy Dorsey and Harry James orchestras to his own musical and dramatic programs, Sinatra proved himself to be one of the greatest and most versatile entertainers of all time. Sinatra's popularity is evident in that he had a song on the *Billboard* charts every year from 1955 to 1995 (Newsweek, April 27, 1998, p.69). *See* **Sinatra, Frank** *in the* **Index of Names.**

11470 *Frank Watanabe and Honorable Archie.* Eddie Holden and Reginald Sharland played the title roles on the popular West Coast comedy sketch, with Holden playing the Japanese servant to his master, Honorable Archie (KFRC, San Francisco, CA, 1929). Holden first played the role of the Japanese houseboy in 1923, when he appeared on San Francisco radio. Soon Holden began working with Reginald Sharland in the role of his "boss." The team dissolved when Sharland was forced to move to the desert to treat his arthritis. Holden then carried on alone with his own program — *Frank Watanabe* (15 min., KECA, Los Angeles, CA, 1936).

11471 *(The) Frankie Avalon Show.* Singer Avalon hosted and sang on the music show for teenagers sponsored by Charles Pfizer Company. Al Caiola's Orchestra and regular guests such as Paul Anka performed weekly (30 min., Saturday, 7:00–7:30 P.M., ABC, 1959).

11472 *(The) Frankie Laine Show.* Singers Frankie Laine and Peggy Lee performed on the show backed by the Freddy Martin Orchestra. The announcer was Stuart Metz. The show was sponsored by the U.S. Army (30 min., Sunday, 4:30–5:00 P.M., CBS, 1951).

11473 Frankburg, Mary. COM-HE (KGDE, Fergus Falls, MN, 1949).

11474 Franke, Dorothy. COM-HE (WLAV, Grand Rapids, MI, 1951).

11475 Frankel, Clara. Singer (WCOA, Pensacola, FL, 1926).

11476 Frankish, Grant. Newscaster (WJAX, Jacksonville, FL, 1941, WOBS, Jacksonville, FL, 1948).

11477 Franklin, Bob. Newscaster (KTKC, Visalia, CA, 1944).

11478 Franklin, Don. DJ (*Melody Lane*, WTMC, Ocala, FL, 1947).

11479 Franklin, Dorothy. "Assistant Shopping Reporter" (WEEI, Boston, MA, 1928).

11480 Franklin, Fred. DJ (KTRF, Thief River Falls, MN, 1956).

11481 Franklin, Isabelle. Soprano (WGY, Schenectady, NY, 1924).

11482 Franklin, Joe. Announcer (WPAT, Paterson, NJ, 1942). DJ (*Joe Franklin's Record Shop*, WJZ, New York, NY, 1948; *Antique Record Shop* and *Echoes of the Big Time*, WMCA, New York, NY, 1948; *Joe Franklin Record Shop*, ABC, 1949; WMCA, 1950). Franklin, one time an assistant to DJ Martin

Block on his *Make Believe Ballroom* program, still played the music of the 1920s through the 1950s on local New York radio in 2000.

11483 Franklin, John. DJ (*940 Alarm Clock*, KTKC, Visalia, CA, 1947).

11484 Franklin, Leon. Leader (Leon Franklin and his Orchestra, WSM, Nashville, TN, 1928).

11485 Franklin, Richard. Concert pianist (WEAF, New York, NY, 1925; WEBJ, New York, NY, 1926).

11486 Franklin, Ross. DJ (*Starlight Parade*, KYNO, Fresno, CA, 1948). Sportscaster (KYNO, 1950).

11487 Franklin, Tommy. Newscaster (KLS, Oakland, CA, 1941).

11488 Franklin, William. Sportscaster (WIB, Utica, NY, 1937).

11489 Franklin Dance Orchestra. Dance band directed by Howard Lanin (WLIT, Philadelphia, PA, 1925).

11490 *Frankly Feminine*. Household information and helpful hints were broadcast by Mary Hamman on the sustaining daily show (15 min., Monday through Friday, 9:30–9:45 A.M., NBC-Red, 1942).

11491 Franklyn, Allan. Sportscaster (WLW, Cincinnati, OH, 1938).

11492 Frankovich, Mike. Sportscaster (KFAC, Los Angeles, CA, 1939–1940).

11493 Franscisci, Ivan. Leader (Ivan Franscisci Orchestra, WEAR, Cleveland, OH, 1925).

11494 Franson, Marceille. COM-HE (KAHI, Auburn, CA, 1960).

11495 Frantz, Woody. DJ (*1400 Club* and *Hillbilly Clock Watcher*, WHOC, Philadelphia, MS, 1948).

11496 Franz, Emily and Doris Bolvig. Violinist and vocalist (WRNY, New York, NY, 1932).

11497 Franz, Fred. Tenor (WBBR, Rossville, NY, 1925).

11498 Franz, Jack. Organist at Detroit's Michigan Theater (WJR, Detroit, MI, 1928).

11499 Franzell, Gregoire. Pianist (*An Evening with Gregoire Franzell*, instr. mus. prg., 15 min., Monday through Friday, 6:30–6:15 P.M., WINS, New York, NY, 1932).

11500 Frary, Wayne. Pianist (WGHP, Detroit, MI, 1926).

11501 Frasco, Nicholas. Banjo soloist (WEAF, New York, NY, 1925).

11502 Fraser, Gladys and Raymond Howell. Dual piano team (KWSC, Pullman, WA, 1926).

11503 Fraser, John Gordon. Newscaster (NBC-Blue, 1944–1945; WJZ, New York, NY, 1945; ABC, 1947–1948).

11504 Fraser, Vic. Leader (*Vic Fraser Orchestra*, instr. mus. prg., KGHF, Pueblo, CO, 1934; KARK, Little Rock, AR, 1939).

11505 Frasetto [Frazetto], Joe. Leader (*Silver Slipper Supper Club Dance Orchestra*, WPG, Atlantic City, NJ, 1928; *Joe Frasetto Orchestra*, WIP, Philadelphia, PA, 1935–1936, 1938; KFKA, Greeley, CO, 1942).

11506 Frassen, Bob. Newscaster (KYSM, Mankato, MN, 1947).

11507 Fraternity Tango Orchestra. Thomas Clive directed the scholastic band (WJY, Hoboken, NJ, 1924).

11508 Frauenthal, Grace Leithton. Pianist (WTAM, Cleveland, OH, 1925).

11509 Fray, Jacques. Leader (*Jacques Fray Orchestra*, instr. mus. prg., CBS, 1936; CBS, 1942). DJ (*Listening with Jacques Fray*, WQXR, New York, NY, 1947–1957; *Listening to Music*, WQXR, 1958–1960).

11510 *Fray and Baum*. Dual piano team, instr. mus. prg. (CBS, 1936).

11511 *Fray and Briggiotti*. Instr. mus. prg. by the talented dual piano team of Jacques Fray and Mario Briggiotti (15 min., Weekly, CBS, 1932–1934). This talented instrumental team often appeared on network programs.

11512 Frayne, Pat. Sportscaster (KFRC, San Francisco, CA, 1926–1928).

11513 Frazee, John. Sportscaster (WCCO, Minneapolis–St. Paul, MN, 1934).

11514 Frazer, Gladys and Raymond Howell. Dual piano team (KWSC, Pullman, WA, 1926).

11515 Frazer, Stella. Pianist (KWSC, Pullman, WA, 1927).

11516 Frazer, Robert. Blind gospel singer (WCAU, Philadelphia, PA, 1926).

11517 Frazier, Bob. DJ (*Alarm Clock* and *920 Club*, WMMN, Fairmont, WV, 1947–1950).

11518 Frazier, Dora. Soprano (WGBS, New York, NY, 1923).

11519 Frazier, Jim. DJ (*Record Request Show*, WMNC, Morganton, NC, 1947).

11520 Frazier Mountain Park Orchestra. KFWB, Hollywood, CA, 1926).

11521 Frech, Edward J. Newscaster (WMAN, Mansfield, OH, 1945; KFRE, Fresno, CA, 1947).

11522 *(The) Fred Allen Show*. Many critics have called *The Fred Allen Show* the best comedy program ever to appear on American radio. Regardless of this statement's validity, it can be agreed that Allen's program consistently produced funny moments because of its combination of good writing and the performance of its excellent ensemble performers over the years.

Allen continued to hone his comic skills as writer and performer all through his radio career, which extended from 1932 to 1949. Beginning in 1932 with the *Linit Bath Club Revue*, he was joined on his broadcasts by his wife, Portland Hoffa. Allen's programs with their various cast members were as follows:

The Linit Bath Club Revue (30 min., Sunday, 9:00–9:30 P.M., CBS, 1932–1933). Sponsored by Corn Products, manufacturers of Linit, the cast included: Allen, Hoffa, Roy Atwell and Jack Smart. Music was supplied by the Lou Katzman Orchestra with vocals by Charles Carlisle. The announcer was Ken Roberts.

The Salad Bowl Revue (30 min., Tuesday, 9:00–9:30 P.M., NBC-Red, 1933). Sponsored by Best Foods' Hellman's Mayonnaise, the cast included Allen, Hoffa, Roy Atwell, Jack Smart and Eileen Douglas. Music was by the Ferde Grofe Orchestra with vocals by Phil Duey. Tiny Ruffner was the announcer.

The Sal Hepatica Revue (30 min., Wednesday, 9:30–10:00 P.M., NBC-Red, 1934). Bristol-Myers Company sponsored the show, whose cast included: Allen, Hoffa, Roy Atwell, Jack Smart, Minerva Pious and Irwin Delmore. Music was by the Ferde Grofe Orchestra with vocals by the Songsmiths. The announcer was Tiny Ruffner.

The Hour of Smiles (60 min., Wednesday, 9:00–10:00 P.M., NBC-Red, 1934). Bristol-Myers sponsored the show. The cast included: Allen, Hoffa, Roy Atwell, Jack Smart, Irwin Delmore, Eileen Douglas, Minerva Pious, Walter Tetley and Lionel Stander. Music was by Lenny Hayton with vocals by Theordore Webb, the Songsmiths and the Sal Hepatica Singers. Tiny Ruffner was the announcer. The sales pitch stated that the program was sponsored by "Ipana [a toothpaste] for the Smile of Beauty and Sal Hepatica [a laxative] for the Smile of Health."

Town Hall Tonight (60 min., Wednesday, 9:00–10:00 P.M., NBC-Red, 1934–1939). Bristol-Myers again sponsored the program. The cast included: Allen, Hoffa, Jack Smart, Eileen Douglas, Minerva Pious, John Brown, Walter Tetley and Lionel Stander. Music was by the Lenny Hayton and Peter Van Steeden orchestras with vocals by the Town Hall Quartet, the Sal Hepatica Singers, the Merry Macs and Lynn Murray and the Town Singers. Harry Von Zell was the announcer.

The Fred Allen Show (60 min., Wednesday, 9:00–10:00 P.M., NBC-Red, 1939–1940). Bristol-Myers once more sponsored the show with a cast that included: Allen, Hoffa, Minerva Pious, John Brown, Charlie Cantor and Alan Reed. Music was by Peter Van Steeden and vocals by Wynn Murray, the Merry Macs and Lynn Murray and the Town Hall Singers. Harry Von Zell was the announcer.

The Texaco Star Theater (60 min., Wednesday, 9:00–10:00 P.M. and 9:30–10:00 P.M., CBS, 1940–1944). The Texas Company, manufacturers of Texaco gasoline, sponsored the program whose cast included: Allen, Hoffa, Miverva Pious, Alan Reed, Charlie Cantor and John Brown. Music was by the Al Goodman Orchestra with vocals by Wynn Murray, Kenny Baker and Hi, Lo, Jack and the Dame. Jimmy Wallington and Arthur Godfrey were the announcers.

The Fred Allen Show (30 min., Sunday, 8:30–9:00 P.M. and 8:00–8:30 P.M., NBC, 1945–1949). This program, sponsored by Standard Brands and the Ford Dealers of America, had a cast that included: Allen, Hoffa, Minerva Pious, Alan Reed, Kenny Delmar, Parker Fennelly and Peter Donald. Music was by the Al Goodman Orchestra and vocals by the DeMarco Sisters. The announcer was Kenny Delmar.

Although Allen always did most of his own writing, he was assisted over the years by a talented writing pool that included Arnold Auerbach, Nat Hiken, Herb Lewis, Larry Marks, Albert G. Miller, Harry Tugend, Aaron Ruben and Herman Wouk. One of Allen's most memorable shows, however, did not depend upon skillful writing. It occurred during the 1940 season, when a trained eagle by the name of Captain Ramshaw escaped during a broadcast.

As he flew on high, the startled studio audience was splattered by the soaring eagle with unwanted deposits from above. Hilarious fun was had by almost all, including, it seems, Captain Ramshaw.

The composite cast of this great comedy show over the years included such regulars and guests as: Portland Hoffa (Allen), Fred Allen, Roy Atwell, Tallulah Bankhead, Jack Benny, Edgar Bergen, Shirley Booth, John Brown, Charlie Cantor, Bing Crosby, Kenny Delmar, Irwin Delmore, Eileen Douglas, Phil Duey, Leo Durocher, Maurice Evans, Parker Fennelly, Jack Haley, Oscar Hammerstein II, "Uncle Jim" Harkins, Alfred Hitchcock, Bob Hope, George Jessel, Bert Lahr, Charles Laughton, Sam Levene, Beatrice Lillie, Pamela Mason, James Mason, Lauritz Melchior, Henry Morgan, Minerva Pious, Alan Reed (Teddy Bergman), Doc Rockwell, Richard Rodgers, Jack Smart, Walter Tetley, Helen Traubel and Orson Welles. The orchestras included were those of Al Goodman, Ferde Grofe, Lennie Hayton, Lou Katzman and Peter Van Steeden. The DeMarco Sisters and the Town Hall Quartet (Scrappy Lambert, Bob Moody, Tubby Weyant and Leonard Stokes) vocal groups also appeared. The show was written by Fred Allen, Arnold Auerbach, Nat Hiken, Herb Lewis, Larry Marks, Albert G. Miller, Aaron Ruben, Harry Tugend and Herman Wouk. The directors were Victor Knight and Howard Reilly.

An extended discussion of Allen's radio comedy is included in the **Comedy and Humor** entry. Two excellent book length treatments of Allen's comedy can be found in Havig's *Fred Allen's Radio Comedy* and Taylor's *Fred Allen—His Life and Wit*. Wertheim's *Radio Comedy* also perceptively analyzes Allen's comic genius. *See* **Comedy and Humor** *and* **Comediennes.**

11523 ***(The) Fred Astaire Show.*** Dancing motion picture star Fred Astaire hosted his show sponsored by the Packard Motor Car Company. Although performers such as Astaire, comedians Charles Butterworth and Eddie Moran, singer Francia White and Johnny Green's Orchestra were talented, *Variety* said the show was seldom more than mediocre (60 min., 9:30–10:30 P.M., NBC-Red, 1936). The following season after Astaire left the program, it became *The Packard Hour.*

11524 ***Fred Waring.*** Waring's orchestra first appeared on radio on station WWJ (Detroit, MI) in the early 1920s. His first network show featured his fine music plus humorist J.P. Medbury (30 min., Weekly, 10:00–10:30 P.M., CBS, 1933). After appearing on several network shows, Waring was given his own programs known variously as *The Chesterfield Supper Club, Chesterfield Time, Pleasure Time, Victory Tunes* and *The Fred Waring Show.* On most of these shows his well known opening theme was "I Hear Music" and his closing, "Sleep." Over the years his programs' cast included many talented performers: Gordon Berger, Daisy Bernier, Lumpy Brannum, Stuart Churchill, Ruth Cottingham, Diane Courtney, Donna Dae, Johnny "Scat" Davis, Stella Friend, Livingston Gearhart, Paul Gibbons, Gordon Goodman, Murray Kane, Hal Kanner, Priscilla Lane, Rosemary Lane, Craig Leitch, Poley McClintock, Arthur McFarland, George McFarland, Virginia Morley, Les Paul, Mac Perron, Ida Pierce, Roy Ringwald, Babs Ryan, Charlie Ryan, Robert Ryan, Robert Shaw, June Taylor, Kay Thompson, Tom Waring, Joan Wheatley and Jane Wilson. His several announcers included: Bill Bivens, Bob Considine, Paul Douglas and David Ross. The program's producer-director was Tom Bennett. The writers were Jack Dolph and Jay Johnson (NBC, CBS, ABC, 1933–1957). *See* ***The Fred Waring Show*** *and* ***Fred Waring and His Pennsylvanians.***

11525 ***Fred Waring and His Pennsylvanians.*** Waring and his "55 Pennsylvanians" were joined by vocalists Stuart Churchill, Paul Owens, Gordon Goodman, Patsy Garrett and Jane Wilson on this show sponsored by Chesterfield cigarettes (15 min., 1941).

11526 ***(The) Fred Waring Ford Show.*** Waring's fine orchestra was featured along with Kay Thompson, Priscilla Lane, Rosemary Lane, Tom Waring, Stuart Churchill and Johnny "Scat" Davis on his entertaining show (15 min., CBS, 1935).

11527 (The) ***Freddie Rich Penthouse Party.*** Singer GoGo DeLys performed with the swinging Freddy Rich band on the lively music show (30 min., Sunday, 8:00–8:30 P.M. CST, CBS, 1936).

11528 **Frederic, Marvin.** Leader (*Marvin Frederic Orchestra*, instr. mus. prg., WSB, Atlanta, GA, 1937–1938; WJZ-NBC-Red, 1938).

11529 **Frederick, George.** Announcer (WDAF, Kansas City, MO, 1925).

11530 **Frederick, Harland.** Newscaster (KSPO, San Francisco, CA, 1945–1947).

11531 **Frederick, Pauline.** Newscaster (ABC, 1946–1947). Frederick was one of the earliest and most respected female news commentators. Her commentary on United Nations' activities were both comprehensive and incisive.

Although Frederick was a successful newscaster, her career undoubtedly was hampered by the not too subtle bias against women newscasters and commentators that was common during her professional career. From radio's earliest days there was an anti-female bias that made it difficult for them to work as announcers, newscasters or commentators. Frederick found it necessary to lower the pitch of her voice in order to broadcast. *See* **Gender Discrimination.**

11532 **Frederick, Pauline.** COM-HE (*Pauline Frederick*, WMFR, High Point, NC, 1949).

11533 **Fredericks, Bill.** DJ (*The Honeydrippers*, KWJJ, Portland, OR, 1950).

11534 **Fredericks, C.W.** Violinist (KYA, San Francisco, CA, 1927).

11535 **Fredericks, Carlton.** Nutritionist Fredericks talked on various nutrition and health topics (*Carlton Fredericks*, WMGM, New York, NY, 1956). Fredericks enjoyed a long, successful broadcasting career discussing various nutritional subjects. *See* ***Carlton Fredericks.***

11536 **Fredericks, Dorothy.** Singer (*Dorothy Fredericks*, vcl. mus. prg., WLW, Cincinnati, OH, 1934).

11537 **Fredericks, Jack.** Newscaster (WIBX, Utica, NY, 1946).

11538 **Fredericks, Pat.** Newscaster (WDWS, Champaign, IL, 1937). DJ (*Coffee Time*, WMAY, Springfield, IL, 1952).

11539 **Fredericks, Ruth.** COM-HE (WCSS, Amsterdam, NY, 1956).

11540 **Fredericks, Vic.** Fredericks was billed as an "air comedian" (WBBM, Chicago, IL, 1926).

11541 **Fredericks, Walter "Wally."** Announcer and station owner (WOBU, Charleston, WV, 1928).

11542 **Frederics, Adelle.** Singer (WICC, Bridgeport, CT, 1936).

11543 **Frederics, Frank.** DJ (*Frank Frederics Show*, WTAM, Cleveland, OH, 1947).

11544 **Frederickson, Frances H.** Announcer (WPCC, Chicago, IL, 1927).

11545 **Frederickson, Roxie (Mary Cullen).** COM-HE (KPOJ, Portland, OR, 1949).

11546 **Fredlund, Myrtle.** Girl baritone (KOIN, Council Bluffs, IA, 1928).

11547 **Free, Joseph B.** Baritone (WEAF, New York, NY, 1924–1926).

11548 ***Free World Theater.*** The *Free World Theater*, a public service government sponsored program, was conceived by Arch Oboler as a means to obtain the ideas of famous people about the war then in progress and the peace that would be forthcoming. Oboler wrote to various famous people and world leaders including Aldous Huxley, Henry Wallace, Joseph Stalin and Chiang Kai-shek to seek their ideas. He then wrote approximately one-quarter of the programs that resulted. Music was composed and directed by Gordon Jenkins. The program ran for four months with little critical praise (30 min., Weekly, 1943).

11549 **Freed, Alan "Moondog."** DJ (*Record Review* and *Matinee*, WAKR, Akron, OH, 1947; *Request Review*, WARK, Akron, OH, 1950; *Moon Dog House*, WJW, Cleveland, OH, 1952; *Alan Freed*, WINS, New York, NY, 1956; *Alan Freed's Rock and Roll Party*, WINS, 1957; *The Big Beat*, KDAY, Hollywood, CA, 1960). Sportscaster (WAKR, 1947). Freed opened his popular DJ programs with his characteristic, "Hey, here we go." He introduced Black music and its performers to white teenagers. The "old Moon Dog" Alan Freed was important for the role he played in popularizing rock-and-roll music.

11550 **Freed, Bessie.** Pianist (*Bessie Freed*, instr. mus. prg., WFIL, Philadelphia, PA, 1936).

11551 **Freed, Carl.** Leader (*Carl Freed Harmonica Band*, instr. mus. prg., WGN, Chicago, IL, WLW, Cincinnati, OH and WOR, Newark, NJ, 1935).

11552 ***Freed Orchestradians*** **(aka *Freed-Eisman Orchestradians*).** Phil Spitalny directed the Freed Orchestra. Dick Robertson and guest singers performed on the program (30 min., Monday, 8:00–8:30 P.M., NBC, 1928–1929).

11553 Freede [Freedle], Beatrice A. COM-HE, (WDCL, Tarpon Springs, FL, 1956).

11554 Freedman, Louise. COM-HE (WRR, Dallas, TX, 1951).

11555 Freedman, Max. Chief announcer (WFAN, Philadelphia, PA, 1925).

11556 *Freedom's People.* This was the first network program to depict the culture and history of African-Americans by presenting a review of their contributions to American culture. Ambrose Caliver produced and directed the program, assisted by such Black intellectuals as Elaine Locke and Sterling Brown of Howard University. The first program in the series was devoted to music. Such diverse personalities appeared on the distinguished series as boxer Joe Louis, singer Paul Robeson and union leader A. Phillip Randolph (30 min., Monthly, NBC, 1941–1942).

11557 Freeland, Bill. DJ (*Sweet Peach Show*, WRUF, Gainesville, FL, 1952).

11558 Freeland, (Dr.) Frank. Pianist (WRR, Dallas, TX, 1926).

11559 Freeland, Mildred. COM-HE (WMID, Atlantic City, NJ, 1951).

11560 Freeman, Doris. COM-HE (WDXI, Jackson, TN, 1960). Freeman began her broadcast career at the age of 7 in 1932 on a Saturday morning radio program on which she sang and danced until she was 13 years old. She broadcast on WDXI (Jackson, TN) in 1948, where she did everything from appearing on a *Radio Bingo* show to broadcasting her own woman's show. In 1950 she moved to WJAK (Jackson, TN). Freeman worked in TV from 1955 to 1957, before going back to sales and radio broadcasting. In her career Freeman did just about everything in broadcasting. She was Sales Manager of WJAK in 1977 and also had a studio where she produced her own commercials.

11561 Freeman, (Dr.) Douglas S. News commentator (WRNL, Richmond, VA, 1940–1941; 1945–1946).

11562 Freeman, Florence. Busy actress Freeman appeared on the *Jane Arden*; *John's Other Wife*; *Valiant Lady*; *Wendy Warren and the News*; *Young Widder Brown*; and *Dot and Will* daytime serial programs.

11563 Freeman, George. Leader (George Freeman's Sooner Serenaders, WBAP, San Antonio, TX, 1923–1924).

11564 Freeman, Harry. Sportscaster (KFSA, Fort Smith, AR, 1953–1960).

11565 Freeman, Helaine. Actress Freeman was a member of *The Career of Alice Blair* daytime serial cast.

11566 Freeman, Honeyboy. DJ (WBOK, New Orleans, LA, 1956).

11567 Freeman, Isabelle. Soprano (WQJ, Chicago, IL, 1925).

11568 Freeman, Jay. Leader (*Jay Freeman Orchestra*, instr. mus. prg., CBS, 1938).

11569 Freeman, Jerry. Leader (*Jerry Freeman Orchestra*, instr. mus. prg., WIP, Philadelphia, PA, 1934; CBS, 1935).

11570 Freeman, Lois. COM-HE (WGBF, Evansville, IL, 1935).

11571 Freeman, Mary. COM-HE (WOWL, Florence, AL, 1956).

11572 Freeman, Ollie. DJ (*Jazzland*, KTIM, San Raphael, CA, 1952–1954).

11573 Freeman, Walter. DJ (*Rise 'n Shine*, WULA, Eufaula, AL, 1949).

11574 Freeman, William N. Newscaster (KARV, Mesa, AZ, 1946).

11575 Freese, Ralph. Announcer-tenor (KOA, Denver, CO, 1925–1928). In 1929, Freese was a busy announcer appearing on such NBC network programs as *The Pilgrims*, *Neapolitan Nights*, *Gold Spot Orchestra*, *Dixie Circus*, *Smith Brothers*, *Whyte's Orchestra* program and *In the Spotlight* (WJZ-NBC-Blue, New York, NY, 1929).

11576 Freiman, Paul. DJ (*Records in Review*, KCOK, Tulare, CA, 1947).

11577 French, Bob. Newscaster (WHKC, Columbus, OH, 1937–1940; WHBC, Canton, OH, 1947).

11578 French, Charles "Charlie." DJ (*Hillbilly Jamboree*, WWNR, Beckley, WV, 1947). Sportscaster (WWNR, 1948).

11579 French, Genevieve. French broadcast talks on various health topics (KPLA, Los Angeles, CA, 1929).

11580 French, (Madame) Geo. COM-HE French was a fashion expert (WGBS, New York, NY, 1925).

11581 French, Graham. Sportscaster (KTUC, Tuscon, AZ, 1944). Newscaster (KTUC, 1946).

11582 French, Jack. DJ (*Off the Record*, KILO, Grand Forks, ND, 1947). Sportscaster (*The 10:20 Sports Club*, KILO, 1947–1948; KNOX, Grand Forks, ND, 1949–1955).

11583 French, Jessie M. Contralto (WBZ, Boston-Springfield, MA, 1924).

11584 French, Jim. DJ (KING, Seattle, WA, 1956).

11585 French, John. Newscaster and special events announcer (WKMO, Kokomo, IN, 1942).

11586 French, Kenneth "Ken." Newscaster (WHEC, Rochester, NY, 1937–1942).

11587 French, Mabel. Contralto (KFUU, Oakland, CA, 1925).

11588 French, Ned. Newscaster (WORL, Boston, MA, 1939). DJ (*1360 Club*, WLYN, Lynn, MA, 1950; WOND, Pleasantville, NJ, 1954).

11589 French, Pete. Newscaster (WHAS, Louisville, KY, 1941). Sportscaster (WHAS, 1944).

11590 *French Cooking.* Bernice Bell taught French cuisine (WLAG, Minneapolis, MN, 1924).

11591 *French For Travelers.* Radio French language lessons were taught by Dr. Thatcher Clark (15 min., Saturday, WOR, Newark, NJ).

11592 Frenger, George H. Announcer-program manager (KPSN, Pasadena, CA, 1926–1927).

11593 Frenkel, John. Station WCOA's first announcer and station manager (WCOA, Pensacola, FL, 1926–1927). Frenkel created the station's call leaders that stood for Wonderful City Of Advantages.

11594 Frenkel, Milt. DJ (*Harmony Hall*, KTLW, Texas City, TX, 1948).

11595 Fresch [Fresh], Grace. Vocalist (*Grace Fresch*, vcl. mus. prg., WCAU, Philadelphia, PA, 1935–1936).

11596 *Freshman Orchestradians* (aka *The Freshman Orchestradians Program*). Hugo Mariani conducted the orchestra and contralto Mildred Hunt sang on the program that was sponsored by the Freshman Radio company. Various guest vocal soloists also appeared (NBC-Blue, 1928–1929).

11597 Freudberg, Leo. Leader (*Leo Freudberg Orchestra*, instr. mus. prg., WOR-MBS, Newark, NJ, 1934–1937; CBS, 1938).

11598 Freund, Helen. Soprano (WGN, Chicago, IL, 1925).

11599 Frey, Eugene. A six-year-old organist and pianist, Frey also sang in three languages. He was a unique radio performer (KSTP, Hot Springs, AR, 1928).

11600 Frey, Fran. Leader (*Fran Frey Orchestra*, instr. mus. prg., WIP, Philadelphia, PA, 1935).

11601 Frey, Phillip A. Tenor (WAHG, Richmond Hill, NY, 1926).

11602 Frey, Reta. COM-HE (KALB, Alexandria, LA, 1960).

11603 Frey, Reuben. Leader, Reuben Frey's Saxophone Quartet (KFYR, Bismark, ND, 1935).

11604 Freymark, Frances Klasgye. Organist (WDBO, Orlando, FL, 1928).

11605 Freyre, L. Newscaster (WPRA, Mayaguez, PR, 1940).

11606 Friberg, Alice (Carolyn King). COM-HE (WJHL, Johnson City, TN, 1949).

11607 Friberg, Alice Fairn. COM-HE (WCYB, Bristol, VA, 1957).

11608 Fribourg, Francis. Fribourg conducted the Little Symphony Orchestra of KSCJ (KSCJ, Sioux City, IA, 1928).

11609 Frick, Ford. Sportscaster (*Chesterfield Sports News*, local New York station, 1935). Frick moved from radio sportscasting to accept the position of president of the National Baseball League for the salary of $12,000 a year.

11610 Frick, Leslie. Contralto Frick was featured on the *Jeddo Highlanders* program (NBC, New York, NY, 1928).

11611 Frick, Lucille. COM-HE (KRNR, Rosebury, OR, 1956).

11612 Fricke, (Mrs.) W.A. Soprano (WMAQ, Chicago, IL, 1925).

11613 Friday, Ann. COM-HE (KMAN, Manhattan, KS, 1951).

11614 Fridell, Vivian. Actress Fridell appeared on such daytime serial programs as *Backstage Wife* aka *Mary Noble, Backstage Wife*; *The Road of Life*; and *The Romance of Helen Trent*.

11615 Fridkins, Bob. Leader (Bob Fridkin Orchestra, WEAF, New York, NY, 1923).

11616 Friebus, Florida. Actress Friebus was a cast member of the *Lora Lawton* and *Ellen Randolph* aka *The Story of Ellen Randolph* daytime serial programs.

11617 Fried, Gladys. Violinist (WLW, Cincinnati, OH, 1923).

11618 Fried, Walter J. Violinist (WFAA, Dallas, TX, 1924).

11619 Friedberg, William. Critic (*William Friedberg*, 15 min., Friday, 12:15–12:30 A.M., WMCA, New York, NY, 1940). Friedberg discussed theatrical and motion picture news and gossip.

11620 Friedlander, Percy. Newscaster (WINN, Louisville, KY, 1941).

11621 Friedlander, Philip. Friedlander was a favorite Chicago announcer. He was called "The Voice of the Air" (WBBM, Chicago, IL, 1926).

11622 Friedman, Edith. Pianist (WEVD, New York, NY, 1936).

11623 Friedman, Lenore. Soprano (WIBO, Chicago, IL, 1926).

11624 Friedman, Lottie. Soprano (WHT, Deerfield, IL, 1925).

11625 Friedman, Ruth. Pianist (WEAF, New York, NY, 1923–1926).

11626 Friedman, Stan. DJ (*Jazz Carnival* and *Platter Parade*, WJMJ, Philadelphia, PA, 1948).

11627 Friel, Ed. DJ (*Record Hop*, WCHI, Chillicothe, OH, 1960).

11628 Frieling, Jim. DJ (*Featuring Frieling*, WEBR, Buffalo, NY, 1947; *Morning Pickup* and *Platter Parade*, WXRA, Buffalo, NY, 1950).

11629 Friend, Dorothy. COM-HE (WGOG, Walhalla, SC, 1960).

11630 Friend, George. DJ (*Lake Region Serenade*, WLAK, Lakeland, FL, 1950; *Morning Gospel Music*, WPLA, Plant City, FL, 1954).

11631 Friendly Dentists Orchestra. The Friendly Dentists Orchestra was featured on the *Dr. Ralph Mitchell and Associated Dentists Program* (KFWB, Hollywood, CA, 1926).

11632 *(This) Friendly Earth*. Philosopher-conversationalist Professor T.V. Smith of the University of Chicago conducted the informative and inspirational weekly program (15 min., Sunday, 7:30–7:45 P.M. CST, WLS, Chicago, IL, 1935).

11633 Friendly House Dramatic Players. Radio station drama group directed by Agnes Montanus (WOC, Davenport, IA, 1929).

11634 (The) Friendly Maids. Marjorie Posselt led the quintet (WEEI, Boston, MA, 1929).

11635 *(The) Friendly Philosopher*. Pedro de Cordova broadcast his warm, homey philosophy and Will Osborne sang and led his orchestra on the weekly program sponsored by Mazola Oil (15 min., Monday-Wednesday-Friday, 9:45–10:00 A.M., NBC-Red, 1933).

11636 *(The) Friendly Philosopher*. Homer Griffith broadcast inspirational messages and urged his listeners to undertake good deeds, such as taking needy Chicago tenement children to visit the Chicago World's Fair. When the Cook County Bureau of Public Welfare asked him to take about 10,000 children to visit the Fair during its second year, Griffith's listeners sent in over $3,000 and other items of value to cover the cost. Station WLS (Chicago, IL) then took 9,177 children to the Fair (15 min., Weekly, WLS, Chicago, IL, 1934–1935). Griffith was born January 12, 1893. By 1935, he said he had read more than 10,000 poems on the air and mailed more than 100,000 copies of them to listeners. He produced, wrote, and made electrical transcriptions of his programs that were broadcast by more than 60 stations in 1935 during his fifth year at WLS.

11637 *(The) Friendly Philosopher*. Homer Griffith, formerly of WLS (Chicago, IL), took his inspirational program to Texas (WFAA, Dallas, TX, 1936). The following year Griffith moved back to WLS (15 min., Saturday, 8:30–8:45 A.M., WLS, Chicago, IL, 1937).

11638 *(The) Friends*. Ted and Dorothy Friend brought the husband-and-wife talk show format to San Francisco. Bill Roddy was their announcer (15 min., Tuesday and Thursday, 4:45–5:00 P.M. and Sunday, 3:45–4:00 P.M., KPO, San Francisco, CA, 1946).

11639 *Friendship Town*. According to *Radio Digest*, the program was one of the "foremost characterizations of small town life on the air today." The cast included Don Carney, Virginia Gardiner, Pick Malone, Pat Padgett. Tenor Frank Luther and the Harry Salter Orchestra provided the music (30 min., Friday, 9:00–9:30 P.M., NBC-Blue, 1932).

11640 Fries, Irene. Pianist (WFBH, New York, NY, 1925).

11641 *(The) Frigidaire Frolics*. The Frigidaire Company, manufacturers of refrigerators, sponsored this variety show that featured the return to radio of Clara, Lu and Em, tenor Stanley Hickman and Ted Fiorito's Orchestra. Charles Lyon was the announcer (30 min., Friday, 8:30–9:00 P.M., NBC, 1936).

11642 *(The) Frigidaire Program*. Jane Froman sang on the Friday version and Howard Marsh on the Wednesday show. The Snow Queens vocal group and the Jacques Renard Orchestra performed on both (15 min., Wednesday and Friday, 10:30–10:45 A.M., CBS, 1933).

11643 Friml, Rudolph. Leader (*Rudolph Friml Orchestra*, instr. mus. prg., WTAR, Norfolk News, VA, 1936; WEAF, New York, NY, 1937; NBC, 1942). Friml, a gifted composer of operettas, was also a popular orchestral conductor.

11644 Frink, Helen. Vocalist-banjoist (KWSC, Pullman, WA, 1925).

11645 Frisch, Frankie. Former star baseball player and manager, Frisch broadcast New York Giant baseball games (WMCA, New York, NY, 1947; MBS, 1955).

11646 Frischneckt, Lee. DJ (*Let's Get Together with Records*, KID, Idaho Falls, ID, 1949).

11647 Frisher, Carl. Comedian on the *Jolly German Hour* program (WOR, Newark, NJ, 1927).

11648 Fristoe, Wiltz. DJ (*Breakfast Club* and *The Swing Club*, WJJM, Lewisburg, TN, 1947).

11649 Frith, Linda. COM-HE (WYTI, Rocky Mount, VA, 1960).

11650 Frits [Friis], Betty. COM-HE (WGOV, Valdosta, GA, 1956–1957).

11651 Fritsch, Elwood. DJ (*The Saturday Hit Review*, KXOX, Sweetwater, TX, 1947).

11652 Fritsch, John. Newscaster (WBAL, Baltimore, MD, 1937).

11653 Fritsche, Herbert. Leader (*Herbert Fritsche Orchestra*, instr. mus. prg., WJAS, Pittsburgh, PA, 1935).

11654 Fritz, Alene. COM-HE (KNAF, Fredericksburg, TX, 1956).

11655 Fritz, Carl. Newscaster (WFIA, Tampa, FL, 1938).

11656 Fritz, John. DJ (*Ol' Man Fritz*, WFMJ, Youngstown, OH, 1952; WMFJ, 1954).

11657 Fritze, Louis P. Flutist (WEAF, New York, NY, 1926).

11658 Fritze, Mel. Newscaster (KROW, Oakland, CA, 1944). DJ (KYA, San Francisco, CA, 1952).

11659 Fritzland, Frances. Pianist (KFH, Wichita, KS, 1928).

11660 Frizelle, Nellie. Pianist (KFI, Los Angeles, CA, 1925).

11661 Froeba, Frank. Leader (*Frank Froeba Orchestra*, instr. mus. prg., NBC, 1936).

11662 Froeming, Robert "Bob." DJ (*Requestfully Yours*, WFRW, Eau Claire, WI, 1948; *Happy Days*, WRFW, 1952).

11663 Frogge, John. Newscaster (WGBB, Freeport, NY, 1939–1941, 1945; *News of Nassau*, WGBB, 1947–1948).

11664 From, Joe. Newscaster (WJWC, Hammond, IN, 1942).

11665 *From Dusty Pages*. CBS presented these half-hour programs that dramatized various ancient myths and legends (30 min., 6:00–6:30 P.M., CBS, 1930).

11666 *(The) Fro-Joy Player*. A program combining a mystery melodrama with musical interludes (30 min., 7:00–7:30 P.M., WJAS Pittsburgh, PA, 1930).

11667 Frolkey, Rex. Announcer (KWUC, LeMars, IA,1927).

11668 Froman, Jane. Singer (NBC, 1934).

11669 Fromme, Galen. Newscaster and sometime DJ (WBAL, Baltimore, MD, 1940, 1945–1946).

11670 *Front Page Drama*. The transcribed program began as the *American Weekly Drama* in the 1933–1934 season. The entertaining program dramatized famous newspaper stories of the time.

11671 *Front Page Exclusive*. Randolph Hearst and Edwin Lee provided news commentary on the program (15 min., MBS, 1955).

11672 *Front Page Farrell*. Richard Widmark originated the title role of fearless reporter, David Farrell, on the weekday serial drama produced by the prolific husband-and-wife team Frank and Anne Hummert. The sponsor was Anacin and Hills Cold Tablets. Florence Williams played the role of Farrell's wife, Sally. The Farrells and their friends often found themselves embroiled in murder investigations. After Widmark and Williams left the cast, the roles of David and Sally were played by Staats Cotsworth and Virginia Dwyer. Carleton Young also later played Farrell.

The program was a blend of "soap opera and

evening thriller," a rare combination in a daytime serial drama. The program was introduced daily as "... the unforgettable story of marriage and a newspaper office — the story of a handsome dashing young star reporter on one of New York's greatest newspapers and the girl he marries on impulse to save her from throwing herself away on a rich man twice her age."

Betty Garde played fast-talking Kay Barnett, David Farrell's fellow reporter on the New York *Eagle.* Evelyn Varden played Sally's mother, a "victory gardener" during World War II, who always did her part whenever asked. A worshipful *Eagle* office boy, Sammy Warner, played by George Sturgeon, emulated David Farrell whenever possible.

The program's theme, "You and I," was played by organist Rosa Rio. Over the years the program's cast included: Peter Capell, Frank Chase, Staats Cotsworth, Robert Donley, Virginia Dwyer, Katherine Emmet, Elspeth Eric, Betty Garde, Sylvia Leigh, Athena Lorde, James Monks, William Shelley, Eleanor Sherman, Vivian Smolen, George Sturgeon, James Van Dyk, Evelyn Varden, Richard Widmark, Florence Williams, and Carleton Young. Alvin Boretz, Harold Gast, Bob Saxon, and Robert J. Shaw were the program's writers and Bill Sweets and Blair Walliser the directors. Sound effects were produced by Ross Martindale and Manny Segal. John Buckwalter, Arthur Hanna and Ed Slattery were the announcers. (15 min., Monday through Friday, MBS 1941–42, NBC 1942–54).

11673 ***Front Page Parade.*** The dramatized Minneapolis news program was sponsored by the Minneapolis *Star* newspaper. The cast included Hal Parkes, Sylvia Dahl, Louise Youngerman, Ed Abbott and George Grim (Daily, WCCO, Minneapolis, MN, 1939).

11674 ***Front Porch Serenade.*** The sounds of frogs and katydids could be heard throughout the show, giving it the proper rural atmospheric touches. The format combined a sketch of country life with CW music. The music and dramatic interludes were performed by Eddie Alan, Tex Atchison, Red Foley, Wilma Williams, Salty Holmes, Dan Hosmer, Chick Hurt, Edith LaCrosse, John Lair, Patsy Montana, Betty Romaine and Jack Taylor (WLS, Chicago, IL, 1936).

11675 ***Frontier Days.*** The western historical serial drama included a dramatic sketch and tenor John White singing cowboy songs. Martin [Marthin] Provensen was the announcer (15 min., 11:00–11:15 P.M., NBC-Blue, 1930).

11676 ***Frontier Gentleman.*** John Dehner played the title role of a British newspaper correspondent who traveled the American West in search of stories. As improbable as the show's premise was, Dehner capably played the role, doing everything, as *Variety* pointed out, from doctoring to fighting. Jerry Goldsmith was the program's musical director. The show premiered Sunday, February 16, 1958 (25 min., Sunday, 2:30–2:55 P.M., CBS, 1958).

11677 ***Frontier Town.*** The Bruce Ellis production, an interesting western drama, was syndicated in the late 1940s. Reed Hadley played the leading role of lawyer Chad Remmington, who moved week to week from one exciting adventure to another. He was assisted by Cherokee O'Bannon, his comic sidekick (30 min, Weekly, Syndicated, 1952–1953).

11678 ***Frontiers of Science.*** Distinguished news commentator Quincy Howe narrated the sustaining science news program (15 min., Tuesday, 6:45–7:00 P.M., WCBS, New York, NY, 1947).

11679 **Froos, Sylvia.** Vocalist (*Sylvia Froos*, vcl. mus. prg., NBC, 1932; CBS, 1934, MBS, 1935, 1938). Although Froos was 18 when she appeared three times a week on the NBC-Blue network in 1932, she was referred to as "Baby Sylvia."

11680 **Frosh Vocal Quartet.** The members of the male vocal group included Ronald Rice, Alfred Lechenby, Ray Moen and Epley Boardman (KWSC, Pullman, WA, 1926).

11681 **Frost, Alice.** Busy actress Frost appeared on *Backstage Wife* aka *Mary Noble, Backstage Wife, The Road of Life* and *The Romance of Helen Trent* daytime serial programs.

11682 **Frost, Bill.** DJ (*Dance Time*, KGFN, Grass Valley, CA, 1947). Sportscaster (KGFN, 1947).

11683 **Frost, Don.** DJ (*The Timekeeper*, WIBB, Macon, GA, 1948).

11684 **Frost, Donald M.** DJ (*Gene Autry Time* and *Time to Dance*, WPAY, Portsmouth, OR, 1950).

11685 **Frost, Jack.** Frost was the featured tenor on the *Williams Syncopators Hour* program (WJZ, New York, NY, 1929).

11686 **Frost, Jack.** DJ (*The Clock Watcher*, WGH, Newport News, VA, 1947).

11687 **Frost, Jack.** DJ (*Requestfully Yours*, WMIN, St. Paul, MN, 1947; *Rhapsody in Wax*, KLER, Rochester, MN, 1948)

11688 **Frost, William.** Newscaster (WISH, Indianapolis, IN, 1944).

11689 ***Frostilla Broadcast Rehearsal.*** The program supposedly demonstrated how orchestra leader Harry Salter spent his typical broadcast studio day preparing for a network program. Blues singer Mildred Hunt was also featured on the program (15 min., Monday, 9:15–9:30 P.M., CBS, 1932).

11690 **Fruit Jar Drinkers String Band.** W.W. Wilkerson directed the country music group. They first appeared on the *Grand Ole Opry* on February 17, 1929 (WSM, Nashville, TN, 1929; the *Fruit Jar Drinkers*, CW mus. prg., WSM, Nashville, TN, 1934–1935).

11691 **Fruitville Camp No. 431 (W.O.W.) Orchestra.** Lead drummer Leo Vargas led the lodge orchestra whose members included: Owen Dyer, p.; George Brown, as.; Henry Dierksen, tpt.; John Rendon, s.; Edward Perry, tpt.; Ralph Ericksen, bjo.; and Leo Downey, acc. (1929). The band probably was featured on local Nebraska radio.

11692 **Fry, Betty.** COM-HE, singer and harpist (WGPA, Bethlehem, PA, 1949).

11693 **Fry, Cecil.** Pianologues (KFOX, Long Beach, CA, 1929).

11694 **Fry, Charlie.** Leader (Charlie Fry's Orchestra, WIP, Philadelphia, PA, 1926).

11695 **Fry, Evan.** Newscaster (KANS, Wichita, KS, 1939).

11696 **Fry [Frye], Henry "Hank."** Leader (Hank Fry and his Hotel Virginia Orchestra, KFON, Long Beach, CA, 1926; KGER, Long Beach, CA, 1928).

11697 **Fry, Hilary.** Newscaster (KADA, Ada, OK, 1942).

11698 **Fry, Kay.** COM-HE (KRIS, Corpus Christi, TX, 1955).

11699 **Fry, Suzanne.** Singer (*Suzanne Fry*, vcl. mus. prg., WIP, Philadelphia, PA, 1936).

11700 **Frydenlund, Mera Ballis.** COM-HE (KDHL, Faribault, MN, 1951).

11701 **Frye, Rosalie Barker.** Contralto (KNX, Los Angeles, CA, 1928).

11702 **Frykman, A.** Announcer (KFLV, Rockford, IL, 1927).

11703 **Fryman, A.T.** Announcer (KFLV, Rockford, IL, 1926).

11704 **Frymire, Larry.** DJ (*Dawn Salute*, WKAR, East Lansing, MI, 1947).

11705 **Fu Manchu.** *See* ***The Collier Hour*** *and* ***The Shadow of Fu Manchu.***

11706 **Fucile, Nino.** Baritone (NBC-Red, New York, NY, 1929). Fucile regularly sang on the network's *Evening Stars* music programs in 1929.

11707 **Fuentes, Francisco.** Spanish baritone (WJZ, New York, NY, 1928).

11708 **Fuentes, Pancho.** Baritone (NBC, 1928).

11709 **Fuhrer String Quartet.** Instrumental group (KHJ, Los Angeles, CA, 1923).

11710 **Fuhrman, Clarence.** Leader (*Clarence Fuhrman Orchestra*, instr. mus. prg., WIP, Philadelphia, PA, 1935–1939).

11711 **Fuhrman, John.** Newscaster (WOC, Davenport, IA, 1945).

11712 **Fujak, Rosalie Barker.** Contralto (KNX, Los Angeles, CA, 1928).

11713 **Fuldheim, Dorothy (Dorothy Violet Schnell)** . Newscaster (WJW, Cleveland, OH, 1946; ABC, 1947). Fuldheim was born Dorothy Violet Schnell in 1893 in Paterson, NJ.

11714 **Fullen, Gene.** DJ (*Club 33*, WBNS, Columbus, OH, 1952–1954).

11715 **Fuller, Barbara.** Actress Fuller was a cast member of daytime serial programs *The Road of Life, Scattergood Baines, Stepmother, Whispering Streets, The Guiding Light, Ma Perkins* and *Today's Children.*

11716 **Fuller, Bertha.** COM-HE (KAVE, Carlsbad, NM, 1956).

11717 **Fuller, Betty.** CVOM-HE (WKZO, Kalamazoo, MI, 1949).

11718 **Fuller, Dorothy Harding.** COM-HE (WBET, Brockton, MA, 1949–1951)

11719 **Fuller, Charles E.** Fuller, who was born in 1887, was best known for his *Old Fashioned Revival Hour* program. He began his religious broadcasting career in the middle 1920s. Although he retired in 1967, the *Old Fashioned Revival Hour* remained on the air until the 1980s. *See* ***The Old Fashioned Revival Hour (The Joyful Sound).***

11720 **Fuller, Clint.** Sportscaster (WYRN, Louisburg, NC, 1960).

11721 Fuller, Dick. Leader (*Dick Fuller Orchestra*, instr. mus. prg., NBC, 1935).

11722 Fuller, Garry. DJ (*Garry Fuller Show*, WLIB, New York, NY, 1952; KSON, San Diego, CA, 1960).

11723 Fuller, Jerry. DJ (KSST, Sulphur Springs, TX, 1956–1957).

11724 Fuller, Lenore. COM-HE (WBAT, Marion, IN, 1951).

11725 Fuller, Lorenzo "Larry." DJ (*Harlem Frolics*, WLIB, New York, NY, 1949; *Gospel Train*, WLIB, 1954).

11726 Fuller, Martin. Newscaster (KOMA, Oklahoma City, OK, 1941).

11727 Fuller, Phyllis. DJ (*Telegram Request*, WSLB, Ogdensburg, NY, 1952–1954).

11728 Fuller, R.W. Bass (KFDM, Beaumont, TX, 1928).

11729 Fuller, Ralph. Baritone (WOC, Davenport, IA, 1925).

11730 Fuller, Syd. Newscaster (KHJ, Los Angeles, CA, 1946).

11731 *Fuller Brush* Man. Allyn Joslyn was the MC. Baritone Earl Spicer, soprano Mabel Jackson, and the Don Voorhees Orchestra provided the music. The show was sponsored by the Fuller Brush Company (30 min., Tuesday, 9:30–10:00 P.M., NBC-Red, 1932).

11732 Fullerton, J. Cyril. Pianist (WEBJ, New York, NY, 1926).

11733 Fullerton, Zoe. Reader (WOC, Davenport, IA, 1924).

11734 Fullmar, Allan. DJ (*Hits of the Week*, WFIG, Sumter, SC, 1947; *Let's Dance*, WKIX, Columbia, SC, 1950).

11735 Fulmer, Dale. Sportscaster (*Sports Review*, WHLM, Bloomsburg, PA, 1960).

11736 Fulmer, Jean. Pianist (KWSC, Pullman, WA, 1927).

11737 Fulmer, Sybil. Organist (KGER, Long Beach, CA, 1930).

11738 Fulsom, Craig. Eight-year-old pianist (KHJ, Los Angeles, CA, 1924).

11739 Fulsom, Jerry. DJ (*Melody Roundup*, KADA, Ada, OK, 1947).

11740 Fulton, Bob. Newscaster (KLRA, Little Rock, AR, 1945). Sportscaster (KLRA, 1945–1946; *Sports with Bob Fulton*, KLRA, 1947–1949; KXLR, Little Rock, AR, 1950).

11741 Fulton, Bob. Sportscaster (WNOK, Columbia, SC, 1952).

11742 Fulton, Jack. Leader (*Jack Fulton Orchestra*, instr. mus. prg., CBS, 1935).

11743 Fulton, Jean. COM-HE (WLBZ, Bangor, ME, 1949).

11744 Fulton, John. Tenor (WRW, Tarrytown, NY, 1925).

11745 Fulton, John. Newscaster (WGST, Atlanta, GA, 1938–1942; 1945). Sportscaster (WGST, 1939–1941; WGST, 1945–1949; *Sports Report*, WGUN, Atlanta, GA, 1960).

11746 Fulton, Maude. Actress (KHJ, Wichita, KS, 1929).

11747 Fulton, Paul. Newscaster (KVOO, Tulsa, OK, 1944).

11748 Fulton, Sue. Contralto (KFH, Wichita, KS, 1928).

11749 *Fulton Royal Orchestra*. Gordon Kidder directed the commercially sponsored orchestra (15 min., Thursday, 6:00–6:15 P.M., NBC-Red, 1931).

11750 Fulwider, F.R. Announcer (WEBD, Anderson, IN, 1925).

11751 *Fun and Fancy Free*. Jiminy Cricket (Cliff Edwards) and Donald Duck (Clarence Nash) appeared on the comedy show with Clarence Nash's band (ABC, 1947).

11752 *Fun for All*. Bill Cullen and Arlene Francis hosted the variety show with audience participation, stunts and quizzes. Organists Abe Goldman and Bert German (or Berman) also were cast members of the transcribed show (30 min., Saturday, 1:00–1:30 P.M., CBS, 1952).

11753 *Fun in Print*. Sigmund Spaeth hosted the summer replacement for *The Silver Theater* program. The sponsor was the International Silver Company. Contestants on the quiz could be asked about "any fact in print," an unique concept indeed (30 min, Sunday, 6:00–6:30 P.M., CBS, 1940).

11754 *Fun in Swing Time*. Tim and Irene Ryan, Hal Gordon and D'Artega's orchestra appeared on the weekly variety show. Del Sharbutt was the announcer (30 min., Sunday, 6:30–7:00 P.M., MBS, 1938).

11755 *Fun, Inc*. Dick "Two Ton" Baker broadcast songs and chatter on the popular local show sponsored by Great Western Laundry (30 min., Monday through Friday, 8:00–8:30 A.M., WJJD, Chicago, IL, 1941).

11756 Funderburk, "Bud." Sportscaster (*Sports Prediction*, KSST, Sulphur Springs, TX, 1960).

11757 Funk, Bill. Leader (Bill Funk and his Packard 6 Orchestra, KFI, Los Angeles, CA, 1927).

11758 Funk, Ed. DJ (*Symphonic*, WRSW, Warsaw, IN, 1960).

11759 Funk, Larry. Leader (*Larry Funk Orchestra*, instr. mus. prg., WNAC, Boston, MA, 1934; WXYZ, Detroit, MI, 1935; WOR, Newark, NJ, 1936; WOR-MBS, Newark, NJ, 1938). *See* **(The) Band of a 1,000 Melodies**.

11760 Funk, Mark N. DJ (*Music for Milady*, WMGW, Meadville, PA, 1948).

11761 Funk, (Mrs.) Pauline G. Soprano (WMAQ, Chicago, IL, 1924).

11762 Funk, Wilbur. Conductor-saxophonist of the KFAC Orchestra (KFAC, Glendale, CA, 1922). *See* **KFAC Orchestra**.

11763 Funkhouser, Don. DJ (WSIG, Mt. Jackson, VA, 1960).

11764 Funnell, Mildred. COM-HE (WTAM, Cleveland, OH, 1949).

11765 *(The) Funniest Things*. Comedy sketch in which two comedians, Cecil and Sally, not otherwise identified, engaged in comic dialog (KLRA, Little Rock, AR, 1929).

11766 *Funny Side Up*. Host Bert Parks, Harmione Gingold, Kenny Delmar and Parker Fennelly appeared on the zany comedy show that premiered Monday, August 24, 1959 (30 min., Monday through Friday, 10:30–11:00 A.M., CBS, 1959). Its life span was short.

11767 *(The) Funnyboners*. Tenor Dave Grant and baritone Gordon Graham along with Bunny Coughlin sang and clowned on the pleasantly entertaining program (15 min., Wednesday, CBS, 1932).

11768 Furback, Fay. Crooning composer-pianist (WGBS, New York, NY, 1928).

11769 Furey, Gene. Baritone (KFWI, San Francisco, CA, 1926).

11770 Furnas, Bob. A performer billed as "Bob Furnas and his Uke" (KTAB, Oakland, CA, 1928).

11771 Furness, Alice and Hazel Furness. A singing team that came to radio from vaudeville (WCAE, Pittsburgh, PA, 1923).

11772 Furniss, (Mrs.) Edith Ellis. Mrs. Furniss conducted the *Half-Hour with Famous Women* program (WOR, Newark, NJ, 1923).

11773 Furniss, Walter. Newscaster (WCOL, Columbus, OH, 1942, 1944–1945; *Cruise for News*, WCOL, 1948).

11774 Fursteneau, Ruth. Singer (KFJM, Grand Forks, ND, 1937).

11775 Fusco, Albert. DJ (*Pop Shop*, WPME, Punxsutawney, PA, 1954).

11776 Fusco, Dan "Danny." DJ (*The Timekeeper*, WKAL, Rome-Utica, NY, 1947–1948; *Morning Date with Danny*, WRUN, Utica, NY, 1949; *The Timekeeper*, WKAL, 1950; *Date with Danny*, WRUN, 1952–1956).

11777 Fussell, Sarah. Actress Fussell was a cast member of the daytime serial programs *Just Plain Bill* and *The Right to Happiness*.

11778 *(The) Future Star Review*. Another of the many juvenile radio amateur shows that appeared on local radio, the program was sponsored by the Jack Blue Dance Studio (30 min., Sunday, 2:00–2:30 P.M., WHN, New York, NY, 1936).

11779 *F.W. Woolworth Hour*. F.W. Woolworth five and dime stores sponsored the talent laden music program with an orchestra conducted by Percy Faith and a variety of guest performers. For instance, the show's first broadcast on Sunday, June 5, 1955, presented Jan Peerce, Gisele MacKenzie, Tony Bennett, Ferrante and Teischer, Ray Walston, Shannon Bolin and Stephen Douglass. Howard G. Barnes was the program's producer-director (60 min., Sunday, 1:00–2:00 P.M., CBS, 1955).

11780 Fyler, Theda. Newscaster (WSYR, Syracuse, NY, 1941–1942).

11781 Gabbert, Noble and Pete Bennett. Instrumental duo of pianist Gabbert and violinist Bennett (KSCJ, Sioux, IA, 1928).

11782 *Gabby Gosman*. Garry Morfit — later famous as Garry Moore — performed his comedy routines as "Gabby Gosman." Gosman's Ginger Ale sponsored the popular show on which Garry kidded his commercial copy and local Baltimore politicians. *Variety* (April 29, 1936, p.45) said that Morfit's performance and funny material deserved more than a five-minute show (5 min., Three Times Weekly, WBAL, Baltimore, MD, 1936). *See* ***The Garry Moore Show***.

11783 Gabor, Eva. Glamorous Miss Gabor was a charming DJ on her *A Little Night Music* program. *See* ***A Little Night Music***.

11784 Gabowitz, Martin. Pianist (WIP, Philadelphia, PA, 1924).

11785 Gabriel, Alexander. Newscaster (WEVD, New York, NY, 1945–1946).

11786 Gabriel, Bernard. Pianist (*Bernard Gabriel*, instr. mus. prg., WOR, Newark, NJ, 1934).

11787 Gabriel, Charles H., Jr. Announcer (KLX, Oakland, CA, 1926–1927). Program Director (NBC-Pacific Coast Network, 1928).

11788 Gabriel, Clarence. Tenor (KJBS, San Francisco, CA, 1925).

11789 Gabriel, Don. DJ (*Dawn's Early Light*, WJW, Cleveland, OH, 1947–1950).

11790 Gabrilowitsch, Ossip [Ossyp]. Pianist-conductor Gabrilowitsch directed the Detroit Symphony Orchestra (KSD, St. Louis, MO, 1922). He continued working at KSD through the mid–1920s.

11791 Gackle, Bob. Sportscaster (KSO, Des Moines, IA, 1956).

11792 Gadberry, Robert "Bob." Newscaster (KOAM, Plattsburg, KS, 1940; WFBI, Wichita, KS, 1941; KFBI, Wichita, KS, 1946). Sportscaster (KFBI, 1941; KFBI, 1949).

11793 Gaddis, Ivan L. Sportscaster Gaddis delivered talks on sports (WOAW, Omaha, NE, 1925).

11794 Gadski, (Mme.) Johanna. Great operatic singer (WJZ, New York, NY, 1921).

11795 Gaelitz, Hilda. Soprano (WOV, New York, NY, 1932).

11796 Gaerner, Fred F. Cellist Gaerner broadcast on KDKA since its inception, including many of its experimental broadcasts. He continued on KDKA (Pittsburgh, PA) into the 1930s.

11797 Gaerts, Jan. Violinist (WBZ, Boston-Springfield, MA, 1924).

11798 Gaeth, Arthur. Newscaster (KOVO, Provo, UT, 1939; KLO, Ogden, UT, 1940; KOVO, 1942; MBS, 1944; KLO, 1945; WMCA, New York, NY, 1947, ABC, 1948).

11799 Gaffney, H.E. Announcer (WSAC, Clemson College, SC, 1925).

11800 Gaffney, Pauline. COM-HE (WBBF, Rochester, NY, 1954).

11801 Gage, Frank. Singer and trumpet soloist (WEAF, New York, NY, 1923). Announcer and Assistant Program Director (Pacific Coast Network of the National Broadcasting Company, 1928). Gage appeared later as a performer (*Frank Gage,* singer and pianist, KHJ, Los Angeles, CA, 1931). In the next decade he led an orchestra (*Frank Gage,* instr. mus. prg. with this opening: "Rhythm in Rhyme with Frank Gage and his orchestra from the Hotel Statler in Cleveland, Ohio," NBC, 1942).

11802 Gage Brewer's Hawaiians. Popular Wichita orchestra (KFH, Wichita, KS, 1928).

11803 Gagne, Theresa. Singer (WBRY, Waterbury, CT, 1939).

11804 Gagnon, Ed. DJ (*Midnight in Plattsburg*, WMFF, Plattsburg, NY, 1947).

11805 Gahran, Hazel. COM-HE (KTOH, Lihue Kauai, HI, 1957).

11806 Gailbraith, John. DJ (*Musical Lunch Counter*, KGO, San Francisco, CA, 1950).

11807 Gailey, George. Newscaster (WSTV, Steubenville, OH, 1941).

11808 Gaillard, Katherine. COM-HE (WFIG, Sumter, SC, 1955).

11809 Gaillard, Marshall. DJ (*Dawn in Dixie*, WAIM, Anderson, SC, 1955–1956).

11810 Gailmor, William S. Newscaster (WARD, Brooklyn, NY, 1940; WHN, New York, NY, 1942; NBC-Blue, 1944; WHN, 1945–1947; WMGM, New York, NY, 1948).

11811 Gaines, Bill. Newscaster (WFBC, Greenville, SC, 1937–1941).

11812 Gaines, Carmen. COM-HE (WOKZ, Alton, IL, 1955).

11813 Gaines, Charles. Leader (*Charles Gaines Orchestra*, instr. mus. prg., CBS, 1934).

11814 Gaines, Dick. Leader (Dick Gaines Orchestra, WBAP, San Antonio, TX, 1924).

11815 Gaines, Jerry. DJ (*1360 Club*, WPPA, Pottsville, PA, 1947; *Jerry Gaines Show*, WHAT, Philadelphia, PA, 1949–1952). Sportscaster (*Sports Today*, WHAT, 1951–1955).

11816 Gaines, Myrtle. COM-HE (WOKZ, Alton, IL, 1956).

11817 Gaines, Sammy. Newscaster (WAIM, Anderson, SC, 1942; *Uncle Sammy's Serenade*, WLET, Toccoa, GA, 1949).

11818 Gaines, Zeke. DJ (*Good Morning Circle*, WGAU, Athens, GA, 1950).

11819 Gainey, Evelyn. COM-HE (WCKB, Dunn, NC, 1955).

11820 Gainsborg, (Mme.) Lolita Cabrera. Pianist (NBC-Blue, New York, NY, 1926; staff pianist, NBC, New York, NY, 1929; *Mme Lolita Cabrera Gainsborg*, instr. mus. prg. with Milton J. Cross as announcer, 15 min., Saturday, 6:00–6:15 P.M., NBC-Blue, 1930; *Mme. Lolita Cabrera*, instr. mus. prg. accompanied by violinist Godfrey Ludlow, 15 min., Sunday, 1:45–2:00 P.M., NBC-Red, 1932).

11821 Gaintner, J.R. Announcer (WGAL, Lancaster, PA, 1925).

11822 Gaither, Frank. Newscaster (WGSI, Atlanta, GA, 1938).

11823 *Gala All-Star Entertainment Direct from the S.S. Leviathan*. The special variety program originated from aboard the luxury liner, S.S. Leviathan (WGBS, New York, NY, 1925).

11824 Galami, Frank. Piano (WHN, New York, NY, 1925).

11825 *Galaxy of Stars*. A transcribed public service program, the *Galaxy of Stars* presented such visiting guest performers as Lawrence Welk, the Lennon Sisters, Ray Price, Jean Shephard, Pat Boone and Guy Mitchell (15 min., Transcribed, Various Statios, 1957).

11826 Gale, Betty. Singer (WDRC, Hartford, CT, 1936).

11827 Gale, Eddie. Singer (WJZ, New York, NY, 1929).

11828 Gale, Gullermo. Leader (*Gale Gullermo Orchestra*, instr. mus. prg., WHAM, Rochester, NY, 1942).

11829 Gale, Howard. Leader (*Howard Gale Orchestra*, instr. mus. prg., WHP, Harrisburg, PA, 1936–1937; WIP, Philadelphia, PA, 1936).

11830 Gale, Jack. DJ (*The Jack Gale Show*, WTBO, Cumberland, MD, 1949; WTMA, Charleston, SC, 1954; WITH, Baltimore, MD, 1957).

11831 Gale, Leta. Pianist (KFXF, Colorado Springs, CO, 1926).

11832 Gale, Marian. Pianist (KFWM, Oakland, CA, 1926).

11833 Gale, Marian E. COM-HE (WWHG, Hornell, NY, 1956).

11834 Gale, Marion Phoebe. Publicist (NBC, 1940s). Gale was the director of the NBC Press Department in Washington, DC.

11835 Gale, Marsha. COM-HE (WIRA, Ft. Pierce, FL, 1960).

11836 Gale, Virginia. COM-HE (WGN, Chicago, IL, 1951–1956).

11837 *Galen Drake*. Drake presented his often rambling conversational comments on a variety of topics of interest to housewives. Regulars performers with Drake were Stuart Foster, Three Beaus and a Peep and the Bernie Leighton Orchestra (WJZ, New York, NY, 1944). His later broadcasting career was with ABC and CBS (30 min., Monday through Friday, 11:30–12:00 noon, ABC, 1947). Drake's format was extended to a daily hour show a year later. At the peak of his popularity on his entertaining 1948 program, Drake played records and engaged in light-hearted conversational talk Doug McNamee was the show's producer (*Galen Drake*, 60 min., Monday through Friday, 11:30–12:30 P.M., CBS, 1948). Several years later, Drake used his old time style and charm once more in still another format (*Galen Drake*, 90 min., Monday through Friday, 10:15–11:00 A.M. and 2:15–3:00 P.M., WOR, New York, NY, 1959).

11838 Galindo, Raphael. Formerly a member of the Madrid Symphony Orchestra, Galindo was a featured violinist on *The Slumber Hour* program (NBC, New York, NY, 1928).

11839 Galipean, Reginald L. Announcer (WGL, Ft. Wayne, IN, 1927).

11840 Gallagher, Betty. Singer (WPCH, New York, NY, 1932).

11841 Gallagher, Bonnie Kay. Actress Gallagher appeared on the *Houseboat Hannah* daytime serial.

11842 Gallagher, Harold. "Midnight announcer" (WTAM, Cleveland, OH, 1928).

11843 Gallagher, Mike. Newscaster (KFPL, Brownsville, TX, 1938–1939).

11844 Gallagher, Roger. DJ (WMCA, New York, NY, 1956).

11845 Gallaher, Edward "Eddie." Sportscaster (KTUL, Tulsa, OK, 1937; WCCO, Minneapolis–St. Paul, MN, 1939; *Sports Thru the Keyhole*, WCCO, 1940–1941; WTOP, Washington, DC, 1946–1947). DJ (*Moondial*, WTOP, 1947–1948; *Sundial*, WTOP, 1948–1954). While at WCCO, Gallaher was a co-host of that station's popular *Quiz of Two Cities* show. Gallaher gained public attention when he began working as an announcer at WCCO, but he gained his greatest fame as a DJ and announcer at Washington's WTOP. *See **Quiz of Two Cities**.*

11846 Gallant, Catherine Rice. COM-HE (WFAU, Augusta, ME, 1956).

11847 Gallant, James. DJ (*1220 Club*, WDEE, New Haven, CT, 1960).

11848 Gallant, Margaret. Pianist (WEAO, Columbus, OH, 1926).

11849 Gallasi, Frank. Leader (*Frank Gallasi Orchestra*, instr. mus. prg., WOR, Newark, NJ, 1935).

11850 Galle, Ludy (Lucy). COM-HE (KHBB, Hillsboro, TX, 1951).

11851 Galleaux, Gig. Leader (*Gig Galleaux Orchestra*, instr. mus. prg., WMBD, Peoria, IL, 1935–1936).

11852 Gallery, Frank. Leader (Frank Gallery Orchestra, WGES, Oak Park, IL, 1925).

11853 Galliart, Melville K. Newscaster (WKBB, Dubuque, IA, 1939).

11854 Gallicchio, Pasquale (Joseph). Leader (Hotel Stevens Symphony Orchestra, WMAQ, Chicago, IL, 1928; *Joseph Gallicchio Orchestra*, instr. mus. prg., NBC, 1936–1940).

11855 Galli-Curci, Amelita. Distinguished opera singer (WJZ, New York, NY, 1928).

11856 Gallo Instrumental Quartet. Instrumental music group that included August Sandbrink, 1st violin; Louis J. Gallo, 2nd violin; Achille V. Gallo, cello; and P.R. Ellsworth, piano (WSMB, New Orleans, LA 1925).

11857 Gallovan, Bill. Newscaster (WJZM, Clarksville, TN, 1947).

11858 Galloway, John. DJ (*Holiday*, WARL, Arlington, VA, 1954).

11859 Gallup, Arlene. Pianist (WORD, Batavia, IL, 1925).

11860 Galster, Agnes Clark. Soprano (KOA, Denver, CO, 1926).

11861 Galth, Frank. Newscaster (WGST, Atlanta, GA, 1940).

11862 Galvin, Grace H. COM-HE (WBRY, Waterbury, CT, 1955–1957).

11863 Gamage, Edward. Tenor (*Edward Gamage*, vcl. mus. prg., NBC, 1935).

11864 Gamba, Celia. Violinist (NBC, 1937).

11865 Gamberg, Allena. Singer (KFUU, Oakland, CA, 1925).

11866 Gamble, Baxter. Newscaster (KGGM, Albuquerque, NM, 1942). DJ (WMRP, Flint, MI, 1955).

11867 Gamble, Bill. DJ (*Pin Up Melodies*, KFRU, Columbia, MO, 1947; WKTL, Cheboygan, WI, 1960).

11868 Gamble, Gail. COM-HE (KOTA, Rapid City, SD, 1951).

11869 Gamble, Jim. Announcer (WKAR, East Lansing, MI, 1927).

11870 Gamble, Lou Bonnie. COM-HE (WCMJ, Palm Springs, CA, 1951).

11871 Gambling, John B. An Englishman just out of the British Navy in 1925, Gambling took a job at WOR, Newark, NJ, as a studio engineer. One day when an announcer for Bernarr McFadden's early morning exercise program failed to arrive on time, Gambling took over the announcing duties on the hour program and easily talked his way through it. When McFadden left the program shortly thereafter in March 1925, Gambling took over for him. The program developed into his long-running *Gambling's Musical Clock* (at times known as *Gambling's Musical Gym Clock*). In 1944, Gambling also served as a newscaster on the program. After broadcasting from 1925 to 1959, he was succeeded, first, by his son, John A. Gambling, who conducted the program from 1959 to 1990, and, later still, by his grandson, John R. Gambling.

September 11, 2000, was as important date in radio history as the *Rambling with Gambling* program that had been heard continuously on WOR (New York, NY) for 75 years was broadcast for the last time (Pristin, New York *Times*, September 12, 2000). John R. Gambling received many sympathetic calls from listeners and such dignitaries as New York City Mayor Rudolf Giulani and New Jersey Governor Christine Todd Whitman. *See* **Appendix A — Chronology, 1906–1960**, Sept. 11, 2000.

11872 Gamelin, F.C. Newscaster (KWLC, Decorah, IA, 1939).

11873 Games, Dolf. Newscaster (KORE, Eugene, OR, 1940).

11874 Gamet, Kenneth. Announcer (WEAU, Sioux City, IA, 1925).

11875 Gamille, Noreen. Character sketches (KFI, Los Angeles, CA, 1929).

11876 Gammell, Sereno B. Newscaster (WTHT, Hartford, CT, 1942, 1945, 1948).

11877 Gammill, Noreen. Monologist Gammill broadcast character sketches (KFI, San Francisco, CA, 1929–1930).

11878 Gammon, Irvin. Newscaster (WAGN, Presque Isle, ME, 1938).

11879 Gandolfi, Alfredo. Metropolitan Opera baritone Gandolfi sang on the *Atwater Kent Hour* (*NBC*, 1929).

11880 Gandy, Art. Newscaster (KHUB, Watsonville, CA, 1942).

11881 Gane, Anita. Pianist (WFIL, Philadelphia, PA, 1935).

11882 *Gangbusters*. Phillips H. Lord created the program and appeared as its first narrator-host. Eventually, Colonel Norman H. Schwarzkopf of the New Jersey State Police and Lewis J. Valentine, the retired New York City Police Commissioner, succeeded him as narrator. Based on actual police cases, *Gangbusters* was a later version of the original *G-Men* program. Originally sponsored by Palmolive Brushless Shaving Cream, the program was heard from 1935 to 1957 in one format or another. *Gangbusters* made the claim that it was "the only national program that brings you authentic police cases. At the end of each program, "clues" were broadcast about criminals at large wanted by the police. These "clues" were said to have resulted in hundreds of criminals being captured. The cast included: Joan Banks, Art Carney, Roger DeKoven, Robert Dryden, Helene Dumas, Elspeth Eric, Anne-Marie Gayer, Larry Haines, Leon Janney, Raymond Edward Johnson, Adelaide Klein, Bill Lipton, Frank Lovejoy, Don MacLaughlin, James McCallion, Santos Ortega, Ethel Owen, Byrna Raeburn, Alice Reinheart, Grant Richards, Linda Watkins and Richard Widmark. The program's narrators included Dean Carlton, John C. Hilley, Phillips H. Lord, Colonel J. Norman Schwarzkopf and Lewis J. Valentine. The announcers were Charles Stark, Roger Forster, Frank Gallop, Don Gardiner and H. Gilbert Martin. Leonard Bass, Harry Frazee, Jay Hanna, Paul Munroe, Bill Sweets and George Zachary were the directors. The show's writers were Brice Disque, Jr., Phillips H. Lord, John Mole and Stanley Niss (30 min., NBC-Blue, ABC, 1936–1957).

11883 Ganic, Sylvia. Soprano (WBBM, Chicago, IL, 1925).

11884 Ganley, Gertrude O'Neill. Impersonator (WCCO, Minneapolis–St. Paul, MN, 1928).

11885 Gann, (Cantor) Moses. Baritone (WOR, Newark, NJ, 1924).

11886 Gannon, Feland. Announcer (WRC, Washington, DC, 1925).

11887 Gannon, Frances F. COM-HE (WNYC, New York, NY, 1951).

11888 Gannon, Joe. DJ (KWPC, Muscatine, IA, 1960).

11889 Gannon, Mike. Sportscaster (WCRS, Greenwood, SC, 1945–1946; *Sports Final*, WIS, Columbia, SC, 1947–1948).

11890 Gannon, Naomi Weaver. Pianist (KPO, San Francisco, CA, 1923).

11891 Gans, Alan. Sportscaster (*Inside Angle on Sports*, KYW, Philadelphia, PA, 1951).

11892 Ganton, John. Tenor (KFWB, Hollywood, CA, 1927).

11893 Gapen, Ken. Newscaster (*National Farm and Home Hour*, NBC, 1947–1948).

11894 Gar, Grace. DJ (*America's Youngest Negro Disc-Jockey*, WBCO, Birmingham-Bessemer, AL, 1949).

11895 Gar, Larry. DJ (*Tempo*, WLBG, Laurens, SC, 1960).

11896 Garacusi, Nicholas. Violinist Garacusi was a member of the Detroit *News* orchestra (WWJ, Detroit, MI, 1925).

11897 Garafalo, Pietro. Newscaster (WHOM, Jersey City, NJ, 1938).

11898 (The) Garay Sisters from Hungary. Singing team (KMA, Shenandoah, IA, 1927).

11899 Garbell, Rosemary. Actress Garbell appeared on the daytime serial program *Mary Marlin* aka *The Story of Mary Malin*.

11900 Garber, Jan. Garber was an Army band leader during World War I. After the war, he and co-leader pianist, Milton Davis, formed a dance band known as the Garber-Davis Orchestra. After Davis left the band in 1924, Garber remained a busy bandleader on the air: (Garber's Swiss Garden Orchestra, WLW, Cincinnati, OH, 1922; Jan Garber and his Musical Clowns, WLW, Cincinnati, OH, 1926 and WABC-CBS, New York, NY, 1929; *Jan Garber Orchestra*, instr. mus. prg., NBC, 1933; KLRA, Little Rock, AR, 1934; WOR, Newark, NJ, 1935–1936; MBS, 1939). Garber was often called the "Idol of the Airways."

11901 Garber, Mary. COM-HE (WTYM, Springfield, MA, 1951).

11902 Garbiel, Charles H. Announcer (KLX, Oakland, CA, 1926).

11903 Garcia, Caridad. Vocalist (*Caridad Garcia*, vcl. mus., prg., WLOK, Lima, OH, 1942).

11904 Garcia, Eva M. Pianist (KGO, Oakland, CA, 1925–1928).

11905 Garcia, Gene. DJ (*Uncle Gene*, WALT, Tampa, FL, 1947–1952).

11906 Garcia, Hector. Newscaster (*Community News*, KPAB, Laredo, TX, 1947).

11907 Garcia, May E. Miss Garcia conducted the *Dance to Health* program (KFWI, San Francisco, CA, 1926).

11908 Garcia, Squeezer. DJ (*Border Bombshell*, KBOR, Lansing, TX, 1949).

11909 Garcia, Woody. DJ (WTSP, St. Petersburg, FL, 1957).

11910 *Garcia's Mexican Marimba*. Ethnic band (Instr. mus. prg., NBC-Red, 1933).

11911 Gard, Margaret. Contralto (KLDS, Independence, MO, 1927).

11912 Garde, Betty. Talented actress Garde appeared on the *Jane Arden*, *Lorenzo Jones*, *Mrs. Wiggs of the Cabbage Patch*, *We the Abbotts* and *Front Page Farrell* daytime serial programs.

11913 Garden, Amanda. Reader (KFSG, Los Angeles, CA, 1925).

11914 Garden, Mary. In 1922, opera star Garden headed the Chicago Opera Company, which later became the Chicago Civic Opera Company. Chicago claimed her as "Our Mary" in 1923, when for the first time in a year she sang in the Chicago Civic Opera's production of "Cleopatra" broadcast (KYW, Chicago, IL, 1923). When she appeared on NBC's inaugural program in 1926, Garden sang "Annie Laurie," "Open Thy Blue Eyes" and "My Little Gray Home in the West." Her role in the development of early Chicago radio is discussed in the **Opera** and **Stations Growth and Development** entries. *See* **Opera** *and* **Stations Growth and Development**.

11915 *(The) Garden Club*. John Baker conducted the informative program for gardeners. Ralph Waldo Emerson provided organ interludes (15 min., Saturday, 11:15–11:30 A.M. CST, WLS, Chicago, IL, 1937).

11916 Garden Pier Dance Orchestra. Club band (WPG, Atlantic City, NJ, 1926).

11917 *Gardening*. Miss Elizabeth Lennox conducted the program for gardeners (WMBD, Peoria, IL, 1935).

11918 *Gardening the Luther Burbank Way*. Mrs. Luther Burbank discussed gardening techniques on the transcribed series (15 min., Transcribed, Various Stations, 1933).

11919 Gardiner, Dick. Leader (*Dick Gardiner Orchestra*, instr. mus. prg., CBS, 1934–1935).

11920 Gardiner, Don. Newscaster (NBC-Blue, 1944–1945; WJZ, New York, NY and *Monday Morning Headlines*, ABC, 1946–1948).

11921 Gardiner, Dorothy. COM-HE (KTLA, Los Angeles, CA, 1957).

11922 Gardiner, Evelyn. COM-HE (KDKA, Pittsburgh, PA, 1951).

11923 Gardiner, Jean. Blues singer (KOIN, Council Bluffs, IA, 1928).

11924 Gardiner, Virginia. Dramatic actress Gardiner appeared on the *Empire Builders* program (NBC, 1929).

11925 Gardner, Carrol. Sportscaster (WMBR, Jacksonville, FL, 1937–1941; WSNY, Schenectady, NY, 1944).

11926 Gardner, Dave. Leader (*Dave Gardner Orchestra*, instr. mus. prg., CBS, 1935).

11927 Gardner, Dick. Leader (*Dick Gardner Orchestra*, instr. mus. prg., WLW, Cincinnati, OH, 1939).

11928 Gardner, Don. Sportscaster (WKBN, Youngstown, OH, 1937–1942; WKBN, 1947–1956; *The Sports Tonight*, WKBN, Youngstown, OH, 1960).

11929 Gardner, Earl. Leader (*Earl Gardner Orchestra*, instr. mus. prg., WOWO, Fort Wayne, IN, 1936).

11930 Gardner, Guy. DJ (*Guy's Guests*, KCOH, Houston, TX, 1949). Sportscaster (*Sports Parade*, KOGT, Orange, TX, 1949).

11931 Gardner, Hazel. Singer (*Hazel Gardner*, vcl. mus. prg., WMBD, Peoria, IL, 1935).

11932 Gardner, Hy. Newscaster (*Twin Views of the News, MBS,* 1947–1948).

11933 Gardner, Jack. Manager (Jack Gardner's Honey Boys Orchestra directed by John McFall, WFAA Dallas, TX, 1923–1924; Jack Gardner's Orchestra, WRR, Dallas, TX, 1926).

11934 Gardner, Jack. DJ (*Sagebrush Symphony*, WHIP, Booneville, MS, 1949–1952).

11935 Gardner, Jan. COM-HE and writer (WMPS, Memphis, TN, 1943). Gardner grew up admiring the *Jane Arden* comic strip that told the story of a glamorous newspaper woman. Lying about her age at 15, she got a job on the Memphis *Commercial Appeal* newspaper. After she was interviewed on WMPS as Teenager of the Week on the *Kay Allen* (Katherine Vaderbrougie) program, Allen asked her if she would like to "get into" radio. When Gardner joined WMPS, she was taught continuity writing by Anne Howard Bailey — who later went on to write the *Lassie*, *The Armstrong Fireside Theater* and other television programs.

When Kay Allen went on assignment to the West Coast, she asked Gardner to take over her program for a week. Not yet 16 years old in 1943, Gardner did the 30-minute program five times a week and was "hooked." The following year Gardner and Jerry Thompson did a teenage DJ show on WMPS, a program that she continued on the air while she attended Memphis State College.

After World War II, she went to work as a copywriter on WJPR (Greenville, MS), where she wrote copy, sold time, did traffic and broadcast for two hours in the afternoon. The versatile Miss Gardner was only 19 when she went to work at WJPR. She left the small Mississippi station to work, first, at a 50,000 watts Buffalo, New York, station and then for a Boston advertising agency. She got into early television in 1949 with a 30-minute Monday through Friday *Kitchen Party* program.

She left radio work in 1949 and "always missed it." Commenting on her radio work, she said (Gardner, 1977), "I always got equal pay for equal work." Gardner returned home to Memphis in 1955 and started her own advertising agency the next year.

11936 Gardner, Ouita Johnson. Soprano (KVOO, Tulsa, OK, 1928).

11937 Gardner, Russell. Newscaster (WHIZ, Zanesville, OH, 1940). Sportscaster (WCED, DuBois, PA, 1941).

11938 Garenas, Maxine. Actor Garenas appeared on the *Mary Noble* aka *Mary Noble, Backstage Wife* daytime serial.

11939 Garfunkel, Leonard. Pianist (WGBS, New York, NY, 1926).

11940 Gargan, Howard. Singer (WRNY, Richmond Hill, NY, 1926).

11941 Gargano, Bill. DJ (*Sunny Side of the Street*, WHTC, Holland, MI, 1954).

11942 Garland, Charlie. Announcer-pianist (WBBM, Chicago, IL, 1925). Director (*Nutty Club*, *Tomahawk Club* and the *Old Gray Mare Club*, WBBM, Chicago, IL, 1928). When WBBM was short of talent in 1925, Garland played the piano for singer Kay Davidson to fill the broadcast schedule. Garland was under somewhat of a handicap, however, since he could only play in the key of C.

11943 Garland, (Mrs.) E.V. Pianist (KVOO, Tulsa, OK, 1928).

11944 Garland, Elbert. Pianist (KVOO, Tulsa, OK, 1928).

11945 Garland, Hamlin. Famous American author read from his own writings (KDKA, Pittsburgh, PA, 1923; KQV, Pittsburgh, PA, 1923).

11946 Garland, Howard. DJ (*Juke Box Revue*, *Wax Museum* and *Midnight Serenade*, WDVA, Danville, VA, 1947).

11947 Garland, Ken. DJ (*WPOR Night Club*, WPOR, Portland, ME, 1954–1957).

11948 Garmony, Eugene. Violinist (WCAE, Pittsburgh, PA, 1924).

11949 Garn, Pearl. Vocalist (*Pearl Garn*, vcl. mus. prg., WIP, Philadelphia, PA, 1935).

11950 Garner, Charlotte. COM-HE (WSAZ, Huntington, WV, 1949).

11951 Garner, J.E. "Pat." Newscaster (KFPW, Fort Smith, AR, 1942–1945; *Behind the Headlines*, 1948).

11952 Garner, Jim. Sportscaster (*Sports Parade*, WJW, Cleveland, OH, 1948).

11953 Garner, Mark. Announcer (WFDF, Flint, MI, 1925).

11954 Garner, Mary Lou. COM-HE (WZYX, Cowan, TN, 1960).

11955 Garner, Robert "Honeymoon." Black DJ (WDIA, Memphis, TN, late 1950s). Garner was a versatile broadcaster, who had been a student of A.C. Williams at Manassas High School. Demonstrating his versatility, Garner was also a skilled singer, musician, announcer, board man and engineer. *See* **Williams, A.C.**

11956 Garnes, C.M. Sportscaster (KBST, Big Spring, AR, 1937). Newscaster (KRIG, Odessa, TX, 1946).

11957 Garnes, Clarence. Newscaster (KANS, Wichita, KS, 1940; KOMA, Oklahoma City, OK, 1941; KPDN, Pampa, TX, 1938). Sportscaster (KANS, 1940; KOMA,

1941; WDOD, Chattanooga, TN, 1944; WSAV, Savannah, GA, 1945; *Spotlight on Sports*, WSAV, 1952–1955).

11958 Garnet, K. Announcer (WEAV, Sioux City, IA, 1924).

11959 Garnett, Leon. Announcer (WFOT, Wichita, KS, 1926).

11960 Garo, Mary. COM-HE (WIZZ, Streator, IL, 1956).

11961 Garr, Bill. DJ (*Bill Garr Show*, KWKW, Pasadena, CA, 1948–1954). Sportscaster (*Hollywood Park Racing*, KDAY, Hollywood, CA, 1960).

11962 Garred, Robert C. "Bob." News analyst (KSFO, San Francisco, CA, 1938; *Bob Garred Reporting*, CBS, 1939–1942; CBS, 1945; KNX, Los Angeles, CA, 1940, 1946–1947).

11963 Garretson, Joseph. Newscaster (WKRC, Cincinnati, OH, 1941; *Shell Oil News*, WSAI, Cincinnati, OH, 1947; *Joe Garretson and the News*, WSAI, 1948).

11964 Garrett, Alfred B. Newscaster (WOSU, Columbus, OH, 1945).

11965 Garrett, Buck. Guitarist (*Buck Garrett and his Guitar*, instr. mus. prg., KUOA, Fayetteville, AR, 1933–1934).

11966 Garrett, C.H. Announcer (WRR, Dallas, TX, 1925).

11967 Garrett, Jimmy. Leader (*Jimmy Garrett Orchestra*, instr. mus. prg., WENR, Chicago, IL, 1937).

11968 Garrett, June. DJ (WAHR, Miami Beach, FL, 1955).

11969 Garrett, Mary Bell. Pianist (WHAS, Louisville, KY, 1923).

11970 Garrett, Norma. Soprano (KPO, San Francisco, CA, 1926).

11971 Garrett, Patsy. Singer (*Here's Patsy*, vcl. mus. prg., WRVA, Richmond, VA, 1953).

11972 Garrett, Tom "Snuff." DJ (KSYD, Wichita Falls, TX, 1957).

11973 Garrett, Zola. Contralto (KVOO, Tulsa, OK, 1928).

11974 *(The) Garrick Gaieties*. Singer Edith Meiser was featured on this music program (1930).

11975 Garrick Theater Symphony Orchestra. Theater band (WAMD, Minneapolis, MN, 1926).

11976 Garrigan, Jimmie. Leader (*Jimmie Garrigan Orchestra*, instr. mus. prg., NBC, 1935).

11977 Garris, Sid. DJ (*Symphony Sid Show*, WJEL, Springfield, OH, 1948).

11978 Garris [Garres], Maurice. Singer (*Maurice Garris*, vcl. mus. prg., WPG, Atlantic City, NJ, 1934–1936).

11979 Garrison, Beth. Singer (*Ye Old Type Fest*, WOOD, Grand Rapids, MI, 1926).

11980 Garrison, Gary. DJ (WHYN, Springfield, MA, 1957).

11981 Garrison, Iliff. Pianist (KOA, Denver, CO, 1925).

11982 Garrison, John. Newscaster (WFUN, Huntsville, AL, 1946; *On the News Front*, WFUN, 1948). Sportscaster (WFUN, 1948).

11983 Garrison, Mabel. Operatic and concert soprano Garrison was frequently heard on the *Atwater Kent Hour* (NBC, 1927–1929).

11984 Garrity, Bob. DJ (WHON, New York, NY, 1947; *Relaxing with Garrity*, WGBB, Freeport, NY, 1948). Traffic news (WOR, New York, NY, 1955). Garrity was one of the first broadcasters to give traffic news from a propeller driven airplane.

11985 Garrity, Charlotte. Actress Garrity was a cast member of *Life Begins* aka *Martha Webster* and *Valiant Lady* daytime serial programs.

11986 Garrity, Margaret. Pianist (WEBH, Chicago, IL, 1924).

11987 Garrity, Vince. Sportscaster (WAAF, Chicago, IL, 1948; *Sports Review*, WAAF, 1954–1955). DJ (WAAF, 1960).

11988 Garroway, David "Dave." DJ (*The 1160* and *Dave Garroway Show*, WMAQ, Chicago, IL, 1947–1948). Sportscaster (WMAQ, Chicago, IL and WENR , Chicago, IL, 1940–1941; WMAQ, 1942–1945). *The Dave Garroway Show* was a variety show broadcast on a sustaining basis on NBC. Emanating from Chicago, it was a summer replacement for *Ellery Queen*. Vocalists Nancy Martin and Jack Haskell appeared with Joseph Gallicchio's orchestra on this pleasant variety show (30 min., Saturday, 6:30–7:00 P.M., NBC, 1947). *See **The Dave Garroway Show**.*

11989 Garroway, Will. Concert pianist (KFI, Los Angeles, CA, 1926). Garroway also performed on other Los Angeles stations such as KNX, KMTR, KFWB and KHJ in the 20s.

11990 *(The) Garry Moore Show*. Garry Moore was the comedian-host of this sustaining comedy-music show. His partners in fun were Kathryn Card, Arthur Kohl, Joe Rockhold and Hugh Studebaker. Rex Mauphins's orchestra and singer Marion Mann also were featured. Michael Roy was the announcer (30 min., Wednesday, 9:00–9:30 P.M., NBC, 1942). After teaming with veteran star Jimmy Durante on *The Jimmy Durante Show* (aka *The Rexall Show*), Moore once more starred on his own show when he hosted an entertaining 60-minute program broadcast by CBS on a sustaining basis. The program featured the singing of Ken Carson and Eileen Woods and the twin piano team of Irving Miller and Bill Wardell. The announcer was Howard Petrie (*The Garry Moore Show*, 60 min., Monday through Friday, 3:30–4:30 P.M., CBS, 1950).

11991 Gartland, John. Cornetist and bandmaster, 106th Infantry Band (WJZ, New York, NY, 1922).

11992 Gartner, Florence. Singer (WAAT, Newark, NJ, 1936).

11993 Garvin, Val. Leader (*Val Garvin Orchestra*, instr. mus. prg., WCAE, Pittsburgh, PA, 1936).

11994 Garvin, Walter M. Newscaster (KLBM, La Grande, OR, 1945).

11995 Gary, El. Tenor (*El Gary*, vcl. mus. prg., WBAL, Baltimore, MD, 1934–1936).

11996 Gary, Lora. COM-HE (WJLD, Birmingham, AL, 1956; KVPI, Ville Platte, LA, 1957).

11997 Gary, Sid. Baritone (*Sid Gary*, vcl. mus. prg, WOR, Newark, NJ, 1934; WIP, Philadelphia, PA, 1936).

11998 *(The) Gary Crosby Show*. Bing's oldest son, Gary, did a good job of crooning, hosting and talking with program guests on his show. The Dreamers vocal group and Buddy Bregman's Orchestra were also program regulars (30 min., Sunday, 8:30–9:00 P.M., CBS, 1955).

11999 Gask, Cecil. Newscaster (WEBR, Buffalo, NY, 1938).

12000 *Gaslight Gayeties [Gaities]* (aka *The Gay Nineties Revue*). The program began as *The Gay Nineties Revue* in 1941 with Joe Howard. Beatrice Kay joined the *Gay Nineties Revue* in 1943. Kay previously had sang at Billy Rose's Diamond Horseshoe night club in New York. The program's name was changed to *The Gaslight Gayeties* in 1944. On *Gaslight Gayeties*, Kay was joined by Michael O'Shea as the singing host, Sally Sweetland and the Charles "Bud" Dant Orchestra. The announcer was Perry Ward (30 min., Saturday, 8:00–8:30 P.M., NBC-Red, 1945). In a later version of the program Jack Smith and Martin Sperzel and Marshall Hall were featured (NBC, 1945).

12001 *Gasoline Alley*. Frank King's comic strip was the basis for this daily serial drama, the story of Skeezix, a young automobile mechanic, his wife and their friends. The program's cast included: Mason Adams, Hazel Dopheide, Janice Gilbert, Jean Gillespie, Billy Idelson, Bill Lipton, Junius Matthews, Jimmy McCallion, Irna Phillips and Cliff Soubier. The program was directed by John Cole and Charles Schenck and written by Kane Campbell and Kay Chase.

Gasoline Alley was a popular family comic strip that first appeared in the Chicago *Tribune* in 1919. The strip started as a weekly meeting of automobile enthusiasts who met in an alley behind the members' respective apartment buildings — therefore, the strip's name. Soon, however, a dramatic change took place when a baby was left on Walt Willet's doorstep. The baby was given the name of Skeezix. After that the plot became a serious, well-written story of a family that matured and aged as time went on.

12002 Gasoline George. George was an unidentified performer who talked authoritatively on such automotive topics as "Intakes and Exhausts" (KFRC, San Francisco, CA, 1925).

12003 Gasparre, Dick. Leader (*Dick Gasparre Orchestra*, instr. mus. prg., NBC, 1935–1938; WLW, Cincinnati, OH and NBC, 1939).

12004 Gaston, Lela Ward. Reader-impersonator (WHB, Kansas City, MO, 1926; WEBH, Chicago, IL, 1927). Gaston also broadcast interesting character sketches.

12005 Gaston, Marcus "Mark." DJ (*Oklahoma Jamboree*, KSIW, Woodward, OK, 1949; *Musical Moments*, KSIW, 1952).

12006 Gaston, Orin. Leader (WSM Concert Orchestra, WSM, Nashville, TN, 1929).

12007 Gately, Robert. Baritone (*Robert Gately*, vcl. mus. prg., NBC-Blue, New York, NY, 1936–1937).

12008 Gates, Connie. Singer (*Connie Gates*, vcl. mus. prg., CBS, 1934–1936; NBC, 1936).

12009 Gates, Edith. Mezzo-soprano (WGI, Medford Hillside, MA, 1922).

12010 Gates, Hilliard. Sportscaster (WOWO, Fort Wayne, IN, 1941–1946; *Gateway to Sports*, WKJG, Fort Wayne, IN, 1947–1949).

12011 Gates, Robert W. Newscaster (WFMJ, Youngstown, OH, 1939).

12012 Gates, Ruth. Actress Gates appeared on the *Amanda of Honeymoon Hill* daytime serial.

12013 Gates, Ted. Newscaster (KROD, El Paso, TX, 1941).

12014 Gatewood, E.J. Baritone, pianist and cellist (WLAC, Nashville, TN, 1928). Gatewood was the Director of Music at the George Peabody College for Teachers.

12015 Gatling, Bill. DJ (*Ready for Music*, WLPM, Suffolk, VA, 1950).

12016 Gaty, Alice. COM-HE (KVPI, Villa Platte, LA, 1957).

12017 Gau, Rheiny. Vocalist (*Rheiny Gau*, vcl. mus. prg., WLW, Cincinnati, OH, 1934).

12018 Gaudet, Laura C. Pianist (WTIC, Hartford, CT, 1925–1926).

12019 Gauenhorst, Mort. Banjoist (KFAB, Lincoln, NE, 1925).

12020 Gause, Thomas S. Newscaster (WMFD, Wilmington, NC, 1945).

12021 Gauss, Chuck. Newscaster (WTMV, East St. Louis, MO, 1948).

12022 Gauss, Katherine. Violinist (WGHB, Clearwater, FL, 1926).

12023 Gautheir, Eva. Soprano (WJZ, New York, NY, 1929).

12024 Gauvin, Aime. DJ (*It's a Woman's World*, WMGM, New York, NY, 1955).

12025 Gavere, (Mrs.) Jane. Mrs. Gravere broadcast a weekly news review program over the University of North Dakota's station (KFJM, Grand Rapids, ND, 1923).

12026 Gavitt, Dick. Newscaster (KANS, Wichita, KS, 1948).

12027 Gawler, Ethel Holtzelaw. Soprano (WRC, Washington, DC, 1924–1925).

12028 Gay, Angela. Singer (WOR, Newark, NJ, 1925).

12029 Gay, Betty. COM-HE (KTBC, Austin, TX, 1957).

12030 Gay, (Mrs.) Charles. Pianist (WEAF, New York, NY, 1925).

12031 Gay, Connie B. DJ and country music entrepreneur (*Let's Be Gay*, WARL, Arlington, VA, 1947; *Town and Country Time*, WARL, 1948–1949).

12032 Gay, Don. DJ (*High Jinks* and the *Early Worm*, KRUL, Corvallis, OR, 1949; KUTI, Yakima, WA, 1955).

12033 Gay, Dottie. COM-HE (WDOK, Cleveland, OH, 1955).

12034 Gay, Eucaste. Newscaster (WHAT, Philadelphia, PA, 1948).

12035 Gay, Mary. COM-HE (KTBC, Austin, TX, 1957).

12036 Gay, Pat. COM-HE (KLZ, Denver, CO, 1956).

12037 *(The) Gay Classics*. The weekly music program was broadcast 10:00–11:00 P.M. on the NBC-Pacific Coast Network. It was described by *Broadcast Weekly* (December 22–28, 1929, p. 23) as: "Classical selections of a gay nature which have captured the fancy of many a music lover comprises the entire presentation, which has for its artists an orchestra and a vocal soloist."

12038 *(The) Gay Nineties Revue*. *See* ***The Gaslight Gayeties***.

12039 Gayer, Marie. Actress Gayer was a cast member of the *Katie's Daughter* daytime serial.

12040 Gayle, Ann. Organist (WCOA, Pensacola, FL, late 1920s).

12041 Gayle, Diana (Dyana). Singer (WTHT, Harford, CT, 1939; WHIP, Harrisburg, PA, 1942; KFBI, Wichita, KS, 1942).

12042 Gayle, Isleta. COM-HE (WCKY, Cincinnati, OH, 1951).

12043 Gayle, Pat. COM-HE (WWXL, Peoria, IL, 1951).

12044 Gaylord, Chester. Announcer-saxophonist (WDBH, Worcester, MA, 1924–1925; WCTS, Worcester, MA, 1925–1928). Singer (WJZ, New York, NY, 1929).

12045 Gaylord, Stephen. Baritone and chief announcer (KGW, Portland, OR, 1928).

12046 Gaylord, Tina. Violinist (WNAD, Norman, OK, 1926).

12047 Gaylord-Young Orchestra. Popular New York City band (WMCA, New York, NY, 1925).

12048 Gayloso Hotel Orchestra. Professor Gaspar Pappalardo directed the hotel band (WMC, Memphis, TN, 1924).

12049 Gayman, L. Vaughn. Newscaster (WKBB, Dubuque, IA, 1939–1945; *Noon-Time News*, WKBB, 1947).

12050 Gayman, Parker. Newscaster (KFRC, San Francisco, CA, 1942).

12051 Gayner, Dot. COM-HE (WGIG, Brunswick, GA, 1960).

12052 "GCA." Designation for announcer G.C. Arnoux (WBAP, Fort Worth, TX, 1923). *See* **Arnoux, G.C.**

12053 *(The) GE Program*. The General Electric Company sponsored the variety show that presented such diverse features as Walter Damrosch conducting a symphony orchestra and Floyd Gibbons fast talking his way through a news commentary (60 min., Saturday, 9:00–10:00 P.M., NBC-Red, 1929). *See* **Gibbons, Floyd.**

12054 GE Publicity Department Male Quarter. Company(General Electric) vocal group (WGY, Schenectady, NY, 1923).

12055 Gearhard, Mary Alice. COM-HE (WHFB, Benton Harbor, MI, 1957).

12056 Gearhart, Lynn. Announcer (WWJ, Detroit, MI, 1925). Newscaster (WSUN, St. Petersburg, FL, 1938; WDAE, Tampa, FL, 1942).

12057 Gearhart, Nick. Newscaster (KTBS, Shreveport, LA, 1947–1948).

12058 Gearhart, Val. DJ (*Open House*, KFXM, San Bernardino, CA, 1947; KRNO, San Bernardino, CA, 1957).

12059 Geary, William. Newscaster (WBRK, Pittsfield, MA, 1944).

12060 Geary's Missourians. Popular regional band (WDAF, Kansas City, MO, 1924).

12061 Gebbart, Sue. COM-HE (KRTR, Thermopolis, WY, 1956).

12062 Gebhardt Mexican Players. Orchestra specializing in Mexican music (WOAI, San Antonio, TX, 1926).

12063 Gedner, Irene. Pianist (WHAM, Rochester, NY, 1936–1937).

12064 *Gedney and Hemings*. Instr. mus. prg. featuring a duo piano team (1936).

12065 Gee [Geen], Stan. Sportscaster (WFMJ, Youngstown, OH, 1944; WGAR, Cleveland, OH, 1949). DJ (*Impressions in Wax*, WGAR, 1947–1950; *Motor Melodies*, WGAR, 1950).

12066 Geer, Charlotte. Writer and program host (NBC, 1920s and 1930s). Geer supposedly was America's first radio newspaper editor. She began a daily radio column in 1924 in the *Newark Evening News* that ran for 12 years. She founded the Newark *News* Radio Club in 1927. Eventually Geer stopped working as a critic and became a broadcaster herself. She had her own *Twilight Hour* program on NBC. She also wrote such programs as *Silas of the Hills*, *The Hammerstein Music Hall* and *The Sweetest Love Songs* program featuring Frank Munn.

12067 Geertsen, (Miss) Edna. Xylophonist (KDYL, Salt Lake City, UT, 1923).

12068 Gegna, Misha. Cellist (KGO, Oakland, CA, 1925). Leader (Misha Gegna Orchestra featured on the *Walter M. Murphy Motors Company Program*, KFI, Los Angeles, CA, 1926).

12069 Gehman, M.W. Announcer (WKJC, Lancaster, PA, 1925).

12070 Geif's Orchestra of New York. Metropolitan dance band (KDKA, Pittsburgh, PA, 1923).

12071 Geiger, Elvira Rose. Pianist (WHN, New York, NY, 1926; WGCP, New York, 1926).

12072 Geiger, George. Newscaster (WMRP, Flint, MI, 1946).

12073 Geirs-Dorf, Irene. Leader (Geirs-Dorf Jazz Band, WCAE, Pittsburgh, PA, 1923).

12074 Geis, Bos. Newscaster (WHBC, Canton, OH, 1941).

12075 Geise, "Happy Harry." Known as the "How-Do-You-Do Man," in 1929 Geise was the chief announcer, continuity department manager, entertainer and "piano composer" at KSTP (Minneapolis–St. Paul, MN). After beginning his radio career in 1921, he had worked at more than fifteen stations by 1929, including WIBO (Chicago, IL), WQJ (Chicago, IL) and WMAQ (Chicago, IL). In 1926 he was WIBO's staff pianist. The employment history of this much traveled and highly successful performer during radio's first decade is impressive:

KYW, Chicago, IL (1921–1922);

WEAF, New York, NY; WJZ, New York, NY; WDAR, Worcester, MA (1923);

WQJ, Chicago, IL (1924);

WIBO, Chicago, IL (1924–1925);

KNX, Los Angeles; KFWB, Hollywood, CA; KHJ, Los Angeles, CA; KFI, Los Angeles, CA; KFQZ, Hollywood, CA (1925);

WIBO, Chicago, IL; WMAQ, Chicago, IL 1926;

WWAE, Pittsburgh, PA; WQJ, Chicago, IL (1927); and

KSTP, Minneapolis–St. Paul, MN (1929).

12076 Geiser, Harold. Geiser was a sometime director of the Vincent Lopez Orchestra (WGR, Buffalo, NY, 1924).

12077 Geisie Brothers. Harmony singing duo (WHT, Deerfield, IL, 1925).

12078 Geisser, Albert. Pianist (WJAZ, Chicago, IL, 1923).

12079 Geissler, (Mrs.) Charles. Bridge expert Geissler conducted her *Contract Bridge* program (WEEI, Boston, MA, 1933).

12080 Gelabert, Clarence. Tenor (WHN, New York, NY, 1923).

12081 Gelder, Marie. Contralto (KFI, Los Angeles, CA, 1928).

12082 Geller, Jules. Newscaster (WMIN, St. Paul, MN, 1937).

12083 Gellert, Max. Virtuoso violinist (WPG, Atlantic City, NJ, 1928).

12084 Gellespie, Bob. Newscaster (WWCO, Waterbury, CT, 1948).

12085 Gelson, Molly. Pianist, member of the May Piano Trio (WJAX, Cleveland, OH, 1924).

12086 Geltz, Harry. Singer (*Harry Geltz*, vcl. mus. prg., WORK, York, PA, 1936).

12087 Gemmon, Irvin. Newscaster (WAGM, Presque Isle, ME, 1939).

12088 *Gems of Melody*. Father John's Medicine sponsored the network music show featuring baritone John Herrick and the Harold Sanford Orchestra (15 min., Tuesday, 7:15–7:30 P.M., NBC, 1933).

12089 Gender Discrimination. From radio's earliest days women faced many barriers and prejudices in broadcasting. Hilmes (1997) in her book, *Radio Voices, American Broadcasting, 1922–1952,* discusses the problems women faced when working in radio during the 20s and the later development of daytime network scheduling as a "ghetto for female listeners." In addition, she comments on the "exclusion" of women from radio history. Hilmes' perceptive analysis of the discrimination against women in radio clearly reflects the views still held by some male broadcast executives. Douglas in another recent study, *Listening In: Radio and the American Imagination,* blames the scarcity of women in broadcast journalism upon "the deeply sexist industry" that believed that listeners would neither like, nor trust the female voice over the air (Douglas, 1999, p. 164). Arguably, it can be concluded that some bias against women in broadcasting still is present.

Although female vocal and instrumental soloists readily found employment in radio by 1939, Ruth Adams Knight observed at the time that opportunities for women in other music department positions behind the microphone were limited (Knight, 1939, p. 114). There were still clerical and secretarial positions available but they seldom offered advancement, and female musical arrangers were practically unknown in radio as were executives.

Knight (1939, p.115) cites the observations of veteran CBS music executive Lucille Singleton in 1939:

> Lucile Singleton, out of her many years of studio experience feels that the radio musical field only demonstrates the great discrimination which exists against women in the business world. Miss Singleton says frankly that she believes that in order to hold a major position a woman must not only be a better executive than a man, but that she must win the confidence and endorsement of some man in order to be allowed to prove it.

Other broadcast pioneers such as Mary Lou Moore and Agnes Law provide other evidence of the problems women faced in radio. Moore (1976) said that when she started in radio in the 1940s most women were receptionists, secretaries or clerks in the music library. There was one exception, she said, because there were a few women doing continuity writing "simply because it paid so badly, they couldn't get men to do the job" (Moore, 1976, p.1). *See* **Moore, Mary Lou.**

Agnes Law (1976) was a 30-year CBS employee, who spent most of her career in executive positions. Working at the network from its first days, Law saw CBS and her responsibilities grow and develop. After establishing and building such CBS departments as the Employment Office, Program Analysis Department and Special Library, Law saw men named to take them over. She (Law, 1976, p. 5) observed that "as always was the case at CBS, after a woman developed a department, they usually hired a man to take over." *See* **Law, Agnes.**

Opportunities for women increased somewhat in the late 1940s, due primarily to the increase in the amount of "women's programming." As late as 1974, however, women held less than 30 percent of all broadcasting jobs. Women held 26 percent of all part and full time jobs, but at the executive (managerial) level the ratio was ten men to one woman.

One woman who escaped the usual restrictions faced by most women was Mary Margaret McBride. When she began working at WOR (Newark, NJ) in 1934, she was told to pretend to be "a wise old grandmother" and broadcast "homey philosophy" using the station's name *Martha Deane.* When she could no longer stand the restrictions, McBride, in the middle of a broadcast, suddenly said: "Oh, what's the use? I can't do it! I'm not a grandmother! I'm not a mother. I'm not even married. Nothing about all this I'm saying sounds real to me and that's because it isn't. The truth is I'm a reporter and I would like to come here everyday and tell you about places I go and people I meet. Write me if you'd like that. But I can't be a grandmother anymore" (Crane, 1993, p. 165). Hilmes (1997, p. 279) gives a slightly different version of the McBride statement, but its tone and content are the same: "I find it necessary to kill all my family. I'm not a grandmother. I don't have any children. I'm not even married. I'm not interested in telling you how to take spots out of Johnny's suits or how to mix all the leftovers in the ice box. I'm a reporter and I've just been to the flea circus. If you would like to hear about it, I'll tell you." When her listeners responded positively, she went on to have a highly successful program that included interviews with people from all walks of life. When she left WOR and the *Martha Deane* role to go to CBS, her success was even greater. Mary Margaret McBride became one of radio's most popular broadcasters, who combined commercial success with a program of serious content for women listeners. She virtually added public service elements to a "women's magazine of the air." *See* **Pioneers; McBride, Mary Margaret** and ***Mary Margaret McBride*.**

Broadcast executives' were still expressing their negative views that women's voices lacked the authority needed to broadcast the news. Elmer Lawler, the ABC president in charge of news, special events and public affairs expressed these views clearly:

> Many women may possess the knowledge and authority but they seldom can convey this through their voices. Even the best-trained actress can't compare with men in this respect. Her voice is naturally thinner, with less timbre and range. It's not as appropriate for reporting crucial events. For hard-core news, the depth and resonance of the male voice are indispensable (Lee Graham, "Women Don't Like to Look at Women, New York *Times*, May 24, 1964, p. 53).

Vice president of the NBC Radio Network, Robert Wogan, suggested that something happened to women when they got in front of a microphone. They become "affected, over dramatic, high-pitched (Graham, New York *Times*, May 24, 1964, p. 53). Wogan, however, admitted that women sounded fine in everyday conversation. A NBC vice-president in charge of television programming was even more blunt when he said, "A woman's manner is not suited to news and serious discussion." Even worse, he added, that she couldn't ask probing questions or be tough with unruly guests, explaining, "She'd rather have her hair in place than her brains" (Graham, New York *Times*, May 24, 1964, p.53).

Later in 1971, Reuven Frank, NBC News president bluntly stated, "I have the strong feeling that audiences are less prepared to accept news from a woman's voice than from a man's" (*Newsweek*, August 30, 1971, pp. 62–63). Professional women in 1974 publicly began to describe their working conditions and the exploitation they suffered in such diverse media as broadcasting, newspapers and book publishing in an effort to bring about needed reforms. The Media Women's Association compiled a series of essays published as *Rooms with No View: A Woman's Guide to the Men's World of the Media,* edited by Ethel Strainchamps. Sixty-five women who worked in the publishing and broadcast industries discussed their working conditions, mostly anonymously, in the book.

Targeting the television networks, the report suggested that sexism was rampant in television broadcasting and particularly disappointing, it said, since television started in the 1950s supposedly with a clean slate uncluttered with the old myths of radio. The results were disappointing: "At local stations," the report said, "women do much of the essential drudgery, but they are effectively barred from the prestigious high-paying jobs" (Strainchamps, 1947, p.4). Network by network, the discouraging facts were reported.

In the sections devoted to ABC News, CBS News, NBC News and NET(National Educational Television), the description of women's roles was grim. For example, in 1973, there were 600 ABC News employees in the United States. Women employees, mostly in secretarial positions, numbered 150. ABC's employment record showed 7 female news writers or editors; 5 female associate producers in contrast to 20 males in that position; 13 female researchers and 2 men; 6 full time female producers and 32 males; and 5 female television correspondents versus 42 men.

CBS News was shown to be a conservative network. In the fall of 1973, only 3 women filled the 50 highest level positions at CBS News. These three were the director of special events; director of religious broadcasting; and the associate archivist. There were only 5 women among the more than 60 reporters and network correspondents. At New York station WCBS, there were 3 women and 22 men. Fewer than 10 women were associate producers, 20 others were men. Among the 22 researchers, only 4 were women. All the secretaries were women. It was said that the picture was the same at other CBS network news bureaus in other cities and at station WCBS (New York). Although some progress was noted, essentially at CBS News the atmosphere essentially was said to be "clubby — male clubby."

The essay on NBC begins with the blunt statement that it was a "man's corporation," where women were relegated to subordinate positions such as: "coffee-snack-meal-getter, personal maid, details-organizer, mail opener and morale booster"(Strainchamps, 1947, p. 11). It was noted that women were barred from such positions as cameraman, engineer, radio program host, technical director, stagehand, soundman, unit manager, supervising editor and from top management. Although there was a few female associate producers, it is said that NBC benefited from women working longer and harder for less pay.

While National Educational Television (NET) had considerable prestige, the corporation allowed few opportunities for female mobility. There was a greater proportion of men to women in the highest levels of management and production at NET. The NET corporate employees included: a male president; five male vice presidents; ten male department directors; and three male attorneys. By far, most women languished in the lowest level jobs and behind the typewriter. The report said this was one of the "blatant facts" of discrimination, based on "deep-seated male prejudices" (Strainchamps, 1947, pp. 18–19). Most direct was this statement from a woman employee: "While it was relatively simple to perceive discrimination as it was laid out on payroll sheets and personnel forms, it was more wrenching to perceive the thousand subtle ways in which we [women] were constantly relegated to inferior positions and conditioned to accept our own inferiority" (Strainchamps, 1947, p. 19).

While all the essayists in *Rooms with No View* (Strainchamps, 1947) reported some improvements at ABC, CBS, NBC and NET, all unanimously judged them to be too small and insufficient. Few women were broadcasting the news even in 1971 either on radio or television. Helen Epstein (Quoted by Strainchamps, 1947, p. 226) described the case of an Ohio radio station manager who refused to hire a woman as newscaster because "news coming from a woman sounds like gossip." Epstein observed that some 20 years previously Pauline Frederick, with a M.A. in International Law, was kept off the air, because as her boss told her "women's voices lack authority."

Years earlier during the World War II era, CBS hired Betty Wason as a foreign correspondent to cover the war from Stockholm, Sweden. When the Germans invaded Norway, Wason managed to get there and report on the fighting. However, CBS soon informed her that her voice was "too young and too feminine" to report war news. They told her that she should find a man to report the news. (Hosley and Yamada, 1987, p. 19).

Despite the strong resistance to women as announcers, pioneer DJ Halloween Martin proved this bias was unfounded. Halloween Martin was born in 1902 in El Paso, Texas, on Halloween. After graduating from De Paul University in 1926, she went to Chicago where she found employment on a newspaper. Martin worked on the Chicago *American*, conducting an advice to the lovelorn column. Located on the upper floor of the newspaper building was station KGY (Chicago, IL). Frequently the station manager would send down to the paper for a substitute announcer and often got Halloween Martin. She did such a good job that Homer Hogan, the station manager, asked her to take a regular announcing job and also host a morning program, *The Musical Clock*, playing records and telling the time every five minutes.

Martin's KYW program was so popular that she was soon asked to add temperature and weather to her time and record announcements. *The Musical Clock* began on April 14, 1930, running from 7:00 to 9:00 A.M. The program was immediately so popular that the Marshall Field department store became its sole sponsor. Martin always picked her own music, with an emphasis on musical comedy, light classics and a bit of jazz. Her program attracted a large and loyal audience that sent her a large volume of complimentary mail: "most pleasant voice we ever heard on radio," "[her] voice sounds natural and unaffected," "[her delivery is] simple, frank and straight forward," and "[she has] a voice with a smile" (Passman, 1971, p. 51).

Halloween Martin's success was directly in opposition to what so many broadcast executives believed to be possible, but they did not change their minds after hearing her. They still believed that women's voices were affected and unpleasant on radio, and, furthermore, that women could not sell convincingly.

When station KYW was moved to Philadelphia, *The Musical Clock* switched to WBBM (Chicago, IL) on December 17, 1934. Halloween's sponsor, Marshall Field, said that by 1938, Martin had played more than 70,000 musical selections during her almost 4,700 hours on the air. Although Marshall Field had conducted an extensive publicity campaign for the program, in 1939 a blunder lost them the "Lady of the Musical Clock."

When Marshall Field by some quirk failed to renew sponsorship of *The Musical Clock* program on time, Sears-Roebuck quickly made a successful bid for it. Realizing their blunder, Marshall Field tried to buy back the program from Sears for a million dollars, but much to their dismay their effort failed.

The Musical Clock program finally ended its run on WBBM in 1944, when it moved to WCFL (Chicago, IL). It was on WCFL that station that Halloween Martin's pioneering broadcast career ended two years later, when her doctor advised her that she should retire to avoid unnecessary stress.

Halloween Martin's successful morning program produced many imitators on Chicago radio and in other large cities. Such popular Chicago DJ's as Norman Ross, Sr., on WMAQ and Bob Hawk on WCFL and WAAF were probably her most famous imitators. Martin's achievements demonstrated that a woman could be an effective announcer, sell products and conduct a popular early morning DJ program. Other women followed her example. One of them was WNEW's (New York, NY) Bernice Judis, known to her public as "La Mama." Later, during the second World War Martha Wilkerson, in the role of *GI Jill*, conducted a morale building DJ program on Armed Forces Radio. *GI Jill* was probably the biggest morale booster Armed Forces Radio provided for servicemen. *See* **Pioneers, Wilkerson, Jill** *and* ***G.I. Jills***

Despite the many barriers they encountered, some women were able to enter the restricted area of news and newscasting. Pioneer women news personnel who successfully worked in radio despite the handicaps they faced were: Dorothy Thompson, Dorothy Kilgallen, Florence Conley, Muriel Draper, Alice Weel, Beth Zimmerman, Ann Gillis, Kay Campbell, Fran Harris, Jo Denman, Helen Heitt, Helen Guy, Irene Kuhn, May Craig, Kathryn Cravens, Lisa Sergio, Margaret Rugli, Mary Breckinridge and Pauline Frederick. Nevertheless, there were many women whose professional careers were blocked completely, or more frequently, frustrated by the obstacles placed in their way by existing male bias. One prime example is Pauline Frederick.

The career of Pauline Frederick provides an example of how a gifted journalist was handicapped by the bias she encountered. Overcoming many of the obstacles she faced, Frederick was the distinguished NBC news' United Nations commentator; author of *First Ladies of the World*; and the recipient of 15 honorary doctorates and many awards, including the George Foster Peabody Award, Dupont's, McCall's, the University of Missouri School of Journalism, the University of Southern California and the Golden Globe broadcasting honors twice. These well deserved honors came at the price of being a woman in network news.

Pauline Frederick was born in Harrisburg, Pennsylvania, to middle class Methodist parents. A staunch religious faith and strong ethical guidelines were her major family influences. During her high school years, Frederick showed a talent for public speaking and journalism and wrote society pieces for the Harrisburg *Telegraph*. After graduating from high school she declined a job offer on the Harrisburg newspaper, deciding, instead, to attend American University in Washington, DC After majoring in Political Science at the university, she earned a master's degree in International Law.

She then began to conduct a series of interviews with the wives of diplomats that was bought by the Washington *Star* newspaper as a weekly feature. Shortly thereafter, her articles were syndicated by the North American Newspaper Alliance (NANA). Frequently her articles appeared in Sunday's New York *Times*.

Frederick's entrance into radio came at the suggestion of Margaret Cuthbert, the head of NBC's programming in New York. Cuthbert, believing Frederick's interviews with diplomat's wives would be good radio, arranged an interview with H.R. Baukhauge for her. With the further suggestions, encouragement and assistance of Cuthbert, she was hired as Baukhauge's assistant. The following week she went on the air with her interviews, which continued to be broadcast by NBC until the beginning of World War II, when other news programs took their place.

Working with veteran commentator Baukhauge was not her happiest experience, since he wanted to keep her out of the newsroom. She was kept her off the air with "real news" stories by Baukhauge. Her interview programs were acceptable, since they were not considered to be "real news stories" (Diliberto, 1975, p. 8). She was kept busy by Baukhauge doing his legwork and writing his news scripts.

At the end of World War II, Frederick decided to leave NBC and go to Germany to freelance at the Nuremberg Trials for the Western Newspaper Alliance and ABC Radio. Despite the magnitude of the news event, she was able to broadcast only once when Herman Goering committed suicide because no other network reporter was available (Diliberto, 1975, p. 9).

When she returned to New York City in 1946 following the trials, Frederick tried to get a job with one of the networks without success. One particularly unhappy event was her audition at CBS News in 1946, where she was turned down by Edward R. Murrow. Inexplicably, one of Murrow's assistants handed her a memorandum that subsequently she saved for many years (Diliberto, 1975, p. 10):

> I have listened to the records submitted by Pauline Frederick. She reads well and her voice is pleasing, but I would not call her material or manner particularly distinguished. We have a long list of women applicants and, as you know, little opportunity to use them. I am afraid that Miss Frederick's name cannot be put near the top of the list. E.R.M.

Murrow's hiring of women was limited. Murrow's "boys in the news division" included no women. Stanley Cloud and Lynne Olson's book, *The Murrow Boys: Pioneers on the Front Lines of Broadcast Journalism*, contains an account of only one woman in the news division. That was the work of Mary Marvin Breckinridge on the *World News Roundup* for some 50 broadcasts in 1939–1940. Cloud and Olson said she [Breckinridge] was the only woman to crack the fraternity of the Murrow Boys (Cloud and Olson, 1996, p. 63). Breckinridge broadcast as part of the *World News Roundup* briefly before leaving for marriage. An alternative story reported by Cloud and Olson was that Breckinridge actually was asked to leave CBS because of her "sensational reporting" of the travail of displaced war refugees. *See* **Breckinridge, Mary Marvin.**

Paul W. White, Murrow's predecessor at CBS News, was willing to hire women in the division. White said that it was unfair to say that women couldn't handle news assignments as well as men. Women, White said, were good reporters. Furthermore, he said there was no truth in the old cliche that women had no news judgment (White, 1947, p. 364). Among the women he welcomed into the news division were Jane Dealy, Patricia Lochridge, Margaret Miller, Alice Weel and Beth Zimmerschied.

Although Murrow rejected her for the CBS News Division, Frederick was offered a few radio assignments at CBS. Among them was covering a forum on how to get a husband and the coverage of the nylon stockings shortage. While doing these "woman's features" for CBS, she was also working for ABC as a stringer, covering much the same "women's features" for that network.

After covering these "women's stories," Frederick finally was hired by ABC News in 1946, but even there she got "real news stories" only if no regular male reporter was available. She remembered, "I was told by my editor that there were great objections to a woman being on the air for serious issues, and he had orders not to use me. But he said if, by chance, I got an exclusive he'd have to use me, adding 'though I'll slit your throat if you tell anyone I gave you this advice'" (Diliberto, 1975, p. 11).

Frederick took the advice and worked hard to obtain exclusive interviews at the United Nations. For example, she got the first interview with King Michael of Romania immediately after his arrival in the United States and another with diplomat Seldon Chapin. She believed, correctly it turned out, that there was great opportunity for her at the UN if she applied herself.

Another example of her treatment at ABC is instructive. After successfully covering a New York local story when no male reporter was available, Frederick felt she should be given an opportunity to cover "real news." Her editor bluntly refused her request, "Oh, no, Pauline. We have to keep our regular news staff all male. It isn't that you haven't proved yourself, but when listeners hear a woman's voice, they'll turn off their radios, because a woman's voice just doesn't carry authority"(Diliberto, p. 11).

When the big names in radio news wanted nothing to do with television, Frederick was assigned to report the televised 1948 national political conventions and, frequently, to report them on the *Today Show*. Incidentally, she always preferred radio reporting to that of television, because radio allowed her more time for background and in-depth news coverage. Between 1946 and 1953, she broadcast various events on ABC radio and television. She had a regular Saturday radio show, *Pauline Frederick's Guest Book*, but in 1947 she began sharing the UN beat with Gordon Fraser, and the UN soon became her favorite assignment.

Despite her UN assignment, Frederick, still not happy at ABC, accepted an offer to move to NBC as a political reporter in 1953. After some frustration at the new network, she eventually was assigned to cover the United Nations for the network, an assignment she loved. Before 1960, most of Frederick's radio work was on NBC. In addition to her frequent radio and TV appearances, she had two radio shows, *Pauline Frederick Reporting* and a Sunday interview show *Listen to the Witness* that was similar in format to *Meet the Press*. After accessing her distinguished career, it is her dedication and fearless reporting at the United Nations for which she is best known, remembered and respected.

Unfortunately, Pauline Frederick's successful struggle to cover "real news" stories in the 1940s and 1950s did not herald the end of bias against women in news' departments. Nancy Dickerson (1976) experienced similar negative attitudes in the 1950s when she tried to break into network news. She felt hurt when men asked her (Dickerson, 1976, p. 3): "Why do you want to go on the air? You're not supporting a family. Why do *you* want to go on the air?" Another embarrassing incident occurred in 1960, when she was scheduled to go on the *Face the Nation* program for the first time, and a CBS vice-president in charge of news called to say, "Listen, you're going to go on a program, and we've never had a woman on it before. Now don't giggle" (Dickerson, 1976, p. 3). Nevertheless, Dickerson went on to have successful career in radio and television news. *See* **Dickerson, Nancy**.

An example of some of the gender discrimination that still persists is provided in John Mainelli's New York *Post* (March 19, 2000, p. 116–117) article about talented women on New York City radio. His article begins in this manner: "Forget Dr. Laura, Joy Browne and Robin Quivers. Radio is still a man's world. Stubbornly resistant to change, radio has never embraced women on the air the way TV has. The old knock on women in radio was that women wouldn't listen to another woman. No radio boss would be caught dead making that argument today. But in the last few years, more female voices have started to come out of the radio and they weren't laughing at Howard Stern jokes." Mainelli said he went looking for top women on New York radio who were breaking the mold and identified Lisa Taylor, Shaila, Valerie Smaldone and Lisa Evers as prime examples.

The role of women in broadcasting has always been questioned. Exactly what jobs should they perform? The earliest gender discrimination appears to have its origin in a combination of "supposed" scientific evidence and ideas, often mistaken, of listener preference. Even though some slight evidence for each exists, their exaggeration no doubt formed the basis for most of the negative bias that occurred.

As late as the 1960s, three widely held notions by many program directors about women's role in radio persisted: First, women's voices didn't carry the authority of men's. Second, women didn't like to hear other women on radio. Three, records by two female vocalists should never be played back-to-back by DJs. The last one lacks any possible shred of objective research evidence. Any possible rational explanation for this particular bit of pernicious wisdom does not exist.

An early statement of bias against women appeared in the *Radio Broadcast* magazine issue of August, 1924. It was included in the regular "Listeners Point of View" feature written by Jennie Irene Mix (Mix,1924a) under the title, "Are Women Undesirable — Over the Radio?" Her curiosity was piqued by a letter she had published the previous month from a man in the phonograph business. Mix raised the question: "What do listeners think of women on the radio?" The writer of the letter published by Mix in the August issue of *Radio Broadcast*, said that it was his opinion and that of others that the listening public found a woman's voice unpleasant *unless she could be seen as she speaks*. He concluded from this observation that women should not be used on the radio as announcers or lecturers. The basis for his opposition to women as speakers was based on the fact that records of women speaking invariable sold very poorly. He said his fellow phonograph sellers joined him in his observation about women being ineffective speakers. Manufacturers, the man stated, learned that "the public will not pay money to listen to the talking record of a woman's voice" (Mix, 1924a, p. 332).

Mix responded by saying that although this was an interesting point of view, "some of the highest paid women in vaudeville are the women heard only in monologues." She (Mix, 1924a, p. 332) followed by asking, "Does this mean that when a woman is speaking she may be fascinating as long as she remains in sight, and becomes displeasing the moment she cannot be seen although she may go right on talking just as delightfully as the moment before?" Her argument was logical. Since more and more women were appearing daily before the microphones, she suggested, that psychologists will certainly study the subject. At present, she noted, that many women broadcast on WOR [Newark, NJ], and that at WGY [Schenectady, NY] there is almost a dramatic presentation each week with such actors as Rosaline Greene, Lola Summers, Marie Prott, Charlotte Paulos, Mildred Stanyon and Gemma Votties. If women's voices were so unpleasant, she explains, WGY would have received many letters of protest from listeners by this time.

Not entirely satisfied with all women speakers on the air, Mix suggested that when they spoke over the radio they sometimes made one of two mistakes: First, they either spoke in a patronizing tone or, second, they were precise to the point of exasperation (Mix, 1924a, p. 334). She also went on to suggest that women radio speakers also were often lacking in humor, but that men were inclined to be too preachy.

She discussed in detail the qualities she considered that made a good announcer:

> There are a few announcers in the country — all men — who are beyond criticism. They are consequently an unfailing pleasure to hear, from their first greeting to their final, "good night." They know just how far to carry familiarity in their speech — a trait that is the final test of the announcer's adaptability to his position. The men who are continually "jollying" their listeners, become extremely tiresome. A little of this sort of thing may be agreeable and effective, but more than a little becomes a surfeit. This is not an individual opinion, but one that has been expressed by large numbers of people.
>
> If Mr. Henry Ford ever loses his job as a maker of automobiles he could undoubtedly get a position as announcer without half trying. This was proved when, at the close of the recent automobile race at Indianapolis, he was lured to the microphone by the genial Mr. Kaney [Sen Kaney] who, for five hours, had himself been at the microphone announcing the progress of the race which was broadcast by WDAP and WGN, Chicago.
>
> Although Mr. Ford had been busy for many hours in his capacity as referee, his voice came through the air as fresh and vigorous as if fatigue were something unknown to him. It was a perfectly poised, finely modulated, clear cut voice that would have held the attention even had the speaker been unknown. And Mr. Ford in a few seconds said as much as some radio speakers would have taken five minutes to say, and without saying it as well, at that (Mix, 1924a, pp. 334–335).

For the next month's edition (*Radio Broadcast*, September, 1924), she sought the opinion of several male broadcast executives as to whether a woman's voice was always displeasing over the radio and published the results. W.W. Rogers of the publicity department of Westinghouse Electric and Manufacturing Company, the owner of station KDKA said: "Women as radio entertainers were pioneers at KDKA. They have had a definite place on the radio schedule since, and I cannot remember a radio program presented by KDKA which did not have at least one woman participating. As I remember, the worst lecturer and the best singer I ever heard by radio were women. But a woman speaker is rarely a success, and if I were a broadcast manager, which I am not, I would permit few women lecturers to appear. The reason is that their voices do not carry the appeal, and so, whatever the effect desired, it is lost on the radio audience. One of the chief reasons for this is that few women have voices with distinct personality. It is my opinion that women depend upon everything else but the voice for their appeal. Their voices are flat or they are shrill, and they are usually pitched far too high to be modulated correctly. Another reason is that women on the radio somehow don't seem to become familiar with their audiences to have that 'clubby' feeling toward the listeners which is immediately felt and enjoyed. Still another thing that is lacking in most women before the microphone is summed up in that trite old phrase, 'sense of humor.' I didn't believe this at one time, but now — well I think its true. We need quite a bit of light and airy stuff, or humorous quirks by radio. To sum the matter up, women who are heard by radio seem unable to let themselves go. They are too self-contained to carry a real friendly feeling out past the transmitting station, through the ether, and into the homes of the radio audiences"(Mix, 1924b, pp. 391–392).

Another negative voice raised against women on the air was that of Corley W. Kirby, director of station WWJ, Detroit. Kirby dismissed the idea that no woman under any conditions would be acceptable to a radio audience when speaking. However, he did say: "I do not believe that women are fitted for radio announcers. They need body in their voices, and this is the most important thing, I think. I grant though that some of the women announcers have better sense than some of the men announcers. I look at the announcer in very much the same light that I would consider the old show announcer. He has something to tell the people, and what he has to tell them they want to hear. His announcements should be short, business-like, and to the point. When women announcers try to be congenial in their announcements, they become affected; and when they attempt to be business-like they are stiff. There also seems to be an offensive nasal quality in their announcements. Their voices are pitched too high. As for women readers, they are as a rule simply terrible. This applies both to those we have had at our station and those I have heard from scores of others" (Mix, 1924b, pp. 392–393).

M.A. Rigg, manager of Buffalo's station WGR suggested that announcing and voice in most cases are "concerned with the individual and not with sex." He went on to say: "Although we have a woman announcer at this station, it is not my intention to feature a woman in this capacity. There are many reasons why to my mind, it seems advisable to use a man as announcer, especially during the heavier part of the work" (Mix, 1924b. p. 393).

Charles B. Popenoe, manager of New York stations WJZ and WJY, limited his statement solely to the quality of transmission of a woman's voice. "We use, of course, just as every other station, a great many women speakers on various subjects, but in no case does a female voice transmit as well as that of the man. As a general thing it does not carry the volume of the average male voice. As far as women announcers are concerned, we have never used them with the exception of Miss Bertha Brainard, who occasionally broadcasts theatrical material or announces a play being broadcast directly from the stage. In this case she is used because she knows a great deal about the theater" (Mix, 1924b, p. 393).

Martin P. Rice, Manager of WGY, Schenectady, NY, said: "It would be about as logical arbitrarily to condemn all women's voices for radio broadcasting as it would be to ascribe all the known virtues to women and all the vices to men. Women, as a class, have not had opportunities to adapt their voices to varying audiences and auditoriums. An insistent high-pitched voice may readily develop unpleasant characteristics, but this is just as true when the speaker appears in person as when she addresses an audience by radio. Women have decided to take a part in public life as well as in domestic life, and they will master the technic of radio if they have not already done so" (Mix, 1924b, p. 391).

J.M. Barrett, station director, WOR, Newark, NJ, was more moderate in tone and response. Mix noted that station WOR probably featured more women speakers than any other station in the nation. Barrett observed: "To my mind, a woman's voice on the radio is not generally considered uninteresting. It depends upon the work that she is doing and the way she does it. It is the same with a man's voice. There are many male voices that are very uninteresting. For certain types of radio work I consider a woman's voice is very essential; but for announcing, a well modulated male voice is the most pleasing to listen to. I have absolutely nothing against a woman's announcing, but really do believe that unless a woman has the qualifications known as "showman's instinct," it really does become monotonous. As a general thing, a woman's voice is considerably higher pitched than a man's voice and sometimes becomes distorted. This, of course, is simply my personal opinion in the matter." (Mix, 1924b, p. 393). Barrett's statement led Mix to state that since WOR had not been deluged with complaints against woman speakers, she remained an advocate of woman broadcasters.

Despite the relatively moderate statements of Rice and Barrett and the logical argument of Mix, the seeds of bias had already been implanted in the minds of many broadcast executives and the listening public, and the biased suggestion did not disappear. After Mix died in 1925, John Wallace took over her column and revived the debate by citing a WJZ (New York, NY) poll. The WJZ poll of 5, 000 listeners reported a hundred-to-one preference of men's voices over women's. Since there was no adequate explanation offered for the unreasonable finding of preference by only 50 persons for women's voices of the 5,000 persons polled, the poll's methods are questionable at least. Nevertheless, the bias against women was reinforced by its publication.

Martin Codell in a 1933 article reported that women were not considered by broadcast executives to be physically or temperamentally suited to be announcers or newscasters (Hilmes, 1997, p. 143). Another aspect by which women were supposedly handicapped was the technical limitations of early radio transmission equipment. Such equipment was not sufficiently sensitive to transmit the higher pitched frequencies without distortion or dropout, resulting in a failure to reproduce and transmit these sounds with the fullest fidelity. Marzolf, a strong advocate of women's rights, explained it this way: "Radio sound production was best with low pitched voices, and when women pitched their voices low it usually sounded forced and unnatural. When they spoke naturally, the high tones became weak, thin and unpleasant on radio" (Marzolf, 1977, p. 123).

Ruth Crane, in her assessment of the opportunities for women during the early days of radio observed: "With the advent of commercial radio in the 1920s, women found their opportunities severely limited. News casting was reserved for men because station mangers and advertisers held that men's voices alone carried authority and believability (Crane, 1993, p. 165).

As early as 1925 when the role of women in radio was seriously being questioned, even Bertha Brainard, then the assistant manager of station WJZ (New York, NY), herself an important broadcast pioneer, went on record to say: "The very qualities that make a woman's speaking voice pleasant — its softness, nuances, inflections and medium pitch — are against her in announcing" (Brainard quoted by Marzolf, 1977, p. 123). Brainard even went so far to suggest that women would find their best opportunities in radio as administrators or in other behind the microphone positions. She suggested that women could be good executives because of their superior "people skills." Women, Brainard said, could succeed in radio because of their research skills, their interviewing ability to gather raw material for broadcasts and their skills at being a hostess (Marzolf, 1977, p. 124).

Brainard later in 1928 provided further advice for women who wished to work in radio. Radio's pioneer nature, she said, offered many opportunities for women. Men and women, she argued, had equal opportunities for equal pay. Realistically, she said that stations were willing to hire both men and women who could make money for them. Furthermore, Brainard continued, many opportunities existed for women, since networks and stations needed many women's feature programs on food, fashions, beauty, child care, education, culture and music. Although positive in nature, the statement relegated women chiefly to *women's work* [women's programs], an unfair discriminatory attitude.

Although based on questionable ideas and opinion, a certain bias against women in radio persisted well into the 1940s when it received a "scientific" bolstering by the research of Cantril and Allport. In the 1940s with the bias against women already firmly established in the minds of many broadcast executives, an extensive research study by Cantril and Allport, in their book *The Psychology of Radio* (1941), supposedly provided a "scientific" basis for the belief that women should play a limited role on radio. They suggested that women were out of place as newscasters and announcers.

Social psychologists Hadley Cantril and Gordon W. Allport, unhampered by false modesty, ambitiously stated that the objective of their study was a "first attempt on the part of psychology to map from their point of view the new mental world created by radio." Some of their experimental studies were conducted in the Harvard Psychological Laboratory and at Boston station WEEI.

The Cantril-Allport study contains several potential pitfalls for those unsophisticated in research methodology. A careful reading of their research methods and findings is an absolute necessity if their study is to be fully understood. One potential problem of interpretation is that a preference for one alternative necessarily means a dislike for other possible responses. Therefore, the *preference* for a male voice on the radio in certain situations does not necessarily mean a *strong dislike* for women in the same situations.

In the introduction to their study, the authors state that many people would rather hear a man speaking over the radio than a woman, although few persons can explain why. Even station managers seldom could give a reason why their announcing staff was entirely male, and neither could they explain why women were freely employed as actresses and singers, but were "virtually barred as announcers" (Cantril and Allport, 1941, p. 127). The authors say they wanted to find the reason for male preference, whether it was a "social prejudice" or a "combination of many factors." Unfortunately, they never provide either an answer to their question, or even a satisfactory explanation.

Among the diverse results of their study were the following:

1. Contralto and baritone voices were preferred to soprano and tenor.
2. Alto and baritone voices were preferred to soprano and bass.
3. More persons would rather hear a man over the radio than a woman.
4. Men were rated "higher" (preferred) or "better" as more natural and persuasive except when reading poetry and abstract passages.
5. Male speakers seemed more interested in the material they read.
6. Males were preferred when reading nonpolitical scripts, weather reports, expository scripts, advertisements and the news.
7. Women were favored when reading abstract scripts (theoretical passages of philosophy, physics, psychology or biology) and poetry.
8. Listeners said one reason for the unpopularity of female voices was their affectation and unnaturalness.
9. Listeners preferred male voices because they were more persuasive and reflected more interest in the material read.

The social psychologists' conclusions, although somewhat contradictory, are enlightening. Even though they state the subjects studied were equally divided by sex, education differences, age and occupations, they admit that when their study began 95 percent of their subjects had already stated that men's voices were more attractive (Cantril and Allport, 1941, p. 131). Apparently, there was a built in bias before the experimentation even began.

A major contradiction appears when the investigators conclude that although listener preference for the male voice to a certain degree might be due to the lower pitch, which makes it more "agreeable in mechanical transmission, " most of the preference of male voices was due to various forms of "antagonism and prejudices" (Cantril and Allport, 1941, p. 208). But then the authors went on to say that engineers state that both male and female voices are transmitted with equal fidelity and, "The problem [the preference for male voices], therefore, is not primarily one of mechanics but of psychology" (Cantril and Allport, 1941, p. 136). Despite the qualification, selective misinterpretation of the Cantril-Allport findings, unfortunately, further served to reinforce the bias that already existed against women as announcers and newscasters by some broadcast executives.

It is generally agreed that the passing years have brought about some decrease in gender discrimination. However, some still remains as recent news stories remind us. The Washington *Post* (March 23, 2000, p.1) headlined: **US Settles Job Bias Cases: A Record $508 Million is Due Women in USIA Dispute.** *USA Today*(March 23, 2000, p. 1) headlined: **Sex Discrimination Suit Costs $508 M: Federal Government Agrees to Settle 23 year-old Lawsuit**; and the New York *Times* (March 23, 2000, p. Al) captioned the story: **U.S. Offers $508 Million in Sex-Bias Case.** The story presented a grim picture. The federal government agreed to pay the largest award ever made in an employment discrimination case against the U.S. Information Agency and the Voice of America, after Carolee Brady applied for a job as a USIA editor of the agency's *Horizon* magazine and was told they were looking for a man for that position. Some 1,100 women joined Brady in a class action suit claiming sex discrimination.

The Washington *Post* described some of the complaints of the plaintiffs that were seeking broadcasting positions:

> The plaintiffs included women who sought work as international radio broadcasters, radio broadcast and electronic technicians, writer/-editors and production specialist between 1974 and 1984. The women said they were relegated to jobs as hostesses instead of commentators on the USIA's broadcasting arm Voice of America and put on the air to break the monotony of the many male announcers. In the technical field, they said jobs were nearly nonexistent.
>
> One woman, a translator and journalist, contended she was turned down in favor of a man who worked as an encyclopedia salesman. Another, who had a doctorate and radio experience, said she lost out to the son of a Voice of America official
>
> "It breaks your heart," said Rose Kobylinski, now 79, who once hosted a Voice of America music program targeted at Poland. "The men kept getting upgraded, not me."

Bruce Frederickson, one of the women's lawyers, explained some of the alleged sex discrimination (New York *Times*, March 23, 2000, p. A22).

> "There were open and hostile comments from men," Mr. Frederickson said.
>
> "There was manipulation of the system. Tests were rigged, scored were changed, less qualified men were hired and men were preselected before the jobs were posted."
>
> "At other times," he said, "Women were told, 'We have enough women.' 'It is not good to have too many women' and 'We need male voices.'"

Other examples of alleged discrimination described in the *Times* story told of Donna DeSanctis, a writer and broadcaster with a Ph.D., who took a test and was told that a man got the job because of his "terrific score." However, the man never took the test. Another job went to a Voice of America official when the test was rigged. The *Times'* story ended with more dramatic examples of federal sex discrimination that the suit uncovered:

> Carolee Brady, who was listed as the lead plaintiff under her former married name of Hartman, has a Ph.D. and applied in 1977 for a job as a writer at the United States Information Agency.
>
> According to her suit, she was told by an editor, "Well they were thinking about hiring a man for the position."
>
> She [Brady] said today: "A man told me he was not going to hire me because I am a woman. It's delicious victory."
>
> Rose Kobylinski, a Polish-language broadcaster, recalled today she was denied a job after being told by the Voice of America that "your voice is too old."

That was 20 years ago and Ms. Kobylinski, now 79, got the settlement and the last laugh. "I now have a radio program in Chicago," she said, "and my voice is not too old."

Certainly the advent of television brought more opportunities for women as newscasters, sportscasters and program hosts, but here, too, there were charges of gender discrimination, based this time on age and possibly physical appearance. Former Olympian swimming gold medal winner Donna deVarona brought a $50 million dollar suit against ABC, charging she was fired because she was over 50 (New York *Post*, April 12, 2000). Ms. deVarona claimed a network executive told her she should look elsewhere for a position because "the network was trying to recapture the young 18-to-39 male market." The *Post* in the same story noted that Janet Peckinpaugh, age 49, the previous year had won an $8.3 million judgment against the local CBS station in an age discrimination suit.

Many years ago Paul W. White welcomed women into CBS radio's news division, which was previously off-limits to them. He attributed the discovery that women could be capable reporters to their employment by radio during World War II because of the severe manpower shortage. His last word on the subject, expressed in his excellent *News on the Air* book, was a strong vote for women's presence in radio news in a sub-division of his book entitled **SEX REARS ITS COMPETENT HEAD** (White, 1947, p. 364):

> I believe, too, that the presence of women on a radio news staff working on easy terms with men and with completely comparable salaries, is a constructive force in office morale. So long as women understand they are to be treated as equals, with the same opportunities and responsibilities as their male colleagues, then they are not apt to request extra privileges such as days off or lighter hours. In the presence of women, an office becomes less slovenly and in between broadcast bull sessions there's more serious discussion of one's work and actual study of the news itself. There doesn't seem to be so much concern about what happened in the Fifth at Aqueduct or, for that matter, about what the G.I.'s called "Topic A." Besides, they're good looking and nice to have around.

White's sentiments were unquestionably right, but they were not universally accepted. Not all broadcast executives, *then or now* shared or accepted his view. Some progress was made by Pauline Frederick and other determined women news reporters, but radio is still not free of gender discrimination. Despite judiciary appeals won by some women, undoubtedly some gender discrimination still exists in 2002. One New York broadcast executive, who shall remain anonymous, says, "It's never spoken of publicly, but I know a few male executives who have privately expressed concern about hiring women in this day and age: (1) You can face a sex discrimination lawsuit if you fire a woman and don't replace her with another woman; (2) You run a risk of being accused of sexual harassment if things go wrong; (3) Pregnancy, because of recent laws, requires that jobs be held open during long periods of absence." Furthermore, he adds, "Some programmers believe that women can be sidekicks but can't actually anchor, humor-driven morning shows. They believe that many people are put off by wisecracking, smart ass women."

12090 Gendron, Henri. Leader (*Henri Gendron Orchestra*, instr. mus. prg., WGES, Chicago, IL, 1935–1936; CBS, 1939).

12091 *Gene and Glenn*. Gene Carroll and Glenn Rowell were popular radio veterans, whose songs and comedy attracted a large listening audience to their Gillette Razor Blades sponsored show (15 min., Monday, 7:15–7:30 P.M., NBC, 1934). The close harmony singing and comedy team began their broadcasting career on Chicago radio in the 1920s. They enjoyed continued popularity over a long professional career. The team reunited in 1954 with a MBS network show, *Gene and Glenn*. The comedy-vocal team were great listener favorites whenever they worked. Gene Carroll had once been part of the Jake and Lena comedy-vocal team. Previously, Carroll had conducted his own local DJ show, *Jake's Juke Box*. In 1954 he once again teamed with Glenn Rowell, who played piano, on a MBS network show originating from Cleveland. Brian Hodgkinson was their announcer. This show reunited these two pioneering radio entertainers late in their careers (15 min., Monday through Friday, MBS, 1954). *See* ***Jake's Juke Box***.

12092 *Gene Arnold and the Commodores*. Gene Arnold was the host who introduced the Commodores, an excellent male vocal quartet, by reciting a bit of verse before each of their musical numbers. The sponsor was the Crazy Water Hotel Company, makers and promoters of Crazy Water Crystals (laxative). The program had a split broadcast schedule (15 min., Wednesday through Friday, 12:00–12:15 P.M. and Sunday, 1:15–2:30 P.M., NBC, 1933).

12093 *Gene Autry*. Autry, a soon to be successful cowboy movie star, came to Chicago in the early 1930s and immediately became a local radio favorite. Billed as "the Oklahoma Singing Cowboy," Autry appeared on WJJD (*Gene Autry—the Oklahoma Singing Cowboy*, 15 min., Monday through Friday, WJJD, Chicago, IL, 1932). He also worked on WLS and the *National Barn Dance* program (WLS, Chicago, IL, 1933), where he gained the national prominence that led to his movie career.

Smiley "Frog" Burnett appeared with Autry when both were featured on the *National Barn Dance*. Burnett went to Hollywood with Autry and appeared in many of his western movies. Burnett also provided the animated cartoon voices of Barney Google, Snuffy Smith, Krazy Kat and others on various *Loony Tunes* motion picture cartoons.

12094 ***Gene Autry's Cowboy Band.*** Autry starred on his CW music show that also featured the Ranch Girls singing group with Louise Rothenberg (WHAS, Louisville, KY, 1931).

12095 ***Gene Autry's Melody Ranch.*** Autry, the singing cowboy motion picture star, both narrated and was featured in the weekly western drama. There were also many opportunities on the show for Gene and his musical associates to sing and play western songs. Wrigley's Doublemint chewing gum was the program sponsor. The cast included: Autry, Jim Boles, Pat Buttram and Tyler McVey. Bill Burch was the producer. The Cass County Boys, a vocal trio led by Carl Cortner, the King Sisters vocal quartet and vocalist Mary Ford also were program regulars. George Anderson, Irwin Ashkenazy, Carroll Carroll and Doris Gilbert were the writers. Lou Crosby was the announcer.

12096 ***Gene Carroll and Jack Grady.*** Guitarist Carroll and pianist Grady met in 1924 and teamed as a vaudeville singing team before coming to radio (WLS, Chicago, IL, 1928). *See* ***Gene and Glenn.***

12097 ***(The) Gene Rayburn Show.*** Rayburn, who billed himself as "a poor man's Henny Youngman," was the host and comedian on the local sustaining variety show. Singer Peggy Ann Ellis and the Ray Ross Orchestra also performed (30 min., Monday through Friday, 12:00–12:30 P.M., WNEW, New York, NY, 1948). Rayburn left former DJ partner Dee Finch to do his own thing on his local DJ show, *The Gene Rayburn Show* on New York's WNBC. Oddly enough, when Rayburn's show was first listed in the New York *Times*, he was incorrectly listed as "Gene Raymond" (150 min., Monday through Saturday, 6:00–8:30 P.M., WNBC, New York, NY, 1952).

12098 ***General Electric Circle.*** Each week a different Metropolitan Opera star was presented on this music program sponsored by the General Electric Company (15 min., Sunday, 5:30–5:45 P.M., NBC-Red, 1932).

12099 ***General Electric Hour.*** Nathaniel Shilkret directed the orchestra for the vocal trio and soloists that regularly appeared on the weekly program (60 min., Saturday, 5:00–6:00 P.M., NBC-Pacific Coast Network, 1929). Another version of the program presented guest stars such as Australian pianist-composer Percy Grainger playing his own compositions with an orchestra conducted by Walter Damrosch. In a later version of the show, Floyd Gibbons delivered eight-minute talks on the "Adventures in Science" segment included on each program (30 min., Saturday, 9:00–9:30 P.M., NBC-Red, 1929–1930).

12100 ***(The) General Electric Theater.*** Although broadcast in 1963, this hour long dramatic anthology series was *one of the last reminders of radio's golden age*. The program presented a talented repertory company with the great stage actress Helen Hayes as the host (CBS, 1963).

12101 ***General Independents Program.*** Four pianists (William Cowles, Joyce Barthelson, Arthur Schwartzman and Charles Hutchinson) and a popular male quartet (the Rounders) performed on the popular music program (NBC-Pacific Coast Network, 1928).

12102 ***(The) General Mills Concert.*** The good music program was sponsored by General Mills and included various guest performers (Weekly, NBC, 1929).

12103 ***General Motors Concert.*** The excellent program of good music was broadcast from the Radio City Music Center, New York City, before an audience of 3,600 persons (NBC, 1935).

12104 ***(The) General Motors Family Party.*** A symphony orchestra and weekly guests vocalists were presented on the good music show (30 min., Monday, 9:30–10:00 P.M., NBC-Red, 1930).

12105 ***(The) General Motors Hour.*** The General Motors Company sponsored the program of classical and semi-classical music with such distinguished performers appearing as composer-pianist George Gershwin (60 min., Monday, 9:00–10:00 P.M., NBC-Red, 1928).

12106 **Genet, Rosalalind.** Book Reviews (WOR, Newark, NJ, 1933).

12107 **Geneva, Emma Butler.** Organist (WJJD, Mooseheart, IL, 1925).

12108 ***Genevieve.*** Instr. mus. prg. by a pianist not otherwise identified (WOR, Newark, NJ, 1934).

12109 **Genevieve's Cave Women.** Genevieve led the all girl orchestra featuring Charlotte Nagel (WTAM, Cleveland, OH, 1925).

12110 **"Genial Gene."** DJ (*The Genial Gene Show*, WGVI, Charlotte, NC, 1948–1949).

12111 **Gensel, Carl.** Organist (KOWW, Walla Walla, WA, 1927).

12112 **Gensel [Gensler], Carl.** Newscaster (WXYZ, Detroit, MI, 1937). Sportscaster (*The Sports Review* and Michigan State football games play-by-play, WXYZ, Detroit, MI, 1937).

12113 **Genshaw, Adele.** Pianist (WIBA, Madison, WI, 1937–1939).

12114 **Gentile, Larry.** DJ (*Gentile Houseparty*, WJBK, Detroit, MI, 1948–1949).

12115 **Gentry, Bob.** Sportscaster (KOMO, Seattle, WA, 1939).

12116 **Gentry, Tom.** Leader (*Tom Gentry Orchestra*, instr. mus. prg., NBC, 1934).

12117 **Geoghardt Mexican Players.** Tex-Mex music orchestra (WOAI, San Antonio, TX, 1926).

12118 **Geordan, Norman.** DJ (*Chime Time* and *Housewives' Music Shop*, WTHI, Terre Haute, IN, 1949; *Teen Tattle*, *Chime Time* and *The Classical Hour*, WTHI, 1952; WFMJ, Youngstown, OH, 1954).

12119 **George, Abner H.** Newscaster (KOBH, Rapid City, SD, 1939; *Tri-State News*, KOTA, Rapid City, SD, 1947; *Rapid City Chevrolet News*, KOTA, 1948).

12120 **George, Al.** Banjoist (WOK, Chicago, IL, 1925).

12121 **George, Angeline.** Singer (WJJD, Mooseheart, IN, 1925).

12122 **George, Carl.** Newscaster (WGAR, Cleveland, OH, 1938–1941).

12123 **George, Don.** Organist (KFI, Los Angeles, CA, 1927).

12124 **George, Florence.** Soprano (NBC, 1937).

12125 **George, Elvira.** Pianist (WGCP, Newark, NJ, 1926).

12126 **George, Francis.** Newscaster (KGBS, Harlingen, TX, 1942).

12127 **George, Harry H.** Banjoist (KPO, San Francisco, CA, 1927).

12128 **George, Lee.** Newscaster (WTMV, East St. Louis, MO, 1939). Sportscaster (KWTO-KGBX, Springfield, MO, 1939–1942; KGBX, 1940–1942; KWTO, 1945; *Sports Spotlight*, KWTO, 1947; *Sports News*, KWTO, 1948). DJ (*Yawn Patrol*, KWTO, 1950).

12129 **George, Lee Elwood.** Sportscaster (*Dick's Beer Sportscast* and *Hamlin's Wizard Oil Sports*, General Mills' baseball broadcasts, Cardinal Brewing Company's baseball broadcasts; Coca-Cola boxing shows; Sieberling Tires auto racing broadcasts, KWTO and KGBX, Springfield, MO, 1937; *Sports Highlights*, KFEQ, St. Joseph, MO, 1949).

12130 **George, Leslie.** Banjoist (WSMB, New Orleans, LA, 1925).

12131 **George, Nelson.** DJ (*Yawn Patrol*, WDBO, Orlando, FL, 1947).

12132 **George, Ruth.** Contralto (WNAC, Boston, MA, 1923).

12133 **George, Steve.** Newscaster (KCRA, Sacramento, CA, 1947). Sportscaster (*Strictly Sports*, KCRA, 1947–1948; *Strictly Sports with Steve George*, KCRA, 1949; *Strictly Sports*, KGMS, Sacramento, CA, 1953–1956).

12134 **George, Tim.** Newscaster (KMA, Shenandoah, IA, 1942–1945.

12135 **George, Tom.** DJ (WJBK, Detroit, MI, 1957).

12136 **George, Tony.** Sportscaster (*Sports by George*, KOME, Tulsa, OK, 1952–1955).

12137 ***George and Bess.*** George Bove sang and Beatrice Woods provided fashion information on their weekly program sponsored by the Worth Department Store (15 min., Friday, 7:30–7:45 A.M., WTIC, Hartford, CT, 1938).

12138 ***George and Rufus.*** The *Christian Science Monitor* (May 3, 1930, p. 2) said this program was a copy of the *Amos 'n' Andy* show. George and Rufus operated the "Speedy Messenger Service" on the show, instead of the Fresh Air Taxicab company. Even the program's announcer copied the style of Bill Hay (15 min., Monday, Thursday and Friday, 7:30–7:45 P.M., WPCH, New York, NY, 1930).

12139 ***George Fisher's Hollywood.*** Fisher broadcast movie gossip weekly and interviewed such stars as Monte Woolley and Nanette Fabray (15 min., KECA, Los Angeles, CA, 1946).

12140 ***George Givot—The Greek Ambassador of Good Will.*** Dialect comedian Givot starred on the evening variety program. Tommy Mack was Givot's stooge (Weekly, CBS, 1935). Leader (*George Givot Orchestra*, instr. mus. prg., CBS, 1936).

12141 ***George Goebel.*** "Little Georgie" Goebel, later a successful television comedian, was a yodeling country music singer in his youth (WDOD, Chattanooga, TN, 1937). His later programs were usually broadcast in the Chicago area. In 1938, he moved to WLS (Chicago, IL), where he often appeared on the *National Barn Dance* program.

12142 ***(The) George Jessel Show.*** Jessel's first network variety show was broadcast on a sustaining basis. Comedian Jessel was joined on the show by the Four Eton Boys and the Freddie Rich Orchestra (30 min., Saturday, 9:30–10:00 P.M., CBS, 1934). A 1937 format presented comedian Jessel assisted by such guest stars as Norma Talmadge, Polly Moran, Man Mountain Dean, Lee Wiley, Burt Kalmar, Harry Ruby, Buster Crabbe, Jackie Cooper, Gus Edwards, Weber & Fields, the Our Gang Kids, Johnny Downs, Judy Garland, Bert Wheeler, George Raft and Smith and Dale (30 min., Weekly, CBS, 1937). Jessel later hosted a transcribed variety show that featured weekly guests including Gus Edwards, Sigmund Romberg, Smith and Dale, Jackie Cooper, Weber and Fields and Al Bernie (15 min., Transcribed, Various Stations, 1938).

12143 ***George Jessel Jamboree.*** Comedian Jessel hosted a variety show (NBC, 1939).

12144 ***George Jordan, Jr.*** Hecker H-O Cereal Company sponsored Jordan, an astrologer who headed the Evangeline Adams Astrological Studios. On the show, Jordan read letters from listeners and offered them advice, but spent most of his time discussing daily horoscopes (15 min., Tuesday, 9:00–9:15 A.M., WOR, Newark, NJ, 1933).

12145 ***(The) George O'Hanlon Show.*** O'Hanlon played a none too smart husband with Lurene Tuttle in the role of his patient, long-suffering wife. Also in the story was a chiseling best friend played by Cliff Young and a sarcastic boss played by Alan Reed (Teddy Bergman). On the amusing, sustaining situation comedy music was provided by Harry Zimmerman's Orchestra (30 min., Tuesday, 8:00–8:30 P.M., MBS, 1948).

12146 ***George "The Real" McCoy.*** George McCoy had a variety of careers. Before World War II, he conducted man-in-the-street interviews. McCoy worked in the Armed Forces Radio Service during World War II. After the war, he drove a taxi cab. On the sustaining New York local program he interviewed patrons at Diamond Dan O'Rourke's club in the Bowery section of New York (15 min., Monday through Friday, 11:00–11:25 P.M., WOV, New York, NY, 1946).

12147 ***George Reed.*** Reed was literally a one-man minstrel show. He played both Mr. Bill and the comedy role of Pussyfoot on the novel program. In addition, Reed sang very well. He was accompanied on the unique show by Sam Small's Rhythm Band (15 min., Tuesday, 10:30–10:45 P.M., WMCA, New York, NY, 1935).

12148 **Georgette, Jeanne.** COM-HE (WCOH, New York, NY, 1932).

12149 ***Georgia Crackers.*** CW mus. prg. performed by a group not otherwise identified (WHP, Harrisburg, PA, 1936).

12150 **Georgia Minstrel Boys.** Minstrel group (WGY, Schenectady, NY, 1927).

12151 **Georgia Sirens Orchestra.** Local musical group (WMAZ, Macon, GA, 1926).

12152 **Georgia Tech Band.** Frank Roman conducted the collegiate band (WBBF, Atlanta, GA, 1925).

12153 ***Georgia Wildcats.*** CW mus. prg. (WRVA, Richmond, VA, 1939). The Georgia Wildcats country-western music group later returned to radio with another CW music show sponsored by Roddy Electric Company. Clayton "Pappy" McMichen, the group's leader, was one of country music's genuine pioneers. He returned to Louisville, KY, and put the group back on the air in 1956. Junior Gilliam appeared with him on the show. Ken Rowland was the announcer (60 min., Sunday, 3:00–4:00 P.M., WKLO, Louisville, KY, 1956).

12154 **Georgian Orchestra.** H.N. Paradies directed the musical organization (WGR, Buffalo, NY, 1923).

12155 ***Georgie and Juanita.*** Georgie and Juanita Mahoney (*Georgie and Juanita*) were a popular singing team who specialized in country-western songs (15 min., Weekly, WNAC, Boston, MA, Yankee Network, 1937).

12156 **Georgievskaia, Maria.** Russian gypsy contralto (WLWL, New York, NY, 1931).

12157 **Georini, Giorgio.** Tenor (WEAF, New York, NY, 1928).

12158 **Geraghty, Larry.** Newscaster (WAGM, Presque Isle, ME, 1944).

12159 **Gerard, Bella.** Contralto (WEAF, New York, NY, 1923).

12160 **Gerard, James.** Tenor (KGO, Oakland, CA, 1926).

12161 **Gerard, James W.** Newscaster (WINE, New York, NY, 1942).

12162 **Gerard, Marie.** Soprano (WOR, Newark, NJ, 1933).

12163 **Gerard, Yvonne.** Pianist (KFI, Los Angeles, CA, 1926).

12164 **Gerben, Stan.** DJ (WBRN, Big Rapids, MI, 1956).

12165 **Gerbini, Francis M.** COM-HE (WBNX, Bronx, NY, 1936).

12166 **Gerding, Geraldine.** Pianist (KFAE, Pittsburgh, PA, 1925).

12167 **Gerdon, Earle.** Newscaster (KRKO, Everett, WA, 1946)

12168 **Gerhard, Romona and Geraldine Gerhard.** Instrumental duo of violinist Ramona and pianist Geraldine (WCCO, Minneapolis–St. Paul, MN, 1928). .

12169 **Gerhardt, Mary Alice.** COM-HE (WHFB, Benton Harbor, MI, 1956).

12170 **Gerken, Dennis.** Newscaster (WJAC, Johnstown, PA, 1945).

12171 **Germ, Bud.** DJ (*Polka Party*, WHLB, Virginia, MN, 1947).

12172 **German, George B.** CW singer German was billed as the "Cowboy balladeer" (WNAX, Yankton, SD, 1928).

12173 ***German and Toy Band.*** Instr. mus. prg. featuring a novelty band (KUOA, Siloam Springs, AR, 1934).

12174 ***(The) German Band.*** The program's popular Chicago music group consisted of "Herr Oscar" Tengblad, Cousin Lou Klatt, trombonist Gerry Vogt, Chris Steiner on tuba and Emilio Silvestre (WLS, Chicago, IL, 1936).

12175 **Germanich, Sophia.** Singer Germanich was known as the "Prairie Farmer Girl" (*Sophia Germanich*, vcl. mus. prg., WLS, Chicago, IL, 1936).

12176 **Gernoets [Gemoets], Louis.** Announcer (WDAH, El Paso, TX, 1927).

12177 **Gerovich, Jack.** Pianist (KPO, San Francisco, CA, 1923).

12178 **Gerrold, Fred.** Baritone (WAHG, Richmond Hill, NY, 1926).

12179 **Gershwin, George.** Distinguished pianist-composer (*General Motors Hour*, NBC, 1928).

12180 **Gerson, Betty Lou.** Gerson, a busy, talented and versatile actress, appeared on such daytime serial programs as *The Guiding Light*; *Girl Alone*; *Last of the Lockwoods*; *Mary Marlin* aka *The Story of Mary Marlin*; *Lonely Women*; *Today's Children*; *The Woman in White*; *Shoestring Castle*; *Midstream*; *The Woman in White*; and *The Road of Life*.

12181 ***Gertrude Niesen.*** Miss Niesen, a fine singer and commedienne, sang and did clever imitations of Lupe Valez and other stars (15 min., Wednesday, 10:00–10:15 P.M., CBS, 1933).

12182 **Gerun, Tom.** *See* **Gerunovich, Tom.**

12183 **(The) Gerun Orchestra.** *See* **Gerunovich, Tom.**

12184 **Gerunovich, Tom.** Using his own name, Gerunowich led the Tom Gerunovich and his Ballroom Entertainers Orchestra (KFWI, San Francisco, CA, 1925; Tom Gerunovich and his Weird Jazz Orchestra broadcasting from the Jungle Town club, KFWI, 1927; Tom Gerunovich's Roof Garden Orchestra, KHJ, Los Angeles, CA, 1929). After he shortened his name, he led the fine Tom Gerun Orchestra that broadcast regularly from San Francisco's Roof Garden Club (KHJ, 1928–1929). Gerun's band included: George Wendt, t.; Frank McMuir, t. and v.; Gary Nottingham, tb. and v.; Dave Gensal, clr. and as.; Eddie Swarthout, as. and ts.; Otto Claire, p.; Jimmy Davis, bj., g. and tba.; Steve Bowers, d. and vcls.; and Lindsay Green, Philip Campbell and Jack Woody. Gerun's band remained active in the 1930s: *Tom Gerun Orchestra*. (WGN, Chicago, IL, 1933; *Tom Gerun's Bal Tabarin Orchestra*, NBC, San Francisco, CA, 1933; NBC, 1935).

12185 **Gervais, Sidney.** Newscaster (*News Roundup*, KATL, Houston, TX, 1947).

12186 **Geste, Helen.** Singer Geste appeared on *The Midnight Frolics* program (KFI, Los Angeles, CA, 1927).

12187 ***Get Rich Quick.*** Johnny Olsen was the MC on the audience participation quiz. One element of the show was Olsen making a phone call and asking the person contacted to answer a question about a skit that had just been performed on the show. Jimmy Blaine was the announcer (30 min., Monday, 9:30–10:00 P.M., ABC, 1948).

12188 Gething, (Major) Peter. Newscaster (WTMA, Charleston, SC, 1940–1942).

12189 Gettelf, Manfred. Pianist (WHT, Deerfield, IL, 1925).

12190 Gettinger, Esther G. Soprano (WBZ, Boston-Springfield, MA, 1926).

12191 Gettings, Matt. Newscaster (WPDQ, Jacksonville, FL, 1942).

12192 Gettys, Norma. Psychologist (WMAQ, Chicago, IL, 1925).

12193 Getz, Billie. COM-HE (KVIC, Victoria, TX, 1956).

12194 Gewinner, Holt. Newscaster (WMAZ, Macon, GA, 1937–1939, 1945).

12195 Geyer, George. DJ (*Cinderella Ballroom*, WARA, Attleboro, MA, 1949; *The George Geyer Show*, WMUR, Manchester, NH, 1952; *Geyer's Sportlite*, WMUR, 1952; WJDA, Quincy, MA, 1954).

12196 Geyer, Marion. COM-HE (WAKR, Akron, OH, 1956).

12197 Gezon, Marie. COM-HE (WHVH, Henderson, NC, 1957).

12198 Ghiorse, Larry. DJ (*Turntable Terrace*, WBET, Brockton, MA, 1947; *Platter Patter*, WBET, 1949–1952).

12199 Ghrist, Eva Kurtz. Organist (KTBI, Los Angeles, CA, 1925).

12200 *G.I. Jill*. Martha Wilkerson, as GI Jill, sang and performed the duties of a DJ on Armed Forces Radio during World War II. *Variety* noted that Wilkerson had sung for more soldiers and sailors on AFRS during the World War II years than Dinah Shore, Jo Stafford and Ginny Sims combined. *See* **Wartime Radio**.

12201 *G.I. Joe*. Lawson Zerbe, Bill Sterling, Horace Graham, Bill Gray, Jack Arthur and Peggy Sanford were cast members of this dramatic series broadcast during World War II (30 min., Weekly, NBC, World War II era).

12202 *G.I. Journal*. *See* **Wartime Radio**.

12203 Gianaris, Harry. Sportscaster (WHAN, Charleston, SC, 1947–1949).

12204 Gianelli, Antonio. Guitarist (WOR, Newark, NJ, 1925).

12205 Giannecchine, William. Pianist-accordionist (KFOB, Burlingame, CA, 1925).

12206 Giard, Mary Lou. COM-HE (WHVH, Henderson, NC, 1957).

12207 Gibbens, Zetta. Soprano (KFSG, Los Angeles, CA, 1926).

12208 Gibbons, Floyd. Gibbons was a newscaster famous for his rapid speech delivery measured at 127 words per minute (3.6 words per second). He had been a war correspondent who had lost an eye in World War I. Gibbons was first heard on the *Headline Hunters* program (NBC, 1929–1931). He told entertaining stories and always was more of a color commentator than a news reporter or analyst. His second series on radio was on WEAF with the "House of Magic" portion of General Electric's *Adventures in Science* program.

12209 Gibbons, Grace. Leader (Grace Gibbons' Italian Village Orchestra, KFI, Los Angeles, CA, 1925).

12210 Gibbons, James L. "Jim." Sportscaster (WMAL, Washington, DC, 1945; *Arrow Sports Review*, WMAL, 1947–1951; WMAL, 1954; ABC, 1949). DJ (*The Town Clock*, WMAL, 1947–1954; WOL, Washington, DC, 1957).

12211 Gibbons, Jim. DJ (KTNM, Tumcumcari, NM, 1947).

12212 Gibbons, John. Newscaster (*Night Extra*, WCAP, Asbury Park, NJ, 1947).

12213 Gibbons, Molly. Newscaster (KLZ, Denver, CO, 1937).

12214 Gibbons, Tommy. Sportscaster (WPIC, Sharon, PA, 1939–1941). Newscaster (WPIC, 1942–1944; *Hourly News*, WPIC, 1947).

12215 Gibbons, William "Bill." DJ (*Club 1570*, WFGN, Gaffney, SC, 1952; WANT, Richmond, VA, 1956).

12216 Gibbs, Agnes. COM-HE (WCSH, Portland, ME, 1949).

12217 Gibbs, Elba. COM-HE (KIUN, Pecos, TX, 1960).

12218 Gibbs, Elizabeth. Contralto (WJZ, New York, NY, 1925).

12219 Gibbs, Genelle. Actress Gibbs was a cast member of *The Woman in White* daytime serial program.

12220 Gibbs, John. DJ (KQV, Pittsburgh, PA, 1949).

12221 Gibbs, Rowland. Sportscaster (KALI, Pasadena, CA, 1948–1949).

12222 *Gibbs and Finney, General Delivery*. Raymond Knight wrote the warm, dramatic serial in which Parker Fennelly and Arthur Allen played their familiar roles of cantankerous old-timers with hearts of gold beating beneath grim exteriors. On the sustaining show, they played Gideon Gibbs and Asa Finney, the proprietors of a rural general store. Patsy Campbell also appeared on the show (15 min., Saturday, 8:15–8:30 P.M., NBC-Blue, 1942). As Buxton and Owen (1972, p. 219) point out, Fennelly and Allen did several programs that essentially were the same and on which they played old characters living in a small New England village. These were: *Four Corners, USA; Gibbs and Finney; The Simpson Boys of Sprucehead Bay; Smalltown Boys; The Stebbins Boys;* and *Uncle Abe and David*.

12223 Gibney, Frank. Tenor (KGO, San Francisco, CA, 1925).

12224 Gibney, J.B. "Jack." Sportscaster (WRBL, Columbus, GA, 1940–1942). Newscaster (WRBL, 1939–1942).

12225 Gibney, Joe. DJ (*Poe's Click Club*, KLIX, Twin Falls, ID, 1947; *Old Joe's KLIX Klub*, WKIX, 1948–1954).

12226 Giboney, Betty O'Neal. COM-HE (WCTW-FM, 1949).

12227 Gibson, Alec. DJ (*Burnt Toast and Coffee*, WVCG, Coral Gables, FL, 1948).

12228 Gibson, Avery. COM-HE (WTOB, Winston-Salem, NC, 1951).

12229 Gibson, Don. DJ (*Midnight Dancing Party*, WJRI, Lenoir, NC, 1947).

12230 Gibson, Eva. COM-HE (WZOB, Fort Payne, AL, 1956).

12231 Gibson, Evelyn. COM-HE (KTKT, Tucson, AZ, 1951).

12232 Gibson, Gerry. DJ (*4:45 Special*, WJOY, Burlington, VT, 1947).

12233 Gibson, Jack "Jockey Jack." Black DJ (Various Stations, 1940s-1960s). Before becoming a DJ, Gibson had been an assistant to Al Benson in Chicago and an actor in various WJJD (Chicago, IL) daytime serials. He also appeared on *Here Comes Tomorrow*, a daytime serial based on the "real life experiences of a black family."

A popular DJ at WERD (Atlanta, GA) in the 1940s, Gibson teamed with Jewish DJ Herb Gershon on the station for their popular noon *Herb and Jack Lunch Call* show (WERD, Atlanta, GA, 1949). The team played classical music as well as popular records. Gibson often made announcements for Dr. Martin Luther King while working at WERD, since the station was located in the same building as Dr. King's Southern Christian Leadership organization. Gibson eventually moved on to become a "morning man" at Cincinnati's WCIN in 1960, where he opened his popular show with the greeting, "This is the morning man in Cincinnati, Jockey Jack."

12234 Gibson, Jane. COM-HE (WKCV, Philadelphia, PA, 1949).

12235 Gibson, Jim. Newscaster (KGB, San Diego, CA, 1941). Sportscaster (KGB, 1941).

12236 Gibson, Judy. COM-HE (WHRV, Ann Arbor, MI, 1949).

12237 Gibson, Phil. Newscaster (WMBD, Peoria, IL, 1945).

12238 Gibson, Riley R. Newscaster (*Behind the News*, KOPP, Odgen, UT, 1948).

12239 Gibson, Ross. Newscaster (KUOA, Siloam Springs, AR, 1940). Sportscaster (KUOA, 1941).

12240 Gibson, Wynne. Actress Gibson appeared on the *When a Girl Marries* daytime serial.

12241 *(The) Gibson Family* (aka *The Gibsons*). Procter and Gamble sponsored the program that was unique in that its music and lyrics were written especially for it by Howard Dietz and Arthur Schwartz, the successful composers of Broadway musicals. The program told the story of two young people, played by Jack and Loretta Clemens, who wanted to enter show business. Also in the cast were: Bill Adams, Al Dary, Anne Elstner, Warren Hull, Kate McComb, John McGovern, Adele Ronson and Ernest Whitman. The singing portions of the show — when the two leads were supposed to sing — were performed by Loretta Clemens, Conrad Thibault, Al Dary and Lois Bennett. Owen Davis succeeded the show's originator and writer, Courtney Riley Cooper. The show was produced by Carlo DeAngelo. Don Voorhees conducted the orchestra. Jimmy Wallington was the announcer (60 min., Sunday, 10:00–11:00 P.M., NBC-Red, 1935).

12242 Gibson Mandolin and Guitar Club. Instrumental club band (WFAA, Dallas, TX, 1922).

12243 Giddings, Natalie. Miss Giddings was the announcer and director of the *Crosley's Woman's Hour* (WLW, Cincinnati, OH, 1928.)

12244 Gieseking, Walter. Distinguished concert pianist (NBC, 1928).

12245 Gifford, Alec. DJ (*Southwest Stampede*, KTBC, Austin, TX, 1948).

12246 Gifford, Alexander. Newscaster (WBAL, Baltimore, MD, 1938–1939).

12247 Gifford, Claude. Newscaster (WOI, Ames, IA, 1940).

12248 Gifford, Dick. Newscaster (KWNO, Winona, MN, 1939).

12249 Gifford, Joseph. Reader (WHO, Des Moines, IA, 1926).

12250 Gifford, Phyllis Knight. COM-HE (WHAS, Louisville, KY, 1957).

12251 Gifford, Sam. Newscaster (WOWO, Fort Wayne, IN, 1945).

12252 *Gigantic Pictures, Inc.* *Gigantic Pictures, Inc.* had a musical comedy format that featured comedian Sam Hearn, actress Alice Frost, singers Betty Jones, George Buechler and Larry Grant. Both the Johnny Blue and the Reggie Childs Orchestras appeared on the show. The show eventually was replaced by the *Tastyeast Amateurs* program (30 min., Sunday, 12:00–12:30 P.M., NBC-Blue, 1935). Comic Sam Hearn was probably best known for his portrayal of "Schlepperman" on the *Jack Benny Show*.

12253 Gigli, Beniamino. Distinguished operatic tenor Gigli sang on the *Atwater Kent Hour* and many other programs (NBC, 1928).

12254 Gignilliat, (General) Leigh R. The Superintendent of Culver Military Academy, General Gignilliat discussed various subjects on the military academy's own station (WCMA, Culver, IN, 1928).

12255 Gilbert, A.V. Newscaster (WIBA, Madison, WI, 1939).

12256 Gilbert, Alma. COM-HE (KYND, Tempe, AZ, 1960).

12257 Gilbert, Delores. Actress Gilbert appeared on the *Lone Journey* daytime serial.

12258 Gilbert, Dick. DJ (*Dick Gilbert*, WHN, New York, NY, 1940; *Dick Gilbert*, 60 min., 5:15–6:15 P.M., WOV, 1941; *Dick Gilbert*, WHN, New York, NY, 1940; *The Latin American Hour* and *The Dick Gilbert Show*, KRUX, Phoenix-Glendale, AZ, 1947; *Dick Gilbert Show*, KTYL, Mesa, AZ, 1949; *Record Parade*, KRDU, Dinuba, CA, 1950; KTYL, 1954; KYND, Tempe, AZ, 1960). Gilbert was a popular DJ, who played recordings of big name bands and frequently sang along with them. Before becoming a DJ, he had been featured as a singer on his own program (*Dick Gilbert*, vcl. mus. prg., WNEW, New York, NY, 1940). Gilbert's death in 1997 prompted the New York *Post* to report his contributions to broadcasting (February 28, 1997, p. 33): Abel Green, *Variety's* editor, first applied the term DJ to Dick Gilbert. He was also said to have been the first to broadcast from a night club. In 1946, Gilbert moved to Arizona where he built and operated KYND in Tempe, AZ. He also operated KPOK-KDOT in Scottsdale, AZ.

12259 Gilbert, Ethel. Managerial staff (NBC, 1940s). Gilbert was a member of NBC's Artists Service Staff that handled the affairs of the network's singers, actors, comedians and musicians it managed.

12260 Gilbert, Genieve. Soprano (KGW, Portland, OR, 1923).

12261 Gilbert, Harry. Leader (*Harry Gilbert Orchestra*, instr. mus. prg., WTIC, Hartford, CT, 1937–1938).

12262 Gilbert, J.J. Flutist (KHJ, Los Angeles, CA, 1923).

12263 Gilbert, Jane. Actress Gilbert was a cast member of the *Stepmother* daytime serial program.

12263a Gilbert, Janice. Busy actress Gilbert appeared on the daytime serial programs *Doc Barclay's Daughter*, *Her Honor, Nancy James*, Hilltop House, *Bachelor's Children* and *The O'Neills*.

12264 Gilbert, Jim. DJ (*Beachcombers' Almanac*, WNDB, Daytona Beach, FL, 1960).

12265 Gilbert, Joe. Leader (*Joe Gilbert Orchestra*, instr. mus. prg., KFEL, Denver, CO, 1934).

12266 Gilbert, Josephine "Jo." Actress Gilbert appeared on the daytime programs *Kitty Keene* aka *Kitty Keene, Incorporated*, *Today's Children* and *Midstream*.

12267 Gilbert, L. Wolse. Pianist (WEAF, New York, NY, 1925).

12268 Gilbert, Lauren. Actress Gilbert was featured on the *Romance of Helen Trent* program.

12269 Gilbert, Livingston. Newscaster (WAVE, Louisville, KY, 1942, 1945).

12270 Gilbert, Virginia. Pianist (WLW, Cincinnati, OH, 1923).

12271 *Gilbert and Sullivan Gems*. The music of Gilbert and Sullivan was masterfully performed on the show by Alma Kitchell, contralto; Muriel Wilson, soprano; Fred Hufsmith, tenor; John Barclay, baritone; Charles Pearson, bass; and an orchestra conducted by Harold Sanford (30 min., Various times, NBC-Blue, 1933).

12272 Gilchrest, Charles. Newscaster (WBZ-WBZA, Boston-Springfield, MA, 1939).

12273 Gilchrest, T.S., Jr. Newscaster (WTMC, Ocala, FL, 1942, 1948).

12274 Gilchrist, Norma. COM-HE (KPOL, Los Angles, CA, 1954).

12275 *Gilda Audrey's Beauty Chats*. Peter Krug was the straight man for Ruth Paige, who in the role of beauty expert Gilda Audrey supplied information and tips on her specialty. The J.M. Adam Beauty Salon sponsored the program (10 min., Wednesday 4:05–4:15 P.M., WEBR, Buffalo, NY, 1939).

12276 Giles, Art. Leader (Art Giles' Everglad Orchestra, KDKA, Pittsburgh, PA, 1926; *Art Giles Orchestra*, instr. mus. prg., WJAS, Pittsburgh, PA, 1935–1939; NBC, 1936; CBS, 1937).

12277 Giles, Erva. Soprano Giles was featured on the *Stars of Melody* program (NBC-Blue, New York, NY, 1929; *Erva Giles*, vcl. mus. prg., WOR, Newark, NJ, 1934).

12278 Giles, Lauretta. Soprano (WQJ, Chicago, IL, 1925).

12279 Gill, A. Cloyd. Newscaster (WMCA, New York, NY, 1934).

12280 Gill, Bo. Sportscaster (WGNY, Newburgh, NY, 1940; *Orange County Sports*, WGNY, 1941; WGNY, 1946).

12281 Gill, Emerson. Leader (Emerson Gill Orchestra, a "sweet sounding dance orchestra" said *Variety*, WTAM, Cleveland, OH, 1927; Bamboo Gardens Orchestra, WTAM, Cleveland, OH, 1928). Gill's Bamboo Gardens Orchestra included: Gill, ldr. and v.; Joe Aumend and Duke Krovonas, t.; Don Dupre, tb.; Menden Frye and Willard Pott, clr. and as.; Jim Harry, clr. and ts.; Eddie Robinson, p.; Imo Smith, tba.; Pinky Hunter, bj. and vcls.; and Andy Pickard, d. Gill's band also broadcast in the next decade (*Emerson Gill Orchestra*, instr. mus. prg., NBC, 1934, 1936; WENR, Chicago, IL, 1937; NBC, 1938).

12282 Gill, Ernest. Violinist (KOMO, Seattle, WA, 1928; *Ernest Gill Orchestra*, instr. mus. prg., NBC, 1939).

12283 Gill, Jane "Janie." COM-HE (WJPD, Ishpenning, MI, 1956).

12284 Gill, Joaquin. Leader (*Joaquin Gill Orchestra*, instr. mus. prg., MBS, 1939).

12285 Gill, Paul. DJ (*Time to Remember*, WCSH, Portland, ME, 1948).

12286 Gill, Rusty. Leader (*Rusty Gill's Saddle Pals*, CW mus. prg., KDKA , Pittsburgh, PA, 1942).

12287 Gilleland, Herbert. Newscaster (WTOL, Toledo, OH, 1939).

12288 Gillen, Anne. Organist (WGBS, New York, NY, 1929).

12289 Gillen, Delores. Actress Gillen appeared on the daytime serial programs *Mary Marlin* aka *The Story of Mary Marlin*, *When a Girl Marries* and *Against the Storm*.

12290 Gilles [Giles], Frank. Announcer (KFUM, Colorado Springs, CO, 1927.

12291 Gillespie, Bob. DJ (*Turntable Memories*, WONS, Hartford, CT, 1947).

12292 Gillespie, Courtney Waggoner. Pianist (WSM, Nashville, TN, 1928).

12293 Gillespie, Dave. Newscaster (WLTC, Gastonia, NC, 1948).

12294 Gillespie, Ethelyn Mills. Lyric soprano (1928).

12295 Gillespie, Frank. Sportscaster (KBMC, Jamestown, ND, 1939; KTAR, Phoenix, AZ, 1942). Newscaster (KTAR, 1942).

12296 Gillett, Helen. Singer from Southwestern University, Georgetown, Texas (WFAA, Dallas, TX, 1924).

12297 Gillette, Albert W. Baritone (KGO, Oakland, CA, 1925–1926).

12298 Gillette, Mickey. Leader (Mickey Gillette's Romanciers Orchestra, KFRC, San Francisco, CA, 1928).

12299 *(The) Gillette Razor Blade Hour*. The Gillette Company sponsored this variety show. Kenneth Pickett was the announcer (Weekly, NBC, 1929).

12300 *Gillette Summer Hotel*. Milton Berle hosted the summer replacement variety show. Andy Sanella's orchestra supplied the music. The announcer was Wendell Hall (30 min., Sunday, 8:00–8:30 P.M., CBS, 1937).

12301 *(The) Gillette Tire Program*. Soprano Grace Wilson and bass John Neher, the DeZurik Sisters, the Hilltoppers and the

Gillette Bears (male) Quartet vocal groups were featured on the music program. Jack Stillwill was the announcer (30 min., WLS, Chicago, IL, 1937).

12302 Gillham, Art. The pioneer announcer, Lambdin Kay also known as "The Little Colonel," gave Gillham the name of the "Whispering Pianist." Gillham had a long career in radio that began on WDAP, Chicago, IL in 1922 and continued on many other stations (WFAA, Dallas, TX, 1924; WMC, Memphis, TN, 1925; and WMCA, New York, NY 1926). He continued to perform in the 1930s (*Art Gillham*, instr. mus. prg., 15 min. Monday, 5:00–5:15 P.M., CBS, 1931; *Art Gillham, the Whispering Pianist*, instr. mus. prg., WDBJ, Roanoke, VA, 1935–1936).

12303 Gilliam, Robert "Bob." DJ (*Off the Record*, WKBB, Dubuque, IA, 1947; *Platters and Patter*, KWNO, Winona, MN, 1949).

12304 Gillick, Pat. Organist (WLW, Cincinnati, OH, 1929).

12305 Gilliland, M. COM-HE (KIBH, Seward, AR, 1957).

12306 Gillin, John J. Chief announcer (WOW, Omaha, NE, 1929). During 1927–1928 Gillin had worked on Chicago's WHT.

12307 Gillis, Anne. Publicist (CBS, 1939). Gill directed the CBS Press Department in Washington, DC.

12308 Gillis, Earle. Newscaster (WHKC, Columbus, OH, 1948).

12309 Gilman, Edith. Soprano (KGO, Oakland, CA, 1925).

12310 Gillis, Hal. Gillis was a singer of "character songs" (WLS, Chicago, IL, 1925).

12311 Gilman, Hal. DJ (*At Your Request*, WSLB, Ogdensburg, NY, 1947–1954).

12312 Gilman, Lucy. Actress Gilman appeared in the *Song of the City* daytime serial program.

12313 Gilman, Page. Actor Gilman, born April 18, 1918, first appeared on radio in a juvenile role in 1927 on the *Memory Lane* program sponsored by General Petroleum (NBC-Red network). Gilman's greatest fame, however, came from his long-time appearance in the 1930s and 1940s as Jack on *One Man's Family* and various roles on *I Love a Mystery*, both popular productions of Carlton E. Morse.

12314 Gilman, Toni. Actress Gilman appeared on the early daytime serial program *Sue and Irene* (WGN, Chicago, IL, 1930).

12315 Gilmer, Betty. COM-HE (KGBX, Springfield, MO, 1956).

12316 Gilmer, Elmora [Elnora]. COM-HE (KSLV, Monte Vista, CA, 1956–1957).

12317 Gilmore, Ann. COM-HE (WSOC, Charlotte, NC, 1949).

12318 Gilmore, Anne. COM-HE (WGST, Atlanta, GA, 1956).

12319 Gilmore, Bruce. DJ (*Matinee at Club 1500*, WABJ, Adrian, MI, 1947; *WGH Digest*, WGH, Newport News, VA, 1952–1954; WKAN, Kankakee, IL, 1956).

12320 Gilmore, Eddy. Newscaster (NBC, 1946).

12321 Gilmore, Gloria. COM-HE (WEEB, Southern Pines, NC, 1957).

12322 Gilmore, Patricia. Singer, (*Patricia Gilmore*, vcl. mus. prg., NBC, 1942).

12323 Gilmour, Eleanore. Soprano (WHT, Decatur, IL, 1925).

12324 Gilmour, Florence. Soprano (WEAF, New York, NY, 1923).

12325 Gilreath, Howard C. DJ (*Gospel Song Time*, WVOP, Vidalia, GA, 1952; *Hoedown Party*, WVOP, 1954).

12326 Gilroy, Peggy. Ukulele soloist (WSOM, New York, NY, 1927).

12327 Gilroy, Ralph. Sportscaster (WNAC, Boston, MA and WAAB, Boston, MA, 1937).

12328 Gil's Musical Mechanics. Popular Portland, OR, orchestra (KXL, Portland, OR, 1929).

12329 Gilstrap, Karine. COM-HE (KTAE, Taylor, TX, 1956–1957).

12330 *(The) Gin Rummy School.* Harold Davis conducted the novel program designed to teach listeners the fundamentals of Gin Rummy (15 min., Weekly, WDAS, Philadelphia, PA, 1942).

12331 Ginger and Bill. Vcl. team (WCAU, Philadelphia, PA, 1933). Ginger was Virginia Baker.

12332 Gingras, Eva. Singer (WBZ, Boston, MA, 1932).

12333 Gingrich, Reba. Pianist (*Reba Gingrich*, instr. mus. prg., WHP, Harrisburg, PA, 1936).

12334 Ginn, Ann. COM-HE (WSAL, Loganport, IN, 1951).

12335 *(The) Ginny Simms Show.* Borden Company sponsored the show featuring the lovely singer, Ginny Simms, as hostess. She was joined by the Sportsman vocal group and Frank DeVol's Orchestra. Guest stars appearing on the program included Danny Thomas, Billy deWolfe, Frank Sinatra, Eddie Cantor, Gene Kelly, Phil Baker, Charles Coburn, Jerry Colonna and Sonny Tufts (CBS, 1946).

12336 *(The) Ginny Sims Song Shop.* Singer Sims was accompanied by the Buddy Cole Trio on the music show sponsored by Botany Clothes (15 min., Sunday, 10:00–10:15 P.M., ABC, 1950).

12337 Ginsberg, Harry. Sportscaster (WNBC, New Britain, CT, 1937).

12338 Ginsburg, Norman Jay. News commentator (WCAU, Philadelphia, PA, 1940).

12339 Ginsburgh, Arnie "Woo Woo." Rock-and-roll DJ (WBOS, Boston, MA, 1957; WMEX, Buffalo, NY, 1960).

12340 Ginsburgh, Ralph. Leader (*Ralph Ginsburgh Orchestra*, instr. mus. prg., WGN, Chicago, IL, 1934; *Ralph Ginsburgh's Concert Orchestra*, instr. mus. prg., MBS, 1939; WGN, 1942).

12341 Gionfriddo, Al. Sportscaster (KONG, Visalia, CA, 1956). Former Brooklyn Dodger baseball star Gionfriddo is best remembered for his spectacular catch of Joe DiMaggio's long drive in one of the many hard fought World Series baseball games between the Dodgers and the New York Yankees.

12342 Girad, Mary. COM-HE (WHVH, Henderson, NC, 1960).

12343 Giralt, Kay. COM-HE (KYOU, Greeley, CO, 1957).

12344 Girard, Adele. Singer, (*Adele Girard*, vcl. mus. prg., CBS, 1934).

12345 Girard, Armand. Bass-baritone (*Armand Girard*, vcl. mus. prg., NBC, 1934).

12346 Girard, Paul. Newscaster (WBAL, Baltimore, MD, 1939–1940).

12347 Gire, Lorraine. Singer (WMBH, Joplin, MO, 1937).

12348 *Girl Alone.* Betty Winkler played the title role of Patricia Rogers, the girl who was alone on the daytime dramatic serial. After a series of misunderstandings, Patricia, much to her dismay, found that her former fiancé had married another woman. The situation compounded her difficulties and provided many opportunities for conflict and plot twists. The program was written by Fayette Krum. The directors were Gordon Hughes and Axel Gruenberg. Kellogg's cereals and Quaker Oats were the sponsors during its five-year broadcast run (1935–1941). The cast included: Don Briggs, Herbert Butterfield, Betty Caine, Kathryn Card, Fran Carlon, Jack Chalbeck, Les Damon, Sidney Ellstrom, Laurette Fillbrand, Don Gallagher, Earl George, Betty Lou Gerson, Stanley Gordon, Jane Green, John Hodiak, Henry Hunter (Arthur Jacobson), Bob Jellison, Raymond Edward Johnson, Ian Keith, Arthur Kohl, Janet Logan, Ted Maxwell, Pat Murphy, Herbert Nelson, Frank Pacelli, Charles Penman, Fern Persons, Arthur Peterson, Michael Romano, Syd Simons, Hope Summers, Dan Sutter, June Travis, Willard Waterman, Karl Weber, Betty Winkler and Joan Winters (15 min., 9:15–9:30 A.M., NBC-Red, 1935).

12349 *(The) Girl Friends.* Vcl. mus. prg. by an otherwise unidentified female trio (WXYZ, Detroit, MI, 1935).

12350 *(The) Girl from Paris.* Jane Morgan sang on the weekly sustaining vocal music program (15 min., Sunday, 2:45–3:00 P.M., NBC, 1951).

12351 *Girl Meets Boy.* Miss Jo Hipple and Ed Cooper asked questions of the three girl and three boy contestants who wanted to meet members of the opposite sex for dating. Their questions supposedly brought out each participant's likes and dislikes. At the end of each program a jury of five persons selected from the audience paired the participants off as best they could. After the pairings were completed, the sponsor, Bit-O-Honey Candy Company, paid for their evening dates (30 min., Friday, 9:00–9:30 P.M., WGN, Chicago, IL, 1947).

12352 *Girl Reporter.* Newspaper reporter and author Alma Sioux Scarberry and her husband, Ted Klein, wrote the program, a dramatic serial based on her own career as a "sob sister." The program began on local Chicago radio (WENR) before going on the network (15 min., Tuesday and Thursday, 7:45–8:00 P.M., NBC, 1931).

12353 *Girl Reporter* (aka *Bernardine Flynn—Girl Reporter*). Actress Bernardine Flynn, as herself, reported the news of the day (15 min., Chicago, IL, 1941).

12354 *Girls of the Golden West.* CW vcl. mus. prg. (WLS, Chicago, IL, 1937). Millie and Dolly Good were talented CW music performers known as the Girls of the Golden West. Their 1937 programs were produced at the border station of XERA, Mexico, and broadcast by many stations throughout the United States by transcription.

12355 ***(The) Girls Story Hour.*** Eunice L. Randall prepared and told stories especially for girls (WGI, Medford Hillside, MA, 1923).

12356 **Giroux, Lee.** Sportscaster (KSAN, San Francisco, CA, 1945). DJ (*Dollars or Donuts*, KGO, San Francisco, CA, 1948; *Sunrise Roundup*, KGO, 1950).

12357 **Girvin, Hal.** Leader (Hal Girvin's Hotel Oakland Dance Orchestra, KGO, Oakland, CA, 1928).

12358 **Girvin-Devel's California Collegians Orchestra.** Popular California band (KGO, San Francisco, CA, 1925).

12359 **Gisburne, Edward.** Announcer (WEEI, Boston, MA, 1928–1930).

12360 **Giselman, Marshall W.** Organist (KPO, San Francisco, CA, 1925–1926). Giselman broadcast organ recitals from the California Memorial Palace of the Legion of Honor, San Francisco, CA.

12361 **Gish, Eddie.** DJ (*KLIX Ballroom*, KLIX, Twin Falls, ID, 1952).

12362 **Giskin, Ossip.** Cellist-leader of the Lubovisky String Quartet (KHJ, Los Angeles, CA, 1923).

12363 **Gismondi, James.** Sportscaster (WMBS, Uniontown, PA, 1946; *Sportlights*, WMBS, 1947–1948; *Sports Tonight*, WMBS, 1952; *Sports Today*, WMBS, 1954). Newscaster (*Gismondi Edits*, WMBS, 1948).

12364 **Gissler, C.** Broadcast talks on bridge (WEEI, Boston, MA, 1931).

12365 **Githens, Dorothy.** Soprano (*Roxy and his Gang*, NBC, 1929).

12366 **Gitman, Simon.** Pianist (WIP, Philadelphia, PA, 1924).

12367 **Gittelson, Frank.** Violinist (WBAL, Baltimore, MD, 1926).

12368 **Gittus, Art.** DJ (*Record Shop*, WABJ, Adrian, MI, 1947).

12369 **Giuriani, Orlando.** Tenor (KFWM, Oakland, CA, 1927).

12370 ***Give and Take.*** John Reed King hosted this quiz show that was sponsored by Cannon Mills. Contestants attempted to answer questions correctly to win the prize they had previously selected. Jack Carney produced and directed the show with sound effects created by Art Strand (30 min., Saturday, 11:30–12:00 noon, CBS, 1951).

12371 **Givan, Marjorie.** COM-HE (KLER, Rochester, NY, 1949).

12372 **Given, Joe.** DJ (*Band Parade*, WOV, New York, NY, 1948).

12373 **Given, Ken D.** Sportscaster (WCHS, Charleston, WV, 1941; WLBJ, Bowling Green, OH, 1944–1946; WLBJ, 1952). Newscaster (WLBJ, 1944–1945).

12374 **Given, Marge.** COM-HE (WLBK, DeKalb, IL, 1956).

12375 **Givney, John J.** Newscaster (*On Capitol Hill*, WTRY, Troy, NY, 1948).

12376 **Giza, Wanda M.** COM-HE (*It's Delightful to be Married*, WARE, Ware, MA, 1949)

12377 **Glackin, W.O.** DJ (*Morning Music*, WWWB, Jasper, AL, 1947).

12378 **Glacy, Robert.** Newscaster (WKBW, Buffalo, NY, 1948). DJ (WGR, Buffalo, NY, 1955).

12379 **Gladding, Al.** Newscaster (*York Journal of the Air*, WNOW, York, PA, 1948).

12380 **Gladney, Norman.** DJ (*Tune Inn*, WWDC, Washington, DC, 1947).

12381 **Gladstein, Bobby.** COM-HE (KTMC, McAlester, OK, 1957).

12382 **Gladstone, Eve.** Pianist (*Eve Gladstone*, instr. mus. prg., WXYZ, Detroit, MI, 1935).

12383 **Gladstone, Henry.** Sportscaster (General Mills' baseball broadcasts, WHN, New York, NY, 1937 and Socony-Vacuum baseball broadcasts, WHN, 1937). News analyst (*The World We Make*, WHN, 1939; *Transradio News*, WOR, New York, NY, 1941, 1944–1948; WOR, 1952).

12384 **Gladstone, Lon.** Leader (*Lon Gladstone Orchestra*, instr. mus. prg., WFIL, Philadelphia, PA, 1936).

12385 **Glaenzer, Anita G.** Mezzo-soprano (WJZ, New York, NY, 1924–1925).

12386 **Glancy, Shirley.** COM-HE (WIMS, Michigan City, IN, 1951).

12387 **Glans, Helen.** Pianist (KFAE, Pullman, WA, 1925).

12388 **Glanville, Roberta.** Soprano Glanville specialized in American Indian songs. She had formerly sung with the Metropolitan Opera Company (WBAL, Baltimore, MD, 1927–1928).

12389 **Glass, Beatrice.** Singer (WMMN, Fairmont, WV, 1936).

12390 **Glass, Dorine.** Newscaster (WSAV, Savannah, GA, 1940).

12391 **Glass, Julia.** Pianist (NBC-Red, New York, NY, 1927).

12392 **Glass, Louis.** DJ (*Hoedown Harmonies*, WTRC, Elkhart, IN, 1948).

12393 **Glass, Margaret.** Organist (KTHS, Hot Springs National Park, AK, 1928).

12394 **Glass, Robert.** Announcer (KRLD, Dallas, TX, 1927).

12395 **Glasser [Glaser], Ben.** Leader (Ben Glasser Orchestra, WJZ, New York, NY, 1925).

12396 **Glasser, Don.** Leader (Don Glasser Orchestra broadcasting from the Skyway above the Hotel Peabody in Memphis, TN, 1950s).

12397 **Glasser and Cross.** Duo piano team (WFBH, New York, NY, 1925).

12398 **Glassman, Juliette.** Concert pianist (WEAF, New York, NY, 1926).

12399 **Glauser and Cross.** Duo piano team (WFBH, New York, NY, 1925).

12400 **Glave, Russell.** Leader (*Russell Glave Orchestra*, instr. mus. prg., KYW, Chicago, IL, 1933).

12401 **Glawson, Grace.** Soprano (KDKA, Pittsburgh, PA, 1924).

12402 **Gleason, Bob.** DJ (*Requestfully Yours Coffee Club*, WMSL, Decatur, AL, 1948).

12403 **Gleason, Bob.** DJ (*Nye Beachcomber*, KNPT, Newport, OR, 1950).

12404 **Gleason, Peco.** Sportscaster (WCHV, Charlottesville, VA, 1937; WRTD, Richmond, VA, 1939).

12405 **Gleaves, J.** Newscaster (WLAC, Nashville, TN, 1937).

12406 **Gleba, Tom.** DJ (*Mr. Melody*, WBNS, Columbus, OH, 1949).

12407 **Glee, Banjo and Mandolin Clubs of Cornell University.** Collegiate music groups (WLW, Cincinnati, OH, 1924).

12408 **Glee Club, Denver Chapter 2 (Masonic) Lodge.** Edwin Richards directed the fraternal organization's vocal music group (KOA ,Denver, CO, 1925).

12409 **Glen, Allan.** British baritone (WOR, Newark, NJ, 1924).

12410 **Glen, Irma (Irma G. Becklenberg).** Organist Glen, born August 3, 1908, was touring the vaudeville circuits at the age of 14 as a pianist. She organized her all-girl orchestra — the Melody Maids — the following year. Glen first appeared on radio over KYW (Chicago, IL, 1922). She joined WENR, Chicago, IL in 1927 and WBCN, Chicago, IL in 1928. Later, she became staff organist at NBC in Chicago. It was said that Glen appeared in over 10,000 programs, sometimes as an actress, but most often as an organist. In 1931, it was reported that Glen appeared on the air at least a dozen times each week (*Irma Glen*, organ recital each weekday, 15 min., Monday through Friday, 2:15–2:30 P.M., NBC-Blue, 1931; *Irma Glen*, inst. mus. prg., NBC, 1937).

12411 ***Glen Echo Orchestra.*** Mus. prg. (WJSV, Washington, DC, 1936). The band was from the Glen Echo amusement park.

12412 **Glenn, Amy Jo.** COM-HE (WSLS, Roanoke, VA, 1951).

12413 **Glenn, Charles "Charlie" G.** Whistler (KFI, San Francisco, CA, 1928). Singer Glenn sang "the old songs" (KFWI, San Francisco, CA, 1929).

12414 **Glenn, Charles.** Sportscaster (WNAX, Yankton, SD, 1935).

12415 **Glenn, Charles.** Newscaster (KGBX and KWTO, Springfield, MO, 1937).

12416 **Glenn, Hazel.** Soprano (*Hazel Glenn*, vcl. mus. prg., NBC, 1934).

12417 **Glenn, Ivo.** Tenor (WSM, Nashville, TN, 1926–1928).

12418 **Glenn, Joe.** Newscaster (WMMN, Fairmont, WV, 1939).

12419 **Glenn, Mary.** COM-HE (KFJI, Klamath Falls, OR, 1949).

12420 **Glenn, Rich.** DJ (*Hillbilly Supper Club* and *Swing Shift*, KXOL, Fort Worth, TX, 1952).

12421 **Glenn, Ward.** Newscaster (WTOL, Toledo, OH, 1941).

12422 **Glenn, Wilfred.** Bass (WEAF, New York, NY, 1927–1929). Glenn sang on many NBC network programs.

12423 ***Glenn Miller's Moonlight Serenade.*** Chesterfield cigarettes sponsored the excellent big band music show that featured singers Ray Eberle, Marion Hutton, Paula Kelly and the Modernaires, saxophonist-singer

Tex Beneke and the great Glenn Miller Orchestra (15 min., Monday through Friday, 1940). During the era of Big Band music, only the Benny Goodman band on his *Let's Dance* and *Camel Caravan* programs approached the consistently high level of music broadcast by the Glenn Miller band.

The Miller band played a major role in the *Sun Valley Serenade* and *Orchestra Wives* motion pictures. Another of their memorable sponsored radio shows was *The Chesterfield Supper Club*. The band's personnel during its great 1939–1940 years included: Leigh Knowles, John Best, Dale McMickle, Clyde Hurley, t.; Paul Tanner, Jim Priddy, Frank D'Anolfo, tb.; Willie Schwartz, Al Klink, Hal McIntyre, Ernie Caceres, Tex Beneke, s.; Maurice Purtill, d.; Rolly Bundock, sb.; and Chummy MacGregor, p. Vocalists who sang with the Miller band were: Marion Hutton, Dorothy Claire, Gail Reese, Linda Keene, Skip Nelson, Tex Beneke and Ray Eberle.

Miller led a talented service band during World War II and made some German language propaganda broadcasts to Germany [*See* **Wartime Radio**]. He was presumably killed when a plane carrying him from England to France apparently crashed into the English Channel.

12424 **Glenn's Cornhuskers Orchestra.** Regional CW band (WLS , Chicago, IL, 1925).

12425 **Glickman, Marty.** Sportscaster (*Sports Resume, Today's Baseball* and *Sports Fanfare*, WHN, New York, NY, 1939–1942; WHN, 1945–1947; WMGM, New York, NY, 1948–1956). Glickman had been a star athlete at Syracuse University. His first radio job was at WHN in 1939, when he worked with Bert Lee and Dick Fishel to broadcast the Brooklyn Dodgers baseball games. After he returned from service following World War II, he did basketball play-by-play for WHN. It was then that he began his famous call after a successful basket, "Swish ... and good like Nedicks." Nedicks, a maker of soft drinks, was his sponsor.

12426 **Glickstein, Dave.** Trumpet soloist Glickstein frequently appeared on the *Music While You Dial* program (WOR, Newark, NJ, 1925).

12427 **Glidden and Snyder.** Piano team (WOKO, Albany, NY, 1942).

12428 **Glieber, Frank.** Sportscaster (WRR, Dallas, TX, 1956).

12429 ***Glimpses Through the Stage Door.*** Mort Eiseman broadcast news about plays and their players (WHAR, Atlantic City, NJ, 1926).

12430 **Glissman, Rex.** Leader (Rex Glissman Orchestra playing from the Taverne de Paris, KFRC, San Francisco, CA, 1925).

12431 ***(The) Globe Theater.*** The program broadcast many fine dramatic presentations such as *One Life to Give* with Joseph Cotten; *Turnip's Blood* with Herbert Marshall and Rosemary DeCamp; *The Little Foxes* with Bette Davis, Robert Walker and Otto Kreuger; *Sitting Pretty* with Garry Moore and Jimmy Wallington; and *Shop Worn Angel* with Adolphe Menjou and Robert Marshall. Bill Johnstone was initially the host before he was replaced by Herbert Marshall (30 min., Weekly, 1945).

12432 ***(The) Gloom Chasers.*** Tastyeast sponsored the comedy show featuring Colonel Lemuel Stoopnagle (F. Chase Taylor) and Budd (Wilbur Budd Hulick), a zany comedy team sometimes billed as "The Fun Makers." The story is told that this successful radio team got their start in 1931 on Buffalo's radio station WMAK. When announcer Wilbur Budd Hulick supposedly found himself with 15 minutes of air time to fill and no way to fill it, he rushed out into the studio and found F. Chase Taylor, another announcer. The 15 minutes of nonsense they produced caused them to team up for further comedy ventures. Taylor had previously performed in a comedy team, *Nip and Tuck*, on WMAK in 1925 (15 min., Monday through Thursday, 8:45–9:00 P.M., CBS, 1931).

12433 ***(The) Gloom Chasers.*** Comedian Dutch Haid hosted the local Philadelphia comedy show featuring pianist Kenny Martin, guitarist Eddie Nash, trumpeter Toby Seeley and the vocal team of the Two B's — Beeby and Betty Wise (30 min., Wednesday, 12:00–12:30 P.M., WWSW, Philadelphia, PA, 1936).

12434 ***(The) Gloom Dodgers.*** The variety show was sponsored by MGM (Monday through Friday, WHN, New York, NY, 1945). The show featured Kay Stevens, also known as Kay Lorraine (Kay Lorraine Grim). She previously had sung on *The Chamber Music Society of Lower Basin Street, Vaudeville Theater, The Ford Summer Hour, The Song of Your Life* and *The Pursuit of Happiness* programs

12435 **Gloomy (Gayle Grubb) and Eddie (Eddie Ellington).** A popular comedy singing team, whose program in early 1927 began: "Hello Everybody! This is Gloomy speaking for Eddie and Gloomy, the Harmony Boys of KFAB. We've been harmonizing for about eighteen months and everytime we get blue, we dig through the two hundred thousand letters we have received since the first day" (*Radio Digest*, April 1, 1927). The boys were great listener favorites (KFAB, Lincoln, NE, 1927).

12436 **Gloomy Gus.** Singer-entertainer Gayle Grubb (KFAB, Lincoln, NE, 1926). *See* **Gloomy and Eddie**.

12437 **Glorch, George.** Announcer (WMBB, Homewood, IL and WOK, Chicago, IL, 1928).

12438 ***Gloria.*** Gloria Call talked about clothes and grooming on her local woman's program (15 min., Monday through Friday, WOKO, Albany, NY, 1953)

12439 ***Glorious One.*** Irene Rich starred in the daytime serial that told the story of the ups and downs of a marriage. Rich, a fine actress, *Variety* said, was the best thing about the program. In addition to Miss Rich, the program's cast included: Florence Baker, Gale Gordon, Gladys Gwynne, John Lake, Jane Morgan, Larry Nunn and Anne Stone (15 min., Monday-through-Friday, Network, Mid-1930s).

12440 **Glover, Al.** Banjoist (WMAK, Buffalo, NY, 1928).

12441 **Glover, Alice A.** Pianist Glover accompanied the WBZ String Quartet (WBZ, Springfield, MA, 1926).

12442 **Glover, Herbert B.** Announcer Glover was sometimes designated as "ATN" (WJZ, New York, NY and WJY, New York, NY, 1925).

12443 **Glover, Virginia.** Pianist (WEAF, New York, NY, 1924).

12444 **Glover, Willard.** DJ (*Request Express*, WMBS, Uniontown, PA, 1947).

12445 **Glover, (Professor) William L.** Professor Glover was the director of the Troy, New York, Vocal Society (WHAZ, Troy, NY, 1926).

12446 **Glover Watson Old Time Dance Orchestra.** Old fashioned dance band (WJR, Detroit, MI, 1926).

12447 **Gloyne, Richard Featherstone.** Newscaster (KFOR, Lincoln, NE, 1937).

12448 **Glucksman, Erwin.** Leader (*Erwin Glucksman Orchestra*, instr. mus. prg., WBEN, Buffalo, NY, 1937).

12449 **Gluriani, Orlando.** Tenor (KFWM, Oakland, CA, 1927).

12450 **Gluskin, Lud.** Leader (*Lud Gluskin Orchestra*, instr. mus. prg., CBS, 1935–1936; KFEQ, St. Joseph, MO, 1942). Gluskin's band was featured on many network programs.

12451 **Glynn [Glyn], Eleanor.** Pianist (WRC, Washington, DC, 1923–1924).

12452 **Glynn, Jack.** DJ (*Coffee Club*, KIUL, Garden City, KS, 1947).

12453 ***(The) G-Men* (aka *Gangbusters*).** Phillips H. Lord produced and wrote of the dramatic adventure series that glorified the adventures of Federal Bureau of Investigation agents. It was first broadcast July 20, 1935, when it dramatized the death of John Dillinger. The series was supposedly based on the official files of the FBI. The program was sponsored by the Chevrolet Motor Car Company (30 min., Saturday, 9:00–9:30 P.M., NBC-Red, 1935). Eventually, the series became *Gangbusters*. *See* ***Gangbusters***.

12454 ***Go for the House.*** What made *Go For the House* different from the many other radio quiz shows on the air was its prize. The lucky husband-and-wife team who answered all the necessary questions won a six-room house and lot. John Reed King was the MC, George Benninger the organist and Doug Browning the announcer (30 min., Wednesday, 9:30–10:00 P.M., ABC, 1948).

12455 ***Goat Island Goats.*** The zany variety program featured Bellwether Goat, Jack L. Everson; Chinese Goat, William J. Seroy; Japanese Goat, Samuel Wachsman; Swedish Goat, Frank Olson; African Goat, Charley "Rastus" Faust; Contralto Goat, Marguerite Vogel; Tenor Goat, Ernest Grey; Baritone Nanny Goat, Gertrude Tracy; and the miscellaneous goats, Lois Cullen and Adele Steinbeck. The program was broadcast by KTAB (Oakland, CA) in 1926–1927.

12456 **Gobber-Tripplett Orchestra.** Popular local band (WHAS, Louisville, KY, 1923).

12457 **Gobbi, Caterina.** Dramatic soprano (WEAF, New York, NY, 1925).

12458 **Gober, Jim.** DJ (*Rhythm Roundup*, KNOW, Austin, TX, 1947). Sportscaster (KOBE, Las Cruces, NM, 1956).

12459 **Goble, (Mrs.) John T.** Soprano (WHO, Des Moines, IA, 1925).

12460 **Godberry, Robert.** Newscaster (KFH, Wichita, KS, 1948).

12461 **Goddard, Betty.** COM-HE (WISR, Butler, PA, 1951).

12462 **Goddard, Don.** Newscaster (NBC, 1940–1941; WEAF, New York, NY, 1942; NBC, New York, NY, 1945; WMCA, New York, NY, 1946; WINS, New York, NY, 1947–1948).

12463 **Goderson, Mae M.** Pianist (WHN, New York, NY, 1925).

12464 **Goderson, Raymond.** Newscaster (KUSD, Vermillion, SD, 1945).

12465 **Godetz, Tony.** Zither player (KYW, Chicago, IL,1922).

12466 **Godfred, Arthur Morton.** Announcer (NBC, 1931).

12467 **Godfrey, Arthur.** Singer, musician and MC Godfrey was born August 31, 1903. Godfrey began his radio career in 1929 on an amateur show (WFBR, Baltimore, MD). He found immediate listener approval and soon gained national popularity with his CBS network *Arthur Godfrey Show*. *See* ***The Arthur Godfrey Show***.

12468 **Godfrey, Marty.** COM-HE (KYME, Boise, ID, 1956).

12469 **Godfrey, Merele.** DJ (*Sweet and Lovely*, WDOB, Jackson, MS, 1954).

12470 **Godman, Carolyn.** COM-HE (WMCT, Memphis, TN, 1957).

12471 ***God's Half-Hour***. Reverend John B. Andrews conducted the religious program sponsored by the John Brown Schools (KUOA, Fayetteville, AR, 1933).

12472 **Godt, Gene.** Newscaster (WHO, Des Moines, IA, 1940–1942, 1946).

12473 **Godwin, Al W.** Sportscaster (WWL, New Orleans, LA, 1940–1941; KRLD, Dallas, TX, 1942; WHN, New York, NY, 1944; *Spotlight on Sports*, WNDR, Syracuse, NY, 1947).

12474 **Godwin, Cyril.** Violinist (KFWB, Hollywood, CA and KELW, Burbank, CA, 1928).

12475 **Godwin, Earl.** Newscaster (WMAL, Washington, DC, and WRC, Washington, DC, 1938; WRC, 1939; NBC, 1940–1941; *Watch the World Go By*, NBC, 1942; NBC-Blue, 1944–1945; WMAL and ABC, 1945–1948). Godwin's conservative *Watch the World Go By* program was sponsored by the Ford Motor Company. His customary sign-off phrase was, "God bless you one and all."

12476 **Goeb, Paula.** COM-HE (KICO, Calexico, CA, 1956).

12477 **Goehlich, Herman.** Pianist (WLW, Cincinnati, OH, 1925).

12478 **Goerch, Carl.** Newscaster (WPTF, Raleigh, NC, 1939, 1942, 1945–1948).

12479 **Goerner, Bob.** DJ (*Curfew Club*, KWQ, San Jose, CA, 1947–1950; *Showtime*, KCBS, San Francisco, CA, 1955; *The Music Scene*, KCBS, 1960).

12480 **Goerss, Jon.** Newscaster (WJLS, Beckley, WV, 1939).

12481 **Goettsche, Nettie.** Violinist (WOW, Omaha, NE, 1927).

12482 **Goggino, (Maestro) Antonio.** Director (Hillsborough Band, WDAE, Tampa, FL, 1927).

12483 **Gohmann, Margaret.** COM-HE (WLRP, New Albany, NY, 1951).

12484 **Goke, Frances.** COM-HE (WSWW, Platteville, WI, 1956–1957).

12485 **Golas, Jean.** COM-HE (WICH, Norwich, CT, 1956).

12486 **Golbring, Arlette.** COM-HE (KBOM, Bismark-Mandan, ND, 1957).

12487 **Golconda Orchestra.** West Coast band (KHQ, Seattle, WA, 1929).

12488 **Gold, Bill.** Newscaster (WINX, Washington, DC, 1946).

12489 **Gold Dragon Orchestra.** Club band (WHAS, Louisville, KY, 1927).

12490 **Gold, Frances.** Singer (WGBS, New York, NY, 1928).

12491 **Gold, Lou.** Leader (Lou Gold's Wigwam Club Orchestra, WHN, New York, NY, 1924).

12492 **Gold Leaf Music Masters.** George Lipschultz directed the orchestra (KYA, San Francisco, CA, 1928).

12493 **Gold, Mara.** Pianist (WKBQ, New York, NY, 1927).

12494 ***(The) Gold Dust Twins***. Goldy and Dusty, the Gold Dust Twins, featured such songs as "Honey, I'm in Love With You," "Happy Little Moke" and "Solomon Levi" on their popular show (WEAF, New York, NY, 1925–1926). *The Gold Dust Twins* program also featured William Stoess conducting the Johnston Orchestra (WLW, Cincinnati, OH, 1927).

12495 **Gold Medal Band.** Conway King directed the popular band (WBAP, Fort Worth, TX, 1924).

12496 ***(The) Gold Medal Express***. The variety show sponsored by General Mills, the makers of Wheaties cereal, presented a talented array of performers that included a novelty orchestra, comic impersonator and many guest artists. Weekly regulars included the Victor Arden-Phil Ohman piano team and the Wheaties Trio, comprised of Joe Shuster, Johnny Tucker and Monroe Silver. Ford Bond was the announcer (30 min., 8:30–9:00 P.M., NBC-Red, 1931).

12497 ***(The) Gold Medal Fast Freight* (aka *The General Mills Fast Freight*)**. The program was announced as "a cargo of melody by the Wheaties Quartet" (30 min., Weekly, 8:00–8:30 P.M., CBS, 1930; 15 min., Wednesday, 9:00–9:15 P.M., CBS, 1931–1932). The popular Wheaties (male) Quartet was sponsored by General Mills, the makers of Wheaties, and Gold Medal flour. They were accompanied by organist Eddie Dunstedter. The Wheaties Quartet first appeared Christmas Eve, 1926, on WCCO, Minneapolis, MN. The quartet's members were Bill Elliott, William Oppenrath, Ernest Johnson and Philip C. Schmidt. Years later, Nels Swensen took the place of William Oppenrath. The group was famous for the "Wheaties Song" sung to the tune of "She's a Jazz Baby." The song that later served as a theme for the *Jack Armstrong* program began:

"Have you tried Wheaties?
They're whole wheat with all of the bran.
Won't you try Wheaties?
For wheat is the best food of man."

The program may have sometimes been listed as *The General Mills Fast Freight* program.

12498 ***(The) Gold Medal Hour***. Not really one program but a block of four different programs broadcast on different days, it contained, for example, daytime serials *Betty and Bob* and *Broadway Cinderella* broadcast each weekday, while *The General Mills (News) Program*, *The Worry Clinic*, *Hymns of All Churches* and the *Betty Crocker Cooking School* programs alternated on other days. The block of programming made its debut on June 1, 1936. *See* ***Betty and Bob***, ***The Worry Clinic*** *and* ***Hymns of All Churches***.

12499 **Gold Medal Krackers' Dance Orchestra.** Popular dance band (KFH, Wichita, KS, 1926).

12500 ***Gold Medal Minstrels***. General Mills Bisquick sponsored the show that presented old gags and songs performed by unidentified entertainers (15 min., Monday, 11:45–12:00 noon, MBS, 1935).

12501 ***Gold Medal Radio Cooking Course***. General Mills sponsored the early radio cooking school program (WGR, Buffalo, NY, 1925).

12502 ***(The) Gold Star Minstrels***. Roland Winters hosted the lively sustaining variety show that featured singers Jimmy Carroll and Betty Mulliner, comedians Happy Jim Parsons and Gee Gee James, the Gold and Silver Quartet and Ray Bloch's Orchestra. Ted Brown was the announcer (30 min., Saturday, 9:00–9:30 P.M., MBS, 1946).

12503 ***Gold Strand Crusaders***. The Merle Johnson Orchestra and vocalists Veronica Wiggins and Freddie Vettel performed on the concert music program (30 min., 10:30–11:00 P.M., NBC, 1930).

12504 ***(The) Gold Strand Group***. The Sunday afternoon music program was broadcast 1:00–2:00 P.M. and presented a studio orchestra, tenor Gwynfi Jones, saxophonist Walter Beban and soprano Barbara Blanchard (NBC-Pacific Coast Network, 1928).

12505 ***(The) Gold Strand Group***. Another version of the program featured the Gold Strand Orchestra playing both popular and semi-classical music (Weekly, NBC-Blue, 1927–1928).

12506 **Gold Strand Orchestra.** Local band (WFAA-NBC, Dallas, TX, 1929).

12507 **Goldbahn, Richard "Dick."** Vocalist (*Richard Goldbahn*, vcl. mus. prg., WFIL, Philadelphia, PA, 1935; *The Yodeling Troubadour*, vcl. mus. prg., WIP, Philadelphia, PA, 1936).

12508 **Goldberg, Gertrude.** Singer (KGFJ, Los Angeles, CA, 1929).

12509 **Goldberg, Lou.** Director (Britlings Dallas Cafeteria Orchestra, WFAA, Dallas, TX, 1923).

12510 Goldberg, M.G. Announcer (KFOY, St. Paul, MN, 1927).

12511 Goldberg, Rubin. Newscaster (WLTH, Brooklyn, NY, 1939).

12512 *(The) Goldbergs*. Originally called *The Rise of the Goldbergs*, the show grew out of Gertrude Berg's first program, *The House of Glass*, broadcast on the network in 1929 in a 15-minute daily version. Gertrude Berg, who played Mollie Goldberg, created and wrote the show. On the program, she and Jake Goldberg, played by James R. Waters, faced the normal problems of a poor Jewish family living in New York. Despite the fact that the actors spoke with heavy New York Jewish accents, the program achieved national popularity because of its realistic portrayal of human relationships. Many notable performers and actors appeared on the program. When Mme. Ernestine Schumann-Heink, for example, asked to appear on the show, Gertrude Berg wrote her in for three special appearances (Buxton and Owen, 1973, p. 98). Metropolitan opera star Jan Peerce also appeared on the show to sing on Yom Kippur and Passover.

In addition to Berg and Waters the program's cast included: Tito Aguglia, Mimi Vuolo, Artie Auerbach, Jeannette Chinley, Cecile Evans, Eddie Firestone, Jr., George Herman, Raymond Edward Johnson, Garson Kanin, Howard Merrill, Zina Provendie, Alfred Ryder (Alfred Corn), Roslyn Silber, Menasha Skulnik, Everett Sloane, Sidney Slon, Arnold Stang, Anne Teeman, Joan Tetzel, Edward Trevor, Joan Vitez, Bertha Waldon, Carrie Weller and Bruno Wick. The director was Wes McKee.

When the program returned to the air in 1949, it was the same show that currently was running on television. Although the 1949 show was not a simulcast, Friday's radio script was broadcast Monday night on the TV show. The long radio run was carried by all the major networks (NBC-Blue, MBS, CBS, 1929–1947, 1949–1950). *See* ***The House of Glass***

12513 Goldcrest Five. Saxophonist Harris Owen directed the Goldcrest Five, station KLRA's staff orchestra, featuring vocals by Mrs. Owen (Mina) Madden (KLRA, Little Rock, AR, 1927).

12514 Golde, Walter. Pianist (WEAF, New York, NY, 1926).

12515 Golden, Bob. Leader (*Bob Golden Orchestra*, instr. mus. prg., WCAU, Philadelphia, PA, 1939, 1942).

12516 Golden, Ernie. Leader (Ernie Golden and his Hotel McAlpin Orchestra, WMCA, New York, NY, 1925–26). *Variety* praised the Golden band for its "humor and musicality."

12517 Golden, Florence. Actress Golden appeared on the *Life of Mary Southern* daytime serial program.

12518 Golden, G. Evelyn. Reader (WBZ, Boston-Springfield, MA, 1924).

12519 Golden, Kenneth. "Nebraska's leading tenor" (KOIL, Council Bluffs, IA, 1929).

12520 Golden, Marie. Pianist (KNX, Los Angeles, CA, 1928).

12521 Golden, Ray. DJ (*Ray Golden Show* and *Memory Melodies*, KSTN, Stockton, CA, 1949). Sportscaster (KSTN, 1953–1956).

12522 Golden, Robert C. Golden was the violinist-director of the Wanamaker Crystal Tea Room Orchestra (WOO, Philadelphia, PA, 1924).

12523 *Golden Bars of Melody* (aka *Golden Bars of Music*). Fels Naptha Soap Company sponsored the local music show that presented songs by soprano Rhona Lloyd plus poetry and prose selections read by announcer Fred Temple (15 min., Monday, Wednesday and Friday, 10:00–10:15 A.M., WFIL, Philadelphia, PA, 1940).

12524 *(The) Golden Bird*. Nathan Provol was the owner and trainer of 16 canaries, one of whom — the Golden Bird — was the "leader." The bird chorus under the latter's "direction," whistled and tweeted their melodic way through the songs Mr. Provol played on the piano. Fittingly, the show was sponsored by the Kemper Canary Seed Company (15 min., Wednesday, 9:00–9:15 A.M., WMCA, New York, NY, 1934).

12525 *(The) Golden Blossom Honey Orchestra*. Instr. mus. prg., (15 min., Saturday, 7:15–7:30 P.M., CBS, 1931).

12526 *(The) Golden Blossom Revue*. J.A. Paton Company, makers of Golden Blossom Honey, presented tenor Fred Hufsmith and contralto Julie Pursell with Harold Levey's Orchestra on the entertaining music show. Jimmy Wallington was the announcer (60 min., Sunday, 1:30–2:30 P.M., NBC-Blue, 1933).

12527 *(The) Golden Canary*. Just-Rite Company Pet Food sponsored the singing canary, who would perform on his owner's signal (WIP, Philadelphia, PA, 1932).

12528 *(The) Golden Crown Quartet*. The Black gospel quartet broadcast regularly on Hampton Roads, VA, radio in 1928.

12529 Golden Echo Quartet. Singing group specializing in spirituals (WSM, Nashville, TN, 1926).

12530 Golden Gate Amphions. Frank Stetanik directed the club orchestra (KYA, San Francisco, CA, 1927; *Golden Gate Ampions Goldcoasters Orchestra*, instr. mus. prg., WGN, Chicago, IL, 1935).

12531 Golden Gate Quartet. Male vocal group (*Golden Gate Quartet*, vcl. mus. prg., WJR, Detroit, MI and WCKY, Cincinnati, OH, 1942). The popular Black vocal group first broadcast their own regular program on WIS (Columbia, SC) in 1942, before attaining national popularity by appearing on many network programs.

12532 Golden Gate Syncopators. Popular Virginia band (WRVA, Richmond, VA, 1926).

12533 *Golden Gems*. Contralto Elsie Baker and baritone Theodore Webb sang with Hugo Mariani's Orchestra on the music program. Alwyn E.W. Bach was the announcer (30 min., Thursday, 8:00–8:30 P.M., NBC-Blue, 1930). Contemporary records indicate that the program was also broadcast at a later time during the same year (30 min., Tuesday, 10:30–11:00 P.M., NBC-Blue, 1930).

12534 *Golden Legends*. The dramatic program was hosted by playwright-actor-producer Ted Maxwell. In 1928, Maxwell dramatized Longfellow's poem "Hiawatha" over the NBC-Pacific Coast Network. The program's musical interludes were provided by the National Concert Orchestra (NBC-Pacific Coast Network, 1928).

12535 *(The) Golden Pheasant Orchestra*. Instr. mus. prg. (NBC, 1933).

12536 *(The) Golden State Blue Monday Jamboree*. The early variety show contained a little something for everyone. Among the featured performers were Harry "Mac" McClintock and his Haywire Orchestra; the comic-singing team of Al and Cal Pearce; singer Juanita Tennyson; tenor Robert Olsen; and contralto Hazel Warner — "The Sweetest Voice on the Air." The orchestra was conducted by Meredith Willson, musical director of KFRC, who formerly was solo flutist with the New York Philharmonic Orchestra.

Some comedians and the roles they played on the show were Bill Wright (Professor Hamburg), Tommy Monroe (Lem the Scowler) and Arnold McGuire (Lafe the Thinker). After Harrison Holliway became the manager of the Don Lee Network station, he continued to announce the show (KFRC, San Francisco, CA, 1930).

12537 *Golden West Cowboys*. CW mus. prg. by otherwise unidentified CW performers (WSM, Nashville, TN, 1936–1939).

12538 *(The) Golden West Girl and her Orchestra*. The traveling CW music group from Portland's KGW was broadcast on both KFOA (Seattle, WA) and KHQ (Spokane, WA) in 1928.

12539 Goldenberg, H.E. Announcer (WHB, Kansas City, MO, 1928).

12540 *(The) Goldenrod Revue*. Goldenrod Beer sponsored the variety show that emphasized music. Comedian Julius Tannen hosted the show that featured Phil Spitalny's Orchestra, singer Ethel Pastor, a male vocalist, the Goldenrod Singers (a mixed chorus), and such guest performers as contralto Marjorie Logan. Harry Von Zell was the announcer (30 min., Friday, 8:30–9:00 P.M., CBS, 1933).

12541 Golder, Harry. Newscaster (WXYZ, Detroit, MI, 1937–1941). Sportscaster (WXYZ, 1940).

12542 Goldermann, Robert. DJ (*Your DJ RG*, WFAU, Augusta, ME, 1949).

12543 Goldfarb, Ben. Leader (Ben Goldfarb and his Bluebird Orchestra, WOR, Newark, NJ, 1925).

12544 Goldfeather, Rose. Pianist (WEAF, New York, NY, 1925).

12545 Goldkette, Jean. Goldkette was a busy band leader (Jean Goldkette Orchestra, WWJ, Detroit, MI, 1924; Jean Goldkette's Breeze Blowers, WCX, Detroit, MI, 1926; Goldkette Ensemble, WCX, 1926; Jean Goldkette's Petite Symphony Orchestra, WJR, Detroit, MI, 1926; Jean Goldkette's Serenaders, WJR, 1926; Jean Goldkette's Victor Recording Orchestra, WJR, 1926; Pla-Mor Ballroom Orchestra, WDAF, Kansas City, MO, 1928). In 1929, the Goldkette band appeared on programs sponsored by two companies, Mallory Hats and Studebaker Motors. The band also appeared on another program (*Jean Goldkette Orchestra*, instr. mus. prg., 30 min., Saturday, 9:00–9:30 P.M., MBS, 1945).

12546 **Goldman Band (aka the Edwin Franco Goldman Band).** Led by the famous bandsman, Edwin Franko Goldman, the band appeared on the first *Cities Service Program* broadcast on February 18, 1927. In the same year it appeared on the *General Motors Family Party* (NBC, 1927; *Pure Oil Company Program,* NBC-Red, New York, NY, 1929; *The Goldman Band Concert*, 45 min., Saturday, 9:30–10:15 P.M., NBC-Blue, 1934). The band was a great favorite among listeners for many years on NBC's later broadcasts of the *Goldman Band Concert* programs. The annual radio (park) summer concert series was a gift to New York City by the Daniel Guggenheim Foundation (Tuesday and Thursday, 7:30–8:00 P.M., NBC-Blue, 1935–1936 and Saturday, 6:30–7:00 P.M., NBC-Blue, 1935–1936). The series of occasionally broadcast open air concerts from New York City's Central Park Promenade were first offered in 1921 by WEAF.

12547 **Goldman, Leon.** Violinist (WAHG, Richmond Hill, NY, 1926; *Leon Goldman*, instr. mus. prg., CBS, 1935; WABC, New York, NY, 1937; *Leon Goldman Orchestra*, instr. mus. prg., CBS, 1938).

12548 **Goldman, Meyer.** Leader (*Meyer Goldman Orchestra*, instr. mus. prg., WFBR, Baltimore, MD, 1935).

12549 **Goldman, Queenie.** Pianist (WAHG, New York, NY, 1925).

12550 **Goldosi Trio.** Music group consisting of violin, piano and cello (WBZ , Boston-Springfield, MA, 1926).

12551 **Goldsborough, Murray.** Sportscaster (WFMD, Frederick, MD, 1945).

12552 **Goldsborough, Winfred Lee.** Soprano (WDAF, Kansas City, MO, 1925).

12553 **Goldschein, (Mrs.) H.H.** Soprano (WSM, Nashville, TN, 1928).

12554 **Goldsmith, Amy.** Eighteen-year-old lyric coloratura soprano Goldsmith sang on the *Atwater Kent Hour* (NBC, 1928–1929).

12555 **Goldsmith, Ethel.** Actor (WLW, Cincinnati, OH, 1926).

12556 **Goldsmith, Lee.** Newscaster (KSAN, San Francisco, CA, 1939).

12557 **Goldstein, (Dr.) A.** Talked on care of the eyes (KDKA, Pittsburgh, PA, 1923).

12558 **Goldstein, Jack.** Pianist-accordionist Goldstein frequently appeared on the *Saturday Midnight Program* (WAHG, New York, NY, 1926).

12559 **Goldstein, Sam.** Tenor (KYW, Chicago, IL, 1924).

12560 **Goldtrap, George.** DJ (*Morning Melodies*, KWNA, Winnemucca, NV, 1960).

12561 **Goldwaithe, Chandler.** Leader (*Chandler Goldwaithe Orchestra*, instr. mus. prg., NBC, 1935; *Chandler Goldwaithe's Ensemble*, instr. mus. prg., NBC, 1935).

12562 **Goldsworthy, John.** Newscaster (WAIT, Chicago, IL, 1945).

12563 **Goldwater, Antoinette [Antonette].** Reader (WEAF, New York, NY, 1924).

12564 **Goldwater, Lon.** Leader (Lon Goldwater Orchestra, KFQZ, Hollywood, CA, 1927).

12565 ***Golf Lessons.*** Joe Novak broadcast radio golf lessons (KGO, Oakland, CA, 1925).

12566 ***(The) Golf School of the Air.*** Dick Walsh conducted the sustaining series of golfing instruction programs (15 min., Weekly, WBRY, Waterbury, CT, 1938).

12567 **Golightly, W. Grover, Jr.** Sportscaster (WSPA, Spartanburg, SC, 1945–1946). Newscaster (WSPA, 1948).

12568 **Golub, Marie.** Violinist (*Marie Golub*, instr. mus. prg., KSD, St. Louis, MO, 1936).

12569 **Goluboff, Sidney.** Newscaster (WELI, New Haven, CT, 1938).

12570 **Gomo, (Professor) Gracinto.** Singer (WLW, Cincinnati, OH, 1922).

12571 **Gomon, Ed.** DJ (*Supper Serenade*, WHMA, Anniston, AL, 1947).

12572 **Gompers, Mabel.** Soprano (WHN, New York, NY, 1925).

12573 **Gomph, Martha.** Harpist (WGR, Buffalo, NY, 1924).

12574 **Gonce, Chet L.** Newscaster (KNEW, Hobbs, NM, 1942).

12575 ***(The) Gondoliers.*** The Gondoliers were the Stoneberger brothers, Manon and Clyde, a CW music team that played the mandolin and guitar (WJSV, Mount Vernon Hills, VA, 1931).

12576 ***(The) Gondoliers.*** Vcl. mus. prg., by an otherwise unidentified vocal group (WXYZ, Detroit, MI, 1935).

12577 **Gonella, John.** Newscaster (WPTR, Albany, NY, 1948).

12578 **Gonnella, Eva.** Soprano (KXA, Seattle, WA, 1928).

12579 **Gonzales [Gonzalez], Aaron "Chief."** Leader (Chief Gonzales Texas Hotel Orchestra, WBAP, San Antonio, TX, 1926; Chief Gonzales and his Arabian Room Orchestra, KOA, Denver, CO, 1927–1928; Chief Gonzales and his Barcelonians Orchestra playing from the El Patio Ballroom, Lakeside Park, Denver, CO, KOA, 1927; Aaron Gonzales Orchestra, instr. mus. prg., KFEL, Denver, CO, 1934). Pianist (KFI, Los Angeles, CA, 1929).

12580 **Gonzales, Ed.** DJ (*Clock Watchers Society*, WCMB, Lemoyne, PA, 1949; *Big Rig Serenade*, WCMB, Harrisburg, PA, 1952).

12581 **Gonzales, Napoleon "Nap."** Newscaster (KVSF, Santa Fe, NM, 1945). DJ (*Santa Fe Hour*, KVSF, 1947).

12582 **Gonzalez, Jean.** COM-HE (KTRI, Sioux City, IA, 1949).

12583 **Gonzalez, Jose T.** DJ (KCCT, Corpus Christi, TX, 1955–1957).

12584 **Gonzelman, Marie.** Organist (*Marie Gonzelman*, inst. mus. prg., KFBI, Abilene, KS., 1936).

12585 **Goo Chong, Peter [Peter Chong].** Actor-comedian Chong was born December 2, 1898. His first radio appearance was on the *Collier's Radio Hour* (NBC, 1929).

12586 **Good, Dolly and Millie Good (aka The Girls of the Golden West).** The Good Sisters were a popular CW singing team who began singing on station WLS (Chicago, IL,1933). They appeared on several of that station's shows, including the *National Barn Dance*. Eventually, they moved to Cincinnati radio in 1949. *See* ***The Girls of the Golden West***.

12587 **Good, Gene, Jr.** DJ (*Good Wanderin'*, KOCO, Salem, OR, 1949). Sportscaster (*Good Reports on Sports*, KOCO, 1951).

12588 **Good, Harry G.** Newscaster (WOSU, Columbus, OH, 1945).

12589 ***Good as Gold.*** Organist William Meeder provided a weekly concert of organ music. One of his typical programs included: "Dragon Flies" by Gillette; "Ave Maria" by Bach-Gounod; and "Swan Song" by Wagner (30 min., Sunday, 7:00–7:30 A.M., NBC, 1935).

12590 ***Good Housekeeping Studio.*** Victoria Williamson discussed interior decoration topics on the informative program for women (NBC-Blue, New York, NY, 1928).

12591 ***Good Morning, Neighbors.*** Tom Breneman hosted the local program for housewives. Elma Latta Hackett contributed recipes and household hints (15 min., Tuesday, 10:15–10:30 P.M. KFRC, San Francisco, CA, 1936).

12592 ***Good Neighbor Time.*** Cedric Adams, a great local favorite, hosted this show that combined farm information, music and news. Singers Bob DeHaven and the Red River Valley Boys sang with Wally Olson's Orchestra. Farm information was supplied by WCCO's Farm Editor, Maynard Speere (45 min., Monday through Friday, 12:00–12:45 P.M., WCCO, Minneapolis–St. Paul, MN, 1954).

12593 ***Good News.*** Pittsburgh Paints sponsored the transcribed music show featuring Kay Costello, Harold Vanderberg, Paul Robinson, Dick Keith, Frances Nevin, James Landry, the Southern Singers and the Cosmopolitan Singers. Fred Graham was the program's announcer (15 min., Transcribed, Various Stations, 1930s).

12594 ***(The) Good Will Court.*** A.L. Alexander conducted the unique program that provided legal advice for a variety of legal and personal problems. When the sustaining program began broadcasting locally in 1935, *Billboard* called it one of the most unusual and interesting shows on the air (45 min., Sunday, 9:45–10:30 P.M., WMCA, New York, NY, 1935). With Chase and Sanborn as sponsor the following year, the show ran into legal problems of its own. After only two months of network exposure, the New York State Supreme Court barred lawyers and judges from appearing on the program. Chase and Sanborn then dropped its sponsorship and the program went off the air. A.L. Alexander later (1943) returned to network radio with the *A.L. Alexander's Mediation Board. See* ***A.L. Alexander's Mediation Board***.

12595 **Goodale, Esther.** Newscaster (WXYZ, Detroit, MI, 1939).

12596 **Goodall, Ulna.** Newscaster (WHP, Harrisburg, PA, 1942).

12597 Goodding, Ken. Sportscaster (*Reports from the World of Sports*, KVAK, Atchison, KS, 1947; *Sports Parade*, KRES, St. Joseph, MO, 1948–1949).

12598 Goode, Agatha. Soprano (WOV, New York, NY, 1932).

12599 Goode, Nancy. COM-HE (KFRM, Kansas City, MO, 1951; KMBC, Kansas City, MO, 1951).

12600 Goode, Michael J. Newscaster (WELI, New Haven, CT, 1938–1942, 1945; *The Political Scene*, WNHC, New Haven, CT, 1945–1947; *People's Lobby*, WNHC, 1948).

12601 Goode, Richard. Newscaster (WRDW, Augusta, GA, 1942).

12602 Goodelle, Niela [Nina]. The former singing star of the *Ziegfeld Follies* appeared on her own program (*Niela Goodelle*, vcl. mus. prg.,15 min., Sunday, 7:45–8:00 P.M., CST, NBC-Blue, 1935–1936).

12603 Goodfellow, Helen. Pianist (KFWM, Oakland, CA, 1926).

12604 Goodfellow, Johnny. DJ (WIRE, Indianapolis, IN, 1960).

12605 Goodhart, Al. Pianist (WMCA, New York, NY, 1925).

12606 Goodheart, Myrtle. Blues singer (WBAP, Fort Worth, TX, 1928).

12607 Goodin, Del. Newscaster (KSRO, Santa Rosa, CA, 1941).

12608 Goodkin, Alice. Actress Goodkin was a cast member of the daytime serials *Romance of Helen Trent*, *Bright Horizon* and *Dan Harding's Wife*.

12609 Goodman, Benny. Leader (*Benny Goodman Orchestra*, instr. mus. prg., NBC, 1934–1936; CBS, 1938–1939; WGN, Chicago, IL, 1942). The Goodman band was one of the best orchestras of the "Big Band Swing Era." The band became nationally known for its numerous radio appearances, beginning with the *Let's Dance* programs of 1935 on NBC. After many remote broadcasts, the band began its second sponsored program, *The Elgin Revue*, for the Elgin Watch Company in March 1936. Following appearances on the *Hollywood Hotel* program and the band's own *Camel Caravan* programs (CBS, 1937–1938), the Goodman group broadcast a popular series of programs originating from New York's Manhattan Room (CBS, 1937).

The band's radio and recording personnel during this time included: Benny Goodman, clr.; Harry James, Gene Goodman, Charles Griffin, t.; Vernon Brown, tb; Hymie Schertzer, George Koenig, as.; Art Rollini, Vido Musso, ts.; Jess Stacy, p.; Allan Reuss, g.; Harry Goodman, sb.; and Gene Krupa, d.

12610 Goodman, Betty. COM-HE (WTAO, Boston, MA, 1955).

12611 Goodman, Dave. DJ (*Fun Time*, WFUN, Huntsville, AL, 1947; *Humor Club*, KANE, New Iberia, LA, 1949).

12612 Goodman, Frank. DJ (*Evening Music*, KSFE, Needles, CA, 1960).

12613 Goodman, Genevieve. Pianist (WLW, Cincinnati, OH, 1923–1925).

12614 Goodman, Hal. Leader (*Hal Goodman Orchestra*, instr. mus. prg., WTAM, Cleveland, OH, 1935–1937).

12615 Goodman, Harold. Leader (*Harold Goodman's Tennessee Valley Boys*, CW mus. prg., 1939).

12616 Goodman, Henry. Newscaster (KMBC, Kansas City, MO, 1945).

12617 Goodman, Herald. Singer-comedian-MC Goodman appeared on the *Yeast Foamers* program (NBC, 1929) and the *Montgomery Ward Program (*NBC, 1929–1930).

12618 Goodman, Juanita. COM-HE (KICA, Clovis, NM, 1951–1954).

12619 Goodman, Lawrence. Pianist (WSM , Nashville, TN, 1928; *Pianologues*, instr. mus. prg., WSM, 1938).

12620 Goodman, Mischa. Violinist (WGBS, New York, NY, WOR, Newark, NJ; WNYC, New York, NY and WEAF, New York, NY, 1925).

12621 Goodman, Morris. Violinist (WEAF, New York, NY, 1924).

12622 Goodman, Ruth M. COM-HE (WTOC, Savannah, GA, 1954–1960).

12623 Goodman, Sam. DJ (*Yawn Patrol*, WCOM, Parkersburg, WV, 1949).

12624 Goodman, Sidney. Sportscaster Goodman broadcast sports news and football play-by-play (KTBR, Portland, OR, 1928).

12625 Goodman, Zeta. Pianist (KGO, Oakland, CA, 1926).

12626 Goodmurphy, Alice. Pianist (KPO, San Francisco, CA, 1925).

12627 Goodney, John. Violinist (WJAZ, Chicago, IL, 1923).

12628 Goodnight, Al. DJ (KCBD, Lubbock, TX, 1957).

12629 Goodnight, Clyde. Sportscaster (*Pigskin Parade*, KUBA, Yuba City, CA, 1949).

12630 Goodnight, Jeanie. COM-HE (KDMS, El Dorado, AR, 1957).

12631 Goodnough, Helen. COM-HE (WHDL, Olean, NY, 1955).

12632 Goodrich, Bill. Pianist-organist (15 min., Weekdays, 8:45–9:00 A.M., KOIL, Council Bluffs, IA, 1928). Goodrich broadcast a request music program weekdays sponsored by Black and White Grocery Stores.

12633 Goodrich, Bill. Sportscaster (*Let's Look at Sports*, WRBC, Jackson, MS, 1947–1948; sports play-by-play, WRBC, 1949; *Tops in Sports*, WSLI, Jackson, MS, 1952; WSPA, Spartanburg, SC, 1953; *Sports World*, WORD, Spartanburg, SC, 1955; *Looking at Sports*, WLBT, Jackson, MS, 1960).

12634 Goodrich, Nancy. COM-HE (WCHV, Charlottesville, VA, 1951).

12635 Goodrich, Roger. Newscaster (WOLF, Syracuse, NY, 1940).

12636 *(The) Goodrich Zippers*. The Goodrich Tire and Rubber Company sponsored this hour long musical variety program (60 min., Weekly, NBC-Red, 1926).

12637 Goodsell, B.M. Violinist (KSD, St. Louis, MO, 1923).

12638 Goodson, Mark. Newscaster (KFRC, San Francisco, CA, 1939).

12639 Goodstein, Arthur. Blues singer (KHJ, Los Angeles, CA, 1926).

12640 Goodwin, Barbara. COM-HE (WMAG, Forest, MS, 1957).

12641 Goodwin, Betty. Fashion editor (NBC, 1930s). The first fashion editor for the NBC network, Goodwin was succeeded by Amelia Umnitz.

12642 Goodwin, (Mrs.) Boyd. Violinist (KTHS, Hot Springs National Park, AR, 1927).

12643 Goodwin, Dorothy. Book reviewer (KMOX, St. Louis, MO, 1936).

12644 Goodwin, Gretchen. COM-HE (WHKK, Akron, OH, 1949).

12645 Goodwin, Hal. Newscaster (WHAI, Greenfield, MA, 1938–1940). Sportscaster (WHAI, 1940). DJ (KRLA, Los Angeles, CA, 1959).

12646 Goodwin, Harry D. Newscaster (WBZ-WBZA, Boston-Springfield, MA, 1938–1939).

12647 Goodwin, Hugo Philler. Organist (WCCO, Minneapolis–St. Paul, MN, 1925–1928).

12648 Goodwin, Jerry. Pianist (WMAK, Buffalo, NY, 1928).

12649 Goodwin, John Paul. Newscaster (KPRC, Houston, TX, 1937).

12650 Goodwin, Leroy. Tenor (WNAC, Boston, MA, 1923).

12651 Goodwin, Sidney L. Sportscaster (KTBR, Portland, OR, 1927).

12652 *(The) Goodyear Program*. Goodyear Tire and Rubber Company sponsored this fine music program starring soprano Grace Moore, the Revelers Quartet — known here as the Goodyear Quartet (James Melton, Lewis James, Wilfred Glenn and Phil Dewey), Victor Young's Orchestra and various guest performers (30 min., Wednesday, NBC-Red, 1932). The following year the Arthur Pryor Concert Orchestra and John Philip Sousa's band were also presented on the program.

12653 Goodyear Silvertown Cord Orchestra. Popular commercial orchestra directed by Joseph Knecht (WEAF, New York, NY, 1925).

12654 *(The) Goofy Birds Frolic*. One of the many zany variety shows that was broadcast during the 1920s (150 min., Sunday, 10:00 P.M. to Monday 12:30 A.M., KJR, Seattle, WA, 1927).

12655 Goosby, Bill. DJ (KDEN, Denver, CO, 1956).

12656 *(The) Goose Creek Parson* (aka *The Country Church of Hollywood*). The dramatic serial with an inspirational, if not outright religious emphasis, told the story of Josiah Hopkins, an ordained minister and Army Chaplain, who displayed his simple philosophy and showmanship. On a typical program, the Parson took a buggy ride with Old Dan, his horse, down a country road where he swapped talk with the people he met. A trademark of the rural serial drama was Old Dan's hoof beats as he pulled Parson Josiah Hopkins' buckboard (15 min., Monday through Thursday, 5:30–5:45 P.M. and Sunday, 5:15–5:30 P.M., CBS, 1936). The program's cast included Reverend W.B. Hogg and Mrs. Hogg as the Reverend and Mrs. Josiah Hopkins. They were assisted by: Mary Hogg Michael, Elvia Allman, Tom Baxter, Leonard Harlan, Robert Gordon,

Thural A. Rosencraft, John F. Knox and Rudolf Atwood. A male quartet and a women's choir were also regular cast members. The announcer was Paul Rickenbacker. The show was sponsored by Super-Suds Laundry Soap. A later version of the program appeared on Pacific Coast radio (15 min., Monday, Wednesday and Friday, 7:30–7:45 P.M., KNX, Los Angeles, CA, 1940).

12657 **Gootenberg, Phil.** Environmentalist who spoke on wild life and their survival (WMCA, New York, NY, 1939).

12658 **Gorden [Garden], Amanda.** Reader (KFSG, Los Angeles, CA, 1925).

12659 **Gordon, Alma Frances.** Contralto (KFI, Los Angeles, CA, 1926–1927).

12660 **Gordon, Anilee.** COM-HE (KIAS, Las Vegas, NV, 1951).

12661 **Gordon, Anna S.** Violinist (WIP, Philadelphia, PA, 1924; KFI, Los Angeles, CA, 1925).

12662 **Gordon, Bertie.** Soprano (WGES, Oak Park, IL, 1925).

12663 **Gordon, Bill.** Newscaster (WAIR, Winston-Salem, NC, 1940).

12664 **Gordon, Bill.** DJ (*1340 Club*, WHHM, Memphis, TN, 1947; WHBQ, Memphis, TN, 1948).

12665 **Gordon, Bruce.** Vocalist (*Bruce Gordon*, vcl. mus. prg., KSD, St. Louis, MO, 1936–1937).

12666 **Gordon, Childe.** Violinist (WBBM, Chicago, IL, 1926).

12667 **Gordon, Darline.** COM-HE (KROS, Clinton, IA, 1949).

12668 **Gordon, Dorothy.** Famous producer-writer of children's programming, Gordon also conducted her own programs (*Dorothy Gordon's Children's Corner*, CBS, 1937). See **Pioneer Women Broadcasters.**

12669 **Gordon, (Mrs.) Drayton H.** COM-HE (WFTR, Front Royal, VA, 1954).

12670 **Gordon, (Professor) E.B.** In the winter of 1921–1922, Professor Gordon began experimentation with broadcasts of music appreciation courses on 9XM, experimental station of the University of Wisconsin. His later experimental efforts were attempted during the *Wisconsin School of the Air's Journey* segments of the *Music Land* program broadcast in the 1940s.

12671 **Gordon, Elsie Mae.** Monologist and actress who played Maybelle on *Showbelle* (CBS, 1931). She also appeared on the *Valiant Lady* daytime serial.

12672 **Gordon, Frank.** Leader (*Frank Gordon Orchestra*, instr. mus. prg., WCCO, Minneapolis–St. Paul, MN, 1936–1937).

12673 **Gordon, Fred.** Newscaster (WIRE, Indianapolis, IN, 1946).

12674 **Gordon, Georgene.** Contralto (*Georgene Gordon*, vcl. mus. prg., WOR, Newark, NJ, 1935).

12675 **Gordon, Gloria.** Actress Gordon was a cast member of the *Dr. Paul* daytime serial.

12676 **Gordon, Gray.** Leader (*Gray Gordon Orchestra*, instr. mus. prg, WLW, Cincinnati, OH, 1936; NBC, 1939).

12677 **Gordon, Hal (Harold L. Hollinsworth).** Tenor Gordon was born October 20, 1906. His extensive singing career on radio began on KFAB (Lincoln, NE) in 1928, when he was a member of a college quartet during his freshman year at the University of Nebraska.

12678 **Gordon, Herb.** Leader (*Herb Gordon Orchestra*, instr. mus. prg., WFBL, Syracuse, NY, 1942).

12679 **Gordon, (Reverend) I.H.** DJ (WLOK, Memphis, TN, 1957).

12680 **Gordon, J. "Red."** Sportscaster (KELD, El Dorado, AR, 1939; KELD, 1946–1947; *According to the Rules*, KELD, 1948; sports play-by-play, KELD, 1949).

12681 **Gordon, Jeanne.** Metropolitan Opera contralto (KPO, San Francisco, CA, 1927; WEAF, New York, NY, 1928).

12682 **Gordon, Jim.** Sportscaster (WMGM, New York, NY, 1954).

12683 **Gordon, Jimmy.** Sportscaster (WLW, Cincinnati, OH, 1936).

12684 **Gordon, Kathleen.** Singer (WOR, Newark, NJ, 1932).

12685 **Gordon, Keith.** Newscaster (*Midday News*, KXO, El Centro, CA, 1947).

12686 **Gordon, Lee.** Leader (*Lee Gordon Orchestra*, instr. mus. prg, NBC, 1935–1936; NBC, 1940; WTAM, Cleveland, OH, 1942).

12687 **Gordon, Lee.** Newscaster (KICD, Spencer, IA, 1945; *World's Pictures in Words*, KAYL, Storm Lake, IA, 1948).

12688 **Gordon, Lindy.** COM-HE (KWIN, Ashland, OR, 1956; KWIL, Albany, OR, 1957).

12689 **Gordon, Lloyd.** DJ (*Luncheon Club* and *Kiddie Korner*, WESB, Bradford, PA, 1949). Sportscaster (*Sports Special*, WESB, 1954).

12690 **Gordon, Lore.** Tenor (KFAB, Oakland, CA, 1929).

12691 **Gordon, Mace.** Operatic baritone (WIBO, Chicago, IL, 1926).

12692 **Gordon, Marion.** Soprano (WIP, Philadelphia, PA, 1925).

12693 **Gordon, Mary.** Gordon was a reader of children's stories (KFOA, Seattle, WA, 1926). She also broadcast news and information for women (*Household Hints* and *Fashion*, KFOA, 1928).

12694 **Gordon, Mary.** Actress Gordon appeared on the *Those We Love* daytime serial.

12695 **Gordon, Mimi.** COM-HE (WPRC, Lincoln, IL, 1951–1954).

12696 **Gordon, Phil.** DJ (*1280 Club*, WOV, New York, NY, 1949; *Afternoon Swing Session*, WWRL, Woodside, NY, 1949–1950).

12697 **Gordon, Philip Keyne.** Newscaster (WJW, Akron, OH, 1942).

12698 **Gordon, Sally.** COM-HE (WJLD, Bessemer, AL, 1951).

12699 **Gordon, Sarah.** Reader (KHJ, Los Angeles, CA, 1924).

12700 ***Gordon String Quartet.*** Instr. mus. prg. (WBZ-WBZA. Boston-Springfield, MA and WTIC, Hartford, CT, 1939).

12701 **Gordon, Stubby.** Leader (*Stubby Gordon Orchestra*, instr. mus. prg., NBC, 1935).

12702 **Gordon, Virginia.** Soprano (WMBD, Peoria, IL, 1935).

12703 **Gordon, W.C.** Announcer (KJR, Seattle, WA, 1927).

12704 **Gordon, (Dr.) W.D.** Scots bagpiper (KGO, Oakland, CA, 1926).

12705 **Gordon, Westell.** British lyric tenor, composer and cellist (WHN, New York, NY, 1926). Gordon also appeared on the *Major Bowes Capitol Theatre Family* program (NBC, 1929).

12706 **Gordone, Lillian.** Contralto (WGCP, Newark, NJ, 1925).

12707 **Gore, Del.** DJ (*Del Gore Show*, KYA, San Francisco, CA, 1948). Sportscaster (*Sports Desk*, KROW, Oakland, CA, 1952).

12708 **Goren, Channah Spector.** COM-HE (WEVD, New York, NY, 1951).

12709 **Goren, Oscar.** Newscaster (WEVD, New York, NY, 1944).

12710 **Gorin, Igor.** Baritone (*Igor Gorin*, vcl. mus. prg., NBC, 1934).

12711 **Gorin, Katherine.** Pianist (WDAP, Chicago, IL, 1923).

12712 **Goris, Albert (Howard R. Goris).** Goris, author of the entertaining *Uncle Wiggly* children's stories, read them on the air for young listeners (1920s-1930s).

12713 **Gorman, Al.** Pianist-leader (Al Gorman's Novelty Orchestra, WHAS, Louisville, KY, 1923). The band included Henry Miller, as.; Cliff Gorman, bj.; Homer Muth, tb.; and Hubert Elkins, d.

12714 **Gorman, Cliff.** Banjoist (WHAS, Louisville, KY, 1923).

12715 **Gorman, Johnny.** COM-HE (KVMC, Colorado City, TX, 1955).

12716 **Gorman, Lydia.** Newscaster (KFAM, St. Cloud, MN, 1938).

12717 **Gorman, Ross.** Leader (Ross Gorman Orchestra, WEEI ,Boston, MA, 1925; leader, Ross Gorman's Earl Carroll Vanities Orchestra broadcasting from the Earl Carroll Theater, WEAF, New York, NY, 1925; WGR, Buffalo, NY, 1925; *Ross Gorman Orchestra*, broadcasting from New York's Monte Carlo restaurant, WEAF, New York, NY, 1926; *Ross Gorman and his Biltmore Orchestra*, instr. mus. prg., CBS, 1932).

12718 **Gorman, Vivette.** Miss Gorman broadcast home economics talks (KYW, Chicago, IL, 1924).

12719 **Gorman, Wendy.** DJ (WIHR, Hood River, OR, 1955).

12720 **Gorner, Joseph.** Director, Venetian Room Orchestra (WJR, Detroit, MI, 1928).

12721 **Gorno, Giacinto.** Tenor Gorno sang on WLW's first broadcast. He was accompanied by his brother, Romeo Gorno, on the piano and William Morgan Knox on the violin (WLW, Cincinnati, OH, 1922).

12722 **Gorodonsky, Noy.** Leader (*Noy Gorodonsky Orchestra*, instr. mus. prg., WOR, Newark, NJ, 1935).

12723 **Gorrell, Henry.** Newscaster (NBC-Blue, 1945).

12724 **Gorst, Martha.** Pianist (WTRC, New York, NY, 1927).

12725 Gorsuch, Ken. Newscaster (KGGM, Albuquerque, MN, 1939; KFXJ, Grand Junction, CO, 1941).

12726 Gosar, Donald. COM-HE (KEYY, Provo, UT, 1957).

12727 Gosar, Donna. COM-HE (KOVO, Provo, UT, 1954; KEYY, Pocatello, ID, 1957).

12728 Gosden, Cy. DJ (WMT, Cedar Rapids, IA, 1960).

12729 Gosden and Correll. Freeman Gosden and Charles Correll, later famous as the creators of *Amos 'n' Andy,* were featured on the *Kinky Kids Parade* show (WEBH, Chicago, IL, 1926). Songs and patter were their first radio contributions. *Sam and Henry* soon followed and started them on the road to achieve spectacular success. *See* ***Sam and Henry*** *and* ***Amos 'n' Andy***.

12730 Goskin, Charles. Tenor (WHN, New York, NY, 1926).

12731 Goslin, Johnny. DJ (*Hi Jinks,* KRUL, Corvallis, OR, 1947).

12732 *(The) Gospel Lesson (German).* The foreign language program was broadcast by the Concordia Lutheran Seminary station (KFUO, St. Louis, MO, 1927).

12733 *(The) Gospel Singer.* Edward McHugh was known as "The Gospel Singer." Accompanied by organist Rosa Rio, McHugh claimed to have sang more than 3,000 gospel songs on his program (NBC-Blue, 1933–1942).

12734 *(The) Gospel Singers.* The program of religious songs was broadcast daily for 30 minutes, except Sunday when it was an hour in length. The singers included Dent Holcomb, tenor; Mrs. H.H. Johnson, soprano; Mrs. Mildred Packard, contralto; and Fred N. Hodges, bass (KMMJ, Grand Island, NE, 1930).

12735 *(The) Gospel Travelers.* "Cousin" Eugene Walton was featured with the Black gospel singing group (KWEM, West Memphis, AR, 1950s).

12736 Goss, Bailey. Sportscaster (WBAL, Baltimore, MD, 1940–1942; WBAL, 1945–1946).

12737 Goss, Frank. Newscaster (KFWB, Los Angeles, CA, 1940). Sportscaster (KFWB, 1940).

12738 Goss, Gene. DJ (*Platter Party,* KLRA, Little Rock, AR, 1948).

12739 Goss, Kay. Violinist (*Kay Goss,* instr. mus. prg., WSM, Nashville, TN, 1934).

12740 *(The) Gossip Behind the Mike.* Norsee Toothpaste sponsored the radio gossip show that purported to tell the inside story of broadcasting. After Wallace Butterfield delivered the gossip, he interviewed such radio stars as Donald Novis, who often appeared on the show (15 min., Monday, 12:30–12:45 P.M., CBS, 1935).

12741 *(The) Gothamaires.* Vcl. mus. prg. by a male quartet not otherwise identified (WXYZ, Detroit, MI, 1935).

12742 *Gotham String Quartet.* Instr. mus. prg. (MBS, 1937).

12743 Gotteig, Ruth. COM-HE (WMSC, Columbia, SC, 1957).

12744 Gotthberg, Ozelle G. COM-HE (WEPA, Ft. Payne, AL, 1960).

12745 Gottleib, Ethel. Operatic soprano (WPCH, New York, NY, 1932).

12746 Gottlieb, (Mrs.) Ralph. COM-HE (WMSC, Columbia, SC, 1956).

12747 Gottlieb, Ruth. COM-HE (WMSC, Columbia, SC, 1954–1957).

12748 Gottlieb, Richard. Newscaster (*Varner News,* WTAW, College Station, TX, 1947; *Shell Reporter,* KTHT, Houston, TX, 1948).

12749 Gottsche, Dora Boedeker. Mezzo-soprano (WBZ, Springfield, MA, 1925).

12750 Gotwald, Helen. Newscaster (*Looking Around,* WSBA, York, PA, 1948).

12751 Gotwalk, Helen Miller. COM-HE (WSBA, York, PA, 1949).

12752 Gough, Gaines. DJ (WMRA, Myrtle Beach, SC, 1949).

12753 Gough, L.B. Announcer (KFDM, Beaumont, TX, 1928).

12754 Gough, Sandy. DJ (WTTH, Port Huron, MI, 1955–1956).

12755 Gough, Walter. Leader (Walter Gough Orchestra, KGO, Oakland, CA, 1926).

12756 Gould, Alice. COM-HE (KIMN, Denver, CO, 1954).

12757 Gould, Barbara. Gould broadcast beauty talks for women (WJZ, New York, NY, 1929).

12758 Gould, Betty. Organist (*Betty Gould,* instr. mus. prg., WIP, Philadelphia, PA, 1935).

12759 Gould, Caterina. Soprano (WEAF, New York, NY, 1925).

12760 Gould, Darrell. DJ (*Adventures in Sound,* WCCC, Hartford, CT, 1960).

12761 Gould, Dick. DJ (*Who's Singing that Song,* WLOW, Norfolk, VA, 1947; *Alarm Clock Club,* WLOW, 1950).

12762 Gould, Dorothy R. COM-HE (KFMA, Davenport, IA, 1957).

12763 Gould, Jay. DJ (*11th Hour Dancetime* and *National Record Mart,* WMCK, McKeesport, PA, 1949).

12764 Gould, John. Newscaster (WLAM, Lewiston, ME, 1948).

12765 Gould, Lawrence. Singer (*Lawrence Gould,* vcl. mus. prg., WIP, Philadelphia, PA, 1935).

12766 Gould, (Mrs.) Lester L. COM-HE (WJNC, Jacksonville, NC, 1949).

12767 Gould, Lloyd. Baritone (WQJ, Chicago, IL, 1925).

12768 Gould, Mitzi. Talented actress Gould appeared on the daytime serial programs *Life Can Be Beautiful, Nona from Nowhere, Romance of Helen Trent, The Story of Bess Johnson* and *We Love and Learn.*

12769 Gould, (Master) Morton. Twelve-year-old pianist Gould played classics (WOR, Newark, NJ). He later gained prominence as conductor, arranger and composer (*Morton Gould Orchestra,* instr. mus. prg., MBS, 1934; WCAE, Pittsburgh, PA, 1935; MBS, 1937–1940).

12770 Gould, Rita. Singer Gould appeared on the *Vitality Shoes* and *Evening in Paris* programs (1932).

12771 Gould, William. DJ (*Harmony Lane,* KODL, The Dalles, OR, 1954).

12772 *Gould and Shefter.* Dual piano team (instr. mus. prg., NBC, 1935).

12773 Gould Family Orchestra. Family music group (KFON, Long Beach, CA, 1926).

12774 Goulding, P.H. Newscaster (WEEI, Boston, MA, 1942).

12775 Goulding, Phil. DJ (*Your Hits of the Week,* WMGM, New York, NY, 1955).

12776 Gouldy, Ted. DJ (*Saturday Morning Round-Up,* WBAP, Fort Worth, TX, 1947).

12777 Goulet, Philleas. Baritone (KYA, Oakland, CA, 1927).

12778 Gove, Clifford. Sportscaster (*Sports Newsreel* and *Rod and Gun Club,* WLAM, Lewiston, ME, 1949).

12779 Gover, Tim. DJ (WLBH, Mattoon, IL, 1955).

12780 Gow, George. Newscaster (WCHS, Charleston, WV, 1939; WLW, Cincinnati, OH, 1944; KPH, Wichita, KS, 1945–1948). Sportscaster (WCHS, 1939).

12781 Gowan, John. Vocalist (WTIC, Hartford, CT, 1935).

12782 Gowan, Lerlyne V. COM-HE (WDIX, Jackson, TN, 1951).

12783 Gowans, Al. Sportscaster (*Before the Kickoff* and *Football Score Roundup,* WTCN, St. Paul–Minneapolis, MN, 1939–1940).

12784 Gowdy, Curt. Sportscaster (KFBC, Cheyenne, WY, 1944; KOMA, Oklahoma City, OK, 1945–1946; *Sports by Gowdy,* KOMA, 1947; *Sports by Gowdy,* KOCY, Oklahoma City, OK, 1948; WHDH, Boston, MA, 1951; *Report on Sports,* WHDH, 1952–1960; *Football Roundup,* NBC, 1955; Boston Red Sox baseball play-by-play, WHDH, 1960).

12785 Gowen, John K., 3rd. Newscaster (WCOP, Boston, MA, 1938).

12786 "GR." Designation for announcer Gene Rouse (WOAW, Omaha, NE, 1925). *See* **Rouse, Gene.**

12787 *G.R. Kenney Company's Story Teller.* Miss Blanche Elizabeth Wade wrote and told stories for young listeners (WEAF, New York, NY, 1924).

12788 Grabau, Bill. Leader (Bill Grabau's Hotel Cosmopolitan Dance Orchestra, KOA, Denver, CO, 1929).

12789 Grabe, Earl C. Newscaster (WSPD, Toledo, OH, 1946).

12790 Grabiel, Dick. Leader (Dick Grabiel's Arkansas Travelers Orchestra, KFDV, Fayetteville, AR, 1923). The band included leader Grabiel on drums, Tommy Warner on piano, Bob Lacey and Alton Hart on saxophone, Price Dickson on banjo and trombone and trumpeter Dwight Stroupe.

12791 Grable, Marian. Grable conducted her *Helen of Hollywood* program on which she talked about stars and the movies they made. She also frequently conducted interviews with the stars in their Hollywood homes by telephone from her Dallas studio (WFAA, Dallas, TX, 1928).

12792 Grace, Dorothy. Singer (WOV, New York, NY, 1936).

12793 Grace, E.R., Jr. Newscaster (WJR, Detroit, MI, 1946).

12794 *Grace and Eddy*. Vcl. mus. prg. by an otherwise unidentified singing team (KYW, Philadelphia, PA, 1936).

12795 *Grace Hayes*. Hayes, a popular vaudeville and Broadway singing star, had her own NBC radio program in 1932. One of her listening audience's particular favorites was her rendition of "You've Got Me Between the Devil and the NBC" (NBC, New York, NY, 1932).

12796 Grace Little Symphony Orchestra. Symphonic group from the Grace Methodist Church of Dallas, Texas (WFAA, Dallas, TX, 1929).

12797 Gracey, Bill. Newscaster (KTRC, Visalia, CA, 1944).

12798 Gracey, Stuart. Baritone (*Stuart Gracey*, vcl. mus. prg., WOR, Newark, NJ, 1936).

12799 *(The) Gracie Fields Show*. England's "Our Gracie" appeared with the Keynotes and Billy Ternent's Orchestra on this pleasant transcribed music show. The MC was Bernard Braden (30 min., Transcribed, Various Stations, 1951). During the World War II years, singer Fields frequently performed on American radio networks in a variety of formats (NBC-Blue, ABC and MBS).

12800 Gracy, Willie Mae. COM-HE (KATZ, St. Louis, MO, 1957).

12801 Gradova, Gitta. Pianist (WJZ, New York, NY, 1923).

12802 Gradstein, Norma. Pianist (WJZ, New York, NY, 1924).

12803 Grady, Jack. DJ (*Ramblin' Bob*, KXOA, Sacramento, CA, 1948; *Sports Roundup*, KXOA, 1949; KYNO, Fresno, CA, 1952–1956).

12804 Grady, Jim. Sportscaster (*Bowling*, KSRO, Santa Rosa, CA, 1960).

12805 Grady, Joe. DJ (*950 Club*, WPEN, Philadelphia, PA, 1947–1954).

12806 *Grady Cantrell*. Cantrell was a popular Midwest radio personality. He patterned his sustaining show after the *Voice of Experience* program, by offering advice to listeners with personal problems (15 min., Wednesday, 7:00–7:15 A.M., KWK, St. Louis, MO and KWOS, Jefferson City, MO, 1939).

12807 Graeber, Charles F. Leader (Charles F. Graeber's Mandolin Club Orchestra, KYA, San Francisco, CA, 1928).

12808 Graeppel, Ernest. Leader (Ernest Graeppel and his Castle House Orchestra broadcasting from the Punch and Judy Theater, WHN, New York, NY, 1923–24).

12809 Graf, Mamie. COM-HE (KGYW, Vallejo, CA, 1956–1957).

12810 Graff, Johnny. Leader (*Johnny Graff Orchestra*, instr. mus. prg., WIP, Philadelphia, PA, 1938).

12811 Graff, Shirley. COM-HE (KLGN, Logan, UT, 1955).

12812 Grafton, Gloria. Soprano (*Gloria Grafton*, vcl. mus. prg., WCBM , Baltimore, MD, 1934).

12813 Grafton, Samuel. Newscaster (WOR, New York, NY, 1945).

12814 Graham, Bill. Newscaster (WDGY, Minneapolis–St. Paul, MN, 1944–1945).

12815 Graham, C.W. Announcer (WOO, Philadelphia, PA, 1924).

12816 Graham, Catherine. COM-HE (KOOL, Phoenix, AZ, 1956).

12817 Graham, Donald R. Newscaster (*The Town Crier*, KVOA, Tuscon, AZ, 1947).

12818 Graham, Dorothy. COM-HE (KFEQ, St. Joseph, MO, 1951).

12819 Graham, Evelyn. COM-HE (KBOY, Medford, OR, 1960).

12820 Graham, Frank. Graham, a New York *Sun* sports reporter, talked on baseball topics (WBAY, New York, NY, 1922). Station WBAY later became WEAF (New York, NY).

12821 Graham, Gordon. Tenor (WBZ, Boston-Springfield, MA, 1925).

12822 Graham, Gordon. Newscaster (WIBC, Indianapolis, IN, 1947).

12823 Graham, Henry W. Reader (KYW, Chicago, IL, 1924).

12824 Graham, Herb. DJ (*KFEQ Disc Derby*, KFEQ, St. Joseph, MO, 1947).

12825 Graham, Hilda. Actress Graham was featured on the *Romance of Helen Trent* daytime serial program.

12826 Graham, Howard C. Announcer (WREO, Lansing, MI, 1927).

12827 Graham, Lola. Violinist (KFAE, Pullman, WA, 1925).

12828 Graham, Lucille. COM-HE (WPAY, Portsmouth, OH, 1949).

12829 Graham, Margery. Book reviewer (WGN, Chicago, IL, 1936).

12830 Graham, Marguerite. COM-HE (KDIX, Dickinson, ND, 1951).

12831 Graham, (Mrs.) Marion. Pianist (WBZ, Boston-Springfield, MA, 1925).

12832 Graham, Mildred. Soprano (WNJ, Newark, NJ, 1929).

12833 Graham, Nettie. COM-HE (WBHP, Harrisburg, PA, 1954).

12834 Graham, Peg. COM-HE (WLCR, Torrington, CT, 1949).

12835 Graham, Ross. Bass (KTHS, Hot Springs National Park, AK, 1928; *Ross Graham*, vcl. mus. prg., NBC, 1935–1936). Graham was also sometimes identified as a baritone. Another facet of the interesting Ross career was his winning appearance in the 1931 Atwater Kent auditions and his broadcasts with *Roxy's Gang (NBC)*.

12836 Graham, Vance. Newscaster (KMPC, Los Angeles, CA, 1945–1946).

12837 Graham, Vera. Organist (WFOX, Long Beach, CA, 1930).

12838 Graham, Virginia. Singer Graham was known as the "Little Irish Crooner" (WLS, Chicago, IL, 1929).

12839 Graham, Walter. Newscaster (WMAZ, Macon, GA, 1941; WBML, Macon, GA, 1945). Sportscaster (WBML, 1945–1948; *Sports Review*, WBML, 1949–1954; WRBL, Columbus, GA, 1955–1956).

12840 Graham, Walter H. Baritone (WOAW, Omaha, NE, 1924).

12841 Graham, William. Newscaster (KOTA, Rapid City, SD, 1945).

12842 *(The) Graham-Paige Hour*. The Graham-Paige Motor Company sponsored the Detroit Symphony Orchestra conducted by Ossip Gabrilowitsch. Edgar A. Guest sometimes appeared as guest narrator on the program (Weekly, 9:30–10:30 P.M., CBS, 1931). The orchestra was occasionally conducted by Victor Kolar.

12843 Grainger, Sharon. Actress Grainger appeared on the daytime serial programs *The Guiding Light*, *Mary Marlin* aka *The Story of Mary Marlin* and *Midstream.*

12844 Gramlich, George. Tenor (KNX, Los Angeles, CA, 1928).

12845 *Gramps*. Craig McDonnell played the role of a small-town newspaper editor with a wife, played by Anne Seymour, and two children on the sustaining summer replacement for the *Dennis Day* program. The editor's troubles began when Gramps, played by Edgar Stehli, arrived to spend some time with his family. The listener usually wondered: How can Gramps possibly get into so much trouble? Joan Lazer and Edwin Bruce were also in the cast (30 min., Wednesday, 8:00–8:30 P.M., NBC, 1947).

12846 Gran, Hulda Frisk. COM-HE (KEYD, Minneapolis, MN, 1949).

12847 Granas, Mort. DJ (*Platter Parade*, WTBC, Tuscaloosa, AL, 1947).

12848 Granberry, Katherine. Soprano (WOR, Newark, NJ, 1924).

12849 *Granby's Green Acres*. Gale Gordon played the title role of John Granby on the sustaining situation comedy. As the story unfolded, Granby bought a farm to get away from his dull bank clerk's job. Unfortunately, he knew nothing whatsoever about farming, and the show's comedy situations arose from his many fumbling mistakes. The summer replacement for *The Egg and I* was the basis for the successful *Green Acres* television show that starred Eddie Albert and Eva Gabor. Joining Gordon in the radio cast were : Bea Benadaret, Louise Erickson, Parley Baer and Opie Cates, who both acted and led the orchestra (30 min., Monday, 6:30–7:00 P.M., CBS, 1950).

12850 Grand, Mitchell. Pianist (Mitchell Grand, instr. Mus. Prg., WHP, Harrisburg, PA, 1938, 1942.

12851 *Grand Central Station*. The sound of a steam locomotive rushing into New York's Grand Central Station opened the program, followed by the announcer's dramatic statement: "As a bullet seeks its target, shining rails in every part of our great country are aimed at Grand Central Station, heart of the nation's greatest city. Drawn by the magnetic force of the fantastic metropolis, day and night great trains rush toward the Hudson River, sweep down its eastern bank for 140 miles, flash briefly by the long red row of tenement houses south of 125th Street, dive with a roar into the two-and-one-half mile tunnel which burrows beneath the glitter and swank of Park Avenue and then..." The sound of steam being released from an engine was heard and the announcer loudly proclaiming with stress on each syllable,

"Grand Central Station ... crossroads of a million private lives ... gigantic stage on which are played a thousand dramas daily!"

The program was narrated by Jack Arthur and Alexander Scourby. The separate and complete dramatic episodes broadcast weekly were about life in New York City — exciting, romantic and, sometimes, funny. The cast included: Jim Ameche, Beverly Bayne, Nancy Coleman, Hume Cronyn, Mary Mason, McKay Morris and Arnold Moss. The writers were Ethel Abby, Jay Bennett, Martin Horrell, Elinor Lenz and Dena Reed. Himan Brown and Martin Horrell were the producers. The directors were Ira Ashley, Ray H. Kremer and William Rousseau. Ken Roberts and Tom Shirley were the announcers.

12852 Grand Dutchess Marie of Roumania. The Grand Dutchess discussed various aspects of manners and etiquette (CBS, 1936).

12853 *Grand Hotel*. Based on Vicki Baum's novel of the same name, the program presented a series of dramatized episodes in the lives of a hotel's guests. The sponsor was Campana's Hand Balm. The program replaced the company's *Vanity Fair* variety program. The show debuted October 1, 1933 (30 min., Sunday, 5:30–6:00 P.M., NBC-Blue, 1935). Among the cast members over the years were many talented veteran radio actors: Don Ameche, Jim Ameche, Don Briggs, Raymond Edward Johnson, Phil Lord, Barbara Luddy, Anne Seymour, Olan Soule and Betty Winkler. George Vandel was the writer and Joe Ainley the producer.

12854 *Grand Marquee*. George Stone was the announcer on the sustaining program that was an imitation of the *First Nighter* program. Jim Ameche, Olan Soule, Beryl Vaughn, Herbert Butterfield, Charles Egleston, Ray Suber and Hope Summers were in the cast. Joseph Gallichio's Orchestra supplied the music (30 min., Tuesday, 9:00–9:30 P.M., NBC-Red, 1946).

12855 *Grand Ole Opry* (Began as the *WSM Barn Dance*). From November 18, 1925 to 1926 the program was known as the *WSM Barn Dance*. It became the longest running radio program of all time — still on the air in 2007. On the first program broadcast November 28, 1925 Uncle Jimmie Thompson, a seventy-seven year old fiddler from Tennessee, was one of two musicians who performed. The other was a pianist, his niece Eva Thompson Jones. After playing for an hour without a break, Thompson was asked if he was tired. He replied that he was just getting warmed up. For several Saturday nights George Hay, the announcer-director, Uncle Jimmy Thompson and his niece were the only performers. The response from WSM (Nashville, TN) listeners was enthusiastic. An editorial writer in the Nashville *Tennessean* of December 27, 1925, reviewed the show:

> "Old tunes like old lovers are the best at least judging from the applause which the new Saturday night features at WSM receive from listeners from all parts of the country. Jazz has not completely turned the tables on such tunes as *Turkey in the Straw* and *Pop Goes the Weasel*. America may not be swinging its partners at a barndance, but it seems to have the habit of clamping on earphones and patting its feet as gaily as it ever did when the oldtime fiddlers get going."

The name of the program, the *WSM Barn Dance*, was changed to the *Grand Ole Opry* in 1926. According to a frequently repeated story, it was given its name by announcer-director George Hay in 1926. From 7:00 to 8:00 P.M. on Saturday evening, WSM carried the *Music Appreciation Hour* conducted by Dr. Walter Damrosch. After Damrosch concluded his program with a musical composition that depicted an on coming train, Hay said: "Friends, the program which just came to us was devoted to the classics. Dr. Damrosch told us that it is generally agreed that there is no place in the classics for realism. However, from here on out for the next three hours we will present nothing but realism. It will be down to earth for the earthy. In respectful contrast to Dr. Damrosch's presentation of the number which depicts the onrush of the locomotive, we will call on one of our performers, DeFord Bailey, with his harmonica to give us the country version of the "Pan American Blues." Bailey then played this country music tune that contained a section that sounded like a train. After Bailey finished, Hay returned to the microphone and said: "For the past hour, we have been listening to music taken largely from grand opera. But from now on, we will present the *Grand Ole Opry*."

George D. Hay was an important figure in the program's history. Called the "Solemn Old Judge," Hay developed and hosted the program for almost 30 years, before Grant Turner took over the announcing duties in 1944. Hay first became aware of country music shortly after World War I, when as a newspaper man he traveled to an Ozark town to cover the funeral of a war hero. While there, he heard some of the region's genuine American music. His appreciation for this music led to his development of both the *National Barn Dance* and the *Grand Ole Opry* programs.

After a successful career at Chicago's WLS, where he inaugurated the *National Barn Dance* program, Hay moved to Nashville's WSM as station manager and announcer. In 1926, soon after Uncle Jimmy Thompson's initial broadcast on the *WSM Barn Dance*, he put together the performers and format that became the *Grand Ole Opry*. Hay opened the shows with a blast on his old steam boat whistle called Huckpuckena, named for a small Mississippi town. Although he was called the Solemn Old Judge, there was a joke around the *Opry* crew that Hay was neither old, solemn, nor a judge.

Some of the earliest and greatest performers on the program were Uncle Dave Macon, DeFord Bailey and Dr. Humphrey Bate and his Possum Hunters. DeFord Bailey, a skilled harmonica player, was famous for playing "The Fox Chase," a song that simulated the sounds of a pack of hounds chasing a fox. Bailey, an African-American was the first member of his race to perform on the *Grand Ole Opry*. Dr. Humphrey Bate, leader of Dr. Humphrey Bate and his Possum Hunters string band, was a harmonica player and a busy surgeon from Tennessee. In 1924, he had appeared on WDAD, Nashville, TE. He joined the *WSM Barn Dance* on October 24, 1925 to lead the Possum Hunters, the first string band to be featured on the program. The members of Bate's band were Oscar Stone, Walter Liggett, Staley Waltron, Paris Pond, Oscar Albright, Bert Hutcherson, James Hart and Stringbean. Sisters Sarie and Sally (Mrs. Eva Wilson and Mrs. Margaret Waters), a talented singing team, should also be mentioned for they were the first female stars of the *Grand Ole Opry* when they appeared in 1925.

Uncle Dave Macon (David Harrison Macon) became the *Grand Ole Opry's* first star when he joined the *Opry* at the age of 56. Uncle Dave operated a Tennessee company, the Macon Midway Mule and Wagon Transportation Company, that carried goods between Woodbury and Murfeesboro, Tennessee before he began his professional career. Before joining the Opry, Uncle Dave had been a professional for more than eight years and a busy local entertainer for many years before that.

During his teamster years, Uncle Dave had performed at picnics and various social affairs in rural Tennessee singing and playing the banjo. He learned his songs, stories and how to play the banjo from the many vaudevillians who at various times stayed in his mother's boarding house. Uncle Dave, himself, appeared in vaudeville before coming to radio, always a great champion for and performer of American country music. "The Dixie Dewdrop Uncle Dave Macon," as he was affectionately called, was unique. He died at the age of 88, three weeks after his last appearance on the show and became the first Opry legend.

Other early bands on the *Opry* were the Gully Jumpers (guitarist-leader Paul Warmack; fiddler Charlie Arrington; Burt Hutcherson and Roy Hardison); the Fruit Jar Drinkers (leader-fiddler Grandpappy Wilkerson; guitarist Claude Lampley; mandolinist Tommy Leffew and bass fiddler H.J. Ragsdale); and the Crook Brothers Band (leader-harmonica performer Herman Crook; Mathew Crook; banjoist-singer Lewis Crook; guitarist Blythe Poteet; guitarist Bill Etters and fiddler Kirk McGee). Most of these bands were named by program director George D. Hay.

In 1928, Harry Stone was hired as a WSM announcer and associate program director to assist Hay. Eventually, Stone became the station's program director and proved himself to be a masterful promoter of both the *Grand Ole Opry* and station WSM.

Over the years the program grew and continued to gain popularity. Even the length of the show grew until it extended to four hours. WSM advertised in 1942 that the show was a "... four-hour presentation of the down-to-earth, clean headed, clean minded America that will triumph because it is America." Appearing in the August 17, 1942, issue of *Broadcasting*, the advertisement also carried the familiar patriotic flavor that so often prevailed during World War II. The program's popularity was enhanced by the talent of another great star — Roy Acuff. In 1935, Roy Acuff and the Crazy Tennesseans (leader-fiddler Acuff; guitarist Jess Easterday; bass fiddler Red Jones; Cousin Jody (James Clell Summey); blackface comic Jake Tindell and Kentucky Slim were broadcasting daily on WROL (Knoxville, TN, 1935), before coming to Nashville and getting their own show on WSM (1938). After several unsuccessful attempts, Acuff and his band, now known as Roy Acuff and the Smokey Mountain Boys, made their first *Grand Ole Opry* appearance on February 26, 1938. The *Opry's* second great star had arrived.

Like the *National Barn Dance*, the *Grand Ole Opry* eventually became a network program on NBC in 1939, sponsored by Prince Albert smoking tobacco. It continued on that network until 1957. Like the *National Barn Dance* program, the *Grand Ole Opry* also used wrap-around local programming that featured *Opry* performers both before and after the network show. They also sent groups of performers on the road to perform at schools, theaters and fairs in various northeastern and southern towns throughout the country.

Hundreds of performers appeared on the program during the many years the show was on the air from 1925 to 1960. Some of these performers in addition to those already mentioned were: Uncle Ed Poplin and the Poplin Band from Lynchburg, Tennessee (Papa Ed Poplin on fiddle, pianist A. Poplin, guitarist Jack Woods, guitarist Louise Poplin and Frances Poplin, mandolinist); blind pianist and accordion soloist Fred Shriver; Asher and Little Jimmie Sizemore, a five-year-old singer; Binkley Brothers (Gayle and Amos); fiddler Curley Fox and Ruby Owens, "Radio's Original Yodeling Cowgirl"; blue grass music pioneer Bill Monroe and his Blue Grass Boys; Pee Wee King (Julius Frank Anthony Kuczynski) and the Golden West Cowboys (Milton Estes; Curley Rhodes; singer Texas Daisey; Long John Miller; Jack Scaggs and Abner Sims); Arthur Smith and his Dixie Liners; Zeke Clements and the Bronco Busters; fiddler Oscar Stone; Jack Shook and his Missouri Mountaineers band (guitarist-leader Shook; Dee Simmons; accordionist Bobby Cartleman; Fiddlin' Arthur Smith and guitarist Nap Bastian); Dorris Macon; singer Miss Lou Hesson; Theron Hale and his daughters Elizabeth and Mamie Ruth; blind fiddler Uncle Joe Mangrum; the Pickard Family led by Obed "Dad" Pickard; pianist Sue McQuiddy; mezzo-soprano Louise Harsh, fiddler Mellie Dunham; pianist Alycone Bate; Lonie and Tommy Thompson, the Singing Range Riders; Jack Shook and the Dixie Dons vocal quartet; the Delmore Brothers — Alton and Rabon; the Lakeland Sisters; Sam McGee; Robert Lunn; banjoist W.L. Totty; Buster Bate; Claude Lampley; H.J. Ragsdale; Tom Leffew; George Wilkerson; Charlie Arrington; Tom Andrews; Gayle and Amos Kinkley; Oscar Stone; Oscar Albright; Walter Liggett; Paul Warmack; Roy Hardison; Burt Hutcherson; Herman Crook, Kirk McGee, Bill Etter; Stanley Walton, Blythe Poteet, Lewis Crook, Dee Simmons, Fiddlin' Sid Harkreader, David "Stringbean" Akeman, Nap Bastian, Carl Smith, the Carter Sisters, Hank Snow the "Singing Ranger," Eddy Arnold, Zeke Clements the Dixie Yodeler, Kay Carlisle, Little Jimmie Dickens, Jimmy Selph, George Morgan, Clyde Julian "Red" Foley; Ernest Tubb and the Texas Troubadours; Bob Wills and the Texas Playboys; Lloyd "Cowboy" Copas; singer-comic Lew Childre; guitar virtuoso Chet Atkins, Paul Howard and the Arkansas Cotton Pickers; the Bales Brothers — John and Walter; the Poe Sisters — Nell and Ruth, Hank Williams and many others.

Many great country comedians appeared on the *Opry*. There was Whitey Ford the Duke of Paducah and Rod Brasfield, but perhaps the best loved and remembered was Cousin Minnie Pearl (Sarah Ophelia Cannon), whose cheap hat with a $1.98 price tag dangling from its rim and friendly greeting of "*How-dee*" started *Opry* listeners laughing before she said a word. Colley, an educated woman, played the role of a country bumpkin. She was down to earth and funny. Although Rod Brasfield and Minnie Pearl probably were the best country comedy team on the *Opry*, there were other talented country comedians and groups.

Among them were banjoist-comic Rachel Veach, billed as "Rachel, Queen of the Hills. Rachel sometimes teamed with others like guitarist Lonnie Wilson and Pete Kirby, as "Pap and Oswald, Rachel's Two Country Comedian Boy Friends." At other times it was "Rachel and her Great Big Bashful Brother Oswald (Pete Kirby)." Then, too, there was Smilin' Joseph (Joe Zinkan) and Odie (Oral Rhodes), sometimes billed as "Papa and Odie" or "Pap and his son Odie." Another funny team was "Cicero (Lloyd George) and Oscar (Rollin Sullivan)," later better known as "Lonzo and Oscar." Before Cousin Minnie Pearl, two great *Opry* favorites had been Sarie and Sally (Mrs. Edna Wilson and Mrs. Margaret Walters) whose comedy mainly consisted of Sarie's wisecracking gossip about their hometown neighbors. Sarie and Sally appeared both on the *Grand Ole Opry* and the *National Barn* Dance. An example of a Sarie and Sally routine is given in the *National Barn* Dance entry [*See* ***National Barn Dance***].

Blackface comedy routines often appeared on the early *Grand Ole Opry* radio programs. In the early 1930s, Leroy "Lasses" White came to WSM to conduct his *Lasses White's Minstrels* show. White later teamed with Lee Davis "Honey" Wilds and appeared on the *Opry*. After White left to work in Hollywood, a new blackface team was created of Bunny Biggs and "Honey" Wilds.

Although the program was dropped from the NBC network schedule in 1957, it still remains a popular WSM program (*WSM Barn Dance*, WSM, Nashville, TN, 1925–1926; *Grand Ole Opry*, 30 min., Saturday, NBC, 1939–1957; WSM, 1926-Present).

12856 ***Grand Opera Album***. The Saturday evening program of operatic selections featured soprano Dorothy Talbot; contralto Margaret O'Dea; tenor E. Harold Spalding; and baritone Harold Dana, accompanied by the National Concert Orchestra conducted by Max Dolin (NBC-Pacific Coast Network-KFI, San Francisco, CA, 1928).

12857 ***Grand Opera from Victor Red Seal Records***. Fred Smith told the story of the opera between records played.

12858 ***Grand Rapids' Librarian Club***. (WOOD, Grand Rapids, MI, 1939).

12859 ***Grand Slam***. Continental Baking Company sponsored the musical quiz show. Singer Irene Beasley was the host, assisted by pianist Bob Downey, organist Abe Goldman and announcer Dwight Weist. The contestants listened to Beasley sing several songs and then attempted to answer a series of questions about them. If they correctly answered five, they achieved a "Grand Slam" and received a $100 savings bond as a prize. The quiz program replaced the long-running *Bachelor's Children* daytime serial (15 min., Monday through Friday, 11:30–11:45 A.M., CBS, 1946).

12860 **Grandberry, Enla.** Soprano (KGO, Oakland, CA, 1925).

12861 **Grandin, Thomas.** Newscaster (NBC-Blue, 1945).

12862 ***Grandma's Hymn Hour***. Vcl. mus. prg. of religious songs and hymns (WMBD, Peoria, IL, 1935).

12863 ***Grandpa Bulger's Children's Hour***. The children's program was hosted by an unidentified "Grandpa" (KXL, Portland, OR, 1929).

12864 ***Grandpa Burton***. Bill Barr played all the characters on the unusual show, on which Grandpa Burton told his grandson the story of his life and adventures. If the old man exaggerated some of his adventures a bit, it only provided more fun for his listeners — young and old (15 min., Monday, Wednesday and Friday, 4:15–4:30 P.M., NBC, 1935).

12865 ***Grandpa Jones***. CW vcl. mus. prg. featuring Louis Marshall "Grandpa" Jones (WWVA, Wheeling WV,1938). This talented CW performer played a "grandpa" character even as a young man just starting his career. Jones later was a *Grand Ole Opry* regular.

12866 **Grandpappy.** DJ (*County Store*, WTXL, Springfield MA, 1949).

12867 ***Grandstand Quarterback***. Dick Enroth hosted the show and welcomed his guests, who talked about the University of Minnesota's football game played the previous day (30 min., Sunday, 12:00–12:30 P.M., WTCN, Minneapolis, MN, 1952).

12868 ***Grandstand Thrills***. Lester Weinrot directed the program that dramatized current news events. Elinor Harriot was a member of the cast (15 min., Weekly, 7:30–7:45 P.M. CST, WGN, Chicago, IL and WLW, Cincinnati, OH, 1935).

12869 **Graney, Jack.** Sportscaster (WCLE, Cleveland, OH and WHK, Cleveland, OH, 1937; WCLE, 1939–1941; WHK, 1940–1941; WCLE and WHK, 1942; WEWS, Cleveland, OH, 1954). Graney also broadcast Cleveland Indians baseball games for the Standard Oil Company on WHK in 1935.

12870 **Grange, Red.** Sportscaster Grange, a former college and professional football great, known as the Galloping Ghost, supplied football commentary on his own show that was broadcast twice weekly on the NBC-Red Network in 1936. On Friday, Grange predicted the winners of the following day's games. Saturday, he would broadcast the scores of more than 70 football games. On Monday evening, Grange would appear on the *Greater Sinclair Minstrels* to supply further analysis of the games (15 min., Friday, 8:30–8:45 P.M., NBC-Red, 1936 and 15 min., Saturday, 5:00–5:15 P.M.,

NBC-Red, 1935). Grange also appeared on many other stations and programs in the years that followed (*Red Grange's Sports Gossip*, WGN, Chicago, IL, 1937; WCLE, Cleveland, OH and WHK, Cleveland, OH, 1940; WMAQ, Chicago, IL, 1945; WJJD, Chicago, IL, 1948; *Football Huddle*, WJJD, 1949).

12871 Granger, Betty. COM-HE (WLIB, New York, NY, 1956).

12872 Granger, Florence. Contralto (KFDM, Beaumont, TX, 1928).

12873 Granger, Percy. Famous Australian pianist-composer (WJZ, New York, NY, 1921; WEAF, New York, NY, 1927).

12874 Granlund, Nils Thor (aka "NTG" or "Granny"). Broadway showman and publicity man for Loews' Theaters, Granlund began his career as a New York newspaperman. When Loew's, Incorporated began operation of station WHN (New York, NY), Granlund left his paper to head their press and publicity department. Loew's planned to use station WHN to broadcast their vaudeville acts and to promote Metro-Goldwyn-Mayer motion pictures.

Granlund began announcing on WHN early in 1922 to further Loew's objectives. He also hosted numerous broadcasts from Broadway clubs, ballrooms, cafes and restaurants. His bosses were not particularly happy when he began to clown and do comedy bits, but they were overjoyed when he recited poetry to fill interludes in WHN's broadcast programming. Kipling and Robert Service were particular favorites of Granlund's listeners. He was often forced to recite "Boots" five times a day on the air and "The Shooting of Dan McGrew" almost as often. Granlund was the first radio performer to receive a thousand fan letters a day. He also apparently was the first to introduce the concept of the radio variety show and it was his idea to bring composers to radio to introduce their own songs. Granlund began broadcasting in 1922, flourished in it in 1923 and continued to enjoy great popularity for the rest of the decade (WHN, New York, NY, 1922–1929). He also did blow-by-blow fight broadcasts in 1927 (WHAP, New York, NY). *Variety* characterized NTG's 1924 radio style when he was broadcasting remote broadcasts for WHN (New York, NY) as tough and aggressive. When he hosted the broadcast of Dan Gregory's orchestra from New York's Crystal Palace Ballroom, Granlund said that it was a "nifty place to learn how to dance" and called Gregory's band "24 punks." *See* ***NTG and His Girls.***

12875 Grannatt, Harry. Concert pianist (KOIN, Portland, OR, 1928).

12876 Grant, Alexander. Baritone (KOA, Denver, CO, 1926).

12877 Grant, Allan. Pianist (*Allan Grant*, instr. mus. prg., WGN, Chicago, IL, 1934).

12878 Grant, Austin. Newscaster (WWJ, Detroit, MI, 1938–1945; WXYZ, Detroit, MI, 1946–1947).

12879 Grant, Bob. Newscaster (WOAK, Oak Park, IL, 1948). DJ (*Night Watch*, KRNR, Roseburg, OR, 1949; *World of Sports*, KRNR, 1951–1952). He celebrated 50 years in radio on WOR (New York) in 1998 as a popular conservative talk show host.

12880 Grant, Brenton. Newscaster (WSAI, Cincinnati, OH, 1946).

12881 Grant, Bruce. Newscaster (KRNT-KSO, Des Moines, IA, 1942). DJ (WGRD, Grand Rapids, MI, 1957).

12882 Grant, Douglas B. Gospel baritone (WMT, Cedar-Rapids, Waterloo, IA, 1938. Newscaster (WMT, 1937–1945; KRNT-KSO, Des Moines, IA, 1945).

12883 Grant, Ethel. Pianist (WRC, Washington, DC, 1924).

12884 Grant, Felix. DJ (*Tune Inn*, WWDC, Washington, DC, 1948). Grant, a relaxed, low-keyed jazz specialist became a great Washington, DC, favorite on WMAL from the late 1940s through the next few decades.

12885 Grant, Hal. Sportscaster (WGBR, Goldsboro, NC, 1944–1946). DJ (*Musical Clock*, WDBJ, Roanoke, VA, 1948–1952).

12886 Grant, Harold. DJ (*Wax Museum*, KBMW, Wahpeton, ND, 1949).

12887 Grant, Herman. Violinist (WOC, Davenport, IA, 1928).

12888 Grant, Howard. Newscaster (*County News*, WKIZ, Brainerd, MN, 1947).

12889 Grant, Hubert. Sportscaster (WNOE, New Orleans, LA, 1940–1941; WDSU, New Orleans, LA, 1942). Newscaster (WALA, Mobile, AL, 1945).

12890 Grant, Janet. COM-HE (*Janet Grant's Cooking Talks*, NBC-Red, 1932). Miss Grant's cooking programs were sponsored by the American Kitchen Products Company, manufacturers of Steero Beef Boullion Cubes.

12891 Grant, Jerry. Leader (Jerry Grant Orchestra, KHJ, Los Angeles, CA, 1926).

12892 Grant, Jim. DJ (*The Dream Smasher*, WSPB, Sarasota, FL, 1947).

12893 Grant, Johnny. DJ (*Johnny Grant Show*, KGIL, San Fernando, CA, 1948; *Johnny Grant Show*, KMPC, Los Angeles, CA, 1949–1952; KMPC, 1954).

12894 Grant, Joseph. Newscaster (WMEX, Boston, MA, 1941, 1947).

12895 Grant, Ken. DJ (*Hillbilly Hit Parade*, KMAC, San Antonio, TX, 1947). Sportscaster (KNUZ, Houston, TX, 1952–1955).

12896 Grant, Lee. Leader (*Lee Grant Orchestra*, instr. mus. prg., WIP, Philadelphia, PA, 1939).

12897 Grant, Lee. DJ (*Western Jamboree*, Pryor, OK, 1949).

12898 Grant, Marcellette. Ukulele soloist (WNAD, Norman, OK, 1926).

12899 Grant, Marshall. Organist (*Marshall Grant*, instr. mus. prg., KNX, Los Angeles, CA, 1933).

12900 Grant, Milt. DJ (*Cavalcade*, WINX, Washington, DC, 1949; *The Milt Grant Show*, WOL, Washington, DC, 1949; WOL, 1952–1955).

12901 Grant, Newell. DJ (*Rise and Shine*, KEYJ, Jamestown, ND, 1955).

12902 Grant, Peter. Announcer (WLW, Cincinnati, OH, 1924). Newscaster (1937–1938, *Front Page Parade*, MBS, 1939, 1946–1947).

12903 Grant, Ralph. DJ (*Listen to Lem*, WLEM, Emporium, PA, 1960).

12904 Grant, Taylor. Newscaster (WCAU, Philadelphia, PA, 1938–1945; *Headline Edition*, ABC, 1946–1948). Sportscaster (WCAU, Philadelphia, PA, 1940–1942).

12905 Grant, Ted. Violinist (*Ted Grant*, instr. mus. prg., WMMN, Fairmont, WV, 1942).

12906 Grantham, Billy. Leader (*Billy Grantham Orchestra*, instr. mus. prg., NBC, 1933).

12907 Grantham, Dorothy. COM-HE (WFVA, Fredericksburg, VA, 1957).

12908 *Grantland Rice Sports Stories.* Rice, the dean of American sportswriters, conducted the show that focused on the human interest stories in sports (15 min., Saturday, 10:00–10:15 P.M., NBC-Red, 1945).

12909 *(The) Grantland Rice Story.* Sportswriter Jimmy Powers narrated the sports' program based on the great Grantland Rice's writings. Some poetry and commentary in Rice's own voice was included. Sports stars of past years were also interviewed on the transcribed show (15 min., Transcribed, Various Stations, 1955).

12910 Granville, Charles. Newscaster (KFAC, Los Angeles, CA, 1944).

12911 Granville, Joan. COM-HE (WVEC, Hampton, VA, 1951).

12912 *Graphology.* Louise Rice conducted the program of handwriting analysis (WGBS, New York, NY, 1925).

12913 Gratten, Bernadine. Soprano (WRNY, New York, NY, 1926).

12914 Grau, Phil. Newscaster (WEMP, Milwaukee, WI, 1940; *Radiotorials*, WEMP, 1945–1947; *Topics of the Times*, WEMP, 1948).

12915 Grauenhorst, Matt. Banjoist (KFAB, Lincoln, NE, 1925).

12916 Grauer, Ben. Newscaster (NBC, 1940–1948). Grauer was one of NBC's most active announcers for several decades.

12917 Grauer, Lindell. COM-HE (KNDY, Marysville, KS, 1956).

12918 Gravelin, Katherine. Pianist (WBZ, Boston-Springfield, MA, 1924–1925; WBAL, Baltimore, MD, 1926).

12919 Graver, Ted. Piano and accordion soloist (WBAP, Fort Worth, TX, 1928).

12920 Graves, Catherine. COM-HE (WCMA, Corinth, MS, 1954).

12921 Graves, Constance D. "Connie." COM-HE (WDEV, Waterbury, VT, 1956–1957).

12922 Graves, Don. DJ (*Your on with Don*, WHRV, Ann Arbor, MI, 1948).

12923 Graves, Fran. COM-HE (WKBV, Richmond, IN, 1960).

12924 Graves, Preston. Pianist-manager (WMBB, Homewood, IL and WOK, Chicago, IL, 1926–1928).

12925 Graves, Ted. Pianist (WBAP, Fort Worth, TX, 1928).

12926 Gray, Al. Newscaster (WSTV, Steubenville, OH, 1940–1941).

12927 Gray, Barry. DJ (WOR, New York, NY, 1945–1947; WKAT, Miami Beach, FL,

1947–1950). Newscaster (WKAT, FL, 1948–1950; *The Barry Gray Show*, WMCA, New York, NY, 1949–1950; WKAT, 1950; WMCA, 1952). When Gray first came to New York , he conducted a late night DJ show at WOR but he soon turned it into a "talk" show. After going to Florida and working for a few years at Miami Beach's WKAT, he returned to WMCA to broadcast a talk show from Chandler's Restaurant in Manhattan. At Chandler's, he interviewed the stars including Grace Kelly, Kay Armen, Phil Foster, Irving Berlin, Milton Berle and Danny Thomas. While there he became embroiled in a feud with Walter Winchell as the result of Winchell's alleged bad treatment of Josephine Baker at the Stork Club. As a result of the argument with Winchell, Gray maintained that he lost many of the stars who had previously come by to talk with him on his program from Chandler's. After Chandler's, he broadcast for WMCA from such clubs and restaurants as Bob Olin's, the Town and Country Club and the Seville Hotel in Miami Beach. Gray's long broadcasting career, primarily on New York local radio, extended until shortly before his death in 1996. His quick mind, resonant voice and interviewing skills made him a skillful pioneer in talk radio programming. Only Long John Nebel did more to develop talk radio.

12928 Gray, (Mrs.) Carl R. Bible class leader (WOAW, Omaha, NE, 1926).

12929 Gray, Caroline. Pianist (WEAF, New York, NY, 1924).

12930 Gray, Caroline. Pianist (*Caroline Gray*, instr. mus. prg., CBS, 1934).

12931 Gray, Charles "Charlie." Newscaster (KRBG, Okmulgee, OK, 1947; *Rise and Shine*, KOME, Tulsa, OK, 1950).

12932 Gray, Charles W. Newscaster (*Community News*, WHEB, Portsmouth, NH, 1947–1948).

12933 Gray, Clifford D. Newscaster (WSPA, Spartanburg, SC, 1946). DJ (1947; *Reveille Revels*, WSPA, 1949).

12934 Gray [Grey], Cynthia. Provided romantic advice on her *Advice to the Lovelorn* program (WOAW, Omaha, NE, 1925).

12935 Gray, Dick. Sportscaster (*Pigskin Parade*, WORD, Spartanburg, SC, 1940; WGNC, Gastonia, NC, 1941). Newscaster (WGNC, 1941).

12936 Gray, Earl. Leader (Earl Gray Orchestra with vocals by Jack Bain, KFOA, Seattle, WA, 1924; Earl Gray and his Hotel Butler Orchestra, KSND, Seattle, WA, 1925).

12937 Gray, Edith. Soprano (WOR, Newark, NJ, 1928).

12938 Gray, Eleanor. Pianist (WEAF, New York, NY, 1924).

12939 Gray, Elmer. Pianist. *See also* **Pasadena Orchestra DeLuxe.**

12940 Gray, Ethel. COM-HE (WQUA, Moline, IL, 1949).

12941 Gray, G. Donald. Announcer-baritone (KOMO, Seattle, WA, 1927–1929).

12942 Gray, George. Newscaster (WGBS, Miami, FL, 1946).

12943 Gray, Georgia. Soprano (KJR, Seattle, WA, 1927).

12944 Gray, Gilda. Famous *Ziegfeld Follies* singer and dancer (WOO, Philadelphia, PA, 1924; CBS, 1928–1929).

12945 Gray, Glen. Leader (*Glen Gray Orchestra*, instr. mus. prg., CBS, 1933–1935; NBC-Blue, 1936; WJR, Detroit, MI, 1937; CBS, 1938–1940). Gray was the moving spirit of the great band that was also known as the Casa Loma Crew.

12946 Gray, Gordon. DJ (WJR, Detroit, MI, 1947).

12947 Gray, Grace Viall. COM-HE (WIBO, Chicago, IL, 1926).

12948 Gray, Hardin. Newscaster (WBIG, Greensboro, NC, 1939).

12949 Gray, Harry. Baritone (KSD, St. Louis, MO, 1923).

12950 Gray, Helen. A twelve-year-old child singing star from Montclair, New Jersey, Gray first appeared on radio February 26, 1922 (WJZ, New York, NY).

12951 Gray, Hugh. DJ (WDZ, Decatur, IL, 1948–1950).

12952 Gray, James H. Newscaster (*Weekly Commentary*, WALB, Albany, GA, 1947).

12953 Gray, Jim. Newscaster (WCFL, Chicago, IL, 1948; *Melody Merchant*, WAIT, Chicago, IL, 1950).

12954 Gray, John. Newscaster (WDOD, Chattanooga, TN, 1939–1941, 1946). DJ (*Gray's Army*, WDOD, 1949; *Gray's Array*, WDOD, 1952).

12955 Gray, Kitty. COM-HE (WBOC, Salisbury, MD, 1954).

12956 Gray, Louise. COM-HE (WBBW, Youngstown, OH, 1956).

12957 Gray, Margaret. Pianist (KOL, Seattle, WA, 1929).

12958 Gray, Otto. Leader (Otto Gray and his Oklahoma Cowboy Band, WTAM , Cleveland, OH, 1928). His band was sometimes known merely as Otto Gray's Cowboys, a popular CW radio and recording group that appeared on many stations during the middle and late 1920s.

12959 Gray, Phil A. Newscaster (WEMP, Milwaukee, WI, 1938).

12960 Gray, Phyllis. COM-HE (WPDR Youngstown, OH, 1955–1956).

12961 Gray, Stanley. Baritone crooner (KOIN, Portland, OR, 1928).

12962 Gray, Walter. Walter Gray directed the *Dramatic Club* program (WFI, Philadelphia, PA, 1928).

12963 *Gray (Harriet) and Hughes (Walter)*. Vcl. mus. prg. (KUOA, Siloam Springs, AR. 1939). Gray and Hughes were a popular singing team on local Arkansas radio.

12964 *Graybar's Mr. and Mrs.* (aka ***Mr. and Mrs.***). The program was based on a comic strip by Clare Briggs. A series of dramatic sketches, *Graybar's Mr. and Mrs.* told the story of the events in lives of a married couple, Joe and Vi. The leading roles were played by Jack Smart and Jane Houston. Georgia Backus was also in the cast (15 min., Tuesday, 10:00–10:15 P.M., CBS, 1930). Jack Smart later gained national prominence by playing the title role on *The Fat Man* program.

12965 Graybill, Shirlee. COM-HE (KMON, Great Falls, MT, 1951).

12966 Grayling's String Trio. Instr. mus. prg. (WHT, Chicago, IL, 1926).

12967 Gray's Collegiate Orchestra. College dance band (KFXF, Colorado Springs, CO, 1926).

12968 Grayson, Bob "Bobby." Leader (*Bob Grayson Orchestra*, instr. mus. prg., WCAE, Pittsburgh, PA, 1936; NBC, 1937).

12969 Grayson, Carl. Leader (*Carl Grayson Orchestra*, instr. mus. prg., WLW, Cincinnati, OH, 1934).

12970 Grayson, Gene. Baritone (*Gene Grayson*, vcl. mus. prg., WMAQ, Chicago, IL, 1936).

12971 Grayson, Hal. Leader (*Hal Grayson Orchestra*, instr. mus. prg., MBS, 1934; NBC, 1938).

12972 Grayson, Jay. DJ (*Yawn Patrol*, WANN, Annapolis, MD, 1947; WBAL, Baltimore, MD, late 1940s and 1950s). Grayson was particularly interested in playing jazz recordings. He displayed an impressive knowledge of the music and discriminating taste on his programs.

12973 Grayson, June. COM-HE (KVNI, Coeur D'Alene, ID, 1951).

12974 Grayson, Mel. DJ (*Mood Indigo*, WSSV, Petersburg, VA, 1947; *Request Club*, WSSV, 1950). Sportscaster (*The Sportsman*, WSSV, 1948).

12975 Grayson, Sid. Newscaster (KWFT, Wichita Falls, TX, 1946). Sportscaster (*The Sports Desk*, KFDX, Wichita Falls, TX, 1949–1952). DJ (*Lone Star Theater*, KFDX, 1950).

12976 Grayson, Virginia. Soprano (KGO, Oakland, CA, 1926).

12977 Grayson, W. Norman. Pianist (WAHG, Richmond Hill, NY, 1925).

12978 Graziani, Aurora D. "Rory." COM-HE (WWON, Woonsocket, RI, 1956–1957).

12979 *Great American Applebury's*. Reginald Travers directed the humorous dramatic serial (KYA, San Francisco, CA, 1929).

12980 *(The) Great American Tourist*. Phil Baker was the comedian-host on the variety show. He was assisted by his stooges Beetle and Bottle. Hal Kemp's Orchestra supplied the music. Harry Von Zell was the announcer. The show was sponsored by the Gulf Oil Refining Company (30 min., Sunday, 7:30–8:00 P.M., CBS, 1935).

12981 *(The) Great Day*. John Reed King hosted the quiz program that differed only in that it originated from various armed forces' bases and gave only servicemen a chance at prizes. George Spots directed and Robert Jennings produced the audience participation show (30 min., Friday, 9:30–10:00 P.M., MBS, 1952).

12982 *(A) Great Day for Music*. Recorded music, inspirational prose and romantic poetry were the major components of the program. The prose and poetry was read by Franklyn MacCormack (60 min., Monday through Friday, 9:00–10:00 P.M., WCFL, Chicago, IL, 1948).

12983 ***Great Fires of History.*** John B. Fisher discussed various fiery conflagrations and disasters on the unique sustaining show (15 min., 10:00–10:15 P.M. NBC-Blue, 1941).

12984 ***(The) Great Fraud.*** Each week a different authority was presented on the sustaining program to report what was wrong with the U.S.S.R. The first week's speaker was Mrs. Ada Siegel. The announcer was Jim McKay (15 min., Sunday, 12:15–12:30 P.M., ABC, 1953).

12985 ***(The) Great Gildersleeve.*** *The Great Gildersleeve* was a spin-off from the *Fibber McGee and Molly* show, for it was there that Harold Peary first appeared as the blustering Throckmorton P. Gildersleeve. Gildy was as big a windbag as Fibber McGee and equally warm-hearted. Both were generous pussy cats. Gildy left the quiet little city of Whistful Vista and the *Fibber McGee and Molly* show to become Water Commissioner of Summerfield, where he coped with his newly assumed civic responsibilities and those of rearing his niece and nephew, Marjorie and Leroy.

Summerfield, thanks to writers Virginia Safford Lynne, Sam Moore, John Wheedon and Andy White, was also peopled with such comic characters as druggist Peavey, Floyd the barber, Birdie Lee Coggins the maid, Leila Ransom the marriageable Southern belle and the irascible Judge Hooker.

Over the years that the program was on the air (1941–1958), the cast included: Bea Benadaret, Tommy Bernard, Arthur Q. Bryan, Hans Conreid, Richard "Dick" Crenna, Richard Legrand, Forrest Lewis, Una Merkel, Shirley Mitchell, Hal Peary, Lillian Randolph, Marylee Robb, Earle Ross, Walter Tetley, Lurene Tuttle and Willard Waterman. Waterman replaced Harold Peary in the title role when the latter left the program in 1950. The orchestra was led by Jack Meakin. The announcer was John Wald. Karl Gruener, Fran Van Hartresfeldt and Cecil Underwood were the directors.

12986 ***(The) Great Gunns.*** Forrest Barnes wrote and William A. Backer produced and directed the situation comedy that *Variety* said was loosely based on the life of the Barrymore family. Each of the program's characters was convinced that he or she was a dramatic genius. Brett Morrison played Chris Gunn; Barbara Luddy, his wife, Veronica; Bob Jellison, Buster Gunn; and Phil Lord, Pop Gunn. Other cast members were Rita Ascot, Herb Butterfield, Marvin Miller and Willard Waterman. The announcer was Pierre Andre (30 min., Thursday, 9:30–10:00 P.M., MBS, 1941).

12987 **(The) Great Lakes Mixed Quartet.** The singing group's members were Charlotte Crown, soprano; Lucille Long, contralto; Oscar Heather, tenor; and Martin [Marthin] Provensen, bass (WENR, Chicago, IL and WBCN, Chicago, IL, 1928).

12988 ***Great Moments from Great Plays.*** Herbert Heyes was a featured player in the series that presented dramatic episodes from various plays (Tuesday, KFWB, Hollywood, CA, 1930).

12989 ***Great Moments in History.*** William Rainey directed the weekly dramatic series that portrayed significant episodes of American history. The first hour-long broadcast in the series was "The Monitor and the Merrimac," (NBC-Red, 1927).

12990 ***Great Personalities.*** Newspaper reporter and war correspondent Frazier Hunt broadcast word pictures of various American leaders. Rosario Bourdon's Orchestra provided the music (15 min., Tuesday, 9:30–9:45 P.M., NBC-Blue, 1932).

12991 **(The) Great Scott.** DJ (KLEE, Houston, TX, 1950).

12992 **Great Western Power Company Orchestra.** Commercially sponsored band (KFUU, Oakland, CA, 1925).

12993 **Great Western Silver String Serenaders.** Harry E. Sell directed the orchestra (WHO, Des Moines, IA, 1925).

12994 **Greater Louisville Ensemble.** Mixed quartet and string ensemble that included musicians Esther Metz, Alma Scholtz, Joseph Eisenbeis and William G. Meyer directed by Gustav Flexner (WHAS, Louisville, KY, 1928–1932).

12995 ***(The) Greatest of These.*** A sophisticated series of dramatic episodes, the program told the story of Harvey Desmond, a crusading attorney played by Tom Collins. His fiancé, Betty Crane was played by Mary Lansing (Weekly, 30 min., 1940s).

12996 ***(The) Greatest Story Ever Told.*** Goodyear Tire and Rubber Company sponsored the program on which Biblical stories such as "The Good Samaritan" were dramatized. The show was based on a book of the same name by Fulton Oursler. Members of the cast included: Jack Hartley, Rod Hendrickson, Alan Hewitt, Ray Morgan, Henry Neeley, Warren Parker, Eleanor Sherman, Sidney Smith, John Sylvester, Karl Swenson, Karl Weber and Roland Winters. Only Parker, in the role of Jesus, was a continuing character (30 min., 6:30–7:00 P.M., ABC, 1947).

12997 **Greaves, Alec.** DJ (*All Star Western Revue*, KTOW, Oklahoma City, OK, 1949).

12998 **Greaves, Penny.** COM-HE (KWKC, Abilene, TX, 1957).

12999 **Greb, Harry.** Former professional boxing champion conducted a physical exercise program (KDKA, Pittsburgh, PA, 1922).

13000 **Grebe, Earl C.** Newscaster (WSPD, Toledo, OH, 1941–1942, 1944–1947). Pianist (*Earl Grebe*, instr. mus. prg., WSPD, Toledo, OH, 1942).

13001 **Grebe, Fred.** DJ (*Musical Mailman*, WHAI, Greenfield, MA, 1947).

13002 **Grebe, Jim.** Sportscaster and play-by-play broadcaster of football, baseball and basketball (KMUR, Murray, UT, 1951).

13003 **Grebe Synchrophase String Ensemble.** Instrumental ensemble sponsored by Grebe Radio Manufacturing Company (KFI, Los Angeles, CA, 1926).

13004 **Greeley, Elora.** Pianist (KFWM, Oakland, CA, 1929).

13005 **Green, Art.** DJ (*Make Believe Ballroom*, WMIE, Miami, FL, 1948–1949; *Make Believe Ballroom*, WINZ, Miami, FL and *Curtain Calls*, WTVJ, Miami, FL, 1952; *Make Believe Ballroom*, WKAT, Miami Beach, FL, 1954–1957).

13006 **Green, Bill.** Dulcimer soloist (WEAF, New York, NY, 1925).

13007 **Green, Bill.** DJ (WDUN, Gainesville, GA, 1955).

13008 **Green, Bill.** DJ (WTBC, Tuscaloosa, AL, 1955).

13009 **Green [Greene], Connie.** COM-HE (KBOR, Brownsville, TX, 1956–1957).

13010 **Green, D.J.** Reader (WTIC, Hartford, CT, 1925).

13011 **Green, H.E.** Newscaster (KFKA, Greeley, CO, 1946–1948).

13012 **Green, Halene [Helene].** COM-HE (WMIK, Middletown, KY, 1951).

13013 **Green, (Mrs.) Irving.** Contralto (KOA, Denver, CO, 1925).

13014 **Green, Jacques.** Leader (Jacques Green Orchestra and Jacques Green's Club Deauville Orchestra broadcasting with Clark's Hawaiians, WJZ, New York, NY, 1925).

13015 **Green, Jane.** Actress Green was a cast member of the daytime serial programs *Girl Alone* and *Midstream.*

13016 **Green, Joe.** Vibraphone and xylophone soloist and leader of several popular radio orchestras (WEAF, New York, NY, 1925). Leader (Royal Stenographers Orchestra; the Serenading Shoemakers Orchestra; and the Joe Green Novelty Marimba Band on the *General Motors Family Party* program, NBC, 1927). Joe Green and his brother, George Hamilton Green were among the busiest radio and recording artists during the 1920s and 1930s (*Joe Green Orchestra*, instr. mus. prg., WIP, Philadelphia, PA, 1936; NBC, 1938). *See* **The Green Brothers Orchestra.**

13017 **Green, Johnny (John Waldo Green).** Pianist, composer, orchestra conductor and MC Green was born October 10, 1908. A talented musician, he first appeared on radio as a pianist (WEAF, New York, NY). Leader (*Johnny Green Orchestra,* instr. mus. prg., NBC, 1934; CBS, 1935; WTNJ, Trenton, NJ, 1936).

13018 **Green, La Fawn.** COM-HE (KRBC, Abilene, TX, 1951).

13019 **Green, Lauretta.** Contralto (KFWI, San Francisco, CA, 1927).

13020 **Green, Leland.** Saxophonist (KTBI, Los Angeles, CA, 1925).

13021 **Green, Lindsey.** Tenor (WFAA, Dallas, TX, 1923).

13022 **Green, Lois.** Soprano (KOIL, Council Bluffs, IA, 1926).

13023 **Green, Lynn.** COM-HE (KCOG, Centerville, IA, 1960).

13024 **Green, Margaret.** Pianist (KOIL, Council Bluffs, IA, 1926).

13025 **Green, Marvin.** Pianist (WJY, New York, NY, 1925).

13026 **Green, Mary Francis.** COM-HE (WMDC, Hazlehurst, MS, 1956).

13027 **Green, Patty.** COM-HE (WSOC, Charlotte, NC, 1951).

13028 **Green, Punch.** Pianist-singer (KGW, Portland, OR, 1926).

13029 **Green, Rose.** Pianist (WKBH, Madison, WI, 1937).

13030 Green, Sally. COM-HE (WWRI, West Warwick, RI, 1960).

13031 Green, Terry. Newscaster (KCRC, Enid, OK, 1945).

13032 Green, Thelma. Pianist (KTBI, Los Angeles, CA, 1925).

13033 Green, Thomas, Jr. Green was the announcer on the *Armour Hour* program (NBC-Blue, New York, NY, 1929).

13034 Green, Tommy. Irish tenor (KFXF, Colorado Springs, CO, 1926).

13035 Green, Vera. COM-HE (WAAB, Worcester, MA, 1957).

13036 Green, Vivian. Leader (*Vivian Green Orchestra*, instr. mus. prg., WIP, Philadelphia, PA, 1935).

13037 Green, W.H. Announcer (WKBT, New Orleans, LA, 191927).

13038 *Green Brothers Orchestra*. Instr. mus. prg. (NBC, 1934; WBZ, Boston-Springfield, MA, 1935; NBC, 1935; WIBX, Utica, NY, 1942).

13039 *(The) Green Hornet*. *The Green Hornet*, a famous adventure show, opened with its theme — Rimsky-Korsakov's "Flight of the Bumble Bee" — followed by an announcer dramatically proclaiming, "The Green Hornet." The loud, angry sound of a hornet buzzing was heard as the announcer continued, "He hunts the biggest of all games! Public enemies who try to destroy our America." The sound of the Hornet's car, the Black Beauty was then heard roaring away. Once more the announcer explained, "Ride with Britt Reid in the thrilling adventure, 'The Hornet Returns.' The Green Hornet strikes again!" That exciting opening explained the basis for the dramatic series and told the listener what could be expected.

Another creation from the team of Fran Striker and George W. Trendle at Detroit's WXYZ, the program never failed to deliver on its promise of exciting adventure. The cast included: Lee Allman, Donovan Faust, Bob Hall, Raymond Hayashi, Al Hodge, Jim Irwin, Jack McCarthy, Rollon Parker, Jack Petruzzi, Gil Shea and Mickey Tolon. Bob Hite, Fielden Farrington, Hal Neal, Mike Wallace and Charles Woods were the announcers. Charles Livingstone was the director and James Jewell served as producer-writer-director.

13040 *(The) Green Lama*. A sustaining summer replacement for *Broadway is My Beat*, the good mystery adventure drama was written by Roland Foster and William Froug. Norman Macdonnell was the producer and director. The *Green Lama* was a comic strip and pulp magazine character originally created by Roland Foster. The title character, played by Paul Frees, had developed special powers by studying with the devine Lamas of Tibet. He used these powers to battle for justice and humanity. In the cast with Frees were: Harry Bartell, Paul Dubov, Laurette Filbrandt, Nestor Paiva, Herb Vigran and Ben Wright. Music was supplied by Richard Aurandt. The announcer was Larry Thor (30 min., Sunday, 5:30–6:00 P.M. CBS, 1949).

13041 *(The) Green Mountain Boys*. The Vermont Publicity Center sponsored the show, whose major purpose was to attract tourists to see Vermont. George Ludlam was "The Vacation Counselor," who advanced recommendations on each program to visit Vermont. The Jesters [male singing trio] provided the music on the entertaining local show (15 min., Sunday, 11:15–11:30 A.M., WJZ, New York, NY, 1935).

13042 *Green Valley Line*. An interesting syndicated dramatic serial, the *Green Valley Line* told the story of people who lived in a railroad terminal town named Morristown that was located on the Green Valley Railroad line. The story of the struggle caused by the effort of a large eastern rail conglomerate to take over their small railroad was completed in 52 fifteen-minute episodes The transcribed program featured a group of competent unidentified actors who sounded like the WXYZ (Detroit, MI) acting group that regularly performed on the *Lone Ranger* and *Green Hornet* programs (Transcribed, Various Stations, 1940s).

13043 Greenan, Emilie. Soprano (KFKU, Lawrence, KS, 1926).

13044 Greenberg, Claire. Soprano (WPCH, New York, NY, 1929).

13045 Greenberg, Fanny. Soprano (WELI, New Haven, CT, 1940).

13046 Greenblatt, Ben. Pianist (*Piano Ramblings*, instr. mus. prg., 15 min., Thursday, 6:45–7:00 P.M., WFIL, Philadelphia, PA, 1936). Greenblatt's entertaining talk and piano selections made this a popular local program.

13047 Greendahl, Jeanne. COM-HE (WHB, Kansas City, MO, 1956–1957).

13048 Greene, Alfred. Lyric tenor (WFSG, Los Angeles, CA, 1925).

13049 Greene, (Miss) Bert. Executive (WOR, New York, NY, 1930s). Although she started at WOR to work on the microphone, she went into administration. She became administrative assistant to Alfred J. McCosker, the station manager.

13050 Greene, Bob. Newscaster (KNX, Los Angeles, CA, 1945).

13051 Greene, (Miss) Bobbie L. COM-HE (WSOK, Nashville, TN, 1957).

13052 Greene, Carl. DJ (*Carl Calls*, KSON, San Diego, CA, 1947).

13053 Greene, Edith Michaux. Soprano (WSAI, Cincinnati, OH, 1925).

13054 Greene [Green], Esther Fricke. Miss Greene played the organ and Chinese chimes from the Angeleus Temple on Sister Aimee McPherson's station (KFSG, Los Angeles, CA, 1925).

13055 Greene, June K. COM-HE (WHAI, Greenfield, MA, 1956–1957).

13056 Greene, John C. Newscaster (WGTC, Greenville, NC, 1945). Sportscaster (WGTC, 1945). DJ (*Hillbilly Star Time*, WRHI, Rock Hill, SC, 1949).

13057 Greene, Margaret. Pianist (WHAS, Louisville, KY, 1923).

13058 Greene, Monte. DJ (WLEC, Sandusky, OH, 1955).

13059 Greene, Paul A. Announcer (WSAI, Cincinnati, OH, 1924–1926). Greene was known as "WSAI's Bridge Voice." Station WSAI was owned by the U.S. Playing Card Company, Inc.

13060 Greene, Rachel Fraese. Soprano (WTAM, Cleveland, OH, 1924).

13061 Greene, Richard. Newscaster (WJTN, Jamestown, NY, 1945).

13062 Greene, Robbie L. COM-HE (WSOK, Nashville, TN, 1957).

13063 Greene, Rosaline. Greene was the leading female actress of the WGY Players group. Despite her great popularity she was paid only $5 a week for some time. Two years after she began and gained great popularity with the listening audience, her salary was raised to $7.50 a week (WGY, Schenectady, NY, 1925). Greene was one of radio's finest actresses, who, incidentally, was developed *by* and *for* the medium. In the 1920s, she appeared on the *Eveready Hour* (NBC-Red, 1927–1929) and the *Empire Builders* program (NBC-Blue, 1927–1929). Later, she played Mary Lou on the *Showboat* program and was the announcer for Phil Spitalny's *Hour of Charm* program in 1935. Arguably, Greene was the first and finest actress ever developed by radio. *See* **Drama**.

13064 Greene, William S. Leader (*William S. Greene Ensemble*, instr. mus. prg., WBT, Charlotte, NC, 1937).

13065 Greenhaigh, Natalie. Pianist (WRST, Long Island NY, 1928).

13066 Greenhoe, Robert S. Sportscaster (*Sports Notebook*, WHTC, Holland, MI, 1949–1952).

13067 Greenhouse, Martha. Actress Greenhouse was a cast member of the *Companion* program (ABC, 1954).

13068 Greenlaw, Stanley H. Musical saw performer Greenlaw was accompanied by pianist Edna Gove (WBZ, Boston-Springfield, MA, 1924; WEEI, Boston, MA, 1925).

13069 Greenlead, Edna. Operatic soprano (WGBS, New York, NY, 1928).

13070 Greenlee, Toddy. COM-HE (WANB, Waynesburg, PA, 1960).

13071 Greenley, Charles. Announcer (KGCA, Decorah, IA, 1927).

13072 Greenspan, Bud. Sportscaster (WHN, New York, NY, 1947; WMGM, New York, NY, 1948–1949). Greenspan wrote and produced an excellent auditory documentary of World War II — *The Sounds of War* — for Westinghouse Broadcasting Company. His careful research and discriminating selection of material produced radio documentary at its very best.

13073 Greenwich Village Follies Serenaders Orchestra. Club dance band (WIP, Philadelphia, PA, 1923).

13074 Greenwood, Katherine. COM-HE (WALL, Middletown, NY, 1956–1957).

13075 Greenwood, Warren. Sportscaster (WHAI, Greenfield, MA, 1939; WHAI, 1942). Newscaster (WHAI, 1941). DJ (*Platter Playhouse*, WHAV, Haverhill, MA, 1950; WERI, Westerly, RI, 1954).

13076 Greer, Ben. Newscaster (WSPA, Spartanburg, SC, 1948).

13077 Greer, Bill. DJ (*Night Show*, WNDB, Daytona Beach, FL, 1960).

13078 Greer, Bob. Newscaster (*Between the Lines*, KPRK, Livingston, MT, 1947.

13079 Greer, Lois Genel. COM-HE (KVMA, Magnolia, AR, 1954).

13080 *Greetings from Old Kentucky*. This was a pleasant music variety program (30 min., Thursday, 3:30–4:00 P.M., CBS, 1935).

13081 Grefig, Adam. Leader (Palisades Dance Orchestra, WGBS, New York, NY, 1928).

13082 Gregerson, Albert. Baritone (KGO, Oakland, CA, 1925).

13083 Gregg, Edith. Leader (Edith Gregg and Her King Joy Lo Syncopators Orchestra, WHB, Kansas City, MO, 1926).

13084 Gregg, Mary. COM-HE (KAFY, Bakersfield, CA, 1951).

13085 Gregg, Tom. DJ (*The Nightwatchman*, WREN, Topeka, KS, 1947).

13086 Gregoire, Juliet. COM-HE (KXOC, Chico, CA, 1954–1955).

13087 Gregor, Marty. Leader (*Marty Gregor Orchestra*, instr. mus. prg., KDKA, Pittsburgh, PA, 1934; WJAS, Pittsburgh, PA, 1937).

13088 Gregori, Virginia. Singer on the programs *La Palina Hour*, *Story in a Song* and *Night Club Romance* (CBS, 1929).

13089 Gregorson, Dick. Newscaster (KGO, San Francisco, CA, 1945).

13090 Gregory, Bob. Newscaster (WCBS, Springfield, IL, 1939).

13091 Gregory, Bobby. Accordionist-pianist (KPO, San Francisco, CA, 1925; WHN, New York, NY, 1926; WGBS, New York, NY, 1928).

13092 Gregory, Dan. Leader (Dan Gregory's Orchestra broadcasting from New York City's Crystal Palace Ballroom, WHN, New York, NY, 1924; Dan Gregory's Dancing Carnival Orchestra, WHN, 1929; *Dan Gregory Orchestra*, instr. mus. prg., WHP, Harrisburg, PA, 1937).

13093 Gregory, Doris. COM-HE (KPBM, Carlsbad, NM, 1956).

13094 Gregory, Dorothy. Actress Gregory appeared on the daytime serial programs *Kitty Keene, Incorporated*, *Scattergood Baines* and *Stepmother*.

13095 Gregory, Gregg. DJ (*Music for the Girls*, KVER, Albuquerque, NM, 1947).

13096 Gregory, Helen Felch. Soprano (WEAF, New York, NY, 1923).

13097 Gregory, Keith. Newscaster (WBLJ, Dalton, GA, 1941).

13098 Gregory, Lucy. COM-HE (WHRV, Ann Arbor, MI, 1957).

13099 Gregory, Mary Jane. COM-HE (WBRZ, Baton Rouge, LA, 1957).

13100 Gregory, Paul. Leader (*Paul Gregory Orchestra*, instr. mus. prg., WIP, Philadelphia, PA, 1936).

13101 Gregory, Mark. Newscaster (WJR, Detroit, MI, 1944; *Tomorrow's Headlines*, KSTP, St. Paul–Minneapolis, MN, 1945–1947; WLOL, Minneapolis, MN, 1948).

13102 Gregory, Mary Jane. COM-HE (WBRZ, Baton Rouge, LA, 1957).

13103 Gregson, Jack Dana. Sportscaster (KDYL, San Francisco, CA, 1937–1939; KSFO, San Francisco, CA, 1940). DJ (KFSO, 1947; KROW, Oakland, CA, 1950 and *G.E. Platter Party*, KXOB, Stockton, CA, 1950; *The Jack Gregson Show*, ABC, 1954; *Jack's Place*, ABC, 1955).

13104 Greif, Frank G. Tenor (WGES, Oak Park, IL, 1925 and WEBH, Chicago, IL, 1926).

13105 Greim, Helen. Pianist (WJAZ, Chicago, IL, 1923).

13106 Greiner, Seth. Pianist (*Seth Greiner*, instr. mus. prg., KMOX, St. Louis, MO, 1936).

13107 Greise, Harry. Pianist and recording artist Greise was said by *Variety* to be able to "tickle the ivories skillfully" (KYW, Chicago, IL, 1923).

13108 Grella, Rocco. Leader (Clearwater Scarlet Guards Band, WFLA, Clearwater, FL, 1927–1928; Rocco Grella's Saxophone Octet, WFLA, Clearwater, FL, 1928–1929).

13109 Grel-Meister's Hungarian Orchestra. Popular club band (WMCA, New York, NY, 1927).

13110 Grendell, Lloyd. Singer (KHQ, Spokane, WA, 1928).

13111 Grenet, Eliseo. Leader (*Eliseo Grenet Orchestra*, instr. mus. prg., WIP, Philadelphia, PA, 1936).

13112 Grenier, Cap. Sportscaster (*National Sports Parade*, WHVR, Hanover, PA, 1952).

13113 Grenier, Ethel. Singer (*Ethel Grenier*, vcl. mus. prg., WEEI, Boston, MA, 1934).

13114 Grenier, Helen. COM-HE (KVMC, Colorado City, TX, 1951).

13115 Gressier, Mimi. Australian soprano (WHEC, Rochester, MN, 1927).

13116 Gretes, Inge. COM-HE (KRPL, Moscow, ID, 1956).

13117 Greup, Ernest. Newscaster (*News Digest*, WKRT, Cortland, NY, 1948).

13118 Grew, David. Newscaster (KFPY, Spokane, WA, 1942; KHQ, Spokane, WA and KGA, Spokane, WA, 1945).

13119 Grew, Patricia. Singer and poetry reader (WMCA, New York, NY, 1939).

13120 Grey, Ann. Blues singer (KFWB, Hollywood, CA, 1927–1929).

13121 Grey, Ethel. COM-HE (WSBA, York, PA, 1951–1956).

13122 Grey, Freda. COM-HE (WWIT, Canton, NC, 1957).

13123 Grey, Jane. Singer (*Jane Grey*, vcl. mus. prg., WFIL, Philadelphia, PA, 1936).

13124 Grey, Jerry. DJ (*Wake Up Hot Springs*, KCHS, Hot Springs, NM, 1947).

13125 Grey, Joan. Singer (WMCA, New York, NY, 1936).

13126 Grey, Lanny and Ginger. DJ (*Start the Day with a Smile*, WMGM, New York, NY, 1950).

13127 Grey, Mitchell. DJ (*Breakfast with You*, WJPA, Washington, PA, 1950).

13128 Grey, Nan. Actress Grey was a cast member of the *Those We Love* daytime serial program.

13129 Grey, Peggy Burke. COM-HE (KCRE, Cresent City, CA, 1954).

13130 Grey, Robert. Newscaster (WFNC, Fayetteville, NC, 1948).

13131 Greyson, Carl. Newscaster (*World in Review*, WSM, Nashville, TN, 1948).

13132 Gridley, Dan. Tenor (KMTR, Hollywood, CA, 1926; staff tenor, KNX, Los Angeles, CA, 1929). Gridley also appeared on the *Philco Hour of Theater Memories* (NBC-Blue, New York, NY, 1927–1931).

13133 Gridley, Violet. Singer (WBZ, Springfield, MA, 1924).

13134 Gridley, Violet and Fred Bernier. Popular song team (WBZ, Springfield, MA, 1924).

13135 Griebel, Edna Beatrice. Pianist (WOR, Newark, NJ, 1929).

13136 Grieg, Frank. Tenor (WJAZ , Chicago, IL, 1926).

13137 Grieg, John. Actor Grieg played the continuing role of Professor Lucifer Butts on the *Collier's Radio Hour* program (NBC, 1929).

13138 Grier, Harry. Newscaster (KTRH, Houston, TX, 1942–1945; *World at Large*, KTRH, 1947). Sportscaster (KTRH, 1942; KTRH, 1945–1946).

13139 Grier, Jimmy. Leader (*Jimmy Grier Orchestra*, instr. mus. prg., WBBM, Chicago, IL, 1934; WJSV, Washington, DC, 1934; NBC, 1937–1938).

13140 Grierson, Tom. Organist (*Tom Grierson*, instr. mus. prg., WHAM, Rochester, NY, 1934–1938).

13141 Griest, Irene. Violinist (WDAR, Philadelphia, PA, 1924).

13142 Griffeth, Gail. COM-HE (KMED, Medford, OR, 1956).

13143 Griffin, Alexander. Newscaster (MBS, 1944; *Griffin Reporting*, MBS, 1945).

13144 Griffin, Alia. COM-HE (KHSB, Hemet, CA, 1960).

13145 Griffin, Alice. Pianist (WHAS, Louisville, KY, 1923).

13146 Griffin, Beatrice. Violinist (WWJ, Detroit, MI, 1928).

13147 Griffin, Ben. Tenor (*Ben Griffin*, vcl. mus. prg., KGHI, Little Rock, AR, 1929).

13148 Griffin, (Sister) Bessie. DJ (WMRY, New Orleans, LA, 1957).

13149 Griffin, Betty. COM-HE (WIBX, Utica, NY, 1949).

13150 Griffin, Bob. Singer (*Bob Griffin*, vcl. mus. prg., WOR, Newark, NJ, 1934). Griffin mixed songs with patter on his programs.

13151 Griffin, Bobby [Bobbie]. Griffin was working as an assistant announcer when he took part in a dramatic incident at WHO (Des Moines, IA) in 1925. Shortly after 10:00 A.M. on May 27, 1925, Griffin became the central figure in an interesting bit of radio history when he broadcast the following announcement: "Attention all peace officers, all peace officers, State of Iowa! The Cottage State Bank in Des Moines has just been held up and robbed by four or five men driving a Paige sedan. Their description follows...."

Soon, one of his listeners saw four men change from a Paige sedan to a Marmon at Des

Moines' Woodland Cemetery. Following them until they left town heading south, the listener notified the police. Griffin then broadcast: "Bandits have switched to a Marmon heading south. Be on the lookout." After noon a muffled telephone call came in to the station for Griffin that warned, "If you wanna stay healthy, cut out puttin' them police bulletins on the air" (*Broadcasting*, April 1, 1937, p. 1). Later — there was an attempted attack on him as he left the WHO studio to go to lunch.

By mid-afternoon of May 17 in Bethany, Missouri, Constable Arthur Stanley recognized the bandits' car. When word reached WHO, Griffin broadcast, "Bandits sighted at Bethany, Missouri. Still driving Marmon. Have switched to Missouri license plates." At Avenue City, Mississippi, after a gun battle with police, the bandits' car crashed and two bandits were caught. The other two bandits escaped across the fields. WHO broadcast: "Be on the lookout for two bandits escaped from gun battle with officers at Avenue City, Mississippi, wanted in connection with bank robbery at Des Moines this morning." Sometime later outside St. Joseph, Missouri, a WHO listener was asked for a lift by the two fugitives who had escaped from the Avenue City gun battle. They were soon arrested in Kansas City. A fifth member of the holdup gang, who had been left in Des Moines, was picked up shortly afterward. By December 5, 1925, all five men were convicted and sentenced to the Iowa State Penitentiary with terms ranging from ten years to life. Their swift apprehension, trial and conviction was aided by Griffin and the pioneer broadcasters at WHO.

Griffin enjoyed a successful broadcasting career (WHO, Des Moines, IA, 1925–1927). He moved to KVOO (Bristow, OK) in 1927. In the fall of 1927, he became announcer-director at WJBT (Chicago, IL). Griffin then moved to station WRUF (Gainesville, FL) in 1928 and later was broadcasting the news on KYW (Chicago, IL) in 1931.

13152 Griffin, Catherine. COM-HE (WJVA, South Bend, IN, 1951).

13153 Griffin, Clarence. Newscaster (WBBO, Forest City, NC, 1948).

13154 Griffin, Dan. DJ (*Mail Bag*, WGTM, Wilson, NC, 1947–1949; *Daytime in Dixie*, WGTM, Wilson, NC, 1950).

13155 Griffin, Dean. DJ (*Musical Clock*, WBKH, Hattiesburg, MS, 1955).

13156 Griffin, Florence. Soprano Griffin was billed as "The Radio Florence" (WEAR, Cleveland, OH, 1925).

13157 Griffin, George. Baritone (*George Griffin*, vcl. mus. prg., NBC, 1938–1939; MBS, 1942).

13158 Griffin, Helen. COM-HE (WLBJ, Bowling Green, KY, 1957).

13159 Griffin, Howard. Violinist (KHJ, Los Angeles, CA, 1929).

13160 Griffin, Jerry. DJ (*Music Room*, WDOS, Oneonta, NY, 1954; WNBF, Binghampton, NY, 1956; WGBI, Scranton-Wilkes Barre, PA, 1957).

13161 Griffin, John. Newscaster (KIUP, Durango, CO, 1947).

13162 Griffin, John A. Newscaster (KABR, Aberdeen, SD, 1945–1946).

13163 Griffin, Michael. Newscaster (*The News and You*, WTAQ, Green Bay, WI, 1947–1948).

13164 Griffin, Waymon. Leader (Waymon Griffin Orchestra featuring Will Paris and Clifton Craig, Experimental 5 ACW, Fort Smith, AR, April, 1922). A typical early broadcast of the band included such songs as "The Wabash Blues," "Everybody Step," "Tuck Me to Sleep," "Sweet Lady," "Dream on Eternity," "Tytee," "Dapper Dan" and "There'll Be Some Changes Made." The band was said to be "the first colored orchestra to broadcast in the state of Arkansas."

13165 Griffin, William. Bassist Griffin played with the Swanee Orchestra (WJZ, New York, NY, 1923).

13166 Griffin, Zeke. DJ (*Boogie Beat*, KSAN, San Francisco, CA, 1950–1952).

13167 Griffis, Annette S. COM-HE (WSGN, Birmingham, AL, 1960).

13168 Griffith, Bill. Newscaster (KCKN, Kansas City, MO, 1945; KMBC, Kansas City, MO, 1946–1947).

13169 Griffith, D.W. David Lewelyn Wark Griffith was born January 22, 1875 in LaGrange, KY. Katz (1998, p. 563) says Griffith was the "single most important figure in the history of American film and one of the most influential in the development of world cinema as an art." In addition to contributing such silent motion pictures as *The Birth of* a *Nation*, *Broken Blossoms*, *Intolerance*, *Orphans of the Story*, *Way Down East* and *Judith of Bethulia*, Griffith began in 1909 to develop a company of such future motion picture stars as Mary Pickford, Donald Crisp, Dorothy and Lillian Gish, Harry Carey, Mae Marsh, Mabel Normand and Blanche Sweet. Griffith developed and used such cinematic techniques as dramatic lighting, changing camera angles, the close-up, the full shot, rhythmic editing and parallel action. He used these innovative techniques consciously and creatively (Katz, 1998, p. 563). Famous pioneer motion picture director Griffith occasionally spoke on the *Brooklyn Mark Strand Stage and Studio Program* (WNYC, New York, NY, 1925).

13170 Griffith, Don. Sportscaster (*Sports Page of the Air*, WCOA, Pensacola, FL, 1948–1949; *Sports Page*, WCOA, 1951).

13171 Griffith, Marge. COM-HE (WRTA, Altoona, PA, 1949–1956).

13172 Griffith, Rex. Tenor (*Rex Griffith*, vcl. mus. prg., WLW, Cincinnati, OH, 1935). Griffith also was a talented organist at the station (*Rex Griffith*, instr. mus. prg., WLW, 1936).

13173 Griffith, Robert. Newscaster (KVAK, Atchinson, KS, 1941) Sportscaster (KVAK, 1941).

13174 Griffiths, Bill. Sportscaster (WJW, Akron, OH, 1937–1941; WADC, Akron, OH, 1945–1948).

13175 Griffiths, Dave. Sportscaster (WGBI, Scranton, PA, 1937–1941; *Sportsreel of the Air*, WARM, Scranton, PA, 1947–1954; WSCR, Scranton, PA, 1956).

13176 Griffiths, Virginia F. Soprano (KGO, Oakland, CA, 1926).

13177 Grigg, Becky. COM-HE (WDVA, Danville, VA, 1949).

13178 Griggs, Hazel. Pianist (WQXR, New York, NY, 1937).

13179 Grill, Katherine. Contralto (WAMD, Minneapolis, MN, 1926).

13180 Grilli, Guilia. Soprano (WEAF, New York, NY, 1925).

13181 Grim, Christian A. Pianist-composer (WBBM, Chicago, IL, 1926).

13182 Grim, George. Newscaster (WLOL, Minneapolis–St. Paul, MN, 1940–1941; WCCO, Minneapolis, MN, 1946–1948).

13183 Grimes, Bera Meade. Pianist Grimes appeared on *The Breakfast Hour* program (WFAA, Dallas, TX, 1927–1928).

13184 Grimes, Gertrude. Reader (KXLF, Colorado Springs, CO, 1926).

13185 Grimes, Ida. COM-HE (WYZE, Atlanta, GA, 1957).

13186 Grimes, Jackie. Actress Grimes was a cast member of the *Valiant Lady* daytime serial.

13187 Grimes, James W. Newscaster (WOSU, Columbus, OH, 1945).

13188 Grimes, Min. COM-HE (WNAG, Granada, MS, 1960).

13189 Grimes, Waldo. Newscaster (KSAC, Manhattan, KS, 1941).

13190 Grimm, Charles "Cholly." Sportscaster Grimm was a former baseball manager of the Chicago Cubs baseball club (WBBM, Chicago, IL, 1939).

13191 Grimm, Lorraine. Leader (*Lorraine Grimm Orchestra*, instr. mus. prg., KMOX , St. Louis, MO, 1935).

13192 Grinday, Hilary. COM-HE (WTTS, Bloomington, IN, 1955).

13193 Grindon, Edna M. Soprano (KYW, Chicago, IL, 1925).

13194 Grisette, Etta Mae. COM-HE (WHKY, Hickory, NC, 1956).

13195 Grisez, Georges. Clarinetist (WCCO, Minneapolis–St. Paul, MN, 1928).

13196 Griskey, William. Newscaster (KTOP, Topeka, KS, 1948).

13197 Grissom, Gail. DJ (*Tele-Quest Time*, WTTS, Bloomington, IN, 1948; *Night Special*, WTOM, Bloomington, IN, 1950).

13198 Griswold [Grisswold], Phyllis. Organist (WOAW, Omaha, NE, 1925).

13199 Griswold, George R. Newscaster (WTMA, Charleston, SC, 1940–1942, 1944–1945).

13200 Griswold, Roger. Sportscaster (WCBM, Baltimore, MD, 1946; *Headlines in Sports*, WCAO, Baltimore, MD, 1955; WBMD, Baltimore, MD, 1956).

13201 Griswold, Zona Marie. Lyric soprano (WEAF, New York, NY, 1924).

13202 *Grits and Gravy*. Lulu Vollmer, who previously had written the *Moonlight and Honey Suckle* program, wrote this comedy-drama that told of the adventures of Cabe Crump, a happy-go-lucky mountaineer, who got the call to be a preacher. *Variety* said the program was a good example of homespun

American portraits with fine characterization and good writing. The cast included: George Gaul, Christine Strauss, Fred Stewart, William Janney, Margie Mayne and Catherine L'Eagle (30 min., Thursday, 8:00–8:30 P.M., NBC, 1934).

13203 Grizzard, Herman. Sportscaster (WLAC, Nashville, TN, 1937–1940; WLAC, 1960).

13204 Groat, Carl D. Newscaster (*World Front*, WLW, Cincinnati, OH, 1947).

13205 Grobe, Al. Newscaster (WINS, New York, NY, 1938; WQXR, New York, NY, 1945).

13206 Groce, Rocky. DJ (WFEC, Miami, FL, 1954; WRVM, Rochester, NY, 1957; *Rhythm Express*, WLIB, New York, NY, 1960).

13207 Groeber, Ida. Pianist (WOR, Newark, NJ, 1925).

13208 Groen, Bill. Dulcimer soloist (WNYC, New York, NY, 1926).

13209 Grofe, Ferde. Composer Grofe frequently led his own orchestra (*Ferde Grofe Orchestra*, instr. mus. prg., NBC, 1933; KFEL, Denver, CO, 1934; WLW, Cincinnati, OH, 1935; WHAS, Louisville, KY and KSD, St. Louis, MO, 1936; WGY, Schenectady, NY, 1937–1939).

13210 Groff, Madeline. Soprano (WHN, New York, NY, 1924).

13211 Groff, Will. DJ (*Rise and Shine*, WJEJ, Hagerstown, MD, 1947–1948, 1950).

13212 Grohman, Jim. DJ (*Musical Clock*, WFPG, Steel Pier, Atlantic City, NJ, 1947; *Sleepy Jim*, WMID, Atlantic City, NJ, 1948; *Musical Clock*, WFPG, 1950).

13213 Gromler, Ethel Holtzclow. Soprano (WJZ, New York, NY, 1925).

13214 Groom, Mary. Actress Groom appeared on the *Mr. and Mrs.* program.

13215 Gross, Beryl Mae. Reader (WMAQ, Chicago, IL, 1924).

13216 Gross, Bob. DJ (WANE, Fort Wayne, IN, 1957).

13217 Gross, Clair. Newscaster (*Human Side of the News*, KSIB, Creston, IA, 1947). DJ (*Mystery Melody*, KSIB, 1947).

13218 Gross, Doris. Reader (WQJ, Chicago, IL, 1926).

13219 Gross, (Mrs.) E.W. Soprano (KFDM, Beaumont, TX, 1928).

13220 Gross, H.R. Newscaster (WHO, Des Moines, IA, 1938; WLW-WSAI, Cincinnati, OH, 1941; WISH, Indianapolis, IN, 1944–1945; KXEL, Waterloo, IA, 1945–1946).

13221 Gross, Herman. Sportscaster (*The Sportsman*, WKTM, Mayfield, KY, 1947).

13222 Gross, June. Singer (WTAQ, Green Bay, WI, 1937).

13223 Gross, Lottie. Pianist (KJBS, San Francisco, CA, 1925).

13224 Gross, Mona. COM-HE (KFSA, Fr. Smith, AR, 1960).

13225 Gross, Sheldon. Newscaster (*The Town Crier, Town Topics* and *The Atlantic City Forum of the Air*, WFPG, Steel Pier, Atlantic City, NJ, 1947–1948).

13226 Gross, Sidney. DJ (*International Jazz Club*, ABC, 1949).

13227 Grosse [Grosso], Johanna. Organist (WLW, Cincinnati, OH, 1926–1928; *Johanna Grosse*, inst. mus. prg., WLW, 1934–1936).

13228 Grosso, Elmer. Director (Elmer Grosso Orchestra, WOR, Newark, NJ, 1926).

13229 Grosso, Martha. Soprano (WEVD, New York, NY, 1930).

13230 Grosz, Vera. Newscaster (KUSD, Vermillion, SD, 1945).

13231 *(The) Grouch Club*. Formerly broadcast in Los Angeles over KFWB, the sustaining program came to New York City in 1938 with its original Grouch Master, Jack Lescoulie. The show was a burlesque on those programs that "sold" happiness. Gripes and complaints of Lescoulie as well as those written in by listeners were broadcast. Arthur Q. Bryan, the Novel Airs singing group and Nat Brusiloff's Orchestra were program regulars (30 min., Tuesday, 9:30–10:00 P.M., WMCA, New York, NY, 1938).

13232 Grove, Bill. DJ (*Fort Bragg Hour*, WFNC, Fayetteville, NC, 1947).

13233 Grove, Elliott. DJ (*Club 570*, WSYR, Syracuse, NY, 1947).

13234 Grove, Harry. Newscaster (KBIZ, Ottumwa, IA, 1941). DJ (Harry Grove became a popular Kansas City DJ with his *Meet Mr. Music* program, 25 min., Monday through Friday, 10:35–11:00 P.M., KCMO, Kansas City, MO, 1948).

13235 Grove, Jerry. DJ (*Musical Clock*, WPAY, Portsmouth, OH, 1947).

13236 Grove, Roy. Newscaster (WTTM, Trenton, NJ, 1944; *News at Six*, WTTM, 1948).

13237 Grover, Gertrude. COM-HE (WHCU, Ithaca, NY, 1949).

13238 Grover, Laura. Singer (WBNX, Bronx, NY, 1936).

13239 Grover, Ted. Newscaster (WBYN, Brooklyn, NY, 1944).

13240 Groves, Dorothy. Soprano (KFQW, Seattle, WA, 1928).

13241 Groves, Jean. COM-HE (KBIM, Roswell, NM, 1955).

13242 *Growin' Up*. The daytime serial told the story of teenagers growing up in a "modern American city." As its announcer said the "ever fascinating story of youth finding its way in life is sponsored by Johnson and Johnson." The cast members were not identified (15 min., Monday through Friday, Network, Middle 1930s).

13243 Grsi, Elsa. Actress Grsi was a cast member of the *Valiant Lady* program.

13244 Grubb, Gayle. Announcer-director (KFAB, Lincoln, NE, 1926–1927).

13245 Grubbs, Viola. COM-HE (KVMC, Colorado City, TX, 1951).

13246 Grubbs, Virginia Gartrell. Singer (WRVA, Richmond, VA, 1929).

13247 Gruber, Iris Virginia. Soprano (WIP, Philadelphia, PA, 1925–1926); WLIT, Philadelphia, PA, 1925; WGBS, New York, NY, 1927). Some local periodicals identified Gruber as a contralto.

13248 Grubert, Ron. DJ (*Polka Party*, KNUJ, New Ulm, MN, 1960).

13249 *(The) Gruen Program*. Tom Neeley's Saxophone Quartet was featured on the music show sponsored by Gruen Watches (15 min., Saturday, 6:15–6:30 P.M., NBC-Blue, 1931).

13250 Gruenberg, Irene. Pianist (WNYC, New York, NY, 1939).

13251 Grueter, Larry G. Pianist (WLW, Cincinnati, OH, 1925).

13252 Gruetter, Al. Leader (*Al Gruetter's Greenwich Coliseum Orchestra*, instr. mus. prg., KMO, Tacoma, WA, 1929).

13253 Gruhler, Dick. Singer (*Dick Gruhler*, vcl. mus. prg., WPG, Atlantic City, NJ, 1935).

13254 Gruhn, Rudi. Newscaster (KFRE, Fresno, CA, 1947).

13255 *(The) Grummits*. "Senator" Ed Ford, a good comedian from the vaudeville stage, wrote the script and played the role of Pop on the sustaining situation comedy. Mom, played by Eunice Howard, was a Mrs. Malaprop. Their daughter, Roselle, was in love with a wise cracking show-off played by Peter Donald. The program's director was Roger Bower (15 min., Wednesday, 11:00–11:15 P.M., NBC-Red, 1934).

13256 Grund, Lynn. COM-HE (WAUD, Auburn, AL, 1951).

13257 Grupp, Dave. Xylophonist Grupp appeared frequently on the *Wrigley Review* program (1928). Band leader (Grupp led the orchestra on the *Raybestos Twins* program, NBC-Red, New York, NY, 1929).

13258 Gruppe, Helen. Pianist (WHN, New York, NY, 1924).

13259 Gruza, Larry. Newscaster (WICC, Bridgeport, CT, 1938).

13260 Guardino, Monte J. DJ (*Afternoon Jamboree*, KUIN, Grants Pass, OR, 1947; *Happy Go Lucky Time*, KUIN, 1955–1956).

13261 Guardiola, Carlos. Pianist (KWWG, Brownsville, TX, 1926).

13262 Guarnieri, Isabelle. Soprano (*Isabelle Guarnieri*, vcl. mus. prg., WOR, Newark, NJ, 1935–1936).

13263 Gubbins, George. Announcer (WGES, Chicago, IL, 1927).

13264 Gudelsky, H. Newscaster (WKBZ, Muskegon, MI, 1938).

13265 Guderyahn, Richard. Violinist (WJAZ, Chicago, IL, 1924).

13266 Guenneti [Guennetti], Louis. Leader (*Louis Guenneti Orchestra*, instr. mus. prg., MBS, 1936).

13267 Guerin, Bill. DJ (*That Program* and *Little Folks*, WMFD, Wilmington, NC, 1948).

13268 Guernsey, Alice. Violinist (WQJ, Chicago, IL, 1926).

13269 Guerra, Henry. Newscaster (WOAI, San Antonio, TX, 1939–1941, 1946).

13270 Guerrero, Salvador. DJ (*Mexico Sings*, KECK, Odessa, TX, 1954).

13271 Guertin, Neil. DJ (*On the Record*, WWON, Woonsocket, RI, 1960).

13272 Guess, Bob. DJ (*Request Time*, WLBH, Mattoon, IL, 1947).

13273 Guess, Linnie Lee. Soprano (KNRC, Los Angeles, CA, 1925).

13274 *Guess the Tune.* Howard Jones conducted the quiz show in the role of "Dr. Rhythm." Listeners were asked to guess the titles of the recorded songs played on the program. Movie passes were awarded to winners who sent in the correct answers. If the winners accompanied their answers with a box top of the sponsor's Dr. Jayne's Cough Remedy, they received an additional five dollar cash prize (15 min., 12:00 noon-12:15 P.M., Monday, Wednesday and Friday, WIP, Philadelphia, PA, 1942).

13275 *Guess Where.* Phillip Morris cigarettes sponsored the quiz show that was hosted by June Walker. Contestants were required to listen to a dramatized sketch and then identify the location where it took place. Budd Hulick and Charlie Cantor were the cast members. The program was replaced by *Breezing Along*, a musical review (30 min., Friday, 8:00–8:30 P.M., MBS, 1939).

13276 Guest, Bud. Newscaster (WJR, Detroit, MI, 1936–1941). Guest replaced Billy Repaid as newscaster in 1936 and continued at WJR until he went into service in 1941.

13277 Guest, Edgar A. Guest read his own poetry and that of others on a transcribed program (*Edgar A. Guest*, WASH, Grand Rapids, MI, 1942). He also appeared on many network programs reading his own poetry. *See **It Can Be Done** and **Welcome Valley**.*

13278 Guest, Helen. Ballad singer (KFI, Los Angeles, CA, 1927).

13279 *Guest Star.* A transcribed program, *Guest Star* was sponsored by the United States Treasury Department in an effort to promote the sale of U.S. Savings Bonds. The long-running series, at one time or another, featured almost all the great stars of radio and motion pictures. Regulars on the show were Kenny Delmar, the Savings Bond Singers and Denes Agay's Orchestra. Harry Sosnik's Orchestra also appeared on some programs. Guests during 1947 included Henry Morgan, Jimmy Durante, Garry Moore, Abbott and Costello, the Chordettes, Edith Adams, Andy Williams, Perry Como, Denise Lor, Johnny Desmond, Sarah Vaughan, Alfred Drake, Rise Stevens, the Four Lads, Julie London, Julius La Rosa, Sylvia Sims, Gordon MacRae, Gogi Grant, Curt Massey and Martha Tilton, Peggy King, Eddy Arnold, the Lennon Sisters, Fats Domino, Matt Dennis, Connie Russell, Georgia Gibbs, Burl Ives, Ish Kabibble and Kay Kyser, Art Tatum, Alec Templeton, Dave Barbour, Gloria Swanson, Frances Langford, Bonita Granville, Humphrey Bogart, Dinah Shore, Walter Brennan, Jane Pickens, Hildegarde, Bill Boyd, Olan Soule, Barbara Luddy, Dick Leibert, Bing Crosby, Eddie Cantor, the Ray Anthony Orchestra, the Stan Kenton Orchestra, Rosemary Clooney, Connie Haines, Rudy Vallee, the Xavier Cugat Orchestra, the Sons of the Pioneers, Spike Jones and the City Slickers, Frankie Yankovic, Tony Martin, Marguerite Piazza, Frankie Laine, the Guy Lombardo Orchestra, the Lawrence Welk Orchestra, Russel Nype, the Frank DeVol Orchestra and Tony Perkins (15 min., Transcribed, Various Stations, 1943–1962.)

13280 Guge, Eleanor. COM-HE (KLIL, Estherville, IA, 1954).

13281 Gugenheim, Helen. Writer (NBC, 1939). Gugenheim wrote news and special events scripts for the network.

13282 Guggenmos, Ruth. Pianist (WOAW, Omaha, NE, 1924).

13283 Guidi, Hugh. DJ (*Top Spot*, WTOP, Washington, DC, 1948–1949).

13284 *(The) Guiding Light.* The daytime serial was written by Irna Phillips. It was one of the most admired and durable programs on radio. For its first nine years on the air, announcer Fort Pearson opened the program by saying, "The *Guiding Light*, created by Irna Phillips." From Jan 25, 1937 when it first went on the air until 1946, the central figure, played by Arthur Peterson, was a minister, Dr. John Rutledge, a warm-hearted, nonsectarian preacher, who attempted to assist people with their troubles and teach them how to live the good life. The reading lamp that Reverend Rutledge kept in his window served as a symbolic guide for his parishioners who were in distress. It was, he said, the Friendship Lamp that he kept burning. Figuratively for his parishioners, it was *The Guiding Light.* One of Rutledge's persistent themes on the program was:

> There is a destiny that makes us brothers
> None goes his way alone
> All that we send into the life of others
> Comes back into our own.

When Dr. Rutledge died in 1946, Dr. Charles Matthews entered the story, and the following year he opened the Church of the Good Samaritan. The Bauer family was introduced in 1948 and the program followed their lives from then on. The radio format was discontinued in 1956, but on the television version that began in 1952, the story continued without any loss of continuity. Starting on television with a 15-minute format, the program expanded to 30 minutes September, 1968, and to 60 minutes on November 7, 1977. The program was still being broadcast on the CBS television network in 1998.

Author Irna Phillips, one of the foremost writers of daytime serials, wrote the program until 1947. She said she wrote about the program's locale, characters and plot from her own life experiences. She was an energetic, creative dynamo, who was both proud and aggressively protective of her work. After her radio programs went off the air, she continued to write several successful daytime television serials.

Throughout its entire run on radio, *The Guiding Light's* theme was always the same: If the family will stick together and work hard, happiness and success will be achieved. The program insisted that the American family could *make it* by combining faith and hard work.

The program's cast included: Jone Allison, Betty Arnold, Ruth Bailey, Frank Behrens, Bill Bouchey, Sidney Breese, Muriel Bremner, Phil Dakin, Frank Dane, Sam Edwards, Laurette Fillbrandt, Margaret Fuller, Betty Lou Gerson, Sharon Grainger, Ken Griffin, Annette Harper, Gladys Heen, Gail Henshaw, Raymond Edward Johnson, Eloise Kummer, Mary Lansing, Phil Lord, Sunda Love, Charlotte Manson, Mercedes McCambridge, Carolyn McKay, Marvin Miller, Bret Morrison, Arnold Moss, Arthur Peterson, Ed Prentiss, Michael Romano, Beverly Ruby, Alma Samuels, Mignon Schreiber, Hugh Studebaker, Lyle Sudrow, Henrietta Tedro, Sam Wanamaker, Willard Waterman, Leonard Waterman, Jane Webb, Sarajane Wells, Lesley Woods and Seymour Young. Clayton "Bud" Collyer and Fort Pearson were the announcers and David Lesan and Carl Wester its producers. The program's directors were Harry Bubeck, Gil Gibbons, Gordon Hughes, Howard Keegan, Ted MacMurray and Charles Urquhart.

On CBS on Monday, June 2, 1947, the new writer, Art Glad, attempted to follow the successful format created by Irna Phillips. Dr. Charles Matthews, the new minister, who was the central figure in this version was played by Hugh Studebaker. Matthews was the minister of the Good Samaritan Church of Selby Flats, an under privileged Los Angeles neighborhood. Cast members in the new version were Betty Lou Gerson, Ned DeFener and Willard Waterman. The announcer was Herbert Allen. Duz Soap Power—"Duz Does Everything"—sponsored the program (15 min., Monday through Friday, 1:45–2:00 P.M., CBS, 1947).

13285 Guidry, Beverly. COM-HE (WJBW, New Orleans, LA, 1954).

13286 Guild, Carol. COM-HE (WICK, Scranton, PA, 1960).

13287 Guilford, Fay. Soprano (*Fay Guilford*, vcl. mus. prg., WOR, Newark, NJ, 1935).

13288 Guill, Mary White. Soprano (WSM, Nashville, TN, 1928).

13289 Guinan, Jack. Newscaster (WJTN, Jamestown, NY, 1946). Sportscaster (*Reports on Sports*, WJTN, 1947–1948; *Speaking Sports*, WJTN, 1948; sports play-by-play, WSCR, Scranton, PA, 1949; WQAN, Scranton, PA, 1951; *Athlete of the Week*, WQAN, 1955).

13290 Guion, David. Pianist Guion was on the musical faculty of Southern Methodist University (WFAA, Dallas, TX, 1923). He was known as the "American Cowboy Composer." His weekly program was called *David Guion and his Orchestra.* Baritone Paul Revell was featured (15 min., Tuesday, 11:30–11:45 P.M., NBC-Red, 1932).

13291 *Guitar Lessons.* J.F. Roach broadcast weekly half-hour guitar lessons (15 min., Friday, 1:30–1:45 P.M., WLW, Cincinnati, OH, 1922).

13292 Guiterrez, Leopold. Chilean baritone (WJZ, New York, NY, 1925).

13293 Guizar, Tito. Mexican tenor Guizar starred in motion pictures in the U.S. and Mexico (*Tito Guizar*, vcl. mus. prg., 15 min., Friday, 10:45–11:00 P.M., CBS, 1932; *Tito Guizar*, vcl. mus. prg., 15 min., Monday, 5:45–6:00 P.M., CBS, 1933;CBS, 1934–1935). Guizar studied music at the Mexico City Conservatory of Music in 1925. He appeared in theatricals in Mexico before studying voice for two years in Italy. He returned to Mexico as an opera singer, but finding it too formal, he undertook a career in popular music. After enjoying success in Mexican motion pictures, he appeared as a guest performer on many American radio programs. A short time later, Guizar appeared in American movies and had his own radio show.

13294 Gulch, Bennie. Leader (Bennie Gulch and his Rainbow Orch., WKBO, Jersey City, NJ, 1927).

13295 Guldin, Seel. Soprano (WIP, Philadelphia, PA, 1925).

13296 *(The) Gulf Headliners*. Gulf Oil Refining Company sponsored the good music show hosted by Charles Winninger. The performers included tenor Frank Parker, the Pickens Sisters and the Revelers Quartet. Frank Tours conducted the orchestra. At various times the program was announced by Norman Brokenshire and Harry Von Zell (30 min., Sunday, 7:30–8:00 P.M., CBS, 1935).

13297 *(The) Gulf International Program*. Gulf Oil Refining Company attempted to broadcast shortwave variety programs that emanated from Berlin, London, Vienna and Paris. Although shortwave reception was only fair-to-good, the program's general broadcast quality was satisfactory. *Variety* pointed out that the program's major problem was that its European entertainers tended to be only mediocre (30 min., Sunday, 9:00–9:30 P.M., NBC-Blue, 1934).

13298 *(The) Gulf Program* (aka *Will Rogers' Good Gulf Show* or *The Gulf Headliner Program*). Will Rogers appeared on many of these Gulf programs until 1935, when he was killed with Wiley Post in a plane crash. Singers Carol Deis, Hallie Stiles, James Melton, the Revelers Quartet and Al Goodman's Orchestra were also members of the cast. While Rogers went on vacation in 1935, he was replaced by Bert Lehr. When Rogers did not appear on other shows, Fred Stone and George M. Cohan were featured. Joseph Bell was the program's announcer (30 min., Sunday, 9:00–9:30 P.M., NBC-Blue, 1933). At other times, the program was broadcast Sunday evenings from 8:30–9:00 P.M. *See* **Rogers, Will.**

13299 *Gulf Spring Show*. Mus. prg. with singer Nancy Martin backed by Max Adkins' Saxomaniacs (Tuesday and Thursday, 12:30–12:45 P.M., WCAE, Pittsburgh, PA, 1934).

13300 Gullans, Florence. Mezzo-soprano (WJAZ, Mt. Prospect, IL, 1928).

13301 Gullickson, Charles. Newscaster (WDOD, Chattanooga, TN, 1942).

13302 Gullickson, Florence. COM-HE (WDOD, Chattanooga, TN, 1951).

13303 (The) Gully Jumpers. Paul Warmack led the CW string band that was featured on the *Grand Ole Opry* program (WSM, Nashville, TN, 1925–1939). The group began as amateurs, who worked as mechanics and carpenters in their daytime jobs. The first group of Gully Jumpers consisted of Burt Hutcherson, Charlie Arrington and Paul Warmack.

13304 Gumm, Bill. Sportscaster (*Sports Review*, WRNJ, Racine, WI, 1952). DJ (WRJN, 1957).

13305 *(The) Gumps*. A serial drama, *The Gumps* was based on the popular comic strip of the same name by Sidney Smith. The show appeared on the CBS network in 1934, after originating on WGN (Chicago, IL) in 1931. The original Chicago cast included Jack Boyle, Dorothy Denver and Charles Flynn, Jr., as Andy, Min and Chester Gump respectively. Bess Flynn played their maid, Tilda. The original series was written by Thomas J. Foy assisted by suggestions from the comic strip creator, Sidney Smith (WGN, 1931.) At that time WGN had four programs based on comic strips: *The Gumps*, *Harold Teen*, *Gasoline Alley* and *Little Orphan Annie*. When the show appeared on the CBS network, the cast included Wilmer Walter, Agnes Moorehead and Jackie Kelk as the Gump family members. Lester Jay also appeared on the show. Himan Brown and Irwin Shaw wrote the network version of the program. Ralph Edwards was the announcer (15 min., Wednesday, 11:15–11:30 A.M., CBS, 1934–1937). An interesting event occurred in 1935 when *The Gumps* program made a premium offer to its listeners. In response they received 5,800 letters with a dime enclosed. When the sacks containing the letters were stolen from their office, they announced the theft on the air and asked all who had responded to the offer to send a card and they would make good on the offer. In the next few weeks the company sent out 12,000 premiums to listeners who claimed to have written earlier (CBS, 1934–1937).

13306 Gundaker, Ed C. Sportscaster (WHP, Harrisburg, PA, 1937–1942; WHP, 1946; *Spotlight on Sports*, WHP, 1947–1948). Newscaster (WHP, 1941).

13307 Gundell's Orchestra. Local Boston dance band (WEEI, Boston, MA, 1925).

13308 Gunderman, John F. Pianist (WGR, Buffalo, NY, 1924–1926).

13309 Gunderson, Dale. DJ (*Make Mine Music*, KXRO, Aberdeen, WA, 1947; *Off the Record*, KBKW, 1949; *Make Mine Music*, KXRO, 1950).

13310 Gunderson, Swede. Sportscaster (KYUM, Yuma, AZ, 1952).

13311 Gunn, Ben. Newscaster (WHSC, Hartsville, SC, 1946; WCON, Atlanta, GA, 1947). DJ (*Roll Jordan*, WEAS, Atlanta, GA, 1948). Sportscaster (African-American football play-by-play, WEAS, 1949).

13312 Gunn, Dick. DJ (*1490 Club*, KICO, Calexico, CA, 1950).

13313 Gunn, E. Frank. Newscaster Gunn conducted the *Ye Towne Topics* local news program (KFSD, San Diego, CA, 1926).

13314 Gunn, Eleanor. Miss Gunn hosted *Eleanor Gunn's Fashion Feature* program (WFI, Philadelphia, PA, 1925). She also delivered fashion talks on WJZ (New York, NY, 1925).

13315 Gunn, George. Sportscaster (WMAL, Washington, DC and WRC, Washington, DC, 1939–1940).

13316 Gunn, Janet. COM-HE (KCMJ, Palm Springs, CA, 1954).

13317 Gunn, Jimmie. Leader (*Jimmie Gunn and his Dixie Serenaders Orchestra*, instr. mus. prg., WBT, Charlotte, NC, 1934).

13318 Gunn, Jo Ann. COM-HE (KENO, Las Vegas, NV, 1957).

13319 Gunn, Johnny. DJ (*On KEZY Street*, KEZY, Anaheim, CA, 1960).

13320 Gunnells, Barbara. DJ (*Royalties of Jazz*, WKBK, Detroit, MI, 1947).

13321 Gunning, Betty. COM-HE (WFCI, Providence, RI, 1949; WJAR, Providence, RI, 1956).

13322 Gunning, Cliff. Singer (KFI, Los Angeles, CA, 1928).

13323 Gunning, Elizabeth "Betty." COM-HE (WJAR, Providence, RI, 1951–1956).

13324 Gunnison, Royal Arch. Newscaster (WOR, New York, NY, 1945).

13325 Gunsell, Fred. Pianist (WSKC, Bay City, MI, 1928).

13326 Gunsky, Maurice. Composer-tenor (KPO, San Francisco, CA, 1925–1927). Gunsky was sometimes accompanied in 1925 by pianist Merton Bowes.

13327 *Gunsmoke*. Norman Macdonnell produced and directed the action-filled adult western program that entertained both children and adults. Music was supplied by Rex Koury. The program starred William Conrad as Matt Dillon, the Marshal of Dodge City, Kansas. His deputy, Chester Proudfoot, was played by Parley Baer. Howard McNear played the town's crusty Doc Adams. Georgia Ellis played Miss Kitty, a saloon girl. From its first broadcast in 1952, until its last in 1961, the writing by John Meston and the acting of the cast was uniformly excellent (30 min., Saturday, 7:30–8:00 P.M., CBS, 1952). By 1954, the adult western drama, sponsored by Liggett and Myers Tobacco Company, was part of a fill for *The Lux Radio Theater*, which after 20 years on radio had moved to television. The radio cast also included: Harry Bartell, Lawrence Dobkin, Sam Edwards, Joseph Kearns, Vic Perrin and Barney Phillips. The announcers were Roy Rowan, George Fenneman and George Walsh (30 min., Monday, 9:00–9:30 P.M., CBS, 1954).

13328 Gunst, Naomi. Pianist (*Naomi Gunst*, instr. mus. prg., WJAS, Pittsburgh, PA, 1935).

13329 Gunter, Hardrock. DJ (*Jamboree Matinee*, WWVA, Wheeling, WV, 1954).

13330 Gunter, Rose Ella. DJ (*High School Platter Party*, WTMC, Ocala, FL, 1950).

13331 Gunther, John. Newscaster (NBC, 1939–1945).

13332 Gunther, Ted. DJ (*Rumpus Room*, WFCB, Dunkirk, NY, 1954).

13333 Gunzendorfer [Guznendorfer], Wilton "Wilt." Leader (Wilt Gunzendorfer's Dance Band played every evening from the Hotel Whitcomb, Drury Lane in San Francisco, KFRC, San Francisco, CA, 1925–1927).

13334 Guokas, Matt. Sportscaster (WPEN, Philadelphia, PA, 1949–1956).

13335 Guren, Dora. COM-HE (WHAP, Hopewell, VA, 1951).

13336 Gurewich, Jascha. Leader (Jascha Gurewich's Symphonic Orchestra, WOR, Newark, NJ, 1926).

13337 Gurney, John. Basso (*John Gurney*, vcl. mus. prg., NBC, 1937).

13338 Gurney's WNAX Radio Orchestra. This band was sponsored by the Gurney Seed Company of Yankton, South Dakota, owner and operator of station WNAX (Yankton, SD, 1927–1928). It won the *Radio Digest's* most popular radio orchestra poll in 1928, when the band polled 43,270 votes to lead the second place Walter Krausgrill's Balconades Ballroom Orchestra from KFRC (San Francisco, CA), who polled 30,828 votes and third place Seven Aces orchestra from WBAP (Dallas, TX).

13339 *Gus Van and Arlene Jackson*. Van, an old vaudevillian performer and minstrel man, teamed on this program with female singing star, Arlene Jackson. They talked, joked and sang to the music of the William Wirges Orchestra (15 min., Tuesday, 7:45–89:00 P.M., NBC-Blue, 1934).

13340 Gushee, Oliver W. Organist (KOA, Denver, CO, 1927).

13341 Gusselle, Gertrude. Ballad singer (KECA, Los Angeles, CA, 1930; KFI, Los Angeles, CA,1930).

13342 Gussman, (Mrs.) Frank. Soprano (WSM, Nashville, TN, 1928).

13343 Gustafson, Andy. Sportscaster (WTVJ, Miami, FL, 1949).

13344 Gustavus Adolphus College Choir. Collegiate vocal group (NBC, 1939).

13345 Guth Brothers. The Guth Brothers "sang songs of all nations" (WPG, Atlantic City, NJ, 1929).

13346 Guthrie, Bill. DJ (*Coffee Club*, WTAW, College Station, TX, 1948).

13347 Guthrie, David L.R. Newscaster (*United Nations Commentator*, WGPA, Bethlehem, PA, 1947–1948).

13348 Guthrie, (Major) John B. Major Guthrie was a United Forest Service officer who spoke on "Vacations" (KPO, San Francisco, CA, 1923).

13349 Guthrie, Warren. Baritone accompanied by pianist Hazel Fish (KROW, Oakland, CA, 1930).

13350 Guthrie, Willard. Sportscaster (KWRO, Coquille, OR, 1951).

13351 Gutierez, Lupe. DJ (*Latin Home Hour*, KCSB, San Bernardino, CA, 1952).

13352 Gutleben, Phil. Pianist (KFWM, Oakland, CA, 1927).

13353 Gutkin, Bessie. Pianist (WSBH, Brooklyn Heights, NY, 1928).

13354 Gutting, Raymond. Gutting conducted the weekday *Market Report* program (KMOX, St. Louis, MO, 1928).

13355 Guttman, Elizabeth. Soprano (WBAL, Baltimore, MD, 1926).

13356 Guy, Aubrey. DJ (*Bandstand Serenade*, WMC, Memphis, TN, 1947; *The Dixie Merry-Go-Round*, WMC, 1952; WMPS, Memphis, TN, 1954–1957).

13357 Guy, Barry. DJ (*Spinner Sanctum*, WLAN, Lancaster, PA, 1955).

13358 Guy, Corris. COM-HE (KTLA, Los Angeles, CA, 1957).

13359 Guy, Jay. Organist (*Jay Guy*, instr. mus. prg., WKAR, East Lansing, MI, 1942).

13360 *(The) Guy Lombardo Orchestra Program*. Lombardo and his band were joined by Wendell Hall the "Red-headed Music Maker" on the entertaining musical variety show (60 min., Tuesday, 11:00–12:00 midnight, CBS, 1928–1929). On his own programs the smooth Lombardo band provided dance music (*Guy Lombardo and his Royal Canadians,* instr. mus. prg., 30 min., Saturday, 11:00–11:30 P.M., CBS, 1930). The Lombardo band later was also featured on a Ziv transcribed half-hour program series (1948–1949) and many other remote broadcasts.

13361 Guyan, George. Sportscaster (KFRU, Columbia, MO, 1937–1939).

13362 Guyer, Sanford. Newscaster (WPEN, Philadelphia, PA, 1938).

13363 Guyman, Bill. Sportscaster (KGO, San Francisco, CA, 1944; *Football Warmup*, KSFO, San Francisco, CA, 1947; KFRC, San Francisco, CA, 1960).

13364 Guyon's Paradise Ballroom Orchestra. Club band (WGES, Oak Park, IL, 1926).

13365 "GWW." Designation for announcer George W. Willet (WOC, Davenport, IA, 1924).

13366 Gwynn, Edith. Newscaster (NBC, 1944).

13367 Gwynn, Nell. Soprano (WLS, Chicago, IL, 1926).

13368 Gwynn, Z.V. "Easy." Sportscaster (WFNC, Fayetteville, NC, 1940; WGAC, Augusta, GA, 1942; WIBC, Indianapolis, IN, 1945). DJ (*Easy Does It* and *Easy Listening*, WIBC, 1947–1957).

13369 Gwynne, Gladys. Gwynne appeared on the *Glorious One* program (Network, 1930s).

13370 Gypsy (Elsa Charlotte Musgrove). Gypsy was a contralto who accompanied herself on the piano when she broadcast alone (KPO, San Francisco, CA, 1925). Gypsy, whose maiden name was Elsa Charlotte Kaufman, frequently appeared as part of the Gypsy and Marta singing team. In the 1930s, she appeared alone on her own programs, where she interviewed various stars (*Gypsy Personal Close-Ups,*15 min., Wednesday, KPO, San Francisco, CA, 1931). *See* **Gypsy and Marta.**

13371 Gypsy and Marta. A female singing team — Gypsy was Elsa Charlotte Musgrove (Mrs. Harry George Musgrove), the granddaughter of a Polish noble man. She married an American army officer. Marta was Martha Reavey. The contralto (Gypsy) and soprano (Marta) appeared as a team on the *Mona Motor Oil Company Program* (KPO, San Francisco, CA, 1925; KPO, 30 min., Thursday 11:00–11:30 A.M., 1928–1929).

13372 Gypsy Girl. Singer-accordionist (WPCH, New York, NY, 1932).

13373 *Gypsy Joe*. *Gypsy Joe* was an excellent 15-minute transcribed show, a production of Jimmy Scribner, who played all the parts on the pleasant program. Gypsy Joe with a dialect marked by a faint trace of a southern accent told his animal stories to a child called "Little One." One program started this way: "Ah is Gypsy Joe. I've a good story. A long time ago around a gypsy camp they would sometimes be singing and there would be dancing. Sometimes there would be a story and one of the stories they have tell around the gypsy camp for a long time is the one called "The Mosquito Quartet." Gypsy Joe then went on to tell the story. Despite the fractured pronunciation, it was excellent radio for children. Although he was not usually identified, the talented Jimmy Scribner also wrote the program (Transcribed, Various Stations, late 1940s). *See* ***The Johnson Family*.**

13374 *Gypsy Nina*. Nina was a soprano who sang and played the accordion on the sustaining program. *Billboard* identified her as a feminine version of the Street Singer (15 min., Monday, 10:00–10:15 P.M., NBC-Blue and CBS, 1933).

13375 *Gypsy Sweetheart*. Singer-comedienne Inez Chesterton appeared on the show that mixed good humor with song (15 min., Weekly, WOWO, Fort Wayne, IN, mid–1930s).

13376 *(The) Gypsy Trail*. Emery Deutsch, his orchestra and vocalist Karle Thome supplied romantic gypsy music on the weekly show (30 min., Sunday, 1:30–2:00 P.M., CBS, 1931).

13377 H&S Poque Company Orchestra. Commercially sponsored band (WLW, Cincinnati, OH, 1926).

13378 "(The) Ha Ha Man." Designation for Charles Erbstein, the owner and announcer of station WTAS (Chicago, IL, 1925). *See* **Erbstein, Charles.**

13379 Haag, Hans. Violinist (WBBR, New York, NY, 1926).

13380 Haag, Robert. Actor Haag appeared in *The Sheriff, When a Girl Marries, Young Dr. Malone* and *Young Widder Brown.*

13381 Haagas, Cecilia. Singer (KFWM, Oakland, CA, 1929).

13382 Haaker, Edwin L. Newscaster (NBC, 1945–1946).

13383 Haan, Ruth. COM-HE (WMTC, Vandeve, KY, 1951).

13384 Haas, Al. Leader (Al Haas Orchestra, WGL, Ft. Wayne, IN, 1927).

13385 Haas, Alexander. Leader (*Alexander Haas Gypsy Orchestra*, instr. mus. prg., WOR, Newark, NJ, 1934–1935).

13386 Haas, Karl. Popular classical music commentator on *Adventures in Good Music,* his program was called by the New York *Times* (C19, Tuesday, February 8, 2005) "the most listened to classical music show in the world." His radio career began in Detroit, where he hosted weekly previews of Detroit Symphony concerts. After conducting a weekly music program for the Canadian Broadcasting Corporation, Haas began a weekly hour long program of music and comment in 1959. His program, *Adventures in Good Music,* was Detroit's top rated program in its time slot. The program was nationally syndicated in 1970 and carried by hundreds of stations in the United States, Mexico, Australia, Mexico, Panama and the Armed Forces Network. Haas discontinued broadcasting new shows in 2003 at age 89. The program was broadcast from transcriptions until his death two years later at 91 in 2005.

13387 **Haas, Grant.** Newscaster (WHA, Madison, WI, 1940).

13388 **Haas, Haven.** Announcer (WLBW, Oil City, PA, 1925).

13389 **Haas, M.J.** Newscaster (KFQD, Anchorage, AK, 1938).

13390 **Haas, Theodore.** Newscaster (KOIL, Omaha, NE, 1944).

13391 **Haase, Evelyn.** COM-HE (KSMN, Mason City, IA, 1954).

13392 **Haaser, Charles.** Newscaster (WTHT, Hartford, CT, 1937–1938; WMAS, Springfield, MA, 1940). DJ (*To the Ladies*, WMAS, 1948; *Shoppers' Special*, WMAS, 1952).

13393 **Hack, George.** DJ (*For the Children*, WNOW, York, PA, 1950).

13394 **Hacker, Les.** Newscaster (KVEC, San Luis, Obispo, CA, 1945).

13395 **Hackett, Evelyn.** Actress Hackett was in the cast of *American Women's Jury.*

13396 **Hackett, Jon.** Sportscaster (KRNT, Des Moines, IA, 1945–1946; *Sports of all Sports*, KERO, Bakersfield, CA, 1949).

13397 **Hackett, Neil.** Newscaster (KGKO-WBAP, Fort Worth, TX, 1940).

13398 **Hackscher, Ernie.** Leader (*Ernie Hackscher Orchestra*, instr. mus. prg., WCAE, Pittsburgh, PA, 1942).

13399 **Hadaway, Emmett.** DJ (WMBC, Macon, MS, 1954).

13400 **Haden, Evelyn.** COM-HE (WKWK, Wheeling, WV, 1956–1957).

13401 **Haddock, Ruth.** Contralto (KFI, Los Angeles, CA, 1929).

13402 **Hadfield, Ben.** Announcer (WNAC, Boston, MA, 1925).

13403 **Haden, Evelyn.** COM-HE (WKWK, Wheeling, WV, 1954–1957).

13404 **Haden, Sarah.** Actress Haden was featured on the *Moonlight and Honeysuckle* program.

13405 **Hadley, Cis.** COM-HE (KCJB, Minot, ND, 1957).

13406 **Hadley, Henry.** Conductor (Henry Hadley and his Philharmonic Orchestra, NBC, New York, NY, 1926; New York Philharmonic Orchestra, WJZ, New York, NY, 1927; conductor on the *Gulbranson Hour* program, WABC-CBS, New York, NY, 1929).

13407 **Hadley, Irving "Bump."** Former Yankee pitcher broadcast baseball play-by-play (WBZ-WBZA, Boston-Springfield, MA, 1942–1948).

13408 **Hadley, June.** COM-HE (WANE, Fort Wayne, IN, 1954).

13409 **Hadley, June.** COM-HE (WKWK, Wheeling, WV, 1955).

13410 **Hadley, William H., Jr.** Newscaster (*Final Edition*, KXLR, North Little Rock, AK, 1947).

13411 **Haefner, Louise B.** Contralto (WGY, Schenectady, NY, 1923).

13412 **Haemer, Pearl.** Haemer told stories for children.

13413 **Haenle, Florence.** Violinist (WFI, Philadelphia, PA, 1924).

13414 **Haenschen, Gustave "Gus."** Musical director (*Palmolive Hour* program, 1929; *Gus Haenschen Orchestra*, instr. mus. prg., NBC, 1935).

13415 **Haffey, Thom.** Newscaster (WLAP, Lexington, KY, 1938).

13416 **Hafford, Howard.** Saxophonist Hafford was a member of the Syrian Shrine Band Trio (WLW, Cincinnati, OH, 1923). Tenor (WLW, 1926).

13417 **Hafner, Betty.** COM-HE (WMOG, Brunswick, GA, 1956).

13418 **Hagaman, Josephine.** Soprano and pianist-contralto (WTAM, Cleveland, OH, 1924).

13419 **Hagaman, Josephine.** (WTAM, Cleveland, OH, 1924).

13420 **Hagan, Cass.** Leader (Cass Hagan's Orchestra broadcasting from New York's Park Central Hotel, 1927; Cass Hagan's Hotel Manger Orchestra broadcasting from the New Yorker hotel, WOR, Newark, NJ, 1927; KTM, Santa Monica, CA, 1928). The band in 1927 included: Hagan, ldr.-v.; Bob and Bo Ashford, t.; Eddie Lappe, tb.; Jack Towne, clr., as. bar.; Frank Crum, ts.; Lennie Hayton, p. and or.; Jim Mahoney, bj.; Ed Brader, sb. and tba.; and Chick Condon, d.

13421 **Hagan, Frances.** COM-HE (KIND, Independence, KS, 1956–1957).

13422 **Hagan, Malone.** Newscaster (*News and Views*, KCTX, Childress, TX, 1947).

13423 **Hagan, Stan.** DJ (*Wake Up and Live*, WMAN, Mansfield, OH, 1947; *Sugar and Spice*, KANS, Wichita, KS, 1948; *The Stan Hagan Show*, KANS, 1949; *Top Tune Time*, KFH, Wichita, KS, 1952).

13424 **Hagedorn, Mary Lou.** COM-HE (KURV, Edinburg, TX, 1948).

13425 **Hagelston, Charles.** Leader (*Charles Hagelston Orchestra*, instr. mus. prg., WOR, Newark, NJ, 1935).

13426 **Hageman, Harold L.** Newscaster (WADC, Akron, OH, 1938–1942, 1944–1948).

13427 **Hageman, Jim "Jimmy."** Sportscaster (WCHV, Charlottesville, VA, 1945). DJ (*Musical Clock*, WCHV, 1947–1948; *Platter Parade*, WCHV, 1950).

13428 **Hagen, Olive.** Organist (WKBH, La Crosse, WI, 1957).

13429 **Hagenor, Herb.** Leader (*Herb Hagenor Orchestra*, instr. mus. prg., WBEN, Buffalo, NY, 1942).

13430 **Hager, Kolin.** Sometimes designated as "KH," Hagler was the manager and chief announcer of station WGY (Schenectady, NY, 1924). He was a prize winning high school orator who developed his linguistic, acting and singing skills at Albany (New York) State Teachers College. Proficient in French, German and Italian, Hagler performed in touring musical productions before entering radio.

While at WGY, Hagler established a school for announcers in 1923. One of his students was A.O. Coggeshall, who later became an announcer at WGY (New York, NY). During his early years at WGY (1921), Hager was at times the victim of too much articulateness without thought. Once after a famous singer finished her song, Hager said, "Miss _____ has just sung 'All Through the Night.' We will now stand by for distress signals." Needless to say the singer was not amused despite Hager's profuse apologies for his unintended critical comment.

13431 **Haggard, Pauline.** Pianist-contralto (WEAF, New York, NY, 1926–1929; *Pauline Haggard, Songs*, vcl. mus. prg., 30 min., Saturday, 6:30–7:00 P.M., NBC-Blue, 1930).

13432 **Haggett, Florence.** Soprano (WBZ, Boston-Springfield, MA, 1924).

13433 **Haggin, Ann.** COM-HE (KSET, El Paso, TX, 1954).

13434 **Hagler, Eloise.** COM-HE (WAVU, Albertville, AL, 1956).

13435 **Hague, Earl.** Newscaster (WWDC, Washington, DC, 1942). DJ (WPIX, Alexandria, VA, 1967).

13436 **Hagy, Shirley.** COM-HE (WOPI, Bristol, TN, 1960).

13437 **Hahle, Sharon Ann.** COM-HE (KBOM, Bismark, ND, 1960).

13438 **Hahn, Frederick E.** Violinist (WIP, Philadelphia, PA, 1924).

13439 **Hahn, Helen.** Studio hostess Hahn was one of the earliest female announcers in radio (WBAY, New York, NY, 1921).

13440 **Hahn, Theodore.** Leader (*Theodore Hahn Orchestra*, instr. mus. prg., WLW, Cincinnati, OH, 1934).

13441 **Haid, Allen L.** Newscaster (WHIZ, Zanesville, OH, 1941–1942). Sportscaster (WHIZ, 1941).

13442 **Haidrigo, Juan.** Leader (*Juan Haidrigo and His Americanos Marimba Band*, instr. mus. prg., CBS, 1936).

13443 **Haigis, John W., Jr.** Newscaster (WHAI, Greenfield, MA, 1939).

13444 **Hail, Ewen.** Tenor (WFAA, Dallas, TX, 1926).

13445 **Hailer, Dick.** Announcer (KGW, Portland, OR, 1926).

13446 **Hailes, Viola.** Lyric-soprano (WGY, Schenectady, NY, 1924–1925).

13447 **Hain, William.** Tenor (NBC, New York, NY, 1928; WGBS, New York, NY, 1929; *William Hain*, vcl. mus. prg., NBC, 1934).

13448 **Haine, Norma Allen.** Contralto (WTIC, Hartford, CT, 1927).

13449 **Haines, Charles.** Newscaster (KGHF, Pueblo, CO, 1947).

13450 **Haines, Happy.** DJ (*Moon Dial*, KOEL, Oelwein, IA, 1952).

13451 **Haines, Larry.** Actor Haines appeared on *Big Town, Dimension X, Gangbusters, Joyce Jordan, Girl Interne, The Man Behind the Gun, Pepper Young's Family, Rosemary* and *Young Dr. Malone.*

13452 **Haines, Mary.** COM-HE (WCAM, Camden, NJ, 1949).

13453 **Haines, Mary Lewis.** Miss Haines broadcast household hints for women (KFRC, San Francisco, CA, 1925). Haines was the "domestic science expert" of the San Francisco *Call.*

13454 **Haines, Tom.** Announcer (WTAR, Norfolk, VA, 1925).

13455 **Haines, William.** Newscaster (WCOP, Boston, MA, 1942).

13456 **Hainline, Joseph R. "Joe."** Newscaster (KGBX-KWTO, Springfield, MO, 1939, WJR, Detroit, MI, 1946–1947).

13457 Hairgrove, Se. COM-HE (KBRZ, Freeport, TX, 1960).

13458 Haislip, Walter. Newscaster (WSTP, Salisbury, NC, 1940).

13459 Hait, Mal. DJ (WEOK, Poughkeepsie, NY, 1952–1954; WKIP, Poughkeepsie, NY, 1955–1957).

13460 Haitowitsch, Abraham. Blind violinist (WEAF, New York, NY, 1924).

13461 Hal and Henry. WMAQ's "football team" broadcast all of coach Amos Alonzo Stagg's University of Chicago Maroons football games in 1927. Hal Totten was the leading member of the broadcast team (WMAQ, Chicago, IL, 1927).

13462 Halban, Desi. Soprano (NBC, 1941).

13463 Halbman, Alex. Clarinetist (KMOX, St. Louis, MO, 1926).

13464 Hale, Alan. Newscaster (WISN, Milwaukee, WI, 1938–1940). Sportscaster (WISN, 1939–1940).

13465 Hale, Arthur. Newscaster (WOR, Newark, NJ, 1938–1941; *Confidentially Yours*, MBS-WOR, New York, NY, 1942; MBS, 1944; *Your Richfield Reporter*, MBS, 1945).

13466 Hale, Cecil. Newscaster (WSAI-WLW, Cincinnati, OH, 1942).

13467 Hale, Edith. Pianist (KDKA, Pittsburgh, PA, 1924).

13468 Hale, (Mrs.) Edward Everett. Mrs. Hale talked on topics of interest to and about women including "What Kind of Jurors Will Women Be?" (WGY, Schenectady, NY, 1923).

13469 Hale, Emma. COM-HE (KRIG, Odessa, TX, 1951).

13470 Hale, Florence. Newscaster (*Florence Hale's Radio Column*, NBC, 1938).

13471 Hale, Franc. Versatile actress Hale was a cast member of the daytime serial programs *Aunt Jenny* aka *Aunt Jenny's Real Life Stories, Young Dr. Malone* and *John's Other Wife.*

13472 Hale, (Major) Harry C. Director, Sixteenth Infantry Band (WJZ, New York, NY, 1922).

13473 Hale, Helen. Whistler (KFAE, Pullman, WA, 1925).

13474 Hale, Hot Rod. DJ (WBCO, Birmingham-Bessemer, AL, 1949).

13475 Hale, Ingaborg M. COM-HE (WAMW, Washington, IN, 1956).

13476 Hale, Lucille. Organist (KDKA, Pittsburgh, PA, 1924).

13477 Hale, Marie. COM-HE (WOR, Newark, NJ, 1932).

13478 Hale, Richard. Baritone (WJZ, New York, NY, 1926).

13479 Hale, Ted. Pianist (*Ted Hale*, instr. mus. prg., WIP, Philadelphia, PA, 1935–1936).

13480 Hale and Derry. Comedy singing team known as "Ike and Mike" (WDAF, Kansas City, MO, 1928). The team was not otherwise identified.

13481 Haler's Dance Orchestra. Popular local band (WLW, Cincinnati, OH, 1929).

13482 Haley, Al. Newscaster (WWOL, Lackawanna, NY, 1947).

13483 Haley, Ambrose. Leader (*Ambrose Haley and His Ramblers Orchestra*, instr. mus. prg., KMOX, St. Louis, MO, 1935).

13484 Haley, Elizabeth and Gladys Mick. The team broadcast programs of vocal and piano music (KLCN, Blytheville, AR, 1928).

13485 Haley, Herb. Newscaster (KGO, San Francisco, CA, 1945).

13486 Haley, James. "Old-time fiddler" (KMOX, Knoxville, TN, 1926).

13487 Haley's Hawaiian Trio. Instrumental group (WHB, Kansas City, MO, 1928).

13488 *Half Hour in the Nation's Capitol.* Each week "outstanding thinkers from various walks of life," were presented "under the auspices of the Daughters of the American Revolution" (30 min., Thursday, 7:30–8:00 P.M., NBC-Red, 1930).

13489 *Half Hours with Famous Women.* Mrs. Edith Ellis Furniss talked about the memorable activities and contributions of American women (WOR, Newark, NJ, 1923).

13490 Halk, John. Violinist (KMOX, St. Louis, MO, 1928).

13491 Hall, Al. Newscaster (KGKB, Tyler, TX, 1940). Sportscaster (KGKB, 1940–1941).

13492 Hall, Alfred. Singer (WOV, New York, NY, 1928).

13493 Hall, Anna DeWitte. Celeste soloist (WKAF, Milwaukee, WI, 1926).

13494 Hall, Arty. Leader, Arty Hall's Radio Rubes comedy-singing group (NBC, 1937).

13495 Hall, Barbara. COM-HE (WHCU, Ithaca, NY, 1949–1957).

13496 Hall, Bob. Chief announcer (KOIL, Council Bluffs, IA, 1928).

13497 Hall, Bob. Pianist (*Bob Hall*, instr. mus. prg., WBAL, Baltimore, MD, 1935).

13498 Hall, Bob. DJ (*Tops in Pops*, WVVW, Fairmont, WV, 1950).

13499 Hall, Cody E. COM-HE (WHMA, Anniston, AL, 1960).

13500 Hall, Edith Lucille. Pianist (KDKA, Pittsburgh, PA, 1924).

13501 Hall, Edward W. Announcer (WICC, Bridgeport, CT, 1926).

13502 Hall, Elese. COM-HE (WHAB, Baxley, GA, 1956).

13503 Hall, Frances. COM-HE (WJBF, Augusta, GA, 1955).

13504 Hall, Fred. Leader (Fred Hall's Terrace Orchestra, WJZ, New York, 1925).

13505 Hall, Fred. Newscaster (WDSU, New Orleans, LA, 1944). DJ (WMIE, Miami, FL, 1948).

13506 Hall, George. Busy musician-singer Hall broadcast as "The Fantom Fiddler"; played double piano duets with Hortense Rose; sang duets with Grace Donaldson; and joined the Maids of Harmony to form the Harmony Trio of WSAI (Cincinnati, OH, 1928).

13507 Hall, George. Leader, (George Hall's Arcadians Orchestra, WJZ, New York, NY, 1927). The Arcadians included the following personnel: Frank Comisky and George Knapp, t.; Mike Martini, tb; Jack Linton, Sam Rore, Rudy Reinhart, clr., as. and ts.; Sam Horowitz, p.; Charles Ruoff, bj.; Moe Spivak, d.; and Ben Rapfogel, tba. The band was also busy in the 1930: (*George Hall Orchestra*, instr. mus. prg., CBS, 1933; WJSV, Washington, DC, 1934; CBS, 1936; WHP, Atlantic City, NJ, 1937; WRC, Washington, DC, 1938–1939).

13508 Hall, George. Actor Hall appeared on the *Pepper Young's Family* daytime serial.

13509 Hall, (Mrs.) Gilbert. Soprano (KVOO, Tulsa, OK, 1928).

13510 Hall, Grace. Newscaster (WJAR, Providence, RI, 1937). COM-HE (WJAR, Providence, RI, 1936–1941)

13511 Hall, Halsey. Sportscaster (KSTP, St. Paul–Minneapolis, MN, 1939–1944; WCCO, Minneapolis, MN, 1945–1946; *Time Out for Sports*, WCCO, 1947–1960). Hall worked for several Twin Cities stations, but spent most of his time at WCCO. When he returned to that station in the 1940s, he began a career that eventually saw him broadcast Minnesota Twins' American League baseball games. He broadcast these games into the 1970s and beyond.

13512 Hall, Harriet. COM-HE (WBSM, New Bedford, MA, 1951; WNBH, New Bedford, MA, 1955).

13513 Hall, Harvey. Leader (Harvey Hall and his U.S. Grant Hotel Orchestra, KFSD, San Diego, CA, 1926).

13514 Hall, Hedley. Newscaster (KMYC, Marysville, CA, 1945). Sportscaster (KMYC, 1945).

13515 Hall, Helen. Newscaster (MBS, 1947–1948).

13516 Hall, Jack. Sportscaster (*Sports Scope*, WRDW, Augusta, GA, 1960).

13517 Hall, Jim. DJ (*Corn in Carolina*, WBBB, Burlington, NC, 1948; WWVA, Wheeling, WV, 1957).

13518 Hall, Kendall W. Singing xylophonist (KYW, Chicago, IL, 1922).

13519 Hall, Lee. COM-HE (WHNC, New Haven, CT, 1949).

13520 Hall, Libby. Singer (WIP, Philadelphia, PA, 1937).

13521 Hall, Lois. Actress Hall was a cast member of the *Second Husband* daytime serial program.

13522 Hall, Lorraine. COM-HE (KOOL, Phoenix, AZ, 1949).

13523 Hall, Louis. Actor Hall appeared on *Orphans of the Storm, Our Gal Sunday* and *Young Widder Brown.*

13524 Hall, Lynn. COM-HE (KRBC, Abilene, TX, 1956).

13525 Hall, Margaret. Whistler (KROW, Oakland, CA, 1930).

13526 Hall, Margaret. COM-HE (WCHN, Norwich, CT, 1956).

13527 Hall, Myrtle De Fries. Cornetist (KTAB, Oakland, CA, 1926).

13528 Hall, Norman. Leader (Norman Hall's South Sea Islanders [orchestra], NBC. 1928).

13529 Hall, Norman. DJ (*Strictly Informal*, WOMI, Owensboro, KY, 1947–1948).

13530 Hall, Polly. COM-HE (WBRT, Bardstown, KY, 1956).

13531 Hall, Radcliffe. Sportscaster (WGY, Schenectady, NY, 1939). Newscaster (NBC, 1945).

13532 Hall, Rae Eleanor. Violinist (*Rae Eleanor Hall*, instr. mus. prg., WCAU, Philadelphia, PA, 1936). Hall was billed as possessing a "magic violin."

13533 Hall, Robert F. Announcer (WKAF, Milwaukee, WI, 1927).

13534 Hall, Ruby. Hall was a member of the Harmony Girls singing team (KGA, Spokane, WA, 1928).

13535 Hall, Russ. DJ (*Once Over Weekly*, WFAA, Dallas, TX, 1947; *Russ Hall Show*, WJR, Detroit, MI, 1948; *Russ Hall Show*, KLIF, Dallas, TX, 1950). Sportscaster (KLIF, Dallas, TX, 1948; WCAU, Philadelphia, PA, 1960).

13536 Hall, Shirley. Singer (WMEX, Boston, MA, 1939).

13537 Hall, Sid. Leader (Sid Hall's Orchestra broadcasting from Yoeng's Restaurant, New York City, WJZ, New York, NY, 1928).

13538 Hall, Sid. Sportscaster (*Meet Your Teams*, WTCJ, Tell City, IN, 1949).

13539 Hall, Sleepy. Leader (*Sleepy Hall Orchestra*, instr. mus. prg., WLW, Cincinnati, OH, 1933; NBC, 1934; ABS, 1935; CBS, 1936).

13540 Hall [Hale], Theron and Daughters. The CW music group of fiddles and banjo appeared on the *WSM Barn Dance* program (WSM, Nashville, TN, 1929–1930).

13541 Hall, Wendell W. A popular singer, Hall made his radio debut as the "Red Headed Music Maker on WCCO (Minneapolis, MN). In 1923–1924, he was billed as "KYW's Music Maker (KYW, Chicago, IL). Hall was a great favorite on the *Eveready Hour*, where he was called variously: "The Eveready Red Head," "Eveready Red," "The Eveready Entertainer," and the "Eveready Red-Headed Music Maker."

In 1929, Hall appeared on a program sponsored by Wrigley Chewing Gum with the Guy Lombardo Orchestra (CBS, 1929). In addition, he broadcast many programs in which he alone was featured: *Wendell Hall—the Red Headed Music Man* (vcl. mus. prg., 15 min., Sunday 5:45–6:00 P.M., NBC, 1934–1936; *Wendell Hall*, vcl. mus. prg. sponsored by Fitch Shampoo, 15 min., Friday, 7:15–7:30 P.M., CST, NBC, 1936). Hall's program of Sunday, May 5, 1935, included the following songs: "Hello Blackbird," "Meadowlark," "Listen to the Mocking Birds," "The Burpy Bird," "A Brown Bird Singing" and "Let's All Sing Like the Birdies Sing."

13542 Hall, (Mrs.) William. Contralto (WSM, Nashville, TN, 1928).

13543 Hall, Williams. Newscaster (KECA, Los Angeles, CA, 1945).

13544 *Hall and Gruen*. Instr. mus. prg. by a dual piano team (NBC, 1935).

13545 *Hall of Fantasy*. The horror-fantasy series, sometimes sponsored by Granite Furniture Company, was often broadcast on a sustaining basis. The director was Richard Thorne and the writer Robert Olsen. The cast members included Carl Grayson, Beth Colter, Phyllis Perry, Mel Wyman and Richard Harcourt (30 min., Weekly, MBS, 1947–1953).

13546 *Hall Quartet*. Vcl. mus. prg. (KVOR, Colorado Springs, CO, 1939).

13547 Hallback, Billy. Leader (Billy Hallback's Footwarmers Orchestra, WRR, Dallas, TX, 1926).

13548 Halle, Jane C. COM-HE (WSON, Henderson, KY, 1956–1957).

13549 Halle, Kay. Newscaster (WGAR, Cleveland, OH, 1942). Newscaster Halle originated news broadcasts from Central and South American cities such as Mexico City; Lima, Peru; and Santiago, Chile.

13550 Halleck, Mark. Sportscaster, football play-by-play (WKLO, Louisville, KY, 1951).

13551 Haller, R.V. "Dick." Announcer-host Haller was famous for closing the zany, late night *Hoot Owl* program with the instruction: "Keep growing wiser, order of the Hoot Owls' orchestra, Grand Screech and cast." Haller, of course, was the "Grand Screech" (KGW, Portland, OR, 1925–1927).

13552 Hallet, Richard M. Newscaster (WGAN, Portland, ME, 1946).

13553 Hallett, Mal. Leader (Mal Hallett's Roseland Dance Orchestra, WHN, New York, NY, 1924; Mal Hallett's Orchestra, WGBS, New York, NY, 1926; Mal Hallett's Arcadians, WHN, 1927). Hallett's busy band during this period included: Hallett, ldr. and as.; Bill Carlin, t. and vcls; Carl Swearingen, t.; Andy Russo, tb.; Ollie Ahearn and Nelson Arguesso, clr., as. and ss.; Sam Sherman, ts. and vcls.; Frank Guilfoyle, p.; Vic Mondello, bj.; Frank Friselle, d.; and Larry de Laurence, tba. The band was also active in the following decades: *Mal Hallett Orchestra*, mus. prg., (WOR, Newark, NJ, 1936; NBC, 1940; WSM, Nashville, TN, 1942).

13554 Halliday, Madaleine M. COM-HE (WOTW, Nashua, NH, 1954).

13555 Halligan, Joseph. Halligan was a singer of Irish songs (WGBS, New York, NY, 1925).

13556 (The) Hall-Johnson Singers. The talented African-American singing group frequently appeared on the *Eveready Hour* (NBC, New York, NY, 1927).

13557 Hallman, Abe. Leader (Abe Hallman's Orchestra, KNRC, Los Angeles, CA, 1925).

13558 Hallman, Selma. Singer (*Selma Hallman*, vcl. mus. prg., WIP, Philadelphia, PA and WPG, Atlantic City, NJ, 1936).

13559 *(The) Hallmark Hall of Fame* (aka *The Hallmark Radio Hall of Fame*). Lionel Barrymore hosted the anthology series that presented dramatic productions featuring such stars as: Dana Andrews, Jean Pierre Aumont, Lew Ayres, Lionel Barrymore, Anne Baxter, Charles Bickford, Ann Blythe, Charles Boyer, Bruce Cabot, McDonald Carey, Jeff Chandler, Sarah Churchill, Joseph Cotten, Jeanne Crain, Robert Cummings, Bobby Driscoll, Irene Dunne, Douglas Fairbanks, Jr., Joan Fontaine, Judy Garland, Edmund Gwenn, Ann Harding, Van Heflin, John Hodiak, Van Johnson, Deborah Kerr, Angela Lansbury, Fred MacMurray, Lon McAllister, Dorothy McGuire, Ray Milland, Agnes Moorehead, David Niven, Lloyd Nolan, Ronald Reagan, Rosalind Russell, Martha Scott, Barbara Stanwyck, Dean Stockwell, Elizabeth Taylor, Richard Todd, Richard Widmark, Teresa Wright, Jane Wyman, Loretta Young and Robert Young (30 min., Weekly, CBS, 1953–1955).

13560 Hallock, Mel. Newscaster (KWYO, Sheridan, WY, 1942, 1945).

13561 Halloran, Edwin. Writer Halloran wrote the *Aunt Jenny* and *First Nighter* programs.

13562 Halloren, Ryan. Newscaster (KWNO, Winonah, MN, 1940). Sportscaster (KWNO, 1940).

13563 Halloway, Harrison. Halloway broadcast business information on his *Babson's Statistics* program (KFRC, San Francisco, CA, 1925). Announcer (KFRC, 1927).

13564 (The) Hallroom Boys. Comedy singing team of Tom Breneman and Leroy Kullberg (KNX, Los Angeles, CA, 1928).

13565 Hallroyd String Quartet. Instrumental group (WGR, Buffalo, NY, 1924).

13566 *(The) Halls of Ivy*. Don Quinn was the creator, writer and producer of this program that starred Ronald Colman and his wife, Benita Hume Colman. The Colemans played Dr. William Todhuner Hall, the president of a small liberal arts college, and his wife, Victoria Cromwell Hall. Nat Wolff directed the pleasant situation comedy. Schlitz beer was the sponsor (30 min., Friday, 8:00–8:30 P.M., NBC, 1949).

13567 Hallwood, Dick. DJ (*After Hours Club*, WBBC, Flint, MI, 1947).

13568 Halman, Doris. Actress Halman appeared on the daytime serial programs *Aunt Jenny* aka *Aunt Jenny's Real Life Stories* and *Kitty Foyle*.

13569 Halop, Billy. Actor Halop appeared on *Bobby Benson's Adventures* (title role), *The Children's Hour*, *Home Sweet Home* and *Let's Pretend*.

13570 Halpin, Josephine. Newscaster (KMOX, St. Louis, MO, 1938–1939; *Let's Discuss the News*, KMOX, 1940; *One Woman's Opinion*, KMOX, 1941).

13571 Halprin, George. Pianist (*George Halprin*, instr. mus. prg., WGAR, Cleveland, OH, 1935).

13572 Halse, Ray. Leader (Ray Halse Orchestra, WGY, Schenectady, NY, 1925).

13573 Halsey, Bob. Leader (*Bob Halsey Orchestra*, instr. mus. prg., KFEL, Denver, CO, 1934).

13574 *(The) Halsey-Stuart Program*. The program of semi-classical music also included financial advice by the "Old Counselor." The studio symphony orchestra was under the direction of George Dasch. The Chicago Symphony Orchestra also performed on some programs. Prominent business leaders spoke each week. In 1931, for example, the speakers presented were: Rome C. Stephenson, President of the American Bankers' Association; D.F. Kelley, President, National Retail Dry Goods Association; T. George Lee, President, Armour and Company and T.S. Morgan,

President, F.W. Dodge Corporation (30 min., Wednesday, 9:00–9:30 P.M., NBC-Red, 1928–1931).

13575 Halstead, Antoinette. Contralto (*Antoinette Halstead*, vcl. mus. prg., WGY, Schenectady, NY, 1934).

13576 Halstead, (Mrs.) Charles. COM-HE (KDIA, Auburn, CA, 1951).

13577 Halstead, Henry. Leader (Henry Halstead Orchestra, KGO, San Francisco, CA, 1924–1926; KPO, San Francisco, CA, 1926). When broadcasting over KFWB (Hollywood, CA) in 1925, Halstead's orchestra was reported as "radiocasting over KFWB from the Hollywood Roof Ballroom." Halstead's orchestra included: Halstead, ldr. and v.; Ted Schilling, t.; Ross Dugat, tb.; Ernie Reed and Chuck Moll, clr. and as.; Abe Maule, clr., v., and ts.; Hal Chanslor, p.; and Zeke Mann, bj. and g. In the 1930s: (*Henry Halstead Orchestra*, instr. mus. prg, MBS, 1935; CBS, 1936).

13578 Halteman, Charles. Newscaster (WTOL, Toledo, OH, 1939).

13579 Halverson, Pat. Newscaster (WRBC, Jackson, MS, 1947).

13580 Halverson, Thelma. Soprano (WCCO, Minneapolis–St. Paul, MN, 1927).

13581 Halvorson, Fay. COM-HE (KGCX, Sidney, MT, 1951).

13582 Halyard, Loretta. COM-HE (WCMI, Ashland, KY, 1960).

13583 Ham, J.B. Newscaster (WIZE, Springfield, OH, 1945).

13584 Ham, Lois. COM-HE (KSID, Sidney, NE, 1954).

13585 Ham, Ray and Fred Sommer. Instrumental team of banjoist and guitarist (WHB, Kansas City, MO, 1928).

13586 Haman, Henry. Tenor (KFWI, San Francisco, CA, 1926).

13587 Hamblen, Stuart. CW singer-song writer Hamblen played "Cowboy Joe" on KFI (Los Angeles, CA, 1929), beginning a long, successful career on California radio. In 1930, he became a member of the popular Beverly Hillbillies group, only to leave them to form his own band. He began his *Lucky Stars* (KFWB, Los Angeles, CA, 1932) program. For the next 20 years, it was said, he was probably the most popular western performer on Los Angeles radio (Kingsbury, 1998, p. 226). From 1952 through the late 1970s. The Academy of Country Music in 1972 recognized Hamblen as "the first Western singer on Los Angeles radio" (Kingsbury, 1998, p. 226). Hamblen starred in several western movies as the villain opposite such stars as Roy Rogers and Gene Autry. His best known composition is "This Old House."

13588 Hamblin, Enola. Pianist (WGR, Buffalo, NY, 1926).

13589 Hamil, Alma J. COM-HE (WESC, Greenville, SC, 1956).

13590 Hamil, Gail. Whistler (WOAW, Omaha, NE, 1923).

13591 Hamil, Myrtle. Pianist (WFBH, New York, NY, 1925; WGBS, New York, NY, 1925).

13592 Hamilton, Bill. Newscaster (WCFL, Chicago, IL, 1948).

13593 Hamilton, Billy. Leader (Billy Hamilton's Glanduja Cafe Orchestra, KFRC, San Francisco, CA, 1926).

13594 Hamilton, Bob. DJ (*The Bob Hamilton Show*, WDSU, New Orleans, LA, 1949; *Top Twenty at 1280*, WDSU, 1952).

13595 Hamilton, Dick. Newscaster (KIUL, Garden City, KS, 1940; KGNO, Dodge City, KS, 1942; WAPO, Chattanooga, TN, 1944). Sportscaster (KIUL, 1940).

13596 Hamilton, Edna May. Contralto Hamilton was a "well known pupil of Madame Marguerite Maretzek" (KLS, Oakland, CA, 1923; KTAB, Oakland, CA, 1926).

13597 Hamilton, Gene. Announcer (WAIU, Columbus, OH, 1929).

13598 Hamilton, George. Leader (*George Hamilton Orchestra*, instr. mus. prg., NBC, 1935; WHAS, Louisville, KY, 1936; WGN, Chicago, IL, 1937; MBS, 1939).

13599 Hamilton, James. Baritone (*James Hamilton*, vcl. mus. prg., WAAF, Chicago, IL, 1935; WJJD, Chicago, IL, 1936).

13600 Hamilton, Jan. COM-HE (WMAK, Nashville, TN, 1956).

13601 Hamilton, Jim. Newscaster (WLEU, Erie, PA, 1939–1941, 1945).

13602 Hamilton, Jim. DJ (*Record Shop*, WIND, Chicago, IL, 1948; WTOL, Toledo, OH, 1957).

13603 Hamilton, Joe. Newscaster (WLBJ, Bowling Green, OH, 1945). DJ (*Wake Up and Grin*, WLBJ, 1947).

13604 Hamilton, John. DJ (*Uncle John's Bandbox*, KPRL, Paso Robles, CA, 1947; KSRO, Santa Rosa, CA, 1956).

13605 Hamilton, Kay. COM-HE (WSAI, Cincinnati, OH, 1949).

13606 Hamilton, Kenneth "Ken." Sportscaster (WEBQ, Harrisburg, IL, 1948–1951; *Sports Roundup*, WEBQ, 1952–1956).

13607 Hamilton, Margaret. Pianist-composer (NBC, 1929).

13608 Hamilton, Martha. COM-HE (WJZM, Clarksville, TN, 1949).

13609 Hamilton, Priscilla. COM-HE (WHEB, Portsmouth, NH, 1955).

13610 Hamilton, Roy. Baritone (KFBK, Sacramento, CA, 1926).

13611 Hamilton, Spike. Leader (Spike Hamilton Orchestra, WJAZ, Chicago, IL, 1926).

13612 Hamilton, Vanita. Pianist (KFWI, San Francisco, CA, 1929).

13613 Hamilton, Wade. Organist (KVOO, Tulsa, OK, 1929).

13614 *Hamilton-Brown Sketchbook*. NBC broadcast the interesting series of dramatic sketches (30 min., Friday, 11:00–11:30 P.M., NBC-Blue, 1930).

13615 Hamilton County Knights of the Ku Klux Klan Band. KKK organization band (WLW, Cincinnati, OH, 1923).

13616 Hamilton Orchestra. Atlantic City orchestra (WPG, Atlantic City, NJ, 1926).

13617 Hamlett, Jim. DJ (*Cactus Jim*, KFXM, San Bernardino, CA, 1949; *Cactus Jim Show*, KMON, Great Falls, MT, 1950; *Cactus Jim Show*, KUTA, Salt Lake City, UT, 1952).

13618 Hamlin, Dave. Newscaster (KVAK, Atchinson, KS, 1939).

13619 Hamm, Fred. Leader (Fred Hamm's Orchestra was later replaced by Husk O'Hare's popular band, WTAS, Chicago, IL, 1925; Fred Hamm's Purple Grackle Orchestra, WLIB, Chicago, IL, 1926; Fred Hamm's Victor Recording Orchestra, WLIB, Chicago, IL, 1928). *See* **O'Hare, Husk.**

13620 Hamm, John Bennett. Baritone (WJAZ, Chicago, IL, 1926).

13621 Hamman, Mary. On her sustaining program, *Frankly Feminine*, Mary Hamman provided household information and commentary (15 min., Monday through Friday, 9:30–9:45 A.M., WEAF, New York, NY, 1942).

13622 Hammer, Granville "Granny." Sportscaster "Granny" Hammer was a former Philadelphia Phillies baseball star (*Sports Hi-Lites*, WEZL, Richmond, VA, 1960.

13623 Hammer, Jimmie. Leader (*Jimmie Hammer Orchestra*, instr. mus. prg., WRTD, Richmond, VA, 1939).

13624 Hammer, Muriel. COM-HE (KEXO, Grand Junction, CO, 1951).

13625 Hammerman, Bill. Announcer (WKBN, Youngstown, OH, 1925).

13626 Hammersley, Evadna (Lora Price). COM-HE, writer and director (KOA, Denver, CO, 1930s). Hammersley began work at KOA as a writer. Four years later she became the director of women's programs. On her own program she interviewed such celebrities as Bob Hope, Paul Raymond, Lauritz Melchior, James Melton, Eleanor Roosevelt and Mae West. She left KOA in the mid–1950s to become Director of Education and Information for the American Sheep Producers Council, where she originated and produced a package of programs for the organization that went to 50 stations. Her work at the American Sheep Producers Council was done under the name of Paula Owen. She also used that name to write cookbooks published by Random House.

Hammersley (1975) says that the attitude toward women in broadcasting changed by the 1970s. She said earlier that no matter what experience you had, you always began as a typist. They always asked, "Can you type?" That was the way you got your toe in the door according to Hammersley. In addition, there were two standards of pay for the same job for men and women. That no longer was the case in 1975 she said (Hammersely, 1975).

13627 *Hammerstein Music Hall*. Producer Ted Hammerstein featured Lucy Laughlin on the variety show (30 min., Tuesday, 6:00–6:30 P.M. CST, CBS, 1936).

13628 Hammett, W. Eugene. Leader (Amrad Banjo-Mandolin Club Orchestra, WGI, Medford Hillside, MA, 1923).

13629 Hammond, Carl E. Announcer (KFOA, Seattle, WA, 1924).

13630 Hammond, Elinore. Thirteen-year-old pianist (KHJ, Los Angeles, CA, 1924).

13631 Hammond, Esther. Singer (*Esther Hammond*, vcl. mus. prg., WLW, Cincinnati, OH, 1934).

13632 Hammond, Fred. Newscaster

(KPAB, Laredo, TX, 1939; KONO, San Antonio, TX, 1940; KPRO, Riverside, CA, 1945).

13633 **Hammond, Harvey.** Organist (*Harvey Hammond*, instr. mus. prg., WCAO, Baltimore, MD, 1935).

13634 **Hammond, Jean.** Leader (Jean Hammond's Elks Club Tune Tinkers Orchestra, WTMJ, Milwaukee, WI, 1927).

13635 **Hammond, John.** Organist Hammond broadcast half-hour recitals from the Piccadilly Theatre every Tuesday at midnight (WGBS, New York, NY, 1925).

13636 **Hammond, Madeline.** Singer (WIBO, Chicago, IL, 1926).

13637 **Hammond, Martha.** COM-HE (KVMC, Colorado City, TX, 1951).

13638 **Hammonds, Ina.** COM-HE (KBHC, Nashville, AR, 1960).

13639 **Hammond's Cottage City Dance Orchestra.** Club band (KFXF, Colorado Springs, CO, 1926).

13640 **Hamp, Johnny.** Pianist, band leader and singer Hamp, according to *Variety*, "... pleasantly played and crooned the blues." Leader (Johnny Hamp and his Kentucky Serenaders Orchestra, WIP, Philadelphia, PA, 1926; KFKX, Hastings, NE, 1927). Hamp's Kentucky Serenaders included the following personnel: Lester Brewer, t.; William Benedict, tb.; Ray Stillson and Charles Dale, clr., ss. and as.; Howard Bartlett, clr., as. and ts.; Hal White, v. and vcls.; John Strouse, d.; and Elwood Groff, tba. and vcls. Hamp commuted from San Francisco to Los Angeles weekly by plane to host the *Thirty Minutes of Sunshine* program in 1928 (KNX, Los Angeles, CA, 1928). In the following decade the Hamp band often appeared on radio (*Johnny Hamp Orchestra*, instr. mus. prg., NBC-Red, 1931; WBBM, Chicago, IL, 1933; *Johnny Hamp's Hotel Mark Hopkins Orchestra:* NBC, 1933; WLW, Cincinnati, OH, 1934; WHAS, Louisville, KY and CBS, 1935; NBC, 1937–1939). Hamp's band frequently featured singer June McCloy, who was one of the girls glorified by Florenz Ziegfeld in his productions. The Hamp band often broadcast from San Francisco's Mark Hopkins Hotel,

13641 **Hampden, Burford.** Actor Hampden appeared on *The O'Neills* daytime serial program.

13642 **Hampden Glee Club of Holyoke, Massachusetts.** Norman Dash directed the choral group (WBZ, Boston-Springfield, MA, 1925).

13643 **Hampson, Gordon (Gordon Hampson Light Opera Company).** Light opera group remembered for their broadcast of *The Tales of Hoffman* (WRNY, New York, NY, 1926).

13644 **Hampton, Bonnie Roth.** Reader (KLDS, Independence, MO, 1926).

13645 **Hampton, E.R.** Announcer (WABC, New York, NY, 1928).

13646 **Hampton, Vera Sue.** Pianist (WSB, Atlanta, GA, 1925).

13647 **Hamrick, Tiny.** Newscaster (WBRE, Wilkes-Barre, PA, 1939). DJ (*Tune Time with Tiny*, WKBW, Buffalo, NY, 1948).

13648 **Hanauer, Bert.** Announcer (WCAO, Baltimore, MD, 1929).

13649 **Hance, Kenneth M.** Announcer (WDAY, Fargo, ND, 1925).

13650 **Hancher, George.** Baritone (WIBO, Chicago, IL, 1926).

13651 **Hancock, Don.** Announcer Hancock worked on the *Harvest of Stars, Life Can Be Beautiful, Major Bowes Original Amateur Hour* and *Romance of Helen Trent.*

13652 **Hancock, Hunter.** Newscaster (KPAB, Laredo, TX, 1942). Rock-and-Roll DJ (KGJF, Hollywood, CA, 1954; KPOP, Los Angeles, CA, 1955–1957; KGFJ, Los Angeles, CA, 1960). Sportscaster (KPAB, 1942).

13653 **Hancock, John.** DJ (*Timekeeper Time*, WKTY, La Crosse, WI, 1948; *Barndance Kapers*, WKTY, 1950).

13654 **Hancock, Kingsley.** Announcer-musician (1928).

13655 **Hancock, Shirley.** COM-HE (WMTA, Central City, KY, 1955).

13656 **Hancock, William "Wee Willie."** Singer-organist-pianist (KGO, Oakland, CA, 1925; KPO, San Francisco, CA, 1929).

13657 ***Hancock and Goodheart.*** Piano duo (15 min., Tuesday, 8:30–8:45 P.M., NBC, 1931).

13658 **Hand, Arthur J.** Baritone (WGBS, New York, NY, 1923).

13659 **Hand, Jack.** Sportscaster (WNBF, Binghampton, NY, 1939–1942). Newscaster (WNBF, 1942).

13660 **Handlan, Joe.** Newscaster (WCHV, Charlottesville, VA, 1937).

13661 **Handler, David.** Violinist (WBBM, Chicago, IL, 1926).

13662 **Handley, Gertrude.** COM-HE (WDAK, Columbus, GA, 1949).

13663 **Handley, Lee "Jeep."** Sportscaster Handley was a former Pittsburgh Pirate (NL) baseball player turned broadcaster (KDKA, Pittsburgh, PA, 1954).

13664 **Handman, Edith.** Singer (WRNY, New York, NY, 1932).

13665 **Handrich, Fred.** Newscaster (WQAM, Miami, FL, 1941).

13666 ***Hands of History.*** *Hands of History* was a dramatic series based on various historical events with musical interludes (15 min, Weekly, 11:30–11:45 A.M., NBC-Pacific Coast Network, 1929).

13667 ***Handsome Bob and the Ohioans.*** CW mus. prg. by unidentified performers (WORK, York, PA, 1938).

13668 **Handy, Katherine Eugene.** Singer Handy, a contralto who sang the blues, was the daughter of W.C. Handy (WOR, Newark, NJ, 1926).

13669 **Handy, Truman Bishop.** Pianist (KFWI, San Francisco, CA, 1927).

13670 **Hanefin, Margaret.** Violinist Hanefin was, according to *Radio Digest*, "well known to musical circles in San Francisco and [the] Bay region" (KPO, San Francisco, CA, 1923).

13671 **Hanenseldt, (Madame) Mertzago.** Pianist (WRC, Washington, DC, 1925).

13672 **Hanes, Tom.** Sportscaster (WTAR, Norfolk, VA, 1939).

13673 **Haney, Bill.** Sportscaster (WSFC, Somerset, KY, 1956; WKBJ, Milan, TN, 1956).

13674 **Haney, Lynn.** COM-HE (WKAP, Allentown, PA, 1951).

13675 **Hanford, Delores.** Singer (WEVD, New York, NY, 1937).

13676 **Hanford, E. Mark.** Announcer (KFDD, Boise, IA, 1926).

13677 ***Hank Keene's Gang.*** Popular CW group (WTIC, Hartford, CT, 1931).

13678 ***Hank Simmons' Showboat.*** Old time melodramas were broadcast on this program from the "showboat *Maybelle.*" Harry C. Browne, originated, wrote, produced, directed and starred as Captain Hank Simmons. Singer Edith Thayer and actress Elsie Mae Gordon were program regulars (60 min., Wednesday, 11:00–12:00 midnight, CBS, 1930 and Saturday, 10:00–11:00 P.M., CBS, 1931). A half-hour format was adopted later in 1931. The show opened with the announcer proclaiming: "Tonight Hank Simmons' floating theater, *The Maybelle*, lies moored along the levee of a Mississippi River town. Actors and stage hands are making final preparations for the evening performance, while outside along the levee the crowds are beginning to gather, attracted by Hank's band, which is giving the customary evening concert before the big show begins aboard the showboat."

After the band played a march, the announcer continued: "This way, folks. This way to the big show. See the Hank Simmons Dramatic Comedy Company, playing the popular classical drama, 'Ingomar the Barbarian.' Four acts with specialties between, no waits, show going on all the time. The first performance of this delightful comedy drama ever given aboard the showboat. Act one: The capture. Act two: The hostage. Act Three: The conversion. Act Four: All's well that ends well. See Hank Simmons in the greatest part of his showboat career as Ingomar the Barbarian. See Maybelle as Parthenia, the beautiful Grecian maid. Special scenes and costumes for the beautiful Grecian play. This way folks. Remember the prices — 10-20-30 cents. Box office in the gangway yonder. Come one. Come all. See the great Hank Simmons Quartet and don't forget charming dainty Jane McGrew in their delightful specialties between the acts. This way, everybody!"

13679 ***Hank Williams.*** Williams, a great CW music performer began singing on radio at the age of 14 (WSFA, Montgomery, AL, 1937). He appeared on several local stations before gaining national fame on the *Louisiana Hayride* and the *Grand Ole Opry* programs. His transcribed *Health and Happiness* show was a popular feature on many stations. Williams died of a heart attack January 1, 1953, in the back of a car chauffeuring him to a performance in Canton, Ohio. *See* ***The Health and Happiness Show*****, Country-Western (CW) Music on Radio** *and* **Singers: Crooners, Song Birds, Country Belles, Cow Girls and Hillbillies.**

13680 **Hankel, Freddie.** Leader (*Freddie Hankel Orchestra*, instr. mus. prg., WMAQ, Chicago, IL, 1942).

13681 Hankins, Helen. Singer (WIND, Gary, IN, 1935).

13682 Hankins, Jack P. Newscaster (WORD, Spartanburg, SC, 1944; WBBB, Spartanburg, SC, 1945).

13683 Hankins, W.W. Newscaster (*The Hankins Show*, WEBC, Duluth, MN, 1948).

13684 Hanks, Margaret. COM-HE (WAGM, Presque Isle, ME, 1949).

13685 Hanks, Nancy. COM-HE (KIRX, Kirksville, MO, 1949).

13686 Hanlein, Fritz. Director (Fritz Hanlein's Trianon Ensemble, WDAF, Kansas City, MO, 1924).

13687 Hanley, Lorraine. COM-HE (WROK, Rockford, IL, 1951).

13688 Hanley, Louise. Manager (NBC, 1939). Hanley supervised all the printing services of the network.

13689 Hanlon, John. Sportscaster (WEAN, Providence, RI, 1953–1956).

13690 Hanlon, Tom. Sportscaster (KNX, Los Angeles, CA, 1939–1942). Newscaster (KNX, 1944; *Giant Football Roundup*, KNX, CA, 1952; *Sports Scoreboard*, KNX, 1954). DJ (*Merry-Go-Round*, KNX, 1949).

13691 Hanly, Jack. Organist (WBZ, Boston-Springfield, MA, 1924).

13692 Hann [Haun], Helen. Hann, an employee of the AT&T Long Lines Department at WEAF, started as a studio hostess and became the station manager and announcer (WEAF, New York, NY, 1922).

13693 Hann, Louis M. Baritone (WEAF, New York, NY, 1923).

13694 Hanna, Arthur. Director Hanna directed *Brighter Day*, *David Harum*, *Joyce Jordan, Girl Interne*, *Just Plain Bill*, *Lora Lawton*, *Our Gal Sunday*, *Perry Mason*, *Right to Happiness* and *This Is Nora Drake*.

13695 Hanna, Betty. Actress Hanna appeared on the daytime serials *Ma Perkins* and *Stepmother*.

13696 Hanna, Bob. Singer Hanna performed on the *Hearts in Harmony* program.

13697 Hanna, Bob. Sportscaster (*Sports Review*, WWPB, Miami, FL, 1952).

13698 Hanna, C.A. Baritone (WTAM, Cleveland, OH, 1924).

13699 Hanna, Earl. Newscaster (*Dixie News Cross Section*, WMOX, Meridian, MS, 1947). DJ (WJAM, Marion, AL, 1954).

13700 Hanna, Edna K. COM-HE (WLAN, Lancaster, PA, 1951).

13701 Hanna, Michael R. Newscaster (WIBX, Utica, NY, 1939).

13702 Hanna, Robert. Newscaster (WGFJ, Los Angeles, CA, 1944).

13703 Hanna, Ruth Winter. Soprano (KFSG, Los Angeles, CA, 1925).

13704 Hanna, Ted. Newscaster (WGAR, Cleveland, OH, 1938–1942).

13705 Hannah, Robert "Bob." Newscaster (*Morning News*, WFIG, Sumter, SC, 1947). DJ (*Musical Clock*, WFIG, 1947).

13706 Hannan, Marjorie. Busy actress Hannan appeared on the daytime serials *Bachelor's Children*, *Ma Perkins*, *Mary Marlin* aka *The Story of Mary Marlin*, *We Are Four* and *Sally of the Talkies*.

13707 Hannemann, Jacob. Pianist (WJAZ, Mt. Prospect, IL, 1928).

13708 Hannen, Helen and Ella Thomsen. Hannen and Thompson played flute solos and duets (KFKU, Lawrence, KS, 1926).

13709 Hannes, Arthur. Newscaster (WHDL, Olean, NY, 1940).

13710 *Hannibal Cobb*. An interesting sustaining mystery serial, *Hannibal Cobb* was unusual in that it was broadcast in time slots usually reserved for women's daytime serials. Santos Ortega played the master detective Hannibal Cobb assisted by cast members: Wendy Drew, Ethel Everett, Barry Kroeger, Amy Sedell and James Van Dyke. Ira Marion, Lillian Schoen and Louis M. Heyward wrote the show. Martin Andrews and Charles Powers were the producer-directors. Les Griffith was the announcer. The great radio organist Rosa Rio provided musical interludes (15 min., Monday through Friday, 3:30–3:45 P.M., ABC, 1950).

13711 Hannon, Bob. Vocalist (*Bob Hannon*, vcl. mus. prg., WGN, Chicago, IL, 1936).

13712 Hannon, LaVerne. Pianist (WQJ, Chicago, IL, 1925).

13713 Hannon, Stuart. Newscaster (KROW, Oakland, CA, 1941).

13714 Hannon, Thomas. Baritone (WHN, New York, NY, 1925).

13715 Hannoules, John. Saxophonist (WSB, Atlanta, GA, 1923).

13716 Hannson, Peter. Newscaster (WIZE, Springfield, OH, 1947).

13717 Hanold, Louis. Leader (Louis Hanold and his Appollo Concert and Dance Orchestra, WGBS, New York, NY, 1927).

13718 Hanrahan, Bill. Newscaster (WNHC, New Haven, CT, 1946).

13719 Hansard, David C. Violinist (KFMQ, Fayetteville, AR, 1924). Hansard was accompanied by pianist Mildred Gillespie.

13720 Hanscomb, Olga. COM-HE (WFLA, Tampa, FL, 1956–1957).

13721 Hansen, Carroll. Newscaster (KJBS, San Francisco, CA, 1941; KQW, San Jose, CA, 1941–1942 and KJBS, 1942; KQW, 1946). Sportscaster (KQW, 1946; *Looking 'em Over*, KQW, 1947–1948; *Sports Review*, KCBS, San Jose, CA, 1949–1955).

13722 Hansen, Cliff. Newscaster (KOL, Seattle, WA, 1940).

13723 Hansen, Edith. COM-HE (WNAX, Yankton, SD, 1949).

13724 Hansen [Hensen], Edith. COM-HE (KGLO, Mason City, IA, 1951).

13725 Hansen, Edith. COM-HE (WMAY, Springfield, IL, 1951).

13726 Hansen, Elena. Soprano (WTIC, Hartford, CT, 1925).

13727 Hansen, Flo. COM-HE (KFRE, Fresno, CA, 1951–1954).

13728 Hansen, Harry. Announcer (WSPD, Toledo, OH, 1925). Critic Hansen broadcast talks about books (WMAQ, Chicago, IL, 1925).

13729 Hansen, Howard. Newscaster (WHBY, Appleton, WI, 1946).

13730 Hansen, Jack. Drums-tympani (KOMO, Seattle, WA, 1928).

13731 Hansen, Joe. Newscaster (WTOP, Washington, DC, 1945).

13732 Hansen, Mal. Newscaster (WHO, Des Moines, IA, 1940).

13733 Hansen, Marilyn. Pretty four-year-old blues singer (KMO, Tacoma, WA, 1932).

13734 Hansen, Martin W. Announcer (WGBF, Evansville, IN, 1925). Chief announcer (WGBF, 1929).

13735 Hansen, Ole. Leader (Ole Hansen's Spanish Village Orchestra, KFSD, San Diego, CA, 1926).

13736 Hansen, Robert "Bob." Newscaster (KUTA, Salt Lake City, UT; KSFO, San Francisco, C), 1944; *Business News*, KSFO, 1948).

13737 Hansen, Sally. COM-HE (KSVC, Richfield, UT, 1956).

13738 Hansen, Vern. Newscaster (WGN, Chicago, IL, 1941).

13739 Hansen, Verna. Soprano (WAAW, Omaha, NE, 1924).

13740 Hansen, Zanna. Pianist (WEBJ, New York, NY, 1925).

13741 Hanshaw, Ruth. COM-HE (WAYZ, Waynesboro, PA, 1960).

13742 Hanson, Bob. Newscaster (KUTA, Salt Lake City, UT, 1939).

13743 Hanson, Carl. Actor Hanson was in the cast of *Dan Harding's Wife*.

13744 Hanson, Dee. COM-HE (KRCK, Ridgecrest, CA, 1960).

13745 Hanson, Earl. Leader (*Earl Hanson Orchestra*, instr. mus. prg., WCSH, Portland, ME, 1934).

13746 Hanson, Ed. Sportscaster (WFHR, Wisconsin Rapids, WI, 1951–1956).

13747 Hanson, Eleanor. COM-HE (WHK, Cleveland, OH, 1949).

13748 Hanson, (Mrs.) Ferne. Singer (WHAD, Milwaukee, WI, 1926).

13749 Hanson, Harley. Sportscaster (*The Sports Digest*, KOTA, Rapid City, SD, 1951–1960).

13750 Hanson, (Major) Joseph. Newscaster (WPID, Petersburg, VA, 1941).

13751 Hanson, Michael. DJ (WHA, Madison, WI). Hanson for many years was a popular Madison DJ with his *Asylum* and *Round Midnight* programs.

13752 Hanson, Peter. Pianist (KPO, San Francisco, CA, 1925).

13753 Hanson, Ted. Leader (*Ted Hanson Orchestra*, instr. mus. prg., WNAC, Boston, MA, 1934).

13754 Hanzel, Betty. COM-HE (WBBW, Youngstown, OH, 1951).

13755 *Hap Hazzard*. Ransom Sherman wrote and played the title role on the situation comedy, a summer replacement for *Fibber McGee and Molly. The* sponsor was the S.C. Johnson Company. Sherman played Hap Hazzard, the manager of Crestfallen Manor, a zany hotel that was part of the Stop and Flop Chain, where the comedy took place. Elmira Roesaler played Sherman's scatterbrained secretary and Cliff Soubier his efficiency expert. The announcer was Harlow Wilcox (30 min., Tuesday, 8:30–9:00 P.M., NBC, 1941).

13756 **Happiness Candy Boys.** Comedy singing team of Billy Jones and Ernie Hare (WEAF, New York, NY, 1926). It is reported that the Happiness Boys first gained national prominence with their WEAF (New York, NY) appearances in 1924 and 1925. Exactly when Jones and Hare became a two-man team is not clear. It is clear, however, that Jones, Hare and Briers were paid $300 per appearance by WEAF (*Radio Age*, January, 1925, p. 28). The following year, Jones and Hare broadcast weekly (*The Happiness Boys*, 30 min., Friday, 8:30–9:00 P.M., WEAF, New York, NY, 1926). *See* **Jones, Billy and Hare, Ernie**.

13757 ***(The) Happiness Kids.*** The vocal team of Hortense Rice and George Hall were featured on the vocal music program (WLW, Cincinnati, OH, 1931).

13758 ***Happiness Program.*** The California Crematorium sponsored the program of soothing music and inspirational talk broadcast weekly (KTAB, Oakland, CA, 1927).

13759 ***Happy Bakers.*** Songs were performed by Phil Duey, Frank Luther, Jack Parker and Harriet Lee on the pleasant music show. They were assisted by their arranger-accompanist (15 min., Monday, 8:00–8:15 P.M., CBS, 1933).

13760 ***(The) Happy Chappies.*** Harry Morton and Nat Vincent were the singing friends on the popular program. The talented song and piano team composed the popular "When the Bloom is on the Sage" song (KFRC, San Francisco, CA, 1928; 15 min., 12:00–12:15 P.M., Monday through Friday, KMPC, Beverly Hills, CA, 1931; WMT, Cedar Rapids–Waterloo, IA, 1936–1937).

13761 ***(The) Happy Clarks.*** Mr. and Mrs. Clark sang hymns on the popular local program sponsored by CocoWheats Cereal. John Falls was the announcer (15 min., Monday, 11:00–11:15 P.M., KYW, Philadelphia, PA, 1941).

13762 ***Happy Dan's Radio Folks.*** Happy Dan conducted the early morning program of music and talk (KLRA, Little Rock, AR, 1939).

13763 ***Happy Days.*** The popular network variety show originated from Philadelphia (60 min., Tuesday, 9:00–10:00 A.M., CBS, 1935).

13764 ***Happy Days in Dixie.*** Folk and CW singer Bradley Kincaid conducted the popular music show (30 min., Wednesday, 3:15–3:45 P.M., NBC-Blue, 1934). *See* **Kincaid, Bradley**.

13765 ***Happy Drewry Gang.*** CW mus. prg. by otherwise unidentified performers (WKZO, Kalamazoo, MI, 1942).

13766 ***(The) Happy Gilmans.*** A sustaining daytime dramatic serial about an "average American family," *The Happy Gilmans* remained on the air for only a short time. The story of the Gilman family was about Stan Gilman, a football hero, who had been unfairly prevented from playing in a game by his coach. When mother Gilman worried about this injustice and tried to do something about it, the plot became complex (15 min., Friday, 1:45–2:00 P.M., NBC-Red, 1938).

13767 ***Happy Go Lucky Hour.*** Al Pearce hosted the popular West Coast variety show that featured CW singer "Mac" McClintock, comic Simpy Fitts and singers Edna O'Keefe and Norman Nielsen (KFRC, San Francisco, CA, 1930).

13768 ***Happy Hal's Housewarming.*** Peruna Tonic and Color-Bak, manufactured by Drug Trade Products, Inc., sponsored the CW music show with Hal O'Haloran as genial host and hillbilly philosopher. Patsy Montana and the Prairie Ramblers supplied the CW music (30 min., Monday through Saturday, 9:00–9:30 A.M., MBS, New York, NY, 1934).

13769 ***Happy Hank.*** CW vcl. mus. prg. by an otherwise unidentified performer (WNAX, Yankton, SD and WHO, Des Moines, IA, 1939).

13770 ***Happy Hank's Round Up.*** CW mus. prg. (WTMJ, Milwaukee, WI, 1939).

13771 ***Happy Hanson Haberdashery Trio.*** Music on the program was provided by the instrumental trio of Evelyn Jernberg, Henry Riverman and Louise Schroeder. Vocals were by Fred R. Lyon (KFQW, Seattle, WA, 1927).

13772 ***Happy Hollow.*** Music, drama and commercials were woven into the on-going events of the daytime serial (KMBC, Kansas City, MO, 1929). When it went on the network, the show included such characters as Aaron and Sarah Peppertag, Aunt Lucinda Skinflint, Uncle Ezra Butternut, Little Douglas Butternut and Charity Grubb (15 min., Monday through Friday, 1:45–2:00 P.M., CBS, 1935).

13773 ***(The) Happy Homemaker.*** Ida Bailey Allen conducted her show, one of the most popular women's programs in radio's early years. Carried by both major networks, it was on CBS from 1929 to 1935 and, later, on NBC from 1935 to 1936. *See* **Allen, Ida Bailey**.

13774 **(The) Happy Hoosier Harmonists of New Albany, Indiana.** Charles Harris directed the orchestra that included Harris, s. and clr.; Carson Bard, p.; Stumpe Meyer, d.; Emil Stein, s.; Kenneth Robison, t.; and Albert Koehler, bj. (WHAS, Louisville, KY, 1924–1925).

13775 **Happy Hours Girl.** Singer (KEX, Portland, OR, 1930).

13776 ***Happy Island.*** Ed Wynn played King Bubbles of Happy Island, who sought to help his people solve their problems on the comedy program. (There also was a King Nasty of Worry Park.) Singers Jerry Wayne and Evelyn Knight not only sang, but also played the roles of Prince Richard and Princess Elaine. Music was by Mark Warnow's Orchestra. The Borden Diary Company sponsored the program (30 min., Friday, 7:00–7:30 P.M., NBC, 1944).

13777 ***Happy Jack*** (aka ***Happy Jack Turner***). Vcl. mus. prg. by popular vocalist Turner (15 min, Monday through Friday, 11:00–11:15 A.M., NBC-Red, 1937).

13778 ***Happy Jack's Old Timers.*** CW mus. prg. (WNAX, Yankton, SD, 1939).

13779 ***Happy Jack's Orchestra.*** Instr. mus. prg. (WSM, Nashville, TN, 1926).

13780 ***Happy Johnny.*** CW vocal music program by Happy Johnny (John Zufall) accompanied by his gang of CW musicians (WORK, York, PA, 1935). *See* **Zufall, John A.**

13781 ***Happy Johnny and Bob.*** CW vcl. prg. (WORK, York, PA, 1936). The team led by Happy Johnny (John Zufall) specialized in country songs. *See* **Zufall, John A.**

13782 ***Happy Johnny and Gang.*** Happy Johnny (John Zufall) led the CW group (WBAL, Baltimore, MD, 1939). The gang later moved to WFMD (Frederick, MD), where they broadcast for years. Happy Johnny reemerged as a DJ on WBMD (Baltimore, MD) in 1948. *See* **Zufall, John A.**

13783 ***Happy Landings.*** Young Mitzi Green starred on the children's daytime serial (WBBM, Chicago, IL, middle 1930s).

13784 ***Happy Rambler.*** Veteran performer Irving Kaufman was joined by singer Lucy Allen on the vocal music show that mostly presented old time songs. Sponsor Swift & Company included a cooking talk on each show (15 min., 10:30–10:45 A.M., NBC-Red, 1933).

13785 ***Happy Rose Dance Orchestra.*** Instr. mus. prg. (WTIC, Hartford, CT, 1932).

13786 ***Happy Thought Time.*** COM-HE Ellen Rose Dickey conducted the women's program. In 1928, she began one program this way: "Hello homemakers and mothers. This is *Happy Thought Time* at WJJD. I'm going to talk to you about children's diets — about well-balanced meals for those youngsters of ours that are growing so fast, playing and studying so hard and who are often getting far too little sleep" (WJJD, Chicago, IL, 1928).

13787 ***Happy Trails*** (aka ***The Roy Rogers Show***). Roy Rogers and Dale Evans were the stars on a program that combined their singing with a dramatic western episode. The show began with the announcement: "The dependable Dodge-Plymouth dealer in your neighborhood, the man who sells and services the elegant new 1954 Dodge, presents the new Roy Rogers radio show. Yes, it's the new Roy Rogers radio show for the whole family — adventure, suspense, mystery and music starring Roy Rogers, King of the Cowboys and Dale Evans, Queen of the West, with Pat Brady and the Mellowmen. And now here to greet you with a song and a story are Roy and Dale."

Art Rush produced and Ralph Rose directed the show. The writers were Ralph Rose and Stanley Adams. Music was arranged and conducted by Frank Worth. Virginia White was the production assistant. The cast included: Jane Webb, Byron Kane, Herb Butterfield, Joe Duval, Colleen Collins, Larry Dobkin, Marvin Miller, Paul Parrott, Tom Holland, Leo Clary, Phil Justine, Jay Novello, Bill Johnstone, Frank Nelson, Jack Kruschen, Eddie Marr, Joan Banks, Vic Perrin, Paul McGuire, Paul Frees, Tony Barrett and Parley Baer. Lou Crosby was the announcer (MBS, NBC, 1944–1955).

13788 ***Happy Vagabond.*** Jack Arthur (Arthur Campbell), a good baritone, was featured on the program of popular songs and ballads (15 min., Monday through Saturday, 10:15–10:30 P.M., WOR, Newark, NJ, 1932).

13789 ***Happy Valley Boys.*** CW mus. prg., by unidentified performers (WCAU, Philadelphia, PA, 1936–1938).

13790 ***Happy Wonder Bakers.*** Ed (Edward) Thorgersen was the announcer on the weekly music program sponsored by Wonder Bread. Tenor Frank Parker and pianist Frank Black, who also conducted the orchestra, were featured. Sigmund Spaeth was the program host (30 min 8:30–9:00 P.M., NBC-Red Network, 1929–1931). A later format of the program featured Phil Duey, Frank Luther, Jack Parker and Vivian Roth (15 min., Monday-Wednesday-Friday, 8:00–8:15 P.M., CBS, 1934).

13791 **Har, Ted.** Baritone (*Ted Har*, vcl. mus. prg., WKAR, East Lansing, MI, 1942).

13792 **Harbe, Marie.** COM-HE (WKOA, Hopkinsville, KY, 1955).

13793 **Harber, Harry.** Newscaster (WFAA, Dallas, TX, 1946).

13794 **Harbman, Harry.** Violinist (*Harry Harbman*, instr. mus. prg. (MBS, 1942).

13795 ***Harbor Lights.*** Burr C. Cook wrote the weekly dramatic sketch that told about Captain Jimmy Norton and his young friend, Joe. The Captain spun yarns with bells tolling and ship whistles blowing in the background to provide a maritime atmosphere. Jim Lewis and Fred Hathaway were featured in the cast. Raymond Carter was the announcer.

The show presented a "play within a play," since each week the program opened and closed with a ferry-boat scene. The opening announcement went this way: "The *Harbor Lights.* Once again we go aboard the old New York ferry boat to meet white-haired Captain Jimmy Norton and his young friend, Joe, and hear another of the captain's famous stories of the clipper ships and high adventure. All aboard." The show was consistently a popular network drama (Tuesday, 10:00–10:30 P.M., NBC-Red, 1929–1931).

13796 ***(The) Harbor We Seek.*** In late 1945, station WSB began a series of programs to explore the problems of youth, combat intolerance and prejudice and all anti-American activities. Brad Crandall wrote and directed this Peabody Award winning program (WSB, Atlanta, GA, 1945)

13797 **Harbrecht, Bill.** Leader (Bill Harbrecht Orchestra, WHAZ, Troy, NY, 1927).

13798 **Harcum, Marjorie.** Contralto Harcum appeared on the *Roxy's Gang* program (WEAF, New York, NY, 1925).

13799 **Hard, Anne.** Newscaster Hard broadcast her *Current Events* program five times weekly (9:45–10:00 A.M., WEAF, New York, NY, 1933).

13800 **Hard, William.** News analyst Hard discussed Washington doings on his *Back of the News in Washington* program (15 min., Wednesday, 7:45–8:00 P.M., NBC-Red, 1930–1931). Newspaper correspondent Hard was one of radio's earliest political analysts. Later on his *William Hard* program, he provided news analysis with an emphasis on political commentary (CBS, 1936).

13801 ***Harden and Weaver*** **(Frank Harden and Jackson Weaver).** The early morning team was an entertaining and innovative pair that combined intelligent talk, recorded music and good humor (WMAL, Washington, DC, 1960). Harden and Weaver began broadcasting in 1960 and continued for more than 25 years in Washington, DC. *Harden and Weaver* replaced Bill Malone as the WMAL morning men in March, 1960. The forerunner of the *Harden and Weaver Show* was a 15-minute ABC network evening show that had a brief run in the mid–1950s known as *Frank and Jackson.* Harden and Weaver's warm hearted and gentle humor included skits, jokes and many dialects. Among the characters they created were: gardening expert Phil Dirt; poet Percy Dovehearts, field reporter Chuck Roast; and musicologist Dr. Headcold. When the team began their early morning DJ show in 1960, they were one of the last reminders of radio's golden age. Although great Washington favorites, they failed to achieve the national recognition accorded the popular WRC (Washington, DC) *The Joy Boys* show of Eddie Walker and Willard Scott. *See* ***The Joy Boys.***

13802 **Harden, "Red."** Announcer (WSRF, Breadlands, IL, 1925).

13803 **Harden, Reginald.** Newscaster (WMVA, Martinsville, WV, 1941).

13804 **Harder, Jack.** Newscaster (WAYX, Waycross, GA, 1942).

13805 **Hardin, Dick.** Singer (*Dick Hardin*, vcl. mus. prg., WMBD, Peoria, IL, 1935).

13806 **Harding, Anne.** Manager-researcher (CBS, 1940s). Harding was in charge of the CBS research and files department.

13807 **Harding, Irene.** Organist (*Irene Harding*, instr. mus. prg., WFIL, Philadelphia, PA, 1936).

13808 **Harding, Jim.** Sportscaster (*Hi School Hilites*, WDAK, Columbus, OH, 1955).

13809 **Harding, Joan.** COM-HE (WNLK, Norfolk, CT, 1951).

13810 **Harding, Mathilde.** Pianist Harding appeared on the *Major Bowes Capitol Theatre* program (NBC, 1928).

13811 **Harding, Ted.** Newscaster (WHHM, Memphis, TN, 1946). DJ (*Ted Harding Show*, WNOR, Norfolk, VA, 1949).

13812 **Harding, Vincent.** Newscaster (KWTO, Springfield, MO, 1946).

13813 **Harding, William "Bill."** Sportscaster (WINS, New York, NY, 1939–1942).

13814 **Hardison, Roy.** Hardison was a banjo soloist on the *WSM Barn Dance* (WSM, Nashville, TN, 1928).

13815 **Hardley, Walter.** Organist (WJZ, New York, NY, 1923).

13816 **Hardman, Ben.** Newscaster (KJR, Seattle, WA, 1938).

13817 **Hardman, Benedict E.** Newscaster (KSO, Des Moines, IA, 1937; *Streamlined News*, WDGY, Minneapolis, MN, 1940; WLOL, Minneapolis–St. Paul, MN, 1941).

13818 **Hardy, Doris.** COM-HE (WFGM, Fitchburg, MA, 1956).

13819 **Hardy, Glen.** Newscaster (KHJ, Los Angeles, CA, 1939).

13820 **Hardy, Honeyboy.** DJ (*Sweet Chariot*, WBOK, New Orleans, LA, 1952–1954).

13821 **Hardy, Madeline.** Pianist (*Madeline Hardy*, instr. mus. prg., WCBM, Baltimore, MD, 1934).

13822 **Hardy, R.H.** Newscaster (KPAC, Port Arthur, TX, 1945).

13823 **Hardy, Ruth.** Pianist (WHAZ, Troy, NY, 1923).

13824 **Hare, Clarine.** COM-HE (KOCO, Salem, OR, 1956).

13825 **Hare, Hobart.** DJ (*Breakfast Cabaret*, KPDR, Alexandria, LA, 1947).

13826 **Hare, (Mrs.) Marin Scott.** Singer on the experimental radio station located at Ford Wood on Bedloe Island, New York, 1922).

13827 **Hare, William.** Actor Hare was in the cast of *Lora Lawton.*

13828 **Harger, Earl.** Leader (*Earl Harger Orchestra*, instr. mus. prg., WOR, Newark, NJ, 1935).

13829 **Harger, Lucille Atherton.** Contralto Harger was a "harmony singer" who, according to *Radio Digest*, was a "singer of heart songs and How! [She] has IT in her voice" (KFRC, San Francisco, CA, 1927; KPO, San Francisco, CA, 1928).

13830 **Hargis, Modesta.** Whistler performed "whistlogues"(WCOA, Pensacola, FL, 1930).

13831 **Hargraves, Bobby.** Leader (*Bobby Hargraves Orchestra*, instr. mus. prg., WFIL, Philadelphia, PA, 1939).

13832 **Hargreaves, Randall.** Newscaster (WMCA, New York, NY, 1942).

13833 **Hargrove, Bob.** Newscaster (*Your Labor Report*, KVSM, San Mateo, CA, 1947).

13834 **Hargrove, William.** Baritone (*William Hargrove*, vcl. mus. prg., WOR, Newark, NJ, 1934).

13835 **Haring, Bob.** Leader (*Bob Haring Orchestra*, instr. mus. prg., WCBM, Baltimore, MD, 1934; *Bob Haring Presents*, ABS. 1935).

13836 **Haring, Claude.** Sportscaster (WIBG, Philadelphia, PA, 1944–1946).

13837 **Hariton, Ruth.** *Children's Stories* (WNYC, New York, NY, 1936).

13838 **Harker, Bob and Ted Watterman.** Banjo duet team (KPLA, Los Angeles, CA, 1927).

13839 **Harker, F. Flaxington.** Organist (WRVA, Richmond, VA, 1926).

13840 **Harkness, Eddie.** Leader (Eddie Harkness Orchestra playing from the Marine Room of the Olympic Hotel, KFOA, Seattle, WA, 1925).

13841 **Harkness, Richard.** Newscaster (WNBC, New York, NY and WRC, Washington, DC, 1942, 1944–1947). Later, his program was known as *Harkness of Washington*, in which the emphasis was on political analysis (15 min., Weekdays, 12:15–12:30 P.M., NBC, 1949).

13842 **Harkness, (Mrs.) Robert.** Contralto (KTBI, Los Angeles, CA, 1926).

13843 **Harkreader, Sid.** Fiddler and mainstay of the *WSM Barn Dance* program (WSM, Nashville, TN, 1928).

13844 Harlan, Cynthia. COM-HE (WWTV, Cadillac, MI, 1956–1957).

13845 Harland, Mary. COM-HE (WNAE, Warren, PA, 1956).

13846 *Harlem Amateur Hour*. The local amateur hour broadcast from the stage of Harlem's Apollo Theater was one of the last examples of a programming format that had been extremely popular for many years. Band leader Lucky Millinder was the host. The Apollo Theater audience responded quickly to the performers' efforts, either with cheers of approval or hoots of derision. Special guests such as Ethel Waters and Dizzy Gillespie appeared regularly (45 min., Wednesday, 11:15–12:00 midnight, WJZ, New York, NY, 1952).

13847 *Harlem Amateur Night*. Bill "Bojangles" Robinson hosted the sustaining amateur hour program broadcast from the stage of Harlem's Apollo Theater (60 min., Thursday, 12:00–1:00 A.M., WMCA-ABS, 1934).

13848 *Harlem on Parade*. Joe Bostic hosted the entertaining "all Black" musical show that featured blues singer Marion Miller, singers Dick Porter and Edward Matthews with Jesse Cryor and his Rhythm Rascals Orchestra (30 min., Wednesday, 10:00–10:30 P.M., WHN, New York, NY, 1935).

13849 *Harlem Serenade*. *Radio Stars* (December, 1933, p. 6) described the good music show as presenting "grand, aboriginal rhythms" (Network, 1933).

13850 Harless, Daniel. Newscaster (WSAV, Savannah, GA, 1942).

13851 Harline, Leigh. Organist (KFRC, San Francisco, CA, 1928; KHJ, Los Angeles, CA, 1929).

13852 Harlow, LeRoy. Director of the *Silicon Vanities Miniature Musical Comedies* program (WEEI, Boston, MA, 1928).

13853 Harlow, Mary Louise. COM-HE (WNAV, Annapolis, MD, 1954).

13854 Harluig, H. Newscaster (WHBU, Anderson, IN, 1942).

13855 Harman, Frank. Newscaster (*Farm News*, *Blue Water Farmer* and *Dinner Bell* programs, WTTH, Port Huron, MI, 1948).

13856 Harman, J. Marion, Sr. Newscaster (WGOV, Valdosta, GA, 1941; *The Guest Editor*, WTRR, Sanford, FL, 1948).

13857 Harmes, Frank. DJ (*Swing Class*, WITH, Baltimore, MD, 1947).

13858 Harmo Jazz Orchestra. Popular local dance band (KOIL, Council Bluffs, IA, 1926).

13859 Harmon, David. Writer Harmon wrote the *American Women* and *Chesterfield Supper Club* programs.

13860 Harmon, George K. Tenor (WHAS, Louisville, KY, 1924).

13861 Harmon, Josephine. Singer (WROK, Rockford, IL, 1937).

13862 Harmon, Merle. Sportscaster (*Spotlight on Sports*, KSFT, Trinidad, CO, 1948; NBC, 1960).

13863 Harmon, Raymond. Tenor (KHJ, Los Angeles, CA, 1923).

13864 Harmon, Roy Lee. Newscaster (WWNR, Beckley, WV, 1948).

13865 Harmon, Tom. Sportscaster Harmon was an University of Michigan football All-American who became a good broadcaster (WCAR, Pontiac, MI, 1940; WJR, Detroit, MI, 1941; MBS, New York, NY, 1945; *Here Comes Harmon*, KFI, Los Angeles, CA, 1948; KNX , Los Angeles, CA, 1951–1952). Harmon also appeared regularly on the NBC *Jimmy Durante Show* in 1947.

13866 Harmon, William L. Announcer (WSAJ, Grove City, PA, 1925).

13867 Harmonica Jacks. *Variety* said the instrumental group made their harmonicas "talk pretty" (WLTH, Brooklyn, NY, 1928).

13868 *Harmonica Mac*. Mac (Clarence McCormack) led his trio including fiddler Frank Miller and guitarist Robert Schule on the CW music program (WLW, Cincinnati, OH, 1931).

13869 Harmonica Mike. *See* **Sullivan, Cloyde.**

13870 Harmonica Quintet. Instrumental group (WEEI, Boston, MA, 1926).

13871 *(The) Harmonica Rascals*. Borrah Minevitch led his virtuoso harmonica ensemble on the sustaining show (30 min., Sunday, 8:30–9:00 P.M., NBC-Blue, 1932).

13872 Harmonica Twins. Instrumental team (WFAA, Dallas, TX, 1926).

13873 Harmony Five Orchestra. Orchestra directed by Tom D. Collins (WFAA, Dallas, TX, 1924).

13874 Harmony Four. The popular female singing group included: Hortense McKee, 1st soprano; Helen Starke, 2nd soprano; Frances Minton, 1st contralto and accompanist; and Eva Dell Chamlee, 2nd contralto (KPO, San Francisco, CA, 1926).

13875 Harmony Girls. The *Christian Science Monitor* (April 18, 1925 p. 12) identified the singing team as the "Misses Carpenter and Ingram." They were Grace Ingram and Edith Carpenter (WLS, Chicago, IL, 1924–1925).

13876 Harmony Hounds. Singing team of Stanley Gray and Stanley Bacon (KOIN, Portland, OR, 1928).

13877 *Harmony House*. Organist Irma Glen and baritone Lawrence Salerno performed on the local music program sponsored by the Morris B. Sachs Company. Greg Donovan was the announcer (15 min., Monday through Thursday, 10:15–10:30 A.M., WENR, Chicago, IL, 1946).

13878 Harmony Kings. Popular dance band (WHK, Cleveland, OH, 1927).

13879 *Harmony Land*. A popular sustaining program of quiet, slumber hour music, *Harmony Land* featured baritone Jack Arthur, a mixed vocal harmony group and George Shackley's Orchestra (30 min., Friday, 10:30–11:00 P.M., WOR, Newark, NJ, 1933).

13880 *(The) Harmony Oil Twins*. John and Ned (John Wolfe and Ned Tollinger) exhibited their vocal and comic talents as the Harmony Oil Twins (15 min., Tuesday and Friday, 8:45–9:00 P.M. PST, NBC-Pacific Coast Network, 1930).

13881 Harmony Peerless Orchestra. W.A. Zweifel directed the Denver band that played from the Colburn Hotel (KOA, Denver, CO, 1925–1926).

13882 Harmony Two. Singing team of Sue and Lou, not otherwise identified (WHEC, Rochester, NY, 1929).

13883 Harned, Gladys. Violinist (KFDM, Beaumont, TX, 1925–1928).

13884 (The) Harness Makers. A talented vocal trio of Gus Swanson, Fritz Carlson and Frank Peterson (KMA, Shenandoah, IA, 1928).

13885 Harnish, Robert "Bob." Newscaster (*CTC News*, WLAN, Lancaster, PA, 1948). DJ (*Melody Matinee*, WLAN, 1948). Sportscaster (*The Sports Review* and football play-by-play, WLAN, 1948–1949).

13886 Harold, Jane Caldwell. Soprano (KDKA, Pittsburgh, PA, 1924).

13887 Harold, Lou. Leader (*Lou Harold Orchestra*, instr. mus. prg., WIP, Philadelphia, PA, 1936).

13888 *Harold Davis Presents*. Genial host Davis was the major element that made this local variety show a Philadelphia favorite. Comedian Dick Nelson, tenor Dave Walls and Fred Stahl's Orchestra were program regulars (30 min., Friday, 4:30–5:00 P.M., WDAS, Philadelphia, PA, 1936).

13889 *Harold Teen*. Based on Carl Ed's *Harold Teen* comic strip, the program was first broadcast in 1931 and received critical praise. *Radio Digest* (Vol. 28, No. 5, April, 1932, p. 63) called the program one of the most authentic teen age skits on the air. Blair Walliser and Fred Kress were the writers. Joe Sanders composed the program's theme song that proclaimed, "School days are the best days of your life."

Harold was played by Bill Farnum. The rest of his gang and the actors who portrayed them were: Lilacs, (Wally Colbath); Beezie, (Jack Spencer); Giggles, (Ireene Wicker); and Lillums, (Eunice Yankee). *Harold Teen* was one of several radio programs based on comic strips that originated at Chicago's station WGN. The program's cast in both in its early and later formats included: Willard "Bill" Farnum, Eddie Firestrone, Jr., Charles Flynn, Rosemary Garbell, Ireene Wicker, Bob Jellison, Marvin Miller, Loretta Poynton, Jack Spencer, Beryl Vaughn and Willard Waterman (15 min., Monday through Saturday, 6:15–6:30 P.M. CST, WGN, Chicago, IL, 1931–1932). A later version was broadcast on MBS in 1941–1942.

13890 Haroldson, Gail. Pianist (KFDY, Brookings, SD, 1925).

13891 Haroldson, Ruth. Violinist (KFDY, Brookings, SD, 1925).

13892 *Harp Harmony*. The program offered a joint recital featuring harpist Annie Louise David, violinist Antonio diGrasso and contralto Eva G. Atkinson (15 min., NBC-Pacific Coast Network, 1930).

13893 Harper, Annette. Actress Harper was a cast member on the daytime serial programs *The Guiding Light* and *Mainstream*.

13894 Harper, Chet. Leader (*Chet Harper Orchestra*, instr. mus. prg., KFEL, Denver, CO, 1939).

13895 Harper, Clarence. Tenor (WMBB, Homewood, IL and WOK, Chicago, IL, 1928).

13896 Harper, Hugh. Newscaster (WMC, Memphis, TN, 1939–1941).

13897 Harper, Jean. Contralto (WLAW, Lawrence, MA, 1939; WMEX, Boston, MA, 1939).

13898 Harper, John K. Announcer (WJR, Detroit, MI, 1925).

13899 Harper, Mary E. COM-HE (WEBQ, Harrisburg, IL, 1951).

13900 Harper, Sally. COM-HE (WLAN, Lancaster, PA, 1960).

13901 Harper, Tro. Newscaster (KSFO, San Francisco, CA, 1937–1939; WOR, New York, NY, 1945).

13902 Harper, Viola. Soprano (WRC, Washington, DC, 1924).

13903 Harpole, Mary E. COM-HE (KVOU, Uvalde, TX, 1956).

13904 Harrawood, Nelle. Reader (WOS, Jefferson City, MO, 1925).

13905 Harrice, Cy. Announcer Harrice appeared on the *Ethel and Albert* and *Quick as a Flash* program.

13906 *Harriet Parsons*. Harriet, the daughter of Louella Parsons, like her mother broadcast Hollywood news and gossip on her program sponsored by the Emerson Drug Company (15 min., Wednesday, 8:30–8:45 P.M., NBC-Blue, 1938).

13907 Harrington, Bill. Singer (*Bill Harrington Sings*, vcl. mus. prg., 15 min., Monday through Friday, 11:30–11:45 P.M., MBS, 1947).

13908 Harrington, Bill. DJ (*Tea Time Ballroom*, WESX, Salem, MA, 1947). Sportscaster (*Sports Journal*, WNEB, Worcester, MA, 1952).

13909 Harrington, Claire. Soprano (KTAB, Oakland, CA, 1925).

13910 Harrington, Edward F. "Ted." Announcer-organist-whistler (WCX, Detroit, MI, 1922–1924).

13911 Harrington, Happy Hank. Comedian (WGN, Chicago, IL, 1928).

13912 Harrington, Jack. Newscaster (WSPD, Toledo, OH, 1941).

13913 Harrington, Jerry. Announcer-actor-singer Harrington was one of several actors who played the role of "Tim" on the *Teena and Tim* series on CBS. In the early 1920s on WCCO (Minneapolis–St. Paul, MN), Harrington was called "The Little Irish Tenor."

13914 Harrington, John. Sportscaster (WBBM, Chicago, IL, 1936–1939; WBBM, 1944–1947).

13915 Harrington, John. Newscaster (KOB, Albuquerque, NM, 1944). Sportscaster (KTAR, Phoenix, AZ, 1947–1949).

13916 Harrington, Mary S. COM-HE (WALE, Fall River, MA, 1954).

13917 Harrington, Norman. Newscaster (KGLU, Safford, AZ, 1939–1940, 1944–1946).

13918 Harrington, Reba. Cellist (WBZ, Boston-Springfield, MA, 1924).

13919 Harrington, Ted. Announcer (WCX, Detroit, MI, 1924).

13920 Harriot, Elinor. Actress Harriot appeared on the daytime serial programs *We Are Four* and *Mary Marlin* aka *The Story of Mary Marlin.*

13921 Harris, Alan. Banjo soloist (WGCP, Newark, NJ, 1925).

13922 Harris, Alma. Pianist (*Alma Harris*, instr. mus. prg., WJAS, Pittsburgh, PA, 1935).

13923 Harris, Bass. DJ Harris' *House of Joy* show was said to have been the most popular DJ show in the Seattle area, if not the entire Pacific Coast in 1947 (120 min., Monday through Saturday, 1:00–3:00 P.M., KING, Seattle, WA, 1947).

13924 Harris, Betty. COM-HE (WANT, Richmond, VA., 1954).

13925 Harris, Betty. COM-HE (WHOW, Clinton, IL, 1954–1955).

13926 Harris, Bill. Newscaster (WJZM, Clarksville, TN, 1941).

13927 Harris, Bob. Newscaster (KLZ, Denver, CO, 1939; WMCA, New York, NY, 1941; *New York Times News*, WMCA, 1945).

13928 Harris, Bradley. Newscaster (KGB, San Diego, CA, 1938).

13929 Harris, Bruce "Frosty." DJ Harris was known variously as "The Snowman" and "Frosty the Snowman."(KRLA, Los Angeles, CA, 1959).

13930 Harris, Buddy. Newscaster (WRR, Dallas, TX, 1941). DJ (*Music Bar and Midnight Grinder*, WRR, 1949; KGKO, Dallas, TX, 1954).

13931 Harris, Chaz. DJ (*Rise 'n' Shine*, WJHP, Jacksonville, FL, 1949).

13932 Harris Choral Club. Dallas vocal group (WFAA, Dallas, TX, 1923).

13933 Harris, Chuck. Actor Harris appeared on the *Kitty Keene* daytime serial program.

13934 Harris Company Orchestra. Commercially sponsored band (WFAA, Dallas, TX, 1923).

13935 Harris, Craig. DJ (*Craig Harris Matinee*, KLX, Oakland, CA, 1947).

13936 Harris, Credo Fitch. Announcer and station manager (WHAS, Louisville, KY, 1923–1924).

13937 Harris, Dave. Leader (Dave Harris and his Seven Syncopators, playing from the Majestic Theater in Dallas, WFAA, Dallas, TX, 1922).

13938 Harris, Dean. DJ (*Request Time*, WAGE, Syracuse, NY, 1947; WHEN, Syracuse, NY, 1956).

13939 Harris, Don. Pianist (WCCO, Minneapolis–St. Paul, MN, 1925).

13940 Harris, Dottie. COM-HE (WSAV, Savannah, GA, 1951).

13941 Harris, Edith. COM-HE (WIST, Charlotte, NC, 1960).

13942 Harris, Ellis. Newscaster (KDAL, Duluth, MN, 1939–1940). Sportscaster (KDAL, 1939).

13943 Harris, Elmer. Piano accordionist (WMAK, Buffalo, NY, 1928).

13944 Harris, Ethel Sisson. Cellist with the WEAO Trio (WEAO, Columbus, OH, 1925).

13945 Harris, Fran. Actress Harris appeared in a later version of *Clara, Lu and Em* daytime serial program.

13946 Harris, Frances Kay. Newscaster (*Women's News*, KGBC, Galveston, TX, 1948. COM-HE (KGBC, 1956–1960).

13947 Harris, Francis. Newscaster (WWJ, Detroit, MI, 1944).

13948 Harris, Francis "Fran" Alvord. COM-HE (WWJ, Detroit, MI, 1954–1957). Harris was working as an assistant in the advertising department of Himelhoch Brothers department store, Detroit, Michigan, in 1929, when the store wanted to start a woman's program on a local station. She became "Julia Hayes" for the store on their program that ran from 1929 to 1934. She later conducted another radio show as "Nancy Dixon." Harris became women's editor at WWJ (Detroit, MI) in 1946, where she also broadcast general news. She was on WWJ radio and television until 1964, when she left the station to go into business for herself.

13949 Harris, George. Newscaster (WLS, Chicago, IL, 1935).

13950 Harris, George. Leader (*George Harris Orchestra*, instr. mus. prg., WBZ, Boston-Springfield, MA, 1936).

13951 Harris, Harry. Singer (*Harry Harris*, vcl. mus. prg., KFI, Los Angeles, CA, 1932).

13952 Harris, Herbert J. "Herb." Newscaster (WSB, Atlanta, GA, 1940–1942; *The World at Noon*, WERD, Atlanta, GA, 1948). DJ (WQXI, Atlanta, GA, 1949–1954).

13953 Harris, Jack. Newscaster (*News in Review*, WSM, Nashville, TN, 1938–1940). Sportscaster (WSM, 1939; *Berghoff Sports Reporter*, WSAP, Portsmouth, VA, 1947; *Tidewater Sports Parade*, WSAP, 1948; *Sports Parade*, WNOR, Norfolk, VA, 1951). DJ (WKDA, Nashville, TN, 1956).

13954 Harris, James Lionel. Newscaster (KFI, Los Angeles, CA, 1944).

13955 Harris, Jay. Newscaster (WCKY, Cincinnati, OH, 1939).

13956 Harris, Jean. COM-HE (KWKH, Shreveport, LA, 1960).

13957 Harris, Jean E. Pianist (WHAZ, Troy, NY, 1925).

13958 Harris, Jinx. DJ (*Hi Jinx*, KBLI, Blackfoot, ID, 1952).

13959 Harris, Joanne. COM-HE (KSTA, Coleman, TX, 1951).

13960 Harris, Johanna. Pianist (*Johanna Harris*, instr. mus. prg., WCAU, Philadelphia, PA, 1936–1938).

13961 Harris, John A. Newscaster (KFRU, Columbus, MO, 1940).

13962 Harris, Kilroy. Educational lecturer (WJZ, New York, NY, 1923).

13963 Harris, Lee. Newscaster (WTTM, Trenton, NJ, 1945).

13964 Harris, Lester. Leader (Lester Harris Orchestra, WFAA, Dallas, TX, 1923).

13965 Harris, Lloyd G. Announcer (WMC, Memphis, TN, 1925).

13966 Harris, Mama Lou. COM-HE (WBOK, New Orleans, LA, 1956).

13967 Harris, Marjorie. Singer (WOR, Newark, NJ, 1934).

13968 Harris, Milt. Leader (Milt Harris Society Orchestra, KFUU, Oakland, CA, 1926).

13969 Harris, Nick. Detective-author-lecturer Harris told stories of his true experiences with crime and criminals on his weekly program that always demonstrated that crime does not pay (KFI, Los Angeles, CA, 1924–1925).

13970 Harris, Ozzie. COM-HE (WBOK, New Orleans, LA, 1960).

13971 Harris, Paul. Leader (WFAA Symphony Orchestra, WFAA, Dallas, TX, 1928).

13972 Harris, Paul F. Newscaster (WLIO, East Liverpool, OH, 1948).

13973 Harris, Phil. Leader (*Phil Harris Orchestra*, instr. mus. prg., WBBM, Chicago, IL, 1933; WNAC, Boston, MA, 1934; NBC, 1935–1936; CBS, 1937; MBS, 1940). *See **The Jack Benny Show** and **The Fitch Band Wagon (Phil Harris-Alice Faye Show)**.*

13974 Harris, Polly. COM-HE (KEPO, El Paso, TX, 1954).

13975 Harris, Robert. Newscaster (KALE, Portland, OR, 1940).

13976 Harris, Ruth. COM-HE (WATL, Atlanta, GA, 1951).

13977 Harris, Sallie. Guitarist-singer (WFAA, Dallas, TX, 1927).

13978 Harris, Sara Lou. COM-HE (WLIB, New York, NY, 1954).

13979 Harris, Selwyn. Tenor-pianist (KFI, Los Angeles, CA, 1925).

13980 Harris, Stacy. Actor Harris appeared on *Evelyn Winters*, *Pepper Young's Family*, *Superman* and *This Is Your FBI*.

13981 Harris, Walt. Sportscaster (*Pigskin Preview*, KFRC, San Francisco, CA, 1951–1952; KOVR, Stockton, CA, 1956).

13982 Harris, Wes. Sportscaster (*Sports Circus*, WGAY, Silver Spring, MD, 1951).

13983 Harris, Winder R. Newscaster (WTAR, Norfolk, VA, 1938–1942, 1945).

13984 Harris Adolphus Orchestra. Popular local band (WFAA, Dallas, TX, 1924).

13985 Harrison, Adele. Actress Harrison was featured on *The O'Neills* daytime serial.

13986 Harrison, Bob. Sportscaster (WHNC, Henderson, NC, 1945–1948; *Sports Parade*, WHNC, 1949–1951; *WHNC Sports Parade*, WHNC, 1952). Newscaster (WHNC, 1948).

13987 Harrison, Brad. Newscaster (WIL, St. Louis, MO, 1945).

13988 Harrison, C. Newscaster (WHBF, Rock Island, IL, 1947).

13989 Harrison, Charles. Tenor (CBS staff, 1927–1928; *Charles Harrison*, vcl. mus. prg., NBC, 1935).

13990 Harrison, Charlie. DJ (*The Record Rack*, WTAW, College Station, TX, 1947; *920 Club*, KTLW, Texas City, TX, 1948).

13991 Harrison, Dorothy. Soprano (WGY, Schenectady, NY, 1923).

13992 Harrison, Evelyn. Singer (WRVA, Richmond, VA, 1933).

13993 Harrison, Guy Fraser. Orchestra conductor (*Stromberg-Carlson* program, WABC-CBS, New York, NY, 1929).

13994 Harrison, Harry. Entertainer known as the "Clown of the Air" (WGCP, New York, NY, 1925).

13995 Harrison, Harry. DJ (*Hillbilly Jamboree*, KOGT, Orange, TX, 1952; *Coffee Time*, WPEO, Peoria, IL, 1954–1957; WMCA, New York, NY, 1960).

13996 Harrison, Hilda. Singer Harrison was called the "Whispering Soprano" (WPCH, New York, NY, 1931).

13997 Harrison, Jerome K. Director Harrison directed the *Editor's Daughter* daytime serial program.

13998 Harrison, John. Baritone (WFAA, Dallas, TX, 1926).

13999 Harrison, John W. Announcer (WMAQ, Chicago, IL, 1925). Newscaster (WBBM, Chicago, IL, 1938; KTAR, Phoenix, AZ, 1946).

14000 Harrison, M. Lois. COM-HE (KGLU, Safford, AZ, 1951).

14001 Harrison, Mel. DJ (*Amobalko-Sasnakra Serenade*, KWHN, Fort Smith, AR, 1948).

14002 Harrison, Neil. Actor Harrison was in the cast of *John's Other Wife* daytime serial program.

14003 Harrison, Nilda. Soprano (WPCH, New York, NY, 1932).

14004 Harrison, Ray. Leader (Ray Harrison's WHO Orchestra, KFWB, Hollywood, CA, 1925).

14005 Harrison, Raymond Roy. Pianist-violinist (WFAA, Dallas, TX, 1926).

14006 Harrison, Thelma. Pianist (KFI, Los Angeles, CA, 1923).

14007 Harrison, Virginia. COM-HE (WTRB, Ripley, TN, 1956–1957).

14008 Harrison, Wilbanks. Sportscaster (KWSH, Wewoka, OK, 1960).

14009 Harrison, Zeta. Harrison, a member of the KPO Dramatic Guild conducted the *Children's Hour* program (KPO, San Francisco, CA, 1931).

14010 Harrod, Buddy. Leader (*Buddy Harrod Orchestra*, instr. mus. prg., CBS, 1933).

14011 Harrold, Deen. COM-HE (WRHC, Jacksonville, FL, 1951).

14012 Harrover, Ben. Newscaster (KCRC, Enid, OK, 1945).

14013 Harrow, Tim. DJ (*Tempo*, KWCO, Chickasha, OK, 1960).

14014 Harry, Cousin. DJ (*Cousin Harry*, KIUP, Durango, CO, 1950).

14015 *Harry Hershfield*. Comedian Hershfield, who later became most famous for his appearances on *Can You Top This?*, conducted the sustaining comedy show (15 min., Wednesday, 7:45–8:00 P.M., WMCA-ABS, 1934).

14016 *Harry Hershfield*. On his program, Hershfield moved from one restaurant or club to another to interview the celebrities in them (30 min., Monday through Friday, 12:00–12:30 P.M., WOR, Newark, NJ, 1948).

14017 *Harry Reser's Crew*. Wrigley Company, makers of Spearmint chewing gum, sponsored radio pioneer Reser's band previously known as the Cliquot Club Eskimos. The show also featured contralto Peg LaCentra and baritone Ray Heatherton (15 min., Sunday, 4:30–4:15 P.M., NBC-Red, 1934).

14018 *(The) Harry Richman Show*. Singer Richman began as a vaudeville pianist who accompanied Mae West and the Dolly Sisters. He soon began to make solo appearances that led to his radio audition. In 1923, Richman appeared with Nils Thor Granlund (NTG), at New York City's Loew's State Theater and on radio's *Spearmint Hour*. He opened a New York night club of his own and appeared on Broadway in *George White's Scandals*. During this period he was romantically linked with the motion picture star, Clara Bow. Richman frequently appeared with Ken Murray on *The Dodge Program*. During the middle 1930s, he also made a series of 26 electrical transcriptions for the Florida Citrus Company (*The Harry Richman Show*) on which he sang and clowned with his various guest stars. Some of the performers who appeared with him on these transcribed programs were Frank Crumit and Julia Sanderson, Gertrude Niesen, Tom Howard and George Shelton, Kay Thompson, Frank Parker, Tim and Irene, Judy Starr, the Revelers, the Sisters of the Skillet, Cliff "Ukulele Ike" Edwards, Eve Beck, Lee Wiley and Pick and Pat.

14019 *(The) Harry Savoy Show*. Comedian Savoy hosted the summer replacement program for *Fibber McGee and Molly*. Also featured on the show were Benay Venuta and the Peter Van Steeden Orchestra. The announcer was Jimmy Wallington (NBC, 1944).

14020 Harsch, Joseph "Joe." News analyst (NBC, Early 1940s; CBS, 1942; 1944–1945, WTOP, Washington, DC, 1945; *Meaning of the News*, WTOP and CBS, 1947–1948; *Washington Report*, news commentary, Labor-Liberal FM Network, Washington, DC, 1950). Much traveled commentator Harsh provided consistently intelligent commentary during and after World War II.

14021 Harsha, Paul. Newscaster (*State Reporter* and *Blue Water News*, WTTH, Port Huron, MI, 1948).

14022 Harshberger, Dena. Manager-producer (NBC, 1939). After she had originated and produced her own *Civic Concert Service* program and sold it to NBC, the network offered her a job as the first manager of its Hollywood Artists Service Department.

14023 Harshman, G.E. "Jerry." DJ-Newscaster (WPIC, Sharon, PA, 1938–1940). Newscaster (WPIC, 1938).

14024 Harston, Lynette. COM-HE (KLGN, Logan, UT, 1957).

14025 Hart, Ann. COM-HE (WLS, Chicago, IL, 1939).

14026 Hart, Carroll. DJ (*K Club*, WKSK, West Jefferson, NC, 1960).

14027 Hart, Corrine. Blues pianist (KPRC, Houston, TX, 1926).

14028 Hart, Don. Newscaster (WMFF, Plattsburg, NY, 1939–1949; *Morning Dispatch*, WSNJ, Bridgeton, NJ, 1947). Sportscaster (WMFF, 1940).

14029 Hart, Edith. Soprano (WOR, Chicago, IL, 1925).

14030 Hart, Elizabeth. COM-HE (WMAQ, Chicago, IL, 1949).

14031 Hart, Fred L. Newscaster (WLPM, Suffolk, VA, 1945).

14032 Hart, Helen. COM-HE (WHVR, Hanover, PA, 1949).

14033 Hart, Helene. COM-HE (KFNF, Shenandoah, IA, 1957).

14034 Hart, Hershell. Hart was a reporter for the Detroit *Free Press,* who read the news (WWJ, Detroit, MI, 1925).

14035 Hart, Jim. DJ (*Zanzibar Disc Jockey Show*, KLAS, Las Vegas, NV, 1949).

14036 Hart, Joan. COM-HE (WICA, Ashtabula, OH, 1951).

14037 Hart, Lynn. COM-HE (WMAL, Washington, DC, 1954).

14038 Hart, Maude. COM-HE (WLAG, Minneapolis–St. Paul, MN, 1924).

14039 Hart, Maurice. DJ (*Start the Day Right* and *The Hollywood Bandstand*, KFWB, Hollywood, CA, 1947; *Straight From the Heart*, KFWB, CA, 1948–1952).

14040 Hart, Millie. Singer who broadcast with the Shelley Players' Orchestra (KFI, Los Angeles, CA, 1926).

14041 Hart, Rita. COM-HE (WIBV, Belleville, IL, 1957).

14042 Hart, Ruby. Pianist (WTIC, Hartford, CT, 1927).

14043 Hart, Ruth. COM-HE (WOTW, Nashua, NH, 1949).

14044 Hart, Trula. COM-HE (KEEN, San Jose, CA, 1949).

14045 Hart, W.E. Harmonica soloist (KVOO, Tulsa, OK, 1928).

14046 Hart, William M. Newscaster (WPAY, Portsmouth, OH, 1944–1945).

14047 Hart, William S. One of the best, if not the *greatest* silent motion picture cowboy star, Hart, a formally trained actor, gave a masterful reading of "Invictus" on the April 12, 1924, inaugural broadcast of Sears' WLS (Chicago, IL, 1924).

14048 *Hart, Schaffner and Marx Trumpeters.* Hart, Schaffner and Marx, the famous men's clothing company, sponsored the music and news program. The newscaster on the program was Edwin C. Hill, "The Man in the Front Row" (30 min., Thursday, 10:00–10:30 P.M., CBS, 1932).

14049 Harter, Jane. COM-HE (KBLF, Red Bluff, CA, 1949).

14050 Harter, Mildred. Soprano (WTAM, Cleveland, OH, 1924).

14051 Hartford, Norman. Sportscaster (KGFJ, Los Angeles, CA, 1932).

14052 Hartin, Dorothy. COM-HE (KSCO, Santa Cruz, CA, 1956).

14053 Hartle, Clara Moyer. Singer (KFOA, Seattle, WA, 1925).

14054 Hartle, Polly. COM-HE (WAIR, Winston-Salem, NC, 1951).

14055 Hartley, Betty. COM-HE (WBNS, Columbus, OH, 1937).

14056 Hartley, Fred. Leader (Fred Hartley and his Orchestra, KHQ, Spokane, WA, 1927).

14057 Hartley, Howard. Newscaster (*Florida Reporter*, WCLE, Clearwater, FL, 1947; WTAN, Clearwater, FL, 1948).

14058 Hartley, James A. "Jim." DJ (*Hillbilly Hit Parade* and *1240 Club*, WGGA, Gainesville, GA, 1947–1948; WGGA, 1950; *Alarm Clock Club*, WDUN, Gainesville, GA, 1954).

14059 Hartman, (Reverend) Charles H. Announcer (KFWF, St. Louis, MO, 1927–1928).

14060 Hartman, Hazel. COM-HE (WMID, Atlantic City, NJ, 1956).

14061 Hartman, LaMont. Newscaster (WCBA-WSAN, Allentown, PA, 1948).

14062 Hartman, Marx. Newscaster (NBC-Blue, 1942; KLAC, Los Angeles, CA, 1948).

14063 Hartman, Rhea Lee. Reader (KVI, Tacoma, WA, 1927).

14064 Hartman, Rome John. DJ (*Morning Toast*, WIRK, West Palm Beach, FL, 1947). Sportscaster (*Sportscope*, WIRK, 1948–1955).

14065 Hartman, Urban. Tenor (KPO, San Francisco, CA, 1929).

14066 Hartman, Victoria. Violinist (KFUU, Oakland, CA, 1925).

14067 Hartmann, Myrtle. Soprano (KSD, St. Louis, MO, 1926).

14068 Hartnett, Alice. COM-HE (KTBB, Tyler, TX, 1957).

14069 Hartrick, George. Baritone (WWNC, Ashville, NC, 1928).

14070 Hartrick, George A. Newscaster (WCOP, Boston, MA, 1942; *Evening Edition*, WJLS, Beckley, WV, 1947).

14071 Hart's Cafeteria Concert Orchestra. West Coast restaurant band (KFBK, Sacramento, CA, 1926).

14072 Hartwell, Jimmy. Leader (Jimmy Hartwell Orchestra, KYW, Chicago, IL, 1923).

14073 Hartwell, W.E. Announcer (WAGS, Summerville, MA, 1927).

14074 *Hartz Mountain Radio Canaries.* A transcribed program presenting canaries singing their hearts out for Hartz Pet Foods (15 min., MBS, 1944–1945).

14075 Hartzell, Clarence. Actor Hartzell was in the cast of *In Care of Aggie Horn, Li'l Abner, Today's Children* and *Vic and Sade.*

14076 Hartzell, Nancy. Blues singer (*Nancy Hartzell*, vcl. mus. prg., WHAT, Philadelphia, PA, 1936).

14077 Hartzell, Willie. Leader (*Willie Hartzell Orchestra*, CW mus. prg., KFEL, Denver, CO, 1934; *Willie Hartzell's Fellers*, CW mus. prg., KFEL, Denver, CO, 1939; KFEL, 1940).

14078 Hartzog, Marlyn. COM-HE (WKSK, West Jefferson, NC, 1960).

14079 *Harv[e] and Esther*. Consolidated Cigar Company sponsored the show that combined comedy and music. Singers Jack Arthur and Audrey Marsh played the title roles. Teddy Bergman, later known as Alan Reed, assisted in the comedy. Music was supplied by the Victor Arden Orchestra (15 min., Thursday, 8:30–8:45 P.M., CBS, 1935).

14080 Harvard Freshman Glee Club. College vocal group (WNAC, Boston, MA, 1924).

14081 Harvard Glee Club. College vocal group (KSD, St. Louis, MO, 1923).

14082 Harvey, Dennis and Walter Rosenburg. Tenor Harvey and baritone Rosenburg sang duets (KOMO, Seattle, WA, 1929).

14083 Harvey, Georgette. "Black female bass" singer Harvey led the Running Wild Quartet (WGBS, New York, NY, 1927).

14084 Harvey, H. Clay. H. Clay Harvey broadcast lectures on Shakespeare (WDAF, Kansas City, MO, 1928).

14085 Harvey, Happy. DJ (*Early Risers*, KTLW, Texas City, TX, 1960).

14086 Harvey, Helen. COM-HE (WCOL, Columbus, GA, 1951).

14087 Harvey, J.J. Trumpet soloist (KDKA, Pittsburgh, PA, 1925).

14088 Harvey, James. Tenor (KOMO, Seattle, WA, 1929).

14089 Harvey, James H. Harvey broadcast deep sea fishing news (KFON, Long Beach, CA, 1925).

14090 Harvey, James and Zita Dillon. Readers (KOMO, Seattle, WA, 1929).

14091 Harvey, Lloyd "Moe." DJ (*The Moe Show*, WIRL, Peoria, IL, 1952). Sportscaster (*Hi-Lite Sports Recap*, WIBV, Belleville, IL, 1960).

14092 Harvey, Mary. COM-HE (WGEM, Quincy, IL, 1951).

14093 Harvey, (Mrs.) Morton. Talented pianist, contralto and actress Harvey played the role of "Aunt Betty" and told stories for children (WHAM, Rochester, NY, 1929).

14094 Harvey, Norman. Leader (Norman Harvey Orchestra, KFI, Los Angeles, CA, 1926).

14095 Harvey, Paul (Paul Harvey Aurandt). News commentator (WENR, Chicago, IL, 1948; ABC, 1953). Harvey was still broadcasting in 1998 with his resonant voice and extended pauses. Despite his stylized delivery, he never achieved the dramatic impact produced by the timing of Edward R. Murrow. Harvey is best known for his bland humor, human interest stories and brief commentaries with a conservative bent.

14096 Harvison, Fats. Newscaster (WLAU, Laurel, MA, 1956) Sportscaster (WLAU, 1956).

14097 Harwell, Dick. DJ (*Dreamland Ballroom*, KRGY, Westlaco, TX, 1947). Sportscaster (*Spot Sports*, KRGY, 1947).

14098 Harwell, Ernest "Ernie." Sportscaster (WSB, Atlanta, GA, 1940–1941; WAGA, Atlanta, GA, 1946; *The Sports Show*, WGST, Atlanta, GA, 1947). DJ (WBGE, Atlanta, GA, 1947). After serving in the Marine Corps during World War II, Harwell began his career at WSB by broadcasting the Atlanta Crackers baseball games. He went to Ebbets Field to broadcast the Dodger games with Red Barber and Connie Desmond in 1948. When the St. Louis Browns franchise moved to Baltimore to become Orioles, Harwell broadcast their games. He later became a fixture broadcasting Detroit Tigers' games after he moved to Detroit in the 1960s.

14099 Harwood, Brian. DJ (*Green Mountain Ballroom*, WDEV, Waterbury, VT, 1960).

14100 Harwood, Chris. DJ (*Chris Harwood Showcase*, WBUD, Morrisville, PA, 1947; *1450 Turntable Terrace*, WJMJ, Philadelphia, PA, 1950).

14101 Harwood, Geoffrey. Newscaster (WBZ-WBZA, Boston, MA, 1944–1945; *Background to the News*, WBZ-WBZA, 1947–1948).

14102 Hasbrook, Dick. Newscaster (WJMS, Ironwood, MI, 1937–1939). Sportscaster (WJMS, 1939–1940).

14103 Hase, Ed. Newscaster (WCHV, Charlottesville, VA, 1942, 1945).

14104 Hasel, Joe. Sportscaster (WNYC, New York, NY, 1939.) Hasel was a busy sportscaster in 1940–1941, when he broadcast tennis, track, baseball and football commentary and play-by-play (NBC, CBS, WNYC, New York, NY and WNEW, New York, NY, 1940–1941; WJZ-Blue network, New York, NY, 1942; WJZ, 1945–1946; ABC, 1947–1948; *Joe Hasel Show*, WJZ and ABC, 1949; *Joe Hasel Sports*, ABC, 1951; football play-by-play and the *All American Sports Show*, NBC, 1955).

14105 Haselmire, Carma [Carmen]. COM-HE (KLIX, Twin Falls, ID, 1951).

14106 Hasenbalf, Roy. Announcer (WMAQ, Chicago, IL, 1928).

14107 *Hashknife Hartley*. W.C. Tuttle wrote the western drama series and delivered both the prologue and epilogue. The adventures of cowboys Harshknife Hartley, played by Frank Martin, and his sidekick Sleepy Stevens, played by Barton Yarborough were featured. Music was supplied by Harry Zimmerman. The announcer was Don McCall. The well written and acted program was followed on MBS by *Hopalong Cassidy*. The combination provided listeners with one hour of entertaining western dramatic fare (30 min., Sunday, 3:30–4:00 P.M., MBS, 1950).

14108 Haskett, George W. Newscaster (WCNC, Elizabeth City, NC, 1945).

14109 Haskew, Ann. COM-HE (WTCB, Flomaton, AL, 1960).

14110 Haskins, Dad. Leader (Dad Haskins' Hicktown String Band, WADC, Akron, OH, 1927).

14111 Haskins, (Dr.) Robert. A professor of botany at the University of Cincinnati, Haskins gave informative talks on his *Popular Science Talk* program (WLW, Cincinnati, OH, 1925–1926).

14112 Haslett, Linda. COM-HE (KFSB, Joplin, MO, 1957).

14113 Hass, Emil. Reader (WOC, Davenport, IA, 1926).

14114 Hassell, Betty. COM-HE (KBIO, Burley, ID, 1949).

14115 Hassell, Harry. Cellist (WFAA, Dallas, TX, 1926).

14116 Hassell, Irwin E. Pianist (WGBS, New York, NY, 1925).

14117 Hasselman, J.B. Announcer (WKAR, East Lansing, MI, 1925).

14118 Hasser, Charles. Newscaster (WTHT, Hartford, CT, 1939).

14119 Hassmer, Joseph. Baritone (*Joseph Hassmer*, vcl. mus. prg., WGN, Chicago, IL, 1934).

14120 Hastings [Hastin], Ann. COM-HE (KFTM, Fort Morgan, CO, 1956).

14121 Hastings, Annette. Blues singer (NBC, San Francisco, CA, 1928; *Annette Hastings*, vcl. mus. prg., NBC, 1939).

14122 Hastings, Don. Announcer (WBBM, Chicago, IL, 1927).

14123 Hastings, Fred. Bass (WEAR, Cleveland, OH, 1925).

14124 Hastonians Dance Orchestra. Local Nebraska dance band (KFKX, Hastings, NE, 1925).

14125 Hatch, Bill. Leader (Bill Hatch's Hoot Owl Orchestra, KFWB, Hollywood, CA, 1925; Bill Hatch's Oakmont Country Club Orchestra, KFWB, 1925–1926).

14126 Hatch, Emily. Soprano (WGBS, New York, NY, 1925).

14127 Hatch, Nita. COM-HE (WTVN, Columbus, OH, 1955).

14128 Hatch, Wilbur. Pianist-conductor Hatch first appeared as a pianist (KYW, Chicago, IL, 1922). He began appearing on commercial programs on the network in 1927 and was busy on radio during the following decades.

14129 Hatcher, Betty. COM-HE (WLET, Toccoca, GA, 1951),

14130 Hatcher, Julia Virginia. COM-HE (WPKE, Pikeville, KY, 1955).

14131 Hatchett, Grace. COM-HE (KJAY, Topeka, KS, 1954).

14132 Hatchitt, Reece. Newscaster (NBC, 1942).

14133 Hatfield, Helen G. Announcer (WSBF, St. Louis, MO, 1926–1927).

14134 Hatfield, Larry. Newscaster (WOLS, Florence, SC, 1941).

14135 Hatfield, Ruth. Blues singer and pianist (WHB, Kansas City, MO, 1928).

14136 Hathaway, Charles. Leader (Charles Hathaway's Orchestra, WHN, New York, NY, 1923–1924).

14137 Hathaway, J.H. Announcer (KFEL, Denver, CO, 1927).

14138 Hathaway, Joy. Busy actress Hathaway appeared on the daytime serial programs *Second Husband*, *Stella Dallas*, *Young Widder Brown* and *Amanda of Honeymoon Hill*.

14139 Hatteroth, Genevieve. Pianist (KTAB, Oakland, CA, 1926).

14140 Hatteroth, Virginia. Violinist (KTAB, Oakland, CA, 1926).

14141 Hattic, Woodrow. Newscaster (WWL, New Orleans, LA, 1939).

14142 Hauff, Maddalena. Soprano (WJZ, New York, NY, 1923).

14143 Hauge, Herbert. Saxophonist (WCAL, Northfield, MN, 1925).

14144 Haugen, Jane S. COM-HE (KDUZ, Hutchinson, MN, 1954).

14145 Haugner, Al. Newscaster (WMT, Cedar Raids, IA, 1945; *Times Herald on the Air*, WTTH, Port Huron, MI, 1948).

14146 Haun, Helen. An employee of the AT&T Long Line division, Haun became WEAF's first studio hostess and announcer (WEAF, New York, NY, 1922).

14147 Haupt, James "Jimmie." Announcer-singer Haupt joined the announcing staff of WEAF (New York, NY) in 1924, after an audition was arranged for him by Graham McNamee. Haupt had previously sung with McNamee in church, an event that led to his WEAF audition.

14148 Haupt, Jimmie and Marjorie Horton. Harmony singing team (NBC, 1928).

14149 Hauptmann, Liborious. Pianist and musical director (KGW, Portland, OR, 1928).

14150 Hauser, Herb. Leader (*Herb Hauser Orchestra*, instr. mus. prg., WSAI, Cincinnati, OH, 1942).

14151 Hauserman, Elaine. COM-HE (WMAN, Mansfield, OH, 1949).

14152 Hausman Brothers. "Banjo artists" (KMOX, St. Louis, MO, 1926).

14153 Hausman, Evelyn. COM-HE (WGL, Fort Wayne, IN, 1960).

14154 Hausner, Jerry. Actor Hausner was in the cast of *Big Town*.

14155 Havana Casino Orchestra. Latin music group (WOO, Philadelphia, PA, 1924).

14156 *Have Gun, Will Travel*. John Dehner starred in the program when it came to radio in November 23, 1958, after a successful television version had proved to be extremely popular. On radio, Dehner was Paladin, a former U.S. Army officer turned professional gunman, who hired himself out to protect people who couldn't protect themselves. Paladin, in effect, was a 1875 knight of the old west. He operated from the Hotel Carlton, San Francisco, California, with a calling card that said simply: "Have Gun, Will Travel, Paladin, San Francisco." In addition to Dehner, the cast included: Ben Wright as Hey Boy, Paladin's Chinese servant; and Virginia Gregg as Hey Boy's girl friend.

14157 *Have You Heard?* The quarter-hour program discussed many complex topics in geology, and meteorology in clear, readily understood terms (15 min., Tuesday, 1:45–2:00 P.M., NBC-Blue, 1936).

14158 Havel, Lillian. Soprano (WHN, New York, NY, 1924).

14159 *Haven MacQuarrie*. Host MacQuarrie conducted this sustaining radio amateur program (30 min., Sunday, 10:30–11:00 P.M., NBC-Red, 1937).

14160 *Haven of Rest*. Reverend Paul Myers began his *Haven of Rest* program in 1934 (30 min., KMPC, Beverly Hills, CA, 1934). "First Mate Bob" [Myers] conducted the weekly religious program that contained a sermon and several rousing hymns. Myers' opening consisted of a bosun's whistle, the sound of eight bells and a male quartet singing "I've anchored my soul in the haven of rest" (Erickson, 1992, p.94). Myers hosted the program until he retired in 1968. Others then carried on the program well into the 1990s.

14161 **Havens, Doris.** Organist (*Doris Havens*, instr. mus. prg., WCAU, Philadelphia, PA, 1936–1938).

14162 **Havens, Geraldine Isabelle.** Singer (WBZ, Springfield, MA, 1926).

14163 **Havens, Paul.** Newscaster (WGL, Fort Wayne, IN, 1945).

14164 **Havens, Ruth.** DJ (*Teen Time*, WGL, Fort Wayne, IN, 1952).

14165 **Havenstein, Phyllis.** COM-HE (WVAM, Altoona, PA, 1960).

14166 **Haver, George.** Singer (*George Haver*, vcl. mus. prg., WMBD, Peoria, IL, 1935).

14167 **Haverstock, Charles S.** Chief announcer (KOIL, Council Bluffs, IA, 1927).

14168 **Haverstock, Mildred.** Organist (*Mildred Haverstock*, instr. mus. prg., WORK, York, PA, 1936).

14169 **Haverty, G.W.** Announcer (WHDI, Minneapolis, MN, 1925).

14170 ***(The) Haverty Players.*** The local dramatic group's program was broadcast on Saturday nights. Their first dramatic presentation was "The Grandfather's Clock" (KLRA, Little Rock, AR, 1934.)

14171 **Havrilla, Alois.** Announcer Havrilla was born in Czechoslovakia. He came to Bridgeport, Connecticut, as a child. After becoming a successful professional singer who performed at Carnegie Hall, he became an announcer at WPCH (Atlantic City, NJ, 1926). He then moved to New York (WFBH, New York, NY, 1926) and, eventually, joined the NBC staff in 1928.

It was at Carnegie Hall that Havrilla was "discovered" by Graham McNamee. The famous announcer was so impressed with Havrilla's voice that he invited him to come to New York for the audition that resulted in a position on the NBC announcing staff. Havrilla later became a busy newscaster (WOR, New York, NY, 1941; WHOM, New York, NY, 1944; and WOR,1945). He also appeared as an announcer on many network programs.

14172 ***Hawaii Calls.*** Webley Edwards produced, directed and narrated the long-running popular program of Hawaiian music. Beginning in 1945 on MBS, the program was broadcast by the network into the early 1960s. By 1953, *Hawaii Calls* was carried by more stations than any other radio program. It claimed 600 stations on MBS, Canadian Dominion Network, Australian Network, AFRS Network and by shortwave to Asia, South Africa, Oceania and the Voice of Freedom to Europe. In 1955, on its 20th anniversary the program's format was still unchanged. The anniversary broadcast originated from the Hotel Moana before an audience of hundreds of visitors. *See* **Edwards, Webley**.

14173 ***(The) Hawaiian Beach Boys.*** Ray Canfield led the orchestra that broadcast from Los Angeles (KFI, Los Angeles, CA; KECA, Los Angeles, CA, 1931).

14174 **(The) Hawaiian Beachcombers Orchestra.** Marshall Storey directed the Hawaiian music group (KSTP, Minneapolis–St. Paul, MN, 1928).

14175 **Hawaiian Entertainers.** Merle K. Bennett directed the music group that included: C.M. Smith, G.K. Brewer, and Solomon M. Kaiawe (KFH, Wichita, KS, 1926).

14176 ***Hawaiian Fantasy.*** Instr. mus. prg. of Hawaiian music performed by unidentified musicians (WIP, Philadelphia, PA, 1935).

14177 ***Hawaiian Orchestra of Benton [Arkansas].*** Lloyd F. Nickelson directed the Hawaiian music group (Weekly, Friday P.M., KTHS, Hot Springs National Park, AR, 1931).

14178 **Hawaiian Quintet.** Instrumental music group consisting of Frank Plada, Mrs. Frank Plada, Merritt Lamb, Joseph Scabbares and Clarence Young, (WHAS, Louisville, KY, 1924).

14179 **Hawaiian Serenaders.** A vocal team (May Conley and June Berord) broadcast with the Serenaders, a two-man instrumental team (WOBU, Charleston, WV, 1928).

14180 **Hawaiian Sextet.** Steel guitarist Frank Plada directed the music group (WHAS, Louisville, KY, 1925).

14181 ***Hawaiian Shadows.*** Norman Brokenshire narrated the music program surrounded, as a periodical of the time said, "by ukuleles, grass attire and soft melodies" (*Christian Science Monitor*, August 9, 1929, p.6). The program was broadcast by CBS in 1929.

14182 **Hawaiian Trio.** Mr. C.F. Kaygne directed the instrumental music group (WBZ, Springfield, MA, 1925).

14183 **Hawaiian Trio.** Minyan, Coral and Samuel Hallole were the members of the instrumental trio (KMA, Shenandoah, IA, 1928).

14184 ***The Hawaiians Orchestra.*** Instr. mus. prg. (WGY, Schenectady, NY, 1935).

14185 **Hawis, A.M.** Tenor (KYW, Chicago, IL, 1925).

14186 **Hawk, Helen.** Pianist (WJAZ, Chicago, IL, 1923).

14187 **Hawk, Robert "Bob."** Hawk began his early morning program with, "Hear Ye! Hear Ye!" Before doing the morning show on WJJD (Chicago, IL, 1929), Hawk had worked at WMBB (Chicago, IL). He later gained national prominence as an outstanding radio quizmaster on the *Bob Hawk Show*, *Thanks to the Yanks* and the *Take It or Leave It* programs.

14188 ***Hawk Durango.*** On the western action drama Elliot Lewis played the role of a wanderer, who finally settled down as a businessman in his father's old saloon. The program was a summer replacement for *Maisie*. Barton Yarborough, Lucien Littlefield, Frank Lovejoy, Junius Matthews, Dorothy Peterson and Martha Wentworth were in the cast. Kenneth Perkins wrote and William N. Robson produced and directed the interesting western program. Music was provided by Wilbur Hatch's Orchestra (30 min., Friday, 10:30–11:00 P.M. CBS, 1946). The following year the program's format, including the characters, plot and name, was changed to *Hawk Larabee*. *See* ***Hawk Larabee***.

14189 ***Hawk Larabee.*** This program underwent several interesting transformations. It began as *Hawk Durango* before the title and plot were altered to become *Hawk Larabee*. In the latter format, Barton Yarborough, formerly the lead's sidekick, played the title role and owner of the Black Mesa ranch. Barney Phillips played his comic sidekick, Somber Jones. The show was memorable for its opening of Hawk's whistle and the cry, "The Hawk is on the wing" and the use of musical bridges sung by Bob Crawford, Tookie Croenbold, Fran Mahoney and Rod May. Later the bridges were sung by Andy Parker and the Plainsmen. The program was produced and directed by William Robson. The program in its new format was also short-lived (CBS, 1947–1948).

14190 **Hawkes, Kirby.** Director Hawkes directed *American School of the Air* (segments), *Captain Midnight*, *The Couple Next Door* and *Mary Marlin*.

14191 **Hawkins, Arnold.** DJ (*Western Shindig*, KCRT, Trinidad, CO, 1954).

14192 **Hawkins, Erskine.** Leader (*Erskine Hawkins Orchestra*, instr. mus. prg., NBC, 1934–1935; 1937–1940). Trumpet virtuoso Hawkins was billed as "The Twentieth Century Gabriel."

14193 **Hawkins, Frederick E.** Announcer (WEEI, Boston, MA, 1928).

14194 **Hawkins, Happy.** Leader (Happy Hawkins and his Grand Gardens Orchestra, WEEI, Boston, MA, 1925).

14195 **Hawkins, Harold Franklin "Hawkshaw."** CW singer Hawkshaw Hawkins was born December 22, 1921 in Huntington, WV. In 1936, Hawkins entered and won a talent contest on WSAZ (Huntington, WV, 1936), resulting in a regular program on the station. He worked on stations in Charleston, WV (WCHS) and Lawrence, MA. After leaving service at the end of World War II, he worked at station WWVA (Wheeling, WV, 1946–1954), appeared on CBS radio (1946–1954) and was on ABC's television program, *Jubilee USA*. Hawkins joined the *Grand Ole Opry* in 1955. His life ended tragically in a plane crash in 1963 that also killed Patsy Cline and Cowboy Copas.

14196 **Hawkins, Jack.** Newscaster (*News Roundup*, KIUN, Pecos, TX, 1947). Sportscaster (KIUN, 1947–1949).

14197 **Hawkins, Jesse [Jess].** Leader (*Jesse Hawkins Orchestra*, instr. mus. prg., NBC, 1935–1936).

14198 **Hawkins, Lloyd.** Newscaster (KBST, Big Springs, TX, 1946).

14199 **Hawkins, Louise.** COM-HE (KIUN, Pecos, TX, 1951).

14200 **Hawkins, Robert.** Newscaster (WKAN, Kankakee, IL, 1947–1948).

14201 **Hawkins, Stuart.** Writer Hawkins wrote *Bright Horizon*, *Cavalcade of America* and *City Desk*.

14202 **Hawkins, Tom.** DJ (*Happy Hour*, WFBR, Baltimore, MD, 1949).

14203 **Hawkins, Vern.** Sportscaster (KWTO, Springfield, MO, 1953–1956; *Spotlight on Sports*, KWTO, 1960).

14204 Hawkins, Vivienne. COM-HE (WERI, Atlanta, GA, 1960).

14205 Hawkinson, Frank. Newscaster (KADA, Ada, OK, 1939; KGFF, Shawnee, OK, 1940).

14206 Hawley, Bill and Puss Donahue [Donahoo]. A comedy singing team, Hawley and Donahue were featured on a popular evening program (KFRC, San Francisco, CA, 1926).

14207 Hawley, Joe. Hawley was billed as Joe Hawley and his Triple Guitar (KFQZ, Hollywood, CA, 1926).

14208 Hawley, Mark. Announcer (WMAK, Buffalo, NY, 1925). Newscaster (WOR, Newark, NJ, 1935–1938; *Transradio News*, WOR, 1939; CBS, 1941).

14209 Haworth, Carl. Entertainer Haworth was known as "The Singing Banjoist" (KHQ, Spokane, WA, 1928).

14210 Haworth, Donald. Announcer (KFHL, Oskaloosa, LA, 1927).

14211 Hawthorne, Jim. DJ (*The Hawthorne Thing*, ABC, 1948–1950). On the program sponsored by Regal Beer, Hawthorne played records and mixed bits of his zany humor with the music (KECA, Los Angeles, CA, 1948).

14212 *Hawthorne House*. Pearl King Tanner played the leading role of a once wealthy widow, Mrs. Sherwood, on the daytime serial sponsored by the Snow Drift Company. Widow Sherwood defied the difficult Depression times by turning her home into a boarding house. She had two children, Mel, 19, played by Frank Provo, and Marietta, 15, played by Helen Troy. Among the Widow Sherwood's interesting boarders were Barbara Jo Allen, later famous as Vera Vague, a postgraduate sociology student; Grandma Liston, a sharp- tongued octogenarian, played by Olive West, and her daughter, Lois Liston, played by Natalie Park. Eventually, there arrived upon the scene a hungry would-be author played by John Pickard, who took a romantic interest in Lois. The program's cast members also included: Billie Byers, Bobbie Dean, Donald Dudley, Sam Edwards, Florida Edwards, Eddie Firestone, Jr., Charles Gerard, Don Holloway, Bert Horton, Jack Kirkwood, Earl Lee, Dixie Marsh, Ted Maxwell, Monty Mohn, Jack Moyles, Natalie Park, John Pickard, Ruth Sprague, Pearl King Tanner and Lou Tobin. The program's writers were Ray Buffum, David Drummond and Cameron Prud'Homme (30 min., Monday, 9:30–10:00 A.M., PST, NBC, 1935).

14213 *Hawthorne—TBA*. Jim Hawthorne was featured on his sustaining comedy show with music by Robert Armbruster. Hawthorne and Dick Pedicini wrote the show and Art Jacobsen was the director. The announcer was John Storm (30 min., Saturday, 7:00–7:30 P.M., NBC, 1953).

14214 *Hawthorne's Adventures*. Jim Hawthorne, who *Variety* called a toned down Henry Morgan, hosted the mixture of jokes, comedy sketches and music. Also on the sustaining show with him were: Johnny April, Parker Cornell, Dennis Day and Ike Carpenter. Owen James was the announcer (30 min., Saturday, 7:30–8:00 P.M., ABC, 1948).

14215 Hay, Bill. Announcer (WMAQ, Chicago, IL, 1925). *See* ***Amos 'n' Andy***.

14216 Hay, Beverly. COM-HE (KIST, Santa Barbara, CA, 1957).

14217 Hay, George Dewey. An announcer and station executive known as "The Solemn Old Judge," Hay received that nickname when he wrote a bi-lined column called "Howdy Judge" for the Memphis *Commercial Appeal*, where he worked as police beat reporter. In 1923 when the *Commercial Appeal* founded station WMC (Memphis, TN), Hay was appointed "Radio Editor," and much to his dismay designated "announcer," a task he performed quite well.

In 1924, Hay moved to WLS (Chicago, IL) for $75 a week to create and develop *The National Barn Dance*. His trademark was the sound of a railroad whistle and the line, "WLS Unlimited." Hay's station break announcements also were legendary, "WLS, the Sears-Roebuck Station, Chicago," with the last word prolonged and accented by a blend of southern and midwestern pronunciation. He was the winner of *Radio Digest's* 1924 Gold Cup for Best Announcer (WLS, Chicago, IL).

Hay moved to station WSM (Nashville, TN) late in 1925, where he developed another country music show that met with great success, the *Grand Ole Opry* that is still running (1998). Once more Hay used a steamboat whistle as a trademark as he had done previously when he had worked at WMC. He once remarked, "Then it wasn't so much what you could put on the air, as how far you could hear it." *See* ***Grand Ole Opry***.

14218 Hay, Henrietta. COM-HE (KFXJ, Grand Junction, CO, 1949).

14219 Hay, James. Flutist (KSD, St. Louis, MO, 1923).

14220 Hay, Margaret, and Piegi. Vocalist with piano accompanist (WCOH, New York, NY, 1932).

14221 Hay, (Mrs.) William G. "Bill." Pianist (KFKX, Hastings, NE, 1923).

14222 Hay, William G. "Bill." Announcer Hay was born in Dumfries, Scotland. He came to the United States in 1909. Hay began the study of the violin at the age of seven and received vocal training at seventeen. When station KFKX (Hastings, NE) began operation, Hay was the sales manager and treasurer at a Hastings' piano store. After the store gave the station a piano, Hay began announcing, singing, playing, directing choral groups and arranging programs. Later moving to WGN, Chicago, IL, he met Gosden and Correll, who were then performing as *Sam 'n' Henry*, and began announcing their program. Hay became general manager of WGN, before going to WMAQ, Chicago, IL, where *Amos 'n' Andy* was created. Bill Hay once more became Gosden and Correll's announcer and continued in that role at WMAQ during the program's greatest years. Hay, along with Gosden and Correll as *Amos 'n' Andy* went on the NBC-Red Network in 1929. Although he did other work, Hay's fame was inexorably linked with the *Amos 'n' Andy* program. Later, Hay conducted his own program, *Bill Hay Reads the Bible* (WLAV, Grand Rapids, MI, 1942).

14223 (The) Hay Mow Five. Popular midwestern CW group (KSO, Clarinda, IA, 1928).

14224 Hayde, Alice. Soprano (WNYC, New York, NY. 1936).

14225 Hayden, Augusta. Lyric soprano (KPO, San Francisco, CA, 1923).

14226 Hayden, Ethyl. Lyric soprano (WLAG, St. Paul–Minneapolis, MN, 1924).

14227 Hayden, Happy Harry. Singing comedian (WEAF, New York, NY, 1923).

14228 Hayden, Jean. Soprano (KFI, Los Angeles, CA, and KFWB, Hollywood, CA, 1926).

14229 Hayden Male Quartet of Worcester. Male singing group of Arthur G. Harwood, Carl G. Anderson, Eric A. Anderson and Edward L. Davis, (WGI, Medford Hillside, MA, 1923).

14230 Hayes, Albert. Actor Hayes was in the cast of *Doc Barclay's Daughter* and *Valiant Lady*.

14231 Hayes, Anne. COM-HE (KCMO, Kansas City, MO, 1949).

14232 Hayes, Bernadine [Bernardine]. Blues singer (KMOX, St. Louis, MO, 1929).

14233 Hayes, Billy "Bill." Leader (Billy Hayes and his Cathay Tea Garden Dance Orchestra, WCAU, Philadelphia, PA, 1925–1926; *Billy Hayes Orchestra*, instr. mus. prg., WIP, Philadelphia, PA, 1935–1936, 1938).

14234 Hayes, Bobby. Leader (*Bobby Hayes Orchestra*, instr. mus. prg., NBC-Red, 1936–1937).

14235 Hayes, C.H. Announcer (KDYL, Salt Lake City, UT, 1927).

14236 Hayes, Dorothy. Violinist (WBAP, Fort Worth, TX, 1927).

14237 Hayes, Fern. COM-HE (KVAN, Vancouver, WA, 1949).

14238 Hayes, Florence. Pianist (WLAC, Nashville, TN, 1927).

14239 Hayes, George. Newscaster (*The Esso Reporter*, ABC, 1948).

14240 Hayes, Glenn. Newscaster (WBML, Macon, GA, 1945).

14241 Hayes, Grace. Singer (*Grace Hayes*, vcl. mus. prg., NBC-Red, 1932–1935). Hayes was a popular night club, vaudeville, musical comedy and motion picture singer, who specialized in comedy songs. After making a major appearance at the Palace Theater in 1932, she had her own programs on NBC. After reaching radio stardom in 1932, she introduced her teenage son as Peter Lind. Her son, as Peter Lind Hayes, was on WOR (New York, NY) radio in the late 1950s and early 1960s with his wife Mary Healy. *See* **Hayes, Peter Lind and Mary Healy**.

14242 Hayes, Helen. Distinguished actress Hayes appeared on the *Helen Hayes Theatre*, *New Penny* and *Silver Theatre*.

14243 Hayes, Helen. COM-HE (WRNI, Richmond, VA, 1960).

14244 Hayes, James. Newscaster (KLX, Oakland, CA, 1945).

14245 Hayes, Julia. COM-HE (KPO, San Francisco, CA, 1930).

14246 Hayes, L.J. Singer (WJY, New York, NY, 1925).

14247 Hayes, Larry. Newscaster (KSRO, Santa Rosa, CA, 1941).

14248 Hayes, Margaret. Soprano (WGES, Oak Park, IL, 1925).

14249 Hayes, Marguerite Gilbert. Soprano (WNAC, Boston, MA, 1925).

14250 Hayes, Mary A. COM-HE (WREB, Holyoke, MA, 1957).

14251 Hayes, May Bradshaw. COM-HE (WCHB, Inkster, MI, 1957–1960).

14252 Hayes, Michael. Newscaster (WJMC, Rice Lake, WI, 1942). Seattle, WA, 1949; *Scoreboard*, KIRO, 1952; KIRO, 1954–1960).

14253 Hayes [Hays], Pete. Singer (*Pete Hayes*, vcl. mus. prg., WIP, Philadelphia, PA, 1936).

14254 Hayes, Peter Lind and Mary Healy. Popular husband-and-wife talk show team (WABC, New York, NY, 1959–60). Hayes, the son of Grace Hayes, had a pleasant comic persona. He worked on the stage, in nightclubs, on radio and in several movies. Healy was on television with his wife in 1958–1959 on *The Peter Lind Hayes Show*, a variety program that featured such guests as Frank Sinatra and Lucille Ball. In 1960–1961, he starred with Healy on the TV situation comedy, *Peter Loves Mary*. *See* **Hayes, Grace.**

14255 Hayes, Rex. Leader, Bohemian Band (WNAX, Yankton, SD, 1945).

14256 Hayes, Richard. DJ (*Richard Hayes Show*, vcl. mus. prg., Mutual, 1954).

14257 Hayes, Samuel S. "Sam." Announcer, newscaster and sportscaster Hayes became an announcer on San Francisco radio in 1929. As a newscaster he appeared on many programs (*The Bank of America News Reporter*, CBS, 1937; *Richfield News Reporter*, NBC, 1932 and 1937; *Sperry Breakfast News*, NBC, 1939; *Daily Spectator*, CBS, 1939; *Pointing the Periscope*, CBS, 1939; NBC, 1945–1948; *Touchdown Tips*, NBC, 1952).

14258 Hayes, Ukulele Lou. Musician-singer (WMCA, New York, NY, 1925).

14259 Hayes, W.D. Newscaster (WABI, Bangor, ME, 1938).

14260 Hayes, William. Baritone (KTAB, Oakland, CA, 1927).

14261 *Hayloft Jamboree* aka *WCOP Hayloft Jamboree*. CW music show that was at one time b broadcast three times a day on WCOP (Boston, MA, 1951–1956). The show also was broadcast on a "Jamboree network" in New England. The show's MC was Nelson Bragg, introduced as the "Merry Mayor of Milo, Maine and Mrs. Bragg's skinniest kid. At times the show emanated from Boston's Symphony Hall, the Back Bay Theater, John Hancock Hall and the Boston Area. Some of the show's performers were: Country Al Green, Ruth Senter, Muriel White the "Betty Hutton of the Hillbillies," Gerry Lee (Shore), the LeClair Sisters, Joe Val, Danny Gillis, Lucky Shore, Lou Mondon, Dave Miller, Eddie Fisher, Dave Miller, Dee Rogers, Ray Smith, Jim Senter, Carl Stewart (Ray Shact), Bobby Bobo, Bill Busby, Jack Clement, Eddie Zack and His Dude Ranchers, Ray Dixon, Don Kent, Tex Owens and Little Eddie, the Big Yank Unit, the Bayou Boys (Buzz, Jack, Scott and Scott Stoneman), Jerry Devine, Tex Logan, Lilly Brothers, Lane Brothers, Jack Clements, Tootsie and Jackie, Dee Rogers, Dave Miller, Jimmy and Ruth, Doug Terry and the Roving Cowboys, Lou Mondon, Lucky and Elmo (the Radio Rangers) and Elton Britt. Aubrey L. Mayhew was the program's director.

14262 Haymaker, Margaret. Pianist (KDKA, Pittsburgh, PA, 1924).

14263 *(The) Haymaker's Minstrels*. The early radio minstrel program was a popular local show (WLS, Chicago, IL, 1927).

14264 Hayman, Don C. Newscaster (*Manos Theater News*, WMBS, Uniontown, PA, 1947–1948).

14265 Haymer [Hayner], Rutherford. Announcer (WHAZ, Troy, NY, 1924).

14266 Haymes, Joe. Leader (*Joe Haymes Orchestra*, instr. mus. prg., WDBJ, Roanoke, VA, 1936).

14267 Haymond, Carl E. Announcer (KMO, Tacoma, WA, 1927).

14268 Haynes, Andrew. Tenor (WAAM, Newark, NJ, 1925).

14269 Haynes, Beatrice. Pianist (WBZ, Springfield, MA, 1924).

14270 Haynes, Chuck. Haynes was an end man on the *Weener Minstrels Show* (WENR, Chicago, IL, 1929).

14271 Haynes, Floyd. Tenor (KFWI, San Francisco, CA, 1926).

14272 Haynes, Frank. Leader (*Frank Haynes Orchestra*, instr. mus. prg., WOR, Newark, NJ, 1935).

14273 Haynes, Muriel. Writer Hayes wrote radio commercial copy for the Ruthrauff and Ryan Company agency.

14274 Haynes, Richard. Newscaster (KVOL, Lafayette, LA, 1940).

14275 Haynes, Tina May. Organist (WHT, Chicago, IL, 1928).

14276 Haynes, Trudy. COM-HE (WCHB, Inkster, MI, 1957–1960). Haynes was a pioneer Black broadcaster, who was doing social work in Detroit when she was asked if she would like to work in radio. She began doing secretarial work at WCHV (Detroit, MI) in 1956. When a manager asked her if she would like to go on the air, she accepted and began a women's show on which she did interviews and offered tips and household hints. Later, she did a children's show for the station. She left WCHB to work at WXYZ (Detroit, MI) as a TV weather girl before moving again to a Philadelphia station.

14277 Haynes, Zola. Contemporary papers called Miss Haynes a "Dulcetone" vocal soloist (WSWS, Chicago, IL, 1926). Staff pianist and organist (KYW, Chicago, IL, 1928).

14278 Haynie, Jean. COM-HE (KTEM, Temple, TX, 1954).

14279 Hays, Charles H. Announcer (KDYL, Salt Lake City, UT, 1927; KSL, Salt Lake City, UT, 1927).

14280 Hays, Don. Newscaster (WWNR, Beckley, WV, 1948).

14281 Hays, Florence. Pianist (WLAC, Nashville, TN, 1927).

14282 Hays, Harvey. Actor-narrator Hays was in the cast of *Death Valley Days, Mary Marlin, A Tale of Today* and *Words and Music* (narrator).

14283 Hays, Irene. Pianist (KHJ, Los Angeles, CA, 1924).

14284 Hays [Hayes], Jim. DJ (*Music by Request*, KVOA, Tucson, AZ, 1947). Sportscaster (*Punt Formation Please*, KVOA, 1947–1949).

14285 Hays [Hayes], Larry. Newscaster (KSRO, Santa Rosa, CA, 1940).

14286 Hays, Lois. COM-HE (KIRX, Kirksville, MO, 1960).

14287 Hays, Pat. Sportscaster (*Sullivan Scoreboard*, *High School Sports* and *Rod and Reel*, KIRO,

14288 Hays, Ted. Baritone (*Ted Hays*, vcl. mus. prg., WLW, Cincinnati, OH, 1942).

14289 Hays, Virginia. Contralto (NBC, 1939; WLW, Cincinnati, OH, 1942).

14290 (The) Hayshakers Orchestra. Musical group featuring old-time music (WGHP, Detroit, MI, 1929).

14291 Hayton, Lennie. Leader (*Lennie Hayton Orchestra*, CBS, 1936).

14292 Haywire Mac. *See* **McClintock, Harry.**

14293 Hayward, Joyce. COM-HE (WTWA, Thomson, GA, 1951; WGAC, Augusta, GA, 1954). Actress Hayward also appeared on the daytime serial program *Backstage Wife* aka *Mary Noble, Backstage Wife*.

14294 Haywood, Ross. Leader (*Ross Haywood Orchestra*, instr. mus. prg., WIBX, Utica, NY, 1942).

14295 Hayworth, Herb. DJ (*Good Morning*, WOWO, Ft. Wayne, IN, 1949–1952).

14296 Hayworth, Jay. DJ (*1340 Klamworks*, KWOC, Poplar Bluff, MO, 1947).

14297 Hayworth, Vinton. Actor Hayworth was in the cast of *Archie Andrews, Chaplain Jim, Evelyn Winters, Life Can Be Beautiful, Myrt and Marge* and *Second Husband*.

14298 Hazan, Maurice. Newscaster (KGER, Long Beach, CA, 1941).

14299 Hazelwood, Marjorie. Singer (WFAA, Dallas, TX, 1929).

14300 (The) Hazelwood Ensemble. The ensemble included Hazel Wood, soprano-pianist; Myrtle Wood, alto; Alice Dean, pianist; Albert E. Gross, tenor; and Sidney T. Maar, violinist (KTAB, Oakland, CA, 1925).

14301 Hazen, Ruth. COM-HE (KOFE, Pullman, WA, 1960).

14302 Hazenberg, Robert. Saxophonist Hazenberg teamed with Robert DeJonge as a saxophone duet team (WOOD, Grand Rapids, MI, 1926).

14303 Hazlewood, Lee. DJ (*Hillbilly Heaven*, KCKY, Coolidge, AZ, 1954). Sportscaster (*Coors Parade of Sports*, KCKY, 1954; KTYL, Mesa, AZ, 1956).

14304 Hazlitt, John M. News commentator (*JMH Sounding Off*, KVLH, Pauls Valley, OK, 1948).

14305 "HDM." Designation for H.D. Miller, announcer and director of broadcasting at the Amrad station (WGI, Medford Hillside, MA, 1923).

14306 ***He, She and They***. Vcl. mus. prg. by an otherwise unidentified vocal group (CBS, 1935).

14307 Head, Byron "By." DJ (*Alarm Clock Club*, KOIL, Omaha, NE, 1947–1949; *Coffee Club*, KOIL, 1950; *The KOIL Klock*, KOIL, 1954).

14308 Head, Cloyd. Newscaster (WMAQ, Chicago, IL, 1944–1945).

14309 Head, Elmer. Pianist-singer (KFWI, San Francisco, CA, 1928).

14310 Head, Emma George. "Danseuse" (WLW, Cincinnati, OH, 1925).

14311 Head, Ivan R. Newscaster (KVSF, Santa Fe, NM, 1940; *News Till Noon*, KVSF, 1945–1946). Sportscaster (KVSF, 1945; sports play by play, KVSF, 1947).

14312 ***(The) Headline Hunter***. With eye-patch in place, Floyd Gibbons used his fast paced delivery to broadcast news and personal anecdotes. John S. Young was the announcer (30 min., Monday, NBC, 10:30–11:00 P.M. in 1929). *See* **Gibbons, Floyd**.

14313 ***(The) Headliners***. The popular novelty orchestra broadcast six days a week (15 min., Monday through Saturday, 8:15–8:30 P.M., NBC-Blue, 1930).

14314 ***Headlines***. On the dramatic adventure program, Ted Brown, an energetic *Globe* newspaper reporter, and his photographer assistant, Sleepy Dolan, searched for clues to baffling mysteries. Carl Riblet was the program's writer and leading man (15 min., Monday and Thursday, 8:30–8:45 P.M. CST, WENR, Chicago, IL, 1932).

14315 Heagan, Jimmy. Pianist (KLRA, Little Rock, AR, 1930s).

14316 Heald, Henry M. Baritone (*Henry Heald*, vcl. mus. prg., WBZ, Boston-Springfield, MA, 1935).

14317 Healey, Jay. Sportscaster (WGY, Schenectady, NY, 1934).

14318 Healey, (Col.) Jim. Newscaster (WTRY, Troy, NY and WGY, Schenectady, NY, 1942; WSNY, Schenectady, NY, 1944–1945; WWSC, Glens Fall, NY, 1948).

14319 Healey, Meg. COM-HE (KIXL, Dallas, TX, 1956–1957).

14320 ***Health and Efficiency***. Dr. Thomas Darlington delivered a series of health talks beginning March 14, 1922 (WJZ, New York, NY).

14321 ***Health and Happiness***. Chiropractic doctors Hale and Tena S. Murphy had a 12-year career broadcasting health information and hints (KLRA, Little Rock, AR, 1930–1942).

14322 ***Health and Happiness Show***. CW star Hank Williams and his wife starred on the transcribed series of country music shows (Transcribed, Various Stations, 1940s). See ***Hank Williams.***

14323 ***Health Hints***. Dr. Harriet Van Buren Peckham discussed medical topics on this early health program (WOR, Newark, NJ, 1923).

14324 ***Health Talk***. Dr. R.T. Williams broadcast a series of health talks (KNX, Los Angeles, LA, 1925).

14325 ***Health Talk* (aka *Dr. B.A. Atcheson, M.D.*).** Dr. Atcheson conducted the medical information program (WIND, Gary, IN, 1935).

14326 Healy, Chuck. Sportscaster (WBEN, Buffalo, NY, 1947–1955).

14327 Healy, Dolores [Delores]. COM-HE (KBRC, Mount Vernon, WA, 1954–1960).

14328 Healy, Gary. DJ (*Mid-Day Matinee*, KBUN, Bemidji, MN, 1947; WPBC, Minneapolis, MN, 1949).

14329 Healy, James. Newscaster (WGY, Schenectady, NY, 1937–1941; WHBC, Canton, OH, 1945; *Jim Healey and the News*, WSNY, Schenectady, NY, 1947).

14330 Healy, Marie. Coloratura soprano (WEAF, New York, NY, 1928).

14331 Healy (Marion) and Jolley (Grace). Twin piano team (WGR, Buffalo, NY, 1926).

14332 Healy, (Mrs.) Tim. COM-HE (KIXL, Dallas, TX, 1951).

14333 ***Hear It Now***. Edward R. Murrow and Fred W. Friendly produced and wrote the sustaining current affairs program that premiered in 1951. Broadcast crews traveled all over the country to interview news makers and report current events (60 min., Friday, 9:00–10:00 P.M., CBS, 1951). This was little more than an attempt to improve on the old *March of Time* concept by using actual recordings of persons and events. Murrow and Friendly previously had combined to produce an excellent series of audio history on three *Hear It Now* LP recordings. Unfortunately, the radio program seldom lived up to the recorded audio history set.

14334 Hearn, F.D. "Chick." Sportscaster and football play-by-play (WMRO, Aurora, IL, 1947; *"Chick" Hearn on Sports*, WEEK, Peoria, IL, 1951–1955; KRCA, Los Angeles, CA, 1960).

14335 Hearne, Ben. Harmonica soloist from Palestine, TX (WFAA, Dallas, TX, 1923).

14336 Hearne, Nicholas, Jr. Pianist (KHJ, Los Angeles, CA, 1926).

14337 Hearns, John. Actor Hearns was in the cast of *Sally of the Movies*.

14338 Hearst, John Randolph. News commentator (*John Randolph Hearst, News Commentary*, MBS, 1955). John Randolph Hearst was the son of media mogul, William Randolph Hearst, one of the giants of American news and entertainment. Although personally thought of as a press lord with his chain of newspapers, William Randolph Hearst also owned 11 radio stations and a motion picture company that eventually merged with the Metro-Goldwyn-Mayer Picture Company.

William Randolph Hearst combined all three phases of his business by promoting two of his most popular radio personalities — Adela Rogers St. John, an excellent newspaper reporter, and Hollywood columnist Louella Parsons. St. John and Parsons both broadcast regularly on network radio, indirectly promoting Hearst papers and motion pictures.

14339 Heart-Dreyfus, Estelle. Singer (KFI, Los Angeles, CA, 1927).

14340 ***Heart Songs***. Lois and Reuben Bergstrom were the romantic singing team on the weekly music show (15 min., Weekly, 8:30–8:45 A.M. CST, WLS, Chicago, IL, 1935).

14341 ***Heart Songs***. John Paul Goodman read romantic poetry to the musical background of pianist Dwight Brown (15 min., Sunday, 9:15–9:30 P.M. KTSA, San Antonio, TX, 1946).

14342 ***Heart Throbs of the Hills***. Ethel Park Richardson produced and wrote the interesting program that presented dramatized versions of various folk songs. Elton Britt often sang the songs (30 min., Sunday 9:30–10:00 P.M., WJZ-Blue, 1934).

14343 ***Heartbeat Theater***. C.P. MacGregor hosted the dramatic program until his death in 1968, when he was succeeded by Marvin Miller. The program was produced and transcribed by the C.P. MacGregor Studios for the Salvation Army. Each week the story presented had a strong inspirational theme. Among the many talented actors who appeared in the long running series were: Parley Baer, Bret Morrison, Frank Nelson, Alice Reinheart, Janel Waldo, Jim Boles, Daws Butler, Tommy Cook, Hans Conreid, John Dehner, Joe DiSantis, Lou Krugman, Tyler McVey, Harold Peary, Vic Perrin, Alan Reed, Mike Rye, Olan Soule, Les Tremayne, Herb Vigran, Alice Backes, Jeanette Nolan and Lurene Tuttle.

14344 ***Hearts in Harmony***. Martha Atwell directed the daytime serial that told the story of a World War II female volunteer entertainer in a USO Club. Although some action was set in the club, the stories also contained outside activities. There was a strong patriotic message contained in almost every program. Songs in the club were performed by Bob Hanna and Anne Marlowe, who was the singing voice of the heroine, played by Jone Allison. The club's pianist was Vic Arden. Other cast members were: King Calder, Bill Lipton, Ellen Maher, George Matthews, Bill Redfield, Bob Walker and Alice Yourman. Ed Herlihy was the announcer. Kroger's Tender Grade A Beef was the program's sponsor (15 min., Monday through Friday, World War II era).

14345 Heartsill, Francis P. Bass (WRC, Washington, DC, 1924).

14346 Heath, Harold. Sportscaster and sports play-by-play broadcaster (WOC, Davenport, IA, 1949).

14347 Heath, (Mrs.) Julian. Mrs. Heath broadcast daily menus for her women listeners (WJZ, New York, NY, 1924–1925). She later conducted a daily cooking program (WJZ, 1928).

14348 Heath, Mickey. Sportscaster and Milwaukee Brewers baseball play-by-play broadcaster (WEMP, Milwaukee, WI, 1947–1949).

14349 Heather, Oscar. Tenor (WHT, Decatur, IL, 1925). Assistant announcer

(WENR, Chicago, IL; WBCN, Chicago, IL, 1928).

14350 **Heatherton, Ray.** Baritone (*Ray Heatherton*, vcl. mus. prg., NBC, 1933–1935). Heatherton later became a DJ and interviewed guests on his *Heatherton House* program. Russ Dunbar was his announcer (30 min., Sunday, 12:00–12:30 P.M., WOR, New York, NY, 1951).

14351 **Heathman, Jessie E.** COM-HE (WILL, Urbana, IL, 1949).

14352 **Heatter, Basil.** Newscaster (WOR, Newark, NJ, 1954). Basil was the son of Gabriel Heatter.

14353 **Heatter, Gabriel.** News commentator (*Gabriel Heatter*, WOR, Newark, NJ, 1933–1934; WLS, Chicago, IL, 1938; *Borden's Home News*, NBC, 1938; *We the People*, CBS, 1938–1940; *Peter Paul Presents*, WOR, 1939; MBS, 1940–1941; MBS-WOR, 1942–1944; *Behind the Front Page*, MBS-WOR, 1944–1947, *Behind the Front Page* and *Heatter's Mailbag*, MBS, 1949–1960).

After first writing for periodicals, Heatter was invited to debate socialist Norman Thomas on WMCA (New York, NY) in 1932. This led to him accepting a job as a daily 15-minute news commentator on that station. The following year he went to work for WOR (New York, NY) as a news commentator and gained prominence for his broadcasts on the Mutual Broadcasting System at the trial of Bruno Richard Hauptmann, the kidnaper of the Lindbergh baby. Heatter became even better known when he became host of the *We the People* program. *See* ***We the People***.

Gabriel Heatter is best remembered for his efforts at morale building during World War II. He always seemed to find some little item of cheer even in the war's darkest days, so that he could begin his program each evening, "Good evening, everyone. There's good news tonight." Although clearly a cheer leading propagandist, Heatter contributed greatly to civilian morale. He continued broadcasting until 1965, when at age 75 he gave up his regular MBS news broadcast.

14354 ***Heaven and Home Hour.*** Clarence Erickson created and conducted the religious program in Glendale, California, in the 1930s. The host of the program was Russell Kilamn. The 30-minute program was still on the air in the 1990s.

14355 **Hebenstreit, Carl.** DJ (*Hour of Harm*, KTEL, Walla Walla, WA, 1949).

14356 **Hebestralt, Dorothy and Marjory Hebestralt.** The instrumental team played duets on piano and organ (WLW, Cincinnati, OH, 1925).

14357 **Hecht, Albert.** Actor Hecht was in the cast of *A Woman of Courage*.

14358 **Hecht, Arthur J.** Announcer (WKBH, LaCrosse, WI,1925).

14359 **Heck, Jane.** COM — HE (WLCR, Torrington, CT, 1955).

14360 **Heck, Faith.** COM-HE (WHAP, Hopewell, VA, 1954–1955).

14361 **Heckel, Pearl.** Pianist (WQJ, Chicago, IL, 1924–1925).

14362 **Heckert, Fritz.** Leader (*Fritz Heckert Orchestra*, instr. mus. prg., WORK, York, PA, 1942).

14363 **Heckert, Robert.** Newscaster (WIBG, Philadelphia, PA, 1945; KYW, Philadelphia, PA, 1947).

14364 **Heckler, Doris.** COM-HE (WPTZ, Philadelphia, PA, 1955).

14365 **Heckman, Nan.** COM-HE (WEEU, Reading, PA, 1951).

14366 **Heckt, Lucille.** Pianist (WOW, Omaha, NE, 1927). Leader (Dodge (NE) High School Orchestra (WOW, 1927).

14367 **Hecktel, Margaret.** Soprano (KSD, St. Louis, MO, 1924).

14368 **Hecox, Clarence.** DJ (*Shorty the Hired Hand*, KVAN, Vancouver, WA, 1952–1956).

14369 **Hector, Charles.** Leader (Charles Hector and his St. James Theater Orchestra, WBZ, Boston-Springfield, MA, 1925; Yankee Network Band, 1931–1932; *Charles Hector Orchestra*, instr. mus. prg., CBS, 1936; WEEI, Boston, MA, 1939).

14370 **Hector, Louis.** Actor Hector was in the cast of *Lorenzo Jones*, *Pretty Kitty Kelly* and *Sherlock Holmes*.

14371 **Hedge, Ray.** Actor Hedge appeared on *Myrt and Marge* and *Young Dr. Malone*.

14372 **Hedgens, Inez.** Pianist (WFAA, Dallas, TX, 1929).

14373 **Hedgepeth [Hedgepath], William.** Newscaster (WDNC, Durham, NC, 1945). DJ (*Uncle Zeb*, WCSC, Charleston, WV, 1948). Sportscaster (WGTC, Greenville, NC, 1949).

14374 **Hedges, Ruby W.** Harpist (KOA, Denver, CO, 1926).

14375 **Hedeger, Ted (aka Fred Herman).** Announcer Hedeger was also known as "The Bell Boy" (KWK, St. Louis, MO, 1928).

14376 **Hedgens, Inez.** Pianist (WFAA, Dallas, TX, 1929).

14377 **Hedlund, Guy.** Director, *WTIC Playhouse* (dramas) with Jay and Ranny Ray, Beatrice Battey and Barbara Bangs.

14378 **Hedmon, Sam.** Pianist (WRNY, New York, NY, 1928).

14379 **Hedrick, Lee.** Sportscaster (WSAI, Cincinnati, OH, 1952).

14380 **"HEE."** Designation for Harry E. Ehrhart, station owner and announcer (WDAR, Philadelphia, PA, 1924).

14381 ***Heel Hugger Harmonies.*** Robert Armbruster was the musical director of the music program that featured a string ensemble and male quartet (15 min., Tuesday, 8:30–8:45 P.M., WJZ, New York, NY, 1932).

14382 **Heen, Gladys.** Actress Heen was a cast member of the daytime serial programs *The Guiding Light* and *The Road of Life*.

14383 **Heer, Albert.** Bass-baritone (WBZ, Springfield, MA, 1926).

14384 **Heetderks, Anne.** Known as the Bon Marche Story Lady, Miss Heetderks told children's stories (KJR, Seattle, WA, 1925).

14385 **Heffernan, W.P.** Newscaster (WBTM, Danville, VA, 1937–1939).

14386 **Heffner, Georgia.** Miss Heffner broadcast talks on the topic of reducing (WGBS, New York, NY, 1925).

14387 **Hefflin, Van.** Actor Heflin was in the cast of *Betty and Bob*, *The Court of Human Relations*, *The Goldbergs*, *Man I Married*, *Our Gal Sunday* and *Way Down East* before coming a motion picture star.

14388 **Heflin, Virginia.** COM-HE (KOSA, Odessa, TX, 1951–1954).

14389 **Hegaeth, Grace.** Soprano (KYW, Chicago, IL, 1925).

14390 **Hegard, Ken.** Newscaster (WRJN, Racine, WI, 1938). DJ (*Pancake Parade*, WFOX, Milwaukee, WI, 1947–1948).

14391 **Hegele, Blanche.** Soprano (WIP, Philadelphia, PA, 1925).

14392 **Heger, Nina.** Soprano (WOR, Newark, NJ, 1934).

14393 **Hehne, Irene.** COM-HE (WEST, Easton, PA, 1949).

14394 ***Heidelberg Concert Orchestra.*** Instr. mus. prg. (WGN, Chicago, IL, 1934).

14395 **Heiden, Marion.** COM-HE (WPLY, Portsmouth, WI, 1960).

14396 **Heidman, Vera.** Pianist (WHA, Madison, WI, 1925).

14397 **Heidt, Horace.** Leader (Hotel Claremont Orchestra, KRE, Berkeley, CA, 1925; Horace Heidt and his All-American Orchestra, KGO, San Francisco, CA, 1927; Horace Heidt Orchestra, featured on *The Shell Happy Time Hour*, 1929). Heidt's band remained popular on radio and records for three decades. His early band included: Jerry Browne and Warren Lewis, t.; Paul Know, tb.; Dave Phennig, clr., v., as. and ss.; Clarence Moore, as., ss., and bar.; Harold Plummer, clr., ss., as., ts. and bar.; Harold Moore and Lew Lykins, clr., v., as., ss. and ts. and vcls.; Charles Midgley, p.; Lee Fleming, d.; Art Thorsen, tba.; and Charles Bradshaw, bjo.

Heidt's band continued to be busy and popular through the decades of the 1930s and 1940s on various network programs and his own remote broadcasts (*Horace Heidt Orchestra*, MBS, 1934; CBS, 1935; WOR, Newark, NJ, 1935–1936; NBC-Red, 1939; NBC, 1939. *Horace Heidt's Brigadiers*, instr. mus. prg., CBS, 1936; NBC, 1937–1939; KSD, St. Louis, MO, 1940).

14398 **Heikell, Freddy.** Leader (*Freddy Heikell Orchestra*, instr. mus. prg., WLW, Cincinnati, OH, 1937–1938).

14399 **Heilmann, Harry.** Sportscaster Heilmann was a former Detroit Tiger baseball star (WXYZ, Detroit, MI, 1939–1945). From 1940 to1945 he broadcast Tiger baseball games and Michigan State football games on WXYZ.

14400 **Heilner, Van Campen.** Sportscaster (*Rod and Gun Club*, MBS, 1955).

14401 **Heiman, Sam J.** Conductor (Sam J. Heiman Casino Orchestra, WLAC, Nashville, TN, 1924).

14402 **Heimberger, Eric.** Leader (Eric Heimberger's Hotel Dance Band, WTIC, Hartford, CT, 1925–1926).

14403 **Heimer, Berlotz.** Bandmaster, New York City Police Band (WJZ, New York, NY, 1922).

14404 **Heimrich, George.** Newscaster (KFXM, San Bernardino, CA, 1944).

14405 **Heimueller, Marguerite.** Pianist (KSD, St. Louis, MO, 1923).

14406 Hein, Mabelle. Leader (Mabelle Hein and her Blue Bird Band, KFI, Los Angeles, CA, 1926).

14407 Hein, Mel. Sportscaster (*Highlights in the World of Sports*, CBS, 1939). Hein was a former star professional football great with the New York Giants.

14408 Heinberg, Max H. Violinist (WCOA, Pensacola, FL, 1926).

14409 Heine, Helen Corbin. Pianist (WJZ, New York, NY, 1925).

14410 Heineman, Mildred. Pianist (WWJ, Detroit, MI, 1923).

14411 Heineman, Stuart. Newscaster (KFEL, Denver, CO, 1941–1942).

14412 Heinemann, Eda. Actress Heinemann was a cast member of the *Joyce Jordan, Girl Inerne* daytime serial.

14413 *Heinie and the Grenadiers* (aka *Heinie's Grenadiers*). Instr. mus. prg. (WTMJ, Milwaukee, WI, 1935–1937). The "little German" band, a long time favorite with listeners, was directed by Jack Bundy.

14414 Heinrich, Tommy. Sportscaster Heinrich, former New York Yankee right fielder, broadcast his views on baseball and other sports on his *Tommy Heinrich Show* (WCBS, New York, NY, 1955).

14415 Heinrichs [Heinriche], Hilda. Cellist (WMBB, Homewood, IL, WOK, Chicago, IL, 1928).

14416 Heinroth, Charles. Organist (Instr. mus. prg. of Sunday recitals, KDKA, Pittsburgh, PA, 1927).

14417 *Heintz Magazine of the Air.* The husband-and-wife singing team of Frank Crumit and Julia Sanderson were featured on the music show. They were accompanied by the B.A. Rolfe Orchestra (15 min., Weekly, 1937).

14418 Heiny, (Capt.) J.D. Announcer (WOS, Davenport, IA, 1928).

14419 Heinzelman, Delrose. COM-HE (WGHN, Grand Haven, MI, 1956).

14420 Heiser, Gwenne [Gwen]. COM-HE (KCLO, Leavenworth, KS, 1957).

14421 Heitger, Abby. COM-HE (WBIW, Bedford, IN, 1954).

14422 Heith, Max. Violinist (WGCP, Newark, NJ, 1926).

14423 Heithroth, (Dr.) C. Organist (KDKA, Pittsburgh, PA, 1923).

14424 Helbig, A.M. Pianist (KSD, St. Louis, MO, 1923).

14425 Helebrant, Lucie J. COM-HE (KOEL, Oelwein, IA, 1956).

14426 Helen and Hazel. Harmony singing team (KLX, Oakland, CA, 1929).

14427 *(The) Helen Hayes Show.* Distinguished actress Helen Hayes, known as "The First Lady of the Theatre," played the leading roles opposite various male guest stars in the famous plays broadcast in the series. The plays were presented in serial form on the program sponsored by General Foods, the makers of Sanka Coffee. The program went off the air in 1937, only to reappear again in the 1940 and 1945 seasons (30 min., Tuesday, 9:30–10:00 P.M., NBC-Blue, 1935).

14428 *Helen Morgan.* Talented torch singer Morgan was sponsored on the entertaining music program by Bi-So-Dol antacid powder. She was accompanied by the Albert Bartlett Tango Orchestra (30 min., Sunday, 2:00–2:30 P.M., CBS, 1933). *See* ***Singers***.

14429 *Helen of Hollywood.* Marian Grable (as Helen of Hollywood) broadcast information about various movie stars and pictures that were currently in production. Occasionally, she would interview stars such as Conrad Nagel in their Hollywood homes by telephone (WFAA, Dallas, TX, 1922).

14430 *Helen Trent's Romance* (aka *The Romance of Helen Trent*). Better known as *The Romance of Helen Trent*, the program originated as *Helen Trent's Romance* when it was sponsored by Edna Wallace Hopper, Inc. *See* ***The Romance of Helen Trent***.

14431 Helezer, Walter. Newscaster (WEDC, Chicago, IL, 1938–1942).

14432 Helfer, George "Al." Sportscaster (WOR, Newark, NJ, 1939–1941; MBS-WOR, 1942; *Sports Review*, WLW, Cincinnati, OH, 1949; MBS, 1949; *Sports Digest*, *Mutual Baseball Game of the Day*, MBS, 1951–1954; *Al Helfer Sports Show*, MBS, 1955; NBC, 1956).

14433 Helgesen, Ray. Newscaster (KTUC, Tucson, AZ, 1944–1945). Sportscaster (KTUC, 1944–1945; *Sports Spotlight* and *Football Prophet*, KSUN, Bisbee, AZ, 1949).

14434 Helgeson, Bob. DJ (*Friendly Time* and *Spins and Needles*, KSOO, Sioux Falls, SD, 1949; *Helgy's Place*, KSOO, 1952–1956).

14435 Helgeson, Joe. Actor Helgeson was in the cast of *Ma Perkins* and *We Love and Learn*.

14436 Helie, (Mrs.) W.R. Singer (WCOA, Pensacola, FL, 1926).

14437 Hella Temple Band. Fraternal musical group (WFAA, Dallas, TX, 1922).

14438 Hellenic, Ruth. COM-HE (WCMW, Canton, OH, 1956).

14439 Heller, Little Jackie. Tenor (*Little Jackie Heller*, vcl. mus. prg., NBC, 1934–1936). Leader (*Little Jackie Heller Orchestra*, instr. mus. prg., CBS, 1939).

14440 Heller, Shirley. Singer (WMAQ, Chicago, IL, 1936).

14441 Hellman, Ruth B. Soprano (WEAF, New York, NY, 1925).

14442 *Hello, Americans.* Orson Welles hosted the show that combined Latin American music with information about the culture of the "other Americas." Performers on the program included: Gerald Mohr, Agnes Moorehead, Hans Conreid, Pedro De Cordova, Miguelito Valdes, Ted Reid, Lou Merrill, Norman Feld, John Tucker Battle, Tito Guizar, Laird Cregar and calypso singer, Sir Lancelot (30 min., Weekly, 1942).

14443 (The) Hello Girls. Vocal team of Flo and Edna, who were not otherwise identified (WJR, Detroit, MI, 1928).

14444 *Hello, Peggy.* Following the pattern of the novel *Grand Hotel*, the daytime serial drama followed the stories of the guests and employees of a large metropolitan hotel. The title role was played by Eunice Howard, the hotel's switchboard operator. Other major characters on the program were a newspaper reporter played by Alan Bunce and two bell boys played by Jackie Kelk and Arthur Donnelly (15 min., Wednesday and Friday, 9:45–10:00 A.M., NBC-Red, 1937).

14445 *Hello, Sucker.* The series, originating in Chicago, dramatized various scams and business frauds pulled on unsuspecting citizens (30 min., 1952).

14446 Helman, Sam. Leader (Sam Helman Salon Dance Orchestra, WLAG, Minneapolis, MN, 1924; Sammy Helman Brandeis Store Restaurant Orchestra, WOAW, Omaha, NE, 1925).

14447 Helms, (Reverend) E.E. Pastor Helms of the First Methodist Episcopal Church regularly broadcast sermons and services (KHJ, Los Angeles, CA, 1923).

14448 Helms, Nora. Soprano (WNYC, New York, NY, 1925).

14449 Helpler, Morris. Announcer (KOA, Denver, CO, 1928).

14450 *Helpmate.* Frank and Anne Hummert produced the daytime serial drama written by Margaret Lerwerth. The story followed three couples and how they related to each other in their normal, everyday lives. The program originated in Chicago. The cast members included: Kathryn Card, Sidney Ellstrom, Judith Evelyn, Arlene Francis, John Larkin, Myron McCormick, Fern Persons, Beryl Vaughn and Karl Weber (15 min., Monday through Friday, NBC, 1941–1944).

14451 Helsing, Grace. Pianist (WAMD, Minneapolis, MN, 1926).

14452 Helsby, H.R. Newscaster (WHDL, Olean, NY, 1937–1941, 1944–1945).

14453 Heltman, Hazel. Pianist (WLS, Chicago, IL, 1925).

14454 Helton, Bernie. Newscaster (WACO, Waco, TX, 1939–1941).

14455 Helvey, Wesley. Leader (Wesley Helvey's Troubadours Orchestra, WKRC, Cincinnati, OH, 1925; Wesley Helvey and his La Vista Orchestra, WKRC, 1926).

14456 Helwegen, Chuck. Leader (Chuck Helwegen's Ramona Gardens Orchestra, WOOD, Grand Rapids, MI, 1926).

14457 Hembree, Lawrence. Newscaster (WAIM, Anderson, SC, 1937–1939).

14458 Hemenway, Virginia. Leader (Virginia Hemenway's Harmony Girls Orchestra, KHJ, Los Angeles, CA, 1926).

14459 Heming, Violet. Actress Heming appeared on the *Right to Happiness* daytime serial program.

14460 Hemingway, Frank. News commentator (KGW-KEX, Portland, OR, 1942; *Voice of the Nation*, NBC and *One for the Book*, CBS, 1945; KMPC, Los Angeles, CA, 1945).

14461 Hemingway, Lee. Violinist (KFAB, Lincoln, NE, 1928).

14462 Hemminghaus, Paula. Contralto (WJZ, New York, NY, 1928).

14463 Hemmingway, Norman. Newscaster (WPAR, Parkersburg, WV, 1941; *Local News*, WPAR, 1942, 1947).

14464 Hempel, Frieda. Soprano (WEAF, New York, NY, 1926).

14465 Hemphill, Bob. Newscaster (KVWC, Vernon, TX, 1946).

14466 Hemus, Percy. Singer Hemus was born in Topeka, Kansas. He became famous with his songs, wisecracks and his popular "Darktown Poker Club" number on the *Dutch Masters Minstrels* program (NBC, 1928). Hemus later embarked on a successful career as a radio actor. One of his most famous roles was that of The Old Wrangler on the *Tom Mix* show in the 1940s. He also appeared in the cast of *The Court of Human Relations* and *The Road of Life*.

14467 Hench, John. Actor Hench was in the cast of *Those Happy Gilmans*.

14468 Henderson, A. Lee. Sports news reporter and play-by-play announcer of Ohio State University football games (WEAO, Columbus, OH, 1926).

14469 Henderson, Brooks. Newscaster (KSTP, St. Paul, MN, 1939–1942).

14470 Henderson, Billy. Pianist (KMTR, Hollywood, CA, 1925).

14471 Henderson, D.J. COM-HE (WPAD, Paducah, KY, 1956–1957).

14472 Henderson, Douglas "Jocko." Black DJ (WSID, Baltimore, MD, 1951; WHAT, Philadelphia, PA, 1953; *Big Swing Train*, WDAS, Philadelphia, PA,1953–1956). Influenced by Chuck Richards, a friend who was a Baltimore DJ, Henderson took a job at WSID in 1951. Two years later he moved to Philadelphia's WDAS and still later to WOV (New York, NY). As "Jocko" Henderson, he gained considerable popularity in the City of Brotherly Love. He gained additional fame as a rock-and-roll DJ with his *1280 Rocket Show* (120 min., Monday through Friday, 10:00–12:00 midnight, WOV, New York, NY, 1956).

14473 Henderson, Esther Jane. Pianist (WMAQ, Chicago, IL, 1923).

14474 Henderson, Fletcher. Pianist and band leader (Fletcher Henderson's Happy Harmonists, WDT, Chicago, IL, 1923; Fletcher Henderson's Alabama Club Orchestra, WBZ, Springfield, MA, 1923–1924; WHN, New York, NY, 1924–1927). Henderson was a talented arranger, pianist, and band leader, who made many significant contributions to the development of American jazz (*Fletcher Henderson Orchestra,* instr. mus. prg., NBC, 1936; CBS, 1938; WMAQ, Chicago, IL, 1939; WBBM, Chicago, IL, 1942).

14475 Henderson, Fran. COM-HE (WARU, Peru, IN, 1956).

14476 Henderson, (Mrs.) Freddye. COM-HE (WERD, Atlanta, GA, 1956).

14477 Henderson, Gordon. Leader (Gordon Henderson's Dance Band, KPO, San Francisco, CA, 1928).

14478 Henderson, Harriet. Soprano (KPO, San Francisco, CA, 1927).

14479 Henderson, Isabel. Soprano (WEBJ, New York, NY and WOKO, Albany, NY, 1925).

14480 Henderson, James. Sportscaster (WOI, Ames, IA, 1939).

14481 Henderson, Joe. Newscaster (KFPW, Fort Smith, AK, 1938).

14482 Henderson, Leon. News commentator (NBC-Blue, 1945).

14483 Henderson, Louise. COM-HE (WSNJ, Bridgeton, NJ, 1956).

14484 Henderson, Margaret. COM-HE (WGSV, Guntersville, AL, 1956).

14485 Henderson, Robert. Newscaster (KALE, Portland, OR, 1940).

14486 Henderson, Sally. COM-HE (WCOA, Pensacola, FL, 1956).

14487 Henderson, Skitch. Leader (*Skitch Henderson Orchestra*, KVOD, Denver, CO, 1942). DJ (Orchestra leader Henderson turned DJ in 1949, WNBC, New York, NY, 1949).

14488 Henderson, Tom. Newscaster (WHJB, Greensburg, PA, 1947).

14489 Henderson, W.K. ("Old Man" Henderson). Station owner-announcer Henderson bought a share in WGAQ, a 250-watts station, located in Shreveport, Louisiana when it went on the air in 1923. He soon bought out his other partners and brought the station to prominence with its new call letters — KWKH. His station won the *Radio Digest* Gold Cup as the country's most popular station in 1930.

Henderson opened his programs with such greetings as: " Hello, world. This is KWKH at Shreveport, Louisiana. Don't go away." And: "Hello world, W.K. Henderson speaking. Doggone your buttons." His strong protest broadcasts against chain stores and other "enemies of the people" brought him the nicknames of "Old Man Henderson" and the "Shreveport War Horse." He also fought for the "recognition of the South," and "... a fair and equitable distribution as to radio stations, wave lengths and power throughout the United States and not for any certain part of the country." See **Stations — Growth and Development**.

14490 Henderson, Winston. Newscaster (WOI, Ames, IA, 1941).

14491 Henderson-Bland, R. British soldier-poet broadcast his own poetry (NBC, 1931).

14492 Hendra, Christopher. Tenor (WIBO, Chicago, IL, 1926).

14493 Hendre, Alice J. Pianist (WPG, Atlantic City, NJ, 1925).

14494 Hendrick, Peg. COM-HE (KBUC, Corona, CA, 1951).

14495 Hendricks, Edith. Vocalist (*Edith Hendricks*, vcl. mus. prg., CBS, 1942).

14496 Hendricks, Priscilla. COM-HE (WJAM, Marion, AL, 1956).

14497 Hendrickson, Bob. Newscaster (WAGE, Syracuse, NY, 1947). Sportscaster (WAGE, 1949–1951).

14498 Hendrickson, Joe. Newscaster (KGCU, Mandan, ND, 1938).

14499 Hendrickson, Rod. Actor Hendrickson was in the cast of *Amanda of Honeymoon Hill, Backstage Wife, Bulldog Drummond, Second Mrs. Burton* and *Wendy Warren and the News.*

14500 Hendrickson, Vivian. COM-HE (WDVL, Vineland, NJ, 1960).

14501 Hendrie, Hubert. Baritone (*Hubert Hendrie*, vcl. mus. prg., CBS, 1936).

14502 *Hendrik Willem Van Loon*. Popular author Van Loon discussed various topics of general interest on his program. His wide range of knowledge and clarity of expression made the program an excellent example of how intellectually stimulating radio could be. Van Loon's "air-storming" included perceptive discussions of such disparate personalities as Hitler, Mussolini and Isaac Newton (15 min., Sunday, 7:45–8:00 P.M., NBC, 1935). One example of Van Loon's commentary is the opening of his June 6, 1935, broadcast: "A great English physicist once compared life to a game of chess. Some had complained to him that life was not fair and that Nature was not fair and nothing was fair in the universe anyway. To which he answered (and he was quite right) that life and Nature were both of them eminently fair, just like the game of chess. At times both of them seem to be downright unfair and cruel, for they had no respect whatsoever for the individual. But they were never unfair, in the true sense of the word, because the rules according to which they operated were the same for all of us, for high and for low, for poor and for rich, for the stupid and the bright. It was, however, up to us to acquaint ourselves with those rules." Later in the broadcast he concluded: "Nature is not interested in alibis. Nature is only interested in facts. She plays the game according to the rules, but expects you to do the same. If you fail to know the rules, well, that is just too bad, for then you will be very much out of luck. If you insist upon sitting down on a hot stove, you must also expect a few blisters and that is that, as far as Nature is concerned."

14503 Hendrix, Bettie. COM-HE (WPCC, Clinton, SC, 1960).

14504 Hendrix, Cliff. Newscaster (KGHF, Pueblo, CO, 1945). DJ (*Rise and Shine*, KCSJ, Pueblo, CO, 1949–1952).

14505 Hendrix, Jim. Newscaster (WAPO, Chattanooga, TN, 1941–1942).

14506 Hendrix College Troubadours. The Troubadours were a talented 22-piece college band (KGHI, Little Rock, AR, 1929).

14507 Hendry, Bob. Singer of Scots' songs (WLS, Chicago, IL, 1928).

14508 Henestreit, Marjory. Pianist (WLW, Cincinnati, OH, 1925).

14509 Henke, Elsie. Pianist (WLAG, Minneapolis–St. Paul, MN, 1924).

14510 Henle, Ray. Newscaster (WOL, Washington, DC and NBC-Blue, 1944–1947; NBC, 1948).

14511 Henneberg, Inky. Banjoist (KWSC, Pullman, WA, 1926).

14512 Hennefer, Grace. Soprano (KSD, St. Louis, MO, 1939).

14513 Henneke, Ben. Newscaster (KVOO, Tulsa, OK, 1945).

14514 Henneman, Carl. Newscaster (KFAM, St. Cloud, MN, 1938–1939).

14515 Hennessee, Edna. COM-HE (KSWO, Lawton, OK, 1957).

14516 Hennessey, Frank. DJ (*Timekeeper*, WSYR, Syracuse, NY, 1947). When Al Ross, WBAL Baltimore's popular DJ, moved to WRC, Washington, DC, he was replaced by Frank Hennessey. Previously, Hennessey had conducted morning shows in Syracuse on

WSYR and WNDR. His jovial manner soon earned him a large Baltimore following (180 min., Monday through Saturday, 6:00–9:00 A.M., WBAL, Baltimore, MD, 1955).

14517 **Hennessey, Harry.** Newscaster (KFGO, Fargo, SD and WOR, New York, NY, 1948).

14518 **Hennessy, Ed J.** Newscaster (WRBL, Columbus, GA, 1945).

14519 **Henning, Arthur Sears.** Newscaster (WGN, Chicago, IL, 1939).

14520 **Henninger, George.** Musician Henninger played the organ on the *Modern Romance* daytime serial program.

14521 **Henningsen, Walter.** Orchestra director-flutist (KOMO, Seattle, WA, 1927–1928).

14522 **Henningsen, William.** Hymn singer (WBNX, New York, NY, 1939).

14523 ***(The) Henny Youngman Show.*** Raleigh Cigarettes sponsored the variety show featuring comedian Henny Youngman. Music was supplied by Eddy Howard's band. Carol Bruce sang and performed in comedy sketches with Youngman (30 min., Wednesday, 8:30–9:00 P.M., NBC-Red, 1944).

14524 **Henriques, Betty.** COM-HE (WEIM, Fitchburg, MA, 1957).

14525 **Henry, Al.** DJ (*Midnight Matinee,* 45 min., Monday through Saturday, 11:15–12:00 midnight, WONS, Hartford, CT., 1952).

14526 **Henry, Bill.** Newscaster (WTOP, Washington, DC, and CBS, 1945–1947). An occasional criticism of Henry's work was that he sometimes blurred the lines between news reporter and commentator. Henry also was an actor on the *Those We Love* daytime serial program.

14527 **Henry, Dick.** Newscaster (WOOD, Grand Rapids, MI, 1944–1945; *Standard Oil News, Noon News* and *Morning News,* WOOD, 1946–1947).

14528 **Henry, Dorothy.** COM-HE (KNEM, Nevada, MO, 1951).

14529 **Henry, Dorothy.** COM-HE (WGRN, Grinnell, IA, 1957).

14530 **Henry, F.M.** Announcer (KFKZ, Kirksville, MO, 1927).

14531 **Henry, Gil.** DJ (*Call a Cop,* KOPP, Ogden, UT, 1947; *Spinning Bandstand,* KMUR, Murray, UT, 1948; *KING's Open House,* KING, Seattle, WA, 1949–1952).

14532 **Henry, Gloria.** COM-HE (WSJV, South Bend-Elkhart, IN, 1957).

14533 **Henry, Helen Neil.** COM-HE (WNLA, Indianola, MS, 1956).

14534 **Henry, Hortense.** Soprano (WFBH, New York, NY, 1925).

14535 **Henry, Ione.** COM-HE (KRFO, Owatonna, MN, 1957).

14536 **Henry, Julia.** COM-HE (WKOA, Hopkinsville, KY, 1960).

14537 **Henry, Marion.** Pianist (WQJ, Chicago, IL, 1924).

14538 **Henry, Mary Carolyn.** Soprano (KSD, St. Louis, MO, 1926).

14539 **Henry, Maurice.** Leader (*Maurice Henry Orchestra,* instr. mus. prg., WOR, Newark, NJ, 1935).

14540 **Henry, Pat.** DJ (*Sierra Serenade,* KXRX, San Jose, CA, 1948).

14541 **Henry, Rachel.** COM-HE (WJOT, Lake City, SC, 1957).

14542 **Henry, Tal.** Leader (*Tal Henry Orchestra,* instr. mus. prg., WBIG, Greensboro, NC, 1939).

14543 **Henry, Virginia.** Contralto (KLOS, Independence, MO, 1926).

14544 ***Henry and Jerome.*** Vcl. mus. prg. by male vocal team that was not otherwise identified (WIBW, Topeka, KS, 1939).

14545 ***Henry Burr's Book of Ballads.*** Popular tenor Burr sang his favorite ballads, mostly of the old-fashioned type, on the popular music show (15 min., Tuesday, 11:15–11:30 A.M., WLS, Chicago, IL, 1935–1936). *See* **Burr, Henry** *and* ***The National Barn Dance.***

14546 **(The) Henry Ford Old-Time Dance Orchestra.** Traditional music group (WOOD, Grand Rapids, MI, 1926).

14547 ***Henry George Program*** **(aka *Henry and George*).** Don Clark and Dave Elman wrote and performed on the program of one-minute dramas and comedies with dance music presented in the format of a traveling troupe headed by two bellboys, Henry and George. Primarily, this was a blackface comedy show with Georgia Backus, Brad Browne, Don Clark, Dave Elman and Harriet Lee in the cast. Maudie, the cigar counter girl was played by Harriet Lee. Don, the house detective, was played by Brad Browne (30 min., Monday, 9:00–9:30 P.M., CBS, 1929–1930).

14548 ***Henry Hornsbuckle and Hiram Higsby.*** The team played CW music, sang and told jokes. Hornsbuckle was Merle Housh, who also played guitar. Higsby was Truman Wilder, who played harmonica (WIBW, Topeka, KS, 1927). The team moved to station WLS, Chicago, IL, in 1928.

14549 ***(The) Henry Morgan Show.*** Before comedian Morgan starred on this network program, he appeared on New York local radio on WOR, Newark, NJ and the NBC-Blue network with his creative *Meet Mr. Morgan* and *Here's Morgan* programs. On local radio, Morgan was best known for his insulting and insightful humor. On the network shows, his humor tended to grow from skits and a situation comedy format. After a short run on ABC (30 min., Weekly, ABC, 1946–1947), the *Henry Morgan Show* was broadcast by NBC from 1949 to 1950. In its various formats, the program's cast included: Art Carney, Betty Garde, Maurice Gosfield, Florence Halop, Durward Kirby, Madaline Lee, Alice Pearce, Minerva Pious and Arnold Stang. Carroll Moore, Jr., Henry Morgan, Aaron Ruben and Joe Stein were the writers and Charles Powers the director. Music was provided by the Bernie Green Orchestra and the Billy Williams vocal group. The announcers were Art Ballinger, Ben Grauer, Ed Herlihy, Charles Irving, David Ross and Dan Seymour. *See* ***Here's Morgan*** and **Comedy and Humor.**

14550 ***Henry's Exchange.*** Henry Hornsbuckle (Merle Housh) conducted the quarter-hour program of household hints. Henry claimed that he was the only male on radio broadcasting household hints. During one three-week period, he received 13,3562 letters with household hints included. One of his listeners, in fact, sent him 256 hints that had been gathered by three generations of her family (15 min., Monday through Friday, WLS, Chicago, IL, 1939).

14551 ***Henry's Store.*** Young George Gobel sang, played guitar and performed comic bits on the weekly show. Patsy Montana and the Hired Hands CW music group also performed (15 min., Saturday, 8:45–9:00 P.M., WLS, Chicago, IL, 1937).

14552 **Henshaw, Gail.** Actress Henshaw appeared on the daytime serial programs *The Guiding Light, Backstage Wife* aka *Mary Noble, Backstage Wife* and *The Woman in White.*

14553 **Hensley, Joan.** COM-HE (WTLB, Utica, NY, 1957).

14554 **Henson, Doug.** DJ (*Jive Til Five,* WMVG, Milledgeville, GA, 1947; *7:30 Local,* WJMJ, Philadelphia, PA, 1949; WTEL, Philadelphia, PA, 1950; *Wake Up and Smile,* WJMJ, 1954). Sportscaster (WJMJ, 1952; *Speedway,* WJMJ, 1954–1956).

14555 **Henson, Fred C.** Newscaster (WMT, Cedar Rapids, IA and KRNT-KSO, Des Moines, IA, 1945).

14556 **Henson, Russell.** Newscaster (*Time for the News,* WCTT, Corbin, KY, 1948).

14557 **Hentoff, Nat.** DJ (Jazz expert Hentoff broadcast his critical comment on the music and played the best, WMEX, Boston, MA, 1949).

14558 **Henton, Earl.** Newscaster (*10 O'-Clock News,* WEBC, Duluth, MN, 1947–1948).

14559 ***(The) Hep Cat*** **(aka *The Tom Cat*).** DJ not otherwise identified (KITI, Centralia, WA, 50s).

14560 **Hepburn, Helen.** COM-HE (WMUS, Muskegon, MI, 1951; WKBZ, Muskegon, MI, 1954).

14561 **Hepburn, Winnie.** COM-HE (KVIC, Victoria, TX, 1955).

14562 **Hepner, Arthur.** Newscaster (CBS, 1947–1948).

14563 ***Her Honor, Nancy James.*** First broadcast in 1938 on CBS, the daytime serial focused on a female judge in a large city's Court of Common Problems. Barbara Weeks played the title role of Judge Nancy James. Her life was often complicated by the activities of the city's mayor and the District Attorney. Also in the program's cast were: Joan Banks, Joseph Curtin, Michael Fitzmaurice, Maurice Franklin, Janice Gilbert, James Gilbert, Basil Loughrane, Claire Niesen, Alice Reinheart, Chester Stratton, Kay Strozzi, Barbara Weeks and Ned Wever (CBS, 1938–1939).

14564 **Herald [Herold], Florence.** DJ and newscaster (WTTN, Watertown, WI, 1942). Herald began work at station WTTN as a bookkeeper, but while her boss was away the station received many letters requesting German music. When program announcers couldn't pronounce the names of the selections on the records they played, Herald went on the air to pronounce them. Before the boss came back, she was on the air with her own 15-minute program of German music. Herald

(1975) says that she was the first "German DJ." For two years on the station she broadcast news capsules from the *American Herald*, a German newspaper, and *The Housfrau*, a German magazine in between the records she played.

She followed this by initiating a woman's program that was broadcast for 20 years. On her 45-minute program she provided household information. In addition, she did a 15-minute call-in show on which she answered listener's questions. Her listeners called her the "Ann Landers of Household Hints in Watertown."

14565 ***(The) Herald Reporter***. The weekly drama was sponsored by the Ontario Electric Corporation. Each week the program presented a young newspaper reporter named Jimmy, who was unable to find a suitable topic for a story. In order to solve his problem, he would visit Mrs. Henry Russell, an old friend of his family. Mrs. Russell, an experienced homemaker, was able to work a wealth of information and many commercial plugs into their conversation. Ham Woodle created the role of Jimmy, later played by Leo Eagen. Mrs. Russell's role was played by Helen Cawthorn. Al Zink produced and Mary Dixon wrote the interesting local show (15 min., Monday, 1:30–1:45 P.M., WENR, Chicago, IL, 1938).

14566 **Heramin, Lucille.** Contralto (WEBJ, New York, NY, 1926).

14567 ***(The) Herb Oscar Anderson Show***. ABC inaugurated Anderson's show on Labor Day, Monday September 2, 1957, in order to "get some excitement into radio again." Herb Oscar Anderson hosted the "live" music show that featured the Ralph Hermann's Orchestra, singer Carole Bennett and the Satisfiers vocal group. Glenn Riggs was the announcer (60 min., Monday through Friday, 10:00–11:00 A.M., ABC, 1957).

14568 ***(The) Herb Sheldon Show***. The genial humor of comedian Sheldon was the most entertaining part of the variety show. Unidentified vocalist and musicians appeared with Sheldon (25 min., Monday through Friday, 12:45–1:00 P.M., 1949).

14569 ***Herb Shriner Time***. See ***Alka-Seltzer Time***.

14570 **Herbeck, Ray.** Leader (*Ray Herbeck Orchestra*, instr. mus. prg., CBS, 1935; WCAE, Pittsburgh, PA, 1939; CBS, 1940; NBC, 1942).

14571 **Herbert, Arthur.** Leader (*Arthur Herbert Orchestra*, instr. mus. prg., WDEL, Wilmington, DE, 1939).

14572 **Herbert, Evelyn.** Opera prima donna (WEAF, New York, NY, 1923; WOR, Newark, NJ, 1929).

14573 **Herbert, Jasper.** Newscaster (WHHM, Memphis, TN, 1946).

14574 **Herbert, (Mrs.) T.L.** Pianist (WSM, Nashville, TN, 1928).

14575 **Herbert, Victor.** Leader (Victor Herbert's Cosmopolitan Theater Orchestra, WJZ, New York, NY, 1923). The great operetta composer (*Naughty Marietta*, *Babes in Toyland*, *Mlle. Modiste*, etc.) appeared on early radio as conductor of his own orchestra.

14576 **Herbert, William.** Newscaster (WCHS, Charleston, WV, 1938).

14577 **Herbert, Wilma.** Actress Herbert was a *Ma Perkins* cast member.

14578 **Herbert, Wilms.** Actor Herbert was in the cast of *Ma Perkins* and *Today's Children*.

14579 **Herbert's Diamond Entertainers [Orchestra].** Will Osborne led the band that *Variety* said sounded very much like Rudy Vallee's. The program was sponsored by Herbert's, a Harlem jewelry company (WABC, New York, NY, 1929).

14580 **Herbuveaux, Jules J.** Leader (Jules Herbuveaux Orchestra, WCFL, Chicago, IL, 1927). Two years later the entertaining band included such talented musicians as saxophonists Don and Joe Mangano and trumpeter Rex Mauphin (KYW, Chicago, IL, 1929).

14581 ***Hercule Poirot.*** Among mystery author Agatha Christie's many fictional creations, none was more fascinating and entertaining than her five-feet, four-inch mustached Belgian detective, Hercule Poirot. When he used his "little grey cells," Poirot's detective powers were brilliantly displayed. Often depicted in motion pictures and on television, Poirot's radio run was relatively brief. For the radio series he was relocated from his usual London locale and placed in New York City. Harold Huber portrayed the great detective in 1945 on the MBS series of half-hour programs that presented a complete story each week. The program was directed by Cecil Eastman (30 min., Thursday, MBS, 1945).

14582 ***Here Comes Louis Jordan***. Jazzman Louis Jordan and his Tympani Five were featured on the transcribed show carried by 56 stations. Also appearing with the group on the program were such talented African-American performers as the Mills Brothers, Josh White, Dorothy Donegan, the Delta Rhythm Boys and comedian Pigmeat Markham (15 min., Transcribed, Various Stations, 1946).

14583 **Hereford, Bob.** Newscaster (WIL, St. Louis, MO, 1941).

14584 ***Here's Harriet.*** Newspaper columnist Harriet Van Horne talked about New York life and times on her weekly show (10 min., Saturday, WJZ, New York, NY, 1947).

14585 ***Here's Heidy***. Heidy Mayer told stories for children on her weekly program (25 min., Sunday, 8:30–8:55 P.M., WNYC, New York, NY, 1947).

14586 ***Here's Morgan.*** Sardonic comedian Henry Morgan starred on this funny program. He was assisted by Ralph Bell, Maurice Gosfield, Charles Irving, Madeline Lee, Louis Neistat, Arnold Stang and Susan D'Usseau. Singer Elton Britt and Ross Gorman's Orchestra provided the music (30 min., Tuesday, 8:30–9:00 P.M., NBC-Blue, 1946).

Before World War II, Henry Morgan had a 15-minute show on WOR, also called *Here's Morgan*, on which his biting humor was the major element. None of Morgan's post-war programs equaled the popularity of his earlier *Here's Morgan* show. The original *Here's Morgan* program was broadcast by WOR from 1940 to 1943.

Henry Morgan (Henry Lerner von Ost, Jr.) started his radio career as an announcer. His first program —*Meet Mr. Morgan*— was carried by WOR in 1940. He first gained national attention, however, with his 15-minute evening show, *Here's Morgan*, broadcast Monday through Saturday. Morgan combined his zany, acerbic humor with odd recordings and a liberal dose of sponsor baiting to gain a large following. In many respects, Morgan was a forerunner of Jean Shepherd, although the latter's satire was much gentler in tone.

One of Morgan's early sponsors was Adler's Elevator Shoes, and "Old Man Adler" was a frequent target of the comedian's barbs. *Here's Morgan* left the air in 1943 when he entered military service. After leaving service, Morgan went to work for WJZ (New York, NY), before beginning his *Henry Morgan Show* on ABC. *See* **Comedy and Humor** *and* ***The Henry Morgan Show***.

14587 ***Here's to Veterans.*** A transcribed program, *Here's to Veterans* was used by the Veterans Administration to provide veterans with information they needed. The program featured musicians, singers and bands that were the greatest performers radio had to offer: George Hamilton IV, Guy Lombardo, Eddie Heywood, Frank Sinatra, Jerry Gray, Lou Rawls, Buck Owens, Nancy Wilson, Tommy Leonetti, Josh White, Jr., Andy Russell, Helen Reddy, Dale Evans, Lawrence Welk, Miles Davis, Vicki Carr, Stan Kenton, Art Tatum, Duke Ellington, Charlie Barnet, Jack Benny, Burns and Allen, Kid Ory, Les Baxter, Tex Beneke, Nellie Lutcher, Nelson Eddy, Carmen Cavallaro, Eddie Condon, Chuck Foster, Eddie Dean, Ralph Flanagan, Louis Armstrong, Gordon Jenkins, the Three Suns, Mitch Miller, Firehouse Five Plus Two, Merle Travis, George Auld, the Four Knights, Eartha Kitt, Henri Rene, Les Brown, Eddy Howard, Hugo Winterhalter, Johnny Ray, Bob Hope, Ralph Marterie, Nelson Riddle, the Skylarks, Joe Lilley, Anna Maria Alberghetti and Billy May (15 min., Transcribed, Various Stations, 1940s through 1960).

14588 **Herget, Joe.** Newscaster (WCHS, Charleston, WV, 1939–1942).

14589 **Hering, Florence.** Soprano (KYW, Chicago, IL, 1924).

14590 **Hering, Linda.** Saxophonist (WHAD, Milwaukee, WI, 1926).

14591 **Heritage, Ruby O.** Soprano (WHO, Des Moines, IA, 1925).

14592 **Herlihy, Ed.** Newscaster (NBC, 1947–1948). Newscaster Herlihy also enjoyed a long distinguished career as an NBC announcer. He was a longtime spokesman for Kraft Foods. Among the many programs that he announced were: *America's Town Meeting*, *Army Hour*, *The Big Show*, *Dick Tracy*, *The Falcon*, *Hearts in Harmony*, *Horn and Hardart Children's Hour* (host), *Information Please*, *Inner Sanctum*, *Just Plain Bill*, *Life Can Be Beautiful*, *Melody Puzzles*, *Mr. District Attorney*, *The O'Neills*, *Thanks for Tomorrow*, *The Thin Man*, *Truth or Consequences* and *Vic and Sade*.

14593 **Herling, Elmer.** Baritone (KPO, San Francisco, CA, 1927–1928).

14594 Herman, Charles. Newscaster (*One O'Clock News*, WLAV, Grand Rapids, MI, 1947). DJ (*Music for Milady*, WLAV, 1947).

14595 Herman, Dave. Leader (Dave Herman Cinderella Orchestra broadcasting from New York City's Cinderella Ballroom, WOR, Newark, NJ, 1924–1925; *Dave Herman Orchestra*, instr. mus. prg., WOR, Newark, NJ, 1935).

14596 Herman, Joseph. Violin (WOAW, Omaha, NE, 1923).

14597 Herman, Mary. Organist (WDRC, Hartford, CT, 1937).

14598 Herman, Milton. Actor Herman was born May 12, 1896. His first radio work was on WHN (New York, NY, 1926). He was in the cast of *Bishop and the Gargoyle, Circus Days, Death Valley Days, Texaco Star Theater, Today's Children* and *Valiant Lady*.

14599 Herman, Pete. Leader (*Pete Herman Orchestra*, instr. mus. prg., WMEX, Boston, MA, 1939).

14600 Herman, Sam. Herman was a marimba "stylist" who performed on all the New York stations in 1928 (*Sam Herman*, instr. mus. prg. with xylophonist Herman,15 min., Sunday, 11:45–12:00 midnight, NBC-Red, 1930).

14601 Herman, Sylvan. Leader (*Sylvan Herman Orchestra*, instr. mus. prg., WIP, Philadelphia, PA, 1935; *Sylvan Herman Ensemble*, WIP, 1935).

14602 Herman, Woody. Leader (*Woody Herman Orchestra*, instr. mus. prg., NBC, 1934; NBC-Red, 1937–1938).

14603 *Herman and Banta*. Instr. mus. prg. by a talented piano team of Sam Herman and Frank Banta (NBC, 1935).

14604 Hermann, Cleve. Sportscaster (*Cleve Hermann Sports*, KRCA, Los Angeles, CA, 1953–1954; *The Trophy Room*, KNBH, Los Angeles, CA, 1955; *Life Line to the World of Sports*, KFWB, Los Angeles, CA, 1960). Newscaster (*11th Hour News*, KRCA, 1953–1954).

14605 Hermanson, H.O. Tenor (WSWS, Chicago, IL, 1926).

14606 *Hermit's Cave*. Ghost stories and weird tales were dramatized on the program written by Geraldine Elliott and produced by Eric Howlett. The World War II era program began in this way: "Good evening ladies and gentlemen. The Carter Coal Company and the dealers of Olga Coal present the mummers in the little theater of the air. Well by now we're getting a bit used to winter. We're like soldiers in the midst of a campaign growing hardened to discomfort and better able to take it and looking toward the day when the war is won and there'll be plenty of everything again. Including that good Olga Coal. But like good soldiers we can't afford to let down now that victory is in sight. That can make Hitler's ghost walk, which brings me to the Hermit who's ready with a ghost story for you right now. *An eerie laugh is heard.* Ghost stories — weird stories and murder, too. The Hermit knows all of them. Turn out your light. Turn them out! Have you heard the story of Hanson's Ghost?" After this opening the Hermit, played by Mel Johnson, would tell the evening's story (Syndicated, 1940–1945).

14607 Hern, Arthur. Actor Hern was in the cast of *Captain Midnight, The Road of Life* and *Silver Eagle, Mountie*.

14608 Hernandez, Joseph. Sportscaster (KYA, San Francisco, CA, 1939).

14609 Hernandez, Juano. Actor Hernandez was in the cast of *Amanda of Honeymoon Hill, Jungle Jim, Mandrake the Magician, Tennessee Jed* and *We Love and Learn*.

14610 Hernandez, Patsy. DJ (*Highway of Melody*, WFOY, St. Augustine, FL, 1948).

14611 *Herndan and Hughes*. Instr. mus. prg. by a dual piano team (CBS, 1935).

14612 Herndon, Maurice. Newscaster (WLPM, Suffolk, VA, 1940–1942, 1945) Sportscaster (WLPM, Suffolk, VA, 1941).

14613 Herne, (Captain) E.D.C. Newscaster (WGN, Chicago, IL, 1939; 15 min., Monday through Friday, 7:15–7:30 P.M., CST, NBC, 1940–1941).

14614 *Heroes of the World*. Dana S. Merriman directed the series of dramatic sketches that focused on heroic days and deeds. Musical backgrounds were also directed by Merriman. Alwyn E.W. Bach was the announcer (30 min., Sunday, 7:00–7:30 P.M., NBC-Red, 1929).

14615 Herr, Chic. Leader (*Chic Herr Orchestra*, instr. mus. prg., WABC, New York, NY, 1942).

14616 *Herr Herman and the German Band*. Instr. mus. prg. (WMBD, Peoria, IL, 1935). Leader Henry Moeller mixed comedy with lively music on the popular local program.

14617 *Herr Louie and the Weasel*. Herr Louie (Henry Moeller) and Hal Gilles (the Weasel) were comedians on the popular little German band program (WGN, Chicago, IL, 1931).

14618 *Herr Louie's Hungry Five*. Instr. mus. prg. with comedy bits (WCFL, Chicago, IL, 1935). Leader Henry Moeller mixed comedy and music on the local program.

14619 Herrera, Lorenzo. Tenor (WOR, Newark, NJ, 1929).

14620 Herrick, John. Baritone (*John Herrick*, vcl. mus. prg., NBC, 1934–1935; KWK, St. Louis, MO, 1936).

14621 Herrick, Lee. COM-HE (WSJV, Pekin, IL, 1951).

14622 Herrick, Sherb. Sportscaster (*Sports*, WXKW, Albany, NY, 1951–1952).

14623 Herrin, W. Weldon. Newscaster (WTOC, Savannah, GA, 1941; WRBL, Columbus, OH, 1945). Sportscaster (WTOC, 1941; WCCP, Savannah, CA, 1946–1947).

14624 Herrin, "Windy." DJ (*Musical Clock*, WCCP, Savannah, GA, 1948–1952). Sportscaster (WCCP, 1949).

14625 Herring, Charles. Newscaster (KUJ, Walla Walla, WA, 1942).

14626 Herring, Maude Alyse. Soprano (WJZ, New York, NY, 1925).

14627 Herron, J.D. Announcer (WMBI, Chicago, IL, 1927).

14628 Hersh, Gladys E. COM-HE (WKAP, Allentown, PA, 1956–1957).

14629 Hersh, Ralph. Violinist (WGBS, New York, NY and WGCP, Newark, NJ, 1925).

14630 Hershey, Burnett. Newscaster (WMCA, New York, NY, 1940–1941).

14631 Hershfield, Lillian. Soprano (KYW, Chicago, IL, 1924).

14632 Hershmann, Arthur. Baritone (WEAF, New York, 1925).

14633 Herske, A. R. Announcer (WTAM, Cleveland, OH, 1925).

14634 Herson, Bill. DJ (WBAL, Baltimore, MD, 1930s-1940s; WRC, Washington, DC, 1940s-1950s). Herson was a popular Baltimore morning man who enjoyed the same popularity in Washington when he moved to that city (WRC, Washington, DC, 1947; *The Timekeeper*, WRC, 1948–1950).

Herson began his radio career as a staff announcer in the 1930s at WFBR (Baltimore, MD), where he played the piano and sang on a program called *Who Us?* He later moved to WBAL and became a popular DJ before going on to Washington's WRC. In 1954, at the peak of his popularity he moved to Florida where he worked for a short time on local TV.

14635 Herth, Milt. Leader (*Milt Herth Trio*, instr. mus. prg., WMAQ, Chicago, IL, 1934; *Milt Herth* [organist], instr. mus. prg., WIND, Gary, IN, 1936; *Milt Herth Trio*, 15 min., Monday through Friday, 4:45–5:00 P.M., CBS, 1945).

14636 Hertle, Cliff. Pianist (KGO , Oakland, CA, 1925).

14637 Hertsgaard, Ralph. Newscaster (KOTA, Rapid City, SD, 1944; *Rolf Hertsgaard, News*, 15 min., 5:15–5:30 P.M., WCCO, Minneapolis, MN, 1954).

14638 Hertz, Alfred. Leader (Alfred Hertz and his San Francisco Symphony Orchestra, KPO, San Francisco, CA, 1927).

14639 Hertzer, Agnes. Soprano (KPO, San Francisco, CA, 1925).

14640 Hertzog, (Professor) Walter Sylvester. Professor Hertzog told stories from American history on a weekly children's program (KHJ, Los Angeles, CA, 1925).

14641 Herwig, Wilbur. Tenor (KFSG, Los Angeles, CA, 1925).

14642 Herzog, Rose. COM-HE (KRES, St. Joseph, MO, 1949.

14643 Heser, Harry. Leader (*Harry Heser Orchestra*, instr. mus. prg., WHP, Harrisburg, PA), 1936).

14644 Heslop, Stanley. Newscaster (WNFB, Binghampton, NY, 1938).

14645 Hess, Bill. DJ (*Bill the Bell Boy*, WKRG, Mobile, AL, 1948). Sportscaster (*Football Predictions*, WPMP, Pascagoula, MS, 1954).

14646 Hess, Bob. DJ (*Rural Roundup* and *Sunnyside Up*, KLRA, Little Rock, AR, 1949; *Time and Tune Parade*, KLRA, 1952).

14647 Hess, Bob. DJ (*Coffee Time*, KPAN, Hereford, TX, 1949; KFYO, Lubbock, TX, 1955).

14648 Hess, Clyde G., Jr. Newscaster (WTAG, Worcester, MA, 1947–1948).

14649 Hess, James P. "Jim." DJ (*Cowboy Jubilee*, WKGN, Knoxville, TN, 1948–1949; WIVX, Knoxville, TN, 1954–1955).

14650 Hess, Sue. Contralto (WRC, Washington, DC, 1924).

14651 Hessberger [Hershberger], George. Leader (*George Hessberger Orchestra*, instr. mus. prg., WMAQ, Chicago, IL, 1935; *George Hessberger's Bavarian Orchestra*, instr. mus. prg., NBC, 1935; WENR, Chicago, IL, 1936; WTMJ, Milwaukee, WI, 1936; WTAM, Cleveland, OH, 1937).

14652 Hession, Jean. COM-HE (WLOX, Biloxi, MS, 1954–1955).

14653 Hessler, Fred. Newscaster (WHBY, Green Bay, WI, 1938). Sportscaster (WIBU, Poynette, WI, 1941; *Fred Hessler Sports*, KGER, Long Beach, CA, 1949).

14654 Hessler, William H. Newscaster (WLW-WSAI, Cincinnati, OH, 1941; WLW, 1942; *World Front*, WLW, 1946–1948).

14655 Hessy, Cleota. Guitarist (KFSG, Los Angeles, CA, 1926).

14656 Hessy, Cleota and L.C. Smith. Guitar duets (KFSG, Los Angeles, CA, 1926).

14657 Hester, Jess. DJ (*WVIM Houseparty*, WVIM, Vicksburg, MS, 1948).

14658 Hetherington, William. Newscaster (*Size-Up of the News*, WJJR, Newark, NJ, 1948).

14659 Hetland, Jimmy. Newscaster (KOVC, Valley City, NC, 1940).

14660 Hetu, Ruth. COM-HE (WLYN, Lynn, MA, 1951).

14661 Heubach, Ruth. Soprano (WSAI, Cincinnati, OH, 1925).

14662 Heuer, Herb. Leader (Herb Heuer's Vagabonds Orchestra, WOC, Davenport, IA, 1928). The Heuer band broadcast five times weekly on WOC's weekday evening program schedule.

14663 Heuer, Mike. DJ (KMA, Shenandoah, IA, 1954–1956).

14664 Heuser, Katherine V. Trumpet soloist (WIP, Philadelphia, PA, 1925).

14665 Hewettson, Frances. COM-HE (WFVA, Fredericksburg, VA, 1960).

14666 Hewing, Anne Marie. Writer (CBS, 1940s). Hewing wrote magazine features for CBS.

14667 Hewitt, Alan. Actor Hewitt appeared on *My Son and I*, *Romance of Helen Trent* and *This Is Nora Drake*.

14668 Hewitt, Mr. Mr. Hewitt broadcast a weekly "radio motorlogue resort service" (KFI, Los Angeles, CA, 1925).

14669 Hewitt, Ray. Announcer (KFWB, Los Angeles, CA, 1928).

14670 Hey, Elton. Leader, Elton Hey's Virginia Ballroom Orchestra, KECA, Los Angeles, CA, 1930.

14671 Heyn, Hugo. Marimbaphonist-vibraphonist (WOW, Omaha, NE, 1928).

14672 Heyn, John G. Pianist (KTHS, Hot Springs National Park, AK, 1926).

14673 Heyne, William B. Choral director Heyne was born September 26, 1897. His radio career began in 1925 on a Lutheran Church owned station (KFUO, Clayton, MO). Heyne in the 1930s worked on the long-running *Lutheran Hour* and *Lutheran Laymen's League* programs.

14674 Heyner, Herbert. British baritone (WOR, Newark, NJ, 1928).

14675 Heywood, Bill. DJ (WSID, Baltimore, MD, 1952).

14676 Heywood, (Mrs.) E.B. Soprano (WBZ, Boston-Springfield, MA, 1924–1925).

14677 *Heywood Broun's Radio Column*. The New York *Telegram's* columnist Broun, who wrote the popular "It Seems to Me" column, presented his views on the interesting radio show (15 min., Monday through Friday, 6:15–6:30 P.M., CBS, 1930).

14678 *Hi and Lo*. Dick Teela and Gwyneth Neal were the popular network singing team (15 min., Weekly, NBC, 1937).

14679 *Hi-Boys and the Radio Rangers*. CW mus. prg. by performers not otherwise identified (WGY, Schenectady, NY, 1938).

14680 *Hi Jinks*. *Hi Jinks* was a two-hour weekly variety program (120 min., Friday, 8:00–10:00 P.M., KLX, Oakland, CA, 1929). The regular performers included pianist Helen Wegmen Parmelee; tenor M.J. Goodman; sopranos Jeanne Rabinowitz, Thelma Hill and Nellie Clark Alsing; tenor Fred Bounds; yodeler Bill Simmons; violinists Maybelle Morrison and Elisa Madsen; Machado's KLX Hawaiians; the Lost and Found piano duo; the KLX Dreamers male quartet; xylophonist Howard Peterson; the Happy Hayseed; Togo and Fugit, two Japanese Gentlemen; and the Fleur de Lis Dance Orchestra.

14681 *Hi Jinks at Noon*. The lively comedy show later became *Kitty and Bingo*. The "Bingo" was Garry Moore and "Kitty," Katherine Dierken. They did comedy bits and conducted an interesting man-in-the-street interview segment, in which they hung a microphone out of the window of their fifth floor studio so that it reached the street (30 min, Monday through Friday, 12:00–12:30 P.M., WBAL, Baltimore, MD, mid–1930s). Moore came to WBAL from WFBR (Baltimore, MD) in the mid–1930s lured by a $25 a week salary. Katherine Dierken was a talented comedienne, singer and actress, who previously had appeared in vaudeville and on the legitimate stage. At WBAL she was also "Mary Landis," the station's generic name for their home economist women's commentator.

14682 *Hi Jinx*. Jinx Falkenburg and her husband, Tex McCrary, were another of the many husband-and-wife talk show teams that broadcast a local program from their breakfast table during the post–World War II period. Occasionally, guests stopped in to have breakfast and talk with them on their sustaining program (30 min., Monday through Saturday, 8:30–9:00 A.M., WEAF, New York, NY, 1946).

14683 *Hi There, Audience*. Ray Perkins hosted the variety show that featured Helene Daniels, Sid Gary and Willard Amison (30 min., Sunday, 9:00–9:30 P.M., NBC, 1937).

14684 Hiatt, Alma. COM-HE (WSYD, Mt. Airy, NIC, 1954).

14685 Hibbs, Maude. *Radio Guide* called Hibbs the most popular blues singer on the Pacific Coast (KEX, Portland, OR, 1928).

14686 Hibbs, R.P. Newscaster (WJPF, Herrin, IL, 1944).

14687 Hickernell, W.F. Lecturer on various subjects (WJZ, New York, NY, 1923).

14688 Hickerson, Frances. Reader (WSM, Nashville, TN, 1926).

14689 Hickey and Johnson. Hawaiian guitar team (WDT, Decatur, IL, 1925).

14690 Hickman, Art. Leader (Art Hickman's Orchestra and Art Hickman's Concert Orchestra, KHJ, Los Angeles, CA, 1923–1924; Art Hickman's Biltmore Hotel Concert Orchestra under the direction of Edward Fitzpatrick, Earl Burnett, or Paul Finstein, KHJ, 1925).

14691 Hickman, Herman. Star football player and coach Hickman broadcast sports news (NBC, 1951; WCBS, New York, NY, 1953–1954).

14692 Hickman, Stanley. Leader (*Stanley Hickman Orchestra*, instr. mus. prg., CBS, 1934). Vocalist (*Stanley Hickman*, vcl. mus. prg., CBS, 1942).

14693 Hickok, Bill. DJ (*Bill Hickok Show*, WCOP, Boston, MA, 1947).

14694 Hickok, Bill. DJ (*Harmony House* and *Ansley Supper Club*, WCON, Atlanta, GA, 1947).

14695 Hickok, Bill. Sportscaster (WHIS, Bluefield, WV, 1956).

14696 Hickox [Hicox], Gladys Blanchard. Reader (WAAW, Omaha, NE, 1924).

14697 Hickox, Lucille. COM-HE (WLRP, Albany, IN, 1949).

14698 Hickox, Mary. COM-HE (KFI, Los Angeles, CA, 1954–1957).

14699 Hicks, Cap. Newscaster (WRGA, Rome, GA, 1945–1947).

14700 Hicks [Hix], Don. DJ (WCAO, Baltimore, MD, 1930s). Hicks was a pioneering early morning man in Baltimore on WCAO, who played records and read the news. He later moved on to WBAL (Baltimore, MD), where he was known as "Uncle Jack" and conducted a show presenting child amateurs from the stage of the Hippodrome Theater. Hicks began his radio career as an announcer and DJ at WCAO in 1929.

14701 Hicks, Elsie. COM-HE (Organist, KFXF, Colorado Springs, CO, 1926).

14702 Hicks, George F. Announcer (WRC, Washington, DC, 1925). Later famous as a news reporter, Hicks became a NBC staff announcer in November, 1929 and conducted the *New Business World* program (WEAF-NBC, New York, NY, 1929). Newscaster (*Names Make the News*, NBC, 1939; ABC, 1944–1946; *News by Hicks*, ABC, 1948).

14703 Hicks, (Dr.) H.H. Sportscaster (KPDN, Pampa, TX, 1939).

14704 Hicks, Helen Lee. Pianist (KLDS, Independence, MO, 1926).

14705 Hicks, Jack. Newscaster (WLBJ, Bowling Green, KY, 1945).

14706 Hicks, John "Johnny." Newscaster (KGKO, Fort Worth, TX, 1941; WRR, Dallas, TX, 1942; WTAM, Cleveland, OH,

1946). DJ (*Hillbilly Hit Parade*, KRLD, Dallas, TX, 1954).

14707 **Hicks, Romola Latchenm (Nancy Lee).** COM-HE and singer, (KFKV, Rockford, IL, 1929.

14708 **Hicksa, Joseph.** Pianist (KSD, St. Louis, MO, 1926).

14709 **Hidee, Andy "Old Fiddler."** Country violinist Hidee placed his violin between his legs and bowed it like a cello when performing (WLW, Cincinnati, OH, 1926).

14710 **Hiebert, D.H.** Announcer (WRAL, St. Croix Falls, WI, 1925).

14711 **Hiett, Helen.** Newscaster (NBC, 1940–1942). Born in Chenoa, Illinois, in 1913, Hiett left for Europe after graduating from the University of Chicago. She accepted a job at the Geneva Research Center in Switzerland. When World War II began, she moved to France, where she published a newspaper in an effort to influence Americans to support France in the war. She was hired by NBC after an interview at CBS proved fruitless. She left NBC in 1942 to become a European newspaper correspondent. After the war she worked for the New York *Herald-Tribune* for a short time before returning to broadcasting.

14712 **Higbee. Hilda.** COM-HE (KTRB, Modesto, CA, 1951).

14713 **Higbee, Lynn.** DJ (*The Magic of Music*, KFBI, Wichita, KS, 1954; KRMG, Tulsa, OK, 1956; *Music on the Sunny Side*, KRMG, 1960).

14714 **Higbee, Mona.** COM-HE (KSUB, Cedar City, UT, 1951).

14715 **Higbie, Les.** News commentator (MBS, 1954).

14716 **Higby, Mary Jane.** Busy actress Higby appeared on the *Joyce Jordan, Girl Interne*; *John's Other Wife*; *This is Nora Drake*; *Linda's First Love*, *Mary Marlin* aka *The Story of Mary Marlin*; *Stella Dallas*; *Romance of Helen Trent*; *When a Girl Marries*; and *Thanks for Tomorrow* daytime serials.

14717 **Higgins, Charles.** Newscaster (WORC, Worcester, MA, 1938). Sportscaster (WORC, 1939).

14718 **Higgins, Charlie and Joe Burke.** Harmony singing team (WCAU, Philadelphia, PA, 1926).

14719 **Higgins, Francis.** Newscaster (WDAN, Danville, IL, 1938–1939). Sportscaster (WDAN, 1939–1942).

14720 **Higgins, Helen.** Pianist (WOAW, Omaha, NE, 1926).

14721 **Higgins, Hugh.** Sportscaster (WAAW, Omaha, NE, 1939; play-by-play broadcaster, WMOA, Marietta, OH, 1949).

14722 **Higgins, Jake.** Sportscaster (WDAN, Danville, IL, 1940–1941).

14723 **Higgins, Laurie.** Leader (*Laurie Higgins Orchestra*, instr. mus. prg., CBS, 1936).

14724 **Higgins, Len.** Newscaster (KVI, Tacoma, WA, 1939–1940; KSRO, Santa Rosa, CA, 1945–1946). Sportscaster (KSRO, 1946).

14725 **Higginson, Rebekah.** COM-HE (WMEX, Boston, MA, 1951).

14726 **High, Stanley.** News commentator (NBC, 1935).

14727 ***High Adventure*.** The fate of ordinary people facing unusually dangerous situations were dramatized on the adventure series sponsored by Shulton's Old Spice Toiletries. Inge Adams, Jim Boles, John Larkin and Mort Lawrence were in the cast. Lew Davies was the program's musical director (30 min., Sunday, 4:30–5:00 P.M., NBC, 1950). In an earlier version of the program that was broadcast on MBS the narrator was George Sanders.

14728 **High Twelve Male Trio.** The vocal group of W. Vance McCune, W.J. Schoenfeld and A.E. Wright (WHB, Kansas City, MO, 1928).

14729 ***Highlights of the Bible*.** Dr. Frederick K. Stamm hosted and narrated the program that dramatized Biblical stories and related Biblical themes to everyday life: "Religion must not be a thing apart, but must have something to do with life and conduct and general attitudes." A male quartet under the direction of Charles A. Baker performed (30 min., Sunday, 11:30–12:00 noon, NBC-Blue, 1935).

14730 ***Highroads to Health*.** Jackson Beck narrated the dramatic series that focused on such health topics as "The Mysterious Accomplice," as high blood pressure was called. Frequent cast members included Peggy Allenby, Charles Draper, Bill Lipton and Charles Webster. Dr. Arthur Master, M.D., delivered authoritative commentary at the end of each program (15 min., Saturday, 6:30–6:45 P.M., ABC, 1959).

14731 **Highsmith, Wyatt.** Newscaster (WGTC, Greenville, NC, 1945).

14732 **Hightower, Bill.** Newscaster (WFAA, Dallas, TX, 1937). DJ (*The Bill Hightower Show*, KFJZ, Fort Worth, TX, 1950). Sportscaster (*Sports Records*, KXOL, Ft. Worth, TX, 1949; *Sports Scope*, KXOL, 1951).

14733 **Hightower, Jill.** COM-HE (KTNM, Tucumcari, NM, 1956).

14734 ***Highways in Melody*.** Paul LaValle conducted the Cities Service String Ensemble on the fine music program that premiered in its original format on February 18, 1925. The sponsor was the Cities Service Company (30 min., Friday, 8:00–8:30 P.M., NBC-Red, 1945).

14735 **Hilary, Ann.** Actress Hilary appeared on the *Brighter Day* daytime serial program.

14736 ***Hilda Hope, M.D.*** The sustaining daytime serial drama related the human personal relationships of a female physician with her professional ones. Selena Royle played the title role. Himan Brown and Julian Funt wrote the program. Charles Paul supplied organ interludes (30 min., Saturday, 11:30–12:00 noon, NBC-Red, 1939).

14737 **Hildebrand, Ken.** Sportscaster (KDKA, Pittsburgh, PA, 1954).

14738 **Hildebrant, Lena.** Piano soloist Hildebrant in later years accompanied John Charles Thomas (KFVX, Bentonsite, AR, 1925–1926).

14739 ***Hildegarde*.** Singer Hildegarde (Loretta Sell), famous for playing the piano in long white gloves, was featured on a series of five-minute transcribed programs sponsored by U.S. Rubber Tire Company. Dan Seymour was the announcer. The music was arranged and conducted by Raymond Paige (5 min., Transcribed, Many Stations, 1930s).

14740 ***Hildegarde's Radio Room* (aka *Raleigh's Radio Room* or *Hildegarde's Raleigh Radio Room*).** Song stylist Hildegarde hosted her variety show with Jackie Kelk, Ned Sparks, Hank Greenberg, Paul McGrath, Claudia Morgan and Les Tremayne (30 min., Weekly, 1945). The sponsor was Raleigh cigarettes. The Milwaukee *chanteuse* specialized in French songs. Her theme song was "Je Vous Aime Beaucoup."

14741 **Hildeman, Mae.** Singer (WBNX, New York, NY, 1936).

14742 **Hildreth, George.** Tenor (KPC, San Francisco, CA, 1925).

14743 **Hileman, Marjorie W.** COM-HE (KVOC, Casper, WY, 1956).

14744 **Hill, Alice.** Busy actress Hill appeared on the daytime serial programs *Bachelor's Children*, *The Romance of Helen Trent*, *Betty and Bob*, *We Are Four* and *Sue and Irene*. *See* **Daytime Serials aka "Soap Operas."**

14745 **Hill, Alma Gray.** Reader (WOS, Jefferson City, MO, 1926).

14746 **Hill, Ann.** COM-HE (KFBK, Sacramento, CA, 1955).

14747 **Hill, Barre.** Baritone (NBC, 1929).

14748 **Hill, Bessie.** DJ (WMRP, Flint, MI, 1957).

14749 **Hill, Billy.** CW DJ (*Bill Hill Program*, WXLW, Indianapolis, IN, late 40s).

14750 **Hill, Carolyn Crew.** Soprano (KGO, Oakland, CA, 1925).

14751 **Hill, Charles Leslie.** Four-year-old reader (KHJ, Los Angeles, CA, 1925).

14752 **Hill, Claire [Clare].** COM-HE (WWSR, St. Albans, VT, 1956–1957).

14753 **Hill, Don.** Hill was billed as "Don and his Ukulele" (KOIL, Council Bluffs, IA, 1927).

14754 **Hill, Don.** Sportscaster (WCBS, Springfield, IL, 1939; WAVE, Louisville, KY, 1940–1948; *Spotlight on Sports*, WPAR, Parkersburg, WV, 1951; WKLO, Louisville, KY, 1955).

14755 **Hill, Don.** Sportscaster and play-by-play broadcaster of the baseball games of the Columbus Red Birds of the American Association (WHKC, Columbus, OH, 1955).

14756 **Hill, Earl.** Leader (*Earl Hill Orchestra*, instr. mus. prg., WGN, Chicago, IL, 1935).

14757 **Hill, Eddie.** DJ (WSM, Nashville, TN, 1954–1955; WRR, Dallas, TX, 1956). Sportscaster (WRR, 1956–1960).

14758 **Hill, Edwin C.** News commentator (*Behind the Headlines*, NBC-Blue, 1936; *Your News Parade*, CBS, 1937; *The Human Side of the News*, CBS, 1939–1944; *The Human Side of the News*, ABC, 1945–1948).

14759 **Hill, Eunice.** Actress Hill was a cast member of *When a Girl Marries* daytime serial program.

14760 **Hill, Gladys.** Black DJ (*Dizzy Lizzy*, KYOK, Houston, TX, mid–1950s). Hill, a talented Blues singer, became a popular DJ using the name "Dizzy Lizzy." She, in turn, was succeeded in the "Dizzy Lizzy" role by Novella Doe Smith. See **Smith, Novella Doe.**

14761 **Hill, Inga.** Singer on the *Eveready Hour* (NBC, 1929).

14762 **Hill, Jack.** Vocalist (*Jack Hill*, vcl. mus. prg., WPG, Atlantic City, NJ, 1936).

14763 **Hill, Jean.** COM-HE (WHTC, Holland, MI, 1949).

14764 **Hill, Joe.** Sportscaster (WAGA , Atlanta, GA, 1939–1941; WCOL, Columbus, OH, 1942; WDEF, Chattanooga, TN, 1946; *Gridiron Flashes*, WAPO, Chattanooga, TN, 1947; WNTM, Vero Beach, FL, 1953).

14765 **Hill, Joy.** COM-HE (WAZE, Clearwater, FL, 1960).

14766 **Hill, Johnson.** Newscaster (KWLK, Longview, WA, 1938).

14767 **Hill, Kate Adele.** Soprano (KWWG, Brownsville, TX, 1927).

14768 **Hill, Lillard.** Newscaster (KADA, Ada, OK, 1942; WBAP, Fort Worth, TX, 1945–1947).

14769 **Hill, Max.** Newscaster (NBC, 1945–1946).

14770 **Hill, Melvin.** Pianist (KFUU, Oakland, CA, 1925; KFWM, Oakland, CA, 1927).

14771 **Hill, Pat.** Newscaster (KOB, Albuquerque, NM, 1947).

14772 **Hill, Raymond.** Announcer (WMT, Waterloo, IA, 1925).

14773 **Hill, Roberta.** COM-HE (WBSM, New Bedford, MA, 1949).

14774 **Hill, Roger.** Leader (Roger Hill Dance Orchestra, WLW, Cincinnati, OH, 1923).

14775 **Hill, Sammie.** Actress Hill appeared on the daytime serial programs *Home of the Brave*, *Bright Horizon* and *Little Women*.

14776 **Hill, Taffy.** COM-HE (KSHO, Las Vegas, NV, 1960).

14777 **Hill, Teddy.** Leader (*Teddy Hill Orchestra*, instr. mus. prg., NBC-Blue, 1935–1936).

14778 **Hill, Tiny.** Leader (*Tiny Hill Orchestra*, instr. mus. prg., WGN, Chicago, IL, 1939; WCLE, Cleveland, OH, 1942; MBS, 1945).

14779 **Hill, Walter.** Baritone (*Walter Hill*, vcl. mus. prg., WMBD, Peoria, IL, 1936–1937).

14780 **Hill, Will R.** Poetry reader Hill was called "The Old Home Poet" (KGO, Oakland, CA, 1925). *Neath the Hanging Lamp* (KGO, 1930).

14781 **Hill, Zack.** Newscaster (WLBJ, Bowling Green, KY, 1940).

14782 **(The) Hill Billy Boys Quartet.** The network CW singing group included Charles Marshall, Ben McLaughlin, Virgil Ward and Johnny O'Brien (NBC-Pacific Network, 1928).

14783 **(The) Hill Villains Hawaiian Quartet.** Johnny Collins, "The Blonde Duke," was the leader of the popular Portland music group (KXL, Portland, OR, 1928).

14784 **Hillard, Ann.** COM-HE (WACB, Kittanning, PA, 1951).

14785 **Hillas, Margaret.** Actress Hillas appeared on the *Manhattan Mother daytime* serial.

14786 ***Hillbilly Boys.*** The music team of Frank Gage, who played piano, guitar and harmonica, and Charles Marshall, who played guitar, violin and sax were the Hillbilly Boys. In addition, both sang on the CW music program broadcast (NBC-Pacific Coast Network, 1929). In another format, Ben McLaughlin replaced Frank Gage. Johnny O'Brien on harmonica and the Haywire Orchestra were also added to the program (NBC, 1929).

14787 ***Hillbilly Jamboree.*** CW mus. prg. by unidentified performers (WNAX, Yankton, SD, 1939).

14788 ***Hillbilly Kid.*** CW vcl. mus. prg. by Boyden Carpenter (WFBM, Indianapolis, IN, 1934). *See* **Carpenter, Boyden.**

14789 ***Hillbilly Music.*** CW mus. prg. by unidentified performers (KMBC, Kansas City, MO, 1939).

14790 ***Hillbilly Roundup.*** CW mus. prg. (30 min., 11:30–12:00 noon, KCJB, Minot, ND, 1955).

14791 **Hilleary, Perry.** Newscaster (KINY, Juneau, AK, 1945).

14792 **Hilleboe, Gertrude.** Reader (WCAL, Northfield, MN, 1926).

14793 **Hillebrand, Fred.** Entertainer who sang parody songs and provided patter on the *Dutch Masters Program* (CBS, 1931).

14794 **Hillegas, Fred.** Newscaster (WSYR, Syracuse, NY, 1947).

14795 **Hiller, Elizabeth.** COM-HE (*Household Hour*, WMAQ, Chicago, IL, 1924). Although a foremost cooking authority, on Fridays she presented fashion talks in association with Jeanne Mowatt on the *Household Hour*. In 1924 under the direction of Hiller, WMAQ set aside a daily time slot for women's programming. On Monday through Thursday, the topics she covered were: Monday, "Mothers in Council;" Tuesday, "Nursing" with Estelle Weltman; Wednesday, "Beauty Secrets;" Thursday, "Mrs. Hiller's Cooking School;" and Friday, "Fashions" with Jeanne Mowatt.

14796 **Hillestad, Helene.** COM-HE (KPSO, Falfurrias, TX, 1957).

14797 **Hilliard, Shirley.** COM-HE (WDSG, Dyersburg, TN, 1951).

14798 **Hilliards, Jimmy.** Leader (*Jimmy Hilliards Orchestra*, instr. mus. prg., KFOR, Lincoln, NE, 1942).

14799 **Hillias, Peggy "Peg."** Actress Hillias appeared on the daytime serial programs *Bachelor's Children* and *Kitthy Keene* aka *Kitty Keene, Incorporated.*

14800 **Hilling, Paul.** Blind pianist (WLW, Cincinnati, OH, 1926).

14801 **Hillman, Jack.** Baritone (KPO, San Francisco, CA, 1925).

14802 **Hillman, William "Bill."** Newscaster (WMAL, Washington, DC, 1941; NBC-Blue, 1942–1945; WOL, Washington, DC, 1946; MBS, 1947–1948).

14803 **Hills, Harry.** Leader (*Harry Hills Orchestra*, instr. mus. prg., WMBD, Peoria, IL, 1937).

14804 **Hills, Ted.** Announcer (KFVI, Houston, TX, 1925–1927).

14805 **Hillsborough Band.** Maestro Antonio Goggino directed the instrumental group (WDAE, Tampa, FL, 1927).

14806 ***Hilltop House.*** The announcer said *Hilltop House* was dedicated "... to the women of America. [It is] The story of a woman who must choose between love and the career of raising other women's children." The heroine (Bess Johnson) had to make that choice, since she worked as a caseworker in an orphanage. The program made its debut in 1937.

After being off the air for several years, *Hilltop House* returned in 1941 to CBS, where it had started in 1937. On the original program, Bess Johnson played herself. Then after *Hilltop House* was canceled, a spin-off occurred in 1941 that saw Johnson star in *The Story of Bess Johnson. Hilltop House* returned once more to CBS in 1948 and told the story of Julie of Hilltop House. Julie was first played by Grace Matthews and, later, by Jan Miner. The program's locale was Glendale, a small town "bustling with pride over its new water wagon." Over the years in its different formats the cast members included: Vera Allen, Spencer Bentley, Donald Briggs, Edwin Bruce, Helen Coule, Joe Curtin, Margaret Curtis, Lilli Darvas, Jimmy Donnelly, Jeanne Elkins, Maurice Ellis, Ethel Everett, Janice Gilbert, Richard Gordon, David Gothard, Irene Hubbard, Gee Gee James, Bess Johnson, Lamont Johnson, Jay Jostyn, Jackie Kelk, Estelle Levy, Ronald Liss, Dorothy Lowell, Iris Mann, Norma Mae Marlowe, Grace Matthews, Jan Miner, John Moore, Nancy Peterson, Jack Roseleigh, Evelyn Streich, Alvin Sullum, Alfred Swenson, Jimmy Tansey, Susan Thorne, Jerry Tucker, James Van Dyk, Ray Walker, Wallace Warner, Dickie Wigginton and Carleton Young. Ed Wolfe was the producer and Carlo DeAngelo and Jack Rubin the directors. The writing team of Addy Richton and Lynn Stone wrote the show and Chester Kingsbury was the musical director (1937–1941, 1941–1957, MBS & CBS). *See* ***The Story of Bess Johnson.***

14807 ***(The) Hilltoppers.*** The male trio of singers and instrumentalists specializing in CW music were Doyne (Don) Wilson on steel guitar, singer Tommy Tanner and tenor-bass violinist Ernie Newton. The sponsor was the ABC Washers and Ironers Company, (15 min., Monday, Wednesday and Friday, 10:30–10:45 A.M. CST, WLS, Chicago, IL, 1935–1936). Accordionist Augie Klein and violinist Carl Hunt joined the group in 1937.

14808 **(The) *Hilltoppers.*** Sam DeVincent (Sam DeVincenzo) and "Nancy Lee from Tennessee" (Agnes Gross) formed a group known as "Nancy Lee and the Hilltoppers." Other members of the group included fiddler Jack Carmen and Roy Hansen on bass. When leaving service after World War II, DeVincent learned that station WOWO needed a staff band for their Saturday night *Hoosier Hop* network program. The group got the job and appeared on the network show. They also appeared on the station's local *Little Red Barn*, an early morning program broadcast Monday through Saturday. This daily show ended in

1955, when live music on the radio virtually disappeared. The show was then broadcast weekly on Saturday morning until 1960 when it moved to Sunday. The Hilltoppers group disbanded in 1992, when Nancy Lee retired. DeVincent continued with a DJ show that is still on the air (55 min., Sunday, 6:05–7:00 A.M., WOWO, Fort Wayne, Indiana). Sam continues to play: "The good music of the past 75 years, that includes popular songs, hymns, country songs and the recorded performances of Nancy Lee and the Hilltoppers."

14809 **Hillyard, Margaret.** COM-HE (KDMO, Carthage, MO, 1949).

14810 **Hilo Five Hawaiian Serenaders Orchestra.** Hawaiian music group (WBAP, Fort Worth, TX, 1923).

14811 **Hilpack, Bennett.** Actor Hilpack was in the cast of *Doc Barclay's Daughter* daytime serial program.

14812 **Hilton, Charles.** Newscaster (KGLO, Mason City, IA, 1945).

14813 **Himber, Richard.** Leader (*Richard Himber Orchestra*, instr. mus. prg., WHAM, Rochester, NY, 1934; WFBR, Baltimore, MD, 1935; NBC-Blue, 1936; WDBJ, Roanoke, VA, 1936; MBS and NBC, 1938; WGY, Schenectady, NY, 1939).

14814 **Himebaugh, Keith.** Announcer (WKAR, Lansing, MI, 1925).

14815 **Hinderlie, Comfort.** Pianist (WCAL, Northfield, MN, 1926).

14816 **Hindermeyer, Harvey.** Tenor (WEAF, New York, NY, 1926).

14817 **Hinds, William T.** Newscaster (KDKA, Pittsburgh, PA, 1941).

14818 **Hine, Marie M.** Organist (KVOO, Tulsa, OK, 1928).

14819 **Hiner, Al.** Pianist (KFH, Wichita, KS, 1928).

14820 **Hines, Beatrice.** Soprano (KFBK, Sacramento, CA, 1926).

14821 **Hines, Earl "Fatha."** Leader (*Earl Hines Orchestra*, instr. mus. prg., NBC, 1935–1937, 1939). The Hines band frequently broadcast remotes over the years.

14822 **Hines, Edith.** Singer (WBAA, West Lafayette, IN, 1937).

14823 **Hines, Kay.** COM-HE (KBMY, Billings, MT, 1949–1957).

14824 **Hines, Ken.** Tenor (WMAK, Buffalo, NY, 1928).

14825 **Hines, Lindley.** Newscaster (*Over the Back Fence*, WREN, Topeka, KS, 1947; KMOX, St. Louis, MO, 1948).

14826 **Hines, Mary Alice.** COM-HE (KIMA, Yakima, WA, 1955).

14827 **Hines, Soupy.** DJ (*Soupy Hines Show*, WJW, Cleveland, OH, 1949).

14828 **Hink (Elmer Hinkle) and Dink (G.W. Ross).** Hink and Dink were end men on the *Crosley Burnt Corkers* minstrel show (WLW, 1925–1926).

14829 **Hinkel, George.** Singer (*George Hinkel*, vcl. mus. prg., WTIC, Hartford, CT, 1936).

14830 **Hinkel, Wilda.** Actress Hinkel was a cast member of the daytime serial program *Backstage Wife* aka *Mary Noble, Backstage Wife*.

14831 **Hinkle, Elmer.** *See* **Hink and Dink.**

14832 **Hinkle, Evelyn.** COM-HE (KNET, Palestine, TX, 1956–1957).

14833 **Hinkle, Roland D.** Tenor (WTAS, Elgin, IL, 1925).

14834 **Hinman, Florence Lamond.** Contralto (KOA, Denver, CO, 1925).

14835 **Hinn, Michael.** Newscaster (WWNC, Asheville, NC, 1938).

14836 **Hinnett [Hinett], Arthur.** Organist (NBC, 1936; KYW, Philadelphia, PA, 1938; KDKA, Pittsburgh, PA, 1942).

14837 **Hinriche [Hinrich], Hilda.** Cellist (WMBB, Chicago, IL, 1926).

14838 **Hinshaw, Fred Moore.** Newscaster (WLBC, Muncie, IN, 1947).

14839 **Hinton, Elizabeth Ransom.** Coloratura soprano (WHB, Kansas City, MO, 1922–1928).

14840 **Hinton, William.** Organist (KTHS, Hot Springs Natural Parks, AR, 1926).

14841 **Hippee, (Mrs.) George.** Soprano (WHO, Des Moines, IA, 1926).

14842 **Hipple, James B.** Newscaster (KGFX, Pierre, SD, 1937–1939). Sportscaster (KGFX, 1939).

14843 **Hipple, Robert.** Newscaster (KGFX, Pierre, SD, 1938).

14844 **Hiram and Henry.** The country music team, not otherwise identified, mixed rural comedy routines with their music (WIBW, Topeka, KS, 1929 and WLS, Chicago, IL, 1929).

14845 **Hire, L.J.** Viola soloist (WCBD, Zion, IL, 1923).

14846 **Hire, (Mrs.) L.J.** Pianist (WCBD, Zion, IL, 1923).

14847 **Hire, Richard F.** Pianist-violinist (WCBD, Zion, IL, 1923–1926). Hire also performed violin duets with Sydney Stewart (WCBD, 1923).

14848 **(The) Hired Hand.** See **Hough, Harold**.

14849 **(The) Hired Hand's Little Symphony.** Music group of the popular Texas announcer Harold Hough, who was called "The Hired Hand" (WBAP, San Antonio, TX, 1926).

14850 ***(The) Hired Help Skylark Program.*** Lambdin Kay, widely known as "The Little Colonel," conducted the popular musical variety program (WSB, Atlanta, GA, 1923).

14851 ***Hires' Harvesters.*** Hires Root Beer company sponsored the music variety show that featured a 12-piece orchestra conducted by Eugene Ormandy (30 min., Monday, 8:00–8:30 P.M., NBC-Red, 1926–1927).

14852 **Hiroaka, [Hiraoka], Yoichi.** Japanese xylophonist (NBC-Blue, 1934, 1937–1938).

14853 **Hirsch, Elroy.** Sportscaster "Crazy Legs" Elroy Hirsch was a star college and professional football player. He returned to the scene of his college football heroics to broadcast sports news (WKOW, Madison, WI, 1947).

14854 **Hirsch, Sylvia Marion.** Contralto Hirsch was a Brunswick recording artist (WHPP, Bronx, New York, 1927; WGBS, New York, NY, 1928).

14855 **Hirsh, Bert.** Leader (*Bert Hirsh Orchestra*, instr. mus. prg., NBC, 1936; WCBM, Baltimore, MD, 1939).

14856 **Hirsh, Don.** Newscaster (KDKA, Pittsburgh, PA, 1938–1940).

14857 **Hirsh, Russell.** Newscaster (WCMI, Ashland, KY, 1939).

14858 **Hirst, Noble.** Baritone (WIP, Philadelphia, PA, 1925).

14859 **Hisey, Rhea.** COM-HE (WFIW, Fairfield, IL, 1954).

14860 ***Historical Drama—A Visit to State Parks*** **(aka *Illinois Historyland Dramas — State Parks*).** Raymond Warren wrote and Wyn Orr produced the informative dramatic series that depicted the historical significance of various state parks and historical shrines. For example, these included visits to Old Kaskaskia State Park, site of Fort Kaskaskia captured from the British by George Rogers Clark; Blackhawk State Park at Rock Island, IL; the Old Salem State Park in Pike County, KY; and Lincoln's Tomb in Springfield, IL. The program's cast included: Graydon Goss, Al Halus, Dan Hosmer, Bill Fitzsimmons, Dorothy McDonald, Gene McGillan, Don Merryfield and Jess Pugh. Howard Chamberlain was the program's announcer (30 min., 6:30–7:00 P.M. CST, WLS, Chicago, IL, 1935).

14861 ***Historical Highlights.*** Jack Marsh wrote the series of programs that dramatized various historical events. Marsh combined his dramatic writing skills with careful historical research to make this an interesting and informative series (WLW, Cincinnati, OH, 1930s). Previously, Marsh had written the *Great Adventures* series (WLW, 1929–1930).

14862 ***Hit Makers Orchestra.*** Instr. mus. prg. (WOR, Newark, NJ, 1936).

14863 **Hitchcock, Elizabeth.** Organist (KLDS, Independence, MO, 1926).

14864 **Hitchcock, J.F.** Announcer (WHEC, Rochester, NY, 1925).

14865 **Hitchcock, Jack.** Newscaster (KFAB, Omaha-Lincoln, NE, 1945). Sportscaster (KCOL, Fort Collins, CO, 1946–1948; *Spotlight on Sports*, KCOL, 1949).

14866 **Hitchcock, Ray.** Leader (Ray Hitchcock Orchestra, KFRC, San Francisco, CA, 1926).

14867 **Hite, Bob.** Newscaster (CBS, 1944–1945).

14868 **Hitt, Mary.** Singer (WDRC, Hartford, CT, 1936).

14869 **Hitz, Elsie.** Miss Hitz, who had appeared on Broadway at age 15, first worked on radio with Lionel Atwell in an adaptation of Edna Ferber's *Show Boat* in 1927. In the following decades Hitz worked on many daytime dramatic serial programs including *Life Can Be Beautiful*, *Barry Cameron*, *Ellen Randolph* aka *The Story of Ellen Randolph* and *Follow the Moon*. .

14870 **Hitzel, Mel.** Pianist (*Mel Hitzel*, instr. mus. prg., KYW, Chicago, IL, 1934).

14871 **Hix, Gil.** Newscaster (WLS, Chicago, IL, 1944–1945).

14872 Hixon, Bob. DJ (*Sounds of the Night*, WNDU, South Bend, IN, 1960).

14873 Hixon, Gil. Newscaster (*Today's Top News*, KSOK, Arkansas, KS, 1947).

14874 Hixon, Glen. DJ (*Swingtime*, WJAG, Norfolk, VA, 1948; *Today's Top Tunes*, WJAG, 1949). Sportscaster (*Sports Roundup*, WJAG, 1952–1954).

14875 Hjelte, Grace. Pianist (KTAB, Oakland, CA, 1926).

14876 Hjerne, Bernard. Tenor (KFOB, Burlingame, CA, 1925).

14877 Hjertaas, Ella. Contralto (WCAL, Northfield, MN, 1925).

14878 "HM." Designation for announcer Howard Millholland (KGO, Oakland, CA, 1924).

14879 H.M.S. *Pinafore*. The Dallas Academy of Music broadcast the Gilbert and Sullivan operetta as a special presentation (WFAA, Dallas, TX, 1922).

14880 Hoagland, Everett. Leader (*Everett Hoagland Orchestra*, instr. mus. prg., KFWB, Los Angeles, CA, 1931; CBS, 1940). Hoagland's 1940 broadcasts were introduced in this way: "Music designed for dancing with Everett Hoagland and his orchestra from the Empire Room of the Waldorf-Astoria Hotel in New York City."

14881 Hobart, Charles. Newscaster (WINR, Binghampton, NY, 1946; *Cavalcade of the News*, WDOS, Oneonta, NY, 1948.) DJ (WENY, Elmira, NY, 1954).

14882 Hobart, Henry. Singer Hobart was called by *Radio Digest* a "Tenor Extra-Ordinary" (WFLA, Clearwater, FL, 1928).

14883 Hobbie, Evelyn. Singer (*Evelyn Hobbie*, vcl. mus. prg., WIND, Gary, IN, 1935).

14884 Hobbs, Jean. Miss Hobbs broadcast talks on how to budget and shop wisely (KTAB, Oakland, CA, 1926).

14885 Hobengarten, Pauline. Contralto (KSD, St. Louis, MO, 1925).

14886 Hober, Beal. Lyric soprano (*Major Bowes Capitol Theater Family*, NBC, 1929).

14887 Hobgood, Bob. Newscaster (WOMI, Owensburg, KY, 1939; KLUF, Galveston, TX, 1940). Sportscaster (KLUF, 1940).

14888 Hoboken High School Orchestra. Scholastic music group (WEAF, New York, NY, 1926).

14889 Hochauser, Edward. Newscaster (WING, Dayton, OH, 1944).

14890 Hochberg, Murray. Leader (*Murray Hochberg Orchestra*, instr. mus. prg., WNAC, Boston, MA, 1934).

14891 Hochberger, Bessie B. Soprano (WOR, Newark, NJ, 1925).

14892 Hochstettler, Leo. Newscaster (CBS, 1947).

14893 Hock and Jerome. The singing team of Hock and Jerome specialized in popular songs of the era (WJZ, New York, NY, 1924).

14894 Hockaday, Anne. COM-HE (WMPM, Smithfield, NC, 1954).

14895 Hocking, (Dr.) Sam. Newscaster (WSFA, Montgomery, AL, 1938).

14896 Hockmuth, Florence. Pianist (WTIC, Hartford, CT, 1927).

14897 Hodapp, William. Actor Hodapp was in the cast of *Jane Arden*.

14898 Hodek, Frank. Leader (Frank Hodek and his Nightingale Orchestra, WOAW, Omaha, NE, 1925–1926; *Frank Hodek Orchestra*, instr. mus. prg., KGHF, Pueblo, CO, 1939).

14899 Hodgdon, (Dr.) D.R. Dr. Hodgdon, a physician, gave talks on food and nutrition (CBS, 1929).

14900 Hodge, (Dr.) Frederick A. Newscaster (WBEN, Buffalo, NY, 1944–1945; *Reading Between the Lines*, WBEN, 1946–1947).

14901 Hodge, Ted. Newscaster (WNLC, New London, CT, 1940–1941.) Sportscaster (WNLC, 1941–1942).

14902 Hodges, Charles. Newscaster (WNEW, New York, NY, 1941; MBS, 1944; WOR, New York, NY, 1945).

14903 Hodges, Dorothy. COM-HE (WGTM, Wilson, NC, 1957).

14904 Hodges, Elmer C. Announcer (KWKC, Kansas City, MO, 1927).

14905 Hodges, Genie. COM-HE (WROD, Daytona Beach, FL, 1957).

14906 Hodges, Gilbert. Newscaster (KVOR, Colorado Springs, CO), 1937–1938; WTAG, Worcester, MA, 1939). Sportscaster (KVOR, 1938).

14907 Hodges, Harold H. Baritone (WNAC, Boston, MA, 1923).

14908 Hodges, Hilton. Newscaster (WIBW, Topeka, KS, 1939–1942).

14909 Hodges, Julia. Singer Hodges specialized in Spanish songs (KFI, Los Angeles, CA, 1929).

14910 Hodges, Russ. Sportscaster (WIND, Chicago, IL, 1935; WBT, Charlotte, NC, 1940; MBS, Washington, DC, 1941; WOL, Washington, DC, 1941–1945; WINS, New York, NY, 1946; Hodges and Mel Allen broadcast the New York Yankees [American League] baseball games , WINS, 1946; NBC, 1947; WMCA, New York, NY, 1948; Columbia University football, WINS, New York, NY; New York Giants professional football and baseball games, WMCA, New York, NY, 1949–1954).

Hodges began his professional broadcasting career in his hometown of Covington, KY, where he was employed as an announcer while yearning to be a radio crooner. His career as sportscaster began in 1935 at station WIND in Gary, Indiana. Hodges probably is best remembered for his 1951 broadcast of the Giants-Dodgers baseball game won by Bobby Thompson with his dramatic home run that is often called "The Shot Heard Round the World. ."

14911 Hodgetts, (Mrs.) Harry. Canadian lyric soprano (WEAF, New York, NY, 1926).

14912 Hodiak, John. Before he began his motion picture career, actor Hodiak appeared on *Arnold Grimm's Daughter*, *Bachelor's Children*, *Girl Alone*, *Li'l Abner* (title role), *Lone Journey*, *Romance of Helen Trent* and *Wings of Destiny*.

14913 Hoeberlie, Arlie. COM-HE (WTCN, Minneapolis, MN, 1949).

14914 Hoeffer, Eunice. Organist (WBBM, Chicago, IL, 1926).

14915 Hoeg, Otto. Pianist (KGB, San Diego, CA, 1929).

14916 Hoehn, Elsa. Mezzo-soprano (WJY, New York, NY, 1925).

14917 Hoel, Helen, Travis. Singer (WCAU, Philadelphia, PA, 1926).

14918 Hoelze, Elmer G. Studio director, program manager and announcer Hoelze proclaimed his station's slogan, "Carry Me Back to Ole Virginny." Hoelze was identified as "The Radio Voice from Virginia" (WRVA, Richmond, VA, 1926–1927).

14919 Hoestetter, Hildred Norman. Soprano (KYW, Chicago, IL, 1924).

14920 Hoestetter, John. Newscaster (WOI, Ames, IA, 1941).

14921 Hoey, Dennis. Actor Hoey was in the cast of *Pretty Kitty Kelly*.

14922 Hoey, Fred. A former football official, Hoey in 1925 began broadcasting the National, League Boston Braves and American League Boston Red Sox baseball games on the New England Colonial Network.

14923 Hofbrau, Hans. Leader (Hans Hofbrau Entertainers Orchestra, WMCA, New York, NY, 1926).

14924 Hoff, Billie Allen. Blues singer (WCFL, Chicago, IL and KYW, Chicago, IL, 1928).

14925 Hoff, Bud. Hoff was billed as "Bud Hoff and his Ukulele" (KFI, Los Angeles, CA, 1925).

14926 Hoff, Carl. Leader (*Carl Hoff Orchestra*, instr. mus. prg., WENR, Chicago, IL, 1934; CBS, 1935).

14927 Hoff, (Mrs.) Olaf. Newscaster (*Turners Falls Newspaper of the Air*, WHAI, Greenfield, MA, 1947–1948).

14928 Hoffer, Betty. COM-HE (KXGO, Fargo, ND, 1960).

14929 Hoffman, Alyne. Pianist (WBAP, Fort Worth, TX, 1927).

14930 Hoffman, Betty. COM-HE (WGFS, Covington, GA, 1960).

14931 Hoffman, Caroline. Pianist (WFI, Philadelphia, PA, 1925).

14932 Hoffman, Charles. Announcer (WRAV, Yellow Springs, OH, 1925–1926).

14933 Hoffman, Daisy. Pianist (WSM, Nashville, TN, 1926–1928).

14934 Hoffman, Dan. Announcer (WKBN, Youngstown, OH, 1925).

14935 Hoffman, Dave. Monologist (KOMO, Seattle, WA, 1927).

14936 Hoffman, Earl. Leader (Chez Pierre Orchestra, WJAZ, Chicago, IL,1926; WCFL, Chicago, IL, 1928; *Earl Hoffman Orchestra*, WGN, Chicago, IL, 1933; WBBM, Chicago, IL, 1937).

14937 Hoffman, Emil R. Pianist (WOAW, Omaha, NE, 1926).

14938 Hoffman, Emily G. COM-HE (WPFD, Darlington, SC, 1957).

14939 Hoffman, Fred. Newscaster (WWDC, Washington, DC, 1948).

14940 Hoffman, Gracie. DJ (KWIZ, Santa Ana, CA, 1955).

14941 Hoffman, Helen. Soprano (KFI, Los Angeles, CA, 1925).

14942 Hoffman, Helen Ruth. COM-HE (KYAK, Yakima, WA, 1954).

14943 Hoffman, Howard. Newscaster (WHJB, Greensburg, PA, 1941).

14944 Hoffman, Josef. Distinguished pianist Hoffman performed with the New York Philharmonic Orchestra directed by Dr. Walter Damrosch in a concert series that began October 15, 1925 (WJZ, New York, NY).

14945 Hoffman, Marion. Pianist (WGHB, Clearwater, FL, 1926).

14946 Hoffman, Miriam. Singer (WJZ, New York, NY, 1924).

14947 Hoffman, William. Leader (William Hoffman Orchestra, KJR, Seattle, WA, 1926).

14948 *(The) Hoffman Hour*. Critically praised by *Radio Digest*, this music program featured baritone Nelson Eddy, soprano Lois Bennett, contralto Veronica Wiggins with Joseph Pasternack conducting the orchestra (30 min., Friday, 9:00–9:30 P.M., WOR, Newark, NJ, 1932).

14949 Hoffman's Orchestra. Popular local orchestra (KFOA, Seattle, WA, 1925).

14950 Hoffmayer, Carl. Leader (*Carl Hoffmayer Orchestra*, instr. mus. prg., CBS, 1934).

14951 Hoffpauir, Jay. Newscaster (KSIG, Crowley, LA, 1947).

14952 Hofheinz, Roy. News commentator (*Political and Current Events*, KTHT, Houston, TX, 1948).

14953 Hogan, Bill. Leader (*Bill Hogan Orchestra*, instr. mus. prg., NBC, 1932; CBS, 1935).

14954 Hogan, Catherine. Violinist (WBZ, Boston-Springfield, MA, 1924).

14955 Hogan, Claudine. Newscaster (KRLH, Midland, TX, 1940).

14956 Hogan, Ethel. Organist on the *Tone Pictures* program (Monday, Wednesday and Friday, 11:30–12:00 midnight, KDYL, Salt Lake City, UT, 1930s).

14957 Hogan, Fannie [Fanny]. COM-HE (WHJB, Greenburg, PA, 1949).

14958 Hogan, John. Newscaster (WMAZ, Macon, GA, 1941).

14959 Hogan, Joseph. Newscaster (WTMV, East St. Louis, MO, 1939).

14960 Hogan, Lee. COM-HE (KNBH, Hollywood, CA, 1951).

14961 Hogan, Lucky. DJ (WDUZ, Green Bay, WI, 1957).

14962 Hogan, Marty. DJ (*Merry Go Round, Music Mart* and *Where's Hogan?*, WCFL, Chicago, IL, 1948; *The Celebrity Train*, 120 min., Monday through Saturday, 11:30–1:30 P.M., WCFL, 1948; *Stars on Parade*, WJJD, Chicago, IL, 1948–1949; *Musical Merry Go Round*, WCFL, 1949; *Marty Hogan Show*, WJJD, 1950).

14963 Hogan, Tweet. Leader (*Tweet Hogan Orchestra*, instr. mus. prg., NBC, 1934).

14964 *Hogan's Daughter*. Shirley Booth, in the title role, played a zany New York girl in the situation comedy sponsored by Philip Morris cigarettes. The talented cast included Betty Garde, Everett Sloane and Howard Smith. The program was written by John Whedon and Sam Moore (30 min., Tuesday, 8:00–8:30 P.M., NBC, 1949).

14965 Hogarth, Leona. "Songster" (WQJ, Chicago, IL, 1926 and WMCA, New York, NY, 1926).

14966 Hogg, Herbert. Announcer (WRAX, Philadelphia, PA, 1925).

14967 Hoggard, Frank D. Announcer (WJBY, Gadsden, AL, 1925).

14968 Hoggatt, Jack. DJ (*Wake Up Yakima*, KIT, Yakima, WA, 1948; *Destination Midnight*, KIT, 1950).

14969 Hohengarten, Paulyne. Contralto (KSD, St. Louis, MO, 1925).

14970 Hohenstein, (Reverend) Herman H. Announcer, program director and producer (KFUO, St. Louis, MO, 1926–1927).

14971 Hohl, Claudette. COM-HE (WAME, Miami, FL, 1960).

14972 Hohman, Charles C. Bass-baritone (WEAF, New York, NY, 1923).

14973 Hoier, Tom. Actor Hoier was in the cast of *Young Widder Brown*.

14974 Hoieterhoff, Ralph. Newscaster Hoieterhoff delivered talks on current events (WLW, Cincinnati, OH, 1925–1926).

14975 Hoisington, Paula. COM-HE (KCRB, Chanute, KS, 1954).

14976 Hoke, Doris. COM-HE (WLEU, Reading, PA, 1957).

14977 Holbrook, Jack. Newscaster (WMIN, St. Paul, MN and KYSM, Mankato, WI, 1939; WGTC, Greenville, NC, 1940).

14978 Holbrook, John. Newscaster (WGN, Chicago, IL, 1941–1942).

14979 Holbrook, Lillie. Reader (KOA, Denver, CO, 1926).

14980 Holbrook, Pat. Actress Holbrook appeared on the *John's Other Wife* daytime serial program.

14981 Holbrook, Priscilla. Pianist (WIND, Gary, IN, 1938–1939).

14982 Holcomb, Grant, Jr. Newscaster (KPRO, Riverside, CA, 1941–1942; KQV, San Jose, CA, 1944–1945).

14983 Holcomb, Harry. Director-narrator worked on the *Dr. IQ* (director), *Judy and Jane* (director), *Moon River* (narrator) and *Tena and Tim* (director) programs.

14984 Holcomb, Lawrence. Sound effects man Holcomb worked on the *Jane Arden* program.

14985 Holcomb, Margaret. COM-HE (WRON, Ronceverte, WV, 1954).

14986 Holden, Ann. COM-HE (KFRC, San Francisco, CA, 1949; KGO, San Francisco, CA, 1956).

14987 Holden, Helen. COM-HE (*Household Hints*, 30 min., Monday through Friday, 9:15–9:45 A.M., WHBX, Utica, NY, 1948). Miss Holden broadcast home economics information for women on her popular Utica program.

14988 Holder, Hugh. Newscaster (WGRB, Goldsboro, NC, 1940).

14989 Holder, John. CW musician known as "The Old Fiddler" (KFEQ, St. Joseph, MO, 1930).

14990 Holderman, K.L. Announcer (WPSC, State College, PA, 1925).

14991 Hole, Jonathan. Actor Hole was in the cast of *Ma Perkins*.

14992 Holgate, Helen. COM-HE (KSDN, Aberdeen, SD, 1951–1960).

14993 Holiday, Byron. Baritone (*Byron Holiday*, vcl. mus. prg., WOR, Newark, NJ, 1934).

14994 Holiday, Mary. COM-HE (WACO, Waco, TX, 1949–1956).

14995 Holiday, Molly. COM-HE (WHPB, Benton, SC, 1960).

14996 *Holiday for Music*. Nash-Kelvinator Refrigerators sponsored the music show that replaced the *Andrews Sisters* program. Singers Kitty Kallen and Curt Massey were accompanied by the David Rose Orchestra. Harlow Wilcox was the announcer (30 min., Wednesday, 10:30–11:00 P.M., CBS, 1946).

14997 *Holiday for Strings*. Earle Keller's Orchestra supplied the music on the popular Louisville local program (WAVE, Louisville, KY, 1947).

14998 Holiday and Anniversary Programs. Holiday and anniversary programs were staples of radio. Whether it was the Pope celebrating Midnight Mass from Vatican City or Jack Benny's parsimonious behavior, listeners could count on memorable Christmas radio programming. Although Christmas was the basis for most holiday programming, Easter and Thanksgiving were other holidays that received special attention. Such lesser holidays as Valentine's Day and the Fourth of July also sometimes provided themes for some shows. New Year Eve's musical programs such as the *New Year's Eve Dance Party*, probably initiated by Mutual, used the unusual concept of using big band remote broadcasts from east to west across the country on New Year's Eve to "meet" the New Year in different American time zones.

NEW YEAR'S EVE AND NEW YEAR's DAY

Although it was comedy programs that most often used a New Year's theme, such diverse programs as *Mysterious Traveler*, *Gunsmoke*, *Quiet Please*, *Space Patrol*, *The Whistler*, *Sherlock Holmes* and *Philip Marlowe* also provided some variations on the theme.

Hard boiled detective Philip Marlowe, created by Raymond Chandler, was portrayed on radio by Gerald Mohr. Marlowe's "Old Acquaintance," broadcast on December 16, 1948 is an interesting example of how an ordinary mystery program could broadcast a philosophical message with its New Year's Eve theme.

The diversity of programs celebrating the holiday can be seen by these examples:

Alan Young Show (12-27-1946) "Rose Bowl Parade"

Amos 'n' Andy (12-31-43) "New Year's Show"; (12-29-44) "New Year's Party"

Great Gildersleeve (12-17-1942) "Leroy Makes Nitro"; (12-31-1944) "New Year's Eve"; (1-1-1947) "New Year's Costume"; (12-31-1947) "New Year's Parties"; (12-28-1949)

"Hayride"; (12-27-1950) "Double Date with Bullard"; (12-30-1953) "Happy New Year"

Gunsmoke (1-1-1956) "Puckett's New Year"

Honest Harold (The Harold Peary Show) 12-27-1950 "New Year's Dance"

Jack Benny Show (1-3-1937) "More Buck Benny"; (1-1-1939) "Goodbye, 1938"; (12-31-1939) "Gladys Zybisco Disappoints Jack on New Year's Eve"; (12-29-1940) "Father Time Rides Again"; (1-04-42) ""New Year's Eve Party"; (1-02-1944) "Annual New Year's Eve Show"; (12-31-50) "A New Year's Fantasy"; (12-30-1951) "New Year's Date with a French Girl"; (1-2-1955) "Rose Bowl Parade"

Jimmy Durante Show (12-17-1947)

Life of Riley (12-28-1946) "New Year's Show"; (12-30-1949) "Riley Drives a Cab for Bab's Boy Friend"

Life with Luigi (12-27-1949) "New Year's Phone Call"

Mel Blanc Show (12-31-1946) "Zebra of the Year"

Milton Berle (12-30-1947) "Salute to the New Year"

Mysterious Traveler (12-31-1950) "The New Year's Nightmare"

Our Miss Brooks (1-1-1950) "Baby Sitting on New Year's Eve"; (12-31-1950) "Exchanging Christmas Gifts"

Phil Harris-Alice Faye Show (1-1-1950) "Phil Takes Singing Lessons"

Philip Marlowe (12-26-1948) "Old Acquaintance"

Quiet Please (12-29-1947) "Rain on New Year's Eve"

Red Skelton (1-1-1946) "Bells and Resolutions"; (12-31-1946) "Old Man Winter"; (12-31-1950) "New Year's Puzzle"

Scarlet Queen (12-31-1947) "Hattie McCormick"

Sherlock Holmes (12-18-1947) "New Year's Eve Off the Scilly Islands"

Space Patrol (1-1-1955) "Ambush in Space"

The Whistler (12-31-1947) "The First Year"

Wild Bill Hickok (12-31-1954) "Happy New Year."

VALENTINE'S DAY

Amour was the major ingredient in most Valentine Day broadcasts. Romance, or the search for it, most often occurred on the comedy shows, but there were a few interesting variations on the *Quiet Please* and *Cavalcade of America* programs. An indication of the variety and diversity of the programs can be seen below:

Aldrich Family (2-11-43) "Valentine Day's Party"

Amos 'n' Andy (2-16-1945) "Insulting Valentine" or "Valentine Blues"; (2-16-45) "Sapphire Kicks Kingfish Out"

Cavalcade of America (2-14-1944) "GI Valentine"

Duffy's Tavern (2-16-50) "Mystery Valentine"; (2-9-51)"The Unsigned Valentine"

Honest Harold (The Hal Peary Show) 2-14-51 "Mistaken Valentines"

Life of Riley (4-14-48) "Comic Valentine for Peg"; (2-18-49) "Valentine Locket from Monahan"

Mail Call (2-14-1945)

My Favorite Husband (2-11-1949) "Valentine's Day"

Our Miss Brooks (2-19-1950) "Valentine's Day Date"

Ozzie and Harriet (2-13-1949) "Buying a Valentine"

Phil Harris-Alice Faye Show (2-13-1949) Someone Sends Alice Flowers for Valentines Day"; (2-13-1951) "Tomorrow is Valentine's Day"

Quiet Please (2-13-49) "Valentine"

EASTER

Many of the Easter programs were religious services, mostly originated locally, although some were network broadcasts. Most regular programs with Easter themes were comedies, but mystery programs such as *Quiet Please* and *The Shadow* were also represented. A representative sample of the Easter programming follows:

Amos 'n' Andy (3-30-45) "The Easter Hat"

The Bickersons (Date Unknown) "Easter Parade"

Burns and Allen (3-25-48) "Easter Program"

Fibber McGee and Molly (3-23-48) "Molly's Easter Dress Creation"; (4-16-54) "Twelve Dozen Easter Eggs"

Great Gildersleeve (4-25-43) "Easter Rabbits"; (4-9-52) "Easter Show"; (4-1-53) "Sunrise Easter Service"

Jack Benny Show (4-17-38) "At the Circus Easter Show"; (4-17-49) "Easter Parade"; (4-30-1950) "Easter Show"; (4-13-1952) "Jack and Mary Walk in the Easter Parade"; (4-18-1954) "Easter Parade"

Life of Riley (3-27-48) "The Giant Easter Bunny"

Mel Blanc Show (4-8-47) "The Easter Egg Hunt"

Minnesota School of the Air Old Tales and New (3-16-1951) "The Smallest Easter Angel"; (Date Unknown) "How the Easter Lilies Were Chosen"; (Date Unknown) "The Blue Easter Bunny"

Our Miss Brooks (4-9-1950) "Dyeing Easter Eggs"

Phil Harris-Alice Faye Show (4-9-1950) "The Easter Bunny"

Quiet Please (4-17-49) "The Shadow of the Wings"

Shadow (3-28-1940) "Death and the Easter Bonnet"

HALLOWEEN

A few situation comedy programs featured Halloween shows with comic touches, but it was mostly programs like *Suspense* and *Inner Sanctum* that provided sufficient mystery, fear and horror to mark the holiday. Other programs that provided Halloween chills were: *Murder at Midnight, Quiet Please, Dark Fantasy, Weird Circle, Witch's Tale* and the *Black Museum*. By far, however, the most memorable Halloween broadcast was the Orson Welles' *Mercury Theater* production of H.G. Wells' *War of the Worlds* broadcast October 30, 1938.

The "War of the Worlds" as broadcast by CBS began as a program of dance music that was interrupted by a series of "news bulletins" reporting a Martian invasion of earth, supposedly taking place at Grovers Mill, New Jersey. The result was that a million or more Americans were convinced that there really was a Martian invasion underway. Orson Welles later said the program was his "Halloween present" to the country. Despite this memorable hoax, however, there were some comedy programs with a Halloween theme. *See* **Drama**.

A few examples of Halloween special situation comedy programs were:

Aldrich Family (10-31-1940) "Halloween"

Edgar Bergen & Charlie McCarthy (10-30-1938) "Charlie's Halloween Party"; (10-29-1944) "Halloween with Orson Welles"

Father Knows Best (10-29-1953) "Halloween Blues"

Fibber McGee and Molly (10-24-1938) "Gildersleeve's Halloween Party"; (10-31-1943 "Halloween Party"; (10-29-1947) "Halloween Party"

Halls of Ivy (11-7-1951) "Halloween"

Jack Benny (10-30-1938) "Jack Throws a Halloween Party"; (11-02-1941) "Halloween Celebration"

Mercury Theater (Orson Wells) (10-30-1938) "The War of the Worlds"

Our Miss Brooks (10-30-1949) "Halloween Party"

THANKSGIVING SHOWS

Abbott & Costello (11-25-1943) "Formal Thanksgiving Dinner Party"

Aldrich Family (11-25-1948) "Thanksgiving Dance and Turkey Run"; (11-23-1952) "Thanksgiving Turkey"

Amos 'n' Andy (11-19-1943) "Turkey Trouble"; (11-20-1949) "Turkey Falls Off the Truck; (11-19-1950) "Thanksgiving Dinner"

Answer Man (11-23-1944) "Thanksgiving Questions"

Burns and Allen (11-18-1940) "Thanksgiving Show"; (11-17-1942) "Gracie Buys a Live Turkey"; (11-25-1948) "Thanksgiving Program"

Casey, Crime Photographer (11-27-1947) "After Turkey, the Bill"; (11-15-1948) "Holiday"

Command Performance (1944) "Thanksgiving Special"

Dr. Christian (11-22-1939) "Prelude to Thanksgiving"

Father Knows Best (11-23-1950) "Happy Thanksgiving"; (11-26-1953) "Thanksgiving"

Fibber McGee and Molly (11-19-1940) "Visiting Uncle Dennis"; (11-22-1949) "Tax Bill Thanksgiving"; (12-21-1957) "Thanksgiving"

The Goldbergs (11-23-1941) "Thanksgiving Dinner"

Great Gildersleeve (11-16-1941) "Servicemen for Thanksgiving"; (11-22-1942) "Thanksgiving Ration Book"; (11-21-1951) "Thanksgiving with Mikey"

Honest Harold (The Harold Peary Show) (11-22-1950) "Thanksgiving Play"

Jack Benny (11-19-1939) "Purchases Ostrich for Thanksgiving"; (11-23-1941) "Thanksgiving Day Dinner"; (11-21-1943) "Jack Dreams He is a Turkey"; (11-26-1944) How Jack and the Gang Spent Thanksgiving Day"; (11-23-1947) "Movie of Jack's Life"; (11-28-1948) "How Jack and the Gang Spent Thanksgiving Day"

Jimmy Durante (11-22-1946) "Thanksgiving Pilgrim Opera"

Let George Do It (11-20-1950) " Cause for Thanksgiving"

Life of Riley (11-19-1944) "Turkey Hunt"; (11-

29-1947) "Thanksgiving with Gillis"; (11-19-1948) "Thanksgiving Flashback"

Life with Luigi (11-22-1949) "Thanksgiving Celebration"

Lum and Abner (11-23-1944) "Thanksgiving Dinner"

Mel Blanc Show (Date Unavailable) "Thanksgiving Party"; (11-26-1946) "Mel's Thanksgiving Dinner"

Milton Berle (11-25-1947) "Thanksgiving"

Our Miss Brooks (11-27-1949) "Thanksgiving Weekend"; (11-19-1950) "Thanksgiving Program"

Red Skelton (11-21-1951) "Things to be Thankful For"

Sam Spade (11-24-1950) "The Terrified Turkey Caper"

Tarzan (11-22-1951) "African Thanksgiving"

Vic and Sade (11-20-1941) "Rush Humiliated on Thanksgiving"

CHRISTMAS

Christmas, by far, was the holiday most celebrated on radio year after year. There always, of course, were many religious celebrations, both network and local. From Rome, the Pope's celebration of Midnight Mass was an annual Christmas event, usually transcribed for broadcast to the United States. Local celebrations of the Christmas midnight mass was also frequently broadcast by local stations.

Christmas programming varied from comedy fare to mystery and horror. Even with its wide diversity, the emphasis was usually warm and upbeat. Several programs were so popular they became annual Christmas presentations. The first was Dickens' *A Christmas Carol*, followed by the *Amos 'n' Andy Christmas Show*. A children's series that was broadcast by transcription for many years at Christmas time was *The Cinnamon Bear*. Each of these programs contained elements of universal listener appeal for many different audiences.

First broadcast in 1937 and repeated at Christmas on many stations for several years, the *Cinnamon Bear* series became a children's holiday classic. The opening program of the 26 episode serial was first broadcast November 29, 1937. The program's 26th and final episode's happy ending was broadcast December 24, 1937. Written by Glanville "Glen" Heisch, it was narrated by Bud Heistand.

Heisch's inspiration came from a favorite stuffed bear he recalled from his childhood. When he began writing light verse stories for his daughter, Catherine, one of them featured his childhood favorite — the stuffed bear. When he was asked to write a Christmas program for children, he created *The Cinnamon Bear*, and an annual children's holiday favorite was produced.

The story told of the adventures of Judy and Jimmy Barton, who search for the silver star that always was placed on the top of their Christmas tree. While searching in their attic for the star, they find a teddy bear — Paddy O'Cinnamon, who sets out with them to help search. Their silver star, it seems, was stolen by the Crazy Quit Dragon and taken to Maybeland. The Cinnamon Bear guides them on their successful search that ended on Christmas Eve.

Charles Dickens' *A Christmas Carol*, was another annual classic radio Christmas favorite with Lionel Barrymore playing the role of Ebenezer Scrooge. Barrymore's first portrayal of Scrooge was broadcast by CBS on December 25, 1934. With only a few exceptions, Barrymore played the role until 1953. Only the death of his wife and his own illness allowed John Barrymore and Orson Wells to play the role in 1936 and 1938. Many consider *A Christmas Carol* with Barrymore's portrayal the greatest Christmas program ever broadcast (Dunning, 1976, p. 131).

Another radio classic was *Amos 'n' Andy's* annual Christmas program. First broadcast December, 1940, the 15-minute program included Amos reciting and explaining the Lord's Prayer to his little daughter, Arabella. Andy working as Santa in order to get money to buy a present for Arabella was added in 1943, when the program was expanded to a 30-minute format. The annual Christmas program began in 1940 and continued until 1954. The Christmas show became probably the favorite episode of radio's most popular series. (During the peak of its popularity in the early 1940s, the program was said to have been heard by 40 million listeners. A later version of the Amos 'n' Andy Christmas program (12-23-1951) in addition to Freedman Gosden and Charles Correll, included in the cast Barbara Jean Wong as Arabella and Griff Bennett as Mr. Simmons. Harlow Wilcox was the announcer. Music was provided by Jeff Alexander. The program consisted of two parts: first, Andy underwent the rigors of working as Santa Claus, in order to get enough money to buy a beautiful, talking doll as a present for Arabella. Despite his misadventures he successfully obtained the present for the little girl. In the second part of the program Amos recited and explained the Lord's prayer to Arabella. The humorous antics of Andy augmented by the reverential Lord's Prayer recitation by Amos, produced one of radio's most memorable programs. Christmas was always an important time on the *Amos 'n' Andy* program. For example, Amos proposed to Ruby Taylor on Christmas, 1928. He married her Christmas, 1931.

Any discussion of Christmas programs would be incomplete without mention of the *Jack Benny Program*. Drawing on his radio persona as a skinflint with an overly inflated ego, Benny's radio program each Christmas contained these familiar themes. During his many years on radio, cheapskate Jack's Christmas usually featured his cheapness while shopping for presents for the gang. One example of Jack's shoestring Christmas budget was his purchase of shoestrings as Don Wilson's present. There were hilarious variations on the same them year after year.

Some idea of radio's rich diversity of Christmas programming can be seen by a representative list of its programs:

Abbott & Costello (12-14-1944) "Christmas Shopping"; (12-24-1947) "Christmas Program"

Aldrich Family (12-23-1948) "Christmas Program"

Amos 'n' Andy (12-1940) "Christmas Program — Lord's Prayer"; "Christmas Program"; (12-24-1950) "Annual Christmas Show — Andy Plays Santa, the Lord's Prayer"; (12-23-1951) "Andy Plays Santa Claus"

Archie Andrews (12-13-1947) "Christmas Shopping"

Bing Crosby (12-24-1947) "Christmas Show"; (12-20-1950) "Christmas Show";

Command Performance Christmas Show (1948)

Burns and Allen (12-26-1946) "Christmas Presents with Eddie Cantor"

Cavalcade of America (12-21-1942) "A Child is Born"

Cinnamon Bear Series (1937)

Challenge of the Yukon (12-18-1945) "Christmas Presents"; (12-22-1948) "The Man with the Red Coat"

Dragnet (12-21-1950) A 22 Rifle for Christmas

Duffy's Tavern (12-22-1944) "Christmas Program "; (12-21-1945) "A Christmas Carol"; (12-22-1948) "Miracle on Third Avenue"; (12-23-1948) Archie in Bad Spirits"; (12-29-1948) "Christmas Cards"; (12-22-1950) "Charles Coburn plays Santa Claus"

Eddie Cantor Show (12-20-44) "Christmas Show"

Edgar Bergen-Charlie McCarthy Show (12-24-1944) "The Oversight Before Christmas"

Escape (12-22-1953) "Back for Christmas"

Fat Man (ND) "Murder Sends a Christmas Card"

Father Knows Best (12-21-1950) "Hans Christian Anderson Family Christmas"

Fibber McGee and Molly (12-20-1938) "Christmas Shopping for a Nephew"; (12-19-1939) "Uncle Sycamore's Package Arrives"; (12-10-1940) "Mailing Christmas Packages"; (12-16-1941) "Cutting a Christmas Tree"; (12-21-1943) "Looking for a Christmas Tree"; (12-24-1946) "The Night Before Christmas" (12-25-1951) "The Spirit of Giving" (12-22-1953) "Haggling Over a Christmas Tree";

Great Gildersleeve (12-20-1942) "Christmas"; (12-24-1944) "Christmas Eve Program"; (12-23-1945) "Christmas at Home"; (12-25-1946) "Christmas Caroling at Home"; (12-10-1947) "Christmas Shopping"; (12-24-1947) "Stray Puppy at Christmas"; (12-22-1948) "Family Christmas"; (12-20-1950) "Children's Christmas Party"; (12-12-1951) "Leroy Sells Christmas Trees"; (12-2-1953) "Gildersleeve Raises Christmas Money"

Gunsmoke (12-25-1955) "Twelfth Night"

Jack Benny Program (12-20-1936) "An Old Fashioned Christmas Party"; (12-12-1937) "Christmas Shopping"; (12-11-1938) "Christmas Shopping in New York"; (12-25-1938) "Jack's Christmas Open House"; (12-24-1939) "Christmas Shopping for Perfume and a Necktie"; (12-22-1940) "Christmas Shopping"; (12-28-1941) Jack Tells About His Christmas Party"; (12-26-1943) "Christmas at Jack's House"; (12-8-1946) "Christmas Shopping on a Shoestring Budget — Jack Buys Don Shoe Strings for Christmas"; (12-22-1946) "Party at Birmingham Hospital"; (12-21-1947) "Last Minute Christmas Shopping"; (12-19-1948) "Jack Buys a Wallet for Don as Christmas Gift"; (12-18-1949) "Mary Buys Jack a Pencil Sharpener for Christmas"; (12-17-1950) "Jack Buys Don Golf

Tees for His Present"; (12-2-1951) "Jack Buys Don Cuff Links for his Christmas present"; (11-23-1951) "Decorating the Christmas Tree"; (12-7-1952) "Sending Christmas Cards"; (12-13-1953) "Christmas Show from Palm Springs" (12-20-1953) Cactus Christmas Tree"; (12-5-1954) "Christmas Shopping"; (12-26-1954) The Day After Christmas"

Life with Luigi (12-20-1949) "Pasquale Takes Christmas Money"

Lights Out (12-22-1937) "Christmas Story"

Lux Radio Theater (12-20-1948) "Miracle on 34th Street"

Nero Wolfe (12-22-1950) "The Case of the Slaughtered Santas"

One Man's Family (12-25-1949) "A Touch of Christmas Spirit"; (12-25-1950) "Christmas at the Barbours"

Phil Harris-Alice Faye Show (12-11-1949) "A Dishwasher or a Mink"; (12-18-1949) "Cutting a Christmas Tree"; (12-25-1953) "French Refugee Children Children's Christmas"

Red Skelton Show (12-25-1946) "Christmas Trees"; (12-26-1946) "Christmas Stories"; (12-19-1951) "A Christmas Story"

Shadow (12-22-1940) "Joey's Christmas Story"; (12-21-1947) "Gift of Murder"

Sherlock Holmes (12-24-1945) "The Night Before Christmas"; (12-21-1947) "Christmas Bride"; (3-13-1955) "The Blue Carbuncle"

Suspense (12-23-1943) "Back for Christmas"; (12-21-1953) "The Night Before Christmas"; (12-20-1959) "Korean Christmas Carol"

This Is Your F.B.I. (12-24-1949) "Return of St. Nick"

Vic and Sade (11-21-1939) "Smelly Clark Solicits Christmas Gifts"; (11-26-1943) "Christmas Presents"

Yours Truly, Johnny Dollar (12-23-1956) "The Missing Mouse"; (12-22-1957) "Carmen Kringle"; (12-13-1959) "Sudden Wealth"

ANNIVERSARY PROGRAMS

Another special broadcasting format was the anniversary program, mostly of the national networks or large network stations. By far the most interesting and informative were those produced by the National Broadcasting Company, whose operations spanned most of the historic events of radio history. An early anniversary program, *Seven Years of NBC*, was broadcast on the network 10:00–11:00 P.M., November 11, 1933. Written by George Ludlum, the program featured segments from network broadcasts, including many segments of the poetry of Edgar A. Guest, a popular poet of the era. The program began with a portion of Guest's "Radio" poem:

> A thing of tubes and wires, and lo,
> The miracle of radio.
> The simple dial turning around
> Searches the atmosphere for sound
> And captures from the silent air
> Song, music, eloquence and prayer.

Guest's poetry was followed by a narrator, who described NBC's inaugural broadcast in 1926, from a small studio high in the Waldorf-Astoria, located at Fifth Avenue and 34th Street in New York City. That first program featured Mary Garden singing from Chicago, Will Rogers joking from Kansas City and Dr. Walter Damrosch conducting the New York Symphony Orchestra. Although no recordings from the original broadcast were available, the program did contain parts of broadcasts from the years 1927, 1928 and 1929, reporting such political, sports and world events as: Lindbergh's return from Paris following his historic solo flight across the Atlantic in 1927, the Stanford-Alabama Rose Bowl football game, the finale of *Faust* from the stage of the Chicago Civic Auditorium and the Dempsey-Tunney heavyweight championship bout famous for the "long count." Following broadcasts of these events spanning 1927 and 1929, the program described the beginning of the Great Depression. After another segment of Edgar Guest's poetry, the program ended with FDR's reassuring optimist and promise to re-open the banks (following his imposed bank holiday). His optimistic words ended the program:

> After all, there is an element in the readjustment of our financial system more important than currency, more important than gold. and that is the confidence of the people.
>
> Confidence and courage are the essentials of success in carrying out our plan. You people must have faith. You must not be stampeded by rumors or guesses. Let us unite in banishing fear. We have provided the machinery to restore our financial system; and it is up to you to support and make it work. It is your problem, my friends, your problem no less than it is mine. Together we cannot fail.

A chorus in the distance sang "America" as the program ended.

Another informative anniversary program, *WEAF Birthday Celebration*, was broadcast by the National Broadcasting Company on Sunday, August 16, 1942. The program told of WEAF's first broadcast of Wednesday, August 16, 1922. The first WEAF program originated from an improvised studio on the 24th floor of 24 Walker Street. Begun at 7:00 P.M., the program was three hours in length. George Peck was the announcer of this first broadcast that included Victor phonograph records and several unpaid amateur performers. Announcer Peck brought WEAF on the air with this announcement: "This is station WEAF. This is the world's first toll broadcasting station, with studios located at 24 Walker Street in New York City. Heretofore, broadcasting has been gratis to all. Now, due to the great demand by those who wish to use the air waves for good will purpose and with only one wave length available, 360 meters, we are operating a toll broadcasting service. You are now about to hear some Victor phonograph records."

A featured performer on the program was singer Helen Graves, an employee of American Telephone and Telegraph's Long Lines Plant Department, who was accompanied by pianist Mrs. May Swayze and Edna Cunningham of A.T.&T gave a talk and recited a James Whitsomb Riley poem. Violin solos were performed by Joseph Koznik and Frank Graham supplied baseball reports.

Twelve days after its initial broadcast, WEAF transmitted the first radio commercial. The ten-minutes long announcement sponsored by the Queensborough Corporation, a real estate company. On the first commercial, "Mr. Blackwell" urged listeners to hurry to the "apartment house near the green fields." As part of a closing statement at the end of the commercial, Mr. Blackwell proclaimed, "Dr. Royal S. Copeland, Health Commissioner of New York City, recently declared that any person who preached leaving the crowded city for the open country was a public spirited citizen and a benefactor to the race." *Text of the first commercial program and additional details can be found in the August 28, 1922, entry in* ***Appendix A — Chronology, 1906–1960.***

A brief description of the great WEAF programs were given, including their opening themes. The rapid growth of the network provided a problem for such early station announcers as Graham McNamee and Phillips Carlin. In the 1920s these two fine announcers found the station's network, then called the Broadcasting Company of America, was rapidly expanding. In the early days the announcer was required at the end of each program to give the call letters of all the stations in the chain [network] for that broadcast. Carlin, for example, at the end of a program may have ended it with: "This program came to you through stations WEAF, WMAF, WEEI, WJAR, WTAG, WGR, WLIT, WRC, WCSH, WCAE, WTAM, WWJ and WSAI." When the station list became too long to announce, the network substituted for it the familiar NBC chimes at program's end.

All in all, the program was chiefly a celebration of the NBC network and WEAF's pioneer role in its growth. Written by Neal Hopkins and directed by James Haupt, the program's announcer was Ben Grauer with occasional narration by Pedro de Cordoba. Frank Black conducted the NBC orchestra.

Another interesting NBC anniversary program, *NBC, 25 Years of Broadcasting: An Historic Impression in Celebration of RCA's Twenty-Fifth Anniversary*, written by Charles Speer, was broadcast December 2, 1944. Announced and narrated by the talented Ben Grauer, the program presented the themes, brief description and number of years various programs were broadcast by the National Broadcasting Company. The program was informative, but perhaps most important was its prophetic view of broadcasting's future. Grauer summarized its past and predicted the future:

> That's it, Mr. Listener. A series of highlights of radio broadcasting. It's a bigger story than we can ever tell. Radio took opera, the rich man's toy, and brought it into your living room. It gave you a front seat on the dramatic ever changing fronts of this war-ridden world. It has brought into your home music, comedy, talks, drama, debate, education, religion, public events. Now, for the war effort it brings you vital information from your government, ration news, enlistment appeals, bond drives [and] weather reports. It has served you, all 130,000,000 of you in every emergency. And above all, it has lived up to the American tradition.
>
> Oh, I grant you American radio is not perfect. It's made mistakes in the past. It will make more in the future. But it strives con-

stantly to improve itself for your advantage. It exists only to create in the highest measure — a complete justification of the term — Public Service!

Grauer then prophesied broadcasting's future: "Yes I can. In the past 25 years past radio has actually come from the stone age of communications to a super streamlined promise of tomorrow. For our final scene, let's visit the broadcast of tomorrow — television." The program concluded with a brief statement of the promise of television.

One of the best anniversary programs was, *Recollections at Thirty* series of half-hour programs, celebrating 30 years of NBC broadcasting. Narrated by Ed Herlihy assisted by Fred Collins, the programs contained portions of the network's memorably programming of its first 30 years. An audition of the *Recollections at 30* program was broadcast in a 60-minute version as part of the regular NBC *Biography in Sound* series (5-15-1956). The series was broadcast 1956–1957, beginning June 20, 1956. A brief description of some of the programs in the series and their content follows. The references to the *Rudy Vallee Program* usually refers to the *Fleishmann Hour* or the *Royal Gelatin Hour.*

Program 1 (6-20-1956). The program began with Frank Black and His Victor Recording Orchestra playing on *The Radio City Party* program in 1934. A segment of a John B. Kennedy news program (1930s) was followed by Charles Winninger as Captain Henry on the *Maxwell House Showboat* program (1930s). From the mid–1940s Fred Allen and Don McNeil engaged in a humorous exchange. Following Allen and McNeil was Graham McNamee giving a blow-by-blow account of the conclusion of the Max Baer-Primo Carnera heavyweight championship bout (June 14, 1934). A segment from an early husband and wife show, *Coffee and Doughnuts* (1934) and a portion of *Information Please* with Clifton Fadiman, F.P. Adams, Oscar Levant and John Kiernan concluded the first program.

Program 2 (6-27-1956). The second program began with *The NBC Minstrels* (1937) featuring Gene Arnold and Vance McHugh and a segment from *Easy Aces* with Jane and Goodman Ace from the early 1930s. Al Jolson on the *Shell Chateau* (1935) then interviewed boxer Slapsy Maxie Rosenbloom. Major Bowes on his *Major Bowes Amateur Hour* presented a fife, drum and bugle corps followed by a singer who "got the gong." Leslie Howard and his 10-year-old daughter, Leslie Ruth Howard, performed a dramatic scene. The second program concluded with a portion of Rosa Ponselle (1933) celebrating her 15th year at the Metropolitan Opera hosted by Graham McNamee.

Program 3 (7-4-56). Rudy Vallee on the *Rudy Vallee Hour* sang "Kansas City Kitty." The famous burlesque and vaudeville team (Bobby) Clark and (Paul) McCullough performed on a mid–1930s program. A *Lum and Abner* segment featuring Frances Langford was followed by a conversation between Fred Allen and Portland Hoffa on their March 20, 1940 program. Musical selections from the Tom Coakley Orchestra playing from San Francisco on their *Memories and Melodies* program in 1936 and a Al Jolson song on a 1936 *Shell Chateau* show concluded the program.

Program 4 (7-11-1956). Ralph Edwards as *Truth or Consequences* host gave a five dollar prize to a contestant for making love to a seal. In May, 1937, Bob Burns appeared on the *Kraft Music Hall* playing a bazooka solo and Bing Crosby from the sane program sang "Time on My Hands." August, 1936, Douglas Williams on board the Queen Mary in mid Atlantic interviewed Jesse Owens who had become an Olympic champion only a few days before in the Berlin Olympics. The program concluded with a song by the DiMarco Sisters appearing on the *Professional Parade* program in 1936 and a comedy bit by Tom Howard and George Sheldon on the July 4, 1935 *Rudy Vallee Show.*

Program 5 (7-18-1956). Mary Boland, W.C. Fields, Don Ameche, Edgar Bergen and Charlie McCarthy appeared in a segment from a 1937 *Chase and Sanborn Program.* Little Jack Little (1936) sang "What's New?" Jerry Belcher and Parks Johnson conducted a *Vox Pop* interview in the lobby of the old Hotel Pennsylvania in New York City (January, 1936). Bill Comstock at Tizzie Lish described her troubled day on *The Al Pearce Show* in the late 1930s. The last segments were Bobby Breen singing "Tell Everybody" on the *Ben Bernie Show* in 1936 and Dixie Lee Crosby's appearance on the *Shell Chateau* (1936) singing "I'll Never Say Never Again."

Program 6 (7-25-1956). Gene and Glenn as Jake and Lena talked and sang (middle 1930s). Kate Smith, Harry Von Zell and Abe Lyman appeared on a 1936 Jack Benny show. Kate sang "This Time it's Real." John J. Anthony on the *John J. Anthony Goodwill Hour* in the late 1930s provided advice for a young man's personal problems. Ken Christy and a tap-dancing chorus perform "When You Wore a Tulip" on the *NBC Minstrels* (1937)program. Fibber McGee and the Old Timer (probably Cliff Arquette) have a brief conversation in the early 1930s and McGee tries to lead an orchestra. Ben Bernie appeared on his own program in the late 1930s.

Program 7 (8-1-1956). The program began with a selection by the singing team of Billy Jones and Ernie Hare from a late 1920s program. A NBC news bulletin from May 6, 1937, announced the burning of the dirigible *Hindenberg*, followed by Herb Morrison's eye witness on the spot account of the disaster. Julia Sanderson and husband Frank Crumit sang "Did You Say Good Morning this Morning?" on *The Blackstone Plantation Party* (1930s). Phil Baker, Bottle and Beetle perform a comic routine from Baker's 1935 program. Parker Fennelly and Arthur Allyn appear on the last segment of their *Snow Village Sketches* program from the World War II era. The program concluded with Jo Stafford singing "I Can't Give You Anything But Love" and Frank Sinatra performing "Melancholy Baby" and "Time on My Hands" on a 1940 *Tommy Dorsey* show.

Program 8 (8-8-1956). All segments broadcast on program 8 were from NBC broadcasts of Friday, March 4, 1938, beginning with a guest appearance of actor Walter Huston on the *Amos 'n' Andy* program. His appearance was followed by a duet by Lucille Manners and Robert Finnan singing with Frank Black conducting the *City Service Concert* orchestra. Ben Gage, flying in a plane, then described the severe flooded conditions he observed in Southern California. Frank Munn sang with the Abe Lyman Orchestra on a *Waltz Time* program. Jimmy Fiddler broadcast the latest Hollywood news, followed by a dance band remote by the Blue Barron Orchestra featuring a vocal by Cheerful Charlie Fisher.

Program 9 (8-15-1956). The program began with Harry Horlick in the early 1930s conducting "Let's Have Another Cup of Coffee" with Frank Parker doing the vocal. Pick and Pat (mid–1930s) then discussed government subsidies. Eddie Cantor in the 1930s sang "O Gee, O Gosh, O Golly, I'm in Love." On February 6, 1938, Father Coughlin discussed problems with Asia. Rudy Vallee on his own show sang "If There is "Someone Lovelier Than You." Husband and wife Bebe Daniels and Ben Lyon appeared on a *Ben Bernie Show* in the mid–1930s. Deanna Durbin sang "Ave Maria" on the *Eddy Cantor Show* in the 30s.

Program 10 (8-29-1956). December 7, 1935, during the opening of the NBC Hollywood Studio, Al Jolson introduced Bing Crosby who sang "Treasure Island" accompanied by the Victor Young Orchestra. In the same decade, Ed Wynn, "The Perfect Fool," performed a comedy routine. Nelson Eddy sang "Ah, Sweet Mystery of Life" on a 1937 *Maxwell House Program.* An excerpt from Franklin Delano Roosevelt's 1936 Labor Day in his Fireside Chat format was broadcast. January, 1937, Dr. Walter Damrosch presented educational musical examples for children on his *Music Appreciation Hour.* June, 1937, the Sisters of the Skillet (Ed East and Ralph Dumke) performed in an excerpt from a *Chamber Music Society of Lower Basin Street* broadcast the following year announcer Jack McCarthy introduced host Gino Hamilton, who, in turn, introduced Dinah Shore who sang "I'm Coming Virginia."

Program 11 (9-5-1956). All items broadcast on program 11 came from one June 11, 1939 program, that were highlights of a Bon Voyage salute, by British subjects in the United States, to King George and his Queen. The King and Queen were leaving the United States after a visit. Gertrude Lawrence was the program's hostess. The Ray Noble Orchestra played two songs, after which Vivien Leigh and Basil Rathbone read love poems by Elizabeth Barrett Browning and Robert Browning. Sir Cecil Hardwicke, Nigel Bruce and C. Aubrey Smith formed a trio and sang "Three Little Fishes." Greer Garson and Leslie Howard appeared in a scene from *Goodbye, Mr. Chips.* Gertrude Lawrence sang a medley of songs that she had introduced on the stage. The program concluded with a Bon Voyage wish by Gertrude Lawrence and a toast to the King from the American theater by George M. Cohan.

Program 12 (9-12-1956). Mary Martin made her first radio appearance on the *Rudy Vallee Program* (1939) singing "My Heart Belongs to Daddy." Milton Berle performed his comedy routine on the Vallee program of June 4, 1936. Eleanor Powell dances on a 1935 *Magic Key of Radio* program. John Barrymore read "Advice to the Players" from a 1937 *Streamlined Shakespeare* program. Fats Waller played a medley of his hits on a *Rudy Vallee Program* of 1936.

Program 13 (9-19-1956). On the June, 1936, *Magic Key of Radio* program, Ruth Etting sang "You." A portion of the December 11, 1936, abdication speech of Edward VIII was broadcast. The Revellers Quartet sang "Lindy Lou" (1930s), and Julia Sanderson and Frank Crumit sang on their 1930s show, *The Battle of the Sexes.* The program concluded with a segment from Cheerio in the Depression Years and Eddy Cantor late in 1941 spoofed Mr. Anthony in a skit called, "The Court of Inhuman Relations."

Program 14 (10-3-1956). The program opened with the Vincent Lopez Orchestra playing an unidentified melody in the 1930s. Boris Karloff appeared in a brief excerpt from a 1930s *Lights Out* program. Ben Grauer on the Oct. 23, 1936 *Your Hit Parade* program announced that "Just the Way You Look Tonight," sung by Buddy Clark with the Freddy Rich Orchestra, was the number one song on the Hit Parade. February, 1942, Graham McNamee provided an on the spot description of the fire on the French liner *Normandie* anchored in New York harbor. The program's last item was the Marek Weber Orchestra playing "The Beautiful Blue Danube" from a May, 1938 *Contented Hour* program.

Program 15 (10-3-1956). The Pickens Sisters (Jane, Helen and Patty) in the early 1930s sang "Broadway Rhythm" on the *Magic Key of Radio* program. Comedian Joe Cook appeared on the March 7, 1939, *Rudy Vallee Program.* Jeanette MacDonald and Allen Jones sing excerpts from *The Firefly.* Dorothy Thompson on an October 24, 1938, news program commented on the Fair Labor Standards Act that had just gone into effect. Fredda Gibson (Georgia Gibbs) sang on the *Melody Puzzles* program with the Harry Salter Orchestra. Fred Uttel was the quizmaster on the show. The program ended with the Richard Himber Orchestra ("The Music that Speaks for Itself") playing "A Kiss in the Dark."

Program 16 (10-10-1956). Dance Music of the Thirties was the theme of the program, beginning with the Kay Kyser Orchestra playing "Flat Foot Floogie" on his *Kollege of Musical Knowledge* program (1938). It was following by the Glenn Miller Orchestra on a *Carnegie Hall Concert* broadcast playing "Jumping Jive" with vocal by Marion Hutton. Next there was a segment from an *Inside Story* program interpreting swing music and jitterbugging. Roy Shields' Orchestra provided the music. Milton Cross introduced the piano team of Arden and Arden playing "Dardanella" on a *Manhattan Merry-Go-Round* program. Bing Crosby sang "Let's Waltz for Old Times Sake" on a 1937 *Kraft Music Hall* program, followed by the Glenn Miller orchestra playing "Danny Boy." The program concluded with the novelty of Benny Goodman doing the vocal on "Tain't What You Do" and his band playing the tune in the various styles of the Kay Kyser, Fred Waring, Tommy Dorsey and Guy Lombardo bands.

Program 17 (10-17-1956). Fanny Brice in her pre–Snooks days appeared in a skit of the mid–1930s. She also sang "My Man." Joe Penner in the same era clowned and sang "When the Pussy Willow Whispers to the Catnip." Ginger Rogers sang "Isn't It a Lovely Day?" in the 1930s and Mickey Rooney in 1937 sang "When I Grow Up to be a Man." Brenda and Cobina appeared on a *Bob Hope Show* of the 30s. In October, 1935, Wallace Beery on the *Shell Chateau* program introduced 12-year-old Judy Garland who sang "Broadway Rhythm."

Program 18 (10-24-1956). November 2, 1935, Sophie Tucker sang and recited "I'm the Lady in Red." A segment of a *Vic and Sade* program of the 1930s was broadcast. Al Jolson sang a medley of his favorites on the *Shell Chateau* (1930s) accompanied by the Victor Young Orchestra. Ben Bernie on his own show sang "The Horse with the Lavender Eyes." Bill "Bojangles" Robinson danced in 1935 on the broadcast of the opening of the NBC Hollywood Studios. Finally, Ben Grauer introduced Nick LaRocca and the Original Dixieland Jazz band on a 1936 Magic Key of Radio broadcast.

Program 19 (10-31-1956). All segments broadcast on this program was originally part of the 1939 25th ASCAP Anniversary broadcast from Carnegie Hall. The program included famous composers singing their own songs: Jack Norwood sang "Take Me Out to the Ballgame" and "Shine on Harvest Moon." Harry Armstrong sang "Sweet Adeline. Ernie Burnett played "Melancholy Baby" on the piano. Billy Hill sang "I'm Heading for the Last Round-Up." George Whiting sang "My Blue Heaven." New York City's ex-mayor Jimmy Walker introduced Irving Berlin who sang "Alexander's Ragtime Band." Joe Howard sang "I Wonder Who's Kissing Her Now?" William C. Handy played "St. Louis Blues." The program concluded with George M. Cohan singing his "Give My Regards to Broadway" and "I'm a Yankee Doodle Dandy."

Program 21 (11-14-1956). November 16, 1935, Wallace Beery introduced Judy Garland on the *Shell Chateau* program, who sang "Zing Went the Strings of My Heart." Rudy Vallee on his own program introduced Edgar Bergen for his first radio appearance in December, 1936. In 1936, Jan Sablon sang on the *Magic Key of Radio* program. Sigmund Spaeth on the November 16, 1935 *Tune Detective* program was included. Finally, John McCormack sang "Londonderry Air" in November, 1936.

Program 22 (11-21-1956). Jack Benny, Fred Allen and Portland Hoffa appeared on a 1937 *Town Hall* program. Helen Kane ("The Boop Boop a Doop Girl") in the 1930s sang "I Want to be Kissed by You." On a Fall, 1935 *Rudy Vallee* program, Vallee broadcast an introduction to the music of Billy Rose's *Jumbo.* Vallee sang, Richard Rodgers played piano and Gloria Grafton sang "Little Girl Blue." A Fred McMurray and Dorothy Lamour vocal duet performed in 1938 concluded the program.

Program 23 (12-12-1956). Lanny Ross sang on an early 1930s *Maxwell House Showboat* program. A year later Jack Pearl as Baron Munchausen appeared on the *Rudy Vallee* program. Floyd Gibbons in 1936 reported on the New England floods. Carmen Miranda (1939) sang two songs on the *Rudy Vallee* show. Pianist Art Tatum played on a 1935 *Magic Key of Radio* program. John Barrymore meets Charlie McCarthy on *a Chase and Sanborn Program* and the Lenny Hayton Orchestra played "Honeysuckle Rose."

Program 24 (12-19-1956). Cliff Edwards (Ukulele Ike) sang "Paper Moon" in 1933. Red Skelton guested on the August, 1937, *Rudy Vallee Program.* Red Skelton performed a comedy routine from a 1937 *Rudy Vallee Program.* Gloria Swanson in the middle 1930s sang "If I Should Love You." The *Rudy Vallee Program* presented a scene from the Broadway success *Knickerbocker Holiday* with Walter Huston and the original cast members. They sang "September Song." Dick Powell in 1934 sang "Lullaby of Broadway."

Program 25 (12-26-1956). The program consisted entirely of early NBC broadcasts. The first segment presented was from the earliest network program available. Originally broadcast June 11, 1927, it included President Calvin Coolidge welcoming Charles A. Lindberg back from Europe and awarding him the Distinguished Flying Cross. The announcer was Graham McNamee. The Cliquot Club Eskimos in 1927 played "When You and I Were Young Maggie." Joseph White ("The Silver Masked Tenor") in 1927 sang "Mary Lou." In 1927, Lindberg spoke at the National Press Club in Washington, DC. Later that year the George Olsen played and Billy Murray sang a popular song of the day.

Program 26 (1-2-1957). Ethel Merman sang "We're Having a Heat Wave" on NBC in 1938. Judy Holliday sang and was in a skit (1940). In 1938, Bea Wain sang "My Reverie" with Larry Clinton's Orchestra. Judy Canova with brother Zeke and sister Annie sang "St. Louis Blues." Ginny Sims sang "I'll Never Smile Again" with Kay Kyser's orchestra from Chicago's Blackhawk Hotel. Martha Raye appeared with Cary Grant on a NBC program in 1936.

Program 27 (1-9-1957). Gene Autry in 1937 sang "Tumbling Tumbleweeds." August 5, 1937, Rudy Vallee on his program introduced Tommy Rigs and Betty Lou on their first radio appearance. Lillian Roth (1936) sang "Tormented." Rudy on his *Rudy Vallee Program* conducted an announcers' fast talking contest featuring Graham McNamee, Milton Cross and Ben Grauer. The program concluded with a November 3, 1935, appearance of the Tommy Dorsey Orchestra on the *Magic Key of Radio* program.

Program 32 (1-30-1957). Irene Dunne (1935) sang "Lovely to Look At." Joan Davis clowned and sang on the *Shell Chateau* program. She also talked with Ben Blue. July 18, 1938, Douglas "Wrong Way" Corrigan is interviewed in Dublin, Ireland, after his "unauthorized" flight across the Atlantic from New York. The Sweetheart of the Airwaves, Vaughn DeLeath, sang "I Feel Like a Feather in the Breeze." Sam Lanin (1929) leads the Ipana Troubadours in a musical selection, followed by a segment from *Tony Wons Scrapbook* (1930s). The program concluded with Russ Columbo singing "Auf Wiedersehen, My Dear."

Program 33 (2-6-1957). Milton Cross on the *American Album of Familiar Music* introduced Frank Munn and the Bert Hirsh orchestra (June, 1939). Ethel Barrymore appears on the *Rudy Vallee Program* in 1938 and performed a scene from *The White Oaks.* Barry Wood with the Mark Warnow Orchestra on a 1942 *Your Hit Parade* program sang "I Don't Want to Set the World on Fire." Bing Crosby in the 1930s sang "River Rock and Roll" on the *Kraft Music Hall.* Will Rogers in the early 30s talks about the American scene. Tom Waring with *Fred Waring's Pennsylvanians* sang "Ah, Sweet Mystery of Life" in 1928. Finally, the Duncan Sisters sing "Happy Go Lucky Days" in the 20s.

Program 34 (2-13-1957). The program celebrated Lincoln's birthday with all items related in some manner. For example, a 1938 segment from a Rudy Vallee broadcast featured Raymond Massey presenting the closing speech from the *Abe Lincoln in Illinois* play. This was followed from an excerpt from the Feb. 12, 1939 *Magic Key of Radio* broadcast with Alexander Woolcott presenting an oral essay on Lincoln's Gettysburg Address. (The program was originally broadcast 75 years after Lincoln delivered the speech.) The program concluded with two musical selections. First, the Jay Rosamund Johnson Choir sang "Joshua Fit De Battle of Jericho," followed by Frank Black conducting the NBC Orchestra playing "Two Hearts in 3/4 Time."

Program 35 (2-20-1957). "The Cinderella Girl of Radio" Jessica Dragonette sang on a *Cities Service* program (February, 1936). Helen Hayes as Queen Victoria in *Victoria Regina* appears with Vincent Price in a scene from the play on June 14, 1937. Perry Como with the Ted Weems Orchestra on the *Fibber McGee and Molly* (1936) sang "You Turned the Tables on Me." Fall, 1937, Rudy Vallee on the *Rudy Vallee Program* introduced the Stroud Twins—Clarence and Claude. Al Jolson on the August, 1935, *Shell Chateau* program sang "I Feel a Song Coming On."

Program 36 (2-27-1957). Harriet Hill on the *Shell Chateau* (1935) program sang "You Have a Habit." Bob Burns appeared as a guest on the *Rudy Vallee Program* (1935). Bunny Berigan and His Orchestra appeared on a *Magic Key of Radio* program. Elsie Janis (1939) recited, sang and imitated Sophie Tucker and Fanny Brice. Gene Raymond (1936) sang "Twinkle, Twinkle Little Star."

Program 37 (3-6-1957). Dinah Shore accompanied by the Bobby Sherwood Orchestra on the *Eddy Cantor Show* sang "Yes, My Darling Daughter." Charles Laughton performed scenes from his motion picture *Rembrandt* (November 15, 1936). Wyn Murray and Ray Heatherton sang on the *Rudy Vallee Program* (April, 1937). Babe Dedricksen Zacharias talked with Smith Ballew on a 1936 *Shell Chateau* show. John Boles (1930s) sang "The Desert Song," and Harry Lauder (1929) sang two songs.

Program 38 (3-13-1957). John McCormack is introduced by Rudy Vallee on a 1938 *Rudy Vallee Program.* McCormack then sang an Irish song. The Silver Masked Tenor (Joe White) sang "They Called It Ireland." Bea Lillie (1935) appeared in a comic skit. A special remote broadcast from the mission at Capistrano reported the returning of the swallows. Ignace Padrewski performed a piano solo on the September 25, 1938, *Magic Key of Radio* program. Tenor Morton Downey (1938) sang "Christopher Robin."

Program 39 (3-20-1957). Radio Highlights of 1933 was the theme of the program. It included Connee Boswell singing "I Cover the Waterfront" and part of FDR's first inaugural address. Announcer Alois Havrilla on the *Voice of Firestone* introduced Richard Crooks who sang "My Wild Irish Rose." Excerpts from the *Maxwell House Showboat* included comedy from Captain Andy (Charles Winninger), Mary Lou (Lois Wilson) singing, Molasses and January in a comedy skit, and the Maxwell Quartet singing. Ed Wynn clowned with Graham McNamee on the *Ed Wynn Fire Chief* show (1930s). Frances Langford (1930s) sang "The Boulevard of Broken Dreams."

Program 40 (3-27-1957). The program began with Arthur Tracy the Street Singer (1934) singing "Marta" and "When Day is Done." Nellie Revell on *Neighbor Nell* (1936) talked about love. Host Deems Taylor, June Walker and conductor-composer Sigmund Romberg appeared on the *Armour Studio Party* (1936). Edwin C. Hill on the December 10, 1935, *Human Side of the News* discussed the question of naval disarmament. Jack Benny on November 3, 1935, introduced tenor Kenny Baker on his program for the first time. Baker then sang "The Rose in Her Hair." Johnny Green, Don Wilson and Mary Livingston also appeared. March 1, 1936, Jesse Crawford ("The Poet of the Organ") inaugurated the new pipe organ installed in the WMAQ, Chicago, IL, studio by playing two songs.

Program 41 (4-3-1957). The program focused on the 35th anniversary of H.V. Kaltenborn as an NBC news broadcaster. Kaltenborn discussed his beginnings in radio with Mary Margaret McBride on her 1952 program. He described how in April 4,1922, he came to make his first broadcast for the *Brooklyn Eagle* newspaper and talking for 30 minutes on current events. He recalled his 12 hour coverage of the Munich Crisis. His 1941 announcement of the Japanese attack on Pearl Harbor, the death of FDR and the election of 1948 with his incorrect statement that Dewey defeated Truman is included. Later Kaltenborn and Eddie Cantor traded quips on the latter's program. They are joined by Bert Gordon—"The Mad Russian." Mary Margaret McBride expressed her appreciation of Kaltenborn's work, and Chet Huntley discussed his appreciation of Kaltenborn from a contemporary (1957) view.

Program 42 (4-10-1957). Paul Whiteman's orchestra with the Rhythm Boys, including a young Bing Crosby, opened the program playing "From Monday On." A scene from the motion picture, *Camille*, with Greta Garbo and Lionel Barrymore followed from a 1936 broadcast. Shirley Temple singing "On the Good Ship Lollypop" from 1934 was followed by Bill "Bojangles" Robinson dancing. "Grand opera with the bunions" was how Bojangles described it on the Jan. 2, 1937 *Shell Chateau* program. Next, was the May 17, 1938, premiere program of *Information Please.* The first question asked by Clifton Fadiman was "What kind of fat head can be boiled in oil with impunity?" (The answer was a fish by that name.) An interesting fact was that only Franklin P. Adams (FPA) was on the panel of experts of that first *Information Please* program. A 1926 excerpt of the Coon-Sanders Orchestra playing "Night Hawk Blues" concluded the program.

Program 43. This program featured only songs written by Irving Berlin. Ex-New York City Mayor Jimmy Walker introduced Irving Berlin on a 1939 broadcast. Berlin sang "Alexander's Ragtime Band." "Oh, How I Hate to Get Up in the Morning" was sung by Arthur Fields. John Steele sang "A Pretty Girl is Like a Melody" and Vaughn DeLeath in 1924 sang "All By Myself." Lewis James sang "All Alone by the Telephone." In 1925, Henry Burr sang "Always." The Paul Whiteman Orchestra (1927) play "Blue Skies." "Marie" was sung by Franklyn Bauer in 1928. Morton Downing, Singing Sam and Annette Henshaw in 1932 sang "Say It Isn't So." Frank Parker with the A&P Gypsies sang "Let's Have Another Cup of Coffee." Ethel Waters in 1933 sang "Heatwave." The program concluded with Clifton Webb singing "Smile and Show Your Dimples," before it became "Easter Parade."

Finally, recognition should be given to perhaps the finest patriotic anniversary program—*We Hold These Truths.* Naturally, the program's content and performers were important, but the temporal context added to its significance and importance. Broadcast simultaneously by NBC-Red, NBC-Blue, CBS and MBS, *We Hold These Truths* was broadcast December 15, 1941, eight days after the Japanese attacked Pearl Harbor.

The program was narrated by Jimmy Stewart. Its cast included Edward Arnold, Lionel Barrymore, Walter Brennan, Bob Burns, Walter Huston, Elliott Lewis, Marjorie Main, Edward G. Robinson, Rudy Vallee and Orson Welles. Music was under the direction of Bernard Herrman. The program was written by Norman Corwin.

Crossley surveys estimated that the program was heard by more than 60 million listeners (Barnouw, 1968, p. 153). Corwin's writing dramatically presented the Constitutional principles for which the American nation stood. At an hour of national emergency, *We Hold These Truths* proudly celebrated the Constitution and the American spirit.

Some of radio's most entertaining and inspirational moments came from its holiday and anniversary programs. They depended upon the magnificent *audio* medium that was radio in order to achieve their greatest effects.

There were a wide diversity of anniversary programs broadcast over the years. For example, the *National Barn Dance* program presented two anniversary programs in successive years. On October 2, 1943, the program celebrated its tenth full year with Alka-Seltzer as sponsor. Joe Kelly was the host and Jack Holden the announcer. The performers included the Hoosier Hot Shots, the Arkansas Woodchopper, Lulu Belle, Grace Wilson and the Dinning Sisters. The following year on April 15, 1944, the *National Barn Dance* celebrated the twentieth year anniversary of Chicago station WLS. As usual, the program was high-spirited, highly polished and entertaining.

Another example of an unusual radio anniversary program was the March 3, 1939, *March of Time* program. The program celebrated the

16th anniversary of the *first* publication of *Time* magazine. This program included re-enactments of the trial conviction of Jimmy Hines; Adolf Hitler's invitation of Marian Daniels to sing *The Merry Widow* at Munich; the DAR's refusal to allow Marian Anderson to sing at Constitution Hall; the Supreme Court's decision against the steel workers' sit-down strike; Harry Hopkins campaigning in his home state of Iowa; and the election of a new Pope.

14999 **Holister, (Mrs.) Johnnie.** COM-HE (WCIL, Carbondale, IL, 1954).

15000 **Holl, (Dr.) Walter E.** Dentist Holl conducted the *Dentistry of Today* program (KFRC, San Francisco, CA, 1925).

15001 **Holland, Charlotte.** Busy actress Holland appeared on the daytime serial programs *Joyce Jordan, Girl Interne, King's Row, Lone Journey, Open Door, Against the Storm, This Is Nora Drake* and *Big Sister.*

15002 **Holland, Clyvus.** "Five-year-old Shakespearean reader" (KHJ, Los Angeles, CA, 1926).

15003 **Holland, Dick.** Actor Holland was in the cast of *The Barton Family* and *The Road of Life.*

15004 **Holland, Elsie John.** Violinist (WEAF, New York, NY, 1925).

15005 **Holland, Gloria.** COM-HE (WEEU, Reading, PA, 1956–1957).

15006 **Holland, Jo.** COM-HE (WLBT, Jackson, MS, 1955).

15007 **Holland, (Reverend) John W.** Reverend Holland came to WLS in 1933, when he was appointed by Bishop Waldorf to be that station's pastor. He was the first minister ever to have held such a position. Holland appeared on many WLS programs in the years that followed.

15008 **Holland, Leonard.** Newscaster (KPAC, Port Arthur, TX, 1940).

15009 **Holland, Luther.** DJ (*Progressive Serenade,* WFTL, Ft. Lauderdale, FL, 1954–1955).

15010 **Holland, Marion O'Neil.** Violinist (WJAZ, Chicago, IL, 1926).

15011 **Holland, Ruth.** COM-HE (WNOW, York, PA, 1956).

15012 **Holland, (Reverend) W.W.** Minister of the Mt. Lookout Methodist Church, Cincinnati, OH, Reverend Holland conducted a *Radio Chapel Service* program (WLW, Cincinnati, OH, 1922).

15013 **Hollander, Adolph.** Concert violinist (WHAG, New York, NY, 1925).

15014 **Hollander, Will.** Leader (*Will Hollander Orchestra,* instr. mus. prg., WCBM, Baltimore, MD, 1934).

15015 **Hollenbeck, Don.** Newscaster (WJZ, New York, NY, 1945; CBS, 1946–1947).

15016 **Hollenden Hotel Orchestra.** Hotel dance band (WTAM, Cleveland, OH, 1926).

15017 **Hollensworth, Marie.** COM-HE (WLAY, Muscle Shoals, AL, 1951).

15018 **Holler, Carl.** DJ (*Whoopin Holler,* WITZ, Jasper, IN, 1950).

15019 **Holles, Everett.** Newscaster (CBS, 1944–1945; WBBM, Chicago, IL, 1945–1947; MBS, 1954).

15020 **Holliday, Byron.** Tenor (WABC, New York, NY, 1929).

15021 **Holliday, Johnny.** DJ (WHK, Cleveland, OH, 1960).

15022 **Holliday, Mary.** COM-HE (KIRX, Kirksville, MO, 1957).

15023 **Holliday, Mary.** COM-HE (WACO, Waco, TX, 1957).

15024 **Hollingshead, Miriam.** Pianist (WCBD, Zion, IL, 1925).

15025 **Hollingsworth, Mayme.** COM-HE (KWRF, Warren, AR, 1957).

15026 **Hollinshead, Redferne.** Tenor (WDAF, Kansas City, MO and WEAF, New York, NY, 1926).

15027 **Hollinstead, Waldemar.** Baritone (KOIN, Portland, OR, 1928).

15028 **Hollis, Mae.** Soprano (KLD, Independence, MO, 1926).

15029 **Hollis, Steve.** Ancr. (WAAT, New York, New York, 1940s & early 50s). DJ (WBNX, New York, NY, 50s).

15030 **Hollister, Herb.** Newscaster (KANS, Wichita, KS, 1939). Sportscaster (KANS, 1940).

15031 **Hollo, Jo.** COM-HE (WJQS, Jackson, MS, 1960).

15032 **Holloway, Lillian.** Saxophonist (WOAW, Omaha, NE, 1923).

15033 **Holloway, Muriel.** Soprano (KFAE, Pullman, WA, 1924).

15034 **Hollowell, Frank.** Pianist (WSM, Nashville, TN, 1928).

15035 **Hollums, Ellis.** Newscaster (WQAM, Miami, FL, 1942, 1945).

15036 **Holly, Vera.** Singer (*Vera Holly, Songs,* 15 min., Sunday, 3:45–4:00 P.M., MBS, 1947).

15037 ***Holly Sloan*** (aka ***The Story of Holly Sloan***). Gale Page played the title role on the daytime serial. Also in the cast were: Marlene Ames, Louise Arthur, Bob Bailey, Georgia Backus, Helene Burke, Joe Forte, Bob Griffin, Vic Perrin, Charles Seel and B.J. Thompson. General Mills was the sponsor (15 min., Monday through Friday, NBC, 1947–1948).

15038 ***Hollywood Airport.*** A sustaining summer replacement for the *Philco Radio Playhouse,* the dramatic series followed the story of a columnist for *Photoplay* magazine, who each week managed to get involved in some type of Hollywood adventure. Joe Jeigesen hosted and starred as columnist Joe Yorke. Also in the cast were Vera Allen, Anne Pitoniak and Grant Richards. Ira Marion was the writer and Joe Graham the show's producer-director (30 min., Wednesday, 9:00–9:30 P.M., ABC, 1954).

15039 ***Hollywood American Legion Band.*** Instr. mus. prg. by a military style brass band (KWTO, Springfield, MO, 1934).

15040 ***Hollywood Barn Dance.*** CW variety show (KNX, Hollywood, CA, 1932; CBS–Pacific, 1943–1948), first broadcast in 1932, at times featured such stars as Eddie Dean, Jimmy Wakely, Merle Travis, Ken Curtis, Cotton Clark, Andy Parker and the Plainsmen and Foy Willing and the Riders of the Purple Sage. Other performers on the *Barn Dance* were Cliffie Stone, Joe Maphis, Ken Card, Maureen O'Connor, Cottonseed Clark, Kirby Grant, Johnny Bond, Jimmy Walker, Clem Smith and Charlie Linvalle. Guest stars appeared frequently such as Roy Rogers and Bob Hope. The program enjoyed a five year run on the CBS network.

15041 ***Hollywood Bowl Symphony Concerts.*** The Union Oil Company sponsored the series of symphonic concerts. The fourth program in the series featured the Italian pianist-composer Alfredo Casella (90 min., Saturday, 8:30–10:00 P.M., KFI-NBC-Pacific Coast Network, 1928).

15042 ***Hollywood Brevities.*** George Fisher broadcast Hollywood gossip in the form of a letter to his listeners on the weekly transcribed show. Stellar jazz pianist Art Tatum and the Playboys furnished the music (15 min., Transcribed, 1938).

15043 ***Hollywood Chatterbox.*** Barbara Young provided gossip about movies and their players on the weekly show (15 min., Weekly, WFIL, Philadelphia, PA, 1936).

15044 **Hollywood Community Orchestra.** Music group (KFI, Los Angeles, CA, 1924).

15045 ***Hollywood Dateline.*** Irwin Allen interviewed motion picture stars and talked about their latest movies (15 min., Weekly, 5:30–5:45 P.M., KECA, Los Angeles, CA, 1945).

15046 ***Hollywood Dreams.*** Ted Steele and Phyllis Creone in the roles of "Bob and Mary" played two talented young professionals who aspired to a Hollywood career on the daytime serial. The sponsor was the Gordon Baking Company (15 min., Tuesday, 11:00–11:15 A.M., CBS, 1940).

15047 ***Hollywood Fashions.*** Stephanie Diamond broadcast fashion talks on the local program (15 min., Sunday, 6:30–6:45 P.M., WCAE, Pittsburgh, PA, 1936).

15048 **Hollywood Girls Quartet.** Hollywood vocal group (KFI, Los Angeles, CA, 1923).

15049 ***Hollywood Harmonies.*** Jean Rogers delivered what *Variety* called mostly "fan magazine material." Romantic tenor Ralph Elsmore sang with Anthony Candelori's Orchestra. The Freihofer Baking Company sponsored the show (15 min., Monday, 6:45–7:00 P.M., KYW, Philadelphia, PA, 1936).

15050 ***Hollywood Headlines.*** Frank Clark broadcast film news and gossip (KYW, Chicago, IL, 1925).

15051 ***Hollywood Headlines.*** Eddie Hoyle (Eddie Felbion) broadcast Hollywood gossip. The sponsor was the Marco Animal Food Company (15 min., Monday, 10:45–11:00 P.M., WIP, Philadelphia, PA, 1940).

15052 ***Hollywood High Hatters Orchestra.*** Instr. mus. prg. (WEAF-NBC-Red, 1936).

15053 ***Hollywood Highlights.*** Sam Hayes talked about films and their stars on his weekly show (15 min., Weekly, CBS-Pacific Coast Network, 1939).

15054 ***Hollywood Hotel.*** Gossip columnist Louella Parsons hosted and Dick Powell was the MC on the variety program that combined music with dramatic segments. The format was similar to *Grand Hotel*, in that a female telephone operator played by Miss Duane Thompson, opened each program. After Dick Powell left the show, Fred MacMurray, Herbert Marshall and William Powell acted as MC. Music was provided by singers Anne Jamison, Frances Langford, Rowene Williams, baritone Igor Gorin and the orchestras of Raymond Paige and Ted Fiorito. Various guests appeared each week including Leo Carrillo, Jerry Cooper, Frank Parker and Jean Sablon. Victor Chevigny and Ed James were the writers; Bill Bacher the producer; and George MacGarrett the director of the hour show that originated from Hollywood (30 min., Friday, 9:30–10:00 P.M., CBS, 1934).

15055 ***Hollywood in Person.*** Margaret Morton McKay broadcast film news and gossip (KFI, Los Angeles, CA, 1937).

15056 ***Hollywood Jackpot.*** Whitehall Pharmaceutical Company sponsored the quiz conducted by Kenny Delmar and assisted by announcer Bill Cullen. Ralph Murphy's Orchestra provided the music (30 min., Monday, Wednesday and Friday, 4:30–5:00 P.M., CBS, 1946).

15057 **Hollywood McCosker.** McCosker conducted the *Current Motion Pictures* program on which he discussed current motion pictures (WOR, Newark, NJ, 1924).

15058 ***Hollywood Mardi Gras.*** Don Wilson was the announcer on the lively variety show that featured Lanny Ross, Charles Butterworth, Florence George, Jane Rhodes and the Raymond Paige Orchestra (30 min., Tuesday, NBC-Red, 1938).

15059 ***Hollywood Newsreel.*** Bert Wayne was the purveyor of film news and gossip on the sustaining show (15 min., 4:00–4:15 P.M., WNEW, New York, NY, 1947).

15060 ***Hollywood on the Air.*** A star studded, quarter-hour show, *Hollywood on the Air* featured Russ Columbo and the Harry Jackson orchestra. Guest stars who frequently appeared were: Bette Davis, Zasu Pitts, Buck Jones, Bruce Cabot, Bing Crosby, the Pickens Sisters, Ruth Etting, Phil Harris, Jimmy Fiddler, Joan Blondell, Ginger Rogers, Boris Karloff, Maxine Doyle, Alice White, Wallace Ford, Dave Marshall, Dolores Del Rio, Fuzzy Knight and Phil Ohman (15 min., Network, 1933).

15061 ***Hollywood Players*** **(aka *The Cresta Blanca Hollywood Players*)**. *Variety* called the show an imitation of the *Theatre Guild of the Air* program. Various Hollywood stars were presented in dramatizations of motion pictures and plays. Guests included Gregory Peck, Paulette Goddard, Claudette Colbert, Joan Fontaine and John Garfield. Music was supplied by the Bernard Katz Orchestra. Frank Bingham was the announcer (30 min., Tuesday, 9:30–10:00 P.M., CBS, 1946).

15062 ***(The) Hollywood Ramblers.*** Early morning (6:30 A.M.) CW music program (KLRA, Little Rock, AR, 1930s).

15063 ***Hollywood Rendezvous.*** Connie Boswell and Johnny Mercer accompanied by the Lennie Hayton Orchestra provided the songs and music on the pleasant show. The program's first guest was Bing Crosby's valet, George Washington Duke. The show premiered June 12, 1938 (30 min., Weekly, CBS, 1938).

15064 **(The) Hollywood Rhythm Kings Orchestra.** The band was billed as a "Gennett recording orchestra" (KFWB, Hollywood, CA, 1925).

15065 **Hollywood Serenaders.** Jack McGuire directed the California band (KFI, Los Angeles, CA, 1925).

15066 ***Hollywood Show Time.*** The sustaining program replaced the short-lived *Shorty Bell* show.

Mickey Rooney starred, but this time he was the host. Singer Julie Wilson, pianist Buddy Cole, Lud Gluskin's Orchestra and various guest performers entertained. A board of judges selected the "most promising [guest] talent" on each show (30 min., Sunday, 10:00–10:30 P.M., CBS, 1948).

15067 ***Hollywood Showcase.*** Mary Astor hosted and appeared in a weekly dramatic sketch on the program sponsored by Richard Hudnut Cosmetics. Barry Kroeger also performed romantic songs (30 min., Tuesday, 9:30–10:00 P.M., CBS, 1941).

15068 ***Hollywood Showcase.*** Robert Armbruster's Orchestra and a guest vocalist each week, such as Skip Farrell, entertained on the sustaining summer replacement program. Jimmy Wallington was the announcer (15 min., Monday, 10:15–10:30 P.M., NBC, 1953).

15069 ***Hollywood Sketchbook.*** Joan Adams, played by Joan Whitehead, broadcast movie gossip (5 min., Monday through Friday, WEEI, Boston, MA, 1941).

15070 ***Hollywood Spotlight.*** The transcribed Transco program featured the music of Phil Harris and his band, singers Leah Ray, Larry Burke and Tom Jeffries. Cliff Arquette added humor with his portrayal of Aunt Addie. Don Wilson was the program's announcer (15 min., Transcribed, Various Stations, 1930s).

15071 ***Hollywood Star Time.*** Frigidaire and General Motors sponsored the dramatic show that presented many Hollywood motion pictures as radio plays. A typical opening of the show went like this: "You're twice as sure with two great names: Frigidaire and General Motors. Frigidaire presents *Hollywood Star Time* direct from Hollywood. Tonight the radio production of *Elmer the Great.*" The program presented such shows and stars as: *The Lodger* with Vincent Price and Cathy Lewis; *Murder My Sweet* with Dick Powell and Mary Astor; *Double Indemnity* with Alan Ladd; *The Suspect* with Charles Laughton; *It Happened Tomorrow* with Robert Young; and *Christmas in July* with Eddie Bracken and Diana Lynn. Harold Peary, Vanessa Brown, Mickey Rooney, Jane Wyman, Cary Grant, Herbert Marshall, Van Heflin and Ann Todd also starred (30 min., Weekly, CBS, 1947).

15072 **Hollywood String Quartet.** Instrumental group (KFI, Los Angeles, CA, 1926).

15073 **Hollywood Sunnybrook Orchestra.** Popular local band (WWJ, Detroit, MI, 1928).

15074 ***Hollywood Theatre.*** Different motion pictures stars appeared each week in the series of chilling dramas sponsored by Tums. Stewart Jerome and Milton Geiger wrote and Jack Johnstone produced the programs. Barbara Stanwyck made a guest appearance on the first program of the series. Music was supplied by Jeff Alexander. Don Wilson was the announcer (30 min., Tuesday, 8:30–9:00 P.M., NBC, 1951).

15075 ***Hollywood, U.S.A.*** Paula Stone interviewed guests from the motion picture industry and dispersed Hollywood gossip on the transcribed program (15 min., Monday through Friday, Various stations, 1950).

15076 ***Hollywood Whispers.*** This was another of George Fisher's programs on which he broadcast movie gossip. The sponsor was Dr. Strasska's Tooth Paste (15 min., Monday, 7:30–7:45 P.M. CST, Don Lee Network, 1936).

15077 **Hollywoodland Orchestra.** Popular Los Angeles band (KNX, Hollywood, CA, 1925).

15078 **Holm, Bill.** Newscaster (WEED, Rocky Mount, NC, 1941).

15079 **Holm, Clayt [Clate].** DJ (*Out West Special*, KOVE, Lander, WY, 1948; KIUP, Durango, CO, 1956).

15080 **Holman, Al.** Newscaster (WALA, Moline, AL, 1941–1942). Sportscaster (WALA, 1942).

15081 **Holman, Helen.** Soprano (WQJ, Chicago, IL, 1926).

15082 **Holman, Knox.** DJ (*Holman's Hoedown*, WSFA, Montgomery, AL, 1948).

15083 **Holman, Libby.** Singer with the Linit Orchestra (WNAC, Boston, MA, 1931).

15084 **Holman, Lucille E.** Soprano (KFI, Los Angeles, CA, 1923).

15085 ***Holman Sisters.*** Instr. mus. prg. featuring a sisters' piano duo (NBC, 1934).

15086 **Holmes, Alfred.** Ballad singer (WSWS, Chicago, IL, 1926).

15087 **Holmes, Audrey.** COM-HE (WLAC, Nashville, TN, 1960).

15088 **Holmes, Bedford.** Pianist (*Bedford Holmes*, instr. mus. prg., WPG, Atlantic City, NJ, 1936).

15089 **Holmes, Bernie Ash.** COM-HE (KRMG, Tulsa, OK,1954).

15090 **Holmes, Carter.** Newscaster (WFTL, Ft. Lauderdale, FL, 1948).

15091 **Holmes, Charlie.** DJ (MBS, 1956–1957).

15092 **Holmes, Connie.** COM-HE (WAVI, Dayton, OH, 1954).

15093 **Holmes, George R.** Political news commentator (*George K. Holmes News*, 15 min., Friday, 10:00–10:15 P.M., NBC, 1935–1936; *Washington News*, NBC, 1938). Holmes was the Washington bureau chief of INS (International News Service).

15094 **Holmes, Herbie.** Leader (*Herbie Holmes Orchestra*, instr. mus. prg., MBS, 1935; CBS, 1939; WBBM, Chicago, IL, 1942).

15095 **Holmes, J.P.** Announcer (WORD, Chicago, IL, 1925).

15096 Holmes, James G. Newscaster (*Sidelines From Headlines*, WMON, Montgomery, WV, 1948).

15097 Holmes, Lois. COM-HE (KSLA, Shreveport, LA, 1954). Actress Holmes appeared on the *Second Mrs. Burton* daytime serial program.

15098 Holmes, Margaret. COM-HE (KYNO, Fresno, CA, 1951).

15099 Holmes, Mary. COM-HE (WACO, Waco, TX, 1960).

15100 Holmes, R.D. Newscaster (KAST, Astoria, OR, 1945).

15101 Holmes, Ted. Newscaster (WBRK, Pittsfield, MA, 1946).

15102 Holmes, Thurston. Newscaster (WHOM, Jersey City, NJ, 1941).

15103 Holmes, Virginia. COM-HE (KIBS, Bishop, CA, 1957).

15104 Holmes, Wendell. Actor Holmes was in the cast of *Myrt and Marge* and *Sally of the Movies.*

15105 Holmgren, Lois R. COM-HE (WJPD, Ishpeming, MI, 1951).

15106 Holmgren, Rod. Newscaster (WOI, Ames, IA, 1940).

15107 Holmlund, James. Newscaster (*Community News*, WDLB, Marshfield, WI, 1948).

15108 Holmquist, H. Announcer (WLSI, Providence, RI, 1925).

15109 Holmquist, Harry. News commentator (*News Digest*, KDBA, Santa Barbara, CA, 1948).

15110 Holper, Annette. Violinist (*Annette Holper*, instr. mus. prg., WIBG, Greensboro, NC, 1936).

15111 Holst, Ernie. Leader (*Ernie Holst Orchestra*, instr. mus. prg., NBC and CBS, 1933; KDKA, Pittsburgh, PA, 1934; WJR, Detroit, MI, 1937; WMAQ, Chicago, IL, 1940).

15112 Holst, Rudolph H. Announcer (WGAZ, South Bend, IN, 1924).

15113 Holstead, Grace. Soprano (WCAL, Northfield, MN, 1926).

15114 Holt, Alva. COM-HE (KOTN, Pine Bluff, AR, 1956).

15115 Holt, Anita. Violinist (KFI, Los Angeles, CA, 1926).

15116 Holt, Dorothy. COM-HE (WTMC, Ocala, FL, 1960).

15117 Holt, Elissa. COM-HE (WHAW, Weston, WV, 1957).

15118 Holt, Fred. Newscaster (WOWO, Ft. Wayne, IN, 1944; WIRE, Indianapolis, IN, 1946–1947; WCKY, Cincinnati, OH, 1948).

15119 Holt, H. Rush. Sportscaster (WOLS, Florence, SC, 1940; WGGA , Gainesville, FL, 1946). Newscaster (WOLS, 1941–1942, *Inside Washington*, WHAW, Weston, WV, 1948).

15120 Holt, Jeff. DJ (WSSO, Starkville, MS, 1956).

15121 Holt, Jim. DJ (WICE, Providence, RI, 1956).

15122 Holt, Leah. COM-HE (KWJJ, Portland, OR, 1954).

15123 Holt, Mildred. Soprano (WOR, Newark, NJ, 1929).

15124 Holter, Louise. Soprano (WBBC, Brooklyn, NY, 1930).

15125 Holton, Bob. Actor Holton was in the cast of *Dr. Paul.*

15126 Holton, Brick. Tenor (*Brick Holton*, vcl. mus. prg., NBC, 1935).

15127 Holton, Erwin. Tenor (KTAB, Oakland, CA, 1925).

15128 Holton, Peck. Leader (Peck Holton's Orchestra, KGW, Chicago, IL, 1924).

15129 Holtz, Ruth. Soprano (WJY, New York, NY, 1924).

15130 Holtz, Thomas. Newscaster (WDAF, Kansas City, MO, 1942).

15131 Holtz, Thomson. DJ (*Pot Luck*, WOW, Omaha, NE, 1948).

15132 Holtzman, Pearl. Pianist (WIBO, Chicago, IL, 1926).

15133 Holub, Josephine. Violinist (KGO, Oakland, CA, 1925).

15134 Holzberg, William. Violinist (WNYC, New York, NY, 1925).

15135 Holzhauser, Krin. Newscaster-actress Holzhauser after graduating from Louisiana State University was hired by a Shreveport, Louisiana, station as a diction coach. She began her own broadcasting career by doing a few commercials and some dramatic radio roles. After this, she began her newscasting career on KWKH (Shreveport, LA). She performed heroic duties in the 1940s when a cyclone hit an area 40 miles from Shreveport to the sea by broadcasting for 63 hours with only black coffee to keep her going. She was sent out on the job to cover the story, she said, because only herself and one man were available (Holzhauser, 1978). "They never would have taken a woman [otherwise] in those days, you know." Some of her work covering the cyclone was a network feed.

15136 Homan, Virginia. Pianist (KWK, St. Louis, MO, 1936).

15137 Home, Clare. COM-HE (KELO, Sioux Falls, SD, 1955).

15138 Home Brew Orchestra. A country-western music group from Decatur, Texas (WBAP, San Antonio, TX, 1923).

15139 *Home Care of the Sick*. Unidentified performers appeared on the sustaining show that included both an informative talk and a dramatic sketch (15 min., Monday, 11:00–11:15 A.M., WLW, Cincinnati, OH, 1933).

15140 *Home Decoration*. Economics expert Grace Vaill Gray broadcast decorative information and the J. Oliver Riehl Orchestra provided music on the weekly program (15 min., Thursday, 4:00–4:15 P.M., WJZ, New York, NY, 1932).

15141 *Home Economics*. Jeanette Cramer was the home economics specialist on the program (KGW, Portland, OR, 1924).

15142 *Home Economics Talk*. Vivette Gorman delivered talks for women (KYW, Chicago, IL, 1924).

15143 *Home Edition*. Albert W. Warner and Robert Gardner broadcast the news on the quarter-hour program (15 min., WOR, Newark, NJ, 1947).

15144 *Home Folks Frolic*. CW mus. prg. by unidentified performers (WCBM, Baltimore, MD, 1939).

15145 *Home Folks Hour*. People flocked from all over Missouri and Illinois to see this program and sit in the audience. The music and comedy was supplied by organist Ken Wright; the Ozark Moutaineers, a five-piece studio band; and comedian-singer Aunt Sarah, who was a hilarious busy body. One example of the selling power of the show was the sales record it set for the Interstate Nurseries of Haburg, Iowa. When the nursery offered ten gladioli bulbs for a quarter, listeners sent in 4,380 quarters, averaging 146 responses daily for 30 consecutive days (90 min., Monday through Saturday, KMOX, St. Louis, MO, 1933).

15146 *Home Folks Jamboree*. CW music prg. by unidentified performers (WHAS, Louisville, KY, 1939).

15147 *Home Helps*. Bernice Redington of the Seattle *Post Intelligencer* staff broadcast household hints for women (KJR, Seattle, WA, 1925).

15148 *Home Hints*. Marjorie Presnell provided informative hints on the women's show (15 min., Thursday, 9:45–10:00 P.M., WOR, Newark, NJ, 1930).

15149 *Home Hour*. Children's program (KMTR, Hollywood, CA, 1920s).

15150 *Home of the Brave*. Joe, a telephone lineman with romantic problems, was the major figure in the daytime serial first broadcast in 1940. The cast included: Jone Allison, Joan Banks, Alan Bunce, Ted de Corsia, Vincent Donehue, Sammie Hill, Ed Latimer, Tom Tully and Richard Widmark. Organ interludes were performed by Charles Paul (CBS, 1940–1941).

15151 *Home Service Club*. Jane Tucker conducted the weekday program that featured different topics daily:

Monday: Fresh fruits and vegetables
Tuesday: Food suggestions and recipes
Wednesday: Parents Forum
Thursday: Food suggestions and recipes
Friday: Home Bureau speakers.

An orchestra and vocalists also appeared on the program (Monday through Friday, WLS, Chicago, IL, 1937).

15152 *Home Sweet Home*. The domestic affairs of Frank and Lucy Kent and their child, as they struggled to attain a *home sweet home* of their own, formed the basis for the story presented on this daytime serial sponsored by Crisco. The major roles were played by Cecil Secrest, Harriet McGibbon and Billy Halop. Joe Latham also appeared on the program. George Ansbro and John Monks were the announcers. The father, played by Secrest, was a salesman in a haberdashery shop, who didn't seem too bright. Perhaps this was the beginning of the portrayal of the bumbling husband on radio, before Blondie's Dagwood made his appearance (15 min., Monday through Friday, 2:30–2:45 P.M., NBC-Blue, 1934).

15153 ***Home Symphony Orchestra.*** Symphonic mus. prg. by an orchestra conducted by Ernest LaPrade (NBC, 1937).

15154 ***(The) Home Town Boys.*** Nu-Enamel Company sponsored the popular singing group formerly known as the Tastyyeast Jesters (15 min., Weekly, 8:45–9:00 A.M., WOR, Newark, NJ, 1935). *See* ***The Tastyyeast Jesters.***

15155 **Homeier, Skippy.** Actor Homeier was in the cast of *Reg'lar Fellers* and *Second Husband.*

15156 ***Homemakers Club of the Air.*** Martha Goldstein, home economist of the Nebraska Power Company, conducted the program (WOW, Omaha, NE, 1943).

15157 ***Homemakers Half Hour.*** Mary Gordon was featured on the program for women (KFOA, Seattle, WA, 1926).

15158 ***Homemakers Hour.*** Pioneer broadcaster Ida Bailey Allen conducted the women's show (WMCA, New York, NY, 1926). *See* **Ida Bailey Allen.**

15159 ***Homemakers Hour.*** Lois Schenck, editor of the *Prairie Farmer* magazine, and Martha Crane hosted the women's program in 1928 on WLS (Chicago, IL). When Schenck returned to her duties at the *Prairie Farmer*, Crane conducted the program alone until 1934. From 1928–1930 nearly 300 persons appeared on the informative program to discuss such topics as baby care, dental care for school pupils, hot school lunches for rural children, rural recreation, running water in homes and good reading. Home economists and commentators such as Mary Wright, Mrs. Walter Buhlig, Martha Crane, Marjorie Gibson and Helen Joyce provided information for women. The program also included entertainment by organist Elsie May Emerson, pianist John Brown, Evelyn Allan, the singing DeZurick Sisters, Roy Anderson and the Hilltoppers among others. Marjorie Gibson delivered the news bulletins, Mrs. William Sherman conducted the book review segment and Sarah Catlin Weig read her original poetry. Even dramatic segments were included in the program. For example, in 1926 the program contained a Little Theater segment with Marian Gray and Ellen Rose Dickey presenting a one-act play, "Cleopatra — Yesterday and Today." The program enjoyed great local popularity for many years in the greater Chicago area (60 min., Saturday, 1:00–2:00 P.M., WLS, Chicago, IL, 1928–1937).

15160 **Homer, Charlotte H.** Pianist (WGY, Schenectady, NY, 1923).

15161 **Homer (Henry Doyle) and Jethro (Kenneth Burns).** CW comedy team consisting of Henry Doyle and Kenneth Burns worked on the Midday Merry-Go-Round (WNOX, Knoxville, TN, 1932–1937) as the String Dusters. Focusing on their song parody comedy routines as Homer and Jethro, they joined the *Renfro Valley Barn Dance* (NBC, 1939). During this period they appeared on several other programs on NBC and CBS. After serving in the armed forces during World War II, they joined WLW (Cincinnati, OH) to appear on its *Plantation Party.* Returning to Chicago, the team became popular Saturday night regulars on the *National Barn Dance* (WLS, Chicago, 1950s) and during the day on the *Breakfast Club* (NBC, 1950s). Around this time Homer and Jethro were frequent guest stars on many network television programs. Famous for their parodies of hit songs, perhaps their best known was "How Much Is That Hound Dog In The Window?"

15162 ***Homespunogram.*** Tex Taylor, the Lone Star Philosopher, read poetry and delivered his home spun philosophy on the popular Philadelphia sustaining program (15 min., Sunday, 11:00–11:15 P.M., KYW, Philadelphia, PA, 1936).

15163 **Homesteaders Orchestra.** The popular orchestra included: Joe Justiana, ldr.-tb.; Ben Paul, reeds; Don La Sclala, reeds and v.; Jack Marsala, bj., v., and g.; Henry Collins, p.; Ernest Finley, d., x. and p.; Frank Pulsmo, g.; and Jack McWhirter, t. and m. (WHAM, Rochester, NY, 1928).

15164 ***Hometown Jamboree.*** CW music show broadcast five days a week on radio (KXLA, Hollywood, CA, 1949 and on Saturday on television (KCOP, Los Angeles, CA, 1949). The show's performers included: Roy Hawke, Billy Liebert, Ray Merrill, Herman the Hermit, Billy West, Al Williams, Tennessee Ernie Ford, Molly Bee, Gene O'Quinn, Jimmy Bryant, Bucky Tibbs, Jonelle McQuade, Joan O'Brien, Harold Hensley, Cliffie Stone, Charlie Aldrich, Joe Maphis, Johnny Horton, Curley Collins, Harry Rodcay, Billy Strange, Larry Tice, and Roy Harte.

15165 ***Hometown Memories.*** Red Foley and Carol Hammond were the featured entertainers on the interesting program that mixed music and human interest features. The Gillette Razor Company sponsored the popular program. Chuck Acree, the Hometown Reporter, gave interesting facts about various towns. For example, on December 25, 1937, Acree told about Santa Claus, Indiana and Christmas, Florida. Other entertainers who appeared were the Hilltoppers, the singing DeZurik Sisters and veteran vocalist Grace Wilson (30 min., Saturday, 9:30–10:00 P.M., WLS, Chicago, IL, 1936–1937).

15166 ***Hometown Reunion.*** The sustaining CW music show featured an excellent cast that included singer Eddy Arnold, the Willis Brothers Trio, Annie, Lou and Danny and the Hometown Band and Choir. The show originated from Nashville (30 min., Saturday, 10:00–10:30 P.M., CBS, 1948).

15167 ***(The) Hometowners.*** Tenors Paul Nettinga and Jack Eliot, baritone-accordionist Phil Kalar and bass William "Rocky" Rachenbaumer comprised the popular CW quartet that sang and played old tunes on various odd instruments (WLS, Chicago, IL, 1936).

15168 ***Honest Harold.*** Gene Stone and Jack Robinson wrote the situation comedy where Harold Peary played the title role of Honest Harold Hemp, a radio announcer on a small town radio station. Peary's role on the sustaining program was much like the one he played on *The Great Gildersleeve.* Other cast members were Parley Baer, Kathryn Card, Gloria Holiday, Joe Kearns, Jane Morgan, Norman Jean Nillson and Anne Whitfield. Jack Meakin supplied the music. The announcer was Bob Lemond (30 min., Sunday, 7:30–8:00 P.M., CBS, 1950).

15169 **Honey Boys' Orchestra.** Local Texas band (WFAA, Dallas, TX, 1926).

15170 **Honey Girls.** Vocal team consisting of Jean East and Carol Lynn (WIBO, Chicago, IL, 1929).

15171 ***Honey Deane.*** Singer (vcl. mus. prg., 30 min., Tuesday, 9:30–10:00 A.M., NBC-Red, 1934).

15172 ***Honeyboy (George Fields) and Sassafras (Bobbye Shreves).*** Blackface comedy team (WGBS, New York, NY, 1929; KSAT, Fort Worth, TX, 1930). Later, Sassafras was played by Johnnie Welsh (15 min., Saturday, 12:15–12:30 P.M., NBC-Red, 1934; 15 min., Monday through Friday, 12:15–12:30 P.M., 1935). The team "worked" at their own Black Panther Detective Agency. Whether the Sassafras character was originated by Shreves or Welsh is uncertain. Honeyboy explained the team's characters in this way: "You see, Sassafras is the levee type of Negro — lean, lanky, active. I am the Alabama blue gum Negro — slow, sloppy, lazy. Humor in Negro skits depends upon three situations. A Negro to be funny must be either broke, hungry or scared and the problem for the creator of blackface comedy is to stick to these situations and still furnish sufficient variety" (*Radio Digest*, March, 1930, p.77).

15173 **Honeychurch, Dick.** Pianist (WSM, Nashville, TN, 1928).

15174 ***Honeyside Minstrels of Riverside.*** E. Robert Jones conducted and directed the early radio minstrel show (WGR, Buffalo, NY, 1926).

15175 **Honolulu Strummers.** The popular band featured "Hawaiian selections" (WHB, Kansas City, MO, 1926).

15176 **Honti, Josef.** Leader (*Josef Honti Orchestra*, instr. mus. prg., NBC-Red, 1934–1936; NBC, 1942).

15177 **Hood, Adelyn.** Primarily a CW singer, Hood was featured with Vernon Dahlhart on the *Bring and Crystal* program (WOR, Newark, NJ, 1934). She also recorded with the popular balladeer.

15178 **Hood, Elmo C.** Pianist (WSM, Nashville, TN, 1928).

15179 **Hood, Ina Harrison.** Contralto (KOW, Denver, CO, 1928).

15180 **Hood, W.P.** Newscaster (KWFT, Wichita Falls, TX, 1939).

15181 ***(The) Hoofinghams.*** Murray Forbes and Helene Page played the title roles of a married, ex-vaudeville team now retired on the sustaining situation comedy. Arthur Jacobson and Mignon Schreiber were also in the cast of the entertaining show (15 min., Monday-Wednesday-Friday, 11:45–12:00 noon, NBC-Red, 1935).

15182 **Hoogenhouse, Mary.** COM-HE (WCOW, Sparta, WI, 1956–1957).

15183 **Hook, Henry "Hank."** Newscaster (KGLO, Mason City, IA, 1937–1939).

15184 **Hook, J. Nelson.** Singer (WLW, Cincinnati, OH, 1923).

15185 Hook and Jerome. Singing team specializing in harmony songs (WJZ, New York, NY, 1924).

15186 *Hook, Line and Sinker.* The Entz and Rucker Sports Shop sponsored the informative show for fishermen. The program featured talks by outdoors authority Calvin B. Harrison on how to catch fish and provided a "Forum for Fibbing Fishermen" (KEHE, Los Angeles, CA, 1937).

15187 Hooke, Winifred. Pianist (KFI, Los Angeles, CA, 1927).

15188 Hooker, Joe. Newscaster (WLAV, Grand Rapids, MI, 1944–1945; *Breakfast Table News*, WGRD, Grand Rapids, MI, 1948). Sportscaster (WLAV, 1944).

15189 Hooks, Mary. COM-HE (KLVT, Levelland, TX, 1960).

15190 Hoon, (Reverend) Carl. Minister of the Hyde Park Methodist Episcopal Church, Cincinnati, OH, who appeared on the *Thrift Talk* program (WLW, Cincinnati, OH, 1926).

15191 Hooper, Hale. Ballad singer (KTM, Santa Monica, CA, 1928).

15192 Hooper, Jack. Sportscaster (WMBG, Richmond, VA, 1939–1941; *Sports Observer*, WHGB, Harrisburg, PA, 1947–1948; *Report on Sports*, WHGB, 1949–1954). Newscaster (WHGB, 1942).

15193 Hooper, Opal. Saxophonist (WEMC, Barrien Springs, MI, 1925).

15194 Hoopii, Sol. Leader (Sol Hoopii's Hawaiian Trio, KFWB, Hollywood, CA, 1925; Sol Hoopii's Hawaiians, a popular music group, KFWB, 1926).

15195 *Hoosier Hop* aka *WOWO Hoosier Hop.* CW mus. prg. (WOWO, Fort Wayne, IN, 1932; CBS, 1932; NBC, 1939–1940, 1945–1946). First originated at WOWO, the *Hoosier Hop* twice appeared on the NBC network schedule and once on CBS. "Happy Herb" Hayworth was the MC. He was assisted by ventriloquist George Troxel and his "dummy" Danny O'Grady, Nancy Lee and the Hilltoppers, Penny West, Andy Anderson, the Harmony Twins, comedian Uncle Fezz, Judy and Jen, the Blackhawk Valley Quartet and yodeler Kenny Roberts.

15196 *Hoosier Hot Shots and Arkie.* The Hoosier Hot Shots novelty music group first appeared on WOWO (Ft. Wayne, IN). They joined the staff of WLS in 1933 and were heard regularly on the *National Barn Dance*, *Station E-Z-R-A* and other WLS programs. The group consisted of Hezzie Trietsch, Ken Trietsch, Gabe Ward and Gil Taylor.

15197 *(The) Hoosier Housewarmers.* Mus. prg. by otherwise unidentified performers (WLW, Cincinnati, OH, 1937).

15198 *Hoosier Merrymakers and Grandpa Jones.* The CW music program featured a lively music group and the talented Louis Marshall "Grandpa" Jones at the beginning of his career (WWVA, Wheeling, WV, 1936). *See* ***Grandpa Jones.***

15199 *Hoosier Philosopher.* Carlton Clay played the role of Cobadiah Quakenbush, the Hoosier Philosopher, who talked about local, state, national and world events with a warm, homey view point (15 min., Tuesday-Thursday-Saturday, 7:00–7:15 A.M. CST, WLS, Chicago, IL, 1938).

15200 *Hoosier Poet.* Frank Carleton Nelson read his original poetry on the weekly show (15 min., Sunday, 10:30–10:45 A.M., WLS, Chicago, IL, 1937).

15201 *Hoosier Songster.* Vcl. mus. prg. by an unidentified performer (WOWO, Fort Wayne, IN, 1933).

15202 *Hoosierland Barn Dance* aka *WLBC Hoosierland Barn Dance.* CW musical program *Hoosierland Barn Dance* (WLBC, Muncie, IN, 1952) featured Chuck Smith, Jesse Rhode, the Midwestern Trailriders, the Brown County Jamboree Gang, Georgie Riddle, Van and Lorraine Spears and the Western Swing Boys.

15203 (The) Hoot Owls (Orchestra). Musical group featured on the *Pantages Frolic Program* aka the *Hoot Owls Lodge* or the *Hoot Owl Club* program (KGW, Portland, OR, 1924). *See* ***The Hoot Owls Lodge.***

15204 Hoot Owls Dance Orchestra. Popular local dance orchestra (KFOB, Burlingame, CA, 1926).

15205 *(The) Hoot Owls Lodge* (aka *Hoot Owl Club* or *The Pantages Frolic Program*). The unusual variety program was typical of the "wild" and "zany" late evening shows of the period. The program was broadcast simultaneously on two stations from 1923 to 1925 (KGW, Portland, OR and KHQ, Spokane, WA, 10:30 P.M. to midnight). The first programs were broadcast to a remote audience of 600 persons who were eating an eight-course meal. They supposedly were listening to a "lodge meeting" of the Hoot Owls. The program essentially provided an audio floor show for its dining listeners, who heard Pantages vaudeville acts, comedians, musicians and singers. Soprano Kathleen Duffy and vaudeville singer Helen Lewis often appeared on the lively show. The Hoot Owls Orchestra were program regulars.

15206 Hoover, (Mrs.) Elizabeth. Pianist (WBZ, Springfield, MA, 1923).

15207 Hoover, Faye. COM-HE (WBCR, Christianburg, VA, 1956).

15208 Hoover, Helen. Soprano (KJR, Seattle, WA, 1928).

15209 Hoover, Ione. Violinist (WHAS, Louisville, KY, 1926).

15210 Hoover, Jo. COM-HE (WNCT, Greenville, NC, 1955).

15211 Hoover, Mary Josephine. COM-HE (WNCT, Greenville, NC, 1956).

15212 Hoover, Roberta. COM-HE (WLDS, Jacksonville, IL, 1955).

15213 (The) Hoover Orchestra. The Hoover Orchestra was a music group directed by Louis Katzman, featuring the Katzman family: Louis' son Henry played the piano at times and his father Philip Katzman played the cornet (NBC, 1927–1929).

15214 *(The) Hoover Sentinels.* Hoover Vacuum Cleaners Company sponsored the music program featuring the Chicago a Cappella Choir and the Joseph Koestner Orchestra (NBC, 1934).

15215 Hope, Bob. Newscaster (WSFA, Montgomery, AL, 1940–1942). DJ (*WGMA Party*, WGMA, Hollywood, FL, 1954).

15216 Hope, Edward S. Newscaster (KGB, San Diego, CA, 1945).

15217 Hope, Emma. Soprano (WWJ, Detroit, MI, 1924).

15218 Hope, Helen. COM-HE (WHYN, Holyoke, MA, 1951).

15219 Hope, May McDonald. Pianist (KNX, Hollywood, CA, 1926).

15220 Hope, Winkie. DJ (*Midnight Ballroom*, WTAR, Norfolk, VA, 1948–1950).

15221 Hope Orchestra. Mrs. Faye F. Hope directed the orchestra whose member's ages ranged from 12 to 18 years. The musicians included: saxophonist Velma Reynolds; cornetists Howard Williams and Vernon Alexander; clarinetist Charles Warriner; violinists Claude Haskins and Earl Williams; and trombonist Sanford Hope (WOK, Pine Bluff, AR, 1922).

15222 Hopkins, A.F. Newscaster (WJEF, Grand Rapids, MI, 1944).

15223 Hopkins, Al. Leader (Al Hopkins and the Hillbillies, a country music group, WRC, Washington, DC, 1925–1928). The Hopkins group consisting entirely of musicians born in the mountain counties of North Carolina and Virginia: Al Hopkins, Joe Hopkins, Tony Alderman and John Rector. They were the first hillbilly group to settle in Washington, DC, and appear regularly on radio in that city. At that time a recording company executive gave them the name of the "original" hillbillies and under that name they became local Washington, DC, favorites.

15224 Hopkins, Claude. Leader (*Claude Hopkins Orchestra*, mus. prg., CBS, 1934–1935; MBS, 1936).

15225 Hopkins, Doctor Howard "Doc." CW singer-musician "Doc" Hopkins along with Karl Davis and Harry Taylor as the Krazy Kats broadcast on WHAS (Louisville, KY, 1931). When he moved to Chicago he joined the Cumberland Ridge Runners and performed on the *National Barn Dance* (WLS, Chicago, IL). He was featured on the *Suppertime Frolic* (WJJD, Chicago, IL, 1935). Hopkins returned to WLS to work on the *National Barn Dance* once more and have his own show.

15226 Hopkins, Don. Newscaster (WRJN, Racine, WI, 1937; WIBW, Topeka, KS, 1944).

15227 Hopkins, Dorothy. COM-HE (KDRO, Sedalia, MO, 1956).

15228 Hopkins, Gordon. Sportscaster (KXA, Seattle, WA, 1939).

15229 Hopkins, John. Newscaster (WLAV, Grand Rapids, MI, 1940).

15230 Hopkins, John. Newscaster (KFJZ, Fort Worth, TX, 1940, 1945–1946).

15231 Hopkins, L.T. [L.L.]. Book reviewer Hopkins conducted the *A Few Minutes with New Books* program (WGY, Schenectady, NY, 1924–1925).

15232 Hopkins, Lyman. Sportscaster (KGY, Olympia, WA, 1950s).

15233 Hopkins, Phil. Newscaster (WRR, Dallas, TX, 1938).

15234 Hopkins, Ross. Dancer, banjoist and singer (WJBL, Decatur, IL, 1926).

15235 Hopkins, Wes. Newscaster (WTTM, Trenton, NJ, 1944). DJ (*920 Club* and *Lucas Bandstand*, WTTM, 1948; *Name It and Play It*, WTTM, 1950–1955; WCOL, Columbus, OH, late 1950s).

15236 Hopkinson, Sarah. Contralto (WFAA, Dallas, TX, 1927).

15237 Hoppenstein, Archie. Newscaster (KWBU, Corpus Christi, TX, 1946).

15238 Hopper, Hedda. Hollywood columnist Hopper specialized in Hollywood news and gossip (NBC-Blue, 1944; ABC, 1945).

15239 Hopper, John. Pianist (KJR, Seattle, WA, 1928).

15240 Hopple, Mary. Contralto (*NBC Light Opera Company*,1928; *Philco Hour ofTheater Memories*, NBC-Blue, New York, NY, and the *Armstrong Quakers* program, NBC-Blue, 1929).

15241 Hopps, Hiram. DJ (*WOLF Buckaroos*, WOLF, Syracuse, NY, 1947).

15242 Hopton, Tommy. Leader (*Tommy Hopton Orchestra*, instr. mus. prg., WTAM, Cleveland, OH, 1937).

15243 *Horace Heidt's Brigadiers*. Orchestra leader Heidt's music program featured the Heidt band and the King Sisters (Louise, Donna, Alyce and Yvonne Diggs) vocal group (30 min., Tuesday, 10:00–10:30 P.M. CBS).

15244 *Horace Heidt's Treasure Chest*. The Lewis-Howe Company sponsored this small quiz show, a companion to Heidt's more famous *Pot of Gold* program (30 min., Tuesday, 8:30–9:00 P.M., NBC-Red, 1940).

15245 Horan, Edna. Violinist (KPO, San Francisco, CA, 1925).

15246 *Horatio Hornblower*. Phil Higley adapted and wrote the action filled adventure series based on the novels of C.S. Forester. The fine transcribed series was produced and directed by Harry Alan Towers and starred Michael Redgrave. Music was provided by Sidney Torch's Orchestra (30 min., 8:00–8:30 P.M., Transcribed, ABC, 1952).

15247 Horich, Harry. Leader (Harry Horich's Orchestra, KSD, St. Louis, MO, 1926).

15248 Horgan, W.S. Announcer (WGBF, Evansville, IN, 1927).

15249 Horley, Harry. Musical director, *Stars of Melody* program (NBC-Red, New York, NY, 1929).

15250 Horlick, Harry. Leader (A&P Gypsies Orchestra, WOO, Philadelphia, PA, 1925; leader, Harry Horlick's Peerless Reproducers, WEAF, New York, NY, 1928; conductor of the orchestra on the *Stars of Melody* show, 1929). In the next decade Horlick was equally busy: (*Harry Horlick Orchestra*, instr. mus. prg., KUOA, Siloam Springs, AR, 1934; NBC, 1935; KSD, St. Louis, MO, 1940; KSAL, Salinas, KS, 1942; *Harry Horlick's A&P Gypsies*, instr. mus. prg., NBC, 1935). *See* ***The A&P Gypsies***.

15251 Horn, Arthur Van. Newscaster (WOR, New York, NY, 1941).

15252 Horn, Bob. DJ (*Midnight Bandwagon*, WIP, Philadelphia, PA, 1947; *Valley Forge Stardust Time*, WFIL, Philadelphia, PA, 1949).

15253 Horn, Bob. DJ (KIMA, Yakima, WA, 1949; *1460 Club*, KIMA, 1952).

15254 Horn, Elaine. COM-HE (KPUG, Bellingham, WA, 1957).

15255 Horn, Eleanor. Pianist (WSM, Nashville, TN, 1928).

15256 Horn, Reba. COM-HE (WIEL, Elizabethtown, KY, 1956).

15257 Horn, Robert. Newscaster (WCAM, Camden, NJ, 1938–1939).

15258 Horn, Robert. Newscaster (WPAY, Portsmouth, OH, 1939; WMAN, Mansfield, OH, 1940–1942, 1944–1945).

15259 *Horn and Hardart Children's Hour*. Sponsored by Horn and Hardart's automated restaurants (colloquially known as the automats), this Philadelphia local program was on the air for 29 years. Begun in the early 1930s, the program presented for the first time many child performers who became show business stars. Although Ralph Edwards and Paul Douglas also hosted the program, Ed Herlihy, who performed the chore for 17 years, is most often associated with the program. Alice Clements wrote, produced and directed the show. Among the performers who appeared on the program were: the Blackstone Twins, Carol Bruce, "Termite" Daniels, Billy Daniels, Paul Douglas (Host-Announcer), Ralph Edwards (Host-Announcer), Eddie Fisher, Connie Francis, Joey Heatherton, Ed Herlihy (Host-Announcer), Bobby Hookey, Mortimer Howard, Roy Langer, Arthur Q. Lewis, Marion Loveridge, Nicholas Brothers, Arnold Stang and Bea Wain. The piano accompanist was W.M. "Billie" James. The program was a great radio favorite for some 29 years (WCAU, Philadelphia, PA, 1930s to 1950s).

15260 Hornaday, John R. Newscaster (WFAA, Dallas, TX, 1945; WLAQ, Rome, GA, 1947).

15261 Hornbecker, Gloria Jean. COM-HE (WING, Dayton, OH, 1951).

15262 Horne, George D. Singer (WLS, Chicago, IL, 1924).

15263 Horner, Gordon. Sportscaster (*Your Sportscaster*, KTRI, Sioux City, IA, 1940).

15264 Horner, Jack. Sportscaster (KILO, Grand Forks, ND, 1942; KSAL, Salinas, KS, 1944–1945; KSTP, St. Paul–Minneapolis, MN, 1946–1948; *Horner's Corner*, KSTP, 1951; WTCM, Minneapolis, MN, 1960).

15265 Horner, Marion. Contralto (WBZ, Springfield, MA, 1926).

15266 Horning, Dutch. Sportscaster (*Hornin' in on Sports*, KSIB, Creston, IA, 1947–1949).

15267 Horning, E.F. Announcer (WGR, Buffalo, NY, 1925).

15268 Horning, June. COM-HE (WALA, Mobile, AL, 1956).

15269 Hornik, Joseph. Austrian concert violinist and orchestral conductor (San Francisco stations, 1929–1930).

15270 *(The) Horoscope Program*. Famous astrologist Evangeline Adams discussed the significance of horoscopes on the program she conducted. *See* **Adams, Evangeline.**

15271 Horowitz, Fanny. Pianist (WGCP, Newark, NJ, 1925).

15272 Horowitz, Willie. Horowitz performed in various comedy sketches (WMBB, Chicago, IL, 1926).

15273 *Horse Fly and His Wranglers*. Fiddler and singer Horse Fly, not otherwise identified, was the leader of the CW group that featured cowboy music and fun (KNX, Hollywood, CA. 1930).

15274 *Horse Sense Philosophy*. Andrew Kelly as the "Philosopher" combined a homey down to earth philosophy with good humor. Kelly played Mr. Dooley, the proprietor of a country store. He talked with Danny, a young man who came into the store each week. Mr. Dooley talked about the problems of the world in general and economic ones in particular (15 min., Sunday, 7:15–7:30 P.M., NBC-Red, 1933; 15 min., Sunday, 5:45–6:00 P.M., NBC, 1935).

15275 *Horseshoe Mike and Cowboy Joe*. CW mus. prg. by a singing team that specialized in cowboy songs (WWVA, Wheeling, WV, 1936; WEEU, Boston, MA, 1942).

15276 Horstman, Bob. Sportscaster (*You and Conservation*, KFEQ, St. Joseph, MO, 1955–1956; *Sportswatch*, KFEQ, MO, 1960).

15277 Horstmeir, Franklin. Bass (WGES, Oak Park, IL, 1925).

15278 Horten, Marie. COM-HE (KELO, Sioux Falls, SD, 1951).

15279 Horton, Harlan. Newscaster (*Under the Capitol Dome*, KOTA, Rapid City, SD, 1948).

15280 Horton, Marie. COM-HE (KELO, Sioux Falls, SD, 1949).

15281 Horton, Marjorie. Soprano on *The Wrigley Review* program (1928).

15282 Horton, Murray. Leader (Murray Horton Dance Orchestra, WLW, Cincinnati, OH, 1924;. *Murray Horton Orchestra*, instr. mus. prg., WLW, Cincinnati, OH, 1931; WLW, 1934; WOR, Newark, NJ, 1935).

15283 Horton, R.J. Horton, the Director of the Detroit YMCA, broadcast a setting-up exercise program (WWJ, Detroit, MI, 1925).

15284 Horton, Ted. Newscaster (WGBR, Goldsboro, NC, 1939).

15285 Horvet, June. COM-HE (KGHF, Pueblo, CO, 1956).

15286 Horwitz Brothers Orchestra. Los Angeles dance band (KFQZ, Hollywood, CA, 1927).

15287 Hoskins, Phyllis. COM-HE (WMMB, Melbourne, FL, 1956).

15288 Hoskins, Roy. Newscaster (KTOK, Oklahoma City, 1942).

15289 Hosley, Pat. Actress Hosley was a cast member of the *Brighter Day* daytime serial program.

15290 Hosmer, Dan. Actor Hosmer was in the cast of *Pa and Ma Smithers*.

15291 Hosmer, (Mrs.) Page. Book reviewer (KMO, Tacoma, WA, 1929).

15292 Hot Foot Orchestra. Local jazz band (WJAD, Waco, TX, 1926).

15293 Hot Harlemite Orchestra. John G. Smith directed the hot jazz band (WGBS, New York, NY, 1929).

15294 *Hot 'n' Kold Shops Review.* Kold [Food] Shops sponsored the variety program hosted by Al Pearce. A few years later Pearce went on to demonstrate his comic skills on network programs (KFRC, San Francisco, CA, 1928). *See **The Al Pearce Show and His Gang.***

15295 *(The) Hot Spot of Radio.* Henry Starr's piano playing and singing was featured on the music show (15 min., 10:30–10:45 P.M., NBC, 1930).

15296 Hotaling, Earl. Newscaster (WBTM, Danville, VA, 1942). Sportscaster (WBTM, 1942; WBTM, 1945).

15297 *Hotan Tonka.* A member of the Chippewa (Ojibway) Indian tribe, Hotan Tonka told various Indian legends and tales three times a week. His informative program combined nature study, historic facts and Indian legends (Monday-Wednesday-Friday, WLS, Chicago, IL, 1935–1936).

15298 Hotchkiss, Tom. Newscaster (KTUC, Tucson, AZ, 1940).

15299 Hotel Alms Orchestra. Local Cincinnati hotel dance band (WKRC, Cincinnati, OH, 1926).

15300 Hotel Ambassador Concert Orchestra. Hotel band (WPG, Atlantic City, NJ, 1926).

15301 Hotel Astor Orangtine Orchestra. New York hotel band (WJZ, New York, NY, 1926).

15302 Hotel Band Trio. Instrumental group (WTIC, Hartford, CT, 1926).

15303 Hotel Bossert Marine Roof Orchestra. Hotel dance band (WEAF, New York, NY, 1925).

15304 *Hotel Bossert Orchestra.* Instr. mus. prg. (WABC, New York, NY, 1931; WNAC, Boston, MA, 1932; WEAN, Providence, RI, 1932).

15305 Hotel Bretton Hall String Quartet. Instrumental group (WOR, Newark, NJ, 1926).

15306 Hotel Brunswick Orchestra. Hotel dance band (WBZ, Springfield, MA, 1925).

15307 Hotel Chicsa Philharmonic Orchestra. Miss Clara Ahern directed the hotel band (WMC, Memphis, TN, 1923).

15308 Hotel Cleveland Orchestra. Hotel band directed by Ivan Francisi (WEAR, Cleveland, OH, 1925).

15309 Hotel Commodore Concert Orchestra. Hotel orchestra (WJZ, New York, NY, 1925–1926).

15310 Hotel Gayoso Orchestra. Prof. Gasper Pappalardo conducted the hotel orchestra (WMC, Memphis, TN, 1924).

15311 Hotel George Washington Orchestra. John Lucy directed the popular local band (WJAX, Jacksonville, FL, 1929).

15312 Hotel Gibson Orchestra. Cincinnati hotel orchestra directed by Robert Visconti (WLW, Cincinnati, OH, 1925–1926).

15313 Hotel Kimball Orchestra. Springfield, MA, hotel band (WBZ, Boston-Springfield, MA, 1926).

15314 Hotel Kimball Trio. Violinist Jan Gaerts led the trio that also included Arnold Janser, cellist and Lloyd Stoneman, pianist (WBZ, Boston-Springfield, MA, 1924).

15315 Hotel La Salle Orchestra. Chicago hotel band (WMAQ, Chicago, IL, 1926).

15316 Hotel Lassen Orchestra. Local dance band (KFH, Wichita, KS, 1926).

15317 Hotel Lenox Ensemble. Springfield, MA, hotel orchestra (WBZ, Springfield, MA, 1926).

15318 *Hotel Lexington Dance Orchestra.* Instr. mus. prg. (WEAF, New York, NY, 1933).

15319 Hotel Lorraine Grill Orchestra. New York City hotel band (WOR, Newark, NJ, 1925; WJZ, New York, NY, 1926).

15320 Hotel Lowry Orchestra. Hotel band led by Morris Jeffry (WCCO, Minneapolis–St. Paul, MI, 1928).

15321 Hotel Majestic Dance Orchestra. New York City hotel band (WJZ, New York, NY, 1924).

15322 Hotel Manger Dance Orchestra. Howard Phillips directed the Denver dance band (KOA, Denver, CO, 1929; *Hotel Manger Orchestra,* 30 min., Wednesday, 11:00–11:30 P.M.; WDAF, Kansas City, MO, 1930).

15323 Hotel Manitowoc Jazzters. Fourman orchestra led by Al Ehnert, who was identified by *Radio Digest* (November, 1930) as the "Paul Ash of Manitowoc, Wisconsin" (WOMT, Manitowoc, WI, 1929).

15324 Hotel Mayflower Orchestra. Washington hotel band (WRC, Washington, DC, 1926).

15325 Hotel McAlpin Orchestra. New York City hotel orchestra led by Ernie Golden (WMCA, New York, NY, 1926; *Hotel McAlpin Orchestra*, instr. mus. prg., WEAF, New York, NY, 1933).

15326 Hotel Morton Dinner Music. Hotel orchestra (WPG, Atlantic City, NJ, 1926).

15327 Hotel Onandaga Orchestra. Local dance band (WGY, Schenectady, NY, 1926).

15328 *Hotel Paramount Orchestra.* Instr. mus. prg. (30 min., Friday and Saturday, 6:00–6:30 P.M., CBS, 1930).

15329 Hotel Pennsylvania Concert Orchestra. New York City hotel band (WJZ, New York, NY, 1926).

15330 Hotel Pennsylvania Dance Orchestra. Directed by Louis Baer (WCAU, Philadelphia, PA, 1926).

15331 Hotel President String Ensemble. Hotel concert group (WDAF, Kansas City, MO, 1928).

15332 Hotel Richmond Orchestra. Popular Richmond, VA, band (WRVA, Richmond, VA, 1928).

15333 Hotel Richmond Winter Garden Orchestra. Hotel dance band (WRVA, Richmond, VA, 1926).

15334 Hotel St. Francis Concert Orchestra. Edward J. Fitzpatrick directed the hotel band (KGO, Oakland, CA, 1929).

15335 *Hotel St. Regis Orchestra.* Instr. mus. prg. of dance music announced by Martin [Marthin] Provensen (60 min, Friday, 11:00–12:00 P.M., NBC-Red, 1930).

15336 Hotel Sinton Dance Orchestra. Cincinnati hotel dance band (WWJ, Detroit, MI, 1923).

15337 *Hotel Shelton Orchestra.* Mischa Raginsky directed the orchestra in a program of concert music (30 min., Thursday and Saturday, 6:00–6:30 P.M., CBS, 1930).

15338 Hotel Statler Concert Orchestra. Maurice Spitalny conducted the Cleveland hotel orchestra (WTAM, Cleveland, OH, 1928).

15339 Hotel Stevens Symphony Orchestra. Joseph Gallicchio conducted this symphonic orchestra (WMAQ, Chicago, IL, 1928).

15340 *Hotel Taft Orchestra.* Instr., mus. prg. (WABC, New York, NY, 1931; WAAB, Boston, MA, 1932).

15341 Hotel Traymore Grill Dance Orchestra. Atlantic City hotel dance orchestra led by Doc Daughterty (WPG, Atlantic City, NJ, 1926).

15342 Hotel Van Curler Orchestra. New York City hotel band (WGY, Schenectady, NY, 1926).

15343 Hotel Washington Orchestra. Washington dance band (WRC, Washington, DC, 1926).

15344 Hotel Winthrop Dinner Hour Orchestra. Kansas City, MO, hotel band (KMO, Tacoma, WA, 1928).

15345 Hott, Nora. COM-HE (KDFY, Brookings, SD, 1937).

15346 Hottelet, Richard C. News analyst (CBS, 1944–1948).

15347 Houchins, Ken. Singer (*Ken Houchins*, vcl. mus. prg., WIND, Gary, IN, 1935).

15348 Houck, Joe. Singer (*Joe Houck*, vcl. mus. prg., WORK, York, PA, 1936).

15349 Houdek, (Mrs.) Carl. Whistler (WOC, Davenport, IA, 1928).

15350 Houfberg, Holly. DJ (*Holly's Sun-Up Follies*, KLIX, Twin Falls, ID, 1949).

15351 Hough, Bob. DJ (*Off the Record*, KVNI, Coeur d'Alene, ID, 1954). Sportscaster (*Sports Eye View*, KVNI, 1954–1955).

15352 Hough, Harold (aka "The Hired Hand" and "HH"). Hough was born in Kansas in 1887. As a boy he lost a foot when dragged under a train. At 27, he became circulation manager of the Fort Worth *Star-Telegram*, the newspaper that owned station WBAP (Fort Worth, TX). In 1922 the chief—and only—announcer at WBAP was Cam Arnoux. When Arnoux had to go to the hospital for surgery, Hough volunteered to do the station's announcing.

A man with a keen sense of humor, Hough soon attained national popularity. His on the air personality elicited enthusiastic responses from listeners. He identified himself on the air as "HH." When he was asked by listeners what it meant, Hough answered, "Hired Hand," someone who was merely filling-in until Arnoux returned. From then on the station billed him as "The Hired Hand." When Arnoux returned to work, Hough continued his announcing duties.

Arnoux and Hough were responsible for one of the major gimmicks of radio — the phony "feud" — that performers frequently employed in the decades that followed. Hough and Arnoux planned and carried out their "feud" to the amusement of their listeners. Another of Hough's many activities was his role as President of the Radio Truth Society that enrolled ten thousand members, whose purpose was "... to see that the truth is not abused or overworked (*Radio Digest,* March 10, 1927)." Hough's career at WBAP both as announcer and executive was a long and successful one that afforded him numerous opportunities to open and close programs with the trademark sound of cowbells, symbolic of the great southwest Texas cattle empires.

15353 **Houghton, James.** Baritone, (KLDS, Indianapolis, IN, 1926).

15354 **Houglum, Mimi.** COM-HE (KUGN, Eugene, OK,1954).

15355 **Houle, Julette.** Pianist (WEEI, Boston, MA, 1928).

15356 **Houlihan, Bill.** DJ (*Dawnbuster*, WWXL, Peoria, IL, 1947).

15357 ***(The) Hour Glass.*** The Harold Sanford Orchestra, chorus and soloists performed light opera and musical comedy music on the weekly show (60 min., Monday, 10:00–11:00 P.M., NBC, 1933).

15358 ***(An) Hour in Memory Lane.*** The interesting music program directed by Jerome Stewartson presented specially selected favorite music for each age — grandfather, grandmother, mother, father and children (NBC-Pacific Coast Network, 1927).

15359 ***Hour of Charm.*** The music program featured Phil Spitalny and his All-Girl Orchestra. It is said that when Spitalny heard violinist Evelyn Kaye Klein play, he got the idea of an all-girl band. He formed the band and featured Miss Klein as "Evelyn and her Magic Violin" and later married her. Beginning in 1935, his all-girl orchestra was sponsored by General Electric on NBC. Arlene Francis acted as the program's mistress of ceremonies for many years, as did Rosaline Greene. Some other featured members of the Spitalny band were cornetist Katharine Smith, percussionist Viola Schmidt and vocalists Jeannie, Maxine and Vivien. The program's writer was Alton Alexander and the director was Joseph Ripley. Ron Rawson and Richard Stark were the announcers (NBS and CBS, 1935–1948).

15360 ***Hour of Decision.*** The Reverend Dr. Billy Graham, the most popular American evangelist of the time, was a regular on radio during the 1950s. He was assisted by George Beverly Shea, the Crusade Choir and Jerry Beavan, the Crusade's newscaster. Graham's dedication, magnetism and oratorical skills were apparent in all of his programs (*Hour of Decision,* ABC, MBS, NBC, 1953–1963).

15361 ***Hour of Musical Gems.*** Music for the show was provided by the Pacific Salon Orchestra conducted by Liborius Hauptmann with vocals by Dorothy Lewis, Elbert Bellows and Albert Gillette (NBC-Pacific Coast Network, 1929).

15362 ***Hour on Broadway.*** The 60-minute late evening music program's performers included tenor Sidney Dixon, soprano Agatha Turley, contralto Ellen Reep, baritone Jean Kantner and the Broadway Trio (KGA, Spokane, WA, 1929).

15363 **House, Bromley.** Baritone (*Bromley House*, vcl. mus. prg., NBC, 1937).

15364 **House, Colonel.** Announcer House on WMBB (Chicago, IL, 1926) broadcast the station's slogan, "World's Most Beautiful Ballroom."

15365 **House, Eddie.** Singing organist (*Eddie House*, instr. and vcl. mus. prg., CBS, 1935–1937). House played the organ on the *Myrt and Marge* daytime serial program.

15366 **House, Edwin.** Baritone (WMBB, Chicago, IL, 1926).

15367 **House, Judson.** Tenor House was featured on *The Stars of Melody* program (NBC-Red, New York, 1928).

15368 **House, Lee.** Leader (The Lee House Trio broadcast dinner music, WRC, Washington, DC, 1925).

15369 **House, Marguerite.** Cellist (KVOO, Tulsa, OK, 1928).

15370 **House, Mary Thrash.** Pianist (WQJ, Chicago, IL, 1926).

15371 ***House by the Side of the Road.*** Music, inspirational poetry and prose were the major elements of the program sponsored by the S.C. Johnson and Sons Company. Tony Wons spoke most of the soft words. *Variety* observed that Wons provided tacky poetry and homey philosophy. The singing team of Ronnie and Van contributed songs and comedy. Baritone Emery Darcy and soprano Ginna Vanna sang accompanied by an orchestra conducted by Ulderico Marcelli. Guest stars such as Xavier Cugat and Carmen Castello frequently appeared (NBC, 1934–1935).

15372 ***(A) House in the Country.*** On the sustaining daytime serial, a young married couple, played by John Raby and Frances Chaney, moved to the country after living for a year in a small city apartment. They found a suitable house and rented it from their landlord, played by Parker Fennelly, for $30 a month. The program dramatized the many problems they encountered. Other members of the cast were Joan Banks, Patsy Campbell and Ray Knight, who also wrote the program. Lyle Sudrow later replaced John Raby. Joseph S. Bell produced the show, whose announcers were Bud Collyer and Hugh James (15 min., Monday through Friday, 10:30–10:45 A.M., NBC-Blue, 1941).

15373 ***(The) House of Glass.*** Gertrude Berg wrote and directed this forerunner of *The Goldbergs* program. Sponsored by the Colgate-Palmolive Company, the story told of life in a small country hotel (Wednesday, 8:30–9:00 P.M., NBC-Blue, 1935). The cast of the *House of Glass* included Gertrude Berg, Joe Greenwood (Joe Greenwald), Paul Stewart, Helene Dumas, Bertha Walden, Sanford Meissner, Arthur Auerbach, Ann Lubowe, George Tobias, Celia Babcock, Arline Blackburn, Bertha Walden and Bill Artzt and his orchestra. Gertrude Berg wrote the show conveniently set in a hotel, so that there could always be some entertainment going on. *Billboard* said the show contained "a little music, a little heart throb, humor [and] philosophy." The program's warm humanity and good humor made it a national favorite.

Gertrude Berg returned to radio in 1953 with a new version of *The House of Glass*, about Barney Glass, who owned a resort hotel in the Catskills "one hour from New York City — three hours to be exact." Once again between the dramatic episodes there were many opportunities for listeners to hear the hotel's entertainment offerings. In addition to Gertrude Berg, the cast included Gene Baylos, Joseph Buloff, Arnold Stang, Harold Stone and Ann Thomas. Mrs. Berg wrote the show. The show's director was Ken MacGregor. Cherney Berg was the producer-composer. Original lyrics were written by Arnold B. Horwitt. The musical director was Milton Katime (30 min., Friday, 9:30–10:00 P.M., NBC, 1953). *See* ***The Goldbergs***.

15374 ***(The) House That Jack Built.*** This unique show told the "real life" experiences of Sally and Jack Howard, a "modern American couple," who actually were having a house built in the Northwood section of Baltimore. The concept was developed and the program produced by WBAL's Purnell W. Gould, Elinor McCurley and Edward Wacsche, Jr. The cast members included: Mary Spots wood Warren, Leonie Redue and Walter Linthicum. The program was sponsored by many local Baltimore companies connected with the construction trades (WBAL, Baltimore, MD, 1931–1932).

15375 ***(The) House That Music Built.*** Rex Mauphin's Orchestra was featured on the sustaining music program. Jack Lester was the program's announcer (30 min., Tuesday, 9:30–10:00 P.M., WENR, Chicago, IL, 1947).

15376 ***(The) House Undivided.*** True Boardman produced and Herb Conner wrote the daytime serial that *Variety* said was an imitation of *One Man's Family*. This particular family included an elderly man, his wife and children of various ages. Also in the story were their elderly housekeeper and their neighbors (15 min., Monday through Friday, 10:15–10:30 A.M. PST, Don Lee Network, 1937).

15377 ***Houseboat Hannah.*** Frank and Anne Hummert produced the daytime serial followed the story of Hannah, whose husband was crippled by the accidental loss of an arm. Beset by financial problems, the couple were forced live on a houseboat in San Francisco Bay. The roles of Hannah and her husband were originated by Henrietta Tedro and Norman Gottschalk. Other cast members included: William Amsdell, Jim Andelin, Les Damon, Frank Derby, Nancy Douglas, Virginia Dwyer, Donald Gallagher, Bonnie Kay, Carl Kroenke, John Larkin, Doris Rich, William Rose, Henry Saxe and Margaret Shallett. Gene Baker and Olan Soule were the announcers (MBS and NBC-Blue, 1937–1941).

15378 ***Household Economics.*** Kate Brew Vaughn conducted her home economics program (KNX, Hollywood, CA, 1928).

15379 ***Household Hour.*** The program of home economics information was conducted by Mrs. Elizabeth O. Hiller (WMAQ, Chicago, IL, 1925).

15380 **Houser, Lionel.** Book reviewer (KFWI, San Francisco, CA, 1926).

15381 ***Housewives' Half-Hour.*** The popular local "housewives' program" began on February 2, 1935 (KSAC, Manhattan, KS, 1935).

15382 ***(The) Housewives' Hour.*** An early regularly scheduled program for women (WEAF, New York, NY, 1925).

15383 ***Housewives' Musical Program.*** Begun on September 26, 1927, the program was broadcast until September 1, 1937. It was designed to acquaint the listeners with the appreciation of good music (KSAC, Manhattan, KS, 1927–1937).

15384 **Houston, George.** Houston was a baritone who performed on the *Theatre Magazine* program (WGBS, New York, NY, 1928).

15385 **Houston, Harold.** DJ (*1490 Club* and *The Old Chisholm Trail*, KBLF, Red Bluff, CA, 1947). Sportscaster (*Sports Spotlight*, KBLF, 1947).

15386 **Houston, Jane.** Actress Houston was a cast member of *Stella Dallas* daytime serial.

15387 **Houston, Jean.** COM-HE (KGHF, Pueblo, CO, 1957).

15388 **Houston, Josephine.** Soprano (*Josephine Houston*, vcl. mus. prg, NBC-Blue, 1945).

15389 **Houston, Katie.** COM-HE (KTHT, Houston, TX, 1951).

15390 **Houston, Maggie.** COM-HE (KVOR, Colorado Springs, CO, 1960).

15391 **Houston, Marie.** Pianist (WMH, Cincinnati, OH, 1924).

15392 **Houston, (Mme.) Marie.** Soprano (WGCP, Newark, NJ ;WHN, New York, NY, 1925).

15393 **Houston, Ruby.** COM-HE (KDRS, Paragould, AR, 1949).

15394 **Houston, Stanley.** Chief announcer known as "Curley Bond" (KFKX, Chicago, IL, 1928).

15395 ***Houston Hometown Jamboree.*** CW musical program (KNUZ, Houston, TX, 1954), the *Houston Hometown Jamboree* was simulcast on KNUZ-TV (Houston, TX, 1954). Paul Hunter and Biff Collie, who also provided comic routines, served as MC's. Artie Duff, Hank Locklin, Bill Potter, Sonny Burns, Tommy Collins and Patsy Elshire were featured performers.

15396 **Houy, Neyda.** Soprano (KPO, San Francisco, CA, 1924).

15397 **(The) How Do You Do Boys** Comedy singing team of Grady and Doc, not otherwise identified on the program (KMA, Shenandoah, IA, 1926). Grady was high school principal Grady Fort and Doc was Dr. J.D. Bellamy, a dentist.

15398 ***How I Met My Husband.*** As the title suggests, the program focused on how wives met their husbands. Eddie Simmons wrote the interesting program of dramatic sketches. Two letters were read on each program and served as a basis for the romantic dramas presented. The first program, broadcast July 20, 1937, told the story of how a woman met her husband at the 1904 St. Louis World's Fair. The actors on the first program were Harry Eldersveldt and Kay Campbell. Another interesting program presented 17-year-old Lorraine Plachote enacting the story of her grandmother, who was then 78 1/2 years of age (15 min., Tuesday and Friday, 10:25–10:30 A.M. and 10:45–11:00 P.M., WLS, Chicago, IL, 1937–1938).

15399 ***How to Be Charming.*** The women's program was conducted by an unidentified broadcaster (WJSV, Washington, DC, 1936).

15400 **Howard, Allen.** Newscaster (WSPR, Springfield, MA, 1944).

15401 **Howard, Bess E.** News analyst (*Bess E. Howard Looks at the News*, KYW, Philadelphia, PA, 1940–1941; WCAU, Philadelphia, PA, 1945).

15402 **Howard, Betty.** Producer-casting director (agency). Howard worked for the Pedlar and Ryan Agency estimating the wishes of radio's daytime serial audience and attempting to produce and cast programs that would be successful.

15403 **Howard, Bob.** Tenor (*Bob Howard*, vcl. mus. prg., WBAL, Baltimore, MD, 1935).

15404 **Howard, Bob.** Leader (*Bob Howard Orchestra*, instr. mus. prg., WTIC, Hartford, CT, 1942).

15405 **Howard, Bob.** DJ (*The Music Room*, WLEC, Sandusky, OH, 1949).

15406 **Howard, Clare.** Actress Clare was featured on the *I Love Linda Dale* daytime serial program.

15407 **Howard, Dale.** DJ (*Juke Box Review*, KVOX, Moorhead, MN, 1947).

15408 **Howard, Eddy.** Leader (*Eddy Howard Orchestra*, instr. mus. prg., WGN, Chicago, IL, 1942).

15409 **Howard, Ernest.** Newscaster (KVWC, Vernon, TX, 1946).

15410 **Howard, Eunice.** Actress Howard appeared on the daytime serial programs *Hello Peggy*, *Mary Marlin* aka *The Story of Mary Marlin*, *Pages of Romance*, *Pepper Young's Family* and *Red Davis*.

15411 **Howard, Everett.** Newscaster (WIBC, Indianapolis, IN, 1945).

15412 **Howard, (Mrs.) Frank.** Mezzo-soprano (KMOX, St. Louis, MO, 1926).

15413 **Howard, Fred (Fred Howard Wright).** Actor, singer and composer Howard was born September 30, 1896. He appeared in many musical and dramatic stock productions before he made his first radio appearance (KFRC, San Francisco, CA, 1929).

15414 **Howard, Hank.** DJ (*Little Symphony*, WATR, Waterbury, CT, 1947).

15415 **Howard, Harry.** Popular singer Howard appeared December 14, 1921, on the first broadcast of station WDAY (Roselle Park, New Jersey).

15416 **Howard, Henry.** Impersonator-comedian (*Henry Howard*, a comedy program, WPG, Atlantic City, NJ, 1935–1936).

15417 **Howard, Herb.** Howard was part of the DJ team of *Midge and Herb* (WJHL, Johnson City, TN, 1952).

15418 **Howard, Jean.** Pianist (KFI, Los Angeles, CA, 1925).

15419 **Howard, Joe.** Singer-composer (NBC, 1929). Howard later starred on the *Gay Nineties Review* program. *See* ***The Gay Nineties Review.***

15420 **Howard, Joe.** Newscaster (KFBB, Greta Falls, MT, 1938).

15421 **Howard, John.** Newscaster (WHJB, Greenburg, PA, 1947). Sportscaster (WHJB, 1947–1948).

15422 **Howard, Lucy.** COM-HE (WWXL, Manchester, KY, 1957).

15423 **Howard, Mary.** Texas soprano (WEAF, New York, NY, 1925).

15424 **Howard, Nancy.** COM-HE (KMUS, Muskogee, OK, 1956).

15425 **Howard, Ned.** DJ (WMAQ, Chicago, IL, 1949).

15426 **Howard, Paul.** Leader (Paul Howard's Quality Serenaders Orchestra, KFI, Los Angeles, CA, 1926).

15427 **Howard, Paul.** DJ (WTRX, Bellaire, OH, 1955).

15428 **Howard, Peg.** COM-HE (WTOL, Toledo, OH, 1949).

15429 **Howard, Ralph.** Newscaster (NBC, 1945; KNBC, San Francisco, CA, 1947).

15430 **Howard, Robert "Bob."** DJ (*House Party*, WWSO, Springfield, OH, 1949). Sportscaster (WTVN, Columbus, OH, 1952; WVKO, Columbus, OH, 1953–1956).

15431 **Howard, Ruth.** Pianist in the Clare Trio (KFRC, San Francisco, CA, 1926).

15432 **Howard, Shirley.** Singer (*Shirley Howard*, vcl. mus. prg., NBC, 1935).

15433 **Howard, Tex.** Leader (Tex Howard's Davenport Hotel Orchestra, KHQ, Spokane, WA, 1927).

15434 **Howard, Wed.** DJ (WMAQ, Chicago, IL, 1954).

15435 **Howard, Wilbur.** Leader (*Wilbur Howard Quartet*, vcl. mus. prg., KUOA , Siloam Springs, AR, 1939).

15436 **Howard, William.** Sportscaster (*The Realm of Sports*, WJPG, Green Bay, WI, 1960).

15437 ***Howard Dandies.*** The music program sponsored by Howard Clothes featured the Freddie Rich Orchestra, contralto Betty Smart and tenor Ben Alley (15 min., Sunday, 6:30–6:45 P.M., CBS, 1931). When it went on the air April 27, 1929, the band was called the Howard Fashion Plate Orchestra. *See* ***The Howard Fashion Plates.***

15438 ***Howard Fashion Plates.*** The popular music program was sponsored by Howard Clothes. *What's on the Air* magazine (April, 1930, Vol. 1, No. 6, p. 38) described it as "Beau Brummel set to music." Tenor Ben Alley was the featured singer accompanied by the Freddie

Rich band (30 min., Friday, 7:30–8:00 P.M., CBS, 1930). *See **The Howard Dandies**.*

15439 **Howatt, Louise.** Pianist-contralto Howatt was known as the "Happiness Girl" (KFWB, Hollywood, CA, 1925; KMTR, Hollywood, CA, 19280–1930).

15440 **(The) Howdy Boys** The Boys were the entertaining singing team of Harry Geise and Joe Allabaugh (WMAQ, Chicago, IL, 1928).

15441 ***Howdy Doody***. *Variety* said that after he had gained national popularity with his *Howdy Doody* television show for children, Bob Smith made a successful transition with the program to radio. The Howdy Doody character first appeared on the *Triple B Ranch* program at WEAF (New York, NY) conducted by Big Brother Bob Smith. In addition to Buffalo Bob Smith, the program presented Dayton Allen playing Mr. Bluster, Bill Cornac as Flubadub and Judy Tyler as Princess Summerfall-Winterspring. Clarabelle the Clown also was a cast regular. Bob Smith played both Buffalo Bob and produced the voice of the puppet star, Howdy Doody. Each week guests such as Milton Berle and Helen Hayes appeared. Eddie Kean and Bob Cone were the program's writers and Simon Rady the producer-director (60 min., Saturday, 8:30–9:30 A.M., NBC, 1951–1954). Bob Smith said that Howdy Doody grew out of a character he had used previously on his *Big Brother Bob* radio show, aka the *Triple B Ranch* program. On that show Smith had used a "Mortimer Snerd voice" to create a character by the name of Elmer. Elmer said, "Ho, ho, ho, howdy dowdy." Children who came to see the show often asked Smith where Howdy Doody was. Therefore, a radio character came to television before making a transition back to radio.

15442 **Howe, Eleanor.** COM-HE (WBBM, Chicago, IL, 1937; CBS, 1937).

15443 **Howe, Harold.** Newscaster (KSAC, Manhattan, KS, 1941).

15444 **Howe, Joyce.** COM-HE (KSUE, Susanville, CA, 1949).

15445 **Howe, Kay.** COM-HE (KHOW, Denver, CO, 1960).

15446 **Howe, Leonard "Len."** Newscaster (WHO, Des Moines, IA, 1938–1942, 1948).

15447 **Howe, Nancy (Nancy Osgood).** HE-COM/DJ (WNAC, Boston, 1927). Combining shopping reports with records, Howe could have been the first female DJ. News reporter (WBIS, Boston, MA, 1928).

15448 **Howe, Quincy.** News analyst and author (WQXR, New York, NY, 1939–1942; *Quincy Howe and the News*, CBS, 1942–1950; ABC, 1954–1966). One of the most intellectually gifted and objectively honest news broadcasters, Howe wrote several significant books in addition to delivering his uniformly excellent analytic news broadcasts. His radio career began when moonlighting from his editor's job at Simon and Schuster, he began to broadcast the news for station WQXR (New York, NY) in the summer of 1939. He left both WQXR and Simon and Schuster to join CBS radio in 1939. Howe said that his broadcasting career was made possible by the friendship of Max Schuster with Elliott Sanger at WQXR, since the former had always believed that all media were closely related. Schuster maintained that what was good for Simon and Schuster was also good for WQXR.

Howe was a keen observer of the American scene and a perceptive historian. His insights into the broadcasting news business were also particularly penetrating [*See* **News on Radio**]. In a letter to the author written June 9, 1975, Howe commented: "For thirty years I was broadcasting news commentaries, mostly by radio, sometimes by TV, but the day of the all-purpose news analyst has long since vanished. It filled its purpose at the time but has gone the way of the wheelbarrow."

15449 **Howe, Richard H.** Announcer (WJD, Granville, OH, 1924–1925).

15450 **Howe, Trayer.** Newscaster (WJEJ, Hagerstown, MD, 1940).

15451 **Howel, Maud.** Soprano (KFOB, Burlingame, CA, 1926).

15452 **Howell, Bert.** Singer (WGCP, Newark, NJ, 1925).

15453 **Howell, Bobby.** Leader (*Bobby Howell Orchestra*, instr. mus. prg., WDBJ, Roanoke, VA, 1935–1936).

15454 **Howell, Charlie.** *Radio Digest* called Howell a "Golden Tenor" (KMA, Shenandoah, IA, 1928).

15455 **Howell, Clifton "Cliff."** Announcer and singer (KFI, Los Angeles, CA, 1928–1929).

15456 **Howell, H.H.** Announcer Howell frequently broadcast his station's slogan, "We extend Buffalo's regards"(WEBR, Buffalo, NY, 1925–1927).

15457 **Howell, Henry.** Newscaster (WOAI, San Antonio, TX, 1945–1946).

15458 **Howell, Hilton.** Organist (WBZ, Boston-Springfield, MA, 1925).

15459 **Howell, J. A.** Announcer (WCAM, Camden, NJ, 1927).

15460 **Howell, Jim.** Sportscaster (*Sports Desk*, WQAM, Miami, FL, 1960).

15461 **Howell, Lois M.** Pianist (WORD, Batavia, IL, 1925).

15462 **Howell, Lottice.** Singer Howell appeared on the *Roxy's Gang* program (NBC, 1931). Previously she had appeared in a motion picture with Ramon Novarro.

15463 **Howell, Rex G.** Announcer Howell began his radio career while still a high school senior (KFEL, Denver, CO, 1925). His long broadcasting career also included work as a newscaster (KFXJ, Grand Junction, CO, 1938–1942, 1945; *Radiotorial*, KFXJ, 1946–1947).

15464 **Howell, Wayne.** Sportscaster (WTMA, Charleston, SC, 1940). DJ (NBC, 1950).

15465 **Howells, Hamilton.** Cellist (KTAB, Oakland, CA, 1928).

15466 ***Howells and Wright***. Instr. mus. prg. by a talented piano duo (KYW, Philadelphia, PA, 1934; CBS, 1936).

15467 **Howells' Concert Band of Howells, Nebraska.** Town band directed by J.E. Sindelar (WOAW, Omaha, NE, 1925).

15468 **Howerton, George.** Organist (KLDS, Independence, MO, 1926).

15469 ***Howie Wing***. The Kellogg Company sponsored the children's daytime adventure series about Howie Wing, a flying inventor. Howie faced many dangers placed in his path by the villainous Burton York. The cast included: William Janney in the title role assisted by Richard Bishop, Raymond Bramley, John Griggs, Neil O'Malley, Mary Parker and Robert Strauss (15 min., Monday through Friday, 6:30–6:45 P.M., CBS, 1938).

15470 **Howington, Jimmy.** Singer (*Jimmy Howington*, vcl. mus. prg., WTAR, Norfolk, VA, 1936).

15471 **Howison, Elizabeth.** Soprano (WRC, Washington, DC, 1925).

15472 **Howland, Nellie.** Harpist (KFDM, Beaumont, TX, 1927). Director (Magnolia Glee Club, KFDM, 1928).

15473 **Howland Brothers.** A family music group including banjo, violin and ukulele (WCOA, Pensacola, FL, 1926).

15474 **Howle, Conrad.** Newscaster (WMBG, Richmond, VA, 1937–1939).

15475 **Howse, L.B.** Newscaster (WHOP, Hopkinsville, KY, 1942).

15476 **Hoy, Wallace.** DJ (*Wake Up Lenoir*, WJRI, Lenoir, NC, 1950).

15477 **Hoyle, Dorothy.** Violinist (WEAF, New York, NY; WOO, Philadelphia, PA, 1925; WHAP, New York, NY, 1926).

15478 **Hoyos, Rudolfo.** Mexican baritone (WEAF, New York, NY, 1927).

15479 **Hoyt, Betty.** COM-HE (KNBH, Hollywood, CA, 1951).

15480 **Hoyt, Isabelle.** COM-HE (KVAN, Vancouver, WA, 1955).

15481 **Hoyt, Julia.** COM-HE Hoyt conducted a popular fashion program (*Julia Hoyt Fashions,* NBC, 1936).

15482 **Hoyt, Lee.** Newscaster (WIBW, Topeka, KS, 1939).

15483 **Hoyt, Waite.** Sportscaster Hoyt was a former New York Yankee pitching star (WNEW, New York, NY, 1939; *According to Hoyt,* WABC, New York, NY, 1939). In 1942 he broadcast Cincinnati Reds baseball play-by-play (WKRC, Cincinnati, OH, 1942–1945; *Sports Review* and baseball play-by-play, WCPO, Cincinnati, OH, 1947; *According to Hoyt*, WCPO, 1948–1951; WSAI, Cincinnati, OH, 1953; NBC, 1960). Hoyt's broadcast career began when he bounced from one New York station after another broadcasting sports, after his baseball career with the Yankees was over. He worked briefly on WMCA, WNEW, WABC and WOR before finally going to Cincinnati to begin a long successful career. During his early years, Hoyt unsuccessfully tried to join the extensive Wheaties team of baseball broadcasters [*see* **Sports**], but was turned down because they felt that ex-athletes did not have either a sufficient or suitable vocabulary to do baseball broadcasts.

One of the most informative and entertaining aspects of Hoyt's work was his broadcasts during a rain delayed ball game. Called "Waite in the Rain," the rain delay interlude allowed him ample opportunity to use his large stock of baseball anecdotes that listeners greatly appreciated hearing. Known for his crisp articulation and excellent grammar, Hoyt was never the target of English teachers as was his fellow broadcaster — Dizzy Dean. Smith in his comprehensive book on baseball broadcasters, *Voices of the Game*, says that Hoyt was one of the first ex-athletes to become a broadcaster and quite possibly was the best (Smith, 1987, p. 73).

15484 **Hruby, John.** Trumpet soloist (WTAM, Cleveland, OH, 1924).

15485 **Hsiang, C.L. and J.S. Yong.** Two Chinese students from Peking who attended the University of Minnesota, Hsiang and Yong played jazz on the hu-chin — a two-stringed Chinese fiddle. Hsiang also sang (WCCO, Minneapolis–St. Paul, MN, 1928).

15486 **Huan, Marty.** News analyst (*News for Neighbors*, KDMO, Carthage, MO, 1947).

15487 **Huarte, Juan.** Leader (*Juan Huarte Orchestra*, instr. mus. prg., WEAN, Providence, RI, 1936).

15488 **Hubati, Jan.** Leader (*Jan Hubati Ensemble*, instr. mus. prg., WIP, Philadelphia, PA, 1937).

15489 **Hubbard, Alice.** Actress Hubbard appeared on the *Bright Horizon* daytime serial program.

15490 **Hubbard, Betty.** COM-HE (KWBG, Boone, IA, 1951).

15491 **Hubbard, Dorothy.** Pianist (KFQW, Seattle, WA, 1928).

15492 **Hubbard, Elaine.** COM-HE (KSUN, Bisbee, AZ, 1954).

15493 **Hubbard, Helen.** Singer (WDRC, Hartford, CT, 1936).

15494 **Hubbard, Helen M.** Bridge expert (*Helen Hubbard's Auction Bridge Matinee*, KGO, San Francisco, CA, 1926).

15495 **Hubbard, Irene.** Actress Hubbard, a busy and versatile performer, appeared on the *Hilltop House*; *John's Other Wife*; *Joyce Jordan, Girl Interne*; *Little Women, Lorenzo Jones*; *Pepper Young's Family*; *Right to Happiness*; *This is Nora Drake*; *Woman of America*; *Young Widder Brown*; *By Kathleen Norris*; *Our Gal Sunday*; *Amanda of Honeymoon Hill* and *Dot and Will* daytime serial programs.

15496 **Hubbard, John T.** Newscaster (WAGF, Dothan, AL, 1940).

15497 **Hubbard, Marjorie (Margie) Lou.** COM-HE (KPLT, Paris, TX, 1956–1957).

15498 **Hubbell, J. Wesley.** Tenor Howell was on the music faculty of Southern Methodist University (WFAA, Dallas, TX, 1923).

15499 **Hubbs, Frank.** Newscaster (WAGA, Atlanta, GA, 1942; WMAZ, Macon, GA, 1946).

15500 **Huber, Beal.** Soprano (*Beal Huber*, vcl. mus. prg., NBC-Red, 1934).

15501 **Huber, Helen R.** COM-HE (KRMS, Osage Beach, MO, 1954).

15502 **Huber, Justin.** Leader (Justin Huber Dance Orchestra, WLW, Cincinnati, OH, 1924).

15503 **Huber, Richard.** Newscaster (WROW, Augusta, GA, 1942).

15504 **Huber, Russell.** Newscaster (WKBH, La Crosse, WI, 1941).

15505 **Huber, Wynn.** Newscaster (WNAX, Yankton, ND, 1940s). Huber was one of the first female newscasters in the north central part of the United States, where she conducted a daily 10:00 A.M. newscast on station WNAX, Yankton, SD.

15506 **Hubert, Ann.** COM-HE (WAVE, Louisville, KY, 1951).

15507 **Hubner, Gladys.** Harpist (WCCO, Minneapolis, MN, 1926; KOMO, Seattle, WA, 1929).

15508 **Huddleston, Bill.** Newscaster (WBEJ, Elizabethton, TN, 1946).

15509 **Huddleston, Hayden.** Announcer (WDJB, Roanoke, VA, 1924).

15510 **Huddleston, Paul.** Newscaster (WBBB, Burlington, NC, 1941–1942).

15511 **Huddleston, Russ.** Newscaster (WLAC, Nashville, TN, 1940).

15512 **Huder, Fred F.** Bass-baritone (WEAF, New York, NY, 1924).

15513 **Hudgins, Virginia.** COM-HE (WLOE, Leaksville, NC, 1956).

15514 **Hudkins, Ace.** DJ (KCMJ, Palm Springs, CA, 1954).

15515 **Hudson, Dean.** Leader (*Dean Hudson Orchestra*, instr. mus. prg., MBS, 1937).

15516 **Hudson, Harry.** Newscaster (WOPI, Bristol, TN, 1938–1940, 1945).

15517 **Hudson, Harvey.** Tenor (KOIN, Portland, OR, 1928).

15518 **Hudson, Harvey.** Sportscaster (WRVA, Richmond, VA, 1941). DJ (*1450 Club*, WLEE, Richmond, VA, 1947; *Harvey Hudson Show*, WLEE, 1949–1956).

15519 **Hudson, Helen.** Contralto (WENR, Chicago, IL, 1929).

15520 **Hudson, Irish.** CW singer (WMT, Cedar Rapids–Waterloo, IA, 1935).

15521 **Hudson, Patricia.** COM-HE (KTHE, Thermopolis, WY, 1956).

15522 **Hudson, Rollo.** Leader (*Rollo Hudson Orchestra*, instr. mus. prg., WOR, Newark, NJ, 1934).

15523 **Hudson, Ruby Stein.** DJ (WHHM, Memphis, TN, 1949).

15524 **Hudson, Will.** Leader (*Will Hudson Orchestra*, instr. mus. prg., KOWH, Omaha, NE, 1940; WOOD, Grand Rapids, MI, 1942).

15525 **Hudson and Essex Orchestra.** Commercial band (KGW, Portland, OR, 1925).

15526 **Hudson Ramblers Orchestra.** Commercial dance band (WRW, Tarrytown, NY, 1925).

15527 ***Hudson-DeLange Orchestra.*** Instr. mus. prg. (WOR, Newark, NJ, 1936).

15528 ***Hudson-Essex Challengers.*** The Hudson-Essex Automobile Company sponsored this musical variety show featuring an orchestra and choral group (30 min., Tuesday, 10:00–10:30 P.M., NBC, 1928).

15529 **Hudson-Essex Orchestra.** Commercial studio orchestra (WJAR, Providence, RI, 1927).

15530 **Huebel, Gladys.** Contralto (WCCO, Minneapolis–St. Paul, MN, 1928).

15531 **Huebner, Paul.** Newscaster (KWG, Stockton, CA, 1946). DJ (KWG, 1955).

15532 **Huebner, Ruth.** Pianist (KWSC, Pullman, WA, 1925).

15533 **Huesley, Larry.** Sportscaster (KMO, Tacoma, WA, 1939).

15534 **Huessler, Edith.** Contralto (WGBS, New York, NY, 1928).

15535 **Huey, Charlie.** Singer Huey, an early Chicago radio favorite, was widely known as "The Washerwoman of the Air." Huey was brought to station WBBM by station owner Les Atlass (WBBM, Chicago, IL, 1925).

15536 **Huey, Lois M.** COM-HE (WRYO, Rochester, PA, 1951).

15537 **Huff, Joan.** COM-HE (KANS, Wichita, KS, 1949).

15538 **Huff, Sally Canady.** Leader (Sally Huff and Her Sunset Ensemble, KFSD, San Diego, CA, 1926).

15539 **Huffman, Helen M.** COM-HE (WAYB, Waynesboro, VA, 1951–1955).

15540 **Hufsmith, Fred.** Tenor (*Fred Hufsmith*, vcl. mus. prg., NBC-Red, 1936–1937).

15541 **Hug, Lorraine.** Pianist (WSOE, Milwaukee, WI, 1926).

15542 **Hugg, Jeff.** Newscaster (WDSU, New Orleans, LA, 1944).

15543 **Huggins, Bill.** Singer (*Bill Huggins*, vcl. mus. prg., CBS, 1934). *See **Lazy Bill Huggins***.

15544 **Huggins, Hank.** DJ (*No Name Show*, WENK, Union City, TN, 1954).

15545 **Hugh, John.** Newscaster (WHIT, New Berne, NC, 1942).

15546 ***Hugh Cross and Pals.*** CW mus. prg. (WLW, Cincinnati, OH, 1938).

15547 ***(The) Hugh Cross Radio Gang.*** Cross, whose group was also known as the Smokey Mountain Boy and His Georgie Porgie Boys, were an entertaining CW music group (60 min., daily, 10:00–10:30 A.M. and 4:40 P.M., WWVA, Wheeling, WV, 1935–1936.)

15548 **Hughes, Alex.** Pianist (WFAA, Dallas, TX, 1925).

15549 **Hughes, Alice.** Newscaster (WMCA, New York, NY, 1945).

15550 **Hughes, Arthur.** Actor Hughes played the title role of the villainous Dr. Fu Manchu on the *Collier Radio Hour* program (WJZ, New York, NY, 1927–1932). *See **The Collier Radio Hour***. He also was in the cast of *East if Cairo, I Love Linda Dale, Jungle Jim, Just Plain Bill* (title role), *Mr. Keen, Tracer of Lost Persons* and *The Orange Lantern*.

15551 **Hughes, Bertram L.** Newscaster (WHCU, Ithaca, NY, 1940–1942; KXOK, St. Louis, MO, 1944; KWK, St. Louis, MO, 1946).

15552 **Hughes, Bess McLennan.** Contralto (KVOO, Tulsa, OK, 1928).

15553 Hughes, Bessie Dade. Contralto (KOA, Denver, CO, 1926).

15554 Hughes, Betty. COM-HE (KWSH, Holdenville, OK, 1951).

15555 Hughes, Claire. COM-HE (KWKW, Pasadena, CA, 1951–1954).

15556 Hughes, Don. Twelve-year-old dramatic actor Hughes appeared on the *Arabesque* program (WABC-CBS, New York, NY, 1929).

15557 Hughes, Gordon. Director Hughes worked on *Girl Alone, Guiding Light, Just Neighbors, Midstream* and *Woman from Nowhere.*

15558 Hughes, Gwendolyn. Pianist (KGO, Oakland, CA, 1925).

15559 Hughes, Haller Jim. Host of the *Haller Hour* (KDKA, Pittsburgh, PA, 1928).

15560 Hughes, Helen. Leader (Helen Hughes Orchestra, WOC, Davenport, IA, 1926).

15561 Hughes, Helen. Soprano (*Helen Hughes*, vcl. mus. prg., WIP, Philadelphia, PA, 1935).

15562 Hughes, James. Tenor (WLWL, New York, NY, 1928).

15563 Hughes, Janette. COM-HE (WLSC, Loris, SC, 1960).

15564 Hughes, Jim. Announcer (WJAS, Pittsburgh, PA, 1925).

15565 Hughes, John. Actor Hughes was in the cast of *The Other Woman's Diary.*

15566 Hughes, John B. Newscaster (KFRC, San Francisco, CA, 1938; MBS-WOR, New York, NY, 1941–1942; KFWB, Los Angeles, CA, 1944; KHJ, Los Angeles, CA, 1945).

15567 Hughes, Judd. Newscaster (WNBF, Binghampton, NY, 1938).

15568 Hughes, Lola L. and Otto Rauhut. Violin duets (KPO, San Francisco, CA, 1925).

15569 Hughes, Lon. Newscaster (KYA, San Francisco, CA, 1941).

15570 Hughes, Margaret. Soprano (KFI, Los Angeles, CA, 1925).

15571 Hughes, Margo. Pianist (KGO, Oakland, CA, 1925).

15572 Hughes, Maude. Piano (KHJ, Los Angeles, CA, 1930).

15573 Hughes, Paul. Newscaster (KVOR, Colorado Springs, CO, 1937–1938; KTAR, Phoenix, AZ, 1942, 1946). Sportscaster (KTAR, 1942).

15574 Hughes, Ray. Leader (*Ray Hughes Orchestra*, instr. mus. prg., KCKN, Kansas City, MO, 1942).

15575 Hughes, Robert. Leader, Harmony Six Orchestra (KDKA, Pittsburgh, PA, 1922).

15576 Hughes, Rosemary. Soprano (WDAP, Chicago, IL, 1923; *Rosemary Hughes*, vcl. mus. prg., WHAS, Louisville, KY, 1934).

15577 Hughes, Rupert. News analyst (NBC, 1945).

15578 Hughes, Rush. Sportscaster (WMCA, New York, NY, 1941). DJ (*Rush Hughes Show* and *The Song and Dance Parade*, WXOK, St. Louis, MO, 1947; WCFL, Chicago, IL, 1948).

15579 Hughes, Shirley. COM-HE (WTAN, Clearwater, FL, 1954–1955).

15580 Hughes, "Sunny" Jane. Singer (KHJ, Los Angeles, CA, 1925).

15581 Hughes, T.C. Baritone (KFWM, Oakland, CA, 1926).

15582 Hughes, T.W. Newscaster (KMTR, Hollywood, CA, 1938).

15583 Hughes, Tommy. Actor Hughes was in the cast of *Coast-to-Coast on a Bus, Life and Loves of Dr. Susan, Young Dr. Malone* and *Young Widder Brown.*

15584 Hughes, Tory. Sportscaster (WTAW, College Station, TX, 1956).

15585 Huisizer, Madeline. Soprano (WOR, Newark, NJ, 1925; WAHG, Richmond Hill, NY, 1926).

15586 Hulbert, Maurice "Hot Rod." Black DJ (*Tan Town Jubilee* and *Sepia Swing Club*, WDIA, Memphis, TN, 1948; *Hot Rod Hulbert*, WITH, Baltimore, MD, late-1940s).

15587 Hulbert, Ray. Saxophonist-clarinetist (KGW, Portland, OR, 1928).

15588 Hulick, Budd. DJ Hulick was a former member of the popular comic team of Stoopnagle and Budd (WJJL, Niagara Falls, NY, 1950). *See* ***Stoopnagle and Budd.***

15589 Hulick, Helen. COM-HE (WPTV, Palm Beach, FL, 1957).

15590 Hull, Dick. DJ (*Make Believe Danceland*, WFRP, Savannah, GA, 1952–1954). Sportscaster (*Let's Talk Sports*, WFRP, 1951–1955).

15591 Hull, Doc. Newscaster (WCAZ, Carthage, IL, 1938).

15592 Hull, F.F. COM-HE (WKLA, Ludington, MI, 1951).

15593 Hull, Fredericka Sims. Soprano (WGHP, Detroit, MI, 1926).

15594 Hull, Harwood, Jr. Newscaster (WAPI, Birmingham, AL, 1938; NBC, 1942, 1946). DJ (*Caribbean Matinee*, WAPA, San Juan, PR, 1948).

15595 Hull, Henry, Jr. Director Hull directed the *Bright Horizon* daytime serial program.

15596 Hull, Josephine. Actress Hull was a cast member of *The O'Neills* daytime serial.

15597 Hull, Joy. DJ (*For You From JOY*, KCID, Caldwell, ID, 1952).

15598 Hull, (Mrs.) M.C. Pianist (WFAA, Dallas, TX, 1926).

15599 Hull, Martha. COM-HE (KSAL, Salinas, KS, 1949).

15600 Hull, Niki. DJ (KCID, Caldwell, ID, 1954).

15601 Hullinger, Betty. Newscaster (KVCV, Redding, CA, 1944).

15602 Hulsizer, Madeline. Soprano (WOR, Newark, NJ, 1926).

15603 Hulwi, James. Newscaster (WEAU, Eau Claire, WI, 1945).

15604 *Hum and Strum.* The singing team, a longtime radio favorite, consisted of Tom Currier and Max Zides (15 min., Thursday, 10:15–10:30 A.M., WBZ, Boston, MA, 1941). They broadcast under such names as the Flufferettes, Vigor Yeast Collegians, Cleercoal twins, Country Club Boys with the Vincent Lopez orchestra and the Ginger Boys. They also appeared on *Gentle's Homeliters* program.

15605 Human, Sylvan. Leader (*Sylvan Human Orchestra*, instr. mus. prg., WIP, Philadelphia, PA, 1935).

15606 *Humbard Family.* The Humbards presented evangelistic preaching and gospel music on their weekly program. The family included the Reverend and Mrs. A. E. Humbard and their children Rex, Ruth, Leona, Clement, Mary and Juanita. Son Rex later became a nationally known TV evangelist. The *Humbard Family* program began broadcasting on an Arkansas, station (KLRA, Little Rock, AR, 1930s).

15607 Humbert, Don. Leader (*Don Humbert's Strings*, instr. mus. prg., WHDH, Boston, MA, 1939).

15608 Humble, John. Newscaster (WAYX, Waycross, GA, 1942).

15609 Hume, Fabian. Newscaster (WRIB, Providence, RI, 1947).

15610 Humiston, Hod. Sportscaster (*Sports News of the Day* and play-by-play broadcasts of all local sports, KWHK, Hutchinson, KS, 1947–1949; *Sports Roundup*, KWHK, 1948–1949).

15611 Hummel, Mildred. COM-HE (KKIN, Visalia, CA, 1951).

15612 (The) Humming Birds. Vocal trio of three beautiful girls (WRNY, New York, NY, 1928).

15613 *Humor From Judge Magazine.* Comic material was read directly from a magazine on the interesting example of early American radio comedy (10 min., 8:05–8:15 P.M., KDKA, Pittsburgh, PA, October 6, 1923).

15614 Humphrey, Dorothy Stevens. Operatic soprano (WEAO, Columbus, OH, 1926; NBC, 1939; WOR, Newark, NJ, 1940; MBS, 1942).

15615 Humphrey, Helen. COM-HE (WHCU, Ithaca, NY, 1949; WWSC, Glens Falls, NY, 1956–1957).

15616 Humphreys, Bill. Newscaster (CBS, 1947)

15617 Humphreys, Mary Lou. COM-HE (WHRN, Syracuse, NY, 1951).

15618 Humphreys, Ruth. COM-HE (WWSC, Glen Falls, NY, 1955).

15619 Humphries, Dorothy. Soprano (*Dorothy Humphries*, vcl. mus. prg., NBC, 1939; MBC, 1942).

15620 Humphries, Jerllyn. COM-HE (WRWH, Cleveland, GA, 1960).

15621 (The) Humphries Brothers (Jess and Cecil Humphries). Two country fiddlers (KUT, Austin, TX, 1929).

15622 *Humpty Dumpty.* The California Dairy Council sponsored Humpty Dumpty the "Health Clown of California" on the program for young people (KQW, Sacramento, CA, 1926).

15623 Hung, Josephine. News commentator (*American Chinese Program*, WARD, Brooklyn, NY, 1940).

15624 *Hungarian Gypsies Orchestra.* Instr. mus. prg. (WTNJ, Trenton, NJ, 1936).

15625 Hungarian Harmonic Twins. Instr. mus. duo (WJJD, Mooseheart, IL, 1926).

15626 Hungarian Orchestra of the Hotel Astor. Fred Rich directed the New York based band (WJZ, New York, NY, 1926).

15627 Hungerford, Mona. Actress Hungerford appeared on the *Against the Storm* daytime serial.

15628 Hungry Hank. DJ (*Ranch House Roundup*, WMLO, Milwaukee, IL, 1950).

15629 Hunkins, Maurel. Violinist (KRE, Berkeley, CA, 1926).

15630 Hunneryager, (Mrs.) A.E. Pianist (WCBD, Zion, IL, 1925).

15631 Hunnes, Fred. Sportscaster (*Tip Off on Sports*, KATL, Miles City, MT, 1960).

15632 Hunt, Adele. COM-HE (*Hunt for Happiness*, WPAT, Paterson, NJ, 1949).

15633 Hunt, Arthur Billings. Baritone (WEAF, New York, NY, 1929).

15634 Hunt, Audrey. COM-HE (WMRC, Greenville, SC; WIS, Columbia, SC, 1960).

15635 Hunt, Betty Jo. COM-HE (KBIM, Roswell, NM, 1956–1957).

15636 Hunt, Brad. Leader (*Brad Hunt Orchestra*, instr. mus. prg., WLAV, Grand Rapids, MI, 1942).

15637 Hunt, Connie. COM-HE (WGAI, Elizabeth City, NC, 1951).

15638 Hunt, Frazier. Newscaster (CBS, 1941–1942; MBS, 1945).

15639 Hunt, Gabrielle. Leader (*Gabrielle Hunt Orchestra*, instr. mus. prg., WIP, Philadelphia, PA, 1935).

15640 Hunt, Hamlin. Organist (WCCO, Minneapolis–St. Paul, MN, 1924–1928).

15641 Hunt, Jean. COM-HE (KRES, St. Joseph, MO, 1951).

15642 Hunt, Josephine. Soprano (WNYC, New York, NY, 1936).

15643 Hunt, Madeline. Singer known as the "Girl from Mexico" (WEAF, New York, NY, 1926).

15644 Hunt, Mildred. Contralto Hunt appeared on the *Freshman Orchestradiana* program (WJZ, New York, NY, 1929).

15645 Hunt, Paul. Newscaster (WJW, Akron, OH, 1940–1941).

15646 Hunt, Raymond J. "Ray." Newscaster (KONO, San Antonio, TX, 1945; *News at Nine*, KONO, 1947). DJ (*Cowboy Jamboree* and *Saddle Pals*, KONO, 1947; *Saddle Pals*, KONO, 1954).

15647 Hunt, (Dr.) Robert A. Pastor of the First Methodist Church of Dallas, TX, Dr. Hunt preached sermons and performed song recitals with his daughters, Margaret and Marion (WFAA, Dallas, TX, 1924).

15648 Hunt, (Mrs.) S. Soprano (WHAS, Louisville, KY, 1926).

15649 Hunt, Ted. News analyst (*Between the Lines*, KROD, El Paso, TX, 1947).

15650 Hunter, Ben. DJ (KFI, Los Angeles, CA, 1956).

15651 Hunter, Dean. DJ (*Early Birds*, WKMF , Flint, MI, 1950s; *Best Sellers*, WMGM, New York, NY, 1957).

15652 Hunter, Edna. COM-HE (WCHO, Washington Court House, OH, 1956).

15653 Hunter, Eva. Violinist (KVOO, Tulsa, OK, 1928).

15654 Hunter, Fern J. COM-HE (KSUB, Cedar City, UT, 1956).

15655 Hunter, Frances. Soprano (KYW, Chicago, IL, 1925).

15656 Hunter, George W. Announcer (WRVA, Richmond, VA, 1928).

15657 Hunter, Guy. "Blind entertainer" (WOR, Newark, NJ, 1929; *Guy Hunter*, vcl. mus. prg., WIP, Philadelphia, PA, 1935–1936).

15658 Hunter, Harry. DJ (WMVG, Milledgeville, GA, 1947). Sportscaster (*The Sportsman*, WMVG, 1947).

15659 Hunter, Henry (Arthur Jacobson). Actor Hunter was in the cast of *Affairs of Anthony*, *Attorney-at-Law* (title role), *Barton Family*, *Girl Alone*, *Lone Journey*, *Midstream*, *Mary Marlin* and *Wings of Destiny*.

15660 Hunter, Herbert "Herb." Sportscaster (*Baseball Bench*, KMON, Great Falls, MT, 1955; KGA, Spokane, WA, 1960).

15661 Hunter, Joe Louis. DJ (*Modern Sounds*, WCEC, Rocky Mount, NC, 1955–1960).

15662 Hunter, Louise. Metropolitan Opera and Atlanta Municipal Opera Company soprano (WSB, Atlanta, GA, 1926).

15663 Hunter, Mary. Pianist (WHAS, Louisville, KY, 1924).

15664 Hunter, Mary. Actress Hunter was a cast member of the *Against the Storm* and *Barry Cameron* daytime serial programs.

15665 Hunter, Pinky. Leader (*Pinky Hunter Orchestra*, instr. mus. prg., NBC, 1934; WTAM, Cleveland, OH and NBC, 1936; WHK, Cleveland, OH, 1937). Sportscaster (*Bowling News*, WCLE-WHK, Cleveland, OH, 1940–1941).

15666 Hunter, Raymond O. Baritone (WJZ, New York, NY, 1924; WGY, Schenectady, NY, 1925).

15667 Hunter, Sarah Harding. COM-HE (WDOK, Cleveland, OH, 1951).

15668 Hunter, Todd. Newscaster (WBBM, Chicago, IL, 1938–1942; *News and Rhythm*, CBS, 1939–1941).

15669 *Hunter College on the Air.* One of several adult education programs station WNYC produced in association with various New York City colleges and universities (WNYC, New York, NY, 1939–1940).

15670 Hunters' Cabin Orchestra. Club band (WEEI, Boston, MA, 1926).

15671 *Hunter's the Name.* Veteran vaudeville and nightclub performer George Hunter hosted the sustaining variety show that featured the Joe Rines' Orchestra, the Songsmiths and guest vocalists including Edith Karen. Bill O'Connell was the announcer (27 min., Weekly, 9:03–9:30 P.M., WMCA, New York, NY, 1942).

15672 Huntington, Clay. Sportscaster (*Heidelberg Sports Highlights*, KTAC, Tacoma, WA, 1952–1956; KMO, Tacoma, WA, 1960).

15673 Huntington, Gertrude Childs. Soprano (KFI, Los Angeles, CA, 1925).

15674 Huntington, Johnnie. Leader (*Johnnie Huntington*, instr. mus. prg., WTAM, Cleveland, OH, 1936).

15675 Huntington, Mary. "Pianologist" (WBNX, Bronx, NY, 1937). Singer (WIP, Philadelphia, PA, 1937).

15676 Huntley, Chet. Newscaster (KLZ, Denver, CO, World War II era; KNX, Los Angeles, CA, 1945). Huntley later became nationally known for his work on the *Huntley-Brinkley* television program on NBC.

15677 Huntley, Lester. Writer Huntley wrote the *Kitty Keene* and *Ma Perkins* daytime serial programs.

15678 Huntley, Lloyd. Leader (*Lloyd Huntley Orchestra*, instr. mus. prg., WKRC, Cincinnati, OH, 1933; KDKA, Pittsburgh, PA, 1934; NBC, 1935; MBS, 1936).

15679 Hunton, Perley. Clarinetist (WLAK, Bellows Falls, VT, 1922–1923).

15680 Hunton, Theodore. Director Hunton directed the *Big Sister* daytime serial program.

15681 Huntoon, Winifred. Soprano (WGHP, Detroit, MI, 1926).

15682 Hunt's Imperial Orchestra from Tulsa, Oklahoma. Local dance orchestra that broadcast from the Lake Cliff Dancing Pavilion (WFAA, Dallas, TX, 1925).

15683 Huntspon, Neil. COM-HE (WJAK, Jackson, TN, 1956–1957).

15684 Hurd, Dr. and Mrs. Hawaiian guitar instrumental team (WHO, Des Moines, IA, 1926).

15685 Hurd, Leslie. Announcer (KFI, Los Angeles, CA, 1927).

15686 Hurd, Robert. Announcer-tenor (KFI, Los Angeles, CA, 1926).

15687 Hurlburt, Ruth. Soprano (KFQW, Seattle, WA, 1927).

15688 Hurlbut, Jim. Newscaster (WMAQ, Chicago, IL, 1947).

15689 Hurleigh, Robert F. "Bob." Newscaster (WFBR, Baltimore, MD, 1937–1940; WBBM, Chicago, IL, 1944; WGN, Chicago, IL, 1947).

15690 Hurley, Jim. Sportscaster (*The Fishing and Hunting Club of the Air*, ABC, 1945).

15691 Hurley, Monty. Actor Hurley was in the cast of *Careless Love*.

15692 Hurr, Ben. Leader (Ben Hurr Orchestra, WFBG, Altoona, PA, 1925).

15693 Hursley, Frank and Doris. The Hursley writing team wrote *American Women*, *Service to the Front* and *Those Websters*.

15694 Hurst, Cecil. Leader (*Cecil Hurst Orchestra*, instr. mus. prg., WCCO, Minneapolis–St. Paul, MN, 1937).

15695 Hurst, Connie. COM-HE (WCHV, Indio, CA, 1960).

15696 Hurst, Ed. DJ (WPEN, Philadelphia, PA, 1947; *The Ed Hurst Show*, WPEN, 1948; *Ed Hurst and Joe Grady 950 Club*, WPEN, 1949; *950 Club*, WPEN, 1950–1954).

15697 Hurst, Evelyn. Soprano (WGBS, New York, NY, 1926).

15698 Hurst, George. Violinist (WMAK, Buffalo, NY, 1926).

15699 Hurt, Jerry. Ukulele soloist (KVOO, Tulsa, OK, 1928).

15700 Hurt, Marlin. Tenor Hurt was featured on many broadcasts with various orchestras (KYW, Chicago, IL, 1929). Hurt was a member of the popular Tom, Dick and Harry male vocal trio that appeared on many network shows originating from Chicago. He then went on to play the role of Beulah the cook on the *Fibber McGee and Molly* program, before his own *Beulah* show was spun-off. *See* ***Fibber McGee and Molly*** *and* ***Beulah***.

15701 Hurt, Zack. Sportscaster (KFJZ, Fort Worth, TX, 1939; *Texas Sport Spotlight*, KFJZ, 1940; KFJZ, 1945–1951).

15702 Husak, Melva. Soprano (WHAS, Louisville, KY, 1924).

15703 Husband-and-Wife Talk Shows. Ed and Pegeen Fitzgerald inaugurated the first husband-and-wife talk show, *The Fitzgeralds*, in 1937 (WOR, Newark, NJ). Their format was soon copied by many other married couples including such prominent personalities as Tex McCrary and Jinx Falkenburg (*Tex and Jinx*); Mike Wallace and Buff Cobb (*Mike and Buff* aka *The Chez Show*), Binnie Barnes and Mike Frankovich (*Breakfast with Binnie and Mike*), Andre Baruch and Bea Wain (*Mr. and Mrs. Music*), Irma Lemke and David Kroman (*Breakfast with the Brooks*), Jeffrey Lynn and Robin Chandler (*Breakfast with the Lynns*), Myrtle Cooper and Scotty Wiseman aka Lulu Belle and Scotty (*Breakfast in the Blue Ridge*), Alfred and Dora McCann (*The McCanns at Home*), Peter Lind Hayes and Mary Healy (*Peter Lind Hayes and Mary Healy*), and Dorothy Kilgallen and Richard Kollmar (*Breakfast with Dorothy and Dick*).

At one time there was reported to be 78 imitators of the Fitzgeralds on the air, most of whom were on regional networks or local stations. At its worst, this type of program degenerated into little more than saccharin talk and a long parade of commercials without much information or entertainment provided for listeners.

The Fitzgeralds' story and how they originated and conducted the first husband-and-wife talk show is a fascinating one. Margaret "Pegeen" Worrall, a retail store executive met motion picture publicist Ed Fitzgerald in San Francisco and married him in the early 30s. Ed had been a World War I flying ace. Each had radio careers earlier in San Francisco before they came to New York City in 1936. Ed began two programs at WOR (Newark, NJ), an early morning book review program and *Almanac de Gotham*, a late night program. Pegeen went to work as Advertising Manager of McCreery's department store, where she broadcast a program called *Pegeen Prefers*, on which she discussed fashion for the department store.

One day in 1940 when Pegeen was ill, the station manager suggested that she broadcast her program from home until she recovered. Pegeen agreed, but she did not like the idea of Henry Morgan, her regular announcer, seeing her in a bathrobe. A solution was found, by having husband Ed sit with her at their breakfast table and simply begin talking. They had no script, only a microphone on their breakfast table. Numerous letters poured in from listeners who liked what they heard, and the husband-and-wife talk show format was born. The Fitzgeralds aired both their own individual opinions and their domestic squabbles. It was reported that during the 40s the couple was the highest paid husband-and-wife team in radio with their $160,000 yearly salary.

When the Fitzgeralds left station WOR in 1945 to move to WJZ (New York, NY), they were the most popular couple on New York radio. As the replacement for the Fitzgeralds, WOR scheduled *Breakfast with Dorothy and Dick*. The following year WEAF (New York, NY) introduced the *Tex and Jinx* program. Husband-and-wife programs were popular and their number was increasing.

The *Tex and Jinx* show was quite different from *The Fitzgeralds* and most of the other husband-and-wife morning talk programs. Newspaperman and political operative John Reagan "Tex" McCrary first appeared with his multi-talented wife Jinx Falkenburg on local New York radio as *Tex and Jinx* before moving the show to NBC (1947–1948). Beautiful Jinx Falkenburg was a stellar athlete who excelled in tennis and swimming . She had been a successful model and a motion picture starlet, who enjoyed a short-lived career in such less than memorable pictures as *Big Brown Eyes*, *The Singer of Naples*, and *The Lady and the Butler*. It was her marriage to Tex McCrary that led to her successful radio and television career.

Tex was a tough, hard-headed, no nonsense newsman with political ties and interests, who talked primarily about important public affairs topics, while wife Jinx brought a quick intelligence, a warm charm and a light touch that counter balanced McCrary's blunt seriousness and made the program entertaining. This couple didn't pretend they were having breakfast. They simply carried on a conversation that was serious, enlightening and entertaining. Jinx was particularly adept at interviewing prominent people from all walks of life, but it was with those in the entertainment field that she was at her best. Their November 4, 1947, program was typical with its usual ingredients and polished presentation. It began with Tex giving a digest of the news of the day. In addition to discussing Walter Lipmann's column, "Europe Revisited," he reflected on the suicide of American diplomat John J. Winant and ended by asking, "Why does a brilliant, able man take his own life?" He then interviewed newspaperman Richard Kenny, who had observed Howard Hughes initial flight in his "Spruce Goose." The program concluded with Jinx's recorded interview with Walt Disney. Jinx, as usual, was a bright, enthusiastic interviewer who did her homework in preparation for the interview. In response to her intelligent questions, Disney talked about his past and future films and discussed the technical aspects of combining voice with animation. Disney's humor was on display as he referred to Mickey Mouse by saying, "He's the mouse that made me the man I am." Jinx was always comfortable interviewing show business personalities. In 1947, in addition to their daytime program, they also hosted a *Tex and Jinx* variety show on NBC as a summer replacement for *Duffy's Tavern*.

Although Jinx had a good radio voice and precise articulation, it was her sensitivity plus a willingness to ask difficult questions that made her a good interviewer. One example of her ability to ask questions that could embarrass her occurred on the November 24, 1954, *Tex and Jinx* program on which she interviewed Fred Allen. Broadcasting on a NBC station (WRCA, New York, NY), Jinx extensively questioned Allen about his humorously negative opinions on how NBC executives frequently lacked judgment and intelligence. Allen was also given ample time to express his barbed comments about the effects of television. *Tex and Jinx* joined New York's station WOR in 1958 with their same daytime talk format (45 min., Monday through Friday, 2:15–3:00 P.M., WOR, New York, NY, 1958). Once more Jinx interviewed prominent personalities both in and outside the entertainment world, while Tex commented on the news. *See* ***The Tex and Jinx Show (1947)*** and ***The Tex and Jinx Show (1958)***.

Mike Wallace, another no nonsense newsman, was also part of a husband-and-wife talk show. In 1951, Wallace *then* a busy announcer and radio actor along with his actress wife, Buff Cobb, conducted an evening talk program *The Mike and Buff Show* aka *The Chez Show* from Chicago on NBC. Originating from the Sapphire Bar of the Chez Paris club, the couple played records requested by listeners and engaged in light banter. The program was broadcast before Wallace moved on to New York where he eventually gained fame on the *Sixty Minutes* television show.

A talk program with a distinctive Southern California emphasis was conducted by motion picture actress Binnie Barnes and radio sportscaster Mike Frankovich. During their morning show they engaged in the usual husband-and-wife breakfast table talk, concentrating on Hollywood news and gossip (KFVD, Los Angeles, CA, 1947). Their program attracted a loyal local audience, but was relatively short-lived. *See* ***Breakfast with Binnie and Mike***.

Distinguished pioneer announcer Andre Baruch and wife Bea Wain conducted a two hour a day Monday through Friday show of recorded music and informative talk (*Mr. and Mrs. Music*, WMCA, New York, NY, 1948). Bea Wain met her husband while performing on Kate Smith's evening radio variety show where Andre Baruch was the announcer. They later were married on the air on Smith's program.

Bea Wain had been a big band singing star with the Larry Clinton band. Clinton, perhaps the first great "swing" arranger, had arranged for the Glen Gray and Tommy Dorsey orchestras before forming his own band. Wain's warm voice and thoughtful phrasing closely matched Clinton's superior arranging style and the music they produced was extraordinary. An example of their collaboration can be heard on the July 2, 1938, *RCA Victor Campus Club* program that broadcast from the Glen Island

Casino. Joining Bea Wain on that program was Canadian born baritone, Dick Todd, a Bing Crosby sound alike, and tenor Gene McNulty, who later became famous as Dennis Day. When Baruch and Wain left their talk show in 1949, they were replaced by another musical husband-and-wife team, Ted and Doris Steele, whose talk was less "homey" and even more musical. *See* ***Mr. and Mrs. Music***.

Irma Lemke and David Kroman were a popular local husband-and-wife talk team in the Schenectady area. Their *Breakfast with Brooks* program (WGY, Schenectady, NY, 1946) featured casual breakfast table talk. *See* ***Breakfast with the Brooks***.

Myrtle Cooper and Scotty Wiseman supplied rural husband-and-wife talk and music for country-western music fans in the late 40s with their transcribed *Breakfast in the Blue Ridge*. Cooper and Wiseman were known professionally as Lulu Belle and Scotty, the singing sweethearts on NBC's *National Barn Dance* program. They made their many fans happy when their on the air romance became real and culminated in marriage. *Breakfast in the Blue Ridge* combined family talk with pleasant country music. The transcribed show broadcast by many stations in the late 40s was popular with rural and city listeners alike.

On their morning talk show, show business personalities Peter Lind Hayes and Mary Healy broadcast light, pleasant conversation from their Westchester, New York, home (WOR, New York, NY, 1960). Hayes was the son of nightclub, vaudeville and motion picture star Grace Hayes, who also was a radio star in her own right (*Grace Hayes*, NBC, 1932). Actress Mary Healy complimented her husband nicely on the program, as well as later in two television programs on which they starred. *See* ***Grace Hayes*** *and* ***Peter Lind Hayes and Mary Healy***.

Dorothy Kilgallen and Richard Kollmar with their *Breakfast with Dorothy and Dick* were probably the greatest rival of and competitor to *The Fitzgeralds*. Dorothy Kilgallen was a nationally syndicated columnist, later more famous for her regular appearance on the *What's My Line?* television program. Richard "Dick" Kollmar was an actor-producer, who was the host of the *Radio Reader's Digest* program and played the title role on the *Boston Blackie* radio show. He was, however, probably most famous for his roles in such favorite daytime serials as *Big Sister, Bright Horizon, Claudia, John's Other Wife, Pretty Kitty Kelly, When a Girl Marries* and *Life Can be Beautiful*.

Breakfast with Dorothy and Dick was almost the exact opposite of the Fitzgeralds' program. Columnist Kilgallen and her husband, actor-producer Richard Kollmar were sophisticates. On one of their 1956 programs the couple displayed their usual sophisticated range of topics. They opened the show with his, "Hi, darling" and her, "Hi, sweetie." Immediately they began to exchange catty remarks about attending Talullah Bankhead's show, her piano playing and singing with Dorothy concluding, "She just shouldn't sing unless she was doing it for laughs."

Hearing the show, the listener at times probably felt the couple's fun was artificially forced. On most of their 1956 programs, Dorothy and Dick discussed their several extensive trips to Europe, talking at length about Harry's Bar and the Taverna restaurant in Venice. Incidentally, they spent most of their time lavishly praising Angelo, their favorite waiter at Harry's Bar. On other programs they talked mostly about first nights at the theater, the latest "in" restaurant and various show business and entertainment topics. Perhaps it was this difference that played some small part in the rivalry that grew up between them and the other talk programs' couples.

Motion picture star Jeffrey Lynn and actress Robin Chandler replaced the *Breakfast with Dorothy and Dick* program when Kilgallen and Kollmar went on vacation. Their program was short-lived. *See* ***Breakfast with the Lynns*** and ***Breakfast with Dorothy and Dick***.

Despite the major style differences of each, there was considerable rivalry among *Breakfast with Dorothy and Dick, Tex and Jinx*, and *The Fitzgeralds*. While Dorothy and Dick were sophisticated, the Fitzgeralds, Ed and Pegeen, talked about ordinary things at their breakfast table such as the electric bill and the freshness of vegetables at their grocers, much like the ordinary breakfast table talk of ordinary listeners with one exception. There also could be lengthy discussions of Fraidy Cat Plushbottom and Mrs. Dirty Nose, their cats. Listeners also would sometimes be serenaded with the loud purring of the cats as they roamed around the microphone. Although husband-and-wife talk shows were plentiful and their number increasing, no other radio couple matched the Fitzgeralds' style or popularity.

Tex and Jinx stayed clear of the mild on the air feud that erupted between Dorothy and Dick and the Fitzgeralds. The sniping between the couples became particularly strong when Ed and Pegeen returned to WOR in the late 1950s. Finally, station management ordered that all on the air bickering stop.

By the early 1960s, *Breakfast with Dorothy and Dick* and *Tex and Jinx* were off the air, but the Fitzgeralds were still going strong and they continued for almost 20 more years. WOR dropped the program the year following Ed's death in 1982 at the age of 89. Pegeen went back to work in 1983 on WNYC (New York, NY) and continued to broadcast for another five years, chatting mostly about her cats, animal rights and vegetarianism. When her health failed, she left WNYC in April, 1988, and died the following year at age 78.

As early as 1946, when Talullah Bankhead visited the *Fred Allen Show*, Allen directed his satirical barbs against the husband-and-wife shows. On the program Allen and Bankhead portrayed "Talu and Freddy" to deliver one of the most devastating radio satires ever perpetrated. As this sketch illustrates, Allen's satires frequently contained references to contemporary show business personalities, prominent politicians and controversial best selling novels such as *Forever Amber*. The spoof began with an ultra-sweet "regular" talk segment to satirize what these programs normally were like. A "grumpy" section then followed with both spouses waking up out of sorts one morning. Fred and Talu became more and more annoyed with each other until they were shouting and letting the program get completely out of control.

The satire started with Fred and Talullah discussing possible radio opportunities they might explore.

FRED: Talullah, why do you bother with the theater? Rehearsals, one night stands, critics. Have you ever thought about radio?

TALULLAH: What could I do on radio, Fred? Duz does everything.

FRED: But the industry can use new talent.

TALULLAH: Radio's all right for you, Fred, but I have friends I have to face after each program.

FRED: Oh, you and I could go on the air together.

TALULLAH: You mean we'd be another Lum and Abner?

FRED: Well not right away. We'd have to work up to it. The new trend in radio is the husband-and-wife program. The husband and wife just sit at breakfast and chew the fat for half an hour.

TALULLAH: These couples broadcast from their own homes?

FRED: Yes, just jump out of bed around six in the morning.

TALULLAH: Six in the morning? That's for roosters. In the theater actors sleep until noon. Why, Fred, I was 24 years old before I knew what Wheaties were.

FRED: Talullah, all we'd have to do is eat 18 sponsor's products and talk about them for half and hour and the money would roll in.

TALULLAH : Money? I think I'm weakening.

FRED: Why we'd be a cinch, Talullah. Imagine our program. First, the listeners would hear the chime.

Chimes

ANNOUNCER: The current time is six A.M. and now *Talu and Freddy*, that happy, homey couple. We now take you to their apartment where they broadcast direct from their homey little breakfast table. Meet Talu and Freddy.

Sound of organ and canary chirping

TALU: Good morning, Freddy darling.

FREDDY: Good morning, Talu angel.

TALU: Sweetheart, I must say you look particularly well rested this morning.

FREDDY: Yes, thanks to our wonderful factory tested Pasternack Pussy Willow mattress — the mattress that takes all the guess work out of sleeping. So soft and so restful.

TALU: And just $17.50 at Bambergers.

FREDDY: And only in this mattress are the tender hearts of pussy willow used. Well, is breakfast ready, angel face?

TALU: Yes, sweetems, here's your coffee.

FREDDY: Thank you, doll. Umm, what coffee. What aromatic fragrance. It must be....

TALU: You're right, lovey.

FREDDY: I knew it. I knew it.

TALU: It's McKeaster's Vita-Fresh Coffee. The coffee with that locked up goodness. For every body — grind or drip.

TALU: Peach fuzz, you've spilled some on your vest.

FREDDY: Goodie, now I can try some of that Little Panther Spot Remover. No harsh rubbing. Just spray some Little Panther on your vest and watch it eat the spot out.

TALU: And imagine, darling, a big two ounce bottle for only 35 cents.

FREDDY: Or — if you're a congenital messy eater, you can get the handy economical 40 gallon vat.

TALU: Angel eyes darling, I have so much juicy gossip to tell our listeners this morning.

FREDDY: Stop! Don't you dare move, Talu.

TALU: What, darling?

FREDDY: What have you done to your hair? Your hair this morning is breath taking. That sheen! That brilliance!

TALU: Well, I went to Madame Yvonne's Hair-Do Heaven.

FREDDY: Yes.

TALU: It's on Madison Avenue. You go to the back of the orange juice stand, knock three times and ask for Antoine.

FREDDY: Antoine? Well I must say it's devine. It's bunny fluff.

TALU: Madame Yvonne uses that new sensational hair dressing that contains that new mystery ingredient — chicken fat.

FREDDY: I hear it's on sale at all the better swap shops. But go on, darling.

Canary chirping

FREDDY: Our canary, little Yasha.

TALU: Doesn't little Yasha sound glorius this morning?

FREDDY: Yes, and I bet he's saying "Gee Willikers, Mommy and Daddy, thanks for feeding me Gruber's Three-Way Bird Seed that comes in 15- and 25-cent packages tailored to fit the beak.

TALU: Little Yasha's so happy and so carefree.

FREDDY: And why shouldn't he be? He knows that the newspaper on the bottom of his cage is New York's leading daily — *The Morning Record*. The New York *Morning Record* has 32 columnists, 18 pages of comics and all the news that no other newspaper sees fit to print.

TALU: Excuse me, honey. I have a letter here from T.S. Button from Mole Hole, Idaho. Mrs. Button has had a splitting headache for 40 years until she heard about Pepto-Bepto on our program.

FREDDY: Yes, Pepto-Bepto is guaranteed to fizz twice — once before you drink it and once after.

TALU: And here's another interesting letter from a kleptomaniac. He writes....

Child's voice is heard

CHILD: Good morning, mumsy and daddy.

FREDDY: Oh, it's our little three-year-old daughter, Amber.

TALU: Good morning. Isn't she cute? Amber darling, I just love the way your tooth is shining this morning.

CHILD: Yes, mommy. I brushed it with Dr. Pratt's Homogenized Tooth Paste.

FREDDY: And what does Dr. Pratt's Toothpaste do, baby?

CHILD: It freshens your mouth, rolls up its sleeves and really does a job on your dirty old teeth.

FREDDY: Isn't she cute?

TALU: You run along to school, baby. Mommy and Daddy have oh so many things to tell our listeners.

FREDDY: Especially about the celebrities we saw at the Stork Club last night.

TALU: Wasn't it wonderful, Freddy? Tyrone Power, J. Edgar Hoover and Nick Kenny, all waving to us. Now what are you laughing about, lovey darling?

FREDDY: I was just thinking how witty Oscar Levant was last night when he poured that bottle of piccalilli over Jim Farley's head.

TALU: *Laughs.* Dear Oscar's so clever.

FREDDY: With piccalilli especially.

TALU: And wasn't Mr. Farley a good sport? He just sat there grinning and smacking his lips.

FREDDY: And you, too, will smack your lips if you taste Pinkerton's Pre-Shrunk Piccalilli — the only pickalilli that bears the *Hobo News* seal of approval.

Canary chirping

TALU: That's little Yasha telling us it's time to say goodbye.

FREDDY: We'll be back tomorrow morning at six. Until then, this is Freddy and

TALU: Talu.

FREDDY: Saying —

FREDDY AND TALU: Goodbye.

Organ Music

—

After this segment, Fred and Talullah agreed that the husband-and-wife program was an easy radio program format, but they decide nobody could possibly be that happy every day.

FRED: Wasn't that simple, Talullah? With a program like this we could make a fortune.

TALULLAH: But it's ridiculous, Fred. Nobody can possibly be that cheerful every morning.

FRED: Well, that's true. If one of these happy couples woke up grouchy one morning the listeners would probably hear something like this.

Organ Music

FREDDY: *Sleepily* Ahhhhhh.

TALU: Hey, knuckle head, get out of that bed. You've got a program to do.

FREDDY: Will you stop yapping? Six o'clock in the morning. Who's up to hear us? A couple of garbage collectors and a couple of burglars, maybe.

TALU: Well if you want to go back hustling gardenias in front of Macy's, go right ahead.

FREDDY: And what were you? The Queen of the Powder Room at the Brass Rail. My mouth feels like a sand hog just pulled his foot out of it. Gad, I'm sleepy.

TALU: Well, why don't you stay home at night and try sleeping?

FREDDY: Sleeping on that Pasternack Pussy Willow mattress? Pussy willow? It's stuffed with cat hair. Every time I lay down on that cat hair, my back arches.

TALU: Oh, stop beefing. Here's your coffee.

FREDDY: Well, it's about time. PSST! What are you trying to do poison me?

TALU: It's that McKeaster's Coffee. It won't poison you.

FREDDY: It won't, eh? Why do you think the government makes them put the skull and crossbones on the can. Look at that. I spilled some coffee on my vest.

TALU: You're such a slob. I'll get a bottle of Little Panther Spot Remover.

FREDDY: You're not putting any of that atom juice on me. The last time it ate away my shirt and I still have the spot left. Where do you find these sponsors? In the police line-up?

TALU: Look, gruesome, if you keep your bazoo shut for one minute....

FREDDY: YAAH!

TALU: What is it?

FREDDY: Your hair. It looks as though you just took your head out of a Mix- Master.

TALU: I know. That hag Madame Yvonne with her chicken fat. My hair keeps sliding off my head.

Canary chirping

FREDDY: Ah, that bird again. Shut up, you molting pest. I thought I told you to give that shrunken sparrow some of Dr. Gruber's Bird Seed.

TALU: I did. Now Misha is the only canary in the country with an ulcer.

FREDDY: The way Gruber palms off that chopped up beaver board on bird lovers.

TALU: What's in the mail today, chowder head?

FREDDY: A stomach. Someone took that Pepto-Bepto and dropped dead. Why don't you?

TALU: Look here, pan face.

FREDDY: Shut up.

Canary chirping

FREDDY: And, Yasha, you shut up, too.

Child's voice is heard

CHILD: Good morning, mommy and daddy.

Sound of a slap and child crying

FREDDY: That will teach you sneaking up on your parents with that one tooth like an old elf, little Amber.

TALU: Can the kid help it if she looks like you? Well, I told you we should have read the book before we named her.

CHILD: I want my breakfast.

Sound of a slap and child crying

FREDDY: Go gum a doughnut.

TALU: Pipe down. I want to mention some celebrities we saw last night at the Stork Club.

FREDDY: What celebrities? We ate last night at the Automat and you know it. I'm going back to bed.

TALU: The program isn't over yet, dope. We still have 160 products to mention.

FREDDY: Yeah, well you mention them. I've had enough of this six o'clock racket with you and that kid and that canary yapping around. I've got a gun.

Shot

TALU: You rat. You shot Yasha.

FREDDY: Yes, and you're next.

Shot

TALU: Ohhhhhh.

CHILD: Daddy, you killed Mommy.

FREDDY: Yes, Amber.

Shot

AMBER: Am I going, Daddy?

FREDDY: Yes, *Forever Amber*. Tune in tomorrow, folks, for something new in radio programs — *One Man's Family* without the family.

—

The satires of Fred Allen, however, were not more interesting or entertaining than their original target. Ben Gross, the radio critic of the New York *Daily News*, said that the Fitzgeralds were radio's first husband-and-wife talk team and set the example for the many imitators that followed (Gross, 1954, p. 91). He reported that the Fitzgeralds did not always use the "Dear" and "Darling" means of address like so many of their imitators. In fact, Gross (1954, p. 91) observed that although Ed's acerbic remarks were sometimes directed at Pegeen, the respect and devotion that each had for the other was always obvious. At times, Ed would endearingly call Pegeen "Mrs. FitzG honey." Pegeen's nickname for her husband was "Lord Edward."

Two former employees, early and late, of the Fitzgeralds, Jeanne Toomey and Lori Cassels, have provided valuable information about these interesting broadcasters. Jeanne Toomey was a New York crime reporter and columnist, whose book, *Assignment Homicide*, contains a wealth of interesting anecdotes about the Fitzgeralds. At age 21, Toomey was covering police headquarters for the Brooklyn *Daily Eagle*. In 1952, on the way to Europe aboard the super liner U.S. United States, she decided that a possible topic for her *Harbor Lights* column was how pampered dogs and cats traveled across the Atlantic.

When Toomey went down to the ship's kennel, she met a distinguished couple, Ed and Pegeen Fitzgerald visiting their cats, Pussy Willow and Half-is-Alley, who were traveling to Europe with them. This chance meeting led to a life long friendship and work on *The Fitzgeralds* radio program. When Toomey returned from Europe to Brooklyn and the *Eagle*, she received a phone call from Pegeen asking her to visit them. They offered her a job. Eventually Toomey become director of Pegeen's Last Post Animal Sanctuary, located in Falls Village, Connecticut.

At the time Toomey went to work for them, the Fitzgeralds lived in a brownstone on East Seventy-Eighth Street in Manhattan. The town house contained a number of homeless animals, an elderly Shakespearian actor, who both worked as a caretaker there and at the Fitzgeralds' weekend house on Nay Island and his granddaughter who doubled as a maid. This arrangement was typical of the pair's generosity and humane instincts.

While working for the program, Toomey also performed many small chores for Pegeen and Ed. Toomey, who was not adverse to taking a wee drop now and then, recalls that Ed's remarks on the program were frequently outspoken and caustic. During one of the programs, Toomey recalls, Ed queried his wife, "Madam, I demand an explanation. Every time I take that new dog for a walk, it pulls me down to Third Avenue, turns sharp left and drags me into an Irish bar where everyone seems to know it, and the bartender feeds it bologna. Can you explain this?" In her book, Toomey reveals that she could have provided Ed with an explanation, but chose to remain silent (Toomey, 1998, pp. 75–76).

After Ed died in 1982, Pegeen carried on the program alone until she was unceremoniously dropped by WOR in 1983. Her faithful listeners created a storm of protest, but unfortunately they were well beyond the age that the station wanted to attract.

Toomey's autobiography tells the story of a distinguished female journalist, who found an exciting and rewarding journalistic career on the Brooklyn *Eagle* and with King Features plus a lasting friendship with the Fitzgeralds. It includes Toomey's description of her duties at the Last Post Animal Sanctuary as the "chief of operations and concierge of a cat hotel and retirement home" (Toomey, 1989, p. 156) established and funded by Pegeen through the two nonprofit organizations she [Pegeen] had founded.

Lori Cassels, now a singer, songwriter and teacher of the visual impaired, was an employee of the Fitzgeralds during their later years. She was a college girl from the Bronx when she went to work for Pegeen in 1975 and continued on and off as "part secretary and part producer and two parts slave" until 1982. During this time Cassels also worked for the Vivisection Investigation League and the Mercy Animal Clinic that provided low cost spaying and neutering service; and the Millenium Guild, a society of vegetarians that promoted the ethical treatment of animals, all projects of Pegeen. Although people sent donations, essentially these were organizations Pegeen directed and financed when necessary to keep them going. In addition, Pegeen frequently supported other projects, such as documentaries on animal rights and numerous other causes.

Cassels performed various duties for the Fitzgeralds, including traveling down to station WOR to pick up commercial copy and their mail. The Fitzgeralds at that time still conducted the program from their own house on East Seventy-Eighth Street. Cassels eventually stayed with the couple during their broadcasts to assist them with their radio guests and sometimes to speak on the air. Her insights into the couple's broadcasting activities is illuminating, but equally important are the insights she provided about Pegeen as a humanitarian and constant advocate for animals and animal rights.

A particularly interesting story is Cassels' account of Pegeen's faithful volunteer Butterfly McQueen during one of Pegeen's campaigns against cruelty to animals. One of Pegeen's practices was always to have a personal assistant, one of whom was Kathy Novak. After Novak left the Fitzgeralds, she went on to become producer of WOR's *Sherrye Henry Show* and then the *John Gambling Program,* before moving on to work at TV's Public Broadcasting Corporation. Kathy Novak was generally appreciated and well remembered, particularly by Butterfly McQueen, who continued to call all of Pegeen's later assistants "Kathy." Long on spirit, but short on memory, McQueen always called Ms. Cassels and the four other young women who worked for the Fitzgeralds—"Kathy." It was "Thank you, Kathy" and "Goodbye, Kathy" to all the girls.

Lori Cassels recalls that one of the major events that occurred while she worked for the Fitzgeralds was the protest again the Museum of Natural History's bizarre experimentation on cats. Pegeen's campaign was successful in rallying many supporters to protest against these experiments. Sometimes more than a hundred people would come into Manhattan on an weekend to protest. From Pegeen's office, Lori and others passed out signs reading FREE THE CATS and STOP THE TORTURE.

One of the frequent protesters was Butterfly McQueen, whose role as Prissy in *Gone with the Wind* made her famous. Cassels said McQueen, unlike other volunteer protesters, would not telephone to say she was participating. She would just appear at the Museum of Natural History to carry her FREE THE CATS sign.

A year passed and animal experimentation ceased at the museum. The campaign had been successful long ago. One day when Ms. Cassels was driving down Central Park West she spotted a lone woman on the museum's steps with a FREE THE CATS sign. When she walked up to the single protester, she saw that it was Butterfly McQueen, who immediately greeted Lori with a smile and said in her high pitched singsong voice, "Kathy, so good to see you."

Like others who came in contact with Pegeen, Cassels admired her energy, humanity and kindness. Pegeen once described her radio show as, "Book talk, back talk and small talk" (Cassels, 2000). Along with the banter between Pegeen and "Lord Edward," there was some talk of current events, some reminiscences and Ed's book reviews. Usually there was a liberal amount of animal stories accompanied by a constant appeal from Pegeen for their humane treatment. Pegeen also often talked about the antics of her own animals and broadcast a list of animals that needed good homes. When interviewed by J.D. Reed for *People* magazine (August 18, 1986), she was asked what kept her on the air for 50 years. Pegeen responded that she didn't have the faintest idea, and that when her sister, Eve, who lived on the West Coast visited her she said, "I don't think you're very talented. You seem just like you do at home." Pegeen did go on to suggest that her program was a "true-to-life soap opera" (*People*, August 18, 1986, p. 88).

Ms. Cassals summed up her five years of part-time work with the Fitzgeralds by writing that her job was formative in the way that "first jobs, new friends, and working in Manhattan can [be]." Although she did recall how tedious the office work was and how answering the telephone could sometimes be mind numbing, she also learned that "Manhattan was exhilarating and [that]radio personalities could be generous, exacting, irascible and downright bizarre" (Cassals, 2000).

Anecdotes illustrating Pegeen's kindly and optimistic approach to life are numerous. Cassals says that sometimes her job was to pick up animals that needed homes. Once in a home of a kind, visually impaired elderly woman, she found well fed rats, mistaken by the woman for cats, eating from cans of sardines that she had placed on the kitchen floor. When Cassals reported this to Pegeen, her response was, "Rats can be quite docile when given regular meals."

After Ed's death in 1982, Pegeen continued broadcasting alone, but she seemed to recognize that her broadcast career was coming to an end. The time of the program's broadcast changed from 11:00–12:00 noon, to 2:00–3:00 P.M., then, finally, from 8:00–10:00 P.M. Pegeen took the changes in stride, adjusting her work and personal schedules accordingly each time. Then on a Thursday in 1983, WOR informed her that Friday would be her last show. Although the young women who worked for her were sad, unflappable Pegeen took the firing like the good trooper she was. Pegeen's fans protested, but WOR continued its seemingly endless pursuit of a "young" listening audience. Pegeen ended her career by co-hosting with Marty Wayne a daily, 90-minute public radio program (WNYC, New York, NY, 1983), beginning two months after WOR terminated her.

After her death in 1989, Pegeen's love for animals was further demonstrated by the considerable legacy she provided in their behalf. One of her contributions, Last Post Sanctuary for animals located in Falls Village, CT, was predominantly a cat shelter, but also included a few goats, dogs and three pot-bellied pigs. Although the some 350 cats were up for adoption, many of the older ones would spend the rest of their lives there.

Last Post is located on a 37- acre site that cost an estimated $300,000 in 1984 when it was established. The Vivisection Investigation League, a group founded and financed by Pegeen, provided the money for its establishment. The Post's operation is funded entirely by contributions.

Another contribution Pegeen made was the Pegeen Fitzgerald Wildlife Preserve, located near Williamstown, New York, which she funded. She gave the 125-acre wildlife preserve, located near Pulaski, New York, the Salmon River and Lake Ontario, to the Millennium Guild in 1985. In 2001, the Millennium Guild honored the great jazz singer by renaming the 125-acre parcel the Mabel Mercer Wildlife Preserve.

The husband-and-wife talk format the Fitzgeralds originated is gone. Only a few listeners still remember the rapid ebb and flow of husband-and-wife conversation that passed between Pegeen and Lord Edward on their broadcasts. Two non-profit organizations that Pegeen founded and originally funded are still in existence, the Millenium Guild and the Vivisection Investigation League. It is through them that the warmth of Pegeen's humanity and love of animals lives on.

15704 ***Husbands and Wives.*** Sedley Brown and Allie Lowe Miles conducted a program that allowed husbands and wives to discuss publicly their domestic problems on this summer replacement for *The Bakers Broadcast with Robert Ripley* on NBC in 1936. The program first appeared on WOR on a sustaining basis with the same hosts. *Variety* praised it as an entertaining forum on which married couples discussed various domestic topics (30 min., Wednesday, 10:30–11:00 P.M., WOR, Newark, NJ, 1935).

15705 **Huse, Bertha.** COM-HE (WLAW, Lawrence, MA, 1949).

15706 **Huseby, Larry.** Newscaster (KMO, Tacoma, WA, 1939). Sportscaster (KVI, Tacoma, WA, 1942; KVI, 1944–1945).

15707 **Husen, Harvey.** DJ Husen conducted a *P.M. Platter Party* (60 min., Monday through Friday, WABY, Albany, NY, 1949).

15708 **Huser, William A.** Newscaster (WGBG, Greensboro, NC, 1945).

15709 **Husing, Edward Britt "Ted."** Husing was born in 1902 in Deming, New Mexico. He began his announcing career by answering a WJZ (New York, NY) advertisement for an announcer. In 1924 he joined the WJZ staff that already included such distinguished announcers as Milton J. Cross, J. Milton Reid, John B. Daniel and Norman Brokenshire. Husing began broadcasting sports in 1925, by assisting Major Andrew White cover the Pennsylvania-Cornell football game and providing effective "color." Husing left WJZ to join WBET (Boston, MA), the station of the Boston, *Evening Transcript* newspaper but he soon returned to New York to work at WHN (New York, NY). When Major Andrew White became ill in 1928, William Paley appointed Husing as the Columbia Broadcasting System's junior announcer and chief sportscaster.

A high point of Husing's career was his opportunity to broadcast Herbert Hoover's presidential inauguration ceremony in 1929. Husing appeared on CBS from 1939 to 1945. His work there included his *Ted Husing's Sports Slants* (30 min., Saturday, 6:30–6:45 P.M., CBS, 1930) and the *Ted Husing* sports program (CBS, 1936). He later broadcast *Ted Husing Sports* on WMGM (New York, NY, 1951–1952). Husing also worked as a DJ: (*Ted Husing's Bandstand*, WHN, New York, NY, 1947; *Ted Husing's Bandstand*, WMGM, New York, NY, 1948–1954). *See **The Ted Husing Bandstand***.

15710 **Huss, J.W.** Sportscaster (WJMS, Ironwood, MI, 1944). Newscaster (WJMS and WATW, Ashland, WI, 1945; WJMS, 1945–1947 and WIBK, Iron Mountain, MI, 1947).

15711 **Hussery, Charles.** Bass (WHT, Chicago, IL, 1926).

15712 **Hussey, Court.** Leader (*Court Hussey Orchestra*, instr. mus. prg., WMT, Cedar Rapids–Waterloo, IA, 1937).

15713 **Husted, K.W.** Announcer (WCCO, Minneapolis–St. Paul, MN, 1928).

15714 **Hustler, Horace.** Organist (WABQ, Haveford, PA, 1926).

15715 **Husting, Lucille.** Actress Husting was a cast member of the daytime serial program *Mary Marlin* aka *The Story of Mary Marlin*.

15716 **Huston, Theodore.** Newscaster (WMAS, Springfield, MA, 1940).

15717 **Hustow [Huston], George Fleming.** Baritone (NBC, 1934).

15718 **Hutch, Nita.** COM-HE (WTVN, Columbus, OH, 1956–1957).

15719 **Hutchenson, Kenneth.** Newscaster (KGA-KHQ, Spokane, WA, 1941).

15720 **Hutchins, Alice.** Leader (*Alice Hutchins Orchestra*, instr. mus. prg., WRC, Washington, DC, 1935).

15721 **Hutchins, Clair.** Evangelist (WABC, New York, NY, 1959).

15722 **Hutchins, Dave.** Sportscaster (*Sports Desk*, WCHI, Chillicothe, OH, 1960).

15723 **Hutchins, Minabell.** COM-HE (WPTW, Piqua, OH, 1956–1957).

15724 **Hutchinson, Dorothy.** Singer (KWSC, Pullman, WA, 1926).

15725 **Hutchinson, Jimmie.** DJ (*The Boogie Man*, WHSY, Hattiesburg, MS, 1948).

15726 **Hutchinson, Lola.** Soprano (WENR, Chicago, IL, 1938).

15727 **Hutchinson, Martha.** Soprano (WEMC, Berrien Springs, MI, 1925).

15728 **Hutchinson, Mary.** Singer (WNYC, New York, NY, 1936).

15729 **Hutchinson, Ray.** DJ (KOL, Seattle, WA, 1957–1960).

15730 **Hutchison, Burt.** Guitarist on the WSM *Barn Dance* (WSM, Nashville, TN, 1928).

15731 **Hutchinson, Dorothy.** Singer (KWSC, Pullman, WA, 1926).

15732 **Hutchison, Elizabeth S.** COM-HE (WGVM, Greenville, MS, 1956–1957).

15733 **Hutchison, Emily.** COM-HE (WILK, Wilkes-Barre, PA, 1957).

15734 **Hutchison, Fred.** DJ (*Record Session* and *Musical*, WHUN, Huntington, PA, 1947).

15735 **Hutchison, Phyl.** DJ (*Breakfast Club*, WRON, Ronceverte, WV, 1947).

15736 **Hutler, Ana.** Soprano (WEAF, New York, NY, 1923).

15737 **Hutmaker, Barbara.** COM-HE (KUEN, Wenatchee, WA, 1957).

15738 **Hutson, John D.** Newscaster (WFIN, Findlay, OH, 1945).

15739 **Hutson, Lee.** COM-HE (WSAC, Radcliff, KY, 1955).

15740 **Hutton, Bernice.** Pianist (KWWG, Brownsville, TX, 1926).

15741 **Hutton [Hotton], Gordie.** COM-HE (KXGN, Glendive, MT, 1949).

15742 **Hutton, Ina Ray.** Leader (*Ina Ray Hutton Orchestra*, instr. mus. prg., MBS, 1939, 1942).

15743 **Hutton, Joan.** Singer (WBEN, Buffalo, NY, 1936).

15744 **Hutz, Jake.** Leader (Jake Hutz and his Pumpkin Vine Orchestra, WLW, Cincinnati, OH, 1925).

15745 ***Hy Gardner Calling.*** Broadway columnist Hy Gardner broadcast show business news and gossip (15 min., Friday, 10:00–10:15 P.M., NBC, mid–1930s).

15746 **Hyams, Isabel J.** News commentator (*News for Women*, KLIZ, Brainerd, MN, 1947).

15747 **Hyatt, Marion.** DJ (*The Alarm Clock Club*, WJHO, Opelika, AL, 1947).

15748 **Hycke, Ad.** Sportscaster (KGY, Olympia, WA, 1950s).

15749 **Hyde, Bill.** Newscaster (KFIZ, Fond-du-Lac, WI, 1939).

15750 **Hyde, (Mrs.) Clarence R.** Lecturer (*Historical Houses*, WEAF, New York, NY, 1925).

15751 **Hyde, Don.** Newscaster (WGAR, Cleveland, OH, 1947).

15752 **Hyde, George.** Leader (George Hyde Orchestra, KMIC, Inglewood, CA, 1928).

15753 **Hyde, Henry.** Hyde delivered talks on astronomy (NBC-KPO, San Francisco, CA, 1928).

15754 **Hyde, Susan.** COM-HE (WKOA, Hopkinsville, KY, 1956).

15755 ***(The) Hyde Park Alarm Clock.*** The Hyde Park Brewery Company sponsored the unusual morning program that featured Van Vanschoick, an ex-burlesque comic who *really* was the station's janitor. Each morning the janitor stopped his janitorial duties and performed with straight man, Randall Jessee, the KWOS program manager (*Billboard*, January 15, 1938, p. 8). They sang duets, joked and discussed current events (30 min., Daily, 7:00–7:30 A.M., KWOS, Jefferson City, MO, 1938).

15756 **Hyde Park High School Girls' Glee Club.** Scholastic vocal group (WMAQ, Chicago, IL, 1926).

15757 **Hyden, Vic, Jr.** Sportscaster (KTSW, Emporia, KS, 1944).

15758 **Hyder, Doc.** Leader (*Doc Hyder Orchestra*, instr. mus. prg., WIP, Philadelphia, PA, 1935).

15759 **Hydrick, Betty.** COM-HE (WDIX, Orangeburg, SC, 1957–1960).

15760 **Hydrick, (Mrs.) J.C., Jr.** COM-HE (WDIX, Orangeburg, SC, 1957).

15761 **Hyer, (Dr.) Robert Stewart.** Dr. Hyer broadcast Sunday School Lessons (WFAA, Dallas, TX, 1925).

15762 **Hyland, Dan.** Newscaster (WHAI, Greenfield, MA, 1942).

15763 **Hylland, Miriam.** COM-HE (KMMT, Austin, MN, 1955).

15764 **Hylton, Jack.** Leader (*Jack Hylton Orchestra*, instr. mus. prg., CBS, 1935; NBC, 1936).

15765 **Hyman, Maxine.** COM-HE (WYMB, Manning, SC, 1957).

15766 **Hymes, Joe.** Leader (*Joe Hymes Orchestra*, instr. mus. prg., CBS, 1934).

15767 ***Hymn Time.*** *Hymn Time* was an early morning religious program originating from the Chicago Gospel Tabernacle (WLS, Chicago, IL, 1933).

15768 ***Hymns of All Churches.*** Singer Joe Emerson and a choir performed spirituals and sacred songs of various creeds and denominations on the long-running program sponsored by General Mills (15 min., Monday through Friday, 9:00–9:15 A.M., MBS, 1935).

15769 ***Hymns We Love.*** The program of church hymns honored requests from listeners (KWLC, Decorah, IA, 1927).

15770 **Hynd [Hyrd], June.** News commentator (*Guest Book* and *Let's Talk It Over*, NBC, 1938–1939).

15772 ***(The) I.G. Glee Club.*** The glee club was a Black gospel quartet whose first weekly broadcasts made the program an immediate favorite with Memphis listeners. The group included C.H. Evans, R.S. Saunders, E.L. Rhodes and L.S. Brown. The sponsor was the Illinois Central Railroad (Weekly, WREC, Memphis, TN, 1927–1930s).

15773 ***I Deal in Crime.*** William Gargan starred on the adventure series as private eye, Ross Dolan. Music was supplied by Skitch Henderson. The announcer was Dresser Dahlstead (ABC, 1945–1947).

15774 ***I Give You My Life.*** Molly Picon starred on the program that combined music and dramatic episodes that purported to be the story of her life. General Foods was the program's sponsor (30 min., Tuesday, 7:30–8:00 P.M., WMCA, New York, NY, 1938).

15775 ***I Love a Mystery.*** Carleton E. Morse created and wrote the adventure series that told the story of three friends who operated the A-1 Detective Agency. They were: Jack Packard, a rugged, clear thinking stalwart played by Michael Raffetto; Reggie Yorke, a strong, precise British gentleman, played by Walter Paterson; and Doc Long, a tough, devil-may-care Texan, played by Barton Yarborough. Their adventures, crafted by the prolific Morse with his love of language and dramatic daring do, took them all over the world and placed them in some of the most memorable stories broadcast during the so-called Golden Age of Radio. Few listeners can forget how an organ mysteriously played "Brahm's Lullaby" without anyone at the keyboard, how the ghostly baby cried in a house without children whenever some horrible deed was committed, or the strange doings and dangers the three friends encountered in the Temple of the Vampires. Although it began with a 15-minute format broadcast daily during the World War II years, the show eventually evolved into a 30-minute weekly program. Over the years the cast included: Gloria Blondell, Jim Boles, Elliott Lewis, Cathy Lewis, Mercedes McCambridge, John McIntire, Jay Novello, Walter Paterson, Michael Raffetto, Tony Randall, Russell Thorson, Luis Van Rooten, Barbara Jean Wong and Barton Yarborough. The director was Mel Bailey. Michael Raffetto also performed some writing duties with the program's creator-writer, Carlton E. Morse.

When the series was repeated in 1949, the cast included Russell Thorson, Jim Boles and Tony Randall in the cast as the three friends (15 min., Monday through Friday, 7:45–8:00 P.M., MBS, 1950). For more information about Carlton E. Morse and his writing, see the ***One Man's Family*** program entry and also **Drama**.

15776 ***I Love Linda Dale.*** Helen Shields played the title of role of Linda Dale on the daytime dramatic serial. Her husband, Eric Dale, was played, in turn, by Raymond Edward Johnson and James Meighan. Other members of the cast included: Claire Howard, Arthur Hughes, and Kay Strozzi.

15777 ***I Sustain the Wings.*** The U.S. Air Force sponsored the transcribed dramatic show with music and the message: Victory in Europe has been achieved, now let's finish the job (30 min., Saturday, 6:00–6:30 P.M., NBC-Red, 1945). *See* **Wartime Radio.**

15778 ***I Was a Communist for the FBI.*** Dana Andrews played the role of Mart Cvetic, a FBI agent who infiltrated the Communist Party. For nine years, Cvetic was a member of a Communist cell and reported to the FBI on its operation. The syndicated adventure series, sponsored by the Kingston Cake Company, was produced by the Frederick W. Ziv Company (30 min., Sunday, 6:00–6:30 P.M., Transcribed, WIP, Philadelphia, PA, 1952).

15779 ***I Was There.*** Knox Manning narrated dramatized accounts of various headline events. Four events were featured on each program. The first program presented the political contest in 1916 between President Wilson and Charles Evans Hughes.

15780 **Iane, Mary.** Soprano (WELI, New Haven, CT, 1937).

15781 **Iatone, Leone.** Pianist (KTHS, Hot Springs National Park, AK, 1928).

15782 **Iceland Orchestra.** Local music group (WHN, New York, NY, 1926).

15783 ***Ici Paris.*** French talent was presented on the weekly series, sponsored by the Canadian Radio Commission (30 min., Wednesday P.M., 9:00–9:30 P.M., NBC). Jacques Lenoir was the host. Contralto Lucienne Deval and a tenor duo of Jules and Gaston provided the vocal selections.

15784 **Ickes, Harold.** Politician Harold Ickes, former Secretary of the Interior for FDR, delivered a commentary on the news with incisiveness, humor and a definite political slant. The sponsor was Chevrolet (15 min., WGAY, Silver Spring, MD, 1947).

15785 ***Ida Bailey Allen.*** *See* ***The Happy Homemaker.***

15786 **Ide, Carl.** Sportscaster (WKNE, Keene, NH, 1941). DJ (*Pittsburgh's First Favorites*, KDKA, Pittsburgh, PA, 1947; *Carl Ide Calling*, WNJR, Newark, NJ, 1948; *Jazz Revue*, WNJR, 1949; *S S Cool*, WNJR, 1950).

15787 **Idelson, Billy.** Actor Idelson was in the cast of *Gasoline Alley*, *One Man's Family*, *Secret City*, *That Brewster Boy* and *Vic and Sade*. On the latter program, Idelson played the role of the son — Rush Gook.

15788 **Ideal Novelty Orchestra.** Popular novelty band (WHN, New York, NY, 1924).

15789 **Ihlenfeld, Warren.** DJ (*Take It Easy Time*, WISR, Butler, PA, 1948–1949). Sportscaster (*Sports Spotlight*, WISR, 1951).

15790 ***Il Progresso Program.*** Newscaster Gino Pagliari broadcast international, national and local news (WHOM, New York, NY, 1946).

15791 **Ilch, Charley.** Leader (Charley Ilch's Sunset Canyon Country Club Orchestra, KFWB, Hollywood, CA, 1925).

15792 **Iler, George.** Iler was the director in charge of station WSB, Atlanta, GA, when it first went on the air in 1922. Iler and Walter Tison, both licensed radio operators, were station WSB's first employees.

15793 ***(The) Ilka Chase Show.*** Ilka Chase talked about a variety of topics with charm and intelligence on her sustaining show (30 min., Monday, Wednesday and Friday, 2:00–2:30 P.M., WJZ, New York, NY, 1951).

15794 ***I'll Never Forget.*** *True Story* magazine sponsored the program and provided some dramatic material. Listener letters were also dramatized each week. Most letters were about the trials and tribulations involved with the listeners' romantic entanglements. Pat Barnes served as the program narrator. He frequently read Bernarr MacFadden's editorials. Songs by Frank Luther were regular features of the program (15 min., Wednesday, 1:00–1:15 P.M., MBS, 1940).

15795 **(The) Illinois Four.** Male quartet (WHT, Chicago, IL, 1928).

15796 ***Illinois Historyland.*** Illinois state history was the subject of a series of dramatic sketches on the educational program. The cast included Orin Brandon, Hazel Dopheide, Graydon Goss, Dan Hosmer, Dorothy McDonald, Jack Reidy and Bill Vickland. Raymond Warren Christorion wrote the series (WLS, Chicago, IL, 1935).

15797 ***Iloma Islanders Orchestra.*** Instr. mus. prg. (WTIC, Hartford, CT, 1936).

15798 **Imholtz, Dorothy.** COM-HE (KRBC, Abilene, TX, 1954–1955).

15799 ***Immortal Dramas.*** The Montgomery Ward Company sponsored the series of dramatic episodes based on Biblical stories. Unidentified performers appeared on the series (30 min., Monday, 1:00–1:30 P.M., NBC, 1935).

15800 ***Imperial Hawaiians Orchestra.*** Instr. mus. prg. (30 min., Sunday 2:30–3:00 P.M., CBS, 1935). The program was sponsored by the Wyeth Chemical Company.

15801 ***Imperial Male Choir.*** Vcl. mus. prg. (KUOA, Siloam Springs, AR, 1939).

15802 **(The) Imperial Sextet of Harmony.** Local vocal group (KDKA, Pittsburgh, PA, 1923).

15803 ***In a Beer Garden.*** The pleasant comedy told of the pleasures of beer and presented good music and talk. William Lundell and Henry L. Mencken were featured along with Frank Black's orchestra (30 min., Weekly, WJZ, New York, NY, 1933).

15804 ***In a Poet's Workshop.*** Dr. John W. Holland read two or three of his original poems after first explaining how he had decided on the subject matter of each. Many of the Reverend Dr. Holland's poems were published in his book, *Mother's Thimble and Other Poems* (15 min., Thursday, 11:00–11:15 A.M., WLS, Chicago, IL, 1935). *See* **Holland, John W.**

15805 ***In a Russian Village.*** Peter Biljou and his Russian musicians provided the music on the popular network program (30 min., Sunday, 8:30–9:00 P.M., CBS, 1929–1930).

15806 ***In Chicago Tonight.*** Dramatic sketches and musical selections were the major elements of the program. Music was provided by the Harold Stokes Orchestra and singers Annette Stewart and Bruce Foote (30 min., 10:30–11:00 P.M., MBS, 1940).

15807 ***In Danceland.*** Joseph Hornik conducting the orchestra and pianist Henry Starr were regulars on the weekly music program (NBC-Pacific Coast Network, 1929).

15808 ***In the Modern Manner.*** Johnny Green's orchestra played the music on the program that featured singers Sylvia Froos and Evelyn MacGregor and pianist Herman Wasserman. The program's announcer was Carlisle Stevens (15 min, Weekly, CBS, 1934).

15809 ***In the Spotlight.*** Soprano Rosalie Wolfe and baritone Philip Steele were featured on the music show. Ralph Freese was the announcer (15 min., NBC-Blue, 1929).

15810 ***In the Time of Roses.*** A women's vocal octet and tenor soloists, none of whom were identified, appeared on the show (15 min., Monday, 9:45–10:00 P.M., NBC-Red, 1930).

15811 **Inch, Merrill.** Newscaster (KOH, Reno, NV, 1939–1942). Sportscaster (KWRN, Reno, NV, 1949).

15812 ***Indiana Hoedown.*** CW musical program (WFBM, Indianapolis, IN, 1955). A popular "jamboree" program, the *Indiana Hoedown* featured such performers as: the Kentucky Briarhoppers, the Junior Kentucky Briarhoppers, Louise Innis, the Rangers, Judy and Jen, the Ranch Boys and Lee Jones.

15813 **(The) Indianians Orchestra.** Popular local dance band (WGCP, Newark, NJ, 1925).

15814 ***(The) Indigo Girl.*** Vcl. mus. prg. by an unidentified vocalist (WWVA, Wheeling, WV, 1935).

15815 ***Information Please.*** The panel quiz program with a high IQ provided listeners with an opportunity to test its erudite panelists. An unlikely listening audience favorite, the program remained on the air from 1938 to 1951, an extremely long run for an intellectual showcase.

After their first broadcast on May 17, 1938, on NBC-Blue, 2,500 letters were received. In 1945, after being on the air for five years, as many as 28,000 were received weekly.

The program opened with the sound of a rooster crowing and the announcer saying: "Wake up, America. Time to stump the experts. Why not join the rest of the great American public that is doing its best to upset our mental giants." Clifton Fadiman posed the questions to regular panel members including Franklin P. Adams, columnist of the New York *Post;* John Kiernan, sportswriter of the New York *Times*; and pianist Oscar Levant. Each week they were joined by a guest panelist that sometimes was Basil Rathbone, Walter B. Pitkin, Christopher Morley, Albert Spalding, Harkness Duffield, Gracie Allen, Fred Allen, Boris Karloff, Orson Welles, Deems Taylor, Groucho Marx or some other interesting personality. If the listeners' questions stumped the experts, they received a set of the *Encyclopaedia Brittanica* and a small cash prize. After five years on NBC, the program proudly announced that it had given away 1,142 editions of the *Enclyclopaedia Brittanica* and about $50,000. The show's sponsors over the years were Canada Dry, Lucky Strike cigarettes and H.J. Heintz.

15816 **Ingalls, Yodeling Jim.** CW yodeler (WDRC, Harford, CT, 1938).

15817 **Ingalls, Mary.** COM-HE (KGRH, Fayetteville, AR, 1956).

15818 **Ingalls, Wallie.** Sportscaster (KGRH, Fayetteville, AR, 1952–1954).

15819 **Ingebrigtsen, Len.** DJ (*Friendly Time,* KOY, Phoenix, AZ, 1954).

15820 **Ingersoll, C.H.** Newscaster (WLTH, Brooklyn, NY, 1939).

15821 **Ingham, Bob.** Sportscaster (*Highlights in the World of Sports,* WTOL, Toledo, OH, 1940–1941; WJW, Akron, OH, 1942; KTOK, Oklahoma City, OK, 1946; *Sportsviews,* KSD, St. Louis, MO, 1954–1956). Newscaster (WTMV, East St. Louis, IL, 1945).

15822 **Ingle, Yolande.** Contralto (KFXF, Colorado Springs, CO, 1926).

15823 **Inglis, Charles.** Sportscaster (KLZ, Denver, CO, 1939; WKY, Oklahoma City, OK, 1940–1941).

15824 **Ingraham, Eunice.** Soprano (KFSG, Los Angeles, CA, 1925).

15825 **Ingraham, Frances.** Miss Ingraham conducted a cooking show (WJZ, New York, NY, 1929).

15826 **Ingraham, Gene.** Leader (Gene Ingraham's Hotel Berwick Orchestra, WOR, Newark, NJ, 1923; Gene Ingraham's Bell Recording Orchestra, WOR, 1924; WRW, Tarrytown, NY, 1925).

15827 **Ingraham, Roy.** Leader (Roy Ingraham Orchestra, CBS, 1929).

15828 **Ingram, Arthur "Art."** Sportscaster (WLEU, Erie, PA, 1939; WERC, Erie, PA, 1941–1942). Newscaster (WBNY, Buffalo, NY, 1940; *World Wide and Local News,* WERC, 1947).

15829 **Ingram, Bill.** DJ (*Matinee at Melody Lane,* KSYL, Alexandria, LA, 1948).

15830 **Ingram, Corinne.** Singer (WCFL, Chicago, IL, 1926).

15831 **Ingram, Dan.** DJ (WNCH, New Haven, CT, 1957).

15832 **Ingram, Frances.** COM-HE (WOR, Newark, NJ, 1934).

15833 **Ingram, Inez.** Singer Ingram accompanied herself on the ukulele (KFI, Los Angeles, CA, 1929).

15834 **Ingram, Lillian.** Pianist (WGBS, New York, NY, 1925).

15835 **Ingram, Mary Margaret.** COM-HE (KSU, Gladwater, TX, 1949).

15836 **Ingram, Meriam.** COM-HE (WJWS, South Hill, VA, 1956–1957).

15837 **Ingram, Michael.** Actor Ingram was in the cast of *Against the Storm* and *Columbia Presents Corwin.*

15838 **Ingram, Rex.** Actor Ingram appeared on the *Against the Storm* daytime serial program.

15839 **Ingram, Roy.** DJ (WOOW, New Bern, NC, 1955).

15840 ***Ingram Shavers Program.*** Ingram Shaving Cream Company sponsored the program that featured the barber shop trio of Henry Shope, Walter Preston and Taylor Bucley (30 min., Wednesday, 9:00–9:30 P.M., NBC-Red, 1928–1929).

15841 **Ingstad, Bob.** Sportscaster (KOVC, Valley City, ND, 1939–1941; KOVC, 1945–1949; play-by-play, KOVC, 1951). Newscaster (*Noon News,* KOVC, 1945–1960).

15842 **(The) Ink Spots.** Popular Black male singing group and recording artists (*The Ink Spots,* vcl. mus. prg., NBC-Blue, 1935–1939). *See* **King, Jack.**

15843 **Inman, Anne.** COM-HE (WRUN, Utica, NY, 1951).

15844 **Inman, (Mrs.) S.D.** Soprano (WCBD, Zion, IL, 1924).

15845 ***Inner Sanctum*** (aka ***Inner Sanctum Mysteries).*** Radio's best remembered horror program was *Inner Sanctum,* with its host, Raymond Edward Johnson, who invited listeners to enter the program's famous *squeaking door.* Although the stories were sometimes mediocre, the atmosphere of horror was always present.

The program's opening included a brief

organ interlude, the squeaking door and Raymond Edward Johnson saying: "Good evening, friends. This is Raymond, your host, welcoming you in to the *Inner Sanctum*. Ed Herlihy, Allen C. Anthony and Dwight Weist were the announcers. The show's director-producer was Himan Brown. Its writers included Harry and Gail Ingram, Milton Lewis, Sigmund Miller, Robert Newman, John Roeburt and Robert Sloane. Jack Amerine was the busy sound effects man. Paul McGrath and House Jameson also hosted the program.

Guest stars frequently appeared on the program such as: Boris Karloff, Athur Vinton, Peter Lorre, Paul Lukas, Raymond Massey, Claude Rains and Richard Widmark (30 min., NBC, CBS, ABC, 1941–1952).

15846 Innes, Helen Pulaski. Pianist (WIP, Philadelphia, PA, 1924).

15847 Innes, Jane. COM-HE (KWBM, Williston, ND, 1954).

15848 ***(The) Inquiring Reporter.*** Veteran announcer and station executive Steve Cisler interviewed people on the streets of Atlanta (WJTL, Atlantic, GA, 1935). *See* **Cisler, Steve.**

15849 ***(The) Inquiring Reporter.*** France Laux conducted the local program on which each person who could answer a question correctly received a large can of fruit or vegetables (Three times weekly, KMOX, St. Louis, MO, 1936).

15850 ***(The) Inquiring Reporter.*** DJ Lanny Starr, with wire recorder in hand, traveled to S. Klein's department store several times a week to interview shoppers and give them cash prizes (30 min., Tuesday and Thursday, 9:00–9:30 P.M. and Saturday, 5:00–5:30 P.M., WNEW, New York, NY, 1947).

15851 ***Inside Football.*** Cleveland Browns' coach Paul Brown and Bob Neal talked football on their popular sports show (15 min., WGAR, Cleveland, OH, 1948).

15852 ***Inside News from Hollywood.*** Jay Sims broadcast Hollywood gossip. Hazel Bishop lipstick was the sponsor (15 min., Weekly, NBC, 1952).

15853 ***(The) Inside Story.*** Edwin C. Hill, who conducted the program, was a distinguished news reporter, who had never made a public speech before be began broadcasting. In 1930, Hill tried out for the position of newscaster on the *Literary Digest* program, but lost out to Lowell Thomas. The following year he began to broadcast the news for station WOR (Newark, NJ, 1931). Hart, Schaffner and Marx Clothing Company later sponsored his news program on a national CBS network. On the *Inside Story* for the Socony Vacuum Oil Company, Hill interviewed notables from all walks of life including Jack Dempsey, Ethel Barrymore, Grace Moore, Babe Ruth and Gene Tunney. He endeavored to give his listeners greater insight into the lives of those he interviewed and he was successful in doing so. *See* **Hill, Edwin C.**

15854 ***Inspector Thorne.*** Karl Weber played the title role of police inspector Thorne, and Danny Ocko played his assistant, Sergeant Muggins, on the sustaining crime drama. The program opened with the announcer proclaiming, "Tonight the National Broadcasting Company presents the exploits of the spectacular young Inspector Thorne of the homicide bureau, whose investigations rank with many of the most celebrated cases in the annals of crime fiction. An investigator smart enough to claim he is dumb and smart enough to believe it. And now the National Broadcasting Company presents Inspector Thorne in 'The Defrosted Refrigerator Case.'" On the first program of the series, Thorne and Muggins tracked down a millionaires's widow who had killed her husband. When the victim was killed, he fell to the floor screaming, "You killed me." After the case was successfully solved, Inspector Thorne summarized, "Murder is murder, and the price is execution." With dialogue of this nature, the cast had a serious obstacle to overcome. Eugene Edward Francis wrote and Kenneth MacGregor directed the program that was produced by Frank and Anne Hummert (30 min., Friday, 9:00–9:30 P.M., NBC, 1951).

15855 (The) Inspiration Boys. Al Cameron and Pete Bontsema were a popular singing comedy team (WMAQ, Chicago, IL, 1929). *See* ***Al and Pete*** *and* ***The Red Apple Club.***

15856 (The) Instrumental Trio. Pianist Geraldine McNeely directed the trio that included flutist William Fries and violinist Edward Lurton (WHAS, Louisville, KY, 1924).

15857 ***Insurance Court.*** A dramatic sketch and an informative talk were broadcast weekly on the sustaining program. "Real" cases were dramatized and listeners' letters answered by Morris H. Siegel. The program sought reform in the insurance business (30 min., Tuesday, 7:30–8:00 P.M., WENX, New York, NY, 1936).

15858 ***Interdenomination Services.*** The Reverend Claude C. Coile conducted the church services and the Federated Quartet provided vocal selections (WEAF, New York, NY, 1925).

15859 ***International Airport.*** Mason Adams, Everett Sloan and Gilbert Mack starred in the sustaining mystery drama series with a flying background. The first mystery broadcast was "Flight from Fear" (30 min., Thursday, 8:30–9:00 P.M., 1949).

15860 ***International Broadcast from Austria—the Salzburg Music Festival.*** The Vienna Philharmonic conducted by Bruno Walter was featured on the excellent music program (30 min., Sunday, 10:00–10:30 A.M., NBC, 1935).

15861 ***International Broadcast from Russia.*** This was another in a series of excellent music programs from overseas that featured the Moscow Radio Orchestra, its soloists, and singers Katherine Katulskaja, Nicholas Ossipiv and Anatoloj Sadonov. The National Folk Instruments Orchestra also performed with Peter Alexaev conducting (30 min., Sunday, 8:30–9:00 P.M., NBC, 1935).

15862 ***International Liars' Fraternity.*** Bill Green was the MC on the sustaining show. He told tall tales and wildly fanciful yarns. Music was supplied by William Stoess' Musical Prevaricators Band (15 min., Tuesday, 11:45–12:00 midnight, MBS, 1938).

15863 International Novelty Orchestra. The popular radio and recording orchestra was directed by Nathaniel Shilkret (WEAF, New York, NY, 1925; *Victor Hour* program, NBC-Blue, New York, NY, 1926). Although personnel for his band varied, often included were: Mike Mosiello, t.; Chuck Campbell, tb.; Andy Sanella, as. and stg. guitar; Lou Raderman, v.; Herb Borodkin, cl.; and Milt Rettenberg, p., bj., and tba.

15864 ***International Tidbits.*** Gregory Stone conducted the orchestra on the sustaining music program (30 min., Wednesday, 7:30–8:00 P.M., NBC-Blue, 1933).

15865 ***(The) Interwoven Pair.*** Billy Jones and Ernie Hare toured the continent in 1929 and originated some programs of their *Interwoven* [socks] *Pair* series from the NBC-Pacific Coast Network stations. Their program's orchestra on the tour was conducted by William Perry (30 min., Friday, 9:00–9:30 P.M., WJZ-Blue, 1930). *See* **Jones and Hare** *and* **The Happiness Candy Boys.**

15866 ***Intimate Interviews.*** Phil Anderson selected a theme and conducted interviews about it. For example, on one program he interviewed two eye-witnesses of the 1871 Chicago fire — Mrs. Ellen Boening and Walter Thine (15 min. Tuesday, 11:00–11:15 A.M., WLS, Chicago, IL, 1935).

15867 ***(The) Intimate Revue.*** Weekly guests appeared on the variety show that featured Dwight Fiske, the Al Goodman Orchestra and weekly guest stars (30 min., Thursday, 8:30–9:00 P.M., NBC, 1940s).

15868 Intropidi, Ethel. Actress Intropidi appeared on the daytime serial programs *Portia Faces Life, Pretty Kitty Kelly, Valiant Lady* and *Young Widder Brown.*

15869 ***(The) Invisible Microphone.*** The novel variety show took its microphone anywhere to find human interest stories or those with an odd twist. Ruppert Brewery sponsored the show that also featured comedian Arthur Boran, singer Jack Arthur and Lou Katzman's Orchestra (60 min., Friday, 9:00–10:00 P.M., WOR, Newark, NJ, 1933).

15870 ***Invitation to Learning.*** Lyman Bryson conducted the stimulating discussion program that each week focused on a classic work of fiction or nonfiction. Alfred Kazin and Leon Edel were among the panelists who regularly joined Bryson in the discussions. Some of the topics covered over the years were *The Letter of William James*, William Savage Landor's *Imaginary Conversations* and Arthur Conan Doyle's *Sherlock Holmes*. The program celebrated its 15th anniversary on May 19, 1955 (30 min., Sunday, 11:30–12:00 noon, CBS, 1959).

15871 ***(The) Iodent Program.*** Singer Jane Froman and the Roy Shields' Orchestra entertained on the show sponsored by Iodent tooth paste (15 min., Sunday, 3:00–3:15 P.M. CST, NBC, 1932). An earlier music program of the same name was broadcast on the NBC-Red network in 1926.

15872 Iodine, Leon. Organist (WTAL, Toledo, OH, 1926).

15873 Iona, Andy. Leader (*Andy Iona Orchestra*, instr. mus. prg., NBC, 1937).

15874 Iooss, Walter A. Novelty pianist (WAHG, Richmond Hill, NY, 1926).

15875 Iovino, Charles R. Newscaster (WLAW, Lawrence, MA, 1940–1941).

15876 *Iowa Barn Dance Frolic.* CW musical program, the *Iowa Barn Dance Frolic* (WHO, Des Moines, IA, 1931–1958) begun in 1931, was one of the earliest "jamboree" and "barn dance" programs on the air. Originated by J.O. Maland, the program's first sponsor was the Alladin Lamp Company. Stan Widney produced the show for many years. The program's featured performers were primarily those that filled the daily WHO broadcast schedule, including Lem Turner, the Buckaroos, the Crack-O-Dawners and Cliff Carl.

15877 *Iowa Cornhuskers.* CW mus. prg. by unidentified performers (WMT, Cedar Rapids–Waterloo, IA, 1937).

15878 Iowa Wesleyan Glee Club. Collegiate vocal group (WHO, Des Moines, IA, 1925).

15879 (The) Ipana Troubadours. Popular broadcast orchestra led by Sam Lanin (WEAF, New York, NY, 1925–1926; WJZ, New York, NY, 1926–1929). The band included: Hymie Farberman and Red Nichols, t.; Chuck Campbell, tb.; Dick Johnson and Alfie Evans, clr., as. and bar.; Lucien Smith, ts.; Harry Horlick, v.; Arthur Schutt, p.; Tony Colucci, bj. and g.; Vic Berton, d.; and Joe Tarto, tba. The band's theme, "Smiles," was appropriate for one that was featured on a program sponsored by Ipana Toothpaste.

15880 *(The) Ipana Troubadours—Ingram Shavers.* Bristol-Myers Co., makers of Ipana toothpaste and Ingram shave cream, sponsored the music show that featured a male trio and the Sam Lanin Orchestra (30 min., 8:30–9:00 P.M., NBC-Blue Network, 1930). A later format was that of a variety show with an emphasis on music (30 min., Wednesday, 9:00–9:30 P.M., NBC-Red Network, 1934).

15881 *(The) Ira Staden Show.* Municipally owned station WNYC (New York, NY) in 1948 established a precedence. For the first time in its 25 years of operation, the station broadcast a comedy show that *Variety* said was a good one. Ira Staden wrote and performed in a manner similar to Henry Morgan's satirical style. In the cast with Staden were Rene Paul, Doris Parker, Mike Lewin and Naomi Lewis. Herb Ross was the announcer (30 min., Monday, 9:15–9:45 P.M., WNYC, New York, NY, 1948).

15882 Irby, Bill. Sportscaster (WFEB, Sylacauga, AL, 1945).

15883 Ireland, Millard. Newscaster (KOMO, Seattle, WA, 1946).

15884 Ireland, Ward. Assistant announcer (KFOA, Seattle, WA, 1928).

15885 *Irene Beasley's RFD No. 1.* Singer Beasley performed and provided comment targeted for a farm audience on her sustaining program (15 min., Tuesday, 12:15–12:30 P.M., CBS, late–1930's). Later, Beasley also appeared on a program devoted entirely to her singing *Irene Beasley* (15 min., Monday, 3:15–3:30 P.M., CBS, 1945).

15886 *Irene Franklin.* Franklin, a former vaudeville comedienne, performed on her own sustaining comedy show (15 min., Wednesday, 10:15–10:30 P.M., NBC-Blue, 1933).

15887 *Irene Rich Dramas.* Miss Rich appeared with many radio stars in various dramatic presentations. Ry-Krisp sponsored most of the programs. Her announcers were: Frank Goss, Ed Herlihy and Marvin Miller (NBC, 1933; CBS, 1943–1944).

15888 *Irene Ryan's Toy Town Revue.* Comedienne-singer Ryan hosted her variety program (WIND, Gary, IN, 1935). She later played the crusty Granny on *The Beverly Hillbillies* TV show.

15889 Irish and His Uke. Ukulele performer not otherwise identified (KFBF, 1924).

15890 *Irish Blackbirds Orchestra.* Instr. mus. prg. by an orchestra directed by Martin Beirne (NBC, 1936).

15891 (The) Irish Minstrel. Singer Cornelius O'Sullivan was a popular Irish tenor (WGBS, New York, NY, 1927).

15892 Irland, George A. Announcer (WJBU, Lewisburg, PA, 1925).

15893 Irvin, Paul R. Leader, Irwin's Pep Orchestra (KDKA, Pittsburgh, PA, 1922).

15894 Irvin, Shirley. Whistler Irvin specialized in performing Rubenstein's "Melody in F" (KFUU, Oakland, CA, 1925).

15895 *Irvin S. Cobb's Paducah Plantation (aka Paducah Plantation).* Humorist Cobb hosted his variety show in the role of a southern colonel, who owned a large Kentucky plantation. The show's excellent cast included the Hall-Johnson Choir, baritone Clarence Muse, the Four Blackbirds vocal quartet, singer Dorothy Page, the Henry Jackson Orchestra and actors Norman Fields and John Mather. Guest stars such as Gertrude Niesen appeared weekly. Gayne Whitman was the announcer (NBC, 1936).

15896 Irvine, James. Pianist (WCAU, Philadelphia, PA, 1925).

15897 Irvine, Jane. COM-HE (KOOS, Coos Bay, OR, 1951).

15898 Irving, Alice. Soprano (WHAS, Louisville, KY, 1927).

15899 Irving, Bertie. COM-HE (WKO, Bluefield, WV, 1955).

15900 Irving, Bob. DJ (*Platter Chatter*, WLAP, Lexington, KY, 1947–1948; *Irving Serving*, WMAY, Springfield, IL, 1949; *Platter Chatter*, WLAP, 1950; WMAY, 1952).

15901 Irving, Charles. Newscaster (WGN, Chicago, IL, 1942). Announcer-actor Irving appeared on *Bobby Benson's Adventures* (actor), *Breakfast Club* (announcer), *Henry Morgan Show* (announcer), *This is Nora Drake* (announcer) and *Those Websters* (announcer).

15902 Irving, George. DJ (*GI Jive*, WCMA, Corinth, MS, 1947; *1230 Club*, WCMA, 1950).

15903 Irving, Jane. News commentator (*Woman's Side of the News*, WSAI, Cincinnati, OH, 1947).

15904 Irving, Jay. DJ (*Music for Moderns*, KVON, Napa, CA, 1949).

15905 Irving, Jim. DJ (*Radio Bazaar*, WESX, Salem, MA, 1947).

15906 Irving, Paul. DJ (*Evening Heatwave*, WEDC, Chicago, IL, 1947; *Midnight Flyers*, WEDC, 1947–1949).

15907 Irving, Peggy. COM-HE (WMAY, Springfield, IL, 1956).

15908 Irving, Philip. Baritone (*Philip Irving*, vcl. mus. prg., WIP, Philadelphia, PA, 1935).

15909 Irwin, Don. Leader (*Don Irwin Orchestra*, instr. mus. prg., KYW, Chicago, IL, 1933).

15910 Irwin, George. Newscaster (KFJZ, Fort Worth, TX, 1941).

15911 Irwin, Jim. Leader (Jim Irwin's Boston Society Orchestra, WKAV, Laconia, NH, 1922). Irwin's band made the first remote broadcast by WKAV, a week after the station went on the air.

15912 Irwin, John B. Newscaster (KRNT, Des Moines, IA and KSO, Des Moines, IA, 1945).

15913 Irwin, Mae. COM-HE (WFRA, Franklin, PA, 1960).

15914 Irwin, Roberta P. COM-HE (KYUM, Yuma, AZ, 1960).

15915 Irwin, Theodore. Organist (KPO, San Francisco, CA, 1925).

15916 Irwin, Victor "Vic." Leader-pianist (Vic Irwin Hollywood Orchestra, WOR, Newark, NJ; WMCA, New York, NY, 1929).

15917 *Irwin and Davis.* Instr. mus. prg. by a duo piano team (KYW, Philadelphia, PA, 1934).

15918 *Irwin Elliot the Wordcaster.* Irwin Elliot broadcast English grammar lessons on his program sponsored by L. Grossman & Sons, Inc. (15 min., Monday and Thursday, 8:00–8:15 P.M., WMEX, Boston, MA, 1937).

15919 Isaac, Billy. Leader (*Billy Isaac Orchestra*, instr. mus. prg., WCAO, Baltimore, MD, 1934).

15920 Isaac, Rose. COM-HE (WJMS, Ironwood, MI, 1949).

15921 Isaacs, Ethel. Violinist (KGO, Oakland, CA, 1925).

15922 Isaacs, Etta. Pianist (WGBS, New York, NY, 1925).

15923 Isabel, Jeannette. COM-HE (WILD, Birmingham, AL, 1956).

15924 Isbell, Harold. Announcer (KYW, Chicago, IL, 1925). Isbell moved to KNX (Hollywood, CA, 1928) after working at KFI (Los Angeles, CA, 1926). At KNX, Isbell was called "The Town Crier of the Night Watch."

15925 Isbell, Lelia. Pianist (KFI, Los Angeles, CA, 1925).

15926 Iseminger, Audrey. Pianist (*Audrey Iseminger*, instr. mus. prg., WDBJ, Roanoke, VA, 1935–1936).

15927 Ish, Milton. Pianist (KFWM, Oakland, CA, 1929).

15928 Isherwood, James. Baritone (KGO, Oakland, CA, 1925–1926).

15929 **Island City Lodge Symphony Orchestra.** Fraternal musical group (WGBS, New York, NY, 1926).

15930 ***Isle of Golden Dreams.*** Johnnie Walker created and hosted the Pacific Coast variety program (1932).

15931 **Isley, James.** DJ (*Chocolate Jam*, WBBB, Burlington, NC, 1960).

15932 **Ison, Happy ["Hap"].** DJ (*Orange Blossom Special*, WORZ, Orlando, FL, 1952; *Sports Review*, WORZ, 1953).

15933 **Ison, Janis "Jan."** COM-HE (WKOA, Hopkinsville, KY, 1956–1957).

15934 **Ison, S.W.** Sportscaster (WORZ, Orlando, FL, 1953).

15935 **Ison, Steve.** DJ (*Magic Valley Jamboree*, WTIP, Charleston, WV, 1948).

15936 **Israel, Abner.** Newscaster (WGPC, Albany, GA, 1941; *It Happened During the Week*, WALB, Albany, GA, 1945–1947).

15937 **Israel, Ann.** COM-HE (WJNO, West Palm Beach, FL, 1957).

15938 **Israel, Joseph.** Newscaster (WIP, Philadelphia, PA, 1936).

15939 **Israel Temple Choir.** The choir sang appropriate music and Rabbi Louis Brav delivered the address on the early religious program broadcast (WOK, Pine Bluff, AR, 1922).

15940 **Itturlda, (Prof.) Maxine.** Educator (*YMCA Spanish Lessons*, WOR, Newark, NJ, 1933).

15941 ***It Can Be Done* (aka *It Can Be Told*).** Edgar A. Guest hosted the program sponsored by Household Finance Company, on which he also read his own inspirational poems and commented upon the dramatic sketches presented. Most of the program's poems and dramatic episodes shared an inspirational theme that was appropriate for the Depression era show. Often the emphasis was how to obtain wealth. For example, one show dramatized how Mr. John S. Redshaw of Granville, Illinois, made his fortune in merchandising (30 min., Tuesday, 8:30–9:00 P.M., NBC, 1937; CBS, 1937–1939).

Guest was born in Northampton, England, August 20, 1881. He came to the United States at eight years of age and started work at the Detroit *Free Press* newspaper as an office boy. He later became a police reporter, exchange editor, columnist and popular writer of verse on the paper.

Although he was known as the "Poet Laureate of Radio," Guest modestly scoffed at the practice of calling his rhymes poetry, preferring instead to call them verse.

15942 ***It Can Happen to You.*** Eddie Cantor hosted the show that featured the Victor Young Orchestra. Harry Von Zell was the announcer (30 min., Weekly, ABC, 1950s). The show presented a theme of inspiration, love and hope.

15943 ***It Happened in Hollywood.*** Vincent Palmieri, assisted by Muriel Kingsbury, delivered film gossip and commentary (15 min., Wednesday, 4:00–4:15 P.M., WELI, New Haven, CT, 1938).

15944 ***It Happened in Hollywood.*** The Eddie Dunstedter Orchestra, John Conte, Helen Troy and Martha Mears were featured on the quarter-hour dramatic show (CBS, 1939).

15945 ***It Happened in the Service.*** The dramatic series presented dramatizations of the feats of America's heroic servicemen during World War II. Ben Alexander hosted the program. Earl Ebi was the producer (15 min., Tuesday, 7:30–7:45 P.M., NBC, 1942). Some papers indicate that the program also appeared on ABC in 1942.

15946 ***It Pays to Be Ignorant.*** The pseudo-quiz show that parodied intellectual quiz shows such as *Information Please* was hosted by quizmaster Tom Howard. The program usually contained nothing more than the hilarious antics of its regular panel that included George Shelton, Harry McNaughton and Lulu McConnell. Puns, insults and the raucous shrieks of Miss McConnell were always heard on the wildly funny, low-brow show. The cast included: The Esquires (Vocal Group), vocalist Al Madru, Tom Howard, Lulu McConnell, Harry McNaughton and George Shelton. Music was supplied by the Korn Kobblers in the MBS version, followed by Doc Novak's band when the show moved to CBS. On the air from 1942 to 1949, the show was created by Robert and Ruth Howell (the daughter of Tom Howard, the show's producer) and directed by Herbert S. Polesie. Ken Roberts and Dick Stark were the announcers. *It Pays to be Ignorant* began as a local show on WOR (New York, NY, 1942). Tom Howard always asked his daffy panel such questions as these:

> What is a bread knife used for?
>
> What is the best time of year for winter sports?
>
> In what room of the house would you find the kitchen range?

Usually these difficult brain teasers stumped the panel, but they invariably produced hilarious answers (WOR, MBS, CBS, 1942–1949).

15947 ***(The) Italian Street Singer.*** Vcl. mus. prg. by an unidentified vocalist (WLW, Cincinnati, OH, 1935).

15948 ***It's Always Albert.*** Irving Mansfield produced the sustaining situation comedy written by Jacqueline Susann and Beatrice Cole. Arnold Stang played the title role of ignorant Albert, whose antics kept his brother, played by Jan Murray, and his girl friend, played by Pert Kelton, always in the middle of a baffling muddle. Jack Miller's Orchestra supplied the music. George Bryan was the announcer (30 min., Friday, 8:30–9:00 P.M., CBS, 1948).

15949 ***It's Always Sunday.*** A sustaining situation comedy, the program told the story of a clergyman's family. *Variety* noted that although it seemed to be straight out of *Ozzie and Harriet*, at least the Reverend Parker on this show was not ineffectual. Coleen Collins, John Stephenson and Nancy McCullom were in the cast. Frank Fox and Jesse Goldstein were the writers. Norman MacDonnell was the producer/director (30 min., Sunday, 4:30–5:00 P.M., CBS, 1951).

15950 ***It's Fun to Keep House.*** Home economist Helen Adams tried to do the convincing (15 min., Wednesday, 1:00–1:15 P.M. KWK, St. Louis, MO, 1939).

15951 ***It's Higgins, Sir.*** Harry McNaughton capably played the role of a British butler inherited by a middle-class American family. When the family inherited a rare silver set, Higgins the butler came with it to provide the fun on this sustaining situation comedy. A summer replacement for the *Bob Hope Show*, the show was conceived and produced by Paul Harrison. In addition to the critically praised McNaughton, other cast members included: Denise Alexander, Peggy Allenby, Vinton Hayworth, Pat Hosley, Adelaide Klein and Charles Nevil (30 min., Tuesday, 9:00–9:30 P.M., NBC, 1951).

15952 ***It's Joan Davis Time.*** Comedienne Joan Davis starred on the situation comedy show with Lionel Stander, Mary Jane Croft and Bob Jellison. Music was supplied by the John Rarig band. Ben Gage was the announcer (30 min., Weekly, CBS, 1948). *See* **Comediennes**.

15953 ***It's Show Time from Hollywood.*** The Freddy Martin Orchestra was featured on the transcribed show. Clyde Rogers, Stuart Wade, Glen Hughes and the Martin Men sang with the Martin band (15 min., Transcribed, Various Stations, 1950s).

15954 ***It's the Barry's.*** Serutan—"Nature's Remedy " (for constipation)—Laxative sponsored the routine talk show featuring Jack Barry, his wife Marcia Van Dyke and their son Jeff (15 min, Monday through Friday, 9:15–9:30 P.M., NBC, 1953). The slogan of "Serutan is Nature's spelled backward" was often heard in the program's commercials.

15955 ***It's Up to Youth.*** A panel of teen-aged boys and girls talked about such problems of youth as teacher infatuations, friction with older and younger sisters and liars on the sustaining program (30 min., 8:30–9:00 P.M., MBS, 1947).

15956 ***(The) Itty Bitty Kiddy Hour.*** Perry Charles and Ward Wilson burlesqued almost everything about radio on this entertaining sustaining comedy show. Charles narrated the show and Wilson played many roles in the comedy sketches. Their alleged sponsors were a firm of criminal lawyers, whose radio premium giveaway was a set of crime tools. The set of tools, they said, would be mailed free to any listener for $1000, plus the top of a moving van. All in all, *Variety* said, the show was one of radio's brightest efforts (30 min., Sunday, 10:00–10:30 P.M., WHN, 1935).

15957 **Ivan, Gloria.** Russian opera star (WGBS, New York, NY, 1929).

15958 **Ivans, Elaine.** Actress, announcer and MC Elaine Ivans appeared on *The Majestic Hour*. The Majestic Radio Company was the sponsor (CBS, late 1920s).

15959 **Ivantzoff, Ivan.** Baritone (WOR, Newark, NJ, 1929).

15960 **Iverson, Earl.** DJ (*The Music Hall*, WRJN, Racine, WI, 1960).

15961 **Ives, Anita.** COM-HE (WMCA, New York, NY, 1937).

15962 **Ives, Ann.** COM-HE (WSRO, Marboro, MA, 1960).

15963 **Ives, Bob.** Newscaster (*Late Evening News*, WFBL, Syracuse, NY, 1947).

15964 Ives, Burl Icle Ivanhoe. Folk singer Ives also achieved success as a recording artist, motion picture star and Broadway actor. In addition to guest appearances on many network radio programs, he had his own show, *The Wayfaring Stranger* (CBS, 1940–1942). Ives was probably the most popular folk singer of radio's golden age.

15965 Ives, D.H. Announcer (WHAS, Louisville, KY, 1927).

15966 Ives, Jim. DJ (*You Name It*, WINR, Binghampton, NY, 1949).

15967 Ives, Raymond. Actor Ives was in the cast of *Henry Aldrich* (title role), *Land of the Lost*, *Portia Faces Life* and *Reg'lar Fellers*.

15968 Ivey, Butch. DJ (WGFS, Haleyville, AL, 1956).

15969 *(The) Ivory Tent Show*. The variety show, sponsored by Procter & Gamble's Ivory Soap, was the final form taken by *The Gibson Family Show*. Presumably the show was influenced by the success of the *Maxwell House Showboat* program. Supposedly, the Gibson family was now traveling with a tent show troupe headed by Uncle Charlie, who was played by Charles Winninger. Vocal selections were performed by Jack and Loretta Clemens, Conrad Thibault and Lois Wilson. Music was supplied by the Don Voorhees Orchestra (60 min., Sunday, 10:00–11:00 min., NBC-Red, 1935). *See* ***The Gibson Family***.

15970 Izerillo, Guiseppe. Operatic tenor (WRNY, New York, NY, 1928).

15971 Izzard, Wesley S. "Wes." Newscaster (KGNC, Amarillo, TX, 1938–1942, 1945–1946).

15972 *J. Akuhead Pupule Show*. DJ Hal Lewis took this Hawaiian name that translated means "crazy fish head." He conducted a popular Honolulu morning show of news, times, music and community announcements (210 min., Monday through Saturday, 5:30–9:00 A.M., KGU, Honolulu, HI, 1956). His broadcasting rival in Honolulu at the time was KPOA's Lucky Luckman's *Lucky Luck* program. *See* ***Lucky Luck***.

15973 Jabenis, Elaine. COM-HE (WOW, Omaha, NE, 1951).

15974 Jaccard, (Mrs.) E.L. Organist (WBAP, Fort Worth, TX, 1925)

15975 Jack, Elizabeth. Gardening authority (*Gardening Talks*, WMBD, Peoria, IL, 1935). .

15976 *Jack and Ethyl the Motor Mates*. Jack and Ethyl spent many months on an extended honeymoon on the dramatic series. Their travels led them to visit practically all the places of historic, romantic or scenic interest in the states of Washington, Oregon and California (30 min., Wednesday, 8:00–8:30 P.M., NBC-Pacific Coast Network, 1930s).

15977 *Jack and Gene, the Harmony Boys of WLS*. Gene Carroll and Jack Grady first appeared on WLS on January 13, 1928. They broadcast daily. Both played the piano and harmonized. Gene also played the guitar, harmonica and jew's harp (WLS, Chicago, 1928).

15978 *Jack and His Buddies*. Vcl. mus. prg. (WSM, Nashville, TN, 1935).

15979 Jack and Jean. Harmony singing team (KFI, Los Angeles, CA, 1926).

15980 Jack and Jill. Vocal team, not otherwise identified, WHK, Cleveland, OH, 1935).

15981 Jack and Jill. Jack Steck and Florence Bendon comprised the entertaining singing team (15 min., Weekly, WFIL, Philadelphia, PA, 1937).

15982 (The) Jack and Jill Dance Band aka Jack and Jill Tavern Band. Popular local band (KEX, Portland, OR, 1929–1930).

15983 Jack and Paul. Little Jack Little and Paul Small sang on many radio stations (WGBS, New York, NY, 1928).

15984 Jack Rabbits Dance Orchestra. (KFQZ, Hollywood, CA, 1926).

15985 *Jack and Velma*. Vcl. mus. prg. by vocal team (WWVA, Wheeling, WV, 1935).

15986 *Jack Armstrong*. General Mills, makers of Wheaties, sponsored the juvenile daytime serial. Jack Armstong, "The All-American Boy," was an outstanding athlete at Hudson High who possessed sterling character. Jack always found adventure while traveling the world with his friends Billy and Betty Fairfield and their Uncle Jim. Whether it was in Tibet, the Philippines or the jungles of Africa, the group found thrilling adventures. Although the title role was originated by St. John Terrell, Charles Flynn is best remembered as Jack Armstrong. Over the years the program's cast included: Don Ameche, Jim Ameche, Robert Barron, Frank Behrens, Herb Butterfield, Roland Butterfield, Kenneth Christie, Frank Dane, Jack Doty, Charles Flynn, John Gannon, James Goss, William Green, Milton Guion, Stanley Harris, Ann Shepherd (Scheindel Kalish), Butler Manville, Naomi May, Art McConnell, Murray McLean, Marvin Miller, Loretta Poynton, William Rath, Michael Rye (Rye Billsbury), Olan Soule, St. John Terrell, Arthur Van Slyke, Sarajane Wells and Dick York.

The program's writers were Irving J. Crump, James Jewell, Lee Knopf, Talbot Mundy and Colonel Paschal Strong. The theme was sung by the Norsemen Quartet (Kenneth Shon, Al Revere, Ed Lindstrom and Ted Kline. James Peterson was the quartet's pianist-arranger). Robert Hardy Andrews was the program's creator-writer. At different times the program was directed by James Jewell, Ted MacMurray, Pat Murphy, Ed Morse and David Owen. Truman Bradley, Paul Douglas, Franklyn MacCormack, Bob McKee, David Owen and Tom Shirley were the announcers (30 min., Monday through Friday, 5:30–6:00 P.M., CBS, 1935).

15987 *(The) Jack Berch*. Berch and a group of talented musicians and singers were featured on the sustaining program (30 min., Tuesday, 8:30–9:00 P.M., CBS, 1938). Later in a different format of the *Jack Berch* show, Berch alone was featured (15 min., Monday through Friday, 11:45–12:00 noon, NBC-Blue, 1945).

15988 *(The) Jack Benny Show* (aka *The Canada Dry Ginger Ale Program, The Chevrolet Program, The General Tire Show, The Jell-O Program, The Jack Benny Program, The Grape Nuts Program* and *The Lucky Strike Show*). Jack Benny was one of radio's greatest comedians. He is best known for his masterful timing and skillful use of silence as a comedy technique. Benny first appeared on the *Ed Sullivan* program of March 29, 1932 by saying: "Ladies and gentlemen, this is Jack Benny talking. There will be a slight pause while you say, 'Who cares?" Later in 1932, he was given his own show. His many radio shows included the *Canada Dry Ginger Ale Program* broadcast by NBC; *The Chevrolet Program*; *The General Tire Program; The Jello Program*; *The Grape Nuts Program*; and *The Jack Benny Program*.

Jack Benny was born Benny Kubelsky on February 14, 1894. Although Waukegan, Illinois, is well known as Benny's hometown, his mother insisted that he was born in a metropolitan Chicago hospital, a more suitable birthplace for the show business giant he became. Beginning as a vaudeville star, he made the successful transition to radio and television to become the most popular and best loved comedian of radio's Golden Age. It was on radio that Benny and his talented ensemble was best represented, for it was here that Mel Blanc could best add his touch of genius to produce the vocal sound effects Jack used in so many of his routines. Television could never adequately visually reproduce Blanc's vocal characterization on these comic bits.

Always praised as a master of comedy timing, it was precisely Benny's use of pauses and vocal inflections that made him a master comedian. On his show, Benny always played the role of a vain, stingy know-it-all, who mistakenly thought he was sharper and more intelligent than all those around him. Another secret of Benny's success was the talented ensemble of performers who appeared with him for many years. Mary Livingstone, his real life wife, always proved to know more than Benny, as did band leader Phil Harris, tenor Dennis Day and his Black valet, "Rochester" played by Eddie Anderson.

"Rochester," one of radio's foremost comics, was sometimes criticized as perpetuating such Black stereotypes as doing "too much drinking and gambling." Despite these infrequent complaints, "Rochester" was always ahead of "Mr. Benny." Even though he paid verbal deference to his "boss," there never was any doubt that "Rochester" was the smarter of the two and always in charge no matter what Jack might think.

Don Wilson, Benny's long time announcer, in fact, was the only one who always treated him with true respect. Phil Harris, Dennis Day and Mary Livingstone rarely did. Other talented contributors to the program over the years were dialect comedians Sam Hearn and Artie Auerbach, who played the roles of Schlepperman and Mr. Kitzel, respectively. But of all the members of Benny's ensemble the most memorable was Mel Blanc, the master of vocal sound effects and funny characters.

Blanc vocally produced the wheezing, gurgling, coughing and sputtering sound of Benny's antique Maxwell car and the growling menace of Carmichael, the polar bear who guarded the money vaults in Benny's basement. A running gag on the show was how the polar bear had apparently eaten the gas man, since he was never seen after he went to the basement to read the gas meter. Once on the program, when Rochester answered the door bell, Benny asked, "Who was it?" Rochester replied, "It's the gas man." Jack triumphantly shouted, "You see? It's the gas man. I told you Carmichael didn't eat him. What does he want?" "He wants to know where the other gas man is," Rochester replied.

One of Blanc's best comic moments with Jack was his "Cy-Si" routine in which all his responses were answered "Cy," "Si," "Sue," or "Sew."

> BENNY: Excuse me, are you waiting for the train?
> BLANC: Si.
> BENNY: You're meeting someone on the train?
> BLANC: Si.
> BENNY: A relative?
> BLANC: Si.
> BENNY: What's your name?
> BLANC: Cy.
> BENNY: Cy?
> BLANC: Si.
> BENNY: This relative you're waiting for — is it a woman?
> BLANC: Si.
> BENNY: Your sister?
> BLANC: Si.
> BENNY: What's her name?
> BLANC: Sue.
> BENNY: Sue?
> BLANC: Si.
> BENNY: Does she work?
> BLANC: Si.
> BENNY: She has a regular job?
> BLANC: Si.
> BENNY: What does she do?
> BLANC: Sew.
> BENNY: Sew?
> BLANC: Si.

Perhaps the funniest joke ever broadcast on radio appeared on a Benny program. Growing out of Jack's stingy radio persona and his masterful sense of timing, the following routine occurred when he was accosted by a hold-up man:

> HOLD UP MAN: Your money or your life.
> *There is a long, long pause.*
> HOLD UP MAN: Quit stalling — I said your money or your life.
> BENNY: (*With a loud, frustrated whine*) I'm thinking it over.

Another memorable series of comedy events on the Benny show grew from his "feud" with fellow comic, Fred Allen. The supposedly bitter feud began on the *Fred Allen Show*, when a ten-year-old violinist, Stuart Canin, played Rimski-Korsakov's "Flight of the Bumble Bee"(Josefsberg, 1977, p. 240). After Allen complimented the young man on his performance, he remarked that a certain "alleged violinist should hang his head in shame." The Allen-Benny "feud" ran for years. Benny, who was a talented violinist, went along with the gag even to the extent of playing badly on the show for comic effect. At other times, however, he would play with various symphony orchestras on their benefit concert programs. The "feud" was a great listener favorite for both comedians.

After his radio show ended on May 22, 1955, Benny made the successful transition to television with his ensemble mostly intact. For the rest of his life, Benny retained the popularity he had achieved over the years. In addition, he greatly influenced the style of such television stars as Jack Paar and Johnny Carson. Many recordings of his programs are still available as proof of his comedic greatness.

Benny's fine cast always played a major role in his program's success. During his 23-year radio career, his program's cast included: Eddie Anderson, Artie Auerbach, Bea Benaderet, Jack Benny, Sara Berner, Mel Blanc, Ronald Colman and Benita Hume Colman, who played Jack's neighbors, Joel Davis, Dix Davis, Dennis Day, Andy Devine, Verna Felton, Frank Fontaine, Gloria Gordon, Phil Harris, Sam Hearn, Sheldon Leonard, Mary Livingstone, Jane Morgan, Frank Nelson, Ethel Shutta, Blanche Stewart and Don Wilson. Benny's vocalists and vocal groups included the Sportsmen Quartet (Bill Days, Thurl Ravenscroft, Max Smith, John Rarig and, at times, Marty Sperzel), Kenny Baker, Michael Bartlett, Dennis Day, James Melton, Frank Parker and Larry Stevens. His writers were Bill Morrow, Sam Perrin and John Tackaberry and his directors were Robert Ballin and Hilliard Marks. George Balzer, Ed Beloin, Jack Douglas, Milt Josefsberg, Irving Fein and Hilliard Marks were his producers. Several orchestras were featured: Don Bestor, Frank Black, Bob Crosby, Johnny Green, Phil Harris, George Olsen and Ted Weems. The announcers were: Paul Douglas, Alois Havrilla, George Hicks and Don Wilson (NBC, CBS, 1932–1955).

15989 ***(The) Jack Carson Show.*** Comedian Carson delivered funny stand-up comedy material on his show. He was joined by singer Doris Drews, the Taylor Maids singing group, guitarist Tony Romano and the Walter Gross Orchestra. Bob Steward was the announcer (30 min., Tuesday through Friday, 9:30–10:00 P.M., CBS, 1954).

Although he is remembered primarily as a comedian, Carson was a versatile actor, who had a long career in motion pictures. He showed his range by playing villains and gangsters, singing and dancing with Esther Williams in such films as *Dangerous When Wet* (1953) and playing Paul Newman's brother in Tennessee Williams' *Cat on a Hot Tin Roof.*

15990 ***Jack Cooper's All-Colored Review.*** Weekly variety program (WSBC, Chicago, IL, 1935). *See* **Cooper, Jack.**

15991 ***Jack Eigen.*** Eigen introduced a combined DJ-talk show format broadcast from a cafe in New York City (180 min., Monday through Friday, 12:00–3:00 A.M., WMGM, New York, NY, 1951).

15992 ***Jack Eigen's News Reel.*** Eigen broadcast the latest Broadway gossip on his sustaining show (15 min., Monday, 9:15–9:30 P.M., WGN, Chicago, IL, 1936).

15993 ***(The) Jack Frost Melody Moments.*** Eugene Ormandy conducted the orchestra on the good music program (30 min., Thursday, 9:00–9:30 P.M., NBC-Red, 1929; 30 min., Thursday, 9:30–10:00 P.M., NBC-Red, 1931). Tenor Oliver Smith was a program regular and Alois Havrilla was the announcer. The program later returned to the air with Josef Pasternack conducting the orchestra (30 min., Monday, 9:30–10:00 P.M., NBC, 1933).

15994 ***Jack Haley's Log Cabin*** **(aka *The Jack Haley Show, The Log Cabin Jamboree* or *The Wonder Show*).** For the program's first season on the air (1937–1938), the sponsor was Log Cabin Syrup. Artie Auerbach, Lucille Ball, Wendy Barrie, Warren Hull, Virginia Verrill and the Ted Fiorito Orchestra were regularly featured. When Wonder Bread became the sponsor during the final season on the air (1938–1939), the name was changed to *The Wonder Show*. Comedian Haley's particular type of humor never fully succeeded on radio (30 min., Saturday, 8:30–9:00 P.M., NBC-Red, 1938). Hollywood song and dance man Haley is best remembered for his starring role as the Tin Man in the 1939 film, *The Wizard of Oz.*

15995 ***(The) Jack Kirkwood Show.*** Corny jokes and outrageous puns made the program interesting. Jack Kirkwood was the chief comic and the major domo who kept the show moving. A typical interchange between Kirkwood and Gray Seebrook was as follows:

> JACK: I took my sweetheart out to Lover's Leap.
> GRAY: What did she do?
> JACK: She leaped.

Kirkwood's comic associates on the show were Don Reed, Bob Sherry, Gray Seebrook and his wife, Lillian Lee. The music was by the Irving Miller Orchestra and singers Julie Conway and Connie Haines. Jimmie Wallington was the announcer (30 min., Monday through Friday, 9:00–9:30 A.M., 1943). The program grew out of an earlier Kirkwood morning show, *Mirth and Madness* on NBC, that also had featured the music of the Irving Miller and Jerry Jerome orchestras. Kirkwood later was featured on his *New Jack Kirkwood Show* with a supporting cast that included: Bill Gray, Lillian Lee, John Brown, Gloria Blondell, Dick Ryan, Doris Day and the Lud Gluskin Orchestra (30 min., Weekly, CBS, 1946). When the show was revived, comedian Kirkwood told old jokes, assisted by many talented cast members such as singers Lillian Lee, Lee Albert and organists Gaylord Carter and George Wright. Steve Dunne was the announcer on the sustaining show (*The Jack Kirkwood Show*, 30 min., Monday through Friday, 4:00–4:30 P.M., MBS, 1952).

15996 ***Jack Major One-Man Show.*** Major provided music and comedy on the network program (CBS, 1935).

15997 ***Jack Oakie's College.*** Movie comedian Oakie hosted the lively variety show that also featured Stuart Erwin, William Austin, Raymond Hatton, Helen Lynd, Harry Barris, Billy Benedict and the George Stoll orchestra (30 min., Tuesday P.M., CBS, 1938).

15998 ***(The) Jack Paar Show.*** This was Jack Paar's first network radio show. It was part of NBC's efforts to present new talent to a national audience. For several years, the show was a summer replacement for the *Jack Benny Show*. Paar's supporting cast members included Trudy Erwin, Henry Fielding, Hans Conried, Florence Halop, Jud Conlon's Rhythmaires, the

Page Cavanaugh Trio and Jerry Fielding's Orchestra. Guest stars such as Dennis Day appeared each week. The announcers were Hy Averback and Frank Nelson (30 min., Sunday, 7:00–7:30 P.M., NBC, 1947). Paar later had a late night television talk show on NBC for many years, until it was taken over by Johnny Carson.

15999 ***(The) Jack Pearl Show.*** Born on New York City's lower East side, Pearl became famous for his German dialect. He entered show business on Gus Edwards' children's revue, *School Days*. By the middle 1920's, Pearl was a major vaudeville star. He appeared in many guest spots on Ed Sullivan's radio show and in 1931 appeared in the *Ziegfeld Follies of the Air*. Lucky Strike cigarettes signed him to host the *Jack Pearl Show* for the 1932–1933 season.

He became famous with his Baron von Munchausen characterization on the *Jack Pearl Show*, in which he told long, fanciful tales in German dialect. When Cliff Hall, as Charlie his stooge, doubted the Baron's veracity, Munchausen would use his famous line, "Vas you dere, Sharlie?" Jack Pearl and Cliff Hall returned to radio many times later for brief periods, but they never again achieved the popularity and listening audience their earlier program had brought them (30 min., NBC, 1932). Pearl later starred on a similar show sponsored by Raleigh and Kool cigarettes that also featured tenor Milton Bowe, the Tommy Dorsey Orchestra with vocalist Edythe Wright, Robert Bernard, Clayton "Bud" Collyer, John McIntire and Jeanette Nolan. Paul Stewart was the announcer. The theme song was "Two Cigarettes in the Dark." The program opened in this way: "Raleigh and Kool cigarettes present their new show starring Jack Pearl as Baron Von Munchausen with Cliff Hall as Charlie (30 min., Weekly, NBC, 1936).

16000 ***(The) Jack Rabbit Stories.*** David Cory told charming animal stories for children (WJZ, New York, NY, 1923).

16001 ***(The) Jack Smith Show.*** Oxydol soap powder sponsored "Smiling Jack" Smith, a pleasant vocalist, who performed with guests such as the DeMarco Sisters to the music of Earl Sheldon's Orchestra. Don Hancock was the announcer (15 min., Monday through Friday, 7:15–7:30 P.M., CBS, 1946).

16002 ***Jack the Bell Boy.*** DJ Ed MacKenzie conducted the show that was popular with Detroit's bobby soxers (110 min., Monday through Saturday, 3:30–5:20 P.M., WJKB, Detroit, MI, 1947).

16003 ***Jack the Sweet Singer from the West.*** Jack, not otherwise identified, was one of the most popular singers on early Southern radio. He was accompanied by pianist Doris Hauser. Jack's favorite songs were "Where the Colorado River Flows" and "Honey, Stay in Your Own Backyard." (WLBN, Little Rock, AR, 1927).

16004 ***Jack West Cowboys.*** CW mus. prg. (WJR, Detroit, MI, 1935).

16005 ***(The) Jackie Robinson Show.*** Rheingold Beer sponsored Jackie Robinson, the former baseball great. Robinson talked about sports, but he also interviewed such celebrity guests as Steve Allen (30 min., Sunday, 6:30–7:00 P.M., WRCA, New York, NY, 1959).

16006 ***Jacks and Marbles Finale.*** KDAL (Duluth, MN, 1937) in conjunction with the Duluth's City Recreation Department broadcast the final "contests" to determine the jacks and marbles champions that were held on the station's carpets.

16007 ***Jack's Missouri Mountaineers.*** CW mus. prg. with unidentified performers (WSM, Nashville, TN, 1936–1938).

16008 ***Jack's Place.*** Jack Gregson hosted his show of music and celebrity interviews. Other cast regulars included singer Mary Mayo and the Bobby Hackett Quintet (85 min., Monday through Friday, 2:35–4:00 P.M., ABC, 1953).

16009 **Jackson, Alice.** COM-HE (WPRO, Providence, RI, 1949).

16010 **Jackson, Amelda.** COM-HE (WCKB, Dunn, NC, 1960).

16011 **Jackson, Arlene.** Blues singer (*Arlene Jackson*, vcl. mus. prg., NBC, 1934).

16012 **Jackson, Audrey.** COM-HE (WKCT, Bowling Green, KY, 1951).

16013 **Jackson, Beatrice.** COM-HE (WEAV, Plattsburgh, NY, 1951).

16014 **Jackson, Betty.** COM-HE (WEPG, South Pittsburg, TN, 1956).

16015 **Jackson, Bill.** Sportscaster (KVIC, Victoria, TX, 1955; WPTF, Raleigh, NC, 1956–1960).

16016 **Jackson, Dorothy.** COM-HE (WPUB, Bellingham, WA, 1956).

16017 **Jackson, Gretchen.** COM-HE (WPUB, Bellingham, WA, 1956).

16018 **Jackson, Hal.** DJ (WLIB, New York, NY, 1949; *The House that Jack Built*, WLIB, 1954).

16019 **Jackson, Harry (Alan).** Newscaster Jackson, long a fixture at CBS, began as a newscaster-announcer at station KTHS (Hot Springs Natural Park, AR, 1935). He eventually went on to work at WLW, Cincinnati, OH; WHAS, Louisville, KY; and WMC, Memphis, TN, before joining CBS.

16020 **Jackson, Jean.** COM-HE (WJNC, Jacksonville, NC, 1960).

16021 **Jackson, Jill.** COM-HE (WWL, New Orleans, LA, 1949).

16022 **Jackson, Jimmy.** Leader (*Jimmy Jackson Orchestra*, instr. mus. prg. (WMT, Cedar Rapids–Waterloo, IA, 1936; WLW, Cincinnati, OH, 1937).

16023 **Jackson, Joseph Henry.** Jackson was the Literary Editor of the San Francisco *Chronicle*. He broadcast book reviews on various San Francisco stations (San Francisco, 1932).

16024 **Jackson, Judy.** COM-HE (WJXN, Jackson, 1951).

16025 **Jackson, Keith.** Sportscaster (*Sport Spots*, KLER, Lewiston, ID, 1954; KOMO, Seattle, WA, 1960). Jackson later became a busy college football play-by-play man on television.

16026 **Jackson, Libby.** COM-HE (WMDC, Hazlehurst, MS, 1955).

16027 **Jackson, Lillie.** COM-HE (WHED, Washington, NC, 1951).

16028 **Jackson, Loretta.** Singer, (*Loretta Jackson*, vcl. mus. prg., WMMN, Fairmont, WV, 1942).

16029 **Jackson, (Mrs.) Louis.** COM-HE (KOS, Merced, CA, 1951).

16030 **Jackson, Mable Cole.** Contralto (KOA, Denver, CO, 1926).

16031 **Jackson, Marjorie.** COM-HE (KERG, Eugene, OR, 1956).

16032 **Jackson, Norman W.** Hawaiian guitarist (KFXF, Colorado Springs, CO, 1926).

16033 **Jackson, Pat.** COM-HE (KADA, Ada, OK, 1955).

16034 **Jackson, Paul.** DJ (*Speaking of Jazz*, WSNY, Schenectady, NY, 1947).

16035 **Jackson, Ralph.** Leader (Ralph Jackson and his Blue Grass Music, WCAU, Philadelphia, PA, 1926).

16036 **Jackson, Ruth.** Whistler (KFWM, Oakland, CA, 1926).

16037 **Jackson, Sally.** COM-HE (WTTS, Bloomington, IN, 1949).

16038 **Jackson, Sandy.** DJ (*Rhythm Inn*, KBON, Omaha, NE, 1947–1948; *Sandy Jackson Show*, KOWH, Omaha, NE, 1949–1957).

16039 **Jackson, Tom.** DJ (*T-N-T*, WKAB, Mobile, AL, 1947; *Time 'N' Tunes*, WKAB, 1948–1957). Sportscaster (*Sports Interview*, WKAB, 1949).

16040 **Jackson, Willard.** Newscaster (WJMC, Rice Lake, WI, 1942).

16041 **Jackson, William H.** Organist (*W.H. Jackson*, instr. mus. prg., WPG, Harrisburg, PA, 1935–1936).

16042 **Jackson, (Mrs.) William Henry.** Pianist (WSM, Nashville, TN, 1928).

16043 **Jackson's Satisfied Jazz Syncopators.** Dance orchestra (KNRC, Los Angeles, CA, 1926).

16044 **Jackson's Society Orchestra.** Club band (KVOO, Tulsa, OK, 1928).

16045 **Jacob, Hans.** Newscaster (WAAT, Jersey City, NJ, 1941; WOV, New York, NY, 1942, 1944).

16046 **Jacobs, Al.** Pianist (KPO, San Francisco, CA, 1925).

16047 **Jacobs, Betty.** Organist (WJBO, New Orleans, LA, 1929).

16048 **Jacobs, Bob.** Newscaster (WCBI, Columbus, OH, 1945). Sportscaster (WCBI, 1945).

16049 **Jacobs, Dave.** DJ (*Jazz, Inc.*, WSID, Baltimore, MD, 1950).

16050 **Jacobs, Don.** DJ (*Clockwatchers' Society*, WCBM, Lemoyne, PA, 1950).

16051 **Jacobs, Helen DeWitt.** Violinist (WAHG, Richmond Hill, NY, 1926).

16052 **Jacobs, Jacques.** Leader (Jacques Jacobs' Hotel Shelton Ensemble, WOR, Newark, NJ, 1926).

16053 **Jacobs, Lee.** Newscaster (KBKR, Baker, OH, 1945). Sportscaster (KBKR, 1945).

16054 **Jacobs, Leo.** Pianist (WHN, New York, NY, 1924).

16055 **Jacobs, Louise.** COM-HE (KIMO, Carthage, MO, 1951).

16056 Jacobs, M.H. "Max." Newscaster (KPRC, Houston, TX, 1940–1942).

16057 Jacobs, Marvin. DJ (WEGP, Presque Isle, ME, 1960).

16058 Jacobs, Max. Leader (Max Jacobs' Symphony Orchestra, WEAF, New York, NY, 1925).

16059 Jacobs, Paul. Leader (Paul Jacobs' Male Quartet, WSMB, New Orleans, LA, 1926).

16060 Jacobs, Sylvia. Actress Jacobs appeared on the *Midstream* daytime serial program.

16061 Jacobs, Thomas B. "Tom." Newscaster (KTRH, Houston, TX, 1942, 1944–1945). Sportscaster (KTRH, 1942).

16062 Jacobs, William. "Irish Radio Tenor" (WJBL, Decatur, IL, 1927).

16063 Jacobsen, Dick. DJ (*1230 Club*, KXO, El Centro, CA, 1948; *Call a KOPP* and *Wax Works*, KOPP, Odgen, UT, 1950).

16064 Jacobsen, Eva Garcia. Pianist (KFWB, Hollywood, CA, 1925).

16065 Jacobsen, J. W. Announcer (WEW, St. Louis, MO, 1927).

16066 Jacobson, Andy. Leader (*Andy Jacobson Orchestra*, instr. mus. prg., WCLE, Cleveland, OH and KFEL, Denver, CO, 1942).

16067 Jacobson, Arthur. *See* **Hunter, Henry.**

16068 Jacobson, Dorothy. COM-HE (KPUB, Bellingham, WA, 1954–1955).

16069 Jacobson, Evelyn. COM-HE (KGEZ, Kalispell, MT, 1956).

16070 Jacobson, Fred. Monologist (WQJ, Chicago, IL, 1925).

16071 Jacobson, Gene. DJ (*Musical Merry Go Round*, KFGR, Forest Grove, OR, 1949).

16072 Jacobson, Joseph George. Violinist (KPO, San Francisco, CA, 1925).

16073 Jacobson, Lou. Director Jacobson worked on *Backstage Wife* and *Play Broadcast*.

16074 Jacoby, (Miss) Frances. Singer-entertainer (KGY, Lacey, MI, 1926).

16075 Jacques, Pauline. Organist (*Pauline Jacques*, instr. mus. prg., WIND, Gary, IN, 1935).

16076 Jacquillard, Augustine. Soprano (WOR, Newark, NJ, 1928–1929).

16077 Jacquinot, Jules. Organist (KMOX, St. Louis, MO, 1926).

16078 Jadden, Audrey. COM-HE (KWKW, Pasadena, CA, 1949).

16079 Jaeger, Bill. DJ (*Sunrise Patrol*, WBOC, Salisbury, MD, 1950; *Bright Side*, WJWL, Georgetown, DE, 1952).

16080 Jaffe, Arnold. Newscaster (WHOM, Jersey City, NJ, 1941).

16081 Jaffe, Frank. Newscaster (KMA, Shenandoah, IA, 1939).

16082 Jaffe, Moe. Leader (*Moe Jaffe Orchestra*, instr. mus. prg., WIP, Philadelphia, PA, 1936).

16083 Jaffe, Syd. DJ (*Night Club of the Air*, WNHC, New Haven, CT, 1950). Sportscaster (*Sportscope*, WNHC, 1955).

16084 Jaffey, Gilbert. Director (Gilbert Jaffey's Music Makers, WHB, Kansas City, MO, 1924). The Music Makers band was sometimes known as the Sweeney Radio Orchestra, named for R.J. Sweeney, owner and founder of radio station WHB. Jaffey was also the leader of another group (Gilbert Jaffey and his Orchestra, WOAW, Omaha, NE, 1925).

16085 Jafola, (Captain) Tom. Singer (*Captain Tom Jafola*, vcl. mus. prg., WIP, Philadelphia, PA, 1936).

16086 Jagel, Frederick. Jagel, a Metropolitan Opera tenor, performed on the *Atwater Kent Hour* (NBC, 1928).

16087 Jagt, Guy Vander. DJ (*Sunnyside of the Street*, WHTC, Holland, MI, 1949).

16088 Jahn, Al. Leader (*Al Jahn Orchestra*, instr. mus. prg., NBC, 1937–1938).

16089 Jahrl, Edwin. Accordionist (WGBS, New York, NY, 1927).

16090 Jaike, Cherrie. Violinist (WOW, Omaha, NE, 1927).

16091 Jaimes, Marie. Violinist (KLCN, Blytheville, AR, 1928).

16092 *Jake's Juke Box*. Gene Carroll, formerly of the *Gene and Glenn* team, assisted by Marty McNeeley, was a DJ on a popular early morning Cleveland show (180 min., Monday through Saturday, 6:00–9:00 A.M., WJMO, Cleveland, OH, 1947).

16093 *Jake Taylor's Railsplitters*. CW music program (WWVA, Wheeling, WV, 1939).

16094 Jalaya [Jalava], Martha. Soprano (KTAB, Oakland, CA, 1926).

16095 Jalma, Michael. Conductor (University of Minnesota Dance Band, WCCO, Minneapolis–St. Paul, MN, 1928).

16096 Jalmeyfield, Marguerite. Pianist (KYW, Chicago, IL, 1925).

16097 *Jam Session*. A transcribed quarter-hour jazz show, *Jam Session* was broadcast by many stations at various times. Among the many great jazz musicians who appeared on the show were: Wild Bill Davison, Roy Eldridge, James P. Johnson, Miff Mole and his Dixieland Orchestra, the Red Norvo Sextet, Red McKenzie, Eddie Condon, the Art Hodes Trio, Joe Marsala, Ben Webster, the Edmond Hall Sextet and Muggsy Spanier.

16098 *Jamboree*. Originating from Chicago, this variety show presented Don McNeill as host. His fellow performers included the comedy team of the Hoofinghams (Murray Forbes and Helene Page), the Kings Jesters, soprano Mary Steele, the singing Morin Sisters, baritone Edward Davies and the orchestra of Harold Stokes (30 min., Saturday, 9:00–9:30 P.M., NBC-Blue, 1934).

16099 Jamerson, Peter. DJ (*Make Believe Ballroom*, WAVZ, New Haven, CT, 1947; *1230 Club*, WNEB, Worcester, MA, 1948–1949).

16100 James, A.M. DJ (*Howdy Neighbor*, WFRP, Savannah, GA, 1947).

16101 James, Andy. DJ (*Record Review*, WCRA, Effingham, IL, 1947; *Easy Listening*, WGEM, Quincy, IL, 1950). Newscaster (WGEM, 1948).

16102 James, Annie. Soprano (*Annie James*, vcl. mus. prg., WDBJ, Roanoke, VA, 1935).

16103 James, Bob. DJ (*Hi School Hop*, WMAN, Mansfield, OH, 1948).

16104 James, Dale. Announcer (WQAM, Miami, FL, 1925).

16105 James, Donnelly. Leader (*Donnelly James Orchestra*, instr. mus. prg., KVOD, Denver, CO, 1939).

16106 James, Frances. COM-HE (KIEM, Eureka, CA, 1951).

16107 James, Gee Gee. Actress James appeared on the daytime serial programs *The O'Neills* and *Hilltop House*.

16108 James, Gene. Leader (Gene James and the Palace Hotel Dance Orchestra, KPO, San Francisco, CA, 1926).

16109 James, Glen. Newscaster (WBBO, Forest City, NC, 1948).

16110 James, Harry. Leader (*Harry James Orchestra*, instr. mus. prg., CBS, 1939; WMAQ, Chicago, IL, 1940; WCKY, Cincinnati, OH, 1942). Virtuoso trumpeter James led his band on several network radio programs, among them *The Danny Kaye Show*, *The Chesterfield Show* and Coca Cola's *Spotlight Bands Show*. James enjoyed the distinction of appearing on both the first *Spotlight Band Show* in September 1942 and the last in November 1946 (Walker, 1989, p. 209).

Although the band's personnel changed over the years, the members of the fine 1942 band included: Harry James, ldr-t.; Claude Bowen, Nick Buono, Alexander Cuozzo, t.; Dalton Rizzotto, Hoyt Bohannon, Harry Rodgers, tb.; Claude Lakey, Sam Marowitz, as.; Corky Corcoran, ts.; Clint Davis, bar.; Alex Pevsner, Samuel Caplan, John de Vogdt, Leo Zorn, v.; Bill Spears, vl.; Elias Friede, vc.; Al Lerner, p.; Ben Heller, g.; Thurman Teague, sb.; and Mickey Scrima, d. The band's many talented vocalists during its great years were Helen Humes, Connie Haines, Helen Forrest, Jimmy Saunders, Dick Haymes and Frank Sinatra.

16111 James, Hepzibah C. Soprano (WGY, Schenectady, NY, 1924).

16112 James, Hugh. Distinguished announcer James was the long-time announcer for Lowell Thomas' news program. In addition he worked on *Famous Jury Trials*, *Parker Family*, *Second Mrs. Burton*, *The Voice of Freedom*, *Wendy Warren and the News* and *When a Girl Marries*.

16113 James, Jimmy. Leader (*Jimmy James Orchestra*, instr. mus. prg., WLW, Cincinnati, OH, 1937–1938, 1942).

16114 James, John M. Actor James appeared on *Amanda of Honeymoon Hill*, *Backstage Wife* and *FBI in Peace and War*.

16115 James, Joseph. Actor James appeared on *The O'Neills* daytime serial program.

16116 James, Judy. COM-HE (WAXX, Chippewa Falls, WI,1960).

16117 James, Lewis. Tenor James sang on the *General Motors Family Party* (NBC, 1927) and the *Maxwell Coffee Hour* (NBC, 1928).

16118 James, Madame. Leader (Madame James and Her All-Specialty Symphony Orchestra (KHJ, Los Angeles, CA, 1927).

16119 James, Marianne. COM-HE (WFRV, Green Bay, WI, 1960).

16120 James, Nanette Annabelle. Reader (KFH, Wichita, KS, 1926).

16121 James, Paul. Sportscaster (*Sports Final*, KCPX, Salt Lake City, UT, 1960).

16122 James, (Mrs.) R. Rovello. Contralto (KFWM, Oakland, CA, 1926).

16123 James, Rembert. Newscaster (NBC, 1946).

16124 James, Ruth Ellington. COM-HE (WLIB, New York, NY, 1951).

16125 James, Stephen. Newscaster (WEEI, Boston, MA, 1944). DJ (*Once Over Lightly*, WBMS, Boston, MA, 1950).

16126 James, Sylvia. News analyst (WCAM, Camden, NJ, 1941).

16127 James Salt Water Taffy Boys Dance Orchestra. Commercial Atlantic City band (WPG, Atlantic City, NJ, 1926).

16128 James, Vee. COM-HE (WCKY, Cincinnati, OH, 1954).

16129 *(The) James*. John S. Young was the announcer on the dramatic series created by Percy Hemus that depicted "average" American family life. In the cast were: Wade Arnold, Percy Hemus, Jeanne Owen, Katherine Renwick, John Shea and Marcella Shields (15 min., Saturday, 7:15–7:30, P.M., NBC-Red, 1930).

16130 *(The) James and Pamela Mason Show*. *Variety* reported that Arch Oboler, the producer-writer-director of the sustaining dramatic show, resigned before the program premiered. Nevertheless, three transcribed shows had been completed before he did so. The program itself did not remain on the air long. James Mason and his wife (Pamela Kellino Mason) were assisted by Lurene Tuttle in the dramatic portions. Frank Barton was the announcer (30 min., Thursday, 9:30–10:00 P.M., NBC, 1949).

16131 Jameson, House. Actor-host James appeared on the *Aldrich Family*, Brave Tomorrow, *By Kathleen Norris*, *Columbia Presents Corwin*, *Crime Doctor*, *Innter Sanctum* (host), *Renfrew of the Mounted* (title role), *This Day is Ours* and *Young Widder Brown*.

16132 Jameson, Keith. Newscaster (WKBN, Youngstown, OH, 1941; WSAM, Saginaw, MI, 1948).

16133 Jameson, Ruth G. COM-HE (WATO, Oak Ridge, TN, 1957).

16134 Jamesworth, Alfred. Leader (Blue and White Marimba Band, NBC, 1929).

16135 Jamieson, Ruth. COM-HE (WATO, Oak Ridge, TN, 1949).

16136 *(The) Jamineers*. Vcl. mus. prg. by unidentified performers (WNAX, Yankton, SD, 1939).

16137 Jamison, Anne. Soprano (*Anne Jamison*, vcl. mus. prg., NBC, 1936).

16138 Jamison, Steele. Tenor Jamison sang on the *Dutch Masters Minstrels* (1928).

16139 Jamond, Walter. DJ (*Serve Yourself Jamboree*, KROW, Oakland, CA, 1948).

16140 Jamup and Honey. DJ team (*Stop, Sit and Listen*, WSM, Nashville, TN, 1947).

16141 Janasen, Ingrid. Soprano (KFWI, San Francisco, CA, 1929).

16142 Jandeson, Ruth G. COM-HE (WATO, Oak Ridge, TN,1957).

16143 *Jane Ace, Disk Jockey*. The clever sustaining program presented Jane Ace as a DJ, assisted by her sardonic husband, Goodman Ace. The show was written by Goodman Ace and directed by Walter McGraw. Don Pardo was the announcer (30 min., Saturday, 8:00–8:30 P.M., NBC, 1951). *See also* **Ace, Goodman; Comedy** *and* ***Easy Aces***.

16144 *Jane Arden*. William Hodapp adapted the daytime serial drama from the comic strip created by Monte Barrett. Ruth Yorke played the title role of a female newspaper reporter who found adventure in a big city. Other members of the cast were: Bill Baar, Spencer Bentley, Helene Dumas, Maurice Franklin, Florence Freeman, Betty Garde, Richard Gordon, Frank Provo, Howard Smith and Henry Wadsworth. Howard Smith provided the music. The sponsored was the Ward Baking Company (15 min., Monday through Friday, 9:45–10:00 A.M., NBC, 1938).

16145 *(The) Jane Pickens Show*. Soprano Pickens sang with baritone Jack Kilty and the Norman Cloutier Orchestra on her sustaining music show (30 min., Sunday, 5:30–6:00 P.M., NBC, 1948).

16146 Janes, Ardoth Jones. Pianist (WTAY, Oak Park, IL, 1925).

16147 Janes, Dolf. Newscaster (KORE, Eugene, OR, 1941).

16148 Janes, Hal. Sportscaster (WMCA, New York, NY, 1939).

16149 Janis, Eddie. Veteran vaudeville singer and violinist (WJZ, New York, NY, 1921).

16150 Janis, Elsie. Broadway and vaudeville star Janis was known as the "Sweetheart of the A.E.F.," for her work entertaining troops in World War I. She frequently appeared on the radio in the 1920s and 1930s. Veteran entertainer Janis depended chiefly upon humorous monologs on her short-lived sustaining program (*Elsie Janis*, 15 min., Wednesday, 10:00–10:15 P.M. NBC-Red, 1934).

16151 Janiss, Vivi. Actress Janiss appeared on the *Lora Lawton* daytime serial.

16152 *(The) Janitor and His Son*. Two unidentified musical performers conducted their early morning show. The "Janitor" played the harmonica (WFAA, Dallas, TX, 1924). The pair — Rushey and Bill — were also known as "The Gloom Chasers of the Lone Star State."

16153 Jankowski, Mary Lou. DJ (WBIS, Bristol, CT, 1954).

16154 Janness, Katherine. Soprano (*Katherine Janness*, vcl. mus. prg., WCAU, Philadelphia, PA, 1931.

16155 Janney, Leon. Actor Janney appeared on *Charlie Chan*, *Chick Carter, Boy Detective*, (title role), *Ethel and Albert*, *Gangbusters*, *Life of Mary Southern*, *Parker Family* and *Pepper Young's Family*.

16156 Janney, William. Actor Janney was in the cast of *We Are Always Young*.

16157 Jannusch, Ruth. COM-HE (KBIZ, Ottumwa, IA, 1960).

16158 Jansen, Barbra. COM-HE (KBVB, Reno, NV, 1960).

16159 Jansen, Mark. Newscaster (KFEL, Denver, CO, 1945).

16160 Jansen, (Mrs.) Romeyn. Contralto (KFGA, Seattle, WA, 1924).

16161 Janssen, Wilf. Sportscaster (*Local Bowling*, KTVB, Boise, ID, 1960).

16162 Janssen's Hofbrau Haus Orchestra. German music group (WHN , New York, NY, 1925–1926).

16163 Jarman, Frances. COM-HE (WDNC, Durham, NC, 1948–1957).

16164 Jarmunian, Elijah. Armenian pianist (WCAU, Philadelphia, PA, 1925).

16165 Jarmus, Benjamin. Tenor (WEBJ, New York, NY, 1926).

16166 *(The) Jarr Family*. Roy McCardell wrote this show about middle class life based on a comic strip published in the New York *American* (15 min., Thursday and Saturday, 7:45–8:00 P.M., WOR, Newark, NJ, 1932).

16167 Jarrell, W.W. News commentator (*Opinions of the News*, WKTG, Thomasville, GA, 1948).

16168 Jarrett, Art. Tenor (*Art Jarrett*, vcl. mus. prg., 15 min., Monday, Wednesday and Friday, 3:00–3:15 P.M., Tuesday, 6:15–6:30 P.M. and Saturday, 6:00–6:15 P.M., CBS, 1932). Leader (*Art Jarrett Orchestra*, instr. mus. prg., WLW, Cincinnati, OH, 1935; CBS, 1935; NBC, 1936).

16169 Jarrett's Orchestra. Local Boston band (WBZ, Boston-Springfield, MA, 1924).

16170 Jarris, Bob. DJ (WSBA, York, PA, 1959).

16171 Jarvis, Al. DJ (*Make Believe Ballroom*, KLAC, Hollywood, CA, 1948–1957). Jarvis is often credited with originating the *Make Believe Ballroom* concept in 1935, later popularized by Martin Block. *See* ***The Make Believe Ballroom***.

16172 Jarvis, Bill J. Sportscaster (KVGB, Great Bend, KS, 1941; *Bill Jarvis Reports*, KVGB, 1949; *Today in the World of Sports*, KVGB, 1947; *Bill Jarvis Reports Sports*, KVGB, 1951). Newscaster (KVGB, 1946).

16173 Jarvis, Dick. Newscaster (KSIG, Crowley, LA, 1947).

16174 Jarvis, Jan. COM-HE (KSJO, San Jose, CA, 1951).

16175 Jarvis, Johnny. DJ (*Breakfast Melodies*, WJVA, South Bend, IN, 1949).

16176 Jarzebowski, Casimir. Newscaster (WHOM, Jersey City, NJ, 1941).

16177 Jason, Barbara. Singer (WOR, Newark, NJ, 1935).

16178 Jason, (Mrs.) Louise. COM-HE (KYOS, Merced, CA, 1951).

16179 *Jason and the Golden Fleece*. Jason, played by motion picture star McDonald Carey, took many pleasure cruises on his 60 foot cabin cruiser, the Golden Fleece. He was said to be a "philosophic adventurer," who also owned a club on New Orleans' Bourbon Street. His club and his boat provided Jason and his friend, played by William Conrad, with many adventures on the sustaining adventure series. Herb Ellis and Cleve Hermann wrote and Art Jacobson directed the show. Frank Worth supplied the music (30 min., Wednesday,. 10:00–10:30 P.M., NBC, 1952).

16180 Jasper, Al. Violinist (KWTC, Santa Ana, CA, 1928).

16181 Jasper, Art. Leader (*Art Jasper Orchestra*, instr. mus. prg., WBIG, Greensboro, NC, 1938).

16182 Jasper, Frank. Baritone (WAHG, Richmond Hill, NY, 1926).

16183 Jass, Melvin. Newscaster (KUTA, Salt Lake City, UT, 1942).

16184 Javeau, Suzanne. COM-HE (WWL, New Orleans, LA, 1949).

16185 *(The) Javits at Home*. According to *Variety* (September 3, 1958, p. 25), the transcribed program presented Senator Jacob and Marion Javits in a *Dorothy and Dick* format, and further noted that although the Senator made speeches, his wife was much more informal in her conversational style (15 min., Sunday, 8:45–9:00 A.M., WINS, New York, NY, 1958).

16186 Jaxon, Half Pint. Leader (*Half Pint Jaxon Orchestra*, instr. mus. prg., WBBM, Chicago, IL, 1933).

16187 Jay, Dick. DJ and sportscaster (KIUN, Pecos, TX, 1937).

16188 Jay, Harry. Newscaster (WBLY, Lima, OH, 1938; WLOK, Lima, OH, 1939–1942; *World News*, WLOK, 1948).

16189 Jay, Jesse H. Announcer (WIOD, Miami, FL, 1925).

16190 Jay, Lilyan. Pianist Jay was known as the "Lady of the Ivories" (WOR, Newark, NJ, 1929).

16191 Jay, Norman. Newscaster (WCAU, Philadelphia, PA, 1942).

16192 (The) Jayhawker Girl. Singer of popular songs otherwise unidentified (KFH, Wichita, KS, 1928).

16193 Jayne, Betty. Singer (*Betty Jayne*, vcl. mus. prg., WCBM, Baltimore, MD, 1934).

16194 Jayne, Mary. Singer (WTAS, Chicago, IL, 1924).

16195 Jaynes, Vi. COM-HE (WJCD, Seymour, IN, 1956).

16196 Jayson, Vernon. Baritone (NBC, 1928).

16197 *Jazz Goes to College*. Jazz authority and college professor Marshall Stearns skillfully combined his duties as a DJ and critic of the local jazz scene on the informative sustaining program (25 min., Sunday, 4:35–5:00 P.M., WNEW, New York, NY, 1951).

16198 *Jazz Jubilee*. Bob Maltz was the announcer on the rare sustaining entertainment show broadcast by New York's municipal radio station. The good jazz show included such great jazz musicians as James P. Johnson, Freddy Moore, Danny Barker and Tony Parenti's Ragtimers (30 min., Saturday, 6:15–6:45 P.M., WNYC, New York, NY, 1948).

16199 Jazz Nomads. Five Northwestern University students comprised the hot jazz band (WDAP, Chicago, IL, 1923).

16200 *Jazz vs. Classics*. The interesting program contrasted classical music in competition with popular jazz selections. Maurie Sherman's orchestra and the Little Symphony Orchestra of Chicago were featured (WLS, Chicago, IL, 1927). An earlier version of the show was broadcast in 1925 (KOA, Denver, CO, 1925).

16201 *Jazz with List*. Classical pianist Eugene List acted as a jazz DJ on the local sustaining show (25 min., Sunday, 8:35–9:00 P.M., WNEW, New York, NY, 1951).

16202 *J.B. and Mac*. The dramatic serial that was broadcast Monday through Friday told the story of the "typical" life experiences of two people. The show was sponsored by Crazy Water Crystals (15 min., Monday through Friday, WBBM, Chicago, IL, middle 1930s).

16203 *(The) Jean Shepherd Show*. After a career as a DJ in the Midwest, Shepherd came to WOR, where he proved to be an off-beat DJ, who talked more than he played records. It was with this show that Shepherd began to develop a legion of loyal fans (150 min., Saturday, 4:30–6:00 P.M., WOR, Newark, NJ, 1955). *See* **Shepherd, Jean.**

16204 *(The) Jean Shepherd (Evening) Show*. This late evening show allowed Shepherd to spend almost all his time telling his nostalgic yarns about his Midwestern adolescence and hilarious Army experiences. He had now become an engaging monologist who deserved recognition as a humorist (WOR, 1957). *See* **Shepherd, Jean.**

16205 *Jeanne Bowman*. Bowman Diary sponsored the show on which "Miss Bowman" told entertaining animal stories for children (15 min., Monday, 5:15–5:30 P.M., WIBA, Madison, WI, 1941).

16206 Jeannette, Beverly. COM-HE (WHGR, Houghton Lake, MI, 1960).

16207 Jecker, Anne. Soprano (WAAM, Newark, NJ, 1925).

16208 Jedezerek, Theresa. COM-HE (KAWT, Douglas, AZ, 1955).

16209 *(The) Jeddo Highlanders*. Tenor Milton Cross sang and acted as announcer on the good music show in 1930. Contralto Leslie Frick and baritone Frederick Wyatt also performed regularly on the program. The orchestra was conducted by Paul Van Loan (30 min., Wednesday, 7:00–7:30 P.M., NBC-Red, 1929–1930).

16210 Jefferies, David W. Newscaster (KINY, Juneau, AK, 1945).

16211 Jeffers, Sleepy. DJ (*Magic Valley Jamboree*, WTIP, Charleston, WV, 1949–1956).

16212 Jeffersonians Orchestra. Local dance band (WFAA, Dallas, TX, 1925).

16213 Jeffery, Pervis. Singer Pervis was known as the "Radio Tenor" (WOOD, Grand Rapids, MI, 1926).

16214 Jefferys, Allan. DJ (*Midnight Platter Party*, WFPG, Atlantic City, NJ, 1950; *Starlight Salute*, WTOP, Washington, DC, 1952; *In the Land of Music*, ABC, 1960).

16215 Jeffrey, Morris. Director (Hotel Lowry Orchestra, WCCO, Minneapolis–St. Paul, MN, 1928).

16216 Jeffries, Allen. Newscaster (WOWO, Fort Wayne, IN, 1945; WIRE, Indianapolis, IN, 1947–1948).

16217 Jeffries, Helen. Singer (WIP, Philadelphia, PA, 1926).

16218 Jeffries, James. Tenor (WFAA, Dallas, TX, 1929).

16219 "JEK." Designation for Miss Jessie E. Koewing, the busy announcer, violinist and program director of station WOR (Newark, NJ, 1923).

16220 Jellison, Harry. Bass (KSL, Salt Lake City, UT, 1928).

16221 Jellison, Otto J. Tenor (WCCO, Minneapolis–St. Paul, MN, 1928).

16222 Jellison, Robert D. "Bob." Pioneer sound effects man Jellison was born August 21, 1908. His first work as a sound effects man was at WCCO (Minneapolis–St. Paul., MN, 1928). About nine years later he began work as a radio character actor. Actor Jellison was in the cast of *Barton Family*, *Chicago Theater of the Air*, *Girl Alone*, *Great Gunns*, *Harold Teen*, *Lone Journey*, *Midstream*, *Tale of Today*, *That Brewster Boy* and *Tom Mix*.

16223 Jello, Ann. Singer (WMCA, New York, NY, 1936).

16224 Jencks, E.W. Announcer (WWJ, Detroit, MI, 1928).

16225 Jencks, Hugh. Newscaster (KVGB, Great Bend, KS, 1948).

16226 Jendrek, Edward. Station staff tenor (WBAL, Baltimore, MD, 1926–1928).

16227 Jenke, Helen. Contralto (WEAF, New York, NY, 1929).

16228 Jenkins, (Reverend) Andrew "Blind Andy." Born in 1885, Jenkins became blind in middle age. He played banjo, guitar, mandolin and the French harp. He became a preacher in 1910. His radio debut with his daughters, Irene Spain and Mary Lee Eskew, took place August 14, 1922, on station WSB (Atlanta, GA). He was famous as a performer, recording artist and composer. His best selling recordings were "Little Marian Parker," "Billy the Kid" and "The Death of Floyd Collins." Jenkins frequently performed with another pioneer CW performer, Fiddlin' John Carson on WSB.

16229 Jenkins, Bill. DJ (*Corn Squeezing*, WTOP, Washington, DC, 1947).

16230 Jenkins, Bob. DJ (*For Members Only*, KONO, San Antonio, TX, 1950).

16231 Jenkins, (Dr.) Burris A. Radio minister (WHB, Kansas City, MO, 1928).

16232 Jenkins, Ed. Sportscaster (*Sports Parade*, KOEL, Oelwein, IA, 1951). DJ (*Open House*, KOEL, 1952).

16233 Jenkins, Eleanor. Contralto (WNYC, New York City, NY, 1936).

16234 Jenkins, Frank. Newscaster (KFLW, Klamath Falls, OR, 1946).

16235 Jenkins, Gordon. Versatile pianist, conductor, composer and arranger Jenkins was born May 12, 1910. He played ukulele and banjo in his brother's orchestra as a boy and frequently appeared with the band on St. Louis radio. Station staff pianist (KMOX, St. Louis, MO, 1927). Leader (*Gordon Jenkins* Orchestra, instr. mus. prg., NBC, 1935; KGHF, Pueblo, CO, 1939; *Gordon Jenkins Music*, NBC, 1940; KFI, Los Angeles, CA, 1942).

16236 Jenkins, (Mrs.) J. Elliott. Mrs. Jenkins conducted a children's program under the name of "The Lullaby Lady" (WMAQ, Chicago, IL, 1925).

16237 Jenkins, Louise. Violinist (WJAZ, Chicago, IL, 1923–1924).

16238 Jenkins, Polly. CW musical group leader (*Polly Jenkins and Her Playboys*, KDKA, Pittsburgh, PA, 1939).

16239 Jenkins, Ronald. Newscaster (WJNO, West Palm Beach, FL, 1939).

16240 Jenkins, Walter. Bass (KOIL, Council Bluffs, IA, 1926).

16241 Jenkins, Wayne. DJ (*Variety Hour*, WBOW, Terre Haute, IN, 1948).

16242 Jenkins, (Dr.) William P. Dr. Jenkins was a missionary who worked in China. He broadcast religious services (WFAA, Dallas, TX, 1923).

16243 Jenks, Mary Ellen. COM-HE (WMTV, Madison, WI, 1955).

16244 Jennemann [Jenneman], Doris. COM-HE (KSTL, St. Louis, MO, 1956–1957).

16245 Jennings, A.B. Director, St. Stephen's Church Choir, Sewickey, PA, 1923).

16246 Jennings, Al. Newscaster (WTMC, Ocala, FL, 1940–1941). Sportscaster (WTMC, 1940–1941).

16247 Jennings, Al. Newscaster (WMSL, Decatur, AL, 1941). DJ (*Al's Wax Works*, WCCP, Savannah, GA, 1947; *The AJ Show*, WCCP, 1948). Sportscaster (WMSL, 1941; WCCP, 1948; *Coastal Sports*, WCCP, 1949–1954).

16248 Jennings, Dessa Anderson. *Radio Guide* reported that Anderson had sung on 150 radio programs by 1928 (WADC, Akron, OH, 1928).

16249 Jennings, Gordon. DJ (*Hillbilly Fever*, WKOY, Bluefield, WV, 1949–1956).

16250 Jennings, Helen Massey. COM-HE (WJBO, Baton Rouge, LA, 1956).

16251 Jennings, Jay. DJ (*Farmyard Frolics*, WMIS, Natchez, MS, 1952).

16252 Jennings, Mabelle. News commentator Jennings specialized in discussing the personalities and events in the Washington, D.C., area (CBS, 1936).

16253 Jennings, Mrs. COM-HE (KGYO, Missoula, MT, 1949).

16254 Jennings, Sunny. COM-HE (WRGB, Schenectady, NY, 1957).

16255 Jenny, Gerald. Newscaster (WAJR, Morgantown, WV, 1945).

16256 Jenny, Jack. Leader (*Jack Jenny Orchestra*, instr. mus. prg., CBS, 1934; NBC, 1939, CBS, 1942).

16257 *Jenny Peabody*. Olan Soule and Virginia Jones played the leading roles on this daytime serial (15 min., Monday through Friday, WBBM, Chicago, IL, 1937).

16258 Jensen, Allan. Newscaster (KUTA, Salt Lake City, UT, 1941; KSL, Salt Lake City, UT, 1947).

16259 Jensen, Dagny. Soprano (WJAZ, Chicago, IL, 1923).

16260 Jensen, Fred. DJ (*Freddie's File*, KXRN, Renton, WA, 1949).

16261 Jensen, Helen. Organist (*Helen Jensen*, instr. mus. prg., 15 min., Sunday, 11:45–12:00 noon, WLS, Chicago, IL, 1937).

16262 Jensen, J.C. Announcer (WCAJ, University Place, NE, 1927).

16263 Jensen, Kathleen. COM-HE (KWHO, Salt Lake City, UT, 1960).

16264 Jensen, Ken. DJ (*Jam Session*, KUTA, Salt Lake City, UT, 1950).

16265 Jensen, Luther. Announcer (KFOA, Seattle, WA, 1927).

16266 Jensen, M.C. Newscaster (WCAL, Northfield, MN, 1939).

16267 Jensen, Paul. DJ (*Paul's Platter Party*, KOLN, Lincoln, NE, 1948; *Gloombusters*, KOLN, Lincoln, NE, 1949).

16268 Jensen, Ran. DJ (*RCA Victor Varieties*, WOC, Davenport, IA, 1948; *Package from Parkers*, WOC, 1949).

16269 Jensen, Ruth. COM-HE (WLSD, Big Stone Gap, VA, 1954).

16270 Jensen, Sam. DJ (*The Sam Jensen Show*, KCRG, Cedar Rapids, IA, 1948).

16271 Jensen, Russell. Newscaster (KROP, Brawley, CA, 1946).

16272 Jensen, Walt. DJ (*Record Rendezvous*, KSJB, Jamestown, ND, 1949; KWOA, Worthington, MN, 1956).

16273 Jensen and Lettow. A male harmony singing team, Jensen and Lettow were sometimes known as the Harmony Boys (WHB, Kansas City, MO, 1928).

16274 Jenson, Peg. COM-HE (KILO, Grand Forks, ND, 1951).

16275 Jentes, Harry. Jazz pianist (WEAF, New York, NY, 1924–1925).

16276 Jepson, Helen. Soprano, (Networks, 1930–1940s). Glamorous blonde soprano Jepson went from radio stardom to the Metropolitan Opera in 1934. Selected by Met impresario Gatti-Casazza, she was frequently hailed as "one of the most beautiful women on the Met stage." Jepson was a lyric soprano with sufficient volume to fill a hall without amplification (*Radio Guide*, July 28, 1934, p. 5). She was the first female radio star to be signed by the Metropolitan Opera. Tenor Nino Martini was the first. During her second season at the Met she was scheduled to sing Eva in *Die Meistersinger*; Juliet in *Romeo and Juliet*; Violetta in *La Traviata*; and Melisande in *Pelleas and Melisande*.

During her early working life, Jepson had sold everything from hairpins to corsets. Her first singing job was performing solos in a church. She first sang over the radio at the age of 18 over Cleveland's station WTAM in 1924. Her first professional singing contract was with a Chautauqua company that played 81 times in a few weeks under the "big tent." Jepson gained national recognition singing on *Paul Whiteman's Music Hall* aka the *Kraft Music Hall* broadcasts (1933–1934, NBC). Expressing her appreciation of radio, Jepson said, "Radio to me always will be as important as any other branch of my work" (*Radio Guide*, July 28, 1934, p. 3).

16277 Jerde, O.J. Newscaster (*Night Time News*, KFAM, St. Cloud, MN, 1948).

16278 *(The) Jergens Journal*. *See **Walter Winchell**.*

16279 *(The) Jergens Program*. Cornelia Otis Skinner starred on this show in what *Variety* described as "one woman theater" (15 min., Weekly, 7:00–7:15 P.M., NBC-Blue, 1936).

16280 Jeritza, Maria. Metropolitan Opera soprano (WGY, Schenectady, NY, 1926).

16281 Jermaine, Jerry (Margaret Jarman). "Crooning contralto" (KPO, San Francisco, CA, 1928–1929). After making her first radio appearance in 1927, Miss Jermaine remained a San Francisco favorite into the next decade.

16282 Jernberg, George. Cornetist (WIBO, Chicago, IL, 1925).

16283 Jerome, Doreta. Singer (WJZ, New York, NY, 1925).

16284 Jerome, Edwin "Ed." Actor Jerome appeared in *Aunt Jenny*, *Blackstone the Magic Detective* (title role), *By Kathleen Norris*, *Carol Kennedy's Romance*, *Cavalcade of America*, *Man I Married*, *The March of Time*, *Rich Man's Daughter*, *Theatre Guild of the Air*, *When a Girl Marries* and *Woman of America*.

16285 Jerome, Elmora. Contralto (WHAZ, Troy, NY, 1937).

16286 *Jerry at Fair Oaks*. The transcribed show followed the *Jerry at the Circus* program. This show told of Jerry's adventures at school (15 min., Transcribed, 1930s).

16287 *Jerry at the Circus*. *Jerry at the Circus* was a transcribed show that dramatized a young boy's adventures with the circus (15 min., Transcribed, 1930s).

16288 Jerry's Hayshakers. CW music group (WHDH, Boston, MA, 1941).

16289 Jersey's Blue Serenaders of Medvale, NJ. Local orchestra (WJZ, New York, NY, 1922).

16290 Jeske, Fred. Announcer-director Jeske began his radio career in 1926 (WBBM, Chicago, IL), moved on to WTMJ (Milwaukee, WI) and from there back to Chicago's WGES in 1928.

16291 Jesse, Bill. DJ (*Dance Time*, KGDE, Fergus Falls, MN, 1947).

16292 Jessee, Blair. DJ (*Hayloft Jamboree*, WROM, Rome, GA, 1950).

16293 Jessee, Randall. Sportscaster (KWOC, Poplar Bluff, MO, 1939).

16294 *(The) Jessel Jamboree*. Read's Ice Cream sponsored the variety show hosted by comedian George Jessel. Mary Small, Stuart Allen, Sam Calton and the Richard Himber Orchestra were featured. The announcer was Ernest Chappell (30 min., Weekly, 1930s).

16295 Jesson, Johnny. Leader (Johnny Jesson Orchestra, KFQW, Seattle, WA, 1928).

16296 Jessup, Margaret. Producer-director (advertising agency 1930s) Jessup was a member of the McCann-Erickson advertising agency's production staff. She both produced and directed numerous programs.

16297 Jester, Carl. Announcer designated as "CJ" (WGY, Schenectady, NY, 1923–1924).

16298 Jester, O. Pike. Soprano (WQJ, Chicago, IL, 1926).

16299 *(The) Jesters*. The Jesters were a comedy singing trio that had a long running network program sponsored by Tastyeast. The popular male trio specialized in novelty and comic songs and were sometimes known as the Tastyeast Jesters. Since eating Tastyeast was said to provide pep, vim and vigor, the trio's members were known as Pep (Dwight Latham), Vim (Wamp Carlson) and Vigor (Guy Bohman). An earlier program was also known as *The Jesters* (NBC, 1934–1935), featured a trio that had appeared on the NBC network since 1931. *See* ***The Tastyeast Jesters***.

16300 Jeter, F.H. Newscaster (WPTF, Raleigh, NC, 1945).

16301 Jeter, Goetze. Newscaster (*City Journal*, KVOR, Colorado Springs, CO, 1947).

16302 Jewel, Isabel. Actress on the *Eno Crime Club* program (CBS, 1931).

16303 Jewel, Izetta. COM-HE (KCBQ, San Diego, CA, 1949).

16304 *Jewel Cowboys* (aka *The Jewel Cowboys Hillbilly Singers*). CW voc. mus. prg. by a popular Western music band. First begun in 1934, the program was sponsored by Swift & Company, makers of Jewel Shortening. Smiling Bill Thompson was the host. Singer-guitarist Jose Cortes and singer Slim Hall, the "Original Jewel Cowboy," were also featured (30 min., Monday, 8:14–8:45 P.M., WREC, Memphis, TN, 1942). An earlier network series was broadcast on CBS with Roy Wooten as the announcer (30 min., Saturday, 10:30–11:00 A.M., CBS, 1938).

16305 *(The) Jewel Tea Program*. The Jewel Tea Company sponsored the unusual combination of music and recipes (CBS, 1928).

16306 Jewell, Helen J. Organist (KFWM, Oakland, CA, 1928).

16307 Jewell, James. DJ (*Yawn Club*, KTBI, Tacoma, WA, 1949).

16308 Jewell, James "Jim." DJ (*Hub Cap Caravan* and *Eight O'Clock Date*, WBBC, Flint, MI, 1949; KNBX, Kirkland, WA, 1955).

16309 Jewell, Joan. COM-HE (WBBC, Flint, MI, 1956–1957).

16310 Jewell, Mary Ann. COM-HE (WILD, Birmingham, AL, 1954).

16311 Jewell, Joan. COM-HE (WBBC, Flint, MI, 1956).

16312 Jewell, Tony. DJ (*Variety Capers*, KIUL, Garden City, KS, 1948).

16313 Jewell, Mary. COM-HE (WNOE, New Orleans, LA, 1949).

16314 Jewett, Clyde. Pianist (KHJ, Los Angeles, CA, 1926).

16315 Jewett, Ted. Actor Jewett was in the cast of *Cavalcade of America* and *Ellen Randolph*.

16316 *(The) Jewett Jesters*. The Jewett Radio and Phonograph Company sponsored the music show that was organized and conducted by Leo Fitzpatrick ("The Merry Old Chief'"). One of the listeners' special favorites was blind singer, Harold Kean, who was known as the "Sunshine Boy." Others who appeared on the program were Ted de Turk the Play Boy; Newell Struck, linguist deluxe; Elizabeth Swanson; pianist Mary Tudor; singers Muriel Kyle and Romaine Johns; and Johnny Kaaihue and his Hawaiians orchestra. The Jewett Company not only sponsored the program, but also owned the station (Weekly, WJR, Detroit, MI, 1925).

16317 *(The) Jewish Hour*. A brief address by Rabbi Samuel M. Cohen and musical selections by string and woodwind ensembles were broadcast weekly on the sustaining religious program (60 min., Sunday, 3:00–4:00 P.M., NBC-Red, 1928–1930).

16318 *(The) Jewish Poker Game*. Dialect comedians Harry Hershfield, Milt Gross, Jimmy Hussey and Max Fleischer provided the fun on the comedy show (WGBS, New York, NY, 1926).

16319 Jim and Jesse (Jim and Jesse McReynolds). The CW harmony singing brothers team performed on many local radio stations in the 1950s, including the *Swanee River Jamboree* in Live Oaks, FL, the *WDVA Barn Dance* (Danville, VA), the *Mid-Day Merry-Go-Round* (WNOX, Knoxville, TN) and the *WWVA Jamboree* (WWVA, Wheeling, WV). The brothers joined the *Grand Ole Opry* in 1964.

16320 *(The) Jim Backus Show*. Comedians Backus, Harry Housner, Frances Robertson and Dick Trout were featured on the sustaining show. The announcer was Frank Graham (30 min., Sunday, 9:30–10:00 P.M., WOR, Newark, NJ, 1947). A later *(The) Jim Backus Show*, was an ABC program originating from Nashville, TN. Comedian Jim Backus was the host of the variety show. He was joined by singers Betty Ann Grove and Jack Haskell, the Honeydreamers vocal group and the Elliott Lawrence Orchestra. Del Sharbutt was the announcer (55 min., Monday through Friday, 2:00–2:55 P.M., ABC, 1947).

16321 Jim, Jack and Jean. Singing group (KFI, Los Angeles, CA, 1926).

16322 *Jim Lewis' Hillbillies*. CW mus. prg. (WBIG, Greensboro, NC, 1938).

16323 *Jim Poole's Mid-Morning Chicago Hog and Sheep Market News*. Poole broadcasting direct from the Chicago Stock Yards was sponsored by the Chicago Stock Yards Exchange (Monday through Friday, WLS, 1937).

16324 *(The) Jim Reeves Show*. *Variety* said ABC added the *Jim Reeves* CW music show in an effort to improve its schedule. The show originated from Nashville with country singing star Reeves starring along with Dolores Watson, Buddy Hall, the Anita Kerr Singers and Owen Bradley's Orchestra. Dave Cobb was the program's announcer (55 min., Monday through Friday, 1:00–1:55 P.M., ABC, 1957).

16325 *Jimmie and Eddy—the Dean Brothers*. Billed as the "Two Deans of Harmony," Jimmie and Eddy Dean were a favorite singing team of Chicago listeners. Eddy soon left radio to travel to Hollywood and begin a career as a cowboy singing star (15 min., Sunday, WGN, Chicago, IL, 1936; *Jimmie and Eddy Dean*, CW mus. prg., 15 min., Monday through Friday, 8:30–8:45 A.M., WCKY, Covington, KY, 1937). Both brothers also made many *National Barn Dance* appearances on WLS (Chicago, IL).

16326 (The) Jimmie Rodgers Entertainers. *See* **Rodgers, Jimmie.**

16327 *Jimmy and Dad*. One man dramatic show with Pat Barnes playing all the parts (WBZ, Boston, MA, 1931).

16328 *Jimmy Corbin*. Comedian Corbin's sustaining local program was a Des Moines favorite (15 min., Weekly, KRNT, Des Moines, IA, 1937).

16329 *(The) Jimmy Durante Show* (aka *The Rexall Drug Program*.) Durante and Garry Moore had been an entertaining comedy team since 1943, when they replaced Abbott and Costello on the *Comedy Caravan*. The teaming of the younger Moore ("the Haircut") and Durante ("the Schnozz") proved to be an entertaining contrasting pair. The successful team worked together until 1945 with the show's title alternating weekly between *The Jimmy Durante Show* and *The Garry Moore Show*. When Rexall Drug Company became the sponsor, the program was called either *The Rexall Drug Program* or *The Jimmy Durante Show*.

After the departure of Moore, Durante successfully continued alone. His warm, comedy style ensured the show's continued popularity. His new cast members included Barbara Jo Allen, Elvia Allman, Don Ameche, Sara Berner, Candy Candido, Florence Halop, Joseph Kearns, Arthur Treacher and Tommy Halloran. Singers Georgia Gibbs and Peggy Lee and the orchestras of Roy Bargy and Xavier Cugat. Guests such as Greer Garson appeared on the show weekly. Phil Cohan directed the show. The writers were Stanley Davis, Sid Reznick, Jack Robinson, Jay Sommers and Sid Zelinka (30 min., Wednesday, 10:30–11:00 P.M., NBC, 1947).

16330 *Jimmy Fiddler*. Fiddler was one of the most popular of all the Hollywood gossip columnists on the radio (15 min., Wednesday, 10:00–10:15 P.M., NBC-Blue, 1935). In a later format *Jimmy Fiddler* (aka *The Hollywood Reporter*), once more broadcast Hollywood news and gossip (15 min., Weekly, ABC, MBS, 1948).

16331 *Jimmy, June and Jack*. Venida Hair Nets sponsored the vocal trio of June Emmett, Hal and Murray Kane on the popular local show (15 min., Thursday, 11:00–11:15 P.M., WMCA, New York, NY, 1935).

16332 *Jimmy the Talking Bird*. Jimmy, a "crow-like" bird, did the talking on the weekly sustaining program. One of his favorite lines was, "What are you doing Monday night?" Although in person Jimmy's salty language drove little old ladies away, on the air he remained on his best behavior (15 min., Weekly, KHJ, Los Angeles, CA, 1935).

16333 *Jimmy Walker*. Walker, an ex-Mayor of New York, was sponsored by the Paul Lefton Company, makers of Crawford Clothes. Walker was a short-lived network news commentator (15 min., Friday, 8:15–8:30 P.M., NBC-Blue, 1939).

16334 *Jimmy Walker's Opportunity Hour*. Ex-Mayor Walker hosted the local radio amateur hour sponsored by Princess Pat Cosmetics. Henry Gladstone was the announcer (60 min., 9:00–10:00 P.M., WHN, New York, NY, 1940). See **Walker, Jimmy**

16335 ***Jimmy's Hawaiians Orchestra.*** Instr. mus. prg. (KMMJ, Grand Island, NE, 1942).

16336 **Jimmy's Joys.** Popular Dallas orchestra (WFAA, Dallas, TX, 1926).

16337 **Jines, Martha.** Pianist (KFI, Los Angeles, CA, 1925).

16338 **Jiras, Ruby.** Accordionist (*Ruby Jiras*, instr. mus. prg., WHP, Harrisburg, PA, 1936–1938).

16339 **"JJF."** Designation for Major John F. Fanning, one of the most popular of all the pioneer radio announcers (WNAC, Boston, MA, 1923).

16340 **Jo, Peggy.** COM-HE (KGDE, Fergus Falls, MN, 1951).

16341 ***(The) Jo Stafford Show.*** Talented vocalist Stafford was joined on the good music program by tenor Clark Dennis and the Starlighters vocal group. Stafford's husband, Paul Weston led the program's orchestra. The sponsor was the Revere Camera Company (30 min., Thursday, 8:30–9:00 P.M., ABC, 1948).

16342 ***Joan and the Escorts.*** Vcl. mus. prg. (NBC-Blue, 1936).

16343 ***Joan and Kermit.*** Milton Geiger wrote the weekly dramatic serial featuring Fran Carlon and Olan Soule (30 min., Sunday P.M., CBS, 1938).

16344 ***Joanne.*** Vcl. mus. prg. by a contralto not otherwise identified (WAAF, Chicago, IL, 1936).

16345 **Jobes, Herb.** DJ (*Afternoon Showcase*, KIUP, Durango, CO, 1960).

16346 **Jobes, James N.** Sportscaster (*Sinclair Sportscast*, KOFO, Ottawa, KS, 1951).

16347 **Joe, Don.** Sportscaster (KMA, Shenandoah, IA, 1954).

16348 ***Joe and Ethel Turp.*** A situation comedy produced and directed by Larry Berns, its cast included Jackson Beck and Patsy Campbell in the title roles supported by Jack Smart and Art Carney.

16349 ***Joe and Jack—The Piano Twins.*** This was an instrumental music program by a dual piano team (KGHI, Little Rock, AR, 1929).

16350 ***Joe Cook's Cookoo Comedy.*** Comic Joe Cook hosted his variety show that was sponsored by the Colgate-Palmolive Company. Music was supplied by tenor Donald Novis and the Don Voorhees Orchestra (30 min., Monday, 9:30–10:00 P.M., NBC, 1935).

16351 ***(The) Joe DiMaggio Show.*** Former baseball great DiMaggio interviewed sports celebrities and emphasized the importance of clean living on his children's sports show written by Mike Oppenheimer. Jack Barry co-hosted with DiMaggio. Dramatized episodes from the lives of various athletes were presented with such performers as Jackson Beck, Charles Irving, Leon Janney, Mandel Kramer and Everett Sloane. In addition, a young quizmaster conducted a quiz with the young members of the audience. The announcer was Ted Brown. The sponsor was M&M Candies (30 min., Saturday, 10:00–10:30 A.M., CBS, 1950).

16352 ***Joe Moss and the Three California Nuts.*** J.B. Williams Company sponsored the show that combined music and comedy. Joe Moss conducted the orchestra, Vivian Ross sang and the humor was supplied by the Three California Nuts. The "Nuts," formerly were known as the Three Public Enemies, not otherwise identified (15 min., Sunday, 7:30–7:45 P.M., NBC-Red, 1933).

16353 ***Joe Palooka.*** A children's serial drama based on Ham Fisher's cartoon strip, *Joe Palooka* told the story of Joe, a clean living heavyweight boxing champion. The title role, at various times, was played by Teddy Bergman (Alan Reed), Norman Gottschalk and Karl Swenson. Knobby Walsh, Joe's manager, was played by Frank Readick. Other members of the cast were Mary Jane Higby, Elsie Hitz and James Marr. Sportscaster Ted Husing was the announcer (15 min., Tuesday and Thursday, 5:45–6:00 P.M. CST, CBS, 1932).

16354 ***(The) Joe Penner Show*** **(aka *The Baker Broadcast*).** Joe Penner (Joseph Penta) was born in Nadgybeck, Hungary November 11, 1904. He was ten when he arrived in the United States. At an early age he worked as a burlesque comedian in Baltimore's Gayety Theater, where he was discovered by Mike Porter, a staff member of *Radio Guide* magazine. Penner's frenetic comedy routines featured such catch phrases as "You nasty man" and his frequent query, "Do you want to buy a duck?" On the program Penner was joined by: Margaret Brayton, Stephanie Diamond, Monk Monsel, Dick Ryan, Gay Seabrook and Martha Wentworth. The writers were Matt Brooks, Carroll Carroll, Eddie Davis, Hal Finberg, Parke Levy, Arnold G. Maguire, Don Pringle and George Wells. Gordon Thompson was the director. Ozzie Nelson directed the orchestra and Harriet Hilliard was the featured vocalist. Although Penner enjoyed considerable success and critical praise, he quit the program in 1935 and was replaced by "Believe it or Not" Robert Ripley. Penner returned to radio in 1936 with his own *Park Avenue Penner* show that ran until 1940. This show featured the band of Jimmy Grier and singers Gene Austin and Joy Hodges. The next year, Penner died of a heart attack at the age of 37.

16355 ***Joe Powers of Oakville.*** This "boy meets girl" daily serial drama was broadcast on a sustaining basis. Draper Lewis and Jacques Fink wrote the program that was produced by James Hart and directed by Howard Barnes. The cast members included David Anderson, Elizabeth Keller, Richard Leone and Julian Noa. Organ interludes were provided by George Seaman (15 min., Monday through Friday, CBS, 1946).

16356 ***Joe Rines' Dress Rehearsal.*** The program was a simulated rehearsal of a show that contained both music and drama. In addition to maestro Rines and his band, vaudevillian Mable Albertson, comedian Pinky Lee and tenor Morton Bowe were featured, (NBC, 1936).

16357 ***Joe Wesp the Ironic Reporter.*** Although Wesp's commentary was timely, *Variety* said he was rarely ironic. Household Finance sponsored the local news program (10 min., Monday through Friday, 11:05–11:15 A.M., WBEN, Buffalo, NY, 1938).

16358 **Joelsohn, Zinaida.** Pianist (KYW, Chicago, IL, 1925).

16359 **Joelson, Edith.** Soprano (WLWL, New York, NY, 1932).

16360 **Joens, Margaret.** Soprano (KOIL, Council Bluffs, IA, 1927).

16361 ***Joey in the Underworld.*** Convicted ex-bandit Joseph Taylor, now rehabilitated, conducted the unusual series on which he told of crimes and criminals (WJZ, New York, NY, 1923).

16362 **Johansen, Chris.** Newscaster (WGKJ, Charleston, WV, 1939).

16363 **John, Alma.** COM-HE (WWRL, New York City, NY, 1956–1957).

16364 **John, Cousin.** DJ (*Crazy House*, WBRW, Welch, WV, 1947).

16365 **John, Louise.** Horoscope reader (KNX, Hollywood, CA, 1927).

16366 **John and Ned.** John (Wolfe) and Ned (Tollinger) were a versatile duo billed as singers, instrumentalists and comedians. They sometimes were also known as "The Union Station Team" (NBC-Pacific, 1929). The team began broadcasting in 1927 and continued into the early 1930s.

16367 ***John B. Gambling.*** This was yet *another* WOR Gambling show on which John A. Gambling joined his father—John B. They talked and played records (30 min., Monday through Saturday, 11:15–11:45 P.M., WOR, New York, NY, 1954). *See* **Gambling, John B.**

16368 ***(The) John B. Gambling Club.*** John B. and his son, John A. Gambling, played records and engaged in interesting conversation (60 min., Monday through Friday, 3:00–4:00 P.M., MBS, 1952). *See* **Gambling, John B.**

16369 ***(The) John B. Gambling's Saturday Sociable.*** Busy Gambling, in addition to his weekday early morning show that had begun in the 1920s, played records and made small talk on his local Saturday morning program (45 min., Saturday, 8:15–9:00 A.M., WOR, New York, NY, 1950). *See* **Gambling, John B.**

16370 ***John B. Kennedy-Edwin C. Hill News.*** Veteran commentators Kennedy and Hill broadcast the news, each with his own uniquely authoritative style (15 min., MBS, 1956). *See* **Kennedy, John B.** *and* **Hill, Edwin C.**

16371 ***John Charles Thomas and his Neighbors.*** Distinguished singer Thomas, guest vocalists and an orchestra performed on the music program (30 min., Wednesday, 8:00–8:30 P.M. CST, NBC, 1935). *See* **Thomas, John Charles.**

16372 ***(The) John Charles Thomas Show*** **(aka *The Westinghouse Sunday Concert* or *The Westinghouse Program*).** Distinguished baritone Thomas of the Metropolitan Opera Company sang a diverse program of American songs accompanied by the Victor Young Orchestra. Songs were also performed by the Ken Darby Singers. Each week John Nesbitt contributed a spoken segment similar to his popular *Passing Parade* motion picture features. The program was sponsored by the Westinghouse Electric Company (30 min., Weekly, 1943–1946, NBC). *See* **Thomas, John Charles.**

16373 ***(The) John Conte Show.*** Motion picture star Conte conducted a modified DJ show, since he sang a few songs in addition to playing records (45 min., Monday through Friday, 5:15–6:00 P.M., ABC, 1953).

16374 ***John Henry, Black River Giant.*** Juano Hernandez had a leading singing and speaking role on the program that adapted various African-American legends, songs and material drawn from the writings of Roark Bradford. The result was a fine cultural program. George Burke, Geraldine Gerrick and Rose McClendon also appeared in the program's "all Negro cast" (15 min., Sunday, 8:00–8:15 P.M., CBS, 1933). Later, the format was expanded (30 min., Sunday, 6:30–7:00 P.M., CBS, 1933).

16375 ***John Henry Faulk.*** After Faulk's *Johnny's Front Porch* had been dropped from the network schedule, he was successful with his local sustaining DJ show, on which he dispensed his homey philosophy and incisive wit (50 min., Monday through Friday, 5:05–5:55 P.M., WCBS, New York, NY, 1951).

16376 **John R.** Black DJ not otherwise identified (WLAC, Nashville, TN, 1940s-1950s).

16377 ***John Reed King's Best Girl.*** On his novel audience participation show, King interviewed studio audience members and a guest celebrity. His goal was to discover what qualities they wanted their "best girl" to possess (30 min., Monday through Friday, 3:30–4:00 P.M., WOR, Newark, NJ, 1949).

16378 **Johnen, Louis John.** Poetry reader (WLW, Cincinnati, OH, 1926).

16379 **Johnny and Ginny.** DJ team (WEXL, Royal Oak, MI, 1950).

16380 ***Johnny and the Foursome.*** Vcl. mus. prg. (CBS, 1935).

16381 ***Johnny at the Piano.*** Fourteen-year-old pianist Johnny Rudd was a local radio favorite (15 min., Wednesday, 5:00–5:15 P.M., WHO Des Moines, NE. 1938).

16382 ***Johnny Lujack of Notre Dame.*** The sustaining daytime adventure show told the "story" of college (Notre Dame) and professional (Chicago Bears) star football quarterback, Johnny Lujack. The summer replacement for *Armstrong of the S.B.I.* was not limited to Lujack's football exploits. On one of the first stories, for example, he successfully proved the innocence of a 16-year-old accused of stealing. Lujack played himself on the show. Other cast members included Boris Aplon, Jack Evans, Art Hern, Angelyn Orr and Ed Prentiss. Art Ward was the program's announcer (30 min., Monday-Wednesday-Friday, 5:30–6:00 P.M., ABC, 1948).

16383 ***Johnny Mercer's Music Shop.*** Mercer, the talented singer-composer hosted his entertaining music show that also featured singer Jo Stafford, the Pied Pipers and Paul Weston's orchestra (15 min., 1944).

16384 ***Johnny Modero, Pier 23.*** Jack Webb played the title role of a San Francisco waterfront character, who each week somehow became embroiled in solving a mystery. The show bore a strong resemblance to *Pat Novak for Hire*, a program on which Webb had starred previously. In addition to Webb, the program's cast included Francis X. Bushman, William Conrad and Gale Gordon. The show was created by Richard Breen and written by Herb Margolis and Louis Markeim (30 min., Wednesday, 8:30–9:00 P.M., MBS, 1947).

16385 ***(The) Johnny Morgan Variety Show.*** Johnny Morgan hosted the variety show that featured vocalist Milena Miller (Weekly, CBS, 1945).

16386 ***Johnny Olsen's Get Together*** **(aka *Johnny Olsen's Rumpus Room*).** The show kept the versatile Olsen busy conducting guest interviews, a community sing and even singing himself. The show was produced by Jack Cleary (60 min., Saturday, 10:00–11:00 A.M., ABC, 1949).

16387 ***Johnny Presents the Rudy Vallee Show.*** Philip Morris Cigarettes sponsored the entertaining variety show that featured Vallee, Margaret Whiting, Doris Day, Billie Burke, Ruth Etting, the Tune Toppers, Margo and Eddie Albert, Dave Barry and the Wesson Brothers (30 min., Weekly, NBC, 1946–1947).

16388 ***Johnny Thompson and Ilene Woods.*** Thompson and Woods were a talented singing team (30 min., 10:30–11:00 A.M., ABC, 1945).

16389 ***Johnny's Front Porch.*** Homey philosopher John Henry Faulk was not overly successful with his sustaining network show, on which he delivered his commentary in a folksy style (15 min., Sunday, 5:30–5:45 P.M., CBS, 1946). See ***John Henry Faulk.***

16390 **Johns, Brooke.** DJ (*Morning in Maryland*, WBCC, Bethesda, MD, 1948).

16391 **Johns, Florence.** Lyric soprano (WEEI, Boston, MA, 1925).

16392 **Johns, W.M.** Newscaster (WMFJ, Daytona Beach, FL, 1945).

16393 ***John's Other Wife.*** Frank and Anne Hummert produced the daytime serial that told the story of John Perry, a wealthy department store owner and his "other wife," his secretary. His faithful wife, Elizabeth Perry's ups and downs generally were caused by her concerns about the "other wife." First heard on NBC in 1936, the program ran for six years. The cast included: Stella Adler, Joan Banks, Don Beddoes, Ethel Blume, Milo Boulton, Alan Bunce, Macdonald Carey, Mary Cecil, Kingsley Cotton, Matt Crowley, Joseph Curtin, Helene Dumas, Florence Freeman, Franc Hale, Neil Harrison, Mary Jane Higby, Pat Holbrook, Irene Hubbard, Rita Johnson, David Jordan, John Kane, Lyda Kane, Elaine Kent, Alexander Kirkland, Richard Kollmar, James Krieger, Erin O'Brien-Moore, Margaret O'Connell, Vivia Ogden, William Post, Jr., Alice Reinheart, Adele Ronson, Hanley Stafford, Edward Trevor, Luis Van Rooten, Linda Watkins, Phyllis Welch and Ruth Yorke. Bill Sweets was the writer. The program's theme ("The Sweetest Story Ever Told") was whistled, sung, and strummed on the guitar by Stanley Davis.

16394 **Johnson, A.W. "Wally."** Newscaster (KVOA, Tucson, AZ, 1945).

16395 **Johnson, Arnold.** Leader (*Arnold Johnson Orchestra*, instr. mus. prg., CBS, 1935).

16396 **Johnson, Art.** Chief announcer and singer (WOAI, San Antonio, TX, 1922).

16397 **Johnson, Ava.** Newscaster (KXEL, Waterloo, IA, 1945–1946).

16398 **Johnson, Bea.** COM-HE (KMBC, Kansas City, MO, 1949–1957; KFRM, Concordia, KS, 1957).

16399 **Johnson, Bess.** Actress Johnson was the leading lady on *The Witching Hour*, a drama about dreams of the supernatural (Saturday, 5:30–6:00 P.M., CBS, 1930s). Johnson later was a busy daytime serial actress appearing on such programs as *Hilltop House*, *Mary Marlin* aka *The Story of Mary Marlin*, *The Story of Bess Johnson*, *Today's Children* and *True Confessions.*

16400 **Johnson, Betty.** COM-HE (KBTN, Neosho, MO, 1957).

16401 **Johnson, Bill.** Leader (Bill Johnson Orchestra, WFBH, New York, NY, 1925).

16402 **Johnson, Bill.** DJ (*Musical Clock*, WNAX, Yankton, SD, 1952).

16403 **Johnson, Bill.** DJ (*Morning Serenades*, WRHC, Jacksonville, FL, 1952).

16404 **Johnson, Bill.** DJ (*Dinner Bell*, WROL, Knoxville, TN, 1952; *Time for Everybody*, WLAC, Nashville, TN, 1955).

16405 **Johnson, Bonnie.** COM-HE (WBHB, Fitzgerald, GA, 1956).

16406 **Johnson, Carl.** DJ (*Nightcap Revue*, KDIX, Dickinson, ND, 1948).

16407 **Johnson, Carmen.** COM-HE (KCOL, Fort Collins, CO, 1949).

16408 **Johnson, Carol.** Pianist-singer (KECA, Los Angeles, CA, 1930).

16409 **Johnson, Carol.** COM-HE (WSYR, Syracuse, NY, 1960).

16410 **Johnson, Carolyn.** Blues singer (WPCH, New York, NY, 1932).

16411 **Johnson, Charles.** Leader (Charles Johnson and His Victor Recording Orchestra, popular black jazz band broadcasting from Small's Paradise, a Harlem night club, WMCA, New York, NY, 1928).

16412 **Johnson, Charles.** Musician Johnson was billed as the "Duke of the Uke" (*Charles Johnson the Duke of the Uke*, instr. mus. prg., WAAF, Chicago, IL, 1935).

16413 **Johnson, Charles.** Newscaster (KEVE, Everett, WA, 1941).

16414 **Johnson, Charlotte.** COM-HE (WFI, Philadelphia, PA, 1925).

16415 **Johnson, Christine.** Soprano (NBC, 1937).

16416 **Johnson, Clarence.** Tenor (WOC, Davenport, IA, 1928).

16417 **Johnson, Cliff.** Sportscaster (KLX, Oakland, CA, 1945). DJ (*Cactus Jack Show*, WXOB, Stockton, CA, 1950).

16418 **Johnson, Clint.** Newscaster (WFIL, Philadelphia, PA, 1938).

16419 **Johnson, Connie.** Pianist (WDAF, Kansas City, MO, 1928).

16420 **Johnson, D.M.** DJ (*1450 Club*, KVCK, Wolf Point, MN, 1960).

16421 Johnson, Dianne. COM-HE (WCIA, Champaign, IL, 1956).

16422 Johnson, Dick. DJ (*Polka Time*, WIGM, Medford, WI, 1947; *Swing Shift*, WHLB ,Virginia, MN, 1949).

16423 Johnson, Dean. DJ (*Club 970*, KLER, Rochester, MN, 1948).

16424 Johnson, Dora. Actress Johnson was a cast member of the *Ma Perkins* daytime serial program.

16425 Johnson, Dorothy. Soprano (*Popular Bits*, NBC, 1931).

16426 Johnson, Dottie. DJ (*Dottie's Daily*, KSON, San Diego, CA, 1948–1950).

16427 Johnson, Doug. Newscaster (WAGE, Syracuse, NY, 1947).

16428 Johnson, Duane. Newscaster (*Mid-Day News*, KCOY, Santa Maria, CA, 1947). DJ (*Johnson's Folly*, KCOY, 1947).

16429 Johnson, E.S. Announcer (WJAX, Cleveland, OH, 1924).

16430 Johnson, Elbert. Newscaster (WRBL, Columbus, OH, 1945).

16431 Johnson, Elizabeth Morrison. Director of the *Goodnight Children* program (WHN, New York, NY, 1924).

16432 Johnson, Elmer. Newscaster (WHIP, Hammond, IN, 1941).

16433 Johnson, Elmer G. Announcer Johnson was known as "The Voice of the South," because of his deep-voiced authoritative tone (WJAX, Jacksonville, FL, 1923).

16434 Johnson, Erskine. Film news and gossip broadcaster (KECA, Los Angeles, CA, 1944; *Erskine Johnson in Hollywood*, MBS, 1945).

16435 Johnson, Evelyn. Soprano (WOK, Chicago, IL, 1925).

16436 Johnson, Evelyn. COM-HE (WDSR, Lake City, FL, 1955).

16437 Johnson, Fern. COM-HE (KSUB, Cedar City, UT, 1954–1955).

16438 Johnson, Frank. Bass (WEAF, New York, NY, 1926).

16439 Johnson, Gene. Organist (WLW, Cincinnati, OH, 1925).

16440 Johnson, Gene. COM-HE (KEEN, San Jose, CA, 1951).

16441 Johnson, George. Organist (WOW, Omaha, NE, 1928).

16442 Johnson, Gerry. COM-HE (KRLD, Dallas, TX, 1954).

16443 Johnson, G.I. Banjo soloist and member of the Swanee Orchestra (WJZ, New York, NY, 1923).

16444 Johnson, Gladys. Cellist (KGW, Portland, OR, 1927).

16445 Johnson, Gladys Lee. Staff violinist-cellist (KGW, Portland, OR, 1927–1928). Although broadcasting on the same station in the same year, neither Gladys Johnson was related to the other.

16446 Johnson, Glen. Newscaster (WHOP, Hopkinsville, KY, 1944).

16447 Johnson, Gwen. COM-HE (KROS, Clinton, IA, 1949).

16448 Johnson, Harold. Newscaster (WWNY, Watertown, NY, 1941–1942).

16449 Johnson, Harrison Wall. Pianist (WCCO, Minneapolis–St. Paul, MI, 1928).

16450 Johnson, Harry. DJ (*KGNO Request Hour* and *The 1340 Dance Club*, KGNO, Dodge City, KS, 1947).

16451 Johnson, Hazel. Pianist (KSCJ, Sioux City, IA, 1928).

16452 Johnson, Herb. DJ (*Rise 'n' Shine*, WMAZ, Macon, GA, 1950).

16453 Johnson, Herbert. "Boy organist" (KLDS, Independence, MO and KLOS, Independence, MO, 1926).

16454 Johnson, Herbert. Pianist (WGN, Chicago, IL, 1928).

16455 Johnson, Herman C. Leader (Herman Johnson and his Elks Band, WOOD, Grand Rapids, MI, 1926).

16456 Johnson, (General) Hugh. News commentator, military man and politician Johnson enjoyed a brief radio career (15 min., Monday, 8:00–8:15 P.M., NBC-Blue, 1938).

16457 Johnson, Irwin. DJ (*The Early Worm*, WBNS, Columbus, OH, 1941–1942; 1947–1956).

16458 Johnson, J. Howard. Tenor (KNX, Los Angeles, CA, 1928).

16459 Johnson, J. Rush. Announcer (KFXH, El Paso, TX, 1927).

16460 Johnson, Jane. Soprano (WELI, New Haven, CT, 1937).

16461 Johnson, Jason. Actor Johnson was in the cast of *The Married Life of Helan and Warren.*

16462 Johnson, Jay Jay. DJ (*Harlem Express*, WWPB, Miami, FL, 1952).

16463 Johnson, Jennie F.W. Singer (WJAZ, Chicago, IL, 1926).

16464 Johnson, Jerry. Leader (Jerry Johnson Orchestra, WBAP, Fort Worth, TX, 1929).

16465 Johnson, Jimmy. DJ (Eleven-year-old DJ Johnson conducted the *Children's Classic Hour*, WTRR, Sanford, FL, 1950).

16466 Johnson, Joe. Leader (Coronadians Orchestra, KMOX, St. Louis, MO, 1928).

16467 Johnson, John B. Newscaster (WWNY, Watertown, NY, 1941).

16468 Johnson, John N. Sportscaster (*Sports Parade*, KWRW, Guthrie, OK, 1960).

16469 Johnson, Johnnie. Leader (*Johnnie Johnson Orchestra*, instr. mus. prg., WGY, Schenectady, NY, 1936; WOR, Newark, NJ, 1936; WLW, Cincinnati, OH, 1936–1938).

16470 Johnson, Joyce. COM-HE (WOCB, West Yarmouth, MA, 1951).

16471 Johnson, Justine. COM-HE (WEOA, Evansville, IN, 1954).

16472 Johnson, Katherine. Soprano (KYW, Chicago, IL, 1925).

16473 Johnson, Kimberley. DJ (*Top of the Morning*, WLNA, Peekskill, NY, 1949; *Top of the Morning*, WCSH, Portland, ME, 1952).

16474 Johnson, Lamont. Actor-MC Johnson appeared on *Amanda of Honeymoon Hill, Hilltop House* and *Wendy Warren and the News.*

16475 Johnson, Larry C. Newscaster (WDNC, Durham, NC, 1945).

16476 Johnson, Leland. Pianist Johnson was "a finished pianist and greatly appreciated," said *Variety.* The manager of the retail sales department of the Baldwin Piano Company, Johnson was known as the "talking baritone" (WFAA, Dallas, TX, 1923–1926).

16477 Johnson, Len. DJ (*Music Moods*, WIKB, Iron River, MI, 1949). Sportscaster (*WIKB Sports Mike*, WIKB, 1951).

16478 Johnson, Leonard. Newscaster (KFDA, Amarillo, TX, 1940–1941).

16479 Johnson, Leroy. Basso (KSL, Salt Lake City, UT, 1929).

16480 Johnson, Leroy. DJ, singer and musician (*Sing for Joy*, 180 min., Monday through Friday, WAAA, Winston-Salem, NC, 1950). Johnson sang and played sacred music.

16481 Johnson, Lilas. Pianist (*Lilas Johnson Finale,* instr. mus. prg. that presented a concert of piano music, KGB, San Diego, CA, 1930).

16482 Johnson, Lois. COM-HE (KXRO, Aberdeen, WA, 1949).

16483 Johnson, Loring. Tenor (WJAZ, Chicago, IL, 1924).

16484 Johnson, Lou. DJ (KTOE, Mankato, MN, 1949).

16485 Johnson, Louis John. Baritone (WGBS, New York, NY, 1925).

16486 Johnson, Louise. Soprano (WBAL, Baltimore, MD, 1926).

16487 Johnson, Louise. Astrologist (*Louise Johnson the Astroanalyst*, astrology program, KNX, Los Angeles, CA, 1927–1930).

16488 Johnson, Mahlon B. Newscaster (KFKA, Greely, CO, 1938–1939).

16489 Johnson, Margaret. Pianist (WMT, Cedar Rapids–Waterloo, IA, 1932).

16490 Johnson, Margaret. COM-HE (KCRG, Cedar Rapids, IA, 1955). This may be the same Margaret Johnson (pianist) identified in the previous item.

16491 Johnson, Martin. Newscaster (*Early Bird News*, WFBM, Indianapolis, IN, 1940–1941).

16492 Johnson, Mary. Contralto (WAHG, New York, NY, 1925).

16493 Johnson, Maurice "Boss." Johnson conducted the *R.F.D. Farm Program* (WLS, Chicago, IL, 1928–1929).

16494 Johnson, Merle. Saxophonist-leader of the popular 7-11 orchestra, a NBC house band that derived its name from NBC's New York address, 711 Fifth Avenue (WJZ, New York, NY, 1928–1929). Johnson, billed as "The Wizard of the Saxophone," was also the leader of the Merle Johnson Orchestra featured on the *Two Troupers* program (WJZ, New York, NY, 1929).

16495 Johnson, Min. COM-HE (WMON, Montgomery WV, 1954–1955).

16496 Johnson, Monk. Sportscaster (*Sports on Parade*, KUSD, Vermillion, SD, 1947; *Sports of All Sorts*, KDSJ, Deadwood, SD, 1949).

16497 Johnson, Mott. Announcer (KMMJ, Clay Center, NE, 1928). Sportscaster (KMA, Shenandoah, IA, 1940–1941; KMA, 1946).

16498 Johnson, Mozart. Tenor (KGEF, Los Angeles, CA, 1929).

16499 Johnson, Nora. Musician who played the carillon (CBS, 1937).

16500 Johnson, Owen. COM-HE (KROS, Clinton, IA, 1951).

16501 Johnson, Parks. Announcer and newscaster (*Radio Newsreel*, NBC, 1938). *See* ***Vox Pop***.

16502 Johnson, Patricia "Pat." COM-HE (WAVZ, New Haven, CT, 1949; WHAV, Haverhill, MA, 1954–1957).

16503 Johnson, Paul. When station WLAF (Minneapolis, MN) went on the air Labor Day, 1922, Johnson was its first announcer. After WLAG became WCCO on October 2, 1924, Johnson stayed on as staff announcer, a position he filled until 1928. He later left broadcasting to become a physician.

16504 Johnson, Paul. Sportscaster (WTAG, Worcester, MA, 1948).

16505 Johnson, (Mrs.) Paul. Singer (KFUS, Oakland, CA, 1925).

16506 Johnson, Philip N. Newscaster (WHEB, Portsmouth, NH, 1944).

16507 Johnson, Pop. Leader (*Pop Johnson Orchestra*, instr. mus. prg., WIP, Philadelphia, PA, 1936).

16508 Johnson, Ray. Sportscaster (KGY, Olympia, WA, 1942).

16509 Johnson, Raymond Edward. Busy actor-MC appeared on *Bachelor's Children, Brave Tomorrow, Candid Microphone* (MC), *Cavalcade of America, Cloak and Dagger, Curtain Time, Dimension X, Don Winslow of the Navy* (title role), *Ethel and Albert, Everyman's Theater, Famous Jury Trials, First Nighter, Gangbusters, Girl Alone, Goldbergs, Grand Hotel, Guiding Light, I Love Linda Dale, Joyce Jordan, Girl Interne, Kate Hopkins, Angel of Mercy, Lights Out, Mandrake the Magician* (title role), *Mary Marlin, Mr. District Attorney* (title role), *Myrt and Marge, National Farm and Home Hour, Nick Carter, Master Detective, Of Human Bondage, Philip Morris Playhouse, Quick as a Flash, Roger Kildare, Public Defender* (title role), *Stella Dallas, Telephone Hour, Tennessee Jed, There was a Woman, Today's Children, Treasury Agent* (title role), *Valiant Lady, Welcome Valley, Young Hickory* (title role) and *Your Family and Mine*.

16510 Johnson, Rita. Actress Johnson appeared on the daytime serial programs *John's Other Wife* and *Joyce Jordan, Girl Interne*.

16511 Johnson, Robert "Bob." DJ (*The Alarm Clock Club*, KFOR, Lincoln, NE, 1948; *Musical Clock*, KFOR, 1949; *Music Till Noon*, KFGT, Freemont, NE, 1955).

16512 Johnson, Rollie. Sportscaster (*Sports Through the Keyhole*, WCCO, Minneapolis–St. Paul, MN, 1940–1942; WTCN, Minneapolis–St. Paul, MN, 1944–1946; *Sports Review*, WTCN, 1947; *The World of Sports*, WTCN, 1948–1949).

16513 Johnson, Ron. DJ (*1230 Club*, KALG, Alamorgordo, NM, 1949).

16514 Johnson, Ron. DJ (*Ye Olde Record Shoppe*, WBEX, Chillicothe, OH, 1949).

16515 Johnson, Roosevelt. DJ (*Roosevelt's Record Club*, WERD, Atlanta, GA, 1949–1960).

16516 Johnson, Rosemary. COM-HE (WFAA, Dallas, TX, 1955).

16517 Johnson, Ross. Accordionist (WMCA, New York, NY, 1929).

16518 Johnson, (Dr.) Samuel. News analyst (KMOX, St. Louis, MO, 1945–1947).

16519 Johnson, Stan. Newscaster (KWSC, Pullman, WA, 1945).

16520 Johnson, Stute. Announcer (KMMJ, Clay Center, NE, 1928).

16521 Johnson, Ted. Newscaster (KMMJ, Grand Island, NE, 1939–1940; KFBI, Wichita, KS, 1941–1942, 1944). DJ (*Sleepyhead Ted*, WXYZ, Detroit, MI, 1949; WTAC, Flint, MI, 1954–1955).

16522 Johnson, Tetlow. Sportscaster and sports play-by-play (WCLD, Cleveland, MS, 1952).

16523 Johnson, Thelma. Pianist (KFAE, Pullman, WA, 1925).

16524 Johnson, Therese. Organist (WSYR, Syracuse, NY, 1939).

16525 Johnson, Thomas. Johnson was billed as "California's Golden Voiced Baritone" (KFSG, Los Angeles, CA, 1926).

16526 Johnson, Tiny. DJ (*Afternoon Jamboree*, WLPO, La Salle, IL, 1949). Sportscaster (*Sports Parade*, WLPO, 1951).

16527 Johnson, Toki. COM-HE (WHOD, Homestead, PA, 1954).

16528 Johnson, Travis. DJ (*Blue Dreamer*, WIRK, West Palm Beach, FL, 1949–1955).

16529 Johnson, Verne. DJ (*Hold Everything*, KRSC, Seattle, WA, 1947). DJ (*Mail Call*, KRSC, 1950).

16530 Johnson, Violet. Singer-violinist (KSO, Des Moines, IA, 1929).

16531 Johnson, Virginia. Soprano Johnson appeared on the *Chicago Theater Revue* program (WMAQ, Chicago, IL, 1923).

16532 Johnson, Virginia. Soprano (*Virginia Johnson*, vcl. mus. prg., WOR, Newark, NJ, 1936).

16533 Johnson, Waldine. *Variety* called violinist Waldine Johnson "a pioneer Cincinnati radio artist" (WDAF, Kansas City, MO, 1924; WSAI, Cincinnati, OH, 1925).

16534 Johnson, Walfred (Wilfred). Newscaster (KTKC, Visalia, CA, 1940–1941).

16535 Johnson, Wally. Leader (*Wally Johnson Orchestra*, instr. mus. prg., WLAV, Grand Rapids, MI, 1942).

16536 Johnson, Wally. DJ (*Platter Parade*, KFEQ, St. Joseph, MO, 1949).

16537 Johnson, Walter. Announcer (WTIC, Hartford, CT, 1928).

16538 Johnson, Wayne. Newscaster (WTAM, Cleveland, OH, 1945).

16539 Johnson, Willard. Newscaster (*Religion in the News*, NBC, 1945–1948).

16540 Johnson, (Mrs.) William. Soprano (WBZ, Boston-Springfield, MA, 1925).

16541 Johnson, William M. Announcer (WBES, Tacoma Park, MD, 1927).

16542 (The) Johnson Sisters. Vocal team who also played piano and ukulele (WMAK, Buffalo, NY, 1928).

16543 *(The) Johnson and Johnson Orchestra.* The band that appeared on the weekly music program was actually that of Gene Rodemich (30 min., Weekly, NBC-Blue, 1929).

16544 *(The) Johnson and Johnson Program.* The program presented a series of "musical melodramas" featuring Joyce Meredith (NBC, 1929–1930).

16545 *(The) Johnson Family.* Talented Jimmy Scribner created, wrote and produced all the voices — sometimes as many as 22 — for the characters on the clever show. The good natured comedy show presented the story of an entire African-American community in a small town, presumably located in Virginia. Versatile Scribner even played the banjo and produced any sound effects needed. The entertaining show and the creative Scribner never received the recognition both so richly deserved (15 min., Monday through Friday, 5:15–5:30 P.M. CST, WLW, Cincinnati, OH, 1936 and 15 min., Monday through Friday, 4:15–4:30 P.M., MBS, 1947).

16546 *Johnson's Happy Pals.* CW mus. prg. (WRVA, Richmond, VA, 1939).

16547 Johnston, Alvin. DJ (WOOH, Newman, GA, 1956).

16548 Johnston, Arnold. Leader (Arnold Johnston Orchestra, WOR, Newark, NJ, 1928; CBS, New York, NY, 1929).

16549 Johnston, Arthur. Baritone (WAAM, Newark, NJ, 1925).

16550 Johnston, Coralie. COM-HE (KSYL, Alexandria, LA, 1956).

16551 Johnston, Doc. DJ (*Date with Doc*, WBIR, Knoxville, TN, 1949–1950).

16552 Johnston, Frances. COM-HE (KCLO, Leavenworth, KS, 1951–1954).

16553 Johnston, Gertrude. Pianist (WWNC, Asheville, NC, 1928).

16554 Johnston, Janis. Ukulele soloist and vocalist (WNAD, Norman, OK, 1926).

16555 Johnston, Jimmy. DJ (*Cousin Jim*, WNDB, Daytona Beach, FL, 1948).

16556 Johnston, Johnny. Leader (*Johnny Johnston Orchestra*, instr. mus. prg., NBC, 1939). Baritone (*Johnny Johnston*, vcl. mus. prg., CBS, 1939).

16557 Johnston, Johnny. DJ (*Platter Party*, WGAD, Gadsen, AL, 1947).

16558 Johnston, Ken. DJ (*Sunrise Serenade*, WCED, Dubois, FL, 1950).

16559 Johnston, Margaret. Writer (KVOO, Tulsa, OK, 1942). Johnston was one of several re-write women working in the KVOO News Department.

16560 Johnston, Marguerite. Violinist (KFI, Los Angeles, CA, 1925).

16561 Johnston, Mary. Soprano (WBAA, West Lafayette, IN, 1939).

16562 Johnston, Merle. COM-HE (KAND, Corsicana, TX, 1949).

16563 Johnston, Mescal. COM-HE (KLRA, Little Rock, AR, 1954).

16564 Johnston, Patti. Pianist (KVOO, Tulsa, OK, 1928).

16565 Johnston, Terry. DJ (WFEC, Miami, FL, 1956–1957).

16566 Johnston, Wayne. DJ (KAMQ, Amarillo, TX, 1948; KSET, El Paso, TX, 1949).

16567 Johnston Orchestra. William Stoess conducted the orchestra on *The Gold Dust Twins* program (WLW, Cincinnati, OH, 1927).

16568 Johnstone, Alice Roberta. Violinist (WQJ, Chicago, IL, 1925).

16569 Johnstone, Frank. DJ (*Open House*, KFRC, San Francisco, CA, 1952).

16570 Johnstone, Fred. Newscaster (WSLS, Roanoke, VA, 1941).

16571 Johnstone, James H. Mandolin and tenor banjo soloist (KSD, St. Louis, MO, 1923–1924).

16572 Johnstone, Johnny. "Hot" piano player Johnstone also served as a control engineer and press agent (WEAF, New York, NY, 1925–1926).

16573 Johnstone, William "Bill." Actor Johnstone was in the cast of *Casebook of Gregory Hood, Cavalcade of America, Five Star Jones, The Line Up, Mrs. Wiggs of the Cabbage Patch, Philip Morris Playhouse, Portia Faces Life, The Shadow* (title role), *Story of Bess Johnson, Valiant Lady* and *Wilderness Road.* Newscaster (*One of the Finest*, NBC, 1939).

16574 *Joie Theater Program*. Singers Billy Friech, Hal Burton, Bernie Grossman and Bobbie Jones joined pianists Otis Spencer, Nat Osburn, Leon Flatow and Tom Eliot on this early music program broadcast Saturday evenings at 7:30 P.M. by experimental station 5 ACW (Fort Smith, AR, 1922).

16575 Joiner, Jerry. DJ (*Good Yawnin'* and *Joiner's Corner*, WTOK, Meridan, MS, 1949–1954).

16576 Jolly, Jim. Newscaster (WLBJ, Bowling Green, KY, 1945).

16577 *Jolly Bill and Jane*. Jolly Bill Steinke played the role of Jolly Bill who talked with his little niece, Jane, played by Muriel Harbater. They were joined by various characters such as the Bugle Man and Fritzie the Fiddler on the entertaining children's show (15 min., Monday through Friday, 5:30–5:45 P.M., NBC-Red, 1928–1933). Jolly Bill told Jane the story of how "the little mouse took the great big elephant for a long, long ride in his wheelbarrow." Often he opened the program by saying, "Oooh — just listen to that clatter of hoof beats. It must be those wonderful horses, Harry, Dobbin and Prince, coming to take us for a trip to the jolly land of pixies."

In a later version of the program on their popular San Francisco local show, Steinke was joined by Pat Pritchard, who used a juvenile falsetto voice to imitate that of young Jane (15 min., Monday through Saturday, 5:00–5:15 P.M., KPO, San Francisco, CA, 1947). Jolly Bill was widely known as the "story teller extraordinary to American children." An example of the program's story line in 1933 told how Jolly Bill and Jane traveled to the moon on a fantastic rocket, where they were menaced by the King of the Moon and his army. The Moon King enjoyed using powerful rays to shatter neighboring planets. The King, who resided on the dark side of the moon, next planned to direct his devastating ray on the earth. When Jolly Bill and Jane asked their listeners to send in plans as to how the Moon King could be captured and destroyed, they received more than 2,000 suggestions.

Jolly Bill was the Commander of a club that contained several thousand young members. Each member was given a "gold" scarab that granted them a wish whenever they rubbed it. There is no report of any complaints that Jolly Bill received from unfulfilled young listeners who had rubbed their scarab without results.

16578 *Jolly Bill's Cable Car Capers*. Jolly Bill Steinke and organist Eloise Rowan began the popular children's program in 1947 (15 min., Monday through Friday, KNBC, San Francisco, CA, 1947–1949).

16579 *(The) Jolly Cowboy*. An otherwise unidentified singer was featured on the CW music show (KTHS, Hot Springs National Park, AR, 1936).

16580 Jolly Five Orchestra from Egg Harbor City. Popular local band (WFI, Philadelphia, PA, 1923).

16581 *(The) Jolly German Hour*. Carl Frisher conducted the variety show of music and comedy (WOR, Newark, NJ, 1927).

16582 Jolly Jesters Dance Orchestra. California dance band (KGER, Long Island, CA, 1929).

16583 *Jolly Joe*. Vcl. mus. prg. featuring a tenor not otherwise identified (MBS, 1937).

16584 *Jolly Joe and His Pet Pals*. Joe Kelly, as Jolly Joe, conducted the popular Chicago children's program sponsored by Little Crow Milling Company, makers of Coco-Wheat cereal. After three programs, his young listeners sent in 20,000 jokes as entries for a contest for the best jokes. Louis Davis played piano for the Kelly show (15 min., Monday through Friday, 7:00–7:15 P.M., WLS, Chicago, IL, 1935–1937).

16585 *Jolly Joe's Junior Jamboree*. Joe Kelly hosted the show that featured young amateurs singing, playing instruments and performing imitations, etc. (WLS, Chicago, IL, 1940).

16586 *Jolly Journers*. NBC broadcast the program containing "piano sketches for children" in 1935.

16587 *(The) Jolly Jugglers*. A team of baritone Phil Brae and tenor Billy Scholtz provided comedy and songs on their weekly show (15 min., Wednesday, 5:45–6:00 P.M., CBS, 1930s).

16588 *Jolly Lumberjacks*. CW mus. prg. (KWK, St. Louis, MO, 1936).

16589 *(The) Jolly Wonder Bakers*. Wonder Bread sponsored the weekly music program (NBC-Red, 1926).

16590 Jolson, Al. Jolson, the great entertainer, made his first radio appearance on KYW (Chicago, IL) in 1921. He later appeared on such network shows as The Kraft Music Hall. *See **The Kraft Music Hall** and **Shell Chateau**.*

16591 Jolson, Edith. Singer (WICC, Bridgeport, CT, 1937).

16592 *Jonathan Trimble, Esq*. Donald Crisp originated the title role, later played by Gale Gordon, of a 1905 publisher of a newspaper located in a city of 60,000. Trimble was an old, crotchety conservative, who was opposed to any change in his city. Jean Gillespie, Art Gilmore, Jack Mather, Victor Rodman, Earl Ross, Irene Tedrow and Roderick Thomas were also in the cast. The announcer was Tony LeFranco. Mort Green wrote the short-lived sustaining program (30 min., Saturday, 9:30–10:00 P.M., MBS, 1946).

16593 Jones, Adelaide. Singer (WORD, Batavia, IL, 1925).

16594 Jones, Albert. Newscaster (WABZ, Albemarle, NC, 1947).

16595 Jones, Alice. Singer Jones was a member of the Jones Quartet (WTAM, Cleveland, OH, 1924).

16596 Jones, Allen B. Newscaster (WLPM, Suffolk, VA, 1946).

16597 Jones, Ann. COM-HE (WLAP, Lexington, KY, 1957).

16598 Jones, Archdale. DJ (WBAL, Baltimore, MD, 1949).

16599 Jones, Armand. DJ (*K-Bar Round Up*, KVET, Austin, TX, 1948).

16600 Jones, Art. DJ (*Jones Jamboree*, WKOX, Framingham, MA, 1947; *Commuters' Special*, WBKA, Brockton, MA, 1950).

16601 Jones, Arthur. Announcer-director Jones was the announcer on the *Empire Builders* program sponsored by the Great Northern Railroad (NBC-Blue, 1929). *See **Empire Builders**.*

16602 Jones, Arthur T. Newscaster (WEW, St. Louis, MO, 1938–1939).

16603 Jones, Bess. COM-HE (WJEH, Galliplis, OH, 1955).

16604 Jones, Betty. Singer (*Betty Jones*, vcl. mus. prg., WNBR, Memphis, TN, 1930).

16605 Jones, Bill. CW singer (*The Silver Yodeling Bill Jones*, CW vcl. mus. prg., WWVA, Wheeling, WV, 1942).

16606 Jones, Bill. DJ (KLZ, Denver, CO, 1948–1954).

16607 Jones, Bill. DJ (*Danceland*, WIBG, Philadelphia, PA, 1960).

16608 Jones (Billy) and (Ernie) Hare. The popular singing team began broadcasting as "The Happiness Boys" for Happiness Candy on WEAF (New York, NY) in 1923, but their first radio appearance was on October 18, 1921 on WJZ (New York, NY). When the Happiness Boys first gained their greatest national prominence with their WEAF broadcasts in 1924). Exactly when Jones and Hare decided to be a two-man team is not clear. It is known, however, that Jones and Hare were paid a total of $300 for their half-hour program on WEAF (*Happiness Boys*, 30 min., Friday, 8:30–9:00 P.M., WEAF, New York, NY, 1924–1925). When sponsored by the Happiness Candy Company, Jones and Hare used the song, "That's My Hap-Hap-Happiness" to popularize the candy. Another favorite song they frequently sang was "When Lindy Comes Home to his Mother."

Later the team worked for other sponsors that gave them names such as "The Interwoven [socks] Pair," "The Flit [fly spray] Soldiers," "The Taystee [bread] Loafers" and "The

Best Food [mayonnaise] Boys." In the 1920's their programs were known as *The Happiness Boys*, sponsored by the Happiness Candy Company (WEAF, 1923–1929) and *The Flit Soldiers*, sponsored by Standard Oil of New Jersey (WJZ, New York, NY, 1928). Their later programs also kept them busy (*Jones and Hare*, vcl. mus. prg., WLW, Cincinnati, OH, 1934; WGAR, Cleveland, OH, 1935). *See the* **Happiness Boys**.

16609 Jones, Bob. Announcer (WFAA, Dallas, TX, 1923).

16610 Jones, Bob. DJ (*Groans by Jones*, WBIG, Greensboro, NC, 1947–1950).

16611 Jones, Bob. DJ (WSAL, Annapolis, MD, 1947). Sportscaster (*Sports Review*, WEAM, Arlington, VA, 1949).

16612 Jones, Bob. DJ (*Time for a Song*, KFAB, Omaha, NE, 1948; *Jones Junction*, KFAB, 1949–1952).

16613 Jones, Bobby. DJ (*One Night Stand*, WSGC, Elberton, GA, 1947; *Teentimers' Special*, WWWB, Jasper, AL, 1950).

16614 Jones, Broadway. Leader (Broadway Jones and the Royal Poinciana Orchestra, WHN, New York, NY, 1924).

16615 Jones, C.R. Announcer (WMAC, Cazenovia, NY, 1927).

16616 Jones, (Mrs.) Charles. Pianist (KFAB, Lincoln, NE, 1925).

16617 Jones, Chauncy. DJ (*The Swing Shift*, KWBT, Hutchinson, KS, 1947).

16618 Jones, Clarence. Marimbaphone soloist (WBJ, 1925–1926).

16619 Jones, Cleane. Leader (Cleane Jones' Novelty Dance Orchestra broadcasting from the Orpheum Dance Studio, WHN, New York, NY, 1924).

16620 Jones, Dana. DJ (*Yours for the Asking*, WBEC, Pittsfield, MA, 1947–1949; *Sunny Side of the Street*, WBEC, 1952–1956).

16621 Jones, Daniel Boone. Interstate "old fiddling" champion (WOS, Jefferson City, MO, 1926–1928).

16622 Jones, David Rees. Pianist (WMAC, Cazenovia, NY, 1926).

16623 Jones, Dick. Newscaster (WJOL, Joliet, IL, 1945).

16624 Jones, Dixie Farrior. Singer (*Dixie Farrior Jones*, vcl. mus. prg., KGHI, Little Rock, AR, 1929).

16625 Jones, Don. Newscaster (KGVO, Burlington, NC, 1941, 1945).

16626 Jones, Don. Newscaster (KGY, Olympia, WA, 1951). Jones remained at the station and became program director in 1977.

16627 Jones, E. Robert. Jones directed and hosted an early radio minstrel show (*The Honeyside Minstrels of Riverside,* WGR, Buffalo, NY, 1923).

16628 Jones, E.Z. Newscaster (WBBB, Burlington, NC, 1941, 1945). Sportscaster (WBBB, 1941).

16629 Jones, (Coach) Earl D. Sportscaster (WFTM, Maysville, KY, 1948; *Sports Review*, WFTM, 1949; *Sports Edition,* WFTM, 1951–1953).

16630 Jones, Earlene. COM-HE (KIMO, Independence, MO, 1956).

16631 Jones, Elizabeth Gay. Pianist (WFAA, Dallas, TX, 1924).

16632 Jones, Elliot. Newscaster (WPIC, Sharon, PA, 1940–1941, 1946).

16633 Jones, Ev. Leader (Ev Jones' Merrymakers, WTAM, Cleveland, OH, 1924). The band participated in an unique radio broadcast in 1924. Listeners danced in the open air under the WTAM antenna and listened with crystal receivers mounted on their heads as the Ev Jones Orchestra played. The band broadcast frequently on WTAM through the late 1920s.

16634 Jones, (Mrs.) Eva Thompson. Contralto (WSM, Nashville, TN, 1928).

16635 Jones, Forrest. Announcer who proclaimed his station's slogan, "The World Redeemed by Christ" (WRBC, Valparaiso, IN, 1925–1926). WRBC was operated by the Immanuel Lutheran Church.

16636 Jones, Ginger. Busy actress Jones appeared on the *Joyce Jordan*, *Girl Interne*, *Bachelor's Children*, *Kitty Keene* aka *Kitty Keene, Incorporated*, *Backstage Wife* aka *Mary Noble, Backstage Wife*; *Portia Faces Life*, *Carters of Elm Street* and *The Romance of Helen Trent* daytime serials programs.

16637 Jones, Ginny. DJ (*Just for You*, KTBS, Shreveport, LA, 1954).

16638 Jones, Glad Hall. COM-HE (KRRD, Los Angeles, CA, 1949).

16639 Jones, Glenn. Newscaster (KWSC, Pullman, WA, 1939).

16640 Jones, Gwen. Managerial staff (CBS, 1939). Jones was a network production assistant who helped develop new ideas for programs.

16641 Jones, Gwynfi. Tenor (KPO, San Francisco, CA, 1924; KGO, Oakland, CA, 1925; KTAB, Oakland, CA, 1926). Jones also appeared on the *Spotlight Hour* (NBC-Pacific Coast Network, 1928).

16642 Jones, H. Conger. News analyst (*Over the Coffee Cups*, KDLK, Del Rio, TX, 1948).

16643 Jones, Harold. Poetry readings and recitations (WCOU, Lewiston, ME, 1942).

16644 Jones, Haskell. DJ (*Request Club*, KWTX, Waco, TX, 1952).

16645 Jones, Helen. Singer Jones sang on *The Hoot Owls* late night program (KGW, Portland, OR, 1925).

16646 Jones, Helen. COM-HE (WEDC, Chicago, IL, 1957).

16647 Jones, Helen Louise. Contralto (*Helen Louise Jones*, vcl. mus. prg., WPG, Atlantic City, NJ, 1936).

16648 Jones, Howard. Newscaster (WIP, Philadelphia, PA, 1937). DJ (*Here's Howard*, WFIL, Philadelphia, PA, 1950).

16649 Jones, Imogene. Pianist (WCOA, Pensacola, FL, 1926).

16650 Jones, Irene. Pianist (WEAF, New York, NY, 1925).

16651 Jones, Isham. Leader of the popular jazz band known as the Isham Jones Orchestra (KYW, Chicago, IL, 1923). The following year the band performed on the evening entertainment programs broadcast daily by WLS (Chicago, IL, 1924). Later, the band broadcast on various stations live and by transcription (WDAE, Tampa, FL, 1926; *Isham Jones Orchestra*, CBS, 1933–1935; WIP, Philadelphia, PA, 1936). In late 1936, the remnants of this band became the Woody Herman Orchestra, often called "The Band that Plays the Blues."

16652 Jones, Ivan. Announcer-bass (KOMO, Seattle, WA, 1927 and KYW, Chicago, IL, 1928).

16653 Jones, J. Announcer (WQAQ, Scranton, PA, 1925).

16654 Jones, Janet. Singer (WMEX, Boston, MA, 1938).

16655 Jones, J.D. DJ (*1340 Club*, KJAM, Vernal, UT, 1947; *Ranch Boys*, KJAM, 1950; *Alarm Clock Club*, WMLS, Sylacauga, AL, 1952). Sportscaster (KJAM, 1948).

16656 Jones, Jenny. WMON (Montgomery, WV, 1949).

16657 Jones, James D. "Jimmy." Sportscaster (KSAM, Huntsville, TX, 1940; KAND, Corsicana, TX, 1941). DJ (*Music and Madness*, KGVL, Greenville, TX, 1947–1950; *Dr. Pepper Time*, KGVL, 1952).

16658 Jones. Josephine Wilslon. Soprano (KTAB, Oakland, CA, 1925).

16659 Jones, Kathryn. COM-HE (WJET, Erie, PA, 1957).

16660 Jones, Lee. COM-HE (KIRX, Kirksville, MO, 1951).

16661 Jones, Llewellyn. Reviewer of the latest books (KYW, Chicago, IL, 1924; WEBH, Chicago, IL, 1923–1925). Jones was the Literary Editor of the Chicago *Evening Post.*

16662 Jones, L.W. Announcer (WGBA, Baltimore, MD, 1925).

16663 Jones, L.W. Announcer (KFEC, Portland, OR, 1927).

16664 Jones, Lois. News commentator (*Morning Column*, WPAR, Parkersburg, WV, 1948–1949). COM-HE (WPAR, 1956).

16665 Jones, Lora. COM-HE (KBBB, Borger, TX, 1960).

16666 Jones, Louis Marshall "Grandpa." CW music performer Grandpa Jones began his radio career with an early morning show on WJW (Akron, OH, 1930). He was billed on that station as "The Young Singer of Old Songs." Later, when working on a Bradley Kincaid program, he was presented with a pair of old boots, a fake moustache, grease paint, had aging lines painted on his face and given the name "Grandpa Jones." From that time on, he made himself up to appear "old." After working at WWVA (Wheeling, WV), WCHS (Fairmont, WV) and WMNN (Fairmont, WV), he moved to WLS (Cincinnati, OH) to appear on their *Boone County Jamboree* in 1942. When he left the service at the end of World War II, he joined the *Grand Ole Opry.*

16667 Jones, Lucy Lee. COM-HE (WEDO, McKeesport, PA, 1951).

16668 Jones, Martha. Pianist (KFI, Los Angeles, CA, 1925).

16669 Jones, Mary. COM-HE (WFIL, Philadelphia, PA, 1949–1956).

16670 Jones, Mary May. Violinist (WLW, Cincinnati, OH, 1924).

16671 Jones, Maurice. Leader (Maurice Jones' Dance Orchestra, WHAH, 1923–1924).

16672 Jones, Mendel. Newscaster (WCKY, Cincinnati, OH, 1938).

16673 Jones, Meredith. COM-HE (WCOU, Lewiston, ME, 1955).

16674 Jones, Merwin. Newscaster (KOOS, Marshfield, OR, 1937).

16675 Jones, Mimi. COM-HE (WHOS, Decatur, AL, 1956).

16676 Jones, Paul M. Newscaster (WFLA, Tampa, FL, 1945–1947).

16677 Jones, Pearl. Singer Jones was a member of the Jones Quartet (WTAM, Cleveland, OH, 1924).

16678 Jones, Pearl Benedict. Contralto (WJZ, New York, NY, 1927).

16679 Jones, (Mrs.) Rae Lee. Soprano (KOA, Denver, CO, 1926).

16680 Jones, Ray. Tenor (*Ray Jones*, vcl. mus. prg., WBZ, Boston-Springfield, MA, 1935).

16681 Jones, Ray. Actor Jones was in the cast of *Molly of the Movies*.

16682 Jones, Richard. Pianist (WJAZ, Chicago, IL, 1923).

16683 Jones, Robert. Organist (WJAX, Cleveland, OH, 1924).

16684 Jones, Rod. DJ (*1240 Club*, WJNC, Jacksonville, NC, 1948–1950).

16685 Jones, Roy. DJ (*Request Granted*, WMOC, Covington, GA, 1948; *Walton Special*, WMOC, 1950). Sportscaster (*Sports Round-Up*, WMOC, 1948–1949).

16686 Jones, Ruth. COM-HE (WDAD, Indiana, PA, 1957).

16687 Jones, Sam. "Mouth organ" soloist (WKRC, Cincinnati, OH, 1926).

16688 Jones, Sid and Harriet Ferch. Piano team (KOL, Seattle, WA, 1929).

16689 Jones, Silver Yodelin.' CW singer (WWVA, Wheeling, WV, 1942).

16690 Jones, Slew. Sportscaster (WAPF, McComb, MS, 1950–1951).

16691 Jones, Sue. COM-HE (WCOS, Columbia, SC, 1957).

16692 Jones, Tad. DJ (*Alarm Clock Club*, KAVR, Havre, MT, 1948).

16693 Jones, Tom. Newscaster (KYA, San Francisco, CA, 1938).

16694 Jones, Tom. DJ (*Spotlight*, WRFS, Alexander City, AL, 1947; *Dizzy Fingers*, WRFS, 1948; *Music Makers*, WFRS, 1950). Newscaster (WRFS, 1948). Sportscaster (*Tom Jones Predicts*, WFRS, 1947; *The World in Sports*, WFRS, 1948; *Final Sports*, WRFS, 1949).

16695 Jones, (Miss) V.A.L. Announcer and program director (KSD, St. Louis, MO, 1924).

16696 Jones, Venezuela. Actress Jones appeared on the *Our Gal Sunday* daytime serial program.

16697 Jones, Venida. Organist (*Venida Jones*, instr. mus. prg., CBS, 1936).

16698 Jones, Verlaine. COM-HE (KXAR, Agre, AR, 1960).

16699 Jones, Virginia. Actress Jones was in the cast of the *Jenny Peabody* daytime serial program.

16700 Jones, Wes. Sportscaster (KTBS, Shreveport, LA, 1944–1945). Newscaster (KTBS, 1945).

16701 Jontry, Spec. Sportscaster (*Football Scoreboard*, WJBC, Bloomington, IN, 1947).

16702 Joos, Steve. DJ (*Club Savoy*, WHOK, Lancaster, OH, 1954–1955).

16703 Jordan, Al. DJ (*Sunshine Hour*, WCKB, Dunn, NC, 1947).

16704 Jordan, Barbara. COM-HE (WSYR, Syracuse, NY, 1957).

16705 Jordan, Bill. DJ (*Polka Time*, WDAD, Indiana, PA, 1949).

16706 Jordan, Bruce. Newscaster (KFWB, Los Angeles, CA, 1940).

16707 Jordan, Charles. Singer (WFBH, New York, NY, 1925).

16708 Jordan, Charles R. DJ (Sportscaster, WRR, Dallas, TX, 1937–1942).

16709 Jordan, Corrine. Pianist and contralto (WBBM, Chicago, IL, 1926; WCCO, Minneapolis–St. Paul, MN, 1928).

16710 Jordan, David. Actor Jordan was in the cast of *John's Other Wife* daytime serial program.

16711 Jordan, Ed. DJ (*World of Modern Sound*, ABC, 1960).

16712 Jordan, Elaine. Blues singer (*Elaine Jordan*, vcl. mus. prg., WOR, Newark, NJ, 1934).

16713 Jordan, Frank. DJ (*680 Club*, WRNY, Rochester, NY, 1947).

16714 Jordan, Gene. Announcer (KFVE, St. Louis, MO, 1925–1927).

16715 Jordan, Gene. Tenor (*Gene Jordan — the Southland Tenor*, vcl. mus. prg., WJR, Detroit, MI, 1933).

16716 Jordan, Harry. Newscaster (KMO, Tacoma, WA, 1938; KEVR, Seattle, WA, 1945–1946). Sportscaster (KEVR, 1946).

16717 Jordan, Homer. Leader (Homer Jordan and the Southern Melody Chasers, WRR, Detroit, MI, 1926).

16718 Jordon, J.E. Baritone (KPO, San Francisco, CA, 1923).

16719 Jordan, Jack "Jackie." Actor Jordan appeared on *County Seat, Ellen Randolph* and *Let's Pretend*.

16720 Jordan, Jim and Marian Jordan. Jim Jordan was born November 16, 1896 and Marian in April, 1898. After their marriage, they became a singing team with Marian playing the piano and began working the vaudeville circuits. Eventually they managed to get work on WIBO (Chicago, IL) in 1924 at a salary of ten dollars per week. They worked on *The Smith Family* program on Chicago radio for many years and *The Smackouts* and *Kaltenmeyer's Kindergarten* before becoming famous as *Fibber McGee and Molly* in the 1930s. After their first programs on WIBO, they moved to WENR (Chicago, IL, 1929). *See* ***Fibber McGee and Molly*** *and* **Comediennes**.

16721 Jordan, Joan. Singer (WCFL, Chicago, IL, 1939).

16722 Jordan, Kathryn. Singer (WCAU, Philadelphia, PA, 1926).

16723 Jordan, Maitland. Newscaster (KJR, Seattle, WA, 1938).

16724 Jordan, Mark. DJ (*Requestfully Yours*, KGO, San Francisco, CA, 1947).

16725 Jordan, (Dr.) Max. News analyst (NBC, 1936 and 1946).

16726 Jordan, Murray. Sportscaster (WLIB, New York, NY, 1946; *Candlelight and Silver* and *This is Romance*, WLIB, 1950–1954).

16727 Jordan, Pat. DJ (MBS, 1957).

16728 Jordan, Peggy. Singer (WRFL, New York, NY, 1927).

16729 Jordan, Ross. Baritone (*Ross Jordan*, vcl. mus. prg., CBS, 1939). Leader (*Ross Jordan Orchestra*, instr. mus. prg., CBS, 1942).

16730 Jordan, Sarah (Vella Reeves). COM-HE (WBZ, Boston, MA, 1930–1931).

16731 Jordan, "Tiny" Joe. Sportscaster (WKMO, Kokomo, IN, 1947; *Sports Edition*, WSAL, Loganport, IN, 1951).

16732 Jordan, Tony. DJ (*Tony Jordan Show*, KELK, Elko, NV, 1949).

16733 Jordan, Vernon. Organist (*Vernon Jordan*, instr. mus. prg., WBIG, Greensboro, NC, 1936).

16734 Jordan-Lewis Dance Orchestra. Popular local band (WIP, Philadelphia, PA, 1923).

16735 Jorgennsen, Fred. Newscaster (KLS, Oakland, CA, 1945).

16736 Jorgensen, Ed. Newscaster (KFI, Los Angeles, CA, 1945).

16737 Jorgensen, Fred. DJ (KGO, San Francisco, CA, 1955).

16738 Jorgenson, Phil. Pianist (KFAB, Lincoln, NE, 1928).

16739 *Jose Ferrer Presents Shakespeare*. Distinguished actor Ferrer discussed various Shakespearean plays and broadcast the Bard's work as recorded by John Barrymore, Maurice Evans and John Gielgud on the sustaining program (30 min., Sunday, 10:00–10:30 P.M. WNEW, New York, NY, 1951).

16740 Joseph, Al. DJ (*Blues, Bop and Boogie*, WCBT, Roanoke Rapids, NC, 1952) Sportscaster (*Sports Roundup*, WCBT, 1952; WAIM, Anderson, SC, 1956).

16741 Joseph, Bertha. COM-HE (WOOK, Silver Spring, MD, 1949).

16742 Joseph, Eddy. DJ (*The Eddy Joseph Show*, WHLD, Niagara Falls, NY, 1948–1952).

16743 *Josephine Gibson*. Miss Gibson conducted a program about food and its preparation twice weekly (15 min., Twice Weekly, NBC-Blue, 1929–1931).

16744 Josephy, Alvin M. News analyst (*The Hines Trial*, MBS, 1938).

16745 Josh and Si. Josh (Ed Dunham) and Si (Bennett Kilpack) were a popular comedy team (WTIC, Hartford, CT, 1929).

16746 *Josh Higgins of Finchville*. Joe Dumond originated, wrote and played the role of Josh Higgins on the show. Finchville was a fictional counterpart of Finchville, Iowa, Dumond's birthplace. Josh dispensed homey philosophy and sang with a sturdy baritone. Larry Larsen played the organ. The show came to

NBC in 1936 and by 1938 had become a national favorite (15 min., Thursday, 9:30–10:00 P.M., NBC, 1936–1938). The show first appeared on a Waterloo, Iowa, station before coming to Chicago's WLS.

16747 **Joskowitz [Jaskowitz] Rudolph.** Violinist (WGBS, New York, NY, 1925–1926).

16748 **Joslyn, Allyn.** Actor Joslyn appeared on *Court of Human Relations, Dot and Will, Marie the Little French Princess, Pages of Romance, Showboat* and *Time Flies.*

16749 **Joslyn, Charlie.** Leader (Charlie Joslyn Orchestra, KFOX, Long Beach, CA, 1929).

16750 **Joslyn, Henry.** Newscaster (KVOR, Colorado Springs, CO, 1940). Sportscaster (KVOR, 1940).

16751 **Jospe Woodwind Ensemble.** Excellent instrumental group directed by Samuel Jospe (Weekly, Sunday, NBC, 1928).

16752 **Jostyn, Jay.** Actor-narrator Jostyn was in the cast of *Foreign Assignment, Hilltop House, Life of Mary Southern, Moon River* (narrator), *Mr. District Attorney* (title role), *Our Gal Sunday, Second Husband* and *This Day is Ours.*

16753 **Josue, Margaret.** Soprano-pianist (KPO, San Francisco, CA, 1925).

16754 **Joung, Jessie.** Conducted the *KMA Sewing Circle* program (KMA, Shenandoah, IA, 1928).

16755 ***(The) Journal Ranch.*** The unusual musical program had a western setting. The sponsor was the Milwaukee *Journal.* William H. Coffin, the Circulation Manager of the paper, conducted the program and played the role of the ranch boss. Fifteen *Journal* newsboys appeared as junior cowhands. Each week the program contained a story told by Coffin and some pleasant CW music (Sunday afternoon, WTMC, Milwaukee, WI, 1930's).

16756 **Journay, Warren.** Newscaster (WFEA, Manchester, NH, 1946).

16757 ***Journeys in Music Land.*** Professor E.B. Gordon of the University of Wisconsin, known to friends as "Pop" Gordon, began experimenting with music appreciation radio programs in the winter of 1921–1922 on the university's experimental station, 9XM. When *Journeys in Music Land* began, the announcer said: "The Wisconsin School of the Air presents *Journeys in Music Land.*" After this initial announcement, Professor Gordon said: "Good afternoon, boys and girls. Here we are on a bright and sunny afternoon. Let's start out today by singing." Music would then begin and Gordon would continue: "Here's that starting tone. Everyone sit up straight." As a studio vocal group began singing, the school children in the studio would join them by singing loudly. This was an excellent music appreciation program conducted with enthusiasm (WHA, Madison, WI, 1930s and 1940s).

16758 **Jovial Jasper.** A comedian-singer, not otherwise identified, appeared on the *Crosley Variety Hour* program (WLW, Cincinnati, OH, 1928–1929).

16759 **Joy, Alice.** Contralto (*Alice Joy*, vcl. mus. prg., NBC, 1931–1936; *Prince Albert Hour*, NBC, 1930–1931). Ms. Joy, billed as "The Dream Girl," was born Frances Holcombe in Streator, Illinois. She started her singing in vaudeville, but soon came to radio where she enjoyed a successful career.

16760 **Joy, Art.** DJ (*Doug Pitch*, KIEM, Eureka, CA, 1949).

16761 **Joy, Dick.** Announcer Joy announced *The Danny Kaye Show, Forever Ernest, The Saint, Sam Spade, Silver Theater, The Telephone Hour, Those We Love* and *Vox Pop.*

16762 **Joy, Jack.** Leader (*Jack Joy Orchestra*, instr. mus. prg., WXYZ, Detroit, MI, 1935).

16763 **Joy, Jimmy.** Leader (Jimmy Joy's Orchestra and Jimmy Joy's St. Anthony Orchestra, WOAI, San Antonio, TX, 1925). The band included: Joy, ldr.-clr.; Rex Preis, c.; Jack Brown, tb.; Gilbert O'Shaughnessy and Collis Bradt, as. and ts.; Lynn Harrell, p.; Clyde Austin, bj.; Dick Hammell, d.; and Johnny Cole, tba. The band continued to broadcast in the 1930s (*Jimmy Joy Orchestra*, instr. mus. prg., MBS, 1935; WCAE, Pittsburgh, PA, 1936).

16764 **Joy, Lavelle.** COM-HE (KMOR, Oroville, CA, 1954).

16765 **Joy, Leslie.** Bass-baritone (WEAF, New York, NY, 1923).

16766 **Joy, Richard "Dick."** News analyst (*Newspaper of the Air* and *Goodyear Sun-Up News*, CBS and KNX, Los Angeles, CA, 1937; KNX, 1938–1942; CBS, 1942).

16767 **Joy, Terry.** Actress Joy appeared on the *Your Family and Mine* daytime serial program.

16768 ***(The) Joy Boys.*** Willard Scott teamed with blind DJ Ed Walker on WRC (Washington, DC) on this hilarious program of records, chatter and funny bits. Some of the pair's best creations were the Arthur Codfish Program, a biting satire on the Godfrey phenomenon and that of a drummer, whose solo rendition of "The Waltz You Saved For Me," lacked the important element of a melody. The show originated in Washington, DC and remained a great favorite there for more than 16 years. It also gained popularity on the NBC network and the Armed Forces Radio Service (AFRS).

The *Joy Boys'* familiar theme began with the words, "We are the Joy Boys of Radio. We chase electrons to and fro." Eddy Walker explains they got their theme from some of their studio engineers who had graduated from the Capitol Radio Institute and sang it to the tune of *The Billboard March.* Walker and Scott began some of the routines that eventually were expanded on the *Joy Boys* show, when they worked together on the *Two at One* show on WRC broadcast 1954–1956. *Two at One* went off the air in 1956 when Scott went into the Navy. After Scott returned from service in 1958, he and Walker began the *Joy Boys* show on WRC. Beginning as an afternoon show, it eventually became a three-hour evening show from 1963–1971. It became a drive time show in 1971–1972. When WRC changed its format, the *Joy Boys* moved to WWDC (Washington, DC) where the show ran from 1972 to 1974. *See* **Scott, Willard** *and* **Walker, Ed.**

16769 ***(The) Joy Digger Club.*** The early children's program had as its motto, "Dig a little joy out of everything every day. It's there if you dig deep enough." The program was conducted by Nate Cardwell, who used a "whispering singing style" to perform his zany songs (WBBM, Chicago, IL, 1925), Schaden (1988, p. 12) says the program "consisted of songs, stories and instrumental numbers, some of which were performed by children who were members of the Club. Boy Scouts took over the program once a week and from time to time, prominent people gave short talks of interest to youngsters." Membership cards were sent out to the young listeners who "paid" their club dues by writing a letter a month.

16769a **Joy, Jack.** Pianist Joy broadcast pianologues (KTAB, Oakland, CA, 1928).

16770 **Joyce, Bill.** Newscaster (WJTN, Jamestown, NY, 1948).

16771 **Joyce, Howard.** DJ (*Melody Merchant*, WLAV, Grand Rapids, MI, 1947).

16772 **Joyce, Johnny.** Leader (*Johnny Joyce Orchestra*, instr. mus. prg., WGAR, Cleveland, OH, 1937).

16773 **Joyce, Johnny.** Sportscaster (WPAQ, Mt. Airy, NC, 1949–1951). DJ (WPAQ, 1949; *740 Club*, WPAQ, 1950).

16774 **Joyce, Riza.** Actress Joyce was a cast member of the *Young Widder Brown* daytime serial program.

16775 ***Joyce Jordan, Girl Interne.*** After Jordan completed her medical education, the program became *Joyce Jordan, M.D.* Beginning as a general practitioner in the small town of Preston, the program's plot eventually transformed her into a brilliant surgeon. The long-running daytime serial (1937–1955) was broadcast on all the major networks at one time or another. It was first broadcast from 1937 to 1948. A later version resumed broadcasting Monday 10, 1951, starring Fran Carlon and Ethel Owen. The writer was David Driscoll. Himan Brown was the show's producer-director (15 min., Monday through Friday, CBS, 1951). Over the years, the show's cast included: Vera Allen, Ed Begley, Frank Behrens, Ethel Blume, Horace Braham, Carlton Brickert, Kay Brinker, Edwin Bruce, Fran Carlon, Boyd Crawford, Alan Devitt, Virginia Dwyer, Elspeth Eric, Louise Fitch, Michael Fitzmaurice, Jack Grimes, Larry Haines, Eda Heinemann, Mary Jane Higby, Charlotte Holland, Irene Hubbard, Rita Johnson, Raymond Edward Johnson, Ginger Jones, Joe Julian, Virginia Kay, Ed Latimer, Frank Lovejoy, Myron McCormick, Ruth McDevitt, James Monks, Santos Ortega, Ethel Waite Owen, Aileen Pringle, John Raby, Amanda Randolph, Larry Robinson, Erik Rolf, Pat Ryan, Stefan Schnabel, Ann Shepherd (Scheindel Kalish), Les Tremayne, Gertrude Warner, Elizabeth Watts, Charles Webster, Richard Widmark, Betty Winkler, Lesley Woods, Herbert Yost and Bill Zuckert. Ken Roberts was the announcer and Mende Brown, Ted Corday and Arthur Hanna the directors. The writers were Ralph Berkey, David Driscoll, Julian Funt and Henry Selinger.

16776 **Joye, Betty Jean.** COM-HE (WPRY, Perry, FL, 1957).

16777 Juanita and Hillbilly George. CW comedy singing team (YN, 1936).

16778 Jubilante Singers. Vocal group directed by Mme. Beatrice Ferris-Hinz (KFWM, Oakland, CA, 1929).

16779 *Jubilee.* *See* **Radio in Wartime.**

16780 Jubilee Singers (Texas College, Tyler, Texas). Collegiate singing group (WFAA, Dallas, TX, 1926).

16781 Judas, Bernice. Executive (WNEW and WINS,, New York, NY, 1939). Judas began her broadcasting career at station WNEW. Reputedly, she knew more about New York radio than any other station manger in the city.

16782 *(The) Judge.* The sustaining mystery program, written by Henry Lee and Richard Pedicini, was produced and directed by Norman Macdonnell. The story was based on the concept of a retired judge who solved crimes. John Dehner played the title role. Larry Dobkin, Georgia Ellis, Vivi Janiss, Byron Kane, Sarah Selby and June Whittley were also in the cast. The announcer was Dan Cubberly (30 min., Thursday, 9:30–10:00 P.M., CBS, 1952).

16783 *Judge Rutherford—Jehovah's Witnesses.* The transcribed religious program appeared on many stations at various times (15 min., Sunday, 10:00–10:15 A.M., WWVA, Richmond, VA, 1935).

16783a Judges, Fred. Radio spokesman for the Automobile Club of Washington (KFOA, Seattle, WA, 1928).

16784 *Judith Allen.* Ms. Allen broadcast stage and screen news and gossip (15 min., Weekly, WPAT, Paterson, NJ, 1942).

16785 *(The) Judson Radio Corporation Program.* The Judson Radio Manufacturing Company sponsored the music program that presented, among others, mandolin virtuoso Sam Siegel and the Edison Recording Orchestra directed by Herman Newell (CBS, 1928).

16786 *(The) Judy Canova Show.* Comedienne-singer Canova came out of the *Ziegfeld Follies* to begin her radio career on Paul Whiteman's *Musical Variety* program, where she was a great listener favorite. *Variety* called her a female Bob Burns, a genuine compliment that stressed the unsophisticated "hillbilly" role she assumed. Actually, she had been in grand opera. She was joined on the show by her sister, Anne, and brother, Zeke. Music was provided by Paul Whiteman's orchestra (45 min., Sunday, 9:45–10:30 P.M., NBC-Blue, 1936). A later program showed Canova in better form. In the later version, Miss Canova was surrounded with a superior cast on a half-hour comedy show. Written by Fred Fox and Henry Hoople, her cast included Mel Blanc, Verna Felton, Ruby Dandridge, Joe Kearns, Hans Conried, Sheldon Leonard, Ruth Perrot, Gale Gordon, the Sportsmen Quartet and the Charles "Bud" Dant Orchestra. One of Mel Blanc's comedy lines in his character as Pedro that endured was, "Pardon me for talking in your face, senorita." Howard Petrie was the program's announcer (*The Judy Canova Show*, 30 min., Weekly, CBS, NBC, 1943–1953).

16787 *Judy 'n' Jill 'n' Johnny.* Singers Johnny Desmond, Susan Douglas and Susan Thorne were featured in the title roles accompanied by the Casa Loma Orchestra. Bert Parks was the announcer (30 min., Saturday, 12:00–12:30 P.M., MBS, 1946) A later version the following year presented the three singers with Tex Beneke and the Glen Miller Band.

16788 Juele, Frank. Leader (*Frank Juele Orchestra*, instr. mus. prg., WIP, Philadelphia, PA, 1935–1937).

16789 *Juke Box Jury.* Originally a television program, *Juke Box Jury* came to CBS radio in 1954. Each week a different panel of guests passed judgments on various recordings. The show was hosted by Peter Potter. His first guest panel included Robert Wagner, Ann Sheridan, Mitzi Gaynor and Art Linkletter. The announcer was John Jacobs (30 min., Sunday, 7:00–7:30 P.M., CBS, 1954).

16790 Jukes, Mary Lou. COM-HE (KCKT, Great Bend, KS, 1956).

16791 *Jules Allen the Singing Cowboy.* Allen, a genuine cowboy, was sponsored by the Griffin Grocery Company on his popular CW music show (KTUL, OK, 1935). *See* **Allen, Jules.**

16792 Jules Klein's Symphonic Ensemble. Classical music group (WWJ, Detroit, MI, 1928).

16793 Julian, Joseph "Joe." Actor Julian was in the cast of *Big Sister, Bright Horizon, Columbia Presents Corwin, Joyce Jordan, Girl Interne, Life Can Be Beautiful, Life of Mary Southern, The O'Neills, Orphans of Divorce* and *The Sparrow and the Hawk.* DJ (*Moonlight Serenade*, WKOP, Binghampton, NY, 1954; WINR, Binghampton, NY, 1955; WKOP, 1956–1957).

16794 *Julie and Red.* Julie Conway and Red Benson broadcast songs and lively chatter on their sustaining local program (25 min., Saturday, WOR, New York, NY, 1949).

16795 *Jumbo.* Texas Company, makers of Texaco Fire Chief Gasoline, sponsored the replacement for Ed Wynn's *Fire Chief* program. The basic concept came from Billy Rose's successful Broadway production, *Jumbo.* Rose transferred the property into a spectacular radio program starring comic Jimmy Durante. Rose's eye for the colossal and the special was clearly visible, for the program was broadcast before a live radio audience of 4,500. The dramatic sketch with musical episodes was written by Ben Hecht and Charles MacArthur with music by Lorenz Hart and lyrics by Richard Rodgers. Adolph Deutsch led a 32-piece orchestra and Charles Henderson a choir of 30 males called the Razorbacks. Durante played the role of Claudius B. "Brainy" Bowers, a press agent for a small circus who meant well, but always seemed to cause trouble for his boss, John L. Considine, played by Arthur Sinclair, who owned Considine's Wonder Show Circus. Donald Novis played the role of Matt Mulligan, the son of a rival circus owner, who was in love with Considine's daughter, Mickey, played by Gloria Grafton. Additional comedy was added by Considine's cockney secretary, Mae, played by A.P. Kaye. Louis Witten was the program's announcer (30 min., Tuesday, 9:30–10:00 P.M., NBC-Red, 1935).

16796 Jump, Mary Elizabeth. Violinist (KTAB, Oakland, CA, 1926).

16797 Jung, Dorothy A. Soprano (WEAF, New York, NY, 1924).

16798 Junger Maunerchor of Philadelphia. Vocal group conducted by Charles H. Martin, featuring tenor William Ringele, bass Adolph Murta and other soloists (WIP, Philadelphia, PA, 1925).

16799 *Jungle Jim.* Based on Alex Raymond's comic strip, *Jungle Jim* was broadcast by transcription. It was immediately followed by *Flash Gordon*, another Hearst Syndicate comic strip drawn by Alex Raymond. The adventure series told the story of Jungle Jim Bradley, an adventurer who was accompanied by Kolu, his "native" friend. Matt Crowley played the title role for almost the entire run of the program, and Juano Hernandez played Kolu. The program's cast included: Matt Crowley, Kenny Delmar, Franc Hale, Juano Hernandez, Arthur Hughes, Owen Jordan, Jack Lloyd, Vicki Vola and Irene Winston. Jay Clark was the program's writer and producer. The directors were Stuart Buchannan and Irene Fenton. Gene Stafford also wrote some of the episodes. The announcers were Roger Krupp and Glenn Riggs.

16800 *Junior G-Men.* The children's adventure series was sponsored by Fischer Baking Company. Mysterious events occurred to the kids featured on the show. For example, they found a man who mysteriously has been knocked unconscious. Clasped in his hands was a piece of cloth and they soon noticed a man with his clothing ripped. Many other mysterious characters appeared and other strange events took place to make the situation even more baffling (15 min., Wednesday, 6:30–6:45 P.M., MBS, 1936).

16801 *Junior Junction.* The show was for teenagers who discussed their problems and gave possible solutions. Written by Dick York and Larry Gilmore and produced by Phil Patton, the show was hosted by 18-year-old Elizabeth Woodward, who answered questions written in by young girls. The orchestra was led by eighteen-year-old Mary Hartline. Songs were by seventeen-year-olds Tony Trankina and Lola Ameche. Jackie Dvorak, who was also under 20, talked about fashions, manners and lonely heart matters.

16802 *Junior Miss.* The situation comedy dealt with the many problems faced by an adolescent girl. It was based on the short story written by Sally Benson. After first broadcasting with Shirley Temple in the starring role as Judy Graves, the program went off the air. In 1948, it reappeared on CBS in 1948 to begin a successful six year run with Barbara Whiting playing Judy Graves. Over the years the cast included: Barbara Eiler, Gale Gordon, Peggy Knudsen, Margaret Lansing, Elliott Lewis, Priscilla Lyon, Myra Marsh, Sarah Selby, K.T. Stevens, Shirley Temple, Barabara Whiting and Beverly Wills. The producer was Fran Van Hartesfeldt and the director, William Royal. Herbert Little, Jr., Jack Rubin, David Victor and Charlie Sinclair were the writers.

16803 *Junior Nurse Corps.* Angelo Patri, an authority on child rearing, authenticated each program's script before it was broadcast.

The first chapters of the inspirational children's dramatic serial dramatized the life of Florence Nightingale. Sunda Love played the leading role, assisted by Ray Appleby, John Daly, Lucy Gilman, Helena Ray and Donald Weeks. Swift & Company Meat Products sponsored the show (15 min., Monday, 8:15–8:30 P.M., CBS, 1936).

16804 Junkin, George. Announcer-director (KMOX, St. Louis, MO, 1927–1928).

16805 Junkin, Joy Ann. COM-HE (WDSK, Cleveland, OH, 1960).

16806 Junod, Connie. COM-HE (KWBW, Hutchison, KS, 1955).

16807 Juray, Jack. Newscaster (WKBN, Youngstown, OH, 1942, 1948).

16808 Jurgens, Dick. Leader (*Dick Jurgens Orchestra*, instr. mus. prg., WGN, Chicago, IL, 1934; 1937; MBS, 1939; WGN, 1940–1942).

16809 Just, Amanda. Pianist (KWSC, Pullman, WA, 1926).

16810 *Just Entertainment*. When his doctor ordered Gene Autry to rest, the *Just Entertainment* program replaced his *Melody Ranch* program. Wrigley's Double Mint Chewing Gum also sponsored the variety show hosted by Burgess Meredith. He was joined by singers Mahalia Jackson and George Grant, the Four Lads vocal group, comedians Lenny and Colyer and the Caesar Petrillo Orchestra. Joe Foss was the announcer (25 min., Sunday, 9:05–9:30 P.M., CBS, 1956). On a later version of the program, Pat Buttram replaced Burgess Meredith as host. Other members of the cast included Paul Richards, the Jack Halloran Quartet, Bill Kanad, Garry Wells, Betty Martin and Marion Morgan (15 min., Monday through Friday, 1:45–2:00 P.M., CST, CBS, 1956–1959).

16811 *Just Plain Bill*. Robert Hardy Andrews first wrote the story of small town life that was originally called *Bill the Barber*. Frank and Anne Hummert produced the story of barber Bill Davidson, who lived in Hartville. Arthur Hughes played the title role during the entire 22 years the program was broadcast. Bill Davidson, in his own way was similar to the character played by *Ma Perkins*. He was kind, understanding, but above all, he was always humane. The program in 1954 began with the announcement: "Now *Just Plain Bill*. The story of a man who might be living right next door to you. The real life story of people just like people we all know."

During its long run, the program's cast included: Curtis Arnall, Macdonald Carey, Cliff Carpenter, Ray Collins, Clayton "Bud" Collyer, Elizabeth Day, Audrey Egan, Charles Egleston, Sarah Fussell, Ara Gerald, Arthur Hughes, Teri Keane, Elaine Kent, Joe Latham, Charlotte Lawrence, Bill Lytell, James Meighan, Madeleine Pierce, Bill Quinn, Ruth Russell, Ann Shepherd (Scheindel Kalish), Guy Sorel, Helen Walpole and William Woodson. Robert Hardy Andrews, Barbara Bates, Peggy Blake, Evelyn Hart and Jack Kelsey were the program's writers. Martha Atwell, Gene Eubank, Arthur Hanna, Ed King, Norman Sweetser and Blair Walliser directed the program. The opening theme ("Darling Nellie Gray") and closing theme ("Polly Wolly Doodle") were played by Hal Brown on harmonica and guitar. Andre Baruch, Fielden Farrington, Ed Herlihy and Roger Krupp were the announcers. The program was sponsored by Anacin.

16812 Juster, Evelyn. Veteran actress Juster appeared on the daytime serial programs *Amanda of Honeymoon Hill* and *Don Ameche's Real Life Stories*.

16813 Justiana, Joe. Leader (Homesteaders Orchestra, WHAM, Rochester, NY, 1928).

16814 *Justice Triumphs*. The program dramatized "true" police stories drawn from the New York Sunday *News*. Supposedly the stories originated each week from a different large city police force. Jock MacGregor was the program's producer and director. The series had good production values, but the plots were often weak. The cast included Don Douglas, Nancy Sheridan, Ralph Carmargo, Joan Shea, Humphrey Davis, Jim Boles, Joe Latham, Byrna Raeburn, Sidney Smith, Cameron Prud'homme, Paul Conrad and Grace Carlson. Music was conducted by Emerson Buckley. George Carlson Putnam was the narrator and Frank McCarthy the announcer (30 min., Weekly, MBS, 1947).

16815 Justus, Margaret. Soprano (WHKC, Columbus, OH, 1937).

16816 Juvelier, Jeanne. Actress Juvelier appeared on the daytime serial programs *Myrt and Marge* and *The Woman in White*.

16817 *Juvenile Jury*. Jack Barry hosted the show that featured a panel of children (the "jury"), who gave their opinions on various questions sent in to them by their listeners. They discussed such topics as allowances, keeping their room clean, doing chores at home and suitable punishments. Various guest stars as Milton Berle, Eddie Cantor and Red Skelton frequently appeared. The program was first broadcast in 1946 by MBS. The cast included: Glenn Mark Arthur, Jack Barry, Peggy Bruder, Charlie Hankinson, Billy Knight, Laura Mangels, Johnny McBride, Robin Morgan, Dickie Orlan, Patsy Waller, Elizabeth Watson and Jerry Weinsbard. The producer was Dan Ehrenreich (Dan Enright) and John Scott the announcer (30 min., Weekly, MBS and NBC, 1946–1953). *See **Life Begins at Eighty***.

16818 *Juvenile Roundup*. Betty Dugan conducted the popular local sustaining show that featured the singing and dancing of children from Pittsburgh and its surrounding areas (30 min., Monday, 3:00–3:30 P.M. WWSW, Pittsburgh, PA, 1936).

16819 Jyles, Johnny. Newscaster (KGKL, San Angelo, TX, 1940).

16820 K&I Railroad Orchestra. Orchestra directed by J. Clark Martin (WHAS, Louisville, KY, 1925).

16821 *K-7 (K-7 Spy Stories)*. *See **K-7 Spy Stories***.

16822 Kabatnick's Dance Orchestra. Local dance band (WEBJ, New York, NY, 1926).

16823 Kaber, Russell V "Russ." Newscaster (KGCU, Mandan, ND, 1941–1942). Sportscaster (KGCU, 1941; KABR, Aberdeen, SD, 1947; *Today in Sports*, KOVC, Valley City, ND, 1951–1952; *Sports Parade*, KOVC, 1953; *Today in Sports*, KOVC, 1954–1956).

16824 Kabram, Etta and Pauline Sternlicht. Pianists (WEAF, New York. NY, 1926).

16825 Kackley, Olive. COM-HE (WCKY, Cincinnati, OH, 1942). Kackley, the station said, provided her listeners with friendly advice delivered with sharp wit and good humor.

16826 Kackson, (Reverend) O.E. DJ (*Spiritual Echoes*, WYNN, Florence, SC, 1960).

16827 Kadderly, W.L. Announcer (KOAC, Corvallis, OR, 1927).

16828 Kadel, Georgette. COM-HE (KWSO, Wasco, CA, 1951).

16829 Kadell, Bert. Newscaster (KWBU, Corpus Christi, TX, 1945).

16830 KaDell, Carlton. Actor KaDell was in the cast of *Armstrong of the SBI*, *Backstage Wife*, *Jonathan Kegg* (title role), *Kitty Keene*, *Masquerade*, *Red Ryder*, *Road of Life*, *Romance of Helen Trent*, *Tarzan* (title role) and *Wings of Destiny*.

16831 Kader, Al. Leader (Al Kader's Shrine Band, KOIN, Portland, OR, 1928).

16832 Kaderly, Katherine. Organist (WPAP, Brooklyn, NY, 1929).

16833 Kadon, F.M. Announcer (WOMT, Manitowac, WI, 1925).

16834 Kadow, F.M. Newscaster (WOMT, Manitowoc, WI, 1945).

16835 Kadowski, Frank. Leader (Frank Kadowski Orchestra broadcast from the St. Nicholas Hotel's Ballroom or the Orpheum Ballroom, Springfield, Illinois, WCBS, Springfield, IL, 1927).

16836 Kahakalau, William. Leader (*William Kahakalau's Hawaiians Orchestra*, WEEI, Boston, MA, 1934).

16837 Kahl, George. DJ (*Groovology 54*, WMAJ, State College, PA, 1950).

16838 Kahl, Regina. Soprano (WEBJ, New York, NY, 1926).

16839 Kahler, Jean. COM-HE (WFIN, Findlay, OH, 1955).

16840 Kahm, Esther. Pianist (KGFJ, Los Angeles, CA, 1929).

16841 Kahn, Art. Leader (Art Kahn's Senate Theater Orchestra, WLS, Chicago, IL, 1925; Art Kahn and his Sonatrons Orchestra, CBS, 1929). Pianist (*Art Kahn*, instr. mus. prg., WBBM, Chicago, IL, 1936).

16842 Kahn, Earl. Leader (*Earl Kahn Orchestra*, instr. mus. prg., WEBR, Buffalo, NY, 1935).

16843 Kahn, Joseph "Joe." Pianist (WJZ, New York, NY, 1928; *Joseph Kahn*, instr. mus. prg., NBC-Blue, 1936; *The Piano Dances*, NBC-Red, 1941). Kahn also performed regularly on *Information Please* and *Mary Marlin*.

16844 Kahn, Roger Wolfe. Leader (Roger Wolfe Kahn Orchestra featured on *The Victor Hour*, WJZ, New York, NY, 1926; broadcasting from the Hotel Pennsylvania, New York, WJZ, 1927; *Roger Wolfe Kahn Orchestra*, instr. mus. prg., WIP, Philadelphia, PA, 1936; WMCA, New York, NY, 1936).

16845 Kahne, Dorothy. COM-HE (WEKY, Richmond, KY, 1954).

16846 Kahyton, Lewis. Whistler (KYW, Chicago, IL, 1922).

16847 Kaiihue, Johnny. Leader (*Johnny Kaiihue Orchestra,* Hawaiian instr. mus. prg., WTAM, Cleveland, OH, 1942).

16848 Kail, Margaret. Singer (WIND, Gary, IN, 1935).

16849 *Kaima's Hawaiians Orchestra.* Instr. mus. prg. (WHAS, Louisville, KY, 1933).

16850 Kain, Paul. Leader (*Paul Kain Orchestra,* instr. mus. prg., WJSV, Washington, DC and CBS, 1939).

16851 Kain, Red. Newscaster-announcer (WSBA, York, PA, 1943).

16852 Kaiser, Doren. COM-HE (WBEV, Beaver Dam, WI, 1957).

16853 Kaiser, Elmer. Leader (Elmer Kaiser's Riverview Park Melody Masters Orchestra, WHT, Deerfield, IL, 1925).

16854 Kaiser, Lucille. COM-HE (KIUL, Garden City, KS, 1956).

16855 Kaiser, Ronal "Ron." DJ (*Musical Reveille,* KWOC, Poplar Bluff, MO, 1948). Sportscaster (KWOC, 1949; KBTM, Jonesboro, KY, 1953).

16856 Kaiser, Lucille. COM-HE (KIUL, Garden City, KS, 1956).

16857 Kalani, Sam. Leader (Sam Kalani's Hawaiian Trio, KFQZ, Hollywood, CA, 1928). Hawaiian baritone (KFI, Los Angeles, CA, 1928).

16858 Kalar, Phil. Baritone (*Phil Kalar,* vcl. mus. prg., WGN, Chicago, IL, 1934; *Phil Kalar,* popular songs with the WLS Orchestra sponsored by the Evans Fur Company, 15 min., Sunday, 11:15–11:30 A.M., WLS, Chicago, IL, 1935).

16859 Kalashian, Paul. DJ (*Dance Time,* WGGG, Gainesville, FL, 1948).

16860 Kalbach [Kalback], Zac. Saxophonist and band leader, Zac's Home Towners Band (KGA, Spokane, WA, 1929–1930).

16861 Kalber, Floyd. Sportscaster (KMTV, Omaha, NE, 1951).

16862 Kalberer, George. DJ (*5:30 Local,* KDAL, Duluth, MN, 1947–1948; *Vacationland Calling,* KDAL, 1949).

16863 Kalfus, Max. Tenor (WJZ, New York, NY, 1925).

16864 *Kalico Kat Orchestra.* Instr. mus. prg. (KFH, Wichita, KS, 1939).

16865 Kalinofsky, Sammy. Leader (Sammy Kalinofsky and his Sinfonico Band, KHJ, Los Angeles, CA, 1923).

16866 Kalish, Scheindel *See* **Sheperd, Ann.**

16867 Kalkins, Bernard. Organist (WGBS, New York, NY, 1926).

16868 Kalla, Maria. Singer (WGCP, New York, NY,1926).

16869 Kallao, Louis. Cellist Kallao was billed as a 14-year-old Hungarian gypsy (KDKA, Pittsburgh, PA, 1922).

16870 Kallay, Ed. DJ (*Your Saturday Morning Swing Club,* WINN, Louisville, KY, 1947). Sportscaster (*Sports Special,* WAVE, Louisville, KY, 1949–1950; *Sports Headlines,* WAVE, 1951–1960).

16871 Kallenmeyen, Ruth. Singer (KFAB, Lincoln, NE, 1925).

16872 Kallis, Henry. Director (Lido Venice Orchestra, WEEI, Boston, MA, 1928).

16873 Kalmus, Bea. DJ (WHN, New York, NY, 1947; *The Bea Kalmus Show,* 30 min., Monday through Saturday, 8:30–9:00 P.M., WMGM, New York, NY, 1950–1952).

16874 Kalmus, Lee. DJ (*Stairway to the Stars,* WMGM, New York, NY, 1948).

16875 Kalohi, Kimbo. Leader (Kimbo Kalohi's Hawaiian Moonlight Orchestra, WSB, Atlanta, GA, 1924; *Kalohi's Hawaiians Orchestra,* instr. mus. prg., WSB, 1937).

16876 Kalteis, (Professor) Otto. Pianist (WCAE, Pittsburgh, PA, 1925).

16877 Kaltenborn, Hans V. (Von). News commentator Kaltenborn, an outstanding broadcaster and the dean of commentators, was born July 9, 1878. A Harvard Phi Beta Kappa, Kaltenborn was a reporter and associate editor of the *Brooklyn Eagle* when he began a series of half hour news talks on WEAF (New York, NY) in 1923 sponsored by his paper. His "clipped" style of speech drew favorable response from listeners who also had critical praise for his commentary. In 1924, he moved to WAHG (Richmond Hill, NY). WAHG received thirty thousand letters praising his broadcasts.

Kaltenborn became the first radio broadcaster to conduct a presidential interview on the air when he interviewed Calvin Coolidge from the White House's Oval Room in 1924. After being denounced by local politicians and officials for his commentaries, Kaltenborn moved to WOR (Newark, NJ) in 1925. Despite protests and pressure brought by New York mayor James J. Walker, WOR gave him freedom of speech and encouraged his broadcast efforts. Kaltenborn also broadcast for WJZ (New York, NY). In 1928, he discussed the news on his *Current Topics Talk* program (WAHG, 1928). A year later, he appeared on CBS with his *Current Events* program of news analysis that he broadcast weekly (30 min., Monday, 7:00–7:30 P.M., CBS, 1929).

He became more famous when he made the first radio broadcast from a battlefield of the Spanish Civil War in 1936 and for his broadcast of the Munich Crisis in 1938. Kaltenborn's later career as commentator was equally full (*Headlines and Bylines,* CBS, 1938; *Kaltenborn Edits the News,* NBC, 1939–1942; WNBC, New York, NY, 1946–1947; NBC, 1945–1948).

Kaltenborn was known for his rapid, staccato speech delivery that varied from 150 to175 words per minute with occasional bursts of up to 200 words per minute. In addition, his integrity and authoritativeness was recognized. When CBS declared in 1939 that all news analysts should be neutral and objective, Kaltenborn responded honestly by saying that no commentator could meet that standard. The selecting or omitting of news items, the shading or emphasis given the events selected for description and every editorial judgment of the commentator, Kaltenborn noted, was an expression of opinion (Fang, 1977, p. 10). *See* **News.**

16878 Kaltenborn's Orchestra. Local New York dance band (WNYC, New York, NY, 1925).

16879 *Kaltenmeyer's Kindergarten.* Bruce Kamman, as Professor August Kaltenmeyer, attempted to preside over his zany "kindergarten kids," who unfailingly took advantage of him on his comedy show. The professor's pratfalls enriched the hilarious juvenile comedy sponsored by Quaker Oats Aunt Jemima Pancakes. Kaltenmeyer sputtered in his heavy German accent as his kindergarten kids raised havoc. The kids were: Merrill Fugit as Percy Van Schuyler; Cecil Roy as Daisy Dean; Thor Ericson as Yohnny Yohnson; Johnny Wolfe as Izzy Finkelstein; and Jim and Marian Jordan — who later gained fame as Fibber McGee and Molly — as Mickey Donovan and Gertie Gump, respectively. The program was described as "The Nonsense School of the Air" and it always lived up to that billing. *Variety* (October 9, 1935) said this funny show was a radio descendent of an old vaudeville routine — "Nine Crazy Kids." The program's personnel included: Sidney Ellstrom, Thor Ericson, Merrill Fugit, Jim Jordan, Marian Jordan, Bruce Kamman, Cecil Roy, Billy White and Johnny White. The vocal group of the Escorts and Betty (Betty Olson, Ted Claire, Cliff Petersen and Floyd Holm) and Harry Kogen's orchestra performed the musical selections. Douglas Craig was the arranger and accompanist (30 min., Saturday, 5:30–6:00 P.M. NBC, 1937). When anti-German sentiment arose in the United States in 1940, the program's name was changed to *Kindergarten Kapers* and Professor Kaltenmeyer's to Ulysses S. Applegate, a name that clearly said USA. In addition, the Professor's customary closing line, "*Auf widesehen und adieu*" was dropped.

16880 *Kalua Hawaiians Orchestra.* Instr. mus. prg. (WNBH, New Bedford, CT, 1939).

16881 Kalusche, Earle. Newscaster (WFAA, Dallas, TX, 1938).

16882 Kamaka, Charles. Hawaiian composer and guitarist (WFRA, 1926).

16883 Kaminer, Blanche. Miss Kaminer performed pianologues (KFWB, Hollywood, CA, 1926).

16884 Kamm, Herb. Sportscaster (WCAP, Asbury Park, NJ, 1939–1941).

16885 Kamman, Leigh. DJ (*1280 Club,* WOV, New York, NY, 1952; WLOL, Minneapolis, MN, 1957).

16886 Kammerman, J. O. Announcer (WCAT, Rapid City, SD, 1927).

16887 Kamoku, Duke. Leader (Duke Kamoku's Hawaiian Players Orchestra, KGO, Oakland, CA, 1925–1926; Duke Kamoku's Royal Hawaiians, KPO, San Francisco, CA, 1925).

16888 Kampe, Mel. Newscaster (WIL, St. Louis, MO, 1941–1942).

16889 Kampf, Ed. Announcer (WMBF, Miami Beach, FL, 1926).

16890 Kampus Kollegians Orchestra. Collegiate band (WGES, Oak Park, IL, 1925).

16891 Kane, A.J. The owner of the Kane Detective Agency, Kane told weekly detective stories (KFRC, San Francisco, CA, 1926).

16892 Kane, Barbara. COM-HE (KMEL, Wenatchee, WA, 1960).

16893 Kane, David "Dave." DJ (*Clockwatcher*, WLAU, Laurel, MA, 1947–1948; *Rhythm Matinee*, WLAU, 1952).

16894 Kane, Fred. Violinist (WGN, Chicago, IL, 1929).

16895 Kane, Hal. Leader, Hal Kane Orchestra (WBZ, Boston, MA, 1931).

16896 Kane, Helen. Singer Kane was known as "The Boop-Boop-a-Doop Girl" (CBS, 1929). Actress Kane was a member of the *Today's Children* daytime serial program.

16897 Kane, John. Actor Kane was in the cast of *Five Star Jones* (title role), *John's Other Wife*, *Nick Carter, Master Detective*, *Pepper Young's Family*, *Red Davis* and *When a Girl Marries*.

16898 Kane, Johnny. DJ (WINS, New York, NY and WHOM, New York, NY, 1947).

16899 Kane, Lyda. Actress Kane appeared on the *John's Other Wife* daytime serial program.

16900 Kane, Sugar. Vocalist (*Sugar Kane*, vcl. mus. prg., WOR, Newark, NJ, 1935).

16901 Kane's Hawaiians. Instrumental trio (KPO, San Francisco, CA, 1926–1928).

16902 Kaney, Sen. Famous pioneer announcer (KYW, Chicago, IL, 1924; WGN, Chicago, IL, 1925). Kaney became announcer and program director at NBC- Chicago in 1928. Some claim that Kaney was the first to broadcast a baseball and football game and describe a circus performance. .

16903 Kannard, Keith. Leader (Keith Kannard and his Kentucky Ramblers, WHAS, Louisville, KY, 1925).

16904 Kanoff, Efim. Tenor (KPO, San Francisco, CA, 1925).

16905 *Kansas* City Artist Trio. Instrumental group of pianist-director S.F. Rendina; cellist, Anthony Guerra and violinist, Charles Tiabe (WHB, Kansas City, MO, 1927).

16906 Kansas City Athletic Club Orchestra. Eddie Kuhn directed the club band (WDAF, Kansas City, MO, 1928).

16907 Kansas City Star's Radio Orchestra. Commercially sponsored dance band (WDAF, Kansas City, MO, 1924–1926).

16908 *Kansas Roundup*. CW music show (WIBW, Topeka, KS, 1947–1955). The weekly program included such performers as: Bud Davis, Slim Phillips, Lois Pierson, Doc Embree, Dude Hank (LeRoy Carlson), Catherine McKay, Miss Maudie, Colonel Combs, Little Jimmy Dickens, the Rangers Quartet and the Al Clauser Oklahoma Cowboys.

16909 Kanter, Ben. Pianist (*Ben Kanter*, instr. mus. prg., WJJD, Chicago, IL, 1936).

16910 Kantzer, Gay. COM-HE (WSAL, Logansport, IN, 1957).

16911 Kanz, Patricia H. COM-HE (KGNB, New Braunfels, TX, 1956).

16912 Kaplan, Eleanor. Violinist (WMBB, Chicago, IL, 1926).

16913 Kaplan, Ida. Pianist (WTIC, Hartford, CT, 1927).

16914 Karan, Tony. DJ (*Serenatas Mexicanas*, KRIO, McAlen, TX, 1952).

16915 Karber, Ethel. Pianist (WHP, Harrisburg, PA, 1937).

16916 Karch, Hank. A veteran vaudeville performer billed as a "banjokester," Karch mixed his wise cracks with the music he played on his seven string banjo (WLW, Cincinnati, OH, 1928–1929).

16917 Karcher, Sarah. Violinist (KFSG, Los Angeles, CA, 1925).

16918 Kardos, Gene. Leader (*Gene Kardos Orchestra*, instr. mus. prg., WCBM, Baltimore, MD, and CBS, 1934).

16919 Karelle [Karrelle], Ruth. Singer (WEVD, New York, NY, 1936; WIP, Philadelphia, PA, 1936; WMCA, New York, NY,1937).

16920 Karen, Edith. Soprano (*Edith Karen*, vcl. mus., prg., WLW, Cincinnati, OH, 1936).

16921 Karin. COM-HE (*Coffee with Karin*, WTCN, Minneapolis, MN, 1949).

16922 *Karl and Hardy*. The CW team was a long time Chicago favorite. Karl Davis and Hartford Connecticut Hardy, a guitarist and mandolinist respectively, came to WLS in 1931 as members of their former school teacher, John Lair's Cumberland Ridge Runners, before going out on their own (WLS, 1935; WJJD, Chicago, IL, 1936–1937).

16923 *Karl Krug*. On his weekly show Karl Krug broadcast theatrical news and reviews (15 min., Weekly, WJAS, Pittsburgh, PA, 1938).

16924 Karlbom, Barbara. COM-HE (WJRD, Tuscaloosa, AL, 1956–1957).

16925 Karlen, Agatha. Reader (WEBH, Chicago, IL, 1924 and WQJ, Chicago, IL, 1925).

16926 Karlin, Fay. COM-HE (KXXX, Colby, KS, 1955).

16927 Karloff, Boris. DJ Karloff displayed his own true charming self on his interesting sustaining show — not the menacing movie persona he had made famous. Karloff acted as a DJ for children and even told them a bedtime story (30 min., Sunday, 7:00–7:30 P.M., WNEW, New York, NY, 1950).

16928 Karlton, Gerry. Newscaster (KWLC, Decorah, IA, 1947).

16929 Karney, Beulah. COM-HE (WENR, Chicago, IL, 1949).

16930 Karnes, Joe. Pianist (*Joe Karnes*, instr. mus. prg., KMOX, St. Louis, MO, 1936).

16931 Karnes, Robert. Sportscaster (WSIX, Nashville, TN, 1941). Newscaster (WKY, Oklahoma City, OK, 1945).

16932 Karney, Beulah. COM-HE. After Karney hosted a home economics program in 1935 on KMBC (Kansas City, MO), she became the station's program director. She later moved to Chicago to join the NBC-Blue Network in 1941.

16933 Karns, Wimpy. Singer (*Wimpy Karns*, vcl. mus. prg., WAIU, Columbus, OH, 1935).

16934 Karnstedt, Cal. Newscaster (KSTP, St. Paul, MN, 1945; *5:45 News*, KSTP, 1947; *Noon News*, KSTP, 1948).

16935 Karpinski, Stephan. Newscaster (WHOM, Jersey City, NJ, 1941).

16936 Karr, Kathleen. Soprano (WEBJ, New York, NY, 1925).

16937 Karr Brothers Orchestra. "Hot band" broadcasting from the U.S. Grant Hotel (KFSD, San Diego, CA, 1927).

16938 Karraker, Moneda. COM-HE (WRAJ, Anna, IL, 1960).

16939 Karrelle, Ruth. Singer (*Ruth Karrelle*, vcl. mus. prg., WIP, Philadelphia, PA, 1936).

16940 Karrenbauer, Bill. DJ (WHBC, Canton, OH, 1949).

16941 Karson, Lee. Newscaster (KFBC, Cheyenne, WY, 1940; KTAR, Phoenix, AZ, 1940–1941). Sportscaster (KTAR, 1941).

16942 Karver, Wally. DJ (WILK, Wilkes-Barre, PA, 1957).

16943 Kasch, Hy. Leader (Hy Kasch and his Dance Orchestra, KFWB, Hollywood, CA, 1926).

16944 Kaseman, Joanne. COM-HE (WISL, Shamokin, PA, 1957).

16945 Kasin, Rose. Pianist (WOR, Newark, NJ, 1929).

16946 *Kaskaria Ramblers*. CW mus. prg. (WDZ, Tuscola, IL, 1937).

16947 Kaskas, Anna. Lithuanian concert singer (WTIC, Hartford, CT, 1931).

16948 Kasoor's Orchestra. Band from Port Huron, Michigan (WWJ, Detroit, MI, 1923).

16949 Kasper, Tad. DJ (KDAL, Duluth, MN, 1957).

16950 *(The) Kasper Girls*. The vocal music program featured the Kasper Girls (WDOD, Chattanooga, TN, 1937).

16951 Kassel, Art. Leader (*Art Kassel Orchestra*, instr. mus. prg., NBC, 1934; MBS, 1936–1937; WGN, Chicago, IL, 1940–1942). In 1940, one of his programs began with the announcer saying, "Castles in the Air with Art Kassel and his orchestra from the Walnut Room of the Bismark Hotel in Chicago, Illinois."

16952 Kasten, Ruth. COM-HE (WOMT, Maniwotec, WI, 1957).

16953 Kaster, Dolph. Singer (WOK, Pine Bluff, AR, 1922).

16954 Kastner, Irene. COM-HE (WMBR, Jacksonville, FL, 1954).

16955 Kastyluck, Maxim. Russian baritone (WKRC, Cincinnati, OH, 1925).

16956 *Kate MacMullan's Party*. Miss MacMullan, a member of one of Philadelphia's socially prominent families, broadcast etiquette information and tips (15 min., Thursday, 1:30–1:45 P.M., KYW, Philadelphia, PA, 1941).

16957 *Kate Smith and her Swanee Music*. See ***LaPalina Presents Kate Smith***.

16958 *(The) Kate Smith Hour*. Popular singer and famous personality Kate Smith eventually became a DJ on her own sustaining show (55 min., Friday, 8:00–8:55 P.M., WOR, Newark, NJ, 1950).

16959 ***(The) Kate Smith Show.*** Talented singer Smith hosted this hour long variety show for many years, introducing along the way many performers who later would become nationally known stars such as Abbott and Costello, Ezra Stone as *Henry Aldrich*, Henny Youngman and many others. Smith, known by many as "The Songbird of the South," never failed to please her many listeners with her songs. She was famous for introducing Irving Berlin's "God Bless America" and also for popularizing her theme, "When the Moon Comes Over the Mountain." Both her opening ("Hello, everybody") and the show's closing ("Thanks for listening. Good night, folks") were well known trademarks. The Jack Miller Orchestra accompanied her. Ted Collins, Smith's manager, acted as the host on her programs. Bunny Coughlin and Bob Lee served as directors. The writers included: Jay Bennett, Al Garry, Doris Gilbert, Art S. Henley, Jean Holloway and Edward Jurist. Andre Baruch was the announcer (45 min., Thursday, 7:15–8:00 P.M., CBS, 1935). Smith had several other shows over the years.

Some of the personnel who participated in Smith's many shows were: Abbott and Costello, the Aldrich Family cast, John Barrymore, Mary Boland, Ted Collins (Host), Greta Garbo, Grace George, Bert Lahr, Bert Lytell, Helen Menken, Edward G. Robinson, Kate Smith, Margaret Sullivan and Henny Youngman. In 1950, like many other personalities, she became a DJ on *The Kate Smith Hour*. See ***Kate Smith Speaks, The A&P Hour, The Kate Smith Hour*** and **Singers**.

16960 ***Kate Smith Speaks*** **(aka *Kate Smith Talks*).** At the end of her radio career, Smith conducted talk shows with such names as *Kate Smith Speaks* and *Kate Smith Talks* in 1957–1958 on ABC. She commented on various topics chiefly of interest to women.

16961 **Kath, Delores.** COM-HE (KGOS, Torrington, WY, 1960).

16962 **Kathe, Richard.** DJ (*Song Shop*, WMRN, Marion, OH, 1947).

16963 ***Katie's Daughter***. A theatrical background provided the scene of conflict on this daytime serial sponsored by the Manhattan Soap Company. Just as the leading character was about to open as the lead in a Broadway production, she had a quarrel with her boy friend. Does she succeed despite her personal problem? *Variety* observed that the show didn't remain on the air long enough for listeners to discover the answer. In the cast were Martin Blaine, Grace Coppin and Marie Gayer. The announcer was Ken Banghart (15 min., Monday through Friday, 10:00–10:15 A.M., NBC, 1947).

16964 **Katime, Milton.** Conductor Katime was musical director of the *House of Glass* program.

16965 **Katinka Orchestra.** Musical group (WOR, Newark, NJ, 1926).

16966 **Kathan, Marjorie.** Singer (WOW, Omaha, NE, 1927).

16967 **Katlhoff, Ruth.** Soprano (WGES, Oak Park, IL, 1925).

16968 **Katt, George.** DJ (*The Cat's Meow*, WMRO, Aurora, IL, 1950).

16969 **Katz, Al.** Leader (Katz and His Kittens, WOK, Homewood, IL and WPG, Atlantic City, NJ, 1926, WMAQ, Chicago, IL and KRLD, Dallas, TX, 1927; *Al Katz Orchestra*, instr. mus. prg., MBS, 1936). *See* **Katz and His Kittens.**

16970 **Katz, Milton.** Pianist (WEAF, New York, NY, 1925).

16971 **Katz and His Kittens.** Leader Katz had what *Variety* called "a hot band." His 1926 band's personnel consisted of Katz, ldr.-d.; Eddie Kooden, Fred Rollinson, clr.; Jerry Bump, tb.; Joe Magliatti, clr., as. and ss.; Lewis Story, clr., as. and vcls.; George Schectman, clr. and ts.; Jess Stacy, p.; Joe Bishop, tba.; and Tracy Brown, bj.

16972 **Katzman, Louis.** Leader of the Whithall Anglo-Persians, an orchestra strongly praised by *Variety*, that was featured on a program sponsored by the Whithall Carpet and Rug Company (WJZ, New York, NY, 1926). Katzman also led studio bands both for radio and recording sessions. He played both trumpet and violin during a long prolific career (*Louis Katzman Orchestra*, instr. mus. prg., WIP, Philadelphia, PA, 1935).

16973 **Kauffman, Ted.** DJ (*Record Rendezvous*, WCMI, Ashland, KY, 1949).

16974 **Kaufman, Arnold C.** DJ (*Bandstand*, WMBM, Miami Beach, FL, 1948).

16975 **Kaufman, Arthur.** Leader (Arthur Kaufman Serenaders Orchestra, WGBS, New York, NY, 1925).

16976 **Kaufman, Bud.** DJ (*First Call*, WILS, Lansing, MI, 1947).

16977 **Kaufman, C.H.** Kaufman delivered talks on various topics of current interest (WLW, Cincinnati, OH, 1925).

16978 **Kaufman, Irving.** Talented popular baritone, announcer, actor, comedian and MC Kaufman was born February 8, 1900. After touring in vaudeville at the age of seven as a "Russian Midget," he became, in turn, a musician in a circus band, a singer in theaters and a song plugger. Kaufman then began a successful recording career with 22 different companies, including Emerson, Gennett, Crown, Banner, Regal, Harmony, Pathe, Edison, Vocalion, Brunswick, Columbia and Victor, under at least ten aliases. His radio career began when he first appeared on WJZ (New York, NY, 1922) as a vocalist with Gus Haenschen's orchestra. His many radio appearances included the *Champion Sparklers* program in 1928 and several other appearances on WJZ (New York, NY, 1929) the following year. He was also on radio as "Salty Sam." He appeared on Broadway in two versions of *The Passing Show*.

16979 **Kaufman, Lena.** Violinist (WOR, Newark, NJ, 1924).

16980 **Kaufman, Louis L.** News analyst (KQV, Pittsburgh, PA, 1945–1947; *Louis Kaufman News*, KQV, 1948).

16981 **Kaufman, Murray.** DJ (WMCA, New York, NY, 1954–1956).

16982 **Kaufman, Robert.** Newscaster (WISR, Butler, PA, 1941, 1946). Sportscaster (WISR, 1942).

16983 **Kaufman, Sam.** Sportscaster (WOL, Washington, DC, 1951–1953; *Human Side of Sports*, WOL, 1954–1956).

16984 **Kaufman, Schlma [Schalma].** Singer (WLW, Cincinnati, OH, 1923).

16985 **Kaufman, Whitey.** Leader (*Whitey Kaufman Orchestra*, instr. mus. prg., WFBR, Baltimore, MD, 1935).

16986 **Kaufman, Yvonne.** COM-HE (WVSC, Somerset, PA, 1957).

16987 **Kaufmann, Harry J.** Leader-violinist (Kaufmann's Aladdin Hotel Merrymakers, WDAF, Kansas City, MO, 1928).

16988 **Kaufmann's Sni-A-Bar Gardens Orchestra.** Club dance band (WDAF, Kansas City, MO, 1928). This band may have been led by Harry J. Kaufmann. *See* **Kaufmann, Harry J.**

16989 **Kaule, Mary Katherine.** Delivered inspirational talks (KFRC, San Francisco, CA, 1925).

16990 **Kaulfuss, Grace.** COM-HE (WEEZ, Chester, PA, 1960).

16991 **Kaun, Bernard.** Leader (Bausch & Lomb Concert Ensemble, WHAM, Rochester, NY, 1927).

16992 **Kavelin, Al.** Leader (*Al Kavelin Orchestra*, instr. mus. prg., CBS, 1934; WLW, Cincinnati, OH and WGN, Chicago, IL, 1935; MBS, 1936; WGN, Chicago, IL, 1936–1937; NBC, 1939).

16993 **Kay, Andy.** DJ (*Top of the Morning*, KVEC, San Luis Obispo, CA, 1949; KGST, Fresno, CA, 1955).

16994 **Kay, Beatrice.** Soprano (WCOH, New York, NY, 1932). *See* ***(The) Gay Nineties Revue***.

16995 **Kay, Bonita.** Actress Kay appeared on the daytime serial program *Backstage Wife* aka *Mary Noble, Backstage Wife*.

16996 **Kay, Dick.** DJ (*Overture*, WAAP, Peoria, IL, 1960).

16997 **Kay, Donna.** COM-HE (KFIR, North Bend, OR, 1957).

16998 **Kay, Dorothy.** COM-HE (KYSM, Mankato, MN, 1949).

16999 **Kay, Ethel.** Pianist on the *Piano Twins* program with Marie Golden (KNX, Los Angeles, CA, 1930).

17000 **Kay, Evelyn.** Blues singer (WOV, New York, NY, 1932; WPCH, New York, NY, 1932).

17001 **Kay, Geraldine.** Actress Kay appeared on the *Orphans of Divorce* daytime serial program.

17002 **Kay, Harry.** Newscaster (KCKN, Kansas City, MO, 1940).

17003 **Kay, Herbie.** Leader (*Herbie Kay Orchestra*, instr. mus. prg., CBS, 1935–1936; WCCO, Minneapolis–St. Paul, MN, 1937; NBC, 1939; KFEL, Denver, CO, 1942).

17004 **Kay, Hilda.** Pianist (WAAM, Newark, NJ, 1925).

17005 **Kay, Janice.** Singer (WCAU, Philadelphia, PA, 1936).

17006 Kay, Jay. Leader (*Jay Kay Orchestra*, instr. mus. prg., WOWO, Ft. Wayne, IN, 1936).

17007 Kay, Joan. Actress Kay was in the cast of *Those Happy Gilmans*.

17008 Kay, Kathryn. COM-HE (KVOA, Tucson, AZ, 1951–1955).

17009 Kay, Lambdin. Famous pioneer announcer known as "The Little Colonel," Kay was chosen to be the first full time manager of WSB (Atlanta, GA, 1922). He worked at WGN (Chicago, IL, 1925), where he became a popular wit on his *Hired Help Skylark* program.

17010 Kay, Lucy. COM-HE (WBKH, Hattiesburg, MS, 1956).

17011 Kay, Ray. Newscaster (WJRD, Tuscaloosa, AL, 1940). Sportscaster (WJRD, 1940).

17012 Kay, Robert "Bob." Newscaster (WAVE, Louisville, KY, 1941; 1946, WAVE, 1946). DJ (*Cheer Up Party*, WAVE, 1948; *Disc Jockey Contest*, WAVE, 1949–1957).

17013 Kay, Rose. Kay was her station's "Society Editor" (WHKC, Columbus, OH, 1937).

17014 Kay, Scotty. Leader (Scotty Kay Orchestra, WHN, New York, NY, 1925).

17015 Kay, Theodora. COM-HE (WTEL, Philadelphia, PA, 1954).

17016 Kay, Walter. Newscaster (WHA, Madison, WI, 1942). DJ (*Melody Time*, WJW, Cleveland, OH, 1947; *Walt Kay Show*, WDOK, Cleveland, OH, 1949).

17017 *Kay Kyser's Kollege of Musical Knowledge*. The "Ol' Professor" Kay Kyser conducted his happy combination of music, comedy and quiz program. Kyser's band accompanied vocalists Harry Babbitt, Ginny Simms and Sully Mason. Comedian Ish Kabibble, portrayed by trumpeter Mervyn Bogue, supplied zany humor each week. The quiz portion of the program usually had the "Ol' Professor" giving away either broad hints to the correct answer or giving the answer away completely. The good natured program appeared on all the major networks while it was on the air from 1938 to 1949. The cast included: Harry Babbitt, Mervyn Bogue, Georgia Carroll, Trudy Erwin, the King Sisters (Alyce, Donna, Yvonne and Louise), Kay Kyser, Sully Mason, Shirley Mitchell, Ginny Simms and the Town Criers. Frank O'Connor was the producer and Ed Cashman, John Cleary, Harry Sax and William Warwick the directors. Richard Dana and Martin Stark were the writers.

17018 *Kay Parker in Hollywood*. Miss Parker conducted a short program devoted to Hollywood gossip and interviews with such motion picture personalities as Betty Furness, Clara Bow, Zeppo Marx, Anita Louise, Tom Brown, Toby Wing, Claudette Colbert, William Gargan, John Carradine and Lillian Harvey. The program was sponsored by Tangee Lipstick (5 min., Transcribed, 1933).

17019 Kaye, A.T. Actor Kaye was in the cast of *Valiant Lady*.

17020 Kaye, Barbara. COM-HE (WKRG, Mobile, AL, 1954–1955).

17021 Kaye, Barry. DJ (*Barry Kaye Show*, WBMD, Baltimore, MD, 1950; WJAS, Pittsburgh, PA, 1955–1956).

17022 Kaye, Elena. DJ (*Rhythm and Blues*, WJOB, Hammond, IN, 1955).

17023 Kaye, Emily. COM-HE (KXEO, Mexico, MO, 1956).

17024 Kaye, Evelyn (Evelyn and her Magic Violin). While playing with Phil Spitalny's All Girl Orchestra in the 1930s and 1940s, she became famous as "Evelyn and Her Magic Violin." Violinist Kaye was born October 19, 1917. She was a scholarship and fellowship graduate of the Damrosch Institute of Musical Art and the Juilliard School of Music. She first appeared on radio at the age of ten as a soloist on WJZ (New York, NY, 1927). *See* ***The Hour of Charm***.

17025 Kaye, Jane. Singer, (*Jane Kaye*, vcl. mus. prg., WJJD, Chicago, IL, 1936).

17026 Kaye, Lillian. Singer (WTIC, Hartford, CT, 1936).

17027 Kaye, Mary. COM-HE (WBUZ, Fredonia, NY, 1960).

17028 Kaye, Milton. Pianist (*Milton Kaye*, instr. mus. prg., WOR, Newark, NJ, 1934).

17029 Kaye, Sammy. Leader (*Sammy Kaye Orchestra*, instr. mus. prg., NBC, 1935–1936; MBS, 1938; CBS, 1937–1942).

17030 Kaye, Sylvia. COM-HE (KONG, Visalia, CA, 1956).

17031 Kaye, Tony. Newscaster (WEBR, Buffalo, NY, 1942).

17032 Kayser, Joseph. Baritone (NBC, 1928).

17033 Kazounoff, Bernice. Concert pianist and music teacher (WEAF, New York, NY, 1923).

17034 K.C.B. A famous newspaper columnist, who conducted a program about radio programs and performers (*Radio Breezes*, KGO, Oakland, CA, 1925). He was not otherwise identified.

17035 *KDKA Kiddies Club*. Uncle KayDee (C.A. "Tony" Wasserman) presided over the show for children (15 min., Monday through Friday, 5:30–5:45 P.M., KDKA, 1931).

17036 KDKA Little Symphony Orchestra. Victor Saudek conducted the fifteen-piece symphony orchestra founded exclusively for broadcast purposes on December 4, 1921 (KDKA, Pittsburgh, PA, 1921–1925).

17037 *KDKA Players*. Station KDKA presented a series of dramatic productions under the name of the *KDKA Players* with casts that included Elizabeth Drake, Sondra Kostner, Claude Marrio and Helen Wayne among others. The programs were directed by Ed Harvey (KDKA, 1932).

17038 KDYL Dance and Concert Orchestra. Popular band directed by Johnny Rosell (KDYL, Salt Lake City, UT, 1929).

17039 Kealy, Ruth. Reader (KDKA, Pittsburgh, PA, 1923–1924).

17040 Kean, Harold. Baritone (WJR, Detroit, MI, 1928).

17041 Keane, Charlotte. Actress Keane was a cast member of the daytime serial *Backstage Wife* aka *Mary Noble, Backstage Wife*.

17042 Keane, Ed. Sportscaster (*Sports Parade*, KGBS, Harlingen, TX, 1950).

17043 Keane, Jack. DJ (*Hi Time*, KGBS, Harlingen, TX, 1947).

17044 Keane, Rose. Actress Keane appeared on the *Little Italy* dramatic program.

17045 Keane, Terri. Talented actress Keane was a cast member of the daytime serial programs *Just Plain Bill*, *Life Can Be Beautiful*, *Marriage for Two*, *The Second Mrs. Burton* and *Big Sister*.

17046 Kearl, Wayne. Newscaster (KSL, Salt Lake City, UT, 1947).

17047 Kearn, Marion. Soprano (WAHG, New York, NY, 1925).

17048 Kearney, Gerald. DJ (*Merry-Go-Round*, WFEA, Manchester, NH, 1947).

17049 Kearns, George. Actor Kearns was in the cast of the *Rosemary* daytime serial program.

17050 Kearns, Joey. Leader (*Joey Kearns Orchestra*, instr. mus. prg., CBS, 1940).

17051 Kearns, Joseph "Joe." Newscaster (CBS, 1944; KFVL, Hollywood, CA, 1946).

17052 Kearns, June. COM-HE (WTOC, Savannah, GA, 1956–1957).

17053 Kears, Edith. Lyric soprano (KRE, Berkeley, CA, 1923).

17054 Kearson, Grace. COM-HE (WTOC, Savannah, GA, 1956–1957).

17055 Keast, Paul. Baritone (*Paul Keast*, vcl. mus. prg., CBS and WOR, Newark, NJ, 1934).

17056 Keates, Henri A. Organist playing from Cincinnati's McVickers Theatre (WLW, Cincinnati, OH, 1926).

17057 Keath, Donna. Actress Keath appeared on the *Young Dr. Malone* daytime serial program.

17058 Keath, Ed. DJ (*Record Review*, KFRU, Columbia, MO, 1947).

17059 Keating, Buster. Leader (Buster Keating and his Orchestra, WBRL, Manchester, NH, 1928). The Keating band was featured on the station's "Claremont Night."

17060 Keating, John. Tenor (WJZ, New York, NY, 1925).

17061 Keating, Lillian. Singer (WLRH, Brooklyn, NY, 1930).

17062 Keating, Lola. COM-HE (KTEL, Walla Walla, WA, 1960).

17063 Keating, Ray. Leader (*Ray Keating Orchestra*, instr. mus. prg., MBS, 1937).

17064 Kecki, Michael. Newscaster (WHOM, Jersey City, NJ, 1941).

17065 Keddy, Grace. Actress Keddy appeared on the daytime serial programs *Lorenzo Jones* and *We Love and Learn*.

17066 Kedis, James. Tenor (WHN, New York, NY, 1924).

17067 Keech, Kelvin. NBC-New York staff announcer who announced on *The Eveready Hour* (WEAF-NBC-Red, New York, NY).

17068 Keefe, Howard S. Newscaster (WSPR, Springfield, MA, 1937–1938, 1944–1945).

17069 Keefe, Jack. Harvard graduate and former performer on both the Orpheum and Keith vaudeville circuits, Keefe became the first announcer on station WSM (Nashville, TN) in the mid–1920s and associate announcer in 1928.

17070 Keefe, Vera. COM-HE (KLER, Rochester, MN, 1951).

17071 Keefer, Flora McGill. Contralto (WRC, Washington, DC, 1924).

17072 Keefer, Lubov Breit. Pianist (WBAL, Baltimore, MD, 1926).

17073 Keefer-Kocker Orchestra. Commercial band (WLW, Cincinnati, OH, 1925).

17074 Keegan, Howard. Director Keegan directed the *Guiding Light, Tale of Today* and *Woman in White* daytime serial programs.

17075 Keel, Van. Newscaster (WBEN, Buffalo, NY, 1945–1946).

17076 Keele, Hester. Pianist (WSM, Nashville, TN, 1928).

17077 Keeler, Eloise. COM-HE, writer and director (KDAC, Fort Bragg, CA, 1951). After studying drama in high school, Keeler appeared in many little theater plays at the University of California's Greek Theater. She appeared on KGO (San Francisco, CA) in 1924 in a play, *The Superior Miss Callender*, as part of the Little Theatre group directed by Mrs. Roger Noble Burnham at the Claremont Hotel. She was also in the Little Theatre group in Claremont, California, directed by Wilda Wilson Church. While still a school girl she participated with the Church group in reading plays over KGO for which she was paid $5.00 a broadcast.

She appeared in Broadway productions for several years beginning in 1927. She returned to Los Angeles radio in 1938, writing radio shows and advertising copy for the Raymond Morgan Agency. From that beginning she was hired to write for station KFBK (Sacramento, CA), where she worked for five years during the World War II era. She had her own programs at that station, including one in which she interviewed people working for the war effort. Another of her programs was the *Khaki-Wac Quiz* with soldiers and WACs. She also did a *Meditation Program* with organ music and, sometimes, broadcast the news.

After the war, Keeler went to Chicago to work for Marion Claire at station WGNB-FM. She stayed in Chicago for several years writing ten of the station's programs. Her own program was *The World of Tomorrow*, on which she interviewed experts on their predictions of things to come. Keeler (1977) reported the experts' predictions were remarkably accurate.

17078 Keeler, Margie. Singer Keeler was the sister of motion picture star Ruby Keeler (*Margie Keeler*, vcl. mus. prg., WMCA, New York, NY, 1935).

17079 Keeley, Walter. Reader (KOA, Denver, CO, 1926).

17080 Keeling, Jon N. COM-HE (WTRR, Sanford, FL, 1956).

17081 Keen, Harold. Newscaster (KGB, San Diego, CA, 1945).

17082 Keen, Jeff. DJ (*Along the Rialto*, KYW, Philadelphia, PA, 1947).

17083 Keene, Alexander. Violinist (WFAA, Dallas, TX, 1925).

17084 Keene, Day. Writer Keene was the creator-writer of *Kitty Keene* and the writer of *Orphan Annie*.

17085 Keene, Hank. Leader (*Hank Keene's Radio Gang*, CW mus. prg., WTIC, Hartford, CT, 1936).

17086 Keene, Sherman. Leader (*Sherman Keene Orchestra*, instr. mus. prg., WOR, Newark, NJ, 1934).

17087 Keener, Marion. Soprano (NBC, 1928).

17088 Keeny, Mort. Leader (*Mort Keeny Orchestra*, instr. mus. prg., WOR, Newark, NJ, 1935).

17089 Keep, Barney. Sportscaster (*Keeping Up with Sports*, KEX, 1947–1949; *Keep Smiling*, KEX, 1950). DJ (*Barney Keep Show*, KEX, Portland, OR, 1949–1960).

17090 *Keep Joy Radiating Order of the Bats*. The Seattle *Post-Intelligencer* newspaper presented the weekly meeting of the "lodge," whose broadcasts were typical of the zany, late evening variety programs of early radio (KJR, Seattle, WA, 1925).

17091 *Keeping Up with Daughter*. The humorous daytime serial told the story of the daily events in the life of a modern girl. The leading roles were played by Nan Dorland and Janet Kling (15 min., Wednesday, 11:00–11:25 A.M., NBC-Red, 1932).

17092 Kegley, William. Imitations (WCCO, Minneapolis–St. Paul, MN, 1926).

17093 Keglovich, Albert. Thirteen-year-old violinist (KFWB, Hollywood, CA, 1925).

17094 Kehm, Horace. Announcer (WFRB, Chicago, IL, 1927).

17095 Kehner, Suzanne. Metropolitan Opera soprano (NBC, New York, NY, 1928).

17096 Kehrt, Jennie. Miss Kehrt played piano solos and broadcast movie reviews (WLW, Cincinnati, OH, 1923–1924).

17097 Keicher, George. Announcer (WGES, Chicago, IL, 1925).

17098 Keim, Anne. Soprano (WQJ, Chicago, IL, 1925).

17099 Keim, Ralph. Pianist (WQJ, Chicago, IL, 1925).

17100 Keinpeter, Irene. Soprano (WEBR, New York, NY, 1925).

17101 Keirsey, Al. Newscaster (KROD, El Paso, TX, 1940).

17102 Keiser, Della. Contralto (WOO, Philadelphia, PA, 1925).

17103 Keiser, Patricia. Pianist (WBAA, West Lafayette, IN, 1939).

17104 Keisker, Marion (Kitty Kelly). COM-HE (WREC, Memphis, TN, 1949).

17105 Keister, Howard. Trombonist (KDKA, Pittsburgh, PA, 1922).

17106 Keitel, James "Jim." DJ (*Western Matinee*, KMUS, Muskogee, OK, 1948; *Dinnerbell Ramble*, KMUS, 1950).

17107 Keiter, Lester "Les." Sportscaster (KELA, Centralia-Chehalis, WA, 1941–1947; KYA, San Francisco, CA, 1950–1952; *Sports Wire*, WINS, New York, NY, 1954; KYA, 1955).

17108 Keith, Bob. DJ (*Bob Keith Show*, WLOF, Orlando, FL, 1948–1955).

17109 Keith, Dick. Actor Keith was in the cast of *Bright Horizon*.

17110 Keith, Don. Newscaster (KUJ, Walla Walla, WA, 1946).

17111 Keith, Ian. Actor Keith was in the cast of *The Barton Family, Girl Alone, Kitty Keene, Woman in White* and *Your Dream Has Come True*.

17112 Keith, Joe. DJ (*Joe Keith Show*, KLIF, Dallas, TX, 1947).

17113 Keith, Maxine. Newscaster (WOR, New York, NY, 1947–1948).

17114 Keith, Richard "Dick." Actor Keith was in the cast of *Bright Horizon, Mr. Chameleon, Orphans of Divorce* and *True Detective Mysteries*.

17115 Keithley, E. Clinton. Tenor (WMBB, Homewood, IL and WOK, Chicago, IL, 1928).

17116 Keithley, Lennore. Soprano (KGO, Oakland, CA, 1926).

17117 Keitzel, Helen. COM-HE (WBNY, Buffalo, NY, 1957).

17118 Kekeris, Gus. Sportscaster (*March of Sports*, KSGM, Ste. Genevieve, MO, 1949).

17119 Kelch, Norman. Baritone (KFI, Los Angeles, CA, 1924).

17120 Kelford, Trevor. Newscaster (WJMA, Covington, VA, 1943; KXEL, Waterloo, IA, 1945).

17121 Kelk, Jackie. Actor Kelk appeared on *The Aldrich Family, Amanda of Honeymoon Hill, Coast-to-Coast on a Bus, Dick Tracy, The Gumps, Hello, Peggy, Hilltop House, Mother of Mine, Rosemary, Superman, Terry and the Pirates* (title role) and *Valiant Lady*.

17122 Kellam, Cliff. Trombonist (WGHB, Clearwater, FL, 1926).

17123 Kellar, Art. DJ (*Request-a-Record*, WRON, Ronceverte, WV, 1947).

17124 Kelleher, Alberta. Violinist (WBZ, Springfield, MA, 1925).

17125 Kelleher, Phil. Newscaster (WQAM, Miami, FL, 1945).

17126 Kellem, Milton. Leader (*Milton Kellem Orchestra*, instr. mus. prg., CBS, 1934; WCAU, Philadelphia, PA, 1935; WIP, Philadelphia, PA, 1936; CBS, 1936–1937).

17127 Keller, Ann. Soprano (WEBH, Chicago, IL, 1924).

17128 Keller, Connie. COM-HE (WCBK, Battle Creek, MI, 1951).

17129 Keller, Elizabeth. Actress Keller was featured on the *Joe Powers of Oakville* program.

17130 Keller, Helen. Blind and deaf from birth, Helen Keller learned to communicate after working for many years with her teacher and companion, Anne Sullivan. Her inspirational story was dramatized on stage and in film in *The Miracle Worker*. On the *Collier Radio Hour* (NBC, 1929), this remarkable woman delivered short talks on current events. She also made guest appearances on many other radio programs.

17131 Keller, Henry. DJ (*E for U*, KGFW, Kearney, NE, 1950).

17132 Keller, Jo Ann. COM-HE (WKKS, Vanceburg, KY, 1960).

17133 Keller, Leonard. Leader (*Leonard Keller Orchestra*, instr. mus. prg., NBC, 1935; WCCO, Minneapolis–St. Paul, MN, 1937).

17134 Keller, Nan. COM-HE (KBYE, Oklahoma City, OK, 1957).

17135 Keller, Norm. DJ (*As You Like It*, WCNH, Quincy, FL, 1948; WMOH, Hamilton, OH, 1949; *Record Shop*, WMOH, 1952).

17136 Keller, O.J., Jr. DJ (*Juke Box Serenade*, WTAX, Springfield, IL, 1947–1957).

17137 Keller, Robert. Organist (*Robert Keller*, instr. mus. prg., WIP, Philadelphia, PA, 1935–1936).

17138 Kelley, A. Boyd. Newscaster (KRLH, Midland, TX, 1940–1942; KFJZ, Fort Worth, TX, 1944; KBST, Big Spring, TX, 1945). Sportscaster (KRLH, 1940–1942).

17139 Kelley, Bob. Sportscaster (WGAR, Cleveland, OH, 1940–1941).

17140 Kelley, Bob. Sportscaster (KMPC, Los Angeles, CA, 1946; *Parade of Sports*, KMPC, 1947–1954).

17141 Kelley, Buddy. DJ (*Hillbilly Hoedown*, KSUN, Bisbee, AZ, 1948).

17142 Kelley, Don. Sportscaster (WGAR, Cleveland, OH, 1939).

17143 Kelley, Don. Sportscaster (*Don Kelley's Sports Review*, Sunday, Monday through Friday, WLS, Chicago, IL, 1938–1939). Kelley's show was sponsored by the Quaker Oats Company's Little Kurnels cereal.

17144 Kelley, Marian. COM-HE (WKLO, Louisville, KY, 1951).

17145 Kelley, (Mrs.) Marion Booth. News commentator (*Current Topics*, WOR, Newark, NJ, 1933).

17146 Kelley, Marj [Marge]. COM-HE (KORE, Eugene, OR, 1960).

17147 Kelley, Welbourn. Writer Kelley wrote *King's Row.*

17148 Kelli, Paul. Leader (Paul Kelli's Orchestra playing from the Il Trovatore Roof Garden Cafe with intermission solos by singer Mort Harris, KFRC, San Francisco, CA, 1925).

17149 Kellick, I.F. Newscaster (WCAX, Burlington, VT, 1948).

17150 Kellman, Lillian. Violinist (WARS, New York, NY, 1927).

17151 Kellner, Murray [Maury]. Violinist (WJZ, New York, NY, 1927). Leader (Murray Kellner's Orchestra featured on the *Checker Cabbies* program, WOR, Newark, NJ, 1929).

17152 Kellogg, Esther. Violinist (WFLA, Clearwater, FL, 1928).

17153 Kellogg, Jack. Newscaster (KJBS, San Francisco, CA, 1942).

17154 Kellogg, Mary Ryan. Pianist (KJBS, San Francisco, CA, 1925).

17155 Kellogg, May Belle. Pianist (WIND, Gary, IN, 1934).

17156 Kellogg, Mildred. Singer (WBRY, Waterbury, CT, 1941).

17157 Kellogg, Ray and Bill Hatch. Violinist and pianist duo (KFWB, Hollywood, CA, 1925–1926).

17158 *Kellogg's Melody Time*. Charles A. Noble hosted the musical program sponsored by Kellogg's cereals. Tony Russell, the Happy Sisters and xylophonist Salvy Cavicchio were featured (15 min., Wednesday, 6:15–6:30 P.M., WBZ-WBZA, Boston-Springfield, MA, 1937).

17159 Kelly, Andrew. Radio philosopher (*Horse Sense Philosopher*, Sunday, 7:15–&:30 P.M., NBC, 1933).

17160 Kelly, Betty. Soprano (KLX, Oakland, CA, 1929).

17161 Kelly, Bob. Sportscaster (WGAR, Cleveland, OH, 1937).

17162 Kelly, Caryll. Singer (WEEI, Boston, MA, 1936; WICC, Bridgeport, CT, 1930).

17163 Kelly, Charles. Newscaster (WJHL, Johnson City, TN, 1941).

17164 Kelly, Dan. Organist (*Dan Kelly*, instr. mus. prg., WHP, Harrisburg, PA, 1936).

17165 Kelly, Dan. Singer (*Dan Kelly*, vcl. mus. prg., WCAU, Philadelphia, PA, 1935). Leader (*Dan Kelly Orchestra*, instr. mus. prg., WCAU, 1936–1937).

17166 Kelly, Dan L. "Danny." Newscaster (WRDO, Augusta, ME, 1946). DJ (*1400 Club*, WRDO, 1949–1955).

17167 Kelly, Dick. Leader (Dick Kelly Orchestra, WTIC, Hartford, CT, 1926).

17168 Kelly, Ed. Tenor (KFWB, Hollywood, CA, 1925).

17169 Kelly, Edith. Soprano (WHAA, Iowa City, IA, 1924).

17170 Kelly, Frank. Announcer (WHAM, Rochester, NY, 1925).

17171 Kelly, Gene. Sportscaster (WIBC, Indianapolis, IN, 1946–1947; *Kelly's Klubhouse*, WXLW, Indianapolis, IN, 1949).

17172 Kelly, Gene. DJ (*Saturday Serenade*, WNDR, Syracuse, NY, 1947; WPEN, Philadelphia, PA, 1950; WPTZ, Philadelphia, PA, 1953).

17173 Kelly, George. Leader (George Kelly and his Record-Recording Orchestra, WIP, Philadelphia, PA, 1923).

17174 Kelly, George. Pianist (WFAA, Dallas, TX, 1925).

17175 Kelly, Gordon. Newscaster (KGGC, San Francisco, CA, 1937).

17176 Kelly, Grace. COM-HE (WBAT, Marion, IL, 1951).

17177 Kelly, H.A. Leader (*H.A. Kelly's Gospel Singers*, vcl. mus. prg., KGHI, Little Rock, AR, 1928).

17178 Kelly, Hazel. COM-HE (WEEU, Reading, PA, 1949).

17179 Kelly, Jack. Leader (*Jack Kelly Orchestra*, instr. mus. prg., WCFL, Chicago, IL, 1936).

17180 Kelly, Jack. Sportscaster (KMA, Shenandoah, IA, 1942).

17181 Kelly, James. Actor Kelly was in the cast of *Nona From Nowhere.*

17182 Kelly, Joe. Newscaster (KILO, Grand Forks, ND, 1948).

17183 Kelly, Joseph. Newscaster (WHDH, Boston, MA, 1944).

17184 Kelly, Joyce. COM-HE (WBBW, Youngstown, OH, 1957).

17185 Kelly, Karen. COM-HE (WBBW, Youngstown, OH, 1957).

17186 Kelly, Kathleen. Violinist (KLDS, 1926).

17187 Kelly, Marie. Reader (WEBH, Chicago, IL, 1924).

17188 Kelly, Michael. Newscaster (KNX, Hollywood, CA, 1931).

17189 Kelly, Mildred. Pianist (WTAM, Cleveland, OH, 1924).

17190 Kelly, Nancy. COM-HE (KRIB, Mason City, IA, 1956).

17191 Kelly, Nancy. Actress Kelly was a cast member of the daytime serial program *Aunt Jenny* aka *Aunt Jenny's True Life Stories.*

17192 Kelly, Ned. Sportscaster and ice hockey play-by-play broadcaster (KROW, Oakland, CA, 1941).

17193 Kelly, Pat. Sportscaster (*Kentucky Sports Review*, WSFC, Somerset, KY, 1949).

17194 Kelly, Patrick. Announcer on the *Halsey Stuart* program (NBC-Red, New York, NY, late 1920s.

17195 Kelly, Peacock. Leader (*Peacock Kelly Orchestra*, instr. mus. prg., WCFL, Chicago, IL, 1937).

17196 Kelly, Robert. Newscaster (WMAN, Maranette, WI, 1942). Sportscaster (WMAN, 1942).

17197 Kelly, Roger S. Newscaster (WMBS, Uniontown, PA, 1941).

17198 Kelly, Tom. Newscaster (KCMO, Kansas City, MO, 1937–1938; *Sears Global News*, *Butternut News Roundup*, WOOD, Grand Rapids, MI, 1947). DJ (*Wax Works*, WOOD, 1947; WJMS, Ironwood, MI). Sportscaster (WCMO, Kansas City, KS, 1937–1939).

17199 Kelly, Walter C. Vaudeville star who appeared on the *General Motors Family Party* (NBC, 1927) and other network shows in the 1920s. A great vaudeville favorite, Kelly was famous for his racial and often racist comedy routines. An example of his racist stories was the one in which a Black came into his "court" and said, "I didn't do nothing, judge. The railroad ran over my mule and they won't pay me, and they won't give me back my rope. When Kelly asked, "What rope?" The man replied, "De rope I done tied de mule on the track with."

17200 Kelly, Warren Michael. Newscaster (WBNY, Buffalo, NY, 1940). DJ (WJR, Detroit, MI, 1947; *Music Hall*, WJR, 1950).

17201 Kelman, Ed. DJ (*Record Time*, KBMN, Bozeman, MT, 1949).

17202 Kelpe, Henry. Newscaster (KOIL, Omaha, NE, 1947). DJ (KOIL, 1949).

17203 Kelsey, John. Newscaster (WHOM, Jersey City, NJ, 1941).

17204 Kelsey, John D. "Jack." Writer Kelsey wrote *Just Plain Bill* and *My Best Girls.*

17205 Kelsey, LeRoy H. Reader of his original poems (WOS, Jefferson City, MO, 1925).

17206 Kelsey, Maude Q. COM-HE (WGCD, Chester, SC, 1951).

17207 Kelsey, Norman. Newscaster (WCHV, Charlottesville, VA, 1945–1947). DJ (WCHV, 1954).

17208 Kelsey, Walter. Leader (*Walter Kelsey Orchestra*, instr. mus. prg., NBC, 1938).

17209 Kelso, Bill. Sportscaster (KMTR, Hollywood, CA, 1937). DJ (KOPO, Tucson, AZ, 1956).

17210 Keltner, Bill. DJ (WAYE, Baltimore, MD, 1957).

17211 Kelton, Dick. Sportscaster (*Sports Digest* and *Diamond Dust*, WBIS, Bristol, CT, 1950).

17212 Kelton, Pert. Talented comic actress Kelton was featured on the *Blondie* situation comedy with Penny Singleton and Arthur Lake. *It's Always Albert* with Arnold Stang and Jan Murray; *The Magnificent Montague* with Monty Wooley and Anne Seymour; the *Milton Berle Show* with Berle, Arnold Stang and Bert Gordon; and *The Stuart Erwin Show* with Erwin and Peggy Conklin. Unfortunately, Kelton's broadcast career was shortened when *Red Channels* magazine accused her of Communist sympathies.

17213 Kelty, William H. Newscaster (NBC, 1945).

17214 Kelvin, John. Tenor (*John Kelvin*, vcl. mus. prg., 15 min., Thursday, 5:30–5:45 P.M., CBS, 1931; *John Kelvin, Irish Tenor*, vcl. mus. prg., 15 min., Weekly, 5:00–5:15 P.M., CBS, 1935). Kelvin was accompanied by the Vincent Sorey orchestra.

17215 Kemp, Ed. Tenor (WHT, Chicago, IL, 1926).

17216 Kemp, Evelyn. Pianist (KFWB, Hollywood, CA and KNX, Los Angeles, CA, 1928).

17217 Kemp, Hal. Leader (Hal Kemp's University of North Carolina Orchestra, featuring the singing sisters team of Leota and Lola Lane "the Queens of Harmony," WMAK, Buffalo, NY, 1926; Hal Kemp and his Recording Orchestra, WHAS, Louisville, KY, 1927; Hal Kemp Orchestra, WLS, Chicago, IL, 1928). In 1928, Kemp's radio and recording band included: Kemp, ldr.-clr.-as. and vcl; Bob Mayhew and Earl Geiger, t.; Wendell "Gus" Mayhew, tb. and vcls.; Jack Mayhew, clr. and as.; Ben Williams, clr., as. and bar.; Saxie Dowell, cl., ts. and vcls.; Brom Sulser, v.; John Scott Trotter, p. and a.; Ollie Humphries, bj.; Skinny Ennis, d. and vcls.; and Jim Mullen, tba. The band continued broadcasting in the 1930s (*Hal Kemp Orchestra*, mus. prg., CBS, 1934; NBC, 1935; MBS, 1935–1936).

17218 Kemp, Russ. Leader (Russ Kemp's Orchestra, KFWA, Odgen, UT, 1926 and KFXF, Colorado Springs, CO, 1926).

17219 Kemper, Lou. Newscaster (KVOO, Tulsa, OK, 1938; WFAA, Dallas, TX, 1946).

17220 Kemper, Robert S. DJ (*Fan Fare*, KSGM, Ste. Genevieve, MO, 1950).

17221 *(The) Ken Maynard Show*. Popular cowboy motion picture star Ken Maynard starred on the dramatic sketch about western life that was sponsored by Round-Up Soda. There was plenty of action for Maynard and even some love interest on the program (15 min., Monday-Wednesday-Friday, 6:45–7:00 P.M., KFWB, Los Angeles, CA, 1936).

17222 *(The) Ken Murray Show*. Comedian Murray was supported by tenor Phil Regan and the Russ Morgan Orchestra on the variety show (CBS, 1936). Cast for the *Ken Murray Show* over the years included: Eve Arden, Tony Labriola, Ken Murray, Phil Regan, Shirley Ross and Marlyn Stuart. Music was by the Lud Gluskin and Russ Morgan orchestras. Ken England and David Freedman were the program's writers. On Murray's later 1938 show, he was assisted by a stooge named Oswald, played by Tony Labriola. An example of their humor was this:

> MURRAY: What do you mean the name of the song is part of an auto? You mean oil? I've got that oil feeling.
>
> OSWALD: O-O-O-H No! I got it. It's four wheel brakes.
>
> MURRAY: Four wheel brakes?
>
> OSWALD: Yeah, Four Wheel Brake the News to Mother.

*See **Laugh with Ken Murray**.*

17223 Kenan, Dan C. Newscaster (*Tomorrow's Headlines Tonight*, KHBG, Okmulgee, OK, 1948).

17224 Kendall, Cy. Actor Kendall was in the cast of *Aunt Mary*, *Big Town* and *Tarzan*.

17225 Kendall, Jenny G. Pianist (WGR, Buffalo, NY, 1925).

17226 Kendrick, Alexander. News analyst (CBS, 1947–1948).

17227 Kendrick, D. E. Announcer (WFIW, Hopkinsville, KY, 1925).

17228 Kendrick, Dorothy. Pianist (*Dorothy Kendrick*, instr. mus. prg., NBC, 1935).

17229 Kendrick, Elmer. Singer (KTBI, Los Angeles, CA, 1926).

17230 Kendrick, James. Announcer (KFRC, San Francisco, CA, 1928).

17231 Kendrick, Rexford. Announcer (WCGU, Brooklyn, NY, 1928).

17232 Kendrick, Richard. Actor Kendrick was in the cast of *Portia Faces Life*.

17233 Kenin, Herman. Leader-guitarist (Herman Kenin and his Multinomah Hotel Orchestra, KGW, Portland, OR, 1926–27). The band's personnel included: Joe Barris and Ellis Kimball, t.; Vernon Leathers, tb.; Glen Johnston, as.; Press Watkins, as. and vcls.; Tom Sandoval, clr. and ts.; Jack Scott, p.; Van Fleming, bj. and vcls.; Jim Taft, sb.; and Harry Logan, d.

17234 Kennard, Ellen Thompson. Soprano on the *Sea Memories* program (WPG, Atlantic City, NJ, 1929).

17235 Kennard, Ken. Leader (Ken Kennard and his Kentucky Ramblers Orchestra, WHAS, Louisville, KY, 1925).

17236 Kennard, S. R. Announcer (WFBR, Baltimore, MD, 1925).

17237 Kennard, Stewart. Sportscaster (WFBR, Baltimore, MD, 1940–1947).

17238 Kennebrew, Dick. Newscaster (WDEC, Americus, GA, 1947).

17239 Kennedy, Banks. Pianist (WEBH, Chicago, IL, 1925).

17240 Kennedy, Bill. Actor Kennedy was in the cast of *Nobody's Children* daytime serial program.

17241 Kennedy, Bob. Newscaster (WDSM, Superior, WI, 1941).

17242 Kennedy, Cecil. Bass (WHN, New York, NY, 1928).

17243 Kennedy, Dion. Organist (*Dion Kennedy*, instr. mus. prg., NBC, 1934).

17244 Kennedy, Ed. Sportscaster (WSPR, Springfield, MA, 1939).

17245 Kennedy, Ed. Sportscaster (*Sports Eye*, WKRC, Cincinnati, OH, 1953–1959; *Sports Vue*, WKRC, 1960).

17246 Kennedy, (Mrs.) Frank. Blues singer (WFLA, Clearwater, FL, 1928).

17247 Kennedy, Glen. Leader (Glen Kennedy Dance Orchestra featured on the *Pajama Party Program*, KFWI, South San Francisco, CA, 1926).

17248 Kennedy, Irving. Tenor (*Irving Kennedy*, vcl. mus. prg., NBC, 1935).

17249 Kennedy, John B. Announcer-newscaster (WJZ, New York, NY, 1926). Announcer-host Kennedy played the role of the "Editor," (Uncle Henry, the host), on the *Collier Radio Hour* (NBC,1929). In the following decades Kennedy remained busy (*John B. Kennedy, News*, NBC-Red, 1934; news commentator, *RCA Magic Key of Radio*, NBC, 1937; *People's Rally*, NBC, 1938–1940; *Here's John B. Kennedy*, CBS, 1942, NBC-Blue, 1944–1945; WNEW, 1945; *Eye-Witness News*, WFIL, Philadelphia, PA, 1948).

17250 Kennedy, Kevin. Sportscaster (WNYC, New York, NY, 1946; *Sports Panel*, WNYC, 1947).

17251 Kennedy, Lew. Singer (WCAE, Pittsburgh, PA, 1924).

17252 Kennedy, Lou. Newscaster (*News and Farm Review*, WORZ, Orlando, FL, 1947). DJ (*Studio Party*, WORZ, 1948).

17253 Kennedy, Marie. COM-HE (WEEB, Southern Pines, NC, 1956).

17254 Kennedy, Michael. DJ (*Sports and Jive*, WEPM, Martinsburg, WV, 1947).

17255 Kennedy, Pat. Tenor (*Pat Kennedy*, vcl. mus. prg., CBS and NBC, 1935).

17256 Kennedy, Ralph. Newscaster (KUOA, Siloam Springs, AR, 1940–1941).

17257 Kennedy, Ray. DJ (*Rhyme Does Pay*, WRVA, Richmond, VA, 1947).

17258 Kennedy, Reed. Baritone (*Reed Kennedy*, vcl. mus. prg., NBC, 1934).

17259 Kennedy, Terry. DJ (*Spins and Needles*, WBCK, Battle Creek, MI, 1949).

17260 Kennedy, Vann M. Newscaster (KTCB, Austin, TX, 1939).

17261 Kennedy, Walter B. Organist (KGO, Oakland, CA, 1925).

17262 Kennedy, Willard. Newscaster (WWJ, Detroit, MI, 1940).

17263 Kennelly, John. Sportscaster (WNBF, Binghampton, NY, 1960).

17264 Kenney, Andy. Leader (*Andy Kenney Orchestra*, instr. mus. prg., WCCO, Minneapolis–St. Paul, MN, 1930s).

17265 Kenney, Edward. Newscaster (WCPO, Cincinnati, OH, 1945).

17266 **Kenney, Fred.** Newscaster (WAGA, Atlanta, GA, 1942; WROL, Knoxville, TN, 1944; *News Hi-Lights*, WAOV, Vincennes, IN, 1948).

17267 **Kenney, Paul.** Newscaster (*Sunday Noon News*, WMOA, Marietta, OH, 1948). Sportscaster (*Sports Eye*, WMOA, 1949).

17268 **Kennison, Lois.** Actress Kennison appeared on the *Today's Children* daytime serial program.

17269 **Kenny, H.B.** Newscaster (WMBR, Jacksonville, FL, 1944; WSSV, Petersburg, VA, 1945; WLEE, Richmond, VA, 1947).

17270 **Kenny, Mardi.** Soprano (WGY, Schenectady, NY, 1924).

17271 **Kenny, Mart.** Leader (*Mart Kenny Orchestra*, instr. mus. prg., WOR, Newark, NJ, 1936).

17272 **Kenny, Tom.** Baritone (KFRC, San Francisco, CA, 1925).

17273 ***Kenrad Cabin Nights.*** Singer William Burns, the Cotton Pickers vocal quartet, the piano team of Retting and Platt and an orchestra conducted by J.J. Herbuveaux were featured on this variety show. The program usually contained a dramatic sketch with a musical background (30 min., Monday, 10:00–10:30 P.M., NBC-Blue Network, 1929).

17274 **Kenski, M.** Newscaster (WHOM, Jersey City, NJ, 1940).

17275 **Kent, Alan (Bradley).** Announcer-newscaster and writer Kent worked on *Blackstone the Magic Detective* (announcer), *Duffy's Tavern* (writer), *Frank Crumit and Julia Sanderson* (announcer), *Hobby Lobby* (announcer) and *Pepper Young's Family* (announcer). DJ (WOR, New York, NY, 1949).

17276 **Kent, Bob (Robert).** Newscaster (WHIS, Bluefield, WV, 1944–1945). Sportscaster (WHIS, 1945).

17277 **Kent, Bob.** DJ (*Night Owl Show*, WBUD, Morrisville, PA, 1947).

17278 **Kent, Carl, Jr.** Newscaster (WAKR, Akron, OH, 1941–1942). Sportscaster (WAKR, 1940–1942).

17279 **Kent, Elaine.** Actress Kent appeared on the daytime serial programs *John's Other Wife*, *Just Plain Bill*, *Little Women*, *Stella Dallas*, *Our Gal Sunday* and *Valiant Lady*.

17280 **Kent, George.** News analyst (*Texas and World News*, KTBB, Tyler, TX, 1948).

17281 **Kent, Hal.** DJ (*The Brighter Side*, WGBS, Miami, FL, 1952–1954).

17282 **Kent, Harold.** News analyst (*I See By the Paper*, WENE, Endicott, NY, 1947).

17283 **Kent, Herb.** DJ (WBEE, Chicago, IL, 1957).

17284 **Kent, John.** Newscaster (WWL, New Orleans, LA, 1944–1945).

17285 **Kent; Lee.** Leader (Lee Kent and his Terrapache Orchestra, KFWB, Hollywood, CA, 1925).

17286 **Kent, Mona.** Writer Kent worked on the *Carters of Elm Street* program.

17287 **Kent, Patsy.** DJ (*Night Flight*, WMIE, Miami, FL, 1948).

17288 **Kent, Rikel.** Actor-director Kent worked on *Life of Mary Southern* (actor), *Man I Married* (actor) and *Valiant Lady* (director).

17289 **Kent, Stella.** Soprano (WSAI, Cincinnati, OH, 1925).

17290 **Kent, Susan.** COM-HE (WFBR, Baltimore, MD, 1951).

17291 **Kentgen, Selma.** Soprano (WEAF, New York, NY, 1925).

17292 **Kentner Green Hill Farms Orchestra.** Commercial band (WDAR, Philadelphia, PA, 1924).

17293 **Kenton, Stanley "Stan."** Leader (*Stan Kenton Orchestra*, instr. mus. prg., KFEL, Denver, CO, 1942).

17294 ***Kentucky Club Orchestra.*** Instr. mus. prg. (WHAS, Louisville, KY, 1933).

17295 **Kentucky Hotel Orchestra.** Hotel dance band (WHAS, Louisville, KY, 1928).

17296 **Kentucky Serenaders.** Orchestra (KYW, Chicago, IL, 1928).

17297 **(The) Kentucky Wonderbean.** CW music singer Walter Peterson accompanied himself on the harmonica and guitar on his popular music show (WLS, Chicago, IL, 1926–1930). *See* **Peterson, Walter**.

17298 **Kenward, Jack.** DJ (*Once Over Lightly*, WMID, Atlantic City, NJ, 1947).

17299 **Kenwood Club Orchestra.** Club band (WEBJ, New York, NY, 1926).

17300 **Kenworthy, Robert D.** Tenor (KOA, Denver, CO, 1926).

17301 **Kenyon, Adele.** COM-HE (WLNA, Peekskill, NY, 1951).

17302 **Kenyon, Douglass Morrow.** Sportscaster (WBAP, Fort Worth, TX, 1937).

17303 **Kephart, Margaret.** Pianist (KOA, Denver, CO, 1926).

17304 **Kephart, Victor and Marjorie Kephart.** Harmony singing (WHT, Chicago, IL, 1928).

17305 **Kepler, A. Howard.** Singer (KFWM, Oakland, CA, 1927).

17306 **Keplinger, Dick.** Newscaster (KJR, Seattle, WA, 1938–1942; KOMO, Seattle, WA, 1942).

17307 **Keppler, (Mrs.) A.E.** Violinist (WKAF, Milwaukee, WI, 1926).

17308 **Kerchival, Mary.** COM-HE (WSAZ, Huntington, WV, 1956).

17309 **Kerk, Loretta [Lorita].** Pianist (WFI, Philadelphia, PA, 1923–1928).

17310 **Kerlin, J.C.** Newscaster (WGBF, Evansville, IN, 1945; *What Goes On Here*, WGBF, 1947–1948).

17311 **Kerman, David.** Actor Kerman was in the cast of *Those We Love*.

17312 **Kern, Carolyn.** COM-HE (KERN, Bakersfield, CA, 1956).

17313 **Kern, Eleanor.** Night club singer (WOR, Newark, NJ, 1928).

17314 **Kern, Genetta.** COM-HE (WKBV, Richmond, IL, 1951).

17315 **Kern, Henrietta.** Concert soprano (WBAL, Baltimore, MD, 1928).

17316 **Kern, Margaret.** Soprano (WBAL, Baltimore, MD, 1927).

17317 **Kerner's Crazy Water Hotel Orchestra.** This country music group was sponsored by the Crazy Water Crystals company. They broadcast regularly on *The Midnight Frolic* program from the lobby of the Crazy Wells Hotel located in Mineral Wells, Texas (WBAP, San Antonio, TX, 1925).

17318 **Kerns, Vay [Fay].** Soprano (KFAE, Pittsburgh, PA, 1924).

17319 **Kerowitz, Esther.** Violinist (KFWB, Hollywood, CA, 1926).

17320 **Kerr, Alfred.** Sportscaster (WHBQ, Memphis, TN, 1944). Newscaster (WHBQ, 1945).

17321 **Kerr, Charlie.** Leader (Charlie Kerr Orchestra broadcasting from Philadelphia's Cafe L'Aiglon, WIP, Philadelphia, PA 1922, one of the first "band remote" broadcasts; Hotel St. James Orchestra, WIP, 1923–24; Charlie Kerr and his Orchestra, WCAU, Philadelphia, PA, 1926). Kerr's early band included: Kerr, ldr. and d.; Leo McConville, t.; Joe de Luca, tb.; Jerry de Nasi and Vincenzo d'Imperio, clr., ss., and as.; Mike Trafficante, tba.; and Robert McCracken, p. Kerr's band also was active in the 1930s: (*Charlie Kerr Orchestra*, mus. prg., WCAU, Philadelphia, PA, 1935–1936).

17322 **Kerr, Doris.** Singer (*Doris Kerr*, vcl. mus. prg., CBS, 1936–1937).

17323 **Kerr (Doris) and Phillips (Howard).** Singing team (*Kerr and Phillips*, vcl. mus. prg., CBS, 1937).

17324 **Kerr, Jane.** COM-HE (KIDO, Boise, ID, 1949).

17325 **Kerr, Myrl.** COM-HE (KTKR, Taft, CA, 1955).

17326 **Kerr, Rex.** DJ (*Teen Age Party Time* and *Request Granted*, KEPO, El Paso, TX, 1950).

17327 **Kerr, Ruth.** Contralto (WTIC, Hartford, CT, 1927).

17328 **Kerr, Shirley.** COM-HE (WKST, New Castle, PA, 1951).

17329 **Kerr, Stewart.** DJ (*Morning Call*, WANN, Annapolis, MD, 1947).

17330 **Kerr, Thompson B.** Pianist who performed frequently on the *Two Boys and a Girl* music program (WOR, Newark, NJ, 1929).

17331 **Kerr, William.** Baritone (WGHP, Detroit, MI, 1926).

17332 **Kerr, William.** Newscaster (WHBQ, Memphis, TN, 1945).

17333 **Kerr and Phillips (Doris Kerr and Howard Phillips).** Singing team, CBS, 1937).

17334 **Kerry, Katherine.** News commentator (KQW, San Jose, CA, 1948).

17335 **Kerry's Creole Orchestra.** Popular California band (KFI, Los Angeles, CA, 1925).

17336 **Kerrick, Lee.** COM-HE (WSIV, Pekin, IL, 1949).

17337 **Kershner, Dad.** Kershner conducted *Devotions*, a half-hour morning program broadcast six days a week (WLW, Cincinnati, OH, 1928–1929).

17338 **Kertchbaum, Marjorie.** Violinist (KHJ, Los Angeles, CA, 1924).

17339 **Kesch, Katherine.** Reader (KDKA, Pittsburgh, PA, 1923).

17340 Kessel, Harry. Singer (WHB, Kansas City, MO, 1928).

17341 Kesselman, Louis C. Newscaster (WOCU, Columbus, OH, 1945).

17342 Kesselring, Joseph O. Tenor (WGR, Buffalo, NY, 1925).

17343 Kessen, Bill. DJ (*Insomnia Serenade*, WRUF, Gainesville, FL, 1947).

17344 Kesseng, Helene. Soprano (WSAI, Cincinnati, OH, 1925; KSD, St. Louis, MO, 1926).

17345 *(The) Kessinger Brothers*. The Kessingers — Clark and Luke — were a CW singing team who accompanied themselves on the guitar and fiddle (WOBU, Charleston, WV, 1930).

17346 Kessinger, Glen. DJ (WMBD, Peoria, IL, 1950).

17347 Kessler, Blanche Reynolds. Reader (WCBD, Zion, IL, 1925).

17348 Kessler, David E. Newscaster (WHAM, Rochester, NY, 1944–1945; *Today and Yesterday*, WHAM, 1946–1948).

17349 Kessler, Thelma. Leader (*Thelma Kessler Orchestra*, instr. mus. prg., WCAU, Philadelphia, PA, 1934).

17350 Kethley, Agnes. Newscaster (KRGV, Weslaco, TX, 1941).

17351 Kettering, Frank. Leader (*Frank Kettering Orchestra*, instr. mus. prg., KMOX, St. Louis, MO, 1942).

17352 Ketts, Mary. COM-HE (KKOG, Odgen, UT, 1956–1957).

17353 Keulander, Edith. Soprano (WMBB, Homewood, IL and WOK, Chicago, IL, 1928).

17354 Kever, Bonnie. COM-HE (KCPX, Salt Lake City, UT, 1960).

17355 Key, Barbara. DJ (*Coffee Time*, KWSH, Wewoka, OK, 1952).

17356 Key, Jerry. DJ (*Make Way for Music*, WPRE, Prairie Du Chien, WI, 1954).

17357 Key, Jim "Jimmy." DJ (*Mountain Music*, KLPR, Oklahoma City, OK, 1947; *Jimmy's Program*, KANS, Wichita, KS, 1948; *Sunnyside Up*, KLRA, Little Rock, AR, 1952).

17358 Key, Opal. Reader (KHJ, Los Angeles, CA, 1925).

17359 *Key Men Quartet*. Vcl. prg. by otherwise unidentified performers (WOR, Newark, NJ, 1936).

17360 Keyes, Alice. Miss Keyes told children's stories (WJAR, Providence, RI, 1925).

17361 Keyes, Baron. Popular singer (KHJ, Los Angeles, CA, 1928). In the early 1930s on the Pacific Coast, Keyes appeared on the popular children's program, *Clackety Clack the Little Wooden Man.*

17362 Keyne-Gordon, Philip. Mr. Keyne-Gordon was an imaginary conservative commentator who loudly ranted and raved against communism, government spending and food subsidy programs. The "hoax" was perpetrated by five Ohio radio employees before the joke was discovered and the program discontinued (MBS, 1942).

17363 Keys, Ennis. COM-HE (WAAG, Adel, GA, 1955).

17364 *Keys to Happiness*. Dr. Sigmund Spaeth — later famous as "The Tune Detective" — taught radio piano lessons for beginners on his program (15 min., Saturday, 11:30–11:45 A.M., NBC-Red, 1932).

17365 Keyser, (Mrs.) J.H. Soprano (KGO, Oakland, CA, 1924).

17366 Keyser, Lakki. COM-HE (WEKY, Richmond, KY, 1956).

17367 Keyser, Warren. DJ (*Musical Nightcap*, WILM, Wilmington, DE, 1948–1949).

17368 *(The) Keystone Barn Dance Party*. Lulu Belle and various other stars of the *National Barn Dance* program and WLS station performers appeared on this program sponsored by the Keystone Steel and Wire Company. The performers included Chuck, Roy and Christine, the Prairie Ramblers, Sod Busters, DeZurik Sisters and Archie and the Kentucky Girls (30 min., Saturday, 8:30–9:00 P.M., WLS, Chicago, IL, 1936).

17369 *(The) Keystone Chronicle*. The daytime dramatic serial portrayed the lives of employees of a small rural newspaper (15 min., Saturday, 1:30–1:45 P.M., NBC-Blue, 1930).

17370 KFAB Symphony Orchestra. Station's classical group (KFAB, Lincoln, NE, 1928).

17371 KFAC Orchestra. The station orchestra led by Wilbur Funk included Edward Moniot, bj.; Marion Jones, p.; Eldin Benge, c.; Morris Burke, bh.; and Herbert Brooks, v. (KFAC, Glendale, CA, 1922).

17372 *KFI Midnight Follies*. An early version of the program presented by Don Meaney was broadcast from 11:00 P.M. to 3:00 A.M. on KFI (Los Angles, CA). Various stars of the stage and screen were featured. William Beaudine, Carey Wilson and Harry Franklin served as the program's host at different periods (KFI, Los Angeles, CA, 1925–1926). Later, Paul Roberts hosted the late evening music program featuring hot blues singers Helen Geste and Gladys Palmer (KFI, Los Angeles, CA, 1927).

17373 KFI Oratorio Society. Vocal group directed by Mrs. Harry K. Brown (KFI, Los Angeles, CA, 1925).

17374 KFI's Women's Interest Program. Alice White, head of the station's Women's Interest Department, conducted the program. One of the topics she discussed was the making of "Cream Soups and Cream Sauces" (KFI, Los Angeles, CA, 1926).

17375 KFRC Concert Orchestra. Station band directed by Frank Moss (KRFC, San Francisco, CA, 1928–1929).

17376 KFRC Dance Orchestra. Harry Simon directed the station dance band (KFRC, San Francisco, CA, 1928).

17377 KFRC Hawaiians Orchestra. Hawaiian music group (KFRC, San Francisco, CA, 1927).

17378 KFRC Little Symphony Orchestra. Station musical organization directed by Frank Moss (KFRC, San Francisco, CA, 1926).

17379 KFSG Ukulele Band. Thirty-five member instrumental group directed by Essie Brinkley (KFSG, Los Angeles, CA, 1925).

17380 KFWI Male Quartet. The quartet contained tenors Gwynfi Jones and Edwin Stott, baritone P.H. Ward and bass Henry L. Perry (KFWI, San Francisco, CA, 1926).

17381 KFWI Players Trio. Violinist Bernice Perrington, cellist Gertrude Adams and pianist Rachel Ward were members of the studio music group (KFWI, San Francisco, CA, 1926).

17382 KFWM Trio. Trio of pianist Evelyn Ware, violinist Violet Matkovich and vocalist Frachon Seyer (KFWM, Oakland, CA, 1926).

17383 KGO Little Symphony. Station music group directed by Carl Rhodehamel assisted by Arthur S. Garbett. Henry Spies, the orchestra's first horn soloist, was frequently featured (KGO, Oakland, CA, 1925).

17384 KGO Players. The dramatic group broadcast such plays as George Bernard Shaw's four act comedy, "You Can Never Tell." The play was directed by Wilda Wilson Church. Rose Brown was one of the featured players (KGO, Oakland, CA, 1925–1929). *See* **Church, Wilda Wilson.**

17385 *KGY Western Show*. Each morning announcer Ray Harris hosted the early morning CW music show that featured such performers as Tex Mitchell, the Slater Children and the Fat Davis band (Weekdays, KGY, Olympia, WA, 1950s).

17386 "KH." Designation for announcer Kolin Hager (WGY, Schenectady, NY, 1923). *See* **Hager, Kolin.**

17387 Khariton, Michael. Pianist (NBC, 1928).

17388 Kibbe, Charlena. COM-HE (WSPR, Springfield, MA, 1949).

17389 Kibbey, Jean. Singer on the *Nite Caps on Lake Erie* program (WJAX, Cleveland, OH, 1924).

17390 Kibby, Gordon. DJ (*Gordon Kibby Show* and *Knights of the Turntable,* WFUR, Grand Rapids, MI, 1949; *Anything Goes*, WFUR, 1950).

17391 Kibler, Garnet. Blues singer (KFI, Los Angeles, CA, 1926).

17392 Kiczales, Hyla. Executive (WOV, New York, NY, 1930s). Kiczales was the general manager of station WOV; she was another talented woman who ran a New York radio station.

17393 Kidd, Franklin. Tenor (WMBB, Chicago, IL, 1926).

17394 Kidd, Pat. COM-HE (WMOK, Metropolis, IL, 1954).

17395 Kidder, Frank J. Bass (WGI, Medford Hillside, MA, 1922).

17396 Kidder, Walter. Baritone (WEEI, Boston, MA, 1928. *Songs of Yesteryear*, vcl. mus. prg., WNAC, Boston, MA, 1934).

17397 *Kiddies Club*. An early children's program conducted by an unidentified performer (WNAC, Boston, MA, 1925).

17398 *(The) Kiddies Hour*. Uncle Bill, not otherwise identified, conducted the early children's program (WBAP, Fort Worth, TX, 1925).

17399 *Kiddies Hour*. The program by

and for children first appeared on WKBH (LaCrosse, WI) in 1926 and continued well into the 1940's.

17400 ***(The) Kidoodlers*** (aka ***The Kidoodlers Quartette***). Mus. prg. with humor — a cross between the Hoosier Hot Shots and Spike Jones (NBC, 1934; NBC-Blue, 1937; 15 min., Tuesday, NBC-Blue, 1938).

17401 ***(The) Kids Club.*** Announcer-salesman Bill Foss played the role of "Uncle Billy," who conducted the children's program. He was assisted by "Uncle Jimmy" Nicholson, who eventually took over the program (WCSH, Portland, OR, late 1920s).

17402 **Kiehl, Corynn.** Pianist (KJR, Seattle, WA, 1925).

17403 **Kielman, Lucy Jane.** Singer on the *Comy Time* program with Mary Jane Morrison and Uncle Dave (WIBW, Topeka, KS, 1929).

17404 **Kieny, Marie.** Announcer, pianist and program director (WOW, Omaha, NE, 1925–1929). Kieny had worked at WOW since its opening in 1923, when she began employment as the station's studio hostess.

17405 **Kienzle, George.** Newscaster (WHP, Harrisburg, PA, 1946; *1:55 News*, WLAN, Lancaster, PA, 1948).

17406 **Kierman, Ray.** Newscaster (WEEI, Boston, MA, 1941–1942, 1944–1945).

17407 **Kiernan, Walter.** News commentator (NBC-Blue, 1944–1945; *Kiernan's News Corner*, ABC, 1945; WJZ, New York, NY and ABC, 1946–1947; *Kiernan's Corner*, ABC, 1948). DJ (ABC, 1947). Kiernan displayed dry wit and interesting insights on his quarter-hour *Kiernan's Corner* talk show.

17408 **Kiersten, Dorothy.** Singer (WINS, New York, NY, 1936).

17409 **Kieselbach, Walter.** Baritone (WEAF, New York, NY, 1925).

17410 **Kievsky, Lena.** Pianist (WOR, Newark, NJ, 1925).

17411 **Kiff, Claude.** Leader (Claude Kiff's Tavern Band, KSL, Salt Lake City, UT, 1929).

17412 **Kihn, Ed.** Newscaster (KDAN, Oroville, CA, 1948).

17413 **Kiker, Becky.** COM-HE (WJMX, Florence, SC, 1957).

17414 **Kilbes, Dorothy.** Pianist (WIP, Philadelphia, PA, 1926).

17415 **Kilbourne, Gordon.** Leader (Gordon Kilbourne's Orchestra, KJR, Seattle, WA, 1925).

17416 **Kildare, (Mrs.) Owen.** Mrs. Kildare talked about developments in radio, its programs and performers (WEBH, Chicago, IL, 1925).

17417 **Kiler, Bob.** Zither player Kiler had been an entertainer for 21 years in the cafes and clubs of San Francisco before appearing on radio (KFRC, San Francisco, CA, 1928).

17418 **Kiley, Tim.** DJ (*Tim and Ed*, WNMP, Evanston, IL, 1948).

17419 **Kilgallen, Dorothy.** News commentator and gossip columnist (*Star Time with Dorothy Kilgallen*, ABC, 1947–1948). Kilgallen also appeared with husband, Richard Kollmar, on their husband and wife talk show, *Dorothy and Dick*. Columnist Kilgallen later appeared on the popular *What's My Line* television program.

17420 **Kilgo, Jimmy.** DJ (WSOC, Charlotte, NC, 1957).

17421 **Kilgore, Gene.** DJ (*Time to Dance*, KRUL, Corvallis, OR, 1947).

17422 **Kilgore, Joe.** DJ (*Milkman's Matinee*, KRES, St. Joseph, MO, 1947; KUSN, St. Joseph, MO, 1956).

17423 **Kilgore, Shirley.** Newscaster (WDSU, New Orleans, LA, 1944).

17424 **Killeen, J.W.** Newscaster (WSAU, Wassau, WI, 1938–1940).

17425 **Killian, Lenore.** Contralto (KHJ, Los Angeles, CA, 1925).

17426 **Killian, Rudy.** Leader (*Rudy Killian Orchestra*, instr. mus. prg., WCAO, Baltimore, MD, 1936).

17427 **Killick, Lawrence F.** Newscaster (WCAX, Burlington, VT, 1945; *Views of the News*, WCAX, 1947).

17428 **Killoran, Mary.** Soprano (WEAF, New York, NY, 1926).

17429 **Kilman, Ed.** Newscaster (KPRC, Houston, TX, 1945).

17430 **Kilmer, Bess [Beth].** COM-HE (KFI, Los Angeles, CA, 1930).

17431 **Kilmer, Bill.** Newscaster (WSGN, Birmingham, AL, 1941).

17432 **Kilmer, (Mrs.) Kilburn.** Reader Kilmer read her son's poetry (*The Poetry of Joyce Kilmer*), WEAF, New York, NY, 1925).

17433 ***(The) Kilmer Family.*** A daytime dramatic serial, the *Kilmer Family* told the story of another "average American family" (15 min., Monday through Friday, 12:15–12:30 P.M., NBC, 1935).

17434 ***Kilowatt Orchestra.*** Instr. mus. prg. (WTMJ, Milwaukee, WI, 1937).

17435 **(The) Kilowatt Twins.** Harmonizing singing team consisting of Maude and Zona Sheridan (WFLA, Clearwater, FL, 1929).

17436 **Kilpack, Bennett (William B. Kilpack).** Actor Kilpack was born in England, February 6, 1888. He began his long radio career in 1927 by appearing on one of NBC's earliest serial dramas, *Wayside Inn*.

17437 **Kilpatrick, Frank.** DJ (*Club 1500*, KXRX, San Jose, CA, 1948).

17438 **Kilpatrick, Reid F.** Sportscaster (*Kilpatrick's Sport Shorts*, professional football play-by-play and boxing blow-by-blow broadcasts, KEHE, Los Angeles, CA, 1937; *Golf Clinic* and *Today in Sports*, KEHE, 1939; KMTR, Hollywood, CA, 1944).

17439 **Kilwen, Leo.** Viola soloist with the WGY Orchestra (WGY, Schenectady, NY, 1925).

17440 **Kimball, Ann.** COM-HE (KDSH, Boise, ID, 1951).

17441 **Kimball, Edward P.** Organist of the Mormon Tabernacle Choir (KSL, Salt Lake City, UT, 1929).

17442 **Kimball, Elizabeth "Betty."** COM-HE (WHAY, New Britain, CT, 1949–1957).

17443 **Kimball, Emerson.** DJ (*Home Songs*, WCOL, Columbus, OH, 1949–1950).

17444 **Kimball, Frederick.** Newscaster (WWNY, Watertown, NY, 1941–1942).

17445 **Kimball (Mr. and Mrs.) Harry.** Tenor and contralto husband and wife singing team (WHO, Des Moines, IA, 1925).

17446 **Kimball, Helen.** COM-HE (WHAY, New Britain, CT, 1954).

17447 **Kimberley, Helene.** Singer (WROK, Rockford, IL, 1939).

17448 **Kimble, Ralph.** Talked about stamp collecting (WMAQ, Chicago, IL, 1931).

17449 **Kimbo Kalohi's Hawaiian Moonlight Five.** Hawaiian music group (WSB, Atlanta, GA, 1924).

17450 **Kimbrel, Joan.** COM-HE (WIPC, Lake Wales, FL, 1955).

17451 **Kimbrell, Fritz.** Newscaster (KDNT, Denton, TX, 1941).

17452 **Kimbrough, (Mrs.) Herbert.** Mrs. Kimbrough performed vocal solos and pianologues (KWSC, Pullman, WA, 1925).

17453 **Kimbrough, LaVerne Askin.** Contralto (KFAE, Pittsburgh, PA, 1924).

17454 **Kimmel, Emma.** Soprano (WFI, Los Angeles, CA, 1925–1927).

17455 ***(The) Kimmel Kiddies.*** A group of children, ages from 4 to 15, sang together and individually and played musical instruments on the program (KMOX, St. Louis, MO, 1926).

17456 **Kinard, Lee W.** DJ (*Rock and Roll Party*, WABZ, Albemarle, NC, 1955).

17457 **Kincaid, Bradley.** Folk singer Kincaid was one of the brightest stars of the *National Barn Dance* program, a show that began as the *WLS Barn Dance* program. He was born in Garrard County, Kentucky in 1895. Kincaid, a graduate of Berea College, began singing on the radio while taking classes at Chicago's YMCA.

His radio career started with a fifteen-minute program on WLS (Chicago, IL,1926) that became so popular that in the fall he became a regular on *The National Barn Dance*, where he stayed for four years. Each year at WLS (1926–1929), where he was billed as "The Kentucky Mountain Boy," Kincaid received more than 100,000 letters. He sold his own song folios, and by the time he left WLS he had sold 400,000 copies. Kincaid always resented the term "hillbilly." Instead he preferred to be called a "singer of mountain songs." Because of his recordings and radio broadcasts, Malone (1968, p. 56) said of Kincaid that he "probably did more to popularize old-time songs and ballads among Americans than any other individual." He was the first country-music radio star. As McCloud (1955, p. 444) puts it, he was the "first major Country music star created by the medium of radio."

Kincaid later had programs on several stations (*Bradley Kincaid*, CW vcl. mus. prg., WCKY, Cincinnati, OH, 1933; NBC, 1934; WBZ, Boston-Springfield, MA, 1935–1936; and WTAM, Cleveland, OH, 1938).

17458 **Kincaid, Clare.** COM-HE (KASH, Eugene, OR, 1957).

17459 **Kincaid, Earsley F.** COM-HE (WILY, Pittsburgh, PA, 1954–1955).

17460 Kincaid, Fred. Sportscaster (WRR, Dallas, TX, 1945–1946; football, hockey and basketball play-by-play, WRR, 1947–1948; WPLT, Paris, TX, 1950; *Sports Extra*, WPLT, 1951–1956).

17461 Kincaid, Margaret. COM-HE (KNIA, Knoxville, IA, 1960).

17462 Kincaid, Mary Joseph. Station director of the dramatic players group (KFWI, San Francisco, CA, 1928).

17463 Kindall, Edna. Pianist (KTHS, Hot Springs, AR, 1937).

17464 *Kindergarten Kapers*. See ***Kaltenmeyer's Kindergarten***.

17465 Kindley, Charles. Newscaster (KVOV, Redding, CA, 1945).

17466 King, Alice. Soprano (KDKA, Pittsburgh, PA, 1927).

17467 King, Annette. Contralto (*Annette King*, vcl. mus. prg., WCFL, Chicago, IL, 1937).

17468 King, Art. Sportscaster (WEEI, Boston, MA, 1949).

17469 King, Belle. Pianist (KTHS, Hot Springs, AR, 1937).

17470 King, Bert. Leader (*Bert King Orchestra*, instr. mus. prg., WOR, Newark, NJ, 1935).

17471 King, Betsy. COM-HE (WIP, Philadelphia, PA, 1935).

17472 King, Bob. DJ (*Wax Works*, KSOO, Sioux Falls, SD, 1948; *Night Editor*, WNAX, Yankton, SD, 1952).

17473 King, Brad. DJ (*Hit the Deck*, WHAN, Charleston, SC, 1947).

17474 King, Cal. King conducted "health exercises" (KFWI, San Francisco, CA, 1927).

17475 King, Carlton "Dad." Announcer and station supervisor "Dad" King was a former motion picture actor and producer (KMTR, Hollywood, CA, 1926).

17476 King, Carol. COM-HE (WCAX, Burlington, VT, 1956).

17477 King, Charles. Tenor (KNX, Los Angeles, CA, 1928).

17478 King, Charles. DJ (*Platter Shop*, WKAL, Utica, NY, 1948–1950).

17479 King, Charlie and Peggy Flynn. Harmony singing team (*Charlie King and Peggy Flynn*, vcl. mus. prg., NBC, 1934).

17480 *King Cowboy Revue*. CW mus. prg. (KFI, Los Angeles, CA, 1939).

17481 King, Cy. Newscaster (WBEN, Buffalo, NY, 1937–1939; WEBR, Buffalo, NY, 1939–1942, 1944–1948).

17482 King, Dave. Newscaster (WIND, Gary, IN, 1945). DJ (*King Komes Kalling*, WBPZ, Loch Haven, PA, 1947).

17483 King, Delmer Randolph "Del." King began his broadcasting career as singer and staff announcer (KMBC, Kansas City, MO, 1927).

17484 King, Dennis. Singer (*Dennis King*, vcl. mus. prg., NBC, 1934).

17485 King, Dennis. Announcer King worked on the *When a Girl Marries* daytime serial program.

17486 King, Dick. DJ (*The Old Town Square*, KITO, San Bernadino, CA, 1950). Sportscaster (KITO, 1955).

17487 King, Doris. Pianist (KPO, San Francisco, CA, 1925).

17488 King, Dorothea. COM-HE (WSPR, Springfield, MA, 1949).

17489 King, Dub. Sportscaster (*Football Time*, WTAW, College Station, TX, 1949).

17490 King, Earl. DJ (*Lem Hawkins Show*, KFGO, Fargo, ND, 1948).

17491 King, Eddie. Newscaster (KGO-KPO, San Francisco, CA, 1941). Sportscaster (KGO-KPO, 1941).

17492 King, Edward "Ed." Director King directed *Believe It or Not*, *David Harum*, *Dimension X*, *Frank Merriwell* and *Just Plain Bill*.

17493 King, Emeline. COM-HE (KBTK, Missoula, MT, 1956).

17494 King, Ethel Jane. COM-HE (KFH, Wichita, KS, 1949).

17495 King, Frances Rockefeller. Managerial (NBC, 1939). As manager of the NBC Artists and Service Department, King was responsible for handling the affairs of the network's singers, actors, comedians and musicians.

17496 King, Fulton A. Newscaster (WTON, Staunton, VA, 1946). Sportscaster (WTON, 1946). DJ (*Coffee Pot*, WTON, 1947–1952).

17497 King, Gene. DJ (*Dr. Jazz*, 30 min., Friday, 10:15–10:45 P.M., WEVD, New York, NY, 1938).

17498 King, Glen. Newscaster (KLX, Oakland, CA, 1945). DJ (*Glen King Show*, KLX, 1947).

17499 King, H.E. DJ (*Studio Party*, WORZ, Orlando, FL, 1947).

17500 King, Harry. Leader (*Harry King Orchestra*, instr. mus. prg., WOR, Newark, NJ, 1936).

17501 King, Harry. DJ (WMAY, Springfield, IL, 1957).

17502 King, Hazel. Soprano (WJZ, New York, NY, 1927).

17503 King, Helen. Graphologist (WOR, Newark, NJ, 1932).

17504 King, Helen. Actress King was in the original cast of *Clara, Lu and Em* (NBC, 1934).

17505 King, Henry. Leader (*Henry King Orchestra*, instr. mus. prg., WFI, Philadelphia, PA, 1934; NBC, 1935–1936; CBS, 1938–1939).

17506 King, Hermie. Leader (Hermie King and his Supersoloists Orchestra, KTCL, Seattle, WA, 1925).

17507 King, J.D., Jr. DJ (*Western Serenade*, WJRD, Tuscaloosa, AL, 1947). Sportscaster (WJRD, 1949).

17508 King, Jack. Leader of Jack King and the Jesters, an extremely popular vocal trio in the 1930's. They later changed their name to the Ink Spots and appeared on many network programs (Networks, 1930s and 1940s).

17509 King, Jack. Newscaster (WJR, Detroit, MI, 1938–1941).

17510 King, Jan. Newscaster (WMFF, Plattsburg, NY, 1945). Sports director and sportscaster (WEAV, Plattsburg, NY, 1951).

17511 King, Jane. Soprano (*Jane King*, vcl. mus. prg., WJJD, Chicago, IL, 1936). Actress King also appeared on the *Married Life of Helen and Warren* daytime serial.

17512 King, Jean Paul. Actor-director King was featured on NBC's *Great Moments in History* program (NBC, 1927). He also worked as a newscaster (*Hecker HO Daily Information Service*, MBS, 1937), before becoming a distinguished network announcer. He later worked as a DJ (*Confidentially It's Off the Record* show, 15 min., 4:45–5:00 P.M., WABC, New York, NY, 1942; *King's Truth*, KENO, Las Vegas, NV, 1952; KABC, Hollywood, CA, 1955).

17513 King, Jim. DJ (*Needlework at Your Request*, KDMO, Carthage, MO, 1948). Sportscaster (*Sports Parade*, KDMO, 1951).

17514 King, Joanne. COM-HE (WSPB, Sarasota, FL, 1951; WCFR, Springfield, VA, 1960).

17515 King, Joe. Newscaster (CBS, 1945).

17516 King, John E. DJ (*Musical Clock*, WROB, West Point, MS, 1948).

17517 King, Julius. Newscaster (WJTN, Jamestown, NY, 1942, 1945–1948).

17518 King, June. COM-HE (WLBT, Jackson, MS, 1956–1957).

17519 King, Karl L. Conductor of the popular Karl L. King Band (WHQ, Rochester, NY, 1928). King was one of the outstanding brass band conductors and march composers of his era.

17520 King, Kay. COM-HE (KQAQ, Austin, MN, 1960).

17521 King, Larry. Sportscaster (WKAT, Miami Beach, FL, 1960).

17522 King, Mabel. Contralto (KDKA, Pittsburgh, PA, 1926).

17523 King, Margo. COM-HE (KXLY, Spokane, WA, 1951).

17524 King, Marguerietta A. Pianist (WHAS, Louisville, KY, 1924).

17525 King, Marjorie. COM-HE (KNBC, San Francisco, CA, 1956).

17526 King, Mary Burke. COM-HE (KXLA, Pasadena, CA, 1951).

17527 King, Mercer. DJ (KVOP, Vidalia, GA, 1948).

17528 King, Mildred. Pianist (WSM, Nashville, TN, 1928).

17529 King, Nelson. DJ (*Hit Parade Jamboree*, WCKY, Cincinnati, OH, 1946–1948; *Daily Hit Parade*, 1948–1957). King was one of the most popular CW DJ's of the 1930–1950 era. He was, probably the leading CW DJ in the late 1940s.

17530 King, Norma. COM-HE (KEPS, Eagle Pass, TX, 1960).

17531 King, Norman. Newscaster (WTAQ, Green Bay, WI, 1941).

17532 King, (Dr.) O.H. Baritone (KTHS, Hot Springs National Park, AK, 1928).

17533 King, Pat. COM-HE (WRBL, Columbus, OH, 1949).

17534 **King, Pee Wee (Julius Frank Anthony Kuczynski).** CW band leader-songwriter-accordionist King had first professional radio appearances on WRJN (Racine, WI, 1928) and WHBY (Green Bay, WI, 1928). He formed a band at an early age and by 19 as Frankie King had his own program on WJRN (Racine, WI, 1933) and also was featured on the *Badger State Barn Dance* (WJRN, Racine, WI, 1933). He moved to WHAS (Louisville, KY, 1934), where he worked played with the Log Cabin Boys on the *Crazy Water Barn Dance* (WHAS, Louisville, KY, 1935). The following year he formed his Golden West Cowboys band (WHAS, Louisville, KY, 1936) and began a long run on the *Grand Ole Opry* (1937–1947). At the same time he had his own show on KNOX (Knoxville, TN, 1937–1947) called the *Midday Merry-Go-Round.*

His Golden West Cowboys, at one time or another, contained such stars as Ernest Tubb, Eddy Arnold, Minnie Pearl, Redd Stewart and Cowboy Copas. As a songwriter, King was the co-writer with Chilton Price of "Slow Poke" and with Redd Stewart of "Tennessee Waltz." He went to WAVE (Louisville, KY, 1947) to work on both radio and television programs at that station. His busy career also included featured roles in motion pictures with Gene Autry, Charles Starrett and Johnny Mack Brown.

17535 **King, Rea.** COM-HE (WTOR, Torrington, CT, 1960).

17536 **King, Riley "B.B."** Black DJ, musician and singer (*Bee Bee's Jeebies*, WDIA, Memphis, TN, 1951; *Sepia Swing Club*, WDIA, 1950–1951). Born Riley King, he got the name "B.B." from his show business billings of "The Beale Street Boy" and "The Boy from Beale Street" that eventually was shortened to "B.B." On the air, B.B. identified himself as "Dr. King, musical chosen of the blues and heebie jeebies." After King persuaded Sonny Boy Williamson to allow him to appear on the *King Biscuit Flour Show*, he got an opportunity to perform in a West Memphis club that led to a weekly engagement there. He then decided that he also wanted a radio career and began to appear regularly on a segment of Williamson's show as a singer. Shortly afterward King got a show of his own sponsored by Lucky Strike cigarettes. His first DJ job occurred when Hot Rod Hulbert left Memphis to work in Baltimore in 1950. King became a DJ on his *Sepia Swing Club* and stayed at WDIA as a DJ for several years, as his popularity as a performer grew steadily.

17537 **King, Robert.** DJ (*Kaffe Klatsch*, WMOH, Hamilton, OH, 1950).

17538 **King, Ted.** Leader (*Ted King Orchestra*, instr. mus. prg., MBS, 1939).

17539 **King, Tom.** Banjoist (*Tom King*, instr. mus. prg., WPG, Atlantic City, NJ, 1936).

17540 **King, Una.** COM-HE (WTHT, Hartford, CT, 1951).

17541 **King, Vern.** DJ (*Platter Parade*, WIL, St. Louis, MO, 1948).

17542 **King, W.O.** DJ (*Juke Box Review*, WTOC, Savannah, GA, 1947–1955).

17543 **King, Wallace "Wally."** DJ (WATR, Waterbury, CT, 1947; *Fun and Frolics*, WATR, 1948–1950). Sportscaster (*Sports of the Day*, WATR, 1947).

17544 **King, Wayne.** Orchestra leader King was born February 18, 1901. He formed his own band at the request of the owners of Chicago's Aragon Ballroom. His first radio appearances were remote broadcasts from that ballroom (KYW, Chicago, IL,1923). They were followed by many others (Wayne King Orchestra, KVI, Tacoma, WA, 1929; *Wayne King and his Sonatrons*, sponsored by the Sonatron Tube Company, WABC-CBS, New York, NY, 1929–1930; *Wayne King Orchestra*, NBC, 1933–1935; CBS, 1935; MBS, 1936; CBS, 1938; KMOX, St. Louis, MO, 1942).

17545 **King, William.** Director of the *Sunday Symphony Orchestra* [program] featuring musicians from the Cincinnati Symphony Orchestra (WLW, Cincinnati, OH, 1924).

17546 **King, (Mrs.) William.** Organist (WOC, Davenport, IA, 1928).

17547 **King Barry Hawaiians Orchestra.** Hawaiian music group (WGBS, New York, NY, 1925).

17548 **(The) King of Hosts.** *See* **John S. Daggett.**

17549 ***(The) King Biscuit Flour Show.*** Sonny Boy Williamson II (Rice Miller) was the main performer on the 15-minute show that eventually was expanded to a half-hour and broadcast Saturday evening (KFFA, Helena, MS, 1941–1960). Williamson played the harmonica and led his blues band that included Robert Lockwood, Jr. and Pinetop Perkins, among others. John "Sonny" Payne was the show's longtime announcer. The sponsor was the King Biscuit Flour Company. The program became so popular that the sponsor developed a new product called Sonny Boy Corn Meal.

17550 **(The) *King Cole Trio*.** Nat "King" Cole led his talented music group and occasionally sang (15 min., Saturday, 5:45–6:00 P.M., NBC-Red, 1946–1947). Although Cole is often thought to have been the first black performer to have his own television show on NBC, both Hazel Scott and Billy Daniels preceded him.

17551 ***King Kalohi's Hawaiians Orchestra.*** Hawaiian mus. prg. (WSB, Atlanta, GA, 1942).

17552 ***King Kill Kare.*** This was a breezy entertaining one-man-show filled with pleasant songs and witty monologues by an unidentified entertainer (15 min., Monday, 8:15–8:30 A.M., NBC-Blue, 1932).

17553 **King Tut's Melody Artists.** Tut's Friday, September 7, 1923, program (KLS, Oakland, CA) from 8:00–9:00 P.M. included the following musical selections: "All Night Long," "Don't Be Too Sure," "You've Got to See Mamma Every Night," "Stories," "Bebe," "Tell Me a Story," "Swinging Down the Lane," "Wonderful One." "Yes, We Have No Bananas," "Hot Lips," "Barney Google," "Carolina Mammy," "Stella," "Day by Day in Every Way I Love You More and More," "Blue Hoosier Blues," "Louisville Lou" and "Red Moon Waltz."

17554 **Kingan, Joy.** Soprano (KFI, Los Angeles, CA, 1925).

17555 **Kingbay, Meg.** COM-HE (WCCO, Minneapolis, MN, 1956).

17556 **Kingdon, (Dr.) Frank.** News commentator (WMCA, New York, NY, 1944–1945; WOR, New York, NY, 1945–1947).

17557 ***King's Guard*** **(aka *King's Guard Quartet* and *King's Men*).** Vcl. mus. prg. by a male quartet that formerly had sung with Paul Whiteman's orchestra. Usually introduced as having been "discovered in California by Paul Whiteman," the group consisted of pianist-bass Ken Darby, baritone Rod Robinson and tenors Bud Lynn and John Dodson (15 min., NBC-Blue and NBC-Red, 1934–1936). Later the talented group was a summer replacement for *Fibber McGee and Molly* (30 min., Tuesday, 9:30–10:00 P.M., NBC, 1949).

17558 ***King's Jesters Orchestra.*** Instr. mus. prg. (WMAQ, Chicago, IL and NBC, 1937; MBS, 1938).

17559 ***King's Jesters Quartet.*** Vcl. mus. prg. (NBC, 1936).

17560 ***King's Men. See King's Guard.***

17561 ***King's Row.*** The daytime serial, sponsored by the Colgate-Palmolive-Peet Company, was based on Henry Bellamann's novel of the same name and its sequel, *Parris Mitchell of King's Row.* Parris Mitchell, a doctor in his home town of King's Row, was played by Francis DeSales. The radio version of the novel was updated to include contemporary topics. For example, Dr. Mitchell offered to give the United States Government real estate to build a war plant, while villain Foster Green blocked his effort, because he wanted to make a killing by selling the government his own worthless land. These were only some of the complexities encountered by the hero in this adaptation written by Welbourn Kelley, produced by Arlene Lunny and directed by Edward Downes. Joining DeSales in the cast were Jim Boles, Doris Dalton, Charlotte Holland and Charlotte Manson. Lee Vines was the program's narrator and John MacDougall the announcer (15 min., Monday through Friday, 3:15–3:30 P.M., CBS, 1951).

17562 **Kingsbury, Chester "Chet."** Musician Kinsbury was organist on *Backstage Wife* and *Hilltop House.* He also was musical director of the *Second Mrs. Burton* daytime serial program.

17563 **Kingsbury, Gilbert "Gil."** Newscaster (WLW, Cincinnati, OH, 1944; *Washington Front*, WLW, 1948).

17564 **Kingsley, Myra.** Astrologist (WBZ, Boston, MA, 1940).

17565 **Kingsley, Paul.** Newscaster (WGBS, Miami, FL, 1948).

17566 **Kingsley, (Mrs.) Ruby T.** Pianist (WBZ, Springfield, MA, 1923).

17567 **Kingston, Bud.** Cartoonist Kingston taught cartooning on his weekly program (WTIC, Hartford, CT, 1926).

17568 **Kingston, Lenore.** Actress Kingston was a cast member of the daytime serial programs *Midstream* and *Against the Storm.*

17569 ***(The) Kinky Kids Parade.*** The two-man minstrel show featured Gosden and

Correll (WGN, Chicago, IL, 1926). *See* ***Amos 'n' Andy***.

17570 Kinnamon, Ray. DJ (*Record Round-Up*, WBHF, Cartersville, GA, 1947; WTJH, East Point, GA, 1955–1956).

17571 Kinney, Nancy. COM-HE (WPDR, Portage, WI, 1960).

17572 Kinney, Phyllis. Soprano (*Phyllis Kinney*, vcl. mus. prg., WKAR, East Lansing, MI, 1942).

17573 Kinney, Ray. Leader (*Ray Kinney Orchestra*, instr. mus. prg., NBC, 1934, 1939–1940; WLAV, Grand Rapids, MI, 1942).

17574 Kinney, Ruth Lloyd. Mezzo-contralto (WBZ, Boston-Springfield, MA, 1925).

17575 Kinney, Sue. COM-HE (WLWI, Indianapolis, IN, 1957).

17576 Kinsella, J.E.S. Baritone (WRC, Washington, DC, 1924).

17577 Kinsella, Walter. Actor Kinsella as in the cast of *Abie's Irish Rose, Circus Days, Dick Tracy, Jor and Mabel, Leave It to Mike, Martin Kane, Private Eye, Mr. and Mrs. North, Peewee and Windy* and *Stella Dallas.*

17578 Kinsey, Curly. DJ (*Cornbread Jamboree*, WGTA, Summerville, GA, 1952–1956).

17579 Kinsey, Mark E. Newscaster (WHO, Des Moines, IA, 1940–1941).

17580 Kinsley, Vera. COM-HE (WTOT, Marianna, FL, 1960).

17581 *K.I.O. Minstrels*. Gaylord Anderson as "Red Hat" teamed with "Golden Rod," the other end man, to supply the fun on the radio minstrel show (WLW, Cincinnati, OH, 1930).

17582 Kious, Roberta. COM-HE (WLDS, Jacksonville, IL, 1956).

17583 Kipeck, Anthony W. Announcer (WNAB, Boston, MA, 1926).

17584 Kirbery, Ralph. Baritone (*Ralph Kirbery*, vcl. mus. prg., 15 min., 11:15–11:30 P.M., NBC-Red, 1930–1931; *Ralph Kirbery the Dream Singer*, vcl. mus. prg., NBC, 1934–1936). Kirbery was born in Paterson, NJ, August 24, 1900. After a brief stint in the Army during World War I and work as an automobile salesman and flour broker, Kirbery happened to sing for his buddies at the Paterson Legion Post. From that point on, it was only a short time before he began singing on sustaining radio shows in New York. When NBC offered him a contract in 1930, Kirbery began singing on the network's midnight radio shows, thereby earning the billing of "The Dream Singer."

17585 Kirby, Anastasia. Monologist (WBZ, Boston, MA, 1940).

17586 Kirby, Ann. COM-HE (WGAF, Valdosta, GA, 1957).

17587 Kirby, Bea. COM-HE (WTTM, Trenton, NJ, 1954).

17588 Kirby, Bill. DJ (*Music in the Afternoon*, WHCU, Ithaca, NY, 1948; *Alarm Clock Club*, WJOC, Jamestown, NY, 1950).

17589 Kirby, Corley F. Announcer known as "CFK" (WWJ, Detroit, MI 1924); director-announcer, WGHP, Detroit, MI, 1928). Kirby had worked at other Detroit stations previously: WWJ for three years and WJR for one and a half.

17590 Kirby, Clifford. Banjo soloist (WAHG, New York, NY, 1925).

17591 Kirby, Dorothy. Sportscaster on the Georgia Tech campus station (*The Sports Show*, WGST, Atlanta, GA, 1947).

17592 Kirby, Durward. Newscaster (*Press Radio News*, NBC, 1937; WENR, Chicago, IL and WMAQ, Chicago, IL, 1939–1940). Kirby later worked as an announcer and "second banana" on many network radio and TV programs. Some of the radio programs on which he worked were *Breakfast Club, Club Matinee, Henry Morgan Show, Li'l Abner* and *Lone Journey.*

17593 Kirby, Fred. CW singer, musician, and DJ Kirby first appeared on radio on WIS (Columbia, SC, 1927). He later went on to work on WBT (Charlotte, NC, 1932–1939) , WLM (Cincinnati, OH, 1939–1940), WIP (Philadelphia, PA), WFIL (Philadelphia, PA); WLW (*Boone County Jamboree*, Cincinnati, OH) and WLW (*National Barn Dance*, Chicago, IL). He was a DJ on WBT (Charlotte, NC) in the 1950s, while appearing on *Dixie Jamboree* and *Carolina Hayride.*

17594 Kirby, Gene. Sportscaster on the baseball game of the day broadcast (MBS, 1951).

17595 Kirby, Jane. Soprano (*Jane Kirby*, vcl. mus. prg., WBAL, Baltimore, MD, 1934).

17596 Kirby, Jerry. Sportscaster (*Sports Flash*, WKBB, Dubuque, IA, 1947–1948; *Sports Spotlight*, WKBB, 1949–1950). DJ (*Two-Thirty Session*, WKBB, 1948).

17597 Kirby, Jimmy. DJ (*Alabama Hayloft Jamboree*, WAPI, Birmingham, AL, 1948; *Georgia Hayride*, WAGA, Atlanta, GA, 1950).

17598 Kirby, Kleve. Newscaster (WWL, New Orleans, LA, 1938–1939).

17599 Kirby, (Robert) Lee. Sportscaster (football play-by-play, WBT, Charlotte, NC, 1937–1946; *Sports Spotlight*, WBT, 1947–1951).

17600 Kirby, Marji. COM-HE (KVOY, Yuma, AZ, 1960).

17601 Kirch, Frances. Soprano (WFBH, New York, NY, 1925).

17602 Kircher, Irene. Singer (*Irene Kircher*, vcl. mus. prg., WMBD, Peoria, IL, 1935).

17603 *Kiriloff's Orchestra*. Instr. mus. prg. (NBC, 1936).

17604 Kirk, Andy. Leader (*Andy Kirk Orchestra*, instr. mus. prg., NBC-Blue, 1936; MBS, 1939).

17605 Kirk, Cuppy. DJ (*Tivy Jive*, KEVT, Kerrville, TX, 1952).

17606 Kirk, Dorothy Ann. COM-HE (KILO, Grand Forks, SD, 1956–1957).

17607 Kirk, Harry. DJ (*At Your Command*, KORE, Eugene, OR, 1950).

17608 Kirk, Henrietta. COM-HE (WAJF, Decatur, AL, 1954–1955).

17609 Kirk, Lena. Soprano (WQJ, Chicago, IL, 1926).

17610 Kirk, Mary. COM-HE (KBTV, Denver, CO, 1957).

17611 Kirk, Penny. COM-HE (WENT, Gloversville, NY, 1951).

17612 Kirk, "Red." DJ (*Saturday Night Jamboree*, WOPI, Bristol, VA, 1952).

17613 Kirkham, Arthur. Tenor (KOAC, Cornvallis, OR, 1926).

17614 Kirkland, Alexander. Actor Kirkland was in the cast of *Big Sister, John's Other Wife* and *Life and Loves of Dr. Susan.*

17615 Kirkland, (Mrs.) L.A. Singer (KWSC, Pullman, WA, 1925).

17616 Kirkland, Muriel. Actress Kirkland appeared on the daytime serial program *Mary Marlin* aka *The Story of Mary Marlin.*

17617 Kirkman, Arthur. Newscaster (WMFR, High Point, NC, 1948).

17618 Kirkpatrick, Bill. DJ (*Sunrise Serenade*, WSBB, New Smyrna Beach, FL, 1960).

17619 Kirkpatrick, Eloise. Coloratura soprano (KHJ, Los Angeles, CA, 1929).

17620 Kirkpatrick, Helen. Newscaster (WHO, Omaha, NE, 1943).

17621 Kirkpatrick, Jess. Sportscaster (*Old Gold Baseball News*, WGN, Chicago, IL, 1937). News analyst (WGN, Chicago, IL, 1941).

17622 Kirkwood, John. Newscaster (WIL, St. Louis, MO, 1945).

17623 Kirkwood, Leonard. Pianist (WHO, Des Moines, IA, 1925).

17624 Kirnsey, Wade. Announcer (WQAO, New York, NY, 1927).

17625 Kirsch, Frances. Soprano (WGBS, New York, NY, 1925).

17626 Kirsch, Lucien. Cellist (WJZ, New York, NY, 1928).

17627 Kirschner, Al. Pianist (WKRC, Cincinnati, OH, 1925).

17628 Kirschner, Eva Walker. Pianist (KFRC, San Francisco, CA, 1927).

17629 Kirsh, Helen. COM-HE (KMOP, Ocala, FL, 1955).

17630 Kirtley, Lucille. Soprano (KGW, Portland, OR, 1928).

17631 Kirwan, Dennis "Denny." Sportscaster (*Sports Quiz* and *Sports Round-Up*, WINZ, Miami Beach, FL, 1950; KJOY, Stockton, CA, 1956–1960).

17632 Kiser, Jimmy. DJ (*Pajama Jamboree*, WSOC, Charlotte, NC, 1947; *Luncheon with Music*, WSOC, Charlotte, NC, 1948; *Dance Hour*, WSOC, 1950).

17633 Kiss, Mina. Soprano (WEAF, New York, NY, 1924).

17634 Kiss, Robert. Pianist (WOR, Newark, NJ, 1925).

17635 *Kiss and Make Up*. The sustaining giveaway show was a summer replacement for the first half of the *Lux Radio Theater* program. The contestants were married couples with grievances who described their domestic problems to a panel drawn from the audience, who then rendered a decision as to who was at fault. Host Milton Berle would then enforce their penalty that was "to kiss and make up." The Murphy Sisters vocal group and Harry Salter's

Orchestra supplied the music (30 min., Monday, 9:00–9:30 P.M., CBS, 1946).

17636 Kissel, Samuel "Sam." Violinist (*Samuel Kissel*, instr. mus. prg., WHP, Harrisburg, PA, 1936; WJTN, Trenton, NJ, 1937).

17637 Kissell, Gustave. Clarinetist in the WGN Concert Orchestra (WGN, Chicago, IL, 1928).

17638 Kister, George. Newscaster (KMMJ, Grand Island, NE, 1939–1942, 1945).

17639 Kistinger, Dorothy. COM-HE (WKIP, Poughkeepsie, NY, 1949).

17640 Kistler, Gleason. Newscaster (WDAN, Danville, IL, 1939; KFNF, Shanandoah, IA, 1945). .

17641 Kistler, Jack. DJ (*Call and Collect*, WFPB, Middletown, OH, 1948).

17642 Kit, (Mrs.) W. COM-HE (WKIT, Mineola, NY, 1956).

17643 *Kit and Kay*. Vcl. mus. prg. by an otherwise unidentified vocal team, KMBC (Kansas City, MO, 1939).

17644 Kit Kat Klub Band. Jazz band broadcasting from one of New York's hot night spots (WHN, New York, NY, 1926).

17645 Kitchell, Alma. Contralto (*Alma Kitchell*, vcl. mus. prg., NBC, 1935–1937; CBS, 1936). News commentator (*Let's Talk It Over*, NBC, 1938–1939; *Alma Kitchell's Case Book*, NBC, 1939). Kitchell, a pioneer radio and TV performer, lived to the age of 103. In 1927, she began singing on radio, and for the next two decades she was known as "The Golden Voice of Radio." She hosted some of radio's earliest talk shows with such programs as *Let's Talk It Over*, *Alma Kitchell's Brief Case* and *Women's Exchange* on NBC and ABC. She sang on early television programs in the 1930s and appeared in *The Pirates of Penzance*, the first televised operetta. She continued working in television until her retirement in 1949.

17646 Kitchen, Katherine. COM-HE (*Katherine Kitchen*, KWG, Stockton, CA, 1949).

17647 Kitchen, Kenneth. Leader (Kenneth Kitchen's Club Orchestra, WOR, Newark, NJ, 1924).

17648 Kitchen, Mary. COM-HE (KSOO, Sioux Falls, SD, 1936).

17649 Kitchen Klenzer Entertainers. Music group sponsored on radio by a cleaning product (WHT, Chicago, IL, 1926).

17650 *Kitchen Party*. Warren Hull hosted the music program featuring contralto Martha Mears, baritone Jimmy Wilkinson, soprano Frances Lee Barton and the piano team of Al and Lee Reiser (30 min., Friday, 1:30–2:00 P.M., NBC, 1935).

17651 Kitson, (Dr.) Harry D. News analyst (*On Your Job*, NBC, 1939).

17652 Kittell, Clyde. Newscaster (NBC, 1946–1948).

17653 Kittelson, Elaine. Singer (KFJM, Grand Forks, ND, 1937).

17654 Kitterman, Bob. Newscaster (WWSR, St. Albans, VT, 1941).

17655 Kittleson, Curt. DJ (*Scandinavian Melody Time*, KXLF, Butte, MT, 1948).

17656 Kittner, Pauline. Soprano (WEAF, New York, NY, 1927).

17657 Kitts, Edward. Newscaster (WHIS, Bluefield, WV, 1938).

17658 Kitts, Evelyn. A studio hostess at KOIL in 1928, Kitts delivered the *Aunt Sammy* talks on the station. Busy Miss Kitts also sang and played the piano when called upon (KOIL, Council Bluffs, IA, 1928). *See* ***Aunt Sammy***.

17659 Kittson, Norma. Soprano (WJAZ, Chicago, IL, 1926).

17660 *Kitty and Bingo*. Baltimore entertainers Kitty Dierken and Garry Moore talked and clowned on their entertaining noon time show (WBAL, Baltimore, MD, early 1940s). *see* ***The Garry Moore Show***.

17661 *Kitty Keene* (aka *Kitty Keene, Incorporated*). Kitty was a private detective in business for herself, but her personal problems usually were upper most in her mind on this daytime serial. First broadcast in 1937 by MBS, it was another of the Frank and Anne Hummert's many productions. The talented cast included: Bob Bailey, Cheer Brentson, Herbert Butterfield, Fran Carlon, Louise Fitch, Josephine Gilbert, Chuck Grant, Dorothy Gregory, Ken Griffin, Chuck Harris, Peggy Hillias, Ginger Jones, Carlton KaDell, Ian Keith, Janet Logan, Phil Lord, Angeline Orr, Loretta Poynton, Dick Wells and Beverly Younger. Day Keene and Wally Norman were the program's creators and writers. George Fogle and Alan Wallace were the producers-directors. Lester Huntley also was the writer and Win Orr the director at one time (MBS, 1937).

17662 Kitzmiller, Florence. Soprano (KFI, Los Angeles, CA, 1925).

17663 KJBS Pupils of Joseph George Jacobson. Music students of Jacobson were featured on the San Francisco program (KJBS, San Francisco, CA, 1925).

17664 KJR Orchestra. Studio orchestra directed by Henri Damski (KJR, Seattle, WA, late 1920s).

17665 KJR Trio. Instrumental music group consisting of Mischa Levienne, Kola Levienne and John Hopper playing violin, cello and piano (KJR, Seattle, WA, 1927).

17666 Klages, (Mrs.) R.W. Soprano (KFSG, Los Angeles, CA, 1924).

17667 Klamer, Arlene. COM-HE (WICA, Ashtabula, OH, 1955).

17668 Klammer, Hulda. Reader (WCBD, Zion, IL, 1926).

17669 Klann, Marie. COM-HE (WHAK, Rogers City, MI, 1951).

17670 Klaser [Klaeser] , Edith. COM-HE (WLAV, Grand Rapids, MI, 1956).

17671 Klassen, Bern. Tenor (*Bern Klassen*, vcl. mus. prg., 15 min., 10:30–10:45 A.M., NBC-Red, 1945).

17672 Klavan, Gene. News commentator (*Klavan Comments*, WCBM, Baltimore, MD, 1947). DJ (*Three Shades of Dawn*, WCBM, 1947–1948; *Swing Class*, WITH, Baltimore, MD, 1950). Klavan later teamed with **Dee Finch** to form a popular New York DJ team (WNEW, New York, NY, 1956–1960).

17673 Kleckner, Doc. Sportscaster (KFRB, Fairbanks, AK, 1950).

17674 Kleckner, Ruth. Pianist (WMAK, Buffalo, NY, 1928).

17675 Klee, Lawrence. Writer Klee wrote *Aunt Jenny*, *Chaplain Jim*, *Man Against Crime*, *Mr. Keen, Tracer of Lost Persons* and *Valiant Lady*.

17676 Kleeb, Helen. Actress Kleeb was in the cast of *Dr. Kate*.

17677 Kleesewetter, Elsie. Soprano (WEAF, New York, NY, 1924).

17678 Kleibe, Karla. Violinist (WEAF, New York, NY, 1925).

17679 Klein, Adelaide. Actress Klein appeared in *Arabesque* and many other CBS programs (CBS, 1931) She also appeared in *Life Can Be Beautiful*, *Valiant Lady*, *Big Sister* and *We the Abbotts* daytime serial programs.

17680 Klein, Arthur. Pianist (*Arthur Klein*, vcl. mus. prg., WOR, Newark, NJ, 1935).

17681 Klein, Betty. COM-HE (KOGT, Orange, TX, 1956–1957).

17682 Klein, Cornell. Singer-banjoist (KFI, Los Angeles, CA, 1928).

17683 Klein, Don. Newscaster (KEVR, Seattle, WA, 1941). Sportscaster (KEVR, 1941; *Baseball and Sports Review*, KSFO, San Francisco, CA, 1949; KSFO, 1950; sports play-by-play, KIBE, Palo Alto, CA, 1951; KCBS, San Francisco, CA, 1956–1960).

17684 Klein, Ed. DJ (*Cousin Ed Show*, WWXL, Peoria, IL, 1948)

17685 Klein, Edna and Ethel Prokesl. Instrumental duo (WRNY, New York, NY, 1925).

17686 Klein, Joanne. COM-HE (WMIE, Miami, FL, 1960).

17687 Klein, Jules. Leader (Jules Klein Hotel Statler Orchestra, broadcasting from Detroit's Statler Hotel, WWJ, Detroit, MI, 1925–1926; Jules Klein's Symphonic Ensemble, WWJ, 1928).

17688 Klein, (Dr.) Julius. Dr. Klein talked about world business on his weekly fifteen-minute program (CBS, 1929).

17689 Klein, Louis. Autoharp and harmonica soloist (KHJ, Los Angeles, CA, 1925; KMIC, Inglewood, CA, 1928). Klein was billed as the "King of Harmonica Artists."

17690 Klein, Margie. Trombonist Klein played in the *Boys and Girls Farm Bureau Review* program orchestra (WHO, Des Moines, IA, 1924).

17691 Klein, Pat. DJ (*Yawn Patrol*, WKYB, Paducah, KY, 1947).

17692 Klein, Virginia. Pianist (WCAU, Philadelphia, PA, 1925).

17693 Kleinhans, Forrest. Baritone (WBBR, New York, NY, 1926).

17694 Kleinpeter, Irene. Soprano (WBBR, New York, NY, 1925–1926).

17695 Klein's Serenading Shoemakers. Commercially sponsored band led by the busy Joe Green (WOR, Newark, NJ, 1926–1927).

17696 Klemp, Lloyd. Sportscaster (KDAN, Oroville, CA, 1949; *Sports Finals*,

KUBA, Yuba City, CA, 1950; KUBA, 1953–1956).

17697 **Kleunter, Beatrice.** Organist (WNYC, New York, NY, 1936).

17698 **Kleser, Ernest H.** Announcer (WOCL, Jamestown, NY, 1925).

17699 **Kley, Herbert.** Sportscaster (WHBL, Sheboygan, WI, 1947; *Sports Parade*, WHBL 1949; *Sports Roundup*, WLIP, Kenosha, WI, 1949). DJ (*Polka Platter Parade*, WLIP, Kenosha, WI, 1948).

17700 **Klier, Bob.** Musician Klier was billed as "Bob Klier and his zither" (KFRC, San Francisco, CA, 1928).

17701 **Kline, Mary Smith.** Organist (*Mary Smith Kline*, instr. mus. prg., WHP, Harrisburg, PA, 1942).

17702 **Kline, Ted.** Tenor (WCCO, Minneapolis–St. Paul, MN, 1928).

17703 **Klinefelter, Lee M.** Announcer (WBBW, Norfolk, VA, 1927).

17704 **Kling, Buddy.** DJ (*Night Train*, WWDC, Washington, DC, 1954).

17705 **Kling, Herbert.** Oboist Kling teamed with Gustave Kissell to form a talented musical team (WGN, Chicago, IL, 1928).

17706 **Kling, Janet.** Actress Kling was in the cast of *Keeping Up with Daughter.*

17707 **Kling, Jeanette.** Reader (WLS, Chicago, IL, 1926).

17708 **Kling, Norman.** Baritone (WGES, Oak Park, IL, 1925).

17709 **Klingermann, Dale.** DJ (*Midnight Frolic*, KMAC, San Antonio, TX, 1948).

17710 **Klise, Roderic A.** Newscaster (WUJ, Walla Walla, WA, 1937). Sportscaster (KRLC, Lewiston, ID, 1941).

17711 **Klooster, Mary W.** Pianist (WQJ, Chicago, IL, 1925).

17712 **Klos, Louise.** Leader (Louise Klos Trio consisting of harpist-leader Klos, cellist Hazel Babbage and violinist Evelyn Pickerell, KTAB, Oakland, CA, 1925–1926). Klos also was a harp soloist billed as the "Harp de Los Angeles" (KFI, Los Angeles, CA, 1926).

17713 **Klose, Al.** DJ (*Melody Time*, WBRW, Welch, WV, 1947).

17714 **Klossner, Jane.** COM-HE (KBRV, Boonville, NY, 1955).

17715 **Klottsmier, Ingrid.** COM-HE (KKID, Pendleton, OR, 1960).

17716 **Klowden, Nina.** Actress Klowden appeared on the *Midstream* daytime serial program.

17717 **KLRA Musical Talent.** Little Rock, AR, amateur performers appeared on the program (KLRA, Little Rock, AR, 1928–1929).

17718 **Kluck, Carol.** COM-HE (WRIG, Wassau, WI, 1960).

17719 **Klucz, Joe.** Announcer (WTAR, Norfolk, VA, 1925).

17720 **KLX Mixed Quartet.** Vocal group consisting of soprano Barbara Blanchard, contralto Ruth W. Anderson, tenor Albert E. Gross and baritone Desaix McCloskey accompanied by Beatrice L. Sherwood (KLX, Oakland, CA, 1926).

17721 **Klyectoneers.** Either Max Dolin or Vincent Lopez conducted the studio orchestra (NBC-Pacific, 1929).

17722 ***KMA Country School.*** CW variety-music program, the *KMA Country School* (KMA, Shenandoah, IA, 1928–1948) was originated by Earl May. The show focused around a fictional country school. Its announcers were the *teachers*. One of the *teachers* was Toby Stewart. Broadcast either from Shenandoah or Council Bluffs, the program was said to have attracted more than a million visitors to see the show. Some of the performers on the show were: Zeke Williams, the Shumate Brothers (Raymond, Paul, Lewis and Don), Harness Bill and the Harness Makers (Frank "Pete" Peterson, Gus Swanson, Fritz Carlson), the Dixie Girls (Opal and Alta Dixie), Gretta Bellamy, Faylon Geist, Mickey Gibbons, Bill Alexander, Edith Jennings, Frank Jennings, Twylia Danielson, Kay Stewart, Lindy Stewart, Paul Greenlee, Jerry Smith, Joan Williams, Steve Wooden, Elmer Axelbender, Joan Williams, Jeanie Pierson, Mack Sanders, Merl Douglas, Harpo Richardson, Ike Everly, Wayne Van Horn and the Old Time Dance Orchestra. In 1948 the announcer was Glenn Harris. The writer at that time was Max Olive.

17723 ***KMA Roaming Barn Dance.*** Howard Chamberlain was the MC for this typical barn dance program that featured CW performers (KMA, Shenandoah, IA, 1937).

17724 **KMA String Trio.** Instrumental group consisting of Bernice Currier, Birdie Baldwin and Doc Bellamy (KMA, Shenandoah, IA, 1928).

17725 ***KMBC Brush Creek Follies*** **aka** ***Brush Creek Follies.*** CW music-variety show (KMBC, Kansas City, Mo, late 1930s and 1940s; CBS, 1939–1941). Veteran CW host-comedian Hiram Higsby was the show's MC. Other performers were: the Rhythm Riders, Jack Dunnigan, magician Tim West, black-face comedian George Washington White, Colorado Pete, Don Sullivan, comic Jed Starkey, the Tune Chasers, Rusty Marion and Curly Edminster and his Kansas Corral Gang.

17726 ***KMO Novelty Hour.*** An early variety show that combined music and comedy (KXL, Portland, OR, 1928).

17727 **KMOX Junior Orchestra.** An unidentified KMOX staff artist, who was a high school student, conducted the orchestra of 11 boys all below the age of 16 (KMOX , St. Louis, MO, 1928).

17728 **KMOX Melody Maids.** An eleven-piece all-girl orchestra (KMOX, St. Louis, MO, 1928).

17729 **KMOX Ramblers and Ethel Arnold.** A "hotsy-totsy flapper band" said *Radio Digest* (October, 1928, p. 33). Singer Arnold was featured (KMOX, St. Louis, MO, 1928).

17730 **KMTR Concert Orchestra.** Edmund Foerstel usually directed the station orchestra. At other times Loren Powell was the director (KMTR, Hollywood, CA, 1926).

17731 **Knapp, Bert.** Sportscaster (*Bert Knapp's Sports Roundup*, *On the Fifty Yard Line*, *Baseball Almanac* and *Between the Games*, WMCA, New York, NY, 1950).

17732 **Knapp, Del.** Sportscaster (*Rod and Gun*, WNLK, Norfolk, CT, 1955).

17733 **Knapp, La Vonne.** COM-HE (WATK, Antigo, WI, 1955).

17734 **Knapp, Merrill.** Newscaster (WBTA, Batavia, NY, 1947).

17735 **Knapp, Orville.** Ldr. (*Orville Knapp Orchestra*, instr. mus. prg., CBS, 1934–1935; WGN, Chicago, IL; WOR, Newark, NJ, 1935–1936; WFAA, Dallas, TX, 1936). Knapp's vocalist on many of these programs was Edith Caldwell.

17736 **Knapp, Robert "Bob."** DJ (*Wake Up Time*, WRVA, Richmond, VA, 1950). Sportscaster (WRVA, 1954).

17737 **Knatvold, Naida.** Newscaster (WCAL, Northfield, MN, 1939).

17738 **Kneale, Beatrice.** Singer (WOR, Newark, NJ, 1929).

17739 **Kneass, Don.** Newscaster (KIRO, Seattle, WA, 1937; KGW-KEX, Portland, OR, 1942–1945; KGW, 1946).

17740 **Knecht, (Prof.) Amanda Lopez.** Professor Knecht broadcast radio instruction in conversational Spanish (KOA, Denver, CO, 1925).

17741 **Knecht, Joseph.** Leader (Waldorf-Astoria Concert Orchestra, WJZ, New York, NY and WGY, Schenectady, NY, 1925; Goodyear Silver Cord Orchestra, WJZ, 1926).

17742 **Kneeland, Eileen.** COM-HE (WHAV, Haverhill, MA, 1949).

17743 **Kneeland, Vere.** COM-HE (KLOR, Portland, OR, 1955).

17744 **Kneip, Anita Dietrich.** Soprano (WEAF, New York, NY, 1925).

17745 **Kneisel, Bob.** DJ (KWTC, Barstow, CA, 1952).

17746 **Kneisel, Jack.** Leader (Jack Kneisel and his Gypsy Barons Orchestra, WWJ, Detroit, MI, 1928–1930).

17747 **Kneiss, (Professor) Henry.** Violinist-director (Lincoln Salon Orchestra and the KFAB Symphony Orchestra, KFAB, Lincoln, NE, 1928).

17748 **Knell, Jack.** Newscaster (WBT, Charlotte, NC, 1941–1942; WBT, 1944–1945; *News Digest*, *News* and the *Story Behind the News*, WBT, 1946–1947; *News Digest*, WBT, 1948).

17749 **Knell's Tokyo Dance Orchestra.** Local club band (WGR, Buffalo, NY, 1925).

17750 **Knettle, Alma Beckett.** Dramatic soprano (WOW, Omaha, NE, 1927).

17751 **Knetzger, Beatrice.** Pianist (KSD, St. Louis, MO, 1925).

17752 **Knick [Knicks], Walter.** Pianist (*Walter Knick*, instr. mus. prg., CBS, 1937–1938; WBNS, Columbus, OH, 1942).

17753 **Knickerbocker, H.R.** Newscaster (WOR, New York, NY, 1948).

17754 **Knickerbocker Grill Orchestra.** Popular restaurant band (WJZ, New York, NY, 1926).

17755 **Knickerbocker Orchestra.** Local band directed by Bert Estelow (WPG, Atlantic City, NJ, 1925).

17756 **Knickerbocker Trio.** The Coast Radio Supply Company sponsored this string trio that included Walter Gough, Emilee McCormick and Flori Gough (KGO, San Francisco, CA, 1926).

17757 **Knierlin [Knierin], Carl F.** Announcer (KFQW, North Bend, WA, 1926).

17758 **Knierr, Marcella.** Soprano Knierr was a member of the KPO Opera Company (KPO, San Francisco, CA, 1925).

17759 **Knieval, John.** DJ (*Rocket Rhythms*, KIMA, Yakima, WA, 1952).

17760 **Knight, Adrian "Ken."** Black DJ and program director (WERD, Atlanta, GA, 1950s). Ken Knight began his DJ career on radio in 1947 and became one of the South's most popular personalities. He was the Program Director, DJ and news commentator at WERD. In his later years he moved to Jacksonville, Florida, and made his TV debut on Jacksonville's WJXT. He was honored in Jacksonville by having Ken Knight Drive named for him.

17761 **Knight, Al.** DJ (*All Night with Al Knight*, KITO, San Bernardino, CA, 1952; KJAY, Topeka, KS, 1957).

17762 **Knight, Billy.** Announcer (WIL, St. Louis, MO, 1925).

17763 **Knight, Bob.** DJ (WOL, Washington, DC, 1947).

17764 **Knight, Delos.** Sportscaster (WIKC, Bogalusa, LA, 1953). DJ (*Magic City Matinee*, WIKC, 1955).

17765 **Knight, Dick.** DJ (*Dick Knight Show*, KYNO, Fresno, CA, 1948–1950).

17766 **Knight, Doris.** COM-HE (WBBQ, Augusta, GA, 1956).

17767 **Knight, Frances.** COM-HE (WKLX, Lexington, KY, 1949).

17768 **Knight, Frank.** Distinguished announcer Knight worked on the *Longines Symphonette*, *Superman* and *Uncle Don* programs.

17769 **Knight, Frank.** Sportscaster (*Sports Roundup*, WARE, Ware, MA, 1950). DJ (*Parade of Bands*, WARE, 1952).

17770 **Knight, Fred.** DJ (*Knight Club*, WIBG, Philadelphia, PA, 1948; *Music Hall*, WIBG, 1954; WSPA, Spartanburg, SC, 1957; WAVY, Norfolk, VA, 1960).

17771 **Knight, Harold.** Leader (Harold Knight's Singing Orchestra, WIP, Philadelphia, PA, 1925; *Harold Knight Orchestra*, instr. mus. prg., WCAU, Philadelphia, PA and CBS, 1934; WIP, 1936). Organist (*Harold Knight*, instr. mus. prg., WIP, Philadelphia, PA, 1936).

17772 **Knight, Joe.** DJ (*Tulsa Ballroom*, KRMG, Tulsa, OK, 1952–1956).

17773 **Knight, Ken.** DJ (*Musical Clock*, WTCO, Campbellsville, KY, 1948; *Music 'Til Sundown*, WKYW, Louisville, KY, 1954).

17774 **Knight, Kirk.** News commentator (WEXL, Royal Oak, MI, 1946; *Kirk Knight and the News*, WKMH, Dearborn, MI, 1947).

17775 **Knight, Larry.** DJ (*Mostly Music*, WTWN, St. Johnsbury, VT, 1960).

17776 **Knight, Lee.** COM-HE (WSPD, Toledo, OH, 1956).

17777 **Knight, Margaret.** Singer (WFAA, Dallas, TX, 1925).

17778 **Knight, Mary.** COM-HE (KTOW, Oklahoma City, OK, 1956).

17779 **Knight, Muriel.** A musical reader in early radio, Knight read prose and poetry with a musical background (KPO, San Francisco, CA, 1923).

17780 **Knight, Norvell.** Leader (*Norvell Knight Orchestra*, instr. mus. prg., NBC, middle 1940s).

17781 **Knight, Paul.** Director Knight directed the *First Piano Quartet* and *Portia Faces Life* programs.

17782 **Knight, Phyllis.** COM-HE (WHOW, Clinton, IL, 1951).

17783 **Knight, Raymond "Ray."** Actor-writer Knight worked on the *Cuckoo Hour* (actor-writer) *House in the Country* (actor) and *Wheatenaville* (writer-actor). See ***Cuckoo Hour*** *and* ***Wheatenaville***.

17784 **Knight, (Mrs.) Stuart.** Pianist (WGY, Schenectady, NY, 1924).

17785 **Knight, Ted.** DJ (WFNS, Burlington, NC, 1948).

17786 **Knight, Tom.** DJ (*Alarm Clock Club*, WDSM, Superior, WI, 1950).

17787 ***Knight at the Movies.*** Movie critic Arthur Knight interviewed guests and conducted the entertaining program about motion pictures (25 min., Sunday, 3:30–3:55 P.M., WNYC, New York, NY, 1958).

17788 **Knightlinger, Ted.** Newscaster (KMO, Tacoma, WA, 1939).

17789 ***Knights of the Road.*** Hank Lawson — probably a pseudonym for Hank Keene — hosted this program of CW music and comedy (15 min., Monday, 10:15–10:30 A.M., NBC, 1941).

17790 **Knoep, Francis.** Singer (KTAB, Oakland, CA, 1925).

17791 **Knoernschild, Elmer.** Newscaster (KFUO, Clayton, MO, 1940–1941).

17792 **Knoles, Tully.** Newscaster (KWG, Stockton, CA, 1940).

17793 **Knoll, Alma.** Pianist (WEEI, Boston, MA, 1925).

17794 **Knopp, Virginia.** COM-HE (KFJB, Marshalltown, IA, 1949).

17795 **Knorr, Reg.** Actor Knorr was in the cast of *Myrt and Marge* and *Og, Son of Fire*.

17796 **Knotschwar, (Miss) Jackie.** COM-HE (KBRL, McCook, NE, 1956).

17797 **Knott, Jack.** Newscaster (WIS, Columbia, SC, 1945–1946).

17798 **Knott, Martha.** DJ (KBYE, Oklahoma City, OK, 1955–1956).

17799 **Knotti, Frank.** Pianist (*Frank Knotti*, instr. mus. prg., WMMN, Fairmont, WV, 1937–1938).

17800 **Knouse, Anita.** COM-HE (KETX, Livingston, TX, 1957).

17801 **Knouse, Ray.** DJ (*Juke Box and Record Bar*, KCLE, Cleburne, TX, 1947).

17802 **Knowles, Joyce.** COM-HE (WBMC, McMinnville, TN, 1957).

17803 **Knowles, Lillian.** Contralto (WOK, Chicago, IL, 1926; WMAQ, Chicago, IL, 1927).

17804 **Knox, Anita.** Pianist (WORD, Batavia, IL, 1925).

17805 **Knox, Bob.** DJ (*Here's Everything*, WIBG, Philadelphia, PA, 1947–1954).

17806 **Knox, Delores.** DJ (WLAU, Laurel, MA, 1956).

17807 **Knox, Edith.** Pianist (KTAB, Oakland, CA, 1925).

17808 **Knox, Esther M.** Whistler (WAAM, Newark, NJ, 1924).

17809 **Knox, Fannie.** Soprano (KFWM, Oakland, CA, 1926).

17810 **Knox, Harry C.** Flutist (KHJ, Los Angeles, CA, 1923).

17811 **Knox, James F.** Violinist (WBZ, Springfield, MA, 1925).

17812 **Knox, Jim H.** Newscaster (WTFL, Fort Lauderdale, FL, 1939).

17813 **Knox, Lena B.** Pianist (WBZ, Springfield, MA, 1924).

17814 **Knox, Robert B.** Newscaster (WDAS, Philadelphia, PA, 1939–1940).

17815 **Knox, Roger.** Tenor (WJZ, New York, NY, 1925).

17816 **Knox, Sandy.** Newscaster (*The Local News*, KVVC, Ventura, CA, 1948).

17817 **Knox, William Morgan.** Violinist on the faculty of the Cincinnati College of Music (WLW, Cincinnati, OH, 1922).

17818 **KNRC Clowns.** Happy Dodge, Allan Fairchild and Clarence Juneau were the singing comedians known as the KNRC Clowns (KNRC, Los Angeles, CA, 1925).

17819 **Knudsen, Peggy.** Actress Knudsen was in the cast of *The Woman in White* daytime serial program.

17820 **Knutson, Daryl.** DJ (*The Bandstand*, WDSM, Superior, WI, 1947).

17821 **Knutson, Erling.** Violinist (WDAF, Kansas City, MO, 1928).

17822 **Knutson, Hal.** DJ (*Keniters Klub*, WENI, Anchorage, AK, 1948; *Early Bird Show*, WENI, 1952; *Anything Goes*, KBOI, Boise, ID, 1955).

17823 **Knutson, Ken.** DJ (*Afternoon Tune Time*, KLPM, Minot, SD 1948).

17824 **Knutson, Milo.** Newscaster (KROC, Rochester, MN, 1942; KFBI, Wichita, KS, 1944–1945). Sportscaster (KROC, 1942).

17825 **Knutson, Muriel.** COM-HE (KROC, Rochester, MN, 1951).

17826 **KNX Concert Orchestra.** Station band (KNX, Los Angeles, CA, 1928).

17827 ***KNX Morning Gym.*** J.C. Casey conducted the early morning exercise program (KNX, Los Angeles, CA in 1926).

17828 **KNX Rounders.** A five-man vocal group led by Dudley Chambers (KNX, Los Angeles, CA, 1929).

17829 **KOA Minstrel Players (aka *Dark, Dark Secrets*).** Minstrel group that included interlocutor Freeman H. Talbot; Stewart A. Houseman as "Tambo"; H. Gerald Sherman as "Bones"; and H. Gerald Sherman as "Rastus" (KOA, Denver, CO, 1926). The following year the minstrels consisted of H. Gerald Sherman as interlocutor supported by Art Higgins, Freeman H. Talbot and F.A. Franklin (KOA, Denver, CO, 1927). When interlocutor Freeman H. Talbot directed the program, it was called *Dark, Dark Secrets* and had the following cast: Stewart A. Houseman as "Tambo"; F.A. "Shorty" Franklin as "Bones"; Art Higgins as "Rastus" and musicians of the KOA Orchestra directed by Henry Trustman Ginsberg (KOA, 1927).

17830 **KOA Mixed Quartet.** The station's vocal group included Bernice W. Doughty, soprano; Lucille Fowler, contralto; Ralph Freese, tenor; Everett E. Foster, baritone; and director Freeman H. Talbot (KOA, Denver, CO, 1928).

17831 **KOA Orchestra.** Dr. Lewis H. Chernoff directed the station's band (KOA, Denver, CO, 1925–1928).

17832 **KOA Players.** Station KOA's acting group included Otis B. Thayer, Gertrude M. Richards, Iris Ruth Pavey, John Connery, Clayton C. Cowan and Clarence C. Moore (KOA, Denver, CO, 1925).

17833 **KOA Quartet.** Station KOA's vocal group consisted of soprano Margaret Fell; contralto Frances Joseph; tenor Paul Packer; and bass Ross Buckstraw (KOA, Denver, CO, 1926).

17834 ***KOA's Invisible Stage Beauty.*** Iris Ruth Pavey was station KOA's beauty expert who conducted this program for women (KOA, Denver, CO, 1926).

17835 **Koachman, Andy.** Newscaster (WADC, Akron, OH, 1942).

17836 **Kobak, Ed.** Sportscaster (*Sports Review* and football play-by-play, WTWA, Thomson, GA, 1949). *Sports Round Up* (WTWA, 1950; *Sports Review*, WTWA, 1952). DJ (*Kobak's Korn*, WTWA, 1952; WGAC, Augusta, GA, 1954–1955; WBBQ, Augusta, GA, 1957; KRIC, Beaumont, TX, 1960).

17837 **Kober, Eulale.** Pianist (KYW, Chicago, IL, 1926).

17838 **Kobusch, Harry.** Leader (Harry Kobusch and his Orchestra, KPRC, Houston, TX, 1926).

17839 **Koch, Arthur.** Pianist (KSD, St. Louis, MO, 1924). As an organist, Koch broadcast from the Capitol Theater, Des Moines, IA (1928).

17840 **Koch, Clarence.** Announcer (KFEQ, St. Louis, MO, 1925).

17841 **Koch, Herbert "Herbie."** Organist (*Herbie Koch*, instr. mus. prg., WHAS, Louisville, KY, 1935–1938).

17842 **Koch, Ory.** DJ (*Corn Crib Frolics*, KFNF, Shenandoah, IA, 1947–1948).

17843 **Koch, Richard.** Newscaster (WIOD, Miami, FL, 1941).

17844 **Kochanski, Paul.** Russian violinist Kochanski appeared on the *Atwater Kent Hour* program (NBC, 1928).

17845 **Kochendarfer, Therese.** Staff contralto (WFDF, Flint, MI, 1929).

17846 ***(The) Kodak Hour.*** The good music program featured singers Marie Girard, Helen Oelheim, other guest artists and an orchestra conducted by Nathaniel Shilkret (Friday, Weekly, CBS, 1930).

17847 **Koehl, Julius.** Pianist (WOR, Newark, NJ, 1925).

17848 **Koehler, (Mrs.) Herman [Lisbet Hoffman].** Concert pianist (WJZ, New York, NY, 1922).

17849 **Koehne, Freida.** Violinist (KYW, Chicago, IL, 1928).

17850 **Koenig, Frederick.** Announcer (WRW, Tarrytown, NY, 1925–1926).

17851 **Koenig, Mildred.** Organist-singer (*The Ray of Radio*, WJKS, Gary, IN, 1929).

17852 **Koenig, Nicholas.** Violinist (1925).

17853 **Koerner, Esther C.** Reader (KDKA, Pittsburgh, PA, 1922).

17854 **Koernmann, Miriam.** Contralto (WGN, Chicago, IL, 1924).

17855 **Koester, Maria C.** COM-HE (WJAR, Providence, RI, 1924).

17856 **Koester, Tony.** Sportscaster (KFBK, Sacramento, CA, 1937–1945; KFBK, 1950; *Sports Final*, 1951–1955). Newscaster (KFVK, 1938, 1946).

17857 **Koestner, Arthur J.** DJ (*Musical Melodies*, WCRW, Chicago, IL, 1950).

17858 **Koestner, Josef.** Leader of the orchestra on the *Williams Syncomatics* program (NBC-Blue, New York, NY, 1929). Pianist (*Joseph Koestner*, instr. mus. prg., WENR, Chicago, IL, 1942).

17859 **Koetter, (Mrs.) Louis.** Contralto soloist Koetter of the Presbyterian Church of Cincinnati, Ohio, broadcast each Sunday (WLW, Cincinnati, OH, 1923).

17860 **Koewing [Koweing], Jessie (aka "JEK").** Violinist, announcer and program director Koewing was said to have been the only woman announcer at WOR in 1923 (WOR, Newark, NJ, 1923).

17861 ***(The) Koffee Club.*** Cooperative Coffee Distributors sponsored the music program that featured the orchestra of Richard Himber with vocalists GoGo deLys and Stewart Allen (30 min., Friday, 8:00–8:30 P.M., MBS, 1937).

17862 **Kofoed, Jack.** News analyst (*Behind the Headlines*, WIOD, Miami, FL, 1940–1942).

17863 **Kogel, Oscar.** Leader (*Oscar Kogel Orchestra*, instr. mus. prg., WHAS, Louisville, KY, 1935).

17864 **Kogen, Harry.** Musical director, *Yeast Foamers* program (NBC-Red, New York, NY, 1929). Leader (*Harry Kogen Orchestra*, instr. mus. prg., NBC-Blue, 1934–1938).

17865 **Kohl, Alma Pratt.** Pianist (KFI, Los Angeles, CA, 1928–1929).

17866 **Kohl, Arthur "Art."** Actor Kohl was in the cast of *Archie Andrews*, *Bachelor's Children*, *The Barton Family*, *Girl Alone*, *Right to Happiness*, *Road of Life* and *Mary Marlin.*

17867 **Kohl, James.** DJ (*Early Risers Club*, WBOW, Terre Haute, IN, 1948–1950).

17868 **KOIN Light Opera Ensemble.** Station's singing group (KOIN, Portland, OR, 1926).

17869 **KOIN Male Quartet.** Vocal group consisting of Emil Brahms, bass; Bud Abbott, baritone; Denton Denman, tenor; and Lloyd Warren, tenor (KOIN, Portland, OR, 1928).

17870 **KOIN Radio Players.** Miss Jean Macaulay directed this station's dramatic group (KOIN, Portland, OR, 1927).

17871 **Koki, Sam.** Leader (*Sam Koki Hawaiians Orchestra*, instr. mus. prg., MBS, 1934, 1940).

17872 **Kolarek, Tony.** Newscaster (WCAO, Baltimore, MD, 1938).

17873 **Kolb, Fletcher.** DJ (*The Whistlin' Man*, WMRY, New Orleans, LA, 1954).

17874 **Kolb, Harold.** Newscaster (WSAY, Rochester, NY, 1942). DJ (*Musical Showcase*, WARC, Rochester, NY, 1948; *Second Breakfast*, WARC, 1950).

17875 **Kolb, Vivian.** Singer (WHN, New York, NY, 1923).

17876 **Kolberg, Margaret.** Ten-year-old pianist (WOAW, Omaha, NE, 1924).

17877 **Kolby, Cal.** Newscaster (WMAS, Springfield, MA, 1945). DJ (*Make Believe Ballroom*, WAVZ, New Haven, CT, 1947; WDRC, Hartford, CT, 1956).

17878 **Kolence, Nikki.** COM-HE (KPRK, Livingston, MT, 1956).

17879 **Kolisch [Kotitsch] Vlado.** Young Croatian violinist (WEAF, New York, NY, 1925–1926).

17880 **Kollins, Kay.** DJ (*Tea Time at Ten*, KFEQ, St. Joseph, MO, 1950).

17881 **Kollmar, Richard "Dick."** Actor-host Kollmar appeared on *Big Sister*, *Boston Blackie* (title role), *Bright Horizon*, *Claudia*, *John's Other Wife*, *Life Can Be Beautiful*, *Pretty Kitty Kelly*, *Radio Reader's Digest* (host) and *When a Girl Marries.*

17882 **Kolodin, Irving.** DJ (WHN, New York, NY, 1942). Kolodin was the music editor of the weekly New York *Sun*. He presented show business guests, musical celebrities and music lovers from various fields and allowed them to play their favorite recordings and give the reasons for their choices. Kolodin's first guest was Oscar Levant.

17883 **Kolomoku, Walter.** Director, (Walter Kolomoku's Honoluluans Orchestra, WABC, New York, NY, 1929).

17884 **Kolster Dance Orchestra.** Popular dance band (CBS, 1929).

17885 ***(The) Kolster Hour.*** The Ben Selvin Orchestra, singers Mac and Lennie and Rae Samuels were featured on the music program (CBS, 1940).

17886 ***(The) Kolster Radio Hour.*** A weekly concert music program (60 min., Wednesday, 9:00–10:00 P.M., CBS, 1927–1929).

17887 **Koltum, Ruth.** COM-HE (WJBO, Baton Rouge, LA, 1949).

17888 **Komasa, Andy.** Sportscaster (*Sports Bill*, WTWT). DJ (WTWT, Stevens Point, WI, 1950).

17889 **Komole, Eleanor.** COM-HE (WLAD, Danbury, CT, 1951).

17890 ***Komedy Kapers.*** A syndicated comedy and music program, *Komedy Kapers* was hosted by Tom Post. At times the performers were: Bob Burns, Elvia Allman, Shirley Reed, Martha Raye, the Three Stars and others (15 min., Transcribed, 1930s).

17891 **KOMO Orchestra.** Station band conducted by Emil Birnbaum (KOMO, Seattle, WA, 1928).

17892 KOMO Trio. Constance Cook, Rhena Marshall and Fred Lynch were members of the vocal trio (KOMO, Seattle, WA, 1929).

17893 Kondor, (Mme.) Mariska and Eugen Medgyaszay. These singers from the Hungarian Opera Company specialized in Hungarian folk songs (KPO, San Francisco, CA, 1926).

17894 Konecky, Eugene. Announcer-entertainer Konecky started the station's *Blah* Club (WOAW, Omaha, NE, 1925–1928). In 1928, Konecky was known as the "Grand Champion Staller," for his "stalling" through the Dundee-Hudkins fight that *did not take place.* For many years on WOAW he played "Dizzy Izzy" on his *Blah Club* program. Konecky in 1928 also broadcast book reviews for WOW (Omaha, NE).

17895 Kong, W.O. DJ (*1290 Harmony Lane*, WTOC, Savannah, GA, 1950).

17896 Konopacki, Felix. Newscaster (WHOM, Jersey City, NJ, 1941).

17897 Konz, Karl. Sportscaster (KFIZ, Fond-du-Lac, WI, 1940–1942; *Football Prophet*, KFIZ, 1948).

17898 Kooker, Ethel. Book reviewer (WFI, Philadelphia, PA, 1928).

17899 Koons, Bob. DJ (*Jazz Show*, KMO, Tacoma, WA, 1947–1950).

17900 Koons, Eva Seipe. Singer (*Eva Seipe Koons*, vcl. mus. prg., WORK, York, PA, 1936).

17901 Koontz, Marie. Contralto (WRC, Washington, DC, 1924).

17902 Koop, Theodore F. Newscaster (CBS, 1947–1948).

17903 Kooreman, Jean. COM-HE (KBIZ, Ottumwa, IA, 1956).

17904 Kopac [Kopec], Mike. Pianist Kopac was billed as the "King of the Ivories" (KFAB, Lincoln, NE, 1926).

17905 Kopel, Herman. Violinist (WFBH, New York, NY, 1925).

17906 Kopp, Winifred. Contralto (KTBI, Los Angeles, CA, 1929).

17907 Kopp, William J. Leader (William J. Kopp Concert Orchestra, WLW, Cincinnati, OH, 1923).

17908 Kopp, Winifred. Contralto (KTBI, Los Angeles, CA, 1929).

17909 Koppel, Sydney. Pianist (WJZ, New York, NY, 1926).

17910 Kopriver, Terry. COM-HE (WWGP, Sanford, NC, 1951).

17911 Korbel, Winifred. Contralto (KBMW, Wahpeton, ND, 1951).

17912 Korbin, Doc. Leader (Doc Korbin's Orchestra, WEBJ, New York, NY, 1926).

17913 Korff, Arnold. Actor Korff was in the cast of *Young Dr. Malone.*

17914 Korkbridge, Bradford. Actor Korkbridge appeared with Claire Stratton in *Sue Dear*, a musical play broadcast by WJZ (New York, NY, June 24, 1922).

17915 Koretzky, Vitali. Russian tenor (NBC, 1928).

17916 Korey, Kay. COM-HE (KORE, Eugene, OR, 1955).

17917 Korman, Howard. Baritone (WMCA, New York, NY).

17918 Korman, Seymour. Newscaster (MBS, 1942). Foreign correspondent Korman of the Chicago *Tribune's* London bureau was also Mutual's London correspondent.

17919 Korn, Erna. Contralto (WJZ, New York, NY, 1927).

17920 *Korn Kobblers (Orchestra).* Instr. mus. prg. with comic flourishes (WCCO, Minneapolis–St. Paul, MN, 1942; *Korn Kobblers*, instr. mus. prg, MBS, 1947). The comedy music group was reminiscent of Spike Jones, the Kidoodlers and the Hoosier Hot Shots bands.

17921 *Kornienko's Oriental Orchestra.* Instr. mus. prg. (NBC, 1935–1936).

17922 Korsmo, Perdin. Tenor (KVOS, Bellingham, WA, 1928).

17923 Korzelius, Gene. Sportscaster (WBNY, Buffalo, NY, 1945–1954).

17924 Kosowicz, Edward. Newscaster (WHOM, Jersey City, NJ, 1941).

17925 Kossell, Johnny. Leader (KDYL Dance and Concert Orchestra, KDYL, Salt Lake City, UT, 1929).

17926 Kost, Henry. Tenor Kost formerly was billed in vaudeville as "Cody the Singing Cartoonist" (WOR, Newark, NJ, 1927).

17927 Kost, Neva. COM-HE (KYSM, Mankato, MN, 1949).

17928 Kostelanetz, Andre. Assistant conductor of Howard Barlow' symphonic orchestra on the Columbia Broadcasting System's inaugural program (CBS, 1927).

17929 Kosut, Hal. Newscaster (WLIB, Brooklyn, NY, 1946).

17930 Kotera, John. Saxophonist (WOAW, Omaha, NE, 1923).

17931 Kotera, William. Announcer (WIAK, Omaha, NE, 1925).

17932 Kotschwar, Jackie. COM-HE (WBRL, McCook, NE, 1956).

17933 Kott, Lillian. Gospel singer (KFSG, Los Angeles, CA, 1926).

17934 Kounovsky, Rosella. COM-HE (KLPM, Minot, ND, 1956–1957).

17935 Kountz [Koontz], Buzzy. Leader (*Buzzy Kountz Orchestra*, instr. mus. prg., WCAE, Pittsburgh, PA, 1935–1936).

17936 Kovacs, Ernie. DJ (*Coffee with Kovacs*, WTTM, Trenton, NJ, 1948; *Chickenfoot Junction*, WTTM, 1950; WABC, New York, NY, 1955). Comic Kovacs showed his great visual and comic creativity during his television career, where he was a great influence on the media. Kovacs also appeared in films such as *Bell, Book and Candle* (1958) with James Stewart and Kim Novack. His career was shortened by his death in an automobile accident.

17937 Kovacs, Martha. Violinist (WNYC, New York, NY, 1932).

17938 Kovar, Ima Dell. COM-HE (KNAL, Victoria, TX, 1957).

17939 Kowalski, Jacuelyn. COM-HE (WBKV, West Bend, WI, 1960).

17940 Kowing, Shirley. COM-HE (WRRR, Rockford, IL, 1955).

17941 Kozak, Jimmie. Pianist (*Jimmie Kozak*, instr. mus. prg., WAAF, Chicago, IL, 1935).

17942 Kozak, Raymond. Sportscaster (KMMJ, Grand Island, NE, 1942).

17943 Kozalka, Alexander. Violinist (WGY, Schenectady, NY, 1923).

17944 Kozel, Pat. COM-HE (WWIZ, Lorain, OH, 1960).

17945 Kozias, Ethel. Soprano (KFSG, Los Angeles, CA, 1925).

17946 Kozlow, Bucky. DJ (WLIB, New York, NY, 1947).

17947 KPO Carolers. The vocal group that featured ballads and semi-classical numbers consisted of Urban Hartman, Refa Miller, Mildred Bailey and Harvey Orr (KPO, San Francisco, CA, 1929).

17948 KPO Orchestra. Station band (KPO, San Francisco, CA, 1928).

17949 KPO Symphony Orchestra. Symphonic music organization conducted by Nathan Abas (KPO, San Francisco, CA, 1929).

17950 (The) KPO Trio. Instrumental trio including violinist Cyrus Trobbe, cellist George von Hagel and pianist Jean Campbell (KPO, San Francisco, CA, 1926).

17951 Kraatz, Donald. Actor Kraatz was in the cast of *The Barton Family* and *Road of Life* daytime serial programs.

17952 Kraber, Ethel. Pianist (WHP, Harrisburg, PA, 1937).

17953 Krable, Shirley. COM-HE (WQXI, Atlanta, GA, 1951).

17954 Kraemer, Agnes. Dramatic soprano (KFI, Los Angeles, CA, 1925).

17955 Kraemore, Howard. Leader (*Howard Kraemore Orchestra*, instr. mus. prg., WMT, Cedar Rapids–Waterloo, IA, 1936).

17956 Kraeuter, Phyllis. Cellist (WJZ, New York, NY, 1924).

17957 Krafft, Bob. DJ (*Disc Derby*, KXXX, Colby, KS, 1948).

17958 Kraft, Edwin Arthur. Organist (1923).

17959 *(The) Kraft Music Hall.* Before Bing Crosby made the program famous, Paul Whiteman was host. Whiteman's program featured members of his band and such guest performers as pianist Roy Bargy, Ramona, the King's Men, Lee Wiley, William Gargan, Helen Jepson, Johnny Mercer, John Dunbar, Morton Downey and Peggy Nealy. Ford Bond was the announcer (60 min., Weekly, NBC, 1934–1935).

Bing Crosby took over the *Kraft Music Hall* show in 1935 and made it one of radio's most popular programs until he left in 1946. With Crosby as the singing-host, many talented performers were introduced to the American radio public for the first time and gained stardom from that introduction. Prior to Crosby's entrance on the scene, Deems Taylor was co-host with the Paul Whiteman band the program's major feature. Al Jolson took over the show in 1934 when both Taylor and Whiteman departed. Crosby took over from Jolson in 1935. After Crosby left in 1946, Jolson returned to the program for a short time. Nelson Eddy and

Dorothy Kirsten took over several summer *Kraft Music Hall* versions. The final version had Rudy Vallee acting chiefly as a DJ. The program's cast during the Bing Crosby era included: Victor Borge, Connee Boswell, Bob Burns (The Arkansas Traveler), Peggy Lee, Jerry Lester, Mary Martin , George Murphy and the Music Maids and Hal vocal group. Jimmy Dorsey's band appeared one year, but John Scott Trotter provided the music for the remainder of Bing's tenure. The show's writers were Bob Brewster, Carroll Carroll, David Gregory, Ed Helwick and Manny Mannheim. Ed Gardner, Cal Kuhl and Ezra MacIntosh were the directors. The announcers were Ken Carpenter, Roger Krupp and Don Wilson (NBC, 1933–1949).

By 1955, radio was in transition, harassed as it was by the competition of television. *Variety* reviewed that year's version of *The Kraft Music Hall* and found it wanting by noting that the once great *Kraft Music Hall* had fallen on bad days. Rudy Vallee appeared on this version as a DJ, playing recordings and interviewing such celebrities as Gwen Verdon, Julie Andrews, Eddie Condon and Steve Allen. The announcer in this format was Charles Stark. *Variety* concluded this was an indication of the low estate to which radio had descended (60 min., Sunday, 8:00–9:00 P.M., CBS, 1955).

17960 ***(The) Kraft Program.*** Deems Taylor was the host on this music variety show sponsored by the Kraft Food Company. He introduced such performers as Al Jolson, Peggy Healy, the Rhythm Boys, Roy Bargy, Jack Fulton, Ramona and the talented members of the Paul Whiteman band. From the performers listed, it is clear that most of them came from the Whiteman band. Whiteman himself played a major role in the program's creation and production (60 min., Thursday, 10:00–11:00 P.M., NBC-Red, 1933). This program was a forerunner of the *Kraft Music Hall* program. *See* **Singers: Crooners, Canaries, Cow Girls and Hillbillies.**

17961 ***Krakowska Orchestra.*** Instr. mus. prg. (WTIC, Hartford, CT, 1935).

17962 Kraman, Sophie. Violinist (WAHG, New York, NY, 1925).

17963 Kramer, Ben. Newscaster (WDEF, Chattanooga, TN, 1941).

17964 Kramer, Claude. DJ (*Make Believe Ballroom*, KVAK, Atchison, KS, 1947).

17965 Kramer, Curt. Pianist (KFUU, Oakland, CA, 1925; KGW, Portland, OR, 1926).

17966 Kramer, Frances Bauman. COM-HE (WVCG, Coral Gables, FL, 1949).

17967 Kramer, Harry. News analyst (*New York Lighting Electric Stores News*, WNEW, New York, NY, 1937).

17968 Kramer, L.J. Guitarist (KVOO, Tulsa, OK, 1928).

17969 Kramer, Louise. Staff violinist (WFAA, Dallas, TX, 1927).

17970 Kramer, Mandel. Busy actor Kramer was in the cast of *Backstage Wife*, *Counterspy*, *Dimension X*, *The Falcon*, *Famous Jury Trials*, *Mr. and Mrs. North*, *Perry Mason*, *Quick as a Flash*, *The Shadow*, *Stella Dallas*, *Superman*, *This is Your FBI*, *True Detective Mysteries* and *Yours Truly, Johnny Dollar* (title role).

17971 Kramer, Wilford J. News analyst (*Upon Reflection*, WCVS, Springfield, IL, 1948).

17972 Kramins, Robert. News analyst (*The News and You*, WKAR, East Lansing, MI, 1947).

17973 Kramp, Larry. Newscaster (WCBS, Springfield, IL, 1939).

17974 Kranert, L.W. and Dwight Harned. Piano duet team (WHO, Des Moines, IA, 1925).

17975 Krantz, Audrey. Violinist (WHO, Des Moines, IA, 1925).

17976 Krantz, Pat. COM-HE (KLIZ, Brainerd, MN, 1951).

17977 Krash, Abe. Sportscaster (KFBC, Cheyenne, WY, 1940).

17978 Krasof, Wanda. Pianist (KTAB, Oakland, CA, 1925).

17979 Kratz, Ella Jacquette. Pianist (WCAU, Philadelphia, PA, 1926).

17980 Krauel, John. DJ (*Birthday and Anniversary Club*, KFAM, St. Cloud, MN, 1947).

17981 Kraus, Betty. COM-HE (WIRY, Plattsburg, NY, 1956).

17982 Krause, Harvey. Organist (*Harvey Krause*, KOY, Phoenix, AZ, 1933).

17983 Krausgrill, Walter. Leader (Walter Krausgrill's Balconades Ballroom Orchestra, KFRC, San Francisco, CA, 1925–1929).

17984 Krauss, Katherine. Pianist (WBBC and WCGU, Brooklyn, NYC, 1929).

17985 KRE Players. The dramatic group was directed by Ruth Taft. In 1926, they presented a widely praised production of Oscar Wilde's *Lady Windemere's Fan*. Another of its notable broadcasts was Taft's production of Ridgly Torrence's three one-act *Negro Plays* and a program of Negro spirituals sung by James Thomas, billed as "America's own colored baritone." Incidental music for the program was supplied by the KRE String Ensemble (KRE, Berkeley, CA, 1925–1926).

17986 KRE Players Ensemble. Instrumental group directed by Willa Conzelman (KRE, Berkeley, CA, 1925).

17987 Kreamer, Kaye. Newscaster (WROK, Rockford, IL, 1937).

17988 Krebs, S. Walter. Pianist (WEAF, New York, NY, 1923).

17989 Krebs, Veronica. Contralto (WMBB, Chicago, IL, 1926).

17990 Krebsbach, E.E. Announcer (KGCX, Vida, MT, 1927). News analyst (*Between the Lines*, KGCX, Sidney, MT, 1945).

17991 Kreeder, Maurice. Baritone (KRFC, San Francisco, CA, 1928).

17992 Kregeloh, Hubert. News commentator (WSPR, Springfield, MA, 1940–1942, 1944–1945; *Understanding the Peace*, WSPR, 1947–1948).

17993 Kreger, Elwyn. Newscaster (KUSD, Vermillion, SD, 1945).

17994 Kreger, Rosella. COM-HE (WFRM, Coudersport, PA, 1956).

17995 ***Kreimer String Quartet.*** Instr. mus. prg. (CBS, 1936).

17996 Kreindler, Sarah. Violinist (KOA, Denver, CO, 1930).

17997 Kreisler, Fritz. Distinguished violinist Kreisler broadcast concert selections from Pittsburgh's Carnegie Music Hall (KDKA, Pittsburgh, PA, 1922). Kreisler also made numerous network appearances in the following years.

17998 Krell, Fred. DJ (*Krell's Carnival*, WSAM, Saginaw, MI, 1950; *Krell Show*, WSGW, Saginaw, MI, 1952–1956).

17999 ***(The) Kre-Mel Gang.*** Uncle Ollie, "a Swede," told stories for children. The Four Mountaineers from the Blue Ridge Mountains of Virginia sang CW songs on the program. The sponsor was the Corn Products Refining Company (1931).

18000 Kremer, Curt. Leader (Curt Kremer Orchestra, KXL, Portland, OR, 1929).

18001 Kremer, Isa. Ballad singer (WJZ, New York, NY, 1926).

18002 Kremer, Marion. Soprano (WHAP, New York, NY, 1927).

18003 Krenz, Bill. Leader (*Bill Krenz Orchestra*, instr. mus. prg., NBC, 1936; WHAM, Rochester, NY, 1937; NBC-Red, 1938–1939).

18004 Kretecshman [Kretesman], Lorraine. COM-HE (KUBC, Montrose, CO, 1956).

18005 Kretsinger, Jack. Newscaster (WJBC, Bloomington, IN, 1940). Sportscaster (WJBC, 1940).

18006 Kreuger, Art. Leader (*Art Kreuger Orchestra*, instr. mus. prg., WNAC, Boston, MA, 1932).

18007 Kreuger, Benny. Leader (Benny Kreuger's Gold Seal Band, WABC, New York, NY, 1929; *Benny Kreuger Orchestra*, instr. mus. prg., WKBW, Buffalo, NY, 1938; MBS, 1940). Marshall Dane, who was the later show's network announcer, introduced Kreuger as "The master of the saxophone and his orchestra."

18008 Kreuger, Florence. Soprano (WOC, Davenport, IA, 1928).

18009 Kreuger, Frank. Newscaster (WHOM, Jersey City, NJ, 1940).

18010 Kreuger and Dillon. Instrumental duo known as the "Banjo Barons" (WMBB, Chicago, IL, 1926).

18011 Kreutzinger, Ernie. Leader (*Ernie Kreutzinger Orchestra*, instr. mus. prg., CBS, 1934).

18012 KRFU Catfish String Band. Eight-man country music band led by Jimmie Wilson (KRFU, Bristol, OK, 1925).

18013 Krick, Irving. Pianist (KFUU, Oakland, CA, 1925).

18014 Krick, Jeanne. Pianist (KFWM, Oakland, CA, 1926).

18015 Krick, Mabel. Soprano (YN, 1937).

18016 Krickett, Ernie. Leader (Ernie Krickett's Cinderella Orchestra, WOR, Newark, NJ, 1924).

18017 Kriegel, Gil. Newscaster (WLIB, Brooklyn, NY, 1946). DJ (*Laff with Lunch*,

WITH, Baltimore, MD, 1948–1952). Sportscaster (WITH, 1955).

18018 Krieger, Ed. DJ (*WSOO Varieties*, WSOO, Saulte Ste. Marie, MN, 1947–1949; *Coffee Club*, WSOO, 1950).

18019 Krieger, James. Actor Krieger was in the cast of *John's Other Wife*, *Orphans of Divorce* and *Pepper Young's Family*.

18020 Krieger, Vivien. COM-HE (WESB, Bradford, PA, 1956–1957).

18021 Kriens, Christian. Leader (*Christian Kriens and his WTK Concert Orchestra*, instr. mus. prg., WTK, Cleveland, OH, 1931).

18022 Krigger, William B. Baritone (WHN, New York, NY, 1925).

18023 *Krilikowski's Polish Band*. Instr. mus. prg. (WELI, New Haven, CT, 1939).

18024 Kristel, Leon. Tenor (WJY, New York, NY, 1925).

18025 Kritz, (Cantor) Aron. Born in the Ukraine, Cantor Kritz broadcast weekly lectures (WBBM, Chicago, IL, 1927).

18026 Kriz, Bob. Newscaster (WOSH, Oshkosh, WI, 1942).

18027 Kroeck, Louis F. Newscaster (KTMS, Santa Barbara, CA, 1945).

18028 Kroeger, Barry. Actor Kroeger was in the cast of *Big Sister*, *The Falcon* (title role) and *Young Dr. Malone*.

18029 Kroen, Edward J. "Ed." Newscaster (WWSW, Pittsburgh, PA, 1937; WKPA, New Kensington, PA, 1941, 1945).

18030 Kroenke, Carl. Actor Kroenke appeared on *Arnold Grimm's Daughter*, *Houseboat Hannah*, *Ma Perkins*, *Tom Mix* and *Vic and Sade*.

18031 Krohn, S.M., Jr. Announcer (WSMK, Dayton, OH, 1925).

18032 Kroll, Lillian. Pianist (WEBJ, New York, NY, 1926).

18033 Kronenberg, (Rabbi) Aaron. Inspirational broadcasts daily (WBYN, New York, NY, 1940s).

18034 Kronlik, Frank L. Announcer (WGCM, Gulfport, MI, 1925).

18035 Kross, Dick. Newscaster (WGES, Chicago, IL, 1938). Sportscaster (WGES, 1939).

18036 Kroulik, Frank J. Announcer and station manager (WGCM, Gulfport, MS, 1929).

18037 Krouser, Caryl. News analyst (*Local Views of the News*, KWTC, Barstow, CA, 1947).

18038 *Kroy Club Orchestra*. Instr. mus. prg. (WORK, York, PA, 1936).

18039 Kruck, Marion. COM-HE (KCHA, Charles City, IA, 1960).

18040 Kreuger, Jackie. COM-HE (KVET, Austin, TX, 1951).

18041 Krug, E.H. Baritone (WGHB, Clearwater Beach, FL, 1926).

18042 Krugall, Nita. COM-HE (KRES, St. Joseph, MO, 1955).

18043 Kruger, Alma. Actress Kruger was in the cast of the daytime serial programs *Pages of Romance* and *Those We Love*.

18044 Kruger, Kathryn. Newscaster (*4-H Club News*, KLIZ, Brainerd, MN, 1947).

18045 Kruger, Otto. Violinist (WIP, Philadelphia, PA, 1926).

18046 Krugman, Louis "Lou." Actor Krugman was in the cast of *Buster Brown's Gang*, *Dear Mom* and *Romance of Helen Trent*.

18047 Kruh, Bob. Leader (Bob Kruh's College Club Orchestra, WGBS, New York, NY, 1925).

18048 Krulee, Max. Leader (Max Krulee's Orchestra, WBZ, Springfield, MA, 1926).

18049 Krum, Fayette. Daytime serial writer and producer (Network, 1930s). Krum was the writer of the *Girl Alone* daytime serial and producer of *Right to Happiness* and *Road of Life* programs. .

18050 Krum, Tyrell. News analyst (*Veterans' Advisor*, NBC, 1947–1948).

18051 Krumholtz, Phillip. Baritone (WEBJ, New York, NY, 1926).

18052 Krupa, Gene. Leader and virtuoso jazz drummer (*Gene Krupa Orchestra*, instr. mus. prg., NBC, 1940; MBS, 1944). Announcer Bob Martin on MBS introduced the Krupa band with vocalist Anita O'Day in this way: "Gene Krupa from the Hotel Astor Roof in the heart of Times Square, New York City." Krupa was one of the outstanding drummers of his era.

18053 Krupp, Ida. Soprano (KPI, Los Angeles, CA, 1927).

18054 Krupa, Jan. Organist (*Jan Krupa*, instr. mus. prg., WWVA, Wheeling, WV, 1932).

18055 Krupitsky, Clara. Singer (WEVD, New York, NY, 1937–1939).

18056 Krupp, Larry. Newscaster (WJW, Akron, OH, 1940–1941). DJ (*Bandstand*, WJW, Cleveland, OH, 1947; *Anything Goes*, WJW, 1948). Sportscaster (WJW, 1954). By 1947, WJW had moved from Akron to Cleveland.

18057 Krupp, Nita. COM-HE (KRAY, Amarillo, TX, 1956).

18058 Krupp, Roger. Announcer Krupp worked on the *American Album of Familiar Music*, *Arnold Grimm's Daughter*, *Backstage Wife*, *Counterspy*, *Dunninger Show*, *Ellery Queen*, *Famous Jury Trials*, *Jungle Jim*, *Just Plain Bill*, *Kraft Music Hall*, *Lum and Abner*, *Manhattan Merry-go-Round*, *Modern Cinderella*. *Mr. Chameleon*, *Quiz Kids*, *Scattergood Baines*, *Silver Theater*, *Stella Dallas*, *Stepmother*, *Vic and Sade* and *Vox Pop* programs.

18059 Kruschen, Jack. Actor Kruschen was in the cast of *One Man's Family* and *Romance*.

18060 Kruse, Edward and Miss Knolte. Vocal duets (WLW, Cincinnati, OH, 1923).

18061 Kruse, Gladys Herrick. Pianist-organist (WLW, Cincinnati, OH, 1925).

18062 Kruse, Virginia. Teacher of French language (WSUI, Iowa City, IA, 1938).

18063 Krushberg, Roy. J. DJ (WRLD, West Point, GA, 1948).

18064 Kruzan, Edith. Soprano (WBOW, Terre Haute, IN, 1939).

18065 *K-7 Spy Stories* (aka *K-7*). Burke Boyce and George F. Zimmer wrote these stories of espionage during the first world war. Glamour and mystery added interest to the intrigue when the villain didn't always pay for his vile deeds (30 min., Sunday, 5:00–5:30 P.M. or Sunday, 6:00–6:30 P.M., NBC, 1933–1935).

18066 KTAB Choir. The choir members included sopranos Laura Broderick, Helen Holmes, Constrance Morgan and Mrs. W.A. Sorenson; contralto Mrs. J.E. Bowersmith; and basses B.E. Calvin and Dean Gross (KTAB, Oakland, CA, 1925).

18067 KTAB Quartet. The station's vocal group was made up of soprano Dorothy Raegan Talbot; contralto Frances Chamberlain Duncan; tenor Glen Chamberlain; and bass Albert Gillette. Alice Gray Padel was their accompanist (KTAB, Oakland, CA, 1926). At other times during that year, the quartet contained soprano Laura Broderick; contralto Mary Groom Richards; tenor Gwynfi Jones; and baritone Oliver Jones.

18068 KTAB Trio. The vocal group included soprano Helen Cutter; mezzo-soprano Mrs. Jack Davis; and contralto Mrs. Herbert L. Smith. Mrs. Minna Fleissner-Lewis was their accompanist (KTAB, Oakland, CA, 1925).

18069 KTAB Trio. Instrumental trio of violinists Glenwood Walsh and Grace Waldman and pianist Ruth Jenkins (KTAB, Oakland, CA, 1927).

18070 *KTAB Zooks*. The *KTAB Zooks* program combined a minstrel show format with that of a lively popular music program (120 min., Friday, 8:00–10:00 P.M., KTAB, Oakland, CA,1928). Charley Faust was the announcer. The cast included Antone Trempt as Baron von Pretzel; William J. Savoy as Ling; Sam Wachsman as Jappy; and J. Herbert Knowles as Swede. The singers and musicians included Marguerite Vogel, Maude Nickerson, Carl Dietz and Scotty Boyd. Lois Cullen played piano.

18071 KTHS Orchestra. Conductor Dan LeBow led the station band (KTHS, Hot Springs National Park, AR, 1928).

18072 Kuab, Betty. COM-HE (WBEX, Chillicothe, OH, 1956).

18073 *Kuban Cossack Choir*. Vcl. mus. prg. (CBS, 1935).

18074 Kuckein, A. H. Announcer (WOWO, Fort Wayne, IN, 1925).

18075 Kueck's Orchestra of Pine Bluff (Arkansas). For several days after WOK (Pine Bluff, AR) first went on the air February, 1922, concert music was broadcast from 7:00–9:00 P.M. by Kueck's Orchestra under the direction of E.J. Kueck. The members of the band were Professor J.A. Hoffnagle, piano; J.K. Scott, cornet; Carl Bledsoe, clarinet; C.O. Williams, trombone; and King Ritchie, drums.

18076 Kuehn, Vera. Pianist (WHA, Madison, WI, 1925).

18077 Kuehne, John. Baritone (WOR, Newark, NJ, 1927).

18078 Kuehner, Earle. DJ (*Afternoon Ballroom*, WIL, St. Louis, MO, 1947).

18079 Kuhl, Frank. Leader (Frank Kuhl's Original Edgewater Beach Orchestra, featured on the *Candygram Follies* program, WSOE, Milwaukee, WI, 1926).

18080 Kuhlman, Fay. COM-HE (KOOK, Billings, MT, 1960).

18081 Kuhn, Dick. Leader (*Dick Kuhn Orchestra*, instr. mus. prg., network, 1940). Kuhn's band was introduced as follows: "When good fellows get together, the music of Dick Kuhn and his orchestra from the Broadway Cocktail Lounge of the Hotel Astor in New York City."

18082 Kuhn, Eddie. Leader (Kansas City Athletic Club Orchestra, WDAF, Kansas City, MO, 1925–1928).

18083 Kuhn, Ethel. Actress Kuhn appeared on the *Betty and Bob* daytime serial program.

18084 Kuhn, Irene. COM-HE (*Irene Kuhn,* Miss Kuhn delivered talks designed for modern women, 15 min., Weekly, MBS, 1939). *See **(The) Kuhns.***

18085 Kuhn, K.C. Violinist (KYW, Chicago, IL, 1923).

18086 Kuhn, Leo. DJ (*Breakfast with Leo*, WXLT, Ely, MN, 1950).

18087 Kuhn, Vincent. Baritone (WSM, Nashville, TN, 1928).

18088 *(The) Kuhns.* After the trend to husband-and-wife talk shows had become widespread, it was reasonable that the Kuhns — Irene and Rene, mother and daughter — should initiate a sustaining show on which they genially talked about New York local, state and world affairs (15 min., Saturday, 1:00–1:15 P.M., WNBC, New York, NY,1947).

18089 *Kukla, Fran and Ollie.* Like some other children's programs such as *Howdy Dowdy*, for example, *Kukla, Fran and Ollie* came to radio from television. Burr Tillstrom did all voices for his Kuklapolitan puppet creations, who talked to Fran Allison on a variety of humorous topics. Jack Fascinato was this sustaining show's musical director (10 min., Monday through Friday, 1:45–1:55 P.M., NBC, 1952).

18090 Kulick, Marcia. Pianist (WCOH, Yonkers, NY, 1931).

18091 Kulin, Edwin. Pianist (WCAP, Asbury Park, NJ, 1928).

18092 Kulla, S. Frank. Tenor (KSD, St. Louis, MO, 1925).

18093 Kullberg, LeRoy. Musician Kullberg was billed as "LeRoy Kullberg and his Uke" (KFWB, Hollywood, CA, 1927).

18094 Kult, Irving "Irv." Newscaster (WIBA, Madison, WI, 1945). DJ (*Irv's Morning Parade*, WDLB, Marshfield, WI, 1952; *Anything Goes*, WFHR, Wisconsin Rapids, WI, 1954).

18095 Kuma, Tanaka. Japanese soprano (KGY, Lacey, WA, 1922).

18096 Kumler, Mary. Soprano (KOA, Denver, CO, 1926).

18097 Kummer, Eloise. COM-HE (WBBM, Chicago, IL, 1956). As an actress Kummer also appeared in such daytime serial programs as *American Women, The Guiding Light, Backstage Wife* aka *Mary Noble, Backstage Wife, Mary Marlin* aka *The Story of Mary Marlin, Right to Happiness, Road of Life* and *Betty and Bob.*

18098 Kun, Agnes. Pianist (WPCH, New York, NY, 1932).

18099 Kunesh, Joyce. COM-HE (WMAM, Marinette, WI, 1960).

18100 Kunitz, Luigi Von. Violinist (KDKA, Pittsburgh, PA, 1924).

18101 Kuntz, Joe. Accordionist (KTHS, Hot Springs National Park, AR, 1926).

18102 KUOA Men's Glee Club Quartet. Professor Harry E. Shultz directed the vocal group (KUOA, Fayetteville, AR, 1926).

18103 *Kup's Column of the Air.* Chicago *Sun Times* columnist Irv Kupcinet conducted interviews with various celebrities on the show that greatly influenced the many talk shows that followed it. The show was sponsored by Turner Brothers Clothes (15 min., Sunday, 10:30–11:00 P.M., WMAQ, Chicago, IL, 1950).

18104 Kuralt, Charles "Charlie." Sportscaster (*Junior Sports Parade*, WAYS, Charlotte, NC, 1948; *Sports Final*, WAYS, 1949). Kuralt later had a successful television career at CBS.

18105 Kurkenknabe, Don James. Sportscaster (WKNX, Saginaw, MI, 1956).

18106 Kurkidje, Nazar [L. Nazar Kurkdue]. Leader (*Nazar Kurkidje's Concert Orchestra*, instr. mus. prg., CBS, 1935).

18107 Kurland, Patricia. COM-HE (WKNR, New Britain, CT, 1955).

18108 Kurtz, Clara. Pianist (KOIL, Council Bluffs, IA, 1926). Kurtz also directed and hosted a comedy program known as *Clara Kurtz' Chocolate Cake Eaters*, a popular radio minstrel show. One of the show's blackface comics was Frank Hall.

18109 Kurtz, Jack. Pianist-whistler (KFWB, Hollywood, CA, 1925–1926).

18110 Kurtz, Mary Ellen. COM-HE (WLBR, Lebanon, PA, 1956).

18111 Kurtz Karnival Kings Orchestra. Popular New York band (WMCA, New York, NY, 1926).

18112 Kushel, Mel. DJ (*Juke Box Serenade*, WSBA, York, PA, 1947).

18113 Kutta, Rose. Soprano (WJAZ, Chicago, IL, 1926).

18114 Kutz, Edward C. Newscaster (WSPD, Toledo, OH, 1944).

18115 Kuyendall, Jo. COM-HE (WAKP, Hendersonville, NC, 1960).

18116 Kuznitsof, William. Newscaster (WLBJ, Bowling Green, KY, 1946).

18117 Kvalden, Greta. Actress Kvalden appeared on the *Pepper Young's Family* daytime serial program.

18118 Kvale, Al. Leader (*Al Kvale Orchestra*, instr. mus. prg., WMAQ, Chicago, IL, 1934–1935).

18119 KWEM Black Gospel Quartet Programming. The extremely popular gospel station broadcast all through the decade of the 1950s with such popular Black gospel quartets as the Jollyaires, Evening Doves, Harps of Melody and the Keystone Masters of Harmony (KWEM, West Memphis, TN, 1950s).

18120 *KWGB Rhythm Jamboree Bandwagon* aka *Rhythm Jamboree Bandwagon.* CW music program (KWGB, Goodland, TX, 1954). This popular CW jamboree program featured essentially the same performers that previously had made up the WGY *Radio Ranch* show a few months previously. Begun on KWGB radio in 1954, it was simulcast. The performers included Bob and Marion Heck (Marion Bruno), Helen Fish, Stan Fish, Tommy Reilly and singer-comedian Jim Jarose, Jarose, incidentally, was also an announcer and DJ at KWGB, performed his comic capers under the name Crazy Waldo.

18121 *Kwitchurkickin Klub.* The popular variety show (Quit Your Kicking Club) was broadcast weekly (180 min., Saturday, 9:00–12:00 midnight, KFOB, Burlingame, CA, 1925). *Radiocast Weekly* (December 20–26, 1925, p. 59) described it this way: "The fun makers of this program are increasing the quality of entertainment every week; this week will be better. They have arranged a three-hour program that promises an array of vocal, instrumental, and dance music, along with wit and humor."

18122 KWTC Classical Trio. The classical music group included Harold Mathews, oboe; Adeline Cochens, piano; and Lyle Roberts, clarinet. Kinsley Hancock was the program's announcer (KWTC, Santa Ana, CA, 1927–1928).

18123 *KWTO Barn Dance.* CW music program (KWTO, Springfield, MO) probably was broadcast in the early 1950s. One of its performers was pretty female singer Boots Faye.

18124 KYA Orchestra. Gregory W. Golubeff directed the station orchestra (KYA, San Francisco, CA, 1927).

18125 KYA Trio. Instrumental group of violinist Agnes Stevens; cellist Tolida Hicks; and pianist Dell Perry (KYA, San Francisco, CA, 1928).

18126 Kyffin, Mildred. Contralto soloist Kyffin sang with the KOA Light Opera Company (KOA, Denver, CO, 1929).

18127 Kyle, Alastair. Actor Kyle was in the cast of *Our Gal Sunday* and *Portia Faces Life.*

18128 Kyle, Forrest. DJ (*Time to Smile*, KOPP, Ogden, UT, 1947; *MusicalTrain*, KLO, Odgen, UT, 1950; KERO, Bakersfield, CA, 1954). Sportscaster (*Sports Review*, KLO, 1948).

18129 Kyle, Merlin. Flutist (KFSG, Los Angeles, CA, 1926).

18130 Kyle, Muriel M. Soprano (WJR, Detroit, MI, 1928).

18131 Kyle, Peggy. COM-HE (WELS, Kinston, NC, 1956–1957).

18132 Kyler, Benny. Leader (*Benny Kyler Orchestra*, instr. mus. prg., NBC, 1935).

18133 Kyler, Hester. Children's program broadcaster, musician and director (Various stations, 1920s and 1930s). In the early 1920s, Kyler sang with another girl on the *Half Century Club* on a Grand Rapids station, a program on which listener birthdays were celebrated when they reached the age of 50.

She began her own career as a musician playing the piano and accordion twice a week on WSIX (Springfield, TN). Kyler was hired as musician and program director at WSM (Nashville, TN) in 1929. She eventually married and became owner of station WTNT (Ashland, KY), where she was also the program director, traffic manager and conducted a children's program. During her career she conducted children's programs all over the country including Jackson, MI; Grand Rapids, MI; Evansville, IN; Denver, CO; and Milwaukee, WI.

18134 Kyler, James F. Sportscaster (WCMI, Ashland, KY, 1937).

18135 Kyllingstrad, Bob. Newscaster (KGOU, Mandan, NH, 1941).

18136 Kynett, (Mrs.) Xenophen. Contralto (KOIL, Council Bluffs, IA, 1928).

18137 Kyser, Kay. Leader (*Kay Kyser Orchestra*, instr. mus. prg., WIP, Philadelphia, PA, 1935; WCAE, Pittsburgh, PA, 1935–1936; MBS, 1937–1939). Kyser's was a show band par excellence. Although Kyser used singing song titles to introduce selections at times, the band had a big, full bodied sound. The orchestra often was introduced this way: "The Make-You-Want-to-Dance Music of Kay Kyser." *See* ***Kay Kyser's Kollege of Musical Knowledge***.

18138 Kyte, Benny. Leader (*Benny Kyte Orchestra*, instr. mus. prg., WLOK, Lima, OH, 1942).

18139 LaBarr, Frank. DJ (*Music after Midnight* and *Musical Waiter*, WBRE, Wilkes-Barre, PA, 1949–1952).

18140 Labby, Len. DJ (*Who's Labby?*, KSJO, San Jose, CA, 1950).

18141 LaBelle, Rupert. Actor LaBelle was in the cast of *Mary Marlin* and *Today's Children*.

18142 LaBoe, Arthur "Art." DJ (*Sundialers Club*, KCMJ, Palm Springs, CA, 1947; *Teen Timers Matinee*, KGFJ, Hollywood, CA, 1949; *Musical Marathon*, KCMJ, 1950; *Wake Up to Music*, KDAY, Hollywood, CA, 1960).

18143 LaBranche, Ernest "Ernie." DJ (WLLH, Lowell, MA, 1937–1939; WCCM, Lawrence, MA, 1949). Sportscaster (*Today in Sports*, WCCM, 1950–1952).

18144 LaBrayere, Vern. DJ (*Requestfully Yours*, KCIM, Carroll, IA, 1954).

18145 LaCall, Kitty V. COM-HE (KVLC, Little Rock, AR, 1954).

18146 LaCentra, Peg (Margherita LaCentra). Singer (*Peg LaCentra*, vcl. mus. prg., NBC, 1934; *The Mello-O-Roll Ice Cream Show*. Miss Centra was the featured singer on the program. She was accompanied by the Dick McDonough Orchestra, NBC, 1935–1936; *The Peg LaCentra Show*, NBC 1939). Miss LaCentra was Artie Shaw's first vocalist when he formed his own band in 1936.

18147 Lacey, Anne. Child soprano (KFSG, Los Angeles, CA, 1924).

18148 Lacey, Eleanor. COM-HE (KRFC, Rocky Ford, CO, 1956).

18149 Lachenmeier, Rudy H. Sportscaster (KXL, Portland, OR, 1942, 1947; *Sports Page Final*, KGW, Portland, OR, 1948–1952). Newscaster (KXL, 1945).

18150 Lackey, F. Ernest, Jr., "Dutch." Sportscaster (WPAD, Paducah, KY, 1939–1940; WHOP, Hopkinsville, KY, 1941–1942, 1944; *Sportscast*, WHOP, 1947–1948). Newscaster (WHOP, 1940–1942, 1944–1945).

18151 Lackey, Hecht S. Newscaster (WHOP, Hopkinsville, KY, 1940; WSON , Henderson, KY, 1942, 1944–1947).

18152 Lackey, Pierce. Sportscaster (WPAD, Paducah, KY, 1939–1940).

18153 LaCom, Al. DJ (*Al's Hour*, KNEW, Spokane, WA, 1950).

18154 *La Conga*. This sustaining program of South American music presented the music of Joe Frasetto's Orchestra, vocalist Adele Norella and the singing team of Pepita and Lucia (15 min., Monday, 5:15–5:30 P.M., WIP, Philadelphia, PA, 1940).

18155 LaCossit, Henry. News analyst (MBS, 1947–1948).

18156 LaCroix, (Mrs.) Eleanor. Organist (KFXF, Colorado Springs, CO, 1926).

18157 Lacy, Jack. Newscaster (KOKO, La Junta, CO, 1944).

18158 Lacy, Jack. DJ (*Listen to Lacy*, WINS, New York, NY, 1947; *Listen to Lacy* and *Bushels of Fun*, WINS, 1948; *Listen to Lacy*, WINS, 1949–1960).

18159 Lacy, Nick. DJ (KQTY, Everett, WA, 1960).

18160 Lada, Anton. Leader (Anton Lada and his Louisiana Five Orchestra, KNRC, Los Angeles, CA, 1925).

18161 Ladd, Bert. Singer Ladd, known as "The Silver Voice of Dixie," was accompanied by Miss Jewel Shannon (WCOC, Columbus, MS, 1929).

18162 Ladd, Ed. DJ (*Hi Neighbor*, WPAT, Paterson, NJ, 1947–1950; MBS, 1956).

18163 Ladd, Jane. COM-HE (WLWA, Atlanta, GA, 1960).

18164 Laderoute, Joseph. "Boy soprano" (WLWL, New York, NY, 1928).

18165 *Ladies Be Seated*. Ed and Polly East hosted the show that allowed female contestants to compete for small prizes. For example, one of the tasks the contestants were asked to perform was to repeat three times such tongue twisters as: "Little Lily lisps less lately," "Coffee crumb cake crumbles," and "Sing a silly, sunny, summer sonnet." Such games as Train Calling and Pass the Box were also played. The announcers on the pleasant show were Doug Browning, Glenn Riggs, Gil Martyn and George Gunn (ABC, 1944–1950).

18166 *Ladies Fair*. Tom Moore conducted the sustaining quiz program for women. Porter Heaps and Herbert Foote supplied organ interludes. The announcers were Holland Engle and Don Gordon (30 min., Monday through Friday, 1:30–2:00 P.M., MBS, 1950).

18167 Ladies Orchestra. Novel Dallas band (WFAA, Dallas, TX, 1926.)

18168 Ladon, Beulah. Violinist (WEBH, Chicago, IL, 1925).

18169 LaDonne, Jeanne. Mezzo-soprano (KYW, Chicago, IL, 1925).

18170 *Lady Bugs*. The twin piano team of Muriel Pollack and Vee Lawnhurst were featured on the instrumental music program (15 min., Saturday, 9:00–9:15 P.M., NBC-Blue, 1930).

18171 *Lady Esther Serenade*. Lady Esther Cosmetics sponsored the program of good music supplied by the orchestra of Wayne King the Waltz King (30 min., Weekly, Transcribed, 1939).

18172 Lady from Mother Goose Village. Unidentified broadcaster told children's stories (KDKA, Pittsburgh, PA, 1925).

18173 *(The) Lady Next Door* [Madge Tucker]. Miss Tucker conceived, produced and conducted her program of dramatized stories for children broadcast six times weekly (30 min., Monday through Saturday, 5:30–6:00 P.M., NBC-Red, 1929).

18174 *Lady of Millions*. The dramatic serial starred May Robson (WGN, 1937).

18175 Lady of the Ivories. *See* **Lilyan Jay**.

18176 LaFerrara, Vincent. Leader (The Hotel St. Francis Concert Orchestra, KGO, Oakland, CA, 1925; Trocaderians orchestra, Pacific Coast Network, NBC, 1928).

18177 Laffer, Jack. Newscaster (KANS, Wichita, KS, 1939).

18178 Lafferty, Harry. Leader (Harry Lafferty's Orchestra broadcast on the *Music While You Dine* program, WOR, Newark, NJ, 1925).

18179 LaFlamme, Bernice. Pianist (KRE, Berkeley, CA, 1923).

18180 Lafler, Alan. DJ (*Strictly Off the Record*, WNAV, Annapolis, MD, 1952–1956).

18181 Lafon, Emelle. Pianist (KFWM, Oakland, CA, 1927).

18182 LaFontaine, Professor. Ukulele soloist (WHN, New York, NY, 1924).

18183 LaForce, Charles. Newscaster (WEMP, Milwaukee, WI, 1938–1942; *Home Edition*, WFOX, Milwaukee, WI, 1947). Sportscaster (WEMP, 1941).

18184 LaForge, Frank. Composer-pianist (WRC, Washington, DC, 1926).

18185 *LaForge Berumen Musicale*. A weekly program of classical music (30 min., Thursday, 3:00–3:30 P.M., WABC, 1933).

18186 LaFrance, Evelyn. Violinist (WBBR, New York, NY, 1925).

18187 LaFrance Radio Band. Commercially sponsored radio band directed by Anna C. Byrne (WEAF, New York, NY, 1926–1928).

18188 LaFranchise, Charles. DJ (*Platter Patter*, KALE, Portland, OR, 1947; *The Hop*, KPOJ, Portland, OR, 1949). Sportscaster (KALE, 1947; *Sports Forum* and *Pigskin Predictions*, KPOJ, Portland, OR, 1948–1951; *Sports Hi-Lites*, KPOJ, 1952; KLOR, Portland, OR, 1953; *Sport Hi-Lites*, KPOJ, 1954).

18189 LaFranconi [LaFrancone], Terri. Tenor (*Terri LaFranconi*, vcl. mus. prg., NBC, 1935–1936).

18190 LaFreniere, Esther. Soprano (WHDH, Boston, MA, 1939).

18191 LaGallienne, Eva. Famous actress LaGallienne performed with her company in a sponsored one-act play "The Swan" (WEAF, New York, NY, 1923).

18192 LaGrange Baptist Church Quartet. Religious vocal group (WORD, Batavia, IL, 1925).

18193 LaGrave, Ed, Jr. Sportscaster (KUSD, Vermillion, SD, 1940).

18194 LaGuardia, Fiorello H. Former mayor of New York Fiorello LaGuardia worked as a news commentator (*Fiorello H. LaGuardia Speaks for Liberty*, ABC, 1945–1946).

18195 LaHatche, S.L. Singer (WCOA, Pensacola, FL, 1926).

18196 LaHay, Judson. Announcer (WICC, Bridgeport, CT, 1926).

18197 Laidley, Isobel. Cellist (WIBO, Chicago, IL, 1928).

18198 Laing, Gill. Newscaster (KSRO, Santa Rosa, CA, 1939–1940).

18199 Laing, Gordon. Announcer (WPAK, Fargo, ND, 1925–1926).

18200 Lainsberg, Lida. Soprano (WHKC, Columbus, OH, 1937).

18201 Laird, Josephine. Contralto (WBZ, Springfield, MA, 1925).

18202 Laird, Stephen. Newscaster (CBS, 1947–1948).

18203 Lait, Jack. Announcer and master of ceremonies (WBBM, Chicago, IL, 1926).

18204 Lajoie, Alec. Leader (*Alec Lajoie Orchestra*, instr. mus. prg., MBS, 1936).

18205 Lake, Berry. DJ (WHO, Des Moines, IA, 1944–1946).

18206 Lake, Charles. Newscaster (WKST, New Castle, PA, 1938). Sportscaster (WKST, 1939).

18207 Lake, Ed. DJ (*Dixie Disc Review*, WEAR, Pensacola, FL, 1950).

18208 Lake, Horace A. Singer (WRC, Washington, DC, 1924).

18209 Lake, John. Actor Lake was in the cast of *The Glorious One* daytime serial program.

18210 Lake, Nancy [Nanci]. COM-HE (WLEC, Sandusky, OH, 1956).

18211 Lake City Orchestra of Dunkirk. Local band (WGR, Buffalo, NY, 1926).

18212 Lake Norconian Club Orchestra. Club band (KFVD, Culver City, CA, 1929).

18213 Lakeside Methodist Church Choir. Vocal group directed by Mrs. Ray Patterson (WOK, Pine Bluff, AR, 1922).

18214 Lakewood Farm Ensemble. Commercial music group (WJZ, New York, NY, 1925).

18215 Lakewood Terrace Orchestra. Clearwater, Florida, band (WGHB, Clearwater, FL, 1926).

18216 Lale, Max. Newscaster (KMHT, Marshall, TX, 1948).

18217 LaLiberta, Roger. DJ (*The Morning Show*, WWRI , West Warwick, RI, 1960).

18218 Lally, Ed. Leader (Ed Lally's Rendezvous Cabaret Orchestra, WCAE, Pittsburgh, PA, 1925).

18219 Lally, Howard. Leader (*Howard Lally Orchestra*, instr. mus. prg., NBC, 1935–1936).

18220 LaMae, Florence. Organist (KNX, Los Angeles, CA, 1929; *Florence LaMae*, instr. mus., prg., KFAC, Los Angeles, CA, 1932).

18221 LaMar, Bill. DJ (*Housewives' Serenade*, WCAM, Camden, NJ, 1948).

18222 LaMar, (Mrs.) J.W. Violinist (WCOA, Pensacola, FL, 1926).

18223 LaMar, Leona. Psychic (WHN, New York, NY, 1925).

18224 LaMar, Lew. Newscaster (WGN, Chicago, IL, 1941).

18225 *LaMarba Predicts*. Al Abrams, sports writer of the Pittsburgh *Post-Gazette*, in the role of LaMarba attempted to predict college football scores (15 min., Weekly, WWSW, Pittsburgh, PA, 1936).

18226 LaMarca, Maria. Soprano (WGBS, New York, NY, 1929).

18227 LaMariquita and Her Castillians. Excellent string orchestra led by LaMariquita (WFAA, Dallas, TX, 1927).

18228 LaMarr, Alma. COM-HE (KTAB, Oakland, CA, 1930).

18229 LaMarr, Barbara. Contralto (*Barbara LaMarr*, vcl. mus. prg., WFIL, Philadelphia, PA, 1936; WOR, Newark, NJ, 1936).

18230 LaMarr, Frank. Leader (*Frank LaMarr Orchestra*, instr. mus. prg., CBS, 1933; NBC, 1936).

18231 LaMarr, Gladys. Miss LaMarr, who was billed as "The Girl with the Radio Voice," sang with Harvey's Entertainers Orchestra (KJBS, San Francisco, CA, 1925; KFWI, San Francisco, CA, 1926).

18232 LaMay, Lee. Singer, "baritonette" (WEAN, Providence, RI, 1931).

18233 Lamb, Bill. DJ (*Jam for Breakfast*, WBBC, Flint, MI, 1947-1950-1957). Newscaster (*Deadline Headlines*, WBBC, 1948).

18234 Lamb, Britt. Newscaster (WLAY, Muscle Shoals City, AL, 1944).

18235 Lamb, Christine. Miss Lamb, a contralto known as the "Tennessee Lark," won an Atwater Kent Singing Competition (WSM, Nashville, TN, 1928).

18236 Lamb, Eugene. Pianist (KFSG, Los Angeles, CA, 1925).

18237 Lamb, Lois. COM-HE (WSDR, Sterling, IL, 1951).

18238 Lamb, Russ. Sportscaster (KFJZ, Fort Worth, TX, 1940–1941). Newscaster (KFJZ, 1941).

18239 Lambert, (Reverend) B.D. DJ (WRMA, Montgomery, AL, 1957).

18240 Lambert, Ed. DJ (*Off the Record*, WCAW, Charleston, WV, 1947–1950; *The E.L. Show*, WEAT, Lake Worth, FL, 1952).

18241 Lambert, George. Actor Lambert was in the cast of *Amanda of Honeymoon Hill* and *Stella Dallas* daytime serial programs.

18242 Lambert, Harold "Scrappy." Tenor Lambert was a prolific recording artist. Born May 12, 1901, he gave up his legal studies to pursue a career in concert and musical comedy work. After appearing on many recordings with the Ben Bernie Orchestra paired with Billy Hillpot, the two teamed to appear on *The Smith Brothers* program, where they became a popular radio team.

18243 Lambert, Jean. Soprano (WOR, Newark, NJ, 1925).

18244 Lambert, Ken. Newscaster (WJPF, Herrin, IL, 1941 and WLDS, Jacksonville, IL, 1941–1942, 1946). DJ (*Wake Up and Live*, WLDS, 1947).

18245 Lambert, Norman. Pianist-organist Lambert played on station WLBZ when it first went on the air in 1928 (WLBZ, Bangor, ME, 1928). He always wore a tuxedo when playing his theme, "I'm Always Chasing Rainbows." One of his broadcasting feats was to play the piano and the organ simultaneously. He later became the station's traffic and music director.

18246 Lambert, Sally. Newscaster (WGBB, Freeport, NY, 1942).

18247 Lambert, Roger. Sportscaster (*The Sports Notebook*, KORN, Freemont, NE, 1948).

18248 Lambert, Tom. DJ (WISN, Milwaukee, WI, 1957).

18249 Lamberti, Edith. Soprano (WEAF, New York, NY, 1924).

18250 Lamberti, Mikail. Concert cellist with the Symphony Society of New York (WEAF, New York, NY, 1924; WAHG, New York, NY, 1925).

18251 Lambeth, Ralph M. Newscaster (WGBG, Greensboro, NC, 1942).

18252 Lamborn, Betty Jane. Announcer (WGHP, Mt. Clemens, MI, 1925). COM-HE Lamborn conducted the *Women's Hour* program (WGHP, Mt. Clemens, MI, 1928).

18253 LaMere, Roy. Sportscaster (WIGM, Medford, WI, 1946). DJ (*Anything Goes*, WDLB, Marschfield, WI, 1947; *Your Bad Boy*, WFHR, Wisconsin Rapids, WI, 1948–1949).

18254 LaMond, Gene. Tenor (WFAA, Dallas, TX, 1929).

18255 LaMoineau. French singer introduced as the "Sparrow from Montmarte" (WRNY, New York, NY, 1926).

18256 Lamont, Edward. Baritone (*Major Bowes Capitol Theater Family*, NBC, 1928; *Edward Lamont*, vcl. mus. prg., WIP, Philadelphia, PA, 1935).

18257 Lamont, Joyce. COM-HE (WCCO, St. Paul, MN, 1960).

18258 Lamont, Ray. DJ (*Manhattan Melodies*, KBIO, Burley, ID, 1952).

18259 LaMother, Gertrude. Actress (WEEI, Boston, MA, 1928).

18260 LaMotte, George. Bass (KVOO, Tulsa, OK, 1928).

18261 LaMotte, Ruth. Singer (WORK, York, PA, 1937).

18262 LaMountain, Noah. News analyst (*Notebook*, WMAS, Springfield, MA, 1947).

18263 Lamour, Dorothy. Soprano (*Dorothy Lamour*, NBC, 1935). Ms. Lamour later gained fame as a motion picture star. Her sarong and her "Road" pictures with Bob Hope and Bing Crosby probably brought her the greatest popularity. Miss Lamour also starred on radio with Bergen and McCarthy on the *Chase and Sanborn Show* in its early days. *See **The Chase and Sanborn Show**.*

18264 Lampe, Del. Leader (Trianon Orchestra, WMBB, Chicago, IL, 1925). The band was billed as the "World's Most Beautiful Orchestra [playing] in the World's Most Beautiful Ballroom." The group was praised by *Variety* (WOK, Homewood, IL, 1927).

18265 Lampel, Harold. Newscaster (WCBA-WSAN, Allentown, PA, 1940; KTAR, Phoenix, AZ, 1942).

18266 Lamph, Jean. Contralto (KFI, Los Angeles, CA, 1928).

18267 Lampkin, Phil. Leader (Phil Lampkin's Musical Bears [orchestra] playing from the Paradise Ball Room, KGO, Oakland, CA, 1926).

18268 *(The) Lamplighter.* Rabbi Jacob Tarshish broadcast inspirational talks and provided advice on his popular program (MBS, 1935–1941). Tarshish's program was said to have been the Mutual Broadcasting System's first commercially sponsored program. His goal, he said, was to "bring all creeds, all nations, all classes closer together in love and understanding." He certainly had a worthy goal, considering the troubled 1935–1941 era in which he was broadcasting.

Tarshish first appeared on radio in 1926. His listeners always sought his help and advice in solving their problems of a religious, medical, legal and marital nature (15 min., Monday through Thursday, 11:45–12:00 noon and 15 min., Sunday, 2:30–2:45 P.M., MBS, 1935–1938).

18269 *(The) Lamplighter.* In a far different format from the show above, the Los Angeles *Daily News* sponsored Ted Yerza in the title role of *The Lamplighter.* He played records, talked about music and conducted interviews with musicians and singers. Charlie Arlington was the announcer (15 min., Saturday, 10:15–10:30 A.M., KHJ, Los Angeles, CA, 1942).

18270 Lamson, Mary. Reader (WEMC, Berrien Springs, MI, 1925).

18271 Lanahan, Mabel. Blues singer (KFI, Los Angeles, CA, 1927).

18272 Lanasa, Antonio. Tenor (WEAF, New York, NY, 1926).

18273 *Lancaster Central Orchestra.* Instr. mus. prg. (WOWO, Fort Wayne, IN, 1933).

18274 Lancaster, Margaret. Contralto (KFWB, Hollywood, CA, 1925).

18275 Lance, Bonnie Jean. Pianist Lance performed piano duets with Elizabeth Simpson (KFWM, Oakland, CA, 1926).

18276 Lance, Henry. Conductor of the WFAA Staff Orchestra (WFAA, Dallas, TX, 1927; Henry Lance's Gunter Hotel Orchestra, WOAI, San Antonio, TX, 1928).

18277 Lance, Herb. Black DJ (WERD, Atlanta, GA, 1960). Lance later moved to WIGO (Atlanta, GA).

18278 Lancel, Emilie. Concert singer (KGO, San Francisco, CA, 1927).

18279 Lancey, Loraine. Pianist (WJR, Detroit, MI, 1928).

18280 Lanctot, Cliff. DJ (*770 Record Club*, WEW, St. Louis, MO, 1947).

18281 *Land o' Make Believe.* Dr. Arthur Torrance and actress Frances Collette appeared on the program for children (60 min., Sunday, 10:00–11:00 A.M., CBS, 1930).

18282 *Land O' Memories.* Chuck Acree hosted the popular music show featuring singers Grace Wilson, John Neher, Kenny Stevens, Paul Nettinga, the DeZurik Sisters and the Hilltoppers (30 min., Saturday, 9:00–9:30 P.M. CST, WLS, Chicago, IL, 1938).

18283 *Land of Beginning Again.* Poet Rod Arkell read poetry and provided the narration on the inspirational musical series that featured organist Lew White, tenor Harrison Knox, soprano Ruth Everets and the Louis Katzman Bohemian Orchestra (30 min., Sunday, 4:30–5:00 P.M., CBS, 1935). The previous year the program was carried on the NBC network (1934).

18284 *Land of Health* (aka *Da-Ra-No*). The character "Da-Ra-No," a wise man and ruler of the Land of Health, told stories to children as they hiked through the Slumber Forest with him. The children's program was broadcast by KGO (Oakland, CA, 1927) before becoming a network program that also featured the "Singing Sandman" and the "Rock-a-Bye Lady," who offered advice for healthy living to young listeners (NBC-Pacific Coast Network, 1929).

18285 *Land of Make Believe.* Miss Zel DeCyr told charming stories for children and played all the parts in them on the popular local show. Dick Sugar was the announcer (15 min., Saturday, 3:30–3:45 P.M., WEVD, New York, NY, 1949).

18286 *Land of the Lost.* The interesting children's program told the story of two children, Isabel and Billy, played by Betty Jane Tyler and Ray Ives, respectively. They found adventures in an enchanted undersea kingdom, where they were guided by a talking fish named Red Lantern. Isabel Manning Hewson was the producer, director and writer of the unique adventure program. The cast included: Jim Boles, Art Carney, Tom Eldridge, Ray Ives, Athena Lorde, Lee Marshall, Kay Marshall, Junius Matthews, Ann Thomas and Betty Jane Tyler. The announcer was Michael Fitzmaurice and Cyril Armbrister was the director (ABC, MBS, 1943–1948).

18287 Landay Ensemble. Classical musical group (WJZ, New York, NY, 1925).

18288 Lande, Jules. "Violinist to the late President Warren G. Harding" was how he was billed (WDAR, Philadelphia, PA, 1925; *Jules Lande*, instr. mus. prg., NBC, 1934). Leader (*Jules Lande Concert Orchestra*, instr. mus. prg., KFEL, Denver, CO, 1934; *Jules Lande Concert Ensemble*, instr. mus. prg., NBC, 1936; *Jules Lande Orchestra*, instr. mus. prg., WIP, Philadelphia, PA, 1938; WTIC, Hartford, CT, 1939). Lande also was sometimes known as the "Troubadour of the Violin."

18289 Lander, Mae Rose. Soprano (WEBR, Chicago, IL, 1924).

18290 Landers, (Miss) Billie. Blues singer (KEX, Portland, OR, 1930; KJR, Seattle, WA, 1930).

18291 Lander(s), Manny. Leader (*Manny Lander Orchestra*, instr. mus. prg., MBS, 1938–1939).

18292 Landfear, Dean. DJ (*Off the Record*, WMT, Cedar Rapids, IA, 1947–1950).

18293 Landi, Erberto. Newscaster (WHOM, Jersey City, NJ, 1941).

18294 Landine, Robert. Tenor (*Robert Landine*, vcl. mus. prg., WOR , Newark, NJ, 1935).

18295 Landino, Signor. Operatic tenor (WHN, New York, NY, 1924).

18296 Landis, DeWitt. Newscaster (KFYO, Lubbock, TX, 1938–1942). Sportscaster (KFYO,1939–1940, 1944–1946).

18297 Landis, Joyce Royce. Actress Landis appeared in the *We Are Always Young* daytime serial program.

18298 Landis, Louise. Newspaper woman who conducted her own *As a Woman Thinketh* program (KGO, Oakland, CA, 1925). In the 1930s, Landis handled photographs, fashions and fan magazines in the NBC Hollywood Press Department.

18299 Landis, Mary. COM-HE (WBAL, Baltimore, MD, 1937). Mary Landis was a generic name owned by station WBAL and used for many years.

18300 Landis, Meade. Newscaster (WSMJ, Bridgton, NJ, 1948).

18301 Landma, Gertrude. Soprano (KFI, Los Angeles, CA, 1926).

18302 *Landmarks of Music.* General Electric Company sponsored the program of classical music. Nathaniel Shilkret conducted the orchestra (NBC-Red, New York, NY, 1929).

18303 Landon, Harry F. Newscaster (WWNY, Watertown, NY, 1941–1942).

18304 Landon, Jud. Landon delivered talks on outdoor life topics such as hunting and fishing (WGY, Schenectady, NY, 1923).

18305 Landowski, Wanda. Harpsichordist (WJZ, New York, NY, 1927).

18306 Landree, (Mrs.) Jacques. Organist (WMOX, St. Louis, MO, 1926).

18307 Landrey, James. Leader (*James Landrey Orchestra*, instr. mus. prg., WKUO, Siloam Springs, AR, 1934).

18308 Landry, Art. Leader (Art Landry Orchestra, WOAW, Omaha, NE, 1925).

18309 Landry, Jimmy. DJ (*Breakfast Jam*, WDSO, New Orleans, LA, 1947).

18310 Landry-Dooley Cinderella Roof Orchestra. Club dance band (KFXB, Los Angeles, CA, 1927).

18311 Landsberg, Nathan J. Violinist (KGO, Oakland, CA, 1926).

18312 Landstrom, Arthur J. Announcer (KFQU, Alma, Holy City, CA, 1926–1927).

18313 Landt, Ella May. Soprano (WEAF, New York, NY, 1924).

18314 *Landt Brothers Trio.* Popular music group (WJZ, New York, NY, 1929; *Landt Trio*, mus. prg., NBC, 1936).

18315 *Landt Trio and White.* Jack, Dan and Karl Landt teamed with Howard White on the music show that was broadcast six times weekly (NBC, 1930–1932).

18316 Lane, Alice. DJ (WOOK, Silver Spring, MD, 1948).

18317 Lane, Andy. DJ (*All Night Club*, KRIZ, Phoenix, AZ, 1954).

18318 Lane, Arthur. Tenor (*Arthur Lane*, vcl. mus. prg., WGY, Schenectady, NY, 1935).

18319 Lane, Barbara. COM-HE (WISC, Madison, WI, 1956).

18320 Lane, Bill. Organist (*Bill Lane at the Organatron*, WCAX, Lewiston, ME, 1942).

18321 Lane, Bob. Newscaster (KVOO, Tulsa, OK, 1939).

18322 Lane, Carl. Producer Lane produced the *Road of Life* daytime serial program.

18323 Lane, Carol. COM-HE (WRUM, Rumford, ME, 1954).

18324 Lane, Carole. COM-HE (WKIX, Raleigh, NC, 1956).

18325 Lane, Clara. Soprano (WBZ, Boston-Springfield, MA, 1924; WNAC, Boston, MA, 1925).

18326 Lane, Dick. Newscaster (KFBC, Cheyenne, WY, 1944).

18327 Lane, Dick. Sportscaster Lane later became a comedian in motion picture "shorts." He also broadcast descriptions of wresting matches and boxing bouts (KTLA, Los Angeles, CA, 1951–1955).

18328 Lane, Doris. Singer (KCMO, Kansas City, 1937).

18329 Lane, Drury. Newscaster (KICA, Clovis, NM, 1941).

18330 Lane, Eddy. Leader (*Eddy Lane Orchestra*, instr. mus. prg., WOR, Newark, NJ, 1934).

18331 Lane, Eleanor. Pianist (WMT, Cedar Rapids–Waterloo, IA, 1939).

18332 Lane, Eleanor. Singer (*Eleanor Lane*, vcl. mus. prg., NBC, 1939).

18333 Lane, Frank S. Announcer (KFRU, Bristol, OK, 1925–1927). After leaving KFRU, Lane became an announcer-director at WDOD (Chattanooga, TN, 1928). Lane began his career at KFRU before the call letters were changed to KVOO when the station moved to Tulsa, OK.

18334 Lane, Janet. COM-HE (WFIL, Philadelphia, PA, 1935).

18335 Lane, Judith. COM-HE (KIRO, Seattle, WA, 1949–1956).

18336 Lane, Laura. COM-HE (WMRY, New Orleans, LA, 1956).

18337 Lane, Linda. COM-HE (WLOG, Logan, WV, 1949).

18338 Lane, Marian. COM-HE (WRKD, Rockland, ME, 1956–1957).

18339 Lane, Martha. COM-HE (KFJZ, Fort Worth, TX, 1949).

18340 Lane, Mary. Sportscaster and forecaster (WOWO, Fort Wayne, IN, 1937).

18341 Lane, Mary. COM-HE (KERG, Eugene, OR, 1955).

18342 Lane, Marie. DJ (*Jaybird Jamboree*, WJAY, Mullins, SC, 1954).

18343 Lane, Maxie. DJ (*Jaybird Jamboree*, WJAY, Mullins, SC, 1954).

18344 Lane, Milly. COM-HE (WWCA, Gary, IN, 1955).

18345 Lane, Norma. COM-HE (KUMA, Pendleton, OR, 1956).

18346 Lane, Prescott. Leader (*Prescott Lane Orchestra*, instr. mus. prg., KFEL, Denver, CO, 1934).

18347 Lane, Richard. Leader (*Richard Lane Orchestra*, instr. mus. prg., WOR, Newark, NJ, 1942).

18348 Lane, Rilla. Pianist (KFWM, Oakland, CA, 1928).

18349 Lane, Roy. Singer (*Roy Lane*, vcl. mus. prg., WIP, Philadelphia, PA, 1936).

18350 Lane, Tom. Newscaster (WLOF, Orlando, FL, 1941).

18351 Lane, Vance. DJ (*Musical Roundup*, KGER, Long Beach, CA, 1947).

18352 Lang, Ann. Miss Lang was known as the "Crooning contralto" (WGBS, New York, NY, 1927).

18353 Lang, Arthur. Baritone (*Arthur Lang the Gypsy Prince*, vcl. mus. prg., WOR, Newark, NJ, 1934).

18354 Lang, Barbara. Newscaster (WINN, Louisville, KY, 1942).

18355 Lang, Boris. Concert pianist (WOR, Newark, NJ, 1927).

18356 Lang, Clifford. Pianist Lang was known as "The Prince of the Ivories" (WLW, Cincinnati, OH, 1925).

18357 Lang, (Dr.) Ethan A. DJ (WCAM, Camden, NJ, 1937). Sportscaster (WCAM, 1937).

18357a Lang, Fred. Newscaster (WNAC, Boston, MA and WAAB, Boston, MA, 1940–1941, 1945). DJ (*Record Revue*, WNAC, 1952).

18358 Lang, Harry. Leader (Arcadians Orchestra, KMOX, St. Louis, MO, 1928).

18359 Lang, Louise. COM-HE (WIS, Columbia, SC, 1951).

18360 Lang, Polly. COM-HE (WNOP, Newport, KY, 1957).

18361 Lang, William "Bill." Newscaster (KYW, Philadelphia, PA, 1937–1939; *Spotlighting the News*, KYW, 1940; MBS, 1944; WHN, New York, NY, 1945–1947).

18362 Langdon, Ed. Newscaster (WKBN, Youngstown, OH, 1942).

18363 Langdon, Harriet. COM-HE (WARN, Fort Pierce, FL, 1956).

18364 Langdon Brothers. Hawaiian guitar duo (WEBH, Chicago, IL, 1924–1925).

18365 Lange, (Mrs.) Albert G. Pianist (KPO, San Francisco, CA, 1923).

18366 Lange, B. [Bel or Bill]. Newscaster (KGDM, Stockton, CA, 1947). Sportscaster (KOVR, Stockton, CA, 1954–1956).

18367 Lange, Dorothy. COM-HE (KEYJ, Jamestown, NY, 1956).

18368 Lange, Verne. Tenor (KFAB, Lincoln, NE, 1928).

18369 Langerman, Rose. Soprano (KMIC, Inglewood, CA, 1928).

18370 Langeus, Gustav. Clarinetist (WEAF, New York, NY, 1925).

18371 Langford, Frances. Singer (WOR, Newark, NJ, 1932). *See (The) Bob Hope Show.*

18372 Langford, Paul. Newscaster (KRKD, Los Angeles, CA, 1941).

18373 Langhorst, Elizabeth Durland. Soprano (WSAI, Cincinnati, OH, 1925).

18374 Langley, Ralph. DJ (*Morning Watch with Ralph Langley*, KECA, Los Angeles, CA, 1947).

18375 Langlinais, Laura. COM-HE (KVOL, Lafayette, LA, 1949).

18376 Langsam, (Dr.) Walter C. News analyst (WGY, Schenectady, NY, 1941–1942).

18377 Lansing, Charlotte. Singer (*Charlotte Lansing*, vcl. mus. prg., NBC-Blue, 1935).

18378 Langston, Harry. DJ (*Harry the Hoosier*, WWCA, Gary, IN, 1949).

18379 *Langworth Gauchos.* Transcribed South American style music program (KVOA, Tucson, AZ, 1939).

18380 *Langworth Hillbillies.* Transcribed CW music program (KVOA, Tucson, AZ, 1939).

18381 *Langworth Novelty Orchestra.* Transcribed music program (KUOA, Siloam Springs, AR, 1934).

18382 *Langworth Salon Orchestra.* Another example of a transcribed music program (WBIG, Greensboro, NC, 1938).

18383 Langworthy, Mildred. Lyric soprano (WEAF, New York, NY, 1923).

18384 Lanier, Sydney. Newscaster (WJAX, Jacksonville, FL, 1941).

18385 Lanin, Howard. Leader (Howard Lanin Orchestra, WDAR, Philadelphia, PA, 1921; Howard Lanin's Arcadia Cafe Dance Orchestra, WDAR, 1923; Howard Lanin's Dance Orchestra, WDAR, 1924; WIP, Philadelphia, PA, 1925; *Howard Lanin Orchestra*, instr. mus. prg., WIP, 1935).

18386 Lanin, Sam. Sam Lanin was the leader of the Ipana Troubadours, the popular radio and recording band (NBC-Red, New York, NY, 1926–1929 and music director on the *Ingram Shavers* program, NBC-Blue, New York, NY, 1929). Lanin was one of the busiest and most prolific broadcasting and recording band leaders. Between 1920 and 1931, for example, it is reported that he directed almost 400 recording sessions. In 1927, Lanin's Troubadours probably included the following musicians: Red Nichols and Hymie Farberman, t.; Sam Lewis, tb.; Andy Sanella, clr., as. and sg; Larry Abbott, clr. and as.; Norman Yorke, ts.; Murray Kellner, v.; William Wirges, p.; Harry Reser, bj.; Joe Tarto, tba.; and Lanin, ldr.-d.

18387 Lankagel, Hazel. Violinist (KFSG, Los Angeles, CA, 1924).

18388 Lankford, Virginia "Ginny." COM-HE (WZOB, Ft. Payne, AL, 1954–1955).

18389 Lanning, (Dr.) R.L. Minister Lanning broadcast Sunday school lessons (KDKA, Pittsburgh, PA, 1924).

18390 *Lanny Ross.* Tenor Ross appeared on his weekly musical variety show (15 min., Sunday, NBC-Red, 1929–1931).

18391 *(The) Lanny Ross House Show Boat Show.* Another musical variety show presided over by tenor Ross (30 min., Thursday, 7:00–7:30 P.M., NBC-Red, 1935).

18392 *(The) Lanny Ross Show.* Handsome Lanny Ross was the singing host on his program sponsored by Procter & Gamble. He was joined by singer Evelyn Knight, the Herman Chittison Trio and Will Larin's Orchestra. Nelson Case was the announcer (15 min., Monday through Friday, 7:00–7:15 P.M., CBS, 1946).

18393 ***(The) Lanny Ross Show.*** The Gulf Oil Company sponsored veteran radio tenor Lanny Ross on the entertaining music show, not to be confused with his show above. Singer Louise Carlyle and the Buddy Weed Quintet were program regulars. Jimmy Blaine was the announcer (15 min., Monday through Friday, 12:15–12:30 P.M., MBS, 1949–1950).

18394 ***(The) Lanny Ross Showtime.*** After a long and distinguished radio career on such programs as *Showboat, The Log Cabin Inn, The Packard Hour*, the *Lanny Ross State Fair Concert* and the various programs known as *The Lanny Ross Show*, Ross became a DJ, who occasionally sang. He was accompanied by pianist Milton Kaye (30 min., Monday through Friday, 4:30–5:00 P.M., WCBS, New York, NY, 1954).

18395 ***(The) Lanny Ross State Fair Concert.*** Tenor Ross, contralto Helen Oelheim and various guest artists performed on the Ross good music program. Howard Barlow conducted the program's orchestra (30 min., Sunday, 6:00–6:30 P.M., CBS, 1935).

18396 **Lansing, Charlotte.** Singer (NBC, 1935–1937).

18397 **Lansing, Gerry.** DJ (*Tune Factory*, KWTX, Waco, TX, 1947).

18398 **Lansing, Hal.** Ukulele soloist (WQJ, Chicago, IL, 1926).

18399 **Lansing, Hal.** Newscaster (WTCN, Minneapolis, MN, 1941).

18400 **Lansing, Larry.** Newscaster (KVEC, San Luis Obispo, CA, 1941).

18401 **Lansing, Larry.** DJ (*Musical Timekeeper* and *The Music Hall*, WPLH, Huntington, WV, 1947).

18402 **Lansing, Mary.** Actress Lansing was in the cast of *The Guiding Light* daytime serial program.

18403 **Lansley, Mickey.** COM-HE (WNDR, Syracuse, NY, 1954).

18404 **Lanson, Snooky.** Singer (*Songs by Snooky*, vcl. mus. prg., 15 min., Saturday, 5:15–5:30 P.M., NBC, 1947). DJ (*Snooky's Song Shop*, WSM, Nashville, TN, 1947–1950).

18405 **Lanter, Helyn.** COM-HE (KHHH, Pampa, TX, 1960).

18406 **Lantry, C.C.** Announcer (KHQ, Spokane, WA, 1928).

18407 **Lantry, Harry.** Sportscaster (KHQ, Spokane, WA, 1937).

18408 **Lantz, Ada.** Soprano (KFSG, Los Angeles, CA, 1925).

18409 **Lantz, James, Jr.** Sportscaster (KSAL, Salinas, KS, 1940).

18410 **Lantz, Stanley.** Newscaster (WJBC, Bloomington, IN, 1941).

18411 **Laockwood [Lackwood], (Reverend) W.T.** Announcer (KFAU, Boise, ID, 1927).

18412 ***LaPalina Concert.*** LaPalina Cigar Company sponsored the weekly music show (30 min., Sunday, 8:30–9:00 P.M., CBS, 1938).

18413 ***LaPalina Presents Kate Smith* (aka *Kate Smith and her Swanee Music*).** The popular singer, known as "The Songbird of the South," was sponsored by LaPalina Cigars. The program also featured the Nat Brusiloff Orchestra (15 min., Monday through Thursday, 8:30–8:45 P.M., CBS, 1931–1933).

18414 ***LaPalina Rhapsodizers.*** LaPalina Cigars sponsored the musical show directed by Claude MacArthur. The featured singers were Zinaida Nicolina and Ben Alley (30 min., Sunday, 8:00–8:30 P.M., CBS, 1929–1930).

18415 ***(The) LaPalina Smoker.*** The program consisted of the informal entertainment and music supposedly presented at a smoker. William Paley, owner of the LaPalina Cigar Company, developed the program's format. Leading entertainers of the stage and screen frequently appeared. Pianist Harry Link was a regular performer, as were comedians Raymond Hitchcock, Louis Mann and the blackface team of Miller and Lyles. Hitchcock and Mann cohosted the show and provided running patter and chatter. The program was broadcast on a different night after 1929 (30 min., Friday, 9:30–10:00 P.M., CBS, 1928–1929; 30 min., Wednesday, 9:30–10:00 P.M., CBS, 1930).

18416 **Lapetina, Elizabeth.** Coloratura soprano (WCAU, Philadelphia, PA, 1926).

18417 **Lapham, Claude.** Pianist (WGBS, New York, NY, 1927).

18418 **Lapham, George.** Tenor (*George Lapham*, vcl. mus. prg., WFIL, Philadelphia, PA, 1935).

18419 **LaPlante, Roy.** Newscaster (WFIL, Philadelphia, PA, 1941). Announcer LaPlante announced *The Married Life of Helen and Warren* daytime serial program.

18420 **LaPointe, Armand.** Newscaster (WFEA, Manchester, NH, 1946–1947).

18421 **LaPorte, Manny.** Leader (*Manny LaPorte Orchestra*, instr. mus. prg., NBC, 1935; WIP, Philadelphia, PA, 1936).

18422 **Lapp, Bruce.** DJ (*Music 'Til Midnight*, WSAV, Savannah, GA, 1960).

18423 **LaPrade, Ernest.** LaPrade was the orchestra conductor on the *Collier Radio Hour*, a program sponsored by the Crowell Publishing Company (NBC-Blue, 1927–1932).

18424 **LaPrade, Malcolm.** Malcolm LaPrade delivered travel talks on *Cook's Travelogue* program (WJZ, New York, NY, 1926 and NBC, 1927–1928; *Travelogues*, NBC, 1938).

18425 **Lara, R. Carta.** When he was Mexican consul at Dallas, Texas, Lara delivered a series of talks about various Mexican cities and geographical areas (WFAA, Dallas, TX, 1927).

18426 **Larabee, Louise.** Actress Larabee was featured on the *Woman of America* program.

18427 ***Laraine Day.*** Motion picture star Day initiated her "talk" show from New York City's Hutton Restaurant, where she interviewed various celebrities (180 minutes, Monday through Friday, 12:00–3:00 P.M., WMGM, New York, NY, 1952).

18428 **Largay, Ray.** Actor Largay was in the cast of *Ma Perkins* and *Young Widder Brown.*

18429 **Large, Don.** Leader (*Don Large Orchestra*, instr. mus. prg., WJR, Detroit, MI, 1932).

18430 **Largent, (Mrs.) D.W.** Soprano (KFDM, Beaumont, TX, 1928).

18431 **Largy, Paul.** Tenor (WRNY, New York, NY, 1926).

18432 **Larimer, Dan.** Newscaster (WDAF, Kansas City, MO, 1941).

18433 **Larimer, Marion Lowell.** Soprano (WJZ, New York, NY, 1954).

18434 **LaRiwiere, (Mme.) Alba.** Canadian soprano (WOR, Newark, NJ, 1926).

18435 **Larkan [Larkin], "Uncle" Bob.** Leader (Uncle Bob and his Music Makers, KFKB, Milford, KS, 1924–1929; KGHI, Little Rock, AR, 1929).

18436 **Larkin, Don.** DJ (*Night Time Frolic*, WAAT, Newark, NJ, 1948; *Hometown Frolics*, WAAT, 1954).

18437 **Larkin, Frank.** Newscaster (WROL, Knoxville, TN, 1946).

18438 **Larkin, Jean.** COM-HE (WATS, Sayre, PA, 1955).

18439 **Larkin, John.** Busy actor Larkin appeared on *Backstage Wife, Brighter Day, Chicago Theater of the Air, Helpmate, Houseboat Hannah, Lone Journey, Ma Perkins, Mark Trail* (title role), *Perry Mason, Portia Faces Life, Radio City Playhouse, Right to Happiness, Road of Life, Romance of Helen Trent, Stepmother* and *Under Arrest.*

18440 **Larkin, William.** Tenor (*William Larkin*, vcl. mus. prg., WOR, Newark, NJ, 1934).

18441 **Larkin Orchestra.** Popular local orchestra (WNYC, New York, NY, 1925).

18442 **LaRose [LaRosa], Joe.** Leader (*Joe LaRose Orchestra*, instr. mus. prg., WMMN, Fairmont, WV, 1937–1938).

18443 **LaRowe, Phillip.** Central High School organist (KVOO, Tulsa, OK, 1928).

18444 ***Larraine Day.*** Motion picture star Day initiated her "talk" program from New York City's Hutton Restaurant, where she interviewed various celebrities (180 min., Monday through Friday, 12:00–3:00 P.M., WMBM, New York, NY, 1952).

18445 **Larremore, T.** Soprano (KFKU, Lawrence, KS, 1926).

18446 **Larrison, Helen J.** Soprano (WORD, Batavia, IL, 1925).

18447 **Lars the Plumber.** Comic character played by an unidentified performer on various WHO (Des Moines, IA) programs in the mid–30s. His opening line invariably was, "Hello dere."

18448 **Larsen, Alice.** Pianist (KPSN, Pasadena, CA, 1926).

18449 **Larsen, Ambrose.** Organist (WLIB, Chicago, IL, 1926).

18450 **Larsen, Bob.** Leader (Bob Larsen Orchestra, KFSD, San Diego, CA, 1928).

18451 **Larsen, Dorothy.** Pianist (WSM, Nashville, TN, 1928).

18452 **Larsen, Larry.** Organist (*Larry Larsen*, instr. mus. prg., NBC, 1936).

18453 **Larson, Beatrice.** COM-HE (WBIZ, Eau Claire, WI, 1957).

18454 Larson, Evelyn. COM-HE (WCMP, Pine City, MN, 1960).

18455 Larson, Gus. DJ (*Suwannee Swingtime*, WDSR, Lake City, FL, 1954).

18456 Larson, Kay. COM-HE (WHEN, Syracuse, NY, 1956–1957).

18457 Larson, Lillian. Soprano (WMBH, Joplin, MO, 1937).

18458 Larson, Mignon and Phyllis Larson. Piano duets (WLS, Chicago, IL, 1925).

18459 Larson, Mildred. Pianist Larson accompanied the Mellotone Quartet (KFLV, Rockford, IL, 1930).

18460 Larson, Nell. Staff organist and pianist (KHJ, Los Angeles, CA, 1924–1930). Larson began working at KHJ, the Don Lee Station in Los Angeles, in 1924. After working at several other stations, she returned to KHJ in 1926 and appeared on most of the station's programs.

18461 Larson, Ole and Charles Agne. "Comedy songsters" (WMBB, Chicago, IL, 1926).

18462 Larson, Paul. DJ (*Timekeeper*, WNEB, Worcester, MA, 1947–1948; WNEB, 1952; WORC, Worcester, MA, 1956).

18463 Larson, Ruby. COM-HE (WQJ, Chicago, IL, 1935).

18464 Larson, Whitey. Newscaster (WNAX, Yankton, SD, 1942, 1944–1946).

18465 LaRue, Jack. Newscaster (WAKR, Akron, OH, 1946).

18466 LaRue, Marguerite. COM-HE (KBIG, Odessa, TX, 1957).

18467 LaRugga, Charles. Banjo soloist (WHN, New York, NY, 1926).

18468 Lasater, Martha. COM-HE (WTPR, Paris, TX, 1949).

18469 Lascelles [Lescelies], John. DJ (*Musical Clock*, WGR, Buffalo, NY, 1954–1955; *Morning Personality*, WGR, 1960).

18470 Laserow Quartet. Musical group consisting of violinist Max Laserow; cellist Leopold Laserow; violinist Julia Laserow; and pianist Sarah Laserow Hunter (WIP, Philadelphia, PA, 1925).

18471 Lashanska, Hulda. Soprano on the *Atwater Kent Hour* program (NBC, 1927).

18472 Lashbrook, Bob. DJ (*Wake Up and Smile*, WHOT, South Bend, IN, 1947; KPLC, Lake Charles, LA, 1954).

18473 Lasher, Sid. DJ (*590 Express*, WAGA, Atlanta, GA, 1947).

18474 Lask, Mac. Ballad singer (KFI, Los Angeles, CA, 1928).

18475 Laskey, Jesse. Sportscaster (CBS, 1939).

18476 Laskowski, Clement. Tenor (WOK, Chicago, IL, 1925).

18477 Lassell, Leo. Sportscaster (KRSC, Seattle, WA, 1939).

18478 Lassell, Robert. Newscaster (KFIO, Spokane, WA, 1940).

18479 Lassen, Leo. Sportscaster (KRSC, Seattle, WA, 1940–1942, 1944–1945; *Signal Sports*, KRSC, 1947; *Sports Page of the Air*, KING, Seattle, WA, 1948; KOL, Seattle, WA, 1952–1956; KOMO, Seattle, WA, 1957–1960). Despite Lassen's shrill, rapid-fire delivery of baseball play-by-play, he nevertheless earned the title of "Mr. Baseball of Puget Sound." He was the outstanding radio personality of the Pacific Northwest in his time. Lassen began his career by re-creating baseball games on KVL (Seattle, WA) in the 1930s.

18480 *(The) Lasses White-Honey Weil Minstrel Show.* The program contained the blackface minstrel show humor of White and Weil and the Old Harmony Slaves (Chuck Haynes and Ray Ferris) singing old-time ballads (WSM, Nashville, TN, 1934).

18481 *Lassie.* Lassie, the beautiful collie dog of motion pictures, was the star of this dramatic action series. Although the famous collie was on hand to bark and growl on the cue of her trainer, Rudd Weatherwax, the dog's other sounds were produced by animal imitator, Earl Keen. Red Heart Dog Food sponsored the wholesome family program targeted primarily for young listeners. The cast included: Betty Arnold, Earl Keen (imitating animal noises) and Marvin Miller. Frank Ferrin and Harry Stewart were the producers. The organist was John Duffy. Hobe Donovan was the writer and Charles Lyon the announcer. Harry Stewart was the program's director (15 min., Weekly, ABC, NBC, 1947–1950).

18482 Lassiter, Chad. DJ (*Whatcha' Doin'*, WCMA, Corinth, MS, 1947; *Chad Lassiter Show*, WDXI, Jackson, TN, 1948; KNEA, Jonesboro, AR, 1954; WEW, St. Louis, MO, 1957).

18483 *(The) Last of the Lockwoods.* The daytime serial, written by Bill Meredith, told the story of a distinguished old family of the American theater — the Lockwoods. Included with the dramatic episodes were inspirational observations on life and quotations from Shakespeare. The cast included Macdonald Carey, Betty Lou Gerson and Judith Lowry (15 min., 2:00–2:15 P.M. CST, NBC-Blue, 1938).

18484 LaTarte, Alice. Pianist (WLS, Chicago, IL, 1925).

18485 Lateau, Herbert. Newscaster (KARK, Little Rock, AR, 1938).

18486 Latell, Ethel. Contralto (WGBS, New York, NY, 1927).

18487 Lateuser, Geneva. Harpist (KMOX, St. Louis, MO, 1928).

18488 Latham, Darlene. COM-HE (KIFI, Idaho Falls, ID, 1954).

18489 Latham, Iris. COM-HE (WTNS, Coshocton, OH, 1951).

18490 Latham, Jack. Newscaster (KFI, Los Angeles, CA, 1944–1945).

18491 Latham, Vera. Pianist (KWSC, Pullman, WA, 1926).

18492 LaTille, Gilda. Soprano LaTille was known as the "Shamrock Lady" (WGN, Chicago, IL, 1928).

18493 Latimer, Ed. Actor Latimer was in the cast of *Adventures of Topper, Ellery Queen, Home of the Brave, House in the Country, Joyce Jordan, Girl Interne, Nick Carter, Master Detective, Romance of Helen Trent, Rosemary and Wings for the Martins.*

18494 Latimer, Jay. News commentator (*Inside New York*, WINS, New York, NY, 1947).

18495 Latimmer, David K. Newscaster (WOSU, Columbus, OH, 1945–1947).

18496 La Torra, Carmel. Pianist (KOA, Denver, CO, 1926).

18497 Lattery, Fran. Actress Lattery appeared in the cast of the *Marriage for Two* daytime serial program.

18498 *(The) LaTouraine Concert* (aka ***The LaTouraine Coffee Concert Orchestra Program***). Augusto Vannini directed the orchestra on this weekly concert music program (NBC-Blue, 1928).

18499 Latto, Douglas. Violinist (WOOD, Grand Rapids, MI, 1926).

18500 Latz, (Mrs.) Charles. Contralto (WTAM, Cleveland, OH, 1924).

18501 Laub, Kenneth. Newscaster (WWJ, Detroit, MI 1941).

18502 Laubach, Betty. COM-HE (WHLM, Bloomsburg, PA, 1957).

18503 Laubengayer, Ed. Sportscaster (KSAL, Salina, KS, 1937).

18504 Lauder, (Sir) Harry. Distinguished Scots entertainer (NBC, 1929).

18505 Lauder, Jane. Soprano (*Jane Lauder*, vcl. mus. prg., WGY, Schenectady, NY, 1935).

18506 Lauferty, Lillian. After playing *Beatrice Fairfax* on the network, Lauferty developed her own programs *Big Sister* and *Your Family and Mine.*

18507 *(The) Laugh Clinic.* Comedy on this show was supplied by Russell Pratt and Ransom Sherman as the "Two Doctors." Organist Eddie Dunstedter and Al Roth's Laughing Trombones also were featured (30 min., Tuesday, 10:30–11:30 A.M., CBS, 1935).

18508 *Laugh with Isuan.* A combination of music and comedy, *Laugh with Isuan* featured the comic sketches of Bill and Bertie and the music of the Max Dolin Orchestra . (NBC-Pacific Coast Network, 1928).

18509 *Laugh with Ken Murray.* Rinso Soap Powder and Lifebuoy Soap sponsored the short-lived comedy series hosted by comedian Ken Murray. He was joined by Eve Arden, Tony "Oswald" Labriola, tenor Phil Regan, Russ Morgan's Orchestra and weekly guest stars. Phil Uttal was the announcer (30 min., Tuesday, 8:30–9:00 P.M., CBS, 1936).

18510 Laughin, Vivian. COM-HE (KGFW, Kearney, NE, 1956).

18511 Laughinghouse, Lucille. COM-HE (WLAS, Jacksonville, NC, 1956).

18512 Laughlin, Clara E. Broadcaster of travel talks (WMAQ, Chicago, IL, 1925).

18513 Laughlin, Ken. Newscaster (WKQD, Anchorage, AK, 1941).

18514 (The) Laughlin Brothers. Instrumental duo of violinist Connie L. Laughlin and pianist John L. Laughlin (KGER, Long Beach, CA, 1927).

18515 Laughner-Harris Hotel St. Francis Dance Orchestra. Carroll Laughner and Phil Harris were co-directors of the hotel dance band (60 min., Nightly, 11:00 P.M. to 12:00 midnight, NBC-Pacific Network, 1929).

18516 Laughton, Eddy. Leader (*Eddy Laughton Orchestra*, instr. mus. prg., WLW, Cincinnati, OH, 1934–1935).

18517 Laughton Family Orchestra. Local Tulsa band (KVOO, Tulsa, OK, 1928).

18518 Laugman, Oscar. Violinist (WDAR, Philadelphia, PA, 1924).

18519 Lauke, Mary Katherine. Inspirational talks (KFRC, San Francisco, CA, 1925).

18520 *Launderland Lyrics* (aka *Laundryland Lyrics*). This music program presented soprano-tenor duets by Barbara Blanchard and Myron Niesley with an orchestra conducted by Walter Beban (30 min., Saturday, 9:00–9:30 P.M., NBC-Pacific Coast Network, 1929). When the program was later broadcast as *Laundryland Lyrics*, it featured soprano Bernice Taylor, tenor Fred Waldner and the Josef Koestner Orchestra. Ted Pearson was the announcer (NBC-Red, 1929).

18521 Launer, Ed. Newscaster (KODY, North Platte, NE, 1944).

18522 Lauren, Jane. Actress Lauren appeared on the *Wendy Warren and the News* daytime serial program.

18523 Lauri, Alice. Soprano (WAAM, Newark, NJ, 1925).

18524 Lauria, Frank. Leader (Frank Lauria Orchestra, WAHG, Richmond Hill, NY, 1925).

18525 Lauria, Vic. The singer-musician was billed as "Vic Lauria and his Ukulele" (WHN, New York, NY, 1924).

18526 Lauria, Vic and Jack Lauria. Vocal and instrumental team (WHN, New York, NY, 1924).

18527 Laurie and His Serenaders. The musical ensemble was led by pianist Lawrence Nordshom (KFLV, Rockford, IL, 1930).

18528 Laurie, Joe, Jr. Vaudeville comic Laurie, who later became a star of the *Can You Top This?* program, first appeared on various network shows (NBC, 1929).

18529 Laurie, Mary. Contralto (WNBC, New Britain, CT, 1937).

18530 Laurie, William "Bill." Newscaster (KONO, San Antonio, TX, 1941; WINN, Louisville, KY, 1942; KNET, Palestine, TX, 1945).

18531 Laurier, Ludwig. Former first violinist and manager of the Metropolitan Opera Orchestra, Laurier succeeded Cesare Sodero and Harold Sanford as orchestral conductor on *The Slumber Hour* program (NBC-Blue, New York, NY, 1928–1929).

18532 Lauten, Jane C. COM-HE (WGAN, Portland, ME, 1956–1957).

18533 Laux, Ed. Newscaster (WAAT, Jersey City, NJ, 1941). DJ (*Requestfully Yours*, WINZ, Hollywood, FL, 1948). Sportscaster (WAAT, 1946).

18534 Laux, J. France [Francis]. Announcer and sports reporter (KVOO , Tulsa, OK, 1926–1929). After leaving his announcing job at KVOO, Laux came to St. Louis in 1929 to begin an eighteen-year career broadcasting the baseball games of the National League Cardinals and the American League Browns. His sports broadcasting career was spent in St. Louis (KMOX, St. Louis, MO, 1932–1939; *Dope From the Dugout*, *Sports Quiz* and *The Sports Review*, KMOX, 1940–1941; *Il-Mo Hunting and Fishing Club*, KXOK, St. Louis, MO, 1947; *Sports Extra*, KXOK, 1950; *Sports Gallery*, KXOK, 1952–1955).

18535 Lauzau, Fran. DJ (*Rise and Shine*, WMMN, Fairmont, WV, 1952–1954).

18536 LaValle, Al. Newscaster (WEDC, Chicago, IL, 1940–1941). Sportscaster (WEDC, Chicago, IL, 1940–1941; KXEL, Waterloo, IA, 1949).

18537 LaValle, Paul. Leader (*Paul Lavalle Orchestra*, instr. mus. prg. NBC, 1934).

18538 Laveer, Charles. Pianist (*Charles Laveer*, instr. mus. prg., NBC, 1935).

18539 *Lavender and Old Lace*. The quality music program featured various vocal artists and musicians during the short time it was on the air. Sponsored by Bayer Aspirin, the program was introduced as presenting the "songs of other days." Initially, Frank Munn and soprano Muriel Wilson, a male trio and Gus Haenschen's Orchestra were featured (30 min., Tuesday, 7:30–8:00 P.M., CBS, 1934). A later version with the same format featured tenor Munn, soprano Lucy Monroe, Fritzi Scheff and organist William Meeder. The Gus Haenschen Orchestra still provided the music. Frank and Anne Hummert produced the program (Tuesday, 7:30–8:00 P.M., CBS, 1935).

18540 LaVerne, Violet. Miss LaVerne "performed musical readings accompanied by T. Eugene Goudey at the piano" (KPO, San Francisco, CA, 1923).

18541 Lavery, Don. Announcer, pianist, actor and assistant director Lavery played the role of "Jiggs" on the *Maggie and Jiggs* program (WGES, Chicago, IL, 1928–1930).

18542 Lavery, Don L. Newscaster (WEDC, Chicago, IL, 1940–1941). Sportscaster (WEDC, 1940–1941).

18543 Lavign, Leona. Soprano (WOR, Newark, NJ, 1932).

18544 Lavigne, Clare. COM-HE (WATR, Waterbury, CT, 1954).

18545 LaVigne, Richard. DJ (*Musical Reveille*, WHYN, Holyoke, MA, 1947).

18546 Lavitan, Gladys. COM-HE (WIST, Charlotte, NC, 1949–1956).

18547 Lavong, Reginald N. DJ (*Jive Show*, WWRL, New York, NY, 1960; *Snap Club*, WHAT, Philadelphia, PA, 1960; *Reggie Lavong Show*, WBEE, Chicago, IL, 1960; *Reggie Lavong Show*, WRAP, Norfolk, VA, 1960). Lavong also hosted a syndicated DJ program.

18548 Lavque, Maurice. Russian baritone Lavque was known as the "Challiapin of the West" (WMCA, New York, NY, 1927).

18549 Law, Agnes. Executive, producer and director (CBS, 1920s and 1930s). Law was a musician with business experience. She went to work first for the Judson Radio Division when they needed a person with knowledge of musical titles and composers in 1927. Since she could type and use shorthand, she was hired as a secretary for $35 a week. She produced ten hours of musical programs weekly, including the symphonic music conducted by Howard Barlow, salon music directed by Don Voorhees, Red Nichols and His Five Pennies and other Columbia recording artists. Law later developed the *True Story Hour* written by Jules Seebach with Howard Barlow providing the music.

Her work expanded when William Paley bought the company in September, 1928. As CBS, the company expanded rapidly by acquiring more stations, announcers and performers. Law's responsibilities expanded also to include program statistics and data recording. After establishing several departments at CBS, including the Employment Office, Program Analysis Department and the Special Library, Law saw men named to take them over. As Law (1976) said, "...about two years and then as always the case at CBS, after a woman developed a department, they usually hired a man to take over." She observed in 1976, however, that woman's opportunities had increased at CBS and in the broadcasting industry generally.

Law received the George Ehrenz Medal from Syracuse University for her Pioneer Achievement in Broadcasting. When the American Women in Radio and Television organization was established in 1950, five honorary members were named: Eleanor Roosevelt, Judith Waller, Margaret Cuthbert, Dorothy [Doris] Lewis and Agnes Law.

18550 Law, Edith. Soprano (WEAF, New York, NY, 1924; WEBJ, New York, NY, 1925).

18551 Law, Glen. Newscaster (KRNT-KSO, Des Moines, IA, 1938–1945).

18552 Lawbaugh, Vera. COM-HE (WEAR, Pensacola, FL, 1951).

18553 Lawder, Sam. Sportscaster (WRTD, Richmond, VA, 1939; WINX, Washington, DC, 1941).

18554 Lawdis, (Dr.) Leonard Lincoln. Dr. Lawdis conducted a controversial health program that was considered by some to have been chiefly a self-advertisement (WFBH, New York, NY, 1925).

18555 Lawhead, Gordon. DJ (*The Clock Watchers*, WHBQ, Memphis, TN, 1947).

18556 Lawler, Boyd. Young newscaster billed as the "Boy Reporter" (WCAU, Philadelphia, PA, 1939).

18557 Lawler, Grace. Singer (*Grace Lawler*, vcl. mus. prg., WIP, Philadelphia, PA, 1936).

18558 Lawler, Mary. Singer (WGBS, New York, NY, 1926).

18559 Lawler, Tom. Newscaster (*Morning News*, WHBS, Huntsville, AL, 1947); DJ (*Musical Clock* and *Hillbilly Hits*, WHBS, 1947).

18560 Lawless, Andy. Tenor (KFI, Los Angeles, CA, 1928).

18561 Lawley, Lee. DJ (*Hall of Records*, KGER, Long Beach, CA, 1947).

18562 Lawlor, Tom. Newscaster (WNDR, Syracuse, NY, 1946).

18563 Lawlor, William. Baritone (WEAF, New York, NY, 1926).

18564 Lawnhurst, Vee. Pianist (WEAF, New York, NY, 1925). Later, *Variety* called Lawnhurst a "trick piano soloist" (WOR, Newark, NJ, 1928).

18565 Lawrence, Betty. Contralto (WMAQ, Chicago, IL, 1926).

18566 Lawrence, Bob. Leader (Bob Lawrence Orchestra, WCAP, Washington, DC, 1925).

18567 Lawrence, Bob. DJ (*Reveille Roundup*, KTFS, Texarkana, TX, 1947; *Bob Lawrence Show*, KVIC, Little Rock, AR, 1952).

18568 Lawrence, Bruce. DJ (*Turntable Bandstand*, KXOB, Stockton, CA, 1947).

18569 Lawrence, Charlotte. Actress Lawrence was in the cast of the *Just Plain Bill* and *Our Gal Sunday* daytime serial programs.

18570 Lawrence, David. News commentator who broadcast weekly talks on politics (NBC, 1929). On *Our Government* he presented his authoritative commentary on politics (*Our Government*, 15 min., Sunday, 9:00–9:15 P.M., NBC-Red, 1932–1933). Lawrence for many years was also a columnist for and editor of *U.S. News and World Report*.

18571 Lawrence, Elizabeth. Actress Elizabeth Lawrence appeared on the *Right to Happiness*, *Our Gal Sunday* and *The Road of Life* daytime serial programs.

18572 Lawrence, George H. Announcer (WSIX, Springfield, TN, 1925).

18573 Lawrence, J. Pianist (KPO, San Francisco, CA, 1923).

18574 Lawrence, J. Harold. Blind pianist Lawrence was also a band leader (Harold Lawrence Band, WRVA, Richmond, VA, 1926–27).

18575 Lawrence, Jack. Newscaster (WGIL, Galesburg, IL, 1945). DJ (*Friendly Time*, WIRL, Peoria, IL, 1948).

18576 Lawrence, James H. "Jimmy." Sportscaster, football, basketball and baseball play-by-play broadcaster (KOVO, Provo, UT, 1951–1960).

18577 Lawrence, Josephine. Writer Lawrence wrote many of the stories told by Bill McNeery, "The Man in the Moon," on his program for children (WOR, Newark, NJ, 1924–1925).

18578 Lawrence, Larry. Newscaster (WTMJ, Milwaukee, WI, 1937).

18579 Lawrence, Lawrence "Larry" Q. DJ (*Lawrence Q. Lawrence Show*, WCOP, Boston, MA, 1949; *Midnight Milkman*, WCOP, 1952).

18580 Lawrence, Lee. Singer (*Lee Lawrence*, vcl. mus. prg., WCAU, Philadelphia, PA, 1934; WIP, Philadelphia, PA, 1935–1936).

18581 Lawrence, Margaret. Singer (*Margaret Lawrence*, vcl. mus. prg., WPG, Atlantic City, NJ, 1935–1936).

18582 Lawrence, (Mrs.) May F. Pianist (WSM, Nashville, TN, 1928).

18583 Lawrence, Paul. Pianist (WBZ, Springfield, MA, 1924).

18584 Lawrence, Raymond. Actor Lawrence was in the cast of the *Romance* daytime serial program.

18585 Lawrence, Sydney. Baritone (KFWI, Los Angeles, CA, 1928).

18586 Lawrence, Tedd. Sportscaster (WBYN, Brooklyn, NY, 1944). DJ (*Swingtime Session*, WHN, New York, NY, 1947–1950; ABC, 1955; *Man About Music*, ABC, 1960).

18587 *Lawrence Quintet*. Instrumental music group (CW mus. prg., KFEL, Denver, CO, 1939).

18588 Lawrie, Justin. Tenor (NBC, 1928).

18589 *Laws That Safeguard Society*. Dean Gleason Archer discussed American law and its legal system on this informative series of programs. Beginning with his 75th broadcast on January 2, 1932, he began a sequence devoted to *Marriage and the Home*. His first lecture covered "Blood Relationship as a Barrier to Marriage." The concluding three programs in the series were:

> 76th Program: "May First Cousins Marry?"
> 77th Program: "May Relatives-in-Law Marry?"
> 78th Program: "Marriage During Lifetime of Ex-Spouses."

Archer's broadcasts were critically praised (15 min., Saturday, 7:15–7:30 P.M., NBC-Red, 1932). *See* **Archer, Gleason**.

18590 Lawshe, Eleanor. COM-HE (KFNF, Shenandoah, IA, 1956).

18591 Lawson, Reuben. Actor Lawson was in the cast of the *We are Four* daytime serial program.

18592 Lawson, Tex. Sportscaster (*High School Sports*, KWNW, Wenatchee, WA, 1949).

18593 Lawson and McClain Hawaiian String Quartet. Instrumental music group (WLW, Cincinnati, OH, 1926).

18594 Lawton, Elsie. Leader (*Elsie Lawton Orchestra*, instr. mus. prg., KUOA, Siloam Springs, AR, 1934).

18595 Lawton, Fleetwood. Newscaster (KMPC, Los Angeles, CA and KFI, Los Angeles, CA, 1940; KMJ, Fresno, CA, 1942–1944; KFI and NBC, 1945–1947).

18596 Lawton, Reed. Baritone (*Reed Lawton*, vcl. mus. prg., WOR, Newark, NJ, 1935).

18597 Lawton, Sidney. Announcer (WEAJ, Vermillion, SD, 1925).

18598 *Lawyer Q Is on the Air*. The unusual quiz program was presented in two parts. In the first, a court case was dramatized. Then Lawyer Q, billed as the "Quizzical Questioning Counselor of the Law," asked contestants whether the defendant was guilty or innocent. If the contestants answered the same way as had the actual jury, they won small cash prizes. Actors in the dramatized portion included Tony Berger, Sidney Smith and Peter Lord. Dennis James was the program's announcer (30 min., Weekly, MBS, 1947).

18599 *Lawyer Tucker*. The summer replacement for the *Dick Haymes Show* was sponsored by the Auto-Lite Company. The program starred Parker Fennelly in the title role of a big hearted lawyer with an idealistic sense of justice. David Howard and Howard Breslin were the writers and Knowles Entrikin was the producer. The cast also included Arthur Anderson, Cameron Andrews, Ted Osborne, Mae Shultz and Maurice Wells (30 min., Thursday, 9:00–9:30 P.M., CBS, 1947).

18600 Lay, Joel. Baritone (*Joel Lay*, vcl. mus. prg., 15 min., Monday, 7:00–7:15 P.M., WGES, Chicago, IL, 1932). *Radio Digest* praised Lay for his rich baritone voice.

18601 Layden, Beulah. Violinist (WGES, Oak Park, IL, 1925).

18602 Laye, Robert. Newscaster (WMJM, Cordele, GA, 1942).

18603 Layman, Carrol. Newscaster (WDAN, Danville, IL, 1940).

18604 Layne, Jerry. COM-HE (WMBG, Richmond, VA, 1951).

18605 Laz, Jack. Sportscaster and football play-by-play (WGBR, Goldsboro, NC, 1947).

18606 Lazare, Jack. DJ (*Disk Date*, WNYC, New York, NY, 1947; *Milkman's Matinee*, WINS, New York, NY, 1956).

18607 Lazaro, Gus. Leader (*Gus Lazaro Ensemble*, instr. mus. prg., KWK, St. Louis, MO, 1934; *Gus Lazaro Orchestra*, instr. mus. prg., MBS, 1939).

18608 Lazarow, Art. DJ (*Sagebrush Melodies*, WEXL, Royal Oak, MI, 1947).

18609 Lazarow, Joan. COM-HE (WDDY, Gloucester, VA, 1950).

18610 LaZarrora, Eleanor Turner. Pianist (WBZ, Springfield, MA, 1923–1924).

18611 Lazell, J. Arthur. Newscaster (WNAR, Norristown, PA, 1948).

18612 Lazer, Joan. Actress Lazer appeared on the daytime serial programs *Rosemary*, *Valiant Lady* and *Young Dr. Malone*.

18613 *Lazy Bill Huggins*. Huggins, a "dreamy baritone," was accompanied by guitar, violin and piano on his program of pleasant vocal music (15 min., Monday through Friday, 4:00–4:15 P.M., CBS, 1934).

18614 *Lazy Dan the Minstrel Man*. Irving Kaufman played Lazy Dan and all the other characters on his blackface comedy show sponsored by the A.S. Boyle Company. The scene of the show was set in a hardware store, where the boss was the straight man. Whenever it was time to have a song, someone simply said, "Turn on the radio." Kaufman was a talented singer-comedian and he skillfully displayed these talents on the program (30 min., Sunday, 1:30–2:00 P.M., CBS, 1933). Later, the show was broadcast at the same time on either Thursday or Sunday (1935).

18615 *(The) Lazy Ranch Boys Barn Dance*. One of the most popular mid-western shows was the *Lazy Ranch Boys Barn Dance* (WXYZ, Detroit, MI, 1954). The major attraction on the program was the Lazy Ranch Boys band (Casey Clark, fiddle; Herb Williams, vocals and guitar; and comic musician Barefoot Brownie Reynolds. Herb Williams also acted as MC. Other regulars on the show were Chuck Carroll, Mary Ann Johnson, Mary Lynn, Nat and Bill the Kentucky Boys, May Hawks, Don Large, Charlie and Honey the "West Virginia Sweethearts" and Little Evelyn, a 12-year-old singer. Famous guest stars frequently appeared such as: Jimmy Dean, Lulu Belle and Scotty, Moon Mullican, Ken Marvin, Ernie Lee, Hawkshaw Hawkins, Tommy Sosebee, Neal Burris, Jonnie and Jack, Kitty Wells, the York Brothers and Smiling Max Henderson.

18616 Lazzari, Carolina. Contralto (KSD, St. Louis, MO, 1923).

18617 Lea, Sandra. COM-HE (WHB, Kansas City, MO, 1949).

18618 Leach, Edward. Newscaster (WRRF, Washington, NC, 1942). DJ (*Good Morning Man*, WEWO, Laurinburg, NC, 1947). Sportscaster (WRRF, 1942; WHKP, Hendersonville, NC, 1946; WEWO, 1947).

18619 Leach, Margaret. Soprano (WHO, Des Moines, IA, 1926).

18620 Leach, Mary C. Autoharpist (KLX, Oakland, CA, 1923).

18621 Leaf, Ann. Famous radio organist Leaf was born in Omaha, Nebraska, June 28, 1906. The little musician (4' 11" tall, weighing 99 lbs.) began her long radio career in 1929 at CBS at the recommendation of Boris Morros. "Mitey," as some of her friends called her, was a popular organist at New York City's Paramount Theatre for many years (WABC-CBS, New York, NY, 1929; *Ann Leaf*, instr. mus. prg., CBS, 1934–1938).

18622 Leafer, Allan. Leader (*Allan Leafer Orchestra*, instr. mus. prg., CBS, 1934–1935; NBC-Red, New York, NY, 1936–1937).

18623 Leafer, Woodrow. DJ (*Heat Wave*, WJMR, New Orleans, LA, 1947).

18624 Leahy, Adele. Singer (KJBS, San Francisco, CA, 1925).

18625 Leahy, Elizabeth. Whistler (WOR, Newark, NJ, 1924).

18626 Leake, Audred S. "Bus." Sportscaster (*Sports Review* and basketball and football play-by-play, WDNE, Elkins, WV, 1951–1952).

18627 Leakos, Katherine. COM-HE (WGHM, Waterville, ME, 1956).

18628 Leaming, Jim. Sportscaster (*Sports Shots* and basketball, football and baseball play-by-play, WIP, Philadelphia, PA, 1951–1960; *Sports Parade*, MBS, 1955)

18629 Learn, Charlotte. Actress Learn was in the cast of the daytime serial program *Mary Marlin* aka *The Story of Mary Marlin.*

18630 *Learn to Play an Instrument in 26 Lessons by Radio*. The unique program sought to interest children in playing a musical instrument. Dr. Joseph Mady, assisted by various professional musicians, broadcast elementary instruction in playing such instruments as flute, oboe, cornet, French horn, alto horn, sousaphone, piccolo, bassoon, trumpet, mellophone, trombone, tuba, clarinet and saxophone. Separate instruction was provided for each instrument (Weekly, NBC-Red, 1936).

18631 Leary, Margaret. Soprano (WHN, New York, NY, 1925).

18632 Leary, Marion. Soprano (WHN, New York, NY, 1925).

18633 Leaska, (Mme.) Leah. Operatic and concert soprano (KGW, Portland, OR, 1928).

18634 Leason, Ray. Newscaster (WHBY, Green Bay, WI, 1932).

18635 *Leave It to Joan*. Comedienne Joan Davis starred in the funny sustaining situation comedy, assisted by cast members Joseph Kerns and Elvia Allman. The announcer was Bob Lemond. Music was supplied by Lud Gluskin's Orchestra (30 min., Monday, 9:00–9:30 P.M., CBS, 1949). A later version of the sustaining show had Joan playing a bungling department store clerk who was frantically searching for a man. The cast included Mary Jane Croft, Gerald Mohr and Willard Waterman. The orchestra was conducted by Lyn Murray. Bob Stevenson was the announcer (30 min., Monday, 10:00–10:30 P.M., CBS, 1950).

18636 *Leave It to Mike*. The short-lived situation comedy starred Walter Kinsella in the title role. The program was written by Howard Merrill and directed by Roger Bower. Other cast members included: Joan Alexander, Arthur Elmer, Hope Emerson, William Keene and Jerry Macy (MBS, 1945–1946).

18637 Leavitt, Mel. Sportscaster (WDSU, New Orleans, LA, 1949; *Great Moments in Sports*, WDSU, 1950–1955).

18638 Leavitt, Robert "Robin." DJ (*Tunes for Teens*, WWSR, St. Albans, VT, 1954; WJOY, Burlington, VT, 1957).

18639 Leazor, Perry. DJ (*1400 Club*, WSTP, Salisbury, NC, 1949).

18640 LeBaron, Eddie. Leader (*Eddie LeBaron Orchestra*, instr. mus. prg., NBC-Blue, New York, NY, 1937; NBC, 1940).

18641 LeBlanc, Barbara. COM-HE (KALB, Alexandria, LA, 1956–1957).

18642 LeBlanc, Barbara. COM-HE (KALB, Alexandria, LA, 1956–1957).

18643 LeBow, Dan. Conductor-violinist, KTHS Orchestra (KTHS, Hot Springs National Park, AR, 1928).

18644 LeBow, Guy. Sportscaster (WHN, New York, NY, 1947; NBC and CBS, 1953).

18645 LeBrun, Harry. Newscaster (WHEC, Rochester, NY, 1937–1942).

18646 Lechner, Lucille. Singer (WFAA, Dallas, TX, 1923).

18647 LeClaire, Mary Jean. COM-HE (KODI, Cody, WY, 1949).

18648 LeClaire, Violet. Actress LeClaire was in the cast of the *Myrt and Marge* daytime serial program.

18649 LeClaire Hotel Orchestra. Hotel dance band (WOC, Davenport, IA, 1926).

18650 Lecock, Mary Lou. Soprano (WEMC, Berrien Springs, MI, 1925).

18651 LeCot, Amanda Schmidt. Soprano (WOC, Davenport, IA, 1927).

18652 L'Ecuyer, Jack. Organist (KFEQ, St. Joseph, MO, 1929).

18653 Lederer, (Mrs.) A.C. COM-HE (KINE, Kingsville, TX, 1949).

18654 Lederer, John [Jack]. Pianist-leader (John Lederer Orchestra, sometimes billed as the Marylanders Orchestra, WBAL, Baltimore, MD, 1927–1928; *John Lederer Orchestra*, instr. mus. prg., WCAO, Baltimore, MD, 1938–1939).

18655 Ledford, Lily May. CW musician-singer (WLW, Cincinnati, OH, 1937). Country music pioneer Ledford was the leader, vocalist, banjoist and fiddler of the Coon Creek Girls, the first all-female string band. Born in Big Gorge in eastern Kentucky in 1917, she grew up listening to the string band music her family members played. As a teenager, she joined her family's band known as the Red River Ramblers. After a WLS (Chicago, IL) talent scout invited her to come to Chicago for an audition, Ledford made frequent appearances on the station's popular *WLS Barn Dance* program. After she signed a personal management contract with John Lair, she moved to WLW (Cincinnati, OH). When Lair decided to form an all-girl string band with Ledford as the leader, the Coon Creek Girls was formed. The band made its first appearance on WLW in 1937 and immediately became a great listener favorite. The Coon Creek Girls were heard nationwide on the *Renfro Valley Barn Dance* program. Although the group made several recordings, it enjoyed its greatest success on the radio. The band, the first all-girl string band, originally consisted of leader-banjoist Lily May Ledford; guitarist Rose Ledford; mandolinist Esther "Violet" Koehler; and fiddler and bassist Evelyn "Daisy" Lange.

18656 Ledos, Marion F. Soprano (WEAF, New York, NY, 1925).

18657 Lee, Annabelle. Singer (WHN, New York, NY, 1936).

18658 Lee, Anne. COM-HE (KYW, Philadelphia, PA, 1951).

18659 Lee, Audrey. Blues singer (KWTO, Springfield, MO, 1937).

18660 Lee, Barbara. Actress Lee was in the cast of *The Man I Married* daytime serial program.

18661 Lee, Bernard "Barney." Sportscaster (WRBL, Columbus, GA, 1941; *Leeward Side of Sports*, WBBC, Flint, MI, 1949–1950; *Sports Roundup*, WJLB, Detroit, MI, 1951; *Time for Sports*, WJLB, 1952–1956; *Sports Beat*, WJLB, 1960). Newscaster (WRBL, Columbus, GA, 1941).

18662 Lee, Bert. Sportscaster (WMCA, New York, NY, 1939; *Today's Baseball*, *Sport's Fanfare* and professional football and hockey play-by-play, WMCA, 1940; WHN, New York, NY, 1941–1942, 1944–1948; WMGM, New York, NY, 1949; *Take a Tip From Me*, *Warm-Up Time* and *Sports Extra*, WMGM, 1951–1955).

18663 Lee, Bert, Jr. Sportscaster (WMGM, New York, NY, 1948; WMGM, 1954).

18664 Lee, Beth. COM-HE (WPTR, Albany, NM, 1949).

18665 Lee, Betty. COM-HE (WCED, DuBois, PA, 1956).

18666 Lee, Billy. Actor Lee was in the cast of *Ma Perkins.*

18667 Lee, Bob. Newscaster (KFFA, Helena, AR, 1941). Sportscaster (KFFA, 1941).

18668 Lee, Bob. Sportscaster (*Springfield Sports Review*, KICK, Springfield, MS, 1960).

18669 Lee, Bobbie. Leader of Philadelphia jazz band (Bobbie Lee and his Cotton Pickers, WDAR, Philadelphia, PA, 1924; WFBH, New York, NY, 1925).

18670 Lee, Buddy. Leader, Buddy Lee's Cotton Pickers orchestra (WFBH, New York, NY, 1925).

18671 Lee, Burt. Director Lee directed the *Bachelor's Children* daytime serial program.

18672 Lee, Canada. Actor Lee also took a turn as a DJ in 1948. *See **The Canada Lee Show**.*

18673 Lee, Carol. COM-HE (KTAN, Sherman, TX, 1951; KECK, Odessa, TX, 1954–1957).

18674 Lee, Caroline. Singer known as "The Virginia Girl with her Spanish guitar" (WGHB, Clearwater, FL, 1926).

18675 Lee, Carol. COM-HE (KECK, Odessa, TX, 1957).

18676 Lee, Cliff. Newscaster (KFXM, San Bernadino, CA, 1939).

18677 Lee, Cordelia MacClure. Contralto (WBZ, Springfield, MA, 1925).

18678 Lee, David. Three-year-old singer (NBC, 1928).

18679 Lee, David "Dave." Newscaster (WIBC, Indianapolis, IN, 1945). DJ (*Records on Parade*, WKJG, Fort Wayne, IN, 1947; *Dave Lee Show*, WKJG, 1948; *Record on Parade*, WKJG, 1950).

18680 Lee, Dave. DJ (*Hi Neighbor*, WLOK, Lima, OH, 1948).

18681 Lee, Donna. Newscaster (WTMV, East St. Louis, IL, 1944–1945).

18682 Lee, Dick. Newscaster (WHBU, Anderson, IN, 1944–1945). Sportscaster (WHBU, 1945).

18683 Lee, Dixie. Vocalist-band leader (*Dixie Lee and the Dixieland Band*, instr. mus. prg., WRVA, Richmond, VA, 1936).

18684 Lee, Donna. Newscaster (WTMV, East St. Louis, IL, 1944–1945).

18685 Lee, Doris. Pianist (KGO, Oakland, CA, 1926).

18686 Lee, Doris. Miss Lee broadcast beauty talks (KDKA, Pittsburgh, PA, 1927).

18687 Lee, Dorothy. COM-HE (KPQ, Wenatchee, WA, 1957).

18688 Lee, D'Voe. COM-HE (KOLE, Cleburne, TX, 1949).

18689 Lee, Earl. Leader (*Earl Lee Orchestra*, instr. mus. prg., WXYZ, Detroit, MI, 1935).

18690 Lee, Earl. Actor Lee appeared on the *Hawthorne House* and *One Man's Family* programs.

18691 Lee, Edwin. Newscaster (MBS, 1955).

18692 Lee, (Mrs.) Fitz-Hugh. Lecturer (*Indian Lore,* WCAE, Pittsburgh, PA, 1937).

18693 Lee, Frank. Newscaster (WMMN, Fairmount, WV, 1944–1945). Sportscaster (WMMN, 1944–1950; *Sports Journal*, WMMN, 1951–1955).

18694 Lee, George. Sportscaster (KGBX, Springfield, MO and KWTO, Springfield, MO, 1937).

18695 Lee, Glenn. Leader (*Glenn Lee Orchestra*, instr. mus. prg., WLW, Cincinnati, OH, 1935).

18696 Lee, Gretchen. COM-HE (WOOD, Grand Rapids, MI, 1951).

18697 Lee, Harriet. Contralto (WABC, New York, NY, 1929). Singer on the *Ceco Couriers* program (WABC, New York, NY, 1929).

18698 Lee, Harry W. Newscaster (WMFD, Wilmington, NC, 1939–1940, 1945). Sportscaster (WMFD, 1940).

18699 Lee, J.W. "Joe." Newscaster (KGFF, Shawnee, OK, 1939, 1945).

18700 Lee, Jack. DJ (*R.F.D. 1090*, WCRA, Effingham, IL, 1952).

18701 Lee, Jane. COM-HE (KNBC, San Francisco, CA, 1949).

18702 Lee, Janet. COM-HE (WTTM, Trenton, NJ, 1949).

18703 Lee, Jean. Soprano (WCAL, Northfield, MN, 1936).

18704 Lee, (Miss) Jerry. Contralto (WMEX, Boston, MA, 1939).

18705 Lee, Jerry. COM-HE (WKLX, Paris, KY, 1960).

18706 Lee, Jetta Sue. COM-HE (KBTO, El Dorado, KS, 1955).

18707 Lee, Josephine. COM-HE (WNCT, Greenville, NC, 1957).

18708 Lee, June. "The singing vagabond" (WGCP, New York, NY, 1926).

18709 Lee, June. COM-HE (KFEL, Grand Junction, CO, 1951; KSTR, Grand Junction, CO, 1957–1960).

18710 Lee, Larry. Leader (*Larry Lee Orchestra*, instr. mus. prg., WLW, Cincinnati, OH, 1934).

18711 Lee, Letha. COM-HE (KPAC, Port Arthur, TX, 1957).

18712 Lee, Lila. DJ (*Mail Bag*, WEDO, McKeesport, PA, 1947).

18713 Lee, Linda. COM-HE (KTBC, Austin, TX, 1956).

18714 Lee, Loretta. Soprano (WBAL, Baltimore, MD, 1926–*1927; Loretta Lee*, vcl. mus. prg., CBS, 1935). Miss Lee was a graduate of Baltimore's Peabody Conservatory of Music.

18715 Lee, Lydia. The "Little Blue Bird," Lydia Lee talked about radio and other entertainment topics (WENR, Chicago, IL, 1929).

18716 Lee, Lyle. Newscaster (WLOK, Lima, OH, 1948).

18717 Lee, Madaline. Actress Lee appeared on the *Second Mrs. Burton* daytime serial program.

18718 Lee, Margery. COM-HE (WRBC, Jackson, MS, 1951).

18719 Lee, Marion. Reader (WCBD, Zion, IL, 1925).

18720 Lee, Martha. COM-HE (KLX, Oakland, CA, 1929).

18721 Lee, Martha. COM-HE (WAAB, Boston, MA, 1931–1936).

18722 Lee, Mary D. Newscaster (KGFF, Shawnee, OK, 1950s).

18723 Lee, Merrill. Vocalist (*Merrill Lee*, vcl. mus. prg., WIP, Philadelphia, PA, 1936).

18724 Lee, Norma. Contralto (KFWI, San Francisco, CA, 1929).

18725 Lee, Pat. Guitarist-singer (KFI, Los Angeles, CA, 1928).

18726 Lee, Pat. COM-HE (WBT, Charlotte, NC, 1956–1957).

18727 Lee, Patricia. COM-HE (WRGS, Rogersville, TX, 1957).

18728 Lee, Peggy. Singer (WDAY, Kansas City, MO, 1937).

18729 Lee, R.E. Newscaster (KWLC, Decorah, IA, 1939).

18730 Lee, Raymond. Baritone (KPRC, Houston, TX, 1926).

18731 Lee, Rosa. Soprano (*Rosa Lee*, vcl. mus. prg., NBC, 1935–1936; WLW, Cincinnati, OH, 1936; KGHF, Pueblo, CO, 1939; WXYZ, Detroit, MI, 1942).

18732 Lee, Rose. Soprano (NBC, 1937).

18733 Lee, Ruth. Soprano (WEMO, Berrien Springs, MI, 1925).

18734 Lee, Ruth. Soprano (WRNY, Richmond Hill, NY, 1925).

18735 Lee, Sair. Contralto (NBC, 1937).

18736 Lee, Sarah. Soprano (WOR, Newark, NJ, 1932).

18737 Lee, Shepard. Newscaster (*1st National Bank News*, WTWA, Thomson, GA, 1948).

18738 Lee, Sue Austin. Mezzo-soprano (KFI, Los Angeles, CA, 1927).

18739 Lee, Suzanne. Pianist (*Suzanne Lee*, instr. vcl. mus. prg., WIP, Philadelphia, PA, 1935).

18740 Lee, Ted. Newscaster (WISH, Indianapolis, IN, 1944).

18741 Lee, Ted. DJ (WJJD, Chicago, IL, 1960).

18742 Lee, Thelma. Soprano (KEX, Portland, OR, 1928). Miss Lee was known as the "Golden West Girl" (KGW, Portland, OR, 1928).

18743 Lee, Tom. Leader (Tom Lee's Concert Band, WKRC, Cincinnati, OH, 1926).

18744 Lee, Toni. COM-HE (WHJB, Greensburg, PA, 1955).

18745 Lee, Vanston. Baritone (WEAF, New York, NY, 1925).

18746 Lee, Viola K. Organist Lee played from the Alladin Theater in Denver (KOA, Denver, CO, 1927).

18747 Lee, Virginia. Soprano (WOC, Davenport, IA, 1928).

18748 Lee, Virginia. COM-HE (WLEE, Richmond, VA, 1956–1957).

18749 Lee, W.C. DJ (*680 Club*, WCLE, Clearwater, FL, 1947).

18750 Lee, William. Newscaster (WBZ-WBZA, Boston-Springfield, MA, 1938).

18751 Lee, William. Newscaster (KRIG, Odessa, TX, 1946).

18752 Lee, William A. "Billy." Actor Lee was in the cast of *Flying Time*, *Ma Perkins* and *Mary Marlin.*

18753 Lee, Wilma. Singer (KWBG, Hutchinson, KS, 1937).

18754 Lee, Zeb. Sportscaster (WSKY, Asheville, NC, 1947–1956).

18755 *Lee Adams*. Adams was a homespun philosopher (15 min., Saturday, 10:15–10:30 A.M., CBS, 1947).

18756 *Lee Mace's Ozark Opry*. CW music show (KRCG, Jefferson City, MO, 1953; KMOS, Sedalia, MO, 1953). Founded by CW musician Lee Mace and his wife Joyce as a live show presented from near the Lake of the

Ozarks. By 1957 the show was a popular item on the broadcast schedules of both KRCG-TV and KMOS-TV. The live show continued after the death of Lee in 1985, was presented six nights a week from its own Ozark Opry auditorium during the summer months.

18757 ***Lee Sullivan's Vest Pocket Varieties.*** The sustaining variety show featured entertainers Frank Maxwell, Florence MacMichael, the Smoothies and announcer Tex Antoine (15 min., Monday through Friday, 10:00–10:15 A.M., WNBC, New York, NY, 1946).

18758 ***Lee Wiley.*** Great jazz and ballad singer Wiley starred on her own program (15 min., Wednesday, 6:00–6:15 P.M., CBS, 1936).

18759 **Leedon [Leedom], Mary and Helen Leedon [Leedom].** Singing team (WIP, Philadelphia, PA, 1926).

18760 **Leeds, David.** Newscaster (WAAT, Jersey City, NJ, 1942).

18761 **Leeds, Jerry.** DJ (*Bunkhouse Jamboree*, KVSM, San Mateo, CA, 1952).

18762 **Leeds, Norman.** DJ (*Request, Please*, WHUM, Reading, PA, 1947).

18763 **Leefers, Robert.** Newscaster (WMT, Cedar Rapids–Waterloo, IA, 1940–1941).

18764 **Leek, Helen.** Soprano (WLAC, Nashville, TN, 1927).

18765 **Leeland, Betty.** Eight-year-old singer (WDGY, Minneapolis, MN, 1929).

18766 **Leen, Carthilla.** Reader (KFSG, Los Angeles, CA, 1936).

18767 **Leen, Fanny Ashby.** Singer (KFSG, Los Angeles, CA, 1926).

18768 **Leeper, Raymond.** Leader of a 20-piece string band (KVOO, Bristow, OK, 1926).

18769 **Leeper, Thekla.** COM-HE (WMRF, Lewistown, PA, 1956).

18770 **Lees, Jean.** Broadcast travelogûes (KOMO, Seattle, WA, 1927).

18771 **Leest, Maurice.** Leader (Maurice Leest String Quartet, WJZ, New York, NY, 1926).

18772 **LeFarge, Maurice.** Pianist (WJZ, New York, NY, 1922).

18773 **LeFebre, Channing.** Organist (WBAL, Baltimore. MD, 1926). LeFebre also played on the *Seiberling Singers Hour* (NBC, 1928).

18774 **Lefevre, Bill.** Sportscaster (WFBR, Baltimore, MD, 1953).

18775 **Lefevre, Carolyn.** Violinist (KHJ, Los Angeles, CA, 1926).

18776 **LeFevre, Eva Mae.** Singer (*Gospel Songs*, WGST, Atlanta, GA, 1950).

18777 **Lefferts, Florence.** Soprano (WFI, Philadelphia, PA, 1925).

18778 **Leftwich, Jelly.** Leader (*Jelly Leftwich Orchestra*, instr. mus. prg., WRVA, Richmond, VA, 1938).

18779 **Leg, Dorothy.** COM-HE (KPQ, Wenatchee, WA, 1949).

18780 **Legare, John E.** DJ (*Supper Dance Hour*, WAYX, Waycross, GA, 1947).

18781 ***Legends of America.*** Herbert J. Bilberman, who also appeared in the cast, and Earl C. Hildreth wrote the dramatic episodes from American history presented on this sustaining program. Also in the cast were Ted De Corsia, Allyn Joslyn and Gale Sondergaard (30 min., Tuesday, 10:00–10:30 P.M., CBS, 1933).

18782 **Legette, (Lt.) James V.** Announcer on the U.S. Army Experimental Station (AT 9, Fort Bragg, North Carolina, 1926).

18783 **Leggett, Barbara.** COM-HE (WPNC, Plymouth, NC, 1960).

18784 **LeGrand, (Mrs.) H.N.** Musician LeGrand played tenor saxophone, drums and marimba and was the director of the orchestra on the *Boys and Girls Farm Bureau Review* program (WHO, Des Moines, IA, 1924).

18785 **LeGrand, Oats.** Sportscaster (KOTE, Fergus Falls, MN, 1960).

18786 **Lehay, Pearl.** Pianist (WBZ, Springfield, MA, 1926).

18787 ***Lehn & Fink Serenaders.*** Jack Shilkret directed the commercial orchestra featured on the *Lehn & Fink Serenaders* program of light concert music (30 min., Weekly, NBC-Blue, 1928–1929).

18788 **Lehnhoff, Bill.** DJ (*Your Program*, KTW, Seattle, WA, 1947; *Moments with the Masters*, KTW, 1948; *Music For You*, KTW, 1955).

18789 **Lehnhoff, Henry.** DJ (*Um-Pa-Pa*, KWED, Seguin, TX, 1954).

18790 **Lehvinne, Mischa.** Concert pianist who filled the intermissions between local election returns broadcast 8:00–10:00 P.M., November 6, 1923 (KPO, San Francisco, CA, 1923).

18791 **Leibert, Richard "Dick."** Organist (*Dick Liebert*, instr. mus. prg., NBC, 1935–1938). Organist Leibert played on the *Big Sister*, *Life and Loves of Dr. Susan*, *Second Mrs. Burton*, *Stella Burton*, *Stella Dallas* and *When a Girl Marries* daytime serial programs.

18792 ***Leibert's Musicale.*** Organist Dick Leibert performed along with a female singer and a male quartet on the music program sponsored by Luden's Incorporated (15 min., Friday, 8:15–8:30 P.M., NBC-Blue, 1934).

18793 **Leich, Walter.** Newscaster (WGBF, Evansville, IN, 1938–1939).

18794 **Leidendeker, Maxine.** (COM-HE, KBIZ, Ottumwa, IA, 1951–1954).

18795 ***Leider Singers.*** Vcl. mus. prg. (NBC-Blue, 1935).

18796 **Leidy, William.** Singer (WIP, Philadelphia, PA, 1924).

18797 **Leigh, Sara.** Conducted the *Sara Leigh's Hour for Ladies* (KHQ, Spokane, WA 1927).

18798 **Leigh, Sylvia.** Actress Leigh was in the cast of the *Ma Perkins* and *Front Page Farrell* daytime serial programs.

18799 **Leighton, Ben.** Newscaster (WEBC, Duluth, MN and WHLB, Virginia, MN, 1939–1941).

18800 **Leighton, George.** DJ (*White Tower Show*, WROW, Albany, NY, 1952).

18801 **Leighton, Jean King.** Songs, stories and impersonations of stage stars (KYW, Chicago, IL, 1922).

18802 **Leighton, Ruth.** Mezzo-soprano (WEEI, Boston, MA, 1925).

18803 **Leighton's Arcade Cafeteria Orchestra.** Music group directed by Jack Cronshaw (KHJ, Los Angeles, CA, 1925; KNX, Los Angeles, CA, 1926).

18804 **Leimbach, Louis.** Tenor (KPO, San Francisco, CA, 1923).

18805 **Leimert, Tim.** Newscaster (CBS, 1944).

18806 **Leipsic, Doris and Emma Normand.** Dual piano team (KLX, Oakland, CA, 1928).

18807 **Leiser, Stella.** COM-HE (WMOH, Hamilton, OH, 1949).

18808 **Leisure, Clarence.** Newscaster (KHSL, Chico, CA, 1938). DJ (*Voice in the Night*, KNBC, San Francisco, CA, 1954). Sportscaster (KHSL, 1939).

18809 **Leitch, Albert.** Newscaster (WJSV-CBS, Washington, DC, 1942; NBC-Blue, 1944; CBS, 1945).

18810 **Leitch, Roberta.** Soprano (KPO, San Francisco, CA, 1927).

18811 **Leithner, Frank.** Jazz pianist (WEAF, New York, NY, 1923–1924).

18812 **Leland, Cy.** Sportscaster (WBAP, Fort Worth, TX, 1937).

18813 **Leland, (Mrs.) Morton.** Reader Leland frequently broadcast "The Ballad of the Reading Gaol" (WJZ, New York, NY, 1923).

18814 **Lellman, Jack.** Newscaster (KDAL, Duluth, MN, 1940; WISH, Indianapolis, IN, 1941; WJR, Detroit, MI, 1945).

18815 **Lelong, Lise.** COM-HE (WJMR, New Orleans, LA, 1951).

18816 **LeLovelace, Charlotte.** Blues singer (KFWB, Hollywood, CA, 1927).

18817 **Lemaire, Jean.** Pianist (WAHG, Richmond Hill, NY, 1926).

18818 **Lem and Lafe.** A blackface comedy team, not otherwise identified (KPO, San Francisco, CA, 1928).

18819 **Lem Hawkins Hillbillies.** CW musical group (WDAY, Fargo, ND, 1936).

18820 ***Lem Perkins' Rough Riders.*** Cowboy music was the specialty of the CW group (Thursday P.M., KFEL, Denver, CO, 1931).

18821 **LeMaire, Jean.** Pianist (WAHG, Richmond Hill, NY, 1926).

18822 **Leman, J.W.F.** Conductor of the Women's Symphony Orchestra (WFI, Philadelphia, PA, 1925).

18823 **LeMarr, Leila.** Pianist (WKRC, Cincinnati, OH, 1925; WSAI, Cincinnati, OH, 1925).

18824 **LeMay, Mary Ann.** COM-HE (WISN, Milwaukee, WI, 1956).

18825 **LeMeadows, Fay.** COM-HE (WHIO, Dayton, OH, 1937).

18826 **Lemen, Matt.** Newscaster (*News at Noon-Fifteen*, KOPO, Tucson, AZ, 1947). DJ (*Tempo Rendezvous*, KOPO, 1948; *Juke Box Jubilee* and *Tempo Rendezvous*, KOPO, 1950; KOLD, Tucson, AZ, 1960).

18827 **Lemieux, Mel.** Leader (Mel Lemieux Dance Orchestra, KLX, Oakland, CA, 1928).

18828 **Lemma, Joyce.** COM-HE (KBWD, Brownwood, TX, 1951).

18829 LeMoine Orchestra. Popular local orchestra (WGCP, New York, NY, 1926).

18830 Lemon, Doc. DJ (*Ol' Doc Lemon Show*, WLOK, Lima, OH, 1952; KSO, Des Moines, IA, 1955; WCUE, Akron, OH, 1957).

18831 LeMon, Mel. Announcer (KFWB, Hollywood, CA, 1928).

18832 Lemond, Lee. DJ (*Goodwill Dawnbuster*, WJR, Detroit, MI, 1950).

18833 Lemons, Wishard. Newscaster (KOCY, Oklahoma City, OK, 1946). DJ (*Voice vs. Voice*, KOCY, 1947).

18834 Lenard, Grace. Actress Lenard appeared on *The Road of Life* daytime serial program.

18835 Lenay, Will. DJ (*Morning Star*, WLW, Cincinnati, OH, 1947; *Will Lenay Show*, WCPO, Cincinnati, OH, 1952; WSAI, Cincinnati, OH, 1954–1957).

18836 Lencioni, C. Accordionist (KFOB, Burlingame, CA, 1925).

18837 Lenhard, Bill. News analyst (*News in Review*, WFUR, Grand Rapids, MI, 1948).

18838 Lenhart, Garrett "Garry." News analyst (WHO, Des Moines, IA, 1945; *World Events Commentary*, WHO, 1946–1947).

18839 Lenington, Drury. Tenor (KFI, Los Angeles, CA, 1925).

18840 Lenni, Francesca. Actress Lenni was in the cast of the *Your Family and Mine* daytime serial program.

18841 Lennon, Paul. Sportscaster (*Sports Review* and football and basketball play-by-play, WSUA, Bloomington, IN, 1947; WTOM, Bloomington, IN, 1948–1950).

18842 Lennox, Betty. COM-HE (WGY, Schenectady, NY, 1937). Newscaster (WGY, Schenectady, NY, 1945).

18843 Lennox, Elizabeth. Contralto (Columbia network staff, New York, NY, 1927; the *Palmolive Hour*, WEAF-Red-New York, NY, 1927–1931; and WEAF, New York, NY, 1929).

18844 Lennox, James. Sportscaster (KHBG, Okmulgee, OK, 1939).

18845 Lennox, John, Jr. Newscaster (KHBG, Okmulgee, OK, 1947).

18846 Lennox String Quartet. This instrumental group broadcast a weekly half-hour program of light concert music (30 min., Weekly, NBC-Blue, New York, NY, 1928–1929).

18847 LeNoir, Irene. Singer (KTAB, Oakland, CA, 1925).

18848 Lenox, Bonnie. COM-HE (KGKB, Tyler, TX, 1951).

18849 Lenrow, Bernard. Actor Bernard was in the cast of *Casey, Crime Photographer, Ellen Randolph, Eternal Light, Mystery Theater* and *Valiant Lady.*

18850 Lent [Lento], Caroline. Mezzo-soprano (WOV, New York, NY, 1932).

18851 Lent, Jimmy. Leader (Jimmy Lent's Society Orchestra, WOR, Newark, NJ, 1925).

18852 Lentell, (Mrs.) Lulu. Contralto (KLDS, Independence, MO, 1925).

18853 Lentz, Al. Leader (Al Lentz and his Tuneful Comedians Orchestra were described in *Broadcasting* (Feb. 19, 1927, p. 23) as "strutting their static over WMC," WMC, Memphis, TN, 1927). The Lentz band included: Lentz, ldr.-bj.-vcls.; Ted Eddy and Sid Peltyn, t.; George Schaute, tb.; Penny Holder, Bill Manning and Irving Loonan, clr. and as.; Carl Oarech, clr. and ts.; Mac Ceppos, v.; Harry Cohen, p.; Buddy Burtson, d.; and Jack Vaughn, tba.

18854 Lentz, Arthur "Art." Sportscaster (WIBA, Madison, WI, 1940–1941, 1945–1950; WISC Madison, WI, 1951–1952).

18855 Lenz, Dorothy Smith. Soprano (WTAM, Cleveland, OH, 1924).

18856 Lenz, Elinor. Actress Lenz appeared in the *Aunt Jenny* aka *Aunt Jenny's True Life Stories* daytime serial programs.

18857 Lenz, Jack. Tenor (*Jack Lenz*, vcl. mus. prg., WOR, Newark, NJ, 1935).

18858 Lenz, Ted. Newscaster (KSAN, San Francisco, CA, 1940; KVAK, Atchison, KS, 1945). DJ (KGFJ, Hollywood, CA, 1950).

18859 Leo, Fred K. Sportscaster (WMRO, Aurora, IL, 1941; WMBD, Peoria, IL, 1944–1945; KDEN, Denver, CO, 1956–1960).

18860 *Leo J. Meyberg Company Program.* The commercial program presented musical comedies and dramatic presentations. One example broadcast in 1926 was *The Geisha*, a Japanese musical comedy written by Owen Hall and Sidney James. Directed by Carl Anderson, the cast included: Jane Gates, Alice E. Hansen, Margaret O'Dea, James Gerard, Ira D. Moran, Edwin Heinsohn and Waldemar Engberg (KGO, Oakland, CA, 1926).

18861 Leon, Edward. French language lessons were taught by Leon (KNX, Los Angeles, CA, 1928).

18862 Leon, Frank. Pianist (KOMO, Seattle, WA, 1928).

18863 Leonard, Agnes. Singer of songs for children on Friday evenings (WJZ, New York, NY, 1924).

18864 Leonard, Archie L. Newscaster (KTHS, Hot Springs, AR), 1946).

18865 Leonard, Bill. Announcer Leonard conducted a program in which he interviewed the "ordinary little man" (CBS, mid–1940s). Leonard went to TV and later to network executive positions.

18866 Leonard, Dell. Leader (*Dell Leonard Orchestra*, instr. mus. prg., WCKY, Cincinnati, OH, 1935).

18867 Leonard, Dodee. COM-HE (KGFW, Kearney, NE, 1957).

18868 Leonard, Elizabeth. COM-HE (KING, Seattle, WA, 1956–1957).

18869 Leonard, Gene. Actor Leonard was in the cast of *American School of the Air, Trouble House* and *Valiant Lady.*

18870 Leonard, Hal. Leader (*Hal Leonard Orchestra*, instr. mus. prg., WGN, Chicago, IL, 1942).

18871 Leonard, Harold. Director (Harold Leonard's Red Jackets Orchestra from the Club Madrid, WIP, Philadelphia, PA, 1923). The Harold Leonard Orchestra's daily half-hour radio shows in 1928 probably made it the most frequently heard band on the air (WABC, New York, NY, 1928).

18872 Leonard, Harry. Leader (Harry Leonard's Waldorf-Astoria Orchestra, WJZ, New York, NY, 1926).

18873 Leonard, Helen. Pianist (WSGH, Brooklyn Heights, NY, 1928).

18874 Leonard, Inez. Singer known as "The Masked Soprano" (WMAQ, Chicago, IL, 1926).

18875 Leonard, Jesse. Newscaster (KEX, Portland, OR, 1945). DJ (*Sunnyside Up*, KEX, 1947).

18876 Leonard, Jimmy. DJ (*The Jimmy Leonard Show*, WSAI, Cincinnati, OH, 1950).

18877 Leonard, Joseph J. Newscaster (KNOX ,Knoxville, TN, 1944).

18878 Leonard, Lee. Sportscaster (WFMJ, Youngstown, OH, 1945–1947; *Speaking of Sports* and *Sports Final*, WFMJ, 1949–1950). DJ (*Lee Leonard Show*, WLOW, Norfolk, VA, 1952; KLAN, Leemore, CA, 1956–1960).

18879 Leonard, Mabel. After a successful tour on the Orpheum vaudeville circuit, organist Leonard began working at KFWB (Los Angeles, CA, 1927). Leonard also was an excellent pianist.

18880 Leonard, Mac. DJ (*Please Play*, KHUZ, Borger, TX, 1947).

18881 Leonard, Myrtle. Singer (KPO, San Francisco, CA, 1929).

18882 Leonard, Richard "Dick." Director-writer Leonard with the exception of one program directed *Backstage Wife, Barry Cameron* (writer) *Chaplain Jim, Front Page Farrell, Mr. Chameleon, Mr. Keen, Tracer of Lost Persons, Romance of Helen Trent, Stella Dallas* and *Young Widder Brown.*

18883 Leonard, Steve. Leader (*Steve Leonard Orchestra*, instr. mus. prg., WGN, Chicago, IL, 1934; MBS, 1942).

18884 Leonard and Hinds. Harmony singing team (KFRC, San Francisco, CA, 1926).

18885 Leone, Eva. Director, Children's Opera Company (WNYC, New York, NY, 1939).

18886 Leone, Leo. Tenor (WTIC, Hartford, CT, 1931).

18887 Leone, Richard. Actor Leone was in the cast of *Woman of America.*

18888 Leonhardt, Paul A. Leonhardt conducted a morning exercise program (KYW, Chicago, IL, 1925).

18889 Leopold, J. Walter. Pianist-composer (KFI, Los Angeles, CA, 1927).

18890 Leotta, Mme. Reader (KOIN, Portland, OR, 1928).

18891 LePage, Grace. Soprano (KGO, Oakland, CA, 1925).

18892 LePage, Jean. Sportscaster (*Sports Review*, WMSA, Massena, NY, 1947).

18893 *LeParadis Dance Band.* Instr. mus. prg. (WAAB, Boston, MA, 1932).

18894 LePere, Raymond. Organist LePere broadcast from the Dallas Palace Theater five mornings each week (WFAA, Dallas, TX, 1929).

18895 Lepgold, Herman. Tenor (WHAD, Milwaukee, WI, 1925).

18896 Lepper, (Captain) J.H. Announcer (WIBS, Jersey City, NJ, 1925; WFBR, Baltimore, MD, 1925).

18897 Lerner, Eva. Singer (WPCH, New York, NY, 1932).

18898 Leroux, Joe. Newscaster (*News from Home*, KELD, El Dorado, AR, 1947–1948).

18899 *Leroy*. Instr. mus. prg. performed by Leroy, a pianist not otherwise identified (WXYZ, Detroit, MI, 1935).

18900 LeRoy, Harry. DJ (KGGC, San Francisco, CA, 1937). Sportscaster (KGGC, San Francisco, CA, 1937; KQW, San Jose, CA, 1940).

18901 LeRoy, Howard. Leader (*Howard LeRoy Orchestra*, instr. mus. prg., WCCO, Minneapolis–St. Paul, MN, 1939).

18902 Lerwerth, Margaret. Writer Lerwerth worked on the *Mrs. Miniver* program.

18903 Les Ambassadeurs. Comedy singing group consisting of Lou Clayton, Eddie Jackson and Jimmie Durante. This was the team in which Jimmie Durante first began his rise to stardom. Their exuberant comedy was particularly well suited to the Prohibition Era in which they began broadcasting (WMCA, New York, NY, 1929).

18904 Lesar, David "Dave." Producer Lesar produced *Brighter Day, Guiding Light* and *Young Dr. Malone.*

18905 *Les Paul and Mary Ford*. Guitarist Paul and his vocalist wife Mary Ford appeared on this inventive music program that probably was transcribed (10 min., 7:30–7:40 P.M., KLPM, Minot, ND and MBS, 1955).

18906 Lescoulie, Jack. DJ (Mutual-WOR, New York, NY all night show, 1947; WOR, 1950). Although Lescoulie began his broadcasting career in radio, it was his television work that brought him national prominence.

Lescoulie's extensive television career began with his acting appearance on *Volume One*, a dramatic anthology series on NBC in 1949. After this program, he presented sports and general features with Dave Garroway on *The Today Show* (NBC, 1952–1961). In addition to co-hosting the *Brains and Brawn* (NBC, 1957–1958) TV game show and the *1-2-3*-GO! educational show (NBC, 1961–1962), Lescoulie followed Steve Allen in hosting *The Tonight America After Dark Show* before hosts Jack Paar and Johnny Carson took over the duties and transformed *The Tonight Show* into the tremendously popular program it eventually became.

18907 Lescoulie, Sylvia. COM-HE (KVAR, Mesa, AZ, 1955).

18908 Leseur, Larry. News commentator (CBS, 1944–1948).

18909 Lesick, Edward Michael. Newscaster (WXYZ, Detroit, MI, 1941).

18910 Leskowitz, Fannie. Pianist (KFI, Los Angeles, CA, 1928).

18911 Leslie, Ann. COM-HE (WISN, Milwaukee, WI, 1957).

18912 Leslie, Chuck. Newscaster (WENR, Chicago, IL, 1946).

18913 Leslie, Florence. Singer (WGBS, New York, NY, 1927).

18914 Leslie, Grace. Contralto (WAHG, Richmond Hill, NY, 1925).

18915 Leslie, Jack. DJ (*Tip Top Spot*, KTIP, Porterville, CA, 1947).

18916 Leslie, Jean. COM-HE (WJMR, New Orleans, LA, 1949).

18917 Leslie, John. Newscaster (WOW, Omaha, NE, 1942–1945; *REX News*, WREX, Duluth, MN, 1948).

18918 Leslie, Laura. Born in Finksburg, Maryland, singer Leslie had a commercially sponsored show, while still attending high school (WBAL, Baltimore, MD, mid–1930's).

18919 Leslie, Maybelle. Pianist (KFWB, Hollywood, CA, 1925).

18920 Lesnevich, Gus. Lesnevich, a former light heavyweight boxing champion, performed as a DJ and talked with his sustaining program's announcer, Bob Emerick (30 min., Saturday, 4:30–5:00 P.M., WOR, New York, NY, 1951).

18921 Lesser, Jerry. Actor Lesser appeared on the *Life of Mary Southern* daytime serial program.

18922 *(A) Lesson in English*. Wilda Wilson Church conducted a program dedicated to the "improvement of our native tongue" (KGO, San Francisco, CA, 1925).

18923 *Lessons in Loveliness*. Nell Vinick delivered beauty talks on the popular network show (CBS, 1930).

18924 Lester, Ann. Contralto (*Ann Lester*, vcl. mus. prg., NBC, 1935).

18925 Lester, Bill. DJ (*Off the Record*, KOY, Phoenix, AZ, 1947; *Record Matinee*, KOY, 1952).

18926 Lester, Frank C. Newscaster (KFXD, Nampa, ID, 1938).

18927 Lester, Helen. Soprano (WOO, Philadelphia, PA, 1925).

18928 Lester, Jack. Sportscaster (WNOE, New Orleans, LA, 1946). DJ (*Jack Lester Show*, WENR, Chicago, IL, 1949).

18929 Lester, Les. DJ (KANE, New Iberia, LA, 1960).

18930 Lester, Rita. Contralto (*Rita Lester*, vcl. mus. prg., NBC, 1935).

18931 Lesters, Gary. DJ (*Breakfast with the Record Man*, WRIB, Providence, RI, 1947).

18932 *Let George Do It*. Bob Bailey played the role of George Valentine, a hard boiled private investigator, who prided himself on taking the "tough jobs." The program opened with him saying, "Danger is my stock in trade. If the job's too tough for you to handle, you've got a job for me, George Valentine. Write full details." The program announcer then added, "Standard Oil of California on behalf of independent Chevron gas stations and Standard stations throughout the west invites you to *"Let George Do It."* Cast members of the program included Eddie Firestone, Jr., Shirley Mitchell, Joe Kearns, Howard McNear, Horace Murphy and Frances Robinson. Organist Eddie Dunstedter provided the music (30 min., Weekly, CBS, 1951).

18933 Letocsky, Stanley Jan. Pianist (WOAW, Omaha, NE, 1925).

18934 *Let Yourself Go*. Milton Berle hosted the variety show featuring Joe Besser, Connie Russell and the Ray Bloch Orchestra (30 min., CBS, 1944–1945). *See **The Milton Berle Show**.*

18935 *Let Yourself Go*. The local music show was sponsored by Borden's Milk. Singer Peggy Ann Ellis, pianist Teddy Wilson and the Roy Ross Orchestra were featured (30 min., Monday through Friday, 12:00–12:30 P.M., WNEW, New York, NY, 1950).

18936 *Let's Compare Notes*. Sally Selby sometimes conducted the daily women's program (KMOX, St. Louis, MO, 1936).

18937 *Let's Dance*. The Saturday night music program, containing three hours of dance music, began broadcasting in the mid–1930's. In 1935, Don Carney was the MC of the program that presented the bands of Xavier Cugat, Kel Murray and Benny Goodman (180 min., NBC, 1935).

18938 *Let's Dance, America*. Fred Robbins hosted the sustaining show featuring Tex Beneke's Orchestra and pianist Skitch Henderson (30 min., Saturday, 10:00–10:30 P.M., CBS, 1948).

18939 *Let's Draw*. James Schwalbach, a Milwaukee high school teacher, conducted the art program on which he claimed that children showed more imagination when instructed by radio than from television (WHA, Madison, WI., 1958). Schwalbach was on WHA radio for more than 30 years.

18940 *Let's Follow Forducy*. H.L. Ripley wrote these excellent mystery stories for the revised version of the *Forducy Minute Mysteries*. The first 15 minutes of the show presented a mystery and conducted a contest. The mystery was then solved in the last quarter-hour segment. Richard Gordon, who previously had played the master sleuth on the *Sherlock Holmes* program, was the featured actor (30 min., Monday, 8:30–9:00 P.M., MBS, 1935).

18941 *Let's Get Acquainted*. Lee Bennett portrayed character analyst Dr. Blake, whose aim on the program was to inform listeners as to the cause and effects of human personality traits. Soy Food Mills sponsored the program (5 min., Monday through Friday, WGN, Chicago, IL, 1942).

18942 *Let's Go to the Opera*. The Book-of-the-Month Club sponsored the music appreciation program that presented Lawrence Tibbett and Marie Rogndahl performing operatic selections. The music was conducted by Thomas Scherman. Frank Waldecker was the announcer (30 min., Sunday, 7:00–7:30 P.M., WOR, Newark, NJ, 1946).

18943 *Let's Go to Town*. The transcribed music program's cast included Gale Storm and the Tony Pastor Orchestra alternating with Perry Como and the Mitchell Ayres band (15 min., Transcribed, 1950s).

18944 *Let's Have Rhythm*. The entertaining Saturday evening program featured the Top Hatters Orchestra (30 min., Saturday, 3:00–3:30 P.M., NBC, 1936). Although identified only as the Top Hatters Orchestra on the show, they were actually Jan Savitt's band. Savitt, who had originally played violin in Leopold Stokowski's Philadelphia Symphony Orchestra, first became a Philadelphia and, later, a national favorite. The band featured vocalist Carlotta Dale, clarinetist Joe "Buddy" Kearns and the "King of the Organ," Arthur Hinnett.

18945 ***Let's Learn Spanish.*** Sixteen stations carried the transcribed series of 39 instructional programs. Joel Sayre, Pedro Domec and Duncan Pirnie performed the language teaching (Transcribed, Various Stations, 1946).

18946 ***Let's Listen to Harris.*** The Northam-Warren Company sponsored the lively music show that featured Phil Harris, his band and vocalist Leah Ray (30 min., Friday, 9:00–9:30 P.M., NBC, 1934). When the Harris band played at Hollywood's Cocoanut Grove, he hired Miss Ray as his band vocalist for $50 a week. She went on to star in motion pictures with Maurice Chevalier in *Bedtime Story* and Bob Hope in *Going Spanish.* Harris later became nationally known as a funny cast member on the *Jack Benny* program. Harris later had a motion picture career and his own radio show with his wife, the *Phil Harris-Alice Faye* program. *See* ***Jack Benny.***

18947 ***Let's Pretend*** **(aka *In the Land of Let's Pretend* and *The Adventures of Helen and Mary*).** The famous children's program originally was known as *The Adventures of Helen and Mary* with the title roles played by Estelle Levy and Patricia Ryan. The name was changed to *In the Land of Let's Pretend* in 1934. Shortly thereafter, the title was shortened to *Let's Pretend,* the one by which it is best known. The program was on the air 13 years without a sponsor because CBS refused to allow it to be commercially sponsored. The network finally relented and allowed sponsorship by Cream of Wheat in 1943. The program's cast over the years included: Bill Adams, Denise Alexander, Albert Aley, Julian Altman, Arthur Anderson, Brad Barker (animal imitator), Maury Benkoil, Vivian Block, Butch Cavell, Kingsley Colton, Ivan Cury, Gwen Davies (Estelle Levy), Elaine Engler, Marilyn Erskine, Dick Etlinger, Anne-Marie Gayer, Jack Grimes, Billy and Florence Halop, Donald Hughes, Lester Jay, Jack Jordan, Robert Lee, Bill Lipton, Ronald Liss, Rita Lloyd, Sidney Lumet, Bobby and Billy Mauch, Michael O'Day, Patricia Peardon, Bob Readick, Patricia Ryan, Eddie Ryan, Jr., Alan Shea, Jimsey Sommers, Harry Swan (animal imitator), Walter Tetley, Sybil Trent, Betty Jane Tyler and Miriam Wolfe. Music was provided by the Maurice Brown orchestra (CBS, 1930–1957). Nila Mack, the program's creator and director, was a star of the stage and silent motion pictures, where she had appeared with Mme. Nazimova.

18948 ***Let's Sing.*** Colgate-Palmolive Company sponsored the audience participation community sing program. The first program host was Jack Arthur, but he soon was replaced by Homer Rodeheaver, formerly the song leader for evangelist Billy Sunday. Rodeheaver did an excellent job as both singing song leader and host (30 min., Wednesday, 9:30–10:00 P.M., CBS, 1936).

18949 ***Let's Visit the Zoo.*** Roger Conant, Curator of the Philadelphia Zoological Gardens, told animal stories and provided little known facts about them on his entertaining and educational sustaining show (15 min., Saturday, 11:30–11:45 A.M., KYW, Philadelphia, PA, 1941).

18950 ***Let's Write Songs.*** Sigmund Spaeth, known as the "Tune Detective," conducted the program for aspiring songwriters. He analyzed various popular songs and provided suggestions for listeners who wanted to write their own songs (15 min., Weekly, WNYC, New York, NY, 1939).

18951 **Letson, Ed.** Newscaster (KFOR, Lincoln, NE, 1938; KFAB, Lincoln, NE and KFOR, 1939).

18952 ***Letters of the Cartwright Family.*** A daytime serial drama that told its story in a format by means of family member's letters to each other. When the letters were presented, they were broadcast in the voice of their writers (WTMJ, Milwaukee, WI, 1937–1938).

18953 **Leucke, Herschel.** Organist Leucke played on the *Life Can Be Beautiful* and *We Love and Learn* daytime serial programs.

18954 **Levant, Phil.** Leader (*Phil Levant Orchestra,* instr. mus. prg., WTMJ, Milwaukee, WI, 1931; *The Phil Levant Orchestra,* instr. mus. prg., WMAQ, Chicago, IL, 1934; NBC, 1936–1937; WGN, Chicago, IL, 1940).

18955 **Levee, Edward.** Tenor known as the "Singing Milkman," accompanied on the piano by his 11-year-old son, Myron Levee (KYW, Chicago, IL, 1922).

18956 **Leverone, Maria.** Pianist (WEAF, New York, NY, 1925).

18957 **Levers, Warren.** Baritone (*Warren Levers,* vcl. mus. prg., WIP, Philadelphia, PA, 1935–1936).

18958 **Leverton, Buck.** Leader (*Buck Leverton and His Lumberjacks,* CW music program, WROK, Rockford, IL, 1936).

18959 **Leverton, O.M.** Newscaster (WLBL, Stevens Point, WI, 1942).

18960 **Levey, Arthur.** Guitarist (WEBJ, New York, NY, 1926).

18961 **Levi, Arthur, Jr.** DJ (*Music Women Love,* WJMR, New Orleans, LA, 1952).

18962 **Levienne, Kola.** Cellist (KJR, Seattle, WA, 1928).

18963 **Levienne's Concert Orchestra.** Local musical group (KOMO, Seattle, WA, 1926).

18964 **Levin, Frederic E.** Bass (KPO, San Francisco, CA, 1923).

18965 **Levin, Harry.** Newscaster (WHOM, Jersey City, NJ, 1942).

18966 **Levin, Natalie.** Violinist (KGO, Oakland, CA, 1924).

18967 **Levin, Sylvan.** Pianist (*Sylvan Levin,* instr. mus. prg., WBAL, Baltimore, MD, 1935) DJ (Talented maestro Levin, WOR's music director, became a "long-haired DJ," who presided over his own show with informative commentary, 55 min., Saturday, 1:30–2:25 P.M., MBS, 1952).

18968 **Levine, Albert.** Newscaster (WCAM, Camden, NJ, 1938).

18969 **Levine [Levint], Gertrude.** Violinist (KFWI, San Francisco, CA, 1926).

18970 **Levine, Hershel.** Newscaster (WHOM, Jersey City, NJ, 1941).

18971 **Levine, (Mrs.) Matty.** Concert pianist (WHN, New York, NY, 1924).

18972 **Levine, Sheppard.** Tenor (WQJ, Chicago, IL, 1924; WIBO, Chicago, IL, 1925).

18973 **Levinson, Bud.** DJ (*Gloom Busters,* KOLN, Lincoln, NE, 1947).

18974 **Levinson, Joe.** Actor Levinson was in the cast of *The Married Life of Helen and Warren.*

18975 **Levitow, Bernard.** Conductor (Bernard Levitow and his Hotel Commodore Ensemble, WABC-CBS, New York, NY, 1929). *See* ***Bernard Levitow and His Commodore Ensemble.***

18976 **Levitski, Mischa.** Pianist (*Misha Levitski,* instr. mus. prg., NBC, 1934).

18977 **Levitsky, Mitchell.** News analyst (WHOM, Jersey City, NJ, 1938; *Jewish News,* WEVD, New York, NY, 1941).

18978 **Levitt, William.** Violinist (WGN, Chicago, IL, 1928).

18979 **Levitzky, Sandia.** Pianist (*Sandia Levitzky,* instr. mus. prg., NBC, 1936).

18980 **LeVoir, Babe.** Sportscaster (WCCO, Minneapolis–St. Paul, MN, 1937, 1946).

18981 **Levy, Bernard.** Sportscaster (WRDW, Augusta, GA, 1939).

18982 **Levy, Estelle.** Actress Levy was in the cast of the *Hilltop House* daytime serial program.

18983 **Levy, George.** Newscaster (WCAP, Asbury Park, NJ, 1939–1940).

18984 **Levy, Hal.** Leader (*Hal Levy Orchestra,* instr. mus. prg., WGY, Schenectady, NY, 1934).

18985 **Levy, Jerome.** Director (Palmer House Symphony Players, WJJD, Chicago, IL, 1926).

18986 **Levy, Milton.** Newscaster (KBKR, Baker, OR, 1945).

18987 **Levy, Si.** DJ (*Sandman Serenade,* KVER, Albuquerque, NM, 1952).

18988 **Lewallen, Dorothy.** COM-HE (WGWR, Asheboro, NC, 1957).

18989 **Lewellhyn Novelty Orchestra.** Popular local orchestra managed by Arthur J. Werner (WJZ, New York, NY, 1922).

18990 **LeWerth, Margaret.** Writer (CBS, 1936). LeWerth was the only woman on the eight member continuity staff at CBS. Her program *Americans at Work* was one of the first to combine dramatization and narrative techniques.

18991 **Lewin, Jack.** Newscaster (WFDF, Flint, MI, 1939; 1944–1945).

18992 **Lewin, Richman.** Newscaster (*Noon News,* KTRE, Lufkin, TX, 1948).

18993 **Lewis, Abby.** Actress Lewis appeared on the *Road of Life* daytime serial program.

18994 **Lewis, Agnes.** Soprano (WMRJ, New York, NY, 1930; ballad singer, WNYC, New York, NY, 1932).

18995 Lewis, Ann. DJ (*Shopping the Town*, WCVA, Culpepper, VA, 1952).

18996 Lewis, Art. Sportscaster (WHA, Madison, WI, 1945).

18997 Lewis (Mme.) Belle Jacobs. Contralto Lewis was a "pupil of Mme. Isabelle Marks" (KPO, San Francisco, CA, 1923).

18998 Lewis, Betty. Singer (WPG, Atlantic City, NJ, 1935).

18999 Lewis, Bill. DJ (*Red's Club*, WKOX, Framingham, MA, 1947–1950).

19000 Lewis, Bill. DJ (*Midnight in Minot*, KLMP, Minot, ND, 1947; *Afternoon Tune Time*, WLMP, 1950).

19001 Lewis, Bob. Newscaster (WFPG, Atlantic City, NJ, 1940; WIBX, Utica, NY, 1946).

19002 Lewis, C.M. Lewis was the radio spokesman for the Washington [state] Manufacturers Association (KFOA, Seattle, WA, 1928).

19003 Lewis, Cara. COM-HE (WLOU, Louisville, KY, 1956).

19004 Lewis, Celia. Fifteen-year-old pianist (KFI, Los Angeles, CA, 1925).

19005 Lewis, Charles A. Newscaster (KSAL, Salina, KS, 1945).

19006 Lewis, (Mrs.) Clarke. Soprano (KGO, Oakland, CA, 1926).

19007 Lewis, D.H. Tenor (WHO, Des Moines, IA, 1924).

19008 Lewis, Don. Newscaster (WWL, New Orleans, 1941–1945).

19009 Lewis, Dorothy. Contralto (KJR, Seattle, WA, 1928).

19010 Lewis, Dorothy. COM-HE (WKAT, Swainsboro, GA, 1954).

19011 Lewis, Earl. Newscaster (WHNC, Henderson, NC, 1945; *News Roundup*, WMBL, Morehead City, NC, 1948). DJ (*Record Bar*, WGBR, Goldsboro, NC, 1952).

19012 Lewis, Ed. DJ (*1240 Club* and *Turntable Talk*, KRDO, Colorado Springs, CO, 1947; *920 Club*, KFXJ, Grand Junction, CO, 1948). Sportscaster (*Nightcap of Sports*, KRDO, 1947; *Sports Resume of the Day*, KFXJ, 1948; *Sports Reel*, KFXJ, 1949–1950; *Sports Digest*, KFXJ, 1951; KIT, Yakima, WA, 1956).

19013 Lewis, Ednyfed. Tenor (WFI, Philadelphia, PA, 1923).

19014 Lewis, Ervin. Newscaster (WLS, Chicago, IL, 1938–1939; WLS, Chicago, IL, 1941–1948).

19015 Lewis, Forrest. Actor Lewis appeared on *Betty and Bob, The Great Gildersleeve, Ma Perkins, Meet the Meeks, One Man's Family, Scattergood Baines, Stepmother* and *Tom Mix*.

19016 Lewis, Franklin. Sportscaster (WGAR, Cleveland, OH, 1939).

19017 Lewis, Fulton, Jr. A popular conservative radio commentator, Lewis began his radio career while working for the Washington, (DC) *Herald* and broadcasting its news bulletins (WMAL, Washington, DC, 1927; WOL, Washington, DC, 1937–1938; MBS, 1939–1941; NBC, 1941; WHN, New York, NY, 1942; WOL, 1945; *Top of the News*, MBS, 1942–1948). Usually Lewis' program began with an announcer saying, "Fulton Lewis, Jr., bring you the *Top of the News*."

No radio commentator probably elicited more ambivalent reactions of approval and disapproval than did Fulton Lewis, Jr. His *Top of the News* program had 529 sponsors. In 1939, Lewis was Washington's best known political commentator. The Charles A. Lindbergh "Baby" Kidnapping case and the Munich Crisis brought him national prominence for his broadcast coverage of them. During World War II, Lewis exposed many government scandals and examples of corruption by defense contractors. FDR, "big labor," and government corruption were his prime targets through the years. He continued broadcasting after the end of the war, but his strong conservative views kept him under almost constant attack by his rivals and the politicians he angered.

19018 Lewis, Gene. Actor Lewis appeared in early radio dramas (WFAA, Dallas, TX, 1923).

19019 Lewis, Gene. DJ (KTHT, Houston, TX, 1947; *Teen Canteen*, KTHT, 1950).

19020 Lewis, George. DJ (*Music by Request*, WCBM, Baltimore, MD, 1948; WOND, Pleasantville, NJ, 1955).

19021 Lewis, Gertrude. Newscaster (WDGY, Minneapolis–St. Paul, MN, 1937; WLOL, Minneapolis–St. Paul, 1940).

19022 Lewis, Gladys. Soprano (WGY, Schenectady, NY, 1926).

19023 Lewis, Harriet. Pianist (KFWI, San Francisco, CA, 1927).

19024 Lewis, Harry. Singer (WHO, Des Moines, IA, 1926).

19025 Lewis, Helen. Vaudeville singer Helen Lewis was featured on *The Hoot Owls Program* (KGW, Portland, OR, 1925).

19026 Lewis, Helen. Actress Lewis appeared on the *Dick Tracy, Kate Hopkins, Angel of Mercy, Ma Perkins, The Mighty Show, Road of Life* and *This is Your FBI*.

19027 Lewis, Henry. Hawaiian guitarist Lewis frequently teamed with Norman Jackson (WHO, Des Moines, IA, 1926).

19028 Lewis, J. Leonard. Leader (*J. Leonard Lewis Orchestra*, instr. mus. prg., WPG, Atlantic City, NJ, 1936).

19029 Lewis, Jack. Leader (Jack Lewis and his Ocean Pier Orchestra, WIP, Philadelphia, PA, 1923; *Jack Lewis Ensemble*, instr. mus. prg., WIP, 1938).

19030 Lewis, Jack. Newscaster (KARK, Little Rock, AK, 1937; KARK, 1939; WALA, Mobile, AL, 1941).

19031 Lewis, John. Announcer (WLAC, Nashville, TN, 1928).

19032 Lewis, John. Baritone (*John Lewis*, vcl. mus. prg., WSM, Nashville, TN, 1935).

19033 Lewis, John. Sportscaster (WJTN, Jamestown, NY, 1939).

19034 Lewis, John. Sportscaster (WCAO, Baltimore, MD, 1949; *Spotlight on Sports*, WCAO, 1950).

19035 Lewis, John W. Lewis, an officer of the Cincinnati Better Business Commission, delivered talks on various business topics and the threat of Communism to the American way of life (WLW, Cincinnati, OH, 1925–1926).

19036 Lewis, Johnny. Leader (*Johnny Lewis Orchestra*, instr. mus. prg., WIP, Philadelphia, PA, 1936 and WLW, Cincinnati, OH, 1936).

19037 Lewis, Joseph. Leader (Joseph Lewis Orchestra, WIP, Philadelphia, PA, 1923).

19038 Lewis, Josephine. COM-HE (WNCT, Greenville, NC, 1957).

19039 Lewis, June. COM-HE (WJEJ, Hagerstown, MD, 1949).

19040 Lewis, June. COM-HE (WJEF, Grand Rapids, MI, 1949).

19041 Lewis, Kay. COM-HE (WGAI, Elizabeth City, NC, 1949).

19042 Lewis, Kitty. COM-HE (WKTK, Chehalis-Centralia, WA, 1956).

19043 Lewis, LaNaomi Coffin. Violinist (WQJ, Chicago, IL, 1925).

19044 Lewis, Lyle. DJ (*Luncheon Dance Time*, WABZ, Albemarle, NC, 1947).

19045 Lewis, Madge Terry. Pianist (WHAS, Louisville, KY, 1924).

19046 Lewis, Mark. DJ (*Spin and Chin*, WWOD, Lynchburg, VA, 1947). Newscaster (*Radio Journal*, WWOD, 1948).

19047 Lewis, Mary. Metropolitan Opera soprano (WEAF, New York, NY, 1926. *Mary Lewis*, vcl. mus. prg., WHP, Harrisburg, PA, 1935).

19048 Lewis, Milton. Writer Lewis wrote the *Inner Sanctum, The Thin Man* and *This is Nora Drake* programs.

19049 Lewis, Pat. DJ (*Open House*, KING, Seattle, WA, 1960).

19050 Lewis, Phyllis. COM-HE (WCNB, Connersville, IN, 1949).

19051 Lewis, R.P. Newscaster (KOKO, La Junta, CO, 1944).

19052 Lewis, Ralph. Violinist (New York radio, 1936).

19053 Lewis, Robert. Newscaster (CBS, 1945; WTOP, Washington, DC, 1946).

19054 Lewis, Robert Q. DJ (*Robert Q's Waxworks*, CBS, 1949). *See* ***The Robert Q. Lewis Show***.

19055 Lewis, Rose. Singer (WELI, Boston, MA, 1939).

19056 Lewis, Sabry. DJ (*Rhythm 'n' Blues*, WBMS, Boston, MA, 1952).

19057 Lewis, Sol. Newscaster (NBC-Blue, 1942).

19058 Lewis, Stanford. Newscaster (WIP, Philadelphia, PA, 1941).

19059 Lewis, Ted [Theodore Friedman]. Famous band leader and entertainer Lewis led his band on the *All-Night International Program* (WHB, Kansas City, MO, 1923). He also led the Ted Lewis and his Synchrophonic Clowns orchestra on the *Revue Intime* broadcast from New York's Parody Club the following year (WHN, New York, NY, 1924). The 1924 Lewis band's personnel probably included the following: Lewis, ldr., clr., as. and vcls.; Dave Klein, c.; George Brunies and Harry Raderman, tb.; Sol Klein, v.; Dick Reynolds, p.; Vic Carpenter, bj.; John Lucas, d.; and Harry Barth, tba.

Lewis' trademark was his battered top hat

and frequent inquiry, "Is *everybody* happy?" Both served him well for many decades. Among many other broadcasts, the Lewis band appeared later on CBS in 1929 and WLW (Cincinnati, OH, 1935).

19060 Lewis, Terese [Theresa]. Writer (Agency, 1930s). Lewis was a writer in the Radio Department at the Young and Rubicam advertising agency.

19061 Lewis, Texas Jim. CW singer and band leader (Leader, *Texas Jim Lewis Band*, CW mus. prg., MBS, 1942). Lewis first broadcast on WTAW (College Station, TX, 1929), before appearing on KPRC (Houston, TX, early 1930s) and WJR (Detroit, MI, early 30s). He and his music group appeared in several western movies with such stars as Johnny Mack Brown, Gene Autry, Eddie Dean and Charles Starrett.

19062 Lewis, Walter. Newscaster (WTNJ, Trenton, NJ, 1941–1942).

19063 Lewis, Welcome. Contralto crooner (WEAF, New York, NY, 1929).

19064 Lewis, Wilma. COM-HE (KAVL, Lancaster, CA, 1956–1957).

19065 Lexington Theater Orchestra. Theater band (WHN, New York, NY, 1925).

19066 Ley, Martha. News analyst (WHOM, Jersey City, NJ, 1941). COM-HE (WHOM, 1957).

19067 Leyden, Bill. DJ (*Music Hall*, KMPC, Los Angeles, CA, 1947; *The Bill Leyden Show*, KFWB, Los Angeles, CA, 1949–1952).

19068 Lias, Jim. News commentary (*Names in the News*, WCED, Dubois, PA, 1948).

19069 Libby, Edward F. "Ed." Newscaster (WJMA, Covington, VA, 1941). DJ (*Ad Lib with Ed Libby*, WAYB, Waynesboro, VA, 1950; WINA, Charlottesville, VA, 1954). Sportscaster (WKEY, Covington, VA, 1947; WKRC, Cincinnati, OH, 1950).

19070 Libby, John C. Newscaster (WCOU, Lexington, ME, 1940). Sportscaster (WCOU, 1940–1942, 1946–1960).

19071 Libby, (Dr.) O.G. Dr. Libby told American Indian stories on his *Story Telling Hour* over the University of North Dakota's station (KFJM, Grand Forks, ND, 1923–1925).

19072 Libby Band. Toscha Seidel, an excellent classical violinist, performed on the *Around the World in Music* program sponsored by Libby, McNeil and Libby canning company and conducted its band (NBC-Blue, New York, NY, 1929).

19073 *Libby, McNeill and Libby Program.* Mus. prg. featuring Mme. Kupenko singing with an orchestra conducted by Claude McArthur (NBC, 1929).

19074 *Library of Congress Chamber Musicale Program.* Good music program series broadcast from Washington, D.C. (NBC, 1935).

19075 LiButti, George. Newscaster (WSAY, Rochester, NY, 1945).

19076 Lichtenstein, Ida. Pianist (WJZ, New York, NY, 1925).

19077 Lichtensul, Elsie. COM-HE (KDKA, Pittsburgh, PA, 1929).

19078 Lido Club Orchestra. Club band (WHEC, Rochester, NY, 1928).

19079 Lido Venice Orchestra. Club orchestra led by Henry Kallis (WEEI, Boston, MA, 1928).

19080 Lieb, Frederick. Lieb broadcast baseball news (WNYC, New York, NY, 1925).

19081 Liebbe, (Robert) Bob "Spike." Sportscaster (KWPC, Muscatine, IA, 1946; *Muscatine Sports Review*, KWPC, 1947–1948; *Sterneman Sports* and *Ten Minutes with Ten Pins*, KWPC, 1949; *All Sports*, KWPC, 1950).

19082 Lieberfeld, Dan. Leader (*Dan Lieberfeld Orchestra*, instr. mus. prg., WRVA, Richmond, VA, 1939).

19083 Lieberknecht, Katherine. Pianist (WOC, Davenport, IA, 1923).

19084 Lieberman, Harold. Leader (Harold Lieberman's Melody Nine, KFI, Los Angeles, CA, 1925).

19085 Lieberson, Gershon. Tenor (KFWI, San Francisco, CA, 1927).

19086 Liedemedt, Theodore. Violinist (WIP, Philadelphia, PA, 1926).

19087 *Liederkranz Chorus.* Vcl. mus. prg. (WFBL, Syracuse, NY, 1935).

19088 Lien, Lorraine. COM-HE (KDIO, Ortonville, MN, 1960).

19089 Lierman, Gay. COM-HE (KLEX, Lexington, MS, 1960).

19090 Lifschitz, Ruth. Pianist (WSBH, Brooklyn Heights, NY, 1928).

19091 *(The) Life and Loves of Dr. Susan.* Lever Brothers' Lifebouy Soap sponsored the daytime serial that told the story of the troubles encountered by Dr. Susan Chandler, a widow who lived with her in-laws in a small town. Eleanor Phelps played the title role. Also in the cast were: Fred Barron, Mary Cecil, Elspeth Eric, Tommy Hughes, Alexander Kirkland, Gloria Mann, Mary Mason and Allie Lowe Miles. The director was Ed Rice. Dick Leibert was the program's organist. The show was written by Edith Meiser. Frank Luther was the announcer who also sang the Lifebouy commercial (15 min., Monday through Friday, 2:15–2:30 P.M., CBS, 1939).

19092 *Life Begins* (aka *Martha Webster*). Bess Flynn wrote the daytime serial first broadcast in 1940 by CBS. Later the name was changed to *Martha Webster* (CBS, 1940–1941). The cast included: Ray Collins, Donald Cook, Gretchen Davidson, Jimmy Donnelly, Helene Dumas, Ralph Dumke, Bess Flynn, Charlotte Garrity, Toni Gilman, Margaret MacDonald, Agnes Moorehead, Jeanette Nolan, Ethel Waite Owen, Patricia Peardon, Betty Philson, Janet Rolands, Eddie Ryan, Everett Sloane, Edgar Stehli, Tom Tully and Carleton Young. The director was Diana Bourbon.

19093 *Life Begins at 80.* This panel show was based on age. On the show, host Jack Barry quizzed oldsters, instead of the youngsters he had confronted previously on *Juvenile Jury*. The geriatric panel show, appropriately enough, was sponsored by such products for the older generation as Geritol, Campbell's soup and Serutan Laxative. The panelists commented on various personal problems faced by the older generation. The program was produced by Dan Ehrenreich (Dan Enright). Diana Bourbon was the director. Ken Roberts was the announcer. The program appeared on both MBS and ABC (1948–1953).

19094 *Life Can Be Beautiful.* An idealistic daytime serial drama, this long running show (1938–1954) told the story of Chichi Conrad and her adopted father, Papa David Solomon, roles that were originated by Alice Reinheart and Ralph Locke. Papa David owned the Slightly Read Bookshop, through which most of the show's characters passed. Some idea of the general tenor of the show can be drawn from the familiar opening intoned by its announcer: "John Ruskin wrote this, 'Whenever money is the principal object of life, it is both got ill and spent ill, and does harm both in the getting and spending.' *Life Can Be Beautiful* is an inspiring message of faith drawn from life, written by Carl Bixby and Don Becker, and brought to you by Spic and Span. No soap, no other cleaner, nothing in America cleans painted walls, woodwork and linoleum like Spic and Span."

Over the years, the inspirational program's cast included: Peggy Allenby, Ed Begley, Clayton "Bud" Collyer, Humphrey Davis, Roger DeKoven, Carl Eastman, Gavin Gordon, Mitzi Gould, Vinton Hayworth, Elsie Hitz, John Holbrook, Joe Julian, Waldemar Kappel, Teri Keane, Adelaide Klein, Richard Kollmar, Earl Larrimore, Ralph Locke, Ian Martin, John Moore, Agnes Morehead, Dick Nelson, Ethel Waite Owen, Minerva Pious, Alice Reinheart, Sidney Smith, Paul Stewart, Charles Webster, Ruth Weston and Ruth Yorke. The directors were Oliver Barbour and Chick Vincent. Don Becker and Carl Bixby were the writers and Don Becker the producer-director. The announcers on the program were Bob Dixon, Ralph Edwards, Don Hancock, Ed Herlihy and Ron Rawson. Herschel Leucke was the organist.

19095 *Life in New York.* Sidney Garfield described wartime life in New York on the quarter-hour show (15 min., Weekly, WJZ, 1942).

19096 *(A) Life in Your Hands.* Earle Stanley Gardner created the character of Jonathan Kegg, a wealthy retired lawyer, who frequently acted as a friend of the court [*amicus curiae*]. Whenever he thought justice was threatened, Kegg redressed the balance to avert the potential injustice. Myron Wallace (Mike Wallace) was the program's narrator and Ken Nordine the announcer. Kegg was played at various times by Carlton KaDell, Ned LeFevre and Lee Bowman. Other cast members included: Boris Aplon, Marianne Berthrand, Maurice Copeland, Everett Clark, Harry Eders, Carl Grayson, Art Hern, Geraldine Kay, Ed Prentiss and Beverly Younger. The program was written by Bob and Billie McKee. Brown and Williamson Tobacco Company, makers of Raleigh Cigarettes, sponsored the summer replacement show for *People are Funny* (30 min., Tuesday, 10:30–11:00 P.M., NBC, 1949–1952).

19097 *Life Is a Song.* From 1934 to 1936, lovely Countess Olga Albani was the featured singer on the music program with the Charles Previn Orchestra (30 min., Sunday, 8:00–8:30 P.M., CST, NBC-Blue, 1935). After the Countess left the show, her place was taken by baritone Edward Nell.

19098 ***Life Is Worth Living.*** The Admiral Corporation, makers of Admiral television sets, sponsored the series of inspirational and spiritual talks by Bishop Fulton J. Sheen. After achieving success on TV, Sheen came to radio to deliver his inspirational talks. Previously Bishop Sheen had appeared on *The Catholic Hour* for more than 20 years (55 min., Thursday, 9:05–10:00 P.M., MBS, 1953).

19099 **Life of Antoine Cadillac.** Popular dramatic series competed in 13 weeks (WMAQ, Chicago, IL, 1931).

19100 ***(The) Life of a Student Nurse in a Hospital.*** The program consisted of a series of talks describing how student nurses were trained (WOO, Philadelphia, PA, 1923).

19101 ***(The) Life of Mary McCormie.*** Based on the life of opera star, Mary McCormie, the program sponsored by the Lumberman's Mutual Casualty Insurance Company, starred the singer herself. McCormie sang and performed in the 13-week dramatic series. Also in the cast were Vincent Coleman, Angeline Hedrick and Isabel Randolph. The program was written by Miss McCormie and Fritz Blocki (15 min., Weekly, 8:00–8:15 P.M. CST, WBBM, Chicago, IL, 1935).

19102 ***(The) Life of Mary Southern.*** Hinds Honey and Almond Cream and Pebeco toothpaste sponsored the daytime serial drama. The story concerned a modern woman who sought love and happiness, despite the many difficulties she encountered. The cast included: Minabelle Abbott, Betty Caine, Linda Carlon, Jeanne Colbert, Florence Golden, Leon Janney, Jay Jostyn, Joseph Julian, Rikel Kent, Jerry Lesser, Bess McCammon, Charles Seel and Jack Zoller. Don Becker wrote and Chick Vincent directed. The announcer was Ken Roberts (15 min., Monday through Friday, 5:15–5:30 P.M., MBS, 1935–1938).

19103 ***(The) Life of Riley.*** William Bendix played the role of Chester A. Riley on the weekly situation comedy sponsored by Prell Shampoo and Teel for a beautiful smile. Later, the title role of Riley was played by Jackie Gleason and Lionel Stander. Other program sponsors over the years the show was on the air were Pabst Blue Ribbon beer, Dreft and the American Meat Institute.

Riley each week had to meet and contend with Gillis, his neighbor, a gloomy Digger O'Dell who called himself "Your Friendly Undertaker;" and his understanding and frequently frustrated wife, Peg. John Brown played both the roles of Riley's neighbor and that of the "Friendly Undertaker." Peg was played by Grace Coppin and Paula Winslowe. Other members of the cast were: Scotty Beckett, Conrad Binyon, Peggy Conklin, Hans Conreid, Tommy Cook, Sharon Douglas, Barbara Eiler and Jack Grimes (30 min., Weekly, ABC, NBC, 1944–1951).

19104 ***(The) Life of Uncle Ned.*** A dramatic sketch broadcast weekly (Sunday, NBC, 1935).

19105 ***(The) Life Saver Rendezvous.*** Life Savers candy sponsored the pleasant music show that featured tenor Phil Duey, singer Jane Williams, a male vocal trio and the orchestra of Aldo Ricci and his Rhythm Strings (30 min., Wednesday, 8:00–8:30 P.M., NBC-Blue, 1935).

19106 ***(The) Life Time Review.*** Shaeffer Pen Company sponsored the music program that featured the music of the Harold Stokes Orchestra and guest vocalists (15 min., Monday, 8:00–8:15 P.M., MBS, 1938).

19107 ***Life with Luigi.*** J. Carrol Naish played the title role on the situation comedy sponsored by Spearmint chewing gum. Luigi was an Italian immigrant who with his friends sought and found the good life in the United States. Naish was assisted by such veteran radio character actors as Alan Reed and Hans Conreid. Others in the cast were: Joe Forte, Jody Gilbert, Ken Peters and Mary Shipp. The show was directed by Cy Howard. The writer-director was Mac Benoff. Bob Lemond, Charles Lyon and Bob Stevenson were the announcers (30 min., Weekly, CBS, 1948–1953).

19108 ***(The) Lifebuoy Show.*** *See **Al Jolson Lifebuoy Show**.*

19109 **Liggett, Lucy.** COM-HE (WLEC, Sandusky, OH, 1957).

19110 **Light, Enoch.** Leader (*Enoch Light Orchestra*, instr. mus. prg., WSJV, Washington, DC, and CBS, 1934; WGN, Chicago, IL, NBC, 1936 and WOR, Newark, NJ, 1936; CBS, 1939).

19111 **Light, Ethel.** Pianist (WEAF, New York, NY, 1925).

19112 **Light and Power Concert Orchestra.** Commercially sponsored orchestra (WDAF, Kansas City, MO, 1928).

19113 ***Light Crust Doughboys.*** CW mus. prg. (KARK, Little Rock, AR, 1939). *The Light Crust Doughboys* celebrated their twentieth year on the air in 1950, when they appeared with Slim Whitman, Jack and Ruth Perry. The Doughboys were still an outstanding CW music group at that time (KMAC, San Antonio, TX, 1950).

The band originated in 1929 when it was formed by Bob Wills, Herman Amspiger and Milton Brown. Sponsored by the Aladdin Mantle Lamp Company, they appeared on WBAP (Fort Worth, TX, 1930) under the name of the Alladin Laddies. The next year they broadcast two programs daily on KFJZ (Fort Worth, TX, 1931) advertising Light Crust Flour, calling themselves the Fort Worth Doughboys. After assuming the Light Crust Doughboys name, the group's programs were broadcast on WBAP (Fort Worth, TX), WOAI (San Antonio, TX), KPRC (Houston, TX), KTAT (Fort Worth, TX) and KOMA (Oklahoma City, OK). The popular western swing band through the 1950s was the regular band on the *Big D Jamboree* (KRLD, Dallas, TX, 1940s-1950s).

19114 ***(The) Light of the World.*** Frank and Anne Hummert produced the series of dramatized stories from the Old Testament written for radio by Katharine and Adele Seymour. The program was narrated by Bret Morrison. Among the frequent cast members were: Bill Adams, Peggy Allenby, Jack Arthur, Sanford Bickart, Humphrey Davis, Eric Dressler, Louise Fitch, Barbara Fuller, Mitzi Gould, Ernest Graves, Iris Mann, James McCallion, James Monks, Bret Morrison, Virginia Payne, Lynne Rogers, Elaine Rost, Chester Stratton, Daniel Sutter and Florence Williams. Basil Loughrane was the producer-director. Don Becker was the creator-producer. The directors were Oliver Barbour and Don Cope. Clark "Doc" Whipple was the organist and musical director. Stuart Metz and Ted Campbell the announcers. The Seymours were assisted in their writing by Noel B. Gerson and Margaret Sangster. The program ran from 1940 to 1950 on both NBC and CBS.

19115 ***Light Opera Gems.*** Channon Collinge conducted the program of operatic music (30 min., Friday, 4:00–4:30 P.M., CBS, 1934).

19116 ***Light Opera Hour.*** Mus. prg. with soprano Emma Kimmel, tenor Charles Beauchamp and an orchestra conducted by Vincenzo Pometti (KFWB, Hollywood, CA, 1929).

19117 ***Lights Out*** **(aka *The Devil and Mr. O*).** The weekly dramatic series was created by Wyllis Cooper in 1935. The program was best known for the writing and direction of Arch Oboler, who took over from Cooper the following year. Suspense, horror and gruesome sounds were the major elements of the popular show. The program frequently disappeared from the air only to reappear again on a different network in a different time slot (NBC, CBS, MBS, 1935–1947). Originally presented in a 15-minute format, the show eventually was extended to 30 minutes. Often broadcast in the late evening, it was at one time appropriately broadcast at midnight. The cast included: Sidney Ellstrom, Templeton Fox, Raymond Edward Johnson, Ted Maxwell, Lou Merrill and Betty Winkler. The tales of horror were written by Arch Oboler, Wyllis Cooper and Ferrin N. Fraser. Some of the *Lights Out* shows were repeated in 1970 in *The Devil and Mr. O* series.

19118 ***Light Up and Listen.*** The Imperial Tobacco Company sponsored the transcribed music program. In its various formats the show featured such performers as the Jesters, Delta Rhythm Boys, John Gart Trio, Peg LaCentra, Felix Knight, Ted Steele Novatones, Tony Mottola, Jean Ellington, Joan Brooks, Gwen Williams, Frank Banta and the Men of Music, Allen E. Riser and the Evening Serenaders, the Four Belles, Four Flames, Four Showmen, Joan Edwards, the Spring Wheel Singers, Ramona, Peter deRose and May Singhi Breen, Al and Lee Reiser and Jimmy Sears. The announcer was Milton Cross (15 min., Transcribed, NBC, early 1930s).

19119 ***Light Up Time.*** Frank Sinatra, Dorothy Kirsten and Jeff Alexander's Orchestra appeared on the entertaining musical program sponsored by the American Tobacco Company. Don Wilson was the announcer (30 min., Monday through Friday, 7:00–7:30 P.M., NBC, 1949).

19120 **Lightbody, Charles.** Newscaster (WSLB, Ogdensburg, NY, 1946).

19121 Lightcap, Jack. Sportscaster (*Parade of Sports*, NBC, 1951; WINS, New York, NY, 1952).

19122 Lighthall, (Mrs.) Ray. Soprano (KFDM, Beaumont, TX, 1928.)

19123 Lighthouse Pete. CW soloist on the banjo and harmonica (KFWM, Oakland, CA, 1927).

19124 Lightner, Dorothy. Pianist (*Dorothy Lightner*, instr. mus. prg., KLX, Oakland, CA, 1929).

19125 *Lightning Jim.* A western adventure series, *Lightning Jim* told the story of Marshall Jim Whipple and his deputy, Whitey Larson (30 min., 1950s).

19126 Lightstone, Gertrude. Pianist (NBC, 1928).

19127 Like, Jap. Sportscaster (WILO, Frankfort, IN, 1956).

19128 *Li'l Abner.* The weekday comedy serial was based on Al Capp's satirical comic strip. It told the story of Abner Yokum, a big, handsome good-hearted hillbilly, played by John Hodiak. Mammy and Pappy Yokum added to the fun, as did Daisy Mae, who actively pursued Abner for romantic reasons. The program's cast included: Hazel Dopheide, Laurette Fillbrandt, Clarence Hartzell and John Hodiak. Its producer was Wynn Wright and Ted MacMurray its director. The radio adaptation was by Charles Gussman. Durward Kirby was the announcer (15 min., Monday through Friday, 5:30–5:45 P.M., NBC-Red, 1940).

19129 *Lilac Time.* Romantic music was the chief ingredient offered on the program. Baron Swen von Hallberg's string ensemble and a baritone identified only as "The Night Singer" were featured. The sponsor was Pinaud, Inc. (30 min., Monday, 10:30–11:00 P.M., CBS, 1935).

19130 Liles, Mardi. Newscaster (WWNC, Asheville, NC, 1941).

19131 Lillianette. Singer (WMBQ, Brooklyn, NY, 1931).

19132 Lillie, Beatrice. Glamorous musical comedy star of *Andre Charlot's Revue of 1924*, Miss Lillie could both charm and entertain with her songs and comedy (WOR, Newark, NJ, 1924).

19133 Lilligard Trio. Instrumental group (WJAZ, Chicago, IL, 1924).

19134 Lilly, Gladys. Violinist (WTIC, Hartford, CT, 1926).

19135 Lillyquist, Clifford. Bass (KTBI, Los Angeles, CA, 1925).

19136 (The) Limerick Minstrel. *See* **Ferguson, David.**

19137 Lincoln, Bessie. Pianist (KFSG, Los Angeles, CA, 1925).

19138 Lincoln, Ed. DJ (WSBA, York, PA, 1956–1957).

19139 Lincoln Salon Orchestra. Club band (KFAB, Lincoln, NE, 1928).

19140 Lind, George. Baritone (KFDM, Beaumont, TX, 1928).

19141 Lind, Octo. Baritone (KTAB, Oakland, CA, 1929).

19142 Lind, Rose. Contralto Lind was known as the "KGO Melody Girl" (KGO, Oakland, CA, 1927–1928).

19143 Lind, Waldemar. Leader (Waldemar Lind States Restaurant Orchestra, KPO, San Francisco, CA, 1925–1926).

19144 Linda, Rosa. Concert pianist (*Rosa Linda*, instr. mus. prg., NBC, 1935–1936, 1938).

19145 Lindamood, Linda. COM-HE (WSVA, Harrisonburg, VA, 1960).

19146 Lindberg, Ben. Singer-ukulele soloist (KFPY, Spokane, WA, 1928).

19147 Lindbert, Aileen. COM-HE (WABJ, Adrian, IN, 1948).

19148 Lindemann, Big Bud. DJ (WGRD, Grand Rapids, MI, 1957).

19149 Linden, Emily. Pianist-leader (*Emily Linden Ensemble*, instr. mus. prg., KTAB, Oakland, CA, 1927). The group consisted of Liden, violinist Edna Horan, flutist Alene Dickson, cellist Vernel Deane and soprano Alice Miriam.

19150 Linden, Jane. COM-HE (WASK, Lafayette, IN, 1949).

19151 Linden, Patria. Newscaster (WOAI, San Antonio, TX, 1945).

19152 Lindenman, Lillian. Soprano (WBBC, Brooklyn, NY and WCBU, Brooklyn, NY, 1929).

19153 Linder, Arthur. Tenor (*Arthur Linder*, vcl. mus. prg., WCFL, Chicago, IL, 1937).

19154 Linder, Helen M. COM-HE (WBUY, Lexington, NC, 1957).

19155 Linder, Morton. Newscaster (WSBT, South Bend, IN, 1944–1946).

19156 Linderman, Jane. COM-HE (KCRE, Crescent City, CA, 1956).

19157 Lindgren, Irene. COM-HE (WFBM, Indianapolis, IN, 1956).

19158 Lindhe, Vin. Staff pianist, organist and reader (WFAA, Dallas, TX, 1927).

19159 Lindholm, Bert. Pianist (WGBS, New York, NY, 1925).

19160 Lindig, Lee. Tenor (WQJ, Chicago, IL, 1926).

19161 Lindley, Ernest K. News analyst (WRC, Washington, DC, 1942; NBC, 1945).

19162 Lindley, Kathryn. Pianist (*Kathryn Lindley*, instr. mus. prg., WIBA, Madison, WI, 1935).

19163 Lindman, George. Newscaster (KGFF, Shawnee, OK, 1945).

19164 Lindsay, Art. Announcer (KFOA, Seattle, WA, 1928).

19165 Lindsay, Bill Frank. DJ (*Soap 'n' the Saddle*, KELT, Electra, TX, 1949). Sportscaster (KELT, 1951).

19166 Lindsay, Charles K. Leader, Cavaliers Dance Orchestra (WGER, Long Beach, CA, 1930).

19167 Lindsay, Estelle Lawton. Miss Lindsay broadcast *Talks to Women* (KNX, Los Angeles, CA, 1925).

19168 Lindsay, Gladys. Soprano (WGR, Buffalo, NY, 1926).

19169 Lindsay, Grove. Baritone (KFI, Los Angeles, CA, 1925).

19170 Lindsay, Jack. DJ (*Platter Plant*, WCEC, Rocky Mount, NC, 1947).

19171 Lindsey, James H. DJ (*Roy's Record Room*, KWSL, Lake Charles, LA, 1948).

19172 Lindsey, Lou. COM-HE (WROY, Carmi, IL, 1949).

19173 Lindstrom, Everett. Lindstrom was a crooner known as the "KSTP Troubadour." He accompanied himself on his 16-string Gibson harp-guitar (KSTP, St. Paul, MN, 1930s). Formerly Lindstrom sang on WAMD (Minneapolis, MN) and WCCO (Minneapolis, MN) in the 1920s.

19174 Lindstrom, (Mrs.) Lillian Dahl. Pianist (WCCO, Minneapolis–St. Paul, MN, 1925).

19175 Lineberry, Betty. COM-HE (WKSR, Pulaski, TN, 1951).

19176 Linepeter, Irene. Soprano (WBBR, New York, NY, 1924).

19177 Liner, Sammy. Leader (*Sammy Liner Orchestra*, instr. mus. prg., WBZ-WBZA, Boston-Springfield, MA, 1934).

19178 *(The) Lineup.* Bill Johnstone played the role of Lt. Ben Guthrie and Wally Maher was his assistant, Sgt. Matt Greb, on the dramatic series that dramatized "actual" police cases. The show was written by Blake Edwards and produced by Jaime Del Valle. The program opened this way: "Ladies and gentlemen, by electrical transcription, we take you now behind the scenes of a police headquarters in a great American city, where under the cold glaring lights will pass before us the innocent, the vagrant, the thief, the murderer. This is *The Lineup.*" Organist Eddie Dunstedter supplied the music (30 min., Weekly, CBS, 1950–1953).

19179 Linfrio, A.V. Announcer (WGBS, New York, NY, 1925).

19180 Ling, Harry. Baritone (KGA, Spokane, WA, 1929).

19181 Lingard, Peggy. Pianist (WOO, Philadelphia, PA, 1925).

19182 Lingeman, Caspar J. Radio minstrel show entertainer (WJR, Detroit, MI, 1928).

19183 Lingeman, Johann. European cellist (WGN, Chicago, IL, 1928).

19184 Lingerfelt, Francis. COM-HE (WCGC, Belmont, NC, 1956).

19185 Lingle, Kitty. COM-HE (WMOG, Brunswick, GA, 1956).

19186 Linhoff, Lenore. Soprano (WGBS, New York, NY, 1928).

19187 Linick, Art. Comic actor who played the role of KYW's "Mrs. Schlagenhauer" (KYW, Chicago, IL, 1926). He later was the Dutch comic actor who presided over *The Dunkers Club* program, (KYW, 1928).

19188 *(The) Linit Show.* Corn Products Company sponsored the musical program hosted by Julius Tannen. Singers Nino Martini and Jane Froman performed with Erno Rapee's Orchestra. Ted Husing was the announcer (60 min., Sunday, 9:30–10:30 P.M., CBS, 1933). Fred Allen, among others, also appeared on still another program that was known as *The Linit Show*. *See* ***The Fred Allen Show.***

19189 Link, Norman. Pianist (WOWO, Fort Wayne, IN, 1928).

19190 Link, Wally. Newscaster (WCOL, Columbus, OH, 1937).

19191 ***Link Boline's Cowboy Band.*** CW band (KVOO, Tulsa, OK, 1928).

19192 Linkowski, Edna. Pianist (KPO, San Francisco, CA, 1923).

19193 Links, Harry. Popular song writer Links discussed American popular music (WCAU, Philadelphia, PA, 1925).

19194 Linn, Bandel. DJ (*At Home with Bandel Linn*, WSPB, Sarasota, FL, 1949; *Bandel Linn Show*, WSPB, 1952–1957; *Yawn Patrol*, WHFB, Benton Harbor-St. Joseph, MN, 1960).

19195 Linn, Clare. DJ (*Clare "Shoulders" Linn*, WKMH, Dearborn, MI, 1949).

19196 Linn, Eddie. Tap dancer and entertainer Linn conducted a radio calisthenics program (WLW, Cincinnati, OH, 1928). Baritone (*Eddie Linn*, vcl. mus. prg., WLW, 1934).

19197 Linn, Johnny. DJ (*Sunset Express*, KAVR, Apple Valley, CA, 1960).

19198 Linn, Ken. Newscaster (KOME, Tulsa, OK, 1940; KTBI, Tacoma, WA, 1941). DJ (*Music Room*, WLW, Cincinnati, OH, 1949; *Platter Time*, WLW, 1950).

19199 Linn, Martha. Daytime announcer (WHT, Chicago, IL, 1928).

19200 Linn, Vann. Leader, Wolverine Syncopators orchestra (KYW, Chicago, IL, 1923).

19201 Linnell, Mildred. Pianist (WBZ, Springfield, MA, 1924).

19202 Linner, Carl. Pianist (WQJ, Chicago, IL, 1924; KYW, Chicago, IL, 1925).

19203 Linsley, (Prof.) E.G. Professor Linsley of Mills College and Chabot Conservatory lectured on Biblical subjects (KTAB, Oakland, CA, 1925)

19204 Linthicum, Walter. Talented announcer-baritone Linthicum was a soloist on many WBAL (Baltimore, MD) programs in the late 1920s. In addition to radio, Linthicum did a great deal of concert and oratorio performances and appeared as soloist at two of Baltimore's largest churches (WBAL, Baltimore, MD, 1928). The versatile Linthicum also served as announcer, sportscaster and newscaster (WBAL, 1940–1949).

19205 Linton, William. Tenor (*William Linton*, vcl. mus. prg., WFIL, Philadelphia, PA, 1936).

19206 Lionquist, Irene. Contralto (WTIC, Hartford, CT, 1925).

19207 Lipez, Harris. DJ (*Platter Chatter*, WBPZ, Lock Haven, PA, 1947). Sportscaster (WBPZ, Lock Haven, PA, 1947–1948; *Sports Parade*, WBPZ, 1949–1952; *Inside of Sports*, WBPZ, 1951–1952).

19208 Lipker, Charles H. Newscaster (WFIN, Findlay, OH, 1943–1945).

19209 Lippi, Eda Scatena. Soprano (KPO, San Francisco, CA, 1926).

19210 Lippich, Richard. Leader (Richard Lippich and his Mandolin Trio, WGR, Buffalo, NY, 1923).

19211 Lippincott, Elwood. Newscaster (KELA, Centralia-Chehalis, WA, 1941–1942). DJ (*Mugumps*, KELA, 1947).

19212 Lippy, Earl. Singer (*Earl Lippy*, vcl. mus. prg., WBAL, Baltimore, MD, 1934; WLW, Cincinnati, OH, 1935).

19213 Lipsey, Elsa. COM-HE (WGBA, Columbus, GA, 1954).

19214 Lipshultz, George. Leader (George Lipshultz and his Music Orchestra, KPO, San Francisco, CA, 1923).

19215 Lipshutz, Morris. Violinist (WDAR, Philadelphia, PA, 1924).

19216 Lipston, Ben "Benny." Lyric tenor (KFWI, San Francisco, CA, 1926; KYA, San Francisco, CA, 1927).

19217 Lipton, Bill "Billy." Actor Lipton was in the cast of *Chick Carter, Boy Detective* (title role), *Coast-to-Coast on a Bus, Everyman's Theater, Gangbusters, Gasoline Alley, Hearts in Harmony, Let's Pretend, Nick Carter, Master Detective, Radio City Playhouse, Right to Happiness, Road of Life, Mary Marlin, Young Dr. Malone* and *Your Family and Mine.*

19218 Lipton, David. Announcer on the *Balaban and Katz Theatre Program* (WMAQ, Chicago, IL; WGN , Chicago, IL and WEBH, Chicago, IL, 1926).

19219 Lipton, James. Actor Lipton was in the cast of *Evelyn Winters* and *The Lone Ranger.*

19220 Lishman, Harold. Leader (Harold Lishman and the Bessie Keau Nut Hawaiian Players Orchestra, KHJ, Los Angeles, CA, 1924).

19221 Lishon, Henri. Leader (*Henri Lishon Orchestra*, instr. mus. prg., WMAQ, Chicago, IL and NBC, 1936).

19222 Lisman, Edward. Baritone (WFAA, Dallas, TX, 1922).

19223 Liss, Ronald. Actor Liss was in the cast of *Bright Horizon, Buck Rogers in the 25th Century, Coast-to-Coast on a Bus, Dimension X, Hilltop House, Let's Pretend, Mark Trail, Superman* and *Two on a Clue.*

19224 List, Eugene. Classical pianist List was a jazz DJ on his sustaining local New York show, *Jazz With List* (25 min., Sunday, 8:35–9:00 P.M., WNEW, New York, NY, 1951).

19225 List, Jacob. Psychologist (WMCA, New York, NY, 1939).

19226 List, Jay. COM-HE (WDUH, Gainesville, GA, 1954).

19227 ***(The) Listen-In-Er.*** Radio critic Harrison Holloway supplied knowledgeable news and criticism and included a weekly "Cheers and Jeers" segment on the intelligent weekly sustaining program (15 min., Thursday, 10:15–10:30 P.M. PST, KFI, Los Angeles, CA, 1938).

19228 ***Listen, Ladies.*** COM/HE Florence Lehmann conducted her women's show (WCCO, Minneapolis, MN, late 1930s).

19229 ***Listen to a Love Song.*** Tenor Tony Martin and his excellent guests such as Lena Horne, performed with Al Sack's Orchestra. Jimmy Wallington was the announcer (30 min., Saturday, 7:30–8:00 P.M., CBS, 1946).

19230 ***Listen to Cliff.*** Chicago listeners enjoyed listening to Cliff Johnson and his wife and children on their early morning talk show (30 min., Monday through Saturday, 7:30–8:00 A.M., WBBM, Chicago, IL, 1947).

19231 ***Listeners' Letters.*** Letters from listeners, pro and con, were broadcast by E.B. Heaton and Fred Petty (WLS, Chicago, IL, 1926).

19232 Listengart, Benjamin. Violinist (WJY, New York, NY, 1925).

19233 ***(The) Listening Post.*** Bret Morrison and Clayton "Bud" Collyer narrated the series of dramatized stories from *The Saturday Evening Post* magazine. Radio adaptations of the magazine's stories were written by Noel B. Gerson, Gerald Holden and Ben Kagan. The 15-minute program was broadcast by ABC from 1944 to 1948. Henry Klein and James Sheldon were the directors. Members of the cast included: Clayton "Bud" Collyer, Nancy Douglass, Mary Jane Higby, Fredric March, Myron McCormick, Ethel Owen, Martha Scott, Everett Sloane and Joan Tetzel.

19234 Lister, Bill. DJ (*Hillbilly Hit Parade*, KABC, San Antonio, TX, 1947).

19235 Lister, Lydia Warren. Ms. Lister conducted the regularly scheduled "club radiocast" of the California Federation of Women's Clubs (KTAB, Oakland, CA, 1925).

19236 ***(The) Listerine Hour.*** A 60-minute concert music program (CBS, 1927).

19237 Liston, Carole Ann. COM-HE (WGIL, Galesburg, IL, 1956).

19238 Litch, Jack. Newscaster (KROX, Sacramento, CA, 1945).

19239 Litchfield, Dorothy M. Singer-whistler (WBCN, Chicago, IL, 1925).

19240 Litchfield, Litch "Uncle Litch." DJ (*Cornfield Frolics*, WPAI, Charleston, SC, 1948; *The Uncle Litch Daybreak Jamboree*, WKBC, North Wilkesboro, NC, 1949; WFAK, Charleston, SC, 1950).

19241 ***Literary Digest Topics in Brief.*** Lowell Thomas discussed the news and events of the day (15 min., Monday through Friday, 6:45–7:00 P.M., NBC-Blue, 1932).

19242 ***Literary Hour.*** Wilda Wilson Church conducted the morning program devoted to literary topics (45 min.,10:45–11:30 A.M., KGO, Oakland, CA, 1926).

19243 ***Lithox Oldtime Fiddlers.*** CW music program (KTHS, Hot Springs Natural Park, AR, 1928).

19244 Litsky, Joyce. Pianist (WBNX, Bronx, NY, 1937).

19245 Littau, Joseph. Pianist (NBC, 1928). Leader (*Joseph Littau Orchestra*, instr. mus. prg., NBC, 1936; *Joseph Littau Orchestra*, instr. mus. prg., NBC-Red, New York, NY, 1936).

19246 Littell, Margaret J. Soprano (WGY, Schenectady, NY, 1925).

19247 Litterer, (Dr.) Henry. Guitarist (WSM, Nashville, TN, 1928).

19248 Little, Bill. DJ (*Songs of Range Capers*, KADA, Ada, OK, 1947).

19249 Little, Charles. Violinist (*Charles Little*, instr. mus. prg., WsBZ, Boston-Springfield, MA, 1935).

19250 Little, (Dr.) George. Dr. Little discussed various breeds of dogs, i.e., "Airdales" (WOR, Newark, NJ, 1925).

19251 Little, Jack. Sportscaster (KQW, San Jose, CA, 1940).

19252 Little, James A. Newscaster (WTAG, Worcester, MA, 1937–1941, 1947).

19253 Little, "Little" Jack. Little was a popular radio singer who originally was a song plugger (WIP, Philadelphia, PA, 1926). Leader (*Little Jack Little Orchestra*, instr. mus. prg., WMT, Waterloo, IA and WGY, Schenectady, NY, 1934 and CBS, 1935; *Little Jack Little*, instr-vcl mus. prg., CBS, 1934–1936; WGY, Schenectady, NY, 1935).

19254 Little, Lou. Sportscaster Little was a famous Columbia University football coach, who coached at that prestigious university when it was a pigskin powerhouse (*Football Forecasts* program, MBS, 1937).

19255 Little, (Miss) Merry. Singer of "heart songs for children" (KDKA, Pittsburgh, PA, 1924).

19256 Little, Richard Henry (R.H.L.). Famous Chicago *Tribune* columnist Little, who wrote the well known "A Line O' Type or Two," was a talented columnist, humorist and poet. He broadcast a weekly *Air Line* program (15 min., Sunday evening, WGN, Chicago, IL, 1928).

19257 Little, Robert "Bob." Newscaster (WGL-WOWO, Ft. Wayne, IN, 1940; WCPO, Cincinnati, OH, 1942).

19258 Little Bear Balalaika Orchestra. Russian music group (WGBS, New York, NY, 1926).

19259 *Little Bits from Life*. Bill Vickland brought some information, humor and philosophy to his listeners twice weekly. Organist Ralph Waldo Emerson and the Dean Brothers (Jimmy and Eddy) supplied the music and songs (15 min., Wednesday and Friday, WLS, Chicago, IL, 1935).

19260 *(The) Little Brown Church*. Dr. John Holland, a Methodist minister, conducted the favorite WLS non-sectarian program, begun in 1925, that had only one creed: "Thou shalt love thy neighbor as thyself." The Little Brown Church Quartet was a regular feature. In 1929, the Little Brown Church Quartet consisted of Lucille Magill, Bernice Ozmun, Eugene Leonardson and William O'Connor. In 1936, the Quartet was composed of Reuben Bergstrom, Lois Bergstrom, Ruth Slater and Vernon Gerhardt (WLS, Chicago, IL, 1930s).

A typical 1926 *Little Brown Church* program began with chimes played by Grace Clark. Next, Sam Guard, the first lay minister of the *Little Brown Church of the* Air, read and preached the sermon. Other singers and musicians that appeared on the show in its early years were singer Grace Wilson, the George Goforth band and organist Ralph Waldo Emerson.

19261 (The) Little Brown Church Quartet. Singing group consisting of Lucille Magill, soprano; Bernice Ozmun, contralto; Eugene Leonardson, baritone; and William O'Connor, tenor (WLS, Chicago, IL, 1928).

19262 *(The) Little Church Around the Corner*. The dramatic serial, a half-hour in length, was broadcast Tuesday and Friday mornings. Irna Phillips and Walter Wicker were the writers. The program supposedly was based on stories dramatizing events that took place in New York's Church of the Transfiguration (WMAQ-NBC, Chicago, IL, 1934).

19263 (The) Little Colonel. Designation for popular announcer, Lambdin Kay (WSN, Nashville, TN, 1925). *See* **Kay, Lambdin**.

19264 *Little German Band*. Instr. mus. prg. (WBIG, Greensboro, NC, 1936).

19265 *Little Herman*. The entertaining comedy-adventure show was sponsored by Cheeseborough Manufacturing Company. Bill Quinn played the title role of Little Herman, an ex-convict who ran a candy store and tracked down racketeers in his spare time. While pursuing criminals, Little Herman picked pockets and cracked safes in order to further justice. The cast of the entertaining show included: Edwin Bruce, William Podmore, Cameron Prud'homme and Barry Thompson. Dan Donaldson was the announcer (30 min., Saturday, 9:00–9:30 P.M., ABC, 1948).

19266 *Little Italy*. *Little Italy* was a daytime serial that portrayed life on the lower East Side of New York. The central characters of the story were the Moreno family. Father and mother Marino were played by Himan Brown and Ruth Yorke. Rose Keane, Ned Wever and Alfred Corn played their children (15 min., Tuesday and Thursday, 6:45–7:00 P.M., 1934).

19267 *Little Kitty Kelly*. Frank Dahm wrote the daytime serial that probably originated from Chicago.

19268 *Little Known Facts About Well Known People*. Popular motivational author Dale Carnegie, who wrote the best seller, *How to Win Friends and Influence People*, hosted the informative show. Music was supplied by the Harold Sanford Orchestra. John Holbrook was the announcer (15 min., Sunday, 5:30–5:45 P.M., NBC-Red, 1933). In 1935, the program was sponsored by the American Radiator Company (5 min., Monday through Friday, 1:45–1:50 P.M. CST, NBC, 1935).

19269 *Little League*. Hal Goodnough broadcast Boston Little League baseball news on his sustaining local show (15 min., 6:00–6:15 P.M., WEEI, Boston, MA, 1953).

19270 *(The) Little Maids*. Eva, Evelyn and Lucille Overstake sang old fashioned songs on their program (WLS, Chicago, IL, 1930s).

19271 *Little Miss Babo's Surprise Party* (aka *Little Miss Babo*). B.T. Babbit, Inc., makers of Babo Cleanser sponsored child singing star, Mary Small, who was Little Miss Babo. The music program featured such popular guests as baritone Mario Cozzi, contralto Francis Langford, tenor Frank Parker and the Sizzlers vocal group each week. Blackface comedians Molasses and January supplied the humor and the William Wirges Orchestra the music. Ford Bond was the announcer, (30 min., Sunday, 1:30–2:00 P.M., NBC-Red Network, New York, NY, 1934–1935).

In 1934, 12-year-old Mary Small of Baltimore, Maryland, made her debut on this program. Previously little Miss Small had been a great hit when she sang on Rudy Vallee's Fleischmann program.

19272 *(A) Little Night Music*. Eva Gabor was a glamorous and charming DJ on her show, written, produced and directed by Bill Kalland (25 min., Tuesday through Thursday, 11:35–12:00 midnight, WNEW, New York, NY, 1952).

19273 *Little Orphan Annie*. The famous children's daytime serial program was first broadcast on the NBC-Blue network in 1931. Based on Harold Gray's comic strip, the show was sponsored by Ovaltine. While it was on the air a great many premiums were offered to listeners who sent in a seal from an Ovaltine can and a dime. Shake-up mugs for Ovaltine and secret decoder badges were favorite premiums the program offered its young listeners. A familiar part of the show was Annie's dog, Sandy, whose bark was supplied by famous animal imitator, Brad Barker.

The program opened with its famous theme:

Who's that little chatterbox?
The one with pretty auburn locks?
Who can it be?
It's Little Orphan Annie.
She and Sandy make a pair.
They never seem to have a care.
Cute little she,
It's Little Orphan Annie.
Bright eyes
Cheeks a rosy glow
There's a store of healthiness handy.
Pint-size
Always on the go
If you want to know
"Arf," goes Sandy.
Always wears a sunny smile.
Now wouldn't it be worth your while,
If you could be
Like Little Orphan Annie?

The program's cast included: Hoyt Allen, Stanley Andrews, Boris Aplon, Brad Barker (Imitated Sandy), Allan Baruck, Shirley Bell, Harry Cansdale, Janice Gilbert, Jerry O'Mera, Henry Saxe, Olan Soule, Henrietta Tedro and St. John Terrell. The director was Alan Wallace. Originally written by Frank Dahm, the show later was written by Ferrin N. Fraser, Day Keene, Roland Martini and Wally Norman. The announcer was Pierre Andre. The title role was originated by Shirley Bell (Monday through Friday, 15 min., 4:45–5:00 P.M., NBC, 1935).

19274 *Little Red Apple Club*. Variety program conducted by C.D. "Neal" Tomy in the mid–1920s.

19275 *(The) Little Red Barn*. *See* **The Hilltoppers**.

19276 *(The) Little Red Book*. Columnist Paul Yawitz broadcast metropolitan gossip. The sponsor was the Ansonia Shoe Company. Entertaining music was supplied by Vincent Sorey (15 min., Monday, 6:30–6:45 P.M. WINS, New York, NY, 1934).

19277 *(The) Little Red Schoolhouse*. The weekly program was said to have been the first educational program of its type ever broadcast in Chicago (60 min., Weekly, 2:00–3:00 P.M., WLS, Chicago, IL, 1925).

19278 Little Symphony. Orchestra conducted by Frances Fribourg (KSCJ, Sioux City, IA, 1928)

19279 Littlefield, Herb. Leader (*Herb Littlefield Orchestra*, instr. mus. prg., NBC, 1935).

19280 Littlefield, Jimmy. Leader (*Jimmy Littlefield Orchestra*, instr. mus. prg., KYW. Philadelphia, PA, 1936).

19281 Littlefield, Maudellen. Miss Littlefield was the "Tell-Me-a-Story Lady" (WDAF, Kansas City, MO, 1925). She also taught "radio piano lessons" for children on the station (WDAF, 1925).

19282 Littlehales, Elmer. Newscaster (KAST, Astoria, OR, 1944–1945).

19283 Littlejohn, John "Johnny." DJ (*Record Rendezvous*, WJXN, Jackson, MS, 1947; WMIS, Natchez, MS, 1956).

19284 Littleton, Buck. News analyst (*Alabama Today*, WKLF, Clanton, AL, 1947). DJ (*Musical Clock*, WKLF, 1947).

19285 *(The) Littman Orchestra Program.* The orchestra was joined by tenor Byron Holiday and contralto Helen Richards on the program (15 min., 1:30–1:45 P.M., WWJ, Detroit, MI, 1930).

19286 Littman's Employees Orchestra. Commercial dance band (WHN, New York, NY, 1925).

19287 Liufrio, A.V. Pianist (WMCA, New York, NY, 1925).

19288 Liuzza, Ted R. Newscaster (WSMB, New Orleans, LA, 1930).

19289 *Live Like a Millionaire.* Jack McCoy hosted the giveaway show sponsored by General Mills. *Variety* noted the show gave "away everything but the kitchen sink." Ivan Ditmars was the show's musical director and John Nelson the announcer (30 min., Monday through Friday, 2:30–3:00 P.M., NBC, 1950).

19290 Lively, Lee. News analyst (*News Here at Home*, WLOW, Norfolk, VA, 1948). DJ (*The Lively Show*, WLOW, 1948; *The Juke Box Review*, WLOW, 1950).

19291 *(The) Lively Arts.* Perceptive critic and gifted writer Gilbert Seldes conducted his informative sustaining show. Dick Bradley was its announcer (25 min., Sunday, 10:00–10:25 P.M., WNEW, New York, NY, 1948).

19292 Livengood, C.G. Announcer (WSBT, South Bend, IN, 1925–1927).

19293 Liverance, Robert. Newscaster (WMVA, Martinsville, VA, 1941; WAIM, Anderson, SC, 1945).

19294 Livermore, Mercer. COM-HE (WKKO, Cocoa, FL, 1956–1957).

19295 *(The) Lives of Harry Lime.* Lang-Worth [Langworth] Features distributed the transcribed series produced by Harry Allan Towers and written and directed by Orson Welles, who also played the title role. Harry Lime was a shrewd confidence man, always on the side of right, but inevitably on all sides of the law. McDonald Park and Irene Prador were also in the cast (30 min., Wednesday, 9:00–9:30 P.M., NBC-Blue, 1951). Welles previously played Harry Lime in the 1949 British film, *The Third Man*. Leonard Maltin in his *Movie and Video Guide* (1992, p. 1235) concludes that [novelist] Graham Greene's account of the mysterious Harry Lime in post–World War II Vienna was a bona fide classic, and that the Anton Karas' zither rendition of "The Third Man Theme" added the right touch. On radio, Harry Lime was portrayed as a more heroic, less sinister figure.

19296 *(The) Lives of Jewish Composers.* Both music and narration were used to tell the stories of Jewish composers on the show sponsored by Maxwell House Coffee. Music was performed by George Touller's Orchestra (30 min., Wednesday, 7:15–7:45 P.M., WMCA, New York, NY, 1935).

19297 Livesay, Danae. Pianist (KWSC, Pullman, WA, 1925).

19298 Livingston, Charles. Baritone (WHT, Chicago, IL, 1928).

19299 Livingston, Jerry. Leader (*Jerry Livingston Orchestra*, instr. mus. prg., WOR-MBS, Newark, NJ, 1938; MBS, 1940).

19300 Livingston, Jimmy. Leader (*Jimmy Livingston Orchestra*, instr. mus. prg., WBT, Charlotte, NC, 1937).

19301 Livingston, Marion. Organist (WELI, New Haven, CT, 1939).

19302 Livingston, Sam. Sportscaster (*Down Sports Avenue*, WKYB, Paducah, KY, 1947–1951).

19303 Livingstone [Livingston], Mabel. Miss Livingstone conducted a children's program on which she was known as "The Children's Poet" (WHN, New York, NY, 1924).

19304 Livingstone, Margo. Newscaster (*Woman Reporter*, WELI, New Haven, CT, 1939).

19305 Livosi, Joseph. Violinist (WGBS, New York, NY, 1925).

19306 *Lizabeth Ann's Sunday School.* First broadcast on Louisville's WHAS, the program provided Sunday School services for shut-in children. Children of many races and denominations came before the microphone (15 min., Sunday, 12:00–12:15 P.M., WOR, Newark, NJ, 1932).

19307 Lloyd, Archie. Singer (WCAU, Philadelphia, PA, 1926).

19308 Lloyd, Dollye. COM-HE (KJOE, Shreveport, LA, 1955).

19309 Lloyd, Jack. Sportscaster (WTHT, Hartford, CT, 1940). Newscaster (WAGE, Chicopee, MA, 1946).

19310 Lloyd, John. Sportscaster (WTHT, Hartford, CT, 1939).

19311 Lloyd, Margaret. Violinist (WLW, Cincinnati, OH, 1925).

19312 Lloyd, Norman. Actor Lloyd was in the cast of *The Marriage*.

19313 Lloyd, Robert E. Newscaster (KOB, Albuquerque, NM, 1944–1946).

19314 Lloyd, Rhona. COM-HE (Miss Lloyd conducted a popular talk show for women, *Rhona Lloyd*, 15 min., Monday, 1:30–1:45 P.M., KYW, Philadelphia, PA, 1942).

19315 Lloyd, Ruth. Mezzo-soprano (WBZ, Boston-Springfield, MA, 1925).

19316 Lloyd, Ted. Producer Lloyd produced the *Whispering Streets* daytime serial program.

19317 Lloyd, Vincent "Vince." Newscaster (WMBD, Peoria, IL, 1941). Sportscaster (WMBD, 1946–1948; *Sports Digest*, WMBD, 1948; WGN, Chicago, IL, 1949–1956).

19318 *Lloyd Pantages Covers Hollywood.* Pantages broadcast news and gossip about films and film stars (15 min., Weekly, 1:45–2:00 P.M., CBS, 1938).

19319 *Loahna and Her Dolls.* PTA officials, educators and civic leaders praised this novel program that featured Loahna, a 13-year-old collector of dolls from all parts of the world. She described a doll on each program and told something about the customs of the country from which it came. Loahna corresponded with girls of her own age from all over the world and included their thoughts and comments into her broadcasts. Three college girls ("We Three") also appeared on the program to read poetry (KOA, Denver, CO, 1940).

19320 Loar, Lloyd. Musical saw performer (WWJ, Detroit, MI, 1928).

19321 Lobanoff, Paul. Tenor (KFI, Los Angeles, CA, 1926).

19322 *Lobby Interviews.* Announcer Walter Framer conducted *Vox Pop*-type interviews from the lobby of Pittsburgh's Penn Theater on the sustaining program (15 min., Wednesday, 3:00–3:30 P.M. WWSW, Pittsburgh, PA, 1938).

19323 Lobler, (Dr.) B.Z. News analyst (*An Economist Views the News*, WJOY, Burlington, VT, 1948).

19324 Loblov (Lobov), Bela. Leader (Bela Loblov's Lombardy Hotel Orchestra, NBC-Blue, New York, NY, 1928; conductor of the Candlelight Dance Orchestra on the *Alice Foote MacDougal Hour*, WABC-CBS, New York, NY, 1929).

19325 Lochman, Walt. Sportscaster (WCMO, Kansas City, MO, 1945–1947; *Spotlight on Sports*, KJAY, Topeka, KS, 1950). DJ (*Walt's Wax Works*, WCMO, 1947).

19326 Locke, Ed. DJ (*Dawn Patrol*, WIP, Philadelphia, PA, 1952).

19327 Locke, Francis P. Newscaster (WIOD, Miami, FL, 1937–1939).

19328 Locke, G.B. Announcer (WBAP, San Antonio, TX, 1925).

19329 Locke, Gene. DJ (*Mailbag Show*, WMMT, McMinnville, TN, 1947; WRUS, Russellville, KY, 1955–1956; *Stickbuddy Jamboree*, WRUS, 1960).

19330 Locke, (Mrs.) Iona Towne. Soprano (KFDM, Beaumont, TX, 1928).

19331 Locke, Ralph. Actor Locke was in the cast of *Dot and Will*, *Life Can Be Beautiful* and *Second Husband*.

19332 Locklayer, Johnny. Leader (*Johnny Locklayer Orchestra*, instr. mus. prg., WDBJ, Roanoke, VA, 1939).

19333 Lockner, Louis P. News commentator (NBC, 1945).

19334 Lochner, Lydia. Contralto (WEBH, Chicago, IL, 1925).

19335 Locke, (Mrs.) Iona Towne. Soprano (KFDM, Beaumont, TX, 1928).

19336 Lockhart, Ina. Contralto (WWJ, Detroit, MI, 1925).

19337 Lockser, Judith. Actress Lockser was in the cast of the *Ma Perkins* and *Brighter Day* daytime serial programs.

19338 Lockwood, Arlen. COM-HE (WBSE, Hillsdale, MI, 1956).

19339 Lockwood, Della. COM-HE (WVEC, Hampton, VA, 1949).

19340 Lockwood, Doty. Newscaster (WCON, Atlanta, GA, 1947).

19341 Lockwood, Grace. Actress Lockwood appeared on the *Betty and Bob* daytime serial program.

19342 Lockwood, Ken. Newscaster (KBKR, Baker, OR, 1942, 1945–1946).

19343 Lockwood, Pat. COM-HE (WDAX, McRae, GA, 1957).

19344 Lockwood, Roy. Director Lockwood directed the *Valiant Lady* daytime serial program.

19345 Locy, Essie Blinkley. Cornetist (KFSG, Los Angeles, CA, 1924).

19346 Loder, Kenneth. Cellist (KFAB, Lincoln, NE, 1928).

19347 Lodge, Karyl. COM-HE (Miss Lodge talked mainly about fashion, WKAT, Miami Beach, FL, 1942).

19348 Loeb, Marx. Director Marx directed *American School of the Air, Counterspy, Greatest Story Ever Told, The Life of Riley* and *This Life is Mine.*

19349 Loeb, Sophie Irene. Expert Loeb talked on various child welfare topics (WRNY, New York, NY, 1928).

19350 Loeben, Emillie. Pianist (WIP, Philadelphia, PA, 1924).

19351 Loeffler, Sandra. COM-HE (KRLD, Dallas, TX, 1956).

19352 Loew, Lou. Leader (*Lou Loew Orchestra*, instr. mus. prg., WOWO, Ft. Wayne, IN, 1935).

19353 Loew's 83rd Street Orchestra. Theater band (WHN, New York, NY, 1926).

19354 Loew's Metropolitan [Theater] Orchestra. Theater orchestra (WHN, New York, NY, 1926).

19355 Loey, Rita. COM-HE (WBSS, New Smyrna Beach, CA, 1956).

19356 Lofback, Bill. Newscaster (WSAM, Saginaw, MI, 1946).

19357 Loftield, Keith. Newscaster (KTUC, Tucson, AZ, 1945).

19358 Loftus, Florence. Soprano (WGBS, New York, NY, 1926).

19359 *Log Cabin Bar Z Ranch.* General Foods sponsored the lively CW music show featuring Louise Massey and the Westerners, Red Foley, Eva O. Foley and Paul Race (30 min., Tuesday, 7:00–7:30 P.M. CST, WLS, Chicago, IL, 1937).

19360 *Log Cabin Boys.* CW mus. prg. (WWVA, Wheeling, WV, 1936–1938).

19361 *(The) Log Cabin Inn* (aka *Lanny's Log Cabin Inn*). General Foods, makers of Log Cabin Syrup, sponsored the variety show hosted by tenor Frank Crumit. Music was supplied by Harry Salter's Orchestra and singers Conrad Thibault and Eva Taylor (30 min., Wednesday, 10:00–10:30 P.M., NBC-Red, 1935). In another version of the show, *The Log Cabin Inn* (aka *Lanny's Log Cabin Inn*), talented tenor Ross hosted and sang. The Harry Salter Orchestra was also featured. The show's writer was Carolyn Strouse (30 min., Wednesday, 8:30–9:00 P.M., NBC-Red, 1935).

19362 *Log Cabin Jamboree.* Comedian Jack Haley hosted the variety show that featured Wendy Barrie, Virginia Varo and the Ted Fiorito Orchestra. Warren Hull was the announcer. Log Cabin Syrup was the program's sponsor (30 min., Saturday P.M., NBC, 1937–1938).

19363 Logan, Betsy. Betsy Logan provided advice for the lovelorn on her *Affairs of the Heart* program (WDAR, Philadelphia, PA, 1923). She also conducted a women's program, *Betsy Logan's Household Hints* (WDAR, 1923).

19364 Logan, Ella. Singer (*Ella Logan*, vcl. mus. prg., NBC, 1936).

19365 Logan, Janet. Busy actress Logan was in the cast of the daytime serial programs *Girl Alone, Kitty Keene* aka *Kitty Keene, Incorporated, Road of Life, Romance of Helen Trent, Stepmother* and *Dr. Paul.*

19366 Logan, Jim. DJ (*For You By Request*, WGPA, Bethlehem, PA, 1947).

19367 Logan, Judy. COM-HE (WAAF, Chicago, IL, 1949).

19368 Logan, Martha. COM-HE (WHB, Kansas City, MO, 1941).

19369 Logan, Mary. COM-HE (WTTM, Trenton, NJ, 1960).

19370 Logan, Sarah. Contralto (KDKA, Pittsburgh, PA, 1926).

19371 Logan, Walter. Leader (*Walter Logan Orchestra*, instr. mus. prg., NBC, 1936).

19372 Loge, Hazel Fleemer. Soprano (WEAF, New York, NY, 1924).

19373 Logsdon, Pauline. Soprano (KHJ, Los Angeles, CA, 1930).

19374 Lohikar, Marie. Contralto (*Marie Lohikar*, vcl. mus. prg., KFI, Los Angeles, CA, 1929).

19375 Lohman, P.H. News commentator (*An Economist Views the News*, WJOY, Burlington, VT, 1947).

19376 Lohmann, Paula. COM-HE (WMBD, Peoria, IL, 1957).

19377 Lohmiller, Grace Huber. Soprano (WOC, Davenport, IA, 1925).

19378 *Lola the Mystic.* Lola, a mentalist, told fortunes on the half-hour Saturday afternoon program (30 min., Saturday P.M., KNRC, Santa Monica, CA, 1928).

19379 Loma Brothers Colored Quartet. Vocal quartet (NBC, 1935).

19380 Lomax, (Professor) A.L. Professor Lomax of the University of Oregon's Extension Division spoke on "Oregon Resources" (KGW, Portland, OR, 1923).

19381 Lomax, Henry S. "Stan." Sportscaster (WOR, Newark, NJ and New York, NY, 1939–1946; *Stan Lomax.* Sports news show, 15 min., Monday through Saturday, 6:45–7:00 P.M., WOR, Newark, NJ, 1947; *Stan Lomax Sports*, WOR, New York, NY, 1947–1948 and WHN, New York, NY, 1947–1948, MBS, 1955, WOR, 1949–1960). Lomax began his career at WOR in 1930 as an announcer. He soon began working as an assistant to Ford Frick at the station. When Frick left broadcasting to become president of the National [baseball] League in 1934, Lomax took over Ford's sportscasting program. During his long broadcasting career Lomax also broadcast professional football play-by-play.

19382 Lombardo, Anthony and John Paulis. Accordion and banjo team (WGR, Buffalo, NY, 1926 and WOCL, Jamestown, NY, 1926).

19383 Lombardo, Frank. Leader (*Frank Lombardo Orchestra*, instr. mus. prg., WBRE, Wilkes-Barre, PA, 1942).

19384 Lombardo, Guy. Leader (Guy Lombardo and his Royal Canadians Orchestra, WTAM, Cleveland, OH, 1925–1928). Later his band was featured on the *Guy Lombardo and His Royal Canadians* program, sponsored by the General Cigar Company. The program was sometimes referred to as the *Robert Burns Panatella Country Club* (CBS, 1929–1932). The band also appeared on the *Wrigley Gum* program with Wendell Hall, the "Red-Headed Music Maker" (WABC-CBS, New York, NY, 1929). Lombardo organized his band in Canada in 1921 and brought it to the United States in 1923. The earliest personnel of the popular band was: Guy Lombardo, ldr. and v.; Lebert Lombardo, t.; Jack Miles, tb.; Carmen Lombardo, clr., as. and vcls.; Fred Higman, t.; Fred Kreitzer, p.; George Gowans, d.; and Francis Henry, bj. The band was equally busy on radio in the 1930s and 1940s (*Guy Lombardo Orchestra*, instr. mus. prg., WNAC, Boston, MA, 1932; *Lombardo Land*, instr. mus. prg., NBC, 1934; NBC, 1935; MBS, 1936–1937; CBS, 1934–1939; MBS, 1940; KMOX, St. Louis, MO, 1942). Over the years the Lombardo band contained many family members. Brother Carmen was the arranger, vocalist and composer; brother Liebert played the trumpet; and brother Victor played the baritone saxophone.

19385 Lombardo, Pete. DJ (*A Guy Named Lombardo*, KPMO, Pomona, CA, 1954).

19386 (The) Lombards. The comedy-singing team of Leia and Harry Lombard offered entertaining musical selections and comedy sketches (WLS, Chicago, IL, 1928).

19387 London, Jack. DJ (KPRC, Houston, TX, 1960).

19388 London, Joe. Newscaster (KTOK, Oklahoma City, OK, 1941). Sportscaster (KTOK, 1941).

19389 London, Rex. DJ (*1240 Club*, KHOZ, Harrison, AR, 1947).

19390 *London Singers.* Vcl. mus. prg. (KUOA, Siloam Springs, AR, 1939).

19391 *Lone Cowboy.* CW vcl. mus. prg. with an unidentified singer (WIBA, Madison, WI, 1936).

19392 *Lone Journey.* *Lone Journey* was a daytime dramatic serial that had three different incarnations, first on NBC, then CBS and, finally, ABC. The last version told the story of Wolfe Bennett, played by Staats Cotsworth, a successful Chicago business man who left city life to live on a Montana ranch. The cast included Joan Alexander, Cameron Andrews, Fran Carlon, Olive Deering, Charlotte Holland and Delores Gilbert. Sandra Michael wrote the program from 1940 to 1942, but then left to write other shows. She and her brother, Peter Michael, later returned to again write *Lone Journey*. *Variety* noted that with their return, the program's characters became more human and the serial's quality greatly improved. The announcers were Nelson Case, Durward Kirby, Henry Morgan and Charles Woods. Axel Gruenberg, Ted MacMurray and Martin Magner were the directors (15 min., Monday through Friday, 11:45–12:00 noon, ABC. 1951).

19393 ***(The) Lone Ranger.*** The best known and most loved hero of radio by both children and adults was the Lone Ranger. With his faithful Indian companion, Tonto, the Lone Ranger fought outlaws in the "thrilling days of yesteryear" astride his great horse Silver. Station WXYZ (Detroit, MI) was the source of three of radio's greatest heroes who battled against crime in their own special way. These super heroes were the Lone Ranger, the Green Hornet and Sgt. Preston on the *Challenge of the Yukon*. Of all of them none was as popular as the Lone Ranger.

The cast included: Elaine Alpert, Dick Beals, Brace Beemer, Jack Deeds, Earle Graser, John Hodiak, Amos Jacobs (Danny Thomas), Ted Johnstone, James Lipton, Bob Maxwell, Herschel Mayal, Jay Michael, Rollon Parker, Jack Petruzzi, Frank Russell, George Seaton, Ernie Winstanley and John Todd. The producer-director-writer was James Jewell. The show was also directed by Al Hodge and Charles Livingstone. Fran Striker and Georger W. Trendle were the program's creators. The announcer-narrators included Brace Beemer, Fred Foy, Harry Golder, Bob Hite, Harold True and Charles Woods. Fran Striker was the program's chief writer and story editor. The other writers were Dan Beatty, Tom Dougall, Gibson Scott Fox, Bob Green, Felix Holt, Bob Shaw and Shelley Stark. Although the title role was played by George Seaton, Jack Deeds, Earle Graser, it is Bruce Beemer who is best remembered in the role. Tonto, the Lone Ranger's faithful Indian companion was played by John Todd during the program's entire run (30 min., MBS, ABC, 1933–1955).

19394 ***Lone Star Boys.*** CW mus. prg. (WIRE, Indianapolis, IN, 1936).

19395 ***(The) Lone Star Cowboy.*** Tex Ritter starred in the dramatic serial in the title role. The program also contained comedy and music. The show replaced the *Cowboy Tim's Roundup* program (15 min., Monday through Friday, WHN, New York, NY, 1933–1934).

19396 ***(The) Lone Star Cowboys.*** CW music program with a Texas music group that included the Shelton Brothers (Bob and Joe Attlesey) and Leon Chappalear (KGKB, Tyler, TX, 1929).

19397 **Lone Star Five Orchestra.** Local Dallas band (WFAA, Dallas, TX, 1925).

19398 ***(The) Lone Star Ranger.*** Tex Ritter sang cowboy songs and told western yarns on his CW music show (WOR, Newark, NJ, early 1930s).

19399 ***(The) Lone Wolf.*** Writer Mike Barry's (Barry N. Malzberg) stories of a dashing ex-jewel thief named Michael Lanyard—the *Lone Wolf*—turned detective was adapted for radio by Louis Vittes. He was played initially by Gerald Mohr before Walter Coy took over the role. Mohr, incidentally, also played the role in several motion pictures. Dick Auranot and Jay Novello were also in the cast of the sustaining show. The producer was Frank N. Danzig and the director was Larry Hays (30 min., Saturday, 5:00–5:30 P.M., MBS, 1948–1949). The *Lone Wolf* character of the radio series is related to stories by that name written by Louis Joseph Vance *only* by name.

19400 ***Lonely Cowboy.*** CW mus. prg. with an otherwise unidentified performer (WOR, Newark, NJ, 1936).

19401 ***Lonely Troubadour.*** Voc. mus. prg. by an otherwise unidentified singer (KWTO, Springfield, MO, 1939).

19402 ***Lonely Women.*** General Mills sponsored the daytime serial that dramatized the loneliness of women separated from their men during World War II. The story described the lives of a group of women living in a women's apartment run by a kindly manager played by Viola Berwick. Barbara Luddy, Betty Lou Gerson, Eileen Palmer, Virginia Payne, Norma Jean Ross, Cliff Soubier, Les Tremayne, Willard Waterman and Harriette Widmer were in the cast. Marvin Miller and Fort Pearson were the announcers and Bernice Yanocek the organist. The show was written by Irna Phillips (15 min., Monday through Friday, 1:15–1:30 P.M., NBC, 1942).

19403 **Lonergran, Angela G.** Cellist (WBZ, Springfield, MA, 1924).

19404 **(The) Lonesome Cowboy.** *See* **John White.**

19405 ***Lonesome Cowboy.*** The lonesome cowboy was Roy Faulkner, a popular CW singer with a long radio career (WIBW, Topeka, KS, 1937). Faulkner had previously broadcast over stations KFKB (Abilene, KS); WFAA (Dallas, TX); WBAP (Fort Worth, TX); WBOW (Terre Haute, IN); (WHO, Des Moines, IA); and several of the Mexican border stations during the early and mid–1930s.

19406 ***Lonesome Gal.*** DJ Jean King talked to her male listeners with a mellow, seductive voice that they liked very much. Typical of her remarks was: "Sweetie no matter what anybody says, I love you more than anybody in the whole world." Often calling her listeners "baby" and "muffin," she wore a kitten mask when appearing in public. King did not abandon the kitten mask until 1953. She made her eastern debut on Monday, May 27, 1950 (15 min., Monday through Friday, 11:15–11:30 P.M., WOR, Newark, NJ, 1950). Her broadcasting career lasted from 1947 to 1951.

19407 ***Lonesome Ranger.*** CW mus. prg. by a singer, not otherwise identified (WTNJ, Trenton, NJ, 1939).

19408 ***Lonesome Yodeler.*** CW singer Lee Morse was the popular Lonesome Yodeler (WPAY, Portsmouth, OH, mid–1940s).

19409 **Long, Arthur.** Baritone (*Arthur Long*, instr. mus. prg., NBC, 1935).

19410 **Long, Ben.** Leader (*Ben Long Orchestra*, instr. mus. prg., WGR, Detroit, MI, 1942).

19411 **Long, Buck.** DJ (*Buck's Back Room*, WABB, Mobile, AL, 1949).

19412 **Long, Chet.** Newscaster (WCOL, Columbus, OH, 1944; *Chet Long News*, WBNS, Columbus, OH, 1946–1948).

19413 **Long, Deane S.** Newscaster (WSAL, Salisbury, MD, 1938; WAKR, Akron, OH, 1939; KXEL, Waterloo, IA, 1945). Sportscaster (WSAL, 1939).

19414 **Long, Dick.** Leader-violinist (Dick Long Orchestra, WLAG, Minneapolis, MN, 1924; Dick Long's Nakin Cafe Band, WCCO, Minneapolis–St. Paul, MN, 1926–28; Dick Long's Trio, WCCO, 1926; Dick Long Orchestra, WCCO, 1928; *Dick Long Orchestra*, instr. mus. prg., WCCO, 1936).

19415 **Long, Dick.** DJ (*Matinee at Radio Center*, KROD, El Paso, TX, 1950).

19416 **Long, Emmet.** Leader (Emmet Long's Golden Pheasant Orchestra, WCCO, Minneapolis–St. Paul, MN, 1926–28).

19417 **Long, "Fiddlin' Sam."** Fiddler Long specialized in old time country tunes (KVOO, Tulsa, OK, 1928).

19418 **Long, Happy.** CW singer (*Happy Long*, CW vcl. mus. prg., WIRE, Indianapolis, IN, 1936).

19419 **Long, Harry.** Newscaster (KVI, Tacoma, WA, 1941, 1943–1945).

19420 **Long, Huey.** *See* **Charlatans, Demagogs and Politicians.**

19421 **Long, James J.** Sportscaster (*Sports Review*, KDKA, Pittsburgh, PA, 1924).

19422 **Long, Joe B., Jr.** Newscaster (WROL, Knoxville, TN, 1945).

19423 **Long, Johnny.** Leader (*Johnny Long Orchestra*, instr. mus. prg., NBC, 1935; WRVA, Richmond, VA, 1936; WCAE, Pittsburgh, PA, 1938; KMA, Shenandoah, IA and KMOX, St. Louis, MO, 1942).

19424 **Long, Johnny.** DJ (*1400 Club*, KDWT, Stamford, TX, 1947).

19425 **Long, Ken.** DJ (*Late Riser's Club*, WGAN, Portland, ME, 1949–1950).

19426 **Long, Lucille.** Born May 5, 1902, Long began her radio career as a singer on KYW (Chicago, IL, 1924). She later performed on WQJ (Chicago, IL, 1926). *Variety* noted her versatility by saying she was also a "popular woman harmonica player" (WQJ, 1926).

19427 **Long, Mary.** COM-HE (WFMD, Frederick, MD, 1956).

19428 **Long, Paul.** Bass (*Paul Long*, vcl. mus. prg., WDBJ, Roanoke, VA, 1935).

19429 **Long, Paul.** News commentator (*Plain Talk from Iron City*, *Studebaker News*, *Keystone Lumber News*, KDKA, Pittsburgh, PA, 1947–1948).

19430 **Long, Russell "Russ."** Newscaster (WCSC, Charleston, SC, 1940–1942; WCSC,

Charleston, SC, 1944–1945). Sportscaster (WCSC, 1942).

19431 Long, Stuart. News commentator (KTBC, Austin, TX, 1945; *Texas at Ten*, KVET, Austin, TX, 1947–1948).

19432 Long, Terry. Sportscaster Long specialized in broadcasting soccer news (WBNX, New York, NY, 1939).

19433 Long Beach Municipal Band. Distinguished cornetist and band leader Herbert L Clark led the community band (KFON, Long Beach, CA, 1925–1926).

19434 *Long John Nebel.* Although he often sounded like a fast talking New York con man, Long John Nebel's primary training was as a Manhattan sidewalk pitchman, band leader, photographer and New Jersey auctioneer. John Nebel (Jack Knebel) is important because he was one of the first and certainly one of the very best radio talk show hosts. Even though Barry Gray preceded him in the New York area, Long John's creativity and imagination made him the model talk show host. Early in his career Nebel took listeners' telephone calls and put them on the air live, thanks to a seven-second delay mechanism.

Long John's guests ranged from some truly great actors, novelists or musicians to an interplanetary traveler just returned from a journey to the planet Venus. Nebel's first radio show on WOR was with Charlie Holmes (*The Charlie and John Show*, 30 min., 4:40–5:00 P.M., MBS, 1956). This show ran for 13 weeks on 23 of the 260 MBS stations. When it was not renewed for network broadcast, the *New Charlie and John Show* ran on WOR alone. A little later Nebel had his own show (John Nebel, 30 min., Monday through Friday, 1956). When Jean Shepherd was dropped mid-show for talking too much and playing too few records, Nebel replaced him with a format that allowed him to develop his own entertaining talk show style (*Long John Nebel*, 300 min., Midnight–5:00 A.M., WOR, 1956). He moved to the NBC network in 1963 (*Long John Nebel*, 300 min., Midnight–5:00 A.M., NBC, 1963).

Nebel was among the first to discuss topics such as UFOs (Unidentified Flying Objects), extra-sensory perception, witchcraft, voodoo, the occult, interplanetary travel and the experiences of the ambassador from Venus. He chose the right program topics at the right time. In addition, he added a panel of interesting participants to discuss a topic with a guest. Among the interesting guests Long John introduced were:

> Dr. Wallace Musto, the inventor of a machine to read a person's aura;
>
> Thomas G. Hieronymous, the inventor of a machine to analyze "eloptic radiation" in minerals;
>
> Orfeo Angelucci, who had ridden in a space ship at the speed of ten million miles per hour;
>
> Andy Sinatra, a barber who communicated with outer space creatures by mental telepathy. Nebel called him the "mystical tonsorial artist from Brooklyn";
>
> George Van Tassel, who hosted an annual Interplanetary Spacecraft Convention at Van Tassel's California spacecraft landing strip; and
>
> Buck Nelson, who had entertained visitors from Venus and received from them a Venusian dog named "Bo."

The topics that Nebel, his panelists and guests discussed included: women's place in the world; Middle East relations; modern philosophy; one world ideologies; Houdini; famous courtroom trials; building pipe organs; Paris and Rome travel; spiritualism; the Sacco–Venzetti controversy; jazz; folk music and narcotics. Nebel's wide range of interests, topical and universal, made him a late night favorite. Another added feature were the panelists that regularly appeared with Nebel such as: Donald Bain, Lester del Rey; Sanford Teller; Lyle Stuart, Ed Springarn and Al Lottmann.

Long John moved to WMCA (New York, NY) in 1971 to begin a show with his wife, ex-model Candy Jones (*The Long John and Candy Jones Show*, 240 min., 8:00–12:00 midnight, WMCA, New York, 1971). That same year Nebel learned he had developed the prostate cancer that eventually killed him. Nebel's contribution as a talk show host far overshadowed his brief stint as a DJ early in his career. *See* **Nebel, Long John**.

19435 *(The) Long Sisters and the Piano Pals.* Local music program (WGY, Schenectady, NY, 1935).

19436 *Longhorn Luke and his Cowboys.* Jules Verne Allen led the popular CW music group (WOAI, San Antonio, TX, 1932). *See* **Allen, Jules Verne**.

19437 *(The) Longine Symphonette.* Mishel Piasto conducted the fine orchestra on the transcribed music program sponsored by the Longine-Whittnauer Watch Company. Frank Knight was the announcer (30 min., Sunday, 4:30–5:00 P.M., CBS, 1950).

19438 Longley, Mary. Singer and ukulele soloist (*Mary Longley*, vcl. mus. prg., WPG, Atlantic City, NJ, 1935).

19439 Longlois, Doris. COM-HE (KNOC, Natchitoches, LA, 1960).

19440 Longmire, Cary. Newscaster (NBC-WRC, Washington, DC, 1942; WLIB, New York, NY, 1944; NBC, 1945; WMAL, Washington, DC, 1946; WOR, New York, NY, 1947).

19441 Longo, Ester Vela. Concert violinist (WMCA, New York, NY, 1932).

19442 Longwell, Robert "Bob." Newscaster (*Orange Crush News* and *Christian Science Monitor Newscast*, WJBK, Detroit, MI, 1937; WIBC, Indianapolis, IN, 1938; WCAR, Pontiac, MI, 1942; WJR, Detroit, MI, 1945). Longwell also worked as a sportscaster during his early years of broadcasting on his *Premier Beer Hockey Resume* (WWJ, Detroit, MI; *Tiger Tales*, WJBK, 1937).

19443 Lono [Lano], James L. Leader (James Lono's Hawaiian Orchestra, KPO, San Francisco, CA, 1925–1926). The group consisted of leader Lono, Bob Lee, John Liu, Nicholas Keola, Jesse Fisher and Sylvester Luhan.

19444 Look, Elsie May. Organist (WLS, Chicago, IL, 1926).

19445 Loomis, Ernest. Loomis lent his name to the Ernest Loomis and his Victor Recording Orchestra (KOA, Denver, CO, 1927–1928), but the band was actually led by Earl Donaldson.

19446 Loomis Garden Dancing Palace. Local dance band (KHQ, Spokane, WA, 1926).

19447 Loos Brothers. Singing team (WEBH, Chicago, IL, 1925).

19448 Loose, Carl. Newscaster (WPAR, Parkersburg, WV, 1946).

19449 Looss, Walter A. Pianist (WAHG, Richmond Hill, NY, 1926).

19450 Lopa, Professor. Leader (Professor Lopa's Royal Hawaiian Orchestra, KPO, San Francisco, CA, 1923).

19451 Loper, Dan. Leader (*Dan Loper Orchestra*, instr. mus. prg., NBC, 1935).

19452 Lopez, A.J. Announcer (WNBH, New Bedford, MA, 1926–1927).

19453 Lopez, Joe. DJ (*Memory Song Man*, WIOD, Miami, FL, 1952).

19454 Lopez, Joseph. Announcer (WNAC, Boston, MA, 1925).

19455 Lopez, Laurie. COM-HE (KIFN, Phoenix, AZ, 1951).

19456 Lopez, Lucio Barrios. DJ (*Lucky Lager Dance Time*, KGST, Fresno, CA, 1960).

19457 Lopez, Vincent. Leader (Vincent Lopez Orchestra, WJZ, New York, NY, 1921–1926; WGR, Buffalo, NY, 1923–1924; Vincent Lopez Orchestra broadcasting from Pittsburgh's Davis Theater, KDKA, Pittsburgh, PA, 1924; Vincent Lopez Hotel Statler Dance Orchestra, directed by Harold Gieser, WGR, 1924–25; WOR, Newark, NJ, 1925; Vincent Lopez and his Hotel Pennsylvania Orchestra, WEAF, New York, NY, 1924–1926). The Lopez orchestra is said to have been the first to broadcast "live." Lopez first broadcast regularly in 1921 over WJZ from the Hotel Pennsylvania Grill Room, New York City. Some of the band's sessions from the Hotel Statler on WGR in 1924–25 were said to have been directed by Harold Geiser. Later, as Lopez always used to say, he was broadcasting from the Hotel Taft: "Just a stone's throw from Times Square — the Hotel Taft."

In the following decades the Lopez band was very active on radio (*Vincent Lopez Orchestra*, KYW, Philadelphia, PA, 1933; WBZ-WBZA, Boston-Springfield, MA, 1934; NBC, 1935; CBS, 1936–1939; KGBX, Springfield, MO, 1942).

19458 Lopriore, Michael. DJ (*The Italian Hour*, WJOC, Jamestown, NY, 1954).

19459 *Lora Lawton.* Frank and Anne Hummert were the producers of the daytime serial drama in which Lora Lawton left her native Midwest to work as a housekeeper for Peter Carver, a wealthy shipbuilder in Washington, DC. When Lora eventually married Carver, her trials and tribulations really began. First broadcast in 1943, the program ran on NBC for seven years. The cast included: Charita Bauer, Fran Carlon, Marilyn Erskine, Florida Friebus, Walter Greaza, William Hare, Vivi Janiss, Alan MacAteer, Kate McComb, Paul McGrath, James Meighan, Jan Miner, Carol Summers, Joan Tompkins, James Van Dyk, Ned Wever, Ethel Wilson and Lawson Zerbe. The directors were Martha Atwell, Arthur Hanna and Fred

Weihe. Jean Carroll, Elizabeth Todd and Helen Walpole wrote the program. The announcer was Ford Bond (NBC, 1943–1950).

19460 Loranger, William F. Newscaster (WSAM, Saginaw, MI, 1945).

19461 Lorber, (Dr.) Z. News analyst (WSBC, Chicago, IL, 1946).

19462 Lorch, Carl. Leader (*Carl Lorch Orchestra*, instr. mus. prg., WLW, Cincinnati, OH, 1934).

19463 Lorcher, Lillian. Soprano (WFBH, New York, NY, 1925).

19464 Lord, Christine. COM-HE (WNMP, Evanston, IL, 1949).

19465 Lord, Phil. Actor Lord appeared on *Chicago Theatre of the Air*, *Flying Time*, *Grand Hotel*, *Great Gunns*, *Guiding Light*, *Kitty Keene*, *Mary Marlin*, *Tom Mix* and *Woman in White*.

19466 Lord, Phillips H. Actor, producer and writer Lord was born July 13, 1902. After a career in education and a failure at fiction writing, Lord built a program around a Sunday Evening Singing School that by 1928 was being carried by 32 stations. The following year (1929), NBC decided the program was worth network presentation and *Sunday Evening at Seth Parker's* was broadcast nation wide. Lord, himself, played "Seth Parker" and the program attained a large listening audience. In the decades that followed, Lord wrote and produced many other popular programs such as *By Kathleen Norris* (producer), *Counterspy* (producer), *Gangbuser* (producer-director), *Mr. District Attorney* (producer), *Sky Blazers* (producer), *Treasury Agent* (producer) and *We the People* (producer). *See* ***Sunday Evening at Seth Parker's***.

19467 Lordan, Margaret. COM-HE (KSEM, Moses Lake, WA, 1955).

19468 Lorde, Athena. Actress Lorde was in the cast of the daytime serial programs *Young Widder Brown* and *Front Page Farrell*.

19469 Lorelei Quartet. Vocal group that included Flora Howell Bruner, Blanche Hamilton Fox, Easton Kent and Harry Truax (KFRC, San Francisco, CA, 1925–1926). Tenors Hamilton Fox and Gwynfi Jones replaced Kent and Truax in 1926.

19470 Loren, William H. DJ (*Turntable Windup* and *It's the Tops*, WLVA, Lynchburg, VA, 1947).

19471 Lorenz, Sherwood. Newscaster (*Cook and Brown Newscast*, WOSH, Oshkosh, WI, 1947).

19472 *Lorenzo Jones.* Another production of Frank and Anne Hummert, this daytime serial drama followed the life of good-hearted, impractical Lorenzo Jones, whose inventions and schemes never quite seemed to work out well for him. The long-running NBC program (1937–1955) featured Karl Swenson in the title role throughout the entire run. Over the years, the program's cast also included: Frank Behrens, John Brown, Art Carney, Betty Garde, Louis Hector, Irene Hubbard, Joe Julian, Grace Keddy, Jean McCoy, Kermit Murdock, Ethel Waite Owen, Elliott Reid, Ann Shepherd (Scheindel Kalish), Nancy Sheridan, Chester Stratton, Lucille Wall, Helen Walpole, Coleen Ward, Mary Wickes and Roland Winters. The directors were Stephen Gross, Frank Hummert, and Ernest Ricca. Theodore and Mathilde Ferro were the writers. Don Lowe was the announcer (15 min., Monday through Friday, NBC, 1937–1955).

19473 Lorig, Marvin C. Newscaster (WGPC, Albany, GA, 1941–1942).

19474 Lorin, Harold A. Lorin talked about "The American Indian in Story and Song" (KOA, Denver, CO, 1926).

19475 Loring, August. Tenor (WCCO, Minneapolis–St. Paul, MN, 1928).

19476 Loring, Michael. Singer (*Michael Loring*, vcl. mus. prg., CBS, 1935; WCAU, 1939; WCAU, Philadelphia, PA, 1942).

19477 Loring, Rod. Leader (Rod Loring's Tavern Orchestra, KHJ, Los Angeles, CA, 1925).

19478 Lorraine, Carl. Leader (Carl Lorraine's Pershing Palace Orchestra, WOK, Chicago, IL, 1926).

19479 Lorraine, Doris. Mezzo-soprano (WBBM, Chicago, IL, 1935).

19480 Lorraine, Florence. Ballad singer (KFWI, San Francisco, CA, 1929).

19481 Lorraine, Mitzi. Singer (*Mitzi Lorraine*, vcl. mus. prg., WIP, Philadelphia, PA, 1936).

19482 *Lorraine Sherwood's Travel-Go-Round.* Miss Sherwood delivered travel talks. The sponsor was Hillman Minx Automobiles (30 min., 12:00–12:30 P.M., WOR, Newark, NJ, 1950).

19483 Lorring, Joan. Actress Lorring appeared on the daytime serial programs *Stella Dallas* and *This is Nora Drake*.

19484 *Los Angeles Concert Hour.* Soprano Patricia Ann, baritone William Kalani and tenor Paul Roberts performed on the West Coast music program (60 min., Thursday, 7:00–8:00 P.M., NBC-Pacific Coast Network, 1928).

19485 Los Angeles Fire Department Orchestra. Municipal band (KFI, Los Angeles, CA, 1927–1929).

19486 Los Angeles Grand Opera Association. The operatic company broadcast such operas as "La Traviata" with Claudia Muzio, Jose Mohjica and Giuseppe de Luca. The company at times featured such artists as Tito Schipa, Thalia Sabaniera and Myrtle Donnelly (KFI, Los Angeles, CA, 1924).

19487 Los Angeles Philharmonic Orchestra. Walter Henry Rothwell and George Schneevough conducted the orchestra on various broadcasts (KFI, Los Angeles, CA, 1927). The Los Angeles Philharmonic was unique in that it appeared on a program sponsored by the White King Soap Company as early as October 9, 1924 over station KHJ, Los Angeles, CA.

19488 Los Angeles Railway Orchestra. Commercial band (KFQZ, Hollywood, CA, 1927).

19489 Los Angeles Rose Room Orchestra. Club dance band (KFI, Los Angeles, CA, 1925).

19490 *Los Angeles Symphony Band.* Instr. music program (Saturday, 4:00–5:00 P.M., MBS, 1947).

19491 *Los Angeles Symphony Orchestra.* Symphonic music program (WTAR, Norfolk, VA, 1938).

19492 Los Angeles Trio. Instrumental group consisting of May McDonald Hope, piano; Calmon Luberski, violin; and Ilya Bronson, cello (KHS, Los Angeles, CA, 1923).

19493 Los Angeles Trio. Singing group that included Bud Van Gorden, Ralph Metser and Gordon Van Gorden (KWK, St. Louis, MO, 1928).

19494 Los Caballeros. Spanish orchestra (KPO, San Francisco, CA, 1927).

19495 *Los Charros.* The music of Mexico was featured. Singers Tito Guizar and Chago Rodriquez were accompanied by guitarist Juariz Garcia (15 min., Friday, 8:15–8:30 P.M., WOR, Newark, NJ, 1932).

19496 Los Gatos High School Orchestra. Scholastic orchestra (KGO, Oakland, CA, 1926).

19497 Los Serranos Country Club Orchestra. California club band (KFWB, Hollywood, CA, 1926).

19498 *(The) Loser.* The interesting program's concept was introduced: "You are listening to *The Loser* and the sound of prisoners being locked up for the night. On this program you will hear the actual voice of the prisoner as he tells his crime story." The program's purpose was to prove that crime did not pay (30 min., Weekly, NBC, 1955).

19499 Losser, Ernie. Tenor (KTAB, Oakland, CA, 1925).

19500 Lossez, Bill. Leader (*Bill Lossez Orchestra*, instr. mus. prg., WBZ-WBZA, Boston-Springfield, MA, 1934).

19501 *Lossez Biltmore Orchestra.* Instr. mus. prg. (WNAC, Boston, MA, 1932).

19502 *Lost and Found.* Station KGEZ (Kalispell, MT, 1944) inaugurated the unique service program. It is estimated that while on the air the program returned to listeners approximately $27,000 worth of their lost items.

19503 *(The) Lost Angels of KHJ.* This was one of the many loosely structured late night variety programs of music and comedy broadcast by early radio stations. It featured the Majestic Six orchestra, the Lost Angels orchestra, the KHJ String Quartet and other local favorites (KHJ, Los Angels, CA, 1925) *See* **The Lost Angels Orchestra**.

19504 Lost Angels Orchestra. The station band appeared on the popular *Lost Angels of KHJ* program (KHJ, Los Angeles, CA, 1925). The band featured among many others harpist Walter Biddick. At times, the Majestic Six orchestra was featured on the *Lost Angels of KHJ* program. *See* ***The Lost Angels of KHJ***.

19505 *(The) Lost Legion.* Wyllis Cooper wrote and acted in the dramatic romantic-adventure series. Each program told a complete story about the French Foreign Legion stationed in Algeria. This program was highly praised by the *Radio Digest* (Vol. 28, No. 5, April, 1932, p. 64). Don Ameche, Marigold Cassin, Vinton Haworth and Sunda Love were in the cast (1932).

19506 Lothian, Eleanor. Actress-writer (WHEC, Rochester, NY, 1929).

19507 Lott, Stokes. Organist (*Stokes Lott*, instr. mus. prg., WOR, Newark, NJ, 1934).

19508 Lotus Male Quartet. Vocal group (WGI, Medford Hillside, MA, 1922).

19509 Lotz, Emma. Pianist (WGY, Schenectady, NY, 1923).

19510 Lou, Anita. COM-HE (WASA, Havre De Grace, MD, 1924).

19511 Louann, Helen. Mezzo-soprano (WOR, Newark, NJ, 1924).

19512 Loucks, Barbara. COM-HE (WADS, Ansonia-Derby, CT, 1957).

19513 Loud, Einer. Newscaster (KWLC, Decorah, IA, 1942).

19514 Loud, Ted. Newscaster (KSRV, Ontario, OR, 1946).

19515 Loudon, Gordon. Newscaster (KALK, Alexandria, LA, 1938).

19516 *Louella Parsons Show.* Columnist Parsons was a Hollywood powerhouse who broadcast film business news weekly on her show sponsored by Woodbury Soap (15 min., Weekly, Transcribed, 1951). She wrote an important Hollywood gossip column for the Hearst newspapers.

19517 Loughrane, Basil. Producer-director-announcer Loughrane worked on *Beyond these Valleys* (director), *Her Honor, Nancy James* (announcer), *Light of the World* (producer-director), *Sherlock Holmes* (director), *Mary Marlin* (director) and *Young Doctor Malone* (producer).

19518 Loughrin, Dick. Newscaster (WDEV, Waterbury, CT, 1941).

19519 Louie's Hungry Five. The little German band featured broad ethnic comedy routines. Louie the leader was often frustrated by the Weasel, another member of the band. Weasel would say, "Vel, goodness gracious mercy sakes, Herr Louie! Ven do we eat?" Louis would respond, "Shot op, Veasel, der dodaker iss looking you at." Chicago listeners liked what they heard (WGN, Chicago, IL, 1928–1929). *See* ***Herr Louie and the Weasel.***

19520 *Louis Sobol.* Broadway columnist Sobol dispensed news and gossip on his network show (15 min., Weekly, MBS, 1940).

19521 *Louise Benay Entertains.* Miss Benay conducted interviews with guests and presided over her popular local variety show (60 min., Monday through Friday, WROW, Albany, N.Y., 1947).

19522 *Louise Massey and the Westerners.* A popular CW music group, the Westerners consisted of Louise, Dott and Allen Massey, Larry Wellington and Milt Mabie (WLS, Chicago, IL, 1937). The group was often featured on the *National Barn Dance* program.

19523 *Louisiana Hayride.* The *Louisiana Hayride* was one of the outstanding CW music shows that for many years rivaled the *Grand Ole Opry*. Begun in 1948 at KWKH (Shreveport, LA), the program ran until 1958. The show's manager was Horace Logan. Known as the "The Cradle of Stars," the *Louisiana Hayride* featured CW music greats such as Hank Williams, Webb Pierce, Jim Reeves, Floyd Cramer, Faron Young, Elvis Presley, Johnny Cash, David Houston, Slim Whitman, Kitty Wells, Johnny and Jack (Johnny Wright and Jack Anglin) and Johnny Horton (30 min., Saturday, 9:00–9:30 P.M., MBS, 1940s and 1950s). *See* **Country-Western Music.**

19524 Lounsbury, Jim. Newscaster (KSO, Des Moines, IA, 1945). DJ (*Record Shop*, WIND, Chicago, IL, 1949; WLEX, Lexington, KY, 1950; WGN, Chicago, IL, 1954). Sportscaster (KSO, 1945).

19525 Loury, Francis G. Pianist (WBZ, Springfield, MA, 1926).

19526 Louth, Mary. Violinist (WGN, Chicago, IL, 1924).

19527 Love, Aileen H. COM-HE (WRLD, West Point, GA, 1956).

19528 *(The) Love Doctor.* An unidentified performer dispensed advice to the lovelorn (15 min., Friday, 12:00–12:15 P.M., MBS, 1935).

19529 Love, Elizabeth. Actress Love was in the cast of the daytime serial programs *Big Sister* and *Amanda of Honeymoon Hill.*

19530 Love, Harry J. Newscaster (*Home Edition*, WENE, Endicott, NY, 1948).

19531 Love, Hazel Fleener. Soprano (WEAF, New York, NY, 1924).

19532 *Love Letters.* While Ennio Bolognini and Dave Bacall supplied a romantic musical background, announcer Franklyn MacCormack read anonymous love letters. The program was transcribed (15 min., Monday-Wednesday-Friday, 11:15–11:30 P.M., WENR, Chicago, IL, 1947).

19533 Love, (Mrs.) Louis. COM-HE (*The Care of Children.* WDAR, Philadelphia, PA, 1924; WLIT, Philadelphia, PA, 1925).

19534 Love, Mark. Basso Love was a concert singer who directed a vocal group (WGN, Chicago, IL, 1928–1930; *Mark Love*, vcl. mus. prg., WGN, 1934; KFEL, Denver, CO, 1939). Announcer Quin Ryan of WGN proudly called him "The Big Buffalo of the Bass Octaves."

19535 Love, Martha. COM-HE (WHIO, Dayton, OH, 1939).

19536 Love, Nancy. COM-HE (WAGC, Chattanooga, TN, 1955).

19537 Love, Richard. Leader (*Richard Love Orchestra*, instr. mus. prg., WOR, Newark, NJ, 1942).

19538 Love, Steve. Leader (Steve Love Orchestra, KFWB, Hollywood, CA, 1929).

19539 Love, Sunda. Busy and versatile actress Love appeared in such daytime serial programs as *Bachelor's Children, The Guiding Light, Myrt and Marge, Right to Happiness, Stepmother, Tale of Today* and *Today's Children.*

19540 *Love Scenes in Music.* A program of romantic concert music (30 min., Thursday, 11:00–11:30 P.M., NBC-Red, 1930).

19541 *Love Story Theatre.* Jim Ameche starred in the weekly sustaining show that presented a complete romantic drama with various actors and actresses. Sylvan Levin's Orchestra provided the music (30 min., Friday, 8:30–9:00 P.M., WOR, Newark, NJ, 1946).

19542 Lovegren, Robert W. Baritone (KGO, Oakland, CA, 1925).

19543 Lovejoy, Frank. Before becoming a motion picture star, Lovejoy was a busy radio actor appearing on *Amazing Mr. Malone* (title role), *Blue Play House, Brave Tomorrow, Bright Horizon, Calling All Detectives, Deadline Drama, Gangbusters, Joyce Jordan, Girl Interne, Man Behind the Gun, Mr. and Mrs. North, Murder and Mr. Malone, Night Beat, Stella Dallas, Theatre Guild on the Air, This is Your FBI, Valiant Lady, We Love and Learn, Young Widder Brown* and *Your Family and Mine.*

19544 Loveless, Faye. DJ (KANV, Shreveport, LA, 1955).

19545 Loveless, Wendell. Announcer (WMBI, Chicago, IL, 1925).

19546 Loveless and King. Male vocal team (WMBI, Chicago, IL, 1928).

19547 Lovell, Bob. Newscaster (*Local News*, WNDR, Syracuse, NY, 1948).

19548 Lovell, J.J. Banjo soloist (WLAC, Nashville, TN, 1929).

19549 Lovell, (Mrs.) Nettie Wheeler. Pianist (WLAK, Bellows Falls, VT, 1922).

19550 Loveton, John. Director Loveton directed *Aunt Jenny, Court of Missing Heirs* and *Mr. and Mrs. North.*

19551 Loving, Reguge Ray Soprano (KFDM, Beaumont, TX, 1928–1929).

19552 Low, Rambling. DJ (*Rainbow Ridge*, WJJL, Niagara Falls, NY, 1948).

19553 Lowden, Dorothy Chenoweth. Harpist (WOAW, Omaha, NE, 1926).

19554 Lowe, Alfred. Violinist (WAPI, Auburn, AL, 1929).

19555 Lowe, Bert. Leader (*Bert Lowe Orchestra*, instr. mus. prg., WNAC, Boston, MA, 1934).

19556 Lowe, Billie. Singer known on the Pacific Coast as the "California Radio Favorite" (WOC, Davenport, IA, 1925).

19557 Lowe, Billy. Lowe was a popular New York City DJ (*Uptown Skyline*, 60 min., Monday, through Saturday, 7:00–8:00 A.M., WLIB, New York, NY, 1950).

19558 Lowe, Bryan. Newscaster (WLBJ, Bowling Green, KY, 1945).

19559 Lowe, David. Newscaster (WNEW, New York, NY, 1938).

19560 Lowe, Don. Announcer on the programs of Peter DeRose and his wife, May Singhi Breen (NBC-Blue, New York, NY, late 1920s). In addition he worked on *The Dunninger Show, Ethel and Albert, The Fishing and Hunting Club of the Air, Lorenzo Jones* and *The Moylan Sisters.*

19561 Lowe, Frank M., Jr. Newscaster (KGB, San Diego, CA, 1940).

19562 Lowe, Guy W. Newscaster (KFRU, Columbia, MO, 1939).

19563 Lowe, Helen. Soprano (KPO, San Francisco, CA, 1929).

19564 Lowe, Jackson "Jack." DJ (*1450 Club*, WWDC, Washington, DC, 1947; *Jackson Lowe Program*, WINX, Washington, DC, 1949; *1450 Club*, WWDC, 1950; WUST, Bethesda, MD, 1954).

19565 Lowe, Jim. DJ (*Disc Derby*, KFRU, Columbia, MO, 1947; *The Lowe Down*, WIRE, Indianapolis, IN, 1948; *The Lowe Down*, WENR, Chicago, IL, 1949; *Best by Request*, KWTO, Springfield, MO, 1950; WRR,

Dallas, TX, 1954–1956; *Jim Lowe,* 25 min., Monday through Friday, 9:05–9:30 A.M., WCBS, New York, NY, 1956; and for the second time on the same day, *Jim Lowe Again,* 15 min., Monday through Friday, 11:30–11:45 P.M., WCBS, 1956; *Jim Lowe's Hideaway Show,* WCBS, New York, NY, 1957).

19566 Lowe, Jimmy and Norm Alden. DJ team (*The Juke Box,* KXOL, Fort Worth, TX, 1947).

19567 Lowe, Kay. COM-HE (WKLO, Louisville, KY, 1951–1954).

19568 Lowe, Ken. Newscaster (*Merit News,* KWY, Oklahoma City, OK, 1947–1948).

19569 Lowe, Louis "Louie." Leader (*Louis Lowe Orchestra,* instr. mus. prg., WFBM, Indianapolis, IN, 1934–1936).

19570 Lowe, Maxim. Leader (*Maxim Lowe Ensemble,* instr. mus. prg., NBC, 1933; WPAR, Parkersburg, WV, 1937; CBS, 1937–1938).

19571 Lowe, Mona. Blues singer (*Mona Lowe,* vcl. mus. prg., WOR, Newark, NJ, 1935).

19572 Lowe, Richard. News analyst (*City Edition,* WBEX, Chillicothe, OH, 1948).

19573 Lowe, Ruth. Pianist (*Ruth Lowe and Sair Lee,* 15 min., Weekly, NBC-Blue, 1942). Singing piano duo Lowe and Lee broadcast on the network weekly.

19574 Lowell, Dorothy. Actress Lowell appeared on the daytime serial programs *Hilltop House, Our Gal Sunday* and *The Man I Married.*

19575 Lowell, Maurice "Maury." Director Lowell directed the *When a Girl Marries* daytime serial program.

19576 Lowell Electric Corporation Employees Orchestra. Company band (WEEI, Boston, MA, 1925).

19577 Lowenhein [Lowenheince], Mary Jane. Pianist (WLAC, Nashville, TN, 1929).

19578 Lower, Gaydon. Euphonium soloist (WLS, Chicago, IL, 1926).

19579 Lowery, Bill. Newscaster (WBEJ, Elizabethton, TN, 1946). DJ (*Let's Have Fun,* WGRV, Greeneville, TN, 1947; *Let's Have Fun,* WGST, Atlanta, GA, 1949–1954). Sportscaster (*Sports Round-Up* and local football and baseball games play-by-play, WGRV, 1947; WQXI, Atlanta, GA, 1948).

19580 *Lowe's Mandolin Serenaders.* Instr. mus. prg. by a string group directed by Hugh Lowe (KFWM, Oakland, CA, 1926–1928).

19581 Lown, Bert. Leader (*Bert Lown Orchestra,* instr. mus. prg., NBC, 1933).

19582 Lowrance, Bomar. Sportscaster (WSOC, Charlotte, NC, 1939–1941, 1946).

19583 Lowrey, Meador. Newscaster (*Streitmann Biscuit Company Newscast* and *News of the World,* WHAS, Louisville, KY, 1937–1938; KRLD, Dallas, TX, 1940–1945). Sportscaster (WHAS, 1937).

19584 Lowry, Betty Jean. COM-HE (WGEM, Boise, ID, 1951).

19585 Lowry, Ed. Singing comedian (*Ed Lowry,* music and comedy prg., NBC, 1934).

19586 Lowry, Freda. COM-HE (KWOA, Worthington, MN, 1956).

19587 Lowry, Judith. Actress Lowry appeared on the daytime serial programs *Last of the Lockwoods, Mary Marlin* aka *The Story of Mary Marlin, Masquerade, Shoestring Castle, Today's Children, Valiant Lady* and *Dan Harding's Wife.*

19588 Lowry Male Quartet. Vocal group (WCCO, Minneapolis–St. Paul, MN, 1928).

19589 Loyd, Keith. Newscaster (KVOP, Plainview, TX, 1945).

19590 Loyet, Paul. Announcer (WOC, Davenport, IA, 1928).

19591 Lozano, Guillermo. Sportscaster (KCOR, San Antonio, TX, 1953).

19592 Lozano, R. Newscaster (KGFI, Brownsville, TX, 1938).

19593 Lozier, Jack. DJ (*General Store,* KRIS, Corpus Christi, TX, 1949).

19594 "LP." Designation for announcer Lester Palmer (WOAW, Omaha, NE, 1925).

19595 Luboviski, Calmon. Russian "master violinist" (KHJ, Los Angeles, CA, 1925–1926; KNX, Los Angeles, CA, 1927–1930).

19596 Lubowe, Ann. Actress Lubowe appeared on the *Hour of Glass* program.

19597 Lucas, Ben. Newscaster (WRBL, Columbus, OH, 1941; WRDW, Augusta, GA, 1942). DJ (WRGA, Rome, GA, 1947; *Talk of the Town,* WRGA, 1949–1960).

19598 Lucas, Clyde. Leader (*Clyde Lucas Orchestra,* instr. mus. prg., NBC, 1934; CBS, 1936; MBS, 1939; KLZ, Denver, CO, 1940).

19599 Lucas, Ernest. Violinist (KFWM, Oakland, CA, 1929).

19600 Lucas, Harley. Newscaster (WLOK, Lima, OH, 1946). DJ (*Hart Beats,* WLOK, Lima, OH, 1947).

19601 Lucas, Jackie. Blues singer (KFI, Los Angeles, CA, 1926).

19602 Lucas, Lee. DJ (KVI, Seattle, WA, 1960).

19603 Lucas, (Mrs.) Lucian L. Pianist (WFLA, Clearwater, FL, 1928).

19604 Lucas, Marjorie C. Pianist (WWJ, Detroit, MI, 1924).

19605 Lucas, Martin. DJ (*Hi Neighbor,* KWBU, Corpus Christi, TX, 1947).

19606 Lucas, Nick. Popular singer (WEBH, Chicago, IL, 1924; CBS, 1929; *Nick Lucas, Songs,* vcl. mus. prg., 15 min., Sunday, 6:00–6:15 P.M., CBS, 1934).

19607 Lucas, Silas. Newscaster (WGTM, Wilson, NC, 1941–1942).

19608 Lucatorto, Benjamin. Pianist (WEAF, New York, NY, 1924).

19609 Lucca, Peggy Jayne. COM-HE (WOND, Pleasantville, NJ, 1954).

19610 Lucchese, Josephine. Coloratura soprano Lucchese was prima donna of the San Carlo Opera Company (WIP, Philadelphia, PA, 1924–1925).

19611 Luce, Dean. Newscaster (WCHV, Charlottesville, VA, 1945; WDRC, Hartford, CT, 1946). Sportscaster (WMAL, Washington, DC, 1950).

19612 Luce, Roy. Newscaster (KWPC, Muscatine, IA, 1948).

19613 Lucia, Helen. Soprano (WSOM, New York, NY, 1927).

19614 Luchansky, James. Austrian tenor (WIBO, Chicago, IL, 1925).

19615 *Lucille and Iva.* Vcl. mus. prg. (KFEQ, St. Joseph, MO, 1929).

19616 *Lucille and Lanny.* Vcl. prg. featuring a talented singing team that was not otherwise identified (WBAL, Baltimore, MD, 1935).

19617 *Lucille Buhl.* Miss Buhl delivered beauty care talks five times weekly (15 min., Monday through Friday, 2:00–2:15 P.M., NBC-Blue, 1927).

19618 Lucille Phillips' Royal Gypsy Orchestra. Popular Cleveland band (WKK , Cleveland, OH, 1922).

19619 *Lucius Beebe.* Critic Beebe broadcast weekly dramatic criticism (15 min., Weekly, MBS, 1940).

19620 Luck, Lucky (Lucky Luckman). DJ (*Wake Up Hawaii,* 210 min., Monday through Saturday, 5:30–9:00 A.M., KPOA, Honolulu, HI, 1952). Lucky Luck conducted a popular Honolulu morning show on which he broadcast the news, time and weather, as well as playing records in an effort to out draw his rival Hal Lewis on KGU. *See **J. Akuhead Pupule Show.***

19621 Luck, Lydia. Singer (*Lydia Luck,* vcl. mus. prg., WOR, Newark, NJ, 1935).

19622 *Lucky Rangers.* CW mus. prg. (WIP, Philadelphia, PA, 1935–1936).

19623 *Lucky Smith.* Heavyweight boxing champion Max Baer played a detective in these dramatic sketches, sponsored by Gillette Blue Blades and broadcast by NBC in 1935. The program conducted a contest that provided winners with free tickets and transportation to New York City to attend the Baer-Braddock heavyweight championship fight that was scheduled to take place. The program ceased broadcasting immediately after Baer lost his fight and the heavyweight championship to James J. Braddock. *See **Max Baer.***

19624 *Lucky Strike Dance Orchestra.* Instr. mus. prg. (WBZ-WBZA, Boston-Springfield, MA, 1932).

19625 *Lucky Strike Hour.* B.A. Rolfe conducted the Lucky Strike Dance Orchestra on the musical variety show sponsored by Lucky Strike cigarettes. At various times Bert Lahr, Walter Winchell and Jack Pearl also appeared. The program enjoyed continued popularity well into the mid–1930s (60 min., 9:00–10:00 P.M., NBC, 1928–1931). Later, Paul Whiteman hosted the show that featured his orchestra along with Peggy Healy, Jack Pearl and his stooge Cliff Hall and Ramona. Howard Claney was the announcer (30 min., Weekly, NBC, 1933).

19626 *(The) Lucky Strike Hours.* This was a series of three programs sponsored by Lucky Strike Cigarettes that presented different elements on each day of the week it was broadcast. Walter O'Keefe was the MC on all three nights. On Tuesday night, the orchestras of Jack Denny and Joe Sanders performed and

Jack Curtin presented dramatized police cases. Walter Winchell delivered the latest gossip on Thursday night with the music performed by the bands of Anson Weeks and Joe Moss. On Saturday, comedian Bert Lahr was featured with George Olsen's Orchestra. Despite the apparent abundance of talent, critical reviews of the program were never enthusiastic (60 min., Tuesday-Thursday-Saturday, 10:00–11:00 P.M., NBC-Red, 1932).

19627 ***Lucky U Ranch.*** The Sons of the Pioneers, Shug Fisher and Betty Taylor appeared on the entertaining CW music show broadcast on a sustaining basis (30 min., Monday through Friday, 12:30–1:00 P.M., ABC, 1951).

19628 **Lucy, C.T.** Special features announcer (WRVA, Richmond, VA, 1928).

19629 ***Lucy Jane* (Kielman) *and Mary Jane* (Morrison).** The singing team was featured with Uncle Dave on a WIBW music show (WIBW, Topeka, KS, 1930s).

19630 **Ludden, Florence.** Singer (WHA, Madison, WI, 1925).

19631 **Luddy, Barbara.** Talented actress Luddy appeared on the *Lonely Women*; *Margot of Castlewood* aka *Margo of Castlewood*; *Road of Life*; and *The Woman in White* daytime serial programs. She also appeared on such night time dramatic shows as *The Chicago Theater of the Air*; *First Nighter*; *Grand Hotel;* and the *Great Gunns* situation comedy.

19632 ***Luden's Novelty Orchestra.*** Instr. mus. prg. (WNAC, Boston, MA, 1931–1932). The orchestra was directed by Dan Rybb.

19633 **Ludes, Edward.** Announcer (KJBS, San Francisco, CA, 1926–1927). Entertainer as the Chief Herring and host of the Royal Order of the Smoked Herring (KIBS, 1926).

19634 **Ludlam, George.** News commentator (*For Men Only*, NBC, 1938).

19635 **Ludlam, Kennedy.** News commentator (*America United*, NBC, 1947).

19636 **Ludlam, Lillian.** COM-HE (WLCR, Torrington, CT, 1951).

19637 **Ludlum, George.** Accordionist (KOMO, Seattle, WA, 1927).

19638 **Ludlow, Godfrey.** Australian violinist (WIP, Philadelphia, PA, 1925; staff announcer and violinist, WJZ, New York, NY, 1925–1928; *Godfrey Ludlow*, instr. mus. prg., WOR, Newark, NJ, 1934).

19639 **Ludwig, Margaret.** Contralto (WJZ, New York, NY, 1924).

19640 **Ludwig, Preston.** Percussionist (KGW, Portland, OR, 1928).

19641 ***Ludy West and Trio.*** CW mus. prg. (WLW, Cincinnati, OH, 1937).

19642 **Luebke, Grace.** COM-HE (WFRO, Fremont, OH, 1957).

19643 **Luecke, Herschel.** Organist (*Herschel Luecke*, instr. mus. prg., WLW, Cincinnati, OH, 1942).

19644 **Lueth, Charles.** Newscaster (WCLO, Jonesville, WI, 1937).

19645 **Lugar, Jack [Joe].** Orchestra leader-saxophonist (WLW, Cincinnati, OH, 1923–1928).

19646 **Luhken (Mrs.) Albert.** Contralto (KVOO, Tulsa, OK, 1928).

19647 ***Luke Slaughter of Tombstone.*** The western adventure series premiered Sunday, February 23, 1958, sharing an hour with the *Frontier Gentleman* program. Luke Slaughter was a tough ex-calvary man who moved to Arizona to become a cattle rancher. On the first program, he ran a herd from Mexico to Texas assisted by a motley crew of cowhands and a runaway girl. Sam Buffington's portrayal of Slaughter was popular with many listeners. The show opened with Buffington saying, "Slaughter's my name — Luke Slaughter. Cattle's my business. It's a big business. I got a big stake in it. And there's no man west of the Rio Grande can take it from me." Robert Stanley wrote, Lucian Davis produced and William Robson directed the show (25 min., Sunday, 2:05–2:30 P.M., CBS, 1957–1958).

19648 **Lukens [Luken], Ned.** DJ (*Jumpin' with Jack*, WEAS, Decatur, GA, 1947; *Jack the Bell Boy*, WEAS, 1948–1952; *The Nite Owl Show*, WAOK, Atlanta, GA, 1954–1955).

19649 **Lukens, Stella.** Pianist and program director (WMBH, Joplin, MO, 1936–1939). Program director Lukens also played the piano and organ on broadcasts. As program director, she planned and scheduled every program, selected all the music for commercial programs, originated new program ideas and conducted all studio auditions.

19650 **Lukesh, Joe.** Leader (*Joe Lukesh Orchestra*, instr. mus. prg., KMMJ, Grand Island, NE, 1942).

19651 ***Lukewela's Royal Hawaiians Orchestra.*** Instr. mus. prg. (WHP, Harrisburg, PA, 1939; WHP, 1942).

19652 **Lukins, Harry.** Newscaster (WAVE, Louisville, KY, 1939–1942; *Noon News*, KDMO, Carthage, MO, 1947).

19653 **Lull, Lucia.** COM-HE (WMBS, Huntsville, AL, 1957).

19654 ***(The) Lullaby Lady.*** Mrs. J. Elliott Jenkins told bed-time stories and sang songs for children (WMAQ, Chicago, IL, 1925).

19655 ***(The) Lullaby Lady.*** May Sprintz sang sleepy time songs, read poems and told stories for children on her popular children's show. She told many Mother Goose stories (15 min., Monday through Saturday, 7:00–7:15 P.M., WINS, New York, NY, 1932).

19656 ***(The) Lullaby Lady* (aka *Lullaby Time*).** Miss Val McLaughlin conducted the popular children's program that also was sometimes known as *Lullaby Time* (WLS, Chicago, IL, 1926). *See* **Val McLaughlin.**

19657 ***Lullaby Lester and the Old Timers.*** CW mus. prg. (KFEQ, St. Joseph, MO, 1939).

19658 ***(The) Lullaby Man.*** Tiny Renier provided bedtime songs and stories for little listeners (WDAF, Kansas City, MO, 1931).

19659 ***Lullaby Time* (aka *Lullaby Twins*).** The veteran radio team of Ford and Glenn provided their usual entertaining songs and chatter. *The Lullaby Twins*, Ford Rush and Glenn Rowell, were a comedy singing team that charmed children on their evening program (WLS, Chicago, IL, 1924–1925). *See* **Ford and Glenn.**

19660 ***Lulu Belle and Scotty.*** CW husband and wife singing team (WLS, Chicago, IL, 1935–1937). Although the husband and wife team had many different sponsors over the years, one of their longest standing ones was the Morton Salt Company (15 min., Saturday, 9:15–9:30 P.M., WLS, Chicago, IL, 1936). Another sponsor was Foley's Store (15 min., Monday through Friday, 7:15–7:30 P.M., WLS, Chicago, IL, 1936). The team were long time favorites on the *National Barn Dance* for 25 years, where they gained national prominence (WLS). Scotty wrote many popular songs, including "Have I Told You Lately That I Love You?" *See* **Husband-and-Wife Talk Programs** *and* **Breakfast in the Blue Ridge.**

19661 **Lum, Bruce.** Announcer (WDAE, Tampa, FL, 1927).

19662 ***Lum and Abner.*** Chester Lauck and Norris Goff, two sophisticated gentlemen, for 22 years portrayed the roles of the two kind-hearted owners of the rural Jot 'Em Down Store located in Pine Ridge, Arkansas. The team got their start in the 1920s at station WBAP (Forth Worth, TX) before going on to network fame. These two supposed oldsters at first played all the roles themselves, but this soon changed. Their easy going humor lasted on radio from 1931 to 1953. The show's cast included: Cliff Arquette, Edna Best, Andy Devine, Norris Goff, Chester Lauck and Zasu Pitts. The directors were Bill Gay, Robert McInnes and Forrest Owen. Betty Boyle, Roz Rogers, Howard Snyder, Jay Sommers and Hugh Wedlock, Jr. wrote the program. Larry Berns was the producer-director and Sybil Bock the organist. Gene Baker, Carlton Brickert, Lou Crosby, Gene Hamilton, Roger Krupp, Del Sharbutt and Wendell Niles were the announcers (15 min., Monday, Wednesday and Friday, 7:15–7:30 P.M., CBS, 1940). *Lum and Abner* eventually appeared on all the major networks — ABC, CBS, MBC and NBC.

One familiar show opening went this way. After the sound of a telephone ring was heard, the announcer said: "That's our ring. Time for *Lum and Abner* brought to you by Miles Nervine and Alka-Seltzer." In order to honor the men, the town of Waters, Arkansas, changed its name to Pine Ridge in 1936.

19663 **Lummis, Dayton.** Newscaster (WCAM, Camden, NJ, 1941).

19664 **Lumpkin, Anne.** COM-HE (KLRA, Little Rock, AR, 1960).

19665 **Lumsden, Elizabeth.** Contralto (WNYC, New York, NY, 1936; WBNX, Bronx, NY, 1936).

19666 **Lunceford, Jimmy.** Leader (*Jimmy Lunceford Orchestra*, instr. mus. prg., NBC, 1934–1936; WTAR, Norfolk, VA, 1938; CBS, 1940).

19667 ***Luncheon at Sardi's.*** Roger Bower hosted the interesting sustaining program that was broadcast from Sardi's restaurant, a favorite meeting place for many Broadway show people. On a typical program, Bower interviewed such personalities as Vincent Sardi, Jr., Harry Hershfield, Roscoe Karns, Jan Murray, Paula Lawrence, Johnny Long, Judith Evelyn and

Bert Wheeler. George Hogan was the announcer (30 min., Saturday, 1:00–1:30 P.M., WOR, Newark, NJ, 1947). A later version of *Breakfast at Sardi's* used a similar format. Bill and Tom Slater were co-hosts on the 1954–1955 broadcast series. This quarter-hour interview show was broadcast on MBS with Gary Stevens as the producer-director.

19668 ***Luncheon at the Waldorf.*** Ilka Chase hosted the variety show broadcast from the Empire Room of New York's Waldorf Hotel. The Paul Baron Orchestra supplied music. Bert Parks was the announcer (30 min., Saturday P.M., NBC-Blue, 1941).

19669 ***Luncheon at the Waldorf: 45 Minutes on Broadway.*** Ed and Pegeen Fitzgerald brought their bright, entertaining chatter to the Waldorf Hotel, where they interviewed celebrity guests such as James Donald and Carol Burnett (45 min., Monday through Friday, 12:15–1:00 P.M., WOR, Newark, NJ, 1958).

19670 ***Luncheon Date with Ilka Chase.*** Actress Chase always conducted a lively show on which she discussed cultural and public affairs (NBC, 1942).

19671 ***Luncheon Song Review.*** Norman White conducted the program that each week featured the vaudeville entertainers currently playing at Detroit theaters (WJR, Detroit, MI, 1928).

19672 ***Luncheon with Lopez.*** Pianist-orchestra leader Vincent Lopez conducted his interesting show that combined good talk, celebrity interviews and music (15 min., 1:15–1:30 P.M., MBS, 1945). *See* **Lopez, Vincent.**

19673 **Lund, Dick.** DJ (*Corn Lovers' Hour*, WFRP, Savannah, GA, 1950).

19674 **Lund, Ed.** DJ (*1450 Club* and *Wax Works*, WGOV, Valdosta, GA, 1947).

19675 **Lund, Einer.** Newscaster (KWLC, Decorah, IA, 1941, 1945).

19676 **Lund, Eric F.** Newscaster (WLVA, Lynchburg, VA, 1940).

19677 **Lund, Howie.** DJ (*Here's Howie*, WJMO, Cleveland, OH, 1947–1948).

19678 **Lund, Jack.** DJ (*920 Club*, KFXJ, Grand Junction, CO, 1947; *Sweet and Sentimental*, KXRX, San Jose, CA, 1952–1954).

19679 **Lund, Ronald.** Newscaster (KJR, Seattle, WA, 1940).

19680 **Lund, Victor "Vic" H.** Sportscaster (WIRE, Indianapolis, IN and WAOV, Vincennes, IN, 1940–1941, 1946). Newscaster (WAOV, 1941).

19681 **Lundberg, Syl.** Leader (Syl Lundberg Orchestra, WJAX, Cleveland, OH, 1924).

19682 **Lunday Sisters.** Instrumental string quintet (WFAA, Dallas, TX, 1925).

19683 **Lunde, Laurette Reitz.** Soprano (WLAG, Minneapolis–St. Paul, MN, 1924).

19684 **Lundell, Jenny.** Soprano (KTAB, Oakland, CA, 1926).

19685 **Lundquist, Bill.** Newscaster (WCAL, Northfield, MN, 1945).

19686 **Lundquist, Eldon "Eldy."** Sportscaster (WTRC, Elkhart, IN, 1939–1942, 1944–1949; *Sports Today*, WTRC, 1950–1956).

19687 **Lundquist, George.** Organist (*George Lundquist*, instr. mus. prg., WJTN, Trenton, NJ, 1937–1938).

19688 **Lundquist, Vernon.** DJ (*Readin' and Writin'*, WKGN, Knoxville, TN, 1947; *620 Club*, WROL, Knoxville, TN, 1949).

19689 **Lundquist-Lilly Quartet.** Singing group specializing in old-time songs (KJR, Seattle, WA, 1926).

19690 **Lundy, Dan.** Newscaster (KXLA, Los Angeles, CA, 1947).

19691 **Lung, Charles "Charlie."** Actor Lung appeared on the *Romance* daytime serial program.

19692 **Lung, Phyllis.** COM-HE (KYNO, Fresno, CA, 1960).

19693 **Lunn, Robert.** CW singer (*Robert Lunn*, CW mus. prg., WSM, Nashville, TN, 1936–1938).

19694 **Lunzar, Jean.** COM-HE (KING, Seattle, WA, 1949).

19695 **Lupton, Danny.** Actor Lupton was in the cast of *In Care of Aggie Horn.*

19696 **Lupton, (Mrs.) H.M.** Pianist-soprano (WLAC, Nashville, TN, 1928–1929).

19697 **Lupton, John "Johnny."** Sportscaster (WLAN, 1946). DJ (*Remote Control*, WLAN, Lancaster, PA, 1947; *Rhythm by Request*, WLAN, 1948; *Lupton's Matinee* and *Spinner Sanctum*, WLAN, 1949; *Midnight Snack Bar*, WLAN, 1950; *Lupton's Matinee*, WLAN, 1952; *All Night Watch*, WCAU, Philadelphia, PA, 1954–1956).

19698 **Lusinchi, Victor.** Newscaster (MBS, 1939).

19699 **Lusk, Bernie.** Sportscaster (*Sports Review* and *Sports Cap*, KROC, Rochester, NY, 1950–1960).

19700 **Lusk, Irving.** Newscaster (KEVR, Seattle, WA, 1945).

19701 **Lusk, Milan.** Violinist (KYW, Chicago, IL, 1923).

19702 **Lustgarden, Alfred.** Violinist (KWSC, Pullman, WA, 1925).

19703 **Lustgarden, Ruth.** Pianist (WGN, Chicago, IL, 1924).

19704 **Luther, Aida.** Soprano Aida Luther specialized in Spanish and Latin American songs. She was accompanied by Lupe Luna (30 min., Weekly, 7:00–7:30 P.M., KTAB, Oakland, CA, 1920s).

19705 **Luther, Deacon.** DJ (*Red, Hot and Bluesy*, WBCO, Bessemer, AL, 1954).

19706 **Luther, Frank.** Tenor (*Frank Luther*, vcl. mus. prg., NBC, 1935; WBIG, Greensboro, NC, 1936). In his broadcast performances Luther also played the harmonica, jews harp, ukulele and celeste. He was mostly on radio during the early 1930s and into the 1950s. Other programs on which he appeared were *I'll Never Forget* (singer), *The Life and Loves of Dr. Susan* (announcer) and *Your Lover* (conversation and songs).

19707 **Luther, John.** Sportscaster (*Pennzoil Sports Desk*, WERC, Erie, PA, 1960).

19708 **Luther, Paul.** Actor Luther was in the cast of *Backstage Wife* and *The Man Behind the Gun.*

19709 **Lutman, (Dr.) Thomas.** Dr. Lutman delivered inspirational lectures on such up beat topics as "How to Make Your Ship Come In" (KHJ, Los Angeles, CA, 1924).

19710 **Luton, (Mrs.) Horace.** Soprano (WLAC, Nashville, TN, 1929).

19711 **Lutz, Charles V.** Newscaster (WKRC, Cincinnati, OH, 1938–1939).

19712 **Lutzi, Gertrude.** Soprano (WKBW, Buffalo, NY, 1936–1937). Lutzi performed in 1937 on a program with violinist David Cheskin (WKBW, Buffalo, NY, 1937).

19713 **Lux, Lillian.** Soprano (WBNX, Bronx, NY, 1936).

19714 ***(The) Lux Radio Theatre.*** George Wells wrote motion picture and Broadway play adaptations for the program for almost ten years (1934–1944), establishing him as one of the best adaptors for radio. The *Lux Radio Theatre* was first broadcast in 1934 on the NBC network, originating from New York City under the direction of Antony Stanford. In its earliest version, Broadway stars were used in broadcasts of Broadway plays. The program took on the different format that made it famous in 1936, when it moved to Hollywood and was directed by Cecil B. DeMille. In the Hollywood format, radio versions of motion pictures were broadcast weekly featuring motion picture stars. DeMille's first program, *The Legionnaire and the Lady* (*Morocco*) with Clark Gable and Marlene Dietrich, was broadcast June 1, 1936.

DeMille's showmanship and the glamour of Hollywood made the program a national favorite that was said to attract some 40 million listeners weekly at the peak of its popularity. DeMille's casting indicates both his favorite actors and his flair as a showman. For instance, in relatively minor roles he would cast such famous people as Mary Garden, Jesse L. Lasky, Daniel Frohman and Theda Bara. Among the leading ladies who appeared most often on the program, Barbara Stanwyck had 15 appearances, and Claudette Colbert and Loretta Young tied with 14 starring roles. Don Ameche with 18 and Fred MacMurray with 17 leading roles led all male actors in appearances.

Although the program continued until 1955 with William Keighley and Irving Cummings acting as host, much of its glamour and verve disappeared when DeMille left in 1945. DeMille's departure was due to his refusal to accept something that was antagonistic to his beliefs. He gave up his position on the show that paid him almost $100,000 yearly to maintain his integrity. DeMille refused to contribute a dollar to his local AFRA (American Federation of Radio) union for the purpose of fighting a California election proposition that would create a "right to work" open shop law. Although the sponsor would have paid the dollar contribution for him, DeMille refused to allow them to make the contribution for him on principle. His refusal to contribute banned him from any further radio appearances, and the Lux Radio Theatre was never the same again although it continued on the air until 1955. Music for the program was provided by the Louis Silvers Orchestra (NBC, 1934–1936; CBS, 1936–1955).

19715 Luxford, Nola. Newscaster (*Four Star News*, NBC, 1939).

19716 *Luxury Shop.* Jurgens Lotion sponsored this summer replacement for the *Walter Winchell* program, a dramatic program that starred famous actress, Cornelia Otis Skinner (NBC, 1936).

19717 Lwoitz, William. Pianist (*William Lwoitz*, instr. mus. prg., WIP, Philadelphia, PA, 1936).

19718 Lybarger, Bruce. Violinist (WHO, Des Moines, IA, 1926).

19719 Lybarger, William. Sportscaster (WBRB, Red Bank, NJ, 1939).

19720 Lychenheim, Marion. Pianist (WJAZ, Chicago, IL, 1926).

19721 Lyle, Edith. Reader (KDKA, Pittsburgh, PA, 1924).

19722 Lyle, Gladys. Organist (WGH, Newport News, VA, 1942).

19723 Lyle, Robert. Newscaster (WLS, Chicago, IL, 1948).

19724 Lyles, Johnnie. DJ (*Blues, Bounce and Boogie*, KALB, Alexandria, LA, 1948).

19725 Lyles, O. Sportscaster (*Tops in Sports*, WHSC, Hartsville, SC, 1960).

19726 Lyman, Abe. Leader (Abe Lyman's Coconut Grove Orchestra, KNX, Los Angeles, CA, 1925–1926; Abe Lyman's Dance Orchestra, WABC-CBS, New York, NY, 1929; *Abe Lyman Orchestra*, instr. mus. prg., WNAC, Boston, MA, 1932; WMAQ, Chicago, IL, 1934; CBS, 1935–1938; WTAM , Cleveland, OH, 1936; NBC, 1937–1939; MBS, 1938; WLW, Cincinnati, OH, 1942).

19727 Lyman, Clara Oglesby. Organist (WHIO, Dayton, OH, 1936–1938).

19728 Lyman, Peter. Newscaster (KDAL, Duluth, MN, 1945).

19729 Lyn, Pel. Newscaster (WKAT, Miami Beach, FL, 1945).

19730 Lynady, Jean. COM-HE (WCDL, Carbondale, PA, 1957).

19731 Lynagh, James. Newscaster (WEEU, Reading, PA, 1945).

19732 Lynch, Bill. After beginning as a junior announcer (WOR, Newark, NJ; CBS, 1928), Lynch became prominent as an announcer when he helped cover Herbert Hoover's presidential inauguration for NBC in 1929.

19733 Lynch, Cecil. Newscaster (KTRB, Modesto, CA, 1939, 1944).

19734 Lynch, Charles T. DJ (*Platter Party*, WFGF, Kalamazoo, MI, 1947–1950).

19735 Lynch, Doris. COM-HE (KWSO, Wasco, CA, 1957).

19736 Lynch, Fred. West Coast radio tenor (KOMO, Seattle, WA, 1927–1928).

19737 Lynch, James "Jim." Lynch provided the sound effects for *The Goldbergs*, *Joe DiMaggio Show*, *Perry Mason* and *The Romance of Helen Trent*.

19738 Lynch, Kenneth "Ken." Actor Lynch was in the cast of *Backstage Wife*, *Bishop and the Gargoyle*, *Hap Harrigan*, *Portia Faces Life* and *Woman of America*.

19739 Lynch, Leo. Tenor (WNYC, New York, NY, 1925).

19740 Lynch, Mary. Singer and tap dancer on *The Farmer's Fiddler Hour* (WCFL, Chicago, IL, 1929).

19741 Lynch, Montgomery. Baritone (KOMO, Seattle, WA, 1928).

19742 Lynch, (Mrs.) Montgomery. Organist Montgomery played on the great organ of the First M.E. Church of Seattle (KJR, Seattle, WA, 1925–1926).

19743 Lynch, Patrick. Accordionist (WJY, New York, NY, 1925).

19744 Lynch, Peg. Writer-actress Lynch wrote and starred in the popular *Ethel and Albert* program. *See* ***Ethel and Albert***.

19745 Lynch, Rudd. Newscaster (CKLW, Detroit, MI and Ontario, Canada, 1946).

19746 Lynch, Steve. Singer (WWNC, Asheville, NC, 1929).

19747 Lynch, William S. Announcer (WOR, Newark, NJ and CBS, New York, NY, 1928).

19748 Lynd, Jane. COM-HE (WEAF, New York, NY, 1939).

19749 Lyndymond, Virginia. COM-HE (WSVA, Harrisonburg, VA, 1956).

19750 Lynker, John. DJ (WSKN, Saugerties, NY, 1957).

19751 Lynn, Andy. DJ (*Open House*, KAYL, Storm Lake, IA, 1952–1956).

19752 Lynn, Carol. COM-HE (WIRL, Peoria, IL, 1957).

19753 Lynn, Catherine "Kay." COM-HE (WIRL, Peoria, IL, 1957).

19754 Lynn, Fred. DJ (KWTO, Springfield, MO, 1954–1960).

19755 Lynn, Jane. COM-HE (WLW, Cincinnati, OH, 1954).

19756 Lynn, Janet. Singer (WAAF, Chicago, IL, 1938).

19757 Lynn, Kathryn. COM-HE (KFAL, Fulton, MO, 1957).

19758 Lynn, Loretta (Loretta Webb). CW singer. Loretta Webb was born in Butcher Holler, Kentucky in 1935. Although raised in a poor family, she was greatly influenced by the rich folk music she heard around her. Two years after she made her first recordings as Loretta Lynn, she was invited to join the *Grand Ole Opry*. Nationwide recognition soon followed. Her many honors and awards were well-deserved by this great country music artist. *See* **Singers**.

19759 Lynn, Lorna. Actress Lynn was in the cast of the *Brighter Day* daytime serial program.

19760 Lynn, Melda G. COM-HE (WBCM, Bay City, MI, 1954).

19761 Lynn, Merrie. COM-HE (KVOD, Denver, CO, 1954).

19762 Lynn, Peggy. COM-HE (WEST, Easton, PA, 1954).

19763 Lynn, (Mrs.) Ralph. COM-HE (WPLH, Huntington, WV, 1949).

19764 Lynn, S. Ken. DJ (*Ken Lynn Calling* and *Saturday Party*, WLW, Cincinnati, OH, 1948).

19765 *Lynn Murray.* Squibb Laboratories sponsored this transcribed show that featured the Lynn Murray chorus and orchestra (15 min., Transcribed, Weekly, 1944).

19766 *Lynne, Your Personal Shopper.* Miss Lynne supplied news about rationing and conservation for her World War II listeners. In addition, she offered to shop for those whose gas ration supply prevented them from driving to town to do their own (KIDO, Boise, ID, 1943).

19767 Lynton, Pelham. Newscaster (WKAT, Miami Beach, FL, 1941).

19768 Lyon, Charles "Charlie." Announcer Lyon worked on the *Curt Massey and Martha Tilton Show* and *Lassie* programs. Newscaster (WMAQ, Chicago, IL, 1942).

19769 Lyon, Eddie "Ed." Newscaster (KGGM, Albuquerque, NM, 1938; KTUL, Tulsa, OK, 1940–1942).

19770 Lyon, Eva Nora. Pianist (WAHG, Richmond Hill, NY, 1926).

19771 Lyon, Harry. Leader (Harry Lyon Orchestra, WNOX, Knoxville, TN, 1927).

19772 Lyon, Hartzell. Baritone (KMOX, St. Louis, MO, 1928).

19773 Lyon, (Dr.) J. Sproles. Dr. Lyon was minister of Atlanta's First Presbyterian Church. He made it possible for WSB to claim that it was the first station to broadcast a complete church service. Begun in 1922, the program's more than 50 year broadcast run made it the oldest continuous religious program in America (WSB, Atlanta, GA, 1922).

19774 Lyon, Jack. Organist (*Jack Lyon*, instr. mus. prg., WMBD, Peoria, IL, 1936).

19775 Lyon, Len. DJ (*Hillbilly Request*, KWCO, Chickasha, OK, 1947).

19776 Lyon, Leonard. Newscaster (KBST, Big Spring, TX, 1941).

19777 Lyon, Priscilla. Actress Lhyon was in the cast of the *Those We Love* daytime serial program.

19778 Lyon, Russ. Newscaster (WBCM, Bay City, MI, 1941).

19779 Lyon, Ruth. Soprano (WMBB, Homewood, IL and WOK, Chicago, IL, 1928; *Ruth Lyon*, vcl. mus. prg., WLW-NBC, Cincinnati, OH, 1935).

19780 Lyon, Ted. Newscaster (KWBG, Hutchinson, KS, 1939).

19781 Lyon and Healy. Organ recital team (WGN, Chicago, IL, 1926).

19782 Lyons, Al. Leader (*Al Lyons Orchestra*, instr. mus. prg., NBC, 1935).

19783 Lyons, Blanche Bliss. Soprano (WWJ, Detroit, MI, 1923).

19784 Lyons, Bob. DJ (*Florida Special*, KSDJ, San Diego, CA, 1947).

19785 Lyons, Bobby. Leader (*Bobby Lyons Orchestra*, instr. mus. prg., WHAM, Rochester, NY, 1938).

19786 Lyons, Eugene. Newscaster (WMCA, New York, NY, 1939).

19787 Lyons, Jim. Newscaster (KVOE, Santa Ana, CA, 1940–1941). Sportscaster (KVOE, 1940–1941).

19788 Lyons, Jimmy. DJ (*Disapades*, KSDJ, San Diego, CA, 1947; *Disapades*, KNBC, San Francisco, CA, 1949; *Disapades*, KGO, San Francisco, CA, 1952; KDON, Salinas, CA, 1955; KNBC, San Francisco, CA, 1956).

19789 Lyons, John. Newscaster (WSAR, Fall River, MA, 1945).

19790 Lyons, Mary Ann. COM-HE (WANS, Anderson, SC, 1960).

19791 Lyons, Mel. Pianist (KPO, San Francisco, CA, 1925).

19792 Lyons, Milton. Leader (*Milton Lyons Orchestra*, instr. mus. prg., WCAO, Baltimore, MD, 1935).

19793 Lyons, Robert. DJ (*1240 Club*, WHIZ, Zanesville, OH, 1947).

19794 Lyons, Ruth. COM-HE (WLW, Cincinnati, OH, 1949).

19795 Lyons, Sylvia D. Pianist (WEAF, New York, NY, 1926).

19796 Lyons, Tom. DJ (*Dancing in the Dark*, WJHL, Johnson City, TN, 1952). Sportscaster (WJHL, 1952–1955).

19797 Lyons, William. Harmonica soloist (WOC, Davenport, IA, 1928–1930). Newspapers called Lyons "a harmonicist."

19798 ***Lyons and Lyons Present.*** This variety show featured many vaudeville and theatrical stars weekly (30 min., Friday, 11:30–12:00 midnight, WOR, Newark, NJ, 1930).

19799 ***Lyric Challengers.*** The network series dramatized incidents in the lives of various great men. John S. Young was the program's announcer (NBC-Red, New York, NY, 1929).

19800 (*The*) *Lyric Duet.* The singing team of Norma Leyland and Alma Keller were a regular midnight feature on WMCA (New York, NY, 1926).

19801 (The) Lyric Quartet. Vocal group consisting of Sarah Peck, soprano; Jane Packham Alexander, contralto; Gilbert Morris, tenor; and baritone Almet B. Jenkinson. They were accompanied by Agnes P. Schaffer (KDKA, Pittsburgh, PA, 1923).

19802 Lyser, Herbert. Newscaster (KFOR, San Francisco, CA, 1938).

19803 Lytell, Bill. Actor Lytell was in the cast of *Just Plain Bill.*

19804 Lytle, Ed. Newscaster (WHAM, Rochester, NY, 1942).

19805 Lytle, Harry. Sportscaster (WMAN, Mansfield, OH, 1942).

19806 Lytton, Ed. Baritone (WHO, Des Moines, IA, 1925).

19807 ***M.A. Gospel Singers.*** The Black gospel singing group consisted of R.D. Rogers, Ozell Webster, Silas Hughes, Will Rodgers, Andrew Keely, Nathaniel Breakenridge, Roosevelt Webster and Roosevelt Muse (WMPS, Memphis, TN, 1946).

19808 ***Ma and Pa.*** Parker Fennelly and Margaret Dee were featured in the title roles as a Cape Cod couple who operate a sandwich shop in this dramatic sketch. First heard on CBS as a weekly half-hour show (30 min., Sunday, 4:00–4:30 P.M. CST, CBS, 1936), the following year it became a quarter-hour show broadcast five times a week (15 min., Five times weekly, CBS, 1937).

19809 ***Ma Fraser's Boarding House.*** The weekly dramatic serial told the story of a group of people living at Ma Fraser's boarding house (15 min., 6:30–6:45 P.M., WGY, Schenectady, NY, 1934).

19810 ***Ma Perkins*** **(aka *Oxydol's Own Ma Perkins*).** "Oxydol's [soap powder] own *Ma Perkins*" was one of the best remembered and respected daytime serial dramas. The program featured two radio performers, whose record for longevity in a single role has never been challenged. During the entire 27 years the program was on the air with its 7,065 broadcasts, the roles of Ma Perkins and her son-in-law, Willie, were played by Virginia Payne and Murray Forbes. Almost as remarkable, the role of Ma's old friend, Shuffle, was played by Charles Egleston for 25 years. Notable, too, is the fact that Oxydol sponsored the show for its entire broadcast. Kindly and wise Ma helped her family and many friends through long years of tensions and troubles.

The program's cast included: Casey Allen, Rita Ascot, Clare Baum, Cheer Brentson, Jack Brinkley, Herbert Butterfield, Kay Campbell, Fran Carlon, Maurice Copeland, Constance Crowder, Mary Frances Desmond, Nancy Douglass, Margaret Draper, Barry Drew, Patricia Dunlap, Charles Egleston, Bobby Ellis, Gilbert Faust, Laurette Fillbrandt, Louise Fitch, Murray Forbes, Margaret Fuller, Don Gallagher, Rene Gekiere, Earl George, Stanley Gordon, Betty Hanna, Marjorie Hannan, Joe Helgeson, Wilma Herbert, Jonathan Hole, Fred Howard, Dora Johnson, Carl Kroenke, Ray Largay, John Larkin, Billy Lee, Sylvia Leigh, Forrest Lewis, Helen Lewis, Judith Lockser, DeWitt McBride, Stuart McIntosh, McKay Morris, Dolph Nelson, Marilou Neumayer, Angeline Orr, Virginia Payne, Jack Petruzzi, Glen Ransom, Mary Marren Rees, Curtis Roberts, Elmira Roessler, Bill Rose, Cecil Roy, Rye Billsbury, Nanette Sargent, Ray Suber, Dan Sutter, Les Tremayne, Beryl Vaughn, Duke Watson, Stanley Waxman, Lillian White, Edwin Wolfe, Arthur Young and Beverly Younger. The producer was Lester Vail and Doc Whipple the organist and music director. Robert Hardy Andrews was the creator and Lee Gebhart, Lester Huntley, Natalie Johnson and Orin Tovrov were the writers. The program's directors were Philip Bowman, George Fogle, Roy Winsor and Edwin Wolfe. The announcers were Jack Brinkley, Dan Donaldson, Marvin Miller and Dick Wells.

19811 Maar, Gene. DJ (*Youth Today*, KGDN, Edmonds, WA, 1960).

19812 Maas, Bill. DJ (*Tea Time Tunes*, WBAA, West Lafayette, IN, 1947).

19813 Maas, Don. DJ (*1450 Club*, KSEM, Moses Lake, WA, 1948).

19814 ***Mabel at the Music Counter.*** Blues singer and pianist Corinne Jordan starred on her entertaining music show (KSTP, St. Paul, MN, 1928). Jordan was also the station's program director.

19815 Mabie, Beatrice. COM-HE (WJZ, New York, NY, 1932).

19816 Mable, Kit. COM-HE (WBNR, Beacon, NY, 1960).

19817 Mably, Elsie Addison. Contralto (WGY, Schenectady, NY, 1927).

19818 Mabry, Bob. DJ (*All Hit Request Program*, WIBG, Philadelphia, PA, 1947).

19819 Mabry, Dick. DJ (*A Man and his Music*, WIBG, Philadelphia, PA, 1947–1948).

19820 Mabry, Joe. Sportscaster (WHUB, Cookeville, TN, 1940–1942). Newscaster (WHUB, 1946).

19821 Mac, Billy. Sportscaster (WBML, Macon, GA, 1941).

19822 Mac, Kim DJ (WACT, Tuscaloosa, AL, 1960).

19823 ***Mac and Bob*** **(Lester McFarland and Robert A. Gardner).** McFarland and Gardner, blind singers and musicians, were extremely popular CW music performers (15 min., Daily, including Sunday, 9:15–9:30 A.M., KDKA, Pittsburgh, PA, 1935). They also appeared on a South Carolina station among many others (KFBC, Greenville, SC, 1937). On 1925 they appeared on WNOX (Knoxville, TN, 1925) and joined the *National Barn Dance* (WLW, Chicago, 1931). *See* **McFarland, Lester and Robert A. Gardner.**

19824 Mac and Gert. Harmony singing team (WENR-WBCN, Chicago, IL, 1928).

19825 ***Mac and His Gang.*** CW mus. prg. conducted by Harry "Mac" McClintock (KFRC, San Francisco, CA, 1927). *See* **McClintock, Harry Kirby "Mac."**

19826 ***Mac Round the Campfire.*** CW mus. prg. conducted by Harry "Mac" McClintock (KFRC, San Francisco, CA, 1925). *See* **McClintock, Harry Kirby "Mac."**

19827 MacAide, Virginia. COM-HE (WICH, Norwich, CT. 1960).

19828 MacAllister, Charles. Actor MacAllister was in the cast of *Dr. Kate.*

19829 MacArthur, Lee. Newscaster (KIEV, Glendale, CA, 1941).

19830 MacArthur, Peter. Announcer known as the "Scotsman Perfecto" (WOC, Davenport, IA, 1925–1928).

19831 MacAteer, Alan. Actor MacAteer was in the cast of *Backstage Wife* and *Lora Lawton.*

19832 Macauley, Ed. Sportscaster (WEW, St. Louis, MO, 1952).

19833 MacAuley, Paul R. Sportscaster (KOKO, La Junta, CO, 1941).

19834 Macbeth, Alex C. Sportscaster (WLAW, Lawrence, MA, 1939; WCCM, Lawrence, MA, 1949–1950).

19835 MacBeth, W.W. Harmonica virtuoso (WFAA, Dallas, TX, 1924).

19836 MacBride, Doris. COM-HE (KEYY, Pocatello, ID, 1949).

19837 MacBryde, John "Jack." Actor MacBryde was in the cast of *Amanda of Honeymoon Hill*, *Death Valley Days* (played "The Old Ranger"), *Eno Crime Club*, *Peewee and Windy*, *Texaco Star Theater* and *Young Widder Brown.*

19838 MacCallum, Boone. News analyst (*Tell It to the Judge*, KFXJ, Grand Junction, CO, 1948).

19839 MacClain, Leonard. Organist (*Melody Mac*, instr. mus. prg., WCAU, Philadelphia, PA, 1936).

19840 MacCue, Beatrice. Contralto (WEAF, New York, NY, 1925).

19841 MacCullough, Bess. COM-HE (WHLS, Port Huron, MI, 1954).

19842 MacDill, Wilfred. Sportscaster (WTAD, Quincy, IL, 1939).

19843 MacDonald, Angus. Baritone (WBZ, Boston-Springfield, MA, 1925).

19844 MacDonald, Avis. Vibraphone soloist (KYW, Portland, OR, 1928).

19845 MacDonald, Bill. Newscaster (KFAB, Omaha-Lincoln, NE, 1945).

19846 MacDonald, Bruce. Newscaster (WJW, Cleveland, OH, 1946).

19847 MacDonald, Claudine. Newscaster (NBC, 1933).

19848 MacDonald, Dolly. *See* **McDonald, Dolly.**

19849 MacDonald, Donald. Tenor (WJAR, Providence, RI, 1925).

19850 MacDonald, Dorothy. COM-HE (WRFC, Athens, GA, 1954).

19851 MacDonald, Ed. Actor MacDonald was in the cast of *Aunt Jenny* and *Big Town.*

19852 MacDonald, George. Sportscaster (*Sports Hilites*, KAVR, Havre, MT, 1950; *Radio Sportpage*, KBIO, Burley, ID, 1952).

19853 MacDonald, Gerry. COM-HE (WCBY, Cheboygan, MI, 1954).

19854 MacDonald, Jean. Teenage pianist MacDonald played duets with her brother (WBBM, Chicago, IL, 1925).

19855 MacDonald, John. Weatherman (*John MacDonald—Yankee Weatherman,* WNAC-Yankee Network, Boston, MA, 1947).

19856 MacDonald, Margaret. Actress MacDonald was in the daytime serial program's cast of the *Life Begins* aka *Martha Webster.*

19857 MacDonald, Marie. COM-HE (KFBI, Wichita, KS, 1949).

19858 MacDonald, Ray. Tenor (KJBS, San Francisco, CA, 1925).

19859 MacDonald, Sandy. DJ (*Sunny Side Up*, WGAT, Gate City, VA, 1960).

19860 MacDonnell, Dan. Newscaster (CBS, 1944).

19861 MacDougall, Bertha. Mezzo-soprano (KSTP, St. Paul, MN, 1929).

19862 MacDougall, John. Newscaster (WLOL, Minneapolis, MN, 1945).

19863 MacDougall, Ranald. Writer MacDougall wrote *Man Behind the Gun, Passport for Adams* and *There was a Woman.*

19864 MacDougall, William. Scots singer-comedian (KFI, Los Angeles, CA, 1925–1926).

19865 MacDowell, Bert. Leader (*Bert MacDowell Orchestra,* instr. mus. prg., KYW, Pittsburgh, 1932).

19866 MacDowell, Peggy. COM-HE (WHFB, Benton Harbor, MI, 1949).

19867 (The) MacDowell Quartet. Vocal group including soprano Caroline Bracey; contralto Mrs. L. Wallace Ohl; tenor Arthur Ray Davis; and bass Clair Anderson. The director-accompanist was Lyman Almy Perkins assisted by violinist Pierre de Backer (KDKA, Pittsburgh, PA, 1924).

19868 Mace, Alice. Pianist (KMOX, St. Louis, MO, 1928).

19869 Mace, Max. DJ (WMRB, Greenville, SC, 1956).

19870 Mace, Ray. Leader (*Ray Mace Orchestra*, instr. mus. prg., WBEN, Buffalo, NY, 1942).

19871 MacEachron, Peg. COM-HE (WQXT, Palm Beach, FL, 1957).

19872 MacFarlane, David L. Newscaster (KTSW, Emporia, KS, 1944).

19873 MacFarlane, Margaret. Mezzo-soprano (WBZ, Springfield, MA, 1925).

19874 MacFerran, J.D. Assistant announcer and publicity man MacFerran was known as "Radio Mac" (WMBB, Homewood, IL and WOK, Chicago, IL, 1928).

19875 MacGinsey, Bob. Famous whistler who appeared on the *Empire Builders* program (WJZ, New York, NY, 1929).

19876 MacGregor, Evelyn. Mezzo-soprano (WCDA, New York, NY, 1929).

19877 MacGregor, J.C. Newscaster (KOB, Albuquerque, NM, 1939–1940).

19878 MacGregor, Joan. COM-HE (WCSS, Amsterdam, NY, 1949).

19879 MacGregor, Jock. Director-producer-writer MacGregor worked on *Brownstone Theater* (director), *Cisco Kid* (director), *Mysterious Traveler* (director), *Nick Carter, Master Detective* (producer-writer-director) and *Strange Dr. Weird.*

19880 MacGregor, Kenneth W. "Ken." Actor MacGregor appeared on *Archie Andrews, Chicago Theater of the Air, City Desk, Grand Ole Opry, Mystery Theater, Palmolive Beauty Box Theater, Show Boat, Thanks to the Yanks* and *When a Girl Marries.*

19881 MacGregor, R.J. News analyst (*City Hall*, WFBR, Baltimore, MD, 1947).

19882 Machado's KLX Hawaiians Orchestra. Local music group (KLX, Oakland, CA, 1929).

19883 MacHarrie, Lindsay. Born in 1900, MacHarrie was a multi-talented announcer, actor, writer, producer and director, who worked primarily on Pacific Coast radio. He began work at KHJ, Los Angeles, CA, in 1928 and soon thereafter became the chief announcer and continuity writer at the station (1929–1930). Among the national network programs on which he worked were *House of Glass* (director) and *Second Mrs. Burton* (producer).

19884 Machetti, Tilda. Soprano (KFI, Los Angeles, CA, 1925).

19885 Macias [Macia], Pete. Leader (Pete Macias L'Aiglon Orchestra, a popular Washington, D.C., dance band, WRC, Washington, DC, 1924; *Pete Macias Orchestra*, instr. mus. prg., WMAL, Washington, DC, 1936).

19886 MacIntyre, Dorothy. Pianist (WJAR, Providence, RI, 1925).

19887 Mack, Ann. Soprano (WDAF, Kansas City, MO, 1926).

19888 Mack, Austin. Leader (*Austin Mack Orchestra*, instr. mus. prg., WBBM, Chicago, IL, 1935–1937).

19889 Mack, Beatrice. Soprano (NBC, 1936).

19890 Mack, Bernie. DJ (*Radio Juke Box* and *Groovin' at the Grove*, WMUR, Manchester, NH, 1947).

19891 Mack, Bill. DJ (*The Bill Mack Show*, KWFT, Wichita Falls, TX, 1949; KLTI, Longview, TX, 1956).

19892 Mack, Bill. Newscaster (WEDC, Chicago, IL, 1945–1946). DJ (*Hot and Bothered*, WEDC, 1947; *Stomp Time*, WEDC, 1948; *Denemark Music Time*, WEDC, 1949; *Hot and Bothered* WEDC, 1950–1957).

19893 Mack, Billie. Leader (Billie Mack Orchestra, KPRC, Houston, TX, 1926).

19894 Mack, Bruce. DJ (*Night Owl Club*, KOSA, Odessa, TX, 1947).

19895 Mack, Ellyn. COM-HE (KBUR, Burlington, IA, 1954–1955).

19896 Mack, Floyd. Newscaster (NBC, MBS, 1942).

19897 Mack, Harry. Chief announcer (WNJ, Newark, NJ, 1925).

19898 Mack, Helen. Actress Mack appeared on the *Myrt and Marge* daytime serial program.

19899 Mack, Jack. DJ (*Country Store*, WULA, Eufaula, AL, 1948).

19900 Mack, Jim. DJ (*Yawnin' in the Morning*, WHFB, Benton Harbor, MI, 1947–1948; *Matinee at 1060*, WHFB, 1948–1949).

19901 Mack, Jimmie. Jimmie Mack was a teller of "humorous tales" (KNX, Los Angeles, CA, 1926; KTAB, Oakland, CA, 1926). .

19902 Mack, Johnny. Known as "Uncle Jay of WJAY." *Radio Digest* (December 1, 1927) said Mack was the "first radio Santa Claus in Pittsburgh" (WJAY, Pittsburgh, PA, 1927).

19903 Mack, Lois. COM-HE (WWKY, Winchester, KY, 1955).

19904 Mack, Nila. Producer-direct (CBS, 1940s-1950s). One of radio's most outstanding producers and directors of children's programs, Mack's major contribution was her *Let's Pretend* program. She gave up a promising dramatic career to write, produce and direct the program. Mack auditioned 25 children weekly for each program and had a permanent working list of 50. She also was the producer-director of the *Mrs. Miniver* program.

19905 Mack, Pete. Leader (*Pete Mack Moosickers*, instr. mus. prg., NBC, 1935–1936).

19906 Mack, Robert. Leader (*Robert Mack Orchestra*, instr. mus. prg., WCAU, Philadelphia, PA, 1936). Vocalist (*Robert Mack*, vcl. mus. prg., WCAU, 1936).

19907 Mack, Russell. DJ (*The Musical Clock*, KROD, El Paso, TX, 1947).

19908 Mack, Wally. Film news commentator (*Movie and News Views*, WBBB, Burlington, NC, 1948). DJ (*Jive at Five*, WBBB, 1948; *Music from Graham*, WBBB, 1950; *Dawnbusters*, WFNS, Burlington, NC, 1950; *Dawnbusters*, WBUY, Lexington, NC, 1954).

19909 Mack, Wayne. Newscaster (WGAR, Cleveland, OH, 1940–1942).

19910 MacKay, Florence. Pianist (KOA, Denver, CO, 1926).

19911 MacKay, Sadie. Soprano (WTIC, Hartford, CT, 1927).

19912 MacKaye, Frederic. Actor MacKaye was in the cast of *Brent House.*

19913 MacKenzie [McKenzie], Ed. MacKenzie was a DJ who conducted the *Jack the Bellboy* program (110 min., Monday through Saturday, 3:30–5:20 P.M., WJBK, Detroit, MI, 1947–1950; *Record Matinee*, WXYZ, Detroit, MI, 1954–1957). *Variety* said he was very popular with Detroit's bobby soxers.

19914 MacKenzie, Honey. Actress MacKenzie was a cast member of the *Married Life of Helen and Warren* daytime serial program.

19915 MacKenzie, Jock. Sportscaster (*Sports Parade*, KYJC, Medford, OR, 1950).

19916 MacKenzie, Joseph C. Baritone (WBZ, Boston-Springfield, MA, 1924).

19917 MacKenzie, Margaret. Soprano (WAAM, Newark, NJ, 1925).

19918 MacKenzie, Pat. COM-HE (WNDU, South Bend, IN, 1960).

19919 *MacKenzie River Ranch.* Hal O'Halloran and his Rangers supplied the music on the CW music program sponsored by the MacKenzie Milling Company (Monday through Friday, 15 min., 6:15–6:30 A.M., CST, WLS, Chicago, IL, 1936).

19920 MacKercher, John. Newscaster (WMMN, Fairmont, WV, 1942).

19921 Mackie, Alice. Soprano (WOR, Newark, NJ, 1924).

19922 Mackie, Jeanette. COM-HE (WFIE, Evansville, IN, 1956).

19923 MacKinnon, Alice. Soprano (WBZ, Springfield, MA, 1926).

19924 Mackintosh, Gloria. COM-HE (KULE, Ephrata, WA, 1960).

19925 MacKnight, John. Newscaster (WDGY, Minneapolis–St. Paul, MN, 1942).

19926 MacKown, Marjorie Truelove. Pianist (WTAM, Cleveland, OH, 1928).

19927 MacKrell, (Reverend) James. MacKrell, who formerly conducted the station's *Uncle Mac* radio programs for children, later conducted religious programs that attracted thousands of listeners. He set a record by sending out 350 Bibles in one day and receiving mail from 36 states in response to his program. During this time, MacKrell was the pastor of the Scott, Arkansas, All Souls Community Church. His program was broadcast by KLRA (Little Rock, AR, 1939). *See* ***Uncle Mac's Booster Club*** *and* ***Uncle Mac Reads the Comics.***

19928 MacLaclan, Marguerite. Violinist (KFAE, Pullman, WA, 1925).

19929 MacLaughlin, Don. Actor MacLaughlin was in the cast of *Chaplain Jim* (title role), *Counterspy* (title role), *Ethel and Albert, Gangbusters, Road of Life, Romance of Helen Trent, Tennessee Jed* (title role) and *We Love and Learn.*

19930 MacLean, Alice. Lyric soprano (WOMO, Seattle, WA, 1927–1928).

19931 MacLean, Jean. DJ (*Mystery Music Shop*, KBIO, Burley, ID, 1947; *It's Up to You* and *The 1240 Club*, KAVR, Havre, MT, 1948; KGAE, Salem, OR, 1955).

19932 MacLean, John. Newscaster (WHEC, Rochester, NY, 1944).

19933 Maclee, Gerry. COM-HE (KGMC, Englewood, CO, 1960).

19934 MacLeod, Duncan. Newscaster (KALE, Portland, OR, 1940).

19935 MacLeod, Leslie. Ukulele soloist (WGCP, Newark, NJ, 1925).

19936 MacMahon, Tom. Newscaster (WWJ, Detroit, MI, 1948).

19937 MacMasters, Dan. Newscaster (WWNY, Watertown, NY, 1941–1942).

19938 MacMillan, Conchita. Soprano (WRC, Washington, DC, 1925).

19939 MacMillan, (Mrs.) George W. Soprano (KGO, Oakland, CA, 1924).

19940 MacMillan, Lowell H. Announcer (WGR, Buffalo, NY, 1925). Sportscaster (WHEC, Rochester, NY, 1939–1941, 1945–1947; *Gulf Sports Reporting*, WHEC, 1948; *Sports Roundup*, WHEC, 1949–1951; *Sports Reporter*, WHEC, 1952).

19941 MacMillen, Don. News analyst (*Radio Extra*, KCSJ, Pueblo, CO, 1948).

19942 MacMurray, Frederick. Violinist (KHJ, Los Angeles, CA, 1926).

19943 MacMurray, Phil. Newscaster (KECA-KFI, Los Angeles, CA, 1941).

19944 MacMurray, Ted. Director MacMurray directed *Guiding Light* and *Lone Journey.*

19945 MacNeil, Marion. COM-HE (WERI, Westerly, RI, 1949).

19946 Macon, David Harrison "Uncle Dave." Legendary singer-banjoist Macon appeared regularly on the *Grand Ole Opry* from his first appearance on the WSM *Barn Dance*, which later became the *Grand Ole Opry*, in 1927 until shortly before his death in 1952. Before his radio appearances, Uncle Dave had appeared in vaudeville and traveled with medicine shows (WSM, Nashville, TN, 1925; *Uncle Dave Macon*, CW mus. prg., WSM, 1937). On the latter program, Uncle Dave was accompanied by his son Dorris and the Possum Hunters music group. *See* ***The Grand Ole Opry.***

19947 Macpeake, Agnes. Soprano (WHN, New York, NY, 1924).

19948 Macpherson, Fred. News commentator (*The Editor Looks at the News*, KOY, Phoenix, AZ, 1948).

19949 Macpherson, John. Cooking commentator Macpherson dispensed cooking information and advice as "The Mystery Chef." He was always pictured wearing a black mask. His program *The Mystery Chef* was sponsored by Davis Baking Powder Company and broadcast on both the NBC Red and Blue networks at various times between 1929 and 1938. *See* ***The Mystery Chef.***

19950 MacPherson, Olive. Pianist (WBZ, Springfield, MA, 1925).

19951 MacPherson, Olive Marty. Soprano (WPG, Atlantic City, NJ, 1925).

19952 MacPherson, Stewart. Sportscaster (WCCO, Minneapolis, MN, 1950).

19953 MacRae, Johnny. DJ (*Rise and Shine*, WABI, Bangor, ME, 1947).

19954 MacRae, Johnny. Sportscaster (*Highlights on Sports*, WTSB, Lumberton, NC, 1947).

19955 Macrae, Kay. Coloratura soprano (WMCA, New York, NY, 1925; WGBS, New York, NY, 1925).

19956 Macredie, (Mrs.) George. Macredie and Mrs. Roy Nol were a piano duet team (WCAE, Pittsburgh, PA, 1924).

19957 *Mac's Haywire Band.* CW mus. prg. with a band led by Mac McClintock (KFRC, San Francisco, CA, 1927). *See* **McClintock, Harry Kirby "Mac."**

19958 Maculay, Dick. Announcer (WHAD, Milwaukee, WI, 1925).

19959 MacVane, John. Newscaster (NBC, 1942, 1945–1948).

19960 MacWhorter, (Reverend) Gardner A. Conducted chapel services (KYW, Chicago, IL, 1923).

19961 MacWilliams, Don. Sportscaster (*Sports Journal*, WCSH, Portland, ME, 1950–1960).

19962 Macy, G. Underhill. Entertainer Macy was well known for his work in vaudeville, musical comedy and light opera. He starred in such programs as the *Co Co Couriers* and *Hank Simmons' Showboat* (CBS, New York, NY, 1929).

19963 Macy, Jerry. Actor Macy was in the cast of *Right to Happiness* and *Valiant Lady.*

19964 Macy, Marty. COM-HE (KONP, Port Angeles, WA, 1949).

19965 Macy, Olma. COM-HE (WHMA, Anniston, AL, 1960).

19966 (The) Mad Irishman. DJ (WIMS (Michigan City, IN, 1949). The identity of the Mad One was not identified.

19967 *Madame Marie.* An otherwise unidentified performer who broadcast beauty talks (KNX, Los Angeles, CA, 1929).

19968 *Madame Nadya Olyanova.* Madame Olyanova was an extremely popular "graphologist psychologist." Her billing was both unusual and unbelievable (MBS, 1935).

19969 *Madame Sylvia.* The Madame was "Hollywood's beauty expert." She gave beauty information and tips to her audience and also interviewed movie star guests (15 min., Tuesday, 10:30–10:45 P.M. NBC, 1933).

19970 Madame Zelaine. Fortune teller (WCAX, Burlington, VT, 1942).

19971 Madden, George S. Baritone (WJZ, New York, NY, 1922).

19972 Madden, Gertrude. COM-HE (WWPA, Williamsport, PA, 1956–1957).

19973 Madden, William J. Leader (*William Madden Concert Orchestra*, instr. mus. prg., WPG, Atlantic City, NJ, 1934; WIP, Philadelphia, PA, 1935).

19974 Maddock, Zelda. Pianist (WHB, Kansas City, MO, 1926).

19975 Maddox, Bill. DJ (KBHS, Hot Springs National Park, AR, 1960).

19976 Maddox, Dean. Sportscaster (KROW, Oakland, CA, 1941). Newscaster (KFRC, San Francisco, CA, 1942).

19977 Maddox, Kathy. DJ (WMCK, McKeesport, PA, 1956–1957).

19978 Maddox, Lois. Singer (WPAR, Parkersburg, WV, 1937).

19979 Maddox, Mari-Lou. COM-HE (WROY, Carmi, IL, 1951).

19980 Maddox Brothers and Rose. CW family band featuring vocalist sister Rose. The group's early station broadcasts included those on KTRB (Modesto, CA, 1937); KFBK (Sacramento, CA, 1939; and KGDM (Stockton, CA, 1945). They played on the *Grand Ole Opry* (WSM, Nashville, TN, 1956–1957). *See* **Singers.**

19981 Maddux, Pee Wee. DJ (WVMI, Biloxi, MS, 1956).

19982 Madison, Bob. DJ (*Sunrise Serenade*, WMAW, Milwaukee, WI, 1948).

19983 Madison, Larry. DJ (*Larry's Roundtable*, KVRS, Rock Springs, WY, 1948).

19984 Madison, Peggy. Vocalist (*Peggy Madison*, vcl. mus. prg., WIP, Philadelphia, PA, 1936).

19985 Madison, Thurber. Violinist (WEMC, Berrien Springs, MI, 1926).

19986 *Madison Singers.* A weekly choral music program (30 min., Sunday, 10:00–10:30 P.M., CBS, 1933).

19987 Madley, Madge. Singer (NBC, 1935).

19988 *(The) Madrigal Club of San Francisco.* Choral music program directed by Maynard S. Jones with first sopranos Carmen Brock, Josephine Carberry, Lillian Evans, Helen Crombie, Millie Mills and Mary Rochefort; second sopranos Vita M. Jones, Mae Spurgeon, Minnie Wragby, Dora Slater; and altos Elizabeth Scully. Amy Butler, Kate Dobbin, Margaret Leckey, Evelyn Leckey and Ilyeen Remeck (KPO, San Francisco, CA, 1927).

19989 Madriguera, Enrique (Enric). Leader (*Enric Madriguera Orchestra*, instr. mus. prg., NBC, 1935; MBS, 1936).

19990 Madsen, Connie. COM-HE (KSID, Sidney, NE, 1957).

19991 Madsen, Harold. Singer Madsen was an original member of the Nifty Three Trio and a cast member of the Broadway musical "Just a Minute," before taking a position as staff vocalist at station KOIL (Council Bluffs, IA, 1929–1930). Before joining KOIL, Madsen had also played trumpet with several popular dance orchestras.

19992 Madson's Midshipmen Dance Orchestra. Local dance band (KGO, Oakland, CA, 1926).

19993 Mae, Helene. Soprano (*Helene Mae*, vcl. mus. prg., NBC, 1935).

19994 Maegle, Eleanor. Violinist (KFSG, Los Angeles, CA, 1925).

19995 Maehl, Charles. Pianist (KSD, St. Louis, MO, 1923).

19996 *Maestro's Hour.* Instr. mus. prg. with Cesare Sodero's Orchestra, contralto Alma Kitchell, soprano Astride Fjelda, tenor Guiseppe de Benedetto and basso Theodore Webb (NBC-Blue, 1929).

19997 *(The) Magazine Rack.* An educational program that focused on the content of current magazines, *The Magazine Rack* originated in 1936 at WOI, the Iowa State University's station. The program was re-broadcast by WSUI, the State University of Iowa's station.

19998 Magee, George. News commentator (WINS, New York, NY, 1939).

19999 Magee, Jackie. COM-HE (WCOH, Newman, GA, 1960).

20000 Maggio, Charles. Leader (Charles Maggio's Irwana Dance Orchestra, KFWI, San Francisco, CA, 1929).

20001 Maggio, Joe. DJ (*Musical Merry-Go-Round, Six to Seven Club* and *The Little Show*, KIDO, Boise, ID, 1947–1950).

20002 Maggio, Theresa. Singer (WBRY, Waterbury, CT, 1937).

20003 *(The) Magic Hour.* A transcribed music show, *The Magic Show* was broadcast five times weekly. The featured singers were Jane Pickens, Virginia Rea, Connie Boswell and Conrad Thibault. Dave Rubinoff, his violin and orchestra, supplied the music (15 min., Tuesday, Thursday and Saturday, 8:15–8:30 A.M. CST and 15 min., Wednesday and Friday, 11:15–11:30 A.M., CST, WLS, Chicago, IL, 1935).

20004 *Magic Island.* The opening of the syndicated adventure story transcribed in the 1930s explained its plot: "A wealthy and beautiful California woman, Mrs. Patricia Gregory, has spent 14 years searching the world over for her little daughter, Joan Gregory. Fourteen years ago, Mrs. Gregory, her husband and baby daughter were shipwrecked in the South Pacific. Everyone on board was believed lost except Mrs. Gregory. But she has always felt that her little girl was also saved. This belief has caused Mrs. Gregory to offer a large reward for news of any young, white girl found in the south sea islands, who might prove to be her daughter. Fourteen years she has waited in vain. But now the story begins in Los Angeles." Needless to say, the story became complex and filled with many dangers (15 min., Transcribed, Many Stations, 1930s).

20005 *(The) Magic Key* (aka *The Magic Key of RCA* or *The Magic Key of Radio*). NBC used this quality program to demonstrate the cultural contribution radio could make. Although popular entertainment was stressed, many classical musicians and vocalists were also featured. Among the performers that appeared were: Ruth Etting, Fibber McGee and Molly, John B. Kennedy, Rudolf Ganz, the Frank Black orchestra, harpist Casper Beardon, Paul Robeson, Jane Froman, Doris Weston, Frank Forrest, Paul Taylor Chorus, harpist Margaret Brill, Rudy Vallee, Irving Berlin, Darryl Zanuck, Jan Peerce, Tommy Dorsey, Jack Harris orchestra, Ann Jamieson, Sonja Henie, Tyrone Power, Walter Abel, Whitney Bern and George Shelley. Milton Cross and Ben Grauer were the announcers (60 min., Sunday, 2:00–3:00 P.M., NBC-Red, 1935–1939).

The National Broadcasting Company (1935) described the quality program this way:

> Famous stars and entertainers of the radio, stage and screen, and musicians of opera, symphony, the concert and the dance will be starred in a new series of Sunday matinee programs to be inaugurated over an NBC-WJZ network on Sunday, September 29, at 2:00 P.M., EST.
>
> The artists will be "co-featured" with technical developments in broadcasting, in receiving and long distance transmission equipment, in motion pictures and in recording under the sponsorship of the Radio Corporation of America. The series is to be known as *The Magic Key of RCA.*
>
> The full hour broadcast will be an "RCA Family" program. The talent to be presented will include broadcast stars from NBC, recording artists of RCA Victor and screen stars known to the public through the medium of RCA sound picture equipment. Their broadcasts will be available to the entire world through the world-wide communication facilities of RCA. Some of the broadcasts will be picked up from foreign countries and from ships at sea. The coast-to-coast NBC-WJZ network will include stations in Canada and the westernmost NBC affiliate KGU in Honolulu, Hawaii.
>
> The series will present such outstanding artists as Kirsten Flagstad, Lauritz Melchoir, Lotte Lehmann, Helen Jepson and Giovanni Martinelli of the Metropolitan Opera Company; the Boston and Philadelphia symphony orchestras; Paul Whiteman and his orchestra; John B. Kennedy, NBC commentator; Albert Spalding, violinist; Dr. Walter Damrosch and Dr. Frank Black conductors; Conrad Thibault, baritone; and Fats Waller. There will be an array of stage, screen and radio favorites. The list of dance bands will include those of Ray Noble, Richard Himber, Benny Goodman, Enric Madriquera, Jan Garber, Jolly Coburn and Xavier Cugat.
>
> Among those definitely scheduled to participate in the inaugural broadcast on September 29 will be Dr. Damrosch, Frank Black, Paul Whiteman and John B. Kennedy. Others will be announced at an early date. Kennedy will act as master of ceremonies and introduce the stars who will parade before the microphone during the series. A new group will be heard each week.
>
> The "Magic Key" used as the title of the broadcast signifies radio knowledge, research and experience, which has unlocked the doors through which the talent of these artists, in broadcasting and the allied arts of phonograph and the sound motion picture, reaches a vast audience.
>
> The "co-starring" of radio development and facilities in the "Magic Key" series will come incidentally in the quality of the broadcast and reception facilities in the ease with which radio reaches out to the world. The fact that a famous artist happens to be half way around the globe will be no handicap to his appearing as a headliner, brought in on short wave by RCA Communications, Inc.

20006 *(The) Magic Kitchen.* Jane Porter conducted the popular St. Louis cooking program (KMOX, St. Louis, MO, 1934).

20007 *Magic Mirror.* Donald Novis and the Ted Royal Orchestra were featured on the Wednesday evening music program (CBS, 1936).

20008 *Magic Moments.* A variety show, sponsored by Borden Company, *Magic Moments* combined music and comedy with cooking tips provided by Jane Ellison. Marcella Shields and Frank Scanlon supplied comedy and the piano team of Pollock and Lawnhurst the music (15 min., Thursday, 10:45–11:00 A.M., NBC, 1933).

20009 *Magic of Romance.* Eddie Duchin's orchestra and the vocals of Stanley Worth were featured on the music show (30 min., Weekly, 8:00–8:30 P.M., NBC-Blue, 1938).

20010 *Magic of Speech.* Begun in 1925, the self-improvement program featured speech and diction authority Vida Ravenscroft Sutton broadcasting hints on how to improve voice and speech habits. The program was broadcast on the NBC network from 1929 to 1937. The 1927–1929 program was broadcast weekly (15 min., Thursday, 3:15–3:30 P.M., NBC-WEAF, 1927–1929).

When Miss Sutton came to NBC in 1929, she conducted a school for all network announcers, who attended in order to improve their speech and diction. Sutton stressed that in order to improve speech one must, "Listen—Listen—Listen." Because of Sutton's influence, the American Academy of Arts and Letters began awarding an annual prize for the best diction on radio. Some winners of these awards were Milton J. Cross in 1929; Alwyn Bach in 1930; John Wesley Holbrook, 1931; David Ross, 1932; and Jimmy Wallington in 1933.

20011 Magidoff, Robert. Newscaster (NBC, 1941, 1945–1946).

20012 Magnante, Charles. Accordionist (WBT, Charlotte, NC, 1942).

20013 Magnavox Radio Orchestra. Commercial band (KNX, Los Angeles, CA, 1927).

20014 Magner, Martin. Director Magner directed the *Lone Journey* daytime serial program.

20015 *Magnificent Montague.* Monty Wooley played a former Shakespearian actor, now a member of a thespians' club, who spent much of his time on the program attempting to keep his fellow members from learning that he was currently portraying Uncle Goodheart on a children's program. Wooley's deception often landed him in embarrassingly hilarious situations. Other cast members included Pert Kelton and Anne Seymour. Music was performed by organist Jack Ward (30 min., Weekly, NBC-Blue, 1950–1951).

20016 Magno, Nina. COM-HE (WADC, Akron, OH, 1951–1954).

20017 Magnolene Mike. Announcer not otherwise identified (KFDM, Beaumont, TX, 1926–1927).

20018 Magnolia Glee Club. Singing group directed by Miss Nellie Howland (KFDM, Beaumont, TX, 1928).

20019 Magnolia (Magnoleum) Petroleum Company Band. Fifty-piece company band directed by Dr. Harry Cloud. On January 1, 1924, the band broadcast a concert over WFAA, Dallas, TX, that the Dallas *News* reported drew more than 7,500 letters and cards from listeners all over the country. As a result, the band's concerts continued to be broadcast over WFAA. The band also broadcast over station KFDM (Beaumont, TX, 1925). In 1928, the band was directed by Prof. R.A. Dhossche (KFDM, 1928).

20020 Magnolia Petroleum Company Orchestra. Company band (WRR, Dallas, TX, 1926).

20021 *Magnolia Time.* Dan Hosmer was featured on the early morning CW music show that also presented the Hometowners, Helene Brahm and the Hoosier Sod Busters (15 min., Tuesday and Thursday, 8:15–8:30 A.M. CST, WLS, Chicago, IL, 1936).

20022 Magnus, John. DJ (KGFJ, Los Angeles, CA, 1955–1960).

20023 Magnuson, J. Woodrow. Newscaster (WHBF, Rock Island, IL, 1939).

20024 Magoun, Bessie. Violinist (WOW, Omaha, NE, 1927).

20025 Magoun, Milly. Violinist (WOW, Omaha, NE, 1927).

20026 Magrath, Edith. Contralto (WBZ, Springfield, MA, 1926).

20027 Magrini, Bud. Sportscaster (*Bud Magrini's Previews of Reviews*, KSRO, Santa Rosa, CA, 1948–1950; sports play-by-play, KSRO, 1951).

20028 Magruder, Don G. Magruder talked on agricultural topics such as "Milking Machines" (KWSC, Pullman, WA, 1925).

20029 Maguire, Dick. News analyst (KQW, San Jose, CA, 1944; KFRC, San Francisco, CA, 1945). Sportscaster (KFJI, 1946). DJ (*Ricky's Request*, KFJI, Klamath Falls, OR, 1947).

20030 Maguire, H. Thomas. Newscaster (WLYN, Lynn, MA, 1948).

20031 Maguire, Kathy. COM-HE (WTNT, Tallahassee, FL, 1960).

20032 Maguire, Paula (Betty Newton). COM-HE (WBMS., Columbus, OH, 1949).

20033 Maguire, Thomas. Sportscaster (*Eastern Shore Sports Roundup*, WCMD, Cambridge, MD, 1948).

20034 Maguire, Walt. Newscaster (WCAM, Camden, NJ, 1941).

20035 *Magyar Gypsy Orchestra.* Instr. mus. prg. (WEEU, Boston, MA, 1938).

20036 Mahaffey, Margaret. Singer-pianist (WJAG, Norfolk, VA, 1929).

20037 *Mahalia Jackson Show.* Miss Jackson, an excellent gospel singer, was joined on her transcribed program by the Jack Halloran Quartet and the Falls-Jones group (25 min., Sunday, 9:05–9:30 A.M. CST, CBS, 1954).

20038 Mahan, Johnny. Sportscaster (WDAS, Philadelphia, PA, 1952).

20039 Mahaney, Bob. Newscaster (WGY, Schenectady, NY, 1937; WIBX, Utica, NY, 1941, 1946).

20040 Maher, Ellen. Actress Maher appeared in the *Hearts of Harmony* daytime serial program.

20041 Maher, Mont. Actor Maher was in the cast of the *Dr. Kate* daytime serial.

20042 Maher, Raymond. Baritone (WMCA, New York, NY, 1925; WAHG, Richmond Hill, NY, 1926).

20043 Maher, Walter A. "Wally." Dramatic and character actor Maher was born August 4, 1908. After appearing in stock theatricals, Maher was featured on WLW dramatic programs (Cincinnati, OH, 1929). Later, he appeared on *Brent House*, *Circus Days*, *The Line-Up*, *One Man's Family* and *The Tommy Riggs and Betsy Lou Show.*

20044 Mahlenbrock, Martha. Pianist (WOR, Newark, NJ, 1924).

20045 Mahon, William. Announcer (KOIN, Portland, OR, 1928).

20046 Mahoney, Claude. News analyst (WTOP, Washington, DC, 1941, 1944–1947).

20047 Mahoney, George. One-man band performer (WAAB, Boston, MA, 1931).

20048 Mahoney, John. DJ (*Harlem Hit Parade*, KFRD, Rosenberg, TX, 1948).

20049 Mahoney, Julia. Soprano (WBEN, Buffalo, NY, 1927).

20050 Mahoney, May. Pianist (WHY, Martinsville, IL, 1924).

20051 Mahoney, Ralph. Newscaster (KOY, Phoenix, AZ, 1944).

20052 Mahoney, William. Baritone (WGCP, Newark, NJ, 1925).

20053 Mahoney, William "Bill." Announcer (KOIL, Council Bluffs, IA, 1928).

20054 Mahr, Beverly. Singer (WMBG, Richmond, VA, 1942).

20055 Mahra the Mind Reader. Early radio "mentalist" (KFI, Los Angeles, CA, 1928; *Mahra—Radioland's Psychic*, KJBS, San Francisco, CA, 1929).

20056 Maids of Melody. Singing team consisting of Hortense Rose and Grace Donaldson (WSAI, Cincinnati, OH, 1926; WLW, Cincinnati, OH, 1927).

20057 Maier, Walter A. Newscaster Maier began a weekly series of broadcasts of news and current affairs on March 13, 1926 (KFJO, St. Louis, MO, 1926). At the age of 29, Maier delivered a keynote address to a religious convention broadcast by WHAS (Louisville, KY). Soon after he delivered the speech, Maier became a professor at Concordia Seminary in St. Louis, MO. Convinced of the power of radio, he raised sufficient funds to enable the Seminary to operate its own station KFUO—"Keep Forward Upward Onward," which began broadcasting on December 14, 1924. On October 2, 1930, Maier began broadcasting *The Lutheran Hour* on CBS from WHK, Cleveland, Ohio.

His first program began with ten minutes of religious music sung by the Cleveland Bach Choir, followed by a 19-minute sermon by Maier. Listener response to the *Lutheran Hour was* enthusiastic. CBS estimated that the program reached a weekly audience of more than five million. *See* ***The Lutheran Hour***.

20058 *Mail Call.* *See* **Wartime Radio**.

20059 Mailander, H.C. Announcer (KFWA, Odgen, UT, 1926).

20060 *Main Street Music Hall.* Earl Wrightson used his great baritone voice on the weekly music show. He was accompanied by an orchestra conducted by Alfredo Antonini (30 min., Saturday, 4:00–4:30 P.M., CBS, 1950). The following year there was a cast change on the sustaining program, in which Russ Emery and Nancy Evans replaced Wrightson (30 min., Sunday, 5:00–5:30 P.M., CBS, 1951).

20061 ***Main Street Sketches.*** This popular dramatic series contained sketches of small town life. In the cast were Don Carney (later famous as Uncle Don), who played the role of Luke Higgins, Lida Ward Gaston, Allyn Joslyn, Eunice N. McGarrett, Edith Thayer, Roger Bower, Elsie McCormack, Tad Stout, Claire Stenz and Reynolds Brooks. The program was first broadcast on CBS in 1927 and on WOR, 1929–1930.

20062 Maine, Gordon. Leader (*Gordon Maine Orchestra*, instr. mus. prg., WLW, Cincinnati, OH, 1938).

20063 Mainer, J.E. and Wade Mainer. Brothers leaders CW string band (*Mainer's Mountaineers*, WWNC, Ashville, NC, 1941). The popular CW music group also consisted of Jack Shelton, Curly Shelton, Howard Dixon and Tiny Dotson among others. The announcer on its 1941 Ashville show was Monty Ayles. The Mainers came from a large mountain family in Buncombe County, North Carolina. They began broadcasting early in the 1930s over WSOC (Gastonia, NC) and WBT (Charlotte, NC), with infrequent excursions to WWL (New Orleans, LA) and WWNC (Asheville, NC). Under the sponsorship of Crazy Water Crystals, the Mountaineers were featured on the *Crazy Barn Dance* (WBT, Charlotte, NC, 1934). The Mainers' radio theme was "Way Down Yonder in the Cumberland Mountains." After 1936 Wade left the group to form his own band, the Sons of the Mountaineers, and broadcast over WPTF (Raleigh, NC), WBT (Charlotte, NC), WWNC (Asheville, NC) and WROL (Knoxville, TN).

The original Mountaineers went on to broadcast over WPTF (Raleigh, NC), WSPA (Spartanburg, SC), WIS (Columbia, SC); the Border Stations for a short period and, finally, over KMOX (St. Louis, MO).

20064 Maines, Marlin. Leader (*Marlin Maines Orchestra*, instr. mus. prg., WLW, Cincinnati, OH, 1938).

20065 ***Maisie.*** Versatile motion picture star Ann Sothern played Maisie on this entertaining situation comedy. In addition to Sothern, the cast included such talented radio actors as John Brown, Norman Field, Elliott Lewis, Wally Maher, Lurene Tuttle and Donald Woods. The announcer was Ken Niles. Cal Kuhl and William Rousseau were the directors and Art Phillips the writer of the show. Eversharp was the program's sponsor during most its broadcast run (30 min., Weekly, CBS, 1945–1946; Sustaining, MBS, 1949–1952).

20066 ***Maison Russe Orchestra.*** Instr. mus. prg. (MBS, 1936).

20067 Maitland, Arthur. Actor Maitland was in the cast of *Archie Andrews*, *David Harum* and *Your Family and Mine*.

20068 Maitland, Patrick. Newscaster (MBS, 1939).

20069 Maitland, Robert. Leader (*Robert Maitland Orchestra*, instr. mus. prg., WLW, Cincinnati, OH, 1936).

20070 ***Majah, Son of India.*** A professional entertainer in vaudeville, Majah had appeared on 67 radio stations before coming to KMA. Majah chiefly told fortunes on the air (KMA, Shenandoah, IA, 1926–1927). His successor at KMA, the Great Kharma, was a "master of the Bombay Seance and an expert at radio hypnosis."

20071 Majestic Ballroom Orchestra. Club band directed by Philip Sapiro (KGO, Oakland, CA, 1927; KFON, Long Beach, CA, 1928).

20072 ***Majestic Curiosity Shop.*** The Sunday evening music program was sponsored by the General Household Utilities Company. The first broadcast was on October 14, 1928 and the last December 21, 1930 (Weekly, Network, 1928–1930).

20073 Majestic Orchestra. Commercial band directed by Lester Harris (WFAA, Dallas, TX, 1925).

20074 Majestic Orchestra. William A. Hage led the commercial band (KLRA, Little Rock, AR, 1928).

20075 ***(The) Majestic Tenor and his Banjo.*** Singer-musician who was not otherwise identified — possibly Arthur Craft (KHQ, Spokane, WA, 1928).

20076 ***Majestic Theater of the Air.*** **(aka** ***The Majestic Hour*** **or** ***The Majestic Theater Hour*****).** The Majestic Radio Corporation sponsored the popular variety program featuring the music of the Arnold Johnson Orchestra, singer Belle Baker and the comedy of the Two Black Crows, also known as Moran and Mack (CBS, 1927–1930). At various times, different stars were presented, including Eddie Cantor, Ruth Etting, Wendell Hall, minstrel man Eddie Leonard, Edgar Guest, Grace LaRue, Lee Morris, Scrappy Lambert, Redferne Hollinshead, Grace LaMar and blues singer Lee Morse. Later, the program was reduced to 30 minutes in length. At that time the Majestic Tenor Arthur Craft and the Majestic Orchestra were featured.

20077 Majewski, Sandra. COM-HE (WNDU, South Bend, IN, 1960).

20078 Major, Clare Tree. Director of a series of half-hour dramatic programs (*The Threshold Players Program*, WGBS, New York, NY, 1926).

20079 Major, Jack. Singer (*Jack Major*, vcl. mus. prg., NBC, 1935).

20080 (The) Major and his Orchestra of Ocean Park. Popular local band (KHJ, Los Angeles, CA, 1923).

20081 ***Major and Minor.*** This otherwise unidentified piano team was a popular Rochester feature (WHAM, Rochester, NY, 1929–1930).

20082 ***Major Bowes Original Amateur Hour.*** Major Edward E. Bowes' long running amateur hour gained popularity at the height of the Great Depression, but eventually faded as did that national economic trauma. Graham McNamee was the program's most popular announcer. Bowes began each program by saying, "Thank you, Graham and good evening friends. Once more the wheel of fortune spins and where it stops nobody knows." From the hundreds of amateurs who auditioned for the program no more than 20 "acts" were included on each program. One of the famous singers who appeared on the show was Frank Sinatra in 1937, when he was a member of the Hoboken Four. Although the young Frank Sinatra's appearance with the Hoboken Four is generally well known, that of another young singer, Maria Callas, is not. Using the pseudonym Nina Foresti, the eleven-year-old Callas sang Puccini's "Un Bei di" from *Madame Butterfly.*

Bowes was a brilliant showman whose threatened use of the "gong" for those performers not doing well added an additional appeal for his listeners. In 1946, the show was discontinued when Bowes died, but it returned shortly thereafter as the *Original Amateur Hour* hosted by Ted Mack (60 min., NBC, CBS, 1935–1946, 1948). Mack took the show to television as *Ted Mack's Original Amateur Hour* on January 18, 1948.

20083 ***Major Bowes Family*** **(aka** ***The Major Bowes Capitol Family Hour*** **or** ***The Family Hour*****).** Major Edward E. Bowes hosted this music program with his "family" of performers. The program, sponsored by General Mills and Swanson Foods, first appeared on the network July 26, 1925. The *Major Bowes Family* program developed from the *Roxy's Gang* program, originated by showman Roxy Rothafel, first broadcast November 19, 1922, from the stage of New York City's Capitol Theater. Originally, Rothafel, assisted by Bowes, conducted the show. Bowes took over the program when Rothafel left it in 1926. Bowes and Ted Mack acted as hosts from that time on. J. Robert Blum and Lloyd Marx directed the show. The 1930 version included Yasha Bunchuk conducting the Capitol Theater Orchestra and announcer John S. Young (30 min., Sunday, 8:00–8:30 P.M., NBC-Red, 1930).

One early featured performer was Belle "Bubbles" Silverman, who later gained fame as opera singer Beverly Sills. A 1933 program presented soprano Maria Silveira; tenor Nicholas Consentino; pianist Hannah Klein; baritone Tom McLaughlin; a male quartet, the Four Minute Men; and a symphonic orchestra (60 min., Sunday, 11:15–12:25 P.M., NBC, 1933). On Sunday, May 5, 1935, the performers included Waldo Mayo, violinist and orchestra conductor; baritone Tom McLaughlin; soprano Helen Alexander and the Sizzlers vocal group (60 min., Sunday, 7:00–8:00 P.M., NBC, 1935). The program's time slots and lengths varied over the years. On August 18, 1935, the talent presented included baritone Tom McLaughlin, tenor Nicholas Consentino, soprano Helen Alexander, Roy Campbell's Royalists and the orchestra directed by violinist-conductor Waldo Mayo (30 min., Sunday, 10:30–11:00 A.M., NBC, 1935). Among the other performers who appeared on the show were tenors Colin Moore, Wesley Boynton, Carlo Ferette, Westell Gordon and Will Osborne; baritones Edward LaMonte and Dudley Wilkinson; sopranos Natalie Alt, Louise Dave, Hober Beal, Sylvia Miller and Rella Wynn; contraltos Betty Poulus and Gertrude Wood; the Wandering Minstrels, Artie Dunn and Lee Reis; pianists Jacques Pintel and Dave Schooler; trumpeter Robert Denti; saxophonist Clyde Doerr; xylophonist William Dorn; clarinetist Charles C. Thetford; and music glass virtuoso Wesley Ossman. *See* **Roxy Rothafel** *and* ***Roxy's Gang.***

20084 Major Minor. Theater pianist (WAAM, New York, NY, 1929).

20085 *Major Silly and Colonel Nut.* The comedy team of Charlie Egleston and George Lloyd broadcast weekly (WCKY, Covington, KY, early 1930s).

20086 *Major V.* The interesting dramatic adventure series was written by Charles Gussman. The story concerned an American trapped in Berlin during World War II, when the United States and Germany declared war. He immediately became a leader in the German underground movement to overthrow Hitler. None of the performers on the sustaining program were identified (30 min., Sunday, 4:30–5:00 P.M. WWJ, Detroit, MI, 1942).

20087 Makaehu, William. Steel guitar soloist (KTBI, Los Angeles, CA, 1926).

20088 *Make Believe.* Singers Bill Perry and Ruth Carhart sang on the 15-minute music program, accompanied by Johnny Augustine's Orchestra (15 min., CBS, 1936).

20089 *Make Believe Ballroom.* When WNEW (New York, NY) was carrying the trial of Bruno Richard Hauptmann, the accused kidnapper of the Lindbergh baby, there were long intervals that had to be filled. Martin Block, then a staff announcer at the station, suggested that by playing records the station could eliminate the expense of keeping musicians standing by to provide musical fills. His idea was accepted and this led to Block's highly successful *Make Believe Ballroom* show. Block talked about the music and the bands as though the broadcast was indeed originating from the ballroom where they were playing (WNEW, New York, NY, 1935). It has been suggested that in 1935 Al Jarvis at KFWB (Los Angeles, CA) used the format before Block.

20090 *Making Merry with Sperry.* Popular Hugh Barrett Dobbs conducted the show with his musical partner Wee Willie (William H. Hancock). The program included setting-up-exercises, songs, patter and musical interludes. Also on the show were Irish tenor, Kevin Ahearn and pianist Art Fadden. The show was carried on the NBC-Pacific Coast Network on Monday, Wednesday and Friday mornings in 1930. The remainder of the week—Tuesday, Thursday and Saturday—it was carried locally by KPO (San Francisco, CA, 1930). Hugh Barrett Dobbs was a great West Coast radio favorite. *See* **Dobbs, Hugh Barrett**.

20091 Malchiodi, Carolyn. COM-HE (WGMA, Hollywood, FL, 1956).

20092 Malchman, Nathan. Newscaster (WNBH, New Bedford, CT, 1939).

20093 Malcolm, Howard. DJ (*Morning Watch* and *The Record Rack*, WCOP, Boston, MA, 1948; *Malcolm's Morning Watch*, WCOP, 1950).

20094 *Malcolm Claire.* Claire told fairy tales and folk legends on his excellent children's show. Claire changed his voice to portray all the characters in the stories he told. He had first become famous for his comic portrayal of the blackface character Spareribs on the *National Barn Dance* program. Claire's famous comedy characters also included the Old Witch, Whitewash and the Old Man, but Spareribs was the one for which he is best remembered (15 min., Monday through Saturday, 6:00–6:15, NBC, 1936–1939).

20095 Maledon, Bernice. Singer (KWTO, Springfield, MO, 1937).

20096 Malek, Clementine. Station staff soprano (WHAD, Milwaukee, WI, 1926).

20097 Malerich, Jack. Leader (*Jack Malerich and his Singing Strings Orchestra*, instr. mus. prg., WCCO, Minneapolis–St. Paul, MN, early 1930s; *Jack Malerich Orchestra,* WCCO, 1935).

20098 Maleville, Buddy. Leader (*Buddy Maleville Orchestra*, instr. mus. prg., KOA, Denver, CO, 1940).

20099 Malicke, Irene. Pianist (WWJ, Detroit, MI, 1923).

20100 Malin, Alice. News commentator (*The Woman of Tomorrow*, NBC, 1938).

20101 Malin, Donald F. Announcer-music director (WLS, Chicago, IL, 1928). Malin came to WLS in 1926 and became music director in 1928. Malin saw radio as a means to further listener appreciation of good music. *Radio Guide* praised him for his efforts to provide quality music shows. Malin, himself, conducted a series of piano and talk shows on *Personalities in Music* (WLS, 1929–1930).

20102 Malin, Margaret. COM-HE and newscaster (WMBH, Joplin, MO, 1939). Malin conducted a 30-minute weekday program on which she broadcast recipes and household hints. She also broadcast a once a week program, *The Magic Kitchen*, from a local Joplin theater before a large audience.

20103 Malin, Ronald F. Announcer (WLS, Chicago, IL, 1927).

20104 Maliwons, Jane. Newscaster (KVCV, Redding, CA, 1941).

20105 Mallants, Salty. Sportscaster (*Salty Says—Boating and Fishing News*, WIOD, Miami, FL, 1950).

20106 Malle, Eddie "Dixie Boy." Singer (WCAU, Philadelphia, PA, 1925).

20107 Malle, Eddie and Danny Dougherty. Singing team (WCAU, Philadelphia, PA, 1926).

20108 Mallin, Dorothy Gay. COM-HE (WDOK, Cleveland, OH, 1956).

20109 Mallin [Malin], Theda. COM-HE (WEBR, Buffalo, NY, 1957).

20110 Mallon, Dwight. Newscaster (WKRC, Cincinnati, OH, 1940).

20111 Mallon, Neva. Vocalist (KFWM, Oakland, CA, 1929).

20112 Mallory, Martha. COM-HE (WWNH, Rochester, NH, 1949–1956).

20113 Mallory, Virginia. COM-HE (WTVR, Richmond, VA, 1956).

20114 Mallory, Walter. Tenor (WCCO, Minneapolis–St. Paul, MN, 1928). Mallory had appeared as the featured singer on WCCO's local *Pence Buick Program* in the early 1920s.

20115 Mallory Hatters. Commercially sponsored fourteen piece orchestra conducted by Les Stevens (WJZ, New York, NY, 1929).

20116 Mallotte, Albert Jay. Organist (KYW, Chicago, IL, 1925; *Albert Jay Mallotte*, instr. mus. prg., KHJ, Los Angeles, CA, 1932).

20117 Mallotte, Stanleigh. Vocalist (*Stanleigh Maliotte*, vcl. mus. prg., NBC, 1934). Newscaster (*Rhyming the News*, WAPI, Birmingham, AL, 1940).

20118 Malloy, (Mrs.) John. Soprano (WOC, Davenport, IA, 1927).

20119 Malloy, Les. DJ (*Les Malloy Show*, KGO, San Francisco, CA, 1947; *1260 Club* and *Request By Wire*, KYA, San Francisco, CA, 1948–1950).

20120 Malm, Edith. COM-HE (WLEM, Emporium, PA, 1960).

20121 Malneck, Matty. Leader (*Matty Malneck Orchestra*, instr. mus. prg., NBC, 1935; KMA, Shenandoah, IA, 1942).

20122 Malone, Bill. Sportscaster (WMAL, Washington, DC, 1952–1954; *Sports Review*, WMAL, 1955).

20123 Malone, Bob. Tenor (WKRC, Cincinnati, OH, 1926–1928).

20124 Malone, Danny. Tenor (*Danny Malone*, vcl. mus. prg., NBC, 1934).

20125 Malone, Florence. Actress Malone was a cast member of the daytime serial programs *Kitty Kelly*, *Against the Storm*, *Young Widder Brown* and *Amanda of Honeymoon Hill.*

20126 Malone, Francis P. "Frank." News analyst (WIOD, Miami, FL, 1937–1939; *News and Views*, WIOD, 1940–1942).

20127 Malone, Hal. Singer (*Hal Malone*, vcl. mus. prg., WMBD, Peoria, IL, 1935).

20128 Malone, Mary Cornelia. Soprano (WSM, Nashville, TN, 1926).

20129 Malone, (Major General) Paul B. News analyst (*Weekly War Journal*, NBC-Blue, 1942, 1945).

20130 Malone, Steve. DJ (*Rock 'n' Roll Wythm*, WYTH, Madison, GA, 1960).

20131 Malone, Ted (pseudonym for Alden Russell). Ted Malone began work as an announcer-ukulele soloist at KMBC, Kansas City, MO, in 1929. Once when a group of musicians failed to appear, he was told to fill the time by reading poetry. When he insisted upon being introduced with a pseudonym, another announcer called him *Ted Malone.* After that, Ted Malone was regularly scheduled to read poetry. This eventually became the main element of his popular network feature of later years, *Between the Bookends.* Malone also broadcast the news (NBC-Blue, 1944, 1948). *See* ***Between the Bookends***.

20132 Maloney, James. Newscaster (WBRK, Pittsfield, MA, 1941).

20133 Maloof, Alexander. Director of the Alexander Maloof Oriental Orchestra (NBC, 1928).

20134 Maloy, Hettie. Singer (WNAD, Norman, OK, 1926).

20135 Maloy, Jack. Sportscaster (WORL, Boston, MA, 1937; WEEI, Boston, MA, 1944, 1949–1950).

20136 *Maltex Program.* The Frank Pinero Orchestra was featured on the weekly music program (15 min., Thursday, 5:30–5:45 P.M., NBC-Red, 1932).

20137 ***Mammoth Carolina Jamboree.*** CW mus. prg., (WBIG, Greensboro, NC, 1938).

20138 ***Man About Hollywood.*** George McCall broadcast movie gossip on a national network on his sustaining program (30 min., Friday, 8:00–8:30 P.M., CBS, 1940).

20139 ***Man About Town.*** A Buffalo brewery sponsored the program of local gossip dispensed by Charlie Bailey (5 min., Wednesday, 6:55–7:00 P.M., WGR, Buffalo, NY, 1939).

20140 ***Man Behind the Gun.*** Jackson Beck narrated the offshoot of the *This is War* program. *Man Behind the Gun* was a series of dramatized historically correct events designed to boost citizen morale during World War II. The radio documentary was written by Ranald MacDougall. The cast included: Larry Haines, Frank Lovejoy, Paul Luther, Myron McCormick, William Quinn and Elizabeth Reller. The music director was Van Cleave. The producer-director was William N. Robson (1943–1944, CBS).

20141 ***(The) Man Called X.*** Herbert Marshall starred as detective Ken Thurston, who was assisted in his adventures by Leon Belasco. The program's opening explained the show: "Wherever there is mystery, intrigue, romance, in all the strange and dangerous places of the world, there you will find The Man Called X." In addition to Marshall, the cast included: Leon Belasco and GeGe Pearson. The writer was Milton Merlin. The producers were Jack Richard Kennedy, Jack Johnstone and William N. Robson. The show was sponsored variously by Chesterfield cigarettes, Anacin and RCA. (30 min., Weekly, ABC, NBC, CBS, 1944–1952).

20142 ***Man from Homicide.*** Dan Duryea played the role of plain clothes policeman Lou Dana, who worked the homicide beat. The sustaining program was a summer replacement for *Inner Sanctum.* The program was written by Louis Bitties, produced by Helen Mack and directed by Dwight Hauser. Basil Adlam supplied the program's music. Bill Bouchey assisted Duryea in his battle against crime. Also in the cast were: Jim Backus, Joan Banks, Larry Dobkin, Maggie Morley, Lamont Johnson, Tom Tully and Arthur Q. Bryan (30 min., Monday, 8:00–8:30 P.M., ABC, 1951).

20143 ***(The) Man I Married.*** Frank and Anne Hummert produced the daytime serial drama that first aired in 1939 on the NBC-Red network. The story told of Evelyn Waring, whose major troubles arose because of the personal weakness of her husband, i.e., his drinking, lack of discipline and inability to persevere. The program was broadcast from 1939 to 1942. The cast included: Fanny May Baldridge, Spencer Bentley, Frances Carden, Clayton "Bud" Collyer, John Gibson, Jackie Grimes, Van Heflin, Ed Jerome, Raymond Edward Johnson, Rikel Kent, Barbara Lee, Fred Irving Lewis, Dorothy Lowell, Arnold Moss, Santos Ortega, Ethel Waite Owen, Walter Vaughn, Vicki Vola, Gertrude Warner, Betty Winkler and Betty Worth. The program was written by Don Becker and Carl Bixby and directed by Oliver Barbour. Howard Petrie was the announcer.

20144 ***(The) Man in the Moon.*** Bill McNeery, "The Man in the Moon," told stories for children on WOR (Newark, NJ, 1924–1925). Thomas Cowan said that McNeery's *Man in the Moon* program broadcast on WJZ (Newark, NJ) in 1923 was probably the first children's program on radio.

20145 ***Man in the Stands.*** The Duke of Paducah (Benny Ford) interviewed fans at Sportsman's Park when the St. Louis Browns and the St. Louis Cardinals baseball teams were playing at home. He asked fans questions about baseball. *Variety* said Ford did particularly well on Ladies Day, when an average of 15,000 women attended games by paying only a 25-cent service charge. Ford was sponsored by the Columbia Brewing Company (15 min., Daily, KWK, St. Louis, MO, 1936).

20146 ***Man in the Street.*** Announcer Don Kelley interviewed natives of Omaha who came his way in the city's streets (KOIL, Omaha, NE, 1937).

20147 ***Man on the Farm.*** The Quaker Oats Company, makers of Ful-O-Pep Feeds, sponsored the program broadcast from the Ful-O-Pep Experimental Farm of the Quaker Oats Company located in Libertyville, IL. Chuck Acree conducted the informative and entertaining program primarily for farmers and their families. Acree interviewed farmers. In addition, Dr. O.B. Kent, Director of the Experimental Farm, delivered poultry news and advice on raising poultry. Music was provided by the Hoosier Sodbusters, Reggie Cross and Howard Black (30 min., Saturday, 12:30–1:00 P.M., CST, WLS, Chicago, IL, 1938). In 1949, the program returned on a sustaining basis with a radical format change. Chuck Acree returned as host, but this time it was an audience participation show. Acree asked such questions as: "Do Holsteins give more milk than Jerseys?" The program's announcer was George Menard (30 min., Saturday, 12:00–12:30 P.M., MBS, 1949).

20148 **Manaco, Hugh.** Leader (*Hugo Manaco Orchestra,* instr. mus. prg., MBS, 1939).

20149 **Manahan, Fred.** DJ (*Bumper to Bumper,* WATG, Ashland, OH, 1954–1956).

20150 **Manahan, Tommy.** Leader (*Tommy Manahan Orchestra,* instr. mus. prg., WOR, Newark, NJ, 1935).

20151 **Manbeck, (Mrs.) W.H.** Director, First Presbyterian Church Choir, Batavia, IL, WORD, Batavia, IL, 1925).

20152 **Mandarin Cafe Orchestra.** Cafe band directed by Lynn Pryor (KPO, San Francisco, CA, 1926).

20153 **Manderson, Steve.** Newscaster (WGAC, Augusta, GA, 1945).

20154 **Mandeville, Butler.** Actor Mandeville was in the cast of *Masquerade.*

20155 **Mandeville, Jessie.** Soprano (KYW, Chicago, IL, 1925).

20156 **Mandolin Musicians.** CW music group (KMA, Shannandoah, IA, 1928).

20157 **Mandrake, Chuck.** Sportscaster (*Sportraits,* WICA, Ashtabula, OH, 1951).

20158 ***Mandrake the Magician.*** The transcribed daytime adventure serial was broadcast from November 11, 1940 to February 6, 1941. Raymond Edward Johnson played the title role on the program based on the comic strip by the same name by Lee Falk and Phil Davis. The story featured Mandrake — a super magician who had learned his magic arts from a Tibetan master. He was assisted in his battle against crime and criminals by Lothar, his giant Black servant and the beautiful Princess Narda, played by Juano Hernandez and Francesca Lenni. Laddie Seaman was also in the cast. The program was produced by Henry Souvaine and directed by Carlo De Angelo (15 min., Monday through Friday, 1940–1941). Somehow, Mandrake's escapes from the clutches of various villains by means of his magic powers always seemed to make it a little too easy. Incidentally, Raymond Edward Johnson went on to play the role of Raymond the host behind the *Inner Sanctum's* creaking door.

20159 **Manecchia, I.A.** Newscaster (WHOM, Jersey City, NJ, 1940s).

20160 **Manessy and Herring Hawaiian Entertainers.** Hawaiian music group (WGBS, New York, NY, 1928).

20161 **Mangan, Buddy and Bertie Mayors.** Comedy team (CBS, 1932).

20162 **Mangini, Johnny.** DJ (*Sunday Sports,* WKBS, Oyster Bay, NY, 1950).

20163 **Manguso, Mike.** Saxophonist with Harold Gleser in the Vincent Lopez orchestra (WJZ, New York, NY, 1925).

20164 **Manhattan Beach Orchestra.** Popular local band (WSOE, Milwaukee, WI, 1926).

20165 ***Manhattan Guardsmen Orchestra.*** Instr. mus. prg. with a 28-piece orchestra broadcasting from New York's Radio City studios (NBC-Red, New York, NY, 1935).

20166 ***Manhattan Maharajah.*** George Ansbro, "The Manhattan Maharajah," was a glorified DJ. Before playing each record, Ansbro would read some classic poetry or original verse against the background of "oriental-sounding music." *Variety* said the program was reminiscent of radio's earlier days (30 min., Monday through Friday, 4:30–5:00 P.M., ABC, 1951).

20167 ***Manhattan Merry-Go-Round.*** Ford Bond and Roger Krupp were the announcers for the program that took listeners on an imaginary trip of New York's night clubs and supper clubs. The memorable opening lines proclaimed by Ford Bond clearly identified the program's format: "Here's the *Manhattan Merry-Go-Round* that brings you the bright side of life, that whirls you in music to all the big night spots of New York town to hear the top songs of the week sung so clearly you can understand every word and sing them yourself." At each location visited, one of the program's vocalists would sing a song. The long-running entertaining show was sponsored by Dr. Lyon's Tooth Powder. The cast changed considerably over the years. For example, in the program's early days Jean Sargent and David Percy were the vocalists singing with the Gene Rodemich Orchestra (30 min., Sunday, 9:00–9:30 P.M., NBC-Red, 1933–1949). A few years later the cast had expanded somewhat with tenor Pierre LeKreeun and soprano Raquel de Corlay and the Men About Town singing with the Andy Sannella Orchestra (30 min., Sunday, 8:00–8:30 P.M., NBC, 1935). The program was produced by Frank and Anne Hummert and directed by Paul Dumont.

20168 ***Manhattan Mother.*** A separated career woman with a daughter to raise was the problem faced by the dramatic serial program's leading character. Margaret Hillas and Kay Brinker were in the cast. Procter & Gamble's Chipso Soap Flakes sponsored the program (15 min., Wednesday, 9:15–9:30 P.M., CBS, 1939).

20169 Manhattan Orchestra. Local New York band (WMCA, New York, NY, 1925).

20170 Manhattan Serenaders. Club band (WHN, New York, NY, 1925).

20171 Manhattan String Trio. Instrumental group (WOAW, Omaha, NE, 1926).

20172 ***Manhattan Trivia.*** As the title suggested, Richard Brooks dispensed trivial information on his novel series (15 min., Thursday, 5:15–5:30 P.M., WNEW, New York, NY, 1938).

20173 ***Manhatters Orchestra.*** Instr. mus. prg. (NBC, 1936–1937).

20174 Manier, Will R. News analyst (*Undercurrents and Current Events*, WSM, Nashville, TN, 1940).

20175 Manierre, Margaret. Soprano (WJZ, New York, NY, 1925).

20176 Manlove, Dudley. Newscaster (KSAN, San Francisco, CA, 1939).

20177 Manly, Irving. Baritone (WHN, New York, NY, 1924).

20178 Mann, Alan. DJ (KFWB, Hollywood, CA, 1947).

20179 Mann, Arthur. Newscaster (MBS, 1939; 1942). During World War II, Mann was Mutual's correspondent in Africa.

20180 Mann, Bernard. Pianist (WMCA, New York, NY, 1925).

20181 Mann, Dick. Announcer (WRJN, Racine, WI, 1925).

20182 Mann, Gloria. Actress Mann appeared on the *Life and Loves of Dr. Susan* daytime serial.

20183 Mann, Gordon L. Leader (Gordon L. Mann's Saxophone Quintet, WBAP, Fort Worth, TX, 1926).

20184 Mann, Helen. Singer (WEAN, Providence, RI, 1937).

20185 Mann, Herbert. Newscaster (WRJN, Racine, WI, 1938).

20186 Mann, Iris. Actress Mann was a cast member of the *Hilltop House* daytime serial program.

20187 Mann, Joe. Leader (Joe Mann and his Rainbow Lane Orchestra broadcasting from Denver's Shirley-Savoy Hotel, KOA, Denver, Co, 1925).

20188 Mann, Joseph. Newscaster (WKWK, Wheeling, WV, 1944; WJAS, Pittsburgh, PA, 1945).

20189 Mann, Margaret. Contralto (KTAB, Oakland, CA, 1928).

20190 Mann, Marion. Singer (*Marion Mann*, vcl. mus. prg., WBIG, Greensboro, NC, 1936).

20191 Mann, Milton. Leader (*Milton Mann Orchestra*, instr. mus. prg., WOR, Newark, NJ, 1936).

20192 Mann, Muriel. Organist (KOIL, Council Bluffs, IA, 1926).

20193 Mann, Ned. Newscaster (WHK, Cleveland, OH, 1944–1946).

20194 Mann, Paul. Actor Mann was in the cast of *The Adventures of Topper* and *Passport for Adams.*

20195 Mann, Peggy. Singer (*Peggy Mann, v*cl. mus. prg. featuring Miss Mann singing from the Park Central Hotel's Coconut Grove Room, New York City with Henry Halstead's Orchestra, 15 min., Three Times Weekly, CBS, 1936).

20196 Mann, Peggy. COM-HE (WTVD, Durham, NC, 1956–1957).

20197 Mann, Sandra. Singer (WBNX, Bronx, NY, 1936; WELI, New Haven, CT, 1937).

20198 Mann, Si. Newscaster (WJAS, Pittsburgh, PA, 1945).

20199 Mann, Stu. Sportscaster (*In the Bleachers*, WDGY, Minneapolis, MN, 1940–1942; WLOL, Minneapolis–St. Paul, MN, 1944–1946; *In the Bleachers*, WLOL, 1947–1951).

20200 Mann, Suzanne. COM-HE (KEEN, San Jose, CA, 1957).

20201 Manna Kea Trio. Instrumental music group (WOAW, Omaha, NE, 1926).

20202 Manners, Jane. Singer (KSAL, Sioux City, IA, 1942).

20203 Manners, Lucille. Soprano (*Lucille Manners*, vcl. mus. prg., NBC, 1935–1936).

20204 Manners, Mae. COM-HE (KCSJ, Pueblo, CO, 1949).

20205 Manners, Marjorie. COM-HE (WIS, Columbia, SC, 1949).

20206 Manners, Martha. COM-HE (WKTV, Utica, NY, 1956).

20207 Manners, Zeke. Leader (*Zeke Manners Gang*, a hillbilly CW music program of highly sophisticated "hillbillies," WIBX, Utica, NY, 1937; WGR, Buffalo, NY, 1938). DJ (Manners played recordings on his *Zeke Manners Show*, WINS, New York, NY, 1956).

20208 Manning, Bernice. Soprano (WPCH, New York, NY, 1932).

20209 Manning, Carolyn. Contralto (WRC, Washington, DC, 1924).

20210 Manning, Day. DJ (*Dawn Patrol*, WIL, St. Louis, MO, 1950).

20211 Manning, Jack. Actor Manning was in the cast of *Young Dr. Malone.*

20212 Manning, Knox. News analyst (KHJ, Los Angeles, CA, 1937–1940; *Headlines on Parade*, CBS, 1939; CBS-KNX, Los Angeles, CA, 1941).

20213 Manning, Mary. COM-HE (WHKC, Columbus, OH, 1949).

20214 Manning, Mary. COM-HE (WLAC, Nashville, TN, 1949–1957).

20215 Manning, Ray. DJ (*Platter Parade*, WIL, St. Louis, MO, 1947; *Ray Manning Show*, WIL, St. Louis, MO, 1948; *Ray Manning Show*, KSTL, St. Louis, MO, 1949; *Platter Parade* and *Breakfast Club*, WIL, 1950).

20216 Manning, Ruth. COM-HE (WCTT, Corbin, KY, 1949).

20217 Manning, Tom. Sportscaster Manning began broadcasting play-by-play baseball games of the Cleveland Indians in 1925 (WJAY, Cleveland, OH) and, later, regularly on WJAM, (Cleveland, OH) for many years beginning in 1928. Manning also broadcast play-by-play of Ohio State University's football games, the National Air Review, Western Open Golf Tournament and the National Open Golf Tournament for NBC in 1937 as well as his regular *Leisy's Beer Sport Resume* (WTAM, 1937–1939; baseball World Series and the All Star Baseball game, NBC, 1939; WTAM, 1940–1950; *Sports Revue*, WNBK, Cleveland, OH, 1951–1952; WTAM, 1953–1954; Ohio State football games, WTAM, 1955; WNBK, 1955; KYW, Pittsburgh, PA, 1956–1960). Newscaster (WTAM, 1942).

20218 Manning Hawaiian and Jug Orchestra. Instrumental group that included Clarence F. Manning, leader-sg.; J. W. Manning, g.; V. E. Manning, jug; and E. V. Manning, g. (1930s).

20219 Manno, Gaetano. Singer (WJAX, Cleveland, OH, 1924).

20220 Manns, William. Newscaster (WCAM, Camden, NJ, 1939).

20221 Mansfield, Andy. Versatile Mansfield was a pianist, arranger, singer, orchestra leader, program director, comedian and announcer (WLS, Cincinnati, OH, 1929–1930). Before coming to WLW, Mansfield had played with the Little Jesse James Orchestra over Miami's WGBU, WIOD, WMBF and WJAX in 1924. He later joined Ray Miller's Orchestra and Blue Steele's Recording Band in 1926 before joining the WLW staff that same year. In 1930, Mansfield conducted *Mansfield's Morning Gazette,* a program that included music and news reports. On Saturday evenings Mansfield performed entertaining pianologues. In addition, he appeared in such comedy sketches as "Josephine the Terrible Traveling Piano." Mansfield later *may* have worked with his wife, Virginia, as DJs in Pasadena, CA.

20222 Mansfield, Andy. DJ (*Notes to You*, KWKW, Pasadena, CA, 1947; *The Andy Mansfield Program*, KWKW, 1950).

20223 Mansfield, Dick. Leader (*Dick Mansfield Orchestra*, instr. mus. prg., WIP, Philadelphia, PA, 1934; NBC-Red, 1936).

20224 Mansfield, Joseph "Joe." Director Mansfield directed the *Backstage Wife, Colgate Sports Newsreel* (with Bill Stern) and *Mirth and Madness.*

20225 Mansfield, Mike. Newscaster (KGVO, Missoula, MO, 1941).

20226 Mansfield, Olga. Contralto (WBZ, Springfield, MA, 1924).

20227 Mansfield, Roberta. COM-HE (WEKR, Fayetteville, TN, 1954).

20228 Manship, Mary Ann. COM-HE (WHSC, Hartsville, SC, 1955).

20229 Manson, Charlotte. Versatile, talented and busy actress Manson appeared in such divergent programs as *The Guiding Light*;

King's Row; *Backstage Wife* aka Mary *Noble, Backstage Wife*; *Road of Life*; *Romance of Helen Trent*; *Stepmother* and *Brighter Day* daytime serials and, in addition, the *American Women; Fu Manchu; Hotel for Pets; Joe DiMaggio Show; MGM Screen Test; Nick Carter, Master Detective, Parade of Progress, Society Girl, True Confessions* and *Twenty Question*.

20230 Mansur, Charlotte C. COM-HE (KXGN, Glendive, MT, 1951).

20231 Mansuy, Frank P. Newscaster (WENY, Elmira, NY, 1945; *News You Need*, WSCR, Scranton, PA, 1947).

20232 Mantia's Symphony Orchestra. Symphonic band (WMCA, New York, NY, 1925).

20233 Mantz, Wanda. COM-HE (KWCR, Cedar Rapids, La, 1949).

20234 Manuel, Ken. Newscaster (WWJ, Detroit, MI, 1942; WWJ, 1944–1945; *News by Manuel*, WWJ, 1947–1948).

20235 Manuel and Williamson. Harpsichord ensemble (*Past Masters*, NBC, 1937).

20236 Manuel Cigar Girls. Female singing group with Charlotte Myers and Mary Tudor that previously had appeared on the *Red Apple Club* (NBC, 1927 and WJR, Detroit, MI, 1927–1928). Lucille Burke was with the group when it first appeared on WCX, before the station became WJR.

20237 Manzanares, Jose. Leader (*Jose Manzanares Orchestra*, instr. mus. prg., CBS, 1935–1936).

20238 Manzel, Jan. COM-HE (WJOC, Jamestown, NY, 1940).

20239 Manzi, Thomas. Blind pianist (WHN, New York, NY and WEAF, New York, NY, 1925).

20240 Maple, Barbara Jane. Pianist (WJAX, Jacksonville, FL, 1924).

20241 Maple City Four. The male harmony singing vocal quartet began their radio career on WMBD (Peoria, IL, 1926). They came to Chicago from LaPorte, IN, and went to work on WLS. When the group first appeared on Chicago radio, the members included Fritz Clark, Al Rice, Art James and Pat Patterson (WLS, Chicago, IL, 1929). By 1931, the group consisted of Pat Patterson, Art James, Al Rice and Fritz Meissner. In 1937, the group included Pat Patterson, Fritz Meissner, Art James and Dewey Kistler and was accompanied by pianist Reggie Peele. When James became ill in 1940, he was replaced by Chuck Kerner. The group was a long-time favorite on Chicago's WLS and that station's famous *National Barn Dance* program.

20242 Maples, Franklin Grady. News analyst (KICA, Clovis, NM, 1942; *World's Eye View of the World Wide News*, KTNM, Tucumcari, NM, 1947–1948). Sportscaster (KICA, 1942; KTNM, 1948–1949).

20243 Maples, Nelson. Leader (Nelson Maples and his U.S. Leviathan Orchestra cruise ship band, WIP, Philadelphia, PA, 1926).

20244 *Marathon Melodies.* The local music show was sponsored by the Ohio Oil Company and "its many Marathon dealers." Dan Riss hosted the show that featured the Jimmy James Orchestra, singer Sylvia Rhodes and the Three Devore Sisters vocal group (30 min., Friday P.M., WLW, Cincinnati, OH, 1941).

20245 Maraveas, George. Singer (WFBH, New York, NY, 1925).

20246 Marble, Alice. Sportscaster (WNEW, New York, NY, 1940). Marble was a former tennis champion.

20247 Marble, Harry. News analyst (*Greystone News*, WCAU, Philadelphia, PA, 1938; CBS, 1939–1944).

20248 Marble, Mary. Newscaster (WHOB, Gardner, MA, 1946).

20249 Marble, Smiling Eddie. Tenor, known as "The Boy with the Green Hat." His accompanist was pianist Dorothy Richardson (KGER, Long Beach, CA, 1929–1930).

20250 Marburger, Harvey. Leader (Harvey Marburger and his Keith Vaudeville Entertainers Orchestra, broadcasting from the Cafe L'Aiglon, Philadelphia, PA; WIP, Philadelphia, PA; Harvey Marburger Orchestra, WIP, 1925).

20251 Marcelle, Lou. DJ (*All Star Western Jamboree*, KFWB, Hollywood, CA, 1947).

20252 Marcelli, Mme. Clementine. Singer (KFWM, Oakland, CA, 1929).

20253 March, Donna. COM-HE (WADK, Newport, RI, 1956–1957).

20254 *(The) March of Events.* Charles Martin, one of the developers of *The March of Time*, originated this similar program for WMCA (30 min., Sunday, WMCA, New York, NY, 1932).

20255 *(The) March of Games.* The sustaining quiz show originally was co-hosted by Jane Martin and ex-vaudevillian Norman Frescott on the *Town Hall Big Game Hunt*. The children's quiz show portion of the program was hosted by 14-year-old McArthur Ross and 11-year-old drum major Sybil Trent. Portions of the show also included the "Musical Memory" segment, on which contestants identified songs played by the orchestra. There were tongue twisters such as, "A crop of poppies in copper coffee pots" and Topsy-Turvy Teasers in which contestants were asked to correct such statements as, "William Tell shot an arrow through an orange while it was sitting on his son's head."

20256 *(The) March of Time.* *Time* magazine originated and sponsored the broadcast, one of radio's best remembered news programs. The half-hour program made its debut March 1931 as a half-hour program featuring 30 actors, 19 musicians and 8 production service personnel. They claimed that 11 editorial and research workers were also involved. Each program contained from six to eight dramatized recreations of contemporary historical events. On the first program, for example, the renomination of Big Bill Thompson as Mayor of Chicago was dramatized.

Fred Smith, *Time's* managing editor in 1931 created the program. The scripts were written by Tom Everitt. The director was Don Stauffer. Thomas Harrington was the casting director. Howard Barlow conducted the orchestra. At times, Arthur Pryor, Jr., conducted a brass band when the program required it. The original cast included imitations of historical figures. For example Franklin D. Roosevelt was imitated by Bill Adams; President Hoover by Ted De Corsia; James J. Walker by Frank Readick; Joseph Stalin by Teddy Bergman (Alan Reed); Samuel Seabury by Wilmer Walter; Benito Mussolini by Porter Hall; King Alphonso of Spain by Pedro de Cordoba; Ramsey MacDonald by Alfred Shirley and Alfred E. Smith by Charles Slattery. Ted Husing and William Adams were the announcers (30 min., Friday, 8:30–9:00 P.M., CBS, 1931–1932).

In 1935, there was a time and format change. Although the content and mode of presentation stayed the same, the program became a quarter-hour program broadcast five times a week. Howard Barlow remained as orchestral director, but Arthur Pryor, Jr. became program director. The *March of Time* concept and format was copied by Pathe Company. On their program the motion picture company played soundtracks of historic events from its own newsreels.

The *March of Time* cast included: Bill Adams, Georgia Backus, Art Carney, Staats Cotsworth, Ted de Corsia, Kenny Delmar, Peter Donald, Martin Gabel, Edwin Jerome, Nancy Kelly, Adelaide Klein, Myron McCormick, John McIntire, Hershel Mayal, Gary Merrill, Agnes Moorehead, Claire Niesen, Jeanette Nolan, Elliott Reid, Charles Slattery, Everett Sloane, Jack Smart, Lotte Stavisky, Karl Swenson, Maurice Tarplin, Louise Wall, Dwight Weist, and Agnes Young. The directors were Homer Fickett, Lester Vail, William Spier and Don Stauffer. Arthur Pryor, Jr. was the producer-director and Tom Harrington the assistant producer. The news editor was Bill Geer. The writers were Carl Carmer, Richard Dana, Brice Disque, Jr., Paul Milton and Garrett Porter. Howard Barlow and Donald Voorhees were the program's musical directors.

20257 Marchan, George. Singer (*George Marchan*, vcl. mus. prg., WGES, Chicago, IL, 1936).

20258 Marchand, Alex. Newscaster (KALB, Alexandria, LA, 1941).

20259 Marchant, Rae. Violinist (KGO, Seattle, WA, 1925).

20260 Marchbanks, Lois. COM-HE (WFDM, Beaumont, TX, 1949).

20261 Marchetti, Berta. Contralto (WJZ, New York, NY, 1929).

20262 Marchetti, Gilda. Soprano (KFI, Los Angeles, CA, 1925).

20263 Marchetti Concert Quartet. Instrumental group (KFI, Los Angeles, CA, 1925).

20264 Marconi, Gugliamo. Marconi, a Nobel Prize winning physicist, invented and developed an efficient means for the wireless transmission (wireless telegraphy) of messages. Marconi's invention was later developed by Armstrong, De Forest and Fessenden, among others, into what became commercial broadcasting. As Lewis (1993, p. 2) said radio was the creation of three men possessing "genius, vision, determination and fascinating complexity"—Lee De Forest, Edwin Howard Armstrong and David Sarnoff. If radio was an outgrowth of Marconi's *product*, it was Lee De Forest and Dr. Frank Conrad who developed the *process* of broadcasting and the business acumen of David Sarnoff and William Paley that made it commercially viable. *See* **Armstrong, Edwin Howard; Conrad, Frank; De Forest, Lee; Paley, William S.;** *and* **Sarnoff, David.**

20265 Marconi Brothers. Brother act that performed accordion duets (WHN, New York, NY, 1925).

20266 Marcos, Madeline. Astrologer (WHEC, Rochester, NY, 1936).

20267 Marcotte, Don. Director (Don Marcotte and his Vagabonds Orchestra, WEAF, New York, NY, 1927; NBC, 1930).

20268 Marcotte, John. Pianist billed as "The Vagabond Pianist" (WEAF, New York, NY, 1927).

20269 Marcotte, Paul. DJ (*Platter Patter*, KPOJ, Portland, OR, 1948).

20270 Marcoux, Henri. Baritone (WLWL, New York, NY, 1928).

20271 Marcus, Leslie. Newscaster (KWJJ, Portland, OR, 1942).

20272 Marcus, Lillian. Singer (WELI, New Haven, CT, 1937).

20273 Marcussen, (Miss). Soprano ("pupil of Mme. Armand Cailleau," KPO, San Francisco, CA, 1923).

20274 Marden, Adrienne. Actress Marden appeared on the *Story of Bess Johnson* daytime serial program.

20275 Marden, Orison S. Marden told "bedtime stories for grown-ups" (WBZ, Springfield, MA, 1924).

20276 ***Mardi Gras Hour.*** Vcl. mus. prg. featuring tenor Ben Alley (CBS, 1930).

20277 ***Mardi Gras of Melody.*** On this program sponsored by the Public Service Company of Illinois, Dudley Crafts Watson talked about home maintenance. Music was provided by tenor Bob Hannon, vocalist Sally Jo Nelson, the Four Grenadiers male vocal group, the Doring Sisters and Harold Stokes' Orchestra (30 min., Wednesday, 9:30–10:00 P.M., WGN, Chicago, IL, 1936).

20278 Mareen, Mary. Actress Mareen appeared on *The Road of Life* daytime serial program.

20279 Maren, Milton. Leader (*Milton Maren Orchestra*, instr. mus. prg., WOR, Newark, NJ, 1936).

20280 Marengo, Joe. Leader (Joe Marengo's Harmony Five Orchestra that broadcast from Hollywood's Green Mill Cafe, KFQZ, Hollywood, CA, 1926).

20281 Mares, Jerry. News commentator (*Journal*, WCBM, Baltimore, MD, 1947).

20282 Margana, Nina. Soprano (WJZ, New York, NY, 1925).

20283 Marget, M.M. "Manny." Tenor-violinist-monologist (WDAY, Fargo, ND, 1929–1930). Formerly Marget was heard on KWK (St. Louis, MO). Sportscaster (WVOX, Moorhead, MN, 1942; *Sports Shorts*, WVOX, 1950–1956).

20284 Marggraff, Norm. DJ (*Fritz the Plumber*, WMIL, Milwaukee, WI, 1952–1955).

20285 Margie Make-Believe. Unidentified entertainer who told stories for children (WAHG, Richmond Hill, NY, 1926).

20286 Margot, Marie. Harpist (WBBM, Chicago, IL, 1925).

20287 ***Margot of Castlewood*** **(aka** ***Margo of Castlewood*****).** The daytime serial was sponsored by the Quaker Oats Company. The story dramatized the conflict in the Carver family. The Margot of the title was Margot Carver, played by Barbara Luddy, who felt torn between her family and her desire to live her own life. Other cast members included Francis X. Bushman, Ethel Waite Owen and Charles Carroll. Basil Loughrane was the program's director (15 min., Monday through Friday, 9:00–9:15 A.M., CST, NBC-Blue, 1937).

20288 Margraff, Irving. Director (Blackstone String Quartet, WGN, Chicago, IL, 1928).

20289 Margraff, Irving. Leader (*Irving Margraff Ensemble*, instr. mus. prg., WCFL, Chicago, IL, 1937).

20290 ***Margy the Steno.*** Elizabeth Todd, Secretary to Burke Boyce, NBC Continuity Editor, wrote the weekly comedy serial program. The story began when Margy, played by Marcella Shields, walked into the office of her boss, Mr. Harrison, at the Pearly Dew Rice Company. Other cast members were Helene Handin and Jack McBride (15 min., Saturday, 7:30–7:45 P.M., NBC-Blue, 1931).

20291 Maria, Juana. COM-HE (KIWW, San Antonio, TX, 1957).

20292 ***Maria's Matinee.*** The entertaining variety program featured singers Lanny Ross, Conrad Thibault and Mary Lou (60 min., Friday, 3:00–4:00 P.M., NBC-Red, 1934).

20293 Marian, Edith. Soprano (NBC, 1928).

20294 Mariana, Nick. Sportscaster (KGVO, Missoula, MT, 1937–1940; KXLK, Great Falls, MT, 1948).

20295 Mariani, Hugo. First orchestral conductor on the famous *Slumber Hour* program (NBC, 1928. Mariani also conducted the orchestra on the *Dutch Masters Minstrels* program, NBC, 1928; leader of the Mediterraneans Dance Band, NBC-Blue, New York, NY, 1928; the *Freshman Orchestradiana Hour* orchestra, WJZ, 1929; the *Voice of Firestone*, WABC-CBS, New York, NY, 1929; *Hugo Mariani Orchestra*, instr. mus. prg., MBS, 1936).

20296 Mariani, John. DJ (*Italian Melodies*, WAVZ, New Haven, CT, 1948; *Morning Man*, WAVZ, 1950).

20297 Marie, Joan. COM-HE (WAPC, Riverhead, NY, 1960).

20298 Marie, May. Broadcast news of style and fashion (KOA, Denver, CO, 1926).

20299 ***Marie the Bargain Hunter.*** An unidentified female conducted her program of shopping information for women (KFBI, Abilene, KS, 1936).

20300 ***Marie the Little French Princess.*** The daytime serial told the story of a girl from a royal family, who was living her life as would any American woman. Ruth Yorke played the title role assisted by James Meighan. Andre Baruch was the announcer (15 min., CBS, 1935). The program was said to have been one of the first "soap operas" to be broadcast nationally by a network.

20301 Marigold Garden Dance Orchestra. Club dance band (WCCO, Minneapolis, MN, 1926).

20302 Marimba Band. Popular orchestra that included Arthur Forcade, Edward Stanley, Bill Bradley, Ross Peterson, Harry Nassau, Evelyn Nassau and "Doc" Willats (KPO, San Francisco, CA, 1925).

20303 Marin, Fina. COM-HE (KWKW, Pasadena, CA, 1956–1957).

20304 Mariner, Marjorie. COM-HE (WFMJ, Youngstown, OH, 1951).

20305 ***Mariners Quartet.*** The racially mixed male singing group first gained popularity when they appeared on the *Arthur Godfrey Show*. The members of the group were Martin Bougham, Homer Smith, Thomas Lockard and James Smith (15 min., Weekly, NBC-Red, 1946).

20306 Marino, Rosa. Singer (WMAQ, Chicago, IL, 1927).

20307 Mario, Queena. Soprano (*Queena Mario*, vcl. mus. prg., NBC, 1934).

20308 ***Mario Lanza Show.*** Lanza starred on his variety show sponsored by the Coca-Cola Company. Giselle MacKenzie and the Ray Sinatra Orchestra were regular performers on the summer replacement for the *Edgar Bergen-Charlie McCarthy Show*. Bill Baldwin was the announcer (30 min., Sunday, 8:00–8:30 P.M., CBS, 1951).

20309 Marion, Don. Leader (*Don Marion Orchestra*, instr. mus. prg., WXYZ, Detroit, MI, 1935).

20310 Marion, Ira. Writer Marion wrote *Hannibal Cobb*, *Modern Romances* and *Mr. President.*

20311 Marion, John. Newscaster (WGAT, Utica, NY, 1947).

20312 Marion, Russell "Russ." Newscaster (WMFR, High Point, NC, 1941; WBTM, Danville, TX, 1947). DJ (WBTM, Danville, VA, 1947).

20313 Mariotti, Dolores. COM-HE (WLSV, Wellsville, NY, 1957).

20314 Maris, Paul V. Broadcast talks for farmers (KGW, Philadelphia, PA, 1923).

20315 Marita, Marion. Soprano (WOR, Newark, NJ, 1932).

20316 ***Marjah the Mystic.*** Marjah was a mentalist, who broadcast nightly while he was appearing at Little Rock's Cinderella Gardens. Listeners sent in questions and the mystic would answer them. The program's announcer proclaimed that Marjah was able to "see all, know all and tell all" (KLRA, Little Rock, AR, 1929).

20317 ***(The) Marjorie Mills Hour.*** The "domestic science" program began on the New England network in 1933. "Marjorie Mills" was a "generic" name used by many performers during the life of the program (30 min., Monday through Friday, New England Network, 1933–1942).

20318 ***Mark Trail.*** Kellogg's Pep cereal sponsored the dramatic adventure series for children, that told the story of a forest ranger,

Mark Trail. The title role was originated by Matt Crowley, who was always involved in hair-raising cliff-hanging adventures. The program, first written by Max Ehrlich, was adapted from a comic strip by Ed Dodd. The cast included: Ben Cooper, Staats Cotsworth, Matt Crowley, Joyce Gordon, John Larkin and Ronald Liss. Drex Hines was the director. The program's other writers were Albert Aley, Gilbert Braun, Elwood Hoffman and Palmer Thompson. Jackson Beck and Glenn Riggs were the announcers (30 min., Monday-Wednesday-Friday, 5:00–5:30 P.M., MBS, 1950).

20319 Markel, Michael. Leader (Michael Markel's Society Orchestra, WJZ, Newark, NJ and WEAF, New York, NY, 1926). In 1917, Markel had recorded for Victor with a group billed as Sergeant Markel's Orchestra.

20320 *Market Basket.* Radio pioneer Vaughn deLeath and announcer Bill Elliott provided information about the best food buys. The sponsor was Park City Laundry (15 min., Monday, 10:00–10:15 P.M., WICC, Bridgeport, CT, 1938).

20321 *Market Basket.* Three members of the station KOL staff conducted the morning program devoted to shopping information. They were station manager Ricky Bras, Kathy McArdle and announcer Earl Thomas. One feature of the show was the awarding of a market basket as a prize to the listener who correctly answered an interesting puzzle: a jar of beans was shaken before the microphone and listeners asked to guess how many beans it contained (KOL, Seattle, WA, 1930s).

20322 Markey, Arthur. Sportscaster (WJAR, Providence, RI, 1937–1941; 1944).

20323 Markey, Enid. Actress Markey appeared on the *Woman of Courage* daytime serial.

20324 Markey, Ralph. Leader (Ralph Markey and his Musical Keys Orchestra, KMTR, Hollywood, CA, 1926; KPLA, Los Angeles, CA, 1927).

20325 Markey, Ray. Sportscaster (WTHT, Hartford, CT, 1937–1940).

20326 Markin, Eddie. Leader (*Eddie Markin Orchestra*, instr. mus. prg., WMAQ, Chicago, IL, 1934).

20327 Markley, Peggy. COM-HE (WRTA, Altoona, PA, 1949).

20328 Markowitz, Bert. Leader (Bert Markowitz Orchestra, KFUV, Oakland, CA, 1925).

20329 Marks, Beatrice. COM-HE (KVER, Albuquerque, NM, 1949).

20330 Marks, Florence. Publicist (NBC and CBS, 1930s and 1940s). Marks joined CBS as a publicist in 1935. Three years later she joined NBC in the same position, where she stayed for five years. Before entering radio, she had worked for the *New York Times.*

20331 Marks, Garnett. Sportscaster (KMOX, St. Louis, MO, 1932; WMCA, 1939–1940; KGFN, Grass Valley, CA, 1947). Newscaster (WMCA, New York, NY, 1937; *Roma Wine News* and *Community Opticians News*, WMCA, 1938–1939). Marks was the announcer of the first St. Louis big league baseball game broadcast on radio in 1927.

20332 Marks, Gerald. Leader (Gerald Marks and his Orchestra and the Gerald Marks' Hotel Fuller Orchestra, WGHP, Detroit, MI, 1926).

20333 Marks, Judy. COM-HE (WXIX, Milwaukee, WI, 1957).

20334 Marks, Kate. Pianist (WLIT, Philadelphia, PA, 1925).

20335 Marks, Louise. COM-HE (KMHL, Marshall, MN, 1955).

20336 Marks, Regina. Violinist-musical director (WAPI, Birmingham, AL, 1929–1930).

20337 Marks, Sherman. Actor-director Marks worked on *Backstage Wife* (actor), *Captain Midnight* (actor), *Cloak and Dagger* (director) and *The Whistler* (director).

20338 Markward, William "Bill." Sportscaster (WCAM, Camden, NJ, 1937–1941; WIBG, Philadelphia, PA, 1944).

20339 Marley, Madge [Morley]. Singer (*Madge Marley*, vcl. mus. prg., NBC, 1937).

20340 Marley, Phil. Leader (*Phil Marley Orchestra*, instr. mus. prg., WGBI, Scranton, PA 1937).

20341 Marlin, Albert W. Chief announcer and studio manager before coming to WAAB, Boston, MA, 1931 as announcer.

20342 Marlow, June. COM-HE (WMAQ, Chicago, IL, 1949).

20343 Marlowe, Betty. Leader (*Betty Marlowe Orchestra*, instr. mus. prg., NBC, 1935).

20344 Marlowe, Brenda. Blues singer (*Brenda Marlowe*, vcl. mus. prg., WOR, Newark, NJ, 1942).

20345 Marlowe, Fran. COM-HE (WBUX, Doylestown, PA, 1949).

20346 Marlowe, Hugh. Actor Marlowe was in the cast of *Brenda Curtis, Ellery Queen* (title role), and *Our Gal Sunday.*

20347 Marlowe, Norma Mae. Actress Marlowe was in the cast of the *Hilltop House* daytime serial.

20348 Marlowe, Paul. Newscaster (WAYB, Waynesboro, VA, 1947; *Sizing Up Sports*, WLOF, Orlando, FL, 1950).

20349 Marlowe, Ralph. Tenor (KLX, Oakland, CA, 1929).

20350 Marlowe , Raymond (Raymond Metz). Tenor-reader Marlowe was born January 21, 1893. He was an oratorio and opera singer, synagogue soloist, choir director and voice teacher. Marlowe first worked in radio in 1925 (WOR, Newark, NJ; WABC, New York, NY, 1925).

20351 Marlowe, Sylvia. Folk singer (NBC, 1941).

20352 Marner, Will R. Newscaster (WSM, Nashville, TN, 1940).

20353 Marques, Luis. Newscaster (CBS, 1947).

20354 Marquette Mandolin Club. Music club directed by Professor R.C. Bryant (WLS, Chicago, IL, 1924).

20355 Marr, Art. Leader (Art Marr's Imperial Dance Orchestra, KOIL, Council Bluffs, IA, 1926).

20356 Marr, Dale. Newscaster (*Luncheon News*, WBBC, Flint, MI, 1947).

20357 Marrero, Luis E. Newscaster (WNEL, San Juan, PR, 1948).

20358 *(The) Marriage.* This transcribed program announced its purpose with its opening: "With the conviction that marriage remains one of the most popular domestic arrangements between friendly people, NBC takes pleasure presenting one of the most distinguished couples of the American theater, Jessica Tandy and Hume Cronyn, as Liz and Bob Marriott, bringing you the love and laughter of *The Marriage.*" Despite the program's constant proclamation of self-righteous humanity, it was entertaining fare directed by Edward King. In addition to Tandy and Cronyn, the cast included Sylvia Davis, Denise Alexander, Kermit Murdock, Ann Thomas, Norman Lloyd, Byrna Raeburn, James Stevens, William Redfield and David Anderson (30 min., Transcribed, NBC, 1950s).

20359 *Marriage for Two.* Elaine Sterne Carrington produced the sustaining daytime dramatic serial written by Winifred Wolf. It told the story of a young woman, played by Teri Keane, who was both romantic and wise. She had a romance with an irresponsible young man and married him. In the story she was primarily concerned about her husband's lack of financial responsibility. Marian Barney, Staats Cotsworth, Fran Lattetry, Evelyn Varden and Gertrude Warner were in the cast. Organ music was played by Fred Feibel. The announcer was John Tillman (15 min., Monday through Friday, 2:30–2:45 P.M. CBS, 1948).

20360 *(The) Marriage License Bureau.* Veteran WGN announcer Quin Ryan hosted the program, on which he interviewed those who had just received their marriage licenses. He asked such questions as, "How did you meet?" and "What are your plans?" (15 min., WGN, Chicago, IL, 1935).

20361 *Married Life of Helen and Warren.* Don Martin produced this good daytime serial sponsored by the Philadelphia *Evening Bulletin.* The story revolved around the domestic problems faced by a young married couple. Jane King and Jason Johnson played the title roles assisted by other cast members such as Joe Levinson and Honey MacKenzie. Don Martin was the producer and Roy LaPlante the announcer (15 min., Monday and Wednesday, 11:30–11:45 A.M., WFIL, Philadelphia, PA, 1940).

20362 Marrion, Frank E. Newscaster (KAST, Astoria, OR, 1939).

20363 Mars, (Mrs.) Edna G. Pianist (KDKS , Pittsburgh, PA, 1924).

20364 Marsala, Joe. Leader (*Joe Marsala Orchestra*, instr. mus. prg., CBS, 1940; MBS, 1942).

20365 Marsden, Ruth Roberts. COM-HE (WICY, Malone, NY, 1956).

20366 Marsh, Addie. Blues singer (WCFL, Chicago, IL, 1935).

20367 Marsh, Audrey. Pianist, singer, MC and actress Marsh, after singing as part of a harmony team in vaudeville from 1922 to 1928, appeared solo on the *Shell Happy Time* program sponsored by Shell Union Oil Company on the NBC-Red network.

20368 **Marsh, Carol [Caroline].** Pianist (CBS, 1940–1941).

20369 **Marsh, Dixie.** Actress Marsh was in the cast of the *Hawthorne House* daytime serial program.

20370 **Marsh, Dorothy.** COM-HE (WJZ, New York, NY, 1922).

20371 **Marsh, E.E.** Announcer (KFJI, Astoria, OR, 1926–1927).

20372 **Marsh, Herbert.** Leader (*Herbert Marsh Orchestra*, instr. mus. prg., WBZ-WBZA, Boston-Springfield, MA, 1932).

20373 **Marsh, Isabel.** Soprano (WFLA, Clearwater, FL, 1929).

20374 **Marsh, Jan.** COM-HE (WCRB, Waltham, MA, 1951).

20375 **Marsh, Jerry.** Tenor (*Jerry Marsh*, WOR, Newark, NJ, 1935).

20376 **Marsh, John.** Newscaster (WCOU, Lewiston, ME, 1942).

20377 **Marsh, Judy.** Singer (WROK, Rockford, IL, 1938).

20378 **Marsh, Lee.** Newscaster (KGVO, Missoula, MT, 1938).

20379 **Marsh, Louis T.** Newscaster (WMRN, Marion, OH, 1941–1942, 1945).

20380 **Marsh, Maggie.** Violinist (WOC, Davenport, IA, 1924).

20381 **Marshall, Bob.** Newscaster (WDBO, Orlando, FL, 1942). DJ (*Party Line*, WGBS, Miami, FL, 1948; *Record Jury*, WGBS, 1952–1954). Sportscaster (WDBO, 1942).

20382 **Marshall, Caryl.** Soprano (WGY, Schenectady, NY, 1925).

20383 **Marshall, Charles.** Singer-producer (NBC-San Francisco, CA, studios, 1929–1930).

20384 **Marshall, Dave.** Leader (*Dave Marshall Orchestra*, instr. mus. prg., WXYZ, Detroit, MI, 1942).

20385 **Marshall, Don.** Newscaster (KFIZ, Fond du Lac, NY, 1940–1941).

20386 **Marshall, Duane.** Leader (*Duane Marshall Orchestra*, instr. mus. prg., WHDH, Boston, MA, 1939).

20387 **Marshall, (Mrs.) Fred.** Soprano (WHO, Des Moines, IA, 1926–1927).

20388 **Marshall, Gene.** Newscaster (WBML, Macon, GA, 1941–1942, 1945; *C & S News*, WDAR, Savannah, GA, 1948).

20389 **Marshall, George.** News commentator (*Report to Ashland*, WCMI, Ashland, KY, 1948).

20390 **Marshall, H.A.** Announcer (KFLZ, Atlantic City, NJ, 1926–1927).

20391 **Marshall, Honey.** COM-HE (WAKR, Akron, OH, 1951).

20392 **Marshall, Howard.** Newscaster and commentator (NBC, 1937–1939).

20393 **Marshall, Hugh.** Tenor (WDAP, Chicago, IL, 1923).

20394 **Marshall, Jane.** COM-HE (WTTH, Port Huron, MI, 1951–1957).

20395 **Marshall, Jerry.** DJ (WNEW, New York, NY, 1947; *The Music Hall*, WNEW, 1948–1954).

20396 **Marshall, John.** Newscaster (WLAV, Grand Rapids, IA, 1941). Sportscaster (WLAV, 1941; WGRD, Grand Rapids, MI, 1948).

20397 **Marshall, (Mrs.) John.** Reader (WCBD, Zion, IL, 1925).

20398 **Marshall, Kyser.** Leader (*Kyser Marshall Orchestra*, instr. mus. prg., WIP, Philadelphia, PA, 1936).

20399 **Marshall, Marian.** Newscaster (WTNJ, Trenton, NJ, 1942).

20400 **Marshall, Mary Louise.** COM-HE (WOC, Davenport, IA, 1949).

20401 **Marshall, Major, Jr.** DJ (WEEB, Southern Pines, NC, 1954–1957).

20402 **Marshall, Maud Graham.** Newscaster (*KGY's Town Crier*, KGW, Lacey, WA, 1928).

20403 **Marshall, Nancy.** Actress Marshall appeared on the daytime serial programs *The Story of Bess Johnson* and *Big Sister*.

20404 **Marshall, Olive.** Operatic soprano (NBC, New York, NY, 1928).

20405 **Marshall, Peggy.** Singer (WPCH, New York, NY, 1928).

20406 **Marshall, R.E. "Rusty."** Sportscaster (WPAY, Portsmouth, NH, 1945–1946; *Time Out for Sports*, WPAY, 1947).

20407 **Marshall, Ray.** Newscaster (WHOM, Jersey City, NJ, 1941).

20408 **Marshall, Rhena.** Mezzo-soprano (KOMO, Seattle, WA, 1927–1928).

20409 **Marshall, Sue.** COM-HE (WDEC, Americus, GA, 1951).

20410 **Marshall, Virginia.** Organist (KWWG, Brownsville, TX, 1927).

20411 **Marshall, Warren.** DJ (*This is My Song*, KDIX, Dickinson, ND, 1947).

20412 **Marshall, William.** Director Marshall worked on the *Modern Romances* and *Whispering Streets* daytime serial programs.

20413 **Marshall Fields Tea Time Orchestra.** Department store sponsored band (WGN, Chicago, IL, 1926).

20414 ***Marshall Jamboree* aka *KMHT Marshall Jamboree*.** CW music show, the *Marshall Jamboree* (KMHT, Marshall, TX, 1952) was sponsored by the Marshall Chamber of Commerce and broadcast from the Marshall City Hall stage. The show's manager was A.T. Young with famous CW DJ T. Tommy Cutrer as MC. Some of the show's performers included: Buddy Young and His Texas Ramblers, Don Holt, Rhett Grant, Glenda Grant, A.B. Moore, Earl Woods, Russell Cooner and Carol Williams. Guest stars such as Martha Carson, Dicie and Jean Nettles, Blue Mountain Sweethearts and Norman Nettles and His Blue Ridge Mountain Boys and Girls.

20415 **Marshard, Jack.** Leader (*Jack Marshard Orchestra*, instr. mus. prg., CBS and NBC, 1939).

20416 **Marshman, Mary Margaret.** COM-HE (KSFA, Nacogdoches, TX, 1951).

20417 **Marsho, (Mrs.) Zola.** Pianist, violinist and soprano vocalist (KRFU, Columbia, MO, 1925).

20418 **Marston, A.D.** Announcer (WABI, Bangor, ME, 1923–1924).

20419 **Marston, Adelaide (Addy Richton and Lynn Stone).** Writer Marston often wrote under the names of Addy Richton and Lynn Stone. She wrote *Hilltop House*, *This Life is Mine* and *Valiant Lady*.

20420 **Marta.** Soprano soloist who frequently sang as part of the Gypsy and Marta vocal team (KPO, San Francisco, CA, 1925–1926). *See* ***Gypsy and Marta*.**

20421 **Martell, Paul.** Leader (*Paul Martell Orchestra*, instr. mus. prg., WIP, Philadelphia, PA, 1936; WOR, Newark, NJ, 1939).

20422 **Martell, Rose.** Singer (WPCH, New York, NY, 1932).

20423 **Martell, Tony.** COM-HE (WEJL, Scranton, PA, 1956).

20424 **Marten, Judy.** DJ (*The Judy Marten Show*, WTIK, Durham, NC, 1950).

20425 **Martens, Thora.** Contralto (WENR, Chicago, IL; KMOX, St. Louis, MO and WOW, Omaha, NE, 1929). Busy Martens previously sang on Chicago's KYW, WQJ, WHT, WEBH and WIBO, KMOX (St. Louis, MO) and WCCO (Minneapolis–St. Paul, MN). Martens had first appeared on KYW (Chicago, IL) singing with Dorothy Wilkins in the early 1920s.

20426 **Martenson, Luella.** COM-HE (WKOW, Madison, WI, 1949).

20427 ***Martha and Hal*. .** Singing team (WOR, Newark, NJ, 1937).

20428 ***Martha Deane*.** Copyrighted name for the home economist owned by station WOR (New York, NY). The first Martha Deane role was played by Mary Margaret McBride from 1934 to 1937. Bessie Beatty followed in the role at WOR from 1940 to 1941. The last Martha Deane was Marion Young Taylor, who began in 1941 and continued in the role for decades. *See* **Beatty, Bessie; McBride, Mary Margaret; *Mary Margaret McBride and* Taylor, Marion Young.**

20429 ***Martha Roundtree's Capitol Close-Ups*.** Miss Roundtree interviewed such Washington notables as Vice-President Richard Nixon, FBI Chief J. Edgar Hoover, Speaker of the House Sam Rayburn and Attorney General William Rogers on her interesting program (45 min., Weekly, 3:15–4:00 P.M., WOR, 1959). Martha Roundtree's major contribution to radio was her creation with Lawrence Spivak of the *Meet the Press* program. *See* ***Meet the Press*.**

20430 **Martin, Ann.** COM-HE (WKBC, North Wilkesboro, NC, 1949).

20431 **Martin, Arthur.** Newscaster (WIZE, Springfield, OH, 1945).

20432 **Martin, Bob.** News analyst (KGVO, Missoula, MT, 1944–1945).

20433 **Martin, Browne.** Violinist (WSM, Nashville, TN, 1928).

20434 **Martin, Bud.** Newscaster (KVCV, Redding, CA, 1941).

20435 **Martin, Carl.** Newscaster (WIL, St. Louis, MO, 1945).

20436 Martin, Carol. COM-HE (KTUX, Pueblo, CO, 1951).

20437 Martin, Carroll. Trombonist (WIBO, Chicago, IL, 1925).

20438 Martin, Cecil. Newscaster (KEPI, Dublin, TX, 1939).

20439 Martin, Clara. COM-HE (WBIG, Greensboro, NC, 1956–1957).

20440 Martin, Dan. DJ (*Morning Neighbor*, WFMD, Frederick, MD, 1947).

20441 Martin, Della. DJ (*Teen Tattle Time*, KPHO, Phoenix, AZ, 1952).

20442 Martin, Dick. Newscaster (KGNC, Amarillo, TX, 1938).

20443 Martin, Dolph. Orchestra ldr. who featured singer Clare Willis (CBS, 1933).

20444 Martin, Don. Producer Martin produced *The Married Life of Helen and Warren*.

20445 Martin, Don. Sportscaster (Cornell University football play-by-play, WHCU, Ithaca, NY, 1955).

20446 Martin, Donna. Soprano (KGO, Oakland, CA, 1926).

20447 Martin, Dude. CW ldr. of Dude Martin and His Nevada Night Herders (KLX, Oakland, CA, 1939).

20448 Martin, Edra Paula. COM-HE (WEBK, Tampa, FL, 1956).

20449 Martin, Esther. COM-HE (KDTH, Dubuque, IA, 1956–1957).

20450 Martin, Florence. Clarinetist on the *Boys and Girls Farm Bureau Review* program.

20451 Martin, Freddy. Leader (*Freddy Martin Orchestra*, instr. mus. prg., WGN, Chicago, IL, 1935–1937; WFIL, Philadelphia, PA, 1936; MBS, 1936–1937; NBC, 1939–1940).

20452 Martin, Gene. Newscaster (WTAM, Cleveland, OH, 1952).

20453 Martin, George. Newscaster (WMSD, Muscle Shoals, AL, 1940; KEEW, Brownsville, TX, 1941; WRFF, Washington, DC, 1942–1945).

20454 Martin, George Wellington. Baritone (KFWB, Hollywood, CA, 1927).

20455 Martin, Georgia. COM-HE (WCEN, Mt. Pleasant, MI, 1957–1960).

20456 Martin, Gil. Newscaster (NBC-Blue, 1944).

20457 Martin, Grace. Soprano (WWJ, Detroit, MI, 1924).

20458 Martin, Hal. Newscaster (KGNC, Amarillo, TX, 1948).

20459 Martin, Halloween. One of the earliest female announcers and DJs, Martin was born on Halloween in Texas in 1902. She came to Chicago directly from college to work in the Home Economics department of the Chicago *Herald Examiner*. When station KYW (Chicago, IL, late 1920s), owned by the newspaper, needed a substitute for another female announcer, Prudence Penny, Martin filled in. She went on from these first broadcasts about interior decoration to conduct the station's popular *Musical Clock* program by playing records, giving the time and weather reports. Listeners enjoyed Martin's musical choices that ranged from the classics to jazz. Soon Miss Martin was known as "Miss Musical Clock." She continued conducting the program through the mid–1940s. *See* **Gender Discrimination**.

20460 Martin, Harris. Newscaster (WRRN, Warren, OH, 1941).

20461 Martin, Henry. CW fiddler (*Henry Martin*, CW instrumental prg. with Martin, who was billed as "the one-finger old-time fiddler" KGHI, Little Rock, AR, 1928).

20462 Martin, Howie. Announcer (KOIL, Council Bluffs, IA, 1928).

20463 Martin, Ian. Actor Martin was in the cast of *Against the Storm*, *Big Sister*, *Chandu the Magician*, *Life Can Be Beautiful* and *Right to Happiness*.

20464 Martin, Jack. Newscaster (WKBH, La Crosse, WI, 1940–1942). Sportscaster (WKBH, 1941, 1944–1945; *Sports Flash*, WKBH, 1952).

20465 Martin, Jack Bennett. Newscaster (KIUL, Garden City, KS, 1945).

20466 Martin, James "Jim." Newscaster (WGAR, Cleveland, OH, 1944–1948).

20467 Martin, Jean. COM-HE (KEEN, San Jose, CA, 1951–1960).

20468 Martin, Jeanette. Soprano (WJAZ, Chicago, IL, 1923).

20469 Martin, Joan. Soprano (WNAC, Boston, MA, 1933).

20470 Martin, Joe. Leader (*Joe Martin's Studio Six Orchestra*, instr. mus. prg., KFI, Los Angeles, CA, 1925).

20471 Martin, Joe. DJ (*Music Shop*, WTMV, East St. Louis, MO, 1948–1955; WOW, Omaha, NE, 1956–1957; *Breakfast Bandstand*, WOW, 1960).

20472 Martin, Jolly Joe. DJ Martin had a popular early morning music show (WNAX, Yankton, SD,1945).

20473 Martin, Johnny. Musician Martin was billed as an "uke artist" (WMCA, New York, NY, 1926).

20474 Martin, Josephine (Emily Barton). COM-HE (*Emily Barton, Home Reporter*, KFRC, San Francisco, CA, 1949).

20475 Martin, Juan. Tenor (WGBS, New York, NY, 1927).

20476 Martin, Kathryn. Soprano (KFWB, Hollywood, CA, 1925).

20477 Martin, Kathryn. Pianist (WFI, Philadelphia, PA, 1926).

20478 Martin, Kay. COM-HE (WHIN, Gallatin, TX, 1949).

20479 Martin, Ken. Martin conducted an early children's program (*Ken Martin's Evening with Children*, KDKA, Pittsburgh, PA, 1923).

20480 Martin, Kitty. COM-HE (WAYX, Waycross, GA, 1951).

20481 Martin, Lee. COM-HE (KSIM, Sikeston, MO, 1951).

20482 Martin, Lewis D. Newscaster (WDSM, Superior, WI, 1942, 1945).

20483 Martin, Louis "Lou." Newscaster (KOAM, Pittsburg, KS, 1940–1942). Sportscaster (KOAM, 1941–1942).

20484 Martin, Lu. DJ (*Time Out for Gospel Music*, WCMR, Elkhart, IN, 1960).

20485 Martin, Luther. Newscaster (WGAA, Cedartown, GA, 1945).

20486 Martin, M.L. Announcer (WGBC, Memphis, TN, 1925).

20487 Martin, Margaret. COM-HE (WSLM, Salem, IN, 1955; WOWI, New Albany, IN, 1960.

20488 Martin, Marian. News analyst (*News for Women*, KMOX, St. Louis, MO, 1941).

20489 Martin, Marion. Pianist (WWJ, Detroit, MI, 1928).

20490 Martin, Mary Anne. COM-HE (WDEC, Americus, GA, 1951).

20491 Martin, Mary Hale. Miss Martin conducted the *Household Period* program for housewives sponsored by Libby-McNeil-Libby (15 min., Wednesday, 10:35–11:00 A.M., NBC-Blue, 1929).

20492 Martin, Maurine. Violinist (WBAA, West Lafayette. IN, 1999).

20493 Martin, Molly. COM-HE (WBAL, Baltimore, MD, 1956–1957).

20494 Martin, Monica. COM-HE (WTIP, Portersville, CA, 1951).

20495 Martin, Nancy. Singer (*Nancy Martin*, vcl. mus. prg., WCAO, Baltimore, MD and WOR, Newark, NJ, 1935).

20496 Martin, Nat. Leader (Nat Martin's Orchestra, WGBS, New York, NY, 1925; WIP, Philadelphia, PA, 1926).

20497 Martin, Nat R. "Tiny." Sportscaster (WHCV, Charlottesville, VA, 1944; WHBQ, Memphis, TN, 1945; WFNC, Fayetteville, NC, 1946; *Highlights in Sports*, WFNC, 1947–1948; *Highlights in Sports*, WFNC, 1949; *Tiny Martin's Sports Show*, WFNC, 1951).

20498 Martin, Paul. Leader (*Paul Martin Orchestra*, instr. mus. prg., NBC, 1934, 1938–1939).

20499 Martin, Paul. News analyst (*Youth in the News*, WIP, Philadelphia, PA, 1938).

20500 Martin, Paul. Producer Martin produced *Right to Happiness*.

20501 Martin, Ray. Sportscaster (*Sports Review*, WALL, Middletown, NY, 1947).

20502 Martin, Reginald B. "Reggie." Announcer (WSBT, South Bend, IN, 1925). Sportscaster (KFAB, Lincoln, NE and KFOR, Lincoln, NE, 1936–1937; WHB, Kansas City, MO, 1937, WGBS, Miami, FL, 1944). Newscaster (WIZE, Springfield, OH, 1945).

20503 Martin, Rita. COM-HE (KALV, Alva, OK, 1960).

20504 Martin, Robert "Bob." DJ (*Record Roundup*, WALT, Tampa, FL, 1948–1952).

20505 Martin, Rosemary. COM-HE (WNOP, Newport, KY, 1951).

20506 Martin, Sara. Singer (WHB, Kansas City, MO, 1926).

20507 Martin, Suzanne. COM-HE (KING, Seattle, WA, 1949).

20508 Martin, Thomas Emmet. Newscaster (WIBX, Utica, NY, 1937; WWNY, Watertown, NY, 1942, 1944–1945). Sportscaster (WIBX, 1937).

20509 Martin, Tiny. Sportscaster (*Sports Parade*, KGLC, Miami, OK, 1949).

20510 Martin, Victor G. Announcer (WHAM, Rochester, NY, 1927).

20511 Martin, Virginia. Pianist (WLAC, Nashville, TN, 1929).

20512 Martin, Wilton. Newscaster (WAIM, Anderson, SC, 1942).

20513 Martin, Zeke. Leader (*Zeke Martin and the Boys*, CW mus. prg., WNAX, Yankton, SD, 1939).

20514 *Martin Block Presents.* Block used his *Make Believe Ballroom* format on this West Coast version (180 min., Monday through Friday, 10:00–1:00 P.M., KFWB, Los Angeles, CA, 1940s).

20515 *Martin Gosch.* Gosch, with a style that sounded remarkably like Walter Winchell, discussed movies, their stars and radio programs on his RCA-Victor sponsored show (5 min., Wednesday, 6:40–6:45 P.M., WFIL, Philadelphia, PA, 1935).

20516 *Martin Kane, Private Eye.* Ted Hediger wrote and directed the exciting mystery drama starring William Gargan. As a New York private investigator, Gargan attracted a large audience with this fast paced adventure show sponsored by the U.S. Tobacco Company on radio and TV. Also in the cast were Walter Kinsella and Nicholas Saunders. Lloyd Nolan replaced Gargan in 1951 on radio and TV. Fred Uttal was the announcer (30 min., Sunday, 4:30–5:00 P.M., NBC, 1949).

20517 Martindale, Ross. Martindale provided the sound effects on the *Front Page Farrell* daytime serial program.

20518 Martindale, Winston ("Wink" or "Winkie"). Sportscaster (WDXI, Jackson, TN, 1952) and country music performer Martindale became a popular Memphis DJ, who played recorded music, gave time signals and supplied pleasant early morning chatter on his *Clock Watchers* program (240 min., Monday through Saturday, 5:00–9:00 A.M., WHBQ, Memphis, TN, 1955–1956). Later, in a highly unusual radio event, after Martindale had established a large following with a DJ stint at KHJ (Los Angeles, CA, 1958–1960), he was "traded" to KRLA, another Los Angeles station, for DJ Perry Allen. When traded to KRLA, Martindale brought along his Rubber Duckie and Wink Awake contests. Late in 1960, highly successful Martindale became KRLA's regular morning man.

20519 Martineau, Lorraine. COM-HE (WKNB, West Hartford, CT, 1960).

20520 Martinelli, Giovanni. Metropolitan Opera tenor (WJZ, New York, NY, 1927).

20521 Martinez, Al. DJ (*Discapades*, WKIP, Poughkeepsie, NY, 1949; *Music Unlimited*, WKIP, 1952–1955).

20522 Martinez, Doris. Soprano (WSMB, New Orleans, LA, 1926).

20523 Martinez, E.J. Announcer (KPO, San Francisco, CA, 1923).

20524 Martinez, Providencia. COM-HE (WVJP, Caguas, PR, 1960).

20525 Martinez, Ralph. Leader (Ralph Martinez and the Chamber of Commerce Band, KWWG, Brownsville, TX, 1926; Ralph Martinez's Concert Orchestra, KFWB, Hollywood, CA, 1929).

20526 Martini, Nino. Tenor (*Nino Martini*, vcl. mus. prg., CBS, 1933–1936). Martino had previously sang on the *Grand Opera Concert* program (CBS, 1929).

20527 Martino, Gilbert. Sportscaster (WDRC, Hartford, CT, 1937).

20528 Martin's Melody Orchestra. Popular radio band (WEAO, Columbus, OH, 1926).

20529 Martsoff, (Mrs.) J.E. Soprano (KDKA, Pittsburgh, PA, 1923).

20530 Martinsen, Thelma. Soprano (KLDS, Independence, MO, 1927).

20531 Martinson, Doug. News analyst (*News of the Week*, WFUN, Huntsville, AL, 1948).

20532 Martucci, Q. Bellevoice. Soprano (KFWI, San Francisco, CA, 1926).

20533 *Marty May.* Comedian May was joined on the sustaining variety show by Carol Dee, his "straight girl," crooner Jerry Cooper, rhythm singer Loretta Lee and the Johnny Augustine Orchestra (30 min., Thursday, 9:30–10:00 P.M., CBS, 1935).

20534 Martyn, Gilbert. News analyst (NBC-Blue, 1944; *This Moving World*, ABC, 1945; *Magazine of the Week*, KTLA, Los Angeles, CA, 1948).

20535 Martyn, Stan. Sportscaster (*Behind the Sports Desk*, WBCM, Levittown, PA, 1960).

20536 Martz, Gayle. COM-HE (WHLM, Bloomsburg, PA, 1955).

20537 Marucci, Virginio. Violinist (WLW, Cincinnati, OH, 1926–1928).

20538 Marvey, Gene. Leader (*Gene Marvey Orchestra*, instr. mus. prg., NBC, 1935).

20539 Marvin, Betty. Ukulele soloist (WBNY, New York, NY, 1926).

20540 Marvin, Bill. Sportscaster and play-by-play broadcasts (KSON, San Diego, CA, 1947). DJ (*Off the Record*, KSON, 1948; *1240 Time*, KSON, 1950).

20541 Marvin, Jane. DJ Marvin, identified only as "Janie," broadcast as a late night female DJ. She emphasized romance as she played soothing music on her *Two at Midnight* show (60 min., Monday through Friday, 12:00–1:00 A.M., WPTR, Albany, NY, 1952).

20542 Marvin, Johnny. Tenor (*Johnny Marvin*, vcl. mus. prg., NBC, 1933–1934; WLS, Chicago, IL, 1935).

20543 Marvin, Nancy. Singer (*Nancy Marvin*, vcl. mus. prg., WOR, Newark, NJ, 1935).

20544 Marvin, Tony. Newscaster (CBS, 1942). Marvin was probably most famous for his announcing assignments on many *Arthur Godfrey Show* programs on CBS in the 40s and 50s. DJ (Marvin tried his hand as a DJ on his daily show, *The Tony Marvin Show*, 120 min., Monday through Saturday, 2:00–4:00 P.M., WABC, New York, NY, 1958).

20545 Marx, Elzer. Sportscaster (WITY, Danville, IL, 1953–1960).

20546 Marx, Harpo. Harpist (WOR, Newark, NJ, 1929). The "silent" Marx brother was a talented musician.

20547 Marx, Jerry. Newscaster (KOMA, Oklahoma City, OK, 1944–1945).

20548 Marx, Regina. Leader (Concert Orchestra. WAPI, Birmingham, AL, 1929).

20549 *Marx Brothers Show.* The talking members of the brothers' team, Groucho and Chico, appeared on the short-lived show. Music was supplied by the Raymond Paige Orchestra (30 min., Weekly, 1937).

20550 Mary Christine Albin Trio. Instrumental group consisting of violinist Evelyn Pickerel, cellist Hazel Babbage and soprano Florence Kitzmiller (KFI, Los Angeles, CA, 1925).

20551 *Mary Ellen and Al.* Vcl. mus. prg. by harmony singing team (KGNF, North Platte, NE, 1939).

20552 *Mary Foster—the Editor's Daughter* (aka *Mary Foster, Editor's Daughter* and *Editor's Daughter*). Joan Banks played the title role on the daytime serial drama. Also featured in the cast were Parker Fennelly and Effie Palmer. At the conclusion of each show, Parker Fennelly as the editor, shared a bit of his daily wisdom. One of his observations was that "Folks in a small town live a much more relaxed life." In 1942, after the serial had been on the air for a year, a brief news segment was added to each program. The program had a seven year run. Sponsored by Kroger's Bread, the show exemplified the values of small town life (MBS, 1941–1947).

20553 Mary Jane and her Ukulele. Ukulele soloist (KMOX, St. Louis, MO, 1926).

20554 Mary Ruth. COM-HE (WYOM, Brookline, MA, 1949).

20555 *Mary Margaret McBride.* One of radio's most famous and gifted interviewers, Mary Margaret McBride never possessed an exceptionally good radio voice. Despite this, she rightfully enjoyed great popularity because of her skillful and intelligent interviewing techniques. She talked about every possible topic from the arts, motion pictures, Broadway plays, books, politics and world affairs. Politicians, stars of the entertainment world, artists and famous personages from the literary world appeared on her various programs.

McBride was working for the Newspaper Enterprise Association in New York when she auditioned for a job at WOR (New York, NY) in 1935. She immediately was hired and became *Martha Deane*, the station's copyrighted name for the person who conducted their woman's show. She began a successful broadcasting run that lasted from 1935 to 1940. At WOR, she frequently was joined on her program by Marjorie Moffet, who wrote and recited poetry; monologist Islay Benson; and Juliette "Nikki" Nicole speaking on fashion topics. Vincent Connolly and Dick Willard were her announcers (*Martha Deane*, Daily, 2:30–3:00 P.M., WOR, New York, NY, 1935–1940). She left the WOR and the role of Martha Deane in 1940, when her sponsor requested that her time slot be changed. McBride then went to work at NBC under her own name After leaving WOR, she continued interviewing famous persons such as Bob Hope, Jimmy Durante, Danny Kaye, the Dionne Quints, Elizabeth Taylor, Admiral Richard E. Byrd, James Thurber, Eleanor Roosevelt, General Omar Bradley, John Hersey, Henry Morganthau, Eddie Cantor, Bette Davis, Jinx Falkenburg, Tex McCrary, Fred Waring, Dinah Shore, George Montgomery, Olsen and Johson, Thor Hegerdahl, Carl Van Doren, Fannie Hurst, Quentin Reynolds, Mary Garden, Poppy Cannon and Jean Thomas. (*Mary Margaret McBride*, Monday through Friday, NBC; ABC, 1940–1954). *See* **Pioneers; Gender Discrimination; Martha Deane;** *and* **McBride, Mary Margaret**.

20556 ***Mary Marlin*** **(aka *The Story of Mary Marlin*).** Life was fairly ordinary for Mary Marlin on the daytime serial until her young lawyer husband, Joe Marlin, was elected the junior senator from Iowa. Mary, her Senator husband and their young son moved to Washington, DC, to meet many new trials and tribulations. Among the complications Mary faced in the serial was her husband's plane crash in Russia, his amnesia and the many snares set for him by attractive women in the Washington social and political scene. After originating in Chicago in 1934, the show was carried by the NBC-Red network in 1935. Joan Blaine created the title role during its Chicago run on WMAQ (Chicago, IL, 1935). On the network the title role was played by Anne Seymour, Betty Lou Gerson, Muriel Kirkland, Eloise Kummer and Linda Carlon. Other cast members included: Bill Adams, Charme Allen, Bob Bailey, Clare Baum, Helen Bemiller, Judy Blake, Carlton Brickert, Gene Burke, Francis X. Bushman, Betty Caine, Fran Carlon, Constance Crowley, John C. Daly, Frank Dane, Peter Donald, Barry Drew, Eddie Firestone, Jr., Bob Fiske, Murray Forbes, Templeton Fox, Rosemary Garbell, Earl George, Delores Gillen, Sharon Grainger, Robert Griffin, Marjorie Hannan, Elinor Harriot, Harvey Hays, Mary Jane Higby, Eunice Howard, Lucille Husting, Arthur Jacobson, Raymond Edward Johnson, Bess Johnson, Arthur Kohl, Rupert LaBelle, Charlotte Learn, William A. Lee, Bill Lipton, Phil Lord, Judith Lowry, Bobby Dean Maxwell, DeWitt McBride, Jay Meredith, June Meredith, Gene Morgan, Bret Morrison, Arnold Moss, Patsy O'Shea, Frankie Pacelli, Arthur Peterson, Loretta Poynton, Jess Pugh, Isabel Randolph, Olga Rosenova, Gerta Rozan, Jerry Spellman, Fred Sullivan, Joan Vitez and Bob White. Created and written by Jane Crusinberry, the program was directed by Don Cope, Kirby Hawkes, Ed Rice and Basil Loughrane. The "Clair de Lune" theme was played by pianists Allan Grant and Joe Kahn (15 min., Monday through Friday, 11:30–11:45 P.M., WMAQ, Chicago, IL, 1934–1935; NBC, 1935–1943;CBS, 1944–1945; ABC, 1951–1952).

20557 ***Mary Pickford*** **(aka *Mary Pickford's Stock Company*).** On her program silent movie star Pickford, who was known as "America's Sweetheart," chose plays in which she took the leading roles. The program broadcast on October 3, 1934, presented "The Church Mouse." Royal Deserts was the sponsor of the program, an evening replacement for the *Jack Pearl Show* (30 min., Wednesday, 8:30–9:00 P.M., NBC-Red, 1935).

20558 ***(The) Mary Small Revue.*** Small, who had entered radio as a child singing star ("Little Miss Bab-O") starred on this entertaining variety show (30 min., Sunday, 5:00–5:30 P.M., NBC-Blue, 1945). *See* ***Little Miss Bab-O***.

20559 **Maryland Artists Ensemble.** J. Van Praag directed the musical group that broadcast from the Hotel Maryland, Pasadena, California (KPSN, Pasadena, CA, 1925).

20560 **Maryland Hotel Dance Orchestra.** Hotel dance band (KPSN, Pasadena, CA, 1926).

20561 ***Maryland Mysteries.*** Good local folk lore was presented on these dramatizations of strange tales from various regions of Maryland. The cast included: David Kurland, Katherine Dierken, Lois Benson, Shelton Young, Tom O'Connell, Rex Reynolds and Garry Morfit—later famous as Garry Moore (30 min., Weekly, WBAL, Baltimore, MD, 1936). Both Morfit and Dierken were on the WBAL station staff. They appeared together as Bingo and Kitty on the station's comedy shows.

20562 ***Maryland Six Orchestra.*** Instr. mus. prg. with orchestra conducted by Jacque Cohen (KJBS, San Francisco, CA, 1925).

20563 **Marylanders Orchestra.** John Lederer was the leader (Marylanders Orchestra, WBAL, Baltimore, MD, 1928).

20564 **Marylin Trio.** Instrumental group consisting of Helen Bennett, violin; Marion Matthews, cellist; and Mildred Carroll, pianist and soprano (KNX, Los Angeles, CA, 1928–1930).

20565 **Marscho, (Mrs.) Zola.** Pianist, violinist and soprano vocalist (KRFU, 1925).

20566 ***Ma's Sewing Circle.*** Elmo Ellis created and produced the hour long comedy show. Brad Crandall, Jimmy Bridges, Frank Caron, Roy McMillan, Bob Van Camp and Jane Sparks Willingham were featured (60 min., WSB, Atlanta, GA, 1947).

20567 **Masestra, Emile.** Spanish cellist (WGBS, New York, NY, 1927).

20568 **Masi, Marie E.** DJ (WHBI, Newark, NJ, 1948; *Rhythm Parade Time*, WHBI, 1949–1955).

20569 **Masi, William A.** DJ (WHBI, Newark, NJ, 1948).

20570 **Masinek, Tosca.** COM-HE (KWRN, Reno, NV, 1951).

20571 **Masingale, Luther.** DJ (*Loafing with Luther*, WDEF, Chattanooga, TN, 1948–1949; *Sun Dial*, WDEF, 1949).

20572 **(The) Masked Soprano.** *See* **Leonard, Inez.**

20573 **Maslin, Alice G.** Pianist (KMOX, St. Louis, MO, 1928).

20574 **Mason, Art.** Newscaster (KMPC, Bakersfield, CA, 1944). Sportscaster (KMPC, 1946; KMPC, 1954–1955).

20575 **Mason, Bernice.** Soprano (WOC, Davenport, IA, 1923).

20576 **Mason, Betsy.** COM-HE (WHED, Washington, DC, 1956).

20577 **Mason, Bill.** DJ (*Mason's Mixer*, WDBQ, Dubuque, IA, 1956–1967).

20578 **Mason, Bobbye.** COM-HE (KROT, Baytown, TX, 1949).

20579 **Mason, Buck.** DJ (*Buck Mason* featured only Mason on the show, but he talked to the imaginary members of a large cast and played recorded western music, 40 min., Friday, 12:05–12:45 P.M., WBNY, New York, NY, 1941).

20580 **Mason, David.** Trombonist (WCBD, Zion, IL, 1923).

20581 **Mason, Dorothy.** Miss Mason broadcast weekly dancing lessons (WDAE, Tampa, FL, 1926).

20582 **Mason, Edith.** Prima donna soprano on the *Atwater Kent Hour* (NBC, New York, NY, 1927–1928).

20583 **Mason, Gerald and Daniel Mon.** Cornet and trombone soloists (WCBD, Zion, IL, 1925).

20584 **Mason, Greg.** DJ (KRLA, Los Angeles, CA, 1959).

20585 **Mason, Kathryn.** Pianist (WHO, Des Moines, IA, 1924).

20586 **Mason, Lee.** COM-HE (KCSJ, Pueblo, CO, 1949).

20587 **Mason, Lena.** Operatic soprano (WGBS, New York, NY, 1928).

20588 **Mason, Louise.** Soprano (KLDS, Independence, MO, 1927).

20589 **Mason, Marion.** COM-HE (KTOE, Mankato, MN, 1956).

20590 **Mason, Mary.** Home economist Mason conducted the *Home Forum* program (WRC, Washington, DC, early 1920s). She later directed the *Women's Club* program on WNAC (Boston, MA, 1925–1928). In 1928, Mason was Ida Bailey Allen's assistant on the *Homemakers' Club* (CBS, 1928). The following year she was the director of women's programs for WBZ (Boston, MA. 1929).

20591 **Mason, Mary.** COM-HE (WJVB (Jacksonville Beach, FL, 1951).

20592 **Mason, Mary.** COM-HE (WHAT, Philadelphia, PA, 1957–1960).

20593 **Mason, Mary.** Actress Mason appeared on the daytime serial programs *Life and Loves of Dr. Susan, Betty and Bob* and *Evelyn Winters* aka *The Strange Romance of Evelyn Winters.*

20594 **Mason, Max.** French horn soloist (WJAR, Providence, RI, 1925).

20595 **Mason, Maude.** Pianist (WAHG, New York, NY, 1925–1926).

20596 **Mason, Mildred "Dixie."** Singer (WLS, Chicago, IL, 1934).

20597 **Mason, Pamela.** COM-HE (KABV, Los Angeles, CA, 1960).

20598 **Mason, Paul.** Leader (*Paul Mason Orchestra*, instr. mus. prg., CBS, 1933–1934; WIP, Philadelphia, PA, 1935).

20599 **Mason, Roy.** Newscaster (KEVE, Everett, WA, 1941). Sportscaster (KEVE, 1941).

20600 **Mason, Ruth.** COM-HE (WREB, Holyoke, MA, 1940).

20601 **Mason, Sherman.** DJ (WEW, St. Louis, MO, 1960).

20602 Mason, Shirley. Soprano (WMEX, Boston, MA, 1940).

20603 Mason, Shirley. COM-HE (KFRU, Columbia, MO, 1951).

20604 Mason, William. Newscaster (WBRB, Red Bank, NJ, 1939).

20605 Mason-Heflin Male Quartet. Vocal group that contained tenors Roy MacClellan and Frederick Ainne, baritone Albert Hirst and bass Henry L. Booth. The accompanist was Flora Ripka (WIP, Philadelphia, PA, 1924).

20606 Masquelet, Eleanor. Blues singer (WCFL, Chicago, IL, 1929).

20607 *Masquerade.* Irna Phillips wrote the daytime dramatic serial. *Variety* said the program was "too talky" and identified its basic themes as: "Life is only an illusion" and "Things are not what they seem." *Variety* praised the cast that included: John Deering, Fay Warren, Gale Page, Judith Lowry, Betty Winkler, Don Briggs, Phil Lord, Butler Mandeville, Dan Sutter and Joan Winters. After running for 13 weeks the program was taken off the air, but a flood of letters from listeners brought it back September 9, 1935 (15 min., Monday through Friday, 2:30–2:45 P.M., NBC-Red, 1935).

After another long interval off the air, the program returned to the NBC schedule in 1946. The cast included Marguerite Anderson playing the leading role of a war widow who faced many romantic problems. She was supported by Conrad Binyon, Jack Edwards, Jr., Carlton KaDell and Ted Maxwell (NBC, 1946–1947).

20608 *Masquerade.* Impersonators were the featured performers on this novel program. The performers and those they imitated were: Paul Berry (Bing Crosby); Agnes Moorhead (Bea Lillie); Cleander Four (Mills Brothers); Frank Gould (George Burns); Bert Parks (Dick Powell); Alice Frost (Gracie Allen); Arthur Kay (Bert Lahr); Dwight Weist (Fred Allen); Kay Hogan (Morton Downey); Ruth Goetz (Betty Boop); Edna Harris (Eve Sully); Paul Douglas (W.C. Fields); Cameron Andrews (Ed Wynn); and Jean Rowe (Mae West). Even the Mark Warnow orchestra joined in the fun by imitating the styles of the Duke Ellington, Eddie Duchin, Wayne King and Ted Weems bands (60 min., Weekly, WABC, New York, NY, 1935).

20609 *(The) Masqueraders.* The vocal quartet of young college men included, among others, tenor Roger Robinson from Northwestern University and bass Winford Stracke from the University of Iowa (WBBM, Chicago, IL, 1930's).

20610 Massare, Domenick. Tenor (WTIC, Hartford, CT, 1925).

20611 Masselink, Virginia. Pianist (WEAF, New York, NY, 1925).

20612 Massell, Robert. Newscaster (NBC-Blue, 1944).

20613 (The) Massengales. Singers Clyde and Florence Massengale were a popular harmony team (WBAP, Fort Worth, TX, 1928).

20614 Massengill, Luther. Newscaster (WDEF, Chattanooga, TN, 1941–1942).

20615 Massey, Bill. Newscaster (KANS, Wichita, KS, 1940).

20616 Massey, (Mrs.) Guinn. Pianist (KTHS, Hot Springs National Park, AR, 1928).

20617 Massey, Louise and the Westerners. CW singer Victoria Louise Massey as part of the Massey Family CW group, including her father (Henry "Dad" Massey), two brothers (Allen and Curt Massey) and her husband (Milt Mabie). They played the Chautaqua circuit in 1928 until they arrived at Kansas City, MO, where they got their own program on KMBC (Kansas City, MO, 1928–1933) as the Westerners. After joining the *National Barn Dance* (WLS, Chicago, IL, 1933–1935), the group enjoyed a long recording and personal appearance career, including many guest appearances on network radio programs. Both Louise and younger brother, Curt Massey, recorded extensively. After the Westerners retired, Curt had his own network and transcribed radio series (*Curt Massey Show*, KNX, Los Angeles, CA, 1950s). Louise's songwriter career was marked by her composition of the popular, "My Adobe Hacienda." Her career, McCloud (1995, p. 512) says, ranks her with Patsy Montana and the Girls of the Golden West as a popularized of "Cowgirl and Western songs."

20618 Massey, Vera. Singer (*Songs by Vera Massey*, vcl. mus. prg., 15 min., Saturday, 5:45–6:00 P.M., WOR, Newark, NJ, 1947).

20619 Massey, Vera. COM-HE (WSDU, New Orleans, LA, 1954).

20620 Massies, Eddy. Leader (Eddy Massies' Orchestra, KFUU, Oakland, CA, 1925).

20621 Mast, Benny. DJ (*Hillbilly House Party*, WATA, Boone, NC, 1949; *1450 Club*, WATA, 1952). Sportscaster (*Around the Sports World*, WATA, Boone, NC, 1952).

20622 *Master Musicians.* The early music program featured many vocal soloists and an 18-piece concert orchestra directed by Hugo Mariani (45 min., Sunday, 10:25–11:00 P.M., WJZ-Blue, 1930).

20623 *Master Singers.* Vcl. mus. prg. (KVOR, Colorado Springs, CO, 1939).

20624 Master Six Orchestra. Commercial dance band (KFAB, Lincoln, NE, 1926).

20625 *Masterpieces of Charles Dickens.* The WPA (Works Progress Administration) Players broadcast a series of seven dramatizations of the works of novelist Charles Dickens (WOV, New York, NY, 1939).

20626 Masters, Bob. DJ (*Invitation to Dream*, KXOA, Sacramento, CA, 1948).

20627 Masters, Ed. Newscaster (WOC, Davenport, IA, 1945).

20628 Masters, Frankie. Leader (*Frankie Masters Orchestra*, instr. mus. prg., NBC, 1934; CBS, 1935–1937; WENR, Chicago, IL, 1937; KFEL, Denver, CO, 1940–1942; MBS, 1942).

20629 Masters, Harold. Leader (*Harold Masters Singers*, vcl. mus. prg., WEEU, Boston, MA, 1937).

20630 Masters, Len. Sportscaster (*Little League Salute*, WCOP, Boston, MA, 1955).

20631 Masters, Les. Sportscaster (WCOP, Boston, MA, 1952).

20632 Masters, Margaret. COM-HE (KSL, Salt Lake City, UT, 1956–1957).

20633 Masterson, Paul. Newscaster (KOY, Phoenix, AZ, 1940).

20634 *Masterwork Hour.* In 1929, a young lawyer approached Herman Neuman, the music director of WNYC, to donate a large collection of records with the request that they be broadcast for the enjoyment of New York listeners. Neuman readily agreed and initiated the *Masterwork Hour* program that was broadcast daily from 11:00–12:00 noon. The station claimed that this was the first program of classical music regularly scheduled for broadcast (60 min., Monday through Friday, 11:00–12:00 noon, WNYC, New York, NY, 1929).

20635 Mastin, Charlie. DJ (WEKY, Richmond, VA, 1956).

20636 Maston, George. News analyst (*Noon Newspaper*, KPDR, Alexandria, LA, 1947).

20637 Matatesla, Maria. Singer (WGES, Chicago, IL, 1936).

20638 Materi, Stacy. COM-HE (KROD, El Paso, TX, 1956).

20639 Mathay, Nicholas. Leader (*Nicholas Mathay Orchestra*, instr. mus. prg., NBC, 1935–1936).

20640 Mathers, Helen. Soprano (WTIC, Hartford, CT, 1925).

20641 Matheson, Daddy. Matheson conducted a children's program, *Daddy Matheson's Nature Stories for Children* (KFON, Long Beach, CA, 1925).

20642 Matheson, Mac. DJ (*Dude Ranch Roundup*, KTUC, Tucson, AZ, 1948–1954).

20643 Mathews, Bill. Newscaster (KMYC, Marysville, CA, 1940).

20644 Mathews, Dean. Pianist (WCBS, Springfield, MA, 1927).

20645 Mathews, Dorothy. Newscaster (WFOY, St. Augustine, FL, 1945).

20646 Mathews, Gertrude. Pianist (WQJ, Chicago, IL, 1925).

20647 Mathews, Lucille. Violinist (WQJ, Chicago, IL, 1925).

20648 Mathews, May. COM-HE (KRXL, Roseburg, OR, 1951).

20649 Mathews, P. Arlow. Leader (Wheat's Ice Cream Company Orchestra, WGR, Buffalo, NY,

20650 Mathews, Peggy. Blues singer (KFWB, Hollywood, CA, 1926).

20651 Mathewson, Margaret. Soprano (WOC, Davenport, IA, 1925).

20652 Mathias, Wally. Leader (*Wally Mathias Orchestra*, instr. mus. prg., WTAM, Cleveland, OH, 1942).

20653 Mathiebe, B. Singer (WHN, New York, NY, 1925).

20654 Mathiot, J.E. Announcer (WGAL, Lancaster, PA, 1925).

20655 Mathiot, Luther. Announcer (WGAL, Lancaster, PA, 1925).

20656 Mathis, Lyle. Newscaster (KVCV, Redding, CA, 1944). Sportscaster (KVCV, 1944–1946).

20657 Mathis, Sue. COM-HE (KVOP, Plainview, TX, 1955).

20658 Mathison, Sig. News analyst (*6 PM News*, KRIC, Beaumont, TX, 1948).

20659 Matinee Musical Club Chorus. Vocal group directed by Helen Pulaski Innes in association with the Matinee Club Orchestra and class conducted by Alexander Smallens (WIP, Philadelphia, PA, 1925).

20660 *Matinee Musicale*. Tenor Ben Klassen and soprano Carol Deis were featured on the weekly music show (15 min., Thursday, 4:15–4:30 P.M., NBC, 1935).

20661 *Matinee with Bob and Ray*. Bob Elliot and Ray Goulding, two station staff announcers who were experienced DJ's, teamed up to play records and produce an excellent daily combination of satire and nonsense. Their comic genius was just beginning to be appreciated when the program began (30 min., Monday through Friday, 1:00–1:30 P.M., WHDH, Boston, MA, 1948).

20662 Matlock, Ruth Russell. Versatile soprano Matlock sang, danced and acted on radio (WFBH, New York, NY, 1926).

20663 Matlock, Sam. DJ (*Magazine of the Air*, WKRC, Cincinnati, OH, 1953).

20664 Matson, Betty. DJ (WEAW, Evanston, IL, 1954).

20665 Matt, M. Leonard. News analyst (WDAS, Philadelphia, PA, 1938–1940, 1945; *Column of the Air*, WDAS, 1948).

20666 Matteson, Ruth. Actress Matteson appeared on the *Against the Storm* daytime serial program.

20667 Matthews, A.J. Old-time fiddler whose specialties were "The Chicken Crowed for a Day," "Somebody Ran Away with Dinah," and "Flowers From My Mother's Grave" (WOK, Pine Bluff, AR, 1922).

20668 Matthews, Alice. Pianist (WNAC, Nashville, TN, 1928).

20669 Matthews, Bately. Newscaster (KGGM, Albuquerque, NM, 1937).

20670 Matthews, Bill. DJ (*Record Room*, WMIS, Natchez, MS, 1948; *Red River Roundelay*, KALB, Alexandria, LA, 1952).

20671 Matthews, Blanche Moore. Pianist (WSM, Nashville, TN, 1928).

20672 Matthews, Buck. DJ (WJR, Detroit, MI, 1957).

20673 Matthews, Don. DJ (*Teen Time*, WIDE, Biddleford, ME, 1960).

20674 Matthews, E.B. Announcer and director of the *Farmers' Radio Chautauqua* (KTHS, Hot Springs National Park, AR, 1928).

20675 Matthews, Gail. Singer (WCOP, Boston, MA, 1939).

20676 Matthews, Gay. Singer (*Gay Matthews*, vcl. mus. prg., WAAF, Chicago, IL, 1936).

20677 Matthews, Georgie. Leader (Georgie Matthews Orchestra, WGBS, New York, NY, 1928).

20678 Matthews. Grace. In addition to portraying Margo Lane on *The Shadow* program, actress Matthews appeared on the daytime serials *Hilltop House*, *Big Sister* and *Brighter Day*.

20679 Matthews, Joe B. Newscaster (WGKV, Charleston, WV, 1939–1940). Sportscaster (WGKV, 1942).

20680 Matthews, Junius. Actor Matthews was in the cast of *Buck Rogers in the 25th Century*, *David Harum*, *Gasoline Alley*, *Land of the Lost* and Sherlock Holmes.

20681 Matthews, Marion. Cellist in the Marylin Trio (KNX, Hollywood, CA, 1929).

20682 Matthews, Marion. Organist (WNAX, Yankton, SD, 1937).

20683 Matthews, Marion. Pianist and organist (WNAX, Yankton, SD, 1945).

20684 Matthews, May. COM-HE (KRNR, Roseburg, OR, 1949).

20685 Matthews, Peggy. Blues singer (KFWB, Hollywood, CA, 1926).

20686 Matthews, Tom. Newscaster (WLAK, Lakeland, FL, 1939; WFLA, Tampa, FL, 1945–1947). Sportscaster (WLAK, 1940; WFLA, 1946–1949).

20687 Matthews, Sallie Belle. Leader (Sallie Belle Matthews Orchestra, WBAP, Fort Worth, TX, 1924).

20688 Matthews Sisters. Harmony singers who also played the uke (KGW, Portland, OR, 1928).

20689 Mattman, Theodore. Cellist (WEAF, New York, NY, 1923, WCAE, Pittsburgh, PA, 1924; WGBS, New York, NY, 1925).

20690 Matts, Warren. Newscaster (KOB, Albuquerque, NM, 1940–1941).

20691 Mattson, P.J. COM-HE (WARE, Ware, MA, 1954).

20692 Matz, Dody. COM-HE (WHLF, South Boston, VA, 1957).

20693 Matzenhauer, (Madame) Margaret. Metropolitan Opera soprano (WRC, Washington, DC, 1926).

20694 Mauck, Freddy. Leader (*Freddy Mauck Orchestra*, instr. mus. prg., WMT, Cedar Rapids–Waterloo, IA, 1937).

20695 Mauck, Vivienne. COM-HE (KBBS, Buffalo, WY, 1957).

20696 *"Maudie."* Mrs. Boyd Shreffler was "Maudie," a popular pianist in 1929–1930. *Radio Guide* said she was WIBW's most popular entertainer. "Maudie" played listener requests and received more fan mail in 1930 than any other WIBW entertainer (WIBW, Topeka, KS, 1929–1930).

20697 *Maudie's Diary*. The Continental Baking Company, manufacturers of Wonder Bread, sponsored the situation comedy based on the events in the life of Maudie Mason as she described them in her diary. During the two years of the program's run, the leading roles were played by Mary Mason and Charita Bauer. Also in the cast were Betty Garde, William Johnstone, Caryl Smith and Robert Walker. The announcer was Art Millett (30 min., Thursday, CBS, 1941).

20698 Maughn, Flora. Contralto (WIP, Philadelphia, PA, 1925).

20699 Maul, Herbie. Leader (Herbie Maul and his Medleys Orchestra broadcasting from the Westwood Club, KLRA, Little Rock, AR, 1939).

20700 Maule, Mary Katherine. Broadcast inspirational talks (KFRC, San Francisco, CA, 1925).

20701 *Maumee Valley Jamboree*. CW music program (WTOD, Toledo, OH, 1947). One of the program's featured singers was Marge Engler.

20702 Mauney, Ruth. COM-HE (WCTT, Corbin, KY, 1951).

20703 Mauphin, Rex. Leader, Rex Mauphin's Original Texas Hotel Orchestra (WBAP, San Antonio, TX, 1923; *Rex Mauphin Orchestra*, instr. mus. prg., NBC, 1934). In 1930, Maupin played trumpet with the Jules Herbuveaux's KYW (Chicago, IL) Orchestra. Versatile Maupin also played piano, cello and conducted the band at times. Before coming to KYW, Mauphin had played with Pryor's band and also with those of Paul Ash, Mark Fisher, Benny Meroff, Charles Kaley, Verne Buck and Charley Straight.

20704 Maurer, Hazel. Pianist (WDBO, Winter Park, FL, 1929).

20705 Mauri, Mauro. Tenor (WOR, Newark, NJ, 1927).

20706 Maurice, Janet. Elocutionist (WJZ, New York, NY, 1923).

20707 *Maurice*. Instr. mus. prg. by organist Maurice, who was not otherwise identified (WFBL, Syracuse, NY, 1938).

20708 *Maurice Chevalier* (aka *The Chase and Sanborn Show*). Chevalier, a famous French entertainer, performed on the music show accompanied by David Rubinoff conducting the orchestra. Jimmy Wallington was the announcer (30 min., 8:00–8:30 P.M., NBC-Red, 1931). *See* ***Chase and Sanborn Show***.

20709 *Maurice's Orchestra*. Instr. mus. prg. (KFI, Los Angeles, CA, 1934).

20710 Maurine Trio. Vocal trio consisting of Florence Hertzog, soprano; Maurice Miller, violinist; and Elvira Johnson, pianist (KTAB, Oakland, CA, 1926).

20711 Mauritz, Claire. Pianist (KHJ, Los Angeles, CA, 1925).

20712 Mauser, Cora. COM-HE (WKBH, LaCrosse, WI, 1949).

20713 Maust, (Mrs.) Joseph. Pianist (WRVA, Richmond, VA, 1926).

20714 Mauthe, Chick. Leader (*Chick Mauthe Orchestra*, instr. mus. prg., KWK, St. Louis, MO, 1942).

20715 *Maverick Jim*. This was an unusual children's western adventure drama, in that a story began on Thursday and concluded on Friday. Sterling Stewart wrote the interesting show. The cast included John Battle, Artells Dickson, Anne Elstner, Alice Frost and Margaret West. Occasionally, Dickson and West performed western songs. Runkel Brothers, makers of Runko Malt Beverages, sponsored the show (30 min., Thursday and Friday, 7:45–8:15 P.M., WOR, 1933).

20716 Maves, Dorothy. COM-HE (WCSI, Columbus, IN, 1951).

20717 ***Max Baer.*** Heavyweight boxer Max Baer starred as taxi driver Al Harper, who wanted to become a boxer, in this series sponsored by Goodrich Tire and Rubber Company. The series led up to the actual heavyweight championship bout that Baer had with the champion, Primo Carnera, which, incidentally was also broadcast with Goodrich's sponsorship. *Variety* noted that Baer did an acceptable job meeting the adventures he found on the program. At the conclusion of each show, Baer came on to tell of his training in preparation for the title bout with Carnera. Baer went on to win the heavyweight title easily, before losing it to an underdog boxer by the name of James J. Braddock (15 min., Monday-Wednesday-Friday, 7:45–8:00 P.M., NBC-Blue, 1934). *See* ***Lucky Smith***.

20718 ***(The) Max Baer Show.*** Baer, the former heavyweight boxing champion, was assisted on his show by Jerry Morton. Baer was a DJ, who also conducted celebrity interviews and delivered clever ad libs. *Variety* said that Max was almost as good a radio performer as he was a champion boxer (55 min., Monday, 11:05–12:00 midnight, KNX, Los Angeles, CA, 1953). *See* ***Lucky Smith***.

20719 **Maxemin, Juan.** Singer of Spanish songs (KFI, Los Angeles, CA, 1928).

20720 **Maxey, (Mrs.) John, Jr.** COM-HE (WLVA, Lynchburg, VA, 1951).

20721 ***Maxine.*** Contralto Maxine Marlowe was featured on the vocal music show (CBS, 1934).

20722 **Maxon, Roy.** Leader (*Roy Maxon Orchestra*, instr. mus. prg., NBC, 1935).

20723 **Maxson, John.** Newscaster (KWJJ, Portland, OR, 1942).

20724 **Maxwell, Bette.** COM-HE (WLAP, Lexington, KY, 1949; WLEX, Lexington, KY, 1956).

20725 **Maxwell, Bob (adult actor).** Actor Maxwell appeared on *The Lone Ranger* and *The Shadow* programs.

20726 **Maxwell, Bob.** Sportscaster (*Sports Revue*, WKNX, Saginaw, MI, 1947). DJ (*Bob Maxwell Show*, WWJ, Detroit, MI, 1948–1949; *Luke the Spook*, WWJ, 1950; *Man About Town*, WWJ, 1952–1954; *Music with Melody*, WWJ, 1955–1957).

20727 **Maxwell, Bobby Dean (child actor).** Actor Maxwell was in the cast of *Mary Marlin*.

20728 **Maxwell, Chuck.** DJ (*Variety Matinee* and *Night Watchman*, WREN, Topeka, KS, 1948)

20729 **Maxwell, Ed.** Actor Maxwell was in the cast of *Masquerade*. .

20730 **Maxwell, Edward C.** Newscaster (WERD, Atlanta, GA, 1948).

20731 **Maxwell, Elsa.** Society and entertainment commentator (MBS, 1945).

20732 **Maxwell, Jocko.** Newscaster (WWRL, Woodside, NY), 1937). Sportscaster (WWRL, 1937–1941, 1945–1946; *WWRL Sports Club*, WWRL, 1947–1948; *Sports Page*, WWRL, 1949; *Sports Review*, WWRL, 1950–1951; *Sports Digest*, WWRL, 1952; WNJR, Newark, NJ, 1953; *Football Scoreboard*, WWRL, 1954–1955; WNJR, 1956).

20733 **Maxwell, Preston.** Newscaster (KNEW, Hobbs, NM, 1942).

20734 **Maxwell, Richard.** Tenor (WOR, Newark, NJ, 1928 and WJZ, New York, NY, 1929; *Richard Maxwell*, vcl. mus. prg., CBS, 1936–1939). Maxwell on these programs was billed as a philosopher-tenor.

20735 **Maxwell, Robert.** Producer-writer-director Maxwell worked on *The Superman* program.

20736 **Maxwell, Ted.** Announcer (NBC-Pacific Network, 1928).

20737 **Maxwell, Ted.** Actor Maxwell was in the cast of *Flying Time*, *Girl Alone*, *Hawthorne House*, *Lights Out*, *Masquerade* and *Welcome Valley*.

20738 **Maxwell, Virginia.** COM-HE (WEBC, Erie, PA, 1951).

20739 **Maxwell Coffee House Orchestra.** Commercial band led by Nat Shilkret (NBC, 1927).

20740 ***Maxwell House Coffee Concert Program.*** A good hour-long concert music program, that featured such popular vocal performers as tenor Richard Crooks, crooners Gene Austin and Willard Robison and Marguerite Namara (NBC-Blue, 1926–1927).

20741 **Maxwell House Coffee String Quartet.** Instrumental group directed by violinist-leader Harry Jackson; violinist H.G. Frerike; cellist Phillip Musgrave; and pianist Harold Shellhorn (KFWB, Hollywood, CA, 1925).

20742 ***Maxwell House Coffee Time.*** Maxwell House Coffee was one of radio's most prolific sponsors and, generally, their programs were of the highest quality. The *Maxwell House Coffee Time* show was no different. It was an extension of the earlier *Good News* program, also sponsored by Maxwell House Coffee. Primarily a comedy, the program presented both Frank Morgan as a bumbling blow-hard and Fanny Brice as her hilarious Baby Snooks character. The writing was always clever and the performances outstanding. The cast included: Jack Arthur, Fanny Brice, John Conte, Cass Daley, Hanley Stafford, Frank Morgan and Alan Reed (Teddy Bergman). The writers were Keith Fowler, Paul Henning, Ed James, Phil Rapp. Robert Young and John Conte were the announcers. Music was supplied by the Meredith Willson orchestra (NBC, 1940–1944).

20743 ***Maxwell House Ensemble.*** This good music program had a similar format in the two versions of the show broadcast during the 1931 and 1932 seasons, but the performers were different. In the former, tenor Frank Parker, contralto Helen Rowland, pianist Arthur Schutt, a male quartet and an orchestra conducted by Don Voorhees were featured (30 min., Thursday, 9:30–10:00 P.M., NBC-Blue, 1931). The latter version, on the other hand, featured tenor Lanny Ross, the Songsmiths Male Quartet (Scrappy Lambert, Randolph Weyant, Leonard Stokes and Bob Moody) and the Don Voorhees Orchestra (30 min., Friday, 9:30–10:00 P.M., NBC-Blue, 1932).

20744 ***Maxwell House Melodies.*** Maxwell House Coffee sponsored the music program that featured the Dixie Vocal Trio consisting of Victor Hall, Leonard Stokes and Tubby Weyant singing with an orchestra conducted by David Mendoza. The announcer was Alwyn E.W. Bach (NBC-Blue, 1929). The following year the program featured soprano Muriel Wilson, a male quartet, a mixed vocal ensemble of eight voices and the Harold Sanford Orchestra. Edmund "Tiny" Ruffner was the announcer (30 min., Thursday, 9:30–10:00 P.M., NBC-Blue, 1930).

20745 ***Maxwell House Showboat.*** *See* ***Showboat***.

20746 ***Maxwell House Summer Show.*** General Foods, makers of Maxwell House Coffee, sponsored the excellent music show that was a summer replacement for the *Burns and Allen Show*. The cast included Frances Langford, Eloise Dragon, Myra Marsh and the Dick Davis Choir. Carmen Dragon conducted the orchestra. The announcer was Toby Reed (30 min., Thursday, 8:30–9:00 P.M., NBC, 1947).

20747 **May, Agnes Clark.** COM-HE (WJR, Detroit, MI, 1956).

20748 **May, Andrew.** Baritone (WOR, Newark, NJ, 1923).

20749 **May, Arlene [Arline].** COM-HE (WXRA, Buffalo, NY, 1956).

20750 **May, (Dr.) Arthur.** News analyst (WHEC, Rochester, NY, 1945).

20751 **May, Bea.** COM-HE (WITV, Ft. Lauderdale, VA, 1955).

20752 **May, Darrell.** Cornetist (KDKA, Pittsburgh, PA, 1923).

20753 **May, Earl E.** Owner-announcer (KMA, Shenandoah, IA, 1928.) News analyst and commentator (1939–1941, 1944–1946). May was also owner of the May Seed and Nursery Company. *See* **Stations — Growth and Development**.

20754 **May, Edward C.** Organist (WHEC, Rochester, NY, 1929).

20755 **May, Florence.** Pianist (KELW, Burbank, CA, 1928 and KFWB, Hollywood, CA, 1928).

20756 **May, Foster.** Newscaster (WOW, Omaha, NE, 1938–1942). Foster was a popular newscaster and special events announcer on WOW before moving on to KECA (Clayton, MO, 1946).

20757 **May, Lena.** Pianist (KQW, Chicago, IL, 1927).

20758 **May, Mary Ruth.** COM-HE (WMTN, Morristown, TN, 1957).

20759 **May and June.** The harmony singing team May and June, not otherwise identified, were popular local favorites (WMBB, Homewood, IL, and WOK, Chicago, IL, 1928).

20760 ***Maybelline Musical Romance.*** Spanish tenor Don Mario, an orchestra conducted by Harry Jackson and guest stars such as motion picture star Bebe Daniels were featured on the variety program (WEAF-NBC-Red, 1934).

20761 **Mayehoff, Ed "Eddie."** Leader (*Ed Mayehoff Orchestra*, instr. mus. prg., MBS, 1940). Actor Mayehoff was in the cast of *Against the Storm*.

20762 Mayer, Alfred [Albert]. Announcer (KFIZ, Fond du Lac, WI, 1926).

20763 Mayer, Bill. DJ (*Mayer of the Morning*, WGAR, Cleveland, OH, 1948–1954; WTAM, Cleveland, OH, 1955; WRCV, Philadelphia, PA, 1956).

20764 Mayer, Estelle. Violinist (WAHG, Richmond Hill, NY, 1925).

20765 Mayer, Henrietta. Coloratura soprano (WGBS, New York, NY, 1928).

20766 Mayer, Jack. Sportscaster (*Football Prophet*, WALB, Albany, GA, 1947; *Spotlight on Sports*, WALB, 1948).

20767 Mayer, Marilyn. Soprano (*Marilyn Mayer*, vcl. mus. prg., WOR, Newark, NJ, 1936).

20768 Mayer, Maurice. Announcer (WPEP, Waukegan, IL, 1927).

20769 Mayer, Purcell. Violinist (KFI, Los Angeles, CA, 1928–1929).

20770 Mayer, William. Newscaster (WGAR, Cleveland, OH, 1945–1946).

20771 Mayer, William J. Baritone (WIP, Philadelphia, PA, 1924).

20772 Mayh, Frank. Violinist (WHN, New York, NY, 1925).

20773 Mayhew, F.E. "Tiny." Sportscaster (KASA, Elk City, OK, 1940–1942). Newscaster (KASA, 1941–1942, 1945).

20774 Mayhew, Nye. Leader (*Nye Mayhew Orchestra*, instr. mus. prg., WOR, Newark, NJ, 1936).

20775 Mayhew, Ralph. Reader (WJZ, New York, NY, 1923).

20776 Maylott, Jack. News analyst (*Torrington and the World*, WTOR, Torrington, CT, 1948).

20777 Maynard, Bill. Sportscaster (*Sports Round-Up*, KTTS, Springfield, MO, 1947–1952). DJ (*Disc Jockey Jamboree*, KAMD, Camden, AR, 1948).

20778 Maynard, H.H. Newscaster (WOSU, Columbus, OH, 1945).

20779 Maynard, Jake. Sportscaster (WFVA, Fredericksburg, VA, 1960).

20780 Maynard, Robert K. "Bob." News analyst (*Highlights and Shadows of the News*, WSVS, Crewe, VA, 1947–1948).

20781 Mayne, Professor. Mayne talked about various aspects of self-improvement, i.e., "Everyday Speech" (WAHG, Richmond Hill, NY, 1925).

20782 Mayo, Pauline Lucille. Reader-impersonator (KDKA, Pittsburgh, PA, 1922).

20783 *Mayor S. Davis Wilson.* Philadelphia's Mayor Wilson broadcast weekly talks on civic problems and progress on his sustaining program (10 min., Thursday, 6:00–6:10 P.M., KYW, Philadelphia, PA, 1937).

20784 Maypole, Roy, Jr. Write Maypole worked on the *Hobby Lobby* and *Stepmother* programs.

20785 Mays, Esmeralda Berry. Violinist (KMOX, St. Louis, MO, 1928).

20786 Mays, Zilla Florine Horton. Black DJ (WAOK, Atlanta, GA, 1954). Mays was a silky-voiced pioneer female DJ — the only woman in 1954 on Atlanta radio with her own program. She began as "The Mystery Lady" and later "The Dream Girl." Later she began to feature gospel music on her programs. Mays devoted a large part of her life to promoting civic and humanitarian activities.

20787 May's Mandolin Musicians. Novelty music group (KMA, Shenandoah, IA, 1926–1928). The group of 12 musicians appeared variously as the May Flower Trio, Kay Tire Orchestra, KMA Coffee Orchestra, the Jig and Reel Orchestra, the Elysian Symphony Orchestra and the Corn Pickers' Gang on Earl E. May's station.

20788 *Maytag Frolic.* Maytag Washing Machine Company sponsored the popular Coon-Sanders orchestra on the lively music show. The Coon-Sanders orchestra used its own theme as the program's signature, "The Nighthawk Blues" (1929). This probably was one of the early transcribed programs that achieved a large audience.

20789 *Maytag Orchestra.* Instr. mus. prg. (WBZ-WBZA, Boston-Springfield, MA, 1932).

20790 Maytin, Herbert. Violinist (WOR, Newark, NJ, 1925).

20791 Maytire Orchestra. Club dance band (WKM, Shenandoah, IA, 1928).

20792 Maywood, Pat. COM-HE (KOGA, Ogallala, NE, 1957).

20793 Mazer, Bill. Sportscaster (*Sports Extra*, WKBW, Buffalo, NY, 1948–1951; WGR, Buffalo, NY, 1954; *Sports Roundup*, WGR, 1960).

20794 Mazurek, Maas. DJ (KCHS, Truth or Consequences, NM, 1956).

20795 Mazzucchi, Oswald. Cellist Mazzucchi, a one-time member of the New York Philharmonic Orchestra, was the leader of the orchestra on WJZ's famous *Slumber Hour* program (WJZ, New York, NY, 1929).

20796 McAdam, David. Tenor (KLX, Portland, OR, 1929).

20797 McAdams, Harry. Sportscaster (KWEW, Hobbs, NM, 1960).

20798 McAdams, Lou. Bass McAdams appeared on the *Weed Chain Program* and other CBS programs (1930).

20799 McAdow, Sciota. Soprano (WHO, Des Moines, IA, 1924).

20800 McAdoo, Dick. DJ (*Yawn Patrol*, WGBG, Greensboro, NC, 1947–1948; *Musical Showcase*, KFDM, Beaumont, TX, 1954–1955). Sportscaster (*Sports Roundup*, WGBG, 1951).

20801 McAfee, Marion. Soprano (*Marion McAfee*, vcl. mus. prg., NBC, 1934).

20802 McAleece, Gerald "Red." Sportscaster (KDTH, Dubuque, IA, 1950–1953; *Sideline Sports Chatter*, KDTH, 1954–1956).

20803 McAlister, R.B. Sportscaster (KFYO, Lubbock, TX, 1937–1942).

20804 McAllister, (Mrs.) A.B. and Mme. Beatrice Ferrio Hinz. Singing team (KFWM, Oakland, CA, 1926).

20805 McAllister, Don. DJ (*Rise and Shine*, WDBO, Orlando, FL, 1947; *Yours Sincerely*, WDBO, 1949–1950). Sportscaster (WDBO, 1949; *Sports Roundup*, WDBO, 1950; *Sports in Review*, WDBO, 1952–1955).

20806 McAllister, Grady. Sportscaster (WKKO, Cocoa, FL, 1955).

20807 McAllister, M. Actor McAllister was in the cast of *Young Dr. Malone*.

20808 McAllister, Ruth. COM-HE (KRPL, Moscow, ID, 1949).

20809 McAllister, William. DJ (*Valley Bandstand*, KREO, Indio, CA, 1950).

20810 McAndrew, Bill. DJ (*Swing Session*, WARM, Scranton, PA, 1947).

20811 McAndrew, Hilda. Singer (*Hilda McAndrew*, vcl. mus. prg., WBRE, Wilkes-Barre, PA, 1942).

20812 McArdle, Rodney. Newscaster (KXA, Seattle, WA, 1942).

20813 McArt, W.J. Tenor (KVOO, Tulsa, OK, 1928).

20814 McArthur, Doug. Sportscaster (KTAC, Tacoma, WA, 1956–1960).

20815 McAnulty, Bob. DJ (*Robert's Roost*, KWJJ, Portland, OR, 1952; KGW, Portland, OR, 1954–1955).

20816 McBride, Alys Mae. COM-HE (WHLB, Virginia, MN, 1956).

20817 McBride, Bonnie. News analyst (*News for Women*, KUOA, Siloam Springs, AR, 1940).

20818 McBride, DeWitt. Actor McBride appeared on *Famous Jury Trials*, *Lone Journey*, *Ma Perkins*, *Mary Marlin* and *Tom Mix* programs.

20819 McBride, Forrest. DJ (*Studio House Party*, WOKE, Oak Ridge, TN, 1954).

20820 McBride, Lester. Newscaster (KGLU, Safford, AZ, 1941–1942). DJ (KGLU, 1949). Sportscaster (KGLU, 1942).

20821 McBride, Mary Margaret. Popular commentator on topics of particular interest to women (NBC, 1942). *See* ***Mary Margaret McBride***.

20822 McBride, Robert "Bob." Newscaster (WPIK, Alexandria, VA, 1946). DJ (*Early Birds*, WPIK, Alexandria, VA, 1947).

20823 McBride, W.G. Newscaster (WDBO, Orlando, FL, 1941, 1945).

20824 McBroom, Hazel. Contralto (WIBO, Chicago, IL, 1926).

20825 McCabee, C.B. News analyst (*The Editor Talks It Over*, WCMA, Corinth, MS, 1947).

20826 McCabe Jubilee Singers. Vocal group specializing in "Negro spirituals" (WSUN, St. Petersburg, FL, 1928).

20827 McCachren, W.S. Announcer (WHP, Harrisburg, PA, 1925).

20828 McCaffrey, Joseph "Joe." Newscaster (CBS, 1944; WTOP, Washington, DC, 1945; MBS, 1954).

20829 McCaffrey, Tom. Sportscaster (*Sports Whirl*, WSSB, Durham, NC, 1950).

20830 McCain, W.H. "Bill." Newscaster (WBRC, Birmingham, AL, 1938–1941, 1944; WAGA, Atlanta, GA, 1945).

20831 McCaleb, Louise. COM-HE (HLP, Centerville, TN, 1956).

20832 McCaleb, Mildred. COM-HE (KLMX, Clayton, NM, 1951).

20833 McCall, Bettie. COM-HE (WCAO, Baltimore, MD, 1949).

20834 McCall, Bill. News analyst (*News Roundup*, WHAT, Philadelphia, PA, 1948).

20835 McCall, Bob. DJ (*Chariot Wheels*, WCRE, Cheraw, SC, 1955).

20836 McCall, Don. Newscaster (WEBC, Duluth, MN, 1940).

20837 McCall, George. Hollywood news and gossip broadcaster (*Hollywood Screenscopes*, CBS, 1937).

20838 McCall, Jack. Sportscaster McCall broadcast wrestling matches (KSYL, Alexandria, LA, 1950).

20839 McCall, L.C. DJ (*800 Club*, WWPF, Palatka, FL, 1947). Sportscaster (WWPF, 1947).

20840 McCall, Lawson. News analyst (*Currently Speaking*, KEX, Portland, OR, 1947; *McCall News*, KEX, 1948).

20841 McCall's Snappy Six Orchestra. Popular local orchestra (KFQZ, Hollywood, CA, 1926).

20842 McCallion, James "Jimmy." Actor McCallion appeared on *Billy and Betty*, *The Children's Hour*, *City Desk*, *Coast-to-Coast on a Bus*, *Gangbusters*, *Gasoline Alley*, *Light of the World* and *One Man's Family*.

20843 McCallister, Paul. Newscaster (KFDA, Amarillo, TX, 1941).

20844 McCallum, Lee. Poet McCallum read his own poetry and stated his own philosophy. He was the author of the "History and Rhymes of the Lost Battalion" (WBZ, Boston, MA, 1931).

20845 McCambridge, Mercedes. Talented, busy and versatile radio and motion picture actress McCambridge appeared on such programs as *Abie's Irish Rose*; *Dick Tracy*; and *I Love a Mystery*, as well as *This Is Nora Drake*; *The Guiding Light*; *Midstream*; *Tale of Today*; *Betty and Bob*; and *Big Sister* daytime serials.

20846 McCammon, Bess. Actress McCammon appeared on the daytime serial program *Backstage Wife* aka *Mary Noble, Backstage Wife*, *Life of Mary Southern*, *Romance of Helen Trent*, *Stepmother* and *Young Widder Brown*.

20847 McCampbell, Ursula. Violinist (WSM, Nashville, TN, 1928).

20848 McCandless, Paul B. "Mac." Newscaster (WDAD, Indiana, PA, 1946). Sportscaster (WDAD, 1947). DJ (*Music with Mac*, WDAD, Indiana, PA, 1947).

20849 McCann, Alfred W., Sr. McCann was an early broadcaster specializing in food and nutrition (*The Philosophy of Nutrition*, WJZ, New York, 1925). In later years, his son, daughter-in-law and grand daughter carried on his work on the air. *See* ***The McCann Pure Food Hour***.

20850 McCann, Bob. DJ (*Matinee Melodies*, KBMY, Billings, MT, 1947). Sportscaster (*Sportsreel*, KBMY, 1947; *Sports Review*, WBMY, 1949; *Sports Parade*, KBMY, 1950–1955).

20851 McCann, Dora and Alfred McCann. COM-HE (AM nutrition program, WOR, New York, NY, 1950). *See* **Husband-and-Wife Talk Shows**.

20852 McCann, E.G. Newscaster (KGCU, Mandan, ND, 1937–1938).

20853 McCann, Jim. Newscaster (WIBG, Glenside, PA, 1940; KYW, Philadelphia, PA, 1946). Sportscaster (WIBG, 1940).

20854 McCann, Mildred. Soprano (WFLA, Clearwater, FL, 1929).

20855 *(The) McCann Pure Food Hour*. Alfred W. McCann, Jr., took over the show in 1931, when his father, Alfred W. McCann, Sr. died. The elder McCann had begun the program in 1925 and established a laboratory to test foods (60 min., 10:00–11:00 A.M., WJZ, 1926). A commercial success, the program stressed the necessity to eat right to prevent disease. Wife Dora joined her husband on the show in the 1950s. Begun on WJZ, the McCanns completed their broadcasting career on WOR (New York, NY) with their *McCanns at Home* program. *See* ***The McCanns at Home***.

20856 McCann, Richard. Newscaster (KBON, Omaha, NE, 1946).

20857 McCann, Tom. Newscaster (WKRC, Cincinnati, OH, 1942). DJ (*Serenade to Seattle*, 30 min., Thursday, 6:30–7:00 P.M., KHR, Seattle, WA, 1948; *Easy Listening*, KJR, Seattle, WA, 1949).

20858 *(The) McCanns at Home*. Alfred and Dora McCann, husband and wife, added an afternoon talk session to their weekday morning food and nutrition program (15 min., Monday-Tuesday-Wednesday-Friday, 12:45–1:00 P.M., WOR, Newark, NJ, 1953). When Alfred, Jr. died, wife Dora carried on with the assistance of daughter, Patsy. When Dora died, Patsy carried on the program until well into the 1980s. See ***The McCann Pure Food Hour** and* **Husband-and-Wife Talk Shows.**

20859 McCarthy [McCarty] , Burl. Newscaster (WTSP, St. Petersburg, FL, 1941). DJ (*Wake Up Tampa*, WDAE, Tampa, FL, 1947).

20860 McCarthy, Charles. Announcer (WSAR, Fall River, MA, 1925).

20861 McCarthy, Charles F. Newscaster (WRAL, Raleigh, NC, 1939; NBC, 1946–1948; *The Sunday News Desk*, NBC, 1952).

20862 McCarthy, Clem. Sportscaster McCarthy's skillful blow-by-blow boxing broadcasts for NBC in 1937 included the Louis-Schmeling heavy weight championship bout and the Louis-Braddock championship fight. In that same year, he broadcast the Kentucky Derby and Preakness Stakes races, as well as conducting his regular *All Sports Program*. His other work included (*Sports News* WINS, New York, NY, 1934; *Sports*, NBC, 1936; *Krueger Sports Reel* program, NBC, 1940; *Racing Scratches*, NBC and WHN, New York, NY, 1940; WHN, 1941; NBC and WHN, 1944; WNBC, New York, NY, 1946; *Clem McCarthy Sports Show*, NBC, 1947–1949; horse racing broadcasts, NBC, 1952). Gravel-voiced McCarthy was perhaps most famous for his horse racing calls and his broadcast of the second Joe Louis-Max Schmeling heavyweight title boxing bout.

20863 McCarthy, Helen. Pianist (WIP, Philadelphia, PA, 1925).

20864 McCarthy, J.B. DJ (WJR, Detroit, MI, 1960).

20865 McCarthy, Jack. Newscaster (WXYZ, Detroit, MI, 1940).

20866 McCarthy, Jim. Sportscaster (*On the Sports Scene*, WBRE, Wilkes-Barre, PA, 1951–1954).

20867 McCarthy, Josephine. COM-HE (WMIE, Miami, FL, 1949).

20868 McCarthy, Margaret. Soprano (KDKA, Pittsburgh, PA, 1926).

20869 McCarthy, Red. DJ (*Platter Chatter*, WHGB, Harrisburg, PA, 1947–1950; *The Red McCarthy Show*, WHGB, 1952–1957; WCMB, Harrisburg, PA, 1960).

20870 McCarthy, Tom. Newscaster (WCPO, Cincinnati, OH, 1939–1941; WKRC, Cincinnati, OH, 1944–1947).

20871 McCarthy, Vivian. Soprano (WMAQ, Chicago, IL, 1924).

20872 McCartney, Maida H. COM-HE and newscaster (KOJM, Havre, MT, 1947–1968). McCartney conducted more than 5,000 broadcasts from her home in Chinook, MT, on KOJM (Havre, MT) from 1947 to 1968 on her program, *The Chinook Hour*. She came to Chinook, MT, in 1931 and wrote a regular column for the Chinook *Opinion* called "The Sugar City Silhouettes." Her daughter, who also was a writer, asked her why she didn't do a *Chinook Hour*. The following year she began writing news, announcements, etc. for KOJM. When they asked her if she would do a news program, she agreed if she could broadcast from her home.

She broadcast her program from a bedroom overlooking the prairie land that she loved so much. On the program she interviewed more than 3,000 guests, including exchange students from Scotland, Ireland, Sweden, Iceland, Norway, Turkey and Italy. When KOJM complained there was too much background noise in her house, she put a sign on her front door reading: PLEASE DO NOT RING THE BELL, COME IN QUIETLY DURING MY BROADCAST. One day a person who had a little too much to drink read the note, came up the stairs and saw her broadcasting the news. He said, "What're you doing talking to yourself?" She called her engineer at the station in Havre and told him to put on some records. She then lead the man downstairs, gave him some money to go down town and eat and *locked* her door.

When her program started in 1947, it was before the rural telephone was available. The program provided listeners with information about what roads were open and also broadcast police reports. Her theme was Bing Crosby's "Dear Hearts and Gentle People." Her personal motto was "Give the roses to the living." In 1975 (McCartney, 1975) said, "Well, I think it's amazing that I could just come right out of the kitchen, wipe the soup suds off my hands and go up and do the program. I didn't have any training. I just always liked to talk." This great pioneer retired in 1967 at the age of 72.

20873 McCarty, Donald E. DJ (*Off the Record*, WBOW, Terre Haute, IN, 1947).

20874 McCarty, Harold. Newscaster (KVOV, Redding, CA, 1945).

20875 McCarty, Jack. Newscaster (KORE, Eugene, OR, 1938–1939). Sportscaster (KORE, 1939–1940).

20876 McCarver, Rachel. COM-HE (WCPC, Houston, MS, 1960).

20877 McCarville, Barney. Announcer, sportscaster and newscaster (KYW-KFKX, Chicago, IL, 1929–1930).

20878 McCaskill, (Mrs.) Harold. Singer (WCOA, Pensacola, FL, 1927).

20879 McCauley, Helen. Pianist (WHP, Harrisburg, PA, 1942).

20880 McCauley, Joe. DJ (*Dawn Patrol*, WIP, Philadelphia, PA, 1947–1959; *Morning Show*, WIP, 1960).

20881 McChesney, (Mrs.) L. Conducted a children's program as the "*Tell Me a Story Lady*" in the 1920s.

20882 McChuthan, Dot Echols. Musician in the Palace Theater String Orchestra (WBAP, Fort Worth, TX, 1925).

20883 McClanahan, Eleanor. Pianist (WEMC, Berrien Springs, MI, 1926).

20884 McClanahan, Rosalind. Soprano (WBAA, West Lafayette, IN, 1939).

20885 McClanahan, Steele. DJ (*Musical Clock*, KGBS, Harlingen, TX, 1947). Sportscaster (KGBS, 1942).

20886 McClary, Hy. McClary taught a radio art course (KFWI, San Francisco, CA, 1927).

20887 McClean, (Mrs.) C.Z. Violinist (WOK, Pine Bluff, AR, 1922).

20888 McClean, Elizabeth. Actress McClean was a cast member of the daytime serial program *Aunt Jenny* aka *Aunt Jenny's Real Life Stories*.

20889 McCleary, (Mrs.) John. Violinist (KWWG, Brownsville, TX, 1926).

20890 McClellan, (Mrs.) James. Pianist (WOK, Pine Bluff, AR, 1922).

20891 McClelland, Charles. Lyric baritone (WOR, Newark, NJ, 1928).

20892 McClelland, Van Der Veer. Newscaster (WAAB, Boston, MA, 1941).

20893 McClellen, (Mrs.) George. Singer-whistler (WFAA, Dallas, TX, 1924).

20894 McClendon, Gordon. Station owner McClendon was an important contributor to the development of Top-40 programming. Best known for his broadcasts of re-creations of baseball games, McClendon also helped pioneer the Top-40 format. Unlike the Storz programming pattern, the McClendon format was best known for its rock and roll music. Like Storz, McClendon employed extensive promotional activities and sufficient creative programming to be called the "Orson Welles of radio." *See* **Stations.**

20895 McCleod, Mercer. Actor McCleod was in the cast of *Second Husband*.

20896 McClintock, Harry Kirby "Mac"/"Haywire Mac." CW singer-songwriter McClintock was born in Knoxville, Tennessee, this pioneer country-western singer had an early career that included work as a merchant seaman and soldier and travel as a hobo. He became a popular Victor recording star under the name of "Haywire Mac." McClintock claimed to have composed such songs as "Big Rock Candy Mountain" and "Hallelujah, I'm a Bum Again."

He first sang cowboy songs on KFRC (San Francisco, CA) in 1925 and continued doing so into the 1930s on several highly popular programs such as the daily *Mac and His Gang*, *Mac Round the Campfire* and *Mac's Haywire Band*, all on KFRC from 1925 through 1928 and into the next decade (*Mac McClintock*, KFRC, 1933). McClintock was an important figure in the development of American country-western music. *Radio Guide* (February, 1930, p. 97) said that Mac was also a popular entertainer on KFRC's *Children's Hour* program.

He was said to have probably "wrecked the old 97 more than anyone else." McClintock's songs ranged from country-western to children's tunes. An idea of his range can be seen from the 78 R.P.M. recordings he made for Victor such as: VI 21343: "The Bum Song" and "Hallelujah! I'm a Bum"; VI 21421: "The Old Chisholm Trail" and "Red River Valley"; VI 21567: "The Circus Days" and "The Man on the Flying Trapeze"; VI V-40016: "The Trail to Mexico" and "Get Along Little Doggies." McClintock sometimes recorded as "Radio Mac" singing with Mac's Haywire Orchestra.

20897 McClintock, Mary. COM-HE (WHBQ, Memphis, TN, 1956).

20898 McCloskey, Katherine. COM-HE (KDB, Santa Barbara, CA, 1954).

20899 McCloy, Ruth and Dick Keplinger. Husband and wife talk and commentary program (KOMO, Seattle, WA, 1949).

20900 McCluer, Paul. Announcer (WENR, Chicago, IL, 1928–1929). McCluer was also a continuity writer for the station and the announcer on *The Sunshine Hour* program (WENR, 1929–1930).

20901 McCluney, Richard. Baritone (WJBY, Gadsden, AL, 1929–1929).

20902 McCluny, Isabelle. COM-HE (KVOR, Colorado Springs, CO, 1951).

20903 McClure, Al. DJ (*Dance Time*, KOAM, Pittsburg, KS, 1947).

20904 McClure, Jean. COM-HE (WFCT, Knoxville, TN, 1960).

20905 McClure, Ken. DJ (*Jukebox Serenade*, WHB, Kansas City, MO, 1954).

20906 McClure, Marie. Pianist (WMH, Cincinnati, OH, 1924).

20907 McColl, Helen. Blues singer (KOMO, Seattle, WA, 1929).

20908 McCollough, Mary. COM-HE (KTIS, Hobart, OK, 1951).

20909 McCollum, Audrey. COM-HE (KWAT, Watertown, SD, 1951).

20910 McComb, Kate. Actress McComb was in the cast of the daytime serial programs *Lora Lawton*, *The O'Neills*, *Valiant Lady* and *Evelyn Winters* aka *The Strange Romance of Evelyn Winters*.

20911 McComb, Patricia. COM-HE (WSAM, Saginaw, MI, 1951).

20912 McCombs, Verna. Contralto (WJAZ, Chicago, IL, 1926).

20913 McConnell, Bryan. DJ (*We Congratulate*, WKST, New Castle, PA, 1947–1950).

20914 McConnell, Elizabeth. Violinist (WLAC, Nashville, TN, 1929).

20915 McConnell, Jane. Contralto (WHT, Decatur, IL, 1925).

20916 McConnell, Jim. DJ (*Music for Moderns*, KLOU, Lake Charles, LA, 1947).

20917 McConnell, (Bishop) Francis. Bishop of the Pittsburgh area Methodist Church, McConnell broadcast sermons on KYW (Chicago, IL, 1923).

20918 McConnell, Jane. Contralto (WHT, Decatur, IL, 1925).

20919 McConnell, Smiling Ed. Comedian, pianist and singer McConnell was born January 12, 1892. McConnell, the son of a minister, became a song leader for several evangelists before going into vaudeville and touring the lyceum circuits. In 1922, he went to work for WSB (Atlanta, GA). Eventually he performed on WJAX (Jacksonville, FL, 1926) and WSUN (St. Petersburg, FL, 1928).

McConnell broadcast as part of the singing team of *Ed and Mama* (WSUN, 1929–1930). He was active in the following years with his own programs (*Smiling Ed McConnell*, vcl. mus. prg., KUOA, Fayetteville, AR, 1933–1934; CBS, 1935; WLW, Cincinnati, OH, 1936; NBC, 1939).

20920 McConnell, Terry. COM-HE (WSTN, St. Augustine, FL, 1957).

20921 McCord, Erma R. COM-HE (WHBU, Anderson, IN, 1956–1957).

20922 McCord, Nancy. Soprano (WEAF, New York, NY, 1924–1926).

20923 McCord, Walter. Tenor (KFI, Los Angeles, CA, 1928).

20924 McCorey, Fern. Reader (WOAW, Omaha, NE, 1923).

20925 McCormack, Jack. DJ (*Mac's Wax Works*, WIRK, West Palm Beach, FL, 1952).

20926 McCormack, Joe. Leader (*Joe McCormack Orchestra*, instr. mus. prg., WGBI, Scranton, PA, 1937–1938, 1942).

20927 McCormack, John. Great Irish tenor (WEAF, New York, NY, 1925). On his 1925 broadcast on WEAF, McCormack appeared with Lucrezia Bori. He often appeared on the *RCA Victor Hour* program (WEAF, 1927–1929). McCormack's second series of radio recitals were broadcast on Wednesday evenings from 7:30–8:00 P.M. with an orchestra conducted by William Daley. Later, McCormack appeared on CBS: *John McCormack*, vcl. mus. prg. (7:30–8:00 P.M., CBS, 1934).

20928 McCormick, (Mrs.) Harold. *See* **Walska, Ganna.**

20929 McCormick, John. DJ (*London House Show*, WJJD, Chicago, IL, 1954–1955).

20930 McCormick, Leo. Baritone (KSTP, St. Paul, MN, 1929–1930).

20931 McCormick, Myron. Broadway and motion picture actor McCormick appeared on radio in *Central City*, *Helpmate*, *Joyce Jordan*, *Girl Interne*, *Listening Post*, *Man Behind the Gun*, *The March of Time*, *Passport for Adams* and *Portia Faces Life*.

20932 McCormick, Peggy. Contralto (KVOO, Tulsa, OK, 1928–1930).

20933 McCormick Fiddlers. CW music group consisting of Pa and Ma McCormick, Frank Mills, Ohmar [Omar] Castleman and Jerry Foy (WLW, Cincinnati, OH, 1927–1930).

20934 McCould, Keith. Staff announcer-pianist (WJZ, New York, NY, 1925).

20935 McCoy, Bill. DJ (*McCoy's Mad House*, KWNW, Wenatchee, WA, 1948).

20936 McCoy, Clyde. Leader (*Clyde McCoy Orchestra*, instr. mus. prg., WGN, Chicago, IL, 1934; WIP, Philadelphia, PA, 1936; KNX, Los Angeles, CA, 1939).

20937 McCoy, Marlys. COM-HE (WMOD, Moundsville, WV, 1957).

20938 McCoy, Mary. Soprano (NBC, 1929).

20939 McCoy, Mary. DJ (*Triple H Roundup*, KMCO, Conroe, TX, 1960).

20940 McCoy, Rita. COM-HE (WMRF, Lewiston, PA, 1949).

20941 McCoy, Sid. DJ (WGES, Chicago, IL, 1955).

20942 McCoy, Walter. Singer McCoy was billed as "The Man with Two Voices" (KGO, San Francisco, CA, 1927).

20943 McCracken, Chester. Writer McCracken wrote *Kate Hopkins, Angel of Mercy.*

20944 McCracken, Hal. Pianist (KOIN, Portland, OR, 1928).

20945 McCracken, Jarrell. Sportscaster (*May's Sports Cast*, KGNO, Dodge City, KS, 1947; KWTX, Waco, TX, 1951).

20946 McCracken, Ward. Violinist (KTAB, Oakland, CA, 1925).

20947 McCrae [McCravy], Margaret. Vocalist (*Margaret McCrae*, vcl. mus. prg., CBS, 1935–1936).

20948 McCraine, C.H. Announcer (WCBH, Oxford, MS, 1927).

20949 McCraine, Thelma. COM-HE (WGLC, Centerville, MS, 1956).

20950 McCraney, Betty. COM-HE (KSEL, Lubbock, TX, 1956).

20951 McCrary, "Jinx" Falkenburg. COM-HE (WRCA, New York, NY, 1956–1957). *See* ***Tex and Jinx*** *and* **Husband-and-Wife Talk Shows**.

20952 McCrary, Judith. COM-HE (WJSB, Crestview, FL, 1957).

20953 McCreary, Mac. DJ (*1400 Club*, KEBE, Jacksonville, TX, 1947–1948).

20954 McCreath, Ray. Announcer (WTFF, Washington, DC, 1927–1928).

20955 McCristall, Marie. Soprano (WHN, New York, NY, 1925).

20956 McCrocklin, Angeline. Contralto (WAPI, Birmingham, AL, 1929–1930).

20957 McCroy, Jannette. COM-HE (WBAC, Cleveland, TN, 1955).

20958 McCrudden, Marilyn. COM-HE (WSHB, Stillwater, MN, 1951).

20959 McCue, Dorothy. COM-HE (KULE, Ephrata, WA, 1956).

20960 McCulley, Maurine. Actress in a KFWB mystery serial (KFWB, Hollywood, CA, 1929).

20961 McCulloch, Sybyl. COM-HE (WETB, Johnson City, TN, 1954).

20962 McCullough, Annette. Contralto (WGY, Schenectady, NY, 1936).

20963 McCullough, Dan. DJ (*Musical Matinee*, MBS, 1955–1956; WOR, New York, NY, 1960).

20964 McCullough, Katie. COM-HE (KMHT, Marshall, TX, 1960).

20965 McCully, June. COM-HE (WKXP, Lexington, KY, 1957).

20966 McCune, Bill. Leader (*Bill McCune Orchestra*, instr. mus. prg., WOR, Newark, NJ, 1934–1936; CBS, 1940).

20967 McCune, Dorothy. Newscaster (KVOO, Tulsa, OK, 1938). McCune broadcast news and special events programs at KVOO, Tulsa, OK, in 1938.

20968 McCune, Katherine. Actress McCune was born August 20, 1917. She began her radio career at the age of twelve (WDAF, Kansas City, MO, 1929). One of her notable appearances was her role on the *Scattergood Baines* daytime serial program.

20969 McCune, Mildred. COM-HE (KTHV, Little Rock, AR, 1956).

20970 McCune, Will. Leader (*Will McCune Orchestra*, instr. mus. prg., CBS, 1938).

20971 McCurdy, Barbara J. COM-HE (WTCB, Flomaton, AL, 1956).

20972 McCurdy, Marsh. Leader (Marshland Dance Orchestra, WHN, New York, NY, 1923). Organist at Loew's Lexington Theater, New York City (WHN, New York, NY, 1926).

20973 McCurley, Lanse. Sportscaster (WDAS, Philadelphia, PA, 1939–1941).

20974 McCuskey, Alice. DJ (*Music Librarian, Music to Remember, Morning Melodies* and *World Famous Music*, WOSU, Columbus, OH, 1947).

20975 McCutcheon, Don M. DJ (*Sunday Musicale*, KASH, Eugene, OR, 1947). Sportscaster (*Sports Final*, KIHR, Hood River, OR, 1951–1953).

20976 McCutcheon, Dot. Leader (Dot McCutcheon's Orchestra, WBAP, San Antonio, TX, 1924).

20977 McCutcheon, W.A. Announcer who proclaimed his station's slogan, "We're on Chataugua Lake" (WOCL, Jamestown, NY, 1926–1927).

20978 McDade, Marian Dual. Pianist (KDKA, Pittsburgh, PA, 1923–1924).

20979 McDaniel, Ann. COM-HE (KWFC, Hot Springs, AR, 1954).

20980 McDaniel, Carl. Sportscaster (KLUF, Galveston, TX, 1940–1941). DJ (*Martins Music Shop*, KOCY, Oklahoma City, OK, 1947).

20981 McDaniels, Ace. DJ (*Trailers Trail*, KALE, Richland, WA, 1949).

20982 McDaniels, Roy. Yodeling cowboy singer (*Roy McDaniels*, vcl. mus. prg., KFXM, Beaumont, TX, 1932).

20983 McDaniels, Winifred. DJ (*Mac at the Record Rack*, KLFY, Lafayette, LA, 1949; KSYL, Alexandria, LA, 1957).

20984 McDermott, Marian. Soprano (WICC, Bridgeport, CT, 1936).

20985 McDermott, Tom. Singer-pianist (WHB, Kansas City, MO, 1929–1930).

20986 McDermott, Tom. Director-producer McDermott worked on the *Perry Mason* (producer), *Portia Faces Life* (producer), *Rosemary* (producer), *Wendy Warren and the News* (director) and *When a Girl Marries.*

20987 McDevitt, Leo. DJ (*Accent on Rhythm*, WAAB, Worcester, MA, 1947; *1230 Club*, WBSM, New Bedford, MA, 1949–1952).

20988 McDevitt, Ruth. Actress McDevitt appeared on the *Joyce Jordan, Girl Interne* daytime serial program.

20989 McDonald, A.S. Announcer (KFI, San Francisco, CA, 1923).

20990 McDonald, Al. DJ (*Al Mac's Music-Al*, KOTA, Rapid City, SD, 1949; *Spinners Sanctum*, KOTA, 1954).

20991 McDonald, Arch. Sportscaster and Washington Senators baseball play-by-play (WJSV, Washington, DC, 1934–1942; WTOP, Washington, DC, 1944–1947; *Speaking of Sports*, WTOP, 1949–1956). When McDonald began broadcasting Washington Senators' baseball in 1934, his engineer at Griffith Stadium was Granville Klink, Jr. McDonald and Klink worked the games from a small corrugated tin booth located on top of Griffith Stadium directly in line with home plate, where they had a good view. Since they were completely out of sight of the fans, on many hot Washington afternoons when the tin booth sweltered like a small oven, both McDonald and Klink stripped down to their shorts to broadcast the games (Klink, 1996).

Klink recalls how McDonald recreated Senators' games when they were out of town. He said a local telegraph operator with a typewriter sat next to McDonald. The telegrapher at the ball park sent a description of the plays and the studio telegrapher would then type out the results so McDonald could announce them. McDonald used a bell to indicate base hits. One, two, three or four bells sounded to indicate a single, double, triple or home run. He was known by his colleagues as "the Rembrandt of Baseball Reconstructions."

McDonald was such a local favorite that his favorite song—"They Cut Down the Old Pine Tree"—was played on the Griffith Stadium public address system before each home game. When McDonald went to New York to broadcast Yankee games in 1939, he was replaced by Walter Johnson, the former great Senators pitcher, to do the team's play-by-play broadcasts.

An example of the McDonald sense of humor can be found on the calling card he carried:

Nylon Hosiery Sirloin Steaks
Gasoline Coupons Race Tips Clubhouse Badges
Pullman Tickets Sugar New Tires
Cigarettes Cigars Chewing Gum
Hotel Reservations
ARCH McDONALD
CBS Washington, DC
TOASTMASTER MASTER OF CEREMONIES
Gin Rummy Expert World's Finest Whiskies
NO SEATS FOR OKLAHOMA
Cannot Clear With Sydney

McDonald, who always claimed to be an expert on gin rummy, ironically, died playing the game. One afternoon after broadcasting a

Washington Redskins professional football game in New York, McDonald took the train back to Washington. En route he was playing gin rummy with friends, when he suddenly slumped to the table. His death in 1961 was a shock to his many friends and listeners.

20992 McDonald, Avis. Leader (*Avis McDonald Orchestra*, mus. prg., WCFL, Chicago, IL, 1935).

20993 McDonald, Bob. Newscaster (KGNC, Amarillo, TX, 1941–1942, KRGV, Weslaco, TX, 1945). Sportscaster (KGNC, 1941–1942; KRGV, 1944).

20994 McDonald, Bryan [Brian]. Announcer (WJAS, Pittsburgh, PA, 1925–1927).

20995 McDonald [MacDonald], Dolly. Blues singer (KFI, Los Angeles, CA, 1926–1927).

20996 McDonald, Dorothy Day. COM-HE (WRFC, Athens, GA, 1955). Actress McDonald also appeared on the daytime serial programs *Painted Dreams* and *Aunt Abbey Jones.*

20997 McDonald, Frank. DJ (*Merry-Go-Round*, WCOP, Boston, MA, 1948).

20998 McDonald, Garf. DJ (*Music As You Like It*, KWSL, Lake Charles, LA, 1947).

20999 McDonald, Geri. COM-HE (WCBY, Cheboygan, MI, 1957).

21000 McDonald, Grace. Contralto (WSAI, Cincinnati, OH, 1929).

21001 McDonald, Grant. Singer (KSD, St. Louis, MO, 1925).

21002 McDonald, Irving T. Newscaster (WEEI, Boston, MA, 1942, 1944–1948).

21003 McDonald, James G. Broadcast talks on international affairs (NBC-Red, New York, NY, 1929; NBC-Blue, 1942).

21004 McDonald, James G. Tenor (*James G. McDonald*, vcl. mus. prg., WXYZ, Detroit, MI, 1942).

21005 McDonald, Jay. DJ (*Record Club*, WEW, St. Louis, MO, 1948; *770 Record Club*, WEW, 1950).

21006 McDonald, Jean. Actress McDonald appeared on the *Pained Dreams*, an early daytime serial program.

21007 McDonald, (Dr.) John J. News analyst (*Average Opinion*, WLBR, Lebanon, PA, 1948).

21008 McDonald, Julian. DJ (*Piggie Park Panorama*, WFIG, Sumter, SC, 1960).

21009 McDonald, June. COM-HE (KHEY, El Paso, TX, 1960).

21010 McDonald, Margaret. Actress McDonald was in the cast of *Kate Hopkins, Angel of Mercy* (title role).

21011 McDonald, Marie Chapman. Violinist (KGW, Portland, OR, 1924).

21012 McDonald, Marion. COM-HE (WOW, Omaha, NE, 1949).

21013 McDonald, Mary. COM-HE (KOB, Albuquerque, NM, 1956–1957).

21014 McDonald, Monty Margetta. Miss McDonald was the first network TV cooking show host. Although she had a long career as a television and motion picture actress, her chief claim to radio fame came when NBC signed her in 1945 to become the first female network announcer.

21015 McDonald, Norman. Newscaster (WJLS, Beckley, WV, 1941).

21016 McDonald, Rex. Banjo soloist and director (Silver King Dance Orchestra, WSUN, St. Petersburg, FL, 1928).

21017 McDonald, Rosa. DJ (*No Name Jive*, KLVK, Pasadena, TX, 1952).

21018 McDonald, Tex. DJ (*Ripley Request Time* and *Mason, Fleming and Brown County Matinee*, WFTM, Maysville, KY, 1948).

21019 McDonald, Ukulele Bob. Ukulele soloist (WGCP, New York, NY, 1926).

21020 McDonnell, Craig. Actor McDonnell was in the cast of *Bobby Benson's Adventures, Bringing Up Father, Daddy and Rollo, David Harum* (title role), *Official Detective, Second Mrs. Burton, Under Arrest* and *Valiant Lady.*

21021 McDonnell, Gene. Newscaster (KELO-KSOO, Sioux Falls, SD, 1939–1941). Sportscaster (KELO-KSOO, 1941).

21022 McDonnell, Margaret. COM-HE (KOSA, Odessa, TX, 1951; KTFS, Texarkana, TX, 1954).

21023 McDonnell, Mary. COM-HE (WGEM, Quincy, IL, 1949).

21024 McDonnell, Roberta Butler. Soprano (KTAB, Oakland, CA, 1927).

21025 McDonough, Dick. Sportscaster (WAAB, Boston, MA and WNAC, Boston, MA, 1937).

21026 McDougal, Cherie. COM-HE (WCHS, Charleston, WV, 1954).

21027 McDowall [McDowell], John H. Announcer (WMAY, St. Louis, MO, 1925).

21028 McDowell, Bill. Newscaster (WPIC, Sharon, PA, 1939–1942, 1945).

21029 McDowell, Goodloe. Newscaster (WLAP, Lexington, KY, 1938). Sportscaster (KENO, Las Vegas, NV, 1941).

21030 McDowell, Grace. Hawaiian guitarist McDowell was a member with Edith McDowell of a Hawaiian guitar duo (WEAF, New York, NY, 1923; WFAA, Dallas, TX, 1924).

21031 McDowell, Jan. COM-HE (WIRA, Ft. Pierce, FL, 1949).

21032 McDowell, Rachel K. Broadcast religious news (WEVD, New York, NY, 1939).

21033 McDowell, Roddy. DJ (Movie star McDowell tried his hand as DJ on *The Roddy McDowell Show,* KMPC, Los Angeles, 1948).

21034 McDuffee, Kane. Whistler (WQJ, Chicago, IL, 1926).

21035 McEachern, Cecilia. COM-HE (WHBQ, Memphis, TN, 1949).

21036 McEachern, Lee. DJ (*The Clock Watchers*, WHBQ, Memphis, TN, 1947).

21037 McEldowney, Todd. Sportscaster, hockey, football and basketball play-by-play (WOBT, Rhinelander, WI, 1960).

21038 McElhone, Alice. Pianist (WFI, Philadelphia, PA, 1925).

21039 McElmurray, Al. Newscaster (WFAA, Dallas, TX, 1946).

21040 McElroy, Alicia. Leader (Alicia McElroy's String Quartet, KGW, Portland, OR, 1926).

21041 McElroy, Cole. Leader (Cole McElroy's Dance Orchestra, KGW, Portland, OR, 1926; Cole McElroy's Columbia Recording Dance Band, KOIN, Portland, OR, 1928; Cole McElroy's Oregonians Orchestra, KOIN, 1928; and Cole McElroy's Own Dance Band, KOL, Seattle, WA, 1929).

21042 McElroy, Mac. DJ (*The Timekeeper* and *The 1230 Club*, WERC, Erie, PA, 1947; *Top of the Morning*, WIKK, Erie, PA, 1948–1950; WIRO, Ironton, OH, 1954–1956).

21043 McElroy, Michael. Sportscaster (WMT, Cedar Rapids–Waterloo, IA, 1941).

21044 McElroy, Peter. Newscaster (WINX, Washington, DC, 1940).

21045 McElroy, Rosalie. COM-HE (KVOA, Tucson, AZ, 1957).

21046 McElroy Saxophone Quintet. Instrumental group (WCBD, Zion, IL, 1926).

21047 McElroy, W.F. Announcer (WHBQ, Memphis, TN, 1927).

21048 McElveen, Henry, Jr. DJ (*Boogie Man*, WJOT, Lake City, SC, 1954).

21049 McElveen, Moody. Newscaster (WCOS, Columbia, SC, 1941, 1944–1945). Sportscaster (WCOS, 1945–1946).

21050 McElwain, George. Announcer (KGO, Oakland, CA, 1928).

21051 McElwee, Russ. DJ (*Dance Time*, WKDK, Newberry, NC, 1947).

21052 McEnelly's Singing Orchestra. Edwin McEnelly was a violinist in and leader of this unique music organization that specialized in semi-classical and popular dance music (WBZ, Springfield, MA, 1924–1925).

21053 McEntire, Walter F. Lecturer who spoke on "Mission San Luis de Francis" (KHJ, Los Angeles, CA, 1923).

21054 McEven, Sam. DJ (*Capitol Caravan*, WOL, Washington, DC, 1954).

21055 McEwen, Charles. Newscaster (WOPI, Bristol, TN, 1941).

21056 McEwen, Velma. COM-HE (KWBC, Ft. Worth, TX, 1954).

21057 McFadden, A.T. DJ (*A.T.'s Night Club*, WPLI, Jackson, TN, 1949). Sportscaster (WJAK, Jackson, TN, 1956).

21058 McFadden, Frances. Pianist (WSM, Nashville, TN, 1928).

21059 McFall, John. Leader (McFall's Dance Orchestra, WFAA, Dallas, TX, 1923; Gardner's Honey Boys Orchestra, WFAA, 1924).

21060 McFarlan, Charles. Tenor (KFI, Los Angeles, CA, 1928).

21061 McFarland [MacFarland], Dan L. Organist (KFI, San Francisco, CA, 1925–1926).

21062 McFarland, Dorothy. COM-HE (KCHA, Charles City, IA, 1951).

21063 McFarland, Grace. COM-HE (KGON, Oregon City, OR, 1949).

21064 McFarland, Lester and Robert A. Gardner (Mac and Bob). Singer-guitarist Lester McFarland and singer-mandolin player, Robert A. Gardner, both blind, became famous in country music as Mac and Bob. They performed on station WMOX (Knoxville, TN, 1927–1930), before going on to become part of the *National Barn Dance* cast on WLS (Chicago, IL). McFarland and Gardner began performing as Mac and Bob in 1924 (WNAV, Nashville, TN, 1924). The team later moved to WMOX and later still to Chicago's WLS. *See* ***Mac and Bob***.

21065 McFarland, Muriel. Pianist (WMH, Cincinnati, OH, 1924).

21066 *McFarland Twins Orchestra.* Instr. mus. prg. (NBC, 1939).

21067 McFarlane, Ian Ross. Newscaster (WFMD, Frederick, MD, 1939–1940; WJEJ, Hagerstown, MD, 1941–1942; WITH, Baltimore, MD, 1944–1946; WFBR, Baltimore, MD, 1947).

21068 McFawn, Rita. Soprano (WEBH, Chicago, IL, 1924 and WHT, Decatur, IL, 1925).

21069 McFawn and Belber. Harmony singing team (WMBB, Chicago, IL, 1926).

21070 McFeaters, Dale. Newscaster (KDKA, Pittsburgh, PA, 1938).

21071 McFeeters, Raymond. Tenor (KFI, Los Angeles, CA, 1925).

21072 McGann, Hugh. Baritone (KOIL, Council Bluffs, IA, 1928).

21073 McGarry, Jones Dana. DJ (*Requestfully Yours*, WBEC, Pittsfield, MA, 1947).

21074 McGarry, Mac. DJ (*The Mac McGarry Show*, WBEC, Pittsfield, MA, 1948; *The Mac McGarry Show*, WRC, Washington, DC, 1949).

21075 *McGarry and his Mouse.* Movie star Wendell Corey initiated the role of bumbling, none too bright detective Dan McGarry on the summer replacement for the *Eddie Cantor Show* that was sponsored by Bristol-Myers. The bumbling McGarry was frequently saved only by the quick intercession of his girl friend, Kitty Archer, who he affectionately referred to as his "mouse." The cast members included: Patsy Campbell, Peggy Conklin, Wendell Corey, Ted de Corsia, Carl Eastman, Betty Garde, Jack Hartley, Jerry Macy, Shirley Mitchell, Roger Pryor and Thelma Ritter. Music was by the Peter Van Steeden Orchestra. Milton J. Kramer wrote the show. Bert Parks was the announcer (30 min., Wednesday, 9:00–9:30 P.M., NBC-Red, 1946).

21076 McGavren, Marge. COM-HE (KMMJ, Grand Island, NE, 1956).

21077 McGaw, Helen. COM-HE (KBOL, Boulder, CO, 1951; KMMJ, Grand Island, NE, 1956).

21078 McGay, Bob. Newscaster (KPRO, Riverside, CA, 1944).

21079 McGeary, Ruth. COM-HE (WPAR, Parkersburg, WV, 1949).

21080 McGee, Art. DJ (*Let's Get Together with Records*, WALB, Albany, GA, 1952). Sportscaster (WALB, 1952).

21081 McGee, Beulah. Contralto (WOC, Davenport, IA, 1928).

21082 McGee, C. Martin. Musician McGee taught radio ukulele lessons (WCAP, Washington, DC, 1925).

21083 McGee, Frank. News analyst (KGFF, Shawnee, OK, 1946).

21084 McGee, Johnny. Leader (*Johnny McGee Orchestra*, instr. mus. prg., MBS, 1934; NBC, 1940).

21085 McGee, Kirk and Sam McGee. The McGee brothers were leaders of a country string music band featured on the *Grand Ole Opry* (WSM, Nashville, TN, 1925–1930; *Sam and Kirk McGee*, CW mus. prg., WSM, Nashville, TN, 1938). The brothers continued to perform on the *Grand Ole Opry* program for several decades.

21086 McGee, Laura. COM-HE (WCHK, Canton, GA, 1960).

21087 McGeehan, Bill. McGeehan broadcast the first three games of the October, 1923, baseball World Series before Graham McNamee took over to broadcast the remaining series games. Pioneer sportscaster McGeehan later broadcast the Harry Greb-Johnny Wilson boxing bout (WEAF, New York, NY, November 24, 1923).

21088 McGeehan, Mary Lee. COM-HE (WAZL, Hazleton, PA, 1951).

21089 McGenty, Dennis. Newscaster (WJMC, Rice Lake, WI, 1941).

21090 McGhee, Addison F. Sportscaster (WKAT, Miami Beach, FL, 1939).

21091 McGhee, Fred. Newscaster (KGBX, Springfield, MO and KWTO, Springfield, MO, 1939; KGBX, 1942).

21092 McGibbon, Harriet. Actress McGibbon was in the cast of the *Home Sweet Home* daytime serial program.

21093 McGibeny, Donald. Newscaster (WMAQ, Chicago, IL, 1935; WAIT, Chicago, IL, 1947–1948).

21094 McGiffin, Norton. Newscaster (WBAP, Fort Worth, TX, 1945).

21095 McGill, J.H. Newscaster (KGHF, Pueblo, CO, 1944).

21096 McGill, Mary. Popular pianist (KFVX, Bentonville, AR, 1926–1928).

21097 McGill, Morrey [Maury]. DJ (*Tip Top Tunes*, WCMW, Canton, OH, 1947; WLIO, East Liverpool, OH, 1950).

21098 McGill, W.E. "Windy." Sportscaster (WTJS, Jackson, TN, 1937).

21099 McGinley, A.B. Sportscaster (WTIC, Hartford, CT, 1936).

21100 *McGinty Oklahoma Cowboy Band* (aka *McGinty Cowboy Band*). The country-western music group played such songs as "Break the News to Mother" and "My Darling Nellie Gray" (WLW, Cincinnati, OH, 1927–30).

21101 McGivern, Frank. Newscaster (WJBC, Bloomington, IN, 1940–1941). Sportscaster (WJBC, 1940–1941).

21102 McGlone, Louise. Organist (KMA, Shenandoah, IA, 1928).

21103 McGovern, John. Actor McGovern was in the cast of *Backstage Wife, Case Book of Gregory Hood, East of Cairo, Ellen Randolph, Gibson Family, Highway Patrol, The O'Neills, Our Gal Sunday, Pages of Romance* and *Tennessee Jed*.

21104 McGowan, Dru. COM-HE (WOOF, Dorhan, Al, 1960).

21105 McGowan, George L. Sportscaster (KFPY, Spokane, WA, 1940–1941). Newscaster (KINY, Juneau, AK, 1945.)

21106 McGowan, Grace. Coloratura soprano (KMOX, St. Louis, MO, 1928).

21107 McGrady, Jeannette. Actress McGrady was in the cast of *Valiant Lady* daytime serial program.

21108 McGranahan, Thomas. Tenor (WEAF, New York, NY, 1925).

21109 McGrane, Don. Leader (*Don McGrane Orchestra*, instr. mus. prg. (MBS, 1940).

21110 McGrath, Audrey. Actress McGrath was in the cast of *The Romance of Helen Trent* daytime serial program.

21111 McGrath, Edwin "Ed." Sportscaster (*Sports Roundup*, WSPA, Spartanburg, SC, 1940–1941, 1945–1946; *Duke's Sports Show* and *Pigskin Highlights*, WSPA, 1947; *Duke Power Company Sports Show*, WSPA, 1950–1954). News analyst (*News in Review*, WSPA, 1946–1948).

21112 McGrath, Frank. Director (Parker House Concert Orchestra, WEEI, Boston, MA, 1928).

21113 McGrath, Leonard. Announcer (WSAR, Fall River, MA, 1925).

21114 McGrath, Marjorie. Pianist (WMSG, New York, NY, 1929).

21115 McGrath, Paul. Actor McGrath was in the cast of *Big Sister, Brighter Day, Casebook of Gregory Hood* (title role), *Inner Sanctum, Lora Lawton, This Life Is Mine, When a Girl Marries* and *Young Dr. Malone*.

21116 McGrath, William A. Announcer (WSAR, Fall River, MA, 1926).

21117 McGraw, Helen. Pianist (WBAL, Baltimore, MD, 1927).

21118 McGraw, Mac. Sportscaster (*UP Sports*, KFTM, Fort Morgan, CO, 1952–1954). DJ (*Western Roundup*, KFTM, 1954).

21119 McGreevy, John. Baritone (WOC, Davenport, IA, 1926).

21120 McGregor, Blanche. Contralto (KSD, St. Louis, MO, 1925).

21121 McGregor, Horace. Newscaster (WMSD, Shefield, AL, 1938). Sportscaster (WMSD, 1939).

21122 McGregor, Jean. Soprano (WAHG, New York, NY, 1926).

21123 McGregor, Jean. Actress McGregor appeared on the *Today's Children* daytime serial program.

21124 McGregor, Marguerite. COM-HE (WPEP, Taunton, MA, 1957).

21125 McGregor, Rosemary. COM-HE (KBNZ, La Junta, CO, 1955).

21126 McGrew, Bob. Leader (*Bob McGrew Orchestra*, instr. mus. prg., NBC, 1935–1937).

21127 McGrew, Dangerous Dan. DJ (WLBG, Laurens, SC, 1949).

21128 McGrew, Eva. COM-HE (WMTL, Leitchfield, KY, 1960).

21129 McGrew, Jack. Newscaster (KPRC, Houston, TX, 1939–1942).

21130 McGrew, Janet. Actress-executive assistant (NBC, 1939). Actress McGrew was in the cast of the *Young Dr. Malone* daytime serial program. McGrew in 1939 was an executive assistant to NBC president Lenox Lohr.

21131 **McGuire, Dorothy.** Motion picture star McGuire was in the cast of the *Big Sister* daytime serial program.

21132 **McGuire, Kathryn.** Actress (WOC, Davenport, IA, 1925).

21133 **McGuire, Mary.** COM-HE (KDTH, Dubuque, IA, 1954).

21134 **McGuire, Ray.** Newscaster (WGRM, Grenada, MS, 1939–1940). Sportscaster (WNOE, New Orleans, LA, 1946; *Sports 5:30 PM*, WNOE, 1947).

21135 **McHale, Jimmy.** Leader (*Jimmy McHale Orchestra*, instr. mus. prg., WIP, Philadelphia, PA and WORK, York, PA, 1938).

21136 **McHan, Bill.** News analyst (*Noon Edition*, WJPR, Greenville, MS, 1947).

21137 **McHenry, Alice Jane.** Child singer (*Alice Jane McHenry*, vcl. mus. prg., WHN, New York, NY, 1935) McHenry was a 12-year-old who had undergone a series of operations for an inverted stomach. She was a good, young soprano billed as the "upside down tummy girl."

21138 **McHugh, Edward.** Singer McHugh specialized in gospel songs (*Edward McHugh*, NBC-Blue, 1935–1937).

21139 **McHugh, Mary.** Contralto (NBC, 1938).

21140 **McHugh, Phil.** Newscaster (KMPC, Bakersfield, CA, 1939–1941).

21141 **McIlvaine, Don.** DJ (*Juke Box Review*, WHWL, Nanticoke, PA, 1947).

21142 **McInnes, Marion Keisker.** Producer-director, writer, COM-HE (WREC, Memphis, TN, 1926–1950s). McInnis first appeared on WREC (Memphis, TN) in 1929, when Martha Burns organized a children's "strolling" dramatic group to give performances at various city playgrounds. Miss Burns persuaded the manager of WREC to broadcast a weekly story hour program, *Winken, Blinken and Nod*, on which each of the three sailed in their boat each week with a story for children. McInnis was on the program when she was 14-years-old. The program was on WREC for a year.

During her college years, McInnis wanted to be a singer, but she appeared again on WREC in a dramatic series with the Memphis Little Theater group. At this time she evolved into more of a writer than performer. During her freelancing days in Memphis from the mid–1940s through the early 1950s, she had at least one broadcast each day on some Memphis station. She continued making dramatic appearances during these years, working mostly in dramatic productions and comedy shows. One example of her shows was a popular feature similar to television's *Hee-Haw* with many rural jokes and humor. Another was her portrayal of Auntie Bilious on a program on which she told bedtime stories in garbled language.

After many years of freelancing, she took a permanent job at WREC. She began writing and producing two programs in 1946. One was an afternoon show *Set Your Dial*; another was a morning quiz show, *The Pleasure Hour*. For the network she directed, wrote, produced and cleared the music for local orchestra "feeds" from the Hotel Peabody.

She was best known for her *Meet Kitty Kelly* program that ran for ten years. (Kitty Kelly was her professional name). When the station manager suggested that she do a woman's show, McInnis (1977) said, "Well, I will do a program that I hope everyone will listen to and not [just] because I'm a woman. I will not do recipes and the typical home show things." She didn't, but, instead, broadcast interviews and provided varied information. Although she originally disliked television, she eventually worked extensively in that medium.

21143 **McIntire, Fay.** Newscaster (KGBM, La Grande, OR, 1945).

21144 **McIntire, John.** Before becoming a motion picture and television star, actor McIntire appeared on *The Adventures of Mortimer Meek, Cavalcade of America, Ellen Randolph, March of Time, Mercury Theatre on the Air, The O'Neills* and *Philip Morris Playhouse* programs.

21145 **McIntire [McIntyre], Katherine [Katheryne].** Violinist, contralto and monologist (KMOX, St. Louis, MO, 1928).

21146 **McIntire, Lani.** Leader (*Lani McIntire Orchestra*, instr. mus. prg., NBC, 1938; KFEL, Denver, CO, 1942).

21147 **McIntosh, Bob.** Newscaster (WLLH, Lowell, MA, 1937).

21148 **McIntosh, Burr.** McIntosh was an early pioneer broadcaster of warm, cheerful bits genial of philosophy. His program consisted of homilies and gentle talk. Generally, McIntosh was billed as "*The Cheerful Philosopher*" (WJZ, New York, NY, 1923). Later his program, *Half-Hour with Burr McIntosh the Cheerful Philosopher,* was broadcast on KHJ (Los Angeles, CA, 1926). McIntosh had enjoyed an adventurous life, previously having served as a war correspondent with Teddy Roosevelt's Rough Riders in Cuba.

21149 **McIntosh, Stuart.** Actor McIntosh was in the cast of *Ma Perkins.*

21150 **McIntosh, Ezra.** Announcer (WOW, Omaha, NE, 1925). Newscaster (WWNC, Ashville, NC, 1938–1941).

21151 **McInturf, Lucille.** Organist (WWNC, Asheville, NC, 1928).

21152 **McIntyre, Anita Hopper.** Ms. McIntyre's broadcasts were similar to those of Burr McIntosh. She was known for her efforts to "bring a message of comfort and cheer to the sick" (KFSG, Los Angeles, CA, 1926). *See* **McIntosh, Burr**.

21153 **McIntyre, Doris.** Pianist (WBZ, Springfield, MA, 1925).

21154 **McIntyre, Frank.** News analyst (KGVO, Missoula, MO, 1940; KRBC, Abilene, TX, 1941; WKY, Oklahoma City, OK, 1942; KUTA, Salt Lake City, UT, 1945).

21155 **McIntyre, Frank.** DJ (*Mid-Morning Melody Matinee*, KLIX, Twin Falls, ID, 1947).

21156 **McIntyre, Hal.** Leader (*Hal McIntyre Orchestra*, instr. mus. prg., WCCO, Minneapolis–St. Paul, MN, 1937; KMOX, St. Louis, MO, 1942).

21157 **McIntyre, Mildred "Millie."** COM-HE (WRCO, Richland Center, WI, 1954–1957).

21158 **McIntyre, Susie.** COM-HE (WBTV, Charlotte, NC, 1954–1955).

21159 **McIver, Ernest.** Newscaster (WTOP, Washington, DC, 1944–1945).

21160 **McJoynt, Pat.** COM-HE (WJAZ, Troy, NY, 1951).

21161 **McKay, Betty.** Singer (KMTR, Hollywood, CA, 1925).

21162 **McKay, Carolyn.** Actress McKay appeared on *The Guiding Light* daytime serial program.

21163 **McKay, Cheri.** Contralto (*Songs and Smiles of Chri McKay*, KMOX, St. Louis, MO, 1929; NBC, 1934).

21164 **McKay, Harry.** Singer (*Harry McKay*, vcl. mus. prg., WIP, Philadelphia, PA, 1936).

21165 **McKay, J.C.** Baritone-violinist (WBZ, Boston-Springfield, MA, 1925).

21166 **McKay, James.** Baritone (KFWI, San Francisco, CA, 1926).

21167 **McKay, Janet.** Singer (*Janet McKay*, vcl. mus. prg., WIP, Philadelphia, PA, 1935).

21168 **McKay, Jim.** Sportscaster (WCBS, New York, NY, 1955).

21169 **McKay, Marion.** Leader (Marion McKay's Orchestra broadcast from Cincinnati's exclusive Swiss Gardens restaurant, WKRC, Cincinnati, OH, 1925–26; Marion McKay's Bond Hill House Orchestra, WKRC, Cincinnati, OH, 1925). The band's personnel included: McKay, ldr. and bj.; Paul Weirick and Izzy George, t.; Terry George, tb.; Ernie McKay, clr., as. and ss.; Skinny Budd, ts.; Russell Mock, as; Harry Bason, p.; Jack Tillson, d. and vcls.; and Ed Johns, tba.

21170 **McKay, Richard.** Actor McKay was in the cast of *David Harum.*

21171 **McKay, Scott.** Actor McKay was in the cast of *Barry Cameron.*

21172 **McKean, Ed.** Newscaster (KFH, Wichita, KS, 1937). Sportscaster (KFH, 1939).

21173 **McKechnie, Bill.** Baritone McKechnie later was a major league baseball player and manager of the Cincinnati Reds baseball team (KDKA, Pittsburgh, PA, 1922).

21174 **McKechnie, Jim.** Sportscaster (*Sport Slants* and *The Sport Report*, WENE, Binghampton-Endicott, NY, 1950–1951; WNDR, Syracuse, NY, 1954; *Sports Final*, WNDR, 1955–1956).

21175 **McKee, A.L.** Announcer (WHBU, Anderson, IN, 1925.

21176 **McKee, Allan.** Newscaster (KFAC, Los Angeles, CA, 1944).

21177 **McKee, Bob.** Newscaster (*Mobiloil News*, WCAE, Pittsburgh, PA, 1939).

21178 **McKee, Edna.** Pianist and blues singer (KVOO, Tulsa, OK, 1928; KMOX, St. Louis, MO, 1929–1930). McKee was known as "The Oklahoma Melody Girl." Previously she had sung on many stations: KPLA (Los Angeles, CA); KNX (Hollywood, CA); KFI (Los Angeles, CA); and KFWB (Los Angeles, CA).

21179 McKee, Hudson. Newscaster (KFEL, Denver, CO, 1945).

21180 McKee, Margaret "Mickey. " A whistler who performed on the *Roxy and His Gang* program (NBC-Blue, New York, NY, 1927).

21181 McKee, Thomas F. "Tom." Newscaster (WJTN, Jamestown, NY, 1938–1940).

21182 McKeehan, Harry M. Leader (Jack O'Lantern Orchestra, WCBE, New Orleans, LA, 1927).

21183 McKeever, John. Baritone (*John McKeever*, vcl. mus. prg., WOR, Newark, NJ, 1935).

21184 McKellar, Doug. Newscaster (KECA, Los Angeles, CA, 1946).

21185 McKellar, Mildred. COM-HE (WLOX, Biloxi, MS, 1955).

21186 McKellar, Nan. Contralto (KFI, Los Angeles, CA, 1926).

21187 McKellen, Annette. COM-HE (KBMX, Coalinga, CA, 1956–1957).

21188 McKelvey, June. Singer McKelvey accompanied herself with her uke (KJBS, San Francisco, CA, 1925).

21189 McKelvey, June and Virgil McElmoyle. Vocal harmony team (KJBS, San Francisco, CA, 1925).

21190 McKelvie [MacKelvie], Art. DJ (*Music Shop*, KHQ, Spokane, WA, 1947; *The Art McKelvie Show*, KHQ, 1948; *Saturday Matinee*, KHQ, 1952).

21191 McKenna, Genevieve. Soprano (WEAF, New York, NY, 1925).

21192 McKenna, Jim "Scottie." Singer (KTAB, Oakland, CA, 1928).

21193 McKennan, (Mrs.) Leora Sage. Soprano (KDKA, Pittsburgh, PA, 1925).

21194 McKenzie, (Reverend) J.A. Minister McKenzie broadcast weekly Bible School lessons (KMA, Shenandoah, IA, 1928).

21195 McKenzie, Kay. COM-HE (WSJB, Jamestown, NY, 1960).

21196 McKenzie, Maggie. COM-HE (KGNC, Amarillo, TX, 1954).

21197 McKenzie, R.T. Newscaster (KFXD, Nampa, ID, 1937).

21198 McKeon, Marion. Soprano, (WGY, Schenectady, NY, 1925).

21199 *McKesson Musical Magazine*. McKesson-Robbins Drug Company sponsored the music program featuring tenor Fred Hufsmith and a concert orchestra (30 min., Tuesday P.M., NBC-Red, 1931). A later version of the program featured Erno Rapee as orchestral conductor (30 min., Tuesday, 9:00–9:30 P.M., WABC, New York, NY, 1932).

21200 *McKesson Newsreel of the Air*. Another McKesson-Robbins Drug Company sponsored program, this one featured a discussion of the news events of the day with appropriate music (60 min., Sunday, 5:00–6:00 P.M., WMAL, Washington, DC, 1930).

21201 McKevitt, H.W. Sportscaster (KRE, Berkeley, CA, 1937).

21202 McKevitt, Liz. COM-HE (KNPT, Newport, OR, 1960).

21203 McKey, Wibby. Newscaster (WMJM, Cordele, GA, 1941).

21204 McKiernan, Jerry. Newscaster (WRRN, Warren, OH, 1941).

21205 McKiernan, Vivian. COM-HE (KXRO, Aberdeen, WA, 1955).

21206 McKinley, Barry. Baritone (*Barry McKinley*, vcl. mus. prg., WJZ, New York, NY and NBC-Red, 1936; NBC, 1939).

21207 McKinley, (Mrs.) D.B. Contralto specializing in Canadian songs (KPO, San Francisco, CA, 1924).

21208 McKinley, Ethel Dorr. Cellist (WIP, Philadelphia, PA, 1926).

21209 McKinley, Gertrude. Soprano (WBNX, Bronx, NY, 1936).

21210 McKinley, Larry. Sportscaster (*Sports Briefs*, WMRY, New Orleans, LA, 1955–1956).

21211 McKinley, Verona. COM-HE (KSCB, Liberal, KS, 1949).

21212 McKinney, C.F. Announcer (WFMA, Culver, IN, 1927).

21213 McKinney, Carl J. [Alexis]. Newscaster (WGTC, Greenville, NC, 1941–1942, 1944–1945). Sportscaster (WGTC, 1945).

21214 McKinney [McKiney], Fred. Singer (KFRC, San Francisco, CA, 1925).

21215 McKinney, Maurice. Newscaster (WJOI, Florence, AL, 1946).

21216 McKinney's Cotton Pickers. A popular radio and RCA Victor recording orchestra, that began as the Synco Septet and, later still, the Synco Jazz Band playing in and around Springfield, Ohio, in the early 20s. Saxophonist Milton Senior organized the band. Ex-circus drummer William McKinney, stopped playing drums in 1926 to become the band's manager.

McKinney's Cotton Pickers, contained some conservatory trained musicians, none of whom came from the south. The group was one of the finest bands of the period, due chiefly to the musical direction and arrangements of Don Redman, who had left the Fletcher Henderson Orchestra in 1927 to join it. After playing in such cities as Detroit, Baltimore, and Dayton, the band attracted the attention of orchestra leader-entrepreneur, Jean Goldkette, head of his National Amusement Corporation.

Goldkette took control of the band, while McKinney remained the business manager. Since Detroit's Graystone Hotel was the musical headquarters of Goldkette's management organization, he arranged for the band to play at the Graystone Hotel Ballroom, broadcast frequently, and obtain a RCA recording contract. After this send-off, the Cotton Pickers toured extensively to New York, Philadelphia, Chicago, and Atlantic City. After the tour and numerous broadcasts, the band enjoyed national popularity until about 1931. When the Goldkette organization terminated its relationships with the band in 1930, the group began to deteriorate, disbanding and regrouping several times in the following years. Changing musical tastes and internal problems caused the band to play its final engagement in Baltimore at Carlin's Amusement Park in the summer of 1934. The band's personnel in 1928 at the height of its popularity included: Cuba Austin, Langston Curl, Ralph Escudero, J. Horley, George Jones, John Nesbitt, Todd Rhodes, Prince Robinson, Milton Senior and arranger-musical director Don Redman (WJR, Detroit, MI, 1928).

21217 McKinnie, Peggy. COM-HE (WTJS, Jackson, TN, 1954).

21218 McKinnon, Bill. Newscaster (WBNS, Columbus, OH, 1946). Sportscaster (*Sports Digest*, WBNS, 1947–1950; *Shell Sports Digest*, WBNS, 1951).

21219 McKinnon, Bob. Sportscaster (*Sports Round Up*, WRFS, Alexander City, AL, 1947; *First Sports*, WRFS, 1949). Newscaster (WRFS, 1948). DJ (*1050 Club*, WRFS, 1948).

21220 McKinnon, Mattie Laura. COM-HE (WLAU, Laurel, MS, 1955).

21221 McKinstry, (Mrs.) Robert. Contralto (KGER, Hollywood, CA, 1929).

21222 McKitrick, Fred L. Announcer (WFDF, Flint, MI, 1925).

21223 McKittrick, Dorothy "Dotty." COM-HE (WEIM, Fitchburg, MA, 1949).

21224 McKlean [McClean], (Mrs.) C.Z. Violinist (WOK, Pine Bluff, AR, 1922).

21225 McKnight, Eddie. Leader (Eddie McKnight's Dance Orchestra, WPG, Atlantic City, NJ, 1926).

21226 McKnight, John. Newscaster (WDOD, Chattanooga, TN, 1941).

21227 McKown, David A. Newscaster (WMBS, Uniontown, PA, 1941).

21228 McLanahan, Frances. COM-HE (WBOR, Brownsville, TX, 1949).

21229 McLane, Jean. COM-HE (WCAO, Baltimore, MD, 1954–1955).

21230 McLaughlin, Ben Walker. Under the name of "Ben Walker," McLaughlin conducted NBC's *Women's Magazine of the Air* program. The entertaining and informative program was divided into several segments that might contain anything from jazz to an organ recital. With respect to these various segments of his program, McLaughlin said, "Three sponsors a day keep the blues away" (60 min., Monday through Saturday, NBC, early 1930s).

21231 McLaughlin, Bob. DJ (*570 Club*, KLAC, Hollywood, CA, 1948–1950).

21232 McLaughlin, Francis. Newscaster (WBRE, Wilkes-Barre, PA, 1946).

21233 McLaughlin, James. Sportscaster (*St. Croix Sports Round Up*, WSHB, Stillwater, MN, 1951–1954; WAVN, Stillwater, MN, 1956).

21234 McLaughlin, Manus. Violinist (McLaughlin's transcribed program, *Manus McLaughlin and His Old Time Fiddle*, appeared on many stations in the 1920s).

21235 McLaughlin, Val. A popular teller of children's tales, Miss McLaughlin started at WOW (Omaha, NE) before coming to WLS (Chicago, IL) in 1926. In Chicago, she conducted the popular *Lullaby Time* program for children (WLS, 1926). *See* **(The) Lullaby Lady**.

21236 McLaurin, Frank. DJ (*Homemakers Harmonies*, KFXM, San Bernardino, CA,

1948; *Open House*, KFXM, 1950). Sportscaster (*Sports Review*, KFXM, 1949).

21237 McLean, Betty (Betty Stevens). COM-HE (*Betty Stevens*, WENE, Endicott, NY, 1949).

21238 McLean, Dean. DJ (*Hillbilly DJ*, KWBC, Ft. Worth, TX, 1948).

21239 McLean, Jack. Leader (*Jack McLean Orchestra*, instr. mus. prg., MBS, 1934).

21240 McLean's Dance Orchestra. Popular radio band (WEBJ, New York, NY, 1926).

21241 McLellan, Annette. COM-HE (KBMX, Coalinga, CA, 1956–1957).

21242 McLemore, Morris. Sportscaster (*McLemore Sports*, WIOD, Miami, OH, 1949–1951; *Sports News and Views*, WIOD, 1952–1955).

21243 McLendon, Gordon. Newscaster (KNOE, Monroe, LA, 1945; KLIF, Dallas, TX, 1948). Sportscaster and sports play-by-play broadcaster (KLIF, Dallas, TX, 1949–1955).

21244 McLendon, Norwood. Newscaster (KTEM, Temple, TX, 1942).

21245 McLeod, Keith. Pianist (WJZ-NBC, New York, NY, 1925). Vibraphone soloist (NBC-Blue, New York, NY, 1929).

21246 McLeod, Leslie. Tenor (WHN, New York, NY, 1925).

21247 McLinn, George "Stoney." Sportscaster (WIP, Philadelphia, PA, 1937–1946; *Sports Shots*, WIP, 1947–1949; *Sports Parade*, WIP, 1950–1952).

21248 McLouth, Louis. Tenor (WGR, Buffalo, NY, 1924).

21249 McMahan, Mac. Newscaster (KSRO, Santa Rosa, CA, 1938).

21250 McMahon, Alice. Contralto (WBCN, Chicago, IL, 1926).

21251 McMahon, Charles. Newscaster (WCSC, Charleston, SC, 1939–1942; WNOX, Knoxville, TN, 1946).

21252 McMahon, Coletta. Actress McMahon appeared on *The Woman of America* program.

21253 McMahon, Leah. Pianist, blues singer and program director (1929).

21254 McMahon, Marge. COM-HE (KYRO, Potosi, MO, 1960).

21255 McMahon, Pat. DJ (WOC, Davenport, IA, 1957).

21256 McMahon, Tom. Newscaster (WWJ, Detroit, MI, 1946).

21257 McManus, Gertrude. Pianist (WOC, Davenport, IA, 1926).

21258 McManus, Maureen. Actress McManus appeared on the *Pepper Young's Family* daytime serial.

21259 McMartin, D. Cole. Newscaster (KVFD, Fort Dodge, IA, 1940–1941; KSIB, Creston, IA, 1946; WMT, Cedar Rapids, IA, 1948).

21260 McMaster, John [Jay]. DJ (Sports Matinee, WMEX, Boston, MA, 1948–1950; *Music Hall*, WMEX,1954–1955).

21261 McMaus, Mercedes. Blues singer (WRR, Dallas, TX, 1926).

21262 McMeen, Jo. COM-HE (WMRF, Lewistown, PA, 1957).

21263 McMichael, Marie. Organist (KFNF, Shenandoah, IA, 1936).

21264 McMichen, Clayton. Legendary Georgia country music violinist McMichen joined the famous Skillet Lickers CW music group in 1926 (WSB, Atlanta, GA, 1926).

21265 McMillan, Marvelle. Newscaster (KVOL, Lafayette, LA, 1945).

21266 McMillen, Dick. Leader (*Dick McMillen Orchestra*, instr. mus. prg., WREN, Lawrence, KS, 1939).

21267 McMillin, (Mrs.) Benton. Reader (WSM, Nashville, TN, 1928).

21268 McMillin, (Reverend) Frederick. Minister McMillin of the First Presbyterian Church of Walnut Hills, Cincinnati, Ohio, broadcast religious services (WLW, Cincinnati, OH, 1928–1929).

21269 McMinnville Exchange Club Male Quartet. Local vocal group (WLAC, Nashville, TN, 1928).

21270 McMoran, Lynn. Newscaster (KEVE, Everett, WA, 1941).

21271 McMullen, Blanche. Soprano (WFLA, Clearwater, FL, 1929).

21272 McMullen, Gretchen. COM-HE (YN, 1936; WEAN, Providence, RI, 1939).

21273 McMurray, Barbara. COM-HE (WLRP, New Albany, IN, 1956–1957).

21274 McMurray, DeWitt. McMurray, an editor of the semi-weekly *Farm News*, broadcast regularly. McMurray's broadcasts were identified by the Dallas *Daily News* as "a medley of humor, pathos and wisdom" (WFAA, Dallas, TX, 1924–1925).

21275 McMurray, Emmet H. Newscaster (WHBQ, Memphis, TN, 1942; WJPB, Greenville, MS, 1944).

21276 McMurray, James. Newscaster (WSIX, Pierre, SD, 1939).

21277 McNabb, Fred. McNabb broadcast talks on various gardening topics (KHJ, Los Angeles, CA, 1928).

21278 McNabb, Mary. Contralto (KFI, Los Angeles, CA, 1925).

21279 McNally, Mary Anne. COM-HE (KANS, Wichita, KS, 1954–1955).

21280 McNally, Ray. Sportscaster (KGNC, Amarillo, TX, 1956).

21281 McNally, Walter. Irish baritone (NBC, 1928).

21282 McNamara, Jim. Newscaster (KLAC, Los Angeles, CA, 1948).

21283 McNamara, Joe. Leader (Joe McNamara and his Twin Elms Orchestra, WJAR, Providence, RI, 1926).

21284 McNamara, John. Newscaster (WLPM, Suffolk, VA, 1947).

21285 McNamara, Lawrence "Larry." Sportscaster (*Sports News*, WNHC, New Haven, CT, 1951–1955).

21286 McNamara, Tom. Football news and conjecture were presented by McNamara (KOA, Denver, CO, 1925).

21287 McNamee, Graham. McNamee, a famous pioneer announcer, was born in Washington, D.C., July 10, 1888. He arrived in New York City with his divorced mother and began studying piano and voice. In 1921, the New York *Sun* reported his stage debut favorably by writing: "He performed with apparent justness, care and style" (Smith, 1992, p. 10). Furthermore, he performed with apparent success in more than 150 recital programs during his first season for which he also received praise from the New York *Times* (Smith, 1992, p. 11).

In May, 1923, seeking additional opportunities, McNamee was hired by WJZ. McNamee broadcast a blow-by-blow account of the middle weight championship boxing bout between Harry Greb and Johnny Wilson on August, 1923. His meteoric rise was assisted in September, 1923, when he was teamed with Grantland Rice, who was to do play-by-play, while McNamee provided color commentary at the World Series. After four innings, Rice passed the microphone to McNamee to do the play-by-play (Smith, 1987, p. 11). McNamee's performance caught the fancy of the nation and his popularity rose quickly.

He soon began to broadcast other sports events — football games, boxing bouts, tennis matches, etc. — President Calvin Coolidge's 1923 address to Congress, foreign coronations and both 1924 political conventions. The historic 1924 Democratic Convention in New York's Madison Square Garden lasted through 103 ballots. McNamee broadcast the convention almost continuously for the grueling fourteen days it lasted. After broadcasting his third World Series in 1925, he received more than fifty thousand letters or telegrams.

When the National Broadcasting Company became a network in 1926, McNamee's usual openings and closings became known to millions of listeners. He opened with: "Good evening, ladies and gentlemen of the radio audience" and closed with, "This is Graham McNamee speaking. Good Night all." By 1939, McNamee was also broadcasting the news on NBC.

After McNamee's death in 1942 at the age of 53 from a cerebral embolism, columnist Heywood Broun wrote of him: "McNamee justified the whole activity of radio broadcasting... . A thing may be a marvelous invention and still dull as ditch water. It will be that unless it allows the play of personality. A machine amounts to nothing more unless a man can ride. Graham McNamee has been able to take a new medium of expression and through it transmit himself— to give it vividly a sense of movement of feeling. Of such is the kingdom of art" (Smith, 1992, p. 12).

21288 McNaughton, H. Bliss. Newscaster (WTBO, Cumberland, MD, 1938).

21289 McNaughton, Peggy. COM-HE (WCRA, Effingham, IL, 1949).

21290 McNay, Ione. Newscaster (WOI, Ames, IA, 1941–1942, 1945).

21291 McNeel, Sherri. COM-HE (KOCA, Kilgore, TX, 1955).

21292 McNeeley, Marty. DJ (*McNeeley and Music*, WJR, Detroit, MI, 1949; *Music Hall*, WJR, 1954).

21293 McNeely, Beth. COM-HE (WTSP, St. Petersburg, FL, 1951–1960).

21294 McNeery, Bill. McNeery became "The Man in the Moon" after a curious mishap. A woman who wrote a series of children's stories in the Newark *Ledger*, was planning to broadcast them on station WOR, Newark, NJ. The woman had to climb an iron ladder and go through a hole in the roof to reach the studio that was located on top of a factory building. As studio personnel were helping her up the ladder, the lady fainted. McNeery, a reporter who happened to be present, said, "Now what do we do?" Announcer Tommy Cowan handed him the children's stories and at that moment McNeery became "The Man in the Moon," a role he played for many years (Gross, 1954, p. 58–59). It should be noted, however, that during the early years of radio there was more than one "Man in the Moon" broadcasting children's stories in the greater New York area.

21295 McNeil, Dave. Sportscaster (*Sportscope*, WCRB, Walham, MA, 1951).

21296 McNeil, Dean. DJ (*Blues at Sunrise*, KWBC, Ft. Worth, TX, 1949–1954).

21297 McNeil, Donald. Announcer (WTMJ, Milwaukee, WI, 1925).

21298 McNeil, Ida A. A pioneer in radio, McNeil began as announcer and manager of station KGFX (Pierre, SD, February, 1922). She continued in that position well in the 40s. She was still working on KGFX in 1948 as a DJ.

21299 McNeil, Robert J. Newscaster (KGFX, Pierre, SD, 1937).

21300 McNeill, Donald Thomas "Don." Best remembered as host of the popular long-running *Breakfast Club* program, McNeill studied journalism at Marquette University. It was during his sophomore year as a journalism major that McNeill first became an announcer at WISM (Milwaukee, WI). At that time he was also working at the Milwaukee *Sentinel* where, among his many chores he drew cartoons. In 1933, he took over as host of the *Smiles Before Breakfast* program. Later in the same year the program was transformed into *The Breakfast Club*. *See **The Breakfast Club**.*

21301 McNellis, Maggi. Miss McNellis was a lively and charming DJ (60 min., 10:30–11:30 P.M., WINS, New York, NY, 1956). She later gained national prominence as a TV panelist.

21302 McNerney, Francis. Newscaster (WTOL, Toledo, OH, 1945–1946).

21303 McNulty, Lymore. Mezzo-soprano (WIP, Philadelphia, PA, 1924).

21304 McNutt, Lona. COM-HE (KTSW, Emporia, KS, 1951).

21305 McNutt, Ruth. Reader (WGY, Schenectady, NY, 1922).

21306 McPeak, Mary Jane. COM-HE (KGRO, Gresham, OR, 1960).

21307 McPhee, John C. Newscaster (KARV, Mesa, AZ, 1946).

21308 McPherson, Aimee Semple. Billy Sunday and Aimee Semple McPherson were the most prominent evangelists of the Twenties. Glamorous Sister Aimee Semple McPherson in her long, flowing white robes preached to thousands who attended her Angelus Temple in Los Angeles. Her dynamic preaching style, physical attractiveness and her striking religious settings made virtually each of her sermons a dramatic presentation. At one service, for example, she dressed as a traffic cop, blew a whistle, and bellowed, "Stop! You are all going to Hell!" Along with Paul Rader in Chicago and New York's Paul Roach Stratton, she was a pioneer religious broadcaster.

Her first radio sermons were broadcast from San Francisco during the winter of 1921–1922. Her second sermon there was devoted to divine healing. Early in 1924, while alternating with other Protestant ministers broadcasting sermons, she soon realized that radio could be used to expand her ministry. In order to do so, she established her own station in Los Angeles, KFSG —*K*alling *F*our *S*quare *G*ospel (Los Angeles, CA). The third Los Angeles station to go on the air, KFSG began operations February 6, 1924. KFSG went on the air with the words of Priscilla Owens' hymn, "Jesus Saves."

> Give the winds a mighty voice,
> Jesus saves! Jesus saves!
> Let the nations now rejoice,
> Jesus saves! Jesus saves!

The Angelus Temple's organist, Esther Fricke Green, played both religious and classical musical numbers on that first broadcast day.

Every weekday morning, Sister Aimee conducted *The Sunshine Hour* program broadcast at 7:00 A.M. from her temple in Los Angles. She began her programs by saying, "You thousands of people here, you in the orchestra, you in the first balcony, you in the second balcony, you crowds standing in the rear, you thousands over the radio." Her station's first programming consisted of her many converts giving their testimonies plus such controversial features as broadcasting the addresses of gambling halls, speakeasies and the names of persons engaging in "white slavery."

One of the high points in Sister Aimee's broadcasting career took place on June 19, 1925, when a caller from Santa Barbara told her of the devastating earthquake the city had just experienced. Sister Aimee immediately entered her studio, stopped the program then in progress and began to tell her listeners of the disaster. Sister Aimee asked them to collect clothing, canned and cooked food. She told anyone with a truck to fill it with gas and come to the Temple. She said, "Be prepared to drive emergency supplies to Santa Barbara ... If you have nothing to give, give yourself. Come on over and help sort clothing and pack boxes." Her appeal was enthusiastically answered. Her listeners responded generously. By the time the Red Cross met to organize aid for Santa Barbara, two truck convoys from Angelus Temple had already arrived in Santa Barbara with blankets and food for the homeless.

A typical Sunday program broadcast January 18, 1925, on KFSG was as follows:

> 10:30–12:30 P.M. Complete morning services of the Angelus Temple with a sermon by pastor-evangelist Aimee Semple McPherson.
>
> 2:30–4:30 P.M. Afternoon worship service with the Silver Band, Temple Choir and sermon by Aimee Semple McPherson.
>
> 7:00–9:45 P.M. Evening service with a special musical hour program and sermon by Aimee Semple McPherson.
>
> 10:00–11:00 Organ recital by Esther Fricke Greene.

Sister Aimee lost favor with Secretary of Commerce Herbert Hoover in 1927, because she often changed her station's frequency. When Hoover warned her to stop this practice, she immediately shot back a telegram:

> PLEASE ORDER YOUR MINIONS OF SATAN TO LEAVE MY STATION ALONE STOP YOU CANNOT EXPECT THE ALMIGHTY TO ABODE BY YOUR WAVE LENGTH NONSENSE STOP WHEN I OFFER MY PRAYERS TO HIM I MUST FIT INTO HIS WAVE RECEPTION STOP OPEN THIS STATION AT ONCE.

Later, public perception of the luster of McPherson's evangelistic zeal was dimmed somewhat by the scandal surrounding the alleged hoax of her "disappearance-kidnapping," believed by many, instead, to really have been a sojourn with a male assistant from her radio station. To the modern ear Sister Aimee's sermons sound old fashioned, but her personal magnetism attracted a large radio listening audience. She used a vigorous delivery style and an extension of her vowels for added emphasis. She mixed humor with a keen insight of human nature. When she died in 1944, her congregation included 22,000 members and 600 churches.

21309 McPherson, Charlotte. COM-HE (WTTM, Trenton, NJ, 1956–1957).

21310 McPherson, Clyde. DJ (*Ranch Party Time*, WROB, West Point, MS, 1948).

21311 McPherson, (Mrs.) Elvira. Mrs. McPherson broadcast talks on "How to Raise Bees" (WOR, Newark, NJ, 1922).

21312 McPherson, Gaylord A. Newscaster (WDOD, Chattanooga, TN, 1939; WBLJ, Dalton, 1941; WDOD, 1944–1945). DJ (*Morning Serenade*, WDOD, 1948).

21313 McPherson, Hugh. DJ (WCHS, Charleston, WV, 1955–1957).

21314 McPherson, Marie. COM-HE (WEAM, Arlington, VA, 1951).

21315 McQuhae, Allen. Irish tenor (*Atwater Kent Hour*, 1926–1927).

21316 McRae, Don C. Announcer (KFOO, Salt Lake City, UT, 1926).

21317 McRae, Duane. DJ (*Breakfast in Bedlam* and *The Album of Musical Memories*, KROY, Sacramento, CA, 1948).

21318 McRae, June. DJ (*Wake Up Miami*, WFEC, Miami, FL, 1952; WMBM, Miami, FL, 1954).

21319 McRae, Tom. Newscaster (WJMS, Ironwood, MI, 1940).

21320 McReynolds, Jane. COM-HE (KFTM, Ft. Morgan, CO, 1960).

21321 McRorie, Janet. Continuity editor (NBC, 1930s). McRorie came to NBC in 1934 and created her own department as continuity acceptance editor. Some people called her the network "censor," since her staff of six checked from 60 to 105 scripts daily. Dorothy McKemble was a member of her department.

21322 McShane, Elizabeth. COM-HE (WOR, Newark, NJ, 1933–1934).

21323 McShane, Joe B. Announcer (KGDR, San Antonio, TX, 1927).

21324 McShane, Lu. COM-HE (KFXD, Nampa, ID,1955).

21325 McShane, Lucille. COM-HE (KSRV, Ontario, OR, 1951).

21326 McSloy, Sid. Newscaster (KGVO, Missoula, MT, 1945).

21327 McSpadden, H.W. Talks on insect life were broadcast by McSpadden (KNX, Los Angeles, CA, 1925).

21328 McSwain, Pat. Newscaster (WGNC, Gastonia, NC, 1941).

21329 McTavish, Blanche. Contralto (WOR, Newark, NJ, 1929).

21330 McTigue, Harry. Sportscaster (WHAM, Rochester, NY, 1939; WLOL, Minneapolis–St. Paul, MN, 1941; WINN, Louisville, KY, 1944–1945). Newscaster (WINN, Louisville, KY, 1944–1945).

21331 McVay, Bob. Sportscaster (*Speaking of Sports*, KFJI, Klimath Falls, OR, 1951; *Sports Final*, KFJI, 1952).

21332 McWain, Wes. DJ (MBS, 1957).

21333 McWhorter, John. Sportscaster (*Sports Spotlight*, WDKD, Kingstreet, SC, 1950).

21334 McWilliams, Hal. Sportscaster (KCMC, Texarkana, TX, 1951; KCKY, Coolidge, AZ, 1956).

21335 McWilliams, Megan H. COM-HE (WNRV, Narrows, VA, 1960).

21336 Mead, Doris. Actress Mead was in the cast of *The Road of Life* daytime serial program.

21337 Mead, Dorothy "Dottie." COM-HE (WSPB, Sarasota, FL, 1956–1957).

21338 Mead, Grace. Soprano (KFI, Los Angeles, CA, 1927).

21339 Mead, Myrtle. Singer (WPAR, Parkersburg, WV, 1937).

21340 Meade, Charles. Actor (WLW, Cincinnati, OH, 1926).

21341 Meade, Mary. Singer (WIND, Gary, IL, 1935).

21342 Meade, Merrill. Newscaster (KXL, Portland, OR, 1945).

21343 Meade, Ruth. Pianist Meade played regularly on *The Night Owls* program (KGW, Portland, OR, 1924–1925).

21344 Meader, George A. Metropolitan Opera tenor (WEAF, New York, NY, 1928).

21345 Meader, Raymond. Announcer (WDBR, Boston, MA, 1924–1925; WSSH, Boston, MA, 1925).

21346 Meadowmere Club Orchestra. Club band (WBAP, Fort Worth, TX, 1923).

21347 Meadows, (Miss) Frankie. Blues singer (WHN, New York, NY, 1928).

21348 Meadows, Marcia. COM-HE (WQJ, Chicago, IL, 1924).

21349 Meadows, V.E. COM-HE (ABS, 1935).

21350 Meakin, Jack. Leader (*Jack Meakin Orchestra*, instr. mus. prg., NBC-Blue, 1938).

21351 *Meakin Theatrical News.* Jack Meakin broadcast theatrical chatter and gossip on his sustaining show. Al Kavelin's Orchestra provided the music (30 min., Monday, 9:00–10:00 P.M. PST, NBC, 1937).

21352 *(The) Meal of Your Life.* The unusual transcribed program was broadcast by 63 stations. The show took place at an imaginary dinner at New York's Waldorf-Astoria in honor of some celebrity guest. The celebrity told the story of his most memorable meal. After he began his narrative, there was a fadeout to a dramatization of the story. The guests who told their story included Elsa Maxwell, George Jessel, Ned Sparks, Ilka Chase and Rosemary Lane. David Ross was the program's host (30 min., Transcribed, Various Times and Stations, 1946).

21353 Meaney, Charlotte. Reader (WBNX, New York, NY, 1937).

21354 Meaney, Ed. Sportscaster (WESX, Salem, MA, 1946). Newscaster (WESX, 1947).

21355 Mears, Martha. Contralto (*Martha Mears*, vcl. mus. prg., NBC, 1934–1936).

21356 *(The) Measles Club.* Conrey Bryston, the station's publicity director, originated the program after his daughter had to stay home from school with the measles. She was forced to listen to daytime radio fare that was designed for adults. At Bryston's suggestion, the children's program was initiated. Recorded music for children was broadcast and Roy Chapman, the station's program director, supplied stories and commentary (30 min., KTSM, El Paso, TX, 1938).

21357 Meath, Ed. Sportscaster (WHEC, Rochester, NY, 1949–1952).

21358 Mechlin, Ruth. News analyst (*For Women Only*, KRMD, Shreveport, LA, 1947).

21359 Mecker, Louise. Broadcast weekly book reviews (WDAF, Kansas City, MO, 1928–1929).

21360 Medcalfe, Roy. L. Organist (WFOX, Long Beach, CA, 1929).

21361 Meddars, Elizabeth. Violinist in the WMH String Trio (WMH, Cincinnati, OH, 1924).

21362 Medert, Elizabeth. Violinist (WSAI, Cincinnati, OH, 1925).

21363 *Medical Question Box.* Dr. John R. Brinkley, the famous and infamous "radio doctor," broadcast his medical information program on his own station (KFKB, Medford, KS). Brinkley first went on the air September 23, 1923. The program was the beginning of a long and controversial career in American radio. *See* **Brinkley, John R.** *and* **Charlatans, Demagogues and Politicians.**

21364 Mediterraneans Dance Band. Hugo Mariani directed the popular radio band (WJZ, New York, NY, 1928).

21365 Medland, Jack. Pianist (KDYL, Salt Lake City, UT, 1929).

21366 Medley, Louise. COM-HE (WHUB, Cooksville, TN, 1956).

21367 Medrow, Virginia. COM-HE (WDWS, Champaign, IL, 1956).

21368 Meecham, Malcolm. Actor Meecham was in the cast of *Backstage Wife* daytime serial program.

21369 Meechy, Montana. Leader (*Montana Meechy's Band*, instr. mus. prg., MBS, 1942).

21370 Meeder, William. Organist (*William Meeder*, instr. mus. prg., NBC-Blue, 1936–1938; leader, *William Meeder Ensemble*, instr. mus. prg., WEAF-NBC-Red, 1938). Meeder played the organ of acted as musical director on *Big Sister*, *Brighter Day*, *Pepper Young's Family* and *Right to Happiness*.

21371 Meehan, Lewis. Tenor (KYW, Chicago, IL, 1926–1928; KFI, Los Angeles, CA, 1929).

21372 Meek, Sandy. In 1925, Tenor Meeks specialized in Scots and popular songs on many Chicago stations such as WBBM, WQJ, KYW and WEBH. *Radio Age* (August, 1925, p. 17) called his voice "McCormick-like."

21373 Meeker, Bobby. Leader (Bobby Meeker Orchestra, WLIB, Elgin, IL, 1927; Drake Hotel Dance Orchestra, WGN, Chicago, IL, 1928; *Bobby Meeker Orchestra*, instr. mus. prg., CBS, 1936; KMOX, St. Louis, MO, 1937).

21374 Meeker, Louise. Miss Meeker broadcast weekly book reviews (WDAF, Kansas City, MO, 1928).

21375 Meekes, Fay. Contralto (KFWI, San Francisco, CA, 1926).

21376 Meeks, Carl. DJ (*Tiny's Platter Party*, WRLC, Toccoa, GA, 1947).

21377 Meeks, Don. Newscaster (WWVA, Wheeling, WV, 1945).

21378 Meeks, Max. DJ (*Max in the Morning*, WFMR, High Point, NC, 1949–1960). Meeks broadcast his early morning program for many more decades.

21379 Meenam, William T. Newscaster (WGY, Schenectady, NY, 1938).

21380 Mees, Dick. Leader (Dick Mees Orchestra, WLW, Cincinnati, OH, 1923).

21381 *Meet Corliss Archer.* *Meet Corliss Archer* was a situation comedy that dramatized the trials and tribulations encountered by an intelligent adolescent girl. It was based on the writings and original creation of F. Hugh Herbert. Each week Corliss Archer and her boy friend found themselves embroiled in the hilarious situations (to everyone else) that adolescents find so frustrating. The program showed an adolescent girl's struggle with maturity, while *Henry Aldrich* paralleled the adjustments and frustrations of adolescence on the male side. Although Priscilla Lyon and Lugene Sanders also played the title role, Janet Waldo is best remembered, for she played Corliss for ten of the twelve years the program was on the air. Also in the cast were: Arlene Becker, Tommy Bernard, Sam Edwards, David Hughes, Fred Shields, Irene Tedrow and Barbara Whiting. The writers were Jerry Adelman, Carroll Carroll and F. Hugh Herbert. Bert Prager was the director.

21382 *Meet Frances Scott.* Mrs. Frankie Basch (Frances Scott) conducted her program of informal talks and interviews of interest to women (WHN, New York, NY, 1942). Previously she had been heard on such network shows as *It Takes a Woman* and *What Burns You Up?*

21383 *Meet Me at Melton's.* Ina Bradley was the hostess of the program broadcast from James Melton's Antique Auto Museum in Bridgeport, CT. Opera star James Melton and Philip Langner appeared regularly on the show. Mike Merrill was the announcer (30 min., Saturday, 11:30–12:00 noon, WICC, Bridgeport, CT, 1952).

21384 ***Meet Me at Parky's.*** Harry Einstein played the role of Nick Parkyarkarkas, the owner of Parky's, a small restaurant, on the situation comedy sponsored by Old Gold Cigarettes. Einstein had played the Parkyarkarkas character earlier on the *Eddie Cantor Show* and the *Al Jolson Lifebouy Show.* It was Einstein's comic character that was the primary focus of the program. The talented cast included: Jean Barton, Leo Cleary, Harry Einstein, Sheldon Leonard, Frank Nelson and Ruth Perrott. The program was written by Harry Einstein and Hal Fimberg. The directors were Hal Fimberg and Maurice Morton. Music was by the Opie Cates Orchestra accompanying the Short Order Chorus and vocalists Dave Street, Patty Bolton, Peggy Lee and Betty Jane Rhodes. The announcer was Art Gilmore.

21385 ***Meet Me at the Copa.*** Celebrity interviews with celebrities from New York's Copacabana night club were the sole ingredients of the all-night local program (210 min., Tuesday through Saturday, WINS, New York, NY, 1947).

21386 ***Meet Me in St. Louis.*** Russell Beggs wrote the entertaining situation comedy about a 15-year-old heroine's doings in turn of century St. Louis. Ann Gardner played the role of the teenager. Brook Bryon, Jack Edwards, Vinton Hayworth, Raymond Edward Johnson, Billy Redfield, Ethel Wilson and Agnes Young were also in the cast. Vladimir Solinsky's Orchestra supplied the music (30 min., Sunday, 10:30–11:00 P.M., NBC, 1950). The program was based on a book by Peggy Benson. The 1944 movie by the same name starred Judy Garland and Margaret O'Brien and featured such music as "The Trolley Song."

21387 ***Meet Millie.*** Audrey Trotter, initially, and Elena Verdugo, later, played the title role of Brooklyn secretary, Millie Bronson. Also in the cast of the sustaining situation comedy were Earle Ross and Bill Tracey. Music was by Irving Miller's Orchestra. Bob Lemond was the announcer (30 min., Monday, 9:30–10:00 P.M., CBS, 1951).

21388 ***Meet Miss Sherlock.*** Jane Sherlock, an apartment store buyer, played detective on the summer replacement show written and produced by Don Thompson and Lee Jack Newman. Music was composed and performed by organist Milton Charles (30 min., Weekly, CBS, 1946).

21389 ***Meet the Artist.*** Bob Taplinger interviewed various radio stars on his weekly program (15 min., Saturday, 6:00–6:15 P.M., CBS, 1933).

21390 ***Meet the Artist.*** Nancy Russell interviewed artists on the New York local program. Later, she conducted a show called *Meet the Songwriter*, using the same concept and format (15 min., Weekly, WJZ, New York, NY, 1938). *See* ***Meet the Songwriter***.

21391 ***Meet the Folks.*** Performers of the popular *National Barn Dance* were interviewed. Ed Paul was the host who conducted the cast interviews back stage at Chicago's Eighth Street Theater. He would then go to the theater lobby to interview visitors to the program. A typical gag Paul would use was to ask a visitor to describe Red Foley. After the guest made his best effort, Paul would introduce him to Red Foley and ask him to describe him once more (30 min., 7:00–7:30 P.M. CST, WLS, Chicago, IL, 1937–1938). The *Bar-N-Frolic* program replaced the *Meet the Folks* program in 1938 and featured performances by the *National Barn Dance* stars.

21392 ***Meet the Menjous.*** Motion picture stars Adolf Menjou and his wife, Vera Teasdale, literately discussed current affairs on their sustaining show, that *Variety* noted was better than many of the other husband-and-wife talk shows so prevalent at the time (15 min., Monday through Friday, 9:15–9:30 A.M., WOR, Newark, NJ, 1949).

21393 ***Meet the Press.*** Martha Roundtree originated the program in 1945 and served as its first host. A panel of journalists were brought together each week to interview a news maker, usually a politician. The program made a successful transition to television on November 6, 1947. The television version of *Meet the Press* celebrated its 50th anniversary in 1997.

The radio version introduced the format of several journalists questioning a newsworthy person each week. The same format is used today by all the networks and many local television stations with such programs as ABC's *Today (with Sam Donaldson and Cokie Roberts)* and *Face the Nation* on CBS.

Lawrence Spivak, editor of the *American Mercury* magazine, was the program's best known radio host. Spivak conducted the television version until 1975, when he was succeeded as host by such broadcast journalists as Bill Monroe, Marvin Kalb, Chris Wallace, Garrick Utley and Tim Russert. Unfortunately, not all the television hosts who succeeded him were as consistently unbiased and as fearlessly willing to ask the "hard" question as was Spivak.

21394 ***Meet the Songwriter.*** Nancy Russell interviewed songwriters who lived in or were visiting New York City on her sustaining program. She previously conducted the *Meet the Artist* program (15 min., Tuesday, 12:00–12:15 P.M., WJZ, New York, NY, 1939). See ***Meet the Artist.***

21395 ***Meet Your Boys in Uniform.*** Young Army men were interviewed at the Indian Town Gap, PA, army base on the sustaining World War II program (15 min., Monday, 10:30–10:45 P.M., WCAE, Pittsburgh, PA, 1941). *See* **Wartime Radio**.

21396 ***Meet Your Lover.*** Thickly coated with sentiment, singer Frank Luther was very popular on the 1933–1934 program. He would say, "Darling, you are the only one in the world for me. I love you — really I do. I love you so much." Luther always drew great quantities of fan mail (15 min., Network, 1933–1934). Frank Luther entered radio in 1926. He later became part of the famous Revelers Quartet and in 1934 was one of the *Happy Wonder Bakers.*

21397 ***Meet Your Match.*** An audience participation quiz show conducted by Tom Moore, whose only unique characteristic was that the winner of a quiz round was allowed to pick the next opponent from audience volunteers (30 min., Thursday, 9:00–9:30 P.M., MBS, 1949). The sustaining program went off the air for a few years before NBC brought it back for the 1952–1953 season.

21398 ***Meet Your Navy.*** The amateur talent of sailors based at the Great Lakes Training Station was featured on the sustaining program hosted by Jack Stillwell (30 min., Tuesday, 7:30–8:00 P.M., NBC, 1942). *See* **Wartime Radio**.

21399 ***Meet Yourself.*** Psychiatrist Louis J. Lewis conducted the sustaining program in the style of *The Voice of Experience.* He provided advice on the mental and spiritual problems of the listeners who wrote him (15 min., Wednesday, 3:15–3:30 P.M., WIP, Philadelphia, PA, 1938).

21400 ***Meeting of Protective Order of Lake Merritt Ducks.*** This was another example of the interesting late evening variety programs broadcast in the mid–1920s that featured zany doings (KLX, Oakland, CA, 1925).

21401 **Megarle, Ralph H.** Announcer known as "TOD" (WDAE, Tampa, FL, 1926).

21402 **Mehaffey, (Mrs.) John.** Reader (WCBD, Zion, IL, 1925).

21403 **Mehan, Bob.** DJ (*Around the Bay After Midnight*, KWBR, Oakland, CA, 1947).

21404 **Mehan, Louis.** Tenor (KNX, Hollywood, CA, 1928).

21405 **Meheir, Martha.** Contralto (WLS, Chicago, IL, 1925).

21406 **Mehl, Ernie.** Sportscaster (WDAF, Kansas City, MO, 1952).

21407 **Mehl, Frances.** Whistler (KHJ, Los Angeles, CA, 1926).

21408 **Meier, L. Carlos.** Organist (WHO, Des Moines, IA, 1924). Meier broadcast organ recitals from the Capitol Theatre, Des Moines, Iowa (WCBD, Des Moines, IA, 1925; WHO, Des Moines, IA, 1926).

21409 **Meighan, Malcolm.** Busy actor Meighan appeared on *Alias Jimmy Valentine*, *Backstage Wife*, *By Kathleen Norris*, *City Desk*, *Dot and Will* (title role), *Falcon* (title role), *Flash Gordon* (title role), *I Love Linda Dale*, *Just Plain Bill*, *Lone Journey*, *Lora Lawton*, *Marie the Little French Princess*, *Orphans of Divorce*, *Romance of Helen Trent*, *Second Husband* and *Special Agent* (title role).

21410 **Meinhard, (Miss) Cecil.** Soprano (WFJC, Akron, OH, 1928).

21411 **Meinhold, Kitty.** Pianist (WGY, Schenectady, NY, 1923).

21412 **Meiser, Edith.** Writer-actress (Networks). Although also an actress, Meiser is best known as the writer of *New Penny*, Helen Hayes' first dramatic series for radio and the adventures of Sherlock Holmes.

21413 **Meisle, Kathryn.** Contralto on the *Atwater Kent Hour* program (NBC, 1927).

21414 **Meisler, Beatrice.** Miss Meisler broadcast various recitations (WGBS, New York, NY, 1925).

21415 **Meisner, Charlene.** COM-HE (WCBZ, Bangor, ME, 1949).

21416 **Meisner, Joan (Betty Lane).** COM-HE (WSOY, Decatur, IL,1949; WTAX, Springfield, IL, 1960).

21417 Meissner [Meisner], O.W. Announcer (WSOE, Milwaukee, WI, 1925–1927). Singer (WSOE, Milwaukee, WI, 1926).

21418 Meissner, Sanford. Actor Meissner was in the cast of *House of Glass.*

21419 Meister, Bob. News analyst (*Three Star Edition,* WMAM, Marinette, WI, 1947). DJ (*Hitchin' Post,* WMAM, 1947).

21420 Meister, Don. Newscaster (WDSU, New Orleans, LA, 1944).

21421 Meksin, Arnold. Russian pianist (WGBS, New York, NY, 1925).

21422 Mekuda, Lydia. COM-HE (KFOR, Lincoln, NE, 1951).

21423 *Mel Blanc Show* (aka *Mel Blanc's Fix-It Shop* or merely the *Fix-It Shop*). Mel Blanc, one of radio's most gifted performers, was featured on the situation comedy sponsored by Colgate-Palmolive Company. Blanc played the roles of both the owner of a Fix-It shop and his hapless helper, Zookie. Also in the cast were: Jim Backus, Bea Benadaret, Hans Conreid, Mary Jane Croft, Joe Kearns, Alan Reed (Teddy Bergman) and Earle Ross. The program was written by David Victor, Herb Little, Jr. and Mac Benoff. The producer was Joe Rines and the director was Sam Fuller. Music was supplied by the Victor Miller Orchestra. Bud Heisland was the announcer (30 min., Tuesday, 8:30–9:00 P.M., CBS, 1946).

21424 Meland, Mildred Langtry. Contralto (WCCO, Minneapolis–St. Paul, MN, 1925).

21425 Melaney, Howard. Tenor (WLS, Chicago, IL, 1928–1930). Melaney was known as "The Singing Fireman." It was said that he traveled 4,000 miles weekly singing for his employer at Northern Pacific Railroad railway stations from coast to coast.

21426 Melatz, Wilma. Soprano (WOW, Omaha, NE, 1927).

21427 Melbourne, John P. Newscaster (KXL, Portland, OR, 1942).

21428 Melbourne, Rex. Leader (*Rex Melbourne Orchestra,* instr. mus. prg., WIBX, Utica, NY, 1942).

21429 Mele, Violet. Pianist (*Ragging the Black and Whites,* WPCH, New York, NY, 1932).

21430 Melgard, Al. Organist (WLS, Chicago, IL and WBBM, Chicago, IL, 1926; *Al Melgard,* instr. mus. prg., 15 min., Saturday, 10:30–10:45 A.M. CST, WLS, Chicago, IL, 1937).

21431 Melges, Douglas. Newscaster (KSTP, St. Paul, MN, 1945).

21432 Melhrie, Thelma. Soprano (KFSG, Los Angeles, CA, 1925).

21433 Melledge, (Mrs.) Edgar Cecil. Conducted a women's program (*The Women's Hour,* WRNY, New York, NY, 1924).

21434 Mellonino, Claire. Pianist (KHJ, Los Angeles, CA, 1925; KNX, Los Angeles, CA, 1927–1929).

21435 Mellor, Ethel Rust. Singer of Camp Fire Girls' songs (WJZ, New York, NY, 1922).

21436 Melloy, Jack. Newscaster (WDAS, Philadelphia, PA, 1945). DJ (*Rainbow Rendezvous,* WHOT, South Bend, IN, 1948).

21437 *Melodiana.* The Abe Lyman Orchestra and vocalists Bernice Claire and Oliver Smith were featured on the music program (30 min., Sunday, 4:00–4:30 P.M., CBS, 1935).

21438 Melodians. Male vocal trio consisting of Laurie, Eddie and Bennie, not otherwise identified (WGES, Chicago, IL, 1928).

21439 (The) Melodie Boys Orchestra. Popular radio band (WGY, Schenectady, NY, 1925).

21440 *Melodie Musings.* Lyons Wickland narrated the program that featured the songs of Warren White and the Carlton Kelsey Orchestra. Ted Bliss wrote and produced the program (15 min., Tuesday, 8:45–9:00 P.M., Mutual-Don Lee Network, 1938).

21441 *Melodies de France.* George Barrerre and his symphony orchestra performed on the French music program (NBC, 1931).

21442 *Melodies of Not So Long Ago.* Joseph Sweiker narrated the popular music program (Weekly, WBAL, Baltimore, MD, 1926).

21443 *Melodies with the Music Master.* The Anthony Candelori Orchestra was featured on the sustaining program (15 min., WFIL, Philadelphia, PA, 1938).

21444 Melody, Joe. DJ (*Spins and Needles,* KBKI, Alice, TX, 1949). Sportscaster (WOAI, San Antonio, TX, 1956).

21445 Melody Belles Orchestra. The all female band was billed as the "The Melody Belles Orchestra, the Clover Gardens' Girls Orchestra" (WHN, New York, NY, 1923–1924).

21446 Melody Five Boys. The band performed in clown's dress as they played Dixieland jazz (WSY, Birmingham, AL, 1923).

21447 *Melody Highways.* Milton Cross narrated the sustaining music show that featured vocalist Stuart Foster, concert pianist Earl Wild and Bernard Green's Orchestra. The program was directed by Leonard Blair and produced by William Marshall (30 min., Sunday, 9:15–9:45 P.M. ABC, 1952).

21448 *Melody Hour.* The pleasant evening music show featured soprano Amy Goldsmith, baritone Garfield Swift and an unidentified orchestra (Weekly, Sunday, 8:00 P.M., NBC-Red, 1934). *See* ***The Contented Hour.***

21449 *Melody in the Night.* The Paul LaValle Orchestra was featured on the late night music show (30 min., Weekly, NBC-Blue, 1940).

21450 *Melody Lane.* Organist Don Voegel performed on the weekly instrumental music show (15 min., Monday, 12:15–12:30 P.M. CST, WIBA, Madison, WI, 1942).

21451 *Melody Maids* (aka *The Maids of Melody*). The singing team of Hortense Rose and Grace Donaldson sang on the program (WSAI, Cincinnati, OH, 1928–1929). George Hall, billed as "The Phantom Fiddler," was also featured.

21452 *Melody Mainliner.* The wartime program originating from Turner Field included music, comedy bits and interviews with servicemen. Hosted by Private Matthew Huttner. The producer was Lieutenant Starr Smith (30 min., Weekly, WALB, Albany, GA, 1942). *See* **Wartime Radio.**

21453 *Melody Master.* A weekly dramatic sketch and several musical selections were the ingredients of the show sponsored by General Electric. The cast included William P. Adams, Charme Allen, Virginia Howard, Edwin Jerome, Allyn Joslyn, Frances Nordstrom, William Stickles and Robert Straus (30 min., Sunday, 11:00–11:30 P.M., NBC-Red, 1935).

21454 *Melody Matinee.* The music show first went on the air in 1926 and was one of radio's oldest sponsored programs. In 1938, the show's performers included soprano Muriel Dickson, tenor Morton Bowe, the Cavaliers Quartet and the Victor Arden Orchestra (30 min., Sunday, 12:30–1:00 P.M. CST, NBC-Red, 1938).

21455 *Melody Memories.* Soprano Gail Taylor and an orchestra directed by Mort Grauenhorst were featured on the music show (30 min., Saturday, 8:30–9:00 P.M., NBC-Pacific Coast Network, 1930).

21456 *Melody Mountaineers.* CW mus. prg. (WMT, Cedar Rapids–Waterloo, IA, 1937).

21457 *Melody Musketeers.* The weekly music program featured unidentified performers (30 min., Monday, 7:00–7:30 P.M., NBC-Red, 1929).

21458 *Melody Parade.* Vocalist Sophia Germanich and an unidentified orchestra performed on the music show (15 min., Monday-Wednesday-Friday, 1:45–2:00 P.M., WLS, Chicago, IL, 1937).

21459 *Melody Puzzles.* Fred Uttal conducted the audience participation quiz, on which some members of the audience were seated on the stage. A dramatic cast performed several skits in which phrases of popular songs were hidden. Each phrase that was identified earned a contestant a prize. Buddy Clark and Freda Gibson (Georgia Gibbs) performed the songs accompanied by the Harry Salter Orchestra. The announcer was Ed Herlihy (30 min, 7:00–7:30 P.M., NBC-Blue, 1937–1938).

21460 *Melody Ranch* (aka *Gene Autry's Melody Ranch*). The 15th anniversary of the popular show was celebrated on September 1, 1955, a year before it left the air. Popular singing cowboy movie star Gene Autry hosted, sang and starred in a complete western story dramatized each week. The program was sponsored by Wrigley's Chewing Gum throughout its entire run. Pat Buttram supplied comedy relief. In addition to Autry, other singers and musicians who appeared on the show included: Cass County Boys, the King Sisters, Alvino Rey, Johnny Bond and the Blue Jeans. The announcers were Lou Crosby and Charlie Lyon (CBS, 1940–1956). *See* **Autry, Gene** *and* **Singers: Crooners, Song Birds, Country Belles, Cow Girls and Hillbillies.**

21461 *Melody Tenor.* Vcl. mus. prg. (WPG, Atlantic City, NJ, 1936).

21462 *Melody Theatre.* Don Agar and Frederick Mayhew wrote, Frank Armour produced and Alan Jacoby directed the novel combination of music and drama. The program claimed to present the greatest tales of melody and romance. Each quarter-hour program presented a complete story. Bret Morrison narrated the transcribed program. The announcer was Phil Tonken (15 min., Monday through Friday, MBS, 1947).

21463 **Melody Three.** Vocal trio not otherwise identified (WIBO, Chicago, IL, 1926).

21464 **Melody Trio.** Vocal trio of Sid Lippman, Dale Imes and Sally Farnsworth (KNX, Los Angeles, CA, 1928–1930).

21465 **Melody Twins.** Vocal team of Dorothy Maddox and Vera Trueblood (WHB, Kansas City, MO, 1928–1930).

21466 **Melodyland Syncopators.** Dance band directed by Ed Berliant (WHN, New York, NY, 1923).

21467 **Melotone Male Quartet.** Vocal group consisting of Francis Kaye, Willard Newburg, Earl Johnson and Carl Johnson (KFLV, Rockford, IL, 1929–1930).

21468 **Melrose, Edythe Fern.** COM-HE (WXYZ, Detroit, MI, 1949–1956).

21469 **Melrose, Margaret F.** Soprano (KHJ, Los Angeles, CA, 1923–1926).

21470 **Melsing, Melba.** Singer (KFWB, Hollywood, CA, 1925).

21471 **Melton [Milton], Billy.** Billy Melton, a "one man band," played harmonica and guitar simultaneously (KSTP, Hot Springs National Park, AR, 1928).

21472 **Melton, Charles F.** Musician Melton was billed as "Charlie the French Harp King" (WLAC, Nashville, TN, 1929–1930).

21473 **Melton, Dave.** DJ (*Melton's Mad House*, KOEL, Oelwein, IA, 1949; KLIK, Jefferson City, MO, 1955).

21474 **Melton, Frank.** Newscaster (WJZM, Clarksville, TN, 1941). DJ (*Frank Melton Show*, WDXI, Jackson, TN, 1948; KGUL, Greenville, TX, 1956).

21475 **Melton, James.** Tenor Melton was born January 2, 1904. He was a Metropolitan Opera tenor who enjoyed great popularity on radio (WEAF, New York, NY, 1929). Melton first appeared on radio in 1927 with *Roxy's Gang* (NBC, 1927). Later, he was a soloist on the *Seiberling Singers* program (NBC-Blue, New York, NY, 1928–1931) sponsored by the Seiberling Rubber [tire] Company. Among the many programs on which he appeared was the *Mobil Oil Concert.* Melton's career blossomed in the 1930s and 1940s both on the radio, the opera stage and motion pictures. *See* ***Roxy and His Gang***.

21476 **Melton, Jimmie.** DJ (KBHS, Hot Springs National Park, AR, 1960).

21477 **Melton, Orrin.** Newscaster (KYSM, Mankato, MN, 1940–1942).

21478 **Meltzer, Theodore.** Newscaster (WMIN, St. Paul, MN, 1940).

21479 **Melville, John.** Newscaster (WNOC, Norwich, CT, 1946).

21480 **Melvin, Charles.** Organist (WLW, Cincinnati, OH, 1929).

21481 **Melvin, Dorothy.** COM-HE (*Dorothy Melvin's Charm Mirror*, WAAB, Boston, MA, 1936).

21482 ***Memories and Melodies.*** Memories in the form of prose and poetry were supplied by Ed Maul. Ralph Waldo Emerson provided him with an organ background (15 min., Thursday, 11:15–11:30 A.M., WLS, Chicago, IL, 1937).

21483 ***Memories of Jenny Lind and Claire Schumann.*** Soprano Anna Barbash was one of the performers on the fine musical program (WPG, Atlantic City, NJ, 1926).

21484 ***Memory Lane.*** *Memory Lane* was a daytime comedy-drama serial based on small town midwestern life at the beginning of the Twentieth Century. The writer was Eileen Piggott. The cast included Bernice Berwin, Richard LaGrand, Ben McLaughlin, Billy Page, Constance Temple, Billy Temple and George Rand (NBC-Pacific network, 1929).

21485 **Memory Orchestra.** Radio dance band (WRW, Tarrytown, NY, 1925).

21486 ***Memory Song Man.*** Joe Lopez, the station manager of WICC, sang old fashioned songs on the weekly music show (15 min., Weekly, WICC, Bridgeport, CT, 1939).

21487 **Memphis Plectrum Orchestra.** Music group (WMC, Memphis, TN, 1926).

21488 ***Men About Town.*** Paul Pelletier conducted the entertaining "Biggest Little Band in the Town" (15 min., Weekly, WMAS, Springfield, MA, 1941).

21489 ***Men of Manhattan.*** Vcl. mus. prg. by male quartet (CBS, 1935).

21490 ***Men of the West.*** Vocal quartet (NBC-Blue, 1936; NBC, 1939).

21491 ***Men of Vision.*** The transcribed program presented dramatizations of the life of such famous persons as Gutenberg, Isaac Newton, Marco Polo, Nero, Galileo, Theodore Roosevelt, Benjamin Franklin and Leonardo DeVinci (15 min., Transcribed, Various Stations, 1937–1938).

21492 ***Men with Batons.*** Bill Gottlieb, record reviewer of the Washington *Post*, played records and supplied knowledgeable comments on jazz, swing and popular music in general on the sustaining show (30 min., Saturday, 9:30–10:00 P.M., NBC, 1940).

21493 **Menacoff, "Coach."** Sportscaster (*Sports Payoff*, WTTT, Coral Gables, FL and WCSC, Charleston, SC, 1950).

21494 **Menchaca, Jose.** Newscaster (WHOM, Jersey City, NJ, 1941).

21495 **Mencken, Grace.** Singer, who was actress Helen Mencken's sister (WOR, Newark, NJ, 1929).

21496 ***Mend Your Manners.*** Ed and Pegeen Fitzgerald produced and hosted a panel discussion program on manners. Claude Phillippe, Victor van der Linde, Mme. Nichole and Irene Hayes were panel regulars (30 min., Monday, 8:30–9:00 P.M., NBC-Blue, 1952).

21497 **Mendel, Joe.** Leader (Joe Mendel and his Pep Band, KFRC, San Francisco, CA, 1925–1928).

21498 **Mendelson, Jean.** COM-HE (WJNC, Jacksonville, NC, 1955).

21499 **Mendelson, Wallace.** Newscaster (WROL, Knoxville, TN, 1947).

21500 **Mendelssohn Trio.** Instrumental group (KJR, Seattle, WA, 1926).

21501 **Mendez, Raphael.** DJ (Mendez, the virtuoso trumpet player, played some of his own recordings on his *Raphael Mendez Program*, KWKW, Pasadena, CA, 1947).

21502 **Mendoza, David.** Leader (David Mendoza Orchestra, WJAX, Cleveland, OH, 1929 and the Fada Orchestra, WABC-CBS, New York, NY, 1929).

21503 **Menefee, Allen R.** Newscaster (KVAK, Atchison, KS, 1946).

21504 **Menefee, Robert "Bob."** Newscaster (WSLS, Roanoke, VA, 1941, 1946).

21505 **Menge, Maurice.** Leader (Maurice Menge and his El Patio Orchestra, KGFJ, Los Angeles, CA, 1928–1929).

21506 **Mengelberg, Willem.** Distinguished orchestra conductor Mengelberg led the *General Motors Family Party's* orchestra (NBC, 1927).

21507 **Menkes, Sally.** Pianist who *Variety* called "one of the station's pioneer entertainers" (KYW, Chicago, IL, 1924–1925). Menkes later was a member of a vocal trio that included Jack Baus and Sterra Feigen (WENR, Chicago, IL, 1929–1930).

21508 ***Mennen Men Program.*** Mennen Shaving Cream sponsored the musical variety show. Curt Peterson was the announcer (1929).

21509 ***Men's Conference Program.*** The Reverend S. Parkes Cadman conducted the weekly religious program (90 min., Sunday, 4:00–5:30 P.M., NBC-Red, 1923–1929). The program later was known as *The National Radio Pulpit*. *See* ***The National Radio Pulpit***.

21510 **Mentor, Art.** Newscaster (KNET, Palestine, TX, 1947).

21511 **Mentzer, Earl.** Singer (*Earl Mentzer*, vcl. mus. prg., WORK, York, PA, 1936).

21512 **Menzer, Carl.** Announcer (WSUI, Iowa City, IA, 1925–1927).

21513 **Merande, Dora.** Actress Merande appeared on the *Woman of Courage* program

21514 **Mercado, Bob.** DJ (KWKW, Pasadena, CA, 1954–1955).

21515 ***Mercado's Mexican Fiesta Orchestra.*** Instr. mus. prg., (WWJ, Detroit, MI, 1935).

21516 **Mercer, Harry Yeazell.** Tenor (WOC, Davenport, IA, 1928).

21517 **Mercer, Hazel N.** COM-HE (WPAR, Parkersburg, WV, 1960).

21518 **Mercer, Martha.** COM-HE (WKKO, Cocoa, FL, 1955).

21519 **Mercer, Ruby.** DJ (*Ruby Mercer Show*, MBS, 1954).

21520 **Mercer, Sylvia.** COM-HE (WHYS, Ocala, FL, 1957).

21521 **Merchant, Helen.** Pianist (KGO, Oakland, CA, 1924–1925).

21522 **Mercier, Art.** Newscaster (KOIL, Omaha, NE, 1937).

21523 **Mercier, Joseph.** Newscaster (WCAR, Pontiac, MI, 1940).

21524 **Mercier, Ray.** DJ (WCSH, Portland, ME, 1955).

21525 Mercier, Roselle. Book reviewer (WJZ, New York, NY, 1924).

21526 Mercier, Woodrow. Sportscaster (WRUM, Rumford, ME, 1954).

21527 Mercurio, Joe. Singer (*Joe Mercurio*, vcl. mus. prg., WHLS, Port Huron, MI, 1942).

21528 *(The) Mercury Theater* aka *The Mercury Theater of the Air.* The young Orson Welles created the series of drama productions best known for the H.G. Wells' *War of the Worlds* program that caused widespread hysteria in 1938 [*See* **Drama**]. Some of its other productions were dramatizations of *The Count of Monte Cristo, Hell on Ice, Around the World in 80 Days, The Man Who Was Thursday, Three Short Stories, Seventeen, Dracula, Treasure Island, A Tale of Two Cities, The 39 Steps, Abraham Lincoln, The Affairs of Anatole* and *Jane Eyre.*

The program was produced by Welles, directed by John Houseman and written by Howard Koch. The cast included Everett Sloane, Martin Gabel, George Coulouris, Agnes Moorehead, John McIntire, Karl Swenson, Alice Frost, Frank Readick, Kenny Delmar, Ray Collins and Richard Widmark and, of course, Welles (60 min., 8:00–9:00 P.M., CBS, 1938). The program was on the air for only one season. The following season the name was changed to *The Campbell Playhouse* (1939–1940) and still later a similar show by Welles, the *Lady Esther Theatre* (or the *Orson Welles Theater*), was broadcast 1941–1943 on CBS.

21529 Meredith, Burgess. Distinguished Broadway and motion picture actor appeared on radio on *The Campbell Playhouse, Pursuit of Happiness* (MC), *Red Davis* (title role) and *We the People* (host).

21530 Meredith, Georgia. COM-HE (WRFB, Schenectady, NY, 1951).

21531 Meredith, (Mrs.) J. COM-HE (WMMN, Fairmont, WV, 1954).

21532 Meredith, Jay. Actress Meredith appeared on the *Amanda of Honeymoon Hill, Brighter Day, By Kathleen Norris; Ellen Randolph, The Mighty Show, Our Gal Sunday* and *Mary Marlin* daytime serial programs.

21533 Meredith, Joyce. Actress on the *Johnson and Johnson Program* (NBC, 1929).

21534 Meredith, June. Pianist (WEEI, Boston, MA, 1931).

21535 Meredith, June. Actress Meredith was in the cast of *Mary Marlin* aka *The Story of Mary Marlin*; *Stepmother*; and *Tale of Today* daytime serial programs.

21536 Meredith, Lee. Newscaster (WOMI, Owensburg, KY, 1939). DJ (*Listen with Lee*, KATE, Albert Lea, MN, 1950).

21537 *Meredith Willson Show.* Willson led the orchestra and hosted the pleasant variety show, sponsored by General Foods' Jello with an emphasis on fine music performances. Among the show's featured performers were South African folk performers Marais and Miranda, Pauline Carter, Betty Allen, Norma Zimmer, Marxwell Smith, Bob Hanlon and John Rarig (30 min., Wednesday, 10:30–11:00 P.M., ABC, 1948).

21538 Mereness, Edna. Soprano (WGY, Schenectady, NY, 1926).

21539 Meresco, Joe. Pianist on the *Music that Satisfies Program* with the Nat Shilkret orchestra (NBC, 1932).

21540 Merideans Orchestra. Emery Deutsch led this band that broadcast at noon on weekdays (WABC, New York, NY, 1929).

21541 *Meridian Hustlers Orchestra.* The CW music group was from Meridian, MS (WAPI, Birmingham, AL, 1929–1930).

21542 Merino, John. Newscaster (KGLU, Safford, AZ, 1939).

21543 Merkel, F. Cornetist (WJZ, New York, NY, 1922).

21544 Merker, Harry. Leader (Harry Merker Orchestra, NBC, 1928).

21545 Merkey, Maryland. Soprano (KFRC, San Francisco, CA, 1926).

21546 Merkin, Sylvia. Singer (*Sylvia Merkin*, vcl. mus. prg., WFIL, Philadelphia, PA, 1936).

21547 Merkle, Walter W. Announcer (WGST, Atlanta, GA, 1927).

21548 Merna, John. Sportscaster (WIBX, Utica, NY, 1940). Newscaster (WIBX, 1941).

21549 Meroff, Benny. Leader (*Benny Meroff Orchestra*, instr. mus. prg., WOR, Newark, NJ, 1936; WLW, Cincinnati, OH, 1937).

21550 Merrell, A.F. Merrell conducted a program on stamp collecting (*A.F. Merrell and His Stamp Club*, KFRC, San Francisco, CA, 1926).

21551 Merrell, Steve. Organist (*Steve Merrell*, instr. mus. prg., WLW, Cincinnati, OH and WSAI, Cincinnati, OH, 1936).

21552 Merrick, Bob. Singer (*Bob Merrick*, vcl. mus. prg., WIP, Philadelphia, PA, 1935).

21553 Merrick, Mahlon. Leader (Davenport Hotel Orchestra, KHQ, Seattle, WA, 1927; KHQ Concert Orchestra, KHQ, 1928).

21554 Merridew, Reg. Newscaster (WKOK, Sunbury, PA, 1938–1940; WGAR, Cleveland, OH, 1945).

21555 Merrifield, Don. Actor Merrifield was born December 6, 1872. After thirty years of theatrical experience, Merrifield made his first radio appearance in Chicago (WLS, Chicago, IL, 1924). Merrifield experienced almost twenty-five years of continuous radio employment after that first broadcast.

21556 Merrill, Claucus G. Newscaster (*AM Edition*, WHAR, Clarksburg, WV, 1947).

21557 Merrill, Cosette. Ms. Merrill was a stimulating female news commentator (*Cosette Merrill*, news analyst, 15 min., WBEN, Buffalo, NY, 1939). *Variety* said Ms. Merrill talked of many things "from shoes and ships and sealing wax to cabbages and kings."

21558 Merrill, G.G. Newscaster (KVNU, Logan, UT, 1939). Sportscaster (KVNU, 1941).

21559 Merrill, Gary. Motion picture actor Merrill previous appeared on radio in *The March of Time, Right to Happiness, Second Mrs. Burton* and *Superman.*

21560 Merrill, Lou. Actor Merrill was in the cast of *Buster Brown's Gang, Latitude Zero, Lights Out, Parties at Pickfair* and *Those We Love.*

21561 Merrill, Paul. Newscaster (KGLU, Safford, AZ, 1941).

21562 Merriman, Dana S. Musical conductor on *The Pilgrims* program (NBC-Blue, New York, NY, 1929).

21563 Merriman, Slick. Pianist (KFAB, Lincoln, NE, 1926).

21564 Merrin, Dick. Sportscaster (WMAN, Mansfield, OH, 1944). News analyst (*Morning Edition*, WHBC, Canton, OH, 1948).

21565 Merrion, Bob. Singer (*Bob Merrion*, vcl. mus. prg., WIP, Philadelphia, PA, 1936).

21566 Merritt, Betty L. COM-HE (WAGA, Atlanta, GA, 1956–1957).

21567 Merritt, Dorothy. COM-HE (WSTC, Stamford, CT, 1949).

21568 Merritt, Lenore. COM-HE (KIHR, Hood River, OR, 1956).

21569 Merritt, Margaret. COM-HE (WCOL, Columbus, OH, 1954).

21570 Merritt, Wesley. Pianist (WBZ, Springfield, MA, 1926).

21571 Merrow, Chester. Newscaster (WHEB, Portsmouth, NH, 1939–1942).

21572 Merry, Edward. Newscaster (WFCL, Orangeburg, NY).

21573 *Merry-Go-Round.* Hal Culver hosted and sang Irish songs on the pleasant music show. He was joined by CW singing star, Patsy Montana (WLS, Chicago, IL, 1938).

21574 *Merry Macs.* Popular vocal group (NBC, 1935). The group originally consisted of older brothers Judd and Ted McMichael, younger brother Joe McMichael and Virginia Rees. When Joe was killed in World War II, his place was taken by Lynn Allen.

21575 Merry Madcaps. Dance band conducted by Norman Cloutier, featuring Tiny Berman on tuba, specialized in "hot tunes" (NBC, 1931).

21576 Merry Made Music Makers. Utah dance band (KFWA, Ogden UT, 1926).

21577 Merry Musical Maids. Orchestra whose business manager, drummer and contralto vocalist was Mabel Moran (WOAW, Omaha, NE, 1925).

21578 Merry Old Chief. *See* **Fitzgerald, Leo.**

21579 Merryfield, Mary. COM-HE (WMAQ, Chicago, IL, 1956–1957).

21580 Mertens, Louis. Violinist (WSM, Nashville, TN, 1928).

21581 Mertens, Mary. COM-HE (KFGO, Fargo, ND, 1951).

21582 Mertens, Pete. Newscaster (KIRO, Seattle, WA, 1939–1940).

21583 Mertz, Joseph. Lyric tenor (KNRC, Los Angeles, CA, 1925).

21584 *Merv Griffin Show.* Singer Merv Griffin hosted his entertaining variety show that also featured Darla Hood, Scott Vincent, the Spellbinders and Jerry Bresler's Orchestra. Guests such as Jaye P. Morgan added to the program's fun and good music (40 min., Monday through Friday, 7:15–7:55 P.M., ABC, 1957). Griffin later hosted a popular TV talk show.

21585 Mervine, Frank. DJ (*Out of the Night*, WCBM, Baltimore, MD, 1947).

21586 Meserand, Edythe. Executive, DJ and newscaster (NBC, 1927; WGBS, New York, NY, 1931; WOR, New York, NY, 1940s. Meserand was a pioneer whose broadcasting career spanned the first 50 years of network broadcasting. After beginning work at NBC in 1927, she went to WGBS (New York, NY, 1931) as the station's *Musical Clock Girl*. During World War II, she worked as a newscaster at WOR (New York, NY). She worked in television in 1949. *See* **Gender Discrimination**.

21587 *Meservey's Orchestra*. Instr. mus. prg. (WESG, Elmira, NY, 1938).

21588 Meservy, Maye. COM-HE (KVNU, Logan, UT, 1957).

21589 Meskill, Bob. DJ (*After Hours*, WBBQ, Augusta, GA, 1947; *1230 Club*, WJBC, Bloomington, IN, 1950). Sportscaster (*Sports Special*, WBBQ, 1947; *Sports Spotlight*, WJBC, 1948).

21590 *Message of Israel*. Rabbi Joseph Wise hosted the religious program that began its long network run on NBC in 1934. The program was a production of the New York Board of Rabbis.

21591 Messengale, (Mrs.) Florence. Pianist (WBAP, Fort Worth, TX, 1926).

21592 Messenheimer, Sam. Leader (Sam Messenheimer String Orchestra, KMTR, Hollywood, CA, 1926).

21593 Messer, Frank. DJ (*Juke Box Revue*, WSKY, Asheville, NC, 1947; *Spinner Sanctum*, WSKY, 1948; *Dance Time* and *Magic Ballroom*, WSKY, 1950). Sportscaster (*World of Sports*, WRNL, Richmond, VA, 1953–1960).

21594 Messersmith, Rex. Farm news reporter (WNAX, Yankton, SD, 1957).

21595 Messing, Ruth. COM-HE (WMAM, Marinette, WI,1949).

21596 Messinger, Johnny. Leader (*Johnny Messinger Orchestra*, instr. mus. prg., NBC, 1939).

21597 Messmer, Ruth. Blues singer (KOIN, Portland, OR, 1929).

21598 Messner, Dick. Leader (*Dick Messner Orchestra*, instr. mus. prg., CBS, 1934–1935; WLW, Cincinnati, OH, 1936; WOR, Newark, NJ, 1935–1936). *See* **Messner Brothers Dance Orchestra**.

21599 Messner, Johnny. Leader (*Johnny Messner Orchestra*, instr. mus. prg., MBS, 1938; NBC, 1939–1940). *See* **Messner Brothers Dance Orchestra**.

21600 Messner Brothers Dance Orchestra. New York dance band (WEAF, New York, NY, 1924). There were five Messner brothers who went on New York radio in 1924.

21601 Metcalf, Dean. Newscaster (KARM, Fresno, CA, 1940–1942). Sportscaster (KARM, 1941).

21602 Metcalf, Max. Newscaster (WAAM, Rochester, NY, 1947).

21603 Metcalf, Peggy. Blues singer (WWNC, Asheville, NC, 1929).

21604 Metcalf, William. Organist (WTAM, Cleveland, OH, 1925).

21605 Metheney, Frank. Pianist (KNRC, Los Angeles, CA, 1925).

21606 Metropolis Trio. Popular singing group consisting of messers King, Butler and Ellis, who were not otherwise identified (WHN, New York, NY, 1924).

21607 *Metropolitan Echoes*. Soprano Erva Giles, contralto Devora Nadorney, tenor Robert Simmons, violinist and musical director Arcadie Birkenholz and accompanist Joe Kahn were featured on the good music program. The announcer was George Hicks (30 min., Sunday, 4:00–4:30 P.M., NBC-Blue, 1930). Milton Cross was the program's announcer in 1929.

21608 Metropolitan Male Quartet. Male vocal group (KVOO, Tulsa, OK, 1928).

21609 Metropolitan Male Singers. Popular radio vocal group (KGO, Oakland, CA, 1926).

21610 *(The) Metropolitan Opera*. NBC carried the first Metropolitan Opera broadcasts on a sustaining basis. Lucky Strike cigarettes became the first sponsor in 1933. Listerine in 1934 was the second. RCA took over the sponsorship in 1936 and remained through the Depression years, until Texaco (the Texas Company) took over the Saturday matinee series sponsorship in 1940. *See* **Opera**.

21611 *Metropolitan Opera Auditions of the Air* (aka *Metropolitan Auditions of the Air*). Sherwin-Williams Paint Company sponsored the musical program on which aspirants to an operatic career performed. The host was Edward Johnson and the orchestra was conducted by Wilfred Pelletier (30 min., Sunday, 6:30–7:00 P.M., NBC-Blue Network, 1942). Later the program was sponsored by Farnsworth Radio & TV, Inc. In that format, Pelletier still conducted the orchestra, but Milton Cross took over as host.

21612 *Metropolitan Opera, USA*. Operatic baritone Lawrence Tibbett hosted the program on which young operatic artists performed (30 min., Thursday, 7:30–8:00 P.M., NBC-Blue Network, 1942).

21613 Metropolitan Quartet. Vocal group consisting of Charles Bolin, 1st tenor; Bert Folsom, 2nd tenor; Chester Craig, baritone; and B.J. Richards, bass. Pianist Amelia Lowe Richards was the accompanist (KPO, San Francisco, CA, 1923).

21614 Metropolitan Theatre Orchestra. Theater orchestra directed by Creatore (KFI, San Francisco, CA, 1925).

21615 Metz, Bernice. Pianist (KWSC, Pullman, WA, 1927).

21616 Metz, Henrietta. Banjoist (KWSC, Pullman, WA, 1927).

21617 Metz, Lucius. Tenor (*Lucius Metz*, vcl. mus. prg., WLW, Cincinnati, OH, 1936).

21618 Metz, Lora. COM-HE (WMOU, Berlin, NH, 1949).

21619 Metzger, Emily. Soprano (KGER, Long Beach, CA, 1928).

21620 Metzger, Jeanne [Jean]. COM-HE (KVAR, Mesa, AZ, 1955; KTVK, Phoenix, AZ, 1955–1956).

21621 Meuser, Hans. Bass (WLW, Cincinnati, OH, 1925).

21622 *Mexican Marimba Orchestra*. Instr. mus. prg. (NBC, 1935; KGNF, North Platte, NE, 1940).

21623 *Mexican Musical Tours*. Musical program featuring the Angell Mercado Orchestra (NBC, 1935).

21624 *Mexican Typica Orchestra*. Instr. mus. prg. (WBZ-WBZA, Boston-Springfield, MA, 1932; NBC, 1934).

21625 Meyer, Alice. Pianist Meyer was a "pupil of George Kruger" (KPO, San Francisco, CA, 1923).

21626 Meyer, Allen. DJ (*Polka Party*, WJAG, Norfolk, NE, 1952).

21627 Meyer, Ann. COM-HE (WGGA, Gainesville, GA, 1954–1955).

21628 Meyer, Ches. Leader (Ches Meyer Orchestra, WHAS, Louisville, KY, 1923).

21629 Meyer, Don. DJ (*Jughead's Juke Box*, WRVA, Richmond, VA, 1947).

21630 Meyer, Earl. Leader (*Earl Meyer Orchestra*, instr. mus. prg., WIP, Philadelphia, PA, 1936).

21631 Meyer, Edward Lee. Actor (WLW, Cincinnati, OH, 1926).

21632 Meyer, Edward V. Flutist on *Major Bowes Capitol Theater Family* program (NBC, 1928).

21633 Meyer, Elsa. Pianist (WPG, Atlantic City, NJ, 1926).

21634 Meyer, Eugene. Concert pianist (WIL, St. Louis, MO, 1926).

21635 Meyer, (Mrs.) Eugene. Pianist (WSM, Nashville, TN, 1928).

21636 Meyer, Frederick G. "Fred." Sportscaster (WHDL, Olean, NY, 1937; football play-by-play, WHDL, 1940–1941). Newscaster (WHDL, 1940).

21637 Meyer, Harriet. COM-HE (WLLY, Richmond, VA, 1956).

21638 Meyer, Harry. Leader (*Harry Meyer Orchestra*, instr. mus. prg., NBC, 1935).

21639 Meyer, [Myers] Jack. Leader (Jack Meyer's Musical Architects Orchestra, WCAU, Philadelphia, PA, 1925; WFAN, Philadelphia, PA, 1927).

21640 Meyer, Rose. Pianist (WRNY, New York, NY, 1932).

21641 Meyer, Ruth. Singer (*Ruth Meyer the Melody Girl*, vcl. mus. prg., WFBE, Cincinnati, OH, 1933).

21642 Meyer, Ruth and Janet Meyer. Jazz pianist Janet Meyer and her singing partner, Ruth, were a popular radio team (WHN, New York, NY, 1923).

21643 Meyer, Sig. Banjo soloist. *See* **Pasadena Orchestra DeLuxe**.

21644 Meyer, Vic. Leader (Butler Hotel Orchestra, KJR, Detroit, MI, 1928 and Vic Meyer's Orchestra, KJR, 1928).

21645 Meyer, Woody. Leader (Woody Meyer Orchestra, WLW, Cincinnati, OH, 1923–25).

21646 Meyer Davis Orchestra. Popular orchestra directed by Meyer Davis and, occasionally, by Lon Chassy (Meyer Davis Bellevue

Stratford Orchestra, WFI, Philadelphia, PA, 1923).

21647 ***Meyer the Buyer.*** Harry Hershfield played the title role in the situation comedy based on Jewish humor. New York City's garment center was the focus of the program's action, where Meyer interacted with various garment industry workers. Featured in the cast in addition to Hershfield were: Nick Adams, Alan Reed (Teddy Bergman), Geoffrey Bryant, Paul Douglas, Dot Harrington, Ethel Holt and Adele Ronson (30 min., Syndicated, Various Stations and Times, mid–1930's).

21648 **Meyerinck, Herb.** Director (Clift Hotel Dance Orchestra, KPO, San Francisco, CA, 1926; Herb Meyerinck's Mandarin Orchestra, KFRC, San Francisco, CA, 1929).

21649 **Meyers, Eddie.** Leader (Eddie Myers Orchestra, a versatile band broadcasting from New York's Amoy Restaurant, WHN, New York, NY, 1929). Sometimes the band broadcast an entire hour of Chinese music.

21650 **Meyers [Myers], George Nelson.** Newscaster (KFAR, Fairbanks, AK, 1937–1940).

21651 **Meyers, Joseph.** Humorous readings (KDKA, Pittsburgh, PA, 1922).

21652 **Meyers, Lois.** COM-HE (KTLW, Texas City, TX, 1960).

21653 **Meyers, Stan.** Leader (*Stan Meyers Orchestra*, instr. mus. prg., NBC, 1935).

21654 **Meyers, Sullivan.** Actor Meyers was in the cast of *Young Dr. Malone.*

21655 **Meyers, Ted.** News analyst (KFAC, Los Angeles, CA, 1938–1939; KECA-KFI, Los Angeles, CA, 1940–1942; KFI, Los Angeles, CA, 1944–1948). Sportscaster (KECA-KFI, 1941).

21656 **Meyers, Wayne.** Reader (WEBH, Chicago, IL, 1925).

21657 ***Meyers Kiddie Club Jamboree.*** The Saturday morning feature presented the musical performances of local youngsters (KLRA, Little Rock, AR, 1941).

21658 **Meyn, Ted.** Organist (WDAF, Kansas City, MO, 1926).

21659 ***MGM Radio Club.*** Radie Harris provided Hollywood news and gossip on this show that also featured musical selections by Jack Whiting, Frank Hernandez and the Johnny Green Orchestra (30 min., Weekly, WHN, New York, NY, 1936).

21660 **Micaud, Nancy.** COM-HE (WCHV, Charlottesville, VA, 1960).

21661 **Micciche, Joe.** Sportscaster (KRKD, Los Angeles, CA, 1937).

21662 **Michael, George.** DJ (*Morning Watch*, WROW, Albany, NY, 1947).

21663 **Michael, Jay.** DJ (WCAE, Pittsburgh, PA, 1952–1957).

21664 **Michael, Mike.** Newscaster (WAYS, Charlotte, NC, 1946).

21665 **Michael, Millie.** COM-HE (WATS, Sayre, PA, 1960).

21666 **Michael, Milton.** Tenor (KFDM, Beaumont, TX, 1928).

21667 **Michael, Peter.** Writer Michael wrote the *Lone Journey* daytime serial program.

21668 **Michael, Raymond "Ray."** Sportscaster (WMAL, Washington, DC and WRC, Washington, DC, 1940–1941; WMAL, 1942; WRC, 1954–1960). Michael for many years was Washington's most respected and beloved announcer and sportscaster.

21669 **Michael, Robert.** DJ (*Midnight Dancing Party*, WRTA, Altoona, PA, 1947; *Variety Matinee*, WRTA, 1949–1950).

21670 **Michael, Susie.** Director-host of a children's program that featured Inez Caplan, pianist, and "Aunt Nell," the story teller (KGW, Portland, OR, 1923).

21671 **Michael, Terry.** Newscaster (KRAL, Rawlins, WY, 1948).

21672 ***Michael Shayne, Private Detective.*** Jeff Chandler played the title role on the mystery drama series based on the character created by Brett Halliday (Davis Dresser). Over the years, the program frequently disappeared only to reappear on another network. Cast members in the different formats included Louise Arthur, Kathy Lewis, Wally Maher and Robert Sterling (30 min., Transcribed Weekly, 5:00–5:30 P.M., WOR, Newark, NJ, 1949).

21673 **Michaelis, Arnold.** Director Michaelis directed *Amanda of Honeymoon Hill* and *Twenty Thousand Years in Sing Sing.*

21674 **Michaelman, Ed.** DJ (*Na Lei O Hawaii [Song of the Islands]*, KGMB, Honolulu, HI, 1954).

21675 **Michaelson, Bill.** Newscaster (KRAL, Rawlings, WY, 1948).

21676 **Michaelson, Winifred.** Pianist (WRC, Washington, DC, 1924).

21677 **Michaud, Vietta.** Singer (WABI, Bangor, ME, 1942).

21678 **Michaux, Elder Lightfoot.** Minister Michaux, whose programs featured his own excellent choir, possessed both speaking and singing vocal skills that were excellent (WJSV, Washington, DC, 1936). His religious programs on radio and, later, on television attracted a large audience.

21679 **Michel, Al.** Sportscaster (WTAQ, Green Bay, WI, 1937–1941).

21680 **Michel, Bob.** DJ (*Let's Dance*, WJSW, Altoona, PA, 1947; *Bob Michel Show*, WKRT, Cortland, NY, 1948).

21681 **Michel, Marti.** Leader (*Marti Michel Orchestra*, WOR, Newark, NJ, 1935).

21682 ***Michelin Hour.*** Michelin Tires sponsored the musical variety program (30 min., Tuesday, 8:30–9:00 P.M., NBC-Blue, 1928).

21683 **Michelini, Alma.** Soprano (KYA, San Francisco, CA, 1927).

21684 **Michelson, (Mrs.) P.E.** Singer (KFDY, Brookings, SD, 1925).

21685 ***Michigan Barn Dance.*** CW music show (WKNX, Saginaw, MI, probably mid–1950s). This barn dance program included such performers as Tex Ferguson and His Drifting Pioneers, Little Jimmy Dickens and Dusty Owens.

21686 **Mickel, Harold.** Newscaster (WERC, Erie, PA, 1945).

21687 **Mickelson, Siegfried.** News analyst (KFKU, Lawrence, KS, 1940; WCCO, Minneapolis–St. Paul, MN, 1944).

21688 ***Mickey Mouse*** **(aka** ***The Mickey Mouse Theater*** **or** ***The Mickey Mouse Theater of the Air*****).** Dramatized cartoon sketches made this an entertaining children's program. The antics of Mickey and Minnie Mouse, Donald Duck, Goofy and Clarabelle Cow were presented. The title role of Mickey was played by Walt Disney. Others in the cast were Clarence Nash as Donald Duck; Thelma Boardman as Minnie; Stuart Buchanan as Goofy; and Florence Gill as Clarabelle Cow. Bill Demling was the show's writer. Felix Mills conducted the orchestra and, generally, was responsible for the other music groups that appeared on the program such as Donald Duck's Swing Band and the Minnie Mouse Woodland Choir. Pepsodent Toothpaste sponsored the program (30 min., Sunday, 5:30–6:00 P.M., NBC-Red, 1938).

21689 ***Mickey Mouse Club.*** Manager Harold Murphy of Seattle's Liberty Theater, conducted the Saturday morning show for children that consisted of songs, games, funny skits and organ music played by Sam Totten [Totter]. The program was a great local favorite (KGY, Seattle, WA, 1930s).

21690 **Mickles [Mickley], Lillian.** COM-HE (WHGB, Harrisburg, PA, 1956–1957).

21691 **Micklin, Harold.** Conductor-violinist of the station orchestra (WFL, Philadelphia, PA, 1928).

21692 ***Mid-Afternoon Madness.*** Thomas Garrison Morfitt, who became better known as Garry Moore, was the host-comedian on the entertaining show. Gary told old jokes and demonstrated his wit on the sustaining show. Music was supplied by a good band called the Gentlemen of Jam (60 min., Tuesday, 3:00–4:00 P.M., KWK, St. Louis, MO, 1940). The program was one of Moore's first after he left station WBAL (Baltimore, MD). *See* ***Bingo and Kitty.***

21693 ***Mid-Day Merry-Go-Round (Midday Merry-Go-Round).*** The CW variety show was a popular Knoxville feature for many years, running from the1937 until into the 1959. Among its performers over the years were: Molly O'Day, Lost John Miller, Johnny and Jack, Chet Atkins, the Carlisle Brothers, Smilin' Eddie Hill, the Tennessee Hillbillies, Pee Wee King, Charlie Monroe, Don Gibson, the Stringbusters, Don Gibson, Arthur Q,. Smith, Roy Acuff and comedians Archie Campbell and Homer and Jethroe (WNOX, Knoxville, TN, 1937–1959).

21694 **Middleman, Herman.** Leader (*Herman Middleman Orchestra*, instr. mus. prg., KDKA, Pittsburgh, PA, 1936–1938).

21695 **Middlemast, Jessie.** COM-HE (WHLI, Hempstead, KY, 1954).

21696 **Middleton, B.N.** News analyst (*Middleton and the News*, WUSN, Charleston, SC, 1948).

21697 **Middleton, Charles.** Announcer who broadcast his stations's self designation as

"The Voice of the Maple City" (WRAF, La Porte, IN, 1925–1927).

21698 **Middleton, Mary Sue.** COM-HE (WHLN, Harlan, KY, 1957).

21699 **Middleton, Robert "Bob."** DJ (*1450 Club*, WWSC, Glens Falls, NY, 1947; *Best on Wax*, WWSC, 1952–1957). Sportscaster (WIPS, Ticonderoga, NY, 1956).

21700 ***Midget Automobile Races.*** Bill Thompkins talked about the sport on the local show sponsored by the Beverwyck Brewing Company (15 min., Wednesday, 11:15–11:30 P.M., WROW, Albany, NY, 1949).

21701 ***Midland Minstrels.*** CW mus. prg., KMBC (Kansas City, MO, 1939).

21702 ***Midnight at the Goghans.*** Goghan, a gossip columnist for the Philadelphia *Daily News*, and his wife added a new twist to the husband-and-wife talk show format by greeting the listening public at midnight and interviewing a guest each evening on their popular local show (15 min., Monday through Friday, 12:00–12:15 A.M., WIBG, Philadelphia, PA, 1947).

21703 ***Midnight Dance.*** Charles Strickland's New York Park Central Hotel Orchestra were featured on the program (NBC-Red, New York, NY, 1929).

21704 ***Midnight Frolic.*** Kerner's Crazy Water Hotel Orchestra appeared on the program sponsored by Crazy Water Crystals. Mainly CW music was played. The show was broadcast from the lobby of the Crazy Wells Hotel in Mineral Wells, Texas (WBAP, Fort Worth, TX, 1925).

21705 ***Midnight Frolic.*** Packard Automobile Company sponsored the spirited late night music and comedy program. The Packard Dance Band and singer Helen Geste were featured (KFI, Los Angeles, CA, 1927).

21706 ***Midnight Frolic of KPO.*** Music and comedy were the major elements of the late night broadcast. Various stars of musical comedy fame, vaudeville and the movies were featured, for example, Rosetta and Vivian (Topsy and Eva), who appeared on the March 26, 1926 program (KPO, San Francisco, CA, 1926).

21707 ***Midnight Heralds (L.I.F.E. Band and Choir).*** Religious concert from Aimee Semple McPherson's Angelus Temple with an orchestra and chorus conducted by Nolan Tucker (60 min., Sunday, 12:00 midnight to 1:00 A.M., KFSG, Los Angeles, CA, 1928).

21708 ***Midnight Jamboree.*** See ***Ernest Tubbs' Record Shop;*** **Tubb, Ernest** *and* **Singers: Crooners, Song Birds, Country Belles, Cow Girls and Hillbillies.**

21709 ***Midnight Revue.*** Variety program broadcast from Cleveland's Allen Theater (Weekly, 11:10–12 midnight, WTAM, Cleveland, OH, 1927).

21710 **Midnight Sons Orchestra.** Local dance band (WEAF, New York, NY, 1925).

21711 ***Midnight Stage and Screen Frolic.*** Variety program broadcast from the Hotel Gibson with celebrities appearing at Cincinnati theaters (Thursday, 12 midnight to 1:00 A.M., WLW, Cincinnati, OH, 1926).

21712 ***Midstream.*** On the daytime dramatic serial, a middle-aged married couple faced their mid-life crises and the marital problems they encountered. The adverse effects upon their children were many. Procter & Gamble sponsored the program written by Pauline Hopkins and directed by Gordon Hughes. Originating in Chicago, the program premiered on NBC in 1939. Over the years the cast included: Bill Bouchey, Elia Braca, Sidney Ellstrom, Willard Farnum, Laurette Fillbrandt, Betty Lou Gerson, Josephine Gilbert, Sharon Granger, Jane Green, Annette Harper, Henry Hunter (Arthur Jacobson), Sylvia Jacobs, Bob Jellison, Lenore Kingston, Nina Klowden, Mercedes McCambridge, Marvin Miller, Pat Murphy, Connie Osgood, Olan Soule, Hugh Studebaker, Russell Thorson and Lesley Woods.

21713 **Midway Gardens Orchestra.** Club music group (WBCN, Chicago, IL, 1925).

21714 ***Midway Jamboree.*** CW music program (WGWD, Gadsden, AL, 1952). The CW music show included such performers as: Lee Bonds and the Shady Side Playboys, Rita Faye, Smiley Wilson, Lucky Joe Almond, Bobby Cox, Bill Roberts, Al Ferrel, Sonny Sims, Johnny Herrin, Larry Garmon and Junior Scott.

21715 ***Midweek Hymn Sing.*** The popular program featured baritone soloist Arthur Billings Hunt and a mixed quartet consisting of Hunt and Clyde Dengler, tenors; Helen Janke, contralto; and Muriel Wilson, soprano. George Vause provided the piano accompaniment. The program was first broadcast in 1926 (30 min., Thursday, 7:00–7:30 P.M., NBC-Red, 1930). The format changed the following year to 15-minutes and was sometimes listed as *The Midweek Federation Hymn Sing*. The mixed quartet at this time consisted of Arthur Billings Hunt, baritone; Richard Maxwell, tenor; Helen Janke, contralto; and Muriel Savage, contralto. Accompanist George Vause remained (15 min., Tuesday, 7:00–7:15 P.M., NBC-Red, 1931).

21716 ***(The) Midwestern Hayride (aka Boone County Jamboree*** **and** ***Country Hayride).*** The CW music show, formerly known as *The Boone County Jamboree*, continued until well into the 1960s (WLW, Cincinnati, OH, 1938–1960s). It became the *Midwestern Hayride* in 1945. Among the CW music stars that appeared on the show were the Drifting Cowboys group that consisted of Merle Travis, Bill Brown, Morris "Sleepy" Marlin and Walter Brown; Boone County Buccaneers; Sunshine Sue and Her Rangers; Happy Valley Girls; the Girls of the Golden West; Hugh Cross, Hank Penny, Curly Fox and Texas Ruby, Lulu Belle and Scotty, Bradley Kincaid; Grandpa Jones; the Delmore Brothers; and the Brown's Ferry Four.

The radio program was simulcast on television in 1948. The radio program ended in the late 1950s, but the television program lasted until 1974. Its name was changed to *Country Hayride* in the early 1970s. *See* ***The Boone County Jamboree.***

21717 **Midwood Orchestra.** Local dance band (WRNY, New York, NY, 1925).

21718 **Midyett, Dorothy.** COM-HE (WTJS, Jackson, TN, 1956).

21719 **Mieras, Wes.** Newscaster (KVI, Tacoma, WA, 1940). Sportscaster (*Sports Sparks*, KVI, 1940).

21720 **Mierhauser, Fran.** COM-HE (KJAM, Madison, SD, 1960).

21721 **Miesle, Kathryn.** Contralto (NBC, 1928).

21722 **Mighahan Oriental Trio.** Instrumental music group (WGBS, New York, NY, 1925).

21723 **Mignolet, Jeanne.** Singer Mignolet was a member of *Roxy's Gang* (NBC, 1928–1930).

21724 **Mihm, Lydia.** Soprano (WAAF, Chicago, IL, 1935).

21725 ***Mike and Buff's Mail Bag.*** Mike Wallace and Buff Cobb discussed such momentous domestic questions on the transcribed sustaining show as, "Should husbands and wives have separate vacations?" A segment of each program was a recorded portion by Hollywood commentator George Fisher, who conducted an interview with a motion picture star. Harry Kramer was the program's announcer (15 min., Monday through Friday, 3:34–4:00 P.M., CBS, 1954). *See* **Husband-and-Wife Talk Shows.**

21726 **Mike (Arthur Wellington) and Herman (Jimmy Murray).** Mike and Herman were a popular comedy team (WENR, Chicago, IL and WBCN, Chicago, IL, 1928–1930).

21727 **Mikkalo, Evelyn.** COM-HE (KLBM, LaGrande, OR, 1949).

21728 **Mikkalson, Bob.** Sportscaster (State University of Iowa basketball play-by-play, WMT, Cedar Rapids, IA, 1960).

21729 **Mikus, Alice.** Harpist (WBZ, Springfield, MA, 1924).

21730 **Milam, Lena.** Violinist (KFDM, 1925).

21731 **Milburn, Emory.** Newscaster (KVCV, Redding, CA, 1939).

21732 ***Mildred Bailey.*** Singer Bailey, known as the "Rocking Chair Lady," was accompanied by such fine musicians as Red Norvo, Roy Eldridge, Teddy Wilson and Specs Powell on her good music show. Weekly guests included such singers and musicians as Vaughn Monroe and Tony Pastor (15 min., Weekly, CBS, 1944–1945).

21733 **Miles, Allie Lowe.** Actress Miles was in the cast of the cast of the *Life and Loves of Dr. Susan* daytime series program.

21734 **Miles, Bill.** DJ (*Sunnyside Up*, KDRS, Paragould, AR, 1955).

21735 **Miles, Dottie.** COM-HE (WJOT, Lake City, SC, 1956).

21736 **Miles, Eddie Mae.** COM-HE (WLSM, Louisville, KY, 1957).

21737 **Miles, Jack.** Leader (*Jack Miles Orchestra*, instr. mus. prg., WGY, Schenectady, NY, 1934; WTAM, Cleveland, OH, 1936).

21738 **Miles, Jim.** Newscaster (WCKY, Cincinnati, OH, 1937).

21739 **Miles, Ogden.** Actor Ogden was in the cast of *Woman of America*.

21740 Miles, Robert. News analyst (*Radio Town Mirror*, KIXL, Dallas, TX, 1947).

21741 Miles, Rory. COM-HE (WBRE, Wilkes-Barre, PA,1954).

21742 Miles, (Mrs.) T.E. Contralto (WSM, Nashville, TN, 1926).

21743 Miley, Bill. Comedian (KFWM, Oakland, CA, 1927).

21744 Milford, Skip. DJ (*Melodies for Millions*, WCRW, Chicago, IL, 1947).

21745 Milhauser, Fred. Violinist (KFWM, Oakland, CA, 1927).

21746 Milhill, Floyd. Newscaster (WMBG, Richmond, VA, 1945).

21747 Milholland, Howard L. Announcer (KGO, Oakland, CA, 1926).

21748 Milholland, Vida. Soprano (WEAF, New York, NY, 1927).

21749 *Milkman's Matinee.* Stan Shaw conducted this all-night DJ show that probably was the first one with this particular title (mid–1940's).

21750 *Milkman's Matinee.* Art Ford was the DJ on the popular New York show. Ford claimed 400,000 listeners to whom he provided 43 hours of recorded requests weekly. His program content ranged from boogie-woogie to the New World Symphony. He often got requests from a group of Columbia University professors who called themselves "The Grant's Tomb Jazz and Chowder Society" (360 min., daily except Sunday — Monday through Saturday, 12:00 midnight to 6:00 A.M.; 420 min., Sunday, 12:00 midnight to 7:00 A.M., WNEW, New York, NY, 1947).

21751 *Milky Way Winners.* Mars Candy Company, makers of Milky Way candy bars, sponsored the weekly dramatic serial with a racing theme. The story featured Mrs. Darrow, the owner of the Milky Way Stables, who had a three-year-old horse entered in an important race. The program's cast included: Bob Blakeslee, Frank Dane, Angie Herrick, Bob Jellison, Eugenie McGillan and Betty McLean (15 min., Monday, 6:30–6:45 P.M., CST, WGN, Chicago, IL, 1935).

21752 Millan, L.H. "Mac." Sportscaster (*Mac Millan Sports*, WHEC, Rochester, NY, 1955).

21753 Millar, Adele. Broadcast beauty talks (KGFJ, Los Angeles, CA, 1928).

21754 Millar, Lee. Millar was an animal imitator. He imitated a dog on the *Those We Love* daytime serial program.

21755 Millar, Marie. Soprano (KFI, San Francisco, CA, 1925).

21756 Millar, Scottie. Singer Millar was an "authorized" Harry Lauder impersonator (WTIC, Hartford, CT, 1926).

21757 Millay, Edna St. Vincent. Poet-author (Networks, 1930s and 1940s). Millay was born in Rockland, ME, in 1892. After graduating from Vassar College in 1917, she went to New York City to pursue a free lance writing career. She settled in the city's Greenwich Village and lived the bohemian life of the 1920s. She wrote her much acclaimed poem, "Renascence," while still an undergraduate. Millay was said to have blended the freshness of nature with the Greenwich Village bohemian's "burning of the candle at both ends." Critics wrote that F. Scott Fitzgerald's *Far Side of Paradise*, Millay's "A Few Figs From Thistles" and Ernest Hemingway's *The Sun Also Rises* were typical example of the fresh new American literature produced in the 1920s (Spiller, Thorp, Johnson, Canby and Ludwig, 1963).

Millay in 1939 appeared on a New York *Herald-Tribune Forum* program (WJZ, New York, NY) with James Conant, the president of Harvard University, where she voiced strong disapproval of the German political philosophy and strong approval for those of France and Great Britain. The Allies, she said, had civilized concepts like our own, adding that we hope they will win the war. In conclusion, she read her poem, "Underground System."

During World War II, Rex Strout, the creator of the Nero Wolfe mysteries, asked her to write a poem about the atrocities the Nazis committed at Lidice in Czechoslovakia, where they killed 173 men and boys; deported 203 women to a concentration camp; gassed 81 of Lidice's 104 children and sent the rest to orphanages. They then burned the entire village. This outrage was perpetrated because they thought the villagers were harboring the underground leaders responsible for the assassination of the Nazi commander known as "Heydrich the Hangman." Millay responded by writing "The Murder of Lidice," a verse play that was broadcast by NBC on October 19, 1942, and short waved to England and Europe and to South and Central America in Spanish and Portuguese translations.

21758 Millender, Lucky. Leader (*Lucky Millender Orchestra*, instr. mus. prg., WOWO, Ft. Wayne, IN, 1942).

21759 Miller, Albert. Tenor (WEAF, New York, NY, 1925).

21760 Miller, Albert G. Writer Miller wrote for *The Ben Bernie Show, Buck Rogers in the 25th Century, Eno Crime Club, Fred Allen Show, Maudie's Diary* and *Those Websters.*

21761 Miller, Alice. Violinist (WJZ, New York, NY, 1925).

21762 Miller, Andrew. A lecturer from the Oregon Bankers Association, Miller spoke on "The Relation of the Farmer and the Banker" (KGW, Portland, OR, 1923).

21763 Miller, Barbara. COM-HE (WAMS, Wilmington, DE, 1954).

21764 Miller, Big Freddy. Baritone (*Big Freddy Miller*, vcl. mus. prg., CBS, 1933, 1936).

21765 Miller, Bill. DJ (WMON, Montgomery, WV, 1955).

21766 Miller, Bill. DJ (KGGF, Coffeyville, KS, 1955–1956).

21767 Miller, Bob. Singer (WHN, New York, NY, 1925).

21768 Miller, Bob. Sportscaster (*Sports Page of the Air*, WARC, Rochester, NY, 1949).

21769 Miller, Campbell. Newscaster (WJBC, Bloomington, IN, 1939).

21770 Miller, Carl. Leader (*Carl Miller Orchestra*, instr. mus. prg., WORK, York, PA, 1936).

21771 Miller, Chester H. Announcer (WEAN, Providence, RI, 1927).

21772 Miller, Claude. Pianist (WRC, Washington, DC, 1924).

21773 Miller, Curley. Leader (*Curley Miller's Plow Boys*, CW mus. prg., KDKA, Pittsburgh, PA, 1935; WMMN, Fairmont, WV, 1938).

21774 Miller, Daisy. Monologist Miller specialized in "Negro dialect" stories (WJZ, New York, NY, 1922).

21775 Miller, Dave. Leader (*Dave Miller Orchestra*, instr. mus. prg., WISN, Madison, WI, 1935).

21776 Miller, David L. "Dave." Newscaster (WAAT, Jersey City, NJ, 1941, 1944). DJ (*Home Town Frolic*, WAAT, 1947–1948; *Bar 93 Ranch* and the *Dave Miller Show*, WPAT, Paterson, NJ, 1949).

21777 Miller, David "Moose." Sportscaster and play-by-play man who broadcast Flathead County's basketball and football games (KGEZ, Kalispell, MT, 1958–1960).

21778 Miller, Dean. DJ (*Glassdoor Melodies*, WCOL, Columbus, OH, 1947).

21779 Miller, Diane. COM-HE (WEDO, McKeesport, PA, 1951).

21780 Miller, Dick. Tenor (WMAK, Buffalo, NY, 1928).

21781 Miller, Dick. DJ (*The Ole Hep Cat*, WRBC, Jackson, MS, 1949).

21782 Miller, Dorothy. Soprano Miller appeared on the *Roxy and His Gang* (WJZ-NBC, New York, NY, 1927).

21783 Miller, Dorothy. DJ (*A Miss with the Hits*, WBBQ, Augusta, GA, 1952).

21784 Miller, Dorothy "Dottie" Mae. COM-HE (WTAC, Flint, MI, 1954–1955).

21785 Miller, Dorothy Ruth. Concert pianist (KFI, Los Angeles, CA, 1926).

21786 Miller, Dot. Singer Miller was a member of *Roxy's Gang* (WEAF, New York, NY, 1925).

21787 Miller, Dotty. COM-HE (WSGW, Saginaw, MI, 1954).

21788 Miller, Earl. Banjoist (*Earl Miller's Banjo*, instr. mus. prg., WHP, Harrisburg, PA, 1936).

21789 Miller, Ed. Farm news reporter (*Farm Fair*, WMFT, Florence, AL, 1948).

21790 Miller, Eda. Pianist (WFBH, New York, NY, 1925).

21791 Miller, Eddie. Singer (*Eddie Miller*, vcl. mus. prg., WIP, Philadelphia, PA, 1935).

21792 Miller, Edward "Ed." DJ (*Bring Back the Bands*, WLAN, Lancaster, PA, 1955–1957).

21793 Miller, Eddy. Leader (Eddy Miller's Dixie Boys Orchestra, KFQZ, Hollywood, CA, 1926).

21794 Miller, Elsie. Pianist (WBPI, New York, NY, 1925).

21795 Miller, Elwanda. COM-HE (WICO, Campbellville, KY, 1951).

21796 Miller, Fanny Ward. Reader (KRE, Berkeley, CA, 1926).

21797 Miller, Fay. Pianist (WHN, New York, NY, 1924).

21798 Miller, Frances. Soprano (WHN, New York, NY, 1923; WGBS, New York, NY, 1925).

21799 Miller, Fritz. Leader (*Fritz Miller Orchestra*, instr. mus. prg., CBS, 1934–1935).

21800 Miller, George. Sportscaster (WGY, Schenectady, NY, 1946).

21801 Miller, George P. DJ (*Club 1560*, KWCO, Chickasha, OK, 1947; *Mystery Matinee*, KADA, Ada, OK, 1949).

21802 Miller, (Dr.) George R. Announcer (KGBZ, York, NE, 1927).

21803 Miller, Gerald. Announcer (WBRS, New York, NY, 1927).

21804 Miller, Glenn. Leader (*Glenn Miller Orchestra*, instr. mus. prg., CBS and MBS, 1935; NBC, 1940; KANS, Wichita, KS, 1942). Many popular music critics would argue that the orchestras of the great Glenn Miller and that of Benny Goodman were the best radio big bands of the era. During World War II, Miller led an Air Force Orchestra that did some propaganda broadcasting beamed at German listeners. *See* **Wartime Radio** *and* ***Glenn Miller***.

21805 Miller, Grant R. DJ (*Musical Melodies*, WCRW, Chicago, IL, 1947).

21806 Miller, Hal. Newscaster (WHEB, Portsmouth, NH, 1938).

21807 Miller, Halsey. Leader (Halsey Miller's Newark Athletic Club Orchestra playing on the *Music While You Dine* program, WOR, Newark, NJ 1923–1924 and Halsey Miller's Orchestra, WOR, Newark, NJ, 1925).

21808 Miller, Harold. Sportscaster (WORK, York, PA, 1937).

21809 Miller, Hazel. Contralto (KFAB, Lincoln, NE, 1925).

21810 Miller, Helen. COM-HE (WSTP, Salisbury, NC, 1954).

21811 Miller, Henry. Saxophonist (WHAS, Louisville, KY, 1923).

21812 Miller, Herbert Dwight. Miller was an instructor of English at Tufts College before becoming an announcer and director of broadcasting at WGI (Medford Hillside, MA, 1923). He sometimes was designated as "HDM."

21813 Miller, Howard. DJ (WIND, Chicago, IL, mid–1950s). Miller's popular program was broadcast for more than two decades.

21814 Miller, Howard B. Announcer (WIAD, Philadelphia, PA, 1925).

21815 Miller, Hugh. Bass (KFDM, Beaumont, TX, 1928).

21816 Miller, (Dr.) I.M. Announcer (KFIQ, Yakima, WA, 1926).

21817 Miller, Irene. Singer (KWSC, Pullman, WA, 1925).

21818 Miller, Irene. Pianist (KTAB, Oakland, CA, 1926).

21819 Miller, Irving. Leader (*Irving Miller Orchestra*, instr. mus. prg., NBC, 1940).

21820 Miller, J.W. News analyst (*Aggie News*, WTAW, College Station, TX, 1947).

21821 Miller, Jack. Leader (*Jack Miller Orchestra*, instr. mus. prg., WAAB, Boston, MA, 1932).

21822 Miller, Jack. Sportscaster (*Morning Line and Sports Digest*, KGGF, Coffeyville, KS, 1952).

21823 Miller, Jack. Sportscaster (KDLR, Devils Lake, ND, 1952–1955).

21824 Miller, Jan. COM-HE (WDUX, Waupaca, WI, 1957).

21825 Miller, Janet. COM-HE (WARM, Scranton, PA, 1956).

21826 Miller, Jay. Sportscaster (NBC, 1960).

21827 Miller, Jeff. Whistler (WGHB, Clearwater, FL, 1926).

21828 Miller, John G. Leader of the Railite YMCA Band (WLAC, Nashville, TN, 1929).

21829 Miller, John W. Newscaster (WREX, Duluth, MN, 1948).

21830 Miller, John Z. Newscaster (*AP News*, KGCU, Mandan, ND, 1940s).

21831 Miller, June. COM-HE (WSAR, Fall River, MA, 1955).

21832 Miller, Kate. Whistler (WHO, Des Moines, IA, 1924–1926).

21833 Miller, Ken. News analyst (KVOO, Tulsa, OK, 1937–1942, 1944–1945; *Assignment for the Southwest*, KVOO, 1948).

21834 Miller, Larry. Musical director-staff organist (WSBA, York, PA, 1945).

21835 Miller, Leah. Miller conducted the *Women's Exercise Program* (KSTP, St. Paul, MN, 1930). She was the Physical Director of the St. Paul Y.M.C.A.

21836 Miller, Leo. Violinist (WQJ, Chicago, IL, 1926).

21837 Miller, Leroy. DJ (*The Leroy Miller Club*, WFIL, Philadelphia, PA, 1947; *The Breakfast Club*, WFIL, 1948; *The LeRoy Miller Club*, WFIL, 1949–1950).

21838 Miller, Lew. Leader (Lew Miller Dance Orchestra, KYA, San Francisco, CA, 1928).

21839 Miller, Lois. Organist (WTAM, Cleveland, OH, 1937; KDKA, Pittsburgh, PA, 1934–1938).

21840 Miller, Lou. Miller was "Uncle Jack" on his station's children's program (KOIL, Council Bluffs, IA, 1928).

21841 Miller, (Mrs.) M. *Child Study Report* (WEAF, New York, NY, 1932).

21842 Miller, Mamie. Miss Miller was KMA's "Domestic Science Lady" (KMA, Shenandoah, IA, 1928).

21843 Miller, Margaret. Singer (KFAE, Pullman, WA, 1925).

21844 Miller, Marvin. Newscaster (NBC, 1944). Actor-announcer Miller had a busy career in radio. His appearances include *The Affairs of Anthony* (actor), *Andrews Sisters Eight-to-the-Bar Ranch* (announcer), *Armchair Adventures* (announcer), *Aunt Mary* (announcer), *Backstage Wife* (actor), *Beat the Band* (announcer), *Beulah* (announcer), *Billie Burke Show* (actor), *Buster Brown Gang* (actor), *Captain Midnight* (actor), *Chicago Theatre of the Air* (actor), *Cisco Kid* (actor), *Coronet Storyteller* (announcer), *Date with Judy* (announcer), *Dear Mom* (actor), *Don Ameche Show* (announcer), *Duffy's Tavern* (announcer), *Family Theater* (actor), *First Nighter* (actor), *Gay Mrs. Featherstone* (actor), *Great Gunns* (actor), *Guiding Light* (actor), *Harold Teen* (actor), *Irene Rich Dramas* (announcer), *Jack Armstrong* (actor), *Jeff Regan* (actor), *Judy and Jane* (actor), *Knickerbocker Playhouse* (actor), *Lassie* (actor), *Louella Parsons* (announcer), *Ma Perkins* (announcer), *Marvin Miller, Story Teller* (narrator), *Midstream* (actor), *Moon Dreams* (narrator), *Name the Movie* (MC), *Old Gold Show* (announcer), *One Man's Family* (actor), *Peter Quill* (title role), *Play Broadcast* (actor), *Press Club* (actor), *Railroad Hour* (announcer), *Red Skelton Show* (announcer), *Right to Happiness* (actor), *Road of Life* (actor), *Romance of Helen Trent* (actor), *Rudy Vallee Show* (announcer), *Scattergood Baines* (actor), *Songs by Sinatra* (announcer), *Stars over Hollywood* (announcer), *Stepmother* (actor), *Strange Wills* (actor), *Tell It Again* (narrator), *That Brewster Boy* (announcer), *Today's Children* (actor), *Treat Time* (narrator), *Uncle Walter's Dog House* (actor), *The Whistler* (title role), *Wings of Destiny* (announcer) and *Woman from Nowhere* (announcer).

21845 Miller, Marty. COM-HE (WRAW, Reading, PA, 1949).

21846 Miller, Mary. Pianist-singer (WGBS, New York, NY, 1925).

21847 Miller, Mary Liz. COM-HE (WKBV, Richmond, IN, 1951).

21848 Miller, Neil. Tenor, KFRC (San Francisco, CA, 1926).

21849 Miller, Norma T. Violinist (KLOS, Independence, MO, 1926–1927).

21850 Miller, Paul. DJ (*Paul Miller Show*, WCKY, Cincinnati, OH, 1951–1954).

21851 Miller, Paul J. Announcer (KQV, Pittsburgh, PA, 1924).

21852 Miller, Pearl. Soprano (WNYC, New York, NY, 1925).

21853 Miller, Peter. Newscaster (WSNY, Schenectady, NY, 1945).

21854 Miller, Phyl. COM-HE (KGVO, Missoula, MT, 1951).

21855 Miller, R. Glover. Newscaster (WAIM, Anderson, SC, 1937).

21856 Miller, Ray. Leader (Ray Miller Orchestra that appeared on the *Sunny Meadows Radio Show* in 1929).

21857 Miller, Refa. Soprano (KPO, San Francisco, CA, 1929).

21858 Miller, Rex. Newscaster (KHJ, Los Angeles, CA, 1945–1947).

21859 Miller, Robert. Organist (KLDS, Independence, MO, 1925–1926).

21860 Miller, Robert. Singer Miller was billed as "KRE's Singing Realty Man" (KRE, Berkeley, CA, 1926).

21861 Miller, Robert. News analyst (*Over the Line Fence*, WFRD, Worthington, OH, 1948).

21862 Miller, Robert. DJ (*The Koly Klub*, KOLY, Mobridge, SD, 1960).

21863 Miller, Roger. Black DJ (WAAA, Winston-Salem, NC, 1950). Miller conducted two shows one in the morning and the other in the afternoon on WAAA. He formerly had been a popular DJ on WGOG (Greensboro, NC).

21864 **Miller, Ross.** DJ (*Juke Box Jingles* and *Your Box at the Opera*, WTIC, Hartford, CT, 1948–1955).

21865 **Miller, Roy.** Leader (*Roy Miller Orchestra*, instr. mus. prg., WGBI, Scranton, PA, 1938).

21866 **Miller, Russell.** Newscaster (KTOK, Oklahoma City, OK, 1941–1942).

21867 **Miller, Sarah.** Newscaster (KPAB, Laredo, TX, 1945).

21868 **Miller, Skip.** Sportscaster (*A Look at Sports*, WJSW, Altoona, PA, 1949–1951).

21869 **Miller, Stretch.** Sportscaster (WJBC, Bloomington, IL, 1937; WIL, St. Louis, MO, 1949; *Sports Extra*, WIL, 1950–1952; WIRL, Peoria, IL, 1953; WIRL, 1956).

21870 **Miller, Sylvia.** Sixteen-year-old soprano Miller (WGCP, Newark, NJ, 1925) later sang on the *Major Bowes Capitol Family* program (NBC, 1928).

21871 **Miller, Ted.** Leader (Ted Miller's Crazy Water Crystals Hotel Orchestra, WBAP, Fort Worth, TX, 1925).

21872 **Miller, Troy S [C].** Announcer (WRHM, Minneapolis, MN, 1925–1927).

21873 **Miller, (Mrs.) Verne.** Contralto (WOAW, Omaha, NE, 1923).

21874 **Miller, Violet.** Contralto (WJZ, New York, NY, 1925).

21875 **Miller, Vivian.** Organist (WWVA, Wheeling, WV, 1937).

21876 **Miller, Walter.** Conductor (Walter Miller and his Ritz-Carlton Dance Orchestra, WOO, Philadelphia, PA, 1924).

21877 **Miller, Wayne.** Newscaster (*The Richfield Reporter*, NBC, 1940).

21878 **Miller, William B. "Skeets."** Famous for broadcasting "live" accounts of Floyd Collins ordeal when that young man was trapped in a Kentucky cave during the mid–1920s.

21879 **Miller, Wyman.** Cellist (WOR, Newark, NJ, 1925).

21880 **Miller's Lafayette Concert Orchestra.** California concert band (KMTR, Hollywood, CA, 1926).

21881 **Millhauser, Fred.** Violinist (KFWM, Oakland, CA, 1928).

21882 **Millhauser, Sigrid.** Soprano (KFWM, Oakland, CA, 1927).

21883 **Millholland, Howard L.** Announcer sometimes designated as "HM" (KGO, San Francisco, CA, 1924–1930). Millholland later became studio manager and program director. He was famous for his *Radio Vaudeville* program. In addition he performed as a reader, impersonator and singer.

21884 **Millhouse, Glenn.** Newscaster (KGEZ, Kalispell, MT, 1945–1946). Sportscaster (KGEZ, 1945–1950s). In the 1950's Millhouse broadcast newscasts (8:00 A.M., 9:00 A.M., 12:00 noon and 5:00 P.M., KGEZ, 1950s).

21885 **Millican, Ken.** Newscaster (KXYZ, Houston, TX, 1945–1947; *Ken Millican News*, KXYZ, 1948).

21886 ***Millie Considine.*** Millie, the wife of Bob Considine, herself a newspaper columnist, interviewed personalities from show business and others in the news on her transcribed show (15 min., Monday through Friday, 12:15–12:30 P.M., MBS, 1956).

21887 **Millier, Marian.** COM-HE (KFYO, Lubbock, TX, 1949).

21888 **Milligan, June.** COM-HE (WRLC, Lewiston, ME, 1955).

21889 **Milligan, Marian.** COM-HE (WTAD, Quincy, IL, 1957).

21890 ***Milligan and Mulligan.*** Don Ameche played a detective on this show that blended comedy and adventure. His assistant was Bob White. Tom Shirley was the announcer (1935).

21891 **Million, Mary E.** Pianist (KLX, Oakland, CA, 1923).

21892 **Million, Peg.** COM-HE (WHFB, Benton Harbor, MI, 1951).

21893 ***Million Dollar Band.*** Barry Wood was the regular vocalist on the half-hour program presenting top musicians who played for a different band leader each week. The Double Daters Quartet and Ruth Doring also performed (30 min., Saturday, P.M., 1943).

21894 **Million Dollar Four Orchestra.** Band featured on the *Starr Motor Car Company Program* (KFWB, Hollywood, CA, 1926).

21895 **Million Dollar Pier Orchestra.** Atlantic City dance band (WPG, Atlantic City, NJ, 1926).

21896 **Millrood, George B.** Violinist (WJR, Detroit, MI, 1928).

21897 **Mills, Arthur.** Accordionist (*Arthur Mills*, KLRA, Little Rock, AR, 1930s).

21898 **Mills, Betty.** COM-HE (WFTG, London, KY, 1956).

21899 **Mills, Billy.** Leader (*Billy Mills Orchestra*, instr. mus. prg., CBS, 1935–1936).

21900 **Mills, Bob.** Tenor (KPCB, Seattle, WA, 1927).

21901 **Mills, Byron.** Announcer (KGO, Oakland, CA, 1928). Baritone (KGO, 1928).

21902 **Mills, Dick.** DJ (*The Dick Mills Show*, 240 min., Monday through Friday, 7:00–9:00 A.M. and 4:00–6:00 P.M., WPTR, Albany, NY, 1950).

21903 **Mills, Dick.** DJ (KMA, Shenandoah, IA, 1955).

21904 **Mills, E.M.** Trumpet soloist (WOAW, Omaha, NE, 1926).

21905 **Mills, Felix.** Musical director-composer-arranger Mills was born July 28, 1901. He first worked on radio in 1928 (KHJ, Hollywood, CA, 1928).

21906 **Mills, Floyd.** Leader (*Floyd Mills Orchestra*, instr. mus. prg., WDEL, Wilmington, DE, 1938).

21907 **Mills, Frank.** Newscaster (KGKO, Fort Worth, TX, 1938). Sportscaster (KGKO, 1939; KGKO and WBAP, Forth Worth, TX, 1940, 1945).

21908 **Mills, Harry Q.** Organist (KFWB, Hollywood, CA, 1929).

21909 **Mills, Jay.** Leader (*Jay Mills Orchestra*, instr. mus. prg., NBC, 1934).

21910 **Mills, Jim.** DJ (WMAQ, Chicago, IL, 1957).

21911 **Mills, Ken "Kenny."** Newscaster (WPIC, Sharon, PA, 1941–1942).

21912 **Mills, (Professor) Lennox.** Newscaster (WCCO, Minneapolis, MN, 1941–1946).

21913 **Mills, Marjorie.** COM-HE (*The Marjorie Mills Hour*, 30 min., Monday through Friday, 1:30–2:00 P.M., WNAC, Boston, MA, 1941). Miss Mills broadcast household hints for women.

21914 **Mills, Nancy.** COM-HE (KVEC, San Luis Obispo, CA, 1954).

21915 **Mills, Nellie Callendar [Callender].** Violinist (KFI, Los Angeles, CA, 1928–1929).

21916 **Mills, Noel.** Actress Mills was in the cast of *When a Girl Marries* daytime serial program.

21917 **Mills, Patricia.** COM-HE (KWVY, Waverly, IA, 1960).

21918 **Mills, Russ.** Sportscaster (WFOM, Marietta, GA, 1947–1948). Newscaster (WFOM, 1948).

21919 **Mills, Ruth Ticknor.** Contralto (KFLV, Rockford, IL, 1929–1930). Miss Mills was said to specialize in "heart songs."

21920 **Mills, Wilma.** Singer (WBAA, West Lafayette, IN, 1938).

21921 ***Mills' Blue Rhythm Band.*** Instr. mus. prg. (NBC, 1934–1935).

21922 **Mills Brothers.** Vocal group (*The Mills Brothers*, vcl. mus. prg., CBS. 1931; WPIC, Sharon, PA, 1942). The group, consisting of John, age 21; Herbert, 19; Harry, 18; and Don, 17, was said to be "radio's most popular find" of 1931. One of the offers made to listeners on their show 1931 show was a mail order guitar for $6.25.

21923 **Mills College Choir.** Vocal group directed by Luther B. Marchant that featured soloists: Genevieve Sweetser, Mary Chaddock, Elizabeth Thomas and Lauren Wilson. Ethel Whytal provided organ accompaniment (KTAB, Oakland, CA, 1925).

21924 **Mills College Quartet.** Members of the collegiate vocal group included: sopranos Genevieve Sweetser and Ethel Eves singing with contraltos Elizabeth Thomas and Pauline Mendenhall (KTAB, Oakland, CA, 1925).

21925 ***Mills' Play Boy Orchestra.*** Instr. mus. prg. (NBC, 1933).

21926 **Millwee, Daphne.** COM-HE (KCKY, Coolidge, AZ, 1951).

21927 **Mills-Welsh, (Mrs.) Rose.** Soprano (WIP, Philadelphia, PA, 1924).

21928 **Milne, Dorothy.** Violinist (KOA, Denver, CO, 1926).

21929 **Milne, James T. "Jim."** DJ (*Yawn Club* and *Polka Party*, WNHC, New Haven, CT, 1947–1951). Sportscaster (Basketball, hockey and football play-by-play, WHNC, 1947).

21930 **Milo [Mio], Henry.** Newscaster (WINS, New York, NY, 1945–1946).

21931 ***Milshaw and Crowley.*** Harmony singing team (Vcl. mus. prg., KFQZ, Hollywood, CA, 1928).

21932 **Miltner, Jack.** Newscaster (WKBN, Youngstown, OH, 1942). DJ (*Musical Clock*, WTAM, Cleveland, OH, 1950).

21933 Milton, Jud. Sportscaster (KSJB, Jamestown, ND, 1951; *Sports Review*, KSJB, 1952). DJ (KROD, El Paso, TX, 1957.)

21934 Milton, Kathy. COM-HE (WMCK, McKeesport, PA, 1960).

21935 Milton, Lew. Newscaster (WHBU, Anderson, IN, 1940, 1948).

21936 Milton, Peggie. DJ (*Pleasantly Your Peggie*, WMAZ, Macon, GA, 1952).

21937 *Milton Berle Show.* Although Milton Berle enjoyed some success in the medium of radio, it was in television that he enjoyed his greatest popularity. On radio, Berle was unable to use his considerable talents as a physical comic that made him so popular in vaudeville and on television. Radio never allowed him to become an "Uncle Miltie" or achieve the status of a "Mr. Television." He made his radio debut in 1934, but did not become a regular performer until 1936 with the *Community Sing* program broadcast by CBS. He followed this with a 1944 series, *Let Yourself Go*, broadcast by CBS in 1945 and *Kiss and Make Up* the same year on that network. Berle's radio cast on the *Milton Berle Show* included some of radio's finest actors: Jack Albertson, Eileen Barton, Jackson Beck, John Gibson, Bert Gordon, Pert Kelton, Mary Shipp, Arnold Stang and Roland Winters. The program's writers were Hal Block and Martin A. Ragaway. Music was supplied by Ray Bloch's orchestra. Frank Gallop was the announcer (30 min., Weekly, ABC, 1947–1948). When the *Milton Berle Show* went on television the following year, Berle soon became "Mr. Television."

21938 *Milton Brown and the Musical Brownies.* The early CW band played jazz with a southwestern flavor. After playing with the Light Crust Doughboys, Brown formed his Brownies band in 1932. They became famous with their daily broadcasts on San Antonio's KTAT and WBAP in the early 1930s. Although an influential western swing band, Brown's career was brief. He was killed in an automobile accident in 1936.

21939 *Milton C. Work.* As bridge hands were being played, Work commented upon them on his unique bridge show (NBC, 1930).

21940 *Milton Cross Opera Album.* After the 1949 Metropolitan Opera season was completed, Cross played operatic recordings and discussed them intelligently. Ed. Reimers was the program announcer (30 min., Sunday, 4:30–5:00 P.M., ABC, 1949). *See* **Cross, Milton.**

21941 Milvihill, Joseph P. DJ (*1100 Club*, WTAM, Cleveland, OH, 1948).

21942 *Milwaukee District Court.* Actual cases were broadcast from the city's courtrooms on the program sponsored by the Milwaukee Safety Commission. Two microphones were placed at the judge's bench. Except for a brief introduction by the program's announcer, the only other voices heard were those who actually were participating in the cases. No one was forced to go on the air, but it was reported that few ever declined (WTMJ, Milwaukee, WI, 1935).

21943 Milwaukee Turnvarein Symphony Orchestra. Symphonic music group (WHAD, Milwaukee, WI, 1926).

21944 Mims, Bill. DJ (*Night Owl*, WHAN, Charleston, SC, 1947; *The A Train*, WCON, Atlanta, GA, 1948; *Yawn Patrol*, WATL, Atlanta, GA, 1949). Sportscaster (*Sports of the Day*, WATL, 1950).

21945 Mims, Ernie. DJ (WOC, Davenport, IA, 1960).

21946 Mims, Slim. DJ (*Uncle Ugly*, WJMX, Florence, SC, 1949).

21947 Minahan, Ann D. COM-HE (WCCM, Lawrence, MA, 1957).

21948 Minahan, Julia. COM-HE (WCCM, Lawrence, MA, 1956).

21949 Minard, Frank. Banjoist (WKRC, Cincinnati, OH, 1926).

21950 Mincowski, Pete. Violinist (WKRC, Cincinnati, OH, 1925).

21951 *Mind Your Manners.* Allen Ludden wrote and hosted the audience participation show about etiquette for teenagers (30 min., 10:00–10:30 A.M., WTIC, Hartford, CT, 1947).

21952 Mineo, Sam. Pianist (WMAK, Buffalo, NY, 1928).

21953 Miner, Don. Singer (KFQZ, Hollywood, CA, 1926).

21954 Miner, Jan. Versatile actress Miner appeared in such diverse programs as *Boston Blackie*; *Casey, Crime Photographer*; *Dimension X*; and *Perry Mason*, as well as *Hilltop House* and *Lora Lawton* daytime serials.

21955 Miner, Paul. Newscaster (WINS, New York, NY, 1946).

21956 *Miner Mike.* Ted Rogers, in the role of "Miner Mike," was sponsored by the Utah Mining Association. He told stories about people who had made significant contributions, but never made the headlines (15 min., Sunday, 12:45–1:00 P.M., KALL, Salt Lake City, UT, 1952).

21957 Minevich, Borrah. Harmonica virtuoso Minevich performed brilliantly (*The Theater Magazine* program, WGBS, New York, NY, 1928; *Borrah Minevich's Harmonica Rascals*, instr. mus. prg., NBC, 1933; WENR, Chicago, IL, 1934).

21958 Mingle, Yvonne. COM-HE (WMTS, Murfeesboro, TN, 1954–1955).

21959 Miniard, Julia E. DJ (WATM, Atmore, AL, 1955). COM-HE (WATM, 1956).

21960 *Miniature Biographies.* Grace Sanderson Mitchie wrote the weekly half-hour dramas based on the lives of famous personages (30 min., Weekly, 9:30–10:00 P.M., NBC-Pacific Coast Network, 1929).

21961 *Miniature Theatre.* An hour dramatic program, *Miniature Theatre* featured stories by great writers such as George Ade (30 min., Saturday, 10:30–11:30 P.M., NBC-Blue, 1930).

21962 Minium, James. Newscaster (WHIZ, Zanesville, OH, 1940; WMAN, Mansfield, OH, 1942).

21963 Minneapolis Symphony Orchestra. Symphonic orchestra directed by Henri Verbruggen (WCCO, Minneapolis–St. Paul, MN, 1928; *Minneapolis Symphony Orchestra*, sometimes known as the *Minneapolis-Honeywell Wonder Hour*, 1930–1932). In 1935 the orchestra broadcast a 14-week series of classical music programs. The orchestra at this time was conducted by Paul Lamay and Eugene Ormandy (60 min., Thursday, 10:30–11:30 P.M. CST, NBC-Red, 1935).

21964 *Minnie and Maud.* The unique daytime serial of "human appeal and native comedy" was probably the first to focus on the lives, customs and idioms of the Pennsylvania Dutch in Lancaster Country, Pennsylvania (10 min., Wednesday, Thursday and Saturday, 9:05–9:15 A.M. CST, NBC-Blue, 1936).

21965 Minnie Pearl. CW comedienne and singer. *See* **Comediennes, Singers and Pearl, Cousin Minnie.**

21966 Minnich [Minnick], Rosemary. COM-HE (KEYS, Corpus Christi, TX, 1949).

21967 Minnick, Frances. COM-HE (WBIW, Bedford, IN, 1951).

21968 Minor, Dick. DJ (*Platter Prevue*, WDUK, Durham, NC, 1947).

21969 Minor, Vernon. Newscaster (KWBW, Hutchinson, KS, 1942).

21970 *Minstrels of 1938.* Interlocutor Gene Arnold was assisted by endmen Vance "Catfish" McCune and Bill Thompson, who provided typical radio minstrel show humor (NBC-Chicago, 1938).

21971 Minstrels Shows, Vaudeville, Burlesque and Radio. Minstrel shows, vaudeville and burlesque were important early influences on American radio, providing as they did both material and performers. When Jolson sang "Mammy" in blackface, Weber and Fields performed their ethnic "Dutch" act and Abbott and Costello their familiar "Who's on First" routine, all three of these forms of entertainment were represented.

The minstrel show tradition that began about 1830 in the United States reached its "golden age" in1850. Thomas Dartmouth "Daddy" Rice has been called the "father of the American minstrel show." About 1839, Rice saw a crippled Black man perform an odd dance while singing a strange song. When Rice blacked his face, copied the crippled man's clothes and performed what he called his "Jim Crow dance" on New York City stages, its popularity increased immediately. Soon, however, the focus moved from individual minstrel performers, moving, instead, toward the ensemble show. Another important minstrel of the era was Dan Decatur Emmett, who composed many popular minstrel songs. Emmett created a show with three other entertainers singing and dancing in blackface that he called the Virginia Minstrels.

Popularity of the minstrel show declined after 1870. By the time of World War I only a few minstrel companies remained active and those that did had lost most of their audience to vaudeville. Minstrel shows on radio, however, remained popular through the 1930s. Jolson's blackface performances on the Broadway stage were reminiscent of the old minstrel show format. Jolson had performed previously with Lew Dockstader's Minstrels, a famous minstrel show troupe. The demise of the minstrel show paved the way for vaudeville, a more modern entertainment form that contained a little bit of everything.

The typical vaudeville program consisted of a series of acts of from approximately 15 to 20 minutes in length. These acts included a diverse group of performers, but the shows invariably were "clean." They included scores of singers, musicians, hypnotists, mentalists, escape artists, eccentric dancers, strong men and regurgitators, who drank liquids to put out fires. In addition, the vaudeville stage displayed celebrities from the sports world, the movies and the world of crime's criminals and their victims.

Great vaudevillians such as W.C. Fields and Will Rogers made the successful transition from vaudeville to motion pictures and radio. Some others who easily made the move to radio were such stars as Eddie Cantor, Sophie Tucker, Webber and Fields, George Burns and Gracie Allen, Kate Smith, Al Jolson and Jack Pearl, Jim and Marian Jordan (Fibber McGee and Molly) and Bob Hope. Singing teams such as Billy Jones and Ernie Hare and Scrappy Lambert and Billy Hillpot easily moved into radio as the Happiness Boys (and many other names) and the Smith Brothers, also known as Trade and Mark. Although many vaudeville comedians successfully made the move into radio, others, whose comedy was largely visual such as Ed Wynn, Bert Lahr and Jimmy Durante, struggled with the transition.

If vaudeville was family entertain for middle and working class families, burlesque has come to be thought of as a risque working class entertainment primarily for males. However, burlesque shows when they started in the 1840s contained a wide variety of entertainment. The term "burlesque" apparently comes from the entertainment's early content of spoof and satire. Some 20 years later, however, the British form of burlesque began to feature pretty young women on stage in tights, instead of the usual Victorian bustles and hoop skirts. It was, in fact, the tour of Lydia Thompson's troupe that brought immodestly clothed pretty women and sex into American burlesque. By 1880 the standard American burlesque show contained scantily clad women and frequent sexual innuendo.

Many vaudeville performers reluctantly worked in burlesque, but more often it was burlesque performers who "advanced" to perform in vaudeville. A number of celebrated vaudeville stars got their training and experience in burlesque before successfully moving into vaudeville and radio. Some of them were W.C. Fields, Red Skelton, Jackie Gleason, Bert Lahr, Milton Berle and Phil Silvers.

Burlesque like vaudeville suffered a serious loss of audience to motion pictures in the 1920s, but a new element was added to the former — strip tease performers such as Ann Corio, Sally Rand and Gypsy Rose Lee. After interminable scuffles with the law, the change in sexual mores and American society's standards made burlesque little more than a naughty, old-fashioned anachronism. Still — many fine comedians went into radio from the dying format.

21972 **Minter, Dan.** DJ (*Ladies Night Out*, WOWO, Ft. Wayne, IN, 1952).

21973 **Minter, Elkin.** COM-HE (KSFA, Nacogdoches, TX, 1949).

21974 **Minton, Linda.** COM-HE (WHVH, Henderson, NC, 1960).

21975 **Mintz, Dave.** DJ (*Dave's Ditties*, KVOS, Bellingham, WA, 1952).

21976 **Mintz, Herbie.** Pianist (KYW, Chicago, IL, 1923–1924). DJ (WLS, Chicago, IL, 1955).

21977 **Mintz, Herbie and "Our Sally" Menkes.** Piano team (KYW, Chicago, IL, 1924). *See* **Menkes, Sally.**

21978 ***Minute Men Quartet.*** Vcl. mus. prg. (NBC, 1937).

21979 ***Miracles of Magnolia.*** First heard in 1931, Fanny May Baldridge played all the roles in the dramatic serial about southern life (NBC-Blue, 1931–1933).

21980 **Miranda, Erma H.** Leader (Beloit College Choir, WBBW, Norfolk, VA, 1925).

21981 **Mirova, Juliette.** Pianist (WEVD, New York, NY, 1939).

21982 **Mirsch, Hazel.** *Variety* called her "the official station organist who it was claimed [was] the first woman to broadcast from the station in 1922" (KYW, Chicago, IL, 1922–1924).

21983 **Mirth, Mildred.** COM-HE (KOEL, Oelwein, IA, 1960).

21984 ***Mirth and Madness.*** Jack Kirkwood was the featured performer on the comedy-variety show. Funny sketches and running gags were the main ingredients of the show first broadcast by NBC in 1943. The cast included: Lee Brodie, Billy Grey, Tom Harris, Jack Kirkwood, Lillian Lee, Jean McKean, Mike McTooch, Don Reid (Reed), Herb Sheldon, Ransom Sherman and Bob Sherry. The show was written by Jack Kirkwood and Ransom Sherman. The director was Joseph Mansfield. Music was supplied by the Jerry Jerome and the Irving Miller orchestras (NBC, 1943). A typical example of the Kirkwood humor about elections and politicians who wanted to be elected follows:

> JACK: We now bring you the voice of the man in the street.
>
> DRUNK: I ain't getting up to vote for nobody.
>
> JACK: Is there a cocker spaniel out here who wants a kiss?
>
> DRUNK: Would you kiss a cocker spaniel to get a vote?
>
> JACK: Why not? They go to the polls, too.

See ***The Jack Kirkwood Show.***

21985 ***Mirth and Melody.*** The show opened with the announcement: "*Mirth and Melody* from New Orleans brings you the Merry Minstrels." Each week the program supposedly originated from a different city and the opening changed accordingly. The radio minstrel show was one of the last of its kind. The featured endmen were William "Algernon" Jefferson and Mr. Ernie "Iodine" Whitman. Ken Christy was the interlocutor and Mr. Nichodemus Brown a cast regular. Tenor Harry Babbitt and the Dark Town Quartet were accompanied by the Buzz Adlam band. Owen James was the announcer (30 min., weekly, late 1940s).

21986 ***Mirthful Melodies.*** Simpy Fitts conducted the half-hour program that mixed fun with music (KFRC, San Francisco, CA, 1928). *See* **Simpy Fitts.**

21987 **Mischke, Virginia.** COM-HE (WHFB, Benton Harbor, MI, 1951).

21988 **Miserando, Illumento.** Violinist (WJZ, New York, NY, 1923).

21989 ***Miss Broadway.*** Miss Broadway was Leona Hollister, who broadcast theatrical news and gossip (15 min., Weekly, WBRB, Red Bank, NJ, 1939).

21990 **Miss Jane.** Not otherwise identified, Miss Jane was a favorite announcer of St. Louis listeners (KSD, St. Louis, MO, 1924). *See* **Miss Jones.**

21991 **Miss Jones.** Miss Jones was one of the first female announcers on radio in the early 1920s (KSD, St. Louis, MO). She might have been the **Miss Jane** previously listed.

21992 **Miss Maiden Dallas.** Weekly talks on what "*Milady of the Southwest*" should wear were delivered by Miss Dallas. Her program was sponsored by the Manufacturer's Division of the Dallas Chamber of Commerce (WFAA, Dallas, TX, 1927).

21993 ***Miss Moonbeam.*** Maurice Barrett wrote the charming little story of Miss Moonbeam, a little bit of the moon who occasionally dropped in on Harvey Graham to help him solve his problems. None of the cast members of the sustaining show were identified (15 min., Sunday, 11:15–11:30 P.M., WHN, New York, NY, 1936).

21994 **Miss Nancy.** The otherwise unidentified performer broadcast "book chats" (KFI, Los Angeles, CA, 1925).

21995 ***Miss Patricola.*** Miss Isabella Patricola was a talented singer who specialized in blues and jazz (WMCA, New York, NY, 1929).

21996 ***Miss Patti and the Boys.*** CW mus. prg. (WMBD, Peoria, IL, 1937).

21997 **Miss Yvette.** Concert pianist (KTHS, Hot Springs, AK, 1928).

21998 **Mission Bell Orchestra.** Pryor Moore directed the local band (KFI, Los Angeles, CA, 1927).

21999 ***Mission Secret.*** Frances Rathburn wrote, Alan Beaumont produced and Howard Keegan directed the live, local show originating from Chicago. On the adventure series, Charles Flynn played a State Department courier who found many exciting adventures in Mexico. Clare Baum and Sandra Gair were also in the cast (15 min., Monday through Friday, 9:30–9:15 P.M., WMAQ, Chicago, IL, 1953).

22000 **Missouri Hill Billies.** Country music group (WOS, Jefferson City, MO, 1926).

22001 **Missouri Ramblers.** Dance orchestra (WHB, Kansas City, MO, 1928).

22002 **Missouri State Prison Concert Band.** Virgil W. Combs conducted the famous early radio band that was comprised entirely of prison inmates (WOS, Jefferson City, MO, 1923).

22003 **Missouri State Prison Dance Orchestra.** Prison orchestra directed by Hugh C. French (WOS, Jefferson City, MO, 1924).

22004 ***Mr. Ace and Jane.*** The situation comedy was not as entertaining as their earlier *Easy Aces* program, but it still demonstrated the acerbic humor of Goodman Ace and the considerable comic skill of his wife, Jane. The program was sponsored by Army Air Force Recruiting (30 min., Saturday, 7:00–7:30 P.M., CBS, 1948). *See* **Comediennes** *and* ***Easy Aces.***

22005 ***Mr. Alladin.*** Paul Frees played the title role of a private investigator with the ability to perform miracles on the unusual show. *Variety* criticized the show for containing too many utterly fantastic elements. Music was supplied by Marlin Skiles' Orchestra (30 min., Saturday, 9:30–10:00 P.M., CBS, 1951).

22006 ***Mr. and Mrs.*** **(aka *Graybar's Mr. and Mrs.*).** The popular situation comedy was sponsored by the Graybar Company. Jane Houston and Jack Smart starred. The program was based on a comic strip written by Clare Briggs. These dramatic sketches told of the eventful life of a young married couple (30 min., Tuesday, 10:00–10:30 P.M., CBS, 1929–1931).

22007 ***Mr. and Mrs.*** Old fashion songs and comic dialogue were the chief ingredients in the weekly program (30 min., Friday, 10:00–10:30 P.M., NBC-Pacific Coast Network, 1929). Each program was hosted by "Mr. and Mrs. Sylvester Updike," who were visited by Mr. Whossis and others. The cast included: Ben McLaughlin, Bobbe Deane and Charles Marshall.

22008 ***Mr. and Mrs.*** Henry Fisk Carlton and William Ford Manley wrote this early series on which Joe and Vi — the main characters — talked like an ordinary married couple. The series always was amusing and never unrealistic. The cast included: Mary Groom, Gail Taylor, George F. Field, Eddie Albright and Irving Kennedy.

22009 ***Mr. and Mrs. Blandings.*** When Mr. and Mrs. Blandings moved to the country, they encountered a series of problems transplanted urban couples often faced. The situation comedy told their story. Cary Grant played Mr. Blandings, the same role he had played in the movie, *Mr. Blandings Builds His Dream House,* upon which the program was based. His wife, Muriel, was played by Grant's real life wife, Betsy Drake. The capable actors assisting them were Gale Gordon and Sheldon Leonard (30 min., Sunday, 5:30–6:00 P.M., NBC, 1951).

22010 ***Mr. and Mrs. Go to the Theater.*** Drama critics Ethel and Julius Colby reviewed the latest Broadway plays and motion pictures on their irregularly scheduled program. The critics broadcast their reviews each evening after they had attended a first night performance of either a play or motion picture (WMCA, New York, NY, 1942).

22011 ***Mr. and Mrs. Music.*** Bea Wain, a former big band singer with the Larry Clinton orchestra and her husband, veteran announcer Andre Baruch, joined the already large number of DJ's and soon attracted a large local listening audience (204 min., Monday through Friday, 12:03–2:00 P.M. and 4:03–5:30 P.M., WMCA, New York, NY, 1948). *See* **Husband-and-Wife Talk Shows**.

When Andre Baruch and Bea Wain left the show, their place was taken by Ted and Doris Steele, another husband-and-wife team. *Variety* noted that with the change there still was a "lot of homey talk" but the emphasis by far was put on the recorded music (150 min., Monday through Friday, 9:15–11:45 A.M., WMCA, New York, NY, 1949).

22012 ***Mr. and Mrs. North.*** The dramatized mystery show was based on fictional characters created by Frances and Richard Lockridge. Humor invariably was part of the well-written show. In its various formats the show appeared, on and off from 1941 to 1955, on both CBS and NBC. The cast over the years included: Staats Cotsworth, Joseph Curtin, Francis DeSales, Alice Frost, Walter Kinsella, Mandel Kramer, Frank Lovejoy and Betty Jane Tyler. Charles Paul conducted the orchestra. Joseph King was the announcer.

22013 ***Mr. Andre—Mr. Radio.*** Veteran radio announcer Pierre Andre was a DJ on the sustaining show. He played all types of music ranging from John Philip Sousa's "Stars and Stripes Forever" to Jelly Roll Morton playing his own "Tiger Roll" (25 min., Thursday, 7:30–7:55 P.M., WGN, Chicago, IL, 1951).

22014 ***Mr. Boston.*** James M. Curley, the former Governor of Massachusetts and four times the Mayor of Boston, talked about politics and philosophy. He even read poetry on his local sustaining program (30 min., Monday through Friday, 5:30–6:00 P.M., WBMS, Boston, MA, 1952). This is additional evidence that politicians on radio are not a modern idea.

22015 ***Mr. Broadway.*** Ira Marion wrote and Martin Andrews directed the sustaining program with a clever concept. The program was a dramatic anthology series based on the concept that a Broadway columnist, played by Anthony Ross, told stories to a nightclub singer played by Irene Manning about "the most lovable, most hateful street." The stories, somewhat reminiscent of the Damon Runyon yarns, were then dramatized. Nightclub singer Manning sang three or four times on each program to the music of Glen Osser's band (30 min., Thursday, 8:00–8:30 P.M., ABC, 1952).

22016 ***Mr. District Attorney.*** Bristol-Myers sponsored the long-running (1939–1954) crime drama with a memorable opening. The program began with the stern voice of the announcer proclaiming: "Mr. District Attorney ... Champion of the People ... Defender of Truth ... Guardian of our fundamental rights to life, liberty and the pursuit of happiness." After a musical interlude the authoritative voice of *Mr. District Attorney* stated: "And it shall be my duty as District Attorney not only to prosecute to the limit of the law all persons accused of crimes perpetrated within this county but to defend with equal vigor the rights and privileges of all its citizens." This statement of purpose and its reiteration of American principles were particularly appropriate for 1939, a late Depression-era year in which the ominously troubled European scene had begun to disturb many thoughtful Americans.

22017 ***Mr. Feathers.*** Parker Fennelly played the title role of a middle-aged drugstore soda jerk unhappy with his lot in life. In addition to Fennelly, Don Briggs, Mert Coplin, Robert Dryden, Ralph Locke and Elinor Phelps were in the cast of the sustaining program. Music was provided by the Ben Ludlow Orchestra. The announcer was Bob Emerick (30 min., Wednesday, 10:00–10:30 P.M., MBS, 1950).

22018 ***Mr. Fixit.*** An unidentified performer broadcast fixer-upper tips (KFRC, San Francisco, CA, 1929).

22019 ***Mr. Fixit.*** This home repair show was novel in that it dramatized the problems of a "typical domestic couple" who needed help. The couple, played by Loretta Ellis and Art Van Horn, sought the advice of Mr. Fixit, who was played by Jim Boles. The typical couple wanted to learn "how to fix up their home themselves." Greystone Press sponsored the show. There were many suggestions on the program that listeners should purchase a book on home repairs written by Hubbard Cobb published by Greystone Press (MBS, 1949).

22020 ***Mr. Good.*** *Mr. Good* was a daytime serial drama sponsored by Lydia Pinkham Tablets (15 min., Network).

22021 ***Mr. Hobby Lobby.*** Dave Elman, who was associated with the *Hobby Lobby* program, also joined the large number of radio personalities turned DJ (60 min., Monday through Friday, 4:00–5:00 P.M., WFDR, Manchester, GA, 1950).

22022 ***Mr. Hollywood.*** Julius Colby broadcast movie gossip on his weekly show sponsored by RKO Theaters (15 min., Tuesday, 6:25–6:30 P.M., WMCA, New York, NY, 1941).

22023 ***Mr. I.A. Moto*** **(aka *Mr. Moto*).** Peter Lorre played the title role of the fictional Japanese detective created by John P. Marquand. Mr. Moto was "a man of mystery, culture and sensitivity — a man who, while hating violence, ruthlessly fights communism at home and abroad with his courage, his brain and his fabulous knowledge of international persons, places and things." Later, the opening was altered as follows: "Once again, NBC brings you Pulitzer Prize winner John P. Marquand's fabulous and mysterious Mr. Moto — international agent extraordinary — the inscrutable, crafty and courageous little oriental, whose exploits have endured him to millions of Americans in another adventure in the world of international intrigue." James Monks later played the role of Mr. Moto. John Larkin, Gavin Gordon and Scott Tennison were also in the cast (30 min., Weekly, NBC, 1951).

22024 ***Mr. Information.*** Veteran announcer Mendel Jones of Cleveland's WJAY played the role of the information man on the weekly program. Listeners called in their questions and Jones would provide the information they sought. The local show became so popular that it soon expanded to 45 minutes after beginning as a half-hour show (45 min., Weekly, WJAY, Cleveland, OH, 1935).

22025 **Mr. Jubes and His Sunshine Serenaders Orchestra.** A popular nine-piece local band (WBRL, Manchester, NH, 1928).

22026 ***Mr. Keen, Tracer of Lost Persons.*** Frank and Anne Hummert produced the show that began in 1937 on the NBC-Blue network in a quarter-hour format. In that format, kindly old Mr. Keen actually did seek "lost" persons. When the format changed in 1943, the program became a weekly half-hour mystery drama, in which Mr. Keen attempted to solve murders along with his assistant, Mike Clancy. The cast included: Phil Clarke, Arthur Hughes, Jim Kelly, Bennett Kilpack and Florence Malone. The program was directed by Richard Leonard. Barbara Bates, Stedman Coles, David Davidson, Charles J. Gussman, Lawrence Klee and Robert J. Shaw were the writers. Al Rickey was the musical director.

22027 ***Mr. Manhattan.*** Newspaper columnist and author Charles Hanson Towne was an entertaining raconteur on this sustaining local program, on which he talked about Manhattan of yesterday, today and tomorrow (15 min., Wednesday, 9:00–9:15 P.M., WNEW, New York, NY, 1934).

22028 ***Mr. Mercury.*** Ken Pettus and Lou Scofield wrote the blend of crime fighting and circus lore presented on the dramatic adventure serial. The show featured John Larkin in the title role of a circus acrobat who used his skills to battle against crime and criminals. One example of his daring acrobatic escapes was his leap from a 25th floor terrace to safety in order to escape from the bad guys. Also in the cast were Raymond Edward Johnson, Teri Keane and Gil Mack (30 min., Tuesday, 7:30–8:00 P.M. ABC, 1951).

22029 **Mr. Morning.** DJ, not otherwise identified (WCOL, Columbus, OH, 1949).

22030 ***Mr. Pep's Pep Meeting For Sales People.*** A motivational program presented by unidentified personnel (KYA, San Francisco, CA, 1927).

22031 ***Mr. President.*** Crucial events in the life of different American President were dramatized each week on the sustaining dramatic program. Edward Arnold always played the *Mr. President* role. The program was written by Jean Holloway and Ira Marion and produced by Dick Woollen. Although Arnold's supporting cast members varied each week, William Conrad and Betty Lou Gerson made frequent appearances (30 min., Weekly, ABC, 1947–1951).

22032 **Mr. Radiobug.** Mr. Radiobug was an otherwise unidentified performer who told children's stories on his *Skypictures for Children* program (WOR, Newark, NJ, 1922).

22033 ***Mr. Zipp [Zip].*** Xylophone soloist with personality (WGN, Chicago, IL, 1928).

22034 **Mistletoe Melody Maids.** Nine female singers plus the director made up the vocal group (WOAI, San Antonio, TX, 1926).

22035 **Mistovich, Mike.** Sportscaster (*Local Sports*, KORA, Bryan, TX, 1948–1950; *Sports Mike*, KORA, 1952–1956).

22036 **Mitchell, Al.** Leader (*Al Mitchell Orchestra*, instr. mus. prg., CBS, 1936).

22037 **Mitchell, Al.** Newscaster (KGLO, Mason City, IA, 1937; WOI, Ames, IA, 1941). Sportscaster (KGLO, 1937; WOI, 1941).

22038 **Mitchell, Albert.** Musician-conductor Mitchell was born May 31, 1893. During the decades of the 1930's and 1940's, Mitchell enjoyed popularity as "*The Answer Man,*" on the program of that name (WOR, Newark, NJ). His first radio appearances were in 1923 as an orchestra leader and as announcer for Paul Whiteman.

22039 **Mitchell, Barbara Jane.** Five-year-old singer (KHJ, Los Angeles, CA, 1923).

22040 **Mitchell, Bendita.** COM-HE (WTOB, Winston-Salem, NC, 1956).

22041 **Mitchell, Bertha.** Pianist (WSUN, Clearwater, FL, 1929).

22042 **Mitchell, Betty.** COM-HE (WGAN, Portland, ME, 1949).

22043 **Mitchell, Betty.** DJ (*Betty Mitchell Show*, WKAB, Mobile, AL, 1952).

22044 **Mitchell, Bo.** Sportscaster (WBSR, Pensacola, FL, 1952–1956).

22045 **Mitchell, Bob.** DJ (WMSN, Raleigh, NC, 1956).

22046 **Mitchell, Bob.** DJ (WBCR, Christianburg, VA, 1956).

22047 **Mitchell, Bud.** Newscaster (WJR, Detroit, MI, 1945).

22048 **Mitchell, Courtney.** COM-HE (WDEM, Providence, RI, 1951).

22049 **Mitchell, Dave.** Newscaster (KTUL, Tulsa, OK, 1944).

22050 **Mitchell, Dolly.** Singer (WICC, Bridgeport, CT, 1937).

22051 **Mitchell, Don.** Newscaster (KGYW, Vallejo, CA, 1948). Sportscaster (KGYW, 1948).

22052 **Mitchell, Ed B.** Cornetist (WIP, Philadelphia, PA, 1925).

22053 **Mitchell, Elsie Breese.** Soprano (KDKA, Pittsburgh, PA, 1924).

22054 **Mitchell, Evelyn.** COM-HE (WVEC, San Luis Obispo, CA, 1951).

22055 **Mitchell, Everett G.** Ex-bank clerk and insurance adjuster turned concert singer, Mitchell was hired to sing on KYW (Chicago, IL, 1926). He became chief announcer and farm director at station WENR (Chicago, IL, 1926) later that year, a move that eventually led to his fame. He also appeared on station WIBO (Chicago, IL, 1926).

When the *National Farm and Home Hour* began its long broadcast run on NBC and became known as "the nation's agricultural bulletin board," Mitchell was the program's host. His famous opening for the program was: "It's a *beautiful* day in Chicago. It's a great day to be alive, and I hope it is even more beautiful wherever you are." If the weather was damp and rain falling, Mitchell said, "Oh, yes! It may be raining out doors and a little damp, but it is a great day to be alive." The opening brought him national recognition. Mitchell also worked as a newscaster (WMAQ, Chicago, IL;WENR, Chicago, IL, 1940 and WMAQ, 1944). *See* ***The National Farm and Home Hour***.

22056 **Mitchell, Gordon.** Newscaster (WSLS, Roanoke, VA, 1945).

22057 **Mitchell, Greenwood.** Baritone (KOMO, Seattle, WA, 1929).

22058 **Mitchell, Harold "Red."** Sportscaster (*Seeing Red with Mitchell*, KSIG, Crowley, LA, 1947–1950).

22059 **Mitchell, Helen.** Pianist (WHAS, Louisville, KY, 1923).

22060 **Mitchell, Hugh.** Newscaster (WHBQ, Memphis, TN, 1946).

22061 **Mitchell, Jack.** Sportscaster (WRR, Dallas, TX, 1939; KOMA, Oklahoma City, OK, 1941).

22062 **Mitchell, James.** Newscaster (WCLS, Joliet, IL, 1941).

22063 **Mitchell, Joe.** Newscaster (KIDO, Boise, ID, 1939).

22064 **Mitchell, Kenneth.** Leader (Kenneth Mitchell's Hollywegians Orchestra, KFI, Los Angeles, CA, 1925).

22065 **Mitchell, Leona.** Soprano (WGHP, Detroit, MI, 1926).

22066 **Mitchell, Marge.** COM-HE (WIRL, Peoria, IL, 1954).

22067 **Mitchell, Mary Webster.** Contralto (KGO, Oakland, CA, 1924).

22068 **Mitchell, Merrie Boyd.** Soprano (KYW, Chicago, IL, 1924; WQJ, Chicago, IL, 1925).

22069 **Mitchell, Milford.** Newscaster (KAND, Corsicana, TX, 1941).

22070 **Mitchell, (Dr.) Nicholas P.** News analyst (*World Today*, WFBC, Greenville, SC, 1942, 1946–1947; *Nick's Notebook*, WFBC, 1948).

22071 **Mitchell, Nita.** Singer (KYA, San Francisco, CA, 1929).

22072 **Mitchell, Norma.** COM-HE (WJFJ, Webster City, IA, 1957).

22073 **Mitchell, Owens.** Leader (*Owens Mitchell Orchestra*, instr. mus. prg., KFMQ, Fayetteville, AR, 1924).

22074 **Mitchell, Ruth.** COM-HE (WTTB, Vero Beach, FL, 1956).

22075 **Mitchell, S.W.** Newscaster (KBUR, Burlington, IN, 1941).

22076 **Mitchell, Sybil.** *Variety* said Pianist Mitchell played "syncopated piano selections and plantation songs" (WCOA, Pensacola, FL, 1926).

22077 **Mitchell, Tom.** Baritone (KNX, Los Angeles, CA, 1928).

22078 **Mitchell, Verlee.** COM-HE (WEOA, Evansville, IN, 1955).

22079 **Mittelstadt, Harriet.** Soprano (WJZ, New York, NY, 1925).

22080 **Mitten, Ralph.** Played the chimes (WJAZ, Chicago, IL, 1926).

22081 **Mitten, William.** Newscaster (WFEA, Manchester, NH, 1945).

22082 **Mittendorf, Eugene S.** Announcer (WKRC, Cincinnati, OH, 1927).

22083 **Mittendorg, Virginia.** COM-HE (KOPO, Tucson, AZ, 1951).

22084 **Miura, Tamaki.** Japanese soprano (WEAF, New York, NY, 1928).

22085 **Mix, Doris.** COM-HE (KRPL, Moscow, ID, 1954–1960).

22086 **Mize, Eileen.** Reader (WRNY, New York, NY, 1926).

22087 **Mizer, Frederick W.** Announcer Mizer broadcast his station's slogan, "The Most Southern Radiocasting Station in the U.S." (WQAM, Miami, FL, 1925–1927).

22088 **Mizner, Connie.** COM-HE (KVNC, Winslow, AZ, 1956–1957).

22089 **Mladenka, Joy.** COM-HE (KXYZ, Houston, TX, 1956).

22090 Moan, Hal. DJ (KOMO, Seattle, WA, 1956–1957).

22091 *Moana Hawaiians Orchestra.* Instr. mus. prg. (WGY, Schenectady, NY, 1938).

22092 Moats, Andy. Leader (*Andy Moats Orchestra*, instr. mus. prg., WJAG, Norfolk, NE, 1939).

22093 Mobley, Ernest. Newscaster (KVWC, Vernon, TX, 1940).

22094 Mobley, Preston. DJ (WERD, Atlanta, GA, 1956).

22095 *Mobil Oil Concert.* A concert orchestra conducted by either Nathaniel Shilkret or Erno Rapee. Violinist Yacob Zayde and cornetist Del Staigers were featured on the good music program. Operatic tenor James Melton was a frequent guest (30 min., Wednesday, 8:30–9:00 P.M., NBC-Red, 1930).

22096 *Mobiloil Magazine.* Dramatic recreations of current news events and music were regular components of the radio magazine show sponsored by the General Petroleum Corporation. Tenor Robert Snyder was joined by singers Maurine Marseilles, Nadine Connor, Marshall Sohl and a mixed choir. Music was provided by David Broekman's orchestra (30 min., Thursday, 9:00–9:30 P.M., KHJ, Los Angeles, CA, 1935).

22097 Mobiloil Quality Orchestra. Fifty musicians performed weekly in the largest commercial orchestra on radio of the period. Erno Rapee conducted the orchestra (NBC, 1929).

22098 Mock, Bill Russell, Jr. Newscaster (KVOS, Bellingham, WA 1937). Sportscaster (KVOS, 1937; KGW, Portland, OR, 1938–1941; KEX, Portland, OR, 1938–1941).

22099 Mock, Nancy. COM-HE (WNAR, Norristown, PA, 1949).

22100 Moder, Dick. Leader (Dick Moder and his Bandoliers Orchestra, KGFJ, Los Angeles, CA, 1928–1929).

22101 *Modern Cinderella.* The daytime dramatic serial starred Laine Barklie, Eddie Dean, Rosemary Dillion, Ben Gage and also David Gothard, formerly of the *Romance of Helen Trent* and *Bachelor's Children* program. Roger Krupp was the announcer (CBS, 1936–1937).

22102 *Modern Dance.* Agnes DeMille conducted the program on which she discussed modern dance news and trends (NBC, 1931).

22103 *Modern Minstrels.* A blackface chorus of 35 men and two unidentified endmen were in the large minstrel company with Harry Von Zell as interlocutor. Gordon Whyte produced the radio minstrel show featuring Lou Lubin. Music was provided by Leith Stevens' Orchestra (60 min., Saturday, 8:00–9:00 P.M., CBS, 1935).

22104 *Modern Woodman Orchestra.* Instr. mus. prg. (WJBC, Bloomington, IN, 1936).

22105 *Modernists.* Billy Hamilton, director of the WBT orchestra, conducted the weekly program devoted to the works of modern composers (WBT, Charlotte, NC, 1933).

22106 Moe, Helen. Soprano (KOA, Denver, CO,1925).

22107 Moehlman, A.H. Newscaster (WOSU, Columbus, OH, 1940).

22108 Moeller, Katherine. Reader Moeller appeared on *The Children's Hour* program (KSTP, St. Paul, MN, 1929).

22109 Moen, Joe. Sportscaster (*Moen 'Em Down*, WBEL, Beloit, WI, 1951–1954).

22110 Moffatt, Ralph. Newscaster (WDGY, Minneapolis–St. Paul, MN, 1942). DJ (*Say It with Music* and *Music Is No Mystery*, WCCO, Minneapolis, MN, 1948; *Nite Notes*, WDGY, Minneapolis, MN, 1949).

22111 Moffett, Ray. *DJ (Morning Musical Clock*, WCAO, Baltimore, MD, 1947).

22112 Mofield, Ray. Newscaster (WPAD, Paducah, KY, 1948. *Football Forecast*, WPAD, 1948; *Sport Hi-Lites*, WPAD, 1949; *Ole Colonel*, WPAD, 1950; *Sports Hi-Lites*, WPAD, 1951–1955).

22113 *Mohawk Treasure Chest.* James Meighan narrated the program featuring Ralph Kirbery, later billed as "The Dream Singer," and Harold Levey's Orchestra. Each week Martha Lee Cole discussed interior decoration topics. Frank Singhiser was the announcer (30 min., Sunday, 2:00–2:30 P.M., NBC-Red, 1934).

22114 Mohawk Valley Singer. Vocalist not otherwise identified (WGY, Schenectady, NY, 1942).

22115 Mohnkern, Leonard. DJ (*Polka Date*, WKRZ, Oil City, PA, 1950).

22116 Mohr, Gerald. Actor Mohr was in the cast of *Dear John.*

22117 Mohr, Gertrude. Musical director (WCAE, Philadelphia, PA, 1929).

22118 Moir, Joyce. COM-HE (KGEZ, Kalispell, MT, 1957).

22119 Moir, William. Tenor (KTAB, Oakland, CA, 1927).

22120 Molasses and January (Pick Malone and Pat Padgett). The popular blackface comedy team first appeared on the *WOR Minstrels*, WOR (Newark, NJ). Malone and Padgett became Molasses and January in 1932, when they appeared on the *Maxwell House Showboat* program. They became Pick and Pat later for CBS. In 1942, they returned to the air as Molasses and January. In September, 1942, they became *America's Advisors on the Home Front* (5 min., Monday through Friday, NBC-Blue network, 1942). As part of their advice the boys provided "advice for husbands of defense workers." *See* **Wartime Radio.**

22121 Mole, (Mrs.) George. Pianist (WBZ, Springfield, MA, 1924).

22122 Mole, Miff. Great jazz trombonist of the Columbia Broadcasting System's dance band (NBC, 1928–1929).

22123 Moleler, James. Harpist-guitarist (WFAA, Dallas, TX, 1922).

22124 Moles, F.J. Announcer (WFAV, Lincoln, NE, 1924).

22125 Molhollen, Harold and Yorke Copelen. Violin duet team (KFI, Los Angeles, CA, 1927).

22126 Molina, Carlos. Leader (*Carlos Molina Orchestra*, instr. mus. prg., NBC, 1934; CBS, 1934; WLW, Cincinnati, OH, 1936).

22127 Moline Plowboys. CW music male quartet (WOC, Davenport, IA and WOAW, Des Moines, IA, 1926).

22128 Moll, Allen. Newscaster (KDYL, Salt Lake City, UT, 1945).

22129 Mollard, Margaret. COM-HE (WBUT, Butler, PA, 1951).

22130 *Molle Minstrels.* Veteran radio comics Al Bernard and Paul Dumont were the endmen on this radio minstrel show sponsored by Molle shaving cream. Milton Rettenberg conducted the orchestra. On Friday evening, the cast was supplemented by tenor Mario Cozzi. *Variety* noted that sometimes the jokes on the show were as snappy as its songs (15 min., Monday through Thursday, 7:15–7:30 P.M. and Friday, 10:00–10:30 P.M., NBC-Blue, 1934–1935).

22131 Mollinari, Bob. Leader (Bob Mollinari Orchestra, WHN, New York, NY, 1923).

22132 *Molly of the Movies.* Thompson Buchanan wrote the script for the dramatic daytime serial sponsored by the Wonder Company, the makers of Ovaltine. Gene Byron, Betty Caine and Ray Jones starred in the story of a young girl starting out in the motion picture business (15 min., Thursday, 3:00–3:15 P.M., WOR, Newark, NJ, 1935).

22133 *Molly Picon's Parade.* Molly Picon starred in the variety show, sponsored by General Foods, that *Variety* said had a Jewish flavor. It was necessary to know Yiddish to appreciate all of the humor. Tenor Seymour Rechtzeit and announcer-straight man Alan Williams were regular cast members. Each week various visiting comics were on hand (30 min., Tuesday, 8:00–8:30 P.M., WMCA, New York, NY, 1940).

22134 Molyneaux, Peter. Broadcast book reviews (WBAP, San Antonio, TX, 1925). Newscaster (WFAA, Dallas, TX, 1940).

22135 *Moments of Melody.* Various orchestra conductors led a network orchestra in familiar classical and operetta selections (15 min., Weekly, NBC, 1935).

22136 Momeyer, John. Newscaster (WKMH, Dearborn, MI, 1948).

22137 Mon, Mae. Soprano (WNYC, New York, NY, 1925).

22138 *Mona Motor Oil Company Program.* A variety program that featured musical numbers by contralto Lilyan May Challenger and the Mona Motor Oil String Quartet directed by William Baffa (KFWB, Hollywood, CA, 1927).

22139 Mona Motor Oil Harmony Team. Vocal team of Gypsy and Marta (KPO, San Francisco, CA, 1926). *See* **Gypsy and Marta.**

22140 *Mona Motor Oil Merrymakers Orchestra.* Tenor Robert Olsen sang with the Merrymakers (KFRC, San Francisco, CA, 1927).

22141 *Mona Motor Oil Mixed Quartet.* Vcl. mus. prg. by a quartet consisting of soprano Mrs. Will Cutler; contralto Mrs. X. Kynett; tenor Howard Steberg and bass Philip Helgren (KOIL, Council Bluffs, IA, 1929–1930).

22142 Mona Motor Oil Orchestra. Commercial band (KOIL, Council Bluffs, IA, 1928).

22143 Mona Motor Oil Trio. Instrumental group including violinist Mischa Gluschkin; cellist George von Hagel; and pianist Jean Campbell (KPO, San Francisco, CA, 1925; KNX, Los Angeles, CA, 1926).

22144 Mona Motor Oil Twins. Critically praised female vocal team (KOIL, Council Bluffs, IA, 1927).

22145 Mona Motor Oil Twins. Singing team of John Wolfe and Ned Tollinger (KOIL, Council Bluffs, IA, 1928). The year before a female vocal team had broadcast on KOIL using this name.

22146 Mona Motor Oilers Orchestra. Band directed by Felix Mills (KFWB, Hollywood, CA, 1928).

22147 Monaco, Del. DJ (*Coffee Time*, WJJL, Niagara Falls, NY, 1954–1955).

22148 Monaco, Jimmy. Leader (*Jimmy Monaco Orchestra*, instr. mus. prg., WOR, Newark, NJ, 1936).

22149 Monaghan, George. DJ (*Monaghan's Morning Watch*, WOR, New York, 1947–1950).

22150 Monahan, Billy. Twelve-year-old tenor (WNAC, Boston, MA, 1925).

22151 *Monahan Post American Legion Band.* G. Emerson Smith directed the brass band consisting of Paul Roserg, Jr., Frank Beals, Harold Royky, Dudley Knutson, Leo Vincent, Leroy Kudrele, Paul Hinrichs, Eugene Rohr and Clayton E. Mitchell (KSCJ, Sioux City, IA, 1928).

22152 *Monarch Mystery Tenor.* The "mysterious singer" was Charles J. Gilchrest (15 min., Sunday, 2:15–2:30 P.M., NBC-Blue, 1933).

22153 Moncrief, Adiel. Announcer (WMAZ, Macon, GA, 1925).

22154 Monday, Raymond "Ray." Newscaster (KPDN, Pampa, TX, 1938–1941; WACO, Waco, TX, 1946; WRUN, Utica, NY, 1948).

22155 *Monday Musicale.* Coloratura soprano Margaret King sang on the sustaining show. She was accompanied by Ralph Paul on piano and solovox (15 min., Monday, 9:00–9:15 P.M., WBRE, Wilkes-Barre, PA, 1941).

22156 Moneak, Eleana. Leader (*Eleana Moneak Ensemble*, instr. mus. prg., CBS, 1935–1936).

22157 *Monica's Music Box.* Singer Monica Lewis and her weekly guests entertained on the sustaining music show. Ray Bloch's orchestra supplied the music (15 min., Friday, 8:15–8:30 P.M., WOR, Newark, NJ, 1946).

22158 *Monitor.* Faced with a crisis in lower Hooper ratings and the subsequent negative effects on advertising revenues, radio network executives sought alternative programming formats to reverse the adverse effects of the declines and the impact of television. One innovative programming genius, who also possessed the requisite skills of a persuasive salesman and a dynamic showman, was Sylvester "Pat" Weaver, president of the NBC network. It was Weaver's creative genius that was responsible for the revolutionary radio concept of the *Monitor* programming format.

Monitor, it should be recognized, was not a *single* program, but a broadcasting format, a continuous service that began Saturday morning at 8:00 A.M. and ended Sunday night at midnight, a 40-hour broadcasting service, that was a complete departure from previous patterns of programming. As Weaver explained it on a line presentation to affiliate stations on April 1, 1955, *Monitor* was designed to reverse radio's loss in listening audience and in advertising revenues.

As Weaver described it, *Monitor* would utilize radio's ability to go anywhere on short notice to cover news events and present special events without previous scheduling restrictions. *Monitor* had no strict time segments. One segment might have a 10-second one-liner by a comedian, a five-minute news interview; a live big band remote broadcast, coverage of a sporting event; a few minutes from a Broadway play or a current motion picture; or a few minutes of music from the Lido Night Club in Paris. Weaver's vision was an ambitious one that was skillfully executed by *Monitor's* executive producer, Jim Fleming.

It seemed that almost all the famous NBC newsmen and sportscasters appeared on the service, as did such great comedians as Fred Allen, Milton Berle, Henny Youngman, Jimmy Durante, Bob Hope, Fibber McGee and Molly and Bob and Ray. Vignette was one of Weaver's favorite words that he used to characterize *Monitor's* programming. If a listener didn't like a particular segment (vignette), he or she knew that what was coming later might be more interesting. Weaver said that *Monitor* would look at the whole world, and that its only criterion was: Will it interest the listener?

Monitor began June 12, 1955 as a 40-hour weekend programming format that offered a little something for everyone, with genial Dave Garroway as one of its most engaging hosts. In November 1955, the format was expanded to five hours Monday through Friday with a *Weekday* format title. Other networks such as MBS, ABC and CBS also experimented with the *Monitor* programming format, but none were as imaginative, informative or as entertaining as their model. After a little more than a decade NBC dropped the *Monitor* format (1955–1967).

22159 *Monitor Views the News.* Various newscasters delivered news from the editorial room of the *Christian Science Monitor* (15 min., Saturday, 8:00–8:15 P.M., WBZ, Springfield-Boston, MA, 1934).

22160 Monk, Alfred. Leader (Alfred Monk Orchestra, WHAM, Rochester, NY, 1926).

22161 Monk, Benny. Talented jazz pianist Monk performed on *The Village Grove Nut Club* program (WMCA, New York, NY, 1929).

22162 Monk, Izabelle [Isabel]. COM-HE (WRJN, Racine, WI, 1957).

22163 Monkman, Bob. Sportscaster (WRJN, Racine, WI, 1948). DJ (*Requestfully Yours*, WRJN, 1950; *Robins Nest*, WRJN, 1952–1954).

22164 Monks, James. Actor Monks was in the cast of *Against the Storm*, *Front Page Farrell*, *Joyce Jordan*, *Girl Interne*, *Light of the World*, *Little Orphan Annie*, *Our Gal Sunday*, *Theatre Guild of the Air* and *Woman of America*.

22165 Monks, John. Actor-announcer Monks worked on *America's Hour* (actor), *Buck Rogers in the 25th Century* (actor) and *Home Sweet Home* (announcer).

22166 Monotti, Theresina. Coloratura soprano (KFRC, San Francisco, CA, 1926).

22167 Monroe, Bill. News analyst (*New Orleans and the World*, WNOE, New Orleans, LA, 1947–1948).

22168 Monroe, Cal. Newscaster (*Noon News*, WCAP, Asbury Park, NJ, 1948). DJ (*Record Rendezvous*, WCAP, 1948; *Voices in the Night*, WCAP, 1950).

22169 Monroe, Charlie. Leader (CW music group, WPTF, Raleigh, NC, 1939).

22170 Monroe, Clark. DJ (*The Clark Monroe Show*, WTAW, College Station, TX, 1947).

22171 Monroe, Clyde. Billed as a "blind artist of expression," Monroe broadcast popular recitations (WJZ, New York, NY, 1923).

22172 Monroe, Freddie. Leader (*Freddie Monroe Orchestra*, instr. mus. prg., KARK, Little Rock, AR, 1934).

22173 Monroe, Hank. DJ (*Juke Box Serenade*, WOLF, Syracuse, NY, 1948; *Bing Crosby Sings*, WOLF, Syracuse, NY, 1950).

22174 Monroe, Jacqueline. Violinist (WJAZ, Chicago, IL, 1923).

22175 Monroe, James "Jim." Newscaster (KCMO, Kansas City, MO, 1940–1942, 1944–1946).

22176 Monroe, Joe [John]. DJ (*Camptown Radio*, *Tea and Trumpets* and *Monroe's Ayem Mayhem*, KENT, Shreveport, LA, 1948–1952; KJOE, Shreveport, LA, 1955).

22177 Monroe, Larry. DJ (WNOE, New Orleans, LA, 1956).

22178 Monroe, Lucy. Soprano (*Lucy Monroe*, vcl. mus. prg., NBC, 1935).

22179 Monroe, Odessa. COM-HE (WCIN, Cincinnati, OH, 1954).

22180 Monroe, R.A. Sportscaster (*Fish and Tiller*, WJNO, West Palm Beach, FL, 1956).

22181 Monroe, Vaughn. Leader (*Vaughn Monroe Orchestra*, instr. mus. prg., NBC, 1934; WCCO, Minneapolis–St. Paul, MN; KFH, Wichita, KS, 1942; CBS, 1942). A popular recording artist, Monroe's strong nasal baritone voice brought him great popularity. Among his many hit records were the best-selling "Ghost Riders in the Sky" and "Racing With the Moon."

22182 Monroe, Willa. COM-HE (*The Tan Town Homemakers Show*, WDIA, Memphis, TN, 1949–1957). Monroe was hired by WDIA as the station's first female announcer in 1949, and she immediately began her daily weekday homemakers' show. Her 9:00–9:45 A.M. show often enjoyed a higher Hooper rating than did Arthur Godfrey's popular network show broadcast in the same time period.

Beginning with her theme, "Sweet and Lovely," her show included quiet music, recipes and news of interest to women. She allowed her listeners to come to her office personally to receive information on nutrition, budgeting and child care *on her own time without charge.*

22183 Monroe, William Smith "Bill." Leader CW music group Monroe with brothers Birch and Charlie, as the Monroe Brothers, gained listener popularity on WBT (Charlotte, NC, 1935; *Bill Monroe and the Kentuckians,* CW music program, KARK, Little Rock, AR, 1938). Pioneer Blue Grass musician Monroe appeared on many local radio stations. After several months on Omaha (Nebraska) radio in the middle 1930s, Monroe's band went on tour for Crazy Water Crystals (laxative). Monroe later worked on Atlanta radio's *Crossroads Follies,* where he formed the Blue Grass Boys band that consisted of Chubby Wise, Earl Scruggs, Cedric Rainwater and Ken "Lonzo" Martin. Monroe and the Blue Grass Boys joined the *Grand Ole Opry* in 1939 and performed there until his death in 1996. Monroe is widely recognized as the "Father of Bluegrass."

22184 Monroe, Wilson. Newscaster (KTKC, Visalia, CA, 1944).

22185 Monroe Jockers' Orchestra. Popular Los Angeles band (KNX, Los Angeles, CA, 1928).

22186 Monsees, Anita. COM-HE (WHCU, Ithaca, NY, 1949).

22187 Montagne, Imelda. Contralto Montagne was a member of the Pepper Maids harmony singing group. The group sang with the Musical Musketeers orchestra (NBC, 1929).

22188 Montague, Winston. Sportscaster (WRVA, Richmond, VA, 1941).

22189 Montana, Janet. Singer (WBBR, Brooklyn, NY, 1936).

22190 Montana, Patsy (Ruby Blevins). Singer, guitarist, fiddler and songwriter, she first appeared on Los Angeles radio as Rubye Blevins, the Yodeling Cowgirl from San Antone in 1931. She sang with Stuart Hamblen and Monty Montana on KMIC (Los Angeles, CA, early 1930s). After a brief time on KWKH (Shreveport, LA, 1932), she moved to Chicago (WLS, Chicago, 1933) and joined the Kentucky Ramblers, a group that later became the Prairie Ramblers. The original band that included Charles "Chick" Hurt, Jack Taylor, Floyd "Salty" Holmes and Shelby "Tex" Atchison were long time regulars on the *National Barn Dance* (WLS, Chicago, IL). With Montana moved they had their own show on WOR (Newark, NJ, 1934).

Montana had her own network show (1946–1947) and worked on the *Louisiana Hayride* (KWKH, Shreveport, LA, 1948). An important CW pioneer, she was elected to the Country Western Hall of Fame in 1996. Patsy is probably best remembered for her hit, "I Want to Be a Cowboy's Sweetheart."

22191 Montana, Wally. Montana was billed as "The singing cowboy" (WMSG, New York, NY, 1928).

22192 *Montana Meechy's Cowboys.* CW mus. prg. (WFBR, Baltimore, MD, 1939).

22193 Montana Slim (Wilf Carter). Canadian Wilf Carter was a popular CW singer (*Montana Slim the Yodeling Cowboy,* vcl. mus. prg., CBS, 1936–1939).

22194 Montani, Nicola. Singer (WIP, Philadelphia, PA, 1926).

22195 Montano, Carlos. Newscaster (KPHO, Phoenix, AZ, 1944).

22196 Montanus, (Mrs.) Agnes (Mrs. Agnes Montanus and her Friendly House Dramatic Players). Radio drama group (WOC, Davenport, IA, 1928–1930).

22197 Montell, Doug. Sportscaster (KSFO, San Francisco, CA, 1939).

22198 Montezuma Club Orchestra. Club dance band (KWSC, Pullman, WA, 1926).

22199 Montgomerie, Angie. Contralto (WHT, Chicago, IL, 1928).

22200 Montgomery, Bob. DJ (*Music 'til Sign-Off,* WFHR, Wisconsin Rapids, WI, 1947).

22201 Montgomery, John. Newscaster (WFPG, Atlantic City, NJ, 1940).

22202 Montgomery, Lynn Carol. COM-HE (KXOB, Stockton, CA, 1951).

22203 Montgomery, Ray. Actor Montgomery was in the cast of *Dear John.*

22204 Montgomery, Richard G. Montgomery broadcast book chats (KGW, Portland, OR, 1926).

22205 Montgomery, Ruth. Soprano (WDAF, Kansas City, MO, 1929).

22206 Montgomery Ward and Company Orchestra. Band on the company's *Montgomery Ward's Trail Blazers* program (WBAP, San Antonio, TX, 1926).

22207 *Montgomery Ward's Trail Blazers.* Montgomery Ward, the mail order company, sponsored the program of popular music. The Montgomery Ward and Company Orchestra and many popular CW performers were featured (WBAP, San Antonio, TX, 1926).

22208 *Monticello Party Line.* On the unique daytime serial, listeners supposedly listened in on a telephone party line in the Midwestern community of Monticello. The program told the story of small town life, where there were no villains or heart-broken wives. Peggy Wall played the leading role of Lorrie Ellis, a telephone operator on the Monticello party line.

Each program began with the buzz of the switchboard in Lorie Ellis' telephone office. Lorrie, incidentally, was the center of most of the program's love interest. Other characters on the show were the town gossips, Sara and Aggie, and Clem, Aggie's public spirited husband (15 min., Monday through Friday, 9:00–9:15 A.M. CST, WLS, Chicago, IL, 1935; 15 min., Monday through Friday, 10:00–10:15 A.M., WLS, 1936).

22209 Montmarte Cafe Dance Orchestra. Vince (Vincent) Rose directed the club band (KFWB, Hollywood, CA, 1925–1928).

22210 *Montreal Symphony Orchestra.* Performing primarily in Montreal, Canada, the excellent symphonic group was heard on various American stations in 1930 (WMAL, Washington, D.C., 1930).

22211 Montreras, Manual. Leader (*Manual Montreras Orchestra,* instr. mus. prg., WTAM, Cleveland, OH, 1936).

22212 Montz, Wanda. COM-HE (KWCR, Cedar Rapids, IA, 1951).

22213 *Moo Cow.* The late evening variety show was conducted by "Moo Cow, the radio bossy." Featured musical performers on the show were the Dairy Maids and the Cow Boys, Mike Decker's Old Timers, the Hill Villain Hawaiians and pianist-violinist-guitarist Archie Hewitt (60 min., Tuesday, 10:00–11:00 P.M., WOW, Omaha, NE, 1930).

22214 Moody, Emily Winston. COM-HE (WFLA, Tampa, FL, 1949–1951).

22215 Moody, June. Singer (*June Moody,* vcl. mus. prg., WSM, Nashville, TN, 1934).

22216 Moody, Lorna. COM-HE (WBGE, Atlanta, GA, 1954).

22217 Moody, Marian McCook. COM-HE (KRNO, San Bernardino, CA, 1957).

22218 Moody, Olympia. COM-HE (KURY, Brookings, OR, 1960).

22219 Moody, Robert "Bob." Singer Moody sang bass in the Town Hall Quartet on the *Fred Allen Show* and in the Show Boat Four on *Showboat.*

22220 Moon, Hal. Newscaster (KQW, San Jose, CA, 1945). DJ (*Music for Milady,* KGBD, Lubbock, TX, 1952).

22221 Moon, Virginia. COM-HE (KTRM, Beaumont, TX, 1957).

22222 *Moon Glow Melodies.* The Moon Glow Company sponsored the weekly music show featuring romantic tenor Wayne Van Dyne (15 min., 7:30–7:45 P.M. CST, WMAQ, Chicago, IL, 1936).

22223 *Moon Magic.* Musical program featuring songs by the "Maid of the Moon," harpist Kajetan Ahl and the Arion Trio (30 min., Thursday, 9:30–10:00 P.M., NBC-Pacific Network, 1927–1928).

22224 *Moon Mullins.* Frank Willard's comic strip provided the basis for this comedy show that told the story of Moonshine Mullins, his brother Kayo and his Uncle Willie, who were some of the inhabitants of Lord Plushbottom's boarding house run by the Lord's wife, Mamie. The Willard comic strip was created in 1923 for the New York *News Syndicate.* Moon (Moonshine) Mullins was a roughneck. His Uncle Willie was a man who always wore an undershirt and dropped cigar ashes on the carpet of Lord and Lady Plushbottom's boarding house.

22225 *Moon River.* *Moon River* was a popular syndicated program of soothing music and poetry that originated from WLW (Cincinnati, OH). Created by Edward Byron, the show was narrated by many different broadcasters, including Don Dowd, Peter Grant, Harry Holcomb, Jay Jostyn, Palmer Ward and Charles Woods, who read the poetic selections (15 min., Syndicated, 1935).

22226 Mooney, Art. Leader (*Art Mooney Orchestra,* instr. mus. prg., MBS, 1935).

22227 Mooney, Dow. Newscaster (WFAA, Dallas, TX, 1940; WLAG, Nashville, TN, 1941–1942; WKY, Oklahoma City, OK, 1945).

22228 Mooney, Jack. Singer-instrumentalist (*Jack Mooney and His Banjo,* KGB, San Diego, CA, 1927).

22229 Mooney, Tom. Baritone (WSM, Nashville, TN, 1928).

22230 *Moonlight Savings Time.* The program consisted of a series of recordings of daytime programming broadcast at night for war workers (WOR, New York, NY, World War II period).

22231 *Moonshine and Honeysuckle* (aka *Moonlight and Honeysuckle*). The early serial drama was created and written by Lulu Vollmer and directed by Henry Stillman. The story of the Botts family, who lived in the little southern town of Lonesome Hollow, was told. Ann Sutherland played the role of Ma Botts; John Mason that of her husband; and Louis Mason their son, Clem. Claude Cooper played Pegleg Gaddis and Anne Elstner the role of Cracker Gaddis. Also in the cast were Jeanie Begg, Bradley Barker, Sara Haden, John Milton and Therese Witler (NBC, 1930–1932).

22232 Moorad, George. News commentator (CBS, 1944; *George Moorad Comments*, KGW, Portland, OR, 1947–1948).

22233 Moore, Alice. Soprano (*Alice Moore*, vcl. mus. prg., WDBJ, Roanoke, VA, 1935).

22234 Moore, Ann Carroll. Teller of children's stories (WEAF, New York, NY, 1926).

22235 Moore, Archie. Basso (KFI, Los Angeles, CA, 1925).

22236 Moore, Babs. COM-HE (WORD, Spartanburg, SC, 1956).

22237 Moore, Barbara. COM-HE (WMBD, Peoria, IL, 1949).

22238 Moore, Barbara. COM-HE (KFST, Ft. Stockton, TX, 1956).

22239 Moore, Beri. DJ (*Guess Who?*, WCTA, Andalusia, AL, 1947). Sportscaster (Football, basketball and baseball play-by-play, WCTA, 1947; WMOX, Meridian, MS, 1950).

22240 Moore, Beth. News commentator (*News in a Woman's World*, KTHS, Shreveport, LA, 1942).

22241 Moore, Betty. COM-HE (*Interior Decorating*, NBC, 1934). Her program was sponsored by the Moore paint company. *She might have been the "Betty Moore" who broadcast later in 1940.*

22242 Moore, Betty. COM-HE (*Clean Up and Paint Your Home*, NBC, 1940). Betty Moore was sponsored by the Moore paint company.

22243 Moore, Betty. COM-HE (WGAD, Gadsden, AL, 1960).

22244 Moore, Bob. Newscaster (WCNC, Elizabeth City, NJ, 1945).

22245 Moore, Carl Deacon. Leader (*Deacon Moore Orchestra*, CW mus. prg., WLW, Cincinnati, OH, 1934; NBC, 1938).

22246 Moore, Carlton. Leader (*Carlton Moore Orchestra*, instr. mus. prg., WXYZ, Detroit, MI, 1935).

22247 Moore, Charles. Director (Chicago Symphony Orchestra, NBC-Red, New York, NY, 1929).

22248 Moore, Charles. News analyst (*Top of the News*, WASA, Havre de Grace, MD, 1948).

22249 Moore, Clarence. Newscaster (KOA, Denver, CO, 1938).

22250 Moore, Coleen. Silent screen star Moore spoke to her "radiophans" (KHJ, Los Angeles, CA, 1924).

22251 Moore, Cora. COM-HE (WJZ, New York, NY, 1924).

22252 Moore, Dave. Newscaster (KLS, Oakland, CA, 1944).

22253 Moore, Don, Jr. Announcer (KGCG, Newark, AR, 1927).

22254 Moore, Duncan. Newscaster and farm editor (WJR, Detroit, MI, 1938–1940, 1945).

22255 Moore, Edna. Soprano (WFI, Philadelphia, PA, 1925).

22256 Moore, Edna. COM-HE (WJWL, Georgetown, DE, 1954–1955).

22257 Moore, Eileen. COM-HE (WRUM, Rumford, ME, 1956).

22258 Moore, Eleanor. COM-HE (WSBT, South Bend, IN, 1949–1957).

22259 Moore, Ellie. COM-HE (WBIR, Knoxville, TN, 1956).

22260 Moore, Frank. Director (Frank Moore's Studio Players that broadcast dramatic productions, KFAB, Lincoln, NE, 1927). One of Moore's critically praised presentations was *Romeo and Juliet.*

22261 Moore, (Mrs.), Frank J. Contralto (WBZ, Springfield, MA, 1927).

22262 Moore, Fred. Newscaster (WOW-WLG, Fort Wayne, IN, 1942).

22263 Moore, Frensley. Leader (Frensley Moore's Black and Gold Serenaders Orchestra, WBAP, Fort Worth, TX, 1925).

22264 Moore, (Reverend) Gatemouth. DJ (*Light of the World*, WDIA, Memphis, TN, 1948).

22265 Moore, George Austin. Monologist and comic vocalist who specialized in dialect stories (WHAS, Louisville, KY, 1932).

22266 Moore, Gladys F. Soprano (KYW, Chicago, IL, 1923).

22267 Moore, Hal. Newscaster (NBC, 1937). Sportscaster (KRE, Berkeley, CA, 1937; *Tanforan Races*, KSAN, San Francisco, CA, 1949).

22268 Moore, Hal. DJ (*The Bugle Call*, WCAU, Philadelphia, PA, 1947).

22269 Moore, Henry. Newscaster (KPLT, Paris, TX, 1937). Sportscaster (KPLT, 1939).

22270 Moore, Heyward. Newscaster (WGNS, Murfeesboro, TN, 1947).

22271 Moore, Homer. Operatic baritone (WFLA, Clearwater, FL, 1928).

22272 Moore, (Mrs.) Howard. Organist (WFHH, New York, NY, 1927).

22273 Moore, J.B. Tenor (KFEF, Los Angeles, CA, 1929).

22274 Moore, Jack. Sportscaster (*Piedmont Sports*, WELP, Easley, SC, 1960).

22275 Moore, James. Singer (WOK, Pine Bluffs, AR, 1922).

22276 Moore, Jesse. Pianist (KTAB, Oakland, CA, 1926).

22277 Moore, Jimmie. Newscaster (KBWD, Brownwood, TX, 1941).

22278 Moore, Joe. Leader (Joe Moore Astor Roof Band, WOR, Newark, NJ, 1929).

22279 Moore, John. Actor Moore appeared on *Evelyn Winters, Hilltop House, Mrs. Miniver* and *Terry and the Pirates.*

22280 Moore, John Trotwood. Reader (WSM, Nashville, TN, 1926).

22281 Moore, Lee. DJ (WNLK, Norfolk, CT, 1950).

22282 Moore, Lee. DJ (WWVA, Wheeling, WV, 1956).

22283 Moore, Leslie. News analyst (*Views of the Week*, WTAG, Worcester, MA, 1947).

22284 Moore, Lindle. Newscaster (WEBQ, Harrisburg, IL, 1939).

22285 Moore, Marjorie. Leader (Marjorie Moore's Melody Maids, a ten-piece, all girl orchestra, specializing in both classical and jazz numbers, WEAF, New York, NY, 1925).

22286 Moore, Mary. COM-HE (WJAG, Norfolk, VA, 1949).

22287 Moore, Mary. COM-HE (WEBJ, Brewton, AL, 1951).

22288 Moore, Mary. COM-HE (WJAG, Norfolk, NE, 1956–1957).

22289 Moore, Mary Louise. COM-HE (WHED, Washington, DC, 1957).

22290 Moore, Mat. COM-HE (WMPA, Aberdeen, MS, 1956).

22291 Moore, Meade. COM-HE (WCNC, Elizabeth City, NY, 1956–1957).

22292 Moore, Morrill. Organist Moore performed at the Linwood Theater, Kansas City, Missouri (WHB, Kansas City, MO, 1926). In 1928, Moore was organist for the Rockhill Theater and staff organist at WHB.

22293 Moore, Mozelle. COM-HE (WHVH, Henderson, NC, 1956).

22294 Moore, Otto. Baritone (WEBH, Chicago, IL, 1924; WQJ, Chicago, IL, 1926).

22295 Moore, Paul. Newscaster (KIT, Yakima, WA, 1937; WTJS, Jackson, TN, 1945).

22296 Moore, Pryor. Leader (Pryor Moore Orchestra, KFI, Los Angeles, CA, 1926).

22297 Moore, Ralph. Announcer (KLS, Oakland, CA, 1927).

22298 Moore, Sally. Contralto (*Sally Moore*, vcl. mus. prg., 15 min., Monday and Friday, 6:30–6:45 P.M., CBS, 1945).

22299 Moore, Sally. COM-HE (WAMM, Flint, MI, 1957).

22300 Moore, Templeton. Tenor (WWJ, Detroit, MI, 1924).

22301 Moore, Terry. COM-HE (WEDO, McKeesport, PA, 1954).

22302 Moore, Vern. Newscaster (KIDO, Boise, ID, 1939–1941, 1945). Sportscaster (KIDO, 1941).

22303 Moore, Warren. Baritone (*Warren Moore*, vcl. mus. prg., WIP, Philadelphia, PA, 1935).

22304 Moore, Winnie Fields. Miss Moore broadcast "travelogues" (KFI, Los Angeles, CA, 1929).

22305 Moore, Yvonne. DJ (WWON, Woonsocket, RI, 1950).

22306 Moorehead, Agnes. Actress Moorehead entered radio in 1925 as a singer on KMOX (St. Louis, MO). After working on the Broadway stage, Moorehead began dramatic work in radio in the 1930's and 1940's. She appeared frequently on the *Evening in Paris* program on CBS in 1929 and 1930. Some of her most memorable radio performances were on the *Mercury Theater* and *Suspense* programs. Among the diversified programs in which she appeared were *The Adventures of Mister Meek, America's Hour, Ben Bernie Show, Brenda Curtis, Bringing Up Father, Bulldog Drummond, Cavalcade of America, Dot and Will, The Gumps, Life Can Be Beautiful, March of Time, Mayor of the Town, Mercury Theatre of the Air, Mighty Show, Orange Lantern, Phil Baker Show, The Shadow, Sherlock Holmes, Story of Bess Johnson, Suspense, Terry and the Pirates, This Day Is Ours* and *Way Down East.* In these programs she was featured in such roles as "Margo Lane" on *The Shadow* and on *Terry and the Pirates* as the "Dragon Lady."

Miss Moorehead was one of radio's finest actresses, whose work spanned the Golden Age of Radio. She also enjoyed a successful career in motion pictures and on television. She gained national prominence late in her career in the role of Elizabeth Montgomery's mother, Endora, on the *Bewitched* television program.

22307 Moorehead, Dora Bryan. Singer (KDKA, Pittsburgh, PA, 1924).

22308 Moorehead, Tom. Sportscaster (WFIL, Philadelphia, PA, 1946–1950; *The Tom Moorehead Sports Show*, WFIL, 1951–1956).

22309 Moorehouse, Ward. Drama critic Moorehouse discussed the New York theater scene (WGBS, New York, NY, 1925).

22310 Moorman, Covey. COM-HE (WFAL, Fayetteville, NC, 1954).

22311 Mooseheart Novelty Orchestra. Lodge band (WJJD, Mooseheart, IL, 1925).

22312 Moosman, Beal. Dramatic actor (KOMO, Seattle, WA, 1928).

22313 MoPac Band. J. Roger Gould directed the commercial musical organization (KLRA, Little Rock, AR, 1929).

22314 MoPac Saxophone Band. The novel music group was directed by George T. Hitch (KGHI, Little Rock, AR, 1929).

22315 Moquette, Hector. Sportscaster (*Sports Carnival*, WWRL, New York, NY, 1960).

22316 Moraga, Pedro. DJ (*Melodias Mananeres*, KIFN, Phoenix, AZ, 1949).

22317 Morain, Ota. COM-HE (WMVO, Mt. Vernon, OH, 1956).

22318 Morales, Joe. DJ (*Pasadena Hour*, KLVL, Pasadena, TX, 1954).

22319 Moran, Betty. Actress Moran was in the cast of the daytime serial programs *Dear John, Today's Children* and *The Career of Alice Blair.*

22320 Moran, Florence. COM-HE (WLBR, Lebanon, PA, 1954).

22321 Moran, Gussie. Glamorous tennis player conducted a sports news program (WMGM, New York, NY, 1958).

22322 Moran, Jack. DJ (*Pitchin' Kurva*, KURV, Edinburg, TX, 1948–1950; *Sports Beat and Football Forecasts*, KVER, Albuquerque, NM, 1951–1952).

22323 Moran, Jack. DJ (WMON, Montgomery, WV, 1948–1949; *The World of Sports*, WMON, 1950).

22324 Moran, Mabel. Versatile drummer, contralto singer and business manager of the Merry Musical Maids music group (WOAW, Omaha, NE, 1925).

22325 Moran, Nellie Lee. Soprano (WSM, Nashville, TN, 1928).

22326 *Moran and Mack* (aka "The Two Black Crows") The team originally consisted of George Moran and Charles Mack. They were a popular blackface vaudeville act that frequently appeared on the *Majestic Theater Hour*, a musical variety program (CBS, 1929) and the *Eveready Hour* (NBC, 1929). Although Moran and Mack were the original team members, others such as Bert Swor, George Searchey and Charles Sellers took over at various times.

The *Moran and Mack* comedy show combined their comedy routines with the music of Tom Waring and Babs Ryan singing with the Fred Waring's Orchestra. The program was sponsored by P. Lorrilard Tobacco Company (30 min., Wednesday, 10:00–10:30 P.M., CBS, 1933).

22327 Morand, Edward V. Newscaster (WLTH, New York, NY, 1940).

22328 Morand, June. Leader (June Morand Orchestra, CBS, 1941).

22329 Morantz, Annette. Managerial staff (WOR, New York, NY, 1930s). Morantz worked with Stella Berthoff and (Ms.) Bert Greene on WOR's Artists Bureau's staff/

22330 Morath, Max. DJ (Critically praised pianist Morath played records on his *Max Unpax the Wax* program, KVOR, Colorado Springs, CO, 1947; KGHF, Pueblo, CO, 1950).

22331 Moravia, Harold. Tenor (WOK, Chicago, IL, 1925).

22332 Morbio, Patricia O'Connor. Irish soprano (KPO, San Francisco, CA, 1924).

22333 More, Uncle Tom. DJ (*Club 99 Jamboree*, WNOX, Knoxville, TN, 1948–1949; *Jamboree*, WNOX, 1950–1955).

22334 *More For Your Money.* This program featured a series of talks by various expert economists such as Salmon O. Levinson. They tried to help listeners with various economic problems (CBS, 1935).

22335 Morehouse, Leslie C. Announcer (WSBT, South Bend, IN, 1925).

22336 Morehouse, Marguerite. Organist (KOIL, Council Bluffs, IA, 1928).

22337 Moreland, Harry. Sportscaster (WROL, Knoxville, TN, 1940). Newscaster (WDOD, Chattanooga, TN, 1941–1942). DJ (*Cousin Harry's Hayloft*, WROL, Knoxville, TN, 1948).

22338 Moreland, Helen. COM-HE (KTEN, Ada, OK, 1954).

22339 Moreland, Nick "Peg." Singer-guitarist whose specialty was country-western music, Moreland was the first full-time music performer to join the staff of WFAA (Dallas, TX, 1924).

22340 Morelli, Giovanni. Tenor (WOR, Newark, NJ, 1925).

22341 Morelli, Jean. Soprano (WHDH, Boston, MA, 1941).

22342 Morelli, Mario. Leader (*Mario Morelli Orchestra*, instr. mus. prg., KUOA, Siloam Springs, AR, 1934).

22343 Morelli, Whitfield. Pianist (WSM, Nashville, TN, 1928).

22344 Morely, Bill. Minstrel show endman (WGBS, New York, NY, 1928).

22345 Moreno, Buddy. DJ (WJJD, Chicago, IL, 1955–1956; WHHM, Memphis, TN, 1957).

22346 Moreno, Elizabeth. Pianist (WCOA, Pensacola, FL, 1926).

22347 Morenson, Luella. COM-HE (WKOW, Madison, WI, 1957).

22348 Morenzo, Paul. Tenor (WJY, Hoboken, NJ, 1924).

22349 Morey, Art. Newscaster (KWJJ, Portland, OR, 1938). Sportscaster (KWJJ, Portland, OR, 1939–1942).

22350 *Morey Amsterdam.* Comedian-cellist Amsterdam had his own radio program in 1930 (KNX, Hollywood, CA, 1930). Amsterdam used his cello playing as part of his comic routine, often interrupting his playing with rapid fire quips. Although he started out early in radio, Amsterdam gained his greatest prominence in television. *The Morey Amsterdam Show* was broadcast from 1948 to 1950 on the CBS and Dumont television networks. The show featured Vic Damone and Jacqueline Susann and was directed by Irving Mansfield. Next, Amsterdam shared hosting *America at Night* on Tuesday and Thursday nights, while Jerry Lester hosted on Monday, Wednesday and Friday. *America at Night,* network television's first late night program, was transformed by Sylvester "Pat" Weaver into *The Tonight Show* television program.

Perhaps it was Amsterdam's role as Buddy Sorrell, a fast-talking comedy writer, on the Dick Van Dyke television show that brought him his greatest recognition and fame and continues to do so with the show's reruns on the Nick at Night cable network. Amsterdam was also a regular television panel member or host on three radio programs that eventually enjoyed a brief TV run: *Can You Top This?, Who Said That?* and *Stop Me If You've Heard This. See* ***The Morey Amsterdam Show, Stop Me if You've Heard This One*** *and* ***The Morey Amsterdam Matinee.***

22351 *Morey Amsterdam Matinee.* Amsterdam was a DJ on this show, although he called himself a "Josh Jockey." Phil Goulding was the announcer (30 min., Monday through Friday, 3:00–3:00 P.M., WHN, New York, NY, 1947).

22352 *Morey Amsterdam Show.* Amsterdam hosted his local variety show that featured Liza Morrow and Vic Damone singing with Joel Herron's Orchestra. Phil Goulding was the announcer (55 min., Monday through Saturday, 1:05–2:00 P.M., WHN, New York, NY, 1946).

Two years later veteran comedian Amsterdam hosted another network variety show with the same name. Featured on the show with him were Charles Irving, Betty Garde, Jackson Beck, Millard Mitchell, Art Carney and Ginney Powell. Music was by Henry Sylvern's Orchestra (30 min., Saturday, 9:00–9:30 P.M., CBS, 1948).

22353 Morgan, Alice Adams. COM-HE (KMHT, Marshall, TX, 1956–1957).

22354 Morgan, Arthur. Violinist (WBAL, Baltimore, MD, 1928).

22355 Morgan, Buford. DJ (*Parade of Bands*, KEBE, Jacksonville, TN, 1947).

22356 Morgan, Cindy. COM-HE (KVON, Napa, CA, 1954).

22357 Morgan, Clarke. Morgan was the musical director of the *Wendy Warren and the News* program.

22358 Morgan, Claudia. Actress Morgan appeared on the daytime serial programs *Right to Happiness*, *Against the Storm* and *David Harum*.

22359 Morgan, Constance. Soprano (KTAB, Oakland, CA, 1925).

22360 Morgan, Dale. DJ (KLZ, Denver, CO, 1956).

22361 Morgan, Dick. News analyst (*Five-Star Final*, KTUC, Tucson, AZ, 1947). DJ (*Swingtime*, KTUC, 1947). Sportscaster (*Speaking of Sports*, KTUC, 1947).

22362 Morgan, Edward P. News commentator (*Edward P. Morgan and the News*, Monday through Friday, early 1950s). Liberal commentator Morgan was sponsored by the AFL-CIO. He was introduced by his announcer, Frank Harden, with this identification: "Fifteen million Americans bring you *Edward P. Morgan and the News*."

22363 Morgan, Elizabeth. Actress Morgan was in the cast of the *Stella Dallas* daytime serial program.

22364 Morgan, Em. Sportscaster (*Sports Story*, KPGW, Pasco, WA, 1951–1956).

22365 Morgan, Gene. Actor Morgan appeared on *Carol Kennedy's Romance*, *Myrt and Marge*, *Mary Marlin* and *Today's Children*.

22366 Morgan, George. CW singer-songwriter Morgan had shows on WAKR (Akron, OH), WWST (Wooster, OH), WIBW (Topeka, KS) and WKNX (Saginaw, MI) before he starred on WLW's *Midwestern Hayride* (WLW, Cincinnati, OH) and the *WWVA's Jamboree* (WWVA, Wheeling, WV) programs. Morgan joined the *Grand Ole Opry* in 1948.

22367 Morgan, Hal. Newscaster (WGAR, Cleveland, OH, 1942). DJ (*Morgan's Musical Inn*, WGAR, 1947–1949; *Morgan's Manor*, WGAR, 1949; *Musical Inn*, WGAR, 1950–1957).

22368 Morgan, Hank. Sportscaster (*Sports Review*, *Sports Preview* and *Sports Scoreboard*, WNOA, Raleigh, NC, 1948; WOBS, Jacksonville, FL, 1950; WQXI, Atlanta, GA, 1960).

22369 Morgan, Helen. Morgan was a great torch singer (WGBS, New York, NY, 1927; *Helen Morgan, Songs*, CBS, 1933). A great blues singer, Helen Morgan starred on stage and in films. Perhaps she is best remembered for singing "Along Came Bill" from the musical, *Showboat*. She appeared in several other Ziegfeld productions. Renowned for singing while sitting on a grand piano, a film of her life, *Both Ends of the Candle*, was made in 1957. *See* **Singers**.

22370 Morgan, Henry. DJ and comedian Henry Morgan played records on his *Here's Morgan* program (WMGM, New York, NY, 1952). Announcer (*Lone Journey*). *See* ***Here's Morgan*** *and* ***The Henry Morgan Show***.

22371 Morgan, Ira D. Baritone (KELW, Burbank, CA, 1928).

22372 Morgan, Jack. Newscaster (*Mid-Day News*, WMAW, Milwaukee, WI, 1948).

22373 Morgan, Jane. Actress Morgan appeared on the serial programs *Glorious One* and *Bent House*.

22374 Morgan, Jane. Singer (*Jane Morgan*, vcl. mus. prg., NBC, 1951).

22375 Morgan, John. Newscaster (WTAR, Norfolk, VA, 1941).

22376 Morgan, John Carl. Newscaster (WINC, Winchester, VA, 1945).

22377 Morgan, Lorraine. COM-HE (WULA, Eufaula, AL, 1949).

22378 Morgan, Louise. COM-HE (WNAC, Boston, MA, 1956).

22379 Morgan, Lucille. Violinist (KRE, Berkeley, CA, 1926).

22380 Morgan, Madge. Soprano (KVOO, Tulsa, OK, 1928).

22381 Morgan, Marion. Soprano (WEEI, Boston, MA, 1925).

22382 Morgan, Mary. COM-HE (WJAG, Norfolk, NE, 1956).

22383 Morgan, Melvena H. COM-HE (KWSK, Pratt, KS, 1956).

22384 Morgan, Mona [Maude]. Shakespearean reader (WJZ, New York, NY, 1923).

22385 Morgan, Pearl Wilson. COM-HE (KWFR, San Angelo, TX, 1955).

22386 Morgan, Ray. Newscaster (WPG, Atlantic City, NJ, 1939; WCOP, Boston, MA, 1940). Sportscaster (WBAB, Atlantic City, NJ, 1940; WWDC, Washington, DC, 1946; baseball, basketball, football and hockey play-by-play, WWDC, 1947–1949; *Sports School of the Air*, WWDC, 1950).

22387 Morgan, Robert. Newscaster (WKRC, Cincinnati, OH, 1940).

22388 Morgan, Robin. DJ (Robin at age five almost certainly was the youngest DJ on American radio, WOR, New York, NY, 1947).

22389 Morgan, Roy E. News analyst (WILK, Wilkes-Barre, PA, 1947; *It Seems to Me*, WILK, 1948).

22390 Morgan, Russ. Leader (*Russ Morgan Orchestra*, instr. mus. prg., NBC, 1935–1939; *Music in the Morgan Manner*, NBC, 1936; KSD, St. Louis, MO, 1940).

22391 Morgan, Ruth. Pianist (KFWM, Oakland, CA, 1926).

22392 Morgan, Slim. DJ (WGIL, Galesburg, IL, 1955).

22393 Morgan, Thomas "Tom." Newscaster (WOV, New York, NY, 1944, 1947).

22394 *(The) Morgan Trio* (aka Le Morgan Trio). Instr. mus. prg. (30 min., Wednesday, 4:00–4:30 P.M., NBC-Red, 1931). The members of the trio were pianist Marguerite Morgan, violinist Frances Morgan and harpist Virginia Morgan.

22395 Morgrace, Dick. Newscaster (WABI, Bangor, ME, 1941).

22396 Morin Sisters. Family vocal trio (*The Morin Sisters*, vcl. mus. prg., NBC, 1935; NBC, 1939).

22397 Morissee, Jack. Tenor (WHN, New York, NY, 1924).

22398 Moritz, John. Newscaster (WCBS, Springfield, IL, 1938).

22399 Mork, Carol. COM-HE (WPDR, Portage, WI, 1957).

22400 Morley, Felix. News analyst and cultural commentator (NBC, 1947).

22401 *Mormon Tabernacle Choir*. The excellent choir broadcast from the Mormon Tabernacle that was located on Temple Square in Salt Lake City, Utah. The choir first appeared on radio on a NBC affiliate (KSL, Salt Lake City, UT, 1929). The program moved to CBS in 1932. The directors of the choir through the years were Anthony C. Lund and J. Spencer Cornwall. Richard L. Evans was the program's producer, director and announcer. The famous organists who appeared on the program were Alexander Schreiner and Frank Asper. A regular feature of the program was the inspirational "The Spoken Word" segment delivered by either J. Spencer Cornwall or Richard L. Evans. Early listings of programs give various days and times: *The Mormon Tabernacle Choir and Organ*. Organist and a choir of 300 voices directed by George B. Durham (30 min., Monday, 6:00–6:30 P.M., NBC-Blue, 1930). *The Mormon Tabernacle Choir and Organ* program featured the Choir with organ. The director was Anthony C. Lund (15 min., 2:45–3:00 P.M., NBC-Blue, 1932).

22402 *Morning at McNeill's*. A variety program hosted by Don McNeill (Thursdays, 9:15–9:45 A.M., NBC, 1936). Vocalist Gale Page and the band of Roy Shields were featured. McNeill conducted the show in addition to his regular *Breakfast Club* program.

22403 *Morning Devotions*. The program of inspirational music was performed by soprano Katherine Palmer; contralto Joyce Allmand; tenor John Jamison and baritone John Wainman. Organist Lowell Pator directed the program (30 min., Saturday, 7:00–7:30 A.M., NBC, 1935).

22404 *Morning Devotions*. Jack Holden conducted the early morning program of inspirational readings and music. Tenor William O'Connor and organist Howard Petersen were program regulars with Tom Hargis sometimes also singing on the program (15 min., Monday through Friday, 7:30–7:45 P.M., WLS, Chicago, IL, 1937).

22405 Morning Glory Dance Orchestra. Local California band (KMIC, Inglewood, CA, 1928).

22406 *Morning Homemakers Program*. Information for women and pleasant music were the ingredients of the program whose cast included pianist John Brown, the Hometowners Quartet and a studio orchestra. The information for women segment was provided by Julia Hayes, Helen Joyce and Martha Crane

(30 min., Monday through Friday, 10:30–11:00 A.M., WLS, Chicago, IL, 1937).

22407 ***Morning Matinee.*** R.H. Macy Company sponsored the early morning music and talk show that featured the Ben Bernie Orchestra and Nellie Revell interviewing such guests as Edna Woolman and Gladys Swarthout (45 min., Thursday, 9:00–9:45 P.M., MBS, 1936).

22408 ***Morning Minstrels.*** A daily radio minstrel show, that always presented station WLS regulars doing their thing. An early cast featured announcer Jack Holden, the Home Towners Quartet, comedians Chuck and Ray and endman Possum Tuttle (Vance McCune). The program was sponsored by the Olson Rug Company (15 min., Monday through Friday, 8:00–8:15 A.M., WLS, Chicago, IL, 1935). Later that year the program included Merton Minnich, Walter Tuite, Lew Storey, Clyde Moffett, Osgood Wesley, Eddie Dean, Tiny Stowe and Cousin Toby (15 min., Monday through Friday, 8:45–9:00 A.M., WLS, Chicago, IL, 1935).

Still later — Joe Kelly, as "Swampy Sam" and Henry Hornsbuckle playing "Morpheus Mayfair" replaced comedians Chuck and Ray. One of "Morpheus"often repeated line was, "I ain't lazy — I'se tired." Other cast members on the later program included: Ted Gilmore, Bill Thall, Chuck Haynes, Ray Ferris, Paul Nettings, Jack Eliot, Phil Kalar, Rocky Racherbaumer, Possum Tuttle, Ken Wright, Otto Morse and Zeb Hartley. Jack Holden remained the announcer. The program characteristically ended with Al Boyd producing the sound effect of train sounds (15 min., 8:45–9:00 A.M., WLS, Chicago, IL, 1936). The program continued into 1937, still sponsored by the Olson Rug Company, with essentially the same cast. However, a little German band, Otto and the Novelodeons, was an important addition.

22409 ***Morning Philosopher—Coleman Cox.*** Cheery commentary on life for his listeners was provided by Cox (NBC, 1935).

22410 ***Morning Round-Up.*** Patsy Montana and the Prairie Ramblers sang and played their pleasant brand of CW music (8:30 A.M., WLS, Chicago, IL, 1937).

22411 ***Morning Services of the Church of the Covenant.*** Religious services (Sunday, 11:00–12 noon, WLW, Cincinnati, OH, 1923.

22412 **Morningside String Quartet.** Instrumental music group (WAHG, Richmond Hill, NY, 1925).

22413 **Morola Orchestra.** Popular radio band (KFWB, Hollywood, CA, 1926).

22414 **Morrell, Katherine.** Soprano (KOA, Denver, CO, 1925).

22415 **Morrey, Grace Hamilton.** Pianist (WAIU, Columbus, OH, 1928).

22416 **Morris, Carl.** Saxophonist, Pasadena Orchestra DeLuxe. *See* **Pasadena Orchestra DeLuxe.**

22417 **Morris, Colton "Chick."** Sportscaster (WBZ-WBZA, Boston-Springfield, MA, 1940). Newscaster (WBZ-WBZA, 1941).

22418 **Morris, Dewitt "Bud."** Newscaster (KELA, Centralia and Chehalis, WA, 1937–1939).

22419 **Morris, Don.** Newscaster (WMBC, Detroit, MI, 1938).

22420 **Morris, Dudley.** Newscaster (KOAM, Pittsburg, KS, 1941–1942).

22421 **Morris, Ed.** DJ (*Evening Serenade*, WFST, Caribou, ME, 1960).

22422 **Morris, Fay.** Banjoist (KWSC, Pullman, WA, 1925).

22423 **Morris, Frank.** Yodeler (WKY, Chicago, IL, 1922).

22424 **Morris, G.F.** Newscaster (WBRB, Red Bank, NJ, 1940).

22425 **Morris, Grace.** COM-HE (WBIZ, Eau Claire, WI, 1955).

22426 **Morris, Harriet.** Pianist (WLW, Cincinnati, OH, 1924).

22427 **Morris, Helen.** Soprano (WEAF, New York, NY, 1924; WMCA, New York, NY, 1925).

22428 **Morris, Herman.** Baritone (WOR, Newark, NJ, 1925).

22429 **Morris, (Mrs.) J.W.** Xylophone soloist (WBZ, Springfield, MA, 1926).

22430 **Morris, Jack.** Newscaster (KTUL, Tulsa, OK, 1944–1945, 1948). Sportscaster (KTUL, 1942).

22431 **Morris, James M.** Newscaster (KOAC, Corvallis, OR, 1942). Sportscaster (KOAC, 1944–1946).

22432 **Morris, James N.** Newscaster (WSTP, Salisbury, NC, 1945).

22433 **Morris, Jerry.** Newscaster (KOL, Seattle, WA, 1942, 1945).

22434 **Morris, Jesse.** DJ (*Swingship*, WFPG, Atlantic City, NJ, 1955).

22435 **Morris, (Mrs.) Joe.** COM-HE (WAGS, Bishopville, SC, 1956).

22436 **Morris, Louise.** COM-HE (WTOR, Torrington, CT, 1954).

22437 **Morris, Louise.** COM-HE (WDAK, Columbus, GA, 1956).

22438 **Morris, Margaret Messer.** Soprano (KNX, Los Angeles, CA, 1928).

22439 **Morris, Mary.** COM-HE (WBEX, Chillicothe, OH, 1957).

22440 **Morris, McKay.** Actor Morris was in the cast of *Dodsworth*, *Grand Central Station* and *Ma Perkins.*

22441 **Morris, Mitchell.** Newscaster (WHAS, Louisville, KY, 1932; WFAM, South Bend, IN and WSBT, South Bend, IN, 1939).

22442 **Morris, Monte.** DJ (*Wastebasket Review*, KSYC, Yreka, CA, 1952; *Yawn Patrol*, KYJC, Medford, OR, 1954).

22443 **Morris, Paul R.** Newscaster (WCAO, Baltimore, MD, 1938–1941).

22444 **Morris, Robert.** Ex-football player Morris conducted a program of sports news and commentary (WBZ-WBZA, Boston-Springfield, MA, 1928).

22445 **Morris, Skeets.** Leader (*Skeets Morris Orchestra*, WHAS, Louisville, KY, 1938).

22446 **Morris, (Dr.) V.P.** News analyst (*World in Review*, KOAC, Corvallis, OR, 1947).

22447 **Morris, Willie.** Soprano (WOR, Newark, NJ, 1939).

22448 ***Morris H. Siegel.*** Siegel delivered talks about various aspects of insurance (15 min., Weekly, WMCA, New York, NY, 1938).

22449 **Morrisey, Marie.** Contralto (WLS, Chicago, IL, 1926).

22450 **Morrison, Bret.** Actor Morrison was in the cast of *Arnold Grimm's Daughter*, *Best Sellers*, *Chicago Theatre of the Air*, *First Nighter*, *Great Gunns*, *Guiding Light*, *Light of the World*, *Listening Post*, *Parties at Pickfair*, *Road of Life*, *Romance of Helen Trent*, *The Shadow* (title role), *Song of the Stranger* and *Woman in White.*

22451 **Morrison, Carlton.** Newscaster (WSB, Atlanta, GA, 1948).

22452 **Morrison, Chester.** Newscaster (NBC, 1945).

22453 **Morrison, Clair E.** Announcer-manager (KYA, San Francisco, CA, 1927–1928). Morrison formerly was announcer-station director at KPO (San Francisco, CA, 1926).

22454 **Morrison, Eddie.** DJ (WEBB, Baltimore, MD, 1960).

22455 **Morrison, Edris.** Director (KOIN Players, KOIN, Portland, OR, 1928).

22456 **Morrison, Ethel.** Actress Morrison was in the cast of the *Young Dr. Malone* daytime serial program.

22457 **Morrison, (Mrs.) Florence Denny.** Pianist (KOA, Denver, CO, 1925).

22458 **Morrison, Gary [Garry].** Newscaster (WDNC, Durham, NC, 1942; WPTF, Raleigh, NC, 1944–1945). Sportscaster (WPTF, 1945).

22459 **Morrison, (Mrs.) George.** Violinist (KOA, Denver, CO,1926).

22460 **Morrison, Gordon.** Guitarist (KMOX, St. Louis, MO, 1926).

22461 **Morrison, Grace.** COM-HE (WERC, Erie, PA, 1957).

22462 **Morrison, Herbert.** Newscaster (KQV, Pittsburgh, PA, 1948).

22463 **Morrison, Marilyn.** COM-HE (WELC, Welch, WV, 1956).

22464 **Morrison, Mary Jane.** Pianist-singer on *The Comy Time* program (WIBW, Topeka, KS, 1929).

22465 **Morrison, Maybelle.** Violinist (KLX, Los Angeles, CA, 1929).

22466 **Morrison, P. Harold.** Baritone (WBZ, Boston-Springfield, MA, 1924).

22467 **Morrison, Stu.** Newscaster (KTNM, Tucumcari, NM, 1941).

22468 **Morrison, Wilbur.** News analyst (WGY, Schenectady, NY, 1938; *News Analyst*, WRUN, Utica, NY, 1948).

22469 **Morrissey, Jack.** DJ (*Star Spotlight*, WHKK, Akron, OH, 1947; *Musical Clock*, WARK, Akron, OH, 1950).

22470 **Morrissey, Jim.** Morrissey broadcast market news and reports (*Mid-Morning Chicago Cattle, Hog and Sheep Market*, 5 min., Monday through Friday, 10:10–10:15 A.M., WLS, Chicago, IL, 1936). Morrissey broadcast from Chicago's Union Stock Yards on this program sponsored by the Chicago Livestock Exchange.

22471 **Morrissey, Mary.** Soprano (WNBC, New Britain, CT, 1937).

22472 **Morros, Boris.** Leader (*Boris Morros String Quartet*, instr. mus. prg., CBS, 1938).

22473 **Morrow, Ben.** Sportscaster (WCBY, Cheboygan, MI, 1956).

22474 **Morrow, David.** Newscaster (WCAP, Asbury Park, NJ, 1940–1942).

22475 **Morrow, Estelle.** Pianist (KTAB, Oakland, CA, 1929).

22476 **Morrow, Marjorie.** Director (CBS, 1930s). Before becoming an assistant director for CBS, Morrow had prior experience in radio publicity, production and direction. As a casting director at CBS, she conducted practically all the network's auditions.

22477 **Morrow, Russ.** Leader (*Russ Morrow Orchestra*, instr. mus. prg., WIP, Philadelphia, PA, 1936).

22478 **Morrow, Thelma.** Xylophonist (WHO, Des Moines, IA, 1925).

22479 **Morsch, Fern.** COM-HE (KOVC, Valley City, ND, 1954).

22480 **Morse, Bob.** Newscaster (KSIM, Salem, OR, 1948).

22481 **Morse, Carleton E.** Writer-director-producer Morse's productions included *His Honor the Barber*, *I Love a Mystery*, *I Love Adventure* and *One Man's Family.*

22482 **Morse, Clyde.** Announcer (WHAM, Rochester, NY, 1925). Pianist (*Clyde Morse*, instr. mus. prg., KDKA, Pittsburgh, PA, 1934).

22483 **Morse, F. Wellington, Jr.** Announcer (KFWH, Chino, CA, 1926; KFWI, San Francisco, CA, 1927).

22484 **Morse, Gwendolyn.** Pianist (KFI, Los Angeles, CA, 1929).

22485 **Morse, Helen.** Contralto (KVOO, Tulsa, OK, 1929).

22486 **Morse, Jane.** Blues singer (KMO, Tacoma, WA, 1928–1929).

22487 **Morse, Janeen.** COM-HE (WTNT, Tallahassee, FL, 1954).

22488 **Morse, Kenneth.** Leader (Kenneth Morse Orchestra, KFI, Los Angeles, CA, 1926 and Kenneth Morse and his Venice Ballroom Orchestra, KFI, 1926).

22489 **Morse, Lee.** Popular female singer (CBS, 1929) Morse, who was an excellent song stylist was described as that "decorative little red-haired singer of musical comedy fame." She had sung for two years on the Pantages vaudeville circuit and appeared opposite Raymond Hitchcock in the Broadway play *Hitchy-Koo.* She wrote more than 200 songs and made more than 235 phonograph records. After signing an exclusive CBS contract, Morse made many radio appearances including one on the *Van Heusen Show* (CBS, mid–1930s).

22490 **Morse, Margaret.** COM-HE (WSNY, Schenectady, NY, 1951).

22491 **Morse, Molly.** COM-HE (KFMB, San Diego, CA, 1956–1957).

22492 **Morse, Olive.** Soprano (*Olive Morse*, vcl. mus. prg., 15 min., 8:30–8:45 P.M. CST, WLS, Chicago, IL, 1935).

22493 **Morse, Sybil Jane.** Pianist (WEEI, Boston, MA, 1934).

22494 **Morse, Tony.** Newscaster (KGO, San Francisco, CA, 1944–1945).

22495 **Morson, Leslie.** Newscaster (WNLC, New London, CT, 1946).

22496 ***Mort Sahl Show.*** Sahl delivered thoughtful comic monologs that blended satire and irony, as he looked into every aspect of American life (30 min., Tuesday, 12:00–12:30 P.M., KGO, San Francisco, CA, 1954). Sahl's timely political and social commentaries were unique radio fare that unfortunately was short-lived.

22497 **Mortensen, Modesta.** Violinist (KGO, Oakland, CA, 1926).

22498 **Mortensen [Morenson], Luella.** COM-HE (WKOW, Madison, WI, 1957–1960).

22499 **Morton, Dorothy.** Pianist (WSM, Nashville, TN, 1928).

22500 **Morton, Fannie Bess.** Soprano (WHAS, Louisville, KY, 1923).

22501 **Morton, Harriet.** Soprano (KTAB, Oakland, OH, 1925).

22502 **Morton, Harry.** Tenor (KOA, Denver, CO, 1925).

22503 **Morton, Imogene.** Pianist (WMBH, Joplin, MO, 1937).

22504 **Morton, James.** Baritone (WBZ, Springfield, MA, 1923).

22505 **Morton, Lew.** DJ (*Salty Morton's Matinee*, WJNO, West Palm Beach, FL, 1948).

22506 **Morton, Mava.** COM-HE (WKNA, Charleston, WV, 1954).

22507 **Morton, (Mrs.) R.H.** Lyric soprano (WFAA, Dallas, TX, 1922).

22508 **Morton, Ray.** Tenor (*Ray Morton*, vcl. mus. prg., NBC-Red, 1936).

22509 **Morton, Shirley.** Pianist (WPAR, Parkersburg, WV, 1937).

22510 ***Morton Downey.*** Tenor Downey was featured on his own program broadcast on a sustaining basis by CBS four times weekly (CBS, 1929). Downey later was sponsored by Coca-Cola.

22511 ***Morton Downey's Studio Party.*** Popular tenor Downey, the Henry Busse orchestra and weekly guest artists performed on his entertaining music show (30 min., Saturday, 8:00–8:30 P.M., CBS, 1934).

22512 **Morwood, William.** Writer Morwood wrote *Road of Life.*

22513 **Mosby, A.J.** Newscaster (KGVO, Missoula, MO, 1941).

22514 **Mosby, Ruth Greenough.** COM-HE (KGVO, Missoula, MO, 1956).

22515 ***Moscow Radio Orchestra.*** The excellent Russian orchestra broadcast from Moscow by short wave. The conductor was Peter Alexeev. The program also presented singers Katherine Katulskaja and Anatolij Sadomov and balaika soloist, Nicholas Ossipiv (30 min., Sunday, 7:30–8:00 P.M. CST, NBC-Red, 1935).

22516 **Mose (Harold Hughes) and Cholly (Joe Simonson).** A blackface comedy singing team, Mose and Cholly specialized in "plantation songs," on their *Mose and Cholly from Sootville* program (KOIL, Council Bluffs, IA, 1927). Sometimes the team was known as **Mose and Charlie**.

22517 **Mose and Henry.** Blackface comedy team (WKBE, Worcester, MA, 1929–1930 and WORC, Worcester, MA, 1930). Mose was Armand LaPointe and Henry was Ralph Warren.

22518 **Moseby's Blue Blowers Orchestra.** Popular jazz band (KNRC, Los Angeles, CA, 1926; KPO, San Francisco, CA, 1927).

22519 **Moseley, June.** COM-HE (WACL, Waycross, GA, 1957).

22520 **Moseley, Shiela S.** COM-HE (KABB, Hot Springs, AR, 1960).

22521 **Moseley, Shirley.** COM-HE (WOWL, Florence, AL, 1954–1960).

22522 **Mosely, L.O. "Lasso."** Announcer Mosely sometimes was also known as "The Sheik," apparently because he was a great favorite among female listeners (1923).

22523 **Mosely, Lois.** Singer (WFAA, Dallas, TX, 1929).

22524 **Mosely, Max.** Sportscaster (*Friday Night Quarterback*, WAPX, Montgomery, AL, 1949).

22525 **Mosely, Sidney.** Newscaster and commentator (WMCA, New York, NY, 1940–1942; WOR, New York, NY, 1945). British born news commentator Mosely, a correspondent for the New York *Times* and the *London Daily Express*, was an author who broadcast the news from the distinctly different point of view of a British Conservative (Middle 1940s and 1950s).

22526 **Mosely, Wallace.** Newscaster (WAIM, Anderson, SC, 1937).

22527 **Mosely, Wayne.** Newscaster (WDIG, Dothan, AL, 1948).

22528 **Mosena, Richard.** Newscaster (KBUR, Burlington, IA, 1945–1946).

22529 **Moser, Gene.** Newscaster (KSAL, Salinas, KS, 1946).

22530 **Moser, (Reverend) M.L.** A popular Little Rock, Arkansas preacher, Moser conducted a weekly religious program (KLRA, Little Rock, AR, 1935).

22531 **Moses, Emanuel.** Violinist (WEAF, New York, NY, 1925).

22532 **Moses, Frank S.** Past Grand Master of Iowa's Masonic Lodge Moses spoke on "Americanism" (WAC, Davenport, IA, 1923).

22533 **Moses, John B.** Newscaster (WHKC, Columbus, OH, 1941–1942, 1945).

22534 **Moses, Lucille.** COM-HE (KWIZ, Santa Ana, CA, 1954).

22535 **Moses, Stanford.** Bass (KGO, Oakland, CA, 1926).

22536 **Mosher, Alice Forsythe.** Soprano (KPO, San Francisco, CA, 1926).

22537 **Moshier,, Jeff.** Sportscaster (WSUN, St. Petersburg, FL, 1939–1940).

22538 **Mosler, Sue.** COM-HE (KFKA, Greeley, CO, 1956).

22539 **Mosley, Don.** Newscaster (KQW, San Jose, CA, 1945).

22540 **Mosley, Herky.** Sportscaster (WDAK, West Point, GA, 1941).

22541 **Moss, Arnold.** Actor Moss was in the cast of *Against the Storm*, *Big Sister*, *Columbia Presents Corwin*, *Grand Central Station*,

Guiding Light, The Man I Married and *Mary Marlin.*

22542 **Moss, Dick.** Leader (Dick Moss's Virginians Orchestra, KFXB, Los Angeles, CA, 1927). Moss was a concert pianist, station musical director and conductor of the KFRC Concert Orchestra (KFRC, San Francisco, CA, 1928–1929). He was a recording artist, who formerly had served as director of music at the University of Hawaii.

22543 **Moss, Elizabeth.** COM-HE (KSEY, Seymour, TX, 1951–1954).

22544 **Moss, Frank.** Pianist (1930) and director of the KFRC Little Symphony Orchestra (KFRC, San Francisco, CA, 1926).

22545 **Moss, Gwendolyn.** Violinist (WLAC, Nashville, TN, 1927).

22546 **Moss, Harry.** Leader (Harry Moss Orchestra, WHN, New York, NY, 1925).

22547 **Moss, Jean.** Contralto (*Jean Moss*, vcl. mus. prg., WAAF, Chicago, IL, 1935).

22548 **Moss, Nora LaMarr.** Contralto (WHB, Kansas City, MO, 1926).

22549 **Moss, Seeburn.** Sportscaster (*Saturday Scoreboard*, WFPM, Ft. Valley, GA, 1960).

22550 ***Moss Covered Melody Period.*** Musical program with many unidentified musicians and vocalists in addition to the Moss Covered Melody Orchestra (WBBM, Chicago, IL, 1926).

22551 **Mossman, Sally.** COM-HE (WMCK, McKeesport, PA, 1956–1957).

22552 **Mossman, Sara.** COM-HE (WLBR, Lebanon, PA, 1951).

22553 **Most, Johnny.** Sportscaster (*Most in Sports*, WNAO, Raleigh, NC, 1949; WMGM, New York, NY, 1952–1954; WCOP, Boston, MA, 1955; WVDA, Boston, MA, 1956).

22554 **Mosteller, Jerry.** Newscaster (WMRC, Greenville, SC, 1946).

22555 ***Mother Ethel.*** An otherwise unidentified female broadcaster delivered informative chats for "homemakers" (KVI, Tacoma, WA, 1927).

22556 ***Mother Goose.*** Winifred Olson in the title role pleased Olympia, WA, children with her Saturday morning program. She incorporated creative play activities for children in her program by means of stories, games and music (Saturday A.M., KGY, Olympia, WA, 1948–1956).

22557 ***Mother Knows Best.*** Kellogg's Corn Flakes sponsored the quiz conducted by MC Warren Hull and Isabelle Beach. Ralph Paul was the announcer (30 min., Saturday, 5:30–6:00 P.M., CBS, 1950).

22558 ***Mother Love.*** The program, sponsored by Carson Brothers, was aimed at a Jewish audience. Each Sunday a dramatic sketch was combined with music. During the first half of the program, singers Mischa Rose and Sarah Gorden performed with Yascha Mushnitsky's orchestra. In the last 15 minutes the dramatic sketch, *Married Love*, written by Oscar Ostroff, was presented. Performed in English, the sketch was a melodrama about Jewish customs and morality. Rose Wallerstein, Abe Almar, Herbert Plot, Jerry Jarvis and May E. Freedman were in the cast (30 min., Sunday, 4:00–4:30 P.M., WFIL, Philadelphia, PA, 1935).

22559 ***Mother of Mine.*** Mother Morrison, played by Agnes Young, was the main character on the daytime serial drama. She faced many problems when she moved in with her son and daughter-in-law. The interpersonal frictions that might be expected were precisely the ones she encountered. The program's cast included: Arthur Allen, Pattee Chapman, Donald Cook, Jackie Kelk, Paul Nugent, Ruth Yorke and Agnes Young (15 min., Monday through Friday, NBC-Blue, 1940).

22560 ***Mother Randall and the Blue Ribbon Melodies.*** CW mus. prg. (KOA, Denver, CO, 1939).

22561 ***Mother Spencer.*** The early afternoon daytime serial featured Mother Spencer, an elderly Southern California personality, who sang and played the guitar (15 min., Monday through Saturday, KTYM, Los Angeles, CA, 1932).

22562 **Motor Six Orchestra.** Leader (George Belshaw, KFAB, Lincoln, NE, 1928).

22563 **Motor Town Trio.** Popular local musical group (KNX, Hollywood, CA, 1926).

22564 **Motschenbacker, Nelle [Neile].** COM-HE (KRXL, Roseburg, OR, 1956–1957).

22565 **Mott (Reverend) George.** The Reverend Mott broadcast Sunday services from the First Congregational Church of Springfield, VT (WBNX, Springfield, VT, 1927).

22566 **Mott, (Dr.) John R.** Broadcast talks on religious topics (WHA, Madison, WI, 1923).

22567 **Mottard, Elaine.** COM-HE (WMAW, Menominee, MI, 1954).

22568 **Motz, Leora.** COM-HE (KAYS, Hays, KS, 1949).

22569 **Moulan, Frank.** Comedian (NBC, 1929).

22570 **Moulin Rouge Orchestra.** Chicago club band (WBBM, Chicago, IL, 1926).

22571 **Moulton, Percy.** Newscaster (WHEB, Portsmouth, NH, 1937).

22572 **Mounce, Earl B.** Musical director and orchestra conductor (WFBM, Indianapolis, IN, 1928).

22573 **Mound City Orchestra.** Popular music group (KDKA, Pittsburgh, PA, 1923).

22574 **Mount, (Mrs.) W.C.** Reader (KOA, Denver, CO, 1926).

22575 **Mt. Ida Presbyterian Baptist Choir.** Church Choir from Davenport, Iowa (WOC, Davenport, IA, 1923).

22576 **Mount Morris College Male Quartet.** Collegiate vocal group (WLS, Chicago, IL, 1926).

22577 **Mount Olive Jubilee Singers.** Singing group featuring "Negro spiritual songs" (WCOA, Pensacola, FL, 1926).

22578 **Mountain, Archie.** Sportscaster (WCNL, Hewport, NH, 1960).

22579 **Mountain, Delaine.** DJ (*Mountains of Music*, WAVU, Albertville, AL, 1960).

22580 **Mountain, Pete.** Singer (*Pete Mountain*, vcl. mus. prg., WXYZ, Detroit, MI, 1935).

22581 **Mountain, Rose.** Contralto (WJZ, New York, NY and WGY, Schenectady, NY, 1925).

22582 ***Mountain Melody Boys.*** CW mus. prg. (WPAR, Parkersburg, WV, 1938).

22583 ***Mountain Memories.*** John Lair hosted the program of CW music sponsored by Big Yank Overalls. The Cumberland Ridge Runners CW group was featured (15 min., Saturday, 6:00–6:15 P.M. CST, WLS, Chicago, IL, 1935).

22584 ***Mountain Merry-Makers.*** Announcer Jack Holden hosted the daily CW music show sponsored by Pinex Cough Syrup. The Girls of the Golden West (Dolly and Molly Good), violinist Lily May and the talented singer, "Rambling Red" Foley were featured (15 min., Monday through Friday, 11:00–11:15 A.M., WLS, Chicago, IL, 1936).

22585 ***(The) Mountaineers.*** CW mus. prg. (KFOR, Lincoln, NE, 1939).

22586 ***Mountainville True Life Sketches.*** Station WABC (New York, NY) constructed a Tiny Tots Theater of the Air specifically for the program in order that its young audience could see the performers broadcast in full costume. Frank Knight and Yolanda Langworthy appeared on the children's show. Music was supplied by Milt Shaw's Detroiters Orchestra (30 min., Monday, 7:00–7:30 P.M., CBS, 1929–1930).

22587 **Mounts, Wyletta.** COM-HE (KCOW, Alliance, NE, 1954).

22588 **Mourton, Leona.** Contralto (KGW, Portland, OR, 1924).

22589 **Moutrey, Mary.** Soprano (KPO, San Francisco, CA, 1926).

22590 ***Movie Chats.*** Peggy Patton broadcast news about current films and their stars (WISN, Madison, WI, 1935).

22591 ***Movie-Go-Round.*** Kathleen Lamb presented movie reviews and Hollywood gossip on the local program (15 min., Sunday, 6:30–6:45 P.M., WCOP, Boston, MA, 1936).

22592 ***Movie Starr Dust.*** Martin Starr dispensed movie reviews and Hollywood gossip on his sustaining local show (15 min., Wednesday, WMCA, New York, NY, 1948).

22593 **Movieland Dance Orchestra.** Popular radio band (KFI, Los Angeles, CA, 1926).

22594 ***Movietone Radio Theater.*** The program was an effort to achieve the success that previously had been achieved by the *Lux Radio Theater.* This series, however, presented other stories as well as those adapted from motion pictures. The show starred such performers as Jeanne Cagney, Ann Rutherford, Pat O'Brien, Jeff Chandler, Lurene Tuttle, Eddie Bracken, Marjorie Reynolds, Virginia Bruce, Caesar Romero, Ann Dvorak, John Howard and Gale Storm (30 min., Weekly, 1930s).

22595 **Mowat, Jean.** Commentator on fashions (WMAQ, Chicago, IL, 1925).

22596 **Mower, June.** COM-HE (KOVO, Provo, UT, 1949).

22597 Mower, Millicent. Vaudeville singer (WGBS, New York, NY, 1928).

22598 Mowers, Beulah. Concert pianist (WBBM, Chicago, IL, 1926).

22599 Mowrer, Edgar Ansel. Newscaster (WMCA, New York, NY, 1944).

22600 Mowry, Gloria. COM-HE (*Dorothy from Doerflingers*, WKBH, La Crosse, WI, 1949).

22601 Moxon, Florence. Pianist (WBRK, Pittsfield, MA, 1939).

22602 Moyer, Earl. Leader (*Earl Moyer Orchestra*, instr. mus. prg., WIP, Philadelphia, PA, 1936–1939).

22603 Moyer, Goof. Leader (Goof Moyer and his New Yorkers Orchestra, a vaudeville band that appeared regularly on the *Southern Radio Program*, WLBN, Little Rock, AR, 1927).

22604 Moyer, Lillian. Soprano (WEBH, Chicago, IL, 1924).

22605 Moyle, Paul. Sportscaster (WCNC, Elizabeth City, NC, 1940–1941). Newscaster (WCNC, 1940–1941).

22606 Moyle, Will. DJ (WVET, Rochester, NY, 1957).

22607 Moyles, Jack. Actor Moyles was in the cast of *Hawthorne House*.

22608 Moynihan, James D. Whistler Moynihan was accompanied by John S. O'Connell (WBZ, Boston-Springfield, MA, 1924).

22609 Mozart Choral Club. Vocal group directed by Earle D. Behrends (WFAA, Dallas, TX, 1924–1926).

22610 Mozley, Don. Newscaster (KLX, Oakland, CA, 1942; CBS, 1947–1948).

22611 Mozley, Lois. Singer (WNAD, Norman, OK, 1926).

22612 Mroz, W. Newscaster (WEDC, Chicago, IL, 1945).

22613 *Mrs. Montague's Millions.* A weekly serial drama (15 min., Saturday, 10:15–10:30 P.M., NBC-Blue, 1934).

22614 *Mrs. Murphy's Boarding House.* The comedy drama starred comedienne Dot Harrington (CBS, 1930).

22615 Mrs. Savage's Mandolin Club. Group of amateur musicians (WGI, Medford Hillside, MA, 1924).

22616 *Mrs. Thrifty Buyer.* An unidentified performer provided female listeners with shopping information (15 min., Tuesday, 10:30–10:45 A.M., WHAM, Rochester, NY, 1935).

22617 *Mrs. Wiggs of the Cabbage Patch.* Frank and Anne Hummert produced the daytime serial drama based on the novel of the same name by Alice Caldwell Rice. After beginning on NBC, the show moved to CBS, where it remained for the duration of its run. Betty Garde and Eva Condon played the title role of a poor woman who struggled to keep her family together in a poor city area known as the Cabbage Patch. The cast included: Marjorie Anderson, Eva Condon, Andy Donnelly, Alice Frost, Betty Garde, Bill Johnstone, Joe Latham, Frank Provo, Robert Strauss and Agnes Young. The program was produced by Frank and Anne Hummert. George Ansbro was the announcer (15 min., Monday through Friday, 9:45–10:00 A.M., CBS, 1935).

22618 Mrs. "WJC." Designation for announcer Mrs. William C. Cramb (WGY, Schenectady, NY, 1923).

22619 *Mu Rho Phi Epsilon.* Fraternity program of comedy and music (WIP, Philadelphia, PA, 1925).

22620 *Much About Doolittle.* Jack Kirkwood starred in this combination of situation comedy and stand-up comic routines. The sustaining program was a summer replacement for the *Red Skelton Show*. Verna Felton, Bob Jellison, Joe Kearns, Hal March and Marylee Robb were also in the cast. The Leith Stevens Orchestra supplied the music (30 min., Sunday, 9:00–9:30 P.M., CBS, 1950).

22621 Mueller, Hattye. Composer-pianist (KHJ, Los Angeles, CA, 1923).

22622 Mueller, Marvin. Newscaster (KDRO, Sedalia, MO, 1940; NBC, 1944).

22623 Mueller, Merrill. News analyst (NBC, 1945–1946).

22624 Mueller, Rodger. Newscaster (WHBY, Appleton, WI, 1945).

22625 Muenzer, Hans. Violinist (WDAP, Chicago, IL, 1923).

22626 *Mufti the Man of Magic.* Hugh Studebaker starred on the children's daytime adventure serial. Mufti, the program's main character, found adventures in the Himalayan Mountains, where he encountered the crazy inventor of the "wings of doom," a villain who always caused trouble of one sort or another (WBBM, Chicago, IL, early 1930s).

22627 Mugford, Gertrude. Soprano (WOK, Chicago, IL, 1925).

22628 Mugford, Jimmy. Newscaster (WSPA, Spartanburg, SC, 1938).

22629 Muir, Frances. Newscaster (CBS, 1942).

22630 Muir, G.R. Announcer (WDZ, Tuscola, IL, 1927).

22631 Muir, James H. Musical saw performer (KFWI, San Francisco, CA, 1926).

22632 Muirhead, James E. Harmonica soloist (WAAM, Newark, NJ, 1925).

22633 Mulcahy, Henry. Newscaster (WLAW, Lawrence, MA, 1946).

22634 Mulherin, Mary Jo. COM-HE (WTIS, Jackson, TN, 1949).

22635 Mulhall, Robert C. Sportscaster (WOI, Ames, IA, 1944). Newscaster (WOI, 1945).

22636 Mulholland, Flo. Singer Mulholland appeared on the *Roxy's Gang* program (WEAF, New York, NY, 1925).

22637 Mulholland, Frances. Violinist (KOIL, Council Bluffs, IA, 1926).

22638 Mull, Trudy. COM-HE (KMDO, Fort Scott, KS, 1940s).

22639 Mullally, Don. DJ (*Caledonia Capers*, WTWN, St. Johnsbury, VT, 1949; *1340 Club*, WTWN, 1952; *Rhythm at Random*, WTWN, 1954).

22640 Mullen, Esther. COM-HE (WGAR, Cleveland, OH, 1949).

22641 Mullen, Frank E. Sioux City, Iowa, newspaper farm editor Mullen broadcast "chats with farmers," (KDKA, Pittsburgh, PA, 1921–1927). As a young farm editor of the *National Stockman and Farmer* journal, he was picked to develop KDKA's farm programming. Mullen is credited as beginning the first daily program for farmers on radio. His program is often thought to have been the forerunner of the popular *National Farm and Home Hour*. Mullen met with NBC president Merlin H. Aylesworth and David Sarnoff, head of the Radio Corporation of America. Mullen successfully persuaded them to broadcast a national network program for farmers. This led to the first broadcast of *The National Farm and Home Hour* on October 2, 1928, sponsored by Montgomery Ward Company. The program was carried by the entire NBC network of 13 stations. By mid–1929, the program was moved from Pittsburgh to Chicago, and it was there in 1930 that Everett Mitchell became associated with it. Mullen and Mitchell worked together to make it the outstanding agricultural program it became. *See* ***The National Farm and Home Hour***.

22642 Mullen, Jack. Irish bagpiper (KDKA, Pittsburgh, PA, 1922).

22643 Mullen, Miriam. COM-HE (WOSA, Wausau, WI, 1955).

22644 Muller, Gertrude. Singer (WFBH, New York, NY, 1925).

22645 Muller, Helen. Singer (WFBH, New York, NY, 1925).

22646 Muller, Wayne. Newscaster (KOB, Albuquerque, NM, 1945).

22647 Mullholland, Frank. Comedian Mullholland appeared on the *Roxy and His Gang* program (NBC, New York, NY, 1927).

22648 Mullholland, Ross. DJ (*The Barefoot Society*, WXYZ, Detroit, MI, 1947–1950; WWJ, Detroit, MI, 1952–1956; WHRV, Ann Arbor, MI, 1957).

22649 Mullican, Aubrey Wilson "Moon." CW musician Mullican was known as the "King of the Hillbilly Piano Players." After working for years with various groups, he played with Jimmie Davis (KWKH, Shreveport, LA, 1943). He later worked at KLAC (Port Arthur, TX, 1943), KPBX (Beaumont, TX, 1945), and KECK (Odessa, TX, 1950). He joined the *Grand Ole Opry* in 1951.

22650 Mulligan, Ray. DJ (*Anthracite Club*, WPAM, Pottsville, PA, 1952).

22651 Mulligan, William E. Newscaster (KEPY, Spokane, WA, 1941).

22652 Mullin, Esther. COM-HE (WGAR, Cleveland, OH, 1951).

22653 Mullinan, Ed. Sportscaster (WJBY, Gadsden, AL, 1937).

22654 Mullinax, Ed. Sportscaster (*Sports Panorama*, WLAG, LaGrange, GA, 1946–1952; *Sports Revue*, WLAG, 1954; *Sports Final*, WLAG, 1955).

22655 Mullinger, Keith. Newscaster (WOI, Ames, IA, 1942).

22656 *Mullini's Girl Syncapators Orchestra.* Instr. mus. prg. (KFQZ, Hollywood, CA, 1928).

22657 Mullins, Louise. Reader (KOA, Denver, CO, 1925).

22658 Mullins, Moon. DJ (*Moon's Music*, WJMO, Cleveland, OH, 1949; KGW, Portland, OR, 1954; KITT, Yakima, WA, 1956).

22659 Mullins, Ray. Leader (Ray Mullins Orchestra broadcasting several nights per week from the Jack O'Lantern Eat Shoppe, KTHS, Hot Springs National Park, AR, 1924–1925). Mildred Cobb was the vocalist with the band.

22660 Mullon, Hop. Sportscaster (WSNJ, Bridgeton, NJ, 1950).

22661 Mulready, Tom. Newscaster (WHO, Des Moines, IA, 1942).

22662 Mulroney, Dorothy Birchard. Pianist (WBZ, Boston-Springfield, MA, 1925).

22663 Mulrooney, Margaret M. COM-HE (WQAN, Scranton, PA, 1949).

22664 Mulroy, Bert. Newscaster (WFHR, Wisconsin Rapids, WI, 1942).

22665 Mulvey, Daniel. Newscaster (WAVZ, New Haven, CT, 1948).

22666 Mulvihill, George. Newscaster (KGUO, Missoula, MO, 1944).

22667 Mulvihill, Joe. DJ (*Collegiate Party*,105 min., Saturday, 11:15–12:55 P.M., WTAM, Cleveland, OH, 1948). DJ Mulvihill spun records and interviewed guests on his popular local show.

22668 Muncy, Hugh. Newscaster (KXEL, Waterloo, IA, 1945).

22669 Munday, William C. "Bill." A sports writer on the Atlanta *Journal* newspaper, Munday broadcast sports news (WSB, Atlanta, GA, 1925). Munday shared the 1929 broadcast of the Georgia-California Rose Bowl game from Pasadena, California, with Graham McNamee. Later in 1929, he joined the NBC announcing staff.

22670 Mundell, Esther. Soprano (KGO, Oakland, CA, 1925).

22671 Mundt, Nelva. Contralto (WEMC, Barrien Springs, MI, 1925).

22672 Mundt, (Mrs.) S.E. Pianist (WMC, Memphis, TN, 1923).

22673 Mundy, Carolyn. COM-HE (WRIB, Providence, RI, 1957).

22674 Mundy, Fred. Leader (*Fred Mundy Orchestra*, instr. mus. prg., WDBJ, Roanoke, VA, 1936).

22675 Mundy, John. Cellist Mundy appeared frequently on the *Ampico Series of Distinguished Artists* program (WJZ, New York, NY, 1923).

22676 Munger Place Methodist Church Choir of Dallas, Texas. Church vocal group directed by J. Abner Sage (WFAA, Dallas, TX, 1928).

22677 *Munger Place Methodist Church Service.* The Reverend J. Abner Sage conducted the church service and vigorously sang hymns with the Munger Place Methodist Church Choir (Weekly, Sunday, WFAA, Dallas, TX, 1928).

22678 Munhall, Grace. Pianist (WJAS, Pittsburgh, PA, 1935).

22679 Muni, Scott. DJ (*The Sandman*, WJBO, Baton Rouge, LA, 1952).

22680 Municipal Instrumental Trio. Pianist Herman Neuman directed the instrumental trio that also included violinist William Holzberg and flutist Alfiere Pierno (WNYC, New York, NY, 1925).

22681 *Municipal Traffic Court.* Actual Chicago traffic cases were broadcast in an effort to promote safety and reduce traffic accidents. Judge John Gutknecht presided (WBBM, Chicago, IL, 1936).

22682 Munn, Frank. Popular tenor Munn sang under the name Paul Oliver on *The Palmolive Hour* (NBC, New York, 1927). He formerly was a member of the Rudd Light Opera Group (NBC, New York, NY, 1928–1929).

22683 Munn, Robert. Organist (WGR, Buffalo, NY, 1923).

22684 Munnerlyn, Mildred. Singer (WFAA, Dallas, TX, 1929).

22685 Munoz, Margarita. COM-HE (KTXN, Austin, TX, 1956).

22686 Munro, Florence Luedeke. COM-HE (WMBD, Peoria, IL, 1951–1954).

22687 Munro [Munroe], Hal. Leader (*Hal Munro Orchestra*, instr. mus. prg., WOW, Omaha, NE, 1934; CBS, 1936).

22688 Munro, Jim Lee. DJ (KVOM, Morrilton, AR, 1955).

22689 Munro, Margaret. Pianist (WHAS, Louisville, KY, 1923).

22690 Munro, Red. DJ (*The Record Rack* and the *Night Owl Club*, WCOG, Greensboro, NC, 1948; *Fun Dial*, WTMA, Charleston, SC, 1949; *Record Rack* and *The Night Owl Club*, WCOG, Greensboro, NC, 1950).

22691 Munsch, Louise. COM-HE (WES, St. Louis, MO, 1949).

22692 Munsell, James. Violinist (WLW, Cincinnati, OH, 1925).

22693 Munson, Beulah Beach (Mrs. Henderson Van Surdan). Concert singer (WGB, Buffalo, NY, 1928).

22694 Munster, Elena. Soprano (WRR, Dallas, TX, 1926).

22695 Munyan, Harry. News analyst (*The Rambler*, WIOD, Miami, FL, 1948).

22696 Mura, Corinna. Spanish vocalist (*Carinna Mura*, vcl. mus. prg., WOR, Newark, NJ, 1935–1936–1937). Mura was billed as an "exotic songstress."

22697 Muralov, Eugene. Newscaster (KWBU, Corpus Christi, TX, 1945).

22698 *Murder and Mr. Malone.* Frank Lovejoy and Frances Robinson played the roles of a smart detective and his loyal secretary, who successfully trapped the bad guys each week on the program sponsored by Guild Wines. The program was written by Miss Craig Rice, well known for her mystery novels. The producer was Bill Rousseau. Tom Collins, William Conrad, Betty Lou Gerson, Frank Graham and Pete Leeds were also in the cast. Dick Aurant's orchestra supplied the music. Art Gilmore was the announcer (30 min., Saturday, 9:30–10:00 P.M. NBC-Blue, 1947).

22699 *Murder at Midnight.* The syndicated dramatic series presented eerie tales of the supernatural. The exciting show premiered on May 1, 1950. The first story was "The Dead Hand" with Betty Caine, Barry Hopkins, Barry Kroeger and Frank Readick. Organ music was provided by Charles Paul (30 min., Syndicated on Various Stations, 1950).

22700 *Murder by Experts.* Mystery writer Dickson Carr was the first host and narrator on the sustaining mystery program. Each week a guest expert told his favorite mystery story and it would be dramatized. Cast members included Cameron Andrews, Frank Behrens, Ian Martin, Byrna Raeburn, Lawson Zerbe, Ann Shepherd (Scheindel Kalish), Ralph Camargo and Bill Zuckert. Robert A. Arthur and David Kogan were the show's producer and director. Music was supplied by Emerson Buckley. After Carr left the show, the other host-narrators who followed him were Brett Halliday and Alfred Hitchcock (30 min., Monday,9:00–9:30 P.M., MBS, 1949).

22701 *Murder Will Out.* William Gargan and Eddie Marr starred as Chief of Homicide Inspector Burke and his assistant, Detective Nolan, on the unusual combination mystery and quiz program. After the mystery was dramatized, four contestants from the studio audience were asked to identify the murderer. If they answered correctly, they were awarded a Gold Detective Certificate certifying that they were expert amateur detectives. The program was sponsored by the Ranier Brewing Company of San Francisco and Los Angeles. Larry Keating was the program's announcer. (30 min., ABC, 1946).

22702 Murdoch, Virginia. Soprano (WRR, Dallas, TX, 1926).

22703 Murdock, Alice. Soprano (KTAB, Oakland, CA, 1928).

22704 Murdock, Charlie. Sportscaster (WRVA, Richmond, VA, 1956). DJ (*The Top Forty Show*, WQAM, Miami, FL, 1960).

22705 Murdock, Edith. COM-HE (*Zales' Bridal Consultant*, KBST, Big Spring, TX, 1949).

22706 Murdock, (Mrs.) Henry. Violinist (Army Radio Station, Fort Wood, Bedloe Island, NY, 1922).

22707 Murdock, Kermit. Actor Murdock appeared on *Columbia Presents Corwin*, *Lorenzo Jones* and *Under Arrest.*

22708 Murdock, (Mrs.) W. Pianist Murdock was a member with Ivan Strough of a dual piano team (WGY, Schenectady, NY, 1923).

22709 Murley, James E. Sportscaster (WBZ, Boston, MA, 1926).

22710 Murphey, Josephine. COM-HE (WCOR, Lebanon, TN, 1956).

22711 Murphree, Jack. DJ (*Strictly Informal*, WOMI, Owensboro, KY, 1952–1956).

22712 Murphree, Leon. DJ (*Morning Percolator*, WKUL, Cullman, AL, 1952; WFMH, Cullman, AL, 1954).

22713 Murphy, Bill. Newscaster (*Shell News Reporter*, WGBS, Miami, FL, 1947).

22714 Murphy, Bob. DJ (*The Bob Murphy Show*, WJBK , Detroit, MI, 1948). Sportscaster (*Sports Column of the Air*, WJR, Detroit, MI, 1948).

22715 Murphy, Bob. DJ (*Hi Neighbor*, WJMR, New Orleans, LA, 1948).

22716 Murphy, C.T. COM-HE (KELT, Electra, TX, 1951).

22717 Murphy, David. Newscaster (WKNY, Kingston, NY, 1941).

22718 Murphy, Doris. COM-HE (KMA, Shenandoah, IA, 1956).

22719 Murphy, Ed. DJ (*The Ed Murphy Show* and *Platter Party*, WSYR, Syracuse, NY, 1947; *Timekeeper*, WSYR, 1949–1960).

22720 Murphy, Edward. Announcer (KFI, Los Angeles, CA and KFWB, Hollywood, CA, 1925).

22721 Murphy, Ella. Miss Murphy broadcast weekly book reviews (KMA, Shenandoah, IA, 1928–1930).

22722 Murphy, Florence. Newscaster (WCCO, Minneapolis–St. Paul, MN, 1940).

22723 Murphy, Howard and Herbert Rodgers. Harmonica duo (KFSG, Los Angeles, CA, 1925).

22724 Murphy, Jimmy. Newscaster (*World News*, WBYS, Canton, OH, 1948).

22725 Murphy, John. Newscaster (WTOL, Toledo, OH, 1938).

22726 Murphy, Louise. COM-HE (WQUA, Moline, IL, 1951).

22727 Murphy, Lambert. Tenor on the *Maxwell Coffee Hour* (WJZ, New York, NY, 1927).

22728 Murphy, Margaret. COM-HE (WCMC, Wildwood, NJ, 1954).

22729 Murphy, Mickey. Newscaster (KFPL, Dublin, TX, 1939). DJ (*Cool School*, KWAP, Ft. Worth, TX, 1960).

22730 Murphy, Orlando J. Announcer (KUT, Austin, TX, 1927).

22731 Murphy, Pat. Director-actor Murphy worked on *Girl Alone* (actor), *Jack Armstrong* (director), *Midstream* (actor) and *Silver Eagle, Mountie* (actor).

22732 Murphy, Robert Leo "Bob." Sportscaster (KSTP, St. Paul–Minneapolis, MN, 1937). Newscaster (KSTP, 1940–1942).

22733 Murphy, Thelma. Organist (WLW, Cincinnati, OH, 1929).

22734 Murphy, Walter. Newscaster (WINN, Louisville, KY, 1945).

22735 Murphy, William. Newscaster (WGBS, Miami, FL, 1948).

22736 *Murphy Barnyard Jamboree.* Murphy Products sponsored the weekly CW music show that featured the Prairie Ramblers; the Hilltoppers; Otto and the Novelodeons; the Winnie, Lou and Sally vocal group; the WLS Quartet; and comic Pat Buttram (30 min., 9:00–9:30 P.M. CST, WLS, Chicago, IL, 1938).

22737 Murr, Emma. Contralto (WCOH, New York, NY, 1932).

22738 Murray, Alcibia. COM-HE (WUST, Bethesda, MD, 1954).

22739 Murray, Arthur. Dance master Murray broadcast radio dancing lessons (WDAR, Philadelphia, PA, 1924 and WHO, Des Moines, IA, 1924). His programs also appeared on many other stations.

22740 Murray, Billy. Popular comic singing recording star (WEAF, New York, NY, 1925; WJZ, New York, NY, 1927).

22741 Murray, Dick. Murray broadcast market and stock reports (WFAA, Dallas, TX, 1928).

22742 Murray, Don. Newscaster (WAZL, Hazleton, PA, 1937, 1946). Sportscaster (WAZL, 1946; *Sports Chat*, WAZL, 1947; *Spotlight on Sports*, WDBJ, Roanoke, VA, 1948–1949; *Sports Review*, WDBJ, 1950–1951; *Sportslants*, WDBJ, 1952–1955; WAZL, 1956).

22743 Murray, Dub. DJ (*Downbeat*, KLUE, Longview, TX, 1960).

22744 Murray, Edith. Singer (*Edith Murray*, vcl. mus. prg., CBS, 1934).

22745 Murray, Estelle Swearingen. Murray broadcast stories for children (KFBK, Sacramento, CA, 1925).

22746 Murray, Franny. Sportscaster (WIBG, Philadelphia, PA, 1944–1946; *Sporting Page*, WIBG, 1947–1948, WPEN, Philadelphia, PA, 1949).

22747 Murray, George. DJ (*Make Believe Ballroom*, KECK, Odessa, TX, 1955).

22748 Murray, (Mrs.) H.M. Violinist (KLDS, Independence, MO, 1926).

22749 Murray, Hal. DJ (*Murray-Go-Round*, WKAT, Miami Beach, FL, 1947; *Murray-Go-Round*, KLIF, Dallas, TX, 1948; *Sweet Corn Serenade*, WSKY, Asheville, NC, 1952; WLOS, Asheville, NC, 1954; WKAT, 1955).

22750 Murray, J.K. Tenor (WBZ, Boston-Springfield, MA, 1924–1925).

22751 Murray, Jack. Leader (Jack Murray's Italian Village Orchestra, KFI, Los Angeles, CA, 1926).

22752 Murray, James. Tenor (WEBH, Chicago, IL, 1926).

22753 Murray, James. Baritone (KPLA, Los Angeles, CA, 1928).

22754 Murray, James. Newscaster (WWON, Woonsocket, RI, 1948). Sportscaster (WWON, 1948; WBKA, Brockton, MA, 1949).

22755 Murray, James "Jim." Sportscaster (WCAE, Pittsburgh, PA, 1939–1941).

22756 Murray, Johnny. Newscaster (KFI, Los Angeles, CA, 1944).

22757 Murray, Lee. COM-HE (WJR, Detroit, MI, 1960).

22758 Murray, Lyn. Leader (*Lyn Murray Orchestra*, instr. mus. prg., CBS, 1936, 1939).

22759 Murray, Mal. DJ (WNAX, Yankton, SD, 1945).

22760 Murray, Margaret. Contralto (WOOD, Grand Rapids, MI, 1926).

22761 Murray, Maude. Contralto (WNAC, Boston, MA, 1925).

22762 Murray, Michael. Newscaster (WCBM, Baltimore, MD, 1946).

22763 Murray, Norine. Singer of Irish songs (WOC, Davenport, IA, 1928).

22764 Murray, Phil. DJ (WSBA, York, PA, 1955).

22765 Murray, Rachel Nell. Guitarist (WSM, Nashville, TN, 1928).

22766 Murray, Rae. Leader (*Rae Murray Orchestra*, instr. mus. prg., KFEL, Denver, CO, 1934).

22767 Murray, Rita. COM-HE (*The Voice of Friendship*, 15 min., Twice Weekly, 3 California CBS stations, 1942). Miss Murray entered radio in 1929 and for several years was the investment counselor of the air for several CBS Pacific Coast stations.

22768 Murray, Thomas "Tom." Newscaster (WHAM, Rochester, NY, 1938–1941, 1946).

22769 Murrell, Glenda. COM-HE (KDBS, Alexandria, LA, 1955).

22770 Murrie, David H. Newscaster (WTBO, Cumberland, MD, 1938–1941).

22771 Murrow, Edward (Egbert) R. "Ed." Distinguished news commentator on CBS, 1941–1948, Murrow first gained fame with his World War II Sunday afternoon (1:30–1:45 P.M.) broadcasts from London and his famous exaggerated pause trademark opening, "This — is London."

Murrow changed his name to Edward and joined CBS as director of talks and education in 1935. In 1937, he was appointed the network's European News Director. Upon arriving in London, Murrow played down intellectual content in programming, choosing, instead, to emphasize what the "people want" (Fang, 1977, p. 307). At this stage of his broadcast career, drama and human interest were already his goals. He saw the need and value of radio correspondents reporting daily from the major European capitals.

After a distinguished broadcasting career at CBS and losing a corporate power struggle there, Murrow left to become director of the USIA (United States Information Agency) during the Kennedy administration. Among his last radio productions was *Hear It Now*, jointly produced with Fred W. Friendly. This program sought to bring the actual sounds of news events to radio. Unfortunately, what the program usually brought to the microphone was only a series of "talking head" experts and politicians. *See* ***Hear It Now***.

Murrow left lasting impressions on broadcast news programming — both positive and negative — that still are found today in radio and television. It has been said that he defined radio-TV broadcast journalism with the intelligence, drama, human interest, ideology and the chill of corporate culture he brought into broadcast news departments. Ironically, some of the fine broadcast newsmen that Murrow ("Murrow's boys") brought to CBS to make CBS radio news the excellent department it was, eventually left or retired from the network with bitterness, frustration and disappointment about what the broadcasting news business had become (Cloud and Olson, 1997, pp. 390–393).

Bob Edwards, host of National Public Radio's *Morning Host* program, described Murrow's significant contributions to broadcast journalism in his book, *Edward R. Murrow and the Birth of Broadcast Journalism* (John Wiley, 2004). Although the book is a valuable contribution, its title is somewhat misleading since it contains the phrase of "Birth of Broadcast Journalism," without a mention in the text of such pioneer radio broadcasters as Floyd Gibbons, Lowell Thomas, Edwin C. Hill, H.V. Kaltenborn, H.R. Baukhage or Quincy Howe. Despite the oversight, Edwards' book contributes to an understanding of Murrow's significant influences upon contemporary broadcast journalism.

22772 **Murrow, Janet.** (CBS, World War II era). Janet Murrow, the wife of Edward R. Murrow broadcast feature news programs during World War II on such topics as "Christmas Shopping in London." Usually her broadcasts were preceded by a man giving the "hard" news. He work ended just prior to the Allied D-Day invasion.

22773 **Murry, Patty.** COM-HE (KRAL, Rawlins, WY, 1960).

22774 **Murton, Harriet.** Soprano (WTAB, Oakland, CA, 1925).

22775 **Musche, Marguerite.** Soprano (KFWB, Hollywood, CA, 1927).

22776 **Musche, Ruth.** COM-HE (WOTW, Nashua, NH, 1949).

22777 **Muse, Orene.** COM-HE (WJBO, Baton Rouge, LA, 1949).

22778 **Musgrave, Carol.** Music reviews (KFWB, Hollywood, CA, 1925).

22779 ***Music All America Loves to Hear.*** Singer Marion Talley and a concert orchestra were featured on the good music program that presented opera arias and light opera selections, along with favorites from the concert repertoire (15 min., Friday, 9:30–9:45 P.M. CST, NBC-Red, 1936).

22780 ***Music and American Youth.*** The unique weekly broadcast presented the performances of American public school children's orchestras, bands and choruses (30 min., Sunday, 9:30–10:00 A.M., NBC-Red, 1936).

22781 ***Music and Moondog.*** Louis "Moondog" Hardin was a blind, robed New York City street musician, who usually wore a Viking helmet. He was joined on his program by Jim Coyans. Moondog beat out rhythms on his various percussion instruments, discussed his philosophy and read his prose. Earl Cobb and Bud Brandt wrote the strange, but interesting, local program (15 min., Sunday, 10:15–10:30 P.M. WNEW, New York, NY, 1951).

22782 ***(The) Music and Musings of Dr. Mu.*** Sage comments by a "mysterious Chinese philosopher," not identified, and soothing music were the main ingredients of the popular network program (CBS, 1928). The "Chinese philosopher" was one of early radio's pioneers. Dr. Mu's tone was not always philosophical, as an early example from 1922 in poetic form illustrates (*Radio News*, June, 1922, p. 1059):

The right path is near
says Mencius
Yet men seek it afar off,
The right receiver is here—
—the Glebe CR-5
The wise radioist need seek no further.

22783 ***(The) Music Appreciation Hour.*** Professor Hywel C. Rowland, Head of the Music Department of the University of North Dakota, played recordings of the classics and supplied his commentary on the educational program originating from the university's radio station (KFJM, Grand Forks, ND, 1940s).

22784 ***Music by Al Goodman.*** Maestro Goodman conducted a 17-piece orchestra on his weekly music show (15 min., Sunday, 4:50–5:00 P.M. CST, NBC-Red, 1935).

22785 ***Music by Gershwin.*** The music of distinguished American composer, George Gershwin, was featured on the program. His music was performed by tenor Dick Robertson, sopranos Rhoda Arnold and Lucille Peterson and a male sextet. Harry Von Zell was the program's host. The music was provided by the Louis Katzman Orchestra (30 min., Sunday, 6:00–6:30 P.M., CBS, 1935).

22786 ***Music by Rosemary.*** DJ Rosemary Stanger wrote and conducted her show that featured recorded music and intelligent commentary (15 min., Monday through Friday, 6:45–7:00 P.M., CWT, WLS, Chicago, IL, 1942).

22787 ***Music Everyone Loves.*** Honey Krust Bakery sponsored the program, first broadcast in 1943. The program featured hymns sung by a trio consisting of Clarence Locke, John Frederick and Don Cavins accompanied by Marion Locke on the pipe organ. Frank Berger was the announcer (30 min., Saturday, 5:00–5:30 P.M. WAVE, Louisville, KY, 1947).

22788 ***Music for a Half Hour.*** Frank J. McCarthy produced and narrated the sustaining program that featured music from light operas and musical comedies. The regular cast included pianist Al Fanelli and the Emerson Buckley Orchestra. Different guest stars such as operatic tenor Mario Berini appeared weekly (30 min., Sunday, 3:00–3:30 P.M., WOR, Newark, NJ, 1949).

22789 ***Music from the Heart of America.*** Falstaff Brewing Company sponsored the entertaining music show originating from Chicago. Singers Jack Haskell and Anne Hershey performed to the music of Joseph Gallichio's Orchestra. John Holtman was the announcer (30 min., Weekly, 8:30–9:00 P.M., NBC, 1948).

22790 ***Music Guild Program.*** The good music program featured various musicians such as composer-pianist, Earl Lawrence (NBC, 1935).

22791 ***Music Magic.*** Joan Blaine was the program's narrator. She also performed readings of various prose selections. Music was performed by tenor Charles Sears, Joan and the Escorts vocal group and the Harry Kogen Orchestra (30 min., Thursday, 9:30–10:00 P.M., NBC-Blue, 1936). An earlier version, broadcast on Saturday afternoon, had featured soprano Ruth Lyon and tenor Cyril Pitts and an unidentified orchestra (30 min., Saturday, 2:30–3:00 P.M., NBC-Blue, 1935).

22792 ***(The) Music Man.*** Karl Bonawitz played the organ and piano on the music show sponsored by the F.A. North Piano Company. Bill Lang was the program announcer (15 min., Tuesday, 1:30–1:45 P.M., KYW, Pittsburgh, PA, 1938).

22793 **Music Masters.** Popular twenty-five piece concert orchestra (WBAP, Dallas, TX, 1928–1930).

22794 **Music on Radio.** From radio's earliest days when its "cat's whisker" crystal receivers, relatively speaking, provided only fair-to-poor quality sound, music has been one of radio's most popular elements. Literally, thousands of amateurs, semi-professionals and professional singers and musicians appeared before its microphones and filled the air with music of great variety and quality. All kinds of music filled the broadcast schedules of early stations and despite crystal set reception and varying performance quality, the audience loved what they heard.

Early popular singers such as the Silver Masked Tenor Joseph M. White and Jessica Dragonette led the way for the talented singers who soon followed such as Rudy Vallee, Bing Crosby, Russ Columbo, the Street Singer and Kate Smith. The Coon-Sanders Nighthawk Orchestra from Kansas City; the Cliquot Club Eskimos Orchestra merrily playing from New York; and the country music performers on the *Grand Ole Opry* and the *National Barn Dance* entertained millions each week.

The Atwater Kent Hour, Metropolitan Opera weekly broadcasts and the KYW broadcasts of the Chicago Civic Opera Company were some examples of the distinguished programming early radio brought into the home [*See* ***Atwater Kent Hour*** *and* **Opera**.]. Semi-classical favorites, operettas and musical theater selections were broadcast by the *Chicago Theater of the Air*, the *Voice of Firestone* and the *Railroad Hour*. Lighter fare was available to listeners on *The American Album of Familiar Music*, the *Coronation Hour* and the *Manhattan Merry-Go-Round* programs [*See* ***Chicago Theater of the Air, Voice of Firestone, Railroad Hour, American Album of Familiar Music, Coronation Hour*** *and* ***Manhattan Merry-Go-Round***.]. Popular big band music was supplied by the *Victory Parade of Spotlight Bands* and the *One Night Stand* programs, on which virtually all the nation's most popular bands were presented [*See* ***The Victory Parade of Spotlight Bands*** *and* **Radio in Wartime**.]. Country-western music programs were also plentiful [*See* ***Grand Ole Opry, National Barn Dance*** *and* **Country-Western (CW) Music on Radio**.], as was good classical music appreciation programming by Dr. Walter Damrosch and Arturo Toscanini [*See* **Walter Damrosch** *and* ***The NBC Symphony***.]. Appreciation of jazz and the blues was presented tongue-in-cheek by the *Chamber Music Society of Lower Basin Street* program. Rhythm, blues and gospel performers were also plentiful [*See* ***The Chamber Music Society of Lower Basin Street*** *and* **Black Radio**.]. All this music and more came into American homes day and night. Listeners enjoyed it and asked for more.

In radio's early years, most music was performed "live." As years went by, however, DJs and recorded music virtually replaced all "live" musicians and singers. *See* **Transcriptions**.

22795 ***Music Over Your Radio.*** Atwater Kent sponsored the series of programs that demonstrated how different sections of a "symphony orchestra combine to form a composite tonal entity" (NBC-Red, 1929).

22796 ***Music Shop.*** In 1925, Andy Woolfries inaugurated this show that was broadcast at 7:15 A.M. and ran until 9:00 A.M. Woolfries talked in an informal manner with a pleasant conversational style about the weather between the classical and semi-classical recordings he played. Woolfries' original theme was Liadov's "A Musical Snuff Box." After Woolfries left WOI in 1941, a number of announcers took over the program. Today (1997) the program is conducted by WOI's program director, Doug Brown (WOI, Ames, IA, 1926–1997).

22797 ***Music That Endures.*** The sustaining musical concert program was written by Henry Barbour and produced by Lewis James. It replaced *The Affairs of Tom, Dick and Harry* program. Henry Walker conducted the orchestra. Guests such as Attillio Bagiore performed weekly. The announcer was Pierre Andre (30 min., Monday, 9:30–10:00 P.M., WGN, Chicago, IL, 1942).

22798 ***Music That Satisfies.*** Singer Ruth Etting hosted the early variety show, sponsored by Chesterfield cigarettes, featuring baritone Alex Gray, United Press sportswriter Henry L. McLemore and Nat Shilkret's 35-piece orchestra. Leona Hagarth was the announcer (30 min., Monday through Saturday, 10:30–10:45 P.M., CBS, 1932). An earlier version of *Music that Satisfies* had presented the Boswell Sisters singing group, "The Street Singer" Arthur Tracy and Norman Brokenshire as the program's announcer. Shilkret's orchestra was a regular feature (NBC, 1932).

In 1944, the program reappeared on CBS once more with a music format. This time the Paul Barron Orchestra was featured with vocalists Monica Lewis and Harry Prime. In 1945, *Music that Satisfies* starred singer Johnny Johnston, a tall, handsome baritone, who in the early 1930's had played the guitar and sang with the Art Kassel band. Chesterfield was still the show's sponsor (15 min., Tuesday, Wednesday and Thursday, 7:15–7:30 P.M., CBS, 1945).

22799 ***Music Till Past Midnight.*** Al Bueltner was the DJ on the popular show (120 min., Monday through Saturday, 10:30–12:30 A.M., 1947).

22800 ***Music While You Dial.*** Trumpet virtuoso Dave Glickstein and other talented musicians were featured on the music show (WOR, Newark, NJ, 1925).

22801 ***Music You Love.*** The Pittsburgh Symphony Orchestra conducted by Antonio Modarelli and various guest artists appeared weekly on the good music program sponsored by the Pittsburgh Plate Glass Company (45 min., Sunday, 2:00–2:45 P.M., CBS, 1936).

22802 ***Musical Almanac.*** "The old almanac explorer," not otherwise identified, supplied information on various topics on the entertaining show. Music and singing was provided by Pat Petterson, Art Janes, Al Rice, Fritz Meissner, Sally Foster, Joe Fredkin, Jack Daly and Lou Klatt (15 min., Tuesday and Thursday, 12:45–1:00 P.M. CST, WLS, Chicago, IL, 1936).

22803 ***Musical Americana.*** Tenor Clyde Barrie and sopranos Ruby Elzy and Vivian Collier sang the songs on the special program devoted to the "music of and about the American Negro" (CBS, 1937).

22804 **(The) Musical Chefs.** The *Musical Chefs* were the singing team of Don Traveline and Max Freedman (WBAP, Fort Worth, TX, 1928; WCAU, Philadelphia, PA, 1929–1930).

22805 ***Musical Clock.*** Halloween Martin, one the earliest and best female announcers ever to conduct a morning program, did her thing for WBBM (Chicago, IL) from the late 1920's until well into the 1930's. In 1937, for example, she was known as the "Musical Clock Girl." On her first popular early morning program, she played records and supplied time and weather reports (KYW, Chicago, IL, 1929). *See* **Martin, Halloween** *and* **Gender Discrimination**.

22806 ***Musical Clock.*** Bill O'Toole, a great Baltimore favorite, conducted the early morning DJ show. He played records and read the news. He also had a popular segment called "Uncle Bill and Snowball," on which he played both the roles of a kindly old man and that of Snowball, a small Black boy. The brief comedy segment was always concluded with the playing of a recording of "Tin Pan Parade" sung by Vaughn de Leath. Brent Gunts recalls that de Leath's version was a particularly moving ("tear-jerker") rendition. The "Uncle Bill and Snowball" segment was a regular feature broadcast late in each program to get children to brush their teeth (WCAO, Baltimore, MD, 1930s).

22807 ***Musical Clock.*** The Marshall Field department store sponsored the time, weather and music show conducted by Marie Auer (120 min., Monday through Saturday, 7:00–9:00 A.M., WBBM, Chicago, IL, 1936).

22808 ***Musical Clock.*** Don Kelley ran the musical clock show for Omaha, Nebraska, listeners (KOIL, Omaha, NE, 1937).

22809 ***(The) Musical Clock Girl.*** Angela Warde, known as "New York's Sweetest Voice on Radio," played records and provided the time and weather news (WINS, New York, NY, 1932).

22810 ***Musical Comedy Memories.*** The nostalgic program was written by announcer Bob Brown. It featured singer Belle Forbes Cutter in 1927 and tenor Chauncey Parsons in a later version (15 min., Sunday, WBBM-NBC, Chicago, IL, 1927).

22811 ***Musical Cruiser.*** Pat Barnes hosted a mythical radio cruise with the music of the Guy Lombardo Orchestra (30 min., Wednesday, 10:00–10:30 P.M., WEAF-Red, 1934).

22812 ***Musical Diary.*** Contralto Gale Page, tenor Clark Dennis and organist Jesse Crawford performed on the weekly music program (15 min., Sunday, 3:00–3:15 P.M. CST, NBC-Red, 1935).

22813 ***Musical Footnotes.*** Footsaver Shoes sponsored the half-hour music program with soprano Vivian Della Chiesa, tenor Franz Imhof and the Ralph Ginsburgh String Ensemble (15 min., Sunday, 11:30–11:45 A.M., CBS, 1935).

22814 ***Musical Foursome.*** A program of semi-classical music (15 min., Friday, 6:00–6:15 P.M., CBS, 1930).

22815 ***Musical Headliners.*** Frank Tours conducted the orchestra for the talented singers that regularly performed on the music show. The performers included tenor James Melton, soprano Helen Stiles, the Revelers Quartet and the Pickens Sisters (30 min., Sunday, 7:30–8:00 P.M., CBS, 1935).

22816 ***Musical Kilowatts.*** Baritone Russell McIntryre, who sounded something like Bing Crosby, pianist Jane Bartlett, organist Jack Phipps and guitarist Don White entertained on the program sponsored by the Duke Power Company. The announcer was Clair Shadwell (15 min., Monday, 11:45–12:00 noon, WBT, Charlotte, NC, 1938).

22817 ***Musical Klass.*** The American Tobacco Company sponsored Kay Kyser and his band on the program, a forerunner of Kyser's *Kollege of Musical Knowledge*, which was to come later (45 min., Tuesday, 8:00–8:45 P.M., MBS, 1938). *See* ***Kay Kyser's Kollege of Musical Knowledge***.

22818 ***Musical Melodrama.*** The musical variety program was broadcast weekly (30 min., Tuesday, 9:00–9:30 P.M., NBC-Red, 1929).

22819 ***Musical Memories.*** *Musical Memories* was a variety show that was a forerunner of *Welcome Valley*. *See* ***Welcome Valley***.

22820 ***Musical Mirth Makers.*** Boston listeners enjoyed the music and humor provided on the program by such performers as pianist George Benson, saxophonist Austin Rosmer and violinist-vocalist Bert Dolan (WBZ, Boston, MA, 1926).

22821 ***Musical Moments.*** Sponsored by Chevrolet, the music show was hosted by Hugh Conrad, who later became famous as Westbrook Van Voorhis. The transcribed program featured the music of David Rubinoff and vocalists Virginia Rea and Jan Peerce (15 min., Thursday, 9:00–9:15 P.M., WMCA, New York, NY, 1935–1936).

22822 ***Musical Mountaineers.*** CW mus. prg. (WFBR, Baltimore, MD, 1939).

22823 **Musical Musketeers Orchestra.** California band directed by Walter Beban (60 min., 11:00 P.M. to Midnight, Saturday, NBC-Pacific Network, 1929).

22824 ***Musical Newsy.*** The orchestras of Tommy Tucker and Seegar Ellis provided the music on the transcribed quarter-hour show (15 min., Transcribed on Various Stations, 1938).

22825 **Musical Nighthawks.** Jazz band directed by Harry Moll (KFBK, Sacramento, CA, 1927).

22826 ***Musical Reveries.*** Orson Welles contributed dramatic readings to the variety program that also featured tenor Stuart Churchill and the Ken Woods Orchestra (CBS, 1936).

22827 ***Musical Revue.*** Music program with tenor Ben Alley and organist Ann Leaf (Wednesday, 3:15–3:30 P.M., CBS, 1932).

22828 ***(A) Musical Romance.*** Romantic elements on the program were supplied by tenor Don Mario Alvarez and the music of Harry Jackson's Orchestra. Jimmy Fiddler provided gossip about the movies and their stars (NBC-Red, 1934).

22829 ***Musical Round-Up Program.*** The pleasant CW music show featured such performers as the Kentucky Girls (Alma and Winona "Jo" Taylor) on WLS (Chicago, IL,1937).

22830 ***Musical Steelmakers.*** Employees from the Wheeling Steel Corporation were the performers featured on the weekly program that originated on WWVA (Wheeling, WV), before it become a network feature. The hosts on the show were Lois Mae Nolte and John Winchell. Regular performers included the Singing Millmen, soprano Sara Rehm and the Old Timer (MBS, NBC, ABC, 1938–1944).

22831 ***Musical Steeplechase.*** Joseph Cherniavsky created the musical quiz on which each contestant was given the name of a different race horse (30 min., MBS, 1930s).

22832 ***(A) Musical Toast.*** Vocalists Jerry Cooper and Sally Singer backed by an unidentified orchestra performed on the weekly music show (CBS, 1936).

22833 ***Musical Travelog Program.*** Pianist J. Van Cleft Cooper was featured on the program that contained musical selections and travel information. Deane H. Dickason was the announcer (KPO, San Francisco, CA, 1926).

22834 ***Musical Variety.*** The Paul Whiteman Orchestra, comic Judy Canova and tenor Frank Parker were featured on the variety show (30 min., Weekly, CBS, 1935).

22835 **Musick, Helen.** Dramatic soprano (WMOX, St. Louis, MO, 1926).

22836 **Musing, Burt.** Announcer (KDKA, Pittsburgh, PA, 1925).

22837 **Muskens, H.** Dutch tenor (KMOX, St. Louis, MO, 1926).

22838 **Musselman, Blossom.** Pianist (KYW, Chicago, IL, 1922).

22839 **Mustard, Fred.** Newscaster (WKMO, Kokomo, IN, 1945).

22840 **Mustarde, Herbert.** Baritone (WJY, New York, NY, 1925).

22841 **Mustin, Brent.** Dialect monologs and songs (KDKA, Pittsburgh, PA, 1922).

22842 **Muth, Homer.** Trombonist (WHAS, Louisville, KY, 1923).

22843 **Mutual Stores Male Quartet.** Vocal group consisting of tenor Orrin Leon Padel; tenor Ray B. Nealan; baritone Francis P. Watts; and bass Charles L. Delmar. Alice Gray Padel was the group's accompanist (KTAB, Oakland, CA, 1925).

22844 **Muzio, Claudio.** Soprano (NBC, 1929).

22845 **Muzzy, James "Jim."** Sportscaster (*Today's Sports Today* and *Sports Whirl*, WHBC, Canton, OH, 1946–1956).

22846 **Muzzy, Ray.** Leader (Ray Muzzy's Carter Lake Club Orchestra, WOAW, Omaha, NE, 1925).

22847 ***My Book House Story Time.*** The children's program was conducted by an unidentified performer (15 min., Monday, Wednesday and Friday, 5:45–6:00 P.M., CBS, 1930).

22848 ***My Diary.*** Patricia Ann Manners wrote the daytime dramatic serial (WBBM, Chicago, IL, 1938).

22849 ***My Favorite Husband.*** Lucille Ball starred in the funny situation comedy based on Isabel Scott Rorick's novel, *Mr. and Mrs. Cugat*. The show essentially was the basis for Miss Ball's classic television show, *I Love Lucy*, for it was here that she portrayed a zany housewife. The show's cast included: Lucille Ball, Lee Bowman, Richard Denning, Gale Gordon and Ruth Perrott. Jess Oppenheimer was the writer-director. Bob Carroll, Jr. and Madalyn Pugh assisted Oppenheimer with the writing (CBS, 1948).

22850 ***My Friend Irma.*** Motion picture star Marie Wilson was the "dumb, good-hearted blonde" on the sustaining situation comedy. Her friend, played by Cathy Lewis, was often driven to distraction by her antics. The writers of the funny show were Stanley Adams, Parke Levy and Roland MacLane. The director was Cy Howard. Sound effects were produced by James Murphy. The show's announcers included Frank Bingman, Johnny Jacobs and Wendell Niles. Music was supplied by Lud Gluskin's orchestra with vocals by the Sportsmen Quartet. The cast included: Joan Banks, John Brown, Hans Conreid, Leif Erickson, Gloria Gordon, Cathy Lewis, Myra Marsh, Alan Reed (Teddy Bergman) and Marie Wilson (30 min., Friday, 10:30–11:00 P.M., CBS, 1947).

22851 ***My Good Life.*** Sam Taylor and Russell Beggs wrote and Wynn Wright produced and directed the situation comedy that contained many old jokes about hen-pecked husbands and women drivers. The fine acting cast included John Conte, Arlene Francis and Joe Bell (30 min., Friday, 9:30–10:00 P.M., NBC, 1949).

22852 ***My Little Margie.*** Making the transition from TV to radio, the situation comedy was sponsored by Philip Morris Cigarettes. It told the story of widower Verne Albright, played by Charles Farrell, as he tried to cope with the antics of a scatterbrained daughter in her twenties. Gale Storm played the title role of daughter, Margie Albright. Also in the cast of the funny comedy show were Verna Felton, Gil Stratton, Jr., Doris Singleton and Will Wright. Lud Gluskin's Orchestra supplied the music (30 min., Sunday, 8:30–9:00 P.M., CBS, 1952).

22853 ***My Name is Logan.*** Newscaster Arthur Van Horne talked to his audience in a folksy manner much in the style of Galen Drake about life and the current scene on his novel program (30 min., Sunday, 10:30–11:00 P.M., WOR, Newark, NJ, 1949).

22854 ***My Silent Partner.*** A sustaining situation comedy, *My Silent Partner* followed the actions of a small town girl, played by Faye Emerson, who moved to New York City. The funny problems she encountered were provided by such talented cast members as: Cameron Andrews, Ruth Gilbert, Harold Stone and Lyle Sudrow. Dick Dudley was the announcer (30 min., Thursday, 8:00–8:30 P.M., NBC, 1949).

22855 ***My Son Jeep.*** The half-hour weekly show concerned a small town doctor, a widower with a ten-year-old son and a thirteen-year-old daughter. The doctor's son, Jeep, caused most of his funny problems and tribulations . The program's cast included: Lynn Allen, Donald Cook, Martin Huston, John Lazah and Leona Powers. The announcer was Fred Collins. Walter Black and Bill Mendrek wrote and Dan Sutter directed the program. Music was supplied by John Geller (30 min., Sunday, 7:00–7:30 P.M., NBC, 1953). A later, 15-minute daily version of the program was broadcast in 1955. This time the cast included Bobby Alford, Cameron Andrews, Joyce Gordon, Joan Lazer, Paul McGrath and Leona Powers. Walter Black and Bill Mendrek once again wrote the show. Edwin Duerr was the producer-director. Gaylord Avery was the announcer (15 min., Monday through Friday, 8:00–8:15 P.M., CBS, 1955). This was another program that made a successful transition from TV to radio.

22856 **Myatt, (Mrs.) Herman.** Soprano (WSM, Nashville, TN, 1928).

22857 **Myberg, Gertrude.** COM-HE (KGHL, Billings, MT, 1957).

22858 **Myer, Dick.** DJ (*Schooltime*, WAGM, Presque Isle, ME, 1950).

22859 **Myer, Pauline.** Choral director, New Britain Normal School Glee Club, WTIC, Hartford, CT, 1925).

22860 **Myers, Denny.** Sportscaster (*Denny Myers Talks Football*, WEEI, Boston, MA, 1949).

22861 **Myers, Earl.** Sportscaster and sports play-by-play (KTHE, Thermopolis, WY, 1960).

22862 **Myers, Ed.** Leader (Ed Myers and his Peony Park Orchestra, WOAW, Omaha, NE, 1926).

22863 **Myers, Ed.** DJ (WCHL, Chapel Hill, NC, 1956).

22864 **Myers, Gene.** Newscaster (KLEE, Houston, TX, 1948). DJ (*KLEE Club*, KLEE, 1950).

22865 **Myers, Hubert.** DJ (WDAN, Danville, IL, 1947).

22866 **Myers, J. Clarence.** Newscaster (KYA, San Francisco, CA, 1937–1939).

22867 **Myers, Joe.** Newscaster (KOA, Denver, CO, 1938). Sportscaster (KOA, 1937–1940).

22868 **Myers, Kent.** Sportscaster (KSUB, Clay City, UT, 1956).

22869 **Myers, Pete.** DJ (WNEW, New York, NY, 1960).

22870 **Myers, Robert.** Newscaster (WMBH, Joplin, MO, 1944).

22871 **Myers, Uncle Tom.** Harmonica soloist Myers, who wore a white moustache and a full beard, was called by *Variety* "the best known harmonica player in the country" (KRFU, Columbia, MO, 1925).

22872 **Myers, Vic.** Leader (Vic Myers Melody Orchestra, WSB, Atlanta, GA, 1924).

22873 **Myers, Wayne.** Monologist (WIBO, Chicago, IL, 1926).

22874 **Myerson, Bess.** COM-HE (WABC, New York, NY, 1955).

22875 **Mylie, Meg.** Actress Mylie was in the cast of the *Wendy Warren and the News* daytime serial program.

22876 **Mylins [Mylus], Ella.** Lyric soprano (WEAF, New York, NY, 1924).

22877 Myra, Isabel Pirie. Chautauqua-lyceum lecturer on such topics as "Not Who You Are But What You Are" (WMAQ, Chicago, IL, 1922).

22878 *Myra Kingsley—Astrologer.* Astrologer Kingsley discussed astrological topics and interviewed motion picture stars and pointed out the events taking place in "their stars." Jean Paul King was the program announcer (15 min., Monday through Friday, 11:45–12:00 noon, MBS, 1938).

22879 Myric(k), Thelma. Soprano (KFWI, San Francisco, CA and KYA, San Francisco, CA, 1927).

22880 Myronoff, Boris. Concert pianist (KFI, Los Angeles, CA, 1927).

22881 *Myrt and Marge.* The title roles of the popular daytime serial were played by the program's writer, Myrtle Vail, and her daughter, Donna Damerel Fick. Although daytime serials frequently have tragedy as one their major elements, this one's first run ended tragically with the death of one of its principals. One of radio's most memorable daytime serials, *Myrt and Marge* went off the air in 1941 when Donna Damerel Fick died in childbirth.

Written by Myrtle Vail (Myrt), it began as an evening program before becoming a daytime serial in 1937. The story told of two show girls, Myrt Spear and her sister, Marge Minter. Myrt, the older sister, did her best to guide her sister through the many problems she faced in show business. Originally, the cast included: Ray Appleton, Cliff Arquette, Jackson Beck, Ed Begley, Alan Reed (Teddy Bergman), Cliff Bunston, Marjorie Crossland, Matt Crowley, Joseph Curtin, John C. Daly, Dorothy Day, Roger DeKoven, Alan Devitt, Arthur Elmer, Edith Evanson, Lucille Fenton, Donna Damerel Fick, Michael Fitzmaurice, Lucy Gillman, Ken Griffin, Vinton Hayworth, Ray Hedge, Wendell Holmes, Raymond Edward Johnson, Jeanne Juvelier, Reg Knorr, Joe Latham, Violet Le Claire, Sunda Love, Helen Mack, Warren Mills, Gene Morgan, Marie Nelson, Santos Ortega, Eleanor Rella, Dick Sanaver, Henry Saxe, Olan Soule, Maurice Tarplin, Henrietta Tedro, Betty Jane Tyler, Myrtle Vail, James Van Dyk, Robert Walker and Karl Way. The show's writers were Cliff Thomas and Myrtle Vail. Eddie House, Rosa Rio and John Winters were the organists. The directors were John Gunn and Lindsay MacHarrie. Andre Baruch, David Ross and Tom Shirley were the announcers.

The show returned in 1946 as a transcribed program broadcast by 40 stations. This version was directed by Myrtle Vail and Roy Hedge and produced by John Green. Some early segments of the later version were almost identical with the original program. In the later cast were Alice Goodkin, Vinton Hayworth, Ray Hedge and Alice Yourman. Andre Baruch was the program's announcer (15 min., Monday through Friday, Transcribed on Various Stations, 1946).

22882 Myrtil, Odette. French singer and orchestra leader, Odette Myrtil and Her Orchestra (NBC, 1931).

22883 Mytock, Ross D. Leader, Philippine Orchestra from the S.S. *Lone Star State* (WJZ, New York, NY, 1922).

22884 *(The) Mysteries of Paris.* This early mystery drama told the story of the pursuit by a daring American heiress and a titled Englishman, who was a member of the British Secret Service, of "The Octopus," a sinister, powerful leader of the Paris Underworld. The cast included Elsie Hitz, John McGovern and Agnes Moorehead. Music was produced by an orchestra directed by Billy Artzt (30 min., Monday, 9:30–10:00 P.M., CBS, 1932).

22885 Mysterious Duo. An unidentified "masked" singing team (WRR, Dallas, TX, 1926).

22886 (The) Mysterious Soprano of KHJ. Popular singer not otherwise identified.

22887 *(The) Mysterious Traveler.* Maurice Tarplin was the Mysterious Traveler, who each week invited listeners to take a train ride with him into the realm of the supernatural. Each half-hour program presented episodes that told of weird and terrifying events. At the end of each program, the Mysterious Traveler concluded with, "I take this train every week at this time." In addition to Tarplin, the program's cast included: Jackson Beck, Ed Begley, Shirley Blank, Lon Clark, Roger DeKoven, Bill Smith and Bill Zuckert. Jock MacGregor was the director. The creators and writers were Robert A. Arthur and David Kogan. Organist Doc Whipple and the orchestra of Al Pinella supplied the music. Jimmy Wallington was the announcer (30 min., Weekly, MBS, 1943–1952).

22888 *(The) Mystery Chef.* The mysterious culinary expert was John MacPherson. By 1946, his transcribed series of 280 recorded quarter-hour programs were broadcast by 28 stations. The popular show that gave women recipes and cooking tips afforded him an excellent opportunity to attract sponsors. The "mysterious one" enjoyed a long, successful radio career. His entire broadcast career extended from 1929 to 1948 on NBC-Red and NBC-Blue.

22889 *Mystery House.* The dramatic mystery-adventure series featured Agnes Moorehead. The announcer was Neil Enslen (30 min., Friday, 10:30–11:00 P.M., NBC-Red, 1930).

22890 *Mystery House.* The series of half-hour dramatized mysteries starred horror motion picture star Bela Lugosi who also hosted each show (MBS, 1951).

22891 *Mystery Is My Hobby.* Private investigator Barton Drake, played by Glenn Langan, found himself involved in crime each week as he prowled the streets and haunts of New York City. Since Drake was a private investigator, the program's title is not accurate. Rod O'Connor was the program's announcer (30 min., Weekly, MBS, 1945).

22892 *Mystery Tales.* The Marlin Fire Arms Company sponsored the dramatized series drawn from *True Mystery* magazine. Radio's pioneer acting troop, the WGY Players, provided good performances on these mysteries. The troop included: Eugene O'Haire, Marjorie Tyler, John Sheehan, Irma Lehmke, Alexander McDonald, Chester Vedder and John Allen (30 min., Sunday, 4:00–4:30 P.M., WGY, Schenectady, NY, 1936).

22893 *Mystery Theatre.* Inspector Mark Saber, played by Les Damon, was the leading character in the mystery-adventure series sponsored by Sterling Drug Company. Saber and his assistant solved crimes each week on the show written by Ken Field. Gene Patterson produced and Frank Papp directed the show. In addition to Les Damon, the cast included Joan Alexander, Walter Burke, Bob Hague, Luis Van Rooten and Santos Ortega (30 min., Wednesday, 9:30–10:00 P.M. ABC, 1953).

22894 (The) Mystery Three. A Chicago vocal trio that unfortunately still remains mysterious and unidentified (WEBH, Chicago, IL, 1928).

22895 *Mystery Without Murder.* The sustaining show with a clever concept program featured a tall, easy going detective, Peter Gentle, played by Luther Adler, who couldn't stand violence. When embroiled in the midst of a case, he often returned to his office to think while bowing his bass fiddle. Teri Kean was also in the cast of the unique program (30 min., Saturday, 10:00–10:30 P.M., NBC, 1947). The novel program was designed for the radio listener who wanted mystery without gore and homicide.

22896 *Mystic Nights of the Sea Friday Night Minstrel Show.* Gosden and Correll conducted the weekly radio minstrel show (WMAQ, Chicago, IL, 1936). *See* ***Amos 'n' Andy***.

22898 *N&W Imperial Quartet.* The Norfolk and Western Railroad sponsored the talented black gospel quartet's vocal music program (WDBJ, Norfolk, VA, 1928).

22899 N. Shellenburg and Company Symphony Orchestra. John A. Carroll conducted the commercial symphonic orchestra (WCAU, Philadelphia, PA, 1925).

22900 *N.T.G. and His Girls.* Nils Thor Granlund, well known Broadway producer, "presented show girls on radio" on the show that was sponsored by the Emerson Drug Company. He hosted the program and presented six or seven girls on each show. They told something about themselves and then played an instrument, sang or read some dramatic selection. N.T.G., as he was always known, wanted to demonstrate the talent possessed by the showgirls. Carroll Carroll wrote the show and Herb Polesie was the director. Harry Salter's Orchestra supplied the music. *Variety* said that the idea of presenting chorus girls on radio had been started a month earlier by Dan Healey on WNEW (New York, NY, 1935). In addition, they commented that after N.T.G. introduced each girl, he made wisecracks that were totally lacking in humor. *Variety* did note that the girls' talent generally was good. (30 min., Tuesday, 9:00–9:30 P.M., NBC-Blue, 1935).

Nils T. Granlund was born in Korpilombolo, Sweden in 1892. He came to the United States at the age of nine. After becoming the press agent for Marcus Loew, he later became publicity director for the entire Loew's theater chain. He started in radio in 1922 and by 1924 he had announced several boxing bouts and served as host on several stations. *See* **Granlund, Nils T.**

22901 Nabors, Chick. DJ (*Musical Spree*, WQBC, Vicksburg, MS, 1948).

22902 Nabors, Pat. Sportscaster (*Sports Review*, WSOC, Charlotte, NC, 1948–1949; *BC Sports Review*, WSOC, 1950).

22903 Nabors [Nobors], Ted. Newscaster (KTRH, Houston, TX, 1942, 1944–1945). DJ (*Top of the Morning* and *At Your Service*, KTHT, Houston, TX, 1948–1952).

22904 Nacos, Mary J. COM-HE (WGTM, Wilson, NC, 1925).

22905 Nadig, Henry Davis. Newscaster (WKNE, Keene, NH, 1942).

22906 Nadworney, Devora. Strikingly beautiful opera singer Nadworney was the first person to broadcast opera over a "national hook-up" on January 4, 1923. After that time she was affiliated with WJZ where she broadcast (NBC-Blue, New York, NY, 1923–1928; *Devora Nadworney*, vcl. mus. prg., NBC, 1934).

22907 Naffzigler, Esther. Pianist (WCBD, Zion, IL, 1925; WCBS, Springfield, IL, 1926).

22908 Nafus, Marv. DJ (*Top Twenty*, WKCT, Bowling Green, KY, 1955).

22909 Nagel, Charlotte. Pianist Nagel was a member of a music group known as Genevieve's Cave Women orchestra (WTAM, Cleveland, OH, 1925).

22910 Nagel, Conrad. Motion picture actor Nagel was interviewed by Marian Grable from his Hollywood home by telephone on her *Helen of Hollywood* program (WFAA, Dallas, TX, 1928). Nagel became a DJ in 1952 (*The Conrad Nagel Show*, 30 min., Monday through Friday, 1:30–2:00 P.M. NBC, 1952). As a DJ, Nagel mixed theatrical gossip with the music he played.

22911 Nagel, Harold. Leader (*Harold Nagel Orchestra*, instr. mus. prg. (NBC, 1936, 1938).

22912 Nagel, Teresa Rose. Nagel conducted early interview programs (WGBS, New York, NY, 1925). She interviewed such silent screen stars as Marie Dressler and Gloria Swanson.

22913 Nagle, Dave. DJ (*The Record Man*, WCHV, Charlottesville, VA, 1947).

22914 Nagle, Evelyn Petzner. Singer (WTIC, Hartford, CT, 1926).

22915 Nagle, (Mrs.) Harry H. Performed musical saw selections (WLW, Cincinnati, OH, 1925).

22916 Nagle, Jack. DJ (*Skyline Patrol*, WMFR, High Point, NC, 1950).

22917 Nagler, Al. Sportscaster (WJBK, Detroit, MI, 1937; *Al Nagler Sports*, WJBK, 1947–1949; *Sports Spotlite*, WJBK, 1950–1955; Detroit Red Wings hockey matches, WXYZ , Detroit, MI, 1956).

22918 Nahas, Fred. News analyst (*Tomorrow's History*, KXYZ, Houston, TX, 1948).

22919 Nahhas, Adele. Soprano (KFQW, Seattle, WA, 1927).

22920 Nahorn, Ted. Newscaster (KTRH, Houston, TX, 1946).

22921 Naill, George S. Announcer (KFI, Los Angeles, CA, 1923).

22922 Naimo, John [Jack]. DJ (*Bedford Bandstand*, WBIW, Bedford, IN, 1952). Sportscaster (WJOB, Hammond, IN, 1953–1960).

22923 Naiseth, Franz. Newscaster (WMFG, Hibbing, MN, 1941).

22924 Naiss, Elsa. Pianist (KTAB, Oakland, CA, 1928).

22925 Najamey, Abe. DJ (*800 Radio Show*, WLAD, Danbury, CT, 1954–1956).

22926 Najarian, Mabel. Pianist (WNAC, Boston, MA, 1925).

22927 Nalder, (Dr.) Frank F. Lecturer (KWSC, Pullman, WA, 1928).

22928 Nalley, Velva. Blues singer (WDAF, Kansas City, MO, 1929).

22929 Nalte, Carolyne. Soprano (WMAQ, Chicago, IL, 1926).

22930 Namara, Marguerite. Soprano (*Maxwell House Coffee Hour*, WJZ, New York, NY, 1927). Earlier Namara sang in *Cavalleria Rusticana* on the *Edison Hour* (WRNY, New York, NY, 1926).

22931 *Name That Tune*. Red Benson hosted the sustaining show on which two contestants attempted to correctly name songs after they heard parts of them performed by singer June Valli and the Harry Salter Orchestra. Both Salter and Valli were graduates of the popular *Stop the Music* show. Wayne Howell was the announcer. By 1976, the show was running on television (30 min., Friday, 9:30–9:00 P.M. NBC, 1952).

22932 Nance, Evelyn. COM-HE (WRR, Dallas, TX, 1956).

22933 Nance, Laurita. Blues singer (KGFJ, Los Angeles, CA, 1929).

22934 Nance, Laurita and Mildred Brotzman. Blues singing team (KGFJ, Los Angeles, CA, 1929).

22935 Nance, Lee. DJ (*Lee Nance Show*, WATL, Atlanta, GA, 1952).

22936 Nance, Ray. Leader (*Ray Nance's Rhythm Barons Orchestra*, mus. prg., WIND, Gary, IN, 1936).

22937 Nancy Lee (Romola Latchem Hicks). Singer and conductor of a homemakers' program (KFLV, Rockford, IL, 1929).

22938 Nannini, Nita. COM-HE (KLAS, Las Vegas, NV, 1956).

22939 Napier, Byron "By." DJ (*Ballads and Byron*, KCRC, Enid, OK, 1948; *Night Watch*, KCRC, 1949; WEAU, Eau Claire, WI, 1956).

22940 Napoli, Olivia. COM-HE (WELO, Tupelo, MS, 1949).

22941 Narber, Elizabeth Roehr. Soprano (WGY, Schenectady, NY, 1926).

22942 Nardi, Nalda. Contralto (WMCA, New York, NY, 1932; WIP, Philadelphia, PA, 1935).

22943 Narel, Dorothy. COM-HE (WKNY, Kingston, NY, 1954).

22944 Narz, Jack. Sportscaster (*Sports Mirror*, KWIK, Burbank, CA, 1947).

22945 Narz, Jim. DJ (*Yawn Patrol*, WLOU, Louisville, KY, 1948; *Musical Comedy a la Carte*, KPOL, Los Angeles, CA, 1954).

22946 Nash, (Dr.) Albertine Richards. Consulting psychologist (KGO, Oakland, CA, 1929).

22947 Nash, Alleta Jo. Pianist (WHIS, Bluefield, WV, 1942).

22948 Nash, Barnes H. Newscaster (WJIS, Beckley, WV, 1939).

22949 Nash, Bob. Newscaster (KDSH, Boise, ID, 1948). Sportscaster (KDSH, 1948).

22950 Nash, Bob. DJ (*Club 800*, KSEL, Lubbock, TX, 1947).

22951 Nash, (Mrs.) Charles A. Pianist, musical director and singer (KFUL, Galveston, TX, 1929).

22952 Nash, Eleanor. COM-HE (NBC, 1941).

22953 Nash, Joey. Leader (*Joey Nash Orchestra*, instr. mus. prg., KMOX, St. Louis, MO, 1936). .

22954 Nash, Len. Leader (Len Nash and the Original Country Boys, a country-western group, KFWB, Hollywood, CA, 1926; KNX, Los Angeles, CA, 1928).

22955 Nash, Marjorie. Organist Nash performing from the Rialto Theater in Denver, Colorado (KOA, Denver, CO, 1926).

22956 Nash, Noble. Newscaster (WCBS, Springfield, IL, 1939).

22957 Nash, R.J. Newscaster (KRNT, Des Moines, IA, 1944; *12 O'Clock News*, KSO, Des Moines, IA, 1947).

22958 Nash, Ralph. Newscaster (WBRW, Welch, WV, 1945).

22959 Nash, Roger. DJ (*Music Women Love*, WJMR, New Orleans, LA, 1952; WNOE, New Orleans, LA, 1954).

22960 Nash, William, Jr. Sportscaster (KOH, Reno, NV, 1937–1941).

22961 Nash-Finch Orchestra. Popular local radio band (WCCO, Milwaukee-St. Paul, MN, 1926).

22962 Nash Plantation Orchestra. An orchestra that specialized in Mexican and popular music (WFAA, Dallas, TX, 1926).

22963 *Nashville Conservatory of Music*. The Nashville Conservatory sponsored the weekly good music show. The director was Signor Guetona S. DeLuca (WLAC, Nashville, TN, 1928).

22964 Nashe, Carol. COM-HE (WILD, Boston, MA, 1960).

22965 Nasmyth, Louise. Pianist (KFAE, Pullman, WA, 1924–1925).

22966 Nason, Harold. Pianist (*Atwater Kent Hour*, NBC, 1928).

22967 Nassau, James A. Nassau broadcast motion picture reviews (WDAR, Philadelphia, PA, 1923).

22968 Nassau, Joseph N. "Joe." Announcer (WOO, Philadelphia, PA, 1925–1926). Sportscaster (WIBG, Glenside, PA, 1938).

22969 Nasser, Mildred. Billed as broadcasting a "female baritone recital" by the *Christian Science Monitor* (April 18, 1925, p. 12), Nasser appeared on, KFI (Los Angeles, CA) in 1925.

22970 Nast, Frankie. Violinist (KOA, Denver, CO, 1925).

22971 Nathan, C. Henry. Actor Nathan was in the cast of *Woman in White.*

22972 Nathan, Norman. DJ (*Platter Chatter*, WMEX, Boston, MA, 1948–1950).

22973 Nathanson, B. Violinist and saxophonist of the Sewanee Orchestra (WJZ, New York, NY, 1923).

22974 Nation, Buck. CW singer (*Buck Nation—Songs of the West,* 15 min., 6:45–7:00 P.M., WMCA, New York, NY, 1934).

22975 Nation, Herschel. DJ (*Disko Nation*, WAGC, Chattanooga, TN, 1948). Sportscaster (*Sports Hour*, WAGC, Chattanooga, TN, 1948; *The Sportsman Hour*, WAGC, 1948).

22976 Natten, Ina. Soprano (WTIC, Hartford, CT, 1927).

22977 *National Amateur Night.* Ray Perkins was the host on the amateur hour. If a contestant performed badly, Perkins blew a whistle. This was in contrast to Major Bowes who on his amateur hour gave poor performing contestants a gong. The Arnold Johnson Orchestra provided music for the amateur contestants (30 min., Sunday, 5:00–5:30 P.M., CBS, 1935).

22978 (*The*) *National Barn Dance* (aka *Old Fiddlers Hour* and *The Aladdin Play Party*). The *National Barn Dance* had its modest beginning shortly after station WLS (Chicago, IL) went on the air, when a fiddler by the name of Tommy Dandorand made a series of broadcasts that influenced George D. Hay to begin a "barn dance" program. Listener response was immediate and enthusiastic. The program, first known as *The Old Fiddlers Hour*, became the *Alladin Play Party* sponsored by the Alladin Kerosene Lamp Company. In 1926 the name was changed to the *National Barn Dance.* The program was broadcast from a studio with an auditorium seating an audience of only 100 until 1930, when the program moved to a 1,200 seat theater that was filled for each weekly broadcast with *paying* customers.

In addition to Hay, who later moved to WSM (Nashville, TN), where he was instrumental in developing the *Grand Ole Opry*, other behind the scene workers such as John Lair, Edgar Bill and George Biggar labored tirelessly and successfully to develop and promote the program. Their skill, faith and perseverance made it a local favorite at first, and soon thereafter a national institution when it went on the network in 1933.

The show's first performers were host George D. Hay, fiddler Tommy Dandorand, square dance caller Tom Owen, a Chicago hospital worker; Ford and Glenn; organist Ralph Waldo Emerson; Bob Hendry; and Ed Goodreau. In 1936, station WLS received 1,515, 901 pieces of mail praising the *National Barn Dance.* An indication of how the show's popularity grew with the years was shown by the September 19, 1937 broadcast from Chicago's Soldiers Field when more than 20,000 fans showed up for a celebration of Farm Week.

What was special about the program was its interesting mix of personalities, judicious choice of musical selections and comedy routines and its constant attention to its audience's taste. Among the major performers and personalities that made the show a radio favorite for so many years were: George D. Hay, the first host; Jolly Joe Kelly, the host who succeeded Hay; resonant voiced announcers such as Steve Cisler and Jack Holden; Arkie the Woodchopper (Luther Ossenbrink), the all-purpose singer and square dance caller; Grace Wilson the beloved ballad singer; Henry Burr the legendary tenor; Otto (Ted Morse) and the Novelodeons band; and the goofy Hoosier Hot Shots novelty band. Some other *National Barn Dance* performers were: veteran radio performers Al and Pete (Al Bernard and Pete Botsema); concertina soloist Albert Blaha; pianist Alec Templeton; singer Bill O'Connor; cowboy singer Bob Atcher; the Buccaneers (Captain Stubby Fouts, Jerry Richards, Dwight "Tiny" Stokes and Sonny Fleming); Charley Marshall and his Mavericks (Johnny O'Brien, Johnny Charley Marshall and Abe Wright); Arizona Hopi singer Chief Taptuka; singer Christine the Little Swiss Miss (Jack Holden's wife, Christine Smith); singer-instrumentalist Chubby Parker; singer-banjoist Cousin Emmy; cowboy singer Bill Newcomb; the [later] Cumberland Ridge Runners (Ed Goodreau, John Lair, Doc Hopkins, Karl Davis, Gene Rupp, Hartford Taylor); the *original* Cumberland Ridge Runners (Linda Parker, Slim Miller, John Lair, Karl Davis, Red Foley and Hartford Taylor); whistler Delia Ann Ragland; the yodeling DeZurik Sisters (Mary Jane and Carolyn); singer Dorothy Sanwald; the Dixie Hamonica King Eddie Allan; the homespun Hoosier poet, Edgar Guest; singer Evelyn (Mary) Wood; veteran radio singing team Ford and Glenn; Russian harmonica virtuoso Fred Zimbalist; comic Cousin Ephrem Z; cowboy singers Gene Autry and Smiley Burnett; the "Little Cowboy" singer, George Goebel; dance caller Gus Colby; singer-whistler Hal "Buddy" Brooks; the Hilltoppers; the Hired Hands; jug, song whistle and harmonica performer Don Gackett; Fred LaCabe on harmonica and spoons; Ben Pigotti on accordion; Tony Pacionelas on uke; comedy team Jimmy James and Cousin Tilford (Holly Swanson); singer Joe Parsons; dance caller John Dolce; singer John Neher; pianist John Brown; five-year-old singer Joy Miller; violinist Karl Schulte; singer Ken Stevens; the Kentucky Girls singing team; singer Lily May (Lily May Leonard), Cousin Emma (Joy Founier) and the Lindner Twins; Louise Massey and the Westerners; singer Mary Jane Johnson; Hoosier mimic Max Terhune (Max Scully); the Neighbor boys vocal trio (Lawrence Quiram, Louis Quiram and Caroll Hollister); the Ole Harmony Slaves (Chuck Haynes and Ray Ferris) vocal team; comic-musician Otto (Ted Morse) in the role of "Uncle Otto" or "Genevieve"; Otto Clausen, director of Chicago's Norwegian Singing Society; Pat Buttram, the comic pride and joy of Winston County—the "Winston County Flash"; singer Phyllis Brown; singer Polly of the Range (Pauline Beane); organist Ralph Emerson; the Ranch Boys (Curly Bradley, Jack Ross and Shorty Carson); Rex and the Cornhuskers; Rock Creek Wranglers; Roy Leathen, the 13-year-old yodeler; the Sage Riders (Dolph Hewitt, fiddler; Donald "Red" Blanchard, bass and Don White, singer-fiddler-guitarist); singer Sally Foster; Shirley Graham and her Carolina Vagabonds ("a group of colored singers" who specialized in "spirituals and plantation songs"); Simmons and Clifford; singer Smiling Ed McConnell; the Three Wisconsin Honey Bees a female vocal trio; Tom, Dick, and Harry, popular male vocal trio; singer Tom Hargiser; Tom Corwine expert producer of animal, poultry and wildlife imitations; square dance caller Tom Owens; singer Tommy Tanner; old-time fiddler Tommy Dandurand; Irish baritone Tony Corcoran; the Vass Family (Emily, Louisa, Virginia, Sally, and Frank Vass); Verne and Lee Hassell; Walter Peterson; Douglas Perkins, a 13-year-old fiddler; Gid Tanner and the Skillet Lickers; the Girls of the Golden West; Sigmund Spaeth, the "Tune Detective"; singer Betty Jones (Jane Schultz); singer Ezbai Wells; singer Grace Wilson; Ralph Dunbar's Bell Ringers (featuring almost 100 bells); cowboy singer Romaine Lowdermilk; mimic Purv Pullen; Normaendes Sangforening and the Norwegian Singing Society of Chicago; Olaf the Swede (William Sorenson); the Sodbusters (Reggie Cross and Howard Block); W.B. "Dad" Chenoweth and his Fiddlers; the Maple City Four; Henry Burr; Verne, Lee and Mary (Verne and Lee Haskell and Mary Evelyn Wood); Uncle Ezra; Spare Ribs, Lulu Belle and Scotty (Myrtle Cooper and Scotty Wiseman); the Masqueraders, a masked singing group; whistler Elmer Esping; Otto's Novelodeons (Little German band led by Ted "Otto" Morse consisting of Zeb Hartley, Art Wenzel, Bill Thall and Buddy Gilmore); the Hoosier Hot Shots (Paul "Hezzie" Trietsch, Otto "Gabe" Ward, Paul Kettering and Kenneth "Ken" Trietsch); the Ahn Sisters (singing group of Jean, age 18, Miriam, 16, Virginia, 14, and Mary 12), the Three Stooges Trumpet Trio (William Beamish, Harold Doolittle and Norman Weinberg); cowboy singer Tumbleweed; singer Lucille Long; singer Shelby Jean Davis; dance caller Bob Lough; banjo virtuoso Eddy Peabody; singer Skip Farrell; the Dinning Sisters (Jean, Ginger and Lou), harmony singing team; band leader Glen Welty; and the WLS female vocal trio of Winnie (W), Lou (L) and Sally (S), whose initials just happened to be the station's call letters. Over the years the program had many announcers who acted as MC in addition to Joe Kelly: Harold Safford, Dudley Richards, George Ditlay, Hal O'Halloran, Jack Holden, Steve Cisler and Bill Bailey.

WLS on its Saturday night schedule wrapped its music programs around the *National Barn Dance* network broadcast. These programs featured regular WLS performers and members of the *National Barn Dance* crew. Incidentally, this was a pattern also used by the *Grand Ole Opry* show at WSM. Some examples of the WLS programming and sponsors are given below:

Saturday evening, January 11, 1936

7:00–7:15—*Prairie Ramblers and Patsy Montana; Henry Hornsbuckle and the Hoosier Sod Busters* (G.E. Conkey Company).

7:15–7:30—*Hoosier Hot Shots* and guest artists (Morton Salt Company).

7:30–8:00—*Keystone Barn Dance Party* featuring Skyland Scotty (Keystone Steel and Wire Company).

8:00–8:30—*National Barn Dance* NBC Hour with Uncle Ezra; Maple City Four;

Verne, Lee and Mary; Hoosier Hot Shots; Lucille Long; Sally Foster; Skyland Scotty and other Hayloft favorites with Joe Kelly master of ceremonies (Alka-Seltzer).

8:30–9:00—*Aladdin Hayloft Theater.*

9:00–9:30—*Barn Dance Frolic* with Hilltoppers; Patsy Montana; Possum Tuttle (Gillette Rubber Company).

9:30–10:00—*Prairie Ramblers and Red Foley* (Jelsert).

From 10:00 to 10:30 P.M., the *Prairie Farmer-WLS National Barn Dance* continued until 12:00 midnight with varied features, including the Prairie Ramblers; Otto and his Tune Twisters; Patsy Montana; Hometowners Quartet; Christine the Little Swiss Miss; Girls of the Golden West; Red Foley; Hilltoppers; Bill O'Connor; Grace Wilson; Hoosier Sod Busters; Eddie Allan; Arkie (The Arkansas Traveler) and many others.

In 1937, many *National Barn Dance* performers augmented their income by selling song books for half a dollar each. Two favorites were *Lulu Belle and Scotty's Songbook* and the *Prairie Ramblers and Patsy Montana Songbook.* Like the performers of its counterpart, the *Grand Ole Opry*, the *Barn Dance* stars appeared around the country at various theaters and county fairs. Appearances by WLS Artists for the week of September 6, 1936 were reported by the station's *Stand By* magazine as follows.

Sunday, September 6, 1936

Luxemburg, WI—Kewaunee Co. Fair—Night Show Only—WLS ON PARADE: Uncle Ezra; Hoosier Hot Shots; Tom Corwin; Ralph and Helen Sternerd; Rube Tronson and his band.

Toluca, IL—St. Ann's Picnic—Matinee and Night—The Four Hired Hands.

Chilton, WI—Calumet Co. Fair—(Night Show Only)—*WLS BARN DANCE*: Lulu Belle and Skyland Scotty; Bill McCluskey; Tom Owens' Entertainers; Winnie Lou and Sally; Pat Buttram; Miss Pauline.

Beaver Dam, WI—Central Labor Union Show—(Matinee and Night)—Three Neighbor Boys.

Monday, September 7, 1936 (Labor Day)

Cedar Grove, WI—Cedar Grove Fire Department—Matinee and Night—*Prairie Ramblers and Patsy Montana.*

Rock Island, IL—Douglas Park—Matinee and Night—*WLS BARN DANCE*: Lulu Belle and Scotty; Otto and His Novelodeons; Georgie Goebel; Miss Christine; Bill McCluskey; Possum Tuttle; Hoosier Sod Busters; Henry Hornsbuckle.

Beaver Dam, WI—Central Labor Union Show—Matinee and Night—The Bergstroms and Eddie Allan.

Newton, KS—Harvey County Fair—*WLS BARN DANCE*: Arkansas Woodchopper; Radke Sisters; The Barn Dance Band; Olaf the Swede; Billy Woods; The Hayloft Trio; Pokey Martin.

Galesville, WI—Trempealeau Co. Fair—Night Show Only—*WLS BARN DANCE*: Rube Tronson's Band; The Hayloft Dancers; Tom Corwine; Flannery Sisters and the Sternards.

Norway, MI—Dickinson Co. Fair—Matinee and Night—WLS ON PARADE: Winnie, Lou and Sally; Tom Owens' Entertainers; Chuck and Ray; Three Neighbor Boys; Pat Buttram.

Tuesday, September 8, 1936

Hart, MI—Oceana Co. Fair—Matinee and Night—*WLS BARN DANCE*: Winnie, Lou and Sally; Tom Owens' Entertainers; Three Neighbor Boys; Chuck and Ray; Ralph and Helen Sternard.

Fairbury, NE—Bonham Theater—Matinee and Night—*WLS BARN DANCE*: Arkansas Woodchopper; The Barn Dance Band; Hayloft Trio; Radke Sisters; Olaf the Swede; Billy Woods; Pokey Martin.

Olney, IL—Richland Co. Fair—Matinee and Night—*WLS BARN DANCE*: Maple City Four; Georgie Goebel; The Hayloft Fiddlers; Possum Tuttle; Miss Christine; Owens Sisters.

Fremont, OH—Sandusky Co. Fair—Night Only—*WLS BARN DANCE*: Lulu Belle and Skyland Scotty; Hoosier Hot Shots; Hoosier Sod Busters; Ramblin' Red Foley and Eva; The Flannery Sisters; Bill McCluskey; Miss Pauline.

Rhinelander, WI—State Theater—Matinee and Night—WLS MERRY-GO-ROUND: Prairie Ramblers; Patsy Montana; The Hayloft Dancers; Tom Corwine; Pat Buttram.

Wednesday, September 9, 1936

Indianapolis, IN—Fair Grounds—Afternoon Only—Lulu Belle and Skyland Scotty.

Gladstone, MI—Rialto Theater—Matinee and Night—WLS MERRY-GO-ROUND: Prairie Ramblers; Patsy Montana; Hayloft Dancers; Tom Corwine; Pat Buttram.

Goodland, KS—Sherman Theater—Matinee and Night—*WLS BARN DANCE*: Arkansas Woodchopper; The Barn Dance Band; Olaf the Swede; Hayloft Trio; Radke Sisters; Billy Woods; Pokey Martin.

Thursday, September 10, 1936

Marshfield, WI—Central Wisconsin State Fair—Matinee and Night—WLS ON PARADE: Lulu Belle; Skyland Scotty; Prairie Rambler and Patsy Montana; Bill McCluskey; Pat Buttram; Tom Corwine; Miss Pauline; Exhibition Dancers.

Shawano, WI—Shawano Country Fair—Night Only—WLS ON PARADE: Winnie, Lou and Sally; Tom Owens' Entertainers; Chuck and Ray; The Hayloft Dancers; Ralph and Helen Sternard.

Clay Center, KS—Clay County Fair—Night Only—*WLS BARN DANCE*: Arkansas Woodchopper; The Barn Dance Band; Hayloft Trio; Olaf the Swede; Billy Woods; Pokey Martin; Radke Sisters.

Beaver Dam, WI—Dodge County Fair—WLS ARTISTS: Otto and his Novelodeons; Flannery Sisters; Henry Hornsbuckle; Hoosier Sod Busters; Delia Ann and Betty.

Friday, September 11, 1936

Waukon, IA—Allamakee Co. Fair—Night Only—*WLS BARN DANCE*: Lulu Belle, Skyland Scotty, Bill McCluskey, Hoosier Sod Busters; Miss Pauline; Tom Corwine; Flannery Sisters.

Jefferson, WI—Jefferson Co. Fair—Night Only—*WLS BARN DANCE*: Prairie Ramblers and Patsy Montana; Jolly Joe Kelly; Winnie, Lou and Sally; Exhibition Dancers; Chuck and Ray; Delia Ann and Betty; The Sternards.

Alpena, MI—Alpena Co. Fair—Matinee and Night—*WLS BARN DANCE*: Rube Tronson's Band; Georgie Goebel; Miss Christine; Barn Dance Fiddlers; Possum Tuttle; Owens Sisters.

Gays Mills, WI—Crawford Co. Fair—Night Only—*WLS BARN DANCE*: Ramblin' Red Foley and Eva; Pat Buttram; Tom Owens' Entertainers; Ozark Sisters; Hayloft Dancers.

Saturday, September 12, 1936

Gays Mills, WI—Crawford Co. Fair—Night Only—WLS MERRY-GO-ROUND: The Barn Dance Band; Tom Owens' Entertainers; Billy Woods; Pokey Martin; Radke Sisters.

Sunday, September 13, 1936

Quincy, IL—Washington Theater—Matinee and Night—Uncle Ezra and the Hoosier Hot Shots.

Ilgair Park—Chicago, IL—Matinee and Night—*WLS BARN DANCE*: Lulu Belle and Skyland Scotty; Bill McCluskey; Otto and his Novelodeons; Tom Corwine; Miss Pauline; Billy Woods; Flannery Sisters; Hoosier Sod Busters.

Ottawa, OH—Ottawa Theater—Matinee and Night—*WLS BARN DANCE*: Arkansas Woodchopper; Miss Pauline; Tom Owens' Entertainers; Hayloft Trio; Olaf the Swede; Pokey Martin; Ralph and Helen Sternard.

Hoopeston, IL—McFerren Theater—Matinee and Night—WLS ROUND-UP: Prairie Ramblers; Patsy Montana; Winnie, Lou and Sally; Ralph and Helen Sternard; Pat Buttram, Hayloft Dancers.

Although the program began by broadcasting old-time and country music, over the years the format became more and more sophisticated. Country music was judiciously intermixed with the current song hits of the day and were performed in a smooth, highly professional manner. When someone referred to the *National Barn Dance* hillbillies, a cynic replied: "If they're hillbillies, why do they live in penthouses, eat caviar and ride in Cadillacs?" The program's ability to change over the years undoubtedly accounted for its continued popularity among both urban and rural listeners. The program's long time announcer was Jack Holden. Glen Welty conducted the orchestra.

22979 ***National Barn Dance Fiddlers.*** Tommy Dandorand and Rube Tronson on fiddles, banjoist Sam Mack and dance caller Ed Goodman made up the popular CW music group (WLS, Chicago, IL, 1929–1930). They also played regularly on the *National Barn Dance* for many years.

22980 ***National Battery Girls.*** The popular local female vocal trio consisted of Grace Epperson, Olive Stageman and Rachael Salisbury (KOIL, Omaha, NE, 1930).

22981 ***National Battery Symphony Program.*** The National Battery Symphony Orchestra featured, among others, clarinetist and saxophonist George Rice and violinists, Fred Ruhoff and Herman Ruhoff (KSTP, St. Paul, MN, 1929–1930). Also featured in the orchestra were H.C. Woempner, dir.-f.; Max Scheliner, v.-librarian; John Lamber, v.-ss.; Frank Obermann, v.-vl.-p.; James Messear, vc.; Alan Warren, vc.-s.; Frank Kuchynka, sb.; John Stamp, t.; Con Derus, t.; Spence Adkins, tb.;

Earl Handlon, clr.-s.; Marion Teschion, clr.-s.; Marion Cooke, d.; Harry Cunningham, bss.; Alexander Duvoir, o.; Burton Speakman, bj.; and Alan Hustana, f.

22982 ***National Broadcasting Company Concert Bureau Hour.*** The Landt Trio, the Bonnie Ladies, the Colonials, the Three Kings and a Queen, crooner Mildred Hunt and tenor Lanny Ross appeared on the popular concert music program. The concert orchestra was directed by Hugo Mariani (NBC-Red, New York, NY, 1929).

22983 ***National Broadcasting Company Opera Program.*** Max Dolin directed the weekly hour long operatic music program. Condensed operas were broadcast. For example, Massenet's *Manon* with Harold Spaulding, William Rainey, Mary Groom Richards, Harold Dana, Barbara Blanchard, Harrison Ward, Maynard Jones, Elfrieda Wayne, J.H. Stewartson, G. Chatfield and Margaret O'Dea was broadcast in 1927. Dolin also provided piano accompaniment (NBC, 1927).

22984 ***National Carbon Company Program.*** Operettas were presented such as Franz Lehar's *The Merry Widow* on the two-hour music program. Directed by Carl Anderson with Franz Vinton LaFerrera's Concert Orchestra, the program's cast included: Elfrieda Wynne, Albert Gillette, Claire Harsha Upshur, James Girard and Grace LePage (KGO, Oakland, CA, 1925).

22985 ***National Church of the Air*** **(aka *The National Religious Service Program*).** Reverend Harry Emerson Fosdick conducted the weekly network religious program (30 min., Weekly, NBC-Blue, 1927–1928).

22986 ***National Farm and Home Hour.*** The *National Farm and Home Hour* was a long running variety and information show that combined news, music, dramatizations and information specifically designed for farmers and their families. The program was broadcast on NBC from 1928 to 1958. Important in its early development was Frank E. Mullen. *See* **Mullen, Frank E.**

During its early days, the program was broadcast six times weekly (45 min., Monday through Saturday, 1:15–1:00 P.M., NBC-Blue, 1929). The customary opening by host Everett Mitchell was, "It's a beautiful day in Chicago." At one time Baukhage broadcast the news on the program. A favorite part of the program was the dramatized "Uncle Sam's Forest Rangers" segment. Actors in the segment were Raymond Edward Johnson, Harvey Hays, Judith Lowry and Lucille Harding. Don Ameche also performed with the group at one time. Music was provided by Harry Kogen and The Homesteaders, Jack Baus and the Cornbusters vocal group and the Cadets male quartet. Mirandy of Persimmon Hollow added a comic touch.

The program was supervised by W.E. Drips and produced by Herbert Lateau. Sponsors of the show at various times included the Montgomery Ward mail order company and the United States Department of Agriculture.

22987 ***National Grand Opera Company*** **(aka *The National Broadcasting Grand Opera Company*).** During 1929, the radio opera company performed *The Secret of Suzanne*, *Martha*, *Aida* and *Hansel and Gretel*. The program at that time was known as the *National Broadcasting Grand Opera Company*. The company included Paula Heminghaus, Genia Zielinska, Devora Nadworney, Julian Oliver and Astride Fjelde. The orchestra was conducted by Cesare Sodero (NBC-Red, New York, NY, 1929). The program's name was changed to *The National Grand Opera Program* in 1930.

22988 **National Light Opera Company.** Operettas were broadcast on Sunday evenings by the group (7:15–8:15 P.M., NBC-KOA, Denver, CO, 1929). A similar program presented by the same group the following year was called *The NBC Light Opera Program* (60 min., Sunday, 1:00–2:00 P.M., NBC, 1930). *See* ***The NBC Light Opera Program.***

22989 ***National Male Four.*** The vocal quartet consisted of tenors Earl Stockdale and Raymond D. Waller, baritone Leo Hemminghaus and bass Nels Swenson. They were sometimes known as "Ye Merry Men of Windsor" (KSTP, St. Paul, MN, 1929–1930).

22990 ***National Music Camp at Interlochen, Michigan.*** High school orchestras, bands and other smaller instrumental groups from the music camp under the direction of Dr. Joseph E. Maddy were featured (60 min., Sunday, 2:00–3:00 P.M., NBC-Blue, 1935).

22991 ***National Musical Comedy Theater.*** The program's major emphasis was the presentation of musical comedy selections. Among the featured performers was bass soloist, Charles Robinson (NBC-Red, 1928).

22992 ***National Opera Concert.*** Wilfred Pelletier conducted the symphonic orchestra on the classical music program. Various operatic singers appeared each week (30 min., Sunday, 2:00–2:30 P.M., NBC-Blue, 1933).

22993 **National Players.** William Rainey directed the NBC network dramatic group. A typical production was their 1927 broadcast of O. Henry's "Mamon and the Archer" with M.E. Harlan, Emilie Melville, Wheaton Chambers, Jean Paul King, Doris Cannery and Benjamin Purington (NBC, 1927).

22994 ***National Radio Home Hour.*** "Betty Crocker" was the major contributor to the program of homemaking information (60 min., Wednesday, 11:00–12:00 noon, NBC-Red, 1928–1929).

22995 ***National Radio Homemakers Hour.*** Begun in 1927, the women's program was conducted by Ida Bailey Allen, one of the most popular female broadcasters in radio history. She was assisted by Mrs. Louise Baker, Joan Barrett, Grace White and Janet Lee. Musical selections were performed by contralto Elizabeth Wood and baritone Richard Hale. Ralph Christian was the program's musical director. The program was broadcast each weekday in 1930. From Monday through Friday, the major topics were food and cooking; beauty hints were also addressed on Tuesday; and some interior decoration topics added on Wednesday (NBC-Blue, 1927–1930).

22996 ***National Radio Pulpit*** **(aka *The Men's Conference*).** In 1923, the Greater New York Federation of Churches began its radio division and originated the *first* national religious radio program — *The Men's Conference*— later renamed the *National Radio Pulpit*. The program was broadcast by WEAF (New York, NY, 1923) from New York City's Park Avenue Christ (Methodist) Church. Dr. S. Parkes Cadman was the chief speaker from 1923 until 1936, when Reverend Ralph Washington Sockman took over. Harry Emerson Fosdick, in turn, replaced Sockman. The program, which was broadcast for a little more than four decades, was said to have been the first religious program broadcast from a network studio.

22997 ***National Radio Symphony Orchestra.*** Walter Damrosch conducted the orchestra on the symphonic music program (60 min., Saturday, 9:00–10:00 P.M., NBC-Red, 1926–1928).

22998 ***National Spelling Bee.*** Dr. Harry Hagen conducted the spelling bee sponsored by Standard Brands. Five dollars were awarded to the winner and medals to some of the runner-ups (60 min., Saturday, 7:00–8:00 P.M., WMCA, New York, NY, 1937). Spelling Master Paul Wing also conducted a national radio spelling bee, a network broadcast that attracted a surprisingly large listening audience (NBC, 1937–1940).

22999 ***National Vespers.*** Dr. Paul Scherer delivered the sermon on the religious program that took the place of *The National Religious Service Program*, sometimes known as *The National Church of the Air* (60 min., Sunday, 5:00–6:00 P.M., NBC-Blue, 1934).

23000 ***National Youth Conference.*** Rev. Dr. Daniel A. Poling conducted the inspirational program for young people broadcast on Sundays from noon to one P.M. on the NBC-Pacific Coast network in 1929. A mixed quartet was featured that included soprano Muriel Wilson, contralto Helen Janke, tenor Richard Maxwell and baritone Earl Waldo. George Shackley conducted the orchestra (60 min., Sunday, 3:00–4:00 P.M., NBC, 1929–1930).

23001 ***Natural Bridge Dancing Class.*** The Natural Bridge Shoe Company sponsored the program that attempted to teach dancing by radio. Arthur Murray, the famous dancing teacher, conducted the program (15 min., Friday, 8:45–9:00 P.M., NBC-Blue, 1931).

23002 ***Natural Bridge Program.*** Stories of famous loves and lovers were dramatized with a romantic musical background. The program was sponsored by the Natural Bridge Shoe Company (15 min., Friday, 8:45–9:00 P.M., NBC-Blue, 1930).

23003 ***Nature Sketches.*** First begun in 1941, the program ran for more than eight successive years on the NBC network. The format consisted of various persons extolling the many glories of nature and the great outdoors (15 min., Saturday, 3:00–3:15 P.M., NBC, 1948).

23004 **Naughton, Russell "Russ."** Sportscaster (WDRC, Hartford, CT, 1942). DJ (*Music off the Record*, WDRC, 1947; *Shoppers Special*, WDRC, 1949; *Music off the Record*, WDRC, 1950; *Yawn Patrol*, WDRC, 1954).

23005 **Naugle, Dave.** DJ (KFJZ, Fort Worth, TX, 1949; *Off the Record*, KFJZ, 1950).

23006 **Nauhas, Bertie.** COM-HE (WHIM, Bloomsburg, PA, 1951).

23007 **Nauman, Dick.** Newscaster (KWFT, Wichita Falls, TX, 1940–1941). Sportscaster (KWFT, 1940–1941; *Sports Resume*, WRR, Dallas, TX, 1947).

23008 **Nausbaum, Mort.** DJ (WHAM, Rochester, NY, 1948).

23009 ***(The) Naval Air Reserve Show.*** Jim Ameche hosted the show that told the story of the Naval Air Reserve's mission and performance. Others who appeared on the show were singers Skip Farrell and Connie Russell and the King's Jesters vocal group. Jack Carson, Georgie Gobel and pianist Skitch Henderson were also program regulars (15 min., Weekly, Various Stations, early 1950s).

23010 **Navara, Jimmie.** Leader (*Jimmie Navara Orchestra*, instr. mus. prg., WXYZ, Detroit, MI, 1935).

23011 **Navara, Leon.** Leader (*Leon Navara Orchestra*, instr. mus. prg., CBS, 1935).

23012 **Navarette, Victor.** Pianist (KFWI, San Francisco, CA, 1928).

23013 **Navarro [Navaro], Al .** Leader (*Al Navarro Orchestra*, instr. mus. prg., WFBR, Baltimore, MD, 1936).

23014 **Navigato, Jennie.** Soprano (KYW, Chicago, IL, 1925; WIBO, Chicago, IL, 1926).

23015 ***Navy Wife.*** A World War II program that told the story of Mrs. Richard Walker, a recently evacuated wife of a Navy Lieutenant. The program recounted the various activities and problems faced by wives of servicemen (KGO, San Francisco, CA, 1942). *See* **Wartime Radio**.

23016 **Naylon, Larry.** DJ (*Sunrise Serenade*, KPRC, Houston, TX, 1947; *Requestfully Yours*, KOPO, Tucson, AZ, 1949).

23017 **Naylor, Josephine.** COM-HE (WQJ, Chicago, IL, 1925).

23018 **Naylor, Oliver.** Leader (Oliver Naylor Band, a group that *Variety* said offered "bright jazzique" on their CBS broadcasts originating from Philadelphia's Palais Royal Club, CBS, Philadelphia, PA, 1929; *Oliver Naylor Orchestra*, instr. mus. prg., WIP, Philadelphia, PA, 1933, 1936; NBC, 1935; CBS, 1942).

23019 **Naylor, Tony.** DJ (*Tony's Time*, WBTM, Danville, VA, 1952).

23020 ***Nazi Jazz.*** Robert Garden's orchestra played from Berlin, Germany on the program that included a liberal dose of political propaganda (30 min., Sunday, 11:30–12:00 noon, WJZ-NBC, 1936).

23021 **NBC Balalaika Orchestra.** String music group directed by Gregory Golubeff and tenor Enrico Martinelli were featured (NBC, 1929).

23022 ***NBC Cinema Theatre Program.*** The novel program presented the typical parts of a metropolitan movie theater's show, including an overture, newsreel, stage show (vaudeville), a comedy short and a "feature story" (30 min., Wednesday, 9:00–9:30 P.M. CST, NBC-Blue, 1935).

23023 ***NBC Club Matinee.*** *NBC Club Matinee* was a forerunner of what later became *Club Matinee*. The early version featured guitarist Sunny Jim Wolverton and singer Betty Bennett (NBC, 1937). *See **Club Matinee***.

23024 ***NBC Green Room.*** Mus. prg. (NBC-Pacific Coast Network, 1929). The show was a 60-minute weekly program featuring soprano Gail Taylor, tenor Irving Kennedy and organist Elmer Crowhurst (60 min., Friday, 7:00–8:00 P.M., NBC, Pacific Coast Network, 1929).

23025 ***NBC Light Opera Program.*** The NBC network presented productions of operettas, including Gilbert and Sullivan's *H.M.S. Pinafore* (60 min., Sunday, 1:30–2:30 P.M., NBC, 1935).

23026 ***NBC Star Playhouse*** **(aka *NBC University Theater*).** John Chapman, the drama critic of the New York *Daily News*, hosted the program on which great plays were dramatized. For example, the program presented Frederic March and Florence Eldridge in *A Farewell to Arms;* Rex Harrison in *The Second Man;* and Angela Lansbury and Dan O'Herlihy in *Cashel Byron's Profession.* Other presentations were *The Heart of Darkness, Great Expectations, The Way of All Flesh, Lord Jim, Passage to India, The Grapes of Wrath, Portrait of the Artist as a Young Man, The Heart of Midlothian, Sons and Lovers, Babylon Revisited, Ministry of Fear, Henry Esmond, Pickwick Papers, The Marble Fawn, Huckleberry Finn, Gulliver's Travels, Tom Jones* and *All the King's Men.* Some other stars that performed on the program were John Lund, John Dehner, Preston Foster and Jane Darwell (60 min., NBC, 1953).

23027 ***NBC Symphony Orchestra.*** Symphonic mus. prg. series with maestro Arturo Toscanini conducting these distinguished classical music programs (NBC, 1939). Although Toscanini is generally considered to have been the orchestra's first conductor, Pierre Monteaux conducted the radio debut of the orchestra November 13, 1937 as a combined Red and Blue networks' presentation (9:00–10:00 P.M.). David Sarnoff, NBC's head, had a special studio, 8H, constructed especially for the orchestra. Although Frank Black also conducted the orchestra on some programs, it should be recognized that Arturo Toscanini was the first *regular conductor to lead a full symphony orchestra created for radio.* Ben Grauer was frequently the program's announcer.

23028 ***NBC Troubadours.*** Maynard Jones was the musical director of the half-hour music program (NBC, 1929). The dual piano team of Marion Hunter and Doris Blaney was featured.

23029 ***NBC University Theater.*** *See **NBC Star Playhouse**.*

23030 **Neal, Bill.** DJ (WGTM, Wilson, NC, 1948).

23031 **Neal, Don.** Newscaster (KEX, Portland, OR, 1945). Sportscaster (KFLW, Klamath Falls, OR, 1947; KWLK, Longview, WA, 1948).

23032 **Neal, Eleanor.** COM-HE (WMBM, Miami Beach, FL, 1957).

23033 **Neal, James "Jim."** Newscaster (KOME, Tulsa, OK, 1940–1941). DJ (*RFD 93*, WSLI, Jackson, MS, 1948; WAPO, Chattanooga, TN, 1956). Sportscaster (KOME, 1940).

23034 **Neal, Kay.** Singer (WHO, Des Moines, IA, 1937).

23035 **Neal, Lee.** Newscaster (WPAR, Parkersburg, WV, 1942).

23036 **Neal, Roger.** Neal was a musician billed as "Roger Neal and his Ukulele" (KHJ, Los Angeles, CA, 1926).

23037 **Neal, Roy.** Newscaster (WIBG, Philadelphia, PA, 1942).

23038 **Neal, Si.** Leader (*Si Neal Orchestra*, instr. mus. prg., WORK, York, PA, 1936).

23039 **Neal, Tom.** DJ (*Ticker Toons*, WCOM, Parkersburg, WV, 1948). Sportscaster (*Let's Talk Sports*, WTAP, Parkersburg, WV, 1954).

23040 **Nealan, Ray.** Tenor (*Ray Nealan*, vcl. mus. prg., KFWI, San Francisco, CA, 1926).

23041 **Neale, Floyd.** Chief announcer (WGBS, New York, NY, 1927–1928).

23042 **Neale, Louis "Lou."** Sportscaster (*Sports Roundup*, WFGN, Gaffney, SC, 1948). DJ (*You Name It—We Play It*, WFGN, 1950).

23043 **Nealon, T.V.** Announcer Nealon often proclaimed his station to be "The Voice of the Anthracite" (WQAN, Scranton, PA, 1925–1927).

23044 **Neapolitan Four.** Instrumentalists, opera singers, and comedians were presented on the variety show (KPO, San Francisco, CA, 1927).

23045 ***Neapolitan Moments.*** Typical Neapolitan folk songs were played by an orchestra of mandolins and violins. Tenor Nicola Mercorelli and soprano Esther Liquori were featured (WCDA, New York, NY, 1930).

23046 ***Neapolitan Nights.*** Milton Cross was the announcer on the program that featured Neapolitan music. The performers included soprano Delores Cassinelli, tenor and musical director Giuseppe de Benedetto, accordionist Joe Biviano and a mandolin quartet (30 min., Sunday, 12:00–12:30 P.M., NBC-Red, 1930). An earlier version consisted of only vocal selections with accordion accompaniment (30 min., Monday, 9:00–9:30 P.M., NBC-Blue, 1928–1929).

23047 **Neapolitan Quartet.** Vocal group consisting of tenors E. Vallett and D. Carra; baritone E. Porcini; and bass F. Figone (KPO, San Francisco, CA, 1927).

23048 **Nearn, Joe.** DJ (*1490 Club*, KFFA, Helena, AR, 1947).

23049 **Neatherly, John W.** DJ (*Swing Shift*, KSAM, Huntsville, TX, 1947).

23050 **Neatour, Harold.** Announcer (WRVA, Richmond, VA, 1928–1929).

23051 ***(The) Nebbs.*** The situation comedy was based on the comic strip of the same name created by Sol Hess and W.A. Carlson in 1923. The comic strip offered a continuous story, not a daily gag. Both in the strip and on the radio program, Rudy Nebb, the husband, was a strong family man. The program was a pleasant, light hearted comedy serial. Announcer Tommy Dixon introduced the show with: "Cystex presents *The Nebbs* starring Gene and Kathleen Lockhart as Rudy and Fannie Nebbs—straight from America's comic strips with Junior, Obie and all the others you've laughed and adventured with for 22 years." Music was supplied by Bud Carlton (30 min., Sunday, 4:30–5:00 P.M., MBS, 1945).

23052 Nebel, Long John. DJ (WOR, New York, NY, 1956). *See* ***Long John.***

23053 Neblett, Johnny. Sportscaster (KWK, St. Louis, MO, 1941).

23054 Nebraska State Hospital Orchestra. State orchestra directed by Peter Thordsen (KFKX, Hasting, NE, 1925).

23055 *Neck of the Woods.* CBS brought authentic Americana to the radio listening public with the *Neck of the Woods* program. The writer was Carl Carmer, author of *Stars Fell on Alabama* and *Listen for a Lonesome Drum.* The first program dealt with the Ohio River Valley by presenting folk yarns and songs of the region (30 min., Monday, 8:30–9:00 P.M., CBS, 1930s).

23056 *Ned Jordan, Secret Agent.* The detective serial was written by Fran Striker, creator of the *Lone Ranger.* The producer was George W. Trendle, who was also closely associated with that radio favorite. *Ned Jordan, Secret Agent* was a sustaining program featuring Jack McCarthy in the title role, who also provided necessary narration to clarify and advance the plot. Dick Osgood and Shirley Squires were also in the cast (30 min., Saturday, 8:00–8:30 P.M., WXYZ, Detroit, MI, 1939).

23057 *Ned Sparks Show.* Dead-pan movie comedian Sparks' comedy show was sponsored by the Travel and Publicity Bureau of the Ontario Provincial Government. Vocalists Sair Lee, Dave Davies and Romanelli's Orchestra appeared with Sparks (30 min., Sunday, 5:30–6:00 P.M. CBS, 1941).

23058 Nedbalova, Marianne. Violinist (WOR, Newark, NJ, 1925).

23059 Nedin, Richard "Dick." DJ (*Song Shop*, WKNY, Kingston, NY, 1948; *RL Juke Box*, WWRL, New York, NY, 1950; WEOK, Poughkeepsie, NY, 1954; WKNY, Kingston, NY, 1955).

23060 Nedry, Roger. Sports commentator (*The Sportsman*, KPAS, Banning, CA, 1948). DJ (*Chinnin' and Spinnin',* KPAS, 1950).

23061 Nedvesky, Chester. DJ (KIYI, Shelby, MT, 1948).

23062 Neece, Helen. COM-HE (KRES, St. Joseph, MO, 1956).

23063 Needham, Ed. DJ (*Concord Ballroom*, WKXL, Concord, NH, 1954).

23064 Needham, Leo. Actor Needham appeared on the *Lowney Sweethearts* program sponsored by Lowney Chocolates (NBC-Blue, 1928; the *Gold Spot Pals* program sponsored by Grafton & Knight Company, NBC-Blue, 1928; and *Empire Builders* sponsored by the Great Northern Railroad, NBC, 1929).

23065 Needham, W.C. Newscaster (WTFB, Troy, AL, 1948).

23066 Neeham, Marion. COM-HE (WTBF, Troy, AL, 1949).

23067 Neel, Clive Lee. Newscaster (KASA, Elk City, OK, 1942).

23068 Neeld, Jimmie. DJ (*Spinner's Sanctum*, KYER, Albuquerque, NM, 1949).

23069 Neeley, Bert. Violinist (WLW, Cincinnati, OH, 1926–1929).

23070 Neeley, Henry M. Actor-composer-announcer Neeley originally was a theater and film critic for the Philadelphia *Evening Ledger.* He also published and edited one of radio's first fan magazines, *Radio in the Home.* Neeley founded and became the first secretary of the Philadelphia Opera Society. He became director of WIP (Philadelphia, PA) in 1921. He played the role of the "Old Stager" when he hosted the *Philco Hour of Theater Memories* (NBC-Red, New York, NY, 1925). Neeley also was in the cast of *Orphans of Divorce* and *Stella Dallas. See* ***The Philco Hour of Theater Memories.***

23071 Neely, Jack. DJ (*Mailbox Roundup*, WKTM, Mayfield, KY, 1948–1950).

23072 Neer, Chuck. DJ (*Plantation Time*, WIAM, Williamston, NC, 1954).

23073 Neff, Ernie. Newscaster (KQV, Pittsburgh, PA, 1940; WHJB, Greenburg, PA, 1941; WCAE Pittsburgh, PA, 1944).

23074 Neff, Helene. Soprano (WNLC, New London, CT, 1937).

23075 Neff, Joan. COM-HE (WBNY, Buffalo, NY, 1955).

23076 Neff, Marie K. Conducted a women's club program (KDKA, Pittsburgh, PA, 1924).

23077 Neff, Walter. Announcer (WPCH, New York, NY 1929; WOR, Newark, NJ, 1925–1929).

23078 Negin, Kolia. Tenor (NBC-Pacific Network, 1927).

23079 Negri, Rino. Newscaster (WHOM, Jersey City, NJ, 1940).

23080 Negrin, Lucille. Concert violinist (WOR, Newark, NJ, 1929).

23081 *Negro Dialect Songs and Stories.* Comedian-singer Al A. Reynolds sang and told dialect and stories (KTHS, St. Paul, MN, 1925).

23082 Negro Melody Singers. Vocal group (WNYC, New York, NY, 1939).

23083 Negus, Neva. "Artistic bird warbler" (KFI, Los Angeles, CA, 1929).

23084 *Nehi Program.* Norman Brokenshire hosted the music program that was sponsored by the Nehi Bottling Company, makers of Nehi soft drinks. Music was supplied by singer Veronica Wiggins, the Rondoleers vocal group and the George Shackley orchestra (15 min., 1931).

23085 Nehrlick, Ruth. Violinist (KWSC, Pullman, WA, 1926).

23086 Nehrling, Wally. DJ (*Dawn Patrol* and *Platter Chatter*, WIRE, Indianapolis, IN, 1947).

23087 Neibling, Daisy. Soprano (WBBC, and WCBU, Brooklyn, NY, 1929).

23088 Neibling, Ed. Newscaster (KTUL, Tulsa, OK, 1948).

23089 Neibur, Eddie. Leader (*Eddie Neibur Orchestra*, instr. mus. prg., WBBM, Chicago, IL, 1935).

23090 Neidig, Joe. DJ (KFDA, Amarillo, TX, 1948).

23091 *Neighbor Nell* (aka *The Nellie Revell Show* and *Nellie Revell Interviews*). *See* ***Nellie Revell Interviews.***

23092 Neighbors, Dorothy. COM-HE Neighbors broadcast "menu hints" (KOL, Seattle, WA, 1929).

23093 *Neighbors.* Zona Gale and Marion DeForest wrote the dramatic sketch based on Gale's *Friendship Town* novels. The sustaining program dramatized the doings of Main Street characters in an average American town. The cast included Effie Marsh, Elsie Mae Gordon, Mary Buckley, Marion Barney, Helen Lowell, Arthur Aylesworth and Lorna Elliott. The program's theme was "Old Fashioned Garden" (30 min., Weekly, 10:30–11:00 P.M., NBC-Red, 1933).

23094 Neil, (Mrs.) F.H., Jr. Pianist (KSD, St. Louis, MO, 1925).

23095 Neil, Jack. Newscaster (KRIC, Beaumont, TX, 1942, 1945; KTRM, Beaumont, TX, 1948).

23096 Neilan, Ray. DJ (*Bernie and Ray Matinee* and *Request Matinee*, WKNB, New Britain, CT, 1948–1952; *Musical Showcase*, WKNB, New Britain, CT, 1955).

23097 Neill, Amy. Violinist (WBAL, Baltimore, MD, 1926).

23098 Neilsen, Jay. DJ (WITH, Baltimore, MD, 1947).

23099 Neilson, (Mrs.) C.L. Soprano (KGW, Portland, OR, 1924).

23100 Neilson, Ellen. Singer billed as "The GE Girl" (WGY, Schenectady, NY, 1923).

23101 Neilson, Paul. Newscaster (WJBO, Baton Rouge, LA, 1939; NBC-Blue, 1945; WGN, Chicago, IL, 1947).

23102 Neime, Walder. DJ (*Breakfast Club*, WMBL, Morehead City, NC, 1949).

23103 Neithamer, (Lt. Colonel) William F. Newscaster (KTSA, San Antonio, TX, 1944–1947).

23104 Nekuda, Lydia. COM-HE (KFOR, Lincoln, NE, 1949).

23105 Nelin, Cecil. DJ (KNEL, Brady, TX, 1948).

23106 *Nell Vinick.* Miss Vinick broadcast beauty hints for women listeners (15 min., Friday, 11:00–11:15 A.M., CBS, 1929).

23107 Nelles, Marvin "Marv." DJ (*1490 Club*, KORN, Mitchell, SD, 1948; WSAU, Wausau, WI, 1955; *Rise and Shine*, WRIG, Wausau, WI, 1960).

23108 Nelles, Maurice. Announcer (KUSD, Vermillion, SD, 1927).

23109 *Nellie Revell Interviews* (aka *Nellie Revell, Nellie Revell at Large, Neighbor Nell* and *The Nellie Revell Show*). Revell was a veteran news reporter, *Variety* columnist and broadcaster. She originated one of the first and best radio "talk" shows. Her frank, inquiring interviews were examples of early American radio's programming at its best. On her 1931 program she was billed as "The Voice of *Radio Digest*" (15 min, NBC-Red, 1931). Over the years her program had various names and was broadcast at different times, but remained essentially the same (15 min. Sunday, 9:45–10:00 A.M., NBC, 1935). Revell's programs usually included "cheer-up" material of inspirational talk, poetry and music. Using "Love Thy Neighbor" as her theme, Revell was always an up-beat host. Music was supplied by organist Chandler Goldwaithe and vocalist Jimmy Wilkinson

23110 ***Nellie Revell the Voice of Radio Digest.*** Revell, who wrote for *Radio Digest*, was sponsored by the weekly radio magazine. Revell interviewed various show business personalities and told stories about radio, stage and motion picture stars (15 min., NBC-Red, 1931).

23111 Nellums, (Mrs.) M.E. Soprano (WLAC, Nashville, TN, 1929).

23112 Nelsen, Esther. Poetry readings (WROK, Rockford, IL, 1937).

23113 Nelsen, Mel. Newscaster (WLB, Minneapolis, MN, 1941).

23114 Nelskog, Wally. DJ (*Wally's Music Makers*, KRSC, Seattle, WA, 1949; KJR, Seattle, WA, 1955).

23115 Nelson, Albi. DJ (*Matinee of Music*, KRLC, Lewiston, ID, 1954).

23116 Nelson, Ann. COM-HE (KPOR, Quincy, WA, 1960).

23117 Nelson, Art. DJ (*Sunny Side Up*, KLIF, Dallas, TX, 1949, 1955).

23118 Nelson, Bert. Sportscaster (WIND, Chicago, IL, 1945).

23119 Nelson, Professor Bertram. Nelson was a Professor of Public Speaking at the University of Chicago. He broadcast lectures on good speech (WMAQ, Chicago, IL, 1929–1930).

23120 Nelson, Bette. COM-HE (WBRD, Bradenton, FL, 1957).

23121 Nelson, Billie Jean. COM-HE (WTIK, Durham, NC, 1956).

23122 Nelson, Blanche Beaumont. Soprano (KYW, Chicago, IL, 1923).

23123 Nelson, Bob. DJ (*Coffee Cup Club*, KOVC, Valley City, ND, 1947–1949; *Band Parade*, KOVC, 1950; *Music for You*, KSJB, Jamestown, ND, 1954).

23124 Nelson, Bob. DJ (*Swing Clinic*, WBBQ, Augusta, GA, 1948–1950).

23125 Nelson, Bob. DJ (*Music For You*, WBBZ, Ponca City, OK, 1948).

23126 Nelson, Bob. DJ (*Musically Yours*, WSUN, Charleston, SC, 1948).

23127 Nelson, Carl. DJ (*Masters of Rhythm*, WTMJ, Milwaukee, WI, 1948–1950).

23128 Nelson, Charles. DJ (*Platter Parade*, KOLE, Port Arthur, TX, 1948; *Harlem Echoes*, KGBC, Galveston, TX, 1950).

23129 Nelson, Chet. Leader (*Chet Nelson Orchestra*, instr. mus. prg., WIP, Philadelphia, PA, 1936).

23130 Nelson, Cy. Newscaster (WGIL, Galesburg, IL, 1946). DJ (*Half Music—Half Nelson*, WGIL, 1949; *Half Music—Half Nelson*, KXEL, Waterloo, IA, 1952).

23131 Nelson, David "Dave." DJ (*Dave Nelson Show*, WSAP, Portsmouth-Norfolk, VA, 1948; *The Dave Nelson Show*, WWAP, Portsmouth, VA, 1950).

23132 Nelson, Dick. Actor Nelson was in the cast of *Life Can Be Beautiful* and *Second Husband*.

23133 Nelson, Dick. Newscaster (WPIC, Sharon, PA, 1941).

23134 Nelson, Dolph. Actor Nelson appeared on *Dear Mom* and *Ma Perkins*.

23135 Nelson, Earl. Ukulele soloist (WEEI, Boston, MA, 1925).

23136 Nelson, Earle. Crooning "fur trapper" Nelson sang on the *Fox Fur Trappers* program (CBS, New York, NY, 1929).

23137 Nelson, Emelia. Pianist (WCBD, Zion, IL, 1924–1926).

23138 Nelson, Emilie. COM-HE (KLTZ, Glasgow, MT, 1957).

23139 Nelson, Esther. Organist (WTIC, Hartford, CT, 1926).

23140 Nelson, Florence. Soprano (WJAZ, Chicago, IL, 1923).

23141 Nelson, Ford. Black DJ (*Let's Have Fun, Tan Town Jubilee, Highway to Heaven, Hallelujah Jubilee*, WDIA, Memphis, TN, 1950s). Nelson was a talented hot pianist who had backed up B.B. King. As a DJ, he played more serious music and many gospel songs. He was sometimes called the "Grand Old Pappa of Gospel Music." Cantor (1992, p. 102) describes Nelson's *Let's Have Fun*, his rhythm and blues show, as "cerebral, subdued and sophisticated."

23142 Nelson, Frank. DJ (*1340 Club*, WLDY, Ladysmith, WI, 1948).

23143 Nelson, Gene. Newscaster (*Noon News*, KFAM, St. Cloud, MN, 1948).

23144 Nelson, Gene. DJ (*Start the Music*, WLCS, Baton Rouge, LA, 1950). Sportscaster (WLCS, 1956).

23145 Nelson, George. Chief announcer-bass (KOMO, Seattle, WA, 1928).

23146 Nelson, (Mrs.) George. COM-HE (WLIP, Kenosha, WI, 1956).

23147 Nelson, George B. DJ (*1450 Club*, WHIT, New Bern, NC, 1948). Sportscaster (WRNB, New Bern, NC, 1960).

23148 Nelson, Gertrude "Gert." COM-HE (WAOK, Atlanta, GA, 1956).

23149 Nelson, Gordon. DJ (*Alarm Clock Club*, KOVE, Lander, WY, 1948).

23150 Nelson, Grace. 14-year-old pianist (WQJ, Chicago, IL, 1924–1925).

23151 Nelson, Harriet Hilliard. Harriet Hilliard was a popular big band singer before marrying band leader Ozzie Nelson. On *The Adventures of Ozzie and Harriet*, both on radio and TV, she displayed a warm presence with skillful humorous touches. *See* ***The Adventures of Ozzie and Harriet***.

23152 Nelson, Herbert "Herb." Actor Nelson was in the cast of *Betty and Bob, Carters of Elm Street, Dan Harding's Wife, Girl Alone* and *Young Dr. Malone*.

23153 Nelson, Howard. News analyst (WDAY, Fargo, ND, 1945; *News as it Happens*, WAKR, Akron, OH, 1948).

23154 Nelson, Irene. COM-HE (WLIP, Kenosha, WI, 1957).

23155 Nelson, Jack. Announcer (WJJD, Mooseheart, IL, 1925–1927).

23156 Nelson, Jack. One of radio's first singing stars (WDAP, Chicago, IL, 1927).

23157 Nelson, Jack. DJ (*590 Club*, WLVA, Lynchburg, VA, 1949).

23158 Nelson, Jaline. COM-HE (KWBW, Hutchinson, KS, 1949).

23159 Nelson, Jerry. DJ (*Afternoon Show*, WMSR, Manchester, TN, 1960).

23160 Nelson, Karl. News analyst (*The Town Crier*, WTOL, Toledo, OH, 1940–1941).

23161 Nelson, Kathryn. COM-HE (KNOW, Austin, TX, 1949).

23162 Nelson, Leonard. Leader (Leonard Nelson Orchestra broadcasting from the Knickerbocker Grill, WGY, Schenectady, NY, 1924).

23163 Nelson, Lindsey. Sportscaster (WKGN, Knoxville, TN, 1947; *Sports Time*, WKGN, 1948; WROL, Knoxville, TN, 1949; *This Week in Sports* and *Ask the Sports World*, NBC, 1952–1960).

After broadcasting football games at the University of Tennessee, Nelson received battle stars for seven campaigns while serving with the Ninth Infantry Division in World War II. His national exposure came when he began broadcasting baseball games for the Liberty Broadcasting System. He joined NBC in 1952 and worked college and professional football games for more than ten years.

23164 Nelson, Lois Curtis. Pianist (WQJ, Chicago, IL, 1925).

23165 Nelson, M.L. News analyst (*The Billboard*, WHO, Des Moines, IA, 1947–1948).

23166 Nelson, Madame. Psychologist (KFI, Los Angeles, CA, 1926).

23167 Nelson, Marie. Actress Nelson appeared on the daytime serial programs *Aunt Abby Jones* (1938); *Bachelor's Children, Myrt and Marge, Romance of Helen Trent* and *Chickie* (WBBM, Chicago, Il, 1933).

23168 Nelson, Maurine. COM-HE (WGET, Gettysburg, PA, 1951).

23169 Nelson, Myrtle. COM-HE (KFAD, Fairfield, IA, 1954).

23170 Nelson, Nancy. Singer (*Nancy Nelson*, vcl. mus. prg., KMOX, St. Louis, MO, 1935).

23171 Nelson, Nancy. COM-HE (WFIN, Findlay, OH, 1951).

23172 Nelson, Ozzie. Leader (*Ozzie Nelson Orchestra*, instr. mus. prg., MBS, 1936, 1938; CBS, 1935–1942). In 1940, the announcer introduced the Nelson band by saying, "Young America's favorite from the Blackhawk in Chicago, Illinois, Ozzie Nelson."

Nelson first organized a band while in law school at Rutgers. His successful band appearances caused him to give up a law career for one in music. The Nelson band appeared frequently on radio and motion pictures, in addition to a prolific recording record. In addition to many remote broadcasts, the band appeared on the *Baker's Broadcast*, first, with Joe Penner and, later, with Robert Ripley. The early Nelson band of the 1930s during its busiest radio years included: Nelson, ldr.-vcls.; Holly Humphreys, t.; Harry Johnson, t.; Bo Ashford, t.; Abe Lincoln, tb.; Elmer Smithers, tb.; Charlie Bluebeck, clr.-as.; Bill Stone, clr.-as.; Bill Nelson, clr.-ts.; Sid Brokaw, v.-vb.; Harry Gray, p.; Chauncey Gray, p.; Sandy Wolfe, g.; Fred Whiteside, sb.; Joe Bohan, d. and Harriet Hilliard, vcls.

After many radio appearances, Ozzie and wife, Harriet Hilliard (Peggy Lou Snyder), his former band vocalist, began a successful radio program — *The Adventures of Ozzie and Harriet.* After the radio program became an even greater success on television, Nelson was unable to meet the demands of leading a band and disbanded it. *See* ***The Adventures of Ozzie and Harriet.***

23173 **Nelson, Paul.** Pianist (KFOB, Burlingame, CA, 1925).

23174 **Nelson, Ralph.** Sportscaster (KCKN, Kansas City, KS, 1938).

23175 **Nelson, Ramona H.** COM-HE (KRAL, Rawlins, WY, 1957).

23176 **Nelson, Robert C.** Newscaster (WOSH, Oshkosh, WI, 1944–1945).

23177 **Nelson, Ross.** Sportscaster (WGRM, Greenwood, MS, 1940). Newscaster (WOPI, Bristol, TN, 1941).

23178 **Nelson, Sally Jo.** Singer (WGN, Chicago, IL, 1936).

23179 **Nelson, Shirley.** COM-HE (WHWB, Rutland, VT

23180 **Nelson, Stan.** DJ (*Radio Almanac*, KITE, San Antonio, TX, 1948–1952; *Musical Clock*, KITE, 1954–1956).

23181 **Nelson, Stub.** Sportscaster (KEX, Portland, OR and KGW, Portland, OR, 1940).

23182 **Nelson, Tank.** Sportscaster, WBBB, Burlington, NC, 1944).

23183 **Nelson, Ted.** Announcer-general manager Nelson came to station WRNY (New York, NY) after working at WMCA (New York,.NY) and WPCH (Hoboken, NJ). Nelson also broadcast boxing bouts (WRNY, 1929–1930).

23184 **Nelson, Ted.** DJ (*Music Matinee* and *After Hours*, KVET, Austin, TX, 1950).

23185 **Nelson, Ted.** DJ (*Merry-Go-Round*, WHYN, Holyoke, MA, 1950).

23186 **Nelson, Thomas.** Newscaster (KHSL, Chico, CA, 1945).

23187 **Nelson, Vernon.** DJ (KTRI , Sioux City, IA, 1950).

23188 **Nelson, Violet.** Pianist Nelson accompanied such CW music groups as the Happy Jacks, the Sunshine Four and the Old Time Fiddlers (WNAX, Yankton, SD, 1928).

23189 **Nelson, Walt.** DJ (*Barnyard Jamboree*, WUSN, Charleston, SC, 1948).

23190 **Nelson, Wayne.** Announcer and director (WNRC, Greensboro, NC, 1929).

23191 **Nelson, Wilford.** DJ (*Music Shoppe*, WHSC, Hartsville, SC, 1952).

23192 **Nelson, William Warvelle.** Station orchestra leader (WCCO, Minneapolis–St. Paul, MN, 1928).

23193 **Nelster, Lucille.** Violist (WKAF, Milwaukee, WI, 1926).

23194 **Nelton, Edward.** Singer (WHN, New York, NY, 1925).

23195 **Nemeth, Margaret.** COM-HE (WCPA, Clearfield, PA, 1956).

23196 **Nemeth, William.** News analyst (*The Federal Index*, WARL, Arlington, VA, 1947).

23197 ***Nemo and Eddie's Orchestra.*** Instr. mus. prg. (WLW, Cincinnati, OH, 1936).

23198 **Nenick, Ruth.** Actress (KHJ, Los Angeles, CA, 1929–1930).

23199 **Nenno, Robert.** DJ (*Matinee Mailbag*, WGVA, Geneva, NY, 1952).

23200 **Neo-Russian String Quartet.** Instrumental group (NBC-WFAA, Dallas, TX, 1929).

23201 **Nero, Jim.** DJ (*980 Club*, KFRD, Roshenberg, TX, 1948).

23202 **Nesbit, Carolyn.** Singer (WSB, Atlanta, GA, 1925).

23203 **Nesbit, Jean.** COM-HE (KCKN, Kansas City, MO, 1957).

23204 **Nesbitt, Dick.** Sportscaster (WKRC, Cincinnati, OH, 1941,1945–1946; *Dick Nesbitt Sports*, WKRC, 1947; WJJD, Chicago, IL, 1954).

23205 **Nesbitt, Jane.** COM-HE (WJMA, Orange, VA, 1956).

23206 **Nesbitt, John.** News commentator (*The Passing Parade*, MBS, 1937).

23207 **Nesbitt, Norman.** News commentator (KHJ, Los Angeles, CA, 1939, 1944; *What's New with Norman Nesbitt*, ABC, 1945).

23208 **Nesbitt, Phil.** DJ (WITH, Baltimore, MD, 1947).

23209 **Nesselroad, Paul.** DJ (KVOR, Colorado Springs, CO, 1960).

23210 ***Nestle Chocolateers.*** The music group led by Nat Brusiloff was sponsored by Nestle's Chocolate Company. Singer Chick Farmer regularly appeared with Brusilloff's band. Ethel Merman and Mary Spencer also appeared with the band on the program at times (NBC-Blue, 1931). Two years later, the program's cast included Walter O'Keefe as announcer, host and performer. Singer Ethel Shutta and the Don Bestor Orchestra also were featured. When not singing, O'Keefe and Shutta performed various comedy bits (30 min., Friday, 8:00–8:30 P.M., NBC-Blue, 1933).

23211 **Netherland, Joel.** DJ (*Record Ranch*, WAZF, Yazoo City, MS, 1954).

23212 **Netherly, Carol.** COM-HE (KOSY, Texarkana, TX, 1955).

23213 **Nette, Vera.** Operatic prima donna (WGBS, New York, NY, 1929).

23214 **Nettleton, Dick.** DJ (*At Your Command*, KVAN, Vancouver, WA, 1949).

23215 **Networks.** Networks had their formal beginnings in 1926 with the formation of the National Broadcasting Company (NBC). The inception of NBC began when the Radio Corporation of America (RCA) purchased New York's pioneer radio station, WEAF, from the American Telephone & Telegraph Company (AT&T). WEAF had pioneered "chain broadcasting" in which stations were linked by AT&T telephone lines to form temporary networks for such special events programming as the Dempsey-Carpentier fight, World Series baseball games, election events, etc. All of these "network" events, however, were one-time presentations. By February 12, 1924, the *Eveready Hour* was transmitted over a telephone system from WEAF in New York to WJAR (Providence, RI). As a result of this successful "chain broadcasting," the telephone system was extended the following year to include twelve stations, including one as far west as Chicago.

When station WJZ, operated by RCA, was unable to use rival AT&T's telephone lines for chain transmission, the station was forced to use Western Union Company's telegraphic lines. Because of the nature of Western Union's lines, WJZ experienced inferior transmission in quality of voice and music. WJZ immediately sought improved means to transmit their chain broadcasts. Sponsors approved the concept of chain (network) broadcasting in order to increase the number of listeners who would hear their commercials. Broadcasters also favored networks because they helped station program directors to fill their daily broadcast schedules with much needed talent (Chase , 1942, p. 28).

In January, 1926, RCA approved the formation of a new company that was to become the National Broadcasting Company. RCA owed 50 percent of the new company; General Electric, 30 percent; and Westinghouse, 20 percent. George McClelland became general manager of NBC and Bertha Brainard the program manager. NBC's formal beginning was on November 1, 1926, when it linked nineteen stations in a gala inaugural broadcast from the Grand Ballroom of New York's Waldorf-Astoria Hotel before an audience of a thousand invited guests. Participants on this spectacular broadcast included: Mary Garden singing from Chicago; Will Rogers speaking from Kansas City, Missouri; pianist Harold Bauer; Metropolitan Opera tenor, Tito Ruffo; the comedy team of Weber and Fields; the New York Symphony conducted by Dr. Walter Damrosch; Cesare Sodero conducting a light opera company; the Edwin Franko Goldman band; and remote broadcasts by the orchestras of Ben Bernie, B.A. Rolfe, George Olsen and Vincent Lopez. The era of network radio had begun.

By the following year, NBC had both the Red and Blue networks in operation, originating from WEAF and WJZ, respectively. Chase (1942, p. 40) noted differences in the Red and Blue networks in 1942, by suggesting that the Red network carried mostly commercial programs, while the Blue network became the "cultural network."

Where RCA, GE and Westinghouse had provided a solid financial foundation for the National Broadcasting Company network, the next to be developed — the Columbia Broadcasting Company — did not enjoy this luxury. From the start, severe financial problems beset United Broadcasters, Inc., the company that became CBS. In the spring of 1926, a group of eastern broadcasters met in New York's Astor Hotel to discuss their mutual problems. George A. Coats, who happened to be staying at the hotel at the time of the broadcasters' conference, saw radio as a potentially profitable business. Coats happened to meet with Arthur Judson, the president of the Columbia Concert Bureau, the company that managed most of the leading concert stars of the day. The two men joined with Major Andrew J. White, who was then working at General Electric's WGY (Schenectady, NY) station, a song broker by the name of Francis Marsh and Edward Ervin, the assistant manager of the New York Philharmonic Association to form United Broadcasters, Inc., in January, 1927.

United Broadcasters, Inc. was formed with great enthusiasm but limited financial resources. After suffering many financial hardships, Major Andrew White, director of the company, negotiated the sale of the company's rights to the Columbia Phonograph Company, who fearing rival Victor Recording Company's joining with RCA, decided to protect their own interests by investing in radio broadcasting. White then organized the Columbia Phonograph Broadcasting Company. On September 18, 1927, the new Columbia Company inaugurated its own spectacular inaugural broadcast day with a symphonic concert by an orchestra directed by Howard Barlow, followed by a presentation of an original American opera, *The King's Henchman* with music by Deems Taylor and libretto by Edna St. Vincent Millay.

Financial difficulties persisted and the Columbia Phonograph Broadcasting Company sold the network back to Major White and his group after operating for the first three months at a monthly loss of $100,000. Badly needing an infusion of additional cash, White used the influence of a Philadelphia dentist, Dr. Leon Levy, to persuade Jerome H. Louchheim to invest in the network. By chance, another major figure in the development of network radio — William S. Paley — then entered the picture because he was related by marriage to Leon Levy.

Paley, the brother-in-law of Dr. Levy, was the son of the owner of the Congress Cigar Company. Suffering from the competition of cigarettes, Congress Cigars had experienced a drastic loss of sales. In order to stem this continued sales decline, the company tried radio advertising by sponsoring the popular *LaPalina Smoker* program. After twenty-six weeks of radio advertising, Congress Cigar sales zoomed from 400,000 to more than a million sold daily (Chase, 1942, p. 43). Enthused by the effect of the company's radio advertising and the opportunities radio provided, Paley urged Louchheim to sell his interest in United Broadcasters to him. Paley then became president of United Broadcasters, while White remained president of the Columbia Phonograph Broadcasting Company. In January, 1929, the two companies merged and Paley became president of the Columbia Broadcasting System, the company that was created. CBS had formally begun.

Some other networks were:

1. The Quality Network was organized in 1929 with stations WOR (Newark, NJ), WLW (Cincinnati, OH), WLS (Chicago, IL) and WXYZ (Detroit, MI). It became the Mutual Broadcasting System in 1934.

2. The Don Lee Network began in 1929 as the West Coast branch of CBS.

3. The Yankee Network was begun in 1929 by John Shepard III with stations WNAC (Boston, MA), WAAB (Boston, MA), WICC (Bridgeport, CT) and WEAN (Providence, RI) participating. General Tire and Rubber Company purchased the network in 1943.

4. The RKO Network, founded in 1928, was an outgrowth of the Radio-Keith-Orpheum theater chain. It was purchased by the General Tire and Rubber Company in 1955.

5. Gordon McLendon operated the Liberty Broadcasting system, best known for its broadcasts of baseball games, about half of which were studio recreations. It went national in 1950 with 240 affiliated stations. At its peak it achieved a network of 458 affiliated stations before ceasing operations in 1952.

The radio networks that flourished during radio's golden years began to fade in importance with the coming of television. After World War II there were hundreds of stations that were not affiliated with networks. This meant they had many hours of programming to fill at little expense. DJs and recorded music supplied many of the answers as local radio programming began to become more important

During radio's golden age, there were 56 million radio sets in American homes. By 1951, the number of sets had grown to 99 million sets, but the Hooper ratings showed the medium's popularity was fading. A comparison of some of radio's biggest shows in 1948 and 1951 shows this clearly:

Program	1948	1951
Jack Benny Show	26.5	4.8
Bob Hope Show	16	3.2
Groucho Marx Show	12	5.0
Bing Crosby Show	18	3.8
Amos 'n' Andy	13.6	5.9
Arthur Godfrey's Talent Scouts	20.3	5.9

The old favorites had lost much of their audience. Quiz and giveaway shows enjoyed a limited success, but they were merely temporary stopgaps. Network radio was on its last legs in 1960. The only old favorites still on the air were the *Breakfast Club* and the *Arthur Godfrey Show.* These disappeared in 1968 and 1972.

23216 Netzorg, Benedetson. Organist (WWJ, Detroit, MI, 1932).

23217 Neu, J. Alfred. Tenor (*Alfred J. Neu*, vcl. mus. prg., WJBC, Bloomington, IN, 1936).

23218 Neubauer, Von. DJ (KLEE, Ottumwa, IA, 1956).

23219 Neumayer, Marilou. Actress Neumayer was in the cast of the *Ma Perkins* daytime serial.

23220 Neumeyer, Joyce. COM-HE (KRSL, Russell, KS, 1956).

23221 Neumiller, Howard. Pianist (WEBH, Chicago, IL, 1925–1926 and musical director, WENR, Chicago, IL and WBCN, Chicago, IL, 1928; *Howard Neumiller*, instr. mus. prg., CBS, 1936).

23222 Neuschwander, John. DJ (*Music 'Til Midnight*, KOOS, Coos Bay, OR, 1952).

23223 Neuschwander, Kathryn. Pianist (WEAF, New York, NY, 1925).

23224 Nevada, Charles. Sportscaster (WTMJ, Milwaukee, WI, 1937–1940).

23225 Nevers, Ernie. Sportscaster (*Scout Report*, KSAN, San Francisco, CA, 1949).

23226 Neville, Bill. Newscaster (KROC, Rochester, MN, 1940).

23227 Neville, Harry. Actor Neville was in the cast of *East of Cairo*, *The O'Neills* and *Sherlock Holmes.*

23228 Neville, Helen. COM-HE (WKBW, Buffalo, NY, 1951; WGR, Buffalo, NY, 1954–1955).

23229 Nevin, Olive [Olvin]. Soprano (KDKA, Pittsburgh, PA, 1924).

23230 Nevins, Belle. Singer (KCMO, Kansas City, MO, 1937).

23231 Nevins, George. Tenor (WSM, Nashville, TN, 1928).

23232 New, James H. "Jimmy." Sportscaster and play-by-play broadcaster of Cartersville High School sports events (WBHF, Cartersville, GA, 1947; *Jimmy New's Sports Show*, WBHF, 1948–1949; *Today in Sports*, WBHF, 1950).

23233 *New Adventures of Nero Wolfe.* A fictional creation by Rex Stout, obese detective Nero Wolfe was more comfortable sitting in an easy chair contemplating the orchids he loved to grow than chasing criminals. Nevertheless, Wolfe was the intelligent sleuth whose orders were carried out by Archie Goodwin, his tough, smart assistant. Archie got the facts and performed the acts that brought criminals to justice, but it was Wolfe's brain and logic that actually solved the crimes. Santos Ortega portrayed the fat master detective on the first *Adventures of Nero Wolfe* radio series broadcast by NBC-Blue in 1943. Himan Brown was the producer of the first Wolfe radio series. A second series with Francis X. Bushman as Wolfe and Elliott Lewis as Archie was broadcast in 1945 (MBS, 1945–1946). A third series with Sydney Greenstreet was broadcast in 1950 (NBC, 1950). Greenstreet portrayed Wolfe as a traveling detective, completely opposite to Rex Stout's easy chair bound sleuth. Archie Goodwin over the years was played by some five or six actors in the various formats broadcast.

23234 New Arlington Hotel Orchestra. Instr. musical group (KTHS, Hot Springs National Park, AK, 1926).

23235 *New Baby of 1939.* From the time of its birth, the progress of a baby was reported periodically on the program. The first two programs of the series were broadcast from the hospital where the baby was born. The others were from the baby's home. Broadcast in cooperation with the Milwaukee Medical Society, the program included the baby's parents, doctors and nurses in "how-to-do-it situations" about the "radio baby" (WTMJ, Milwaukee, WI, 1939).

23236 *New Big Show.* A Pacific Coast music program the *New Big Show* featured host Frank Gage introducing vocal solos, instrumental trios and quartets and musical selections by Frank Ellis and his Trocadero Orchestra. Vocal selections were performed by Clarence Hayes, "the Voice of the South," with his guitar, Cookie the Sunshine Girl and the Charles Marshall Singers (NBC-Pacific Network, 1929).

23237 New Britain Normal School Glee Club. Vocal group directed bu Pauline Myer (WTIC, Hartford, CT, 1925).

23238 ***New Business World.*** Merle Thorpe conducted the information service program for business men (30 min., Saturday, 8:00–8:30 P.M., NBC-Red, 1930).

23239 **New Century Brass Quartet.** The brass quartet included: Harry Kisselman, 1st t.; Walter MacDowell, 2nd t.; Ralph Binz, 1st tb.; James Walde, 2nd tb.; and Loretta Kerk, accompanist (WFI, Philadelphia, PA, 1925).

23240 ***New Deal on Main Street.*** Don Carney, later famous as Uncle Don, played the leading role of Uncle Luke on the serialized drama of rural life sponsored by Kopper's. Some programs took place at the village's brass band practices, giving the "boys" a chance to play their old fashioned musical selections (WOR, Newark, NJ, 1933).

23241 ***(The) New Jack Kirkwood Show.*** Comedian Kirkwood hosted the network variety show that featured Lillian Lee, Bill Gray, John Brown, Gloria Blondell, Dick Ryan, Doris Day and the orchestra of Lud Gluskin (30 min., CBS, 1946).

23242 ***New Mail Bag.*** Roy Baret and Jack Benkey answered listeners' questions about radio personalities, sang and told jokes on their sustaining weekly show (15 min., Wednesday, 2:45–3:00 P.M., KQV, Pittsburgh, PA, 1936).

23243 **New Method Laundry and Petroleum Dye Works Orchestra.** Company sponsored instrumental group (KTCL, Seattle, WA, 1925).

23244 **New Monterey Society Orchestra.** Popular club band directed by Elmer L. Cook (WOR, Newark, NJ, 1926).

23245 **New Orleans Harmony Kings.** New Orleans jazz band (WSMB, New Orleans, LA, 1925).

23246 ***New Penny.*** Actress Helen Hayes starred in the dramatic series written by Edith Meiser. Joseph Bell also appeared in the cast (30 min., Monday, 7:00–7:30 P.M. CST, NBC-Blue, 1936).

23247 **New Shanghai Orchestra.** San Francisco restaurant band (KFWI, San Francisco, CA, 1929).

23248 **New Willard Hotel Orchestra.** Hotel dance band (WRC, Washington, DC, 1926).

23249 ***New World a Coming.*** The distinguished series by and about African-Americans starred such performers as Canada Lee, Maxine Sullivan, Hazel Scott, Marian Anderson, Art Tatum, Ben Webster, Roy Eldridge, the Hall-Johnson Choir, Josh White, Charlie Shavers, Roy Wilkins and Georgia Burke. The topics presented in the series were: "The American Negro Theatre," "The Negro Reporter," "The Story of Negroes and Health," "A Statement by the Black Community on D-Day," "The Negro in Early American History" and "The Meaning of V-E Day to Negroes.

Partially based on a book by Black writer, Roy Otley, the series was broadcast as a local New York program. The series always presented dramatic and documentary programs featuring famous Black performers (30 min., Weekly, WMCA, New York, NY, 1944–1945).

23250 ***New York by a Representative New Yorker.*** Newspaper gossip columnist and radio commentator Walter Winchell began his broadcasting career in 1929 with his lively program about New Yorkers and New York life. It was the beginning of a long successful broadcasting career. *See* **Winchell, Walter** *and* ***The Jergens' Journal.***

23251 ***New York Civic Orchestra.*** Symphonic music program (WTAR, Norfolk, VA, 1938).

23252 ***New York Close Up.*** Jinx Falkenburg and husband Tex McCrary talked about big city doings and interviewed such famous guests as Rise Stevens, Jim Robinson, Laraine Day and Vic Damone on their hour show (1952). *See* **Husband-and-Wife Talk Shows, "Jinx" Falkenburg and** ***Tex and Jinx.***

23253 ***New York Edison Hour.*** The good music program presented classical and semi-classical music selections weekly (WJZ, New York, NY, 1925).

23254 ***New York Herald Tribune Observer.*** The *Herald Tribune* [newspaper] sponsored the news commentary program (30 min., Monday and Friday, 11:00–11:30 P.M., CBS, 1930).

23255 **New York Oratorio Society.** Singing group directed by Albert Stoessel (NBC, New York, NY, 1926).

23256 **New York Philharmonic Orchestra.** Symphony orchestra founded in 1925 (WGY, Schenectady, NY, 1925). The *New York Philharmonic Orchestra*, inst. mus. prg. began broadcasting in 1927 on Sundays for a variable period that might extend from 45 minutes to two hours (CBS, 1927). In 1930, the orchestra was conducted by Bernardino Molinari (60 min., Sunday, 1:00–2:00 P.M., NBC-Red, 1930; CBS, 1935). For the 1936 broadcast season, guest conductors from November through April were John Barbirolli, Igor Stravinsky, Georges Enesco and Arthur Rodzinski. Soloists during this period were Metropolitan opera soprano Marjorie Lawrence; soprano Hulda Dashanska; pianist Frank Sheridan; Spanish cellist Yaspar Cassado; pianist Robert Serkin; violinist Joseph Sziegeti; and British pianists Ethel Bartlett and Rae Robertson (120 min., Sunday, 2:00–4:00 P.M., CBS, 1936). Prior to joining NBC, Arturo Toscanini also conducted the New York Philharmonic in the mid–1930s.

23257 ***New York Soap Box.*** John Wingate stood in front of WOR's studios to get the views of passing people, who were willing to speak on microphone for the listening audience (15 min., Saturday, 12:15–12:30 P.M., WOR, New York, NY, 1947).

23258 ***New York Spotlight.*** John Hamilton Coombs interviewed celebrities Monday through Thursday from a New York restaurant on Park Avenue. On Friday, Norton Mockridge, crime reporter of the New York *World-Telegram-Sun*, did the show with the focus on criminal investigative news (180 min., Monday through Friday, 12:00–3:00 P.M., WJZ, New York, NY, 1952).

23259 **New York Symphony Orchestra.** Symphonic orchestra conducted by Dr. Walter Damrosch (NBC, New York, NY, 1926).

23260 ***New York Times Youth Forum.*** Dorothy Gordon moderated the long-running program, on which some famous person discussed various topics with a group of young people. For example, the *Times* film critic, Bosley Crowther, discussed with them the question: "Is the influence of the movies still great?" This was an example of good radio programming directed toward young people (45 min., Saturday, 10:15–11:00 P.M., WQXR, New York, NY, 1951).

23261 **New York Trio.** The instrumental group included: pianist Clarence Adler, clarinetist Cornelius Van Vliet and violinist Louis Edlin, v. (WNYC, New York, NY, 1925).

23262 ***New Yorkers Trio.*** The vocal trio included Bob Meyer, Bill Baker and Cal Gooden sang "from the Zebra Room of the Town House on Wilshire Boulevard, Los Angeles, California." Roger Carroll was the announcer (ABC, 1951).

23263 **Newby, Mildred.** Pianist (KFRU, Lawrence, KS, 1926).

23264 **Newcomb, Alan.** DJ (WBT, Charlotte, NC, 1956–1959; *Tempo*, WBT, 1960).

23265 **Newcomb, Carl.** Announcer (KFYF, Oxnard, CA, 1926–1927).

23266 **Newcomb, Charles W. "Charlie."** Sportscaster (*The Sports WORD*, WORD, Spartanburg, SC, 1948–1950).

23267 **Newcomb, Edith Fern.** Contralto (KLX, Oakland, CA, 1929).

23268 **Newcomb, Genevieve.** COM-HE (WFAX, Falls Church, VA, 1949).

23269 **Newcomb, H.J.** Announcer (WRJN, Racine, WI, 1925).

23270 **Newcomber, Maxine and Eileen Newcomber.** These two blind girls were a popular singing team that WWVA's announcers introduced as, "The girls with a song in their hearts." After first appearing on the station in 1941, the girls were soon given their own program (*Maxine and Eileen Newcomber*, vcl. mus. program, WWVA, Wheeling, WV, 1941–1943).

23271 **Newcomer, Carl.** Saxophonist (WCBD, Zion, IL, 1926).

23272 **Newcomer, P.R. and Carl Newcomer.** Vocal duet team (WCBD, Zion, IL, 1926).

23273 **Newell, Dave.** Sportscaster (*Fishing and Hunting Club of the Air*, ABC, 1945).

23274 **Newell, Elwood.** Newscaster (KRMC, Jamestown, ND, 1938).

23275 **Newell, Ernest S.** Announcer who proudly proclaimed the station's slogan, "The Pioneer Broadcasting Station of Vermont" (WQAE, Springfield, VT, 1925–1927).

23276 **Newell, Herman.** Leader (the Edison Recording Orchestra featured on the *Judson Radio Corporation Program*, WABC, New York, NY, 1928).

23277 **Newell, Polly.** COM-HE (WABV, Abbeville, SC, 1960).

23278 **Newell, Verna.** COM-HE (KFGO, Fargo, ND, 1956).

23279 **Newhall, (Col.) Bob.** Sportscaster (WLW, Cincinnati, OH, 1935; WSPB, 1946). News analyst (WSPB, Sarasota, FL, 1945; *Radio Times*, WSPB, 1947–1948).

23280 Newhall, Gene. Newscaster (KYSM, Mankato, MN, 1939).

23281 Newhall, Scott. Newscaster (KGO, San Francisco, CA, 1945).

23282 Newhouse, Jean. Singer (WPCH, New York, NY, 1932).

23283 Newkirk, Alfred R. "Al." Newscaster (WICA, Ashtabula, OH, 1941–1942, 1944–1945). Sportscaster (WICA, 1942, 1945–1946; *Speaking of Sports*, WICA, 1947).

23284 Newkirk, Grace Lee. COM-HE (KXXX, Colby, KS, 1949).

23285 Newkirk, Ted. Leader (Ted Newkirk's Harmonica Band, WHN, New York, NY, 1924).

23286 Newlan, Will. Saxophonist (WBBM, Chicago, IL, 1925).

23287 Newland, Dwight. Newscaster (WWSR, St. Albans, VT, 1941).

23288 Newlun, Bill. DJ (KIT, Yakima, WA, 1954).

23289 *(The) Newlyweds.* Virginia Morgan and Santos Ortega played the title roles on the dramatic serial that included many humorous moments. Their maid was played by Essie Palmer (CBS, 1930).

23290 *(The) Newlyweds.* Mrs. and Mrs. Jack Orrison engaged in comic dialog on the sustaining show that *Variety* said sounded like an imitation of *Easy Aces* (15 min., 7:30–7:45 P.M., KDKA, Pittsburgh, PA, 1938).

23291 Newman, Alma. Soprano (WGBS, New York, NY, 1925).

23292 Newman, Bernie. DJ (*Breakfast Party*, WENE, Binghampton-Endicott, NY, 1949).

23293 Newman, Cy. Sportscaster (WJBW, New Orleans, LA, 1946; *Cy Speaks of Sports*, WLIO, East Liverpool, OH, 1949).

23294 Newman, Ed. DJ (WEVD, New York, NY, 1947).

23295 Newman, Erie. Newscaster (*Noontime Reporter*, WCLE, Clearwater, FL, 1947).

23296 Newman, Eula. COM-HE (KLPT, Paris, TX, 1951).

23297 Newman, Harriet E. Pianist (WGR, Buffalo, NY, 1926).

23298 Newman, Helen Wetmore. Soprano (WJZ, New York, NY, 1923).

23299 Newman, Herbert. Pianist (WNYC, New York, NY, 1926).

23300 Newman, Ida. COM-HE (WIDA, Quincy, MA, 1954–1955).

23301 Newman, James A. DJ (*Tops in Pops — Nonsense with Newman*, KFAL, Fulton, MO, 1949).

23302 Newman, M. Pearl. Broadcaster of beauty hints (KFWI, San Francisco, CA, 1927).

23303 Newman, Mildred. Singer (WHN, New York, NY, 1925).

23304 Newman, Morrie. Leader (*Morrie Newman Orchestra*, instr. mus. prg., WLW, Cincinnati, OH, 1942).

23305 Newman, Robert. Writer Newman wrote *Big Sister*, *Inner Sanctum* and *The Thin Man* programs.

23306 Newman, Robert "Bob." DJ (*Musical Echoes*, WEEU, Reading, PA, 1952; *Your Lucky Star*, WEEU, 1954; WKAP, Allentown, PA, 1956–1957).

23307 Newman, Rose. Singer of Russian songs (WPG, Atlantic City, NJ, 1929).

23308 Newman, Ruby. Leader (*Ruby Newman Orchestra*, instr. mus. prg., NBC, 1936; NBC-Red, 1938).

23309 Newman, Virginia. Pianist (WBBM, Chicago, IL, 1926).

23310 Newman, Zipp. Sportscaster (WSGN, Birmingham, AL, 1945–1947).

23311 Newport, Bill. DJ (*Beale Street Jive*, WMFT, Florence, AL, 1950).

23312 Newport, Joan. COM-HE (KSCB, Liberal, KS, 1957).

23313 *News Comes to Life.* The local New York program, sponsored by the Remington-Rand Company, was another of the many shows of the period that dramatized the week's news (30 min., Sunday, 6:30–7:00 P.M., WINS, New York, NY, 1936).

23314 *News Digest.* News commentator Scotty Mortland interpreted the news (KPO, San Francisco, CA, 1929).

23315 *News Here and Abroad.* Commentators William Hillman and Ernest K. Lindley supplied their analysis of daily events (15 min., Monday through Thursday, 10:00–10:15 P.M., NBC-Blue Network, 1942).

23316 *News — No War.* During World War II, the innovative program presented city, state and national news *only*. No war news was ever broadcast (KFRC, San Francisco, CA, 1942).

23317 *News of the World.* CBS called in their correspondents in the major world capitals to cover the news. The program was broadcast prior to World War II and during most of the war years as well.

23318 News on Radio. American social and cultural life was filled with momentous events during the years from 1920 to 1960, and all of it was chronicled by radio. After the first World War came the Great Depression, World War II and the Korean War, events that inexorably influenced and paved the way for the great changes in social attitudes and behavior that followed.

Many competent radio newscasters reported the day-to-day events during these four memorable decades. There also were a few brilliant analysts, whose thoughtful and objective commentary on the news brought understanding to their listeners. Far too many, however, were little more than rip-and-readers, who took their news broadcasts directly from their teletype machines.

Although some similarities may be found, most radio and television broadcasters today lack the best qualities possessed by the early giants of radio news broadcasting. Few electronic journalists can equal the scholarly preparation of Quincy Howe, the resonant voice and dramatic delivery style of Edward R. Murrow, or the honestly and integrity of Lowell Thomas. Perhaps this is the reason the public has lost so much respect for both print and broadcast journalists.

The issue of bias among early radio commentators was not identified as a problem by many listeners. A 1938 study, for example, conducted by the Columbia University School of Journalism reported that out of 300 radio commentators studied, only 1 of 7 were considered biased (Fang, 1977, p. 6). When CBS declared that news analysts should be neutral and objective, Hans von Kaltenborn, the dean of commentators, responded honestly that no commentator could possibly meet that standard. He noted that the selecting or omitting of news items, the shading of emphasis given to the bits he selects to describe, and every editorial judgment was an expression of an opinion. Kaltenborn's view would not be acceptable in most modern broadcasting newsrooms. Today we see the former employees of powerful members of the House of Representatives, the Senate and even the White House easily move into what is known as "broadcast journalism."

The names of many early newscasters and their radio broadcasts have been dimmed by time. Pittsburgh's KDKA broadcast the results of the Harding-Cox presidential election in 1920. Years earlier in 1916, Dr. Frank Conrad conducted experimental broadcasts from his garage on which he talked and played records. Perhaps Conrad at times even commented upon local and national news, but it is not certain that he did. Only his small listening audience of wireless operators heard him.

Regardless of who were the very first, certain pioneering newscasters, analysts and commentators of the 1920s can be identified. One such newsman was Frederic William Wile with his *The Week in Washington* (WRC, Washington, DC, 1923–1925; NBC, 1926–1928; CBS, 1929–1938). Another was H.V. Kaltenborn, who first broadcast his *Current Topics* program on WAHG (New York, NY) in 1926. Kaltenborn gained national prominence with his report of the 1938 Munich Crisis — an event he described in his book, *I Broadcast the Crisis*. Eating and sleeping in CBS Studio 9, Kaltenborn made 85 broadcasts during the 18 day crisis. Kaltenborn's feat was admirable, even though the Munich Crisis preserved world peace for only a year. During the Spanish Civil War in 1936, Kaltenborn described a battle, while hidden in a haystack located between the combatants (Sterling and Kitross, 1978, p. 176). Unfortunately, today Kaltenborn is generally remembered only as the radio newscaster who erroneously reported Dewey's victory over Truman in the 1948 presidential election.

Another early newsman was the swashbuckling, picturesque Floyd Gibbons. A figure right out of adventure novels, Gibbons wore a white patch over his left eye, which he had lost in the World War I battle of Belleau Wood. On his *Headline Hunters* program, Gibbons used his rapid fire machine gun delivery to recount his feats with Pancho Villa in the 1916 Mexican Revolution, his later pursuit with General John J. Pershing of Villa in Mexico and his World War I adventures. A genuine hero, Gibbons had received the Croix de Guerre and a Chevalier of the Legion of Honor ribbon from France. After an embarrassing episode that may have resulted from too much imbibing, Gibbon was replaced on his news program by Lowell Thomas.

If Gibbons was the adventuring soldier-of-fortune type newsman, Thomas was an adventuring intellectual, scholar and journalist, whose integrity and objectivity was never questioned. Even though Thomas was a conservative Republican, his listeners never got a hint of partisanship or lack of honest objectivity in his reporting.

Edward R. Murrow first came to national attention during World War II with his broadcasts from London at the peak of the German aerial blitz. Murrow's dramatic opening of "This ... is London" with his characteristic long pause added drama to his insightful account of the courage and perseverance of the British people. Equally important was Murrow's expert executive ability to attract and hire a group of newsmen that evolved into the prestigious CBS News division. If some of the division's luster eventually dimmed in the television era, none of the responsibility for its deterioration can be blamed on Murrow.

Sports events in radio's early days were always treated as news events, not merely as "sports." The Dempsey-Carpentier fight of July 2, 1921, and the broadcasts in 1923 of the Army-Notre Dame football game and World Series were considered news broadcasting "firsts." After the novelty of broadcasting sports events faded, an era of special features and stunt broadcasting began. There were broadcasts from airplanes in the heavens and from submarines beneath the sea. All of them, however, were more demonstrations of technical capabilities than legitimate reporting of the news. One of the stunts most frequently broadcast was the frying of an egg on a sidewalk during a blistering hot July or August day.

Some early broadcasts deserved to be called special features for their coverage of breaking news events. WGN's Quin Ryan broadcast many of them in the 1920s. It was Ryan who broadcast the Scopes Monkey Trial from Dayton, Tennessee, in which the "old time religion" was championed by William Jennings Bryan against the advocate of modern scientific thought — Clarence Darrow. Another special event described by Ryan was Floyd Collins' death as a result of his accidental entombment in a mountain cave.

Another historic special broadcasting event was Herb Morrison's description of the dirigible *Hindenburg* disaster at Lakehurst, New Jersey. Morrison of WLS (Chicago, IL) was making a recording of the airship's arrival when the great ship burst into flames and was entirely destroyed. Morrison's recording of the event provided radio with one of its most memorable as-it-happened broadcast moments. Although Morrison's account was recorded, three networks suspended their policy against playing recordings to broadcast it.

As early as 1922, the friction between newspapers and radio became obvious when the Associated Press warned its members that any use of AP news by "radio telephone" was strictly forbidden. Furthermore, the AP carried out its restriction by fining the Portland *Oregonian* a hundred dollars for using AP bulletins on radio to report the 1924 election. Other news services placed similar restrictions on the use of their material by networks and stations in 1933.

Radio and newspapers had not always been in conflict. In radio's early days newspapers frequently owned and operated stations. In fact, it could be argued that newspapers were vitally important in advancing radio's early development. In 1933 when it became clear that radio was in competition with newspapers for advertising, the wire news services, controlled by the newspaper industry, took action to forbid the use of their news services by radio in any unauthorized manner. The American Newspaper Publishers Association in accord with the AP, UP, INS, CBS, NBC and the Press-Radio Bureau agreed to limit radio to only two daily news reports of five minutes or less duration that could be broadcast only before 9:30 A.M. or after 9:00 P.M. Other restrictions placed on radio were that it was forbidden to broadcast sponsored news programs; not be allowed to perform news gathering activity; could not use any news not provided by the Press-Radio News Bureau, or do anything other than broadcast original interpretation and commentary. No hard news was permitted other than that broadcast during the prescribed time periods.

Public demand for more radio news eventually broke the 1933 agreement. United Press (UP) and the International News Service (INS) began providing radio stations with news that could be sponsored. The following year the Associated Press (AP) took similar action. Radio had won the battle. Stations could now gather and broadcast the news and comment upon it.

World War II presented radio with the challenge to not only report the news, but also to maintain and boost civilian morale whenever possible. In England, civilian morale was boosted by the work of such entertainers as Vera Lynn ("The Sweetheart of the Forces") and Gracie Fields ("Our Gracie"). Even more important were the BBC speeches of prime minister Winston Churchill, whose stirring rhetoric personified the tradition of British bravery and tenacity at its best. By contrast, President Roosevelt's radio Fireside Chats were effective in combating the paralyzing economic fears of Americans during the Depression years. Oddly enough, Doctor New Deal never made a fully successful transition to Doctor Win-the-War on radio.

During the war morale was raised by newscasters like Edward R. Murrow with his descriptions of the stubbornly heroic resistance of the British and by Gabriel Heatter's proclamation each evening of "Ah, there's good news tonight." Even radio gossip columnist Walter Winchell became a weekly morale booster with his patriotic commentaries.

Radio readily demonstrated its creativity and technical facility during the war. Broadcasts originated from fox holes in the midst of combat and from the tail gunner's nest of a bomber on a mission. Broadcasts of this nature plus the many programs on which servicemen appeared to talk with their family and friends back home were powerful morale boosts. *See* **Wartime Radio**.

Radio voluntarily submitted to wartime censorship during World War II. Any mention of weather conditions, troop locations or their movements that might help the enemy were not broadcast. Radio proved its value in World War II with its coverage by so many talented correspondents. Perhaps the most outstanding group of correspondents and analysts during World War II were those of CBS. Some of that network's correspondents and analysts were: Carroll Alcott, John Adams, Melvin Allen, Hubert Anderson, John Anderson, Charles Barbe, Dave Baylor, George Bryan, Griffing Bancroft, Mary Marvin Breckinridge, Philip Brown, Robert Best, Winston Burdett, Cecil Brown, Mallory Brown, Curtis Butler, Charles Collingwood, Ed Chorlian, George Cushing, Herbert Clark, Joe Congress, Ned Calmer, Tris Coffin, Bill Costello, W.W. Chaplin, Erskine Caldwell, Wells Church, Hugh Conover, Norman Corwin, Ted Collins, Harry Cramer, Eve Curie, Bill Cullen, Elmer Davis, John Charles Daly, Rex Davis, Bill Downs, William J. Dunn, Robert Emerick, Douglas Edwards, Erlin Ecklin, George Fielding Eliot, H.B. Elliston, John Evans, Robert Evans, Victor Eckland, Webley Edwards, William Ewing, Edward Fleming, Fransworth Fowle, George Folster, Harry W. Flannery, James Fleming, John Fisher, Louis Fischer, Noel Field, Felden Farrington, Jack Findell, Charles Griffin, Thomas Grandin, Chet Huntley, Don Hancock, Edwin Hartrich, John Harrington, John B. Hughes, Joseph C. Harsch, Mark Hawley, Quincy Howe, Russell Hill, Ralph Harder, Richard C. Hottelet, Tom Hanlon, Bill Henry, George Herman, Chester Holcomb, Everett Holles, Ralph Ingersoll, Alan Jackson, Albin Johnson, Hugh Jenks, Russell Jones, Alexander Kendrick, H.V. Kaltenborn, Jack Knell, John Reed King, Walter Kerr, James King, Albert Leitch, Dan Lundberg, Larry Lesueur, Morley Lister, Robert Lewis, Tim Leimert, Bill Lang, Arthur Menken, Alice L. Moats, Arnim Meyer, Chester Morrison, Don Moseley, Edward Montgomery, Edward R. Murrow, George Moorad, Harry Marble, Janet Murrow, Kenneth Meeker, Larry Meyer, Paul Manning, Thompson Moore, Walton Moore, Tony Marvin, Dennis McEvoy, Joe McCaffrey, Paul Niven, Don Pryor, Ernest Pope, Fred Painton, George Putnam, John Purcell, Nelson Pringle, Capt. Felix Reisenberg, Gene Rider, John M. Raleigh, Quentin Reynolds, Bill Rodgers, Charles Shaw, Dana Schmidt, Eric Sevareid, Frank Stevens, Glen Stadler, Harry Smith, Howard K. Smith, James Stewart, John Cameron Swayze, Kent Stevenson, Neil Strawser, Robert Spence, Vincent Sheean, Warren Sweeney, William L. Shirer, David Schoenbrun, Daniel Schorr, Willian Shadel, William Slocum, Jr., Clarence Sorensen, Courtney Terrett, Ed Taylor, Frank Tremaine, Henry J. Taylor, John Tillman, Bob Trout, Bernard Valery, David Vale, Albert W. Warner, Betty Wason, Ford Wilkins, Jackson Wheeler, Linton Wells, Margaret Bourke-White, Paul Ward, Phil Woodyat, Spencer Williams, Sven Wilson, Tom Worthen, William Winter, William L. White, W.R. "Bud" Wills, Leigh White, Stan Wilson and Alexander Woolcott. Other war correspondents from various stations and networks are listed in the **Wartime Radio** entry.

The Korean War that followed World War II was a "television war." Radio news correspondents still performed their duties and reported to their listeners, but now they played only a secondary role. Radio analysts and commentators were rapidly disappearing. Instead television newsmen, their camera men and television anchor men had replaced them at center stage. Television was now the chief medium the public used to receive its news.

A significant contribution to broadcasting seen on television today (1997) was radio's *Meet the Press* program. Developed and brought to radio in 1945 by producer-director Martha Roundtree in association with Lawrence Spivak, editor of the *American Mercury* magazine. The program brought news makers, usually politicians, each week to be quizzed by guest journalists. This program format currently (1998) is used by all national networks and many local television stations.

Television in 2004 displayed many influences exerted by Edward R. Murrow.

Walter Cronkite's work provides an example. Walter Cronkite did not emphasize many "feature" entertainment stories during his years as CBS television anchorman from 1962 to 1981, but he did add to the image of the anchorman as a personality bigger than the news and the program on which he appeared. These perceptions can be traced directly to the tradition of Edward R. Murrow and the status he achieved during his radio and television days. This is not intended to disparage Murrow, but only an attempt to understand Murrow's important influence on contemporary (2006) news broadcasting.

Murrow's rooftop reporting during the London Blitz, Fenton (2005, p. 25) says, was more than great reporting, but also was propaganda (Fenton, 2005, p. 25) designed to show Americans that the war could not be won without their participation. There is no reason to doubt Fenton's conclusion. Arguably, this was propaganda in a good cause, but it was not objective reporting of the news. America's entrance even into a "good" war should not have been influenced by biased news broadcasts.

Fenton's generally reverential treatment of Murrow in his book shows his own bias, but he includes some comments from Don Hewitt about the "high Murrow" and the "low Murrow" that are enlightening. Hewitt, the CBS director who was the creative force behind the highly successful *60 Minutes* television program, emphasized the importance of blending entertainment with the news to achieve a *successful* news program. Hewitt noted the "high Murrow" and "low Murrow," could be found in Murrow's *See It Now* television program. On that show, Hewitt, pointed out, you could look into both Marilyn Monroe's closet and Robert Oppenheimer's laboratory. The CBS director emphasized the need to combine entertainment [features] with the news (Fenton, 2005, p. 56).

Still later, Hewitt contributed some advice on how to help the network's evening news programs regain their previously large viewing audience. In his Op-Ed article, "News with Views" (New York *Times*, Op-Ed, Wednesday, April 20, 2005, p. A33), Hewitt recommended that the networks simply copy the format of his own CBS show, "*60 Minutes*": "Now if the networks are looking for ways to re-energize their news, the formula may be as simple as taking a page from the "*60 Minutes*" book and offering some audacious commentary." Some contemporary critics would contend there is already too much opinion — audacious or otherwise — on news programs and too little "hard," factual news.

Edward R. Murrow generally received critical acclaim for his television work on the *See It Now* and *Person to Person* programs and his various news documentaries, although some of his work consisted of light, feature material instead of hard, factual news. It was, however, Murrow's assembling of many distinguished broadcast journalists that enabled the CBS News Division to reach a level of excellence unequaled by either ABC or NBC. Not all of Murrow's influences on broadcast journalism in the television era, however, were positive ones.

Some of the influences exerted by Murrow on broadcast journalism were:

1. The emergence of the broadcaster as a personality and the rise of the "anchorman" as a TV star and broadcast personality. (An era of "personality" anchormen came to an end in 2005 with the departure of Dan Rather, the retirement of Tom Brokaw and the death of Peter Jennings.)
2. The mixture of "soft news" and features with "hard, objective news."
3. The emphasis upon vocal quality, presentation style and physical appearance as contrasted with content and informative value.
4. The greater appeal to the emotions through the introduction of dramatic themes, incidents and presentation style.
5. The introduction of editorial comment along with the factual treatment of the news.

Although these changes came about gradually, they were noted by some critical observers by 2004. In addition, there was a growing perception among some television viewers that broadcast and cable networks such as ABC, CBS, NBC and CNN were to some degree biased in their presentation of the news. Right or wrong, the perception of bias resulted in some loss of viewers. The perception of bias along with increased popularity of other sources of information such as additional cable sources and the internet produced still more listener (viewer) loss. The question of bias at CBS was discussed by Bernard Goldberg in his book, *Bias: A CBS Insider Exposes How the Media Distorts the News*. The critical appraisal of network news departments culminated in 2004, with Dan Rather's use and defense of allegedly forged documents critical of President Bush's Air National Guard service. Coming as it did only a few weeks before the 2004 presidential election, even the staunchest defenders of network news were embarrassed by the incident.

Even CBS stalwarts criticized Rather and the network's news programming. The revered Murrow even received mild criticism (Fenton, 2005, p.56). At the time of Rather's alleged use of forged materials just prior to the 2004 presidential election, Fenton asked Walter Cronkite if he watched the *CBS Evening News* on television. Cronkite emphatically said he did not, explaining that it was mostly crime and "sob sister" stuff. He further amplified his answer by saying the program contained mostly "scandal sheet" and "tabloid material" (Fenton, 2005, p. 149).

After the Rather incident, the New York *Times* (January 10, 2005) reported that CBS chairman Leslie Moonves said he planned to "introduce significant, potentially revolutionary changes in the format of *Evening CBS News* when Dan Rather departs in March (Carter and Steinberg, January 10, 2005, B1,5). Moonves indicated that the shift would be "away from the 'voice of God' single anchor" format that had been used throughout the history of network television news (Carter and Steinberg, January 10, 2005, B 1,5).

Even television's Public Broadcasting Service has been accused of bias. A front page story of the May 2, 2005 New York *Times* headlined, Chairman Exerts Pressure on PBS, Alleging Bias with the sub-head of, Cites a Need for Balance. The story reported that Chairman of the Corporation for Public Broadcasting Kenneth Y. Tomlinson seeks to correct possible liberal bias (Labaton, Manly and Jensen, New York *Times*, May 2, 2005, p. 1). Tomlinson was quoted as saying: "My goal here is to see programming that satisfies a broad constituency. I'm not after removing shows or tampering internally with shows."

The *Times'* story continued to report that Bill Moyer, a former moderator of the PBS *Now* program has been a target of "conservative criticism" for a lack of balance in his program content and commentary. For example, Moyer was quoted as saying: "The entire federal government was 'united behind a right-wing agenda that included the power of the state to force pregnant women to give up control over their bodies'" (Labaton, Manly and Jensen, New York *Times*, May 2, 2005, p. A19). Longtime PBS executives, on the other hand, see Tomlinson's acts as a threat to the independence of their programming. *See* **Howe, Quincy; Murrow, Edward R.; Ryan, Quin; Thomas, Lowell; Wile, Frederic William; Winchell, Walter; *Meet the Press*** *and* **Wartime Radio.**

23319 ***News Testers.*** Leonard M. Leonard conducted the quiz show that gave each winning participant five dollars. Leonard compiled and selected the questions that he used on the program from newspapers (15 min., Weekly, MBS, 1938).

23320 ***News with Edward Bierstadt.*** News analyst Bierstadt broadcast his regularly scheduled news program (WOR, Newark, NJ, 1925).

23321 **Newsom, Oscar.** DJ (*Rise and Shine*, WWGS, Tifton, GA, 1949).

23322 **Newsom, Rita.** COM-HE (KDXE, Little Rock, AR, 1960).

23323 **Newsome, Buck.** DJ (*Melody Corner*, KYMA, Yuma, AZ, 1949).

23324 **Newsome, Gil.** DJ (*Bandstand Revue*, KWK, St. Louis, MO, 1948–1960; *First Five*, KWK, 1948–1960). Newsome, a former announcer on Coca-Cola's popular *Spotlight Bands* program, left that show to become a well known St. Louis DJ.

23325 **Newsome, (Mrs.) Francis.** Pianist (WNAC, Boston, MA, 1923).

23326 ***Newspaper of the Air.*** M. Buten Company, manufacturers of Hawk Paints, sponsored the news show that presented Lee Vines broadcasting straight news; Howard Brown providing editorial commentary; and Zelda Cotton women's news (15 min., Monday-Tuesday-Wednesday and Friday, 8:00–8:15 P.M., WIP, Philadelphia, PA, 1940).

23327 **Newstrom, Elmer.** Leader (*Elmer Newstrom Orchestra*, instr. mus. prg., WIND, Chicago, IL, 1935).

23328 **Newton, David.** Newscaster (WKWF, Key West, FL, 1948).

23329 **Newton, Dwight.** Newscaster (KPO, San Francisco, CA, 1945).

23330 **Newton, Ernie.** Tenor (KHQ, Spokane, WA and KHJ, Los Angeles, CA, 1928).

23331 **Newton, (Mrs.) Fleming.** Whistler (KWWG, Brownsville, TX, 1927).

23332 **Newton, Gay Richard.** DJ (*Classical Music*, KELT, Electra, TX, 1949).

23333 **Newton, Phyllis.** Pianist (WTIC, Hartford, CT, 1925).

23334 **Ney, Chuck.** DJ (*At Your Request*, WDSG, Dyersburg, TN, 1950). Sportscaster (KAYL, Storm Lake, IA, 1952–1955).

23335 **Ney, Elly.** Pianist Ney was the wife of Willem Van Hoodstraten, assistant conductor of the New York Philharmonic Orchestra. She appeared on *The Brunswick Hour* in 1925.

23336 **Niccoli, Alessandro.** Violinist (WBZ, Springfield, MA, 1926).

23337 **Nicholas [Nickolas], Mary.** Singer (WHP, Harrisburg, PA, 1937).

23338 **Nichols, Bob.** DJ (*My Favorite Records*, KOMO, Seattle, WA, 1952).

23339 **Nichols, Bob.** DJ (*Blues 'n' Boogie*, WPAL, Charleston, SC, 1952–1955).

23340 **Nichols, Deno.** Newscaster (KROZ, Harrison, AR, 1946). Sportscaster (*Sports Roundup*, KLRA, Little Rock, AR, 1949; KWRF, Warren, AL, 1954).

23341 **Nichols, Dorothy.** Cellist Nichols was the sister of jazz trumpeter Loten "Red" Nichols (KTAB, Oakland, CA, 1929).

23342 **Nichols, G.B.** Spanish speaking announcer (KFDM, Beaumont, TX, 1928).

23343 **Nichols, Hal G.** Announcer (KFON, Long Beach, CA, 1927; KFOX, Long Beach, CA, 1929).

23344 **Nichols, Harry O.** Organist (WREC, Memphis, TN, 1925–1929).

23345 **Nichols, Hazel.** Pianist (KGO, Oakland, CA, 1925).

23346 **Nichols, Jack.** DJ (*Harlem Hive*, KSAM, Huntsville, TX, 1952).

23347 **Nichols, Loren "Red."** Leader ("Red" Nichols Jazz Band, CBS, 1927; CBS, 1935, CBS, 1942).

23348 **Nichols, Nick.** Leader (Nick Nichols Dance Orchestra broadcasting from the Garden Pier, WPG, Atlantic City, NJ, 1926).

23349 **Nichols, Nick.** DJ (*Rhythm Ranch*, WPLA, Plant City, FL, 1949).

23350 **Nichols, Ray.** Leader (Ray Nichols Recording Orchestra, WAAM, Newark, NJ, 1925; WEAF, New York, NY, 1926; broadcasting from the Palais Royal, WOR, Newark, NJ, 1928; WMCA, New York, NY, 1929).

23351 **Nichols, Robert.** Violinist (KFWI, San Francisco, CA, 1926).

23352 **Nichols, Robert.** Associate announcer-baritone (KOMO, Seattle, WA, 1928).

23353 **Nicholls, John N.** Versatile announcer-baritone-staff pianist (KOIN, Portland, OR, 1928).

23354 **Nicholson, Don.** Newscaster (KGLO, Mason City, IA, 1945; WTAD, Quincy, IL, 1948).

23355 **Nicholson, John.** Sportscaster (*Sports Special*, WTMC, Ocala, FL, 1947–1950). DJ (*Club 1290*, WTMC, 1949–1950; *Wake Up Time*, WTMC, 1950).

23356 **Nicholson, Marie.** Lyric soprano (WEAF, New York, NY, 1924).

23357 **Nicholson, Nick.** DJ (*The Farm Roundup*, KROW, Oakland, CA, 1948; *Records and Stuff*, KROY, Sacramento, CA, 1954).

23358 **Nicholson, Trudi.** COM-HE (WLBT, Jackson, MS, 1957).

23359 **Nicholson, Uncle Jimmy.** *See* **Foss, Bill.**

23360 **Nicholson, W. Curtis.** Nicholson gave talks on the improvement of speech, i.e., "The Right Word" (WMCA, New York, NY, 1925).

23361 **Nicholson, Williams B.** Tenor (WSM, Nashville, TN, 1928).

23362 **Nick and Noodnick.** DJ team not otherwise identified (KROW, Oakland, CA, 1954).

23363 ***Nick Carter, Master Detective.*** Nick Carter was the fictional creation of John Russell Coryell. When Carter came to MBS radio in 1943, he was jointed by his assistants, Patsy and Scrubby. Nick was portrayed by Lon Clark. His assistants were played by Helen Choate, Charlotte Manson and John Kane. Organist Hank Sylvern supplied the music (MBS, ABC, 1943–1955). Carter's adopted son, Chick, also appeared on his own mystery adventure program, (*Chick Carter, Boy Detective*), fighting a villainous character known as the Rattler. The *Nick Carter, Master Detective* program's cast included: Helen Choate, Lon Clark, Raymond Edward Johnson, John Kane, Ed Latimer, Bill Lipton, Charlotte Manson, John Raby and Bryna Raeburn. The producer-director was Jock MacGregor. Alfred Bester, Norman Daniels, Ferrin N. Fraser, Milton J. Kramer, David Kogan and John McGreevey were the writers. Michael Fitzmaurice was the announcer (MBS and ABC, 1943–1955). *See* ***Chick Carter, Boy Detective.***

23364 **Nickel, Betty.** DJ (*Nickelodeon*, WHK, Cleveland, OH, 1948).

23365 **Nickel, Phil.** DJ (*Melody by Moonlight*, KSEL, Lubbock, TX, 1952; *Recess for Rhythm*, KENM, Portales, NM, 1954).

23366 **Nickell, G.E.** Sportscaster and football and baseball play-by-play (KUIN, Grants Pass, OR, 1947).

23367 **Nickell, Joe.** Announcer (WIBW, Topeka, KS, 1925). Newscaster (WIBW, Topeka, KS, 1939–1940).

23368 ***Nickelodeon.*** This program presented a radio burlesque of "old five-cent moving pictures" (30 min., Monday, 8:30–9:00 P.M., NBC-Blue, 1936). Earlier in the year, *Nickelodeon* was broadcast one half-hour earlier on Tuesdays by the NBC-Red Network.

23369 **Nickels, Jack P.** Sportscaster (*The Sports Special*, KTRC, Santa Fe, NM, 1947).

23370 **Nickerson, Gene.** Leader (*Gene Nickerson Orchestra*, instr. mus. prg., WHDH, Boston, MA, 1939).

23371 **Nickle, Margaret.** Pianist (WFLA, Clearwater, FL, 1929).

23372 **Nickson, Nick.** DJ (*950 Club* and *Musical Showcase*, WARC, Rochester, NY, 1948–1950; WBBF, Rochester, NY, 1955–1957).

23373 **Nicolaevskaya, Rasna.** Russian soprano (WPCH, New York, NY, 1932).

23374 **Nicolina, Zinaida.** Pianist-singer Nicolina was known as the "Gypsy Princess" (WOR, Newark, NJ, 1929). She also was featured on the *La Palina* program.

23375 **Nicoll, Irene Howland.** Contralto (KGO, Oakland, CA, 1925).

23376 **Nidas, Dan.** News analyst (KFKA, Greeley, CO, 1940).

23377 **Niday, Kaghleen.** Actress Niday was in the cast of the *Brenda Curtis* daytime serial program.

23378 **Nidever, Laura.** COM-HE (KASH, Eugene, OR, 1951).

23379 **Nidiffier, Randolph.** DJ (WBEJ, Elizabethton, TN, 1949).

23380 **Niebling, Albert.** News analyst (KOME, Tulsa, OK, 1941; *News of the Week*, KRRV, Sherman-Denison, TX, 1947).

23381 **Niedermier, Rosanna.** COM-HE (WPLY, Plymouth, WI, 1957).

23382 **Niedholt, Ruth.** Violinist Niedholt was a member of the Claire Trio (KFRC, San Francisco, CA, 1926).

23383 **Niese, George.** Actor Niese was in the cast of *Backstage Wife.*

23384 **Niesen, Claire.** Talented actress Niesen appeared in such daytime serial programs as *Her Honor, Nancy James, Backstage Wife* aka *Mary Noble, Backstage Wife* (title role), *The O'Neills* and *The Second Mrs. Burton* (title role).

23385 **Niesen, Gertrude.** Singer (CBS, 1935).

23386 **Nielsen, E.A.** Announcer who broadcast his station's slogan that was based on its call letters, "Kind Friends Come Back" (KFCB, Phoenix, AZ, 1926–1927).

23387 **Nielsen, Paul.** Newscaster (WGN, Chicago, IL, 1948).

23388 **Nielsen, Sweyn Hildiry.** Baritone (KPO, San Francisco, CA, 1923).

23389 **Nielson, Al and Bill Moss.** Piano team (WBBM, Chicago, IL, 1941).

23390 **Nielson, Paul.** Newscaster (WBBM, Chicago, IL, 1945).

23391 **Niersbach, Bill.** DJ (*Breakfast with Bill*, WKBV, Richmond, IN, 1949–1960).

23392 **Niesen, Gertrude.** Vocalist (*Gertrude Niesen*, vcl. mus. prg., CBS, 1935).

23393 **Niete, Charles.** Newscaster (KTKC, Visalia, CA, 1946).

23394 Nieto, Raquel. Coloratura soprano Nieto was accompanied by Jose Perches (KFWB, Hollywood, CA, 1926).

23395 Nigey, Ruth. Singer (WMCA, New York, NY, 1939).

23396 ***Night Beat.*** Frank Lovejoy played the role of Randy Stone, a newspaper columnist for the Chicago *Star*, who roamed the city streets on the sustaining show in search of interesting stories he found each week. Although most were mysteries, some were diverse adventure tales. Joan Banks, William Conrad and Lurene Tuttle were also in the cast (30 min., Monday, 10:00–10:30 P.M., NBC, 1950).

23397 ***Night Cap Yarns.*** Frank Graham skillfully told adventure tales for adults on the popular Pacific Coast sustaining program (15 min., Monday, 10:15–10:30 P.M. PST, CBS-Pacific Coast Network, 1939).

23398 ***Night Caps on Lake Erie.*** The late evening musical variety show presented, among many others, singers Jean Kibbey and June Ackroyd and banjo soloist Eddie Conner (WJAX, Cleveland, OH, 1924–1925). The program started at midnight and sometimes went on to 4:00 A.M. A rhyme that was repeated frequently on the program was:

A life on the wave from Lake Erie,
A cruise with the Nite Caps' Crew;
It's 2:00 A.M., but I don't give a whoop,
I'll stick till the gang gets through.

The gang of entertainers included: Phil Barker, the Harry Lauder of Cleveland; singer Carrabelle Johnson who led her Neapolitan Orchestra; the Metro Trio (June, Bell and Josephine), a skilled ukulele and vocal trio; operatic soprano Miss Rex Haller; and singers June McMahon, Josephine Peterka and Belle Barrows. The program's orchestra was led by Austin J. Wylie. Talent for the program was selected by Jim Few assisted by Frank Weisenberger.

23399 ***Night Court of the Air.*** Dramatized court cases were presented (CBS, 1936).

23400 ***Night Editor.*** Cardinet Candy Company sponsored the series of dramatizations of news stories narrated by Hal Burdick (15 min., Tuesday, 7:30–7:45 P.M. PST, NBC, 1935).

23401 ***Night Howl* Frolic.** Late night variety show broadcast from Cincinnati's Hotel Gibson (Friday, 12:15 P.M.-1:15 A.M., WLW, Cincinnati, OH, 1926).

23402 ***(A) Night of Opera.*** The Little Rock Community Music Association sponsored the weekly program of operatic music featuring singers: Gracie and Elizabeth Scherer, Billy O'Brien, Conrad Farrell and the Methodist Chorus directed by Mrs. I.J. Steed (KLRA, Little Rock, AR, 1929).

23403 ***(The) Night Owls.*** Ruth Meade and a number of other talented performers were featured on this late night variety show (KGW, Portland, OR, 1924–1925).

23404 ***Night Shift with Rayburn and Finch.*** Gene Rayburn and Dee Finch were DJ's with a difference. They traded witty banter, played records and frequently interviewed celebrity guests (60 min., Saturday, 9:00–10:00 P.M., ABC, 1950). *See* ***Rayburn and Finch.***

23405 ***Night Time on the Trail.*** CW mus. prg. by unidentified performers (KMBC, Kansas City, MO, 1939).

23406 ***(The) Nighthawk Frolic*** **(aka** ***The Night Hawks*** **and** ***The Kansas City Nighthawks*****).** The original *Night Hawk Frolic* began in the early days of radio. The program was conducted by Leo Fitzpatrick, who was known as "The Merry Old Chief." The music was provided by the famous Coon-Sanders Nighthawk orchestra. Listeners could write in to get a card issued by the Merry Old Chief to certify they were WDAF Nighthawks. At the peak of its popularity the Nighthawks Club enrolled two million listeners (WDAF, Kansas City, MO, 1922).

Originating in the early days of radio, *The Nighthawk Frolic* was a lively music and variety show conceived and conducted by Leo Fitzpatrick, "The Merry Old Chief," and his assistant John Patt. Fitzpatrick and the Coon-Sanders Orchestra broadcasting from the Plantation Grill of the Muehlebach Hotel in Kansas City were said by critics to have "half-a-world burning lights at all hours of the night." This was the era of DX (distance) radio listening and two million listeners from all over the country were tuned to their program.

Fitzpatrick explained the program had its inception in the latter part of 1922. He said up to that time at WDAF (Kansas City, MO), they had merely followed the stereotyped formula of introducing a singer or musician in the studio and allowing the performer to sing or play. Fitzpatrick got the idea that he would allow the public to listen to the atmosphere as well. He said, "the hottest thing in town at that time was the Coon-Sanders Orchestra, playing at the local Newman Theatre and at the Hotel Muehlehach. [Therefore] We installed microphones in the hotel, and the next night we were on the air. The listeners had their first taste of transferring a night club into the ether where they heard the chatter of dancers, the playing of the orchestra and such popular pieces of the day as "Gallagher and Sheen" and "Running Wild" (Shurdick, 1946, p.60)."

Fitzpatrick had definite ideas about how and why the program attained such popularity throughout the country: "The band would play fifteen minutes and then there would be a ten minute lull that offered a very difficult problem until we started to read telegrams and make alleged wisecracks, which later proved almost as popular as the music. I think the real success of the *Night Hawks* was that it gave every little town throughout the country its own night club. It was a custom then to gather a few jugs of *corn*, hold a party and wait for the *Night Hawks* to start broadcasting for the evening's entertainment. The *corn* probably contributed as much as the *Night Hawks* did to the evening" (Shurdick, 1946, pp. 60–61).

The program was known variously as *The Night Hawks, The Kansas City Nighthawks* and *The Nighthawk Frolic.* It was one of the most popular programs of early radio. It gained popularity for both Fitzpatrick and the Coon-Sanders Orchestra. The Coon-Sanders Nighthawks Orchestra moved to Chicago in 1923, where they continued to enjoy great popularity broadcasting from that city's Blackhawk Restaurant on station WGN. *See* **Fitzpatrick, Leo** *and* **Coon-Sanders Nighthawk Orchestra.**

Since 1922, when it was initiated by "The Merry Old Chief," station WDAF had a program titled *The Nighthawk Frolic.* Although in the early days of radio the show was a live variety show, it eventually became a show on which the Merry Old Chief, now played by Bill Leeds, acted only as a DJ (*The Nighthawk Frolic*). Despite this drastic change, listeners could still obtain a card issued by the Merry Old Chief— a reminder of radio's early days (25 min., Saturday, 11:30–11:55 P.M., WDAF, Kansas City, MO, 1948). *See* ***The Nighthawk Frolic*** *and* **Fitzpatrick, Leo.**

23407 ***Nightline.*** One of NBC's sustaining radio programs introduced in 1957, *Nightline* contained features, news, theater criticism, news analysis, etc. Walter O'Keefe hosted the program, which also included Joseph C. Harsch, Martin Agronsky, Leon Pearson, David Brinkley and various guests (85 min., Tuesday-Wednesday-Thursday, 8:30–9:55 P.M., NBC, 1957).

23408 Nightingale, Earl. News commentator (WJNC, Jacksonville, NC, 1945). Sportscaster (WJNC, 1946).

23409 Nightingale, Helen. Soprano (KOIL, Council Bluffs, IA, 1928).

23410 Nightingale Orchestra. Popular club band (WOAW, Omaha, NE, 1926).

23411 ***Nights in Spain.*** A music program with Spanish prima donna soprano Francesca Ortega and an orchestra conducted by Max Dolin (NBC-Pacific Network, 1929).

23412 ***Nightwatch.*** A crime show, *Nightwatch* told "real life police stories" about "real" people *on the scene.* Reporter Don Reed traveled with two detectives from the Culver City, California, police department as they answered calls to investigate incidents. Reed recorded the calls for later broadcast (30 min., CBS, 1954).

23413 Nigocia, Harry. DJ (*Mid-Day Serenader*, WJBW, New Orleans, LA, 1948–1952).

23414 Nigro, Ann. Concert pianist (WMEX, Boston, MA, 1939).

23415 Niles, Charles. Newscaster (WTHT, Hartford, CT, 1937–1939).

23416 Niles, David. DJ (*Music You Want*, WEVD, New York, NY, 1949).

23417 Niles, (Reverend) Harold. News commentator (*Current Comment*, WICC, Bridgeport, CT, 1938).

23418 Niles, Harry. Bass (WEAF, New York, NY, 1926).

23419 Niles, Helen. COM-HE (WAPX, Montgomery, AL, 1951).

23420 Niles, Jack. Announcer (WFBH, New York, NY, 1925).

23421 Niles, Ken. Announcer Niles worked on such programs as *Abbott and Costello Show, Beulah, Big Town, Danny Kaye Show* and *Hollywood Hotel.*

23422 Niles, Wendell. Announcer-writer-producer Niles was born December 29, 1904. He broke into radio as an orchestra leader in 1923 and worked in vaudeville with his orchestra for many years. Niles enjoyed a distinguished announcing career the following two decades. He announced such programs as *Bob Hope Show, Lum and Abner* and *When a Girl Marries.*

23423 Nilsson, Christine (Mrs. Carl Chindbloom). Pianist (WRCm Washington, DC, 1925).

23424 Nimmo, Bill. DJ (*Platter Time*, WLW, Cincinnati, OH, 1947–1950).

23425 Nims, L.M. Announcer (WSKC, Bay City, MI, 1926).

23426 *Nine to Five.* A comedy serial glorifying an American secretary, *Nine to Five* was appropriately enough sponsored by the L.C. Smith Corona Typewriter Company. Mary Grey, the secretary, played by Lucille Wall, worked for the R.G. Boggs Company, a small business that supplied fire hose and extinguishers. The company's fortunes and misfortunes rose and fell with the doings of Parker Fennelly, the boss, and his employees played by Lucille Wall, Jack Smith and Willie McCallion (15 min., Thursday, 6:15–6:30 P.M. CST, NBC-Blue, 1935).

23427 Ninon. Fashion critic of the San Francisco *Chronicle* Ninon broadcast on that topic (KPO, San Francisco, CA, 1927).

23428 Ninth Cavalry Band. A military band stationed at Fort Riley, Kansas (KFKB, Milford, KS, 1927).

23429 *Nip and Tuck.* Frederick Chase Taylor, who later gained fame as Colonel Stoopnagle with Wilbur Budd Hulick on the *Stoopnagle and Budd* program, was one-half of the *Nip and Tuck* blackface comedy team that performed frequently on WMAK (Buffalo, NY, 1925–1926).

23430 Nippes, Elmer. Leader (Elmer Nippes Orchestra, WAAM, Newark, NJ, 1925).

23431 Nireman, Sidney. Pianist (WBBM, Chicago, IL, 1926).

23432 Nirenstein, Alfred. Violinist (WEAF, New York, NY, 1925).

23433 *Nisely Dream Shop.* "Ronet the Singing Slave" was featured on the music program (WLW, Cincinnati, OH, 1930).

23434 Nissen, Roger K. Pianist (KPO, San Francisco, CA, 1925).

23435 Nissim, Renzo. Newscaster (WBNX, New York, NY, 1945).

23436 Nissley, Charles H. An extension specialist from the Agricultural and Extension College, New Brunswick, New Jersey, Nissley broadcast agricultural talks (WOR, Newark, NJ, 1922).

23437 Nisted, Christine. Violinist (WGES, Oak Park, IL, 1925).

23438 *(The) Nit Wit Hour* (aka *The Nit Wits*). The zany comedy show was created and directed by Brad Browne who played the role of the Chief Nit Wit. The other nit wits were: Lizzie Twitch played by Yolanda Langworthy; Professor R.U. Musclebound by Harry Swan; Aphrodite Godiva by Georgia Backus; Eczema Succotash by Minnie Blauman; Patience Bumpstead by Margaret Young; Algernon Ashcart by Chester Miller; Mocha de Polka by Lucille Black; and Gabriel Horn by Ernest Naftzer (30 min., Saturday, 9:00–9:30 P.M., CBS, 1930–1931).

23439 Nitz, Al. Tenor (WSOE, Milwaukee, WI, 1926).

23440 Niville, Helen. COM-HE (WKBW, Buffalo, NY, 1949).

23441 Nix, Ed. DJ (*Disc and Chat* and *Campus Review*, KVOE, Santa Ana, CA, 1952). Newscaster (*World of Sports*, KVOE, 1952).

23442 Nixon, Herbert. Organist (KFON, Long Beach, CA, 1927).

23443 Nixon, Hilda. COM-HE (WITN, Washington, DC, 1956).

23444 Nixon, Joe. DJ (*Night Watchman*, WKGN, Knoxville, TN, 1948).

23445 Nixon, Marion. Singer billed as the "Queen of Song" (WTAQ, Green Bay, WI, 1939).

23446 Nixon, Milt. DJ (*Teen-O-Rama*, WDRF, Chester, PA, 1955; WGEE, Indianapolis, IN, 1957).

23447 Nizzoli, Mildred. COM-HE (KROG, Sonora, CA, 1956).

23448 *No School Today.* Jon Arthur played all the roles on the entertaining children's program originating from Cincinnati. One of the characters he created was an elf named Sparky. Ireene Wicker, who had formerly conducted her own *Singing Lady* program, sometimes appeared on the program to tell stories. Occasionally, a shortened version of the program was broadcast called *Big Jon and Sparky*. In different time formats — from one to two hours — and title, Arthur broadcast from 1950 to 1956 (120 min., Saturday, 9:00–11:00 A.M., ABC).

23449 Noa, Julian. Actor Noa was in the cast of *The O'Neills, Right to Happiness, Superman* and *This Day Is Ours.*

23450 Noah's Arkadians Orchestra. Instrumental music group directed by Joe W. Rines (WEEI, Boston, MA, 1925).

23451 Nobbs, George. Announcer (WHN, New York, NY, 1925).

23452 Nobel, Al. DJ (*The Juke Box*, KQV, Pittsburgh, PA, 1948–1956).

23453 Noble, Bob. DJ (*Breakfast with Bob*, WSAV, Savannah, GA, 1949).

23454 Noble, Clinton "Clint." Leader (*Clint Noble Orchestra*, instr. mus. prg., NBC-Red, New York, NY, 1936; WGAR, Cleveland, OH, 1942).

23455 Noble, Daniel. Announcer (WCAC, Mansfield, CT, 1927).

23456 Noble, Deke. Sportscaster (WKMO, Kokomo, IN, 1944).

23457 Noble, Dick. Newscaster (WIBC, Indianapolis, IN, 1939; WMAQ, Chicago, IL, 1942).

23458 Noble, Leighton. Leader (*Leighton Noble Orchestra*, instr. mus. prg., MBS, 1935; WIP, Philadelphia, PA, 1938; CBS, 1939).

23459 Noble, Linda. Soprano (WGY, Schenectady, NY, 1924).

23460 Noble, Ray. Leader (*Ray Noble Orchestra*, instr. mus. prg. that featured the fine British band, WIND, Chicago, IL; CBS, 1935; NBC, 1935–1936, 1939; WTAM, Cleveland, OH, 1937). *See **the Chase and Sanborn Hour**.*

23461 Noble, Roger. DJ (*Music for Today*, WSLI, Jackson, MS, 1948).

23462 Noble, Ruth. COM-HE (WYOM, Brookline, MA, 1949).

23463 Noble, Wendell. News analyst (*Newscope*, MBS, 1947–1948).

23464 Nobles, Gene. Black DJ (*Dance Hour*, WLAC, 1949–1957; *Randy's Record Shop*, WLAC, Nashville, TN, 1936; *The Dance Hour*, WLAC, 1949–1957). Sportscaster (WLAC, 1944).

23465 Nobles, Tom. Newscaster (WDOD, Chattanooga, TN, 1945). Sportscaster (*BC Sports Review, Sports Mirror* and *The Football Prophet*, WDOD, 1947; *Sports Parade*, KCOY, Santa Ana, CA, 1952).

23466 Noe, Thurston. Organist (WJZ, New York, NY, 1923).

23467 Noel, Harold. Announcer-publicity man (WGES, Chicago, IL, 1928).

23468 Noel, Jack. DJ (*Spin the Platter*, WTTS, Bloomington, IN, 1948–1960).

23469 Noel, Tom. Noel was the musical director of KVOO. In addition, he played Hippo and Professor Schnitzelbank on the station's *A.B.C. Safety Club of KVOO* (KVOO, Tulsa, OK, 1929–1930).

23470 Noethans, William. DJ (*Western Roundup*, KSCO, Santa Cruz, CA, 1950).

23471 Noftsinger, Kay. COM-HE (KYAK, Yakima, WA, 1949).

23472 Noggle, Hal. Newscaster (KFWD, Anchorage, AK, 1938).

23473 Nol, (Mrs.) Roy. Pianist Nol was a member with George A. Macredie of a piano-duet duo (WCAE, Pittsburgh, PA, 1924).

23474 Nolan, Bob. Leader (*Bob Nolan Orchestra*, instr. mus. prg., WLW, Cincinnati, OH, 1936; *Bob Nolan's Toy Band*, mus. prg., WLW, 1936).

23475 Nolan, Clara. Pianist (KFWI, San Francisco, CA, 1926).

23476 Nolan, George. DJ (KFDA, Amarillo, TX, 1948).

23477 Nolan, Helen. Publicist (NBC, 1930s). Nolan was a member of the NBC network's publicity staff with Rosellen Callahan and June Aulick.

23478 Nolan, Henrietta. Violinist (WQJ, Chicago, IL, 1925; KYW, Chicago, IL, 1926).

23479 Nolan, Jeanette. Actress Nolan appeared on the daytime serial program *Life Begins* aka *Martha Webster.*

23480 Nolan, Joe. Sportscaster (WABY, Albany, NY, 1942; WOKO, Albany, NY, 1944).

23481 Nolan, Robert H. Announcer-singer Nolan was also known as "BN" (WDAE, Tampa, FL, 1926).

23482 Nolan, Tim. DJ (*Sun Dial*, KXYZ, Houston, TX, 1952).

23483 Nolan, Tom. DJ (WCON, Atlanta, GA, 1950; *Crossroad Store*, WGLS, Decatur, GA, 1952).

23484 Noland, Nancy. Singer (NBC, 1934).

23485 Nolce, Susan. COM-HE (WTRX, Bellaire, OH, 1956).

23486 Nolen, Betty. COM-HE (WREL, Lexington, VA, 1949).

23487 Nolen, Betty Hughes. DJ (*Just For Ladies*, KADA, Ada, OK, 1950).

23488 Noll, Kerman. Sportscaster (WKOK, Sunbury, PA, 1938–1941).

23489 Noll, Lou. Tenor with the Bonnie Laddies singing group (NBC, 1929).

23490 Noll, Ray. DJ (*Cousin Ray*, KALL, Salt Lake City, UT, 1948–1950).

23491 Nolting, Gladys. COM-HE (WJCD, Seymour, IN, 1954; WHDM, McKenzie, TN, 1955–1960).

23492 (The) Nomads. Russian musical group conducted by Paul Zam (NBC, New York, NY, 1928). The string ensemble was directed by Charles Hart in 1929 (NBC-Pacific Coast Network, 1929). On the network, the group was directed by Alexander Kiriloff and Neil Enslen was the announcer (NBC-Blue, 1929). A later version combined music and humor. The veteran vaudeville team of Peg Wynne and Ambrose Parker were featured. Charles Hart directed a string ensemble in light musical selections (NBC-Pacific Coast Network, 1929; KNX, Los Angeles, CA, 1930).

23493 *Non-Sectarian Anti-Nazi League Talk.* Anti-Nazi organization program (Saturday, 2:45–3:00 P.M., WEVD, New York, NY, 1939).

23494 *Nona From Nowhere.* Frank and Anne Hummert produced the daytime serial first broadcast in 1949. Toni Darnay was featured in the title role of an adopted Hollywood actress, who wanted to find her real parents. Her father had once saved the life of a famous Hollywood producer. He asked the producer to "redeem his promise" and help Nona. The plot twist, however, was that the producer, her adoptive father, fell for Nona. The program's cast also included: Mitzi Gould, James Kelly, Florence Robinson and Karl Weber. The writer was Helen Walpole. Ford Bond was the announcer (15 min., Monday through Friday, 3:30–3:45 P.M., CBS, 1949–1950).

23495 *Nondenomination and Nonsectarian Church Services.* Dr. Frank Boyd conducted these services (KPO, San Francisco, CA, 1925).

23496 *Nonsense and Melody.* The variety show featured Frank Gill, Jr., William Demling, Jean Cowen, Charley Wellman, Bernadine Miller, the Jack Tars Trio and the Salvatore Sante Orchestra (15 min., Weekly, middle 1930s). The program consisted entirely of Pacific Coast talent.

23497 *(The) Noon Address.* . During the second week of its operation, station WFAA (Dallas, TX) inaugurated a series of talks by Dallas city officials, visiting experts and various business and professional men. The Dallas *News* printed the topics to be discussed from July 7 through September 2, 1923:

1. The Influence of Modern Day Luncheon Clubs
2. The Return of Prosperity to the Southwest
3. Americanism
4. Electrical Progress in Texas
5. The Southwest Style Pageant
6. Investing at Home
7. Amusements
8. The Modern Woman
9. The Southwest Market
10. Keeping Fit
11. The Weather
12. Traffic Problems
13. Municipal Auditorium
14. The Tractor Industry
15. Seed Bed Preparation
16. What Women Should Wear
17. Dallas, a Music Center
18. What's the Matter with Baseball?
19. True Conditions Existing in Hollywood
20. Real Estate and the Realtor
21. Dallas Parks and Playgrounds
22. Better Business Series
23. The Proper Erection of Aerials
24. Prevention of Cancer
25. Boy Scouts
26. Labor Day
27. Fire Prevention
28. YMCA Educational Activities
29. Dancing, Correct and Improper Latest Steps
30. The Drama and the Little Theater
31. Law Enforcement
32. The Future of Radio Telephony
33. Prospects for Football in the Southwest
34. Water Purification
35. Welfare Council Campaign
36. Safety First
37. Books You Should Know
38. Phases of Einstein Theory
39. Natural History
40. Opportunity of the United States in World Affairs
41. Poultry
42. The Modern Novel
43. The Large Family
44. The Value of Vacation
45. The Cotton Industry.

23498 *Noon Farm Program.* The weekday program began its run on December 1, 1924, and continued for decades. Beginning at 12:30 P.M., the program's structure remained the same throughout: a musical introduction; two seven-minute talks; and a question period in which from 25 to 30 questions sent in by listeners were answered. The program provided farmers with such important information as spraying dates, insect outbreaks and techniques of control, livestock disease warnings, etc. (WLS, Chicago, IL, 1924).

23499 Noone, Jimmy. Leader (*Jimmy Noone Orchestra*, instr. mus. prg., WIND, Gary, IN, 1937).

23500 Norcroff, Mildred. Pianist (KLDS, Independence, MO, 1926).

23501 Nordberg, Carl. Leader (Carl Nordberg's Plantation Players Orchestra, WDAF, Kansas City, MO, 1925).

23502 Norden, Earl. Newscaster (WHDF, Calumet, MI, 1945). DJ (*Disc King*, WSAM, Saginaw, MI. 1954).

23503 Nordin, Ernest, Jr. Director, WOW's Little Symphony Orchestra (WOW, Omaha, NE, 1929). Nordin was a gifted flute and saxophone soloist.

23504 Nordine, Jack. DJ (WADP, Kane, PA, 1955–1956).

23505 Nordstrom, Clarence. Singer (WGBS, New York, NY, 1926).

23506 Nordstrom, Ken. DJ (WPBC, Minneapolis, MN, 1949).

23507 Nordstrom, Lawrence. Leader (Lawrie and his Serenaders Orchestra, instr. mus. prg., Weekly, WFLV, Rockford, IL, 1929–1930).

23508 Nordwall, Beth Woodruff. Mezzo-soprano (KHJ, Los Angeles, CA, 1923).

23509 Norerg, Sven. Newscaster (NBC, 1946).

23510 Norgard, Bob. DJ (*Polka Time*, WFRO, Fremont, OK, 1949).

23511 *Norge Program.* Bunny Berigan and his orchestra were featured on the syndicated music show. Vocals were supplied by Frances Faye. Norge Refrigerator Company was the sponsor (15 min., Syndicated, 1936).

23512 Norgress, Joyce. COM-HE (KOBE, Las Cruces, NM, 1956).

23513 Noriega, Eddie. DJ (*Eddie Spins 'Em* and, in Spanish, *1230 Club*, KWTC, Barstow, CA, 1947).

23514 Norlander, Joan. COM-HE (KNUJ, New Ulm, MN, 1957).

23515 Norman, Adele. COM-HE (WIOU, Kokomo, IN, 1956).

23516 Norman, Alan. DJ (*Minute Man*, WFDF, Flint, MI, 1952–1955; WJIM, Lansing, MI, 1957).

23517 Norman, Beth. COM-HE (KYA, San Francisco, CA, 1954).

23518 Norman, Bob. DJ (*1490 Club*, WESB, Bradford, PA, 1950). Sportscaster (WESB, 1950).

23519 Norman, Charles "Chuck." Sportscaster (KBIZ, Ottumwa, IA, 1942). Newscaster (KBIZ, 1943).

23520 Norman, Don. Newscaster (WCFL, Chicago, IL, 1938).

23521 Norman, Don. DJ (*Music Room*, WLOS, Asheville, NC, 1948).

23522 Norman, Eric. Newscaster (WRRN, Warren, OH, 1941).

23523 Norman, Gene. DJ (*The Eastside Show*, KFWB, Hollywood, CA, 1947; *Mild and Mellow*, KMPC, Los Angeles, CA, 1947; *The Gene Norman Show*, KFWB, 1949; KLAC, Los Angeles, CA, 1954).

23524 Norman, Hal. DJ (KFDM, Beaumont, TX, 1957–1960).

23525 Norman, Henry. Newscaster (*Headline News*, KPAC, Port Arthur, TX, 1948).

23526 Norman, Jess. Leader (Jess Norman's Hot Boys Orchestra, KPO, San Francisco, CA, 1929).

23527 Norman, Kay. COM-HE (KNEA, Jonesboro, AR, 1954).

23528 Norman, Nancy. COM-HE (WDZ, Decatur, IL, 1956–1957).

23529 Norman, Neil. Sportscaster (WIL, St. Louis, MO, 1937–1946; *Sports Review*, WIL, 1947–1948; *Hilites in the World of Sports*, WTMV, East St. Louis, IL, 1949).

23530 Norman, Robert C. DJ (*Mailbag Matinee*, WHDL, Olean, NY, 1949–1952). Sportscaster (WKNY, Kingston, NY, 1956).

23531 Norman, Russ. DJ (*Traffic Jamboree*, KING, Seattle, WA, 1949).

23532 Norman, Stan. DJ (*Hits and Encores*, KTUC, Tucson, AZ, 1949; KOPO, Tucson, AZ, 1956). Sportscaster (University of Arizona sports play-by-play broadcasts, KTUC, Tucson, AZ, 1950).

23533 Norman, Stanley. DJ (*The Stanley Norman Show*, WPIT, Pittsburgh, PA, 1947). News analyst (*Man About Town*, WPIT, Pittsburgh, PA, 1948).

23534 Norman, Wally. Writer Norman wrote *Kitty Keane* and *Little Orphan Annie*.

23535 *Norman Brokenshire Show*. Veteran radio personality Brokenshire talked about gardening on his show (15 min., Various days, WOR, New York, NY, 1953). *See* **Brokenshire, Norman**.

23536 *Norman Vincent Peale*. Minister Norman Vincent Peale, author of the best selling *The Power of Positive Thinking*, answered questions read by Clyde Kettel sent in by listeners. Peale's answers focused on the positive up-beat side and were mostly of inspirational and motivational nature (10 min., Monday through Friday, 10:05–10:15 A.M., NBC, 1955).

23537 Norris, Bob. DJ (*Bandstand*, WGUY, Bangor, ME, 1954).

23538 Norris, Bobby. Sportscaster (WMAZ, Macon, GA, 1937–1938).

23539 Norris, Edgar. Pianist-singer (WFAA, Dallas, TX, 1926).

23540 Norris, Fate. Five-string banjoist from Georgia who joined the Skillet Lickers country music group in 1926 (WSB, Atlanta, GA, 1924–1926).

23541 Norris, Faye. Banjoist (KWSC, Pullman, WA, 1926).

23542 Norris, Florenz. Norris broadcast talks on various psychological topics (KFI, Los Angeles, CA, 1928).

23543 Norris, Joan. COM-HE (WJMJ, Philadelphia, PA, 1954).

23544 Norris, Joe. DJ (*Matinee*, WDWS, Champaign, IL, 1960).

23545 Norris, Kathleen. COM-HE. Best selling novelist Kathleen Norris discussed topics of interest to women (WOR, Newark, NJ, 1925).

23546 Norris, Lulu. Marimbaphone soloist (WBAV, Columbus, OH, 1925).

23547 Norris, Mary. Miss Norris broadcast talks for mothers on her *Tomorrow's Baby* program (CBS, 1929).

23548 Norris, Peggy. Singer (WGBS, New York, NY, 1928).

23549 Norris, Randy. DJ (*Random Ranch*, KEYD, Minneapolis, MN, 1949–1952).

23550 Norris, Ruth. COM-HE (KBKI, Alice, TX, 1955).

23551 Norris, Stan. Leader (*Stan Norris Orchestra*, instr. mus. prg., NBC-Red, New York, NY, 1936; WMAQ, Chicago, IL, 1937).

23552 North, Jack. DJ (*Sunday in the Country*, WAVA, Arlington, VA, 1960).

23553 North, LeRoy. Pianist (WOK, Chicago, IL, 1925).

23554 North, Marcella. Pianist (WLIT, Philadelphia, PA, 1925).

23555 North Carolina Ridge Runners. CW music group (WDEL, Wilmington, DE, 1942).

23556 North Dallas High School Band. Scholastic band (WFAA, Dallas, TX, 1925).

23557 North Texas A&M College Band. Collegiate band directed by Lieutenant L.W. Caine (WBAP, Fort Worth, TX, 1924).

23558 North Texas State Teachers' College Orchestra. College orchestra (WBAP, Dallas, TX, 1923).

23559 *North Little Rock Night*. The one-time special program broadcast January 19, 1928 and featured local talent from Little Rock, Arkansas. The program included piano solos by Billy Weed; banjo solos by Joe Donegan, some unidentified vocalists and Jack Rosenthal and his Night Owl Orchestra (120 min., 9:00–11:00 P.M., WLBN, Little Rock, AR, 1928). The program shared many sponsors, some of whom were the Times Printing Company, North Little Rock Electric Company, Citizen's Furniture Company, Argenta Building and Loan Association, Mayflower Diary, White's Drug Store, Clark Ice Cream Company, Lindsey Coal and Ice Company, Hendershot's Cafe, Owens and Company and the Home Electric Company.

23560 Northcott, Stanley F. Announcer Northcott broadcast his station's slogan, "World's Star Knitting Company (WSKC, Bay City, MI, 1927–1928).

23561 Northcutt, J.R. Dramatic actor (NBC-San Francisco, 1929).

23562 Northe, James Neill. Tenor (KHJ, Los Angeles, CA, 1926).

23563 Northington, Jimmy. DJ (*1450 Swing Club*, WHKP, Hendersonville, NC, 1948; *Coffee Club*, WHKP, 1954).

23564 Northrup, Beulah Clark. Pianist (WREO, Lansing, MI, 1925).

23565 Northrup, Dwight. Announcer (WSPD, Toledo, OH, 1925).

23566 Northrup, Kathryn. Reader (KLX, Oakland, CA, 1929).

23567 Northrup, Robert. Announcer (WLS, Chicago, IL, 1924).

23568 Northup, E.D. Newscaster (WCNC, Elizabeth City, NC, 1947).

23569 Northwest Atwater Kent Dealers All-Artist Orchestra. Commercially sponsored musical group directed by Herbert Preeg (KGW, Portland, OR, 1927).

23570 *Northwestern Chronicle*. Northwestern Yeast Company sponsored the Sunday afternoon dramatic series. The program originated from Chicago and featured Bill Barth, Dolores Gillen, Bernardine Flynn, Loretta Poynton and Merrill Fugit (Sunday P.M., NBC, 1933).

23571 Norton, Ann. Singer (*Ann Noble Sings For You*, WOV, New York, NY, 1936).

23572 Norton, Dick. DJ (*Money Man Show*, WNAV, Annapolis, MD, 1954).

23573 Norton, Dolph. Newscaster (WJBO, Baton Rouge, LA, 1945).

23574 Norton, Frank. Newscaster (WMAS, Springfield, MA, 1938–1940).

23575 Norton, Gene. Leader (Gene Norton Orchestra, WOW, Omaha, NE, 1927).

23576 Norton, Marion. COM-HE (KDMS, El Dorado, AR, 1954).

23577 Norton, (Dr.) O.E. Newscaster (KMOX, St. Louis, MO, 1945).

23578 Norton, Paul. DJ (*Tuneville Trolley*, KAMD, Camden, AR, 1952).

23579 Norval, Bud. DJ (*Rhythm Time*, WFOR, Hattiesburg, MS, 1948; *Breakfast Serenade*, WFOR, 1949; *Rural Roundup*, WFOR, 1950; *Breakfast Serenade*, WFOR, 1954).

23580 Norvell, Caskie. News analyst (*Greensboro Cavalcade of News*, WBIG, Greensboro, NC, 1937). Sportscaster (WBIG, 1937).

23581 Norvell, George. DJ (*Percolator Club*, KGLN, Glenwood, CO, 1952).

23582 Norvo, Red. Leader (*Red Norvo Orchestra*, instr. mus. prg., MBS, 1936; CBS, 1937; WGN, Chicago, IL, 1937; CBS, 1938). Norvo was a great American jazzman.

23583 Norwig, George. Sportscaster (*Spotlight on Sports*, *Let's Talk Sports*, *Pigskin Preview* and *Football Scoreboard*, WCSC, Charleston, SC, 1950; *Spotlight on Sports*, WCSC, 1952–1953).

23584 Norwood, Helen. COM-HE (KOWH, Omaha, NE, 1954).

23585 Norwood, Jack. Pianist (WBAP, Fort Worth, TX, 1923).

23586 Norwood, William "Bill." Newscaster (KGMB, Honolulu, HA, 1942, 1945; CBS, 1947–1948).

23587 Nosco, Henry. Violinist (NBC, 1928).

23588 *Nosey News*. Mildred Ransom portrayed Aunt Sarah whose monologues and character sketches focused on all the news and gossip that came to her attention (15 min., KMOX, St. Louis, MO, 1935).

23589 Nosokoff, John. Leader (John Nosokoff Orchestra, WCAE, Pittsburgh, PA, 1927).

23590 Noss, Luther. Pianist (WCAL, Northfield, MN, 1925).

23591 Notari, Serena. Newscaster (WEDC, Chicago, IL, 1938–1942, 1945).

23592 Notch Inn Orchestra. Club band (WEAF, New York, NY, 1926).

23593 *(The) Notorious Tariq* (aka ***The Notorious Tarique***). Motion picture star Turhan Bey played the title role on the adventure series that told the story of an international collector of antiquities and jewels. Mysterious Tariq, capably played by Bey, weekly found intrigue, romance and crime on the short-lived series (30 min., Weekly, ABC, 1947).

23594 Notto, Eddie. Singer (WFBH, New York, NY, 1925).

23595 Notz, Margaret. Pianist (KGW, Portland, OR, 1924).

23596 Nourse, Gertrude. Pianist (WHO, Des Moines, IA, 1926)

23597 Nourse, Neysa. Singer (WINS, New York, NY, 1936). .

23598 Nourse, William Ziegler. Broadcast poetry and directed the WMAQ players (WMAQ, Chicago, IL, 1929).

23599 Novak, Dick. DJ (KGW, Portland, OR, 1957).

23600 Novak, Frank. Tenor (WCCO, Minneapolis–St. Paul, MN, 1925–1929).

23601 Novak, Jane. Blues singer (WCCO, Minneapolis–St. Paul, MN, 1926).

23602 Novak, Jay. Sportscaster (KOKO, LaJunta, CO, 1948–1950; *Speaking of Sports*, KBNZ, La Junta, CA, 1952).

23603 Novak, Joe. Broadcast golf lessons on the air (KGO, Oakland, CA, 1925).

23604 Novak, Tom. DJ (WOC, Davenport, IA, 1955).

23605 Novak Vaudettes. *Radio Digest Illustrated* described this orchestra as wild women playing fast and scorching blues (KGW, Portland, OR, 1926).

23606 Novales, (Mrs.) Guiomar. Brazilian pianist (WJZ, New York, NY; WGY, Schenectady, NY; WRC , Washington, DC; and KDKA, Pittsburgh, PA, 1925).

23607 Novel, J. Walter. DJ (*Popular Tune Time*, KDJV, Sanger, CA, 1949).

23608 *(The) Noveleers.* The Noveleers group was a popular novelty male vocal quartet (CBS, 1936).

23609 Novella, Alma [Alba]. Soprano (WJZ, New York, NY, 1929; WCDA, New York, NY, 1929).

23610 Novello, Mike. DJ (*The Alarm Clock Club*, WRNL, Richmond, VA, 1947–1948; *Mailbox*, WRNL, 1949).

23611 *(The) Novellodeons.* A "little German band" led by Otto (Ted Morse). Morse was a short—five feet four inches and 200 pounds—trumpet player who led his popular little band. WLS (Chicago, IL) listeners particular liked his "Wedding of the Winds" and "When the Pussy Willow Whispers to the Cat-Nip" songs (WLS, 1937).

23612 Novelty Broadcasters' Orchestra. Popular radio band (WGES, Oak Park, IL, 1925).

23613 Nover, Beatrice. Reader (WEAF, New York, NY, 1926).

23614 Novins, Stuart. COM-HE (KNX, *Women's Forum*, KNX, Los Angeles, CA, 1949).

23615 Novis, Donald. Tenor Novis was the winner of the first place prize in the Atwater-Kent Radio Audition. He appeared on the *Atwater Kent Hour* in 1929 (KMTR, Los Angeles, CA, 1929).

23616 Novor, Florence. Pianist (WIP, Philadelphia, PA, 1924).

23617 Novosi, Pietro. Newscaster (WHOM, Jersey City, NJ, 1941).

23618 Novy, Gus. Leader (Gus Novy and his Orchestra, WTAY, Oak Park, IL, 1925).

23619 Nowlin, Eleanor. COM-HE (WCAX, Burlington, VT, 1949).

23620 Noyes, Helen. Cellist (WJAZ, Cleveland, OH, 1924).

23621 Nuanu, Joseph. Leader (*Joseph Nuanu's Hawaiians*, instr. mus. prg., WLW, Cincinnati, OH, 1942).

23622 Nuccio, Carmen. Prima donna of the New Orleans Grand Opera Company (WSMB, New Orleans, LA, 1925).

23623 Nugent, Helen. Cellist (Singer Nugent sang in five languages (CBS, 1931). Later as the "Old Fashioned Girl," she sang on WLW (Cincinnati, OH, 1935–1937).

23624 Nugent, Jack. DJ (*Jack's Juke Box*, KASM, Albany, MN, 1949). Sportscaster (KASM, 1951).

23625 Nugent, Paul. Actor Nugent was in the cast of *Mother of Mine* and *Stories of the Black Chamber.*

23626 Nugent, Tom. Newscaster (KOVC, Valley City, ND, 1939).

23627 Nunn, Guy. Newscaster (WJR, Detroit, MI, 1945).

23628 Nunn, Paul. Actor Nunn was in the cast of *Brent House* and *Glorious One.*

23629 Nunn, Will. Newscaster (WENK, Union City, TN, 1948).

23630 Nunnallee, Rea A. Director, Mann Singers of Van Alstine (WFAA, Dallas, TX, 1924).

23631 Nunnally, Katherine M. COM-HE (WSSV, Petersburg, VA, 1951).

23632 Nunnelley, Frances. COM-HE (WCRT, Birmingham, AL, 1954).

23633 Nusbaum, Mort. Newscaster (WSAY, Rochester, NY, 1942,1945). DJ (WHAM, Rochester, NY, 1949–1952; *The Mort Nusbaum Show*, WBBF, Rochester, NY, 1954–1955).

23634 Nutley, Pat. COM-HE (WGEZ, Beloit, WI, 1956–1957).

23635 *(The) Nuts of Harmony.* Cliff Arquette and Lolly Gookins were the singing comedy team on the transcribed program (15 min., Transcribed, Various Stations, 1935). *See* ***Cliff and Lolly.***

23636 Nutting, Sue. COM-HE (KNOT, Prescott, AZ, 1957).

23637 *(The) Nutty Club.* One of Chicago's favorite programs during the early 1920s, WBBM's *The Nutty Club*, boasted a "membership" of hundreds of thousands. The show responded to the many music requests they received from their listeners. Schaden (1988, p. 12) describes the show in this way:

> The *Nutty Club* originated at the Granada Cafe on Chicago's south side and was heard every Saturday night from midnight until three in the morning. Celebrities took an informal part in this entertaining session which included both music and comedy. Among those who appeared on the program were Paul Whiteman, Helen Morgan, Guy Lombardo, Olsen and Johnson, and almost every other popular performer of the day who happened to stop in at the Cafe.

23638 NuTymers Orchestra (aka NuTimers). Radio band directed by violinist-pianist S. Erich Hechter (WGR, Buffalo, NY, 1925).

23639 Nuzum, Chuck. Sportscaster (WCAE, Pittsburgh, PA, 1952).

23640 *NYA Varieties.* The National Youth Administration sponsored the variety show that combined music and dramatic sketches with interviews conducted by Stanley L. Stevens. Phil Napoleon's Orchestra and singer Buddy Breeze performed. Billy Gilbert, Virginia Waring and Helen Sofia were also in the cast (30 min., Thursday, 5:00–5:30 P.M., WNYC, New York, NY, 1940).

23641 Nyberg, Gertrude. COM-HE (KGHL, Billings, MT, 1955).

23642 Nydegger, Verne. DJ (*Carnival of Music*, KFBI, Wichita, KS, 1947–1950).

23643 Nye, Ada. Violinist (WNAD, Norman, OK, 1926).

23644 Nye, Bill, Jr. Singer (WWNC, Ashville, NC, 1929).

23645 Nye, Harry G. Nye was the announcer for the Setting-Up Exercise portion of the *Early Risers' Club of KSTP* (St. Paul–Minneapolis, MN, 1928–1930). Nye also was the Physical Director of the St. Paul Y.M.C.A.

23646 Nye, J.P. At 78 years of age, J.P. Nye played ballads on his guitar assisted by his little granddaughter, Mary F. Nye (KMA, Shenanndoah, IA, 1926).

23647 Nye, Louis. Talented comic performer Louis Nye was a DJ on his own *Louis Nye Show* (75 min., Monday through Friday, 8:15–9:35 P.M., WCBS, New York, NY, 1959). In addition to playing records, Nye also did funny dialect comedy bits. He later became a regular performer on several of Steve Allen's network television variety shows.

23648 Nyklicek, George. Organist (*George Nyklicek*, instr. mus. prg., KPO, San Francisco, CA, 1932).

23649 Nyland, Ralph. Leader (*Ralph Nyland Orchestra*, instr. mus. prg., WLW, Cincinnati, OH, 1937).

23650 Nyne, Kay. Organist (WLW, Cincinnati, OH, 1925).

23651 Nyquist, Carroll. DJ (*Turntable Time*, WNMP, Evanston, IL, 1952).

23652 Nyrielle, Georgette. Singer (WRNY, New York, NY, 1926; WGL, New York, NY, 1927).

23653 *Oahu Serenaders.* Hawaiian music program (CBS, 1934).

23654 Oak Cliff Presbyterian Church (Dallas, Texas) Choir. Choral group that frequently broadcast sacred music concerts (WFAA, Dallas, TX, 1923).

23655 Oakes, Barney. Sportscaster (WATL, Atlanta, GA, 1938, 1940). Newscaster (WJPR, Greenville, MI, 1939).

23656 Oakes, Texas Jimmie. DJ (WTCR, Ashland, KY, 1957).

23657 *Oakie Armstrong and the Oakie Armstrong Chamberlain Cowboys.* The weekly CW program was broadcast live from Olympia's Tropics Ballroom (KGY, Olympia, WA, 1940s).

23658 *(The) Oakite Red Wings.* A daytime program of light music (30 min., Weekly, CBS, 1929).

23659 Oakland, Will (Herman Hinrichs). Leader (Will Oakland and his Chateau Shanley Orchestra, WHN, New York, NY, 1925–1927; host and singing star of his own program *Will Oakland's Chateau*, broadcast weekly from his own Manhattan night club, WHN, New York, NY, 1926; *Will Oakland*, vcl. mus. prg., WMCA, New York, NY, 1929;

Will Oakland's Terrace Club, 30 min., Saturday, 11:00–11:30 P.M., WOR, 1931; Will *Oakland's Jesters Orchestra*, instr. mus. prg., WIP, Philadelphia, PA, 1935). Counter-tenor Oakland was said to have had the highest male voice ever heard on the stage. He began his professional career at 24, performing in vaudeville, minstrel shows, night clubs and on radio and television. Oakland recorded hundreds of songs during his professional career.

23660 **Oakland Male Quartet.** Vocal group that included tenors Robert Battison and Hugh Williams, baritone Clarence Oliver and bass Charles Lloyd. The quartet was accompanied by Theodore J. Irwin (KTAB, Oakland, CA, 1925).

23661 **Oakland Orpheus Male Choir.** The male vocal group accompanied by Bess Beatty Roland broadcast from the Oakland Auditorium Theater. The director was Edwin Dunbar Crandall (KTAB, Oakland, CA, 1925).

23662 **Oakland-Pontiac Little Symphony.** Symphonic music group (NBC-WFAA, Dallas, TX, 1928).

23663 **Oakland Real Estate Board Glee Club.** Vocal group directed by Zura E. Bells that consisted of Kenneth M. Morse, Everett Dowdle, Gibson Paull, Edward F. Jones, Frank M. Young, Earl B. Leonard, Ralph E. Wastell, Harry L. Holcomb and Burt R. Shrader. Beth J. Wastell was their accompanist (KGO, Oakland, CA, 1925).

23664 **Oakland Six Dance Orchestra.** Popular music group that broadcast on the *Reeve-Gartzman, Inc.* program (KFWB, Milford, KS, 1926).

23665 **Oakland Tribune Orchestra.** Commercially sponsored band (KLX , Oakland, CA, 1923).

23666 **Oakley, Iris Martinson.** Contralto (KOIN, Portland, OR, 1928–1929).

23667 **Oakley, Jack.** Bass (WEAF, New York, NY, 1926).

23668 **Oakley, John.** Bass (NBC, 1929).

23669 **Oakley, Victor Dale.** Announcer (WFAA, Dallas, TX, 1929–1929).

23670 **Oakley Trio.** Instrumental group consisting of pianist Richard Bailey; violinist Josef Walters; and cellist Niles Cutter (KRE, Berkeley, CA, 1926).

23671 **Oaks, Daisy.** Soprano (WFLA, Clearwater, FL, 1929).

23672 **Oaks, Dallin H.** DJ (*Platter Party*, KCSU, Provo, UT, 1952). Sportscaster (KCSU, 1955).

23673 **Oates, William.** Newscaster (WLBJ, Bowling Green, KY, 1941). Sportscaster (WLBJ, 1941).

23674 **O'Bannon, Gene.** DJ (*680 Music Shop*, KABC, San Antonio, TX, 1949; *Houston Hit Parade*, KTHT, Houston, TX, 1950; *Music for Mom*, KITE, San Antonio, TX, 1955).

23675 **Ober, Josephine.** Educational talks (WGBS, New York, NY, 1929).

23676 **Oberd, Matilda.** Soprano (WRST, Long Island, NY, 1928).

23677 **Oberg, Arthur.** Tenor (*Arthur Oberg*, WGN, Chicago, IL, 1934).

23678 **Oberg, Paul.** Pianist and music director (WLAG, Minneapolis, MN, 1922).

23679 **Oberlin, Richard.** Newscaster (WHAS, Louisville, KY, 1946).

23680 **Obermann, Frank.** Soloist on violin, viola and piano in the National Battery Symphony Orchestra (KSTP, St. Paul, MN, 1929).

23681 **Oberndorfer, (Mrs.) Mara E.** Announcer (WMAQ, Chicago, IL, 1923).

23682 **Oberndorfer, Marx and Anne Oberndorfer.** A talented couple who were musicians, composers and commentators, the Oberndorfers provided their listeners with stories of the romance in the lives of famous composers and the music they wrote (WGN, Chicago, IL, 1928; WMAQ, Chicago, IL, 1929).

23683 **Oberto, Betty.** COM-HE (WLPO, La Salle, IL, 1951).

23684 **Oblinger, Jackie.** COM-HE (WHIS, Bluefield, WV, 1954–1957).

23685 **Obolensky, (Princess) Ivanova.** Singer on the *Paris Night Life* program (NBC, 1931) and broadcast beauty talks on her *Princess Obolensky Youth Matinee* (WNAC, Boston, MA, 1931).

23686 **Oboler, Arch.** Distinguished radio writer, director and producer Oboler was one of radio's most prolific writers. See **Drama.**

23687 **O'Brian, Donald P.** DJ (*Western Jamboree* and *Ten Ten Club*, KCHI, Chillicothe, MO, 1949).

23688 **O'Brian, Pat.** Sportscaster (KMAC, San Antonio, TX, 1941).

23689 **O'Brian, Tex.** DJ (*Western Jamboree*, KCHI, Chillicothe, MO, 1952).

23690 **O'Brien, Adrian.** Organist (*Adrian O'Brien*, instr. mus. prg., WLW, Cincinnati, OH, 1936).

23691 **O'Brien, Barbara.** COM-HE (KTVW, Tacoma, WA, 1955).

23692 **O'Brien, Bernard.** Baritone (KGO, Oakland, CA, 1925).

23693 **O'Brien, Bill.** DJ (*Time to Dance*, WBET, Brockton, MA, 1950). Sportscaster (WSAR, Fall River, MA, 1952–1955).

23694 **O'Brien, Carlos.** Xylophonist (WDAR, Philadelphia, PA, 1924).

23695 **O'Brien, Catherine.** Reader (WBCN, Chicago, IL, 1925).

23696 **O'Brien, Dave.** DJ (*Dixieland Matinee*, WDXI, Jackson, MS, 1952).

23697 **O'Brien, David J.** Newscaster (WSTP, Salisbury, NC, 1945). Sportscaster (WSTP, 1945).

23698 **O'Brien, Dolores Dohrman.** Contralto (KFUU, Oakland, CA, 1925).

23699 **O'Brien, Don.** Sportscaster (*The Sports Parade*, KTUL, Tulsa, OK, 1940).

23700 **O'Brien, Don.** Sportscaster (KIOA, Des Moines, IA, 1947–1949).

23701 **O'Brien, Don.** Sportscaster (*Sports Page of the Air*, WNAX, Yankton, SD, 1947).

23702 **O'Brien, Dorothy.** Pianist (WLW, Cincinnati, OH, 1924).

23703 **O'Brien, Eddie.** Actor O'Brien was in the cast of *Aunt Jenny.*

23704 **O'Brien, Edmond.** Before becoming a motion picture star, O'Brien was in the cast of *Betty and Bob.*

23705 **O'Brien, Eleanor.** Soprano (WIP, Philadelphia, PA, 1924).

23706 **O'Brien, Ellis "Ellie."** DJ (*At Home and Away*, WCSH, Portland, ME, 1954–1956).

23707 **O'Brien, Frederick.** Author, lecturer and teacher broadcast travel talks (KPO, San Francisco, CA, 1930).

23708 **O'Brien, George.** Tenor (WEAF-NBC, New York, NY, 1926–1929).

23709 **O'Brien, Gerry.** News analyst (KTUC, Tucson, AZ, 1945; *The Editor Speaks*, KTUC, 1947). DJ (*Gerry O'Brien*, WTUC, 1948).

23710 **O'Brien, Hazel.** Contralto (KDKA, Pittsburgh, PA, 1924).

23711 **O'Brien, Howard Vincent.** Literary editor of the Chicago *Daily News*, O'Brien conducted a book review series (WMAQ, Chicago, IL, 1929).

23712 **O'Brien, Jack.** DJ (*Melody Corner*, KVOR, Colorado Springs, CO, 1950).

23713 **O'Brien, Jim.** DJ (*Morning Jamboree*, WMRO, Aurora, IL, 1949; *1280 Club*, WMRO, 1950; *Cat's Meow*, WMRO, 1952).

23714 **O'Brien, Joe.** Sportscaster (WMCA, New York, NY, 1941–1947). DJ (WMCA, 1954–1960).

23715 **O'Brien, Johnny.** Harmonica soloist (NBC, San Francisco, CA, 1929; *Johnny O'Brien's Harmonica High Hats*, instr. mus. prg., NBC, 1937).

23716 **O'Brien, Kay.** COM-HE (WOCB, West Yarmouth, MA, 1960).

23717 **O'Brien, Larry.** Leader (*Larry O'Brien Orchestra*, instr. mus. prg., WIBA, Madison, WI, 1935).

23718 **O'Brien, Lee.** COM-HE (KIUP, Durango, CO, 1956).

23719 **O'Brien, Libby.** COM-HE (WSTC, Stamford, CT, 1954).

23720 **O'Brien, Madeline.** Soprano (KGO, Oakland, CA, 1925).

23721 **O'Brien, Margaret.** COM-HE (*Shopping Highlights with Marge*, KFBC, Cheyenne, WY, 1949).

23722 **O'Brien, Margie.** COM-HE (KFBC, Cheyenne, WY, 1954–1955).

23723 **O'Brien, Mary Lou.** DJ (KTBS, Shreveport, LA, 1956).

23724 **O'Brien, (Miss) Nell.** Popular soprano (KHB, Kansas City, MO, 1922–1924).

23725 **O'Brien, Pat.** DJ (KIUP, Durango, CO, 1948).

23726 **O'Brien, Patsy.** COM-HE (WHLM, Bloomsburg, PA, 1956).

23727 **O'Brien, "Philadelphia Jack."** O'Brien conducted a physical education and conditioning program (WRNY, New York, NY, 1928).

23728 **O'Brien, Raymond.** Tenor (WEAF, New York, NY; WOO, Philadelphia, PA, 1925; WOR, Newark, NJ, 1926).

23729 **O'Brien, Sherry.** Sportscaster (WDAS, Philadelphia, PA, 1940, 1944–1947; *The Sports Show*, WDAS, 1948–1950; *Report on*

Sports, WDAS, 1952–1956; WJMJ, Philadelphia, PA, 1960).

23730 O'Brien, Tom. DJ (*Club 93*, WPAT, Paterson, NJ, 1960).

23731 O'Brien, Tommy. Sportscaster (KTRM, Beaumont, TX, 1947–1949; *Morning Sports*, KTRM, 1950; KPNG, Port Neches, TX and KPAC, Port Arthur, TX, 1960).

23732 O'Brien-Moore, Erin. Actress O'Brien-Moore was in the cast of the daytime serial programs *John's Other Wife* and *Big Sister*.

23733 O'Brien Brothers. Guitar duo (WRNY, New York, NY, 1925).

23734 O'Byrne, Joe. Sportscaster (*KYW Hunting and Fishing Club*, WYW, Philadelphia, PA, 1947–1948).

23735 O'Callahan, Gene. Newscaster (WCNW, Brooklyn, NY, 1938). Sportscaster (WCNW, 1938).

23736 Occidental College Men's Glee Club. KHJ (Los Angeles, CA, 1925).

23737 *O'Cedar Time.* This music program, sponsored by O'Cedar Furniture Polish, featured blues singer Bernadine Hayes, who was billed as "The Redhead of the Air" (15 min., Sunday, 5:30–6:00 P.M., CBS, 1930).

23738 Ochmann, Judy. COM-HE (WBOF, Virginia Beach, VA, 1956–1957).

23739 Ocho, Bernard. Violinist (NBC, 1928).

23740 Ochs, Frank H. Tenor (WHN, New York, NY, 1926).

23741 Ochsenhart [Ochsenhirt], Homer. Leader (*Homer Ochsenhart Orchestra*, instr. mus. prg., WJAS, Pittsburgh, PA, 1935).

23742 O'Connell, Bill. DJ (*Song Shop*, WMBL, Morehead City, NC, 1947).

23743 O'Connell, Eileen. DJ (*For Children Only*, WMGM, New York, NY, 1952).

23744 O'Connell, Emory L. Announcer (WGAT, Lincoln, NE, 1923).

23745 O'Connell, Margaret. Actress O'Connell was in the cast of the *John's Other Wife* daytime serial program.

23746 O'Connell, Nancy. COM-HE (WLAM, Lewiston, ME, 1951).

23747 O'Connell, Terry. DJ (WSWN, Belle Glade, FL, 1952).

23748 O'Connor, Bill. DJ (WCFL, Chicago, IL, 1954; WAAF, Chicago, IL, 1956).

23749 O'Connor, Dan. Newscaster (KFDA, Amarillo, TX, 1946).

23750 O'Connor, George. Newscaster (WINR, Binghampton, NY, 1946–1948).

23751 O'Connor, Hazel. Pianist (WIP, Philadelphia, PA, 1925).

23752 O'Connor, Helen. Contralto (WJZ, New York, NY, 1925).

23753 O'Connor, Helen. COM-HE (WCHI, Chillicothe, OH, 1957).

23754 O'Connor, Jack. DJ (*O'Connor's Nervous System*, WOBS, Jacksonville, FL, 1950).

23755 O'Connor, John. Newscaster (WLDS, Jacksonville, IL, 1941).

23756 O'Connor, Rod. Newscaster (KSL, Salt Lake City, UT, 1940; WGN, Chicago, IL, 1942).

23757 O'Connor, Ruth E. COM-HE (WFCB, Dunkirk, NY, 1951).

23758 O'Connor, Stanley. Baritone (KOIN, Portland, OR, 1928).

23759 O'Connor, Thomas. Newscaster (WBAL, Baltimore, MD, 1945).

23760 O'Connor, Tom. Sportscaster (WBIZ, Eau Claire, WI, 1949). DJ (*1400 Club*, WBIZ, 1948–1950).

23761 O'Connor, William "Bill" or "Billy." Irish tenor (WLS, Chicago, IL, 1924; WLS, 1925; WLAC, Nashville, TN, 1929; *William O'Connor*, vcl. mus. prg., WLS, 1935). O'Connor frequently sang novelty and sentimental songs on the *National Barn Dance* in the 1920s. He also was a member of the singing team "Billy and Bob the Singing B.B. Boys" who broadcast on WLAC, 1929.

23762 Odames [O'Dames], Elizabeth. COM-HE (WRUN, Utica, NY, 1956).

23763 O'Day, Billie. COM-HE (WIOD, Miami, FL, 1949; WCKR, Miami, FL, 1957).

23764 O'Day, Happy. DJ (WAKE, Atlanta, GA, 1956; KYES, Roseburg, OR, 1957).

23765 O'Day, Michael. Actor O'Day was in the cast of *Big Sister*, *Big Town*, *Coast-to-Coast on a Bus*, *Let's Pretend*, *Parker Family* and *Robinson Crusoe, Jr.*

23766 O'Day, Pat. COM-HE (WARN, Fort Pierce, FL, 1960).

23767 O'Day, Patti. COM-HE (KGRH, Fayetteville, AR, 1949).

23768 O'Dea, Margaret. Contralto (NBC, 1929).

23769 O'Dean, E.D. Announcer, known as "Radio-dean" (WWT, Buffalo, NY, 1923).

23770 O'Dell, Edna. Contralto (*Edna O'Dell*, vcl. mus. prg., NBC, 1935).

23771 O'Dell, John P. Newscaster (WAAF, Chicago, IL, 1937).

23772 O'Dell, Martha. COM-HE (WTUX, Wilmington, DE, 1957).

23773 O'Dell, Stuart, Jr. Newscaster (WOPI, Bristol, TN, 1939; WHLN, Harlan, KY, 1944).

23774 O'Dell's Hottentots. Jazz orchestra (WLAC, Nashville, TN, 1928–1929).

23775 Oden, Ramon Espanal. Guitarist (KTAB, Oakland, CA, 1925).

23776 Odets, Clifford. Later famous playwright Odets broadcast various readings and recitations (WBNY, New York, NY, 1926).

23777 O'Doherty, Seamus. Irish tenor (WGBS, New York, NY, 1928).

23778 Odom, Raymond "Ray." Sportscaster (KRBC, Abilene, TX, 1949; *Sports Hilights*, KRIZ, Phoenix, AZ, 1952; KRUX, Glendale, AZ, 1954). DJ (*Good Morning Program*, KSTA, Coleman, TX, 1950).

23779 O'Donnell, Bill. Sportscaster (*Parade of Sports*, WJPF, Herrin, IL, 1948).

23780 O'Donnell, Bill Martin. Sportscaster (*WIBX Sports Trail*, WIBX, Utica, NY, 1948–1950; WSYR, Syracuse, NY, 1953–1954; 1960).

23781 O'Donnell, Bob. DJ (*Music off the Record*, WJTN, Jamestown, NY, 1947; *Insomnia Inn*, WSYR, Syracuse, NY, 1949–1952).

23782 O'Donnell, Elizabeth. Soprano (WBBM, Chicago, IL, 1935).

23783 O'Donnell, Gene. Actor O'Donnell was in the cast of *Those We Love*.

23784 O'Donnell, Johnny. DJ (*Club 1270*, WHBF, Rock Island, IL, 1950).

23785 O'Donnell, William M. Newscaster (KDON, Monterey, CA, 1941–1942).

23786 Odson, Robert J. "Bob." Newscaster (*Korbers Noon News*, *Evening Headlines*, KVER, Albuquerque, NM, 1947; *Noontime News*, WBYS, Canton, OH, 1948).

23787 Odum, James "Jim." DJ (*Hillbilly Time*, WHKP, Hendersonville, NC, 1948; *Club Fourteen Double O*, WHKP, 1950).

23788 Oehme, Hans. Leader (*Hans Oehme Orchestra*, instr. mus. prg., WHDH, Boston, MA, 1939).

23789 Oelheim, Helen. Contralto (CBS, 1928).

23790 Oelrichs, Marjorie. COM-HE Oelrichs conducted a twice weekly fashion program (*What to Wear and When to Wear It*, CBS, 1929–1930).

23791 Oettinger, Elmer. Newscaster (WGTM, Wilson, NC, 1942; WGTM, 1945–1946; *Tar Heel News*, WNAO, Raleigh, NC, 1948).

23792 *Of Human Bondage* (aka ***Wheetena Playhouse***). Somerset Maugham's popular novel was the basis for the daytime serial. Raymond Edward Johnson and Jessica Tandy were the featured performers. Carlo De Angelo was the director. Wheetena Cereal was the sponsor (15 min., Monday through Friday, 12:00–12:15 P.M., NBC, 1940–1941).

23793 *Of Many Things.* Erudite Dr. Bergen Evans, a professor at Northwestern University, conducted this interesting discussion show broadcast by all Westinghouse stations (Weekly, 15 min., 1955).

23794 Offen, Lilli. Soprano (WEAF, New York, NY, 1924).

23795 Offenburg, Charlie. Leader (Charlie Offenburg and his Paris Cafe Orchestra, KFQZ, Hollywood, CA, 1926).

23796 Offhaus, Russell "Russ." Newscaster (WCOP, Boston, MA, 1941). DJ (WPIT, Pittsburgh, PA, 1948).

23797 *Official Detective.* *Official Detective* was an exciting adventure show broadcast in association with *Official Detective* magazine. The program began as a sustaining 15-minute program before expanding to a 30-minute format. Originally the cast included Fred Barton, Charlotte Dembo, Dana Hardwicke, Alan Stevenson, Chuck Webster and Bill Zuckert (15 min., Sunday, 8:45–9:00 P.M., MBS, 1947). In its later half-hour format, Ed Begley, Craig McDonnell and Louis Nye played the leading roles. Wynn Wright was the director. The writers were Jack Bentkover and William Wells. Music was by the Sylvan Levin Orchestra. Sound effects were provided by Al April (MBS, 1946–1957).

23798 *Officer Dagnacius Mulcahy.* Under the guise of Officer Dagnacius Mulcahy, Frank L. Madden regularly broadcast talks on traffic safety and current events. One of his many safety tips was: "Watch your wheel and mind your accelerator" (KSTP, Minneapolis–St. Paul, MN, 1928–1930).

23799 **Offmiss, Marty.** DJ (*Pulaski Nite Spot*, WPUV, Pulaski, VA, 1952).

23800 **O'Flynn, Rudy.** Tenor (WHN, New York, NY, 1924).

23801 ***(The) O'Flynn.*** Broadway producer Russell Janney brought the 13-week series of swashbuckling adventures set in 17th century England to radio. Sponsored by the Standard Oil Company of New Jersey, manufacturers of Esso Aero gasoline, the story told of Captain Flynn O'Flynn, played by Milton Watson. O'Flynn was heading home in 1689 after numerous victories on foreign seas, when, by coincidence, he rescues an English lady in distress. Many complications follow. The program's music and acting were both well done. David Ross was the announcer (30 min., Friday, 10:30–11:00 P.M., CBS, 1934).

23802 **Ogden, Alfred W.** Pianist (WDAR, Philadelphia, PA, 1923).

23803 **Ogden, Vivia.** Actress on the *Wayside Cottage* dramatic serial (CBS, 1929).

23804 **Ogle, Lady Ruth.** Ballad and blues singer (WLAC, Nashville, TN, 1928–1929).

23805 **Oglesby, Frank.** Tenor (WIP, Philadelphia, PA, 1924).

23806 **Oglesby, Warwick.** Sportscaster (WHAT, Philadelphia, PA, 1938).

23807 **O'Grady, Joe.** DJ (WKIP, Poughkeepsie, NY, 1956).

23808 **O'Grady, Rosie.** COM-HE (WBRB, Mt. Clemens, MI, 1960).

23809 **O'Grady, William.** Tenor (WCCO, Minneapolis–St. Paul, MN, 1928; KTSP, St. Paul, MN, 1929).

23810 **O'Grady, (Mrs.) William.** Organist (WQJ, Chicago, IL, 1926).

23811 **O'Hara, Hamilton.** Sound effects man O'Hara worked on the *Guiding Light*, *Hilltop House*, *Wendy Warren and the News* and *Young Dr. Malone* programs.

23812 **O'Haire, Eugene "Gene."** Sportscaster (WGY, Schenectady, NY, 1937–1941).

23813 **O'Haire, J.C.** Bible teacher (*J.C. O'Haire*, religious program, WCBD, Waukegan, IL, 1935).

23814 **O'Halloran, Hal.** News analyst (*Looking Things Over*, WHBL, Sheboyan, WI, 1947). Sportscaster (WHBL, 1949–1950; KVOO, Tulsa, OK, 1953–1956).

23815 **O'Halloran, Harold.** Announcer (WLS, Chicago, IL, 1929). Chief announcer and singer (WCFL, Chicago, IL, 1929).

23816 **O'Hara, Bernice.** Violinist (WCAL, Nothfield, MN, 1926).

23817 **O'Hara, Bill.** DJ (KSTN, Stockton, CA, 1956).

23818 **O'Hara, Dick.** Newscaster (WKBN, Youngstown, OH, 1948).

23819 **O'Hara, Don.** DJ (*Portable Bandstand*, KMJ, Fresno, CA, 1947).

23820 **O'Hara, James J.** Organist (*James J. O'Hara*, instr. mus. prg., WBZ-WBZA, Boston-Springfield, MA, 1934).

23821 **O'Hara, John "Johnny."** Sportscaster (WCFL, Chicago, IL, 1930; *Sports News*, WJKS, Gary, IN, 1932; KWK, St. Louis, MO, 1937–1949; KWKL, Peoria, IL, 1949).

23822 **O'Hare, Genevieve.** Harpist (KPO, San Francisco, CA, 1923).

23823 **O'Hare, Geoffrey.** Composer, author and singer O'Hare appeared on the *Roxy and His Gang* program (WJZ-Blue Network, New York, NY, 1927).

23824 **O'Hare, Husk.** Leader (Husk O'Hare's Orchestra replaced the Fred Hamm Orchestra, WTAS, Chicago, IL, 1925; Husk O'Hare's Coconut Grove Orchestra, WOK, Chicago, IL, 1926). O'Hare, billed as "the Genial Gentleman of the Air," and his band later broadcast from the Canton Tea Room during lunch hours and late evenings in the mid–1930s (WBBM, Chicago). O'Hare was more a manager, business man and agent than a "band leader." He "fronted" the band and took care of its business affairs.

23825 **O'Hare, (Rev.) J.C.** Minister of the North Shore Congregational Church (WPCC, Chicago, IL, 1926).

23826 **O'Hare, Lucille.** Soprano (WBBM, Chicago, IL, 1935).

23827 **O'Hearn, Margaret.** Contralto (WCDA, Brooklyn, NYC, 1928).

23828 **Ohl, (Madame) Emmy.** Soprano (WHT, Deerfield, IL, 1925).

23829 **Ohlin, Helen.** Singer (WLAW, Lawrence, MA, 1939).

23830 **Ohlmeier, Bill.** DJ (KAYS, Hays, KS, 1960).

23831 **Ohlson, (Reverend) Frederick.** Newscaster (WHEB, Portsmouth, NH, 1946).

23832 **Ohman, Phil.** Leader (Phil Ohman Trio played on the inaugural broadcast of WEAF in 1923, WEAF, New York, 1923). Ohman later teamed with Victor Arden to form a talented piano duet team (WJZ, New York, NY, 1929) and later organized a popular band (*Phil Ohman Orchestra*, instr. mus. prg., NBC, 1936).

23833 **Ohrt, Ev.** DJ (*Alarm Clock Club*, KMHK, Mitchell, SD, 1947).

23834 **Ohst, Ken.** A veteran newscaster, sportscaster and reader on station WHA (Madison, WI) for many years, Ohst was best known for his pioneer music show *Jazz Classics* that was began in the late 1940s and ran for 17 years (WHA, Madison, WI, 1940s).

23835 **Oikeman, Elizabeth.** COM-HE (WTUL, Tulsa, OK, 1951).

23836 **(The) Oil Twins.** The vocal team of Ned Tollinger and John Wolfe were popular radio entertainers (KOIL, Council Bluffs, IA, 1926).

23837 **Oinchas, Manny.** DJ (*Fiesta Time*, KTKT, Tucson, AZ, 1949).

23838 **O'Kane, Dick.** Singer (WHB, Kansas City, MO, 1928).

23839 **O'Keefe, Jean.** COM-HE (WFIW, Fairfield, IL, 1956).

23840 **O'Keefe, Walter.** Composer-singer (NBC, 1928) O'Keefe was known as "The Broadway Hillbilly." He was best known for singing "The Man on Flying Trapeze." He later had several network programs of his own for which he always wrote his own material.

23841 ***Oklahoma Bob Albright's Hoosier Hop.*** Albright's music group were featured on the CW music show (30 min., Tuesday, 2:30–3:00 P.M., CBS, 1935). Albright had previously conducted another show (WLW, Cincinnati, OH, 1932).

23842 ***Oklahoma Outlaws.*** CW mus. prg. (WIBX, Utica, NY, 1938). Al Clauser led the good country-western music group that included Slim Phillips, Don Austin and Carlos Ruffino. The transcribed half-hour show was broadcast by many other stations at various times in 1938–1939.

23843 **(The) Oklahoma Pepper Bird.** Popular announcer not otherwise identified (KFRU, Columbia, MO, 1925).

23844 ***Oklahoma Round-Up.*** Hiram Higsby hosted the CW music show with Ann Bond and Dick Reinhart. Alan Page was the program's announcer (Weekly, CBS, 1946).

23845 **(The) Oklahoma Yodeling Cowboy.** *See* **Gene Autry.**

23846 **Olah, Paul N., Jr.** Leader (Paul Olah and his Hungarian Gypsy Orchestra, WGBS, New York, NY, 1928).

23847 **Olberts, Leo.** DJ (*Hillbilly Hits*, KALB, Alexandria, LA, 1949).

23848 **Olchi-Albi, Nicholas.** Cellist (KNX, Hollywood, CA, 1928–1929).

23849 **Old, Chuck.** DJ (*Chuckwagon Jamboree*, WMBM, Miami Beach, FL, 1948).

23850 ***(The) Old Colonel's Reflections.*** The sustaining show presented Wes Carr as the "Old Colonel." When the Colonel wasn't discussing his warm, homey philosophy, he was singing oldtime songs with his rich bass voice (15 min., Monday-Wednesday-Friday, 6:30–7:00 P.M., WWSW, Pittsburgh, PA, 1936).

23851 ***(The) Old Company Program.*** Old Company Coal Company sponsored the concert music program featuring tenor Reinald Werrenrath (30 min., Weekly, NBC-Blue, 1929).

23852 ***(The) Old Company Singalong.*** Old Company Coal also sponsored the light music program with a sing-a-long format. The performers included baritone Vernon Archibald, baritone Frank Croxton, tenor Charles Harrison, tenor Lambert Murphy and pianist Arthur Leonard. Milton J. Cross was the announcer (30 min., Sunday, 6:30–7:00 P.M., NBC-Red, 1929). Later the day and time changed (30 min., Friday, 9:30–10:00 P.M., NBC-Red, 1930).

23853 ***(The) Old Counsellor.*** General financial questions were answered by the "Counsellor." Music was supplied by the Andy Sanella Orchestra. The program was sponsored by Halsey, Stewart stock brokers (NBC-Red Network, 1929).

23854 ***Old Cowhand.*** CW vcl. mus. prg. by unidentified singer (WCAU, Philadelphia, PA, 1938).

23855 ***(The) Old Dirt Dobber.*** Joy Floral Company sponsored Tom Williams on the local gardening show. Williams as the Old Dirt Dobber previously had been broadcasting nationally to his loyal gardening listeners for many years (15 min., Monday through Friday, 8:15–8:30 A.M., WLAC, Nashville, TN, 1946).

23856 Old Fashioned Girl. An otherwise unidentified singer (WLW, Cincinnati, OH, 1935).

23857 *(The) Old-Fashioned Revival Hour* (aka *The Joyful Hour*). Charles E. Fuller, who first began broadcasting revival services in 1933 over KGER (Long Beach, CA), initiated his *Old-Fashioned Revival Hour* on KNX (Hollywood, CA) the following year. After attracting a large listening audience, the program switched to MBS in 1937. The program began on only 13 Mutual stations, two years later the program was carried on all 152 network affiliates and heard by an estimated audience of ten million. *See* **Fuller, Charles E.**

23858 Old First Church Orchestra. Religious musical group (WBZ, Springfield, MA, 1926).

23859 *Old Gold All-American Football News.* Thornton Fisher and coach Slip Madigan of St. Mary's College conducted the football news program sponsored by Old Gold cigarettes (NBC, 1935).

23860 *Old Gold Character Reading.* Old Gold cigarettes sponsored numerologist Lorna Fanfin. She broadcast "numerological [sic] observations" on news events of the day, character analysis of the famous — living and dead — plus forecasts of the future. She had listeners send in their full names and birth dates for individual numerology readings (15 min., Tuesday, 8:15–8:30 P.M., CBS, 1931).

23861 *Old Gold Hour.* The music program featuring the Paul Whiteman Orchestra was broadcast from Los Angeles, while the band was in Hollywood filming "The King of Jazz." At the time the Whiteman band included Eddie Lang, Frank Trambauer, Joe Venuti and Bix Beierbecke. Bing Crosby and the Rhythm Boys were kept busy crooning "Mississippi Mud" on these shows. The program was first broadcast January 4, 1928 (60 min., Wednesday, NBC-Red, 1928–1929). *See* **Singers: Crooners, Canaries, Cow Girls and Hillbillies.**

23862 *Old Gold Party Time.* Bert Parks hosted the local talk and music show sponsored by Old Gold Cigarettes. Singer Kay Armen sang and the Buddy Weed Trio played the music. Don Hancock was the announcer (15 min., Monday through Friday, 1:00–1:15 P.M., WJZ, New York, NY, 1949).

23863 *Old Gold Program.* The *Old Gold Program* was a variety show sponsored by Old Gold Cigarettes. Fred Waring's Pennsylvanians [orchestra] was featured. When the program began, humor was supplied by comedian John Medbury. Later, a "Negro mammy" character, Mandy Lou, was added and, later still, comedian George Givot, "the Greek Ambassador of Good Will." Despite the additions of new comedians, John Medbury still wrote all the comic material used (1933). Moran and Mack also performed at times on the show. Later that same year other format changes were made. Music was still supplied by Fred Waring's orchestra, but Harry Richman was added to provide vocals and Milton Berle the comedy. David Ross was the announcer. *Variety* praised the show as very entertaining (30 min., Friday, 10:30–11:00 P.M., WOR, Newark, NJ, 1933).

Still later, the *Old Gold Show's* format changed once again: Don Ameche hosted the new variety show format with regular performers Claire Trevor, Pat Friday, Six Hits and a Miss and Victor Young's Orchestra. Each week Ameche and Trevor acted in a dramatization of a Mark Hellinger short story (30 min., Friday, 10:00–10:30 P.M., NBC-Red, 1940).

In 1947, another format change took place on *The Old Gold Show* (then sometimes referred to as *The Frank Morgan Show*). This version featured the entertaining comedy of Frank Morgan and a sketch about the Bickersons (Don Ameche and Frances Langford). Weekly guests, such as Dinah Shore, appeared. Carmen Dragon's Orchestra and announcer Marvin Miller were other cast regulars. Phil Rapp was the writer-director. The program was produced by Mann Holiner and Frank Woodruff (30 min., Wednesday, 9:00–9:30 P.M., CBS, 1947).

23864 *Old Gold Show.* Herbert Marshall was the host and appeared in dramatic sketches each week with different guest stars such as Virginia Bruce. Comedians Bert Wheeler and Hank Ladd and the Merry Macs singing group appeared each week (30 min., Monday, 7:00–7:30 P.M., NBC-Blue, 1941).

23865 (The) Old Gray Mare Band of Brownwood, Texas. Popular CW music group (WBAP, Fort Worth, TX, 1926).

23866 *Old Hag's Hour Glass.* Noreen Gamill played all the female characters on the show consisting of five vignettes that usually portrayed considerable irony. It was a fine vehicle for the actress, allowing her to play characters of all ages, personality types, classes of society and dialects (15 min., Transcribed, Various Stations, mid–1930s).

23867 *Old Hayloft Theatre.* Each week in the theatre "owned" by Al Halus the Aladdin Players, a WLS station group, was presented in an old-fashioned melodrama. The cast of these dramas included Les Tremayne, Hazel Dopheide, Dorothy McDonald, and Al Halus (30 min., Saturday, 9:30–10:00 P.M. CST, WLS, Chicago, IL, 1935).

23868 *Old Heidelberg.* A Tuesday afternoon program featuring the German music of Ernie Stenam's Orchestra (CBS, 1936).

23869 Old Heidelberg Ensemble. Instrumental group (*Old Heidelberg Ensemble*, instr. mus. prg., WMAQ, Chicago, IL, 1935).

23870 Old Hickory. An Iowa minstrel, not otherwise identified, sang old-time songs and accompanied himself on the guitar (KSTP, St. Paul–Minneapolis, MN, 1929).

23871 *(The) Old Home Town.* The weekly program supposedly broadcast a weekly entertainment held in a village school. Sid Ten Eyck acted as host on the novel program (30 min., Friday, 7:30–8:00 P.M., WCKY, Cincinnati, OH, 1934).

23872 *Old Kentucky Barn Dance.* William Aldridge produced the entertaining country music show featuring such talented singers, musicians and comics as Randy Archer, Janie Workman, the House Sisters, the Red River Ramblers, Robert Fisher, Maggie Mae, Tom "Cactus" Brooks, Tiny Thomwale, Bernie Smith, the Bell Family and Shorty Chesser. The announcer was Bob Lawson. The program originated at station WHAS in Louisville, Kentucky (60 min., Friday, 7:00–8:00 P.M., CBS, 1952). By 1955, the *Old Kentucky Barn Dance* was still a network fixture. The good country music show by this time was hosted by Shorty Chesser who took over the host role from Randy Archer. Others in the cast included Mary Jane Johnson, Sleepy Marlin, Tom Brooks, Tiny Thomwale, Bobby Lewis and Martha Ford. The announcer was Bob Lawrence (60 min., Friday, 7:30–8:30 P.M., CBS, 1955). After being on CBS for four years, the last show on that network was broadcast December 22, 1956. By this time *The Old Kentucky Barn Dance* had been reduced to a 30 minutes format. Randy Archer returned as the host. He was assisted by singer Judy Marshall, violinist Sleepy Martin and guitarist Bernie Smith. Tom Brooks was the announcer (30 min., Saturday night, CBS, 1956).

23873 Old King Cole. Designation for announcer N. Deen Cole (WHO, Des Moines, IA, 1924).

23874 *Old Kitchen Kettle.* Mary Wright dispensed information about fruit and vegetables, including everything from shopping for them to cooking them. Music was supplied by the Hilltoppers and a concert orchestra (15 min., Monday through Friday, 11:15–11:30 A.M. CST, WLS, Chicago, IL, 1936).

23875 *Old Man Adam.* Bud Raney, playing the role of Old Man Adam, was a good DJ. Adam Hats sponsored the show that allowed listeners to phone in requests. Old Man Adam would then mention their names and play the records they wanted to hear (300 min., Thursday, 11:30 P.M. to 4:30 A.M., WHN, New York, NY, 1945).

23876 *Old Man Donaldson.* Donaldson talked with his "niece" about rubies, pearls and diamonds. The sponsor was L. Heller & Sons, who sold various types of precious stones. The program originated in the studios of WEAF (New York, NY, 1926).

23877 (The) Old Missourians. Nine-man country music band plus pretty blues singer, Jean Starr (KFPY, Spokane, WA, 1928).

23878 *Old Man Sunshine.* Bob Pierce sang songs and told stories that were inspirational and up-beat. Milton J. Cross was his program's announcer (NBC-Blue, 1929). *See* **Pierce, Bob.**

23879 *Old Music Chest.* Phil Kalar and organist Ralph Waldo Emerson were featured on the quarter-hour music program (15 min., Tuesday, 11:15–11:30 A.M., WLS, Chicago, IL, 1936).

23880 *Old Music Shop.* Pat Mann wrote the sustaining dramatic sketch about an old German music shop owner, who refused to stock either popular or jazz records. He stuck strictly to the classics, much to the consternation of his daughter and her boy friend. Both tried unsuccessfully to convince him to change his mind and ways. No acting credits were given for the interesting weekly show (15 min., Wednesday, 8:30–8:45 P.M., WEVD, New York, NY, 1935).

23881 ***Old Painter.*** Jack Holden used his rich resonant voice to read inspirational poetry. A soothing musical background helped set the proper mood (15 min., Monday-Wednesday-Friday, 12:30–12:45 A.M., WMAQ, Chicago, IL, 1937).

23882 ***Old Pirate and the Jolly Four.*** Music and jokes were provided by the Old Pirate and his jolly musical shipmates (KUOA, Fayetteville, AR, 1931).

23883 ***Old Skipper.*** Don Hicks in the title role told exciting stories of the early days of sailing ships on the sustaining program. These entertaining little dramas also contained sea chanteys performed by a talented male singing group that was not identified (15 min., Sunday, 11:15–11:30 P.M., NBC-Blue, 1933).

23884 ***Old Songs of the Church.*** Basso Arthur Billings Hunt sang and directed the vocal group in renditions of favorite religious hymns. Other singers such as soprano Kathrine Palmer; contralto Joyce Allmand; and tenor Richard Dennis also performed. The organist accompanying them was Lowell Patton (15 min, Sunday, 1:30–1:45 P.M., KDKA, Pittsburgh, PA, NBC-Blue, 1933–1934).

23885 ***Old-Time Break Downs (Square Dances).*** A.B. Williams of Jefferson City, Missouri, directed the CW music program and supplied dance calls (WOS, Jefferson City, MO, 1923).

23886 ***Old-Time Singing and Old-Fashioned Playing*** **(aka *The Old-Time Fiddling and Singing Program*).** CW music program directed by H.G. Kidduo (WOAW, Omaha, NE, 1923). The program sometimes was also known as *The Old-Time Fiddling and Singing Program.*

23887 **(The) Old Time String Trio.** Instrumental musical group playing barn dance music composed of fiddlers Louie Barton and George Schrimpf and guitarist Bryan Williams (WOS, Jefferson City, MO, 1924).

23888 ***(The) Old Timer.*** Pat Barnes played both roles of the questioner and the Old Timer who provided answers to questions written into him by listeners. Generally, Barnes' replies and commentary focused on "humanity and its foibles" (WGN, Chicago, IL, 1928).

23889 **(The) Old Timers.** Banjo and guitar CW performers (KFKB, Medford, KS, 1925–1926).

23890 ***Old Timers.*** CW mus. prg., probably not the KFKB group from the 1920s (KREQ, St. Joseph, MO, 1939).

23891 **Old Town Duo.** Violinist Rose Vitto Sherman and harpist Marie Ludwig provided dinner music nightly from the Old Town Coffee Room of Chicago's Hotel Sherman (WLS, Chicago, IL, 1929–1930).

23892 **Old Wheat Street Baptist Colored Quartet.** Vocal group that featured "darky spirituals" (WSB, Atlanta, GA, 1923).

23893 **Oldaker, Lynn E.** Sportscaster (KGFX, Pierre, SD, 1937–1941).

23894 **Oldre, Fred.** Leader-banjoist (Fred Oldre and his Gayety Theatre Orchestra, WCCO, Minneapolis–St. Paul, MN, 1927–1929).

23895 **Olds, Dorothy.** Pianist (KVOO, Tulsa, OK, 1928–1929; KTHS, Hot Springs National Park, AR, 1929).

23896 **Olds, E.L.** Announcer designated as "ELA" (WBAP, San Antonio, TX, 1923).

23897 ***(The) Oldsmobile Program.*** Oldsmobile [automobiles] sponsored the combination of sports news and music. Ted Husing was the sportscaster on the show. Music was performed by contralto Barbara Mauel, the Humming Birds vocal group and the Leon Belasco Orchestra (30 min., Wednesday, 8:30–9:00 P.M., CBS, 1933).

23898 ***(The) Oleanders Male Quartet.*** Vcl. mus. prg. by male quartet, (CBS, 1935–1936).

23899 **O'Leary, Alice.** Contralto (WNAC, Boston, MA, 1934).

23900 **O'Leary, James H.** DJ (*Echoes and Encores,* KFXM, San Bernardino, CA, 1948; KBIG, Avalon, CA, 1960).

23901 **O'Leary, Joseph.** Leader (O'Leary's Irish Minstrels, WEEI, Boston, MA, 1928–1929).

23902 **Oleson, Alice.** Pianist (WHIP, Hammond, IN, 1938).

23903 **Oleta, Henrietta.** Contralto (WLTH, Brooklyn, NY, 1930).

23904 **Olin, Grace Bradford.** Singer (WBZ, Springfield, MA, 1924).

23905 **Olin, Jerry.** DJ (WMOU, Berlin, NH, 1956).

23906 **Olinger, Dick.** DJ (*Musical Clock,* WDAD, Indiana, PA, 1949).

23907 **Oliphant, Elmer.** Sportscaster Oliphant was an All-American football player 1915–1917 who discussed the rules of football (WGY, Schenectady, NY, 1922. Oliphant was the Physical Education Director at Union College at the time of his broadcasts.

23908 **Oliphant, H. Duncan.** News analyst (*Editors View the News,* WGAN, Portland, ME, 1947–1948).

23909 **Olive, Gray.** DJ (*Toast and Coffee,* WWOD, Lynchburg, VA, 1948–1952; WMSC, Columbia, SC, 1956–1957).

23910 **Oliver, Alice.** Violinist (WSWS, Chicago, IL, 1926).

23911 **Oliver, Altheda.** Mezzo-soprano (KNX, Los Angeles, CA, 1928–1929).

23912 **Oliver, Bryce.** Newscaster (WEVD, New York, NY, 1937; WHN, New York, NY, 1938–1939; WMCA, New York, NY, 1940–1942; WEVD, 1945).

23913 **Oliver, Cliff.** DJ (*Owl's Club,* WHBC, Canton, OH, 1937; *Hospitality House,* WRFD, Worthington, OH, 1954).

23914 **Oliver, Dennis.** DJ (*Dennis the Menace Show,* WAXX, Chippewa Falls, WI, 1960).

23915 **Oliver, Eddie.** Leader (*Eddie Oliver Orchestra,* instr. mus. prg., CBS, 1936).

23916 **Oliver, Frank.** Actor in the WGY Players (WGY, Schenectady, NY, 1923).

23917 **Oliver, Gerardo.** Singer (WGBS, New York, NY, 1928).

23918 **Oliver, Harold.** Leader (Harold Oliver and his Log Cabin Orchestra, WOR, Newark, NJ, 1925).

23919 **Oliver, Jerry.** DJ (*Open House,* KRXL, Roseburg, OR, 1949).

23920 **Oliver, Josephine.** Violinist (WSWS, Chicago, IL, 1926).

23921 **Oliver, Julian.** Tenor (NBC, 1928–1929).

23922 **Oliver, King.** Legendary jazz trumpeter King Oliver led the influential King Oliver's Jazz Orchestra (WHT, Chicago, IL, 1923).

23923 **Oliver, Paul.** *See* **Munn, Frank.**

23924 **Oliver, Shirley.** COM-HE (WCRE, Cheraw, SC, 1956).

23925 **Oliver, Shirling.** Actor Oliver was in the cast of *Beyond These Valleys* and *Valiant Lady.*

23926 **Oliver, Simeon.** Eskimo pianist (WJJD, Chicago, IL, 1926; KMOX, St. Louis, MO, 1929).

23927 **Oliver, W.** DJ (*Musical Clock,* WJVA, South Bend, IN, 1950).

23928 **Oliver High School Orchestra.** Pittsburgh public school orchestra (WCAE, Pittsburgh, PA, 1926).

23929 **Olivet, Jean.** Actress Olivet was in the cast of the *Dr. Paul* daytime serial program.

23930 **Olivia.** Olivia was billed as "the only child broadcaster in the world telling bedtime stories" (WTAS, Elgin, IL, 1924). She was not otherwise identified.

23931 ***Olivio Santoro.*** Santoro, billed as "The Boy Yodeler," played the guitar and yodeled. He was sponsored by F.G. Volk's Philadelphia Scrapple. To the tune of "Ta-Ra-Ra-Boom-De-Ay," Santoro began by yodeling: "Scrapple o-del-ay-de-ay comes from Phil-a-del-phi-ay" and ended by admonishing his listeners to eat it as long as it was Volk's. His program followed *The Moylan Sisters,* an excellent example of clever programming. Glenn Riggs was the program announcer (15 min., Sunday, 11:45–12:00 noon, NBC-Red, 1942).

23932 **Olivotti, Eva.** Light opera prima donna (WMTR, Los Angeles, CA, 1929).

23933 **Olmstead, Elise.** Children's program host and station owner (KFQX, Seattle, WA, 1924). Canadian born Elise Olmstead, best known to Seattle citizens as "Elsie," married Roy Olmstead in 1924. She was an attractive, intelligent young woman, who had studied music, spoke several languages and traveled widely in Europe. Her husband, Roy, who had recently been dismissed from his position as a Seattle police lieutenant, was the undisputed king of the "Northwest's largest ring of rum-runners and bootleggers" (Richardson, 1981, p. 33). Together Roy and Elise founded and operated station KFQX (Seattle, WA, 1924). It was Elise, however, who actually ran the station. It was as "Aunt Vivian" that Elise attained her greatest *popularity* and *notoriety.* It was generally believed that encoded in her nightly bedtime stories for children were secret messages for her husband's rum running fleets. The Olmstead's KFQX enjoyed great success in 1924, but Prohibition agents soon shut the station down and indicted the couple. *See* **Aunt Vivian.**

23934 **Olmsted, Nelson.** Actor-narrator Olmsted appeared on *Arnold Grimm's Daugh-*

ter, Bachelor's Children, In Care of Aggie Horn and *Stories by Olmstead.*

23935 **Olsen, Al.** Billed as "Al Olsen and his Whispering Guitar" (WBAP, Fort Worth, TX, 1928–1929).

23936 **Olsen, Bruno.** DJ (*Jukebox Serenade*, WLPO, LaSalle, IL, 1950).

23937 **Olsen, Doris.** Pianist (KGO, Oakland, CA, 1925).

23938 **Olsen, Frederic.** Newscaster (WHEB, Portsmouth, NH, 1939–1941).

23939 **Olsen, George.** Leader (George Olsen's Portland Hotel Orchestra broadcasting "direct by telephone" from the Portland Hotel, KGY, Chicago, IL, 1923; George Olsen's Metropolitan Orchestra, KGY, Chicago, IL 1924; George Olsen band directed by Herman Kenin on KGW, Portland, OR, 1923–1924; and featured on the *Victor Hour*, WJZ, 1926).

In 1929, Ethel Shutta, the popular vocalist who was Olsen's wife, sang with the band. Olsen's earliest band included: Olsen, ldr. and d.; Red Nichols, t.; Floyd Rice, t. and vcls.; Chuck Campbell, tb.; George Henkel, f., ss. and as.; Buck Yoder, clr. and ss.; Dave Phennig, ts. and v.; Eddie Kilfeather, p., Jack Hensen, tba.; and Billy Priest, as. and bj. The Olsen band continued to be popular in the 1930s (*George Olsen Orchestra*, instr. mus. prg., NBC, 1934; WXYZ, Detroit, MI, 1935; CBS, 1936–1937).

23940 **Olsen, Hazel.** A student at Yankton College Conservatory, Miss Olsen was accompanist for Herbert Lemke, a singer specializing in German songs, Happy Jack, Nancy and Glenn, John Sloan, Eddie Dean and other singers (WNAX, Yankton, SD, 1926–1929). She also sang with the Esther and Hazel harmony team on the station.

23941 **Olsen, Howard.** DJ (*Club Coeur D'Alene*, KVNI, Coeur D'Alene, ID, 1948).

23942 **Olsen, Joan.** Leader (Joan Olsen Orchestra, CBS, 1933).

23943 **Olsen, Johnny.** DJ (*Johnny Olsen* (60 min., Monday through Friday, 10:00–11:00 P.M., WMLO, Milwaukee, WI, 1947; *Johnny Olsen's Rumpus Room*, ABC, 1949–1950). Olsen was a very popular local DJ on Milwaukee radio.

23944 **Olsen, Robert.** Tenor Olsen was a Victor recording artist (KYA, San Francisco, CA, 1927; KFRC, San Francisco, CA, 1927–1929).

23945 **Olsen, Robert.** Newscaster (WKY, Oklahoma City, OK, 1945).

23946 **Olsen, Tom.** Newscaster (KGY, Olympia, WA, 1942).

23947 **Olshewsky, Anne.** COM-HE (WOTW, Nashua, NH, 1960).

23948 **Olson, Alma.** Contralto (WCAL, Northfield, MN, 1924).

23949 **Olson, Betty.** Contralto (*Betty Olson*, vcl. mus. prg., WAAF, Chicago, IL, 1935).

23950 **Olson, Bob.** DJ (WJMS, Ironwood, MI, 1949). Sportscaster (WJMS, 1952–1960).

23951 **Olson, Chuck.** DJ (KSO, Des Moines, IA, 1956).

23952 **Olson, (Mrs.) Clara.** Soprano (WCCO, Minneapolis–St. Paul, MN, 1928–1929).

23953 **Olson, Clarence.** Leader-violinist (Clarence Olson Orchestra, WCCO, Minneapolis–St. Paul, MN, 1927–1929).

23954 **Olson, D.B.** DJ (*Jukebox Serenade*, WGIL, Galesburg, IL, 1948).

23955 **Olson, Dale.** DJ (*Radio Rhythm Ranch* and the *Hillbilly Hit Parade*, KDIX, Dickinson, ND, 1948).

23956 **Olson, Dee.** COM-HE (WABO, Waynesboro, MS, 1955).

23957 **Olson, Donald.** Saxophonist (KWSC, Pullman, WA, 1926).

23958 **Olson, Doris.** Pianist (KTAB, Oakland, CA, 1926).

23959 **Olson, Dwight.** DJ (*Hit Tunes*, WJPS, Evansville, IN, 1949).

23960 **Olson, Elsie.** Accordionist at WLAG (Minneapolis, MN, 1923) and later at WCCO (Minneapolis, MN).

23961 **Olson, Esther.** Reader (KWSC, Pullman, WA, 1926).

23962 **Olson, Fred and Charles Olson.** The Olsons were a dual banjo team (WOC, Davenport, IA, 1928).

23963 **Olson, Gail.** Leader (*Gail Olson Orchestra*, instr. mus. prg., WPTF, Raleigh, NC, 1939).

23964 **Olson, Gladys.** COM-HE (WJZM, Clarksville, TN, 1956).

23965 **Olson, (Mrs.) H.O.** Cellist (WSM, Nashville, TN, 1928; WLAC, Nashville, TN, 1929).

23966 **Olson, Harold.** Baritone (WQJ, Chicago, IL, 1926).

23967 **Olson, Herb.** DJ (KXIC, Iowa City, IA, 1948; *Rumpus Room*, KXIC, 1950).

23968 **Olson, Joan.** Singer (CBS, 1934).

23969 **Olson, Leota.** Singer (*Leota Olson*, vcl. mus. prg., WIND, Gary, IN, 1935).

23970 **Olson, Max.** DJ (*Tippin' Inn*, KULF, Alpine, TX, 1952).

23971 **Olson, Nate.** DJ (*Music of the West*, KOOS, Coos Bay, OR, 1949).

23972 **Olson, Ole.** DJ (*House of Music*, WILS, Lansing, MI, 1952).

23973 ***Olympic Glee Club Program.*** Henry L. Perry directed the vocal music program broadcast from the Ampico Salon of the Wiley B. Allen Company building. The soloists included tenors Frank Mueller and Ray Nealan, baritone Frederick Keast and basso profundo, H. Victor Vogel. Judson Weller was the accompanist (KGO, Oakland, CA, 1926).

23974 **Olympic Hotel Concert Orchestra.** Hotel band (KFOA, Seattle, WA, 1925).

23975 **Olympic Rangers Orchestra.** Radio dance band (WABC, New York, NY, 1929).

23976 ***Olympics of the Air.*** Jack Starr conducted the sustaining sports quiz show (30 min., Monday, 7:00–7:30 P.M., KMBC, Kansas City, MO, 1938).

23977 **O'Malley, Charles "Chick."** Sportscaster (*Sports Matinee*, WACE, Chicopee, MA, 1948; *Sports Page*, WACE, 1949–1953). DJ (*Tel-O-Quester*, WACE, 1950).

23978 **O'Malley, "Happy Jack."** Violinist O'Malley was an old-time fiddler and leader-manager of Happy Jack's Old-Time and New-Time Orchestra (WNAX, Yankton, SD, 1927–1930). O'Malley started his radio career after he won 13 old-time fiddling contests.

23979 **O'Malley, Nan.** Pianist (KFI, Los Angeles, CA, 1926).

23980 **O'Malley, Neil.** Actor O'Malley was in the cast of *Bobby Benson's Adventures, Bringing Up Father* and *Howie Wing.*

23981 **O'Malley, Robert.** Actor O'Malley was in the cast of *Today's Children.*

23982 **Oman, "Coach" Tury.** Sportscaster (*Speaking of Sports*, WTJS, Jackson, TN, 1949).

23983 ***Omar Khayyam.*** Betty Webb and Stuart Buchanan starred on the weekly dramatic show that was heavy on atmosphere, mood and music. Romance was on the air (KHJ, Los Angeles, CA, 1932–1933).

23984 **O'Moore, Barry.** Irish tenor (WCAU, Philadelphia, PA, 1926). Leader (Barry O'Moore and the Bonwit Teller Ensemble, instr. mus. prg., WCAU, Philadelphia, PA, 1926).

23985 **O'Moore, Colin.** Tenor O'Moore sang on the *Philco Hour of Theater Memories* program with Jessica Dragonnette (NBC-Blue, New York, NY, 1927–1931).

23986 ***On a Sunday Afternoon.*** This sustaining variety show featured the Harold Stokes Orchestra, tenor Lawrence Salerno and the Three Graces, a female vocal trio consisting of Kathleen and Anette Bretzlaff and Patricia Clayton (30 min., Sunday, 2:00–2:30 P.M., MBS, 1938).

23987 ***On a Sunday Afternoon.*** Eddie Gallaher hosted the unusual show that combined live and recorded music. Regular cast members included singers Louise Carlyle and Stuart Foster performing with the orchestras of Alfredo Antonini and Russ Case (150 minutes, Sunday, 3:00–5:30 P.M., CBS, 1954).

CBS tried yet another version of the earlier 1954 program with the same name. This time the host was Byron Palmer and the live music was performed by Joan Weldon, the Pied Pipers and Wilbur Hatch's Orchestra (30 min., Sunday, CBS, 1955).

23988 ***On Olympia.*** Students from Olympia High School who were studying radio wrote the program, performed on it and were the announcers (KGY, Seattle, WA, 1930s).

23989 ***On Stage.*** Elliott and Cathy Lewis, a husband and wife team, acted in many of the dramas presented on the series, after already having enjoyed a busy radio career. He also produced and directed the *Suspense* program. She had played the intelligent friend on *My Friend Irma.* Others who sometimes appeared with them on the *On Stage* program were William Conrad, Clayton Post, Peggy Webber and Ben Wright. Lud Gluskin's orchestra supplied the music. The program was written by Richard Chandlee (30 min., Thursday, 8:30–9:00 P.M., CBS, 1953).

23990 ***On the Spot.*** Ray Barrett roamed Manhattan to obtain man-in-the-street interviews *on the spot* (15 min., WEAF, New York, NY, 1934).

23991 ***On Wings of Song.*** Tenor Roy Russell and the piano team of Virginia Johnson and Alma Green were featured on the entertaining music show (30 min., Sunday, 2:00–2:30 P.M. PST, CBS, 1936).

23992 **O'Nan, Pat.** DJ (*Music Library*, WINN, Louisville, KY, 1954–1955).

23993 **Onandaga Hotel Orchestra.** Hotel dance band (WGY, Schenectady, NY, 1926).

23994 ***Once Upon a Midnight.*** Alfred Hitchcock supervised and hosted the mystery show that included all the usual touches of mystery and suspense expected of a Hitchcock production (30 min., Weekly, ABC, early 50s).

23995 **Ondarcho, S.C.** Sportscaster (WBTM, Danville, VA, 1937).

23996 ***One Buck Private's Experiences in World War I.*** Al Rule recounted his war experiences while Ralph Waldo Emerson provided organ background music. The topics Rule discussed were: "Submarine Dangers," "A Funeral at Sea," "A Battle with Submarines," "Landing in England," "Crossing the English Channel," "Training for the Front" and "Our First Battle" (15 min., Thursday, 7:45–8:00 P.M., WLS, Chicago, IL, 1936). Rule's program was changed to Sunday at a later date.

23997 ***101 Ranch Boys.*** Andy Reynolds was the acoustic guitarist and leader of the CW music group that originally consisted of musicians from Oklahoma and Kansas. Smokey Roberts was the accordionist; George Lang the string bassist; and Cliff Brown the violinist. Named for an actual Oklahoma ranch, the group specialized in country-western music and developed a large following with their lively music and entertaining comedy routines (30 min., Monday through Friday, 8:30–9:00 A.M. and 30 min., Monday through Friday, 3:30–4:00 P.M., WSBA, York, PA, 1943–1944). Later in the 1940s the group recorded for Columbia Records and broadcast coast-to-coast on ABC. Eberly (1992, p. 10) notes that the success achieved by station WSBA might not have been reached so quickly if it had not been for the 101 Ranch Boys. Both the group's career and the station's success was advanced when Louis Vyner, the conductor of the York Symphony Orchestra, became station manager of WSBA. Although he had followed a quite different musical path, Vyner liked the CW music the 101 Ranch Boys played and increased their air time on WSBA. The group went on the ABC network in the late 1940s, where their program ran for four years on a sustaining basis. On their network show the group played straight CW music, omitting the comedy routines at which they were so adept (30 min., Saturday, 12:00–12:30 P.M., ABC).

23998 **116th Regimental Band of the Washington National Guard.** Military band that presented weekly radio concerts (KFOA, Seattle, WA, 1924).

23999 **136th Field Artillery Band.** Military band (WHAS, Louisville, KY, 1926).

24000 **172nd Field Artillery Band of Manchester.** The military band joined with the Cotillions Dance Orchestra on station WBRL's first broadcast (Manchester, NH, 1925).

24001 **174th Infantry Band.** Still another military band (WGR, Buffalo, NY, 1926).

24002 ***One Man's Family.*** The distinguished evening serial drama, *One Man's Family* was created and written by Carleton E. Morse. *One Man's Family* was extraordinary for the quality of its writing, acting and longevity. According to Buxton and Owen (1972, p. 179), it was the longest running serial drama on American radio, running as it did from April 19, 1932 to May 8, 1959.

Comfortably situated in the outskirts of San Francisco, just below the Golden Gate Bridge, was Sea Cliff, the comfortable upper-middle class home of Henry and Fanny Barbour, the Mother and Father Barbour of *One Man's Family*. Although his was the title role, Henry Barbour's life was shared and positively influenced by his wife, Fanny. Well-to-do Henry was a retired stockbroker, the family patriarch of a large extended family consisting of numerous children and grandchildren.

The program was first broadcast on the NBC-West Coast network in 1932 on a sustaining basis. It became a national show May 17, 1933, on the NBC-Red network, where it ran with varying time formats until the last broadcast on May 8, 1959. The show was exceptional, not only for its long broadcast run, but also for the high quality of the writing. Morse certainly deserves recognition as one of radio's most prolific and best writers. [Additional comment on Morse's writing is included in the **Drama** entry.] *One Man Family's* characters aged naturally, made mistakes, matured and, generally, faced the usual trials and tribulations — large and small — found in everyday life. Although this was the story of an upper middle class family, despite the Great Depression they suffered no economic deprivation. With the approach of World War II the family had members go into service and even experienced the death of a loved one and the captivity of others by the Nazis. In short, the program's characters seemed to be real members of the class they were portraying. Throughout the entire series Morse's thoughts and philosophy were strongly expressed.

It was probably Morse's philosophy and values that were chiefly responsible for the program's longevity. Perhaps the two chief messages the program stated and reiterated frequently were: The family was the most important factor in maintaining satisfactory levels of individual, national and world standards of living [conduct]; A strong belief in the value of patriotism and American democratic ideals should be encouraged.

A strong expression of these values can be found in a 1938 publication, *One Man's Family Looks at Life* (*1938*), that echoed the program's ideology. In that publication, the family is portrayed as sitting in a comfortable living room discussing the worsening world and national situation. One expresses the thought that it is impossible to isolate oneself from the troubled times: "What's one man's trouble is every man's trouble ." The recurring theme of individual responsibility was begun with Father Barbour's statement: "To begin with, its my opinion that the family is the source whence comes the moral strength of a nation. And the disintegration of any nation begins with the disintegration of the family. The family is the smallest unit in society. Million and millions of these little units make a nation. And the standards of living set up by these units indicate the high or low standards of a nation."

He continued:

> I think that you'll find that today there are more broken homes, more divorced men and women, more children without one of their parents than at any time in the history of the world ... It's a primary cause. The world's in confusion. Why? In my opinion it's mainly because national thought is confused. Why? Because the thoughts of the citizens of each nation are confused. Again why? Because something has happened to the individual ... something that shakes his faith in himself and in all the established institutions he's always believed in.

Father Barbour identified divorce as a major problem:

> If a child's world is wrecked before his eyes, what has he to cling to? It immediately colors his conception of the whole world. Immediately his mind forms the belief that there is nothing solid, nothing stable, nothing that he can ever quite believe in, and he grows to manhood a cynical, unbelieving citizen, certain that the only law of the universe is "every man for himself."

Mother Barbour placed much of the responsibility on women:

> Why, half the wives I know whimper at the least inconvenience. They feel imposed upon if they are forced to spend their time looking after their children. They dodge responsibility, ignore duty, and dissipate a lot more than is good for them. Well, I'm not talking about bad women.... I'm talking about the new generation of young wives. They're not bad and they're not without courage and honor, but they've simply been petted and humored and spoiled until they don't know anything else.

When the discussion turned to economic conditions, younger son, Clifford, discussed the discord between employees and employers. He deplored it and expressed the need for a common meeting ground between them:

> Seriously though, it seems to me that the answer is plain enough ... the reason for unpleasantness between worker and employer is simply a lack of understanding! They're too far apart in their points of view, and naturally if you don't understand a person you're a little suspicious and afraid of him. Everything he does you try to interpret as a move to hurt you. So you've got to find a common meeting ground. I mean a common denominator for employer and employee.

As was so often the case, Paul, the elder son, supplied the final concluding statement. He had served as a fighter pilot in World War I and was wounded when he was shot down. He discussed the grim world situation of 1938 and called for individual responsibility in considering the "prospect of war and the rumors of war facing the world of 1938." He suggested that people all over the world believe that the only way out "of all this mess is to return to the fundamental principles each of us learned at his mother's knee."

When war came, all members of the Barbour family made their contributions no matter how much personal suffering it entailed. Although some critics contended that Morse was frequently too preachy, it was obviously preaching that his audience wanted to hear and believe. His was the voice of middle class American values, hopes and dreams.

Over the years *One Man's Family* was on the air, the program carried several premium offers. Frequently the number of premium requests by listeners were astounding. For example, an offer of a family picture book in 1934, when the program was still being carried only by the NBC-Pacific network, elicited more than 110,000 premium requests. Even though this was a large figure for regional coverage, a later 1937 offer made when the program was on the full NBC network drew more than half a million requests.

The major cast members remained in their original roles for an extended period. There were few changes that took place. The most memorable roles and the actors that originally portrayed them were:

Father Barbour — J. Anthony Smythe
Mother Barbour — Minetta Ellen
Paul — Michael Raffetto
Clifford — Barton Yarborough
Hazel — Bernice Berwin
Jack — Page Gilman
Claudia — Kathleen Wilson

These performers not only originated their roles, but stayed with them during most of the program's run. Over the years the cast members included: Mary Adams, Barbara Jo Allen, Robert (Bob) Bailey, Jeanne Bates, Dawn Bender, Tommy Bernard, Bernice Berwin, Conrad Binyon, Henry Blair, Bill Bouchey, Francis X. Bushman, Herb Butterfield, Michael Chaplin, Tom Collins, Frank Cooley, Lloyd Corrigan, Mary Jane Croft, Dix Davis, Sharon Douglas, Sam Edwards, Jack Edwards, Jr., Minetta Ellen, Norman Field, Laurette Fillbrandt, Eddie Firestone, Jr., David Frankham, Barbara Fuller, Page Gilman, William Green, Virginia Gregg, Mary Lou Harrington, Clarence Hartzell, Bert Horton, Floy Margaret Hughes, Billy Idelson, Cy Kendall, Lou Krugman, Mary Lansing, Leone Ledoux, Earl Lee, Jana Leff, Forrest Lewis, Susan Luckey, Wally Maher, Maurice Manson, Charles McAllister, James McCallion, Mary McGovern, Tyler McVey, Dickie Meyers, Marvin Miller, Helen Musselman, Jeanette Nolan, Jay Novello, Susan Odin, Jill Oppenheim, Dan O'Herlihy, Walter Patterson, Victor Perrin, Ken Peters, George Pirrone, Frank Provo, Michael Raffetto, George Rand, Jean Rouverol, Ann Shelley, J. Anthony Smythe, Marilyn Steiner, Naomi Stevens, Richard Svihus, Russell Thorson, Emerson Tracy, Janet Waldo, Anne Whitfield, Kathleen Wilson, Winifred Wolfe, Ben Wright, Barton Yarborough and Loretta Young. The organists who performed were Paul Carson, Sybil Chism and Martha Green. The directors were by Carlton E. Morse and Charles Buck, George Fogle and Clinton Twiss. Harlan Ware and Michael Raffetto also were the writers at times. The announcers were William Andrews, Frank Barton and Ken Carpenter.

24003 ***One Night Stand.*** The excellent long-running big band remote broadcast series began as part of radio's World War II war effort to promote morale. *See* **Radio in Wartime**.

24004 ***One Night Stands with Pick and Pat* (aka *One Night Stands*).** The comedy team of Pick and Pat was featured along with the orchestra of Joseph Bonime (30 min., Monday, 7:30–8:00 P.M., CBS, 1935).

24005 ***One-String Danny and Banjo Slim.*** Otherwise unidentified instrumental duo (KFQZ, Hollywood, CA, 1926).

24006 ***(The) $1,000 Reward.*** This was an unusual sustaining program that combined a mystery drama with a listener participation quiz. Before the mystery drama was completed, a listener was called and asked to solve the mystery. The correct answer brought the listener a prize of a thousand dollars on this "mystery version" of *Stop the Music*. Ralph Bell, Esther Everett, Ken Lynch and Bill Smith were in the cast. John Sylvester was the program host. Ken Roberts was the announcer (30 min., Sunday, 7:00–7:30 P.M., NBC, 1950).

24007 ***One White Rose.*** Helen Gotwalt Miller wrote the program that was devoted to local Pennsylvania history (WSBA, York, PA, 1945).

24008 ***One World Flight.*** Norman Corwin produced and directed the program based on the trip around the world he took in 1946. During the trip Corwin visited 13 countries to talk with persons there from various walks of life. Although his talks also included interviews with various prominent persons in these countries, Corwin was somewhat disappointed with the documentary-dramas these interviews produced. *One World Flight* was a 13-part series (30 min., Weekly, CBS, 1947).

24009 **O'Neal, Gertrude Ogden.** Pianist-vocalist (KFWM, Oakland, CA, 1927).

24010 **O'Neal, J.B.** Sportscaster (WAYX, Waycross, GA, 1937).

24011 **O'Neal, Pat.** COM-HE (WCPS, Tarboro, NC, 1960).

24012 **O'Neil, Anne.** Singer (WQJ, Chicago, IL, 1924).

24013 **O'Neil, Chuck.** DJ (*The Chuck O'Neil Show*, WFEA, Manchester, NH, 1948; WFEA, 1957).

24014 **O'Neil, Hazel.** Soprano (WMAQ, Chicago, IL, 1924).

24015 **O'Neil, Jim.** Newscaster (KJBS, San Francisco, CA, 1939; KQW, San Jose, CA, 1940).

24016 **O'Neil, Jim.** DJ (*660 Club*, KOWH, Omaha, NE, 1948).

24017 **O'Neil, Kitty.** Soprano O'Neil sang on the *Philco Hour of Theater Memories* (NBC-Blue, New York, NY, 1927–1931) and the *NBC Light Opera Company* (*NBC*).

24018 **O'Neil, Leo.** Tap dancer who performed on radio (WLW, Cincinnati, OH, 1929).

24019 **O'Neil, Lucille.** Soprano (WJAZ, Mt. Prospect, IL, 1928).

24020 **O'Neil, Pat.** Irish baritone (KPLA, Los Angeles, CA, 1928).

24021 **O'Neil, Paul.** DJ (*Commuter's Express*, WNMP, Evanston, IL, 1950).

24022 **O'Neil [O'Neill], Peggy.** Singer, pianist, studio director and actress O'Neil played the role of Maggie on the *Maggie and Jiggs* program (WGES, Chicago, IL, 1928).

24023 **O'Neil, Tom** DJ (*Be Bop Time*, WNAO, Raleigh, NC, 1948).

24024 **O'Neill, Dick.** DJ (*Melody and Rhythm Time*, WCVS, Springfield, IL, 1949).

24025 **O'Neill, Edward G.** Newscaster (WGNY, Newburgh, NY, 1944–1946).

24026 **O'Neill, (Mrs.) Gertrude.** Reader-impersonator O'Neill was best known for her Scandinavian dialect sketch, "Tillie at the Photographer" (WCCO, Minneapolis–St. Paul, MN, 1927).

24027 **O'Neill, Jimmy.** Newscaster (KORN, Fremont, NE, 1944). Sportscaster (KORN, 1944). DJ (*Paging the Stars*, KOWH, Omaha, NE, 1954–1955.

24028 **O'Neill, Jimmy.** DJ O'Neill became the first voice to be heard on KRLA, Los Angeles, CA, at midnight, September 1, 1959. After a musical interlude, O'Neill said, "You have been listening to KXLA. You are now listening to KLRA — Radio for the Young at Heart." Station KXLA, a Los Angeles station with a country-music format, became KRLA in 1959, when a young Jimmy O'Neill, a 19-year-old DJ began his regular program of recorded music (180 min., Monday through Friday, 7:00–10:00 A.M., KRLA, Los Angeles, CA, 1959).

24029 **O'Neill, Johnny.** DJ (WREV, Reidsville, NC, 1949; *Sentimental Serenade*, WAIR, Winston-Salem, NC, 1954). Sportscaster (WMFR, High Point, NC, 1953–1956).

24030 **O'Neill, Virginia.** Singer (WCOH, New York, NY, 1932).

24031 ***(The) O'Neills.*** *The O'Neills* began as an evening program before becoming a daily daytime serial. The sponsor was the Gold Dust Corporation. *Variety* said the program had the potential to develop into an *Abie's Irish Rose* situation with both Irish and Jewish characters on the scene for a potential romance. The program was written by Jack Rubin and Jane West. The director was Carlo DeAngelo and Jack Rubin. The announcer was Ed Herlihy. The cast included: Charme Allen, Marjorie Anderson, John Anthony, Arline Blackburn, James Boles, Betty Caine, Linda Carlton, Charles Carroll, Helen Claire, Roger DeKoven, Jimmy Donnelly, Violet Dunn, Ethel Everett, Roy Fant, Jessie Fordyce, Janice Gilbert, David Gothard, Burford Hampden, Adele Harrison, Josephine Hull, Gee Gee James, Joseph James, Kate McComb, John McGovern, Harry Neville, Claire Niesen, Julian Noa, Vivia Ogden, Santos Ortega, Lawrence Palmer, Selena Royle, Jack Rubin, Chester Stratton, Alfred Swenson, Jimmy Tansey, Gladys Thornton, James Van Dyk, Jane West, Betty Winkler and Lawson Zerbe (MBS, CBS, NBC, 1934–1943).

24032 ***Onli Serenade.*** The good music program was broadcast twice weekly at different times. The orchestra of Joseph Lugar, soprano Edith Karen and baritone Horace Capps was featured (15 min., Tuesday, 10:00–10:15 P.M. and Sunday 2:15–2:30 P.M., WLW, Cincinnati, OH, 1936).

24033 Onslow, Jake [Jack]. Sportscaster (WAAB, Boston, MA and WNAC, Boston, MA, 1937). Veteran professional baseball player and coach Onslow also conducted a series entitled *Jake Onslow's Baseball School* (WEAN, Providence, RI, 1938).

24034 Oosling, Marion. COM-HE (WRLZ, Kalamazoo, MI, 1956).

24035 *(The) Open Door.* Sandra Michael wrote the daytime serial drama that *Variety* called an imitation of *One Man's Family* without that show's easy pace. The leading character of the story was Dean Erik Hansen of Jefferson College. Hansen's daughter, Liza, now a widow, had married the wrong man. Further plot complications began when her son, Jeff, came to live in Dean Hansen's house. The Dean was played by Dr. Alfred Dorf, a minister from Brooklyn. Others in the cast were: Charlotte Holland and Alex Scourby. The narrator was Arnold Moss. Chase and Sanborn Coffee sponsored the show. After Sandra Michael left, the program was written by Doria Folliott (15 min., Monday through Friday, 10:15–10:30 A.M., NBC-Red, 1943).

24036 *Open House.* Baritone Nelson Eddy, soprano Francia White and the Josef Pasternack Orchestra performed on the music program sponsored by the Vick Chemical Company (30 min., Sunday, 7:00–7:30 P.M. CST, CBS, 1936).

24037 *Open House* (aka *The Ona Munson Show*). Movie-radio actress Munson interviewed radio personalities on the quarter-hour show. Anita Ellis sang with the Lud Gluskin Orchestra. The announcer was Jay Stewart (15 min., CBS, 1944).

24038 *(An) Open Letter on Race Hatred.* The program was produced at the suggestion of Walter White, then president of the N.A.A.C.P., with the cooperation of William Paley. This was one of the few times when network radio presented a program that attempted to assess the role of African-Americans in the nation's life (30 min., CBS, 1943).

24039 *(The) Open Road.* Red Quinlan, an 18-year-old, starred in the dramatized story that told how he had traveled some 6,000 miles walking by foot, hitchhiking by thumb, and by rail on trains. *Variety* noted that the program attempted to keep youth from "taking wrong paths" in their search for fortune and gold (15 min., Monday, 10:45–11:00 P.M., NBC, 1935).

24040 *(The) Opera Guild.* Chase and Sanborn Coffee sponsored the broadcast of a condensed grand opera. The series was directed by Deems Taylor with music conducted by Wilfred Pelletier from the Metropolitan Opera (60 min., 8:00–9:00 P.M., NBC-Red, 1935).

24041 Opera on Radio. One of early radio's greatest cultural contributions was the rich treasure trove of operatic fare broadcast. Early radio provided listeners with a varied operatic repertoire. In 1910, Lee De Forest conducted an experimental broadcast of Enrico Caruso singing from the Metropolitan Opera's stage. On May 11, 1922, WEAF broadcast Verdi's *Aida* from the Kingsbridge Armory in the Bronx, New York. Performed by the Metropolitan Opera company, *Aida* was narrated by pioneer announcer, Tommy Cowan (WEAF, New York, 1922).

Chicago's KYW was the first station to present complete operas on a regularly scheduled basis in 1921 and 1922. When KYW was licensed in the fall of 1921, the station's management made the decision to make good music it chief programming. Distinguished radio historian Gleason Archer (1933) has given an account of KYW's decision to broadcast opera. He says that KYW executives needed programming to fill their broadcast schedule and attract listeners. Mary Garden, Director of the Chicago Opera Company, seeking favorable publicity and wishing to strengthen her company, consulted with KYW management and announced that her company's operas would be broadcast on that station. The effect on radio sales in Chicago and the surrounding Midwestern area was phenomenal. Prior to Miss Garden's announcement the number of radios in Chicago was estimated to be approximately 1,500. By the end of the first opera season that was broadcast by KYW, there were 20,000 sets in Chicago alone.

The Chicago Opera Company came to KYW because of the trouble plaguing the company. Director and conductor Gino Marinuzzi had resigned, because of the trouble in the company, which was losing the patronage of a wealthy businessman, experiencing internal conflicts, and, in addition, a drastic loss of attendance. In an effort to overcome all these problems, operatic singing star Mary Garden was persuaded to become the company's director.

True to her dynamic nature and temperament, Mary Garden made her first season as director a memorable one. First, she announced that American singers would be welcomed. Second, she assembled a stellar group of operatic stars such as Tito Schipa, Amelita Galli-Curci, Gadski, Rosa Raisa, Dux, Lipkowska, Schwartz, Muratore and D'Alvarez. Perhaps most important of all, Garden, herself, sang two or three times each week. Third, Miss Garden saw the broadcasting of her company's productions as a means to alleviate the problems she faced of inadequate financing and an alarming loss of attendance. Neither Chicago, nor any other American city had ever enjoyed as rich an opera season. The company was saved and the next year the name was changed to the Chicago Civic Opera Company.

Radio Broadcasting News (January 20, 1923) used its cover to illustrate Ina Bourskayha, Feodor Chaliapin, Claudia Muzio, Amelita Galli-Curci, Anna Ludmila and Amata Grassi under a headline that read: **Chicago Grand Opera Stars Heard Through Station KYW.** The page 3 editorial elaborated on its cover illustrations:

> By the time you receive this issue of RADIO BROADCASTING NEWS the Chicago Civic Opera Association will have finished one of the most successful opera seasons ever experienced in Chicago; a season devoted to popular prices, which resulted in packed houses every night during the entire run of ten weeks. At the same time radio broadcasting station KYW, one of the four large stations operated by the Westinghouse Electric & Manufacturing Company, and the only station in the world to broadcast grand opera, concluded the most important, instructive, and entertaining feature of its daily twelve hour schedule. During the entire opera season KYW put into the air productions of the best known operas of the Chicago Civic Opera Association, whose hearty cooperation made this feature possible.

The editorial went on to note that the station received thousands of letters from every state in the union thanking and praising them. It added that most of the letters were received from people living in more isolated districts where good music was a rare treat and opera only a dream. KYW broadcast a variety of music as the March 17, 1923 issue of the same publication indicated by showing a picture of jazz greats Noble Sissle and Eubie Blake seated at the piano watching Broadway performers Miller and Lyle on the stage performing *Shuffle Along*, a musical play that was broadcast by the station.

Both the Chicago Civic Opera Company and KYW were strengthened by their series of operatic broadcasts. The opera company enjoyed good publicity and KGY's evening listening audience greatly increased. When the opera season ended, there was a demand on the part of its listeners for more music with the same high musical standards they had been enjoying.

Bowing to listener expectations, the station hired a musical director and a group of studio (staff) musicians, among them Polly Willis (Polly Willis Archer). By year's end, KYW was able to maintain a 12-hour broadcast day, the most comprehensive broadcast schedule of any American station (Archer, 1938, p. 21). Beginning at 9:25 A.M., the station signed on with a report of the Chicago Board of Trade market prices, which were then repeated each half hour. News bulletins, musical selections and bedtime stories for children were also broadcast daily.

During the first two years of its affiliation with the Chicago Civic Opera Company, KYW broadcast performances of *Aida*, *Carmen*, *Parsifal*, *Tosca*, *The Snow Maiden*, *Il Trovatore*, *La Boheme*, *The Love of Three Kings*, *The Barber of Seville; Rigoletto*, *Cavalleria Rusticana* and *Madame Butterfly*.

Some of the performers that KYW's listeners heard in those years were Angelo Minghetti in *La Boheme*; Ina Bourskayha in *Carmen*; Mary Garden in *Tosca*; Mary McCormic, *Carmen*; Forest Lamont, *Cavalleria Rusticana*; Edith Mason, *Madame Butterfly*; Louise Homer, *Il Trovatore*; and Ivan Streschenko in *The Barber of Seville*.

After KYW's initial offerings some of the other operas broadcast in 1923 were Verdi's *Rigoletto* and *Othello* and Massanet's *Cleopatra*. The cast of *Rigoletto* included Angelo Minghetti, Giacomo Rimini, Virgilio Lazzari, Doria Fernando, Kathryn Brown, Gildo Morelato, William Beck, Lolia Barr and Max Teft. Pietro Cimini was the conductor. The *Othello* cast included Charles Marshall, Rosa Raisa, Giacomo Rimini, Maria Classens, Jose Mojica, Lodovico Olivero, Alexander Kipnis, Alfred Gandolfi and Milo Luka with Ettore Panizza conducting. The *Cleopatra* cast included

Georges Baklanoff, Desire Deferei, Alexander Kipnis, William Beck, Gildo Morelato, Herman Dresben, Mary Garden, Myrna Sharlow, Alice D'Harmanoy and Jose Mojica. Dances were by Adolph Bohm, Anna Ludmilla and the Corps de Ballet with Ettore Panizza conducting the orchestra.

Other Chicago stations met KYW's challenge by also providing opera broadcasts for their listeners. WMAQ in 1923 presented Ferrier's *Monna Vanna* with a cast that included George Baklanoff, Claudia Muzio, Edward Cotrevil, Fernando Ausseau, Jose Mojica, William Beck, Jane de Keyser and Gildo Morelato. Giorgio Polacco was the conductor. Later on December 25, 1923, WMAQ broadcast the Chicago Civic Opera Company's production of Humperdinck's *Konigs Kinder* at Chicago's Auditorium Theater. The cast included Charles Hart, Claire Dux, Alfredo Gandolfi, Maria Classens, Harry Steir, Vittorio Trevisan, Lucie Weston, Jose Mojica, Milo Luka, Ruth Lewis, Max Teft and Katherine Sutherlin. The orchestra was conducted by Isaac Van Grove.

One controversy concerning early operatic broadcasts remains unresolved. It has been suggested that local stations such as KYW and WMAQ in the early years of radio presented little more than condensations or one hour presentations of operas (Jackson, 1992, p. 4). Contemporary sources of that time do not provide a basis for such a statement. The belief that complete operas were not broadcast until the formation of networks is not borne out by contemporary accounts either. It is reported that network broadcasting of opera began with the Chicago Civic Opera's presentation of the garden scene from *Faust* on January 21, 1927 (Jackson, 1992, p. 4). A publication of the day carried the report that *Faust,* sponsored by the Brunswick-Balke-Collender Company, was broadcast complete from the Chicago Civic Opera Auditorium on the NBC network, January 21, 1927.

KYW was not the only station broadcasting local [non-network] operatic programming. As early as March 15, 1922, Thomas Cowan at WJZ (New York, NY) arranged and announced Mozart's *The Impressario* with a cast that included Hazel Huntington, Regin Vicarino, Tom McGranahan and Percy Hemus. On March 25, 1922, WJZ presented a two-hour broadcast in English of *Martha* by the Bijou Opera Ensemble. The following year (April 2, 1923), WJZ broadcast Gilbert and Sullivan's *The Mikado* from the stage of Newark's Shubert Theater.

West Coast stations also offered early broadcasts of opera. KGY (Olympia, WA), for example, broadcast the complete Bizet's *Carmen* by means of recordings and story continuity on May 28, 1922. *The Bohemian Girl* with a cast of Albert Gillette, Robert Saxe, Waldemar Engborg, Edwin Heinsohn, Grace LePage, Eva Atkinson and violinist Robert Bourke was broadcast by KGO (Oakland, CA, 1926). Beethoven's *Fidelio* with Albert Gillette, Arthur Schmitt, Albert E. Gross, Ruth Louise Hullen, Herman Genes, Irene Weinmann and Gwynfi Jones, a chorus of 30 voices and a 30-piece orchestra conducted by George von Hegel was broadcast by KPO (San Francisco, CA, March 24, 1927). KFRC (San Francisco, CA, 1927) broadcast Gounod's *Faust* with Flora Howell Bruner, N. Garrett, Blanche Hamilton Scott, Georges Simondet, Jose Corra, James Isherwood and the KFRC Little Symphony Orchestra.

The NBC research department offers the conflicting opinion that the first complete opera was broadcast February 17, 1923, from the stage of the Metropolitan Opera (Wood, 1992, p. 4). It is agreed that the opera was Wagner's *The Flying Dutchman,* but primary sources give the date as February 16, 1923. Jackson (1992, p. 4) suggests that another candidate for the first complete opera broadcast was the KDYL (Salt Lake City, UT) presentation of *La Boheme,* performed by an eight-piece orchestra and a cast of amateur singers.

There is no argument, however, that the most important event in operatic broadcasting took place on December 15, 1931, with the Christmas Day broadcast of Humperdinck's *Hansel and Gretel* from the stage of the Metropolitan Opera by NBC over 129 stations. Narrated by Deems Taylor with Milton J. Cross as announcer, it was the first of a long series of Metropolitan Opera broadcasts that over the years provided listeners an opportunity to hear hundreds of great artists singing the great operatic scores. The cast included Editha Fleischer and Queena Mario in the title roles and Dorothee Manski as the Witch. Also in the cast were Henrietta Wakefield, Gustav Schutzendorf, Pearl Besuner and Dorothy Flexer. The orchestra was conducted by Karl Riedel. NBC took over the opera house's box 44, where the engineers and their equipment shared the crowded space with commentator Deems Taylor and narrator Milton J. Cross. It was with this broadcast that Cross began his career as announcer and, later, narrator of the operas, a role that he played brilliantly until his death in 1975.

During much of the depression era, NBC broadcast the Met operas on a sustaining basis. George Washington Hill's American Tobacco Company, makers of Lucky Strike cigarettes sponsored the first series of 15 broadcasts from the Met during the 1933–1934 season. Listerine antiseptic became the second sponsor the following year. RCA was a later sponsor. After running on a sustaining basis for years, the first opera broadcast from the Met sponsored by the Texas Company (Texaco) occurred December 7, 1940, with the production of Mozart's *Le Nozze de Figaro* with Ezio Pinza, Salvatore Baccaloni, Jarmila Novotma, Licia Albanese, John Brownlee and Elizabeth Rethberg with Ettore Panizza conducting.

NBC broadcast the Metropolitan Opera broadcasts until 1943, when they were switched to ABC. In 1960, the Metropolitan Opera and Texaco formed a partnership to establish its own network to broadcast the operas every Saturday afternoon throughout the United States and Canada and to 22 other countries. The network required that stations carry the entire 20 week Met season and also to broadcast each opera live and in its entirety. The first opera heard on the Texaco–Metropolitan Opera network was Verdi's *Nabucco* on December 3, 1960.

The Metropolitan Opera broadcast format has changed very little over the years. Today (1998) it is essentially the same as the one used in 1947. A frequent feature was *Opera News on the Air* conducted by impresario and conductor Boris Goldovsky. The feature presented the news about opera plus many interviews with performers from the worlds of opera, theater and public life. Another intermission feature was the *Opera Quiz.* The Met broadcast of February 22, 1947 used the program's usual format with Milton J. Cross making the opening statement.

> CROSS: Good afternoon, everyone. This is Milton Cross. Again on this Saturday afternoon as on every previous Saturday during the opera season, I am at my place in the broadcasting box of the Metropolitan Opera House in New York City, inviting you on behalf of the Texas Company to listen to the performance of a complete opera as performed at a regular Saturday matinee at this world famous theater. You are also invited to listen to the three Metropolitan radio programs which are brought to you during the intermission periods which occur in the stage presentation.
>
> The matinee opera you will hear today is one of the six operas selected last season by the radio audience as their choice for the season's repertory. It is George Bizet's great masterpiece *Carmen.* This is the sixth and last of your chosen operas. The others have already been heard on Saturday broadcasts earlier in the season. They were *Aida, Faust, Boris Godunoff, Der Rosenkavalier* and *Hansel and Gretel.*
>
> Our cast is headed by famous American mezzo-soprano Rise Stevens, one of the greatest interpreters of the fascinating Spanish gypsy, Carmen. The leading tenor role, that of Don Jose, whose infatuation with Carmen proves disastrous to himself and to her, will be sung today by Ramon Vinay. As this will be Mr. Vinay's first appearance on a Saturday broadcast, let me introduce him to you by saying that he was born in Chile, had a French father and an Italian mother, and that he began his singing career in Mexico. It is interesting to note that — like a number of other tenors — including Lauritz Melchior and Seth Svanholm, Mr. Vinay began his career as a baritone. Mr. Vinay's debut at the Metropolitan was made just a year ago, when he achieved brilliant success in the role in which you will hear him this afternoon — Don Jose. Contrasted with the rather flamboyant Carmen is the simple village maiden, Micaela, sung this afternoon by Nadine Connor. The young American baritone, Robert Merrill, will be entrusted with the role of Escamillo and from him we will hear the famous "Toreador Song." The two soldier friends of Don Jose, Morales and Zuniga, will be sung by John Baker and William Hargrave. There are other gypsies in the story beside Carmen and among them we will find Thelma Votipka, Lucielle Browning, George Cehanovsky and Leslie Chabay. The conductor for Carmen today is Max Rufold.
>
> There are three intermissions in the opera Carmen and our broadcast will include three intermission radio programs. When the cur-

tain falls at the end of the first act, Boris Goldovsky will present another *Opera News on the Air*. Appearing with Mr. Goldovsky in *Opera News on the Air* will be two of the most outstanding American artists at the Metropolitan — Eleanor Steber, a soprano, and Jan Peerce, tenor. Between the second and third acts we will bring you another meeting of the *Opera Quiz*, with our regular quiz master, Olin Downes, throwing in the questions and three well known quiz experts throwing back the answers — Sigmund Spaeth, Robert Lawrence and our special guest for today, Mrs. John DeWitt Peltz, editor of the illustrated opera magazine, *Opera News*. During the third intermission there will be another discussion of a pertinent operatic question in the series known as *The Opera Round Table*. Our Round Table participants today will be the director of the Metropolitan Opera Guild, Mrs. Herbert Witherspoon, the well known musical authority, Huntington Watts and the guiding spirit of *Opera News on the Air*, Boris Goldovsky. Robert Lawrence will be moderator at the "*Opera Round Table*" and the question at issue is as follows: "In an opera singer which is the most important? Voice, musicianship or acting ability?"

This all afternoon broadcast is brought to you directly from the stage of the Metropolitan Opera House in New York City by the Texas Company, whose Texaco petroleum products are well known throughout the world. And now let me give you a brief outline of what happens during the first act of today's opera.

The story of Carmen takes place in Spain, a little over one hundred years ago. The scene of the first act is a public square in the city of Seville. On the right hand side of the stage is a cigarette factory. On the left a guard house with a group of soldiers lounging. Passers-by throng the square and the scene is a brilliant one, with bright-colored Spanish costumes in the bright Spanish sunlight. Lieutenant Morales, one of the soldiers, notices a shy young girl crossing the square and approaches her gallantly. "I am looking for a certain corporal named Don Jose," she says. Morales tells her that Don Jose is not there, but will come in when the guard changes. Micaela is too timid to accept his invitation to wait for Don Jose and she leaves the square.

After the opera was completed, Cross closed the program in this way:

And now a timely winter message brought to you by the Texas Company. Every week that goes by adds to the strain winter has put on America's cars. And many a car may weaken under that strain — break down at a time when it is needed most. So a winter check up at this time would be an important part of every car owner's personal car safety campaign. It is in your own interest to keep your car in condition. It is also in the public interest. A check up now can save many a car — prevent accidents and help save lives.

The Texas Company hopes you have enjoyed the broadcast including the performance of *Carmen*, the *Opera Quiz*, *Opera News on the Air* and *Opera Round Table*. You are cordially invited to be with us every Saturday matinee throughout the New York opera season. This is Milton Cross, saying good-bye until next week at this same time, when the Texas Company brings to opera lovers everywhere another complete Saturday afternoon at the Metropolitan. This is ABC the American Broadcasting Company.

When Texaco had completed its fiftieth year of sponsoring the Metropolitan Opera's weekly broadcasts in 1990, a compilation was made of the operas presented and how many times each was broadcast. There were 133 operas broadcast by Texaco from 1940 to 1990, ranging from such familiar favorites as *La Boheme* broadcast 36 times to *Porgy and Bess*, four times. Favorite operas were broadcast many times. As of 1990, the most often broadcast operas and the number of times they were presented were as follows:

1. *La Boheme* (Puccini), 36.
2. *Aida* (Verdi), 33.
3. *Carmen* (Bizet), 31
4. *Tosca* (Puccini), 29.
5. *Il Trovatore* (Verdi), 25.

Both the diversity and number of operas that were [and are] presented by Texaco and the Metropolitan Opera indicates the significant cultural contributions these broadcasts represent.

Music critic and composer Deems Taylor in 1922 wrote in the New York *World* that radio would essentially be dead in three years, because the terrible reception then possible would never be improved and that performers would demand to be paid. Taylor who was the commentator in 1930–1931 of the Metropolitan Opera broadcasts and, later, the longtime commentator on the New York Philharmonic Symphony Orchestra's Sunday afternoon broadcasts, admitted his mistake in 1937. In his book, *Of Men and Music*, Taylor (1937, p.303–304) estimated that each broadcast of the New York Philharmonic Orchestra reached nine million people. Since the orchestra's founding in 1845, Taylor made what he considered to be a generous estimate that some eight million people had heard the music *live* in the concert hall. Therefore, he said more people hear one of the broadcasts than those who heard a concert in person during the previous 92 years of the orchestra's existence. Consequently, Taylor concluded, radio certainly had made a significant cultural contribution. The same can be said of the Metropolitan Opera broadcasts.

24042 ***Operatic Echoes.*** Music from various operas was performed by contralto Helen Nugent, soprano Rhoda Arnold, bass Charles Robinson and an orchestra conducted by Vincent Sorey (15 min., Tuesday, 9:00–9:15 A.M., WABC, New York, NY, 1932).

24043 **Opfinger, Marie.** Lyric soprano (WABC, New York, NY, 1929).

24044 **Opheim, Don.** DJ (*Record Rack*, KFAM, St. Cloud, MN, 1952).

24045 **Opie, Everett George.** Busy announcer, dramatic reader, continuity writer and director Opie (WQJ, Chicago, IL, 1925; WJJD, Chicago, IL, 1929) began in radio at KYW (Chicago, IL) in 1923 before moving on to WMAQ (Chicago, IL); WQJ (Chicago, IL); WIBO (Chicago, IL); WJZ (New York, NY); and KSTP (St. Paul–Minneapolis, MN). His early years in radio were busy ones.

24046 ***Opie Cates Show.*** Band leader Opie Cates left his band behind to appear in his sustaining situation comedy. *Variety* called him a "rural Dennis Day." The story told how Opie from Clinton, Arkansas, came to live at Mrs. Burdick's boarding house in a nearby town. Soon he encountered problems with life in general and his girl friend in particular. Also in cast with Cates were Francis X. Bushman, Barbara Fuller, Noreen Gamill and Fred Howard. The Buzz Adlam Orchestra supplied the music (30 min., Monday, 8:30–9:00 P.M., ABC, 1947).

24047 ***Opinion.*** On this man-in-the-street interview show, Tex Antoine with his tape recorder collected the opinions on various topics of the New Yorkers he met in the street (25 min., Sunday, 2:05–2:30 P.M., WRCA, New York, NY, 1957).

24048 **Oppegard, Helen.** Newscaster (WBBM, Chicago, IL, 1941). Oppegard was the only woman newscaster at Chicago station WBBM in 1941.

24049 **Oppel, Jerry.** DJ (*Today's Top Tunes*, KOLE, Port Arthur, TX, 1948).

24050 **Oppenheimer, Kitty.** COM-HE (KTIM, San Raphael, CA, 1956–1957).

24051 **Opper, Frederick B.** News analyst (NBC-Blue, 1944–1945; ABC, 1947).

24052 ***Opry Spotlight.*** Ralph Emery conducted the influential all-night CW recorded music and interview show that immediately became a great favorite throughout the country (285 min., Monday through Saturday, 10:15 P.M. to 3:00 A.M., WSM, Nashville, TN, 1939–1957). It was said that Emery combined the skills of a journalist with that of an excellent CW music DJ. See **Emery, Ralph.**

24053 **Optimistic Do-Nuts.** Comedy singing group (KNX, Los Angeles, CA, 1929).

24054 **O'Quinn, Evona.** COM-HE (WHAB, Baxley, GA, 1956).

24055 **Oram, Richard.** Newscaster (WMAN, Mansfield, OH, 1941–1942).

24056 **Oravec, Frank.** DJ (WGBF, Evansville, IL, 1948).

24057 **Oravetz, Jule.** Newscaster (WRJN, Racine, WI, 1938).

24058 **Orbach, Henry.** Newscaster (KFEL, Denver, CO, 1939; KARK, Little Rock, AR, 1940–1941; KFRE, Fresno, CA, 1945).

24059 **Orchard Park High School Orchestra.** Scholastic music group (WGR, Buffalo, NY, 1925).

24060 **Orchestra Romaine.** Popular radio band (KFVE, University City, MO, 1925).

24061 **Orcutt, Eddy.** Newscaster (KGB, San Diego, CA, 1945).

24062 **Ordat, Mary.** COM-HE (WMRI, Marion, IN, 1960).

24063 **Ore, Leigh.** Announcer (WLBW, Oil City, PA, 1925).

24064 **Oregonian Concert Orchestra.**

Popular local band (KGW, Portland, OR, 1925).

24065 O'Reilly, Ed. Harmonica soloist O'Reilly was a former Mississippi riverboat captain (KSTP, St. Paul–Minneapolis, MN, 1929).

24066 O'Reilly, Jay. Sportscaster (WJLS, Beckley, WV, 1940).

24067 O'Reilly, Mike. DJ (*Atomic Boogie*, WJXN, Jackson, MS, 1949).

24068 Oreste's Peck Inn Orchestra. Club band (WOR, Newark, NJ, 1924).

24069 Orfield, Bennett. Newscaster (WTCN, St. Paul–Minneapolis, MN, 1938–1940; *News Reporter*, WLS, Chicago, IL, 1947).

24070 *Organ Concerts.* In 1927, station WJR initiated a series of organ concerts from various motion picture theaters that proved popular. The organists who appeared in the series were Merle Clark, Bob Clark, Arthur Gustow and Armin Franz (WJR, Detroit, MI, 1927).

24071 *Organ Jubilee.* Organist Arthur Hays played from Omaha's World Theater. Dr. Applesauce (Arthur A. Frudenfeld) was the program announcer for WOAW (Omaha, NE) in 1925.

24072 Orgren, Dick. DJ (KLVC, Leadville, CO, 1956).

24073 Oriental Blue Bird Orchestra. Club music group (WEAF, New York, NY, 1924).

24074 *Oriental Fantasy.* Many "different countries of the world" were the scenes of stories dramatized on the half-hour show. Several of the stories presented consisted of six or more episodes. Ardis Long — staff writer of KFOX — originated and wrote the dramatic feature (30 min., 8:00–8:30 P.M., Weekly, KFOX, Long Beach, CA).

24075 Oriental Male Quartet. Radio vocal group (WLS, Chicago, IL, 1928–1929).

24076 Original Bostonians Orchestra. Popular Boston band (WBZ, Springfield, MA, 1927).

24077 Original Charleston Five Orchestra. Local jazz band (WNYC, New York, NY, 1925).

24078 Original Country Boys. *See* **Otto Gray.**

24079 Original Dixieland Jazz Band. Pioneer jazz band (WNJ, Newark, NJ, 1925).

24080 Original Edgewater Beach Orchestra. Frank Kuhl led the hotel band featured on the *Candygram Frolic* (WSOE, Milwaukee, WI, 1926).

24081 Original Highland Syncopators. Local jazz band (WOR, Newark, NJ, 1923).

24082 Original Indiana Fire Department Dance Orchestra. Local municipal band that turned professional (WHN, New York, NY, 1924).

24083 Original Kentucky Night Owls. Jack Seligman directed the band (WHAS, Louisville, KY, 1924).

24084 *(The) Original Make Believe Ballroom.* DJ Al Jarvis' imaginary ballroom format, begun in 1933, was consistently a great Los Angeles favorite. Jarvis used the format before it was made nationally popular by Martin Block on New York radio (180 min., Monday through Saturday, 10:00–1:00 P.M., KLAC, Los Angeles, CA, 1947). *See **The Make Believe Ballroom.***

24085 Original Manford Aces Orchestra. Band directed by John J. Lesko (WHN, New York, NY, 1924).

24086 Original Midnight Serenaders. William A. Seibert directed the jazz group (WHN, New York, NY, 1924).

24087 Original Wonderland Syncopators. Club band directed by Edward L. Watts (WHN, New York, NY, 1924).

24088 O'Riley, Patrick. DJ (WAIT, Chicago, IL, 1956).

24089 Orilkoff, Abrasha. Violinist (KHJ, Los Angeles, CA, 1923).

24090 Oriole Male Quartet. The vocal group's members were tenor Fred H. Dempster; tenor William U. Ellis; baritone Dennis Fox; and bass William K. Kleith (KFWM, Oakland, CA, 1928).

24091 Oriole Marimba Band. Novelty orchestra (WEBH, Chicago, IL, 1926).

24092 Oriole Orchestra. Club band (WEBH, Chicago, IL, 1926).

24093 Oriole Trombone Duo. Brass duet team (WEBH, Chicago, IL, 1926).

24094 Orioles Orchestra. Local band directed by Raymond Atkins (KFI, Los Angeles, CA, 1925).

24095 Oris, Josephine. COM-HE (WJMJ, Philadelphia, PA, 1957).

24096 Orlando, Don. Leader (*Don Orlando Orchestra*, instr. mus. prg., MBS, 1942).

24097 Orlando, Nicholas. Director (Orlando's Concert Orchestra, WRNY, New York, NY, 1925; Roosevelt Concert Orchestra, WRNY, 1926).

24098 Orlando's Orchestra. Orchestra directed by Herbert Somay (WJZ, New York, NY, 1924).

24099 Orlich, Gena. COM-HE (KELO, Sioux Fall, SD, 1960).

24100 Orlofski, Dorothy. Contralto (WFLA, Clearwater, FL, 1929).

24101 Ormandy, Eugene. Director (12-piece Hires' Harvesters Orchestra, NBC-Red, New York, NY, 1927). Violinist-conductor (Jack Frost Musickers Orchestra, featured on a program sponsored by Jack Frost sugar company; musical director, *Jack Frost Melody Moments* program, NBC-Red, New York, NY, 1929). Ormandy's work was often praised by *Variety:* "Ormandy injects a lot of his musical personality into that fiddle when he steps into a cadenza." Ormandy later became the distinguished conductor of the Philadelphia Symphony Orchestra (WABC-CBS, New York, NY, 1929). In 1929, he also recorded several selections under the name of Dr. Eugene Ormandy's Salon Orchestra.

24102 Ornelas, Manuel. DJ (*Fiesta Time*, KTKT, Tucson, AZ, 1952).

24103 Ornest, Stan. Sportscaster (WGBS, Miami, FL, 1950–1956).

24104 Ornstein, Leo. Russian pianist (WJZ, New York, NY, 1928). Ornstein also appeared on *The Ampico Hour of Music* (NBC-Blue, New York, NY, 1929).

24105 O'Rourke, John. DJ (KBNZ, La Junta, CO, 1956; KSOO, Sioux Falls, SD, 1960).

24106 O'Rourke, Leo. Tenor (NBC, New York, NY, 1929).

24107 Orowitz, Eli M. Orowitz conducted the *Weekly Movie Broadcast* programs with its news and reviews (WPG, Atlantic City, NJ, 1928–1929).

24108 *Orphans of Divorce.* Stage star Margaret Anglin and James Meighan starred in the weekly serial drama sponsored by Dr. Lyons' Tooth Powder. The story concerned a middle-aged wife divorced by her husband, who then married a younger woman. She allowed her children to stay with her wealthy ex-husband, while she opened a small shop to support herself. When her daughter experienced trouble with her husband, she re-entered the picture for she had already known the sorrows of divorce. The serial was another of the Frank and Anne Hummert productions. The cast included: Margaret Anglin, Charita Bauer, Warren Bryan, Richard Gordon, Louis Hall, Joseph Julian, Geraldine Kay, Richard Keith, James Krieger, James Meighan, Henry M. Neeley, Vivia Ogden, Effie Palmer, Patricia Peardon and Claire Wilson. The program's familiar theme was "I'll Take You Home Again, Kathleen" (30 min., Monday, 7:00–7:30 P.M., NBC-Blue, 1939).

24109 Orpheus Female Trio. Instrumental trio consisting of violin, cello and piano (WJZ, New York, NY, 1926).

24110 Orpheus Girls Dance Orchestra. Female dance band (KWFI, San Francisco, CA, 1926).

24111 Orpheus Male Chorus. Twenty-five voice male chorus directed by R. Jefferson Hall (KOA, Denver, CO, 1925).

24112 Orr, Angeline. Actress Orr appeared on the daytime serial programs *Kitty Keene* aka *Kitty Keen, Incorporated*, *Ma Perkins* and *Road of Life.*

24113 Orr, Beulah Whitney. Soprano (WBZ, Springfield, MA, 1924).

24114 Orr, Elsie. Soprano (WIBO, Chicago, IL, 1926).

24115 Orr, John T. Newscaster (WHBQ, Memphis, TN, 1944).

24116 Orr, (Mrs.) Jones. Violinist (WLAC, Nashville, TN, 1929).

24117 Orris, Edith Hart. Pianist (KPO, San Francisco, CA, 1926).

24118 Orshorn, F.M. Announcer (KFAJ, Boulder, CO, 1926).

24119 Ort, Kathryn. Soprano (KYW, Chicago, IL, 1928).

24120 Ortega, Santos. A talented and busy actor, Ortega appeared on *Adventures of Nero Wolfe*, *Affairs of Peter Salem*, *Amazing Mr. Smith*, *Big Sister*, *Bright Horizon*, *Bulldog Drummond* (title role), *Charlie Chan* (title role), *Dimension X*, *Ellery Queen*, *Gangbusters*, *Green Valley, USA*, *Hannibal Cobb* (title role), *Joyce Jordan*, *Girl Inerne*, *The Man I Married*, *Myrt and Marge*, *The O'Neills*, *Perry Mason* (title role), *Portia Faces Life*, *Quick as a Flash*, *Roger Kilgore, Public Defender* (title role), *The Shadow* and *This Is Your F.B.I.*

24121 **Ortell, Doris.** COM-HE (WSSB, Durham, NC, 1951).

24122 **Orth, Robert W.** Announcer (WLB, Minneapolis, MN, 1925).

24123 **Ortiz, Emita.** Spanish soprano (WJZ, New York, NY, 1928).

24124 **Orton, Hal.** DJ (KRIC, Beaumont, TX, 1950).

24125 **Orton, Ray.** Singer (KTAB, Oakland, CA, 1925).

24126 **Orton and His Ukulele.** Instrumental soloist (KPLA, Los Angeles, CA, 1927).

24127 **Orum, Bill.** Sportscaster (KFUO, Clayton-St. Louis, MO, 1941, 1945; WEW, St. Louis, MO, 1945–1947; *Sports Review*, WEW, 1948; KCRC, Enid, OK, 1950; *Sports by Bill Orum*, KCRC, 1951; *Sports Report*, KCRC, 1952; *The Sportsman*, KCRC, 1955). DJ (*Platter Time*, KFEQ, St. Joseph, MO, 1948; KGWA, Enid, OK, 1955–1956).

24128 **Orvis, Josephine.** COM-HE (WJMJ, Philadelphia, PA, 1957).

24129 **Ory, Kid.** Leader (Kid Ory and his Creole Band, Various Stations, 1948).

24130 **Osborn (Col.) F.M.** Announcer (KFAJ, Boulder, CO, 1926).

24131 **Osborn, Gene.** DJ (KWWL, Waterloo, IA, 1948). Sportscaster (KWWL, 1949; KXEL, Waterloo, IA, 1951).

24132 **Osborn, Wayne.** Sportscaster (WIND, Chicago, IL, 1944).

24133 **Osborne, Belle.** Contralto (WHN, New York, NY, 1926).

24134 **Osborne, Charles E.** Osborne conducted a regularly scheduled physical fitness program (WFAA, Dallas, TX, 1924).

24135 **Osborne, George.** Cellist and assistant conductor (National Battery Symphony Orchestra and leader of the Casino Orchestra, WEAF, New York, NY; WJZ, New York, NY; KSTP, St. Paul–Minneapolis, MN, 1929). Osborne formerly had played with the popular Ben Bernie orchestra.

24136 **Osborne, Harry.** DJ (*Haphazard Harry's 1450 Club*, KVMV, Twin Falls, ID, 1948).

24137 **Osborne [Osburn], Howard.** Leader (Howard Osborne's Vanity Fair Orchestra, WBBM, Chicago, IL and WEBH, Chicago, IL, 1926).

24138 **Osborne, Jimmy.** DJ (*J.O. Jamboree*, WLEX, Lexington, KY, 1948–1950; *Jimmy Osborne*, 120 min., Monday through Friday, 9:30–11:30 A.M. and 30 min., Saturday, 12:00–12:30 P.M., WKLO, Louisville, KY, 1951).

24139 **Osborne, Len.** DJ (*Len Osborne Show*, WTBO, Cumberland, MD, 1952).

24140 **Osborne, Mary.** Guitarist (KLPM, Minot, ND, 1936).

24141 **Osborne, Ozzie.** DJ (*Ten Thirty Time*, WISH, Indianapolis, IN, 1947–1948; WFBM, Indianapolis, IN, 1949; *Variety Hour*, WISH, 1950).

24142 **Osborne, Roy.** Newscaster (KRBC, Abilene, TX, 1945).

24143 **Osborne, Tim.** DJ (*Tim Time*, KTHT, Houston, TX, 1948–1952; KTHT, Houston, TX, 1956).

24144 **Osborne, Vera.** Soprano (WOR, Newark, NJ, 1932).

24145 **Osborne, Verna.** Contralto Osborne was a first place winner in the Atwater Kent contest in 1929. She also was a member of WOR's vocal group, the Moonbeam Girls (WOR, 1934).

24146 **Osborne, Wayne.** Sportscaster (WJJD, Chicago, IL and WIND, Chicago, IL, 1946; *Sports Roundup*, WOPA, Oak Park, IL, 1955).

24147 **Osborne, Will.** Leader (Will Osborne's Nicollet Hotel Orchestra, WCCO, Minneapolis, MN, 1924; Will Osborne Orchestra, KVI, Tacoma, WA, 1929). Osborne also led the band on the *Herbert's Diamond Entertainers* program that was sponsored by a Harlem jewelry store. He frequently used medleys and announced his numbers against a musical background, closely imitating Rudy Vallee's popular style (WABC, New York, NY, 1929). Ironically, Osborne later subbed for Rudy on the latter's *Villa Vallee* dinner broadcasts in 1929. The band also broadcast on KVI (Tacoma, WA, 1929). In the next decade, Osborne's band appeared frequently (*Will Osborne Orchestra*, instr. mus. prg., 30 min., Tuesday, 11:00–11:30 P.M., CBS, 1930; *Will Osborne Orchestra*, instr. mus. prg., CBS, 1934; NBC, 1934–1935; WOR, Newark, NJ, 1936, 1940). The introduction to his 1940 network program was: "Listen to the glisten of the slide trombone from the Casa Manana in Culver City, California."

24148 **Osburn, Jimmee.** Banjo soloist (*Jimmee Osburn the Barefoot Banjo Boy*, CW music prg., WGBF, Evansville, IN, 1930).

24149 ***Oscar Brand Folksong Festival.*** Folk singer Brand performed on the entertaining sustaining program of folk songs. He was assisted by Ursula Brand and Daniel O'Donnell. Jean Ritchie also appeared frequently with Brand. Hillard Edell was the announcer (30 min., Sunday, 6:00–6:30 P.M., WNYC, New York, NY, 1945). The program was still being broadcast by WNYC in 1961.

24150 **Osgood, Beatrice.** Pianist (*Beatrice Osgood*, instr. mus. prg. (CBS, 1935).

24151 **Osgood, Connie.** Actress Osgood was in the cast of the daytime serial programs *Midstream*, *Stepmother*, *We Are Four* and *Chickie*.

24152 **Osgood, Nancy.** News analyst (WRC, Washington, DC, 1949; *Women in the News*, WXYZ, Detroit, MI, 1937).

24153 **O'Shea, Eddie.** Leader (*Eddie O'Shea Orchestra*, instr. mus. prg., WTIC, Hartford, CT, 1935).

24154 **O'Shea, James.** Newscaster (WLEU, Erie, PA, 1941).

24155 **O'Shea, Oscar.** Actor O'Shea was in the cast of *Those We Love*.

24156 **O'Shea, Patrick.** Tenor (KXLF, Colorado Springs, CO, 1926).

24157 **O'Shea, Patsy.** Actress O'Shea appeared on the daytime serial programs *Mary Marlin* aka *The Story of Mary Marlin* and *The Romance of Helen Trent*.

24158 **O'Shea, Sylvia.** Pianist (KSTP, St. Paul–Minneapolis, MN, 1929).

24159 **Oshel, Val.** Newscaster (WEBQ, Harrisburg, PA, 1946).

24160 **O'Shields, Claude.** Newscaster (WMFD, Wilmington, NC, 1942, 1945).

24161 **Oshins, Milt.** DJ (*Dance Time*, WGGG, Gainesville, FL, 1948).

24162 ***Oshkosh Boys.*** CW mus. prg., commercially sponsored by and named for an overall manufacturer (WCCO, Minneapolis–St. Paul, MN, 1937).

24163 ***Oshkosh Core Gang.*** CW mus. prg. commercially sponsored and named for its sponsor (WHO, Des Moines, IA, 1936).

24164 ***Oshkosh Slim.*** CW music show (KFAB, Lincoln, NE, 1936).

24165 **Osina, Sophia.** Pianist (KVOO, Tulsa, OK, 1928–1929).

24166 **Osmond Aces Dance Orchestra.** Local dance orchestra (WEBJ, New York, NY, 1926).

24167 **Ossenbaugh, (Mrs.) Richard.** Soprano (KOA, Denver, CO, 1925).

24168 **Ossenbrink, Luther (aka "Arkie," "Arkie the Woodchopper" and the "Arkansas Woodchopper.")** Singer and square dance caller Ossenbrink was a favorite singer of mountain and cowboy songs on the *National Barn Dance* (WLS, Chicago, IL) that he joined in 1929. Before he joined the program, Ossenbrink had broadcast on KMBC (Kansas City, MO, 1928–1929), and stations KMOX (St. Louis, MO); KWK (St. Louis, MO); WHB (Kansas City, MO); WFAA (Dallas, TX); and WMBD (Peoria, ILL). Arkie joined the *National Barn Dance* (WLS, Chicago, IL) and stayed with the show until it stopped broadcasting in 1960. He later moved to WGN (Chicago, IL), where he performed on the *WGN Barn Dance* until it went off the air in 1971.

24169 **Ossman, Wesley.** "Musical glass virtuoso" Ossman performed on the *Major Bowes Capitol Theater Family* program (NBC, 1929).

24170 **Ossola, Margaret.** COM-HE (WJAC, Johnstown, PA, 1956–1957).

24171 **Ost, Shirley.** COM-HE (WOTY, Jacksonville, FL, 1960).

24172 **Ostberg, Bob.** DJ (*1580 Club*, WFGM, Fitchburg, MA, 1949).

24173 **Ostenberg, Daisy.** Soprano (KPO, San Francisco, CA, 1923).

24174 **Ostenberg, Minna.** Soprano (WJR, Seattle, WA, 1927).

24175 **Osterberg, Bob.** DJ (*Music Parade*, WMUU, Greenville, SC, 1952).

24176 **Osterberg, Minna.** Soprano (KJR, Seattle, WA, 1927).

24177 **Ostberg, Elin K.** Tenor (WBZ, Springfield, MA, 1926).

24178 **Osterbrock, W.C.** Announcer (WHAG, Cincinnati, OH, 1924–1925).

24179 **Ostranders Plectral String Sextette.** Instrumental music group (KFOA, Seattle, WA, 1923–1925.)

24180 Ostroff, (Sgt.) Bill. Sportscaster (*Sports Quiz*, WMBM, Miami Beach, FL, 1948).

24181 Ostroff, Peter. DJ (*It's Up to Date*, KSUB, Cedar City, UT, 1948).

24182 Ostumo, Mario. Pianist (WEBJ, New York, NY, 1926).

24183 O'Sullivan, Bill. DJ (*The Morning Show*, WRIV, Riverhead, NY, 1960).

24184 O'Sullivan, Bob. DJ (KWIK, Burbank, CA, 1947).

24185 O'Sullivan, Cornelius. Irish tenor known as "The Irish Minstrel" (WGBS, New York, NY, 1927).

24186 O'Sullivan, Tim. Newscaster (WGL, Fort Wayne, IN, 1945–1947). Sportscaster (*The Story of Sports*, WGL, 1948).

24187 Oswald, Alfredo. Brazilian pianist featured on the *At the Baldwin* program (Sunday afternoon, Weekly, NBC, 1929).

24188 Oswitz, Bertha. Lyric soprano (KVOO, Tulsa, OK; KWK, St. Louis, MO, 1929).

24189 Otero, Emma. Soprano (WOOD, Grand Rapids, MI, 1941; NBC, 1941; WORK, York, PA, 1942).

24190 Otey, Florence Walden. Member of the WBAL [instrumental] Trio (WBAL, Baltimore, MD, 1929).

24191 *(The) Other Americas.* Latin America authority and news commentator Edward Tomlinson hosted the program that included news, commentary, classical and popular music of various Latin American countries performed by South American artists (15 min., Friday, 9:30–9:45 P.M., NBC-Blue, 1935).

24192 *(The) Other Woman's Diary.* Jack Van Nostrand wrote the romantic drama series sponsored by Gordon-Allen, Ltd. Each program presented a story complete in itself. Each one began with a female voice saying, "Dear Diary." After the opening, the drama would then unfold. Different actors appeared on the program such as Beatrice "Bea" Benadaret, John Hughes and Lou Tobin (15 min., Weekly, 8:15–8:30 P.M., KFRC, San Francisco, CA, 1936).

24193 Otis, C.W. Announcer (WLAX, Greencastle, IN, 1925).

24194 Otis, Don. DJ (*The Don Otis Show*, 55 min., Daily, 9:05–10:00 P.M., KLAC, Los Angeles, CA, 1947; *Let's Play Records*, KLAC, Hollywood, CA, 1948). Otis was an extremely popular Los Angeles DJ.

24195 Otis, Lehman "Lee." DJ (WCLE, Cleveland, OH; WHK, Cleveland, OH, 1938–1940).

24196 O'Toole, Emmet. Irish tenor (KYW, Chicago, IL, 1922).

24197 O'Toole, Joe. Announcer (WJAY, Cleveland, OH, 1925).

24198 O'Toole, Terry. Tenor (YN, 1937; *Terry O'Toole*, WHDH, Boston, MA, 1946).

24200 O'Toole, William "Bill" or "Uncle Bill." O'Toole was a popular announcer and entertainer on WCAO (Baltimore, MD, 1929). He conducted a morning show and several popular children's shows on the Baltimore's station. On one of them he read the comics.

24201 Otradorsky, La Verne. Soprano (KFWM, Oakland, CA, 1926).

24202 Otstot, Amos. Leader (*Amos Otstot Orchestra*, instr. mus. prg., WIRE, Indianapolis, IN, 1937).

24203 Ott, Ben. Newscaster (KTKC, Visalia, CA,1946). DJ (*940 Nightcap*, KTKC, 1947).

24204 Ott, Tommy. Organist (*Tommy Ott*, mus. prg., WCKY, Covington, KY, 1930s).

24205 Ott, Woodrow "Woody." Sportscaster (WESG, Elmira, NY, 1938; WENY, Elmira, NY, 1940–1941).

24206 Otte, Johnny. DJ (*Tops in Pops*, WJCD, Symour, IN, 1952). Sportscaster (WJCD, 1952).

24207 Otterson (Ottersen), Louise. COM-HE (WJVA, South end, IN, 1951–1960).

24208 Otto, Bob. Newscaster (WKRC, Cincinnati, OH, 1944–1945; *WCPO News*, WCPO, Cincinnati, OH, 1947).

24209 Otto, Evangeline. Cellist (WLW, Cincinnati, OH, 1923).

24210 Otto, George. Leader (George Otto's Hawaiians Orchestra, KLX, Oakland, CA, 1929).

24211 Otto, John. DJ (*Mostly Music with Otto*, WBNY, Buffalo, NY, 1954).

24212 Otto, Walter. Baritone (WFLA, Clearwater, FL, 1929).

24213 *Otto and His Novelodeons.* The little German band led by Ted Morse was a great favorite of Chicago listeners. The show was sponsored by Hamilton Carhart Overalls (15 min., Tuesday, 6:45–7:00 P.M., CST, WLS, 1936). *See Otto's Tune Twisters.*

24214 *Otto Gray and His Oklahoma Cowboys.* One of the most popular CW music groups on radio in the 1930's (15 min., Monday through Friday, 7:15–7:30 A.M. CST, NBC, 1936). *See* **Gray, Otto.**

24215 *Otto's Little German Band.* Otto (Ted Morse), a great Minnesota radio favorite, began his long radio career with the "little German band" in the late 1920s (KSTP, St. Paul, MN, 1928).

24216 *Otto's Tune Twisters.* Otto's (Ted Morse) band furnished the music and Evelyn the Little Maid sang the songs on the popular local program sponsored by Litsinger Motors (WLS, Chicago, IL, 1935). The group was also Otto and the Novelodeons. *See* ***Otto and the Novelodeons.***

24217 Ouellette, Lionel. News analyst (*Community News of Dover*, WHEB, Portsmouth, NH, 1946–1948).

24218 Ouellette, Sonia. COM-HE (WLAM, Lewiston, ME, 1957).

24219 *Our Boys in the Army.* Mrs. Florence W. Kane read letters from men in service on the inspirational and reassuring local sustaining program broadcast during World War II (5 min., Thursday, 12:15–12:20 P.M., WIP, Philadelphia, PA, 1943). *See* **Wartime Radio.**

24220 *Our Daily Food.* The Great Atlantic and Pacific Tea Company (A&P Stores) sponsored the program, on which Colonel Goodbody and Judge Gordon talked about food. Coincidentally, their conversation usually turned to a discussion of the sponsor's products and stores. Cooking authority George Rector was also on hand to dispense recipes. Music was performed by organist Chandler Goldthwaite and the Four Grocers quartet (Frank Parker, Henry Shope, John Seagle and Elliott Shaw) sang the songs (15 min., Saturday, 9:45–10:00 A.M., NBC-Red, 1932).

24221 *Our Gal Sunday.* One of radio's most popular daytime serial dramas, *Our Gal Sunday* was an interesting fantasy blend of romance, riches and social anxiety. The central plot line was stated by the announcer at the beginning of each program. After the "Red River Valley" theme had faded the announcer asked:

> Our Gal Sunday, the story of an orphan girl named Sunday, from the little mining town of Silver Creek, Colorado, who in young womanhood married England's richest, most handsome lord, Lord Henry Brinthrope. The story asks the question: Can a girl from a mining town of the West find happiness as the wife of a wealthy and titled Englishman?

The title role was originated by Dorothy Lowell and that of Lord Henry by Karl Swenson. The cast included: Inga Adams, Charita Bauer, Spencer Bentley, Kay Brinker, Delma Byron, Fran Carlon, Joe Curtin, Alistair Duncan, Katherine Emmet, Roy Fant, Ara Gerald, John Grinnell, Tom Gunn, Louis Hall, Van Heflin, Irene Hubbard, Venezuela Jones, Jay Jostyn, Elaine Kent, Alastair Kyle, Joe Kyle, Joe Latham, Charlotte Lawrence, Dorothy Lowell, Hugh Marlowe, John McGovern, John McQuade, Jay Meredith, James Monks, Louis Neistat, Clyde North, Santos Ortega, John Raby, Florence Robinson, Ruth Russell, Anne Seymour, Ann Shepherd (Scheindel Kalish), Vivian Smolen, Robert Strauss, Joan Tompkins, Vicki Vola, Eustace Wyatt and Carleton Young. The announcers were Art Millett, James Fleming, John A. Wolfe, Bert Parks, Charles Stark and John Reed King. Frank and Anne Hummert were the producers. The directors were Frank and Anne Hummert, Stephen Gross, and Arthur Hanna. Sound effects were produced by John McCloskey. Jean Carroll and Helen Walpole were the writers. The program, evolved from an earlier one called *Rich Man's Darling*, was first broadcast March 29, 1937 (Weekdays, 12:45–1:00 P.M., CBS). *See* ***Rich Man's Darling.***

24222 *Our Gospel Singer.* William Blevins was the featured singer and host of the program broadcast in 1936. He was the first Negro to be featured on an Alabama radio station (Washington *Tribune*, March 3, 1936). Many community leaders who were sponsoring various civic projects. appeared on the program. Blevins also presented many prominent Negro choirs the *Tribune* reported. (Tuesday, Thursday and Sunday, WSGH, Birmingham, AL, 1936).

24223 *Our Government.* David Lawrence provided authoritative commentary on American government and politics on this program (15 min., Sunday, 9:00–9:15 P.M., NBC-Red, 1930).

24224 ***Our Home* (aka *A Workshop of Living Together*).** W.K. Cobb, director of the department of home service for the Parent-Teacher Association, supervised the series of programs devoted to exploring the elements in the home during wartime. The programs were related to child development (15 min., Friday, 1:15–1:30 P.M., PCT, Don Lee Broadcasting System, 1942).

24225 ***Our Home on the Range.*** The Vicks Company sponsored the quality music program starring John Charles Thomas (30 min., Wednesday, 9:00–9:30 P.M., NBC).

24226 ***Our Little Playhouse.*** Yolanda Langworthy, who also wrote many of the scripts, directed the melodramatic matinee program (30 min., Wednesday, 3:00–3:30 P.M., CBS, 1929).

24227 ***Our Miss Brooks.*** Talented motion picture star Eve Arden played the role of Connie Brooks, an English teacher at Madison High School, who yearned for the romantic attention of Mr. Boynton, the shy biology teacher at the school, played by Jeff Chandler. The classic radio situation comedy also featured Dick Crenna, Gale Gordon, Gloria McMillan, Jane Morgan and Leonard Smith in the cast. Al Lewis was the program's director-writer and Larry Bernstein the producer. Wilbur Hatch was the music director. Sound effects were produced by Bill Gould (30 min., weekly, CBS, 1948–1957).

24228 ***Our Neighbors.*** Jerry Belcher, one of the original *Vox Pop* hosts, asked questions of audience members that brought out the problems, humor and sadness found in everyday family life (30 min., 2:30–3:00 P.M. CST, NBC-Red, 1936).

24229 ***Our Own Hardware Program.*** "Our Own Bob" DeHaven conducted the variety show that was broadcast Saturday mornings in the 1940s from different Our Home Hardware stores located throughout the Northwest. Tenors Burt Hanson and Ernie Garvin joined singer Jeanne Arland to provide entertainment.

24230 ***Our Prairie Poet.*** Original poetry was read on the program by an unidentified performer (WDZ, Tuscola, IL, 1936).

24231 **Our Wandering Musician.** A novelty pianist from Punxsutawney, Pennsylvania, not otherwise identified, "jazzed the classics and specialized in various musical parodies" on the irregular feature (WTAM, Cleveland, OH, 1924).

24232 **Oursler, Fulton.** News commentator, author and former editor of *Liberty* magazine (WHN, New York, NY, 1941–1942; WOR, New York, NY, 1945).

24233 ***Out of the Dark Room.*** Maurice Hart conducted the informative photography program (30 min., Monday, 9:00–9:30 P.M., WMCA, New York, NY, 1940).

24234 ***Out of the Deep.*** Ted Maxwell wrote and starred in the original run of the adventure series that followed the story of Captain Gunnar Carlisle, the captain of his ship, *The Blue Falcon*, and a daring deep sea diver. Also in the cast were Charlie Lung and Don Stanley. Organist Joe Enos supplied the music (30 min., Weekly, NBC, 1945–1946). In a later format the main role was played by Wally Maher as the "noted deep sea diver and soldier of fortune" (NBC, 1951).

24235 ***Out of the Ivory Tower.*** Poet-author Eve Mirriam conducted interviews with a poet during the first half of the program and read her own poetry during the second (15 min., WQXR, New York, NY, 1942).

24236 ***Out of the Night.*** Talented organist Phil Raboin broadcast from the state capitol's rotunda and KGY announcer Dyer Downing read poetry. The program was broadcast nightly (30 min., 10:30–11:00 P.M., KGY, Olympia, WA, 1945–1952).

24237 ***Outdoor Girl Beauty Program.*** Blanche Sweet, former silent motion picture star, was the Outdoor Beauty girl on the women's program. She broadcast beauty tips for women (NBC, 1935).

24238 ***Outdoor Life Time.*** The transcribed hunting and fishing program was carried by eight stations. The program was conducted by Raymond J. Brown, the editor of *Outdoor Life* magazine. Also in the cast were C. Blackburn Miller, Edward Rogers and Jim Boles (15 min., Transcribed on Various Stations, 1946).

24239 **Outland, Henry.** Newscaster (KLZ, Denver, CO, 1945).

24240 **Outlaw, Dick.** DJ (WILM, Wilmington, DE, 1949).

24241 ***Over the Back Fence.*** An unidentified performer announced that he would talk of cabbages and kings on the interesting local program, and he did exactly that (15 min., Monday-through-Friday, 9:00–9:15 P.M., WREN, Lawrence, KS, 1947).

24242 **Overbay, Paul.** Newscaster (WKPT, Kingsport, TN, 1942).

24243 ***Overcraft Home Talks.*** A women's homemaking program (15 min., Wednesday, 11:30–11:45 A.M., NBC-Red, 1927).

24244 **Overstreet, Patty.** COM-HE (WAML, Laurel, MA, 1956).

24245 **Overton, Dave.** Sportscaster (WSM, Nashville, TN, 1949).

24246 **Oviatt, Herb.** DJ (WFHR, Wisconsin Rapids, WI, 1956).

24247 **Ovington, Ray.** DJ (WROD, Daytona Beach, FL, 1956). Sportscaster (*Rod and Gun Club*, MBS, 1955; WROD, Daytona Beach, FL, 1956).

24248 **Owen, Alan "Al."** DJ (*Marine Ballroom*, WFPG, Atlantic City, NJ, 1948; *The Music Room*, WMID, Atlantic City, NJ, 1949–1956).

24249 **Owen, Cliff.** Newscaster (KNAK, Salt Lake City, UT, 1945). Sportscaster (KNAK, 1945; KLWT, Ogden, UT, 1946; *Five Star Final*, KOPP, Ogden, UT, 1947).

24250 **Owen [Owens], Don.** DJ (*Melody Roundup*, KADA, Ada, OK, 1948; *10:15 Club*, KADA, 1950; *Postcard Parade*, KWSH, Wewoka, OK, 1952). Sportscaster (KSMI, Seminole, OK, 1950; *Sports Review*, KWSH, 1952).

24251 **Owen, Elwyn.** Organist (WBCM, Bay City, MI, 1942).

24252 **Owen, Em.** Newscaster and pianist (WTAQ, Green Bay, WI and WHBY, Green Bay, WI, 1937–1938).

24253 **Owen, Ethel Waite.** Busy actress Owen appeared in such daytime serial programs as *Joyce Jordan, Girl Interne*; *Backstage Wife* aka *Mary Noble, Backstage Wife*; *Life Begins* aka *Martha Webster*; *Life Can Be Beautiful*; *Lorenzo Jones*; *Man I Married*; *Margot of Castlewood*; *Right to Happiness*; *Against the Storm*; *Second Mrs. Burton*; *Stepmother*; *Tale of Today*; *Today's Children*; *Valiant Lady*; *When a Girl Marries*; and *Betty and Bob*.

24254 **Owen, Forrest, Jr.** Sportscaster (WELL, Battle Creek, MI, 1937; WKAR, East Lansing, MI, 1940). Newscaster (WKAR, 1939).

24255 **Owen, Frances.** Announcer (WJAS, Pittsburgh, PA, 1925).

24256 **Owen [Owens], Frances.** COM-HE (WBLT, Bedford, VA, 1957).

24257 **Owen, Gordon.** Sportscaster (KUTA, Salt Lake City, UT, 1938).

24258 **Owen, Hughetta.** Contralto (WEAF, New York, NY, 1926; WBZ, Boston, MA, 1926).

24259 **Owen, Ken.** Newscaster (KPMC, Bakersfield, CA, 1937).

24260 **Owen, Leiter Dexter.** News analyst (*The Monitor Views the News*, WHIP, Hammond, IN, 1940).

24261 **Owens, Bonnie.** CW singer Owens joined the Buck Owens' band — Mac and the Skillet Lickers — as a teenager and appeared with them on KTYL (Mesa, Arizona, 1947). She married CW singer Merle Haggard after her first marriage to Buck Owens ended in divorce.

24262 **Owens, Dick.** Sportscaster (WISL, Shamokin, PA, 1952).

24263 **Owens, Dottie.** COM-HE (WISL, Shamokin, PA, 1955).

24264 **Owens, Doye "Tex."** Singer-songwriter Owens, a real cowboy, was known as the "Original Texas Ranger." He broadcast on KMBC (Kansas City, MO, 1934) and later on *Red Horse Ranch* on that station and in a syndicated version (KMBC, 1935; syndicated, 1935).

24265 **Owens, Gary.** DJ (WNOE, New Orleans, LA, 1957).

24266 **Owens, Harry.** Leader (Harry Owens and his Orchestra playing from the Rainbow Isle, Mayfair Hotel, KFWB, Hollywood, CA, 1927; *Harry Owens Orchestra*, instr. mus. prg., NBC, 1934; CBS, 1942).

24267 **Owens, Ila Lorbach.** Pianist (WBAV, Columbus, OH, 1924).

24268 **Owens, Irene M.** Soprano (WHN, New York, NY, 1924).

24269 **Owens, Jack.** Newscaster (WBHB, Fitzgerald, GA, 1946; *Alarm Clock Club*, WNEX, Macon, GA, 1952).

24270 **Owens, Jesse.** DJ (WAAF, Chicago, IL, 1957–1960).

24271 **Owens, Josephine.** COM-HE (WEKR, Fayetteville, TN, 1960).

24272 **Owens, Larry.** DJ (*Just Records*, WTOD, Toledo, OH, 1949).

24273 **Owens, Morey C.** Sportscaster (WROK, Rockford, IL, 1937–1946; *Sports Review*, WROK, 1947–1956).

24274 **Owens, Oma.** COM-HE (KWTX, Waco, TX, 1955).

24275 **Owens, Pat.** COM-HE (WCHL, Chapel Hill, NC, 1956).

24276 **Owens, Ray.** News commentator (*Today in Syracuse*, WFBL, Syracuse, NY, 1946–1947).

24277 **Owens, Sheila.** DJ (WEIC, Charleston, IL, 1957).

24278 **Owens, Tex.** CW vcl. mus. prg. (KMBC, Kansas City, MO, 1939).

24279 **Owens, Tom.** Square dance caller on the first *National Barn Dance* program (WLS, Chicago, IL, April 19, 1924). Leader (*Tom Owens and His Cowboys*, WMT, Cedar Rapids, IA, 1930s). *See* ***The National Barn Dance***.

24280 **Owens, Tom.** DJ (*1330 Club*, KFH, Wichita, KS, 1949).

24281 **Owensby, Bill.** DJ (*Matinee Melodies*, WEWO, Laurinburg, NC, 1947).

24282 **Owensville High School Band.** Scholastic band (WGBF, Evansville, IL, 1926).

24283 **Owley, Harry.** Leader (Harry Owley's Cinderella Orchestra, WHN, New York, NY, 1924).

24284 **Owrill, Bob.** DJ (*Polka Party*, WPOR, Portland, ME, 1950–1951; *Matinee Frolic*, WPOR, 1952).

24285 **Oxenrider, Orvan.** DJ (WALD, Walterboro, SC, 1960).

24286 **Oxford, Earl.** Baritone (WEAF, New York, NY, 1929).

24287 **Oxford, George.** Newscaster (WJBW, New Orleans, LA, 1939).

24288 **Oxford, George "Jumping George."** DJ (*Sepia Serenade*, KWBR, Oakland, CA, 1948; *Tastefully Yours*, KWBR, 1950; *Recorded Jazz Concert*, KSAN, San Francisco, CA, 1954–1956). "Jumping George" Oxford became an outstanding rock-and-roll DJ on KSAN.

24289 **Oxford Girls.** Harmony singing team (WQJ, Chicago, IL, 1926).

24290 **Oxiner, Kenneth.** DJ (*Melody Times*, WHOC, Philadelphia, MS, 1952).

24291 **Oxley, Harold.** Leader (Harold Oxley's Warwick Hotel Orchestra, KPRC, Houston, TX, 1926).

24292 **Oxman, Roy.** Baritone (KFQW, Seattle, WA, 1928–1929).

24293 ***(The) Oxol Trio.*** The harmonizing male vocal trio of Dave Grant, Gordon Graham and Bunny Coughlin entertained on the music show (CBS, 1934).

24294 ***Ozark Carnival.*** CW mus. prg. (KMOX, St. Louis, MO, 1936).

24295 **Ozark Inn Orchestra.** Club dance band (WFAA, Dallas, TX, 1926).

24296 ***Ozark Jubilee.*** Red Foley, Grady Martin's Crossroads Gang and other talented country-western performers appeared on the lively music show that originated in Springfield, Missouri (25 min., Saturday, 10:05–10:30 P.M., ABC, 1954). After the show's appearance on the ABC radio network in 1954, it made a successful transition to television.

24297 ***Ozark Mountaineers.*** CW mus. prg. (KUOA, Fayetteville, AR, 1933–1934; CBS, 1937–1938; WRTD, Richmond, VA, 1939).

24298 ***(The) Ozark Smile Girls.*** CW vocal group broadcast by WLBN (Little Rock, AR, 1927). The girls proudly proclaimed they came from Fort Smith, Arkansas.

24299 ***Ozark Varieties.*** CW mus. prg., KMOX (St. Louis, MO), 1939.

24300 **Ozment, Howard.** DJ (*Record Session*, WTMA, Charleston, SC, 1948).

24301 ***P.M. Platter Party.*** Harvey Hudson was the late night DJ on the local show (60 min., Monday through Friday, WABY, Albany, NY, 1949).

24302 **P.O.S. of A. Band.** Fraternal organization band (WIP, Philadelphia, PA, 1926).

24303 **P.S.C. Orchestra.** Popular Iowa band (WOC, Davenport, IA, 1924).

24304 **Pa, J. Landi.** Ukulele soloist (KYW, Chicago, IL, 1922).

24305 ***Pa and Ma Smithers*** **(aka *Ma and Pa Smithers*).** *Pa and Ma Smithers* first appeared on KFBI, Milford, Kansas, in 1932 before moving to WLS, Chicago, Illinois. The basic plot changed little over the years. The couple lived alone on the outskirts of Titusville, Pennsylvania, after their children had gone to the city. Ma kept Pa from getting too cranky and stood up for him at all times. Dan Hosmer and Christine Crans in the title roles provided warm good humor to the picture of rural life. Virginia Temple also appeared on the show. The choir members who attended practice at the Smithers' Fairview Farms each Wednesday evening — all members of the WLS (Chicago, IL) studio family — were the Sod Busters, Sophia Germanich, the Home Towners and the Hilltoppers (15 min., Monday through Friday, 1:00–1:15 P.M., WLS, Chicago, IL, 1935).

24306 ***Pa Perkins and His Boys.*** CW music show (KFBI, Milford, KS, 1932–1936).

24307 **Paar [Parr] , H.F.** Announcer (WKAA, Cedar Rapids, 19251–1926; WCR, Cedar Rapids, 1927).

24308 **Paar, Jack.** Sportscaster — not the television performer (ABC, 1956).

24309 **Paarman [Parman], Mildred.** Violinist (WOC, Davenport, IA, 1925).

24310 **Pabst, Art.** Popular West Coast singer (KNX, Los Angeles, CA, 1925).

24311 **Pace, Betty.** COM-HE (WIUY, Jacksonville, FL, 1951).

24312 **Pace, Bob.** DJ (*Musical Roundup*, KCTX, Childress, TX, 1949).

24313 **Pace, Dorothy Jean.** Pace was a cast member of *Krank's Varieties* and the *KSTP Players* (KSTP, St. Paul–Minneapolis, MN, 1929).

24314 **Pace, Iona.** COM-HE (WHAB, Baxley, GA, 1955).

24315 **Pace, Zena.** COM-HE (WATR, Waterbury, CT, 1956).

24316 **Pacelli, Bob.** Leader (*Bob Pacelli Orchestra*, instr. mus. prg., WGN, Chicago, IL, 1934; WBBM, Chicago, IL, 1935).

24317 **Pacelli, Frank "Frankie."** " Actress Pacelli was in the cast of *Betty and Bob*, *Mary Marlin*, *Tale of Today* and *Today's Children*.

24318 **Pacheco, Enock.** Violinist (KFBK, Sacramento, CA, 1926).

24319 **Pacenisch, Lillian.** Pasenisch discussed art and jewelry on the *Tea Time* program.

24320 **Pachner, Ruth.** Soprano (WEBJ, New York, NY, 1926).

24321 **Pacific Coast Club Orchestra.** Club dance band (KRON, Long Beach, CA, 1926).

24322 ***Pacific Islanders Orchestra.*** Hawaiian instr. mus. prg. (WBAL, Baltimore, MD, 1935; WMMN, Fairmont, WV, 1937).

24323 **Pacific Male Quartet.** Vocal quartet that included Gibson Paul, 1st tenor; Kenneth Morse, 2nd tenor; Ralph Wastell, baritone; and Burt Shrader, bass (KTAB, Oakland, CA, 1926).

24324 **Pacific Salon Orchestra.** Liborius Hauptmann directed the popular band (WABC, New York, NY, 1929).

24325 ***Pacific Serenaders.*** The *Pacific Serenaders* music program featured an orchestra with tenor Hugh Williams (30 min., Saturday, 8:00–8:30 P.M., NBC-Pacific Network, 1929). The following year vocal solos by Edward Randall were added to the program's orchestral selections.

24326 **Pacino, Helen.** Singer (KFWB, Hollywood, CA, 1928).

24327 **Pack, Gene.** Announcer (KDYL, Salt Lake City, UT, 1926).

24328 **Pack, Patti.** COM-HE (KFRE, Fresno, CA, 1957).

24329 **Packard, Charles "Charlie."** Sportscaster (*Sports Album*, KWSI, Council Bluffs, IA, 1948–1949).

24330 **Packard, Lou.** DJ (*Varsity Hour*, WJOR, Bangor, ME, 1947).

24331 **Packard, Margaret O.** COM-HE (KTRC, Santa Fe, NM, 1957).

24332 ***Packard Ballad Hour.*** A popular Pacific Coast musical show, the *Packard Ballad Hour* featured singers Billy Hall, Polly Grant Hall, Barney Weber, the Ashley Sisters and a studio band (120 min., 10:00–12:00 midnight, Weekly, KFI, Los Angeles, CA, 1925).

24333 **Packard Concert Orchestra.** Commercial band directed by Pryor Moore. Violinist Purcell Mayer and soprano Helen Guest were featured (KFI, Los Angeles, CA, 1928–1929).

24334 **Packard Dance Band.** The commercially sponsored (Packard Motor Cars) band appeared on *The Midnight Frolic* (KFI, Los Angeles, CA, 1927).

24335 ***(The) Packard Motor Company Program*** **(aka *The Packard Show* or *The Packard Hour*).** Baritone Lawrence Tibbett was the featured artist when the program originally was broadcast in 1934 in a 30-minute format. In 1936, the format was extended to an hour, and movie star Fred Astaire became the featured performer along with comedian Charlie Butterworth, singer Trudy Woods and Johnny Green's Orchestra (60 min., NBC, 1936). The next year Walter O'Keefe replaced Astaire as host. Butterworth remained on the show, but comedian Cliff Arquette was added along with soprano Florence George and Raymond Paige's Orchestra. Don Wilson was the announcer (NBC, 1937–1938). *See* ***(The) Fred Astaire Show.***

24336 Packard Six Dance Orchestra. Bill Hennessy and Chet Mittendorf directed the Packard Motor Car Company band (KFI, Los Angeles, CA, 1926).

24337 Packer, (Mrs.) Paul C. Pianist (WSUI, Iowa City, IA, 1927).

24338 *Padded Fists.* The dramatic serial told the story of a well-bred college boy, who found himself being trained as a boxer by his female manager and a "pug" trainer. The program's hero was played by Dick Wells (15 min., Monday through Saturday, 10:30–10:45 P.M., KYW, Philadelphia, PA, 1932).

24339 Paddock, Charles W. Champion sprinter Paddock discussed sports news (KPSN, Pasadena, CA, 1926).

24340 Padel, Alice Gray. Pianist (KTAB, Oakland, CA, 1925).

24341 Padgett, Bob. DJ (*Music with a Meaning*, WVSA, McGehee, AR, 1954).

24342 Padilla, Elva. Sportscaster (*Rio Grande Serenade*, KPAB, Laredo, TX, 1947).

24343 Padley, Eleanor. Pianist (WGY, Schenectady, NY, 1923).

24344 Padnick, Dorothea. Pianist (WAAT, Jersey City, NJ, 1927).

24345 Padric, Gerry. DJ (WOOW, Greenville, NC, 1960).

24346 *Paducah Plantation.* Irvin S. Cobb appeared on the variety program playing the role of an old Southern Colonel who owned the Paducah Plantation. The serial drama presented guests and workers on the plantation. Regular music performers on the show included the Hall-Johnson Choir, baritone Clarence Muse, Dorothy Page and an orchestra directed by Harry Jackson. Guests on the program in 1936 included Marion Talley, Ruth Chatterton, Gertrude Niesen and Jane Froman. Actors Norman Fields and John Mather were cast regulars. Gayne Whitman was the announcer (30 min., Saturday, 9:30–10:00 P.M., NBC, 1936).

24347 Padula, Marguerite. Contralto (*Marguerite Padula*, vcl. mus. prg., 15 min., Wednesday, 2:45–3:00 P.M., NBC-Blue, 1936). She was accompanied on the show by the Jerry Sears orchestra.

24348 Pafford, Buck. DJ (WGOV, Valdosta, GA, 1956).

24349 Pagano, Ernie. Broadcast "studio gossip from Hollywood" (KFRC, San Francisco, CA, 1925).

24350 Paganucci, Anthony. Pianist-composer (NBC, 1929).

24351 Page, Anita. Singer on the *Musical Cocktail* program.

24352 Page, Arthur. Page was known as a garrulous, enthusiastic and sentimental announcer, who conducted the long running *Dinner Time* program (WLS, Chicago, IL, 1924).

24353 Page, Beverly. Singer (WMCA, New York, NY, 1939).

24354 Page, Billy. Ten-year-old actor Page appeared in the weekly humorous portrayal of Midwestern life presented on the *Memory Lane* program (NBC, San Francisco, CA, 1928–1929).

24355 Page, Bob. Announcer (WOCL, Jamestown, NY, 1925).

24356 Page, (Mrs.) Clarence. Contralto (KGO, Oakland, CA, 1925).

24357 Page, Dave. Newscaster (KIRO, Seattle, WA, 1948). DJ (*Make Way for Music*, KIRO, 1948; *KIRO Paging*, KIRO, 1952; *Dance Time*, KIRO, 1954–1955; KREM, Spokane, WA, 1956).

24358 Page, Dorothy. Singer (*Dorothy Page*, vcl. mus. prg., NBC, 1936).

24359 Page, Eliott. DJ (*Turntable Terrace*, WCAX, Burlington, VT, 1948; *Saturday Date*, WSKI. Montpelier, VT, 1949; *The Band Box*, WWSR, St. Albans, VT, 1950). Sportscaster (WWSR, 1948; *Page on Sports*, WSKI, 1951–1954).

24360 Page, Evelyn. COM-HE (WTVL, Waterville, ME, 1956–1957).

24361 Page, Fran. COM-HE (KRGV, Weslaco, TX, 1960).

24362 Page, Frank. DJ (*Yours for the Asking*, KWEM, West Memphis, AR, 1947; KWHN, Fort Smith, AR, 1955–1956).

24363 Page, Gale. Motion picture and radio actress Page appeared on the daytime serial programs *Holly Sloan* (title role), *Masquerade* and *Today's Children.*

24364 Page, Helene. Actress Page appeared in the situation comedy program *The Hoofinghams* (NBC, 1935).

24365 Page, John. Sportscaster (*Paging Sports*, WCSS, Amsterdam, NY, 1948–1949; *Pagin' Sports*, WCSS, 1952–1954).

24366 Page, Julia Phillips. Contralto (KGO, Oakland, CA, 1925).

24367 Page, Larry. DJ (WTOC, Savannah, GA, 1955).

24368 Page, Linda. COM-HE (WIKK, Erie, PA, 1954).

24369 Page, Maurice O. Newscaster (WIBU, Poynette, WI, 1941, 1948).

24370 Page, Mrs. COM-HE (WJR, Detroit, MI, 1954–1957).

24371 Page, Norman "Norm." Sportscaster (WHLB, Virginia, MN, 1941). DJ (*Columbia Masterworks*, *Mr. Music* and *Requestfully Yours*, WMIN, St. Paul, MN, 1947; *Music For You*, WMAS, Springfield, MA, 1954).

24372 Page, Pat. COM-HE (WTTM, Trenton, NJ, 1949; WPEN, Philadelphia, PA, 1957).

24373 Page, Phil. DJ (KEYS, Corpus Christi, TX, 1956; KTUL, Tulsa, OK, 1960).

24374 Page, Sam. DJ (*Requestfully Yours*, *Juke Box Revue* and *Anything Goes*, WNBF, Binghampton, NY, 1948; *Page's Party*, WNBF, 1949).

24375 Page, Virginia. Actress Page appeared on the *Today's Children* daytime serial program.

24376 *Pages of Romance.* NBC presented the early daytime serial in 1932 with an exceptionally talented cast of radio actors that included: Peggy Allenby, Alan Reed (Teddy Bergman), Eunice Howard, Allyn Joslyn, Alma Kruger, John McGovern, Hugh Rennie and Ned Wever.

24377 Paget, Barrie. Newscaster (KMPC, Beverly Hills, CA, 1939).

24378 Paget, Joe. Sportscaster (WJDX, Jackson, MS, 1939–1940; KATE, Albert Lea, MN,1941–1944).

24379 Pagliara, Nicholas. Tenor (WHAM, Rochester, NY, 1928). Musical director (WHEC, Rochester, NY, 1929).

24380 Pagliari, Gino. Newscaster (WHOM, Jersey City, NJ, 1941).

24381 Pagnotti, Elle. COM-HE (WPTS, Pittston, PA, 1957).

24382 Pagoda Cafe Orchestra. Instrumental musical group (WIP, Philadelphia, PA, 1926).

24383 Paige, Ann. COM-HE (WILD, Birmingham, AL, 1955).

24384 Paige, Carl. Sportscaster and sports play-by-play (KLAS, Las Vegas, NV, 1950; *Nevada Sports Slants*, KLAS, 1951; *Hames Sports Slants*, KLAS, 1952; KYMA, Yuma, AZ, 1954).

24385 Paige, Dotty. COM-HE (WREN, Topeka, KS, 1954).

24386 Paige, Ellsworth. Bass (WGY, Schenectady, NY, 1929).

24387 Paige, Eric. Newscaster (WMRN, Marion, OH, 1945). DJ (*Mixing It Up*, WWNR, Beckley, WV, 1947; *Juke Box*, WLOW, Norfolk, VA, 1948; *850 Club*, WCAV, Norfolk, VA, 1949). Sportscaster (*Sports Parade*, WWNR, 1947; WLOW, 1949; WCAV, 1951; *Page on Sports*, WCAV, 1952).

24388 Paige, Frances. COM-HE (KCRA, Sacramento, CA, 1951).

24389 Paige, Norman. Newscaster (NBC-Blue, 1944).

24390 Paige, Raymond. A graduate of the American Conservatory of Music, Chicago, IL, Paige directed musical activities at the Los Angeles' Paramount Theatre before assuming the position of musical conductor at KHJ (Los Angeles, CA and KFRC, San Francisco, CA, 1929–1930).

24391 Paine, Fred S. Drummer and xylophonist Paine performed in the Detroit *News* Orchestra (WWJ, Detroit, MI, 1925).

24392 Paine, Gertrude. Pianist and reader known as the "Musical Humorist" (KDKA, Pittsburgh, PA, 1922; KQV, Pittsburgh, PA, 1922).

24393 *Painted Dreams.* The *Painted Dreams* serial drama originally was broadcast on WGN (Chicago, IL) as *Sue and Irene*, with the title roles played by Ireene Wicker and Irna Phillips, the creator and author of the program. *Sue* and *Irene* was considered by WGN to have been the first "soap opera" broadcast on that station in 1930 (Buxton and Owen, 1972, p.

183). The serial dramatized the story of Mother Moynihan's boarding house and its inhabitants. When the program evolved into *Painted Dreams*, Phillips and Wicker continued in the cast with Phillips still the author. When Ms. Phillips left WGN, she originated and wrote *Today's Children* for NBC. *Painted Dreams* remained on WGN where it was written at times by Bess Flynn and Kay Chase. The *Painted Dreams'* cast, in addition to Phillips and Flynn included: Alice Hill, Dorothy Day McDonald and her daughter Jean McDonald, Kay Chase, Olan Soule, Lucy Gilman and Dick Wells (15 min., 11:45–12:00 P.M., 1934).

24394 Painter, Betty. COM-HE (KVGB, Great Bend, KS, 1954).

24395 Painter, Bydell. Pianist (KVOS, Bellingham, WA, 1928).

24396 Painter, Frank. DJ (*The Coonhunter*, WBLJ, Dalton, GA, 1954–1955). Sportscaster (WBLJ, Dalton, GA, 1960).

24397 Paisant, Milton. Paisant was billed as the "Singing guitarist" (NBC, 1929).

24398 *Pajama Party.* *Pajama Party* was a music program that featured the Glen Kennedy Dance Orchestra (KFWI, San Francisco, CA, 1926).

24399 Pal Lido Orchestra. Musical group directed by Allister Wylie (KMOX, St. Louis, MO, 1928).

24400 *Palace Credit Revue.* J. Herbert Angell was the host of the local variety program sponsored by the Palace Credit Store of Pittsburg, PA. Harry Baker's orchestra, vocalist Rudy "Hector" Humbertson and announcer Herbert Morrison were program regulars (30 min., Wednesday, 12:00–12:30 P.M. KQV, Pittsburgh, PA, 1936).

24401 Palace Hotel Rose Room Dance Orchestra. Hotel band directed by Gene James (KPO, San Francisco, CA, 1925–1926).

24402 Palace Theatre String Orchestra. The theatre orchestra led by Don Albert included L.E. Faget, Carl Austermiller, Frank Dawkins, Dot Echols McCuthan, and George C. Drum (WFAA, Dallas, TX, 1923; WBAP, San Antonio, TX, 1925).

24403 Palacios, Senor. Senor Palacios was the director of the Spanish Orchestra that specialized in Hispanic music (KEX, Portland, OR, 1929).

24404 Paladino, G. Mandolin soloist (WOR, Newark, NJ, 1922).

24405 Paland, Henrietta. Reader (KHI, Los Angeles, CA, 1925).

24406 Palange, Angelo. Sportscaster (WCDA, New York, NY, 1928; *Adams Hats Sports Program*, WINS, New York, NY, 1939; WVFW, Brooklyn, NY, 1940).

24407 Pales, Norman. Leader (Norman Pales and his *S.S. Leviathan* Orchestra, WIP, Philadelphia, PA, 1926).

24408 Palen, Dan. DJ (*Wax Works*, WLAU, Laurel, MA, 1947).

24409 Paley, Edith. Pianist (WBZ, Springfield, MA, 1924).

24410 Paley, Ruth. Contralto (WBZ, Springfield, MA, 1924).

24411 Paley, William. Creator and longtime head of the Columbia Broadcasting System, Paley was one of the pioneers of radio's Golden Age. In 1927, he placed an advertisement for his father's cigar company on Philadelphia's station WCAU. When cigar sales doubled, Paley recognized the commercial importance of the medium. Backed financially by his father, Paley purchased a floundering chain of 16 stations that eventually became CBS.

Paley was a skillful executive and an excellent judge of entertainment and popular taste. One of his major coups was the luring of Jack Benny, Edgar Bergen, Red Skelton and many other comedians from NBC to become CBS regulars. He also fostered the development of the CBS news department, one of the best ever created. Aware of the impact of broadcasting upon American culture, Paley did his utmost to combine cultural values with popular and commercial appeal and often succeeded.

24412 Palisades Amusement Park Dance Orchestra. Park dance band led by Adam Grefig (WHN, New York, NY, 1925; WGBS, New York, NY, 1928).

24413 Palisadians Orchestra. Club band (WMCA, New York, NY, 1925).

24414 Pallan, Art. DJ (*Record Hits*, WWSW, Pittsburgh, PA, 1947–1949; *Tune Inn*, WWSW, 1954; KDKA, Pittsburgh, PA, 1957).

24415 Palmer, Alyce. COM-HE (WTAW, Bryan, TX, 1957).

24416 Palmer, Barbara. COM-HE (KRMW, The Dalles, OR, 1955).

24417 Palmer, Betty. COM-HE (WICY, Malone, NY, 1960).

24418 Palmer, Bruce. News analyst (*Oklahoma's Front Page*, WKY, Oklahoma City, OK, 1946–1947).

24419 Palmer, Bryan. Newscaster (KFAC, Los Angeles, CA, 1940).

24420 Palmer, Charles G. DJ (*Open House*, KFXM, San Bernardino, CA, 1947; *Mention Music*, KFXM, 1948).

24421 Palmer, Clark. DJ (*Your Song*, WRFO, Worthington, OH, 1952).

24422 Palmer, Duke. DJ (KBOR, Brownsville, TX, 1954–1956).

24423 Palmer, Effie Lawrence. Actress Palmer appeared in several daytime serial programs such as *Dot and Will*, *Ellen Randolph*, *Five Star Jones*, *Mary Foster the Editor's Daughter*, *The O'Neills*, *Orphans of Divorce*, *Road of Life*, *Seth Parker* and *This Day Is Ours*.

24424 Palmer, Eileen. Actress Palmer was in the cast of the daytime serial programs *Backstage Wife* aka *Mary Noble, Backstage Wife*, *Lonely Women*, *Road of Life* and *Scattergood Baines*.

24425 Palmer, Ethel. Soprano (WJAZ, Chicago, IL, 1923).

24426 Palmer, (Mrs.) Frank. Soprano (KGO, Oakland, CA, 1925).

24427 Palmer, George. Newscaster (WIBC, Indianapolis, IN, 1938–1939).

24428 Palmer, (Mrs.) George. Soprano (WLAG, Minneapolis–St. Paul, MN, 1924).

24429 Palmer, Gladys. Singer (KFOB, Burlingame, CA, 1925).

24430 Palmer, Guelda and Eddie Stott. Singing team (KFRC, San Francisco, CA, 1926).

24431 Palmer, Harold. Announcer (WOW, Omaha, NE, 1928–1929).

24432 Palmer, (Mrs.) Harry. Singer (WOC, Davenport, IA, 1923).

24433 Palmer, Henry. Pianist (WJZ, New York, NY, 1922).

24434 Palmer, Jack and Harry Woods. Piano team (WGCP, New York, NY, 1925).

24435 Palmer, Jim. DJ (*Record Shop*, KSIM, Sikeston, MO, 1952).

24436 Palmer, Katherine. Soprano (NBC, 1928; *Katherine Palmer*, vcl. mus. prg., NBC, 1934).

24437 Palmer, Lester. Announcer known as "LP" (WOW, Omaha, NE, 1923–1930). Palmer was a graduate of Creighton Law School in 1927. Two years later he was elected a municipal judge. When Palmer wrote a personal biography for the station in 1930, he noted that he was a total abstainer and a confirmed bachelor—"no hope of matrimony whatsoever." One of the first announcers on the station, Palmer continued broadcasting weekly on WOW after he became a municipal judge. He often broadcast his station's slogan, "The city surrounded by the United States."

24438 Palmer, Margaret. COM-HE (WCLB, Camilla, GA, 1956).

24439 Palmer, (Dr.) Melchoir. News analyst (WIND, Gary, IN, 1945).

24440 Palmer, Olive. See **Rea, Virginia.**

24441 Palmer, Paige. COM-HE (WEWS, Cleveland, OH, 1954).

24442 Palmer, Pat. COM-HE (KCNA, Tucson, AZ, 1957).

24443 Palmer, Patricia. COM-HE (WIRL, Peoria, IL, 1956).

24444 Palmer, Robert. Sportscaster (*Along the Sports Trail*, KTSW, Emporia, KS, 1952–1954).

24445 Palmer, Ruggles. DJ (WFAA, Dallas, TX, 1948).

24446 Palmer, Sannee. COM-HE (KSVC, Richfield, UT, 1954).

24447 Palmer, Shirley. COM-HE (WORC, Worcester, MA, 1956).

24448 Palmer, Skeeter. Leader (*Skeeter Palmer Orchestra*, instr. mus. prg., WHAM, Rochester, NY, 1938, 1942).

24449 Palmer, Travis. COM-HE (WSSO, Starkville, MI, 1957).

24450 Palmer, W.G. "Bill." Announcer (WCOA, Pensacola, FL, 1928).

24451 *Palmer House Ensemble.* Instr. mus. prg. (MBS, 1935; WGN, Chicago, IL, 1936).

24452 *Palmer House Promenade.* Veteran radio entertainer Ray Perkins hosted the show, sponsored by the Palmer House Hotel, that was intended to boost tourism in 1934 at the Chicago's World Fair—the Century of Progress. Gale Page sang with Harold Stokes' Orchestra. Weekly guests, such as Gladys Swarthout also performed (30 min., Tuesday, 10:00–10:30 P.M., NBC-Blue, 1934).

24453 Palmer House Symphonic Players. Instrumental music group directed by Jerome Levy (WJJD, Mooseheart, IL, 1926).

24454 Palmer House Victorians Orchestra. Hotel band (WJJD, Mooseheart, IL, 1926).

24455 *Palmolive Hour.* The *Palmolive Hour* was a concert music program sponsored by the Colgate-Palmolive Company, manufacturers of Palmolive Soap. The program featured "Olive Palmer" and "Paul Oliver," the names the sponsors used for soprano Virginia Rea and tenor Frank Munn. In addition to these talented performers, contralto Elizabeth Lennox and the Revelers Quarter performed to the music of Gustave Haenschen's orchestra.

The popular Revelers Quartet consisted of tenors Lewis James and James Melton, baritone Elliott Shaw and bass Wilfred Glenn. Guest stars such as Fanny Brice, Claudia Muzio and Nellie and Sara Kouns appeared weekly. The program also popularized such instrumentalists as jazz violinist Murray Kellner, Hawaiian guitarist virtuoso Andy Sanella and Larry Abbott, who produced music with a comb wrapped in tissue paper. Phillip Carlin and Alois Havrilla were the program's announcers (60 min., Wednesday, 9:30–10:00 P.M., NBC-Blue, 1927–1931).

24456 Palmquist, Paul W. Announcer (WKBS, Galesburg, IL, 1925).

24457 Palmquist, Ron. DJ (*Show Time*, KMOR, Littleton, CO, 1960).

24458 Palmquor, Claire. COM-HE (WDVN, Gainesville, FL, 1956).

24459 *Pals of the Prairie.* CW music show (WNAX, Yankton, SD, 1936).

24460 Pam, Anita. COM-HE Pam conducted the *Household Adviser* program (WPAP, Palisades, NJ, 1928).

24461 Panchito. Leader (*Panchito's Orchestra*, instr. mus. prg., CBS, 1934; MBS, 1936; NBC, 1937; MBS, 1938).

24462 Panetta, Genevive. COM-HE (WBOY, Clarksburg, NY, 1957).

24463 Paniagua, Raul. Concert pianist (WEAF, New York, NY, 1925).

24464 Panico, Louis. Leader (*Louis Panico Orchestra*, instr. mus. prg., CBS, 1935; WOR, Newark, NJ, 1936; WEAF, New York, NY, 1936; WENR, Chicago, IL, 1937; NBC-Blue, 1937–1938).

24465 Panka, Toni. COM-HE (WPRE, Prairie Du Chien, WI, 1954).

24466 Pannell, Winnifred. Organist (KTBI, Los Angeles, CA, 1925).

24467 Panner, Ray. News analyst (*Virginia in the News*, WLOW, Norfolk, VA, 1947).

24468 Panny, Frank. Sportscaster (*Racing News*, WOKO, Albany, NY, 1950).

24469 Pantages, Jimmie. DJ (*Yours for the Asking*, KLIF, Dallas, TX, 1947).

24470 Pantages, Lloyd. Pantages dispensed Hollywood news and gossip (*Lloyd Pantages Covers Hollywood*, CBS, 1937).

24471 *Pantages Hippodrome Vaudeville Acts.* Various vaudeville circuit performers appeared (KFBK, Sacramento, CA, 1925).

24472 Panther City Orchestra. Texas band directed by J.N. Wimple (WBAP, Fort Worth, TX, 1923).

24473 Panther Hawaiian Trio. Hawaiian instrumental group (WBAP, San Antonio, TX, 1926).

24474 *Pantry Party.* A cooking show for women, *Pantry Party* also featured lively music. Dick Lawrence was the producer; Eleanor Howe gave the recipes for cookies and cakes; Milton Charles sang the songs; and George Watson did the announcing (WBBM, Chicago, IL, 1937–1938).

24475 Paolineli, Earl. Accordionist (KYA, San Francisco, CA, 1927).

24476 Papagoda, Joann. COM-HE (WAVZ, New Haven, CT, 1960).

24477 Pape, Joe. Leader (*Joe Pape Orchestra*, instr. mus. prg., WJAS, Pittsburgh, PA, 1942).

24478 Paperte, Frances. Contralto (WEAF, New York, NY, 1927–1928).

24479 Papp, Frank. Director Papp directed *Barton Family*, *Eternal Light* and *Right to Happiness.*

24480 Pappalardo, (Professor) Gasper. Leader (Hotel Gayoso Orchestra, WMC, Memphis, TN, 1924; Pappalardo Brothers Orchestra, WMC, 1926).

24481 Pappas, Jim. DJ (WALL, Middleton, NY, 1960).

24482 *Pappy Cheshire.* Pappy Cheshire led a highly popular gang that attracted a large number of CW music lovers (KMOX, St. Louis, MO, 1936). The following year Cheshire's group broadcast twice daily on another station (45 min., Monday through Friday, 6:15–6:30 A.M. and 4:30–5:00 P.M., WBBM, Chicago, IL, 1937).

24483 Paquin, Marge. DJ (*Musical Jamboree*, KSOO, Sault Ste Marie, MI, 1947).

24484 *Parade of Stars.* Comedian Ken Murray hosted the variety show that also featured tenor Kenny Baker and the orchestra of David Broekman (30 min., Friday, 7:30–8:00 P.M., CST, NBC, 1940).

24485 *Parade of the Sponsors.* An unusual sustaining program that broadcast news of the various sponsored shows on radio and advanced promotional material for prospective buyers of radio time (15 min., Weekly, KGYO, Missoula, MT, 1938).

24486 *Parade of the States.* Each week Bruce Barton hosted a tribute to one of the states. Information and music related to the honored state were the major ingredients of the program. Erno Rapee conducted the orchestra (30 min., Monday, 9:30–10:00 P.M., NBC-Red, 1932).

24487 *Paradise Isle.* Each weekday evening a mythical horse race realistically was broadcast. The location was Paradise Isle, supposedly a casino in the Agua Caliente area. The program's Mexican orchestra supplied music. Two of the casino's "colored" servants carried on a funny conversation for program continuity. It was said that local bookies had a daily book on the "race" (KMTR, Hollywood, CA, 1932).

24488 *Paradise Partners.* CW mus. prg. (KGNF, North Platte, NE, 1939).

24489 Parady, William F. Sportscaster (*Sports Highlights*, KGLU, Safford, AZ, 1946–1947; *Along the Sports Trail*, KCKY, Coolidge, AZ, 1948; *Pigskin Party*, KCKY, 1949; KGLU, 1950).

24490 *Parallel.* An interesting program, *Parallel* was NBC's locally broadcast version of the CBS show, *You Are There.* Kenneth Banghart, Bob Wilson, Bob Ryan, Gabe Pressman, Ray Owen, Jimmy Powers and Dr. Louis Hacker were commentators on the show produced by Steve White. Len Weinles was the writer and director. The premiere was Sunday, October 6, 1957 (55 min., Sunday, 1:05–2:00 P.M., WRCA, New York, NY, 1957).

24491 Paramount Five. Musical group consisting of Albert Thomas, John Marshall, Thomas A. Patterson, Charlie Grubbs and Robert Fisher (KPRC, Houston, TX, 1927).

24492 *Paramount-Publix Hour* (aka *Paramount-Publix Radio Hour* or *The Paramount Hour*). The weekly musical program featured an orchestra, vocal soloists and guest stars. The singers, at various times, included tenors Ben Alley and Dennis King. The Apollos Male Quartet — Ray Johnson, L. Dwight Snyder, J. Marshall Smith and Del Porter — also were featured. In its earliest years the show was 60 minutes in length. Later it was decreased to 30 minutes and the day of broadcast changed (60 min., Saturday, 10:00–11:00 P.M., CBS, 1930; 30 min., Tuesday, 10:30–11:00 P.M., CBS, 1931).

24493 *Paramount Symphony Orchestra.* The concert music hour was presented by a theater band (60 min., Saturday, 10:00–11:00 P.M., CBS, 1929).

24494 Parcher, Lola. DJ (KCLX, Colfax, WA, 1954).

24495 Pardo, Maria. Spanish opera singer (WOR, Newark, NJ, 1929).

24496 Pardue, (Mrs.) E.L. Soprano (WLAC, Nashville, TN, 1929).

24497 Parent, Robert. DJ (*Parent's Variety Program*, KCRA, Sacramento, CA, 1948).

24498 Parenteau, Zoel. Leader (*Zoel Parenteau Orchestra*, instr. mus. prg., CBS, 1934).

24499 Paret, Betty. Harpist (WQXR, New York, NY, 1939).

24500 Parham, Virginia. COM-HE (WHNC, Henderson, NC, 1951).

24501 Paris, Morris. Newscaster (WEVD, New York, NY, 1945).

24502 Parise, Julie. COM-HE (WMFG, Mibbing, MN, 1960).

24503 Parish, Guy. Sportscaster (WEBQ, Harrisburg, IL, 1944). DJ (*Rhythm Roundup*, WEBQ, Harrisburg, IL, 1948).

24504 Parish, Ned. Leader (*Ned Parish Orchestra*, instr. mus. prg., NBC, 1934).

24505 Park, Marion. COM-HE (WINC, Winchester, VA, 1957).

24506 Park, Miriam Nelson. Singer (WGY, Schenectady, NY, 1926).

24507 Park, Natalie. Actress Park was in the cast of the *Hawthorne House* daytime serial program.

24508 Park, Ralph. Leader (Ralph Park's Casino Beautiful Dance Orchestra, KPRC, Houston, TX, 1926).

24509 Park, Vera C. Contralto (WPG, Atlantic City, NJ, 1934).

24510 *Park Avenue Hillbillies.* CW mus. prg. (WTMJ, Milwaukee, WI, 1936).

24511 Park Sisters. Ukulele and vocal duets performed by June and Francis Park (KFI, Los Angeles, CA, 1926).

24512 Park Union High School Orchestra and Glee Club. Scholastic instrumental and choral music groups (KHJ, Los Angeles, CA 1926).

24513 Parke, Newt and Gerry. Harmony singing team (KFRC, San Francisco, CA, 1926).

24514 Parker, Al. DJ (*Anything Goes*, WJJD, Chicago, IL, 1949).

24515 Parker, Alan. Newscaster (WSYR, Syracuse, NY, 1938).

24516 Parker, Alice. COM-HE (WHUC, Hudson, NY, 1949).

24517 Parker, (Mme.) Andres. Leader (Mme. Andres Parker Singers, WRNY, New York, NY, 1926).

24518 Parker, Anne. COM-HE (WJBF, Augusta, GA, 1949).

24519 Parker, Ben. Newscaster (KWEW, Hobbs, NM, 1938). Sportscaster (KWEW, 1939).

24520 Parker, Bob. DJ (*Ala Carte*, KLRA, Little Rock, AR, 1952).

24521 Parker, Chubby. Singer-banjoist (WLS, Chicago, IL, 1925). Parker was best known for his song, "My Little Sod Shanty." He joined the *National Barn Dance* in 1925 (WLS, 1925).

24522 Parker, Dorothy. Pianist (WGI, Medford Hillside, MA, 1922).

24523 Parker, Earl. Newscaster (WDZ, Tuscola, IL, 1938). Sportscaster (WDZ, 1939).

24524 Parker, Eddie. DJ (*Morning Express*, WKGN, Knoxville, TN, 1949–1957; WFCT, Knoxville, TN, 1960).

24525 Parker, Eleanor. COM-HE (WBTM, Canville, VA, 1951).

24526 Parker, Elzie. DJ (KAJO, Grants Pass, OR, 1960).

24527 Parker, Eric. DJ (*570 Club*, WMAM, Marinette, WI, 1949).

24528 Parker, Ethel O. COM-HE (WELM, Elmira, NY, 1954–1960).

24529 Parker, Faye. COM-HE (WDAR, Savannah, GA, 1955).

24530 Parker, Frank. Tenor Parker was featured on the *A&P Gypsies* and the *Evening in Paris* programs (NBC, 1929–1930). He was also on *Hollywood Hotel*, *Jack Benny Program* and the *Woodbury Soap Hour.* Parker appeared on the *Those We Love* program as an actor. He also appeared as a guest star on many radio shows. Parker later was featured on some of Arthur Godfrey's radio and television programs.

24531 Parker, Frank. Sportscaster (*The Sportsman*, WCLE, Clearwater, FL, 1948).

24532 Parker, Fred. DJ (*Juke Box*, WJWL, Georgetown, DE, 1952; *Supper Serenade*, WJWL, 1954). Sportscaster (*Tenth Inning*, WJWL, 1952).

24533 Parker, Gail. Banjo soloist (WHT, Chicago, IL, 1927).

24534 Parker, Gene. DJ (*Spin It and Win It*, WCOU, Lewiston, ME, 1947; *T-N-T*, WWCO, Waterbury, CT, 1948).

24535 Parker, Harmony Hick. Instrumentalist billed as "Harmony Hick and his Ukulele" (KGO, Oakland, CA, 1926).

24536 Parker, Helen. COM-HE (WHBQ, Memphis, TN, 1951).

24537 Parker, H.M. Violinist (WGN, Chicago, IL, 1923).

24538 Parker, Horace. Newscaster (KWSC, Pullman, WA, 1945).

24539 Parker, Jack. Tenor (NBC, 1929).

24540 Parker, Jack. Newscaster (WJIM, Lansing, MI, 1938, 1944).

24541 Parker, Janet. COM-HE (KHUZ, Borger, TX, 1957).

24542 Parker, Jesse. DJ (*1450 Club*, WHSC, Hartsville, SC, 1960).

24543 Parker, Joe. Sportscaster (NBC, 1937).

24544 Parker, John. DJ (*Parker's Playhouse*, WBTM, Danville, VA, 1949).

24545 Parker, June. Blues singer (KFWB, Hollywood, CA, 1926; KHJ, Los Angeles, CA, 1926–1927).

24546 Parker, Ken. DJ (*1250 Club*, WDVA, Danville, VA, 1949).

24547 Parker, Laurence "Larry." Newscaster (KMA, Shenandoah, IA, 1947–1948).

24548 Parker, Linda (Genevieve Elizabeth Muenich). CW singer Parker at 17 was singing on WWAE (Hammond, IN, 1929). The following year she had her own program (*Jeanne Munich, the Red-Haired Bluebird*, WAAF, Chicago, IL, 1930). In 1932, John Lair hired her as part of the Cumberland Ridge Runners (WLS, Chicago, IL, 1932). She became a favorite on the *National Barn Dance.* Tragically, she died at the age of 23 following an acute appendicitis attack. *See **National Barn Dance.***

24549 Parker, Lou. Ballad singer (KFWB, Hollywood, CA, 1926). Leader, Lou Parker and His Melody Entertainers (KNRC, Los Angeles, CA, 1926).

24550 Parker, Mac. Newscaster (WCAU, Philadelphia, PA, 1938).

24551 Parker, Marge. COM-HE (KNCY, Nebraska City, NE, 1960).

24552 Parker, Mary. COM-HE (KFFA, Helena, AR, 1949).

24553 Parker, Mary. DJ (KBOP, Pleasanton, TX, 1956; *Wake Up to Music*, KBOP, 1960).

24554 Parker, Mary Elizabeth. COM-HE (KBOP, Pleasanton, TX, 1957).

24555 Parker, Olive. Actress Parker appeared on the *Road of Life* daytime serial program.

24556 Parker, Orin. News analyst (*DTR News*, KCSU, Provo, UT, 1948).

24557 Parker, Pat. COM-HE (WNNT, Warsaw, VA, 1955).

24558 Parker, Paul. Newscaster (WHIT, New Berne, NC, 1942). Sportscaster (WHIT, 1945; WGNI, Wilmington, NC, 1949). DJ (*740 Club*, WMBL, Morehead City, NC, 1947; *Paul Parker Show*, WGNI, 1948; *The Double P Show*, WGNI, 1949).

24559 Parker, Priscilla. Soprano (NBC, 1928).

24560 Parker, Priscilla. COM-HE (WHUM, Reading, PA, 1951).

24561 Parker, Raymond. Tenor (WAHG, Richmond Hill, NY, 1925).

24562 Parker, Robert. Newscaster (WLW, Cincinnati, OH, 1944).

24563 Parker, Royal. DJ (*Royal Record Review*, WASA, Havre de Grace, MD, 1949).

24564 Parker, Virgil "Virg." Sportscaster (*Sports Parade* and *Gridiron Guesses*, KORE, Eugene, OR, 1947; *Sports Revue*, KORE, 1948–1954; KRSN, Los Alamos, NM, 1956).

24565 Parker, Wes. DJ (WSBA, York, PA, 1953).

24566 Parker, Woody. Actor Parker was in the cast of *Rosemary.*

24567 Parker, Z.D. COM-HE (KEN, Ada, OK, 1954).

24568 *(The) Parker Family.* Don Becker created and produced the weekly situation comedy that first appeared in 1939 on the NBC-Blue network. The story involved the typical problems of adolescence faced by Richard Parker and his supportive family. The writers were Ben Kagan, Priscilla Kent, Vera Oldham, Chick Vincent and Ed Wolfe and the directors Oliver Barbour and Chick Vincent. The program's cast included: Marjorie Anderson, Linda Carlon-Reid, Roy Fant, Mitzi Gould, Leon Janney, Jay Jostyn, Michael O'Day, Fern Persons, Aileen Pringle and Pat Ryan. The announcer was Hugh James (NBC-Blue, 1939–1944).

24569 Parker House Concert Orchestra. Instr. mus. group directed by Frank McGrath (WEEI, Boston, MA, 1928).

24570 Parker Store Chorus. Vocal group directed by Mrs. Esther Candill consisting of C.F. Rand, tenor; Edna M. Trine, soprano; D.P. Roberts, tenor; E.J. Shurtz, bass; Carla Holtermann, alto; and Ruth Eckstrand, soprano. Beulah LaFrance was the group's accompanist (WOC, Davenport, IA, 1923).

24571 Parkes, Hal. Newscaster (KUTA, Salt Lake City, UT, 1938). Sportscaster (KUTA, 1939; *In the World of Sports*, KLO, Ogden, UT, 1940; KROW, Oakland, CA, 1942–1944; *Sports Sparks*, KOLE, Port Arthur, TX, 1947–1948). DJ (*Request Performance*, KOLE, 1947).

24572 Parkes, Paul. Baritone (WEAF, New York, NY, 1925).

24573 Parkhurst, Adele. Soprano (WEAF, New York, NY, 1926).

24574 Parkington, Margaret. Contralto (KPRC, Houston, TX, 1926).

24575 Parkins, Bob. DJ (*Dunkers Club*, KOLN, Lincoln, NE, 1947).

24576 Parks, Al. DJ (*Jukebox Serenade*, WKAI, Macomb, IL, 1949).

24577 **Parks, Betty.** COM-HE (WSCR, Scranton, PA, 1956).

24578 **Parks, Daryl [Daryle] E.** Newscaster (WRJN, Racine, WI, 1941). Sportscaster (WRJN, 1941–1942, 1947; *Sports Camera*, WKLO, Louisville, KY, 1949; WKBC, Cincinnati, OH, 1954).

24579 **Parks, Del.** Sportscaster (*Off-Sides*, WILM, Wilmington, DE, 1947; *The Sports Trail*, WAMS, Wilmington, DE, 1948; WPEN, Philadelphia, PA, 1949; *Bandstand and Grandstand*, WPEN, 1950; *10th Inning*, WPEN, 1951; *Sports Caravan*, WEEZ, Chester, PA, 1960).

24580 **Parks, Don.** DJ (*Record Party*, WLCX, LaCrosse, WI, 1949).

24581 **Parks, Erv.** DJ (*Coffepot Capers*, WMIS, Natchez, MS, 1952).

24582 **Parks, Hal.** News analyst (KQW, San Jose, CA, 1945).

24583 **Parks, Harlan.** DJ (*1100 Club*, WLBB, Carrollton, GA, 1960).

24584 **Parks, (Mrs.) Howard.** Contralto (WFAA, Dallas, TX, 1926).

24585 **Parks, Larry.** DJ (WHOC, Philadelphia, MS, 1954; *Miss Jubilee*, WBKN, Newton, MS, 1960).

24586 **Parks, Shirley.** COM-HE (WXXW, Albany, NY, 1951).

24587 **Parlar, Jim.** Sportscaster (*Sportscope*, KWTC, Barstow, CA, 1960).

24588 **Parlin, Albert C. "Al."** Newscaster (WMRN, Marion, OH, 1942; WHKC, Columbus, OH, 1944–1946; *Sohio News*, WTOL, Toledo, OH, 1948).

24589 **Parlow, Vern.** Newscaster (WOMT, Manitowoc, WI, 1937).

24590 **Parmalee, Helen Wegman.** Pianist (KLX, Oakland, CA, 1929).

24591 **Parmelee-Dohrmann Company Orchestra.** Commercial band (KNX, Los Angeles, CA, 1927).

24592 **Parmer, Edith.** COM-HE (WGYV, Greenville, AL, 1949).

24593 **Parmet, Gus.** Sportscaster (*Scoreboard of the Air*, WHIM, Providence, RI, 1951–1954; WICE, Providence, RI, 1957).

24594 **Parnacott, Barney.** Sportscaster and softball play-by-play broadcaster (WDSR, Lake City, FL, 1950).

24595 **Parnassus Trio.** Instrumental group (NBC, New York, NY, 1928–1929).

24596 **Parnell, Eva.** Actress Parnell appeared on the daytime serial programs *Road of Life* and *Young Widder Brown.*

24597 **Parnell, Sarah [Sara].** COM-HE (WJAM, Marion, AL, 1957–1960).

24598 **Parodians Dance Orchestra.** Local dance band (WCAU, Philadelphia, PA, 1926).

24599 **Parody Orchestra.** New York dance band (WMCA, New York, IL, 1926).

24600 **Parr, Dorothy.** COM-HE (*Henrietta Meets the Ladies*, WWNY, Watertown, NY, 1949; WCNY, Carthage, NY, 1957).

24601 **Parr, Fran.** COM-HE (KSOX, Raymondville, TX, 1957).

24602 **Parr, (William) Grant.** Newscaster (NBC, 1941, 1945–1946).

24603 **Parr, W.H.** Newscaster (*Traffic Scoreboard*, WTOC, Savannah, GA, 1947–1948).

24604 **Parre, Dick.** Leader (Dick Parre's Club Plaza Band, WABC, New York, NY, 1929).

24605 **Parrin, Vic.** Actor Parrin was in the cast of *Holly Sloan.*

24606 **Parrino, Ted.** Newscaster (KRLD, Dallas, TX, 1945).

24607 **Parris, Bill.** DJ (WNLK, Norwalk, CT, 1950). Parris' program ran for three decades, combining music, news, sports, weather and humor.

24608 **Parris [Parrish], Helen.** COM-HE (WKLF, Clinton, IA, 1951; WAGA, Atlanta, GA, 1954).

24609 **Parrish, Ann.** COM-HE (KGIV, Charlotte, NC, 1949).

24610 **Parrish, Helen.** COM-HE (KNXT, Los Angeles, CA, 1955–1957).

24611 **Parrish, Hurley, Jr.** DJ (*Hurley's Early Bird*, WDUK, Durham, NC, 1948).

24612 **Parrish, John.** DJ (*Triple R Program*, WLEX, Lexington, KY, 1948; *The Music Man*, WVLK, Versailles-Lexington, KY, 1949).

24613 **Parrish, Kathryn.** Pianist (WQJ, Chicago, IL, 1926).

24614 **Parrish, Wynne.** News analyst (*Women in the News*, WOLF, Syracuse, NY, 1940).

24615 **Parry, Betty.** COM-HE (WXKW, Albany, NY, 1949).

24616 **Parry, Bill.** DJ (*Afternoon Affair*, KTEM, Temple, TX, 1960).

24617 **Parry, Grant.** DJ (*Bing Sings*, KJAM, Vernal, UT, 1947).

24618 **Parry, Leroy.** Leader (Leroy Parry's Elite Orchestra, KNRC, Los Angeles, CA, 1925; Leroy Parry's Orchestra of Seven Smiles, KHJ, Los Angeles, CA, 1926).

24619 **Parsley, Bill.** DJ (*Record Shop*, KSEL, Lubbock, TX, 1948). Sportscaster (KSEL, 1948).

24620 **Parsons, Alfred.** DJ (WNAV, Annapolis, MD, 1949).

24621 **Parsons, Ben.** Sportscaster (WJHO, Opelika, KS, 1944). DJ (*Midnight Dancing Party*, WRBL, Columbus, GA, 1948–1949; *Spinners Sanctum*, WRBL, 1954–1957).

24622 **Parsons, Boyd.** DJ (*Alarm Clock Club*, WGAD, Gadsden, AL, 1952).

24623 **Parsons, Bruce.** DJ (*Ebony Boogie*, WVIM, Vicksburg, MS, 1952; WBRN, Big Rapids, MI, 1955).

24624 **Parsons, C.L. "Poss."** Sportscaster (KOA, Denver, CO, 1941).

24625 **Parsons, Chauncey.** Tenor (KDKA, Pittsburgh, PA, 1923; WEAF, New York, NY, 1929; *Chauncey Parsons*, vcl. prg., NBC-Chicago, IL, 1930).

24626 **Parsons, Jeanne.** COM-HE (WAJR, Morgantown, WV, 1949).

24627 **Parsons, Kathryn.** Singer known as the "Girl O' Yesteryear" (CBS, 1931).

24628 **Parsons, Louella.** Hollywood news and gossip (*Hollywood News*, NBC, 1938; NBC-Blue, 1944; *The Louella Parsons Show*, ABC, 1945–1947; *Hollywood Reporter*, ABC, 1948). Parsons, as the longtime Hearst Hollywood columnist, was a powerful force in the entertainment business. She had *all* the Hollywood gossip and told the story exactly the way the studios wanted it told. Her broadcasting career extended from 1931 to 1951 on both ABC and CBS.

24629 **Parsons, Marshall, Jr.** Sportscaster (WHBB, Selma, AL, 1941; WBRC, Birmingham, AL, 1944; WDOD, Chattanooga, TN, 1945–1946; *Parsons' Sports*, WQAM, Miami, FL, 1948; *Parsons' Sports* and *Tomorrow's Sports Page*, WQAM, 1949–1955; WCKR, Miami, FL and WCKT, Miami, FL, 1957).

24630 **Parsons, Peg.** Newscaster (WLEU, Erie, PA, 1940–1941). Sportscaster (WLEU, 1940–1941).

24631 **Parsons, (Mrs.) Pollard.** Pianist (WLAC, Nashville, TN, 1929).

24632 **Parsons, Robert.** Newscaster (WMBI, Chicago, IL, 1940).

24633 **Partee, Dora Damon.** Cornetist (WEHF, 1923).

24634 **Partido, Fred.** DJ (*Tempo*, KWCO, Chickasha, OK, 1960).

24635 ***Parties at Pickfair.*** Silent screen star, Mary Pickford ("Our Little Mary") was the hostess on the program that originated from Pickfair, her Beverly Hills home. Music was supplied by the Al Lyons Orchestra and the Paul Turner Singers. Cast members included James Eageles, Mary Jane Higby, Lou Merrill, Bret Morrison and Ted Osborne. In addition, guests such as Edward Everett Horton entertained. Each guest was introduced as they arrived by "Alvin the Butler, " played by Eric Snowden. The short-lived series was sponsored by the National Association of Ice Industries (30 min., Tuesday, 10:00–10:30 P.M., CBS, 1936).

24636 **Partner, Dan.** Sportscaster (KSAC, Manhattan, KS, 1939).

24637 **Parton, Claude "Red."** Sportscaster (*Sports Scoop* and *Sports Roundup*, WOLF, Syracuse, NY, 1940–1944; *Sports Scoop*, WOLF, 1947–1954).

24638 **Partridge, Dick.** DJ (*1250 Club*, WTMA, Charleston, SC, 1949; WHIM, Providence, RI, 1957; WNEW, New York, NY, 1960).

24639 **Partridge, Marion.** Pianologues (WWJ, Detroit, MI, 1925).

24640 **Pasadena Orchestra Deluxe.** Six-piece music group consisting of Elmer Gray, p.; Charles Wagg, c.; Charles Elkin, v. and as.; Carl Morris, C-Melody s.; Sig Meyer, bj.; and Jack Wrout, d. (KYW, Chicago, IL, 1923).

24641 **Pasadena Presbyterian Church Quartet.** Religious vocal group whose members included soprano Melba French Barr; contralto Mary Booth; tenor Harold Proctor; and baritone Louis Courcil (KPPC, Pasadena, CA, 1927).

24642 **Paschall, Walter.** Newscaster (WSB, Atlanta, GA, 1941–1942, 1948). Paschall began his career as a newsman at WSB in the 1930s.

24643 **Pascocelle, Robert.** Pianist (WGBS, New York, NY, 1925, NBC, New York, NY, 1929).

24644 Pascoe, Helen. Newscaster (*The Family News*, WGNY, Newburgh, NY, 1940).

24645 Pascoe, Ken. DJ (*Pascoe's Kitchen*, KDB, Santa Barbara, CA, 1948).

24646 Paskman, Dailey. Respected showman, manager and director of station WGBS (New York City, NY), Paskman produced the station's spectacular inaugural broadcast in 1924, featuring Raymond Hitchcock, Rosamond Pinchot, Vincent Lopez, Arthur "Bugs" Baer, Rube Golderg, Mary Ellis, William Kent, Morris Gert, George Gershwin, the Dolly Sisters, Judith Anderson, Louis John Bartels, Dagmar Godowsky, Sigmund Spaeth and Tony Sarg.

Some of the innovations and programs Paskman produced at WGBS were his music dramas, tabloid versions of plays with a music background. For example, the lives of Mozart and Beethoven were presented. Later he introduced "tabloid operas" and long radio plays. In addition, he initiated a regular musical program broadcast from an plane flying above New York, New Jersey, Connecticut and Pennsylvania. The airborne show featured Maxine Brown singing from a Sikorsky biplane. Paskman also produced an early interview program conducted by Sylvia Golden, the Assistant Editor of *Theatre Magazine* on which she interviewed such entertainment stars as Eva LaGalliene, Jean Tennyson, Ruth Baker, Mary Lawlor, Richard Hale, Ruth Etting, Helen Ford, Belle Baker, Clarence Nordstrom, Vivienne Segal, Sophie Tucker and Irene Bordoni. Her informative program presented performers from vaudeville, the musical comedy and dramatic theater. Paskman probably is best remembered for his *Dailey Paskman Minstrels* program, sometimes known as the *WGBS Radio Minstrels*. *See* ***Dailey Paskman Minstrels***.

24647 Pasmore, Mary. Violinist (KGO, Oakland, CA, 1925).

24648 Pasquale, Giovanni. Baritone (WCAU, Philadelphia, PA, 1925).

24649 Pasquale, Mary. Pianist (WGBS, New York, NY, 1925).

24650 Pasquale, Mary. Violinist (KGO, Oakland, CA, 1925).

24651 Pasquali, Joe. Sportscaster (*High School Football*, WSIG, Mt. Jackson, VA, 1960).

24652 Pasquet, Jean. Announcer (WWL, New Orleans, LA, 1925).

24653 Pasquin and Harris Harmony Boys. Harmony singing team (KJR, Seattle, WA, 1927).

24654 Pass, Dana. Newscaster (KWKW, Pasadena, CA, 1947).

24655 Pass, Rosaline. Pianist (WAHG, New York, NY, 1926).

24656 Passage, Alice. COM-HE (KYAK, Yakima, WA, 1955).

24657 Passage, George. Sportscaster (*Sports Album* and *Sports Final*, WRVA, Richmond, VA, 1947–1948). Newscaster (WRVA, 1948).

24658 Passe [Pass], Noel. Sportscaster (*Sports Spotlite*, WKAY, Glasgow, KY, 1948; WVOK, Birmingham, AL, 1949; KTHT, Houston, TX, 1950–1953; KTRE, Lufkin, TX, 1954). DJ (*Passin' Time*, KTRE, 1954).

24659 Passer, Burt. Newscaster (KYSM, Mankato, MS, 1945).

24660 *(The) Passing Parade.* John Nesbitt, a West Coast radio favorite, told interesting human interest stories on the local show sponsored by Dwarf Sales Company (15 min., Sunday, 7:00–7:15 P.M., KFRC, San Francisco, CA, 1936). Nesbitt later broadcast on CBS, NBC and MBS from 1938 to 1949 and, at the same time, enjoyed a lucrative career making motion picture shorts (15 min., Monday through Friday, 9:15–9:30 P.M., MBS, 1948). John Nesbitt entered radio in 1930 when he originated his *Headlines of the Past*, a program that eventually became *The Passing Parade*.

24661 *(A) Passport for Adams.* Norman Corwin produced the adventure series that told the story of a small town editor, Doug Adams, and a New York photographer, Perry "Quiz" Quisinberry. These two men, played by Robert Young and Dane Clark, were sent on assignment by the Consolidated News Syndicate to various countries. The program had a semi-documentary format, by which the culture and customs of various countries were portrayed. The story concerned itself chiefly with Adams, a "county editor who's been sent on a trip around the world to visit various cities and talk to the people of the United Nations." Adams visited Monrovia, Moscow and Tel Aviv. Other cast members were Myron McCormick and Paul Mann. The director was Corwin who also wrote some of the scripts (30 min., CBS, 1943).

24662 Paster, Freda. Pianist (WOR, Newark, NJ, 1925).

24663 Pasternack, Josef. Musical director on the *Atwater Kent Hour (*NBC-Red, New York, NY, 1929).

24664 Pastor, Tony (Anthony Pestritta). Leader (*Tony Pastor Orchestra*, instr. mus. prg., NBC, 1935; WAKR, Akron, OH, 1942).

24665 Pastor School Radio Orchestra. Band directed by Edwin Swindel (WOC, Davenport, IA, 1925).

24666 Paszty, Bertha. Singer (WLW, Cincinnati, OH, 1926).

24667 Pat and Sunshine. Pat Flanagan sang, read his own original verse and provided comic monologues on the weekly 15-minute program. Pianist Marigold Cassin accompanied Flanagan (WOC, Davenport, IA, 1928).

24668 *Pat Barnes.* Veteran radio entertainer Barnes returned to the air with his show sponsored by Procter & Gamble's Dreft. Barnes opened each show with a greeting sung to the tune of "The Isle of Capri." On a typical program Barnes recited poems with a soothing organ background provided by Larry Larsen. His program combined poetry, philosophy, commentary and music (15 min., Monday, 11:00–11:15 A.M., CST, NBC, 1935). *See* **Barnes, Pat.**

24669 *Pat Barnes and Ralph Dumke.* Knox Gelatin sponsored the unusual show featuring these radio veterans. On the show they engaged in a serious discussion of baseball teams and their players and just about every thing else that happened to come to mind (10 min., Saturday, 3:00–3:10 P.M., WOR, Newark, NJ, 1939).

24670 *Pat Barnes' Barnstormers.* Veteran radio entertainer Barnes conducted the variety show whose main ingredients were music and comedy (WRVA, Richmond, VA, 1938).

24671 *Pat Barnes in Person.* Radio veteran Pat Barnes was featured in a solo venture, NBC, 1935.

24672 *Pat Buttram and Melvinny.* Veteran country comic Pat Buttram was the featured performer on the rural comedy show. Supposedly Buttram was working in Chicago on the program and speaking on the telephone to his sweetheart, Melvinny, who he had left back in Harleyville, Alabama (15 min., Monday through Friday, 1:00–1:15 P.M., WLS, Chicago, IL, 1934).

24673 *Pat Buttram's Radio School for Beginners Just Startin'.* Oshkosh Work Clothes sponsored country comic Buttram, who later became Gene Autry's movie and radio sidekick. On the show, Buttram was joined by Henry Hornsbuckle, the Hoosier Sod Busters, the Hired Hands, Reg Kross, Howard Black, Jim and Eddie Dean. Joe Kelly was the show's announcer. Bill Meredith and Pat Buttram wrote the show that was produced by Al Boyd (15 min., Monday through Friday, 6:45–7:00 A.M., WLS, Chicago, IL, 1936).

A typical example of the Buttram humor was the comment he made one day in 1936 about WLS announcer, Jack Holden: "I noted where Holden is a playin' the part of Tom Mix on the air now. Well, it's about time. He's been gettin' mixed up in his scripts for years. Holden says he came from up in Michigan whar 'Men are Men.' Gosh, that's why they ran him out." Buttram also commented on the Chicago scene during Prohibition, "My uncle [in Chicago] was a tail gunner on a beer truck."

24674 Pate, Virginia F. COM-HE (WASA, Havre De Grace, MD, 1960).

24675 Patee, Rita. COM-HE (WOAP, Owosso, MI, 1957).

24676 Patek, Rudy. Concertina soloist Patek was a member with Ben Ray of a concertina duet team (KYW, Chicago, IL and WDAP, Chicago, IL, 1923).

24677 Peterson, (Mrs.) A.W. Reader (WGY, Schenectady, NY, 1923).

24678 *Pathé News of the Air.* The program claimed that it presented the "actual sounds of news events." When this was the case, it was because it was taken directly from the sound tracks of Pathé newsreels (15 min., Twice per week, MBS, 1935).

24679 *Pathfinders.* Dr. William Van Wyck cast a critical eye upon a variety of topics and shared his views with listeners on all of them (15 min., Monday, 8:00–8:15 P.M. PST, KFRC, San Francisco, CA, 1937).

24680 Patio Royal Dance Orchestra of New Orleans. Popular jazz and dance orchestra that included Leslie C. George, dir-bj.; Clarence Broth, p.; William Brevan, Jr., c.; Evans Zevely, as.; and Louis Uhle, d. (WSMB, New Orleans, LA, 1925).

24681 Paton, Clyde. Sportscaster (KGY, Olympia, WA, 1937).

24682 Patrick, Bea. COM-HE (WKNY, Kingston, NY, 1955).

24683 Patrick, Betty. Violinist-singer (KFI, Los Angeles, CA, 1925).

24684 Patrick, Chuck. DJ (WAGN, Menominee, MI, 1960).

24685 Patrick, Chuck. DJ (KUSN, St. Joseph, MO, 1960).

24686 Patrick, Frances. Pianist (WSM, Nashville, TN, 1928–1929).

24687 Patrick, George. DJ (WCKR, Miami, FL, 1960).

24688 Patrick, Henry [Harry]. Leader (*Henry Patrick Orchestra*, instr. mus. prg. (WIP, Philadelphia, PA, 1935–1936).

24689 Patrick, James. Black DJ (WERD, Atlanta, GA, 1950s). James was also known as "Alley Pat." He began his DJ chores at WERD in 1950 and stayed there until 1954, when he moved to station WAOK (Atlanta, GA). Patrick became "Alley Pat" at the result of the station's program director selling two hours of morning air time to Atlantic Beer. Patrick in the morning would say, "Let's get over that hangover with a nice cold bottle of Atlantic Ale." In the afternoon for Steiner Brew, he would say, "Let's go down in the alley and get some beer." His listeners affectionately soon began to call him "Alley Pat" (George, 1997, p. 1).

24690 Patrick, Pat. Leader (Pat Patrick and his Orchestra, WLW, Cincinnati, OH, 1926). Announcer (WFBE, Cincinnati, OH, 1927).

24691 Patrick, Pat. DJ (*Lunch Call*, WERD, Atlanta, GA, 1949; *Dance Party*, WAOK, Atlanta, GA, 1960).

24692 Patrick, Paul. Newscaster (KICM, Mason City, IA, 1948).

24693 Patrick, Robert. Newscaster (WCBS, Springfield, IL, 1945).

24694 Patrick, Roger. Newscaster (KROS, Clinton, IA, 1942).

24695 Patrick, Ruth. COM-HE (KAMQ, Amarillo, TX, 1956).

24696 Patrick, Van. A some time newscaster, Patrick's major achievements were as a sportscaster (KOCA, Kilgore, TX, 1937; KRMD, Shreveport, LA, 1939; WHBF, Rock Island, IL, 1940–1942; WPEN, Philadelphia, PA, 1945; WEBR, Buffalo, NY, 1946; WGAR, Cleveland, OH, 1947; *Strictly Sports*, WGAR, 1948; *Sports Scripts*, WJR, Detroit, MI, 1949–1951; *Sports Final*, WJR, 1951; professional football play-by-play, MBS, 1954; WKMH, Detroit, MI, 1957; WKMH and MBS, 1960).

24697 Patrick-Marsh Dance Orchestra. Hollywood band (KFWB, Hollywood, CA, 1926).

24698 Patricola, Miss. Isabella Patricola was a popular jazz singer of the 1920s. Miss Patricola broadcast on many stations at that time and was also a popular vaudeville and recording star (NBC, 1920s).

24699 Patswold, Dorothy. Singer (WNAD, Norman, OK, 1926).

24700 *Patsy Montana.* Patsy Montana was a famous CW singer who enjoyed great popularity nationally because of her broadcasting and recording success, WLS (Chicago, IL, 1936). In 1949, she was featured on Shreveport, LA, radio. Her biggest radio and recording hit was "I Want to Be a Cowboy's Sweetheart." *See* **Singers.**

24701 Patt, John F. Chief announcer-assistant director (WDAF, Kansas City, MO, 1923; WJR, Detroit, MI, 1925; KFKU, Lawrence, KS, 1926).

24702 Patt, Ralph. Assistant announcer (WDAF, Kansas City, MO, 1926). Announcer (WJR, Detroit, MI, 1929).

24703 Pattee, Betty. COM-HE (WKNB, New Britain, CT, 1951).

24704 Pattee, (Colonel) John A. Musician known as the "Old Soldier Fiddler" (WEAF, New York, NY, 1925).

24705 Patten, Andy. News analyst (*Air Force News*, WLOX, Biloxi, MS, 1948).

24706 Patten, Bob. DJ (WABI, Bangor, ME, 1949).

24707 Patten, (Major) Will A. News analyst (WRGA, Rome, GA, 1939).

24708 *Patterns in Poetry.* Mary Moran read poetry on the weekly program (15 min., 8:00–8:15 P.M., WOKO, Albany, NY, 1950).

24709 *Patterns in Swing.* Vocalist Edith Hedrick was one of the performers that appeared on the network music program (CBS, 1939).

24710 Patterson, (Mrs.) A.H. Soprano (KGO, San Francisco, CA, 1925).

24711 Patterson, Anne [Ann]. Mezzo-soprano (WGHP, Detroit, MI, 1926).

24712 Patterson, Bob. Leader (Bob Patterson's Orchestra, WBZ, Springfield, MA, 1926).

24713 Patterson, Buell. Sportscaster (WIND, Gary, IN, 1935).

24714 Patterson, C.P. DJ (WBCK, Battle Creek, MI and WONS, Hartford, CT, 1948–1949).

24715 Patterson, Coleman. News analyst (*Carolina Reporter*, WTSB, Lumberton, NC, 1947).

24716 Patterson, Edmund. Black DJ (15 min., Monday through Friday, WERD, Atlanta, GA, 1955). A native of Atlanta, Patterson hosted a daily gospel music show that expanded from a quarter hour to a half-hour and, eventually, to a full hour show.

24717 Patterson, Jimmy "Jim." Newscaster (WISE, Asheville, NC, 1942). DJ (*By Jimminy*, WBT, Charlotte, NC, 1949–1954). Sportscaster (WISE, 1948).

24718 Patterson, Joan. COM-HE (KVEC, San Luis Obispo, CA, 1955).

24719 Patterson, Mark. Violinist Patterson was a member of a string band featured on the *WSM Barn Dance* (WSM, Nashville, TN, 1927).

24720 Patterson, Mitzi. COM-HE (KMUR, Murray, UT, 1951).

24721 Patterson, Pat. Newscaster (KGLO, Mason City, IA,1938; WMT, Cedar Rapids, IA, 1944–1947). Sportscaster (WMT, 1944–1946).

24722 Patterson, Ruth. Soprano (KPRC, Houston, TX, 1926).

24723 Patterson, Wade. Newscaster (KGLO, Mason City, IA, 1939). Sportscaster (WMT, Cedar City-Waterloo, IA, 1945).

24724 Patterson, Wanda. COM-HE (KBWD, Brownswood, TX, 1951).

24725 Pattison, Jim. DJ (*1450 Club*, WDAD, Indiana, PA, 1949). Sportscaster (*Sports Parade*, WDAD, 1949; *Sports Review*, WDAD, 1950–1951; *Round Up*, WDAD, 1951).

24726 Patton, Alice. Accordionist (*Alice Patton*, instr. mus. prg., NBC-Blue, 1934).

24727 Patton, Estelle. Soprano (WEAF, New York, NY, 1926).

24728 Patton, Madelyn Y. COM-HE (WMNC, Morganton, NC, 1956).

24729 Patton, Mary. Actress Patton was in the cast of the *Bachelor's Children*, *The Right to Happiness* and the *Road of Life* daytime serial programs.

24730 Patton, Peggy. Miss Patton broadcast movie reviews (WSOE, Milwaukee, WI, 1926).

24731 Patton, Phyllis. Harpist (WROK, Rockford, IL, 1939).

24732 Patty Jean (Louise Huey). COM-HE (WHAS, Louisville, KY, 1932).

24733 Paul, Charles. Organist-orchestra leader Paul appeared on *Mr. and Mrs. North*, *Road of Life*, *The Shadow*, *This Is Nora Drake* and *Young Dr. Malone*.

24734 Paul, Don. DJ (*Noon to Two Point of View*, WNAK, Wilkes-Barre, PA, 1960).

24735 Paul, Ed. Newscaster (WCFL, Chicago, IL, 1939–1940). Sportscaster (*Wiedemann's Sports Eye*, WMRN, Marion, OH, 1949; WCED, DuBois, PA, 1957).

24736 Paul, Herb. Sportscaster Paul did play-by-play of the University of Minnesota's football games (WCCO, MN, 1924). One of Paul's memorable broadcasts was that of November 15, 1924, when the Minnesota Golden Gophers defeated Illinois 20–7 and stopped Red Grange the famous "Galloping Ghost."

24737 Paul, Ida Mae. Soprano (WGY, Schenectady, NY, 1925).

24738 Paul, Les (Lester William Polsfuss) aka Rhubarb Red. Popular CW guitarist and arranger Paul began his radio career playing with Joe Wolverston's Apple Knockers on KMOX (St. Louis, MO, 1932). During the mid–1930s, he was featured on Chicago radio as Rhubarb Red. After turning more toward jazz guitar, Paul married Mary Ford (Iris Colleen Summers), with whom he made several hit records using her vocals with his muti-tracked recorded guitar.

24739 Paul, Mary Jane. Reader (KDKA, Pittsburgh, PA, 1924).

24740 Paul, Nick. DJ (KRLD, Dallas, TX, 1956–1957).

24741 Paul, Sandy. DJ (KIBE-KDFC, San Francisco, CA, 1960).

24742 Paul, Sydney "Syd." Newscaster (WFBR, Baltimore, MD, 1940). DJ (*Coffee Pot*, WHOL, Allentown, PA, 1949–1952).

Sportscaster (*Sportsmen Corner*, WHOL, 1952–1954).

24743 **Paul, Vince.** DJ (*Night Sounds*, KWNO, Winona, MN, 1960).

24744 ***Paul Ash's Stage Show.*** The variety show, hosted by Paul Ash, featured the orchestra of David Mendoza and organist Jesse Crawford plus guest vocalists (30 min., Saturday, 10:00–10:30 CBS, 1930).

24745 ***Paul Bruce Pettit.*** Pettit reported on film and other available entertainment in the Albany, New York, area (10 min., Monday through Friday, 6:45–6:55 P.M., WROW, Albany, NY, 1947).

24746 ***Paul Whiteman Buick Program.*** The talented Whiteman band and singers appeared along with such other stars as Virginia Rae, Frank Munn, the Pickens Sisters, Jack Fulton, Jane Vance, Red McKenzie, Irene Taylor, Mike Pingatore and Roy Bargy (30 min., Weekly, NBC, 1932–1933).

24747 ***Paul Whiteman Orchestra.*** The Whiteman band at the peak of its popularity was featured on a 60-minute music program (60 min., Tuesday, 9:00–10:00 P.M., CBS, 1929).

24748 ***Paul Whiteman Program.*** Paul Whiteman once more was the host who presented his band and weekly guests on the variety show sponsored by Liggett & Myers Company. Although many guest stars appeared, Whiteman's music was the chief attraction (30 min., Friday, 8:30–9:00 P.M., CBS, 1938).

24749 ***Paul Whiteman's Music Hall.*** Paul "Pops" Whiteman presented his excellent band and vocalists on the popular music show sponsored by Kraft Cheese. Cast regulars included Ramona, Johnny Hauser, Peggy Healy, Johnny Mercer, Bob Lawrence, the King's Men vocal group and Metropolitan Opera soprano, Helen Jepson (60 min., Thursday, 10:00–11:00 P.M., NBC, 1935).

24750 ***Paul Whiteman's Musical Varieties.*** Whiteman's Sunday evening musical program featured Ramona and singers Durelle Alexander, Bob Lawrence, Johnny Hauser, the King's Men, great trombonist Jack Teagarden, pianist Roy Bargy and Judy, Anne and Zeke Canova. Whiteman also had weekly guests such as tenors Frank Parker and Morton Downey and Walter Wolfe King, Suzanne Fisher, Helen Ault and Stuff Smith (45 min., Sunday, 7:45–8:30 P.M., NBC, 1936).

24751 ***Paul Whiteman's National Guard Assembly.*** The program was devoted to advancing the National Guard and featured the band with singers Mindy Carson and Johnny Thompson. Guests such as Elton Britt and Earle Wild also appeared (15 min., Transcribed, Weekly, late 1940s and early 1950s).

24752 ***Paul Wing—The Story Man* (aka *The Magic Typewriter Show*).** Paul Wing told entertaining stories for children (15 min., Monday, Wednesday and Friday, NBC-Red, 1933–1935).

24753 ***Paul Wing's Spelling Bee.*** Energine cleaning fluid sponsored this popular spelling bee (WJZ, New York, NY, 1939).

24754 ***Paula Stone.*** Miss Stone broadcast movie comment and conducted interviews with show business personalities (15 min., WNEW, New York, NY, 1942). *Paula Stone* on a later program discussed entertainment news from throughout the world (15 min., Monday through Friday, 12:00–12:15 P.M., WMGM, New York, NY, 1952).

24755 ***Paula Stone and Phil Brito.*** These two talented vocalists appeared on their entertaining music show (15 min., Tuesday and Thursday, 1:30–1:45 P.M., MBS, 1945).

24756 **Paule, Vern.** DJ (*Breakfast Brigade*, WJPS, Evansville, IL, 1948).

24757 **Paulette, Cyprian.** Tenor (*Cyprian Paulette*, vcl. mus. prg. with Mrs. C.C. Paulette as accompanist, KGHI, Little Rock, AR, 1929).

24758 **Pauley, Gay.** COM-HE (MBS, New York, NY, 1957).

24759 **Pauley, Marian.** Miss Pauley was billed as "Marian Pauley and her Steel Guitar" (KFQZ, Hollywood, CA, 1926).

24760 **Paulin, Pierre.** Newscaster (KDKA, Pittsburgh, PA, 1941).

24761 **Paulist Choristers.** Religious singing group that broadcast a two-hour program of choral music sponsored by Gimbel Brothers department store (WEAF, New York, 1923; WLWL, New York, NY, 1929).

24762 **Paull, Ed.** Sportscaster (*Top of the Sports*, WCED, DuBois, PA, 1949).

24763 **Paull [Paul] Sisters.** Julia and Ruth Paull sang accompanied by Phil Spitalny's Orchestra on the broadcast originating from New York City's Pennsylvania Grill (NBC-Red, 1928–1929).

24764 **Paulmann, Alice.** Soprano (WHN, New York, NY, 1925).

24765 ***Paul's Piano Pictures.*** Instr. mus. prg. by an unidentified pianist (WMMN, Fairmont, WV, 1937).

24766 **Paulsgrove, William H.** Sportscaster (WJEJ, Hagerstown, MD, 1940–1941).

24767 **Paulson, Al.** Newscaster (KOBH, Rapid City, SD, 1942; WLOL, Minneapolis, MN, 1944; KOTA, Rapid City, SD, 1945). Sportscaster (KOBH, 1942).

24768 **Paulson, Robert.** Newscaster (KATE, Albert Lea, MN, 1940–1942, 1944).

24769 ***(The) Pause That Refreshes.*** Coca-Cola sponsored the good music program that presented Frank Black conducting a 60-piece orchestra and choir of 35 voices (30 min., Friday, 10:30–11:00 P.M., NBC-Red, 1935). A later program format presented the Andre Kostelanetz orchestra and featured singer John Charles Thomas. Albert Spalding was the narrator (1942). Still later, *The Pause That Refreshes* was hosted by Roger Pryor. Vocalist Ginny Simms and Percy Faith's Orchestra provided the music (30 min., Sunday, 6:30–7:00 P.M., CBS, 1947).

24770 **Pavey, Iris Ruth.** Miss Pavey delivered beauty talks as "KOA's Invisible Stage Beauty" (KOA, Denver, CO, 1926).

24771 **Pavey, Richard.** Announcer and singer Pavey sang with the Angelus Trio and with the famous Fillmore Concert Band (WLW, Cincinnati, OH, 1927–1929).

24772 **Pavid, (Mme.) Emmy.** Travel talks such as "Life in a Swiss Village" (KOA, Denver, CO, 1926).

24773 **Pavioff, Joseph.** Baritone (WGBS, New York, NY, 1925).

24774 **Pavolino, Mary.** Leader (*Mary Pavolino Orchestra*, instr. mus. prg., WICA, Ashtabula, OH, 1942).

24775 **Paxton, Dorothy.** Contralto (WQJ, Chicago, IL, 1926).

24776 **Paxton, Mary.** Newscaster (WIBC, Indianapolis, IN, 1938).

24777 **Paxton, Patricia Ann "Pat."** COM-HE (WDET, Center, TX, 1954–1957).

24778 **Paxton, Tom.** DJ (*Variety Package*, WKY, Oklahoma City, OK, 1952–1957).

24779 **Payette, Marvelle.** Soprano (WGHP, Detroit, MI, 1926).

24780 **Payne, Albert.** Newscaster (WHDF, Calumet, MI, 1945).

24781 **Payne, Art.** Leader (Art Payne Orchestra, WHAS, Louisville, KY, 1926).

24782 **Payne, Doris.** Soprano (KFAE, Pullman, WA, 1924).

24783 **Payne, Ethel.** Singer (WOR, Newark, NJ, 1923).

24784 **Payne, George.** Tenor (WHAM, Rochester, NY, 1928–1929).

24785 **Payne, Howard.** Banjo soloist (WIBO, Chicago, IL, 1926).

24786 **Payne, Ida Mae.** COM-HE (WYNK, Baton Rouge, LA, 1960).

24787 **Payne, Jack.** Sportscaster (*Sports Round-Up* and *Sports Final*, KNOR, Norman, OK, 1950).

24788 **Payne, (Mrs.) Joe.** COM-HE (WDAN, Danville, IL, 1949).

24789 **Payne, Karl.** Violinist (WLW, Cincinnati, OH, 1926–1928).

24790 **Payne, Larry.** Newscaster (WTOL, Toledo, OH, 1939; WJR, Detroit, MI, 1941, 1945).

24791 **Payne, Lloyd "Painless."** DJ (*Hayride*, WDXB, Chattanooga, TN, 1948; *Painless Payne*, WDXB, 1950–1957). Sportscaster (*Sportscope*, WDXB, 1948).

24792 **Payne, Mabel Turner.** Singer (KPO, San Francisco, CA, 1926).

24793 **Payne, Mather.** Newscaster (WRGA, Rome, GA, 1937). Sportscaster (WRGA, 1941).

24794 **Payne, (Mrs.) Rex G.** COM-HE (KDET, Center, TX, 1956–1957).

24795 **Payne, Robert.** Newscaster (WCOU, Lewiston, ME, 1940).

24796 **Payne, Virginia.** Actress Payne began her radio career on WLW (Cincinnati, OH) in 1928. Her greatest fame, however, came decades later when she played the title role on *Ma Perkins* for the entire life of the program. Payne played the role on 2,065 broadcasts during the 27 years *Ma Perkins* was on the air. She also appeared on such daytime serial programs as *Carters of Elm Street*, *Lonely Women* and *Today's Children*. *See* ***Ma Perkins.***

24797 ***Payne's Children's Program.*** Uncle John Daggett told bedtime stories for children on his program (KHJ, Los Angeles, CA, 1924). *See* **Uncle John (Daggett)**.

24798 **Paynter, Teena.** COM-HE (KFTM, Ft. Morgan, CO, 1949).

24799 Payson, Rex. Pianist (KFI, Los Angeles, CA, 1926).

24800 Paysone, E. Leader (E. Paysone and his Orchestra, WEEI, Boston, MA, 1926).

24801 Payton, James "Jim." News analyst (WLOL, Minneapolis–St. Paul, MN, 1940; *Tribune Time*, WDSM, Superior, WI, 1947–1948). Sportscaster (WDSM, 1941).

24802 Pazmor, Radiana. Contralto (WJZ, New York, NY, 1928).

24803 Peabody, Eddy. Great banjo soloist (*Eddy Peabody*, instr. mus. prg., NBC, 1934; *Eddy Peabody*, instr. mus. prg., KFWB, Los Angeles, CA, 1937).

24804 Peabody and Frew. Banjo team (WJAX, Cleveland, OH, 1924).

24805 *Peaceful Valley* (aka *Peaceful Family*). Soothing quiet organ music was played by Milt Spooner. Announcer Fred Webber read inspirational poetry and prose on the weekly program (15 min., Monday through Saturday, 10;45–11:00 P.M., WFIL, Philadelphia, PA, 1940).

24806 Peach, Bob. Sportscaster (*WFBR Sports*, WFBR, Baltimore, MD, 1952).

24807 Peacher, Gwendolyn. Newscaster (KNX, Los Angeles, CA, 1944).

24808 Peacock, Edith Wing. Talked on various "psychological subjects" (WJZ, New York, NY, 1922).

24809 Peacock, Elizabeth. Violinist (KFWM, Oakland, CA,1926).

24810 Peak, E.N. Announcer (KFJB, Marshalltown, IA, 1926–1927).

24811 Peak, Gene. News analyst (WPAD, Paducah, KY, 1942; *D-X News* and *Sterling News*, WPAD, 1945–1947).

24812 Pearce, Albert W. "Al." Comedian, born July 15, 1898. Pearce began his career as a musician and a salesman, before singing on a local station with his brother, Cal, as part of the Real Estate Glee Club. He formed his "gang" and a hosted the *Happy Go Lucky Hour* program on a Pacific Coast station from 1929 to 1932. In the 30's, the "gang" appeared on the NBC-Red network. *See* ***Al Pearce and His Gang*** *and* **Pearce, Clarence "Cal."**

24813 Pearce, Clarence "Cal." A younger brother of Al Pearce, Cal joined with his brother to form a harmony singing team in 1924. Cal sang bass to brother Al's tenor (Pacific Coast radio, 1928). *See* **Pearce, Albert "Al."**

24814 Pearce, Norman. Announcer-reader (WMCA, New York, NY, 1923–1926).

24815 Pearce, Paul. Announcer (WEMC, Berrien Springs, MI, 1927).

24816 Pearch, Violet. Pianist (WJZ, New York, NY, 1923).

24817 Peardon, Patricia. Actress Peardon appeared on the evening dramatic program *Orphans of the Storm* and the daytime serial *Life Begins* aka *Martha Webster.*

24818 Peardon, Ross. Baritone (WMCA, New York, NY, 1925).

24819 Pearl, Clara B. COM-HE (WLBN, Lebanon, KY, 1960).

24820 Pearl, Jim. DJ (*Mr. Music Man*, KBTN, Neosho, MO, 1960).

24821 Pearl, Morey. Leader (Morey Pearl Orchestra, WNAC, Boston, MA, 1925; *Morey Pearl Orchestra*, instr. mus. prg., WEEI, Boston, MA, 1934).

24822 Pearl, Ray. Leader (*Ray Pearl Orchestra*, instr. mus. prg., NBC, 1936; WCAE, Pittsburgh, PA, 1938; WCCO, Minneapolis–St. Paul, MN, 1942). During his network broadcasts in the 1940s, Pearl was introduced in this way: "The sunset music of Ray Pearl and his orchestra from the Casino Gardens in Los Angeles."

24823 Pearl, Sumner. DJ (*Summer Time*, WDEM, Providence, RI, 1949).

24824 Pears, Tom. DJ (*Crossroads Jamboree*, KVOL, Lafayette, LA, 1949–1955).

24825 Pearson, Al. Newscaster (KFQD, Anchorage, AK, 1941). DJ (*Melody Ranch*, KSRO, Santa Rosa, CA, 1949–1952).

24826 Pearson, Drew. Popular newspaper columnist and radio commentator Pearson first broadcast with Robert S. Allen in 1935 before beginning his own program (*The Washington Merry-Go-Round*, 15 min., MBS, 1935). Pearson shortly thereafter began broadcasting his own program (*Listen America*, MBS, 1939; *Sunday Evening News of the World*, NBC, 1940–1941; *The Washington Merry-Go-Round*, NBC-Blue, 1942–1944; ABC, 1945–1947).

Pearson taught briefly at the University of Pennsylvania, before embarking on a series of other occupations. After beginning a career in journalism, Pearson teamed with Robert S. Allen to write an interesting *Washington Merry-Go-Round* column that eventually was syndicated to 620 newspapers. As the result of his columns and radio broadcasts, Pearson was called a liar by FDR, a S.O.B. by President Harry Truman and much worse by senators of such diverse political stances as Joseph McCarthy, Walter George, William Jenner, Theodore Bilbo and columnists Westbrook Pegler and Walter Winchell. It might be concluded that Drew Pearson must have been a valuable commentator if he could attract such a widely diverse set of enemies.

His successful radio career extended from the World War II era through 1953 on ABC. His attacks against perceived wrongs, probably was never more valuable than when he led the charge against Joseph McCarthy.

24827 Pearson, Ed. Sportscaster (WCOP, Boston, MA, 1939).

24828 Pearson, Fort. An announcer on Shreveport radio, before working in Port Arthur, Texas, and at KPRC (Houston, TX), Pearson had a long successful professional career, announcing many network programs such as *Guiding Light* and *Lonely Women.* Later while working as a newscaster, Pearson conducted the *United Press News* program (WMAQ, Chicago, IL, 1937; WMAQ and WENR, Chicago, IL, 1938–1941; WMAQ, 1942). Pearson also worked as a sportscaster during his broadcasting career (*The Football Prophet*, WENR, 1937; football play-by-play, NBC, 1937; WMAQ, Chicago, IL and WENR, 1939–1941; WMAQ, 1942–1945).

24829 Pearson, Gustav. Newscaster (KWJJ, Portland, OR, 1942).

24830 Pearson, James. Newscaster (KFNF, Shenandoah, IA, 1937).

24831 Pearson, James Estel. Newscaster (KWTO, Springfield, MO, 1937).

24832 Pearson, Jane. COM-HE (KTOW, Oklahoma City, OK, 1957).

24833 Pearson, John. Newscaster (KWTO-KGBX, Springfield, MO, 1938).

24834 Pearson, John A. Announcer (KEX, Portland, OR, 1929).

24835 Pearson, Johnny. DJ (*Ranch House Party*, KWWL, Waterloo, IA, 1948; *The Johnny Pearson Show*, KOWH, Omaha, NE, 1949–1952; WHB, Kansas City, MO, 1954).

24836 Pearson, L. Cello (KPO, San Francisco, CA, 1925).

24837 Pearson, Leon. News analyst (WWDC, Washington, DC, 1945; WMCA, New York, NY, 1944).

24838 Pearson, Mary. COM-HE (Kilgore, TX, 1951).

24839 Pearson, Paul. Leader (*Paul Pearson Orchestra*, instr. mus. prg., WLW, Cincinnati, OH, 1935).

24840 Pearson, Peggy. COM-HE (WDXL, Lexington, TN, 1955).

24841 Pearson, Rosemary. DJ (*Kiddie Request Time*, WJPB, Fairmont, WV, 1949).

24842 Pearson, Ted. Announcer, actor and singer Pearson began his radio career as a singer and announcer at WJKS (Gary, IN, 1927). Busy Pearson worked on many network programs (*Empire Builders*, NBC-Blue, 1927–1929, sponsored by the Great Northern Railway; the *Halsey Stuart Program*, NBC-Red, 1927–1931, sponsored by Halsey, Stuart and Company; *The Armour Hour*, NBC-Blue, 1927–1931, sponsored by the Armour Company; *The Studebaker Champions*, NBC-Blue, 1927–1930, sponsored by the Studebaker Corporation; *Conoco Adventures*, NBC, 1928–1929, sponsored by the Continental Oil Company; *Florsheim Frolic*, NBC-Red, 1928–1930, sponsored by Florsheim Shoes; the *Maytag Program*, NBC-Blue, 1928–1930, sponsored by Maytag Washers; and the *Paul Whiteman Painters* program, NBC-Blue, 1929–1930, sponsored by the Allied Paint Groups).

24843 Pearson, Wally. DJ (*1600 Revue*, KCRG, Cedar Rapids, IA, 1950).

24844 Pearson, William. Newscaster (WFCL, Odgensburg, NY, 1937; WWNY, Watertown, NY, 1941).

24845 Peary, Harold. Tenor (NBC, San Francisco, CA, 1929). Peary became more famous by portraying the "Great Gildersleeve." Peary later became a soft-spoken DJ on his local New York program, *The Harold Peary Show* (55 min., 1:00–1:55 P.M., WMGM, New York, NY, 1953). *See* ***The Great Gildersleeve.***

24846 Pease, Charles. DJ (*Strictly Music*, WWHG, Hornell, NY, 1960).

24847 Pease, Ruth. Pianist (KFWM, Oakland, CA, 1927).

24848 Peasley, Betheme. Reader (WOAW, Omaha, NE, 1923).

24849 Pebbles, Ed. DJ (*Sundial*, WBML, Macon, GA, 1952).

24850 ***Pebeco on Parade.*** Radie Harris interviewed motion picture stars and other guests. Singers Katherine Carrington and Milton Watson with Will Osborne's band provided the musical selections on the program. The sponsor was Pebeco Toothpaste (30 min., Friday, 9:00–9:30 P.M., MBS, 1934).

24851 **Pecararo, Dick.** Leader (*Dick Pecararo Orchestra*, instr. mus. prg., WIP, Philadelphia, PA, 1935).

24852 **Pecht, Jerry Lee.** Newscaster (WBAL, Baltimore, MD, 1937).

24853 **Peck, Albert.** DJ (*Juke Box*, KROS, Clinton, IA, 1948). Sportscaster (*Strikes and Spares*, KROS, 1948).

24854 **Peck, Anne S.** Peck broadcast travel talks (WJZ, New York, NY, 1923).

24855 **Peck, Charlotte.** COM-HE (KXOC, Chico, CA, 1955).

24856 **Peck, Clair W.** Sportscaster (KRUL, Corvallis, OR, 1947; *World of Sports*, KRUL, 1951). News analyst (*Jigsaw News*, KRUL, Corvallis, OR, 1948; KGAL, Lebanon, OR, 1953; KGHM, Brookfield, MO, 1957).

24857 **Peck, Curtis D.** Chief announcer (KPO, San Francisco, CA, 1927–1929). Peck frequently announced the station's slogan, "The Voice of San Francisco, The City by the Golden Gate."

24858 **Peck, Emmett.** Pianist (WFAA, Dallas, TX, 1928).

24859 **Peck, Gale.** DJ (*Platter Party*, KTIP, Porterville, CA, 1949).

24860 **Peck, Harry.** Newscaster (KFBI, Wichita, KS, 1940; KOIL, Omaha, NE, 1944–1945).

24861 **Peck, Merlyn.** Monologist (WLAW, Lawrence, MA, 1939).

24862 **Peck, Pauline.** COM-HE (WJZ, New York, NY, 1925).

24863 **Peck, Stanley.** Announcer (KSMR, Santa Maria, CA, 1927).

24864 **Peck, Thomas L.** Gardening talks (WJZ, New York, NY, 1923).

24865 **Peck, Victor.** Sportscaster (KTSW, Emporia, KS, 1945).

24866 **Peckham, (Dr.) Harriet Van Buren.** Dr. Peckham regularly broadcast her *Health Hints* program (WOR, Newark, NJ, 1923–1924).

24867 **Pecora [Pecorara], Joseph.** Pianist (NBC, 1929).

24868 **Pederson, Maurine.** COM-HE (KTOE, Mankato, MN, 1951).

24869 **Pederson, Viola and Ruth King.** Vocal duet team (KFSG, Los Angeles, CA, 1925).

24870 **Pedigo, Speck.** DJ (*Cowboy Serenade*, KCRC, Enid, OK, 1950).

24871 **Pedlow, Marian.** COM-HE (WDRF, Chester, PA, 1957).

24872 **Pedro, Don.** Leader (*Don Pedro Orchestra*, instr. mus. prg., WAVE, Louisville, KY, 1935).

24873 **Pedrosa, Alfonso and Sophia P. Pedrosa.** Spanish bass and soprano (WGN, Chicago, IL, 1928–1929).

24874 ***Pee Wee King and the Golden West Cowboys.*** Accordionist King took over Gene Autry's band after Autry went to Hollywood to begin his movie career. King's group was another CW band that featured western swing music (WSM, Nashville, TN, 1937).

24875 **Peebles, Edith.** Newscaster (KGKL, San Angelo, TX, 1941).

24876 **Peeck, Helen.** Pianist (KSD, St. Louis, MO, 1923).

24877 **Peeler, Doug.** Newscaster (WAYS, Charlotte, NC, 1946).

24878 **Peeples, Cornelius.** Actor Peeples was in the cast of *Road of Life*, *Silver Eagle*, *Mountie*, *Stepmother*, *Those Happy Gilmans* and *Tom Mix*.

24879 **Peeples, Gertrude.** Pianist (WKBW, Buffalo, NY, 1936).

24880 **Peer, Lee.** DJ (*Western Request*, KELK, Elko, NV, 1949).

24881 **Peerless Male Quartet.** Popular radio and recording vocal group (WEAF, New York, NY, 1925).

24882 ***Peerless Reproducers.*** An afternoon half-hour music program, the *Peerless Reproducers* featured an orchestra and male chorus. The sponsor was a radio set manufacturer [Peerless] that boasted about its product: "We are the lowest in an effort to emphasize the lower frequencies on the air." The show achieved a large listening audience (NBC-Pacific Coast Network, 1928).

24883 **Peery, James R.** Newscaster (WJDX, Jackson, MS, 1945).

24884 **Peet Trio.** Instrumental group consisting of John Holder, violin; William Warner, guitarist; and Mrs. Helen Shea, pianist (KOIL, Council Bluffs, IA, 1929).

24885 ***Pegeen Fitzgerald.*** Pegeen Fitzgerald appeared alone on her sustaining program on which she supplied lively chatter on a variety of topics (MBS, 1939). *See* ***The Fitzgeralds*** *and* **Husband-and-Wife Talk Shows.**

24886 ***Pegeen Prefers.*** Once again Pegeen Fitzgerald talked about a variety of topics on her popular program. Her specialty was to advise listeners on how to live better by spending less (25 min., Monday through Friday, 9:00–9:25 A.M., WOR, Newark, NJ, 1942). *See* **Husband-and-Wife Talk Shows,** ***Pegeen Fitzgerald*** *and* ***The Fitzgeralds.***

24887 ***Peggy Flynn and Charles King.*** The mixed singing team's comedy was as entertaining as their singing *Variety* said. King, formerly had been a Broadway star (15 min., Sunday, 9:45–10:00 P.M., NBC-Blue, 1934).

24888 **Peggy Jo.** COM-HE (KGDE, Fergus Falls, MN, 1949).

24889 ***(The) Peggy Lee Show.*** Great song stylist Peggy Lee sang with the Russ Case Orchestra on the music show sponsored by Rexall Drug Company. Program guests also performed weekly. Bill Adams was the announcer (30 min., Sunday, 7:30–8:00 P.M., CBS, 1951).

24890 ***Peggy's Doctor.*** A romantic daytime serial, *Peggy's Doctor* was broadcast three times weekly (15 min., 12:15–12:30 P.M., Monday, Wednesday and Friday, NBC-Red, 1934). Pioneer radio actors Rosaline Greene and James Meighan played the leading roles.

24891 **Pei, Lyn.** Newscaster (WKAT, Miami Beach, FL, 1942).

24892 **Peikin, Helen.** COM-HE (WGLI, Babylon, NY, 1960).

24893 **Peiss, Ed.** DJ (*Ballroom*, KOOK, Billings, MT, 1949; *Sugar and Spice* and *The 1230 Club*, KVOS, Casper, WY, 1950). Sportscaster (*Sports Record*, KOOK, 1952; KOOK, 1954; *Mustang Baseball*, KOOK, 1955).

24894 **Pelia, (Master) Louis.** Fourteen-year old accordionist Pelia was a pupil of Syl Prior (KPO, San Francisco, CA, 1923).

24895 **Pelle, Fred.** DJ (*Requestfully Yours*, WCRK, Morristown, TN, 1952).

24896 **Pellenpa, Carl.** Sportscaster (WJPD, Ishpeming, MI, 1960).

24897 **Pelletier, Julane.** Pianist (WJJD, Chicago, IL, 1936).

24898 **Pelletier, Lillian.** Soprano (KWFI, San Francisco, CA, 1926).

24899 **Pelletier, Paul.** Leader (*Paul Pelletier Orchestra*, instr. mus. prg., WMAS, Springfield, MA, 1941).

24900 **Pelletier, Vincent.** Announcer Pelletier worked on *Aunt Mary*, *Calling All Detectives* (narrator), *Coronation Contented Hour*, *First Nighter*, *Speak Up, America* (quiz) and *This Is Life* (actor).

24901 **Pelletteri, Carlo.** Pianist (WOKO, Peekskill, NY,1925).

24902 **Pellettieri, Vito.** Leader (Vito Pellettieri and his Orchestra, WSB, Atlanta, GA, 1926; WSM, Nashville, TN, 1926–1929).

24903 **Pellow, Marian.** COM-HE (WDRF, Chester, PA, 1956).

24904 **Peloquin, Pete.** DJ (WCHF, Chippewa Falls, WI, 1957).

24905 **Peltier, Bud.** Baritone (WWJ, Detroit, MI, 1923).

24906 **Peluso, Thomas.** Leader (*Thomas Peluso Orchestra*, instr. mus. prg., WHDH, Boston, MA, 1939).

24907 **Pelz, Mischa.** Leader (Mischa Pelz Orchestra, KOIN, Portland, OR, 1927).

24908 **Pemberton, Grace.** *Children's Hour* (KFRU, Columbia, MO, 1926).

24909 **Penberthy's Rambler Orchestra.** Popular California band (KFI, Los Angeles, CA, 1926).

24910 **Pence, Ozzie.** DJ (*Melody Lane*, KTMC, McAlester, OK, 1950).

24911 **Pencke, William.** Baritone (WFLA, Clearwater, FL, 1929).

24912 **Pendarvis, Paul.** Leader (*Paul Pendarvis Orchestra*, instr. mus. prg., WLW, Cincinnati, OH, 1934; NBC, 1935; WIBA, Madison, WI, 1936).

24913 **Pendergrast, William.** DJ (*Requestfully Yours*, WNBH, New Bedford, MA, 1949).

24914 **Pendleton, Andy.** Leader (Andy Pendleton's Dixie Revelers Orchestra, WGBS, New York, NY, 1927).

24915 **Pendleton, Lolly.** COM-HE (WWBG, Bowling Green, OH, 1956).

24916 **Pendleton, Madeline.** Reader (KYW, Chicago, IL, 1923).

24917 **Penfield, Addison "Add."** Newscaster (WDNC, Durham, NC, 1938). Sportscaster (WDNC, 1939; WSB, Atlanta, GA, 1942; *World of Sports* and *Sports Report*, WRNY,

Rochester, NY, 1947–1948; *Sports Quiz*, WRNY, 1949; WBIG, Greensboro, NC, 1952–1960).

24918 Penha, Michel. Cello soloist of the San Francisco Symphony Orchestra (KGO, San Francisco, CA, 1927).

24919 Penhallegon, E.B. Newscaster (WSOY, Decatur, IL, 1945).

24920 Penland, Nell Bates. COM-HE (WAYZ, Waycross, GA, 1957).

24921 Penman, Charles. Actor Penman was in the cast of *Chicago Theatre of the Air*, *Girl Alone*, *Rosemary*, *Stepmother* and *Uncle Walter's Dog House*.

24922 Penn, Bill. Newscaster (WBAX, Wilkes-Barre, PA, 1945).

24923 Penn, David. Newscaster (WCOL, Columbus, OH, 1937–1940).

24924 Penn, Penelope. Newscaster and COM-HE (WSB, Atlanta, GA, 1945).

24925 Pennell, William "Bill." News analyst (KFWB, Los Angeles, CA, 1944; *Bill Pennell Reports*, WORZ, Orlando, FL, 1947; *TNT News*, WMAK, Nashville, TN, 1948).

24926 Penner, Nancy. COM-HE (WLOW, Norfolk, VA, 1951).

24927 Penner, Raymond C. "Ray." News analyst (WGKY, Charleston, WV, 1941–1942; *Virginia in the News*, WLOW, Norfolk, VA, 1948). Sportscaster (WNEX, Macon, GA, 1946; *Sports Parade of the Air*, WLOW, 1947).

24928 Pennewell, Jack. Pennewell was billed as "Jack Pennewell and his Famous Twin Six Guitar" (WIBO, Chicago, IL, 1926).

24929 Pennewell, Ralph. Sportscaster (*Sports Varieties*, WWIN, Baltimore, MD, 1951–1955).

24930 Penney, Ed. DJ (*Penney Serenade*, WTAO, Cambridge, MA, 1949–1954).

24931 Penning, Herbert. "Boy saxophonist" (KMOX, 1926).

24932 Pennington, John. Newscaster (KFJI, Klamath Falls, OR, 1945).

24933 Pennington, Pen. Pennington broadcast book reviews (WFLA, Clearwater, FL, 1929).

24934 Pennsylvania Railroad Chicago Terminal Band. Commercial band (KYW, Chicago, IL, 1923).

24935 Penny, Gail. DJ (*Curfew Capers*, WJRD, Tuscaloosa, AL, 1948–1950; *Swing Your Partner*, WIS, Columbia, SC, 1954).

24936 Penny, Hank. CW singer, musician, songwriter, DJ and band leader Penny was influenced by the western swing movement. His first radio appearance was on WAPI (Birmingham, AL, 1933), followed by work at WWL (New Orleans, LA, 1936). He formed his own band — the Radio Cowboys — in 1936. The band's first broadcasts were on WKBC (Birmingham, AL., 1936) and WAPI (Birmingham, AL, 1936). The following year the band joined the *Chattanooga Playhouse* (WDOD, Chattanooga, TN, 1937). He took a job as early morning DJ on WSB (Atlanta, GA, 1940). A short time later, Penny joined the *Boone County Jamboree* (WLW, Cincinnati, OH, 1940) and the *Midwestern Hayride* (WLW, Cincinnati, OH, 1940). He later worked as a radio DJ (*Penny Serenade*, KGIL, San Francisco, CA, 1948; *Western Hit Parade*, KRKD, Los Angeles, CA, 1940s) and television performer.

24937 Penny, Prudence. Ms. Penny conducted a women's *Home Making Program* (KPO, San Francisco, CA, 1925).

24938 Penny, Prudence. COM-HE (*The Romance of Foods*, WOR, Newark, NJ, 1934).

24939 Penny, Prudence. COM-HE (KING, Seattle, WA, 1949).

24940 Penny, Warren. DJ (*The Music Wagon*, WROM, Rome, GA, 1960).

24941 *(The) Penny Singleton Show.* Penny played a widow with two children to raise on the situation comedy sponsored by Wheaties cereal. She was in the real estate business and this provided most plot situations for the show. The program's good supporting cast included Jim Backus, Bea Benadaret, Gale Gordon, Sheilah Kuehl and Marylee Robb. Music was by Von Urbanski's orchestra. Frank Martin was the announcer (30 min., Tuesday, 9:30–10:00 P.M., NBC, 1950). Penny Singleton starred in the *Blondie* motion picture series.

24942 *Penny Wise.* Ms. Wise chatted, played recorded music and sang a few songs on her pleasant local show. Allen Stratton was the announcer (60 min., Monday through Friday, 1:00–2:00 P.M., WBYN, Brooklyn, NY, 1941).

24943 *Penrod* (aka *Penrod and Sam*). The evening serial drama presented Booth Tarkington's comic novel, *Penrod and Sam*, in 14 chapters. Howard Merrill and Jimmy McCallion played the leading roles of Penrod and Sam. Eddie and Betty Wragge were also in the cast. The 14th and concluding chapter of Tarkington's book was broadcast on Saturday, May 31, 1930 (30 min., Saturday, 9:30–10:00 P.M., NBC-Pacific Network, 1930). In a later version, Billy Halop, Eddie Wragge and Jimmie McCallion played the leading roles (NBC, 1934).

24944 Penrose, Bernard. Newscaster (WBAB, Atlantic City, NJ, 1948).

24945 Penrose, Dixie and Peggy Driscoll. Sister singing team (KDYL, Salt Lake City, UT, 1928).

24946 Pens, Franklin. "Boy soprano" (WLW, Cincinnati, OH, 1924).

24947 Pensacola Philharmonic Orchestra. Local symphonic group (WCOA, Pensacola, FL, 1926).

24948 *Pensacola Speaks.* WCOA (Pensacola, FL) was one of the first stations in the country to have a telephone talk show. *Pensacola Speaks* was first broadcast in 1960 and was still on the air in 1998.

24949 *Penthouse Serenade.* Vocal mus. prg. with tenors Jack Fulton and Don Mario and an orchestra conducted by Charles Gaylord. Emery Hall was the host of the program sponsored by Maybelline Cosmetics. Hollywood beauty adviser Dorothy Hamilton appeared weekly to offer hints and information (NBC, 1935).

24950 *Penzoil Program.* Charles "Chick" Sale, veteran vaudeville comic, played the role of Wheel Wilkins on the early comedy sketch (CBS, 1930). A later version of *The Penzoil Program* became a music program with the Harry Sosnik Orchestra and the King's Jesters male vocal group featured (30 min., Sunday, 7:00–7:30 P.M., CBS, 1932).

24951 *People in the News.* Distinguished news commentator Dorothy Thompson discussed national and international events from the perspective of great personalities currently "making the history of the world" (15 min., Weekly, 8:45–9:00 P.M., NBC-Red, 1937). *See* **Thompson, Dorothy**.

24952 *People Worth Talking About.* Cosmo Hamilton told anecdotes about such famous people as H.G. Wells, Rudyard Kipling, Oscar Wilde and P.G. Wodehouse (45 min., Weekly, WOR, New York, NY, 1932).

24953 *Peoples' Payroll Party.* Sears Roebuck Company sponsored the show in order to boost the U.S. Treasury's War Bond Sales Campaign during World War II. The series of programs featured comedian Owen Dunning, stories by Charles Robison, the mixed vocal chorus of Joseph Sampietro and the studio orchestra. The series was hosted and written by Johnny Carpenter (30 min., Weekly, KOIN, Portland, OR, 1942). *See* **Wartime Radio**.

24954 *Peoples' Poetry.* Herb Newcomb read his own poetry that *Variety* said was of much higher quality than that Edgar Guest had broadcast years previously (15 min., Sunday, 9:45–10:00 P.M., WENR, Chicago, IL, 1949).

24955 *Peoria Ramblers.* CW mus. prg. (WMDB, Peoria, IL, 1937).

24956 Pepe, Johnny. Sportscaster (WPIC, Sharon, PA, 1940–1946; *Sports Review*, WPIC, 1948–1952). Newscaster (WPIC, 1946).

24957 Pepe, Marie. COM-HE (WHXY, Bogalusa, LA, 1955).

24958 Pepper, Ken. DJ (KVER, Clovis, NM, 1960).

24959 Pepper, Vernon. Newscaster (WSJN, Bridgeton, NJ, 1939).

24960 Pepper, William. Newscaster (WPAY, Portsmouth, OH, 1945).

24961 Pepper Maids. Female vocal harmony trio that specialized in blues songs (NBC, San Francisco, CA, 1929).

24962 *Pepper Young's Family.* Originally known as *Red Adams* and *Red Davis* before becoming *Forever Young* in 1935, when the Davis family was transformed into the Young family, the serial became *Pepper Young's Family* in 1936. The program was notable in that Elaine Carrington was the writer throughout the entire broadcast run and that the first leading actor in the title role of Red Adams was a young Burgess Meredith. He was not, however, the only well known actor who appeared on the program during its run: Mason Adams, Bill Adams, Curtis Arnall, Marion Barney, Tony Barrett, Alan Bunce, Thomas Chalmers, Blaine Cordner, Michael Fitzmaurice, Richard Gordon, G. Swaye Gordon, George Hall, Stacy Harris, Eunice Howard, Irene Hubbard, Leon Janney, John Kane, James Krieger, Greta Kvalden, Maureen McManus, Madeleine Pierce, Bob Pollock, Elliott Reid, Jack Roseleigh, Laddie Seaman, Annette Sorell, Jean Sothern, Chester Stratton, Charles Webster, Edwin R. Wolfe, Elizabeth Wragge and Lawson Zerbe. The directors were John Buckwalter, Chick Vincent and Ed Wolfe. William Meeder was the musical director. Martin Block, Alan Kent and Richard Stark were the announcers.

24963 Pepple, Ruth. Pianist (NBC, 1933; WJZ, New York, NY, 1939).

24964 *Pepsi-Cola Hour.* Al Clauser and his Oklahoma Cowboys, an entertaining country-western group and a great San Antonio radio favorite, were featured on the CW program. George Irving was the announcer (30 min., Tuesday, 7:00–7:30 P.M., KABC, San Antonio, TX, 1947).

24965 Perata, Pete. DJ (*Jump Time*, KDON, Santa Cruz, CA, 1948).

24966 Perazzo, Eugene "Gene." Pianist-organist (WMH, Cincinnati, OH, 1925 and WKRC Cincinnati, OH, 1925–1926; *Gene Perazzo*, instr. mus. prg., WLW, 1936).

24967 Perceval, Irene. Harpist (WHAP, New York, NY, 1927).

24968 Perches, Jose. Concert pianist (*Jose Perches*, instr. mus. prg., KFWB, Hollywood, CA, 1927).

24969 Percy, David. Baritone (KFWB, Hollywood, CA, 1928).

24970 Percy, Vincent. Organist (WEAR, Cleveland, OH, 1925).

24971 Perdue, Toby A. COM-HE (WLSD, Big Stone Gap, VA, 1957).

24972 Perea, Tina. DJ (*Latin American Serenade*, KVER, Albuquerque, NM, 1948).

24973 Perfect, George. Organist (WRR, Dallas, TX, 1926).

24974 *Perfect Circle Concert Hour.* The "hour" program was actually a two-hour performance by the Cincinnati Symphony Orchestra conducted by Vladimir Bakaleinkoff (120 min., Saturday, 6:00–8:00 P.M., WLW, Cincinnati, OH, 1929).

24975 Perfetto, John J. Trombonist-baritone with the Columbia Broadcasting System Symphony Orchestra (CBS, 1929).

24976 Pergola Brothers. Accordion and banjo team (WHN, New York, NY, 1925 and WRNY, New York, NY, 1925).

24977 Pericola, Frank. Sportscaster (*Sports Spotlight*, WEAR, Pensacola, FL, 1948; WDLP, Panama City, FL, 1954).

24978 Perkal, Ethel. Soprano (WRST, Long Island, NY, 1928).

24979 Perkins, Bobbye. Actress Perkins appeared on the *Brown-Bilt Footlites* program (CBS, 1929).

24980 Perkins, C.B. Sportscaster (WAAB, Boston, MA, 1931).

24981 Perkins, Ed. DJ (*Mr. Music Man*, WHDM, McKenzie, TN, 1960).

24982 Perkins, Elsie. Pianist (WJZ, New York, NY, 1922).

24983 Perkins, Glen. Sportscaster (*Sports Review*, KANS, Wichita, KS, 1948–1949; *Sports Salute*, KFH, Wichita, KS, 1950).

24984 Perkins, (Reverend) J.R. Station chaplain (KOIL, Council Bluffs, IA, 1928–1929).

24985 Perkins, Jack. Sportscaster (WFKY, Frankfort, KY, 1952).

24986 Perkins, Lyman Almy. Organist (KQV, Pittsburgh, PA, 1922).

24987 Perkins, Maggie. COM-HE (WOCB, West Yarmouth, MA, 1956–1957).

24988 Perkins, Margaret. COM-HE (WKTC, Barstow, CA, 1960).

24989 Perkins, Mona. Contralto (WGHP, Detroit, MI, 1926).

24990 Perkins, Mrs. Mrs. Perkins was known to listeners only as the "KMA Poultry Lady" (KMS, Shenandoah, IA, 1928).

24991 Perkins, Omar. Director (Playmate Orchestra, WHB, Kansas City, MO, 1929).

24992 Perkins, Ray. Pianist-singer-comedian Perkins was born August 23, 1897. After a successful songwriting career, he first appeared on radio in 1923 by creating the character of "Judge, Jr." on the *Judge Magazine* program (WJZ, New York, NY). Later, Perkins appeared with a female performer on his *Ray Perkins and Princess Aloha* program (WGBS, New York, NY, 1925). After his performances on the *Judge* magazine program were completed in 1927, he returned to song writing for Warner Brothers for three years before once more returning to radio in 1930.

24993 *Perkins, Ray and Princess Aloha.* Comedy and music team (WGBS, New York, NY, 1925).

24994 Perkins, Russ. Singer (*Russ Perkins*, vcl. mus. prg., WAAF, Chicago, IL, 1935).

24995 Perl, Betty. COM-HE (WEOK, Poughkeepsie, NY, 1954).

24996 Perl, Dorothy. Pianist (WIP, Philadelphia, PA, 1926).

24997 Perleno, Hilda. Singer (WSPB, Toledo, OH, 1929).

24998 Perlin, Bernie. Sportscaster (KOLD, Tucson, AZ, 1955–1960).

24999 Perlin, Mildred. Reader (WIBO, Chicago, IL, 1925).

25000 Perlman, Maurice. Pianist (WHN, New York, NY, 1926).

25001 Pernin, (Reverend) O.J. Reverend Pernin spoke on self-help topics such as, "Twenty Minutes of Good Reading" (KYW, Chicago, IL, 1924–1929).

25002 Peronto, Mildred. Contralto (WBZ, Springfield, MA, 1927).

25003 Perrazo, Gene. Organist (*Gene Perrazo*, instr. mus. prg., WLW, Cincinnati, OH, 1936).

25004 Perrazzo, Don. DJ (*Sunrise Serenade*, KBON, Omaha, NE, 1948;1952–1954).

25005 Perrie, Don. Sportscaster (*The World of Sports*, WJBO, Baton Rouge, LA, 1954; *Jax World of Sports*, WJBO, 1955).

25006 Perrin, Carolyn. COM-HE (WGWC, Selma, AL, 1956).

25007 Perrin, (Mrs.) Jessie Pugsley. Soprano (KPO, San Francisco, CA, 1923).

25008 Perrin, Keyes. DJ (*Record Riddles*, WOR, New York, NY, 1947; *WROW Ballroom*, WROW, Albany, NY, 1949–1951; *Ruppert Sports Parade*, WROW, 1952).

25009 Perrin, Pat. DJ (*Koffee Kup Kapers*, KRGH, Fayetteville, AR, 1948).

25010 Perrin, Wally. Leader (Wally Perrin's Packard Dance Orchestra, KFI, Los Angeles, CA, 1928).

25011 Perrou, Joan. COM-HE (KALB, Alexandria, LA, 1955).

25012 Perry, Bess. Contralto (WBAL, Baltimore, MD, 1926–1929).

25013 Perry, Betty Sue. COM-HE (WSRK-FM, Shelbyville, IN, 1949).

25014 Perry, Bill. DJ (*The Man Who Came to Breakfast*, WPJB, Providence, RI, 1949).

25015 Perry, Bob. DJ (*Bob Perry's Melody Merry-Go-Round*, WLAW, Boston-Lawrence, MA, 1949; *980 Club*, WCAP, Lowell, MA, 1952; *CAP-980 Club*, WCAP, 1960).

25016 Perry, Charles. DJ (*Music Around the Clock*, WWSR, St. Albans, VT, 1949).

25017 Perry, Dell. Female pianist (*Piano Capers*, instr. mus. prg., NBC, 1930).

25018 Perry, Dick. DJ (WBOB, Galax, VA, 1949; *Pittsburgh Matinee*, WPIT, Pittsburgh, PA, 1950).

25019 Perry, Edith. Actress Perry was in the cast of *The Woman in White* daytime serial program.

25020 Perry, Frances. Soprano (WBZ, Springfield, MA, 1924).

25021 Perry, Fred. Harmonica soloist (*Fred Perry*, instr. mus. prg., KGHI, Little Rock, AR, 1929).

25022 Perry, George. DJ (*Swing Session*, WARM, Scranton, PA, 1947).

25023 Perry, Henry L. Director (KPO Vocal Ensemble, KPO, San Francisco, CA, 1929).

25024 Perry, Jake. DJ (*Woody's Survey*, WDDY, Gloucester, VA, 1960).

25025 Perry, Jay. DJ (WTOP, Washington, DC, 1957).

25026 Perry, Joe. DJ (*The Music Shop*, WGFG, Kalamazoo, MI, 1952).

25027 Perry, Kathryn. Saxophonist (WHO, Des Moines, IA, 1927).

25028 Perry, Kay. COM-HE (KYOU, Greeley, CO, 1956).

25029 Perry, Ken. Sportscaster (*Hemm's Sportcast* and *Campus Sportscast*, KFKA, Greeley, CO, 1948).

25030 Perry, Linc. Sportscaster (*Speaking of Sports*, KBRO, Bremerton, WA, 1950–1952).

25031 Perry, Nick. DJ (WPIT, Pittsburgh, PA, 1948).

25032 Perry, Norman. Sportscaster (WSAI, Cincinnati, OH, 1937).

25033 Perry, Pat. COM-HE (WTTC, Towanda, PA, 1960).

25034 Perry, Portia. DJ (WHAT, Philadelphia, PA, 1957).

25035 Perry, (Mrs.) Robert. Pianist (WFLA, Clearwater, FL, 1929).

25036 Perry, Robert. Singer (WBZ, Springfield, MA, 1925).

25037 Perry, Robert N. Sportscaster (WORL, Boston, MA, 1939–1940).

25038 Perry, Ron. Leader (*Ron Perry Orchestra*, instr. mus. prg., WOR, Newark, NJ, 1936).

25039 Perry, Rush. Sportscaster (*Sports Parade*, WRHP, Tallahassee, FL, 1948).

25040 Perry, Russ. DJ (*Record MC*, WTOL, Toledo, OH, 1947).

25041 Perry, Stuart "Stu." DJ (*Strictly Off the Record*, WWSR, St. Albans, VT, 1950; *Music Around the Clock*, WWSR, 1954).

25042 Perry, T. Stanley. Tenor (WGHP, Detroit, MI, 1926).

25043 Perry, Tom. DJ (*Night Club*, WBCM, Bay City, MI, 1960).

25044 Perry, Tony. DJ (*Juke Box Matinee*, WFRL, Freeport, IL, 1948).

25045 Perry, Tut. DJ (*T.P.'s Wigwam*, WCDL, Carbondale, PA, 1952; *T.P.'s Wigwam*, WHLM, Bloomsburg, PA, 1954). Sportscaster (*Sports Supplement*, WCDL, 1951; WCDL, 1956–1957).

25046 Perry, Wes. Sportscaster (*Sports Review*, KLUF, Galveston, TX, 1950–1951).

25047 Perry, Wib. DJ (*Wib Perry Show*, WCAX, Burlington, VT, 1947).

25048 Perry, Will C. Leader of the orchestra on the *Three-in-One Theater* program (NBC, New York, NY, 1928). The commercially sponsored Will Perry and his Interwoven [men's socks] Orchestra appeared on the network (NBC-Blue, New York, NY, 1929). He also was musical director on the *Songs of the Season* program (NBC-Red, New York, NY, 1929).

25049 Perry, William S. Announcer (WLBW, Oil City, PA, 1925).

25050 Perry, William S., Jr. Tenor (WSM, Nashville, TN, 1928–1929).

25051 Perry and Russell. *Variety* called them a "unique two-man singing orchestra." The two men played the saxophone, French horn, banjo, ukulele and other instruments. *Radio Digest* (Dec., 1924) said of them, "If you happen to have a grouch when you tune in on them, they'll give you a quick hunch toward cheerfulness" (WOR, Newark, NJ, 1924–1925).

25052 *(The) Perry Como Show.* Romantic crooner Como (CBS, 1943–1955) had been on the national scene for many years, but in 1948 he began simulcasting his program on radio and TV. For several seasons, the Fontaine Sisters vocal group were featured with him. Como was one of the top radio crooners of his era. Only Bing Crosby and Frank Sinatra were his real competition for several decades. His relaxed singing style and pleasant personality were his trademarks.

A barber before beginning a professional singing career in 1933, Como came to national attention in 1944 when he made his first record and began appearing on *The Chesterfield Supper Club* radio program. After Como came to television in 1948 with *The Chesterfield Supper Club* radio-television simulcast, it marked the beginning of his 40 year TV career.

25053 *Perry Goes to Town.* Perry Martin sang and the popular piano duo of Al and Lee Reiser played on this sustaining program (15 min., Friday, 11:45–12:00 midnight, NBC-Blue, 1942).

25054 *Perry Mason.* Earle Stanley Gardner created the character of Perry Mason, a crack lawyer whose major function was to defend the innocent, a task he performed consistently with total success on radio from 1943 to 1955. The radio format of *Perry Mason* was as a quarter-hour daytime serial, before it became a popular television program starring Raymond Burr in the title role. John Larkin and Santos Ortega, at times, played Perry Mason on radio. The radio cast included: Joan Alexander, Donald Briggs, Matt Crowley, Frank Dane, Maurice Franklin, Betty Garde, Mary Jane Higby, Mandel Kramer, John Larkin, Jan Miner, Santos Ortega, Bartlett Robinson, Arthur Vinton, Gertrude Warner, and Charles Webster. Earle Stanley Gardner, Dan Shuffman, Irving Vendig and Eugene Wang were the writers. The producers were Leslie Harris and Tom McDermott and the directors were Hoyt Allen, Ralph Butler, Carlo De Angelo, Carl Eastman and Arthur Hanna. Paul Taubman was the musical director. Bob Dixon and Richard Stark were the announcers (15 min., Monday through Friday, CBS, 1943).

25055 Perry's Ye Old New England Choir. Traditional vocal group (WBZ, Springfield, MA, 1924).

25056 Perryman, Tom. DJ (*Hillbilly Hit Parade*, KSIJ, Gladewater, TX, 1952).

25057 Pershing, Estelle. Director, Pershing Choral Club (KYW, Chicago, IL, 1922).

25058 Pershing Palace Orchestra. Club dance band (WOK, Chicago, IL, 1926).

25059 Persico, John. DJ (*Musicross*, WISL, Shomokin, PA, 1952).

25060 Persinger, Elsie. Pianist (*Elsie Persinger*, instr. mus. prg., WDBJ, Roanoke, VA, 1936).

25061 Person, Berdell. COM-HE (KIMN, Denver, CO, 1957).

25062 Person, Violet. COM-HE (WMTC, Vancleve, KY, 1951).

25063 *(The) Person and Mission of Jesus.* This program included a religious lecture delivered by Dr. William Sullivan, the Mission preacher of the Unitarian Layman's League (WFAA, Dallas, TX, 1924).

25064 (The) Personality Twins. Singing team of Mildred McKiney and Ruth McKiney (KOIN, Portland, OR, 1928).

25065 Persons, Fern. Actress Persons appeared on the *Girl Alone* and *Helpmate* daytime serial programs.

25066 Persons, June. COM-HE (WELY, Ely, MN, 1957).

25067 Persons, Johnny. While a junior in the electrical engineering course at the Georgia School of Technology, Persons was "elected" Chief Announcer at station WGST (Atlanta, GA, 1925).

25068 Pesenti, Phyllis. COM-HE (KMED, Medford, OR, 1960).

25069 *Pet Milk Show.* See ***The Bob Crosby Show*** and ***Saturday Night Serenade.***

25070 *Pet Peeves.* Host Jack Shannon collected the peeves of New Yorkers on his sustaining program. They had lots of them and expressed each one vigorously (15 min., Saturday, 8:30–8:45 P.M., WMCA, New York, NY, 1938).

25071 *Pete Kelly's Blues.* Jim Mosher wrote the entertaining series that combined good jazz with the many adventures cornetist and band leader Pete Kelly encountered in the speakeasy era of the Roaring Twenties. Jack Webb played the title role of Pete Kelly, the leader of his Pete Kelly's Big Seven band, on the sustaining program. The excellent dixieland group was led by talented cornetist Dick Cathcart. The six other fine musicians joining him were Marty Carb, Nick Fatool, Matty Malneck, Bill Newman, Elmer Schneider and Ray Schneider. Only a program such as the *Chamber Music Society of Lower Basin Street* consistently offered jazz as good as that broadcast weekly on *Pete Kelly's Blues* (30 min., Wednesday, 9:00–9:30 P.M., NBC, 1951).

25072 *Pete Mack's Moosickers.* Veteran comic Pete Mack played a "German professor" who led a brassy, little German street band on the sustaining program. Tenor Jimmy McManus also appeared on the show (15 min., Thursday, 2:45–3:00 P.M., NBC-Red, 1935).

25073 Peter, Ruth. Soprano (WRC, Washington, DC, 1924).

25074 *Peter Donald Show.* Stanback Headache Powder sponsored the transcribed program featuring dialect comedian, Peter Donald. He was assisted by the Three Flames — an instrumental group consisting of guitar, piano and string bass. The announcer was Dennis James (15 min., Transcribed, Various Stations, 1947).

25075 *Peter Lind Hayes Show.* Al Singer produced and Frank Musiello directed the show that *Variety* said was an attempt to make Peter Lind Hayes a "Saturday Arthur Godfrey." In addition to Hayes, his wife, Mary Healy, was on hand to assist him as were such program regulars as singers Jerry Vale and Leslie Uggams, pianist Teddy Wilson and the Norman Leyden Orchestra. Guests such as the Mariners vocal group appeared regularly (30 min., Saturday, 2:00–2:30 P.M., CBS, 1954).

25076 Peter Pan Society Orchestra. Talented music group (WEBJ, New York, NY, 1926).

25077 *Peter Pfeifer.* This short-lived program was conceived by Jack Pearl, who played the title role. Pearl created the program when he thought that people might be tired of his Baron Munchausen character. When the character of Pfeifer, a German tavern keeper, was not successful, he immediately switched back to the Baron.

25078 Peterman, H.J. Conductor (U.S. Naval Academy Band, WBAL, Baltimore, MD, 1928).

25079 Peterman, Maurice. Baritone (WFAA, Dallas, TX, 1928).

25080 Peters, Alice. Violinist (WCBD, Zion, IL, 1926).

25081 Peters, Ann. COM-HE (KWCJ, Natchitoches, LA, 1949).

25082 Peters, Becky. COM-HE (WJAG, Norfolk, NE, 1955).

25083 Peters, Bill. DJ (*The Breakfast Show*, WESB, Bradford, PA, 1950).

25084 Peters, Bob. DJ (*Weekend in Western Montana*, KGVO, Missoula, MT, 1954).

Sportscaster (WAFB, Baton Rouge, LA, 1954–1955).

25085 Peters, Bobby. DJ (*Bobby Peters Show*, WBAP, Fort Worth, TX, 1949).

25086 Peters, Esther. COM-HE (WLNH, Laconia, NH, 1957).

25087 Peters, Irene. COM-HE (KWLM, Willmar, MN, 1949–1957).

25088 Peters, John. DJ (*Swing Shanty*, WPDX, Clarksburg, WV, 1948; *Dawn Busters*, WPDX, 1949; *Swing Shanty* and *Dawn Busters*, WPDX, 1950–1954).

25089 Peters, Ken. Actor Peters was in the cast of *Aunt Mary*, *Life with Luigi* and *One Man's Family*.

25090 Peters, Ken. Sportscaster (KTMS, Santa Barbara, CA, 1944; play-by-play broadcasting, KTMS, 1947; California league baseball play-by-play, KTMS, 1948; *Ken Peters' Sport News*, KIST, Santa Barbara, CA, 1950).

25091 Peters, Marianne. COM-HE (KMTV, Omaha, NE, 1957).

25092 Petersen, Chester "Chet." Announcer (WBBM, Indianapolis, IN, 1925).

25093 Petersen, Harry. Sportscaster (KOBH, Rapid City, SD, 1941; *Grainbelt Scoreboard*, KOTA, Rapid City, SD, 1947–1948; *The Scoreboard*, KOTA, 1949).

25094 Petersen, Helen. COM-HE (KFH, Wichita, KS, 1960).

25095 Peterson, Alma. Soprano (NBC, New York, NY, 1929).

25096 Peterson, Anna J. COM-HE (Miss Peterson conducted a domestic science program, *Table Talk*, KYW, Chicago, IL, 1923–1925). Peterson, who was known as "Our Radio Mama," was the head of the Home Service Department of the Peoples Light and Coke Company, Chicago, IL. She was considered to be an outstanding authority on American cooking. She later broadcast daily home service items of interest to women (WENR, Chicago, IL, 1929).

25097 Peterson, Arnold. DJ (*Musical Reveille*, WATW, Ashland, WI, 1949–1954).

25098 Peterson, Arthur "Art." Actor Peterson appeared on *Bachelor's Children*, *Barton Family*, *Girl Alone*, *Guiding Light* and *Silver Eagle, Mountie*.

25099 Peterson, Bill. DJ (*Tops in Pops*, KTAR, Phoenix, AZ, 1954).

25100 Peterson, Bob. DJ (*Hi-Fi Holiday*, WSSV, Petersburg, VA, 1960).

25101 Peterson, Carlton. DJ (*East Listening*, KGFW, Kearney, NE, 1948).

25102 Peterson, Curt. Peterson was a singer turned announcer (WJZ, New York, NY, 1925–1926). He announced *The Mennen Men* program and became the supervisor of announcers at NBC in 1929. He was born in Albert Lea, Minnesota, February 12, 1898. After serving in World War I as a lieutenant of infantry, he graduated from Oregon University in 1920. Before entering radio, he was a singer and teacher of voice at Miss Mason's Castle School for Girls.

25103 Peterson, Delece. DJ (*Studio Party*, KASH, Eugene, OR, 1949).

25104 Peterson, Eddy. Sportscaster (*Sportscast*, KSUB, Cedar City, UT, 1948; *Sports Revue and Prevue*, KSUB, 1951).

25105 Peterson, Frank. Tenor (WOAW, Omaha, NE, 1926).

25106 Peterson, Don. DJ (*Musical Scrapbook*, KICM, Mason City, IA, 1950).

25107 Peterson, George. DJ (*Dancing Party*, WBSC, Bennettsville, SC, 1952).

25108 Peterson, Gertrude. Contralto (WEAF, New York, NY, 1923).

25109 Peterson, Gladys. Soprano (WMAQ, Chicago, IL, 1927).

25110 Peterson, Hal. DJ (*Personality Time*, WSAR, Fall River, MA, 1952; WARA, Attleboro, MA, 1954).

25111 Peterson, Helen. COM-HE (WLDY, Ladysmith, WI, 1949).

25112 Peterson, Howard L. Organist (WJJD, Mooseheart, IL, 1926).

25113 Peterson, Ida. Soprano (WCBD, Zion, IL, 1926).

25114 Peterson, James. DJ (*Time and Temperature*, WORZ, Alton, IL, 1950).

25115 Peterson, Janice. COM-HE (KBRC, Freeport, TX, 1954).

25116 Peterson, Juanita. Singer (WOW, Omaha, NE, 1927).

25117 Peterson, Kenneth "Ken." DJ (KIFI, Idaho Falls, ID, 1948; *Playing Favorites*, WOC, Davenport, IA, 1950).

25118 Peterson, Kitty. COM-HE (WVOP, Vidalia, GA, 1954).

25119 Peterson, Laura J. COM-HE (KCVL, Colville, WA, 1960).

25120 Peterson, Lewis W. Concert tenor and organizer of the Brahms Quartet (KSTP, St. Paul–Minneapolis, MN, 1929).

25121 Peterson, Lucille. Singer (WMCA, New York, NY, 1932).

25122 Peterson, Marilyn. COM-HE (WDLB, Mansfield, WI, 1955).

25123 Peterson, Martha. COM-HE (WBZ, Springfield, MA, 1924).

25124 Peterson, May. Metropolitan Opera star Peterson (WJZ, New York, NY, 1921–1923) was said to have been heard by 100,000 listeners when she broadcast in 1923.

25125 Peterson, Nancy. Actress Peterson appeared on the *Hilltop House* daytime serial program.

25126 Peterson, Pete. DJ (*Music for Matinee*, KICD, Spencer, IA, 1950).

25127 Peterson, Rolfe B. DJ (KOVO, Provo, UT, 1949; *Rolfe Peterson Show*, KSL, Salt Lake City, UT, 1952–1957; KGO, San Francisco, CA, 1960).

25128 Peterson, Skip. DJ (KLIZ, Brainerd, MN, 1960).

25129 Peterson, Walter. Harmonica and guitar country music performer known as "The Kentucky Wonderbean" (WLS, Chicago, IL, 1928–1929).

25130 Peterson, Walter. DJ (*Wake Up With Walt*, KELP, El Paso, TX, 1949).

25131 Peterson, Warren. Leader (Warren Peterson's Hollyfornians Orchestra, KFQZ, Hollywood, CA, 1926).

25132 Peterson, Wesley. Nine-year-old flutist who was a pupil of Agnes Peterson (KPO, San Francisco, CA, 1923).

25133 Peterson, William. Mandolin soloist (KYW, Chicago, IL, 1923).

25134 Petit, Maude Hanson. Musician Petit talked on such topics as "What We See and Hear in Music" (WCAU, Philadelphia, PA, 1925).

25135 Petoello, Joan. COM-HE (WPAC, Patchogue, NY, 1954).

25136 Petranka, Joe. Sportscaster (WSFA, Montgomery, AL, 1939–1940).

25137 Petri, Egon. Concert pianist (*Egon Petri*, instr. mus. prg., NBC, 1934).

25138 Petrice, Lenore. Soprano (KFWM, Oakland, CA, 1927).

25139 Petrich, Lee. DJ (*Cowboy Jamboree*, KONO, San Antonio, TX, 1949–1954).

25140 Petrie, Cordia Greer. Reader (WGY, Schenectady, NY, 1924).

25141 Petrie, George. Actor Petrie appeared on *Amazing Mr. Malone*, *Backstage Wife*, *Big Town*, *Call the Police*, *Casebook of Gregory Hood* (title role), *Charlie Wild, Private Eye* (title role), *The Falcon* (title role), *Philo Vance*, *Superman* and *Tennessee Jed*.

25142 Petrie, Howard. Announcer (WBZA, Springfield, MA, 1927–1929). Petrie's network announcing included work on *Abie's Irish Rose*, *Blondie*, *Camel Caravan*, *Jack Carson Show*, *Jimmy Durante Show*, *Judy Canova Show* and *The Man I Married*.

25143 Petronella, Tony. Sportscaster (*Sports Spotlight*, WRIB, Providence, RI, 1947).

25144 Petroskey, La Vonne. COM-HE (WATK, Antigo, WI, 1960).

25145 Petrova, Olga. Actress Petrova read poetry (WEAF, New York, NY, 1925).

25146 Petruzzi, Jack. Actor Petruzzi was in the cast of *Green Hornet*, *Lone Ranger*, *Ma Perkins* and *Road of Life*.

25147 Pettack, Keith. DJ (*Mississippi Valley Concert*, KXGI, Fort Madison, IA, 1949). Sportscaster (*Sports on Parade*, KXGI, 1951).

25148 Pettay, Bob. Leader (*Bob Pettay Orchestra*, instr. mus. prg., WTAM, Cleveland, OH, 1942).

25149 Pettay, Fran. DJ (*Disc Digger*, WHK, Cleveland, OH, 1947; *Music Hall* and *The Hour of Entertainment*, WJR, Detroit, MI, 1948–1949; *Night Watchman*, WJR, 1950).

25150 Pettegrew, C.W. Sportscaster (WOSU, Columbus, OH, 1937–1942; WOSU, 1947).

25151 Pettersen [Petersen], Leon. DJ (*The Big Eight*, WISC, Madison, WI, 1949–1952).

25152 Petti, Dick. DJ (*Music for Birds*, WBCK, Battle Creek, MI, 1952).

25153 *Petticoat on the Air.* The weekly program presented an unidentified female newscaster, who might have been Isabel Manning Hewson (15 min., Weekly, WFIL, Philadelphia, PA, 1936). *See* ***Petticoat Philosopher.***

25154 *Petticoat Philosopher.* Isabel Manning Hewson, the Petticoat Philosopher, broadcast only good news and her commentary about it. She was sponsored by the Good 'n' Rich Cheese Company (15 min., Tuesday and Thursday, 11:45–12:00 noon, WFIL, Philadelphia, PA, 1937).

25155 Pettit, Lorring. Saxophonist (WJAZ, Chicago, IL, 1923).

25156 Pettit, Lloyd. Sportscaster (*The Last Word in Sports*, WTMJ, Milwaukee, WI, 1952).

25157 Petty, Fred. Farm program announcer (WLS, Chicago, IL, 1928). Petty was nationally recognized as an expert farm news reporter.

25158 Petty, Winston. Cellist (KTAB, Los Angeles, CA, 1925).

25159 Petway, (Mrs.) Jake. Pianist and member of the Crystal Quartet (WLAC, Nashville, TN, 1929).

25160 Petya, Margaret A. COM-HE (WWSW, Pittsburgh, PA, 1949).

25161 Peyer, Joe. Leader (Joe Peyer's St. Paul Athletic Club Orchestra, WCCO, Minneapolis–St. Paul, MN, 1925; station orchestra leader, WCCO, 1928–1929).

25162 Peyser, Ethel R. COM-HE (WJZ, New York, NY, 1925).

25163 Peyton, Doc. Leader (*Doc Peyton Orchestra*, instr. mus. prg., WGY, Schenectady, NY, 1934).

25164 Peyton, Eddie. Leader (*Eddie Peyton Orchestra*, instr. mus. prg., WJAS, Pittsburgh, PA, 1935).

25165 Peyton, Stanley. Newscaster (WAKR, Akron, OH, 1940–1941).

25166 Pfaender, Edna. COM-HE (WKLY, Hartwell, GA, 1955).

25167 Pfaff, Ray. Leader (Ray Pfaff Orchestra, WGY, Schenectady, NY, 1923; Ray Pfaff and his Orchestra, WHAS, Louisville, KY, 1923).

25168 Pfahler, Fred. Announcer (WTAR, Norfolk, VA, 1925–1929). Newscaster (WROL, Knoxville, TN, 1941–1942).

25169 Pfau, Franz. Pianist-arranger (WMAQ, Chicago, IL, 1929).

25170 Pfefferkorn, Bettemae. Singer-reader (KHJ, Los Angeles, CA, 1925).

25171 Pfeger, Martha. Pianist (WORD, Batavia, IL, 1925).

25172 Pfeiffer, Bob. Newscaster (WMT, Cedar Rapids, IA, 1947).

25173 Pfeiffer, Keith. DJ (*Western Caravan*, KFJB, Marshalltown, IA, 1949).

25174 Pfeiffer, Mary Lou. COM-HE (WRFD, Worthington, OH, 1956–1957).

25175 Pfeiffer, Rudy. Sportscaster (KGON, Oregon City, OR, 1954). DJ (*Musicman*, KERG, Eugene, OR, 1960).

25176 Pfeil, (Mrs.) E.J. COM-HE (WNMP, Evanston, IL, 1949).

25177 Pfiel, Jack. DJ (*Blackjack's Bedlam*, WMAJ, State College, PA, 1950).

25178 Pfizenmayer, Henry. Organist (WJAY, Cleveland, OH, 1927).

25179 Pflaum, Irving. Newscaster (WBBM, Chicago, IL, 1945).

25180 Pfluke, Enelle. COM-HE (WMIE, Miami, FL, 1957).

25181 Phair, Jean. COM-HE (WKTV, Utica, NY, 1960).

25182 (The) Phantom Clarinetist. The mysterious musician was a high school girl, Luise Reszke (WLW, Cincinnati, OH, 1927).

25183 *(The) Phantom Dancer.* Hennafoam Liquid Shampoo (Liquid Sunshine for Your Hair) sponsored the romantic effort by a tenor to sing and speak sweetly to his "imaginary" female companion. The announcer began the program by saying, "A beautiful girl and a handsome man are dancing. Mayfair knows him as the Phantom Dancer. He sings his songs as he is dancing with his new romance." The Dancer talked sweet talk and sang with a thin voice that lacked emotional color (15 min., Transcribed, early 1930s).

25184 *(The) Phantom Pilot.* Langendorf Bread Company sponsored the transcribed adventure show for juveniles. The story of the entertaining series told of the exciting adventures of the Phantom Pilot and O'Hara, his Irish assistant. None of the show's actors were identified (15 min., Monday through Friday, 6:15–6:30 P.M., KHJ, Los Angeles, CA, 1938).

25185 *Phantom Strings.* *Phantom Strings* was a program of romantic string music conducted by Aldo Ricci (NBC, 1934).

25186 (The) Phantom Violinist. Another "mysterious musician," that we now know was Henry Selinger, virtuoso violinist and director of the Drake Concert Ensemble (WGN, Chicago, IL, 1926).

25187 *(The) Phantom Voice and His Bedtime Story.* The Phantom, not otherwise identified, told stories for children on the early evening program (KTHS, Hot Springs National Park, AR, 1926).

25188 Pharis, Dorothy. COM-HE (WPNX, Phenix City, AL, 1954).

25189 Pheatt, Jack. "Junior announcer" (WSPD, Toledo, OH, 1925–1929).

25190 Pheatt, Merrill. Announcer (WSPD, Toledo, OH, 1925).

25191 Pheiffer, Bill. DJ (*Musical Nightkap*, WKAP, Allentown, PA, 1949; *Polka Parade*, WWNR Beckley, WV, 1952). Sportscaster (WTUX, Wilmington, DE, 1960).

25192 Phelan, Betty Jane. COM-HE (WHOB, Gardner, MA, 1949).

25193 Phelan, John. Sportscaster (KTSM, El Paso, TX, 1954–1955).

25194 Phelan, Tom. DJ (KREM, Spokane, WA, 1957; *Mid-Morning Melodies*, KVOS, Bellingham, WA, 1960).

25195 Phelps, Edith. Soprano (KFXF, Colorado Springs, CO, 1926).

25196 Phelps, Eleanor. Actress Phelps was in the cast of *The Life and Loves of Dr. Susan* (title role) and *Young Dr. Malone* daytime serial programs.

25197 Phelps, G. Allison. Phelps, the "Radio Philosopher," broadcast various philosophic essays (KNX, Hollywood, CA, 1925). Phelps later worked as an announcer (KMTR, Hollywood, CA, 1928–1929).

25198 Phelps, Norman. Leader (*Norman Phelps Hillbilly Rounders Orchestra*, CW mus. prg., WTAR, Norfolk, VA, 1935).

25199 Phelps, Sue. COM-HE (WKOY, Bluefield, WV, 1954).

25200 Phelps, Stuart. Newscaster (KFOX, Long Beach, CA, 1941).

25201 Phi Delta Chi Music Makers. Collegiate music group (KSTP, St. Paul, MN, 1929).

25202 *Phil Baker Show* (aka *The Armour Hour* and *Honolulu Bound*). Veteran vaudeville comedian-accordionist Baker hosted the variety show. Comic situations were provided by Bottle, his British butler, played by Harry McNaughton, and Beetle, an heckling off-stage voice produced first by Ward Wilson and later by Sid Silvers. Baker's cast included: Mabel Albertson, Artie Auerbach, Oscar Bradley, Hank Ladd, Harry McNaughton, Agnes Moorehead, Jack Murray, Sid Silvers, Florence Stewart and Ward Wilson. Music was by the Seven G's (vocal group) and the Hal Kemp and Frank Shields orchestras. The show was written by Phil Baker, Hal Block and Arthur Phillips (30 min., Weekly, 6:30–7:00 P.M. CST, CBS, 1936). Three years later the program was known as *Honolulu Bound*. The sponsor was Dole Pineapples. The Andrews Sisters and the bands of Eddie deLange, Hal Kemp and Frank Shields were featured. Harry von Zell was the announcer. Baker eventually achieved great success as a quizmaster on *Take It or Leave It* and other quiz programs. *See* ***Armour Jester, Beechnut Hour*** *and* ***Take It or Leave It.***

In a later show in 1951, *The Phil Baker Show,* Baker's jokes and commercials were recorded, and a local Baltimore announcer, Buddy Deane, played records, read the news, gave horse race results and hosted the unusual format (120 min., Monday through Saturday, 2:00–4:00 P.M., WITH, Baltimore, MD, 1951).

25203 *Phil Cook Show* (aka *Phil Cook — the Aunt Jemima Pancake Man*). Veteran radio comic Cook appeared in dramatic sketches, played the uke and sang on the quarter-hour show sponsored by Bristol-Myers Company. Music was supplied by the Andy Sanella Orchestra (15 min., Monday, Wednesday and Friday, 8:45–9:00 P.M., NBC-Blue, 1933). In an earlier morning show sponsored by the Quaker Oats Company's Aunt Jemima pancakes, Cook sang, told jokes and stories for 15 minutes each weekday. Much of Cook's program —*Phil Cook the Aunt Jemima Pancake Man*— consisted of rhymed humor about current events presented in the format of his trademark "I See By the Papers" song.

Cook's program began with the sound effects of a rooster crowing, an alarm clock ringing and the sound of a yawn. The announcer then said: "With these familiar morning sounds, the Quaker Oats Company invites you to Aunt Jemima's breakfast table, where Phil Cook, the pancake man, entertains each weekday morning with a fresh batch of his home-cooked ditties."

After singing his opening song, Cook greeted his listeners this way:

> Good morning folks. Get going. It's breakfast time. Did you have a pleasant night? How's your appetite? When the rooster's crowing and alarm clocks chime, it's Aunt

Jemima Pancake time. What a breakfast any man makes when they're in sight. Let a stack of golden pancakes start the day right. Here's one man who's knowing he's in his prime at Aunt Jemima's Pancake time.

Well, here we are again. Now if you'll just pull your chairs up to our breakfast tables, while Aunt Jemima's endeavoring to keep your plates filled with those luscious golden browns, the pancake man will annoy you by dishing out some more of my home-cooked foolishness, using the little ole ukulele for a frying pan.

Well, dad, I suppose you're going to the fair today. What? I never heard of holding 'em in winter, but that's what the paper says, "Fair today and tomorrow." I know the fellow who writes those forecasts and he isn't feeling very well—as the weather hasn't agreed with him lately—which reminds me.

Cook then followed this introduction by singing, "It Don't Do Nothing but Rain."

25204 ***Phil Regan Camp Show.*** During the Korean War, tenor Phil Reagan hosted the music show from various service installations such as the Travis Air Force Base (30 min., Sunday, 5:00–5:30 P.M., NBC, 1951). *See* **Wartime Radio.**

25205 ***Phil Regan Show.*** Tenor Regan performed with Jud Conlon and his Rhythmaires and Dick Valente's Orchestra on the music show sponsored by the United States Steelworkers of America Union (WMCA, New York, NY, 1959).

25206 ***Phil Spitalny's Music.*** Spitalny's orchestra broadcast from New York's Hotel Pennsylvania's Grill (30 min., Saturday, 7:30–8:00 P.M., NBC-Red, 1930). *See* ***Hour of Charm*** *and* **Spitalny, Phil.**

25207 **Philadelphia and Reading Railroad Band.** Forty-five member musical organization (WPG, Atlantic City, NJ, 1925).

25208 **Philadelphia Cafe Orchestra.** Restaurant dance band (WIP, Philadelphia, PA, 1923).

25209 ***Philadelphia Symphony Orchestra.*** The orchestra was sponsored by Philco in one of its earliest radio appearance (CBS, 1931); *Philadelphia Symphony Orchestra*, symphonic concert music program conducted by Eugene Ormandy (CBS, 1938).

25210 **Philbrick and His Younker Tea Room Orchestra.** Restaurant band (WHO, Des Moines, IA, 1926).

25211 ***Philco Amateur Show.*** Philco Radio and Television Company sponsored the local radio amateur show hosted by Jimmie Allen, station WIP's press chief (30 min., Saturday, 8:00–8:30 P.M., WIP, Philadelphia, PA, 1936).

25212 ***Philco Boys.*** Philco Radio Company sponsored the comedy-music program that dramatized an "informal evening" at the home of one of the boys. Captain Ezra Higby told the boys of his trouble with a neighborhood widow, and they gave him helpful advice. Many songs were performed during the half-hour program by the "boys," Irv, Harry, Tom and Ted accompanied by Johnny the accordionist (30 min., Thursday, 9:30–10:00 P.M., NBC-Pacific Coast Network, 1928). *See* ***Philco Camp Fire Program.***

25213 ***Philco Camp Fire Program.*** Begun as the *Philco Boys*, the program changed its format to one in which "Captain Ezra Higby" entertained the "Philco Boys" by telling them his fishing yarns around the campfire. The boys (Irv, Harry, Tom and Ted with Johnny, their accordionist accompanist) listened to the Captain's tales and frequently sang their lively songs (NBC-Pacific Coast Network, 1928).

25214 ***Philco Hour*** (aka ***The Philco Symphony, The Philco Concert Orchestra*** and ***The Philco Symphonic Hour).*** Philco Company sponsored the program of light opera music introduced by Henry M. Neely in the role of the "Old Stager." The program originally featured sopranos Lois Bennett and Barbara Mauel (Manuel). The orchestra was conducted by William Artzt. The announcer was Ted Husing (30 min., Wednesday, 10:00–10:30 P.M., CBS, 1930). When the program began in 1927, it was known as *The Philco Hour of Theater Memories.* In that format it was 60 minutes in length and broadcast by NBC. After the program changed networks and was reduced to 30 minutes in length, it was known variously as *The Philco Symphony, The Philco Concert Orchestra* and *The Philco Symphonic Hour. See* ***The Philco Hour of Theater Memories.***

25215 ***(The) Philco Hour of Theater Memories.*** Philco Radio Corporation sponsored the program that pioneered in the broadcasting of operettas. Henry M. Neely, in the role of "The Old Stager," hosted the program that featured soprano Jessica Dragonette and tenor Colin O'Moore. The cast also included sopranos Emily Woolery and Kitty O'Neal; tenors Dan Gridley and Henry Shope contraltos Mary Hoople and Doris Doe; baritone Walter Preston; and bass Charles Robinson. Harold Sanford was the program's musical director. The program's theme was "Memories," written by Neeley and Sanford.

During its first season on the air the program presented Victor Herbert's *The Only Girl* and *Mlle. Modiste* starring Fritzi Sheff, the operetta's original star, and Donald Brian from the cast of the first American production of *The Merry Widow.* The *Philco Hour of Theater Memories* presented the first radio broadcasts of such operettas as *The Vagabond King, The Student Prince, Blossom Time, My Maryland* and *Maytime.* The program led to the great popularity and national fame of Jessica Dragonette and established her as one of radio's outstanding singers. *See* ***Philco Hour.***

25216 ***Philco Radio Playhouse.*** Joseph Cotten was the executive producer and narrator of the transcribed dramatic series. Each program was an adaptation of plays previously broadcast on the *Philco Television Playhouse.* Eugene Schiess directed and James Burton produced the series, unique in that it came to radio *from* television (30 min., Wednesday, 9:00–9:30 P.M., ABC, 1953).

25217 **(The) Philco Serenaders.** An excellent commercial orchestra (WMAK, Buffalo, NY, 1926).

25218 ***Philharmonic Society of New York Orchestra.*** John Barbirolli conducting the orchestra on the symphonic music program (CBS, 1939).

25219 **Philip, Ray.** Leader (*Ray Philip Orchestra*, instr. mus. prg., WHDH, Boston, MA, 1939).

25220 ***Phillip Morris Playhouse.*** The famous dramatic series presented various stories of suspense and adventure in various broadcast runs from 1939 to 1943 and later from 1948 to 1949 on NBC. William Spier directed the latter broadcast series. NBC again broadcast the program (1951–1952), now called *The Phillip Morris Playhouse on Broadway* with Charles Martin as director. In its various formats, the program usually presented entertaining dramatic fare for listeners. The cast included: Alan Reed (Teddy Bergman), Charlie Cantor, Ray Collins, Raymond Edward Johnson, Bill Johnstone, John McIntire, Jeanette Nolan, Ann Thomas, Barbara Weeks and Ward Wilson. Music was supplied by the orchestras of Ray Bloch, Johnny Green and Russ Morgan. The program was directed by Jack Johnstone, Charles Martin and William Spier.

25221 ***Phillip Morris Program.*** Phillip Morris Cigarettes sponsored the music show that first featured baritone Phil Duey, soprano Barbara Schermerhorn and Leo Reisman's Orchestra (30 min., Wednesday, 9:30–10:00 P.M., NBC-Red, 1933). The following year the day and time of broadcast changed (30 min., Tuesday, 8:00–8:30 P.M., NBC-Red, 1934). Later, the Russ Morgan Orchestra and various vocalists were featured on the show. Johnny Roventini, who was 43-inches tall and weighed less than 50 pounds, was the famous bellboy whose characteristic cry, an extended, "Call for Phillip Morris," was a permanent feature of the program. Roventini was used in print advertising and radio cigarette commercials for many years. Phillip Morris found him in 1933 after searching New York hotels looking for the "best bellhop in town." They found him working at the Hotel New Yorker and transformed his life by making him a nationally known celebrity.

25222 ***Phillip Morris Presents.*** The good music program featured the Johnny Green Orchestra and singers Glenn Cross, Floyd Sherman, Beverly Freeland, Jack Smith, the Six Sea Breezes, the Groove Group, and Charles O'-Connor (30 min., Weekly, NBC-Blue and MBS, 1939–1940).

25223 **Phillippe, Gene.** DJ (WKID-AM and WKID-FM, Urbana, IL, 1949).

25224 **Phillippi, Mary Jane.** COM-HE (KGPH, Flagstaff, AZ, 1951; KBUZ, Phoenix, AZ, 1960).

25225 **Phillippi, Shirley.** DJ (WYVE, Wytheville, VA, 1956).

25226 **Phillips, Ann.** Pianist (WEAF, New York, NY, 1925).

25227 **Phillips, Arthur.** Phillips was a tenor on the *Roxy and His Gang* program (NBC, New York, NY, 1928).

25228 **Phillips, Becky.** COM-HE (WRR, Dallas, TX, 1954).

25229 **Phillips, Bill.** DJ (*Disk Doings,* 120 min., Monday through Friday, 3:00–5:00 P.M.,

WABY, Albany, NY, 1947; *Coffee Club* and *You Name It, We Play It*, WABY, 1948; *Window Shopping*, WABY, 1950; *Bill Phillips Show*, WBAX, Wilkes-Barre, PA, 1952–1957). Sportscaster (WBAX, 1950).

25230 **Phillips, Billie P.** COM-HE (WBLE, Batesville, MI, 1955).

25231 **Phillips, Burns.** Marimbaphone soloist (KFI, Los Angeles, CA, 1928).

25232 **Phillips, C.W.** DJ (*Juke Box Revue*, WBBB, Burlington, NC, 1948–1950).

25233 **Phillips, Charles "Charlie."** DJ (KTBS, Shreveport, LA, 1947–1948).

25234 **Phillips, Charles F.** Announcer (WFBL, Syracuse, NY, 1925).

25235 **Phillips, Chuck.** DJ (*Sunrise Serenade*, WMAW, Milwaukee, WI, 1949; WEMP, Milwaukee, WI, 1954–1957).

25236 **Phillips, Conrad.** Sportscaster (*Sports Time*, WGIV, Charlotte, NC; WSVA, Harrisonburg, VA, 1957). DJ (*1600 Club*, WGIV, Charlotte, NC, 1950).

25237 **Phillips, Curtis.** Announcer (KFWV, Portland, OR, 1927).

25238 **Phillips, Dale.** Sportscaster (*Sports Wire*, KXOB, Stockton, CA, 1955).

25239 **Phillips, Dewey.** DJ (WHBQ, Memphis, TN, 1949; *Red, Hot and Blue*, WHBQ, 1952–1956).

25240 **Phillips, D.G.** Sportscaster (WFBC, Greenville, SC, 1939).

25241 **Phillips, Donald.** Newscaster (WTAL, Tallahassee, FL, 1946). Sportscaster (WTAL, 1946).

25242 **Phillips, Dorothy Ehler.** Soprano (WFXF, Colorado Springs, CO, 1926).

25243 **Phillips, Ed.** DJ (WRUF, Gainesville, FL, 1949).

25244 **Phillips, Elena.** COM-HE (KAFP, Petaluna, CA, 1960).

25245 **Phillips, Forrest.** Tenor (KGO, San Francisco, CA, 1926).

25246 **Phillips, G. Allison.** Announcer (KMTR, Los Angeles, CA, 1928).

25247 **Phillips, George.** DJ (*Top O' the Morning*, WJNO, West Palm Beach, FL, 1952).

25248 **Phillips, (Rev.) George W.** Reverend Phillips broadcast religious messages (KTAB, Oakland, CA, 1928).

25249 **Phillips, Gordon.** Sportscaster, football play-by-play and Roanoke boxing bouts blow-by-blow broadcasting (WROV, Roanoke, VA, 1947).

25250 **Phillips, H.O.** Leader (Bessemer Hawaiian Orchestra, WAPI, Auburn, AL, 1929).

25251 **Phillips, Hazel.** COM-HE (WWNR, Beckley, WV, 1956–1957).

25252 **Phillips, Howard.** Tenor (NBC, 1928–1929).

25253 **Phillips, (Dr.) Hubert.** Newscaster (KMJ, Fresno, CA, 1945).

25254 **Phillips, Irna.** Prolific writer Phillips wrote the evening dramatic show *Welcome Valley* and the daytime serial programs *The Brighter Day, The Guiding Light, Lonely Women, Painted Dreams, The Right to Happiness, The Road of Life, Today's Children* and *The Woman in White*.

25255 **Phillips, Jean.** COM-HE (WARK, Hagerstown, MD, 1956–1957).

25256 **Phillips, Joseph A. "Joe."** DJ (*Carolina in the Morning*, WRNO, Orangeburg, SC, 1952; WDIX, Orangeburg, SC, 1956–1957).

25257 **Phillips, Kay.** Soprano (KFRC, San Francisco, CA, 1926).

25258 **Phillips, Ken.** DJ (*Light 'n' Easy*, KAFP, Petaluma, CA, 1954).

25259 **Phillips, Lee.** DJ (*The Morning Mayor*, WPEC, Washington, DC, 1960).

25260 **Phillips, Len.** DJ (*All Night Revue*, KWBR, Oakland, CA, 1950).

25261 **Phillips, Louise.** Soprano (WSAI, Cincinnati, OH, 1925).

25262 **Phillips, Lulu.** Soprano (WEAF, New York, NY, 1925–1926).

25263 **Phillips, Mary.** Singer (NBC, 1934).

25264 **Phillips, Oral.** Newscaster (KHSL, Chico, CA, 1939).

25265 **Phillips, Pete.** Tenor (KTHS, Hot Springs National Park, AR, 1928–1929).

25266 **Phillips, Phil.** Director (Springtime Serenaders [orchestra], WFLA, Clearwater, FL, 1928–1929).

25267 **Phillips, Phil.** DJ (*1260 Bandstand*, WNXT, Portsmouth, OH, 1949–1954).

25268 **Phillips, Ralph.** DJ (*Tune Shop*, WFBR, Baltimore, MD, 1948; *Encore Matinee*, WFBR, 1952; *Melody Ballroom*, WFBR, 1954).

25269 **Phillips, Ronald.** Clarinetist (KOMO, Seattle, WA, 1928–1929).

25270 **Phillips, Ros.** DJ (*Klub Kare*, KARE, Atchison, KS, 1959).

25271 **Phillips, Rose.** Violinist (WEAF, New York, NY, 1925).

25272 **Phillips, Rubin.** Violinist (WLW, Cincinnati, OH, 1923).

25273 **Phillips, Ruth.** Soprano (*Ruth Phillips*, vcl. mus. prg., WMAQ, Chicago, IL, 1934). Blues singer (WCFL, Chicago, IL, 1935).

25274 **Phillips, Steve.** DJ (*TNT Show*, WJKO, Springfield, MA, 1949).

25275 **Phillips, Thomas C.** Newscaster (WDAK, West Point, GA, 1940). Sportscaster (WDAK, 1940).

25276 **Phillips, Walter.** DJ (WCPO, Cincinnati, OH, 1949; *Mission Midnight*, WLW, Cincinnati, OH, 1952).

25277 **Phillips, Wendy.** COM-HE (WIP, Philadelphia, PA, 1954–1955).

25278 **Phillips, Winnie.** COM-HE (WAYE, Baltimore, MD, 1957).

25279 **Phillipson, Christine.** Violinist (NBC, New York, NY, 1929).

25280 **Philo, Viola.** Miss Philo was a dramatic soprano who performed on the *Roxy's Gang* program (NBC, 1928).

25281 **Philpott, W.A.** Coin specialist Philpott spoke on such topics as, "The Story of American Coins" (WFAA, Dallas, TX, 1923).

25282 **Philson, Betty.** Actress Philson was in the cast of the daytime serial programs *Life Begins* aka *Martha Webster* and *We the Abbotts*.

25283 **Phipps, Jack.** Actor (NBC, San Francisco, CA, 1929).

25284 **Phipps, Jack.** Pianist (*Jack Phipps*, instr. mus. prg., WBT, Charlotte, NC, 1936).

25285 **Phipps, Joe.** Newscaster (KTBC, Austin, TX, 1941, 1945). Sportscaster (KTBC, 1941).

25286 ***Phone Again Finnegan.*** Stu Erwin played the title role of Finnegan, the harassed superintendent of the Welcome Arms apartment house. The sponsor was the Household Finance Company. Finnegan was particularly troubled by his Swedish janitor, played by the show's co-author Harry Stewart. Florence Lake played the apartment house's switchboard operator. Music was supplied by the Lou Kosloff Orchestra. Ken Niles was the announcer (30 min., Thursday, 10:30–11:00 P.M., CBS, 1946).

25287 ***Phonograph Records.*** Although this was not the program's name, it is worthy of inclusion, since it apparently was the first time that phonograph records were played on a regularly scheduled basis. The program was broadcast over St. Louis University's station WEW in 1921. Brother George E. Rueppel, who conducted the "program," may be said to have been the first DJ.

25288 ***Phonograph Records of Popular Music.*** Programs of 15 minutes of recorded music broadcast five times per week in the afternoon (WLW, Cincinnati, OH, 1923. A morning period of recorded music a half-hour in length was scheduled five times per week by WLW.

25289 ***Phrase That Pays.*** Red Benson conducted the quiz sponsored by Colgate-Palmolive Company. Ted Brown later replaced Benson. The show was a replacement for the *Bob and Ray* program (15 min., Monday through Friday, 11:30-ll:45 A.M., NBC, 1953).

25290 **Phreaner, Bill.** Newscaster (KFIO, Spokane, WA, 1941).

25291 ***Phyllis and Her Fiddle.*** Instr. mus. prg. by an unidentified female musician (WBIG, Greensboro, NC, 1939).

25292 ***Physical Culture.*** "Spike" Shannon conducted one of the first early morning exercise programs (KDKA, Pittsburgh, PA, 1924).

25293 ***Physical Culture.*** Bernarr McFadden, publisher of *Physical Culture* and *True Story* magazines, sponsored the program on which Mary (Nora Sterling) and Bob (William Brent), known as "America's Radio's Sweethearts," traveled across the continent several times visiting unusual places and meeting interesting people (30 min., Friday, 9:00–9:30 P.M., CBS, 1930–1932).

25294 ***Physical Culture Magazine Hour*** **(aka *The Physical Culture Hour*).** McFadden Publications, publishers of *Physical Culture Magazine*, sponsored the series of dramatized stories (30 min., Monday, 9:00–9:30 P.M., CBS, 1927–1930).

25295 ***Physical Fitness.*** Charles E. Osborne conducted his exercise program (WFAA, Dallas, TX, 1924).

25296 ***Piano Capers.*** Female pianist Dell Perry provided the musical capers (NBC, 1930).

25297 ***(The) Piano Dances.*** Pianist Joseph Kahn performed on the instrumental music show (15 min., Weekly, NBC-Red, 1940–1941).

25298 ***Piano Pals.*** The piano team of Dorothy Sherman and M. Pitot were featured on the instrumental music program (NBC, 1934).

25299 ***Piano Rambles.*** Pianist Estelle Barnes was the featured performer on the music program (WAAF, Chicago, IL, 1935).

25300 ***(The) Piano Symphony.*** This special program was unique in that it presented 225 pianists playing 125 pianos at the same time from the Indianapolis Music Festival held at the Butler University Field House. Twenty-five of the pianists were teachers. The 200 others were students playing double pianos (30 min., 3:30–4:00 P.M. CST, NBC-Red, 1936).

25301 ***(The) Piano Twins.*** Lester Place and Robert Pasocelle, known as the Piano Twins, were often featured on WJZ's famous *Slumber Hour* music program (WJZ, New York, NY, 1929 and also over WEAF-NBC, New York, NY, 1929). They were busy in the following decade as well: *The Piano Twins*, instr. mus. prg. with Place, Pascocelle and tenor Chick Bullock, (15 min., Monday, 7:30–7:45 P.M., NBC, 1930; *The Piano Twins*, instr. mus. prg., 15 min., 5:45–6:00 P.M., WINS, New York, NY, 1932; *The Piano Twins*, instr. mus. prg., WGR, Buffalo, NY, 1937; WKBW, Buffalo, NY, 1938).

25302 **Pica, Joe.** DJ (*Tunes Before Noon*, WHLM, Bloomsburg, PA, 1954).

25303 **Picard, John.** Writer Picard wrote *Hawthorne House*, *Pretty Kitty Kelly* and *Wendy Warren and the News.*

25304 **Piccolo, Don.** DJ (*Don Piccolo Show*, WKBI, St. Marys, PA, 1949–1952).

25305 ***Pick and Play with Bob and Ray.*** Bob Elliott and Ray Goulding conducted the sustaining quiz show. *Variety* said that the considerable comic talents of Bob and Ray were wasted when they hosted an audience participation quiz like this one (30 min., Friday, 9:30–10:00 P.M., NBC, 1953).

25306 **Pickard, Carey.** Announcer (WMAZ, Macon, GA, 1926–1927).

25307 **Pickard, Obed "Dad."** CW singer Pickard appeared with many of the string bands that appeared on the *Grand Ole Opry* (WSM, Nashville, TN, 1926–1927). This led to Pickard becoming leader of the Pickard Family, a busy family group of CW musicians and singers (WJR, Detroit, MI, 1928). *See* ***The Pickard Family*** *and* ***The Pickard Family and the Missourians.***

25308 **Pickard, Shirley.** COM-HE (WTRB, Ripley, TN, 1955).

25309 **Pickard, Thelma.** COM-HE (WDCF, Dade City, FL, 1957).

25310 ***(The) Pickard Family.*** This was a popular CW music group that in the 1930s was known as a hillbilly group. Southern folk songs were sung on their program accompanied by their own string instruments. During the early days the group consisted of Mom and Dad Pickard, Ruth, Charlie and little Ann Pickard. The announcer was Thomas Breen, Jr. (30 min., Friday, 8:00–8:30 P.M., NBC-Blue, 1928–1930). They also broadcast on WSM (Nashville, TN, 1932) and WCAU, (Philadelphia, PA, Friday, 4:00–4:30 P.M., 1934). Grunow Refrigerators sponsored *The Pickard Family* for a quarter-hour program broadcast Monday, 7:15–7:30 P.M. over WFIL, Philadelphia, PA, in 1936 with Tom Stone as the program announcer. In 1937, the *Pickard Family* program was broadcast each weekday evening on WGN (Chicago, IL). The following year the family's program was broadcast on KYW (Philadelphia, PA).

25311 ***Pickard Family and the Missourians.*** The popular CW music family was teamed with another CW music group (WFIL, Philadelphia, PA, 1935).

25312 **Pickel, Charles.** DJ (*Insomniacs' Record Shop*, WBIR, Knoxville, TN, 1948; *Music Mill*, WBIR, 1949).

25313 **Pickens, E.M.** Pickens came to station WFVX directly from high school and was employed as the station's first announcer (WFVX, Bentonville, AR, 1925).

25314 **Pickens, Francine.** COM-HE (KRLW, Walnut Ridge, AR, 1955).

25315 ***(The) Pickens Party.*** Singer Jane Pickens was featured on the transcribed music program (15 min., Transcribed, Various Stations, 1951).

25316 ***(The) Pickens Sisters.*** The singing Pickens Sisters' specialty was popular songs (15 min., Sunday, 9:45–10:00 P.M., NBC-Blue, 1933).

25317 **Pickerell, Evelyn.** Violinist (KFI, Los Angeles, CA, 1925).

25318 **Pickering, Blanche.** Pianist (WBZ, Springfield, MA, 1925).

25319 **Pickering, Gladys Blackwell.** Singer (KHJ, Los Angeles, CA, 1926).

25320 **Pickering, Helen.** COM-HE (WHJC, Matewan, WV, 1954).

25321 **Pickering, Tom.** DJ (*1150 Club*, WIMA, Lima, OH, 1948).

25322 **Pickett, Bill.** DJ (*Requestfully Yours*, KGPH, Flagstaff, AZ, 1952).

25323 **Pickett, Jack.** Sportscaster (NBC, 1960).

25324 **Pickett, Kenneth.** Pickett was the announcer on *The Gillette Razor Blade Program* (NBC, 1929).

25325 **Pickett, L. Leroy.** Baritone (WGY, Schenectady, NY, 1925).

25326 **Pickett, Lyman.** DJ (*Clockwatcher*, WRUF, Gainesville, FL, 1950).

25327 **Pickett, Roy.** Newscaster (KATE, Albert Lea, MN, 1941).

25328 **Pickett, Wilbur.** Leader (*Wilbur Pickett Orchestra*, instr. mus. prg., WOWO, Fort Wayne, IN, 1934).

25329 **Pickney, Vivian.** COM-HE (KXRO, Aberdeen, WA, 1954).

25330 **Pickrem, Conrad.** DJ (*Rhythm Ramblers*, WFEB, Sylacauga, AL, 1949; *Sunrise Serenade*, WFEB, 1954).

25331 **Pickwickians Dance Orchestra.** Popular Oakland dance band (KTAB, Oakland, CA, 1929).

25332 **Picon, Molly.** Singer-monologist (*Molly Picon Program*, a music and comedy show, 15 min., Weekly, WMCA-ABS Network, 1934).

25333 **Picus, Larry.** DJ (*The A Train*, WCCP, Savannah, GA, 1949; WSTN, St. Augustine, FL, 1957).

25334 **Pidot, George.** Announcer (WGN, Chicago, IL, 1928).

25335 **Pie Plant Pete (Claude Moyle).** Claude Moyle was a folk musician and CW singer who played a harmonica-guitar combination that he called his "Two cylinder Cob-Crusher." His first radio work was on WLS (Chicago, IL, 1927). *Pie Plant Pete* attracted large audiences with his local shows (WLS, Chicago, IL, 1930; WTAM, Cleveland, OH, 1936–1937). In addition, Pie Plant Pie worked on WBZ (Boston, MA) and WHAM (Rochester, NY) in the pre–War period.

25336 ***Pie Plant Pete and Bashful Harmonica Joe.*** Pie Plant Pete (Claude Moye) and Bashful Harmonica Joe (Joseph Troyan) played lively CW music and engaged in funny chatter. Despite the fact they were considered to be "hillbillies," the pair delivered what *Variety* called a polished, sophisticated performance (15 min., Tuesday, 10:15–10:30 A.M., WBZ-WBZA, Springfield and Boston, MA, 1937).

25337 ***Piedmont Concert Orchestra.*** Instr. mus. prg. (WBIG, Greensboro, NC, 1936).

25338 **Piedmont High School Orchestra.** Public school music group directed by Professor W.G. Alexander Bell (KFWM, Oakland, CA, 1927).

25339 **Pieplow, E.C.** Newscaster (KWBG, Hutchinson, KS, 1939; KABR, Aberdeen, SD, 1946).

25340 **Pierce, Art.** DJ (*Turntable Ballroom*, WABM, Houlton, ME, 1952).

25341 **Pierce, Barrett.** DJ (*The Barrett Pierce Show*, KWBU, Corpus Christi, TX, 1949).

25342 **Pierce, Barthol W.** News analyst (KTRB, Modesto, CA, 1946; *Headlines that Make History*, KTRB, 1948).

25343 **Pierce, Bill.** DJ (*The Mayor of Tin Pan Alley*, WBKA, Brockton, MA, 1950).

25344 **Pierce, Bill.** DJ (*Bill Pierce Show*, WSCR, Scranton, PA, 1948–1950).

25345 **Pierce, Bob ("Old Man Sunshine").** As Old Man Sunshine, Pierce sang songs and told stories, (WJZ-Blue, 1929–1931).

25346 **Pierce, Don.** Newscaster (WCNC, Elizabeth City, NC, 1946; *Adams Sports Parade*, WRRF, Washington, DC, 1947).

25347 **Pierce, Edwin.** Newscaster (WDLP, Panama City, FL, 1941). Sportscaster (WDLP, 1941).

25348 **Pierce, Elsie.** Miss Pierce talked on *Beauty and Personality* (WRC, Washington, DC, 1925 and WGBS, New York, NY, 1925).

25349 **Pierce, Frank and Vic Beall.** Comedy singing team (KFWB, Hollywood, CA, 1925).

25350 **Pierce, H.I., Jr.** Sportscaster (KGHL, Billings, MT, 1937).

25351 Pierce, Jackie. COM-HE (WFTL, Ft. Lauderdale, FL, 19489; WTVJ, Miami, FL, 1957).

25352 Pierce, Jennings. "Premier West Coast announcer" Pierce also broadcast agricultural talks (KGO, San Francisco, CA, and the Pacific Coast network of the National Broadcasting Company, 1926–1930). Pierce was the chief announcer at the NBC San Francisco station. His first designation was as "JP." He was the first Westerner to broadcast coast-to-coast from the Pacific Coast to the Atlantic Coast in 1928. Notable broadcast assignments for him included Herbert Hoover's acceptance of the Republican presidential nomination in 1928 and the broadcast of the arrival of the dirigible Graf Zappelin at Los Angeles.

25353 Pierce, Joe. DJ (*Tops in Pops*, WFAA, Dallas, TX, 1949; KVOZ, Laredo, TX, 1956).

25354 Pierce, John. Sportscaster (WTCB, Flint, MI, 1947). DJ (*Record Lounge*, WTAC, Flint, MI, 1950).

25355 Pierce, Madeleine. Actress Pierce appeared on the daytime serial programs *Just Plain Bill*, *Pepper Young's Family*, *When a Girl Marries* and *Ethel and Albert.*

25356 Pierce, Norman. Sportscaster (WOMT, Manitowoc, WI, 1937).

25357 Pierce, Pete. Sportscaster (*The World of Sports*, WBCC, Bethesda-Chevy Chase, MD, 1948).

25358 Pierce, Rachel. Soprano (WFLA, Clearwater, FL, 1929).

25359 Pierce, Ross. Leader (*Ross Pierce Orchestra*, instr. mus. prg., WLW, Cincinnati, OH, 1936).

25360 Pierce, W.B. Announcer (WBBL, Richmond, VA, 1927).

25361 Pierce, Webb. CW singer, musician and songwriter Pierce first had his own show on radio at the age of 16 (*Songs by Webb Pierce*, KLMB, Monroe, LA, 1932). He joined the *Louisiana Hayride* (KWKH, Shreveport, LA, 1950) and began a successful recording career.

25362 Piercey, Gail. COM-HE (WCOR, Lebanon, TN, 1960).

25363 Piercy, Alice. Pianist (KTM, Santa Monica, CA, 1929).

25364 Pierno, Alfiere. Flutist (WNYC, New York, NY, 1925).

25365 Pierre, Lucky. DJ (WEBR, Buffalo, NY, 1956).

25366 Piersen, Eleanor. Soprano (KGO, Oakland, CA, 1926).

25367 Pierson, Dalton. Newscaster (KGVO, Missoula, MT, 1939).

25368 Pierson, James. Newscaster (KFNF, Shenandoah, IA, 1938).

25369 Pierson, Paul. Leader (*Paul Pierson Orchestra*, insr. mus. prg., WLW, Cincinnati, OH, 1934).

25370 Pierson, Violet Warren. Miss Pierson told children's stories (WCAP, Washington, DC, 1924).

25371 Pierson, William T. Announcer (WCAP, Asbury Park, NJ, 1924).

25372 *Pigfoot Pete.* Listeners enjoyed the CW music of Pigfoot Pete (Bill Saunders) and his CW music group (30 min., Monday through Friday, 9:00–9:30 A.M., WTRY, Troy, NY, 1947; *Pigfoot Pete Jamboree.* Bill Saunders talked, sang and told jokes on the popular local show, 30 min., Monday through Friday, 5:00–5:30 P.M., WOKO, Albany, NY, 1948). Saunders later worked as a DJ using the same program name: *Pigfoot Pete's Jamboree* (WOKO, Albany, NY, 1949).

25373 Piggly Wiggly Concert Orchestra. Band sponsored by a Pacific Coast grocery chain (KFON, Long Beach, CA, 1927–1928).

25374 Piggly Wiggly Girls. Music group on Pacific Coast broadcasts that included some talented violinists, pianists, and singers (KHJ, Los Angeles, CA, 1924–1925).

25375 Piggly Wiggly Girls. Female singing trio (KHJ, Los Angeles, CA, 1926).

25376 Piggly Wiggly Hawaiian Trio. Instrumental music group (KHJ, Los Angeles, CA, 1925).

25377 Piggly Wiggly Trio. The male vocal group, originally organized in Denver, Colorado, in 1922, included Don Wilson, Martin Daugherty and Harry Morton. The trio was brought to San Francisco by the Piggly Wiggly Company to appear on KFRC (San Francisco, CA, 1928). They originally sang on KFRC, sponsored by Piggly Wiggly Grocery stores, before moving to KHJ (Los Angeles, CA) later in 1928.

25378 Piggott, Eileen. Soprano Piggott sang on the *Spotlight Hour* and other programs on the Pacific Coast network of the National Broadcasting Company in 1928.

25379 Pigue, Bob. Sportscaster (WMC, Memphis, TN, 1939–1941).

25380 Pihl, Eleanor. Pianist (WCBD, Zion, IL, 1925).

25381 Pike, William. Leader (William Pike's Orchestra, WGBS, New York, NY, 1926).

25382 Pilcher, Bev. DJ (*The Farmer's Daughter*, KRTV, Hillsboro, OR, 1955).

25383 Pilcher, William. Tenor (KFI, Los Angeles, CA, 1925).

25384 Pilgrim Chapel Choristers. Vocal group (WFAA, Dallas, TX, 1925).

25385 (The) Pilgrims. Mary McCoy, Laura Coombs, Ruth Ann Watson, Henry Shope, William Daniels and Earl Waldo were members of the Pilgrims, a mixed vocal sextet directed by Dana S. Merriman (NBC-Blue, New York, NY, 1929–1935). Ralph Freese and Milton Cross were occasionally the program announcers.

25386 *(The) Pilgrims.* An informative program that simulated a trip to the Holy Land. *The Pilgrims* featured music provided by an orchestra conducted by Charles Hart. Gale Sanderson Michie supplied the program's word pictures (45 min., Sunday, 8:15–9:00 P.M., NBC-Pacific Coast Network, 1929).

25387 *Pilgrims Orchestra.* Music program featuring a California orchestra directed by August Hinrichs. Tenor Harry Robertson and baritone Boris Malameth also appeared on the program (KGO, San Francisco, CA, 1928).

25388 Pillar, Jeeter. Leader (*Jeeter Pillar Orchestra*, instr. mus. prg., KMOX, St. Louis, MO, 1937).

25389 Pilley, Jack W. Announcer and station manager (KFCR, Santa Barbara, CA, 1928). Newscaster (KTMS, Santa Barbara, CA, 1942).

25390 *Pillsbury Pageant.* Violinist Toscha Seidel, Arthur Tracy the Street Singer and Sam Lanin's Orchestra performed on the music program sponsored by Pillsbury Cake Flour (30 min., Friday, 9:00–9:30 P.M., CBS, 1930).

25391 Pine, Allan. Sportscaster (*Sports Roundup*, WHLI, Hempstead, NY, 1954).

25392 Pine, Joseph. Clarinetist-saxophonist (KOMO, Seattle, WA, 1928–1929).

25393 *Pine Corners Social.* CW mus. prg. (WCCO, Minneapolis–St. Paul, MN, 1939).

25394 *(The) Pine Mountain Social* (aka ***The Pine Mountain Social at the Renfro Valley Homestead***). John Lair, an authority on American folk music, narrated the community gathering at Renfro Valley Homestead in the Cumberland Mountains of Tennessee. When the old folk songs were performed, Lair would tell their history. Singers Red Foley, Lulu Belle and Skyland Scotty and a supporting cast of 20 singers and musicians performed on the show (30 min., Sunday, 2:15–2:45 P.M., NBC-Blue, 1935).

25395 *Pinebrook Praises.* Religious program with music and a canary chorus (WBNX, New York, NY, late 1940s-early 1950s).

25396 Pinell, Claude. Newscaster (KPAC, Port Arthur, TX, 1947).

25397 Pines, Dora. Singer of Russian songs (WEVD, New York, NY, 1929).

25398 Pingle, Jack. DJ (*Good Music in Hi-Fi*, WECL, Eau Claire, WI, 1960).

25399 Pingre, Earl. Pingre read poetry and brief commentaries (KFI, Los Angeles, CA, 1928).

25400 Pinke, William. Operatic tenor (WFLA, Clearwater, FL, 1929).

25401 Pinkley, Carson. DJ (*Sundialers Club* and *The Party Line*, KSMA, Santa Maria, CA, 1948; KAVL, Lancaster, CA, 1949; *Alarm Klok Klub*, KELK, Elko, NV, 1950).

25402 Pinkney, Ron. DJ (WEBB, Baltimore, MD, 1960).

25403 Pinney, Donald. DJ (*Preview Time* and *Memory Lane*, KBIO, Burley, ID, 1950).

25404 Pinney, Katherine. Pianist (KOMO, Seattle, WA, 1928).

25405 Pintel, Jacques. Russian pianist who appeared on the *Major Bowes Capitol Theater Family* program (NBC, 1928).

25406 Pinto, Anna. Harpist (WJZ, New York, NY, 1925).

25407 Pinto, Jack. DJ (WBUD, Trenton, NJ, 1956).

25408 *Pinto Pete* (aka ***Pinto Pete's Ranch Boys***). The transcribed CW music and humor program by unidentified performers was broadcast by numerous stations in the mid-to-late 1930s (WTMJ, Milwaukee, WI, 1935; KSL, Salt Lake City, UT, 1939). At times the program was listed as *Pinto Pete's Ranch Boys* (WDBJ, Roanoke, VA, 1939).

25409 ***Pioneer Stories.*** The "Old Timer," not otherwise identified, spun yarns about the western cattle country, the Erie Canal and other pioneering topics on the interesting program sponsored by Allis-Chalmers Farm Equipment Company. Special background music added to the program's effectiveness (15 min., Tuesday and Thursday, 6:30–6:45 P.M., WLS, Chicago, IL, 1937).

25410 **Piotti, Prince.** Singer (WHN, Chicago, IL, 1926).

25411 **Pious, Minerva.** Fine comic actress Pious also appeared on the *Life Can Be Beautiful* daytime serial program. Her finest comic work, however, was on the *Fred Allen Show. See* **Comediennes** *and the* ***Fred Allen Show.***

25412 **Piowaty, Deborah.** COM-HE (WIRA, Fort Pierce, FL, 1956–1957).

25413 **Pipkin, Shirley.** COM-HE (KFSA, Fort Smith, AR, 1956).

25414 **Pippert, Paul.** DJ (*Requestfully Yours*, KSMN, Mason City, IA, 1948).

25415 ***Pippo & Poppo.*** Paolo Sereno and Arrigo Columbo, two announcers on WOV, appeared on the entertaining quarter-hour show of jokes and puns (WOV, New York, NY, 1942).

25416 ***Pirate Ship.*** A weekly dramatic adventure program that starred Guy Durrell as "Captain Silver" (KSTP, Minneapolis–St. Paul, MN, 1928).

25417 **Pirnie, Donald.** Baritone (WBZ, Springfield, MA, 1925).

25418 **Pironi, Ruth.** Soprano (KOIN, Seattle, WA, 1928–1929).

25419 **Piroso, Nicholas.** Leader (Nicholas Piroso and his Orchestra, WHN, New York, NY, 1923).

25420 **Piscope's Troubadours.** Popular dance orchestra (WGBS, New York, NY, 1929).

25421 **Pistol Pete's Cowboys.** CW music group (WHP, Harrisburg, PA, 1941).

25422 **Pitblade, Harriet C.** Pianist (WBZ, Springfield, MA, 1924).

25423 **Pitcher, J. Leslie.** Tenor (KJR, Seattle, WA, 1928–1929).

25424 ***Pitching Horseshoes.*** Kreml Hair Tonic and Musterole Salve sponsored Broadway columnist Billy Rose's five-minute program. Rose broadcast the same type of Broadway gossip that he customarily included in his column (5 min., Monday through Friday, 8:55–9:00 P.M., MBS, 1947).

25425 **Pitcock, Bob.** DJ (*Supper Club*, KFSA, Ft. Smith, AR, 1952–1960).

25426 **Pitman, Linwood T.** Announcer (WCSH, Portland, ME, 1927–1929).

25427 **Pitman, Ralph R.** Pitman began work as an engineer at station WOK (Pine Bluff, AR), when it went on the air February 18, 1922. During WOK's first broadcast day, he also did the announcing, broadcast bulletins and asked listeners to call and write to comment on their reception of the program. Pitman later became a regular full-time station announcer.

25428 **Pitoniak, Ann.** Actress Pitoniak appeared on the daytime serial program *Aunt Jenny* aka *Aunt Jenny's Real Life Stories.*

25429 **Pitot, Genevieve.** Pianist (WOR, Newark, NJ, 1933–1934).

25430 **Pittenger, Dick.** DJ (*Amber Room*, WFBM, Indianapolis, IN, 1950). Sportscaster (*Sports Review*, WFBM, 1950; *Sports News*, WFBM, 1951).

25431 **Pittenger, Theodore.** Violinist (KVOO, Tulsa, OK, 1928–1929).

25432 **Pitts, Cyril.** Tenor (NBC, 1928; *Cyril Pitts*, vcl. mus. prg., NBC, 1935).

25433 **Pitts, Jim.** DJ (*Saturday Shindig*, WBIR, Knoxville, TN, 1948).

25434 **Pitts, Margo.** COM-HE (WISR, Butler, PA, 1957).

25435 ***Pittsburgh Amateur Winners Program.*** A local amateur show that was an outgrowth of the *Wilken's Summer Amateur Show* that preceded it, the program was hosted by Brian MacDonald (30 min., Friday, 7:00–7:30 P.M., WCAE, Pittsburgh, PA, 1936).

25436 **Pittsburgh Athletic Association Orchestra.** Music group (KDKA, Pittsburgh, PA, 1924).

25437 **Pittsburgh Civic Quartet.** Vocal group directed by Mrs. Will Earhart (KDKA, Pittsburgh, PA, 1921). The group presented a entire program of Christmas Carols on December 17, 1921.

25438 ***Pittsburgh Symphony Strings.*** The symphonic music program was broadcast weekly (30 min., Sunday, 6:00–6:30 P.M., NBC, 1936).

25439 **Pitzinger, Arthur.** Leader (Arthur Pitzinger Orchestra, KFWB, Hollywood, CA, 1926–1929).

25440 **Piveral, Elizabeth.** COM-HE (WNIM, Maryville, MO, 1956).

25441 **Pizinger, Gertrude.** Mezzo-soprano (WJZ, New York, NY, 1939).

25442 **Pizza, Salvatore.** Leader (Morning Glory Club Dance Orchestra, WDAR, Philadelphia, PA, 1925; Salvatore Pizza Orchestra, WLIT, Philadelphia, PA, 1926).

25443 **Pizzicara, Anna.** Soprano (WEAF, New York, NY, 1925).

25444 **Place, Ed.** Sportscaster (*Playtime on the Air*, WAAB, Boston, MA, 1940).

25445 **Place, Lester.** Pianist (NBC, 1929).

25446 **Place, Lou.** Newscaster (KGFJ, Los Angeles, CA, 1944).

25447 **Placer, Samuel.** Tenor (WGBS, New York, NY, 1928).

25448 **Plamadore, Ray.** Sportscaster (WKBH, LaCrosse, WI, 1940–1941).

25449 **Plambeck, Herbert H.** Newscaster (*Des Moines Farm News Reports*, WHO, Des Moines, IA, 1937–1940).

25450 **Plamer, Bruce.** Newscaster (WKY, Oklahoma City, OK, 1948).

25451 **Plamer, Johnny.** DJ (*Tempos at Ten*, WRCS, Ahoskie, NC, 1950).

25452 **Pla-Mor Ballroom Orchestra.** Jean Goldkette directed the popular ballroom band (WDAF, Kansas City, MO, 1928).

25453 **Plank, John.** Whistler (KSTP, St. Paul–Minneapolis, MN, 1929).

25454 **Plank, Laura.** COM-HE (KASH, Eugene, OR, 1956).

25455 **Plant, Elton.** Singer (WWJ, Port Huron, MI, 1923).

25456 ***Plantation Echoes.*** *Plantation Echoes* was a pleasant musical variety program set in the mansion of Judge Chandler, "somewhere south of the Mason and Dixon Line," where a group of entertainers from the plantation met to sing and talk. The Judge's nieces, Barbara and Ethel, joined Jerry and his Dixie Melodists and Rufus, Rastus and Little Tambo to provide entertainment. The program's cast included Bobbe Deane, Georgia Simmons, Clarence Hayes, Charles Marshall, Sylvano Pale and Johnny Toffoli (30 min., Tuesday, 8:00–8:30 P.M., NBC-Pacific Coast Network, 1929).

25457 ***Plantation Echoes.*** Vicks Chemical Company, manufacturer of products for colds, sponsored the weekly music show that presented blues singer Mildred Bailey, "The Rocking Chair Lady," singing with the Willard Robison and his Deep River Boys Orchestra (15 min., Monday, 7:15–7:30 P.M., NBC, 1935).

25458 ***Plantation House Party.*** Louis Buck was the announcer on the transcribed show. Country comic Whitey Ford, "the Duke of Paducah," hosted the show that also featured the smooth baritone singing of Jack West, the Dixie Dolls vocal group and the music of Owen Bradley and the Colonels orchestra (15 min., Transcribed, Many Stations, late 1940s).

25459 ***Plantation Jubilee* (aka *The Curt Massey Show*).** A sustaining CW music show, *Plantation Jubilee* featured baritone Curt Massey, comic George Beatty, Allen Massey and the Westerners, the Lee Sisters vocal group and the popular vocal trio of Tom, Dick and Harry (Bud Vandover, Marlin Hurt and Gordon Vandover). Charles Lyons was the announcer. The show was created and written by Gordon Vandover, a member of the Tom, Dick and Harry vocal group (30 min., Thursday, 8:00–8:30 P.M., MBS, 1949).

25460 ***Plantation Party.*** Bugle Chewing Tobacco sponsored the country-western music program that also contained broad rustic humor. The program's opening contained, suitably, a bugle call. When the program changed to a transcribed format, only the opening bugle call survived. Whitey Ford, "The Duke of Paducah," was the host and resident country comic. He was assisted by the popular singing trio of Tom, Dick and Harry — Bud Vandover, Marlin Hurt and Gordon Vandover — Louise Massey and the Westerners, the Dining Sisters, the Range Riders and Curt Massey (NBC, 1936–1943).

25461 ***Planters Pickers.*** Planters Peanuts sponsored the weekly 30-minute variety program that featured the Hallelujah Singers and the Billy Artzt orchestra. Edward Thorgersen was the announcer (30 min., Weekly, NBC-Red, 1929).

25462 **Plasencia, Flavio.** Young Mexican baritone (WGN, Chicago, IL, 1928).

25463 **Plasmati, Aelia.** Soprano (WHDH, Boston, MA, 1940).

25464 Plasschaert, Camielle. Violinist (WJZ, New York, NY, 1923).

25465 Platis, George. Sportscaster (KOVO, Provo, UT, 1942; KLIX, Twin Falls, ID, 1948). DJ (*Platis Platter Party*, KLIX, 1948–1950).

25466 Platt, Chuck. DJ (*Varsity Club*, KDSH, Boise, ID, 1952).

25467 Platt, David M. DJ (*Music for a Sunday Evening* and *In Record Time*, WKLV, Blackstone, VA, 1949).

25468 Platt, Dick. Pianist (NBC, Chicago, IL, 1929).

25469 Platt, Evelyn. Recitations (WEAF, New York, NY, 1923).

25470 Platt, Joseph. Sportscaster (*Sports Extra* and *Sports Predictions*, WBBZ, Sulphur Springs, TX, 1949).

25471 Platt, Lillie Maud. Pianist and program director (WCOC, Columbus, MS, 1928).

25472 Platt and Nierman. Piano team (*Platt and Nierman*, instr. mus. prg., NBC, 1934).

25473 Platten, Jack. DJ (*The Jack Platten Show*, WFEC, Miami, FL, 1949).

25474 *Platter Party.* An unidentified DJ played recorded music on the local show (30 min., 5:15–5:45 P.M., KCJB, Minot, ND, 1955).

25475 *(The) Play Boys.* A vocal trio of Felix Bernard, Walter Samuels and Leonard Whitcop was accompanied by an unidentified orchestra on the network music show (30 min., Tuesday, 3:00–3:30 P.M., CBS, 1934).

25476 Playford, John M. Violinist (WGY, Schenectady, NY, 1922).

25477 *(The) Playgoer.* *The Playgoer* (Mrs. Dorothy Fuller) presented dramatic criticism on this sustaining program (15 min., Tuesday, 1:45–2:00 P.M., WMEX, Boston, MA, 1942).

25478 *Plays for Americans.* Arch Oboler wrote and produced the short series of experimental plays, using a stream of consciousness approach and imaginative sound effects. The program was broadcast on an occasional basis by NBC. Stars of motion pictures and plays appeared in them including Joan Blondell, Bette Davis, Olivia DeHaviland, Raymond Massey, Alla Nazimova, Dick Powell, Claude Rains, James Stewart and Robert Taylor (30 min., Weekly, 1938–1942; 1944). *See* **Drama.**

25479 *(The) Play's the Thing.* Bernardine Flynn talked about plays and their players (Chicago radio, 1931).

25480 *Pleasant Valley Folks.* The Crown Overall Manufacturing Company, maker of Headlight Overalls, sponsored the self-styled hillbilly music program. Listener requests and old songs were its major elements. Charles Seel, the Devore Sisters, tenor Charles Waune, the singing sisters trio of Lucy, Martha and Annabelle and Joe Lugar's Orchestra provided the music on the popular CW music show (15 min., Thursday, 7:45–8:00 P.M., MBS, 1936).

25481 Pledger, Douglas "Doug." Sportscaster (WSAU, Wausau, WI, 1942). DJ (KNBC, San Francisco, CA, 1954–1960).

25482 Plimmer, Dennis. Newscaster (WQXR, New York, NY, 1944–1945).

25483 Plock, Troth Tyler. Pianist (KFI, Los Angeles, CA, 1925).

25484 Plogstedt, Lillian. Organist (WLW, Cincinnati, OH, 1923).

25485 Plotke, Joe. Leader (*Joe Plotke Orchestra*, instr. mus. prg., CBS, 1935).

25486 Plotkin, Ben. Leader (Ben Plotkin Orchestra, WOR, Newark, NJ, 1927).

25487 Plotz, Eddie. Leader (Eddie Plotz and his New Yorkers Orchestra, WGBS, New York, NY, 1928; Eddie Plotz and his New York Vagabonds, WGBS, 1928).

25488 *Plow Boys.* CW mus. prg. (KDKA, Pittsburgh, PA, 1936).

25489 Plowman, Marsh W. Sportscaster (KWAT, Watertown, SD, 1940–1941). Newscaster (KWAT, Watertown, SD, 1945).

25490 Plumb, Myrtle. Soprano (WFLA, Clearwater, FL, 1929).

25491 Plumber, Gaylord. DJ (*Musical Matinee*, KOFO, Ottawa, KS, 1949).

25492 Plumlee, Paul. Newscaster (WGLU, Safford, AZ, 1941). Sportscaster (WGLU, 1941).

25493 Plummer, Bill. DJ (*The Wishing Well*, KOPR, Butte, MT, 1948).

25494 Plummer, Ruby. Soprano (WORL, Boston, MA, 1959).

25495 Plumstead, Eugene M. Newscaster (WSGN, Birmingham, AL, 1946).

25496 Plunkett, A. Olive. COM-HE (WZOB, Fort Payne, AL, 1951).

25497 Plunkett, Oliver. Tenor (WLW, Cincinnati, OH, 1923).

25498 Pobers, Michael. Newscaster (WQXR, New York, NY, 1944).

25499 Pobrislo, Joseph. DJ (*Bar-O-Ranch*, KDAC, Fort Bragg, CA, 1948).

25500 *Pocketbook News.* Wilma Soss broadcast economic news of interest to consumers. The sponsor was the Bristol-Myers Company (10 min., Monday, 9:30–9:40 P.M., NBC, 1958).

25501 Podhanski, Pod. DJ (KOEL, Oelwein, IA, 1956).

25502 Podmore, William "Bill." Actor Podmore was in the cast of *Second Husband*, *Terry and the Pirates*, *We Love and Learn* and *Young Dr. Malone.*

25503 Poehler, W. Xylophonist (KFUO, St. Louis, MO, 1926).

25504 Poehling, Joe. Announcer (WOWO, Fort Wayne, IN, 1925).

25505 Poelher, (Mrs.) Eleanor. Managing director Poelher of WLAG (Minneapolis, MN, 1922) stayed with station WLAG until 1927 when it became WCCO.

25506 Poettler, Eleanor. Book reviewer (*Among Good Books*, WCCO, Minneapolis–St. Paul, MN, 1925).

25507 Pohlman, G. Anton. Announcer (KPPC, Pasadena, CA, 1927).

25508 *Poems.* Beatrice Meisler broadcast weekly poetic recitations (WGBS, New York, NY, 1925).

25509 *Poems that Live.* Bill Vickland read poetry as organist Romelle Fay provided a musical background (15 min., Sunday, 11:00–11:15 A.M., WLS, Chicago, IL, 1935).

25510 *(The) Poet of Radioland.* J.M. Seiferth read his original poetry on his popular local program (WSMB, New Orleans, LA, 1932).

25511 *Poet Prince.* Anthony Frome (Abraham Feinberg) was the romantic reader of poetry. Alwyn E.W. Bach was the announcer (NBC, 1934). Frome graduated from the Cincinnati Hebrew Union College and for some time served as a rabbi.

25512 *(The) Poet Scout.* The unusual program was produced by Ray Zaner, a local York Scout executive. The program presented Boy Scouts reading their own original poems (WSBA, York, PA, 1946).

25513 *Poetic Melodies.* Wrigley's Chewing Gum sponsored the program of music and poetry. Franklyn MacCormack read the poetry. Billy Mills' Orchestra and tenor Jack Fulton provided the music. Don Hancock was the program's announcer (15 min., Monday through Thursday, 10:00–10:15 P.M., CBS, 1936 and Tuesday, 7:00–7:15 P.M., CBS, 1936). In 1938, Fulton sang with Kelsey's Orchestra. MacCormack still read the poetry in this format.

25514 *Poetic Paradise.* Allen C. Anthony read poetry against a musical background supplied by organist Rich Hayes on the sustaining program (15 min., Wednesday, 9:00–9:15 P.M., KWK, St. Louis, MO and KWOS, Jefferson City, MO, 1938).

25515 *Poetic Strings.* Leon Goldman conducted the program of light concert music. The program began with the announcement: "We present *Poetic Strings*, a lyrical program of light concert music for the morning hours, gleaned from the melody treasures of many lands. The first number is an oriental air in soft romantic mood — "Chinese Serenade" (15 min., CBS, 1930s).

25516 *Poetry Club.* Mrs. David Hugh read and discussed poetry, KHJ (Los Angeles, CA), 1929.

25517 *Poetry of Our Time.* Distinguished author and poet Katherine Anne Porter read her own poetry on the weekly program (30 min., Sunday, 11:30–12:00 noon, NBC, 1953).

25518 *Poet's Corner.* An unidentified performer read poetry. The sponsor was Hewitt's Bookstore (KFON, Long Beach, CA, 1926).

25519 *Poet's Gold.* David Ross read romantic poetry on the late Sunday afternoon program. Victor Bey's Orchestra provided the music (15 min., Sunday, 5:00–5:15 P.M. CBS, 1933–1934). *Variety* commented that the program was one of the best of the many programs of the 1930's featuring poetry and quiet music. David Ross was also praised for his fine voice.

25520 Pogue, Robert W. [Ralph Pogue]. Pogue talked on business topics such as, "Merchandising for Women" (WLW, Cincinnati, OH, 1925–1926).

25521 Pointel, Charles H. Sportscaster (WFIG, Sumter, SC, 1940–1941; WRDW, Atlanta, GA, 1942). Newscaster (*12:30 Edition*, WFIG, 1947). DJ (*Corn Lovers Hour*, WRDW, 1948).

25522 Pointius, Ernest. Announcer (WREN, Lawrence, KS, 1925).

25523 Points, Freddie. Pianist and "Player of the Mouth Harp" (KOIL, Council Bluffs, IA, 1929).

25524 *Pokie Martin and the Arkansas Woodchopper* (aka ***Pokie Martin and Arkie***). Pokie Martin (Don Allen) and Arkie the Arkansas Woodchopper (Luther Ossenbrink) were a popular team that combined country humor and music (15 min., Monday through Saturday, 1:00–1:15 P.M., WLS, Chicago, IL, 1937).

25525 Pokorn, Julius. Violinist (WHN, New York, NY, 1923).

25526 Poland, Henrietta. Singer (KHJ, Los Angeles, CA, 1925).

25527 Poland, Sam. DJ (*Musical Matinee*, WCHS, Charleston, WV, 1949; *Sam's Show*, WCHS, 1952–1954; *Clockwatchers*, WCHS, 1955–1957).

25528 Polaska, Alva. Soprano (WOR, Newark, NJ, 1924).

25529 Poleman, Dan. Leader (*Dan Poleman and His Dance Orchestra*, instr. mus. prg., WCDA, New York, NY, 1929).

25530 *Police Headquarters.* The 15-minute transcribed program presented "authentic" police cases. Some of the cases dramatized were the "Red Dugan Murder," "The Life Insurance Scheme," "The Boxing Match Death," "Infiltrating the Mob" and "The McKenzie Death" (15 min., Transcribed, Various Stations, 1932).

25531 *Policewoman.* Phillips H. Lord produced and directed the dramatic series based on the 35 years experience of Mary Sullivan of the New York City Homicide Squad. Miss Sullivan appeared at the opening and close of each of these realistic sustaining programs. Betty Garde played the title role, assisted by Frances Chaney, Grace Keddy and Mandel Kramer. Music was supplied by organist Jesse Crawford. The announcers were Ed Herlihy and Dick Dunham (15 min., Weekly, 10:45–11:00 A.M., NBC-Blue, 1946).

25532 Poling, (Dr.) Dan. Dr. Poling conducted the *Young Peoples' Conferences* program (WLW, Cincinnati, OH, 1928–1929).

25533 *Polish Alliance Orchestra.* Instr. mus. prg. (WMMN, Fairmont, WV, 1937–1938).

25534 *(The) Political Education Forum.* Begun in 1932, the program gave free uncensored air time to all legally qualified candidates for public office. All parties, Communists and Prohibitionists included, were given free broadcast time. The program was conceived by Harold Engel (WHA, Madison, WI, 1932).

25535 *(The) Politicians.* Two dialect comics, Frank McInerny and Fred Lundberg, as an Irish policeman and a Swedish politician were the performers on the popular local show of the early 1930s (WCCO, Minneapolis, MN, 1930s).

25536 Polizzotto, Flo. COM-HE (WAFB, Baton Rouge, LA, 1951).

25537 Polk, Bill "Billy." DJ (*Good Morning Man*, WJAT, Swainsboro, GA, 1952–1954; WBAW, Barnwell, SC, 1955).

25538 Polk, Daisy. Soprano Polk specialized in "Negro spirituals" (WFAA, Dallas, TX, 1928).

25539 Polk, George. Newscaster (CBS, 1947).

25540 Polk, Jean. Contralto (WJJD, Chicago, IL, 1935).

25541 Polk, Marshall. Tenor (WSM, Nashville, TN, 1928–1929).

25542 Polk, Oscar. Actor Polk was in the cast of *Big Sister*.

25543 Poll, Jean. Contralto (*Jean Poll*, vcl. mus. prg., WJJD, Chicago, IL, 1935).

25544 Poll, Lillian. Soprano (WILL, Urbana, IL, 1939).

25545 Pollack, Ben. Leader of a fine jazz band (Ben Pollack's Orchestra, WBBM, Chicago, IL, 1927; NBC, 1928; Ben Pollack and his Park Central Orchestra, NBC, Chicago, IL, 1929; *Ben Pollack Orchestra*, instr. mus. prg., NBC, 1934; WENR, Chicago, IL, 1934; WBRE, Wilkes-Barre, PA, 1942).

25546 Pollack, Frank. DJ (*Contrasts in Music*, WEXT, Milwaukee, WI, 1950; *On the House*, KOOL, Phoenix, AZ, 1954; KRUX, Phoenix, AZ, 1956–1957; KRLA, Los Angeles, CA, 1959).

25547 Pollack, Lee and Joe Sherman. Singing team (WGCP, New York, NY, 1925).

25548 Pollack, Marjorie. Soprano (WEBH, Chicago, IL, 1924).

25549 Pollak, Lou. Singer (WHN, New York, NY, 1925).

25550 Pollak, Vic. Leader (*Vic Pollak and His Rhythm Band*, instr. mus. prg., KFWI, San Francisco, CA, 1927).

25551 Pollant, Victor. Violinist (WGHP, Detroit, MI, 1926).

25552 Pollard, Bob. DJ (*Record Review*, KTAR, Phoenix, AZ, 1950).

25553 Pollard, Gwen. Soprano (WHN, New York, NY, 1925).

25554 Pollman, Hank. DJ (*Western Request*, KUIP, Durango, CO, 1952).

25555 Pollman, Harold. Newscaster (KFJM, Grand Forks, SD, 1946).

25556 Pollock, Lee. Newscaster (KGKB, Tyler, TX, 1940).

25557 Pollock, Muriel. Pianist (WTN, Nashville, TN, 1929). Ms. Pollock frequently appeared on the *Broadway Lights* program (NBC-Red, New York, NY, 1929; *Muriel Pollack*, instr. mus. prg., NBC-Red, 1936).

25558 Pollock, Muriel and Lawnhurst, Vee. Piano team (*Pollock and Lawnhurst*, instr. mus. prg., NBC-Blue, 1931–1934).

25559 Pollock, Reed. Newscaster (KDON, Monterey, CA, 1941–1942, 1944–1945).

25560 Pollom, Ray. DJ (*Music with Ray*, WATW, Ashland, WI, 1952).

25561 Polly Anna Serenaders. Local dance band (WFAA, Dallas, TX, 1926).

25562 *Polly Entertains.* Polly Malone talked about various topics of interest to women, and Earl Truxell's orchestra provided the music (30 min., Monday through Friday, 2:00–2:30 P.M., WCAE, Pittsburgh, PA, 1936).

25563 *Polly of the Range.* Singer Pauline Beane was featured on the CW music show (WMBD, Peoria, IL, 1938).

25564 *Polly Paine.* Polly Paine, played by Beatrice McBride, delivered interior decorating talks on the weekly program sponsored by the Paine Furniture Company (15 min., Wednesday, 3:45–4:00 P.M., WEEI, Boston, MA, 1942).

25565 *Polly Preston's Adventures.* The weekly dramatic series contained some elements of mystery (15 min., Tuesday, 7:45–8:00 P.M., NBC-Blue, 1929).

25566 *Polly the Shopper.* Polly Shedlone dispensed shopping hints on the half-hour program (30 min., Monday through Friday, 9:00–9:30 A.M., WHN, New York, NY, 1938).

25567 Polman, Norm. DJ (*Polman Train of Music*, WMMW, Meriden, CT, 1949).

25568 Polokoff, Eva. Violinist (WJAZ, Chicago, IL, 1926; WIBO, Chicago, IL, 1928–1929).

25569 Polonus, Harold. Newscaster (WPIC, Sharon, PA, 1939).

25570 Polos, Louise. Pianist (KGO, Oakland, CA, 1926).

25571 Poltesk, James. Pianist (WJAZ, Chicago, IL, 1923).

25572 Polyzoides, Dr. News analyst (KHJ, Los Angeles, CA, 1945).

25573 Pomeroy, Esta. Organist (KGO, Oakland, CA, 1926). Pianist (KTAB, Oakland, CA, 1927).

25574 Pometti, Vincenzo. Leader (Vincenzo Pometti Orchestra, KFWB, Hollywood, CA, 1929).

25575 *Pompeian Make-Up Box.* The talented Boswell Sisters sang with Bob Haring's band. The sponsor was Pompeian Cosmetics (15 min., Monday and Wednesday, 7:30–7:45 P.M., WCCO, Minneapolis, MN, 1932).

25576 *Pompeian Program.* A jazz band led by Milton Rettenberg and beauty talks by Jeanette de Cordet were featured on the weekly program sponsored by Pompeian Cosmetic Company (30 min., Sunday, 9:00–9:30 P.M., CBS, 1931).

25577 *Pompeian Serenade.* The Pompeian Cosmetics Company sponsored the musical program featuring Jerry Cooper and Ted Royal. Arlene Francis read the cosmetics commercials (15 min., Thursday, 12:15–12:30 P.M., CBS, 1936).

25578 Pomrenze (Dr.) H.M. News analyst (WSBC, Chicago, IL, 1946–1948).

25579 Ponce, Dorothea. Blues singer (*Dorothea Ponce*, vcl. mus. prg., WLW, Cincinnati, OH, 1935).

25580 Ponce Sisters. Harmony singing team of Ethel and Dorothy Ponce (WEAF, New York, NY, 1925; NBC-Blue, New York, NY, 1927).

25581 Poncy, Berthe. Pianist (ABC, 1929).

25582 Pond, Lynn. COM-HE (WMAS, Springfield, MA, 1955).

25583 ***Ponds' Dance Party.*** Betty Council was the announcer on the music program sponsored by Ponds' Face Cream (30 min., Friday, 9:30–10:00 P.M., NBC-Red, 1932).

25584 ***Ponds' Players.*** Maude Adams starred in the series of dramatic presentations. Victor Young's Orchestra also appeared (NBC, 1934).

25585 ***Pond's Program.*** The Leo Reisman Orchestra supplied the music and Mrs. Eleanor Roosevelt an informative talk on each weekly program (NBC, 1932).

25586 ***Ponds' Vanity Fair.*** A drama of "real life" was presented on the show that combined dramatized sketches with good music. Lee Wiley and Paul Small provided vocals and the Victor Young Orchestra the music. Ilka Chase and Hugh O'Connell played the smart wife and the dumb husband on the "real life" program (30 min., Friday, 8:30–9:00 P.M., NBC-Red, 1933).

25587 **Ponte, Ruth Hake.** Pianist (KOA, Denver, CO, 1926).

25588 ***Pontiac Matinee.*** Baritone Don Ross sang with an unidentified orchestra on the music show sponsored by the Pontiac Motor Car Company (15 min., Tuesday, 2:30–2:45 P.M., CBS, 1933).

25589 ***Pontiac Program.*** Stoopnagle and Budd were featured along with singers William O'Neill and Jeanne Lang, a chorus and the Andre Kostelanetz Orchestra (30 min., Wednesday, 9:30–10:00 P.M., CBS, 1933). Several years later, *The Pontiac Program* featured host Don McNeill, contralto Jane Froman, the Modern Choir and Frank Black conducting the Pontiac orchestra (30 min., Sunday, 10:30–11:00 P.M., NBC, 1935). The Pontiac Motor Car Company sponsored these programs.

25590 **Pontius, Ernest.** Announcer (WREN, Lawrence, KS, 1929).

25591 **Pontius, Walter.** Tenor (WGN, Chicago, IL, 1928). A New York *Times* music critic called Pontius "another John McCormack." The versatile Pontius sang everything from arias and oratorios to the popular hits of the day.

25592 ***Pony Express Roundup.*** CW mus. prg. (KFEQ, St. Joseph, MO, 1939).

25593 **Ponzi, Vincent.** Leader (*Vincent Ponzi's Serenaders Orchestra*, instr. us. prg., WPG, Atlantic City, NJ, 1935).

25594 **Poole, Bill.** Newscaster (WGPC, Albany, GA, 1939). Sportscaster (WGPC, 1939).

25595 **Poole, Bob.** DJ (*Poole's Paradise*, 40 min., Monday through Friday, 9:15–9:55 A.M., MBS, 1948; *Poole's Parlor,* WOR, New York, NY, 1948–1950). Poole was a popular DJ on the Mutual Network.

25596 **Poole, Harriet.** Organist-pianist in the Aeolian Trio (KFWM, Oakland, CA, 1929).

25597 **Poole, Henry.** Newscaster (KOY, Phoenix, AZ, 1938).

25598 **Poole, Jim.** The "Dean of livestock market broadcasters," Poole began broadcasting on WLS (Chicago, IL) in 1925 several times a day and continued with that schedule until he retired in 1943.

25599 **Poole, Robert D.** DJ (*Turn Table Roundup*, WMRC, Greenville, SC, 1948; *Poole's Party Line*, WMRC, 1949).

25600 **Poor, John.** Newscaster (WHBQ, Memphis, TN, 1939).

25601 **Poore, Mary Ernest.** Violinist (WHAS, Louisville, KY, 1923).

25602 **Poore, Pearl May.** Soprano (KFWI, San Francisco, CA, 1929).

25603 **Poorman, A.E.** Announcer (WBAK, Harrisburg, PA, 1927).

25604 **(The) Pop Twins.** Female singing team of soprano Dorothy Drakeley and contralto Rose Quigley (WHAM, Rochester, NY, 1928–1929).

25605 ***Pop McDonald.*** CW mus. prg. (KWK, St. Louis, MO, 1939).

25606 **Popaski, Loyal.** Announcer (WJBC, LaSalle, IL, 1925).

25607 **Pope, Anita.** COM-HE (KFYO, Lubbock, TX, 1956).

25608 **Pope, Bette.** COM-HE, (WCPC, Houston, MS, 1957).

25609 **Pope, Bill.** Sportscaster (WESG, Elmira, NY, 1927–1939; WENY, Elmira, NY, 1944–1945; *Sports Front*, WENY, 1947–1948; *The Last Round*, WOKO, Albany, NY, 1949; *Sports Extra*, WOKO, 1950; WABY, Albany, NY, 1951; WENY, 1952; WABY, 1954–1955). DJ (*You Name It—We Play It*, WABY, 1950–1952).

25610 **Pope, Bob.** Leader (*Bob Pope Orchestra*, instr. mus. prg., WBT, Charlotte, NC, 1936).

25611 **Pope, Francois.** COM-HE (WBKB, Chicago, IL, 1951).

25612 **Pope, Georgia.** Guitarist Pope was a member of a guitar trio with Ruth Elder and J. Henry Brady (WHAS, Louisville, KY, 1923).

25613 **Pope, Loren.** Newscaster (WOL, Washington, DC, 1946).

25614 **Pope, Marshall.** Newscaster (KFJZ, Fort Worth, TX, 1940).

25615 **Pope, Russell.** Newscaster (KVCV, Redding, CA, 1944).

25616 ***Popeye.*** A children's dramatic series, *Popeye* was based on E.C. Segar's comic strip. Wheatena sponsored this entertaining show for youngsters. The cast included: Floyd Buckley, Don Costello, Jimmy Donnelly, Jean Kay, James Kelly, Olive La Moy, Charles Lawrence, Det Poppen, Mae Questel, Jack Mercer, Everett Sloane and Miriam Wolfe. Victor Erwin's Cartoonland Band supplied musical backgrounds. Kevin Keech was the announcer. (15 min., Thursday, 7:15–7:30 P.M., NBC-Red, 1935).

25617 **Poplier [Porlier], John.** Tenor Poplier was billed as "The Young Whispering Tenor" (WGBS, New York, NY, 1928).

25618 **Popo, Bill.** Sportscaster (WENY, Elmira, NY, 1941).

25619 **Popora, Titania.** Contralto (*Titania Popora*, vcl. mus. prg., KFWM, Oakland, CA, 1928).

25620 **Poppe, Vera English.** Cellist (WMAQ, Chicago, IL,1923).

25621 **Popper, Daisy.** Soprano (WJY, New York, NY, 1924).

25622 **Popper, Herman.** Leader (Herman Popper's Viennese Trio, WJZ, New York, NY, 1925).

25623 **Popper, Lillian Seckendorf.** Pianist (WJZ, New York, NY, 1925).

25624 ***Popular Classics.*** Leopold Spitalny conducted the orchestra on the good music program (30 min., Sunday, 7:00–7:30 P.M., NBC-Blue, 1938).

25625 **Porch, J.W.** "Harmonica and guitar artist" (WLAC, Nashville, TN, 1929).

25626 **Porcher, W.H., Jr.** Sportscaster (WAYS, Charlotte, NC, 1944).

25627 **Port, Shirley.** Soprano (KTAB, Oakland, CA, 1926).

25628 **Porta, Josephine.** Soprano (WFLA, Clearwater, FL, 1929).

25629 **Porta, Pat.** DJ (*Rural Route 950*, KFSA, Fort Smith, AR, 1948).

25630 **Porter, A.W.** A student at the University of Arkansas, Porter broadcast play-by-play of the football game between the University and the Northeastern Oklahoma Teachers College in 1924 (KFMQ, Fayetteville, AR, 1924).

25631 **Porter, Beatrice J.** COM-HE (WRGA, Rome, GA, 1960).

25632 **Porter, Bob.** DJ (WJJD, Chicago, IL, 1957).

25633 **Porter, C.W.** Sportscaster and play-by-play broadcaster of local football games (WJRI, Lenoir, NC, 1950–1951).

25634 **Porter, Charles.** DJ (*Juke Box Review*, KIRX, Kirksville, MO, 1950).

25635 **Porter, Clarine J.** COM-HE (WCOA, Pensacola, FL, 1956). Porter conducted a mid-afternoon women's program.

25636 **Porter, Don.** DJ (*Swing Soiree*, KUGN, Eugene, OR, 1948; *Don Porter Show*, KGO, San Francisco, CA, 1949; KXL, Portland, OR, 1956–1957).

25637 **Porter, Everett, Jr.** DJ (*Trax on Wax*, WRGA, Rome, GA, 1948). Sportscaster (*Spotlight on Sports*, WGWD, Gadsden, AL, 1950).

25638 **Porter, Hazel.** COM-HE (WRGA, Rome, GA, 1960).

25639 **Porter, Homer.** News analyst (*Community News*, WIGM, Medford, WI, 1948).

25640 **Porter, Irving.** Announcer (WGCP, Newark, NJ, 1925).

25641 **Porter, Jeanne.** COM-HE (WELI, New Haven, CT, 1951).

25642 **Porter, Margaret.** Soprano (WMEX, Boston, MA, 1940).

25643 **Porter, May [Maye].** COM-HE (KVNJU, Logan, UT, 1955–1956).

25644 ***Porter Patter.*** Linda Porter interviewed guests and delivered informative talks for women on her sustaining show (15 min., Thursday, 9:30–9:45 A.M., WMCA, New York, NY, 1942).

25645 **Porter, Ray.** DJ (*Alarm Clock Club*, KRHD, Duncan, OK, 1950).

25646 **Porter, Ross.** Newscaster (KGFF, Shawnee, OK, 1937).

25647 **Porter, Steve.** Singer (*The Dutch Masters Minstrels* program, NBC, 1928).

25648 Porter, Ted. DJ (*Musical Roundup*, KDRS, Paragould, AR, 1952).

25649 Porter, Winslow. Newscaster (WORL, Boston, MA, 1940; WNAB, Bridgeport, CT, 1941). Sportscaster (*Sports Review*, WINC, Winchester, VA, 1948).

25650 Porterfield, Peggy. COM-HE (WNDB, Daytona Beach, FL, 1956).

25651 Porterfield, Walter. Newscaster (KFRU, Columbia, MO, 1937).

25652 *Portia Faces Life.* Portia Blake Manning, the program's heroine, was played by Lucille Wall throughout the entire program's run (1940–1951). Portia Manning was a successful lawyer who constantly faced personal and professional problems on the popular daytime serial. Its opening announcement captured the major theme of the program: "*Portia Faces Life* ... a story reflecting the courage, spirit and integrity of American women everywhere." Over the years the program's cast included: Marjorie Anderson, Joan Banks, Luise Barclay, Donald Briggs, Edwin Bruce, Peter Capell, Les Damon, Nancy Douglass, Rosaline Greene, Ethel Intropidi, Raymond Ives, Bill Johnstone, Ginger Jones, Richard Kendrick, Alastair Kyle, John Larkin, Ken Lynch, Myron McCormick, Santos Ortega, Esther Ralston, Elizabeth Reller, Doris Rich, Larry Robinson, Bartlett Robinson, Selena Royle, Anne Seymour, Alison Skipworth, Cora B. Smith, Lyle Sudrow, Barry Sullivan, Karl Swenson, Henrietta Tedro, James Van Dyk, Walter Vaughn, Lucille Wall and Carleton Young. The program was written by Hector Chevigny and Mona Kent. The producers were Don Cope and Tom McDermott, and the directors were Hoyt Allen, Mark Goodson, Paul Knight and Beverly Smith. The announcers were George Putnam and Ron Rawson.

25653 Portillo, Ernesto. DJ (KEVT, Tucson, AZ, 1954).

25654 Portingall, Dorothy Wallace. Saxophonist-singer (WHN, New York, NY, 1924).

25655 *Portland Fire Department Orchestra.* The "smoke eaters" band broadcast weekly (60 min., Weekly, 9:00–10:00 P.M., KXL, Portland, OR, 1928). Intermission solos were sung by Brad Johnson, who was known as "The Fire Fighting Caruso."

25656 Portman, David. Newscaster (WFAS, White Plains, NY, 1944).

25657 Portola Boys Band. Earl Dillon directed the juvenile band (KPO, San Francisco, CA, 1927).

25658 *Portrait of the Artist.* Brief dramatized lives of various artists and composers such as Johannes Brahms were presented on the sustaining program. Margaret Loworth was the writer and Jack Mosman the director. Dwight Weist was the narrator (10 min., Sunday, WCBS, 1947).

25659 *Portraits of Harmony.* Vincent Lopez and his orchestra presented "tone paintings" of popular songs on the weekly network show (30 min., 8:30–9:00 P.M. CST, NBC-Blue, 1936).

25660 Porwaniecki [Porwaniki], Leo. DJ (*Sunny Side of the Street*, WLIP, Kenosha, WI, 1948; *Music for Today*, WLIP, 1952–1957).

25661 Posenke, Brad. Newscaster (WNMP, Evanston, IL, 1948). Sportscaster (*Game Time Rhythms* and *Hickory House*, WNMP, Evanston, IL, 1948).

25662 Poska, Al. DJ (*Midnight Flyer*, KFI, Los Angeles, CA, 1947–1950; *The Flyer*, KFI, 1954–1957).

25663 Poslam Hawaiians. Hawaiian band (WMCA, New York, NY, 1926).

25664 Posselt, Marjorie. Leader (Friendly Maids [instrumental quintet], WEEI, Boston, MA, 1928–1929).

25665 Post, Dick. Actor Post was in the cast of *Road of Life.*

25666 Post, Gladys. Vocalist (*Gladys Post*, vcl. mus. prg., KMOX, St. Louis, MO, 1935).

25667 Post, Hazel. Soprano (WHAZ, Troy, NY, 1937).

25668 Post, Johnny. Baritone (WQJ, Chicago, IL, 1926).

25669 Post, Myra. Pianist (WFLA, Clearwater, FL, 1929).

25670 Post, William, Jr. Actor Post appeared in *John's Other Wife.*

25671 Post Lodge Orchestra. Fraternal orchestra directed by Harold Oxley (WJZ, New York, NY, 1924).

25672 Posthauer, Mercedes. Soprano (WNYC, New York, NY, 1925).

25673 *Pot of Gold.* The original *Pot of Gold* program was hosted by Horace Heidt and featured his orchestra (NBC, 1939). The program was an early "big money" giveaway show on which $1,000 was given away to the listener who answered the program's weekly telephone call. The random phone number to be called was selected by three spins of the "Wheel of Fortune." The show was conceived by Ed Byron and gained immediate popularity because of the large amount of money it gave away. The show was taken off NBC in 1940 after its first season. *Variety* (October 9, 1946, p.53) said that the *Pot of Gold* program went off the air when the FCC began to investigate its operation. The program returned on ABC in 1946 for one season with Happy Felton as host, Harry Salter's orchestra, singers Vera Holly and Jimmy Carroll and announcers Bob Shephard and Lyn Sterling.

25674 *Potash and Perlmutter.* The program revived two Jewish characters created by Montague Glass. The sponsor was Health Products Company, manufacturers of Feenamint laxative. The program was a warm-hearted, humorous sketch that featured Joseph Greenwald and Lou Welsch, stage and screen comedians, in the title role (15 min., Monday, 8:30–8:45 P.M., NBC-Blue, 1933).

25675 Pote, Garry. DJ (*Classic Corner*, WKMC, Roaring Springs, PA, 1960).

25676 Poteet, Sandy. DJ (*Ricky's Request*, KFJI, Klamath Falls, OR, 1949).

25677 Potes, Eugene. Newscaster (WNAD, Norman, OK, 1938). Sportscaster (WNAD, 1941).

25678 Pothoff, Wilma. Pianist (KFI, Los Angeles, CA, 1927).

25679 Potholm, Dagmar. Reader (WTIC, Hartford, CT, 1926).

25680 Potler, Bob. DJ (*Potler's Platter Party*, KFWB, Hollywood, CA, 1948).

25681 Potter, Alice. COM-HE (WEAV, Plattsburgh, NY, 1960).

25682 Potter, Amy. Violinist (KFWM, Oakland, CA, 1926).

25683 Potter, Andrew. Newscaster (KROW, Oakland, CA, 1939).

25684 Potter, Bob. DJ (KCLO, Leavenworth, KS, 1957).

25685 Potter, Cliffordean. COM-HE (WOMI, Owensboro, KY, 1951–1955).

25686 Potter, Dick. DJ (*Dick's Doghouse*, WMPS, Memphis, TN, 1949).

25687 Potter, Evelyn. Pianist (KHJ, Los Angeles, CA, 1925).

25688 Potter, Francis. Leader (Francis Potter's Banjo Orchestra, WOAW, Omaha, NE, 1925–1926).

25689 Potter, George. DJ (KIYI, Shelby, MT, 1948).

25690 Potter, Grace. COM-HE (WMOU, Berlin, NH, 1954).

25691 Potter, John. Newscaster (KROW, Oakland, CA, 1940).

25692 Potter, Morton. Leader (*Morton Potter Orchestra*, instr. mus. prg., WHAS, Louisville, KY, 1934).

25693 Potter, Paul. Actor Potter was in the cast of *Stella Dallas.*

25694 Potter, Penny. COM-HE (KCOK, Tulare, CA, 1951).

25695 Potter, Peter. DJ (*Peter Potter's Platter Parade*, KFWB, Hollywood, CA, 1948–1949; KLAC, Los Angeles, CA, 1954–1955).

25696 Potter, Sam. DJ (WFKY, Frankfort, KY, 1948).

25697 Potterfield, Peggy. COM-HE (WNDB, Daytona Beach, FL, 1957).

25698 Potts, Porter E. Leader (Porter E. Potts Hotel Van Curler Orchestra, WGY, Schenectady, NY, 1926).

25699 Poucher, J. Wayne. Sportscaster (WSLS, Roanoke, VA, 1944; WCSC, Charleston, SC, 1947; *Looking at Sports*, WUSN, Charleston, SC, 1948; WCOS, Columbia, SC, 1949–1950; *Sports Headlines*, WCOS, 1951–1955).

25700 Pouler, (Mrs.) Charles. Soprano (KGO, Oakland, CA, 1925).

25701 Poulter [Pouler], (Mrs.) Charles. Soprano (KGO, Oakland, CA, 1925).

25702 Poulus, Betty. Contralto (*Major Bowes Capitol Theater Family*, NBC, 1928).

25703 Poulus, Jerry. DJ (KIEM, Eureka, CA, 1950).

25704 Pournelle, Eugene. Newscaster (WHBQ, Memphis, TN, 1941).

25705 Povich, Shirley. Sportscaster (WINX, Washington, DC, 1941; WTOP, Washington, DC, 1952).

25706 Powe, Dorothy. COM-HE (KPLC, Lake Charles, LA, 1955).

25707 Powell, Bill. DJ (*Bounding with Billy*, WSOK, Nashville, TN, 1952).

25708 Powell, Bob. DJ (*Spinner's Sanctum*, WGAN, Portland, ME, 1948).

25709 Powell, Cathy. COM-HE (WADK, Newport, RI, 1960).

25710 Powell, Charles "Charlie." DJ (*Week End Revue* and *Favorite Recordings*, WKJG, Fort Wayne, IN, 1948; *After Breakfast*, WKJG, 1950).

25711 Powell, Dick. After a successful singing career in the movies and on radio, Powell successfully played a tough private investigator. Among his network appearances were those on *Final Edition, Hollywood Hotel, Richard Diamond, Private Investigator* and *Rogue's Gallery*.

25712 Powell, Don. Sportscaster (*Poach the Coach*, KLCB, Libby, MT, 1955).

25713 Powell, Ed. DJ (*Duneland Danceland*, WWCA, Gary, IN, 1952).

25714 Powell, Edith. Singer (WOV, New York, NY, 1936).

25715 Powell, Eleanor and Laurence Powell. Instrumental team that played Hebridean folk music on violin and piano (KUOA, Fayetteville, AR, 1926).

25716 Powell, Helen. Soprano (KWSC, Pullman, WA, 1926).

25717 Powell, Jack "Scat." DJ (*Club Matinee*, WTOD, Toledo, OH, 1948; *2315 Club*, WKY, Oklahoma City, OK, 1950).

25718 Powell, Jesse. COM-HE (KLMO, Longmont, CO, 1956).

25719 Powell, Jimmy. Sportscaster (KVOA, Tucson, AZ, 1940). Newscaster (KVOA, Tucson, AZ, 1941).

25720 Powell, John. Pianist (*Atwater Kent Hour*, NBC, 1927).

25721 Powell, Kenneth C. "Ken." DJ (*1400 Club*, WELM, Elmira, NY, 1947–1950).

25722 Powell, Larry. DJ (WIMS, Michigan City, IN, 1949).

25723 Powell, Lib. COM-HE (WOOW, Greenville, NC, 1960).

25724 Powell, Loren. Director (KMTR Concert Orchestra, KMTR Hollywood, CA, 1926; Loren Powell's Little Symphony, KMTR, 1929).

25725 Powell, Louise. Pianist (WHAS, Louisville, KY, 1925).

25726 Powell, Malvern. Announcer (WGH, Newport News, VA, 1925).

25727 Powell, Max. DJ (*Hits for the Mrs.*, WHIT, New Bern, NC, 1960).

25728 Powell, Neville. DJ (*Harlemania*, KRIC, Beaumont, TX, 1948).

25729 Powell, (Mrs.) Pasco. *See* **Aunt Sally.**

25730 Powell, Paul. Pianist (WFAA, Dallas, TX, 1929).

25731 Powell, Sally. COM-HE (KAMD, Camden, AR, 1955).

25732 Powell, Steve. DJ (KCRC, Enid, OK, 1952).

25733 Powell, Teddy. Leader (*Teddy Powell Orchestra*, instr. mus. prg., MBS, 1942).

25734 Powell, Tom. Recognized as one of the best known Scots dialect singers and impersonators in the amateur ranks, Powell's broadcasts contained a homey philosophy and warm humor that was somewhat reminiscent of Sir Harry Lauder. He appeared on several stations in the late 1920s.

25735 Powell, Verne. Saxophonist (KFAB, Lincoln, NE, 1929).

25736 Powell, Woody. Sportscaster (*Sports Final*, WCVA, Culpepper, VA, 1952).

25737 Power, E.B. Stamp specialist spoke on such topics as, "Hidden Fortunes in Cancelled Stamps" (WJZ, New York, NY, 1924).

25738 Power, Matty. COM-HE (KYUM, Yuma, AZ, 1954).

25739 Power, Tom. DJ (*Sunrise Serenade*, WMUR, Manchester, NH, 1952).

25740 Powers, Alice. Pianist (WFLA, Clearwater, FL, 1929).

25741 Powers, Don. DJ (*Mythical Ballroom*, KIUL, Garden City, KS, 1950).

25742 Powers, Francis J. Sportscaster (*Second Guesser*, NBC, 1937).

25743 Powers, (Dr.) George. Tenor (WMC, Memphis, TN, 1926).

25744 Powers, Jack. DJ (*Club 1150*, WJBO, Baton Rouge, LA, 1947–1950).

25745 Powers, Jim. Sportscaster (WRIV, Riverhead, NY, 1960).

25746 Powers, Jimmy. Sportscaster (WMCA, New York, NY, 1939; *Powerhouse*, WHN, New York, NY, 1940; WOR, New York, NY and WMCA, 1941; *Powerhouse of the Air*, WNEW, New York, NY, 1949–1950; WRCA, New York, NY, 1953–1957).

25747 Powers, John. Tenor (KSD, St. Louis, MO, 1925).

25748 Powers, Joseph "Joe." DJ (WNAV, Annapolis, MD, 1949; *Hillbilly Jamboree*, WBMD, Baltimore, MD, 1954–1957).

25749 Powers, Leighton. Leader (*Leighton Powers Orchestra*, instr. mus. prg., WPTF, Raleigh, NC, 1936).

25750 Powers, Percy. DJ (*62 Club*, WRBC, Jackson, MS, 1947). Sportscaster (*Sports Roundup* and local baseball and football play-by-play broadcasting, WRBC, 1951; *Sports Roundup*, WRBC, 1952–1955; *Spotlight on Sports*, WJQS, Jackson, MS, 1960).

25751 Powers, Ralph. DJ (*Morning in Maryland*, WFBR, Baltimore, MD, 1947; *Ralph Powers Show*, WBMD, Baltimore, MD, 1950).

25752 Powers, Robert W. Leader (Robert W. Powers Orchestra and the Robert W. Powers Hudson-Essex Orchestra, WJAR, Providence, RI, 1926).

25753 Powers, Ted. DJ (*Power House*, WDEV, Waterbury, VT, 1949–1952). Sportscaster (WDEV, 1953; *Sports Final*, WDEV, 1954).

25754 Powers, Tom. DJ (*Second Cup of Coffee*, WADK, Newport, RI, 1960).

25755 Powers, Vern. DJ (WDBL, Springfield, TN, 1949).

25756 Powers, William. Powers was billed as a "Colored" tenor (NBC-San Francisco, CA studio broadcasts, 1929).

25757 *(The) Powers Charm School.* Beauty authority John Robert Powers answered questions on beauty and charm that were sent in by listeners (25 min., Monday through Friday, 12:35–1:00 P.M., NBC-Blue, Sustaining, 1946).

25758 *Powers Gourand.* Yellow Cab Company sponsored radio raconteur Gourand on the popular local program. He was known as a radio man-about-town, who talked about anything and everything (10 min., Wednesday, 12:00–12:10 P.M., WCAU, Philadelphia, PA, 1936). On a later show, once again sponsored by the Yellow Cab Company, Gourand talked mainly about topics with a local Philadelphia flavor (10 min., Tuesday, 11:30–11:40 P.M., WCAU, Philadelphia, PA, 1942).

25759 Powless, Sam. DJ (*Saturday Session*, WHBU, Anderson, IN, 1950).

25760 Poyner, Alice. Violinist (KPO, San Francisco, CA, 1923).

25761 Poyner, Graham. Newscaster (WPTF, Raleigh, NC, 1938). Sportscaster (WPTF, 1939).

25762 Poynton, Loretta. Busy actress Poynton appeared on such daytime serial programs as *Kitty Keene* aka *Kitty Keene, Incorporated*; *Mary Marlin* aka *The Story of Mary Marlin*; *Romance of Helen Trent*; *Betty and Bob*; and *Dan Harding's Wife*.

25763 Prados, (Mrs.) James. COM-HE (KSLO, Monroe, LA, 1951).

25764 *Prairie Dream Boys.* CW mus. prg. (WNAX, Yankton, SD, 1939).

25765 *Prairie Farmer Dinner Bell Program.* *Prairie Farmer* magazine sponsored this long-running show, whose audience consisted mainly of farm families listening at noon. John Baker conducted the program that presented various informative features for farmers and many musical selections. Tenor Otto Marek was one of the WLS regulars that appeared frequently. The program always closed with a hymn and the Rev. Dr. John W. Holland speaking briefly. Holland either read a poem or told of an inspirational incident, but always ended with a brief moment of meditation (45 min., Monday through Friday, 12:00–12:45 P.M., WLS, Chicago, IL, 1937). John Baker also conducted the *4-H Club*, *Future Farmers of America* and *Garden Program* on the WLS Saturday programming schedule that appealed to farmers and their family members.

25766 *Prairie Farmer School Time.* Every school day from 1:00–1:15 P.M., WLS (Chicago, IL) presented the educational program. Each day of the week was devoted to a different educational topic:

Monday: Current Events
Tuesday: Music Appreciation
Wednesday: Business and Industry
Thursday: Touring the World
Friday: Good Manners

An example of the programming presented was a visit to the Chicago Railroad Station with E.S. Buckmaster and J.R. Kastner describing the Railway Express Agency; Javier Cerecedo speaking about his native Puerto Rico; and the "Woodlands Trails" feature by Trailblazer Don, who talked about the migration of birds (15 min., Monday through Friday, WLS, Chicago, IL, 1935).

25767 *Prairie Folks.* Erik Rolf played the leading role in the daytime serial that told the story of the struggles faced by settlers in Minnesota in the 1870's. Rolf was supported by a talented cast including Morris Carnovsky, Cliff Carpenter, Kingsley Colton, Nell Converse, Parker Fennelly, Josephine Fox, Joe Helgeson and Helen Warren (1930s).

25768 ***Prairie President.*** William Vickland directed the program and played Abraham Lincoln on the dramatic series based on Lincoln's life. Raymond Warren wrote the program. Harriet Gordon Bingham played Ann Rutledge. Other cast members included Grace Leonard Bailey, Dolly Day, Theodore Doucet, Douglas Hope, Ellen Vogler and Louis Ramsdell (Weekly, WLS, Chicago, IL, 1930).

25769 ***Prairie Ramblers and Patsy Montana.*** The Prairie Ramblers were a popular CW music group that first was called the Kentucky Ramblers. The band included Chick Hurt, Jack Taylor, Salty Holmes and left-handed fiddler, Shelby "Tex Atchison." The popular country-western singer, Patsy Montana, was a regular performer with the group when they worked for a short period on WOR (Newark, NJ, 1934). The band had its own program backing Gene Autry at WLS in 1933. Their programs, sponsored by the Drug Trade Company (15 min., Monday through Saturday, WLS, Chicago, IL, 1936–1937). The group and Patsy Montana were also regulars on the *National Barn Dance* (WLS, Chicago, 1936–1956). When Patsy Montana left the group in the 1940s, musicians Rusty Gill, George Barnes and Augie Kline joined it.

25770 **Prairie Singer.** CW singer, no other information (WLS, Chicago, IL, 1939).

25771 ***Prairie Sweethearts.*** CW singing team, not otherwise identified (WMMN, Fairmont, WV, 1936).

25772 **Prasek, Winnie.** COM-HE (KVIC, Victoria, TX, 1954).

25773 **Prater, Frank.** DJ (*The No Name Show*, WBNS, Columbus, OH, 1948).

25774 **Prater, George.** Black DJ (*Harlem Express*, KGBC, Galveston, TX, 1949–1960). Prater was a popular DJ who conducted two daily shows. One was his night time (10:00–12:00 midnight) *Harlem Express* program broadcast Monday through Friday. The other was an early morning show that was equally popular.

25775 **Prather, Bob.** DJ (*Hayloft Jamboree*, WIRJ, Humboldt, TX, 1949).

25776 **Prather, Genevieve.** Blues singer (WCFL, Chicago, IL,1935).

25777 **Pratt, Betty.** Actress Pratt was in the cast of the *Young Dr. Malone* daytime serial.

25778 **Pratt, "Bud."** DJ (*1230 Club*, KRES, St. Joseph, MO, 1948–1950). Sportscaster (KSIS, Sedalia, MO, 1957).

25779 **Pratt, Clara.** COM-HE (KSEL, Lubbock, TX, 1951).

25780 **Pratt, Jay.** DJ (*Jay Juke Box*, KLKC, Parsons, KS, 1949).

25781 **Pratt, Jim.** DJ (*Hits and Headlines*, KGBS, Harlingen, TX, 1952).

25782 **Pratt, Molly.** Pianist (KPO, San Francisco, CA, 1923).

25783 **Pratt, Richard B.** DJ (*Midday Melodies*, KSUB, Cedar City, UT, 1947).

25784 **Pratt, Russell.** Originator of the *Topsy Turvy Time* and *Potpourri* variety programs (WMAQ, Chicago, IL, 1928–1929). Along with Ransom Sherman and Joe Rudolph, Pratt was one of the "Three Doctors" and one of the "Phee Dees" on the *Musical Potpourri* show. Pratt's *Topsy Turvy Time Radio Club for Boys and Girls* enrolled more than 300,000 boys and girls.

25785 **Pray, Claude.** Newscaster (KFIZ, Fond-du-Lac, WI, 1939).

25786 **Pray, Erwin M.** Announcer (KFVR, Denver, CO, 1925–1927).

25787 **Preaw, Eddie.** Leader (*Eddie Preaw Orchestra*, instr. mus. prg., WIP, Philadelphia, PA, 1935).

25788 **Pregg, [Preeg], Herbert.** Pregg was the station's orchestra director-violinist (KTCL, Seattle, WA, 1926; KOMO, Seattle, WA, 1928–1929).

25789 **Preisler, Charles.** Preisler was a violinist on the staff of the Central College Conservatory (KFKQ, Conway, AR, 1923).

25790 **Premier Orchestra.** Popular radio band (WGBS, New York, NY, 1925).

25791 ***Premier Salad Dressers.*** Radio veterans Brad Browne and Al Llewelyn were the funny team featured on the show (30 min., Thursday, 9:00–9:30 P.M., CBS, 1931).

25792 **Prendergast, Ed.** DJ (*Man from Mars*, WBOK, New Orleans, LA, 1952).

25793 **Prenevost, Bill.** DJ (*Juke Box Review*, KSDN, Aberdeen, SD, 1952).

25794 **Prenevost, William.** DJ (*Melody Showcase*, WATW, Ashland, WI, 1949).

25795 **Prentice, Joseph "Joe."** DJ (WMRF, Lewiston, PA, 1948; WAEB, Allentown, PA, 1949; *Grab Bag*, WGPA, Bethlehem, PA, 1950).

25796 **Prentiss, Ed.** Actor-announcer Prentiss appeared on *Armstrong of the SBI* (announcer), *Arnold Grimm's Daughter* (actor), *Barton Family* (actor), *Captain Midnight* (actor-title role), *Guiding Light* (actor), *Right to Happiness* (actor), *Romance of Helen Trent* (actor), *Silver Eagle, Mountie* (actor), *Tale of Today* (actor) and *Today's Children* (actor).

25797 **Preper, Lulu E.** Soprano (KGO, Oakland, CA, 1924).

25798 **Prescott, Allen.** DJ (ABC and WJZ, New York, NY, 1948). The "wife-saver" also tried his hand as a DJ. *See* ***Allen Prescott and The Wife Saver.***

25799 **Prescott, Eunice Curry.** Contralto (WGST, Atlanta, GA, 1925).

25800 **Prescott, Lillian.** Soprano (WAAM, Newark, NJ, 1924).

25801 ***Present from Hollywood.*** The Three Suns musical group was featured on the pleasant music show (15 min., NBC-Blue, 1946).

25802 ***Presenting Charles Boyer.*** Each program of the dramatic series began with Boyer earning food and drink by telling stories to affluent visitors (30 min, Weekly, NBC, 1950).

25803 ***Presenting Claude Rains.*** Begun as a one-time special, the transcribed show later was placed on the regular network schedule. Actor Rains read selections about significant events in the lives of famous people (15 min., Monday through Friday, 3:30–3:45 P.M., NBC, 1955).

25804 ***Presenting Mark Warnow.*** Maestro Warnow led his orchestra on the network music program (30 min., Wednesday, 8:30–9:00 P.M., CBS, 1935).

25805 ***Presenting Shakespeare.*** Thomas Dunning Rishworth, director of KSTP's dramatic programs, presented a series of Shakespearian dramas with such actors as Lucille Smith, Wilva Davis, Gould Stevens and Leo Bain. Rishworth also had a daily program on the station designed to improve speech (*The King's English*, 5 min., Monday through Friday, 1:10–1:15 P.M., KSTP, St. Paul, MN, 1932).

25806 **Presossmer, Gertrude.** Soprano (WJZ, New York, NY, 1925).

25807 **Presley, Joyce.** COM-HE (KGYN, Guymon, OK, 1957).

25808 **Presley, R.N. "Bob."** DJ (*Radio Relay Quiz*, KCNY, San Marcos, TX, 1952; KTBC, Austin, TX, 1957; KILT, Houston, TX, 1960).

25809 **Presnell, Marjorie.** COM-HE (WOR, Newark, NJ, 1929).

25810 **Press, Carl.** Newscaster (WKRC, Cincinnati, OH, 1944).

25811 ***(The) Press Box Quarterback.*** Eastern Silk Mills sponsored the weekly sports show, on which the star player of the past weekend's high school or college games was interviewed. This formed the basis for a sports contest that allowed listeners to vote for the "Player of the Year" (KTSM, El Paso, TX, 1942).

25812 **Presser, Ben.** DJ (*Three Ring Circus*, KSFT, Trinidad, CO, 1947).

25813 **Pressey, (Mrs.) Edward.** Talks on law topics for women (WGY, Schenectady, NY, 1923).

25814 **Pressley, Harriet.** COM-HE (WPTF, Raleigh, NC, 1943–1960). After working in a commercial plant as an analytical chemist during World War I, Pressley came to Peach Institute (college) in Raleigh, North Carolina, to teach chemistry. During World War II when many announcers left radio to enter military service, she joined the staff of WPTF. At the station she was responsible for various programs, including *Your Child and You* and the *Institute of Religion*. However, her own program, *The Harriet Pressley Show*, was her major concern. Her program ran on WPTF for 17 years from 1943 to 1960. Some of the people she interviewed on the program was Eleanor Roosevelt, Marian Anderson, Eddie Albert and Dr. Ralph Bunche. In 1979, Pressley (Pressley, 1979) observed that women had many more opportunities in radio than when she began, and that many more women were "doing the news" and finding greater opportunities.

25815 **Prest, Bob.** DJ (*Melody Tune*, WWHG, Hornell, NY, 1949).

25816 **Preston, Art.** News analyst (*Morning News* and *News at Noon*, KTUC, Tucson,

AZ, 1947). DJ (*1400 Club*, KTUC, Tucson, AZ, 1947–1949). Sportscaster (*Sports Parade*, KTUC, 1947).

25817 Preston, C. Newscaster (KWAL, Wallace, ID, 1942).

25818 Preston, Lew. Sportscaster (*Sports Highlights*, KVAI, 1948). DJ (*Saddle Pals*, *940 Trail* and *All Star Western*, KVAI, Amarillo, TX, 1950).

25819 Preston, Violet. Blues singer (KFWB, Hollywood, CA, 1925).

25820 Preston, Walter. Announcer (WIBO, Chicago, IL, 1925; NBC, New York, NY, 1928). Baritone (WJZ, New York, NY, 1928; *Philco Hour of Theater Memories*, NBC-Blue, New York, NY, 1927–1931).

25821 Preston, Walter. Director Preston worked on the *Sally of the Movies* program. He may have been the announcer-baritone described above.

25822 Prestridge, Flo. COM-HE (KDBS, Alexandria, LA, 1957).

25823 *Pretty Kitty Kelly.* Wonder Bread and Hostess Cupcakes sponsored the daytime serial that told the story of Kitty Kelly, an Irish countess, who emigrated to America. A framed murder charge, an attempt to rob her of her heritage and amnesia caused her considerable difficulty. The program's cast included: Charme Allen, Arline Blackburn, Helen Choate, Clayton "Bud" Collyer, Matt Crowley, Artells Dickson, Louis Hector, Dennis Hoey, Ethel Intropidi, Richard Kollmar, Florence Malone, John Pickard, Bartlett Robinson, Charles Slattery, Howard Smith, Luis Van Rooten, Lucille Wall and Charles Webster. The writer was Frank Dahm. Matt Crowley was the program's announcer-narrator (15 min., Monday through Friday, 5:45–6:00 P.M., CBS, 1937). The program was broadcast from 1937 to 1940.

25824 Preuss, Russ. Sportscaster (*Fallstaff Sportscast*, KTTR, Rolla, MO, 1950–1951).

25825 Prevatt, Dennis. DJ (*Swing Shift*, WJHP, Jacksonville, FL, 1949).

25826 Previn, Charlie. Leader (*Charlie Previn Orchestra*, instr. mus. prg., NBC, 1934).

25827 Prewitt, Larry. Leader (Larry Prewitt's Louisvillians Orchestra, WHAS, Louisville, KY, 1926).

25828 Preyer, Carl. Pianist (KFKU, Lawrence, KS, 1925).

25829 Price, Burt. Sportscaster (*Sports News*, KHQ, Spokane, WA, 1929).

25830 Price, C.A. Newscaster (WTAW, College Station, TX, 1945).

25831 Price, Carolyn. COM-HE (KSD, St. Louis, MO, 1939).

25832 Price, Charlie. DJ (*Charlie's Night Train*, WOAY, Oak Hill, WV, 1952).

25833 Price, Clyde. DJ (*Popular Music*, WFMH, Cullman, AL, 1952).

25834 Price, Dan. DJ (*Farm Fair*, WALB, Albany, GA, 1947). Sportscaster (*Sports Round-Up*, WALB, 1947).

25835 Price, (Miss) Elizabeth. Miss Price broadcast piano lessons (WLAC, Nashville, TN, 1929).

25836 Price, Ethel Eaves. Soprano (WBCN, Chicago, IL, 1926).

25837 Price, Georgia. Pianist and harpist (WJAX, Jacksonville, FL, 1929 and NBC, 1929).

25838 Price, Gordon. DJ (*Parade of Bands* and *The WNEX Bandstand*, WNEX, Macon, GA, 1948).

25839 Price, Joe. DJ (*Afternoon Jam Session*, WKSR, Pulaski-Lawrenceburg, TN, 1947).

25840 Price, John. Newscaster (WHP, Harrisburg, PA, 1946–1948).

25841 Price, John. Newscaster (WKAT, Miami Beach, FL, 1948).

25842 Price, Juanita Blair. Soprano (WFAA, Dallas, TX, 1924).

25843 Price, Lillian. Soprano (WGBS, New York, NY, 1925).

25844 Price, Marjorie. COM-HE (WILM, Wilmington, DE, 1949–1957).

25845 Price, Nancy. COM-HE (WINA, Charlottesville, VA, 1956–1957).

25846 Price, Nibs. University of California football coach Price teamed with a "sports expert" and sports editor of the San Francisco *Chronicle* each week to discuss weekly gridiron news (KTAB, San Francisco, CA, 1926).

25847 Price, Norman. Price was the tenor and vocal arranger for the Armchair Quartet. The group appeared on the *Enna Jettick Melodies* program (CBS, 1928–1929) sponsored by Dunn & McCarthy makers of Enna Jettick Shoes.

25848 Price, Pam. COM-HE (WBBQ, Augusta, GA, 1957).

25849 Price, Paul. DJ (*Priceless Hour*, WANE, Ft. Wayne, IN, 1949; *Paul Price Show*, WFTW, Fort Wayne, IN, 1950).

25850 Price, Peggy. Blues singer (KTM, Santa Monica, CA, 1928–1929).

25851 Price, Priscilla. Violinist (KSTP, St. Paul–Minneapolis, MN, 1929).

25852 Price, R.E. Newscaster (WBBO, Forrest City, NC, 1948).

25853 Price, T.W. Delivered talks on his *Dogs* program such as, "The Training of Police Dogs" (WLW, Cincinnati, OH, 1925–1926).

25854 Price, Wiley. DJ (*Rockin' Rhythm*, WTMV, East St. Louis, MO, 1948; *Rhythm and Blues*, KSTL, St. Louis, MO, 1949).

25855 Price Steel Guitar Trio. Steel guitar instrumental group (WMAQ, Chicago, IL, 1923).

25856 Priddy, Marian. Pianist (WCBD, Zion, IL, 1926).

25857 Priest, Don. News commentator (WCOA, Pensacola, FL, 1959–1960). Priest's distinguished broadcast career included work at: WKNE (Keene, NH, 1950); WTSA (Brattleboro, VT, 1951); WNDB (Daytona Beach, FL, 1951); WHWB (Rutland, VT, 1951); WSPB (Sarasota, FL, 1952); WHFB (Benton Barbor, ME, 1958); and WDLP (Panama City, FL, 1959).

25858 Priest, Ward. Announcer (WCAD, Canton, NY, 1927).

25859 Priestley, Harold W. Announcer (WWJ, Detroit, MI, 1929).

25860 Prigge, Mildred. Organist (WLW, Cincinnati, OH, 1926).

25861 Prima, Buddy. Sportscaster (WCEC, Rocky Mount, NC, 1952).

25862 Prima, Louis. Leader (*Louis Prima Orchestra*, instr. mus. prg., CBS, 1935).

25863 Prime, Rosina. COM-HE (KCLV, Clovis, NM, 1954).

25864 Primely, Marjorie. Pianist (KFRC, San Francisco, CA, 1927).

25865 *Primer for Parents.* Miss Lanny Harper offered advice to parents on the sustaining local show. Paul Brentson was the announcer (30 min., Wednesday, 10:00–10:30 P.M., WNEW, New York, NY, 1947).

25866 Primikiris, John. DJ (WHDL, Olean, NY, 1957).

25867 Primm, Art. Newscaster (KTRC, Visalia, CA, 1937–1939; KVI, Tacoma, WA, 1942; KFRC, San Francisco, CA, 1945).

25868 Prince, Bob. Prince, who was best known for his work in sports, also worked as a newscaster (*11th Hour News*, WCAE, Pittsburgh, PA, 1947). Sportscaster (WJAS, 1944–1946; *Bob Prince Sports*, WJAS, 1947; *Case of Sports*, WJAS, 1948–1952; WENS, Pittsburgh, PA, 1955).

25869 Prince, Buck. Sportscaster (*Sports Preview by Prince*, WNBC, New York, NY, 1949).

25870 Prince, Clara. COM-HE (WEWL, Camden, TN, 1960).

25871 Prince, Dave. DJ (*Clock Watcher*, WKBW, Buffalo, NY, 1949).

25872 Prince, Graham. Leader (Graham Prince Orchestra, WGHB, Clearwater, FL and WMBC, Detroit, MI, 1926; Graham Prince and his Tar-Heel Orchestra, WGHB, Clearwater, FL, 1926).

25873 Prince, Lurinda. Contralto (WLAC, Nashville, TN, 1929).

25874 *Prince Albert Quarter Hour.* Singer Alice Joy and Van Loan's Orchestra entertained on the music show sponsored by Prince Albert pipe tobacco (15 min., Monday through Friday, 7:30–7:45 P.M., NBC-Red, 1932).

25875 *Prince Charming.* Johnny Olsen hosted the audience participation show, on which wives lunching at the Rendezvous Room of New York City's Hotel Victoria served as contestants. The wives told why their husbands were great — a "genuine Prince Charming." A group of judges awarded a two-week vacation at a summer resort, a wardrobe and other items to the convincing winner. Mort Lawrence was the announcer (30 min., Monday through Friday, 4:30–5:00 P.M., WOR, New York, NY, 1949).

25876 Prince Joveddah. Mind reader (WHN, New York, NY, 1926).

25877 *Prince of Pep and his Orchestra.* Veteran radio entertainer Charlie Wellman, the "Prince of Pep," hosted the program that featured his humor and his orchestra's music (KHJ, Los Angeles, CA, 1930). *See* **Wellman, Charlie.**

25878 *Princess Midnight.* DJ Nancy Anderson was featured. It was the first time

Boston had a late night female DJ (95 min., Monday through Friday, 11:30–1:05 A.M., WCOP, Boston, MA, 1952).

25879 ***Princess Pat Players.*** Originally a series of dramatic sketches, the program featured various performers. For example, one sketch was titled "Lord Jesse James." The program later became a serial drama, *Tales of Today*, that told the story of one family. Actors on the program were Douglas Hope, Alice Hills, Peggy Davis and Arthur Jacobson (30 min., Monday, 8:30–9:00 P.M., NBC, 1934–1935).

25880 **Prindle, Alice.** Contralto (KEX, Portland, OR, 1928).

25881 **Pringle, Aileen.** Actress Pringle was in the cast of *Joyce Jorday, Girl Interne* daytime serial program.

25882 **Pringle, Nelson.** Newscaster (CBS, 1941; KNX, Los Angeles, CA, 1942; CBS, 1944–1948).

25883 **Pringle, William.** Actor Pringle was in the cast of *Follow the Moon.*

25884 **Pringle, Pete.** Newscaster (KNX, Los Angeles, CA, 1938).

25885 **Prior, Charles E., Jr.** Tenor (WTIC, Hartford, CT, 1925).

25886 **Prior, Eddie.** Leader (*Eddie Prior Orchestra*, instr. mus. prg., WIP, Philadelphia, PA, 1935–1936).

25887 **Priscilla and Her Piano.** Pianist who was not otherwise identified (WJJD, Chicago, IL, 1940).

25888 ***Priscilla Pride.*** Miss "Pride" supplied her listeners with news about downtown Chicago shopping, women's clothing, style and the latest fashions. Songs on the program were performed by the Hometowners Quartet accompanied by organist Ralph Waldo Emerson (15 min., Monday through Friday, WLS, Chicago, IL, 1937).

25889 ***Prison Tales.*** Prison chaplain William Nisson Brenner told stories from inside prison that emphasized the evils of crime and criminals (WIP, Philadelphia, PA, 1925).

25890 **Pritchard, Bob.** Sportscaster (*Your Sports Parade, Pigskin Pickers* and *Wildcat Rally*, KPLT, Paris, TX, 1948–1949).

25891 **Pritchard, Bosh.** DJ (*You Asked For It*, WDAS, Philadelphia, PA, 1948). Sportscaster (*The Eagle's Nest*, WPEN, Philadelphia, PA, 1950; *The Sports Page*, WPEN, Philadelphia, PA, 1954). Bosh Pritchard was a great Philadelphia Eagles professional football star before becoming a broadcaster.

25892 **Pritchard, Wayne.** DJ (KSOO, Sioux Falls, SD, 1956–1960).

25893 **Pritchett, Coe.** Coe Pritchett broadcast talks on topics of interest to farmers (WFEQ, Minneapolis, MN, 1929).

25894 **Pritchett, Mary Alice.** Miss Pritchett was a singer from Bonham, Texas (WFAA, Dallas, TX, 1924).

25895 **Prittie, Don.** DJ (*Musical Mail Bag*, WLEC, Sandusky, OH, 1950).

25896 ***Private Files of Matthew Bell.*** Seabrook Farms Frozen Foods sponsored the mystery drama series starring Joseph Cotten as a police surgeon with a yen for sleuthing. Fran Carlon was also in the cast. The show was written by John Roeburt and produced and directed by Himan Brown. Phil Tonken was the announcer (30 min., Sunday, 4:30–5:00 P.M., MBS, 1952).

25897 ***(The) Private Life of Dr. Dana* (aka *The Private Practice of Dr. Dana* or *Dr. Dana*).** Jeff Chandler played the title role on the Sunday afternoon drama. Dr. Dana not only cured the medical problems of his patients, but their other personal problems as well. Nurse Gorsey, Dr. Dana's steadfast helper, was played by Mary Lansing. The program was written by Adrian Gendot. Sterling Tracy was the producer (30 min., Sunday afternoon, CBS, 1947–1948). Chandler went on to have a successful career in television and motion pictures.

25898 **Pro, Bob.** DJ (KDLK, Del Rio, TX, 1948).

25899 **Probst, Nick.** Leader (Nick Probst Banjo Trio, WBBM, Chicago, IL, 1925).

25900 **Proctor, Bob.** Sportscaster (*Sports Parade*, WLBJ, Bowling Green, KY, 1948; WLBJ, 1955).

25901 **Proctor, Frank.** DJ (WBML, Macon, GA, 1947).

25902 **Proctor, Gene.** DJ (*Proc's Pops*, WSGN, Birmingham, AL, 1952).

25903 **Proctor, Harlan.** DJ (*Hold Everything*, WCAO, Baltimore, MD, 1949).

25904 **Proder, George.** DJ (*Harlem Express*, KGBC, Galveston, TX, 1952).

25905 **Prodis, Paul.** Newscaster (WARD, Brooklyn, NY, 1939).

25906 ***Professor Fishface.*** Elmore Vincent, as Professor Fishface, was a talented comedian and singer. He also created and broadcast as Smilin' Sam from Alabam and Uncle Zeb and his Texas Troubadours (1920s and 1930s).

25907 ***Professor Henry McLemore, Humorist.*** McLemore's humor, *Variety* said, was good, but frequently delivered in a nasalized, rustic manner on the sustaining program (15 min., Friday, 8:00–8:15 P.M., CBS, 1932).

25908 ***Professor McLallen.*** Jack McLallen, a veteran vaudeville comedian, provided good humor and entertainment on the sustaining show. He was assisted by the Sizzlers, a harmony singing trio (15 min., Thursday, 10:45–11:00 P.M., NBC, 1933).

25909 ***Professor Miller and His Guitar.*** Guitarist (KFI, San Francisco, CA, 1930).

25910 ***Professor Quiz.*** Dr. Earl Craig was the quizmaster on this early quiz program. Bob Trout was the announcer and Ed Fitzgerald the director (30 min., Saturday, 7:00–7:30 P.M., CST, CBS, 1937). Along with *Uncle Jim's Question Bee*, this was one of radio's earliest and most popular quiz shows. In various formats the show was on the air from 1936 to 1948 on both CBS and ABC.

25911 ***Professor Schnitzel.*** Professor Schnitzel conducted the program, whose humor depended upon his strange grammatical forms and neologisms. George Stoll and his Rhythm group provided background music (ABC, 1929).

25912 ***Professor Socrates and His Dance Quartet.*** Despite the title, the program was a variety show that featured strong on humor and song. The program was a pastime and avocation of five Charlotte business men. Professor Junk was played by R.S. "Socrates" Rainey, a former school principal. Dago was Norman Childress. Rafe the Dumbbell was Ralph Webb. Smoky was Earl Helms, who also sang bass, and Fats was Cecil Hollifield, who also played guitar and sang humorous solos (local Charlotte, NC, radio probably in the late 1920s).

25913 **Proffen, Elna.** Soprano (WBAL, Baltimore, MD, 1926).

25914 ***Program by the Royal Order of Smoked Herring Held in the Aquarium at the Willard Battery Station.*** The variety show was typical of the late night, "wacky" anything goes programming on radio that was popular in the 1920s (WJBS, San Francisco, CA, 1926).

25915 ***Program of Songs Made Famous by Jenny Lind.*** As its name suggests, the program narrowly focused on particular vocal selections, i.e., "numbers selected from the Freida Hempel program," performed by Juanita Tennyson accompanied by pianist Frank Moss (KFRC, San Francisco, CA, 1927).

25916 **Progressive Music School.** The Progressive Music School's pupils broadcast various variety programs at irregular intervals consisting of vocal and instrumental selections (KSTP, St. Paul–Minneapolis, MN, 1929).

25917 **Prome, (Mme.) Tessie.** Dramatic soprano (WHN, New York, NY, 1923).

25918 ***Promenade Serenade.*** Milton Cross narrated the good musical program with tenor Jan Peerce, concert pianist Earl Wild and Bernard Green's Orchestra (30 min., Monday, 8:30–9:00 P.M., ABC, 1953).

25919 ***(The) Prophecy.*** *The Prophecy* program was actually one big commercial, since the dramatic sketch traced the origin and development of Poland Springs water and the hotel resort associated with it (30 min., Tuesday, 9:00–9:30 P.M., CBS, 1933).

25920 ***Prophylactic Orchestra.*** A popular half-hour music show (30 min., Weekly, NBC-Blue, 1928–1929).

25921 **Prosser, Frances M.** COM-HE (KGMC, Englewood, CA, 1957).

25922 **Prosser, John.** Newscaster (KTHS, Hot Springs, AR, 1939).

25923 **Prosser, Marie.** COM-HE (KATE, Albert Lea, MN, 1956–1957).

25924 **Protsman, Faith M.** COM-HE (WNER, Live Oak, FL, 1957).

25925 **Proudfoot, Frank.** Announcer (WKBN, Youngstown, OH, 1925).

25926 **Prough, Celia.** Saxophonist (KFSG, Los Angeles, CA, 1924).

25927 **Prough, Ed.** Sportscaster (WDAY, Fargo, ND, 1937–1939).

25928 **Provence, Robert "Bob."** Newscaster (WKBN, Youngstown, OH, 1941; *11th Hour News*, WKNA, Charleston, WV, 1947). Sportscaster (*Keystone Sports Review*, WKNA, Charleston, WV, 1947; *Sports Review* and *Sports Final*, WKNA, 1949).

25929 **Provendie, Zina.** Actress Provendie was in the cast of *The Goldbergs* daytime serial.

25930 Provensen, Dick. DJ (*Music in the Night*, WFAA, Dallas, TX, 1950; KGFJ, Los Angeles, CA, 1957).

25931 Provensen, Martin [Marthin]. Announcer (WENR, Chicago, IL, and WBCN, Chicago, IL, 1928–1929).

25932 Provenson, Herley. News analyst (*Pinex News Reel Theatre*, WHN, New York, NY, 1942).

25933 Providence Biltmore Dance Orchestra. Hotel band (WJAR, Providence, RI, 1926).

25934 Providence Dairy "Grade A" Entertainers. Commercially sponsored orchestra (WJAR, Providence, RI, 1926).

25935 Provo, Frank. Actor-writer Provo worked on the *Jane Arden* (actor), *Mrs. Wiggs of the Cabbage Patch* (actor), *One Man's Family* (actor) and *Wendy Warren and the News* (writer).

25936 Provost, Eric. Sportscaster (*Sports Special*, WSPB, Sarasota, FL, 1947).

25937 Prow, E. Leader (*E. Prow Orchestra*, instr. mus. prg., WIND, Chicago, IL, 1935).

25938 Prowell, Dorothy. Violinist (KOIL, Council Bluffs, IA, 1926).

25939 Prudence Brothers Orchestra. Instr. mus. prg. (KNRC, Los Angeles, CA, 1925).

25940 *Prudence Penny.* "Miss Penny" discussed various home economics topics (KFI, Los Angeles, CA, 1925).

25941 Prudence Penny of the San Francisco Examiner. The generic Miss Penny broadcast home making talks (KPO, San Francisco, CA, 1925). The actress who played Miss Penny is unknown.

25942 Prud'Homme, Cameron. Actor-writer Prud'Homme worked on *David Harum* (actor-title role), *Hawthorne House* (writer) and *The Theatre Guild of the Air* (actor).

25943 Prue, Beverly. COM-HE (WDOE, Dunkirk, NY, 1957).

25944 Pruitt, Bernice. COM-HE (WBBB, Burlington, NC, 1960).

25945 Pryce, Kenneth. Newscaster (WALB, Albany, GA, 1941).

25946 Pryor, Arthur. Leader (Arthur Pryor's Band and Pryor's Concert Band, WEBJ, New York, NY, 1925; WCAP, Washington, DC, 1928). Pryor's excellent band was also featured on the popular *General Motors Family Party* and *Shadertown Band* programs (NBC-Red, New York, NY, 1929; *Arthur Pryor's Cremo Military Band*).

25947 Pryor, Bill. Sportscaster (WNBF, Binghampton, NY, 1946; *Spotlight on Sports*, WNBF, 1947–1954). DJ (*Pryor's Party*, WNBF, 1949–1955).

25948 Pryor, Cactus. DJ (*Hoedown*, KTBC, Austin, TX, 1948; *Midway of Music*, KTBC, 1949; *The Music Maker*, KTBC, 1952).

25949 Pryor, Don. Newscaster (WTOP, Washington, DC and CBS, 1944–1947, CBS, 1948).

25950 Pryor, Eleanor. COM-HE (WIPC, Lake Wales, FL, 1956).

25951 Pryor, Lynn. Leader (Mandarin Cafe Orchestra, KPO, San Francisco, CA, 1926; KLX, Oakland, CA, 1929).

25952 Pryor, Richard. DJ (*Austin Hoedown*, KTBC, Austin, TX, 1950).

25953 Pryor, Roger. Leader (*Roger Pryor Orchestra*, instr. mus. prg., CBS, 1936–1937; NBC, 1938).

25954 Pryor Moore Concert Orchestra. Local radio band (KFI, Los Angeles, CA, 1925).

25955 Ptotke, Joe. Leader (*Joe Ptotke Orchestra*, instr. mus. prg., CBS, 1935).

25956 Public Service Programs. Radio from its earliest period carried programs of information for the public good without charge. Some of these included such shows as *The Voice of the Army*, *Here's to Veterans*, *Treasury Star Parade*, etc. Usually 15 minutes in length the transcribed programs featured the biggest names in show business. *See* **Transcriptions.**

25957 *Publix Night Owl's Frolic.* The "frolic" was broadcast from the stage of Brooklyn's Paramount Theater. Various vaudeville, stage and radio stars were featured each week (30 min., 11:30–12:00 midnight, CBS, 1930).

25958 Puccini Opera Company. Operatic group that broadcast such operas as *Aida*, *Carmen* and *The Barber of Seville* (WOR, Newark, NJ, 1923).

25959 *Puck the Comic Weekly Man.* The syndicated program contained the reading and dramatizations of such comic strips from Hearst's *American Weekly* as Hopalong Cassidy, Prince Valiant, Donald Duck, Flash Gordon, Alice in Wonderland, Beetle Bailey and Bringing Up Father (30 min., Weekly, 1950–1953).

25960 Puckett, Bert. Sportscaster (WMT, Cedar Rapids–Waterloo, IA, 1937–1940).

25961 Puckett, Martha. COM-HE (WCBI, Columbus, MS, 1954).

25962 Puckett, (George) Riley. Famous blind country music singer-guitarist Riley Puckett was accidentally blinded at the age of three. When he decided to make music his full time profession, his smooth baritone voice made him a favorite while singing with the Skillet Lickers group (WSM, Nashville, TN, 1923). Puckett was a popular CW recording artist.

25963 Puckett, Truman. DJ (*Southern Jubilee*, WJLD, Bessemer, AL, 1949; *The Truman Puckett Show*, WJLD, 1952–1960).

25964 Pudney, Earle. DJ (*Earle Pudney Show*, WGY, Schenectady, NY, 1952–1957).

25965 Puget Sound Savings and Loan Association Orchestra. Henri Damski conducted the commercially sponsored band (KJR, Seattle, WA, 1925–1926).

25966 Pugh, Ed. DJ (*Melody Merchant*, WPRE, Prairie Du Chien, WI, 1954).

25967 Pugh, Jess. Actor Pugh was in the cast of *Junior Nurse Corps*, *Og, Son of Fire*, *SilverEagle*, *Mountie* and *Mary Marlin*.

25968 Pugia, Joseph. DJ (*Battle of the Bands*, WLIO, East Liverpool, OH, 1949). Sportscaster (*Spotlight on Sports*, WLIO, East Liverpool, OH, 1951).

25969 Puida, Marie. Pianist (KDKA, Pittsburgh, PA, 1924).

25970 Pulido, Juan. Baritone (WEAF, New York, NY, WOR, Newark, NJ and WJZ, New York, NY, 1925).

25971 Pulin, Gladys. COM-HE (WHOS, Decatur, AL, 1955).

25972 Pulis, Virginia. COM-HE (KOJM, Havre, MT, 1960).

25973 Pulitz, Lois Zu. Violinist (CBS, 1929).

25974 Pulley, Guy and Katherine Pulley. Instrumental team of banjoist and guitarist (WLS, Chicago, IL, 1928).

25975 Pulley, Katherine. Pulley, a versatile musician, performed on the guitar, banjo and ukulele (WIL, St. Louis, MO, 1929).

25976 Pulliam, Billie. COM-HE (KPDN, Pampa, TX, 1951).

25977 Pullis, Gordon. Trombonist (WFLA, Clearwater, FL, 1929).

25978 Pullman High School Girls Sextette. Scholastic vocal group (KFAE, Pullman, WA, 1924).

25979 Pullman Porter Band and the Broadway Quartet. Popular metropolitan music groups (WOR, Newark, NJ, 1923).

25980 Pullman Porters. The African-American male vocal quartet was said to specialize in "spirituals and mammy" songs (WGN, Chicago, IL, 1928).

25981 Pulsifer, Fay M. Pianist (WGBS, New York, NY, 1927.)

25982 Pumphrey, Horace. Sportscaster (WKAX, Birmingham, AL, 1946). News analyst (*Behind the World News*, WKAX, Birmingham, AL, 1948).

25983 *Pun and Punishment.* This was one of the first unrehearsed programs on radio. John Cameron Swayse, former columnist and drama critic of the *Kansas City Journal*, hosted the program that was created and developed by Janet Huckins to "glorify the American pun." The show's experts produced puns on the spot in order to help contestants identify secret words and win prizes (30 min., Tuesday, 7:30–8:00 P.M. CST, KMBC, Kansas City, MO, 1941).

25984 *Pupils on Parade.* Singer Eddie Miller hosted the local program on which young music students from Eddie Miller's studio performed (15 min., Sunday, 12:15–12:30 P.M., WMCA, New York, NY, 1936).

25985 Purcell, Burke. Sportscaster (KGFX, Pierre, SD, 1939).

25986 Purcell, Estella. Lyric soprano (WBAL, Baltimore, MD, 1927).

25987 Purcell, James. Sportscaster (KVAK, Atchinson, KS, 1944–1945). Newscaster (KVAK, 1945).

25988 Purcell, Jane. Singer Purcell was known as "The Original KNX Girl" (KNX, Hollywood, CA, 1925–1929). Known as the "Girl with the Ballad Voice," Purcell sang on many NBC network shows (1931–1932).

25989 Purcell, Joan. COM-HE (WCLI, Corning, NY, 1954).

25990 Purcell, John. Newscaster (CBS, 1942).

25991 Purcell [Pursell], June. Singer Purcell was known as the "Original KNX Girl" (KNX, Hollywood, CA, 191925–1929).

25992 Purcell, Woody. DJ (*Flair*, WCHV, Charlottesville, VA, 1960).

25993 Purcer, Jim. DJ (*Wake Up Tri-State*, WCMI, Ashland, KY, 1948).

25994 Purdy, Gladys. COM-HE (KVIN, Vinita, OK, 1957).

25995 Purdy (Mrs.) Guy U. Mrs. Purdy broadcast bridge talks (WAAW, Omaha, NE, 1925).

25996 Purdy, Michael L. Newscaster (KLPM, Minot, ND, 1947).

25997 *Pure Oil Brass Band.* The Pure Oil Company sponsored the excellent brass band conducted by bandmaster Edwin Franko Goldman (30 min., Weekly, NBC-Blue, 1929).

25998 *Pure Oil Potpourri.* Pure Oil Company also sponsored the entertaining variety show hosted by Cedric Adams that featured Clellan Card and the Jack Malerich Orchestra (WCCO, MN, 1938). Clellan Card was a Minneapolis dentist's son who began work at WCCO in the early 1930s.

25999 Purnell, Charles. DJ (WILM, Wilmington, DE, 1949–1952).

26000 Purple Grackle Orchestra. Popular novelty dance band (WTAS, Elgin, IL, 1925).

26001 Purrington, Anna K. COM-HE (WICH, Norwich, CT, 1951).

26002 Purse, Todd. DJ (*Todd Purse Show*, WJLB, Detroit, MI, 1950; WJW, Cleveland, OH, 1954).

26003 *Pursuit.* John Dehner played Inspector Peter Black of Scotland Yard on the mystery show sponsored by Wrigley Gum, that was a summer replacement for the *Gene Autry Show*. Ted de Corsia and Ben Wright played the role of Black at other times. Also in the cast were Herb Butterfield, Jack Edwards, Eileen Erskine, Harold Hughes, Bill Johnstone, Byron Kane and Raymond Lawrence. William N. Robson was the program's producer-director. Music was by Marlin Skiles' Orchestra. The sound effects were produced by Clark Casey and Berne Surrey. Bob Stevenson was the announcer (30 min., Saturday, 8:30–9:00 P.M., CBS, 1949–1950). In later years, Elliot Lewis became the program's producer-director. The music was by organist Eddie Dunstedter and the Leith Stevens Orchestra. The program opened with a voice saying: "A criminal strikes quickly and fades back into the shadows of his own dark world. And then, the men from Scotland Yard begin the relentless pursuit when man hunts man."

26004 Purvis, Bette Lou. DJ (*The Girl Friend*, WPGH, Pittsburgh, PA, 1947–1950).

26005 Pushin, Ruth. Singer (WKRC, Cincinnati, OH, 1926).

26006 Puter, Jack. DJ (*Kitchen Company*, KFXJ, Grand Junction, CO, 1947). Sportscaster (*Sports Round-Up*, KFXJ, 1947).

26007 Putman, Don. DJ (*Put and Jiggs*, WBBZ, Ponca City, OK, 1949–1954).

26008 Putnam, Bob. DJ (*Sun Up in Dallas*, KIXL, Dallas, TX, 1954).

26009 Putnam, George Frederick. Sportscaster (*Tomorrow's Touchdowns* and *Football Preview and Review*, KSTP, St. Paul, MN, 1937). News analyst (*Campbell Condensed News*, *Salute to Saturday* and *Sunday News Highlights*, NBC, 1939; NBC, 1941; NBC-WEAF, New York, NY, 1942; NBC, 1945). Announcer (*Joe and Mabel* and *Portia Faces Life*, network).

26010 Putnam, Jim. DJ (*Musical Clock*, WHIT, New Bern, NC, 1954).

26011 Putnam, Ruth. News analyst (*World Situation*, WESX, Salem, MA, 1945–1948).

26012 Puttman, Charles W. Announcer (WRAV, Yellow Springs, OH, 1927).

26013 Pyatt, Al. Newscaster (KIUL, Garden City, KS, 1942).

26014 Pyle, Howard. Leader (*Howard Pyle Orchestra*, instr. mus. prg., WCAO, Baltimore, MD, 1938).

26015 Pyle, J. Howard. News analyst (KTAR, Phoenix, AZ, 1938–1941, 1945; *Arizona Highlights*, KTAR, 1947; *Arizona Highlights*, KTAR and KGLU, Safford, AZ, 1948).

26016 Pyle, Jack. DJ (*Open House* and *Club 700*, WLW, Cincinnati, OH, 1948; *Musical Clock*, KYW, Philadelphia, PA, 1949–1954; WIP, Philadelphia, PA, 1956–1957; WRCV, Philadelphia, PA, 1960). Sportscaster (WPTZ, Philadelphia, PA, 1953).

26017 Pyle, Jack. Sportscaster (*Sports World Today*, WLAC, Nashville, TN, 1948).

26018 Pyle, W.D. Announcer (KFXF, Denver, CO, 1926–1927).

26019 Pyne, Joe. Sportscaster (WVCH, Chester, PA, 1948). DJ (*Downbeat*, WVCH, 1950; WILM, Wilmington, DE, 1952).

26020 Pyles, Dave. Sportscaster (WMOA, Marietta, OH, 1953–1956).

26021 Pyron, Dick. Newscaster (WATL, Atlanta, GA, 1937; WAGA, Atlanta, GA, 1938–1939).

26022 Q-Tail. Q-Tail was a pet and mascot pig at Oklahoma A & M University that "broadcast" a suitable opening for a noon agricultural news program (KVOO, Tulsa, OK, 1928).

26023 Quaal, Ward. Newscaster, announcer and executive (WGN, Chicago, IL, 1941–1960) Ward Quaal ranks as one of the most enterprising and successful broadcaster both in front of the microphone and in the board room. As an entrepreneur, he helped found the Christine Valmy Cosmetics company, produced a Broadway play and founded a Texas oil company. It was his executive management skill, however, that made WGN radio and television a great national station.

While in high school, Quaal worked for three years as announcer, writer and salesman for WBEO (Marquette, MI). Later, while at the University of Michigan he worked on the staff of WJR (Detroit, MI). After he received his undergraduate degree from the University of Michigan on June 7, 1941, he joined WGN the following day.

His announcing job at WGN lasted only to 1942, when he entered the United States Navy. After leaving the Navy in 1945, Quaal rejoined WGN as a special assistant to the general manager. It was while serving as special assistant that his management skills became apparent. He played a major role in the development of the station's farm and public affair departments; represented the station in Washington, DC; and assisted in the development of WGN-TV that went on the air in 1948.

After taking a leave of absence to serve as executive director of Clear Channel Broadcasting Service, Washington, DC, from 1949 to 1952, Quaal joined the Crosley Broadcasting Company, Cincinnati, Ohio, in 1953 as assistant general manager. The following year he became vice-president and general manager of Crosley's radio, television and short wave properties.

He returned to WGN as vice president and general manager in 1956 and initiated an expansion program that resulted in the station becoming a national broadcasting leader with facilities for radio, television, production companies and cable coast to coast. He remained active with the station for many years, eventually retiring as President of WGN Continental Broadcasting Company — now known as the Tribune Broadcasting Company. He continues to serve the company as a management consultant.

Quaal later accepted commission assignments from Presidents Truman, Kennedy and Johnson. In addition to these government assignments, he has co-authored two books on broadcast management and now heads a broadcast consultant company.

This broadcast pioneer has been awarded many honors including: induction in *Broadcasting* magazine's Hall of Fame; the Illinois Broadcasters Association's Lifetime Achievement in Broadcasting Award; and the Governor's Award of the Chicago Chapter of the National Academy of Television Arts and Sciences for "developing the finest independent station in the United States." For his many contributions to American broadcasting, Quaal richly deserves the numerous honors and awards he has received.

26024 Quade, Warren. DJ (*Quade's Parade*, WJHL, Johnson City, TN, 1947; *Juke Box Review*, KCOY, Santa Maria, CA, 1948–1950; *Request Review*, KCOY, 1950). Sportscaster (*Sports Parade*, KCOY, Santa Maria, CA, 1948).

26025 Quaglin, Edith. COM-HE (KREX, Grand Junction, CO, 1957).

26026 Quail, (Mrs.) John. Soprano (WOC, Omaha, NE, 1927).

26027 Quain, Tom. DJ (WMAX, Grand Rapids, MI, 1957).

26028 Quakenbush, Jack. DJ (*Record Session*, WLRP, New Albany, IN, 1949).

26029 Quackenbush, John. DJ (WBEU, Beaufort, SC, 1956).

26030 *Quality Twins.* Ed East and Ralph Dumke, formerly famous for their broadcasts as the "Sisters of the Skillet," returned to radio on this show to offer their unique brand of humor and silly household advice and hints. The Dick Ballou Orchestra and tenor Gene Ramey provided the music (15 min., Tuesday and Thursday, 10:15–10:30 A.M., CST, CBS, late 1930's).

26031 Qualtrough, Morrison. Sportscaster (KROD, El Paso, TX, 1940–1941).

26032 Quann, Homer. DJ (WSVA, Harrisonburg, VA, 1956).

26033 Quarles, Giles W. *Variety* said that Quarles was billed as the "King of the Mandalie" (WGHB, Clearwater, FL, 1926).

26034 Quartel, Frankie. Leader (*Frankie Quartel Orchestra*, instr. mus. prg., KYW, Chicago, IL, 1934).

26035 Quartin-Schumann, (Mme.) Anna. Coloratura soprano (WNYC, New York, NY, 1932).

26036 Quast, Ina. Pianist (KLPM, Minot, ND, 1936).

26037 Quattlebaum, Andrew. Singer Andrew Quattlebaum of Sherill, Arkansas, a student of Chicago's Bush Conservatory, broadcast a program of vocal music (WOK, Pine Bluff, AR, 1922).

26038 Quattlebaum, Howard. DJ (*Mail Order Music*, WTBF, Troy, AL, 1948; *Best on Wax*, WAGF, Dothan, AL, 1954).

26039 Quave, Mackie. DJ (*In the Groove*, WIS, Columbia, SC, 1950–1957).

26040 Quave, Morris. Newscaster (WDOD, Chattanooga, TN, 1941).

26041 Quay, William. DJ (WESA, Charleroi, PA, 1954).

26042 Queen, Betty. Contralto (WOR, Newark, NJ, 1934).

26043 Queen, Hal. DJ (*Musical Clock*, WMNC, Morganton, NC, 1947; *Hayloft Jamboree* and *Coffee with Queen*, WHKY, Hickory, NC, 1948).

26044 Queen, Roy. DJ (*Western Round-Up*, KXWL, St. Louis, MO, 1947; *Roy Queen Hillbilly Hit Parade*, KXLW, St. Louis, MO, 1948).

26045 Queeney, Jim. DJ (KPAC, Port Arthur, TX, 1957).

26046 Quentin, Gertrude Wolfe. Soprano (WQJ, Chicago, IL, 1925).

26047 Quenzer, Art. Leader (Art Quenzer's Blue Point Syncopators Orchestra, WHN, New York, NY, 1923).

26048 Quick, Clete. Sportscaster (*Football Prophet*, WSUH, Oxford, MS, 1960).

26049 Quick, Gerald. Sportscaster (*Football Review*, WHSC, Hartsville, SC, 1950–1951).

26050 Quick, Jerry. DJ (*Dawn in Dixie*, WHSC, Hartsville, SC, 1952). Sportscaster (*World of Sports*, WHSC, 1952).

26051 Quick, Johnny. DJ (*Red, Hot and Blue*, WDSC, Dillon, SC, 1954).

26052 Quick, Netta. COM-HE (WSUH, Oxford, MS, 1955).

26053 *Quick as a Flash*. This quiz show contained two distinct parts. In the first, its contestants were asked questions with the prizes given to those who answered first. In the second, a brief mystery was dramatized with the cast of such favorite radio mystery programs as *The Shadow*, *Bulldog Drummond*, *Ellery Queen* and *Nero Wolfe*. The contestants then attempted to solve the mystery first. If they did so *Quick as a Flash*, they won a major prize. Among the program's cast members were: Joan Alexander, Jackson Beck, Elspeth Eric, Raymond Edward Johnson, Mandel Kramer, Santos Ortega, Julie Stevens and Charles Webster. The program was directed by Richard Lewis and written by Louis M. Heyward, Mike Sklar and Eugene Wang. The hosts were Bill Cullen, Win Elliot and Ken Roberts. Ray Bloch's orchestra provided the music. The announcers were Frank Gallop and Cy Harrice (MBS and ABC, 1944–1951).

26054 Quigg, Caroline. Organist (WOO, Philadelphia, PA, 1925).

26055 Quiggle, Helen. COM-HE (WKBI, St, Marys, PA, 1956).

26056 Quigley, Don D. DJ (*Discin' with Don*, KCID, Caldwell, ID, 1952; KWEI, Weiser, ID, 1954). Sportscaster (KCID, 1952; KWEI, 1953–1956).

26057 Quigley, E.C. "Ernie." Sportscaster (WIBW, Topeka, KS, 1940–1946; *Ernie C. Quigley Sports*, WIBW, 1947–1948; KLWN, Lawrence, KS, 1953–1955).

26058 Quilan, Tom. DJ (*Requestfully Yours*, KWBG, Boone, IA, 1952).

26059 Quill, Joseph. Newscaster (WBET, Brooklyn, NY, 1947).

26060 Quillian, H.J. Assistant announcer (KOMO, Seattle, WA, 1928).

26061 Quillin [Quillen], Ted. DJ (*Tangle*, KELP, El Paso, TX, 1948; KFWB, Los Angeles, CA, 1957). Sportscaster (WACO, Waco, TX, 1954).

26062 Quimby, John. DJ (KRNO, San Bernardino, CA, 1955–1957).

26063 Quimby, Lee. Sportscaster (WWSC, Glen Falls, NY, 1953–1955).

26064 Quimby, Wilda Grim. COM-HE (WRAC Racine, WI, 1957).

26065 *Quin Ryan Reporter*. News program by veteran radio newsman Ryan (15 min., Saturday, 7:45–8:00 P.M., WGN, Chicago, IL, 1934). See **Ryan, Quin**.

26066 *Quin Ryan's Amateur Hour* (aka *Quin Ryan's Amateurs*). Quin Ryan conducted the Chicago amateur show (15 min., Monday, 6:45–7:00 P.M., WGN, 1935). *See* **Ryan, Quin**.

26067 Quinby, Dan. Reader (KOIN, Council Bluffs, IA, 1928).

26068 Quinby, Edith. COM-HE (KREX, Grand Junction, CO, 1957).

26069 Quinby, Wilda Grim. COM-HE (WRAC, Racine, WI, 1957).

26070 Quinlan, Dick. Leader (Dick Quinlan Golden Derby Orchestra, WHAS, Louisville, KY, 1924).

26071 Quinlan, J.F. Baritone (WGY, Schenectady, NY, 1923).

26072 Quinlan, Jack. Sportscaster (WIND, Chicago, IL, 1952; *Sports Forecast*, WIND, 1954; NBC, 1960).

26073 Quinlan (Texas) String Band. Local Texas band (WFAA, Dallas, TX, 1926).

26074 Quinn, Dominic. DJ (*Polka Hour*, WFDF, Flint, MI, 1952).

26075 Quinn, Elwyn. Newscaster (KDYL, Salt Lake City, UT, 1938).

26076 Quinn, Florence. Actress Quinn broadcast with the Community Players of the Chicago Civic Theater (WMAQ, Chicago, IL, 1922).

26077 Quinn, Frances. Newscaster (KFRE, Fresno, CA, 1942).

26078 Quinn, Frances. COM-HE (WIPC, Lake Wales, FL, 1956).

26079 Quinn, Fred. DJ (WMGW, Meadville, PA, 1954).

26080 Quinn, Harry. News analyst (*Valley News*, KURV, Edinburg, TX, 1948).

26081 Quinn, Hazel. Pianist (KFBK, Sacramento, CA, 1926).

26082 Quinn, Homer. DJ (WNDR, Syracuse, NY, 1956).

26083 Quinn, Inez. Soprano (WHAM, Rochester, NY, 1929).

26084 Quinn, Jack. Sportscaster (*Sports Digest* and *Sports Final*, WMBD, Peoria, IL, 1949–1950; *Sports Editor*, WMBD, 1951). DJ (*The Jack Quinn Show* and *Time and Tempo*, WDZ, Tuscola, IL, 1950).

26085 Quinn, Jack L. Sportscaster (KWIE, Kennewick, WA, 1952).

26086 Quinn, Joe. Sportscaster (*Sports Parade*, WJMA, Orange, VA, 1950).

26087 Quinn, Kay. Singer (WNEW, New York, NY, 1939).

26088 Quinn, Margaret. Pianist (WLW, Cincinnati, OH, 1926).

26089 Quinn, Mel. Newscaster (WBAL, Baltimore, MD, 1945).

26090 Quinn, Mike. DJ (*Highway 850*, KTAC, Tacoma, WA, 1960).

26091 Quinn, Pat. Newscaster (WPAG, Ann Arbor, MI, 1946).

26092 Quinn, Ray. Sportscaster (*Spotlight on Sports*, WBKA, Brockton, MA, 1948). DJ (*A Look at the Records* and *Mid-Morning Merry-Go-Round*, WBKA, 1950).

26093 Quinn, Robert. Newscaster (WKBZ, Muskegon, MI, 1938). Sportscaster (WKBZ, 1946).

26094 Quinn, Rose. Contralto (WQJ, Chicago, IL, 1925).

26095 Quinn, William "Bill." Actor Quinn worked on *Against the Storm*, *Just Plain Bill*, *Man Behind the Gun*, *Right to Happiness*, *Stella Dallas*, *What's the Name of that Song?* (MC) and *Your Family and Mine*.

26096 Quinn, William. DJ (WNDR, Syracuse, NY, 1954).

26097 Quintana, Virginia. DJ (KFLJ, Walsenburg, CO, 1957).

26098 Quinton, Charles. Sportscaster (KGFF, Shawnee, OK, 1944).

26099 Quinty, George. Leader (*George Quinty Orchestra*, instr. mus. prg., WTNJ, Trenton, NJ, 1936).

26100 Quiring, Bette. COM-HE (KSCB, Liberal, KS, 1949).

26101 Quisenberry, T.E. Quisenberry broadcast poultry lectures (WDAF, Kansas City, MO, 1928).

26102 Quist, Phoebe Ann. Singer (KFJM, Grand Forks, ND, 1937).

26103 *Quixie Doodles* (aka *Bob Hawk's Quixie Doodles Quiz*). Two teams competed against each other on the quiz program originally hosted by Bob Hawk. Hawk later was replaced by Colonel Lemuel Q. Stoopnagle (Frederick Chase Taylor). Alan Reed (Teddy Bergman) was the program announcer (30 min., Weekly, MBS, 1938–1941). *Also see* ***The Bob Hawk Show*** *and* ***Take It or Leave It.***

26104 ***Quiz Kids.*** Alex Cowan was the creator-producer of the unique panel quiz show that included intelligent youngsters of ages ranging from four to sixteen. These amazing youngsters answered difficult questions submitted by listeners. The program was a pediatric *Information Please.* An idea of the difficulty of the questions posed to the panel can be gained from the first question asked them by host Joe Kelly on the initial program broadcast June 28, 1940: "I want you to tell me what I would be carrying home if I brought an antimacassar, a dingby, a sarong and a apteryx" The program's cast included: Andre Aerne, Joan Alizier, Mary Ann Anderson, Lois Jean Ashbeck, Jack Beckman, Joan Bishop, Sally Bogolub, Virginia Booze, Claude Brenner, Sheila Brenner, Robert Burns, Nancy Bush, Pat Chandler, Cynthia Cline, Nancy Coggeshall, Joann Cohen, George Coklas, Sheila Conlon, Naomi Cooks, Gerald Darrow, Muriel Deutsch, Ruth Duskin, Ruel Fischman, Harve Bennett, Robert Easton, Inez Fox, Jack French, Richard Frisbie, Arthur Haelig, Geraldine Hamburg, Lois Jean Hesse, Gunther Hollander, Gloria Hunt, Barbara Hutchinson, Anne Israel, Edith Lee James, Nanni Kahn, Lois Karpf, Lucille Eileen Kevill, Paul Kirk, Richard Kosterlitz, Joel Kupperman, Clem Lane, Jr., Rochelle Liebling, Jack Lucal, Lonny Lunde, Frank Mangin, Jr., Joan McCullough, Mary Clare McHugh, Norman D. Miller, Tim Osato, John C. Pollock, Charles Schwartz, Corinne Shapira, Van Dyke Tiers, Robert Walls, William Wegener, Richard Weixler, Lloyd Wells, Richard Williams, Elizabeth Wirth, Davida Wolffson, Nancy Wong and Marvin Zenkere. Maggie O'Flaherty and John Lewellen were the writers. The directors were Jack Callahan, Riley Jackson, Forrest Owen, Ed Simmons and Clint Stanley (30 min., Wednesday, 8:00–8:30 P.M., NBC-Blue, 1941). The program was on the air from 1940 to 1954 on NBC, ABC and CBS. Originally, it began as a summer replacement for the *Alec Templeton Show,* before being regularly scheduled on the NBC-Blue network in 1940.

26105 ***Quiz of Two Cities.*** The program's unique concept of competition between two near-by cities began in 1938. It was produced by Gene Wilkey and conducted by Clellan Card. Ray Tenpenny was the announcer. A team of contestants from Minneapolis competed with one from St. Paul. Max Karl handled the announcing chores in St. Paul and Eddie Gallaher those in Minneapolis (WCCO, Minneapolis–St. Paul, MN, 1938). On the MBS network from 1944 to1945, the show featured contests between teams from New York and Chicago. Michael Fitzmaurice was the host. A similar format had appeared previously on local California radio with teams from Los Angeles and San Francisco competing. Reid Kilpatrick and Mark Goodson were the hosts in the California cities.

26106 ***Quotes from Georgia's Quills.*** Each week concise summaries of the editorial views of the 50 leading Georgia newspapers were broadcast on this program of news and commentary (15 min., Weekly, WSB, Atlanta, GA, 1942).

26107 ***R.G. Dun Rhythm Club.*** Wendell Hall hosted the early music and comedy show (Three times weekly, P.M., WJR, Detroit, MI, 1932).

26108 **R.P.I. Student Band.** The college band from Rensselaer Polytechnical Institute was a great radio favorite (WHAZ, Troy, NY, 1927).

26109 **Raasch, Bunny.** COM-HE (WPEO, Peoria, IL, 1960).

26110 **Rab, Jack.** DJ (WKMO, Kokomo, IN, 1947).

26111 **Rabat, Kenneth.** Sportscaster (*Sports and Weather*, WJRT, Flint, MI, 1960).

26112 **Rabb, John.** Newscaster (WJRI, Lenoir, NC, 1938).

26113 **Rabb, K.** COM-HE (WJRI, Lenoir, NC, 1954).

26114 **Rabb, Stuart.** Newscaster (WSJS, Winston-Salem, NC, 1938).

26115 **Rabbinoff, Benno.** Violinist (WOR, Newark, NJ, 1925; *Benno Rabbinoff*, instr. mus. prg., NBC, 1938).

26116 **Rabell, Fred.** News commentator (*Confidentially Yours*, KSON, San Diego, CA, 1947; *Between the Lines*, KSON, 1948).

26117 **Rabell, Jack.** DJ (*Jackson Calling*, KSON, San Diego, CA, 1947).

26118 **Raber, Alan D.** DJ (*Two for Three Show*, WKAP, Allentown, PA, 1948). Sportscaster (*Sports Highlights*, WKAP, 1949–1950; *Sports Digest*, WKAP, 1951–1956).

26119 **Rabinoff, Anastasia.** Soprano (KYW, Chicago, IL, 1926).

26120 **Rabinoff, Esther.** Violinist (WIBX, Utica, NY, 1937).

26121 ***Raboid.*** Mind reader Raboid, not otherwise identified, offered advice to his lovelorn listeners and sold his "Isis Stone," a good luck charm for a dollar (WBNX, Bronx, NY, 1933). Raboid was a featured performer on WBNX, the keystone New York station of Ed Wynn's Amalgamated Broadcasting Company.

26122 **Raborg, (Major) Paul C.** Newscaster (WHN, New York, NY, 1940; WINS, New York, NY, 1942).

26123 **Raby, John.** Actor Raby was in the cast of *Amanda of Honeymoon Hill, Brighter Day, House in the Country, Joyce Jordan, Girl Inerne, Nick Carter, Master Detective, Our Gal Sunday, Wendy Warren and the News* and *When a Girl Marries.*

26124 **Racine, Shirley.** COM-HE (KSYL, Alexandria, LA, 1957).

26125 **Rackow, Ed.** "Harmonica ace" (WSBC, Chicago, IL, 1925).

26126 **Radar, Jocko.** Sportscaster (WDOR, Sturgeon Bay, WI, 1960).

26127 ***Radarios.*** Announcer-actor Robert Stayman coined the word *radario*, combining *radio* with *scenario* to describe what actor-director Fred Smith was attempting with station WLW's radio dramas in 1922–1923. In addition to Fred Smith, other actors that participated in the station's dramatic productions were Robert Stayman, Mary MacMillan, Mary Sullivan Barnes, Helen Schuster Martin and the program's musical director, Mrs. Thomas Prewitt (WLW, Cincinnati, OH, 1922–1923).

26128 **Radcliffe, John.** Newscaster (KOY, Phoenix, AZ, 1950s).

26129 **Radcliffe Dance Orchestra.** Local dance band (WEBJ, New York, NY, 1925).

26130 **Radeck, Jack.** DJ (*Pat Your Foot*, WORD, Spartanburg, SC, 1948).

26131 **Rader, C.B.** Stock market announcer (KFH, Wichita, KS, 1929).

26132 **Rader, Leonard.** Sportscaster (KTTS, Springfield, MO, 1946).

26133 **Rader, Paul.** Born in 1879, Rader has been called the first great religious broadcaster. After first appearing on the *Radio Church of America* program in New York City, Rader discovered the power of radio when he was invited by the Mayor of Chicago to speak on the inaugural broadcast of that city's station WHT in 1921. The following year Rader founded the Chicago Gospel Tabernacle and began regular broadcasting. In 1922, Rader used an idle station transmitter to broadcast 14 hours of religious programming every Sunday. After broadcasting his gospel service each week, he also broadcast two evening programs — *The March of Ages* and *The Back Home Hour.* He began a series of daily *Breakfast Brigade* programs on CBS in 1930.

26134 **Raderman, Lou.** Leader (Lou Raderman and his Pelham Heath Inn Orchestra, playing from New York's Pelham Heath Inn, WEAF, New York, NY, 1926; *Lou Raderman Orchestra*, instr. mus. prg., WIP, Philadelphia, PA, 1936). Raderman also frequently played violin on *The Radiotrons* program (WJZ, New York, NY, 1927).

26135 **Radford, Margaret.** COM-HE (WARL, Arlington, VA, 1957).

26136 ***Radie Harris.*** Miss Harris talked about Hollywood stars and their films (15 min., Weekly, MBS, 1938).

26137 ***Radio Almanac.*** Orson Welles hosted the program that included music, drama, comedy and informative features. Sponsored by Moboil Oil and Gasoline, the cast members and guests included: Robert Benchley, Lionel Barrymore, Susan Hayward, Kay Thompson, Miguelito Valdez, Verna Felton, Lou Merrill, Hans Conreid, John Brown, Ray Collins, Martha Stewart, Betty Hutton, Dennis Day, Martha Tilton, Monte Woolley, Ella Mae Morse, Lucille Ball, Charles Laughton, Ann Sothern, Charlie Cantor, Ethel Waters, Lana Turner, Keenan Wynn and the King Cole Trio. Music was provided by the Lud Gluskin Orchestra. One of the contributions of this series was the traditional jazz program in 1944, which brought the jazz form to public notice and once more made it popular. The performers who appeared on the all-star traditional jazz group broadcast were: Mutt Carey, Kid Ory, Jimmy Noone, Buster Wilson, Bud Scott, Ed Garland and Zutty Singleton (30 min., Weekly, CBS, 1943–1944).

26138 ***Radio Bible Class.*** The weekly religious program was conducted by Dr. William A. Anderson (WFAA, Dallas, TX, 1923).

26139 ***Radio Bible Hour.*** The Reverend J. Harold Smith began the Bible study program in 1935. He gained his largest listening audience when he began broadcasting on WNOX (Knoxville, TN). After a controversy, Smith left WNOX to found his own station — WBIK (Knoxville, TN). When the FCC charged him with improprieties, he moved his program to Mexico's XERF in 1953 and flourished until the middle–1980s, when the Mexico government banned English language religious programs on their powerful border stations.

26140 ***Radio Book Club.*** In 1930, Iowa State College began a book club program. For a small fee and return postage, club members could borrow books by mail. The club began circulating books February 12, 1930 with 231 members. By June 1, 1939 there were 2,372 members enrolled. The accompanying radio program provided information about new books and extolled the pleasures of reading (WOI, Ames, IA, 1930).

26141 ***Radio Broadcast Dope.*** Monte Cross conducted the novel program that gave listeners the latest news about radio and its performers (WIP, Philadelphia, PA, 1923).

26142 ***(The) Radio Chapel Service.*** The Reverend Robert R. Brown originated the non-denominational religious program in 1923 on WOW (Omaha, NE).

26143 ***Radio Church of the Air.*** The Reverend and Mrs. Joseph Irwin conducted the church of the air program (WSBA, York, PA, 1945).

26144 ***Radio Church of America.*** This was the New York radio program on which famous radio preacher Paul Rader first appeared. His successful experience on the *Radio Church of America*, the first continuing religious broadcast series, encouraged him to continue broadcasting his religious message.

26145 ***Radio Circus.*** Quaker Oats Company sponsored the juvenile quiz with musical selections. Johnny Olsen, assisted by Jess Kilparick, conducted the quiz show from a Chicago theater (60 min., Saturday, 11:00–12:00 noon, CST, WGN, Chicago, IL, 1939).

26146 ***Radio City Music Hall Symphony.*** The Radio City Music Hall Orchestra, an excellent symphonic music group, consistently played such fine music as those offered on their August 18, 1935, program that included: Rossini's "Overture to the Barber of Seville"; Grieg's "The Erl King," "Heart Wounds" and "Last Spring"; Ponchelli's "Cielo E Mar"; and Irving Berlin's "Top Hat," "Piccileno," "No Strings," "Cheek to Cheek" and "Isn't This a Lovely Day?" (60 min., Sunday, 11:30–12:30 P.M., NBC, 1935).

26147 ***Radio City Party.*** John B. Kennedy narrated the music program, sponsored by RCA Radiotron tubes, featuring the Victor Light Opera Company and orchestral conductor Nathaniel Shilkret. Comedian Joe Cook also performed regularly (30 min., Saturday, 9:00–9:30 A.M., NBC, 1934–1935).

26148 **Radio Dance Orchestra.** Radio dance band (WHN, New York, NY, 1924).

26149 ***Radio Dancer.*** The dancer was Drusilla, who tapped out her routines before the microphone for her listeners (WGBS, New York, NY, 1925).

26150 ***Radio Double Quartette.*** Vcl. mus. prg. that included bass Thomas B. Chase (Sunday, P.M., WOW, Omaha, NE, 1929).

26151 **Radio Eight Symphony Orchestra.** Symphonic orchestra conducted by George von Hagel (KPO, San Francisco, CA, 1926).

26152 ***Radio Explorer's Club.*** Bosch, Inc., sponsored the weekly dramatized program that presented the exploits of modern explorers (15 min., Sunday, 5:30–5:45 P.M., NBC, 1935).

26153 **Radio Franks.** The singing comedy team of Frank Wright and Frank Bessinger recorded frequently and often appeared on early radio (WHN, New York, NY, 1924; WJZ, New York, NY, 1925).

26154 ***Radio Godmother.*** Lucy Broadstreet (the "Radio Godmother") conducted her unique program on which she combined songs and stories for children and adult listeners as well (WOK, Pine Bluff, AR, 1922).

26155 ***Radio Gossip Club.*** Veteran radio entertainers Eddie and Fannie Cavanaugh broadcast gossip about radio and its stars (15 min., Monday, 12:25–12:30 P.M., CBS, 1935).

26156 ***Radio Guide Revue.*** *Radio Guide* magazine sponsored the good music program. Blues singer Fannye Rose Shore — later famous as Dinah Shore — performed. She was assisted by Louise and her Dixie Dons singing group and baritone Joseph McPherson (Weekly, WSM, Nashville, TN, 1936).

26157 ***Radio Guild.*** Begun in 1929, the hour-long dramatic series was dedicated to broadcasting 200 years of classics. A 1932 cast included Sheila Hayes, Florence Malone, Harry Neville, Jeanne Owen, Leo Stark, Charles Warburton and Charles Webster. Vernon Radcliffe was the program's director (60 min., Weekly, 4:15–5:15 P.M., NBC-Blue, 1932). The program in a 30-minute format ran until 1940.

26158 ***Radio Hall of Fame*** **(aka** ***The Philco Radio Hall of Fame*****).** The Philco Radio Corporation sponsored the program that presented the best radio performers and programs as selected by *Variety.* All types of programs and performers were represented on the unique program hosted by Deems Taylor. Paul Whiteman's Orchestra provided the music (60 min., Sunday, 6:00–7:00 P.M., NBC-Blue, 1943). When the show was reduced to a 30-minute format the range of its performers was extended to include actors from all forms of entertainment, not merely from radio. Glenn Riggs was the announcer in the half-hour format.

Some of the performers who appeared on the program were: Larry Adler, Brian Ahearne, the Aldrich Family program's cast, Fred Allen, the Andrews Sisters, Kay Armen, Mary Astor, Kenny Baker, Phil Baker, Bonnie Baker, Tallulah Bankhead, Red Barber, Sheila Barrett, Ed Begley, Milton Berle, Irving Berlin, Charles Bickford, Ray Bolger, Victor Borge, Connie Boswell, Charles Boyer, Fannie Brice, Burns and Allen, Bob Burns, Billy Butterfield, Jimmy Carroll, Jerry Colonna, John Conte, Laird Cregar, Hank D'Amico, Gloria DeHaven, the Delta Rhythm Boys, Diana Lynn, Peter Donald, Morton Downey, Jimmy Durante, Eddie Cantor, Ralph Edwards, Joan Edwards, Dale Evans, Frank Fay, Verna Felton, Gracie Fields, Jay C. Flippen, Joan Fontaine, Helen Forrest, Four Chicks and a Chuck, Rudolf Friml, Jane Froman, Reginald Gardiner, Ed Gardner, William Gargan, Georgia Gibbs, Jackie Gleason, Benny Goodman, Bill Goodwin, Bonita Granville, Eddie Green, Reed Hadley, Jack Haley, Sir Cedric Hardwicke, George "Gabby" Hayes, Helen Hayes, Dick Haymes, Harry Herschfield, Milt Herth, Hi, Lo, Jack and the Dame, Hildegarde, Harriet Hilliard, Portland Hoffa, Bob Hope, Willie Howard, Budd Hulick, Betty Hutton, Marion Hutton, Burl Ives, the John Gart Trio, Raymond Edward Johnson, Allen Jones, Jennifer Jones, the King Sisters, Evelyn Knight, Alexander Knox, Carole Landis, Joe Laurie, Jr., Jerry Lester, Frank Lovejoy, Lum and Abner, Jeanette MacDonald, Frederic March, Nora Martin, Mary Martin, Groucho Marx, Lauritz Melchoir, the Merry Macs, Garry Moore, Frank Morgan, George Murphy, Dean Murphy, Bob Nolan, Helen O'Connell, Santos Ortega, Les Paul, Martha Raye, Doc Rockwell, Sue Ryan, Senator Ed Ford, Ginny Simms, Red Skelton, Cornelia Otis Skinner, Smith and Dale, Kate Smith, the Sons of the Pioneers, Alec Templeton, Lowell Thomas, Danny Thomas, the Three Suns, Mel Torme, Frank Tours, Orson Welles, George Wettling, Ernie Whitman, Earl Wild, Mary Lou Williams, Charles Winninger, Barry Wood, Eileen Woods, Nan Wynn, Keenan Wynn, Ed Wynn and Lawson Zerbe.

26159 ***Radio History of the War*** **(aka** ***A History Book Wired for Sound*****).** Jackson Beck narrated the informative sustaining program of recorded history. Ted Cott was the writer and producer. Henry Morgenthau III was the production coordinator. The program premiered in December, 1950 (30 min., Sunday, 5:00–5:30 P.M., WNEW, New York, NY, 1950).

26160 ***Radio Household Institute.*** The *Radio Household Institute* was a network program that combined information on home economics, domestic problems and how to rear a healthy family with music. The home economics expert of the show was Elizabeth Carter. A Mrs. Milton told how to raise healthy family members; Billy Brenton and a Miss Byrnes acted out dramatizations of various family problems and sang, as did a baritone, identified only by the name of Mr. Thomas (15 min., Mornings, Wednesday and Saturday, NBC-Red, 1930–1933). *The Radio Household Institute* previously had been broadcast five times weekly (15 min., Monday through Friday, 10:00–10:15 A.M., NBC-Red, 1927–1928).

26161 ***Radio Movie Man.*** Geoffrey L. Whalen broadcast movie reviews (WGI, Medford Hillside, MA, 1923).

26162 ***Radio Newsreel of Hollywood.*** Mobil gas stations sponsored the transcribed program broadcast on various stations. A different Hollywood star was interviewed each week. The illustrious group included such performers as Loretta Young, Walter Huston, Frank Fay, Richard Bathelmess, Edward G. Robinson and Douglas Fairbanks, Jr. (15 min.,

Monday, 7:45–8:00 P.M., KDKA, Pittsburgh, PA, early 1940's).

26163 ***Radio Piano Lessons.*** Miss Maudellen Littlefield conducted the series of piano lessons (WDAF, Kansas City, MO, 1925).

26164 ***Radio Poet.*** L.H. Wagner read poetry on the weekly program (WGI, Medford Hillside, MA, 1923).

26165 **Radio Ramblers.** Popular radio music group (WFBH, New York, NY, 1925).

26166 ***Radio Ranch.*** Ernie Lindell and his group of CW musicians performed on the transcribed music show (55 min., Transcribed, Various Stations, 1:05–2:00 P.M., 1953).

26167 ***Radio Reader's Digest*** **(aka *The Hallmark Program* or *The Reader's Digest Radio Edition*).** First broadcast in 1942, the program dramatized stories from the *Reader's Digest* magazine. The host-narrators over the years were Richard Kollmar, Conrad Nagel and Les Tremayne. The program was produced by Anton M. Leader and Carl Schullinger. The director was Robert Nolan. Van Cleave was the program's musical director. Ralph Berkey, Carl Bixby, Henry Denker, James Erthein, Josephine Lyons, Peggy Lou Mayer, William N. Robson and Robert Sloane were the writers.

Some of the performers who appeared on the program were: Brian Aherne, Lucille Ball, Tallulah Bankhead, Ethel Barrymore, Wallace Beery, Ralph Bellamy, Constance Bennett, Anne Blyth, Shirley Booth, Charles Boyer, James Cagney, Louis Calhern, Dane Clark, Claudette Colbert, Ronald Colman, Richard Conte, Joseph Cotten, Olivia DeHaviland, Douglas Fairbanks, Jr., Geraldine Fitzgerald, John Garfield, Sidney Greensteet, Helen Hayes, Van Heflin, Ruth Hussey, Dean Jagger, Van Johnson, Dick Kollmar, Otto Kruger, Charles Laughton, Peter Lawford, Gertrude Lawrence, Paul Lucas, Frederic March, James Mason, Raymond Massey, Dorothy McGuire, Burgess Meredith, Robert Mitchum, Wayne Morris, Paul Muni, Laurence Olivier, Pat O'Brien, Michael O'Shea, Susan Peters, William Powell, Roger Pryor, Claude Rains, Gene Raymond, Babe Ruth, Ann Rutherford, Karl Swenson, Jean Tierney, Franchot Tone, Claire Trevor, Orson Welles and Robert Young (30 min., Weekly, CBS, 1942–1948).

26168 ***Radio Realities.*** Leo Fitzpatrick created and conducted the program dedicated to radio itself. Fitzpatrick discussed aspects of radio that were controversial or misunderstood. The major objective of the program, which was expressed at the end of one of the programs, was to provide "a defense of radio." It went on to say that: "If there is any fair minded medium in the world of today, it is American radio broadcasting, which does not alarm with headlines or sway with skillful words, and subtle editorial policy. But it is as direct as one man speaking directly to another must needs be. Radio stands on the record of its own spoken word, ready to give an accounting to its public at any time." This program format was another of Fitzpatrick's several innovations (WJR, Detroit, MI, 1931). *See* **Fitzpatrick, Leo.**

26169 ***Radio Revels.*** Max Dolin and his Grenadiers supplied the music on the network variety show. Also featured on the program were Irving Kaufman, Peg LaCentra, Cameron Andrews, Kent and Kitall and Louise Dawson (30 min., Weekly, NBC, 1935).

26170 ***Radio Sing.*** William Wade Hinshaw conducted the unusual group singing program before a large studio audience on WJZ (New York, NY, 1923).

26171 ***(The) Radio Trio.*** Pianist, whistler and baritone Carson Robison, Steven Cady and Harry Kessel comprised the popular trio. They were assisted by "Mr. R.A. Dio" (Leo Fitzpatrick) who originated and popularized many early programs and entertainers (WDAF, Kansas City, MO, 1922).

26172 ***Radio Typewriting Course.*** WHA was one of the first, if not the first, to broadcast typewriting lessons on radio (WHA, Madison, WI, 1932).

26173 ***Radio Vanities.*** Singer Frank Parker and an unidentified orchestra performed on the weekly music show (30 min., Tuesday, 8:00–8:30 P.M., MBS, 1934).

26174 ***Radiographs.*** A dramatization with narration of various incidents in Arkansas history was presented. The writer was Ewing Canaday and the sponsor the Gilmore Paint and Paper Company (15 min., Monday-Wednesday-Friday, 10:00–10:15 A.M., Arkansas local radio, 1940).

26175 ***Radio-Keith-Orpheum Hour*** **(aka *The RKO Theatre of the Air*).** The variety show originally sponsored by the RKO Theater Chain featured singing star Armida and Leo Reisman's Orchestra. The announcer was Graham McNamee (30 min., Tuesday, 10:30–11:00 P.M., NBC-Red, 1930). The following year film, vaudeville and radio stars once more appeared each week as guests, but in this format the program featured an orchestra directed by Milton Schwartzwald (30 min., Friday, 10:30–11:00 P.M., NBC-Red, 1931).

26176 ***Radio's Greatest Lover.*** An unidentified male performer read romantic prose and poetry (15 min., Wednesday, 10:45–11:00 P.M., NBC, mid–1930's).

26177 **Radio's Harmonica King.** *See* **Sullivan, Cloyde.**

26178 ***Radiotorial.*** George Wilder Cartwright broadcast his opinions on this "radiotorial" series on various topics ranging from local politics to the Constitution of the United States (KFI, Los Angeles, CA, 1927).

26179 ***Radiotron Program.*** The popular musical program featured saxophonist Andy Sanella and his band (NBC-Blue, 1927).

26180 ***Radiotron Varieties.*** Newspaper columnist and humorist Arthur "Bugs" Baer hosted the variety show that also featured Welcome Lewis and Harold Van Emburgh singing to the music of William Daly's orchestra (15 min., Wednesday and Saturday, 8:15–8:30 P.M., NBC-Red, 1931).

26181 ***Radioviews.*** Mrs. Owen Kildare conducted the program that provided her listeners with information about radio programs and their performers (WFBH, New York, NY, 1925).

26182 **Radka, Al.** DJ (KFRE, Fresno, CA, 1957).

26183 **Radley, Verne.** Leader (Verne Radley Orchestra, KTHS, Hot Springs National Park, AR, 1928–29).

26184 **Radlin, Henry L.** Principal Radlin of the Los Angeles Hebrew School occasionally broadcast sermons (KHJ, Los Angeles, CA, 1923).

26185 **Radom, Edyth.** COM-HE (WDRC, Hartford, CT, 1955).

26186 **Radonich, Romeo.** DJ (*La Hora Espanol,* KGLU, Safford, AZ, 1947).

26187 **Radz, Ethel.** Soprano (WHAZ, Troy, NY, 1925).

26188 **Rae, Bob.** DJ (KPMC, Bakersfield, CA, 1957).

26189 **Rae, Janet.** Singer (KFAE, Pullman, WA, 1925).

26190 **Rae, Joan.** Actress Rae was in the cast of the situation comedies *The Adventures of Ozzie and Harriet* and *Blondie.*

26191 **Rae, Shirley.** COM-HE (KRKO, Everett, WA, 1949).

26192 **Rae (Juanita) and Lee (Harriet Lee).** Popular female harmony singing team (WLS, Chicago, IL, 1926).

26193 **Raeburn, Byrna.** Actress Raeburn appeared on the daytime serial program *A Tree Grows in Brooklyn* and on *Casey, Crime Photographer, Dimension X, Gangbusters, Nick Carter, Master Detective* and *Under Arrest.*

26194 **Raeburn, Johnny.** Sportscaster (*Sports Special,* WMIX, Mt. Vernon, IL, 1948).

26195 **Raffensberger, Don.** Sportscaster (WMRF, Lewiston, PA, 1953). DJ (WMRF, 1956).

26196 **Rafferty, Skip.** DJ (WOND, Pleasantville, NJ, 1960).

26197 **Ragatz, Hugh Hammond.** Singer (KOA, Denver, CO, 1925).

26198 **Ragen, Dick.** Director (WIP Philadelphia Little Symphony broadcasting a dinner hour concert, WIP, Philadelphia, PA, 1923).

26199 **Raginsky, Mischa.** Leader (Mischa Raginsky Orchestra, instr. mus. prg., CBS, 1934).

26200 **Ragland, Della Ann.** Newscaster (KWBG, Hutchinson, KS, 1937).

26201 **Ragley, Sally.** COM-HE (WPME, Punxsutawney, PA, 1954).

26202 **Ragsdale, Norman.** DJ (*Slap-Happy-Happy Club,* WCNC, Elizabeth City, NC, 1950).

26203 **Rahders, Paul.** DJ (*Merry Go Round,* KANA, Anaconda, MT, 1949).

26204 **Rahere, Earl.** DJ (*Juke Box,* WLAK, Lakeland, FL, 1949).

26205 **Rahman, Bob.** DJ (WHEN, Syracuse, NY, 1957).

26206 **Raht, Katherine.** Actress Raht appeared on the daytime serial programs *Against the Storm* and *Young Doctor Malone.*

26207 **Raie, Renee.** Singer (WTIC, Hartford, CT, 1936).

26208 **Railing, (Mrs.) Curtis Burnley.** Impersonator (WJZ, New York, NY, 1922).

Railing was best known for her "impersonation of her adorable little girl, Joy."

26209 Railite YMCA Band. YMCA band directed by John G. Miller (WLAC, Nashville, TN, 1929).

26210 *Railroad Hour* (aka *The Summer Railroad Hour*). The American Association of Railroads sponsored the music program that presented operettas, Broadway musical adaptations and special musical dramatizations starring Gordon MacRae. MacRae was assisted by many talented female guests singers such as Dinah Shore, Jane Powell, Jo Stafford, Lucille Norman, Dorothy Kirsten, Ginny Simms, Eileen Wilson, Gladys Swarthout and Rise Stevens.

First broadcast in a 45-minute format in 1948, the program soon was expanded to a full hour. Uniformly high in quality of material and performance, the *Railroad Hour* was one of radio's best music programs. The orchestra was conducted by Carmen Dragon and John Rarig. Norman Luboff conducted the choir. The program was directed by Murray Bolen, Ken Burton and Fran Van Hartesfeldt. The writers were Jean Holloway, Jerry Lawrence and Bob Lee. Marvin Miller was the announcer (ABC and NBC, 1948–1954). There also was a *Summer Railroad Hour* with an identical format, but different singing stars.

26211 Rainbow Girls Glee Club. Vocal group directed by Mrs. Bryon McDonald (KTAB, Oakland, CA, 1926).

26212 *Rainbow House.* *Rainbow House* was a *Let's Pretend* program for the undertwelves (MBS, 1947).

26213 Rainbow Orchestra. Popular local band (WMCA, New York, NY, 1925; WGCP, Atlantic City, NJ, 1926).

26214 Rainbow Orchestra. A popular name for orchestras, this particular Rainbow Orchestra was directed by Eddie Collins (WCOA , Pensacola, FL, 1926).

26215 *Rainbow Rhythms.* Joe Frasetto's band supplied the rhythms on the local sustaining program. Frank Warrington was the announcer (15 min., Thursday, 12:15–12:30 P.M., WIP, Philadelphia, PA, 1940).

26216 Raine, Grace G. Singer (WTIC, Hartford, CT, 1936).

26217 Raines, Jim. DJ (*Chore Time*, WAVL, Apollo, PA, 1950). Sportscaster (*Whirl Around the World of Sports*, WCBS, Anderson, IN, 1952).

26218 Rainey, William. Rainey was a singer on the *Spotlight Hour*, a variety program consisting mainly of musical selections (NBC, 1927).

26219 Rainwater, Jody. DJ (*Sunrise Salute*, WSVS, Crewe, VA, 1954).

26220 Raisa, Rosa. Prima donna Raisa of the Chicago Civic Opera company often appeared on the regular Thursday night broadcasts of that company (WGN, Chicago, IL, 1928).

26221 Raiser, Ada. Reader (WIP, Philadelphia, PA, 1925).

26222 *Raising Junior.* Peter Dixon wrote the daily daytime series about the life and times of an "average" American family. Aline Berry played the mother. Dixon (1931, p. 308) said that his pattern of writing was to have his fictional family have some good luck, followed by some unfortunate events. As he said, "When things look best, something unfortunate happens and when things look bleak, something very pleasant happens just in the nick of time." The daily daytime series was a popular NBC feature (15 min., Monday through Friday, NBC, 1930–1931). The program's opening was as follows:

> *Raising Junior*, the Wheatena serial story comes to you at this time every evening except Monday through the courtesy of the Wheatena Corporation ... maker of Wheatena ... the delicious wheat cereal — sun-browned, roasted and toasted. How frequently you have that hungry empty feeling around eleven o'clock in the morning? Too early for lunch — too late for a snack ... so you just put up with an hour or so of discomfort. But try this interesting experiment. Get a package of Wheatena — the toasty, nut-like wheat cereal from your grocer today and enjoy a steaming, fragrant dish of it for tomorrow's breakfast. Then observe results around eleven o'clock. How much more alert and energetic you feel. How much better without that empty, hungry feeling. For Wheatena supplies plenty of vital strength and energy to carry you through the long period between breakfast and lunch. Just ask your grocer for this delicious nourishing cereal in the familiar yellow and blue package.
>
> And write in this evening for your copy of *Feeding Your Child from Crib to College.*
>
> This little book, you know, was written especially for the Wheatena Corporation by an eminent authority on diet. It contains information on family feeding that every mother should have at hand. And, besides, it provides many attractive menus and delicious recipes to lighten the burden of meal planning. Just send your name and address to the Wheatena Corporation, Rahway — R-A-H-W-A-Y — New Jersey, and you will receive your complimentary copy by mail.
>
> Yesterday, Ken decided to make a study of baby foods, not only in the interest of Junior, but because his firm is anxious to obtain the account of a firm manufacturing such products. Today was a half holiday for Ken and he had all afternoon to spend at home. So let's drop down to the Lee's little apartment and see if he's putting his time to good use.

26223 Raistric, Ernest. Newscaster (WFOY, St. Augustine, FL, 1939).

26224 Rajoan Trio. Instrumental music group (WREO, Lansing, MI, 1925).

26225 *Rajput.* Rajput, a "high caste Hindu with an Oxford degree and more than eight years service with the British secret service in India," was a radio fortune teller. Sponsored by Dr. Strasska's toothpaste, Rajput told his listeners that he would send them a good luck ivory elephant if they would send in a flap from his sponsor's toothpaste (KTRH, Houston, TX, 1931).

26226 Rak, John. Saxophonist (WQJ, Chicago, IL, 1925).

26227 Rakauska, Mariona. Polish folk singer (WYW, Chicago, IL, 1923).

26228 Rakes, Barbara. COM-HE (WHEO, Stuart, VA, 1960).

26229 *Rakov's Orchestra.* Instr. mus. prg. (CBS, 1937; WBZ, Boston-Springfield, MA, 1938; NBC, 1939).

26230 Raleigh, John. Newscaster (WCCO, Minneapolis–St. Paul, MN, 1944–1945).

26231 Raley, H.J., Dr. Announcer (WEBQ, Harrisburg, IL, 1927).

26232 Ralicki, Hank. DJ (*The Timekeeper* and *Mailbag Matinee*, WHDL, Olean, NY, 1947).

26233 Rall, Lavon. Announcer (KFRU, Columbia, MO, 1927).

26234 Ralon, Arsenio. Violinist (WJZ, New York, NY, 1925). Marimba soloist (WRC, Washington, DC, 1925).

26235 Ralph, Donald T. "Don." Newscaster (KGDM, Stockton, CA, 1941). DJ (*Coffee Club*, KSTN, Stockton, CA, 1949).

26236 Ralph, Richard. Tenor (WGHP, Detroit, MI, 1926).

26237 *Ralph and Hal.* CW mus. prg. by a team known as "The Oldtimers" (WLS, Chicago, IL, 1937).

26238 Ralston, Esther. Actress Ralston appeared on the daytime serial programs *Portia Faces Life*, *We the Abbotts* and *Woman of Courage* (title role).

26239 Rambeau, Marjorie. Famous actress Rambeau appeared in a complete production of Shakespeare's *As You Like It* broadcast from the stage of the 44th Street Theater, New York City, on April 23, 1923 (WJZ, New York, NY).

26240 *Rambler and Mary Lou.* . CW mus. prg. by otherwise unidentified performers (KMOX, St. Louis, MO, 1936).

26241 *Ramblin' Mountaineers.* The CW group was headed by Carl Story, often regarded as the father of blue grass country music. Story and his group blended the traditional mountain blue grass style with old-time country church singing (WHKY, Hickory, NC, 1934).

26242 *Rambling Red Foley and the Girls of the Golden West.* The good CW group left WLS, Chicago, IL, to broadcast on WLW (Cincinnati, OH, 1937).

26243 Ramey, C. Harold. Leader (Harold C. Ramey and the Harmony Hounds Orchestra (KFQZ, Hollywood, CA, 1926).

26244 Ramey, Lamar. DJ (*Top 100 Tune Show*, WLET, Toccoa, GA, 1960).

26245 Ramey, Lavarre. Sportscaster (*It's Ten Pin Time*, KWRO, Coquille, OR, 1960).

26246 Ramirez, Joe. DJ (*Latin American Melodies*, KDZA, Pueblo, CO, 1960).

26247 Ramon, Laon. "Boy monologist" (KHJ, Los Angeles, CA, 1926).

26248 *Ramona and the Tune Twisters* (aka *Ramona and Her Mighty Minstrels*). The 15-minute program featured Ramona, who had been a long-time favorite with the Paul Whiteman band (MBS, 1941–1945). Ramona first began playing the piano in Don Bestor's band before moving on to join the Whiteman band as a singer-pianist.

26249 Ramos, Ralph. News commentator (*While You Slept*, KFDM, Beaumont, TX, 1947–1948).

26250 Rampy, C.W. DJ (*1600 Club*, KMAE, McKinney, TX, 1948–1952).

26251 Ramsay, William T. "Bill." DJ (*Club 630*, WIRC, Hickory, NC, 1948; *Songs in Flight*, WVOT, Wilson, NC, 1952). Sportscaster (*Sports Parade*, WVOT, 1953).

26252 Ramsey, Anita. COM-HE (KGA, Spokane, WA, 1960).

26253 Ramsey, Duane. Newscaster (KRBC, Abilene, TX, 1945).

26254 Ramsey, Forrest. Newscaster (WFTC, Kinston, NC, 1946).

26255 Ramsey, Margaret. COM-HE (WJHO, Opelika, AL, 1960).

26256 Ramsey, Nick. DJ (WFAA, Dallas, TX, 1957–1959; *Carnival of Music*, WFAA, 1960).

26257 Ramsey, Pat. COM-HE (KGOS, Torrington, WY, 1956).

26258 Ramsey, Ray. DJ (*Breakfast with the KREM*, KREM, Sunnyside, WA, 1949; KREM, 1956–1960).

26259 Ramsey, Raymond "Ray." DJ (*Spin A Platter*, WHIR, Danville, KY, 1948–1954).

26260 Ramsey, S. Waymond. Newscaster (KOMA, Oklahoma City, OK, 1937; KELD, El Dorado, AZ, 1939; KFDA, Amarillo, TX, 1941). Sportscaster (KOMA, 1937).

26261 Ramsey, Shirley. COM-HE (WSEE, Erie, PA, 1956).

26262 Ramsey, Wayne. DJ (KENA, Mena, AR, 1960).

26263 Ramseyer, J.M.L. Cellist (WBZ, Springfield, MA, 1924).

26264 Ramsley, (Mrs.) Graham. COM-HE (WHED, Washington, SC, 1949).

26265 Ramsperger, Jeanne. COM-HE (KHEP, Phoenix, AZ, 1957).

26266 *Ramus II.* The 1953 program was a feature from out of the early days of radio. Ramus II was "America's outstanding crystal gazer and personal guidance counselor." On the program, he combined prophecy with personal advice. He talked about divorce, separation and cheating wives and husbands in response to letters sent to him by his listeners (15 min., Monday through Friday, 9:30:9:45 P.M., WOKO, Albany, NY, 1953).

26267 *Ranch Boys.* CW mus. prg. (NBC, 1935; WCBM, Baltimore, MD, 1938; WHP, Harrisburg, PA, 1939).

26268 *Ranch House Boys.* The Ranch House Boys were a popular group specialized in CW music (WNAX, Yankton, SD, 1936).

26269 Rand, Edwin. Actor Rand was in the cast of *Today's Children.*

26270 Rand, Fred. Sportscaster (*Spotlight on Sports*, WAZF, Yazoo City, MS, 1950; *Sports Spotlight*, WCLD, Cleveland, MS, 1952).

26271 Rand, George. Actor (NBC-Pacific Coast Division, 1929).

26272 Rand, Gren. Sportscaster (WABY, Albany, NY, 1940–1941; WOKO, Albany, NY, 1942).

26273 Rand, Harry. DJ (*KOBK Musical Clock*, KOBK, Owatonna, MN, 1952).

26274 Rand, Ted. Sportscaster (KBTM, Jonesboro, AR, 1945; play-by-play sports broadcasts, KDRS, Paragould, AR, 1948).

26275 Randall, Arthur "Art." Pianist (WOAW, Omaha, NE, 1926). Director (Royal Fontanelle Orchestra, WOAW, Omaha, NE, 1926–1928; WOW, Omaha, NE, 1928–29).

26276 Randall, Betty. Singer (NBC, 1941; WRDO, Augusta, ME, 1941).

26277 Randall, Charles. Leader (*Charles Randall Orchestra*, instr. mus. prg., WRVA, Richmond, VA, 1938).

26278 Randall, Clyde R. Announcer-program director (WSMB, New Orleans, LA, 1925). Announcer-program director (WIL, St. Louis, MO, 1926).

26279 Randall, Dave. Sportscaster (*Scores*, WTOC, Savannah, GA, 1955).

26280 Randall, Eunice L. (Eunice Randall Thompson). Miss Randall broadcast stories for girls on *The Girls' Story Hour.* She also served as announcer and engineer at the station (WGI, Medford Hillside, MA, 1923).

26281 Randall, Fern. COM-HE (KWRT, Boonville, MO, 1956–1957).

26282 Randall, John. Newscaster (WNAX, Yankton, SD, 1941).

26283 Randall, Peggy. COM-HE (WBAL, Baltimore, MD, 1934).

26284 Randall, Porter. Newscaster (KGKO, Fort Worth, TX, 1939; KGKO-WBAP, Fort Worth, TX, 1940; KFJZ, Fort Worth, TX, 1941–1942, 1945–1948).

26285 Randall, Vischer A. Randall was the first announcer at station WEAF (New York, NY, 1922).

26286 Randall, Wolston. Baritone (WWJ, Detroit, MI, 1923).

26287 Randazza, Ada. COM-HE (WLCR, Torrington, CT, 1954).

26288 Randel, Ted. DJ (*Lucky Lager Dance Time*, KGEM, Boise, ID, 1952).

26289 Randell, Harlan. Baritone (WHT, Chicago, IL, 1928).

26290 Randle, Bill. DJ (CBS, 1955).

26291 Randle, Bill. DJ (WERE, Cleveland, OH, 1955–1956).

26292 Randolph, Amanda. Both a dramatic and comic actress, Amanda Randolph appeared in several daytime serial programs such as *Joyce Jordan*, *Girl Interne* and *Young Dr. Malone*. In addition, she appeared on the *Abie's Irish Rose* and *Beulah* programs. In an early program (1930s), Randolph played the title role of *Aunt Jemima.*

26293 Randolph, Harold. Pianist (WBAL, Baltimore, MD, 1926).

26294 Randolph, Ivan Fitz. DJ (*1-2-3 Club*, WCLO, Janesville, WI, 1947).

26295 Randolph, Isabel. Actress Randolph was in the cast of *Dan Harding's Wife* (title role), *Fibber McGee and Molly*, *One Man's Family*, *Mary Marlin*, *Tale of Today* and *Welcome Valley.*

26296 Randolph, Jack. Baritone (*Jack Randolph*, vcl. mus. prg., WMAQ, Chicago, IL, 1935). Leader (*Jack Randolph Orchestra*, instr. mus. prg., KDKA, Pittsburgh, PA, 1935–1937).

26297 Randolph, James. Newscaster (WWCO, Waterbury, CT, 1947).

26298 Randolph, John. Newscaster (WGBR, Goldsboro, NC, 1945).

26299 Randolph, Leola. COM-HE (KENM, Portales, NM, 1957).

26300 Randolph, Milton. Announcer (WMAZ, Macon, GA, 1927).

26301 Randolph, William. Newscaster (WIOU, Kokomo, IN, 1948).

26302 *Randy's Record Shop.* Gene Nobles was the DJ on the recorded music program (WLAC, Nashville, TN, 1936).

26303 Ranelle, Grace. Soprano (WAAM, Newark, NJ, 1925).

26304 Raney, Bud. DJ (Raney was a popular DJ who called himself *Old Man Adam,* 300 min., Thursday, 11:30–4:30 A.M., WHN, New York, NY, 1945). Raney's program was sponsored by Adam Hats.

26305 Raney, Wayne T. CW musician (harmonica) and singer Raney was known as a "harmonica wizard" (McCloud, 1995, p. 656). At the age of 13, he had his own program on Border Radio (XEPN, Piedras Negras, Mexico, 1933). He later appeared on WCKY (Cincinnati, OH, 1941); WMC, Memphis, TN, 1945); the *California Hayride* (Pacific coast stations); *Grand Ole Opry* (WSM, Nashville, TN, 1949); and *WWVA Jamboree* (WWVA, Wheeling, WV). He also had numerous syndicated programs throughout his career.

26306 *Range Riders.* CW mus. prg. (KWK, St. Louis, MO, 1936–1937; WREN, Lawrence, KS, 1939).

26307 *Range Riders and Billy Doss.* CW music program with a group featuring guitarist Billy Doss (KWK, St. Louis, MO, 1936).

26308 Ranger, James H. "Jim." Sportscaster (*The Sports Editor*, KVSM, San Mateo, CA, 1947–1948; *Sideline Slants*, KAFY, Bakersfield, CA, 1949; KCOY, Santa Maria, CA, 1953; *Time Out for Sports*, KWG, Stockton, CA, 1953).

26309 Ranger, (Capt.) Richard. Organist (*Captain Richard Ranger*, instr. mus. prg., WOR, Newark, NJ, 1932).

26310 *Ranger Bill.* Wallace J. Hutchinson, the Director-Supervisor of the California State Ranger Service, wrote the program to promote forest safety and publicize the hazards of mountain fires. Ranger Bill, played by Barry Hopkins, discussed the dangers and problems forest visitors might face (KPO-NBC, San Francisco, CA, 1928).

26311 *Rangers.* CW mus. prg. (WBT, Charlotte, NC, 1939).

26312 Rankel, John. Baritone (WGES, Oak Park, IL, 1925; WHT, Chicago, IL, 1928).

26313 Rankin, Bill. DJ (KRTR, Thermopolis, WY, 1957).

26314 Rankin, Jean. Violinist (KSAC, Manhattan, KS, 1925).

26315 Rankin, Katherine. Pianist (WOC, Jefferson City, MO, 1923–1924).

26316 Rankin, Mary. COM-HE (KVFD, Fort Dodge, IA, 1949–1957).

26317 Ranney, Mary Aileen. COM-HE (WROW, Albany, NY, 1949).

26318 Ransom, Al. Leader (Al Ransom and his Admirals Orchestra, WADC, Akron, OH, 1928).

26319 Ransom, Betty. Soprano (KWSC, Pullman, WA, 1927).

26320 Ransom, Buddy. Singer (*Buddy Ransom*, vcl. mus. prg., WLW, Cincinnati, OH, 1934).

26321 Ransom, Glen. Actor Ransom was in the cast of *Ma Perkins.*

26322 *Ransom Sherman Presents* (aka *The Ransom Sherman Show* and *The Ransom Sherman Variety Program*). Ransom Sherman, who was one of the original "Doctors" of early radio, hosted this entertaining sustaining variety show. Sherman, with the support of Durward Kirby and Bob Jellison, handled the comedy. Music and songs were performed by the Four Vagabonds, Wayne Van Dyne, Lillian Cornell and Joseph Gallicchio's Orchestra (30 min., Wednesday, 9:00–9:30 P.M., NBC, 1939).

26323 Ransome, (Mrs.) Billy. Pianist (KWWG, Brownsville, TX, 1926).

26324 Rapchak, Mike. Sportscaster (*The Sports Show*, WWCA, Gary, IN, 1950).

26325 Rapee, Erno. Conductor (Moboil Quality Orchestra on *The Moboil Concert Program*, the largest commercial orchestra on the air at the time, NBC-Red, New York, NY, 1929).

26326 *Rapid Transit.* Both the dramatic and humorous incidents of life in a large metropolitan city were dramatized on the program. Music was provided by an orchestra conducted by Enrique (Enric) Madriguera (NBC-Pacific Network, 1929).

26327 Rapieff, Ken. Sportscaster (WICC, Bridgeport, CT, 1940–1941).

26328 Rapley, Anna. Singer (WFAA, Dallas, TX, 1925).

26329 Rapp, Barney. Leader (Barney Rapp's Orchestra, WHAS, Louisville, KY, 1924–1925; *Barney Rapp Orchestra*, instr. mus. prg., WLW, Cincinnati, OH, 1935).

26330 Rapp, Doug. DJ (WDSM, Superior, WI, 1956).

26331 Rapp, Gene. Newscaster (KOAT, Albuquerque, NM, 1948).

26332 Rapp, J.C. Announcer (KMA, Shenandoah, IA, 1929).

26333 Rappelet, A.O. Newscaster (KCIL, Houma, LA, 1947).

26334 Rasberrry, Charlie. DJ (*Musical Roundup*, KDRS, Paragould, AR, 1955).

26335 Rasch, Katherine. Singer from the "Ziegfeld Follies" Broadway production (WGCP, Newark, NJ, 1925).

26336 Rash, Lester R. Sportscaster (WKAM, Goshen, IND, 1953; *Morning Sports Review*, KGOS, Torrington, WY, 1954). DJ (*Sunday Serenade*, KGOS, 1954).

26337 Rashkin, Mary. Pianist (WJY, New York, NY, 1925).

26338 Rasjlos, Theresa Wolfe. Soprano (WEAF, New York, NY, 1923).

26339 Rasmussen, Eric. Rasmussen broadcast a variety of "health training exercises" (KGO, Oakland, CA, 1926).

26340 Rasmussen, Leo G. Newscaster (KICD, Spencer, IA, 1942).

26341 Rasmussen, Lois. COM-HE (KBIA, Columbia, MS, 1960).

26342 Rasmussen, Marie. Violinist (WOAW, Omaha, NE, 1924).

26343 Rasoplo, Enrique. Violinist (1929).

26344 Rasspicjome, Vladimir. Pianist (KGO, Oakland, CA, 1925).

26345 Rast, Malcolm "Mike." DJ (*Club 1400*, WKAY, Glasgow, KY, 1947; WCOS, Columbia, SC, 1948; WCOS, 1954–1955).

26346 *Rastus and His Musical Menagerie.* This was an early morning show that combined comedy and songs (Monday through Friday, six times weekly, 8:00 A.M., WEAF, New York, NY, 1928).

26347 Rastus and Professor I-Know-It. Popular blackface comedy team not otherwise identified (KLX, Oakland, CA, 1929).

26348 Ratcliffe, Clarence. Tenor (NBC, New York, NY, 1929).

26349 Ratcliffe, H.C. Newscaster (WEEI, Boston, MA, 1942).

26350 *Rate Your Mate.* Joey Adams interviewed married couples who participated in the quiz. As the title suggests, each spouse guessed whether the other would answer various questions correctly. In such circumstances, even an incorrect answer by a spouse in response to a question could bring a prize if the other predicted it. Hal Simms was the announcer (30 min., Saturday, 7:00–7:30 P.M., CBS, 1950).

26351 Rathbun, Jack. Sportscaster (WJHP, Jacksonville, FL, 1940; *World of Sports*, WBSR, Pensacola, FL, 1949).

26352 Rathe, Bob. DJ (*1280 Club*, WMRO, Aurora, IL, 1948; *Coffee Time*, WGEZ, Beloit, WI, 1952).

26353 Rathert, Norm. Leader (Norm Rathert and his Trojan Tooters Orchestra, KFI, Los Angeles, CA, 1926).

26354 Ratner, Sol. Sportscaster (WDAR, Savannah, GA, 1955).

26355 *Ratyna's Orchestra.* Instr. mus. prg. (WORL, Boston, MA, 1939).

26356 Raubacher, George. Sportscaster (WCLO, Janesville, WI, 1944).

26357 Rauh [Raul], Helen. Classical pianist (WHT, Chicago, IL, 1926; WIBO, Chicago, IL, 1928–1929).

26358 Rauhut, Jeanette. Violinist Rauhut was a member of the Aeolian Trio (KFWM, Oakland, CA, 1929).

26359 Rauhut, Otto. Director (Otto Rauhut Violin Ensemble consisting of Kathleen Horton, C. William Friedrichs, Jr., Isador Botasof, Emmett Dorman, Jack Murphy, Max Segal, Reuben Schwartz and Edward Veen, KPO, San Francisco, CA, 1925).

26360 Raulerson, Spence. DJ (*Raulerson Rambles*, WMGA, Moultrie, GA, 1952).

26361 Rautavirta. Virginia. COM-HE (WMFG, Hibbing, MT, 1960).

26362 Ravazza, Carl. Leader (*Carl Ravazza Orchestra*, instr. mus. prg., NBC-Blue, 1935–1936).

26363 Ravel, Carl. Leader (*Carl Ravel Orchestra*, instr. mus. prg., CBS, 1937).

26364 Raven, George. DJ (*By George*, KSYC, Yreka, CA, 1952).

26365 Ravenel, Florence [Florence Ray]. HE-COM (*Florence Ravenel*, Saturday, WBBM, Chicago, IL, 1937). Ravenel broadcast a program of interest to women. She also broadcast a women's program on Chicago's WJJD in 1937. Ravenel previously had appeared on the *Homemaker's Hour* (WLS, Chicago, IL). She also played a role on the popular daytime serial, *Ma Perkins.*

26366 Ravenel, John. Newscaster (WSJS, Winston-Salem, NC, 1939).

26367 Rawles, Delly. COM-HE (KMON, Great Falls, MT, 1957).

26368 Rawlings, Julian. Newscaster (WGOV, Valdosta, GA, 1941). Sportscaster (WGOV, 1941).

26369 Rawlings, Phila. COM-HE (WSM, Nashville, TN, 1954).

26370 Rawlinson, Chuck. Sportscaster (*Sizing Up Sports*, WNOW, York, PA, 1950–1952).

26371 Rawls, Charlie. Sportscaster (WSLI, Jackson, MS, 1940; 1945).

26372 Rawson, Margaret. Pianist (KFAE, Pullman, WA, 1924).

26373 Rawson, (Mrs.) Myrtle. Contralto (KTBI, Los Angeles, CA, 1929).

26374 Rawson, Ron. Announcer Rawson worked on *Hour of Charm, Life Can Be Beautiful, Portia Faces Life, Road of Life, The Thin Man* and *Young Dr. Malone.*

26375 Ray, Ben. Concertina soloist Ray performed with Rudy Patek as a concertina duet team (WDAP, Chicago, IL, 1923).

26376 Ray, Betty. Singer (WFIL, Philadelphia, PA, 1935).

26377 Ray, Bob. DJ (*Bob Ray Show*, WIRK, West Palm Beach, FL, 1952).

26378 Ray, Charles. Harmonica soloist (KDKA, Pittsburgh, PA, 1922).

26379 Ray, Curt. DJ (*Curt Ray Show*, KMOX, St. Louis, MO, 1948–1954).

26380 Ray, Del. DJ (WVMA, Magnolia, AR, 1948). Sportscaster (WVMA, 1949).

26381 Ray, Ed. Sportscaster (WDAE, Tampa, FL, 1940).

26382 Ray, Eva. Soprano (KYW, Chicago, IL, 1922).

26383 Ray, Florence. *See* **Ravenel, Florence.**

26384 Ray, Gene. DJ (*Cornfield Frolics*, WPAL, Charleston, SC, 1952).

26385 Ray, Houston. Leader (Houston Ray Orchestra, WHN, New York, NY, 1924).

26386 Ray, Joan. Staff contralto (KTAB, Oakland, CA, 1926–1929).

26387 Ray, Johnnie. Singer and recording star Ray turned DJ (*The Johnnie Ray Show*, 55 min., Saturday, 7:05–8:00 P.M., Network radio, 1959).

26388 Ray, Larry. Sportscaster (*7 P.M. Sports Roundup*, WHB, Kansas City, MO, 1950–1954).

26389 Ray, Melville. Tenor (WLW, Cincinnati, OH, 1926).

26390 Ray, Miriam. Singer (*Miriam Ray*, vcl. mus. prg. (15 min., Thursday,, 3:30–3:45 P.M., CBS, 1931). The Columbia Broadcasting System called her "Columbia's sensational new blues singer"

26391 Ray, Paul D. *Variety* called Ray a "railroad pianist" (WFAA, Dallas, TX, 1926).

26392 Ray, Ruth. COM-HE (KTVO, Ottumwa, IA, 1956).

26393 Ray, Ruth A. Violinist (WBZ, Springfield, MA, 1923).

26394 Ray, Virgil. Leader (Virgil Ray's Winter Garden Orchestra, KFI, Los Angeles, CA, 1927).

26395 Ray, Wendy. DJ (KERG, Eugene, OR, 1956).

26396 Ray, William "Bill." Chief announcer (KFWB, Hollywood, CA, 1927–1929).

26397 *Ray Bolger Rexall Show.* Entertainer Ray Bolger hosted the variety show that featured singer Jeri Sullivan and the Roy Bargy Orchestra. Guests such as Frank Sinatra and Joan Davis frequently appeared with Bolger (30 min., Weekly, CBS, 1945).

26398 *Ray Knight's Cuckoo Clock* (aka *Ray Knight's Cuckoos* and *The Cuckoo Hour*). Ray Knight's early *Cuckoo Hour*, despite its name, was only 30 minutes in length. A later version was a full hour. Adelina Thompson played the role of zany Mrs. Pennyfeather on both versions. On the program, Knight listened to popular songs and interpolated nutty comments throughout and called his show a musical depreciation hour (60 min., Weekly, Monday, 8:00–9:00 P.M., CST, NBC-Blue, 1935). *See* **Knight, Ray.**

26399 *Ray Noble Show.* Bandleader Noble hosted the summer replacement for *The Sealtest Village Store.* Ilene Woods and the Crew Chiefs vocal group appeared with the Noble band. Hy Averback was the announcer (30 min., Thursday, 9:30–10:00 P.M., NBC, 1948).

26400 Raybestos Twins. The veteran radio comedy team of Al Bernard and Billy Beard were featured as the Raybestos Twins on the show sponsored by Raybestos. Tenor Lanny Ross, the Bonnie Laddies vocal trio and Sam Herman's Orchestra also were regular cast members on the variety program (30 min., Friday, 7:30–8:00 P.M., NBC-Red, 1928–1930). During this period they also were sometimes heard at an earlier hour (30 min., Friday, 6:00–6:30 P.M., NBC-Red, 1928–1929).

26401 Rayburn, Alice. Singer (WPAR, Parkersburg, WV, 1937).

26402 Rayburn (Gene) and Finch (Dee). Rayburn and Finch were a popular New York DJ team (*Anything Goes*, WNEW, New York, NY, 1947–1948). After Finch left, Rayburn did his own thing on other radio shows. *See* **Rayburn, Gene.**

26403 Rayburn, Gene. DJ (WNEW, New York, NY, 1950; *Gene Rayburn Show*, Rayburn called himself "a poor man's Henny Youngman," when he hosted his comedy variety show and tried his hand at comedy (WNEW, New York, NY, 1948). Rayburn later returned to DJ duties with a program also called the *Gene Rayburn Show* (150 min., Monday through Saturday, 6:00–8:00 A.M., WNBC, New York, NY, 1952).

26404 Raymon [Raymond], Paul. DJ (*Swing Session*, WJRD, Tuscaloosa, AL, 1947). Sportscaster (WJRD, 1948).

26405 Raymond, Al. Leader (Al Raymond Orchestra, WHN, New York, NY, 1925).

26406 Raymond, Anne. Known as "The Health Fairy," Raymond told health stories for children (WJZ, New York, NY, 1922).

26407 Raymond, Art. DJ (*Rhumba Rendezvous* and *Band Stand*, WVNJ, Newark, NJ, 1948).

26408 Raymond, Betty. COM-HE (WOTW, Nashua, NH, 1955).

26409 Raymond, Carl E. Chief announcer and station manager (KFOA, Seattle, WA, 1925).

26410 Raymond, Charles. Director (Raymond Dance Orchestra, WEBJ, New York, NY, 1926).

26411 Raymond, Clem. Leader (Clem Raymond's Dixie Jazz Band, KGO, San Francisco, CA, 1927).

26412 Raymond, Frank. News commentator (*Just Eavesdropping*, KVSM, San Mateo, CA, 1947–1948).

26413 Raymond, Hal. Leader (*Hal Raymond Orchestra*, instr. mus. prg., WTAM, Cleveland, OH, 1936).

26414 Raymond, Hal. DJ (WEEK, Peoria, IL, 1957).

26415 Raymond, Jack. Sportscaster (WISN, Milwaukee, WI, 1946). DJ (WRIT, Milwaukee, WI, 1947). News commentator (*News of the World*, WISN, 1948).

26416 Raymond, Jimmy. Singer known as the "After Dinner Boy" (KJBS, San Francisco, CA, 1925).

26417 Raymond, Jo Ann. COM-HE (WION, Ionia, MI, 1955).

26418 Raymond, Joseph. Violinist (CBS, 1929).

26419 Raymond, Louise. Blues singer (WLW, Cincinnati, OH, 1936).

26420 Raymond, Ollie. DJ (*Request Granted*, KEPO, El Paso, TX, 1948).

26421 Raymond, Ray. As "Brother Bob," Raymond hosted a program with a group of performers, all of whom were under twenty years of age (KTAB, Oakland, CA, 1929).

26422 Raymond, Stan. Sportscaster (WATL, Richmond, VA, 1946; *Sports Scope*, WATL, 1947; *Sportscope*, WBGE, Atlanta, GA, 1950; *Sportscope*, WATL, Atlanta, GA, 1952; WQXI, Atlanta, GA, 1953–1956; WWOD, Lynchburg, VA, 1960).

26423 *Raymond Scott Show.* Talented Raymond Scott led his orchestra on the weekday music show (15 min., Monday through Friday, 4:45–5:00 P.M., CBS, 1945). Scott earlier had his own show as a solo pianist (*Raymond Scott,* instr. mus. prg., CBS, 1934).

26424 Ray-O-Vac Twins. Russ Wildley and Bill Sheehan were a popular singing team known as the Ray-O-Vac Twins (KFWB, Los Angeles, CA; KFWB, Hollywood, CA; WSM, Nashville, TN, 1927). For a short period in 1926, the Ray-O-Vac Twins broadcast from KTHS (Hot Springs Natural Park, AR, 1926). The popular team was sponsored by the French Battery Company of Madison, Wisconsin, makers of Ray-O-Vac batteries. The Ray-O-Vac Twins came to station KMA late in the 1920s and remained at the station as the *KMA Farm Belt Paint Boys* for many years (KMA, Shenandoah, IA, late 1920s).

26425 Razaf, Andy. Singer-composer (WGCP, Newark, NJ, 1925).

26426 Razzetto, Laura. Soprano (KPO, San Francisco, CA, 1926).

26427 *RCA Educational Hour.* Walter Damrosch conducted the NBC network's orchestra and generally provided instruction in this early national network programming attempt at music appreciation. The program was broadcast at 10:00 A.M. during the 1928 season from October to May. The music appreciation selections played by the orchestra were graded for students from the third grade through college. The program's first half-hour contained music for children in grades three to six, while the last half-hour was for students from grades seven through high school and college. Damrosch soon became a much beloved radio personality whose masterful accomplishments as a teacher were recognized and duly appreciated (NBC-Blue, 1928). *See* ***The Music Appreciation Hour.***

26428 *RCA Hour* (aka *The RCA Victor Hour* or *RCA Victor Program*). The 1928 version of the *RCA Hour* included a dramatic interlude and musical selections performed by baritone Harold Dana with Max Dolin conducting the RCA Orchestra (NBC-Pacific Coast network, 1928). The following year the format changed to that of an informative program that combined an inquiring look at world history, music and philosophy (60 min., Friday, 8:00 to 9:00 P.M., NBC-Pacific Coast Network, 1929). For example, a musical segment of the latter program included the musical compositions of Augusta Holmes with contralto Margaret O'Dea and tenor Harold Spaulding performing them. A later network format in 1930 of 60 minutes length featured the RCA Salon Orchestra conducted by Nathaniel Shilkret. The announcer was John S. Young (60 min., Thursday, 10:00–11:00 P.M., NBC-Red, 1930).

26429 *RCA Radio Matinee.* Performers Rudy Vallee and Hazel Glenn plus the team of Eddie and Ralph appeared on the entertaining weekly variety program (60 min., Weekly, NBC, 1935).

26430 *RCA Radiotrons.* Baritone John Charles Thomas was often featured on the concert music hour (NBC-Blue, 1926).

26431 *RCA Theremin Ether Wave Music.* The Radio Corporation of America sponsored the quarter-hour program of theremin music. Although it was listed as ether, the music did possess an ethereal sound (15 min., Saturday, 7:15–7:30 P.M., NBC-Blue, 1930).

26432 *RCA Victor Hour.* See ***The Victor Hour.***

26433 ***RCA Victor Show.*** The excellent music program presented Arthur Fiedler conducting the Boston Pops Orchestra and baritone Robert Merrill (30 min., Sunday, 5:30–6:00 P.M., NBC, 1948).

26434 **Rea, Bobby.** Newscaster (KFRU, Columbia, MO, 1939).

26435 **Rea, Ethel.** Soprano (WMCA, New York, NY and WRNY, Richmond Hill, NY, 1925).

26436 **Rea, Virginia.** Virginia Rea was a popular performer who sang under the name of "Olive Palmer" on the *Palmolive Hour* (NBC, New York, NY, 1927).

26437 **Read, Brooks.** Sportscaster (*Sports Memories*, KPRK, Livingston, MT, 1947).

26438 **Read, Harlan Eugene.** News commentator (WOR, Newark, NJ, 1934; WBBM, Chicago, IL, 1944–1945).

26439 **Read, Lawrence.** Newscaster (WEXL, Royal Oak, MI, 1944).

26440 **Read, Lillian French.** Soprano (WORD, Batavia, IL, 1925).

26441 **Read, Nancy.** COM-HE (KCBQ, San Diego, CA, 1951).

26442 **Read, Sue.** Actress Read appeared on the *We Love and Learn* daytime serial program.

26443 **Reade, Frances Lawson.** Contralto (WGY, Schenectady, NY and WOKO, Albany, NY, 1925).

26444 **Reade, Laura.** Soprano (WEVD, New York, NY, 1937).

26445 ***Readers' Guide.*** Joseph Henry Jackson broadcast his views on the latest books and events in the literary world (KGO, Oakland, CA, 1929).

26446 **Reading, Nancy.** COM-HE (WMAM, Marinette, WI, 1956).

26447 **Readick, Frank.** Actor Readick appeared on *Adventures of Mortimer Meek, America's Hour, Buck Rogers in the 25th Century, Cavalcade of America, Famous Jury Trials, FBI in Peace and War, Forty-five Minutes from Broadway, Joe Palooka, Let's Pretend, The Shadow* (He was the second actor to play the character when it was broadcast as part of the *Detective Story Program.*) and *Smiling Jack* (title role).

26448 ***Readings.*** John B. Daniels broadcast a series of poetry and prose reading programs (WJZ, New York, NY, 1925).

26449 **Readon, Dan.** Sportscaster (*Speaking of Sports*, WWSC, Glen Falls, NY, 1947).

26450 **Ready, Les.** DJ (*Jukebox Revue*, KUGN (Eugene, OR, 1947).

26451 **Reagan, Neil.** Sportscaster (KFWB, Los Angeles, CA, 1940).

26452 **Reagan, Ronald "Dutch."** Sportscaster Reagan's play-by-play of Big Ten football games were considered some of the most colorful sports' broadcasts in the U.S. (WOC, Davenport, IA; WHO, Des Moines, IA, 1933). Reagan's first major network radio appearance was on *The Warner Brothers Academy Theater* program in 1938.

He became a popular motion picture star after going to Hollywood in 1937. After a bit role in *Hollywood Hotel* (1937), he starred in *Brother Rat* (1938); *Dark Victory* (1939); *Knute Rockne, All American* (1940); *Kings Row* (1942); *This is the Army* (1943); *The Hasty Heart* (1949); *Bedtime for Bonzo* (1951); *The Killers* (1964) and many others.

He also had a busy television career in *Amos Burke, Secret Agent* (1963); as the successor to Stanley Andrews on *Death Valley* (1966) and as host of *The General Electric Theater* (1954–1962). He left television in 1966 to begin a successful career in politics. After serving as Governor of California, Reagan became President of the United States.

26453 **Reager, Judy.** COM-HE (WPDX, Clarksburg, WV, 1954).

26454 **Reagles, Walter.** Tenor (WGY, Schenectady, NY, 1923–1924).

26455 ***Real Folks*** **(aka** ***Real Folks from Thompkins Corner*****).** George Frame Brown wrote the daytime dramatic serial and also played the leading role of Matt Thompkins. Others in the cast and their roles were Phoebe MacKaye as Dorothy Thompkins and Mrs. Watts; Tommy Brown as Elmer Thompkins; and Edwin H. Whitney as Judge Whipple. Also in the cast were: Virginia Farmer, Joyce Benner, Roger Marsh, Geofrey Warwick and G. Underhill Macy. Music was produced each week by the "Thompkins Corner Firemen's Band." Brown said he attempted to show life as it was lived in "any upstate city." The show was one of radio's first dramatic series (30 min., Monday, 9:30–10:00 P.M., NBC-Blue, 1928–1931).

26456 ***Real Silk.*** Real Silk Hosiery Company sponsored the veteran radio comedy team of Dr. Pratt and Dr. Sherman (Russell Pratt and Ransom Sherman) on the variety show that also featured the Vincent Lopez Orchestra (30 min., Sunday, 10:15–10:45 P.M. NBC-Blue, 1933).

26457 **Reams, Hunter.** Newscaster (WJNO, West Palm Beach, FL, 1938; WSTV, Steubenville, OH, 1942; WJPA, Washington, PA, 1945).

26458 **Reams, Ted.** Sportscaster (WRVA, Richmond, VA, 1937–1939).

26459 **Reardon, Helen.** COM-HE (KBOW, Butte, MT, 1960).

26460 **Reardon, Tom.** DJ (*Midnight Revue*, WHHM, Memphis, TN, 1947; WABG, Greenwood, MS, 1956).

26461 **Reavley, Jack.** DJ (*Club 600*, KTBB, Tyler, TX, 1948).

26462 **Rebeo, Margot.** Organist (MBS, 1937).

26463 **Reber, Don.** DJ (KEIO, Pocatello, ID, 1947; *Show Tune Time*, KVNU, Logan, UT, 1948).

26464 **Rechlin, Edward.** Pianist (WGBS, New York, NY, 1925).

26465 **Reckner, Harry.** Sportscaster (*Reports on Sports*, KTSA, San Antonio, TX, 1949).

26466 **Reckow, Cliff.** Reckow was the concert master violinist in the National Battery Symphony Orchestra (KSTP, St. Paul–Minneapolis, MN, 1929).

26467 **Record Boys of WJZ.** The popular singing team consisted of Al Bernard, Frank Kamplain and Sammy Stept (WJZ, New York, NY, 1926).

26468 ***Recording Sessions.*** DJ Art Ford conducted the interesting sustaining show on which he asked various recording artists how they made their records. Ford would then play the records discussed (25 min., Sunday, 12:35–1:00 P.M., WNEW, New York, NY, 1952).

26469 **Rector, Bob.** DJ (*1560 Club*, KSWI, Council Bluffs, IA, 1947; *Best by Request*, KWTO, Springfield, MO, 1952).

26470 **Rector, Gabby.** DJ (*KLIK Clock*, KLIK, Jefferson City, MO, 1954–1955).

26471 ***Red and Black Revue.*** Comedian Dean Vine, pianist Pauline Albert and Merle Johnston's orchestra performed on the sustaining variety program (30 min., Tuesday, 10:30–11:00 P.M. WOR, Newark, NJ, 1934).

26472 ***Red Apple Club.*** Cornelius D. Tomy conducted the popular early radio show that included music and interviews and performances by famous stage and screen stars. Norman White was the program's featured singer (Tuesday, P.M., WCX, Detroit, MI, 1923). The show, Detroit's most popular program for many years, began when Tomy scheduled the Stickles Sisters Orchestra to perform on a Tuesday evening at 10:00 P.M. Announcer Tomy talked on the air with the band leader, described the girls' dresses and hummed along with the band. A Detroit music publisher, Bartlett Holmes, also sang on the first program. Tomy did not give Holmes' name, but announced that he would award a "nice red apple" to the first person who called in the name of the singer. A correct call soon came in and the "red apple" awarded to the winner. Listeners sent hundreds of letters to the station and the Red Apple Club had its beginnings. The Stickles Sisters band returned the following Tuesday, and once more Tomy conducted the program. Some of the popular entertainers who frequently appeared on the *Red Apple Club* were: Bernice, a 16-year-old pianist; Whispering Bill Collins, one of radio's first crooners; Al Cameron and Pete Bontsema (Al and Pete); Charlotte (Myers) and Mary (Tudor), a team of singer and piano player; Doc McPhee, a dentist who had been a "rube comic" in vaudeville and accompanied his stories by playing his five-string banjo; the Wolverine Four band; singer Estelle Forbes, Ann Forbes, Gladys Sanderson, Sister Ruby Jones, Edna Rae and Billy Mack. Incidentally, the *Red Apple Club* singer Norman White became so popular that he later had his own *Luncheon Song Review* program on WJR (Detroit, MI). The *Red Apple Club* program remained on the air for more than five years.

26473 **Red Cross.** Announcer and staff pianist (WWNC, Ashville, NC, 1929).

26474 ***Red Cross Mattress Hour.*** Howard Petrie was the host of the variety program (WBZ, Boston, MA, 1931).

26475 ***Red Davis.*** Sponsored by Beechnut gum, the program was a forerunner of the *Forever Young* and the *Pepper Young's Family* programs. Before Beechnut took over the sponsorship, it had been known as *Red Adams.* Fearing that the name "Adams" would remind listeners of rival Adams' Chewing Gum,

Beechnut insisted upon a name change. The program told a warm human interest story of a young man's trials and tribulations with his girl friend, his buddies and a father who didn't understand him. Burgess Meredith played the title role, supported by Marion Barney, Ethel Blume, Eunice Howard, John Kane, Jack Roseleigh, Jean Sothern and Elizabeth Wragge (NBC, Monday, Wednesday and Friday, 8:45–9:00 P.M., NBC-Blue, 1933–1934). The show also had been broadcast on the same days earlier at 7:15–7:30 P.M. on NBC-Red. *Also See* ***Pepper Young's Family***.

26476 Red Dog Orchestra of Chicago. Popular Midwest band (KYW, Chicago, IL, 1922).

26477 *Red Foley and Lily May* (aka *Red Foley and His Merrymakers*). CW singer Rambling Red Foley and his wife, Lily May, appeared with the Girls of the Golden West on the music show sponsored by Pinex (15 min., Monday through Friday, 11:00–11:15 A.M. CST, WLS, Chicago, IL, 1936). *See* ***Rambling Red Foley and The Girls of the Golden West***.

26478 *Red Goes to Camp*. The dramatic series told the story of a boy attending the Chicago Boys' Club camp at Winona Lake, Indiana. Camp members took all the parts on the show directed by Howard Tooley (15 min., 2:30–2:45 P.M., WLS, Chicago, IL, 1938).

26479 *Red Grange Forecasts*. Football great Red Grange, who in his playing days was known as "The Galloping Ghost," broadcast weekly football forecasts for CBS in 1934. By 1936, Grange was on NBC three times weekly both with football news and his predictions for the coming week's games.

26480 *Red Horse Ranch*. CW mus. prg. (WFBM, Indianapolis, IN, 1935).

26481 *Red Horse Tavern*. Socony Vacuum Company, manufacturer of the gasoline sold at the "Sign of the Flying Red Horse," sponsored the musical show featuring Freddie Rich's orchestra and the Tavern Singers — a 16-voice mixed choir. Osgood Perkins hosted the program, did impersonations, introduced the musical selections and interviewed weekly guests such as Eleanor Powell (30 min., Friday, 8:00–8:30 P.M., CBS, 1935).

26482 Red Peppers. Hot jazz band led by Frank Silsby (KVOO, Tulsa, OK, 1929).

26483 *Red Ramblers*. The Ramblers, a popular CW musical group, appeared on the typical early morning local music show broadcast in Missouri (15 min., Thursday, 6:45–7:00 A.M. CST, KWOS, Jefferson City, MO, 1938).

26484 *Red River Dave (Dave McEnery)*. A real cowboy, CW singer McEnery first appeared on local San Antonio, TX, and Border Radio stations before moving east and broadcasting his own network stations (Mutual and NBC, 1938–1939). He was probably the first CW singer to have his own TV program. A story, perhaps apocryphal is that once during a 12-hour TV broadcast McEnery wrote 52 songs while handcuffed to a piano (*Red River Dave*, CW mus. prg., 15 min., Saturday, 9:30–9:45 A.M., WOR, Newark, NJ, 1939). McEnery enjoyed a brief motion picture career, but a long, profitable recording one.

26485 *Red Ryder*. Fred Harman's western comic strip was the basis for the action packed dramatic series. Ryder was accompanied on his adventures by his young Indian friend, Little Beaver. One of the best remembered parts of the show was the opening delivered by announcer Ben Alexander: "From out of the West comes America's famous fighting cowboy — Red Ryder!" The cast included: Tommy Cook, Reed Hadley, Carlton KaDell and Brooke Temple. Paul Franklin was the program's writer, producer and director (NBC-Blue, 1942–1949).

26486 *Red Skelton Show*. Pantomime comedian Skelton made his successful radio debut in 1939 on the *Avalon Time* show. On his own show in 1941, Skelton introduced such memorable comedy characters as the Junior the Mean Little Kid, Clem Kadiddlehopper, Willy Lump-Lump, J. Newton Numbskull, and the western gun fighter, Deadeye. He was assisted by some fine comedic supporting actors. In the cast were: Verna Felton, Harriet Hilliard, Marlin Hurt, Tommy Mack, GeGe Pearson, "Wonderful" Smith and Lorene Tuttle. The program's writers were Jack Douglas, Ben Freedman, Johnny Murray and Edna Skelton. Jack Simpson was the program's producer and Keith McLeod the director. Music was supplied by the orchestras of Ozzie Nelson and David Rose. The vocalists were Anita Ellis, Harriet Hilliard, Ozzie Nelson and the Four Knights vocal quartet. Truman Bradley, John Holbrook and Pat McGeehan were the announcers. Although Skelton was a talented clown, his skills were displayed to best advantage on television and in films, where his pantomime and physical comedy talent could be best utilized.

26487 *Red Star Rangers*. CW mus. prg. (WOR, Newark, NJ, 1937).

26488 *Red Star Revue*. Heywood Broun, a New York *World-Telegram* columnist, hosted the variety show featuring singer Mabel Jackson, the comedy team of Pick and Pat, a vocal group called the Four New Yorkers and the comedy singing team of Gordon, Dave and Benny (30 min., Wednesday, 8:30–9:00 P.M., WOR, Newark, NJ, 1933).

26489 *Red Steele, Flying Investigator*. Fred Hunter wrote and played the title role on the juvenile adventure serial. G-Man Steele was a Native American Indian, who had been an All-American football halfback and world traveler before becoming a G-Man. In the story, Steele fought crime in all parts of the United States. Paul Gott supplied the program's organ music. Massey's Dairy sponsored the program and offered membership in the Red Steele Membership Club for a milk bottle cap from Massey's Milk. Each program ended with a moral and an injunction to drink the sponsor's milk (15 min., Monday through Saturday, WTMV, St. Louis, MO, 1937).

26490 *Red Trails*. A dramatic series, based on fact, *Red Trails* was researched and written by Stewart Sterling. The story told of the uprising of the Metis (half-breeds) led by Louis Riel in Canada's northwest territory in 1895. *Red Trails* was broadcast weekly (30 min., Tuesday evenings, 9:00–9:30 P.M., NBC-Red, 1929). The program was rebroadcast six years later. Once more the story dramatized the bravery of the Canada's Royal Mounted Police in putting down the rebellion led by Louis Riel in 1895. The latter version, sponsored by the American Tobacco Company, featured Warren Colston as a heroic Mounted Police Sgt. Also in the cast were: Arline Blackburn, Alfred Corn and Victor McLaglen. Graham Harris was the program's musical director (30 min., Thursday, 8:30–9:00 P.M., NBC-Blue, 1935).

26491 *(The) Red Wagon Boys*. The comedy-singing team were popular local favorites (WMAZ, Macon, GA, 1934).

26492 Redabaugh, Red. COM-HE (KRDO, Colorado Springs, CO, 1956).

26493 *Redbook Magazine*. Stories from *Redbook* magazine were dramatized on the 15-minute show. The first two stories presented were "Anything You Want to Know" on May 26, 1932 and "He Knew Women" on June 2, 1932.

26494 Redbord, Rita. Soprano (WGCP, New York, NY, 1926).

26495 Redd, Corrine. Soprano (KNX, Hollywood, CA, 1926).

26496 Reddy, Lawrence. Baritone (WCCO, Minneapolis–St. Paul, MN, 1928–1929).

26497 Redeen, Robert L. "Bob." Newscaster (WOC, Davenport, IA, 1944–1945).

26498 Redell, Emma. Singer (WNYC, New York, NY, 1935).

26499 Redenbaugh, Edna. COM-HE (WDEL, Wilmington, DE, 1949).

26500 Redfern, Gene. Versatile singer, guitarist, violinist and director of the *A.B.C. Safety Club* (KVOO, Tulsa, OK, 1929).

26501 Redfern, Gene and Barney Breene. Harmony singing team (KVOO, Tulsa, OK, 1928).

26502 Redfield, Frank. Newscaster (KWJB, Globe, AZ, 1941).

26503 Redfield, William "Bill" or "Billy. Actor Redfield appeared on *Brighter Day*, *Coast-to-Coast on a Bus*, *David Harum*, *Hearts in Harmony*, *Right to Happiness* and *Young Dr. Malone*.

26504 Redford, Lee. DJ (*1490 Swing Club*, WKAY, Glasgow, KY, 1950).

26505 *(The) Redhead*. R.K. Vollaerts wrote, Leonard Blair produced and Martin Andrews directed the sustaining situation comedy. Mary McCarty played the title role of a brash, wise-cracking young girl from a small Nebraska town, who came to New York City to pursue a career in modeling. Dick Van Patten and Vinton Hayworth were also in the cast. *Variety* said the show was originally planned for Janis Paige, who turned it down because of the plot content (30 min., Thursday, 8:00–8:30 P.M., ABC, 1952).

26506 Redington, Bernice. Miss Redington talked on a variety of home economics topics on her *Home Helps* segments (KJR, Seattle, WA, 1925).

26507 Redington, Jane. Graphologist (WINS, New York, NY, 1932).

26508 Redington, Ruth. COM-HE (WKNE, Keene, NH, 1949–1957).

26509 Redlund, Alice. Organist (KSTP, St. Paul–Minneapolis, MN, 1929).

26510 Redman, George. Leader (George Redman Orchestra, KNX, Los Angeles, CA, 1926; George Redman's Concert Orchestra, KNX, Los Angeles, CA, 1927).

26511 Redmond, A.K. Newscaster (WHP, Harrisburg, PA, 1941).

26512 Redmond, Aldan. Announcer (WBZA, Springfield, MA, 1927–1929).

26513 Redmond, Dick. Newscaster (WHP, Harrisburg, PA, 1945–1947).

26514 Redmond, Don. Leader (*Don Redmond Orchestra,* instr. mus. prg., WIP, Philadelphia, PA, 1935, CBS, 1936).

26515 Redmond, Mary. Violinist (KDKA, Pittsburgh, PA, 1926).

26516 Rednor, Nan. COM-HE (WBUD, Trenton, NJ, 1956).

26517 *Reducing Talks.* Georgia Heffner conducted the series of self-improvement talks on weight reduction (WGBS, New York, NY, 1925).

26518 Reece, Mary Lou. COM-HE (WGBA, Columbus, GA, 1956–1957).

26519 Reece, Sanford "Sandy." DJ (*Sandman Serenade,* WSBT, South Bend, IN, 1947–1950). Sportscaster (*Sports Review,* WSBT, 1947–1948).

26520 Reed, Alan (Teddy Bergman). *See* **Bergman, Teddy.**

26521 Reed, Alan, Jr. Young actor Reed was in the cast of *Falstaff Fables* with his father.

26522 Reed, Art. Sportscaster (*Sports Final,* WMON, Montgomery, WV, 1947).

26523 Reed, B. Mitchel. DJ (KFWB, Los Angeles, CA, 1957).

26524 Reed, Bill. Sportscaster (*Sports Scrapbook,* KYOU, 1948; *Sportscast,* KMYR, Denver, CO, 1949–1950; KFEL, Denver, CO, 1955; KHOW, Denver, CO, 1960). DJ (*Wake Up and Live,* KYOU, Greeley, CO, 1950).

26525 Reed, Bob. DJ (*Tea Time Tunes,* WBAA, West Lafayette, IN, 1947).

26526 Reed, C.D. Newscaster (KNEL, Brady, TX, 1945–1948). Sportscaster (KNEL, 1947).

26527 Reed, Carl. Newscaster (WHEB, Portsmouth, NH, 1942, 1945)

26528 Reed, Crawford. Violinist (WAPI, Auburn, AL, 1929).

26529 Reed, Delis. Newscaster (KNEL, Brady, TX, 1941).

26530 Reed, Dell. "Dixie tenor" (KMOX, St. Louis, MO, 1929).

26531 Reed, Dick. Newscaster (WHIO, Dayton, OH, 1938; WIRE, Indianapolis, IN, 1940, 1946).

26532 Reed, Donna. Actress Reed, later a famous television and motion picture star, appeared in the cast of *The Romance of Helen Trent.*

26533 Reed, Donna. COM-HE (WAXU, Georgetown, KY, 1960).

26534 Reed, Elliott. Actor Reed was in the cast of *Carol Kennedy's Romance.*

26535 Reed, Evelyn. Pianist in the WMH String Trio (WMH, Cincinnati, OH, 1924).

26536 Reed, Glen. DJ (*Town and Country Club,* WMNE, Menomonie, WI, 1952).

26537 Reed, Grace. COM-HE (WIRI, Plattsburgh, NY, 1955).

26538 Reed, Helen. Pianist (WQJ, Chicago, IL, 1925).

26539 Reed, J. Lewis. Announcer designated as "ALN" (WJZ, New York, NY and WHY, Schenectady, NY, 1925).

26540 Reed, Kay. Organist (WNEW, New York, NY, 1935–1937).

26541 Reed, Lynne. DJ (*Gloombusters,* KOLN, Lincoln, NE, 1948). Sportscaster (*Speaking of Sports,* KOLN, 1950).

26542 Reed, Mable Hinzie. Violinist (WOW, Omaha, NE, 1927).

26543 Reed, Madeline. Lyric soprano (WIP, Philadelphia, PA, 1924).

26544 Reed, Marion. Actress Reed was in the cast of the *Bachelor's Children* daytime serial program.

26545 Reed, Mitch. DJ (*Mr. Midnight,* WOR, New York, NY, 1954–1955).

26546 Reed, Norman. Chief announcer (WPG, Atlantic City, NJ, 1929).

26547 Reed, Philip. Actor-singer Reed was in the cast of *David Harum* (actor), *Gay Nineties Revue* (tenor in the Elm City Four singing group) and *Society Girl* (actor).

26548 Reed, Ralph. News commentator (*Top Talk of the Day,* WNYC, New York, NY, 1947).

26549 Reed, Red. DJ (*Club 1450,* WHKP, Hendersonville, NC, 1948–1950). Sportscaster (*Sports Parade,* WHKP, 1948; *Red Reed Sports,* WHKP, 1949).

26550 Reed, Theodore Alan (Teddy Bergman). Actor-comedian Alan Reed was born August 20, 1907. After high school, he worked in many stock companies and toured with his cousin, Harry Green, in vaudeville for years. His first radio appearance was in *True Detective Mysteries* in 1927. Later, he appeared on *The Collier Hour* (NBC-Blue, 1928), sponsored by *Collier's* magazine and the *Eveready Hour* (NBC-Red, 1929), sponsored by the National Carbon Company in 1929. In the next two decades Reed appeared on many programs. He probably gained his greatest fame appearing on *Fred Allen* programs. *See* ***The Fred Allen Show.***

26551 Reed, Virginia. Violinist (WBAA, West Lafayette, IN, 1939).

26552 Reed, William. Newscaster (KXEL, Waterloo, IA, 1945).

26553 Reeder, William. Newscaster (KLCN, Blytheville, AR, 1942).

26554 Reedy, Dorothy Heywood. Pianist (KVOO, Tulsa, OK, 1928–1929).

26555 Reedy, George. News analyst (NBC-Blue, 1945; WOL, Washington, DC, 1947).

26556 Reef, Wally. Newscaster (WFEL, Denver, CO, 1937–1942).

26557 Reeges, Jim. Newscaster (KYW, Philadelphia, PA, 1946).

26558 Reep, Ellen. Contralto (KGA, Spokane, WA, 1929).

26559 Reep, Philip. Tenor (WHAM, Rochester, NY, 1928–1929).

26560 Rees, Mary Marren. Actress Rees appeared on the *Ma Perkins* daytime serial program.

26561 Rees, Robert Max. Newscaster (KMJ, Fresno, CA, 1945–1946).

26562 Reese, Al. Leader (Al Reese and his Broadway Orchestra, KOIL, Council Bluffs, IA, 1926).

26563 Reese, Dorothy. Hostess, announcer and pianist (WRAK, Williamsport, PA,1932).

26564 Reese [Reid], Lewis. Popular announcer Reese came to radio after a career as an actor in silent films (WOR, Newark, NJ, 1929).

26565 Reese, Mary Lou. COM-HE (WGBA, Columbus, GA, 1957).

26566 Reese, Paul. Announcer (KFI, Los Angeles, CA, 1924).

26567 Reese, Paula Carr. COM-HE (WMOA, Marietta, OH, 1956).

26568 Reese, Pearl. Soprano (KOIL, Council Bluffs, IA, 1926–1927).

26569 Reese, Von. DJ (KTHT, Houston, TX, 1947).

26570 Reeve, Grace Fisher. Soprano (WJZ, New York, NY, 1925).

26571 *Reeve-Gartzman Program.* The Oakland Six Orchestra was featured on the music program (KFWB, Los Angeles, CA, 1926).

26572 Reeves, George. Sportscaster (KCRC, Enid, OK, 1941; WSAV, Savannah, GA, 1942; WHAS, Louisville, KY, 1945; WINN, Louisville, KY, 1948; *Sports Review,* WINN, 1949; *George Reeves Reports on Sports,* WINN, 1950). DJ (*The GBR Show,* WINN, 1948).

26573 Reeves, Ida Marie. COM-HE (WAZF, Yazoo City, MS, 1957).

26574 Reeves, James Travis "Jim." Smooth CW singer Reeves began his radio career as an announcer (KSIG, Gladewater, TX, 1952) and later as newscaster and DJ (KGRI, Henderson, TX, 1952). The following year Reeves moved to KWKH (Shreveport, LA) as singer and announcer. He soon became a member of the *Louisiana Hayride* (1953–1963). Reeves' pleasant baritone voice allowed him successfully to "crossover" into the field of "popular" songs. He died in a private plane crash in 1964.

26575 Reeves, Jeanette. Singer (WOW, Omaha, NE, 1927).

26576 Reeves, Jim. DJ (*C'Mon and Dance,* WIP, Philadelphia, PA, 1950).

26577 Reeves, Norma (June Vaughn). COM-HE (KROS, Clinton, IA, 1949).

26578 Reeves, Ollie. Leader (Ollie Reeves Orchestra, KFWA, Ogden, UT, 1926). The Reeves band broadcast from the Berthana Ballroom in Ogden, UT.

26579 Reeves, Ray. Sportscaster (WRAL, Raleigh, NC, 1940–1947; WRAL, 1952). Newscaster (WRAL, 1945).

26580 Reeves, Wayne. Sportscaster (WHBU, Anderson, IN, 1940).

26581 Reeves, Wenona. Contralto (KWK, St. Louis, MO, 1929).

26582 Reeves, William. Newscaster (WELI, New Haven, CT, 1939).

26583 Reeves, William "Bill." Newscaster (WSIX, Nashville, TN, 1939; WHUB, Cookeville, TN, 1940–1941; WHBQ, Memphis, TN, 1945).

26584 *Refreshment Time.* Coca-Cola sponsored the lively music program that featured vocals by Connie Boswell and Babs Ryan and her Brothers. Ray Noble's orchestra were regular performers on the half-hour program (30 min., Weekly, CBS, 1935).

26585 Regal, (Mrs.) Francis. Pianist (WBZ, Springfield, MA, 1923).

26586 Regalbuto, Victoria and Mary Regalbuto. Piano team (WEAF, New York, NY, 1925).

26587 Regan, Bernard. Baritone (WOC, Davenport, IA, 1926).

26588 Regan, Dick. Leader (Dick Regan and his WIP Little Symphony, WIP, Philadelphia, PA, 1923).

26589 Regan, John. Sportscaster (WGBS, New York, NY, 1925).

26590 Regan, Lillian. COM-HE (WGBS, New York, NY, 1925).

26591 Regan, Matt. DJ (*Early Risers Club*, WBTA, Batavia, NY, 1947–1952).

26592 Regan, Tom. Sportscaster (*Your Fishcaster*, KFOX, Long Beach, CA, 1948).

26593 Regas, Virginia. COM-HE (WJKO, Springfield, MA, 1951).

26594 Regensberger, Samuel. Newscaster (WSBC, Chicago, IL, 1948).

26595 Regent, Robert. Newscaster (KOH, Reno, NV, 1942).

26596 Regent, Roger. Actor Regent was in the cast of *Ellen Randolph*.

26597 Regent Roof Orchestra. Local club dance band (WOOD, Grand Rapids, MI, 1926).

26598 *Reggie's Harmonica Ragamuffins.* Reggie Cross was the organizer and leader of the harmonica group that consisted of 12 young Chicago harmonica players between the ages of 14 and 21. The soloist was Ralph Hutchins. Other members of the group were Willard Volquardsen, Ruby Siegel, Paul Kosberg, Stanley Speck, John Pauls, John Thomas, John Eilenfeldt, Anthony Borowicz, Joe Bernie and Raymond Butman (Weekly, WLS, Chicago, IL, 1935).

26599 Regier, Meryl Wolfe. Soprano (KFI, Los Angeles, CA, 1923).

26600 Reginald, Martin Ruell. Sportscaster (Brown and Williamson Tobacco Company football broadcasts, KOIL, Omaha, NE, and KFOR, Lincoln, NE, 1937; Kellogg Co. football broadcasts, KFAB, Lincoln, NE; Drake Relays broadcasts, MBS, 1937).

26601 Regis, Del. Leader (*Del Regis Orchestra*, instr. mus. prg., WCAU, Philadelphia, PA, 1935).

26602 Regis, Gene. Leader (*Gene Regis Orchestra*, instr. mus. prg., WXYZ, Detroit, MI, 1935).

26603 *Reg'lar Fellers.* Gene Byrnes' comic strip was the basis for the short-lived situation comedy about the pranks and problems of adolescents. It was a veritable showcase for the Van Patten family, since both Dickie and sister Joyce were featured. Other cast members were: Skippy Homeier, Dickie Monahan, Patsy O'Shea and Orville Phillips. The program was directed by Joseph Hill (NBC, 1941).

26604 Rehberg, Lillian. Violinist and cellist (KYW, Chicago, IL, 1928–1929).

26605 Reich, Aileen. Soprano (KLDS, Springfield, MA, 1951).

26606 Reich, Hilda. Soprano (WNYC, New York, NY, 1926).

26607 Reichblum, Chuck. Sportscaster (*Sports Daily Double*, WJAS, Pittsburgh, PA, 1953–1955).

26608 Reichenbach, Paul. Reichenbach was a twelve-year-old performer on *The Children's Hour* program (KSTP, St. Paul–Minneapolis, MN, 1929).

26609 Reichert, F.J. DJ (*Disc Jockey Jamboree*, KGCU, Mandan, SD, 1947).

26610 Reichman, Cecilia. Concert pianist (WGBS, New York, NY, 1925).

26611 Reichman, Joe. Leader (*Joe Reichman Orchestra*, instr. mus. prg., WOR, Newark, NJ, WLW, Cincinnati, OH and MBS, 1936).

26612 Reid, Carl Benton. Actor Reid appeared on the *Big Sister* daytime serial program.

26613 Reid, Clark. DJ (*The Record Shop*, WHFB, Benton Harbor, MI, 1948; *1060 Club*, WHFB, 1950; WJR, Detroit, MI, 1954; WJBK, Detroit, MI, 1956–1957).

26614 Reid, Don. Leader (*Don Reid Orchestra*, instr. mus. prg., WHIO, Dayton, OH, 1937).

26615 Reid, Elliott. Actor Reid was in the cast of *Billy and Betty*, *Carol Kennedy's Romance*, *Lorenzo Jones*, *The March of Time*, *Mighty Show*, *Pepper Young's Family* and *Trouble House*.

26616 Reid, Erle "Duke." Newscaster (KOB, Albuquerque, NM, 1945).

26617 Reid, Jim. Newscaster (WPTF, Raleigh, NC, 1941). Sportscaster (WPTF, 1941, 1946; *Sports Review*, WPTF, 1947–1948; *BC Sports Review*, WPTF, 1949–1955; *Duke Football*, WTVD, Durham, NC, 1960).

26618 Reid, J. Lewis. Announcer (WJY, New York, NY, 1925).

26619 Reid, Joseph. Newscaster (WRVA, Richmond, VA, 1941).

26620 Reid, Katherine. Singer (WHA, Madison, WI, 1925).

26621 Reid, Kay. Contralto (WEAF, New York, NY, 1932).

26622 Reid, Lawson. Organist (KTHS, Hot Springs National Park, AK, 1925–1926).

26623 Reid, Linda. Actress Reid appeared on the *Romance of Helen Trent* daytime serial program.

26624 Reid, Marguerite. Pianist (KMOX, St. Louis, MO, 1929).

26625 Reid, Michael. Newscaster (KVRS, Rock Springs, WY, 1942). Sportscaster (KVRS, 1942, 1945–1946; *Sports Review*, WVRS, 1947–1949).

26626 Reid, Paul. News analyst (*6:30 Edition*, WFIG, Sumter, SC, 1947). DJ (*Club Request*, WKLF, Clanton, AL, 1948). Sportscaster (*The Sports Page*, WKLF, 1949–1950).

26627 Reid, Richard S. Sportscaster (*Sports Round-Up* and *Previews in Sports*, WTVL, Waterville, MS, 1947).

26628 Reid, Rosemary. COM-HE (WFPM, Ft. Valley, GA, 1960).

26629 Reid, Shirley. Pianist-singer (KFI, Los Angeles, CA, 1928).

26630 Reid, Sue Bailey. COM-HE (WEAN, Providence, RI, 1956).

26631 Reid, W.L. News analyst (*Washington Today*, WCAP, Asbury Park, NJ, 1948).

26632 Reid, (Mrs.) Wallace. Actress (KHJ, Los Angeles, CA, 1929–1930).

26633 Reider, (Mrs.) J. Organist (WJBC, Bloomington, IN, 1936).

26634 Reidy, Paul. DJ (*1340 Club*, WFIG, Sumter, SC, 1947). Sportscaster (*The Sportsman*, WFIG, 1947).

26635 Reifsnyder, Howard. Newscaster (WALL, Middletown, NY, 1948).

26636 Reig, Howard. DJ (*Howard Reig Show*, WGY, Schenectady, NY, 1947–1950).

26637 Reighley, Joe. DJ (*Crazy Rhythm*, KAMD, Camden, AR, 1947).

26638 Reilley, Ellen. COM-HE (WOLF, Syracuse, NY, 1960).

26639 Reilly, Alex. Organist (KFI, Los Angeles, CA, 1926–1927).

26640 Reilly, Arthur. Newscaster (WLW, Cincinnati, OH, 1942 ; WCPO, Cincinnati, OH, 1945).

26641 Reilly, Ed. Newscaster (WGAA, Cedartown, GA, 1946; *Late Edition*, WGAA, 1948). Sportscaster (WGAA, 1946; *Sports Parade*, WGAA, 1948).

26642 Reilly, Frank. Leader (Frank Reilly Country Club Orchestra, WOR, Newark, NJ, 1923). Baritone (WAAM, Newark, NJ, 1925).

26643 Reilly, J.A. Announcer (WJAR, Providence, RI, 1924–1925).

26644 Reilly, Peggy. COM-HE (WJOC, Jamestown, NY, 1955).

26645 Reilly, R. Edward. DJ (*Swing Time Club*, WGAA, Cedartown, GA, 1947). Sportscaster (*Sports Parade*, WGAA, 1947).

26646 Reilly, Speed. DJ (KLX, Oakland, CA, 1937). Sportscaster (KLX, 1941–1945; *Sports Review*, KLX, Oakland, CA, 1947).

26647 Reily, Charles. DJ (WTAR, Norfolk, VA, 1937).

26648 Reimuth Trio. Vocal group (WCCO, Minneapolis–St. Paul, MN, 1928).

26649 *Reinald Werrenrath.* Werrenrath, the distinguished concert baritone, conducted the sustaining lecture-recital program series (15 min., Thursday, 9:45–10:00 P.M., WQXR, New York, NY, 1940).

26650 Reinberg, Herman. Cellist (KFRC, San Francisco, CA, 1929).

26651 Reinberg, Syd. Leader (Syd Reinberg Orchestra, WABC, New York, NY, 1929).

26652 Reineke, Earl C. Reineke was the founder of station WDAY in 1922, the first station in the northwest. Reineke was the chief announcer, owner and station manager (WDAY, Fargo, ND in 1929).

26653 Reinemund, Adam. Announcer (KINT, Muscatine, IA, 1927).

26654 Reinertsen, Steve. Newscaster (WCAL, Northfield, MN, 1945).

26655 Reinhard, Harry. Sportscaster (WCAU, Philadelphia, PA, 1944).

26656 Reinhardt, Edith. Soprano (WBAL, Baltimore, MD, 1926).

26657 Reinhardt, Fred. Newscaster (WJPF, Herrin, IL, 1941, 1947).

26658 Reinhart, Cy. Leader (Cy Reinhart Orchestra, WHAS, Louisville, KY, 1926).

26659 Reinhart, Ted. DJ (*Merry-Go-Round*, WHUN, Huntington, PA, 1948). Sportscaster (WFBG, Altoona, PA, 1955).

26660 Reinheart, Alice. Actress Reinheart first appeared on radio in 1928, beginning a long career as a dramatic actress (KYA, San Francisco, CA, 1928). Later, she appeared on such daytime serial programs as *Her Honor, Nancy James* and *John's Other Wife*. She played a variety of roles in popular programs as the *Abbott Mysteries*; *Casey, Crime Photographer*; *Gangbusters*; and *One Man's Family*. Perhaps her most famous role was that of Chichi in *Life Can Be Beautiful*.

26661 Reinsch, Leonard. Announcer of studio programs and broadcaster of track meets and football games (WLS, Chicago, IL, 1929).

26662 Reis, (Mrs.) Ignace. COM-HE (WMAQ, Chicago, IL, 1922).

26663 Reis, Lee. Blackface comedy singer who teamed with Artie Dunn to appear on *Roxy's Gang* (NBC, New York, NY, 1928).

26664 Reiser, Al. Leader (Al Reiser Dancing Orchestra, WHN, New York, NY, 1924; Al Reiser's Corinthians, WJY, Schenectady, NY, 1924; Club Ferreu Orchestra, WJZ, New York, NY, 1924).

26665 Reising, Hazel and Eileen. Harmony singing team (KVOO, Tulsa, OK, 1929).

26666 Reising, Marie. COM-HE (WOND, Pleasantville, NJ, 1957).

26667 Reisman, Leo. Leader (Leo Reisman's Egyptian Room Orchestra, WNAC, Boston, MA, 1923; Leo Reisman Ensemble, WBZ, Springfield, MA, 1925 and Leo Reisman Orchestra, WBJ, 1924 and WBZ, Springfield, MA, 1925; Leo Reisman Hotel Lenox Orchestra WJZ, New York, NY, 1925; Leo Reisman and his Hotel Brunswick Orchestra, WBZ, 1926). The Reisman band's smooth style was popular on radio for several decades. Personnel in his early band included: Reisman, dir.-v.; John Jacobson and Herman Brenner, t.; Walter Poole, tb.; Andrew Jacobson, clr., ss. and as.; Allan Lang, ss. and as; Felix Greenbert, clr., as. and ts.; Raymond Pugh, p.; Joseph Tronstein, tba. and sb.; and Harry Sigman, d. In the following decades the Reisman band continued to appear on the air (*Leo Reisman Orchestra*, instr. mus. prg., NBC, 1934; MBS, 1938).

26668 Reiss, (Mrs.) E.C. Contralto (KWWG, Brownsville, TX, 1926).

26669 Reiter, Hilda. Soprano (WIP, Philadelphia, PA, 1927).

26670 Reiter, Fred. Newscaster (WSPB, Sarasota, FL, 1940; WFLA, Tampa, FL, 1946–1947).

26671 Reith, Harry. Sportscaster (*Man About Sports*, WKST, New Castle, PA, 1949; *Sports Roundup*, WKST, 1952–1955).

26672 Reith, Herbert W. Leader, Herbert W. Reith and His Moonlight Serenaders (WJZ, New York, NY, 1922).

26673 Reitman, Bill. DJ (*Music on the QT* and *The Santa Fe Trail*, KVSF, Santa Fe, NM, 1948).

26674 Reitz, R. Newscaster (WLEU, Erie, PA, 1945).

26675 Reitzer, Herman. Sportscaster (WDEL, Wilmington, DE, 1937).

26676 Rejebian, Aram. Newscaster (KVEC, San Luis Obispo, CA, 1940–1941, 1945). Sportscaster (KVEC, 1940–1941, 1945).

26677 Reletina, Elizabeth. Coloratura soprano (WCAU, Philadelphia, PA, 1926).

26678 Relieux, Louis. Leader (*Louis Relieux Orchestra*, instr. mus. prg., KOA, Denver, CO, 1932).

26679 Religious Broadcasting. Religious broadcasting began early in the history of American radio with both Christian and Jewish services provided for listeners. Sterling and Kitross (1978, p. 78) suggest that KDKA (Pittsburgh, PA) probably broadcast the first religious service on January 2, 1921, when it transmitted the vesper service of the Pittsburgh Calvary Episcopal Church conducted by the Junior Associate Reverend Lewis Whittmore (Ward, 1995, p. 208). In New York City the first continuing religious programming began with the *Radio Church of America* on November 27, 1921. Following soon after came WDM, the first licensed religious broadcasting station, located at 18th and W Streets, Washington, DC. The 100-watt station was owned and operated by the Church of the Covenant, now the National Presbyterian Church.

One of the earliest religious broadcasts in the New York City area was a Christmas message delivered by the Reverend George P. Daugherty of the Christ Episcopal Church of Glen Ridge, NJ, on WJZ (New York, NY), December 24, 1921. The success of the broadcast encouraged the Reverend Daugherty to begin regular Sunday services program on WJZ, starting in January, 1922. A few months later on March 1, 1922, a series of Lenten Services conducted by the Rt. Reverend Michael J. Gallagher, the Catholic Bishop of the Diocese of Detroit; the Rt. Reverend Charles D. Williams, Episcopal Bishop; and Bishop Theodore S. Henderson were broadcast by WWJ (Detroit, MI).

Pioneer religious broadcaster Paul Rader by invitation of Mayor William Hale Thompson of Chicago broadcast a message from City Hall in 1922. Rader previously had preached on the *Radio Church of America* program. Encouraged by the enthusiastic responses of his listeners, Rader began his own radio ministry. The following year on April 3, 1923, R.R. Brown began his *Radio Chapel Service* on April 3, 1923. When he realized how large his listening audience was, he decided to form an organization for his listeners and founded the *World Radio Congregation*.

Proof that radio and religion were related in the public consciousness was reported on August 10, 1922, when the Louisville *Courier* wrote: "God is always broadcasting." Even though the message has some suggestion of Babbittry, it nevertheless shows the state of mind at that time. This was also when the Concordia Seminary began operation of its KFUO (St. Louis, MO) station, and Professor Walter Maier began his religious broadcasting career.

One of America's greatest evangelists, Aimee Semple MacPherson, went on the air February 6, 1924. Her station — WFSG (Los Angeles, CA) — was operated by Sister Aimee's Church of the Four Square Gospel. Two years later, on July 28, 1926, the Concordia (Lutheran) Theological Seminary station, WMBI, began its operation under the direction of program manager Wendell Loveless and station manager, Henry Crowell. The station became a major training group for evangelical radio broadcasters (Ward, 1994, p. 209).

Lois Crawford received her operators license from the Federal Radio Commission in 1927. Hers was the first operator's license received by a woman. Crawford worked at religious station KFGQ (Boone, IA). Women like Sister Aimee Semple MacPherson and Lois Crawford were true pioneers of American religious radio. The extent and variety of religious broadcasting on American radio can be seen in tables One and Two.

Table One: Sunday Church Services, October, 1929

8:00 A.M. Methodist — KFKB.
8:30 A.M. Lutheran — WTMJ.
9:00 A.M. Baptist — WSAZ; Catholic Apostolic — WCBD; other services — WCBF, KPOF.
9:30 A.M. Christian — WHB; Evangelical — KFLV; Methodist — WDAG, WHBQ.
10:00 A.M. Baptist — WEBQ, WGBC, KFJF, WSSH, WJR; Catholic — WJBC, WWL, WHBY, WJBC; Episcopal — WIP; Methodist — KFKB, KFWC; Other Services — WORD, WHK, KGW, KGFL, WHEC, WABO, WHAS, KOMO, KFJB; Paul Rader's Chicago Gospel Tabernacle, WJBT 10:00 A.M. to midnight (Independent).
10:15 A.M. Congregational — WBNX; Baptist — KQW.
10:30 A.M. Baptist — WMAN; Christian — WADC; Lutheran — KGDE; Methodist — WLBV, WHBL, WGBB, WMBS, WRAF, WGES; Methodist Protestant — WMPC; Presbyterian — KFYR, KTBR, WJAY; Universalist — WABI; Other services — WENR, WBCN, WHAM, WKBZ, WQAM, WKJC.
10:45 A.M. Baptist — WNBJ; Christian Science — KYW, KFKX; *(continued on next page)*

Sunday Church Services, October, 1929 *(continued)*

Lutheran — WLCI, KFEQ; Methodist — WOAN; Presbyterian — WDBO, WHBD; Unitarian — WKAV; Other Services — WFBG, WMES, WLS, WMBH, KTBI, KFEQ, WOL, WMAQ.
11:00 A.M. Baptist — WPCC, WBT, KOCW, WSAZ, KMIC, WLAP, WABZ, KFXR, KQW, KFDX, WWL; Catholic — KFBU; Christian — KFXD, KGEZ; Christian Science — KFQA, WMCA, WOKO; Congregational — WOC, WREN, KOMO, KSCJ, KSOO; Episcopal — KUT, WTAQ, WIBG, KFBU, WDRC; Evangelical — WNAX; Lutheran — KFBL, WCWK, WRAW, WKY; Methodist — WCFL, KSO, WKY, KGEW, KXL, KYA, KJR, KSBA, WCAJ; Presbyterian — KGRS, KTW, WDOD, KFUM, KGA, KGEW, WSIX, KGFI, KVI, WNRC, KGAR; Unitarian — WNBH; Universalist — WCLS, WNAC, WBIS; Other Services — WCAZ, KGCN, WRR, KOW, KTHS, WJAS, WJAX, KGFL, KMED, KMA, WDAE, KGCX, WSM, WENR, WBCN, KFQU, WKBH.
11:15 A.M. Berachah Church — WRAX.
11:30 A.M. Catholic — WGES; Other Services — WJBT, WCAO.
1:00 P.M. Other Services — WJBT, KWJJ.
1:30 P.M. Other Services — WJBT, WKBS.
2:00 P.M. Baptist — WEBQ, WBAW; Other Services — WENR, WBCN, WOKO, WJAX.
2:30 P.M. Baptist — KFXR; Catholic Apostolic — WCBD; Other Services — WORD, KFGQ.
3:00 P.M. Presbyterian — KTW; Other Services — WNAC, WBIS, KFUO, WBBM, WJBT.
3:30 P.M. Other Services — WFBG, WJBT, WLBW, WJKS.
4:00 P.M. Episcopal — WIBG; Methodist — WGBB; Other Services — KWCR, WENR, WBCN, WCAJ.
4:45 P.M. Presbyterian — WBT.
5:00 P.M. Catholic — WHBY; Congregational — WKAV; Presbyterian — KGFI.
6:00 P.M. Methodist — KFKB; Other Services — WLS.
6:30 P.M. Baptist — KOCW, WKAV, WSSH; Other Services — WNAC, WBIS.
6:45 P.M. Presbyterian — KPPC.
7:00 P.M. Baptist — WEBQ; Christian — WHB; Congregational — WOC; Episcopal — WIP; Lutheran — WRBC, KYW; Methodist — KFWC; Other Services — WORD, WKJC, KFEQ, KOMO, WMAQ.
7:15 P.M. Baptist — KFH; Congregational — WTAD; Presbyterian — KSCJ; Other Services — KTBI, WSM.
7:30 P.M. Baptist — WDAG, WDOD, WCFL, WJAY, WMAN, WGBC, WABZ, KFXR, KFIF, KQW, WNBJ, WSSH; Christian — WKY; Congregational — KRE; Evangelical — KFLV; Lutheran — WRBC, KYW; Methodist — WFBG, WEBE, WENR, WBCN, KOCW, WMBS, KEX, KTBR, KTW, KGA, KVI; Universalist — WABI; Other Services — WHK, KGCN, WRR, KUOA, WNRC, WJBC, WHAS, KFJB, KMED, WQAM, KGGF, WHEC, WABO, WDAE, WBBM, KRLD, WKJC.
7:45 P.M. Baptist — WPCC, KFDX; Episcopal — KFPY; Lutheran — WLCI; Methodist — WOAM; Other Services — WMES, KOW.
8:00 P.M. Baptist — WBT, WLAP; Catholic — WCLS; Catholic Apostolic — WCBD; Christian Science — KOIN, KOMO; Episcopal — WCAO; Lutheran — KGDE; Methodist — KGBX, KSBA; Presbyterian — KGRS, KGAR; Other Services — KTHS, KMIC, WJAX, WMBH, KYA, WMAQ.
9:00 P.M. Presbyterian — WDBO.
9:15 P.M. Other Services — KFH, KFUO.
9:30 P.M. Other Services — KWCR, WJBT.
10:00 P.M. Baptist — WJR.
FRIDAY NIGHT: Jewish Services—7:45—WKJC.
NOTE: OTHER SERVICES includes services conducted by regular denominations alternating from Sunday to Sunday and also sacred services by community churches, undenominational, non-sectarian, International Bible Students Association and others. The time given is the starting time of the service in the time zone where station is located. For example, if the church is located in eastern time zone, the time given is Eastern Standard Time.

Table Two: Selected Religious Broadcasts for the Month of July, 1939

STATION	PROGRAM	DAY OF BROADCAST
WCKY (Cincinnati, OH)	*Lockland Baptist Church*	Sunday
WHAS (Louisville, KY)	*Ausbury College Devotions*	Monday through Saturday
WHO (Des Moines, IA)	*The Boone Family*	Monday through Saturday
WLS (Chicago, IL)	*Morning Devotions*	Monday through Saturday
WHAM (Rochester, NY)	*Kindly Thoughts*	Monday through Saturday
WFAA (Dallas, TX)	*Morning Meditations*	Monday through Saturday
WWL (New Orleans, LA)	*Mass*	Sunday
WWL (New Orleans, LA)	*Ave Maria*	Sunday
WHAM (Rochester, NY)	*Sunday Church Service*	Sunday
WLS (Chicago, IL)	*Old Fashioned Revival Hour* (Charles E. Fuller)	Sunday
WSB (Atlanta, GA)	*In Radioland with Shut-Ins* and *Little Church in the Wildwood*	Sunday
WSB (Atlanta, GA)	*Call to Worship — Peachtree Christian Church*	Sunday
WSB (Atlanta, GA)	*Baptist Tabernacle Agoga Bible Class (Morgan Blake)*	Sunday

(continued on next page)

Donald Grey Barnhouse became the first to purchase network time from CBS to conduct a religious program, but the selling of time by the network was short lived. Preaching on early radio has been characterized as a "record of violent denomination battles on the air" (West, 1941, p. 268) with emphasis on doctrinal correctness as a means to spread particular dogmas and creeds. An early effort to dignify religious broadcasts and eliminate denominational battling was made by NBC in 1927, when it adopted a self-imposed code that banned the sale of network broadcast time for religious purposes, stating that the time should instead be donated by the network.

By 1931, CBS adopted a similar set of principles when it decided to ban the sale of network time for religious broadcasting. This probably was in reaction to the controversy produced by Father Charles E. Coughlin's broadcasts. In place of his broadcasts, the network acted in cooperation with the Council of Churches to produce its own religious programming.

The *Mormon Tabernacle Choir* program, originating from KSL (Salt Lake City, UT) for NBC, began in 1929. The portion of the program carrying a religious message was known as "The Spoken Word."

In addition to the growing number of "radio ministers," there also were the great evangelists of the time who broadcast their religious messages. Probably the best known were Billy Sunday and Aimee Semple MacPherson. Sunday, a former baseball player, appeared on several network programs with his famous song leader Homer Rodeheaver. Sister Aimee, on the other hand, established her own radio station on which she broadcast daily. A later evangelist by the name of Billy Graham became a major religious spokesman thanks to the services he conducted on his weekly radio series, *The Hour of Decision* (ABC, 1950).

Several important religious programs appeared on network after the Reverend S. Parkes Cadman first began his *National Radio Pulpit* in 1926 on the NBC network. Harry Emerson Fordick's *National Vespers* was carried by the same network in 1928. Programs devoted to specific faiths such as *The Catholic Hour*, the *Mormon Tabernacle Choir* program, the *Lutheran Hour* and *The Message of Israel* followed. Another memorable religious program that attracted a large and enthusiastic audience was conducted by Elder Solomon Lightfoot Michaux, an inspiring African-American minister. His talented Happy-Am-I Choir was always featured on his programs. Michaux's dynamic and energetic style inspired many listeners.

Ward (1994, p. 54) in his scholarly treatment of religious broadcasting says that radio's golden age produced a large number of evangelical broadcasters and successful programs:

> Henry Schultze and Peter Eldersveld — *Back to God Hour*
> Theodore Epp — *Back to the Bible*
> T. Myron Webb — *The Bible Fellowship Hour*
> Edna Jean Horn — *The Church by the Side of the Road*
> Clarence Erickson — *The Heaven and Home Hour*

Selected Religious Broadcasts for the Month of July, 1939 *(continued)*

WSB (Atlanta, GA)	*First Presbyterian Church Service*	Sunday
WHAS (Louisville, KY)	*Dr. John Zoller from Detroit*	Sunday
WAPI (Birmingham, AL)	*Call to Worship*	Sunday
WAPI (Birmingham, AL)	*Brotherhood Association*	Sunday
WOAI (San Antonio, TX)	*Bright and Early Coffee Choir*	Sunday
WBAP (Ft. Worth, TX)	*Church Services*	Sunday
WOAI (San Antonio, TX)	*First Presbyterian Church Service*	Sunday
WHO (Des Moines, IA)	*Humanitarian Hour*	Sunday
WHO (Des Moines, IA)	*The Bible Broadcaster*	Sunday
WHO (Des Moines, IA)	*Father Charles E. Coughlin*	Sunday
WHO (Des Moines, IA)	*Little Brown Church*	Sunday
WBAP (Ft. Worth, TX)	*Religion in the News*	Sunday
WHO (Des Moines, IA)	*News and Views about Religion*	Sunday
WHAM (Rochester, NY)	*Christian Science Monitor*	Sunday
WSB (Atlanta, GA)	*Bible School Lesson (Dr. Marion McHull)*	Sunday
WFAA (Dallas, TX)	*Sunday School Lesson*	Sunday
WLS (Chicago, IL)	*Sunday School Lesson*	Sunday
WAPI (Birmingham, AL)	*West End Church of Christ*	Tuesday
WHO (Des Moines, IA)	*Back-to-the-Bible*	Tuesday
WHO (Des Moines, IA)	*National Radio Revival*	Thursday
WHAS (Louisville, KY)	*Week Day Devotions*	Monday through Friday
WOAI (San Antonio, TX)	*Catholic Hour*	Sunday
WOAI (San Antonio, TX)	*Gospel Singer*	Sunday through Thursday
WAPI (Birmingham, AL)	*Church of the Air*	Sunday
WHO (Des Moines, IA)	*Hymns of all Churches*	Monday through Thursday
WOAI (San Antonio, TX)	*The Chuck Wagon Gang*	Sundays
WCKY (Cincinnati, OH)	*Father Charles E. Coughlin*	Sunday

M.R. DeHaven—*Radio Bible Class*
J. Harold Smith—*Radio Bible Hour*
Paul Myers—*The Haven of Rest*
Dale Crowley, Sr.—*The Right Start of the Day*
Jack Wyrtzen—*The Word of Life Hour*
H.M.S. Richards—*The Voice of Prophecy*

See **Coughlin, Charles E.; McPherson, Aimee Semple;** *and* **Charlatans, Demagogs and Politicians.**

26680 Rella, Eleanor. Actress Rella was featured on the *Myrt and Marge* daytime serial program.

26681 Reller, Elizabeth. Actress Reller appeared on the daytime serial programs *Portia Faces Life, Betty and Bob* (title role), *Young Dr. Malone* and *Doc Barclay's Daughter.*

26682 Relyea, Charles. Baritone (WAHG, Richmond Hill, NY, 1925).

26683 Rem, Charlie. DJ (WCOM, Parkersburg, WV, 1957).

26684 Remand, Ollie. Sportscaster (*Grand Prize Sports Review*, KEPO, El Paso, TX, 1948).

26685 *Remember with Joy.* Barry Becker hosted the music program sponsored by Joy Candy Company. Baritone Rush Perkins and pianist Estell Barnes were featured (15 min., Sunday, 4:00–4:15 P.M., WAAF, Chicago, IL, 1937).

26686 Remey, Ethel Young. Actress Remey was in the cast of the daytime serial programs *Young Widder Brown* and *Rich Man's Darling.*

26687 Remick, Dean. Concert pianist (*Dean Remick,* instr. mus. prg., WSBC, Chicago, IL, 1935).

26688 *Reminisences.* An old-time Bostonian shared his memories of old Boston on the ten-minute weekly program Wednesday evenings (10 min., Wednesday, WNAC, Boston, MA, 1925).

26689 Remington, Jack. DJ (WKRC, Cincinnati, OH, 1954).

26690 Remington, O.J. Newscaster (WNOX, Knoxville, TN, 1945).

26691 Remley, Helen. Coloratura soprano (WLW, Cincinnati, OH, 1925).

26692 Remsburg, Bill. DJ (WFMD, Frederick, MD, 1956).

26693 Remsen, Alice. Singer-actress Alice Remsen sang on the *Stromberg-Carlson Hour* sponsored by the Stromberg-Carlson Telephone Manufacturing Company (NBC-Blue, 1927) and the *Palmolive Hour* sponsored by Colgate-Palmolive Company (NBC-Red, 1927–1928).

26694 Remsen, Walter. Leader (*Walter Remsen Orchestra,* instr. mus. prg., WCAE, Pittsburgh, PA, 1936).

26695 Remy, Helen. Pianist (WLBV, Mansfield, OH, 1928).

26696 Renald, Dr. Pianist (*Dr. Renald,* instr. mus. prg., WGR, Buffalo, NY, 1937).

26697 Renald, Josef. Palmist Renald was sponsored by a nail polish company. Despite being a palmist, somehow Renald plied his trade on the air and received some 2,000 letters from listeners weekly (WOR, New York, NY, 1930s).

26698 Renard, Jacques "Jack." Leader (Mansion Inn Orchestra, WEEI, Boston, MA, 1924; Meyer Davis New Arlington Ensemble, KTHS, Hot Springs National Park, AK, 1924). Renard led the ten-piece Meyer Davis Orchestra on the inaugural program of station KTHS (Hot Springs National Park, AR, December 20, 1924). He also was a violinist with the Meyer Davis Orchestra (WEAF, New York, NY, 1925) and the Boston's Coconut Grove Orchestra (WEEI, Boston, MA, 1928–29). Renard later led his own band, as well as those of various network programs (*Jacques Renard Orchestra,* instr. mus. prg., CBS, 1934–1937; MBS, 1939).

26699 Renaut, Frank. Tenor (*Frank Renaut,* vcl. mus. prg., WORK, York, PA, 1936). Organist (*Frank Renaut,* instr. mus. prg., WORK, York, PA,1937–1938).

26700 Renchen, Wilma. COM-HE (WTAY, Robinson, IL, 1956).

26701 Rendall, Esther. Soprano (WCBD, Zion, IL, 1926).

26702 Rendell, Arthur. Clarinetist (WCBD, Zion, IL, 1923).

26703 *Rendezvous.* Popular singer Irene "Bee" Beasley and the Clyde Lucas orchestra appeared on the program (30 min., Wednesday, 7:00–7:30 P.M., NBC-Blue, 1936).

26704 *Rendezvous at 711.* Baritone Norman Sweetser presided over a talented group of NBC artists in the weekly music program (WEAF, NBC-Red, 1929).

26705 *Rendezvous Musical.* This half-hour music program used the clever concept of portraying evenings in a night club, where a romance between the club's two featured singers had begun. The program used actors Eunice Howard and Buford Hampden as the singers. However, the singers who actually sang the songs were Jane Williams and Phil Duey. The Men About Town vocal group also appeared accompanied by the Aldo Ricci Orchestra (Weekly, NBC-Blue, 1935).

26706 *Rendezvous with Ramona.* Veteran singer-pianist Ramona, who first became famous while playing with the Paul Whiteman Orchestra, performed with Joe Lugar's orchestra on the program (15 min., Monday through Friday, 6:30–6:15 P.M., WLW, Cincinnati, OH, 1947).

26707 *Rendezvous with Ruth Moss.* Miss Moss conducted celebrity interviews on this local show (15 min., Friday, 6:30–6:45 P.M., WAAB, Boston, MA, 1936).

26708 Rendina, S.F. Rendina was the pianist-director of the K.C. Artist Trio and conductor of the WHB Concert Orchestra (WHB, Kansas City, MO, 1928–1929).

26709 Rene, Leon. Leader (Leon Rene and his Southern Syncopators, KFI, Los Angeles, CA, 1928; Leon Rene's Kit Kat Club Orchestra, KFI, 1929).

26710 *Renfro Valley Barn* Dance (Different versions of this program known as *The Renfro Valley Gathering* and *The Renfro Valley Country Store* were broadcast at various times). The popular country music program was carried by the Mutual Broadcasting System from 1937–1939. Later, the program was carried on CBS. Announcer Eugene Trace introduced such performers as Clyde J. "Red" Foley, the Girls of the Golden West (Dolly and Molly Good) and country comedian Benjamin "Whitey" Ford, who was known as the Duke of Paducah (60 min., Saturday, 7:00–8:00 P.M., WLW-MBS, 1937). The *Renfro Valley Barn Dance,* created by John Lair in 1937, was located in a replica of a nineteenth century Kentucky town. Lair, who had been born in Renfro Valley, Kentucky, went north in 1927 to become program director and music librarian at station WLS (Chicago, IL). He was one of those who encouraged folk musicians to appear on the *National Barn Dance* and other WLS shows. Lair joined with country comedian Ford and country-western singer Red Foley to buy some Kentucky land in 1937 with the intention of building a music barn.

WLW (Cincinnati, OH) made the decision to increase its CW music programming and persuaded Lair to join the station. Lair then began his *Renfro Valley Barn Dance*, originating the program in Cincinnati from 1937–1939. The following year he moved the program to its own "barn" in Renfro Valley, from which he broadcast the show before a large and appreciative paying audience. Lair later produced another popular CW music show, *The Renfro Valley Gathering*.

Lair said "the barn dance show was the first and only barn dance on the air presented by the actual residents of an actual community." Listener response to the program was enthusiastic. When Lair offered pictures of the barn to those who wrote requesting it, he received some 253,000 requests. Lair was an intelligent entrepreneur, who combined a genuine love of American folk music with a sharp business sense. Located near Mt. Vernon, Kentucky, the Renfro Valley Music Barn attracted a Saturday night paid attendance for the program that averaged 5,000, but sometimes reached as high as 10,000 (*Billboard Music Yearbook*, 1944, pp. 344–345).

Many CW stars were developed on Lair's programs, including: Homer and Jethro, Old Joe Clark, Whitey Ford the "Duke of Paducah," Martha Carson and the Drifting Pioneers (guitarist Merle Travis, fiddler Morris "Sleepy" Marlin, mandolinist Walter Braun and bassist Bill Braun). Lair's programs were particularly memorable for their haunting theme, "Take Me Back to Renfro Valley." *See* ***Renfro Valley Folks***.

26711 ***Renfro Valley Folks.*** The network return of the popular country music program — then known as hillbilly — featured the Duke of Paducah (Whitey Ford), the Brown County Revelers, the Harvest Hands, Aunt Idy and Little Clifford and the Coon Creek Girls. Eugene Trace returned as program announcer (Weekly, NBC-Red, 1941). The show was picked up by CBS when it left NBC, but the cast remained essentially the same (Sunday, CBS, 1947).

26712 Renfrow, Charlie. Sportscaster and sports play-by-play (WAKP, Hendersonville, NC, 1960).

26713 Renick, Jim. Sportscaster (WCOL, Columbus, OH, 1944).

26714 Renier, Tiny. Renier was billed as the "Singing Cowboy" (WDAF, Kansas City, MO, 1928).

26715 Renk, Fritz. Violinist (WORD, Batavia, IL, 1925). Leader-violinist (Mendel Brothers Trio playing lunch hour music, WMAQ, Chicago, IL, 1927; Palmer House Trio playing dinner music, WJJD, Chicago, IL, 1927).

26716 Renn, Sarah. COM-HE (WHIY, Orlando, FL, 1960).

26717 Renner, Earl. Tenor (KDKA, Pittsburgh, PA, 1924).

26718 Renner, Laurette. COM-HE (KSUM, Fairmont, MN, 1949).

26719 Rennick, Louise. Pianist (WEAO, Columbus, OH, 1925).

26720 Rennie, Pauline. Singer (WKBW, Buffalo, NY, 1937).

26721 Renny, Kay. Singer (WEVD, New York, NY, 1937).

26722 Renolds, Rita. COM-HE (KCUL, Ft. Worth, TX, 1960).

26723 Rensch, Ty. DJ (KGFX, Pierre, SD, 1956).

26724 Renwick, Chuck. DJ (WKNX, Saginaw, MI, 1956).

26725 Renwick, Kay. Actress Renwick appeared on the daytime serial programs *Backstage Wife* aka *Mary Noble, Backstage Wife* and *When a Girl Marries.*

26726 REO Male Quartet. Singing group (WREO, Lansing, MI, 1925).

26727 REO Motor Car Company Band. Band commercially sponsored by Reo Motor Car Company (WREO, Lansing, MI, 1926).

26728 ***Reo Wolverine Orchestra.*** Instr. mus. prg. (KPO, San Francisco, CA, 1928).

26729 Repaid, W. Hal "Billy." News analyst (WJR, Detroit, MI, 1933; WMBC, Detroit, MI, 1938; *The Flying Reporter*, MBS-WOL, Washington, DC, 1942–1945; WJLB, Detroit, MI, 1946). Newscaster and analyst Repaid was famous for his rapid fire speech delivery that was perfect for his appearances on the *Household Musical Clock* program sponsored by the Household Finance Company (WJR, Detroit, MI, mid–1930s).

26730 Repco, Joe. Sportscaster (WBKZ, Battle Creek, MI, 1955).

26731 Replogle, Kent. Sportscaster (*Sports Scoreboard*, WVAM, Altoona, PA, 1960).

26732 Repp, Guy. Actor Repp was in the cast of *County Seat* and *Rosemary.*

26733 Repp, Henry. Organist (WEAF, New York, NY, 1925).

26734 Repp, Onalee. Pianist (KGER, Long Beach, CA, 1928).

26735 Reppert, James. Newscaster (WSM, Nashville, TN, 1945).

26736 ***Republic Star Time.*** Marilyn Cantor, Eddie's daughter, took over from DJ Bea Kalmus to host the program sponsored by Republic Stores. Miss Cantor interviewed celebrity guests such as Delores Gray. Bill Lang was the announcer (30 min., Monday through Saturday, WMGM, New York, NY, 1952).

26737 Requard, Jay. DJ (*Tunes at Noon*, WEPM, Martinsburg, WV, 1947; *American Sports Parade*, WSID, Baltimore, MD, 1948).

26738 Reseburg, Walter. Baritone (KOMO, Seattle, WA, 1929).

26739 Reser, Harry. Leader (Harry Reser and his Carolina Melody Boys, WHN, New York, NY, 1923). Musical director-banjoist Reser also appeared with the *Gold Dust Twins*, sponsored by the Gold Dust Corporation (NBC-Red, 1923–1925) and, more prominently, as leader of the Cliquot Club Eskimos, the famous radio orchestra sponsored by Cliquot Club for the Ginger Ale and Sparking Water Company (NBC-Red, 1925–1934) and as orchestra conductor on the *Flit Soldiers* program, sponsored by the Standard Oil Company (NBC-Red, 1929). In the following years, Reser continued to be busy (*Harry Reser Orchestra*, instr. mus. prg., WRC, Washington, DC, 1935; WHP, Harrisburg, PA and KSD, St. Louis, MO, 1936; NBC, 1936–1937; WMAL, Washington, DC and WHP, 1938). When the Cliquot Club Eskimos first went on the air, they supposedly were playing from the Eskimo Night Club. Their program opened with the sound of sleigh bells and the barking of sled dogs.

26740 Reser, Lonely. Leader (*Lonely Reser Orchestra*, instr. mus. prg., WHP, Harrisburg, PA, 1936).

26741 Resnick, Dean. Pianist (WHT, Deerfield, IL, 1925).

26742 Resnick, Helen. Pianologues (KFWI, San Francisco, CA, 1929).

26743 Resnick, Leo. Operatic tenor (WGBS, New York, NY, 1927).

26744 Resorb, Harry. Leader (*Harry Resorb Orchestra*, instr. mus. prg., WCKY, Cincinnati, OH, 1935).

26745 Ress, George F. Announcer-music director (WRC, Washington, DC, 1929).

26746 Ressler, Minella [Manila] T. Contralto (WIP, Philadelphia, PA, 1925).

26747 Resta, Francis. Director (17th U.S. Infantry Band, WOW, Omaha, NE, 1928–1929).

26748 Resta, Luigi A. Clarinetist (WHAS, Louisville, KY, 1929).

26749 Retermel, Rita. Pianist (WEAF, New York, NY, 1924).

26750 Rethberg, Elizabeth. Soprano (MBS, 1941).

26751 Rethenberg, Helen. "Pianiste" (WHN, New York, NY, 1925).

26752 ***Retold Tales.*** Gerald Stopp produced and playwright Henry Fisk Carlton wrote the weekly program on which famous short stories were dramatized. One of the program's best known productions was O. Henry's "Gentle Grafter" with Arthur Allen and Andy Tucker (WJZ, NBC-Blue, 1928).

26753 Rettenberg, Milton. Pianist-orchestra conductor Rettenberg appeared on the *Eveready Hour* (NBC-Red, 1925–1928); *Eastman Kodak Hour* (NBC-Blue, 1928–1933); *Cities Service Concert* (NBC-Red, 1929–1938); and the *B.A. Rolfe Orchestra* instr. mus. program (NBC-Red, 1928–1931).

26754 Retter, Hilda. Soprano (WPG, Atlantic City, NJ, 1926).

26755 Retting, Buryl. Pianist (NBC, Chicago, IL, 1929).

26756 Rettner, Kathleen. Rettner was a nine-year-old singer on *The Children's Hour* program (KSTP, St. Paul–Minneapolis, MN, 1929).

26757 ***Return Engagement.*** Brent Gunts and Ad Weinert (who later became announcer

Lee Stevens on such network television shows as Ed Sullivan's *Toast of the Town*) conducted this show on which they played old records and exchanged entertaining talk (WFBR, Baltimore, MD, 1949–1953). Brent Gunts earlier had produced the *Varsity Club* program with Garry Moore in the middle–1930s at WFBR.

26758 **Reuning, Fred.** Sportscaster (WOPI, Bristol, TN, 1939).

26759 **Reuter, Jerry.** DJ (*Record Shop*, KLRA, Little Rock, AR, 1948).

26760 ***Reveille in Dixie.*** The weekly dramatic series was produced locally. It emphasized the ways and means to achieve victory in World War II (WSB, Atlanta, GA, World War II era). *See* **Wartime Radio**.

26761 ***Reveille with Beverly.*** Jean Ruth Hay conducted the World War II era show of music and talk designed to improve servicemen's morale (KIMN, Denver, CO, World War II). *See* **Wartime Radio**.

26762 **Revel, Arthur.** Leader (*Arthur Revel Orchestra*, insr. mus. prg, WCAE, Pittsburgh, PA, 1937).

26763 **(The) Revelers.** The Revelers were a popular male vocal quartet that appeared on many network programs in the 1920s and 1930s. Initially, the group included Lewis James, Franklyn Baur, Elliott Shaw and Wilfred Glenn. They were augmented later by Ed Smalle, bass, pianist and arranger. In their early days they had recorded extensively as the Shannon Quartet. Their radio and recording work made them nationally known and admired. Tenor James Melton also sang with the Revellers during their earliest years.

26764 **Revell, Nellie.** Known as the "Voice of *Radio Digest*," Miss Revell conducted an interesting radio interview program in 1933. She opened her new series in this way: "Howdy friends, you remember me, don't you? I haven't in all the time I've been on radio had as much pleasure out of a program as I'm having tonight. Of course, everybody who's ever listened to me on the air or read any of my writings know my great admiration and affection of Irwin S. Cobb." Nellie then proceeded to conduct an amusing and informative interview with humorist Cobb.

26765 **Revelle, Orville.** Sportscaster (WKAT, Miami Beach, FL, 1939–1941).

26766 **Revere, Everett.** Basso with the WSUN Quintet (WSUN, St. Petersburg, FL, 1929).

26767 ***Reviewing the Drama.*** Cranston Brenton presented reviews on the weekly program (15 min., Friday, 7:30–7:45 P.M., New York radio, 1926).

26768 **Rex, Joe.** Newscaster (WLOK, Lima, OH, 1948). Sportscaster (*The Buckeye Sportsman*, WLOK, 1949).

26769 ***Rex Cole Mountaineers.*** Cole's group was a popular CW music group (NBC, 1930).

26770 **Rex Serenaders Orchestra.** Local metropolitan band (WHN, New York, NY, 1923).

26771 **Rey, Mario.** DJ (KALT, Pasadena, CA, 1956; KWKW, Pasadena, CA, 1960).

26772 **Rey, Veronica.** Singer (WNYC, New York, NY, 1936).

26773 **Reyes, Henry.** DJ (KRFC, Rocky Ford, CA, 1956).

26774 **Reyes, Juan.** Pianist (*Juan Reyes*, instr. mus. prg., NBC, 1934)

26775 **Reyes, Revua.** Mexican singer accompanied by his father, guitarist Rayo Reyes (NBC, 1932).

26776 **Reymer's R.V. Bees (aka Reymer's R.V.B. Trio).** The comic vocal trio consisted of baritone Jack Thompson, tenor Edgar Sprague and bass Ed Hicks (KDKA, Pittsburgh, PA, 1928–1929).

26777 **Reynard [Reymond], Jeanne, Roberta Mould and Sylvia Holmes.** The trio of female DJs made up the all-female DJ staff of station WYFE (New Orleans, LA) in 1959.

26778 **Reynard, Jeanne.** COM-HE (KYSM, Mankato, MN, 1957).

26779 **Reynold, Jimmy.** DJ (*Blue 'n' Boogie* and *The 730 Club*, WPAL, Charleston, SC, 1948).

26780 **Reynolds, Al A.** Comedian Reynolds specialized in *Negro Dialect Songs and Stories* (KTHS, Hot Springs National Park, AR, 1926–1929).

26781 **Reynolds, Art.** DJ (*Wake Up Mississippi*, WHSY, Hattiesburg, MS, 1948).

26782 **Reynolds, Bee.** COM-HE (KGBX, Springfield, MS, 1960).

26783 **Reynolds, Bob.** Sportscaster (WHAI, Greenfield, MA, 1941; WEIM, Fitchburg, MA, 1942–1944).

26784 **Reynolds, Carter L.** Newscaster (KFDA, Amarillo, TX, 1939; WMT, Cedar Rapids–Waterloo, IA, 1940–1941).

26785 **Reynolds, Carroll.** Newscaster (WHOT, South Bend, IN, 1944). DJ (*1580 Club*, WJVA, South Bend, IN, 1947).

26786 **Reynolds, Dorothy.** Reader (*Negro and Italian Dialect Readings*, KOA, Denver, CO, 1926). Actress Reynolds played the role of Hazel Staton in *Radio Digest's* program, "*A Step on the Stairs*" in the 1920s.

26787 **Reynolds, Erma.** Soprano (WCBD, Zion, IL, 1925–1926).

26788 **Reynolds, F.W.** Announcer (WHAM, Rochester, NY, 1928–1929).

26789 **Reynolds, Frank.** Sportscaster (WJOB, Hammond, IN, 1946; *6:30 Final*, WJOB, 1948; play-by-play, WJOB, 1949).

26790 **Reynolds, Fred.** DJ (*Swinging at the Sugar Bowl*, WGN, Chicago, IL, 1948).

26791 **Reynolds, Jack.** Leader (*Jack Reynolds Orchestra*, instr. mus. prg., WCAE, Pittsburgh, PA, 1935).

26792 **Reynolds, Jack.** DJ (KTOW, Oklahoma City, OK, 1956).

26793 **Reynolds, Jessie.** COM-HE (WBRM, Marion, NC, 1956–1957).

26794 **Reynolds, Jim.** DJ (*1440 Club*, KMLB, Monroe, LA, 1948).

26795 **Reynolds, John M.** Newscaster (*WLOS News*, WLOS, Asheville, NC, 1947). DJ (*Teentimers' Revue*, WLOS, 1950).

26796 **Reynolds, Leo.** Sportscaster (*Sports Review*, KRBC, Abilene, TX, 1947; *Sports Spotlight*, KRBC, 1948–1949; *Sports Spotlight* and *Sports Final*, KFDX, Wichita Falls, TX, 1950).

26797 **Reynolds, Lois.** COM-HE (WACE, Springfield, MA, 1956).

26798 **Reynolds, Marion.** Organist (WNBC, New Britain, CT, 1937; WELI, New Haven, CT, 1939).

26799 **Reynolds, Meredith.** COM-HE (WSTC, Stamford, CT, 1949).

26800 **Reynolds, R. Foster.** Announcer (WEAN, Providence, RI, 1925).

26801 **Reynolds, Ralph.** DJ (*Dance Club*, KGBX, Springfield, MO, 1948; KSIS, Sedalia, MO, 1956).

26802 **Reynolds, Redd.** DJ (*Road Show*, WBLR, Batesburg, SC, 1960).

26803 **Reynolds, Rex.** DJ (*Starlight Serenade*, WTON, Staunton, VA, 1960).

26804 **Reynolds, Rita.** COM-HE (KCUL, Ft. Worth, TX, 1957).

26805 **Reynolds, Robert F.** Sportscaster (*Spotlight on Sports* and *Hats off to Today*, WTAC, Flint, MI, 1948).

26806 **Reynolds, Ronnie "Ron."** DJ (KCVR, Lodi, CA, 1956–1957).

26807 **Reynolds, Russell "Russ."** DJ (*Sundial-Romney Hour*, WCUM, Cumberland, MD, 1952–1956).

26808 **Reynolds, Rusty.** DJ (KDOK, Tyler, TX, 1956–1957).

26809 **Reynolds, "Sentimental Tommy."** Singer (WLW, Cincinnati, OH, 1926).

26810 **Reynolds, Tommy.** Leader (*Tommy Reynolds Orchestra*, instr. mus. prg., WHAS, Louisville, KY, 1938).

26811 **Reynolds, St. John.** Announcer (WFBC, Knoxville, TN, 1927).

26812 **Reynolds, Vera.** Violinist (KOA, Denver, CO, 1926).

26813 **Reynolds, (Mrs.) William.** Announcer (KLZ, Denver, CO, 1926).

26814 **Reynolds, William D. "Doc."** Announcer (KLZ, Denver, CO, 1927).

26815 **Reynolds, William.** DJ (*Impulse*, WPRW, Manassas, VA, 1960).

26816 **Reynolds, (Mrs.) William D.** Announcer (KLZ, Dupont, CO, 1925–1926).

26817 **Reynolds-Kent Hotel Kentucky Orchestra.** Hotel band (WHAS, Louisville, KY, 1926).

26818 **Rezner, Johnny.** Newscaster (WKST, New Castle, PA, 1945). This could be the **John Reznor** of the next entry.

26819 **Reznor, John.** DJ (*Johnny's Matinee*, WPFB, Middletown, OH, 1948–1955).

26820 ***RFD Dinner Bell Program.*** The letters RFD in the program's title represented Radio Farmer's Democracy. It was a daily program of information for farmers (WLS, Chicago, IL, 1924).

26821 ***Rhapsody in Rhythm.*** Singer Connie Haines, the Golden Gate Quartet, pianist Skitch Henderson and Jan Savitt's Orchestra provided the entertainment on the show sponsored by Old Gold cigarettes. Art Gilmore was the announcer (30 min., Sunday, 10:30–11:00 P.M., NBC-Red, 1946). As Old Gold's summer show the following year, *Rhapsody in Rhythm* featured singers Peggy Lee and Johnny Johnson, the Jubalaires vocal group, harpist Robert Maxwell and Jan Savitt's Orchestra. Frank Goss was the announcer (30 min., Wednesday, 9:00–9:30 P.M., CBS, 1947).

26822 ***Rhapsody of the Rockies.*** The weekly music show originated from Denver, Colorado (30 min., Saturday, 6:00–6:30 P.M., NBC, 1947).

26823 **Rhawn, H.G.** Newscaster (WKLK, Clarksburg, WV, 1942).

26824 **Rhea, Larry.** Sportscaster (*Diary of Sports*, KCKN, Kansas City, MO, 1949).

26825 **Rhea, Mary Jane.** Contralto (KLDS, Independence, MO, 1926).

26826 **Rhein, Gene.** Sportscaster (WGNF, North Platte, NE, 1937).

26827 **Rheingold Quartet.** Radio vocal group (WJZ, New York, NY, 1923).

26828 **Rhenish Trio.** The members of the instrumental music group were Mrs. J. Barth, Mrs. L. Appe and Miss L. Velter. Their specialty was German folk songs (KFWM, Oakland, CA, 1927).

26829 **Rhett, Alicia.** COM-HE (WTMA, Charleston, SC, 1949).

26830 **Rheubottom, Harry.** DJ (*Harry's Swing Session*, KCSB, San Bernardino, CA, 1952).

26831 **Rhies, Frank.** Pianist (KVOO, Tulsa, OK, 1928–1929).

26832 **Rhinard, Ethel.** Pianist (KLX, Oakland, CA, 1927).

26833 **Rhoades, Allan.** Leader (*Allan Rhoades Orchestra*, instr. mus. prg., WHP, Harrisburg, PA, 1936–1938).

26834 **Rhoades, Frank.** Newscaster (KALL, Salt Lake City, UT, 1945).

26835 **Rhoads, Dusty.** Sportscaster (*Sports Roundup*, WFAX, Falls Church, VA, 1949).

26836 **Rhoads, Howard.** Sportscaster (KUJ, Walla Walla, WA, 1946).

26837 ***Rhoda Arnold and Charles Carlisle.*** The weekly music program presented Arnold and Carlisle in vocal duets (30 min., Sunday, 11:00–11:30 A.M., CBS, 1933).

26838 **Rhode, Karl.** Leader (*Karl Rhode Orchestra*, instr. mus. prg., WBZ, Boston-Springfield, MA, 1936).

26839 **Rhodenheiser, Dave.** DJ (*Teen Time*, WMVG, Middledgeville, GA, 1960).

26840 **Rhodes, Betty Jean.** COM-HE (WFOM, Fairmont, NC, 1954).

26841 **Rhodes, Billy.** Tenor (WGCP, New York, NY, 1925).

26842 **Rhodes, Bob.** DJ (*Solid Senders Club* and *The Rhodes Record Room*, WHOO, Orlando, FL, 1948–1952).

26843 **Rhodes, David.** Newscaster (WHBY-WTAQ, Green Bay, WI, 1939).

26844 **Rhodes, Dick.** DJ (*Sweet and Smooth*, WELM, Elmira, NY, 1947).

26845 **Rhodes, Dusty.** Tenor (NBC, Chicago, IL, 1929).

26846 **Rhodes, Dusty.** Sportscaster (*Sports Final*, WSGW, Saginaw, MI, 1952; *The Story on Sports*, WAMM, Flint, MI, 1960).

26847 **Rhodes, E.C.** Announcer (WSGH, New York, NY, 1925).

26848 **Rhodes, John.** Newscaster (WHUB, Cookeville, TN, 1941, 1945).

26849 **Rhodes, Joy.** COM-HE (KNET, Palestine, TX, 1955).

26850 **Rhodes, (Mrs.) Laura.** Soprano (WHAZ, Troy, NY, 1923).

26851 **Rhodes, Patti.** *Variety* identified Miss Rhodes as a sultry voiced female DJ (*This Is Patti,* 30 min., Friday and Saturday, 12:00–12:30 P.M., WABC, New York, NY, 1954).

26852 **Rhodes, Roxy [Roxy].** COM-HE (KTTR, Rolla, MO, 1956–1957).

26853 **Rhodes, Roy K.** DJ (*Country Clambake*, KWSL, Lake Charles, LA, 1948).

26854 **Rhodes, Will A.** Tenor (KDKA, Pittsburgh, PA, 1923).

26855 **Rhodes Orchestra.** Popular radio band (WNAC, Boston, MA, 1925).

26856 **Rhody, James B.** News analyst (*This 'N' That*, WFKY, Frankfort, KY, 1947).

26857 **Rhone, Paul.** DJ (*Mailbag* and *Special Request*, WMON, Montgomery, WV, 1947; KPRO, Riverside, CA, 1956). Sportscaster (*World of Sports*, WMON, 1947).

26858 ***Rhubarb Red.*** A CW tenor, guitarist and harmonica player, Rhubarb Red appeared daily at 6:30 A.M. and again at 9:00 A.M. in an all request program (WJJD, Chicago, IL and WIND, Gary, IN, 1935–1937. Red's given name was Lester William Polsfuss, one that he soon changed to Les Paul and gained national fame.

26859 **Rhyno, Lucy.** Soprano (KOIL, Council Bluffs, IA, 1926).

26860 **Rhys-Herbert Male Quartet.** Male vocal group (WCCO, Minneapolis–St. Paul, MN, 1928–1929).

26861 ***Rhythm and Games.*** Fannie Stene conducted the award winning program for kindergarten children for 35 years on WHA (Madison, WI).

26862 ***Rhythm at Eight.*** Singer Ethel Merman was accompanied by the Al Goodman Orchestra on the half-hour Sunday evening music program. Ted Husing was the announcer. When Merman left for Hollywood to begin a movie career, she was replaced by singer Benay Venuta (30 min., Sunday, 6:00–6:30 P.M., CBS, 1935).

26863 ***Rhythm at Midnight.*** Shirley Sadler sang with Hilly Edelstein's orchestra on the sustaining music show (30 min., Wednesday, 12:00–12:30 A.M., WBBM, Chicago, IL, 1938).

26864 ***Rhythm at Random.*** A recorded music program, *Rhythm at Random* was conducted by an unidentified DJ (KCJB, Minot, ND, 1955).

26865 ***Rhythm Boys.*** Fels-Naptha Soap Company sponsored the program featuring an unidentified harmony singing group (15 min., Thursday, 12:15–12:30 P.M., CBS, 1936).

26866 ***Rhythm Makers Orchestra.*** Instr. mus. prg. (WGY, Schenectady, NY, 1938; WPTF, Raleigh, NC, 1939).

26867 ***Rhythm on the Road.*** Amoco gasoline sponsored the program that was said to have been designed for Sunday drivers. Music by Elliott Lawrence's Orchestra, the Honeydreamers vocal group, singers Kay Armen and Bob Manning were featured. Weekly guests also performed. Bob Dixon was the announcer (60 min., Sunday, 4:00–5:00 P.M., CBS, 1955).

26868 ***Rhythm Rangers.*** Violinist George Hall was joined by Hortense Rose and Gina Donaldson on the CW music program (WLW, Cincinnati, OH, 1929).

26869 ***Rhythm Rangers.*** The popular CW music program featured the Rhythm Rangers: guitarist Ozzie Westley; saxophonist Lew Storey; bass fiddler Clyde Moffat; accordionist Eddie Fritz; violinist Joe Stevens; and Bronco Bill played by Jess Kirkpatrick (WWVA, Wheeling, WV, 1936.) The following year the group broadcast on WGN (Chicago, IL).

26870 ***Rhythm Rascals.*** Mus. prg. featuring vocalist Edith Hedrick (CBS, 1939).

26871 **Rhythm Rustlers.** Orchestra directed by Jack Van Cleve (WJBL, Decatur, IL, 1926).

26872 **Rialto Theater Symphony Orchestra.** Harry Brader was the symphony's violinist-conductor. Pianist Frank Strawn was often the featured artist (WOAW, Omaha, NE, 1925).

26873 **Rian, Cliff.** Newscaster (WTCN, Minneapolis, MN, 1946).

26874 **Ribb, Jimmy.** Sportscaster (KNOW, Austin, TX, 1937–1939).

26875 **Ricard, Doris.** COM-HE (WBBB, Burlington, NC, 1951).

26876 **Ricardo, Ric.** DJ (WGES, Chicago, IL, 1960).

26877 **Ricardo, Stan.** DJ (WGES, Chicago, IL, 1956).

26878 ***Ricardo and His Guitar.*** Instr. mus. prg. (WBBM, Chicago, IL, 1935).

26879 **Ricau, Lionel.** Newscaster (WSM, Nashville, TN, 1942, 1945).

26880 **Ricca, Ernest.** Director Ricca worked on *Amanda of Honeymoon Hill, Evelyn Winters, Lorenzo Jones, Mystery Theater, Romance of Helen Trent, Stella Dallas, Time For Love, True Confessions* and *Valiant Lady.*

26881 ***Riccardo, Psychic Prince.*** Psychic forecasts and fortunes were presented by Riccardo (KNX, Los Angeles, CA, 1928).

26882 ***Riccardo's Caballeros Orchestra.*** Instr. mus. prg. (NBC, 1937).

26883 **Ricci, Peter.** Baritone (WCAU, Philadelphia, PA, 1926).

26884 **Rice, Al.** Newscaster (WBIG, Greensboro, NC, 1946).

26885 **Rice, B.M.** Announcer (WORD, Batavia, IL, 1925–1927).

26886 **Rice, Catherine.** COM-HE (WFAU, Augusta, ME, 1957).

26887 **Rice, C.B.** DJ (*Gravy Train*, KLVL, Pasadena, TX, 1954).

26888 **Rice, Dick.** DJ (*Afternoon Melodies*, KYRO, Potosi, MO, 1960).

26889 **Rice, Earl.** Pianist (WGY, Schnectady, NY, 1924).

26890 **Rice, Ed.** Writer-director Rice worked on *The Life and Loves of Dr. Susan* (director), *Mary Marlin* (director), *Shell Chateau* (writer) and *True or False* (writer).

26891 Rice, Ed. Sportscaster (*Sports Final*, KOSF, Nacogdoches, TX, 1950).

26892 Rice, Edward [Edmund]. Violinist (WGY, Schenectady, NY, 1923–1925).

26893 Rice, Effie. Pianist (WADC, Akron, OH, 1929).

26894 Rice, George. Clarinetist and saxophonist Rice played in the National Battery Symphony Orchestra (KSTP, 1929).

26895 Rice, Gladys. Coloratura soprano on the *Roxy and His Gang* program (NBC, New York, NY, 1927; WEAF, New York, NY and WJZ, New York, NY, 1929).

26896 Rice, Grantland. Sports writer Rice on October 5, 1921 broadcast baseball's first World Series (New York Giants against the New York Yankees) over a hook-up of the Westinghouse network. The following year (Oct. 4, 1922), he broadcast the World Series over another early Westinghouse network. As the New York *Times* reported: "For the first time, [radio] carried the opening game of the World Series play-by-play direct from the Polo Grounds to great crowds throughout the eastern section of the country, through the broadcasting station WJZ. Grantland Rice related his story direct to an invisible audience, estimated to be five million, while WGY at Schenectady and WBZ in Springfield relayed every play of the contest. All the sounds of the game could be heard by listeners." In 1923, Rice shared broadcast chores of the World Series on 1923 with Graham McNamee, a chore that propelled the latter into prominence. Rice's fame, however, rests primarily on his newspaper columns and features.

26897 Rice, Herman. Leader (Herman Rice and his Blue Hills Orchestra, WOR, Newark, NJ, 1925).

26898 Rice, Howard ("Uncle Don" Carney). Howard Rice entered vaudeville as "Don the Trick Pianist." In 1925, he worked on New York's WMCA before moving on to WOR, Newark, NJ. He went on the air on WOR with a children's program on which he told stories. The sponsor was a toy manufacturer. Rice enjoyed a long successful career on WOR radio as Uncle Don. *See* **Uncle Don.**

26899 Rice, Jean. COM-HE (WCPK, College Park, GA, 1960).

26900 Rice, Laura [Louise]. Graphologist (WGBS, New York, NY, 1925).

26901 Rice, Lew. Station operator and sportscaster who occasionally assisted Hal Totten with Chicago area sports broadcasts (WMAQ, Chicago, IL, 1928–1929).

26902 Rice, Lillian. Mezzo-soprano (WFAA, Dallas, TX, 1929).

26903 Rice, Louise. Graphologist (WGBS, New York, NY, 1925).

26904 Rice, Marcia. Singer (NBC, 1942).

26905 Rice, Maurice. Newscaster (WDAF, Kansas City, MO, 1941).

26906 Rice, R.M. Announcer Rice at WORD (Batavia, IL, 1926) proclaimed its slogan, "The Watchtower Station WORD."

26907 Rice, Rosemary. Actress Rice appeared on the daytime serial programs *Right to Happiness*, *When a Girl Marries* and *Young Dr. Malone*.

26908 Rice, William. Newscaster (WMBC, Detroit, MI, 1940).

26909 Rice Institute Student Band. College band (KPRC, Houston, TX, 1926).

26910 Rich, Al. Sportscaster (*Baseball*, WLOH, Princeton, WV, 1949; *Sports Roundup*, WLOH, Princeton, WV, 1950–1951).

26911 Rich, Bertha. Pianist (WOR, Newark, NJ, 1925).

26912 Rich, Catherine. COM-HE (WFAU, Augusta, ME, 1955–1957).

26913 Rich, Charlotte W. COM-HE (WLOB, Portland, ME, 1957).

26914 Rich, Doris. Veteran radio actress Rich appeared on the daytime serial programs as *Barry Cameron*, *Houseboat Hannah* (title role), *Portia Faces Life*, *The Road of Life* and *The Romance of Helen Trent*.

26915 Rich, Fred "Freddie." Leader (Fred Rich Astor Band, a group praised by *Variety* for its "corking style of dance music" WJY, New York, NY, 1925–1926). Rich also led the Hungarian Orchestra of the Hotel Astor (WJZ, New York, NY, 1926). Rich's early band included: Rich, dir.-p.; Hymie Farberman, Leo Conville and Mike Mosiello, t.; Earl Kelly, tb.; Ted Klein, clr., ss. and as.; Ken Moyer, clr., as. and m.; Rudy Adler, ts.; Jimmy Johnston, bsx.; Phil Oliwitz, v.; Ray Bauduc, d.; and Jack Hansen, tba. In later years Rich was known as *Freddie Rich*. He became musical director of WABC (New York, NY) in 1928. His later work included: *Freddie Rich Orchestra*, instr. mus. prg. (CBS, 1934–1936; WLW, Cincinnati, OH, 1937).

26916 Rich, Irene. Miss Rich was a distinguished radio actress (KFWB, Hollywood, CA, 1927). She appeared in the *Glorious One* dramatic series (Network, mid–1930s). Her later work included roles on the programs *Dear John*, *Irene Rich Dramas* and *Woman From Nowhere*.

26917 Rich, Jimmy. Theater organist at Loew's Jersey City Theater (WPAP, Brooklyn, NY, 1929).

26918 Rich, Louis. Leader (*Louis Rich Orchestra*, instr. mus. prg., WCLE, Cleveland, OH, 1937; MBS, 1939).

26919 Rich, Margaret. Soprano (WSM, Nashville, TN, 1927).

26920 Rich, Marian. Mezzo-soprano (WOR, Newark, NJ, 1933–1934).

26921 Rich, Mike. DJ (*Platter Playboy*, WTRY, Troy, NY, 1947; WROW, Albany, NY, 1948). Sportscaster (*Five Star Final*, WTRY, 1947).

26922 Rich, Neville. Rich broadcast talks on business topics such as "Talks on Constructive Selling — the Human Element in Industry" (KGO, Oakland, CA, 1925).

26923 Rich, Reba. COM-HE (WBBB, Burlington, NC, 1956).

26924 Rich, Vance. Sportscaster (*Sports Parade*, WENC, Whiteville, NC, 1947).

26925 *Rich Man's Darling.* Kolynos Tooth Paste sponsored the dramatic serial whose theme, *Variety* said, was that of a "girl's sacrifice on the altar of love for her family." The story focused on Peggy Burchard, played by Louise Blocki, a reporter on the *Gotham Press*, who worked because her family had lost their fortune. In order for her brother to go to college and make life easier for her widowed mother and her sister, she married a wealthy suitor, even though she didn't love him. Olan Soule played the role of a fellow reporter who secretly loved her. Peggy Wall and Frank Seay were also in the cast (15 min., Monday, 12:15–12:30 P.M., CST, WGN, Chicago, IL, 1935). The following year the program underwent something of a transformation when it made its network appearance. Peggy, an attractive young woman played by Peggy Allenby, this time was married to a middle-aged business man, Gregory Alden, played by Edwin Jerome. Karl Swenson and Ethel Renney were also in the cast. Art Millett was the announcer (15 min., Monday through Friday, 11:45–12:00 noon, CBS, 1936). The following year still another transformation took place when the program evolved into *Our Gal Sunday*. *See* ***Our Gal Sunday.***

26926 *Richard Lawless.* A dramatic serial, *Richard Lawless* featured Kevin McCarthy, Cathleen Cordell, Neil Fitzgerald, Sidney Smith and Peter Boyles in the cast. Music was supplied by John Gart's orchestra. *Variety* identified the program as radio's ill-advised venture into the swashbuckling period of Charles the Second in 17th century England. The sustaining program was relatively short-lived (30 min., Sunday, 8:00–8:30 P.M., CBS, 1946).

26927 *Richard Maxwell.* Tenor Maxwell broadcast a weekly program of popular songs (30 min., Monday, 9:00–9:30 P.M., NBC-Blue, 1929).

26928 Richard the Riddler. Unidentified performer who broadcast programs "for radio children" (KDKA, Pittsburgh, PA, 1924).

26929 Richards, Amelia Lowe. Pianist (KPO, San Francisco, CA, 1926).

26930 Richards, Art. Actor Richards was in the cast of *When a Girl Marries*.

26931 Richards, Bill. DJ (*Falls City Dancing Party*, WGKV, Charleston, WV, 1947; *Dancing Party*, WGKV, 1948; *Richards' Rendezvous*, WGKV, 1952).

26932 Richards, Bob. Announcer (KHQ, Spokane, WA, 1929).

26933 Richards, Bud. DJ (*Rise and Shine*, KOJM, Havre, MT, 1947).

26934 Richards, Carrie. Leader (Carrie Richards' Hotel Portage Quintet, WADC, Akron, OH, 1926).

26935 Richards, Chuck. DJ (WBAL, Baltimore, MD, 1956).

26936 Richards, Dick. Sportscaster (WTBO, Cumberland, MD, 1942).

26937 Richards, E. John. Organist (WOC, Davenport, IA, 1923).

26938 Richards, Helen. Miss Richards was a blues singer billed as "The Crooning Singer" (WOR, Newark, NJ, 1928–1929; *Vitality Program*, NBC, 1932). When she appeared in vaudeville, she had been billed as the "female baritone."

26939 Richards, Jack. Newscaster (KEUB, Price, UT, 1938). Sportscaster (KEUB, 1939).

26940 Richards, Jack and Billy Church. Comedy team that formerly was featured with the A.G. Fields' Minstrels (WAIU, Columbus, OH, 1928).

26941 Richards, Janet. Cellist in the Claire Trio (KFRC, San Francisco, CA, 1926).

26942 Richards, Jean. COM-HE (WKID, Urbana, IL, 1949).

26943 Richards, Jimmy. Leader (*Jimmy Richards Orchestra*, instr. mus. prg., WOWO, Ft. Wayne, IN, 1934; NBC, 1939).

26944 Richards, Joan. COM-HE (WIPC, Lake Wales, FL, 1954; WHBO, Tampa, FL, 1954).

26945 Richards, Johnny. Leader (*Johnny Richards Orchestra*, instr. mus. prg., WCLE, Cleveland, OH, 1937).

26946 Richards, Lillian. Singer Richards was known as the "Rice Hotel Songbird" (KPC, Houston, TX, 1926).

26947 Richards, Mal. Newscaster (WJHO, Opelika, AL, 1940). Sportscaster (WJHO, 1940).

26948 Richards, Malcolm. DJ (*The Malcolm Richards Show*, WCPO, Cincinnati, OH, 1947–1950).

26949 Richards, Mary Groom. Contralto (KGO, Oakland, CA, 1925; KTAB, Oakland, CA, 1926.) Miss Richards was also featured on NBC's *Spotlight Hour* broadcast in 1927.

26950 Richards, Mel. DJ (WSBA, York, PA, 1951).

26951 Richards, Royce. Sportscaster (*Speaking of Sports*, WMMT, McMinnville, TN, 1947–1950; WLAC, Nashville, TN, 1960).

26952 Richards, Tecla. Soprano (WMH, Cincinnati, OH, 1924).

26953 Richards, Tom. DJ (*Soy Club*, WSOY, Decatur, IL, 1947).

26954 Richards, Tony. DJ (WLVA, Lynchburg, VA, 1957).

26955 Richards, (Mrs.) Verl Stiles. Soprano (WJZ, New York, NY, 1924).

26956 Richardson, Alexander David. Organist (WOR, Newark, NJ, 1929).

26957 Richardson, Betty Joe. Known as the "Sweetheart of WBBZ," the four-year-old singer charmed her listeners (WBBZ, Chicago, IL, 1929).

26958 Richardson, Bill. Sportscaster (*Early Bird Sports*, WITZ, Jasper, IN, 1949).

26959 Richardson, Bob. Sportscaster (KWK, St. Louis, MO, 1937–1939).

26960 Richardson, Bobby. Sportscaster (*Sports Memory*, WFIG, Sumter, SC, 1960).

26961 Richardson, Dick. Leader (Dick Richardson Orchestra, WFAA, Dallas, TX, 1924).

26962 Richardson, Dorothy. Pianist (KGER, Long Beach, CA, 1929).

26963 Richardson, Doug. Leader (Doug Richardson and his Orchestra, KTCL, Seattle, WA, 1926).

26964 Richardson, Earl A. Sportscaster (WASK, Lafayette, IN, 1950–1952, 1955–1956). DJ (WFAM, Lafayette, IN, 1957).

26965 Richardson, Ethel Park. Folk singer and writer Richardson created and produced the *Wayside Cottage* dramatic serial (CBS, 1929) and several other critically praised network programs, such *Heart Throbs of the Hills* aka *Hillbilly Heart Throbs* and *Dreams of Long Ago* (NBC,1933–1939). The various stars who appeared on this program included Tex Ritter, Carson Robison, Frank Luther, the Vass Family, Zora Layman and Texas Jim Robinson.

Richardson, herself, sang mountain songs on WDOD (Chattanooga, TN, 1926), before she came to New York and had her own program on WOR (Newark, NJ, 1930s) and NBC (1930s). Richardson was said to have created and written some dozen radio shows.

26966 Richardson, Fabiola D. Soprano (WBZ, Springfield, MA, 1925).

26967 Richardson, Florence "Flo." Violinist (WOR, Newark, NJ). Leader (Flo Richardson Orchestra, WOR, Newark, NY, 1925; *Florence Richardson Orchestra*, instr. mus. prg., WOR, 1934; NBC, 1935).

26968 Richardson, Frankie. Leader (*Frankie Richardson Orchestra*, instr. mus. prg., WIP, Philadelphia, PA, 1936).

26969 Richardson, Fred. Tenor (KOMO, Seattle, WA, 1927).

26970 Richardson, H. Larry. Newscaster (WIBC, Indianapolis, IN, 1944–1946).

26971 Richardson, Harry K. Announcer-assistant director of continuity and station publicity (KVOO, Tulsa, OK, 1929). Richardson started in radio in 1923. Before working at KVOO, he was the Radio Editor of the *Daily Oklahoman*.

26972 Richardson, (Mrs.) Henry E. Contralto (WSM, Nashville, TN, 1928–1929).

26973 Richardson, J.P. (The Big Bopper). CW DJ, singer and songwriter Richardson joined KTRM (Beaumont, TX, 1949) as a DJ. Shortly after he left station KTRM to devote his entire time to performing, he lost his life in a plane crash that also took the lives of Buddy Holly and Richie Valens.

26974 Richardson, James. Newscaster (WJHL, Johnson City, TN, 1945).

26975 Richardson, Jeannette. Soprano (WEMC, Berrien Springs, MI).

26976 Richardson, Martin. Tenor (WJZ, New York, NY, 1925).

26977 Richardson, Matt. Newscaster (WESG, Elmira, NY, 1938).

26978 Richardson, Sarah Hill. Violinist (WHAS, Louisville, KY, 1923).

26979 Richardson, Shirley. COM-HE (KVWO, Cheyenne, WY, 1954).

26980 Richardson, Stanley. Newscaster (NBC, 1942, 1945).

26981 Richardson, Ted. DJ (*Solid Sendin'*, WMOH, Hamilton, OH, 1947; *Turntable Turnover*, WMOH, Hamilton, OH, 1948; *1450 Club*, WMOH, 1952).

26982 Richardson, Wing. Newscaster (WFOY, St. Augustine, FL, 1945).

26983 Richboug, John. DJ (*Record Parade*, WLAC, Nashville, TN, 1960).

26984 Richerson [Richardson], Ann. COM-HE (WMFC, Monroeville, AL, 1957).

26985 Richey, Joan. COM-HE (KVOA, Tucson, AZ, 1949).

26986 Richey, Tom. Xylophonist and drummer (WLW, Cincinnati, OH, 1926–1929 and WSAI, Cincinnati, OH, 1929).

26987 *Richfield Country Club* (aka *The Country Club*). Music and a talk on golf were the main ingredients of the program sponsored by the Richfield Oil Company. Betty Barthell sang with Jack Golden's orchestra and golf professional Alex Morrison supplied golfing hints. Ernest G. Lendenning was the program host and Ben Grauer the announcer (30 min., Friday, 10:30–11:00 P.M., NBC-Red, 1933). A slightly changed format for the program was broadcast the same year with soprano Mary McCoy, blues singer Betty Barthell, a double vocal quartet and the Jack Golden orchestra. Sports writer Grantland Rice told stories about sports and their performers (30 min., Monday, 7:30–8:00 P.M., NBC-Red, 1933). When broadcast on CBS, the program was known simply as *The Country Club*, but it was the same program (30 min., Weekly, 10:00–10:30 P.M., CBS, 1933). A year later on NBC, the format remained essentially the same with a different time slot (30 min., Monday, 10:00–10:30 P.M., NBC-Blue, 1934).

26988 Richie, Bill. Newscaster (KFYO, Lubbock, TX, 1945).

26989 Richie, George T. Announcer and studio pianist (KOA, Denver, CO, 1929).

26990 Richie, Rona. COM-HE (WAAA, Red Wing, MN, 1951).

26991 Richison and Sons. Country group that specialized in "old time fiddlers' music" (KVOO, Tulsa, OK, 1929).

26992 Richman, Harry. Leader (Harry Richman and his Entertainers Orchestra, WHN, New York, NY, 1926; *Harry Richman*, vcl. mus. prg., NBC, 1934; *Harry Richman Orchestra*, instr. mus. prg., WCAE, Pittsburgh, PA, 1936). Pianist, orchestra leader, singer and motion picture star Richman was a great favorite in the late 1920s and 1930s. He began his radio career as a pianist for NTG (Nils Thor Granlund) and was the brunt of many of Granlund's comic insults. When he gained national popularity in the 1930s, his publicity in 1934 called him "the man of a dozen careers and a hundred romances."

26993 Richmond, Dean. Leader (Dean Richmond Orchestra, KOWW, Walla Walla, WA, 1927).

26994 Richmond, Dick. Sportscaster (*Home Edition Sports*, KRIO, McAllen, TX, 1955).

26995 Richmond, Edna. Soprano (WGBS, New York, NY, 1925).

26996 Richmond, R.W. Newscaster (WHKK, Akron, OH, 1944).

26997 Richmond, Russell. Newscaster (WRRN, Warren, OH, 1942).

26998 Richmond Police String Band. Municipal band from Richmond, Virginia (WRVA, Richmond, VA, 1928).

26999 Richter, Arthur. Organist (WHAD, Milwaukee, WI, 1925–1926).

27000 Richter, Charlotte. COM-HE (WNOP, Newport, KY, 1954).

27001 Richter, (Dr.) Francis. Blind organist (KSTP, St. Paul–Minneapolis, MN, 1929).

27002 Richter, Michael. Flutist (WBAL, Baltimore, MD, 1926–1929).

27003 Richter String Quartet. WOR (Newark, NJ, 1922).

27004 Richters, John. Baritone (KFI, Los Angeles, CA, 1928).

27005 Richton, Addy. Writer Richton wrote under the names of Adelaide Marston and Lynn Stone. The programs she wrote included *Hilltop House, This Life Is Mine* and *Valiant Lady.*

27006 Rickard, Doris. COM-HE (WBBB, Burlington, NC, 1954).

27007 Rickard, Vernon "Tex." A tenor, formerly with Chicago's WGN, Rickard sang on KFWB (Hollywood, CA, 1927–1929).

27008 Ricke, Maryalyce. COM-HE (WMGW, Meadville, PA, 1960).

27009 Rickenbacker, Ace. DJ (*Ace's Platter Chatter,* WSPA, Spartanburg, SC, 1947; *Ace's Postscripts,* WSPA, Spartanburg, SC, 1950–1954; WORD, Spartanburg, SC, 1955).

27010 Ricker, William "Bill." Newscaster (WDEY, Waterbury, CT, 1938–1941).

27011 Rickett, Laverne. Blues singer (KFWI, San Francisco, CA, 1926).

27012 Rickles, Don. Newscaster (KVAN, Vancouver, WA, 1945).

27013 Rickless, Sybil. COM-HE (KXIC, Iowa City, IA, 1949).

27014 Rico, Joe. DJ (*Supper Club,* WWOL, Buffalo, NY, 1948; WHLD, Niagara Falls, NY, 1954–1956).

27015 Riddell, Corwin. Newscaster (WOAI, San Antonio, TX, 1939–1942).

27016 Riddell, Jimmie. Tenor (KOMO, Seattle, WA, 1928).

27017 Riddle, Bill. Sportscaster (*Sports Review,* WNEX, Macon, GA, 1949; WBBQ, Augusta, GA, 1952–1955).

27018 Riddle, Bill. DJ Riddle always began his popular show with his trademark phrase, "Hello, music lovers" (KRLA, Los Angeles, CA, 1959).

27019 Ridenour, Dave. Sportscaster (*Sports Summary,* WLEA, Hornell, NY, 1949; *Sports Showcase,* WTVE, Elmira, NY, 1955).

27020 Ridenour, Gordon M. News analyst (*Afternoon Extra, 6:00 News* and *News Behind the News,* WELM, Elmira, NY, 1947–1948, *Ridenour Checks the News,* WELM, 1948).

27021 Ridenour, Paul. Sportscaster (*Sports Spotlight,* WADE, Wadesboro, NC, 1951–1952).

27022 Rideout, E.B. Meteorologist (WEEI, Boston, MA, 1928–1929). Newscaster (WEEI, 1934).

27023 Rider, Gene. Newscaster (CBS, 1944).

27024 Rider, Maurice "Maury." Sportscaster (KIRO, Seattle, WA, 1939–1941). Newscaster (KIRO, Seattle, WA, 1948). DJ (*Maury's Turntable,* KIRO, 1948; *Angler's Angle,* KJR, Seattle, WA, 1952).

27025 Rider, Richard. Actor Rider was in the cast of *Amanda of Honeymoon Hill.*

27026 Ridge, Jack. DJ (WGAY, Silver Spring, MD, 1947; *Sports Derby,* WEAM , Arlington, VA, 1948). Sportscaster (*Sports Circus,* WGAY, 1947).

27027 Ridgley, Harry. Newscaster (WDAN, Danville, IL, 1942).

27028 Ridgway, Charles B. DJ (WDZ, Tuscola, IL, 1947).

27029 Ridlebaugh, Barbara A. COM-HE (WLCO, Eustis, FL, 1956).

27030 Ridley, Bob. Steel guitar soloist (KVOO, Tulsa, OK, 1929).

27031 Ridley (Bob) and Adkins. Guitar duo (KVOO, Tulsa, OK, 1929).

27032 Ridley, Harriet [Harriette]. Pianist (WOO, Philadelphia, PA, 1924).

27033 Riebe, Fred. Harmonica and French harp soloist (WHB, Kansas City, MO, 1926).

27034 Riedo, Erma French. Singer (WGBS, New York, NY, 1925).

27035 Rieff, Phyllis. Violinist (WOW, Omaha, NE, 1928).

27036 Rieffin, Elsa. Soprano (WJZ, New York, NY, 1923).

27037 Riegel, Ethel A. COM-HE (WKOK, Sunbury, FL, 1954–1955).

27038 Riegel, Rheinhold. Sportscaster (WHA, Madison, WI, 1940–1941).

27039 Riemer, Leroy. Announcer and assistant station manager (KFEQ, St. Joseph, MO, 1929).

27040 Rienhart, Al. Newscaster (WGGM, Albuquerque, NM, 1942). Sportscaster (WGGM, 1942).

27041 Rieschick, Reinhold. Banjo soloist (WAHG, Richmond Hill, NY, 1926).

27042 Riesinger, Hazel. Miss Riesinger was a studio singer known as "The Sooner Girl" (KFJF, Oklahoma City, OK, 1928–1929).

27043 Riestra, Carlos Valle. Pianist (WJY, New York, NY, 1924).

27044 Rietz, William. Singer (WGCP, Newark, NJ, 1925).

27045 Rigby, Loehr. Sportscaster (KPAS, Banning, CA, 1948). DJ (*Diggin' with Rig,* KPAS, 1950).

27046 Riggle, Mary Ann. COM-HE (WLMJ, Jackson, OH, 1960).

27047 Riggs, A.F. "Butch." DJ (WIRO, Ironton, OH, 1957).

27048 Riggs, Leo. Organist (WJZ, New York, NY, 1923).

27049 Riggs, Patricia. COM-HE (WJUN, Redmond, OR, 1954).

27050 Riggs, Tommy. DJ (WCAE, Pittsburgh, PA, 1954–1957).

27051 Riggs, Tubby. Leader (*Tubby Riggs Orchestra,* instr. mus. prg., WHLS, Louisville, KY, 1937).

27052 *(The) Right Start for the Day.* Dr. Dale R. Crowley conducted the daily Bible teaching and religious news program in the mid–1930s and continued broadcasting well into the 1980s.

27053 *Right to Happiness.* Irna Phillips originally wrote the long-running daytime serial drama, before John M. Young became the writer in 1942. The heroine, an ordinary woman with a heart of gold, faced life with a definite philosophy that was best expressed by the program's opening when the announcer said, "Happiness is the sum total of many things — of health, security, friends and loved ones. But most important is a desire to be happy and the will to help others find their right to happiness." The large cast over the years included: Ruth Bailey, Charita Bauer, Joseph Bell, Peter Capell, Staats Cotsworth, Constance Crowder, Les Damon, Luise Barclay, Jimmy Dobson, Helene Dumas, Maurice Franklin, Sarah Fussell, David Gothard, Walter Graeza, Violet Heming, Irene Hubbard, Ginger Jones, Carlton KaDell, Art Kohl, Eloise Kummer, John Larkin, Elizabeth Lawrence, Bill Lipton, Sunda Love, Jerry Macy, Ian Martin, Gary Merrill, Marvin Miller, Claudia Morgan, Julian Noa, Ethel Waite Owen, Mary Patton, Ed Prentiss, Bill Quinn, Billy Redfield, Rosemary Rice, Selena Royle, Anne Sargent, J. Ernest Scott, Alexander Scourby, Anne Sterrett, Hugh Studebaker, Renee Taylor, Leora Thatcher, Gertrude Warner, Charles Webster, Sarajane Wells and Alice Yourman. Fayette Krum, Kathleen Lane, Paul Martin and Carl Wester were the program's producers and William Meeder the musical director. The directors were Gil Gibbons, Arthur Hanna, Frank Papp and Charles Urquhart. Hugh Conover, Michael Fitzmaurice and Ron Rawson were the announcers (NBC-Blue, CBS, 1939–1960).

27054 *(The) Right Word.* W. Curtis Nicholson conducted the self-improvement program devoted to the improvement of speech and diction (WMCA, New York, NY, 1925).

27055 Rigsby, (Mrs.) Byrd. Contralto (KTHS, Hot Springs National Park, AR, 1926).

27056 Rikk, Julius. Leader (*Julius Rikk Orchestra,* instr. mus. prg., WGN, Chicago, IL, 1934).

27057 Rile, Ruth. Contralto (WIP, Philadelphia, PA, 1924–1926).

27058 Riley, Chad. Sportscaster (*Sports Spotlight,* WDYK, Cumberland, MD, 1952–1955; WTBO, Cumberland, MD, 1956).

27059 Riley, Charles. Violinist (KDKA, Pittsburgh, PA, 1923).

27060 Riley, Don. Sportscaster (WBAL, Baltimore, MD, 1937; WCAO, Baltimore, MD, 1940–1944).

27061 Riley, Harry. Sportscaster (*Riley Reports the Sports,* WVVW, Fairmont, WV, 1948–1949). DJ (*Sit and Listen Platter Party,* WVVW, 1950).

27062 Riley, Jack. Leader (Jack Riley Orchestra, WDAF, Kansas City, MO, 1926).

27063 Riley, Jane Adele. Five-year-old reader (WHJ, Los Angeles, CA, 1924).

27064 Riley, Julian C. Announcer and cellist in the KOA Concert Orchestra (KOA, Denver, CO, 1928–1929).

27065 **Riley, Len.** Sportscaster (WFBM, Indianapolis, IN, 1936–1939; *Len Riley Reports the Sports*, WFBM, 1940; WCKY, Cincinnati, OH, 1941).

27066 **Riley, Meuded.** Boy trombonist (WSAI, Cincinnati, OH, 1926).

27067 **Riley, Mickey.** Sportscaster (KMPC, Beverly Hills, CA, 1940).

27068 **Riley, Mike.** Leader (*Mike Riley Orchestra*, instr. mus. prg., WTAM, Cleveland, OH, 1938).

27069 **Riley, Mrs.** COM-HE (WHOT, South Bend, IN, 1949).

27070 **Riley, Susan "Sue."** COM-HE (WNDU, South Bend, IN, 1956–1957).

27071 ***Riley Shephard.*** Shephard, a folksy philosopher, talked about a variety of topics on his daily sustaining program (25 min., Monday through Friday, 4:30–4:55 P.M., 1951).

27072 **Rinaldo, Signor.** Leader (Signor Rinaldo Orchestra, KLX, Oakland, CA, 1929).

27073 **Rinck, Alice.** Violinist (WAAM, Newark, NJ, 1925).

27074 **Rind, Jules.** Sportscaster (WPEN, Philadelphia, PA, 1946–1948).

27075 **Rindon, Charles M.** Leader (Collegians Orchestra, WSM, Nashville, TN, 1928).

27076 **Rinehart, Jack.** Leader (Jack Rinehard's Chinese Garden Orchestra, KFI, Los Angeles, CA, 1926).

27077 **Rinehart, Nolan "Cowboy Slim" or "The King of Border Radio."** Although he seldom appeared on American radio, Rinehart was considered to be the most popular cowboy singer on Border Radio. After broadcasting in the early 1930s on KSKY (Dallas, TX), he gained great popularity on Border Radio stations XEG (Monterrey, MX) and XEPN (Piedras Negras, MX). He made many transcriptions while working at these stations, some of them with Patsy Montana. Rinehart was killed in an automobile accident at the age of 37 in 1948.

27078 **Riner, Bob.** Announcer (WFIW, Hopkinsville, KY, 1927).

27079 **Rines, Joe.** Leader (Noah's Arcadians, WEEI, Boston, MA, 1925; Joe Rines and his Hunters Club Orchestra, WEEI, 1926; Joe Rines and his Elks Hotel Orchestra, WEEI, Boston, MA, 1928–29; *Joe Rines and His Show Boat Orchestra*, WBZ, Boston, MA, 1930). Rines also served as musical director on the *Triadors* program (NBC-Blue Network, New York, NY, 1929 and continued active in the next decade, *Joe Rines Orchestra*, mus. prg., WBZ, Boston-Springfield, MA, 1934–1935; NBC-Red, 1935–1937).

27080 **Ring, Bill.** Sportscaster (KGBX, Springfield, MO and KWTO, Springfield, MO, 1937–1939).

27081 **Ring, Henry.** Leader (*Henry Ring Orchestra*, WCAE, Pittsburgh, PA, 1936).

27082 ***Ringling Brothers, Barnum and Bailey Circus.*** A complete circus performance was broadcast, probably for the *first time* October, 1927 (WDOD, Chattanooga, TN, 1927).

27083 **Ringwood, Roy.** Organist (*Roy Ringwood*, instr. mus. prg., KHJ, Los Angeles, CA, 1932).

27084 ***Rin-Tin-Tin*** **(aka *Rin-Tin-Tin Thriller*).** This children's adventure series was supposedly based on the exploits of Rin-Tin-Tin, the dog who had appeared in numerous silent movies in the previous decade. The program dramatized his adventures and those of other dogs as well. The cast from 1930 to 1932 included Francis X. Bushman, Tom Corwine, Lee Duncan, Betty White, George Opie, Frank Doucet, Bernardine Flynn, Fred Ibbett, Don Ameche and Bob White. The sponsor was Ken-L-Ration (15 min., Thursday, 8:15–8:30 P.M., NBC-Blue, 1932). The following year the program's day and time changed (15 min., Sunday, 7:45–8:00 P.M., CBS, 1933).

27085 **Rio, Rita.** Leader (*Rita Rio Orchestra*, instr. mus. prg., NBC, 1937).

27086 **Rio, Rosa.** Organist *Rosa Rio* was a popular instrumental performer (15 min., ABC, 1947). She provided organ backgrounds and interludes on many programs, including *Between the Bookends, Cavalcade of America, Court of Missing Heirs, Deadline Drama, Ethel and Albert, Front Page Farrell, Hannibal Cobb, Lorenzo Jones, My True Story, Myrt and Marge, Rosa Rio Rhythms, The Shadow* and *When a Girl Marries.*

27087 ***Rio Grande Barbeque.*** CW mus. prg. (KUOA, Siloam Springs, AR, 1939).

27088 **Rion, Virginia.** COM-HE (KCHI, Chillicothe, MO, 1957).

27089 **Rions, Del.** Leader (Del Rions Orchestra, instr. mus. prg., KPO, San Francisco, CA, 1928).

27090 **Riordan, Delia.** Singer (WGCP, New York, NY, 1925).

27091 **Rios, Elvira.** Soprano (KCHI, Chillicothe, MO, 1957).

27092 **Ripa, Louis.** Sportscaster (*Sports Headlines*, KTRB, Modesto, CA, 1949–1950).

27093 **Ripka, Flora.** Pianist (WIP, Philadelphia, PA, 1924).

27094 **Ripley, Fred.** Announcer (WTAM, Cleveland, OH, 1925).

27095 **Ripley, Robert.** Cartoonist, writer and actor Ripley was born December 25, 1893. He originated the *Believe It or Not* series of cartoons and books before he appeared on the *Collier Hour* in 1929 on the NBC-Blue network. Ripley was also on the air in 1931. He was featured on his own *Believe It or Not* program. *See* ***Believe It or Not.***

27096 **Ripley, Ronald.** DJ (*1380 Club*, KBWD, Brownwood, TX, 1947; *Night Watch*, KBWD, 1952; KHOB, Hobbs, NM, 1956; *Coffee Time and Spectrum*, WKTJ, Farmington, ME, 1960).

27097 **Rippetee, Ferrell.** Newscaster (WBOW, Terre Haute, IN, 1944).

27098 **Rippon, Willard.** Junior announcer (WSPD, Toledo, OH, 1925–1929).

27099 **Riquez, Basil.** DJ (*Alegrias*, KTLW, Texas City, TX, 1948).

27100 ***Rise and Shine.*** Wallace "Wally" Butterworth, a radio baritone turned announcer, hosted NBC's *Rise and Shine* program of songs and chatter each weekday morning (NBC-Blue, 1927–1928).

27101 ***Rise and Whine.*** DJ Bob Carter using the name Jim Grouch conducted the daily early morning show (WMCA, New York, NY, 1939).

27102 ***(The) Rise of the Goldbergs.*** Originally broadcast in 1929, the show evolved into the popular daytime serial drama *The Goldbergs* (15 min., Wednesday, 7:00–7:15 P.M., NBC-Blue, 1929). *See* ***The Goldbergs.***

27103 **Riseman, Jules.** Concert Master (WNAC, Boston, MA, 1929).

27104 **Riser, James "Jimmy."** Sportscaster (WJEJ, Hagerstown, MD, 1940, 1946; *Sports Parade*, WJEJ, 1947; *Sports Trail*, WCAV, Norfolk, VA, 1950).

27105 **Rishworth [Rishman], Thomas.** One of the youngest American announcers, Rishworth earned money for his college expenses by announcing and directing the *Early Risers Club* program (KSTP, St. Paul–Minneapolis, MN, 1920s).

27106 ***Rising Musical Stars.*** *Rising Musical Stars*, a half-hour music show, featured Richard Gordon, the Swallows Orchestra and weekly guests (30 min., Sunday, 10:00–10:30 P.M., NBC-Red, 1938).

27107 **Risinger, J.L.** Announcer (KFDM, Beaumont, TX, 1928–1929).

27108 **Risk, Hester.** COM-HE (WMBS, Uniontown, PA, 1954).

27109 **Risman, Anita.** COM-HE (WKAL, Rome, NY, 1954).

27110 **Riss, Daniel "Dan."** Newscaster (WFAA, Dallas, TX, 1939; WLW, Cincinnati, OH, 1944–1946).

27111 **Ristola, George.** DJ (*Platter Party*, KAST, Astoria, OR, 1948).

27112 **Ristola, Mary.** COM-HE (KAST, Astoria, OR, 1957).

27113 **Ritchey, Buck.** DJ (*Harmony Hoedown* and *Sagebrush Serenade*, KVI, Tacoma, WA, 1947–1948; *Chuckwagon Jamboree*, KVI, 1948).

27114 **Ritchie, Albany.** Violinist (KFOA, Seattle, WA, 1928–1929).

27115 **Ritchie, Esther L.** COM-HE (WKLX, Paris, KY, 1957).

27116 **Ritchie, George T.** Pianist (KOA, Denver, CO, 1929).

27117 **Ritchie, Pat.** COM-HE (KWJJ, Portland, OR, 1960).

27118 **Ritchie, Ruth.** COM-HE (WBEJ, Elizabethton, TN, 1956).

27119 **Ritchie, Vera.** Soprano (KXA, Seattle, WA, 1928).

27120 **Ritchie, Willie.** Sportscaster Ritchie was a former world lightweight champion, who broadcast local boxing matches (KYA, San Francisco, CA, 1932).

27121 **Ritine, (Mrs.) Geraldine.** Pianist (WSUI, Iowa City, IA, 1926).

27122 **Ritsema, John.** Newscaster (WKZO, Kalamazoo, MI, 1938).

27123 **Rittenhouse, (Reverend Dr.) Daniel F.** Pastor of the First Baptist Church, Columbus, Ohio (WMAN, Columbus, OH,

1922). Announcer (WMAN, Columbus, OH, 1925).

27124 Ritter, C. Fred. Announcer (WSAN, Allentown, PA, 1925–1927).

27125 Ritter, Diana. DJ (*Teen Time*, KLAN, Renton, WA, 1954)

27126 Ritter, Marian. Newscaster (WEDC, Chicago, IL, 1945).

27127 Ritter, Woodward Maurice "Tex." Texas country-western singer and western movie star, Ritter began singing on radio in 1929 (KPRC, Houston, TX, 1929) while in law school. He went on to appear on New York radio and the Broadway stage before going to Hollywood to star in a series of cowboy movies. On New York radio he appeared on such programs as *Tex Ritter's Campfire* and *Cowboy Tom's Roundup*. On Broadway he appeared in *Green Grow the Lilacs*, the basis for the later hit *Oklahoma*. Tex became a member of the *Grand Ole Opry* in 1965.

27128 Ritz, Anne. Soprano (WMCA, New York, NY, 1925).

27129 Ritz, Myrna. COM-HE (WBTA, Batavia, NY, 1956).

27130 Ritz-Carlton Dance Orchestra. Hotel orchestra conducted by Walter Miller (WOO, Philadelphia, PA, 1924–1926; *Ritz-Carlton Dance Orchestra*, instr. mus. prg., WABC, New York, NY, 1936).

27131 Rivard, Mary Alice. COM-HE (KFOX, Long Beach, CA, 1956–1957).

27132 Rivas, Louis. Sportscaster (*Put It To Pat*, MBS, 1955).

27133 Rivers, Robert. DJ (*Hillbilly Jamboree*, WALD, Walterboro, SC, 1948).

27134 Rives, Winona. Contralto (KWK, St. Louis, MO, 1929).

27135 Rivlin, Jules. Sportscaster (WSAZ, Huntington, WV, 1956).

27136 Rivo, Lee. Tenor (WPCH, New York, NY, 1929).

27137 Rivoli Orchestra. Band directed by assistant conductor, Emanuel Baer (WNYC, New York, NY, 1925).

27138 Rix, Ione Pastori. Soprano (KPO, San Francisco, CA, 1925, 1929).

27139 Rizzo, Henry. Sportscaster (*Sports Roundup*, WWSR, St. Albans, VT, 1954).

27140 Rizzo, Mike. "Boy violinist" (WHT, Chicago, IL, 1926).

27141 Rizzo, Vincent. Leader (Havana Casino Orchestra, WOO, Philadelphia, PA, 1923; Vincent Rizzo Orchestra, WOO, 1925). In 1929, Rizzo was under exclusive contract to Philadelphia's station WCAU (Philadelphia, PA, 1929), but in the next decade he resumed broadcasting on other outlets (*Vincent Rizzo Orchestra*, instr. mus. prg., WIP, Philadelphia, PA, 1935–1936).

27142 Rizzuto, Phil. Sportscaster Rizzuto was a former star New York Yankee shortstop who began his broadcasting career with his *Phil Rizzuto's Sports Caravan (*NBC, 1952, CBS, 1960). Rizzuto enjoyed a long career as Yankee play-by-play broadcaster on local New York television that lasted late into the 1990s.

27143 *RKO Hour.* Leo Reisman's orchestra and French popular singer Irene Bordoni were featured on the musical variety program sponsored by RKO Motion Pictures (60 min., Tuesday, 10:30–11:30 P.M., NBC-Red, 1929).

27144 *RKO Program.* RKO also sponsored the late afternoon music program (30 min., Thursday, 5:00–5:30 P.M., NBC-Red, 1929).

27145 Roach, Hal. Newscaster (KTAR, Phoenix, AZ, 1939).

27146 Roach, J.F. Guitarist (WLW, Cincinnati, OH, 1922).

27147 Roach, Myrtis. Violinist who had previously been selected "Miss Omaha" in the Atlantic City Miss America contest (WOAW, Omaha, NE, 1925).

27148 *Road of Life.* Irna Phillips wrote the daytime serial that told the story of Dr. Jim Brent from his internship through his successful neuropsychiatric practice. Although there was a medical background, the focus was always on Brent's personal life and his romantic relationships. The program's cast included: Peggy Allenby, John Anthony, Betty Arnold, Barbara Becker, Frank Behrens, Viola Berwick, Jack Bivens, Sidney Breese, Muriel Bremner, Dale Burch, Roland Butterfield, Ralph Camargo, Angel Carey, Matt Crowley, Frank Dane, Charles Dingle, Jeanette Dowling, Robert Duane, Harry Elders, David Ellis, Ethel Everett, Louise Fitch, Dick Foster, Dorothy Francis, Vivian Fridell, Barbara Fuller, Betty Lou Gerson, Stanley Gordon, Robert Griffin, Ken Griffin, Bill Griffis, Gladys Heen, Percy Hemus, Arthur Hern, Dick Holland, Carlton KaDell, Arthur Kohl, Donald Kraatz, Eloise Kummer, John Larkin, Joe Latham, Elizabeth Lawrence, Grace Lenard, Abby Lewis, Helen Lewis, Bill Lipton, Janet Logan, Barbara Luddy, Don MacLaughlin, Charlotte Manson, Mary Mareen, Doris Mead, Marvin Miller, Bret Morrison, Angeline Orr, Effie Palmer, Eileen Palmer, Olive Parker, Eva Parnell, Mary Patton, Cornelius Peeples, Dick Post, Terry Rice, Doris Rich, Jack Roseleigh, Dorothy Sands, Nanette Sargent, Marion Shockley, Guy Sorel, Leslie Spears, Julie Stevens, Hugh Studebaker, Ray Suber, Lyle Sudrow, Hope Summers, Reese Taylor, Howard Teichmann, Russell Thorson, Helen Van Tuyl, Evelyn Varden, Beryl Vaughn, Vicki Vola, Sam Wanamaker, Willard Waterman, Sarajane Wells, Lillian White, Ethel Wilson, Joan Winters, Lesley Woods, Lee Young, Lois Zarley and Lawson Zerbe. The show was produced by Walt Ehgott, Fayette Krum, Kay Lane and Carl Wester. Stanley Davis, Gil Gibbons, Walter Gorman, Charles Schenck and Charles Urguhart were the directors. In addition to Irna Phillips the show was written by William Morwood and Howard Teichmann. Charles Paul was the organist. The announcers were George Bryan, Clayton "Bud" Collyer and Ron Rawson. An interesting fact is that the voice of the hospital loud speaker that opened each program by paging Dr. Brent belonged to actress Jeanette Dowling (NBC and CBS, 1937–1959).

27149 *Road to Danger.* Curley Bradley and Clarence Hartzell starred in the dramatic World War II juvenile adventure series that told the story of two heroic Army truck drivers, Stumpy and Cottonseed (30 min., NBC, 1943–1944).

27150 *Road to Fame.* Rocket Gasoline sponsored the Pacific Coast radio amateur hour. Frank Gill and Bill Demling co-hosted the show. The David Broekman Orchestra was also a program regular (30 min., Monday, 8:30–9:00 P.M. PST, KHJ, Los Angeles, CA, 1935).

27151 *Road to Romany.* Gypsy music was played by violinist Maurice Brann and Clarence Fuhrman's orchestra on the popular local music show (15 min., Tuesday, 11:45–12:00 midnight, WIP, Philadelphia, PA, 1937). A program by the same name was broadcast by NBC in 1935.

27152 *Roads That Move.* The Canadian Radio Commission wrote and produced the program for broadcast in the United States and Canada. They said the program "glorified the rivers of the world." Music by the Montreal Symphony Orchestra, entertaining dramatizations and informative narration made this an interesting show. One of the program's narrators was "Genghis Khan," who told of the historic events that occurred on the river Volga (30 min., Thursday, 10:00–10:30 P.M., NBC-Blue, 1934).

27153 *Roads to Romance.* The Associated Motor Company sponsored the dramatic educational series in which Jack and Ethyl Thurston traveled by automobile to various historic sites in the United States. For example, in early 1929 they visited west Seattle to learn the story of Christopher Columbus Simmons, born in that region in 1845 (30 min., Wednesday evenings, 8:00–8:30 P.M., NBC-Pacific Coast Network, 1929.

27154 *Roadshow.* A first of its kind, *Roadshow* was designed by NBC to be heard by those riding in cars. MC Bill Cullen played recorded music and introduced live entertainment. Singer Steve Lawrence and the Johnny Guarneiri (instrumental) Trio were program regulars (240 min., Saturday, 2:00–6:00 P.M., NBC, 1954).

27155 *Roadways of Romance.* Singers Vera Van and Jerry Cooper "traveled" the world on the romantic serial drama. They would stop long enough to sing love songs to each other accompanied by the Freddie Rich band (60 min., Thursday, 3:00–4:00 P.M., CBS, 1935).

27156 Roan, Marcia. COM-HE (WORZ, Orlando, FL, 1949).

27157 Roanoke Fiddle Band. Country-western band (WBAP, San Antonio, TX, 1924).

27158 Roark, C.A. Newscaster (KRLH, Midland, TX, 1941). DJ (KGY, Olympia, WA, 1947).

27159 Roasio, Vernonica. Harpist-soprano (WMAQ, Chicago, IL, 1927).

27160 Robator, Harry. Newscaster (WMAS, Springfield, MA, 1944–1945).

27161 Robb, Bill. DJ (*Robb and the Records*, WKIX, Columbia, SC, 1948).

27162 Robb, Harvey. Pianist (WGY, Schenectady, NY, 1925).

27163 Robb, Major. Newscaster (WSAL, Salisbury, MD, 1939). Sportscaster (WSAL, 1939).

27164 **Robbins, Bette.** DJ (*Robbins' Corner*, WCEM, Cambridge, MD, 1952).

27165 **Robbins, Bill.** Newscaster (WLW, Cincinnati, OH, 1938, WCKY, Cincinnati, OH, 1939–1942, 1948).

27166 **Robbins, Dorothy Lindsay.** Singer (WBZ, Springfield, MA, 1927).

27167 **Robbins, Fred.** Sportscaster (WITH, Baltimore, MD, 1942). DJ (*The Teentimers Club* and *1280 Club*, WOV, New York, NY, 1947–1949;*1280 Club*, WOV, 1950; *The Fred Robbins Show*, 60 min., Monday through Saturday, 11:00–12:00 midnight, WINS, New York, NY, 1950).

27168 **Robbins, Gerry [Jerry].** DJ (KTRF, Thief River Falls, MN, 1955–1956).

27169 **Robbins, Hayden.** Newscaster (*The Heart of the News*, WBBM, Chicago, IL, 1935).

27170 **Robbins, Joanne.** COM-HE (WAVZ, New Haven, CT, 1951).

27171 **Robbins, Max.** DJ (WIRC, Hickory, NC, 1956).

27172 **Robbins, Ruth.** Singer (W1XBX, Waterbury, CT, 1936; WMCA, New York, NY, 1936).

27173 **Robbins, Sam.** Leader (*Sam Robbins Orchestra*, instr. mus. prg., CBS, 1934).

27174 **Roberston, Ruth M.** COM-HE (WIPS, Ticonderoga, NY, 1957).

27175 ***Robert Benchley Show.*** Humorist and author Benchley had gained national popularity from his appearances in several MGM motion picture short features before he began his radio career. He was the host and resident wit on the variety show that also featured the Artie Shaw band and vocalist Dick Todd (NBC, 1938–1939).

27176 ***Robert Montgomery Speaking.*** Motion picture star Montgomery's transcribed commentary was made in London and covered a variety of topics both large and small (15 min., Thursday, 10:10–10:25 P.M., ABC, 1950).

27177 ***Robert Q. Lewis Show.*** Over the year, humorist Lewis' show had many names, but essentially all were similar in nature. Frequently broadcast on a sustaining basis, the program was first heard Saturday, 7:30–8:00 P.M. on NBC-Red. The following year Lewis appeared on the *Robert Q. Lewis Little Show*. Lewis, who formerly had been a DJ on WHN in New York City, was featured on the sustaining show. *Variety* praised him for his "high IQ humor." Florence Robinson, Jackson Beck and William Keene were also in the cast of the comedy show. Music was supplied by Milton Kaye's Orchestra (30 min., Saturday, 7:30–8:00 P.M., CBS, 1947, 1947). The following year *The Robert Q. Lewis Show* assumed a different format, day and time, but it still was broadcast on a sustaining basis. On this variety show, Lewis sang in addition to providing comedy bits. He was assisted by calypso singer, the Duke of Iron, the Mullen Sisters singing team and the music of Howard Smith's Orchestra (30 min., Sunday, 5:00–5:30 P.M., CBS, 1948). A different format was used for *Robert Q's Waxworks*. Here Lewis became a DJ (15 min., Monday through Friday, 7:30–7:45 P.M., CBS, 1951). Not long after, however, even the format of *Robert Q's Waxworks* was slightly changed. On the show, Lewis in addition to being a DJ also conducted interviews with such guests as Eddie Fisher and Moondog (30 min., Sunday, 10:00–10:30 P.M., CBS, 1953). In 1956, Robert Q. once again acted as host on his *Robert Q. Lewis Show*. On the program, comedian Lewis hosted a weekday variety show that featured singers Judy Johnson and Richard Hayes singing with Ray Bloch's orchestra. The show was written by Harvey Bullock and Ray Allen. The producer and director was Bruno Zirato, Jr. (30 min., Monday through Friday, 8:00–8:30 P.M., CBS, 1956).

27178 ***Robert Shaw Chorale.*** Shaw directed an excellent 32-voice mixed choir on the entertaining music show sponsored by Standard Brands. Kenneth Banghart was the announcer (30 min., Sunday, 8:00–8:30 P.M., NBC, 1948).

27179 **Roberts, Albert.** Baritone (WSM, Nashville, TN, 1928–1929).

27180 **Roberts, Art.** DJ (WLS, Chicago, IL, 1960).

27181 **Roberts, Beep.** DJ (*Platter Chatter*, WKAB, Mobile, AL, 1947).

27182 **Roberts, Bill.** Old-time fiddler (WLAC, Nashville, TN, 1929).

27183 **Roberts, Bill.** Newscaster (WMT, Cedar Rapids, IA, 1948).

27184 **Roberts, Bob.** DJ (*The Musical Score Board*, WSID, Baltimore, MD, 1947).

27185 **Roberts, Burton.** Leader (*Burton Roberts Orchestra*, instr. mus. prg., WCAU, Philadelphia, PA, 1934).

27186 **Roberts, Charles.** Newscaster (KVOR, Colorado Springs, CO, 1937).

27187 **Roberts, Clete.** News analyst (KGER, Long Beach, CA, 1938; KMPC, Beverly Hills, CA, 1940–1941; NBC-Blue, 1944–1945; KECA, Los Angeles, CA, 1945; *Clete Roberts Reports*, KMPC, 1947).

27188 **Roberts, Cliff.** Announcer-DJ Roberts in the late 1940s conducted a popular classical music program (*Music of the Masters*, WHA, Madison, WI, 1940s).

27189 **Roberts, Curtis.** Actor Roberts was in the cast of *Ma Perkins*.

27190 **Roberts, Dave.** Newscaster (KDYL, Salt Lake City, UT, 1940; KMPC, Los Angeles, CA, 1945).

27191 **Roberts, Donald "Don."** Newscaster (KTMS, Santa Barbara, CA, 1945; *12:00 News*, KDB, Santa Barbara, CA, 1947). Sportscaster (*The Sportlight*, KDB, 1948).

27192 **Roberts, Ed.** Newscaster (WCBD, Chicago, IL, 1938).

27193 **Roberts, Ford.** DJ (*Hawkeye Hits*, WMT, Cedar Rapids, IA, 1954–1956).

27194 **Roberts, Frank.** Staff tenor (WGN, Chicago, IL, 1928). Roberts was introduced as "Handsome Frank Roberts."

27195 **Roberts, Gail.** Singer (WDRC, Hartford, CT, 1936–1937).

27196 **Roberts, Helen.** Contralto (KOA, Denver, CO, 1925).

27197 **Roberts, Helen.** COM-HE (WMT, Grand Rapids, IA, 1951–1954).

27198 **Roberts, Helen.** COM-HE (WNRC, New Rochelle, NY, 1955).

27199 **Roberts, Helen Buster.** Organist (WBAP, Fort Worth, TX, 1928–1929).

27200 **Roberts, Herb.** Sportscaster (*Sports Roundup*, WHAR, Clarksburg, WV, 1949).

27201 **Roberts, (Mrs.) Henry.** Pianist (KWSC, Pullman, WA, 1927).

27202 **Roberts, Hope LaBarr.** Commentator (*A Woman Looks at the World*, WCAU, Philadelphia, PA, 1933).

27203 **Roberts, Howdy.** DJ, *Musical Clock*, WMT, Cedar Rapids, IA, 1948–1954).

27204 **Roberts, Howie.** DJ (WCFL, Chicago, IL, 1957).

27205 **Roberts, Ingham S.** Newscaster (KGBS, Harlingen, TX, 1942). Sportscaster (KGBS, 1942).

27206 **Roberts, Jack.** Sportscaster (*Off the Sports Wire*, WBIS, Bristol, CT, 1955).

27207 **Roberts, Jay.** DJ (*Night Flight*, WJR, Detroit, MI, 1960).

27208 **Roberts, Juanita.** COM-HE (KLVC, Leadville, CO, 1956).

27209 **Roberts, Jerry.** DJ (WAAT, Newark, NJ, 1947).

27210 **Roberts, Joe.** Banjoist Roberts played in the Vincent Lopez Orchestra (WEAF, New York, NY, 1929).

27211 **Roberts, Joe.** DJ (*Columbia Record Roundup*, KOMA, Oklahoma City, OK, 1947; *Western Jamboree*, KOMA, 1948–1950; KRRV, Sherman, TX, 1955; WFAA, Dallas, TX, 1957).

27212 **Roberts, John.** Newscaster (KIT, Yakima, WA, 1938).

27213 **Roberts, Ken.** DJ (*Tops in Pops*, WMGM, New York, NY, 1952). Before working as a DJ in 1952, Roberts was one of the best and busiest network announcers. He performed announcing chores on such shows as *Al Pearce and His Gang*; *Baby Snooks*; *Easy Aces*, *Grand Central Station*, *It Pays to be Ignorant*; *Joyce Jordan, Girl Interne*, *Life of Mary Sothern*, *The Shadow* and *This Is Nora Drake*.

In his distinguished radio career, Roberts played the role of "Cokie" on *Easy Aces* and served as the quizmaster on the *Quick as a Flash* program. His television appearances included work as host of the *Ladies Before Gentlemen* panel show (Dumont TV, 1951) and with Melvyn Douglas on the *Your Big Moment* audience participation show (Dumont TV, 1953). Roberts was one of the golden voiced announcers of American radio's greatest decades.

27214 **Roberts, Kenneth L.** Sportscaster (KLVC, Leadville, CO, 1956).

27215 **Roberts, Larry.** Sportscaster (*Sports Summary*, WHB, Kansas City, MO, 1948).

27216 **Roberts, Leon.** Newscaster (WJTN, Jamestown, NY, 1944).

27217 **Roberts, Liz.** COM-HE (KCIJ, Shreveport, LA, 1951).

27218 **Roberts, [Robert], Lois.** COM-HE (WFNC, Fayetteville, NC, 1954).

27219 **Roberts, Lyle.** Clarinetist (KWTC, Santa Ana, CA, 1928). *See* **KWTC Trio**.

27220 **Roberts, Lynn [Lyn].** COM-HE (WWOD, Lynchburg, VA, 1949).

27221 **Roberts, Marion.** COM-HE (WRGB, Schenectady, NY, 1954).

27222 **Roberts, Marty.** DJ (*Jamboree* and *Night Riders*, WCKY, Cincinnati, OH, 1951–1953).

27223 **Roberts, Marl L.** Commentator (*Around the World of Events.*)

27224 **Roberts, Matt.** DJ (WWSC, Glens Falls, NY, 1956).

27225 **Roberts, Morgan.** DJ (*1380 Club*, KSWO, Lawton, OK, 1947).

27226 **Roberts, Paul.** Tenor (KFI, Los Angeles, CA, 1926). Announcer (KFI, 1927).

27227 **Roberts, Paul.** Director Roberts directed *Thanks for Tomorrow.*

27228 **Roberts, (Reverend) Paul.** Announcer (KFDD, Boise, ID, 1927).

27229 **Roberts, Paul.** DJ (*Million Dollar Party*, WFBM, Indianapolis, IN, 1948; *Rhythm at Random*, WFBM, 1950).

27230 **Roberts, Rae Potter.** Contralto (WHAM, Rochester, NY, 1929).

27231 **Roberts, Roy.** DJ (WSMB, New Orleans, LA, 1956).

27232 **Roberts, Sandra.** Blues singer (WLW, Cincinnati, OH, 1934).

27233 **Roberts, Sid.** DJ (WJJD, Chicago, IL, 1957).

27234 **Roberts, Stan.** Sportscaster (WARK, Hagerstown, MD, 1954. DJ (WTOW, Towson, MD, 1955).

27235 **Roberts, Warren.** DJ (*Break O' Day* and *Hillbilly Coffee Club*, WEAS, Atlanta, GA, 1948–1955).

27236 **Roberts, Zella.** Harpist (WEAO, Columbus, OH, 1925).

27237 **Roberts Banjo Club.** Amateur instrumental club (WPJ, Philadelphia, PA, 1923).

27238 **Roberts Golden State Band.** Popular radio band (KNX, Los Angeles, CA, 1926).

27239 **Robertson, Alexander Campbell "Eck."** Renowned Texas fiddler Robertson was named for a famous Disciples of Christ minister. He was famous throughout the southwest for continually winning old-time fiddlers' contests long before he made any phonograph records for Victor. When he began broadcasting in 1923 (WBAP, San Antonio, TX), Robertson often played the selections he had recorded for Victor: "Sallie Gooden" and "The Arkansas Traveler."

27240 **Robertson, Arnold.** Actor Robertson was in the cast of *Sally of the Movies* and *This Is Nora Drake.*

27241 **Robertson, B.G.** Newscaster (KTBS, Shreveport, LA, 1940).

27242 **Robertson, Bob.** DJ (*Tune Shop*, WBHF, Cartersville, GA, 1947).

27243 **Robertson, Bruce.** Newscaster (KOAM, Pittsburg, KS, 1939–1940). Sportscaster (KOAM, 1940).

27244 **Robertson, H.M.** Robertson broadcast talks on dogs (KHJ, Los Angeles, CA, 1925).

27245 **Robertson, Jim.** Newscaster (WCLO, Janesville, WI, 1942). Sportscaster (WOKW, Sturgeon Bay, WI, 1952).

27246 **Robertson, Lonnie.** Leader (Lonnie Robertson's Greenback Old Time Fiddlers, KFEQ, St. Joseph, MO, 1929).

27247 **Robertson, Nellie E.** Contralto (WOC, Davenport, IA, 1923).

27248 **Robertson, Randall.** Sportscaster (WEW, St. Louis, MO, 1942).

27249 **Robertson, Ruth M.** COM-HE (WENT, Gloverville, NY, 1954; WIPS, Ticonderoga, NY, 1956–1957).

27250 **Robertson, Shirley.** COM-HE (WKPT, Kingsport, TN, 1954).

27251 **Robertson, T. A.** Announcer (WJSV, Mt. Vernon Hills, VA, 1925).

27252 **Robertson, Ted.** Producer-director Robertson worked on *American Women* (producer-director), *First Line* (producer-director), *Service to the Front* (producer-director) and *Straight Arrow* (director).

27253 **Robertson, Trafton.** DJ (*Sunrise Serenade*, WTAR, Norfolk, VA, 1947–1950).

27254 ***Robertson Hillbilly Band.*** CW mus. prg. (WBT, Charlotte, NC, 1939).

27255 **Robeson, Paul.** Distinguished baritone Robeson broadcast a "program of Negro spirituals" (WJZ, New York, NY, 1926). A graduate of Rutgers University, where he was a star football player, Robeson also enjoyed a successful motion picture career, starring in such films as *Emperor Jones.*

27256 **Robey, Harry.** Sportscaster (*Sports Whirl*, KHUB, Watsonville, CA, 1948).

27257 **Robillard, F.** Sportscaster (WSYB, Rutland, VT, 1960).

27258 **Robillard, Marjorie.** Pianist (KJR, Seattle, WA, 1929).

27259 **Robin, Bob.** DJ (WHB, Kansas City, MO, 1957).

27260 **Robin, Donna.** Pianist (WHEC, Rochester, NY, 1927).

27261 **Robin, Mildred.** Actress Robin was in the cast of the *Doc Barclay's Daughter daytime serial drama.*

27262 **Robin, Rockin'.** DJ (*Rock 'N' Roll Kingdom*, Philadelphia, PA, 1960).

27263 ***Robin Hood Dell Concerts.*** Jose Iturbi conducted the orchestra on this program of classic music. A typical 1935 program contained the following: Tchaikowsky's "Sixth Symphony," Richard Wagner's "Prelude and Liebstod" from *Tristam and Isolde* and the "Overture" to *Die Meistersinger* (120 minutes, Saturday, 8:30–10:30 P.M., CBS, 1934).

27264 **Robinson, Ada.** Soprano (WGY, Schenectady, NY, 1934).

27265 **Robinson, Anna [Ann].** Soprano Robinson was featured on the *Roxy and His Gang* program (NBC, New York, NY, 1927).

27266 **Robinson, Arthur.** Newscaster (WHKC, Columbus, OH, 1942, 1945).

27267 **Robinson, Bartlett "Bart."** Actor Robinson appeared on *Backstage Wife*, *Ellen Randolph*, *Perry Mason* (title role), *Portia Faces Life*, *Pretty Kitty Kelly*, *Romance of Helen Trent*, *Second Mrs. Burton*, *Valiant Lady*, *Woman of America* and *Young Dr. Malone.*

27268 **Robinson, Bert.** Sportscaster (*Time for Sports*, WBET, Brockton, MA, 1949).

27269 **Robinson, Betty.** COM-HE (WYCL, York, SC, 1960).

27270 **Robinson, Blanche.** COM-HE (WOCB, West Yarmouth, MA, 1951–1954).

27271 **Robinson, Blanche E.** Pianist (WQJ, Chicago, IL, 1925).

27272 **Robinson, Bob.** Baritone and talented tap-dancer (WIBW, Topeka, KS, 1929).

27273 **Robinson, Brad.** Sportscaster (WCCO, Minneapolis–St. Paul, MN, 1933).

27274 **Robinson, C.C.** "Old time fiddler" (WOC, Davenport, IA, 1928–1929).

27275 **Robinson, Carl.** Sportscaster (*The World of Sports*, WBCC, Bethesda, MD, 1950).

27276 **Robinson, Charles.** Basso (WEAF, New York, NY, 1926; the *Philco Hour of Theater Memories*, NBC-Blue, New York, NY, 1927–1931 and the *National Musical Comedy Troupe*, NBC-Red, New York, NY, 1928).

27277 **Robinson, Don.** Sportscaster (*Saturday Sportscope*, KIXL, Dallas, TX, 1950).

27278 **Robinson, Dorothy "Dottie" Baker.** COM-HE (WENE, Binghampton, NY, 1956–1957).

27279 **Robinson, Edward G.** Movie star Robinson starred on the *Big Town* program.

27280 **Robinson, Elsie.** Talked on various human relations'(psychology) topics (KFRC, San Francisco, CA, 1925).

27281 **Robinson, Florence.** Actress Robinson appeared on the daytime serial programs *Nona from Nowhere*, *Our Gal Sunday* and *The Romance of Helen Trent.*

27282 **Robinson, Gene.** DJ (*Dancing Party*, WCHS, Charleston, WV, 1948).

27283 **Robinson, Gene.** DJ (WDAN, Danville, IL, 1948).

27284 **Robinson, (Major) George D.** Newscaster (WSUN, St. Petersburg, FL, 1938–1945; WCOA, Pensacola, FL, 1946).

27285 **Robinson, H.L.** Newscaster (KGNC, Amarillo, TX, 1944–1945).

27286 **Robinson, Harold.** Newscaster (WMAN, Mansfield, OH, 1945).

27287 **Robinson, Harry.** Sportscaster and play-by-play sports events (KDSJ, Deadwood, SD, 1947).

27288 **Robinson, Harry.** Actor Robinson was in the cast of *A Woman of Courage.*

27289 **Robinson, Helen.** COM-HE (WAVP, Avon Park, FL, 1957).

27290 **Robinson, Helen Rumsey.** Reader (KOA, Denver, CO, 1926).

27291 **Robinson, (Mrs.) Hester.** Reader (WCBD, Zion, IL, 1923).

27292 **Robinson, Irving B.** Assistant announcer (WNAC, Boston, MA, 1923).

27293 **Robinson, Jackie.** Sportscaster (WMCA, New York, NY, 1948). Robinson, a Hall of Fame baseball star, was the first Black to play major league baseball.

27294 **Robinson, Jane.** Pianist who managed the Robinson Piano Studios (KLCN, Blytheville, AR, 1928).

27295 **Robinson, Jeanne (Kitty Kay).** COM-HE (*Kitty Kay*, WRBL, Columbus, GA, 1949).

27296 **Robinson, Jesse.** Announcer-director (WEHS, Evanston, IL, 1929).

27297 **Robinson, (Miss) Jessie.** Studio director, actress and announcer (WEHS, Chicago, IL, 1926–1929).

27298 **Robinson, Jim.** Sportscaster (*The World of Sports*, KWBE, Beatrice, NE, 1952).

27299 **Robinson, Kathleen.** Singer (WGBS, New York, NY, 1927).

27300 **Robinson, Katherine [Kathryn /Catherine].** Violinist (KWSC, Pullman, WA, 1925–1926).

27301 **Robinson, Katherine.** Pianist (KFGA, Seattle, WA, 1924).

27302 **Robinson, Ken.** Newscaster (WENR, Chicago, IL, 1933).

27303 **Robinson, Ken.** Writer Robinson wrote *Claudia* and *Dan Harding's Wife.*

27304 **Robinson, (Mrs.) L.** COM-HE (KTBC, Austin, TX, 1954).

27305 **Robinson, Lawrence "Larry."** Actor Robinson appeared on *Coast-to-Coast on a Bus, Joyce Jordan, Girl Interne, Portia Faces Life, The Second Mrs. Burton* and *Woman of Courage.*

27306 **Robinson, Lloyd.** Bass (KFAB, Beaumont, TX, 1928–1929).

27307 **Robinson, Marion Brooks.** COM-HE (WFLS, Fredericksburg, VA, 1960).

27308 **Robinson, Martha Pope.** Reader (WHAS, Louisville, KY, 1925).

27309 **Robinson, Max E.** Newscaster and announcer (WSBA, York, PA, 1942). Sportscaster (*Sports Report*, WJTN, Jamestown, NY, 1951–1953; *Sports Roundup*, WJTN, 1954; *Reports on Sports*, WJTN, 1955; *Sports Roundup*, WJTN, 1960).

27310 **Robinson, May.** Soprano (WJZ, New York, NY, 1928).

27311 **Robinson, Pat.** Broadcast sports news (WOR, Newark, NJ, 1925).

27312 **Robinson, Prescott.** Newscaster (WOR, New York, NY, 1941–1942, 1944–1948).

27313 **Robinson, R.** Newscaster (WKAT, Miami, FL, 1946).

27314 **Robinson, Rand.** Bass (KFWM, Oakland, CA, 1921).

27315 **Robinson, Roger.** Baritone (*Roger Robinson*, vcl. mus. prg., WGN, Chicago, IL, 1934).

27316 **Robinson, Sally.** COM-HE (KVOU, Uvalde, TX, 1956).

27317 **Robinson, Sol.** Sportscaster (*Sports Roundup*, WLAD, Danbury, CT, 1955).

27318 **Robinson, Tom.** Newscaster (KBWD, Brownwood, TX, 1941). DJ (*Housewives Club*, KTEM, Temple, TX, 1950).

27319 **Robinson, Valmae.** COM-HE (KPLC, Lake Charles, LA, 1954).

27320 **Robinson, Verba.** Singer Robinson was a member of the Wynken, Blynken and Nod vocal trio (KDYL, Salt Lake City, UT, 1954).

27321 **Robinson, Warner.** DJ (*Best by Request, Birthday Club* and *Request by Telephone*, KVOW, Littlefield, TX, 1947).

27322 **Robinson, Wayne.** Newscaster (WKZO, Kalamazoo–Grand Rapids, IA, 1942).

27323 **Robinson III, Wip.** Newscaster (WDZ, Tuscola, IL, 1940; WSVA, Harrisonburg, VA, 1942; *Wip Robinson and the News*, WVVW, Fairmont, WV, 1948). DJ (WSVA, 1956).

27324 ***Robinson Caruso, Jr.*** Dr. Brown's Cel-Ray soft drink sponsored this exciting adventure series for children. It told the story of some children shipwrecked on a deserted island. Lester Jay, Toni Gilman and Michael O'Day were in the cast (15 min., Tuesday, 5:30–5:45 P.M., WHN, New York, NY, 1938).

27325 **Robischon, James "Jim."** Sportscaster (KGVO, Missoula, MO, 1949). DJ (KXLL, Missoula, MO, 1954).

27326 **Robischon, Tom.** Newscaster (KGEZ, Kalispell, MT, 1941). DJ (*Platter Chatter*, KXLQ, Bozeman, MT, 1947). Sportscaster (KXLQ, 1947).

27327 **Robison, Carson.** Country music singer-composer Robison was born August 4, 1890. He was originally a song plugger, before becoming a vaudeville performer. He gained fame as a radio singer specializing in old time and country songs. When he appeared on WDAF (Kansas City, MO, 1922), Wendell Hall, the "Red-Header Music Maker," heard him and invited him to come to New York. Robison appeared there on the *Eveready Hour* many times (NBC-Red, 1924–1928) and the *Dutch Masters Minstrels* (NBC-Blue, 1928–1930).

He began recording for Victor in 1924. From 1925 to 1928, he worked with Vernon Dahlhart. The collaboration with Dahlhart produced such best selling records as "The John T. Scopes Trial," "Golden Slippers," and "Lucky Lindy [Lindbergh]." A prolific songwriter, Robison's songs included, "Way Out West in Kansas," "Wreck of the Number Nine," and "Carry Me Back to the Lone Prairie." His long radio career extended into the following two decades (*Carson Robison*, CW mus. prg., WHAM, Rochester, NY, 1937; WLW, Cincinnati, OH, 1938; *Carson Robison's Buckaroos*, CW mus. prg., WLW, 1939–1940).

27328 **Robison, Willard.** Tenor-composer (*Maxwell Coffee Hour*,1928). Leader (*Willard Robison Orchestra*, instr. mus. prg., WOR, Newark, NJ, 1934; NBC, 1934–1936).

27329 **Robson, May.** Actress Robson starred on the *Lady of Millions* dramatic program.

27330 **Robson, William N.** Producer-director-writer Robson worked on *Big Town* (director), *Columbia Workshop* (producer), *Escape* (producer-director), *Man Called X* (director), *Prudential Family Hour* (writer) and *Radio Reader's Digest* (writer).

27331 **Roby, Clifton Van.** Sportscaster (*Sports Roundup*, WCUM, Cumberland, MD, 1954).

27332 **Roby, Max.** Newscaster (KSL, Salt Lake City, UT, 1947).

27333 **Roby, Vic.** Newscaster (KOA, Denver, CO, 1944).

27334 **Robyn, Alfred H.** Robyn broadcast piano lessons (WGBS, New York, NY, 1925).

27335 **Robyn, "Wee Willie."** Veteran radio tenor Robyn was first heard on the *Roxy and His Gang* program (NBC, 1927–1928) in the late 1920's. Robyn was also active in the following decade (*Wee Willie Robyn*, vcl. mus. prg., CBS, 1931; *Venida Program*, CBS, 1932).

27336 **Rocap, Billy.** Sportscaster Rocap conducted a program called *Intimate Talks on Current Sports of the Day* (WIP, Philadelphia, PA, 1925).

27337 **Roche, V.B.** Baritone (WOC, Davenport, IA, 1924).

27338 **Roche, William.** Newscaster (WFBR, Baltimore, MD, 1944).

27339 **Rochelie, Tommy.** DJ (*Harlem at Eight*, KREL, Baytown, TX, 1948).

27340 **Rochelle, Dorothy.** Singer (WMCA, New York, NY, 1937; NBC, 1939).

27341 **Rochester, Melvin.** DJ (*1450 Club*, KDSJ, Deadwood, SD, 1947).

27342 ***Rochester Civic Orchestra.*** Instr. mus. prg. (NBC-Blue, 1938–1939).

27343 **Rochester Philharmonic Orchestra.** Symphonic music group (WHAM, Rochester, NY, 1926; *The Rochester Philharmonic Orchestra*, instr. mus. prg., 60 min., Friday, 3:15–4:15 P.M., NBC-Blue, 1929).

27344 **Rochester String Quartet.** Classical music group consisting of Allison MacKown, cello; Cecil Van Hosen, 1st violin; Abram Boone, 2nd violin; and Arthur Stillman, viola (WHAM, Rochester, NY, 1923–1930). In 1930, the *Rochester String Quartet* with the same personnel were given their own program on WHAM.

27345 ***Rochester Symphony Orchestra.*** The Rochester Symphony Orchestra broadcast a weekly program of symphonic music sponsored by the Stromberg-Carlson Radio Company (60 min., Monday, 10:00–10:30 P.M., NBC-Blue, 1929).

27346 **Rochet, Julia.** Soprano (WGBS, New York, NY, 1928).

27347 **Rochon, Lonnie.** DJ (*The Bee-Hive*, KNUZ, Houston, TX, 1948–1953). Rochon, a Louisiana Cajun, was Houston's first black DJ. He specialized in playing rhythm and blues.

27348 **Rochow, Gerrias.** COM-HE (WOKX, Keokuk, IA, 1951).

27349 **Rock, Alan.** DJ (WOTW, Nashua, NH, 1948).

27350 **Rock, Jean Shoulders.** COM-HE (WLOCk, Munfordville, KY, 1960).

27351 **Rock, Joan.** COM-HE (*Jean Rock's Cooking School*, WCCO, Minneapolis, MN, 1934).

27352 **(The) Rock and Roll Hall of Fame and Museum.** Located at One Key Plaza in Cleveland, Ohio, the Rock and Roll Hall of Fame and Museum is dedicated to the preservation of rock music's heritage, to trace its origin and development and honor the men and women who made unique contributions to it. The museum traces rock and roll's birth in the 1950s, its rapid growth in the following decades and its influences on American life and culture. The objective is to be the definitive source for the preservation, interpretation and celebration of the history of rock and roll.

James Henke, music writer, historian and former music editor of *Rolling Stone,* is the Deputy Director and Curator of the museum. David G. Hintz is the museum's Radio Coordinator. An example of the museum's exhibit, "Dedicated to the One I Love," presented April, 1998, honored DJs for their contribution to rock and roll. The exhibit illustrated the work of the following 15 DJs who were active in 1960 and prior years:

Paul Berlin. After being fired for falling asleep on the air, Paul Berlin moved to KNUZ (Houston, TX) in 1950. Always active as a rock and roll DJ, he brought many live shows to Houston, featuring such performers as Jerry Lee Lewis, Chuck Berry and Fats Domino. In 1973, Berlin moved to KQUE (Houston, TX), where he remains on the air.

Dick "The Screamer" Biondi. Legendary rock and roll DJ Biondi started as a sportscaster in the 1940s. In 1950 when he moved to WCBA (Corning, NY), he lasted only three months as a DJ before being fired. His next job at KSYL (Alexandria, LA) was where he began playing rock and roll records. Biondi also worked at WSBA (York, PA) and WJET (Erie, PA), before beginning a four-year run at WHOT (Youngstown, OH). After moving to WKBW (Buffalo, NY), Biondi was fired for playing an Elvis Presley record. This led him to take a job at WLS (Chicago, IL), where he became a DJ legend.

Jerry "The Greeter" Blavat. DJ Blavat began his broadcasting career with a talk show on WCAM (Camden, NJ). Later, in the 1960s when he began playing rock and roll records, he became a great Philadelphia favorite. Blavat is currently on the air on WSSJ (Philadelphia, PA).

Porky "Pork the Tork" Chedwick. Famous as a "white DJ" who played "race records" on his rhythm and blues program on WHOD (Homestead, PA) in 1949. Chedwick, "The Blonde Thunder with the Record Thunder," played "dusky" records for many years on WHOD, which later became WAMO. Chedwick's familiar opening was: "It's the Daddio of the Raddio, your Platter Pushing Papa."

Max Floyd. DJ Max Floyd got his first job in 1957 on KCAR (Clarksville, TX). He worked for several Texas stations until 1961, when he entered military service. He returned to Texas radio in 1965, where he enjoyed great listener popularity.

Jack "The Rapper" Gibson. Distinguished Black DJ Gibson began his broadcasting career as an actor in the "first Black soap opera" on Chicago radio. After beginning work as a DJ at WERD (Atlanta, GA), he worked from 1951–1962 at WLOU (Louisville, KY), WMBM (Miami, FL), WCIN (Cincinnati, OH) and WABQ (Cleveland, OH). In 1962, Gibson left radio to enter the record business at Motown, Decca and Stax. *See* **Gibson, Jack.**

Arnie "Woo Woo" Ginsburg. Arnie Ginsburg was a Boston radio fixture for 40 years. Although his DJ work began in 1956 at WBOS (Boston, MA), he is best known for his 1957–1966 programs at WMEX (Boston, MA). He gained his nickname when one of his sponsors offered a two-for-one special for anyone who came into his shop and said, "Woo Woo sent me."

Dan Ingram. Using catch phrases like "Hi Kemosabe" and "Roll Your Bod," Ingram was known as "The Thinking Man's DJ" and the "only jock with a vocabulary." After beginning his radio career at WNRC (New Rochelle, NY), WALK (Patchogue, NY) and WNHC (New Haven, CT), Ingram moved in 1959 to KBOX (Dallas, TX). A short time later he moved to WIL (St. Louis, MO). Ingram gained his greatest fame for his work at WABC (New York, NY).

Hal Jackson. Jackson's long and varied career began when he broadcast Howard University's baseball games. Starting as a sportscaster before becoming a DJ, he worked at WOOK (Washington, DC), WINX (Washington, DC), WSID (Baltimore, MD) and WANN (Annapolis, MD). During the 1950s, Jackson had DJ shows on three different New York area stations broadcasting *simultaneously* on WMCA (New York, NY), WABC (New York, NY) and WNJR (Newark, NJ). Jackson went on to become a successful broadcast executive and station owner.

Art Laboe. After working in the 1940s at stations in Reno, NV; Pomona, CA; Palm Springs, CA; and San Francisco, CA, Laboe became a prominent rock and roll DJ in 1955 at KXLA (Los Angeles, CA). He is still a successful performer and broadcasting executive.

Hy "Hyski" Lit. Affectionately known as "Hyski," Lit has been a popular DJ on Philadelphia radio for more than 40 years. During the early 1950s, Lit began working at WHAT (Philadelphia, PA), before moving on to WRCV (Philadelphia, PA). When he moved to WIBG (Philadelphia, PA), his career boomed and he emceed shows with Elvis, the Beatles and the Rolling Stones. He opened his programs this way: "Hy ski-o-roomie-mcvouty-o-zoot, the potentate from the keystone, the garden and the diamond state. Going uptown, downtown, round town, crosstown. For all my beats, beards and Buddhist cats ... Hyski's on the scene with the record machine."

Bruce "Cousin Brucie" Morrow. A Brooklyn, NY, native, "Cousin Brucie" began his career at WINS (New York, NY) in 1959. After working for a short time in Miami, FL, Morrow returned to New York to work at WABC. He continues as a successful broadcasting executive and performer.

Pat O'Day. From the beginning of his career, O'Day was both a popular DJ and successful broadcasting executive. After first working at KVAS (Astoria, OR) in 1956, he moved on to stations KLOG (Kelso, WA), KLOQ (Yakima, WA) and KAYO (Seattle, WA), before beginning a long career at KJR (Seattle, WA). At KJR, O'Day worked as DJ, Program Director, Music Director and General Manager. He continues today as a station owner and broadcast consultant.

Martha Jean "The Queen" Steinberg. After starting her broadcasting career in 1954 at WDIA (Memphis, TN), Steinberg became a popular DJ and versatile broadcaster. Today, she is VP and Program Director at WQBH (Detroit, MI), whose call letters, Steinberg says, stands for "Bring the Queen Back Home." *See* **Steinberg, Martha Jean.**

Rufus "Bear Cat" Thomas. "Bear Cat" Thomas met his mentor, Nat D. Williams, while in high school in Memphis, TN. Williams eventually hired him to replace DJ B.B. King in 1950 at WDIA (Memphis, TN). Both as performer and DJ, Thomas enjoyed great success. He opened his early show in this way: "I'm young and loose and full of juice. I got the goose, so what's the use?" Thomas' rhythm-and-blues hit records include "Walking the Dog," "The Funky Chicken" and "The Push and the Pull." After more than 40 years, Thomas is still on the air at WDIA. *See* **Thomas, Rufus** *and* **Williams, Nat D.**

27353 ***Rock Creek Rangers and Sunshine Sue.*** The CW music group consisted of the Rangers who were John, George and Tom Workman and Sunshine Sue, who was Mrs. John Workman (*Rock Creek Rangers and Sunshine Sue*, WLS, Chicago, IL, 1936). The following year the group moved to Shenandoah, IA, where they broadcast as the *Rock Creek Wranglers and Sunshine Sue* (KMA, Shenandoah, IA, 1937).

27354 **Rock Ridge Ramblers.** CW music group (WMT, Cedar Rapids–Waterloo, IA, 1935).

27355 ***Rock-a-bye Dudley.*** By 1948 the airwaves were filled with the talk and recorded music of many talented DJ's, and popular Dick Dudley was one of the busiest (WNBC, New York, NY, 1948).

27356 **(The) Rock-A-Bye Lady.** The talented singer, not otherwise identified, broadcast a weekly program of popular songs (30 min., Friday, 7:30–8:00 P.M., NBC-Blue, 1927).

27357 **Rockdashel, Rock.** DJ (*Mail Train*, WISV, Viroqua, WI, 1960).

27358 **Rocke, Louis.** DJ (*Risin' with Rocke*, WCAX, Burlington, VT, 1948–1950).

27359 **Rockefeller, John D.** Millionaire industrialist Rockefeller often delivered talks on current affairs on the *Collier Hour* program (NBC, 1929).

27360 **Rockenbach, Hiram Hilton.** Popular radio saxophonist Rockenbach toured the central states in 1926, broadcasting from different radio stations approximately four nights a week.

27361 **Rockhold, Joe.** Newscaster (WSPD, Toledo, OH, 1937).

27362 **Rockwell, Al.** DJ (*Al Rockwell Show*, KRNT, Des Moines, IA, 1948–1954).

27363 **Rockwell, Beulah.** Violinist Rockwell was featured regularly on *The Hoot Owls* program (KGW, Portland, OR, 1924–1925).

27364 **Rockwell, Ronald J.** Announcer (WNAL, Omaha, NE, 1926–1927).

27365 **Rockwell, Reverend W.T.** Announcer (KFAU, Boise, ID, 1927).

27366 **Rockwood, Lynn.** Sportscaster (KIXX, Provo, UT, 1954; KOVO, Provo, UT, 1960).

27367 ***Rocky Austin—The Song Rambler of WJAY.*** Austin was a popular Cleveland radio singer (WJAY, Cleveland, OH, 1930).

27368 ***Rocky Fortune.*** *Variety* said that Frank Sinatra played a skinny Sam Spade on the transcribed series that dramatized the adventures of a private eye. Carl Betz, Betty Garde, Hollis Irving, Leon Janney and Charlotte Munson were in the cast of the entertaining mystery show, written by George Lefferts and directed by David Harmon (25 min., Tuesday, 9:35–10:00 P.M., NBC, 1953).

27369 ***Rocky Jordan.*** George Raft played the title role of a Cairo cafe owner with his clipped monotone speech on the show sponsored by Del Monte foods. Jordan always seemed to get involved in one nefarious adventure or another each week. Larry Dobkin, Paul Frees, Lou Krugman, Gerald Mohr and Doris Singleton were also in the cast. Adrian Gendet and Larry Roman wrote the program that was produced and directed by Cliff Howells. Richard Aurandt was the music director (30 min., Wednesday, 8:00–8:30 P.M., CBS, 1951). The weekly program was a re-worked version of *A Man Called Jordan*, a 15-minute daily dramatic serial that had starred Jack Moyles in the title role. When the program went on the weekly national network schedule, motion picture star Raft assumed the title role. The show opened with a voice intoning: "Time now for *Rocky Jordan*. Not far from the Mosque Sultan Hussan in Cairo, stands the Cafe Tambourine run by Rocky Jordan. The Cafe Tambourine, crowded with forgotten men, is alive with the babble of many languages. For this is Cairo, where modern adventure and intrigue unfolds. Today's adventure—"The Lady from Tangier" (30 min., CBS, July 4, 1950).

27370 **Rodda, John.** Tenor (WDBO, Orlando, FL, 1929).

27371 **Rodda, Wally.** Newscaster (WKZO, Kalamazoo, MI, 1938).

27372 **Rodda, Walt.** DJ (*Rat Race*, WKAT, Miami Beach, FL, 1947).

27373 **Roddy, Dave.** DJ (*Bama Beat*, WYDE, Birmingham, AL, 1960).

27374 **Roddy, Ed.** Newscaster (KBIX, Muskogee, OK, 1941). Sportscaster (KBIX, 1941).

27375 **Roddy, Joe.** DJ (KTBC, Austin, TX, 1947; *Coffee Time*, KTBC, 1948; *Midway of Music*, KTBC, 1950).

27376 **Roddy, Pauline.** COM-HE (KODY, North Platte, NE, 1956).

27377 **Roddy, Rod.** DJ (KQV, Pittsburgh, PA, 1960).

27378 **Rodeheaver, Homer.** Baritone-trombonist (KYW, Chicago, IL, 1922). Rodeheaver later traveled with evangelist Billy Sunday as song leader.

27379 **Rodeheaver, Ruth.** Soprano (KYW, Chicago, IL, 1922).

27380 **Rodell, Ruth.** Soprano (WJZ, New York, NY, 1923).

27381 **Rodemich, Gene.** Leader (Gene Rodemich Orchestra, KSD, St. Louis, MO, 1923–1924; musical director of the *Johnson and Johnson* program, NBC-Blue, New York, NY, 1929).

27382 **Rodeo Bill.** DJ (*Rodeo Bill and His Western Hayride*, KWKW, Pasadena, CA, 1948).

27383 **Rodgers, Bob.** DJ (*Tune Topper*, KIUL, Garden City, KS, 1947).

27384 **Rodgers, Cliff.** DJ (*Melody Roundup*, WHKK, Akron, OH, 1947–1950).

27385 **Rodgers, Dave.** Newscaster (WFBM, Indianapolis, IN, 1945).

27386 **Rodgers, Floyd D., Jr.** Newscaster (WIS, Columbia, SC, 1938–1940).

27387 **Rodgers, Jesse.** CW yodeler Rodger's style was influenced by that of his cousin, Jimmie Rodgers. In his early twenties, Jesse appeared on Border Radio—XERA (Mexico City, Mexico, 1932) and XEPN (Piedras Negras, Mexico, 1932). After moving to Philadelphia, he joined the *Hayloft Hoedown* (WFIL, Philadelphia, PA, and ABC, 1945–1949). After that Rodgers appeared on a popular Philadelphia television show as "Ranger Joe."

27388 **Rodgers, Jimmie (aka "The Singing Brakeman" and the "The Blue Yodeler").** Legendary country music singer Rodgers was known as the *first* great country music singing star. His Victor recordings brought great popularity to the music. He began performing as part of the Teneva Ramblers, a country music group that also included Jack Pierce and his brother, Claude, over WWNC (Ashville, NC, 1927). Eventually the group became known as the Jimmie Rodgers Entertainers. Rodgers soon began giving concerts in Washington, D.C., at the Earle Theater and singing his country songs on station WTFF (Washington, DC, 1928). Rodgers had previously appeared on the inaugural program of station WWNC (Ashville, NC, February 22, 1927) and later on its regular broadcast schedule. Much later still, he had a twice a week program on KMAC (San Antonio, TX, 1932).

27389 **Rodgers, Joseph.** Tenor and director of the South Sea Islanders Orchestra (NBC, New York, NY, 1928).

27390 **Rodgers, (Mrs.) R.L.** Coloratura soprano (WFLA, Clearwater, FL, 1928–1929).

27391 **Rodgers, Rienhold.** Newscaster (WFLA, Tampa, FL, 1941).

27392 **Rodgers, Stan.** Sportscaster (WLEU, Erie, PA, 1942).

27393 **Rodgers, Tom.** DJ (KYW, Philadelphia, PA, 1948). Sportscaster (*Inside Angle on Sports*, KYW, 1950; *Sports Review*, WFIL, Philadelphia, PA, 1960).

27394 **Rodgers, Wayne.** Sportscaster (*Warm Up*, WXTN, Lexington, MS, 1960).

27395 **Rodgers, Willie.** DJ (*Western Roundup*, WPEP, San Angelo, TX, 1960).

27396 **Rodig, Dorothy.** Eleven-year-old pianist (WIP, Philadelphia, PA, 1923).

27397 **Rodman, Victor.** Actor Rodman was in the cast of *Those We Love*.

27398 **Rodner, Mort.** Leader (Mort Rodner Orchestra, KSD, St. Louis, MO, 1923).

27399 **Rodolfi, Enrico.** Baritone (KOA, Denver, CO, 1925).

27400 **Rodolfo, Don.** Leader (*Don Rodolfo Orchestra*, instr. mus. prg., NBC, 1935).

27401 **Rodrick, Bob.** DJ (*Rod and His Records*, KGCX, Sidney, MT, 1952). Sportscaster (KGCX, 1952; KVFD, Ft. Dodge, IA, 1955).

27402 **Rodrigo, Marcel.** Spanish baritone (*Marcel Rodrigo*, vcl. mus. prg., NBC-Blue, 1933).

27403 **Rodrigo, Nano.** Leader (*Nano Rodrigo Orchestra*, instr. mus. prg., NBC, 1936).

27404 **Rodriguez, Jose.** News analyst (*Inside the News*, KFI, Los Angeles, CA, 1940; KFI-KECA, Los Angeles, CA, 1942; NBC-Blue, 1945).

27405 **Rodriguez, Mateo.** Newscaster (WHOM, Jersey City, NJ, 1941).

27406 **Rodriguez, Raoul.** Newscaster (*Handy Andy News*, KCOR, San Antonio, TX, 1948).

27407 **Rodriguez the Columbian Troubadour.** Singer (WPCH, New York, NY, 1931).

27408 **Rodstrom, Lloyd.** DJ (KRKO, Everett, WA, 1945). Sportscaster (*Sports Round-Up*, KRKO, 1947–1948).

27409 **Rody, Joan.** COM-HE (WKCW, Warrenton, VA, 1960).

27410 **Roe, Charles.** Newscaster (WBML, Macon, GA, 1942).

27411 **Roe, Florence.** Pianist (KYW, Chicago, IL, 1925).

27412 **Roe, Katherine.** Soprano (KFUS, Oakland, CA, 1925).

27413 **Roe, Russell.** Newscaster (KFAM, St. Cloud, MN, 1944–1945).

27414 **Roe, Thelma.** Violinist (KVOO, Tulsa, OK, 1928–1929).

27415 **Roeder, Charles A.** Newscaster (WCBM, Baltimore, MD, 1940).

27416 **Roehr, Alvin.** Leader (Alvin Roehr's Music Makers, WKRC, Cincinnati, OH, 1925; Alvin Roehr and his Hotel Alms Orchestra, WKRC, Cincinnati, OH, 1926).

27417 **Roelofsma, E.** Clarinetist (CBS Symphony Orchestra, CBS, 1928–1929).

27418 **Roen, Louis.** Announcer Roen was born March 13, 1905. He began his career as staff announcer at WTMJ (Milwaukee, WI, 1927). He was the announcer for the *Today's Children* daytime serial program.

27419 **Roen, Marion.** COM-HE (KMOD, Modesto, CA, 1955).

27420 **Roentgen, Engelbert.** Cellist (WCCO, Minneapolis–St. Paul, MN, 1928–1929).

27421 **Roesch, Anna.** Pianist (WLAC, Nashville, TN, 1929).

27422 **Roesler, Delores.** COM-HE (KWEW, Hobbs, NM, 1957).

27423 **Roesler, George.** Announcer and station manager (KOIL, Council Bluffs, IA, 1929).

27424 **Roesler, Ruby.** Pianist (KPCB, Seattle, WA, 1927).

27425 **Roessler, Elmira.** Actress Roessler appeared on the daytime serial programs *Backstage Wife* aka *Mary Noble, Backstage Wife, Ma Perkins* and *Stepmother*.

27426 **Roetter, Friedroech.** Newscaster (WIBA, Madison, WI, 1941).

27427 **Rogan, Ruth.** Eight-year-old Rogan was a movie actress that frequently appeared on a program featuring young stars of the stage and screen (WOR, Newark, NJ, 1924).

27428 Roger, Sydney. Newscaster (KSFO, San Francisco, CA, 1944–1945).

27429 *Roger Allen.* Allen, a local Grand Rapids, Michigan, architect and daily newspaper columnist, talked about a little of everything on his popular local program (15 min., Sunday, 4:30–4:45 P.M., WJEF, Grand Rapids, MI, 1949).

27430 *Roger Kilgore, Public Defender.* Raymond Edward Johnson, in the title role of the dramatic crime program, each week defended the rights of those unjustly accused. *Variety* noted that he acted like *Mr. District Attorney* in reverse. The sustaining show replaced Theodore Granik's *American Forum*. Charita Bauer, Humphrey Davis, Andy Donnelly, Earl George, Santos Ortega and Bill Smith were also in the cast. Stedman Coles wrote the show and Jock MacGregor was the producer. Music was conducted by Sylvan Levin (30 min., Tuesday, 10:00–10:30 P.M., MBS, 1948).

27431 Roger Williams' Club Quartet. Vocal group (KVOO, Tulsa, OK, 1928).

27432 Rogers and Chapman. Musical team of a harpist and harmonica player (WCAU, Philadelphia, PA, 1926).

27433 Rogers, Ann. COM-HE (WHAM, Rochester, NY, 1949).

27434 Rogers, Ann. COM-HE (WCBA, Culpepper, VA, 1960).

27435 Rogers, Bill. News analyst (CBS, 1947–1948). Announcer (*Brighter Day*, network).

27436 Rogers, Bob. DJ (*Yawn Patrol*, WDEC, Americus, GA, 1948).

27437 Rogers, Burton. Organist (*Burton Rogers*, instr. mus. prg., CBS, 1936).

27438 Rogers, Charles "Buddy." Popular singer and orchestra leader (CBS, 1929; *Buddy Rogers Orchestra*, instr. mus. prg., NBC, 1934; CBS, 1935–1937).

27439 Rogers, Dave. Leader (Hotel Brickman Orchestra, WGBS, New York, NY, 1928).

27440 Rogers, Don. DJ (*The Concert Hour*, WRIB, Providence, RI, 1947; *Star Wagon*, WRIB, 1952).

27441 Rogers, Eddy. Leader (*Eddy Rogers Orchestra*, instr. mus. prg., NBC, 1936, 1938–1939).

27442 Rogers, Eddy. DJ (KALB, Alexandria, LA, 1939). Sportscaster (KALB, 1940).

27443 Rogers, Ellen. Jazz pianist and blues singer (KSTP, Minneapolis–St. Paul, MN, 1928–1929).

27444 Rogers, Ernest. Country-western singer and guitarist (WSB, Atlanta, GA, 1923–1925). Rogers also sometimes performed such comic roles as "Old King Tut the Radio Nut" and "Willie the Weeper" (WSB, Atlanta, GA, 1926).

27445 Rogers, Fay. COM-HE (WCLA, Claxton, GA, 1960).

27446 Rogers, Fey. Newscaster (WOPI, Bristol, TN, 1939–1941, 1945).

27447 Rogers, Floss. COM-HE (WRMN, Elgin, IL, 1955).

27448 Rogers, (Dr.) Frank Sill. Organist (WGY, Schenectady, NY, 1929).

27449 Rogers, Gene. Leader (*Gene Rogers Cowboy Band*, CW instr. mus. prg., KVOA, Fayetteville, AR, 1933–1934).

27450 Rogers, Helen. COM-HE (WHVH, Henderson, NC, 1955).

27451 Rogers, Henry. Pianist (WMCA, New York, NY, 1925).

27452 Rogers, Irv. DJ (KALB, Alexandria, LA, 1939).

27453 Rogers, James A. News analyst (WENC, Whiteville, NC, 1946; *Sunday Commentary*, WJMX, Florence, SC, 1947).

27454 Rogers, Jean. Actress Rogers was in the cast of the *Those We Love* daytime serial program.

27455 Rogers, Joe. Banjoist (KFWM, Oakland, CA, 1929).

27456 Rogers, John. DJ (*Children's Choice*, KUOM, Minneapolis, MN, 1947).

27457 Rogers, Ken. DJ (*Koffee Klub*, KCIL, Houma, LA, 1954).

27458 Rogers, Lee. News analyst (*Our City*, KSAF, Nacogdoches, TX, 1948).

27459 Rogers, Lew. Newscaster (WIBG, Glendale, PA, 1941).

27460 Rogers, Margie. COM-HE (KGB, San Diego, CA, 1957).

27461 Rogers, Ralph. Host of the *Universal Radio Features* program and director of the *Mr. and Mrs.* program (WEEI, Boston, MA, 1928). Newscaster (WJNO, West Palm Beach, FL, 1939).

27462 Rogers, Robert. Newscaster (WSAL, Salisbury, MD, 1938–1939).

27463 Rogers, (Professor) Robert Emmons. Professor Rogers broadcast "Lessons in Modern American Literature" (WHO, Des Moines, IA, 1924). Later, he broadcast book reviews on his *Literary Values in Recent Books* program and presented literature courses on radio (WBZ, Boston-Springfield, MA, 1926).

27464 Rogers, Rockin'. DJ (WTMP, Tampa, FL, 1960).

27465 Rogers, Ronnie. Newscaster (WFLA, Tampa, FL, 1940).

27466 Rogers, Roy (Leonard Franklin Slye). CW singer, songwriter and movie star Rogers began his radio career teaming with his cousin Stanley Slye as the Slye Brothers on KMCS (Inglewood, CA, 1931). Soon thereafter Roy was asked to join the Rocky Mountaineers on KGFJ (Los Angeles, CA). When the group was unsuccessful, he joined two other groups — the International Cowboys and the O-Bar-O Cowboys with no greater success. In 1933, Rogers, Tim Spencer and Bob Nolan formed the Pioneers Trio, and appeared on their own program (*The Pioneers Trio*, KFWB, Hollywood, CA, 1933). The expanded group including Hugh and Karl Farr broadcast as Farley's Gold Star Rangers before they became the Sons of the Pioneers. The group made their movie debut in 1935 in a Gene Autry movie. In addition to many motion pictures, the group was a prolific recording group, whose work included many Thesaurus broadcast transcriptions and syndicated CW music programs. Some of their programs were *Sons of the Pioneers* (Syndicated, WCNW, Brooklyn, NY, 1936); *Sons of the Pioneers* (Mutual, 1939); and Thesaurus transcriptions (1947–1948).

In addition to his highly successful western movie career, as "King of the Cowboys," Rogers was on radio for many years *Roy Rogers Show* (Mutual, 1944–1945 with the Sons of the Pioneers); *Roy Rogers Show* (NBC, 1946–1951 with Dale Evans, Foy Willing and the Riders of the Purple Sage); *Roy Rogers Show* (NBC,1951–1955 with Dale Evans). He and his wife, Dale Evans, made a successful transition to television with their *Roy Rogers Show*. *See* **Evans, Dale; *Farley's Gold Star Rangers;*** *and* ***Happy Trails (aka The Roy Rogers Show).***

27467 Rogers, Ted and Larry Beaumont. Singing team billed as "The Harmonists" (KSL, Salt Lake City, UT, 1929).

27468 Rogers, Tom. DJ (*Tom's Turntable Torture*, WJNC, Jacksonville, NC, 1950).

27469 Rogers, (Reverend Dr.) W.H. The Reverend Dr. Rogers broadcast his church services (KFH, Wichita, KS, 1928).

27470 Rogers, Walter B. Rogers was the conductor of the *Brunswick Hour* program's orchestra (WJZ, New York, NY, 1924).

27471 Rogers, Will. Rogers, the famous American humorist, first broadcast with the *Ziegfeld Follies* showgirls from the Pittsburgh *Post* studio of KDKA (Pittsburgh, PA, 1922). When he appeared on KDKA in 1922, Rogers began by saying: "Hello folks. I've looked at you from the movie screen and stage, but I've never had a chance to talk to you at home before." His warm, down home manner unquestionably was one reason be became one of America's best known and loved personalities and was generally called "America's court jester." After his first appearance, Rogers remarked that radio was too big a thing not to be into.

On NBC in January, 1928, during the network's inaugural broadcast, Rogers performed a controversial satiric imitation of President Calvin Coolidge, "Fifteen Minutes with a Diplomat." He began by saying that he had the privilege of introducing the President who would speak from the White House on national affairs. He said: "Now, folks, we've got a real surprise for you tonight. Something that we didn't put on the program because of the nature of it, we couldn't advertise it. And because he thinks that automobiles have contributed to the success and prosperity of the country, we have a real treat in store for you so get ready for a real surprise. A real announcer should announce this, but I have to do it, and it's nobody but Mr. Coolidge. Mr. Calvin Coolidge from Washington, who wants to take this opportunity to deliver a short message to America. All right, Washington, are you ready? A — ah — all right, Mr. Coolidge, Mr. Coolidge." Rogers then went on to imitate Coolidge's voice: "Ladies and gentlemen, it's the duty of the President to deliver a message to the people on the condition of the country. I am proud to report that the condition of the country as a whole is prosperous. I don't mean that the whole country is prosperous, but as a whole it's — prosperous. That is, it's prosperous for a hole. A hole is not supposed to be prosperous and this country certainly is a whole. There is not a whole lot of doubt about that. Everybody that I come in contact with seems to be doin' well — Hoover, Dawes, Lowden, Curtis, Al Smith, McAdoo — they're all doin' well. Of course, not as they'd like to be doin' by this time next year."

The "President" then continued: "I sent Dwight Morrow down to Mexico. A smart boy, Dwight. He's one of the two smartest boys, in fact, in our class at Amherst where we were preparing for college. Lindbergh is busy in Central America. We seem to get in wrong faster than that boy can get us out. I wish he was twins. I made a statement last fall in which I said I didn't choose to run. It seems to have been misunderstood, or not understood or somethin', so about a month ago I clarified it by saying, 'I still don't choose to run.' If they misunderstood the first 'choose,' I certainly can't see how they could misunderstood this 'un again." Rogers [as Coolidge] then went on to discuss farm relief, foreign debts and international problems in the same humorous vein.

Many listeners who thought Coolidge was actually on the program flooded the White House with protests. Rogers was relieved to learn that the President had enjoyed the joke, but it was Mrs. Coolidge who provided an opportunity for him to apply a clever topper for the incident. When she met Rogers sometime later, she told him she could have given a better imitation of the President. "Well, Grace," Rogers said, "You can imitate Cal's voice better than me, but look what you had to go through to learn it." One of Rogers' favorite targets were politicians. He said the highest praise a humorist can have is to have his remarks included in the *Congressional Record.*

27472 **Rogers, William and Mary Rogers.** The interesting team told funny stories for children and adults (WFAA, Dallas, TX, 1922).

27473 **Rogers, Wilson.** Newscaster (KFIZ, Fond du Lac, WI, 1940).

27474 ***Rogers of the Gazette.*** Norman Macdonnell produced and directed the sustaining dramatic series written by Walter Newman and E. Jack Newman. Will Rogers, Jr. played the title role of a small town newspaper editor. Georgia Ellis and Parley Baer assisted him. Music was supplied by Wilbur Hatch's orchestra. In the role of an editor with an easy-going, folksy philosophy, Rogers was able to convey a brand of humor reminiscent of his late father. Good writing and acting were the major characteristics of the entertaining series (30 min., Wednesday, 9:30–10:00 P.M., CBS, 1953). *See* **Rogers, Will.**

27475 **Rogerson, Gloria.** COM-HE (WWVA, Wheeling, WV, 1957).

27476 **Rogge, Betty.** COM-HE (WING, Dayton, OH, 1957).

27477 **Rohan, Marilyn.** COM-HE (KSTL, St. Louis, MO, 1949).

27478 **Rohn, George "Bill."** Sportscaster (*Sports Gallery*, KSOO, Sioux Falls, IA, 1949–1952).

27479 **Rohner, Charles.** Violinist (WBBR, New York, NY, 1926).

27480 **Rohner, Ron.** DJ (*Ron Rohner's Morning*, WELI, New Haven, CT, 1950s).

27481 **Rohr, Jack.** Leader (*Jack Rohr Orchestra*, instr. mus. prg., WCBM, Baltimore, MD, 1939).

27482 **Rohr, Tilda.** Swiss contralto (WHJ, Los Angeles, CA, 1923).

27483 **Rohrbeck, E. H.** Announcer (WPSC, State College, PA, 1925).

27484 **Rohre, Freddie.** Pianist (WLW, Cincinnati, OH, 1926–1928).

27485 **Rohwer, John.** DJ (*Juke Box*, KROS, Clinton, IA, 1947).

27486 **Rola, Emma.** Singer Rola appeared on the *Ye Old Tyme Fest* program (WOOD, Grand Rapids, MI, 1926).

27487 **Roland, Bessie Beatty.** Organist (KGO, Oakland, CA, 1926).

27488 **Roland, Rusty.** COM-HE (WKOP, Binghampton, NY, 1957).

27489 **Roland, Will.** Leader (*Will Roland Orchestra*, instr. mus. prg., KDKA, Pittsburgh, PA, 1935; WCAE, Pittsburgh, PA, 1936).

27490 **Rolands, Janet.** Actress Rolands appeared on the daytime serial *Life Begins* aka *Martha Webster.*

27491 **Rolf, Erik (Rolf M. Yivisaker).** Announcer-actor Rolf was born June 1, 1911. He joined WDGY (Minneapolis–St. Paul, MN, 1929), where he later became the station's chief announcer and program director. He was the announcer for the *Joyce Jordan, Girl Interne* and *Prairie Folks* network programs.

27492 **Rolfe, B.A. (Benjamin A.).** Leader (B.A. Rolfe and his Palais d'Or Orchestra; the orchestra playing from the Palais d'Or restraurant on Broadway, WHO, Des Moines, IA and the NBC network, 1927; Lucky Strike Orchestra, NBC-Red, New York, NY, 1927–1929). Rolfe had toured Europe as the "Boy Trumpet Wonder" at the age of eleven, before appearing as a soloist with the John Philip Sousa band. He played trumpet in the Vincent Lopez Orchestra before leaving to lead his own radio orchestra in the mid–1920s. Rolfe continued busy in the following decade: *B.A. Rolfe Orchestra*, instr. mus. prg. (NBC, 1934).

27493 **Rolfe, Mary.** Actress Rolfe was in the cast of the *Rose of My Dreams* daytime serial program.

27494 **Rolison, Emily C.** Singer (WGY, Schenectady, NY, 1924).

27495 **Rolkjer, Ethel.** Violinist (KTAB, Oakland, CA, 1925).

27496 **Roll, Richard "Dick."** Newscaster (WHIO, Dayton, OH, 1937–1941; WTAM, Cleveland, OH, 1946). Sportscaster (WHIO, 1939–1940; WTAM, 1946; WLOK, Lima, OH, 1950).

27497 ***Roll Jordan.*** *Roll Jordan* was a popular gospel music program (60 min., Monday through Saturday, WAAA, Winston-Salem, NC, 1950). Black DJ Larry Williams was the host on the popular gospel music show.

27498 **Rolle, Caroline.** Soprano (WIP, Philadelphia, PA, 1925).

27499 **Roller, Larry.** Newscaster (WJNO, West Palm Beach, FL, 1942; WMFJ, Daytona Beach, FL, 1946).

27500 **(The) Rollickers.** Male vocal quartet that consisted of tenors Clark Brewer and Victor Hall, baritone William Scholtz and bass James Davies (CBS, 1928). They had their own program in 1932 sponsored by the Shu-milk Corporation. The host was Henry M Neeley — "The Old Stager" (NBC, 1932).

27501 **Rolling, Bobbie.** Singer-entertainer Rolling was known as the "Million Dollar Personality Girl of Radioland" (KFUL, Galveston, TX, 1927). Her radio career began in 1926, when she was featured over many stations in the south including WSMB (New Orleans, LA) and KPRC (Houston, TX). In 1929 she was featured on KMOX (St. Louis, MO).

27502 ***Rolling Along.*** Organist Ernie Neff and his wife, singer Carole Mansfield, performed on the popular local show (15 min., Sunday, 1:45–2:00 P.M., WCAE, Pittsburgh, PA, 1948).

27503 **Rollini, Adrian.** Leader (*Adrian Rollini Orchestra*, instr. mus. prg., WOR, Newark, NJ, 1937; NBC, 1939).

27504 **Rollins, Carl.** Baritone (WEAF, New York, NY and WDAF, Kansas City, MO, 1926).

27505 **Rollins, Chap.** Farm news reporter (*Valley Farm Reporter* and *Mid-Morning Summary*, KROP, Brawley, CA, 1947). DJ (*Ace of Clubs*, KROP, 1947; KROP, 1956). Sportscaster (KAGH, Pasadena, CA, 1948; *Saturday Scoreboard*, KBUC, Corona, CA, 1950).

27506 **Rollins, Marion.** Announcer (KGDA, Dell Rapids, SD, 1927).

27507 **Rollins, Todd.** Leader (*Todd Rollins Orchestra*, insr. mus. prg., WINS, New York, 1932; WTAM, Cleveland, OH, 1936).

27508 **Rollins, Tom** Sportscaster (*Sports Roundup*, KECK, Odessa, TX, 1950; KVKM, Monahans, TX, 1953).

27509 **Rollins, Wayne.** Sportscaster (*Sports Forecasts*, KYCA, Prescott, AZ, 1952).

27510 **Rolph, Olivette.** COM-HE (WFTM, Maysville, KY, 1957).

27511 **Romance, Ed.** Sportscaster (*Sports Parade*, WPPA, Pottsville, PA, 1947–1949; *Sportsbook of the Air*, WPPA, 1950; *Sports Parade*, WPPA, 1951–1956).

27512 ***Romance.*** Romantic stories such as *Kitty Foyle* were dramatized and broadcast complete on each half-hour program of the series. The Voice of Romance on the program was Doris Dalton. Roy Rowan was the announcer. Organ interludes were supplied by Eddy Dunstedter (30 min., Saturday, 10:30–11:00 P.M., CBS, 1948). A later version of the program also dramatized romantic stories. This time the cast members included: Ben Wright, Raymond Lawrence, Ellen Morgan, Herb Butterfield, Jack Kruschen, Edgar Barrier, Charles Lung, Paula Winslow, Anthony Ellis and Betty Harford. Dan Cubberly was the announcer (CBS, 1955).

27513 ***Romance and Melody.*** A young boy and girl's light patter and clever chatter led into each of the program's musical selections. Jules Lande and his Singing Violin played romantic tunes with the NBC orchestra (15 min., Weekly, NBC, 1935).

27514 ***Romance in Rhythm.*** Les Tremayne played the lead on the variety show broadcast in 1935.

27515 ***Romance, Inc.*** Dexdale Hosiery Mills sponsored the weekly dramatic series that starred Alice Reinheart and Buford Hampden as a man and woman, who started a business as marriage brokers (30 min., Weekly, 9:30–10:00 P.M., NBC-Blue, 1936).

27516 ***Romance Isle.*** A weekly half-hour dramatic series (NBC-Blue, 1927).

27517 ***(The) Romance of Dan and Sylvia.*** A local daytime serial drama with unidentified actors (15 min., Monday, 2:30–2:45 P.M., KDKA, Pittsburgh, PA, 1935).

27518 ***(The) Romance of Helen Trent.*** Frank and Anne Hummert produced the daytime serial, in which Helen, the heroine, constantly attempted to discover whether a woman over 35 could find romance. The daytime dramatic serial was another of the many successful Frank and Anne Hummert productions. The program's cast included: Jay Barney, Spencer Bentley, Bill Bouchey, Sarah Burton, Virginia Clark, Whitfield Connor, Cathleen Cordell, Ken Daigneau, Mary Frances Desmond, Helene Dumas, Patricia Dunlap, Katharine Emmet, Marilyn Erskine, Vivian Fridell, Lauren Gilbert, Lucy Gillman, Alice Goodkin, David Gothard, Mitzi Gould, Hilda Graham, William Green, Alan Hewitt, Mary Jane Higby, Alice Hill, John Hodiak, Ginger Jones, Carlton KaDell, Louis Krugman, Ed Latimer, Janet Logan, Don MacLaughlin, Charlotte Manson, Bess McCammon, Audrey McGrath, James Meighan, Marvin Miller, Les Mitchel, Bret Morrison, Marie Nelson, Patsy O'Shea, Loretta Poynton, Ed Prentiss, Donna Reade, Linda Reid, Doris Rich, Grant Richards, Bartlett Robinson, Florence Robinson, Selena Royle, Klock Ryder, Nanette Sargent, Bernice Silverman, Betty Ruth Smith, Cora B. Smith, Olan Soule, Julie Stevens, Amzie Strickland, Hope Summers, Reese Taylor, William Thornton, Les Tremayne, Peggy Wall, John Walsh, George Ward, Karl Weber and Lesley Woods. Stanley Davis was the producer-director. Martha Alexander, Marie Banner, Ruth Borden, Ronald Dawson were the writers. Richard Leonard, Les Mitchel, Ernest Ricca, Blair Walliser were the producers. Pierre Andre, Fielden Farrington and Don Hancock were the announcers. (15 min., Tuesday, 1:15–1:30 P.M., CBS, 1935). The highly successful program was broadcast from 1930 to 1960.

27519 ***Romance of the Ranchos.*** Frank Graham played the "Wandering Vanquero," who narrated the dramatic series that told of the early history of Southern California. John Dunkel wrote these historical dramas. Bob Lemond was the announcer. The sponsor was the Title Insurance and Trust Company of Los Angeles (30 min., Sunday, 8:30–9:00 P.M., KNX, Los Angeles, CA, 1942).

27520 ***Romance of the Sea.*** A weekly program, the *Romance of the Sea* presented the personal narrative of "The Sea Devil" of World War I, Count Luckner. His adventures and achievements previously had been chronicled by Lowell Thomas. The Roundtowners male quartet opened and closed the program with sea ballads (30 min., Sunday, 9:30–10:00 P.M., CBS, 1932).

27521 ***(The) Romancers.*** A vocal music program that featured romantic songs performed by the singing team of tenor Ben Alley and soprano Helen Nugent (CBS, 1929).

27522 **Romanelli, Leo.** Leader (*Leo Romanelli Orchestra*, instr. mus. prg., MBS, 1937). This might have been a name change by Luigi Romanelli. *See* **Romanelli, Luigi.**

27523 **Romanelli, Luigi.** Leader (*Luigi Romanelli Orchestra*, instr. mus. prg., NBC-Blue, 1935; CBS, 1935).

27524 **Romano, Anita.** Guitarist (KGO, Oakland, CA, 1926).

27525 **Romano, Carla.** Pianist (*Carla Romano*, instr. mus. prg., CBS, 1934–1935).

27526 **Romano, Michael "Mike."** Announcer Romano was in the cast of *Girl Alone, Guiding Light, Silver Eagle, Mountie* and *Today's Children.*

27527 **Romano, Pasquale E.** Baritone (KSTP, St. Paul–Minneapolis, MN, 1929).

27528 **Romano, Phil.** Leader (Phil Romano Orchestra broadcasting from New York's Roseland Ballroom, WHN, New York, NY, 1924; WBZ, Springfield, MA, 1925). Romano and his band had also been heard previously on WGY (Schenectady, NY, 1922–1923).

27529 **Romano, Ralph.** Sportscaster (*Sports Parade*, WWSC, Glens Falls, NY, 1960).

27530 **Romano, Tom.** DJ (WNHC, New Haven, CT, 1948–1949; *Musical Mail Call*, WNHC, 1950).

27531 **Romans, Jackie.** COM-HE (WOVE, Welch, WV, 1960).

27532 ***Romantic Melodies.*** Don Ameche starred as the singing host, who introduced weekly guest performers on the show sponsored by the Campagna Sales Company, makers of D.D.D. Ointment for skin problems. The orchestra was conducted by Eric Sagerquist. Ameche, Sagerquist and the sponsor were all members of the successful *First Nighter* team (30 min., Thursday, 7:30–8:00 P.M., NBC-Blue, 1934).

27533 ***Romantic Rhythm.*** Sally Nelson and Barry McKinley sang with Simon's orchestra on the weekly music show (30 min., Sunday, 6:30–7:00 P.M., CBS, 1935).

27534 **Romany Orchestra.** Popular DC band (WRC, Washington, DC, 1925).

27535 ***Romany Road.*** Contralto Devora Nadworney performed with Harry Horlick's orchestra on the weekly music show (30 min., Wednesday, 9:00–9:30 P.M., NBC-Blue, 1930).

27536 ***Romany Romancers.*** Quality Jewelry Store sponsored the program of romantic melodies sung by Buster King and played on the concertina by Jimmy DePlacito (15 min., Sunday, 12:00–12:15 P.M., WELI, New Haven, CT, 1937). An earlier CBS network version of the program featured soprano Gypsy Nina singing in nine languages — French, Italian, Russian, English, German, Hungarian, Greek, Polish and Spanish — while accompanying herself on the accordion (15 min., Tuesday and Saturday, 1933).

27537 **Romayne, Kay.** Blues singer Romayne appeared on almost every Chicago station in the 1920s, including WEBH (1925); WGES (1927); and WKY (1929). She also was featured on the *Stewart-Warner Theater* program (WBBM, Chicago, IL, 1927).

27538 **Romeo, Juliet.** Singer (WMCA, New York, NY, 1936).

27539 **Romberg, Walter.** Violinist (WFAA, Dallas, TX, 1922).

27540 **Romine, Marion Wakefield.** Miss Romine broadcast literary chats in which she discussed books and dispensed literary gossip (WFAA, Dallas, TX, 1922).

27541 **Romine, Rod.** DJ (*Hillbilly Roundup*, KCJB, Minot, ND, 1954).

27542 **Rommell, (Mrs.) Carl.** Pianist (WBZ, Springfield, MA, 1924).

27543 **Rommel, Ralph R.** Leader (*Ralph Rommel and His Syncopators Orchestra*, KNRC, Los Angeles, CA, 1925).

27544 **Ronan, Honore.** COM-HE (WDAN, Danville, IL, 1949–1957).

27545 **Rondell, Rock.** Sportscaster (KHHH, Pampa, TX, 1960).

27546 **Ronning, Russell.** Saxophonist (KSTP, Minneapolis–St. Paul, MN, 1928–1929).

27547 **Ronson, Adele.** In addition to her appearances on the daytime serial *John's Other Wife*, actress Ronson appeared on such diverse network programming as ***Buck Rogers in the 25th Century, Eno Crime Club, Meyer the Buyer*** and ***Gibson Family.***

27548 **Roof Garden Orchestra.** Popular club dance band (WFI, Philadelphia, PA, 1925).

27549 ***Rookies.*** Successful vaudeville comedians Jay C. Flippen and Joey Faye played the roles of a sergeant and a rookie stationed at Camp Dilemna in the comedy about Army life. Straight man Harry Hiblist and singer Lena Romay were also in the cast. Roger Bower was the program's producer (30 min., Sunday, 7:00–7:30 P.M., WOR, Newark, NJ, 1941).

27550 **Rooney, Pat.** Actor Rooney, a member of the Rosie O'Grady theater group, was interviewed on the *Interview — A.R. Plough* program (WLW, Cincinnati, OH, 1925).

27551 **Roos, Reg.** DJ (*Platter Party*, KRLC, Lewiston, ME, 1950).

27552 **Roosevelt, Eleanor.** Commentator (WNBC, New York, NY, 1951).

27553 **Roosevelt, Elliott.** News analyst (*Commentary*, MBS, 1938–1939). Elliott Roosevelt, a son of FDR, was one the many relations of President Roosevelt who embarked on a career in radio.

27554 **Roosevelt, Emily.** Soprano (WOR, Newark, NJ, 1925).

27555 **Roosevelt, James.** News analyst (KLAC, Los Angeles, CA, 1946), another son of FDR.

27556 **Roosevelt Concert Orchestra.** Music group led by Nicholas Orlando (WRNY, New York, NY, 1926).

27557 **Root, Antha Mussell.** Soprano (WBZ, Springfield, MA, 1925).

27558 **Root, Lucille.** Soprano (KFSG, Los Angeles, CA, 1926).

27559 **Root, Waverly.** Newscaster (MBS, 1939; WINS, New York, NY, 1942).

27560 **Roper, Don.** Sportscaster (*Time Out for Sports*, KBOL, Boulder, CO, 1955).

27561 **Roper, James.** Sportscaster (KRTN, Raton, NM, 1955).

27562 **Roper, Pres.** Newscaster (WCED, DuBois, PA, 1942). DJ (*Wake Up and Live*, WMAN, Mansfield, OH, 1948; *Morning Show*, WMAN, 1954–1957).

27563 **Ropollo, Joe.** DJ (*The 9:30 Express*, KFPW, Fort Smith, AR, 1948; *Musical Clock*, KFPW, 1952).

27564 **Roppolo, Michael "Mike."** Newscaster (KTBS, Shreveport, LA, 1945). Sportscaster (KTBS, 1945). DJ (KTBS, 1947).

27565 **Rorabaugh, Gretta.** COM-HE (WTRN, Tyrone, PA, 1955).

27566 **Rosalak, Boleslaw.** Newscaster (WHOM, Jersey City, NJ, 1941).

27567 ***Rosa Rio.*** Organist Rio was a popular instrumental performer (15 min., ABC, 1947).

27568 **Rosamond, Robert.** Newscaster (WTBO, Cumberland, MD, 1937). Sportscaster (WTBO, 1941).

27569 **Rosario, Rosa.** Singer and flamingo dancer (KMA, Shenandoah, IA, 1927). A popular Spanish singer and flamingo dancer with a "mysterious past," Senorita Rosario fascinated her Iowa listeners. She often appeared on the streets of Shenandoah, IA, in full Spanish dress and ornate jewelry. (Birkby, 1985, p. 54). Supposedly the daughter of a wealthy Spanish family, Rosa was orphaned as a young child. She was one of KMA's most exotic broadcaster performers. Once when she was asked about her life ambitions, she replied that one was that she wanted to be in Movietone films and that the other was to raise chickens. Iowa, at least was the right place to fulfill one of her ambitions. Incidentally, KMA also featured such other exotic performers as the KMA Farm Belt Paint Boys; Majah, Son of India; and the Great Kharma. Unfortunately, little information is available about the latter.

27570 **Roscoe, Michel.** Pianist Roscoe appeared on *Gambling's Musical Clock* program (WOR, Newark, NJ, 1928–1939).

27571 **Roscoe, Paul.** Newscaster (KVAK, Atchinson, KS, 1939–1942). Sportscaster (KVAK, 1941; KFEW, St. Joseph, MO, 1945; *Speaking of Sports*, KJAY, Topeka, KS, 1954).

27572 **Rose, Annabell Jones (aka Reba Swan).** Singer (KGO, Oakland, CA, 1929).

27573 **Rose, Billy.** Leader (Billy Rose's Fifth Avenue Club Orchestra, WOR, Newark, NJ, 1926; Broadway producer Rose later conducted his *Pitching Horseshoes*, a program of show business commentary, MBS, 1947–1948). Speed typist Billy Rose was a long time owner of the famous Diamond Horseshoe night club. Married to Fanny Brice for some time, he later starred his wife, Eleanor Holm, in spectacular swimming shows. He produced the *Jumbo* radio program, as well as the Broadway production of the same name.

27574 **Rose, Bob.** Newscaster (WOOD, Grand Rapids, MI, 1944).

27575 **Rose, David "Dave."** Leader (*David Rose Orchestra*, instr. mus. prg., NBC, 1936).

27576 **Rose, Doreen.** Contralto (WHN, New York, NY, 1936).

27577 **Rose, Fred.** Pianist, tenor and composer (WCFL, Chicago, IL, 1927; KYW, Chicago, IL, 1929).

27578 **Rose, George.** Leader (*George Rose Orchestra*, instr. mus. prg., broadcast from the Indian Grill of the Multnomah Hotel, Portland, Oregon, KGW, Portland, OR, 1926).

27579 **Rose, George.** DJ (WHOS, Decatur, AL, 1948; WMSL, Decatur, GA, 1956).

27580 **Rose, Hazel Conte.** Pianist (WSM, Nashville, TN, 1928–1929).

27581 **Rose, Helen.** Singer (WPCH, New York, NY, 1932).

27582 **Rose, Helen.** News analyst (KFXJ, Grand Junction, CO, 1945).

27583 **Rose, Herm.** DJ (*Variety Show* and *860 Club*, WFHG, Bristol, VA, 1947). Sportscaster (WFHG, 1947).

27584 **Rose, Hortense.** Soprano-pianist (WSAI, Cincinnati, OH, 1929).

27585 **Rose, Iris.** COM-HE (KUEN, Wenatchee, WA, 1960).

27586 **Rose, Irving.** Leader (*Irving Rose Orchestra*, instr. mus. prg., ABS, 1935; WLW, Cincinnati, OH, 1935; KWK, St. Louis, MO, 1936–1937).

27587 **Rose, Johnny.** Singer (*Rose Room*, vcl. mus. prg., WHK, Cleveland, OH, 1947). *See **Rose Room**.*

27588 **Rose, Joseph McKinley.** Tenor (WEAF, New York, NY, 1925).

27589 **Rose, Julia.** COM-HE (WATL, Atlanta, GA, 1951).

27590 **Rose, Kenneth.** Violinist (WSM, Nashville, TN, 1928).

27591 **Rose, Marilyn.** COM-HE (WFIE, Evansville, IN, 1956).

27592 **Rose, May.** Coloratura soprano (KRE, Berkeley, CA, 1923).

27593 **Rose, Mildred.** Soprano (WEAF, New York, NY, 1924; ABS, 1935).

27594 **Rose, Nick.** Leader (Nick Rose and his Revelers Orchestra, WLAC, Nashville, TN, 1928).

27595 **Rose, Patty.** COM-HE (KMED, Medford, OR, 1955).

27596 **Rose, Ralph, Jr.** Violinist (WRNY, New York, NY, 1926).

27597 **Rose, Tony.** Leader (Tony Rose Orchestra, WSM, Nashville, TN, 1928).

27598 **Rose Tree Cafe Orchestra.** Cafe music group (WLIT, Philadelphia, PA, 1926).

27599 **Rose, Vincent "Vince."** Leader (*Vincent Rose Dance Orchestra* broadcasting from the Ritz-Carlton Hotel, WGBS, New York, NY, 1924–1925).

27600 **Rose, William "Bill" or "Billy."** Actor Rose appeared on *Captain Midnight*, *Carters of Elm Street*, *Houseboat Hannah* and *Ma Perkins*.

27601 **Rose Bowl Palace Hotel Orchestra.** Hotel band directed by R. Max Bradfield (KPO, San Francisco, CA, 1925).

27602 ***Rose Marie*** **(aka *Baby Rose Marie*).** Baby Rose (Marie Curley) began her radio singing career on WPG (Atlantic City, NJ) in the summer of 1928 at the age of three, billed as Baby Rose Marie. A daughter of an Italian teamster and a Polish waitress, she soon began touring on the Keith vaudeville circuit. In 1930 at the age of 5, she was earning $100,000 a year. She appeared on both NBC and CBS stations in 1929. *Rose Marie* later sang on her own NBC series (15 min., Weekly, NBC-Blue, 1937–1938). She later co-starred on the *Dick Van Dyke* television series.

27603 ***Rose of My Dreams.*** Peggy Blake wrote and Richard Leonard directed the daytime serial drama, another of the many Frank and Anne Hummert productions. Sponsored by the Manhattan Soap Company, the story followed two sisters with very different personalities, who fought each other for the same man's love. The talented cast included Charita Bauer, James Burke, Joseph Curtin, Mary Rolfe and William Smith. Larry Elliot was the announcer (15 min., Monday through Friday, 2:45–3:00 P.M., CBS, 1946).

27604 ***Rose Room.*** Singer Johnny Rose, a local Cleveland favorite, was featured on the music show (15 min., WHK, Cleveland, OH, 1947).

27605 **Rosebrook, David.** Cornetist (KGO, Oakland, CA, 1925).

27606 **Roseburg, Walter.** Tenor (KOMO, Seattle, WA, 1928).

27607 **Rosehill, David "Dave."** Sportscaster (*Musical Sports Parade*, WDEM, Providence, RI, 1949; *Sports Edition*, WDEM, 1950–1951; *Sports First on Long Island*, WGSM, Huntington, NY, 1954–1955).

27608 **Roseland Dance Orchestra.** Dance hall band directed by Fletcher Henderson (WHN, New York, NY, 1925).

27609 **Roseland Dance Orchestra.** Club band directed by Mel Donahue (KFWI, San Francisco, CA, 1926).

27610 **Rosele, Carmen.** Soprano (WTIC, Hartford, CT, 1935).

27611 **Roseleigh, Jack.** Actor Roseleigh was in the cast of *Buck Rogers in the 25th Century*, *Circus Days*, *Hilltop House*, *Pepper Young's Family*, *Red Davis*, *Road of Life* and *Roses and Drums*.

27612 **Rosell, Johnny.** Director (KDYL Dance and Concert Orchestra, KDYL, Salt Lake City, UT, 1929).

27613 ***Rosemary.*** Elaine Carrington wrote the daytime serial that told the story of Rosemary Harris, who had the misfortune to marry an amnesic war veteran, whose recovered memories included that of a previous marriage. Poor Rosemary faced the bewildering complication from 1944 through 1955. The cast included: Bill Adams, Joan Alexander, Jone Allison, Marion Barney, Patsy Campbell, Helen Choate, Marie DeWolfe, Elspeth Eric, Michael Fitzmaurice, John Gibson, Larry Haines, George Keane, Jackie Kelk, Ed Latimer, Joan Lazer, Woody Parker, Charles Penman, Guy Repp, Sidney Smith, James Van Dyk, Ethel Wilson, Betty Winkler and Lesley Woods. The directors were Hoyt Allen, Ralph Butler, Carl

Eastman, Charles Fisher and Theodora Yates. Tom McDermott was the program's producer and Paul Taubman the musical director. The announcers were Fran Barber, Bob Dixon and Joe O'Brien (15 min, Monday through Friday, 11:15–11:30 A.M., NBC, 1945).

27614 **Rosemary Gardens Dance Music Orchestra.** Colorado Springs club band (KFXF, Colorado Springs, CO, 1926).

27615 **Rosen, Pauline.** Singer of Jewish folk songs (WFAB, New York, NY, 1932).

27616 **Rosenbaum, M. Virginia.** COM-HE (WTBO, Cumberland, MD, 1956).

27617 **Rosenberg, Blanche.** COM-HE (WKRS, Waukegan, IL, 1949).

27618 **Rosenberg, Daryl.** DJ (WIBV, Belleville, IL, 1957).

27619 **Rosenberg, Leo.** Rosenberg was hired by Frank Conrad at KDKA (Pittsburgh, PA) to broadcast the Harding-Cox Presidential election, November 2, 1920. He began work at 6:00 A.M. and stayed behind the microphone until the next day (St. John, 1967, p. 38). This historic event was the first time presidential election results were broadcast.

27620 **Rosenberg, Walter.** Tenor (KOMO, Seattle, WA, 1928).

27621 **Rosenblum, Rosie.** Pianist (KOA, Denver, CO, 1925).

27622 **Rosenfeld, Fred.** Pianist Rosenfeld was identified by *Variety* as "an exclusive WCAE artist" (WCAE, Pittsburgh, PA, 1924).

27623 **Rosenfeld, Joseph.** Leader (Joseph Rosenfeld Orchestra, KNX, Los Angeles, CA, 1928).

27624 **Rosenfield, Big Joe.** DJ (*The Happiness Exchange*, WOR, New York, NY, 1948).

27625 **Rosengren, Alma.** Program director (WJAD, WACO, TX, 1925).

27626 **Rosenova, Olga.** Actress Rosenova appeared on the daytime serial programs *Bachelor's Children* and *Mary Marlin* aka *The Story of Mary Marlin.*

27627 **Rosenstock, Fred.** Pianist (WCAE, Pittsburgh, PA, 1924).

27628 **Rosenthal, Frances.** Bass (WCCO, Minneapolis–St. Paul, MN, 1928–1929).

27629 **Rosenthal, Leroy.** Leader (*Larry Rosenthal and His Night Owl Orchestra,* KGHI, Little Rock, AR, 1927).

27630 **Rosenthal, Yvonne.** Pianist (WQJ, Chicago, IL, 1925).

27631 **Rosenthan, David.** *See* **Ross, David.**

27632 **Rosenwald, Margaret.** Soprano (KSTP, St. Paul–Minneapolis, MN, 1929).

27633 **Roser, Priscilla.** COM-HE (WSFC, Somerset, KY, 1955).

27634 ***Roses and Drums.*** When the dramatic series first began in 1932, it was planned that the program should dramatize important incidents of American history. When the series reached the Civil War, the writers responded to their listening audience's request that episodes about that bloody conflict continue. From that point on, the program's action was laid between 1861 and 1864. The series included a blend of fictional romantic elements with an accurate historical treatment of events.

During the series third year on the air in 1935, the stories occasionally shifted locale from the South to the North to deal with the Northwestern Conspiracy of 1864, a Confederate plot to foster a separatist movement in the North. Another story that year dramatized the adventures of John Yates Beall, who was hung as a member of that conspiracy. When the program ended in 1935, the romantic elements of the plot were resolved with the Southern belle heroine rejecting the suit of a Confederate officer to accept the marriage proposal of a Union captain. Perhaps this symbol of the unification of the North and South was intended to sound the need for reconciliation and the healing of wounds.

The cast included Don Ameche, Reed Brown, Jr., Helen Claire, Walter Connolly, Pedro de Cordoba, Johns Griggs, DeWolf Hopper, Helen Kimm, Elizabeth Love, Mrs. Richard Mansfield, Osgood Perkins, Guy Bates Post, Jack Roseleigh and Florence Williams. Professor M.W. Jernegan from the University of Chicago served as consultant to ensure the program's historical accuracy. The orchestra was conducted by Wilifred Pelletier. Herschel Williams was the program's director (30 min., Sunday, 4:00–4:30 P.M., NBC-Blue, 1935).

27635 **Rosette, George.** News commentator, *George Rosette Comments (*WEVD, New York, NY, 1945–1948).

27636 **Rosine, Beulah.** Conductor (WBBM Concert Ensemble, WBBM, Chicago, IL, 1929).

27637 **Rosing, Vladimir.** Concert singer (1922).

27638 **Ross, Al (Rosser Folks).** DJ (WBAL, Baltimore, MD, 1948–1955; WRC, Washington, DC, 1955–1971). Popular Baltimore DJ Ross played the uke and sang. He came from Charlottesville, Virginia. When Bill Herson left WBAL to move to Washington station WRC, Ross took over his program spot. Ross got the title of "The Timekeeper," because of his method of hitting a chime with a mallet when he announced the time. Like popular DJ Bill Herson before him, Ross eventually moved from WBAL to Washington's WRC in 1955 where he stayed until 1971. After leaving WRC, Ross worked for some time for the Voice of America.

27639 **Ross, Allen.** Sportscaster (WHOC, Philadelphia, PA, 1955).

27640 **Ross, Anthony.** Newscaster (WKBN, Youngstown, OH, 1939–1940).

27641 **Ross, Art.** DJ (*The Clockwatcher*, WWIL, Ft. Lauderdale, FL, 1960).

27642 **Ross, Art.** DJ (WTKO, Ithaca, NY, 1960).

27643 **Ross, Becky.** COM-HE (WWOW, Conneaut, OH, 1960).

27644 **Ross, Betsy.** Betsy Ross of Belding Brothers Company broadcast "sewing talks" in the late 1920's. This may be the Betsy Ross listed below.

27645 **Ross, Betsy.** COM-HE (*Sewing Talk*, KPO, San Francisco, CA, 1925).

27646 **Ross, Bonnie.** COM-HE (WRGB, Schenectady, NY, 1951).

27647 **Ross, Byrne.** Newscaster (KSWO, Lawton, OK, 1945).

27648 **Ross, Dan.** DJ (*Coffee Club*, WWPF, Palatka, FL, 1947).

27649 **Ross, David (David Rosenthan).** Premier announcer Ross was trained by Norman Brokenshire at WABC (CBS, New York, NY, 1929) after he first entered radio in 1926. He became a DJ with his *Rendezvous with Ross* program. Ross was one of the great "golden-voiced" announcers of radio's early days. Both early and late in his career, Ross read poetry on various programs with appropriate music backgrounds. These programs invariably attracted a large listening audience. He turned DJ on his *Rendezvous with Ross* program (15 min., Sunday, 12:45–1:00 A.M., MBS, 1948). Among the many programs he announced were *Coke Club*, *Fred Waring Show*, *Henry Morgan Show*, *Myrt and Marge*, *Old Curiosity Shop* and *Poet's Gold.* As an actor, Ross played one of the title roles on the *True Story Hour with Mary and Bob.*

27650 **Ross, Dorothy.** COM-HE (KTNT, Tacoma, WA, 1957).

27651 **Ross, Eleanor.** Pianist (KFI, Los Angeles, CA, 1928).

27652 **Ross, Elinor.** Singer (WELI, New Haven, CT, 1939).

27653 **Ross, G.W. "Dink."** *See* **Hink and Dink.**

27654 **Ross, George F.** Announcer (WRC, Washington, DC, 1925).

27655 **Ross, Harold.** Newscaster (WBOW, Terre Haute, IN, 1940).

27656 **Ross, J. D.** Announcer (KTW, Seattle, WA, 1927).

27657 **Ross, Jack.** Newscaster (WHAM, Rochester, NY, 1941–1942, 1945–1948).

27658 **Ross, Janet.** COM-HE (KDKA, Pittsburgh, PA, 1956).

27659 **Ross, John R.** Newscaster (WKIP, Poughkeepsie, NY, 1945).

27660 **Ross, Kal.** DJ (*The Filekeeper*, WNDR, Syracuse, NY, 1947–1949; *The Kal Ross Show,*180 min., Monday through Friday, 1:00–4:00 P.M., WOR, New York, NY, 1951. Ross, a popular local DJ, broadcast the *Kal Ross Show* from Monti's Restaurant in New York City's Belmont Plaza Hotel. He took phone call requests from listeners and played records). Sportscaster (*Sports Extra*, WNDR, 1947; WPWA, Chester, PA, 1949; WCAN, Milwaukee, WI, 1955).

27661 **Ross, Lanny.** Tenor Ross was born January 19, 1908. After graduating from Yale University, Ross attended Columbia Law School. As a means to finance his legal education, he made his radio debut on the NBC network on several sustaining programs. Although Ross graduated from Columbia Law school, he never practiced law because his long, successful radio career kept him too busy to join the legal profession. A handsome, talented tenor, Ross was featured on *The Maxwell House Showboat* program in 1929. He also had a fifteen-minute weekly program broadcast Sunday evenings on NBC (New York, NY, 1929–1930). Later Ross performed DJ chores on *The Lanny Ross Show (*WCBS, New York, NY, 1955–1957). Ross also enjoyed a motion picture and television career. *See **The Maxwell House Showboat, The Lanny Ross Showboat Show, The Lanny Ross Showtime, The Lanny Ross State Fair Concert** and **The Lanny Ross Show.***

27662 **Ross, Les.** DJ (*Top of the Morning*, WCNX, Middletown, CT, 1960).

27663 **Ross, Martin.** DJ (*Off the Record* and *Tunes for Teens*, WPTR, Albany, NY, 1950).

27664 **Ross, Martha.** COM-HE (WCVA, Culpepper, VA, 1951).

27665 **Ross, Mary.** COM-HE (KING, Seattle, WA, 1949).

27666 **Ross, Max.** Newscaster (WGTC, Greenville, NC, 1945).

27667 **Ross, Mickey.** Leader (*Mickey Ross Orchestra*, instr. mus. prg., WJAS, Pittsburgh, PA, 1937).

27668 **Ross, Norma Jean.** Actress Ross was in the cast of the daytime serial programs *Scattergood Baines* and *Lonely Women*.

27669 **Ross, Norman.** Ross conducted one of the first early morning programs broadcasting time, weather and music (WMAQ, Chicago, IL, 1929). Sportscaster (WIBO, Chicago, IL, 1932). Newscaster (WCFL, Chicago, IL, 1940; WMAQ , Chicago, IL, 1941). DJ (*Music that Sings* and the *400 Hour*, WMAQ, 1947–1948; *Here's Norman Ross*, WMAQ, 1948; *400 Hour*, WMAQ, 1952; WEAW, Evanston, IL, 1954).

27670 **Ross, Norman De Mille.** News commentator (*News of the Day*, WENR, Chicago, IL, 1937).

27671 **Ross, (Mrs.) R.** Coloratura soprano (WFLA, Clearwater, FL, 1929).

27672 **Ross, Stanley.** Newscaster (NBC, 1942).

27673 **Ross, Wayne.** Sportscaster (*Sports Diary*, KTRI, Sioux City, IA, 1947).

27674 **Ross, Willis "Bill."** Newscaster (KEX-KGW, Portland, OR, 1937–1939).

27675 **Ross, Winston.** Tenor (*Winston Ross*, vcl. mus. prg., WNEW, New York, NY, 1940). Winston Ross, Lanny's brother, never achieved his brother's success on radio.

27676 **Rossa, Erwin.** Violinist (WGY, Lacey, WA, 1922).

27677 **Rossbach, Marlene.** COM-HE (WBRK, Pittsfield, MA, 1956).

27678 **Rossell, Deac.** Newscaster (WTRY, Troy, NY, 1946).

27679 **Rossen, H.B.** Newscaster (KYA, San Francisco, CA, 1945).

27680 **Rossi, George.** DJ (*Hello Show*, WKST, New Castle, PA, 1960).

27681 **Rossi, Olga.** Soprano (WHN, New York, NY, 1925).

27682 **Rossini, Ruby.** Singer (WIBO, Chicago, IL, 1926).

27683 **Rossmiller, Marie.** COM-HE (KSPT, Sandpoint, ID, 1951).

27684 **Rosson, Eddie.** Leader (Eddie Rosson and his Orchestra of Jeffersonville, Indiana, WHAS, Louisville, KY, 1925; Eddie Rosson Orchestra, WHAS, Louisville, KY, 1926).

27685 **Roswell, Faye.** Pianist (KOA, Denver, CO, 1925).

27686 **Rotary Boys Band of Memphis.** Memphis civic organization juvenile band (WBAP, San Antonio, TX, 1924).

27687 **Rote, Kyle.** Sportscaster (Former New York Giants professional football star Rote appeared on radio in 1960 on WNEW, New York, NY, 1960).

27688 **Rotenberger, Otto.** Bass (KLOS, Independence, MO, 1926).

27689 **Roth, Al.** Leader (*Al Roth Orchestra*, instr. mus. prg., CBS, 1935–1936; NBC-Red, 1936–1939).

27690 **Roth, Bob.** DJ (*1-2-5 Club*, KTMS, Santa Barbara, CA, 1947).

27691 **Roth, Bobby.** Pianist (WGBS, New York, NY, 1928).

27692 **Roth, Emmanual.** Newscaster (WNBH, New Bedford, MA, 1941).

27693 **Roth, Gordon.** Newscaster (WSYR, Syracuse, NY, 1941). DJ (*Saturday Juke Box*, KMJ, Fresno, CA, 1947).

27694 **Roth, Jane.** COM-HE (WGSA, Ephrata, PA, 1960).

27695 **Roth, Judith.** Soprano (WRNY, Richmond Hill, NY and WHN, New York, NY, 1926).

27696 **Roth, Judith and Al Wilson.** Singing team specializing in popular songs (WHN, New York, NY, 1924).

27697 **Roth, Judith and James Brennan.** Singing team (WMCA, New York, NY, 1925).

27698 **Roth, Marcella.** Child actress Roth was known as "The Twilight Story Girl of WSMB," who took children's parts on many radio plays (WSMB, New Orleans, LA, 1928).

27699 **Roth, Roy.** Newscaster (WEDC, Chicago, IL, 1945).

27700 **Roth, Sebastian.** Announcer (KGY, Lacey, WA, 1926).

27701 **Rothafel, S.L. "Roxy."** Samuel Lionel "Roxy" Rothafel was born in Stillwater, Minnesota, the son of poor immigrant parents. As a young man he moved to New York City and took a job as a stock boy at a 14th street department store. Bored with that job, he then worked as a book agent, Pennsylvania coal miner and Marine Corps enlistee. Eventually he opened his own small nickelodeon in Forest City, Pennsylvania. When he moved back to New York City he accepted a position as a theater manager. Soon he was working at the Capitol Theater, from whose stage he broadcast his popular *Capitol Theater Family* program (NBC, 1923–1926). Rothafel became extremely active on the New York theater scene. One of his achievements was the help he provided in planning Radio City, before he left RCA after disagreements with upper management.

Rothafel began his Sunday morning program, *Capitol Theater Family*, in 1923. Broadcasting from the stage of New York's Capitol Theater, Roxy brought to his radio public such performers as Erno Rapee, James Melton, Wee Willie Robyn, Caroline Andrews and Marie Gambrelli. From 1927 to 1931, he produced and directed *Roxy and His Gang* (NBC-Blue Network, New York, NY). Roxy broadcast his first program from the AT&T studios on New York's lower Broadway. He concluded that first show with, "Good night, sweet dreams. God bless you." His first program included the following performers: Viola Philo, Bert Shefter, Morton Gould, the Southernaires, Julia Glass, Arturo DeFillipi, Caroline Andrews, Sidor Belarski, Eliazabeth Lennox, Kouznetzoff and Nicolina, the Three Graces vocal trio, Anna Robinson, Geoffrey O'Hara, Dorothy Miller, Wladinna Padwa, Jeanne Lang, Jan Pierce and Evelyn Herbert. Members of his later *Roxy and His Gang* included Eugene Ormandy, Melaine Dowd, Dr. Billy Artzt, Mme. Elsa Stralia, Louis Schearer, Frederick Jaegel, Yascha Bunchuk, Bruce Benjamin, Carl Scheutze, Nada Reisenberg, Edna Baldwin, Betsy Ayres, Evelyn Herbert and Edith Fleischer. When Roxy left the Capitol Theatre to establish a theater of his own, the Roxy on Seventh Avenue in New York, Major Bowes took over the Capitol radio program on WEAF-NBC-Red Network. *See **Roxy and His Gang**.*

27702 **Rothchild, Walter.** Announcer and baritone soloist (KMOX, St. Louis, MO, 1928).

27703 **Rothenberg, Eva [Eve].** Pianist (WHN, New York, NY and WGCP, Newark, NJ, 1925).

27704 **Rothermel, Charles.** Banjo soloist (WGBS, New York, NY, 1928–1929).

27705 **Rothgeb, Paul.** DJ (*Platter Parade Paul*, WJNC, Jacksonville, NC, 1948).

27706 **Rothman, Lee.** DJ (*Record Review*, WSIV, Pekin, IL, 1947; *Jockey's Choice*, WWXL, Peoria, IL, 1948–1950; *Star Time*, WWXL, 1950; WKOW, Madison, WI, 1955).

27707 **Rothman, Marie.** Lyric soprano (WOR, Newark, NJ, 1924).

27708 **Rothrum, William "Bill."** Newscaster (WSYR, Syracuse, NY, 1938–1941). Sportscaster (WSYR, 1940–1946; *Bill Rothrum Show*, WSYR, 1947).

27709 **Rothwell, Alice.** COM-HE (WDRC, Hartford, CT, 1951).

27710 **Rothwell, J.C.** Newscaster (KSAM, Huntsville, TX, 1942).

27711 **Rotthaus, Elena.** COM-HE (KAFP, Petaluma, CA, 1956).

27712 **Rotundo, Joseph.** Newscaster (WGY, Schenectady, NY, 1945).

27713 **Roudybush, Franklin.** Newscaster (WING, Washington, DC, 1941).

27714 **Rough, Frank.** Sportscaster (KWFC, Hot Springs, AR, 1940–1942). Newscaster (KWFC, Hot Springs, AR, 1942).

27715 **Roulstone, Merl.** Newscaster (KICD, Spencer, IA, 1945).

27716 **Roulstone, Tom.** DJ (*Album Time*, WPEP, Taunton, MA, 1960).

27717 **Round, Bill.** DJ (*Musical Clock*, WBMC, McMinnville, TN, 1960).

27718 **Round, William, Jr.** Newscaster (WSIX, Nashville, TN, 1940). Sportscaster (WSIX, 1941).

27719 ***Round and Round Boys.*** The Round and Round Boys, Riley and Forley, not otherwise identified, were featured on the weekly music series (15 min., Wednesday, 1:45–2:00 P.M., CBS, 1936).

27720 ***Round Up Time.*** Rainier Beer sponsored the CW music show with a talented cast that included Texas Jim Lewis and his Rangers, Jack Rivers and Judy Knight. The announcer was Maury Rider (30 min., Friday, 7:00–7:30 P.M., KIRO, Seattle, WA, 1951).

27721 **The Rounders.** A singing group consisting of Myron Neisley, 3rd tenor; Dick Hartz, baritone; Armand Girard, bass; Dudley Chambers, 1st tenor; Bill Cowles, pianist; and Ben McLaughlin, 2nd tenor (NBC Pacific Coast Network, 1928–1929). The group enjoyed great success on the Pacific Coast. Earlier they appeared on NBC's *Eveready Hour* (1927).

27722 ***(The) Roundtowners.*** The popular vocal group consisted of tenors Brad Reynolds and Larry Murphy; baritone Evan Evans; and Lon McAdams (*The Roundtowners*, vcl. mus. prg., NBC, 1932).

27723 **Roundtree, George.** Newscaster (KUOA, Siloam Springs, AR, 1941). DJ (*Peoples' Choice*, WRLC, Toccoa, GA, 1947; *Musical Clock*, KVLH, Pauls Valley, OK, 1954; *Music 'n' Stuff*, KVLH, 1955).

27724 **Rourke, Robert.** Violinist (KGO, Oakland, CA, 1925).

27725 **Rousch, Sig.** DJ (*Blabbermouth Clambake*, WORZ, Orlando, FL, 1952).

27726 **Rouse, Gene.** Pioneer announcer Rouse was born July 14, 1896. He was originally designated as "GR" (WNAL, Omaha, NE, 1922). Rouse had been the sports editor of the Omaha *Daily News*, before he went to work on the paper's station (WNAL) in 1922. He soon became a popular radio personality going on to work at several other stations (WOAW, Omaha, NE, 1923–1924; WJJD, Chicago, IL, 1926–1928; and as announcer-station manager at KYW-KFKY, Chicago, IL, 1928–1929). Rouse specialized in sports and feature broadcasts, although he did serve as newscaster on KYW in 1930. He earned frequent designation as "World's Champion Fight Announcer," but he also broadcast college football and horse races.

27727 **Roush, Charles.** Sportscaster (WIBC, Indianapolis, IN, 1939).

27728 **Roush, Otis.** Newscaster (KBTM, Jonesboro, AR, 1939; WTJS, Jackson, TN, 1945). Sportscaster (WTJS, 1941).

27729 **Roush, Sigel A.** DJ (*Morning Mail*, WBOW, Terre Haute, IN, 1947–1950; WTHI, Terre Haute, IN, 1955).

27730 **Rousmann, Gertrude.** Pianist (WNYC, New York, NY, 1936).

27731 **Rousseau, Porky.** Sportscaster (WSOO, Saulte Ste. Marie, MI, 1944).

27732 **Routh, George.** Newscaster (KIRO, Seattle, WA, 1945).

27733 **Routh, Virginia Young.** Actress Routh was in the cast of the *Young Widder Brown* daytime serial program.

27734 **Routhart, Jules.** Pianist (KPO, San Francisco, CA, 1924).

27735 **Rovello, (Mrs.) R.** Contralto (KFWM, Oakland, CA, 1926).

27736 ***(The) Roving Reporter.*** Martin Starr went into the New York streets to interview the "interesting" people he found there on the sustaining man-in-the-street show (5 min., Thursday, 8:30–8:35 P.M., WMCA, New York, NY, 1936).

27737 ***(The) Roving Reporter.*** Dean Harris and Bob Turner performed man-in-the-street interviews (15 min., Monday and Wednesday, 1:45–2:00 P.M., WHAM, Rochester, NY, 1947).

27738 **Rowan, Roy.** Announcer Rowan appeared on the *Romance* daytime serial program.

27739 **Rowan, Steve.** COM-HE (WMIX, Mt. Vernon, IL, 1956).

27740 **Rowand, Alpha.** DJ (*Paramount Floor Show*, WBLK, Clarksburg, WV, 1950).

27741 **Rowe, C.M.** Sportscaster (WCAT, Rapid City, SD, 1940). Newscaster (WCAT, Rapid City, SD, 1942).

27742 **Rowe, Dave.** Sportscaster (*Along Sports Rowe*, KSEI, Pocatello, ID, 1948–1949).

27743 **Rowe, Flo Beach.** Newscaster (WSLB, Ogdensburg, NY, 1944). COM-HE (WSLB, 1956–1957).

27744 **Rowe, Genevieve.** Soprano Rowe frequently appeared on the *Atwater Kent* program. Ms. Rowe was the first place winner in the *Atwater Kent's National Radio Auditions* of 1929.

27745 **Rowe, Harry.** Baritone (KFI, Los Angeles, CA, 1927).

27746 **Rowe, Jo Anne [Ann].** COM-HE (KVOR, Colorado Springs, CO, 1955; KRDO, Colorado Springs, CO, 1957–1960).

27747 **Rowe, Ken, Jr.** DJ (*Music for Adults*, KJIM, Fort Worth, TX, 1960).

27748 **Rowe, Red.** DJ (*Red Rowe Rancho*, KFWB, Los Angles, CA, 1952).

27749 **Rowe, Samuel G.** Tenor (WHT, Deerfield, IL, 1925).

27750 **Rowens, W.E., Jr.** Newscaster (KRRV, Sherman, TX, 1938). Sportscaster (KRRV, 1939).

27751 **Rowland, Bob.** Sportscaster (*Hall Sports*, KELP, El Paso, TX, 1949).

27752 **Rowland, Carol.** COM-HE (WFBF, Fernandina Beach, FL, 1956).

27753 **Rowland, Rusty.** COM-HE (WKOP, Binghampton, NY, 1956).

27754 **Rowland, W.L., Sr.** Sportscaster (*Along the Sports Trail*, WGWC, Selma, AL, 1947).

27755 **Rowlands, Hugh.** Sportscaster (*Sports Spotlight* and *Speaking of Sports*, WOBT, Rhinelander, WI, 1948). Actor Rowlands appeared on *Dan Harding's Wife*, *Flying Patrol* and *Tom Mix*.

27756 **Rowley, Bob.** Newscaster (WJR, Detroit, MI, 1945–1947).

27757 **Rowley, Jane.** COM-HE (*The Woman's Page of the Air*, WOAI, San Antonio, TX, 1942).

27758 **Rowley, Tom.** Sportscaster (*Sports Slants*, WENE, Binghampton-Endicott, NY, 1952).

27759 **Rowswell, Rosy.** Sportscaster (KDKA, Pittsburgh, PA, 1940).

27760 ***Roxy and His Gang*** (aka ***Roxy and His Original Gang***). S.L. "Roxy" Rothafel began to broadcast his popular variety show, *The Capitol Theatre Family*, from the stage of New York City's Capitol Theatre on February 4, 1923. At that time the Capitol Theatre was New York's largest motion picture palace and routinely produced elaborate stage productions directed by S. L. Rothafel. An off-stage dressing room was used as a radio control room, when WEAF (New York, NY) broadcast the *Capitol Theater Family* program. This was a novel arrangement, since theater owners' generally considered radio to be competition. Roxy left the *Capitol Theater Family* program in 1926, when his announcing technique was criticized by his sponsor, and he began the *Roxy and His Gang* program the following year.

Roxy and His Gang was an extremely popular musical variety show that presented such performers as sopranos Beatrice Belkin, Dorothea Edwards, Jeanne Mignolet, Dorothy Githens, Mary McCoy, Dorothy Miller, Viola Philo, Anna Robinson, Ruth Ann Watmon and Ethel Louise Wright; contraltos Celia Branz and Adelaide DeLoca; tenors Jim Coombs, Adrian DeSilva, David Drollet, Arturo, Fillipi, Agard Lazlo, Geoffrey O'Hare, Arthur Phillips and Harold Van Dusen; baritones Douglas Stanbury and John Gurney; singing teams Lee Reis-Artie Dunn, the Glenn Sisters (Beatrice and Ruth), Ed Smalle-Dick Robertson and the Roxy Male Quartet (Frank Miller, John Young, George Reardon and Frederick Thomas; trumpeter Robert Denti; violinist Joseph Stopak; organist Lew White; harpist Florence Wightman; whistler Mickey McKee; comedienne Nina Gordon; and comedian Frank Mullholland. The program's pianist-arranger was Leo Russoto. Phil Carlin was the announcer (60 min., Monday, 7:30–8:30 P.M., NBC-Blue, 1927–1931).

Other members of *Roxy's Gang* were: coloratura soprano Caroline Andrews, soprano Betsy Ayres, baritone Alva "Bomby" Bomberger, dancer Patricia Bowman, cellist Yasha Bunchuk, dancer Marie Gambarelli, pianist Julia Glass, bass Peter Hanover, tenor James Melton, Gilbert and Sullivan specialist and actor Frank Moulan, contralto Florence Mullholland, tenor Jan Peerce, soprano Gladys Rice, tenor William "Wee Willie" Robyn, baritone Douglas Stanbury, tenor Harold Van Duzee and baritone Leonard Warren.

On this program, Roxy was said to have been the first on radio to broadcast a complete symphony, opera and oratorio (Buxton and Owen, 1973, p. 205). One of the most famous "graduates" of the Roxy shows was tenor James Melton. After graduating from Vanderbilt University, Melton gained a New York reputation through his radio work with the Roxy gang. He soon became a member of the famous Revelers Quartet and, later still, a member of the Metropolitan Opera Company. *Also see* **Rothafel, S.L. "Roxy."**

27761 ***Roxy Symphonic Concert*** (aka ***Roxy Symphony Concert***). Joseph Littau directed the symphonic orchestra on the concert music program. Milton J. Cross was the announcer (60 min., Sunday, 2:00–3:00 P.M., NBC-Blue, 1928–1929).

27762 ***Roxy Theatre Symphony Program.*** Maurice Baron conducted the good music program (30 min., Weekly, 9:00–9:30 P.M., NBC, 1932).

27763 ***Roxy's Guest Stars.*** The usual assemblage of talented performers were presented on one of Roxy's last radio variety programs. The sponsor was Fletcher's Castoria laxatives (1930s).

27764 **Roy, Cecil.** Actor Roy was in the cast of *Amanda of Honeymoon Hill, Kaltenmeyer's Kindergarten, Ma Perkins, Pepper Young's Family* and *The Timid Soul.*

27765 **Roy, Michael.** DJ (KWIK, Burbank, CA, 1947).

27766 **Roy, Nell.** Singer (WOR, Newark, NJ, 1932).

27767 **Roy, Satynananda.** A native of Calcutta, India, Roy broadcast talks about his native country such as, "Benares — the Holy City of the Hindus" (WGI, Medford Hillside, MA, 1923).

27768 **Roy, Ted A.** Tenor Roy, billed as the "Singing Blacksmith," won an Atwater Kent audition contest (KGW, Chicago, IL, 1929). Roy also worked as staff tenor on station KGO (Oakland, CA, 1929).

27769 ***Roy Atwell's Tide Waters Inn.*** Roy Atwell, who was described as a masculine Mrs. Malaprop, performed callisthenics with the English language on the weekday comedy program (15 min., Monday through Friday, 6:30–6:45 P.M., CBS, mid–1930s).

27770 ***Roy Shields and Company.*** The Roy Shields Orchestra was joined by guitarist George Barnes and vocalist Marion Mann on the sustaining music show. Guest singers such as Wayne Van Dyne also performed each week (25 min., Tuesday, 11:05–11:30 P.M. CST, NBC, 1941). A later version of the show featured Jeanne McKenna (1945).

27771 ***Roy Shields Show.*** The musical variety show featured the Shields' orchestra, soprano Ruth Lyon, contralto Gale Page, baritone Edward Davies and the Rangers Male Quartet (30 min., Thursday, 7:30–8:00 P.M. CST, NBC-Blue, 1936).

27772 **Royal, Sue.** Singer (WBNX, New York, NY, 1936).

27773 **Royal, Ted.** Leader (*Ted Royal Orchestra*, instr. mus. prg. (CBS, 1936).

27774 **Royal Ambassador Orchestra.** Popular local music group (WLW, Cincinnati, OH, 1923).

27775 ***Royal Baking Powder Menu Hints.*** Ruth Baker conducted the program on which menus were the main feature (NBC-Pacific Coast Network, 1928).

27776 ***Royal Crown Revue.*** George Olsen's orchestra, vocalist Freda Gibbson, later famous as Georgia Gibbs, the Golden Gate Quartet and the comedy team of Tim and Irene (Ryan) were featured on the variety show. The announcer was Graham McNamee. Nehi Bottling Company sponsored the program (30 min., Friday, 9:00–9:30 P.M., NBC-Blue, 1938).

27777 **Royal Dellwood Tooters.** Bill Stauffiger directed the eleven-man orchestra that broadcast two or three hours on Wednesday afternoons (WMAK, Buffalo, NY, 1927).

27778 **Royal Filipino Orchestra**. Musical organization featuring ethnic music (KSL, Salt Lake City, UT, 1929).

27779 **Royal Fontenelle Orchestra.** Musical group directed by Art Randall (WOW, Omaha, NE, 1928–29).

27780 ***Royal Gelatin Hour.*** Rudy Vallee conducted the 60-minute variety show. The program was Vallee's next endeavor after he completed his run with the *Fleishmann Hour* program, and it followed the same format. Vallee's guests on the *Royal Gelatin Hour* included Tommy Riggs and Betty Lou, Irving Caesar, the Sisters of the Skillet, the Colgate Glee Club, Jimmy Lytell, J.C. Flippen, Rags Ragland, Beatrice Fairfax, Arthur Allen, Dr. William Lyon Phelps, Boris Karloff, Jane Cowl, Grace George, Cecil Humphreys, Misha Auer, Eric Blore, Eddie Green, Wallace Ford, Broderick Crawford, John Barrymore, Hedda Hopper, Kay Thompson and her boys, Lou Holtz, Bill "Bojangles" Robinson, Edgar Bergen and Charlie McCarthy, the Charioteers, Sydney Franklin, Walter C. Kelly "the Virginia Judge," Roland Young, Bernie Bierman, Percy Grainger, Charlies Butterfield, Marjorie Hillis, Walter O'Keefe, Florence Desmond, Bob Hope, Marc Connelly, Bennie Hale, Stanley Holloway, Richard Tauber, J.B. Priestley, Will Fyffe, Ethel Merman, Mary Jane Walsh, Milton Douglas, Mary Boland, Henry Fonda, Sylvia Field, Tyrone Power, Anne Seymour, Charles Laughton, Elsa Lanchester, Maurice Evans, Jean Arthur, Walter Abel, Judith Anderson and Brian Aherne (NBC, 1936–1939). *See **The Fleishmann Hour**.*

27781 **Royal Hungarian Fiddlers from Budapest.** Romanian violinists (KMA, Shenandoah, IA, 1927).

27782 **Royal Mountain Ash Welsh Male Chorus.** Talented vocal group (WIP, Philadelphia, PA, 1926).

27783 ***Royal Music Makers.*** The Royal Typewriter Company sponsored the half-hour music program (30 min., Weekly, NBC-Blue, 1926).

27784 ***Royal Order of Optimistic Doughnuts.*** Comedians Mary Rosetti and Alan Rogers, assisted by Roscoe Ates in the role of Joe Twirp the stuttering reporter, were featured on the zany comedy show (KNX, Los Angeles, CA, 1933).

27785 ***Royal Order of Smoked Herring.*** Another of the many late night music and comedy programs of early radio, the show entertained listeners "with a session of fun, foolishness and folly," (150 min., Friday, 9:00–11:30 P.M., KJBS, San Francisco, CA, 1925). An earlier version broadcast in 1925 was 45 minutes in length.

27786 ***Royal Pacific Islanders Orchestra.*** Instr. mus. prg. (WMMN, Fairmont, WV, 1937).

27787 ***Royal Serbian Gypsies Tamburitza Orchestra.*** The twice weekly gypsy music program was a great listener favorite (KOIL, Omaha, NE, 1932).

27788 **Royal Stenographers Orchestra.** Joe Green directed the commercially sponsored band (1927).

27789 **Royal Typewriter Salon Orchestra.** Commercially sponsored band (WJZ, New York, NY, 1926).

27790 ***Royal Vagabonds.*** Standard Brands' Royal Gelatine sponsored the musical variety show. Ward "Hack" Wilson hosted the show that featured comedian Ken Murray, singer Helen Charleston and an orchestra conducted by Robert Russell Bennett (30 min., Wednesday, 8:00–8:30 P.M., NBC-Red, 1933).

27791 **Royale, Don.** Leader (*Don Royale Orchestra*, instr. mus. prg., WXYZ, Detroit, MI, 1935).

27792 **Royall [Royal], Paul A.** Sportscaster (KSL, Salt Lake City, UT, 1945–1947).

27793 **Royce, Alta King.** Soprano (WGBS, New York, NY, 1927).

27794 **Royce, Robert.** Tenor (*Robert Royce*, vcl. mus. prg., NBC, 1934).

27795 **Roye, (Mrs.) Ruth.** Soprano Roye sang from the stage of Pittsburgh's Davis Theater (KDKA, March 10, 1921).

27796 **Royle, Selena.** Talented actress Royle appeared on several daytime serial programs *Hilda Hope, M.D.* (title role), *The O'Neills, Portia Faces Life, Right to Happiness, Romance of Helen Trent* and *Woman of Courage* (title role) .

27797 **Royle, (Capt.) William "Bill."** World War I flyer Royle was a popular entertainer and master of ceremonies (KPO-NBC, San Francisco, CA, 1929).

27798 **Royster, Myrtle.** COM-HE (KTSN, Austin, TX, 1951).

27799 **Royster, N.L.** Newscaster (WOLS, Florence, SC, 1945).

27800 **Rozan, Gerta.** Actress Rozan appeared on the daytime serial programs *Mary Marlin* aka *The Story of Mary Marlin.*

27801 **Rozell, Ed.** Sportscaster (WKIP, Poughkeepsie, NY, 1940–1941).

27802 **Rozenmaget, Philip.** Violinist (WGR, Buffalo, NY, 1923).

27803 **Rozzelle, Lily.** Soprano (WJZ, New York, NY, 1924).

27804 **Ruark, Dave.** DJ (*Dancing in the Dark*, WGAU, Athens, GA, 1950).

27805 ***Rube Tronson and his Cowboys.*** A popular local CW music show (WLS, 1937).

27806 **Ruben, Bob.** Newscaster (NBC, 1944).

27807 **Ruben, Fabelo.** DJ ("Spanish music programs," WALT, Tampa, FL, 1952).

27808 **Rubens, Jeannette.** Pianist (KFWB, Hollywood, CA, 1925–1926).

27809 **Rubenstein, Babe.** DJ (Sportscaster, WNAC, Boston, MA and WAAB, Boston, MA, 1937).

27810 **Rubenstein, Eve.** COM-HE (KUFD, Ft. Dodge, IA, 1955).

27811 **Rubenstein, Helena.** COM-HE (*Beauty Talks*, WRNY, New York, NY, 1926).

27812 **Rubes of the Rubidoux.** Old-time music duo consisting of Bernard Marnell and Billy Waterworth, KFEQ (St. Joseph, MO, 1929).

27813 **Rubin, Bernie.** DJ (*Twilight Time*, WMID, Atlantic City, NJ, 1947).

27814 **Rubin, Estelle.** Violinist (WHN, New York, NY, 1926).

27815 **Rubin, Herman.** Announcer (WMHA, New York, NY, 1927).

27816 Rubin, Jack. Director-writer Rubin worked on *Break the Bank* (director), *Hilltop House* (director) , *The O'Neills* (director) and *Junior Miss* (writer).

27817 Rubin, Minnie. Rubin told children's stories (WEAF, New York, NY, 1925).

27818 Rubinoff, David. Violinist (WFAA, Dallas, TX, 1928). Rubinoff for many seasons was the orchestra leader on the *Eddie Cantor Show.* He also appeared on his own transcribed show in 1936, *Rubinoff and His Violin.* Pierre Andre was the announcer on the transcribed instrumental music program sponsored by Chevrolet (15 min., Monday, Wednesday and Friday, 6:30–6:45 P.M., WLS, Chicago, IL, 1936).

27819 Rubinoff, Esther. Violinist (WIBW, Topeka, KS, 1937).

27820 *Rubinoff's Orchestra* (aka *Rubinoff's Chevrolet Show*). Instr. mus. prg. (NBC, 1934; WOR, Newark, NJ, 1936).

27821 Rubio, Fernando. Sportscaster (*Southern Select Sports,* KCOR, San Antonio, TX, 1948).

27822 Ruby, Beverly. Actress Ruby was in the cast of the daytime serial programs *The Guiding Light* and *Woman in White.*

27823 *Ruby Mercer and Ted Haig.* Sam Goody's Record Shop sponsored the husband-and-wife DJ program (15 min., Saturday, 11:15–11:30 P.M., WOR, Newark, NJ, 1951).

27824 Ruby Trio. Vocal group consisting of Bernard Ruby, Floyd Ruby and another Ruby (KMA, Shenandoah, IA, 1928–1929).

27825 *Ruby's Orchestra.* Instr. mus. prg. (WNBF, Binghampton, NY, 1938).

27826 Rucezna, Anna. Bohemian contralto (KFI, Los Angeles, CA, 1925).

27827 Ruch, Dan. DJ (*Spins and Needles,* KEPS, Eagle Pass, TX, 1960).

27828 Ruch, Del. Leader (Del Ruch's Orchestra, WIP, Philadelphia, PA, 1925).

27829 Rucker, Foster. Baritone (KFOX, Long Beach, CA, 1929).

27830 Rucker, Joseph B. Bass (WFAA, Dallas, TX, 1923–1928).

27831 Rucker, (Mrs.) Joseph B. Pianist (WFAA, Dallas, TX, 1923–1926).

27832 Rucker, Margaret. COM-HE (WIKC, Bogalusa, LA, 1949).

27833 Rucker, Stanley. Rucker was a member of the Cornhusker Trio (KMA, Shenandoah, IA, 1929).

27834 Ruckle, Robert E. "Bob." DJ (*Cow Bell Club,* WRDW, Augusta, GA, 1948–1949; *Talk of the Town,* WRDW, 1950; *1450 Special,* WRDW, 1952–1954; WBIA, Augusta, GA, 1956). Sportscaster (*Sports Roundup,* WRDW, 1954).

27835 Rudd, Bill. DJ (*Hillbilly Spot Light,* WCCP, Savannah, GA, 1947; KCUB, Tucson, AZ, 1960).

27836 Rudd, Budd. Leader (Budd Rudd Collegian Dance Band, WLW, Cincinnati, OH, 1923).

27837 Rudd, Joe. Pianist (*Joe Rudd,* instr. mus. prg., WCBD, Waukegan, IL, 1936).

27838 Rudd, Luenna. Organist (WKY, Oklahoma City, OK, 1928).

27839 Rudd, Will. DJ (*All Nite Show,* WJMO, Cleveland, OH, 1960).

27840 *Rudd and Rogers.* Vocal and instrumental music program presented by a singing piano team (NBC, 1936).

27841 Ruddock, Merritt. Newscaster (WRNL, Richmond, VA, 1940–1941).

27842 Rudell, Tessie. Singer (WNAD, Norman, OK, 1926).

27843 Rudesille, Ruth Ann. COM-HE (WFHR, Wisconsin Rapids, WI, 1949).

27844 Rudolph, Howard. DJ (*Melody Market,* WITH, Baltimore, MD, 1947–1952).

27845 Rudolph, Jo Ann [Joann]. COM-HE (WKCT, Bowling Green, KY, 1955–1960).

27846 Rudolph, Joe. Versatile announcer, pianist, singer and band leader, who was one of the Three Doctors comic team on the *Potpourri Time* program (WMAQ, Chicago, IL, 1928–1929).

27847 Rudolph, Walter J. Pianist (KTAB, Oakland, CA, 1929).

27848 Rudy, Gerald. Flutist (WEAF, New York, NY, 1924).

27849 *Rudy Seeger's Shell Symphonists Orchestra.* Instr. mus. prg. (60 min., Monday, 8:00–9:00 P.M., NBC-KGO-Pacific Network, San Francisco, CA, 1928). Light classics such as those written by Romberg, Schubert, Lehar and Flotow were performed weekly on the good music show.

27850 *Rudy Vallee Presents the Drene Show.* Drene Shampoo sponsored the entertaining show that combined music, comedy and dramatic sketches. Vallee hosted the show assisted by such cast regulars as comedian Pinky Lee, the Bernie Kreuger Orchestra and announcer Truman Bradley. His numerous talented weekly guests included: Harry the Hipster Gibson, Gloria Blondell, Billie Burke, Virginia Mayo, Dizzy Gillespie, Jean Hersholt, Xavier Cugat, Betty Bradley, Mike Romanoff, Eddie Marr, Ruth Etting, Walter O'Keefe, Celeste Holm, Ella Logan, Robert Alda, Basil Rathbone, Lynn Bari, Audrey Trotter, Patsy Moran, Edward Arnold, Marie MacDonald, Gracie Fields, Peter Lorre, Ingrid Bergman, Ed "Archie" Gardner, the Mel-Tones, Doodles Weaver, Robert Maxwell, Martha Raye, Les Paul, Joan Davis, Benny Carter, Mantan Moreland, Vera Vague, Fred Allen, Shirley Temple, Janis Paige, Tallulah Bankhead, Lionel Stander, Betty Jane Greer, Monte Woolley, Vivian Blaine, Irene Ryan, Abbott and Costello and the Andrews Sisters (30 min., Weekly, NBC, 1944–1946). *See* ***The Rudy Vallee Rehearsal, Fleishmann Hour*** *and* ***The Royal Gelatin Hour.***

27851 *Rudy Vallee Rehearsal.* Vallee also hosted this show that included such cast members and guests as Lionel and John Barrymore, Maxie Rosenbloom, Vera Vague, Billie Burke, Orson Welles, Jose Iturbi, Priscilla Lane, Edna Mae Oliver, Billy Gilbert, Stu Erwin, Joan Davis, Reginald Gardiner and Groucho Marx (30 min., Weekly, NBC, 1940–1941).

27852 Rue, Jim. Sportscaster (*Sports Final,* KSC, Pullman, WA, 1947; KVOE, Santa Ana, CA, 1948). News analyst (*Orange County News,* KVOE, 1948).

27853 Rueb, Louis. Broadcast "Health Exercises" (KECA, Los Angeles, CA, 1929–1930).

27854 Rueppel (Brother) George E. On April 26, 1921, Brother Rueppel, S.J., began daily broadcasting of weather reports and recordings. Some suggest that Brother Rueppel was the first DJ on radio (WEW, St. Louis, MO, 1921). The call letters of WEW stood for "We Enlighten the World"

27855 Ruff, Bill. Sportscaster (*Sportlite,* KOLO, Reno, NV, 1952).

27856 Ruff, Olga. Soprano (KOIN, Portland, OR, 1928–1929).

27857 Ruffin, Edward. COM-HE (KCNY, San Marcos, TX, 1955).

27858 Ruffin, Homer. DJ (*Alarm Clock Club,* KCLE, Cleburne, TX, 1947).

27859 Ruffner, Edmund "Tiny." Six feet four and three-fourths inches tall, Ruffner was ironically known as "Tiny." After leaving the army following World War I, Ruffner worked for Standard Oil Company while planning to become a concert tenor. When his company started a radio program on KFI (Los Angeles, CA), he was selected to be the leading singer. After touring in several musical shows around the country performing in operettas by Victor Herbert and Gilbert and Sullivan, Ruffner applied for an announcing job at NBC in 1927 and got it. His great popularity with listeners assured his success. Ruffner's height at times was stressed by publicists and even exaggerated. For instance, some newspaper stories said he really was six feet, six inches. Certainly he reached the height of fame in his profession. Ruffner worked as announcer on several early network programs.

27860 Ruge, George. DJ (*Make Believe Ballroom,* KYA, San Francisco, CA, 1947; *Koffee Klub,* KYA, San Francisco, CA, 1954).

27861 Rugel, Yvette. Singer (WHN, New York, NY, 1925).

27862 Ruggieri, Nicholas. Newscaster (WFCL, Pawtucket, RI, 1942).

27863 Rugh, Vic. News analyst (KFH, Wichita, KS, 1937; KTUL, Tulsa, OK, 1939; KFBI, Wichita, KS, 1940; KOIL, Omaha, NE, 1941–1942; KANS, Wichita, KS, 1944–1946). Sportscaster (KFH, 1937–1940; KOIL, 1941–1942; KANS, 1944–1946; *Sports Final,* KFBI, Wichita, KS, 1950; KORC, Mineral Wells, TX, 1952).

27864 Ruhl, Oscar. Sportscaster (WMAN, Mansfield, OH, 1940).

27865 Ruhle, Paul. Newscaster (WCLO, Jamesville, WI, 1940–1942).

27866 Ruhoff, Fred. Violinist Ruhoff performed in the National Battery Symphony Orchestra (KSTP, St. Paul–Minneapolis, MN, 1929).

27867 Ruhoff, Herman. Violinist-banjoist Ruhoff performed in the National Battery Symphony Orchestra (KSTP, St. Paul–Minneapolis, MN, 1929).

27868 Ruick, Mel. Actor Ruick was in the cast of *Dear John.*

27869 Ruisi, Nino. Bass (WEAF, New York, NY, 1926).

27870 **Rukeyser, Merle Stanley.** Economic news analyst (NBC and CBS, 1944).

27871 **Rule, Elton.** Sportscaster (KROY, Sacramento, CA, 1940).

27872 ***Rumba Zutty Rumba Band.*** Instr. mus. prg. (WMAQ, Chicago, IL, 1935).

27873 **Rummage, Dorothy Delano.** Soprano (WEAF, New York, NY, 1926).

27874 **Rummer, Al.** Sportscaster (WBAX, Wilkes-Barre, PA, 1942).

27875 **Rumore, Joe.** DJ (*Roundup Time*, WAPI, Birmingham, AL, 1947–1948; *Afternoon Jamboree*, WAPI, 1948; *Roundup Time*, WVOK, Birmingham, AL, 1952–1956).

27876 **Rundle, Ann.** COM-HE (WLAD, Danbury, CT, 1955).

27877 **Runions, Norman "Norm."** Newscaster (KVI, Tacoma, WA, 1938–1939; KIRO, Seattle, WA, 1941).

27878 **Runnels, Gail.** DJ (KOME, Tulsa, OK, 1956).

27879 **Runnions, Guy.** Newscaster (KMOX, St. Louis, MO, 1941, 1945; *News at Noon*, KXLW, St. Louis, MO, 1947).

27880 **Runyon, Bob.** News analyst (*Six O'Clock Edition*, KSDN, Aberdeen, SD, 1948).

27881 **Runyon, Damon.** Sports writer and reporter, he broadcast sports news and commentary (WJZ, New York, NY, 1925). Runyon was famous for his stories of Broadway's "guys and dolls."

27882 **Ruoss, Helen.** Harpist (WJZ, New York, NY, 1923–1924).

27883 **Ruoss, Jane.** COM-HE (WCHS, Charles, WV, 1949).

27884 **Rupert, George P., Jr.** Director (Boston Collegians Band, WGI, Medford Hillside, MA, 1923).

27885 ***Rupert George's Minstrels.*** Many years previously, Rupert George had appeared in several Hal Roach motion picture comedies. He was an endman on the sustaining radio minstrel show. An ex-vaudevillian, Howard Green, was the other. Music was supplied by Lester and his Banjo and the Clarence Fuhrman Orchestra (30 min., Thursday, 11:30–12:00 noon, WIP, Philadelphia, PA, 1936).

27886 **Rupli, Margaret.** Newscaster (NBC, 1942). After graduating Phi Beta Kappa in 1931, Rupli worked for the U.S. Labor Department's Bureau of Labor Statistics. She was hired as a newscaster for NBC by Max Jordan. Her first broadcasts were from Amsterdam. When Holland was invaded by Germany, she escaped to England. She then returned to the United States and made her final broadcast after only six months in radio.

27887 **Rupp, Carl.** Leader (Carl Rupp and his Hotel Hollenden Entertainers Orchestra, WTAM, Cleveland, OH, 1926).

27888 **Rupp, Otto A.** Announcer (WFAM, St. Cloud, MN, 1925–1927).

27889 **Ruppert, Travers.** DJ (WASA, Havre de Grace, MD, 1956).

27890 **Ruppert and McCullough.** Banjoists (WCAU, Philadelphia, PA, 1926).

27891 **Rupple, Vera.** Soprano (WMAK, Buffalo, NY, 1928–1929).

27892 **Rupprecht, Mary K.** COM-HE (KEYE, Perryton, TX, 1960).

27893 ***Rural Route 1170.*** Sam Schneider conducted the daily program of news for farmers (15 min., Saturday, 6:45–7:00 A.M., KVOO, Tulsa, OK, 1942).

27894 **Rurrin, Elward.** DJ (*Spins and Needles*, KVLG, LaGrange, TX, 1960).

27895 **Rush, Al.** DJ (*Sunrisers Club*, KXO, El Centro, CA, 1948).

27896 **Rush, Ford.** Singer (*Ford Rush*, vcl. mus. prg., 15 min., Monday, 8:30–8:45 A.M., WLS, Chicago, IL, 1935). Rush was accompanied by organist Ralph Waldo Emerson.

27897 **Rush, Helen Ball.** Soprano (WEAF, New York, NY, 1923; KDKA, Pittsburgh, PA, 1928).

27898 **Rush, James.** Newscaster (*Just News*, KFDM, Beaumont, TX, 1948).

27899 **Rush, Kent.** Newscaster (KTHS, Hot Springs, AR, 1939–1940).

27900 **Rush, Phillip.** Newscaster (KSAL, Salina, KS, 1940).

27901 **Rush, Red.** Sportscaster (KFXM, San Bernardino, CA, 1953; KCSB, San Bernardino, CA, 1954). DJ (KYA, San Francisco, CA, 1957).

27902 ***Rush (Ford) and Silent Sam.*** Ford Rush starred on the program of CW music and humor (WGY, Schenectady, NY, 1938).

27903 **Rushey and Bill.** A popular blackface comedy team, Rushey and Bill broadcast variously as *The Janitor and His Son* and *The Gloomchasters of the Lone Star State* (WFAA, Dallas, TX, 1926).

27904 **Rushing, Val.** COM-HE (WMOK, Metropolis, IL, 1951).

27905 **Rusk, Clay.** Sportscaster (WOC, Davenport, IA, 1940). News commentator (*Studebaker Commentary*, WHO, Des Moines, IA, 1947).

27906 **Rusnak, Bill.** DJ (*Spotlight*, WDWS, Champaign, IL, 1960).

27907 **Russ, Matilda Bigelow.** Soprano (WGY, Schenectady, NY, 1929).

27908 ***Russ Mulholland.*** DJ Mulholland played records on the sustaining show and conducted a mythical ballroom program, apparently a copy of Martin Block's concept (20 min., Tuesday, 11:40–12:00 midnight, WCAU, Philadelphia, PA, 1942).

27909 **Russak, Leonard.** "Champion boy harmonica player" (WHN, New York, NY, 1924).

27910 **Russell, Alden.** *See* **Malone, Ted.**

27911 **Russell, Ann.** COM-HE (WSM, Nashville, TN, 1949).

27912 **Russell, Ann.** Actress Russell was in the cast of *Carters of Elm Street.*

27913 **Russell, Barclay.** DJ (*Russell's Record Room*, KABC, San Antonio, TX, 1947; WOAI, San Antonio, TX, 1954–1955).

27914 **Russell, Bob.** Newscaster (KTSW, Emporia, KS, 1942).

27915 **Russell, Clarice.** Blues singer (KFI, Los Angeles, CA, 1926).

27916 **Russell, Cy.** Sportscaster (*Sports Summary*, WVCG, Coral Gables, FL, 1950).

27917 **Russell, Dave.** News commentator (*Topline Edition*, KFDM, Beaumont, TX, 1947–1948). Sportscaster (KFDM, 1946; *Southwest Grid Chart*, KFDM, 1947–1949; *Sports Shorts*, KFDM, 1950–1954).

27918 **Russell, I. Earle.** Sportscaster (*Pigskin Parade* and baseball play-by-play, KXOB, Stockton, CA, 1947–1949; *Sports Roundup*, *Sports Letter* and *Great Moments in Sports*, KXOA, Sacramento, CA, 1950; KSJO, San Jose, CA, 1953–1956; KLIV, San Jose, CA, 1960).

27919 **Russell, Elaine.** Blues singer (KWK, St. Louis, MO, 1929).

27920 **Russell, Emerson.** Newscaster (WDZ, Tuscola, IL, 1938).

27921 **Russell, Fran.** Sportscaster (*Strictly Sports*, WMEV, Marion, VA, 1949–1950).

27922 **Russell, Freddie.** COM-HE (WCOR, Lebanon, TN, 1955).

27923 **Russell, George.** Newscaster (WCHV, Charlottesville, VA, 1939).

27924 **Russell, Jack.** Leader (*Jack Russell Orchestra*, instr. mus. prg., WENR, Chicago, IL, 1935; NBC-Red, 1936; WOR-MBS, Newark, NJ, 1938).

27925 **Russell, Joe, Jr.** Newscaster (WELO, Tupelo, MS, 1945).

27926 **Russell, John.** DJ (KMA, Shenandoah, IA, 1960).

27927 **Russell, Jon.** Seventeen-year-old violin prodigy (KGY, Lacey, WA, 1922).

27928 **Russell, Lois Gene.** COM-HE (KVMA, Magnolia, AR, 1957).

27929 **Russell, Luis.** Leader (*Luis Russell Orchestra*, instr. mus. prg., WCAU, Philadelphia, PA, 1934).

27930 **Russell, Marvel.** COM-HE (KXTX, Waco, TX, 1956).

27931 **Russell, Myrtle.** COM-HE (KELT, Electra, TX, 1951).

27932 **Russell, Nell.** Baritone (KMTR, Hollywood, CA, 1926).

27933 **Russell, Paul.** Sportscaster (*Sports Mike*, WHBS, Huntsville, AL, 1948).

27934 **Russell, Roy.** Newscaster (WOPI, Bristol, TN, 1945).

27935 **Russell, Russ.** Announcer (WGN, Chicago, IL, 1925).

27936 **Russell, Ruth.** Pianist (WEAF, New York, NY, 1924).

27937 **Russell, Ruth.** Actress Russell appeared on the daytime serial programs *Just Plain Bill* and *Our Gal Sunday.*

27938 **Russell, Tom.** Sportscaster (WKNE, Keene, NH, 1940).

27939 **Russell, Tony.** Vocalist (*Tony Russell*, vcl. mus. prg., NBC, 1936).

27940 **Russell, William.** Banjoist (WBZ, Springfield, MA, 1926).

27941 **Russey, Harold.** Newscaster (WHMA, Anniston, AL, 1941).

27942 ***Russian Academy Art Trio.*** Pianist Boris Myronoff; violinist Mischa Speigel; and cellist Alex Burrisoff comprised the instrumental trio (KFI, Los Angeles, CA, 1927).

27943 ***Russian Bear Orchestra.*** Instr. mus. prg. (CBS, 1935).

27944 Russian Cathedral Choir. Conducted by Nicholas Vasilieff, the choir's programs originated from the Cathedral at East Ninety-Seventh street in New York City. Many Russian artists appeared with the choir. The choir also sang on *Roxy's Gang* program, (NBC-Blue, New York, NY, 1928; *Russian Cathedral Choir*, voc. mus. program, 30 min., Sunday, 11:15–11:45 P.M., NBC-Red, 1929). The following year the Choir's Sunday program's length was reduced to 15 minutes.

27945 (The) Russian Chorus. Choir directed by Michael Worobrieff (WMAQ, Chicago, IL, 1923).

27946 Russian Eagle Orchestra. Instrumental music group (WGBS, New York, NY, 1924–1925).

27947 Russian Native Orchestra and Art Troupe. Russian music group (WCCO, Minneapolis, MN, 1928–29).

27948 Russian Roggers. The good Midwestern band frequently changed its name for broadcasting purposes (WHO, Des Moines, IA, 1927).

27949 Russian String Quartet. Instrumental music group featured on the *Beverly Hills Nurseries Program* (KNX, Hollywood, CA, 1926).

27950 Russillo, June. Pianist (WPRO, Providence, RI, 1937).

27951 Russo, Dan. Violinist (WIBO, Chicago, IL, 1925–1926; *Dan Russo Orchestra*, instr. mus. prg., NBC, 1934).

27952 Russo's String Quintet. String music group (WDAF, Kansas City, MO, 1929).

27953 Rust, Arthur "Art." Sportscaster (WWRL, New York, NY, 1953; WWRL, 1956; *Sports Roundup*, WWRL, 1960).

27954 Rust, Bill. Sportscaster (KGVL, Greenville, TX, 1949; *Pigskin Preview*, KGVL, 1950–1956).

27955 Rust, Nathan D. Sportscaster (KPAB, Laredo, TX, 1945).

27956 Rust, Sue. COM-HE (WSHE, Sheboygan, WI, 1955).

27957 Rust College Jubilee Singers. Choral group sponsored by the local Robinson Lumber Company (KLCN, Blytheville, AR, 1928).

27958 *Rustic Rhythm Trio.* A CW instrumental trio, previously known as Burke's Country Boys, whose members between themselves played 24 musical instruments. Their names were the Horton Brothers — guitarists Zeb and Elmer Horton — and Paul Robinson who played harmonica (15 min., Tuesday, 12:00–12:15 P.M., CBS, 1936).

27959 *Rusty Draper.* Rusty Draper hosted the variety show that featured Louise O'Brien, the Trends and the Roy Chamberlain Orchestra. Roy Rowan was the announcer (30 min., Transcribed, 1950).

27960 *Rusty Gill and his Boys.* Jack Holden announced the program of the CW music played by Gill and his group. The sponsor was Vita Pills (15 min., Wednesday, 10:30–10:45 P.M., WLS, Chicago, IL, 1942).

27961 Ruth, Charles F. Director, General Electric Band (WGY, Schenectady, NY, 1923).

27962 Ruth, Estelle. Pianist (WADC, Akron, OH, 1929).

27963 Ruth, George Herman "Babe." Sportscaster Ruth, the great "Babe," began broadcasting after he left baseball (*The Babe Ruth Show*, CBS, 1937). Some of Ruth's shows dramatized his "adventures and exploits" on other fronts as well. Ruth's programs also appeared on NBC and MBS.

27964 Ruth, Joan. Metropolitan Opera soprano (WEAF, New York, NY, 1926).

27965 Ruth, (Father) Sebastian. Announcer (KGY, Lacy, WA, 1926–1927).

27966 *Ruth and Ross.* Ruth and Ross — not otherwise identified — mixed song and patter on the NBC network program in 1936.

27967 *Ruth Draper.* Miss Draper, a famous monologist, brought her skills to the short-lived program series sponsored by the American Red Cross (30 min., Tuesday, 10:30–11:00 P.M., WOR, Newark, NJ, 1936).

27968 Rutherford, Ann. Motion picture star Rutherford was one of those who followed Penny Singleton in the title role of the *Blondie* situation comedy.

27969 Rutherford, Jerry. DJ (*The Night Owl Show*, WCMI, Ashland, KY, 1960).

27970 Rutherford, Jim. Sportscaster (*Today's Sports*, KTAT, Frederick, OH, 1950).

27971 Rutherford, (Judge). Leader of Jehovah's Witnesses, Judge Rutherford conducted a Biblical question and answer program for many years well into the 1930s (WBBE, Staten Island, NY, 1925).

27972 *Ruthie and Her Harmonica.* Instr. mus. prg. by an otherwise unidentified performer (WDZ, Tuscola, IL, 1937).

27973 Rutkowski, Tony. Harpist Rutkowski specialized in performing Polish harp music (WBZ, Springfield, MA, 1926).

27974 Rutland, Belle. Soprano (WEAF, New York, NY, 1925).

27975 Rutledge, Buddy. Sportscaster (*Sports Roundup*, WSPC, Anniston, AL, 1955; WHMA, Anniston, AL, 1956).

27976 Rutledge, Don. DJ (*Yawn Patrol*, WEDO, McKeesport, PA, 1947).

27977 Rutledge, Ed. DJ (*Dawn Patrol*, WIL, St. Louis, MO, 1947).

27978 Rutledge, Jack. Newscaster (KGBS, Harlingen, TX, 1941).

27979 Rutledge, Ned. DJ (*In Tune with the Times*, WLAN, Lancaster, PA, 1950; *All Around the Mulberry Bush*, WHVR, Hanover, PA, 1952–1955).

27980 Rutledge, Sunrise. DJ (WBCO, Bessemer, AL, 1956).

27981 Rutz, Uncle Jake. Uncle Jake was a fiddler with the *Pumpkin Vine Orchestra* on their musical program broadcast on a Tuesday evening (WLW, Cincinnati, OH, 1925). *See* **Pumpkin Vine Orchestra.**

27982 Ruysdael, Basil. Announcer Ruysdael was born July 24, 1890. He began work on station WOR (Newark, NJ, 1925). One of Ruysdael's earliest program appearances was as the announcer and poetry reader on the *Red Lacquer and Jade* program (WOR, 1929). He performed a similar role on the *Beggar's Bowl* program the following year. Ruysdael perhaps gained his greatest fame with his work as an announcer on the *Your Hit Parade* program.

27983 Ruziak, Ann. Lyric soprano (WFLA, Clearwater, FL, 1929).

27984 "RW." Designation for announcer Robert Weidaw (WGY, Schenectady, NY, 1923).

27985 Ryan, Agnes. Newscaster (WHEB, Portsmouth, NH, 1939).

27986 Ryan, Al. Daytime announcer and singer (KTAB, Oakland, CA, 1929).

27987 Ryan, Bernie. DJ (WCTC, New Brunswick, NJ, 1947).

27988 Ryan, Bill. DJ (*The Music Hall*, WLBR, Lebanon, PA, 1947; *The Two for Three Show*, WKAP, Allentown, PA, 1948).

27989 Ryan, Bob. DJ (*The Birthday and Anniversary Club*, KFAM, St. Cloud, MN, 1947).

27990 Ryan, Charles. DJ (WKYR, Keyser, WV, 1957).

27991 Ryan, Dave. DJ (*Memory Lane*, WICA, Ashtabula, OH, 1947).

27992 Ryan, Edward J. Newscaster (WATR, Waterbury, CT, 1938).

27993 Ryan, Erica. COM-HE (KUBA, Yuba City, CA, 1954–1955).

27994 Ryan, Eunice. Pianist (WLB, Minneapolis, MN, 1936).

27995 Ryan, Evelyn. Singer (WHN, New York, NY, 1925).

27996 Ryan, Frank. Sports announcer (WEEI, Boston, MA, 1928–1929). Sportscaster (WAAB, Boston, MA, 1937–1940; WNAC, Boston, MA, 1937–1940).

27997 Ryan, Frank. Newscaster (WRDW, Augusta, GA, 1945).

27998 Ryan, George S. [R.]. Announcer (KDKA, Pittsburgh, PA, 1926).

27999 Ryan, Helen. Violinist (WHN, New York, NY, 1925).

28000 Ryan, Helen. COM-HE (KANA, Anaconda, MT; WTHI, Terre Haute, IN, 1949–1960).

28001 Ryan, Helen. COM-HE (WTHI, Terre Haute, IN, 1957).

28002 Ryan, Jack. DJ (*Request Please*, WHUM, Reading, PA, 1948–1955).

28003 Ryan, Jack. DJ (*Matinee* and *Sleepytime Express*, WBRK, Pittsfield, MA, 1960).

28004 Ryan, Jim. Sportscaster (*Speaking of Sports*, KWPC, Muscatine, IA, 1954).

28005 Ryan, Joe. Newscaster (KRNT, Des Moines, IA, 1945).

28006 Ryan, Kathleen. Contralto Ryan was a featured singer at WGN for many years. She also was a member of the WGN Mixed Quartet (WGN, Chicago, IL, 1925–1928).

28007 Ryan, Mike. Sportscaster (*Sports Review*, WCOL, Columbus, OH, 1954).

28008 Ryan, Muriel B. Singer (WHN, New York, NY, 1926).

28009 Ryan, Ned. Newscaster (WHEN, Syracuse, NY, 1948). Sportscaster (WHEN, 1948).

28010 Ryan, Pat. Sportscaster (*Spotlight Sports, Pat Ryan Sports* and football play-by-play, WKY, Oklahoma City, OK, 1947).

28011 Ryan, Patricia "Pat." Actress Ryan appeared on the daytime serial programs *Joyce Jordan, Girl Interne, Little Women* and *Claudia* (title role).

28012 Ryan, Patti. COM-HE (WLWD, Dayton, OH, 1951–1957).

28013 Ryan, Quinlan Augustus N. "Quin." Premier announcer Quin Ryan was born November 17, 1898. After working seven years on the Chicago *Tribune,* he entered broadcasting in 1923, working as program director at WLS (Chicago, IL), program director and announcer WGN (Chicago, IL, 1925) and WMAQ (Chicago, IL). In 1924, Ryan began working at WGN and remained there for decades. Ryan helped contribute to one of early radio's most popular features — the bedtime story — when he portrayed WGN's *Uncle Walt,* first, and then *Uncle Quin.*

Ryan's ingenuity was demonstrated when he "re-created" a heavyweight championship bout that had taken place years before. He researched old newspapers, studied the event carefully and then "broadcast" the James J. Corbett–Bob Fitzsimmons fight "blow-by-blow," as though it was coming to him over the telephone. His most famous broadcasts on WGN probably were the Dayton Scopes' Trial in which Clarence Darrow and William Jennings Bryan argued Darwin's evolution theory in the famous "Monkey Trial"; the ordeal of Floyd Collins trapped in a Kentucky cave; and the Chicago-Illinois football game in which Red Grange scored four touchdowns. *Radio Digest* (October, 1928, p. 78) said that while working at WGN Ryan was known as one of the most vividly graphic and entertaining of the country's sports announcers.

Some early programs conducted by Ryan were *Quin Ryan, Reporter* (15 min., Saturday, 7:45–8:00 P.M., WGN, Chicago, IL, 1935) and an early local radio amateur show, *Quin Ryan's Amateurs* (15 min., Monday, 6:45–7:00 P.M., WGN, Chicago, 1935). In the early 1930s, Ryan served as president of WGN. In 1936, he was broadcasting sports news at WGN and as late as 1939 working as a newscaster at the station. *See* ***Quin Ryan's Amateurs.***

28014 Ryan, Red. News analyst (WCOV, Montgomery, AL, 1947; *News and Analysis,* WJJJ, Montgomery, AL, 1948).

28015 Ryan, Ric. COM-HE (KUBA, Yuba City, CO, 1951).

28016 Ryan, Russell. Assistant announcer (WDAF, Kansas City, MO, 1929).

28017 Ryan, Ruth. Pianist (WEAF, New York, NY, 1924).

28018 Ryan, Ted. Newscaster (KGKB, Tyler, TX, 1937).

28019 Ryan, Tommy. Sportscaster (*Let's Play Ball,* KANA, Anaconda, MT, 1950–1951).

28020 Ryan, Vincent. DJ (*All Thru the Night,* WHAT, Philadelphia, PA, 1950).

28021 Ryan, Waldo. DJ (*Western Star Time,* WFMC, Goldsboro, NC, 1954).

28022 Ryan, Walter. Announcer (WICC, Bridgeport, CT, 1926).

28023 Ryan, William, III. Sportscaster (*Sports Billboard,* WESA, Charleroi, PA, 1948). DJ (*Ryan with Records,* WESA, 1950).

28024 Rybka, Joseph. Leader (Rybka's String Orchestra, KGW, Portland, OR, 1923–1924).

28025 Ryder, Alfred (Alfred Corn). Actor Ryder was in the cast of *Aunt Jenny, The Goldbergs, Little Italy* and *True Confessions.*

28026 Ryder, Klock. Actor Klock was in the cast of *The Romance of Helen Trent.*

28027 Ryder, Les. Sportscaster (WCED, DuBois, PA, 1942, 1946).

28028 Ryder, (Mme.) Theodora Stokow. Pianist (WJZ, New York, NY, 1928).

28029 Ryder, Virginia. COM-HE (KCIL, Houma, LA, 1954–1960).

28030 Ryder, Virginia Wade. COM-HE (WRIC, Beaumont, TX, 1951).

28031 Ryder, William. Baritone (WOR, Newark, NJ, 1927).

28032 Rye, Jack. DJ (*Rye's Record Room,* KTSM, El Paso, TX, 1947; *Rye's Record Room,* KTSM, El Paso, TX, 1948; *Big Record Room,* KTSM, 1952).

28033 Ryel, Floyd. DJ (*Juke Box Review,* WDSC, Dillon, SC, 1947; WSRS, Cleveland Heights, OH, 1950; WICA, Ashtabula, OH, 1955).

28034 Ryerson, Albert. Announcer (WCAR, San Antonio, TX, 1928).

28035 Rykard, Brim. News analyst (WIS, Columbia, SC, 1944; *Journal of the Air,* WCOS, Columbia, SC, 1947).

28036 Rykew, John. DJ (*Rhythm and Rhyme on Record,* KLAS, Las Vegas, NV, 1952).

28037 Ryman, Paul. DJ (*Music for Everyone,* KERG, Eugene, OR, 1952; *Rhyme 'n' Rhythm,* KERG, 1954).

28038 Ryshanek, Will. Leader (*Will Ryshanek Orchestra,* instr. mus. prg., KMOX, St. Louis, MO and ABS, 1935).

28039 Ryte, Rita. COM-HE (WEWO, Laurinburg, NC, 1954).

28040 Ryus, Celeste. Pianist (KHJ, Los Angeles, CA, 1928).